THIRTEENTH EDITION

SCHROEDER'S
ANTIQUES
PRICE GUIDE

Edited by Sharon & Bob Huxford

COLLECTOR BOOKS

A Division of Schroeder Publishing Co., Inc.

The current values in this book should be used only as a guide. They are not intended to set prices, which vary from one section of the country to another. Auction prices as well as dealer prices vary greatly and are affected by condition as well as demand. Neither the Editors nor the Publisher assumes responsibility for any losses that might be incurred as a result of consulting this guide.

Searching For A Publisher?

We are always looking for knowledgable people considered experts within their fields. If you feel that there is a real need for a book on your collectible subject and have a large comprehensive collection, please contact us.

COLLECTOR BOOKS
P.O. Box 3009
Paducah, Kentucky 42002-3009

Introduction

As the editors and staff of *Schroeder's*, our goal is to compile the most useful, comprehensive, and accurate background and pricing information possible. Our guide encompasses nearly seven hundred categories, many of which you will not find in other price guides. Our sources are varied; we use auction results, dealer lists and trade paper ads, and we consult with national collectors' clubs, recognized authorities, researchers, and appraisers. We have by far the largest Advisory Board of any similar publication on the market. Each year we add several new advisors and now have nearly 350 who cover almost 500 categories. They go over our computer printouts line by line, deleting listings that are misleading or too vague to be of merit; they often send background information and photos. We appreciate their assistance very much. Only through their expertise and experience in their special fields are we able to offer with confidence what we feel are useful, accurate evaluations that provide a sound understanding of the dealings in the market place today. Correspondence with so large an advisory panel adds months of extra work to an already monumental task, but we feel that to a very large extent this is the foundation that makes *Schroeder's* the success that it has become.

Our Directory, which you will find in the back of the book, lists each contributor by state. These are people who have allowed us to photograph various examples of merchandise from their show booths, sent us pricing information, or in any way have contributed to this year's book. If you happen to be traveling, consult the Directory for shops along your way. We also list clubs who have worked with us and auction houses who have agreed to permit us the use of photographs from their catalogs.

Our Advisory Board lists only names and home states, so check the Directory for addresses and telephone numbers should you want to correspond with one of our experts. Remember, when you do, *always* enclose a self-addressed, stamped envelope (SASE). Thousands of people buy our guide, and hundreds contact our advisors. The only agreement we have with our advisors is that they edit their categories. They are in no way obligated to answer mail. Some are dealers who do many shows a month. The time they spend at home may be very limited, and they may not be open to contacts. There's no doubt that the reason behind the success of our book is their assistance. We regret seeing them becoming more and more burdened by phone and mail inquiries. We have lost some of our good advisors for this reason, and when we do, the book suffers and consequently, so do our readers. Many of our listed reference sources report that they constantly receive long distance calls at all hours that are really valuation requests. If they are registered appraisers, they make their living at providing such information and expect a fee for their service and expertise.

If you find you need more information than *Schroeder's* provides, there are other sources available to you. Go to your local library; check their section on reference books. Museums are public facilities that are willing and able to help you establish the origin and possibly even the value of your particular treasure. Check the yellow pages of your phone book. Other cities' phone books are available from either your library or from the telephone company office. Look under the heading *Antique Dealers*. Those who are qualified appraisers will mention this credit in their advertisement. But remember that if you sell to a dealer, he will expect to buy your merchandise at a price low enough that he will be able to make an appreciable profit when he sells it. Once you decide to contact one of these appraisers, unless you intend to see them directly, you'll need to get photographs. Don't send photos that are under or over exposed, out of focus, or shot against a background that detracts from important details you want to emphasize. It is almost impossible for them to give you a value judgment on items they've not seen when your photos are of poor quality. Shoot the front, top, and the bottom, describe any marks and numbers (or send a pencil rubbing), explain how and when you acquired the article, and give accurate measurements and any further background information that may be helpful.

The auction houses listed in the Directory nearly all have a staff of appraisal experts. If the item you're attempting to research is of the calibre of material they deal with, they can offer extremely accurate evaluations. Of course, most have a fee. Be sure to send them only professional-quality photographs. Tell them if you expect to consign your item to their auction. Of course, if you disagree with the value they suggest, you are under no obligation to do so.

Nearly five hundred categories are included in our book. We have organized our topics alphabetically, following the most simple logic, usually either by manufacturer or by type of product. If you have difficulty in locating your subject, consult the index. Our guide is unique in that much more space has been allotted to background information than any other publication of this type, and it is easier to read due to the larger-than-average print. Our readers tell us that these are features they enjoy. To be able to do this, we have adopted a format of one-line listings wherein we describe the items to the fullest extent possible by using several common-sense abbreviations; they will be easy to read and understand if you will first take the time to quickly scan through them.

The Editors

Editorial Staff

Editors
Sharon and Bob Huxford

Research and Editorial Assistants
Michael Drollinger, Nancy Drollinger, Patty Durnell, Linda Holycross, Donna Newnum, Loretta Woodrow

Layout
Beth Ray & Gail Ashburn

Cover Design
Beth Summers

On the cover, clockwise from right:
Cookie jar, Snow White, California Originals, marked "©Walt Disney Prod. 866 USA," $500.00+. Courtesy of *Collector's Encyclopedia of Cookie Jars, Book 2* by Fred and Joyce Roerig.

Harlequin dinnerware, regular creamer $13.50; Sugar bowl (lid missing) $10.00. Courtesy of Lydia May.

Hollywood Glo, cardboard sign, $35.00. Courtesy of *Value Guide to Advertising Memorabilia* by B.J. Summers.

Fostoria Wine goblet, Beverly pattern, amber with crystal stem, $20.00. Courtesy of *Fostoria Stemware: Crystal for America* by Milbra Long and Emily Seate.

Santa figural lamp, plastic, 8½", Glo-Light Corporation, 1950's, $12.00. Courtesy of Beth Summers.

Listing of Standard Abbreviations

The following is a list of abbreviations that have been used throughout this book in order to provide you with the most detailed descriptions possible in the limited space available. No periods are used after initials or abbreviations. When two dimensions are given, height is noted first. If only one dimension is listed, it will be height, except in the case of bowls, dishes, plates, or round platters, when it will be diameter. The standard two-letter state abbreviations apply.

For glassware, if no color is noted, the glass is clear. Hyphenated colors, for example blue-green, olive-amber, etc., describe a single color tone; colors divided by a slash mark indicate two or more colors, i.e. blue/white. A number following the last comma in a listing indicates how many items are included in the lot price. Teapots, sugar bowls, and butter dishes are assumed to be 'with cover.' Condition is extremely important in determining market value. Common sense suggests that art pottery, china, and glassware values would be given for examples in pristine, mint condition, while suggested prices for utility wares such as Redware, Mocha, and Blue and White Stoneware, for example, reflect the probability that since such items were subjected to everyday use in the home they may show minor wear (which is acceptable) but no notable damage. Values for other categories reflect the best average condition in which the particular collectible is apt to be offered for sale without the dealer feeling it necessary to mention wear or damage. For instance, advertising items are assumed to be in excellent condition since mint items are scarce enough that when one is offered for sale the dealer will most likely make mention of that fact. The same holds true for Toys, Banks, Coin-Operated Machines, and the like. A basic rule of thumb is that an item listed as VG (very good) will bring 40% to 60% of its mint price (a first-hand, personal evaluation will enable you to make the final judgment); EX (excellent) is a condition midway between mint and very good, and values would correspond.

Am	American	dvtl	dovetail	mahog	mahogany	rstr	restored
appl	applied	drw	drawer	mk	mark	rtcl	reticulated
att	attributed to	emb	embossed, embossing	MIG	Made in Germany	rvpt	reverse painted
bbl	barrel	embr	embroidered	M	mint	rnd	round
bk	back	eng	engraved, engraving	MIB	mint in box	s&p	salt and pepper
bsk	bisque	etch	etched, etching	MOP	mother-of-pearl	sgn	signed
blk	black	EX	excellent	mt, mtd	mount, mounted	SP	silverplated
b3m	blown 3-mold	ft, ftd	foot, feet, footed	mc	multicolor	sz	size
bl	blue	fr	frame, framed	NE	New England	sq	square
brn	brown	Fr	French	NM	near mint	std	standard
bulb	bulbous	G	good	NP	nickel plated	str	straight
C	century	grad	graduated	opal	opalescent	T'print	Thumbprint
c	copyright	grpt	grain painted	orig	original	trn	turned, turning
ca	circa	gr	green	o/l	overlay	turq	turquoise
can	canister	HP	hand painted	o/w	otherwise	uphl	upholstered
cb	cardboard	hdl, hdld	handle, handled	pnt	paint	VG	very good
CI	cast iron	illus	illustration, illustrated by	Pat	patented	Vict	Victorian
compo	composition	imp	impressed	ped	pedestal	wht	white
cr/sug	creamer and sugar	ind	individual	pc	piece	W	width
c/s	cup and saucer	int	interior	pk	pink	w/	with
cvd	carved	irid	iridescent	porc	porcelain	w/o	without
cvg	carving	Invt	Inverted	prof	professional	X, Xd	cross, crossed
dk	dark	lav	lavender	rfn	refinished	yel	yellow
dtd	dated	ldgl	leaded glass	re	regarding	(+)	has been reproduced
decor	decoration	L	length, long	rpt	repainted		
Dmn Quilt	Diamond Quilted	lt	light	rpr	repaired		
dbl	double	litho	lithograph	rpl	replaced		

A B C Plates

Children's plates featuring the alphabet as part of the design were popular from as early as 1820 until after the turn of the century. The earliest English creamware plates were decorated with embossed letters and prim moralistic verses, but the later Staffordshire products were conducive to a more relaxed mealtime atmosphere, often depicting playful animals and riddles or scenes of pleasant leisure-time activities. They were made around the turn of the century by American potters as well. All featured transfer prints, but color was sometimes brushed on by hand to add interest to the design. Braille plates were made for the blind, but these are rather scarce and usually more valuable. You may also find an occasional bowl or mug.

Ceramic

Baker, worker places loaves in brick oven, Staffordshire, 7" 145.00
Base Ball, Running to First Base, gr transfer, 1870s, 8½" 245.00
Bears, 1 w/organ grinder, 2nd w/paw out, Smith-Phillips, 7" 35.00
Behold Him Rising From Grave..., gray transfer/mc, Meakin, 5⅜" ..75.00
Blind Girl, child in doorway, mc transfer, 5¾" 150.00
Boy climbing wall, brn transfer/mc, Staffordshire, 6¾" 125.00
Brighton Beach, bathing pavilion 150.00
Bunnies, stylish clothes, deaf & dumb signs, Aynsley, 8" 135.00
Cat in bowl w/2 cats at side, bl rim, blk transfer, 6" 175.00
Chinonco Watching Departure of Cavalcade 120.00
Clock face, brn transfer, 8" 55.00
Daniel in Lion's Den, mc transfer, Staffordshire 175.00
English newsboy w/papers, mc transfer, Meakin, 6", EX 130.00
Flowers That Never Fade, Staffordshire, 7" 150.00
Girl & 2 dachshunds frightened by bear rug, Dresden 65.00
Hey Diddle Diddle, Bavaria, 7½" 75.00
Importance of Punctuality, gr transfer, Adams, 7" 130.00
John Gilpin's Arrival..., brn transfer/mc, 5⅛" 130.00
Make Hay While..., Franklin's Proverbs, blk transfer/mc, 6" 130.00

Man and child on donkey in landscape, multicolor transfer, 7½", $95.00.

Man w/basket, church at bk, mc transfer, 7", EX 110.00
Miss Muffet, bl transfer, England 88.00
Nations of World, polychrome, Brownhill Pottery, 6½" 185.00
Now I Have a Cow, Franklin Maxim, 5⅛" 125.00
Organ grinder & children, brn transfer/mc, Staffordshire, 7⅛" ...120.00
Poor Richard's Way to Wealth..., blk transfer/mc, 6", NM 120.00
Shepherd w/longhorn & dog, blk transfer/mc, English, 7" 90.00
Soldier w/comic verse, gr transfer, red rim, 5" 140.00
Stable Yard, gray transfer/mc, Staffordshire, 8¼" 85.00
Why Is This...Fishing?, Blks in boat, Staffordshire, 6⅛" 175.00
Zebra, polychrome, Staffordshire, 6", EX 90.00

Glass

Bo Peep w/Bears 55.00
Cane center, 6" 30.00
Clock, Thousand Eye, amber, ABC rim 125.00
Clock & days, vaseline, 7" 75.00
Clock w/Roman numerals in inside border 40.00
Ducks, ABC rim, 6" 50.00
Elephant w/howdah on bk, ABC rim, Ripley & Co, 6" 90.00
Flower bouquet, ABCs on stippled ground, frosted flowers, 6" 75.00
Flying stork & #s, marigold carnival 65.00
Garfield, ABC rim 100.00
Hey Diddle Diddle w/children 55.00
Old Independence Hall, stippled ABCs, scalloped, 7" 100.00

Proud Dog, ABC rim, $65.00.

Quilted center, ABCs & numbers on stippled ground 105.00
Rabbit center, ABC rim, Crystal Glass Co, 6" 55.00
Rooster, hen & chicks, ABC rim 65.00

Tin

Brownies, ca 1893, 8⅞" 160.00
Girl on swing, 6¼" 70.00
Hi-Diddle-Diddle, ABC rim 85.00
Jumbo elephant, ABC rim, 6½" 98.00
Mary Had a Little Lamb, 8" 130.00
Peter Rabbit, animals intertwined in ABC rim, 8½" 75.00
Washington, bust in center, 5⅝" 210.00
Who Killed Cock Robin?, 7⅞", EX 95.00

Abingdon

From 1934 until 1950, the Abingdon Pottery Co. of Abingdon, Ill., made a line of art pottery with a white vitrified body decorated with various types of glazes in many lovely colors. Novelties, cookie jars, utility ware, and lamps were made in addition to several lines of simple yet striking art ware. Fern Leaf, introduced in 1937, featured molded vertical feathering. La Fleur, in 1939, consisted of flowerpots and flower-arranger bowls with rows of vertical ribbing. Classic, 1939-40, was a line of vases, many with evidence of Chinese influence. Several marks were used, most of which employed the company name. In 1950 the company reverted to the manufacture of sanitary ware that had been their mainstay before the Art Ware Division was formed.

Highly decorated examples and those with black, bronze, or red glaze usually command at least 25% higher prices.

Our advisors for Abingdon cookie jars are Joyce and Fred Roerig, authors of *The Collector's Encyclopedia of Cookie Jars*. Their address is in the Directory under South Carolina.

#101, vase, Alpha Classic	30.00
#102, vase, Beta, maroon, 10"	58.00
#104, vase, Delta Classic, 10"	28.00
#110, vase, Beta, bl, 6"	35.00
#116, vase, Classic, 10", from $18 up to	22.50
#126, candle holders, Classic, wht, 2", pr	38.00
#142, vase, Classic, bl, mini, 5½"	25.00
#200, pitcher, ice lip, 2-qt	30.00
#301, jar, Ming, turq	80.00

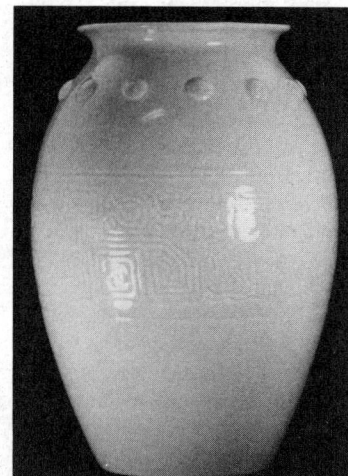

Vase, Lung, turquoise, #302, 11", $165.00.

#305, bookends, sea gull, pr	60.00
#310, jar, Chang, wht matt, 1934-36, 10½"	245.00
#315, vase, Athena Classic, wht, 1934-36, 9"	38.00
#339, plate, salad; dk bl, sq, 7½"	32.00
#351, vase, Capri, Regency gr, 5¾"	44.00
#363, bookends, colt, 5¾", pr	65.00
#375, wall pocket, dbl morning-glory, wht, 7¾"	45.00
#384, candle holders, sunflower, 4½" dia, pr	35.00
#390, vase, morning-glory, turq, 1934-50, 10"	60.00
#3903, seated nude, 7", minimum value	300.00
#3906, shepherdess & fawn, yel w/gold traces, 11½"	95.00
#400, tea tile, geisha, sq, 5"	80.00
#402, vase, Box	65.00
#408, bowl, leaf, beige, 1937, 6½"	65.00
#416, peacock, celadon gr, 7"	45.00
#420, vase, Fern Leaf, no decor, 7¼"	15.00
#429, vase/candle holder, Fern Leaf, 8"	25.00
#434, candle holder, Fern Leaf, 5½x3"	27.50
#437, bowl (window box), Han Pansy, 10½" L	14.00
#442, vase, Laurel, turq matt, 1938-39, 5½"	33.00
#451, candle holders, dbl; Asters, wht, 1934-38, 4½", pr	44.00
#460, bowl, Panel, 8"	40.00
#462, bowl, ribbon, 7½"	12.00
#464, vase, medallion, 8"	30.00
#468, vase, bird, decor, 7½"	35.00
#486, vase, acanthus, gray, 11"	42.00
#491, vase, flower holder; wht, 5"	25.00
#498, window box, Han, lg, 14½" L	25.00
#510, ashtray, donkey, blk, scarce, 5½" dia	95.00
#513, vase, swirl, 9", from 15.00 up to	25.00
#517, vase, Arden, gr, 1934-50, 7"	24.00

#522, vase, Barre, 9"	23.00
#529, bowl, Ti Leaf, 16"	30.00
#540, bowl, flared	30.00
#543, bowl, bulb, rnd, sm	20.00
#544, bowl, Streamliner, sm	15.00
#550, vase, fluted	26.00
#565, cornucopia, blk, 1942-47, 7"	25.00
#568, mint compote, pk, ftd, 1942-47, 6"	28.00
#571, goose, wht, 5"	25.00
#574, heron, 5¼"	25.00
#584, vase, boot form	37.50
#593, vase, bow knot, bl, 9"	25.00
#599, vase, quilted, wht, 9"	30.00
#645, bowl, Contour	22.00
#657, swordfish, decor, 4½"	45.00
#661, swan, chartreuse, 3¾"	35.00
#668, planter, daffodil, 5¼"	20.00
#681/#682, sugar bowl & creamer, daisy	27.50
#700, bowl, pineapple, 14¼"	125.00
#709, bowl, irregular, 13½"	15.00
#712, string holder, mouse	72.50
#716, candlesticks, bamboo, decor, introduced 1939, pr	28.00
A-1, whatnot vase	75.00
Cookie jar, #471, Old Lady, plain or decor, 1942	210.00
Cookie jar, #471, Old Lady, rare gr	195.00
Cookie jar, #495, Fat Boy	240.00
Cookie jar, #549, Hippo, decor, 1942	225.00
Cookie jar, #561, Baby, Blk decor	300.00
Cookie jar, #588, Money Bag, 1947	70.00
Cookie jar, #602, Hobby Horse	185.00
Cookie jar, #611, Jack-in-Box	255.00
Cookie jar, #622, Miss Muffet	205.00
Cookie jar, #651, Choo Choo (Locomotive)	150.00
Cookie jar, #653, Clock, 1949	85.00
Cookie jar, #662, Little Miss Muffet	205.00
Cookie jar, #663, Humpty Dumpty	250.00
Cookie jar, #664, Pineapple	60.00
Cookie jar, #665, Wigwam, minimum value	300.00
Cookie jar, #674, Pumpkin, 1949	310.00
Cookie jar, #677, Daisy, 1949	45.00
Cookie jar, #678, Windmill	185.00
Cookie jar, #692, Witch, minimum value	350.00
Cookie jar, #693, Little Girl	60.00
Cookie jar, #694, Bo Peep	240.00
Cookie jar, #695, Mother Goose	295.00
Cookie jar, #696, Three Bears	90.00
G-1, oil jar, tall	200.00
G-2, palm vase, squat	200.00
G-3, vase, floor; rope	180.00
P-7, jardiniere, 6"	24.00

Adams

Wm. Adams, whose potting skills were developed under the tutelage of Josiah Wedgwood, founded the Greengates Pottery at Tunstall, England, in 1769. Many types of wares including basalt, ironstone, parian, and jasper were produced; and various impressed or printed marks were employed. Until 1800 'Adams Co.' or 'Adams' impressed in block letters identified the company's earthenwares and a fine type of jasper similar in color and decoration to Wedgwood's. The latter mark was used again from 1845 to 1864 on parian figures. Most examples of their product found on today's market are transfer-printed dinnerwares with ornate backstamps which often include the pattern name and the initials 'W.A. & S.' This type of product was made from 1820 until about 1920. After 1890 the word 'England' was included in the mark; 'Tunstall' was added after 1896. From 1914 through 1940, a printed crown with 'Adams, Estbd 1657, England' identified their products. From 1900 to 1965, they produced souvenir plates with transfers of American scenes, many of which were marketed in this country by Roth Importers of Peoria, Illinois. In 1965 the company affiliated with Wedgwood. Although there were other Adams potteries in Staffordshire, their marks incorporate either the first name initial or a partner's name and so are easily distinguished from those of this company. See also Spatter; Staffordshire; Adams Rose.

Bowl, Cries of London, Dr Syntax Reading His Tour, 9" 60.00
Bowl, vegetable; Columbus Discovers Am, gr transfer, 11" L 175.00
Candlesticks, Cries of London, 3½", pr 80.00
Creamer, bl jasper, wht classical figures, 3¼" 45.00
Cup & saucer, floral, dk bl transfer 75.00
Cup & saucer, handleless; stick spatter w/gaudy floral, EX 55.00
Cup & saucer, handleless; The Pet, red transfer, EX 50.00
Jug, 4 panels (seasons), jasper, bl & wht, metal lid, 10" 500.00
Plate, Columbia, red transfer, mk, 10¾" 35.00
Plate, Cupid & maiden, dk bl transfer, 9" 160.00
Plate, fishing/cottage scene, dk bl transfer, 7¾" 78.00
Plate, Palestine, red transfer border, gr center, 9½" 80.00
Platter, bl feather edge, 15", EX 75.00
Platter, Fountain Scenery, red transfer, 11" 130.00
Platter, 2 stags, 3 does, bl transfer, 1850s, 16" 300.00
Urn, coat of arms, wht on cobalt, mini, 2½" 80.00
Vase, Cupid, Venus & Apollo, jasper, bl & wht, hdls, 9" 250.00

Adams Rose, Early and Late

In the second quarter of the 19th century, the Adams and Son Pottery produced a line of hand-painted dinnerware decorated in large, red brush-stroke roses with green leaves on whiteware, which collectors call Adams Rose. Later, G. Jones and Son (and possibly others) made a similar ware with less brilliant colors on a gray-white surface.

Our advisor for this category is Richard Marden; he is listed in the Directory under New Hampshire.

Coffeepot with rare domed lid, repairs, 12", $575.00; Pitcher, scrolled handle and rim, 9", VG, $235.00; Platter, scalloped rim, 20x16½", rare, $2,075.00.

Bowl, early, 2¾x5½", EX 55.00
Bowl, late, England, 5½" 65.00
Bowl, vegetable; late, England, oval, 9¾" 135.00
Bowl, vegetable; late, Staffordshire, England, oval, 8½" 80.00

Chamber pot, early, molded scrolls at rim, mini, 1½", EX 200.00
Coffeepot, early, scroll hdl, dome lid, Adams, 12", EX 575.00
Coffeepot, late, England, rpr, 9", EX 440.00
Creamer, early, 3", EX 150.00
Creamer, early, 5¾", M 285.00
Creamer, late, mk Reg #6154, 5½", VG 70.00
Creamer, late, Staffordshire, England, 5½", NM 240.00
Creamer, late, 3⅜", NM 95.00
Cup plate, early, scalloped, Adams, 4", EX 630.00
Pitcher, early, scalloped rim w/emb scrolls, mk Adams, 8", EX ...450.00
Pitcher, late, 6¾", M 295.00
Pitcher, late, 8½", VG 235.00
Plate, early, beaded rim, mk Adams, 6", NM 95.00
Plate, early, plain rim, mk Adams, 7½" 70.00
Plate, early, scalloped rim, rosette mk, minor wear, 8" 150.00
Plate, early, 9", M 195.00
Plate, late, 12", EX 125.00
Plate, toddy; early, plain rim, mk Adams, 5", EX 120.00
Platter, early, plain rim, mk Adams, 10", EX 290.00
Platter, early, scalloped rim, Adams, 20x16½", NM 2,075.00
Platter, late, Staffordshire, England, 14½", VG 110.00
Platter, late, 12", EX 135.00
Soup plate, early, plain rim, mk Adams, 10¾" 160.00
Soup plate, early, plain rim, mk Adams, 9½", NM 90.00
Soup plate, early, scalloped rim, Adams, 10¾" 200.00
Sugar bowl, early, flared rim, w/lid, 5" 365.00
Sugar bowl, late, England, rpr, 6", EX 200.00
Tea bowl & saucer, early, plain rim, Adams, EX 175.00
Tea bowl & saucer, late, M 125.00
Teapot, early, dolphin hdl, 8x11", VG 475.00
Teapot, early, dome lid, rpr, 11½" 565.00
Teapot, early, rnd body, 5", VG 300.00
Wash bowl, late, emb floral vine at rim, 14½" 160.00

Advertising

The advertising world has always been a fiercely competitive field. In an effort to present their product to the customer, every imaginable gimmick was put into play. Colorful and artfully decorated signs and posters, thermometers, tape measures, fans, hand mirrors, and attractive tin containers (all with catchy slogans, familiar logos, and often-bogus claims) are only a few of the many examples of early advertising memorabilia that are of interest to today's collectors.

Porcelain signs were made as early as 1890 and are highly prized for their artistic portrayal of life as it was then . . . often allowing amusing insights into the tastes, humor, and way of life of a bygone era. As a general rule, older signs are made from a heavier gauge metal. Those with three or more fired-on colors are especially desirable.

Tin containers were used to package consumer goods ranging from crackers and coffee to tobacco and talcum. After 1880 can companies began to decorate their containers by the method of lithography. Though colors were still subdued, intricate designs were used to attract the eye of the consumer. False labeling and unfounded claims were curtailed by the Pure Food and Drug Administration in 1906, and the name of the manufacturer as well as the brand name of the product had to be printed on the label. By 1910 color was rampant with more than a dozen hues printed on the tin or on paper labels. The tins themselves were often designed with a second use in mind, such as canisters, lunch boxes, even toy trains. As a general rule, tobacco-related tins are the most desirable, though personal preference may direct the interest of the collector to peanut butter pails with illustrations of children, or talcum tins with irresistible babies or beautiful ladies. Coffee tins are popular, as are those made to contain a particularly successful or well-known product.

Perhaps the most visual of the early advertising gimmicks were the character logos, the Fairbank Company's Gold Dust Twins, the goose trademark of the Red Goose Shoe Company, Nabisco's ZuZu Clown and Uneeda Kid, the Campbell Kids, the RCA dog Nipper, and Mr. Peanut, to name only a few. Any example of these brings a high price on the market today.

Our listings are alphabetized by company name or, in lieu of that information, by word content or other pertinent description. When no condition is indicated, the items listed below are assumed to be in excellent condition, except glass and ceramic items, which are assumed mint. Remember that condition greatly affects value (especially true for tin items). For instance, a sign in excellent or mint condition may bring twice as much as the same one in only very good condition, sometimes even more. On today's market, items in good to very good condition are slow to sell, unless they are extremely rare. Mint (or near-mint) examples are high.

As a general rule, beer tip trays in near-mint condition are worth $150 to $250. Spool cabinets (depending on condition) may be evaluated at $100 to $150 per drawer.

We have several advertising advisors; Allen Smith specializes in Buster Brown and Red Goose Shoes. He is listed in the Directory under Texas. Our Dr. Pepper advisor is Bill Ricketts, listed under North Carolina. Pepsi-Cola is under the advisement of Craig and Donna Stifter, see Illinois. For further information, we recommend *Huxford's Collectible Advertising,* available at your local bookstore or from Collector Books. See also Advertising Dolls; Advertising Cards; Automobilia; Coca-Cola; Banks; Calendars; Cookbooks; Paperweights; Posters; Sewing Items.

Key:
cb—cardboard	ps—porcelain sign
cl—celluloid	sf—self-framed
lcs—litho on canvas sign	tc—tin container
pp—pre-prohibition	ts—tin sign

Abbott's Angostura Bitters, ts, man, Shonk, 1899, 44x32", G 150.00
AC Allis Chalmers, porc sign, red & bl on wht, 11x11", NM 110.00
Admiration Cigars, rvpt sign, lady, w/silver/gold, 24x18", VG ..2,000.00
Aetna Automobile Insurance, tin sign, 12x24", VG 65.00
Amalie Motor Oil, metal thermometer, glass face, 9" dia, EX 65.00
American Brewing, paper sign, The Philosopher, 20x16", EX 350.00
American Brewing, stoneware match striker, 3x3¾", VG 170.00
American Brewing, tin & glass sign, eagle on shield, 30x41", G ..600.00
American Brewing, ts, Grecian girl & temple, fr, 30x23", EX .2,200.00
Amoco, cloth banner, 5-color, 25x37½", NM 85.00
Anheuser-Busch, cased glass sign, 54½x80"+orig fr, VG 1,750.00
Anheuser-Busch, charger, Say When, 16" dia, EX 400.00
Anheuser-Busch, jackknife, factory scene, 3-blade, 3¼", VG 145.00
Anheuser-Busch, paper sign, girl in red, orig fr, 39x24", G 500.00
Anheuser-Busch, pocketknife, enamel over brass, 3¼", G 145.00
Anheuser-Busch, sf ts, maid w/hops in basket, 38x26", G 600.00
Anheuser-Busch, stained glass window, eagle, 47x32", EX 4,000.00
Anheuser-Busch, tray, cherubs around lady, 16½" oval, EX 450.00
Anheuser-Busch, tray, eagle & 'A,' 12" dia, G 325.00
Anheuser-Busch, tray, factory/eagle/hops, oval, 18½", NM 2,100.00
Anheuser-Busch, tray, factory/eagle/hops, 18½x15½", G 450.00
Anheuser-Busch, tray, Victory, 13x10½", VG 275.00
Anheuser-Busch, ts, factory, later type, orig fr, 16x37", G 500.00
Anthracite Brewing, cl pocket mirror, Santa, 2" dia, EX 250.00
Anthracite Brewing, pocket mirror, lady, 2¾x1¾", VG 65.00
Arnholt Ambersand Chaefer Brewing, tip tray, 4½" dia, EX 160.00
Arnold & Co Brewers, sf ts, man/ladies/carriage, 19x16", VG 350.00
Arrow Beer, sf ts, King Gambrinus, 16½" dia, VG 225.00
Artie Cigars, ts, man on roof, Best...of Year, 10x14", VG 375.00

Ayer's Pills, tin sign, printed by Wells & Hope, 20x14" (excluding frame), VG, $2,100.00.

Atlantic Coastline, ts, blk on yel, 29½" dia, VG 120.00
Aurora Brewing, tray, girl w/glass on tray, 13" sq, G 275.00
Bailey's Pure Rye, sf ts, lady w/tray, Shonk, 1902, 26x18", VG ..215.00
Ballantine Ale, cb sign, lady at Christmas, 12x17", EX 65.00
Baltimore Brewing, tray, stylish lady, 13¼x10½", G 170.00
Barnsdall Super-Gas, porc sign, 2-sided, 30" dia, VG 150.00
Bartel's, sf ts, bold lettering, 22¼x28", G 600.00
Bartel's Beer, canvas sign, professor w/glass, 56x26", G 350.00
Bartholomay, charger, lady toasting, 17½" dia, G 175.00
Beech-Nut Gum, counter display, spring-loaded base, 11x7x7", EX ..600.00
Beech-Nut Gum, tc, pastoral scenes, 6x12¼x11", VG 50.00
Bell of Anderson Whiskey, rvpt sign, topless ladies, 28x20", G ..500.00
Bergner & Engle Brewing, pocketknife, 3-blade, VG 60.00
Berma Shave, wooden jingle signs, complete set, 17x40", VG ..4,500.00
Betsy Ross, sf ts, portrait in oval, 24x20", G 100.00
Beverwyck Beer, tray, The Invitation, 13" dia, VG 150.00
Blatz Beer, cast plaster sign, barmaid & steins, 34x19", VG 50.00
Blatz Beer, chalk & plaster display, barmaid figure, 19", G 175.00
Blatz's Brewing, oilette, man & touring car, 1913, 27x35", EX ...400.00
Blue & Gold Beer, stained glass window, 29x152"+fr, VG 3,500.00
Blue & Gold Lager, stained glass window, 28x68"+fr, VG 5,500.00
Bodegas Franco-Espanolas, ts, lady w/wine, 18½x13", G 50.00
Bonnette Coffee, tc, Dutch kids at table, 5¾x4¼" dia, VG 200.00
Bonnie Bro's Distillers, rvpt sign, factory, fr, 34x45", G 900.00

Bonnie Bros. distiller's ad in original frame, 26x21", VG, $400.00.

Boyce Motor Meters, tin sign, meter diecut, 19x12", EX 825.00
Bradford Brewing, tray, girl w/lei, 16½x13½", VG 300.00
Breidt's Beer, tip tray, lady w/roses, 4¼" dia, VG 160.00
Bremig's Oil Paints, ts, painter & weathervane, 28x20", VG ..9,750.00

Bridal Brand Coffee, tc, man w/donkeys & harbor, 1-lb, VG **250.00**
British America Assurance, tin letter folder, 12½x3", EX **525.00**
Broadway Brewing, tray, hand w/axe, 12" dia, EX **250.00**
Brotherhood Tobacco, cb sign, mc products, 25x17½", VG **125.00**
Brown-Forman Distiller's, tray, Suspects..., dog, 13" dia, VG **225.00**
Buckeye Harvester, paper sign, bee w/mechanical parts, 14x11" ..**125.00**
Buffalo Brewing, tray, lady in straw hat, 12" dia, EX **300.00**
Buffalo Scale, wooden sign, wht on blk pnt, hanging, 16x28", G **85.00**
Buick Motor Cars, porc thermometer, ca 1915, 27", EX **275.00**
Bull Durham, paper sign, bull/fighters, fr, 24x35", NM **600.00**
Bull Durham, paper sign, Teaching Time, Giles, 28x22", VG .**1,500.00**
Burger Beer, clock, emb tin w/wooden case, 15x19x2½", G **75.00**
Burger Beer, clock, pnt tin, 14½x19x2½", VG **130.00**
Burger Brewing, tray, card game, post-pro, 15¼x12½", VG **120.00**
Burley Boy, tin lunch box, Wht Man's Hope, 4x6½x5", EX **2,200.00**
Buscsa L'Ours, cb sign, bears & corsets, 16x22", EX **375.00**

Buster Brown

Buster Brown was the creation of cartoonist Richard Felton; his comic strip first appeared in the *New York Herald* on May 4, 1902. Since then Buster and his dog Tige (short for Tiger) have adorned sundry commercial products but are probably best known as the trademark for the Brown Shoe Company established early in this century. Today hundreds of Buster Brown premiums, store articles, and advertising items bring substantial prices from many serious collectors.

Bandana, mc print on linen, 1940s premium, EX **80.00**
Book, Autobiography of BB, premium, illus, Outcault, 1914 ....**95.00**
Comic book, Andy Devine featured, 1940s **45.00**
Cup & saucer **45.00**
Display, plaster, BB & Tige figural, 17x8" dia, VG **650.00**
Display, tin die-cut stand-up figures of BB & Tige, 33", VG ...**3,500.00**
Doll, compo, mk Brownie, Sept 3, 1915, orig clothes, 32", G **300.00**
Hatchet, BB logo, 13", EX **45.00**
Match holder, BB Bread, tin diecut, EX color litho, 7x2", VG ..**1,000.00**
Mirror, hand-held type in wooden fr, decals, 24x16½", EX **100.00**
Patch, felt, BB, early **15.00**
Patch, felt, 1950s, EX **6.50**
Pocket watch, BB Blue Ribbon Shoes, 1925, EX **350.00**
Poster, linen, BB & Tige, Outcault, Selchow, 17x24" **45.00**
Ring, brass, BB **45.00**
Shoe mirror, metal stand w/wood fr, 15x21½", VG **125.00**
Shoe stretcher, BB figural, 1950s **40.00**
Sign, BB Shoes, tin, BB & Tige, 14x20", EX **800.00**
Stockings, wht, orig top & banding labels, VG orig, pr **30.00**
Tin container, All Spice, BB & Tige on paper label, VG **25.00**
Tin container, BB Cigars, 5x5" dia, VG **650.00**
Valentine, BB & Tige, Tuck, 1904, 5½x3½", unused, EX **35.00**
Whistle, wooden, paper label, G **60.00**
Yo-Yo, tin, color litho, EX **30.00**

C.D. Kenny

C.D. Kenny was determined to be a successful man, and he was. Between 1890 and 1934, he owned seventy-five groceries in fifteen states. He realized his success in two ways: fair business dealings and premium giveaways. These ranged from trade cards and advertising mirrors to tin commemorative plates and kitchen items. There were banks and toys, clocks and tins. Today's collectors are finding scores of these items, all carrying Kenny's name.

Coffee bag **6.50**
Funnel **22.00**

Match holder, elephant figural **28.00**
Plate, child in snow scene, tin **85.00**
Plate, Santa & sleeping child, tin, 10" dia, M **175.00**
Stamp holder, cl, Dutch waitresses **15.00**
Tin container, Tea Party scene, oval **150.00**
Tip tray, girl w/roses, Drink & Enjoy..., 1910, EX **50.00**
Tip tray, raising flag **100.00**
Tray, Geo Washington, rnd, sm **45.00**
Tray, girl w/doll w/holly band, 1910, 10" dia, EX **30.00**

Campbell's Tomato Soup, porc corner sign, 1960s, 22½x15", G ..**1,000.00**
Capital City Brewing, stoneware pitcher, bl & gray, 8¾", G **275.00**
Capt Jack Tobacco, tin letter folder, 9½x3", G **175.00**
Carhartt's Clothing, porc corner sign, 38x23x5½", EX **750.00**
Carter's Inks, oak & glass showcase w/decals, 11x22x14", VG ...**350.00**
Carter's Inks, ts, man at desk, ca 1900, 25x18½", VG **600.00**
Casey & Kelly Beer, tray, King Gambrinus, 13¼" dia, G **250.00**
Casey & Kelly Beer, tray, lady's portrait, 17x14", EX **375.00**
Catlin's Smoking Tobacco, paper sign, hissing cat, 9x12", VG ..**450.00**
Cellarmaster, painting on leather, monk w/glass, 24" dia, G **50.00**
Centlivre Brewing, street & river scenes/factory, 24x38", NM ...**275.00**
Central Beer, cased glass sign, 28½x76½"+orig fr, VG **500.00**
Central Brewing, tray, factory/harbor, 13¾x16¾", EX **700.00**
Central Nat'l Insurance, wood sign, 22x16"+fr, EX **600.00**
Champion Brewery, tray, girl w/wht veil, 16¾" oval, VG **145.00**
Champion Spark Plugs, plastic radio, plug figural, 14½", VG **295.00**
Champion Spark Plugs, tin thermometer, yel/blk/wht, 14", EX ..**600.00**
Chas A Grove's Son's Whiskey, ts, dogs smoking, 14" sq, EX **450.00**
Chas A Grove's Whiskey, tray, Indian/horse/buffalo, 13" sq, VG ..**625.00**
Chas D Kaier, paper sign, girl in oval, 23x17"+fr, VG **700.00**
Chevrolet Trucks, cb sign, mc trucks on creme, 42x63", EX **300.00**
Chrysler Motor Cars, porc sign, 2-sided, 24x35", VG **250.00**
Clark's Peanut Butter, pail, hunter & Indian, 3¾" dia, VG **550.00**
Cleveland & Sandusky Brewing, tray, factory, 14" dia, G **150.00**
Clinton Brewing, tray, 'Bertha' girl w/glass, 13¼" sq, EX **175.00**
Clysmic Waters, tray, bare-chested lady, 13¼x10½", EX **175.00**
Cold Spring Brewing, cloth banner, attached 1898 calendar, 24", EX ..**125.00**
Columbia Beer, tray, Bavarian man w/flagon, 16¾x13½", G **220.00**

Columbia Export Beer, tin litho tray, Henry Weinhard City Brewery, Kaufman & Strauss, 13⅜x16¼", EX, $500.00.

Columbia Brewing, cl pocket mirror, 2¾x1¾", VG **150.00**
Columbia Brewing, oak beer keg, 22x12" dia, EX **100.00**
Columbia Brewing, vitrolite corner sign, patriotic, 18x23", VG .**6,500.00**
Columbus Dispatch, porc thermometer, orange/blk, 27", EX **200.00**

Consumers' Brewing, reverse-grasp labeled mug, 10x7x6", G ..4,500.00
Converse Shoes, cb display, tennis couple, 26x30", VG 300.00
Cook's Beer, ts, lady in red on blk ground, 37x20", G 200.00
Cook's Beer, ts, river boat/dock scene, 22x28", G 115.00
Cook's Water, emb cb sign, lady, She Drinks..., 24x12", NM ..2,750.00
Cooper Tires, tin sign, knight's hat, mc on bl, 15x23", EX 100.00
Cortez Cigars, die-cut ts, girl w/cigars, 1915, 12x16½", EX 500.00
CPF Meerschaum & Briar Pipes, sf ts, smoker, 17x20", G 50.00
Crack-a-Jack Clothes, flanged ts, delivery man, 14x18", EX ...1,950.00
Crisco, porc sign, can shape, Better Than Butter, 20x14", VG ..1,250.00
Crown Brewing, cb diecut, ram w/red jacket, 14x14", EX 1,100.00
Crystal Spring Brewing, stoneware match striker, 5x6¼", EX 300.00
Cumberland Brewing, litho/wood sign, 2 men in car, 16x24", VG .700.00
Daeuffer's Beer, emb & rvpt glass display light, 15" dia, G 100.00
Daeuffer's Beer, porc sign, red/yel/blk shield, 19" dia, EX 225.00
Dallas Engineering Corp, airplane-shaped fan, 1930s, 28", G 300.00
Dazey Butter Churns, cb diecut, lady at churn, 22x27", VG 185.00
De Laval, cloth banner, girl/separator, bl/yel/wht, 8x36", G 170.00
De Laval, flanged porc sign, separator, 27x18", VG 350.00
De Laval, paper sign, girl w/feathered hat, metal fr, 18x14", VG .625.00
De Laval, presentation medallion, 1883-1908, silver, 2" dia, G 45.00
De Laval, ts, counter stand-up type, 19½x13½", VG 500.00
De Laval, ts, lady/boy/calves, rolled edge, 25" dia, G 650.00
Delco Batteries, tin sign, 3-color, 22x30", EX 160.00
Deppen Brewing, rvpt corner sign, elk, copper fr, 13x25", NM ..800.00
Deppen Brewing, wood sign, paper litho, 20x28", G 750.00
Derby Tobacco, emb cb sign, horse/jockey, 23x18"+fr, EX 4,500.00
Diamond Dyes, cabinet, baby in oval, 19x15½x9", G 750.00
Diamond Dyes, cabinet, blond & gold fairy in garden, 31", VG .1,100.00
Diamond Dyes, cabinet, child in oval, 20x16x18", G 450.00
Diamond Dyes, cabinet, children w/balloon, 24½", VG 650.00
Diamond Dyes, cabinet, court jester, 27½x20½x9½", EX 950.00
Diamond Dyes, cabinet, evolution of woman, 30x22½x10", EX .1,050.00
Diamond Dyes, cabinet, evolution of woman, 30x22½x12", VG ..950.00
Diamond Dyes, cabinet, girl w/Kodak/children, 30", G 600.00
Diamond Dyes, cabinet, washer woman, 30x22x10", G 1,000.00
Diamond Dyes, children w/maypole, 30x22½x11", EX 1,350.00
Diamond Wedding Rye, ts, lady w/shot, 12" dia, VG 300.00
Dixon's Pencils, paper sign, lady artist, 29x13", VG 300.00
Dixon's Stove Polish, paper sign, girl in gr, 29x13", VG 150.00
Doan's Pills, thermometer, wooden diecut, worn pnt, 21x5", G ...95.00
Dobler Brewing, gray, horse-drawn wagons, 18½x15¼", G 70.00
Dodge Job-Rated Trucks, metal clipboard, mc pnt, 1940s, 5½", EX .25.00
Dr Daniel's Vet Medicines, Dr w/products, 28½", EX 1,100.00
Dr McNunn's Elixer, paper sign, sick lady/workers, 14x10", EX ..1,000.00
Dr Morse's Indian Root Pills, cb diecut, 5-pc, 27x42", VG 375.00

Dr. Pepper

A young pharmacist, Charles C. Alderton, was hired by W.B. Morrison, owner of Morrison's Old Corner Drug Store in Waco, Texas, around 1884. Alderton, an observant sort, noticed that the drugstore's patrons could never quite make up their minds as to which flavor of extract to order. He concocted a formula that combined many flavors, and Dr. Pepper was born. The name was chosen by Morrison in honor of a beautiful young girl with whom he had once been in love. The girl's father, a Virginia doctor by the name of Pepper, had discouraged the relationship due to their youth, but Morrison had never forgotten her. On December 1, 1885, a U.S. patent was issued to the creators of Dr. Pepper.

Bottle, seltzer; Cheerio-Memphis 165.00
Can, cone top, 1940-50s, 12-oz, G 90.00
Can, cone top, 6-oz, rare, EX 150.00

Clock, light-up, rnd, w/brick wall, 1940s 350.00
Clock, Mountain Herbs, sales presentation, 1982, M 375.00
Dish, cb, dbl-sided, 1950s, EX 75.00
Dispenser, syrup; gr w/NP spigot, 16", G 85.00
Door pull, metal bottle form, EX pnt 50.00
Glass, flared w/1st logo (script), 6", EX 1,700.00
Menu board, tin, Dr Pepper logo along top, vertical, EX 40.00
Pedal car, 1950s, EX 425.00
Radio, wooden cooler shape, 8½x12x8", working, EX 1,200.00
Sign, porc, wht/blk/gr, 27" L, VG 140.00
Sign, tin, convex, 1950s 95.00
Sign, tin, cut-out cap, 28", NM 55.00
Syrup dispenser, urn shape on glass ped, 18x9" dia, VG 7,500.00
Thermometer, rnd, Hot/Cold 90.00
Thermometer, tin, bottle shape, early, 26", NM 160.00
Watch fob, Billiken, brass, EX 120.00

Duesseldorfer Beer, tray, baby beside bird, 21" dia, G 100.00
Duffy Trowbridge Stoves, ts, pig trademark, Shonk, 17x24", VG .550.00
DuPont Denatured Alcohol, tin thermometer, mc, 39", EX 75.00
Dutch Boy Paints, flanged porc sign, 2-sided, 21x14", G 200.00
E Robinson's Sons Beer, tin tray, factory, 13½" dia, NM 450.00
Early Times Distillery, tin charger, bkwoods scene, 24" dia, G ...500.00
Ebbert Wagons, ts, farmer & girl w/apples, 26x38", VG 800.00
Ebling Brewing, tray, factory scene, Shonk, 15¼x18½", EX 1,150.00
Eckart Bro's Brewery, tin/rvpt sign, eagle/world, 24x18", EX 750.00
Edelweiss Beer, stained glass window, fr, 33½x37", EX 3,500.00
Edison Mazda lamps, glass & metal display for bulbs, 13x21x7" .375.00
Electric Auto-Lite Service, porc sign, mc, 26x36", EX 150.00
Emmerling's Brewing, ts, Bavarian couple dine, 1913, 19x27", EX .400.00
Enterprise Brewing, tray, Bavarian man w/glass, 13½x16½", VG ..300.00
Enterprise Brewing, tray, girl w/flower, 1905, 13¼" dia, G 150.00
Eshelman Red Rose Dog & Puppy Food, ts, bag/dog, 36x18", G ...35.00
Eskimo Smoking Tobacco, tc, gold letters on brn, 6", VG 75.00
Esso, plastic shakers, red & wht w/decals, 2¾", pr, EX 20.00
Eureka Harness Oil, ts, red/bl letters on wht, 19x13", G 40.00
Ever-Ready, clock, man w/foamy beard, pendulum, 28", VG ..2,900.00
Ever-Ready, clock, man w/foamy beard, 22x18x4", G 1,000.00
Ever-Ready Batteries, tin display case, 16x9½x11½", G 25.00
Falstaff Beer, sf ts, Peacemaker, 22½x30½", EX 2,000.00
Fashion Cut Plug, lunch bin, couple in auto, 4¼x7¾x5¼", G 150.00
Fecker Beer, tray, beer maid w/growler, 13¼x10½", G 45.00
Fehr's Malt Tonic, sf ts, topless lady, 28x22", EX 1,500.00
Ferdeffinger's Brewing, sf ts, card players, 15x18", EX 400.00
Fern Glen Rye, ts, Blk man w/melon & chicken, 35x23", VG ..1,800.00
Fink Brewing, tray, man pouring, 1913, 16x12½", G 65.00

Ferris Waists, self-framed tin litho sign, sepia-toned domestic scene, Beach Art, ca 1900, 22x16", VG, $800.00.

Fisk Tires, wooden sign, sand finish, 47x31", VG 425.00
Flanagan-Nay Beer, ts, man in overalls, 16½" dia+fr, VG 225.00
Ford, cb display w/neon fr, 1947 car, working, 19x16x6", VG 225.00
Ford Economy Trucks, silk banner w/fringe, 48x39", EX 65.00
Foster Hose, cl sign, lady & buckles, 17x9", EX 275.00
Fox Valley Brewing, pocket watch, Ingersoll, 2½x1¾", VG 250.00
Frank Jones Brewing, paper sign, factory scene, 30x40", G 700.00
Frank Jones Brewing, ts, factory scene, EX color, 30x42", VG ...2,050.00
Freeman Headbolt Engine Heaters, tin thermometer, 15", EX 80.00
French Line, sf ts, ocean liner, 25x37", VG 300.00
Ft Pitt Beer, light-up sign, gr & frosted glass, 7x25x2¾", EX 200.00
Gambrinus Brewery, stained glass window, king/glass, 45x84" ...5,500.00
Gamy Race Cars, print, drivers w/early cars, 23x39", NM 350.00
Garrett's Baker Rye, cl pocket mirror, nude, 2¾x1¾", NM 200.00
Genesee Brewing, tray, 2 Indian ladies/canoe, early, 12" dia, G .135.00
GF Burkhard's Lager Beer, ts, Wells & Hope, early, 17x14", EX ...550.00
Gilbert Rae's Aerated Waters, ts, mc factory scene, 28x20", EX .600.00
Gillette, die-cut ts, 2-sided, 15x13½", EX 2,750.00
Globe Brewing, paper sign, nymph/3 ogling faces, 25x18", G .1,250.00
Globe Tobacco Express, tc, train engine & cars, 8¼" dia, G 350.00
Gluek Brewing, copper-clad corner sign, 24x18", NM 850.00
Goebel Beer, tray, Bavarian man w/product, 12" dia, G 200.00

Gold Dust, embossed tin sign, EX color, minor dents, 19x13½", $650.00.

Gold Medal Motor Oils, metal thermometer, mc, 9⅛" dia, EX ..180.00
Golden Rod Coffee, tc, paper litho, letters/warehouse, 5", G 65.00
Goodyear Tires, porc flange sign, tire/winged shoe, 43x21", G ...600.00
Goodyear Tires, rvpt sign, lights up, wood fr, 8x25", VG 55.00
Great Square Whiskey, tray, bulldog, 13¼x13¼", EX 200.00
Great Western Champagne, ts, bottle form, hangs, 19x13", NM ..300.00
Green River Whiskey, cb sign, Blk man w/mule, 24x15"+fr, VG .25.00
Green River Whiskey, cb sign, Blk man w/mule, 25x20", G 70.00
Green River Whiskey, tray, Blk man w/mule, 12" dia, EX 275.00
Green River Whiskey, ts, Blk man w/mule, fr, 24x33", G 225.00
Green River Whiskey, ts, Blk man w/mule, 31x40½", VG 375.00
Gulf, tin thermometer, wht/blk/brn, 26½x7½", NM 240.00
Gulfpride Aviation, tc, bl/wht/orange, 1-qt, 5½", EX 90.00
Gund's Brewing, cb sign, pioneer family, 14x28"+fr, G 300.00
Gunther's Beer, glass globe, rvpt mc logos, 17x15" dia, EX 1,800.00
Haas Brewing, stained glass transom window, fr, 10x59", G 400.00
Hanley Brewing, photograph, horse-drawn beer wagon, 12x20", G ..85.00
Hanover Whiskey, sf ts, Blk boy & horse's head, 28x39", VG 400.00
Harvard Pure Rye, ts, graduates, bright color, 18x12", EX 400.00
Hastings Oil Filters, cb display, mc, 16" H, EX 55.00
Heinz's Pickling Vinegar, glass jar, 6-sided, emb logo, 12", EX ...225.00
Henry Johnson & Lord Medicine, ts, packages/bottles, 20x14", G .500.00
Hero Coffee, tc, 5 heroes, wood lid, octagonal, 1-lb, VG 170.00
Heurich Brewing, ts, button type w/emb border, 17" dia, G 50.00
HH Carr & Co, wooden sign, I Ship to Chicago, 12x28", G 100.00

Hires

Charles E. Hires, a drugstore owner in Philadelphia, became interested in natural teas. He began experimenting with roots and herbs and soon developed his own special formula. Hires introduced his product to his own patrons and began selling concentrated syrup to other soda fountains and grocery stores. Samples of his 'root beer' were offered for the public's approval at the 1876 Philadelphia Centennial. Today's collectors are often able to date their advertising items by observing the Hires boy on the logo. From 1891 to 1906, he wore a dress. From 1906 until 1914, he was shown in a bathrobe; and from 1915 until 1926, he was depicted in a dinner jacket. The apostrophe may or may not appear in the Hires name; this seems to have no bearing on dating an item.

Bottle, syrup; paper label, w/measuring cap, 12", EX 425.00
Buckle, belt; Drink Hires Root Beer, EX 6.50
Checkerboard, Exhilarating..., Hires boy, blk/yel, 12", VG 350.00
Dispenser, syrup; urn shape, boy w/mug etc, 19x10½", VG ...22,500.00
Dispenser, syrup; w/pump, 12½", EX 150.00
Display, cb diecut, baby crawling, 2-pc, 14x11", G 150.00
Mug, ceramic, boy lifts mug, Mettlach, EX 165.00
Mug, Join Health & Cheer, boy w/mug, Villeroy & Boch, 5", VG ..400.00
Opener, over-the-top, NM 15.00
Punch bowl, ceramic, boy w/mug, Villeroy & Boch, 12x17½", VG .20,000.00
Sign, cb diecut w/easel bk, boy w/package, 1892, 7x5", NM 150.00
Sign, paper, lady in wicker chair, 10½x20", VG 110.00
Sign, paper, 2 men, I Like It..., 1890s, fr, 14x17", EX 2,250.00
Sign, tin, boy points & holds mug, 28x20", G 2,700.00
Sign, tin, girl w/glass, EX color, 19½x13½", VG 500.00
Tire cover, canvas, for spare, 29" dia, EX 225.00
Tray, lady in oval, 13x11", VG 85.00

Hoem Brewing, paper sign, lady, 1903, 29x23", G 350.00
Hohner Harmonicas, cb diecut, boy/25¢ harmonicas, 31x15", VG .300.00
Home Brewing, tin & glass corner sign, early, 16x21", EX 800.00
Honey Moon Tobacco, pocket tin, upright, red, 4½x3x1", VG ..200.00
Hood Tires, wooden thermometer, mc pnt, 15x4", EX 265.00
Hoody's Peanut Butter, tin pail, teeter-totter, 4x3½", VG 125.00
Hoosac Tunnel, paper sign, trains, King litho, 20x23", G 600.00
Horlacher Brewing, cb sign, 2 gnomes w/bbl, 1940s, 24x19", VG .135.00
Hoster's Beer, cb sign, bottle, hanging, 10½x13½", VG 110.00
Hoster's Beer, charger, Something To Crow About, 24" dia, G ..375.00
Hoster's Beer, ts, monks & bbls, 16½x19½"+oval fr, G 290.00
Hubbard's Fertilizers, porc sign, bl & wht, 10x20", EX 35.00
Hudepohl Brewing, sf ts, man w/pipe & bottle, 19x15", VG 110.00
Hudepohl Brewing, vitrolite corner sign, deer, 18x23", EX 1,000.00
Hudson Rambler Sales Service, porc sign, 2-sided, 30x42", EX ..475.00
Illinois Watch Co, ts, Wells & Hope factory, 32x40", G 400.00
Independent Brewing, stoneware pitcher, mc transfer, 12", VG .150.00
Independent Gasoline, porc sign, 2-sided, 30" dia, VG 200.00
Indian Gasoline, porc sign, tepees, 1940, 18x12", VG 155.00
Iron City Brewing, tray, barmaid & shots, 13" dia, VG 75.00
Ivory Soap, cb sign, Busy Day, girl/doll's clothes, 25x17", G 450.00
IW Harper Whiskey, vitrolite sign, men/cabin/dog, 24x18", EX ..900.00
J Widman & Co, tray, Carnation Girl, 13" dia, VG 295.00
J&P Coats, display cabinet, metal & glass, 7x15x10", G 25.00
Jacob Schmidt Brewing, ts, factory & street scene, 28x40", G 600.00
Jap Rose Soap, tin display, 2 children w/soap, 14x18", EX 950.00
Jefferson Brewing..., sf ts, Shakespearean man, 24x18", VG 350.00
John Arnold Brewery, ts, bulldog, 13¼x10¼", VG 250.00
John Deere Farm Implements, porc sign, 2-sided, 24x72", EX 875.00
John Kazmaier, tray, monks playing cards, 16¾x13¾", G 600.00
Jos Schlitz Brewing, ts, factory/portrait, early, 18x15", G 200.00

Justin Gates, cb sign, druggist in gold fields, 21x19", EX 200.00
Kaier's Brewing, tin plate, lady, Vienna Art, 10" dia, VG 75.00
Kaier's Brewing, tray, baby in reserve, 16¾x13½", G 380.00
Kaier's Brewing, tray, girl & horses, 16½" oval, VG 150.00
Kanotex Oil, blimp figural display, electrified, 40" L, VG 600.00
Kansas City Breweries, cl pocket mirror, 2¾x1¾", EX 185.00
Keeley Brewing, tray, Colonials at table, 13" dia, VG 475.00
Kellogg's, cb display, Sweetheart of Corn, 45x21x4", VG 160.00
Kellogg's Corn Flakes, cb diecut, girl w/box, 45x22", G 200.00
Kelly Tires, porc sign, mc, lady in car, 42" dia, EX 8,500.00
Kendall Motor Oil, tc, red/wht/bl, 5-qt, 9½", VG 25.00
Kickapoo Indian Remedies, paper sign, Indian, 24x18", G 2,400.00
Klein Bros Distillers, ts, graduates/ladies, 18x24", G 150.00
Kling's 1911 Beer, stained glass window, fr, 20x28", VG 575.00
Kramer Service Co, schoolhouse regulator clock, 22", EX 400.00

Kuntz Brewery, tin litho tray, Kaufman & Strauss, 13⅛" diameter, EX, $400.00.

Le Roy Cigars, ts, caballero/package, 15x11"+fr, EX 400.00
Lebanon Brewing, rvpt flat-front corner sign, 16x24", EX 700.00
Lee Tires, rvpt sign, lights up, metal case, 7½x32", EX 135.00
Leisy Brewing, tin tray, street scene, 16½x13½", EX 3,650.00
Lemp's Brewing, sf ts, man w/glass, Orig Falstaff, 23x17", VG 450.00
Lenbeck & Betz Eagle Brewery, lady in red, 1911, 13x10½", EX .450.00
Lewis Bergdoll Brewing, pocket mirror, lady, 2¾x1¾", EX 85.00
Lieberman's Beer, tray, Griselda, 1907, 13¼" sq, G 325.00
Lime Kiln Club, paper sign, Blk men, Calvert, 1892, 24x30", EX .800.00
Lincoln Shock Absorbers, tin sign, ca 1920, 24x18", EX 180.00
Lion Beer, tray, lion & bellow trademk, post-pro, 15" oval, G 35.00
Lion Brewing, stained glass window, fr, 23x23", VG 700.00
Log Cabin Syrup, tc, blacksmith, 33-oz 135.00
Log Cabin Syrup, tc, child in door, 4¾" 110.00
Log Cabin Syrup, tc, dog in door, 12-oz, EX 100.00
Log Cabin Syrup, tc, Dr RU Well, cartoon style, rare 250.00
Log Cabin Syrup, tc, Frontier Inn, cowboys & horse, 5-lb 220.00
Log Cabin Syrup, tc, Frontier Jail, 12-oz 150.00
Log Cabin Syrup, tc, Home Sweet Home, 12-oz 150.00
Log Cabin Syrup, tc, pancakes, VG 15.00
London Assurance, sf ts, London street scene, 22x28", G 350.00
Long Life Motor Oil, tc, bl/wht, ca 1940, 2-gal, 10½", VG 85.00
Los Angeles Brewing, tray, factory, 13¼" dia, G 550.00
Louis Obert Beer, tray, portrait/factory, 12" dia, VG 450.00
Lovell & Covel Candies, tin pail, historic scene, 3x3", VG 150.00
Lovell & Covel Candies, tin pail, Peter Cottontail, 3x3", EX 185.00
Lucky Strike, cb sign, couple, 43x26", VG 350.00
Lucky Strike, cb sign, gr & red package, 1934, 18x14", EX 90.00
Lump Beer, tin charger, Falstaff at table, 24" dia, G 150.00
Luzerne Co Brewing, tray, Gettysburg battlefield, 14x17", EX 500.00
LW Harper Whiskey, oilette, couple/touring car, fr, 34x46", G ..150.00
Lyken's Brewing, tray, girl & horse, oval, 16¾x13¾", EX 250.00
Lyken's Cream Topped Lager, pocket mirror, lady, 2¾", VG 45.00
Mac Nicol's Saloon, tin plate, topless lady, Vienna Art, 10", G .245.00

Magic Gasoline, tin sign, emb letters, mc, 24x18", EX 350.00
Magnolia Gasoline, porc sign, flower, 42" dia, G 240.00
Maltosia Pure Food Beer, tip tray, mc on wht, 5" dia, EX 55.00
Marathon Products, porc sign, gr/blk, 2-sided, 29½", VG 355.00
Marathon Tires, ts, couples in touring car, 23x17", G 100.00
Maryland Club Tobacco, pocket tin, upright, 4x3½", VG 350.00
Mathie Brewing, plate, lady in turban, Vienna Art, '05, 10", VG ..50.00
Mauchchunk Beer, metal-cased neon letter sign, 14x26x7", G ..825.00
Mayo's, clock, drop regulator figure-8, Baird, 30½", G 500.00
Mayo's Cut Plug, canvas banner, mc rooster on plug, 30x18", EX ...85.00
McCormick Brewery, tin charger, lobster, 24" dia, G 150.00
McDonald Corp, plastic clock, Ronald figural, electric, 28", EX ..125.00
Merita Bread, ts, Lone Ranger, 36x24", VG 525.00
Miller Beer, neon sign, script logo, 23x29½x13", EX 225.00
Miller Beer, tin diecut, cowgirl w/bottle, 72x36", G 400.00
Minck Brewing, tray, Beauty Contestant, 17¼x12¼", EX 185.00
Mobilfuel Diesel, porc sign, red horse, 1954, 12x12", EX 275.00
Mobilgas, porc-on-tin thermometer, 1920s, 35", EX 240.00
Mobiloil, cb sign, plane/truck/car, mc, 28x20", G 225.00
Mobiloil, porc sign, flying horse, 70x56x3", VG 500.00
Mobiloil, porc thermometer, wht/red/bl, 23x8", EX 250.00
Mobiloil, weathervane, Pegasus, mc pnt, 24", NM 2,700.00
Mobiloil Marine, porc curb sign top, horse, 31" dia, EX 650.00
Mohawk Gasoline, porc neon sign, 47½" dia, EX 2,500.00
Mohawk Tires, metal sign, 3-color, 17x59", VG 75.00
Morans & Budweister, stained glass saloon doors, 24x24", pr 700.00
Morrison Plows, ts, factory/buggies, 13½x19½", G 55.00
Mount Carmel Beer, tip tray, lady w/roses, 4" dia, VG 200.00

Moxie

The Moxie Company was organized in 1884 by George Archer of Boston, Massachusetts. It was at first touted as a 'nerve food' to improve the appetite, promote restful sleep, and in general to make one 'feel better!' Emphasis was soon shifted, however, to the good taste of the brew, and extensive advertising campaigns rivaling those of such giant competitors as Hires and Coca-Cola resulted in successful marketing through the 1930s. Today the term Moxie has become synonymous with courage and audacity, traits displayed by the company who dared compete with such well-established rivals.

Tin litho sign, brilliant colors, Kaufman & Strauss, framed, 28x20", rare, EX, $13,000.00.

Case, wooden, Crystal Lake Bottling, holds 24 7-oz bottles 17.50
Display, Moxie lady in sailor's hat, cb diecut, 17", EX 175.00
Display, 3-D bottle, wood & composition, 35x11½", VG 950.00
Fan, cb, lady w/full glass, 1920s, 9x8", NM 60.00

Fan, cb, man pointing before burst of rays, 2-sided, 8x7", NM **50.00**
Pin, Moxie girl, 1910, scarce **375.00**
Sign, cb diecut, Frank Archer pointing, 2-sided, 16x16", NM **295.00**
Sign, cb diecut, Ted Williams, 3-D, 14" W, EX **125.00**
Sign, tin, Drink..., red w/yel trim, 19x27", EX **325.00**
Sign, tin, Drink..., 2 emb bottle caps, Moxie Man, 19x27", G **210.00**
Sign, tin, elves w/lg case, Learn To Drink..., horizontal, EX **550.00**
Sign, tin, Moxie girl in Horsemobile, 24x12¾", G **350.00**
Sign, tin, Palmer Cox Brownies, Beach, 14x20", EX **1,300.00**
Spinner, metal diecut, Moxie boy, 2-sided, 1911, EX **625.00**
Tip tray, girl on chair, ...Feeds the Nerves, 6" dia, EX **700.00**
Toy, tin Horsemobile, die-cut horse & rider on wheels, 8x9", EX .**1,700.00**
Wooden nickel, M **2.50**

Mulsified Coconut Oil Shampoo, cb sign, lady, 34x22", VG **120.00**
Munsing Wear, ts, 6 kids in union suits diecut, 17x24", VG ...**1,700.00**
Nash, plastic thermometer, 5-color, 15x7½", EX **20.00**
National Beer, tray, cowboy & horse, 16¼x12¾", G **700.00**
National Brewing, milk glass globe, mc rvpt, 17x15" dia, NM **850.00**
National Brewing, tip tray, golfing man & child, 4¼", VG **260.00**
National Brewing, tip tray, man/dog/gun, 4¼" dia, VG **130.00**
National Brewing, tray, A Good Judge, 13¼" dia, G **75.00**
National Brewing, tray, factory scene, 14x10¼", VG **300.00**

Nichols Kola, embossed tin sign, Parker Metal Decorating Co., Baltimore, 38x15", EX, $75.00.

Niggerhair Tobacco, pail, lady w/rings in nose, 6¾x5½", G **120.00**
No-Wax Gulf Motor Fuel, porc flange sign, 18x18", EX **200.00**
Northpole Tobacco, tin lunch pail, pole/man/bear, 6", VG **300.00**
Nu Grape Soda, ts, bottle, red & bl letters on wht, 31x12", G **30.00**
Oak Motor Oil, porc sign, mc, 2-sided, 17x26", EX **750.00**
Oilzum, tin thermometer, blk/orange, 15x7½", EX **425.00**
Old Coon Whiskey, sf ts, hunters at night, 22x28", EX **650.00**
Old Glory Tobacco, tc, eagle on shield on red, 2½x3½", EX **250.00**
Opia Cigar, tip tray, lady w/in crescent moon, 4¼" dia **100.00**
Otto Huber Brewery, tray, Bavarian scene, 16½x13¾", VG **600.00**
P&O Canton Plows, wooden sign, yel/blk plow scene, 10x10", G .**100.00**
Pabst Beer, leaded glass window, 40x38"+fr, EX **6,500.00**
Pabst Beer, paper sign, horse-drawn beer wagon, 14x30"+fr, G **35.00**
Pabst Beer, tray, factory scene, 12¼x17¼", G **90.00**
Pabst Beer, tray, gnomes & flagons, oval, 18½x15¼", G **85.00**
Pabst Brewing, paper sign, girl w/glass, 26½x19", G **400.00**
Paul Jones Whiskey, ts, Temptation of St Anthony, 14x20", VG .**1,600.00**
Peacemaker Coffee, tc, log cabin form, ca 1915, 27½" L, VG **650.00**
Peerless Dyes, cabinet, Bedouin girl/camels, 32x19x11", G **600.00**

Pennsylvania Dutch Beer, clock, glass/metal, electric, 16" dia **175.00**
Pennzoil, tin thermometer, orange & blk, 12" dia, EX **200.00**
Pennzoil Outboard Motor Oil, metal sign, 2-sided, 12x17", NM ..**120.00**

Pepsi-Cola

Pepsi-Cola was first served in the early 1890s to customers of Caleb D. Bradham, a young pharmacist who touted his concoction to be medicinal as well as delicious. It was first called 'Brad's Drink' but was renamed Pepsi-Cola in 1898.

Apron, Pepsi & Pete w/bold logo & bottle, 1930s, VG **250.00**
Bag rack, tin, Pepsi & Pete, 2-sided, 1930s, 13x23", EX **475.00**
Blotter, Deliciously Delightful, 1905, NM **225.00**
Blotter, Pepsi & Pete, 1939, EX **75.00**
Booklet, 38th Anniversary, bottle on front, 1938, EX **90.00**
Bottle, amber glass, str sides, Birmingham AL, NM **55.00**
Bottle, clear glass, paper label, 1950s, 1-qt, EX **95.00**
Bottle, inflatable plastic, 1970s, 66", NM **35.00**
Bottle, seltzer; amber glass, Jacksonville FL, NM **900.00**
Bottle, seltzer; bl glass, ABC Beverage Co, VG **30.00**
Bottle, seltzer; gr glass, Durham NC, EX **100.00**
Bottle opener, celluloid hdl, yel w/bottle logo, 1940s, NM **45.00**
Bottle opener, Drink of Friendship, emb/enameled, 1950s, EX **50.00**
Bottle opener, flat type, 5¢ & logo, 1930s, NM **35.00**
Bottle opener, When Thirsty Try a Bottle, EX patina, 1910-20 ...**80.00**
Bottle opener, wooden hdl, ca 1970s, NM **30.00**
Calendar, lady w/flowers, Armstrong, full pad, '21, 14x25", EX .**2,100.00**
Calendar, lady w/glass by table, full pad, '09, 18½x9½", EX **1,400.00**
Calendar, 6 pgs: 2 months ea page, 13x22", 1950, EX **175.00**
Can, 1976 Bicentennial, cone top, NM **22.00**
Can, 5-bottle cap logo, cone top, 1940s, 12-oz, G **400.00**
Can, 75th Anniversary, musical, 1973, MIB **35.00**
Charm, cap logo & key, 1950s, NM **70.00**
Cigarette lighter, desk type, Lucite, bottle cap,'40s, EX **100.00**
Cigarette lighter, musical, 1950s, NM **130.00**
Clock, bottle cap, yel face, lights up, 1950s, 15" dia, EX **275.00**
Clock, neon, ca 1930, 18" sq, VG **700.00**
Clock, neon w/rvpt glass face, 1930s, 12x16", EX **1,600.00**
Clock, plastic, lights up, caps at numerals, 1951, EX **180.00**
Clock, plastic face w/masonite fr & body, 1945, 14" sq, EX **230.00**
Clock, 3-D plastic bottle cap, lights up, 1950s, 12" dia, EX **140.00**
Coupon, free glass, ca 1910, EX **290.00**
Cup holder, Bakelite, decal ea side, NM **125.00**
Dispenser, china, decor ca 1900-05, EX **6,500.00**
Display, 3-D cb diecut, girl at party, 1950s, 20x18", VG **45.00**
Door pull, metal, Bigger Better, 1940s, NM **125.00**
Fan, cb, Pepsi & Pete on bk, 1940, NM **75.00**
Fan, cb w/wooden hdl, girl w/bottle, 1912, G **500.00**
Fan, paper w/rattan hdl, child w/glass, 1905, NM **1,350.00**
Fountain pen, red/wht/bl, 1930s, NM **45.00**
Hat, soda jerk, yel & red oilcloth, 1930s-40s, VG **80.00**
Jug, syrup; ca 1910-15, 1-gal, NM **500.00**
Lamp shade, stained glass, ca 1970s, NM **95.00**
Menu board, tin, bottle cap logo, 1940s, 27x18½", NM **275.00**
Menu board, wood, ...Goes Great w/Sandwich, 1930s, 24x12", EX .**325.00**
Mirror sign, Have a Pepsi...Light Refreshment, VG **35.00**
Napkin, Pepsi-Cola in yel embr on linen, EX **40.00**
Note pad, w/calendar on bk, 1914, EX **30.00**
Note pad, w/1920-21 calendar inside bk cover, NM **75.00**
Pencil clip, celluloid button, 1940s, EX **15.00**
Plate, 85th Anniversary, Gibson girl, Lenox china, NMIB **75.00**
Pocket mirror, Lillian Russell-type girl, 2¾x1¾", EX **2,750.00**
Poster, cb, Drink...The American Beverage, 1907, 16x24", EX .**8,500.00**

Radio, bl plastic fountain dispenser form, 1964, EX **275.00**
Radio, dispenser-type transistor, leather case, 1964, 7", NM **250.00**
Radio, plastic, bl cooler, 1955, NM **300.00**
Radio, plastic, can form, 1970s, 5", NM **20.00**
Radio, plastic floor-cooler style, electric, 1967, NM **275.00**
Register topper, Please...Don't Forget..., 1940s, VG **275.00**
Shakers, bottle form, 1940s souvenir, MIB, pr **125.00**
Sign, aluminum & litho, Swing Is To..., 1930s, 26x20", VG **350.00**
Sign, cb, couple swimming, 1940s, 26x18", VG **150.00**
Sign, cb, Gibson girl, 1909, 24½x20", VG **600.00**
Sign, cb, girl at beach, 1941, 26x18", VG **325.00**
Sign, cb, girl at table w/bottle & glass, 1910-15, 30x20", VG ..**1,050.00**
Sign, cb, girl in garden, Bottle 5 Cents, 1942, 35x28", VG **400.00**
Sign, cb, girl w/bottle & straw, 1910-15, 24x18", VG **1,000.00**
Sign, cb, girl w/magazine, Light Refreshment, '54, 28x11", VG .**125.00**
Sign, cb, Miss Pepsi-Cola, 1905, 21x27", EX **1,000.00**
Sign, cb, Pepsi's Best, Take No Less, 1949, 24x36", EX **125.00**
Sign, cb, sf, beach girl w/cooler & bottles, 1930s, 29x41", EX **255.00**
Sign, cb, sf, girl in bl w/tan hat, 1940s, 31x24", VG **350.00**
Sign, cb, sf, lady by water, Erbit, 1940s, 31x24", EX **500.00**
Sign, cb, sf, lady in red/wht/bl, 1940s, 31x24", EX **500.00**
Sign, cb, vertical bottle, 1930s, 15x18", NM **180.00**
Sign, cb diecut, bottle, Five Cents, easel bk, 1936, 16", EX **400.00**
Sign, cb diecut, flowers & logo, 1920s-30s, 22x40", G **175.00**
Sign, cb diecut, girl on beach, Pepsi & Pete, 1930s, 40x29", EX .**2,500.00**
Sign, cb diecut, girl on case, 1917, 34x20", VG **3,500.00**
Sign, cb diecut, tennis girl, 1950s, 22x16", NM **150.00**
Sign, cl, bottle cap, 1950s, 9" dia, EX **90.00**
Sign, cl, Drink...Now, red/wht/bl, 1940s, VG **250.00**
Sign, cl, Ice Cold Sold Here, 1940s, 9", EX **260.00**
Sign, cl, More Bounce to the Ounce, 1940s-50s, 9", VG **100.00**
Sign, metal strip, Drink...Bigger & Better, 1x15", EX **50.00**
Sign, porc, dbl dot, 5¢ drink, red/wht/bl, 1940s, 10x30", VG **450.00**
Sign, tin, bottle cap, 1950s, 18" dia, NM **200.00**
Sign, tin, dbl dot, red/gr/yel, Canadians, 1940s, 18x28", VG **300.00**
Sign, tin, die-cut bottle form, 1940s, 45" H, VG **400.00**
Sign, tin, emb bottle cap, 1950s, 18" dia, NM **230.00**
Sign, tin, flanged, Ice Cold Sold Here, 2-sided, 1940s, NM **375.00**
Sign, tin, ribbon & cap logo, 1950s, 27x31", EX **160.00**
Sign, tin, sf, lady w/glass, Shonk litho, '08, 10½x8½", EX **4,000.00**
Sign, tin, vertical bottle, ca 1910-15, 39x13", NM **1,800.00**
Spoon holder, stoneware, w/lid, 1930s-40s, 6", VG **275.00**
Straw holder, stainless steel, ca 1930s, 4x4", VG **180.00**
Straw holder, tin litho, 4-sided, ca 1900s, 6x3x3", EX **6,000.00**
Tap knob, silver w/colored label under plastic, '40s, 12", VG **475.00**
Tape measure, bl & silver, 1950s-60s, EX **30.00**
Thermometer, emb cap logo at bottom, 1950s, EX **100.00**
Thermometer, girl w/straw out of bottle, 1940s, NM **375.00**
Thermometer, glass front, 1951, 12" dia, NM **175.00**
Thermometer, rvpt glass mirrored wall type, '30s, 24x10", NM .**1,000.00**
Thermometer, tin corner type, 1940s, 16x2", NM **100.00**
Tip tray, Gibson girl in soda fountain, 1909, NM **800.00**
Tip tray, lady w/glass, Healthful..., 1910, NM **950.00**
Tip tray, lady w/glass, 1908, NM **2,500.00**
Tip tray, red & gold logo, horizontal, 1906, NM **1,150.00**
Toy truck, compo, Buddy-L, Ry Express decals, 1943, VG **1,500.00**
Toy truck, Fisher-Price look-alike, Hong Kong, 1970s, 5", NM **30.00**
Toy truck, heavy tin, Ny-Lint, EX decals, 1958, 16", NM **175.00**
Toy truck, metal, Tonka, 1978, 8", NMIB....................................**75.00**
Toy truck, plastic, Marx, 1950s-60s, 10", NMIB **350.00**
Toy truck, plastic w/tin litho racks, Marx, 7", NM **325.00**
Toy truck, steel w/open carriers, ca 1950s-60s, 2", EX **85.00**
Toy truck, tin, friction, Lt Refreshment, Japan, 6½", NMIB **500.00**
Toy truck, Tomica, yel, 1947, 2", NM **65.00**

Tray, Enjoy...Hits the Spot, 1940, EX **90.00**
Tray, Hits the Spot, 12 Full ounces, cartoon scene, 1940s, NM **50.00**
Watch fob, capitol building & logo, brass, EX **180.00**
Watch fob, capitol building & logo, silver on brass, EX **300.00**
Watch fob, Delicious, Healthful, enameled, lt wear **200.00**
Watch fob, John Smith & Pocahontas, nickel, ca 1900-05, EX **90.00**
Watch fob, John Smith & Pocahontas, pewter, ca 1900-05, EX ...**85.00**

Perfection Dyes, cb sign, Tuchfarber, early, 13½x9½", EX **50.00**
Perma-Lift Plasters, display, figural corset, 19x25x5½", VG **60.00**
Permit Cigars, cb sign, lady w/match, 28x22"+fr, G **200.00**
Perry Davis' Pain Killer, ts, workers, 18x54", G **1,600.00**
Peter Schoenhofen Brewing, tray, smiling lady, 13" dia, VG **80.00**
Phillip Morris, ts, bellboy calling, 46x16", VG **275.00**
Phillips 66 Ethyl, porc sign, yel/blk/wht, 2-sided, 30" dia, VG **350.00**
Pickwick Ale, sf ts, 3 men at table, 28½x22¼", EX **425.00**
Pierce Oil Corporation, tc, bl/creme, 1920s, ½-gal, VG **75.00**
Pillsbury's Best Feed, ts, red/bl letters on wht, 18x18", EX **30.00**

Planters Peanuts

Mr. Peanut, the dashing peanut man with the top hat, spats, monocle, and cane, has represented the Planters Peanut Company from 1916 to 1961 when the company was purchased by Standard Brands. He promoted the company's product by appearing on premium giveaways, store displays, jars, scales, and in special promotional events. Among the favored treasures of collectors today are the glass display jars. They come in a variety of styles. Some are square, some hexagonal, some barrel-shaped, and others are round. The earliest, issued in 1926, was octagonal and is usually referred to as the 'pennant' jar. Although later reproduced, these are marked 'Made in Italy' on the bottom. The original is embossed on the back panel 'Sold Only in Printed Planters Red Pennant Bags.' In a second octagonal style, this embossed message was replaced with a paper label.

In 1930 a 'fishbowl' jar was introduced, and in 1932 a 'four-corner peanut' jar was issued. The rarest jar of all, the 'football' jar, was also used during the early 1930s. The Planters square jar followed in the 1930s and was replaced by the 'barrel' jar. The six-sided jar with Mr. Peanut decals and the 'pickle' jar were later. All in all, more than fifteen different styles were developed.

In the late 1930s, premiums such as glass and metal figural paperweights, pens, and pencils were distributed. Postwar items were often made of plastic; Mr. Peanut salt and pepper shakers, mugs, and banks were popular. Today's collectors find a treasure trove of advertising memorabilia depicting that debonair gentleman, Mr. Peanut.

Ad, Ladies' Home Journal, Just Look at..., 1919, 10x15" **8.00**
Ad, Saturday Evening Post, Most Popular Nut..., 1929, 10x14" **8.00**
Ashtray, Mr Peanut beside shell tray, bsk, 3x4½", EX **120.00**
Bank, Mr Peanut, pnt CI, recent repro, 8", M **15.00**
Bank, Mr Peanut figural, plastic, NM **15.00**
Blinker, Mr Peanut figural, electrified, 24x8", EX **4,500.00**
Buckle, Mr Peanut figural, metal, EX **20.00**
Car, Mr Peanut driving peanut-shaped car, plastic, 2½x5", EX ..**500.00**
Coin, ltd ed commemorative, Mr Peanut, silver, 1991, 2¼" **55.00**
Coin, Mr Peanut, 1980 Winter Olympics, silver-tone metal, M ...**15.00**
Coloring book, Mr Peanut & Smokey Bear, 1973, M **20.00**
Costume, Mr Peanut, fiberglass, top hat & monocle, 20x50" dia ..**475.00**
Display, Cocktail Peanuts can, cb w/plastic lid, 11x13" dia **25.00**
Display, Mr Peanut, cb, 11¾", EX **12.50**
Divet fixer, Mr Peanut, w/ball marker & tee set, M **45.00**
Doll, Mr Peanut, cloth, 19", EX **18.00**
Doll, Mr Peanut, pnt wood, jtd, 9", VG **155.00**

Figurine, Mr Peanut w/tray, bsk, Japan, 1930s, 4" 120.00
Golf balls, Spalding, box of 3, M 18.00
Jar, Barrel, running Mr Peanut, paper label 275.00
Jar, Chocolate-covered cashews, paper label, 1944, 4½-oz 25.00
Jar, Clipper, orig lid 150.00
Jar, Fish Bowl, rectangular label 150.00
Jar, Fish Bowl, sq paper label 150.00
Jar, Football, peanut finial 300.00
Jar, Leap Year, orig lid 50.00
Jar, mixed nuts, paper label, orig lid, 1940s, 4½-oz 15.00
Jar, octagon, pennant 5¢, 7 sides emb 250.00
Jar, octagon, Pennant 5¢, 8 sides emb 800.00
Jar, peanut butter, early Mr Peanut on tin lid, scarce 25.00
Jar, Pennant 5¢, paper label 175.00
Jar, Please Keep, Mr Peanut, 1930s 65.00
Jar, rnd, frosted label, big knob 45.00
Jar, running peanut, worn silver paint, w/lid, 12x8" dia, VG 250.00

Jar, square, peanut finial, Planters embossed each side, $150.00.

Jar, Streamline, tin lid 65.00
Jar, 4-corner, lg blown-out peanut ea corner, M 300.00
Jar, 6-sided, printed sq label 60.00
Key chain charm, Mr Peanut, 2¼" 5.00
Mechanical pencil, Mr Peanut, EX 40.00
Mug, Mr Peanut, pewter type, Wilton, 1983, M 30.00
Nut chopper, fits 8-oz Planters can 20.00

Paint book, Dedicated to the Children of America, VG, $20.00.

Paperweight, pnt metal Mr Peanut form, 7x3", VG 575.00
Peanut butter maker, 1967, MIB 65.00
Peanut butter pail, Mr Peanut, 1-lb, 4x3½" dia, G 600.00
Pin, Planters 50th Anniversary, enamel 18.00
Playing cards, Planters Tavern Nuts, complete, NM 15.00
Pocketknife, Mr Peanut on wht hdl, EX 15.00

Pop gun, fold-up paper, Mr Peanut on grip, 1930s-40s, 8¾", VG .200.00
Radio, Mr Peanut, Cocktail Peanut can figural, M 45.00
Ruler, wooden, Eat a 5 Cent Bag, 12", EX 18.00
Scale, Peanut figural, 45x20x22", EX 16,250.00
Shakers, Mr Peanut figural, ceramic, 4½", pr, VG 65.00
Shakers, Mr Peanut figural, plastic, tan & blk, 4", pr 18.00
Shakers, Mr Peanut figural, silver plastic, 3", pr 12.00
Spoon, Mr Peanut finial hdl, gold wash 24.00
Spreader knife, Mr Peanut, red plastic, 6¾", EX 6.00
Swizzle stick, Mr Peanut, bl plastic 3.00
Tennis balls, Dunlop, can of 3, M 18.00
Tin container, Cocktail Peanuts, vacuum pack, w/lid, 8-oz 12.00
Tin container, peanut oil, 5-gal, 14x9¼" sq, VG, +box 60.00
Whistle, tan plastic, Mr Peanut, 2½" 8.00

Plymouth Brewing & Malting, tray, girl & phone, 13" dia, G 150.00
Prairie Flower Tobacco, ts, Indian maid/braves, 30x28", G 900.00
Pratt's Veterinary, cabinet, horse/listing, 33x17x7½", EX 1,400.00
Prestone Antifreeze, porc-on-metal thermometer, '40s, 36", EX .100.00
Primley's Chewing Gum, cb sign, bear w/gum, 22x13½", VG .3,200.00
Prince Albert, ts, Chief Joseph, Nez Perce, 26x20", EX 1,150.00
Prince Albert, ts, portrait, 25½x19½", VG 950.00
Prize Penn Motor Oil, tc, gold & wht w/red car, 5½x4" dia, EX ...25.00
Pure Premium, porc pump sign, red/wht/bl, 10x12", EX 45.00
Purina Dog Chow, ts, 2-sided, 40x10", G 20.00
Puritan Motor Oil, tin sign, policeman, 11⅛x35", EX 325.00
Purity Kiss, ts, children/wicker chair, hanging, 8" dia, VG 700.00
Purol Pep Oil, porc sign, bl on wht, 15" dia, NM 425.00
Putnam Dyes, tin cabinet, Gen Putnam/Red Coats, 10x21x9", VG .200.00
Quincy Gasoline, porc sign w/CI fr, 2-sided, 48" dia, G 275.00

RCA Victor

Nipper, the RCA Victor trademark, was the creation of Francis Barraud, an English artist. His pet's intent fascination with the music of the phonograph seemed to him a worthy subject for his canvas. Although he failed to find a publishing house who would buy his work, the Gramaphone Co. saw its potential and adopted Nipper to advertise their product. The company eventually became the Victor Talking Machine Co. and was purchased by RCA in 1929. Nipper's image appeared on packaged accessories, in ads and brochures. If you are very lucky you may find a life-size statue of him; but all are not old, they have been reproduced! Except for the years between 1971 and 1981, Nipper has seen active duty, and with his image spruced up only a bit for the present day, the ageless symbol for RCA still listens intently to 'His Master's Voice.'

Doll, Radio man, jtd wood, Maxfield Parrish, M 1,100.00
Figure, Nipper, compo, 11x5x12", G 125.00
Figure, Nipper, papier-mache, old, 41", EX 1,400.00
Figure, Nipper, papier-mache, 40x42x16", G 300.00
Mirror, Right Partner, silk screened, 22x16", VG 170.00
Needle tin, Nipper, 3-color, NM 28.00
Postcard, hold-to-light, 1907, EX 10.00
Sign, cb, blk & wht w/maroon label, hanging, faded, 20" dia 350.00
Sign, compo board, 78 rpm record w/label, 47" dia, VG 135.00
Sign, paper, His Master's Voice, textured, fr, 25x29", EX 675.00
Sign, porc, Victor Records, 2-sided record shape, 28" dia 400.00
Sign, tin, Victor Talking Machines, dog & Victrola, 13½x19", VG .500.00
Thermometer, porc, NM 485.00

Ralston Cereal, cb box display, red/wht check, 19x14x6", G 145.00

Ranier Beer, ts, girl & bear, rolled corners, 14½" sq, EX 250.00
Reading Brewing, cb sign, girl w/bottles, 20x14½", EX 1,950.00
Recruit Cigarettes, folding chair, 32x17x20", G 25.00
Red Cloud Tobacco, tin strike plate, Indian chief, 6x2", NM 550.00
Red Crown Gasoline, porc sign, red/wht/bl, 2-sided, 42" dia, G .700.00
Red Crown Gasoline, porc sign, 2-sided, 30" dia, VG 450.00

Red Goose Shoes

Realizing that his last name was difficult to pronounce, Herman Giesecke, a shoe company owner resolved to give the public a modified, shortened version that would be better suited to the business world. The results suggested the use of the goose trademark with the last two letters, 'ke,' represented by the key that this early goose held in his mouth. Upon observing an employee casually coloring in the goose trademark with a red pencil, Giesecke saw new advertising potential and renamed the company Red Goose Shoes. Although the company has changed hands down through the years, the Red Goose emblem has remained. Collectors of this desirable fowl increase in number yearly, as do prices. Beware of reproductions; new chalkware figures are prevalent.

Bank, plastic, goose on base w/emb letters, 1960s, 5", M 15.00
Clicker, Red Goose logo on yel, 1950s, M 15.00
Display, nodding papier-mache goose, glass eyes, 24x13x18", G .1,000.00
Horn, cb & wood, The Fun of Having Feet, 6", EX 8.50
Horn, Red Goose Shoes, early, EX 20.00
Shoehorn, metal, pnt logo, EX 15.00
Sign, cb diecut, standup, red goose, 1940s, 11x7", NM 40.00
Sign, porc, goose on yel ground, 17¼x12", EX 300.00
String holder, goose figural, CI, VG pnt 1,400.00
String holder, goose figural, tin diecut, 27x14", VG 825.00
String holder, tin diecut, red/blk/wht goose form, 27x14", VG ...825.00
Thimble, aluminum, name on worn red band 4.00
Thimble, plastic, red logo on creme, EX 4.00

Red Indian Tobacco, tin lunch pail, blk & red, 8" L, VG 650.00
Red Raven, tray, bare-chested child/bottle, 12" dia, VG 300.00
Red Raven Splitz, tray, bird & bottle, 12" dia, VG 80.00
Red Star Line, letter folder, ocean liner, 12x3¼", EX 250.00
Revere Tires, cloth banner, bl/blk/yel, 12x48", EX 140.00
Rex Bitters, paper sign, nude on divan, 9x12"+fr, VG 1,700.00
Richard & Weaver Brewery, cl pocket mirror, 1906, 2¼" dia, G ..275.00
Robert Bosch Pyro Action Spark Plugs, tin sign, 12x19", EX 150.00
Robert Smith Ale, ts, man beside caged tiger, 20x14", VG 350.00
Rochester Brewery, paper sign, maiden/Liberty, 22x32"+fr, VG .450.00
Rockford Watches, ts, girl w/pocket watch, 23x17", G 275.00
Rocky Ford Cigars, paper sign, Indian/canyon, 21x27", EX 200.00
Roi-Tan Cigars, cb sign, couple before fire, 30x39", EX 225.00

Roly Poly

The Roly Poly tobacco tins were patented on November 5, 1912, by Washington Tuttle and produced by Tindeco of Baltimore, Maryland. There were six characters in all: Satisfied Customer, Storekeeper, Mammy, Dutchman, Singing Waiter, and Inspector. Four brands of tobacco were packaged in selected characters; some tins carry a printed tobacco box on the back to identify their contents. Mayo and Dixie Queen Tobacco were packed in all six; Red Indian and U.S. Marine Tobacco in only Mammy, Singing Waiter, and Storekeeper. Of the set, the Inspector is considered the rarest and in excellent condition may fetch more than $1,100.00 on today's market.

Dutchman, Mayo, EX 500.00

Dutchman, Mayo, NM 675.00
Inspector from Scotland yard, Mayo, EX 1,100.00
Mammy, EX 600.00
Satisfied Customer, Mayo, VG 425.00
Singing Waiter, Mayo, EX 600.00
Singing Waiter, US Marine, VG 450.00
Storekeeper, Mayo, NM 695.00
Storekeeper, VG 365.00

Roosevelt Cigars, ts, T Roosevelt portrait, 20x14", EX 13,000.00
Royal Motor Oil, oiler, gr & blk label, crown top, 3½", EX 40.00
Royaline Gasoline, porc sign, mc, 2-sided, 30" dia, EX 1,400.00
RPM Motor Oil, porc sign, bl/red/wht, 2-sided, 28" dia, NM 275.00
RPM Motor Oils & Lubricants, tin sign, 2-sided, 26" dia, EX 100.00
Ruhstaller's Beer, cb sign, mc paddle wheeler, 15x18", EX 500.00
Ruhstaller's Beer, tray, factory, vignettes, 14x17", G 150.00
Ruhstaller's Beer, tray, Purity, girl w/dove, 12¼" dia, G 85.00
Ruhstaller's Lager, tip tray, maid w/flagons, 4¼" dia, EX 225.00
Ryan's Pure Beers, cl pocket mirror, Indian, 2" dia, VG 195.00
Sanford's Inks, display cabinet, wood/glass, 36x22x10", VG 500.00
Santa Claus Soap, wooden crate, Santa label, 10x14x21", G 225.00
Sauer's Extracts, display case, decals on glass, 26x12x7", G 130.00
Schlitz Beer, stained glass window, 31½x58", G 1,000.00
Schmidt's Beer, tin & glass sign, brass bound, 21" sq, G 50.00
Schneider's Beer, tray, Admiral Dewey, 12" dia, G 150.00
Scholl's Axle Grease, tc, red & blk, 6½x5¾" dia, VG 30.00
Schwarzeneach Beer, tray, Jeannette, girl in yel, 13" dia, EX 550.00

Sears, Roebuck and Co., tip tray, factory scene, minor wear, 4½x6", $60.00; Prudential, tip tray, Rock of Gibraltar, 3½x2½", EX, $32.00.

Seitz Beer, tray, bird on crescent, 13" dia, VG 110.00
Seitz Beer, tray, eagle logo, EX color, 13¼" dia, VG 125.00
Seitz Brewing, tray, bulldog, 13¼" sq, EX 195.00
Sheaffer Pens, plastic & brass pen figural display, 1970s, 60" 425.00
Shell Gasoline, metal flange sign, 2-sided, 18x22", EX 450.00
Sinclair Opaline Motor Oil, tin sign, 4-color, 12x20", EX 160.00
Socony Motor Oil, glass bottle, emb letters, 15½", EX 75.00
Sprenger Brewing, tin & glass curved corner sign, 17x23", NM ..1,700.00
Sprenger Brewing, tray, factory on red & blk, 14x17", G 475.00
Sprenger Brewing, ts, Monastery Brew, 3 monks, 12" dia, VG ...500.00
Standard Motor Oil, porc sign, 3-color, 18x36", EX 750.00
Stegmaier Brewing, tray, fishing scene, Shonk, 13¾x10½", VG .125.00
Stegmaier's Beer, glass globe, hangs or stands, 17x16" dia, G 375.00
Sterling Beer, porc sign, man in armour, 19" dia, VG 1,000.00
Stoll Bros, cb diecut, kids in touring car, 12x14"+fr, G 400.00
Stroh's Beer, tray, child w/case, 13¼" sq, VG 250.00
Stroh's Beer, tray, hooded child w/case, 13x10½", VG 200.00

Studebaker, electric clock, gold metal rim, 15¼" dia, EX 115.00
Sunoco Gear Lubricant, tc, bl & orange, 5½x6½" dia, G 30.00
Sunshine Beer, clock, electric, lights up, 22" dia, G 350.00
Sunshine Beer, clock, electric, 15" dia, G 105.00
Supreme Gulf Motor Oil, tc, bl/orange/wht, 1-gal, 10", VG 30.00
Tacoma Beer, rvpt sign, red/bl/milk glass, 36x73", VG 4,000.00
Tacoma Beer, tray, Persian cats w/beer, 13½", VG 500.00
Tannhauser Beer, hanging glass light, orig pnt, 17x16" dia, EX .1,600.00
Terre Haute Brewing, tip tray, dining scene, 4½", EX 80.00
Terre Haute Brewing, tray, Colonials drinking, 15x12½", G 155.00
Texaco, metal thermometer, glass face, 12" dia, EX 500.00
Texaco Aircraft Engine Oil, tc, gr/cream/red, 1-qt, 5½", EX 40.00
Texaco Ethyl, porc sign, mc, 2-sided, 30" dia, EX 375.00
Texaco Golden Motor Oil, porc sign, 4-color, 15" dia, VG 250.00
Texaco Lube, porc sign, red/blk/wht, 15" dia, VG 100.00
Texaco Motor Cup Grease, tin grease can, blk/creme/gr, 5½", VG ..60.00
Texaco Strip Shingles, wood crate, paper label, 12½x36", VG 75.00
Thomas Moore Distilling, ts, cabin scene/card game, 23x31", G .375.00
Thompson's Wild Cherry Bitters, mantel clock, CI, 18", EX 550.00
Tiger Tobacco, lunch pail, red & blk, 7¾x10x5½", VG 65.00
Times Newspaper, clock, figure-8, pendulum, Baird, 31" 500.00
Tirador Cigars, sf ts, musketeer, 28x22", NM 300.00
Tivola Brewing, tray, man w/tray, 12" dia, EX 125.00
Tootsie Rolls, display case, tin & glass, 8x7x5", VG 750.00
Tortoise Shell Cut Roll Tobacco, tc, men/tortoises, 2", EX 125.00
Trommer's Evergreen Brewery, tray, mc scenes, 14x17", G 100.00
Tru-Blu Beer, tray, horse & dog, 13" dia, G 200.00
Turkish Delight Cigarettes, cl sign, bulldog, 18x13", G 130.00
Ulmer Beer, stained glass window, orig fr, 36x96", G 500.00
United Service Motors, porc & neon sign, touring car, 21x36", EX .600.00
US Rubber, boot display, working buckles, 38x10x24", VG 150.00
US Tires, frosted glass sign, yel/wht/dk bl, 12x15", EX 50.00
Utica Club Beer, rvpt & tin lamp, 16x15" dia, G 250.00
Utz & Dunn's Shoes, rvpt stand, wood fr & mirror, 42x42x17" ..400.00
Valvoline, porc sign, gr/wht/red/blk, 30" dia, NM 1,600.00
Veedol Motor Oil, tin flange sign, Flying A diecut, 19x24", EX .100.00
Virginia Dare, tray, Paul & Virginia, 12" dia, G 95.00
Virginia Dare, ts, running couple, 40x30", VG 600.00
Volkswagen Service, porc sign, bl/wht, 30x25", VG 215.00
Walter Baker, plate, serving girl, Vienna Art, 10" dia, EX 225.00
Wayne Brewing, pocket mirror, family at table, 2" dia, VG 175.00
Wayne Brewing, tray, Mad Anthony Wayne, 12" dia, EX 90.00
WE Davy, tray, girl w/medallion, 13¼x10½", G 35.00
Weiland Brewing, tray, lady w/glass, 17x13½", G 175.00
Weiner Plug, lunch box, racing scene, 4½x7¾x5¼", VG 325.00
West Chester Brewing, wood sign, paper litho, 24x34", G 375.00
West End Brewing, tray, Liberty w/flag & eagle, 13" dia, G 60.00
Westmoreland Brewing, stoneware pitcher, mc transfer, 9", G ...350.00
White Label Soup, ts, mc can on shield, 1890s, 14x20", VG 225.00
White Label Soup, ts, wht can/knight's weaponry, 14x19", G 150.00
White Rose Gasoline, porc sign, 3-color, 18x17½", EX 750.00
White Star Gasoline, porc sign, 2-sided, 30" dia, VG 450.00
Wiedemann's Beer, sf ts, 2 showgirls, 23x33", G 450.00
Wieland's Beer, tray, lady w/letter, 13¼x10½", G 100.00
Wieland's Beer, tray, lady w/yel roses, 13¼x10¼", G 75.00
Winchester, silk banner, rider w/rifle, 19x31", EX 450.00
Windisch-Mulhauser Brewing, paper sign, 15x20"+fr, VG 550.00
Wm Peter Brewing, rvpt sign, brewer w/mug, EX gold, 20x14", VG .750.00
Woodlawn Laces, tin cabinet, man & wheeled shoe, 14x12x11", G ..500.00
Worcester Brand Salts, cb sign, bag of salt, 21x15", G 120.00
Yale Brewing, rvpt sign, factory, 24x32", EX 3,000.00
Yankee Boy Tobacco, pocket tin, red & wht, 3½x4x1", EX 550.00
Yosemite Lager, rvpt sign, curved case, 20x66x11", G 6,100.00
Yuengling & Son Lager Beer, rvpt sign, fr, 22x32", G 1,750.00

Yellow Kid Ginger Wafers, tin container, Brinkerhoff & Co., N.Y. Biscuit Co., Illsley litho, 1890s, 14x10¾x10½", G, $11,000.00.

Yuengling's Beer, rvpt corner sign, eagle logo, 16x21", G 3,000.00
Yuengling's Beer, rvpt corner sign, eagle/bbl, 20x28", VG 4,500.00
Yuengling's Beer, rvpt sign, eagle/bbl, 20x16", VG 3,500.00
Yuengling's Beer, sf ts, eagle/bbl/shield, 23" dia, VG 775.00
Yuengling's Beer, tip tray, lady in hat, 4¼" dia, NM 135.00
500 Platolene, porc sign, checkered flag, 12" dia, NM 650.00

Advertising Cards

Advertising trade cards enjoyed great popularity during the last quarter of the 19th century when the chromolithography printing process was refined and put into common use. The purpose of the trade card was to aquaint the public with a business, a product, a service, or an event. Most trade cards range in size from 2" x 3" to 4" x 6"; however, many are found in both smaller and larger sizes.

There are two classifications of trade cards: 'private design' and 'stock.' With private design cards, an individual or company would have a card designed for their use only; no one else could use that design. Stock cards were generics that any individual or company could purchase from a printer's inventory. These cards usually had a blank space on the front in which the individual's name or advertisement could be printed. There were no restrictions on use of these cards, therefore the same card could be used by many different companies. In these listings a stock card is indicated by 'stk.' If there is no such reference, it is assumed the card is a private design. Values are given for cards in near-mint condition.

Four categories of particular interest to collectors are:

Mechanical — a card wich achieves movement through the use of a pull tab, fold-out side, or rotating disk.

Hold-to-light — a card that reveals its design only when viewed before a strong light.

Diecut — a card in the form of something like a box, a piece of clothing, etc.

For a more thorough study of the subject, we recommend *The Advertising Trade Card* by Kit Barry; his address can be found in the Directory under Vermont.

AB Chase Organ Co, 1 playing, 3 watching, factory in bkground ...15.00
Abram French & Co, Pottery, potter at work, brn & wht 38.00
An (Arrow) Escape, boy near archery target, stk 3.00
Arabian Mail Carrier, Arab riding camel in desert, stk 4.00
Ayers Cherry Pectoral, woman in field w/basket of cherries 5.00
Babbitt's Best Soap, boy painting at easel 5.00
Baltimore Oriole w/wing that lifts up, mechanical, stk 35.00
Bell ringer, man ringing bells lined up on table, stk 5.00
Boy & girl dancing in field, friend w/horn on fence, stk 5.00
Chas L Davis as Al Jolsen by man reading newspaper 18.00
Clark's ONT Thread, Columbian Expo view of grounds, buildings ..16.00
Crescent moon w/woman playing mandolin, 2 owls, stk 6.00

Czar Baking Powder, 1 girl w/dinner rolls, 1 w/powder can **8.00**
Dinner party w/frog & 2 mice, gr & gold, stk **4.00**
Division of Labor, stk **7.00**
Donaldson Brothers, Mar 1878 calendar, cherubs on ship **18.00**
Edison Phonograph, 'The Phonograph,' old couple listening **65.00**
Elk standing over dead wolf, stk **2.00**
Estey Organ Co, boy w/tennis racket serenading girl **7.00**
Evertt Piano, 2 women watch man play piano in concert **5.00**
Excelsior Starch, girl holding collar & box **8.00**
Fleischmann & Co, boy on stage, 4 girls w/boxes of yeast **16.00**
Fleischmann & Co, The Sun Is Rising in the Y-East **25.00**
Fleischmann & Co, woman w/flower basket, factory bkground **9.00**
Flower person, girl w/body of morning-glory flower, stk **12.00**
Fruit people, couple w/cherry heads, Clay & Richmond, stk **15.00**
Gilt Edge Shoe Gloss, leaf branches fr 3 swans on water **5.00**
Girl in highchair w/toy rabbit, stk **12.00**
Girl w/bonnet swinging on gate, barefoot boy pushing, stk **3.00**
Girls playing store w/scale & vegetables, stk **5.00**
Harness Race Horse Trinket, c Clay & Richmond, stk **16.00**

Heinz's Keystone Pickles, $35.00.

Home of Gen Benjamin Harrison, Harrison vignette, stk **15.00**
Hood's Sarsaparilla, First Lesson, dog, 3 pups & dead rat **6.00**
Hood's Sarsaparilla, G Cleveland presidential campaign card **10.00**
Hood's Sarsaparilla, James G Blaine presidential campaign **7.00**
Hunting on horsebk, pack of dogs dropping stag, stk **4.00**
Imperial Club Skates, lg skate on front, skaters bkground **25.00**
Johnson, Clark & Co, lion family at home w/sewing machine **6.00**
JS&M Peckham, Art Grand Stove, girl looking at poster **12.00**
Jumbo Objects to Being Put in Irons, stk **7.00**
Jumbo Reaching for Candy, stk **7.00**
Lake Shore Seed Co, red roses **6.00**
Lavine Washing Soap, boy & girl w/donkey & basket of soap **3.00**
Lion Coffee, 2 Chinese boys in bare feet on snow shoes **5.00**
Mason & Hamlin Organ, 2 scenes w/children & adults playing ...**12.00**
McLaughlin's Coffee, baby w/beer stein, Whitsuntide Monday **9.00**
McLaughlin's Coffee, boy in red shirt falling from wagon **12.00**
McLaughlin's Coffee, boy sailor climbing ship's rigging **9.00**
Merchants Gargling Oil, Put It There, baseball batter **16.00**
Musical McGibeney Family, family portrait w/instruments **25.00**
National flag of Holland (or Portugal), stk, ea **7.00**
NY Miniature Opera Co, Silence Be! It Was the Cat **15.00**
Pains Last Days of Pompeii, Albany Theater **16.00**
Pansies & 2 rose buds, c Robert Gair, stk **4.00**
Poole Piano Co, girl playing piano w/girl & boy w/dog **5.00**

Prescott's Universal Stove Polish, 2 puppies in bbl **4.00**
Prudential Ins Co, salesman at door, lady & baby in doorway **12.00**
Red Crown Brand Stove Gas, 2 dogs look at mouse in lantern **4.00**
Redwood Range, Blk woman w/loaf of bread, wht woman & stove ..**26.00**
Romeo & Juliet, kissing couple at window w/pig below, stk **6.00**
Russian Gut Violin String, Thomas Grand Orchestra **36.00**
Sailor boy w/bouquet on stone warf, water in bkground, stk **6.00**
Santa on rooftop dropping packages down chimney, stk **7.00**
Santa w/tree looking in window at 2 girls singing, stk **12.00**
Sterling Organ, woman playing for man & girl **12.00**
Stickney & Poors Spices, woman mixing batter, 2 spice cans **5.00**
Storm King Rubber Boots, I'm in It, boy w/boots in the rain **12.00**
Swans (pr) pulling boy & girl in eggshell boat, stk **12.00**
Ta-Ka-Kake, girl holding corn cake muffin **16.00**
There's Music in the Air, man blowing horn, blk & wht, stk **3.00**
Urchin boy sweeping streets, stk **7.00**
Vegetable person, A Nice Swheat Girl, girl w/wheat body, stk **12.00**
White Swan Soap, girl riding soap bar pulled by swan **12.00**
Young Continental, boy in tricorner hat w/flag & sword, stk **8.00**
3 caged bears w/balloon, stk **7.00**

Advertising Dolls

Whether your interest in ad dolls is fueled by nostalgia or strictly because of their amusing, often clever advertising impact, there are several points that should be considered before making your purchases. Condition is of utmost importance; never pay book price for dolls in poor condition, whether they are cloth or of another material. Restoring fabric dolls is usually unsatisfactory and involves a good deal of work. Seams must be opened, stuffing removed, the doll washed and dried, and then reassembled. Washing old fabrics may prove to be disastrous. Colors may fade or run, and most stains are totally resistant to washing. It's usually best to leave the fabric doll as it is.

Watch for new dolls as they become available. Save related advertising literature, extra coupons, etc., and keep these along with the doll to further enhance your collection. Old dolls with no marks are sometimes challenging to identify. While some products may use the same familiar trademark figures for a number of years (the Jolly Green Giant, Pillsbury's Poppin' Fresh, and the Keebler Elf, for example) others appear on the market for a short time only and may be difficult to trace. Most libraries have reference books with trademarks and logos that might provide a clue in tracking down your doll's identity. Children see advertising figures on Saturday morning cartoons that are often unfamiliar to adults, or other ad doll collectors may have the information you seek.

Some advertising dolls are still easy to find and relatively inexpensive, ranging in cost from $1.00 to $100.00. The hard plastic and early composition dolls are bringing the higher prices. Advertising dolls are popular with children as well as adults. For a more thorough study of the subject, we recommend *Advertising Dolls* by Joleen Robison and Kay Sellers. Joleen is our advisor; she is listed in the Directory under Kansas.

Armour & Co, Internat'l Doll, hard plastic, unmk, 8", M **3.00**
Aunt Jemima Pancake Flour, Aunt Jemima, cloth, 1910, 15", NM .**175.00**
Babbitt Cleanser, Babbitt Boy, compo head, cloth body, 15", EX .**600.00**
Baggie Food Storage Bags, alligator, inflatable, gr, 1974 ....**10.00**
Big Boy Restaurants, Big Boy, Dakin #2040, 1974, 8½", NM **15.00**
Big Boy Restaurants, Big Boy, vinyl, 9½" **12.00**
Blue Ribbon Malt Extract, Lena, uncut cloth, 1930, 14" **185.00**
Borden, Elsie the Cow, vinyl & brn plush, 1977, 15", NM **20.00**
Bradlee Stores, Bruff, gold plush, plastic eyes, 14", NM **12.00**
Bunny Bear Mattress Co, Bunny Bear, cloth, 1973, 12", NM **10.00**
Campbell, Campbell Kid, compo, Horsman, 1948, 12½", EX **300.00**
Carnation Milk, Cry Baby, vinyl, Horsman, 1962, 18", NM **35.00**

Chicken of the Sea, Mermaid, prestuffed cloth, 1976, 15", NM ...30.00
Cookie Crisp, Cookie Crook & Cop, plush, pr 42.50
Cricket Lighters, Cricket, inflatable, 1972, 24", M 12.00
Derby Oil, Derby Man, stuffed cloth, 1960s, 17", NM 15.00
Domino Sugar, Domino Bear, plush, 1975, 15", NM 7.00
Downey's Honey Butter, Honey-Butter Bee, plush, 10½", M 8.00
Eastman Kodak, Champion Retriever, cloth, 1971, 17" L, NM 25.00
Farmer's Brand, J Le Roy Farmer, cloth, 14", NM 150.00
Fels-Naptha Soap, Anty Drudge, cloth, 1933, 11", EX 150.00
Franklin Life Ins, Benjamin Franklin, cloth, 1970s, 12", NM 15.00
General Mills, Boo Boo Ghost, 1975, 7½" 12.00
Gerber, Gerber Baby, Sun Rubber, 1954, 12", EX 25.00
Gorton's Codfish, fisherman, vinyl, all orig, 7½", NM 25.00
Hawaiian Punch, Punchy, stuffed cloth, 1965, 13", NM 10.00
Honeywell, Allergy Annie, stuffed cloth, NM 20.00
Jack Frost Sugar, Jack Frost, stuffed cloth, 20", NM 15.00
Keebler, Keebler Elf, molded/pnt vinyl, 1974, 6½", NM 15.00
Kellogg's, Banana Splits Bingo, cloth, unmk, 10", NM 15.00
Kellogg's, Tony the Tiger, stuffed cloth, 14", NM 15.00
Libby, Libby, cloth, yel yarn hair, Mattel, 14", NM 45.00
Mason Mints, Peppermint Patty, beanbag, Hasbro, 1973, 10" 18.00
MD Bathroom Toilet Tissue, Daisy, cloth, 1977, 17½", EX 10.00
Michelin Tires, Tire Man, inflatable, bl/wht, 25", M 10.00
Munsingware, penguin, vinyl, 7½" 30.00
Nat'l Airlines, Gloria Stewardess, vinyl, 1973, 11½", M 15.00
Nestles, rabbit, brn/tan plush, vinyl eyes & teeth, 1976, M 12.00
Nugget Casino, Nugget Sam, papier-mache nodder, 1953, 5½", NM .20.00
Old Crow Whiskey, Old Crow, hard plastic, 1950, 4½", NM 30.00
Pepperidge Farm, Gingerman, brn cloth, foam filled, NM 10.00
Peter Pan Ice Cream, Peter Pan, cloth, Chase Bag Co, 18", NM ..15.00
Pillsbury, Dough Boy, cloth, deflatable cap/neckerchief, 16" 15.00
Pillsbury, Poppin' Fresh, molded vinyl, 7", M 15.00
Quaker Oats, Cap'n Crunch, hard plastic bank, 1975, 7½", M 35.00
Ralston Purina, Squarecrow, vinyl & cloth, 1965, 23", NM 35.00
Red Barn Restaurant, Big Fish Hungry, plush, 22", NM 20.00
Revlon, Little Miss Revlon, vinyl, Ideal, 1950, 10½", NM 75.00
Royal Crown Cola, Zippy, inflatable, M 12.00
Sambo's Restaurant, Sambo, nylon & felt, Dakin, 10", NM 15.00
Scott Paper, Scottie, plush, plaid bow, 1976, 7", NM 8.00
Sergeant's Sentry IV Flea Collar, Sergeant Dog, plush, 1976, M ..10.00
Sinclair Refining, Dino, inflatable vinyl, 1978, 14", M 7.50
Star-Kist Tuna, Charlie Tuna pillow, 36" L, NM 15.00
Tastykake Bakeries, Baker, prestuffed cloth, 1974, 13", NM 20.00
Texas Dairy Queen, Cheerleader, cloth, 1979, NM 10.00
Tide, Tide Bear, plush, plastic nose & eyes, 1976, 24", NM 8.00
Uncle Mose, oilcloth, 1940s, EX 40.00
United Missouri Bank, tiger, plush, 22", M 10.00
Vermont Maid Syrup, Vermont Maid, vinyl, Uneeda, 15", NM ...70.00
Welch Grape Juice, Wally Welch, plastic hand puppet, 9", NM 2.00
White Front Stores, Friendlee, cloth, 1972, 16", NM 10.00

African Art

African art does not consist of a single class of objects. Rather, these often-powerful sculptures are carved by many varying African tribes and groups across the central continent; each item represents specific cultural and spiritual functions and meanings. Many kinds of materials are used including wood, metal, fiber, ivory, and bone. Considerable numbers of these items are now being reproduced and sold to the tourist trade, but 'authentic' African art is generally considered to consist of objects which were used in cultural and religious activities. The items listed here are authentic, in good condition, and considered to be of average aesthetic quality. Scott Nelson, a collector of African art, is our advisor; his

address is listed in the Directory under New Mexico.

Anklet, Ashanti, open wedge form, bronze, 6" 125.00
Basket, Zaire, open, cowrie shells, fiber, 15" dia 125.00
Beads, trade; ceramic, string of 15 ....75.00
Bell, Yoruba, face, bronze, 4" 275.00
Cloth, Kuba, geometric decor, 18" sq 175.00
Comb, Chockwe, human head surmount, 5" 275.00
Divination board, Yoruba, figures, 16" dia 475.00
Doll, Ashanti, rnd head, simple design, 11" 275.00
Doll, Mossi, abstract human figure, leather covered, 10" 275.00
Door, Dogon, granary, 30 human figures, 2 turtles, 26" 1,250.00
Drum, Hemba, baboon head on side, 40" 600.00
Figure, Bamana, standing male, 24" 475.00
Figure, Baule, standing female, 20" 375.00
Figure, Dogon, male & female couple, 22" 1,250.00
Gold weight, Ashanti, bronze, bird, 3" 125.00
Hat, Kuba, fiber, decor 175.00
Headdress, Bamana, Tchi-wara (antelope), pr 1,500.00
Headrest, Luba, supporting human figure, 8" 375.00
Heddle pulley, Senufo, bird surmount, 7" 475.00
Ibejis, Yoruba, 9", pr 375.00
Knife, Kuba, throwing, str blade, 17" 125.00
Lock, Dogon, door, 2 human figural surmounts, 14" 675.00
Mask, Bamana, N'tomo, 14" 275.00
Mask, Bobo, antelope, polychrome, 24" 475.00
Mask, Chockwe, human face 375.00
Mask, Dan, human face, 16" 375.00
Mask, Dogon, Kanaga, 26" 800.00
Mask, Mende, helmet, female initiation, 12" 675.00
Mask, Pende, human face, 8" 375.00
Pendant, Songye, ivory human figure, ornate cvg, 4" 600.00
Pipe, Makonde, human head bowl, 14" 275.00
Ring, Ashanti, bronze, horse/rider 150.00
Scepter, chief's; Yoruba, figural, 12" 475.00
Stool, Ashanti, crescent seat, 18" 325.00
Stool, Lega, human figural supports, 13" 375.00
Wisk, Tanzania, human figure, horsehair, 14" 200.00

Agata

Agata is New England peachblow (the factory called it 'Wild Rose') with an applied metallic stain which produces gold tracery and dark blue mottling. The stain is subject to wear, and the amount of remaining stain greatly affects the value. It is especially valuable (and rare) when found on peachblow of intense color. Caution! Be sure to use only gentle cleaning methods.

Currently rare types of art glass have been realizing erratic prices at auction; until they stablize, we can only suggest an average range of values. In the listings that follow, examples are glossy unless noted otherwise. Our advisors for this category are Betty and Clarence Maier; they are listed in the Directory under Pennsylvania. See also Green Opaque.

Bowl, 2¾x5" 625.00
Creamer 1,250.00
Finger bowl, ruffled, VG mottling, 2¾x5½" 900.00
Plate, fluted rim, 6½" 850.00
Punch cup, EX mottling, 2¼" 625.00
Spooner, crimped top, allover mottling, matt, 5" 1,550.00
Spooner, sq top, EX color & staining, 4½" 1,200.00
Toothpick holder, sqd rim, 2" 700.00
Toothpick holder, tricorn, EX mottling, 2¼" 600.00
Tumbler, EX color & mottling 950.00

Tumbler, purple hue, NE Glass, 3¾" **1,140.00**
Vase, Morgan; in amber satin glass griffin holder, 10", NM **2,500.00**
Vase, ovoid w/sqd rim, hdls, 4" **775.00**
Vase, pyriform base w/cup-like neck, slender form, 7" **1,350.00**

Agate Ware

Clays of various natural or artificially dyed colors were combined to produce agate ware, a procedure similar to the methods used by Niloak in potting their Mission Ware. It was made by many Staffordshire potteries from abour 1740 until about 1825.

Teapot, typical shape, dolphin handle, lion finial, serpent spout, repair, 5½", $6,600.00; Coffeepot, octagonal with strap handle, faceted spout, repairs, 6½", $11,000.00.

Coffeepot, tankard form, strap hdl, rstr, 6½" **11,000.00**
Cream jug, beak spout, 3 paw ft w/lions' masks, 4½" **3,300.00**
Cutlery hdls, pistol-grip shape, rstr, pr **550.00**
Mug, milk; fluted, cream w/brn marbleizing, 5¼" **1,000.00**
Pitcher, bl/brn/cream clays, ribbed strap hdl, rstr, 6" **465.00**
Pitcher, brn/cream clays, creamware hdl/spout/rim, 6", VG **500.00**
Pitcher, brn/cream clays, ribbed strap hdl, 6½", NM **775.00**
Sauce boat, coal scuttle form, hdl ea side, chips, 5¾" **8,250.00**
Tea caddy, sq w/canted corners, rpl lid, rim chips, 4" **2,600.00**
Teapot, cream/bl/brn clay, scallop shell body, 5", EX **6,000.00**

Akro Agate

The Akro Agate Co. founded in 1914 primarily as a marble maker, operated in Clarksburg, West Virginia, until 1951. Their popular wares included children's dishes, powder jars, flowerpots, and novelty items along with the famous 'Akro Aggies.' Much of their glass was produced in the distinctive marbleized colors they called Red Onyx, Blue Onyx, etc.; solid opaque and transparent colors were also produced. Most of the wares are marked with their trademark, a crow flying through the letter 'A' holding an Aggie in its beak and one in each claw. Other marks include 'J.P.' on children's pieces, 'J.V. Co., Inc.,' 'Braun & Corwin,' 'N.Y.C. Vogue Merc Co. U.S.A.,' 'Hamilton Match Co.,' and 'Mexicali Pickwick Cosmetic Corp.' on novelty items. In 1936 Akro obtained the molds from the Balmer-Westite Co. of Weston, West Virginia. Westite produced a similar line of products for several years. Their ware is drab in color when compared to Akro and is generally unmarked. The embossed Westite logo does appear occasionally on the bottoms of some pieces. Westite is commonly accepted as a companion collectible of Akro.

For more information we recommend *The Collector's Encyclopedia of Children's Dishes* by Margaret and Kenn Whitmyer, available at your local bookstore. Our advisor for miscellaneous Akro Agate is Albert Morin; he is listed in the Directory under Massachusetts.

Chiquita

Creamer, opaque colors other than gr, 1½" **16.00**
Cup, transparent cobalt, 1½" **8.00**
Plate, baked-on colors, 3¾" **3.00**
Saucer, gr opaque, 3⅛" **2.00**
Set, cobalt transparent, 12-pc, MIB **100.00**
Set, cobalt transparent, 16-pc, MIB **127.00**
Sugar bowl, baked-on colors, 1½" **8.00**
Sugar bowl, gr opaque, 1½" **5.00**
Tablecloth, w/4 napkins, set **25.00**

Concentric Rib

Creamer, sm, opaque colors other than gr or wht, 1¼" **14.00**
Cup, sm, gr or wht opaque, 1¼" **5.00**
Set, sm, gr or wht opaque, 10-pc, MIB **53.00**
Teapot, opaque colors other than gr or wht, 3⅜" **14.00**

Concentric Ring

Concentric Ring, 16-piece set, solid opaque colors, small, $105.00.

Cereal, lg, bl marbleized, 3⅜" **45.00**
Creamer, sm, any opaque color, 1¼" **18.00**
Cup, lg, any opaque color, 1¼" **30.00**
Cup, lg, cobalt transparent, 1⅜" **35.00**
Cup, sm, bl marbleized, 1¼" **35.00**
Plate, sm, any opaque color, 3¼" **6.00**
Saucer, sm, bl marbleized, 2¾" **12.00**
Set, lg, cobalt transparent, 21-pc, MIB **540.00**
Sugar bowl, lg, bl marbleized, w/lid, 1⅜" **60.00**
Sugar bowl, sm, any opaque color, 1¼" **18.00**
Sugar bowl, sm, bl marbleized, 1¼" **40.00**
Teapot, sm, cobalt transparent, w/lid, 2⅜" **45.00**

Interior Panel

Cereal, lg, azure bl, 3⅜" **30.00**
Cereal, lg, bl & wht, 3⅜" **30.00**
Creamer, lg, gr transparent, 1⅜" **22.00**
Creamer, lg, red & wht, 1⅜" **32.00**
Creamer, lg, yel opaque, 1⅜" **35.00**
Creamer, sm, red & wht, 1¼" **32.00**
Creamer, sm, yel, 1¼" **32.00**
Cup, lg, azure bl, 1⅜" **35.00**
Cup, lg, bl & wht, 1⅜" **25.00**

Cup, sm, azure bl or yel, 1¼" 22.00
Cup, sm, gr & wht, 1¼" 25.00
Cup, sm, pk lustre, 1¼" 12.00
Cup, sm, red & wht, 1¼" 25.00
Pitcher, sm, topaz transparent, 2⅞" 15.00
Plate, lg, azure bl, 4¼" 10.00
Plate, lg, bl & wht, 4¼" 16.00
Plate, lg, jade lustre, 4¼" 8.00
Plate, sm, azure bl, 3¼" 10.00
Plate, sm, gr & wht, 3¼" 10.00
Plate, sm, pk lustre, 3¼" 7.00
Plate, sm, red & wht, 3¼" 12.00
Plate, sm, topaz transparent, 3¼" 9.00
Saucer, sm, gr & wht, 2⅜" 6.00
Set, lg, gr transparent, 21-pc, MIB 200.00
Set, lg, pk or gr lustre, 21-pc, MIB 320.00
Set, lg, red & wht, 21-pc, MIB 435.00
Set, sm, bl & wht, 16-pc, MIB 265.00
Set, sm, pk or gr lustre, 16-pc, MIB 175.00
Sugar bowl, lg, azure bl, w/lid, 1⅜" 45.00
Sugar bowl, lg, bl & wht, w/lid, 1⅜" 40.00
Sugar bowl, lg, gr & wht, w/lid, 1⅜" 35.00
Sugar bowl, lg, lemonade & oxblood, w/lid, 1⅜" ..55.00
Sugar bowl, lg, pk lustre, w/lid, 1⅜" 35.00
Sugar bowl, lg, topaz transparent, w/lid, 1⅜" ..30.00
Sugar bowl, sm, cobalt, 1¼" 25.00
Sugar bowl, sm, jade lustre or pk lustre, 1¼" ..27.00
Sugar bowl, sm, red & wht, 1¼" 32.00
Sugar bowl, sm, yel, 1¼" 35.00
Teapot, lg, gr & wht, 2⅝" 45.00
Teapot, lg, gr transparent, w/lid, 2⅝" 35.00
Teapot, lg, lemonade & oxblood, w/lid, 3⅜" ...65.00
Teapot, sm, bl & wht, 2⅜" 40.00
Teapot, sm, gr lustre, w/lid, 3⅜" 22.00
Teapot, sm, pk luster, w/lid, 3⅜" 30.00
Teapot, sm, red & wht, 2⅜" 37.50
Tumbler, sm, gr transparent, 2" 8.50
Tumbler, sm, pk lustre, 2" 50.00
Tumbler, sm, topaz transparent, 2" 9.50

J.P. (Made for J. Pressman Company)

Cereal, lg, red or brn transparent, 3¾" 45.00
Creamer, lg, lt bl or crystal, 1½" 30.00
Cup, lg, baked-on colors, 1½" 8.00
Plate, lg, gr transparent, 4¼" 10.00
Plate, lg, lt bl or crystal, 4¼" 10.00
Set, lg, gr or brn transparent, 16-pc, MIB 300.00
Sugar bowl, lg, lt bl or crystal, 1½" 30.00
Teapot, lg, gr transparent, w/lid, 2¾" 60.00

Miss America

Creamer, forest gr 55.00
Creamer, wht 45.00
Cup, orange & wht 45.00
Cup, wht 40.00
Plate, forest gr 45.00
Plate, wht 25.00
Saucer, forest gr 15.00
Saucer, wht 15.00
Set, wht, 17-pc, MIB 495.00
Set, wht w/decal, 17-pc, MIB 600.00
Sugar bowl, orange & wht, w/lid 65.00

Sugar bowl, wht, w/lid 55.00
Teapot, forest gr, w/lid 125.00
Teapot, wht, w/lid 75.00

Octagonal

Cereal, lg, beige & pumpkin, 3⅜" 20.00
Cereal, lg, dk bl, 5⅜" 10.00
Creamer, lg, gr & wht, closed hdls, 1½" 10.00
Creamer, sm, dk gr, 1¼" 14.00
Cup, lg, lemonade & oxblood, closed hdl, 1½" ..25.00
Pitcher, sm, bl, 2⅞" 18.00
Plate, sm, lime gr, 3⅜" 6.00
Set, lg, dk bl, 21-pc, MIB 140.00
Sugar bowl, lg, beige & pumpkin, closed hdl, w/lid, 1½" ..18.00
Sugar bowl, lg, gr & wht w/decal, 1½" 21.00
Tumbler, sm, dk gr, 2" 10.00

Raised Daisy

Creamer, sm, yel, 1¼" 45.00
Cup, sm, bl, 1¾" 45.00
Plate, sm, bl, 3" 14.00
Saucer, sm, beige, 2½" 9.00
Sugar bowl, sm, yel, 1¼" 45.00
Teapot, sm, bl, w/lid, 2⅜" 75.00
Teapot, sm, gr, no lid, 2⅜" 30.00
Tumbler, sm, bl, 2" 55.00
Tumbler, sm, yel, 2" 25.00

Stacked Disc

Creamer, sm, wht, 1¼" 10.00
Cup, sm, any opaque color other than gr or wht, 1¼" ..12.00
Cup, sm, wht, 1¼" 6.00
Pitcher, sm, opaque gr, 2⅞" 12.00
Plate, sm, any opaque color other than gr or wht, 3¼" ..5.00
Saucer, sm, opaque gr, 2¾" 3.00
Set, sm, wht, 21-pc, MIB 120.00
Sugar bowl, sm, opaque gr, 1¼" 10.00
Teapot, sm, opaque gr, w/lid, 2" 12.50
Tumbler, sm, any opaque color other than gr or wht, 2" ..14.00
Tumbler, sm, wht, 2" 7.50

Stacked Disc and Interior Panel

Cereal, lg, bl marbleized, 3⅜" 45.00
Cereal, lg, cobalt transparent, 3⅜" 28.00
Creamer, lg, cobalt transparent, 1⅜" 30.00
Creamer, sm, bl marbleized, 1¼" 40.00
Creamer, sm, gr transparent, 1¼" 28.00
Cup, lg, cobalt transparent, 1⅜" 25.00
Cup, sm, any solid color, 1¼" 12.00
Cup, sm, bl marbleized, 1¼" 37.00
Pitcher, sm, gr transparent, 2⅞" 18.00
Plate, lg, bl marbleized, 4¼" 20.00
Plate, lg, cobalt transparent, 4¼" 15.00
Plate, sm, gr transparent, 3¼" 8.00
Set, lg, gr transparent, 21-pc, MIB 365.00
Set, sm, bl marbleized, 16-pc, MIB 490.00
Set, sm, bl marbleized, 8-pc, MIB 265.00
Set, sm, cobalt transparent, 16-pc, MIB 290.00
Set, water; sm, gr transparent, 7-pc, MIB 90.00
Sugar bowl, lg, cobalt transparent, 1⅞" 50.00

Sugar bowl, sm, any solid color, 1¼" **18.00**
Teapot, lg, cobalt transparent, w/lid, 3¾" **70.00**
Teapot, lg, gr transparent, w/lid, 3¾" **55.00**
Teapot, sm, gr transparent, w/lid, 3⅜" **35.00**
Tumbler, sm, cobalt transparent, 2" **18.00**

Stippled Band

Stippled Band in transparent green: Cup, 1½", $9.00;
Saucer, 3¼", $4.00; Plate, 4¼", $8.00.

Creamer, lg, amber transparent, 1½" **20.00**
Creamer, lg, azure transparent, 1½" **32.00**
Creamer, sm, amber transparent, 1¼" **30.00**
Cup, sm, gr transparent, 1¼" **8.00**
Plate, lg, gr transparent, 4¼" **6.00**
Plate, sm, amber transparent, 3¼" **6.00**
Set, sm, azure transparent, 17-pc, MIB **355.00**
Sugar bowl, lg, amber transparent, w/lid, 1½" **25.00**
Sugar bowl, lg, azure transparent, w/lid, 1½" **45.00**
Teapot, sm, amber transparent, w/lid, 2⅜" **20.00**

Stippled Interior Panel

Creamer, lg, amber transparent, 1½" **20.00**
Creamer, sm, amber transparent, 1¼" **30.00**
Cup, sm, amber transparent, 1¼" **8.00**
Cup, sm, gr transparent, 1¼" **6.50**
Pitcher, sm, amber transparent, 2⅞" **18.00**
Plate, sm, amber transparent, 3¼" **6.00**
Plate, sm, gr transparent, 3¼" **4.00**
Set, lg, amber transparent, 17-pc, MIB **190.00**
Sugar bowl, lg, amber transparent, w/lid, 1⅞" **25.00**
Teapot, sm, amber transparent, w/lid, 3⅜" **20.00**
Teapot, sm, gr transparent, 2⅜" **18.00**

Miscellaneous

Ashtray, gr, Hotel Lincoln **50.00**
Ashtray, gr/wht, Scallop Shell **6.00**
Ashtray, oxblood/wht, sq, 3" **10.00**
Ashtray, Star, mk Victory Safety Tray **150.00**
Basket, bl/wht, 1-hdl **350.00**
Basket, gr/wht, 2-hdl **36.00**
Bell, bl **65.00**
Bowl, bl/wht, Stacked Disc, no ft **85.00**
Bowl, orange, tab hdls, #321 ....**25.00**
Candlesticks, crystal, assembled lamp parts, pr **28.00**
Candlesticks, royal bl, 3¼", pr **250.00**
Cornucopia, bl/wht, NYC Vogue Merc **8.00**
Cup & saucer, demitasse; beige **24.00**

Flowerpot, all colors, Ribbed Top, #291½, 2¼", ea **6.00**
Flowerpot, bl, Plain Band, #298, 1⅞" **18.00**
Flowerpot, bl/wht, Stacked Disk, 3" **10.00**
Flowerpot, blk, Ribbed Top, #300F **20.00**
Flowerpot, Braun & Corwin, #290, 1¼" **25.00**
Flowerpot, gr, Banded Dart, #300 ....**24.00**
Flowerpot, ivory, #1308 ....**135.00**
Flowerpot, ivory, Ribs & Flutes, #296 ....**12.00**
Flowerpot, orange, Combo, #295 ....**110.00**
Flowerpot, orange, factory decor, #1310 ....**165.00**
Flowerpot, orange, Plain Band, 4" **75.00**
Flowerpot, orange/wht, Ribs & Flutes, #297 ....**8.00**
Flowerpot, yel, Banded Dart, #302 ....**50.00**

Jardiniere, yellow, bell
shape, 4¾", $38.50.

J Vivaudou, apothecary jar, wht **24.00**
J Vivaudou, powder box, pk **125.00**
Knife, forest gr, grid style, #739 ....**300.00**
Knife, pk, grid style, #739 ....**65.00**
Lamp, ivory, w/ivory shade **265.00**
Lamp, ivory/brn **65.00**
Marble box, Akro Flinties **350.00**
Marble box, Chinese Checkers **25.00**
Marble box, Kings Game **650.00**
Marble box, 100 #00 glassies **100.00**
Marble box, 100 #1 moss agates **250.00**
Planter, orange, factory decor, #654 ....**28.00**
Planter, orange, Japanese style, #650 ....**150.00**
Powder jar, crystal, Scotty dog form **275.00**
Powder jar, gr, Scotty dog form **175.00**
Powder jar, orange/wht, Mexicali **25.00**
Powder jar, pk, Colonial lady form **50.00**
Powder jar, royal bl, Colonial lady form **250.00**
Vase, bl, Graduated Dart, #312, 8¾" **65.00**
Vase, blk, Graduated Dart, #316, 6¼" **95.00**
Vase, emb wheat on trumpet form, rare, 5" **750.00**
Westite, ashtray, gr, hexagonal **18.00**
Westite, candlesticks, emb floral panel, pr **65.00**
Westite, flowerpot, brn/wht, Graduated Dart **12.00**
Westite, flowerpot, Giant, #304 ....**100.00**
Westite, planter, brn/wht, Japanese style **100.00**

Alexandrite

Alexandrite is a type of art glass introduced around the turn of the
century by Thomas Webb and Sons of England. It is recognized by its
characteristic shading, pale yellow to rose and blue. Although it was
also produced by other companies, only examples made by Webb command premium prices. Amount and intensity of blue determines value.

Our advisors for this category are Betty and Clarence Maier; they are listed in the Directory under Pennsylvania.

Bowl, Honeycomb, ruffled/ftd, 2x5¼"	850.00
Finger bowl, rnd, fluted, w/5½" dia underplate	2,200.00
Match holder, Dmn Quilt, sq top, 3x2½"	650.00
Punch cup, bbl shape, 2¾"	550.00
Tumbler, juice; Honeycomb, EX color, 3"	800.00
Vase, trumpet form w/petal top, 6"	1,550.00
Wine, Optic, citron stemmed ft, rare, 4½x2⅜"	900.00

Wine, distinctive sapphire edge on bowl and base, hollow stem, Webb, 9", $3,000.00.

Almanacs

The earliest evidence indicates that almanacs were used as long ago as Ancient Egypt. Throughout the Dark Ages they were circulated in great volume and were referred to by more people than any other book except the Bible. *The Old Farmer's Almanac* first appeared in 1793 and has been issued annually since that time. Usually more of a pamphlet than a book (only a few have hard covers), the almanac provided planting and harvesting information to farmers, weather forecasts for seamen, medical advice, household hints, mathematical tutoring, postal rates, railroad schedules, weights and measures, 'receipts,' and jokes. Before 1800 the information was unscientific and based entirely on astrology and folklore. The first almanac in America was printed in 1639 by William Pierce Mariner; it contained data of this nature. One of the best-known editions, Ben Franklin's *Poor Richard's Almanac*, was introduced in 1732 and continued to be printed for twenty-five years.

By the 19th century, merchants saw the advertising potential in a publication so widely distributed, and the advertising almanac evolved. These were distributed free of charge by drug stores and mercantiles and were usually somewhat lacking in information, containing simply a calendar, a few jokes, and a variety of ads for quick remedies and quack cures.

Today their concept and informative, often amusing text make almanacs popular collectibles that may usually be had at reasonable prices. Because they were printed in such large numbers and often saved from year to year, their prices are still low. Most fall within a range of $4.00 to $15.00. Very common examples may be virtually worthless; those printed before 1860 are especially collectible. Quite rare and highly prized are the Kate Greenaway 'Almanacks,' printed in London from 1883 to 1897. These are illustrated with her drawings of children, one for each calendar month.

1803, Farmer's, VG	12.50
1813, Farmer's, Robert Thomas, Boston, EX	6.50
1820, Clergyman Minor, Boston, EX	6.50

1827, Christian, preacher on cover, EX	5.00
1852, Farmer & Mechanic, farmer on cover, PA, VG	5.00
1861, Herrick's, EX	8.00
1864, Old Farmer's, RB Thomas Publisher, EX	6.50
1865, Leavitt's Farmer	8.00
1865, Old Farmer's, EX	6.50
1870s, Centaur, mythical creature illus, 20-pg, VG	6.00
1870s, Rush's Almanac & Guide to Health, EX	7.50
1877, Hostetter's Bitters, EX	8.00
1878, Hostetter's US, medicinal remedies, cartoons, etc, EX	25.00
1883, Dr Jayne's Medical, color cover, NM	6.50
1886, Household, EX	12.50
1889, Hostetter's, EX	10.00
1911, Watkins, EX	9.00

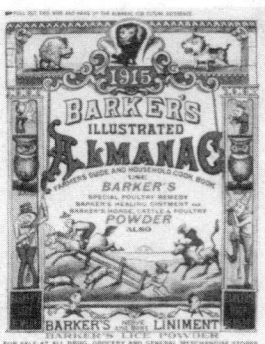

1915, Barker's Illustrated Almanac, NM, $20.00.

1917, Ayer's American, EX	6.00
1928, Swamp Root	4.00
1931, Dr Jayne's, EX	4.00
1940, IL Herb, EX	5.00

Aluminum

Aluminum, though being the most abundant metal in the earth's crust, always occurs in combination with other elements. Before a practical method for its refinement was developed in the late 19th century, articles made of aluminum were very expensive. After the process for commercial smelting was perfected in 1916, it became profitable to adapt the ductile, non-tarnishing material to many uses.

By the late thirties, novelties, trays, pitchers, and many other tableware items were being produced. They were often handcrafted with elaborate decoration. Russel Wright designed a line of lovely pieces such as lamps, vases, and desk accessories that are becoming very collectible. Many who crafted the ware marked it with their company logo, and these signed pieces are attracting the most interest. Wendell August Forge (Grove City, PA) is a mark to watch for; this firm produced some particularly nice examples and upwardly mobile market values reflect their popularity with today's collectors. In general, 'spun' aluminum is from the thirties or early forties, and 'hammered' aluminum is from the fifties.

For further information, refer to *Hammered Aluminum, Hand Wrought Collectibles*, by Danny Woodard, and *Collectible Aluminum, An Identification and Value Guide* by Everett Grist. Our advisor for this category is Ted Haun; he is listed in the Directory under Indiana. See also Russel Wright.

Anglefood cake mold, 3½x11½"	4.00
Basket, acorns, scalloped rim, 6x11¾" dia	15.00
Basket, fruits & flowers emb, Cromwell Hand Wrought, 7¾"	12.00

Basket, handmade, flared sides w/dbl-twist hdl, 10x12x10" **14.00**
Bowl, console; Lucite hdls, Kensington **48.00**

Buffet server, 4-petal flowers on ribbon form handles, hammered lid with applied tulip finial, Rodney Kent, $35.00.

Butter dish, bamboo, clear glass insert, Everlast, ¼-lb **9.00**
Cake basket, tulip form, Rodney Kent, 7x12" **20.00**
Candle snuffer, flower form **10.00**
Casserole, emb tulips & ribbon, hdls, w/lid & undertray **20.00**
Cigarette case, Park, NM **10.00**
Coaster, emb pansy shape, Everlast, 6 for **10.00**
Coaster, golfer, Wendell August Forge **15.00**
Coaster, roses, Everlast, 4 for **5.00**
Hand mirror, Nouveau florals, openwork twisted metal hdl **15.00**
Lazy susan, Ferris wheel type, 3 glass inserts, Everlast, 11" **40.00**
Lazy susan, w/jelly pots & toast rack, Rodney Kent, unused **28.00**
Napkin clip, handmade, set of 6 ....**20.00**
Percolator, ca 1910, 1-cup **22.50**
Plaque, Will Rogers, detailed profile, 1967, 10x16" **48.00**
Relish, sectioned, glass inserts, Continental **32.50**
Syrup server, w/lid **10.00**
Tray, bread; Mum's Continental #566, 11½", NM **20.00**
Tray, hand wrought, hdls, Buenilum, 11" dia **15.00**
Tray, lobster figural, Bruce Fox **45.00**
Tray, pine cones, lg **30.00**
Tray, poinsettia, crimped, loop hdls **10.00**
Tray, shell form, Kensington **25.00**
Tray, wildlife, 4¼x7¼" **6.50**
Tray, wrought, center flower form hdl, Farberware, 4½x8" **17.50**

AMACO, American Art Clay Co.

AMACO is the logo of the American Art Clay Co. Inc., founded in Indianapolis, Indiana, in 1919, by Ted O. Philpot. They produced a line of art pottery from 1931 through 1938 that is today beginning to interest collectors. The company is still in business but now produces only supplies, implements, and tools for the ceramic trade.

Values for AMACO have risen sharply, especially those for figurals, items with Art Deco styling, and pieces with uncommon shapes. Our advisor for this category is Virginia Heiss; she is listed in the Directory under Indiana.

Box, #173, bl gloss, Deco style, w/lid, 2½x5x3" **110.00**
Figure, #199, geisha kneeling, bl gloss, 6½" **225.00**
Temple jar, #132, bl gloss, w/lid, 6" **85.00**
Vase, #1, dk red gloss, Deco style w/hdls, 8½" **95.00**
Vase, #18, matt gr, bulbous w/hdls, early mk, 8x9" **175.00**
Vase, #39, matt yel w/hdls, 6x4½" **72.50**
Vase, #46, pale bl matt, w/hdls, 6½" **65.00**
Vase, #49, gr matt, w/hdls, 9" **95.00**

Vase, #50, gr & red gloss w/tall sq hdls, 7½" **110.00**
Vase, #95, bl gloss, 7" **85.00**

Amberina

Amberina, one of the earliest types of art glass, was developed in 1883 by Joseph Locke of the New England Glass Company. The trademark was registered by W.L. Libbey, who often signed his name in script within the pontil.

Amberina was made by adding gold powder to the batch, which produced glass in the basic amber hue. Part of the item, usually the top, was simply reheated to develop the characteristic deep red or fuchsia shading. Early amberina was mold-blown, but cut and pressed amberina was also produced. The rarest type is plated amberina, made by New England for a short time after 1886. It has been estimated that less than 2,000 pieces were ever produced. Other companies, among them Hobbs and Brockunier, Mt. Washington Glass Company, and Sowerby's Ellison Glassworks of England, made their own versions, being careful to change the name of their product to avoid infringing on Libbey's patent. Prices have been erratic at auction for several months; values given below are in the average range.

Bonbon, sgn Libbey, 7" **350.00**
Bottle, scent; sgn Libbey, 2-oz **450.00**
Bottle, scent; sgn Libbey, 5-oz **300.00**
Bowl, Daisy & Button, Hobbs & Brockunier, +6 ice cream plates .**925.00**
Bowl, Dmn Quilt, 9", +6 4" bowls **700.00**
Bowl, Optic panels, ruffled, sgn Libbey, 4¾x6" **595.00**
Bowl, rectangular top, rnd base, sgn Libbey, 2½x5½" **285.00**
Bowl, sgn Libbey, 11" **450.00**
Bowl, short appl amber hdl, wafer finial on lid, 4¼x5¾" **245.00**
Butter dish, Diagonal Block **235.00**
Butter dish, Dmn Quilt, NE Glass **395.00**
Butter dish, Invt T'print, appl ball finial **235.00**
Butter pat, Daisy & Button, sq, 2¾" **40.00**
Canoe, Daisy & Button, 8" **210.00**
Celery vase, Invt T'print, 5½x3¾" **365.00**
Cheese dish, optic w/12 panels, cut finial, 9½" dia **345.00**
Clock, Daisy & Button, NE Glass **500.00**
Compote, deep, sgn Libbey, 10x7½" **900.00**
Compote, sgn Libbey, 8x6½" **800.00**
Creamer, Invt T'print, sq mouth, amber reeded hdl, 2½" **400.00**
Creamer & sugar bowl, NE Glass **600.00**
Cruet, Reverse Baby T'print, Mt WA **365.00**
Cruet, Swirl, amber hdl, cut amber stopper, Mt WA, 6" **375.00**
Decanter, Dmn Quilt, reverse color, matching stopper, 11" **650.00**
Finger bowl, Honeycomb, scalloped, 5" **155.00**
Mug, lemonade; Swirl, amber snake hdl, 5" **225.00**
Mustard, Invt T'print, bbl form, hinged lid, 3" **275.00**
Pear, w/stem, 3¾" **175.00**
Pitcher, amber hdl, ribbed, bulbous, 7" **200.00**
Pitcher, Drape, sq mouth, bulbous, 7⅛x5½" **300.00**
Pitcher, Herringbone, bulbous, appl amber hdl, 5" **195.00**
Pitcher, Invt T'print, tankard form, NE Glass, 7" **500.00**
Plate, Dmn Quilt, fuchsia, 7" **110.00**
Puff box, sgn Libbey, 4", w/lid **650.00**
Punch cup, NE Glass **120.00**
Punch cup, Wheeling **55.00**
Rose bowl, amber rigaree, NE Glass, 5x4½" **300.00**
Rose bowl, 5-crimp, pale amber ft, 4x4½" **125.00**
Shade, scalloped, 5" fitter, 5¾x7¼" dia **275.00**
Spooner, Daisy & Button, 4" **275.00**
Spooner, Dmn Quilt, EX color, sq scalloped rim, 4½" **500.00**

Toothpick holder, Dmn Quilt, sq mouth, Libbey 235.00
Toothpick holder, fuchsia, sq top, 2½" 160.00
Tumbler, crackled, 4½x2¾" 55.00
Tumbler, Dmn Quilt, 4" 80.00
Tumbler, Invt T'print, 3¾x2⅝" 45.00
Tumbler, juice; Dmn Quilt, 2⅝" 125.00
Tumbler, juice; vertical ribs, corset shape, NE Glass 195.00
Tumbler, lemonade; w/hdl 100.00

Vase, pink hand-painted flowers with green leaves, 8", $225.00.

Vase, appl amber edge, sqd jar form, 8½" 325.00
Vase, Drape, Wheeling, 10" 325.00
Vase, flared, amber ruffle, 10⅛x7⅜" 365.00
Vase, gold twigs/wht floral, swirled, amber ruffle/ft, 12" 325.00
Vase, HP decor on panels, 8½" 250.00
Vase, Invt T'print, everted rim w/amber ruffle, 13x5" 225.00
Vase, lily; 7" 285.00
Vase, lily; 9¾" 350.00
Vase, paneled, gently waisted, att Libbey, 4¼" 175.00
Vase, rigaree neck trim, ribbed, waisted, 3½" 275.00
Vase, ruffled, ribbed trumpet form, sgn Libbey, 10¾" 600.00
Vase, scalloped top, 9" 215.00
Vase, wht flowers/gr leaves w/gold, swirled cylinder, 7" 225.00
Wine, fuchsia, ribbed, 4¾" 335.00

Plated Amberina

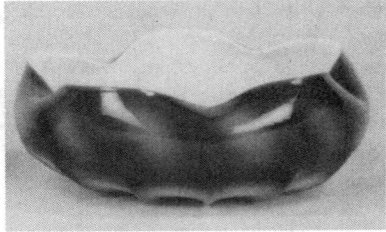

Bowl, 5-lobed form with white interior, 7½", $3,250.00.

Celery vase 2,500.00
Cruet, faceted amber stopper, amber hdl, M 3,000.00
Pitcher, milk; amber hdl, tricorn 5,000.00
Punch cup 1,800.00
Syrup, ridged silver collar/spout/lid/hdl, 6" 7,300.00
Tumbler, M 2,400.00
Vase, bulbous w/trumpet neck, ribbed, EX color, 6" 7,500.00
Vase, 12-rib, flared U-form, 3½" 3,950.00

American Encaustic Tiling Co.

A.E. Tile was organized in 1879 in Zanesville, Ohio. Until its closing in 1935, they produced beautiful ornamental and architectural tile equal to the best European imports. They also made vases, figurines, and novelty items with exceptionally fine modeling and glazes.

Bookends, cupid w/rabbit, mk, 1926, 5x5", pr 145.00
Incense burner, Deco figural 85.00
Paperweight, ram figural 65.00
Temple jar, blk, w/lid, 9" 155.00
Tile, bird, HP, wood fr, 10½x5¼", pr 350.00
Tile, boy w/ram, trees/fence beyond, emb/HP, Meuller, 6½x18" ...625.00
Tile, dedication souvenir, bl, 4" 80.00
Tile, floral, mc on tan, fr, 6" 45.00
Tile, floral, 5-color w/gold, 6x8", pr 75.00
Tile, Harding medallion, wht on bl, 4x4" 65.00
Tile, knight, mc, 10x14x1" 625.00
Tile, lady (full figure) in relief, bl gloss, fr, 3-pc, 18x5½" 225.00
Tile, shepherdess, mc, 18x6" 550.00
Vase, face in relief, allover gold, 5x5" 225.00

American Indian Art

That time when the American Indian was free to practice the crafts and culture that was his heritage has always held a fascination for many. They were a people who appreciated beauty of design and colorful decoration in their furnishings and clothing; and because instruction in their crafts was a routine part of their rearing, they were well accomplished. Several tribes developed areas in which they excelled. The Navajo were weavers and silversmiths, the Zuni, lapidaries. Examples of their craftsmanship are very valuable. Today even the work of contemporary Indian artists — weavers, silversmiths, carvers, and others — is highly collectible. For a more thorough study we recommend *Arrowheads and Projectile Points, Indian Axes,* and *Indian Artifacts of the Midwest.* All three have been written by our advisor, Lar Hothem; you will find his address in the Directory under Ohio.

Key:
bw — beadwork   p-h — prehistoric
dmn — diamond   S — Southern
E — Eastern   W — Western
NE — Northeastern   x — cross

Apparel and Accessories

Before the white traders brought the Indian women cloth from which to sew their garments and beads to use for decorating them, clothing was made from skins sewn together with sinew, usually made of buffalo tendon. Porcupine quills were dyed bright colors and woven into bags and armbands and used to decorate clothing and moccasins. Examples of early quillwork are scarce today and highly collectible.

Early in the 19th century, beads were being transported via pony pack trains. These 'pony' beads were irregular shapes of opaque glass imported from Venice. Nearly always blue or white, they were twice as large as the later 'seed' beads. By 1870 translucent beads in many sizes and colors had been made available, and Indian beadwork had become commercialized. Each tribe developed its own distinctive methods and preferred decorations, making it possible for collectors today to determine the origin of many items. Soon after the turn of the century, the craft of beadworking began to diminish.

Boot moccasins, Kiowa, hard soles, sinew sewn, beadwork uppers and cuffs, yellow pigment-rubbed hide, ca 1890, minor loss, 22", $3,500.00.

Apron, maternity; Cheyenne, bw/fetishes/teeth, 1870 ....600.00
Arm bands, Blackfoot, bw w/ermine, 1880, 26" 475.00
Belt, Sioux, full mc bw on wht, sinew sewn, 1910, 1½x36" 200.00
Breech clout, Nez Perce, bw floral & bear, 1945, 64x12" 150.00
Cuffs, Cree, full bw hide w/lg fleur-de-lis, 1915, 11" 400.00
Dress, Hopi, hand-woven blk ceremonial, Pueblo style, 1950 .....100.00
Dress, Navajo, hand-woven wool w/terrace design, 1950 ....200.00
Dress, Navajo, wool, red/bl terraces, hand-woven sash, '40s 275.00
Dress, Nez Perce, bl trade cloth w/bw yoke, 1945, lg 150.00
Dress, Plateau, hide w/full bw yoke, fringe, 1940 ....650.00
Dress, Plateau, purple velvet w/bw & shells, 1930 ....125.00
Gloves, Metis lady's, buckskin w/contour bw & fringe, 1900 ......250.00
Hat, Haida, plaited cedar bark w/pnt eagle, 1935, 17x7" 350.00
Jacket, Chimayo, made from blanket, 1950s 75.00
Jacket, Cree lady's, buckskin w/fringe, bw on bk, 1935 ....225.00
Leggings, Sioux, sinew-sewn buffalo w/EX geometric bw, 1900 ..800.00
Leggings, Sioux lady's, bw, 1930, 13x7", M 650.00
Mittens, Athabascan, tanned moosehide/floral bw cuffs, 1900 .....60.00
Mittens, buffalo fur w/leather palms, 1890, 15x10" 70.00
Moccasins, Apache lady's, Womanhood Ceremony, w/papers, 1890 .800.00
Moccasins, burial; Santee Sioux, full bw, even on soles, 1900 ..2,200.00
Moccasins, Cheyenne, full bw on sinew-sewn buffalo, 1900 ....350.00
Moccasins, Crow, full geometric bw, rawhide soles, 1930 ....400.00
Moccasins, Kiowa lady's high-tops, ochre, cut beads/conchos .2,200.00
Moccasins, Nez Perce child's, bw on toes, hide soles, 1930 ....300.00
Moccasins, Plains baby's, mc bw on toe & heel, 3⅞" 150.00
Moccasins, Sioux, full bw, sinew-sewn, buffalo soles, 1875 ......1,900.00
Moccasins, Sioux, quilled w/bw, buffalo hide soles, 1800s 2,500.00
Mukluks, Cree child's, moosehide w/floral bw, 1940 ....45.00
Sash, Navajo, hand woven, 1900s, 5x108" 175.00
Sash, Pit River, full bw ceremonial w/butterflies, 1910, 2x62" 100.00
Shawl, dance; lady's, geometric appliques, fringed, 1970s 50.00
Shawl, Kiowa, embr florals on bl trade cloth, 1980, 68x57" 225.00
Shirt, Navajo lady's, velvet w/200+ silver buttons, 1900s 400.00
Vest, Chimayo, Germantown weaving, 1920, 71" 350.00

Arrowheads and Points

Relics of this type usually display characteristics of a general area, time period, or a particular location. With study, those made by the Plains Indians are easily discerned from those of the West Coast. Because modern man has imitated the art of the Indian by reproducing these artifacts through modern means, use caution before investing your money in 'too good to be authentic' specimens.

Abbey Point, AL, made from flake, 1⅞" 3.50
Adena, AR, tan/gray tones, 2¾" 8.50
Adena, TN, lt gray, 2½" 12.00
Anasazi, NM, translucent blk obsidian, convex base, corner notch, 1" .9.00
Beaver Lake, TN, tan, 2¼", EX 45.00
Catacco Creek, AL, brn, 1¾" 4.00
Clovis, NM, pk-brn Alibates flint, hinged flutes, thin, 2½", EX .300.00
Dalton, MO, tan, 2⅛", EX 9.00
Flint Creek, AL, brn, 2⅛" 4.50
Greenbrier, AR, blk flint, 3¼" 120.00
Hardin, AL, tan, 2¼" 18.00
Hardin Barbed, IL, wht flint, thin, 3¼" 130.00
Harrell type, NM, wht agate, side notch, concave base, ⅞" 9.00
Hemphill, MO, wht w/some pk, 4⅛" 160.00
Kalapuyan, WA, wht chalcedony agate, serrated, ¾" 12.00
Levenna, NY, gray, triangular, 1" 4.50
Maud, AR, dk red flint, 1⅛" 15.00
Meserve, AR, lt tan, 2" 20.00
Montell, TX, gray, translucent edge, 2" 25.00
Mulberry Creek, AL, blk, 1¾" 10.00
Nodena, AL, gray, leaf shaped 3.50
Nolan, TX, gray, 2¼", EX 12.00
Paleo, AL, brn tones, elongated triangle, 2¾" 6.00
Scallorn, AR, wht, 1" 12.00
Scallorn, AZ, dk chert, convex base, sm corner notches, 1" 6.00
Scallorn, NM, translucent wht agate, ¾" 12.00
Swan Lake, AL, gray, sm nick, 1¾" 3.50
Table Rock, AR, blk chert, 1¾" 16.00
Table Rock, NY, gray, 2⅛" 5.00
Waubesa, MO, lt purple, 2¼" 7.50

Arts and Crafts

Ashtray, Navajo, hammered silver w/stamped designs, 1960, 5" ...50.00
Ashtray, Zuni, silver top hat shape w/inlaid shells, 1940 ....150.00
Blanket, Tlingit, trade cloth, whale/waves made w/buttons, lg ...500.00
Hide painting, Many Horses, sgn, 1920, 32x24" 200.00
Painting, Chaos, sgn Kabotie, 1975, 14x10" 175.00
Painting, Deer Dancer in full costume, Kai-Sa, 1955, 14x10" 400.00
Pastel, Chief Shot in the Eye, Hans P Luetcke, 1985, 23x17" 100.00
Sand painting, Navajo, Male Mtn Way, story/sgn, 1975, 36x36" ...85.00
Sculpture, Kachina, EX detail/fur robe, sgn Toulouse, 17" 175.00
Tapestry, Daisy Taugelchee, superfine 2 Gray Hills, 21x32" 800.00
Tapestry, Faye Begay, 2 Gray Hills, 1985, 35x27" 500.00
Totem, NW Coast, yel cedar, hand cvd/pnt, 1890, 20" 300.00
Whimsey, Iroquois, floral bw w/Xd Am flags, 1890, 10x3" 150.00

Bags and Cases

The Indians used bags for many purposes, and most display excellent form and workmanship. Of the types listed below, many collectors consider the pipe bag to be the most desirable form. Pipe bags were long, narrow, leather and bead or quillwork creations made to hold tobacco in a compartment at the bottom and the pipe, with the bowl removed from the stem, in the top. Long buckskin fringe was used as trim and complemented the quilled and beaded design to make the bag a masterpiece of Indian Art.

Apache, hide, bw circles w/Xs, long fringe, 1890, 15x7" 275.00
Arapaho, dispatch case, hard leather/fringe/concho, 1870, 15" ...1,750.00
Arapaho, strike-a-lite, full bw/tin cones drops, 1900s, 7" 225.00
Arapaho, strike-a-lite, geometric bw, tin cones, 1900, 9x3" 425.00
Assiniboine, bandolier, floral bw, documentation, 1800, 46" ..2,100.00

Blackfoot, mc spot-stitch bw on lt bl, 6¾x4¾" 295.00
Blackfoot-style, belt pouch, full floral bw, 1900s, 7x5" 160.00
Cheyenne, possible bag, buffalo hide/bw panels, 1890, 21x23" ..1,450.00
Chippewa, full bw w/florals, fringe, 1900, 3¾x2½" 125.00
Chippewa, full/mc bw florals on wht, 1900, 7x6½" 400.00
Cree, deer foot w/hair on, intact dew claws, 1960, 9x7" 50.00
Cree, tobacco, curvilinear beads/porcupine quills, 1900, 36" 950.00
Crow, full bw geometrics, fringed, 1970, 14x5" 85.00
Crow child's, parfleche w/pnt designs, 1800s, 7x10" 200.00
Crow-style, gun case, fringe, classic bw, 1900s, 43" 400.00
Crown, parfleche, pnt motif, trade cloth laced, 1890, 7x9" 400.00
Iroquois, purse, mc flowers/birds bw, 6" 140.00
Nez Perce, belt pouch, corn husk, decor front/bk/flap, 14x7" ...350.00
Nez Perce, corn husk, geometrics on flap, 1930, 16x9" 375.00
Nez Perce, corn husk, twined, red/gr geometrics, 1920, 7x6" 600.00
Nez Perce, corn husk w/pine trees, ca 1900, 7x8" 500.00
Nez Perce/Plateau, allover floral bw, trade cloth, 1935, 15" 1,150.00
Plains, awl case, full bw, w/flap, tin cones, 1900s, 19" 175.00
Plains, knife case, rawhide w/tacks, 1900s, 16", +knife 125.00
Plains, knife case, tin cones/full bw, 1900s, 21", +knife 375.00
Plains, pipe, geometric bw, quilled slats/tassel, 25" 2,420.00

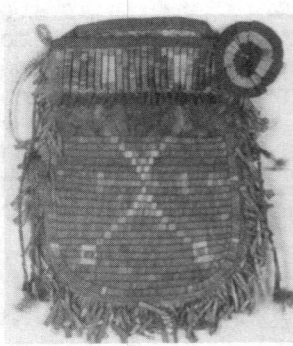

Plains pouch, quill-wrapped parfleche slats with tin cone, multi-colored porcupine quills, 11", $2,200.00.

Plains, Reservation period, 5-color bw, cone dangles, 4½x5" 360.00
Plains, tobacco pouch, rawhide w/5-color bw, 20"+fringe 1,350.00
Plateau, bw elk/floral, 1950, 15x8" 275.00
Plateau, bw w/seed beads curvilinears, 1880, 2½x2" 250.00
Plateau, full bw: lady/2 horses, 1930, 12" dia 250.00
Sioux, pipe, 7-color bw, quilled/fringed, 26", EX 1,100.00
Sioux, tobacco, long fringe, w/ochre, 1800s, 37x6½" 1,150.00
Sioux lady's, tobacco, bw ea side/fringe, 1800s, 8x6" 650.00
Wasco, medicine pouch, loom bw, elk/women, 4x3" 500.00
Yakima, semi-contoured, Elk Dreamer Society, 1900s, 14x12" ...375.00

Baskets

In the following listings, examples are basket form and coiled unless noted otherwise.

Apache, bowl, geometrics, blk martynia/willow, 3½x13" 495.00
Apache, tray, geometric star design, 8" 160.00
Apache, tray, star design in martynia, breaks, 2½x10" 195.00
Apache, tray, woven horsehair, blk/wht w/figures, 2½" dia 130.00
Basin Area, tray, multi-point star in martynia, 13" dia, EX 250.00
Haida, brn spruce fiber w/log crosses & red bands, 3x6" 150.00
Hopi, rnd plaited plaque w/3-color motif, 1910, 2x11" 250.00
Hopi, seed corn basket, 3-color aniline, soiled, 4½x4¾" 60.00
Jicarilla Apache, faint dog figures, minor damage, 3¾x12½" 65.00
Jicarilla Apache, fishing creel, aniline sumac, 7x15½", EX 550.00
Jicarilla Apache, mc zigzags, rim break, 14¼x11½" 880.00
Makah, faded aniline stripes w/star on lid, 3x5½", EX 60.00

Makah, gr & yel bands w/whales/boat/birds, 7¼x7½x7¾" 440.00
Makah, mc bird & whale decor, w/lid, 2⅛x2¼" 100.00
Makah, mc bird design, 2½x4" 50.00
Mission, bowl, geomerics/Xs in redbud, 1920s, 4x15" 1,600.00
Mission, cat & birds pictorial, 4⅜x10", EX 495.00
Mission, gobular w/brn geometrics, soiled, 4¼x7⅜" 198.00
Mission, tray, 2-tone geometrics, 5" dia 85.00
Navaho, wedding basket, 4-color, reed base, 1940s, 12" W 60.00
Paiute, full 4-color bw ext, minor damage, 1⅝x3" 110.00
Papago, bold figures, flared rim, hdls, 12½x18" 600.00
Papago, bowl, yucca w/5 female figures in martynia, 3½x8⅜" 110.00
Papago, bowl, yucca w/8 male figures in martynia, 3⅝x8⅝" 140.00
Papago, olla, geometric frets in yucca & martynia, 4¾x5" 50.00
Papago, olla, terraces in martynia & yucca, 12x9½" 770.00
Papago, plaque, man in maze in martynia & yucca, S Mauw, 18" .105.00
Papago, 19 figures: birds/horses/people, fine weave, 10x13" 580.00
Pima, martynia & willow, fine weave, sm break, 2⅜x3½" 220.00
Pima, olla, willow & martynia w/braid rim, 1910s, 7x9" 1,045.00
Pima, tray, geometric fretwk in martynia & willow, 3x13½" 165.00
Pit River, storage, 8 lines reddish geometrics, 1900, 10x8" 475.00
Pomo, bowl, twined w/half-twist o/l design, 4x10", EX 95.00
Salishan, trunk, imbricated geometrics, 1800s, 12x20x10¼" 330.00
Southwestern/Basin, bowl, 3-rod coil in martynia, 4x11" 195.00
Thompson River, imbricated w/stylized arrows, loop rim, 6½" 75.00
Tlingit, rattle top, mc bracken fern/grass on cedar, 4½x7½" 600.00
Tlingit, 4-color geometrics, tight weave, 4½x5", M 450.00
Wasco, twined corn husk Sally bag, red geometrics, 1890, 7" 400.00
Yurok, hat, geometrics, bracken fern/grass on red, 2⅜x5½" 110.00

Blankets, Navajo

Pueblo Indians first made blankets centuries ago, but today most are made by Navajo Indians. Pendleton and Hudson's Bay blankets became widely available in the 1800s; around the turn of the century, rugs were developed because tourists were more likely to buy them as floor coverings and wall-hangings. Rugs or blankets are made in various regional styles; an expert can usually identify the area where it was made, sometimes even the individual who made it. The colors of wool are natural (gray-white, brown-black), vegetal (from plant dyes), or artificial (aniline, from synthetic chemicals). Value factors include size, tightness of weave, artistry of design, and condition. Examples by artists whose names are well known command the higher prices.

Saddle, blanket weave & design, 1910, 32x27" 50.00
Saddle, dbl, old blanket style, 1920, 58x32" 150.00
Saddle, dbl, transitional twill weave style, 1920, 56x28" 150.00
Saddle, gray w/blk sqs & red lines, borders, 30x28", VG 250.00
Stacked triangles, blk/wht/gray natural wool, 1965, 32x62" 150.00
Transitional, brn/wht dmns, 1910, 81x48" 400.00
Transitional, classic 3-color design, 1910, 76x52" 900.00
3rd Phase Chief's, wht/brn/red/gray, 1910, 53x48" 1,250.00

Ceremonial Items

Cap, Iroquois Glengarry, bw florals, 1870, 10x3½" 400.00
Cvg, Tlingit, cvd wood shaman in full costume, 1910, 9½x3" 300.00
Dance wand, Plains, antlers/beads/hawk bells, 1900s, 33x5" 250.00
Drum, Pueblo, Indian pnt on hide, 1900, 2½x11" 325.00
Drum, Sioux, pnt buffalo/tepee/arrowheads, 1920, 3x22" 475.00
Fetish, cvd stone bear w/arrowhead strapped to bk, 1990, 8" 220.00
Fetish, Plains, full bw turtle w/umbilical cord, 1900s, 5" 150.00
Helmet, NW Coast, pnt wood w/abalone inlay teeth, 1900, 11" ..1,000.00
Knife, Yurok, blk obsidian, from Klamath River, 1800, 15x5" 250.00
Mask, corn husk; Seneca, finely braided/detailed, 14x12" 440.00

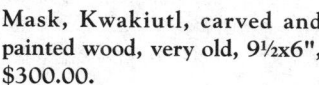

Mask, Kwakiutl, carved and painted wood, very old, 9½x6", $300.00.

Mask, false face; Iroquois, stain/pnt wood, horsehair, 10½" **1,200.00**
Mask, Kwakiult, Wild Woman, cvd/pnt, sgn Antoine, 1985 ......**225.00**
Mask, NW Coast, cvd/pnt, w/hair, sgn Coyote, 1990, 11x8" **300.00**
Medicine bundle, Crow, cloth, 8 medicine/pnt holders, 1930 ....**300.00**
Medicine rock, Crow, beaded, many trade bead drops, 35" **1,000.00**
Rattle, Iroquois, turtle shell, EX patina, 1890, 9x4" **275.00**
Rattle, Navajo, hide/deer hooves 1900, 7x5" **300.00**
Rattle, NW Coast, cvd/pnt bird rattle w/EX designs, 12x3x6" ..**2,000.00**
Rattle, NW Coast, cvd/pnt wood, many figures, inlay, 11x3" **800.00**
Rattle, Sioux, buffalo scrotum, beaded horsetail drop, 1870 ....**500.00**
Shield, Arapaho, Ghost Dance, buffalo hide w/pnt motif, 1880 .**400.00**
Shield, Plains, buffalo hide w/cloth & pnt decor, 24" dia **175.00**
Staff, NW Coast, Speaker's, totemic, human hair, Coyote, '85 ..**250.00**
Switch, sweat house; Sioux, buffalo tail, 1860, 24" **125.00**

Dolls

Apache, fringed bead-work-trimmed hide poncho and skirt, high-top moccasins, cloth body and underskirt, hair ornament, suspensions, shells, and glass beads, 15", $2,900.00; Apache, 4-color painted hide poncho and skirt, tin cone suspensions, cloth body and blouse, high-top moccasins, 14" $4,600.00.

Apache, beaded hide, appl bells/etc, early, 12" **3,000.00**
Beaded hide face, pnt/bw buckskin attire, 1900, 12" **250.00**
Blackfoot, man & lady w/papoose, intricate bw, 1920, 12", pr **300.00**
Chippewa, man & lady, buckskin w/bw attire, 1920, 11", pr **200.00**
Kachina, Butterfly Maiden, flat-cvd, 1900s, 10x8" **175.00**
Kachina, Heyheyos, cvd cottonwood root, 1930, 8" **250.00**
Kachina, mc pnt 'kitten' dancer, S Talahytewa, 10" **150.00**
Kachina, Motsin Dancer, sgn V Namoki, 12½" **85.00**
Kachina, Mudhead, w/blanket, wood base, 1975, 12" **100.00**
Plains, buckskin dress & accessories, 1900s, 12" **200.00**

Plains, muslin, buckskin dress, w/papers+museum mt, 1850, 18" ..**500.00**
Skookum, man & lady, w/blankets, 1920, 12½", pr **200.00**

Domestics

Box, E Woodlands, birch bark/sweetgrass/quillwork, 4½" dia **200.00**
Cradle, Apache, pnt wood, decorated cloth, 1950s, 35", EX **55.00**
Cradle, Flathead, full contour bw, 1800s, museum quality, 25" ..**1,100.00**
Cradle, Pawnee, cvd/pnt stars, brass tacks, fringe, 1932 ....**250.00**
Cradle, Plains, rawhide w/tacked brd, bead/quill trim, 1890 ....**1,250.00**
Spoon, horn, bw hdl, bird effigy tip, 1900s, 9½x2" **80.00**
Spoon, mtn sheep horn, bw hdl, cvd sheep head, 1900s, 21x5" ..**275.00**

Jewelry

   As early as 500 A.D., Indians in the Southwest drilled turquoise nuggets and strung them on cords made of sinew or braided hair. The Spanish introduced them to coral, and it became a popular item of jewelry; abalone and clam shells were favored by the Coastal Indians. Not until the last half of the 19th century did the Indians learn to work with silver. Each tribe developed its own distinctive style and preferred design, which until about 1920 made it possible to determine tribal origin with some degree of accuracy. Since that time, because of modern means of communication and travel, motifs have become less distinct.

   Quality Indian silver jewelry may be antique or contemporary. Age, though certainly to be considered, is not as important a factor as fine workmanship and good stones. Pre-1910 silver will show evidence of hammer marks, and designs are usually simple. Beads have sometimes been shaped from coins. Stones tend to be small; when silver wire was used, it is usually square. To insure your investment, choose a reputable dealer.

Bolo, Buffalo Dancer, inlaid, sgn Beyuka, 1975, 3x5" **550.00**
Bracelet, cuff; Navajo, elaborately hand stamped, 1935, 3" **300.00**
Bracelet, Navajo, heavy, Burnham turq, sgn, 1970, 2" **100.00**
Bracelet, Navajo, 4" turq surrounded by 17 lg turq, sgn NB **200.00**
Bracelet, watch; Navajo, set w/15 natural turq, 1980, 1¾" **70.00**
Bracelet, watch; Zuni, allover coral/MOP inlay, 1980, 1½" **140.00**
Bracelet, Zuni, Devil Dancer/mc inlay, sgn Panteah, 1980, 1½" .**250.00**
Bracelet, Zuni, lg needlepoint cluster w/some petit-point **150.00**
Bracelet, Zuni, 4-row petit-point, 1960, 3" **125.00**
Breast plate, hairpipe bones, Padre beads, 1900s, 12x9" **250.00**
Breast plate, leather w/buffalo teeth/bone beads/medicine pc **200.00**
Breast plate, Sioux, bone hairpipes/brass beads, 1800s, 14x9" **950.00**
Buckle, Navajo, silver w/11 natural turq, sgn RV, 1930, 3½x2" **80.00**
Choker, 3-row, trade beads, cvd bone beads/leather spacers **60.00**
Concho belt, 5 lg ovals+4 butterflies, 4 turq in buckle **1,000.00**
Concho belt, 5 ovals+6 butterflies, turq-set buckle, 3" W **450.00**
Drop, Sioux, bw on hide/buffalo fur/dew claws, 1890, 30" **500.00**
Necklace, Apache, silver beads, X drop, 1940, 32" **70.00**
Necklace, branch coral w/sterling cones, 24" **95.00**
Necklace, lg nuggets of natural spider web turq, 1900s, 24" **450.00**
Necklace, Navajo, all-silver squash blossom, old pawn, 28" **375.00**
Necklace, Navajo, beads/18 mercury dimes, turq naja, 1945 ......**200.00**
Necklace, Navajo, hand-stamped grad handmade beads, '75, 24" .**250.00**
Necklace, Plains, 28 bear claws w/trade bead spacers, 1900s **500.00**
Necklace, Pueblo, turq nuggets/beads, Penetente X drop, 24" **375.00**
Necklace, Santo Domingo, turq nuggets/shell heshi, 23" **75.00**
Necklace, squash blossoms/naja w/Bisbee turq, 1960 ....**175.00**
Necklace, turq/silver cluster squash blossom, sgn Begay, 28" **200.00**
Necklace, Zuni, Lone Mtn turq, Carl Luthey, 1958, 25" **125.00**
Pin, Navajo, turq/silver cluster style, 1930, 3" dia **60.00**
Pin, Zuni, butterfly, turq/jet/shell inlay, 3x5" **100.00**
Ring, Navajo, sq natural turq, filigree edge, 1930 ....**45.00**
Roach, Crow, deer/porcupine hair, 1900, 16x3½" **125.00**

Trade beads, lg grad Venetian chevrons, 1840, 29"	600.00
Trade beads, lg rnd wht Dutch trade beads, 22"	60.00
Trade beads, lg sq bl glass beads w/blk & wht core, 24"	70.00
Trade beads, watermelon chevron beads from Italy, 23"	100.00

Knives and Chipped Blades

The knife was an indispensable tool to the Indian whether he was in battle, hunting game, or doing chores at the campsite. Before the white man's metal blades, all were made of copper, obsidian, flint, or chert. Knife cases, fashioned of leather with intricate decorations of quilling or beadwork, were sometimes suspended from the neck, or they were attached to the belt.

Agate Basin, KY, brn, 10"	450.00
Bk tang, TX, gray, thin, about perfect, 4¼"	175.00
Clovis, MO, tan, 3⅞"	325.00
Kinney, sq bk, TX, tan/off-wht, 2½"	45.00
Kinney sq-bk, TX, off-wht, 3"	65.00
Knife, Kinney, TX, sq bk, tan, 2⅜"	35.00
Knife, TX, gray, 2½"	15.00
Scottsbluff, MO, Late Paleo, common form, 5"	500.00
Spear, Clovis, AR, pk/tan, 4"	265.00
Spear, Etley style, IL, gray, polished, 3⅞", EX	120.00
Spear, Gary, AR, wht chert, 2¾"	10.00
Spear, Smith, KS, tan, 4"	145.00
Spear, TN, brn, ¾"	40.00
St Charles/Dovetail, IL, red chert, EX work, 5¼x1½"	400.00
Stanfield, MO, tan Burlington chert, Early Archaic, 6x1¼"	200.00
Thebes, IA, wht chert, Early Archaic, 4"	85.00

Pipes

Pipe bowls were usually carved from soft stone, such as catlinite or pipestone, an argilaceous sedimentary rock composed mainly of clay. Granite was also used. Some ceremonial pipes were simply styled, while others were intricately designed naturalistic figurals, sometimes in bird or frog forms called effigies. Their stems, made of wood and often covered with leather, were sometimes nearly a yard in length.

Woodlands, dark brown stone elbow-form pipe bowl carved with a bear surmount, 4½" long, $1,300.00.

Blackfoot, blk stone T-bowl, wide flat wood stem, 1910, 26x3"	350.00
Chippewa, blk T-bowl, file-burned wood stem, 1930, 21x2"	75.00
Chippewa, cvd wood L-bowl w/designs, wood stem, 1900, 9x2x1"	50.00
Cloud Blower, blk steatite, from Dalles OR, 1700, 5½x1½"	150.00
Mound Builder, gr-blk stone platform w/bear bowl, p-h, 6x2"	200.00
Pipe tomahawk, brass, copper/tack-trim wood hdl, 1890, 19x7"	800.00
Pipe tomahawk, brass head/beaded wood hdl, 1900s, 17x8"	225.00

Pipe tomahawk, CI w/brass wire-wrapped wood hdl, 1900s, 21"	125.00
Pipe tomahawk, pewter head, bw stem, 1900s, 12x5"	150.00
Plains, platform type cvd from dk brn stone, 1800, 3½x2"	150.00
Plains, wood, pewter band on tip/bowl, twist stem, 1900, 20"	100.00
Sioux, catlinite T-bowl, wood stem/orig quills, 1890, 24x4"	1,100.00
Sioux, red catlinite L-bowl w/pewter inlay, quilled stem, 26"	650.00
Sioux, red catlinite w/brass trim, ca 1860, 12x3"	250.00
Tlingit, seal/raven/eagle/whale-cvd bowl, mc pnt, 2x3¼"	1,550.00

Pottery

Indian pottery is nearly always decorated in such a manner as to indicate the tribe that produced it or the pueblo in which it was made. For instance, the designs of Cochiti potters were usually scattered forms from nature or sacred symbols. The Zuni preferred an ornate repetitive decoration of a closer configuration. They often used stylized deer and bird forms, sometimes in dimensional applications.

Acoma, canteen, stylized parrot, 1900s, 8" dia	175.00
Acoma, effigy, lg owl w/3 sm owls, sgn, 1900s, 6x5½"	150.00
Acoma, jar, blk on wht, 1938, 8x8"	250.00
Acoma, jar, mc decor, 1938, 9x10½"	450.00
Acoma, olla, birds, orange/amber on wht, 1930s, 10⅜"	2,650.00
Acoma, olla, curvilinears/geometrics, 1930, 9x7"	325.00
Acoma, olla, fine lines/curvilinears, 1900, 8x6½"	250.00
Acoma, olla, parrot motif, 1900s, 10x12"	500.00
Casas Grandes, jar, blk on blk geometrics, A Canales, 4½"	65.00
Casas Grandes, jar, tan w/curvilinears, sgn Sambe, 1992, 12"	125.00
Hano, bowl, mc bird designs around inside top, p-h, 4x11"	600.00
Hohokam, olla, red on buff, part of lip gone, p-h, 10"	400.00
Hohokam, pitcher, red on buff, part of lip gone, p-h, 7"	125.00
Hohokam, plate, red on buff, 4 bird designs, p-h, 5½"	450.00
Hopi, bowl, thunderbird w/in, sgn Annette Silas, 1950, 3x8"	125.00
Hopi, canteen, feathers, mc pnt on cream slip, 1930s, 5½"	250.00
Hopi, jar, classic mc migration pattern, N Nampeyo, 1965, 5"	500.00
Hopi, olla, stylized dancer/birds, Nampeyo, 1920, 6½x6"	225.00
Hopi, pot, abstract geometrics, mc slip, 1920-40, 6½x9"	325.00
Hopi, vase, lg stylized birds in blk, 1930, 9x4"	350.00
Hopi, wedding vase, blk/red birds, Frog Woman, 1973, 14"	950.00
Lela & Van, bowl, classic deer motif, hdls, 1970, 4x5"	150.00
Maricopa, vase, blk on red, Ida Redbird, 1970, 8x5"	150.00
Medina, JD; olla, eagle dancer ea side, birds/pueblos, 9x6"	175.00
Quezada, olla, turtle effigy, blk, sgn, 1992, 10x6"	225.00
San Juan, bowl, buff on red, eng linear band, 1960, 5x3"	35.00
Santa Clara, jar, blkware w/curvilinears, sgn Delorita, 4x4"	35.00
Santa Clara, olla, sienna/blk, sgn Stahn-Moo-Whe, 1975, 3"	275.00
Santa Clara, vase, blk w/cvd serpent & arrow, 1930, 5½"	50.00
Santo Domingo, blk on creamy buff, red slip base, 7⅜x8¾"	300.00
Santo Domingo, bowl, blkware w/feathers, 1950, 9x12"	300.00
Santo Domingo, olla, curvilinears, blk/red/cream, 1935, 10"	225.00
Santo Domingo, olla, EX foliate/bird motif, 1920, 10x7"	200.00
Zuni, deer/birds/sunflowers, orange/amber on wht, 1880s, 10"	1,155.00
Zuni, jar, fine line/classic designs, EX quality, 1980, 13"	3,500.00
Zuni, jar, stylized foliage/mc curvilinears, 1900, 10x10"	700.00

Pottery, San Ildefonso

The pottery of the San Ildefonso pueblo is especially sought after by collectors today. Under the leadership of Maria Martinez and her husband Julian, experiments began about 1918 which led to the development of the 'black-on-black' design achieved through exacting methods of firing the ware. They discovered that by smothering the fire at a specified temperature, the carbon in the smoke that ensued caused the pottery to blacken. Maria signed her work (often 'Marie') from the late teens to the 1960s; she died in 1980. Today a piece with her signature may bring prices in the $500.00 to $4,500.00 range.

Bowl, blkware, bear claw design, Maria & Julian, 1935, 3x6" 500.00
Bowl, blkware, incised Marie, w/1930s exhibit tag, 2⅜x7⅜" 685.00
Bowl, blkware, serpent motif, Bl Corn, 1975, 2½x6" 250.00
Bowl, blkware, stylized feathers, sgn Marie, 1940, 3¼x5½" 500.00
Bowl, blkware, 1930s World Exhibit label, sgn Marie, 1½x5" 800.00
Bowl, blkware w/cvd shoulder, Rose Gonzales, 1940, 6x12" 1,000.00
Bowl, Bl Corn, feathers/geometrics all around, 1970, 2¼x10" 500.00
Jar, blkware, Avanya figures, Maria Popovi, '50s, 4½x6¼" 580.00
Jar, blkware, bird tail design, Maria & Julian, 1935, 5" 475.00
Jar, blkware w/geometrics, Maria Popovi, 4x5" 285.00
Plate, blkware, feather border, Maria & Santana, 5¾" 195.00

Rugs, Navajo

Bands of dmns, 4-color, warp/selvage breaks, 1900, 41x48" 195.00
Bird figures in red center, 3-color, 1920s, 67x44", G 900.00
Blocks & dmns, gray/red/blk/orange, regional, 46x65" 400.00
Child's, 4-color, serrated dmns, ca 1870, 40x48", VG 1,200.00
Concentric rectangles, 5-color, hand carded/spun wool, 72x99" .1,320.00
Contemporary serrate, 4-color, Martha Belen, 30½x45" 110.00
Crystal, natural wool w/fishhooks & dmns, 1935, 49x72" 350.00
Eye-Dazzler, 3-color serrations, tassels, 1900s, 60x31", EX 700.00
Fret cross w/stepped terrace, red/brn, fading, 40x62" 230.00
Ganado, blk geometrics w/tan & red, 1920s, 29x49", EX 150.00
Ganado red w/4-color serrated dmns, 1920-40, 42x33", G 250.00

Geometrics, natural and aniline-dyed homespun wool, 4-color, 137x89", $7,150.00.

Germantown, saddle blanket, 5-color, fringe, 1885, 31x25" 2,475.00
Germantown, sawtooth/dmn pattern, 4-color, 46x72", EX 2,900.00
Germantown Chief's, 3-color fine weave, 4 tassels, 56x70" ...10,450.00
Klagatoh, classic design, stepped border, 4-color, 72x108", EX ...875.00
Klagetoh Sunrise, dbl-dye red/dk brn/natural, 39x54", EX 165.00
Navajo, Teec Nos Pos, very fine, 1980, 60x37" 1,050.00
Sawtooth border/dmn motif, 5-color, regional, 46x80" 1,950.00
Spirit line corners, 5-color, 1930s, 35x45" 195.00
Stars/dmns, 5-color, 1910, 78x44", VG 850.00
Storm pattern, 4-color dbl dye, wool, 1920, 25x49" 1,320.00
Teec Nos Pos, co-joined terraced dmns, 1920, 91x38" 3,500.00
Toadlena, brns & tan, 1930s, much wear/stains, 34x62" 250.00
Toadlena, 5-color, hand carded & spun wool, rprs, 33x50" 250.00
Transitional, aniline dyes, 6-color, some bleeding, 56x75" 385.00

Transitional serrate, aniline red/orange/brn, 39x72" 440.00
Two Grey Hills, 4-color, spirit line break, 1960s, 30x58" 330.00
Wearing, Transitional, 4-color, vegetal/aniline, 1890s, lg 800.00
Yei contemporary, 4-color on gray, hand-carded wool, 60x73" ...440.00
Yei Gallup, blk/gr & dbl-dye red on natural, 28½x33½" 95.00

Stoneware

Atl-atl weight, IL, gr granite, grooved/humped, 2¾x¾" 200.00
Bannerstone, IN, angular Geniculate type, oval hole, 2x2½" 350.00
Bannerstone, IN, banded glacial slate, winged, 4¼x2¼" 300.00
Bannerstone, IN, glacial slate, dbl crescent, rstr, 5½x4" 800.00
Bannerstone, OH, dk brn banded/tan slate, Archaic, 2" 125.00
Gorget, maroon hemitite, 2 conical holes, p-h, 2⅛x1⅜" 115.00
Pendant, IL, slate, Archaic period, 3" 45.00
Pestle, OH, quartzite, bell type, miniature, 2½" 45.00
Plummet, PA, hematite, grooved smaller end, 2x1¾" 75.00

Tools

Axe, blk stone head, tapered, from MI, p-h, 8x2" 150.00
Axe, gr-blk stone, dbl-ended, ¾-grooved, p-h, 6x3" 170.00
Axe, striped red stone, ¾-grooved, p-h, 6x3½" 150.00
Drill, AL, gray, stubby w/stemmed base, 1¼" 4.00
Drill, AR, tan, p-h, 1¾" 6.00
Drill, NM, lt gray translucent agate, expanded base, 2" 22.00
Hammer, stone maul head w/cvd human face, from MI, p-h, 6x4" ..200.00
Hoe, AR, 4" 45.00
Hoe, from IL, p-h, 5¼x4¼" 125.00
Scraper, Great Lakes, bone, inlay/cvd human face, 1800, 8x2" ..350.00
Scraper, Plains, steel, leather-wrapped hdl, 1900, 12x2" 50.00
Scraper, Sioux, elk antler/file/buffalo hide, 1880, 11x4x1" 200.00

Weapons

Bow, Plains, red/ochre pnt traces, 1870, 45x1½" 150.00
Club, dbl-point blk stone w/pewter inlay, bw hdl, 24x6" 175.00
Club, flop knob, bw on wood hdl, horsehair drop, 1900s, 52" 200.00
Club, Great Lakes, 'knot' type, wood, 1870, 19x5" 100.00
Club, gun stock-shape wood, brass tacks, steel blade, 36x11" 125.00
Club, Pawnee, gun stock style, steel blade, bird head, 1900s 125.00
Club, Plains, egg-shape stone, wood hdl w/bw, 1880, 23x7" 150.00
Club, Plains, egg-shaped stone, rawhide on hdl, 1870, 43x5" 350.00
Club, Plains, red stone egg shape, hide/wood hdl, 1880, 22x5" ...175.00
Club, Sioux, dbl-end stone head, full bw hdl, 1860, 14x7" 400.00
Club, Sioux, dbl-end stone head, quilled drops, 1900s, 28x4" 250.00

Miscellaneous

Canoe, Chippewa, Woodlands model, birch bark, 1930s, 63", EX ...1,045.00
Flute, bone w/cvd lines, from AZ cave, p-h, 6" 200.00
Flute, Kiowa, hand-cvd bird effigy stop, 1800s, 13x2" 1,100.00
Mortar, Hohokam, basalt stone, p-h, 2x2" 20.00
Peace medal, silver, Andrew Johnson, dtd 1865, 3" 275.00
Peace medal, silver, Zachary Taylor, dtd 1849, w/hole, 3" 400.00
Photogravure, Tonouige-Havasupai, Curtis, 1907, 15" 200.00
Powder horn, buffalo, leather strap w/ornaments, 1880, 25" 350.00
Powder horn, wood/copper ends, bone/antler on strap, 29" 175.00
Rope, Crow, braided horsehair, bw/cloth ends, 1910, 180" 300.00
Saddle, Apache, wood w/lg SW ball horn, 1870, 17x13x11" 175.00
Saddle drape, Yakima, buffalo hide/fringe/bw, 1930, 120x16" 850.00
Trade axe, Hudson Bay type, CI, wood hdl, 1860, 12½x5½" 400.00
Trade axe, iron w/star cutout, leather-wrap hdl, 1880, 21x7" 600.00
Tweezers, Crow, brass, attached to trade bead necklace, 1890 ....100.00

Amethyst Glass

The term amethyst simply describes the rich color of this glassware, made by many companies both here and abroad since the 19th century.

Bottle, scent; deep color, orig stopper, NE Glass, 5½" 260.00
Jar, mc autumn mtn scene w/gold, ped ft, 6½x4⅞" 150.00
Vase, appl mc flowers, amber ft, bl scalloped rim, 12½" 295.00
Vase, corset shape, ftd, 13½" 37.50
Vase, flared, crimped, 8½x9" 48.00
Vase, flint, tulip form, early, 9¾" 375.00
Vase, tulip-like petals form scalloped top, Faroy, 4" 10.00

Amphora

The Amphora Porcelain Works in the Teplitz-Turn area of Bohemia produced Art Nouveau-styled vases and figurines during the latter part of the 1800s through the first few decades of the 20th century. They marked their wares with various stamps, some incorporating the name and location of the pottery with a crown or a shield. Because Bohemia was part of the Austro-Hungarian empire prior to WWI, some examples are marked Austria; items marked with the Czechoslovakia designation were made after the war. Our advisor for this category is Jack Gunsaulus; he is listed in the Directory under Michigan.

Vase, Nouveau lady's profile, trees and foliage background with enameled grapes and leaves, 4-lobed top with gilt, marked, 13", $1,200.00.

Basket, bl w/butterfly, blk hdl, 6½" 200.00
Basket, emb florals, oval, 5½x9½" 250.00
Bottle, water; Greek figures HP on bl, ink stamp, 13½" 120.00
Bowl, appl grapes/vines, tubular upright ea side, 6x9", EX 350.00
Bowl, flowers & lattice, apricot & gr w/gold, ped ft 165.00
Ewer, appl berries/leaves, gr/gold on bl irid mottle, 11x6" 200.00
Ewer, bl & gold irid leaves on cream & gr, vine hdls, mk, 14" 985.00
Ewer, floral, mc on cream, scroll hdl, RS&K, 10½" 150.00
Figurine, lady w/2 baskets, gold trim, 1910s, 17½" 650.00
Figurine, man on camel, Imperial 1908-18 mk, 13x10½" 975.00
Jardiniere, blown-out man/wagon/horses, mc, 10x13" 975.00
Planter, wild duck w/chicks in nest, 1903-18 mk, 8½x10" 625.00
Sculpture, orchid in full detail, gold trim, 10" 1,500.00
Vase, basketweave w/appl flowers, Czech mk, 7" 215.00
Vase, blueberries & pk leaves appl on bl-gr ground, mk, 8¾" 275.00
Vase, butterflies/webs/jewels on dk gr, hdls, RS&K, 8" 500.00
Vase, Deco floral, strong colors, cylindrical, 16" 650.00
Vase, emb Deco flowers, cream w/gold accents, 10½" 125.00
Vase, emb faces/appl flowers on wide swirled top, 6½", EX 1,300.00

Vase, figural, mother lifting sm girl, Imperial mk, 7¾" 250.00
Vase, figural reserve front/bk, 1 w/lady on wht horse, 10½" 300.00
Vase, floral, bl/pk/gr/tan on dk brn, long hdls, 12" 240.00
Vase, floral w/gold trim, stick neck w/ornate hdls, RS&K, 7½" ...60.00
Vase, lily pond w/trees & sun, mc/24k gold, bulbous, 5" 230.00
Vase, maid's profile/trees, gilt, flattened oval w/ribs, 13" 900.00
Vase, mc geometric designs, cobalt trim, sgn, mk, 13½" 800.00
Vase, mc stylized floral bands on ivory, blk rim, mk, 14½" 650.00
Vase, Nouveau lady relief, gold flowers, prof rstr, mk, 18" 750.00
Vase, pk lustre leaves on gr mottled, 4 gold hdls, mk, 8" 225.00
Vase, pnt roses w/gold, conical w/4 angle under-rim hdls, 11" 400.00
Vase, poppies HP on brn, 4 hdls pointing upward, 7" 250.00
Vase, profile: queen in crown w/jewels, gilt, RS&K, 20" 4,600.00
Vase, reserve w/mc birds on tan matt, spout on 1 hdl, 10" 325.00
Vase, stylized flowers, cvd/pnt on brn, sm hdls, 7" 90.00
Vase, sun/bees/flowers, brn/bl w/24k gold, bulbous, 7½" 400.00
Vase, thistles watercolor, rtcl neck, appl hdls, 9x5" 300.00
Vase, webbed w/irid pnt floral band, gold highlights, 9x6" 250.00
Vase, yel roses, gold rim/hdls, Dachel design, 16" 750.00
Vase, 4 appl gr tendrils twist downward, emb floral, 9", NM 375.00

Animal Dishes with Covers

Covered animal dishes have been produced for nearly two centuries and are as varied as their manufacturers. They were made in many types of glass (slag, colored, clear, and milk glass) as well as china and pottery. On bases of nests and baskets, you will find animals and birds of every sort. The most common was the hen.

Some of the smaller versions made by McKee, Indiana Tumbler and Goblet Company, and Westmoreland Glass of Pittsburgh, Pennsylvania, were sold to food-processing companies who filled them with prepared mustard, baking powder, etc. Occasionally one will be found with the paper label identifying the product and processing company still intact.

Many of the glass versions produced during the latter part of the 19th century have been recently reproduced. As late as the 1960s, the Kemple Glass Company made the rooster, fox, lion, cat, lamb, hen, horse, turkey, duck, dove, and rabbit on split-ribbed or basketweave bases. They were made in amethyst, blue, amber, and milk glass, as well as a variegated slag. It is sometimes necessary to compare items in question to verified examples of older glass in order to recognize reproductions.

For more information, we recommend *Covered Animal Dishes* by our advisor, Everett Grist, whose address is in the Directory under Illinois. In the listings below, when only one dimension is given, it is the greater one, usually length.

Key: WS — Westmoreland Specialty

Baby Moses on cattail or reed base, milk glass, unmk, 6¼" 220.00
Cat on lacy base, milk glass, Westmoreland repro 95.00
Cat on wide-rib base, milk glass, 5½" 65.00
Chick in vertical egg, milk glass, 3¾" 125.00
Chicks in oblong basket, milk glass, pnt details, 4¼" 325.00
Dog on wide-rib base, bl opaque w/milk glass head, WS, 5¼" 120.00
Dolphin on sauce dish, milk glass, att Westmoreland, 7¼" 100.00
Duck, Atterbury; any color, unmk Wright repro, 11" 75.00
Duck, Atterbury; milk glass, Pat Apld for on base, 11" 275.00
Duck, Pintail; on dmn basketweave base, WS, 5½" 55.00
Duck, Pintail; on split-rib base, bl opaque, 5½" 110.00
Duck, Swimming; bl opaque, Vallerysthal, 5¾" 100.00
Duck on cattail base, milk glass, unmk, 5½" 85.00
Eagle, Mother; milk glass, Westmoreland 75.00
Eagle, Mother; other than milk glass, Westmoreland 100.00
Elephant w/rider, milk glass, Vallerysthal, 7" 350.00

Fish, Entwined; milk glass, lacy base, dtd lid, 6" dia 200.00
Fish (flat) on ribbed base, gr transparent 45.00
Fish on collared base, clear frosted, unmk 150.00
Fox, on lacy Atterbury base, milk glass, unmk, 6¼" 85.00

Fox on lacy base, milk glass, dated 1889, 7½", $225.00.

Hen, Straight-Headed; clear, red pnt details, IN Glass, lg 10.00
Hen on basketweave base, milk glass, Vallerysthal, 2" 35.00
Hen on cattail base, milk glass, unmk, 5½" 65.00
Hen on dmn basketweave base, bl w/milk glass head, WS, 5¼" 85.00
Hen on lacy base, marbled bk, bl opaque, 6¼" L 300.00
Hen on lacy base, milk glass, Atterbury, 6¼" L 120.00
Horse, milk glass, unmk McKee, 5½" 185.00
Lamb on picket fence, milk glass w/bl opaque head, WS 125.00
Lion, British; milk glass, emb title on base, 6¼" 195.00
Pekingese dog on rectangular base, milk glass, Sandwich, 4¼" ..425.00
Rabbit, Atterbury; bl opaque, glass eyes, dtd base, 6" 425.00
Rabbit, Atterbury; milk glass, glass eyes, dtd base, 9" 195.00
Rabbit, Mule-Eared; on picket base, milk glass, WG 70.00
Rabbit emerging from horizontal egg, milk glass, worn pnt 125.00
Rabbit on wheat base, milk glass, Flaccus 350.00
Rat on egg, pk transparent, lg 225.00
Robin on ped base, bl opaque, unmk late repro 15.00
Robin on ped base, milk glass, Vallerysthal 95.00
Rooster, Standing; clear w/red pnt details, att LE Smith 55.00
Rooster on wide-rib base, milk glass, WS, 5¼" 85.00
Rooster on wide-rib base, wht w/bl head, WS, 5¼" 125.00
Santa on sleigh, milk glass, 5½" L 100.00
Setter on sq base, bl opaque, att Vallerysthal 210.00
Steer's head, milk glass, Challinor Taylor, 7½" 2,200.00
Swan, Block; clear frosted, Challinor Taylor, 7" 145.00
Swan, Block; on basketweave base, milk glass 150.00
Swan, Closed-Neck; on basketweave base, milk glass, WS 75.00
Swan, Raised Wing; milk glass, molded eyes, Westmoreland repro .75.00
Swan, Raised-Wing; milk glass, eye sockets, att Atterbury 185.00
Turkey, standing, clear, unmk, lg 150.00
Turtle, amber transparent, lg 100.00

Appliances, Electric

Kitchen appliances of the electric variety have been around for one hundred years, since the first exhibit of the electric kitchen at the Chicago Exposition of 1893, which introduced a completely new concept in easing the drudgery of kitchen chores. Among the earliest appliances were a water kettle, a sauce pan and a chafing dish. After the turn of the century, patents for resistance wire along with other advances in technology opened up a whole new chapter for the kitchen. Small appliances such as irons, toasters, mixers, coffee percolators and waffle irons were a field in themselves. Later larger appliances such as vacuum cleaners, washing machines and the like were introduced.

Today all early small appliances are being collected. Toasters, irons and percolators top the list. Of special interest are those from the '20s through the '50s, all of which not only make a great collection but wonderful accent pieces for the kitchen.

Prices listed below are for examples in very good to excellent condition and in good working order. Be sure to check them for safety before using old appliances. Our advisor is Jim Barker; he is listed in the Directory under Pennsylvania.

Blender, Knapp Monarch Liquidizer, Deco style, 1940s, EX 50.00
Coffee set, Krome Kraft, golden Bakelite hdls, 3-pc, EX 165.00
Coffee urn, chrome w/yel Bakelite, Manning-Bowman, 14½" 100.00
Coffee urn, Deco globe shape, chrome, cloth cord, 24-cup, EX ..100.00
Deep fryer, Fryrite, EX 12.50
Fan, General Electric, oscillating, desk type, 1938, lg, NM 75.00
Fan, Little Giant, oscillating, electric, 8", EX 52.00
Fan, Luminaire, fancy CI w/brass finish, on stand, 59" 625.00
Fan, Polar Cub, AC Gilbert, 6", EX orig 70.00
Fan/luminaire, cast metal, Cincinnati Victor, 59", VG 225.00
Foot massager, Dr Scholl's, enamel/metal, chrome base 42.50
Hair dryer, Oster, chrome, unused, MIB 50.00
Hair dryer, White Cross, Chicago, electric, 1922, EX in case 20.00
Heater, brass/ceramic/wire, Westinghouse Cozy Glow Jr, 1920 ....48.00
Light bulb, CEL&P Co Hazelton PA on label, 1905, 4½" 18.00
Light bulb, National Mazda, brass base, Tungsten filament 15.00
Light bulb, National Mazda/GE logo, 1915-19 ....15.00
Popcorn popper, Monarch Teenie Weenie, EX 55.00
Popcorn roaster, decaled glass case, counter top, 26", G 300.00
Refrigerator, General Electric, motor on top, 1930, 64" 365.00

Toaster, Hotpoint #159T33, EX, $125.00.

Toaster, El Toasto 150.00
Toaster, L&H #202 or #204, ea 55.00
Toaster, Marian Giant #66 Flip Flop, chrome, EX 55.00
Toaster, Meteor #1220 ....65.00
Toaster, Paragon Electric 200.00
Toaster, Proctor #1405 ....85.00
Toaster, Sampson Tri Matic 150.00
Toaster, Simplex #211 ....150.00
Toaster, Star Rite Extra Fast 50.00
Toaster, Toast-O-Later, EX 160.00
Toaster, Universal E-942 ....85.00
Toaster, Universal E-944 ....65.00
Toaster, Wht Cross #230 ....55.00
Vacuum cleaner, Bellows, EX pnt 110.00

Vacuum cleaner, Fairfax, chrome canister, Deco style, '30s **90.00**
Vacuum cleaner, National, Harvey Stone Sales, 1900s, 52", VG .**80.00**
Waffle iron, Landers, Frary & Clark **45.00**
Waffle iron, Porcelier, EX **150.00**
Waffle iron, Westinghouse #WD-4 ....**50.00**

Arequipa

The Arequipa Pottery operated from 1911 until 1918 at a sanitorium near Fairfax, California. Its purpose was two-fold: therapy for the patients and financial support for the institution. Frederick H. Rhead was the originator and director. The ware, made from local clays, was often hand thrown, simply styled and decorated. Marks were varied but always incorporated the name of the pottery and the state. A circular arrangement encompassing the negative image of a vase beside a tree is most common.

Examples are evaluated according to quality of artwork; size and shape are less important. Those done by Rhead himself are very desirable.

Vase, pink and green decoration on blue matt, marked, ca 1912-13, 8½x4", $1,600.00.

Bowl, incised leaves, brns, glossy, 2¾x4½" **495.00**
Vase, arabesques, cvd/pnt, rust/blk/gr on lt gr, 6x4", EX **4,400.00**
Vase, Arts & Crafts trailings at top, purple matt, 6" **850.00**
Vase, cvd/pnt vine around neck, pk/yel on gr matt, CA, 6" **1,045.00**
Vase, floral/leaf emb on brn-flecked pk-brn semigloss, 8" **900.00**
Vase, gr lava, 8" **550.00**
Vase, gr to blk, wisteria w/rtcl, shouldered, no mk, 11½" **495.00**
Vase, stylized emb leaves/vines, wht/bl/brn/gr, 6¼x3½", NM ..**1,500.00**
Vase, tan matt w/teal at shoulder, #1004, mfg flaw, 3½" **200.00**

Argy-Rousseau, G.

Gabriel Argy-Rousseau produced both fine art glass and quality commercial ware in Paris, France, in 1918. He favored Art Nouveau as well as Art Deco and in the twenties produced a line of vases in the Egyptian manner, made popular by the discovery of King Tut's tomb. One of the most important types of glass he made was pate-de-verre. Most of his work is signed. Items listed below are pate-de-verre unless noted otherwise.

Bowl, lg sunflower front/bk, scaly rim-to-base hdls, 8" **5,100.00**
Bowl, vines/leaves on flared octagon, amber tones, 10" **5,700.00**
Bowl, 4 butterflies encircle rim, lav/gr on wht, deep, 4" **9,750.00**
Bowl, 7 birds around rim, flower center, wine/gr, 4x10" **6,600.00**
Chandelier, as 12" flower blossom, on gilt-metal mt, 32" **18,700.00**

Earrings, Tulipe, tulips on teardrops, lav/rose, 2¾" **2,000.00**
Pendant, Conifere, pine cone/leaves, red/lav, 2½" dia **1,150.00**
Pendant, Violettes de Parma, purple/yel flowers, 2¼" dia **1,265.00**
Plate, lily pads at rim+3 flaring sqs, bl/purple/gr, 12" **3,300.00**
Tray, cameo of lady, ext: dmns/flowers, brn/yel/wine, 7" L **1,800.00**
Vase, Hesperides picks apples, red/purple, ovoid, rstr, 9½" **4,350.00**
Vase, tree trunk/flowers, blk/dk pk/purple on mottle, 6" **5,500.00**
Vase, 2 sq panels w/Egyptian woman w/jug, oranges/brn, 12" ..**40,000.00**
Vase, 3 blk/gr crabs w/red eyes on lav frost, ovoid, 5½" **550.00**
Vase, 3 branches w/berry clusters, red/gr/brn on gray, 2½" **2,400.00**
Veilluse, ovoid shade w/geometrics, brn/tan, 7" **5,200.00**

Art Deco

To the uninformed observer, 'Art Deco' evokes images of chrome and glass, streamlined curves and aerodynamic shapes, mirrored prints of pink flamingos, and statues of slender nudes and greyhound dogs. Though the Deco movement began in 1925 at the Paris International Exposition and lasted to some extent into the 1950s, within that period of time the evolution of fashion and taste continued as it always has, resulting in subtle variations.

The French Deco look was one of opulence — exotic inlaid woods, rich material, lush fur and leather. Lines tended toward symmetrical curves. American designers adapted the concept to cover every aspect of fashion and home furnishings from small inexpensive picture frames, cigarette lighters, and costume jewelry to high-fashion designer clothing and exquisite massive furniture with squared or circular lines. Vinyl was a popular covering, and chrome-plated brass was used for chairs, cocktail shakers, lamps, and tables. Dinnerware, glassware, theaters, and train stations were designed to reflect the new 'Modernism.'

The Deco movement made itself apparent into the fifties in wrought iron lamps with stepped pink plastic shades and Venetian blinds. The sheer volume of production during those twenty-five years provides collectors today with fine examples of the period that can be bought for as little as $10.00 or $20.00 up to the thousands. Chrome items signed 'Chase' are prized by collectors, and blue glass radios and tables with blue glass tops are high on the list of desirability in many areas.

Those interested in learning more about this subject will want to read *Collector's Guide to Art Deco* by our advisor, Mary Frank Gaston. She is listed in the Directory under Texas. See also Bronzes; Chase; Frankart; Furniture; Jewelry; Lalique; Radios; etc.

Ashtray, gold-bronze metal w/lt orange cloisonne, Farberware **15.00**
Ashtray, lady's profile, ceramic, Japan **22.50**
Bedroom suite, blond w/bl glass inserts, 4-poster bed, 3-pc **995.00**
Bookends, nude lady w/man kneeling at ft, Bronzmet, '24, pr **125.00**
Bowl, bl glass, free-form shape, stepped base, unmk, 9" **175.00**
Bowl, chrome, sq ft, unmk, 3¼x8¼"+2 candle holders **150.00**
Box, jewelry, Fr ivory Bakelite, plain, 2x5¼x4" **25.00**
Candelabra, 3-light, rtcl bronze hunt scene, 24½", pr **445.00**
Chandelier, silvered metal w/6 arms, rnd glass shades, 37" **500.00**
Cigarette case, Bakelite & pigskin, sliding top, Rolinx **80.00**
Cigarette case, chrome, Indian chief profile, NY, 3x2" **17.50**
Cigarette case/lighter, silver w/3 gold deer, Elgin, 4¾" **45.00**
Cigarette dispenser, burled maple, wedge shape, 4½" **175.00**
Cigarette holder, blk plastic, 6" **30.00**
Clock, digital, bronze, Silvercrest, mid-1930s, 19" L **225.00**
Clock, gr onyx w/SP brass face/numerals, 8-day, Swiss, 8½" **75.00**
Clock, mantel; gold pnt dog on gr ceramic base, unmk, 11½x10" .**125.00**
Clock, mantel; sq, walnut case, Westminster chimes **225.00**
Clock, violinist rests beside, metal/faux ivory/marble, 27½" L **900.00**
Coffee set, chrome w/blk Bakelite hdls, Heystoneware, 3-pc **40.00**
Compact/cigarette case/lipstick holder, sparkled Lucite, 5x3" **32.50**

Console, Raymond Subes, iron fr w/scrolls, marble top, 35" **2,500.00**
Cup & saucer, demitasse; mc dots on ivory, Hancock Pottery **20.00**
Cup & saucer, Tricorn pattern, Salem China **20.00**
Decanter, clear to gr, notched/beaded ribs, 11", +5 shots **70.00**
Door knocker, brass, Egyptian motif, 6½" L **50.00**
Drawer pulls, butterscotch Bakelite, pr **40.00**
Dresser set, Catalin, 3 ribbed containers on 10½" tray **165.00**
Figurine, birds, gr glossy, Ch Lemanceau **275.00**
Figurine, lady in sarong, Clarke, E Palestine OH, 1940s **130.00**
Hairbrush, brn plastic, stepped shape **7.50**
Incense burner, Egyptian lady, sgn Lisne, ceramic, Fr, 6½" **400.00**
Lamp, boudoir; nude beside amber glass globe, Kelly, 8x8½" **500.00**
Lamp, boudoir; pot metal base w/frosted nude figure top, 8" **250.00**
Lamp, brass, slag glass panels/silk fringe on 8-sided shade **275.00**
Lamp, cobalt & chrome lighthouse form, sailboat on base, 12" ..**175.00**
Lamp, draped nude, pnt metal on blk marble base, Fayral, 21" ..**1,700.00**
Lamp, gr nudes against frosted 5" frosted globe, 11½" **325.00**
Lamp, pyramid geometric frosted shade; wrought base, Degue **925.00**
Lamp, Salterini, skyscraper base, wrought iron/mica, 27" **2,000.00**
Lamp, Saturn w/stars on conical base, satin glass, 12" **465.00**
Lipstick case, sterling w/carnelian stone & eng vines, 2¼" **50.00**
Match holder, brass, brass holder w/attached tray, 4" **70.00**
Mirror, hand; hammered sterling, initials **45.00**
Mirror, iron w/scrollwork & rose bud ea side, oval, 24x35" **575.00**
Mirror, vanity; pot metal nude on faux marble base at front **175.00**
Motion light, mc Indian figural, hammered metal bk, 12" **195.00**
Night light, 4 domed red glass bay windows, chrome **55.00**
Pipe stand, nude diving figure, bronze, unmk **115.00**
Plate, gr-lined profiles & branches on ivory, Iroquois, 9" **30.00**
Sconce, ldgl panels in tassel-shape brass mt, 13", pr **690.00**
Server, 4 chrome trays (2 swivel), Bakelite hdl, 11½" **125.00**
Soap dish, chrome, Manning-Bowman, wall mt **18.00**
Tea set, quadruple SP, SLO Co, ca 1927, 5 lg pcs **150.00**
Toast rack, 4 sections, ball ft, 5" **60.00**
Tray, chrome w/cobalt glass insert, N Bel Geddes, 16x11½" **250.00**
Vase, blk amethest glass w/silver HP decor, 6" **30.00**
Vase, blk glass, trumpet form, unmk, 12" **65.00**
Vase, ceramic, blk spirals trailed on orange, Bazet, 12x10" **350.00**
Vase, Jean Luce, clear glass w/etched overlapping sqs, 7½" **575.00**
Vase, zigzag flames, red/yel/brn/gr, Ditmar Urbach, 8" **300.00**
Wine cooler, Wiskemann, SP cylinder w/angle hdls, 9½" **900.00**

Art Glass Baskets

A popular novelty and gift item during the Victorian era, these one-of-a-kind works of art were produced in just about any type of art glass in use at that time. They were never marked, since these were not true production pieces but 'whimsies' made by glassworkers to relieve the tedium of the long work day. Some were made as special gifts. The more decorative and imaginative the design, the more valuable the basket.

Amber, mc fruit, ormolu hdl & base w/pea pods & leaves, 6½" ..**185.00**
Amberina overshot, hobnail ruffled rim, 9½x7½x8½" **495.00**
Aqua & brn spatter, swirled ribs, ruffled, clear hdl, 6½x5" **255.00**
Butterscotch & opal spangle, crimped, clear V-hdl, 13" dia **285.00**
Gr, wht int, Dmn Quilt, appl dk gr thorn hdl, 6½x4½" **85.00**
Gr opal to red spatter, clear twist hdl, 6½x6" **145.00**
Gr to amber shaded, emb ribs, pk twist hdl, 6x4¾" **95.00**
Gr w/emb swirl & swirl rosettes w/mica, clear hdl, 6½x5" **110.00**
Lime gr to clear opal, emb florals & rope, braided hdl, 7¾" **115.00**
Mc spatter, clear appl leafy branch & hdl, 8-crimp, 5¾x3½" **110.00**
Mc spatter, ruffled rim, clear thorn hdl, 6x5½" **165.00**
Mc spatter, star-shaped top, emb rosettes w/gold, 6x4½" **95.00**

Mc spatter, wht int, ruffled, clear hdl, 5¼x4¾" **95.00**
Mc spatter w/emb hobnails, bl int, twist hdl, 6x5" **100.00**
Mc spatter w/gr mica, clear thorn hdl, 5½x4¼" **105.00**
Orange o/l, 8-crimp top, clear thorn hdl, ftd, 8¼x5¼" **175.00**
Orchid transparent w/emb swirls, clear thorn hdl, 6x5" **95.00**
Pk o/l, ruffled rim, sq amber thorn hdl, 6½x5" **165.00**
Pk opal to vaseline, Drape mold, thorn hdl, 7½x5½x7" **210.00**
Rainbow spatter, Coin Spot, opal cased, 7¼x4½" **435.00**
Rose o/l, amber ruffle, amber crisscross hdl, 8x6½" **210.00**
Tortoise shell, appl amber thorn twist hdl, 8x5" **100.00**
Vaseline, Optic Panels, HP garlands/gold flowers, 7x6" **175.00**
Wht o/l, bl int, ruffled rim, appl hdl, 4½x4½" **55.00**
Wht opaque w/cranberry ruffle, clear twist hdl, 8x5" **145.00**
Yel & wht spatter, emb basketweave, ruffled rim, 5¾x4½" **110.00**
Yel cased w/emb beaded swirl, clear thorn hdl, 6¼x4½" **95.00**
Yel opaque, wht spatter int, gold trim, thorn hdl, 5¼x4⅛" **100.00**

Art Nouveau

From the famous 'L'Art Nouveau' shop in the rue de Provence in Paris, 'New Art' spread across the continent and belatedly arrived in America in time to add its curvilineal elements and asymmetrical ornamentations to the ostentatious remains of the Rococo revival of the 1800s. Nouveau manifested itself in every facet of decorative art. In glassware Tiffany turned the concept into a commercial success that lasted well into the second decade of this century and created a style that inspired other American glassmakers for decades. Furniture, lamps, bronzes, jewelry, and automobiles were designed within the realm of its dictates. Today's market abounds with lovely examples of Art Nouveau, allowing the collector to choose one or several areas that hold a special interest. Our advisor for this category is Steven Whysel; he is listed in the Directory under Arkansas. See also Bronzes; Galle; Jewelry; Loetz; Tiffany; Silver; specific manufacturers.

Mirror, walnut with carved scrolling buds and stems, full-blown poppy at each corner, ca 1900, 24x21", $825.00.

Belt, lady's, SP openwork, lady's head & vintage, EX **200.00**
Box, SP, interlaced foliage, openwork ft, WMF, 7" L **285.00**
Figurine, att WMF, silver metal, nymph beside harp, 12" **350.00**
Figurine, compo, Egyptian girl w/2 baskets, mc/gilt, 22" **250.00**
Figurine, Wiener Keramic, lady w/sm Blkamoor boy, sgn, '07, 16" .**895.00**
Fire screen, copper, iron fr/ceramic insert, English, 29x18" **330.00**
Jardiniere, Villanis, bronze, 3-D maid standing on rim, 31" **4,100.00**
Lamp, Anton K Nelson, gilt bronze, nude in lily pad, 31", NM .**2,500.00**
Lamp, Elias, bronze, winged maid lifts rtcl dome shade, 30" **3,200.00**
Note pad, SP, w/pencil & chain **110.00**

Scissors, brass & steel, 11", in brass sheath **65.00**
Screen, Cutler-Girard, mahog, cvd flowers, ships inlay, 71" **2,185.00**
Tray, sterling, emb iris/naiad busts, Birmingham mks, 9x12" **625.00**
Vanity case, chrome plated, eng flowers, worn mirror, 4x2½" **40.00**
Vase, Charpentier, bronze, 3-D nude, lg grapevine hdls, 16" ...**1,000.00**
Vase, Ditmar, appl leaves/stems, mottled irid, #1/20882, 11" **425.00**
Vase, J Sorram, bronze, slim w/angle hdls, base w/frogs, 15" **1,350.00**
Vase, Mingiot, gilt bronze, cherub at side, hdl, 13", pr **1,400.00**
Vase, Zumbo, nude clings to rim, irid, HP cattails, 13", NM ...**1,900.00**

Arts and Crafts

The Arts and Crafts movement began in England during the last quarter of the 19th century, and its influence was soon felt in this country. Among its proponents in America were Elbert Hubbard (see Roycroft) and Gustav Stickley (see Stickley). They rebelled against the mechanized mass production of the Industrial Revolution and against the cumulative influence of hundreds of years of man's changing taste. They subscribed to the theory of purification of the styles: that designs be geared strictly to necessity. At the same time they sought to elevate these basic ideals to the level of accepted 'art.' Simplicity was their virtue; to their critics it was a fault.

The type of furniture they promoted was squarely built, usually of heavy oak, and so simple was its appearance that as a result many began to copy the style which became known as 'Mission.' Soon factories had geared production toward making cheap copies of their designs. In 1915 Stickley's own operation failed, forced into bankruptcy by the machinery he so despised. Hubbard lost his life that same year on the ill-fated *Lusitania*. Within the decade the style had lost its popularity.

Metalware was produced by numerous crafts people, from experts such as Dirk van Erp and Albert Berry to unknown novices. Prices for Arts and Crafts accessories rose dramatically in 1988, but by the beginning of 1991 leveled off and (in some cases) dropped. Metal items or hardware should not be scrubbed or scoured; to do so could remove or damage the rich, dark patina typical of this period. Our advisor for this category is Bruce Austin; he is listed in the Directory under New York. See also Furniture; Roycroft; Silver; Stickley; specific manufacturers.

Table lamp, Dirk van Erp, hammered copper, ca 1914, 11¾" with 4-panel 11" diameter shade, $6,050.00.

Biscuit jar, Tudric, hammered pewter, emb lily pads at rim **350.00**
Bookends, Old Mission Kopperkraft, appl metal pods/leaves **500.00**
Bowl, Kalo #323, copper, 2x10" dia, VG **250.00**
Bowl, LeBolt #1708/804, silver, goblet form, monogram, 4x5" ...**230.00**
Box, copper w/appl silver fish on lid, fish as hdl, 6½" dia **85.00**
Box, ET Hurley, bronze, sea horses on lid, EX patina, 5" L **400.00**
Box, van Erp, copper, ornate design on lid/bk, mk, 4" W, VG **425.00**
Candle holder, Clarence Crafters, brass w/floral, mk, 3x5½" **140.00**
Candlestick, Jarvie, Iota, brass w/bobeche, no mk, 13½", VG **650.00**

Candlesticks, att Hurley, bronze, sea horse std, 7", VG, pr **325.00**
Candlesticks, Hurley, bronze, 3 stems form heart, 15", pr **1,200.00**
Candlesticks, Jarvie, brass, line on cup/stem, 11", VG, pr **600.00**
Candlesticks, silver/copper, pencil std, wide base, 14", pr **240.00**
Chamberstick, hand-wrought copper w/brass studs, C-hdl, 3x6" ..**45.00**
Chamberstick, Jarvie, angle hdl/ovoid top, EX patina, 6x5" **500.00**
Compote, Kalo #AC2, sterling, petal top/base, 7x9", EX **650.00**
Dish, Liberty/Tudric, pewter, scalloped, peaked lid, 10" **750.00**
Door knocker, ET Hurley, bronze of 2 facing sea horses, mk **600.00**
Frame, Clarence Crafters, copper/brass w/rose motif, 8x6", VG ..**260.00**
Lamp, att van Erp, riveted copper std, mica cone shade, 17" ...**3,750.00**
Lamp, ceiling; 6 slag glass panels in hammered iron fr, 22" **280.00**
Lamp, hammered copper 13½" cone shade w/3 mica panels **1,600.00**
Lamp, Heintz, 9" shade w/rtcl jonquils bkd by mica, 15" **600.00**
Lamp, Old Mission Kopper Kraft, riveted, 18" mica shade, EX ..**4,250.00**
Pen tray, ET Hurley, bronze w/dk gr to blk patina, 7½" L **130.00**
Plant stand, Lakeside Crafters, spindles, 4-leg, brass liner **850.00**
Plaque, emb/hammered copper w/2 horses & man, oak fr, 35x58" .**950.00**
Spoon, Allan Adler, sterling, rnd bowl, wide hdl, 5" **110.00**
Spoon, Kalo #201, long hdl, spade bowl, initial L, 13½" **280.00**
Sugar tongs, Kalo #3996, sterling, 4", EX **260.00**
Tea set, Liberty & Co, hammered copper/brass hdls, 3-pc **375.00**
Tray, Benedict #110, hammered copper w/4 emb spades, 15" dia ..**1,500.00**
Tray, D van Erp, lobed corners w/riveted cutouts, 12" **1,800.00**
Tray, Kalo #G10F, sterling, 5-crimp sides, 10", EX **350.00**
Vase, hand-wrought copper, 3 ornate rtcl areas, 5x5", VG **200.00**
Vase, Heintz, bronze w/dk patina, silver weeds o/l, 11x4½" **450.00**
Vase, Heintz, bronze w/med patina, silver flower o/l, 8x5" **250.00**
Vase, JB #2764, copper, bulbous w/ring foot, 4½", EX **110.00**
Vase, overlapping leaves in Grueby's style, Ohio, 1920, 6" **250.00**
Vase, Silver Crest, bronze w/appl floral, tapered sides, 12" **180.00**
Vase, van Erp, copper w/orig patina, 'warty,' mk, 3x5", EX **850.00**

Austrian Ware

From the late 1800s until the beginning of WWI, several companies were located in the area known at the turn of the century as Bohemia. They produced hard-paste porcelain dinnerware and decorative items primarily for the American trade. Today examples bearing the marks of these firms are usually referred to by collectors as Austrian ware, indicating simply the country of their origin. Of those various companies, these marks are best known: M.Z. Austria; Victoria, Carlsbad, Austria (Schmidt and Company); and O. & E.G. (Royal) Austria.

Though most of the decorations were transfer designs which were sometimes signed by the original artist, pieces marked Royal Austria were often hand painted and so indicated alongside the backstamp.

Of these three companies, Victoria, Carlsbad, Austria, is the most highly valued. Collectors should note that in our listings transfer decorations showing 'signatures' (sgn), such as 'Wagner,' 'Kauffmann,' 'LeBrun,' etc., were not actually painted by those artists but were merely based on their original paintings.

Charger, Von Hindenburgh portrait, cobalt & gold, mk, 12⅜" ..**225.00**
Figurine, chicken, life-like, Keramos, 13x15" **250.00**
Figurine, woman w/vase on shoulder, mc, mk S in circle, 10½" ..**130.00**
Fish set, 10 plates, 22" platter, gravy boat, O&EG Royal **300.00**
Plaque, HP acorns & oak leaves, Royal mk, 9" **48.00**
Plate, Constance portrait, much gold, bl beehive mk, 9¾" **110.00**
Plate, mc roses, sgn Tann, Royal mk, 10" **65.00**
Teapot, flowers/butterflies, rose finial, squat, Herend, 6" **180.00**
Vase, hibiscus cameo, peach on mc ground, Kralik, 5" **350.00**

Autographs

Autograph collecting, also known as 'philography' or 'love of writing,' used to be a hobby shared by a few thousand dedicated collectors. But in recent years, autograph collecting has become a serious pursuit for more than 2,000,000 collectors worldwide. And in the past decade, more investors are adding rare and valuable autograph portfolios to their traditional investments. One reason for this sudden interest in autograph investing relates to the simple economic law of supply and demand. Rare autographs have a 'fixed' supply, meaning that unlike diamonds, gold, silver, stock certificates, etc., no more are being produced. There are only so many Abraham Lincoln, Marilyn Monroe, and Charles Lindbergh autographs available. In the meantime, it's estimated that more than 20,000 new collectors enter the market each year, thus creating an ever-increasing demand. Hence, the rare autographs generally rise steadily in value each year. Because of this scarcity, a serious collector will pay over $10,000.00 for a photograph signed by both Wilbur and Orville Wright, or as much as $25,000.00 for a handwritten letter of George Washington.

But by far, the majority of autograph collectors in the country do it for the love of the hobby. A polite letter and self-addressed, stamped envelope sent to a famous person will often bring the desired result. And occasionally one receives not only an autograph but a nice handwritten letter thanking the fan as well!

In terms of value, there are five general types of autographs: 1) mere signatures on an album page or card; 2) signed photographs; 3) signed documents; 4) typed letters signed; and 5) handwritten letters. The signatures are the least valuable, and handwritten letters the most valuable. The reasoning here is simple: with a handwritten letter, not only do you get an autograph but the handwritten message of the person as well. And this content can sometimes increase the value many times over. A handwritten letter of Babe Ruth thanking a fan for a gift might fetch a few thousand dollars. But if the letter were to mention Ruth's feelings on the day he retired, it could easily sell for $10,000.00 or more.

There are several major autograph collector organizations where members can exchange celebrity addresses or buy, sell, and trade their autographed wares. Philography can be a fun and rewarding hobby. And who knows! In ten or twenty years, those autographs you got for free could be worth a small fortune!

In the listings below, photos are assumed black and white unless noted color. Our advisor for autographs is Tim Anderson; he is listed in the Directory under Utah.

Key:
ADS — handwritten document signed	ins — inscription
ALS — handwritten letter signed	ISP — inscribed signed photo
	LH — letterhead
ANS — handwritten note signed	LS — signed letter, typed or written by someone else
AQS — autograph quotation signed	PLH — personal letterhead
	sig — signature
CS — counter signed	SP — signed photo
DS — document signed	

Alpert, Herb; ISP, 8x10" 10.00
Armstrong, Louis; ISP, 8x10" 370.00
Asimov, Issac; ISP, 8x10" 50.00
Belushi, James; ISP, 8x10" 13.00
Benny, Jack; ins & sig, 3x5" card 55.00
Bernstein, Leonard; ISP, 6x8", 1984 ....100.00
Blanc, Mel; ISP, dtd 1981, 8x10" 135.00
Blocker, Dan; LS, thank you, 1971, 1-pg 150.00
Boyd, William; ISP, as Hopalong Cassidy, 5x7" 100.00

Bradley, Omar; sig on 3x5" card 50.00
Burroughs, John; ALS, June 20, 1887 ....180.00
Burton, Tim; ins & sig on 3x5" card 15.00
Cagney, James; SP, scene w/Bogart from OK Kid, 8x10" 75.00
Cantor, Eddie; sig on 3x5" card 50.00
Chamberlain, Wilt; SP, 8x10" 85.00
Chase, Chevy; ISP, 8x10" 12.00
Christie, Agatha; AQS, Ancient Indian Saying, 1-pg 500.00
Churchill, Winston; LS, Aug 14, 1936, 1-pg 2,400.00
Clay, Cassius; sig on slip of paper 210.00
Collins, Michael; SP, color, in astronaut suit, 8x10" 100.00
Costner, Kevin; SP, scene from Robin Hood, blk/wht, 8x10" 40.00
Crabbe, Buster; ISP, emerging from pool, 3½x5" 50.00
Crosby, Bing; LS, dtd 1952, 1-pg 75.00
Davis, Bette; SP, 8x10" 75.00

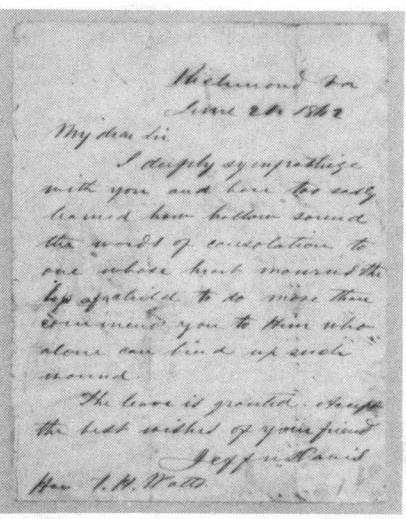

Jefferson Davis, letter written to T.H. Watts, dated 1862, in shadow box frame, $1,250.00.

Dempsey, Jack; SP, 4" sq 125.00
Dickens, Charles; ALS, LH, dtd 1869, 2-pg 2,000.00
Doak, William; sig & ins on lg newspaper photo 22.00
Eddy, Nelson; sig on 3x5" card 55.00
Einstein, Albert; LS, dtd 1945, 1-pg 1,725.00
Eisenhower, Dwight D; LS, White House LH, dtd 1957, 1-pg 200.00
Fleming, Sir Alexander; sig on 3x5" card 325.00
Flynn, Errol; sig & ins on 3x5" card in pencil 125.00
Ford, Gerald; sig on 3x5" card 40.00
Foster, George; SP, 8x10" glossy 25.00
Gere, Richard; SP, 5x7" 20.00
Glenn, John H; ALS, dtd 1959, 1-pg 420.00
Goldberg, Arthur J; SP, 8x10" 165.00
Goldthwait, Bobcat; ISP, 8x10" 10.00
Grant, Cary; sig on 3x5" card 125.00
Grodin, Charles; SP, blk & wht, 8x10" 9.00
Guest, Henry; sig on card 12.00
Guinnes, Alex; SP, as Obi wan Kenobi, 8x10" 38.00
Haley, Alex; SP, 4x6" 100.00
Hayes, Gabby; sig on 3x5" card 125.00
Hayes, Helen; SP, scene w/Gable, 8x10" 42.00
Hayes, Rutherford; ANS, dtd 1884, 1-pg 320.00
Hefner, Hugh; SP, color, ins, 8x10" 15.00
Holmes, Oliver Wendell; AQS, dtd 1880, 1-pg 320.00
Holyfield, Evander; SP, color, in trunks w/belt, 8x11" 30.00
Irving, Dr J; SP, 8x10" 85.00
Jackson, Michael; sig on album cover 150.00

Johansson, Ingemar; SP, 8x10"	35.00
Johnson, Lady Bird; ISP, 8x10"	45.00
Jones, Tom; SP, color, 8x10"	16.00
Jordan, Len; sig on postcard	17.00
Kennedy, Ted; sig on unused banquet ticket	25.00
King, Alan; ISP, 8x10"	10.00
King, Billie Jean; SP, 8x6"	17.00
Ladd, Cheryl; ISP, blk & wht, 8x10"	10.00
Madonna, SP, 8x10" glossy	125.00
Mailer, Norman; sig in book	85.00
Mantle, Mickey; SP, 8x10"	75.00
Michener, James A; SP, dated 1985, 8x10"	60.00
Mitchell, William D; sig on card	22.00
Monroe, Marilyn; SP, 8x10"	2,000.00
Moore, Henry; SP, 6x4"	135.00
Moore, JE; LS on Army War College stationery	22.00
Mother Teresa, LS, reverse of flyer w/her holding child	95.00
Murphy, Audie; SP, 8x10" glossy	100.00
Nixon, Richard M; sig in book, dtd March 1992	100.00
Ono, Yoko; ISP, color, 5x5"	30.00
Orbison, Roy; SP in gold ink, color, in concert, 8x10"	130.00
Peck, Gregory; ISP, 8x10"	38.00
Pickford, Mary; sig on 3x5" card	40.00
Porter, Cole; sig on 3x5 card	175.00
Pryor, Richard; SP, 8x10"	35.00
Remick, Lee; SP, 8x10" glossy	10.00
Rizzuto, Phil; SP, 8x10" glossy	38.00
Rochne, Knute K; sig in yearbook, dtd 1928	1,250.00
Roosevelt, Eleanor; LS, Nov 1, 1957, 1-pg	75.00
Roosevelt, Franklin D; sig on 3x5" card w/picture of FDR	250.00
Rose, Pete; SP, 8x10" glossy	45.00
Ruth, Babe; SP	1,000.00
Rutherford, Johnny; ISP, 8x10"	15.00
Salk, Jonas; SP, lab scene, 8x10"	120.00
Schultz, Charles; ISP, 5x7"	80.00
Shepard, Alan B; ISP, color, 5x4"	22.00
Sousa, John P; ISP, w/Metropolitan Opera program, 8x10"	600.00
Stewart, James; LS, sig on short note	30.00
Stewart, Jimmy; LS, LH, no date, 1-pg	95.00
Truman, Harry S; ins/sig on wine list, dtd 1962	120.00
Unitas, Jonnny; SP, 8x10"	35.00
Wayne, John; SP, 8x10" glossy	350.00
Welles, Gideon; DS, orders from Navy, dtd 1965	88.00
Williams, Ted; SP, 8x10"	75.00

Automobilia

While some automobilia buffs are primarily concerned with restoring vintage cars, others concentrate on only one area of collecting. For instance, hood ornaments were often quite spectacular. Made of chrome or nickel plate on brass or bronze, they were designed to represent the 'winged maiden' Victory, flying bats, sleek greyhounds, soaring eagles, and a host of other creatures. Today they often bring prices in the $75.00 to $200.00 range. R. Lalique glass ornaments go much higher!

Horns, radios, clocks, gear shift knobs, and key chains with company emblems are other areas of interest. Generally, items pertaining to the classics of the thirties are most in demand. Paper advertising material, manuals, and catalogs in excellent condition are also collectible.

License plate collectors search for the early porcelain-on-cast-iron examples. First year plates (e.g., Massachusetts, 1903; Wisconsin, 1905; Indiana, 1913) are especially valuable. The last of the states to issue regulation plates were South Carolina and Texas in 1917, and Florida in 1918. While many northeastern states had registered hundreds of

thousands of vehicles by the 1920s making these plates relatively common, those from the southern and western states of that period are considered rare. Naturally, condition is important. While a pair in mint condition might sell for as much as $100.00 to $125.00, a pair with chipped or otherwise damaged porcelain may sometimes be had for as little as $25.00 to $30.00. See also Gas Globes and Panels.

Air dispenser, Air Scale Co Toledo OH, CI, EX pnt, 49"	850.00
Arm patch, Shell, 2" sq, EX	5.00
Ashtray, Mack, silver metal, 4½", NM	20.00
Ashtray, molded plastic w/Michelin man on edge, 1940s, 6" dia	75.00
Badge, bus; Twin Coach, bus diecut, 1930s	25.00
Booklet, Ford Quick Facts, 1940, EX	18.00
Buckle, Phillips 30-yr service, 3 bl stones	25.00
Catalog, Chervolet Roadster & Pheaton, mc, 1928, 20-pg	20.00
Catalog, Chevrolet, 32-pg, 1934, 8x6", EX	15.00
Catalog, Chevrolet Standard, 1934, 32-pg, 6x9", EX	16.00
Catalog, Dodge showroom, mc, 1958, 8-pg, 12x12", EX	10.00
Catalog, Everything for Your Ford, parts/etc, 1915, 48-pg	17.50
Catalog, Ford, mc, 1935, 16-pg, 7x5", EX	17.50
Catalog, Internat'l Truck Parts Model HS-54 & HS 54C, 1930	35.00
Catalog, Mercury, mc, 1959, 32-pg, 9x6", EX	10.00
Catalog, Model T Ford, 1922	25.00
Catalog, Star Station Wagon & Delivery Trucks, 1922, 6x4"	20.00
Catalog, Studebaker, 1934, 28-pg, 10x11", EX	17.50
Certificate of title, 1931 Ford, IL	10.00
Cigarette lighter, Conoco, cowboy logo, gold/silver, EX	20.00
Display rack, Fisk tires, pnt tin, boy w/candle, EX	70.00
Foldout, Buick, color promo, 1948, opens: 22x24", EX	9.00
Foldout, Oldsmobile, shows 9 models, 1948, opens: 30x34", EX	10.00
Gauge, tire; Buick, ca 1918	20.00
Gearshift knob, orange & wht swirl	45.00
Goggles, wht glass on leatherette, elastic band, 1915, EX	18.00
Guide, Wartime GM Users, 1942, 64-pg, 6x9"	15.00
Handbook, Gasoline Automobiles, Vol 4-18, 1904-18, set of 14	795.00
Headlamp, Dietz Ideal Motor, ca 1897, 11½x6½", pr	310.00

Hood ornaments, stork, bronze, 5" with 13" wingspan, EX, $450.00; Flying crane, brass, 5", EX, $450.00.

Hood ornament, Pontiac Indian head, 1920s	75.00
Hood ornament, Syria Temple Auto Club	75.00
Hood ornament, Winged Flight, triple-plated, Dart Engineering	150.00
Horn, Dixie Model T, brass, mk 1872 Edwards, Pat Pending, 9½"	110.00
Hubcap, Chevrolet, pnt metal, early, 10" dia, EX	20.00
Inkwell, Masters Truck, CI w/emb letters, 5½x7x2¾", VG	210.00
License plate, bl & wht porc, MA, 1908, 5½x10", EX	325.00
License plate, G Wallace & wife w/Confederate flag, plastic	58.00
License plate, Pennsylvania, 1908, M	200.00
License plate attachment, Auto Club of Pittsburgh, porc, 3½", EX	70.00

License plate attachment, IL Farm Bureau, mc porc, 4½x4", EX ..80.00
License plate attachment, Nat'l Chauffeur's Assoc, 1912 ....75.00
License plate reflecter, Dura-Products, lt rust, 4x5½" 10.00
Magazine, Automobile Digest, 1925, 112-pg, 7x10", EX 5.00
Manual, instruction; Packard Motor Cars, 1910, 8½x5½", VG 55.00
Manual, Kawasaki Owner's Workshop, 1975, NM 15.00
Manual, Nash owner's, Series #261, 1925, 79-pg, EX 16.00
Manual, Nash Rambler owner's, 1958, 40-pg, 4x6", EX 10.00
Manual, Overland Model #79T owner's, 1913, 118-pg, EX 55.00
Manual, Your New Hudson, 1940, 31-pg 22.50
Map rack, Calso Gasoline, pnt metal, 3-shelf, 20x12½", EX 95.00
Map rack, wht pnt metal, 15x14", EX 10.00
Mask, Texaco Gasoline, fire chief Ed Wynn paper litho, '34, EX .55.00
Name plate, Hudson, blk plastic, ca 1948-52, 8x3", EX 12.00
Odometer, 1926 Studebaker 35.00
Pamphlet, Chevrolet, foldout, 1925, 8x10", EX 16.00
Pen & pencil set, Maxim Motor Co 75th Presentation, EX 25.00
Photo, albumen of 1908-12 touring car, EX details, 10x8" 15.00
Photo, Pierce Arrow 1920 Roadster, mc, 10x13"+fr 22.50
Photo, showroom, 2-seater sports car, 1912, 10x8", EX 20.00
Postcard, Plymouth Road King, 1939, M 4.00
Promotion item, fire hat, Texaco, celluloid, 5", EX 60.00
Radiator medallion, Chrysler, brass w/red enamel, 1925-29 ....15.00
Radiator medallion, H w/red enamel, 1930-32, EX 15.00
Radio, car; Tucker, speaker, amplifier, etc, MIB 650.00

Autumn Leaf

In 1933 the Hall China Company designed a line of dinnerware for the Jewel Tea Company, who offered it to their customers as premiums. Although you may hear the ware referred to as 'Jewel Tea,' it was officially named 'Autumn Leaf' in the 1940s. In addition to the dinnerware, frosted Libbey glass tumblers, stemware, and a melmac service with the orange and gold bittersweet pod were available over the years, as were tablecloths, plastic covers for bowls and mixers, and metal items such as cake safes, hot pads, coasters, wastebaskets, and canisters. Even shelf paper and playing cards were made to coordinate. In 1958 the International Silver Company designed silverplated flatware in a pattern called 'Autumn' which was to be used with dishes in the Autumn Leaf pattern. A year later, a line of stainless flatware was introduced. These accessory lines are prized by collectors today.

One of the most fascinating aspects of collecting the Autumn Leaf pattern has been the wonderful discoveries of previously unlisted pieces. Among these items are two different bud-ray lid one-pound butter dishes; most recently a one-pound butter dish in the 'Zephyr' or 'Bingo' style; a miniature set of the 'Casper' salt and pepper shakers; coffee, tea, and sugar canisters; a pair of candlesticks; an experimental condiment jar; and a covered candy dish. All of these china pieces are attributed to the Hall China Company. Other unusual items have turned up in the accessory lines as well and include a Libbey frosted tumbler in a pilsner shape, a wooden serving bowl, and an apron made from the oilcloth (plastic) material that was used in the 1950s tablecloth. These latter items appear to be professionally done, and we can only speculate as to their origin. Collectors believe that the Hall items were sample pieces that were never meant to be distributed.

Hall discontinued the Autumn Leaf line in 1978. At that time the date was added to the backstamp to mark ware still in stock in the Jewel warehouse. A special promotion by Jewel saw the reintroduction of basic dinnerware and serving pieces with the 1978 backstamp. These pieces have made their way into many collections. Additionally, in 1979 Jewel released a line of enamel-clad cookware and a Vellux blanket made by Martex which were decorated with the Autumn Leaf pattern. They continued to offer these items for a few years only, then all distribution of Autumn Leaf items was discontinued.

It should be noted that the Hall China Company has produced several limited edition items for the National Autumn Leaf Collectors Club (NALCC): a New York-style teapot (1984); a vase (1987, different than the original shape); candlesticks (1988); a Philadelphia-style teapot, creamer and sugar set (1990); a tea-for-two set and a Solo tea set (1991), a donut jug, and a large oval casserole. New items for the NALCC: small ball jug, 1-cup French teapot, and a set of four chocolate mugs. The NALCC has also given their club members special items over the past few years made for them by Hall China: a sugar packet holder, a chamberstick, and an oyster cocktail. Other items are scheduled for production. All of these are plainly marked as having been made for the NALCC and are appropriately dated. A few other pieces have been made by Hall as limited editions for an Ohio company, but these are easily identified: the Airflow teapot and the Norris refrigerator pitcher (neither of which was previously decorated with the Autumn Leaf decal), a square-handled beverage mug, and the new-style Irish mug. A production problem with the square-handled mugs halted their production. The company then issued a regular conic-style mug with a round handle. Additional items available now are a covered onion soup, tall bud vase, china kitchen memo board, and egg drop-style salt and pepper shakers with a mustard pot. They have also issued a deck of playing cards and Libbey tumblers.

Our advisor for this category is Gwynn Harrison; she is listed in the Directory under California.

Baker, oval, Fort Pitt 90.00
Batter bowl, Saf-Hdl 2,500.00
Bean pot, 1-hdl 500.00
Bean pot, 2-hdl, 2¼-qt 135.00
Bowl, cereal; 6" 10.00
Bowl, coupe soup 12.00
Bowl, cream soup; 2-hdl 30.00
Bowl, fruit; 5½" 4.00
Bowl, metal, enamelware, set of 3 ....200.00
Bowl, mixing; set of 3: 6¼", 7½", 9" 100.00
Bowl, Royal Glas-Bake, set of 4 ....45.00
Bowl, salad 14.00
Bowl, stackette; set of 3: 18-oz, 24-oz, 34-oz, w/lid 75.00
Bowl, vegetable; divided, 10½" 75.00
Bowl, vegetable; oval, w/lid, 10" 35.00
Bowl, vegetable; oval, 10½" 15.00
Bowl, vegetable; rnd, 9" 75.00
Bowl cover set, plastic, 8-pc: 7 assorted covers in pouch 50.00
Bread box, metal 225.00
Butter dish, 1-lb 325.00
Butter dish, ¼-lb 150.00
Butter dish, ¼-lb, Square Top 500.00
Butter dish, ¼-lb, Wings 750.00
Cake plate, 9½" 12.00
Cake safe, metal, motif on top & sides, 5" 35.00
Cake safe, metal, side decor only, 4½x10½" 30.00
Cake stand, metal base, orig box 150.00
Candy dish 350.00
Canister, metal, rnd, w/coppertone lid, set of 4 ....175.00
Canister, metal, rnd, w/ivory plastic lid 10.00
Canister, metal, rnd, w/matching lid, 6" 15.00
Canister, metal, rnd, w/matching lid, 7" 25.00
Canister, metal, rnd, w/matching lid, 8¼" 35.00
Canister, metal, sq, set of 4: 8½" & 4½" 175.00
Casserole, Royal Glas-Bake, deep, w/clear glass lid 25.00
Casserole, Royal Glas-Bake, shallow, w/clear glass lid 20.00
Casserole, Tootsie-hdl, w/lid 22.00
Casserole/souffle, swirl, 3-pt 15.00
Casserole/souffle, 10-oz 10.00

Casserole/souffle, 2-pt 85.00
Cleanser can, metal, sq, 6", M 500.00
Clock, orig works 400.00
Coaster, metal, 3⅛" 4.00
Coffee dispenser/canister, metal, wall type, 10½x19" dia 175.00
Coffee maker, 5-cup, all china, w/china insert 250.00
Coffee maker, 9-cup, w/metal dripper, 8" 35.00
Coffee percolator, electric, all china 225.00
Coffee percolator/carafe, Douglas, w/warmer base, MIB 250.00
Cookie jar, Tootsie 165.00

Creamer and sugar bowl, with lid, 4½", 3¼", $30.00.

Creamer, New Style 8.00
Creamer, Old Style, 4¼" 15.00
Cup & saucer 8.00
Cup & saucer, St Denis 22.00
Custard cup 4.00
Flatware, silverplate, ea 30.00
Flatware, stainless, ea 25.00
Fruit cake tin, metal 10.00
Golden Ray base, to use w/candy dish or cake plate, pr 50.00
Gravy boat 18.00
Hot pad, metal, red or gr felt-like bking, rnd 15.00
Hot pad, oval 12.00
Hurricane lamp, Douglas, w/metal base, pr 400.00
Kitchen utility chair, metal 450.00
Marmalade jar, 3-pc 55.00
Mixer cover, Mary Dunbar, plastic 25.00
Mug, beverage 55.00
Mug, Irish coffee 95.00
Mustard jar, 3½" 55.00
Napkin, ecru muslin 25.00
Pickle dish or gravy liner, oval, 9" 18.00
Picnic thermos, metal 250.00
Pie baker, 9½" 18.00
Pitcher, utility; 2½-pt, 6" 15.00
Place mat, paper, scalloped 25.00
Place mat, set of 8, M in orig package 195.00
Plate, 10" 12.00
Plate, 6" or 7", ea 4.00
Plate, 8" 8.00
Plate, 9" 10.00
Platter, 11½" 15.00
Platter, 13½" 18.00
Playing cards, regular or Pinochle, dbl deck 160.00
Range set, shakers & covered drippings jar 35.00
Sauce dish, serving; Douglas, Bakelite hdl 125.00
Shakers, Casper, pr 18.00
Shakers, range, hdl, pr 18.00

Sugar bowl, New Style 12.00
Sugar bowl, Old Style, 3½" 18.00
Tablecloth, cotton sailcloth w/gold stripe, 54x54" 75.00
Tablecloth, cotton sailcloth w/gold stripe, 54x72" 85.00
Tablecloth, ecru muslin, 56x81" 150.00
Tablecloth, plastic 150.00
Teakettle, metal enamelware 150.00
Teapot, Aladdin 38.00
Teapot, long spout, 7" 45.00
Teapot, Newport 145.00
Teapot, Newport, dtd 1978 ....125.00
Toaster cover, plastic, fits 2-slice toaster 25.00
Towel, dish; pattern & clock motif 45.00
Towel, tea; cotton, 16x33" 35.00
Trash can, metal, red 100.00
Tray, glass, wood hdl, 19½x11¼" 95.00
Tray, metal, oval 55.00
Tray, red w/allover red & yel design, red border 65.00
Tray, tidbit; 2-tier 35.00
Tray, tidbit; 3-tier 55.00
Tumbler, Brockway, 13-oz 18.00
Tumbler, Brockway, 16-oz 20.00
Tumbler, Brockway, 9-oz 16.00
Tumbler, frosted, 14-oz, 5½" 12.00
Tumbler, frosted, 9-oz, 3¾" 18.00
Tumbler, gold frost etched, flat, 10-oz 30.00
Tumbler, gold frost etched, flat, 15-oz 45.00
Tumbler, gold frost etched, ftd, 10-oz 45.00
Tumbler, gold frost etched, ftd, 6½-oz 45.00
Vase, bud; 6" 175.00
Warmer base, oval 150.00
Warmer base, rnd 110.00
Warmer base, rnd, w/4 orig candles, orig mk box 125.00

Aviation

Aviation buffs are interested in any phase of flying, from early developments with gliders, balloons, airships and flying machines to more modern innovations. Books, catalogs, photos, patents, lithographs, ad cards, and posters are among the paper ephemera they treasure alongside models of unlikely flying contraptions, propellers and rudders, insignia and equipment from WWI and WWII, and memorabilia from the flights of the Wright Brothers, Lindbergh, Earhart, and the Zeppelins. See also Militaria. Our advisor for this category is John R. Joiner; he is listed in the Directory under Georgia.

Badge, hat; United Airlines, silver, 1950s 68.00
Beverage server, United Airlines, SP, ice lip, ca 1951 ...35.00
Blanket, Continental Airlines, wool, Pendleton 30.00
Blanket, Southern Air, gray w/bl letters, lap sz 30.00
Blanket, United Airlines, deep maroon, old logo, lap sz ...50.00
Book, Aviation in America, Butterfield, 1957, 64-pg 24.00
Cocktail, Eastern Airlines 12.50
Hatpin, stewardess', Eastern Airlines 25.00
Knife, steak; United Airlines, SP 5.00
Magazine, Popular Aviation, Lindbergh on bk cover, 1927, EX ...16.00
Menu, Air France, Indies cover, 1962 ....2.50
Menu, Pan Am Rainbow Service, 1964 ....2.50
Mug, Am Airlines, blk & wht, sm 5.00
Mug, Eastern Airlines, wht w/gold rim, bottom stamped ...5.00
Photo, Charles Lindbergh, sepia print, 1920s 45.00
Photo, Lindbergh plane leaving airport, Underwood, 11x14" ...78.00
Pin, lapel; TWA, silver 4-engine plane 15.00

Pin-bk, Amelia Earhart in aviator's helmet, 1¼", EX 45.00
Postcard, Am Airlines, DC3, color 11.00
Poster, Northwest, Strato-Clipper, Hong Kong, 25x24", EX 47.50
Program, Long Beach CA 1st Annual Air Show, 1946, EX 6.50
Schedule, TWA, 1947, NM 17.50
Shot glass, Eastern Airlines 2.00
Shot glass, Southern, DC3, Fly Southern, yel 32.50
Shot glass, Southern, 20 Years of Hospitality Country Style 12.50
Timetable, Holiday Airlines, 1986 ....2.00
Travel guide & map, Aloha Lines, M 2.50
Tumbler, Eastern Airlines, side mk & logo 4.00
Wing, Delta Flight Attendant, gold w/mc enamel, 1972 ....40.00
Wing, lapel; Atlantic, sterling, pin-bk, 1940s, EX 15.00
Wings, Delta, plastic 1.50
Wings, Pan Am Jr Clipper Pilot, metal, M 10.00
Wings, United Future Flight Attendant, child's, 1950s 10.00
Wings, United Future Stewardess, plastic, mc, M 3.50

Avon

The California Perfume Company, the parent of the Avon Co., was founded in 1886. Although an 'Avon' line was introduced by the company in the mid-twenties, not until 1939 did it become known as Avon Products, Inc. Collectible Avon items include not only figural bottles and jars but jewelry, awards, product samples, magazine ads, and catalogs as well. For more information concerning the Avon Collectors Club, see the Clubs, Newsletters, and Catalogs section of the Directory. See also California Perfume Company.

For more information, we recommend *Hasting's Avon Collector's Price Guide, 13th Edition*, by Bud Hastings. In the listings that follow, unless noted MIB, prices are for bottles only.

Avon Maid Powdered Cleanser Sample, bl box, 1928, 3-oz 100.00
Bayberry Shaving Cream, tube, 1930-35 ....20.00
Christmas plate, Skaters on the Pond, Wedgwood, 1975, 9" 10.00
Elite Powder, 1930-36, 3-oz 35.00
Headache Cologne, boxed, 4-oz, 1931-34 ....40.00
Jasmine Bath Soaps, 3 cakes, boxed, 1934-36 ....50.00
Kiddie Kennel, 3 molded soaps, boxed, 1955 ....100.00
Lullabye Set, 8-oz baby oil+9-oz powder, boxed, 1955 ....50.00
Mr & Mrs Gift Set, 4 items in box, 1940-42 ....100.00
Rouge, 1930, purse sz 20.00

Station Wagon decanter, green glass with tan plastic top, 1971-73, 7¾", $5.00 ($9.00 MIB).

Spicy Aftershave, 1965, 4-oz 5.00
Tabatha Spray Cologne, blk cat, 1971, 3-oz 5.00
Vanity Book, Dbl Compact & Lipstick, boxed 50.00

Baccarat

The Baccarat Glass company was founded in 1765 near Luneville, France, and continues to this day to produce quality crystal tableware, vases, perfume bottles, and figurines. The firm became famous for the high-quality millefiori and caned paperweights produced there from 1845 until about 1860. Examples of these range from $300.00 to as much as several thousand. Since 1953 they have resumed the production of paperweights on a limited edition basis. Our advisors for this category are Randall Monsen and Rod Baer; their address is listed in the Directory under Virginia. See also Paperweights.

Bottle, scent; Deco-style cut geometrics, w/stopper, 8" 120.00
Bottle, scent; frosted florals, pine cone stopper, 6" 150.00
Bottle, scent; It's You, Elizabeth Arden, crystal hand 1,540.00
Bottle, scent; paneled/bulbous, hollow stopper, sgn, 4½" 125.00
Bottle, scent; Rose Tiente Swirl, swirl stopper, 5½" 70.00
Bottle, scent; Rose Tiente Swirl, 6⅛x2⅜" 75.00
Box, Rose Tiente Swirl, lift-off lid, 2x3" dia 80.00
Compote, Rose Tiente Swirl, gold trim, low ft, 3½x7" 130.00
Decanter, amberina w/poinsettias, swirl stopper, 9" 150.00
Goblet, cameo floral, red on gr w/gold, dbl-knob std, 6½" 325.00
Ink stand, sapphire bl, 3-bottle set, scalloped base, 9" L 395.00
Jar, Swirl, sapphire bl, 6x3" dia 85.00
Lamp, fairy; Rose Tiente, emb Sunburst pattern, 4" 250.00
Tray, Rose Tiente Swirl, 10" L 200.00
Vase, cameo raspberries/leaves, yel-gr on crystal, 6x2½" 375.00
Vase, gr clover in base reflects in paneled sides, 4¼" 50.00
Vase, opal w/gilt, tree trunk form w/snake & insect, 8" 450.00
Wash bowl & pitcher, Rose Tiente Swirl, 13", 5½x15" 1,100.00

Badges

The breast badge came into general usage in this country about 1840. Since most are not marked and styles have changed very little to the present day, they are often difficult to date. The most reliable clue is the pin and catch. One of the earliest types, used primarily before the turn of the century, involved a 't-pin' and a 'shell' catch. In a second style, the pin was hinged with a small square of sheet metal, and the clasp was cylindrical. From the late 1800s until about 1940, the pin and clasp were made from one continuous piece of thin metal wire. The same type, with the addition of a flat back plate, was used a little later. There are exceptions to these findings, and other types of clasps were also used. Hallmarks and inscriptions may also help pinpoint an approximate age.

Badges have been made from a variety of materials, usually brass or nickel silver; but even solid silver and gold were used for special orders. They are found in many basic shapes and variations — stars with five to seven points, shields, disks, ovals, and octagonals being most often encountered. Of prime importance to collectors, however, is that the title and/or location appear on the badge. Those with designations of positions no longer existing (City Constable, for example) and names of early western states and towns are most valuable.

Badges are among the most commonly-reproduced (and faked) types of antiques on the market. At any flea market, ten fakes can be found for every authentic example. Genuine law badges start at $30.00 to $40.00 for recent examples (1950-1970); earlier pieces (1910-1930) usually bring $50.00 to $90.00. Pre-1900 badges often sell for more than $100.00. Authentic gold badges are usually priced at a minimum of scrap value (karat, weight, spot price for gold); fine gold badges from before 1900 can sell for $400.00 to $800.00, and a few will bring even more. A fire badge is usually valued at about half the price of a law badge from the same circa and material. Our advisor for this category is Gene Matzke; he is listed in the Directory under Wisconsin.

AAA Patrol Captain, Auto Club of Michigan, bronze	**20.00**
Auxiliary Police, silvered metal, shield/eagle, 2¾"	**25.00**
CA Special Officer, NP w/blk enameling, 1930s, EX	**22.50**
Deputy Sheriff, Central Falls RI, Lucky 13, silver	**42.50**
Deputy Sheriff, NY, brass, eagle over circular form, NM	**57.50**
Deputy US Marshal AZ District, SP nickel, LAS&SCo, 2½x2"	**.115.00**

F.E. White Chief Engineer, So. Hadley Falls, solid yellow gold, dated May 24, 1886, 4", $400.00.

Highway Patrol, OK, blk & gold	**215.00**
NY City Volunteer Aid, Clean City League, NP, 1910, NM	**30.00**
OH Cloverleaf Security Officer, NP w/red enamel, EX	**20.00**
Phila Fire Insurance Patrol, 14k yel gold shield, 1860s	**425.00**
Police, City of NY Deputy Commissioner, 14k yel gold, 2½"	**525.00**
Police, Hartford CT, eagle/stars/seal, silver, 1860s, EX	**215.00**
Policeman, VA, silver color, eagle atop shield, 1½"	**25.00**
Railroad & Steamboat Police, W Pacific CA, 6-point star, 3¼"	**.175.00**
Retired Police, Billings MT, gold, inscribed/dtd 1925	**65.00**
Special Deputy Sheriff, gold color, ca 1914, EX	**48.00**
Special Police, Boston, silver, early style	**42.50**
Special Police, Kansas City, 1922, hallmk	**65.00**
SWAT, Boise Co ID, Meyer & Wenthe, blk w/wht letters	**125.00**
Texaco 6641 Port Arthur Works, stainless steel, NM	**20.00**
US Guard Corps of Engineers, NP w/blk enameling, 1930s, EX	**...40.00**
US Volunteer Life Saving Corps, sterling, w/ribbon, EX	**40.00**
Veterans Administrative Police, gold color, shield shape	**48.00**
WV School Bus Driver, NP w/blk enameling, ca 1950, EX	**18.00**

Banks

This year the continuing impact of auctions shows in the listings. Again, condition, condition, condition is what is driving the market. In addition, some banks with outstanding provenances were available, and they brought prices that reflect their individual value to a specific collector but distort the real market value of similar banks. The spread between a bank in good condition and an excellent or original condition example continues to widen. It is imperative that you realize the importance of paint and the completeness of a bank. Also some banks have a wide margin of value based on color variations. It becomes more and more important that you attend as many shows and auctions as possible. Direct contact with collectors and knowledgeable dealers is the only way you can get a feel for prices and the desirability of banks, both mechanical and still. Banks continue to hold their value. However, it is becoming extremely important for collectors to understand the market.

Let's take a look at the price variations possible on an Uncle Sam mechanical bank. If you find one with considerable paint missing but with some good color showing, the price would be around $1,000.00. If it has repairs or restoration, the value would drop to something like $800.00 or less. If you had another example, and it had two thirds of its original paint and no repairs, it would be priced around $1,800.00. One with minor nicks and 90% of the original paint could go as high as $3,500.00. Or if you find one that is in near-original paint and has no repairs, $5,000.00 would not be out of line. This should help you see what causes price variations. After considering all of these factors, remember the final price is always determined by what a willing buyer and seller agree on for a specific bank.

Still banks are found in nearly every shape and size, and many types of material have been used in their making. Exactly how many styles were made is unknown; but about three thousand have been identified, and there are thousands more that are unlisted in any book. Cast iron examples are the most popular, but there is increasing interest in early tin and pottery banks made in the United States.

The category of mechanical banks is unique. Along with cast iron bell toys, they are among the most outstanding products of the Industrial Revolution and are recognized as some of the most successful of the mass-produced products of the 19th century. The earliest mechanicals were made of wood or lead; but when John Hall introduced Hall's Excelsior, a cast iron mechanical bank, it was an immediate success. J. & E. Stevens produced the bank for Hall and soon began to make their own designs. Several companies followed suit, most of which were already in the hardware business. They used newly developed iron-molding techniques to produce these novelty savings devices for the emerging toy market. Mechanical banks reflect the social and political attitudes of the times, racial prejudices, the excitement of the circus, and humorous everyday events. Their designers made the most of simple mechanics to produce banks with captivating actions that served not only to amuse but to promote the concept of thrift to the children. The quality of detail in the castings are truly fine examples of industrial art. The most collectible examples were made during the period of 1870 to 1900; however, they continued to be made until the early days of World War II. J. & E. Stevens, Shepard Hardware, and Kyser and Rex are some of the more well-known manufacturers; most made still banks as well.

Still banks are widely collected, and you can literally choose from thousands of banks. No one knows exactly how many different banks were made, but at least three thousand have been identified in the various books published on the subject. Cast iron examples still dominate the market, but the lead banks from Europe are growing in value. Tin and early pottery banks are drawing more interest as well. American pottery banks which were primarily collected by Americana collectors are becoming more important in the still bank field. This market has not been as volatile as the mechanical banks, but the number of collectors is growing. The auction market on still banks is not as extensive as with the mechanicals, but some nice examples do turn up. Collectors and dealers are still the best source.

While the cast iron banks dominate the market, there are examples made from many other materials. Combinations of tin and cardboard and banks made from tin alone are very collectible. Some of the European tin banks are quite rare; England made some fine cast iron mechanicals and many aluminum examples. The popularity of old mechanicals has created a market for reproductions and fakes. Reproductions may have minor value as such, but not as true collectibles. A few of the fakes have attained collectible status but are still not regarded as true mechanical banks.

As both value and interest continue on the increase, it becomes even more important to educate one's self to the fullest extent possible. We recommend these books for your library: *The Dictionary of Still Banks* by Long and Pitman, *The Penny Bank Book* by Moore, and *The Bank Book* by Norman. If you are primarily interested in mechanicals, *Penny Lane*, a book by Davidson, is considered the most complete reference available. It contains a cross-reference listing of numbers from all other publications on mechanical banks.

In the listings that follow, banks are identified by L for Long, G for Griffith, M for Moore, N for Norman, D for Davidson, and W for Whiting.

Key:
CI — cast iron   NPCI — nickel-plated cast iron
EPCI — electroplated cast iron

Advertising

AC Spark Plug, horse in tub form, cast metal/rubber wheels, EX ..**145.00**
Atlantic Premium Motor Oil, tin litho, 2⅞", EX **22.00**
Cinci Stove, CI, lt bl porc enamel, nickel grill, 3½" **50.00**
Cities Service, cb **20.00**
Commercial Travelers, pottery, man w/coin head, 6", NM **125.00**
Electrolux, vacuum cleaner shape, NM **50.00**
Esso, service station man figural, plastic, 5", EX **65.00**
Eureka Gas Heater, M-1350, tin, minor wear, 5¼", EX **75.00**
Ever-Ready Batteries, cat figural, plastic **24.00**
GE Radio, Arcade, M-822, CI, brn pnt, 3¾", EX **250.00**
Hershey's Syrup, can shape, pottery, M **28.00**
Hush Puppy, dog figural, plastic **15.00**
Kelvinator, M-1338, refrigerator shape, door opens, 4", VG **65.00**
Loft's Candies, truck, tin litho, friction, key lock, 10", VG **35.00**
Mellow Furnaces, furnace form, M-1363, bronze pnt, 3⅝", EX ...**125.00**
Mellow Stove, M-1363, stove shape, pnt CI, 3¾", EX **75.00**
Old Dutch Cleanser, tin, NM **38.00**
Radiation Stoves, L-1018, tin, 5¼", EX **140.00**
Red Goose Shoes, M-611, shoes on ped base, Arcade, 5½", EX .**775.00**
Roper Range, M-1341, Arcade, CI, mc pnt, 4", EX **350.00**
Sinclair Power X, EX **12.50**

Snappy Service Copper & Brass Sales, red, white, and blue composition figure, 6¼", $125.00.

Switch to Dodge & Save Money, red tin litho drum shape **35.00**
Tang Robot, plastic, M **6.00**
Tootsie Roll, roll shape **12.00**
Wolf Head Motor Oil, CI, EX **20.00**
Worcester Salt, M-451, elephant, wht metal, gr patina, 4¼" **40.00**
York Stove, M-1351, stove shape, pnt CI, 4", VG **150.00**
Zenith Radio, M-823, wht metal, gold w/paper dial, 3½", EX **65.00**

Mechanical

Two acrobats, cast iron, worn original paint with light repaint at top, 5x7", $3,100.00.

Acrobat, D-1, J&E Stevens, pnt CI, hairline/crack, 5", G **1,650.00**
Always Did 'Spise a Mule, N-250, bench, rpl tail, 9¾", G **450.00**
Always Did 'Spise a Mule, N252, jockey over, pnt CI, 8", G **475.00**
Artillery, D-12, Shepard, pnt CI, rubs, 6", EX **1,200.00**
Atlas Bank, D-13, iron/metal/wood, rpl base, 8", G **800.00**
Bad Accident, D-20, Stevens, CI, VG pnt/lt rust, 10" L, VG .**1,550.00**
Boy on Trapeze, D-50, Barton & Smith, pnt CI, 9¼", G **2,000.00**
Boy Scout Camp, D-52, Stevens, pnt CI, rpr flag, 10", EX **3,200.00**
Bulldog, Standing; D-66, Judd, pnt CI, recast tail, 7", VG **100.00**
Bulldog Savings, D-65, Ives-Blakeslee-Wms, pnt CI, 7", G **1,750.00**
Butting Buffalo, D-90, Kyser & Rex, CI, mc pnt, 7½", EX **7,000.00**
Butting Goat, D-91, Judd, pnt CI, 4¾" L, VG **385.00**
Cabin, D-93, Stevens, CI, yel pnt, 3½", VG **600.00**
Cat & Mouse, Cat Balancing; D-104, Stevens, pnt CI, 11½", EX .**2,200.00**
Chief Big Moon, D-108, Stevens, pnt CI, gold sides, 10" L, EX .**2,750.00**
Clown on Globe, D-227, J&E Stevens, pnt CI, tan base, 9", EX .**1,980.00**
Creedmoor, D-137, Stevens, pnt CI, bl pants, 10", G **550.00**
Creedmoor, N-2000A, J&E Stevens, CI, old rpt, VG **700.00**
Darktown Battery, D-146, Stevens, CI, rpt, 10¾" **550.00**
Dinah, D-153, Harper, CI, worn pnt, long sleeves, 5½", G **250.00**
Dinah, N-2150, CI, minor rpt, EX **625.00**
Eagle & Eaglets, D-165, Stevens, pnt CI, soiled, 8", VG **600.00**
Elephant, D-173, man pops up, Enterprise, rpl tunic, 6", VG **250.00**
Frog on Rnd Base, D-204, pnt CI, recast lattice, 4½", VG **275.00**
Home Bank, N-243, Stevens, CI, rpt, no dormers type, 5", G **250.00**
Humpty Dumpty, D-248, Shepard, pnt CI, 7½", EX **800.00**
Humpty Dumpty, D-248, Shepard, pnt CI, 7½", NM **1,200.00**
Indian & Bear, N-2980, pnt CI, rpl feathers, EX **1,650.00**
Indian Shooting Bear, D-257, Stevens, pnt CI, 10", EX **2,750.00**
Initiating Bank, 2nd Degree; D-220, pnt CI, 7½", EX **4,400.00**
Joe Socko, D-262, Straits, pnt CI, 3½" base, EX **450.00**
Jonah & Whale, D-282, Shepard, pnt CI, 10¼", VG **2,200.00**
Leapfrog, D-292, Shepard, pnt CI, lt fading, 5", EX **2,200.00**
Magic, N-3730A, J&E Stevens, CI, yel pnt, 5¼", EX **3,200.00**
Mammy & Child, D-318, Kyser & Rex, pnt CI, red dress, 9", EX .**5,225.00**
Monkey & Coconut, N-3940, pnt CI, NM **2,600.00**
Mule Entering Barn, D-342, J&E Stevens, pnt CI, 8½", VG ...**1,000.00**
Novelty, N-2460B, J&E Stevens, CI, yel pnt, 4¼", EX **800.00**
Organ Grinder, Boy & Girl; D-368, Kyser & Rex, pnt CI, 7½", EX .**775.00**
Organ Grinder & Performing Bear, N-4350A, pnt CI, 5½", EX ..**6,000.00**
Owl Turns Head, D-375, Stevens, pnt CI, wht variant, 7½", EX ..**990.00**
Paddy & the Pig, N-4400, Stevens, CI, worn pnt, 8", VG **1,600.00**
Professor Pug Frog's...Bicycle Feat, D-400, Stevens, 10" L, EX .**8,250.00**
Pump & Bucket, D-401, pnt CI, bell missing, 6½", VG **600.00**
Rabbit in Cabbage, N-4790, pnt CI, rpl trap, VG **700.00**
Reclining Chinaman, D-410, J&E Stevens, pnt CI, 8" L, EX ...**3,050.00**
Santa Claus, D-428, Shepard, pnt CI, no trap, 6", VG **1,045.00**

Speaking Dog, D-448, Harper, CI, rpt, VG 250.00
Tammany, D-455, Stevens, CI, brn pants/bl jacket, 5½", EX 660.00
Teddy & Bear, D-459, Stevens, pnt CI, lt fading, 7", EX 3,000.00
Trick Dog, D-481, Hubley, pnt CI, yel & maroon base, 8½", EX ..800.00
Trick Dog, D-482, Hubley, pnt CI, 8½", EX 600.00
Trick Pony, N-5640, CI, bronze pnt, NM 525.00
Uncle Remus, D-492, Kyser & Rex, pnt CI, rprs, 4", VG 2,200.00
Uncle Sam, D-493, Shepard, pnt CI, some rpt, 11½", EX 1,200.00
William Tell, D-565, J&E Stevens, pnt (chipped) CI, 10", VG .525.00
World's Fair, D-573, CI, rpt, complete, 8" 500.00

Registering

B&R Mfg, NY, 10¢ register 15.00
Bean Pot, M-951, 5¢ register, pnt CI, NP top, 4", EX 175.00
Daily Dime Clown, EX 20.00
Elves Rolling Coins, EX 65.00
Gem, 10¢ register, emb eagle, EX 22.00
Honeycomb, C-105, 5¼" 110.00
Phoenix Trunk, M-947, 10¢ register, CI, 1890, 3¾x5", EX 255.00
Popeye, 10¢ register, EX 35.00
Snow White, EX 195.00
Statue of Liberty 15.00
TV Bank, W Germany, tin litho, various denominations, 4", EX .22.00
Uncle Sam, 5¢ register 115.00
Uncle Sam's 3-Coin, Durable Toy & Novelty, pnt tin, EX 40.00
Wee Folks Money Box, tin litho, sq, English, 5" 60.00
World Scope, EX 35.00

Still

Amherst Buffalo, M-556, pnt CI, 8" L, EX 385.00
Amish Boy, M-193, J Wright, pnt CI, 1970, 5", M 75.00
Andy Gump, M-217, Arcade, pnt CI, 4⅜", VG 775.00
Apple, M-1621, Kyser & Rex, pnt CI, 5¼", EX 1,275.00
Atlas, L-631, world on shoulders, pot metal, 4½", EX 265.00
Auto, M-1486, Williams, pnt CI, 1910, 5¾" L, EX 1,250.00
Baby in Cradle, M-51, pnt CI, 3¼", EX 1,250.00
Bank of England Safe, M-870, pnt CI, Kyser & Rex, EX 600.00
Baseball Player, M-18, AC Williams, pnt CI, 5¾", NM 625.00
Battleship Maine, L-1581, CI, 4½", EX 350.00
Battleship Maine, M-1441, Grey Iron, pnt CI, 5¼", EX 2,450.00
Battleship Oregon, M-1450, J&E Stevens, pnt CI, 4⅞" L, EX 365.00
Bear, Grisly; M-703, lead, copper pnt, 2¾", EX 50.00
Bear Seated on Log, M-714, pnt CI, VG 650.00

Beauty (embossed on side), M-532, cast iron, 4x5", $110.00.

Billiken on Throne, M-73, Williams, pnt CI, 6½", VG 100.00
Billy Bounce, M-15, Hubley, CI, silver pnt, 4¾", EX 885.00
Bismark Pig, M-602, CI, worn pnt, 1883, 3⅜", VG 265.00
Boss Tweed, M-110, pnt CI, 1870s, 3⅞", EX 3,750.00

Buffalo, M-560, Williams, CI, gold pnt, 3⅛x4¾", EX 195.00
Bulldog, M-372, J Wright, pnt CI, 1960s, 6", M 85.00
Bungalow, M-999, CI, worn mc pnt, 3⅜", EX 400.00
Cadet, M-8, Hubley, pnt CI, gold trim, 5¾", EX 675.00
Camel, Kneeling; M-770, Kyser & Rex, pnt CI, 2½x4¾", EX 775.00
Captain Kidd, M-38, pnt CI, 1900s, 5⅝", VG 350.00
Cat on Tub, M-358, CI, bronze pnt, 4⅛", NM 285.00
Cat w/Ball, M-352, CI, gray & gold pnt, 5⅝" L, EX 300.00
Cat w/Bow, M-350, Hubley, pnt CI, 4⅛", VG 450.00
Century of Progress Building, Arcade, M-1064, 4½x7", EX 1,350.00
Charlie McCarthy, M-209, papier-mache, 9¼", EX 225.00
Chest, Treasure; M-928, CI, worn red & gold pnt, 2¾", EX 200.00

Clown, cast iron, worn silver and red paint, M-211, 1908, 6", $95.00.

Columbia, M-1073, Kenton, CI, bronze pnt, 8¾", EX+ 1,200.00
Columbia Tower, M-1118, Grey Iron, CI, 6⅞", VG 650.00
County Bank, M-1110, brass, 4¼", EX 135.00
Cross, M-1628, pnt CI, 9¼", EX 900.00
Devil, 2-Faced; M-32, Williams, pnt CI, 4¼", EX 1,000.00
Dog on Drum, M-359, Williams, CI, bronze pnt, 4⅛", EX 225.00
Dolphin, M-33, CI, Grey Iron, pnt traces, 4½", EX 450.00
Donkey w/Blanket, M-488, Kenton, CI, mc pnt, 3⅞", EX 885.00
Dormer Bank, M-953, pnt CI, red roof, 4¾", EX 6,250.00
Double Door, M-1125, Williams, pnt CI, gold trim, 5½", EX 395.00
Duck, M-624, Hubley, pnt CI, 4¾", EX 295.00
Dutch Girl, M-16, Grey Iron, CI, bronze pnt, 6½", VG 650.00
Elephant, Circus; M-462, Hubley, CI, mc pnt, 3⅞", EX 345.00
Elephant on Tub, M-484, Williams, pnt CI, 5⅜", EX 215.00
Elephant w/Howdah, M-474, Williams, pnt CI, 4⅞", EX 150.00
Fidelity Safe, M-863, Kyser & Rex, pnt CI, gold trim, 3⅝", NM ..600.00
Flatiron Building, M-1160, CI, dk japanning w/gold, 3", EX 105.00
Football Player, M-11, CI, bronze pnt, 5⅞", EX 450.00
Four Tower, M-1121, J&E Stevens, CI, gold trim, 5¾", EX 400.00
Foxy Grandpa, M-320, Hubley, pnt CI, 5½", NM 485.00
German Helmet, M-1405, tin, worn pnt, 4⅞", VG 175.00
Globe on Arc, M-789, Grey Iron, pnt CI, 5¼", EX 285.00
Globe on Wire Arc, M-785, Arcade, pnt CI, 4⅝", EX 275.00
Globe Savings Fund, M-1199, Kyser & Rex, pnt CI, 7⅛", EX .2,500.00
Gunboat, M-1462, Kenton, CI, mc pnt, 8½" L, EX 1,250.00
Hall Clock, M-1540, Arcade, CI, dk pnt w/gold trim, 5⅝", VG .500.00
Hen on Nest, M-546, CI, bronze pnt, 3", EX 1,800.00
Home, M-1019, Judd, pnt CI, 4", EX 600.00
Home Savings, M-1237, Stevens, dog finial, pnt CI, 5¾", EX 475.00
Honey Bear, M-696, pnt CI, 2½", EX 1,250.00
Horse, Prancing; M-506, CI, gold pnt, lt wear, 4¾", EX 200.00
Horse, Prancing; M-520, CI, old rpt, 7¼", EX 95.00
Horse on Wheels, M-512, Williams, CI, red pnt, 4¼", NM 600.00

Humpty Dumpty, M-42, pnt CI, 5½", NM 975.00
I Hear a Call, M-438, CI, blk pnt, dtd July 20, 1900, 5¼", VG 75.00
Indian w/Tomahawk, M-228, Hubley, pnt CI, 1900s, 5⅞", EX ..445.00
Jewel Safe, M-896, J&E Stevens, CI, no pnt, 5⅜", VG 185.00
Klondyke, M-1610, CI, EX pnt, 3¼", EX+ 1,400.00
Lamb, M-600, J Wright, pnt CI, 1970, 3¼", EX 65.00
Lion, M-737, ears up, Williams, pnt CI, 3⅝", EX 135.00
Lion, Quilted; M-758, pnt CI, 3¾x4¾", EX 450.00
Lion on Tub, M-753, Williams, pnt CI, 7½", EX 215.00
Little Red Riding Hood Safe, M-25, JM Harper, pnt CI, 5", VG .3,200.00
Log Cabin, M-1023, Kyser & Rex, pnt CI, 2½x3¼", NM 750.00
Mailbox on Legs, M-841, Hubley, pnt CI, 5¼", EX 250.00
Mammy w/Hands on Hips, M-176A, pnt CI, EX 115.00
Marshall Stove, M-1362, pnt CI, 3⅞", EX 250.00
Minuteman, M-44, Hubley, pnt CI, ca 1905, 6", NM 585.00
Multiplying Bank, M-1184, J&E Stevens, pnt CI, 1883, 6½", EX .1,800.00
Mutt & Jeff, M-157, Williams, CI, worn gold pnt, 4¼", VG 225.00
Old South Church, M-988, CI, bronze pnt, 10", NM 6,500.00
Our Kitchener, M-1313, CI, 6½", EX 165.00
Palace, M-1116, Ives, pnt CI, 7½", EX 2,950.00
Park Bank Building, M-1157, pnt CI, 4⅜", EX 1,500.00
Plymouth Rock 1620, M-1664, pnt CI, 3⅞" L, EX 1,750.00
Polar Bear, Begging; M-716, Arcade, CI, wht pnt, 5¼", EX 465.00
Possum, M-561, Arcade, silver pnt, 2⅜x4⅜", EX 500.00
Presto, M-1168, Williams, pnt CI, silver & gold pnt, 3⅝", EX 200.00
Pug Dog, Seated: M-405, Kyser & Rex, pnt CI, 3½", EX 500.00
Rabbit, Begging; M-566, Williams, pnt CI, 5⅛", EX 300.00
Radio w/Combination Door, M-833, Kenton, pnt CI/metal, 4½", EX ..365.00
Recording Bank, M-1062, worn NP CI, 6⅝" 185.00
Reindeer, M-737, Williams, CI, bronze pnt, 9½", EX 265.00
Roller Safe, M-880, Kyser & Rex, pnt CI, EX 250.00
Roof Bank, M-1124, Grey Iron, pnt CI, 5¼", G 135.00
Rooster, M-548, CI, mc pnt, 4¾", EX 285.00
Rumplestiltskin, M-75, pnt CI, 1910s, 6", NM 750.00
Shell Out, M-1622, J&E Stevens, pnt CI, 4¾" L, EX 700.00
Soldier, M-45, pnt CI, lt wear, 6", EX 165.00
St Bernard w/Pack, M-439, Williams, pnt CI, 3¾x5½", NM 215.00
Stag, M-737, NP CI, worn pnt, 9½", EX 75.00
Statue of Liberty, M-1165, pnt CI, gold trim, 6⅜", VG 135.00
Stork Safe, M-651, JM Harper, CI, 5½", VG 1,200.00
Sunbonnet Sue, M-257, pnt CI, 1970, 7½", NM 215.00
Teddy Bear, M-694, Arcade, pnt CI, 2½x3⅞", VG 215.00
Thoroughbred, M-526, Hubley, CI, bronze pnt, 5¾", NM 195.00
Trolley Car, M-1474, Kenton, CI, silver pnt, 5¼" L, VG 450.00
Ulysses S Grant Bust, M-116, pnt CI, 1976, 5½", EX 265.00
US Mail, M-835, Kenton, pnt CI, 4¾", NM 525.00
US Treasury, M-1053, Grey Iron, pnt CI, 3¼", EX 465.00
Villa, M-1179, Kyser & Rex, CI, red finial, 5¾", EX 725.00
Wireless Bank, N-5980, CI, lt rust, 6⅝" 80.00

Barber Shop Collectibles

Even for the stranger in town, the local barber shop was easy to find, its location vividly marked with the traditional red and white striped barber pole that for centuries identified such establishments. As far back as the 12th century, the barber has had a place in recorded history. At one time he not only groomed the beards and cut the hair of his gentlemen clients but was known as the 'blood-letter' as well, hence the red stripe for blood and the white for the bandages. Many early barbers even pulled teeth! Later, laws were enacted that divided the practices of barbering and surgery.

The Victorian barber shop reflected the charm of that era with fancy barber chairs upholstered in rich wine-colored velvet; rows of bottles made from colored art glass held hair tonics and shaving lotion. Backbars of richly carved oak with beveled mirrors lined the wall behind the barber's station. During the late 19th century, the barber pole with a blue stripe added to the standard red and white as a patriotic gesture came into vogue.

Today the barber shop has all but disappeared from the American scene, replaced by modern unisex salons. Collectors search for the barber poles, the fancy chairs, and the tonic bottles of an era gone but not forgotten. See also Bottles; Razors; Shaving Mugs.

Blade bank, Dandy Dan, celluloid, mc, w/tool holder, 6½" 18.00
Blade bank, frog figural, ceramic, Listerine advertising 18.50
Blade sharpener, Jogo, NM in silver & blk box 10.00
Bowl, shaving; Currier & Ives, Am Express Train, 1940s, 4⅛" 20.00
Cabinet, sterilizer; NP, 23-compartment, porc lined, 10x4x6" 55.00
Chair, child's, oak & CI w/velvet uphl, Pat 1890, 43" 600.00
Chair, child's, orig wooden horse's head 1,600.00
Chair, child's, w/horse's head in front, sits on lg chair, G 225.00
Chair, Eugene Burninghaus, swan arms, 2-pc, VG 950.00
Chair, Hollstegge-Bauman, oak & CI, cvd swan's head arms, EX ..575.00
Chair, Koch, rnd bk, tufted leather, rstr 3,100.00
Chair, Koken, wht porc w/leather, 52x24x36", VG 200.00
Chair, leather w/pnt oak base, brass ft, reclining, EX 325.00
Chair, Melchior Imperial, oak/leather/chromed CI, rstr, 50" ...1,980.00
Chair, red velvet uphl, porc base, hydraulic, unmk 425.00
Chair, shoeshine; bent wire & CI w/wood seat, 52", EX 440.00
Chair, Universal, oak & nickel fr w/blk leather, 1909, EX 235.00

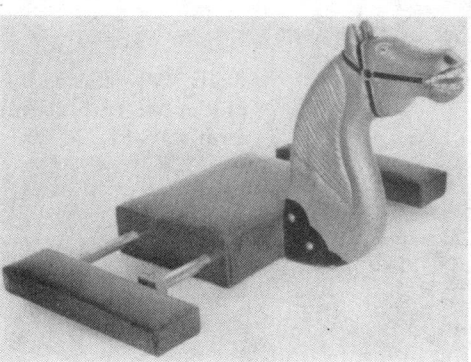

Child's seat with carved horse's head, made to straddle adult's chair, VG, $225.00.

Clippers, Jewel, Boker, hand held, M in worn box 40.00
Clippers, Shapleigh Hardware, St Louis, hand held, EX 35.00
Clippers, Thor Jr, Boker #000, NM 35.00
Clippers, Universal Shear & Novelty #10, lady's, hand held 30.00
Curling iron, Marcel/Repose Acier, insulated hdls, 10½" 8.00
Curling iron, mustache; scarce 20.00
Headrest, for chair, padded, Koken, dtd 1909, EX 35.00
Hot water container, copper, w/tray for instruments, 14x11" 350.00
Jar, Gauze, oval underglass label, Glasco, 7x4½", EX 15.00
Pole, electric, metal & glass, revolves, 3-color, 1930s, 26" 295.00
Pole, electrified, glass & porc on steel, rstr, 96x16" dia 350.00
Pole, leaded glass, Koken, Victorian, 48" 975.00
Pole, leaded glass, red & wht, porc mts, Chisholm NY, 36" 825.00
Pole, pnt tin w/porc top & bottom, some flakes, 33", VG 175.00
Pole, pnt wood, blk & wht w/silver ends, 1850s, 34", VG 1,250.00
Pole, pnt wood, mk Rochester NY, 1920, 34" 300.00
Pole, porc, orig finish, for sidewalk, 90" 2,100.00
Pole, sheet metal on wood, red/wht/blk spiral, 48", EX 235.00

Pole, trn wood, mc pnt, late 1800s, 96", EX 2,300.00
Rack, mug; oak, 40-compartment, 48x48", EX 525.00
Razor, hair trimming; metal, Playtex, NMIB 15.00
Shaving powder stick, Remington, MIB 10.00
Showcase, cvd wood, 2-shelf, fancy door pull, 25x12x7½" 110.00
Sign, Union Barber Shop, eagle on US shield, seal, VG 145.00
Stained glass window, barber pole, contemporary, sgn, 11x20" ..125.00
Station, oak, ornate turnings/moldings, 77x47", EX 825.00
Sterilizer, Herpicide, Bakelite fr & lids, 2 glass containers 125.00
Strop, horsehide, unused, NM 18.00
Stropping tool, Safety Auto Stropper, EX 17.50
Towel steamer, NP copper, Ideal Metal works, 61", EX 425.00

Barometers

Barometers are instruments designed to measure the weight or pressure of the atmosphere in order to anticipate approaching weather changes. Those made prior to the turn of the century (earlier in England and on the continent) were beautifully housed in period cases of mahogany, rosewood, walnut, or cherry, often with brass trim. Pocket barometers/altimeters were produced for surveying and personal use.

Louis XVI giltwood barometer, trophy crest, 18th century, unusual form, 33", $1,320.00.

B Pike & Sons, stick type, eng brass dial, ca 1830, 20" 875.00
CH Farley Portland ME, aneroid, brass, 4¾" dia, VG 100.00
Charles C Hutchinson Boston, brass, 5" dia, EX 115.00
E Kendall New Lebanon...NY, aneroid, 4¾" dia, EX 90.00
EC Spooner Boston, walnut case, mid 1800s, 42", EX 220.00
English, inlaid mahog, scrolled pediment, 1880s, 39", EX 330.00
Friez, Altimore US Navy, aneroid, NM in dvtl box 100.00
H Abraham Optician Liverpool, walnut & walnut veneer, 37" ..935.00
J McAllister & Co Phila, mahog case, 1850s, 13½" 300.00
John M Merrick Worcester MA...Pat Nov 3, 1857, mahog, 38" .880.00
Keuffel & Esser, aneroid, cvd oak case, 7" dia, EX 140.00
P Salvade, rosewood, stick type, 44" 800.00
Unmk, mahog veneer, eng silvered dials, brass trim, 42" 440.00
US Maritime Commission-Friez..., brass, aneroid, 6" dia 90.00
Vanetti & Benzzoni, mahog w/inlay, rpl finial, 39" 770.00
Viking Iver C Weilbach & Co Solver & Svarrer..., on teak base .100.00
W Cray Optician London Bridge, rosewood veneer, 37½" 495.00

Barware

Back in the thirties when social soirees were very elegant affairs thanks to the influence of Hollywood in all its glamour and mystique, cocktails were often served up in shakers styled as miniature airplanes, zeppelins, skyscrapers, lady's legs, penguins, roosters, bowling pins, etc. Some were by top designers such as Norman Bel Geddes and Russel Wright. They were made of silverplate, glass, and chrome, often trimmed with colorful Bakelite handles. Today these are hot collectibles, and even the more common Deco-styled chrome cylinders are often priced at $25.00 and up. Ice buckets, trays, and other bar accessories are also included in this area of collecting. Our advisor for this category is Stephen Visakay, who is listed in the Directory under New Jersey.

Book, The Savoy Cocktail Book, H Craddock, 1930, M 150.00
Cocktail shaker, SP, penguin form, Napier, 12" 1,000.00
Dispenser, Blk bartender, France, 6½x6", NM 750.00
Dispenser, seltzer; Soda King Syphon, ca 1938, 9½x3⅞" 200.00
Ice bucket, aluminum, stamped/emb penguins, West Bend, 1940s ..35.00
Ice bucket, chrome-plated copper, Keystone, 1930s, +tray 95.00
Ice bucket, red anodized aluminum, apple form, Italy, 1950s 35.00
Pinch bottle, SP w/3 eng roosters, Meriden, 1927, 9" 400.00
Pitcher, colored glass, Cambridge, chrome Farber Bros lid 150.00
Rack, tumbler; gyroscopic, 20x4¼" dia rings, +4 tumblers 125.00
Shaker, chrome, penguin form, unmk, 11" 350.00
Shaker, chrome, pitcher form, ped base, Farberware 40.00
Shaker, chrome, vintage etch, slim, form, unmk, 12" 50.00
Shaker, clear glass, w/strainer, horse's head lid, Heisey 200.00
Shaker, clear glass, w/strainer, plain lid, Heisey 40.00
Shaker, clear glass w/chrome, hourglass form, Maxwell Phillip 75.00
Shaker, clear glass w/pk elephants, Hazel Atlas, 10½" 48.00
Shaker, cobalt glass w/silver, dumbbell form, +6 cocktails 450.00
Shaker, cobalt glass w/wht silk-screened recipes, 10½" 38.00
Shaker, cobalt glass w/windmill, chrome top, Hazel Atlas, 10" 28.00
Shaker, nickel silver, NY Stamping Co, 1-gal, 18½" 95.00
Shaker, polished aluminum, skyscraper inspired, 13x3½" 95.00
Shaker, SP, milk can form, Reed & Barton, 10¼" 75.00
Shaker/bar, chrome, Zeppelin, DRGM, MIG, 16-pc, 12" 1,600.00
Tray, flappers w/drinks, Here's How, rectangular, NM 100.00

Basalt

Basalt is a type of unglazed black pottery developed by Josiah Wedgwood and copied by many other companies during the late 18th and early 19th centuries. It is also called 'Egyptian Black.' See also Wedgwood.

Teapot, embossed flowers, 10", $750.00.

Coffeepot, emb motif, dome lid w/widow Warburton, 10", VG ..300.00
Creamer, emb floral/acanthus bands, leaf hdl, oval, 6" L 180.00

Creamer, ribbed, leaf hdl, rnd body, unmk, 4" **100.00**
Jug, swags/ribbons, engine-trn bands, att Yates, 1790, 5" **180.00**
Spill vase, emb cherubs, copper lustre int, 4¾" **200.00**

Baskets

Basket weaving is a craft as old as ancient history. Baskets have been used to harvest crops, for domestic chores, and to contain the catch of fishermen. Materials at hand were utilized, and baskets from a specific region are often distinguishable simply by analyzing the natural fibers used in their construction. Early Indian baskets were made of corn husks or woven grasses. Willow splint, straw, rope, and paper were also used. Until the invention of the veneering machine in the late 1800s, splint was made by water-soaking a split log until the fibers were softened and flexible. Long strips were pulled out by hand and, while still wet and pliable, woven into baskets in either a cross-hatch or hexagonal weave.

Most handcrafted baskets on the market today were made between 1860 and the early 1900s. Factory baskets with a thick, wide splint cut by machine are of little interest to collectors. The more popular baskets are those designed for a specific purpose, rather than the more commonly-found utility baskets that had multiple uses. Among the most costly forms are the Nantucket Lighthouse baskets, which were basically copied from those made there for centuries by aboriginal Indians. They were designed in the style of whale oil barrels and named for the South Shoal Nantucket Lightship where many were made during the last half of the 19th century. Cheese baskets (used to separate curds from whey), herb-gathering baskets, and finely woven Shaker miniatures are other highly-prized examples of the basket weaver's art.

In the listings that follow, assume that each has a center bentwood handle (unless handles of another type are noted) that is not included in the height. Unless another type of material is indicated, assume that each is made of splint. See also American Indian; Eskimo; Sewing; Shaker.

Nantucket, bound oak rim, woven rattan body on oblong wooden base, swing handle, late 1800s, 5x11x7¼", EX, $1,500.00.

Apple, wht oak, old dk gr pnt, bowl shape, 1850s, 9x13½" **125.00**
Apple, wooden band at top, bail hdl, 1910s, ½-bushel **65.00**
Bee keep, rye straw, some age, 17x17" dia **235.00**
Bentwood, rose mall decor, dtd 1873, wear, 5¾x15" **660.00**
Buttocks, bentwood hdl, gr pnt, 5x8½" **75.00**
Buttocks, EX color, 6½x10" **125.00**
Buttocks, EX color & age, 9x11" **215.00**
Buttocks, EX detail, old blk pnt, wear, 9x17x15" **140.00**

Buttocks, old finish, minor damage, 8x15x15" **185.00**
Buttocks, reed & splint, Eye-of-God hdl, old bl pnt, 5x14x8" **150.00**
Buttocks, some age, 5½x11½x10½" **72.50**
Buttocks, weathered gray finish, 8x18x14", EX **95.00**
Buttocks, worn finish, 7x15½x15", NM **200.00**
Cheese, G age & color, minor damage, 7x21" **275.00**
Cheese, well made, 8x12½", NM **325.00**
Feather, oak splint, late 1800s/early 1900s, 29x15" dia **275.00**
Garden, oak, nailed dbl rim, ca 1900, 16½x18½x12" **90.00**
Gathering, low oval, 1800s, 18¼x15½", EX **100.00**
Gathering, 1800s, 23½" dia, EX **110.00**
Laundry, lt natural, bentwood rim hdls, 11x21x26" **75.00**
Laundry, oval, minor damage, 11x27x19" **75.00**
Market, ca 1800s, 16x14", EX **110.00**
Market, wicker w/wooden bottom, wrapped hdl, 8⅜x19½x13" **50.00**
Melon rib, cane-wrapped wooden hdl, 7½x15", EX **50.00**
Melon rib, rim hand holds, EX age & color, 6x12½", EX **100.00**
Nantucket, ca 1900, 7½", EX **600.00**
Nantucket, oval, ca 1900, 12" **880.00**
Nantucket, pocketbook, cvd ivory dolphin plaque on lid, 8" ..**1,100.00**
Nantucket, shaped hdl, incised/trn base, ca 1900, 4¾x3½" **1,045.00**
Nantucket, shaped hdl, reinforced zinc/wood base, 9½x14" **440.00**
Nantucket, swing hdl, ca 1900, 8x6", NM **1,100.00**
Nantucket, swing hdl, incised base, ca 1900, 5x11", EX **600.00**
Nantucket, swing hdl, incised base, 4½x10", EX **550.00**
Nantucket, swing hdl, incised base, 9x4¾", EX **350.00**
Nantucket, swing hdl, trn wooden base, W Hadd, 12¼", EX **715.00**
Pea picking, old red pnt, rectangular, 10" L **220.00**
Pea picking, old wht pnt, rectangular, 6" L **85.00**
Picnic, old bl pnt, dbl swivel hdls, 7x19½x12¾" **35.00**
Picnic, splint appl over wooden liner, bentwood hdls, 8x13x9" ..**110.00**
Rye straw, coiled, ftd, 4⅛x12⅜" **65.00**
Splint, bentwood rim hdls, stains, 5½x9½x8¾" **50.00**
Splint, dk natural patina w/gr & yel decor, 4¼x7¾" **95.00**
Splint, dk varnish, well made, not old, 7x11½" **30.00**
Splint, EX detail/age/color, rim rpr, 7¾x11x11½" **300.00**
Splint, flared sides, red traces, 5x13½x10½", EX **85.00**
Splint, G age, worn finish, 6½x11" **75.00**
Splint, high kick-up, EX color, 6½x12" **77.00**
Splint, mottled stain, 4¼x7x8½" **88.00**
Splint, old mustard-brn pnt, 5x14x11½" **200.00**
Splint, old varnish, 10x17½x9" **125.00**
Splint, oval, some age, 8½x19x13" **60.00**
Splint, pnt starflowers, rim damage, 4½x8" **67.50**
Splint, radiating ribs, oval, old varnish, 6½x16x15" **200.00**
Splint, stamped red/blk watercolor design, 4½x10½x9" **85.00**
Splint, wht pnt w/gr trim, 3¾x11½", EX **140.00**
Splint, 2-tone design, 7½x13x12½" **75.00**
Splint & wicker, stationary wrapped hdl, 3½x7½" **30.00**
Wall hanging, yel pnt over wht & red, 1800s, 9" L, EX **100.00**
Winnowing, wood hdls ea side, minor wear, 4x24" **250.00**

Batchelder

Ernest A. Batchelder was a leading exponent of the Arts and Crafts movement in the United States. His influential book, *Design in Theory and Practice*, was originally published in 1910. He is best known, however, for his artistic tiles which he first produced in Pasadena, California, from 1909 to 1916. In 1906 the business was relocated to Los Angeles where it continued until 1932, closing because of the Depression.

In 1938 Batchelder resumed production in Pasadena under the name of 'Kinneola Kiln.' Output of the new pottery consisted of delicately cast bowls and vases in an Oriental style. This business closed in 1951. Tiles carry a die-stamped mark; vases and bowls are hand incised. Our advisor for this category is Jack Chipman, author of *Collector's Encyclopedia of California Pottery*; he is listed in the Directory under California.

Ashtray, lt bl matt, hexagonal w/emb lettering, 4½", EX	**165.00**
Bookends, 2¾" tiles set in Potter Studio brass mts, pr	**265.00**
Bowl, rose, oval, Pasadena mk, 4x12x7"	**145.00**
Tile, Dutch boy relief, brn w/bl wash, 5¾"	**85.00**
Tile, fruit, bl, 4"	**65.00**
Tile, geometric design, blk & orange, 4"	**45.00**
Tile, Hispanic, 5-color geometric design, mk, 1928, 6"	**75.00**
Tile, La Mayan, terra cotta, 3½"	**65.00**
Tile, peacock, unglazed, impressed mk, 6"	**175.00**
Tile, 2 birds over spigot fountain, 17x12x4"	**275.00**
Vase, gray, cylindrical, 9½"	**250.00**
Vase, mottled Chinese red & gr, 11x4½"	**1,000.00**
Vase, yel, flared rim, 6"	**145.00**

Battersea

Battersea is a term that refers to enameling on copper or other metal. Though originally produced at Battersea, England, in the mid-18th century, the craft was later practiced throughout the Staffordshire district. Boxes are the most common examples. Some are figurals, and many bear an inscription. Values are given for examples with only minimal damage, which is normal. Our advisor for this category is John Harrigan; he is listed in the Directory under Minnesota.

Opera glasses, children hunting and fishing in multicolor enameling, 4¼", in velvet case, $425.00.

Bonbonniere, European scene on underside, 1½x2¾", EX	**625.00**
Bonbonniere, florals/pnt-on 'hdls,' basketweave ground, 2" L	**650.00**
Box, courting scenes on lid, florals on sides, 1½x2½"	**150.00**
Box, grisaille classical scene w/gold, 3½" dia	**500.00**
Box, patch; bluebird on foliage on wht lid, bl base, 1⅝x1½"	**275.00**
Box, patch; foliage/urn/motto, wht beaded border, oval, 1¾" L	**450.00**
Box, patch; lady's torso form, head forms lid, 3"	**1,600.00**
Box, patch; serpent in high relief, 1800s, 2¼", EX	**660.00**
Box, snuff; Esteem the Giver, ca 1780, 2"	**525.00**
Box, snuff; French/English naval battle, 2" L	**750.00**
Box, 2 boxers/10 spectators on lid, cobalt base, ¾x2x1½"	**375.00**
Box, 2 figures in 18th-C landscape on lid, 1800s, 7" L	**1,100.00**
Candlesticks, floral, scalloped drip pans, 9", pr	**1,250.00**
Mirror holders, Gen Washington, pk w/pk banner, 2", pr	**1,225.00**
Needle case, gold floral/pastoral scene on pk, 4½" L	**425.00**
Opera glasses, children hunting & fishing, 4" W, in case	**425.00**

Trays, card; 4 suits decor, pr	**950.00**

Bauer

Originally founded in Paducah, Kentucky, in 1885, the J.A. Bauer Company moved to Los Angeles where it was re-established in 1909. Until the 1920s their major products were terra cotta gardenware, flowerpots, and stoneware and yellowware bowls. During prohibition they produced crocks for home use. A more artful form of product began to develop with the addition of designer Louis Ipsen to the staff in 1915. Some of his work, a line of molded vases, flowerpots, bowls, etc., was awarded a bronze medal at the Pacific International Exposition the following year.

In 1930 the first of many dinnerware lines was tested on the market. Their initial pattern, Plain Ware, was well accepted and led the way to the introduction of the most popular dinnerware in their history and with today's collectors, Ring Ware. It was produced from 1932 into the early 1960s in solid colors of jade green, royal blue, Chinese yellow, light blue, orange-red, and (in very limited quantities) black or white. Its simple pattern was a design of closely-spaced concentric ribs, either convex or concave. Over the years, more than one hundred shapes were available. Some were made in limited quantities, resulting in rare items to whet the appetites of Bauer buffs today. Other patterns were La Linda, produced during the 1940s and 1950s, and Monterey Moderne, introduced in 1948 and remaining popular into the 1950s (made in pink, black, gray, brown, and green.)

After WWII a flood of foreign imports drastically curtailed their sales, and the pottery began a steady decline that ended in failure in 1962. Prices listed below reflect the California market. For more information, we recommend *The Collector's Encyclopedia of California Pottery* by Jack Chipman, our advisor for this category. Mr. Chipman's address may be found in the Directory under California.

Ashtray, plain, blk, 4" sq	**100.00**
Bean pot, plain, blk, 2-hdl, 1-qt	**110.00**
Beater, for beating bowl, metal	**30.00**
Bowl, batter; La Linda, all matt colors, 2-qt	**36.00**
Bowl, cereal; Brusche Al Fresco, speckled grs & gray, 5½"	**5.00**
Bowl, fruit; Brusche Contempo, all colors, 5"	**6.00**
Bowl, fruit; Monterey, all colors but wht, 6"	**13.50**
Bowl, fruit; Ring, jade gr, lt bl or turq, 5"	**15.00**
Bowl, mixing; Ring, yel, lt bl or olive, #12, ½-gal	**50.00**
Bowl, pudding; plain, all colors but blk, #1, 5½"	**22.50**
Bowl, ramekin, La Linda, all matt colors	**8.50**
Bowl, salad; Brusche Al Fresco, coffee brn or Dubonnet, 13"	**27.50**
Bowl, salad; Ring, orange-red, dk bl or wht, low, 9"	**110.00**
Bowl, serving; La Linda, burgundy or dk brn, rnd, 9"	**38.50**
Bowl, serving; Monterey Moderne, blk, 8½"	**50.00**
Bowl, soup; Monterey Moderne, all colors but blk, 5¼"	**11.00**
Bowl, vegetable; Brusche Al Fresco, speckled grs or gray, 7½"	**11.00**
Bowl, vegetable; Brusche Contempo, divided, oval, 7½"	**12.00**
Bowl, vegetable; Ring, olive, gray or red-brn, oval, 8"	**40.00**
Bowl, vegetable; wht, oval, 10½"	**50.00**
Butter dish, Monterey Moderne, all colors but blk, rnd	**35.00**
Candlestick, plain, all colors but blk, hdl	**60.00**
Casserole, La Linda, burgundy or dk brn, 1-qt	**55.00**
Casserole, Ring, blk, #36, 8½"	**170.00**
Casserole, Ring, dk bl, ivory or burgundy, 6½"	**60.00**
Coffee server, Brusche Contempo, all colors, 8-cup	**25.00**
Coffee server, plain, all colors but blk, open	**38.50**
Coffeepot, Ring, chartreuse, gray or red-brn, drip type, 9½"	**145.00**
Cookie jar, Brusche Al Fresco, speckled grs or gray	**30.00**
Cookie jar, Ring, orange-red, ivory or burgundy	**120.00**

Creamer, Brusche Al Fresco, coffee brn or Dubonnet **7.50**
Creamer, La Linda, all matt colors, old shape **11.00**
Cup, jumbo coffee; La Linda, all matt colors **30.00**
Cup & saucer, Brusche Contempo, all colors **10.00**
Cup & saucer, El Chico, all colors **55.00**
Cup & saucer, Monterey, all colors but wht **33.00**
Custard cup, La Linda, burgundy or dk brn **10.00**
Flowerpot, Ring Art & Gardenware, yel or gray, ruffled, 2" **7.50**
Gravy bowl, Monterey Moderne, all colors but blk **27.50**
Honey jar, Ring, yel or lt bl, rare **300.00**
Hostess tray & cup, Brusche Al Fresco, speckled grs or gray **15.00**
Jar, cigarette/cigar; Ring, blk, 4" **240.00**
Jar, refrigerator; Ring, yel, lt bl or olive, complete set **72.50**
Jar, spice; plain, all colors but blk, #1, 4½x3½" **72.50**
Jardiniere, Ring Art & Gardenware, dk bl or wht, 8" **80.00**
Mug, Ring, blk, bbl style, 12-oz **150.00**
Pitcher, Brusche Al Fresco, coffee brn or Dubonnet, ½-pt **8.00**
Pitcher, Monterey Moderne, all colors but blk, 2½-qt **42.50**
Pitcher, Ring, dk bl, ivory or burgundy, bbl style **150.00**
Plate, bread & butter; La Linda, all matt colors, 6" **5.50**
Plate, dinner; plain, blk, 10½" **100.00**
Plate, El Chico, all colors, 9" **30.00**
Plate, grill; Monterey Moderne, rnd **20.00**
Platter, Brusche Al Fresco, speckled grs or gray, 10¼" **6.50**
Platter, Brusche Contempo, all colors **10.00**
Platter, La Linda, burgundy or dk brn, oval, 12" **24.00**
Platter, Monterey, all colors but wht, oval, 12" **22.50**
Platter, Monterey Moderne, blk, oval, 12" **36.00**
Platter, Ring, blk, oval, 9" **50.00**
Relish plate, Monterey, all colors but wht, 10½" **40.00**
Shaker, La Linda, all matt colors **6.00**
Sugar bowl, Brusche Al Fresco, speckled grs or gray **10.00**
Sugar bowl, plain, all colors but blk, w/lid **30.00**
Teacup, Ring, blk **145.00**
Teapot, La Linda, all matt colors, Aladdin style, 8-cup **55.00**
Teapot, Monterey, all colors but wht, 6-cup **55.00**
Teapot, Monterey, wht, 6-cup **70.00**
Teapot, Ring, blk, wood hdl, 6-cup **250.00**
Tumbler, La Linda, burgundy or dk brn, 8-oz **20.00**
Tumbler, Monterey, all colors but wht **20.00**
Tumbler, Monterey Moderne, all colors but blk **15.00**
Tumbler, Ring, lt bl, chartreuse, olive or gray, 3-oz **17.50**
Vase, Ring Art & Gardenware, blk, ruffled, 7" **50.00**
Vase, Ring Art & Gardenware, orange-red, ruffled, 10" **65.00**
Vase, Ring Art & Gardenware, turq or jade gr, ruffled, 7" **25.00**

Bavaria

Bavaria, Germany, was long the center of that country's pottery industry; in the 1800s, many firms operated in and around the area. Chinaware vases, novelties, and table accessories were decorated with transfer prints as well as by hand by artists who sometimes signed their work. The examples here are marked with 'Bavaria' and the logos of some of the various companies which were located there.

Cake plate, floral, pk on white w/gold medallions, sgn, 10" **28.00**
Cookie jar, roses, pk on gr shaded w/gold, mk, 7½x5½" **110.00**
Figurine, girl & goose, pastels, porc, mk, 6½" **50.00**
Figurine, youth chasing geese, pastels, porc, mk, 8½" **75.00**
Pitcher, Grecian ladies, gold tracing, mk, 6x4" **100.00**
Plate, castle scene, floral rim w/gold, Frankenthal, 1700s **600.00**
Tazza w/rtcl bowl, mc floral on porc, mk, 3⅝x5¾" **75.00**
Teapot, pk roses w/gold, ribbed, ZS&Co, +1 c/s **85.00**
Vase, girl w/bonnet, 3½" **110.00**

Bowl, oranges among blossoms and foliage, gold trim, 9½", $75.00.

Beer Cans

When the flat-top can was first introduced in 1934, it came with printed instructions on how to use the triangular punch opener. Cone-top cans, which are rare today, were patented in 1935 by the Continental Can Company. By the 1960s, aluminum cans with pull tabs had made both types obsolete.

The hobby of collecting beer cans has been rapidly gaining momentum over the past ten years. Series types, such as South African Brewery, Lion, and the Cities Series by Schmit and Tucker, are especially popular.

Condition is an important consideration when evaluating market price. Grade 1 must be in like-new condition with no rust. However, the triangular punch hole is acceptable. Grade 2 cans may have slight scratches or dimples but must be free of rust. For Grade 3, light rust, minor scratching, and some fading may be acceptable. When these defects are more pronounced, a can is defaulted to Grade 4. Those in less-than-excellent condition devaluate sharply. In the listings that follow, cans are arranged alphabetically by brand name, not by brewery. Unless noted otherwise, values are for cans in Grade 1 condition.

ABC Extra Dry, cone top, red & blk, 12-oz **110.00**
Alpine, flat top, bl & wht, 12-oz **65.00**
Alta Special Report, flat top, silver/bl/red/cream, 12-oz **350.00**
Bartels, flat top, red/wht/gold, 12-oz **65.00**
Bavarian, pull top, bl & wht, 12-oz **1.50**
Becker's Unita Club, cone top, silver/red/bl, 12-oz **145.00**
Black Horse Ale, pull top, wht/gold/blk, 12-oz **2.50**
Blatz, pull top, brn & lt brn, 11-oz **2.50**
Blue 'N Gold, cone top, bl/wht/gold, 12-oz **250.00**
Bonanza, pull top, red/wht/bl, 12-oz **17.50**
Brau Haus, flat top, people drinking, 12-oz **125.00**
Brown Derby, flat top, wht & gold, 12-oz **15.00**
Buckeye Sparkling Dry, cone top, silver/red/wht, 12-oz **60.00**
Buckhorn, flat top, red, 12-oz **8.00**
Busch Bavarian, flat top, bl & wht, 12-oz **12.50**
Butte lager, flat top, red/wht/gold/bl, 12-oz **45.00**
Canadian Ace Premium, flat top, wht & gold, 12-oz **7.50**
Colt Beer, pull top, wht & bl, 12-oz **10.00**
Colt 45 Malt Liquor, pull top, 10-oz **10.00**
Coors, flat top, gold & blk, 12-oz **90.00**
Copper Club, cone top, 12-oz **65.00**
Drewyr's Extra Dry, flat top, wht, 12-oz **7.50**
Eastside Export, flat top, gold/bl/silver, 12-oz **125.00**
Exeter Beer, flat top, bl & wht, 12-oz, EX **350.00**
Fitzgerald's Pale Ale, cone top, red & wht, 12-oz **175.00**
Fox DeLuxe, flat top, wht & gold, 12-oz **8.50**
GB Bock Dark Beer, flat top, gold/blk/red/silver, 12-oz **65.00**

Goebel Luxury, flat top, red/blk/gold, 12-oz **30.00**
Gold Age, cone top, miner panning gold, 12-oz **400.00**
Golden Glow, flat top, red/gold/wht, 12-oz **180.00**
Grand Prize, flat top, silver & bl, 12-oz **38.00**
Harvard, flat top, gold/red/blk, 12-oz **125.00**
Iron City, pull top, 1972 Christmas can w/gr wreath, 16-oz **27.50**
Lucky Lager Extra Dry, flat top, red & gold, 12-oz **20.00**
Maier Select, cone top, red & wht, 12-oz **135.00**
Miller, pull top, red & wht, 8-oz **4.00**
Milwaukee's Best, flat top, wht/red/gold, 12-oz **5.00**
Ortileb's Lager, cone top, gold & red, 12-oz **95.00**
Pabst Blue Ribbon, flat top, w/o red ribbon, 1953, EX **15.00**
Pearl, flat top, red & tan, 12-oz **27.50**
Pioneer, flat top, brn & wht, 12-oz **35.00**
Playmate Malt Liquor, playmate, flat top, 12-oz, VG **275.00**
Red Top Ale, cone top, NM **65.00**
Regal Amber, flat top, red & wht, 12-oz **300.00**
Schlitz, pull top, 8-oz **4.00**
Tudor Ale, flat top, gr & wht, 12-oz **17.50**
Union Cream Ale, gold/red/brown/'wood grain,' flat top, 12-oz, VG ..**300.00**
Valley Brew Pale Premium, flat top, silver/red/wht/blk, 12-oz **95.00**
Whale's Wht Ale, pull top, blk & wht, 12-oz **22.00**

Belleek, American

From 1883 until 1930, several American potteries located in New Jersey and Ohio manufactured a type of china similar to the famous Irish Belleek soft-paste porcelain. The American manufacturers identified their porcelain by using 'Belleek' or 'Beleek' in their marks. American Belleek is considered the highest achievement of the American porcelain industry. Production centered around artistic cabinet pieces and luxury tablewares. Many examples emulated Irish shapes and decor with marine themes and other naturalistic styles. While all are highly collectible, some companies' products are rarer than others. The best-known manufacturers are Ott and Brewer, Willets, The Ceramic Art Company (CAC), and Lenox. You will find more detailed information in those specific categories. Our advisor for this category is Mary Frank Gaston; you will find her address in the Directory under Texas.

Key:
AAC — American Art China   CAP — Columbian Art Pottery
Company   Works

Ewer, branch-style handle in brown, hand-painted roses on body, marked Beleek (sic), $500.00.

Cream soup, Bouquet, Coxon, w/underplate **175.00**
Creamer, floral band, gold trim, ornate rim & hdl, AAC, 4" **350.00**
Cup, demitasse; Orient pattern, Morgan **150.00**
Letter box, florals w/gold **180.00**
Plate, Boulevard, Coxon, 10½" **200.00**
Salt cellar, sponged gold on scalloped rim & base, AAC, 2½" **125.00**
Teapot, dragon form, gold paste leaves, CAP, 7½x9" **1,200.00**
Tumbler, Souvenir David's Society...1899, CAP, 4¼" **300.00**
Vase, orchids, EX art, sgn, 1903, 13" **395.00**

Belleek, Irish

Belleek is a very thin translucent porcelain that takes its name from the village in Ireland where it originated in 1859. The glaze is a creamy ivory color with a pearl-like lustre. The tablewares, baskets, figurines, and vases that have always been made there are being crafted yet today. Shamrock, Tridacna, Echinus, and Thorn are but a few of the many patterns of tableware which have been made during some periods(s) of the pottery's history. Throughout the years, their most popular pattern has been Shamrock.

It is possible to date an example to within twenty to thirty years of crafting by the mark. Pieces with an early stamp often bring prices nearly triple that of a similar but current item. With some variation, the marks have always incorporated the Irish wolfhound, Celtic round tower, harp, and shamrocks. The first three marks (usually in black) were used from 1863 to 1946. A series of green marks identified the pottery's offerings from 1946 until the seventh mark (in gold/brown) was introduced in 1980 (it was discontinued in 1992). The most current mark, the eighth, is blue. Belleek Collector's International Society limited edition pieces are designated with a special mark in red. In the listings below, numbers designated with the prefix 'D' relate to the book *Belleek, The Complete Collector's Guide and Illustrated Reference, Second Edition* — Wallace-Homestead Book Company, One Chilton Way, Radnor, PA 19098-0230. The author, Richard K. Degenhardt, is our advisor for Belleek; he is listed in the Directory under North Carolina.

Key:
A — plain (glazed only)   I — 1863-1890
B — cob lustre   II — 1891-1926
C — hand tinted   III — 1926-1946
D — hand painted   IV — 1946-1955
E — hand-painted shamrocks   V — 1955-1965
F — hand gilted   VI — 1965-3/31/1980
G — hand tinted and gilted   VII — 4/1/1980-12/22/1992
H — hand-painted shamrocks   VIII — 1/4/1993-current
    and gilted
K — hand painted and gilted
L — bisque and plain
M — decalcomania
N — special hand-painted decoration
T — transfer design

Aberdeen, vase, floral, D55-II, J, lg **900.00**
Aberdeen, vase, floral, D58-IV, D, med sz **300.00**
Appleleaf, candlestick, D270-VII, D **75.00**
Artichoke Tea Ware, breakfast saucer, D1462-I, F, 7" **175.00**
Artichoke Tea Ware, creamer, D719-I, F, 4½" **475.00**
Basket, oval, floral, D118, 4-strand, lg, 12" **1,600.00**
Basket, oval, w/lid, D113, 3-strand, D, lg **6,500.00**
Belleek, flowerpot, floral, D47-II, A, sm **225.00**
Bird's Nest, basket, D123, 4-strand, A, 3¾" **380.00**
Boat ashtray, D229-IV, B, 4⅝" L **38.00**
Boy & Swan, comport, D33-I, F, 10" **5,200.00**

Bust of Lord James Butler, D1128-I, A, 11" 2,800.00
Celtic, cross, D1740-VI, B, lg, 12" 300.00
Celtic Tea Ware, plate, D1435-III, K, 6½" 95.00
Chinese Tea Ware, creamer, D486-I, K 500.00
Chinese Tea Ware, sugar bowl, D485-I, K, 3" 450.00
Christmas plate, 1970, D1850-VI, A 125.00
Cleary, spill, D193-VI, A 35.00
Coral, bell, D2078-VI, D, 5½" 60.00
Dolphin, chamberstick, D343-VI, K 400.00
Double Shell, creamer & sugar bowl, D288-VI/D1301-VI, B 100.00
Echinus, bowl, ftd, D1521-VI, A, 8¼" 475.00
Echinus Tea Ware, teapot, D646-I, F, med sz 750.00
Emerson, mug, D300-II, B 150.00
Erne Tea Ware, teacup & saucer, D445-II, C 225.00
Fern & Flower, wall bracket, D1802-I, A, 11" 1,250.00
Figurine, Crouching Venus, D16-I, F, 17" 8,500.00
Figurine, leprechaun, D1142-III, A, 5½" 325.00
Figurine, Meditation, D20-VII, 7th gold mk, L, 14½" 550.00
Fish, spill, D184-I, B, 7" 850.00
Florence, jug, D813-VII, G, med sz 85.00

**Flowerpot, D51-II, J, 10½",
$2,400.00.**

Frame, floral, D63-II, J, lg, 16x13½" 4,800.00
Grass Tea Ware, honey pot on stand, D755-I, K, 6½" 775.00
Gravy boat, D2083-VII, C, 5" 60.00
Heart, basket, No 3, D1258, 4-strand, D, 6½" 475.00
Henshall, spill, D61-V, D, 5½" 125.00
Hexagon, cake plate, D1263, 4-strand, A, 10" 500.00
Hexagon Tea Ware, dejeuner tray, D395-II, C 1,450.00
Hexagon Tea Ware, teacup & saucer, D622-II, N 300.00
Imperial Shell, D138-II, C, 7" 1,250.00
Irish, pot, D204-II, A, sz 5, 6" 225.00
Island, vase, D88-VI, E, 8" 90.00
Ivy Tea Ware, plate, D1413-III, B, 7" 80.00
Killarney, biscuit jar, D1981-VII, D, 6½" 110.00
Lifford, creamer, D301-I, B, 3¼" 225.00
Limpet Tea Ware, plate, D1372-V, B, 8" 45.00
Limpet Tea Ware, plate, D557-VI, B, 6¼" 30.00
Limpet Tea Ware, teacup & saucer, D549-II, B, 4 sets 480.00
Lithophane, Girl at Wall, D1538-III, A, 8x6½" 3,000.00
Lyre, wall bracket, D1546-I, A, 8½" 1,200.00
Mask Tea Ware, creamer, tall shape, D1484-III, A, sm 90.00
Mask Tea Ware, plate, D1491-III, B, 6¼" 125.00
Nautilus, creamer, D279-II, A, 4" 250.00
Neptune Tea Ware, plate, D423-III, B, 6¾" 70.00
Neptune Tea Ware, tray, D418-II, C, 17¼x14" 1,200.00
Plaque, Praise Ye the Lord, earthenware, D1808-I, D, 8x9" 650.00
Prince of Wales, ice pail, D3-I, F 7,500.00
Rathmore, vase, D1219-III, A, 7½" 100.00

Ribbon, creamer, D243(CR)-III, B, 3½" 60.00
Ribbon, vase, flowered, D1220-III, A, 8" 300.00
Rope Handle, mug, D215-II, B, 2¾" 175.00
Scroll Tea Ware, teacup & saucer, D502-II, G 250.00
Shamrock Tea Ware, dejeuner set (complete), D419-II, C 2,650.00
Shamrock Ware, box, oval, D604-II, E&D, 3¾" 350.00
Shamrock Ware, coffee cup & saucer, D372-II, E 145.00
Shamrock Ware, coffeepot, D1319-V, H, 7" 285.00
Shamrock Ware, dresser tray, D2005-III, E, 10¼x5" 250.00
Shamrock Ware, kettle, D387-II, E, sm 525.00
Shamrock Ware, pin tray, D1563-V, E, 4¾" 85.00
Shamrock Ware, teacup & saucer, low shape, D366-II, E 150.00
Shamrock Ware, teacup & saucer, tall shape, D375-III, E 110.00
Shamrock Ware, teapot, D384-III, E, lg 325.00
Shamrock Ware, trinket box, oval, D604-II, B, E & J, 4" 300.00
Shell, biscuit jar, D599-VI, B, 7" 110.00
Shell Tea Ware, creamer, D590-II, B 350.00
St Matthew Gospel plate, D1811-VI, M&F, ltd ed, 1979 .....125.00
Statue, Blessed Virgin Mary, D1105-IV, L, lg, 18⅜" 800.00
Swan, D254-I, A, lg, 4½" 325.00
Sydenham, basket, D108, 4-strand, A, 10" 1,500.00
Table centre, D56-IV, D 1,400.00
Thistle Top, vase, floral, D1782-V, D, 5⅛" 110.00
Thorn, scent bottle, D335-I, K 375.00
Tobacco, brewer, D176-II, B, 8" 2,900.00
Tridacna Tea Ware, coffee cup & saucer, D462-II, B 135.00
Tridacna Tea Ware, mustard, D1348-III, B, 2½" 55.00
Tridacna Tea Ware, plate, D464-VI, B, 6" 35.00
Tridacna Tea Ware, teacup & saucer, D454-I, C 165.00
Tridacna Tea Ware, teacup & saucer, D454-IV, B 75.00
Trihorse, comport, D37-I, L, 9" 3,000.00
Undine, creamer, D305-VI, B, 5" dia 45.00
Vine, tankard jug, D1314-VI, D, 5½" 140.00
Wild Irish Rose, thimble, D2110-VII, D 27.00

Bells

Some areas of interest represented in the study of bells are history, religion, and geography. Since Biblical times, bells have announced morning church services, vespers, deaths, christenings, school hours, fires, and community events. Countries have used them en masse to peal out the good news of Christmas, New Year's, and the endings of World Wars I and II. They've been rung in times of great sorrow, such as the death of Abraham Lincoln.

Dorothy Malone Anthony is the author of a series of nine books entitled *World of Bells*. Her address is in the Directory under Kansas. All have over two hundred colored pictures covering many bell categories. See also Schoolhouse Collectibles.

Brass, English hand bell, lacquered 100.00
Brass, school type, 6" 50.00
Brass, school type w/wooden hdl, 12" 90.00
Brass, trn wood hdl, 4½x2⅝" 32.50
Bronze, Dutch girl w/jug figural, 4½" 130.00
Cow, steel w/brass-colored solder, crude, 5", EX 20.00
Glass, cranberry swirl, clear hdl, 11x4" 175.00
Glass, cranberry w/wht edge, clear/cranberry hdl, 15x8" 200.00
Glass w/appl hobnails, bird finial atop hdl, loop for hanging 7.50
Pressed glass crystal, hexagonal metal hdl, glass clapper 15.00
Sleigh, brass, 30 bells on leather strap 290.00
Sleigh, brass, 35 on 2 straps 210.00
Sleigh, rump bells, set of 3 (largest 5") on strap 90.00
Sleigh, rump bells, set of 3 on leather strap, 2⅜" dia 60.00

Bennett, John

Bringing with him the knowledge and experience he had gained at the Doulton (Lambeth) Pottery in England, John Bennett opened a studio in New York City around 1877, where he continued his methods of decorating faience under the glaze. Early wares utilized imported English biscuit, though subsequently local clays (both white and cream-colored) were also used. His first kiln was on Lexington Avenue; he built another on East Twenty-Fourth Street. Pieces are usually signed 'J. Bennett, N.Y.,' often with the street address and date. Later examples may be marked 'West Orange, N.J.,' where he retired. The pottery was in operation approximately six years in New York. Pieces signed with other initials are usually worth less. Our advisor for this category is Robert Tuggle; he is listed in the Directory under New York.

Charger, calla lily on cobalt, sgn/1877, 17¾" **6,750.00**
Charger, floral branch/5 insects on apple gr, sgn/1878, 14½" ..**4,620.00**
Charger, insects & flowers on honeycomb, sgn/1878, 14½" **4,620.00**
Vase, crab apple blossoms on cobalt mottle, sgn/1880s, 10" **5,280.00**
Vase, hibiscus, urn form, top missing, sgn/1879 ....**1,200.00**
Vase, peonies on cobalt mottle, sgn/1882, 26" **22,000.00**
Vase, yel flowers on celadon, 10" **1,650.00**

Bennington

Although the term has become a generic one for the mottled brown ware produced there, Bennington is not a type of pottery, but rather a town in Vermont where two important potteries were located. The Norton Company, founded in 1793, produced mainly redware and salt-glazed stoneware; only during a brief partnership with Fenton (1845-47) was any Rockingham attempted. The Norton Company endured until 1894, operated by succeeding generations of the Norton family. Fenton organized his own pottery in 1847. There he manufactured not only redware and stoneware, but more artistic types as well — graniteware, scroddled ware, flint enamel, a fine parian, and vast amounts of their famous Rockingham. Though from an esthetic standpoint his work rated highly among the country's finest ceramic achievements, he was economically unsuccessful. His pottery closed in 1858.

It is estimated that only one in five Fenton pieces were marked; and although it has become a common practice to link any fine piece of Rockingham to this area, careful study is vital in order to be able to distinguish Bennington's from the similar wares of many other American and Staffordshire potteries. Although the practice was without the permission of the proprietor, it was nevertheless a common occurrence for a potter to take his molds with him when moving from one pottery to the next, so particularly well-received designs were often reproduced at several locations. Of eight known Fenton marks, four are variations of the '1849' impressed stamp: 'Lyman Fenton Co., Fenton's Enamel Patented 1849, Bennington, Vermont.' These are generally found on examples of Rockingham and flint enamel. A raised, rectangular scroll with 'Fenton's Works, Bennington, Vermont,' was used on early examples of porcelain. From 1852 to 1858, the company operated under the title of the United States Pottery Company. Three marks — the ribbon mark with the initials USP, the oval with a scrollwork border and the name in full, and the plain oval with the name in full — were used during that period.

Among the more sought-after examples are the bird and animal figurines, novelty pitchers, figural bottles, and all of the more finely-modeled items. Recumbent deer, cows, standing lions with one forepaw on a ball, and opposing pairs of poodles with baskets in their mouths and 'coleslaw' fur were made in Rockingham, flint enamel, and occa-

sionally in parian. Numbers in the listings below refer to the book *Bennington Pottery and Porcelain* by Barret. Our advisors for Bennington (except for parian and stoneware) are Barbara and Charles Adams; they are listed in the Directory under Massachusetts.

Key: c/s — cobalt on salt glaze

Bottle, Coachman's, Rockingham, late, 8⅞" **275.00**
Candlestick, flint enamel, 7¾" **475.00**
Candlestick, Rockingham, 8⅜" **365.00**
Cuspidor, brn w/amber highlights, imp 1849 mk, EX **60.00**
Flask, Ladies' Companion, Rockingham, book form, 5½" **600.00**
Flask, Ladies Suffering G, flint enamel, book form, 1850s, 5¼" ..**600.00**
Flowerpot, flint enamel, 1800s, 4½", EX **300.00**
Flowerpot, molded cattails & attached saucer, 10¼" **150.00**
Flowerpot, redware, mk Bennington Centennial...1877, 3", EX .**140.00**
Inkwell, Rockingham, 1800s **165.00**

Mantel ornament, flint enamel lion with applied coleslaw mane on stepped base, Lymon Fenton & Co., 1849, 5⅞x10⅝x9¼", $7,000.00.

Name plate, Rockingham, corner chips, 3⅜x7¼" **310.00**
Paperweight, mottled flint enamel, rectangle, mk/1849, rpr **375.00**
Paperweight, spaniel reclining, ca 1850, 4½" **350.00**
Pitcher, flint enamel, 1850s, 7¼" **400.00**
Pitcher, milk; face molded at spout, serpent hdl, 8", EX **250.00**
Pitcher, milk; Rockingham, bbl form, ribbed waist, 8", EX **250.00**
Pitcher, Rockingham, emb grapes, Lyman R Fenton, 1844-47, 7" ...**300.00**
Pitcher, Rockingham, mid-1800s, 7½" **330.00**
Pitkin, Rockingham, mid-1800s, 5½" **450.00**
Pitkin, Rockingham, molded ribs, mk, 6¼" **990.00**
Teapot, Rockingham, Rebeccah at the Well, 8½", EX **200.00**
Toby & barrel bottle, Rockingham, emb All for James Crow, 9" ..**395.00**
Toby bottle, Rockingham, mk, 1800s, 10¾" **360.00**
Vase, hand form, flint enamel, 6½" **275.00**
Vase, tulip form, flint enamel, 9" **495.00**

Stoneware

Crock, basket of flowers (detailed), J&E Norton, 1½-gal, NM ...**750.00**
Crock, chicken on dotted ground, J Norton & Co, 5-gal, NM ..**2,250.00**
Crock, chicken pecking corn, c/s, J Norton, 2-gal **1,200.00**
Crock, floral (dotted), E Norton & Co, chip on ear, 2-gal **190.00**
Crock, floral (stylized), c/s, E&LP, 10" **345.00**
Crock, flowers in compote (bold/vivid), J&E Norton, 2-gal, EX ...**675.00**
Crock, leafy floral, c/s, ovoid, L Norton & Co, 1-gal, EX **180.00**
Crock, pheasant pr, c/s, J Norton, 12", EX **1,600.00**
Crock, triple flower, Julius Norton, ovoid, 4-gal, M **350.00**
Jar, #2/stag in field, J&F Norton, chip, 2-gal **4,000.00**
Jar, floral (brushed), c/s, Norton & Fenton, 12¾" **385.00**
Jug, bird in brn brushed slip, L Norton & Son, 11", EX **2,750.00**
Jug, bird on branch (bold), J&E Norton, 1-gal, EX **600.00**
Jug, birds (dbl-crossed/bold), J Norton & Co, 4-gal, NM **900.00**
Jug, floral, c/s, E&LP, flakes/hairline, 15½" **400.00**

Jug, floral (dotted) E Norton & Co, rim chip, 1-gal **120.00**
Jug, flowers in compote (bold/vivid), J&E Norton, rpr, 3-gal **500.00**
Jug, parrot on branch, c/s, J Norton, 11" **700.00**
Pitcher, Albany slip, E&LP, 1½-gal **250.00**

Beswick

In the early 1890s, James Wright Beswick operated a pottery in Longston, England, where he produced fine dinnerware as well as ornamental ceramics. Today's collectors are most interested in the figurines made since 1936 by a later generation Beswick firm, John Beswick, Ltd. They specialize in reproducing accurately detailed bone china models of authentic breeds of animals. Their Fireside Series includes dogs, cats, elephants, horses, the Huntsman, and an Indian figure, which measure up to 14" in height. The Connoisseur line is modeled after the likenesses of famous racing horses. Beatrix Potter's characters and some of Walt Disney's are charmingly recreated and appeal to children and adults alike. Other items, such as character Tobys, have also been produced. The Beswick name is stamped on each piece. The firm was absorbed by the Doulton group in 1973.

Figurine, Afghan hound, med **45.00**
Figurine, Airedale, med **50.00**
Figurine, Alice **65.00**
Figurine, Basset Hound, med **50.00**
Figurine, Beagle, med **50.00**
Figurine, Beagle, sm **37.50**
Figurine, Bull Terrier, med **50.00**
Figurine, Bulldog **38.00**
Figurine, Chickadee, #929 ....**95.00**
Figurine, Collie, sable, med **50.00**
Figurine, Corgi, med **50.00**
Figurine, Dalmatian, med **50.00**
Figurine, Dalmatian, sm **27.50**
Figurine, Dartmoor Pony **55.00**
Figurine, duck, setting, #750 ....**135.00**
Figurine, ducks, flying, #596 1-4 ....**75.00**
Figurine, foal, #1421 ....**25.00**
Figurine, French Poodle, wht, med **185.00**
Figurine, Frog Footman **60.00**
Figurine, Golden Retriever, med **50.00**
Figurine, Labrador **20.00**
Figurine, pheasant, #850 ....**135.00**
Figurine, Queen of Hearts **55.00**
Figurine, Scottie w/ladybug on nose **65.00**
Figurine, Sealyham dog, #1061 ....**75.00**
Figurine, St Bernard **85.00**
Pitcher, palm tree relief, burgundy w/gold, 7½" **75.00**
Shakers, Laurel & Hardy, pr **75.00**

Big Little Books

The first Big Little Book was published in 1933 and copyrighted in 1932 by the Whitman Publishing Company of Racine, Wisconsin. Its hero was Dick Tracy. The concept was so well accepted that others soon followed Whitman's example; and though the 'Big Little Book' phrase became a trademark of the Whitman Company, the formats of his competitors (Saalfield, Goldsmith, Van Wiseman, Lynn, and World Syndicate) were exact copies. Today's Big Little Book buffs collect them all.

These hand-sized sagas of adventure were illustrated with full-page cartoons on the right-hand page and the story narration on the left.

Colorful cardboard covers contained hundreds of pages, usually totaling over an inch in thickness. Big Little Books originally sold for 10¢ at the dime store; as late as the mid-1950s when the popularity of comic books caused sales to decline signaling an end to production, their price had risen to a mere 20¢. Their appeal was directed toward the pre-teens who bought, traded, and hoarded Big Little Books. Because so many were stored in attics and closets, many have survived. Among the super heroes are G-Men, Flash Gordon, Tarzan, the Lone Ranger, and Red Ryder; in a lighter vein, you'll find such lovable characters as Blondie and Dagwood, Mickey Mouse, Little Orphan Annie, and Felix the Cat.

In the early to mid-'30s, Whitman published several Big Little Books as advertising premiums for the Coco Malt Company, who packed them in boxes of their cereal. These are highly prized by today's collectors, as are Disney stories and super-hero adventures. Our advisor for this category is Ron Donnelly; he is listed in the Directory under Florida.

Dick Tracy Solves the Penfield Mystery, VG+, $40.00.

Andy Panda & Pirate Ghosts, Whitman #1459, 1949, EX **22.50**
Apple Mary & Dennie's Lucky Apples, Whitman #1403, 1939, VG ..**17.50**
Aquaman Scourge of the Sea, Whitman #2017, 1968, VG **3.00**
Arizona Kid on Bandit Trail, Whitman #1192, 1936, NM **27.50**
Barney Baxter in Air w/Eagle Squadron, Whitman, 1938, VG **15.00**
Big Chief Wahoo & the Great Gusto, Whitman #1443C, 1938, G .**12.00**
Billy the Kid Western Outlaw, Whitman, Cocomalt, 1935, EX ...**42.50**
Blaze Brandon w/Foreign Legion, Whitman #1447A, 1938, EX ...**28.00**
Blk Silver & His Pirate Crew, Whitman #1414, 1937, VG **20.00**
Blondie, Baby Dumpling & All; Whitman #1487A, 1941, NM ...**42.00**
Blondie, Baby Dumpling & Daisy, Whitman #1429C, 1939, EX ..**30.00**
Blondie, Cookie, & Daisy's Pups, Whitman #1491A, 1943, VG ...**18.00**
Blondie & Dagwood Some Fun, Whitman #703-10, 1949, VG **17.50**
Bobby Benson on H-Bar-Q Ranch, Whitman #1108, 1934, VG ...**17.50**
Brad Turner in Transatlantic Flight, Whitman #1425, 1939, EX **35.00**
Brick Bradford w/Brocco Modern Buccaneer, Whitman, 1938, VG ..**17.50**
Broadway Bill, Saalfield #1580, soft cover, 1935, EX **27.50**
Bronc Peeler Lone Cowboy, Whitman #1417, 1937, EX **25.00**
Buccaneer, Whitman #1470B, movie edition, 1938, VG **30.00**
Buck Jones in Roaring West, Whitman #1174, 1935, VG **25.00**
Buck Rogers & Doom Comet, Whitman #1178, EX **80.00**
Buck Rogers & Planetoid Plot, Whitman #1197, 1936, EX **95.00**
Buck Rogers in War w/Planet Venus, Whitman #1437A, 1938, VG ..**65.00**
Buck Rogers in 25th Century AD, Whitman #742, 1933, VG **95.00**
Buckskin & Bullets, Saalfield #1135, 1938, EX **30.00**
Bugs Bunny & Secret of Storm Island, Dell, 1942, VG **50.00**
Bullet Benton, Saalfield #1169, 1939, EX **22.50**
Burn 'Em Up Barnes, Saalfield #1321, softcover, 1936, VG **22.50**
Captain Easy Soldier of Fortune, Whitman #1128, 1934, VG **27.50**
Captain Midnight & Sheik Jomak Khan, Whitman #1402, 1946, EX .**75.00**
Chandu the Magician, Saalfield #1093, photo edition, 1935, VG ..**35.00**
Chester Gump at Silver Creek Ranch, Whitman, premium, 1933, EX ..**45.00**
Chitty Chitty Bang Bang, Whitman #2025, 1968, NM **8.00**

Dan Dunn...& Border Smugglers, Whitman #1481, 1938, EX **32.00**

Dan Dunn...Trail of Wu Fang, Whitman #1454, 1938, G **25.00**

Danger Trails in Africa, Whitman #1151, 1935, NM **38.00**

Desert Justice, Saalfield #1136, 1938, EX **30.00**

Dick Tracy & the Mad Killer, Whitman #1436D, 1947, EX **40.00**

Dick Tracy Out West, Whitman #723A, 1933, EX **70.00**

Don Winslow & the Giant Girl Spy, Whitman #1408, 1946, EX ...**37.50**

Donald Duck Gets Fed Up, Whitman #1462, 1938, EX **55.00**

Donald Duck Hunting for Trouble, Whitman #14788, 1938, VG ..**24.00**

Flame Boy & Indians' Secret, Whitman #1464B, 1938, EX **35.00**

G-Man in Action, Saalfield #1173, 1940, NM **35.00**

G-Men on the Job, Whitman #1168, 1935, VG **20.00**

Gang Busters Step In, Whitman #1433B, 1939, VG **24.00**

Gene Autry & Raiders of the Range, Whitman #1409, 1946, EX ...**32.50**

George O'Brien & Hooded Riders, Whitman #1457C, 1940, VG ..**22.50**

Ghost Avenger Strikes, Whitman #1462A, 1943, VG **25.00**

Harold Teen Swinging at the Sugar Bowl, Whitman #1418, 1939, EX ..**30.00**

Inspector Wade...Mystery of Red Aces, Whitman #1448A, 1937, NM ..**40.00**

Invisible Scarlet O'Neil Vs King of Slums, Whitman, 1946, VG .**25.00**

Jack Armstrong & Ivory Treasure, Whitman #1435B, 1937, EX ..**50.00**

Jack Swift & His Rocket Ship, Whitman #1102, 1934, VG **30.00**

Jane Arden & Vanished Princess, Whitman #1496B, 1938, VG ..**24.00**

Jim Craig...Trooper & Kidnapped Governor, Whitman, 1938, VG .**22.50**

Jimmie Allen in Air Mail Robbery, Whitman #1143, 1936, EX ...**28.00**

Jungle Jim & Vampire Woman, #1139, 1937, EX **45.00**

Just Kids, Whitman #1401A, 1937, VG **32.00**

Kazan in Revenge of North, Whitman #1105B, 1937, VG **17.50**

Ken Maynard in Western Justice, Whitman #1430B, 1938, VG ..**25.00**

L'il Abner Among Millionaires, Whitman #1401, EX **50.00**

Little Annie Rooney & Orphan House, Whitman #1117, 1936, NM .**50.00**

Little Orphan Annie & Chizzler, Whitman #748, 1933, VG **35.00**

Little Orphan Annie & Ghost Gang, Whitman #1154, '35, NM ..**80.00**

Little Orphan Annie & Movies, Whitman #1416, 1937, VG **30.00**

Little Orphan Annie & Sandy, Whitman #716, 1933, VG **50.00**

Lone Ranger Outwits Crazy Cougar, Whitman #2013, 1968, VG ..**8.00**

Mac of the Marines in Africa, Whitman #1189, 1936, NM **50.00**

Mandrake the Magician, Whitman #1167, 1935, G **12.50**

Mary Lee & Mystery of Indian Beads, Whitman #1438A, '37, EX ..**30.00**

Men of Mounted, Whitman #755, 1934, EX **45.00**

Mickey Mouse & Bat Bandit, Whitman #1153, 1935, VG **55.00**

Mickey Mouse & 7 Ghosts, Whitman #1475, 1940, EX **82.50**

Mickey Mouse in Stolen Jewels, Whitman #1464, 1949, EX **80.00**

Mickey Rooney Himself, Whitman #1427C, 1939, EX **40.00**

Nancy & Sluggo, Whitman #1400A, 1946, EX **45.00**

One Night of Love, Saalfield #1099, photo edition, 1935, VG **30.00**

Pilot Pete Dive Bomber, Whitman #1466, 1941, VG **24.00**

Plainsman, Whitman #1123, movie photo edition, 1936, EX **50.00**

Popeye & Jeep, Whitman #1405C, 1937, EX **65.00**

Popeye Sees the Sea, Whitman #1163, 1936, VG **45.00**

Popeye the Superfighter, Whitman #1406C, 1942, VG **37.50**

Powder Smoke Range, Whitman #1176, movie edition, '35, EX ..**55.00**

Prairie Bill & Covered Wagon, Whitman #758, 1934, EX **45.00**

Radio Patrol, Whitman #1142, 1935, NM **50.00**

Radio Patrol Trailing Safeblowers, Whitman #1173, 1937, VG ...**22.50**

Red Barry Ace... Hero of Hour, Whitman #1157, 1935, EX **35.00**

Red Barry Undercover Man, Whitman #1426A, 1939, VG **22.50**

Red Death on Range, Whitman #1449B, 1940, VG **32.00**

Red Ryder & Squaw-Tooth Rustlers, Whitman #1414A, '46, VG ..**20.00**

Red Ryder in War on Range, Whitman #1473A, 1945, VG **22.50**

Reg'lar Fellers, Whitman #754, 1933, VG **30.00**

Return of Tarzan, Whitman #1102A, 1936, EX **75.00**

Riders of Lone Trails, Whitman #1425A, 1937, EX **30.00**

Secret Agent X-9, Whitman #1144, 1936, VG **27.50**

Sequoia, Whitman #1161, movie edition, 1935, VG **30.00**

Shadow & Living Death, Whitman #1430C, 1940, VG **65.00**

Silver Streak, Whitman #1155, 1935, VG **30.00**

Skeezix in Africa, Whitman #1112A, 1934, VG **25.00**

Skyroads w/Hurricane Hawk, Whitman #1127, 1936, EX **35.00**

Smilin' Jack & Stratosphere Ascent, Whitman #1152A, 1937, EX ...**45.00**

Smitty Golden Gloves Tournament, Whitman, Cocomalt, EX **70.00**

Sombrero Pete, Whitman #1136, 1936, VG **20.00**

SOS Coast Guard, Whitman #1191, 1936, VG **22.00**

Spy, Whitman #768, 1936, VG **22.50**

Story of Shirley Temple, Saalfield #1319, 1934, VG **32.00**

Strawberry Roan, Saalfield #1320, movie edition, 1934, VG **35.00**

Tailspin Tommy & Great Air Mystery, Whitman #1184, 1936, EX ...**65.00**

Tailspin Tommy & Hooded Flyer, Whitman #1423D, 1937, EX ..**50.00**

Tailspin Tommy & Sky Bandits, Whitman #1494, 1936, VG **36.00**

Tarzan & Ant Men, Whitman #1444C, 1945, EX **65.00**

Tarzan & Mark of Red Hyena, Whitman #2005, 1967, EX **12.00**

Tarzan the Fearless, Whitman #769, movie edition, 1934, G **17.50**

Terry & Pirates, Whitman, Lawrie Bros premium, 1935, EX **115.00**

Terry & War in Jungle, Whitman #1420B, 1946, EX **50.00**

Tim McCoy & Sandy Gulch Stampede, Whitman #1490B, 1939, EX .**50.00**

Tim Tyler, Saalfield #1053, 1934, VG **30.00**

Tiny Tim in Big Big World, Whitman #1472, 1945, EX **45.00**

Tom Beatty Ace...Scores Again, Whitman #1165, 1937, VG **27.50**

Tom Mix & Hoard of Montezuma, Whitman #1462C, 1937, EX .**45.00**

Tom Mix & Stranger From South, Whitman #1183, 1936, EX **35.00**

Tom Swift & His Giant Telescope, Whitman #1485C, 1936, EX ..**55.00**

Treasure Island, Whitman #720, 1933, VG **35.00**

Uncle Ray's Story of United States, Whitman #722, 1934, VG ...**30.00**

Walt Disney's Mickey Mouse and the 'Lectro Box, Whitman, 1946, VG, $40.00.

Walt Disney's Pluto the Pup, Whitman #1467A, 1938, VG **30.00**

Wash Tubbs in Pandemonia, Whitman #751, 1934, VG **27.50**

Wells Fargo, Whitman #1471A, movie edition, 1938, EX **55.00**

Will Rogers, Saalfield #1096, photo cover, 1935, VG **25.00**

Winged Four, Saalfield #1131, 1937, EX **30.00**

Woody Woodpecker Sinister Signal, Whitman #2028, 1969, EX ...**7.50**

Wyatt Earp, Whitman #1644, TV edition, 1958, EX **12.50**

Zane Grey's Tex Thorn Come's Out of West, Whitman, 1937, EX .**30.00**

Bing and Grondahl

In 1853 brothers M.H. and J.H. Bing formed a partnership with Frederick Vilhelm Grondahl in Copenhagen, Denmark. Their early wares were porcelain plaques and figurines designed by the noted sculptor Thorvaldsen of Denmark. Dinnerware production began in 1863, and by 1889 their underglaze color 'Copenhagen Blue' had earned them worldwide acclaim. They are perhaps most famous today for their Christmas plates, the first of which was made in 1895. See also Limited Edition Plates.

Creamer, sea gull, w/gold 42.50
Cup & saucer, sea gull, w/gold 42.50
Figurine, boy w/crab, #1870 ....150.00
Figurine, bullfinch, #1909 ....90.00
Figurine, cat, spotted, #2466, 4¾" 95.00
Figurine, cellist, #3032 ....550.00
Figurine, children playing, #1568 ....140.00
Figurine, fish seller, #1702 ....300.00
Figurine, fisher family, #2025 ....400.00
Figurine, girl talking to doll, #2191 ....160.00
Figurine, girl tennis player, #2364 ....165.00
Figurine, lady & child, #1552 ....400.00
Figurine, mandolinist on stool, #1500, 11" 335.00
Figurine, Mary, #1721 ....48.00
Figurine, mason, #1786 ....200.00
Figurine, nude child, wht, #2230, 6½" 55.00
Figurine, nude man asleep on mule, #4026, 9¼" ...675.00
Figurine, penguin, #417, 10½" 355.00
Figurine, Peter, #1696 ....145.00
Figurine, polar bear, 12" 175.00
Figurine, Who Is Calling?, #2251 ....145.00
Plate, sea gull, w/gold, 9⅝" 45.00

Birdcages

Birdcages can be found in various architectural styles and in a range of materials such as wood, wicker, brass, and gilt metal with ormolu mounts. Those that once belonged to the wealthy are sometimes inlaid with silver or jewels. In the 1800s, it became fashionable to keep birds, and some of the most beautiful examples found today date back to that era. Musical cages that contained automated bird figures became popular; today these command prices of several thousand dollars. In the latter 1800s, wicker styles came into vogue. Collectors still appreciate their graceful lines and find they adapt easily to modern homes.

Brass, dome shape w/glass feeders, Hendryx, on orig stand 150.00
Brass, Hendryx, Pat 1906, 9x13" 110.00
Brass, rnd shape, mid 1900s, 16" 275.00
Brass, simple style, mid-1900s, 39x18½" 800.00
Brass, sq shape, mid-1900s, 16" 250.00
Copper & brass, Hendryx, Made in USA, 14" H 175.00
Wicker, cresent moon style, floor stand 425.00
Wicker, hand-cvd fr of fruits/leaves, 1880s, 15x12x9", EX 240.00
Wire & wood w/arched top, wht porc buttons on posts, 20x13x22" .165.00

Wood and wire 2-story building with applied stars and moldings, imperfections, 25x25", $550.00.

Wood, pencil-sz dowels, 3-arch roof, rpl, 13¾" 230.00
Wood & wire, brn-red pnt, arched top, 14" 330.00
Wood Sheraton, trn finials/posts/ft, wire sides, 1820s, sm 1,000.00

Bisque

Bisque is a term referring to unglazed earthenware or porcelain that has been fired only once. During the Victorian era, bisque figurines became very popular. Most were highly decorated in pastels and gilt and demonstrated a fine degree of workmanship in the quality of their modeling. Few were marked. See also Heubach; Nodders; Dolls; Piano Babies.

Boy and girl, Germany, 18", $700.00 for the pair.

Boy & girl, ea w/flower basket, Continental, 1800s, 17", pr 395.00
Boy w/rifle & girl w/doll, pastels, Fr, 17", pr 450.00
Bust, blond girl w/yel bonnet, on floral ped, #327, 8¾" 100.00
Cat, blk, crying w/wht kerchief, basket at side, 4¾" 70.00
Colonial couple on ovoid base, gold trim, 21½" 450.00
Edwardian couple, flowing dress, long coat, Fr, 21", pr 1,200.00
Ewer, Nouveau maiden w/flowing blond hair, lav int, 6" 67.50
Girl on swing w/dog, gold trim, 4⅝x3" 95.00
Girl w/doll, bl coat w/pk trim, 6½x2¼" 80.00
Lady in Renaissance attire, Continental, 1890s, 14" 165.00
Peasant man & lady scanning horizon, 23", pr 1,200.00
Shoe w/mouse atop, baby mouse emerging, 3½x5" 65.00
Tambourine girl, boy w/horn, basket behind, German, 12", pr ...325.00
Toothpick holder, child in fur-trimmed pk coat 48.00
Toothpick/match holder, rabbit figural, open egg, 7" 125.00
Vase, googly-eyed baby w/hands on gr bag, #d, 3¾" 40.00
18th-Century man beside tree, arm out, 6¾" 50.00

Black Americana

Black memorabilia is without a doubt a field that encompasses the most widely exploited ethnic group in our history. But within this field there are many levels of interest: arts and achievements such as folk music and literature, caricatures in advertising, souvenirs, toys, fine art, and legitimate research into the days of their enslavement and enduring struggle for equality. The list is endless.

In the listings below are some with a derogatory connotation. Thankfully, these are from a bygone era and represent the mores of a culture that existed nearly a century ago. They are included only to convey the fact that they are a part of this growing area of collecting interest. Black Americana catalogs featuring a wide variety of items for sale are available; see the Directory under Clubs, Newsletters, and Catalogs for more information. See also Cookie Jars; Postcards; Posters; Sheet Music.

Ad card, Topsy's Restaurant, NY City, 1940s, 5x3¼" **30.00**
Ash pot, man's head, wagging tongue, mc pnt, china, 2½" **125.00**
Ashtray, Amos & Andy, chalkware, 7½", VG **200.00**
Ashtray, boy & goose by fence, 'Early Bird...,' chalkware **35.00**
Ashtray, Butler, CI figural, EX orig pnt, 35x7½x8", VG **525.00**
Ashtray, Coon Chicken Inn, smiling face, 1940-51, 3½" **35.00**
Ashtray, Mammy's Shanty, glass, 1940s, M **80.00**
Ashtray, Mammy w/breast in wringer, chalkware **75.00**
Bank, child w/fruit, googly eyes, bsk nodder, 6¾" **50.00**
Bank, Lucky Joe, glass, 4½" **32.00**
Bank, Mammy, mc, yel turban, ceramic, Japan **35.00**
Bell, Mammy figural, porc, Japan, 1930s, 3½" **75.00**
Book, Little Brn Koko's Pets & Playmates, 1959, 96-pg, EX **55.00**
Book, Little Golden; Little Blk Sambo, 1948, VG **48.00**
Book, Little Pickaninnies, Chubb, Whitman, 1929, 19-pg, G **75.00**
Book, Mamba's Daughters, Novel of Charleston, 1929, EX **40.00**
Book, Nelly Was a Lady, Stephen Foster, illus, 1890, EX **75.00**
Book, Samantha Among the Colored Folks, Kemble, 1894, EX ...**75.00**
Book, Treasury of Stephen Foster, 1st edition, 1946, EX **60.00**
Bottle, milk; Joe Lewis portrait, 1-pt **35.00**
Bowl, baby's cereal; Golliwog, mc, Meakin, 5" **85.00**
Cake plate, Coon Chicken Inn, smiling face, Inca Ware, 5½" ...**195.00**
Card, birthday; Deco-style bellhops, 1933, 5x6", EX **18.00**
Clock, Mammy holding lg pocket watch, pottery, 1940s, M **350.00**
Coffee tin, Mammy litho on red, Luzianne, 3-lb sz, EX **125.00**
Compact, 4 pnt musicians w/sm dog & musical notes, 3x5", G **35.00**
Cookie jar, Aunt Jemima, soft plastic, NM **295.00**
Cookie jar, Mammy, F&F, NM **400.00**
Creamer, Mammy, bsk, Japan, 3½" **125.00**
Creamer & sugar bowl, Aunt Jemima & Uncle Mose, F&F, w/lid .**140.00**
Cruets, oil & vinegar; Mammy & Chef, ceramic, 5¼", EX **125.00**
Cup, Aunt Jemima, cb, 3¼" **35.00**
Doll, child, oilcloth face, mk Poland, 12", EX **65.00**
Doll, Mammy, folk art type, cloth, 6", EX **45.00**
Doll, native, soft rubber, curly hair, Japan, 10", EX **40.00**
Doll, rag; HP face, red & wht dress, carnival prize, '40s, 10" **40.00**
Doll, topsy-turvy, compo, 1920s, 7", EX **245.00**
Egg timer, Chef figural, porc, mc pnt, Germany, 1930s, 3½" **125.00**
Egg timer, native, ceramic, Japan, 6" **90.00**
Envelope, Smoking Sambo Tobacco, 1900 ....**25.00**
Fan, Coon Chicken Inn, smiling face, cb, M **75.00**
Figure, Redcap, cast metal, EX pnt, 1940s, 3¼" **40.00**
Figurine, baby on lustre potty, porc, Germany, 4" **75.00**
Figurine, banjo player, Made in Occupied Japan, 5" **65.00**
Figurine, Golliwog horn player, ceramic, 3" **45.00**
Figurine, Mammy, pnt CI, 2½", EX **110.00**
Incense burner, boy on elephant, bsk, Japan, 3" **60.00**
Incline walker, Mammy, cloth clothes, Wilson Walkie, 1930s, EX ..**85.00**
Key chain/tape measure, Aunt Jemima Breakfast Club, 1940s **65.00**
Kitchen caddy, Mammy figural, 1930s, 6", NM **225.00**
Label, Blk Joe Grapes, 1940s, 13x4" **4.00**
Lawn sprinkler, Sprinklin' Sambo, pnt tin, EX **350.00**
Magnetic board, Mammy holds paper roll, copper, 14x11" **80.00**
Mask, man's face w/exaggerated features, papier-mache, 9½" **50.00**
Measuring cups, graduated face szs, ¼- to 1-cup, set of 4 ....**125.00**
Menu, Coon Chicken Inn, paper, EX **135.00**
Menu, Topsy's, 'Eat w/Your Fingers,' Mammy, 1940, EX **75.00**
Mug, bellhop figural, mc pnt, googly eyes, pottery **45.00**
Napkin, Aunt Jemima, paper **35.00**
Needle book, Mammy on cover, Luzianne premium, 4½" **55.00**
Noisemaker, Cab Callow, Cotton Club..., wooden, 8½", EX **40.00**
Note holder, Aunt Jemima, wood, gr scarf, Japan, 10½" **80.00**
Pamphlet, Message on Segregation, Bishop TX, 1950s, 5-pg **15.00**
Pancake mold, animal shapes, metal, Aunt Jemima premium, 8½" .**145.00**

Pencil, mechanical; face figural, Bakelite, EX **85.00**
Pie bird, Chef, ceramic, Japan **175.00**
Pie bird, Mammy, ceramic, air-brushed mc, 1940s, 4¾" **125.00**
Pin-bk, Aunt Jemima Breakfast Club **20.00**
Pin-bk, Gold Dust Twins, celluloid, 1896, 1¾", EX **125.00**
Place mat, Aunt Jemima's Kitchen, paper, 13¾x9¾" **20.00**
Plate, Aunt Jemima's Restaurant, paper, 1940s, M **50.00**
Plate, Sambo's Restaurant, china, Jackson, 9¾" **68.00**
Postcard, Amos & Andy, fr **30.00**
Postcards, Sambo's Restaurant, full set of 8, M **50.00**
Print, Stuff That Men Are Made Of, Perry, 1904, 8x5½" **35.00**
Puppet, hand; Sammy Davis Jr, rubber head, 10", EX **30.00**
Puzzle, Little Blk Sambo, S Gabriel, ca 1939, EX **50.00**
Recipe cards, Aunt Jemima, set of 16, 1940s, M in mailer **225.00**
Shaker, pancake; Aunt Jemima figural, yel plastic, 9", EX **70.00**
Shakers, body forms holder, nodding head & melon shakers, 3" .**150.00**
Shakers, boy & girl holding ear of corn, ceramic, 2½", pr **75.00**
Shakers, child (resting on elbow) & watermelon, ceramic, pr **70.00**
Shakers, child atop eggplant, ceramic, pr **90.00**
Shakers, child on lettuce, ceramic, pr **90.00**
Shakers, child on potty, ceramic, 5½", pr **100.00**
Shakers, clown plays accordion, ceramic, 6", pr **125.00**
Shakers, girl & hut, ceramic, 4½", pr **95.00**
Shakers, Mammy, Luzianne, gr skirt, F&F, 5¼", EX, pr **225.00**
Shakers, Mammy, very fat, mc pnt, chalkware, 1930s, 2½", pr **90.00**
Shakers, Mammy & Chef, googly eyes, china, 5¾", NM, pr **85.00**
Shakers, Mammy squatting, chalkware, 2½", pr **90.00**
Shakers, mother & baby, exaggerated features, ceramic, 3½", pr ..**55.00**
Shakers, porter, ceramic, Japan, 3½", pr **60.00**
Shakers, Rastus & Liza, wood, 3", pr **27.50**
Sheet music, Auntie Skinner's Chicken Dinner, Blk cover **35.00**
Sheet music, Topsy & Eva, Irving Berlin, 1923, EX **45.00**
Soap dish, Mammy figural, pnt CI, 5¼", EX **225.00**
Spice set, Chef, bow tie hdls, 4 shakers on wooden rack **165.00**
Spoon rest, Mammy, pottery, wall hanging, 8x6", EX **145.00**
Spoon rest, nodding Chef, exaggerated features, Lefton **225.00**
String holder, Butler in blk tails, ceramic, 1930s, M **425.00**
String holder, child w/felt face, wooly hair, MOP eyes, 10" **70.00**
String holder, Mammy face, ceramic, Japan, 6", M **350.00**
Sugar bowl, Mammy, pottery, 1930s, 3½x4¾", M **325.00**
Swizzle stick, Zulu-Lulu, 1940s, set of 6 ....**45.00**
Table card, Aunt Jemima's Restaurant, face diecut, 1953 ....**65.00**
Tin container, Joe Louis Hair Pomade, mc, 1940s, 1x3" dia, EX ..**95.00**
Towel, kitchen; Chef applique, 1930s, EX **60.00**
Towel, kitchen; New Orleans jazz band print, 1940s, EX **42.00**

Toy, bisque baby in wicker carriage, 1930s, $125.00.

Tumbler, Coon Chicken Inn, smiling face, glass, 1940s, 4" **40.00**
Whisk broom, Mammy figural, wooden diecut, w/verse, 7", NM ..**110.00**

Black Cats

Made in Japan during the fifties, these novelty cats may be found bearing the labels of several different importers, all with their own particular characteristics. The best known and most collectible of these cats are from the Shafford line. Even when unmarked, they are easily identified by their red bows, green eyes, and white whiskers, eyeliners, and eyebrows. Relco/Royal Sealy cats are tall and slender, and their bow ties are gold with red dots. Wales is a wonderful line with yellow eyes and gold detailing; Enesco cats have blue eyes, and there are other lines as well. When evaluating your black cats, be sure to inspect their paint and judge them accordingly. 50% paint should relate to 50% of our suggested values, which are given for cats in mint (or nearly mint) paint.

Ashtray, full figure, flat, 'Ashes' in body, 2½x3¾" 7.50
Ashtray, head shape w/open mouth, Shafford, 3" 18.00
Cigarette lighter, Shafford, 5½" 125.00
Condiment set, 2 heads, J&M bows w/spoons, Shafford, 4" 50.00
Cookie jar, lg cat head, Shafford 85.00
Cookie jar, lg cat head, yel eyes, mean face 100.00
Creamer & sugar bowl, cat-head lids are shakers, 5⅜" 45.00
Cruet, oil & vinegar; co-joined cats, 1-pc, Royal Sealy 40.00
Cruets, he w/O eyes, she w/V eyes & hair bow, Shafford, pr 50.00

**Demitasse pot, Shafford, 7½",
$85.00.**

Desk caddy, pen forms tail, spring body holds letters, 6½" 8.00
Egg cup, cat face on bowl, ped ft, Shafford 25.00
Funnel, w/cat face, long wood hdl, Shafford 50.00
Grease jar, sm cat head, Shafford 50.00
Measuring set, 4 cups on wood rack w/cat's face, Shafford 125.00
Mug, cat's face on front, Shafford, 4¼" to top of cat hdl 28.00
Pincushion, cushion on bk, tongue measure 22.50
Pot holder caddy, 'teapot' cat, 3-hook, Shafford 85.00
Shaker, long cat, salt in 1 end, pepper in other, Shafford 65.00
Shakers, rnd-bodied teapot cat, Shafford, pr 35.00
Shakers, seated, bl eyes, Enesco label, 5¾", pr 15.00
Shakers, seated (3") & recumbent (1¾"), lg heads, pr 12.00
Spice set, 6 sq shakers in wood rack, Shafford 125.00
Strainer, w/cat face, long wood hdl, Shafford 50.00
Teapot, bulbous body, head lid, gr eyes, Shafford, 6½" 45.00
Teapot, panther-like, gold eyes, sm 20.00
Teapot, w/creamer & sugar bowl, stacking 50.00
Wall pocket, gr eyes, red bow, Shafford, 5½" 75.00
Wine, emb cat's face, gr eyes, Shafford, sm 20.00

Black Glass

Black glass is a type of colored glass that when held to strong light

usually appears deep purple, though since each glasshouse had its own formula, tones may vary. It was sometimes etched or given a satin finish; and occasionally it was decorated with silver, gold, enamel, coralene, or any of these in combination. The decoration was done either by the glasshouse or by firms that specialized in decorating glassware. Crystal, jade, colored glass, or milk glass was sometimes used with the black as an accent. Black glass has been made by many companies since the 17th century. Contemporary glasshouses produced black glass during the Depression, seldom signing their product. It is still being made today.

To learn more about the subject, we recommend *A Collector's Guide to Black Glass*, written by our advisor, Marlena Toohey; she is listed in the Directory under Colorado. Look for her newly updated value guide. See also Tiffin, L.E. Smith, and other specific manufacturers.

Bottle, scent; France, 1¼" 35.00
Bottle, shoe form, screw cap, unmk, ca 1880-1910, 3½x5¼" 55.00
Bowl, mixing; Hazel-Atlas, 5" 18.00
Bowl, shell shape, gold edge, 5¾" 15.00
Bowl, 6-scallop rim w/gilt, ftd, unknown mfg, 1920s-30s, lg 70.00
Box, stork wading among foliage in wht, brass ft, 6½" dia 375.00
Candlesticks, lg crimped ft, 3", pr 35.00
Candlesticks, molded to imitate crackle glass, 7", pr 45.00
Candy dish, 3-compartment, ornate metal fr, ca 1925-35 ....35.00
Compote, Chatham openwork rim, US Glass, 8½" 85.00
Compote, paneled bowl, tall ped, 6-sided ft, 6x8¾" 45.00
Creamer, Cloverleaf, Hazel-Atlas, 1930s 12.50
Drawer pull 10.00
Flowerpot, attached saucer, 4" 25.00
Match holder, cannon form, HP florals, metal fr, 3½" 95.00
Mayonnaise ladle, ca 1920s 35.00
Paper-cup holder, 2½" 10.00
Plate, ca 1930s, 7½" 10.00
Plate, 2 sides rolled up, hdls, 7" 18.00
Shakers, red plastic tops, att Hazel-Atlas, 3", pr 17.50
Sugar bowl, 6 rings form body, angular hdls, ftd 20.00
Tumbler, clear bowl w/blk domed ft, ca 1929-35, 12-oz 15.00

**Turtle cigarette box, Westmoreland, 1969 (has
been reproduced), 7½", $100.00.**

Vase, frieze w/figures, scalloped/flared rim, 6½" 45.00
Vase, HP floral, ringed neck, ped ft, 15", pr 185.00
Vase, mc leaves, gold highlights, stick neck w/cup rim, 8" 125.00
Vase, stork & foliage enameling, pilgrim-flask form, 9" 98.00

Blown Glass

Blown glass is rather difficult to date; 18th and 19th century examples vary little as to technique or style; it ranges from the primitive to the sophisticated. But the metallic content of very early glass caused tiny imperfections that are obvious upon examination, and these are often indicative of age.

In America, Stiegel introduced the English technique of using a patterned, part-size mold, a practice which was generally followed by many glasshouses after the Revolution. From 1820 to about 1850, glass was blown into full-size three-part molds. In the listings below, glass is assumed clear unless color is mentioned. Numbers refer to a standard reference book, *American Glass* by Helen McKearin. See also Bottles and specific manufacturers. Our advisor for this category is Mark Vuono; he is listed in the Directory under Connecticut.

Bottle, amethyst, globular, 15 swirled ribs, appl lip, 12" **45.00**
Bottle, deep amber, appl hdl & lip, iron pontil, 7¾" **100.00**
Bottle, olive gr, globular, short neck, flared lip, 8" **35.00**
Bowl, aqua, bubbly, tall sides, early, 4½x7" **195.00**
Bowl, aqua, folded rim, NY, 1825-40, 2⅝x7¼" **250.00**
Bowl, cobalt, appl ft w/folded rim, 3⅜" **210.00**
Bowl, dk sapphire, str/slightly flaring sides, 4½x7½" **300.00**
Bowl, fruit; lt yel-gr, appl to inverted cone base, 9x7¾" **275.00**
Bowl, gr-aqua, pontil scar, Am, 1820-50, 1¼x7¾" **165.00**
Bowl, med dk gr, folded rim, pontil scar, Am, 1820-50, 7¾" **550.00**
Bowl, wht opaque w/red amethyst tint, Am, 1850-80, 4¾" **100.00**
Candle holder, hollow, bulbous, appl ft & font, 8½" **50.00**
Compote, cobalt w/wht rim on lip & ft edge, 1800s, 3⅝x5" **450.00**
Compote, cut panel finial, 8⅜x8" **60.00**
Container, deep emerald gr, rolled lip, smooth base, 13¼" **250.00**
Demijohn, amber, 18" **75.00**
Demijohn, deep amethyst, rolled-over lip, pontil scar, 14¾" **365.00**
Demijohn, deep olive-amber, 18¼" **110.00**
Demijohn, olive gr, 19½" **100.00**
Goblet, vertical ribs w/etch design, appl ped & ft, 6¾" **60.00**
Jar, deep aqua, wide mouth, ps, 1820s, 8⅞x3½" dia **200.00**
Jar, dk gr, folded lip, minor burst bubble, 1860s, 11½" **125.00**
Jar, food; yel-olive gr, tooled mouth, Am, 1820-50, 10¾" **180.00**
Jar, med gr w/yel cast, wide mouth, 1820s, 12½x5" dia **160.00**
Jar, med olive, wide flared mouth, 1780-1830, 8¼x4½" **240.00**
Jar, pickle; aquamarine, cathedral arched panels, 12" **225.00**
Jar, storage; gr-aqua, str sides, rolled lip, Am, 1840s, 9" **95.00**
Jar, utility; yel-gr, tooled mouth, crude, Am, 1840-60, 6" **180.00**
Jar, yel olive-amber, wide mouth, flared lip, 1840s, 5" **175.00**
Jar, yel-olive, sheared mouth, Am, 1820-60, 14¼x5¾" **280.00**
Lamp, sparking; globular font w/wine glass stem, 1820s, 4" **300.00**
Mug, mc fox at churn on clear, Europe, 1780-1840, 4¼" **375.00**
Pan, milk; aqua, folded rim, ground pontil, Am, 1840s, 23½" **330.00**
Pan, milk; folded-over rim, sand pontil, 3¼x9½" **275.00**
Pinch bottle, cobalt, 16 vertical ribs, pontil scar, 9" **575.00**
Pitcher, aqua, appl ft, crimped hdl, pontil scar, 7" **250.00**
Salt cellar, swirled ribs, ftd, 1¾" **95.00**
Sugar bowl, aquamarine, 24 vertical ribs, att White, 6⅝" **4,750.00**
Sugar bowl, galleried, folded rim on ft, 1820-40, 7" **715.00**
Sugar bowl, yel-gr, Honeycomb cutting, 6" **85.00**
Tumbler, aqua, rolled lip, pontil scar, 1850s, 5¾" **125.00**
Tumbler, med amethyst, pontiled, tooled lip, 3¼" **65.00**
Tumbler, med olive gr w/aqua lip, str sides, 3¼" **85.00**
Tumbler, pattern molded, 20-rib swirl, Kent, 1820s, 4¾" **5,400.00**
Whiskey jug, dk puce-amber, collared mouth, Am, 1850s, 8" **110.00**
Wine, baluster, stem, 4" **50.00**
Wine, cotton twist stem, bell-form bowl, England, ca 1800, 6" ..**110.00**
Wine, cotton twist stem, 6⅜" **185.00**
Wine, gr-aquamarine, sheared/ground rim, Am, 1830-50, 3½" ...**180.00**
Wine, trumpet bowl, teardrop stem, domed ft, 1750s, 6¼" **220.00**
Wine, wheel eng birds/flowers, folded rim on ft, 4", 3 for **185.00**

Blown Three-Mold Glass

A popular collectible in the 1920s, '30s, and '40s, blown three-mold glass has again gained the attention of many. Produced from

approximately 1815 to 1840 in various New York, New England, and Midwestern glasshouses, it was a cheaper alternative to the expensive imported Irish cut glass.

Distinguishing features of blown three-mold glass are the three distinct mold marks and the concave-convex appearance of the glass. For every indentation on the inner surface of the ware, there will be a corresponding protuberance on the outside. Blown three-mold glass is most often clear with the exception of inkwells and a few known decanters. Any colored three-mold glass commands a premium price.

The numbers in the listings that follow refer to the book *American Glass* by George and Helen McKearin. Our advisor for this category is Mark Vuono; he is listed in the Directory under Connecticut.

Creamer, similar to GV-24, cobalt, sheared rim, 3⅞" **400.00**
Decanter, brandy; flared mouth, matching stopper, 8½" **60.00**
Decanter, flared mouth on bbl form, w/stopper, 1820s, 1-pt **410.00**
Decanter, GII-2 type 1, lt yel-gr, Mt Vernon, 6¾" **6,000.00**
Decanter, GII-28, clear sea gr, sq, att Keene, 1-pt **2,600.00**
Decanter, GII-33, 3 appl rings, 8" **2,250.00**
Decanter, GIII-16, dk forest gr, Keene, 1820-40, 1-pt **2,100.00**
Decanter, GIII-16, yel olive-amber, Keene, 1820-40, ½-pt **400.00**
Decanter, GIII-19, olive-amber, Keene, 1820-40, 1-qt **850.00**
Decanter, GIII-5 or 6, sm stain, 7" **150.00**
Decanter, patterned base & stopper, ca 1880, 13¼" **85.00**
Decanter, T'print, pewter stopper, ca 1880, 10¾" **100.00**
Flip hat, pontiled, folded rim, 1840s, 1⅞" **100.00**
Hat whimsey, GIII-3, folded rim, 2¼" **120.00**
Inkwell, GII-16, olive, 2⅜" **140.00**
Lamp, sparking; cylindrical, Am, 1840-80, 2⅜x1¾" **325.00**
Salt cellar, cobalt, tooled flared rim, pontil scar, 2x3⅛" **135.00**
Syrup, GV-II, appl hdl, tin lid w/pewter thumbpc, 7½" **165.00**
Tumbler, GII-22, 6" **140.00**
Tumbler, pale amethyst, sheared rim, pontil scar, 1820s, 4⅝" **175.00**

Blue and White Stoneware

Blue and white stoneware, much of which was decorated with such in-mold designs as grazing cows and Dutch children, was made by practically every American pottery from the turn of the century until the mid-1930s. Crocks, pitchers, wash sets, rolling pins, and canisters are only a few of the items that may be found in this type of 'country' pottery that has become one of today's popular collectibles.

Roseville, Brush-McCoy, Uhl Co., and Burley Winter were among those who produced it; but very few pieces were ever signed. Naturally, condition must be a prime consideration, especially if one is buying for resale; pieces with good, strong color and fully molded patterns bring premium prices. Normal wear and signs of age are to be expected since this was utility ware and received heavy use in busy households. In the listings that follow, crocks and jars are assumed without lids unless noted otherwise. For further information we recommend *Blue and White Stoneware* by Kathryn McNerney. See also specific manufacturers.

Batter jar, Wildflower, thick appl hdl, 8x7" **275.00**
Bean pot, Boston Baked Beans, Swirl, heavy diffused pattern **300.00**
Beer cooler, Elves, brass spigot, 18x14" **850.00**
Bowl, Apricot, 9½" **85.00**
Bowl, batter; Wildflower, w/hdl **400.00**
Bowl, berry; Diffused Bl, 2½x4½" **75.00**
Bowl, Daisy on Waffle, 10¾" **95.00**
Bowl, Gadroon Arches (Feather Panels), 4½x9½" **150.00**
Bowl, mixing; Flying Bird, 4x7½" **225.00**
Bowl, Reverse Pyramids w/Reverse Picket Fence, 2½x4½" **150.00**
Bowl, Wildflower, 4½x7" **100.00**

Butter crock, Butterfly, orig lid & bail, 6½" 225.00
Butter crock, Daisy & Trellis, orig lid & bail, 4½" 200.00
Butter crock, Eagle, orig lid & bail, M 450.00
Butter crock, Grapes & Leaves, dbl ring around rim, 3x6½" 175.00
Canister, Basketweave, Cereal, orig lid, 7½" 350.00
Canister, Basketweave, Cloves, orig lid, 5" 250.00
Canister, Basketweave, Coffee, orig lid, 7½" 250.00
Canister, Basketweave, Pepper, orig lid, 5" 250.00
Canister, Basketweave, Put Your Fist In, orig lid, 7½" 700.00
Canister, Basketweave, Sugar, orig lid, 7½" 250.00
Canister, Basketweave, Tobacco, orig lid, 7½" 500.00
Canister, Snowflake, rpl lid, 6½x5¾" 150.00
Chamberpot, Wildflower, stenciled pattern, 6x11" 135.00
Coffeepot, Oval, Diffused Bl, bl-tipped knob, str sides, 11x4" 250.00
Coffeepot, Swirl, 'spurs' on hdl, acorn finial, 11½x6" 450.00
Cookie jar, Brickers, flat button finial, 8x8" 325.00
Cookie jar, Turkey Eye color drip, Diffused Bl bands, 9x8" 250.00
Cookie/biscuit jar, Flying Bird, orig lid, 9x6¾" 650.00
Cup, Bow Tie, bird transfer, 3¾x3½" 95.00
Cup, Wildflower w/emb Ribbon & Bow, 4½x2½" 85.00
Custard cup, Fishscale, 5x2½" 75.00
Egg storage crock, Barrel Staves, bail hdl, 5½x6" 185.00
Foot warmer, Diffused Bl, A Warm Friend, 12½x6½" 275.00
Grease jar, Flying Bird, orig lid 650.00
Ice crock, Barrel Staves, rope/tongs/ice block emb, 4½x6" 225.00
Iced tea cooler, Bl Band, flat lid, complete, 13x11" 295.00
Measuring cup, Spearpoint & Flower Panels, 6x6¾" 150.00
Milk crock, Daisy & Lattice, 4x8", NM 125.00
Milk crock, Lovebird, rstr bail & handgrip, 5½x9" 145.00
Mug, Basketweave & Flower, 5x3" 125.00
Mug, beer; advertising, Diffused Bl, sqd hdl 150.00
Mug, Cattails 150.00
Mug, Flying Bird, 5x3" 225.00
Mug, plain 65.00
Mug, Windy City (Fannie Flagg), Robinson Clay Products 200.00
Pickle crock, Bl Band, advertising, recessed lid, 12x9" 225.00
Pickle crock, Heart Band, advertising, rolled rim, 8x8" 225.00
Pie plate, Bl Walled Brick-Edge star emb base, 10½" 100.00
Pitcher, Acorns, stenciled, 8x6½" 135.00
Pitcher, American Beauty Rose, 10" 275.00
Pitcher, Apricot, 8" 165.00
Pitcher, Avenue of Trees, allover bl, 9x7" 200.00
Pitcher, Barrel, +6 mugs 395.00
Pitcher, Basketweave & Flower, 9" 225.00
Pitcher, Bl Band, plain 80.00
Pitcher, Bl Band Scroll 160.00
Pitcher, Bl Sawtooth, Wht Hall 95.00
Pitcher, Bluebird, 9x7" 250.00
Pitcher, Butterfly, 9x7" 250.00
Pitcher, Castle & Fishscale, 8" 195.00
Pitcher, Cattails, 7½" 150.00
Pitcher, Cattails, 9" 185.00
Pitcher, Cherries & Leaves, w/printing, 9½" 350.00
Pitcher, Cherry Cluster, 7½" 195.00
Pitcher, Cherry Cluster & Basketweave, 10" 175.00
Pitcher, Cosmos 195.00
Pitcher, Cow, 8½" 225.00
Pitcher, Doe & Fawn, sparce bl, 8½" 185.00
Pitcher, Dutch Boy & Girl by Windmill, 9" 225.00
Pitcher, Dutch Landscape, stenciled, tall 175.00
Pitcher, Eagle 450.00
Pitcher, Eagle w/Shield & Arrows, rare 500.00
Pitcher, Edelweiss, metal thumb rest, 9x5" 300.00
Pitcher, Fishscale & Wild Rose, 10" 160.00

Pitcher, Flying Bird, 9" 700.00
Pitcher, Grape Cluster on Trellis, allover bl, 7x7" 200.00
Pitcher, Hunting Scene, rare, 7x8" 400.00
Pitcher, Indian Boy & Girl, 6" 350.00
Pitcher, Indian Head in War Bonnet, dk bl, waffled body, 9" 435.00
Pitcher, Iris, 9" 225.00
Pitcher, Leaping Deer, 8½" 175.00
Pitcher, Lincoln, allover deep bl, 10x7" 600.00
Pitcher, Lincoln, allover deep bl, 4¾x4¾" 175.00
Pitcher, Lincoln, allover deep bl, 6x4" 250.00
Pitcher, Lincoln, allover deep bl, 7x5" 300.00
Pitcher, Lincoln, allover deep bl, 8x6" 350.00
Pitcher, Lincoln w/Log Cabin 525.00
Pitcher, Lovebird, arc bands, deep color, 8½" 450.00
Pitcher, Lovebird, pale color, 8½", EX 300.00
Pitcher, Peacock, 7¾x6½" 450.00
Pitcher, Pine Cone, 9½" 200.00
Pitcher, Poinsettia, 6½" 300.00
Pitcher, Rose & Fishscale, 6" 165.00
Pitcher, Rose on Trellis 165.00
Pitcher, Scroll & Leaf, advertising, 8" 250.00
Pitcher, Stag & Pine Trees, 9" 295.00
Pitcher, Swan, long beak, arched neck, deep color, 8½" 275.00
Pitcher, Swan, lt bl, 8½" 295.00
Pitcher, tavern scene, Flemish Jugs...Kinney & Levan, 9" 165.00
Pitcher, Tulip, 8x4" 250.00
Pitcher, Wild Rose, sponged bands, 9" 295.00
Pitcher, Wild Rose, 9x6" 185.00
Pitcher, Wildflower, stenciled 250.00
Pitcher, Windmill & Bush, 9" 225.00
Pitcher, Windy City (Fannie Flagg), Robinson Clay, 8½" 450.00
Pitcher, 2 old men w/canes, dog's-head spout, Germany, 11" 200.00
Roaster, Diffused Bl, appl hdls, flat finial, 9x19" 225.00
Roaster, Wildflower, domed lid, 8½x12" 195.00
Rolling pin, Bl Band, advertising, 14x4" 350.00
Rolling pin, Swirl, orig wooden hdls, 13" 475.00
Rolling pin, Wildflower, w/advertising, 15x4½" 450.00
Rolling pin, Wildflower & Bl Band 250.00

Salt crock, Waffle, wooden lid, 6x6", $165.00.

Salt crock, Apricot, orig lid 145.00
Salt crock, Bl Band, printed letters, 6x5" 135.00
Salt crock, Butterfly, orig lid 185.00
Salt crock, Daisy on Snowflakes, orig lid, 6½x6" 220.00
Salt crock, Flying Bird, orig lid, 9" 350.00
Salt crock, Grapevine on Fence, pale bl, orig lid, 6½x6¾" 225.00
Soap dish, Beaded Rose 125.00
Soap dish, cat's head 150.00
Soap dish, Indian in War Bonnet 150.00

Syrup dispenser, Pep-So, rpl lid, 12x9" 325.00
Teapot, Swirl, dbl wire bail hdl, ball shape, 9x6½" 450.00
Toothbrush holder, Bow Tie, stenciled flower 50.00
Vase, Swirl, cone shape 300.00
Wash set, Rose on Trellis, 2-pc 300.00

Water cooler, Polar Bear, elk in reserve, bear reserve on back, brass spout, 16", $1,000.00.

Water cooler, Apple Blossom, brass spigot, 17x15" 700.00
Water cooler, Bl Band, orig lid 175.00
Water cooler, Cupid, brass spigot, patterned lid, 15x12" 700.00
Water cooler, Polar Bear, NP brass spigot, rare, 17x15" 1,000.00
Water jug, Diffused Bl, cork affixed to stopper, 7x7" 195.00

Bluebird China

Made from 1910 to 1934, Bluebird china is lovely ware decorated with bluebirds flying among pink flowering branches. It was inexpensive dinnerware and reached the height of its popularity in the second decade of this century. Several potteries produced it; shapes differ from one manufacturer to another, but the decal remains basically the same. Among the backstamps you'll find W.S. George, Cleveland, Carrolton, Homer Laughlin, Limoges China of Sebring, Ohio; and there are others.

Bowl, deep, 5" 25.00
Bowl, fruit; Deerwood, 5½" 12.50
Bowl, fruit; Hopewell China, 5" 10.00
Bowl, gravy; w/saucer, Hopewell China 50.00
Bowl, sauce; SP Co, 4½" 12.50
Bowl, soup; PMC Co, 8" 30.00
Butter dish, 4½" holder w/in 7" dia dish, Steubenville 85.00
Casserole, Royal China Internat'l, 7x11½" 125.00
Casserole, w/lid, Ostro China, 10½" dia 95.00
Creamer & sugar bowl, w/lid, Homer Laughlin 45.00
Cup, chocolate; ftd, 3½" 35.00
Cup, coffee; unmk, 3½" 25.00
Cup, tea; unmk 15.00
Ladle, sauce; gold scrolling 40.00
Plate, dessert; Limoges, 6" 8.00
Plate, Homer Laughlin, 8½" 15.00
Plate, National China, 8" 15.00
Plate, rtcl, sq, unmk, 9" 35.00
Plate, Steubenville China, 9" 15.00
Platter, Hopewell China, 13x10" 65.00
Platter, Hopewell China, 17½x13" 95.00

Platter, unmk, 9x7" 35.00
Syrup, unmk, 4" 35.00
Teapot, ELP Co, 8½x8½" 125.00

Blue Ridge

Blue Ridge dinnerware was produced by Southern Potteries of Erwin, Tennessee, from the late 1930s until 1956 in twelve basic styles and two thousand different patterns, all of which were hand decorated under the glaze. Vivid colors lit up floral arrangements of seemingly endless variation, fruit of every sort from simple clusters to lush assortments, barnyard fowl, peasant figures, and unpretentious textured patterns. Although it is these dinnerware lines for which they are best known, collectors prize the artist-signed plates from the forties and the limited line of character jugs made during the fifties most highly. Examples of the French Peasant pattern are valued at double the prices listed below; very simple patterns will bring 25% to 50% less.

Our advisors, Betty and Bill Newbound, have compiled two lovely books, *Blue Ridge Dinnerware, Revised Third Edition,* and *The Collector's Encyclopedia of Blue Ridge,* both with beautiful color illustrations and current market values. They are listed in the Directory under Michigan. For information concerning the National Blue Ridge Newsletter, see the Clubs, Newsletters, and Catalogs section of the Directory.

Chocolate pot, French Peasant, pedestal foot, china, $175.00; Matching creamer and sugar bowl, $90.00 for the pair.

Ashtray, advertising, w/rest 65.00
Ashtray, individual 13.00
Bonbon, flat shell, rare 60.00
Bowl, cereal/soup; 6" 9.00
Bowl, divided, 8" 20.00
Bowl, fruit; 5" 4.00
Bowl, mixing; 8½" 30.00
Bowl, rnd, 8" 15.00
Bowl, salad; 10½" 45.00
Bowl, soup; flat, 8" 15.00
Bowl, vegetable; divided, oval, 9" 22.50
Bowl, vegetable; oval, 9" 20.00
Box, candy; rnd w/lid, rare 95.00
Box, cigarette 65.00
Box, cigarette; w/4 trays 120.00
Box, Dancing Nudes, rare 300.00
Box, Mallard, rare 400.00
Box, Sherman Lily, rare 600.00
Butter dish, ¼-lb, w/lid 45.00
Butter pat/coaster 20.00

Cake lifter	22.50
Carafe, w/lid	60.00
Casserole, w/lid	40.00
Celery, leaf shape, china	30.00
Celery, Skyline shape	25.00
Child's cereal bowl	30.00
Child's feeding dish	30.00
Child's mug	25.00
Child's plate	35.00
Child's play set	275.00
Chocolate pot, pedestal, china	175.00
Coffeepot	100.00
Creamer, demitasse	55.00
Creamer, regular	8.00
Cup & saucer, demitasse; china	30.00
Cup & saucer, Jumbo	35.00
Cup & saucer, regular	10.00
Deviled egg dish	32.50
Dish, baking; 13x8"	25.00
Egg cup, dbl	25.00
Gravy boat	20.00
Gravy tray	18.00
Jug, batter; w/lid	70.00
Jug, character; china, rare	600.00
Jug, syrup; w/lid	80.00
Lamp, china	120.00
Lazy susan, 6-pc w/tray	550.00
Pie baker	25.00
Pitcher, fancy, china	95.00
Plate, aluminum edge, 12"	20.00
Plate, artist sgn, china	750.00
Plate, cake; 10½"	30.00
Plate, Christmas or Turkey	65.00
Plate, dinner; 10"	15.00
Plate, dinner; 9½"	12.00
Plate, party; w/cup well & cup	22.50
Plate, snack; 3-compartment	15.00
Plate, sq, novelty pattern, 6"	45.00
Plate, 11½"	28.00
Plate, 6"	4.00
Platter, artist sgn, 17½"	770.00
Platter, Thanksgiving Turkey	195.00
Platter, Turkey w/Acorns	195.00
Platter, 11"	11.00
Platter, 12½"	15.00
Platter, 15"	22.00
Ramekin, w/lid, 5"	28.00
Ramekin, w/lid, 7½"	32.00
Relish, deep shell, china	50.00
Relish, heart shape, sm	45.00
Relish, loop hdl, china	70.00
Relish, Maple Leaf, china	55.00
Relish, T-hdl, china	40.00
Salad fork	32.00
Salad spoon	28.00
Server, center hdl	25.00
Shakers, Apple, pr	12.00
Shakers, Blossom Top, pr	32.50
Shakers, Bud Top, pr	32.50
Shakers, Chickens, pr	90.00
Shakers, ftd, china, tall, pr	45.00
Shakers, mallards, pr	150.00
Shakers, regular, short, pr	12.00
Sherbet	14.00

Sugar bowl, demitasse; sgn, rare	35.00
Sugar bowl, ped or flare, china	45.00
Sugar bowl, regular, w/lid	13.00
Tea tile, rnd or sq, 6"	32.50
Teapot, china	95.00
Teapot, demitasse; china	125.00
Teapot, demitasse; earthenware	85.00
Tidbit, 2-tier	25.00
Tidbit, 3-tier	30.00
Toast, covered	100.00
Tray, cake; Maple Leaf, rare	45.00
Tray, chocolate pot; china	400.00
Tray, demitasse	90.00
Tray, flat shell, china	80.00
Tumbler, glass	10.00
Vase, boot, 8"	80.00
Vase, bud	80.00
Vase, rnd, china, 5½"	65.00
Vase, ruffled top, 9¼"	90.00
Wall sconce	65.00

Boch Freres

Founded in the early 1840s in La Louviere, Boch Freres Keramis became the foremost producer of art pottery in Belgium. Though primarily they served a localized market, in 1844 they earned worldwide recognition for some of their sculptural works on display at the International Exposition in Paris.

In 1907 Charles Catteau of France was appointed head of the art department. Before that time, the firm had concentrated on developing glazes and perfecting elegant forms. The style they pursued was traditional, favoring the re-creation of established 18th-century ceramics. Catteau brought with him to Boch Freres the New Wave (or Art Nouveau) influence in form and decoration. His designs won him international acclaim at the Exhibition d'Art Decoratif in Paris in 1925, and it is for his work that Boch Freres is so highly regarded today. He occasionally signed his work as well as that of others who under his direct supervision carried out his preconceived designs. He was associated with the company until 1950 and lived the remainder of his life in Nice, France, where he died in 1966. The Boch Freres Keramis factory continues to operate today, producing bathroom fixtures and other utilitarian wares. A variety of marks have been used, most incorporating some combination of 'Boch Freres,' 'Keramis,' 'BFK,' or 'Ch Catteau.' A shield topped by a crown and flanked by a 'B' and an 'F' was used as well. Our advisor for this category is Wayne B. Kielsmeier; he is listed in the Directory under Arizona.

Lamp, 9 penguins incised and colored in black and light green, marked Keramis, wooden base, original 2-socket fittings, 11", $770.00.

Jardiniere, lg deer eating leaves, Catteau, #943, 8" H **1,100.00**
Lamp base, yel/orange sun & rays, 8-panel (4 in ivory), 12" **700.00**
Vase, allover stylized leaves, mc/blk, Catteau, ovoid, 10" **465.00**
Vase, deer, geometric borders, Catteau, 14x8" **1,300.00**
Vase, floral panels on cream crackle, elongated ovoid, 13" **350.00**
Vase, Jacobean floral, mc on ivory, Catteau, pear form, 11" **825.00**
Vase, Persee et les Gorgones, gold on red, flattened, 9" **985.00**
Vase, vertical stripes, ovoid, Catteau, 14" **1,000.00**
Vase, 3 grazing antelopes on wht crackle, drilled, 13½" **850.00**

Boehm

Boehm sculptures were the creation of Edward Marshall Boehm, a ceramic artist who coupled his love of the art with his love of nature to produce figurines of birds, animals, and flowers in lovely background settings accurate to the smallest detail. Sculptures of historical figures and those representing the fine arts were also made and along with many of the bird figurines, have established secondary-market values many times their original prices. His first pieces were made in the very early 1950s in Trenton, New Jersey, under the name of Osso Ceramics. Mr. Boehm died in 1969, and the firm has since been managed by his wife. Today known as Edward Marshall Boehm, Inc., the private family-held corporation produces not only porcelain sculptures but collector plates as well. Both limited and non-limited editions of their works have been issued. Examples are marked with various backstamps, all of which have incorporated the Boehm name since 1951. 'Osso Ceramics' in upper case lettering was used in 1950 and 1951.

Birds

Meadowlark with dandelion and mushroom, #435, 8½x7½", $2,500.00.

American Avocet **1,100.00**
Arctic Tern **2,750.00**
Baby Goldfinch **250.00**
Baby Woodthrush w/butterfly **200.00**
Bobolink **1,450.00**
Catbird **2,000.00**
Chickadee baby **60.00**
Chrysanthemums **1,850.00**
European Goldfinch **1,250.00**
Goldcrest **1,100.00**
Hunter **1,150.00**
Kestrals **2,850.00**
King Fisher Fledgling, 6" **120.00**
Little Wren **250.00**
Nonpareil Buntings **1,000.00**

Peony, dbl **950.00**
Puma **6,500.00**
Raccoons **2,000.00**
Robin baby **120.00**
Robin w/daffodils **5,500.00**
Swan Centerpiece **2,500.00**
Tree Creepers **4,000.00**
Water Lily **650.00**
Yellowhammers **4,000.00**

Bohemian Glass

The term 'Bohemian glass' has come to refer to a type of glass developed in Bohemia in the late 16th century at the Imperial Court of Rudolf II, the Hapsburg Emperor. The popular artistic pursuit of the day was stone carving, and it naturally followed to transfer familiar procedures to the glassmaking industry. During the next century, a formula was discovered that produced a glass with a fine crystal appearance which lent itself well to deep, intricate engraving, and the art was further advanced.

Although many other kinds of art glass were made there, collectors today use the term 'Bohemian glass' to most often indicate clear glass overlaid with color through which a design is cut or etched. (Unless otherwise described, the items in the listing that follows are of this type.) Red or yellow on crystal is common, but other colors may also be found. Another type of Bohemian glass involves cutting through and exposing two layers of color in patterns that are often very intricate. Items such as these are sometimes further decorated with enamel and/or gilt work. Our advisor for this category is Thomas P. Bradshaw; he is listed in the Directory under California.

Beaker, red, deer & trees, 5⅜" **95.00**
Bottle, scent; red, mc florals, 5" **95.00**
Bottle, wine; red, vintage, tall, +2 wines **150.00**
Bowl, cobalt, stylized leaves & flowers, 8" **200.00**
Bowl, red, naturalistic scenes, 5x6" **115.00**
Compote, cobalt, roses allover, 12¾" **300.00**
Decanter, red, animals & castles, late 1800s, 15" **125.00**
Decanter, red, grapevine mid-band & stoppers, 9", pr **150.00**
Goblet, red, stags in forest, cut panels, 6½" **100.00**
Goblet, wine; red, deer & castle, 5⅛" **40.00**
Stein, red, dog in forest, pewter mts, 5½x3¼" **335.00**
Tumbler, red, draped floral bands **70.00**
Urn, amber, nature scene, tall knob std w/eng base, 20" **1,250.00**
Vase, amber, vintage & mitres, bulbous, 6" **90.00**
Vase, red, triple dmn, scalloped top, 10" **85.00**

Bookends

Though a few were produced before 1880, bookends became a necessary library accessory and a popular commodity after the printing industry was revolutionized by Mergenthaler's invention, the linotype. Books became abundantly available at such affordable prices that almost every home suddenly had need for bookends. They were carved from wood, cast in iron, bronze, or brass, or cut from stone. Today's collectors may find such designs as ships, animals, flowers, and children. Patriotic themes, art reproductions, and those with Art Nouveau and Art Deco styling provide a basis for a diverse and interesting collection.

Abraham Lincoln bust, bronze-pnt pot metal, 3¼x2¾" **15.00**
Basket of flowers, CI, orig mc pnt, 5½" **65.00**
Bust of lady, Frankart **175.00**

Camel w/rider, pnt CI 40.00
Cherub, cast metal w/dk bronze finish, 6¼" 350.00
Cocker spaniel, gilt metal, wht onyx base 65.00

Cottage, Ancestral Home of George Washington embossed on base, brass, 4", $35.00 for the pair.

Dog figural, chalkware 45.00
Dutch boy (& girl), Frankart 125.00
Elephant, horseshoe-shape tubular body, Chase, 4½" 275.00
Flamenco dancer, Deco style, sgn Herzel 185.00
Horse, rearing, emerald gr glass, 8" 75.00
Horse head, stylized, Frankart 120.00
Horse rearing, Frankart 115.00
Indian w/full headdress, pnt CI, 1800s, 6" 175.00
Lincoln bust, NuArt 55.00
Monk at library bookcase, HP metal, LUA, c 1922 ....35.00
Nude in shell, pnt chalkware, EX 40.00
Old Ironsides, ship's wheel, bronze finish on brass, 6½" 60.00
Owl, bronze pnt, Frankart, 5½" 125.00
Pagoda, brass, mk China, 6x4" 125.00
Pointer dog, bronze pnt on CI, 8" 75.00
Pointer dog, cream lustre w/gold trim 30.00
Poodle, ceramic 15.00
Scottie, brass, Bradley & Hubbard, paper label 75.00
Scottie, Frankart 145.00
Shakespeare, bronzed bust, 1920s 45.00

Bootjacks and Bootscrapers

Bootjacks were made from metal or wood. Some were fancy figural shapes, others strictly business! Their purpose was to facilitate the otherwise awkward process of removing one's boots. Bootscrapers were handy gadgets that provided an effective way to clean the soles of mud and such. Our advisor for this category is Louis Picek; he is listed in the Directory under Iowa.

Bootjacks

Boss emb on shaft, lacy CI, 15" L 135.00
Cricket, CI, 12" 35.00
Cricket, Webster Bros & Co, Reading PA, 11" 55.00
Hickory, bentwood hdl, hinged/folds, use w/out bending over 85.00
Lever action, wood & CI, EX 85.00
Musselman's Boot-Jack Plug Tobacco, CI, sunflower decor 200.00
Naughty Nellie, CI, mc pnt, 11x5x2½", EX 200.00
Stylized fish, cvd wood, worn finish, 22" L 115.00
Try Me, CI, openwork, no pnt, ca 1890s, 12x4x1¾" 70.00

Bootscrapers

Aunt Jemima figure atop, CI, rpt, 14½" 250.00
CI, on pan w/griffins, worn pnt, 13x17½" 215.00
CI, spool & ball post ea corner, sq, orig pnt, JW Fiske, NY 140.00
Dachshund, CI, old worn wht pnt, 1900s, 7x22x5" 225.00
Dragon finial, CI, early, EX 100.00
Pig silhouette, cut-out eye, CI, 8½x12" 195.00
Scottie dog, CI, orig pnt, EX 65.00
Wrought iron, outward curved ears, primitive, 38x10¼", EX 115.00
Wrought iron, ram's horn scrolls, in marble block 135.00
Wrought iron, twisted posts w/star-emb faceted knobs, 12x8" 150.00
Wrought iron w/detailed scroll finial, 21x24" 770.00
2 quail ea end, CI, rectangular pan, pnt traces, 7x16" 275.00

Boru, Sorcha

Sorcha Boru was the professional name used by California ceramist Claire Stewart. She was a founding member of the Allied Arts Guild of Menlo Park (California) where she maintained a studio from 1932 to 1938. From 1938 until 1955, she operated Sorcha Boru Ceramics, a production studio in San Carlos. Her highly acclaimed output consisted of colorful, slip-decorated figurines, salt and pepper shakers, vases, wall pockets, and flower bowls. Most production work was incised 'S.B.C.' by hand.

Bowl, appl lilies at ruffled rim, 6½" 90.00
Bowl, horse motif, 7" 55.00
Bowl, pussy willows on beige, 10" 45.00
Cup, 3 dinosaur hdls 45.00
Figurine, bluebird, 5x10" 95.00
Pitcher, pk lustre florals w/gold centers, beading, 6½" 65.00
Planter, appl flowers, pr 125.00
Shakers, sailor boy & girl, pr 85.00
Sugar shaker, lady figural, 6" 85.00

Bossons Artware

Bossons artware has been on the international market since 1948 when the first high-relief wall plaques were made to depict English scenes and floral subjects. Though floral plaques are still produced, it is Bossons character wall masks (sculptures) and figurines that have been so popular as gift-store items since they were introduced in 1958/59. Today's collectors appreciate their extremely fine modeling and artistry, and interest is on the increase. Masks most often found are usually subjects of men from all nations and walks of life (women are rare, the three children subjects are extremely rare), and some of the larger wall figurines include an animal. Nearly all are made of a strong plaster medium that is easily chipped or scuffed. Mint or mint-in-box discontinued examples are few.

Except for a rare minority, these masks are marked 'Bossons Copyright Reserved' under the neckline or collar, with a date indicating when the mold was created. Also, on the reverse side of these sculptures will appear the following incision: 'Bossons Copyright Reserved,' and often 'Congleton, England,' with date. Those dates will not change though that model may be issued for years, but collectors seek out the variations in color and modeling that often occur during the mask's span of production. Being modeled in plaster, Bossons are frequently found in deplorable condition, and avid collectors pay the premium prices mentioned here for only the most perfect examples, either in factory 'mint' states or perfectly returned to their original structural and coloring beauty by a restoration artist recommended by Bossons.

Bossons also made a series of both domestic animals and wildlife in plaster as well as a hard plastic called 'Stonite.' Full-length plaster Oriental figures were made in a limited number as were clocks, mirrors and other decorative items. All Bossons products are hand painted by individual artists and highly collectible. The discontinued editions and some of the rarer examples in perfect condition command prices in excess of $1,000.00.

Our advisor for this category is Dr. Don Hardisty; he is recommended by Bossons to restore their products and is listed in the Directory under New Mexico.

Key:
DC — Dickens Character Series   DS — Dog of Distinction

Series A, Bengali, 1970, 10½", very rare, $3,500.00 up to $5,200.00.

Afghan shelf ornament, 1959 Reg Design, 12", $400 up to	900.00
Alsation, DS, 1967, 6¼", current retail	31.00
Basset Hound, DS, 1969, 5", current retail	27.00
Betsey Trotwood, bl collar, DC, 1964	300.00
Betsey Trotwood, pk collar, DC, ca 1965, current retail	42.00
Black Panther, same mold as Golden Puma, 1964, 16"	350.00
Blk or wht Poodle, DS, 1968, 5", current retail	27.00
British Military Mask, orig w/eyes, 1965, extremely rare	600.00
British Military Mask, w/out eyes, 1968, $300 up to	600.00
Caspian Man, 1958 or '59 improved model, 7", ea, $150 up to	200.00
Cheyenne Indian, red fringed jacket, 1967-92	100.00
Deccan Hunters (gr or brn-eyed cheetah), c1959, $175 to	225.00
Dog (Mac, Pooch, Patch, etc), ceramic, unmk, ea, $400 up to	600.00
Dogs & Cats, Series I & II, 1959-61, 3" to 4", $125 up to	300.00
French Military Mask, w/eyes, 1990 reissue, current retail	110.00
French or British Military Mask, w/out eyes, 1965, $300 up to	600.00
Moroccan or Serbian shelf ornament, '63, unmk, 6", $200 up to	400.00
Mr Bumble, DC, 1964, 5½", current retail	42.00
Peon & Sherpa, full-length figures, 18", 15", ea, $250 up to	350.00
Pony Girl, wall figure, c 1968, 7", $400 up to	600.00
Series A, Coolie, c1963, 8", from $165 up to	200.00
Series A, Eskimo, 1968, 8", from $75 up to	125.00
Series A, Kassem, c1966, 8", from $185 up to	275.00
Series A, Montenegrin, c 1959, 8", from $175.00 up to	225.00
Series A, Nigerian Man, c 1959, 5½", from $165 up to	185.00
Series A, Snake Charmer, 1958-59, 10", from $150 up to	750.00
Series B, Albanian, gr hat, 1961, 5½"	125.00
Series B, Corsican, c 1959, 5½", current retail	37.00
Sikh or Himalayan shelf ornament, unmk, 1963, 6", $200 up to	400.00

Warrior panel, Afridi or Berber, 17x11", ea, $350 up to	500.00
Warrior panel, Zulu or Sioux, 17x11", ea, $350 up to	500.00
Wildlife Studies, Birds & Sunflowers, c 1968, 7", $400 up to	600.00
Wildlife Studies, Chaffinches, c 1971, 8", current retail	62.00
Wildlife Studies, Eagle (not Fraser-Art), 1963, 12", $150 to	175.00
Wildlife Studies, Golden Puma, c 1959, 16" L, $200 up to	350.00

Bottle Openers

Around the turn of the century, manufacturers began to seal bottles with a metal cap that required a new type of bottle opener. Now the screw cap and the flip top have made bottle openers nearly obsolete. There are many variations, some in combination with other tools. Many openers were used as means of advertising a product. Various materials were used including silver and brass.

A figural bottle opener is defined as a figure designed for the sole purpose of lifting a bottle cap. The actual opener must be an integral part of the figure itself. A base-plate opener is one where the lifter is a separate metal piece attached to the underside of the figure. The major producers of iron figurals were Wilton Products, John Wright Inc., Gadzik Sales, and L & L Favors. Openers may be free-standing and three-dimensional, wall hung or flat. They can be made of cast iron (often painted), brass, bronze or aluminum.

Numbers within the listings refer to a new reference book printed by the FBOC (Figural Bottle Opener Collectors) organization. Those seeking additional information are encouraged to contact FBOC, whose address can be found in the Directory under Clubs, Newsletters, and Catalogs.

Alligator, head up, CI, Wright, EX pnt, F-135	125.00
Alligator & boy, CI, Wilton, F-134	150.00
Amish boy, CI, F-31	300.00
Beer drinker, CI, Iron Art, F-406	40.00
Bulldog's head, CI, Wilton, F-425, wall mt, NM	100.00
Canada goose, brass-plated CI, Norlin, F-105e, 2⅛x3¾"	30.00
Cockatoo, CI, worn mc pnt, Wright, F-121, 3¼"	100.00
Cocker Spaniel, CI, Wright, F-80	35.00
Cowboy w/guitar, CI, Wright, F-27, VG	90.00
Cowboy w/guitar & cactus, hollow pot metal, F-28, 4⅞"	400.00
Dolphin, chrome, Italy, F-152, 6½"	15.00
Donkey, brass, F-67, lg	40.00
Donkey, brass, magnet in roof of mouth, England, F-64, 3½"	15.00
Elephant, plated aluminum, F-49	25.00
Elephant profile, CI, Wilton, F-48	45.00
Fish, aluminum, F-154	20.00
Fish, pnt pot metal, hollow, Wright, F-158, 2¾"	100.00
Fisherman, brass, EX orig pnt, Riverside, F-30b, 4x2½"	30.00
Flamingo, hollow mold, Wright, F-119	95.00
Foundryman, aluminum, F-29	16.50
Foundryman, CI, F-29, Wright	100.00
Goat, brass, F-73	140.00
Goat, CI, F-71, Wilton	48.00
Indian boy, Iroquois Beverages, pnt aluminum, F-197	40.00
Lobster, CI, F-169	32.50
Lobster, CI, worn red pnt, F-168, 3½"	20.00
Lobster, pnt brass, F-167a, 1¼x3½"	20.00
Mallard, CI, Wilton, F-106	90.00
Man w/straw hat at sign post, F-12, pnt CI, Wright, 4⅛"	15.00
Monkey, aluminum, F-89	30.00
Monkey, CI, Wright, F-89	130.00
Nude standing, brass	48.00
Palm Tree Drunk, CI, Wilton, F-20	40.00
Parrot, CI, Wilton, F-109	25.00

Parrot w/can punch, Wright, F-113 ....**85.00**
Pheasant, CI, EX pnt, Wright, F-104 ....**70.00**
Pretzel, F-230 ....**45.00**
Rooster, CI, Wilton, F-97 ....**40.00**
Sailor w/hands at sides, pnt aluminum, F-18 ......**225.00**
Sea gull, CI, EX pnt, Wright, F-123 ....**55.00**
Sea horse, brass, Canada, F-140 ....**22.50**
Setter dog, CI, Wright, F-79 ....**70.00**
Sign post drunk, CI, Wilton, F-11 ....**7.50**
Skunk, aluminum, NM orig pnt, F-92d, 2⅛x2⅞" **60.00**
Squirrel, CI, brn pnt, Wright, F-92 ....**170.00**
Squirrel, CI, Wright, F-91 ....**80.00**
Squirrel, nickeled CI, Norlin Enterprises, F-91d, 1¾x3" **45.00**
Timberjack Donkey, brass, Walter Ind, F-62 ....**48.00**

Bottles and Flasks

As far back as the 1st century B.C., the Romans preferred blown glass containers for their pills and potions. Though you're not apt to find many of those, you will find bottles of every size, shape, and color made to hold perfume, ink, medicine, soda, spirits, vinegar, and many other liquids. American business firms preferred glass bottles in which to package their commercial products and used them extensively from the late 18th century on. Bitters bottles contained 'medicine' (actually herb-flavored alcohol), and judging from the number of these found today, their contents found favor with many! Because of a heavy tax imposed on the sale of liquor in 17th-century England by King George, who hoped to curtail alcohol abuse among his subjects, bottlers simply added 'curative' herbs to their brew and thus avoided taxation. Since gin was taxed in America as well, the practice continued in this country. Scores of brands were sold; among the most popular were Dr. H.S. Flint & Co. Quaker Bitters, Dr. Kaufman's Anti-Cholera Bitters, and Dr. J. Hostetter's Stomach Bitters. Most bitters bottles were made in shades of amber, brown, and aquamarine. Clear glass was used to a lesser extent, as were green tones. Blue, amethyst, red-brown, and milk glass examples are rare. (Please note that color is a strong factor when pricing bottles. For example, an amber Hostetter's bitters sells for $25.00 or less, but a green variant can bring hundreds of dollars. An aqua scroll flask may bring $50.00, but a cobalt blue variation will command over $1,000.00.)

Perfume or scent bottles were produced abroad by companies all over Europe from the late 16th century on. Perfume making became such a prolific trade that as a result beautifully decorated bottles were fashionable. In America they were produced in great quantities by Stiegel in 1770 and by Boston and Sandwich in the early 19th century. Cologne bottles were first made in about 1830 and toilet-water bottles in the 1880s. Rene Lalique produced fine scent bottles from as early as the turn of the century. The first were one-of-a-kind creations done in the cire perdue method. He later designed bottles for the Coty Perfume Company with a different style for each Coty fragrance. Prices for commercial perfume bottles hinge on condition. Their values appreciate according to these factors: are they still sealed or full; do they retain all factory labels; is the original box or packaging included? Deluxe versions bring premium prices. Example: blue flat Dans La Nuit cologne by Rene Lalique, value for 6" size, $250.00. Dans La Nuit, enameled with stars by Rene Lalique, 3" round ball, $900.00.

Spirit flasks from the 19th century were blown in specially designed molds with varied motifs including political subjects, railroad trains, and symbolic devices. The most commonly used colors were amber, dark brown, and green.

From the 20th century, early pop and beer bottles are very collectible as is nearly every extinct commercial container. Dairy bottles are a relatively new area of interest; look for round bottles in good con-

dition with both city and state as well as a nice graphic relating to the farm or the dairy.

Bottles may be dated by the methods used in their production. For instance, a rough pontil indicates a date before 1845. After the bottle was blown, a pontil rod was attached to the bottom, a glob of molten glass acting as the 'glue.' This allowed the glassblower to continue to manipulate the extremely hot bottle until it was finished. From about 1845 until approximately 1860, the molten glass 'glue' was omitted. The rod was simply heated to a temperature high enough to cause it to afix itself to the bottle. When the rod was snapped off, a metallic residue was left on the base of the bottle; this is called an 'iron pontil.' A seam that reaches from base to lip marks a machine-made bottle from after 1903, while an applied or hand-finished lip points to an early mold-blown bottle. The Industrial Revolution saw keen competition between manufacturers, and as a result, scores of patents were issued. Many concentrated on various types of closures; the crown bottle cap, for instance, was patented in 1892. If a manufacturer's name is present, consulting a book on marks may help you date your bottle.

Among our advisors for this category are Madeleine France (see the Directory under Florida), Mark Vuono (Connecticut), Steve Ketcham (Minnesota), Monsen and Baer (Virginia), and John Tutton (Virginia). In the listings that follow (most of which have been taken from auction catalogs), glass is assumed to be clear unless color is indicated. Numbers refer to a standard reference book, *American Glass*, by George and Helen McKearin. See also Advertising, various companies; Avon; Barber Shop Collectibles; Blown Glass; Blown Three-Mold Glass; California Perfume Company; Czechoslovakia; De Vilbiss; Fire Fighting; Lalique; Medical Collectibles; Steuben.

Key:
am — applied mouth	GW — Glass Works
bbl — barrel	ip — iron pontil
bt — blob top	p — pontil
b3m — blown 3-mold	ps — pontil scar
cm — collared mouth	rm — rolled mouth
fm — flared mouth	sb — smooth base
gm — ground mouth	sl — sloping
gp — graphite pontil	sm — sheared mouth
grd — ground pontil	tm — tooled mouth

Barber Bottles

Bay Rum & mc florals HP on lav opaque, gold trim, 8⅝" **250.00**
Birds & reeds HP on robin's egg bl opaque, ca 1900, 8¾" **250.00**
Cranberry opal w/wht vertical swirl ribs, sb, 1900s, 7¼" **75.00**
Cranberry w/wht herringbone, lt haze, 1900s, 7½" **150.00**
Deep violet-cobalt w/irid o/l, Loetz type, 8⅛" **400.00**
Flying birds, sun & flowers HP on fiery wht opal, 9" **100.00**
Frosted clambroth w/appl bl & wht snake around neck, 7⅝" **350.00**
Hair Tonic & floral HP on fiery wht opal, ca 1910, 9" **100.00**
Hobnail, med yel-amber, tm, sb, lt stain, ca 1900, 6¾" **60.00**
Hobnail, turq, bulbous, polished p, ca 1900, 7", NM **80.00**
House scene HP on milk glass, sb, ca 1900, 8¾" **400.00**
Koken Barber Supply, Bay Rum & florals HP on milk glass, 8" ..**125.00**
Mary Gregory-style child on bright gr, rm, 1900s, 7⅜" **250.00**
Mary Gregory-style seminude on amethyst, rm, 1900s, 8⅞" **350.00**
Mc florals HP on yel-gr frost, sm, ps, 1900s, 8" **175.00**
Mc florals HP on yel-olive, rm, lt stain, ca 1900, 8⅛" **125.00**
Mc florals w/gold HP on amethyst, ps, sm, 1900s, 7¾" **125.00**
Quinine & clovers HP on milk glass, sb, ca 1910, 8¾" **175.00**
Turq opal w/wht fern pattern, rm, sb, 1900s, 6¾" **100.00**
Vegederma & Mary Gregory-style lady on amethyst, 7⅞" **300.00**
Wht floral bands HP on pk-amethyst, sm, 1900s, 6¾" **125.00**

Bitters Bottles

American Life, amber, sl cm, modified log cabin, 9" 475.00
Baker's Orange Grove, lt gold-amber, roped corners, 9½" 180.00
Baker's Orange Grove, yel w/amber tone, am, sb, 9½" 425.00
Big Bill Best, gold-amber, tm, sb, pyramid form, 12" 100.00
Brown's Celebrated Indian Herb, deep chocolate, 12½" 1,250.00
Brown's Celebrated Indian Herb, gold-amber, 12" 550.00
Brown's Celebrated Indian Herb, med amber to yel, 12⅛" 425.00
Burher's Gentian, amber, am, sb, Am, 1870s, 8¾" 75.00
DeMuth's Stomach, lt gold-amber, beveled corners, cm, 9¼" 150.00
Dr AW Coleman's Anti Dyspeptic & Tonic, deep emerald gr, 9" .2,250.00
Dr CW Roback's Stomach, gold-amber, sl cm, bbl form, 9⅜" 210.00
Dr Fisch's, gold-amber, fish form, Am, 1860-80, 11⅝" 200.00
Dr Geo Pierce's Indian Restorative, aqua, lt haze, 8⅞" 160.00
Dr Petzold's Genuine German...Patd 1884, med orange-amber, 7" ..135.00
Dr Thos Hall's CA Pepsin Wine, amber, tm, 1880s, 9" 220.00
Globe Tonic, gold-amber, sq w/columnar corners, 9⅝" 120.00
Godfrey's Celebrated Cordial NY, aqua, ps, am, 10" 775.00
Great Tonic Dr Caldwell's Herb, gold-amber, triangular, 12⅝" ..210.00
Greeley's Bourbon, copper, am, sb, 1860s, 9⅜" 275.00
Greeley's Bourbon, lt copper-puce, sq cm, sb, bbl form, 9¼" 220.00
Greeley's Bourbon, pinkish copper, bbl form, cm, 9" 280.00
Greeley's Bourbon, smoky gray-gr, cm, sb, 1870s, 9¼" 950.00
Greeley's Bourbon Whiskey, med strawberry-puce, sq cm, 9¼" ..300.00
Hall's, lt gold-yel, sq cm, sb, Am, 1860-80, 9" 150.00
Hall's, yel w/faint amber tone, sq cm, sb, bbl form, 9" 210.00
Hibernia, yel-amber, am, sb, 1870s, 9¾" 185.00
Holtzermann's Pat Stomach, gold-amber, cabin form, 9¾" 280.00
HP Berb Wild Cherry, gold-amber, modified cabin, 10" 260.00
JNO Moffat Price $1 Phoenix, olive gr, tm, ps, 5¾", NM 350.00
John W Steele's Niagara Star, dk gold-amber, cabin, 9⅞" 350.00
Kimball's Jaundice, yel-amber w/olive tone, att Stoddard, 7" 250.00
National, deep gold-amber, cm/sb, Am, 1860s, 12½" 220.00
National Pat 1867, med amber, am, sb, sm bruise, 12½" 200.00
Old Sachem...& Wigwam Tonic, dk burgundy, bbl form, 9⅛" ...800.00
Old Sachem...& Wigwam Tonic, gold-amber, bbl form, 9⅜" 500.00
Old Sachem...& Wigwam Tonic, yel-amber, bbl form, 9¼" 150.00
Royal Italian Registered...Genova, med pk-amethyst, 13½" 550.00
Schroeder's Louisville KY, amber, lady's leg, 8¾" 350.00
Schroeder's Louisville KY, med amber, lady's leg, 11⅝" 400.00
Solomon's Strengthening & Invigorating, cobalt, 9⅝" 625.00
ST Drake's Plant'n X Pat 1862, deep red-puce, 6-log, 10" 110.00
ST Drake's 1860 Plant'n X Pat 1862, amber, 4-log, 10⅛" 60.00
ST Drake's 1860 Plant'n X Pat 1862, deep cherry-puce, 10" 200.00
ST Drake's 1860 Plant'n X Pat 1862, yel-amber, 6-log, 10" 200.00

Blown Glass Bottles and Flasks

Apothecary, bright yel w/olive tone, label, 1850s, 10⅝" 375.00
Apothecary, cobalt, wide mouth, tm, blown stopper, 12¾" 200.00
Apothecary, deep olive-amber, sb, rm, sm stain, 1850s, 14" 200.00
Champagne, med olive-amber, ps, sm, France, 1780-1820, 11½" .175.00
Chestnut flask, bright yel-amber, am, ps, New England, 8½" 155.00
Chestnut flask, dk yel-olive, sm w/ring, 1700-1800, 9½" 150.00
Chestnut flask, forest gr, am, ps, New England, 8⅝" 170.00
Chestnut flask, gold-amber, 24 vertical ribs, Midwest, 5" 200.00
Chestnut flask, lt olive-gr, freeblown, appl cm, 9¾" 100.00
Chestnut flask, lt yel-olive, cm, ps, New England, 9⅜" 140.00
Demi-John or storage, yel-amber w/olive tone, ps, 10¾" 70.00
Flask, bright sapphire bl, flat ovoid, appl pewter collar, 8" 350.00
Flask, dk olive w/wht flecks, wide mouth, att Saratoga, 4⅝" 400.00
Flask, GI-22, rm, ps, Am, 1820-40, 1-pt 1,100.00
Gin, yel-olive, sq tapered form, mushroom mouth, ps, 9½" 95.00

Globular, gold-amber, rolled cm, ps, att Wht, 1820-50, 5" 200.00
Ludlow, deep root beer-amber, ps, am, flattened, 1770s, 11" 325.00
Ludlow, med olive gr, ps, rm, 1800-30, 10½x5¼" 100.00
Lutlow, root beer-amber, slightly oval, rm, 1800-30, 8⅜" 100.00
Pitkin flask, bl-gr, 30-rib swirl, New England, ca 1800s, 5" 260.00
Pitkin flask, bright med gr, 32-rib swirl, Midwest, 6⅝" 425.00
Pitkin flask, bright olive gr, 36-rib swirl, New England, 5" 325.00
Pitkin flask, dk yel-olive, 36-rib swirl, New England, 6⅜" 300.00
Pitkin flask, lt gr, 35-rib swirl, sm, ps, 7⅛" 300.00
Pitkin flask, olive gr, 36-rib swirl, 6⅝" 300.00
Pitkin flask, yel-olive, 30-rib swirl, flared sm, 7¼" 325.00
Pitkin flask, yel-olive, 36-rib swirl, New England, 1800s, 5" 350.00
Spirit, free-blown, blk (dk yel-olive), 1700-30, 7⅞" 100.00

Cologne, Perfume, and Toilet Water Bottles

Amethyst, rnd w/sl shoulders, polished p, rm, 1860s, 8¾" 130.00
Amethyst, sq w/vertical rib down ea side, sb, tm, 1860s, 5⅝" 150.00
Aqua, 8-sided corset waist form, rm, haze, 1840-70, 4⅝" 95.00
Clear, beaded flutes, ps, tm, 1860s, 5⅜" 60.00
Clear, T'print, sb, tm, lt haze, 1860s, 5⅝" 45.00
Clear, 5 stars on 3 panels, ribbed corners, 1860s, 10¾" 110.00
Cobalt, beaded flute panels, sb, tm, 1850-70, 8" 475.00
Cobalt, 12-sided, sb, rm, 1860s, 5½" 110.00
Cobalt, 12-sided, sl shoulders, sb, rm, 1860s, 4⅝" 120.00
Deep amethyst, sq w/herringbone in corners, 1860s, 6" 400.00
Deep amethyst, 8-sided corset waist form, 1860s, 4⅝" 350.00

Glass and gilt metal, Louis XV, rococo scrolls and landscape scenes, 1700s, 3½", with fitted case, $1,980.00; Blue overlay and gilt glass with enameling, Bohemia, 1800s, 3½", with fitted case, $275.00; Gold and cut glass, marked with oak leaf in oval, possibly French, 3½", $440.00.

Lav bl, polygonal w/8-sides, sb, tm, 1860s, 4⅝" 240.00
Med pk-amethyst to dk amethyst, 12-sided, sl shoulders, 4½" ...130.00
Med smoky puce, 12-sided, sp, rm, lt haze, 1860s, 7½" 110.00
Milk glass, beaded flutes, sb, rm, 1860s, 5⅝" 95.00
Milk glass, rnd w/beaded flutes, sb, fm, 1860s, 10⅜" 110.00
Pk-amethyst, 12-sided, sb, rm, 1860s, 6¼" 135.00
Powder bl opaque, polygonal w/8 sides, sb, rm, 1860s, 4⅝" 250.00
Sandwich, GI-7, cobalt, b3m, fm, ps, 1820-40, 6" 150.00
Sandwich, GI-7, cobalt, b3m, tm, w/stopper, 1820-40, 7⅛" 260.00
Sapphire bl, Gothic corner columns, sb, tm, 1860s, 5½" 325.00
Sapphire opal, 12-sided, sb, rm, 1860s, 5½" 275.00
Teal gr, polygonal w/8 sides, sb, tm, 1860s, 4⅝" 275.00

Commercial Perfume Bottles

Ave Maria, Matchabelli, crown w/gold, ball stopper, 3¼" 175.00

Cachet, L Lelong, clear & frosted w/molded leaves, 5", +box 230.00
Dans la Nuit, Worth, bl ball form, w/stopper, mini, 1¾" 110.00
Fath de Fath, J Fath, faceted, brass top, 1½", +box 385.00
Futur, Renoir, apothecary shape, ball stopper, 2", +box 110.00
Gardenia, L Lelong, 8-pointed star shape, 2½", MIB 120.00
Gardenia, Mary Chess, pawn shape, gold label & cap, 2", +box ...77.00
Golliwog, Vigney, Golliwog blk glass stopper, 3½", +box 410.00
Heather, Palmyra, faceted, Scotsman face cap, mini, 2¼", +box ..20.00
Heaven Sent, H Rubenstein, frosted angel/ gold cap, mini, 2½" ...55.00
Intoxication, D'Orsay, pleated form/gold cap, mini, 2¼", +box 88.00
It's You, E Arden, triangular, gold label, mini, 2", sealed 88.00
Jasmin, Lander, frosted lady form, label missing, 3¾" 110.00
Mille Fleurs, E Arden, pnt labels, unopened, 2¼", +box 77.00
Passion for Men, E Taylor, purple glass, factice, 11½" 220.00
Safari, Ralph Lauren, cut look, plastic cap, factice, 10¼" 240.00
Sirocco, Lucien Lelong, columnar, glass stopper, 7¾" 200.00
Slumber Song, H Rubenstein, angel w/flowers form, 6½" 220.00
Succes Fou, Schiaparelli, fig leaf form, gr & gold enamel, 3" 770.00
Triomphe, L Laraine, frosted Arc de Triomphe form, 4½" 165.00
Violet Essence, E Arden, bouquet shape, mini, 2", MIB 286.00
Violettes de Cote d'Azure, Berdoues, mini, 1¼", +box 77.00
Xmas Bells, Molinard, blk glass bell form, blk label, 5" 230.00

Dairy

**Ranier's, I Want Ranier's Milk or Nothin',
red pyro, cream top, 1-quart, $26.50.**

Absolutely Pure...Thatcher, man milks, glass lid, 1880s, 1-qt 500.00
AG Smalley & Co Pat Boston MA, clear, tin lid, ½-gal 120.00
AG Smalley Pat Apr 5 1898 Boston & NY, clear, 1890s, 1-qt 85.00
AHS MA Seal 1 Qt...Alta Crest Farms, bright gr, 1930s 700.00
Bowman Dairy Co, orange pyro, metal hdl, cb cap, 1940s, 1-gal ..65.00
Bramlage Dairy Est 1900..., Lincoln bust, amber, 1900, 1-qt 575.00
Brewick Clewell's Creamery God Bless..., orange pyro, 1-qt 75.00
Broadview Vita Lac..., amber, orig cap, 1910s, 1-qt 200.00
Broadview Vita Lac..., amber, sb, orig cap, ½-pt 160.00
Cream Separator...This Side..., 1920s, 1-qt 85.00
Crystal WTCO Milk Jar, 1895-1910, sm bruise, 1-pt 600.00
From Farm...KY Acres...War Bonds..., orange pyro, ½-gal 65.00
Grace Farm...Yonkers NY..., amber, tm, 1900, 1-qt 375.00
Harmony Creamery Buttermilk..., amber, sb, tm, stain, 10-oz 150.00
Howell CM& C...NY...Whitman's Pat...1890..., 1890s, 1-qt 375.00
Huntley...Kazol 2346 W Adams St, amber, sb, 1900s, 6-oz 150.00
Ideal...Borubannais IL...Cream Separator..., 1920s, 1-qt 70.00
Jr Washburn...Wis...Pat Sept 17 89, lt amethyst, 1890s, 1-qt 50.00
Kligerman Dairies...NJ Sour Cream, 1920-40, 1-qt 15.00
KY Acres...Buy War Bonds..., orange pyro, sb, 1-qt 95.00
Lawnfield Farm...Powell & Lockwood...NY, 1890s, 1-qt 110.00
Litchfield...Whiteman's Pat...1890, wire bail, 1890s, 1-qt 350.00

Lyon Brook Dairy...B'klyn, rpl lid, 1890s, 1-qt 350.00
Manorfield Stock Farm..., clear, orig stopper, 1900s, 1-qt 525.00
McCann's Fresh Buttermilk, amber, wire bail, 1910s, ½-gal 270.00
McJunkin-Str Dairy Buttermilk..., amber, 1900s, ½-gal 300.00
Meadow Brook..., JW on sb, amber, tooled lip, 1900s, 1-qt 250.00
Milk for Infants..., Hagerton on base, amber, 1-qt, NM 300.00
Milk for Infants...Dr Brush's Farm..., amber, 1900s, 1-pt 300.00
Olin Hill Providence RI, tm, sb, tin lid, Am, 1880s, 7" 160.00
Polks...Best, amber, sb, 1900s, ½-pt 600.00
Presented for Demonstration Only...Toronto Ont, Imperial qt ..350.00
Property of IL Condensing Co..., Pat...89 on base, 1-qt 170.00
Pure Milk Corp Limited, amber, Canada, 1900, Imperial qt 150.00
RFS RF Stevens..., lt amethyst tint, tin lid, 1910s, 1-qt 70.00
Sanitary...of London..., amber, 1900s, chip, Imperial qt 400.00
Use Sealtest...Products Buy War Bonds..., red & bl pyro, 1-qt 225.00
Warren Creamery 323 Warren St..., smoky aqua, 1900s, 1-pt 80.00
Wm Zeuger Pure Milk & Cream, amber, 1910s, ½-gal, NM 550.00
12½% Standard Cream...Whiteman's...1890, 1890s, 1-qt 125.00

Flasks

Adams/Jefferson, GI-114, bright yel-amber, sm, ps, ½-pt 170.00
Baltimore Monument/Liberty & Union, GVI-3, aquamarine, 1-pt .350.00
Benjamin Franklin/TW Dyott, GI-96, amethystine, 1-qt 1,400.00
Benjamin Franklin/TW Dyott, GI-98, lt gr, sm, 1-pt 2,500.00
Biningers Traveler's Guide, gold-amber, pocket, 6½" 220.00
BP&B, GIX-39, clear, scroll type, sm, ps, ½-pt 450.00
BP&B, GIX-39, moonstone, scroll type, ps, ½-pt, EX 250.00
Bridgeton NJ-Washington/Classical Bust, GI-25, aqua, 1-qt 240.00
Cannon/Little More Grape Capt Bragg, GX-5, aqua, 1-pt 340.00
Clasped Hands/Eagle, GXII-31, gold-amber, am w/ring, ½-pt 140.00
Clasped Hands/Eagle, GXII-43, dk gold-amber, calabash, 1-qt ...220.00
Columbia/Eagle, GI-117, aqua, Kensington Union, 1-pt 625.00
Columbia/Eagle, GI-121, aqua, sm, ps, 1830-50, 1-pt 275.00
Cornucopia/Cornucopia, GIII-2, aqua, Kensington, ½-pt 130.00
Cornucopia/Lg Medallion, GIII-1, lt yel-gr, Midwest, ½-pt 425.00
Cornucopia/Urn, GIII-12, yel-olive, sm, ps, Am, ½-pt 80.00
Cornucopia/Urn, GIII-17, emerald gr, sm, ps, Lancaster, 1-pt 500.00
Cornucopia/Urn, GIII-4, bright med gr, sm, ps, Coventry, 1-pt .290.00
Cornucopia/Urn, GIII-7, emerald gr, sm, ps, ½-pt 150.00
Dbl Eagle, GII-24, aqua, sm, ps, Am, 1830s, 1-pt 110.00
Dbl Eagle, GII-24, copper, sm/ps, att KY, crack, 1-pt 425.00
Dbl Eagle, GII-30, bright aqua, vertical ribs, ½-pt 340.00

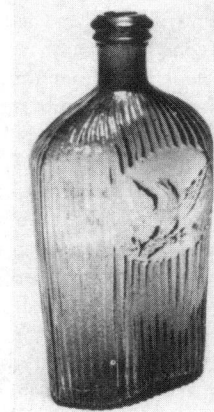

**Double Eagle, GII-31, emerald green, dou-
ble collared lip, pontil scar, Louisville Glassworks, 1855-65, 1-quart, NM, $2,800.00.**

Dbl Eagle, GII-31, aqua, vertical ribs, ps, 1-qt 200.00
Dbl Eagle, GII-70, olive gr, sm, ps, Coventry, 1-pt 145.00

Dbl Eagle, GII-70, yel-olive, sm, ps, Coventry, 1-pt 150.00
Dbl Eagle, GII-71, yel-olive, sm, ps, Coventry, ½-pt 160.00
Dbl Eagle, GII-81, yel-amber, ps, sm, 1840s, 1-pt 240.00
Eagle Liberty/Oak Tree, GII-60, gr, ps, rm, 1830s, ½-pt 850.00
Eagle w/Banner in Beak, GII-143, yel-gr, calabash 200.00
Eagle w/Shield/Dyottville, GII-38, aqua, sm, ps, 1840s, 1-pt 100.00
Eagle/Anchor, GII-67, aqua, dbl cm, New London, ½-pt 260.00
Eagle/Anchor, GII-67, orange-amber, New London, ½-pt 425.00
Eagle/Anchor, GII-68, bright orange-amber, New London, 1-pt ..425.00
Eagle/Anchor, GII-68, lt gr, New London, chip, 1-pt 150.00
Eagle/Anchor, GII-68, yel w/amber streak, New London, 1-pt ...500.00
Eagle/Cornucopia, GII-69, aqua, ps, sm, 1830s, ½-pt 300.00
Eagle/Cornucopia, GII-73, dk gold-yel, Keene, flake, 1-pt 200.00
Eagle/Cornucopia, GII-74, brilliant yel-gr, sm, ps, 1-pt 400.00
Eagle/Flag, GII-48, dk emerald gr, sm, ps, 1830s, 1-qt 2,100.00
Eagle/Medallion, GII-23, aqua, sm, ps, KY, 1-pt 450.00
Eagle/Morning-Glory, GII-19, aqua, Midwest, 1-pt 195.00
Eagle/Morning-Glory, GII-19, brn rockingham, 1850s, 1-pt, NM ..125.00
Eagle/Westford Glass, GII-65, yel-olive, dbl cm, ½-pt 230.00
Eagle/Willington Glass, GII-61, dk olive gr, cm, 1-qt 170.00
Eagle/Willington Glass, GII-61, orange-amber, dbl cm, 1-qt 195.00
Eagle/Willington Glass, GII-61, yel-olive, sb, 1-qt 180.00
Eagle/Willington Glass, GII-62, emerald gr, sl cm, sb, 1-pt 300.00
Eagle/Willington Glass, GII-62, red-amber, dbl cm, 1-qt 280.00
Eagle/Willington Glass, GII-63, dk red-amber, dbl cm, ½-pt 180.00
Eagle/Willington Glass, GII-63, forest gr, dbl cm, sb, ½-pt 130.00
Eagle/Willington Glass, GII-63, olive gr, sm, ps, ½-pt, EX 130.00
Eagle/Willington Glass, GII-63, yel-olive, dbl cm, sb, ½-pt 180.00
Eagle/Willington Glass, GII-64, gold-amber, dbl cm, 1-pt 170.00
Eagle/Willington Glass, GII-64, olive-amber, am, sb, 1-pt 120.00
Eagle/Willington Glass, GII-64, yel-olive, dbl cm, 1-pt 150.00
Flora Temple (horse), GXIII-21, med puce, am, hdl 150.00
Flora Temple (horse), GXIII-22, ginger ale, att Whitney, 1-pt ...425.00
Franklin/Dyott, GI-95, aqua, Kensington, 1-pt, NM 220.00
Franklin/Dyott, GI-96, aqua, sm, ps, Kensington, 1-qt 150.00
Gen Jackson/Eagle, GI-65, aqua, JT& Co, 1829-32, 1-pt 600.00
Gen Lafayette/Eagle, GI-92, aqua, Knox & McKee, 1-pt 4,250.00
Gen Lafayette/Eagle, GI-92, brilliant lt gr, sm, ps, 1-pt 3,700.00
Gen Lafayette/Eagle, GI-93, med emerald gr, 1-pt 2,650.00
Gen Washington/Eagle, GI-16, aquamarine, Kensington, 1-pt ..150.00
Granite Glass Co/Stoddard NH, GXV-7, amber, dbl cm, 1-pt ...125.00
Granite Glass Co/Stoddard NH, GXV-7, gold-amber, dbl cm, 1-pt .160.00
Hard Cider/Cabin, GX-22, ice bl, sm, ps, mouth chips, 1-pt ...1,300.00
Horse & Cart/Eagle, GV-9, bright yel-olive, sm, ps, 1-pt 240.00
Horse & Cart/Eagle, GV-9, olive-amber, sm, ps, Coventry, 1-pt ..160.00
Horseman/Hound, GXIII-17, yel-amber, dbl cm, sb, chip, 1-pt ..150.00
Jenny Lind/Glass Factory, GI-104, powder bl, calabash, 1-qt 360.00
Keene/P&W Sunburst, GVIII-8, yel-olive, sm, ps, ½-pt 225.00
Keene/P&W Sunburst, GVIII-9, olive gr, sm, ps, Keene, ½-pt 250.00
Keene/P&W Sunburst, GVIII-9, yel-olive, sm, ps, Keene, ½-pt .235.00
Kossuth/Sloop, GI-111, aqua, sm, ps, Bridgeton, 1-pt 180.00
Kossuth/Tree, GI-113, lt gr, am w/ring, ip, 1845-60, 1-qt 110.00
Kossuth/Tree, GI-113, lt gray-bl, sl cm, ps, calabash, 1-qt 450.00
Lafayette/DeWitt Clinton, GI-80, lt yel-olive, Coventry, 1-pt ...600.00
Lafayette/Liberty Cap, GI-85, yel-olive, sm, Coventry, 1-pt 225.00
Lafayette/Liberty Cap, GI-86, yel-olive, Coventry, ½-pt 400.00
Lowell Railroad/Eagle, GV-10, olive-amber, bruise, ½-pt 190.00
Lowell Railroad/Eagle, GV-10, yel-olive, sm, ps, ½-pt 230.00
Major Ringgold/Rough & Ready, GI-71, smoky gray tint, 1-pt ..275.00
Masonic Arch/Frigate Franklin, GIV-35, lt gr, sm, ps, 1-pt 1,200.00
Masonic/Eagle, GIV-1, bl-gr, tm, ps, Keene, 1-pt 270.00
Masonic/Eagle, GIV-1a, lt bl-gr, sm, ps, Keene, 1-pt 200.00
Masonic/Eagle, GIV-17, bright olive-gr, Keene, 1-pt 175.00
Masonic/Eagle, GIV-2, bright lt gr, att Keene, 1-pt 335.00

Masonic/Eagle, GIV-20, yel-olive, sm, ps, Keene, 1-pt 150.00
Masonic/Eagle, GIV-24, bright lt yel-amber, Keene, ½-pt 120.00
Masonic/Eagle, GIV-24, bright yel-olive, Keene, ½-pt 170.00
Masonic/Eagle, GIV-3, lt bl-gr, sm, Keene, chip, 1-pt 375.00
Masonic/Eagle, GIV-32, gold-yel w/olive tone, White, 1-pt 1,800.00
Masonic/Eagle, GIV-32, red-amber, sm, ps, White, stain, 1-pt ...260.00
Murdock & Cassel/Zanesville OH, GX-14, lt bl-gr, 1-pt 1,600.00
Scroll, GIX-10, bright bl-gr, sm, ps, flake, 1-pt 175.00
Scroll, GIX-10, gold-amber w/olive tones, sm, ps, 1-pt 350.00
Scroll, GIX-12, bright med olive, crude sm, ps, 1-pt, NM 550.00
Scroll, GIX-45, aqua, corset form, potstone, 1-pt 375.00
Scroll GIX-10, gold-amber, sm, ps, Am, 1840-60, 1-pt 320.00
Seeing Eye Masonic, GIV-43, bright med gr, cm, 1860s, 1-pt 110.00
Sheaf of Wheat/Grapes, GX-3, aqua, sm, ps, ½-pt 130.00
Sheaf of Wheat/Westford Glass, GXIII-35, yel olive-amber, 1-pt .100.00
Sheaf of Wheat/Westford Glass, GXIII-35, yel-amber, 1-pt 125.00
Sheaf of Wheat/Westford Glass, GXIII-37, dk olive gr, ½-pt 110.00
Sheaf of Wheat/Westford Glass, GXIII-37, dk yel-olive, ½-pt 825.00
Sheaf of Wheat/Westford Glass, GXIII-37, gold-amber, ½-pt 110.00
Soldier/Ballet Dancer, GXIII-13, dk yel-olive, Maryland, 1-pt ...750.00
Success to RR, GV-1, dk aqua, Lancaster, 1-pt, NM 220.00
Success to RR, GV-3, bright yel-olive, sm, ps, Keene, 1-pt 220.00
Success to RR, GV-5, forest gr, sm, ps, Mt Vernon, 1-pt 160.00
Success to RR, GV-5, olive-amber, sm, ps, att Mt Vernon, 1-pt .200.00
Success to RR, GV-6, gold-amber w/olive tone, Coventry, 1-pt .180.00
Success to RR, GV-6, yel-olive, sm, ps, Coventry, 1-pt 230.00
Success to RR/Eagle, GV-8, yel-olive, sm, ps, Coventry, 1-pt 230.00
Sunburst, GVIII-16, bright yel-olive, sm, ps, Coventry, ½-pt 260.00
Sunburst, GVIII-18, yel-olive, sm, ps, Coventry, ½-pt 275.00
Sunburst, GVIII-2, clear, sm, ps, New England, 1-pt 290.00
Sunburst, GVIII-2, lt gr, sm, ps, att Keene, 1-pt 400.00
Sunburst, GVIII-29, med emerald gr, beveled corners, 8¼" 150.00
Sunburst, GVIII-5, bright yel-olive, sm, ps, 1815-30, 1-pt 800.00
Taylor/Masterson Eagle, GI-77, aquamarine, Midwest, 1-qt 950.00
Traveler's Companion/Sheaf of Wheat, GXIV-1, gold-amber, 1-qt 95.00
Traveler's Companion/Sheaf of Wheat, GXIV-1, yel-olive, 1-qt ..130.00
Union Glass Works New London CT, GXV-23, lt bl-gr, cm, 1-pt .430.00
Washington/Classical Bust, GI-25, aquamarine, Bridgeton, 1-qt ..200.00
Washington/Eagle, GI-10, aqua, sm, ps, 1830-40, 1-pt 425.00
Washington/Eagle, GI-11, aqua, sm, Am, 1830s, 1-pt 650.00
Washington/Eagle, GI-16, aqua, sm, ps, Kensington, 1-pt 120.00
Washington/Eagle, GI-26, aqua, sm, ps, 1830s, 1-qt 150.00
Washington/Jackson, GI-34, yel-olive, sm, ps, ½-pt 320.00
Washington/Sailing Ship, GI-28, dense amber, Albany, 1-pt 600.00
Washington/Taylor, GI-17, yel-gr, sm, Baltimore, chip, 1-pt 350.00
Washington/Taylor, GI-37, med sapphire bl, Dyottville, 1-qt 475.00
Washington/Taylor, GI-39, med bl-gr, sm, ps, Dyottville, 1-qt ..160.00
Washington/Taylor, GI-40, bright med gr, Dyottville, 1-pt 230.00
Washington/Taylor, GI-42, cobalt, sm, ps, Dyottville, 1-qt 3,400.00
Washington/Taylor, GI-43, dk gold-amber, Dyottville, 1-qt ...1,100.00
Washington/Taylor, GI-43, yel-olive, Dyottville, 1-qt 450.00
Washington/Taylor, GI-51, lt to med sapphire bl, am, 1-qt 450.00
Will You...Drink/...(duck) Swim?, GXIII-27, aquamarine, 1-qt ..110.00

Food Bottles and Jars

Ketchup, Shriver's Oyster...Baltimore, deep emerald gr, 7½" 575.00
Olive, EC Hazard & Co...NY, yel-gr, sb, tm, ca 1870, 9" 70.00
Peppersauce, aquamarine, cathedral arches, hexagonal, 10¾" 265.00
Peppersauce, deep amber, sb, tm, ca 1900, 9⅜" 210.00
Peppersauce, S&P Pat App For, med teal, sb, tm, 8¼" 55.00
Peppersauce, St Louis Spice Mills, lt yel-gr, arches, 8¾" 500.00
Peppersauce, WKL&Co, aqua, cathedral arches, 10" 250.00
Pickle, aqua, cathedral arches, sb, lt haze, 1870s, 14" 130.00

Pickle, med emerald gr, cathedral arches, ca 1870, 13½" **400.00**
Pickle, WK Lewis & Co Boston, med gr, ip, rm, 1845-60, 10¾" .**325.00**
Pickle, Yarnall Bros, clear, 6-sided, sb, rm, 1890s, 13¼" **400.00**
Preserve, WM&P NY, aquamarine, rolled cm, ps, 1840-60, 7¼" ..**90.00**
Sauce, olive-amber, 8-sided, sb, am, European, 1850s, 8" **90.00**

Ink Bottles

Bertinguoit, olive-amber, domed, sm, ps, 2x2⅜" **150.00**
Blown, fiery opal, beveled corners, mc enamel, Germany, 2" **150.00**
Blown, wht opaque, beveled corners, ps, tm, mc enamel, 2¼" **250.00**
Blown, 28 vertical ribs, ps, flared tm, 1830-50, 1½" **170.00**
B3m, GII-18, dk olive amber, cylindrical, 1½x2¼" **125.00**
B3m, GIII-29, med olive-amber, disk mouth, Keene, 1½x2¼" ...**130.00**
Carter's No 1, cobalt, orig pouring cap, NM label, 9½" **95.00**
Carter/Carter, cobalt, sb, am, orig pouring cap, label, 9¾" **140.00**
Cone form, med emerald gr, vertical ribs, label panel, 2¼" **425.00**
Encre de la Grande Vertu Bordaux, dk puce, ps, 1840s, 2" **275.00**
Fahnstocks Neutral Ink, 6 concave panels, 1840-50, 4⅛" **350.00**
Farley, yel-amber, 8-sided, open p, sm, Am, 1830-40, 1¾" **375.00**
Fred D Alling's..., stoneware, molded spout, w/labels, 7⅜" **100.00**
G&R's Am Writing Fluid, aqua, cone shape, 1835-50, 2" **550.00**
Geometric, GIII-29, b3m, yel-amber, tm, ps, 1820s, 1⅝" **110.00**
Harrison's Columbian, cobalt, rm, Am, 1835-1850, 2" **375.00**

Harrison's Columbia Ink, deep sapphire blue, flanged lip, iron pontil, light stain, 1-gallon, 11⅜x6¼", $11,000.00.

Harrison's Columbian Ink/Pat, aqua, 12-sided, am, 7¼" **160.00**
Higgs, lt gr-aqua, 12-sided, rm, ps, 1835-50, 2¾" **400.00**
Hoover Phila, med emerald gr, fm, Am, 1840-50, 6" **200.00**
J Gundry/Cincinnati, aqua, 12-sided, 1835-50, 3" **650.00**
J&IEM, yel-amber, igloo form, 1860-70, 1¾" **250.00**
NE Plus Ultra Fluid, aqua, house form, 2⅝" **350.00**
Pat Harrison's Columbian, aqua, 12-sided, am, 1830-50, 6" **250.00**
Paul's...NY Chicago, cobalt, sb, tm, orig labels, 9¼" **210.00**
Pitkin type, dk olive-amber, 36-rib swirl, sq, 1⅜" **650.00**
Pitkin type, forest gr, 36-rib swirl, New England, 1⅝x2⅛" **500.00**
S Fine Blk Ink, bright med gr, rm, ps, 1830-60, 2⅞" **425.00**
Salt glaze stoneware, gray-brn, 2-hole, 1850s, 1⅞x3½" dia **60.00**
Sewer tile, emb 'button' decor, center filler hole, 4" dia **35.00**
SI Comp, aqua, cottage form, sb, tm, orig label, 2½" **450.00**
Soapstone, blk, 3 quill holes, filler opening, 1790s, 2⅞" **220.00**
SS Stafford's...Made in USA, cobalt, NM labels, 1900s, 9½" **110.00**
Teakettle, cobalt, sb, orig neck ring, 1870-90, 2" **325.00**
Teakettle, dbl font, pottery bird's nest, mc, 1880s, 2" **200.00**
Umbrella, med yel-gr, 8-sided, sb, rm, 1850-70, 2½" **500.00**
Umbrella, olive-amber, 8-sided, sm, Am, 1830-50, 2⅜" **120.00**

Umbrella, orange-amber, 8-sided, sm, 1830-50, 2⅝" **140.00**
Umbrella, yel-amber, 8-sided, ps, sm, Am, 1830-50, 2⅜" **120.00**
Umbrella, yel-olive, octagonal, New England, 1830-60, 2¼" **220.00**
Underwood, cobalt, sb, gm, orig metal cap, 1890s-1910, 7" **80.00**
Underwood Inks 32-oz, cobalt, sb, stain, 1900s, 9⅞" **70.00**
Ward's, deep emerald gr, am w/pour spout, sb, Am, 1860s, 8" **200.00**
Warren's Congress, aqua, 8-sided, ps, rm, 1835-50, 2¾" **400.00**
Wood's Blk Ink Portland, root beer-amber, cone form, 2⅜" **2,800.00**

Medicine Bottles

C Brinckerhoffs Health Restorative, dk olive-gr, ps, 7¼" **350.00**
Couleys Fountain of Health..., aqua, am, haze, 1840s, 9½" **130.00**
CW Merchant Chemist, emerald gr, am, sb, 7¼" **165.00**
DR J Blackman's Genuine Healing Balsam, clear, 8-sided, 5½" **50.00**
Dr Steph Jewett's Celebrated Pulmonary Elixer, aqua, 5⅜" **125.00**
NY College of Medicina Pharmacy..., aqua, rm, cleaned, 5⅝" **75.00**
RRR Radway's Ready Relief $1 NY, aquamarine, sl cm, ps, 8" ..**100.00**
Swaim's Panacea Philada, aqua, am, ps, haze, 1840s, 7¾" **200.00**
Swaim's Panacea Philada, deep olive-gr, am, ps, 1840s, 7¾" **220.00**
Swaim's Panacea Philada, lt apple gr, ps, crude, 1840s, 8" **525.00**
Swaim's Vermifuge Dysentery Cholora..., aqua, rm, 4" **60.00**
USA Hosp Dept, bright sapphire bl w/cobalt streaks, 4⅞" **425.00**
Westlake's Vegetable Ointment, ice bl, sq, rm, 1840s, 3" **80.00**

Mineral Water and Soda Bottles

Registered The City Bottling Co., Peoria, Ill, clear, Hutchinson type, 7⅜", $15.00; McMaster & Derge, IBW, Peoria, Ill, amethyst, Hutchinson type, 6¾", $15.00.

B&G San Francisco Superior Mineral Water, med emerald gr, 7" .**275.00**
BW&Co/NY, cobalt, heavy cm, ip, Am, 1845-60, ½-pt **280.00**
Chase & Co...Water San Francisco Cal, deep emerald gr, 7¼" ...**125.00**
DS&Co San Francisco, cobalt, sb, am, 7⅛" **210.00**
EL Billing's Sac City Geiser Soda, yel-lime gr, sb, am, 7⅛" **275.00**
Highrock Congress Spring, bl-gr, sl cm w/ring, stain, 1-pt **195.00**
Highrock Congress Spring, yel-olive, sl cm, 1860-80, 1-pt, NM .**120.00**
Home Soda Works..., aqua, Hutchinson, mug base, tm, 7⅛" **425.00**
JN Gerdes SF Mineral Water, deep gr-aqua, 8-sided, 7¼" **80.00**
John Clark, yel-olive, sl cm w/ring, sb, high shoulder, 1-qt **110.00**
JP Plummer Boston, cobalt, cm, ip, squat soda form, ½-pt **275.00**
Missisquoi A Springs, emerald gr, cylindrical, 1870s, 1-qt **80.00**
Oahu Soda Works AIEA Oahu..., lt gr, Hutchinson, sb, 7⅝" **110.00**
Owen Casey Eagle Soda Works Sac City, deep yel-olive, 7" **525.00**
Owen Casey Eagle Soda Works Sac City, med cobalt, sb, 7⅜" **60.00**
Superior Mineral Water, cobalt, ip, am, 1855-60, 7¼" **70.00**
Syracuse Springs Excelsior, dk red-amber, sl cm, sb, 1-pt **160.00**
Tarr Smith & Clark Boston Mineral Water, bright gr, ½-pt **145.00**
Taylor & Co Valparaiso Chili Soda..., med bl-gr, ip, 7¼" **275.00**
The Excelsior Water, med yel-gr, 8-sided, ip, am, 7¼" **180.00**
Washington Lithia Well Mineral Water, aquamarine, 1-pt **80.00**

Poison Bottles

GM Rhode's Grand Rapids, Poison on neck, clear, 6½" 75.00
Henry K Wampole & Co Phila, cobalt, orig star label, 2½" 200.00
Hetherington 42nd Street NY CLG&Co..., bright yel-gr, 4⅛" ...250.00
JG Godding...Apothecaries Boston MA, cobalt, 1900s, 7½" 500.00
Mercury Bichloride...Upjohn...MI, yel w/amber tint, 1900, 3¼" ...110.00
Norwich Pharmiacal Co Norwich Conn, cobalt, orig label, 3⅝" ..110.00
Not To Be Taken, deep peacock bl, sb, tm, ca 1900, 7⅝" 95.00
Not To Be Taken Rd No 4617701, yel-gr, sb, 1890-1920, 3" 30.00
Owl Drug Co, owl sitting on mortar, clear, 4¾" 100.00

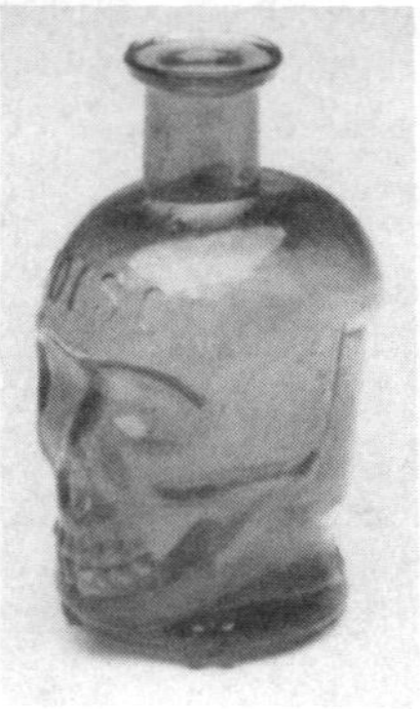

Poison embossed at top of skull figural, cobalt, tooled lip, smooth base, flakes, 4⅛", $1,300.00.

Poison, cobalt, dmn & lattice pattern, 1900s, 7" 115.00
Poison emb on skull form, cobalt, ca 1880-1900, 4⅛", NM 425.00
Poison Sun Drug Co Poison, yel-gr, sb, tm, 1900s, 3⅜" 275.00
Poison Tinct Iodine/skull & crossbones, cobalt, sb, 2⅛" 70.00
Quilted, cobalt, cylindrical, sb, fm, 1880-1900, 10" 350.00
Roman Inc CLG&Co Pat Appl'd For, bright yel-gr, 1900s, 5" ...625.00

Sarsaparilla Bottles

Bush's Smilax, aqua, ps, tm, stain, 1840-55, 10" 275.00
Dr Townsend's...Albany NY, dk olive-amber, am, ps, 1830s, 9⅝" .175.00
Dr Townsend's...Albany NY, emerald gr, ip, am, 9⅞" 140.00
Dr Townsend's...Albany NY, gr w/yel tint, ip, am, 9⅜" 110.00
Dr Townsend's...Albany NY, olive-amber, am, ps, 1840s, 9½" ...135.00
Dr Townsend's...Albany NY No 1, olive gr, ps, am, 9¼" 225.00
Old Dr J Townsend's NY, med emerald gr, am, ip, 1840s, 9½" ...210.00
Old Dr J Townsend's NY, med gr, ip, am, 9¾" 155.00

Snuff Bottles

E Roome Troy NY, med olive-amber, ps, flared tm, 1830s, 4⅜" .125.00
E Roome Troy NY, yel-amber, ps, flared tm, 4¼" 210.00
JJ Mapes No 61 Front St NY, med yel-amber, flared tm, 4⅜" 375.00
JM Venable & Co Petersburg VA, amber, sb, flared tm, 4¼" 160.00
Med amber, sq w/beveled corner panels, ps, flared tm, 4¼" 75.00
Med amber w/olive tone, beveled corners, flared tm, 4½" 45.00
Med yel-amber, beveled corners, ps, flared tm, 4¼" 110.00
Olive-amber, rectangular, beveled corners, 1800s, 6" 125.00
W emb on sb, amber w/yel tone, beveled corners, 4⅛" 75.00
Yel w/amber tone, beveled corners, ps, sm, 1800-20, 4⅜" 135.00

Spirits Bottles

AAA GMCMF Old Valley Whiskey, med gold-amber, 1870s, 8" .525.00
AM Bininger 19 Broad St NY...1848, amber, bbl form, 8⅛" 195.00
AM Bininger...19 Broad St NY, gold-amber, cannon bbl, 12½" .375.00
Baldwin's Celebrated Wines & Brandies, smoky clear, 11⅛" 75.00
Bell of Anderson...Sour Mash, milk glass, emb star, 8⅛" 75.00
Black Cat (seated cat) Rare & Old Whiskey, orange pnt, 11½" .275.00
Budweiser Cafe Bonded Whiskies, sun-colored amethyst, 6¼" ...100.00
Caspers Whiskey...NC People, cobalt, tm, sb, 1890s, 12" 325.00
Chesley's Jockey Club Whiskey, amethyst tone, sb, tm, 12" 200.00
Chestnut Grove Whiskey Co, amber, am & hdl, stain, 8¾" 200.00
CP Moorman...Manuf'r...Bourbon..., amber to yel-amber, 7⅝" ..350.00
Cyrus Eaton & Co Denver, med amber, sb, am, 1880s, 12⅛" 450.00
Davy Crocket Pure Old Burbon, med amber, sb, tm, 1890s, 12" .100.00
EP Middletown & Bro Wheat 1825 Whiskey, olive-amber, 9½" ..130.00
Good Old Bourbon in a Hog's..., med amber, pig form, 6¾" 100.00
Griffith Hyatt & Co Baltimore, med root beer-amber, 7¼" 450.00
H Pharazyn, gold-amber, inward rm, sb, Indian figural, 12½" 375.00
Henry Campe & Co Wholesale Liquor Dealers, amethyst, 11⅞" ..100.00
JT Gayen Altona, dk red-amber, rnd cm, cannon bbl form, 14" .800.00
L Eppinger Portland, clear, sb, tm, 1882-92, 6⅛" 95.00
Loheide & Vorrath Wines & Liquors, orange-amber, sb, 11" 70.00
London Jockey Club House Gin, jockey on horse, gr, cm, 9" 250.00
Miller's Extra...Old Bourbon, gold-amber, 1870s, 7⅜" 425.00
Monongahela CH Old Rye Whiskey, olive-amber, sb, 9½" 170.00
Phoenix Old Bourbon Naber Alfs & Brune, med amber, sb, 11¾" .560.00
Phoenix Old Trade Mark Bourbon, orange-amber, haze, 6¼" 180.00
Phoenix Whiskey Naber Alfs & Brune, med orange-amber, 11⅞" .275.00
The Olive Tree, gin, olive, crude sl cm, Netherlands, 9¾" 220.00
Turner Bros NY, deep root beer-amber, bbl form, 10" 200.00
Wm H Spears & Co Old Pioneer Whiskey, clear, sb, tm, 12" 210.00
1879 Esprit Pour Tous Nouvelle...Depose, book form, 8⅞" 190.00

Miscellaneous

Blacking, olive gr, sq, ps, sm, ca 1830, 4½" 80.00
Blacking, olive-amber, sq, ps, sm, 1830s, 4¼" 60.00
Kidney, deep olive gr, ps, am, Dutch, 1750-1780, 7⅞" 425.00
Lavender salts, Goetting & Co, see California Perfume Co
Mallet, deep olive-amber, ps, am, England, 1740-55, 8¾" 250.00
Mallet, med olive, ps, am, stain, England, 1730-45, 6½x4" 95.00
Mallet, med olive gr, ps, am, England, 1735-55, 9¾" 275.00
Sweet 16, Goetting & Co, see California Perfume Co
Utility, dk amber w/olive tone, cylindrical, 1830s, 6¼" 55.00
Utility, gold amber, expanded neck w/rm, att Stoddard, 8⅜" 120.00
Utility, med emerald gr, beveled corners, ps, 8¼" 220.00
Utility, wht opal, sm, ps, octagonal, Am, 1840-60, 4⅝" 100.00
Utility, yel-amber, cylindrical, fm, 1830s, 5⅝" 90.00
Utility, yel-amber w/olive tone, ps, am, 1830s, 5¾" 75.00

Boxes

Boxes have been used by civilized man since ancient Egypt and Rome. Down through the centuries, specifically designed containers have been made from every conceivable material. Precious metals, papier-mache, battersea, Oriental lacquer, and wood have held riches from the treasuries of kings, snuff for the fashionable set of the last century, China tea, and countless other commodities. See also Toleware; specific manufacturers.

Apple, pine, primitive, some renailing, 11¼x12¼" 130.00
Band, bentwood, worn floral wallpaper, NH, 12x16" 220.00
Band, cb w/Oriental scenic wallpaper, 1700s, damage, 17" 360.00
Band, cb w/wallpaper covering, lt wear/rpr, 18" 195.00
Band, wood/cb/wallpaper, 1833 newspaper lining, 20" 440.00
Beech, mc floral decor, pin hinges on lid, wear, 8⅝" 560.00
Bentwood, bl pnt w/red & gr stripes, pnt rose on lid, 4½" 75.00

Bentwood, bl-gray pnt, bail hdl, w/lid, 11½" dia 70.00
Bentwood, mc birds on old gr rpt, 5¾" dia 35.00
Bentwood, old red pnt, 4¼x8¾" dia 380.00
Bentwood, old red rpt, bail hdl, 11½" dia 200.00
Bentwood, old wht rpt, age cracks, bail hdl, 11¼" dia 250.00
Bentwood, orig blk & red grpt, stencil decor, PA, 11¾" dia 260.00
Bentwood, orig dk gray-bl pnt, w/lid, 8" dia 250.00
Bentwood, orig red pnt w/pnt mc 'jewels,' 3¼" dia 95.00
Bentwood, pine, orig bl w/mc floral, laced seams, 9½" 300.00
Bentwood, red traces, copper tacks, bail hdl, 6¾x12" dia 250.00
Bentwood, red w/blk pnt traces, swivel hdl, w/lid, 5¼x7½" 360.00
Bible, dvtl softwood, cvd design, strap hinges, rpt, 22x17x10" 140.00
Bible, mahog, bracket ft, dvtl, iron strap hinges, 7x18x15" 1,000.00
Bible, oak, relief-cvd facade, rprs, English, 26½" 275.00
Black ball, walnut, trn hdl, w/label & marbles, 9½" 110.00
Brass & jade, mk China, 6" 175.00
Brass covering, tooled decor, losses, 17x19x26" 155.00
Brass filigree, glass jewels, Middle East, 1¾", 3¼", pr 110.00
Brass over wood, emb griffins/foliage, '10s, 2x4½x3½" 50.00
Brass w/eng scene, wooden base, velvet lined, 20th C, 3x10½" 65.00
Brass w/mc Oriental-style floral enameling, 20th C, 6½" 80.00
Bride's, PA Dutch heart/flower/1870 decor, iron hinges, 23", G .200.00
Bride's, pine, orig blk pnt w/mc florals, inscr, 19" 2,500.00
Bride's, pine, orig red pnt w/mc florals, Germany, 19½" 1,100.00
Candle, dvtl, orig brn/red zigzag patterned pnt, 14¼" 550.00
Candle, hardwood, rnd crest, front lid, rpr, 16½" 275.00
Candle, mahog, dvtl, pine bottom, ca 1820s, old rpr, 9¾" 250.00
Candle, pine, orig red pnt w/mc striping, 14" 320.00
Candle, pine, red pnt traces, slant lid, pegs, 6¼x13x6" 110.00
Candle, pine & poplar w/old red, sliding lid, 19¼" 185.00
Candle, tin cylinder, 2 strap hangers, 14x4¼" dia, EX 350.00
Document, pnt pine, New England, 1700s, 7x10½x7½" 825.00
Dome top, beech, orig red-brn pnt w/floral decor, rpr, 13½" 660.00
Dome top, bench w/worn orig pnt, floral & bird decor, 19" 195.00

Dome top box, ochre vinegar paint with umber graining, wrought iron escutcheon and side handles, America, early 1800s, 11½x25¾x13", $750.00.

Dome top, dvtl, orig vinegar grpt, initialed/1822, 13" 360.00
Dome top, dvtl pine, bl sponging on lt ground, lock, 30" 330.00
Dome top, pine, orig bl pnt w/mc floral, wear, 7½" 165.00
Dome top, pine w/grpt & mc foliage, wire nails, 10⅜" 165.00
Dome top, pine w/old red graining, iron hasp, 15" 110.00
Dome top, poplar, orig blk grpt w/red decor, 28" 635.00
Ebonized w/enameled brass Egyptian Revival trim, 8" 115.00
Glass, flowers/bee, wht on ruby, brass hinges & ft, 5" dia 325.00
Hat, covered in swag & tassel wallpaper, ca 1830, 12x19½" 600.00
Jade lid w/ivory floral inlay, brass base, unmk, 11" 300.00
Jewel, gilded brass, beveled glass lid, triangular, 10" 130.00
Knife, dvtl curly maple, handmade repro w/some age, 20x8" 225.00
Knife, Hepplewhite mahog w/inlay medallion, 14" 660.00

Knife, mahog veneer w/inlay, 1800s, 9½x14½x9" 770.00
Knife, oak, dvtl, English, 17¾x10" 95.00
Knife, poplar w/old varnish, brn vertical stripes, 9x13" 50.00
Leather bound w/brass stud trim, bail hdl, lock, 8" 200.00
Mahog w/inlaid marquetry stars on 4 sides & lid, 8x3½x8¾" 180.00
Marquetry, 2 dogs in figured veneer, mirror, 20th-C, 8⅜" 55.00
Metal, painting-on-ivory inset in lid, octagonal, 3½" 325.00
Pine, dvtl, brass hinges & lock, 1850s, 5¾x7⅝x12" 80.00
Pine, orig red pnt w/blk & yel striping, 6x11x17", EX 130.00
Pine w/worn gray & blk rpt, short ft, molded edge, 14x14x15½" ..85.00
Pipe, mahog, truncated case w/cut-out crest, English, 20½" 330.00
Poplar, orig grpt w/gold striping/mc florals, wire nails, 18" 550.00
Poplar, orig yel pnt w/mc striping & foliage, 2-drawer, 16" 1,650.00
Salt, pine w/dk pnt over gr, dvtl, lift lid, 9x9½x7" 138.00
Scouring, pine, gr pnt traces, wire nails, 7x12", EX 30.00
Sewing, pine, chip cvg, trn spool holder, brn grpt, 11x10x10" ...300.00
Spice, cherry, dvtl, 4-part int, sliding lid, rfn, 9" 110.00
Spice, cherry & pine, dvtl, compartmentalized, 10¼x6⅝" 150.00
Spice, hardwood, 11-drawer, porc pulls, wire nails, 25x10" 350.00
Spice, poplar, old red stain, dvtl, hinged lid, 12½" 770.00
Tobacco, brass, tooled lid, rectangular, 3½" 85.00
Verdigris bronze & silver w/monogram, mk, Pat '12, 8¾" 115.00
Writing, ebony inlay w/brass & figured wood, Fr, 10x12½" 250.00
Writing, figured mahog, brass bound, English, 16" 225.00
Writing, mahog w/brass fittings, 15¾" 165.00

Boyd Crystal Art Glass

Boyd Crystal Art Glass is a small but productive glass factory located in Cambridge, Ohio. It was established in 1978 when the Boyd family bought out the Degenhart factory. Over the years Boyd has produced more than 200 molds; while many were their own design, they acquired others from glasshouses no longer in business. All the Boyd pieces are marked with a distinct logo of a 'B' in diamond. Further dating is possible because a line was added under the diamond in 1983, and an additional line was added above the diamond in 1988. In September 1993 another line was added, this one on the right of the diamond. Boyd's glass is prized because of the colors they formulated and the fact that once a piece is produced in a particular color it will not be produced in that color again, even if that color is brought back years later. All pieces are hand pressed from glass that is from a single-day tank. Colors are made for about six weeks or less, thus limiting the number of pieces that can be produced in that color. More than three hundred different colors have been used and developed by the Boyds. Much like Degenhart glass, the colors can be confusing and difficult to identify. Exceptional slags and hand-painted pieces can command up to 50% higher prices. Satin glass variations are priced 10% to 30% higher when they can be found.

In the following listings, (N) indicates a mold that was new in 1993-94. (R) indicates a yearly special edition of a retired piece. Our advisor for this category is Joyce Pringle; she is listed in the Directory under Texas.

Airplane, Cardinal Red, 4x3¼" 17.50
Airplane, Cobalt, 4x3¼" 16.50
Airplane, Vaseline, 4x3¼" 17.50
Artie the Penguin, Alexandrite, 3" 8.25
Artie the Penguin, Vaseline, 3" 12.50
Bingo the Deer, Alexandrite (R) 8.00
Bow Slipper, Cardinal Red 12.00
Bow Slipper, Ruby 24.50
Bow Slipper, Waterloo (Blue) 7.25
Brian Bunny, Cobalt Carnival, 2" (R) 8.25

Brian Bunny, Sky Top Blue, 2" 18.00
Bulldog Head, Heather 12.00
Bunny Salt, Buckeye 6.25
Bunny Salt, Cashmere Pink 7.25
Bunny Salt, Confetti 20.00
Candy the Carousel Horse, Nile Green (N) 6.25
Candy the Carousel Horse, Waterloo 6.25
Cat Slipper, 'OC' 26.50
Cat Slipper, Classic Black Slag 11.00
Cat Slipper, Mint Green 22.50
Cat Slipper, Persimmon Slag 18.50
Cat Slipper, Waterloo (Blue) 8.25
Chick Salt, Alexandrite Carnival 7.25
Chick Salt, Bermuda (Red) 18.00
Chick Salt, Pebble Beige 6.25
Chick Salt, Robin Egg Blue 20.00
Chuckles the Clown, Confetti 12.50
Duck Salt, Cardinal Red, HP 10.00
Duck Salt, Spinnaker Blue 6.25
Elizabeth Doll, Lime Carnival 27.50
Elizabeth Doll, Nile Green 8.25
Fuzzy Bear, Alexandrite Carnival (R) 12.50
Fuzzy Bear, Ruby 30.00
Hand Dish, John's Surprise (Blue) 20.00
Hand Dish, Nile Green 4.00
Heart Jewel Box, Opaline Blue Swirl 38.50
Heart Jewel Box, Waterloo (Blue) 12.50
Heart Toothpick, Vaseline 7.50
Hen Covered Dish, Chocolate, 5" 50.00
Hen Covered Dish, Waterloo (Blue), 5" 20.00
JB Scotty, Cobalt, 3¼x2½" 22.50
JB Scotty, Cobalt Carnival, 3¼x2½" (R) 10.00
JB Scotty, Sunburst, 3¼x2½" 22.50
Jeremy Frog, Cobalt, 2¼" 6.25
Jeremy Frog, Ruby Red, 2¼" 7.25
Jeremy Frog, Vaseline, 2¼" (N) 6.25
Joey the Horse, Alexandrite Carnival, 4" 16.50
Joey the Horse, Sandpiper (Tan), 4" 16.00
Kitten on a Pillow, Dogwood Slag 18.00
Kitten on a Pillow, Firefly 25.00
Louise Doll, Confetti 28.50
Louise Doll, Flame 35.00
Lucky the Unicorn, Custard, 3" 18.00
Mini Vase, Firefly 18.00
Miss Cotton (Kitten Not on Pillow), Celery 8.00
Owl, Candy Swirl 14.50
Owl, Cardinal Red 10.50
Owl Bell, Pocono Blue 10.00
Patrick Balloon Bear, Cashmere Pink 7.50
Patrick Balloon Bear, Country Red 10.00
Patrick Balloon Bear, Enchantment 24.50
Sammy Squirrel, Alexandrite, 3" 10.00
Sammy Squirrel, Autumn Beige, 3" 7.50
Sammy Squirrel, Crown Tuscan Carnival, 3" ...9.25
Skate Boot, Persimmon, 4" 15.00
Skate Boot, Snow Slag, 4" 38.50
Skippy (Dog), Cornsilk (Yellow) 5.00
Skippy (Dog), Mint Green 8.00
Tall Boot, Alexandrite Carnival 10.00
Taxi, Alexandrite 12.50
Taxi, Cobalt (N) 12.50
Tucker (Car), Cashmere Pink 11.00
Tucker (Car), Grape Parfait 12.50
Virgil Reversible Clown, Cobalt 10.00

Virgil Reversible Clown, Waterloo (Blue) (N) 10.00
Willie the Mouse, Classic Black (Satin) 8.00
Willie the Mouse, Primrose 6.00
Zak the Elephant, Flame (1st color in this mold), 3¼x4½" ...45.00
Zak the Elephant, Sandpiper, 3¼x4½" 15.00

Bradley and Hubbard

The Bradley and Hubbard Mfg. Company was a firm which produced metal accessories for the home. They operated from about 1860 until the early part of this century, and their products reflected both the Arts and Crafts and Art Nouveau influence. Their logo was a device with a triangular arrangement of the company name containing a smaller triangle and an Aladdin lamp. Our advisor for this category is Daniel Batchelor; he is listed in the Directory under New York.

Lamps

Table lamp, 16" octagonal shade with linear and geometric gridwork over green slag glass panels on hexagonal metal base, marked, #216, 10", $800.00.

Banquet, wireware shade/std/base, rpl glass insert, 24" 400.00
Chandelier, ldgl 21" spider web wht shade; rtcl bronze skirt 500.00
Conical 16" slag shade w/line & sqs gridwork, #222 base 2,000.00
Paneled 18" shade w/metal floral o/l; base w/glass panels 800.00
Piano, brass/wrought iron, frosted beaded drape 10" shade 550.00
Slag glass 18" 6-sided shade w/palm tree o/l; mk metal std 525.00

Miscellaneous

Andirons, CI winged griffin form, #9537, 20½" 2,500.00
Andirons, wrought iron, griffin face on disk, snake ft, 23" 770.00
Andirons, wrought iron, inverted Y-form w/ball finial, 16" 425.00
Bookends, copper, moon behind owl, dk gr patina, 6x4½" 150.00
Candlesticks, brass, std flares to wide base, mk, 12x6", pr 500.00
Mirror, brass easel bk w/openwork & mythological mask, 12" 225.00

Brass

Brass is an alloy consisting essentially of copper and zinc in variable proportions. It is a medium that has been used for both utilitarian items and objects of artistic merit. Today, with the inflated price of copper and the popular use of plastics, almost anything made of brass is collectible. Our advisor, Mary Frank Gaston, has compiled a lovely book, *Antique Brass and Copper*, with full-color photos; you will find her address in the Directory under Texas. See also Candlesticks.

Blow torch, 7½", $20.00.

Ashtray, bulbous, w/lid, weighted base, Nevasmok NY, 4x4"	15.00
Bottle, scent; crest top w/dauber, unmk, 3½"	47.50
Bowl, center post supports matchbox holder, 1½x5"	12.50
Bowl, eng floral, China, 10" dia	75.00
Box, slipper; emb decor on lid, w/casters, early 1900s	125.00
Bucket, circular, swing hdl, 17½" dia	110.00
Buckle, steel prongs, ornate stampings, Pat 1855, 1½" W	4.00
Can, watering; emb linear decor, hinged lid, Europe, 8x11"	75.00
Candelabra, 3-light, English, 1850s, 20x16", pr	800.00
Candle stand, half-cast w/central iron rod, 1850s, 35½"	300.00
Clock key, brass, E Ingraham & Co Bristol Conn, 2"	5.00
Coach lantern, handmade, mid-to-late 1800s, 15½"	125.00
Coal hod, pattern/punched designs, copper liner, 1850s, 22"	450.00
Coffeepot, sgn TKM, 4¾"	17.50
Colander, pan w/4 circular punched designs, iron hdl	125.00
Creamer & sugar bowl, ornate pewter hdls	150.00
Decanter, musical, glass insert, bail hdl, 8¼x3¼"	47.50
Dipper, 4½" bowl, 13" L	75.00
Dust pan, emb decor, English, 8½x8"	60.00
Ewer, eng decor, riveted hdl, Turkish, unmk, 11"	47.50
Figure, lady in top hat w/opera glasses, worn pnt, 5¾"	150.00
Fire dogs, spherical base, emb florals, Europe, 1850s, 8", pr	400.00
Firebk, sheet brass w/appl decor, English, 1850-90s, 29x18"	350.00
Fork, toasting; cast, British	15.00
Fork, toasting; twist hdl w/cat finial, 18"	40.00
Ginger jar, eng florals, mk India, ca 1900, 8"	48.00
Jardiniere, emb floral band, English, mid-1900s, 4x4"	40.00
Kettle, CI bail, Am, 1850s, 12x19"	300.00
Ladle, sm spout on bowl, pierced hdl, Am, late 1800s, 15"	75.00
Ladle, tasting; hand wrought iron hdl w/hook, 11½"	65.00
Lamp, kerosene, milk glass shade, mk Rayo, late 1800s, 20"	200.00
Lamp, student's, blk metal shade, Am, 1920s, 17½"	275.00
Nutcracker, Naughtie Nellie type, unmk, 4½"	20.00
Pail, milk or water; rim forms loops for bail hdl, 9x10"	100.00
Paper clip, enameled butterfly, recent, 4"	6.50
Roaster, chestnut; octagonal, English, 18½"	150.00
Sconce, emb bird on branch, English, 19x15"	200.00
Sconce, Medusa in high relief, English, 1830s, 26x18"	1,600.00
Spatula, hand-wrought iron hdl w/loop, shaped blade, 15"	70.00
Spittoon, graniteware pan fits beneath, all orig	58.00
Spoon, baptismal; English, late 1800s	12.00
Teapot, whistling bird, handmade, early, EX	75.00
Teaspoon, Am, 1800s	15.00
Tongs, dolphin head jaws, 15½"	125.00
Tongs, simple style, 10½" L	50.00

Tray, stippled decor, 1950s, 11x16"	65.00
Wig holder, 2-arm, porc knobs, trn wood hdl, 14½"	85.00

Brastoff, Sascha

The son of immigrant parents, Sascha Brastoff was encouraged to develop his artistic talents to the fullest, encouragement that was well taken, as his achievements aptly attest. Though at various times he has been a dancer, sculptor, Hollywood costume designer, jeweler, and painter, it is his ceramics that are today becoming highly regarded collectibles.

Sascha began his career in the United States in the late 1940s. In a beautiful studio built for him by his friend and mentor, Winthrop Rockefeller, he designed innovative wares that even then were among the most expensive on the market. All designing was done personally by Brastoff; he also supervised the staff which at the height of production numbered approximately 150. Wares signed with his full signature (not merely backstamped 'Sascha Brastoff') were personally crafted by him and are valued much more highly than those signed 'Sascha B.,' indicating work done under his supervision. Until his death in 1993, he continued his career in Los Angeles, in his latter years producing 'Sascha Holograms,' which were distributed by the Hummelwerk Company.

Another medium he used in his work was resin, and such pieces are also very collectible, though extremely scarce. In the listings below, all items are signed 'Sascha B.' unless otherwise indicated (full signature).

Our advisor for this category is Jack Chipman, author of *Collector's Encyclopedia of California Pottery*; Mr. Chipman is listed in the Directory under California.

Ashtray, bl & gold decor on wht, 5"	26.00
Ashtray, hooded, leaf decor on gr, mk	30.00
Ashtray, 2 igloos, 9½"	25.00
Bowl, Alaska, w/native, 5¾"	60.00
Bowl, ballerina, 3-ftd, 2¼x10"	75.00
Charger, thin wispy figure on platinum, mk front/bk, 17"	210.00
Cigarette holder, stylized bird on pipe shape, +matching tray	72.50
Dish, Alaska, polar bear, 3½" sq	25.00
Figure, circus elephant, platinum on lt bl matt, 7½", 8", pr	315.00
Figure, horse, platinum on pk matt, ca 1957, 10½"	187.50
Figure, poodle, satin-matt crackle, 7x9"	155.00
Mug, prancing horse hdl	120.00
Plaque, native mask, gold & blk, 9½"	155.00
Plate, grape cluster on gr, enamel on copper, 11"	75.00
Plate, pk, gold lustre swirl, dinner sz	10.00
Plate, Star Steed, hand decor by Sascha Brastoff, sgn, 10½"	250.00
Sculpture, horse head on wood base, satin-matt crackle, 7½"	225.00
Vase, abstract geometrics, 12"	100.00
Vase, abstract heads, 10"	160.00
Vase, bl resin, 10"	125.00
Vase, houses, full signature, 10"	185.00

Brayton, Laguna

Durlin E. Brayton made handcrafted vases, lamps, and dinnerware in a small kiln at his Laguna Beach, California, home in 1927. He soon married, and with his wife, Ellen Webster Grieve, as his partner, the small business became a successful commercial venture. They are most famous for their amusing, well-detailed figurines, some of which were commissioned by Walt Disney Studios. Though very successful even through the Depression years, with the influx of imported novelties that deluged the country after WWII, business began to decline. By 1968 the pottery was closed. For more information on this as well as many other potteries in the state, we recommend *The Collector's Ency-*

clopedia of California Pottery by Jack Chipman; he is listed in the Directory under California.

Bowl, serving; solid color, crude/handmade 40.00
Box, raised fruit on all sides, 3¼x5x3" 45.00
Chess piece, Castle, in-mold mk, 1946, 10½" 45.00
Cookie jar, Gingham Dog, +Gingham Dog/Calico Cat shakers .485.00
Dealer sign, Brayton Laguna 350.00

Dinnerware: Plate, 10½",
$30.00; Plate, 7½", $18.00;
Cup and saucer, $45.00.

Figurine, abstract man w/cat, blk satin-matt, ca 1957, 21" 195.00
Figurine, Blackamoor kneels w/bowl at shoulder, 16" 250.00
Figurine, Blk jazz band musicians, 4-pc set 1,100.00
Figurine, boy w/accordion, cobalt trim, ft wide 70.00
Figurine, cow, purple 95.00
Figurine, Gay Nineties, bartender w/2 men at bar, 9x9" 85.00
Figurine, Gay Nineties, Bedtime, couple in nightclothes, 8½" 85.00
Figurine, Gay Nineties, Honeymoon, couple in bathing suits 85.00
Figurine, Gay Nineties, 1 Year Later, couple w/baby 85.00
Figurine, Mexican man, 9" 85.00
Figurine, Mexican peasant couple, bsk & gr glossy, 12½" 80.00
Figurine, mule in harness, 7¼x10" 60.00
Figurine, peasant lady w/flower basket at waist, bl skirt 95.00
Figurine, Pluto howling, 6" 175.00
Figurine, Pluto sniffing, 3¼x5" 125.00
Figurine, Rosita, Mexican girl w/flower basket, 5½" 50.00
Figurine, 2 pirates fighting, stained bsk/color/crackle, 9", pr 275.00
Flower holder, peasant lady 45.00
Flower holder, Sally 30.00
Flowerpot, lightly ruffled rim, Durlin Brayton, 5½" 45.00
Mug, incised mk 25.00
Planter, girl holds apron wide, opening between hands 65.00
Planter, lady w/wolfhound, dtd 1943 ....65.00
Tile, cats on roof, 6-color, D Brayton, 4½" 95.00

Bread Plates and Trays

Bread plates and trays have been produced not only in many types of glass but in metal and pottery as well. Those considered most collectible were made during the last quarter of the 19th century from pressed glass with well-detailed embossed designs, many of them portraying a particularly significant historical event. A great number of these plates were sold at the 1876 Philadelphia Centennial Exposition by various glass manufacturers who exhibited their wares on the grounds. Among the themes depicted are the Declaration of Independence, the Constitution, McKinley's memorial 'It Is God's Way,' Remembrance of Three Presidents, the Purchase of Alaska, and various presidential campaigns, to mention only a few.

'L' numbers correspond with a reference book by Lindsey; 'S' refers to a book by Stuart. Our advisor for this category is Darlene Yohe; she is listed in the Directory under Arkansas.

American Flag, notched border, L-51 ....195.00
Balky Mule 85.00
Bates, L-375 ....65.00
Bible, Give Us This Day, 10¾x8" 60.00
Bunker Hill, L-44, 13¼x9" 75.00
Classic Warrior, 11" 110.00
Columbia, amber, L-54 ....165.00
Columbus 65.00
Constitution, L-43 ....95.00
Continental Hall, Give Us This Day..., 12¾" L 85.00
Crucifix center, Give Us This Day.., 13" L 150.00
Eggs in Sand, 12¼x7¾" 50.00
Eureka, S-1 ....30.00
GAR, L-505, 11" L 90.00
Garden of Eden, Give Us This Day, 12½x9" 35.00
Garfield Drape, We Mourn, dtd, L-303, 11½" 75.00
Garfield Memorial, L-302, 10" L 65.00
Garfield 101, frosted, L-300 ....85.00
George Washington, L-27 ....95.00
Give Us This Day, rosettes in center & border, rnd 75.00
Grant, Let Us Have Peace, vaseline, L-289 ....90.00
Grant Memorial, amber, L-288 ....75.00
Heroes of Bunker Hill 75.00
Horseshoe, single hdls, 13" L 60.00
In Remembrance 50.00
Independence Hall 95.00
It Is Pleasant To Labor, vintage decor, 12¾" dia 55.00
Kansas, plain center 32.00
Kasier Wilhelm, L-445 ....65.00
Knights of Labor, amber, L-512 ....145.00
Knights of Labor, bl, L-512, ca 1889 ....75.00
Last Supper 40.00
Liberty Bell, Signers, L-43 ....85.00
Maple Leaf, vaseline, oval, 13x9½" 85.00
McCormick Reaper, L-229 ....105.00
McKinley, Gold Standard, 10½" 265.00
McKinley, His Will Be Done, clear/frosted 55.00
McKinley, It Is God's Way, oval, 10⅜" 50.00
Mulberry, S-39 ....35.00
Nelly Bly, L-136, 12" L 200.00
Old State House, L-32, 12½" dia 65.00
Old State House, sapphire bl, L-31, rare 195.00
Polar Bear, ship, L-486, 16" 165.00
Pope Leo, S-142 ....45.00
Prescott Stark, Heroes of Bunker Hill, 13" L 100.00
Railroad, L-134 ....75.00
Rock of Ages, milk glass center, oval, L-236 ....165.00
Rose & Snow, 11¼x8¾" 135.00
Ruth the Gleaner, Gillinder 145.00
Scroll w/Flowers, 12" dia 35.00
Stippled Cherry, Our Daily Bread, 9½" 25.00
Symbolic, L-20 ....195.00
Texas Centennial, Alamo center 90.00
Three Presidents, In Remembrance, 12½x10" 95.00
Train, L-134 ....75.00
Victoria Jubilee 1887 ....65.00
Washington Bicentennial, L-258 ....95.00
Waste Not, Want Not, 13¼x8½" 55.00
Westward Ho 95.00
Wheat & Barley, milk glass 65.00
William J Bryan, milk glass 45.00

Bride's Baskets and Bowls

Victorian brides were showered with gifts, as brides have always been; one of the most popular gift items was the bride's basket. Art glass inserts from both European and American glasshouses, some in lovely transparent hues with dainty enameled florals, others of Peachblow, Vasa Murrhina, satin or cased glass, were cradled in complementary silverplated holders. While many of these holders were simply engraved or delicately embossed, others such as those from Pairpoint and Wilcox were wonderfully ornate, often with figurals of cherubs or animals. The bride's basket was no longer in fashion after the turn of the century.

Watch for 'marriages' of bowls and frames. To warrant the best price, the two pieces should be the original pairing. If you can't be certain of this, at least check to see that the bowl fits snuggly into the frame. Beware of later-made bowls (such as Fenton's) in Victorian holders.

In the listings that follow, if no frame is described, the price is for a bowl only.

Enameled wild roses with gold stems and leaves on peach; silverplated frame with sea motif and engraved lobster, 11", $1,700.00.

Bl Dmn Quilt MOP, 3½x10x10½" 325.00
Bl o/l, brn ruffled rim, HP flowers, 5x11" 265.00
Burgundy, gold floral/amber branch hdls, 3-side rim, Webb 350.00
Cranberry, crystal ruffle & wafer ft, 4x9½" 225.00
Cranberry shaded, clear ruffle; SP holder w/ped base, 11" 165.00
Cranberry to mauve o/l, HP decor, 11½" 120.00
Cranberry to pk o/l, emb tassels, bl HP florals, 11½" 350.00
Cream to butterscotch o/l, fluted swirl; Eureka SP fr 280.00
Dmn Quilt MOP, orange, crimped; fancy ftd Meriden fr, 13" 400.00
Gr o/l satin, heavily emb lattice at rim, 3¾x11½" 225.00
Hobnail, pk satin w/bl rim, Mt WA; rstr SP fr, 14" 575.00
Peach to bl to yel opaque, HP decor, crimped rim, 8" 75.00
Pk o/l, gold flowers & scrolls, pleated, 3¾x10¾" 175.00
Pk o/l, mc flowers, wht opaque ribbon edge, 3x10¼" 225.00
Purple o/l satin, HP floral; sgn SP fr, 8½x12¼" 300.00
Red to custard o/l, beaded, clear rim, 10" 80.00
Rose to pk satin, HP florals, ruffled, 2½x10" 225.00
Yel swirl w/floral & gold branches, ruffled; S&W fr, 4x10" 400.00

Bristol Glass

Bristol is a type of semi-opaque opaline glass whose name was derived from the area in England where it was first produced. Similar glass was made in France, Germany, and Italy. In this country, it was made by the New England Glass Company and to a lesser extent by its contemporaries. During the 18th and 19th centuries, Bristol glass was imported in large amounts and sold cheaply, thereby contributing to the demise of the earlier glasshouses here in America. It is very difficult to distinguish the English Bristol from other opaline types. Style, design, and decoration serve as clues to its origin; but often only those well versed in the field can spot these subtle variations.

Biscuit jar, bl w/mc florals, SP lid/rim/hdl, 6⅞x4⅞" 195.00

Biscuit jar, turq bl, w/heron scene, 7½x5½" 225.00
Bottle, scent; gray, glossy, bird & holly, w/stopper, 7⅛" 125.00
Mug, bl w/wht decor, appl hdl, 4½" 50.00
Rose bowl, turq w/gold flowers, 4-crimp, 4x3½" 95.00
Vase, aqua, floral, flared rim, 11¼x4½" 45.00
Vase, bl, florals & gold bands, 4½x2¼" 45.00
Vase, gr, child, brass ormolu hdls & ft, 7¼", pr 165.00
Vase, gr, mc flowers & lg bird, gold trim, 12½x4¼", pr 275.00
Vase, jack-in-pulpit; pk w/mc flowers, 5⅝x4⅝" 85.00
Vase, pk, raised gold leaves, 11½", pr 160.00
Vase, pk, wht int, mc flowers, 13¼x5¾" 295.00
Vase, turq, flowers & bird, w/gold, 10⅛x5½" 145.00
Vase, turq, gold bands & yel florals, 3⅛x2½" 70.00
Vase, turq, gold flowers & bands, 5¼x2¼", pr 125.00
Vase, turq w/heavy gold bands & garlands w/wht enamel, 7x2¾" .150.00
Vase, turq w/many gold leaves & scrolls, 13", pr 265.00
Vase, turq w/mc flowers w/gold, gold hdls, 6¾x3" 95.00
Vase, wht, coach & horses medallion, scrolls, w/gold, 14" 145.00
Vase, wht, cottage in winter scene w/gold, 13½x4⅝" 225.00
Vase, wht to bl, mc coralene florals w/gold, 11x4⅛", pr 350.00

British Royalty Commemoratives

Commemoratives have been issued for royal occasions from Edward VI's 1547 coronation through modern-day events, so it's possible to start collecting at any period of history. Many collectors begin with Queen Victoria's reign, collecting examples for each succeeding monarch and continuing through to modern times.

Some collectors identify with a particular royal personage and limit their collecting to that era, ie., Queen Elizabeth's life and reign. Other collectors look to the future, expanding their collection to include the heir apparents Prince Charles/Princess Diana and their first-born son, Prince William.

Royalty commemorative collecting is often further refined around a particular type of collectible. Nearly any item with room for a portrait and a description has been manufactured as a souvenir. Thus royalty commemoratives are available in glass, ceramic, metal, fabric, plastic and paper. This wide variety of material lends itself to any pocketbook. The range covers expensive limited edition ceramics to inexpensive souvenir key chains, puzzles, matchbooks, etc.

Many recent royalty headline events have been commemorated in a variety of souvenirs. Buying some of these modern commemoratives at the moderate issue prices could be a good investment. After all, today's events are tomorrow's history.

For further study we recommend *British Royal Commemoratives* by our advisor for this category, Audrey Zeder; she is listed in the Directory under California.

Key:
anniv — anniversary	inscr — inscribed
chr — christening	jub — jubilee
com — commemorative	LE — limited edition
cor — coronation	mem — memorial
ILN — Illustrated London News	wed — wedding

Bank, Elizabeth cor, iron crown shape 65.00
Beaker, Edward VII cor, King's Dinner, Royal Doulton 130.00
Beaker, Geo V cor w/gr portrait, ships of war, Whitley 150.00
Beaker, Victoria 1897 jub, enamel, 3¾" 175.00
Bell, Charls/Di wed w/mc portrait, Royal Grafton, 7" 50.00
Bottle, gin; Victoria cor, stoneware; Stephen Greene 700.00
Bust, Queen Mother, LE 500, Royal Staffordshire, 4½" 75.00
Bust, Victoria, milk glass, 1887, 3x3¾x3¾" 165.00

Bust, William IV, inscr Jan 1831, Sam Parker, metal, blk 425.00
Busts, Charles & Di, LE 500, Royal Staffordshire, 4½", pr 150.00
Busts, George V & Mary, parian, EX details, 5½", pr 250.00
Cup & saucer, Elizabeth 1953 cor, mc portrait on mint gr 55.00
Cup & saucer, Victoria/Albert portraits, pk lustre, 1851 ....250.00
Dolls, Charles/Di in wedding clothes, Goldberger, 11", pr 100.00
Egg cup, Elizabeth II/Philip, mc portrait, Bavarian style 25.00
Ephemera, Elizabeth II 1953 cor matchbook cover 12.00
Ephemera, Geo V 1935 Jubilee ILN record number 65.00
Ephemera, Geo VI 1939 Visit, decal w/mc portrait, unused 25.00
Glass, Charles/Di wed, plate, heather, pressed, 3½" 25.00
Glass, Charles/Di 1992 separation, plate, bl, pressed, 3½" 20.00
Glass, Elizabeth II, plate, gr, 3½" 20.00
Glass, Victoria 1897 jub, plate, clear, pressed, 4" 190.00
Glass, Victoria 1937 cor, plate, clear, pressed, 3½" 190.00
Glass, Victoria/Albert 1840 wed plate, clear, pressed, 3½" 190.00
Medal, Princess Charlotte 1820 mem, ¾" 50.00
Medal, Victoria 1897 jub, relief portrait, copper, 2¼" 190.00
Medal, Victoria 1897 jub, sterling silver, Royal Mint, 1" 60.00
Miniature, mug, Elizabeth, mc portrait, 1980s, 1¾" 20.00
Mug, cider; Diana 30th birthday, sepia portrait, LE 250 ....40.00
Mug, cider; Edward VII 1902 cor, gr transfer, Royal Doulton 195.00
Mug, Elizabeth 1992 Annus Horribulus, mc portrait & events 25.00
Mug, Geo VI 1937 cor, relief profile portrait, Burleigh 150.00
Newspaper, King Edward May Marry Mrs Simpson headline 35.00
Novelty, Elizabeth 1953 cor, cigarette lighter, Wedgwood 75.00
Novelty, Victoria/Prince of Wales 1880, royal whist tokens, pr 45.00
Paperweight, Elizabeth 40 Yrs Throne, crystal w/postage stamp 35.00
Photograph, Elizabeth II, bl coat & hat, 1990s, 5x7" 20.00
Pin-bk button, Geo VI cor, family group picture, 1¼" 40.00
Pitcher, Elizabeth 1953 cor, relief profile on pk, Johnson 130.00
Plaque, Elizabeth/Queen Mother/Di/Sara, portrait on blk, 6x8" ...25.00
Plaque, Victoria 1889, relief portrait/details, bronze, 7x10" 375.00

Plate, King V Coronation, Royal Doulton, 10½", $250.00.

Plate, Charles/Di 1981 wed, mc clothes portrait, 10½" 150.00
Plate, Charles/Di 1981 wed, portrait, filigree, Minton, 10½" 195.00
Plate, Elizabeth 40 Yrs on Throne, LE 1000, Wedgwood, 10" 275.00
Plate, Geo VI 1939 Canada Visit, relief portrait, Wedgwood 150.00
Plate, Prince Henry 1984 chr, mc portrait, 6¼" 35.00
Plate, Victoria 1897 jub, portrait & Johnson Bros advertising 250.00
Postcard, George VI 1937 cor, blk & wht, Tuck, set of 4 ....20.00
Postcard, Royal family at Sandringham, mc, 1990 ....10.00
Postcard, Windsor Fire, mc, 1992 ....5.00
Pot lid, Victoria portrait, bottom container for toothpaste 110.00
Print, Elizabeth II 1953 cor, orig matt, 11x14" 35.00
Puzzle, Charles/Di w/wed scene, in box 40.00
Puzzle, Elizabeth II collage of 1953 cor tins, 11x14" 25.00
Spoon, Charles/Di wed, relief portrait & design, SP 25.00
Spoon, Diana, relief portrait & design, SP 15.00
Spoon, George VI 1939 Canada Visit, SP, International 45.00

Spoon, Victoria 1897 jub, relief portrait, sterling 150.00
Stamps, Diana 21 birthday, 3 stamps & souvenir sheet 20.00
Teapot, Edward VII 1901 cor, mc portrait on pk lustre, 2-cup 225.00
Teapot stand, Elizabeth II jub, relief portrait, chrome 25.00
Textile, Edward VII, woven silk, oval, fr, 6x5" 150.00
Textile, Edward VII 1937 cor, flag, blk & wht portrait, 3x5" 35.00
Textile, Elizabeth II 40 Years Throne, towel, linen 12.00
Textile, Victoria 1897 jub, 4 generations, 28x28" 200.00
Thimbles, Royal family members, china, 1983, set of 8 ....60.00
Tin, Charles/Di wed, mc protraits on royal bl, octagonal 35.00
Tin, George V 1910 cor, mc portrait, 2 generations 175.00
Tin, Princesses Elizabeth/Margaret, sepia, Riley's, 5x1½" 50.00
Tin, Victoria & 3 generations, Mazawatte Tea 190.00
Toby Mug, Elizabeth II on throne w/Corgi, HP, LE, K Francis ...275.00
Toby mugs, George V & Queen Mary, pr 495.00
Trading cards, Press Pass, 13 cards in deluxe package 2.00
Tray, Charles/Di wed, engagement portrait, red/wht/bl, 6x7" 25.00
Tray, Elizabeth cor, portrait w/Philip, faux wood sides, 13" 45.00
Tray, Victoria 1887, relief portrait & design, brass, 12" 175.00
Vehicle, Elizabeth II 40th wed anniv, dbl-decker bus, LLEDO 50.00

Broadmoor

In the October of 1933, the Broadmoor Art Pottery was formed and space rented at 217 East Pikes Peak Avenue, Colorado Springs, Colorado. Most of the pottery produced would not be considered elaborate and only a handful was decorated. Many pieces were signed by P.H. Genter, J.B. Hunt, Eric Hellman, and Cecil Jones. It is reported that this plant closed in 1936, and Genter moved his operations to Denver.

Broadmoor pottery is marked in several ways: a Greek or Egyptian-type label depicting two potters (one at the wheel and one at a tile-pressing machine) and the word Broadmoor; an ink-stamped 'Broadmoor Pottery, Colorado Springs (or Denver), Colorado'; and an incised version of the latter.

The bottoms of all pieces are always white and can be either glazed or unglazed. Glaze colors are turquoise, green, yellow, cobalt blue, light blue, white, pink, pink with blue, maroon red, black, and a copper lustre. Both matt and high gloss finishes were used.

The company produced many advertising tiles, novelty items, coasters, ashtrays, and vases for local establishments around Denver and as far away as Wyoming. An Indian head was incised into many of the advertising items, which also often bear a company or a product name. A series of small animals (horses, dogs, elephants, lamb, squirrels, a toucan bird, and a hippo), each about 2" high, are easily recognized by the style of their modeling and glaze treatments, though all are unmarked. Our advisors for this category are Carol and Jim Carlton; they are listed in the Directory under Colorado.

Vase, blue matt, wraparound steer-head handles, 10", $150.00.

Animal figurine, ea...45.00
Ashtray/match holder, Lincoln Zephyr advertising, 1938.............38.00
Bookend, lady's head & shoulders, 6".......................................150.00
Bowl/ashtray, maroon, ruffled...25.00
Cigarette urn, wht tulip cup, 5", on 5" turq leafy pad....................25.00
Paperweight, beetle...35.00
Tile, HP mc parrot, orange border, sgn CJ Jones, mk, 6"..............135.00
Toothpick holder...20.00
Vase, blk gloss, bulbous, orig label, 7½".....................................65.00
Vase, bud; maroon, 8"..45.00
Vase, cobalt, ovoid w/vertical ribbing, orig label, 16"................150.00
Vase, maroon, Indian portrait emb, mk Plains Hotel/1935, 17"..500.00
Vase, maroon, rings & hdls, 5"..65.00
Vase, maroon, urn form, hdls, 7½"..70.00
Vase, turq, shouldered cylinder, 7"..25.00

Broadsides

Webster defines a broadside as simply a large sheet of paper printed on one side. During the 1880s, they were the most practical means of mass-communication. By the middle of the century, they had become elaborate and lengthy with information, illustrations, portraits, and fancy border designs. Those printed on coated stock are usually worth more.

Aikem Knitting Machine Co, Broadway NY, 1850s, 16½x10".....27.50
Aimar's Neurotic Oil..., Charleston SC, 1830s, 8x10".................55.00
Am Cow Milker...Cure for Aching Hands..., 1865, 8x11"............10.00
Cardiff giant, dimensions, exhibition location, 1869, 8x6".........245.00
Central VT RR, Rand, Avery & Co, 22x14"+fr, EX.....................250.00
Death of Pres Wm H Harrison, fancy borders, 1841, 7x15"..........65.00
Dr HC Porter's Tonix Elixer, fancy borders, 5x6".......................12.50
Dr Ward's Vegetable Asthmatic Pills, MA, 1840s, 9x13", EX......45.00
Gro W Smith, Dealer in Dry Goods, etc, Mattawamkeag ME, EX.250.00
Hamilton's Blk Oil, horse illus, 1880s, 24x18"...........................18.50
Indian Sovereign Remedy for Palpitation..., VT, 1840s, 8x12".....28.50
Magic show, Splendid Amusement, Startling..., 1840s, 18x8"......55.00

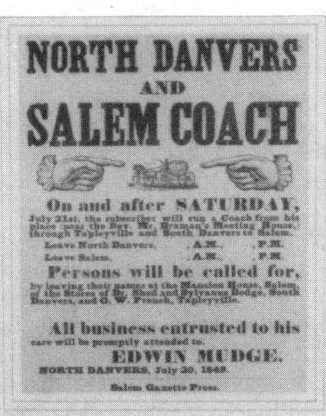

North Danvers and Salem Coach, Salem Gazette Press, 1849, 11x8½", matted and framed, $275.00.

North Danvers & Salem Coach, Salem Gazette, 1948, 9x11"....275.00
Ointment for the Itch, T Hollis, Boston, 1850s, 7x12"..................55.00
Oxegynated Bitters, blk on wht, early, 23x17½", VG.................100.00
Pure Drugs...Gifford Brothers...NJ, 1850s, 15½x7½"..................45.00
Reward, $20,000 for return of abducted boy, 1874, 12x6"..........135.00
Reward, $500 for arrest of murderer, WY, 1893, 11½x8½", VG.200.00
Surrender of Lee, Herald Extra, April 14, 1865, 18x5½".............550.00
Thanksgiving proclamation, Maine emblem at top, 1852, 17x14"..22.50
White's Golden Tonic, illustrated, 1880s, 24x18".......................18.50

Bronzes

Thomas Ball, George Bessell, and Leonard Volk were some of the earliest American sculptors who produced figures in bronze for home decor during the 1840s. Pieces of historical significance were the most popular, but by the 1880s a more fanciful type of artwork took hold. Some of the fine sculptors of the day were Daniel Chester French, Augustus St. Gaudens, and John Quincy Adams Ward. Bronzes reached the height of their popularity at the turn of the century. The American West was portrayed to its fullest by Remington, Russell, James Frazier, Hermon MacNeil, and Solon Borglum. Animals of every species were modeled by A.P. Proctor, Paul Bartlett, and Albert Laellele, to name but a few.

Art Nouveau and Art Deco influenced the medium during the twenties, evidenced by the works of Allen Clark, Harriet Frismuth, E.F. Sanford, and Bessie P. Vonnoh.

Be aware that recasts abound. While often esthetically satisfactory, they are not original and should be priced accordingly. In much the same manner as prints are evaluated, the original castings made under the direction of the artist are the most valuable. Later castings from the original mold are worth less. A recast is not made from the original mold. Instead, a rubber-like substance is applied to the bronze, peeled away, and filled with wax. Then, using the same 'lost wax' procedure as the artist uses on completion of his original wax model, a clay-like substance is formed around the wax figure and the whole fired to vitrify the clay. The wax, of course, melts away, hence the term 'lost wax.' Recast bronzes lose detail and are somewhat smaller than the original due to the shrinkage of the clay mold.

Alliot, L; girl & pheasant, gr-brn patina, 1900s, 16x31".........1,600.00
Austrian, Arab on rug, sits on heels, reads book, 3½"................440.00
Austrian, fox on base, cold pnt, 5"..375.00
Austrian, N African orange vendor, tray on head, 11½".........1,320.00
Austrian, N African runner, mk Geschutz/#2897, 9"................990.00
Austrian, owl standing on book, impressed mk, 6½"................475.00
Austrian, parrot on rooted upright branch, 10½", pr.............3,000.00
Austrian, parrots, EX details & patina, 6¼", 6½", pr...............440.00
Austrian, tiger, 5¼" L..300.00
Austrian, 2 African ivory traders, 1 w/sack of coins, 5"............495.00
Barye, AL; elephant of Senegal, running, mk ZZ, 8½"...........1,650.00
Barye, AL; rabbit, 2½"...275.00
Bitter, Ary; Pan & sleeping goat, silvered, 1900s, 31" L.........1,600.00
Ceribelli, C; bust of young woman, 1880s, 17"......................770.00
Chalice, cast as Bacchus head w/bears & grapevines, 3½".........400.00
Chiparus, Egyptian dancer, arms above, ankles Xd, 29".........7,700.00
Chiparus, Pierrot, cold pnt/ivory, Etling, 20"......................4,000.00
Coustou, Marly Horse, rearing, w/seminude boy aside, 15" L......600.00
Delhomme, Leon-Alexandre; walking panther, 26"...............2,500.00
Demanet, Victor; archer seated on stump pulls bow, 24".........2,100.00
Descomps, Meditation, seated nude, LN&JL seal, #137, 17"...2,000.00
Dubucand, Alfred; group of hunting dogs, 4½x6".....................400.00
Dumaige, Etinne-Henry; nymph by pedestal holds lamp, 18"..1,200.00
Dumaige, H; bust, lady w/flowers in hair, 1800s, 18½"............400.00
Erte, Le Danseur, male dancer holding lasso, c 1980, 18"........1,100.00
Erte, Le Femme et al Panthere, woman w/pet panther, 15".....7,100.00
Garreau, Georges; seated nude w/dove, 1900s, 16"...............1,725.00
Gemito, bust of boy: Mario, 13"..440.00
Godard, hoop-dancer, veined marble base, Etling, 17"...........1,600.00
Gregoire; L; figure of Diana, 1880s, 28"................................660.00
Houdon, bust, lady on sq ped w/circular wreath, 29".............1,500.00
Kelety, Alexandre; sea gull in flight, stepped base, 24"...........575.00
La Porte-Blairsy, standing Breton woman, gilt patina, 9"..........300.00
Lambert-Rucki, Jean; Coupe au Gibus, Blanchet Fondeur, 21"...10,300.00

Laurant, GH; pheasant, on marble/slate base, rpr, 34" L **880.00**
Le Faguays, Pierre; girl w/puppets, blk marble base, 19" **1,700.00**
Le Faguays, Pierre; nude pulls wheel up ramp, 1900s, 20" **1,800.00**
Lorenzl, 2 cavorting nudes, blk patina, marble base, 19" **1,750.00**
Mene, PJ; Moroccan horseman, 21" **1,875.00**
Mene, PJ; stag, miniature, 3½" **195.00**
Millet, F; Les Glaneuses, 3 women in field, oval base, 5x7" **200.00**
Moigniez, Jules; Merino ram & ewe, 9½x12" **770.00**

Moigniez, Jules; cock pheasant, 22⅞", $2,000.00.

Monginot, Charlotte; little girl w/flowers, gilt/ivory, 8" **990.00**
Oliverei, P; nude reclining in open seashell, 18" **2,200.00**
Philippe, Paul; dancer, vest/swirl skirt, ivory/gilt, 15" **550.00**
Pompon, Francois; figure of a grouse, gr patina, 8" **5,500.00**
Rochard, birds in flight, Deco style, 1800s **2,400.00**
Sandoz, Edward Marcel; terrier w/bee on raised paw, 6" **825.00**
Unsgn, owl on branch, detailed casting, 3¼" **40.00**
Vase, gilt fittings, red marble base w/ormolu, 14" **66.00**
Zach, Bruno; dancing couple, wht onyx base, 16" **1,100.00**
Zach, Bruno; nude w/elaborate evening wrap about her, 17" ...**1,900.00**

Brouwer

Theophlis A. Brouwer, recognized as an accomplished artist even before his interests turned to the medium of pottery, started a small one-man operation in 1894 in East Hampton, New York. Two years later he relocated in Westhampton where he perfected the technique of fire-painting, learning to control the effects of the kiln to produce the best-possible results. In 1925 he founded the Ceramic Flame Company in New York, but it is for his earlier work that he is best known. Brouwer died in 1932.

Vase, dk brn metallic w/some copper, gr & purple irid, 5x6" **800.00**
Vase, green/orange/yel/brn fire-pnt mottle, can neck, hdls, 7" **1,200.00**
Vase, rust & gr irid, mk Flame, trumpet neck, ftd, rpr, 12" **4,800.00**

Brownies by Palmer Cox

Created by Palmer Cox in 1883, the Brownies charmed children through the pages of books and magazines, as dolls, on their dinnerware, in advertising material, and on souvenirs. Each had his own personality, among them The Bellhop, The London Bobby, The Chairman, and Uncle Sam. But the oversized, triangular face with the startled expression, the protruding tummy, and the spindlelegs were characteristics of them all. They were inspired by the Scottish legends related to Cox as a child by his parents, who were of English descent. His introduction of the Brownies to the world was accomplished by a poem called *The Brownies Ride*. Books followed in rapid succession, thirteen in the series, all written as well as illustrated by Palmer Cox.

By the late 1890s, the Brownies were active in advertising. They promoted such products as games, coffee, toys, patent medicines, and rubber boots. 'Greenies' were the Brownies' first cousins, created by Cox to charm and to woo through the pages of the advertising almanacs of the G.G. Green Company of New Jersey. Perhaps the best-known endorsement in the Brownies' career was for the Kodak Brownie, which became so popular and sold in such volume that their name became synonymous with this type of camera.

Book, Brownies at Home, 1891, EX **65.00**
Book, Captivating Stories About Animals, Palmer Cox illus, 1908 .**30.00**
Book, Funny Stories About Funny People, 1905, EX **35.00**
Book, Little Goody Two Shoes, 1903, EX **40.00**
Book, Monk's Victory, 1911, EX **32.00**
Box, Log Cabin Brownies, cabin form, Nat'l Biscuit Co, '20s **135.00**
Candlestick, Bobby, 7½" **200.00**
Candlestick, Uncle Sam, 7½" **200.00**
Cigar holder/ashtray, Brownie figural, Pairpoint SP **335.00**
Comic sheet, 1907, lg, EX **30.00**
Cup & saucer, 4 Brownies on cup, 5 on saucer **75.00**
Figurine, Dude, Brownie w/tailcoat & hat, 9" **250.00**
Figurine, Sailor, Defender, 9" **250.00**
Game, Auto Race, tin board **42.50**
Humidor, Bobby, 6" **175.00**
Humidor, Brownie w/Stocking Cap, 6" **185.00**
Napkin ring, SP, Brownie climbs up side **175.00**
Picture frame, paper on wood, 8x10" **40.00**
Pitcher, Brownies playing golf, tan, china, 6" **110.00**
Plate, SP, Brownies on rim, 8½" **50.00**
Plate, 10 action Brownies, 7" **70.00**
Sign, Howell's Root Beer, emb Brownies on tin, EX **175.00**

Brush

George Brush began his career in the pottery industry in 1901 working for the J.B. Owens Pottery Co. in Zanesville, Ohio. He left the company in 1907 to go into business for himself, only to have fire completely destroy his pottery less than one year after it was founded. Brush became associated with J.W. McCoy in 1909 and for many years served in capacities ranging from General Manager to President. (From 1911 until 1925, the firm was known as The Brush-McCoy Pottery Co.; see that section for information.) After McCoy died, the family withdrew their interests, and in 1925 the name of the firm was changed to The Brush Pottery. The era of hand-decorated art pottery had passed for the most part and would soon be completely replaced by the production of commercial lines. Of all the wares bearing the later Brush script mark, their figural cookie jars are the most collectible, and several have been reproduced.

For additional information on Brush cookie jars, we recommend *The Collector's Encyclopedia of Cookie Jars* by our cookie jar advisors, Joyce and Fred Roerig; they are listed in the Directory under South Carolina. See also Brush-McCoy for information on a second reference book.

Cookie Jars

Antique Touring Car, minimum value **375.00**
Boy w/Balloons, minimum value **500.00**
Chick in Nest **450.00**
Cinderella Pumpkin **165.00**
Circus Horse, gr, minimum value **500.00**
Circus Horse, pk, minimum value **600.00**

Clown, yel pants	185.00
Clown Bust	225.00
Cookie House	75.00

Covered Wagon, dog finial, #30, $585.00.

Cow w/Cat on Bk, brn	110.00
Cow w/Cat on Bk, purple, minimum value	500.00
Davy Crockett, gold trim	500.00
Davy Crockett, no gold	200.00
Dog w/Basket	325.00
Donkey w/Cart, #23, brn	285.00
Donkey w/Cart, #33, gray	350.00
Elephant w/Baby Bonnet & Ice Cream Cone, wht	500.00
Elephant w/Monkey on Bk, minimum value	1,000.00
Fish	475.00
Formal Pig, gr hat & coat, minimum value (+)	350.00
Granny, pk apron, bl dots on skirt	225.00
Granny, plain skirt	360.00
Happy Bunny, wht	210.00
Hillbilly Frog (+), minimum value	3,000.00
Hobby Horse, minimum value	500.00
Humpty Dumpty, w/beany & bow tie	235.00
Humpty Dumpty, w/peaked brn hat & shoes	200.00
Lantern, brn/cream, mk K1	65.00
Laughing Hippo	500.00
Little Angel, minimum value	775.00
Little Boy Blue, gold trim, K25 USA, sm, minimum value	650.00
Little Boy Blue, K24 Brush USA, lg	750.00
Little Girl	285.00
Little Red Riding Hood, gold trim, mk, lg, minimum value	700.00
Little Red Riding Hood, no gold, K24 USA, sm	465.00
Nite Owl	95.00
Old Clock	165.00
Old Shoe	85.00
Panda	240.00
Peter Pan, gold trim, lg	800.00
Peter Pan, sm	465.00
Pumpkin w/Lock on Door, W24	325.00
Puppy Police	525.00
Raggedy Ann	465.00
Sitting Hippo	465.00
Sitting Pig	465.00
Smiling Bear	465.00
Squirrel on Log	85.00
Squirrel w/Top Hat, blk coat & hat	235.00
Squirrel w/Top Hat, gr coat	220.00
Stylized Owl	425.00
Stylized Siamese	460.00
Teddy Bear, feet apart	250.00

Teddy Bear, feet together	150.00
Treasure Chest	160.00

Miscellaneous

Bank, pig form, #836, 6½"	35.00
Candlesticks, Florastone, floral medallions on gray, 9", pr	600.00
Casserole, KolorKraft, gr glossy, #561, 7"	52.50
Custard cup, Rainbow Ovenware, 5-oz	12.50
Figurine, bull, Ferdinand, #138, 4x6"	35.00
Figurine, turtle, #487, 5"	50.00
Flowerpot, Rockraft, gr & brn, #811, 8"	75.00
Jardiniere, Floradora, blended glaze, #243, 7"	70.00
Jardiniere, Modern Kolorcraft, bl, 8-sided, #260, 10"	150.00
Light, TV; sailboat form, late 1950s	52.50
Planter, duck, wht w/yel bill & ft, #133	37.50
Planter, Mary & lamb, #291, 6"	17.50
Planter, monkey & open shell, #32, 5x5"	20.00
Planter, police hat, 1950s	30.00
Planter, puppy, #37	20.00
Planter, rabbit w/basket, #147, 7x4½"	22.50
Vase, brn, emb linear decor, #207, 8"	37.50
Vase, GloArt, gr & brn blended, bulbous, #776, 5x7¾"	52.50
Vase, ivory, cornucopia form, #652, 8x6½"	15.00
Vase, pagoda decor, #225, 7½"	35.00

Brush-McCoy

The Brush-McCoy Pottery was formed in 1911 in Zanesville, Ohio, an alliance between George Brush and J.W. McCoy. Brush's original pottery had been destroyed by fire in 1907; McCoy had operated his own business there since 1899. After the merger, the company expanded and produced not only their staple commercial wares but also fine artware. Lines such as Navarre, Venetian, Oriental, and Sylvan were of fine quality equal to that of their larger competitors. Because very little of the ware was marked, it is often mistaken for Weller, Roseville, or Peters and Reed.

In 1918 after a fire in Zanesville had destroyed the manufacturing portion of that plant, all production was contained in their Roseville (Ohio) plant #2. A stoneware type of clay was used there; and as a result, the artware lines of Jewel, Zuniart, King Tut, Florastone, Jetwood, Krakle-Kraft, and Panelart are so distinctive that they are more easily recognizable. Examples of these lines are unique and very beautiful, also quite rare and highly prized!

The Brush-McCoy Pottery operated under that name until after 1925 when it became the Brush Pottery. The Brush-Barnett family retained their interest in the pottery until 1981 when it was purchased by the Dearborn Company. For more information we recommend *The Guide to Brush-McCoy Pottery*, written by Martha and Steve Sanford and edited by David P. Sanford, our advisors for this category. They are listed in the Directory under California. See also Brush.

Bowl, gr matt, #01, 5"	75.00
Candlesticks, Cleo, #020, 1914, pr	375.00
Cookie jar, Kolorkraft, #344, 8½"	175.00
Decanter, Bl Onyx, pinch bottle w/music box, 10"	175.00
Jardiniere, Bluebird, #222, 9"	550.00
Jardiniere, Egyptian, 3 scenes, 1912, 10½"	800.00
Jardiniere, Roman, gladiator holding lion, 1914	700.00
Jardiniere, Vogue, #213, 8½"	250.00
Jardiniere & pedestal, Oriental, #2210, 1913	2,400.00
Pitcher, New Rock, #331, 1926, 4-pt, 7½"	175.00
Stein, Woodland, #133, 16-oz	125.00

Tankard, Corn Line, #50, 1912, 11" 325.00
Umbrella stand, Oakwood, #81, 23" 725.00
Urn, Gr Onyx, #699, 11½" 225.00

Vase, Jewell, #046, 1924, 12", $1,400.00.

Vase, Florastone, #077, 6" 1,200.00
Vase, Jetwood, type 1, #045, 11" 1,000.00
Vase, Jewel, #040, 6" 325.00
Vase, King Tut, scarab design, #050, 1923, 6" 1,125.00
Vase, Kolorkraft, #0162, 12" 200.00
Vase, Panelart, #076, 1924, 7" 1,400.00
Vase, Zuniart #051, 4" 325.00

Buffalo Pottery

The founding of the Buffalo Pottery in Buffalo, New York, in 1901, was a direct result of the success achieved by John Larkin through his innovative methods of marketing 'Sweet Home Soap.' Choosing to omit 'middle-man' profits, Larkin preferred to deal directly with the consumer and offered premiums as an enticement for sales. The pottery soon proved a success in its own right and began producing advertising and commemorative items for other companies, as well as commercial tableware. In 1905 they introduced their Blue Willow line after extensive experimentation resulted in the development of the first successful underglaze cobalt achieved by an American company. Between 1905 and 1909, a line of pitchers and jugs were hand decorated in historical, literary, floral, and outdoor themes. Twenty-nine styles are known to have been made. These have been found in a wide array of color variations.

Their most famous line was Deldare Ware, the bulk of which was made from 1908 to 1909. It was hand decorated after illustrations by Cecil Aldin. Views of English life were portrayed in detail through unusual use of color against the natural olive green cast of the body. Today the 'Fallowfield Hunt' scenes are more difficult to locate than 'Scenes of Village Life in Ye Olden Days.' A Deldare calendar plate was made in 1910. These are very rare and are highly valued by collectors. The line was revived in 1923 and dropped again in 1925. Every piece was marked 'Made at Ye Buffalo Pottery, Deldare Ware Underglaze.' Most are dated, though date has no bearing on the value. Emerald Deldare, made with the same olive body and on standard Deldare Ware shapes, featured historical scenes and Art Nouveau decorations. Most pieces are found with a 1911 date stamp. Production was very limited due to the intricate, time-consuming detail. Needless to say, it is very rare and extremely desirable.

Abino Ware, most of which was made in 1912, also used standard Deldare shapes, but its colors were earthy and the decorations more delicately applied. Sailboats, windmills, and country scenes were favored motifs. These designs were achieved by overpainting transfer prints and were often signed by the artist. The ware is marked 'Abino' in hand-printed block letters. Production was limited; and as a result, examples

of this line are scarce today. Prices only slightly trail those of Emerald Deldare Ware.

The many uncataloged items that have been found over the years indicate that Buffalo Pottery decorators were free to use their own ideas and talents to create many beautiful one-of-a-kind pieces.

Our advisors for this category are Fred and Lila Shrader; they are listed in the Directory under California.

Abino

Ashtray/matchbox holder, sailing scene 850.00
Bowl, windmill scene, 9" 850.00
Candlestick, sailing scene, 9½" 650.00
Hair receiver, sailing scenes, w/lid 675.00
Humidor, sailing scene, 7" 930.00
Pitcher, harbor scene, 8" 900.00
Plaque, unusual sailing scene, 12" 1,350.00
Plate, lakeside scene w/windmills, 9" 600.00
Plate, windmill scene, 6½" 345.00
Tankard, meadow & stream w/windmill, 10½" 1,250.00
Tray, lakeside & windmill scene, 9x12" 1,200.00
Vase, windmill & pond scene, 7" 875.00

Deldare

Ashtray/matchbox holder, Ye Olden Days 525.00
Bowl, fern; no insert, 8" 600.00
Bowl, fruit; Fallowfield, Breakfast, 12" 950.00
Bowl, fruit; Ye Village Tavern, 9" 500.00
Bowl, rim soup; Fallowfield, Breaking Cover, 9" 295.00
Bowl, sauce; Fallowfield, Breaking Cover, 5" 175.00
Bowl, sauce; Ye Olden Days, 5" 150.00
Candle holder, Emerald Art Nouveau, shield-bk 1,400.00
Candlestick, Emerald Art Nouveau, 9" 985.00
Candlestick, Fallowfield scenes, 9" 450.00
Chocolate pot, Emerald, Dr Syntax Reading 1,975.00
Creamer, Emerald, Art Nouveau 385.00
Creamer, Fallowfield Hunt scene 295.00
Cup & saucer, chocolate; Ye Village scenes 420.00
Cup & saucer, demitasse; Ye Olden Days 375.00
Cup & saucer, Fallowfield Hunt scene 265.00
Cup & saucer, Ye Olden Days 240.00
Egg cup, untitled 250.00
Hair receiver, Emerald, Art Nouveau 695.00
Hair receiver, Ye Village Street scenes 375.00
Humidor, Emerald, Old Sailor 890.00
Humidor, Fallowfield Hunt, Supper scene, 8" 950.00
Humidor, Ye Lion Inn, 8" 625.00
Inkwell, Emerald, Art Nouveau, no lid 975.00
Jar, powder; Ye Village Street, w/lid 375.00
Jardiniere, Ye Village Street, 6" 700.00
Mug, Emerald, Dr Syntax scene, 4½" 495.00
Mug, Fallowfield Hunt, Breakfast scene, 4½" 375.00
Mug, Fallowfield Hunt, Breaking Cover, 3½" 350.00
Mug, Fallowfield Hunt scene, 2½" 435.00
Mug, Village scene, 3½" 285.00
Mug, Ye Lion Inn, 4½" 310.00
Pitcher, Emerald, Dr Syntax Bound..., 8" 815.00
Pitcher, Emerald, Dr Syntax Setting Out..., 8¾" 1,150.00
Pitcher, Fallowfield Hunt, The Death, 9" 690.00
Pitcher, To Demand My Annual Rent, 8" 570.00
Pitcher, With a Cane Superior Air, 9" 585.00
Pitcher, Ye Lion Inn, 10" 765.00
Plaque, Fallowfield Hunt, Breakfast scene, 12" 625.00

Plaque, Ye Lion Inn, 12" 525.00
Plate, At Ye Lion Inn, 6¼" 90.00
Plate, cake; Ye Village Gossips, hdls, 10" 475.00
Plate, calendar; 1910, 9½" 1,695.00
Plate, chop; Fallowfield Hunt, The Start, 14" ...625.00
Plate, Deldare Ware, salesman's sample, 6½" ...1,100.00
Plate, Emerald, Dr Syntax Soliloquising, 7¼" ...485.00
Plate, Fallowfield Hunt, The Death, 8¼" 195.00
Plate, Fallowfield Hunt, 6½" 135.00
Plate, Ye Village scenes, 10" 195.00
Platter, Ye Olden Times, 8½x6½" 385.00
Relish dish, Fallowfield, The Dash, 12x6½" 465.00
Sugar bowl, Fallowfield Hunt scenes, w/lid 310.00
Sugar bowl, Village scenes, w/lid 225.00
Tankard, Emerald, Dr Syntax & Becky, 12" 1,450.00
Tankard, Fallowfield, The Hunt Supper, 12" 965.00
Tankard, The Great Controversy, 12" 900.00
Tea tile, Emerald, Dr Syntax Taking Possession ...575.00
Tea tile, Fallowfield Hunt scene, 6¼" 325.00
Teapot, Emerald, Art Nouveau, 5¾" 1,150.00
Toothpick holder, Village decor, 2¼" 250.00
Tray, calling card; Ye Lion Inn, tab hdls, 7¾" ...345.00
Tray, card; Emerald, Dr Syntax Robbed 550.00
Tray, dresser; Dancing Ye Minuet, 12x9" 610.00
Tray, pin; Emerald, Art Nouveau, 6¼x3½" 545.00
Tray, pin; Ye Olden Days, 6¼x3½" 320.00
Tray, tea; Emerald, Dr Syntax, 13x10" 1,250.00
Vase, Emerald w/Art Nouveau floral & birds, 7" ...1,350.00
Vase, Village scenes, 7" 365.00
Vase, Village scenes of Parson Schoolmaster, 8½" ...945.00

Miscellaneous

Pitcher, Cinderella, coach and horses on reverse, 5½", $545.00.

Ashtray, Lune Ware, Lucca's, Los Angeles 45.00
Bowl, Multifleure Lamelle, Sea Cave, 9" 75.00
Bowl, salad; Bl Willow, sq, 9½" 135.00
Butter pat, Bl Willow 25.00
Butter pat, Bluebird pattern 15.00
Butter pat, Davenport's 22.00
Butter pat, Lake Arrowhead Hotel 45.00
Butter pat, Mandalay pattern 12.00
Butter pat, Multifleure Lamelle, Sea Cave 45.00
Butter pat, US Military Academy, West Point 45.00
Butter pat, Vienna pattern 18.00
Canisters, bl & wht floral, no lids, set of 4 ....100.00
Creamer, Bl Willlow, sq, 3½" 55.00
Creamer, Bl Willow, no hdl, 2½" 25.00
Creamer, Roosevelt Bears, 2¾" 120.00

Cup & saucer, Bl Willow 38.00
Cup & saucer, demitasse; Bl Willow 45.00
Cup & saucer, Lune bl, Hotel Leighton, Los Angeles ...25.00
Cup & saucer, The Tacoma, blk on wht 25.00
Gravy boat, Bl Willow, w/underplate 95.00
Mug, Bl Willow 35.00
Mug, Celebration, Expectation, Relaxation, etc, 4¼", ea ...120.00
Mug, Geranium, mc allover pattern, 4½" 65.00
Mug, Odd Fellows, mc, 4½" 110.00
Mug, Smitty's Snappy Service, 4½" 35.00
Pitcher, Bl Willow, 8½" 255.00
Pitcher, Bonrea, 5½" 95.00
Pitcher, Cinderella, 6" 545.00
Pitcher, Geo Washington, bl w/gold trim, 7½" 565.00
Pitcher, Globe Dairy Lunch, Los Angeles, 5½" 45.00
Pitcher, Gloriana, bl & wht, 9¼" 485.00
Pitcher, Holland jug, 6" 465.00
Pitcher, John Paul Jones, bl & wht, 9¼" 625.00
Pitcher, Landing of Roger Williams, mc, 6" 525.00
Pitcher, Old Mill jug, bl & wht, 6" 540.00
Pitcher, Whirl of the Town, mc, 7" 725.00
Plate, Bl Willow, 9" 50.00
Plate, Christmas; 1950-60, 9½", ea 50.00
Plate, Christmas; 1962 ....235.00
Plate, commemorative; White House, Washington DC, 7½" ...65.00
Plate, Historical Series, 10", ea 65.00
Plate, Japan pattern, 10¼" 75.00
Plate, Pasadena Junior League, rose decor, 9½" 65.00
Plate, Roosevelt Bears, 7¼" 265.00
Platter, blk sm-mouth bass, 15x11" 175.00
Platter, Dr Syntax theme, bl & wht, 14x11" 385.00
Platter, Vienna, 11x8" 65.00
Rose bowl, Geraniums, bl & wht, 3½" 110.00
Sauce boat, Arctic Club, Seattle 25.00
Sauce boat, Colorido Ware, Fineview, Phoenix 35.00
Teapot, Bl Willow, 6-cup, 7¼" 175.00
Teapot, Geranium, bl & wht, 6-cup, 6" 185.00
Tureen, Bl Willow, w/lid, 9½" 385.00
Vase, Arrowhead Lodge, Arrowhead Springs, 5½" 28.00
Vase, Indian Tree pattern, 4½" 32.00
Vase, rose decor, HP, gold tracery, 9½" 85.00
Wash set: pitcher, bowl, chamber pot w/lid, sm pitcher ...475.00

Buggy Steps

Recent attention directed torward Western collectibles has stimulated a renewed interest in all horse-drawn memorabilia. American buggy steps fall into this category. American cast iron buggy steps and carriage steps remain one of the important antique prizes of an era long since passed. During the buggy age (1865 through 1910) steps of great variety were invented and patented to assist in vehicle digress and egress. Many steps have their own patented tread design, attachment method, size and shape. A selected group of single steps are listed below. A limited number of new steps can be found on horse-drawn vehicles in some religious communities today, but these steps are easily identified. Prices listed are for steps in mint to good condition. Rust, breaks and pitting reduce value. Our advisor for this category is John Waddell; he is listed in the Directory under Texas.

Beebe Cart, bolts on, 3x3" sq 18.00
Cole, eared oval, slot mt, 3½x2¼" 25.00
CW Co, sq shield, bolts on, 3½x3½" 18.00
Dean & Co, oval, T-mt, 5¼x3½" 45.00

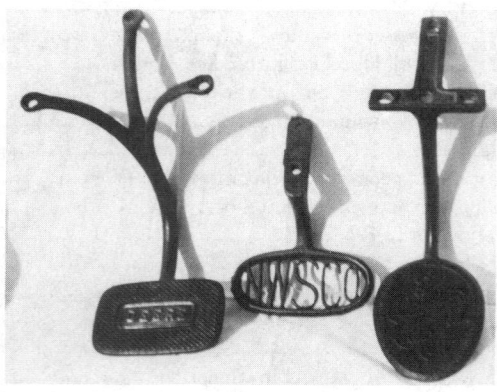

**Deere, brass insert, rectangle, trifork, 4½x3",
$50.00; NWSCO, open oval pad, bolts on,
5x2½", $20.00; Columbia Carriage Co., tri-
fork, oval, T-mount, 5¼x3½", $40.00.**

Emerson, oval, trifork, 5x3½" 40.00
Henry Buggy Co, trifork, oval, 5x3½" 40.00
Moon Bros, oval, trifork, 4½x3½" 40.00
Peru, T-mt, 4½" dia 45.00
Staver, oval, trifork, 4½x3½" 40.00
Studebaker, rectangular, trifork, 5x3¼" 40.00
Thompson Wagon Co, rectangle w/shield, arm 45.00
WG Hesse & Son, T-mt, 4" dia 45.00

Burmese

Burmese glass was patented in 1885 by the Mount Washington
Glass Co. It is typically shaded from canary yellow to a rosy salmon
color. The yellow is produced by the addition of uranium oxide to the
mix. The salmon color comes from the addition of gold salts and is
achieved by reheating the object (partially) in the furnace. It is thus
called 'heat sensitive' glass. Thomas Webb of England was licensed to
produce Burmese and often added more gold, giving an almost fuchsia
tinge to the salmon in some cases. They called their glass 'Queen's
Burmese,' and this is sometimes etched on the base of the object. This
is not to be confused with Mount Washington's 'Queen's Design,'
which refers to the design painted on the object. Both companies added
decoration to many pieces. Mount Washington-Pairpoint produced
some Burmese in the late 1920s and Gunderson and Bryden in the '50s
and '70s, but the color and shapes are different. Our advisors for this
category are Dolli and Wilfred Cohen; they are listed in the Directory
under California. In the listings that follow, examples are assumed to
have the satin finish unless noted 'shiny.'

**Vases, delicate angled han-
dles, Mt. Washington,
10¼", $2,000.00 for the
pair.**

Bowl, berry; Dmn Quilt, Mt WA, 1x6¼" 235.00
Bowl, berry; ruffled, Mt WA, 2¼x9" 750.00
Bowl, brn acorn & gr foliage, hexagonal, Webb, 3⅛x4" 325.00
Bowl, rectangular top, Mt WA, 2x5x4½" 425.00
Bowl, shiny, florals, rigaree collar, flared, 1½x2¾" 250.00
Bowl, tricorn, Mt WA, 2x5" 250.00
Bowl, wide flared rim w/2 spouts, ped ft, Mt WA, 2½x4" 500.00
Bowl, yel appl rigaree, squeezed-in sides, 2½x6½" 750.00
Candlestick, vines/berries, Webb, Queen's, 6" 800.00
Charger, coupe shape, 12" 295.00
Cruet, ribbed, 6½", +pr shakers, in ftd leaf-shape SP fr 1,400.00
Cup, ftd, 2¼", +saucer, 5½" 250.00
Cup & saucer, demitasse; shiny, 2¼x4¾" 275.00
Dish, ice cream; Dmn Quilt, 4", set of 6 ....350.00
Finger bowl, ivy leaves, ruffled, Webb, Queen's, 5" 400.00
Goblet, shiny, 6½" 850.00
Pitcher, lemonade; Egyptian style, sq hdl, 7", +6 4" tumblers ..1,500.00
Pitcher, petticoat shape, duckbill spout, Mt WA, 7½" 965.00
Pitcher, ruffled top, loop hdl, Gunderson, 7x4" 375.00
Pitcher, squatty w/cylinder neck, Mt WA, 7" 325.00
Pitcher, tankard; Mt WA, 9" 800.00
Pitcher, tankard; rose w/Thomas Hood verse, 9" 3,000.00
Plate, coupe shape, 9½" 175.00
Plate, shiny, Mt WA, 9" 175.00
Rose bowl, chrysanthemums, Webb, 3⅜x3⅜" 495.00
Rose bowl, ivy/vines, ruffled sphere w/3 ft, 3¼x2½" 450.00
Rose bowl, scalloped edge, miniature, 2½" 150.00
Rose bowl, shiny, spherical, 2½" 130.00
Salad fork & spoon, orange/gold floral, butterfly, Webb 1,250.00
Shade, shiny, crimped ruffled top, 2½" dia fitter rim, pr 550.00
Shakers, Ribbed Pillar, Mt WA, 4", pr 300.00
Syrup, floral, Mt WA 3,250.00
Toothpick holder, EX color, sq top 295.00
Toothpick holder, yel daises, unfired, 2¾" 395.00
Toothpick holder, 2 yel daisies, vase shape, 2¾" 425.00
Tumbler, juice; Mt WA, 3½" 225.00
Tumbler, lemonade; shiny, Dmn Quilt, loop hdl, 5" 275.00
Tumbler, Mt WA, 3⅞x2¾" 225.00
Tumbler, Mt WA, 4½" 250.00
Vase, allover dots/scrolls/wht flowers, 3-lobe rim, ftd, 11" 4,000.00
Vase, asters, gourd shape, Mt WA, 12" 2,100.00
Vase, asters in wht on leafy vines, tapered, 4½" 450.00
Vase, bottle shape, Webb, Queen's, 7⅞x3⅞" 695.00
Vase, bulbous, flared rim, Mt WA, 5½" 495.00
Vase, bulbous, Mt WA, 6" 495.00
Vase, floral, bl w/gray leaves, squatty w/sq rim, 3½", pr 550.00
Vase, floral, collared 6-sided top, Webb, 3⅛x3" 295.00
Vase, floral, lav, gr & brn, 6-sided top, Webb, 3x3¾" 325.00
Vase, floral, tapered stick neck, Webb, Queen's, 7½" 650.00
Vase, floral & chain bands, Webb, 3¾x3½" 265.00
Vase, florals, gold dots, tapered stick neck, Mt WA, 10" 850.00
Vase, gourd shape, Mt WA, 10¼x5¼" 750.00
Vase, jack in pulpit; crimped rim, Mt WA, 14¼x6" 750.00
Vase, jack-in-pulpit; Mt WA, 7" 345.00
Vase, lily; Gunderson, 1940s, 9½" 365.00
Vase, lily; Mt WA, 9½" 550.00
Vase, lily; shiny, 8" 595.00
Vase, maidenhair fern allover, tapered w/hdls, ftd, 6" 495.00
Vase, trumpet form, Mt WA, 16" 850.00

Butter Molds and Stamps

The art of decorating butter began in Europe during the reign of

Charles II. This practice was continued in America by the farmer's wife who sold her homemade butter at the weekly market to earn extra money during hard times. A mold or stamp with a special design, hand carved either by her husband or a local craftsman, not only made her product more attractive but also helped identify it as hers. The pattern became the trademark of Mrs. Smith, and all who saw it knew that this was her butter. It was usually the rule that no two farms used the same mold within a certain area, thus the many variations and patterns available to the collector today. The most valuable are those which have animals, birds, or odd shapes. The most sought-after motifs are the eagle, cow, fish, and rooster. These works of early folk art are quickly disappearing from the market.

Molds

Acorn & fern, 4¾" 120.00
Cow, glass w/wooden hdl, 4⅝" 85.00
Cow, ½-lb, 3¾" 165.00
Flower design in ea of 4 sqs, dvtl, sq 88.00
Flower designs in each of 2 sqs, brass side hooks, ½-lb 75.00
Flower w/in rope border, EX details, 4½" dia case 125.00
Palm leaves, maple, 4¾" 120.00
Pineapple, deeply cvd, stamped: Pat April 17, 1866, 3¾" dia 125.00
Pomegranate, rnd case, 4¾" 40.00
Rose, EX cvg & details, rectangular, 8x5" 75.00
Rose & bud, 2-pc, rfn, 3½" dia 50.00
Sheaf of wheat, 2-pc, 2" dia 45.00
Sunburst, makes half-rnd ball shape, 1-pc, 2¼x1" dia 68.00
Swan, old finish, 5" dia 110.00
Tulip & leaf, dbl, EX detailed cvg, 1¼x3¾x3⅜" 60.00
3-leaf clovers, fancy, brass mechanism, 4x5½x3¼" 110.00

Stamps

Stylized tulip buds with crosshatching, deep incised leaf carving, notched border, pine, ca 1900, 3⅞", $110.00.

Acorn & foliage, wheel type w/hdl, scrubbed, 5½" dia 50.00
Cow, EX patina, inserted hdl, 3¼" 160.00
Cow, inserted trn hdl, scrubbed, 2½" 140.00
Cow, 1-pc trn hdl, soft dk finish, 4½" dia 330.00
Cow w/tree & flowers, 1-pc trn hdl, 5¼" dia 150.00
Eagle, deeply cvd, EX patina, 3⅜" dia 195.00
Eagle, primitive cvg, 1-pc trn hdl, worn patina, 3" dia 195.00
Eagle, stylized, 1-pc trn hdl, 4½" 220.00
Eagle & shield, 1-pc trn hdl, old dk patina, 3¾" 75.00
Eagle w/star, inserted hdl, 3¾" dia 110.00
Floral, EX cvg, lollipop type, early, EX 300.00
Flower, stylized, boat shape, old patina, 8¾" 160.00
Flower, stylized, w/hdl, lt wear, 3⅝" 80.00
Flower, 1-pc, trn hdl, age crack, 4⅜" dia 165.00
Flower & 2 lg leaves, EX cvg, 1-pc, knob hdl, 3⅞" dia 110.00

Fox, running, 1-pc trn hdl, scrubbed, 3½" dia 635.00
Heart & leaf, lollipop style, 6½" 165.00
Heart & tulip, deeply cvd, walnut, hdl missing, 4½" dia 110.00
Leaf, long hdl, old patina, 4¼" L 65.00
Sheaf of wheat, old dk finish, 2-pc trn hdl, 4" 85.00
Sheaf of wheat, rectangular, scrubbed/worn, 3½x4½" 99.00
Sheaf of wheat, 2½" 55.00
Sheaf of wheat & fern, 3" 65.00
Star, heart & sm hearts around edge, 2½" 65.00
Starflower, scrubbed, inserted trn hdl, 3¾" dia 120.00
Starflower ea side, pine, lollipop style, 8¾" L 550.00
Strawberry, foliage & flower, 1-pc whittled hdl, worn, 4¼" 165.00
Thistle, inserted trn hdl, scrubbed, 2½" dia 85.00
Tulip, stylized, rpl hdl, 1820 on bk, 3⅛x5⅝" 120.00
Tulip, stylized, scrubbed, rectangular, sm cracks, 5½x3½" 105.00
Tulip & stars, hand cvd, 5¼" 195.00
Tulip-like flower, appl stick hdl, 3" 55.00
Tulips & wings, 2¼" 70.00

Buttonhooks

The earliest known written reference to buttonhooks (shoe hooks, glove hooks, or collar buttoners) is dated 1611. They became a necessary implement in the 1850s when tight-fitting high-button shoes became fashionable. Later in the 19th century, ladies' button gloves and men's button-on collars and cuffs dictated specific types of buttoners, some with a closed wire loop instead of a hook end. Both shoes and gloves used as many as twenty-four buttons each. Usage began to wane in the late 1920s following a fashion change to low-cut laced shoes and the invention of the zipper. There was a brief resurgence of use following the 1948 movie 'High Button Shoes.' For a simple, needed utilitarian device, buttonhook handles were made from a surprising variety of materials: from natural wood, bone, ivory, agate and mother of pearl to plain steel, celluloid, aluminum, iron, lead and pewter, artistic copper, brass, silver, gold, and many other materials, in lengths that varied from under 2" to over 20". Many designs folded or retracted, and buttonhooks were often combined with shoehorns and other useful implements. Stamped steel buttonhooks often came free with the purchase of shoes, gloves or collars. Material, design, workmanship, condition and relative scarcity are the primary market value factors. Prices range from $1.00 to over $100.00. Buttonhooks are fairly easy to find, and they are interesting to display. Our advisor for this category is Richard Mathes; he is listed in the Directory under Ohio.

Buttonhook/penknife, ivory side plates, men's 40.00
Glove hook, gold plated, retractable, 3" 75.00
Glove hook, loop end, agate hdl, 2½" 35.00
Shoe hook, colored celluloid hdl, 8" 10.00
Shoe hook, faux ivory celluloid hdl, 8" 5.00
Shoe hook, stamped steel, advertising, 5" 3.00
Shoe hook, wooden hdl, 8" 8.00
Shoe hook/shoehorn combination, steel & celulloid, 9" 20.00

Calendar Plates

Calendar plates were advertising giveaways most popular from about 1906 until the late twenties. They were decorated with colorful underglaze decals of lovely ladies, flowers, animals, birds and, of course, the twelve months of the year of their issue. During the 1950s they came into vogue again, but never to the extent they were originally. Those with exceptional detailing, or those with scenes of a particular activity are most desirable, so are any from before 1906 or after 1930.

Our advisor for this category is Elizabeth M. Stout; she is listed in the Directory under Missouri.

1904, Happy New Year, Cupid & bell, 8"	35.00
1907, Christmas scene & holly	75.00
1907, Santa & sleigh, 9"	55.00
1909, fruit & flowers, 7"	25.00
1909, Gibson Girl, 8½"	30.00
1909, lady driving car, month's border	40.00
1910, Betsy Ross, Jersey City	38.00
1910, girl & horse, 6½"	30.00
1910, holly, Hitchock Hardware, Woodbury CT	38.00
1910, Indian chief's portrait, Imperial China, 8"	25.00
1910, Niagara Falls, NY City	25.00
1911, ducks in flight	30.00
1911, Old Acquaintance	25.00
1912, Indian Maiden	40.00
1912, owl, JR Hess, Leesburg VA	35.00
1914, deer at stream, 7"	35.00
1914, hunting scene, 8"	25.00
1916, flag, 7½"	28.00
1921, dove surrounded by 5 Allied flags, 7¼"	40.00
1924, Happy New Year, Asbury Park	35.00
1930, Dutch boy & dog, 9"	50.00

Calendars

Calendars are collected for their colorful prints, often attributed to a well-recognized artist of the period. Advertising calendars from the turn of the century often have a double appeal when representing a company whose tins, signs, store displays, etc., are also collectible. See also Parrish, Maxfield.

1881, Brooks & Co Varnishes, comic Black scenes, 25x26", EX	350.00
1888, newspaper premium, family scene, 20x15", VG	60.00
1895, Consumers' Brewing, lady in bl, full pad, 19x15", G	400.00
1896, FL Ober Brewing, dogs, cb diecut, w/pad, 17x9½", G	350.00
1897, Lorenz Schmidt's Mt Carbon Brewery, lady/dog, 20x15", G	350.00
1898, Christian Brecht, bathing beauty, 22x15"+fr, EX	900.00
1898, FA Poth & Son Brewers, hunter & dog, 30x20½", EX	800.00
1898, Oriental Brewery, comic boating scene, 28x10", EX	1,100.00
1898, Prospect Brewing, 3 children, printed pads, 21x16", EX	1,100.00
1899, John Kress Brewing, US fleet/Rough Riders, 32x20", G	700.00
1899, Keystone Brewing, sexy barmaid, w/pad, 30x15½", VG	900.00
1899, Listers Fertilizers, lady w/wheat sheaves, 29x19", EX	125.00
1899, Ringler Brewers, girl in flag, 24x16", EX	2,500.00

1899, Ruscher & Co. Lager Beer, lady within floral frame, metal strips, incomplete pad, NM, $950.00.

1899, Schmidt & Sons Brewing, cb diecut, 2 sheets: 15x12", EX	175.00
1899, WP Deppen Brewer, couple by bridge, 15½x20", G	700.00
1900, Sweet Violets, Dutton Nister, 4-panel diecut, 10x5½"	30.00
1900, T Barbey & Son Brewers, girl & dragonfly, 24x20", VG	725.00
1900, US Fidelity & Guaranty, Navy officers & boy, 24x16", EX	476.00
1901, Daisy Air Rifles, child w/air rifle, 22½x15½", VG	3,200.00
1901, Du Pont Smokeless Powder, sgn EH Osthaus, 28x14", EX	1,400.00
1902, Bergdoll's Beer, couple drinking, 22x16½", EX	400.00
1902, Fett & Fett Beer, 3 men at cards, 23x15", VG	400.00
1902, P Barbey & Son Brewers, lady in purple, 24x20", EX	1,000.00

1902, The Little Folks Calendar, diecut, 4-page, 4¾x3¾", EX, $75.00.

1903, John Stocker, lady in chair, Kaufmann/Strauss, 19x15", EX	550.00
1903, Lauer Brewing, Flower's Stock Farm, 29x21", VG	450.00
1903, Loranz Schmidt's Mt Carbon Brewery, 21x17", G	1,100.00
1903, Yuengling Brewery, factory, partial pad, 27x20", VG	575.00
1904, David Stevenson Brewing, Uncle Sam, 28x19½", EX	2,300.00
1904, Plano Harvesting Machinery, girl w/cherries, 21x15", EX	350.00
1905, Lauer Brewing, factory and products, 27½x19½", VG	650.00
1906, Adloff & Hauewaas Beer, cb, lady & lilies, 17x13½", NM	2,000.00
1907, A Scheidt Brewing, sailor ladies, full pad, 30x21", VG	600.00
1907, Lauer Brewing, factory, full pad, 29x20", VG	475.00
1907, Mathie Brewing, cherub diecut, full pad, 16x15", EX	1,300.00
1908, Adloff & Hauerwaas, cb diecut of maids/putti, 20x13"	1,250.00
1908, Ballantines Breweries, factory, no pad, 20x12½", VG	320.00
1908, De Laval, babe & Bessie, 20x13", G	800.00
1908, Kenison, girl in oval, 19½x14", complete, NM	125.00
1909, Geo Zepp Brewery, emb cb, 2 kids w/puppies, 20x20", VG	1,000.00
1910, De Laval Cream Separators, lady in oval, 20x13", VG	350.00
1910, E Robinson's Sons Brewing, lady/roses, w/pad, 22x11", VG	350.00
1911, H Koehler & Co Brewers, lady in evening gown, 18x11", EX	225.00
1911, McCormick Paper, hunters, full pad, 20x13", NM	175.00
1912, Consumers' Brewing, lady in gr & blk, w/pad, 31x16", EX	400.00
1912, Independent Brewing, 3 men at table, 20x14", VG	350.00
1912, Sharples Cream Separator, milk maid & cown, 14x7"+fr, EX	300.00
1913, Ebling Brewing, factory/casino/restaurant, 29x21", VG	500.00
1914, Rieger & Gretz Brewing, lady's portrait, Lunch, 22", VG	450.00
1915, Hohenadel Beer, John L Sullivan, boxing pose, 23x17", G	200.00
1917, US Ammunition, slain game birds, fr, 28x18", EX	260.00
1919, Myers' Pumps, protraits & factory, 48x17", VG	150.00
1922, Sharples Tubular Cream Separators, lady, vertical, EX	110.00
1925, Doe-Wah-Jack, stove/Indian/pioneer lady, 21x11", EX	225.00
1925, Peters Cartridge Co, mallards, fr, 33x18", EX	350.00
1928, Harrisburg Pilot, gypsy girl, 45x22", EX	90.00
1935, Globe Brewing, Indian princess & lilies, 28x14", NM	425.00
1935, Nat'l Life...Insurance, barnyard band, 13½x10½", G	25.00

Caliente

Caliente was a line of colored dinnerware made by the Paden City

Pottery Company in Paden City, West Virginia. It was produced during the 1930s and 1940s in tangerine, yellow, blue, green, and cobalt blue.

Bowl, salad; 10" **25.00**
Bowl, 9" **20.00**
Candle holder **15.00**
Creamer **14.00**
Cup & saucer, cobalt **15.00**
Plate, 6" **5.00**
Plate, 9½" **10.00**
Platter, 14" **25.00**
Shakers, pr **25.00**
Sugar bowl, w/lid **18.00**
Teapot **45.00**

California Faience

California Faience was the trade name used by William V. Bragdon and Chauncy R. Thomas on vases, bowls, and other artware produced at their pottery known as 'The Tile Shop' in Berkeley, California, from 1920 to 1930. Faience tile was the principal product of the business during these years and is the favorite with today's collectors. Items in a glossy glaze are rare and therefore more valuable. Tiles were marked 'California Faience' with a die stamp.

Bowl, bl on turq gloss, turq int, fluted, 2½x6" **165.00**
Figurine, Oriental doing laundry, 4-color, 5x6x6¼" **115.00**
Tile, 4-color floral **325.00**
Vase, maroon, 9x8" **495.00**
Vase, stylized dove band & arrowheads, turq gloss, 6½" **350.00**
Vase, turq, 8" **250.00**
Vase, turq gloss, bulbous, 5½" **185.00**
Vase, yel semimatt, 6" **325.00**

California Perfume Company

D.H. McConnell, Sr., founded the California Perfume Company (C.P. Company; C.P.C.) in 1886 in New York City. He had previously been a salesman for a book company, which he later purchased. His door-to-door sales usually involved the lady of the house, to whom he presented a complimentary bottle of inexpensive perfume. Upon determining his perfume to be more popular than his books, he decided that the manufacture of perfume might be more lucrative. He bottled toiletries under the name 'California Perfume Company' and a line of household products called 'Perfection.' In 1928 the name 'Avon' appeared on the label, and in 1939 the C.P.C. name was entirely removed from the product. The success of the company is attributed to the door-to-door sales approach and 'money back' guarantee offered by his first 'Depot Agent,' Mrs. P.F.E. Albee, known today as the 'Avon Lady.'

The company's containers are quite collectible today, especially the older, hard-to-find items. Advanced collectors seek bottles and other items labeled Goetting & Co., New York; Goetting's; or Savoi Et Cie, Paris. Such examples date from 1871 to 1896. The Goetting Company was purchased by D.H. McConnell; Savoi Et Cie was a line which they imported to sell through department stores. Also of special interest are packaging and advertising with the Ambrosia or Hinze Ambrosia Company label. This was a subsidiary company whose objective seems to have been to produce a line of face creams, etc., for sale through drugstores and other such commercial outlets. They operated in New York from about 1875 until 1954. Because very little is known about these companies and since only a few examples of their product containers and advertising material have been found, market values for

such items have not yet been established. Other items sought by the collector include products marked Gertrude Recordon, Marvel Electric Silver Cleaner, Easy Day Automatic Clothes Washer, pre-1930 catalogs, and California Perfume Company 1909 and 1910 calendars.

There are hundreds of local Avon Collector Clubs throughout the world that also have C.P.C. collectors in their membership. If you are interested in joining, locating, or starting a new club, contact the National Association of Avon Collectors, Inc., listed in the Directory under Clubs, Newsletters, and Catalogs. Those wanting a National Newsletter Club or price guides may contact Avon Times, listed in the same section. Inquiries concerning California Perfume Company items and the companies or items mentioned in the previous paragraph should be directed toward our advisor, Dick Pardini, whose address is given under California. (Please send a large SASE; not interested in Avons, 'Perfection' marked C.P.C.'s, or Anniversary Keepsakes.)

Am Ideal Talcum, tin, left profile of lady, 1911, M **100.00**
Baby Powder, tin, CP trademk, 1905, M **120.00**
Baby Powder, tin, Eureka trademk, 1898, M **125.00**
Bandoline, 1908, 2-oz **100.00**
Bay Rum, glass stopper, 126 Chambers St NY, 1915, 4-oz **130.00**
Cut Glass Perfume, stopper, ribbon, 7-sided rnd label, 1915 ....**225.00**
Daphne perfume, emb glass, flat glass stopper, 1- & 2-oz, 1925 ..**140.00**
Dermol Massage Cream, milk glass, 1923, 1-lb **110.00**
Face Lotion, CP trademk, 1908 ....**115.00**
French Perfumes, 1900s, ¼-oz to 2-oz, ea **125.00**
Lait Virginal, 1900, 2-oz **150.00**
Lavender Salts, gr w/metal top, glass stopper, 1890s **250.00**
Massage Cream, stopper, 1896 ....**160.00**
Mission Garden Talc set, 2 tins in silk-lined box, 1923, M **230.00**
Natoma Rose Perfume, 1-oz w/atomizer, free sample label, '14, M .**180.00**

Natoma Rolling Massage Cream, 1916, $150.00.

Pyrox Toothp Powder, bl tin, M **80.00**
Shampoo Cream, man's face on lid, 1896, 4-oz, M **135.00**
Toothwash, brass stopper, 1921, 2-oz **100.00**
Trailing Arbutus Cream, tubes, 1925, M **40.00**
Travelers Perfume, metal cover, glass stopper, 1900 ....**130.00**
Vernafleur Compact, SP, single & dbl, 1928, M **40.00**
Vernafleur Toilet Soap set, 3 bars in box, 1925, M **115.00**
Violet water, glass stopper, Eureka trademk, '08, 8-oz **200.00**
Witch Hazel, 1896, 8-oz **110.00**

Calling Cards, Cases, and Receivers

The practice of announcing one's arrival with a calling card borne by the maid to the mistress of the house was a social grace of the Victorian era. Different messages (condolences, a personal visit, or a good-by) were related by turning down one corner or another. The custom was forgotten by WWI. Fashionable ladies and gents carried their personally engraved cards in elaborate cases made of such materials as embossed silver, mother-of-pearl with intricate inlay, tortoise shell, and ivory. Card receivers held cards left by visitors who called while the mistress was out or 'not receiving.' Calling cards with fringe, die-cut flaps that cover the name, or an unusual decoration are worth about $3.00 to $4.00, while plain cards usually sell for around $1.00.

Cases

Abalone shell inlay, cvd wht floral medallion, 3⅝" **85.00**
Gold, 14k, Nouveau styling **650.00**
Ivory, cvd figures in garden, 1800s, 3¾x2¾" **195.00**
MOP, deer relief, grapevines, 3⅝" **85.00**
Sterling, chinoiserie relief, grapevines, 3¾" **215.00**
Tin, vertical strap, weekdays in French on pockets, 2x11" **45.00**
Tortoise shell, fishing scene, canted corners, 4" L **82.50**
Tunbridge, mosaic florals, mid-1800s, EX **85.00**

Receivers

Brass, girl's face w/bonnet, 4½x4½" **85.00**
CI, cupped hands w/grapes at wrist, 1865 ....**85.00**
Pewter, lady w/harp beside tray, Archibald Knox, EX **315.00**
Pewter, tiger's head w/bared teeth ea side, 3½x6" **65.00**
Sterling, allover diapering w/monogram, ftd, Schultz, 6" **120.00**
Sterling, woodland courtship scene, Nouveau style **250.00**
Wht metal, Art Nouveau lady emb on fan shape, 5x6" **78.00**

Camark

The Camden Art and Tile Company (commonly known as Camark) of Camden, Arkansas, was organized in the Fall of 1926 by Samuel J. 'Jack' Carnes. Using clays from Arkansas, John Lessell, who had been hired as Art Director by Carnes, produced the initial lustre and iridescent Lessell wares for Camark ('CAM'den, 'ARK'ansas) before his death in December 1926. Before the plant opened in the Spring of 1927, Carnes brought John's wife, Jeanne, and step-daughter Billie to oversee the art department's manufacture of Le-Camark. Production by the Lessell family included variations of J.B. Owens' Soudanese and Opalesce and Weller's Marengo and Lamar. Camark's version of Marengo was called Old English. They also made wares identical to Weller's LaSa. Pieces made by John Lessell back in Ohio were signed 'Lessell,' while those made by Jeanne and Billie in Arkansas during 1927 were signed 'Le-Camark.' By 1928 Camark's production centered on traditional glazes. Drip glazes similar to Muncie Pottery were produced, in particular the green drip over pink. In the 1930s commercial castware with simple glossy and matt finishes became the primary focus and would continue so until Camark closed in the early 1960s. Between the 1960s and 1980s the company operated mainly as a retail store selling existing inventory, but some limited production occurred. In 1986 the company was purchased by the Ashcraft family of Camden, but no pottery has yet been made at the factory.

Our advisor for this category is David Edwin Gifford. He is listed in the Directory under Arkansas. Mr. Gifford is starting an Arkansas Pottery Collector's Society (Camark, Niloak, and others) and seeks those who are interested in joining to write him.

Figurine, cat, blk gloss, climbing, 12" **35.00**
Figurine, cat, wht gloss, beside fishbowl, 8" **30.00**
Jug, mini whiskey, golden brn gloss, 'Pure Corn,' 5" **30.00**
Jug, orange & gr, ball form, clay stopper, 6½" **38.00**
Novelty, cotton dispenser, rabbit, orange, 3" **12.00**
Novelty, dogs, Pointer & Setter, pr **18.00**

Pelican pitcher, green, ball shape, 5¾", **$35.00.**

Pitcher, parrot hdl, bl gloss, 6½" **65.00**
Planter, swans, blk, dbl neck, 8" **15.00**
Shakers, letters S&P, bl, pr **10.00**
Sign, state of Arkansas, gr, 6½" **60.00**
Vase, crackle finish, wht, gold mk, 8" **125.00**
Vase, fish form, orange & brn mottle, 8" **45.00**
Vase, gold lustre palm trees on bronze, sgn Lessell, 12" **500.00**
Vase, Old English, plum & cream, sgn Le-Camark, 8½" **350.00**
Vase, orange & gr, fluted, 5" **25.00**
Wall pocket, flour scoop, pk, 8" **12.00**

Cambridge Glass

The Cambridge Glass Company began operations in 1901 in Cambridge, Ohio. Primarily they made crystal dinnerware and well-designed accessory pieces until the 1920s when they introduced the concept of color that was to become so popular on the American dinnerware market. Always maintaining high standards of quality and elegance, they produced many lines that became best-sellers; through the twenties and thirties they were recognized as the largest manufacturer of this type of glassware in the world.

Of the various marks the company used, the 'C in triangle' is the most familiar. Production stopped in 1958. For a more thorough study of the subject, we recommend *Colors in Cambridge Glass* by the National Cambridge Collectors, Inc.; their address may be found in the Directory under Clubs. *Glass Animals and Figural Flower Frogs of the Depression Era* by Lee Garmon and Dick Spencer is a wonderful source for an in-depth view of this particular aspect of glass collecting. They are both listed in the Directory under Illinois. See also Carnival Glass; Glass Animals.

Apple Blossom, crystal, bowl, low ftd, 11" **25.00**
Apple Blossom, crystal, bowl, pickle; 9" **13.00**
Apple Blossom, crystal, bowl, relish; 4-part, 12" **25.00**
Apple Blossom, crystal, bowl, 13" **30.00**
Apple Blossom, crystal, comport, fruit cocktail; 4" **12.50**
Apple Blossom, crystal, plate, bread & butter; sq **4.00**
Apple Blossom, crystal, plate, dinner; 9½" **40.00**
Apple Blossom, crystal, plate, salad; sq **10.00**
Apple Blossom, crystal, plate, tea; 7½" **9.00**
Apple Blossom, crystal, stem, cocktail; #3130, 3-oz **15.00**
Apple Blossom, crystal, tumbler, #3025, 10-oz **15.00**
Apple Blossom, crystal, tumbler, #3135, ftd, 8-oz **12.00**
Apple Blossom, crystal, vase, rippled sides, 6" **27.50**
Apple Blossom, pk or gr, bowl, finger; #3130, w/plate **37.50**
Apple Blossom, yel or amber, ashtray, heavy, 6" **150.00**

Apple Blossom, yel or amber, bowl, bonbon 25.00
Apple Blossom, yel or amber, bowl, cereal; 6" 25.00
Apple Blossom, yel or amber, bowl, flat, 12" 50.00
Apple Blossom, yel or amber, bowl, relish; 4-part, 12" 45.00
Apple Blossom, yel or amber, creamer, ftd 17.50
Apple Blossom, yel or amber, pitcher, #3130, 64-oz 195.00
Apple Blossom, yel or amber, pitcher, 76-oz 200.00
Apple Blossom, yel or amber, plate, 8½" 20.00
Apple Blossom, yel or amber, saucer 5.00
Apple Blossom, yel or amber, stem, #3025, 10-oz 22.00
Apple Blossom, yel or amber, sugar bowl, ftd 16.00
Apple Blossom, yel or amber, tumbler, #3130, ftd, 5-oz 20.00
Apple Blossom, yel or amber, tumbler, #3135, ftd, 12-oz 32.50
Apple Blossom, yel or amber, tumbler, #3400, ftd, 12-oz 32.50
Apple Blossom, yel or amber, tumbler, 6" 30.00
Candlelight, crystal, bowl, #3900/34, 2-hdl, 11" 60.00
Candlelight, crystal, bowl, #3900/62, 4-toed, flared, 12" 62.50
Candlelight, crystal, candlestick, #3900/67, 5" 37.50
Candlelight, crystal, candlestick, #3900/74, 3-light, 6" 45.00
Candlelight, crystal, comport, #3121, blown, 5⅜" 57.50
Candlelight, crystal, creamer, #3900/40, ind 20.00
Candlelight, crystal, ice bucket, #3900/671 ....100.00
Candlelight, crystal, mayonnaise, #3900/129, 3-pc 57.50
Candlelight, crystal, plate, #3900/26, 4-toed, 12" 55.00
Candlelight, crystal, relish, #3900/120, 5-part, 12" 57.50
Candlelight, crystal, relish, #3900/125, 3-part, 9" 42.50
Candlelight, crystal, stem, cocktail; #3776, 3-oz 25.00
Candlelight, crystal, stem, cordial; #3776, 1-oz 65.00
Candlelight, crystal, stem, oyster cocktail; #3111, 4½-oz 27.50
Candlelight, crystal, stem, water; #3111, 10-oz 30.00
Candlelight, crystal, stem, wine; #3111, 2½-oz 35.00
Candlelight, crystal, vase, #279, ftd, 13" 97.50
Candlelight, crystal, vase, #6004, ftd, 8" 45.00
Candlelight, crystal, vase, bud; #278, ftd, 11" 65.00

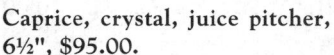

Caprice, crystal, juice pitcher, 6½", $95.00.

Caprice, bl or pk, ashtray, #216, 5" 25.00
Caprice, bl or pk, bowl, #60, crimped, 4-ftd, 11" 100.00
Caprice, bl or pk, bowl, #61, crimped, 4-ftd, 12½" 75.00
Caprice, bl or pk, bowl, almond; #95, 4-ft, 2" 40.00
Caprice, bl or pk, candlestick, #74, 3-light 65.00
Caprice, bl or pk, comport, #130, 6" 60.00
Caprice, bl or pk, creamer, #40, ind 20.00
Caprice, bl or pk, plate, #22, 8½" 32.50
Caprice, bl or pk, plate, #28, 4-ftd, 14" 80.00
Caprice, bl or pk, stem, claret; #5, 4½-oz 175.00
Caprice, bl or pk, tumbler, #188, flat, 2-oz 50.00
Caprice, bl or pk, tumbler, #300, 10-oz 40.00
Caprice, bl or pk, tumbler, #300, 12-oz 40.00
Caprice, bl or pk, vase, #254, 6" 175.00
Caprice, bl or pk, vase, #346, crimped, 7½" 200.00

Caprice, bl or pk, vase, ivy bowl; #232, 5" 150.00
Caprice, crystal, ashtray, #214, 3" 6.00
Caprice, crystal, ashtray, #215, 4" 7.00
Caprice, crystal, bonbon, #133, sq, ftd, 6" 14.00
Caprice, crystal, bottle, bitters; #186, 7-oz 175.00
Caprice, crystal, bowl, #52, crimped, 4-ft, 9½" 30.00
Caprice, crystal, bowl, #65, oval, 2-hdl, 4-ftd, 11" 30.00
Caprice, crystal, bowl, pickle; #102, 9" 20.00
Caprice, crystal, bowl, relish; #124, 3-part, 8" 17.50
Caprice, crystal, bowl, salad; #57, 4-ftd, 10" 32.50
Caprice, crystal, comport, #130, low ftd, 7" 20.00
Caprice, crystal, cracker jar, #202, w/lid 195.00
Caprice, crystal, creamer, #38, med 8.00
Caprice, crystal, oil, #101, w/stopper, 3-oz 22.00
Caprice, crystal, plate, #30, 16" 35.00
Caprice, crystal, plate, cabaret; #26, 11½" 25.00
Caprice, crystal, plate, cabaret; #32, 4-ftd, 11" 22.00
Caprice, crystal, punch bowl, ftd 2,000.00

Caprice, crystal, Flat shaker, $20.00; Footed shaker, $25.00; Creamer and sugar bowl, individual, $40.00.

Caprice, crystal, shakers, #91, ball form, pr 37.50
Caprice, crystal, stem, sherbet; #2, tall, 7-oz 17.50
Caprice, crystal, stem, water; #1, 10-oz 26.00
Caprice, crystal, stem, wine; #6, 3-oz 27.50
Caprice, crystal, sugar bowl, ind, #40 ....10.00
Caprice, crystal, tray, #42, oval, 9" 18.00
Caprice, crystal, tumbler, #10, ftd, 10-oz 18.00
Caprice, crystal, tumbler, #11, ftd , 5-oz 20.00
Caprice, crystal, tumbler, juice; #310, flat, 5-oz 15.00
Caprice, crystal, tumbler, whiskey; #300, 2½-oz 40.00
Caprice, crystal, vase, #252, 4" 45.00
Caprice, crystal, vase, #339, 8½" 50.00
Caprice, crystal, vase, #340, crimped, 9½" 150.00
Caprice, crystal, vase, #345, 5½" 40.00
Chantilly, crystal, bowl, celery/relish; 3-part, 12" 32.50
Chantilly, crystal, bowl, celery/relish; 3-part, 9" 25.00
Chantilly, crystal, bowl, cocktail icer; 2-pc 55.00
Chantilly, crystal, bowl, flared, 4-ftd, 10" 35.00
Chantilly, crystal, bowl, oval, 4-ftd, 12" 35.00
Chantilly, crystal, bowl, relish/ pickle; 7" 20.00
Chantilly, crystal, bowl, relish/pickle; 2-part, 7" 18.00
Chantilly, crystal, bowl, tab-hdld, ftd, 11½" 32.50
Chantilly, crystal, bowl, tab-hdld, 11" 30.00
Chantilly, crystal, butter dish, ¼-lb 200.00
Chantilly, crystal, comport, blown, 5⅜" 37.50
Chantilly, crystal, decanter, ball form 175.00
Chantilly, crystal, decanter, ftd 150.00
Chantilly, crystal, hat, lg 200.00
Chantilly, crystal, hat, sm 150.00
Chantilly, crystal, ice bucket, w/chrome hdl 65.00
Chantilly, crystal, mayonnaise, w/liner & ladle 37.50

Chantilly, crystal, pitcher, upright 175.00
Chantilly, crystal, plate, bread & butter; 6½" 6.50
Chantilly, crystal, plate, salad; crescent form 75.00
Chantilly, crystal, plate, torte; 14" 35.00
Chantilly, crystal, sherbet; #3600, low, 7-oz 15.00
Chantilly, crystal, stem, claret; #3600, 4½-oz 35.00
Chantilly, crystal, stem, claret; #3779, 4½" 35.00
Chantilly, crystal, stem, cocktail; #3625, 3-oz 27.50
Chantilly, crystal, stem, cocktail; #3775, 3-oz 25.00
Chantilly, crystal, stem, cocktail; #3779, 3-oz 25.00
Chantilly, crystal, stem, cordial; #3600, 1-oz 45.00
Chantilly, crystal, stem, cordial; #3775, 1-oz 45.00
Chantilly, crystal, stem, cordial; #3779, 1-oz 55.00
Chantilly, crystal, stem, oyster cocktail; #3775, 4½-oz 15.00
Chantilly, crystal, stem, oyster cocktail; #3779, low, 4½-oz 20.00
Chantilly, crystal, stem, oyster cocktail; low, 4½-oz 16.00
Chantilly, crystal, stem, sherbet; #3600, tall, 7-oz 17.50
Chantilly, crystal, stem, sherbet; #3779, low, 6-oz 15.00
Chantilly, crystal, stem, water; #3779, 9-oz 20.00
Chantilly, crystal, stem, wine; #3600, 2½" 30.00
Chantilly, crystal, stem, wine; #3779, 2½" 30.00
Chantilly, crystal, tumbler, juice; #3779, ftd, 5-oz 15.00
Chantilly, crystal, tumbler, tea; #3600, ftd, 12-oz 20.00
Chantilly, crystal, vase, flower; high ft, 6" 22.00
Chantilly, crystal, vase, flower; ped ft, 11" 45.00
Chantilly, crystal, vase, globe form, 5" 30.00
Chantilly, crystal, vase, keyhole base, 9" 35.00
Cleo, bl, bowl, comport; 4-ftd, 6" 50.00
Cleo, bl, bowl, console; 12" 65.00
Cleo, bl, bowl, oval, 11½" 75.00
Cleo, bl, bowl, pickle; Decagon, 9" 60.00
Cleo, bl, bowl, relish; 2-part 40.00
Cleo, bl, bowl, soup; tab-hdld, 7½" 40.00
Cleo, bl, candlestick, 1-light 35.00
Cleo, bl, comport, #3115, tall, 7" 75.00
Cleo, bl, creamer, Decagon 27.50
Cleo, bl, creamer, ftd 30.00
Cleo, bl, ice tub 85.00
Cleo, bl, mayonnaise, ftd 45.00
Cleo, bl, plate, hdls, Decagon, 7" 20.00
Cleo, bl, plate, 7" 15.00
Cleo, bl, platter, 12" 150.00
Cleo, bl, saucer, decagon 5.00
Cleo, bl, server, center hdl, 12" 65.00
Cleo, bl, sugar bowl, Decagon 25.00
Cleo, bl, tumbler, #3077, ftd, 10-oz 45.00
Cleo, bl, tumbler, #3077, ftd, 5-oz 40.00
Cleo, bl, tumbler, #3077, ftd, 5-oz 40.00
Cleo, colors other than bl, bowl, 8½" 40.00
Cleo, colors other than bl, candy box 75.00
Cleo, colors other than bl, candy dish, w/lid, tall 145.00
Cleo, colors other than bl, pitcher, #3077, w/lid, 63-oz 250.00
Cleo, colors other than bl, pitcher, #38, 3½-pt 175.00
Cleo, colors other than bl, pitcher, w/lid, 22-oz 150.00
Cleo, colors other than bl, salt cellar, 1½" 65.00
Cleo, colors other than bl, tobacco humidor 325.00
Cleo, colors other than bl, tumbler, #3115, ftd, 10-oz 37.50
Cleo, colors other than bl, tumbler, #3115, ftd, 12-oz 35.00
Cleo, colors other than bl, tumbler, #3115, ftd, 8-oz 25.00
Cleo, colors other than bl, vase, 11" 125.00
Crown Tuscan, bowl, flying nude stem, gold trim 250.00
Crown Tuscan, bowl, seashell, #18, 3-toed, 10" 85.00
Crown Tuscan, candlestick, nude stem 125.00
Crown Tuscan, candlesticks, dolphin, 3½", pr 250.00

Crown Tuscan, candlesticks, fish, #66, pr 175.00
Crown Tuscan, candy dish, 3-part, w/lid 50.00
Crown Tuscan, comport, cupped, nude stem 175.00
Crown Tuscan, compote, nude stem, w/pnt decor, 7" 120.00
Crown Tuscan, compote, seashell, floral decor, 7" 145.00
Crown Tuscan, decanter, Nautilus, 40-oz, +5 2-oz shots 500.00
Crown Tuscan, ivy ball, nude stem 255.00
Crown Tuscan, vase, cornucopia; 3¾" 20.00
Crown Tuscan, vase, cornucopia; #3900/575, 10" 65.00
Crown Tuscan/yel, cocktail, nude stem 120.00
Decagon, pastel colors, bowl, almond; ftd, 6" 20.00
Decagon, pastel colors, bowl, bonbon; 2-hdl, 6¼" 10.00
Decagon, pastel colors, bowl, bouillon; w/liner 7.50
Decagon, pastel colors, bowl, cranberry; bell form, 3½" 12.00
Decagon, pastel colors, bowl, fruit; bell form, 5½" 5.50
Decagon, pastel colors, bowl, relish; 2-part, 11" 10.00
Decagon, pastel colors, bowl, relish; 2-part, 9" 9.00
Decagon, pastel colors, bowl, vegetable; oval, 9½" 12.00
Decagon, pastel colors, bowl, vegetable; rnd, 11" 17.00
Decagon, pastel colors, comport, tall, 7" 20.00
Decagon, pastel colors, mayonnaise, w/liner & ladle 18.00
Decagon, pastel colors, plate, bread & butter; 6¼" 3.00
Decagon, pastel colors, plate, service; 12½" 9.00
Decagon, pastel colors, salt cellar, ftd, 1½" 11.00
Decagon, pastel colors, sauce boat, w/underplate 45.00
Decagon, pastel colors, server, center hdl 12.00
Decagon, pastel colors, service; 2-hdl, 13" 20.00
Decagon, pastel colors, stem, sherbet; high, 6-oz 10.00
Decagon, pastel colors, sugar bowl, ftd 9.00
Decagon, pastel colors, sugar bowl, scalloped edge 9.00
Decagon, pastel colors, sugar bowl, tall, ftd, lg 18.00
Decagon, pastel colors, tray, center hdl, 12" 15.00
Decagon, pastel colors, tumbler, service; oval, 15" 20.00
Decagon, red & bl, bowl, cereal; bell form, 6" 15.00
Decagon, red & bl, bowl, fruit; flat rim, 5¾" 11.00
Decagon, red & bl, bowl, vegetable; rnd, 9" 24.00
Decagon, red & bl, comport, low ft, 6½" 25.00
Decagon, red & bl, comport, 5¾" 20.00
Decagon, red & bl, plate, salad; 8½" 10.00
Decagon, red & bl, plate, service; 10" 25.00
Decagon, red & bl, tray, service; oval, 12" 20.00
Decagon, red & bl, tumbler, ftd, 5-oz 10.00
Decagon, red or bl, ice bucket 60.00
Decagon, red or bl, ice tub 45.00
Decagon, red or bl, tray, pickle; 9" 17.50
Diane, crystal, basket, 2-hdl, ftd, 6" 16.00
Diane, crystal, bottle, bitters 125.00
Diane, crystal, bowl, #3122 ....25.00
Diane, crystal, bowl, baker; 10" 40.00
Diane, crystal, bowl, cereal; 6" 25.00
Diane, crystal, bowl, finger; #3106, w/liner 30.00
Diane, crystal, bowl, relish; 2-part, 6" 18.00
Diane, crystal, bowl, relish; 2-part, 7" 20.00
Diane, crystal, bowl, relish; 3-part, 6½" 20.00
Diane, crystal, bowl, 4-ftd, 11" 40.00
Diane, crystal, bowl, 4-ftd, 12" 40.00
Diane, crystal, cabinet flask 185.00
Diane, crystal, candlestick, 5" 17.50
Diane, crystal, cigarette urn 42.50
Diane, crystal, cocktail icer, 2-pc 55.00
Diane, crystal, comport, 5½" 25.00
Diane, crystal, creamer 14.00
Diane, crystal, decanter, ball form 175.00
Diane, crystal, pitcher, Doulton 275.00

Diane, crystal, pitcher, martini 750.00
Diane, crystal, pitcher, upright 150.00
Diane, crystal, plate, dinner; 10½" 60.00
Diane, crystal, plate, 8½" 11.00
Diane, crystal, shakers, flat, pr 28.00
Diane, crystal, stem, wine; #3122, 2½-oz 22.00
Diane, crystal, tumbler, #1066, ftd, 3-oz 15.00
Diane, crystal, tumbler, #3122, 2½-oz 25.00
Diane, crystal, tumbler, juice; ft, 5-oz 27.00
Diane, crystal, tumbler, water; #3122, 9-oz 13.00
Diane, crystal, tumbler, 13-oz 30.00
Diane, crystal, vase, flower; high ft, 6" 32.50
Diane, crystal, vase, flower; high ft, 8" 40.00
Diane, crystal, vase, keyhole base, 12" 65.00
Elaine, crystal, bowl, finger; #3104, w/liner 25.00
Elaine, crystal, bowl, flared, 3-ftd, 10" 30.00
Elaine, crystal, bowl, relish; 2-part, 6" 16.00
Elaine, crystal, bowl, tab-hdld, 11" 30.00
Elaine, crystal, bowl, 2-light, 6" 27.50
Elaine, crystal, candlestick, 3-light, 6" 35.00
Elaine, crystal, comport, 5½" 30.00
Elaine, crystal, cup 20.00
Elaine, crystal, hat, 9" 250.00
Elaine, crystal, pitcher, ball form 125.00
Elaine, crystal, pitcher, Doulton 275.00
Elaine, crystal, pitcher, upright 175.00
Elaine, crystal, plate, bread & butter; 6½" 7.00
Elaine, crystal, plate, dinner; 10½" 60.00
Elaine, crystal, plate, salad; 8" 15.00
Elaine, crystal, plate, torte; 14" 30.00
Elaine, crystal, plate, 2-hdl, 6" 10.00
Elaine, crystal, saucer 3.00
Elaine, crystal, shakers, hdld, pr 35.00
Elaine, crystal, stem, claret; #3500, 4½-oz 30.00
Elaine, crystal, stem, goblet; #1402 ....20.00
Elaine, crystal, stem, goblet; #3104, 9-oz 75.00
Elaine, crystal, stem, wine; 2½-oz 27.50
Elaine, crystal, vase, ftd, keyhole, 9" 45.00
Elaine, crystal, vase, ftd, 8" 40.00
Flower frog, Bashful Charlotte, bl frost, 11" 495.00
Flower frog, Bashful Charlotte, crystal, 11" 155.00
Flower frog, Bashful Charlotte, crystal, 6½" 70.00
Flower frog, Bashful Charlotte, gr, 11" 250.00
Flower frog, Bashful Charlotte, gr, 6½" 145.00
Flower frog, Draped Lady, crystal, 13" 160.00
Flower frog, Draped Lady, crystal, 8½" 97.00
Flower frog, Draped Lady, crystal frost, 13" 150.00
Flower frog, Draped Lady, dk amber, 13" 290.00
Flower frog, Draped Lady, dk amber, 8½" 195.00
Flower frog, Draped Lady, gr, 8½" 120.00
Flower frog, Draped Lady, gr frost, 8½" 125.00
Flower frog, Draped Lady, lt amber, 8½" 165.00
Flower frog, Draped Lady, lt pk, 8½" 100.00
Flower frog, Draped Lady, lt pk frost, 13" 175.00
Flower frog, Draped Lady, med pk, 8½" 100.00
Flower frog, Draped Lady, Moonlight bl, 8½" 325.00
Flower frog, Draped Lady, pk frost, 8½" 125.00
Flower frog, Draped Lady, ½ frost & ½ lt pk, 13" 165.00
Flower frog, Mandolin Lady, crystal 195.00
Flower frog, Mandolin Lady, gr 295.00
Flower frog, Rose Lady, crystal, tall base, 9½" 155.00
Flower frog, Rose Lady, dk amber, tall base, 9½" 245.00
Flower frog, Rose Lady, dk pk, 8½" 190.00
Flower frog, Rose Lady, gr, 8½" 245.00

Flower frog, Two Kids, crystal 150.00
Gloria, crystal, basket, 2-hdl, 6" 16.00
Gloria, crystal, bowl, bonbon; 2-hdl, 5½" 14.00
Gloria, crystal, bowl, cereal; rnd, 6" 12.00
Gloria, crystal, bowl, fruit; sq, saucer type, 5" 7.00
Gloria, crystal, bowl, nut; 4-ftd, 3" 35.00
Gloria, crystal, bowl, oval, 4-ftd, 12" 30.00
Gloria, crystal, comport, low, 7" 30.00
Gloria, crystal, comport, tall, 7" 35.00
Gloria, crystal, comport, 4-ftd, 5" 17.00
Gloria, crystal, creamer, ftd 11.00
Gloria, crystal, plate, dinner; sq 50.00
Gloria, crystal, plate, salad; sq 7.00
Gloria, crystal, plate, 2-hdl, 11" 15.00
Gloria, crystal, saucer, rnd 2.00
Gloria, crystal, shakers, metal tops, ftd, pr 32.50
Gloria, crystal, stem, cocktail; #3035, 3½-oz 17.00
Gloria, crystal, stem, water; #3120, 9-oz 15.00
Gloria, crystal, stem, wine; #3120, 2½-oz 20.00
Gloria, crystal, sugar bowl, tall, ftd 11.00
Gloria, crystal, tumbler, #3115, ftd, 8-oz 12.00
Gloria, gr, pk or yel; bowl, bonbon; ftd 5½" 19.00
Gloria, gr, pk or yel; bowl, cereal; sq, 6" 22.00
Gloria, gr, pk or yel; bowl, cranberry; 4-ftd, 3½" 40.00
Gloria, gr, pk or yel; bowl, vegetable; 2-hdl, 9½" 80.00
Gloria, gr, pk or yel; pitcher, w/lid, 64-oz 275.00
Gloria, gr, pk or yel; plate, cake; sq, ftd, 11" 110.00
Gloria, gr, pk or yel; plate, service; sq 45.00
Gloria, gr, pk or yel; platter, 11½" 95.00
Gloria, gr, pk or yel; saucer, sq 3.00
Gloria, gr, pk or yel; stem, water; #3130, 8-oz 25.00
Gloria, gr, pk or yel; sugar bowl, ftd 18.00
Gloria, gr, pk or yel; tray, relish; center hdl, 4-part 45.00
Gloria, gr, pk or yel; tumbler, #3120, ftd, 10-oz 20.00
Gloria, gr, pk or yel; vase, oval, 4-indent, 9" 125.00
Gloria, gr, pk or yel; vase, 11" 95.00
Imperial Hunt Scene, colors, bowl, 3-part, 8½" 45.00
Imperial Hunt Scene, colors, comport, #3085, 5½" 30.00
Imperial Hunt Scene, colors, decanter 225.00
Imperial Hunt Scene, colors, stem, cocktail; #3085, 2½-oz 40.00
Imperial Hunt Scene, colors, stem, cordial; #3085, 1-oz 150.00
Imperial Hunt Scene, colors, tumbler, #3085, ftd, 5-oz 25.00
Imperial Hunt Scene, crystal, bowl, 8" 35.00
Imperial Hunt Scene, crystal, ice bucket 40.00
Imperial Hunt Scene, crystal, stem, #1402, 18-oz 60.00
Imperial Hunt Scene, crystal, stem, cordial; #1402, 1-oz 55.00
Imperial Hunt Scene, crystal, stem, sherbet; #1402, 6½-oz 35.00
Imperial Hunt Scene, crystal, stem, sherbet; #1402, 7½-oz 40.00
Imperial Hunt Scene, crystal, stem, water; #1402, 10-oz 40.00
Imperial Hunt Scene, crystal, tumbler, #1402, flat, 15-oz 35.00
Imperial Hunt Scene, crystal, tumbler, #1402, flat, 5-oz 20.00
Imperial Hunt Scene, crystal, tumbler, #1402, tall, flat, 10-oz ..25.00
Mt Vernon, amber or crystal, ashtray, #63, 3½" 8.00
Mt Vernon, amber or crystal, ashtray, #68, 4" 12.00
Mt Vernon, amber or crystal, bonbon, #10, ftd, 7" 12.50
Mt Vernon, amber or crystal, bottle, toilet; #18, sq, 7-oz 65.00
Mt Vernon, amber or crystal, bowl, #121, flared, 12½" 32.00
Mt Vernon, amber or crystal, bowl, #126, shallow, 11½" 30.00
Mt Vernon, amber or crystal, bowl, #128, bell form, 11½" 30.00
Mt Vernon, amber or crystal, bowl, #39, 2-hdl, 10" 20.00
Mt Vernon, amber or crystal, bowl, #44, flared, 12½" 32.00
Mt Vernon, amber or crystal, bowl, cereal; #32, 6" 12.50
Mt Vernon, amber or crystal, bowl, fruit; #6, 5¼" 10.00
Mt Vernon, amber or crystal, bowl, pickle; #65, 8" 17.50

Mt Vernon, amber or crystal, bowl, preserve; #76, 6" 12.00
Mt Vernon, amber or crystal, box, #17, sq, w/lid, 4" 30.00
Mt Vernon, amber or crystal, celery, #79, 12" 20.00
Mt Vernon, amber or crystal, comport, #34, 6" 15.00
Mt Vernon, amber or crystal, ice bucket, #92, w/tongs 35.00
Mt Vernon, amber or crystal, lamp, hurricane; #1607, 9" 70.00
Mt Vernon, amber or crystal, mug, #84, stein form, 14-oz 27.50
Mt Vernon, amber or crystal, pitcher, #13, 66-oz 80.00
Mt Vernon, amber or crystal, pitcher, #91, 86-oz 110.00
Mt Vernon, amber or crystal, pitcher, #95, ball form, 80-oz 90.00
Mt Vernon, amber or crystal, plate, bread & butter; #4, 6" 3.00
Mt Vernon, amber or crystal, plate, salad; #5, 8½" 7.00
Mt Vernon, amber or crystal, relish, #200, 3-part, 11" 25.00
Mt Vernon, amber or crystal, relish, #80, 2-part, 12" 30.00
Mt Vernon, amber or crystal, salt cellar, #24, ind 7.00
Mt Vernon, amber or crystal, salt cellar, #24 ....9.00
Mt Vernon, amber or crystal, shakers, #28, pr 22.50
Mt Vernon, amber or crystal, shakers, #88, short, pr 20.00
Mt Vernon, amber or crystal, shakers, #89, tall, pr 25.00
Mt Vernon, amber or crystal, stem, cocktail; #26, 3½-oz 9.00
Mt Vernon, amber or crystal, sugar bowl, #8, ftd 10.00
Mt Vernon, amber or crystal, sugar bowl, #86 ....10.00
Mt Vernon, amber or crystal, tumbler, #58, tall, 10-oz 12.00
Mt Vernon, amber or crystal, vase, #54, ftd, 7" 35.00
Mt Vernon, amber or crystal, vase, #58, 7" 30.00
Nude stem, amber, brandy 95.00
Nude stem, amethyst, cocktail 95.00
Nude stem, amethyst, comport, flared 125.00
Nude stem, carmen, brandy 125.00
Nude stem, carmen, champagne 135.00
Nude stem, carmen, comport, cupped 125.00
Nude stem, carmen, goblet, water 120.00
Nude stem, crystal, comport, cupped 125.00
Nude stem, crystal, comport, flared 95.00
Nude stem, crystal/blk, cocktail 130.00
Nude stem, crystal/frost, ivy ball 250.00
Nude stem, Crystol Optic, brandy 115.00
Nude stem, Crystol Optic/dk gr, ivy ball 200.00
Nude stem, dk gr, brandy 95.00
Nude stem, dk gr, cocktail 95.00
Nude stem, dk gr, comport, cupped or flared 125.00
Nude stem, dk gr, goblet, water 120.00
Nude stem, Gold Crystol, cocktail 110.00
Nude stem, Gold Crystol Optic, brandy 115.00
Portia, crystal, basket, 1-hdl, 7" 195.00
Portia, crystal, bowl, cranberry; 3½" 20.00
Portia, crystal, bowl, pickle or relish; 7" 22.00
Portia, crystal, bowl, relish; 2-part, 6" 16.00
Portia, crystal, bowl, relish; 3-part, 6½" 18.00
Portia, crystal, bowl, 2-hdl, 11" 35.00
Portia, crystal, candlestick, 5" 20.00
Portia, crystal, comport, 5½" 27.50
Portia, crystal, creamer, ball form, hdld 25.00
Portia, crystal, plate, torte; 4-ftd, 13" 35.00
Portia, crystal, plate, 2-hdl, 6" 15.00
Portia, crystal, stem, claret; #3121, 4½-oz 35.00
Portia, crystal, stem, cocktail; #3121, 3-oz 20.00
Portia, crystal, stem, cocktail; #3130, 3-oz 17.50
Portia, crystal, stem, cordial; #3121, 1-oz 55.00
Portia, crystal, stem, cordial; #3126, 1-oz 55.00
Portia, crystal, stem, goblet; #3121, 10-oz 22.50
Portia, crystal, stem, sherbet; #3121, low, 6-oz 13.50
Portia, crystal, stem, sherbet; #3121, tall, 6-oz 15.00
Portia, crystal, stem, sherbet; #3124, low, 7-oz 14.00

Portia, crystal, stem, sherbet; #3126, tall, 7-oz 15.00
Portia, crystal, stem, wine; #3121, 2½-oz 27.50
Portia, crystal, stem, wine; #3124, 3-oz 25.00
Portia, crystal, tumbler, #3124, 3-oz 13.00
Portia, crystal, tumbler, water; #3124, 10-oz 15.00
Portia, crystal, vase, bud; 10" 40.00
Portia, crystal, vase, flower; 11" 50.00
Portia, crystal, vase, flower; 13" 85.00
Portia, crystal, vase, ftd, 6" 40.00
Portia, crystal, vase, keyhole ft, 12" 75.00
Portia, crystal, vase, keyhole ft, 9" 60.00
Rosalie, amber, bowl, bonbon; 2-hdl, 5½" 12.00
Rosalie, amber, bowl, bouillon; 2-hdl 15.00
Rosalie, amber, bowl, cranberry; 3½" 20.00
Rosalie, amber, bowl, soup; 8½" 30.00
Rosalie, amber, bowl, w/lid, 3-part, 3⅝" 35.00
Rosalie, amber, bowl, 10" 25.00
Rosalie, amber, bowl, 11½" 45.00
Rosalie, amber, candy dish, w/lid, 6" 60.00
Rosalie, amber, celery, 11" 20.00
Rosalie, amber, comport, high ft, 6½" 25.00
Rosalie, amber, comport, 6¾" 30.00
Rosalie, amber, icer, w/liner 40.00
Rosalie, amber, marmalade 75.00
Rosalie, amber, plate, 2-hdl, 7" 7.00
Rosalie, amber, sugar bowl, ftd 13.00
Rosalie, amber, sugar shaker 195.00
Rosalie, amber, tumbler, #3077, ftd, 12-oz 25.00
Rosalie, amber, vase, 6" 40.00
Rosalie, bl, pk or gr; bowl, console; 13" 50.00
Rosalie, bl, pk or gr; bowl, decagon; 14" 225.00
Rosalie, bl, pk or gr; bowl, finger; w/liner 35.00
Rosalie, bl, pk or gr; bowl, fruit; 5½" 15.00
Rosalie, bl, pk or gr; bowl, oval, 15½" 95.00
Rosalie, bl, pk or gr; bowl, 11" 40.00
Rosalie, bl, pk or gr; bowl, 2-hdl, 8½" 25.00
Rosalie, bl, pk or gr; nut dish, ftd, 2½" 55.00
Rosalie, bl, pk or gr; platter, 12" 65.00
Rosalie, bl, pk or gr; relish, 2-part, 9" 25.00
Rose Point, crystal, #242, 13½" 135.00
Rose Point, crystal, #3400/59, 9" 60.00
Rose Point, crystal, ashtray, #3500/124, 3¼" 32.50
Rose Point, crystal, ashtray, #721, sq, 2½" 32.50
Rose Point, crystal, bell, dinner; #3121 ....135.00
Rose Point, crystal, bowl, #1401/122, 3-part, 10½" 235.00
Rose Point, crystal, bowl, #3500/50, hdld, 6" 42.50
Rose Point, crystal, bowl, fruit; #1534, blown, 5" 70.00
Rose Point, crystal, bowl, fruit; #3500/10, 5" 42.50
Rose Point, crystal, candlestick, #3121, 7" 70.00
Rose Point, crystal, candlestick, #627, 4" 50.00
Rose Point, crystal, candlestick, #628, 3½" 35.00
Rose Point, crystal, celery, #3400/67, 5-part, 12" 55.00
Rose Point, crystal, comport, #3500/111, 6" 135.00
Rose Point, crystal, comport, #3500/36, 6" 115.00
Rose Point, crystal, creamer, #137, flat 110.00
Rose Point, crystal, creamer, #944, flat 130.00
Rose Point, crystal, dressing bottle, #1261, ftd 295.00
Rose Point, crystal, dressing bottle, #1263, flat 265.00
Rose Point, crystal, marmalade, #147, 8-oz 130.00
Rose Point, crystal, mustard, #1329, ftd, 4½-oz 295.00
Rose Point, crystal, mustard, #151, 3-oz 130.00
Rose Point, crystal, oil, #193, hdld, 6-oz 173.00
Rose Point, crystal, oil, #3400/99, ball form, w/stopper, 6-oz 110.00
Rose Point, crystal, plate, luncheon; #3400/63, 9½" 40.00

Rose Point, crystal, plate, torte; #3500/38, 13" 165.00
Rose Point, crystal, relish, #3500/62, 2-hdl, 4-part, 7½" 55.00
Rose Point, crystal, relish, #3500/71, center hdl, 7½" 125.00
Rose Point, crystal, relish, #3500/86, 2-hdl, 3-part, 10" 52.50
Rose Point, crystal, stem, claret; #3106, 4½-oz 45.00
Rose Point, crystal, stem, cocktail; #3106, 3-oz 30.00
Rose Point, crystal, tumbler, #3400/38, 12-oz 50.00
Rose Point, crystal, tumbler, #3400/38, 5-oz 85.00
Rose Point, crystal, tumbler, #3400/92, 2½-oz 95.00
Rose Point, crystal, vase, #1309, 5" 67.50
Rose Point, crystal, vase, #572, 6" 125.00
Rose Point, crystal, vase, #6004, ftd, 5" 45.00
Rose Point, crystal, vase, #797, flared, flat, 8" 120.00
Rose Point, crystal, vase, globe; #3400/102, 5" 70.00
Rose Point, crystal, vase, ivy; #1066, ball form, ftd, 7" 210.00
Valencia, crystal, ashtray, #3500/124, rnd, 3¼" 10.00
Valencia, crystal, ashtray, #3500/126, rnd, 4" 14.00
Valencia, crystal, bowl, #1402/82, 10" 32.50
Valencia, crystal, bowl, #1402/88, 11" 35.00
Valencia, crystal, relish, #3500/64, 3-part, 10" 27.50
Valencia, crystal, relish, #3500/65, 4-part, 10" 30.00
Valencia, crystal, stem, cocktail; #1402 ....20.00
Valencia, crystal, stem, cordial; #3500 ....65.00
Valencia, crystal, stem, wine; #1402 ....30.00
Valencia, crystal, tumbler, #3500, ftd, 12-oz 18.00
Valencia, crystal, tumbler, #3500, ftd, 13-oz 17.50
Valencia, crystal, tumbler, #3500, ftd, 16-oz 20.00
Wildflower, crystal, bowl, bonbon; 2-hdl, ftd, 6" 17.50
Wildflower, crystal, bowl, relish; #3400/90, 2-part, 6" 17.50
Wildflower, crystal, bowl, relish; 3-part, 6½" 17.50
Wildflower, crystal, butter dish, #3900/52, ¼-lb 165.00
Wildflower, crystal, plate, #3400/176, 7½" 9.00
Wildflower, crystal, plate, #3400/62, 8½" 15.00
Wildflower, crystal, plate, salad; #3900/22, 8" 17.50
Wildflower, crystal, plate, torte; #3900/167, 14" 35.00
Wildflower, crystal, plate, torte; #3900/65, 14" 32.50
Wildflower, crystal, stem, parfait; #3121, low, 5-oz 30.00
Wildflower, crystal, stem, sherbet; #3121, low, 6-oz 15.00
Wildflower, crystal, stem, sherbet; #3121, tall, 6-oz 17.50
Wildflower, crystal, vase, flower; #278, ftd, 11" 42.00
Wildflower, crystal, vase, flower; #6004, ftd, 6" 30.00
Wildflower, crystal, vase, flower; #6004, ftd, 8" 35.00

Cameo

The technique of glass carving was perfected 2,000 years ago in ancient Rome and Greece. The most famous ancient example of cameo glass is the Portland Vase, made in Rome around 100 A.D. After glass blowing was developed, glassmakers devised a method of casing several layers of colored glass together, often with a light color over a darker base, to enhance the design. Skilled carvers meticulously worked the fragile glass to produce incredibly detailed classic scenes. In the 18th and 19th centuries Oriental and Near-Eastern artisans used the technique more extensively. European glassmakers revived the art during the last quarter of the 19th century. In France, Galle and Daum produced some of the finest examples of modern times, using as many as five layers of glass to develop their designs, usually scenics or subjects from nature. Hand carving was supplemented by the use of a copper engraving wheel, and acid was used to cut away the layers more quickly.

In England, Thomas Webb and Sons used modern machinery and technology to eliminate many of the problems that plagued early glass carvers. One of Webb's best-known carvers, George Woodall, is credited with producing over four hundred pieces. Woodall was trained in

the art by John Northwood, famous for reproducing the Portland Vase in 1876. Cameo glass became very popular during the late 1800s, resulting in a market that demanded more than could be produced, due to the tedious procedures involved. In an effort to produce greater volume, less elaborate pieces with simple floral or geometric designs were made, often entirely acid etched with little or no hand carving. While very little cameo glass was made in this country, a few pieces were produced by James Gillender, Tiffany, and the Libbey Glass Company. Though some continued to be made on a limited scale into the 1900s (and until about 1920 in France), for the most part, inferior products caused a marked reduction in its manufacture by the turn of the century. Beware of new 'French' cameo glass from Romania and Taiwan. Some of it is very good and may be signed with 'old' signatures. Watch for stencil-cut designs that are 'disconnected' and segmented. Know your dealer! Our advisor for this category is Don Williams; he is listed in the Directory under Missouri. See also specific manufacturers.

Key: fp — fire polished

English

Bottle, apple blossoms, wht on citron, silver rim/cap, 2x2" 500.00
Bowl, morning-glories, wht on citron, 4-fold rim, 2¾x5½" 750.00
Jam jar, floral, wht on med bl, notched lid, 5¼" 1,650.00
Pitcher, morning-glories, bl on bl, slim form, 8¾" 3,500.00
Vase, anemones, bk: 2 butterflies, wht on red, bulbous, 8" 1,900.00
Vase, apple blossoms, spiked neck band, wht on bl, 4" 800.00
Vase, fairy/knight on horse, dk bl on frost, Sturbridge, 8" 950.00
Vase, ferns, butterfly on bk, rim decor, wht on red, 4" 1,100.00
Vase, fuchsia/butterflies ea side, red/wht on yel, 10" 3,500.00
Vase, lg leaves/flower, wht on lt bl, bulbous, 4½" 895.00
Vase, morning-glories, wht on citron, 5" 750.00
Vase, seasweeds/shells, wht on citron, bulbous, 15" 5,000.00
Vase, 2 nudes, cobalt on textured frost, Sturbridge, 10" 450.00

French

Jardiniere, floral, orange/brn on clear frost, Degue, 7" 400.00
Lamp base, windmill/sailboat on yel-brn, Peynaud, 10" 350.00
Vase, Deco dahlias, fp red, bl cameo border on yel, Degue, 13" ..575.00
Vase, floral, brn/rust on frost, Arsall, 12" 550.00
Vase, floral, gr on pk/yel mottle, bulbous, Arsall, 5" 250.00
Vase, floral pods, pk/dk gr on apricot, ovoid, Arsall, 7¾" 700.00
Vase, freesia, amethyst on frost, Vessiere, 6" 350.00
Vase, fuchsia, ruby on pk mottle, bell form, Docobu, 6" 275.00
Vase, iris, clear w/gold on mottle, Burgun & Schverer, 9" ...7,150.00
Vase, orchids, tan/gr on yel, stick neck, Croismare, 13" 1,000.00
Vase, orchids, wine on orange mottle, cylindrical, Degue, 5" 350.00
Vase, wisteria vines, mulberry on frost, CV Esgiere, 14" 600.00

Canary Lustre

Canary lustre was produced from the late 1700s until about the mid-19th century in the Staffordshire district of England. The body of the ware was of yellow clay with a yellow overglaze; more often than not, copper or silver lustre trim was added. Decorations were usually black-printed transfers, though occasionally hand-painted polychrome designs were also used.

Garniture set, red flowers, gr foliage, line border, 3-pc 1,400.00
Mug, blk cow transfer w/silver lustre trim, 2⅝" 255.00
Mug, Harp for Elisabeth, 2¼" 250.00
Mug, Never Forget an Old Friend 165.00

Mug, Newfoundland Dog for Robert, red transfer, 2⅜" 275.00
Mug, Trifle for Margaret, 2¼" 250.00
Pitcher, silver lustre resist foliage, wear, 5⅜" 300.00
Plate, red flower, line border, 6¼" 350.00

Candle Holders

The earliest type of candlestick, called a pricket, was constructed with a sharp point on which the candle was impaled. The socket type, first used in the 16th century, consisted of the socket and a short stem with a wide drip pan and base. These were made from sheets of silver or other metal; not until late in the 17th century were candlesticks made by casting. By the 1700s, styles began to vary from the traditional fluted column or baluster form and became more elaborate. A Rococo style with scrolls, shellwork, and naturalistic leaves and flowers came into vogue that afforded the individual silversmith the opportunity to exhibit his skill and artistry. The last half of the 18th century brought a return to fluted columns with neoclassic motifs. Because they were made of thin sheet silver, weighted bases were used to add stability. The Rococo styles of the Regency period were heavily encrusted with applied figures and flowers. Candelabra with six to nine branches became popular. By the Victorian era when lamps came into general use, there was less innovation and more adaptation of the earlier styles. See also Silver; specific manufacturers.

Bell metal, trn shaft, sq base, ca 1800, 9½", pr 200.00
Brass, beehive & dmn quilt details, w/push-up, 10", 4 for 240.00
Brass, beehive type, 1800s, 10¾", pr 170.00
Brass, candelabra, 4 open scroll candle arms, claw ft, 20", pr 275.00
Brass, candelabra, 5-light, 4 branch-type arms, 1800s, 19", pr 750.00
Brass, capstan, early, 4¾" 415.00
Brass, drum base, baluster stem, early, rpr, 5" 250.00
Brass, King of Dmns, w/push-up, 12⅜", pr 275.00

Brass, Nuremberg, Germany, late 1600s, one with maker's mark, 10", $1,500.00 for the pair.

Brass, octagonal base/stem/socket, old rpr, early, 7⅜" 165.00
Brass, pan base & side push-up, 7⅝" 360.00
Brass, Prince of Dmns, Victorian, 11¾", pr 300.00
Brass, Queen Anne, resoldered stem, polished, 6¾" 200.00
Brass, Queen Anne, sq base, inverted corners, 6¾", pr 550.00
Brass, Queen Anne, sq base, inverted corners, 7⅜" 185.00
Brass, Queen Anne, 1 mk: Solid English, 12", pr 120.00
Brass, Queen Anne, 1750s, 9⅞", pr 750.00
Brass, Queen of Dmns, w/push-up, Victorian, 11½", pr 385.00
Brass, repousse, SP traces, 11¾", EX 165.00
Brass, rnd tapered shaft, beaded edge base, 1800s, 10½", pr 200.00
Brass, saucer base, push-up tab, 5¾x4", pr 185.00
Brass, saucer base w/push-up, soldered rpr, 5¼" 80.00
Brass, sconce w/gilt, 2-arm w/griffins, 7", pr 275.00
Brass, sq base, early, 6¼" 250.00
Brass, sq base w/circle ring, early, 5¾" 160.00
Brass, stamped detail, SP traces, 12¾", pr 145.00

Brass, w/push-up, mk England, ca 1900, 8¾", pr 90.00
Brass, w/push-up, Victorian, 10½", pr 210.00
Bronze, early style w/scalloped base, 5½" 110.00
Copper, rnd tapered shafts, 1800s, 11", pr 110.00
Glass, bl & wht opaque, dolphin w/dbl-step base, 10¼" 550.00
Glass, canary; loop & petal, 7", pr 225.00
Glass, cobalt, 6-sided, NE Glass, 7⅛", NM 375.00
Glass, flint; wht opaque, crucifix form, 11¼" 85.00
Glass, flint; pressed base, blown socket, dbl-knob stem, 9" 60.00
Glass, flint; pressed base, blown stem, pewter insert, 9" 180.00
Glass, flint; pressed 6-sided base, brass collar, 11" 120.00
Glass, pressed base, free-blown deep socket & extension, 9" 140.00
Iron, gimballed, 9¼" 120.00
Iron, hogscraper, w/push-up, battered brass ring, 7", G 250.00
Iron, hogscraper, w/push-up & lip hanger, brass ring, 7¾" 300.00
Iron, hogscraper, w/push-up & lip hanger, brass ring, 9" 425.00
Iron, hogscraper, w/push-up & lip hanger, pitted, 6¾" 125.00
Iron, hogscraper, w/push-up & lip hanger, worn pnt, 7¼" 185.00
Iron, hogscraper, w/push-up mk Fisher, lip hanger, ring, 7¼" 200.00
Pewter, w/push-up, old rpr, 9", pr 240.00
Pewter, w/push-up & beaded details, 8", pr 330.00
Rose brass, sq base, 8¾" 135.00
Sheet iron, sconce, heavy, primitive, 10½" 140.00
SP w/cut & cranberry flashed hurricane shades, 13¾", pr 330.00
Steel, hogscraper, w/push-up mk Shaw's, blk pnt, 7⅛" 145.00
Tin, hogscraper, w/push-up & lip hanger, worn pnt, 5" 127.50
Tin, hogscraper, w/push-up & lip hanger, 6¼" 110.00
Tin, hogscraper, w/push-up mk Pat 1853, lip hdl, 5⅛" 165.00
Tin, sconce, dmn-shaped reflector w/punched heart, 16½" 185.00
Tin, w/push-up, oblong base, conical snuffer, 6" 150.00
Wire, birdcage type w/trn wooden base, 9½", EX 250.00
Wrought iron, adjustable spiral, trn wooden base, 7", EX 190.00
Wrought iron, rush holder on trn wooden base, 10¾" 425.00
Wrought iron, spring clip, sq base, 3-ftd, twist detail, 8½" 445.00

Candlewick

Candlewick crystal was made by the Imperial Glass Corporation, a division of Lenox Inc., Bellaire, Ohio. It was introduced in 1936, and,though never marked except for paper labels, it is easily recognized by the beaded crystal rims, stems, and handles inspired by the tufted needlework called candlewicking, practiced by our pioneer women. During its production, more than 741 items were designed and produced. In September 1982 when Imperial closed its doors, thirty-four pieces were still being made.

Identification numbers and mold numbers used by the company help collectors recognize the various styles and shapes. Most of the pieces are from the #400 series, though other series numbers were also used. Stemware was made in eight styles — five from the #400 series made from 1941 to 1962, one from #3400 series made in 1937, another from #3800 series made in 1941, and the eighth style from the #4000 series made in 1947. In the listings that follow, some #400 items lack the mold number because that information was not found in the company files.

A few pieces have been made in color or with a gold wash. At least two lines, Valley Lily and Floral, utilized Candlewick with floral patterns cut into the crystal. These are scarce today. Other rare items include gifts such as the desk calendar made by the company for its employees and customers; the dresser set comprised of a mirror, clock, puff jar, and cologne; and the chip and dip set.

Ashtray, eagle form, 1776/1, 6½" 50.00
Ashtray, heart form, 400/172, 4½" 9.00

Ashtray, heart form, 400/173, 5½" 11.00
Ashtray, 400/133, rnd, 5" 8.00
Ashtray, 400/134/1, oblong, 4½" 6.00
Ashtray, 400/652, sq, 4½" 30.00
Basket, 400/273, bead hdl, 5" 185.00
Bowl, bouillon; 400/126, 2-hdl 40.00
Bowl, cottage cheese; 400/85, 6" 25.00
Bowl, finger; 3800 ....25.00
Bowl, finger; 400/1F, 5" 12.00
Bowl, lily; 400/74J, 4-ftd, 7" 60.00
Bowl, lily; 400/75N, bead rim, ftd, 7½" 125.00
Bowl, relish; 400/268, 2-part, 8" 20.00
Bowl, relish; 400/7F, rnd, 8" 20.00
Bowl, 400/183, 3-ftd, 6" 57.50
Bowl, 400/231, sq, 5" 80.00
Bowl, 400/7F, rnd, 8" 35.00
Calender, desk; 1947 ....150.00
Candle holder, flower form, 400/40C, 5" 27.50
Candle holder, flower form, 400/66F, 2-bead stem, 4" 40.00
Candy box, 400/245, sq, rnd lid, 6½" 135.00
Candy box, 400/259, w/lid, 7" 125.00
Clock, rnd, 4" 250.00
Coaster, 400/226, w/spoon rest 13.00
Compote, 400/220, 3-bead stem, 5" 50.00
Compote, 400/45, 4-bead stem, 5½" 22.00
Compote, 400/48F, bead stem, 8" 70.00

Cream soup, $40.00; Underplate, $55.00.

Creamer, 400/122, ind bridge 7.50
Creamer, 400/126, bead hdl, flat 30.00
Creamer, 400/30, bead hdl, 6-oz 7.50
Cup, coffee; 400/37 ....7.50
Decanter, 400/163, w/stopper, 26-oz 275.00
Decanter, 400/18, w/stopper, 18-oz 350.00
Deviled egg server, 400/154, center hdl, 12" 95.00
Fork & spoon, 400/75, set 35.00
Ice tub, 400/168, 2-hdl, 7" 185.00
Knife, butter; 4000 ....200.00
Oil, 400/274, bulb bottom, 4-oz 45.00
Oil, 400/275, bulb bottom, 6-oz 55.00
Pitcher, Manhattan; 400/18, 40-oz 210.00
Pitcher, 400/16, no ft, 16-oz 165.00
Pitcher, 400/18, bead ft, 80-oz 200.00
Pitcher, 400/19, low ft, 16-oz 200.00
Pitcher, 400/419, plain, 40-oz 40.00
Pitcher, 400/424, plain, 80-oz 55.00
Plate, crescent salad; 400/120, 8¼" 42.50
Plate, salad; 400/3D, 7" 8.00
Plate, salad; 400/38, oval, 9" 35.00
Plate, salad; 400/5D, 8" 9.00
Plate, service; 400/13D, 12" 27.50
Plate, service; 400/92D, 14" 30.00

Plate, torte; 400/113D, 2-hdl, 14" 30.00
Plate, torte; 400/20D, 17" 42.50
Plate, 400/124, oval, 12½" 65.00
Plate, 400/145D, 2-hdl, 12" 27.50
Plate, 400/169, oval, 8" 22.50
Plate, 400/266, triangular, 7½" 75.00
Plate, 400/42D, 2-hdl, 5½" 10.00
Plate, 400/50, w/indent, 8" 11.00
Plate, 400/62C, crimped, 2-hdl, 8½" 20.00
Plate, 400/72D, 2-hdl, 10" 17.50
Plate, 400/98, w/indent, oval, 9" 15.00
Platter, 400/124D, 13" 90.00
Platter, 400/131D, 16" 165.00
Stem, brandy; 3800 ....25.00
Stem, claret; 3800 ....30.00
Stem, cocktail; 3800, 4-oz 25.00
Stem, cocktail; 4000 ....22.00
Stem, cordial; 3400, 1-oz 35.00
Stem, cordial; 3800, 1-oz 40.00
Stem, cordial; 4000, 1¼" 30.00
Stem, oyster cocktail; 3400, 4-oz 14.00
Stem, parfait; 3400, 6-oz 45.00
Stem, sherbet; 3400, low, 5-oz 10.00
Stem, sherbet; 4000, tall, 6-oz 14.00
Stem, sherbet; 800, low 25.00
Stem, sherbet; 400/190, tall, 5-oz 15.00
Stem, water goblet; 3400, 9-oz 15.00
Stem, wine; 3400, 4-oz 24.00
Stem, wine; 3800, 4-oz 27.50
Stem, wine; 4000, 5-oz 25.00
Tumbler, 3800, 12-oz 25.00
Tumbler, old-fashioned; 400/18, 7-oz 30.00
Tumbler, parfait; 400/18, 7-oz 40.00
Tumbler, water; 400/18, 9-oz 35.00
Tumbler, 400/19, 10-oz 11.00
Tumbler, 400/19, 12-oz 18.00
Vase, bud; 400/186, ftd, 7" 200.00
Vase, bud; 400/28C, bead ft, 8½" 70.00
Vase, rose bowl; 400/132, ftd, 7½" 150.00
Vase, 400/193, ftd, 10" 150.00

Candy Containers

Figural glass candy containers were first created in 1876 when ingenious candy manufacturers began to use them to package their products. Two of the first containers, the Liberty Bell and Independence Hall, were distributed for our country's centennial celebration. Children found these toys appealing, and an industry was launched that lasted into the mid-1960s.

Figural candy containers include animals, comic characters, guns, telephones, transportation vehicles, household appliances, and many other intriguing designs. The oldest (those made prior to 1920) were usually hand painted and often contained extra metal parts in addition to the metal strip or screw closures. During the 1950s these metal parts were replaced with plastic, a practice that continued until candy containers met their demise in the 1960s. While predominantly clear, they are found in nearly all colors of glass including milk glass, green, amber, pink, emerald, cobalt, ruby flashed, and light blue. Usually the color was intentional, but leftover glass was used as well and resulted in unplanned colors. Various examples are found in light or ice blue, and new finds are always being discovered. Production of the glass portion of candy containers was centered around the western Pennsylvania city of Jeannette. Major producers include Westmoreland Glass, West Bros.,

Victory Glass, J.H. Millstein, J.C. Crosetti, L.E. Smith, Jack Stough, and T.H. Stough. While 90% of all glass candies were made in the Jeannette area, other companies such as Eagle Glass, Play Toy, and Geo. Borgfeldt Co. have a few to their credit as well.

Buyer beware! Many candy containers have been reproduced. Some, including the Camera and the Rabbit Pushing Wheelbarrow, come already painted from distributors. Others may have a slick or oily feel to the touch. The following list may also alert you to possible reproductions:

E&A #149/L #12 Chicken on Nest
E&A #180/L #24 Dog (clear and cobalt)
E&A #539/L #38 Mule and Waterwagon (original marked Jeannette, PA)
E&A #601/L #47 Rabbit Pushing Wheelbarrow (eggs are speckled on the repro; solid on the original)
E&A #618/L #55 Peter Rabbit
E&A #651/L #58 Rocking Horse (original in clear only)
E&A #342/L #76 Independence Hall (original is rectangular; repro has offset base with red felt-lined closure)
E&A #208/L #89 Happifats on Drum (no notches on repro for closure to hook into)
E&A #345/L #90 Jackie Coogan (marked inside 'B')
E&A #349/L #91 Kewpie (must have Geo. Borgfeldt on base to be original)
E&A #546/L #94 Naked Child
E&A #674/L #103 Santa (original has plastic head; repro is all glass and opens at bottom)
E&A #162/L #114 Mantel Clock (originally in ruby flashed, milk glass, clear and frosted only)
#144 Amber Pistol (first sold full in the 1970s, not listed in E&A)
E&A #303/L #168 Uncle Sam's Hat
E&A #111/L #233 Santa's Boot
E&A #132/L #242 Carpet Sweeper (currently being sold with no metal parts)
E&A #133/L #243 Carpet Sweeper (currently being sold with no metal parts)
E&A #177/L #246 Display Case
E&A #521/L #254 Mailbox
E&A #543/L #255 Drum Mug
E&A #661/L #268 Safe (original in clear, ruby flashed, and milk glass only)
E&A #577/L #289 Piano (original in only clear and milk glass, both painted)
E&A #60/L #356 Auto
E&A #33/L #377 Auto
E&A #121/L 238 Camera (original says 'Pat Apld For' on bottom
E&A #56/L #378 Station Wagon (repro 'B. Shakman' or is ground off)
E&A #213/L #386 Fire Engine
E&A #137/L #83 Charlie Chaplin (original has 'Geo. Borgfeldt' on base; repro comes in pink and blue)
Others are possible.

Our advisor for this category is Jeff Bradfield; he is listed in the Directory under Virginia. You may contact him with questions, if you will include an SASE. See Clubs, Newsletters, and Catalogs for the address of the Candy Container Collectors of America. A bimonthly newsletter offers insight into new finds, reproductions, updates, and articles from over four hundred collectors and members, including all authors of books on candy containers.

'L' numbers used in this guide refer to a standard reference series, An Album of Candy Containers, Vols 1 and 2, by Jennie Long. 'E&A' numbers correlate with The Compleat American Glass Candy Containers

Handbook by Eikelberner and Agadjanian, revised by Adele Bowden. Values are given for undamaged examples with original paint and metal parts when applicable or unless noted otherwise. Repaired pieces (often repainted) are worth only a small fraction of one that is perfect. The symbol (+) at the end of some of the following lines was used to indicate items that have been reproduced. See also Christmas; Easter; Halloween.

Lantern, metal foot and top, magnifying glass in top, 3", E&A #438/L #176, $110.00.

Airplane, Army Bomber, w/paper label prop, L #328	32.00
Airplane, US Army B-51, w/wings, L #591	50.00
Amos & Andy, G pnt, L #77 (E&A #21)	435.00
Auto w/Tassels #3, L #362	230.00
Basket, flower design, L #223 (E&A #81)	30.00
Battleship on Waves, L #335 (E&A #96)	175.00
Bear on Circus Tub, orig blades, L #1 (E&A #83)	350.00
Bear Sitting, L #454	185.00
Bell, Hand; wood hdl, L #494	160.00
Bird Cage, L #230 (E&A #94)	225.00
Bird on Mound, w/whistle, L #3 (E&A #95)	555.00
Black Cat for Luck, L #4 (E&A #136-1)	625.00
Boat, w/photograph, L #594	115.00
Bugle or Megaphone, L #278	22.00
Bus, Jitney; closure, L #340 (E&A #114)	365.00
Bus, Rapid Transit; no pnt, L #345 (E&A #116)	550.00
Candy Cane, Mercury Glass; L #613 (E&A #120-1)	80.00
Cannon, cobalt bbl, rpl carriage, L #534 (E&A #122)	300.00
Cannon, sm bbl, orig carriage, L #535	495.00
Car, Electric Coupe #1, L #354 (E&A #49)	60.00
Car, Electric Coupe #2, closure, L #356 (E&A #47)(+)	50.00
Car, Long Hood Coupe #3, L #359 (E&A #51)	110.00
Charlie Chaplin, Smith, G pnt, L #84 (E&A #138)	365.00
Chicken, fancy closure, L #9	500.00
Chicken on Oblong Basket, closure, gr, L #10 (E&A #147)	45.00
Clock, Alarm; #11, L #549	110.00
Clock, Mantel; octagon, paper face/orig pnt, L #116 (E&A #164)	145.00
Coal Car, w/tender, L #402 (E&A #170)	80.00
Coal Car or Tender, orig wheels, L #396 (E&A #171)	200.00
Decorettes, L #655	70.00
Dirigible, Los Angeles; L #322 (E&A #176)	175.00
Dog, Mutt, L #20 (E&A #194)	55.00
Dog, Scotty, L #17 (E&A #184)	15.00
Dog w/Top Hat, L #480 (E&A #194-2)	32.00
Duckling, L-#30 (E&A #197)	115.00
Fire Engine, bl glass, L #381 (E&A #218-1)	110.00
Fire Engine, Little Boiler, L #383 (E&A #217)	75.00
Fish, L #34	400.00
Flatiron, orig pnt, closure, L #249 (E&A #344)	385.00
Flatiron, orig pnt, no closure, L #249 (E&A #344)	325.00
Gas Pump, L #316 (E&A #240)	225.00
Happifats on Drum, G orig pnt, orig closure, L #89 (E&A #208)	350.00
Horn, 3-valve, w/mouthpc, L #281 (E&A #312)	175.00

Hot Doggie, clear w/pnt, L #14 (E&A #320) 465.00
House, orig pnt, closure, L #75 (E&A #324) 165.00
Ice Truck, all orig, L #458 (E&A #784) 665.00
Jackie Coogan, #1, G pnt, L #90 (E&A # 345) 1,200.00
Jackie Coogan, L #521 (+) 1,100.00
Lamp, Hurricane; mini, L #211 (E&A #366) 75.00
Lantern, beveled glass w/gilt & ruby stain, L #175 (E&A #396) ...85.00
Lantern, brass cap, L #184 (E&A #403) 20.00
Lantern, Crosette ribbed base, L #198 (E&A #394) 20.00
Lantern, Japanese paper type, L #572 (E&A #389) 300.00
Lantern, K-600, L #187 (E&A #445) 22.50
Lantern, oval panels, L #570 ....35.00
Limousine, Westmoreland Specialty, L #351 (E&A #45) 175.00
Little Express, L #405 ....300.00
Locomotive, rectangle windows, w/closure, L #413 (E&A #496) .85.00
Locomotive 888, no wheels, L #395 (E&A #485) 45.00
Lynne Doll Nurser, L #72 (E&A #550) 32.00
Mr Rabbit w/Hat, no pnt, L #39 (E&A #610) 1,100.00
Mug, Child's Tumbler, closure, L #256 (E&A #541) 225.00
Mule Pulling Barrel, L #38 (E&A #539) 70.00
Naked Child, Victory Glass, L #94 (E&A #546) 40.00
Owl, glass eyes, closure, L #37 (E&A #566) 110.00
Phonograph, glass record, orig horn, L #288 (E&A #574) 145.00
Poodle Dog, glass head, L #471 ....15.00
Rabbit, Stough's, closure, L #54 (E&A #617)(+) 22.00
Rabbit Begging, orig pnt, closure, L #50 (E&A #611) 82.50
Rabbit in Egg Shell, gold pnt, L #48 (E&A #608) 75.00
Rabbit Nibbling Carrot, L #53 (E&A #609) 35.00
Rabbit on Dome, gold pnt, L #46 (E&A #607) 285.00
Rabbit Pushing Cart, G pnt, L #44 (E&A #602) 285.00
Refrigerator, Victory Glass Co, L #266 (E&A #650) 1,300.00
Rocking Horse #1, L #58 (E&A #651)(+) 350.00
Sedan, 4-door, orig tin wheels, no pnt, L #370 (E&A #57) 85.00
Suitcase, clear, L #217 (E&A #707) 35.00
Swan, L #492 ....130.00
Telephone, lg glass receiver, bl glass, L #580 (E&A #754) 88.00
Telescope, L #270 (E&A #764) 400.00

Toonerville Trolley, L #111, (E&A #767), $700.00.

Train, Overland Limited, L #394 (E&A #778), 4-pc, EX 950.00
Trunk, L #218 (E&A #789) 90.00
Valise, L #220 (E&A #599) 265.00
Volkswagon, L #373 (E&A #58) 40.00
Watch w/Fob, complete w/fob, L #122 ....375.00
Wheelbarrow, tin, L #611 ....65.00
Windmill, pewter top, all orig, L #443 (E&A #840) 415.00

Papier-Mache, Composition

Boot, EX pnt, Germany, 1920s, 5½" 85.00

Chick, mc pnt, wire legs, on cb drum, Germany, 1900s, 5" 180.00
Chinaman sits on log, Germany, 4" 155.00

Dog, glass eyes, head removes, 16½x22", leg repair, $450.00.

Dog, wht rabbit fur, glass eyes, head removes, 9" 350.00
Dog & slipper, appl eyes, worn pnt, minor cracks, 4", VG 195.00
Football player, jtd limbs, wooden base, lt wear, 8½" 465.00
Man in Moon, pnt flakes, 6", VG 200.00
Pig, gr w/blk hat & coat, gr pants, 6x6", EX 215.00
Pug dog, standing, pnt compo, glass eyes, 3½", EX 400.00
Rabbit, appl eyes, Germany, 7¾", VG 325.00
Rabbit, celluloid face, tan mohair, head removes, 5" 195.00
Rabbit on accordion, mechanical, Germany, 10" 1,200.00
Rabbit pulling wooden cart w/cb wheels, 8½" L, NM 185.00
Radio, emb cb w/metal trim, 1¾x3½", EX 100.00
Turkey, compo, hair wattle, head removes, Germany, 7½" 185.00
Turkey, EX feather detail, polychrome worn on base, 5½" 50.00
Washington on horse, worn pnt, 6", VG 295.00

Canes

Fancy canes and walking sticks were once the mark of a gentleman. Hand-carved examples are collected and admired as folk art from the past. The glass canes that never could have been practical are unique whimseys of the glass-blower's profession. Gadget and container sticks, which were produced in a wide variety, are highly desirable. Character, political, and novelty types are also sought after as are those with handles made of precious metals.

For more information we recommend *American Folk Art Canes, Personal Sculpture,* by George H. Meyer, Sandringham Press, 100 West Long Lake Rd., Suite 100, Bloomfield Hills, MI 48304. Our advisor for this category is Bruce Thalberg.

Ash w/cvd vines/acorns/Masonic emblems, dtd 1920, 35½" 330.00
Bamboo, dk stain, sterling silver initials, 36" 60.00
Bamboo, mechanical monkey head sticks out tongue, 36" 375.00
Bamboo, SP hdl opens to glass flask, horn top, 34" 185.00
Blackthorne, thick, root hdl, natural finish, 36" 85.00
Blown glass, lt gr, twisted hdl, triangular shape, 43" 125.00
Burled walnut, sterling knob, mixed metal insect motif, 36" 250.00
Celluloid, horse's hoof, tortoise trim, bamboo shaft, 36" 200.00
Celluloid, 3 bears playing, malacca shaft, 35" 175.00
Ebony w/macrame string, blk pnt, shield cvd in ivory hdl 250.00
Ebony wood, crouching lion hdl, gold ferrule, horn tip, 36" 425.00
Ebony wood, dog's-head ivory hdl, glass eyes, horn tip, 36" 500.00
Ebony wood, horse's-head bone hdl, silver ferrule, 35" 325.00
Fish vertebra, L-shape ebony hdl w/brass tip, 33", VG 225.00
Hardwood, detailed animal/flower/bird cvgs, bird hdl, 35" 385.00
Hardwood w/pistol grip, NP trim, horn tip 95.00
Hickory, cvd snake coiled around, pearl eyes, 36" 100.00

Indian head finial, Dartmouth seal & fraternity names, 1909 .....250.00
Ivory (solid), Japanese, cvd floral motif, wood case, 1880 ....950.00
Ivory hand Torah pointer, removable finger, 1880, 33" 950.00
Ivory knob, cvd multiple heads, Japanese, 1880, 35" 650.00
Leather disks on steel rod shaft, horn hdl, 35" 145.00
Mahog, cvd alligator ivory hdl, silver ferrule, 34" 165.00
Mahog w/horn hdl, silver-colored horn shoe & collar, EX 110.00
Malacca shaft, coat-of arms ivory hdl, 2-section, 35" 450.00
Maple, horn hdl & tip, gold ferrule, 36" 100.00
Pussy willow, blk stain, natural galls, silver tip, 34" 70.00
Riding crop, wrapped shank, silver sprinkler top, 35" 185.00
Riding crop, wrapped shank, stag horn hdl, 28½" 150.00
Rose-stipplewood, copper hdl w/2 compartments, 36" 150.00
Sapling shaft w/tooled silver o/l hdl, PC '94, 35", EX 175.00
Stinkwood, boar's tooth hdl, horn tip, 36" 175.00
Tiger maple, chrome repousse flashlight hdl, Austria, 35" 200.00
Tortoise, cvd boy's head, silver o/l, ebony shaft 800.00
Tortoise, cvd Blk man's head, silver o/l, ebony shaft 900.00
Walnut, baton type, silver & leather ferrule, ash finial, 25" 60.00
Whale vertebrae, wood hdl, 34" 165.00
Whalebone, spiral cvg, whale tooth hdl, 1800s, 30½", EX 550.00
Whalebone w/scrimshaw decor shaft, whale tooth inlay, 34" 350.00
Willow w/stylized dmn-like shapes, dk finish 55.00
Wood, alligator-shaped horn hdl, brass tip, 36" 145.00
Wood, celluloid setter's head hdl, brass ferrule & tip 145.00
Wood, chain-link cvgs w/knob head, curved top, red stain 100.00
Wood, cvd horse's-head hdl w/glass eyes, 34" 155.00
Wood, dog's-head hdl w/glass eyes, brass tip 150.00
Wood, dragon's-head hdl, 32" 100.00
Wood, folk-art primitive figures, knob hdl, 37" 75.00
Wood, gold ball-shaped hdl, MOP paneled collar, brass tip 95.00
Wood, greyhound-shaped horn hdl, horn tip, 37" 145.00
Wood, ivory hdl w/cvd acorn & leaf decor, brass tip, EX 125.00
Wood, knobby shaft w/alligator hdl, inlay eyes, worn pnt 120.00
Wood, man's head w/long beard & elf-type hat hdl, brass tip 125.00
Wood, parrot's head w/glass eyes hdl, leather band, 39" 150.00
Wood, primitive snake cvg, orig worn finish, 33" 110.00
Wood, sm animal heads cvd from branch stubs, 1900s, EX 375.00
Wood, snake's-head hdl, 34" 75.00
Wood, snake w/ball in cage/relief insignia, red varnish 225.00
Wood, stick-like ivory hdl w/sm bear head, brass tip 90.00
Wood, tooth hdl, silver chased leaves ends & ferrule, 34" 200.00
Wood, wht metal hdl shaped as Dickens bust, brass tip, 35" 85.00
Wood w/pearl inlay shapes, brass tipped hdl, 36" 175.00
Zebra wood, clenched hand ivory hdl, 35" 250.00
Zebra wood, eagle's-head hdl w/ivory beak, silver ferrule 350.00
Zebra wood, gold-filled band w/ivory gadrooning, 36" 195.00
Zebra wood, steel hdl opens to monocular, 38" 475.00

Canton

Canton is a blue and white porcelain that was first exported in the 1790s by clipper ships from China to the United States, a practice that continued into the 1920s. Canton became very popular along the East coast where the major ports were located. Its popularity was due to several factors: it was readily available, inexpensive, and (due to the fact that it came in many different forms) appealing to the housewife.

The porcelain's blue and white color and simple motif (teahouse, trees, bridge, and a rain-cloud border) have made it a favorite of people who collect early American furniture and accessories. Buyers of Canton should shop at large outdoor shows and up-scale antique shows. Collections are regularly sold at auction. Collectors usually prefer a rich, deep tone rather than a lighter blue. Cracks, large chips, and major repairs

will substantially affect values. Prices of Canton have escalated sharply over the last twenty years, and rare forms are highly sought after by advanced collectors. Our advisor for this category is Hobart D. Van Deusen; he is listed in the Directory under Connecticut.

Basket, fruit; 10¾", +undertray 600.00
Bowl, scalloped rim, 10¼" 770.00
Bowl, scalloped rim, 7¼" 550.00
Bowl, serving; w/lid, 11¼" 465.00
Bowl, serving; w/lid, 8¼" 275.00
Bowl, shaped sides, 9¾" 880.00
Candlesticks, 11", EX, pr 2,300.00
Candlesticks, 7½", NM, pr 2,200.00
Creamer, 3½" 110.00
Gravy boat, 7¼" 415.00
Hot water dish, 8½" 300.00
Pie plate, 8½" 220.00
Pie plate, 9¼" 250.00
Pitcher, 7½" 935.00

Platter, octagonal, 1800s, 18", $600.00.

Platter, well & tree, 19th C, 12¾" 500.00
Platter, 20" 800.00
Shrimp dish, 10" 495.00
Spoon, 5½", 6 for 220.00
Sugar bowl, w/lid, 6" 275.00
Syllabub, twist hdls (1 rpr), berry finial, 4¾" 150.00
Tazza, sm rpr, 14¾" 990.00
Teapot, pale color, 6" 400.00
Teapot, 5½" 400.00
Tile, canted corners, 4⅝" 360.00
Tile, sq, 4¾" 450.00
Tureen, 10¼", +undertray 770.00
Tureen, 12", EX 770.00
Tureen, 6½", +undertray 550.00
Umbrella stand, 24½" 2,000.00
Vase, cylindrical, 9¾" 440.00

Capo-Di-Monte

Established in 1743 near Naples and sponsored by Charles II, who was King of Naples at that time, Capo-Di-Monte produced soft-paste porcelain figurines and dinnerware usually marked with a 'crown over N' device, though a fleur-de-lis was used on occasion. The factory was closed throughout the 1760s but reopened in 1771 in the city of Naples. There both hard- and soft-paste porcelains were made, sometimes decorated with applied florals in high relief. Their technique as well as their marks were blatantly copied. As a result, this type of encrusted decoration is often referred to today as Capo-Di-Monte. The original factory closed in 1821. Some of their molds were purchased by the Docceia Porcelain factory in Florence which continues to operate to the present time. Most examples on the market today are of fairly recent manufacture. Capo-Di-Monte type wares have been made in Hungary and Germany as well as France and Italy. Many of these pieces continue to bear the 'crown over N' gold stamp. As more collectors recognize and appreciate the quality of the older ware, buyer demand drives prices higher.

Box, armor-making scene, mc w/gilt, gilt brass fittings, 9" 375.00
Box, lady/cherubs/cart of roses, flowers int, 5x6" 300.00
Casket, Bacchic figures in panels, hinged lid, 8x5" 325.00

Ewers, putti and animals, fruit festoons on flared lip, figural handle, late 1800s, 11½", $750.00 for the pair.

Figurine, man w/dog, lady w/sheep, 1900s, 8", pr 150.00
Plate, armorial, sgn Rusconi, 10½" 210.00
Plate, cherub rims, mc enamel & gold, crown/N mk, 8", pr 100.00
Stein, battle scene, crown/N mk, ½-litre, M 350.00
Stein, battle scene, helmet finial, 1-litre, M 895.00
Urn, frolicking cherubs & sea gods, crown/N mk, 7¼", pr 150.00

Carlton

Carlton Ware was the product of Wiltshaw and Robinson, who operated in the Staffordshire district of England from about 1890. During the 1920s, they produced ornamental ware with enameled and gilded decorations such as flowers and birds, often on a black background. In 1958 the firm was renamed Carlton Ware Ltd. Their trademark was a crown over a circular stamp with 'W & R, Stoke on Trent' surrounding a swallow. 'Carlton Ware' was sometimes added by hand.

Card holder, HP Oriental decor on cobalt w/gold 50.00
Cup & saucer, demitasse; blk & wht silhouette w/gold 85.00
Cup & saucer, demitasse; cobalt w/gold int 48.00
Pitcher, Rouge Royale w/gold & chinoiserie, ring hdl 250.00
Sugar bowl, Bleu Royale 38.00
Vase, Rouge Royale, Oriental scene, 6" 95.00

Carnival Collectibles

Carnival items from the early part of this century represent the lighter side of an America that was alternately prospering and sophisticated or devastated by war and domestic conflict. But whatever the country's condition, the carnival's thrilling rides and shooting galleries were a sure way of letting it all go by — at least for an evening.

For further information on chalkware figures, we recommend *The Carnival Chalk Prize* by Thomas G. Morris, who is listed in the Directory under Oregon. Our advisors for shooting gallery targets are Richard and Valerie Tucker; their address is listed in the Directory under Texas.

Carousel ring arm, NP CI w/brass trim, WF Mangels, 49", EX ...150.00
Chalkware figure, Buddy Lee, HP, pk chalk, unmk, '20s, 13½" 85.00
Chalkware figure, bulldog, unmk, 10¼" 55.00
Chalkware figure, Captain Marvel, unmk, 1940-50, 14½" 95.00
Chalkware figure, Charlie McCarthy, c Dummy, Jenkins, 1938, 15" .75.00
Chalkware figure, clown bank, ca 1940-50, 12" 45.00
Chalkware figure, dog w/flower bank, unmk, 10¾" 35.00
Chalkware figure, Donald Duck, 1934-50, 14" 75.00
Chalkware figure, Dutch girl & boy, Jenkins, 1948, 6", pr 20.00
Chalkware figure, Felix the Cat, ca 1922, rare, 12½" 220.00
Chalkware figure, horse w/English saddle, 11" 35.00
Chalkware figure, Hula Hula Girl, unmk, ca 1940-50, 16" 55.00
Chalkware figure, Little Cowboy, unmk, ca 1940, 8½" 25.00
Chalkware figure, Lone Ranger & Silver, mk LR, 10½" 75.00
Chalkware figure, Lotus Chinese girl, Jenkins, 1924, 13¼" 130.00
Chalkware figure, Mae West, Jenkins, 1934, 14" 115.00
Chalkware figure, Oriental lady bust, unmk, 5½" 35.00
Chalkware figure, owl bank, unmk, 16" 55.00
Chalkware figure, Paul Revere, unmk, ca 1935-45, 14½" 35.00
Chalkware figure, Popeye, King Features, 1929-50, 18" 135.00
Chalkware figure, sailor girl, unmk, 1930-40, 12¾" 45.00
Chalkware figure, Scottish Lass, w/bagpipes, unmk, 15" 35.00
Chalkware figure, Snow White, unmk, ca 1937-50, 15" 75.00
Chalkware figure, Tomboy, girl in pants, 1940, #1571, 14½" 35.00
Chalkware figure, Uncle Sam, w/or w/o flat bk, unmk, 15" 75.00
Prop, Houdini figural, glass eyes, EX color, 40x38x18", EX 600.00
Shooting gallery target, battleship, rusted red pnt, 11½" 95.00
Shooting gallery target, bird, CI, pnt traces, 4¼" 65.00
Shooting gallery target, clown in bbl, CI, 12½x5½", G 1,600.00
Shooting gallery target, duck, CI, 5½" 60.00
Shooting gallery target, duck, CI, 7" 95.00
Shooting gallery target, Hitler head, CI, orig pnt, 10½" 400.00
Shooting gallery target, Indian in canoe, CI, rusty 75.00
Shooting gallery target, moose, CI, bl pnt, 7x5x¼" 85.00
Shooting gallery target, owl, stylized, CI, wooden base, 4" 50.00
Shooting gallery target, rabbit, CI, rusted red pnt, 4½" 80.00
Shooting gallery target, running rabbit, pnt CI, CW Parker 2,500.00
Shooting gallery target, Tom turkey, CI, mk Evans, 7" 165.00

Carnival Glass

Carnival glass is pressed glass that has been coated with a sodium solution and fired to give it an exterior lustre. First made in America in 1905, it was produced until the late 1920s and had great popularity in the average American household; for unlike the costly art glass produced by Tiffany, carnival glass could be mass-produced at a small cost. Colors most found are marigold, green, blue, and purple; but others exist in lesser quantities and include white, clear, red, aqua opalescent, peach opalescent, ice blue, ice green, amber, lavender, and smoke.

Companies mainly responsible for its production in America include the Fenton Art Glass Company, Williamstown, West Virginia; the Northwood Glass Company, Wheeling, West Virginia; the Imperial Glass Company, Bellaire, Ohio; the Millersburg Glass Company, Millersburg, Ohio; and the Dugan Glass Company (Diamond Glass), Indiana, Pennsylvania. In addition to these major manufacturers, lesser producers included the U.S. Glass Company, the Cambridge Glass Company, the Westmoreland Glass Company, and the McKee Glass Company.

Carnival glass has been highly collectible since the 1950s and has been reproduced for the last twenty-five years. Several national and state collectors' organizations exist, and many fine books are available on old carnival glass, including *The Standard Encyclopedia of Carnival Glass* by Bill Edwards.

Acorn (Fenton), bowl, amethyst, 7" 140.00
Acorn Burrs (Northwood), bowl, gr, flat, 10" 175.00
Acorn Burrs (Northwood), butter dish, marigold 300.00
Acorn Burrs (Northwood), pitcher, water; marigold 500.00
Acorn Burrs (Northwood), punch cup, bl 75.00
Age Herald (Fenton), bowl, amethyst, scarce, 9¼" 1,200.00
Amaryllis (Northwood), compote, bl, sm 275.00
America (Fostoria), tumbler, gr, rare 125.00
Ancanthus (Imperial), bowl, marigold, 8" 65.00
Apple & Pear Intaglio (Northwood), bowl, marigold, 10" 90.00
Apple Blossom (Northwood), tumbler, bl, enameled 90.00
Apple Blossoms (Dugan), bowl, amethyst, 7½" 58.00
Apple Tree (Fenton), tumbler, marigold 40.00
April Showers (Fenton), vase, marigold 55.00
Arcs (Imperial), bowl, gr, 8½" 50.00
Aztec (McKee), creamer, marigold 250.00
Ball & Swirl, mug, marigold 120.00
Balloons (Imperial), compote, marigold 65.00
Bambi, powder jar, marigold, w/lid 30.00
Banded Diamonds (Crystal), bowl, amethyst, 10" 125.00
Banded Grape (Fenton), pitcher, water; bl 400.00
Banded Grape (Fenton), tumbler, gr 75.00
Banded Grape & Leaf (English), tumbler, marigold, rare 100.00
Banded Panels (Crystal), sugar bowl, amethyst, open 60.00
Banded Portland (US Glass), puff jar, marigold 80.00
Banded Rib, tumbler, marigold 25.00

Beaded Acanthus, milk pitcher, marigold, $75.00.

Beaded Bull's Eye (Imperial), vase, gr, 14" 140.00
Beaded Cable (Northwood), rose bowl, gr 150.00
Beaded Hearts (Northwood), bowl, amethyst 85.00
Beaded Panels (Imperial), bowl, marigold, 5" 25.00
Beaded Panels (Westmoreland), compote, amethyst 55.00
Beaded Shell (Dugan), bowl, amethyst, ftd, 9" 95.00
Beaded Shell (Dugan), mug, marigold 200.00
Beaded Shell (Dugan), sugar bowl, amethyst, w/lid 110.00
Beaded Shell (Dugan), tumbler, amethyst 70.00
Beaded Stars (Fenton), banana boat, marigold 110.00
Beaded Stars (Fenton), bowl, peach opal 90.00
Beaded Stars (Fenton), plate, marigold, 9" 110.00
Beaded Swirl (English), compote, bl 60.00
Beaded Swirl (English), pitcher, milk; bl 90.00
Beads (Northwood), bowl, amethyst, 8½" 60.00
Beads & Bars (US Glass), spooner, marigold 55.00
Bell, paperweight, miniature, 2½" 60.00
Bells & Beads (Dugan), bowl, gr, 7½" 115.00
Bells & Beads (Dugan), compote, amethyst 75.00
Bells & Beads (Dugan), nappy, amethyst 95.00

Bells & Beads (Dugan), plate, amethyst, 8" 170.00
Berry Basket, marigold 55.00
Big Basketweave (Dugan), basket, amethyst, sm 60.00
Big Basketweave (Dugan), vase, marigold, 6" 90.00
Bird w/Grapes (Cockatoo), vase, wall; marigold 75.00
Birds & Cherries (Fenton), bowl, amethyst, rare, 5" 90.00
Birds & Cherries (Fenton), compote, bl 60.00
Black Bottom (Fenton), candy jar, marigold 60.00
Blackberry (Fenton), hat, gr, open edge 50.00
Blackberry (Northwood), bowl, marigold, ftd, 9" 50.00
Blackberry (Northwood), compote, amethyst 65.00
Blackberry Banded (Fenton), hat form, peach opal 90.00
Blackberry Block (Fenton), pitcher, marigold 265.00
Blackberry Bramble (Fenton), bowl, bl 60.00
Blackberry Bramble (Fenton), compote, gr 70.00
Blackberry Spray (Fenton), bonbon, bl 45.00
Blackberry Spray (Fenton), hat form, amethyst 55.00
Blackberry Wreath (Millersburg), bowl, amethyst, 5" 70.00
Blackberry Wreath (Millersburg), bowl, marigold, 9" 65.00
Blocks & Arches, creamer, marigold 42.00
Blocks & Arches, pitcher, crystal, rare 140.00
Blossoms & Band (Imperial), bowl, amethyst, 10" 45.00
Blossoms & Spears, plate, marigold, 8" 52.00
Blossomtime (Northwood), compote, marigold 135.00
Blueberry (Fenton), tumbler, bl, scarce 100.00
Bo Peep (Westmoreland), mug, marigold, scare 125.00
Bouquet, toothpick holder, marigold 75.00
Bouquet (Fenton), pitcher, marigold 385.00
Bouquet (Fenton), tumbler, amethyst 80.00
Bow & English Hob (English), bowl, nut; bl 60.00
Briar Patch, hat form, marigold 40.00
Broken Arches (Imperial), bowl, amethyst, 8½" 50.00
Broken Arches (Imperial), cup, punch; amethyst 30.00
Bubbles, hatpin, amethyst 65.00
Bull's Eye & Leaves (Northwood), bowl, amethyst, 8½" 55.00
Bull's Eye & Spearhead, wine, marigold 90.00
Bulldog, paperweight, marigold 350.00
Bunny, bank, marigold 35.00
Butterflies (Fenton), bonbon, marigold 60.00
Butterfly, lamp, oil; marigold 1,500.00
Butterfly, pin tray, marigold 40.00
Butterfly (Northwood), bonbon, amethyst, regular 75.00
Butterfly & Berry (Fenton), bowl, amethyst, ftd, 10" 200.00
Butterfly & Berry (Fenton), butter dish, marigold 150.00
Butterfly & Berry (Fenton), tumbler, bl 70.00
Butterfly & Berry (Fenton), vase, marigold, rare 40.00
Butterfly & Bower, plate, cake; amethyst, crystal, stemmed 200.00
Butterfly & Fern (Fenton), tumbler, gr 85.00
Butterfly Bower, compote, amethyst, crystal 130.00
Buttermilk (Fenton), goblet, marigold, plain 60.00
Button & Fan, hatpin, amethyst 60.00
Buzz Saw, shade, marigold 45.00
Canada Dry, bottle, marigold 55.00
Cane (Imperial), bowl, marigold, 10" 40.00
Cane (Imperial), wine, marigold 65.00
Cannonball Vt, tumbler, marigold 50.00
Capitol (Westmoreland), bowl, amethyst, ftd, sm 70.00
Captive Rose (Fenton), bonbon, gr 70.00
Captive Rose (Fenton), bowl, marigold, 10" 75.00
Captive Rose (Fenton), plate, amethyst, 7" 190.00
Carnival Honeycomb (Imperial), bonbon, marigold 40.00
Carnival Honeycomb (Imperial), plate, amethyst, 7" 95.00
Carolina Dogwood (Westmoreland), bowl, marigold, 8½" 80.00
Cathedral (Curved Star, Sweden), bowl, marigold, 10" 75.00

Cathedral (Curved Star), chalice, marigold, 7", $145.00.

Cathedral (Curved Star, Sweden), creamer, marigold, ftd 60.00
Cattails, hatpin, amethyst 50.00
Chatham (US Glass), compote, marigold 75.00
Checkerboard (Westmoreland), cup, punch; marigold 90.00
Checkers, ashtray, marigold 47.00
Checkers, bowl, marigold, 9" 40.00
Cherry (Dugan), bowl, marigold, flat, 8" 65.00
Cherry (Millersburg), bowl, marigold, scarce, 9" 90.00
Cherry (Millersburg), bowl, marigold, 4" 60.00
Cherry (Millersburg), butter dish, amethyst 375.00
Cherry (Millersburg), pitcher, milk; marigold, rare 1,100.00
Cherry (Millersburg), sugar bowl, marigold, w/lid 170.00
Cherry & Cable (Northwood), bowl, marigold, scarce, 5" 75.00
Cherry & Daisies (Fenton), banana boat, marigold 950.00
Cherry Blossoms, pitcher, bl 150.00
Cherry Blossoms, tumbler, bl 150.00
Cherry Chain (Fenton), bonbon, bl 55.00
Cherry Chain (Fenton), bowl, amethyst, 6½" 90.00
Cherry Chain (Fenton), compote, bl 80.00
Cherry Chain (Fenton), plate, marigold, 9" 85.00
Cherry Circles (Fenton), bonbon, amethyst 65.00
Cherry Circles (Fenton), bowl, marigold, 8" 50.00
Cherry Smash (US Glass), bowl, marigold, 8" 65.00
Cherry Smash (US Glass), butter dish, marigold 150.00
Chrysanthemum (Fenton), bowl, marigold, flat, 9" 130.00
Circle Scroll (Dugan), bowl, marigold, 5" 40.00
Classic Arts (Czech), rose bowl, marigold 525.00
Cleopatra, bottle, marigold 110.00
Cobblestones (Dugan), bowl, marigold, 5" 40.00
Cobblestones (Imperial), bowl, marigold, 5" 35.00
Coin Dot (Fenton), rose bowl, marigold 90.00
Coin Spot (Dugan), compote, amethyst 60.00
Colonial (Imperial), toothpick holder, gr 95.00
Columbia (Imperial), compote, amethyst 75.00
Concord (Fenton), bowl, amethyst, scarce, 9" 300.00
Connie (Northwood), tumbler, wht pastel 125.00
Coral (Fenton), bowl, marigold, 9" 200.00
Corinth (Westmoreland), bowl, amethyst 60.00
Corning (Corning), insulator, marigold 35.00
Cornucopia (Fenton), vase, marigold, 5" 70.00
Cosmos (Millersburg), bowl, gr, 5" 70.00
Cosmos & Crane, bowl, marigold, 5" 40.00
Cosmos & Crane, spooner, marigold 100.00
Cosmos & Crane, tumbler, marigold, rare 115.00
Cosmos Vt (Fenton), bowl, marigold, 9" 40.00
Country Kitchen (Millersburg), bowl, marigold, rare, 5" 90.00
CR (Argentina), ashtray, marigold 90.00
Crab Claw (Imperial), bowl, marigold, 10" 50.00
Crab Claw (Imperial), cruet, marigold, rare 950.00

Crackle (Imperial), bowl, marigold, 5" 18.00
Crackle (Imperial), bowl, marigold, 9" 25.00
Crackle (Imperial), pitcher, amethyst, dome base 150.00
Crackle (Imperial), plate, amethyst 55.00
Crackle (Imperial), tumbler, amethyst, dome base 30.00
Crocus Vt, tumbler, amethyst 65.00
Crystal Cut, compote, crystal 75.00
Cuba (McKee), goblet, marigold, rare 45.00
Cut Arcs (Fenton), compote, amethyst, 7½" 60.00
Cut Cosmos (Millersburg), tumbler, marigold, rare 450.00
Cut Ovals (Fenton), candlesticks, marigold, pr 175.00
Cut Sprays, vase, peach opal, 9" 75.00
Dahlia (Dugan), bowl, marigold, ftd, 5" 40.00
Dahlia (Dugan), creamer, marigold 75.00
Dahlia (Dugan), spooner, marigold 75.00
Dahlia (Dugan), tumbler, marigold, rare 90.00
Daisy & Cane (English), decanter, marigold, rare 90.00
Daisy & Drape (Northwood), vase, marigold 300.00
Daisy & Plum (Northwood), candy dish, amethyst 90.00
Daisy & Plum (Northwood), compote, marigold 60.00
Daisy Dear (Dugan), bowl, amethyst 48.00
Daisy Squares, goblet, amethyst, rare 900.00
Daisy Wreath (Westmoreland), bowl, marigold, 8" 250.00
Dandelion (Northwood), tumbler, marigold 175.00
Deco Lily, vase, marigold, bulbous 140.00
Deep Grape (Millersburg), compote, gr, rare 1,700.00
Diamond & Daisy Cut (US Glass), compote, amethyst 70.00
Diamond & File, banana boat, marigold 65.00
Diamond Band, sugar bowl, crystal 60.00
Diamond Checkerboard, bowl, marigold, 5" 25.00
Diamond Checkerboard, butter dish, marigold 90.00
Diamond Daisy, plate, marigold, 8" 95.00
Diamond Lace (Imperial), bowl, amethyst, 5" 40.00
Diamond Lace (Imperial), tumbler, amethyst 70.00
Diamond Pinwheel (English), butter dish, marigold 75.00
Diamond Point, rose bowl, marigold 700.00
Diamond Points (Northwood), vase, gr, 14" 80.00
Diamond Ring (Imperial), bowl, fruit; amethyst, 9½" 90.00
Diamond Ring (Imperial), bowl, marigold, 9" 40.00
Diamond Star, vase, marigold, 8" 80.00
Diamond Top (English), spooner, marigold 40.00
Diamonds (Millersburg), pitcher, marigold 285.00
Diving Dolphins (English), bowl, amethyst, ftd, 7" 260.00
Dots & Curves, hatpin, amethyst 55.00
Dotted Daisies, plate, marigold, 8" 90.00
Double Dolphins (Fenton), candlesticks, pastel, pr 90.00
Double Dutch (Imperial), bowl, amethyst, ftd, 9" 75.00
Double Scroll (Imperial), candlesticks, amethyst, pr 80.00
Double Star (Cambridge), tumbler, amethyst, scarce 140.00
Dragon & Lotus (Fenton), bowl, marigold, flat, 9" 185.00
Dragon & Lotus (Fenton), plate, peach opal, rare, 9½" 1,100.00
Dragon's Tongue (Fenton), shade, peach opal 115.00
Dragonfly, shade, pastel 1,800.00
Drapery (Northwood), rose bowl, bl 120.00
Drapery Vt (Fenton), tumbler, marigold, scarce 90.00
Dugan Fan (Dugan), gravy boat, amethyst, ftd 75.00
Dutch, plate, marigold, 8" 55.00
Dutch Mill, ashtray, marigold 65.00
Eagle Furniture (Northwood), plate, amethyst 800.00
Elks (Dugan), nappy, amethyst, rare 4,200.00
Elks (Fenton), bowl, Detroit; bl, scarce 700.00
Elks (Millersburg), paperweight, amethyst, rare 1,500.00
Emu, bowl, marigold, crystal, rare, 5" 75.00
Enamelled Grape (Northwood), tumbler, bl 45.00

English Hob & Button (English), bowl, amethyst, 7" 8.00
Engraved Floral (Fenton), tumbler, gr 95.00
Estate (Westmoreland), creamer, peach opal 90.00
Estate (Westmoreland), vase, bl, stippled, 3" 190.00
Etched Deco, plate, marigold, ftd, 8" 60.00
Exchange Bank (Northwood), plate, amethyst, 6" 500.00
Eye cup, marigold 90.00
Famous, puff box, marigold 75.00
Fanciful (Dugan), plate, bl, 9" 350.00
Fancy Cut (English), tumbler, marigold, miniature 60.00
Fans (English), cracker jar, marigold, w/lid 150.00

Fantail (Fenton), bowl, blue, footed, 9", $275.00.

Fantail (Fenton), compote, bl 195.00
Fashion (Imperial), bowl, marigold, 9" 40.00
Fashion (Imperial), cup, punch; amethyst 40.00
Fashion (Imperial), sugar bowl, amethyst, w/lid 125.00
Feather Stitch (Fenton), bowl, gr, 8½" 90.00
Feathered Serpent (Fenton), bowl, marigold, 5" 30.00
Fentonia, bowl, amethyst, ftd, 9½" 85.00
Fentonia, butter dish, bl 185.00
Fentonia, tumbler, marigold 50.00
Fentonia Fruit (Fenton), pitcher, bl 700.00
Fern (Fenton), bowl, bl, rare, 7" 900.00
Fern (Northwood), compote, amethyst 70.00
Fern Panels (Fenton), hat, gr 60.00
Field Flowers (Imperial), tumbler, amethyst, scarce 60.00
Field Thistle (US Glass), butter dish, marigold, rare 125.00
File (Imperial & English), bowl, amethyst, 5" 40.00
File (Imperial & English), compote, amethyst 50.00
File (Imperial & English), sugar bowl, marigold, w/lid 120.00
File & Fan, bowl, peach opal, ftd, 6" 160.00
Fine Cut & Roses (Northwood), candy dish, bl, ftd 185.00
Fine Cut Flowers & Vt (Fenton), goblet, gr 75.00
Fine Cut Rings (English), creamer, marigold 45.00
Fine Cut Rings (English), jam jar, marigold, w/lid 65.00
Fine Cut Rings (English), vase, marigold 50.00
Fine Rib (Northwood, Fenton & Dugan), bowl, amethyst, 5" 35.00
Fine Rib (Northwood, Fenton & Dugan), compote, peach opal .165.00
Fishscale & Beads (Dugan), bowl, amethyst, 6" 45.00
Five Panel, candy jar, marigold, stemmed 70.00
Flared Panel, shade, milk glass opal 75.00
Flickering Flames, shade, pastel 50.00
Floral & Grape (Dugan), tumbler, bl 50.00
Floral & Optic (Imperial), bowl, marigold, flat, 8" 30.00
Floral & Wheat (Dugan), bonbon, bl, stemmed 45.00
Floral Fan, vase, marigold, etched 57.00
Floral Oval (Higbee), creamer, marigold 60.00
Flower Medallion, tumbler, marigold, very rare 800.00
Flowering Dill (Fenton), hat, marigold 40.00

Flowers & Spades (Dugan), bowl, gr, 5" 27.00
Flute (Millersburg), bowl, amethyst, 5" 40.00
Flute (Millersburg), cup, punch; amethyst 30.00
Flute (Northwood), butter dish, marigold 135.00
Flute (Northwood), sherbet, gr 45.00
Flute & Cane (Imperial), cup, punch; marigold 25.00
Flute & Cane (Imperial), wine, marigold 50.00
Flying Bat, hatpin, gr, scarce 200.00
Footed Drape (Westmoreland), vase, marigold 50.00
Footed Rib (Northwood), vase, marigold 50.00
Footed Shell (Westmoreland), amethyst, sm, 3" 55.00
Forks (Cambridge), cracker jar, gr, rare 500.00
French Knots (Fenton), hat, gr 50.00
Frosted Block (Imperial), celery tray, marigold 40.00
Frosted Block (Imperial), compote, marigold 85.00
Frosted Block (Imperial), plate, marigold, 7½" 70.00
Frosted Ribbon, tumbler, marigold 30.00
Fruit & Flowers (Northwood), bonbon, marigold, stemmed 60.00
Fruit & Flowers (Northwood), bowl, marigold, 5" 40.00
Fruit Lustre, tumbler, marigold 40.00
Fruit Salad (Westmoreland), cup, marigold, rare 30.00
Garden Mums (Northwood), bowl, amethyst, shallow, 5" 200.00
Garden Path (Dugan), bowl, fruit; marigold, 10" 90.00
Garland (Fenton), rose bowl, bl, ftd 60.00
Gay 90s (Millersburg), tumbler, amethyst, rare 1,150.00
Georgia Bell (Dugan), card tray, gr, ftd, rare 95.00
God & Home (Dugan), tumbler, bl, rare 275.00
Gold Fish, bowl, marigold, rare 145.00
Golden Flowers, vase, marigold, 7½" 95.00
Golden Grapes (Dugan), bowl, gr, 7" 60.00
Golden Grapes (Dugan), vase, marigold, 7" 95.00
Golden Harvest (US Glass), wine, amethyst 35.00
Golden Honeycomb (Imperial), bonbon, gr 45.00
Golden Oxen, mug, marigold 90.00
Gooseberry Spray, bowl, amethyst, 10" 85.00
Graceful (Northwood), vase, amethyst 100.00
Grand Thistle (Finland), tumbler, bl, rare 400.00
Grape (Imperial), basket, gr, hdld, rare 90.00
Grape (Imperial), bowl, marigold, 10" 40.00
Grape (Imperial), compote, marigold 50.00
Grape (Imperial), cup, gr 35.00
Grape (Imperial), plate, gr, ruffled, 8½" 50.00
Grape (Northwood's Grape & Cable), bonbon, amethyst 58.00
Grape (Northwood's Grape & Cable), compote, amethyst 375.00
Grape (Northwood's Grape & Cable), cookie jar, amethyst, w/lid .500.00
Grape (Northwood's Grape & Cable), cup, bl 60.00
Grape (Northwood's Grape & Cable), dresser tray, amethyst 250.00
Grape (Northwood's Grape & Cable), hat, amethyst 50.00
Grape (Northwood's Grape & Cable), nappy, amethyst 100.00
Grape (Northwood's Grape & Cable), shot glass, amethyst 285.00
Grape (Northwood's Grape & Cable), tumbler, gr, jumbo 90.00
Grape & Gothic Arches (Northwood), pitcher, amethyst 385.00
Grape Arbor (Dugan), bowl, amethyst, 9½" 400.00
Grape Arbor (Northwood), hat, marigold 75.00
Grape Delight (Dugan), bowl, nut; bl, ftd, 6" 180.00
Grape Heavy (Dugan), bowl, amethyst, 10" 295.00
Grape Heavy (Imperial), cup, custard; amethyst 35.00
Grape Heavy (Imperial), nappy, amethyst 55.00
Grape Wreath (Millersburg), bowl, amethyst, 7½" 75.00
Grapevine Lattice (Dugan), bowl, marigold, 5" 30.00
Greek Key (Northwood), tumbler, amethyst, rare 195.00
Harvest Flower (Dugan), tumbler, marigold 105.00
Harvest Poppy, compote, bl 450.00
Hatchet (US Glass), marigold 150.00

Hattie (Imperial), rose bowl, marigold 95.00
Hawaiian Moon, tumbler, marigold 75.00
Heart & Souvenir (McKee), mug, gr, lg 115.00
Heart & Trees (Fenton), bowl, gr, 8¾" 215.00
Heart & Vine (Fenton), bowl, gr, 8½" 115.00
Hearts & Flowers (Northwood), compote, amethyst 550.00
Heavy Diamond, nappy, marigold 40.00
Heavy Heart (Higbee), tumbler, marigold 150.00
Heavy Prisms (English), celery vase, amethyst, 6" 115.00
Heavy Vine, atomizer, marigold 85.00
Heinz, bottle, red 58.00
Heisey Cartwheel, compote, red 290.00
Heron (Dugan), mug, amethyst, rare 375.00
Hexagon & Cane (Imperial), sugar bowl, marigold, w/lid 90.00
Hobnail (Millersburg), creamer, marigold, rare 275.00
Hobnail (Millersburg), pitcher, amethyst, rare 1,900.00
Hobnail (Millersburg), spittoon, gr, rare 1,800.00
Hobnail Miniature, tumbler, marigold, 2½" 50.00
Hobstar (Imperial), bowl, berry; marigold, 5" 25.00
Hobstar (Imperial), butter dish, marigold 80.00
Hobstar (Imperial), vase, amethyst, flared 200.00
Hobstar & Feather (Millersburg), bowl, diamond; marigold, 5" ..400.00
Hobstar & Feather (Millersburg), creamer, amethyst, rare 800.00
Hobstar & Feather (Millersburg), cup, punch; amethyst, rare 40.00
Hobstar & File, tumbler, marigold, rare 200.00
Hobstar Band (Imperial), celery tray, marigold 85.00
Hobstar Diamonds, tumbler, marigold, very rare 500.00
Hobstar Flower (Northwood), compote, marigold, scarce 55.00
Hobstar Panels (English), creamer, marigold 45.00
Hobstar Reversed (English), butter dish, marigold 55.00
Holiday, bottle, pastel 75.00
Holloween, spittoon, marigold 600.00
Holly (Fenton), compote, amethyst, 5" 50.00
Holly (Fenton), hat, bl 40.00
Holly (Fenton), rose bowl, marigold 400.00
Holly & Berry (Dugan), nappy, gr 60.00
Holly Sprig or Whirl (Millersburg), bonbon, marigold, plain 55.00
Holly Sprig or Whirl (Millersburg), compote, amethyst, rare 625.00
Homestead, shade, marigold 50.00
Honeycomb (Dugan), rose bowl, marigold 190.00
Honeycomb & Clover (Fenton), compote, amethyst 50.00
Honeycomb Ornament, hatpin, bl 90.00
Horn of Plenty, bottle, marigold 60.00
Horses Heads (Fenton), bowl, nut; marigold, rare 250.00
Horses Heads (Fenton), plate, bl, 6½" 800.00
Horseshoe, shot glass, marigold 50.00
Hourglass, vase, bud; marigold 50.00
Humpty Dumpty, jar, mustard; marigold 75.00
Idyll (Fenton), vase, bl, rare 850.00
Illusion (Fenton), bonbon, bl 85.00
Imperial #5 (Imperial), vase, marigold, rare, 6" 95.00
Imperial Daisy (Imperial), shade, marigold 45.00
Inca, bottle, marigold 175.00
Indian Canoe, boat novelty, marigold 100.00
Intaglio Feathers, cup, marigold 25.00
Interior Panels, mug, marigold 75.00
Interior Rays, sherbet, marigold 35.00
Interior Rays (Westmoreland), butter dish, marigold, w/lid 65.00
Interior Swirl, spittoon, peach opal 95.00
Inverted Coin Dot (Northwood-Fenton), rose bowl, marigold 50.00
Inverted Feather (Cambridge), compote, marigold 85.00
Inverted Feather (Cambridge), spooner, marigold, rare 400.00
Inverted Strawberry, bowl, gr, 5" 50.00
Inverted Strawberry, compote, gr, rare, lg 450.00

Inverted Strawberry (Cambridge), sugar
bowl, blue, $150.00.

Inverted Strawberry, pitcher, gr, rare 3,000.00
Inverted Thistle (Cambridge), plate, chop; amethyst, rare 2,600.00
Inverted Thistle (Cambridge), spittoon, amethyst, rare 4,000.00
Inverted Thistle (Cambridge), tumbler, amethyst, rare 300.00
Iowa, mug, marigold, rare, sm 95.00
Iris (Fenton), compote, amethyst 60.00
IW Harper, decanter, marigold, w/stopper 85.00
Jack-in-the-Pulpit (Dugan), vase, amethyst 75.00
Jacob's Ladder, bottle, perfume; marigold 60.00
Jewel Box, inkwell, marigold 150.00
Jeweled Heart (Dugan), pitcher, amethyst, rare 900.00
Jockey Club (Northwood), bowl, amethyst, 7" 600.00
Kitten, paperweight, marigold, rare 250.00
Kittens (Fenton), spooner, marigold, rare, 2½" 175.00
Kittens (Fenton), toothpick holder, bl, 3" 400.00
Kiwi (Australian), bowl, amethyst, rare, 10" 300.00
Knotted Beads (Fenton), vase, gr, 4" 40.00
Lacy Dewdrop (Westmoreland), banana boat, pastel 375.00
Lacy Dewdrop (Westmoreland), banana boat, pearl carnival 375.00
Lacy Dewdrop (Westmoreland), sugar bowl, pearl carnival 180.00
Large Kangaroo (Australian), bowl, amethyst, 10" 210.00
Late Enamelled Grape, goblet, marigold 90.00
Lattice (Dugan), bowl, amethyst 70.00
Lattice & Daisy (Dugan), tumbler, amethyst 60.00
Lattice & Grape (Fenton), tumbler, amethyst 45.00
Lattice & Leaves, vase, bl, 9½" 295.00
Lattice & Prisms, bottle, cologne; marigold, w/stopper 65.00
Laurel, shade, marigold 40.00
Laurel & Grape, vase, marigold, 6" 120.00
Lea & Vt (English), pickle dish, marigold, hdld 45.00
Leaf & Beads (Northwood-Dugan), candy dish, gr, ftd 115.00
Leaf Column (Northwood), vase, gr 45.00
Leaf Swirl (Westmoreland), compote, amethyst 75.00
Leaf Tiers (Fenton), butter dish, marigold, ftd 175.00
Leaf Tiers (Fenton), tumbler, amethyst, ftd, rare 90.00
Lined Lattice (Dugan), hat form, marigold 40.00
Little Beads, compote, marigold, sm 30.00
Little Daisy, lamp, pastel, complete, 8" 500.00
Little Fishes (Fenton), plate, bl, rare, 10½" 850.00
Little Jewel, finger lamp, marigold, rare 650.00
Little Owl, hatpin, marigold, rare 450.00
Little Stars (Millersburg), bowl, amethyst, rare, 10½" 700.00
Little Stars (Millersburg), bowl, marigold, scarce, 7" 100.00
Little Swan, pastel, miniature, 2" 75.00
Long Hobstar, compote, marigold 65.00
Long Horn, wine, marigold 60.00
Long Prisms, hatpin, amethyst 75.00
Long Thumbprint (Dugan), bowl, marigold, 8¾" 40.00
Long Thumbprint (Dugan), butter dish, marigold 70.00

Lotus & Grape (Fenton), plate, gr, rare, 9½" 650.00
Lotus Land (Northwood), bonbon, marigold 1,500.00
Lovebirds, bottle, marigold, w/stopper 575.00
Lucille, tumbler, marigold, rare 750.00
Lustre, tumbler, marigold 45.00
Lustre & Clear (Fenton), vase, marigold, fan form 40.00
Lustre & Clear (Imperial), hat, amethyst 40.00
Lustre & Clear (Imperial), nappy, gr 40.00
Lustre & Clear (Imperial), pitcher, marigold 195.00
Lustre & Clear (Imperial), shakers, marigold, pr 70.00
Lustre Flute (Northwood), bonbon, gr 60.00
Lustre Rose (Imperial), bowl, berry; marigold, 5" 20.00
Lustre Rose (Imperial), fernery, amethyst 60.00
Lustre Rose (Imperial), sugar bowl, gr 55.00
Lustre Rose (Imperial), tumbler, amethyst 30.00
Lutz (McKee), mug, marigold, ftd 60.00
Magpie (Australian), bowl, marigold, 6" 45.00
Majestic (McKee), tumbler, marigold, rare 500.00
Manhattan (US Glass), wine, marigold 40.00
Many Prisms, bottle, perfume; marigold, w/stopper 75.00
Maple Leaf (Dugan), bowl, amethyst, stemmed, 4½" 35.00
Maple Leaf (Dugan), tumbler, bl 40.00
Marilyn (Millersburg), tumbler, amethyst, rare 275.00
Massachusetts (US Glass), vase, marigold 175.00
May Basket (English), basket, gr, 7½" 95.00
Mayflower, compote, amethyst 50.00
Mayflower, hat, peach opal 150.00
Maypole, vase, amethyst, 6¼" 55.00
Melon Rib (Imperial), decanter, marigold 90.00
Melon Rib (Imperial), pitcher, marigold 60.00
Memphis (Northwood), bowl, punch; marigold, w/base ...400.00
Memphis (Northwood), cup, gr 45.00
Mikado (Fenton), compote, gr, lg 2,400.00
Mirrored Lotus (Fenton), bonbon, gr 100.00
Mirrored Lotus (Fenton), rose bowl, bl, rare 480.00

Mitered Ovals (Millersburg), vase, green, rare, $6,700.00.

Moon & Star (Westmoreland), compote, pearl carnival 385.00
Moonprint (English), banana boat, marigold, rare 135.00
Moonprint (English), compote, marigold 50.00
Moonprint (English), pitcher, milk; marigold, scarce 150.00
Muscadine, tumbler, marigold, rare 450.00
My Lady, powder jar, marigold, w/lid 90.00
Near Cut Souvenir (Cambridge), tumbler, marigold, rare 260.00
Nell (Higbee), mug, marigold 75.00
Nesting Swan (Millersnurg), spittoon whimsey, amethyst, rare .5,000.00
Night Stars (Millersburg), bonbon, amethyst, rare 450.00
Nippon (Northwood), plate, gr, 9" 650.00
Northern Star (Fenton), bowl, marigold, 6" 30.00

Northwood's Nearcut, goblet, amethyst, rare 140.00
Northwood's Poppy, pickle dish, bl, oval 175.00
Nu-Art (Imperial), shade, marigold 90.00
Nuggate, pitcher, bl, 6" 90.00
Nugget Beads, beads, amethyst 125.00
Number 2351 (Cambridge), cup, punch; gr 65.00
Number 4 (Imperial), compote, marigold 40.00
Octagon (Imperial), cordial, amethyst 200.00
Octagon (Imperial), goblet, marigold 65.00
Octagon (Imperial), tumbler, gr 35.00
Octagon (Imperial), wine, gr 70.00
Olympus, shade, marigold 60.00
Omnibus, tumbler, bl, rare 795.00
Open Flower (Dugan), bowl, gr, flat or ftd, 7" 50.00
Open Rose (Imperial), plate, amethyst, 9" 180.00
Optic (Imperial), bowl, amethyst, 9" 75.00
Optic & Buttons (Imperial), goblet, marigold 60.00
Optic & Buttons (Imperial), plate, marigold, 10½" 70.00
Orange Tree (Fenton), hatpin holder, bl 290.00
Orange Tree (Fenton), powder jar, marigold, w/lid 95.00
Orange Tree (Imperial), compote, amethyst, sm 60.00
Orange Tree & Scroll (Fenton), tumbler, gr 85.00
Oriental Poppy (Northwood), tumbler, amethyst 75.00
Ostrich (Australian), compote, amethyst, rare, lg 200.00
Oval & Round (Imperial), bowl, gr, 4" 30.00
Oval Prisms, hatpin, amethyst 75.00
Owl, bank, marigold 40.00
Oxford, mustard pot, marigold, w/lid 70.00
Palm Beach (US Glass), bowl, marigold, 5" 30.00
Palm Beach (US Glass), pitcher, marigold 300.00
Panama (US Glass), goblet, marigold, rare 135.00
Panelled Dandelion (Fenton), tumbler, gr 60.00
Panelled Hobnail (Dugan), vase, amethyst, 5" 60.00
Panelled Prisms, jam jar, marigold, w/lid 55.00
Panelled Swirl, bowl, rose; marigold 65.00
Panelled Tree Trunk (Dugan), vase, marigold, rare, 7" ...70.00
Panels & Beads, shade, vaseline opal 55.00
Pansy (Imperial), dresser tray, amethyst 90.00
Panther (Fenton), bowl, whimsey; bl, 10½" 1,000.00
Parlor, ashtray, bl 95.00
Peach (Northwood), butter dish, wht pastel 275.00
Peach & Pear (Dugan), banana bowl, amethyst 95.00
Peaches, bottle, wine; marigold 45.00
Peacock, Fluffy (Fenton), tumbler, amethyst 55.00
Peacock, lamp, carnival base, amethyst 450.00
Peacock, Strutting (Westmoreland); creamer, gr, w/lid ...65.00
Peacock (Millersburg), banana bowl, amethyst, rare ...3,500.00
Peacock (Millersburg), bowl, amethyst, 5" 135.00
Peacock (Millersburg), bowl, ice cream; amethyst, 5" ...90.00
Peacock & Urn (Fenton), compote, amethyst 70.00
Peacock & Urn (Fenton), plate, amethyst, rare, 11" ...1,200.00
Peacock & Urn & Vts (Millersburg), compote, amethyst, lg ...1,500.00
Peacock at the Fountain (Dugan), compote, amethyst, rare 450.00
Peacock at the Fountain (Dugan), cup, marigold 30.00
Peacock at the Fountain (Dugan), tumbler, amethyst 90.00
Peacock Tail (Fenton), bonbon, gr 90.00
Peacock Tail (Fenton), plate, amethyst, 6" 80.00
Pearl & Jewels (Fenton), basket, wht pastel, 4" 200.00
Penny match holder, amethyst, rare 250.00
Pepper Plant (Fenton), hat form, bl 200.00
Perfection (Millersburg), tumbler, amethyst, rare 400.00
Persian Garden (Dugan), plate, chop; peach opal, rare, 13" 4,800.00
Persian Medallion (Dugan), cup, punch; amethyst 35.00
Persian Medallion (Fenton), bonbon, amethyst 55.00

Persian Medallion (Fenton), bowl, orange; bl 275.00
Petals (Dugan), compote, amethyst 60.00
Pickle, paperweight, amethyst, 4½" 65.00
Pigeon, paperweight, marigold 190.00
Pin-Ups (Australian), bowl, amethyst, rare, 8¾" 140.00
Pinched Ribs, vase, marigold 85.00
Pineapple (English), creamer, amethyst 100.00
Pineapple (English), rose bowl, marigold 55.00
Pinwheel (English), bowl, marigold, rare, 8" 50.00
Plaid (Fenton), plate, bl, rare, 9" 450.00
Plain Jane (Imperial), basket, marigold 60.00
Plume Panels, vase, amethyst, 7" 70.00
Poinsettia (Imperial), pitcher, milk; amethyst 950.00
Polo, ashtray, marigold 85.00
Pond Lily (Fenton), bonbon, marigold 45.00
Pony (Dugan), bowl, amethyst, 8½" 260.00
Poodle, powder jar, marigold, w/lid 30.00
Poppy Show (Imperial), lamp whimsey, marigold 2,500.00
Portland (US Glass), bowl, pastel, 8½" 170.00
Prayer Rug (Fenton), bonbon, iridized custard, rare 1,800.00
Pretty Panels (Fenton), tumbler, marigold, hdld 60.00
Pretty Panels (Northwood), tumbler, gr 70.00
Primrose (Millersburg), bowl, ice cream; gr, scarce, 9" 190.00
Primrose Panels (Imperial), shade, pastel 60.00
Prism Band (Fenton), pitcher, gr, decor 395.00
Prisms, tray, marigold, 3" 50.00
Prisms (Westmoreland), compote, gr, scarce, 5" 100.00
Propeller (Imperial), compote, gr 45.00
Pulled Loop (Dugan), vase, amethyst 60.00
Puzzle (Dugan), compote, gr 75.00
Quartered Block, creamer, marigold 60.00
Question Mark (Dugan), compote, amethyst 70.00
Radiance, pitcher, marigold 240.00
Ragged Robin (Fenton), bowl, gr, scarce, 8¾" 100.00
Rainbow (Northwood), compote, gr 150.00
Raindrops (Dugan), banana bowl, amethyst, 9¾" 150.00
Rambler Rose (Dugan), tumbler, amethyst 50.00
Ranger (Mexican), butter dish, marigold 190.00
Ranger (Mexican), shot glass, marigold, rare 425.00
Ranger (Mexican), tumbler, marigold 290.00
Raspberry (Northwood), compote, amethyst 56.00
Raspberry (Northwood), pitcher, milk; gr 275.00
Rays (Dugan), bowl, amethyst, 9" 90.00
Red Panels (Imperial), shade, red 200.00
Regal Swirl, candlestick, marigold, ea 75.00
Rex, pitcher, marigold 375.00
Rib & Panel (Fenton), vase, marigold 50.00
Ribbed Holly (Fenton), compote, amethyst 70.00
Ribbon & Block, lamp, marigold, complete 600.00
Ribbon & Leaves, sugar bowl, marigold, sm 50.00
Rising Sun (US Glass), creamer, marigold 90.00
Rising Sun (US Glass), tray, bl, rare 500.00
Robin (Imperial), mug, marigold, old only 55.00
Rock Crystal (McKee), bowl, punch; amethyst, w/base 600.00
Roll, tumbler, marigold 400.00
Rosalind (Millersburg), compote, amethyst, rare, 6" 550.00
Rose Band, tumbler, marigold, rare 700.00
Rose Bouquet, bonbon, marigold, rare 75.00
Rose Garden (Sweden), rose bowl, bl, rare, lg 700.00
Rose Garden (Sweden), vase, marigold, rnd, 9" 385.00
Rose Panels (Australian), compote, marigold, lg 145.00
Rose Pinwheel, bowl, gr, rare 2,200.00
Rose Show Vt (Northwood), bowl, amethyst, 8¾" 750.00
Rose Tree (Fenton), bowl, marigold, rare, 10" 1,150.00

Rosetime, vase, marigold 100.00
Rosettes (Northwood), bowl, amethyst, ftd, 7" 80.00
Roundup (Dugan), plate, amethyst, rare, 9" 225.00
Ruffled Rib (Northwood), bowl, amethyst, 8" 70.00
Rustic, (Fenton), vase, funeral; gr, 15" 220.00
S-Band (Australian), compote, amethyst 95.00
S-Repeat (Dugan), tumbler, marigold 300.00
Sailboats (Fenton), goblet, gr 275.00
Sailing Ship, plate, marigold, 8" 40.00
Saint (English), candlestick, marigold, ea 300.00
Satin Swirl, atomizer, clear 75.00
Scale Band (Fenton), bowl, marigold, 6" 35.00
Scale Band (Fenton), tumbler, bl 350.00
Scales (Westmoreland), bonbon, amethyst 48.00
Scales (Westmoreland), plate, amethyst, 9" 95.00
Scotch Thistle (Fenton), compote, amethyst 60.00
Scroll Embossed (Imperial), compote, amethyst, lg 450.00
Scroll Embossed Vt (English), ashtray, amethyst, hdld, 5" 60.00
Seagulls (Dugan), bowl, marigold, scarce, 6½" 80.00
Seaweed (Millersburg), bowl, marigold, rare, 5" 400.00

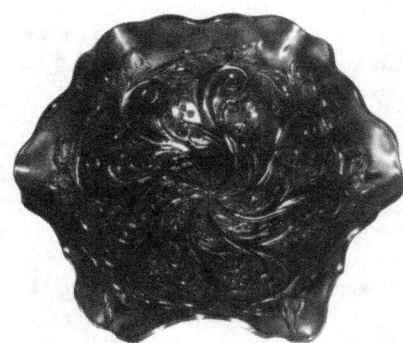

Seaweed (Millersburg), bowl, green, 9", $375.00.

Sharp, shot glass, marigold 50.00
Shell (Imperial), plate, amethyst, 8½" 1,050.00
Shell & Jewel (Westmoreland), creamer, marigold, w/lid 65.00
Sheraton (US Glass), butter dish, pastel 130.00
Ship & Stars, plate, marigold, 8" 40.00
Signet (English), sugar bowl, marigold, w/lid, 6½" 75.00
Silver Queen (Fenton), tumbler, marigold 70.00
Singing Birds (Northwood), mug, amethyst 250.00
Singing Birds (Northwood), sherbet, gr, rare 150.00
Single Flower (Dugan), bowl, amethyst, 8" 40.00
Six Petals (Dugan), plate, amethyst, rare 200.00
Six-Sided (Imperial), candlestick, amethyst, ea 300.00
Ski-Star (Dugan), bowl, amethyst, 5" 50.00
Small Blackberry (Northwood), compote, amethyst 60.00
Small Rib (Dugan), compote, amethyst 45.00
Small Thumbprint, toothpick holder, marigold 70.00
Smooth Panels (Imperial), tumbler, pastel marigold 45.00
Smooth Rays (Northwood-Dugan), rose bowl, amethyst 60.00
Snow Fancy (McKee), bowl, gr, 5" 50.00
Soda Gold (Imperial), pitcher, marigold 240.00
Soutache (Dugan), lamp, marigold, complete 350.00
Sphinx (English), paperweight, amber, rare 595.00
Spiral (Imperial), candlesticks, marigold, pr 165.00
Split Diamond (English), butter dish, marigold, scarce 65.00
Springtime (Northwood), butter dish, marigold 375.00
Square Diamond, vase, bl, rare 750.00
Stag & Holly (Fenton), plate, marigold, ftd, 13" 1,000.00
Star, paperweight, pastel, rare 295.00

Star & Diamond, hatpin, amethyst 75.00
Star & File (Imperial), compote, marigold 45.00
Star & File (Imperial), spooner, marigold 30.00
Star & Hobs, rose bowl, bl, rare, 9" 350.00
Star & Nearcut, hatpin, amethyst 60.00
Star & Rosette, hatpin, amethyst 75.00
Star Medallion (Imperial), bonbon, marigold 45.00
Star Medallion (Imperial), celery tray, marigold 60.00
Star Medallion (Imperial), pitcher, milk; gr 95.00
Star of David (Imperial), bowl, amethyst, scarce, 8¾" ...100.00
Starburst, bottle, perfume; marigold, w/stopper 65.00
Starflower, pitcher, marigold, rare 3,200.00
Stars & Bars (Cambridge), wine, marigold, rare 150.00
Stippled Flower (Dugan), bowl, peach opal, 8½" 85.00
Stippled Rays (Fenton), compote, bl 45.00
Stippled Rays (Imperial), creamer, gr, stemmed 50.00
Stippled Rays (Northwood), compote, gr 65.00
Stippled Strawberry (Jenkins), tumbler, marigold 60.00
Stork (Jenkins), vase, marigold 60.00
Stork ABC, plate, child's; 7½" 60.00
Strawberry (Dugan), epergne, amethyst, rare 900.00
Strawberry (Fenton), bonbon, amethyst 50.00
Strawberry (Millersburg), gravy boat whimsey, vaseline, rare ..1,500.00
Strawberry (Northwood), bowl, bl, 5" 90.00
Strawberry Point, tumbler, marigold 150.00
Strawberry Spray, brooch, bl 175.00
Stream of Hearts (Fenton), compote, marigold, rare 95.00
Studs (Imperial), pitcher, milk; marigold 75.00
Sun Punch, bottle, marigold 30.00
Sunflower & Diamond, vase, marigold, 2 szs, ea 75.00
Sungold (Australian), epergne, pastel 450.00
Sunken Daisy (English), sugar bowl, bl 40.00
Sunray, compote, amethyst 40.00
Swirl (Northwood), tumbler, marigold 110.00
Swirl Vt (Imperial), plate, cake; clear 85.00
Swirled Flute (Fenton), vase, amethyst, 7" 40.00
Swirled Ribs (Northwood), pitcher, marigold 165.00
Sword & Circle, tumbler, marigold, rare 150.00
Target (Fenton), vase, amethyst, 7" 55.00
Ten Mums (Fenton), tumbler, marigold, rare 70.00
Thistle (English), vase, marigold, 6" 45.00
Thistle (Fenton), banana boat, amethyst, ftd, scarce ...400.00
Thistle (Fenton), compote, bl 70.00
Thistle & Lotus (Fenton), bowl, gr, 7" 70.00
Three Row (Imperial), vase, amethyst, rare 1,200.00
Three-in-One (Imperial), toothpick holder, gr, rare 85.00
Tiered Thumbprint, candlesticks, marigold, pr 120.00
Tiny Berry, tumbler, bl, 2¼" 45.00
Toltec (McKee), pitcher, tankard; marigold, very rare ...2,600.00
Top Hat, vase, pastel 50.00
Top O' the Morning, hatpin, amethyst 50.00
Top O' the Walk, hatpin, amethyst 100.00
Tracery (Millersburg), bonbon, gr, rare 650.00
Tree Bark (Imperial), bowl, marigold, 7½" 20.00
Tree Bark (Imperial), candy jar, marigold, w/lid 35.00
Tree of Life (Imperial), plate, marigold, 7½" 40.00
Treebark Vt, tumbler, marigold 20.00
Triads (English), celery vase, marigold 55.00
Tropicana (English), vase, marigold, rare 1,600.00
Tulip (Millersburg), compote, amethyst, rare, 9" 850.00
Tulip & Cane (Imperial), goblet, marigold, rare, 8-oz ...75.00
Twins (Imperial), bowl, fruit; marigold, w/base 60.00
Twitch (Bartlett-Collins), creamer, marigold 30.00
Two Flowers (Fenton), bowl, gr, ftd, 8" 250.00

Umbrella Prisms, hatpin, sm 45.00
Urn, vase, marigold, 9" 65.00
Utility, lamp, marigold, complete, 8" 90.00
Valentine (Northwood), bowl, amethyst, rare, 5" 200.00
Vineyard (Dugan), tumbler, amethyst 50.00
Vining Twigs (Dugan), bowl, gr, 7½" 50.00
Vintage (Dugan), powder jar, amethyst, w/lid 120.00
Vintage (Fenton), bowl, amethyst, 10" 60.00
Vintage (Fenton), bowl, rose; bl 60.00
Vintage (Fenton), plate, bl, 7¾" 130.00
Vintage (US Glass), wine, amethyst 50.00
Vintage Banded (Dugan), pitcher, amethyst 550.00
Vintage Vt (Dugan), plate, amethyst 400.00
Waffle Block (Imperial), bowl, fruit; clambroth, w/base ...200.00
Waffle Block (Imperial), sherbet, smoke 170.00
Waffle Weave, inkwell, marigold 95.00
War Dance (English), compote, marigold, 5" 120.00
Water Lily (Fenton), bonbon, amethyst 55.00
Water Lily (Fenton), plate, chop; very rare, 11" 4,500.00
Water Lily & Cattails (Fenton), pitcher, marigold 340.00
Water Lily & Cattails (Fenton), sugar bowl, marigold ...100.00
Wavy Satin, hatpin, amethyst 95.00
Weeping Cherry (Dugan), bowl, amethyst, flat base ...110.00
Western Thistle, vase, marigold, rare 250.00
Wheat (Northwood), sweetmeat, amethyst, w/lid, rare ...9,500.00
Whirling Hobstar (US Glass), cup, marigold 20.00
Whirling Star (Imperial), compote, gr 85.00
White Oak, tumbler, marigold, rare 300.00
Wide Panel (Northwood-Fenton-Imperial), compote, marigold ...40.00
Wide Panel (Northwood-Fenton-Imperial), goblet, marigold ...40.00
Wide Panel (Northwood-Fenton-Imperial), vase, bl 60.00
Wide Panel (US Glass), salt cellar, marigold 50.00
Wild Berry, jar, marigold, w/lid 250.00
Wild Fern (Australian), compote, amethyst 240.00
Wild Loganberry (Westmoreland), wine, marigold 145.00
Wild Strawberry (Dugan), bowl, amethyst, rare, 6" 95.00
Windmill (Imperial), dish, pickle; marigold 25.00
Windmill (Imperial), tumbler, gr 45.00
Wine & Roses (Fenton), wine, marigold 90.00
Wise Owl, bank, marigold 50.00
Wisteria (Northwood), bank whimsey, wht, rare 2,500.00
Woodlands, vase, marigold, rare, 5" 300.00
Woodpecker (Dugan), vase, wall; gr 90.00
Wreath of Roses (Fenton), bonbon, amethyst 45.00
Wreath of Roses Vt (Dugan), compote, gr 65.00
Wreathed Cherry (Dugan), bowl, amethyst, oval, 5" 40.00
Wreathed Cherry (Dugan), pitcher, amethyst 425.00
Zig Zag (Millersburg), card tray, gr, rare 900.00
Zip Zip (English), flower frog holder, marigold 60.00
Zippered Heart, bowl, amethyst, 9" 110.00
474 (Imperial), cup, marigold 30.00
474 (Imperial), goblet, amethyst 90.00
474 (Imperial), spooner, gr 85.00
474 Vt (Sweden), compote, gr, 9" 90.00
49'er (Imperial), decanter, marigold 125.00
49'er (Imperial), tumbler, marigold 75.00

Carousel Figures

For generations of Americans, visions of carousel horses revolving majestically around lively band organs rekindle wonderful childhood experiences. These nostalgic memories are the legacy of the creative talent from a dozen carving shops that created America's carousel art.

Skilled craftsmen brought their trade from Europe where American carvers took the carousel animal from a folk art creation to a true art form. The 'Golden Age of Carousel Art' lasted from 1880 to 1929.

There are two basic types of American carousels. The largest and most impressive is the 'park style' carousel built for permanent installation in major amusement centers. These were created in Philadelphia by Gustav and William Dentzel, Muller Brothers, and E. Joy Morris who became the Philadelphia Toboggan Company in 1902. A more flamboyant group of carousel animals was carved in Coney Island, New York, by Charles Looff, Marcus Illions, Charles Carmel and Stein & Goldstein's Artistic Carousel Company. These park-style carousels were typically three, four and even five rows with forty-five to sixty-eight animals on a platform. Collectors often pay a premium for the carvings by these men. The outside row animals are larger and more ornate and command higher prices. The horses on the inside rows are smaller, less decorated and of lesser value.

The most popular style of carousel art is the 'country fair style.' These carousels were portable affairs created for mobility. The horses are smaller and less ornate with leg and head positions that allow for stacking and easy loading. These were built primarily for North Tonawanda, New York, near Niagara Falls, by Armitage Herschell Company, Herschell Spillman Company, Spillman Engineering Company and Allen Herschell. Charles W. Parker was also well known for his portable merry-go-rounds. He was based in Leavenworth, Kansas. Parker and Herschell Spillman both created a few large park-style carousels as well, but they are better known for their portable models.

Horses are by far the most common figure found, but there are two dozen other animals that were created for the carousel platform. Carousel animals, unlike most other antiques, are oftentimes worth more in a restored condition. Figures found with original factory paint are extraordinarily rare and bring premium amounts. Typically, carousel horses are found in garish, poorly applied 'park paint' and oftentimes are missing legs or ears. Carousel horses are hollow. They were glued up from several blocks for greater strength and lighter weight. Bass and poplar woods were used extensively.

If you have an antique carousel animal you would like to have identified, send a clear photograph and description along with a LSASE to our advisor, William Manns, who is listed in the Directory under New York. Mr. Manns is the author of *Painted Ponies*, containing many full-color photographs, guides, charts, and directories for the collector.

Key:
IR — inside row   OR — outside row
MR — middle row   PTC — Philadelphia Toboggan
                                 Company

Coney Island Style

Carmel, IR jumper, unrstr	7,000.00
Carmel, MR jumper, unrstr	12,500.00
Carmel, OR jumper w/cherub, rstr	48,000.00
Illions, MR stander, rstr	20,000.00
Illions, OR stander, eagle saddle, rstr	44,000.00
Looff, IR jumper, unrstr	6,000.00
Looff, OR jumper, unrstr	21,500.00
Stein & Goldstein, IR jumper, unrstr	4,500.00
Stein & Goldstein, MR jumper, rstr	17,000.00
Stein & Goldstein, OR stander w/bells, unrstr	35,000.00

European Horses

Anderson, English, unrstr	4,000.00
Bayol, French, unrstr	3,000.00
Heyn, German, unrstr	5,000.00
Hubner, Belgian, unrstr	3,800.00
Savage, English, unrstr	3,500.00

Menagerie Animals (Non-Horses)

Dentzel, bear, unrstr	28,000.00
Dentzel, cat, unrstr	35,000.00
Dentzel, lion, unrstr	55,000.00
Dentzel, pig, unrstr	9,000.00
Dentzel, rabbit, unrstr	40,000.00
E Joy Morris, deer, unrstr	14,500.00
Herschell Spillman, cat, unrstr	17,000.00
Herschell Spillman, chicken, portable, unrstr	7,500.00
Herschell Spillman, dog, portable, unrstr	9,000.00
Herschell Spillman, frog, unrstr	25,000.00
Looff, camel, unrstr	9,000.00
Looff, goat, rstr	18,500.00
Muller, tiger, rstr	30,000.00

Philadelphia Style

Dentzel, IR 'topknot' jumper, unrstr	6,000.00
Dentzel, MR jumper, unrstr	18,000.00
Dentzel, OR stander, rstr	45,000.00
Dentzel, prancer, rstr	9,500.00
Morris, IR prancer, rstr	8,000.00
Morris, MR stander, unrstr	9,500.00
Morris, OR stander, rstr	29,000.00
Muller, IR jumper, rstr	8,900.00
Muller, MR jumper, unrstr	12,500.00
Muller, OR stander, rstr	46,000.00
Muller, OR stander w/military trappings	85,000.00
PTC, chariot (bench-like seat), rstr	8,900.00
PTC, IR jumper, rstr	5,500.00
PTC, MR jumper, rstr	15,500.00
PTC, OR stander, armored, rstr	46,000.00
PTC, OR stander, unrstr	29,500.00

Portable

Allan Herschell, all aluminum, ca 1950	700.00
Allan Herschell, half & half, wood & aluminum head	1,500.00
Allan Herschell, IR Indian pony, unrstr	2,600.00
Allan Herschell, OR, rstr	3,200.00
Allan Herschell, OR Trojan-style jumper	4,700.00
Armitage Herschell, track machine jumper	3,500.00
Dare, jumper, unrstr	3,900.00
Herschell Spillman, chariot (bench-like seat)	3,500.00
Herschell Spillman, IR jumper, unrstr	3,000.00
Herschell Spillman, MR jumper, unrstr	3,200.00
Herschell Spillman, OR, eagle decor	6,000.00
Herschell Spillman, OR, park machine	12,000.00
Parker, MR jumper, unrstr	4,500.00
Parker, OR jumper, park machine, unrstr	14,000.00
Parker, OR jumper, rstr	9,500.00

Carpet Balls

Carpet balls are glazed china spheres decorated with intersecting lines or other simple designs that were used for indoor games in the British Isles during the early 1800s. Mint condition examples are rare.

Allover sm wht dots w/bl centers on bl, 3½", M	150.00

Blk & bl circles around bull's eye on wht, 3", EX 65.00
Blk & wht spatter florals, 3½", NM 225.00
Blk & wht stick spatter florals, 3⅝", EX 170.00
Brn & wht plaid, 3¼" 125.00
Dk gr, emb Henselite Indoor, NM 40.00
Gr & blk stripes wrap around 3 ways on wht, 2⅝", EX 125.00
Pk w/pk dots w/in wht circles, 3½", M 140.00
Purple w/wht polka dots, 3", NM 100.00
Red stick spatter, minor glaze flake, 3¼" 360.00
Yel w/yel dots w/in wht circles, frilled rim, 3", NM 120.00

Cartoon Art

Collectors of cartoon art are interested in many forms of original art — animation cels, sports, political or editorial cartoons, syndicated comic strip panels, and caricature. To produce even a short animated cartoon strip, hundreds of original drawings are required, each showing the characters in slightly advancing positions. Called 'cels' because those made prior to the 1950s were made from a celluloid material, collectors often pay hundreds of dollars for a frame from a favorite movie. Prices of Disney cels with backgrounds vary widely. Background paintings, model sheets, storyboards, and preliminary sketches are also collectible — so are comic book drawings executed in India ink and signed by the artist. Daily 'funnies' originals, especially the earlier ones portraying super heroes, and Sunday comic strips, the early as well as the later ones, are collected. Cartoon art has become recognized and valued as a novel yet valid form of contemporary art.

Key:
ab — airbrushed   cel — celluloid
C — Courvosier   wc — watercolor

Captain Easy, by Roy Crane, 3/30/32, two frames hand colored by Crane, rare, 5½x24", $500.00.

Animation Cel, Full Color

Alice in Wonderland, caterpillar flying, gouache, full cel 920.00
Bluto carries flowers, gouache, full cel, 1930s, 6x7½" 2,760.00
Cinderella, 2 mice & bird sew, gouache, full cel, 9¾x10½" 805.00
Fantasia, purple Centaurette, gouache, partial cel, 7x7" 1,495.00
Fantasia, 2 dewdrop fairies, gouache on C/wc/ab ground, 7x6½" ..2,760.00
Lady & Tramp, gouache, full cel, 1955, 5¾x7½" 1,725.00
Mr Mole leans on cane, gouache on cel on C/ab ground, 8x8" ...635.00
Quick Draw McGraw on train tracks, gouache, wc bkground, 7x9" .253.00
Snow White sings to birds, gouache on C/wc/ab ground, 9x9½" ..4,600.00
Thumper, gouache on laminated cel on C/wc/ab ground, 6x5¼" .1,265.00
Tweedledee & Tweedledum, gouache, full cel, 7x10" 975.00
Winnie the Pooh & Piglet w/tools, gouache, wc bkground, 9x12" .635.00

Animation Drawing

Alice in Wonderland, Queen of Hearts, graphite, 8½x11½" 330.00

Briar Rose, graphite, 1959, 12½x15½", set of 3 ....**1,095.00**
Briar Rose & Prince Phillip, graphite, 12½x15½", 3 for **1,095.00**
Bugs Bunny w/carrot, pencil/crayon, Scribner, 13½x10", pr **2,990.00**
Daffy Duck in scuba gear, pencil/crayon, 1961, 11x8" **865.00**
Fantasia, Mickey as apprentice, graphite/mc pencil, 11x13" **2,420.00**
Fantasia, Pegasus sits on branch, pastel, 10x11½" **2,185.00**
Jiminy Cricket & Gideon, charcoal, 1940, 7x5¼" **550.00**
Jiminy Cricket w/umbrella, graphite/colored pencil, 7½x10" **700.00**
Mickey & Donald w/Goofy, graphite/mc pencil, 1935, 9½x12" .**800.00**
Mickey Mouse, graphite, sgn Walt Disney, 10½x8" **4,600.00**
Mickey Mouse & nephews play w/sweater, graphite, 9½x12" **700.00**
Mickey Mouse on skates, graphite/mc pencil, fr, 8x10", pr **750.00**
Mickey Mouse w/rifle, graphite/colored pencil, '38, 9½x11" **800.00**
Mickey's Service Station, Mickey laughs, graphite, '35, 9x12" ...**700.00**
Mickey w/flowers, graphite/colored pencil, '33, 9½x12" **460.00**
Pepe Le Pew, graphite/colored pencil, 1950s, 11¾x14" **825.00**
Sleeping Beauty, King Hubert, graphite, 12½x15½", pr **460.00**
Waterbabies on fish, graphite/colored pencil, '35, 9½x12" **690.00**
Wolf dressed as Hitler, MGM, colored pencil, 1940s, 9x12" **690.00**

Storyboard

Dumbo, 2 dancing crows, pastel, 1941, 5½x7" **220.00**
Fantasia, lady Centaurette, graphite, 1940, 6x8" **750.00**
Fantasia, pilgrim w/candle, pastel, 1940, 12½x15½" **1,265.00**
Figaro (cat) on banister, graphite, 6x7" **485.00**
Flintstones, Weirdly's, graphite/colored pencil, 10x12", pr **400.00**
Mickey Mouse wallpapers, graphite/colored pencil, '30s, 12x10" ..**350.00**
Music Land instruments run about, bl pencil, '35, 7x9" **700.00**
Pinocchio becomes a boy, graphite/brn pencil, 5x6" **1,265.00**

Miscellaneous

Concept drawing, Centaurettes bathing, pastels, 12x15" **3,680.00**
Concept drawing, Fantasia mushroom dancers, pastels, 10x12" .**3,450.00**
Model drawing, Donald Duck on pony, graphite/red pencil, 9x12" .**350.00**
Model sheet, Mickey Mouse, graphite, 1930s, 8¾x11", pr **1,000.00**
Painting on glass, Bambi & Thumper, Disney Studios, 5½x6" ...**750.00**
Presentation wc, Beany & Cecil, wc/ink on cb, 11x18" **800.00**
Production bkground, Fantasia, flowers, pastel, 12x15½", pr ...**2,860.00**
Publicity drawing, Bugs Bunny w/carrot, pen & ink, 9½x7½" **635.00**
Sunday newspaper comic, Superman, Philadelphia Inquirer, '39 ..**220.00**
Sunday newspaper comic, Tarzan, Celardo, 1954 ....**150.00**
Sunday newspaper comic, Terry & the Pirates, Wunder, 1951 ...**200.00**
Wc on cb, Peg Leg Pete & Mickey Mouse in space, 7x8¼" **520.00**

Cartoon Books

'Books of cartoons' were printed during the first decade of the 20th century and remained popular until the advent of the modern comic book in the late thirties. Cartoon books, printed in both color and black and white, were merely reprints of current newspaper comic strips. The books, ranging from thirty to seventy pages and in sizes from 3½" x 8" up to 11" x 17", were usually bound with cardboard covers and were often distributed as premiums in exchange for coupons saved from the daily paper. One of the largest of the companies who printed these books was Cupples and Leon, producer of nearly half of the two hundred titles on record. Among the most popular sellers were *Mutt and Jeff, Bringing Up Father,* and *Little Orphan Annie.*

Bringing Up Father, #2, Cupples & Leon, NM 80.00
Bringing Up Father, #8, Cupples & Leon, VG 45.00
Bringing Up Father, #15, Cupples & Leon, EX 60.00

Charlie Chaplin Comic Capers, #1, Donohue, 1917, EX **100.00**
Charlie Chaplin Funny Stunts, color, Donohue, NM **110.00**
Charlie Chaplin in the Army, Donohue, NM **150.00**
Curly Tops on Star Island, Cupples & Leon, 1918, G **60.00**
Little Orphan Annie, Willing Helper, Cupples & Leon, 1932, NM ..**65.00**
Little Orphan Annie in Cosmic City, Cupples & Leon, VG **30.00**
Little Orphan Annie the Haunted House, Cupples & Leon, EX ..**40.00**
Mutt & Jeff, #1, Ball, 1910, EX **95.00**
Mutt & Jeff, #5, Ball, 1916, VG **80.00**
Skeezix & Pal, Reilley & Lee, soft cover, 1925, EX **45.00**
Skeezix Out West, Reilley & Lee, hard cover, 1928, NM **75.00**
Winnie Winkle, #4, Cupples & Leon, EX **25.00**

Cash Registers

By 1970 antique cash registers had risen to become blue chip collectibles, joining the ranks of fine paintings, bronzes, firearms, clocks, and other categories having permanent, established worth. Some extremely scarce and elegant cash registers will command up to $25,000.00 on today's market.

Register prices are determined by make, model, size, desirability of pattern and accessories such as add-on clocks, topsigns and personalized nameplates (which may be cast as topsigns or 'lid ovals' and on occasion cast into the register's front or back plates). Of immense consideration is the register's condition.

This column uses 'mint' condition (M) to indicate registers which have been cleaned, oiled, polished and lacquered by a professional and have perfect glass, keytops, and indicators. Some restorers will replace the velvet underneath the lid (where applicable), which is an added touch of elegance. 'Very good' condition (VG) describes unrestored, unpolished registers which are complete and operating. Their values are usually about half of the restored model's value. All prices may vary as much as 20%, depending on geography and demand.

For further information we recommend the highly informative books *Antique Cash Registers, 1880-1920*, by Bartsch and Sanchez (Mr. Bartsch's address may be found in our Directory under Oregon); and *The Incorruptible Cashier*, Vols. I & II, currently available from our other advisor, John Apple, listed in our Directory under Wisconsin.

The first notable 1994 cash register auction was held in January in Springfield, Missouri. The thirty-two machines sold were from the Elwood Sanders Collection and reflect unchanged values for the common models, while the scarce machines showed an increase of about 50%. Some of these are described below.

National Cash Register #321, brass, candy store model with extended base, VG, $1,300.00.

NCR #1000 Class, autographic box attachment, 1910, M **1,200.00**
NCR #1000 Class, autographic box attachment, 1910, VG **650.00**
NCR #129 or #130, bronze, VG, ea **850.00**
NCR #13, Ionic pattern, CI, 1899, G- **225.00**
NCR #2, inlaid mahog cabinet, 1890, scarce, VG **2,100.00**
NCR #2 or #3, detail adder, scroll pattern, VG, ea **900.00**
NCR #215 or #126-5, bronze, fleur-de-lis, VG **850.00**
NCR #250 or #251, bronze, VG **900.00**
NCR #30, NP brass, orig marque & complete int, VG **1,400.00**
NCR #312, #313 or #317, dolphin pattern, 1908-16, M, ea **1,250.00**
NCR #312, #313 or #317, dolphin pattern, 1908-16, VG, ea **750.00**
NCR #322, bronze & brass, $1 maximum sale, M **1,500.00**
NCR #323 to #327, marble 3 sides, extended base, M, ea **1,800.00**
NCR #323 to #327, marble 3 sides, extended base, VG, ea **950.00**
NCR #33, $5.00 maximum, ca 1903, VG **800.00**
NCR #332, #333, #349 or #356, orig top sign, M, ea **1,150.00**
NCR #332, #333, #349 or #356, orig top sign, VG, ea **550.00**
NCR #338, Dogwood pattern, British numerals, ca 1915, VG ...**425.00**
NCR #347-22, inlaid oak, scarce, 1908, VG **3,900.00**
NCR #441, Empire pattern, 1911, VG **500.00**
NCR #441 to #452, M, ea **1,650.00**
NCR #441 to #452, VG, ea **750.00**
NCR #441E to #452E, electric, M, ea **2,250.00**
NCR #441E to #452E, electric, VG, ea **950.00**
NCR #47, wood w/inlay, up to $5, VG **2,250.00**
NCR #50 or #52, Renaissance pattern, VG, ea **1,150.00**
NCR #500 series, floor model, M **4,500.00**
NCR #500 series, floor model, VG **2,250.00**
NCR #52, Renaissance pattern, extended base, 1898, VG **2,900.00**
NCR #522, 2-drw, electric bar model, 1910-16, M **2,500.00**
NCR #522, 2-drw, electric bar model, 1910-16, VG **1,650.00**
NCR #7 or #8, detail adder, fleur-de-lis, VG, ea **800.00**
NCR #711 to #717, factory & mahog grain finish on steel, M, ea ...**275.00**

Cast Iron

In the mid-1800s, the cast iron industry was raging in the United States. It was recognized as a medium extremely adaptable for uses ranging from ornamental architectural filigree to actual building construction. It could be cast from a mold into any conceivable design that could be reproduced over and over at a relatively small cost. It could be painted to give an entirely versatile appearance. Furniture with openwork designs of grapevines and leaves and intricate lacy scrollwork was cast for gardens as well as inside use. Figural doorstops of every sort, bootjacks, trivets, and a host of other useful and decorative items were made before the 'ferromania' had run its course. Our advisor for this category is J.M. Ellwood; he is listed in the Directory under Arizona. See also Kitchen, Cast Iron Bakers and Kettles; and other specific categories.

Armchairs, fern design, 1800s, pr **850.00**
Ashtray/inkwell, crane figural **30.00**
Bench, foliate scrolls/horseshoe openwork bk, w/arms, 62" **1,375.00**
Bench, lyre bk, ca 1850, 48" L **850.00**
Bench, rococo floral details, Minerva head bk, 42x45" **1,750.00**
Bracket, eagle figural, mc pnt, ca 1890s, 13½" **660.00**
Carriage step, CI & wrought, 1970s, EX **25.00**
Chair, swivels, floral scroll details, 32½", EX **550.00**
Cookie board, pineapple, wood hdl, 4½x6", 9" overall **150.00**
Dog, walking, free-standing, Am, 1800s, 29x49" **3,025.00**
Eagle, made to be viewed from below, 31" wingspan **300.00**
Eagle, mc pnt, 24" wingspan, EX **600.00**
Eagle, 14" wingspan, 10-lb, 10", EX **110.00**
Fence post, fluted w/lotus-like bases & capitals, 6 for **100.00**

Frog, I Croak for Jackson Wagon, gr pnt w/mc details, 5¼" 275.00

Garden figures, lions on rectangular bases, bronze paint, America, 1800s, 13x28", $2,300.00 for the pair.

Grate, basting rack, 6 hearts/flowing leaves, 1920s, 19" dia 115.00
Hitching post, Blk boy on sq base, worn silver pnt, 46", EX 3,300.00
Hitching post, horse head atop, fluted, w/lion heads, 70" 500.00
Hitching post, horse head atop, fluted, 67½" 1,100.00
Hitching post, horse head form, EX detail, old blk rpt, 15" 400.00
Hitching post, jockey on sq base, mc pnt, glass eyes, 50", EX 800.00
Horse trough, rectangular, JL Mott...NY, 20½x46x24" 1,400.00
Paperweight, Geo WA bust, sm 40.00
Paperweight, pelican atop patterned dome on sq base, sm 48.00
Paperweight, 3-D heart form, early 1900s, 1x3¾x3¾" 75.00
Pitcher, dolphin heads around base, ornate hdl, 16" 88.00
Plant stand, 3 lacy scroll ft, lacy top, old rpt, 30x14" dia 250.00
Rabbit, wht pnt traces, 12" 350.00
Spider, str sprue, 1800s, 4½x9" 110.00
Swan, wht pnt w/gr base, sm 35.00
Teakettle, gooseneck, Baster, dtd 1863 ....115.00
Teakettle, swan spout, wrought hdl, brass lid, blk pnt, 1800 ....75.00
Tie rod element, fleur-de-lis shape, 1800s, 9¾" 55.00
Urn, cherub heads under flared/serrated rim, mk, 38" 650.00
Urn, classical florals, bird head hdls, silver pnt, 43", pr 880.00
Urn, floral designs, buffalo heads, Kramer, 63x35", pr 7,000.00
Urn, foliage & scroll details, openwork hdls, Kramer, 27", EX ...650.00
Urn, old worn wht pnt, ca 1890s, 18½x14¼" 255.00
Urn, swan base, wht rpt, 38½", VG, pr 925.00

Castor Sets

Castor sets became popular during the early years of the 18th century and continued to be used through the late Victorian era. Their purpose was to hold various condiments for table use. The most common type was a circular arrangement with a center handle on a revolving pedestal base that held three, four, five, or six bottles. Some had extras; a few were equipped with a bell for calling the servant. Frames were made of silverplate, glass, or pewter. Though most bottles were of pressed glass, some of the designs were cut, and on rare occasion, colored glass with enameled decorations was used as well. To maintain authenticity and value, castor sets should have matching bottles. Prices listed below are for those with matching bottles and in frames with plating that is in excellent condition (unless noted otherwise).

Watch for new frames and bottles in both clear and colored glass; these have recently been appearing on the market.

Key: D&B — Daisy and Button

3-bottle, D&B, blown; pressed glass fr w/toothpick on bail 135.00

3-bottle, Gothic Arch, blown; orig stoppers, pewter fr 110.00
4-bottle, cranberry, orig stoppers; pressed glass holder 250.00
4-bottle, Log & Star, amber; orig ped-base fr 150.00
5-bottle, cranberry; orig Pairpoint fr 350.00
5-bottle, etched floral w/cutting, much decor; Meriden fr 250.00
5-bottle, etched wreath/cut dots; rib-trim rstr fr, NM 165.00
5-bottle, etched; Japanese-motif SP fr, bird at top 245.00
5-bottle, Honeycomb; ornate Wilcox fr, EX 265.00
5-bottle, wreath design w/cut dots; decor fr w/call bell 350.00
6-bottle, cut glass; rstr Simpson-Hall-Miller fr, 18" 295.00
6-bottle, D&B, pressed; oversz 18" decor Meriden fr 350.00
6-bottle, etched, rstr ornate Meriden fr w/call bell 425.00
6-bottle, Honeycomb; ornate Tufts fr, 18", EX 315.00
6-bottle, pressed; 18" Simpson-Hall-Miller fr w/VG SP 145.00
6-bottle, Sawtooth; ornate Meriden fr, call bell, dtd 1888, EX ...425.00
7-bottle, Chrysanthemum, cut; Gleason ftd fr w/movable doors .1,500.00
7-bottle, cut crystal; gadrooned/shell-border Geo III fr 495.00
7-bottle, cut crystal; lg ped-ft Gleason fr w/doors 1,500.00

Catalina Island

Catalina Island pottery was made on the island of the same name, which is about twenty-six miles off the coast of Los Angeles. The pottery was started in 1927 at Pebbly Beach, by Wm. Wrigley, Jr., who was instrumental in developing and using the native clays. Its principal products were brick and tile to be used for construction on the island. Garden pieces were first produced, then vases, bookends, lamps, ashtrays, novelty items, and finally dinnerware. The ware became very popular and was soon being shipped to the mainland as well.

Some of the pottery was hand thrown; some was made in molds. Most pieces are marked Catalina Island or Catalina with a printed incised stamp or handwritten with a pointed tool. Cast items were sometimes marked in the mold; a few have an ink stamp, and a paper label was also used.

The color of the clay can help to identify approximately when a piece was made: 1927 to 1932, brown to red clay; 1931 to 1932, an experimental period with various colors; 1932 to 1937, mainly white clay, but tan to brown were also used on occasion.

Items marked Catalina Pottery are listed in Gladding McBean. For further information we recommend *The Collector's Encyclopedia of California Pottery* by our advisor, Jack Chipman; he is listed in the Directory under California.

Dinnerware

Catalina Island, bowl, berry 25.00
Catalina Island, bowl, vegetable; rnd, 8½" 65.00
Catalina Island, candle holder, low 75.00
Catalina Island, custard cup 25.00
Catalina Island, mug, 6" 45.00
Catalina Island, plate, bread & butter; coupe design, 6" 15.00
Catalina Island, plate, dinner; wide rim, 10½" 25.00
Catalina Island, plate, rolled rim, 12½" 75.00
Catalina Island, tumbler, 4" 20.00
Catalina Island, wine cup, hdld 22.50
Rope Edge, casserole, w/lid 50.00
Rope Edge, creamer 35.00
Rope Edge, cup & saucer 35.00
Rope Edge, plate, chop; 13½" 60.00
Rope Edge, plate, salad; 8½" 15.00
Rope Edge, sugar bowl 45.00
Rope Edge, teapot 150.00

Miscellaneous

Ashtray, cowboy hat, matt gr	100.00
Bookends, monk design, matt gr, pr	750.00
Bowl, Indian design, rare	375.00
Bowl, ruffled rim, ink stamp, 2½x9"	60.00
Candelabrum, 3-tier	225.00
Charger, galleon/sea, mc on sky bl over red bsk, 14"	500.00
Charger, HP Mexican scene, mk, ca 1932, 11½"	600.00
Charger, lg figure of banjo player, mc/ivory/bsk, 12½"	400.00
Charger, Submarine Garden, mc fish on bls, 10½"	600.00
Charger, swordfish, HP on lt bl, 14"	395.00
Shakers, cactus, pr	60.00
Tile, Spanish, mc, 6x6"	150.00
Tray, turq, rolled edge, 14½", w/forged iron hdl	125.00

Vase, orange, 8", $250.00.

Vase, bl, ped ft, 4-corner scalloped rim, 8", NM	265.00
Vase, bud; 5"	65.00
Vase, Monterey Brn, flowerpot form, old mk, 5½"	60.00
Vase, stepped design w/hdls, 5"	300.00
Vase, Toyon red, bulbous base, 6"	175.00
Wall pocket, basketweave, 9"	200.00

Catalogs

Catalogs are not only intriguing to collect on their own merit, but for the collector with a specific interest, they are often the only remaining source of background information available, and as such they offer a wealth of otherwise unrecorded data. The mail-order industry can be traced as far back as the mid-1800s. Even before Aaron Montgomery Ward began his career in 1872, Laacke and Joys of Wisconsin and the Orvis Company of Vermont, both dealers in sporting goods, had been well established for many years. The E.C. Allen Company sold household necessities and novelties by mail on a broad scale in the 1870s. By the end of the Civil War, sewing machines, garden seed, musical instruments, even medicine, were available from catalogs. In the 1880s Macy's of New York issued a 127-page catalog; Sears and Spiegel followed suit in about 1890. Craft and art supply catalogs were first available about 1880 and covered such varied fields as china painting, stenciling, wood burning, brass embossing, hair weaving, and shellcraft. Today some collectors confine their interests not only to craft catalogs in general but often to just one subject. There are several factors besides rarity which make a catalog valuable: age, condition, profuse illustrations, how collectible the field is that it deals with, the amount of color used in its printing, its size (format and number of pages), and whether it is a manufacturer's catalog verses a jobber's catalog (the former being the most desirable).

Abbey & Impre, fishing tackle, 1910, 80-pg, EX	75.00
AG Spalding, sporting supplies, 1926, 36-pg, 6x9", VG	50.00

AI Root Beer Supplies, 1936, VG	8.00
Alden's, Chirstmas 1972, NM	40.00
Alden's, 1976 Fall & Winter	40.00
American Carriage Co, carriages, 1894, 74-pg, 5x7"	40.00
American Flyer Trains, color, 1933, 31-pg, 8½x11", EX	50.00
Anchor Electric, telephone supplies, 1897, 25-pg, 5½x8"	40.00
Angelica Uniforms, soda fountain/bellhop/etc, color, 1932, EX	42.00
Army & Navy General Merchandise, 1923, EX	18.00
Assoc Metalcraft Co, ornate items for Catholic church, 1930s	40.00
Baldwin Locomotive Works, 1913, 27-pg, 9x12", VG	70.00
Bausch & Lomb Optical, lenses/etc, 1915, 148-pg, 6½x9¾"	45.00
Belknap, hardware, guns/knives/etc, 1898, 1381-pg, EX	300.00
Birge, furniture & wallpaper, 1909, EX	140.00
Blees-Moore, surgical instruments, 1901, 645-pg, EX	125.00
Bramhill Deane, cooking equipment, 1899, 140-pg, 10x14"	175.00
Bush Co Pianos, illus, 34-pg, 1892, EX	65.00
C Fischer Co, violins, late 1920s, 32-pg, 6x9"	20.00
Curtis-Leger Fixtures, store needs, 1914, 288-pg, 4½x8½"	48.00
DeVry Corp, motion picture cameras etc, 1925, 32-pg, EX	65.00
E Hille Angler Supply, 1971, EX	17.50
Enicott-Johnson, shoes, 1913, 79-pg, 8x10½"	50.00
EW Devoe, artists materials, 1879, 249-pg, 4¼x5½"	65.00
Excelsior Publishing, ABCs or signs/etc, 1921, 49-pg, 6x9"	32.50
FAO Swartz, Christmas Issue, 1962, NM	55.00
Gong Bell Mfg Conn, bells, 1919, 34-pg, 6x9"	50.00
Gould's Pumps, Engines & Rams, 1885, 264-pg, 6x9"	75.00
Grafles, photo equipment, 1827, 32-pg	25.00
Heaney's Magic, #24, ca 1920, 96-pg, EX	10.00
Hooker-Howes, costumes/lighting/etc, 1920s, 48-pg, 4x9½", EX	35.00
Internat'l Harvester, 1923, 456-pg, 7x10", EX	150.00
Ives Trains, color, 1923, 24-pg, 7½x10½", EX	75.00
JC Penney, Christmas 1962, EX	80.00
JC Penney, Christmas 1969, M	22.00
John W Masury & Son, swatches, ca 1892, 33-pg, 4¾x7"	65.00
Ken-Wel Sporting Goods, 1939, EX	45.00
Kingman Farm Machinery, ca 1905, 258-pg, 7x10", EX	140.00
Klausner Co, neckware, 1896, 64-pg, 7x10", EX	20.00
LE Gurley, surveying instruments, 1909, 470-pg, 4½x6¾"	85.00
Leedy, drums, color wraps & illus, 1930, 112-pg, 6x9", M	65.00
Lionel Trains, color, 1931, 50-pg, 9x11"	65.00
LP Ross Shoes, Spring 1905, 72-pg, 6x9½", EX	40.00
Lyon & Healy Violins, color plates, 1917	50.00
Mayer, lady's clothing, 1909, 94-pg, 7¼x10", EX	25.00
McCormick, farm machinery, ca 1900, 32-pg, EX	75.00
Merritt Elliot Co, shoes, Spring 1903, 64-pg, 7x9½"	45.00
Montgomery Wards, Christmas 1982, NM	12.50
Montgomery Wards, monuments/tombstones/mausoleums, 1925	25.00
Motiograph, projectors/stereopticons/etc, 1912, EX	115.00
Murray Line, buggies/wagons/etc, 1909, 192-pg, 8x10"	95.00
Nat'l Builderies #4, Homes for Workers, floor plans, 1918	30.00
Nat'l Tile Co, tiles & floor covering, color, ca 1920	48.00
Ohio Carriage Mfg, color illus, 1915, 143 slick pgs, 8x10"	70.00
Powers Camergraph, 1910, 48-pg, 6x9"	75.00
Remington Modern Firearms Retail Price List for 1935, blk/wht	35.00
Rochester Barrel Machines, ca 1929, 20-pg, 8½x11"	35.00
Rochester Can Co, galvanized items, 1920s, 50-pg, EX	30.00
Santa's Toy Book, Christmas 1954	35.00
Sears, Christmas 1939, EX	48.00
Sears, Christmas 1970, M	22.00
Sears, general merchandise, 1930, EX	50.00
Sears, plumbing & heating, 1930	30.00
Selmer Band Instruments, 1958, EX	8.00
Shapleigh Hardware, guns/knives/etc, 1923, 3098-pg, VG	250.00
Speigel, Christmas 1950, EX	75.00

Taylor Steam Engines, 1885, 68-pg, 7x11", VG **88.00**
Vogue Coiffures, wigs & hair pcs, sepia illus, 1924, 46-pg, EX **60.00**
Wards, Christmas 1950s, EX **75.00**
Warwick & Liberty Bicicles, blk/wht illus, 1893, EX **45.00**
Weeks & Potter, druggist supplies, 1890, 593-pg, 2x7¾" **105.00**
Westcott-Whitmore, Syracuse NY, shoes & buckles, 1916, 40-pg ..**35.00**
Western Auto, mostly toys, Christmas 1956 ....**35.00**
Williams Magneto Telephones, Cleveland, 1887, 18-pg, 6x8" **40.00**

Caughley Ware

The Caughley Coalport Porcelain Manufactory operated from about 1775 until 1799 in Caughley, near Salop, Shropshire, in England. The owner was Thomas Turner, who gained his potting experience from his association with the Worcester Pottery Company. The wares he manufactured in Caughley are referred to as 'Salopian.' He is most famous for his blue-printed earthenwares, particularly the Blue Willow pattern, designed for him by Thomas Minton. For a more detailed history, see Coalport.

Bowl, Oriental motif, bl transfer, 4x10½", EX **250.00**
Creamer, Grecian women, brn transfer, scalloped, 3", VG **37.50**
Creamer, Oriental dragon, blk transfer, bl rim, 4¾", NM **50.00**
Cup & saucer, cottage w/deer, blk transfer, scenic border **25.00**
Cup & saucer, cottage w/family, bl transfer, scenic border **75.00**
Cup & saucer, Liberty & Peace, w/sword/spear/etc, mc, NM **150.00**
Cup & saucer, Oriental motif, bl transfer w/gold, mk **165.00**
Cup & saucer, reaper, blk transfer w/mc, bl rim, EX **80.00**
Cup & saucer, windmill, gray-gr transfer, bl rim, NM **55.00**
Plate, hummingbird, 7", NM **125.00**
Plate, Oriental dragon, blk transfer, bl rim, rosette mk, 7" **45.00**
Plate, shepherds, sheep & cottage, 6¼", NM **125.00**
Plate, soup; elephant scene, 9⅞", EX **110.00**
Sugar bowl, girl in yel milks cow, lid rpr **145.00**

Ceramic Art Company

Jonathan Coxon, Sr., and Walter Scott Lenox established the Ceramic Art Company in 1889 in Trenton, New Jersey, where they produced fine belleek porcelain. Both were experienced in its production, having previously worked for Ott and Brewer. They hired artists to hand paint their wares with portraits, scenes, and lovely florals. Today artist-signed examples bring the highest prices. Several marks were used, three of which contain the 'CAC' monogram. A green wreath surrounding the company name in full was used on special-order wares, but these are not often encountered. Coxon eventually left the company, and it was later reorganized under the Lenox name. See also Lenox. Our advisor for this category is Mary Frank Gaston; she is listed in the Directory under Texas.

Bell, tulip shaped, silver decor on wht, unmk **150.00**
Box, floral, bl w/gold, oval, gr mk, 3¾x2⅜" **75.00**
Box, trinket; lav Delft-style scene, artist sgn, mk, 5¼" **200.00**
Creamer, gold floral, hdl & trim, mk, 3¾" **135.00**
Mug, leaves & nut pods, bbl shape, palette mk, 5" **145.00**
Mug, mc pomegranates, 1890 palette mk, 5½" **195.00**
Mug, monk holding open box on brn, gr mk, 5¾" **110.00**
Pitcher, berries, maroon hdl, gold spout, palette mk, 12½" **225.00**
Pitcher, cider; 3-color grapes, beaded hdl, lg **165.00**
Pitcher, tankard; fruit, yel & gold on lime gr **155.00**
Pitcher, tankard; yel roses, sgn, scalloped, ornate hdl **265.00**
Punch bowl, plums on bl, gr palette mk, 12x15½", 2-pc **985.00**

Salt cellar, scalloped rim, palette mk **25.00**
Sherbet, gold paste florals, ped ft, mk, 3¼" **140.00**
Vase, lady's portrait medallion w/gold, mk, 11½" **285.00**
Vase, portrait, blossoms & gold trim, palette mk, 10" **350.00**
Vase, purple lustre on body, bulbous, gr mk, 3¾" **145.00**
Vase, roses, yel on pk, slim neck, gold hdls, 1889, 12½" **295.00**

Ceramic Arts Studio, Madison

The Ceramic Arts Studio Company began operations sometime prior to the 1940s, but it was about then that Betty Harrington started marketing her goods through this company. Betty Harrington is the designer primarily responsible for creating the line of figurines and knick-knacks that has become so popular with collectors. There were two others — Ulli Rebus, who not only designed several of the animals and various other pieces but taught Betty the art of mold-making as well; and Ruth Planter, who's work may have been very limited. About 65% of these items are marked, but even unmarked items become easily recognizable after only a brief study of their distinctive styling and glaze colors. At least seven different marks were used, among them the black ink stamp and the incised mark: 'Ceramic Arts Studio, Madison, Wisc.' A paper sticker was used in the early years.

After the 1955 demise of the company in Madison, the owner (Ruben Sand) went to Japan where he continued production under the same name using many of the same molds. After a short time, the old molds were retired, and new and quite different items were produced. Most of the Japan pieces can be found with a Ceramic Arts Studio backstamp. The Japan identification was on a paper label and is often missing. Japan pieces are never marked Madison, Wisc., but not all Madison pieces are either. Red or blue backstamps are exclusively Japanese.

Another company that also produced figurines operated at about the same time as the Madison studio. It was called Ceramic Art (no 's') Studio; do not confuse the two.

A second and larger building in the C.A.S. complex in Madison was for the exclusive production of metal accessories. The creator and designer of this related line was Zona Liberace, Liberace's stepmother, who was Art Director for the line of figurines as well. These pieces are rising fast in value and because they weren't marked can sometimes be found at bargain prices. They were so popular that other ceramic companies bought them to complement their own lines, so they may also be found with ceramic figures other than C.A.S.'s.

For those seeking additional information, video tapes (Series 1 and 2) are available from the author, BA Wellman, whose address can be found under Massachusetts. 1995 price guides are also available. Mr. Wellman encourages collectors to write him with any new information concerning company history and/or production. He sends Vera a 'thank you' for helping us with this year's updates.

Ashtray, hippo, 3½" **45.00**
Bank, Tony, razor disposal, 4¾" **48.00**
Bell, Lillibelle, 6½" **65.00**
Bowl, Bonita, 3¾" **40.00**
Bowl, shallow, rectangular, 2¼" **28.00**
Candle holders, Bedtime boy & girl, 4¾", pr **64.00**
Figurine, Adam & Eve (1-pc), 12" **565.00**
Figurine, Alice & wht rabbit, 4½", 6", pr **185.00**
Figurine, angel standing w/star, 5½" **30.00**
Figurine, Bali-Hai, topless, 8" **115.00**
Figurine, Bunny, 1¾" **24.00**
Figurine, Burmese man & woman, 5", pr **75.00**
Figurine, camel, standing, 5½" **60.00**
Figurine, child w/towel, 5" **62.00**
Figurine, Colonial man & lady, 6¾", 6½", pr **65.00**

Figurine, Cupid, 5" 65.00
Figurine, Daisy donkey, 4¾" 48.00
Figurine, drum girl, 4¼" 45.00
Figurine, Dutch Love boy & girl, 5", pr 45.00
Figurine, Fire man & woman, 8¼", pr 235.00
Figurine, flute lady, standing, 8½" 165.00
Figurine, french horn man, sitting, 6½" 165.00
Figurine, frog, 2" 16.00
Figurine, gremlin boy & girl, 4", 2½", pr 165.00

Figurine, guitar boy, 5", $38.00; Little Boy Blue, $32.00.

Figurine, harem girl, sitting, 4½" 35.00
Figurine, Harry & Lillibeth, 6½", pr 68.00
Figurine, Hiawatha, 3½" 85.00
Figurine, Inky skunk, baby girl, 2" 22.00
Figurine, Kabuki dancers, 8¾", 5½", pr 425.00
Figurine, kitten washing paw, wht, 2" 16.00
Figurine, lovebirds (1-pc), 2¾" 24.00
Figurine, Lover Boy, 4¾" 38.00
Figurine, Lutist & Flutist, 12", pr 235.00
Figurine, Madonna w/Bible, 9½" 125.00
Figurine, Madonna w/Child (1-pc), 6½" 85.00
Figurine, mermaid mother on rock, 4" 65.00
Figurine, Minnehaha, 6½" 95.00
Figurine, mouse, 3" L 35.00
Figurine, Mr Monk, 4" 35.00
Figurine, Muff & Puff, 3", pr 55.00
Figurine, palomino colt, 5¾" 75.00
Figurine, panthers, fighting, 8½", 6", pr 195.00
Figurine, Peter Rabbit, 3¾" 35.00
Figurine, Petrov & Petruska, 5¼", 5", pr 45.00
Figurine, Pioneer Sam & Suzie, 5", 5½", pr 65.00
Figurine, Piper girl, singing, 3" 38.00
Figurine, Poncho & Pepita, 4½", pr 68.00
Figurine, Praise & Blessing, 6", 5¾", pr 75.00
Figurine, Ralph the goat w/flower, 4" 35.00
Figurine, red devil imp trio, set of 3 ....285.00
Figurine, saxophone boy, 5¼" 52.00
Figurine, Spaniel mother & pup, 2¼", 1¾", pr 45.00
Figurine, St Francis, sandstone, 9½" 85.00
Figurine, Summer Sally, 3½" 45.00
Figurine, Tembino & Tembo elephants, 6½", 2½", pr ...135.00
Figurine, Ting-a-Ling & Sung-Tu, 5½", 4¼", pr 36.00
Figurine, toadstool, 3" 16.00
Figurine, Toby horse, 2¾" 24.00
Figurine, Tom cat, blk, 4¾" 65.00
Figurine, tortoise w/cane, 3¼" 32.00

Figurine, Violet, ballerina, sitting, 3" 65.00
Figurine, Willing, 4¾" 38.00
Figurine, Winter Willy, 4" 45.00
Figurine, Woody, sitting, wht, 3¼" 75.00
Figurine, Zulu man & lady, 6", 7¼", pr 325.00
Figurine, 19th-Century couple, 6¾", 6½", pr 75.00
Jug, Aladdin, 2" 32.00
Jug, rose motif, 2¾" 32.00
Planter, African man & woman heads, 8", pr 265.00
Planter, bamboo, 2" 25.00
Planter, seashell, 3" 65.00
Planter, Svea & Sven, 6", 6½", pr 125.00
Plaque, Comedy & Tragedy masks, 5¼", pr 95.00
Plaque, Dutch boy & girl, 8", pr 95.00
Plaque, Goosie Gander & Mary Contrary, 4½", 5", pr ...145.00
Plaque, Hamlet & Ophelia, 8¼", pr 265.00
Plaque, Neptune, rare, 6" 135.00
Plaque, Zor & Zorina, 9", pr 95.00
Shakers, Blackamoor, 4¾", pr 95.00
Shakers, Blk Sambo & the tiger, 3½", 5" L 295.00
Shakers, camel, 5½", pr 155.00
Shakers, cats, stylized, 4¼", 2⅝", pr 68.00
Shakers, Chirp & Twirp, 4", pr 68.00
Shakers, crocodile & native boy, 4¼" L, pr 135.00
Shakers, dachshunds, standing & recumbent, 2½", 3½", pr ...68.00
Shakers, Dem & Rep, 4½", pr 85.00
Shakers, Dutch boy & girl, 4", pr 26.00
Shakers, Eskimo boy & girl, 3¼", 3", pr 45.00
Shakers, FiFi & FuFu, 3", 2½", pr 125.00
Shakers, fox & goose, 3¼", 2¼", pr 95.00
Shakers, Indian boy & girl, 3", pr 45.00
Shakers, leopards, 2 fighting, 3½x5¼", pr 195.00
Shakers, ox & wagon, ea 3" L, pr 75.00
Shakers, Paul Bunyan & evergreen, 4½", 2½", pr ...95.00
Shakers, ram & ewe, 2", 1¾", pr 48.00
Shakers, Santa & evergreen, 2¼", 2½", pr 125.00
Shakers, snuggle boy in chair, 2¼", pr 62.00
Shakers, snuggle elephant & native boy, 5", 2¾", pr ...165.00
Shakers, snuggle mouse in cheese, 2½" overall, pr ...24.00
Shakers, snuggle Suzette on pillow, 3" overall, pr ...65.00
Shakers, Sootie & Taffy, 3", pr 55.00
Shakers, Spaniel mother & pup, 2¼", 1¾", pr 45.00
Shakers, Swedish boy & girl, 3¼", pr 38.00
Shelf sitter, Bali boy & girl, 5½", pr 125.00
Shelf sitter, banjo girl, 4" 45.00
Shelf sitter, Billy, w/ball down, blk, 4½" 135.00
Shelf sitter, boy w/dog, girl w/cat, 4¼", pr 65.00
Shelf sitter, canary, left & right, 5", pr 65.00
Shelf sitter, Chinese boy & girl, 4", pr 35.00
Shelf sitter, collie mother, 5" 40.00
Shelf sitter, cowboy & cowgirl, 4¾", pr 75.00
Shelf sitter, Dutch boy & girl, 4½", pr 35.00
Shelf sitter, En Pos & En Repos, 4¾", pr 75.00
Shelf sitter, Greg & Grace, 6", pr 95.00
Shelf sitter, Little Jack Horner, 4½" 45.00
Shelf sitter, Mexican boy & girl, legs crossed, 5¼", 5", pr ...58.00
Shelf sitter, Pudgie & Budgie birds, 5", pr 65.00
Shelf sitter, Young Love boy & girl, 4½", pr 42.00
Vase, bird motif, rnd, 2" 20.00
Vase, Lu Tang on bamboo bud, 7" 42.00

Metal Accessories

Arched window, for Madonna w/child 45.00

Artist palette, left & right, 12", pr 65.00
Artist palette w/shelves, left & right, 12", pr 75.00
Beanstalk for Jack, rare 125.00
Birdcage w/perch, 14" 55.00
Diamond shadow box, for Attitude & Arabesque 55.00
Free-form, left & right, pr 75.00
Free-form w/shelf, left & right, pr 52.00
Pyramid shelves, ea 35.00
Shadow box, w/wood, sq, 13" 30.00
Sofa, for Maurice & Michele 32.00
Star, holds any 1 of angel trio, 9" 35.00
Triple ring shelves, ea 65.00

Chalkware

Chalkware figures were a popular commodity from approximately 1860 until 1890. They were made from gypsum or plaster of Paris formed in a mold and then hand painted in oils or watercolors. Items such as animals and birds, figures, banks, toys, and religious ornaments modeled after more expensive Staffordshire wares were often sold door to door. Their origin is attributed to Italian immigrants. Today regarded as a form of folk art, 19th century American pieces bring prices in the hundreds of dollars. Carnival chalkware from this century is also collectible, especially figures that are personality related. For those, see Carnival Collectibles.

Bank, basket of fruit, worn gr/gold/yel pnt, 6½" 360.00
Bird on base, worn orig 4-color pnt, 5⅛" 330.00
Boy reading, 3-color pnt, PA, 1800s, 16½", EX 1,325.00
Cat, orig blk & wht stripe pnt, w/red bow, 12", EX 165.00
Cat, seated, yel pnt w/red & blk details, rpr, 9½" 990.00
Cat, sleeping, orig brn & wht stripe pnt, bl ribbon, 12", VG 100.00
Dog, blk w/red & yel collar, 3-color features, heavy wear, 10" 120.00
Dog, orig 3-color pnt, minor damage & wear, 6" 365.00
Dove, mc pnt, 1800s, 14¼", EX 220.00
Garniture, fruit & foliage, orig 4-color pnt, 14" 965.00
Pig nodder, orig blk & red pnt, wear/stains, 7½" 770.00
Poodle, orig mc pnt, wear/old rpr, 7¼" 286.00
Rabbit nodder, orig yel/red/blk pnt, EX color, minor wear, 6¼" ..1,100.00
Rooster, orig red/yel/gr pnt, EX color, minor wear, 5⅝" 685.00
Spaniel, seated, yel base, blk ears/tail/legs, wear, 4" 160.00

Stag reclining, original polychrome paint with minor loss, 1800s, 16x16", $935.00.

Watch stand, fruit compote form, mc pnt, 1800s, 14", EX 330.00

Champleve

Champleve, enameling on brass, differs from cloisonne in that the design is depressed or incised into the metal, rather than being built up with wire dividers as in the cloisonne procedure. The cells, or depressions, are filled in with color, and the piece is then fired.

Clock, mantel; gilt bronze w/enameling, urn surmount, 14½" .1,200.00
Clock, mantel; gr onyx, ormolu mts, Tiffany & Co, 19" 2,200.00
Floor lamp, 5 spheres w/mc exotic birds & shrubs, silk shade 450.00
Stand, gr onyx top w/champleve border, onyx ped, 30x18x18" .2,600.00
Teaspoon, flower w/scrolls & lappets, EH, 1891-91, 6¾" 50.00
Teaspoon, red & bl flowers on stem, eng figure in bowl, 6¾" 50.00
Urn, onyx, gilt bronze & enamel, hdls, 10" 250.00
Vase, maidens & cherubs, crystal inserts, hdls, 1800s, 19", pr .3,100.00
Vase, masks & flowers, phoenix roundels, 14½" on stand 775.00

Chase Brass & Copper Company

Americans were shocked in 1923 when an invitation to stage an exhibit at the first major postwar fair, *The 1925 Exposition des Arts Decoratifs et Industriels,* was declined by the American government because the U.S. could not comply with the exposition's requirement that only original work would be exhibited. Even though American industry produced a vast quantity of varied goods, there was very little 'original American' to show, since most design ideas were being brought in from Europe.

This blow to American prestige and the uproar that resulted prompted a dispatch of designers (among them Donald Deskey, Walter Dorwin Teague, and Russel Wright) to the Paris exhibition. They were to determine what steps would be necessary in order for U.S. designs to compete with European standards. They returned championing the new modernist style. By the mid-1930s, products were being designed and marketed that were attractive to the reluctant consumer insistent upon buying a streamline style that was uniquely American. During the decade of the thirties, the Chase Brass & Copper Company offered lamps, smoking acessories, and housewares similar to those Americans were seeing on the Hollywood screen at prices the average buyer could afford. These products are highly valued today not only because of their superior quality but also because of those who created them. Walter von Nessen, Gerth & Gerth, Rockwell Kent, Russel Wright, Laurelle Guild, and Dr. A. Reimann were some of Chases' well-known designers. Emily Post, who served as spokesperson for Chase, promoted a trend away from expensive silver and toward chromium serving pieces.

Besides chromium, Chase manufactured many products in brass, copper, nickel plate, or a combination of these metals; all are equally collectible. Some items had glass inserts which collectors also seek.

Nearly all Chase products were marked, either on the item itself or on a screw or rivet. On sets containing several pieces, the trademark may appear on only one. Be cautious. Check unmarked items to make sure they measure up to Chase's standard of quality, and lighting fixtures that are unmarked may be compared with pictures of verified examples. For safety's sake, replace both cords and internal wiring before attempting to use any electrical product. Not only will you be protected against possible loss from fire, but you will enhance the value of your collectible as well.

For more thorough study we recommend *Art Deco Chrome, The Chase Era,* and *Art Deco Chrome, Book 2, A Collector's Guide, Industrial Design in the Chase Era.* Both are authored by Richard J. Kilbride; Mrs. Kilbride is listed in the Directory under Connecticut. In the listings that follow, examples are polished unless noted satin. Prices are an average of values reported by members of the Chase Collector's Society. See Directory, Clubs and Newsletters.

Ash receiver, Pelican, blk & wht, #17050 ....150.00
Ash receivers, Pentad, chrome, #840, ea 10.00
Ashtray, Aristocrat, chrome, #835, 4" 38.00
Ashtray, Fluted, satin chrome, #17040, 4" 42.00

Ashtray, slide top, nickel w/blk glass, #804A **30.00**
Bank, Clearvue Registering, chrome, #405002, 2x4x2" **105.00**
Bar caddy, chrome, #90141, 6⅛" **15.00**
Bell, Manchu, chrome w/blk compo hdl, #13006, 3¼" **82.00**
Bookends, Octaball, satin brass & copper, #17011, 5½x4", pr ...**625.00**
Bookends, Pilot, brass & walnut, #90138, 6⅜", pr **128.00**
Bookends, Sentinel, brass & red body, #17109, 7¼", pr **425.00**
Bowl, Diana Flower, chrome & walnut, #15005, 10x6¾" **54.00**
Bowl, ice; chrome w/curved hdl, #28002, 7", w/tongs **78.00**
Bowl, sauce; Lotus, chrome w/blk hdl, #17045, w/ladle & tray **53.00**
Box, occasional; brass w/wht heart trim, #90144, 5¼" **56.00**
Bud holder, chrome, 4-tube, #11230, 9" **35.00**
Candlestick, Porpoise, chrome & blk fish, #24008, 4¼", ea **42.00**
Candlestick, Taurus, chrome, J-shape, #24004, 9¾", ea **75.00**
Candlesticks, Bubble, chrome & bl glass, #17063, 2½", pr **85.00**
Candlesticks, Diana, chrome & walnut, #24009, 1⅜x3½", pr **45.00**
Candy dish, brass w/fruit finial, glass insert, #90011, 7" **30.00**
Cheese knife, chrome w/reeded hdl, #17062, 7" **90.00**
Cheese server, chrome w/cutting board, #09009, 14", 3-pc **155.00**
Cigarette box, Connoisseur, satin copper, #842, 7" **90.00**
Cigarette box, Cosmopolitan, chrome w/wht plastic, 5" **85.00**
Cigarette box, Rockwell Kent, bronze, #847, 6½" **1,650.00**
Cigarette server, Ball, chrome & blk, #853, 3⅝" **58.00**
Cigarette server, Cube, red & wht, 2-compartment, #17070 ......**170.00**
Cocktail ball, chrome w/red rubber base, #90071, 3⅜" **30.00**
Cocktail shaker, Bl Moon, chrome w/bl top, #90066 ....**100.00**
Cocktail shaker, Gaiety, chrome w/blk rings, #90034 ....**45.00**
Coffee service, Continental, chrome, #17054, 3-pc **205.00**
Coffee service, Diplomat, chrome, #17029, 3-pc set (no tray) **375.00**
Cruet set, chrome, 2 ribbed glass cruets, #26009, 8x6½" **150.00**
Cup, Bl Moon Cocktail, chrome w/bl glass, #90067, 3½" **35.00**
Cup, Cocktail, chrome hemisphere, #26002, 2¾" **6.00**
Cup, iced drink; chrome w/leaf-hdl stirrer, #90085, 5¼" **35.00**
Cup, old-fashioned cocktail; chrome, w/muddler, #90063, 2⅞" **35.00**
Doorstop, stylized cat form, copper & brass, #90035 ....**245.00**
Fork & spoon, serving; chrome w/wht plastic hdl, #90076 ....**38.00**
Jelly, Duplex, chrome basket w/glass insert, #90062, 5½" **38.00**
Lamp, Circle, chrome, rpl shade, #1004, 14" **75.00**
Lighter, Fire Ball, chrome & red, #851, 2⅜" **75.00**
Lighter, table; automatic, chrome & blk, #825, 3¼x1½" **64.00**
Lighter, Tower, chrome & wht, #872, 3⅝x1¼" **125.00**
Mint & nut dish, chrome, twin bowls, loop hdl, #29003 ....**37.00**
Napkin holder, chrome w/wht hdl, #90148, 6⅛x4⅛" **68.00**
Pitcher, Arcadia, copper w/wht hdl, #90123, 7¼" **82.00**
Pitcher, water; Sparta, chrome, wht plastic hdl, #90055, 8" **76.00**
Salt & Pepper Spheres, chrome, #28004, 1¾" & 1⅛", pr **65.00**
Saucer, Olypmia, chrome, #90072, 6⅜" **26.00**
Silent Butler, chrome w/wht plastic hdl, #17111 ....**42.00**
Smoke stand, 'Lazy Boy,' chrome & red, #17031, 27" **445.00**
Smoke stand, Stratosphere, chrome & blk, #17076, 26" **390.00**
Snack server, Electric, chrome & wht, #90093, 13x6" **205.00**
Sugar Sphere, chrome shaker, #90078, 2⅝" **45.00**
Tray, Cocktail, chrome, #09013, 15⅞x5⅜" **42.00**
Tray, Festivity, chrome w/blk base, #09018, 17x12" **230.00**
Tray, Four-in-Hand, chrome, wht hdl, #17074, 10¼" **95.00**
Tray, Ring, chrome, etched circular design, #90058, 12" **62.00**
Tray, Star Time, chrome w/wht hdls, #09026, 15½x9½" **180.00**
Tray, Triple, chrome (all metal), folding, #09001 ....**34.00**
Vase, Minerva, chrome w/wht plastic, #03012, 6⅜" **48.00**

Chelsea

The Chelsea Porcelain Works operated in London from the middle of the 18th century, making porcelain of the finest quality. In 1770 it was purchased by the owner of the Derby Pottery and for about twenty years operated as a decorating shop. Production periods are indicated by trademarks: 1745-1750 — incised triangle, sometimes with 'Chelsea' and the year added; early 1750s — raised anchor mark on oval pad; 1752-1756 — small painted red anchor, only rarely found in blue underglaze; 1756-1769 — gold anchor; 1769-84 — Chelsea Derby mark with the script 'D' containing a horizontal anchor. Many reproductions have been made; be suspicious of any anchor mark larger than ¼".

Bottle, scent; romantic couple, dove on lid, 3", VG **250.00**

Figurine, boy plays flute with sheep before him and dog at side, all on oval plinth, gold anchor mark, 3¼", $200.00.

Figurine, boy w/flute & dog on plinth, gold anchor mk, 3¼" **200.00**
Figurine, Cavalier holding tricorn hat, gold anchor mk, 9" **500.00**
Figurine, couple w/spyglass, gold anchor mk, late 1700s, 8" **495.00**
Figurine, peacock, appl flowers & gold, anchor mk, 8", pr **400.00**
Plate, floral bouquets, scalloped, gold anchor mk, 8½" **400.00**

Chelsea Dinnerware

Made from about 1830 to 1880 in the Staffordshire district of England, this white dinnerware is decorated with lustre embossings in the grape, thistle, sprig, or fruit and cornucopia patterns. The relief designs vary from lavender to blue, and the body of the ware may be porcelain, ironstone, or earthenware. Because it was not produced in Chelsea as the name would suggest, dealers often prefer to call it 'Grandmother's Ware.'

Grape, bowl, sauce; 6" **8.00**
Grape, bowl, 8" **30.00**
Grape, coffeepot, stick hdl, 2-cup, 7" **65.00**
Grape, creamer **35.00**
Grape, cup & saucer **25.00**
Grape, egg cup **25.00**
Grape, pitcher, milk; 40-oz **50.00**
Grape, plate, 6" **12.00**
Grape, plate, 7" **18.00**
Grape, plate, 8" **20.00**
Grape, sauce boat **30.00**
Grape, sugar bowl, w/lid **40.00**
Grape, teacup **25.00**
Grape, teapot, 2-cup **65.00**
Grape, waste bowl **40.00**
Sprig, cup & saucer **40.00**
Sprig, pitcher, milk **45.00**
Sprig, plate, cake; 9" **40.00**
Sprig, plate, dinner **25.00**
Sprig, plate, 7" **18.00**
Thistle, butter pat **15.00**

Thistle, cup & saucer 35.00
Thistle, plate, 7" 15.00

Chelsea Keramic Art Works

Established in 1872 in Chelsea, Massachusetts, by several members of the Robertson family who later formed the Dedham Pottery, this firm is most noted for its experiments in attempting to re-create the ancient Oriental oxblood-red glaze. They succeeded in this in 1885 and also developed several other outstanding glazes as a result of their perseverance. One was their Oriental crackle glaze which they ultimately used in the manufacture of the very successful Dedham dinnerware. Though their very early artware utilized a redware body, by the late 1870s it was replaced with yellow- or buff-burning clay. A line called Bourgla-Reine (underglaze slip-decorated ware with primarily blue and green backgrounds) was produced, though not to any great extent. Other pieces were designed in imitation of metalware, even to the extent that surfaces were 'hammered' to further enhance the effect. Occasionally live flora was pressed into the damp vessel walls to leave a decorative impression. The pottery closed in 1889. Early wares were not marked; those made from 1875 to 1880 were marked with either two or three lines containing 'Chelsea Keramic Art Works, Robertson and Son,' the 'C-KA-W' cipher, or 'CPUS' in a 4-leaf clover. These were used up to 1889. A paper label was used for a short time on the crackleware. Our advisor for this category is Wayne B. Kielsmeier; he is listed in the Directory under Arizona. See also Dedham.

Plate, apple blossoms and foliage, gray-green, marked Chelsea Keramic Art Works Robertson & Sons, minor chips to applied decoration, 11", $2,000.00.

Charger, woman running in field, bl, A Osbourne, 11" dia 1,800.00
Vase, dragon's blood/olive gr irid, crazing/base pulls, 9½" 1,500.00
Vase, gray crackle (peppering), bulbous bottom, 6¾" 165.00
Vase, mustard, bottle w/4 upright tubes on shoulder, 6½" 825.00
Vase, oxblood w/irid, 4" 425.00

Children's Books

Children's books, especially those from the Victorian era, are charming collectibles. Colorful lithographic illustrations that once delighted little boys in long curls and tiny girls in long stockings and lots of ribbons and lace have lost none of their appeal. Some collectors limit themselves to a specific subject, while others may be far more interested in the illustrations. First editions are more valuable than later issues, and condition and rarity are very important factors to consider before making your purchase.

Alice in Wonderland, 1911, VG, $18.00.

Alice in Wonderland, Cozy Corner, Whitman, 1951, G 25.00
Amusemark Park Pop-Ups, orig cover, 1946 ....75.00
Annie Oakley, Whitman, 1958, NM 17.50
Beverly Gray Freshman, C Blank, Grosset & Dunlap, 1934, EX 5.00
Bill the Broadbill Swordfish, Farrington, 1st edition, 1941, EX 22.00
Billy Whiskers at the Fair, Saalfield, 1930s, VG 20.00
Blkboard Magic, HM Brier, Random House, 1949, 12th print, VG ..9.00
Bobbsey Twins on Houseboat, 1915, EX, +dust jacket..................20.00
Boys & Girls in Bookland, JW Smith illus, dust jacket, 1923 ....50.00
Caleb Cotton, Harrison Cody, 1921, EX 30.00
Candy Land, McLoughlin Bros, 1931, 20-pg, VG 10.00
Castaways of Stratosphere, Dixon, 1935, VG , +dust jacket 27.50
Cheyenne & Lost Gold of Lion Park, Whitman, 1958, VG 10.00
Cinderella, Little Golden Book, 1950, NM 30.00
Country Friends, linen, McLoughlin Bros, 1902, EX 18.00
Dame Trot & Her Comical Cat, Pleasewell, McLoughlin, 1890 ...20.00
Daniel Boone Wilderness Scout, White, Doughery, 1922, EX 95.00
Dogs Grand Dinner Party, Dame Dingle, McLoughlin Bros, 1869 ..35.00
Don Sturdy Across North Pole, Grosset & Dunlap, 1925, VG 8.00
Emerald City of Oz, F Baum, Neill illus, 1932, +dust jacket 65.00
Freckles, Gene Stratton-Porter, 1904, 433-pg, M 7.00
Friendly Fairies, Johnny Gruelle, Volland, 1919, EX 60.00
Fuzzy Duckling, Tell-A-Tale, 1952, EX 7.50
Hans Brinker & Silver Skates, Dodge, Burd illus, 1925, EX 35.00
Hardy Boys Secret of the Old Mill, 1957, VG 10.00
Helen's Babies, Habberton, illus, 1900, EX 20.00
Jeepers the Little Frog, Elf, 1965, NM 16.50
Jolly Animal ABC, McLoughlin Bros, 1888, 7x10", VG 40.00
Just So Stories, Kipling, Gleason & Bransom illus, EX 35.00
Knot Squirrel Tied, A Uttley, Tempest illus, 1969, M 20.00
Loraine & the Little People, Gordon, 1915, EX 12.50
Marco Polo, pop-up, Bancroft & Co, London, NM 100.00
Metropolitan Mother Goose, Watson, Clark illus, EX 25.00
Mickey Mouse, Dean, 4 pop-ups, 1939, 7½x10", EX 350.00
Mickey Mouse, pop-up, Bl Ribbon Books, 1933, EX 230.00
Mickey Mouse in King Arthur's Court, pop-up, 1933, EX 120.00
Mother Goose Rhymes, Lenski, Platt & Monk, 1933, EX 45.00
Over Jungle Trails, Ted Scott #10, Dixon, '29, VG, +dust jacket .12.00
Pebbles Flintstone, Big Golden Book, 1963, NM 35.00
Phantom Treasure, HP Grove, Saalfield, 1928, 235-pg, EX 4.50
Pilgrim's Progress, Bunyon, ca 1920, VG 7.50
Pollyanna at 6 Star Ranch, 1st edition, 1947, VG 22.00
Racing Start, S Beach, Little Brown, 1941, EX, +dust jacket 8.00

Raggedy Ann & Happy Toad, Gruelle, 1944, EX 20.00
Raggedy Ann's Magical Wishes, Gruelle, hardbk, 1928, EX 35.00
Red Randall Over Tokyo, Bowen, Grosset & Dunlap, 1944, EX ..12.50
Snow White, Collins, London, 1939, 80-pg, 9½x13" 27.50
Story of Miss Moppet, B Potter, blk/wht, Graham & Co, EX 20.00
Story of Our Gang..., Whitman, 11 color plates, 1929, EX 16.00
Sunbonnet Babies in Mother Goose Land, Grover, 1927 ....40.00
Sunny Rhymes for Happy Children, Miller, Browne, 1917, EX 25.00
Tales of Mystery & Imagination, Poe, Clark illus, 1933, EX 80.00
Teddy Bears at Circus, Towne, Bray, Reilly & Britton, 1907, EX ...17.50
That Pup, Ellis Parker Butler, 1908, EX 15.00
Tim Swift & His Electric Rifle, Appleton, 1911, +dust jacket 55.00
Tortoise & Hare, Disney, 1935, +dust jacket 50.00
Violet Among the Lilies, Clarkson, 1885, VG 25.00
White Company, AC Doyle, Wyeth illus, ex-library, 1922, EX 25.00
Wild Animals & Their Children, Burgett, 1934 ....15.00
Young Adventurer, Horatio Alger Jr, Burt, no date, VG 18.00
365 Bedtime Bible Stories, Ferguson, Whitman, EX 7.50

Children's Things

Nearly every item devised for adult furnishings has been reduced to child size — furniture, dishes, sporting goods, even some tools. All are very collectible. During the late 17th and early 18th centuries, miniature china dinnerware sets were made both in China and in England. They were not intended primarily as children's playthings, however, but instead were made to furnish miniature rooms and cabinets that provided a popular diversion for the adults of that period. By the 19th century the emphasis had shifted, and most of the small-scaled dinnerware and tea sets were made for children's play.

Late in the 19th century and well into the 20th, toy pressed glass dishes were made, many in the same patterns as full-scale glassware. Today these toy dishes often fetch prices in the same range as those for the 'grown-ups'!

Authorities Margaret and Kenn Whitmyer have compiled a lovely book, *The Collector's Encyclopedia of Children's Dishes*, with full-color photos and current market values; you will find their address in the Directory under Ohio. We also recommend *Children's Glass Dishes, China, and Furniture*, by Doris Anderson Lechler, available at your local bookstore or public library. See also A B C Plates; Canary Lustre; Willow Ware.

Key:
ds — doll size   Fr — French
Emp — Empire

China

Bowl, Bl Marble, bl on wht, oval, 4½" 45.00
Bowl, Calico, oval, 4" 27.00
Bowl, soup; Bl Acorn, English, 4½" 14.00
Bowl, soup; Fishers, dk gr on cream, CE&M, 4" 14.00
Bowl, soup; Scenes From England, bl on wht, England, 3⅝" 50.00
Bowl, Twin Flower, flow bl, oval, England, 5" 85.00
Bowl, vegetable; Athens, bl on wht, w/lid, 2¾" 75.00
Casserole, Bl Willow, Made in Japan, 4" 40.00
Casserole, Forget-Me-Not, flow bl, England, 4¾" 145.00
Casserole, Greek Key, brn/wht, Ridgway, Sparks & Ridgway, 5" ..55.00
Chamber set, wht w/bl trim, bowl, pot & 3" toothbrush holder 38.00
Compote, Bl Banded Ironstone, England, 3¼" 35.00
Creamer, Basket, Salem China, 2¼" 6.00
Creamer, Girls w/Pets, Allerton & Sons, England, 3⅛" 17.00

Creamer, Merry Christmas, pk lustre, Germany, 2⅞" 27.00
Creamer, Punch & Judy, bl transfer on wht, England, 3¼" 30.00
Creamer & sugar bowl, Daffodil, Southern Potteries, 3", 2" 40.00
Cup, Red Willow, Made in Japan, 1⅛" 20.00
Cup & saucer, Bl Willow, Made in Japan, 1½", 3¼" 12.50
Cup & saucer, Teddy Bear, decals, 2", 4¼" 35.00
Cuspidor, wht w/gold leaves 12.50
Fish set, fish on wht w/blk rim, Austria, 7-pc set 275.00
Gravy boat, Gold Floral, England, 5" 35.00
Gravy boat, Kite Flyers, bl transfer on wht, England, 3¼" 100.00
Gravy boat, Pembroke, Bistro England, 2" 35.00
Gravy boat, pk flowers, bl bows, gold trim, Limoges 50.00
Gravy boat, Rosamond, bl on wht w/gold trim, England, 2½" 55.00
Pitcher, wht ironstone, 2" 17.50
Pitcher, wht w/gold leaves 15.00
Plate, Dimity, gr on cream, 3½" 5.00
Plate, Fishers, dk gr on cream, CE&M, 4" 7.00
Plate, Gaudy Floral, England, 3¾" 35.00
Plate, Greek Key, brn on wht, Ridgway, Sparks & Ridgway, 3" 8.00
Plate, Humphrey's Clock, Ridgway's England, 3⅞" 12.00
Plate, Livesley Fern & Floral, England, mid-1800s, 4¼" 10.00
Plate, Silhouette Children, Czechoslovakia 6.00
Platter, Bl Acorn, England, 7¼" 22.00
Platter, Bl Marble, bl on wht, England, 4½" 45.00
Platter, Forget-Me-Not, flow bl, England, 5½" 85.00
Platter, Myrtle Wreath, JM&S, 4" 22.00
Platter, Pagodas, England, 7⅛" 35.00
Platter, Pembroke, Bistro England, 4¼" 25.00
Server, Bl Banded Ironstone, 1-hdl, England, 3" 10.00
Tea set, boy & girl w/flowers & bunnies, Germany, 15-pc 325.00
Tea set, Bridesmaid, decals, Germany, 6-place 350.00
Tea set, Dutch Windmill, decals, 6-place 300.00
Tea set, floral, Noritake, Made in Japan, 4-place 160.00
Tea set, Happy Fats, red trim, Royal Rudolstadt, 20-pc 350.00
Tea set, Mickey & Minnie Mouse, bl lustre, 23-pc, MIB 775.00
Tea set, Nursery Rhyme, Germany, 6-place 180.00
Tea set, pk lustre, Merry Christmas, Germany, 13-pc 625.00
Tea set, pk roses, gr leaves & trim, England, 13-pc 255.00
Tea set, Sunset, Made in Japan, 4-place 100.00
Tea set, wht, unmk, 2" plates, 22-pc set 98.00
Teapot, Basket, flow bl, w/lid, England, 4¼" 145.00
Teapot, Little Bo Peep (Victory), Salem 50.00
Teapot, Orient, bl on wht, w/lid, 4" 95.00
Teapot, Punch & Judy, bl transfer on wht, England, w/lid, 5" 75.00
Teapot, Silhouette Children, Czechoslovakia, w/lid, 3⅝" 27.00
Teapot, stick spatter, brn on wht, Staffordshire, w/lid, 5" 70.00
Teapot, wht ironstone, 3" 25.00
Tray, Dimity, gr on cream, rectangular, 5¾" 18.00
Tureen, Dogwood, flow bl, Minton, 6½" 100.00
Tureen, Kite Fliers, bl transfer on wht, England, 2½x3¼" 150.00
Tureen, Livesley Fern & Floral, England, mid-1800s, 3½" 55.00
Tureen, Myrtle Wreath, JM&S, 4½" 70.00
Tureen, wht ironstone, hdls, w/lid, 2" 20.00
Underplate, Maidenhair Fern, England, 5" 14.00
Wash bowl & pitcher, bl floral on wht 200.00
Waste bowl, Humphrey's Clock, Ridgway's England, 1⅞" 50.00

Furniture

Examples with no dimensions given are child size unless noted doll size.

Armchair, arrowbk, old red rpt, 2½" 127.50

Baby carriage, turned and scrolled wood, with umbrella, iron wheels, 46½" long, $1,675.00.

Bed, hardwood, trn posts, +quilt/mattress/bolster, 28x19x14" 300.00
Bed, red pnt w/HP roses on head & ftboards, ds, 9x23", EX 300.00
Bed, spindle type, folds, +mattress & pillow, 25" 95.00
Bed, tester; trn walnut, 1830s, ds, 29x34" 2,200.00
Chair, arm; ladderbk, woven splint seat, rfn, 22½" 150.00
Chair, cane seat, bentwood bk, 25x12x13" 100.00
Chair, Queen Anne-style repro, 20x11x9", M 165.00
Chair, rocker, oak, pressed bk, 35" 110.00
Chair, rocker, wicker bbl bk, lt bl pnt 125.00
Chair, side; country ladderbk, rpl rush seat, 22½" 40.00
Chair, side; Empire, mahog & veneer, horsehair seat, 19" 450.00
Chair, side; Windsor, bamboo, old rfn, 25½" 99.00
Chest, Empire, curly cherry & walnut, 12½x11x7½" 900.00
Chest, pine, dvtl, 2 drws over 3, brn pnt, 14x14½" 175.00
Chest, 3-drw, porc pulls, wire nails, rpt, 12"+crest 75.00
Cradle, cherry wood, old worn red pnt, dvtl, 42" 300.00
Cradle, curly maple, canted sides, scalloped top, 41", EX 495.00
Cradle, pine, dvtl, well-shaped rockers, rpt, 42" 95.00
Cradle, pine w/hardwood spindles, pnt traces, 39" 95.00
Cradle, poplar, dvtl, shaped rockers, cut-out sides, 42" 275.00
Cradle, poplar, old gr pnt w/silver stencil, rprs, 13½" 85.00
Cradle, splint w/hood, butterfly rockers, buttermilk red 495.00
Cradle, swings on trestle base, pnt wood, 1790s, 37x40x24" 525.00
Cupboard, dining room; glass doors, 4 shelves, 1900, 23x13" 295.00
Cupboard, gr pnt, wire nails, primitive, 20" 75.00
Cupboard, jelly; pine, panel doors, 1-drw, rpl ft, 24x20" 385.00
Cupboard, 2 doors/1 drw/2 doors, 45", 15½" counter height 900.00
Desk, Davenport, top lifts, drws & slots, 7¼x4¾x12½" 700.00
Desk, lap; front drops down, compartments inside, 6¼x8x4" 800.00
Desk, oak & chestnut roll-top, 15x18x9" 900.00
Dresser, ash, w/mirror, orig finish, 30x18" 140.00
Dresser, serpentine top drw, tilt mirror, brass pulls, 26" 600.00
High chair, Mission oak, ds 65.00
High chair, red & blk grpt w/gold, rpt, 1900s, 29" 135.00
Hoosier cabinet, complete, Schoenhut's...USA, 17¼" 2,500.00
Ice box, oak, 3 doors, metal shelves, 16½x11¾x5¾" 900.00
Settee, maple, G Stickley #251, sgn, 30x38" 425.00
Sofa, Empire, horsehair uphl, mahog fr, 20x40x12" 2,000.00
Table, mahog Sheraton, drop leaf, 1-drw, 18½x24½x15" 500.00
Table, pine, star & circle, drop leaf, rnd top, sq legs, 15" 145.00
Table, walnut w/walnut burl octagonal top, 4½x5x5" 375.00

Washstand, red w/mc flowers, towel rack, 1-door, 2-drw, 16" 230.00
Washstand, tiger maple, wooden knobs, 6x4" 675.00

Glassware

Arrowhead-in-Ovals, butter dish 42.50
Bead & Scroll, creamer 27.50
Bead & Scroll, spooner 60.00
Begging Dog, mug 25.00
Birds & Owl, mug, amber 35.00
Button Panel (Duncan & Miller #44), creamer 45.00
Button Panel (Duncan & Miller #44), spooner 67.50
Button Panel (Duncan & Miller #44), sugar bowl, w/lid 125.00
Button Panels, butter dish 100.00
Button Panels, creamer 45.00
Buzz Star (Whirligig), punch bowl+6 cups 50.00
Castor set, 4-bottle (1" shaker & 3 cruets) pewter fr, 6" 195.00
Ceres, mug, turq opaque 35.00
Clear & Dmn Panels, spooner, bl 40.00
Colonial, butter dish, Cambridge 32.00
Colonial, creamer, emerald gr, Cambridge 20.00
Colonial, sugar bowl, w/lid, Cambridge 30.00
Cupid & Venus, mug, lg 30.00
Duncan #42, sugar bowl 40.00
Eastlake, mug, amber 20.00
Elephant, mug, bl 165.00
English Hobnail, pepper bottle, gr 15.00
Fighting Cats, mug 50.00
Fine Cut Star & Fan, butter dish 42.00
Fine Cut Star & Fan, sugar bowl, w/lid 30.00
Galloway, pitcher 30.00
Grapevine w/Ovals, creamer 60.00
Hickman, condiment set, 3-pc on tray 75.00
Hobnail, mug, w/lid 15.00
Horizontal Threads, spooner 40.00
Horned Devil, mug, milk glass 35.00
Inverted Strawberry, punch bowl set, 7-pc 215.00
Lacy Daisy, berry set, 7-pc 65.00
Lamb, sugar bowl, milk glass, w/lid 150.00
Lion, butter dish, frosted 135.00
Martyrs, mug 70.00
Michigan, butter dish, gold trim 125.00
Michigan, creamer 25.00
Michigan, pitcher, gold trim 35.00
Michigan, spooner, gold trim 50.00
Michigan, sugar bowl, gold trim, w/lid 90.00
Monk, stein, crystal or milk glass, sm 25.00
Monkeys & Vines, mug 55.00
Nursery Rhyme, butter dish 85.00
Nursery Rhyme, creamer 40.00
Nursery Rhyme, punch cup, milk glass 22.00
Oval Star, berry dish, sm 10.00
Oval Star, butter dish 20.00
Oval Star, punch bowl 35.00
Oval Star, sugar bowl, w/lid 20.00
Palm Leaf Fan, cake stand 40.00
Pattee Cross, tumbler 15.00
Pennsylvania, creamer, gold trim 50.00
Pennsylvania, creamer, gr w/gold trim 90.00
Pennsylvania, spooner, gold trim 50.00
Rex (Fancy Cut), butter dish 42.50
Rex (Fancy Cut), pitcher 65.00
Rex (Fancy Cut), tumbler 20.00
Rexford, creamer 15.00

Rooster, creamer	135.00
Sawtooth Band, creamer, Heisey	65.00
Sawtooth Band, sugar bowl, w/lid, Heisey	115.00
Stippled Leaf & Grape, cup & saucer	34.00
Style, creamer	15.00
Sultan, creamer, frosted, rare	65.00
Tappan, butter dish, amber, 1950s	37.50
Tappan, creamer, aqua, 1950s	22.00
Tulip & Honeycomb, butter dish, sm	115.00
Tulip & Honeycomb, punch bowl	24.00
Whirligig, butter dish	30.00
Wild Rose, butter dish, milk glass	65.00
Wild Rose, creamer, milk glass	55.00
Wild Rose, punch bowl, milk glass	90.00
Wild Rose, spooner, milk glass	50.00

Miscellaneous

Alphabet board, stencil on wood, dtd Feb 16, '86, EX	85.00
Baby buggy, wicker, all orig, 45"	495.00
Baby buggy, wood/wire/wicker/leather, old red pnt, 31x28"	110.00
Bank, cat figural, Mary Had a Little Lamb decal, ceramic	45.00
Blocks, ABC/Picture, Champion, litho on wood, nested set	500.00
Buggy, curved wooden seat on 4 wheels, blk canopy, 26"	250.00
Candlesticks, brass, 6-sided base, 2½", pr	16.00
Canister, aluminum	10.00
Carriage, wooden wheels, wood/iron fr, bentwood hdl, fringe	295.00
Cash register, Maple Leaf Cash Store Register, 5x4x4½"	32.00
Coal hod, CI, wire bail hdl, 2x3"	24.00
Coffeepot, aluminum, 2-pc	12.00
Coffeepot, Little Dutch Girl & windmills on tin, Ohio Art	24.00
Cup, silver w/eng kittens allover, baby's	30.00

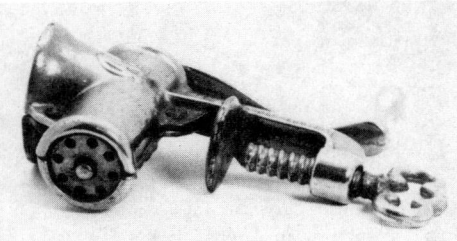

**Food grinder, cast iron, Made in USA, 5",
$40.00.**

Hobby horse, laminated, Appaloosa pnt/horsehair mane, 39"	525.00
Hobby horse, stuffed rag horse head w/button eyes on pole, 47"	125.00
Muffin tin, aluminum, 6-compartment	12.00
Painting, This..Piggy Went to Market, L Tessin, 57x44", EX	715.00
Pan, open, pnt metal, 6½"	40.00
Pans, Cook-N-Serve, Aluminum Specialty Co, 48-pc set	65.00
Pans, Kiddykook Bake Set, Aluminum Specialty Co, M	55.00
Rattle, sterling, Lullaby, dumbbell shape	45.00
Rattle, tin w/bone hdl, ca 1840, 6"	80.00
Rattle, trn wood, wooden rings on shaft	60.00
Rocking horse, cvd/pnt wood, glass eyes, EX mane/tail, 32x59"	935.00
Rocking horse, laminated wood, orig pnt, rprs, 24x46"	660.00
Rolling pin, gr pnt traces on wood, primitive, 10"	30.00
Rolling pin, Mary Had a Little Lamb, ceramic, 9"	145.00
Silverware, bone hdl, ea pc	12.00
Silverware, unmk USA, ea pc	1.50
Sled, Flexible Flyer, striping & decal, 52", EX	200.00
Sled, red pnt w/mc floral spray, Am, 1800s, 35", EX	400.00

Sled, wood & tin w/rpt, uphl seat, primitive, 38"	100.00
Sled, wood w/metal-tipped runner, worn pnt w/gold stencil, 32"	225.00
Sleigh, fold-down wheels, orig decor & pnt, 32x42"	425.00
Sleigh, wood & metal fittings, old red rpt, rprs, 36"	195.00
Stroller, pine & wicker, uphl seat, 23½", EX	165.00
Stroller, wicker bk & sides, wood seat, bentwood hdl, 1890s, ds	185.00
Surrey, curved wooden seat, spoked wheels, blk fringe, 30"	200.00
Tea set, pewter, EX detail, 19-pc	110.00
Teakettle, tin, early, 1½x1½"	48.00
Trunk, dome top, leather straps, decal, tray, 11x16x10"	220.00
Velocipede, steel w/old blk pnt, incomplete seat, 35" L	165.00
Washboard, wooden, 2½x4"	22.00
Yo-Yo, sterling silver w/steel body, foliage decor, EX	95.00

Chocolate Glass

Jacob Rosenthal developed chocolate glass, a rich shaded opaque brown sometimes referred to as caramel slag, in 1900 at the Indiana Tumbler and Goblet Company of Greentown, Indiana. Later, other companies produced similar ware. Only the latter is listed here. See also Greentown. Our advisors for this category are Jerry and Sandi Garrett; they are listed in the Directory under Indiana.

Bowl, sauce; Rose Garland	625.00
Box, Aurora, open, rectangular, 9x5½"	1,450.00
Box, cuff; rnd, 4½" H	485.00
Box, dresser; Venetian, w/lid	365.00
Box, powder; Orange Tree, rnd, w/lid, Fenton	425.00
Butter dish, Geneva	600.00
Carafe, Chrysanthemum Leaf	2,500.00
Compote, jelly; Geneva	175.00
Compote, Melrose, w/lid, 5¾"	350.00
Creamer, File	500.00
Nappy, Chrysanthemum Leaf	675.00
Pitcher, Cattail & Water Lily, Fenton	1,800.00
Pitcher, Wild Rose w/Bow Knot	550.00
Salt cellar, Honeycomb, 3½" dia	575.00
Salt shaker, Beaded Triangle	425.00
Salt shaker, Big Rib	425.00
Spooner, Chrysanthemum Leaf	650.00
Spooner, Geneva	175.00
Sugar bowl, Aldine, w/lid	1,750.00
Sugar bowl, File, w/lid, 4" dia	700.00
Sugar bowl, Touching Squares, w/lid	1,100.00
Sugar bowl, Wild Rose w/Scrolling, w/lid, child's	450.00
Toothpick holder, Kingfisher	750.00
Tray, Wild Rose w/Bow Knot, 10½x8"	375.00
Tumbler, Cattail & Water Lily, Fenton	285.00
Tumbler, Chrysanthemum Leaf	550.00
Vase, Masonic, 6"	450.00

Christmas Collectibles

Christmas past . . . lovely mementos from long ago attest to the ostentatious Victorian celebrations of the season.

St. Nicholas, better known as Santa, has changed much since 300 A.D. when the good Bishop Nicholas showered needy children with gifts and kindnesses. During the early 18th century, Santa was portrayed as the kind gift-giver to well-behaved children and the stern switch-bearing disciplinarian to those who were bad. In 1822 Clement Clark Moore, a New York poet, wrote his famous *Night Before Christmas*, and the Santa he described was jolly and jovial — a lovable old elf who was stern with no one. Early Santas wore robes of yellow, brown, blue, green, red, white, or even purple. But Thomas Nast, who worked as an illustrator for Harper's Weekly, was the first to depict Santa in a red suit instead of the traditional robe and to locate him the entire year at the North Pole headquarters.

Today's collectors prize early Santa figures, especially those in robes of fur or mohair or those dressed in an unusual color. Some early examples of Christmas memorabilia are the pre-1870 ornaments from Dresden, Germany. These cardboard figures — angels, gondolas, umbrellas, dirigibles, and countless others — sparkled with gold and silver trim. Late in the 1870s, blown glass ornaments were imported from Germany. There were over 6,000 recorded designs, all painted inside with silvery colors. From 1890 through 1910, blown glass spheres were often decorated with beads, tassels, and tinsel rope.

Christmas lights, made by Sandwich and some of their contemporaries, were either pressed or mold-blown glass shaped into a form similar to a water tumbler. They were filled with water and then hung from the tree by a wire handle; oil floating on the surface of the water served as fuel for the lighted wick.

Kugels are glass ornaments that were made as early as 1820 and as late as 1890. Ball-shaped examples are more common than the fruit and vegetable forms and have been found in sizes ranging from 1" to 14" in diameter. They were made of thick glass with heavy brass caps, in cobalt, green, gold, silver, red, and occasionally in amethyst.

Although experiments involving the use of electric lightbulbs for the Christmas tree occured before 1900, it was 1903 before the first manufactured socket set was marketed. These were very expensive and often proved a safety hazard. In 1921 safety regulations were established, and products were guaranteed safety approved. The early bulbs were smaller replicas of Edison's household bulb. By 1910 G.E. bulbs were rounded with a pointed end, and until 1919 all bulbs were hand blown. The first figural bulbs were made around 1910 in Austria. Japan soon followed, but their product was never of the high quality of the Austrian wares. American manufacturers produced their first machine-made figurals after 1919. Today, figural bulbs (especially character-related examples) are very popular collectibles. Bubble lights were popular from about 1945 to 1960 when miniature lights were introduced. These tiny lamps dampened the public's enthusiasm for the bubblers, and manufacturers stopped providing replacement bulbs.

Feather trees were made from 1850 to 1950. All are collectible. Watch for newly manufactured feather trees that have lately been reintroduced.

For further information concerning Christmas collectibles, we recommend two highly informative books, *Christmas Collectibles* by Margaret and Kenn Whitmyer and *Christmas Ornaments, Lights, and Decorations, A Collector's Identification and Value Guide*, by George Johnson. Both books are available from Collector Books or your local bookstore.

Bulbs

Andy Gump, mc pnt, milk glass, NM	95.00
Apple, red pnt, milk glass, 1950s, M	15.00
Bear in pajamas, pk, celluloid, EX	75.00
Bird, clear, Japan	25.00
Bird, mc pnt on clear, exhaust tip at beak, European, 4½"	75.00
Birdcage w/2 red birds, milk glass	15.00
Black Forest Clock, milk glass, EX	45.00
Boy in hip boots, worn pnt, milk glass	45.00
Candy cane, red & wht, milk glass, 3", NM	25.00
Cat, dbl-sided, spotted pnt, milk glass, 1920s, EX	45.00
Cat, mc pnt on clear, Mazda, 1920s, 3", NM	60.00
Cat & the Fiddle, mc pnt, milk glass, ca 1930s, NM	30.00
Cat in stocking, mc pnt, milk glass, 1930s, EX	45.00

Choir girl, mc pnt, milk glass, EX	45.00
Clown head w/dunce hat, milk glass, 1930s, VG	40.00
Cottage, mc pnt, milk glass, 2½", EX	12.50
Dog, long ears, EX pnt, milk glass	45.00
Dog hockey player w/stick, milk glass	65.00
Drummer boy, mc pnt, milk glass, EX	55.00
Elephant on ball, mc pnt, milk glass, 1930s, EX	65.00
Father Christmas, mc pnt on clear, ca 1915, 6", EX	175.00
Father Christmas w/tree, red robe, gold staff, Hungary, NM	145.00
Fish, red pnt, milk glass, 1930s, VG	30.00
Flowers in pot, mc pnt on milk glass, England, 1920s, EX	35.00
Frog, lt gr pnt, milk glass, EX	30.00
Geraniums in pot, milk glass, 1930s, EX	45.00
Hound dog, gr bow at neck, pk tones, milk glass, NM	42.50
Jack-o'-lantern, mc pnt, milk glass	65.00
Jester, mc pnt, milk glass, NM	85.00
Lantern, molded swirls, mc pnt, clear, Germany, NM	55.00
Lemon, worn pnt on clear	30.00
Lion w/tennis racquet, mc pnt, milk glass, EX	45.00
Little Jack Horner, mc pnt, milk glass, 1940s, NM	140.00
Little Red Riding Hood, mc pnt, milk glass, EX	85.00
Lucky Lindy, mc pnt, milk glass, NM	55.00
Marshmallow Rabbit, pk pnt, milk glass, EX	40.00

Matchless Star, red with green, plastic, 2½", $40.00.

Minstrel, wht & yel w/orange & red horn, Germany	60.00
Moon Mullins, worn pnt, milk glass, very rare	135.00
Mother Goose, mc pnt, milk glass, EX	75.00
Old Woman in Shoe, mc pnt, milk glass, 1940s, EX	150.00
Peacock, dbl-sided, mc pnt, milk glass, 1950s, NM	65.00
Pig in suit, mc pnt, milk glass, EX	150.00
Rooster w/hockey stick, mc pnt, milk glass, 1930s, VG	65.00
Rose, red pnt, milk glass, sm	30.00
Santa, bright colors, milk glass, 9"	175.00
Santa, full figure, Japan, 8¼", EX	95.00
Santa atop chimney, mc pnt, milk glass, EX	75.00
Santa head, dbl-sided, mc pnt, milk glass, 1930s, EX	35.00
Santa walking up to house, mc pnt milk glass, NM	40.00
Smitty, milk glass, mc pnt, VG	85.00
Snowman w/beret, milk glass, EX	35.00
Spaceman, milk glass, 1930s, EX	65.00
Squirrel, paw to mouth, tan & red pnt, milk glass, NM	48.00
Three Men in a Tub, mc pnt, milk glass, EX	85.00
Tom the Piper's Son, mc pnt, milk glass, EX	245.00
Turkey, mc pnt, milk glass, NM	85.00
Walnut, EX pnt, ivory insulator, European, ca 1915	45.00

Candy Containers

Boy on snowball, bsk & cloth, 5½", VG	98.00
Dwarf, cb, glitter, pnt face, 5"	55.00

Father Christmas, Belsnickle, papier-mache with mica, 9¾", $750.00.

House, bl cb w/cotton Santa w/bag on roof, 4" 95.00
House, cb litho, 1930s, Japan, 5x3¾x3" 40.00
House, pk & gr cb w/cotton Santa, plug in bk, 4" 115.00
Lady's shoe, Dresden, appl bow, 3½" 265.00
Opera glasses, Dresden, dbl, old resilvering, 2x3" 185.00
Santa, compo w/fur beard, in sleigh w/deer, Germany, 5" 350.00
Santa, papier-mache, mc pnt, 1900s, 12½", VG 1,200.00
Santa, papier-mache, red coat, bl pants, 4", EX 695.00
Santa in chimney, fireplace below, papier-mache, 5½" 395.00
Snowman, compo, unmk Japan, 1930s, 4¾" 38.00
Snowman, papier-mache w/cb hat, comic, 7½" 60.00
Star medallion, Dresden, cb & glitter, 3" 115.00
Violin case w/wood violin, Dresden, 3" 215.00
Walnut, Dresden, natural colors, 2½" 85.00

Ornaments

Blown glass ornaments: Christ Child's head, silver with gold hair, 2½", $95.00; Girl with long curls, pearly silver with multicolor details, 3", $110.00.

Accordion, blown, silver/blk/gr/bl/pk/etc, 2¾", M 65.00
Angel, wax, spun glass wings, mesh skirt, sm 100.00
Apple, blown, matt gold & red, 3¼", VG 35.00
Automobile, blown, pearly silver & red, hanger in top, 3¼" 50.00
Baby in snowsuit w/teddy bear, blown, mc pnt, 4" 250.00
Bacchus, blown, mc pnt, on clip, ca 1900, 2½" 350.00
Balloon, blown, mc pnt, scrap Santa face, 3" 165.00
Balloon, blown, red/wht/gold, wire-wrapped, girl w/arrows, 9" ...140.00
Bear coming out of ball, blown, pearly silver/blk/red, 3¼" 335.00
Bear w/hump on bk, standing, blown, silvered, rare, 4½" 450.00
Bear w/muff, blown, bronze/wht/blk/wht frosted, 3¾" 65.00
Bear w/stick, blown, matt pnt, 2½" 98.00
Bell, blown, red/wht/bl, Merry Christmas, clapper, early 40.00
Bird w/trn head, blown w/spun glass tail, on clip, 6¼", EX 25.00

Blowfish, blown, pearly wht/bl/blk/red/gold, 3¾", M 285.00
Brownie, blown, gr pants, pk tie, blk hat, unsilvered, 5" 400.00
Bulldog head, blown, mc pnt, unsilvered, 2¼" 275.00
Butterfly, blown, wire-wrapped pk body, 3¼" 85.00
Butterfly, Dresden, flat, gold lace w/red foil, 3½" 135.00
Car, blown, red & wht, 3" 195.00
Carrot w/leaves, sparkly pk pressed cotton, 3" 50.00
Cat in bag, blown, pearly pk/wht/bl/red, early, 4", NM 150.00
Cat in nightcap, blown, mc pnt, 2½" 265.00
Chandelier, blown, wire wrapped, ca 1890, 7", EX 85.00
Clown, blown, molded inscription: My Darling, flaking, 4¼" 18.00
Clown, blown, wht face, red cb hat, 3¼" 100.00
Clown head breaking through drum, blown, mc pnt, 2½" 165.00
Clown head w/big ears, blown, pearly wht/blk/bl/red, 2½", M 100.00
Comet, Dresden, dbl-sided gold star w/tinsel tail, 4½" 20.00
Comet, spun glass w/scrap angel, 6½", VG 55.00
Comic car, blown, pearly wht/gold/red, 2¼x3x1½", EX 150.00
Cow bell, blown, matt wht/blk/silver/yel, 1930s, 2½", EX 150.00
Doe, leaping, Dresden, 3-D, brn/cream/red, EX 125.00
Dog w/bow tie, blown, mc pnt, 3", G 80.00
Dog w/collar & tie, sitting, blown, mc pnt, 4" 150.00
Drum, blown, pearly wht/gr/gold, 1920s, 2½" dia 40.00
Dwarf, Sleepy, blown, mc pnt, ca 1930s, 2½" 100.00
Elephant, circus; blown, silver/red/gold, 3" 175.00
Explorer, blown, wht frosted hood, gold suit, 4", EX 125.00
Father Christmas w/tree & toys, mc diecut, 5", EX 125.00
Flapper's head, blown, pearly wht/gold/bl, 1930s, 3¼", EX 135.00
Frog, blown, gr & red, early, lt flaking, 4" 90.00
Gazebo, Sebnitz, wire-wrapped, chenille trim, angel diecut, 3" ..150.00
Gnome w/pipe, blown, gr/silver/red, 3½", EX 125.00
Grape cluster, blown, cobalt, EX details, 1½" 15.00
Half moon & cloud, spun glass, w/scrap cherub, 2½" 85.00
Happy Hooligan, blown, peach coat, yel legs, 4½", EX 315.00
Horn, blown, red/silver/bl, 5½", EX 30.00
House w/turkey in front, blown, mc, 1920s, 2½" 25.00
Hummingbird, blown, unsilvered turq, tinsel tail & wings, 10" 65.00
Hunting lodge, blown, shiny yel & bl pnt, 2¼" 35.00
Indian head, blown, bronze/blk/silver/pk, 2½", VG 235.00
Indian in canoe, blown, pearly wht w/red & pk, EX 285.00
Jockey on horse, Dresden, 3-D, EX mc pnt, 3x3" 395.00
Kugel, ball, amber, emb brass cap & ring, 2" 125.00
Kugel, ball, amber, 3" 125.00
Kugel, ball, bl, w/orig MIG label, rpr brass hanger, 5¾" 275.00
Kugel, ball, cobalt, emb brass cap & ring, 2¾" 175.00
Kugel, ball, cobalt, orig metal cap, 10½" 375.00
Kugel, ball, cobalt, ribbed, common hanger, 1⅝" 250.00
Kugel, ball, cobalt, 8-petal hanger, 1½" 110.00
Kugel, ball, gr, orig metal cap, 3" 95.00
Kugel, ball, med bl, 5" 110.00
Kugel, ball, med gr, 2½" 85.00
Kugel, ball, pk-red, orig metal cap, 2" 70.00
Kugel, ball, red, brass hanger, 4¼" 450.00
Kugel, ball, red, 1¾" 110.00
Kugel, ball, red/silver/wht stripes, brass cap, 1890s, 2¾" 350.00
Kugel, ball, silver, 3" 65.00
Kugel, ball, silver, 4¾" 150.00
Kugel, grapes, bl, 6", EX 450.00
Kugel, grapes, gold, orig metal cap, 4½" 250.00
Kugel, grapes, lt gr, brass hanger, 3¼" 450.00
Kugel, grapes, purple, orig metal cap, 2⅞" 575.00

Kugel, grapes, red, orig metal cap, 2⅞" 500.00
Kugel, grapes, silver, orig metal cap, 1880s, 7¼" 425.00
Kugel, grapes, silver, 4¾" 150.00
Kugel, grapes, silver w/gr, 8-petal cap, ca 1890, 4" 250.00
Kugel, grapes w/leaves, dk gr to blk, 4" 225.00
Kugel, pear, red, orig metal cap, 3¼" 250.00
Kugel, pear, silver, brass hanger, 9½" 395.00
Kugel, pear, silver, orig metal cap, 4½" 125.00
Kugel, ribbed pear, gr, orig metal cap, 2⅝" 295.00
Kugel, teardrop, silver, baroque hanger, 3½" 225.00
Lady in cart, chenille, die-cut face, crepe-paper skirt, 4½" 160.00
Lyre, free-blown, w/full-body scrap angel, 4" 150.00
Man in barrel, blown, silver/gold/blk/red, ca 1910, 3" ..165.00
Man's face w/mustache, blown, pearly/wht/pk/gr, 2¾" ..265.00
Mickey Mouse, blown, blk & wht, pipe cleaner tail, 1931, EX ...150.00
Mrs Claus, blown, matt flesh w/blk/pk/red/gold, 4¼" ..225.00
Nude on bell, blown, matt w/gold curls, red bell, 1915, 3" 235.00
Owl, blown, matt pnt, 3½" 98.00
Parasol, blown, red pnt, wire wrapped, 8", VG 110.00
Parrot in ring, blown, spun glass tail, unsilvered, 3¾" 75.00
Partridge, blown, silvered, wire tail, wire wrap, 4" 135.00
Patriotic shield, Dresden, red/wht/bl/gold, 3x1½", VG ..110.00
Peach, blown, covered in crushed glass, mc pnt, 2½" 65.00
Peacock on ball, blown, bl/silver/red, ca 1910, 5" 65.00
Pickle, blown, med gr, 3½" 145.00
Pig w/clover on tummy, blown, mc pnt, ca 1920, 3¼", NM ..115.00
Pine cone, blown, pk w/frost & needles, ca 1900, M 55.00
Pine cone, cb, sparkly finish, 3¼" 40.00
Popcorn head, blown, mc pnt, unsilvered, on clip, 2¼" ..385.00
Rafael angel on ball, blown, mc pnt, 2", EX 120.00
Rattle, blown, pearly wht & pk, 1920s, 5½", NM 30.00
Ringmaster's head, blown, mc pnt, unsilvered, ca 1910, 2¼" ..265.00
Rose w/leaves, blown, pearly wht/gr/pk, 1910x, 3¼", EX 65.00
Rosette, spun glass, w/scrap angel, on clip, M 88.00
Rosette, spun glass, w/scrap kitten, 3½" 80.00
Rosette, spun glass w/scrap cherub, 3½", EX 50.00
Santa, blown, chenille legs, compo boots, mc pnt, 4½" ..195.00
Santa head on spike, blown, mc w/gr hat, 1920s, 5½", EX ..185.00
Santa in automobile, celluloid, 3¾", EX 195.00
Ship, Dresden, flat, EX details, 1½x1¼", NM 185.00
Snowman w/broom, blown, matt wht & red, 3½", VG 85.00
Stocking, red mesh w/Father Christmas diecut, 6" 35.00
Swan, blown, pearly wht/red/bl, tinsel tail, 1930s, 8" 75.00
Table lamp, blown, pearly wht/red/gold/gr/silver, 4", VG ..45.00
Tomato, blown, red pnt, unsilvered, 2½" 55.00
Tree trunk w/bird & leaves, blown, mc, 2¾" 75.00
Umbrella, open, curved hdl, blown, silver/bl/wht/red, 5½" ..110.00
Walnut, blown, orange, unsilvered, 2½" 48.00
Watermelon slice, blown, matt wht w/blk/gr/pk, unsilvered, 4" ..145.00

Miscellaneous

Bells, Silly Symphony, Noma, M in bright box 150.00
Book, Night Before Christmas, Holiday Publishing, 1906, EX 85.00
Fence, feather, Evergreen Hedge, Germany, 65", EX 525.00
Fence, wooden picket style, red & gr pnt, 18" sq 175.00
Garland, lg mc glass beads, ca 1910, 148", EX 185.00
Garland, mc rnd & oval glass beads, 88", EX 100.00
Garland, tinsel w/6 bells & 8 acorns, 120", VG 45.00
Lamb, wooden fr w/cotton-wrapped body, pnt, 2½" 65.00
Lamb, wooly, red bow, Germany, 5" 150.00
Lamb, wooly, red collar, stick legs, 4¼" 110.00
Light, Bust of King Edward, yel-olive, Regd..., 4⅛" 550.00
Light, Bust of Queen Mary, Eclipse Lamps, 4⅛" 675.00

Light, Expanded Dmn, clear w/blk swirls, flared rim, 3" ..130.00
Light, Expanded Dmn, cobalt, pontil scar, 2⅞" 75.00
Light, Expanded Dmn, dk moss gr, flared/folded rim, 2¾" ..100.00
Light, Expanded Dmn, dk pk-amethyst, Pains Pat 1882, 3½" ..70.00
Light, Expanded Dmn, dk red, Brocks...Bohemia, 4" 275.00
Light, Expanded Dmn, dk sapphire bl, flared/folded rim, 2½" ..70.00
Light, Expanded Dmn, med sapphire bl, flared/folded rim, 3" ..90.00
Light, Expanded Dmn, med sapphire bl w/puce, 3" 90.00
Light, Expanded Dmn, med sapphire to puce to amethyst, 3" ..190.00
Light, swirl ribs, aqua, folded rim, Stiegel type, 3" 175.00
Light, swirl ribs, deep amethyst, pontil scar, 2¾" 65.00
Light, swirl ribs, dk sapphire bl, flared/folded rim, 2½" ..70.00
Lights, Mickey Mouse, Noma, w/Mazda lamps, M in display box ..245.00
Lights, Whirl-Glow, revolving, Noma, 1936, MIB 85.00
Mask, Santa, heavy pressed paper, EX pnt, 12" 125.00

Nativity scene, folding creche diecut with red tissue sides, candle holder with asbestos shield on back wall, 15x19x15½", EX, $160.00.

Rattle, Dresden, globe shape, bl w/mc, MIG, 3½" dia 195.00
Rattle, Santa figural, celluloid, mc, Occupied Japan, 4½" ..115.00
Santa, Belsnickle, brn coat w/gold, rare color, 5½" 650.00
Santa, Belsnickle, mustard robe, 11" 850.00
Santa, Belsnickle, wht robe, 10½", EX 600.00
Santa, bsk, red coat & hat, unmk Germany, 2" 110.00
Santa, celluloid face, compo boots, fabric clothes, 6" 115.00
Santa, celluloid wind-up toy, MIB 150.00
Santa, compo & cloth, 5½" 95.00
Santa, compo w/fabric clothes, Japan, 6" 110.00
Santa, papier-mache/wool/cloth, 11", in 12" sleigh 75.00
Santa in sled w/reindeer, bsk, snow base, Germany, 2x3" ..175.00
Santa in sleigh, celluloid, pulled by 3 deer, EX 95.00
Santa in sleigh, compo w/paper suit, 5", sits in sleigh 60.00
Santa jumping jack, red felt over cb, compo mask face, 5½" ..100.00
Santa w/arms around legs, bsk, mc pnt, Japan, 2" 50.00
Santa w/tree, compo & cloth, 4½" 85.00
Tree, aluminum, 6-ft, NMIB 40.00
Tree, bubble lite; 9 sockets on 14" gr tree w/base, EX 150.00
Tree, feather; gr w/red berries, German base, 24", EX 285.00
Tree, feather; lt gr, 13 branches, 6 candle clips, 14" 145.00
Tree, feather; stenciled wood base, 3-part, 1900s, 75", EX ..350.00
Tree, feather; trn wood base, Germany, early, 32", EX 265.00
Tree-top star, metal w/5 candle bulbs, Noma, EX 55.00
Wagon, Putz, gr flat bed w/metal wheels, Germany, 4" 50.00
Wreath, pressed cb, 10½", EX 50.00
Wreath, red chenille w/cotton Santa, 5" 35.00

Chrysanthemum Sprig, Blue

This is the blue opaque version of Northwood's popular pattern, Chrysanthemum Sprig. It was made at the turn of the century and is today very rare, as its values indicate. Prices are influenced by the amount of gold remaining on the raised designs. Our advisors for this category are Betty and Clarence Maier; they're listed in the Directory under Pennsylvania.

Bowl, berry; sm	300.00
Bowl, master fruit; 10½" W	550.00
Butter dish	850.00
Compote, jelly	475.00
Condiment tray, rare, VG gold	750.00
Creamer	385.00
Cruet	1,000.00

Pitcher, 8", $900.00.

Shakers, pr	450.00
Spooner	250.00
Sugar bowl, w/lid	450.00
Toothpick holder	450.00
Tumbler	200.00

Circus Collectibles

The 1890s — the Golden Age of the circus. Barnum and Bailey's parades transformed mundane city streets into an exotic never-never land inhabited by trumpeting elephants with jeweled gold headgear strutting by to the strains of the calliope that issued from a fine red- and gilt-painted wagon extravagantly decorated with carved wooden animals of every description. It was an exciting experience. Is it any wonder that collectors today treasure the mementos of that golden era? See also Posters.

Key:
B&B — Barnum & Bailey   RB — Ringling Bros.

Flashlight, RB B&B, fiber optics, red, wht & bl, NM	24.50
Flyer, Daily Bros, 1940s, 5½x6", EX	7.50
Invitation, VIP; RB B&B, Venice winter quarters, 1990, M	26.00
License plate, RB B&B, plastic, 1985, NM	9.50
Magazine, RB B&B, Emmett Kelly, 1949, 80-pg, VG	20.00
Magazine, RB B&B, Peter Arno illus, 1942	27.50
Magazine, Seagram Spotlight, Herbet Wht clown cover, 1951, EX	16.50
Magazine & review, RB B&B, Flying Concellos, 1939, 72-pg, EX	25.00
Mug, Gunther Gebel-Wms & Kenny, plastic, Farewell Tour, 1988	8.00
Pen, RB B&B, plastic, orange, M	5.00
Poster, Cristiani Bros, Greatest Riding Troup..., 1960, 21x28"	80.00
Poster, Gunther Gebel-Wms, w/schedule, 1989-90	100.00
Poster, King Bros & Cristiani, 3 laughing clowns, 1945, 28x41"	165.00
Poster, Parker & Watts, Kit Carson Jr, ca 1930, 28x40"	175.00
Poster, RB, 1943, 28x41"	275.00
Poster, RB B&B, Prairie Bill...Rough Riders, 1930s, 20x28"	200.00

Program, Hagenbeck-Wallace & Sells Bros, 1935, M	45.00
Program, RB B&B, 101st edition, w/poster, 1972, NM	24.00
Rainsuit, RB B&B, yel & bl unicorn logo, 2-pc, 1980s, EX	27.50
Ring, pewter, emb Jack Earle (Ripley's 8-ft giant)	25.00
Route book, Wallace & Co RR circus, 1888 season, EX	48.00
Sticker, RB B&B, Irvin Feld, 1970s, 1¼x3½", NM, pr	2.50

Clambroth

Clambroth is a term that refers to a type of glass popular in the Victorian period. It was semi-opaque and gray-white in color, said to resemble the broth of the clam. See also Sandwich.

Bottle, scent; gold swag flowers, polished pontil, 11"	195.00
Bowl, scalloped, 3x12"	35.00
Candlesticks, dolphin form w/petal socket, pr	525.00
Cruet, lt bl cuttings in paneled body, step-cut lip, 7"	700.00
Epergne, 1-lily, ftd/ruffled bowl: 6¼x4½"	125.00
Pitcher, appl hdl, 10½"	95.00
Toothpick holder, HP red berries & gr leaves	125.00
Vase, blk horizontal lines, 9x4¾"	32.00
Whiskey taster, lacy, 2"	95.00

Clarice Cliff

Between 1928 and 1935 in Burslem, England, as the director and part owner of Wilkinson and Newport Pottery Companies, Clarice Cliff and her 'paintresses' created a body of hand-painted pottery whose influence is felt to the present time.

The name for the oevre was Bizarre Ware, and the predominant sensibility, style, and appearance was Deco. Almost all pieces are signed and include the pattern names. There were over 160 patterns and more than 400 shapes, all of which are illustrated in *A Bizarre Affair — the Life and Work of Clarice Cliff*, published by Harry N. Abrams, Inc., written by Len Griffen and our advisors, Susan and Louis Meisel, whose address is listed in the Directory under New York.

Clarice Cliff died in 1972, shortly after the Victoria and Albert Museum showed her work in retrospect, and collectors (primarily in England) began seeking and admiring her work. In September of 1982, the Metropolitan Museum of Art in New York acquired and placed on view a selection of six pieces.

Note: Non-hand-painted work (transfer printed) was produced after World War II and into the 1950s. Some of the most common names are 'Tonquin' and 'Charlotte.' These items, while attractive and enjoyable to own, have no value in the collector market.

Charger, Inspiration Bizarre, ribbed, 18"	1,800.00
Isis vase, Gayday, Fantasque, 10x7"	1,100.00
Isis vase, Umbrella & Rain, leaves in panels, 9½", NM	2,300.00
Lotus jug, Bizarre, Coral Firs pattern (trees/hills), 7x6"	700.00
Lotus jug, Fantasque, melon pattern, dbl-hdld	1,500.00
Pitcher, Athens, Fantasque Lily Orange, 8-panel, 7", EX	700.00
Pitcher, Bizarre, Rhodanthe pattern (floral), 7x9"	450.00
Pitcher, Fantasque Melon, flared w/lg angular hdl, 5¾", NM	650.00
Plate, Forest Glen, orange/ivory house on gr hill, 9¾"	500.00
Vase, Bizarre, Delicia pattern (fruit), ftd, 5½x5¾"	650.00
Vase, Bizarre, Secrets pattern (hilly landscape), 8x5¾"	800.00
Vase, Trees & House, Fantasque, #196, flared, 6¼x3¼"	800.00

Cleminson

A hobby turned to enterprise, Cleminson is one of several California potteries whose clever hand-decorated wares are attracting the attention of today's collectors. The Cleminsons started their business at their El Monte home in 1941 and were so successful that eventually they expanded to a modern plant that employed more than 150 workers. They produced not only dinnerware and kitchen items such as cookie jars, canisters, and accessories, but novelty wall vases, small trays, plaques, etc., as well. Though nearly always marked, Cleminson wares are easy to spot as you become familiar with their distinctive glaze colors. Their grayed-down blue and green, berry red, and dusty pink say 'Cleminson' as clearly as their trademark. Unable to compete with foreign imports, the pottery closed in 1963. Our advisor for this category is Jack Chipman, author of *The Collector's Encyclopedia of California Pottery*; he is listed in the Directory under California.

Cookie jar, potbellied stove, $85.00.

Creamer & sugar bowl, Distlefink	24.00
Cup & saucer, There's Something About a Soldier	28.00
Egg cup, lady in apron figural, early	25.00
Gravy boat, Distlefink, brn & gr	25.00
Pancake server, Big Top Circus, juvenile	45.00
Pitcher, Distlefink, 9½"	27.00
Plaque, pastel floral, 5¾", pr	28.00
Plate, Deco fruit, red on ivory, wall hanging	22.00
Plate, rooster crowing, yel decor on rim, 9½"	22.00
Shakers, Distlefink, lg, pr	16.00
Spoon rest, cherries	18.00
Spoon rest, stylized floral on gray, 8½"	18.00
Sprinkler, Chinese boy	35.00
Sugar shaker, girl figural	30.00
Wall pocket, Chef, smiling face, bl eyes, 7¼"	65.00
Wall pocket, mortgage bank	25.00

Clewell

Charles Walter Clewell was a metal worker who perfected the technique of plating an entire ceramic vessel with a thin layer of copper or bronze treated with an oxidizing agent to produce a natural deterioration of the surface. Through trial and error, he was able to control the degree of patina achieved. In the early stages, the metal darkened and, if allowed to develop further, formed a natural turquoise-blue or green corrosion. He worked alone in his small Akron, Ohio, studio from about 1906, buying undecorated pottery from several Ohio firms, among them Weller, Owens, and Cambridge. His work is usually marked. Clewell died in 1965, having never revealed his secret process to others.

Prices for Clewell have advanced rapidly during the past few years along with the Arts and Crafts market in general. Right now, good examples are bringing whatever the traffic will bear.

Bowl, rust/gr patina, sgn/#422-2-6, 3x8"	550.00
Vase, brn/gr patina, tiny opening, #388-2-9, 7x4¾"	800.00
Vase, copper patina, 4"	200.00
Vase, cvd floral w/slim leaves in copper o/l, sgn EJ, 6½", EX	700.00
Vase, dk orange/gr patina, flared/ftd, mk/#120-2-6, 5"	425.00
Vase, dk orange/gr patina, mk/#313-2-7, ovoid, 13"	1,000.00
Vase, dk orange/gr patina, sgn/#459, 8"	850.00
Vase, gr streaky patina, narrow neck, sgn/#435-1-6, 7"	1,000.00
Vase, modeled decor, mk, 3¾"	250.00
Vase, rust/gr patina, milk can shape, #450-26, 22x10"	2,500.00
Vase, rust/gr patina, sgn/#302-2-6, some wear, 11½"	550.00
Vase, strong turq patina, sgn/#277-6, 16"	1,400.00

Clews

Brothers Ralph and James Clews were potters who operated in Cobridge in the Staffordshire district from 1817 to 1835. They are best known for their blue and white transfer-printed earthenwares, which included American Views, Moral Maxims, Picturesque Views, and English Views. A series called *Three Tours of Dr. Syntax* contained thirty-one different scenes with each piece bearing a descriptive title. Another popular series was *Pictures of Sir David Wilkie* with seven prints. (Though we once thought that the Don Quixote series was made by Clews, new information seems to indicate that it was made instead by Davenport.) Both printed and impressed marks were used, often incorporating the pattern name as well as the pottery. See also Staffordshire, Historical. Our advisor for this category is Richard Marden; he is listed in the Directory under New Hampshire.

Cup & saucer, handleless; flower urn, dk bl transfer	140.00
Cup & saucer, Water Girl, dk bl transfer	200.00
Cup plate, Mosaic Tracery, dk bl transfer, 3½"	135.00
Plate, Christmas Eve, dk bl transfer, 8½"	200.00
Plate, Escape of the Mouse, dk bl transfer, 10"	235.00
Plate, Letter of Introduction, dk bl transfer, 5½"	220.00
Plate, man w/lady on burro, dk bl transfer, 8¼"	90.00
Plate, soup; Dr Syntax Mistakes...for an Inn, dk bl transfer, 9⅞"	165.00
Plate, soup; Oriental Sports, med-dk bl transfer, 8½"	185.00
Platter, Dr Syntax Amused, dk bl transfer, 19"	1,400.00
Teapot, floral, dk bl transfer, sm rpr	275.00
Teapot, Setters, dk bl transfer, EX	315.00
Waste bowl, Christmas Eve, dk bl transfer, 6½"	315.00

Clifton

Clifton Art Pottery of Clifton, New Jersey, was organized ca 1903. Until 1911 when they turned to the production of wall and floor tile, they made artware of several varieties. The founders were Fred Tschirner and William A. Long. Long had developed the method for underglaze slip painting that had been used at the Lonhuda Pottery in Steubenville, Ohio, in the 1890s. Crystal Patina, the first artware made by the small company, utilized a fine white body and flowing, blended colors, the earliest a green crystalline. Indian Ware, copied from the pottery of the American Indians, was usually decorated in black geometric designs on red clay. (On the occasions when white was used in addition to the black, the ware was often not as well executed; so even though two-color decoration is very rare, it is normally not as desirable to the collector.) Robin's Egg Blue, pale blue on the white body, and Tirrube, a slip-decorated matt ware, were also produced.

Teapot, Crystal Patina, squat, 3½"	150.00
Vase, Crystal Patina, crystalline w/silver o/l, 6¾"	800.00

Vase, Crystal Patina, lg emb poppies, lt gr, #173, 6¾" **475.00**
Vase, Crystal Patina, vase, wide base, integral hdls, 3¾" **150.00**
Vase, gr matt, emb stylized lily pads, ftd sphere, 2½" **350.00**
Vase, Indian Ware, geometrics in dk brn & cream, #227, 12x9" ..**350.00**
Vase, Indian Ware, geometrics in red & blk, w/hdl, 4x7½" **175.00**

Teapot, Crystal Patina, 5½", $275.00.

Clocks

In the early days of our country's history, clock makers were influenced by styles imported from Europe. They copied the European's cabinets and reconstructed their movements. But needed materials were in short supply; modifications had to be made. Of necessity was born mainspring motive power and spring clocks. Wooden movements were made on a mass-production basis as early as 1808. Before the middle of the century, metal movements had been developed.

Today's collectors prefer clocks from the 18th and 19th centuries with pendulum-regulated movements. Bracket clocks made during this period utilized the shorter pendulum improvised in 1658 by Fromentiel, a prominent English clock maker. These smaller square-face clocks usually were made with a dome top fitted with a handle or a decorative finial. The case was usually walnut or ebony and was sometimes decorated with pierced brass mountings. Brackets were often mounted on the wall to accommodate the clock, hence the name. The banjo clock was patented in 1802 by Simon Willard. It derived its descriptive name from its banjo-like shape. A similar but more elaborate style was called the lyre clock.

Prices have been stable for several years. Unless noted otherwise, values are given for clocks in excellent condition. Clocks that have been altered, damaged, or have had parts replaced are worth considerably less.

Our advisor is Bruce A. Austin; he is listed in the Directory under New York. Our novelty clock advisors are DLK Nostalgia and Collectibles; their address is given under Pennsylvania.

Key:
br — brass	reg — regulator
dl — dial	rswd — rosewood
esc — escapement	T — time only
mcr — mercury	wt — weight
mvt — movement	vnr — veneer
pnd — pendulum	2nds — seconds

Novelty Clocks

Barbie, side profile w/pony tail, bl, wind-up, EX **150.00**

Bayard, Donald Duck, MIB **250.00**
Bayard, Mickey Mouse, MIB **250.00**

Empire mantel clock, Cupid seated on clock with lyre at his side as he pours from ewer, all on ornate rectangular base with four ball feet, ca 1815, 20x15", $2,200.00.

French, scholar & bench, animated, EX **85.00**
Hubley, toy clock disassembles, runs when completed, w/box **75.00**
Ingraham, Roy Rogers, MIB **400.00**
Lux, cuckoo, pendulette **35.00**
Lux, Happy Days, animated **275.00**
Lux, Organ Grinder, animated **125.00**
Lux, Shoeshine Boy, animated **350.00**
Smith, Gambler, animated, M **350.00**
Tezuka, puppy w/moving eyes, dl in 'tummy,' 6" **175.00**

Shelf Clocks

Ansonia, Triumph, walnut, very ornate, new cherubs, 1900, 24" .**475.00**
Brewster-Ingraham, 8-day beehive, 1850, rfn, VG veneer **225.00**
Chauncey Ives, mahog pillar/scroll, wood mvt, rpl rvpt, 30" ...**1,600.00**
China, floral on pk Rococo-style case, Ansonia, 13" **300.00**
Chinese, bracket, 2-fusee, mahog w/MOP, 1800s style, 18" **550.00**
Davis, rosewood, simple style, 8-day calendar, 1860, 25" **325.00**
E Terry & Son, Fed mahog pillar/scroll, ca 1820s, 31" **1,500.00**
EN Welch, ogee, rosewood veneer, brass works, 18¼" **110.00**
English, cvd mahog (ebonized) w/birds, 2-fusee, 1880, 17" **400.00**
Forestville Mfg, acorn style, fusee mvt, ca 1850, 24" **4,125.00**
Fr, china urn form w/ormolu, open esc strikes hrs on bell **800.00**
Fr, regulator, wht marble w/gilt, under glass dome, 18" **425.00**
Fr chinoiserie, damascene dl, lever mvt, 1900, 6" **275.00**
Fr garniture, marble w/EX ormolu ft & trim, 1880, 3-pc **400.00**
Geo Marsh, pillar/scroll, wood works, 1830, pnt gone **140.00**
German for English market, mahog bracket, 15-min strike **700.00**
Germany, traditional style, mahog case, brass works, 17" **85.00**
Gilbert, rnd-top case, 30-hr mvt, 1870 ....**200.00**
Ingraham, Ducat, oak gingerbread, very fancy, 1900 ....**225.00**
Junghans, Westminster bracket, mahog/line inlay, 1920, 15" **200.00**
Kroeber, Versailles, CI w/gilt brass, pk pnt, 1880, 15" **375.00**
Lecoultre, Atmos, brass/glass, self-wind, 1960-dtd plaque **475.00**

Paris, rosewood & ebony w/inlay & brass trim, 9½" 475.00
Seth Thomas, ogee, mahog veneer, rvpt eagle, rfn, pnd, 25" 650.00
Smith-Goodrich, steeple, 3-fusee, orig w/rfn case, 1850 ....700.00
Statue, lady (1 seated) ea side, bronze/ormolu, J Roque, 17" ...1,980.00
Statue of bronze lion on Fr marble/brass/glass case, 19" 800.00
Statue of cherubs, spelter/cloisonne, Fr, lever mvt, boudoir 275.00
Statue of female 'Wisdom,' seated, bronze/marble, Birks 1,000.00
Statue of flapper/dog, spelter, Fr Art Deco, 1920, 3-pc set 225.00
Statue of gilt cherub supporting 30-hr clock, German, 10" 100.00
Statue of horse by dl, marble case/base, New Haven, 1920s 175.00
Statue of Jesus/children, spelter, EX detail, Fr, 1840 ....500.00
Statue of lady/cherub, bronze/onyx, Louis XV style, 14" 750.00
Statue of lady on couch under canopy w/dial, 1830, 18", VG ..4,000.00
Statues of 2 dolphins support clock, bronze, Fr, 1870, 16" 850.00
Waterbury, mahog, key-hole form, porc dl/open esc, 1890, 14" ..250.00

Shelf clock, Birge & Ives, Federal, carved mahogany case, two reverse paintings, early 1800s, 38", $1,600.00.

Tall Case Clocks

Asahel Cheney, Federal, cherry inlay, ca 1800, 84" 5,225.00
Cherry Chpndl, arched top w/fretwork & 3 brass balls, 88" 6,000.00
English, oak, broken arch, 8-day/pnt dl, Masonic, 1840, 87" ...1,500.00
Isaac Brokaw, cherry, NJ, ca 1780, 88" 3,300.00
Juvenaux mvt, mahog/ormolu mts, barometer/temp, 104" 9,000.00
Kerns, oak w/rope moldings, brass works, 84" 715.00
Nathaniel Haneye, pine, wooden mvt, MA, 1700s, 82" 3,025.00

Wall Clocks

Aaron Willard on dl, banjo, re-gilt, rpl tablets, 1840 ....650.00
Austrian, box case, 1-wt Vienna mvt, spun bezel w/emb, 1920 ..250.00
Austrian, regulator, oak, Kronberger dl, 1-wt, 1900, 41" 550.00
Chelsea, banjo, T, silvered br dl, Mt Vernon tablets, mid-sz 475.00
E Howard, #95 banjo, sgn Steel rvpt w/Mt Vernon, 1920, M ..1,200.00
E Taber, banjo, rvpt oak leaves, fishing scene, 31" 1,250.00
Elmer O Stennes, banjo, gilt eagle/acanthus drop/rvpt, 47" 3,250.00
Fr, brass, shaped as watch, 12-pc cartouch dl, 1880, 17" dia 300.00
German, regulator, walnut, EX trn, 3 drops, gong, top gone 270.00
Gilbert, store regulator, rfn oak/rpl Calumet tablet, 1910 ....300.00
Gustav Becker, regulator, rpl hand/case top, eng wts, 1890 ....650.00
Gustav Becker, Viennese-style walnut, mvt w/cut pinions, 1890 ..450.00
Ithaca, #4 dbl-dl calendar, walnut, 30-day, 1880 ....800.00
Ithaca, dbl-dl library w/8" Horton's Pat calendar dl, 1870 ....600.00
Jouout & Angouleme, emb hood, lg pnd, pnt face, 18" 465.00
Lenzkrich, mahog, bracket beneath, T/strike, 1900 ....500.00
Morbier, comptoise, repousse religious motif, rpl pnd, 1800 ......300.00

Morbier, comptoise, 2-wt (rpl), sun/2 cornucopias atop, 1830 ....425.00
New Haven, Columbia, oak, dbl spring, 30-day, 1890, 49" 650.00
New Haven, Thoreau, crystal regulator, open esc, 1910 ....420.00
New Haven, Winsome banjo, Westminster chimes, 1925, 24" ...325.00
S Thomas, Flora, cherry, rfn, paper dl, 1880 ....1,200.00
S Thomas, Office #3, case w/14 brass buttons, rpl tablet/dl 225.00
S Thomas, ship's outside bell, 1890, VG as-found.......................300.00

Cloisonne

Cloisonne is a method of decorating metal with enameling. Fine metal wires are soldered onto the metal body following the lines of a predetermined design. The resulting channels are filled in with enamels of various colors, and the item is fired. The final step is a smoothing process that assures even exposure of the wire pattern. The art is predominately Oriental and has been practiced continuously, except during war years, since the 16th century. The most excellent examples date from 1865 until the turn of the century. The early 20th century export variety is usually lightweight and the workmanship inferior. Modern wares are of good quality and are produced in Taiwan as well as China.

Several variations of the basic art include plique-a-jour, achieved by removing the metal body after firing, leaving only the transparent enamel work; foil cloisonne, using transparent or semitranslucent enameling over a layer of embossed silver covering the metal body of the vessel; wireless cloisonne, made by removing the wire dividers prior to firing; and cloisonne executed on ceramic, wood, or lacquer rather than metal.

Candlestands, elephant form, profuse caparison, 20", pr 1,200.00
Censer, lotus flowers, ftd, dragons on lid, Qianlong mk, 40" ...2,200.00
Censer, ovoid form, 3-leg, gilt bronze hdls, 1900s, 12¼" 1,100.00
Clock, gilt brass trim/HP face, HP portrait pendulum, 19" 350.00
Crane on plinth, wings remove, candle pricket in beak, 35", pr .770.00
Jar, florals in red & bl reserves on bl, w/lid, late, 9" 110.00
Jar, mc flowers & birds on dk bl, late, 9⅜x7" 150.00
Napkin ring, dragons on blk, pr 12.00
Plate, bl fishscale design, China, 8½" 30.00
Teapot, flowers & butterfly in mc panels, late, 4x3" 125.00
Teapot, vintage, mc on 2-tone red w/bl, late, 2⅝", EX 85.00
Tray, floral & bird, late, 5½x9½" 75.00
Urn, flowers & butterfly, hdls, 6" 125.00
Vase, bird on flower branch on dk bl, ft, 1900s, 7", pr 400.00
Vase, birds & blossoms on gray, 6-sided, 1900s, 6⅞", pr 475.00
Vase, blossoming cherry branches, birds on dotted red, 3½" 70.00
Vase, chrysanthumums on wht, 8¾x3⅜" 495.00
Vase, elephant form, profuse caparison, mask hdls, 19", pr 1,650.00
Vase, lotus blossoms, garlic head, lobed form, 1800s, 13½" 800.00
Vase, mc floral on blk, late, 7¼", pr 50.00
Vase, phoenix & dragon lappets below butterflies, 9¾" 400.00
Vase, waves & vining panels on sky bl, 12", pr 550.00
Vase, wisteria on dk bl, classic form, 1900s, 7⅛" 350.00
Vase, wisteria/plum blossom reserves on blk, 1900s, 5⅞", pr 400.00

Clothing and Accessories

'Second-hand' or 'vintage?' It's all a matter of opinion. But these days it's considered good taste (downright fashionable) to wear clothing from Victorian to styles from the sixties. Jackets with padded shoulders from the thirties are 'trendy.' Jewelry from the Art Deco era is just as beautiful and often less expensive than current copies. But why settle for new when the genuine article can be bought for the same price with exquisite lace that no reproduction can rival! When once the 'style' of the day was so strictly obeyed, today, in New York and the larger cities of California and Texas, in particular, nothing well-designed and constructed is 'out of style.' And though costumes by such designers as Chanel, Fortuny, and Lanvin may bring four-figure prices at fine auction houses, as a general rule, prices are very modest considering the wonderful fabrics one may find in vintage clothing, many of which are no longer available. Cashmere coats, elegant furs, and sequined or beaded gowns can be bought for only a small fraction of today's retail. Though some are strictly collectors, many do buy their clothes to wear. Care must be given to alterations, and gentle cleaning methods employed to avoid damage that would detract from their value. Our advisor for this category is Ruth Osborne; she is listed in the Directory under Ohio.

Key:
cap/s — cap sleeves	n/s — no sleeves
embr — embroidery	plt — pleated
hs — hand sewn	s/p — shoulder pads
lgth — length	s/s — short sleeves
l/s — long sleeves	/s — sleeves
ms — machine sewn	

Bathing suit, blk sateen, flower applique, s/s, 1920s, w/cap 75.00
Bathing suit, printed jersey, skirted style, 1940s 20.00
Blouse, cream silk w/pk & bl embr, l/s, collar, 1912, EX 65.00
Blouse, navy silk w/ecru lace, l/s, covered buttons, 1901 ....40.00
Bonnet, blk silk, rpl ties, 1860s-80s 20.00
Bonnet, youth's, brn silk w/cotton lace trim, Civil War era 25.00
Bustle pad, blk 25.00
Camisole, crochet yoke, 1½" W strips, 1900, EX 45.00
Camisole, lacy, embr, Victorian 40.00
Camisole, tucks & lace inserts, fitted bk, drawstrings, 1900 ....110.00
Cap, baby's, Irish crochet 20.00
Cap, boudoir; crochet, ca 1910s, EX 40.00
Cap, leather, Harley Davidson, 1950s 50.00
Cape, blk silk w/velvet cutwork, long, Victorian 150.00
Coat, blk velvet w/wide fox cuffs, 1950s, ¾-length 40.00
Coat, evening; pk velvet, silk lining, shirred sleeves, '20s 200.00
Coat, red wool w/velvet details, Victorian, EX 200.00
Dress, blk crepe, stand-up collar, slit to waist, 1930s 55.00
Dress, blk machine lace, l/s, 2-pc, ca 1910, EX 85.00
Dress, blk mourning style, jet beads, l/s, pleats, 1880s, EX 250.00
Dress, blk satin, crepe/s, lace insert, 1912, EX 45.00
Dress, blk silk chiffon w/lace o/l & pk tucks, long, 1930s 65.00
Dress, cafe-au-lait georgette w/crystal beads, n/s, 1900s, EX 185.00
Dress, child's, batiste & lace, l/s, Victorian 50.00
Dress, child's, cotton brocade, ca 1850 ....85.00
Dress, chocolate panne velvet, beaded silk, l/s, 1930s 65.00
Dress, christening; cambric, handmade, long, ca 1900 ....120.00
Dress, christening; tucking & eyelet, 1910s, 36" 45.00
Dress, christening; tucks & Broiderie Anglaise, long, 1900s 65.00
Dress, cotton, button front, collar, bishop/s, ca 1916, EX 75.00
Dress, crepe, draped front, beads, mandarin neck, l/s, 1940s 75.00
Dress, dbl knit, l/s, collar/cufs, 1950s, EX 30.00
Dress, dk linen, eyelet openwork/embr/tucks, 2-pc, 1890s 150.00
Dress, dk print, 'everyday' type, ca 1890s, EX 115.00
Dress, evening; bl w/rhinestones, Egyptian style, long, 1930s 150.00
Dress, evening; blk moire, ruffled skirt, fishtail bk, flapper 150.00
Dress, evening; pk taffeta, strapless, full skirt, 1950s 45.00
Dress, evening; wht lace, l/s, hs, ca 1910, EX 150.00
Dress, faille, fitted bodice, full skirt, s/s, 1940s 55.00
Dress, figured silk, lace trim, ruffled hem, l/s, 1890s, EX 275.00
Dress, flat crepe, jumper style, s/s, pockets, 1920s 135.00
Dress, lime faille, beaded neck, sheath, '50s, +matching coat 75.00

Dress, maternity; lining adjusts, drop shoulders, l/s, 1920s 235.00
Dress, mourning; blk silk & jet beads, 2-pc, Victorian, EX 300.00
Dress, peach chiffon w/lace top, lg sash, l/s, 1929 ....125.00
Dress, peach silk net, s/s, velvet belt w/rhinestones, '30s 65.00
Dress, sateen, semiprincess style, ¾/s, collar/cuffs, 1910s 195.00
Dress, satin, Harlow type, silver beads/bl sets, long, '30s 65.00
Dress, striped silk, homespun bodice lining, 1820s, VG 145.00
Dress, taffeta, full skirt, short jacket, late 1940s, EX 100.00
Dress, taffeta, ruffled neck, l/s, tight wrists, 1880s, EX 450.00
Dress, velvet w/chinchilla trim, flapper style w/bugle beads 350.00
Dress, voile, lace inserts, l/s, long, 1900 ....165.00
Dress, wedding; fancy embr on net, drop waist, l/s, 1920s 250.00
Dress, wedding; lace, hooped skirt, bolero jacket, 1950s 250.00
Fur cape, monkey, short, w/muff 125.00
Fur coat, Mouton lamb, 1950s, ¾-length, EX 75.00
Fur coat, Persian lamb, blk w/dk brn mink collar, 36", EX 95.00
Fur coat, seal, blk, 42", EX 165.00
Fur hat, seal w/satin trim 25.00
Fur jacket, ermine w/brn mink collar, EX 250.00
Fur jacket, mink, brn, 30", EX 250.00
Fur jacket, silver fox, 26", EX 250.00
Fur muff, monkey, 1930s, 12x14" 35.00
Fur muff, seal w/matching hat 70.00
Fur neck drape, ermine, w/tails 55.00
Fur stole, fox, lt brn w/collar 165.00
Fur stole, mink, EX 165.00
Gloves, child's, wht wool, 1930s, M, pr 14.00
Hat, beaver, gold brushed w/leather banding, Christian Dior 125.00
Hat, beaver, Stetson, EX in box 125.00
Hat, child's, navy velveteen, 1960s, w/drawstring purse 15.00
Hat, cloche, navy bl straw, flapper style, 1920s 45.00
Hat, cloche, wool felt w/sequins & beads 45.00
Hat, Derby, man's, MIB 45.00
Hat, floral brim, lg taffeta bow, 1930s 45.00
Jacket, blk lace, peplum, l/s, 1930s 35.00
Jacket, combing; machine lace & silk ribbon insets, Victorian ...375.00
Jacket, leather, blk police type, 1950s, EX 300.00
Knickers, wool, full legs w/cuffed bottom, 1920s, EX 45.00

Lady's high-top shoes, black leather with white uppers, $50.00.

Nightgown, wide crochet insert at top, l/s, Victorian 50.00
Nightgown, 6" handmade lace bodice w/ribbons, long, 1930s 35.00
Nightshirt, cotton, pearl buttons, crochet-edged l/s, 1880s 115.00
Nightshirt, homespun linen, l/s, crochet at hem, 1850s 120.00
Nightshirt, lady's, homespun, l/s, EX 120.00
Overshoes, child's, blk cloth & rubber, 1-buckle, 1920s, pr 40.00
Pantaloons, eyelet lace hem 30.00
Pantaloons, Victorian 35.00
Parasol, wht linen, bamboo hdl, dtd, Victorian 140.00
Petticoat, cotton w/tucks & lace 50.00
Petticoat, 14" eyelet & tuck hem, long 55.00

Shawl, blk wool, fringe, 64x136", EX 65.00
Shawl, silk, lav, gr & gold embr on cream, long fringe 165.00
Shawl, silk, lg embr flowers, 15" silk fringe, NM 125.00
Shirt, man's, bib front, 1920s, EX 30.00
Shirt, man's, homespun, partial button front, EX 45.00
Shoes, ballet slippers, leather, Victorian, EX, pr 60.00
Shoes, blk fabric w/leather o/l, 1930s, pr 40.00
Shoes, blk moire taffeta, gilt & rhinestones on heels, 1920, pr 65.00
Shoes, blk patent, button strap w/fan, ca 1910, pr 55.00
Shoes, blk patent, pointed toes, button strap, 1910s 50.00
Shoes, blk silk w/strap over instep, 1920s, pr 45.00
Shoes, brn suede & leather, tie over instep, 1940, pr 35.00
Shoes, child's, high-button, red leather, pr 65.00
Shoes, child's, high-top, leather, 18 brass eyes, 1870s, pr 85.00
Shoes, child's slippers, red leather, felt lined, 1900s, pr 60.00
Shoes, high-button, brn suede & leather, pr 95.00
Shoes, high-laced, blk, Victorian, pr 50.00
Shoes, high-laced, taupe leather, Victorian, 1890s, pr 65.00
Shoes, kid, Louis heel, instep button, needle toe, 1920s, pr 60.00
Shoes, lady's, Oxford, brn/tan, spectator toe, pr 25.00
Shoes, sling-bk heels, Lucite w/seashells decor, 1950s 40.00
Shorts, flared 'skort' type, w/belt, mid-1940s, EX 22.50
Skirt, wht, full, lace bottom, long, hs, ca 1900 ....75.00
Slip, lawn, Princess type, circular flounce, ca 1910, EX 175.00
Suit, man's, herringbone wool, 2-button, wide shoulders, '30s 150.00
Vest, Battenburg lace, ca 1900 ....250.00
Vest, man's, brocade, printed cotton lining, 1880s, EX 65.00

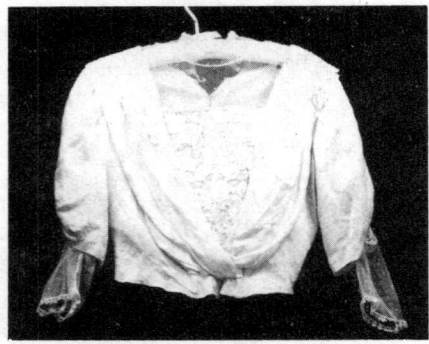

Waist, silk with lace collar and insert,
EX, $40.00.

Waist, silk w/delicate lace, ruffles, l/s, 1900s 75.00
Waistcoat, silk w/mc chain-stitch embr, ca 1780s, EX 725.00

Cluthra

The name Cluthra is derived from the Scottish word 'clutha,' meaning cloudy. Glassware by this name was first produced by J. Couper and Sons, England. Frederick Carder developed Cluthra while at the Steuben Glass Works, and similar types of glassware were also made by Durand and Kimball. It is found in both solid and shaded colors and is characterized by a spotty appearance resulting from small air pockets trapped between its two layers. See also Steuben.

Vase, bl w/clear base, #2011-8, Kimball, 8½" 300.00
Vase, gr, #1812, Kimball, 12" 200.00
Vase, orange/brn/wht in clear, Kimball, 7x8", pr 500.00
Vase, teal/wht, Kimball, 6" 275.00
Vase, wht, #1968, Kimball, 6" 225.00

Vase, yel/opal mottle, ftd cylinder, Kimball, 12½" 250.00
Vase, yel/orange/opal mottle, tapered cylinder, Kimball, 8" 225.00
Vase, yel/orange/opal mottle, trumpet neck, Kimball, 11" 350.00

Coalport

In 1745 in Caughley, England, Squire Brown began a modest business fashioning crude pots and jugs from clay mined in his own fields. Tom Turner, a young potter who had apprenticed his trade at Worcester, was hired in 1772 to plan and oversee the construction of a 'proper' factory. Three years later he bought the business, which he named Caughley Coalport Porcelain Manufactory. Though the dinnerware he produced was meant to be only everyday china, the hand-painted florals, birds, and landscapes used to decorate the ware were done in exquisite detail and in a wide range of colors. In 1780 Turner introduced the Willow pattern which he produced using a newly perfected method of transfer printing. (Wares from the period between 1775 and 1799 are termed 'Caughley' or 'Salopian'; see section on Caughley.) John Rose purchased the Caughley factory from Thomas Turner in 1799, adding that holding to his own pottery which he had built two years before in Coalport. (It is from this point in the pottery's history that the wares are termed 'Coalport.') The porcelain produced there before 1814 was unmarked with very few exceptions. After 1820 some examples were marked with a '2' with an oversize top loop. The term 'Coalbrookdale' refers to a fine type of porcelain decorated in floral bas relief, similar to the work of Dresden.

After 1835 highly decorated ware with rich ground colors imitated the work of Sevres and Chelsea, even going so far as to copy their marks. From about 1895 until the 1920s, the mark in use was 'Coalport' over a crown with 'England A.D. 1750' indicating the date claimed as the founding, not the date of manufacture. From the 1920s until 1945, 'Made in England' over a crown and 'Coalport' below was used. Later, the mark was 'Coalport' over a smaller crown with 'Made in England' in a curve below.

Each of the major English porcelain companies excelled in certain areas of manufacture. Coalport produced the finest 'jeweled' porcelain, made by picking up a heavy mixture of slip and color and dropping it onto the surface of the ware. These 'jewels' are perfectly spaced and are often graduated in size with the smaller 'jewels' at the neck or the base of the vase. Some ware was decorated with very large 'jewels' resembling black opals or other polished stones. Such pieces are in demand by the advanced collector.

It is common to find considerable crazing on old Coalport, since the glaze was thinly applied to increase the brilliance of the colors. Many early vases had covers; look for a flat surface that would have supported a lid (just because it is gilted does not mean the vase never had one). Pieces whose lids are missing are worth about 40% less. Most lids had a finial which have been broken and restored. You should deduct about 10% for a professional restoration on a finial.

In 1926 the Coalport Company moved to Shelton in Staffordshire and today belongs to a group headed by the Wedgwood Company. Our advisors for this category are Henry and Geneva Tyler; they are listed in the Directory under Florida. See also Indian Tree.

Box, jeweled body, S-V1838, ca 1895-1900, 3¼x5¼" 1,650.00
Dish, Japan-style vase & flowers, shell shape w/hdl, 1815, 9" 125.00
Ewer, lg jewels w/gilt, shape #2446C, 1893, 11¾x4¼" 6,000.00
Figurine, Christine, lady w/fan, bl dress, 20th C, 7⅜" 85.00
Figurine, Old Woman's Shoe, 20th C 60.00
Figurine, The Nativity, 20th C 60.00
Plate, Banks of Dee, musical symbols, 1820s, 8" 200.00
Shoe, jewels on gilt, 2½x5" 1,450.00
Teapot, flowers on 'marble,' dog spout, bird hdl, rpr, 8" 150.00

Vase, titled 'Plant,' figural handles, three claw feet, cobalt and white with gilding, S-6798, ca 1895, 16¾x9½", $5,500.00.

Vase, turq & wht jewels in gilt on pk, gold scroll hdls, 7½" 1,100.00

Cobalt Glass

Cobalt glass is characterized by its deep transparent blue color obtained by mixing cobalt oxide and alumina to the batch. It may be found in free-blown, mold-blown, and pressed glassware. See also Blown Glass.

Box, HP flowers w/gold bands & wht dots, 2x3" **55.00**
Cruet, mc florals, appl cobalt hdl, cobalt stopper, 6¼" **85.00**
Jar, gold bands w/mc HP florals, knob finial, 4⅜x3¼" **88.00**
Vase, bulbous, flared rim, 5½" **18.00**
Vase, gold band at top, HP florals, ewer form, 5¼" **75.00**
Vase, gold bands & scrolls, w/lid, 4½x2¼" **75.00**
Vase, 5 blown-out ribs, Deco style, 8½x5⅜" **72.50**

Coca-Cola

J.S. Pemberton, creator of Coca-Cola, originated his world-famous drink in 1886. From its inception the Coca-Cola Company began an incredible advertising campaign which has proven to be one of the most successful promotions in history. The quantity and diversity of advertising material put out by Coca-Cola in the last one hundred years is literally mind-boggling. From the beginning, the company has projected an image of wholesomeness and Americana. Beautiful women in Victorian costumes, teenagers and schoolchildren, blue- and white-collar workers, the men and women of the Armed Forces (even Santa Claus) have appeared in advertisements with a Coke in their hands. Some of the earliest collectibles include trays, syrup dispensers, gum jars, pocket mirrors, and calendars. Many of these items fetch prices in the thousands of dollars. Later examples include radios, signs, lighters, thermometers, playing cards, clocks, and toys — particularly toy trucks.

In 1970 the Coca-Cola Company initialed a multimillion-dollar 'image-refurbishing campaign,' which introduced the new 'Dynamic Countour' logo, a twisting white ribbon under the Coca-Cola and Coke trademarks. The new logo often serves as a cut-off point to the purist collector. Newer and very ardent collectors, however, relish the myriad of items marketed since that date, as they often cannot afford the high prices that the vintage pieces command. For more information we recommend *Petretti's Coca-Cola Collectibles Price Guide*, 1994 edition (available from Nostalgia Publications whose address you will find

under Auctions in the Directory); *Huxford's Collectible Advertising, Second Edition*, and *Collectible Coca-Cola Toy Trucks* by our advisor Gael deCourtivron, who is listed in the Directory under Florida. For further information call the Cocaholics Hotline: 813-355-COLA.

Key: tm — trademark

Reproductions and Fantasies

Beware of reproductions! Prices are given for the genuine original articles, but the symbol (+) at the end of some of the following lines indicate items that have been reproduced. Warning! The 1935 calendar has been reproduced. It is identical in almost every way; only a professional can tell them apart. It is *very* deceiving! Watch for frauds: genuinely old celluloid items ranging from combs, mirrors, knives and forks to doorknobs that have been recently etched with a new double-lined trademark. Still another area of concern deals with reproduction and fantasy items. A fantasy item is a novelty made to appear authentic with inscriptions such as 'Tiffany Studios,' 'Trans Pan Expo,' 'World's Fair,' etc. In reality, these items never existed as originals. For instance, don't be fooled by a Coca-Cola cash register; no originals are known to exist! Large mirrors for bars are being reproduced and are often selling for $10.00 to $50.00.

Of the hundreds of reproductions (designated 'R' in the following examples) and fantasies (designated 'F') on the market today, these are the most deceiving.

Belt buckle, no originals thought to exist (F), up to **5.00**
Bottle, dk amber, w/arrows, heavy, narrow spout (R) **10.00**
Bottle carrier, wood, yel w/red logo, holds 6 bottles (R) **10.00**
Clock, electric, dome style, Ridgway, 1981 (R) **100.00**
Clock, mantel; brass, battery-op, Ridgway Anniv, '80, 6x9" (R) ...**100.00**
Cooler, Glascock Jr, made by Coca-Cola USA (R) **200.00**
Doorknob, glass etched w/tm (F) **3.00**
Knife, bottle shape, 1970s, many variations (F) **5.00**
Knife, fork or spoon w/celluloid hdl, newly etched tm (F) **5.00**
Letter opener, stamped metal, Coca-Cola 5¢ (F) **3.00**
Pocketknife, yel & red, 1933 World's Fair (F) **2.00**
Sign, cb, lady w/fur, dtd 1911, 9x11" (F) **3.00**
Soda fountain glass holder, word 'Drink' not on orig (R) **5.00**
Thermometer, bottle figural, DONASCO, 17" (R) **5.00**
Trade card, copy of 1905 'Bathtub' foldout, emb 1978 (R) **3.00**
Vanity pc (mirror/brush/etc), celluloid, newly etched tm (F) **5.00**
Watch, pocket; often old watch w/new face (R) **10.00**

The following items have been reproduced and are among the most deceptive of all:
Pocket mirrors from 1905, 1906, 1908, 1909, 1910, 1911, 1916, and 1920.
Trays from 1899, 1910, 1913, 1914, 1917, 1920, 1923, 1925, 1926, 1934, and 1937.
Tip trays from 1907, 1909, 1910, 1913, 1914, 1917, and 1920.
Knives: many versions of the German brass model.
Cartons: wood versions, yellow with logo.

These items are currently being marketed:
Brass button, Taiwan, 18", (R)
Brass thermometer, bottle shape, Taiwan, 24"
Cast iron toys (none ever made)
Cast iron door pull, bottle shape, made to look old
Poster, Yes Girl (R)
Button sign, has 1 round hole while original has 4 slots, most have bottle logo, 12", 16", 20" (R)

Bullet trash receptacles (old cans with decals)

Paperweight, rectangular, with Pepsin Gum insert

1949 cooler radio (new)

Straw holders (no originals exist)

Countless trays — most unauthorized (must read 'American Artworks; Coshocton, OH.')

Centennial Items

1986 was the year for the Coca-Cola Company to celebrate its 100th birthday, and amidst all the fanfare came many new collectible items, all sporting the 100th anniversary logo. These items are destined to become an important part of the total Coca-Cola Collectible spectrum. The following pieces are among the most popular centennial items.

Bottle, gold dipped, in velvet sleeve, 6½-oz **50.00**
Bottle, Hutch, amber, Root Co, ½-oz, 3 in case **225.00**
Bottle, International, set of 9 in plexiglas case **275.00**
Bottle, leaded crystal, 100th logo, 6½-oz, MIB **125.00**
Medallion, bronze, w/box, 3" dia **50.00**
Pin set, wood fr, 101 pins **300.00**
Scarf, silk, 30x30" **35.00**
Thermometer, glass cover, 14" dia, M **22.00**

Coca-Cola Originals

Ad, 1905, dbl page, Healthy & Happy, 9x14", VG **150.00**
Ad, 1905, women/children try tonic, 7½x9½", EX **25.00**
Apron, 1930s, Pause...Refresh, bottle, NM **75.00**
Apron, 1960s, Enjoy..., contour logo, 2 pockets, M **22.00**
Ashtray, 1950s, ceramic, w/bottle lighter, NM **85.00**
Ashtrays, 1950s, ruby glass, card suit shape, 4 in box **325.00**

Bank, red plastic with white lettering, 1982, rare, $100.00.

Bank, 1950s, metal, red pnt, battery, Linemar, 10x7x5", VG **250.00**
Bell, 1930s, stamped metal, Refresh Yourself..., 3¼", NM **325.00**
Blotter, 1915, Pure & Healthful, EX **40.00**
Blotter, 1940, clown, Greatest Pause on Earth, NM **60.00**
Book, 1915, Universal Beverage, CC on cover, Elaine, EX **50.00**
Bottle, amber, Huntsville, str sides, NM **45.00**
Bottle, display; 1923, Christmas, clear, w/cap, 20", NM **320.00**
Bottle, flavor; 1950s, Big Chief, lt gr, emb Indian Head **10.00**
Bottle, seltzer; bl, M **90.00**
Bottle, syrup; 1920s, clear w/foil label & pewter lid, NM **425.00**
Bottle, syrup; 1930s, glass w/paper label, EX **100.00**
Bottle ashtray/match holder, 1930s-40s, G decals, w/matches **750.00**
Calendar, 1899, cb, girl at desk in oval, rare, 13x7⅜", VG **6,000.00**
Calendar, 1914, Betty w/bottle, full pad, 32x13" **1,600.00**
Calendar, 1915, w/glass, partial pad, 32x13", EX **1,500.00**
Calendar, 1916, w/glass, partial pad, 32x13", NM **1,150.00**

Calendar, 1917, Constance w/glass, partial pad, 32x13", EX ...**1,000.00**
Calendar, 1918, June Caprice, full pad, 5x9", EX+ **275.00**
Calendar, 1919, M Davis w/glass, partial pad, 6¼x110½", NM .**2,000.00**
Calendar, 1920, girl w/glass, full pad, 32x12", NM **1,200.00**
Calendar, 1921, girl in tam w/glass, full pad, 32x12" **850.00**
Calendar, 1922, girl w/glass at ballgame, no pad, 32x12" **275.00**
Calendar, 1923, girl in bl w/glass, no pad, 27x12", VG **225.00**
Calendar, 1925, girl w/fur, partial pad, VG **400.00**
Calendar, 1926, tennis girl, full pad, rstr to EX **425.00**
Calendar, 1929, girl w/pearls, full pad, EX **500.00**
Calendar, 1930, bathing beauty, full pad, EX **600.00**
Calendar, 1931, boy w/sandwich & dog, full pad, EX **575.00**
Calendar, 1933, man w/dog, full pad, EX **400.00**
Calendar, 1935, boy fishing, dog at side, full pad, NM (+) **425.00**
Calendar, 1937, boy w/pole in hand walks w/dog, full pad, NM .**350.00**
Calendar, 1939, girl pours CC, full pad, NM **300.00**
Carrier, 1920s, cb, diminishing logo, 6-pack, NM **100.00**
Carrier, 1930s, cb, Season's Greetings, 6-pack, EX+ **125.00**
Carrier, 1940s-50s, aluminum, red sides, 6-pack, EX **50.00**
Case, 1920s-30s, yel & red, 24-bottle, tall, VG **40.00**
Case insert, 1954, cb, Eddie Fisher, 12x20", NM **80.00**
Change purse, 1907, gold transfer: When Thirsty..., NM **80.00**
Change purse, 1910s-20s, leather, lt wear, EX **30.00**
Change purse, 1920s-30s, dbl clasp, gold transfer, EX **75.00**
Change receiver, 1890s, Ideal Brain Tonic, 10½", NM **4,500.00**
Cigarette box, 1936, 50th Anniversary, frosted glass, EX **300.00**
Cigarette lighter, Scripto, gas lighter, Sprite, EX **10.00**
Cigarette lighter, Supreme, Drink CC in Bottles, EX **15.00**
Cigarette lighter, 1940s, musical, red & wht logo, EX in box **125.00**
Clip, 1967, brass, 50th Anniversary of Piqua OH Co, NM **50.00**
Clock, 1894-96, figure-8, Ideal Brain Tonic..., Baird, 30", EX .**5,000.00**
Clock, 1903-05, regulator schoolhouse, Ingraham, 25", VG **2,200.00**
Clock, 1910, leather case, bottle form, 8x3", EX **850.00**
Clock, 1950, counter top w/light, brass, Pay When Served, NM ..**500.00**
Clock, 1974, plastic, battery operated, Betty transfer, M **45.00**
Clock, 1975, pocket watch style, wall hanging, MIB **50.00**
Coupon, 1908, free glass of CC, rstr, NM **75.00**
Coupon, 1929, Tickle Toes Wonder Doll, CC premium, NM **90.00**
Diecut, 1932, cb, CC & hot dog, 3-D, 10x20", NM **300.00**
Diecut, 1941, cb, Santa by cooler, easel bk, 32x40", EX **150.00**
Diecut, 1942, cb, Santa w/bag on steps, easel bk, 18x9½", NM .**300.00**
Diecut, 1950s, cb, red picnic cooler, easel bk, 14x18", EX **150.00**
Diecut, 1955, cb, Santa & lamppost, easel bk, 28x14", NM **80.00**
Diecut, 1957, cb, stand-up rocket, Festive Holidays, 33x13", NM .**250.00**
Diecut, 1960s, cb, Santa at tree, easel bk, 24x16", NM **50.00**
Diecut, 1960s, cb, Santa w/sm boy & bottle, 3-D, 24x15", EX ...**50.00**
Dispenser, ceramic, 2 pcs mk Wheeling, +lid/spigot, 18" (+) ..**6,000.00**
Dispenser, dry server; 1930s-40s, red metal, NM **200.00**
Door pull, 1930s, aluminum, Drink..., 1-pc casting, NM (+) **250.00**
Door push, 1930s, porc, complete w/brackets, NM **350.00**
Door push, 1939-41, tin, silhouette girl, EX **350.00**
Door push, 1950s, porc, red & wht, Ice Cold in Bottles, EX **120.00**
Doorknob, 1910s, brass or steel, emb CC, NM **350.00**
Fan, 1900s, bamboo & rice paper, Oriental lady, NM **200.00**
Fan, 1920s, woven bamboo, EX **75.00**
Fan, 1940s-50s, bottle in sun, Sprite boy on bk, EX **60.00**
Fan, 1950s, hand w/bottle, Sprite boy on bk, EX **50.00**
Fly swatter, 1920s, leather paddle, scarce, NM **150.00**
Game, 1938, Steps to Health, 11x26", EX **65.00**
Game board, 1934, Game of Health, Canada, 16¾x17¼", VG **75.00**
Grill plate (truck), aluminum diecut, Drink CC..., 17", NM **375.00**
Hat, driver's, gr w/red patch, EX **90.00**
Hat, soda jerk's, 1950s, paper, red & gr, NM **25.00**
Hat, soda jerk's, 1950s-60s, linen, red & wht, M **50.00**

Jar, gum; glass w/emb lid, CC Pepsin Gum, 11½x4½x4½", G 850.00
Key case, 1950s, Drink CC & wreath, VG 6.00
Menu, 1902, paper, 4⅛x6⅛", EX 400.00
Menu board, 1929, tin, Refresh Yourself, w/bottle, 28x20", EX ..200.00
Menu board, 1932, dmn shape at top w/logo, 28x20", EX 200.00
Menu board, 1950s, tin, fishtail & bottle, 20x28", NM 100.00
Menu card, 1901, Hilda Clark, foldout, 11¾x4", EX 850.00
Menu holder, 1940s-50s, plastic, silhouette girl, EX 80.00
Mug, 1920, ceramic, emb CC, Dan Mercer Pottery, rare, NM 600.00
Music box, 1950s, mini cooler form, w/instructions, NM 150.00
Nature study cards, 1940s-50s, complete set, MIB 50.00
Paperweight, 1930s, heavy glass, Coke is CC over red (+) 45.00
Plate, 1940-50s, Good w/Food, Wellsville China, 6½", NM 350.00
Playing cards, 1909, Gibson girl, single card 80.00
Playing cards, 1939, girl in red sweater, single card 35.00
Playing cards, 1943, Army nurse, no box, EX 50.00
Playing cards, 1943, girls w/wings, EX in box 75.00
Playing cards, 1951, girl at party, NM in box 75.00
Playing cards, 1956, ice skater, EX in box 60.00
Playing cards, 1959, Sign of Good Taste, snowman, sealed, M 90.00
Playing cards, 1961, bowling girl, sealed, M 60.00
Playing cards, 1986, 100th Anniversary, dbl deck, sealed, M 15.00
Pocket mirror, 1910, Hamilton King, 2¾x1¾", EX 60.00
Pocket watch, Time for a Cold Bottle of CC, 2" dia, G 750.00
Postcard, 1910, Hamilton King artwork, VG 200.00
Postcard, 1911, duster girl, VG 230.00

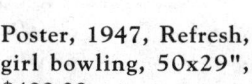

Poster, 1947, Refresh, girl bowling, 50x29", $400.00.

Punch board, 1930s, 2 babies, 1¢ sale price, 9¼x9¼", NM 750.00
Push plate, 1940s-50s, porc, Refresh...in Bottles, 6x4", M 250.00
Radio, 1933, Bakelite, red or brn, bottle form, Crosley, 30" 2,750.00
Radio, 1949-50, plastic/Bakelite, cooler form, 7x12x9½", EX 550.00
Radio, 1950s, vending machine form, transistor, 4½", EX 175.00
Radio, 1970s-80s, bottle form, NM in box 30.00
Sidewalk marker, 1930s-40s, brass, Safety First, NM 210.00
Sign, 1920s, cb w/tin fr, 1915 bottle ea end, 18x54", EX 600.00
Sign, 1920s, celluloid, 'Highballs,' blk w/gold, 6x11¼", VG 525.00
Sign, 1920s, mirror type, Every Bottle Sterilized, 18x8", VG 250.00
Sign, 1927, tin, Sold Here Ice Cold, emb bottle, 19x54", NM ...500.00
Sign, 1930s, plywood, ...in Bottles, 38x23¼", G 200.00
Sign, 1930s, porc, Drink CC, red/blk/wht, 12x28", VG 350.00
Sign, 1930s, porc, Ice Cold, went on truck cab, 18x54", NM 500.00
Sign, 1930s, porc, 1-sided outdoor type, 36x60", NM 300.00

Sign, 1930s, tin, Dasco, trademk under tail of C, 5¾x17¾", EX .180.00
Sign, 1930s, tin, Ice Cold Sold Here, 1923 bottle, 20x28", NM .500.00
Sign, 1930s-40s, neon, CC in Bottles, on orig base, EX 2,000.00
Sign, 1931, cb, Tingling Refreshment, 20x36", VG 280.00
Sign, 1932, tin, Drink CC, trademk in tail of C, 5½x17¼", VG ...175.00
Sign, 1932, tin, Gas Today, CC Sold Here, 54x18", EX 900.00
Sign, 1933, porc, Fountain Service, 2-sided, 22x26", EX 750.00
Sign, 1933, tin, 1923 Christmas bottle, 28x20", EX 350.00
Sign, 1936, cb, Chinese girl on bench, 14½x22", NM 1,000.00
Sign, 1937, cb, girl w/bottle, Face the Sun..., 49x32", EX 650.00
Sign, 1938, cb, bathing girl on rocks, Sunbloom, 50x29", NM ..1,000.00
Sign, 1938, tin, Ice Cold Sold Here, for sidewalk, 28x20", EX ...275.00
Sign, 1939, cb, girl w/bike at rock wall, Niagara, 14x32", VG 200.00
Sign, 1939, porc, Fountain Service, dual taps, 14x27", NM 750.00
Sign, 1940, cb, girl at beach w/bottle, 50x30", EX 650.00
Sign, 1940, cb, girl at drink box, easel bk, 34x42", NM 800.00
Sign, 1940, cb, sailor girl, Good Ol' Pause..., 27x56", NM 650.00
Sign, 1940s, tin, cooler in ring w/arrow, Kay Displays, VG 575.00
Sign, 1942, cb, service girl, I Am Heading..., 27x16", EX 425.00
Sign, 1944, cb, cheerleader, Refresh Yourself, 27x16", NM 500.00
Sign, 1946, cb, boy & girl by pool, 50x29", EX 425.00
Sign, 1946, Yes, hand offers bottle to girl, 11x28", NM (+) 325.00
Sign, 1947, cb, Helene Madison, w/hanger, 13x15", EX 100.00
Sign, 1947, tin, emb bottle on sun logo, 54x18", NM 350.00
Sign, 1948, porc flange, Enjoy CC in Bottles, 2-sided, lg, EX 500.00
Sign, 1949, cb, tennis girl, 27x16", EX 350.00
Sign, 1950, cb, fishing girl, Play Refreshed, 27x56", EX 350.00
Sign, 1950, plastic, Work Safely, 12x14", NM 100.00
Sign, 1950s, celluloid, CC & bottle, 9" dia, NM 175.00
Sign, 1953, cb, Kit Carson, easel bk, 24x16", NM 150.00
Sign, 1954, cb, bird on bell, Come & Get It, 27x16", NM 125.00
Sign, 1954, tin, Refresh w/bottle, 54x18", NM 195.00
Sign, 1956, cb, girl offered bottle, cowboy, 2-sided, 27x16", EX .175.00
Sign, 1960s, tin, fishtail, 18x54", NM 160.00
Sign, 1960s, tin, Ice Cold w/fishtail, MCA, 20x28", EX 150.00
Sign, 1970s, cb, Bill Cosby, Have a...& a Smile, 66x32", EX 25.00
Sign, 1977, mirrored, John Pemberton/Asa Candler, 24x36", M ..350.00
Straw box, 1930s, bottle on 3 sides, cutout on front, EX 150.00
Straw box, 1940s, bottle ea side, Delicious & Refreshing, EX 125.00
Straw box, 1940s, bottle on ea side, torn lid, G 75.00
Straw box, 1950s, holds jumbo Sweetheart straws, NM 50.00
Tablet, 1949, Sprite Boy Safety ABCs, NM 5.00
Tap knob, 1940s-50s, enameled, 2-sided, NM 50.00
Thermometer, 1905, wood, 15x4", EX 350.00
Thermometer, 1915, pnt wood, all orig, 21x5", EX 325.00
Thermometer, 1930, tin, bottle shape, 16½x5", EX 275.00
Thermometer, 1931, emb tin, 1923 bottle, 16x7", EX 225.00
Thermometer, 1950, tin, bottle shape, Robertson, 17x5", EX 100.00
Thermometer, 1950s, glass front, gold bottle, 12" dia, NM 350.00
Thermometer, 1950s-60s, plastic, button top, 7", NM 60.00
Thermometer, 1955, tin, flat, 16", EX 90.00
Thermometer, 1956, gold bottle, 7½", NM in box 35.00
Thermometer, 1958-60, tin, bottle shape, 30", EX 100.00
Thermometer, 1960s, glass front, Enjoy, 12" dia, NM 100.00
Thermometer, 1960s, plastic, fishtail, 6x2½", NM 60.00
Tip tray, 1914, Betty, oval, 4¼x6", EX 165.00
Tip tray, 1959, Swedish smoke glass, 8x6", NM 50.00
Toy train, 1950s-60s, tin wind-up, 6-pc, Japan, EX 350.00
Toy truck, 1930s, Metalcraft, A-frame w/10 bottles, EX 550.00
Toy truck, 1940s, Louis Marx, stake type, red Sprite boy, EX 350.00
Toy truck, 1950s, Buddy L, Pause That Refreshes, VG 100.00
Toy truck, 1970s, Big Wheel, remote control, 10", NM in box ..450.00
Toy truck, 1970s, Buddy L delivery, MIB 65.00
Toy truck, 1970s, friction, Made in Japan, 3½", NM 150.00

Toy truck, 1970s, tin friction, #22 on car, NM	35.00
Wallet, 1920s, leather, gold lettering, 1915 bottle, EX	80.00
Wallet, 1920s-30s, leather, w/note pad inside, VG	20.00
Wallet, 1940s, pigskin, MIB	35.00
Waste paper basket, 1980s, metal, red & wht, M	10.00

Trays

Values are given for trays in excellent condition (C8). Those that have been reproduced are marked with a (+). The 1934 Weismuller and O'Sullivan tray has been reproduced at least three times. To be original, it must have a black back and must say 'American Artworks, Coshocton, Ohio.' It was not reproduced by Coca-Cola in the 1950s.

1901, Hilda Clark, 9¾" dia	3,750.00
1906, Juanita, 10½x13¼"	1,800.00
1907, Relieves Fatigue, 10½x13¼"	450.00
1909, St Louis Fair, 10½x13¼"	1,500.00
1909, St Louis Fair, 13½x16½"	2,000.00
1910, girl in lg hat, Hamilton King, 10½x13¼"	750.00
1913, girl in lg hat, Hamilton King, oval, 12¼x15¼"	750.00
1913, girl in lg hat, Hamilton King, 10½x13¼"	575.00
1914, Betty, oval, 12¼x15¼"	600.00
1914, Betty, 10½x13¼" (+)	575.00
1916, Elaine, 8½x19" (+)	550.00
1920, Garden Girl, oval, 12¼x15¼"	850.00
1920, Garden Girl, 10½x13¼"	725.00
1921, Autumn Girl, 10½x13¼"	625.00
1922, Summer Girl, 10½x13¼"	750.00
1923, Flapper, 10½x13¼"	400.00
1924, Smiling Girl, 10½x13¼"	625.00
1925, Party, 10½x13¼" (+)	400.00
1926, Golfers, 10½x13¼" (+)	500.00
1927, Curbside Service, 10½x13¼"	650.00
1928, Bobbed Hair, 10½x13¼"	500.00
1928, Soda Jerk, 10½x13¼"	625.00
1929, girl in swimsuit w/bottle, 10½x13¼"	450.00
1929, girl in swimsuit w/glass, 10½x13¼"	400.00
1930, Swimmer, 10½x13¼"	400.00

Tray, 1930, telephone, girl on phone, 10½x13¼", EX, $325.00.

1930, Telephone, 10½x13¼"	325.00
1931, boy w/sandwich & dog, 10½x13¼"	675.00
1932, girl in swimsuit on bench, Hayden, 10½x13¼"	575.00
1933, Francis Dee, 10½x13¼"	425.00
1934, Weismuller & O'Sullivan, 10½x13¼", $650.00 to	750.00
1935, Madge Evans, 10½x13¼"	325.00

1936, Hostess, 10½x13¼"	300.00
1937, Running Girl, 10½x13¼"	275.00
1938, Girl in Afternoon, 10½x13¼"	225.00
1939, Springboard Girl, 10½x13¼"	250.00
1940, Sailor Girl, 10½x13¼"	275.00
1941, Ice Skater, 10½x13¼"	250.00
1942, Roadster, 10½x13¼"	250.00
1950, Girl w/Wind in Hair, screened bkground, 10½x13¼"	60.00
1950, Girl w/Wind in Hair, solid bkground, 10½x13¼"	150.00
1955, Menu, 10½x13¼"	40.00
1957, Rooster, 10½x13¼"	125.00
1957, Umbrella Girl, 10½x13¼"	225.00
1961, Pansy Garden, 10½x13¼"	25.00

Vendors

Though interest in Coca-Cola machines of the 1949 — 1959 era rose dramatically over the last few years, values currently seem to have leveled off and actually dropped 15% to 20%. The major manufacturers of these curved-top, 5¢ and 10¢ machines were Vendo (V), Vendorlator (VMC), Cavalier (C or CS), and Jacobs. In the following listings, 'EX' values are for machines in clean, original condition.

Cavalier, model #CS72, EX orig	900.00
Cavalier, model #CS72, M rstr	2,500.00
Cavalier, model #C27, EX orig	1,400.00
Cavalier, model #C27, M rstr	3,000.00
Cavalier, model #C51, EX orig	650.00
Cavalier, model #C51, M rstr	2,000.00
Jacobs, model #26, EX orig	1,500.00
Jacobs, model #26, M rstr	3,000.00
Vendo, model #23, EX orig	650.00
Vendo, model #23, M rstr	1,500.00
Vendo, model #39, EX orig	850.00
Vendo, model #39, M rstr	2,250.00
Vendo, model #44, EX orig	2,000.00
Vendo, model #44, M rstr	3,500.00
Vendo, model #56, EX orig	1,200.00
Vendo, model #56, M rstr	3,000.00
Vendo, model #80, EX orig	650.00
Vendo, model #80, M rstr	1,500.00
Vendo, model #81, EX orig	1,250.00
Vendo, model #81, M rstr	3,000.00
Vendorlator, model #27, EX orig	1,500.00
Vendorlator, model #27, M rstr (on stand)	2,500.00
Vendorlator, model #27A, EX orig	800.00
Vendorlator, model #27A, M rstr	2,000.00
Vendorlator, model #33, EX orig	800.00
Vendorlator, model #33, M rstr	2,000.00
Vendorlator, model #44, EX orig	1,800.00
Vendorlator, model #44, M rstr	3,200.00
Vendorlator, model #72, EX orig	750.00
Vendorlator, model #72, M rstr	2,500.00

Coffee Grinders

The serious collector of kitchenwares and country store items rank coffee mills high on the list of desirable examples. A trend is developing toward preferring items whose manufacturers are easily identifiable. Names to look for include Adams, Arcade, Baldwin Bros., Daisy, Elgin National, Elma, Enterprise, Lane Bros., Parker, Regal, and Sun Mfg. Co.; there are many others. Any of these marks found on coffee mills represent companies who were in business at or before the turn of the century.

Side mills usually have a brass tag located on the tin hopper. If the hopper was made of cast iron, the name was usually cast into the metal. Some of the less expensive versions had no identification. Decals were often used on the front of lap mills and table styles, though sometimes you will find these decals on the inside of the drawer. Because decals are prone to flake off and fade, and since they are often destroyed when the mill is being refinished, lap and table mills are the most difficult types to attribute to a specific manufacturer. Canister mills had names and patent dates molded into the cast iron housing or on the canister itself. Commercial mills used in country and general stores were made of cast iron. Important information such as manufacture and patent dates was usually cast into the wheels, housing, or base of the mill. Such identification contributes considerably toward value.

Good examples of early coffee mills are rapidly becoming difficult to find. Beware of the many imported imposters that are on the market today.

Left to right: Table mill, Charles Parker, $125.00; Table mill, $95.00; Lap mill, Logan & Strobridge, $95.00; Miniature, Daisy, $85.00.

A Kendrick & Sons No 1, lap, CI w/brass hopper, CI drw 125.00
AK & Sons #237707, CI, octagon base, rnd hopper, heavy 185.00
American Beauty, canister, CI & tin, orig cup & papers 65.00
Arcade, Favorite No 7, side, CI w/orig lid 75.00
Arcade, Imperial, lap, CI closed hopper, wood box, EX 110.00
Arcade, Imperial, table, closed CI hopper, wood box 95.00
Arcade, IXL, table, ornate CI hopper, hdl on side, 1-lb, EX 175.00
Arcade, Jewel, canister, rectangular glass hopper, w/lid, EX 135.00
Arcade, table, w/decal, Pat 6-5-1884, 1-lb 95.00
Arcade, Telephone, canister, CI front, Pat Sept 25 '88 ....345.00
Arcade No 40, canister, CI & glass 95.00
Arcade No 700, lap, w/dust cover, Sears 1908 catalog, EX 95.00
Blksmith made, funnel shape, 1-hdl, open hopper, wall mt 225.00
C Ibach stamp on hdl, dvtl walnut, CI hopper 145.00
Coles Mfg No 7, counter, CI, Pat 1887, 16" wheels, 27", EX 675.00
Crescent, table, wood, top-fill, cylinder, 13" 225.00
Daisy No 667, miniature, CI top, wood box & drw, orig decal 80.00
Elgin Nat'l, floor, silver hopper, 24" wheels 1,100.00
Elgin Nat'l No 44, CI/red pnt, w/eagle & pan, 5" wheels, 24" 495.00
Elgin Nat'l No 48, CI w/eagle, orig lily decal, 2-wheel 525.00
Elma, counter, CI, closed hopper, 10" single wheel, 17" 145.00
Enterprise, counter, CI, brass hopper, Pat 1873, 6" wheels, EX ..525.00
Enterprise, counter, CI, eagle on hopper, 2-wheel, Pat 1873 ......525.00
Enterprise, floor, CI, CI hopper, Pat 1898, 39" wheels, VG 1,500.00
Enterprise, table clamp-on, CI w/CI cup, blk w/gold decal 65.00
Enterprise No 1, CI w/CI drw, hdl, covered hopper 225.00
Enterprise No 116½, floor, Pat 1873, 39" wheels, 72", EX 3,500.00
Enterprise No 12, counter, w/eagle, 2-wheel, Pat 1898 ....695.00

Enterprise No 9, CI, brass eagle, Pat 1898, 19" wheels, 28", VG ..750.00
Fairbanks Morse, floor, CI, brass hopper, 2-wheel, 72", EX 2,600.00
Golden Rule, canister, w/orig glass, CI front, wood box, EX 355.00
Grand Union Tea, table, CI sq base, rnd hopper, mfg Griswold .235.00
Griswold, coffee bean roaster, rnd, CI, wood hdl, 3-pc 595.00
Japy Freres, ornate woodwork, brass hopper, ftd 135.00
Juvenile, lap, CI, top, wood box, orig drw & decal, sm, EX 85.00
L'il Tot, miniature, CI hopper & drw front, wood box 80.00
L&S, side, CI, on orig brd 75.00
Landers, Frary & Clark, lap, fancy, CI top, wood box 95.00
Landers, Frary & Clark, Regal No 44, canister, CI & tin, orig 95.00
Landers, Frary & Clark, Universal No 14, table, Pat 1905, VG 85.00
Landers, Frary & Clark No 20, blk, 10" wheels 575.00
Landers, Frary & Clark No 50, counter, CI, 12" wheels, EX+ 550.00
Lees, canister, CI works, rnd glass hopper, EX 70.00
Logan & Strobridge, Franco-American, lap, ornate CI hopper ...125.00
Miniature, canister, boy & girl, 5½x1½" 85.00
Nat'l, coffee & spice counter, CI, 17" wheels, 28", VG 525.00
Nat'l, counter, CI works, covered hopper, wood drw, 1-wheel 85.00
Nat'l Specialty No 0, table clamp-on, CI, covered hopper 85.00
Nat'l Specialty...Philadelphia, CI, 25" wheels, VG 595.00
New Model, lap, CI w/CI drw, bottom opens all 4 sides 75.00
None Such, Bronson Co Cleveland OH, table, tin, pnt 75.00
Parker, Charles; table, tall/thin, CI & tin top, hdl on top 95.00
Parker, side, Pat 1876, CI, on orig brd, grind adj front 75.00
Parker (Chas) No 350, side, CI, orig lid, Pat 4/1876 ....75.00
Parker No 2, counter, CI w/orig decals, 9" wheels, EX 525.00
Parker No 449, canister, CI works, rnd glass hopper, VG 80.00
Parker No 5000, counter, CI, Pat 1897, 12" wheels, 17", VG 525.00
Parker No 555, Challenge Fast Grind, table, 1-lb, orig, EX 95.00
Parker No 60, side, tin hopper, brass eagle, Parker lid 75.00
Persepolis, table, CI & brass, unique 245.00
Primitive, lap, cherry, brass hopper, handmade/unique, 4x4" 175.00
Primitive, lap, dvtl, red buttermilk pnt, orig drw, pewter 165.00
Primitive, lap, dvtl walnut, wrought iron, brass hopper 165.00
PS&W No 3500, side, CI, orig lid, Britannia hopper 75.00
Queen, miniature, CI hopper & drw front, wood box, decal 80.00
Rock Hard, Garant-Sewaarborge, lap, imported 55.00
Russell & Erwin Mfg Co, lap, top adj, CI hopper, wood box 95.00
Russell & Erwin Mfg Co No 1008, CI hopper, wood box 90.00
Russell & Erwin Mfg Co No 60, britannia hopper, wood box 90.00
S&H, counter, CI, w/drw, 19" wheels, 21", VG 475.00
Star, canister, tin w/CI works, Pat 1910, VG 65.00
Star No 7, counter, CI, w/pan, 2-wheel, VG 450.00
Sun Mfg No 1080, Challenge Fast Grind, Columbus OH, table ...80.00
Sun No 1050 Improved, lap, wood, tin hopper 85.00
Swift, side, CI, Pat 1845, Pat Aug 16, 1859, top missing 95.00
Swift No 15, counter, orig decals/pnt, Pat 1875, 19" wheels 875.00
Tin, lap, covered, grind caught in cup underneath 55.00
Universal No 109, blk tin w/gr decal, Pat 1905, EX 95.00
W Cross & Sons, lap, CI w/orig CI drw, brass hopper & pull 85.00
Walton, Bronson, canister, tin & CI, Pat 1911 ....80.00
Wilson, Increase, side, CI & tin 60.00
WW Weaver Warranted, dvtl walnut, pewter hopper, ca 1830 ..195.00

Coin-Operated Machines

Coin-operated machines may be the fastest-growing area of collector interest in today's market. Many machines are bought, restored, and used for home entertainment. Older examples from the turn of the century and those with especially elaborate decoration and innovative accessories are most desirable.

Vending machines sold a product or a service. They were already in common usage by 1900 selling gum, cigars, matches, and a host of other commodities. Peanut and gumball machines are especially popular today. The most valuable are those with their original finish and decals. Older machines made of cast iron are especially desirable, while those with plastic globes have little or no collector value. When buying unrestored peanut machines, beware of salt damage.

The coin-operated phonograph of the early 1900s paved the way for the jukeboxes of the twenties. Seeburg was first on the market with an automatic 8-tune phonograph. By the 1930s Wurlitzer was the top name in the industry with dealerships all over the country. As a result of the growing ranks of competitors, the forties produced the most beautiful machines made. Wurlitzers from this era are probably the most popularly sought-after models on the market today. The model #1015 of 1946 is considered the all-time classic and often brings prices in excess of $7,000.00.

Coin-Op Newsletter; Jukebox Collectors' Newsletter; Chicagoland Antique Amusements, Slot Machine, and Jukebox Gazette; and *Classic Amusements Magazine* are all excellent publications for those interested in coin-operated machines; see the Clubs, Newsletters, and Catalogs section of the Directory for publishing information.

Jackie and Ken Durham are our advisors (for all but jukeboxes); they are listed in the Directory under the District of Columbia. Our advisor for jukeboxes is Norman Nelson; he is listed in the Directory under Ohio.

Arcade Machines

Buckley Jewel Box Digger, floor model, EX 1,600.00
Buckley Treasure Chest Digger, table model, rstr 1,450.00
Caille Mickey Finn Strength Tester, rstr 4,500.00
Exhibit Supply, astrology cards, 12-column, EX 1,500.00
Exhibit Supply Bl Streak 5¢ Digger, rstr 1,995.00
Exhibit Supply Crystal Gazer, floor model, rstr 1,450.00
Exhibit Supply Crystal Palace Digger 1,600.00
Exhibit Supply Grandfather's Clock, ca 1925, VG orig 2,500.00
Exhibit Supply Monarch Digger 1,950.00
Exhibit Supply 1¢ Strength Tester, CI, 50x14x24", EX rstr 600.00
Exhibit Supply 5¢ Merchantman Digger, rstr 2,000.00
Gottlieb Bank-A-Ball, pinball, 1950s, EX orig 425.00
Grandma Fortune Teller, oak, EX orig 3,950.00
Gypsy Fortune Teller, oak, EX orig 3,950.00
Hunter Duck Shooting 1¢, gum, 20x10x24"+stand, VG 275.00
Iron Claw Digger, floor model, early, rstr 3,450.00
Jennings Indian 1¢ Hit the Target, EX orig 595.00
Mercury Strength Tester, rstr 495.00
Mills Punching Bag, rstr 2,500.00
Mutoscope, tin, 1940s style, w/stand, rstr 1,200.00
Mutoscope Model C Clamshell, rstr 4,500.00
Rockola World Series, pinball, EX 2,000.00
Seeburg Coon Hunt, rstr 1,950.00
Shake Hands w/Uncle Sam, EX orig 3,500.00

Jukeboxes

AMI #100, rstr 1,100.00
AMI #1200, EX orig 1,750.00
AMI I, EX orig 2,150.00
AMI Streamliner, 1938, EX orig 2,800.00
Cremona G, rstr 12,000.00
Rockola #1426, rstr 3,500.00
Rockola #1428, EX orig 3,000.00
Rockola #1434, EX orig 1,200.00
Rockola #1468, EX orig 1,600.00
Rockola #1475, G 1,600.00

Rockola #39, counter top, EX orig 2,500.00
Rockola Empress, 1959, EX orig 1,500.00
Rockola Monarch, 1938, EX orig 850.00
Rockola Princess, EX orig 900.00
Rockola Rocket, EX orig 750.00
Seeburg #147, blond trash can, EX orig 1,500.00
Seeburg #222, rstr 2,750.00
Seeburg A, EX 850.00
Seeburg A, rstr 2,500.00
Seeburg B, EX orig 1,500.00
Seeburg B, rstr 2,750.00
Seeburg C, rstr 3,000.00
Seeburg DS-100, EX 1,200.00
Seeburg E, oak w/xylophone, EX orig 8,500.00
Seeburg G, EX 1,600.00
Seeburg HF-100R, M 2,200.00
Seeburg KD-200, M rstr 3,350.00
Seeburg R, EX orig 2,400.00
Seeburg Select-O-Matic 200 Console, complete w/100 records ..880.00
Seeburg V-100, rstr 3,500.00
Seeburg V-200, G orig 1,800.00
Wurlitzer #1100, rstr 6,000.00
Wurlitzer #1250, G 800.00
Wurlitzer #1650, rstr 750.00
Wurlitzer #1700, EX orig 2,250.00
Wurlitzer #1700, NM 2,600.00
Wurlitzer #1900, EX orig 1,500.00
Wurlitzer #2000, EX 2,000.00
Wurlitzer #2150, EX orig 1,650.00
Wurlitzer #24, VG orig 1,800.00
Wurlitzer #3100, EX orig 450.00
Wurlitzer #3800, EX orig 750.00
Wurlitzer #4002, speaker model, EX orig 325.00
Wurlitzer #51, counter top, 1937, NM 1,800.00
Wurlitzer #750, G orig 5,000.00
Wurlitzer #780E, EX orig 3,250.00
Wurlitzer P-12 #9714, walnut case, 1936, EX orig 900.00

Slot Machines

Bally #808, EX orig 1,500.00

Bally 5¢ Spark Plug horse race, wooden case with metal front, 14x16x11", EX, $2,600.00.

Buckley Track Odds, EX orig 2,200.00
Caille Detroit, floor model, 1898, EX orig 7,500.00
Caille 10¢ Superior, EX orig 1,100.00
Caille 25¢ Superior Jackpot, 34x14x14", EX 1,600.00
Dollar Pace, ca 1940s 1,200.00
Fields Five Jacks, EX orig 1,100.00
Jennings Chrome Bell Diamond Front, 1939, VG 1,600.00

Jennings Improved Century Bell, 1933, EX orig 1,800.00
Jennings Little Duke, M rstr 2,650.00
Jennings Today Bell, w/vendor, 1926, EX orig 1,500.00
Jennings 25¢ Standard Chief, EX orig 1,650.00
Jennings 5¢ Club Chief, EX orig 1,650.00
Jennings 5¢ Mint of Quality, EX 1,100.00
Jennings 5¢ Standard Chief, M rstr 2,350.00
Jennings 5¢ Sun Chief, EX orig 1,500.00
Jennings 5¢ Victoria, mints, rstr 1,800.00
Mills Owl Jr, counter top, 1899, EX 3,000.00
Mills QT, M rstr 2,250.00
Mills Roman Head, M rstr 2,950.00
Mills Skyscraper, M rstr 2,350.00
Mills 10¢ Castle Front, M rstr 2,350.00
Mills 10¢ Extra Bell, M rstr 2,950.00
Mills 25¢ Blk Cherry, M rstr 2,150.00
Mills 25¢ Bursting Cherry, M rstr 2,450.00
Mills 25¢ Counter OK, rstr 2,450.00
Mills 25¢ Futurity, EX orig 2,500.00
Mills 25¢ Golden Nugget, open front, EX 950.00
Mills 25¢ Golden Nugget, rstr 2,250.00
Mills 25¢ Hi Top, M rstr 1,950.00
Mills 25¢ Horse Head, M rstr 2,800.00
Mills 5¢ Diamond Front, EX orig 1,400.00
Mills 5¢ Golden Falls, M rstr 2,395.00
Mills 5¢ Golden Nugget, rstr 2,250.00
Mills 5¢ Lion's Head, M rstr 2,450.00
Mills 5¢ Poinsettia, EX orig 1,750.00
Mills 5¢ War Eagle, M rstr 2,750.00
Mills 5¢-25¢ Double Dewey, rstr 26,500.00
Pace All Star Comet, EX orig 1,650.00
Pace All Star Comet, M rstr 2,150.00
Pace Bantam, M rstr 2,150.00
Pace 25¢ Comet, EX orig 1,550.00

Watling 5¢ Brownie Jackpot, 6-coin model, oak case, 27x16x9", EX original, $3,500.00.

Watling Bl Seal, M rstr 2,150.00
Watling Rol-A-Top, M rstr 3,300.00
Watling Treasury, M rstr 3,300.00

Trade Stimulators

Aristocrat Moneymaker 1,200.00
Bluebird 1¢, penny flip, w/gum dispenser, EX orig 300.00
Caille 1¢ Baseball, 1-reel, 1911, EX orig 3,500.00
Caille 1¢ Reliance, 5-reel, 1904, EX orig 1,800.00
Circus motif, penny flip 275.00
Daval Am Eagle, EX orig 300.00
Daval Cent-A-Pack, EX orig 425.00

Daval Clearing House, 3-reel, 1936, VG 495.00
Exhibit Supply Horseshoes, 1935, EX orig 275.00
Groetchen Mercury, EX orig 250.00
Groetchen 1¢ Highstakes, 5-reel, 1936, EX orig 650.00
Groetchen 5¢ Dixie Dominoes, 5-reel, 1937, EX orig 450.00
Jennings 5¢ Good Luck, wooden case, electric console, EX 1,500.00
Kicker-Catcher, skill football game, 18x14x12", VG 550.00
Klix, 5-reel, EX 350.00
Marvel 1¢, cigarettes & gum, 3-reel, 9½x8x11", G 250.00
Mills Commercial, G 4,500.00
Mills Little Perfection, 4-reel, oak, 1926, 16", EX 950.00
Mills Monte Carlo, ca 1900, EX orig 5,000.00
Pace New Deal, 5-reel, 1935, EX orig 495.00
Penny Ante Draw Poker, 1930s, 10x8x9", EX rstr 350.00
Rockola Official Sweepstakes, EX orig 1,200.00
Rockola Radio Wizard, EX orig 600.00
Rockola World Series, pinball, EX orig 1,200.00
Scramball Gambling, mc balls on ramps, 19", EX 175.00
Sparky 5¢ Poker, 5-reel, flat top, EX orig 200.00
Stephen's 5¢ Beer Barrel, counter top, w/pretzel vendor, G 850.00
Sun Bicycle, 2-wheel, EX orig 3,750.00
Wings, 5-reel, EX 350.00

Vendors

Ad-Lee E-Z, gumball, rstr 495.00
Advance 1¢ Matches, glass dome, CI, counter top, 18", G orig ..650.00
Atlas Bantam 5¢, rstr 95.00
Atlas Master, gum, glass globe, 1950s, EX orig 95.00
Blk Baker Boy, gum, animated, 16x8x6", EX orig 4,000.00
Columbus K, gum, EX orig 365.00
Columbus M, hexagonal globe, EX 225.00
Ford 1¢, gum, 1920s, EX orig 75.00
Hanse 1¢ Peanuts, glass globe, 14", EX orig 1,400.00
Lucky 10¢ Horoscope, 18x8x6", G 50.00
Mills 5¢, postage stamps, cast pot metal, oak case, 22x11x8", EX ..1,750.00
Northwestern Tab, gumball, w/key, EX 75.00
Northwestern 1¢, matches, CI w/dolphins, 13½", G orig 250.00
Penny King, 4 in 1, early version, EX orig 825.00
Pulver, clown figure, yel case, EX 700.00
Pulver 1¢ Yel Kid, gum, earliest version, 24x14x11", G 4,750.00
Selmor 1¢, peanuts, CI, EX orig 225.00
Shipman Mfg 10¢, postage cards, 3 cards for 10¢, EX 175.00
Victor Selectorama, capsules, early, EX 85.00
Zeno 1¢, gum, oak case, 16x10x9", VG 700.00

Miscellaneous

Brandt, coin counter 300.00
Caille Washington, scale, wood & CI, full sz, 76", VG 2,900.00
Dayton, 'Moneyweight' marque, platform type, 32x19x20", EX ..800.00
Exhibit Supply Photo Scope, w/stand, EX 475.00
Pace Scale, rstr 445.00
Watling Horoscope Scale, rstr 650.00
Watling Lollipop Scale, EX orig 1,400.00

Comic Books

For almost sixty years, the American public has been thrilled by the monthly adventures of everyone's favorite comic book heroes such as Superman, Captain Marvel, and Spiderman. Each 10¢ comic book issue, featuring a new saga of adventure and mystery, were usually met with excitement and anticipation by the youngsters who eagerly purchased them from their neighborhood candy store or newsstand. Unfortunately, the vast majority of these comic books were eventually discarded in favor of other worldly pursuits. Due to this fact, most comic books from the '30s and '40s did not survive, making them a very scarce and desirable collectible in today's world.

First editions in high-grade condition may bring prices as high as $500.00 or more. Marvel Comics #1, published in October 1939, has sold for the astounding price of $35,000.00. Rarity, age, and quality of artwork are prime factors in determining comic book values. Condition is also very important. A good copy of Showcase #4 (the first appearance of the silver-age Flash) might sell for around $350.00, but a copy of the same book would sell for $7,000.00 in near-mint condition. Some of the better comic books are evaluated below, but many are worth much less. Refer to a good comic book price guide if you decide to buy or sell to any great extent. In the listings that follow, those lines ending with an 'A' describe comics books that recently sold through one of the country's major auction houses.

Human Torch, Volume 1, #38, Chipiden Publishing, August 1954, EX, $120.00.

Action Comics, #28, DC Comics, VG 155.00
Adventures of the Fly, #18, Archie Adventure Series, VG 9.00
All American Men of War, #13, DC Comics, VG 18.00
Amazing Fantasy, #15, Marvel, August 1962, G-, A 800.00
Animal Comics, #5, Mile High, Dell, 1943, NM, A 225.00
Astonishing Tales, #1, Marvel, 1970, NM 20.00
Batman, #210, DC Comics, EX 4.00
Battlefield Action, #23, CDC, 1959, VG 12.00
Best of Donald Duck & Uncle Scrooge, Gold Key, 1964, VG 9.00
Billy the Kid, #3, Toby, 1951, EX, A 50.00
Blackhawk, Son of Blackhawk; #180, Superman DC, 1963, VG ..12.50
Bride's Secrets, #1, Ajax, 1954, EX 12.00
Buck Rogers, #1, Mile High, 1933, M, A 2,200.00
Buck Rogers, #3, Mile High, 1933, EX, A 236.00
Buckskin, #1011, Dell, 1959, G 5.00
Buster Crabbe, #5, Mile High, Famous Funnies, 1952, EX, A 500.00
Captain Marvel, #1, Marvel, 1968, EX 45.00
Captain Marvel Jr, #75, Fawcett, VG 10.00
Conan the Barbarian, #1, Marvel, October 1970, NM, A 88.00
Demon, #1, DC Comics, 1972, EX 15.00
Dennis the Menace TV Special, #1, Fawcett, 1961, EX 17.00
Don Winslow, #1, Fawcett, Captain Marvel cover, VG, A 170.00
Donald Duck, #203, Dell 4-Color, 1948, EX, A 130.00
Donald Duck Adventures, #1, Disney, NM 3.50
Earthman on Venus, Wood art, Avon Fantasy Classic, 1951, G, A .140.00
Ellery Queen Detective, #1289, Dell, 1962, G 5.00
Famous Feature Stories, #1, Dell, 1938, EX, A 150.00
Fantastic Four, #10, Marvel, EX 142.50
Fighting Army, #27, CDC, VG 8.50
Flash Gordon, #1, Harvey, dbl cover, October 1950, EX, A 105.00
Flash Gordon, #10, Dell 4-Color, 1943, G, A 215.00
Flintstones Bigger & Boulder, #1, Gold Key, 1962, EX 20.00

Flip, #1, Harvey, 1954, G 12.00
Forbidden Worlds, #102, 1961, VG 3.50
Gene Autry March of Comics, #39, K&K, 1949, EX, A 50.00
Gene Autry's Champion, #16, Dell, VG 8.50
Gidget, #1, Dell, 1966, EX 18.00
Honah Hex, #1, DC Comics, 1977, NM 14.00
John Wayne Adventure Comics, #1, Toby Press, 1949, EX, A ...625.00
Journey Into Fear, #1, Superior-Dynamic, 1951, G 24.00
Little Lulu, #145, Dell 4-Color, VG 55.00
Lone Ranger, #114, Dell, 1957, G 8.00
Lone Ranger, #82, Dell 4-Color, 1945, G, A 70.00
Man Thing, #1, Marvel, 1974, NM 14.00
Maverick, #980, Dell, 1959, G 5.00
Nomad, #1, Marvel, 1992, M 4.50
Pogo Parade, #1, Mile High, Dell, 1953, NM, A 325.00
Pogo Possum, #9, Dell, 1952, NM, A 65.00
Prince Valiant Feature Book, #26, Ace-David McKay, '37, EX, A .500.00
Rin Tin Tin & Rusty, #31, Dell, 1959, VG 6.50
Roy Rogers, #95, Mile High, Dell 4-Color, 1945, NM, A 285.00
Sergeant Preston of Yukon, #29, Dell, 1959, G 7.00
Shadow, #1, DC Comics, 1973, NM 25.00
Shadow Comics, #1, Mile High, 1940, NM, A 5,400.00
Smiley Burnett Western, #1, Fawcett, 1950, G, A 65.00
Space Busters, #1, Krigstein, Spring 1952, EX, A 270.00
Space Patrol, #1, Krigstein, EX, A 130.00
Space War, #3, CDC, 1960, G 6.50
Spy Thrillers, #1, Atlas, 1954, EX, A 70.00
Star Trek, #2, Gold Key, June 1968, EX, A 100.00
Star Trek, #4, Gold Key, June 1969, EX, A 40.00
Strange Tales, #101, Marvel, October 1962, VG, A 110.00
Strange Worlds, #3, Avon, June 1951, EX, A 390.00
Strange Worlds, #5, Avon, November 1951, EX, A 175.00
Superman, #137, DC Comics, EX 27.50
Superman, #171, Superman DC, VG 16.00
Swamp Thing, #1, DC Comics, Nov 1972, M, A 33.00
Tailspin Tommy, #1, Service Publishing, G, A 40.00
Tales of Asgard, Marvel, 1968, NM 27.50

Tarzan's Jungle Annual #2, 1953, EX, $40.00.

Thunda King of the Congo, #1, Mile High, NM, A 975.00
Undersea Fighting Commandos, #1, Avon, 1952, VG 7.00
US Air Force, #24, CDC, 1962, G 7.50
Walt Disney's Comics & Stories, #57, K&K, 1945, NM, A 90.00
Walt Disney's Comics & Stories, #65, K&K, 1946, VG, A 35.00
Walt Disney's Vacation Parade, #1, Dell Giant, 1950, NM, A ..1,050.00

Compacts

The use of cosmetics before WWI was looked upon with disdain. After the war women became liberated, entered the work force, and started to use cosmetics. The compact, a portable container for cosmetics, became a necessity. The basic compact contains a mirror and a powder puff.

The vintage compacts were fashioned in a myriad of shapes, styles, materials, and motifs. They were made of precious metals, fabrics, plastics, and in almost any other conceivable medium imaginable. Commemorative, premium, patriotic, figural, Art Deco, plastic and gadgetry compacts are just a few of the most sought-after types available today. Those that are combined with other accessories (music/compact, watch/compact, cane/compact) are also very much in demand. Vintage compacts are an especially desirable collectible since the workmanship, design, techniques, and materials used in their execution would be very expensive and virtually impossible to duplicate today.

Our advisor, Roselyn Gerson, has written two highly informative books, *Ladies' Compacts of the 19th and 20th Centuries* and *Vintage Vanity Bags and Purses*, the first book devoted solely to bags and purses that incorporate compacts. She is listed in the Directory under the state of New York. See Clubs and Newsletters for information concerning the compact collectors' club and their periodical publication, *The Powder Puff*.

Ame La May, Victorian lady w/emb flowers, German silver, 2⅛" .35.00
Best, gold plated, horse & pony in smooth gold & wht, 2¾" 35.00
BHS Burlington, gold w/blk enameling & pennant, 2⅝" 20.00
Coty, wht feather on lt bl celluloid, 1⅞x½" 12.50
Coty, Wishbone, dbl vanity, 4x3¾x3¼", M 45.00
Elgin, brushed silver w/gold-tone grapes & blk moire, 4x3" 65.00
Evening in Paris, Bourgois NY, dbl vanity, silver & bl, MIB 100.00
Fitch, blk metal w/lt bl celluloid inlay, rouge, rnd, EX 20.00

Dorothy Gray oval gold-tone compact, lid decorated with rhinestones and black enamel harlequin mask, ca 1940s, $125.00.

Gold mesh w/wht marbleized celluloid lid, 2¼" dia 22.50
Gold plated, center crown over shield, Deco, octagonal, 2x2¼" ...20.00
Houbigant, chrome, Deco diagonal lines, octagonal, 3½" 40.00
Leather, gold w/wht flowers & blk stems, horseshoe shape, 3" 27.50
Leather, metal fr w/snap closure, tooled mc Deco design, 2¾" 38.00
MOP, wht w/3 overlapping dmns in rainbow colors, 2¾x2½" 35.00
Needlepoint, mc flowers on blk fabric, 2¾" sq 38.00
Pocket watch form, HP figures in garden, Fr, 2" dia 125.00
Rex, Zell in gold, gold top w/flowers, bl bottom, 4¼", M 40.00
Rex 5th Ave, SP, w/cloth bag, 4¾", M in bl box w/crown 150.00
Rhinestones & red stone on brn shaded enamel, 2" 22.50
Richard Hudnut, gold & wht w/sunburst, vanity, 3⅜", MIB 45.00
Richard Hudnut, gold top w/decor, 4¼x4⅛", MIB 50.00
Richard Hudnut, gr & gold cloisonne, attached lipstick 250.00
Shields, rhinestones & wht metal figure on blk enamel, 3x2" 38.00
SP, gold map of MA, 2¾x2½" 20.00
Volupte, champleve style w/mc florals, 4" dia 38.00
Yardley, bl & wht enamel w/red clasp, rouge & powder, 3¼x2" 40.00
800 silver, textured finish w/eng flower center, 2¼" 75.00

Consolidated Lamp and Glass

The Consolidated Lamp and Glass Company of Coraopolis, Pennsylvania, was incorporated in 1894. For many years their primary business was the manufacture of lighting glass such as oil lamps and shades for both gas and electric lighting. The popular 'Cosmos' line of lamps and tableware was produced from 1894 to 1915. (See also Cosmos.) In 1926 Consolidated introduced their Martele line, a type of 'sculptured' ware closely resembling Lalique glassware of France. (Compare Consolidated's 'Lovebirds' vase with the Lalique 'Perruches' vase.) It is this line of vases, lamps, and tableware which is often mistaken for a very similar type of glassware produced by the Phoenix Glass Company, located nearby in Monaca, Pennsylvania. For example, the so-called Phoenix 'Grasshopper' vases are actually Consolidated's 'Katydid' vases.

Items in the Martele line were produced in blue, pink, green, crystal, white, or custard glass decorated with various fired-on color treatments or a satin finish. For the most part, their colors were distinctively different from those used by Phoenix. Although not foolproof, one of the ways of distinguishing Consolidated's wares from those of Phoenix is that most of the time Consolidated applied color to the raised portion of the design, leaving the background plain, while Phoenix usually applied color to the background, leaving the raised surfaces undecorated. This is particularly true of those pieces in white or custard glass.

In 1928 Consolidated introduced their Ruba Rombic line, which was their Art Deco or Art Moderne line of glassware. It was only produced from 1928-1932 and is quite scarce. Today it is highly sought after by both Consolidated and Art Deco collectors.

Consolidated closed its doors for good in 1964. Subsequently a few of the molds passed into the hands of other glass companies that later reproduced certain patterns; one such reissue is the 'Chickadee' vase, found in avocado green, satin-finish custard, or milk glass. Our advisor for this category is Jack D. Wilson, author of *Phoenix and Consolidated Art Glass, 1926 - 1980*; he is listed in the Directory under Illinois.

Key: mg — milk glass

Bird of Paradise, ceiling light, custard, sq, 15" 1,450.00
Blackberry, umbrella vase, gold highlights on glossy mg, 18" 500.00
Catalonian, candlestick, #1124 ....35.00
Catalonian, cigarette box, honey, #1107 ....45.00
Catalonian, flower bowl, honey, #1130 ....85.00
Catalonian, vase, pk satin, pinch bottle form, 6" 125.00
Chickadee, vase, brn wash on crystal, 6¼" 110.00
Chintz, vase, lav & blk, #2102, chips, rare 225.00
Chrysanthemum, vase, 2-color highlights on satin mg, 12¼" 150.00
Cockatoo, light shade, pk cased, rare, 10x7", 4" fitter 350.00
Cockatoo, vase, straw opal, ormolu mts, rare, 9" 450.00
Con-Cora, vase, violets decor 45.00
Con-Cora/Tropical Fish, vase, straw opal, 9" 225.00
Dancing Nymph, goblet, frosted, 5¼" 85.00
Dancing Nymph, goblet, pk frosted, 5¼" 100.00
Dancing Nymph, plate, frosted, 8" 75.00
Dogwood, lamp, 3-color highlights on satin mg 125.00
Dragonfly, vase, gold on glossy custard, 6" 175.00
Five Fruits, plate, brn wash, 12" 95.00
Five Fruits, plate, French Crystal, 14" 100.00
Five Fruits, tumbler, gr wash, ftd, 5" 30.00
Florentine, vase, gr, #2201, 6½" 185.00
Hummingbird, powder jar, purple wash, 5" dia 75.00
Jonquil, vase, rose & gr highlighting on satin custard, 6¼" 95.00
Line 700, bowl, lt gr wash, flared rim, 7" 45.00
Line 700, vase, gold highlights on custard, 10" 450.00
Line 700, vase, red w/satin bkground, 7" 300.00

Line 700, vase, yellow wash, 7x8", $120.00.

Lovebirds, table lamp, gr opal, brass fixture, 28"	200.00
Lovebirds, vase, straw opal, ormolu mts, rare	295.00
Mermaid, bowl, plain crystal, 9"	85.00
Ruba Rombic, ashtray, Lilac	325.00
Ruba Rombic, ashtray, Smoky Topaz	400.00
Ruba Rombic, candle holder, Lilac	65.00
Ruba Rombic, ceiling shade, Sunshine, 16" wide, 6" fitter	1,250.00
Ruba Rombic, cigarette box, Jungle Gr	400.00
Ruba Rombic, lamp, metal nude ea side, Kopp cylinder shade	1,500.00
Ruba Rombic, plate, salad; Jade Gr, 8"	85.00
Ruba Rombic, shot glass, Jade Gr, 2¾"	250.00
Ruba Rombic, sugar bowl, Jungle Gr, 3"	150.00
Ruba Rombic, tumbler, Sunshine, 9-oz	75.00
Ruba Rombic, vase, Jade Gr, bottom drilled, 9½"	1,250.00
Ruba Rombic, vase, Jade Gr, 6½"	700.00
Ruba Rombic, vase, Smoky Topaz, 9½"	350.00
Ruba Rombic, whiskey decanter, Smoky Topaz	1,700.00
Screech Owl, vase, wht wash, 6"	85.00
Sea Gulls, vase, ruby-stained reverse highlights on crystal, 11"	225.00
Tropical Fish, bowl, amethyst, flaws, 15¾"	450.00

Cookbooks

Cookbooks from the 19th century, though often hard to find, are a delight to today's collectors both for their quaint formats and printing methods as well as for their outmoded, often humorous views on nutrition. Recipes required a 'pinch' of salt, butter 'the size of an egg' or a 'walnut,' or a 'handful' of flour. Collectors sometimes specialize in cookbooks issued as advertising premiums. Especially desirable are the figurals that were shaped like a jar, a slice of bread, or some other form relative to the product. Others with unique features such as illustrations by well-known artists or references to famous people or places are priced in accordance. Cookbooks written earlier than 1874 are the most valuable and when found command prices as high as $200.00; figurals usually sell in the $10.00 to $15.00 range.

As is true with all other books, if the original dust jacket is present and in nice condition, a cookbook's value goes up by at least $5.00. Right now, books on Italian cooking from before circa 1940 are in demand, and bread-baking is important this year. For further information we recommend *A Guide to Collecting Cookbooks* by Col. Bob Allen and *Price Guide to Cookbooks and Recipe Leaflets* by Linda Dickinson. Our advisor for this category is Charlotte Safir; she is listed in the Directory under New York.

Key:
CB — cookbook   dj — dust jacket

Art of Baking Bread, 1920s	10.00
Betty Crocker, Good & Easy, spiral bound, 1973	7.50
Betty Crocker, Party Book, spiral bound, 1960	8.00
Budget Gourmet, Sylvia V Thompson, 1962	3.00
Camp Cookery, Horace Kephart, 1926	12.00
Campbell's Cooking w/Soup, spiral bound, 1970	7.50
Casserole Treasury, Brunner, w/dust jacket, 1964	8.50
Chafing Dish, Sternau, 1900	16.00
Come to Our Barbeque, Taylor Wine, 1958	6.00
Crescent Baking Powder Recipes for Every Day, 1920s	5.00
Desserts & Salads, Lemcke, 1932	20.00
Easy Meals, Caroline F Benton, 325-pg, 1st ed, 1913	30.00
Fireside Cookbook, James Beard, 322-pg, 1949, VG	12.00
Good Housekeeping's Good Meals & How To Prepare Them, 1927	10.00

Healthful Cookery by Mary Dunbar, Jewel Tea, 1926, VG, $38.00.

Jack Bailey's What's Cookin', 1949, EX	12.00
New Dishes From Leftovers, Coral Smith, 1935	20.00
New York Cookbook, Jane Astor, 1880	45.00
Out of Kentucky Kitchens, Duncan Hines, 1949	12.00
Party Recipe Ideas, Martha Logan, 1962	3.00
Peterson's National Cookbook, Hannah M Peterson, 1891	50.00
Pickle & Relish Recipes, US Dept of Agriculture, 1944	4.00
Pressure Cooking, Ida Bailey Allen, 1949	8.00
Recipe Book, Fisherman's Grotto, 1930	10.00
Settlement Cookbook, Kander, Milwaukee, 1943, 622-pg, EX	12.00
Time-Saving Recipes, Sarah Field Splint, 1922	25.00
Vegetable Cookbook, Cora Rose & Bob Brown, 1939	20.00
101 Desserts, May E Southworth, 1907	40.00

Cookie Cutters

Early hand-fashioned cookie cutters have recently been commanding stiff prices at country auctions, and the ranks of interested collectors are growing steadily. Especially valuable are the figural cutters; and the more complicated the design, the higher the price. A follow-up of the carved wooden cookie boards, the first cutters were probably made by itinerant tinkers from leftover or recycled pieces of tin. Though most of the 18th-century examples are now in museums or collections, it is still possible to find some good cutters from the late 1800s when changes in the manufacture of tin resulted in a thinner, less expensive material. The width of the cutting strip is often a good indicator of age; the wider the strip, the older the cutter. While the very early cutters were 1" to 1½" deep, by the twenties and thirties, many were less than ½" deep. Crude, spotty soldering indicates an older cutter, while a thin line of solder usually tends to suggest a much later manufacture. The shape of the backplate is another clue. Later cutters will have oval, round, or rectangular backs, while on the earlier type the back was cut to follow the lines of the design. Cookie cutters usually vary from 2" to 4" in size, but gingerbread men were often made as tall as 12". Birds, fish, hearts, and tulips are common; simple versions can be purchased for as little as $12.00 to $15.00. The larger figurals, especially those with more imaginative details, often bring $75.00 and up. The cookie cutters listed here are tin and handmade unless noted otherwise.

Animals, aluminum w/stamped-out strap hdl, 1¼", 6 for **7.50**
Animals: elephant/rabbit/rooster/bear/horse/squirrel, open sided ..**125.00**
Bird, tin, flat bk, 6" **60.00**
Bird in flight, tin, w/bk & strap hdl, 3¾x2½" **18.00**
Bird standing, tin, w/bk & strap hdl, 2⅞x1½" **20.00**
Bird w/long neck, tin, flat bk, 5" **40.00**
Boar, tin, w/hdl, 2⅞x5⅞" **35.00**
Cat sitting, tin, w/bk & strap hdl, 3¾x2½" **30.00**
Chick, tin, hdl only **15.00**
Chick, tin, w/bk & strap hdl **23.00**
Dog, tin, w/bk & strap hdl, 4x3" **18.00**
Duck, tin, w/bk & strap hdl, 4x3" **18.00**
Dutchman, tin, w/bk & strap hdl, 5¼x2¾" **40.00**
Eagle w/crimped wings, tin, no hdl, 4⅛x4½" **25.00**
Fish, tin, 5½" **35.00**
Half moon, tin hdl only **12.00**
Heart, tin, hdl only **12.00**
Heart, tin, w/bk & strap hdl, 2⅞x2⅞" **20.00**
Hen, tin, w/bk & strap hdl, 3⅝x3⅞" **22.00**
High-heeled boot, handmade, 1800s, 4⅝" **45.00**
Horse, tin, flat bk, EX workmanship, 6½" L **170.00**
Horse, tin, flat bk, primitive, 7¾" **105.00**
Horse, tin, w/bk & strap hdl, 3½x2¾" **26.00**
Horse running, tin, w/bk & strap hdl, 4⅜x3⅛" **65.00**
Lizard, tin, w/hdl, 3⅛x6½" **45.00**
Penguin standing, tin, w/bk & strap hdl, 3⅝x2½" **24.00**
Rabbit, tin, no hdl, 5x8¾" **30.00**
Rabbit, tin, w/bk & strap hdl, 6½x5" **50.00**
Rabbit running, tin, w/bk & strap hdl, 4x2⅛" **18.00**
Reindeer, tin, no hdl, EX workmanship, 4¾x5" **175.00**
Rocking horse, tin, flat bk, primitive, 1880s, 4x7½" **55.00**
Rocking horse, tin, w/bk & strap hdl, 4¾x4⅜" **45.00**
Round, aluminum w/stamped-out strap hdl, 1¼" dia **2.50**
Santa, tin, open bk, no hdl, Germany, 8½x4⅛" **55.00**
Scalloped rectangle, tin, w/bk & strap hdl, 3⅞x3" **12.00**
Stag, stylized, tin, flat bk, 6½" **135.00**
Stag, tin, flat bk, EX workmanship, 8½" **300.00**
Swan, tin, w/bk & strap hdl, 2⅞x2¾" **35.00**

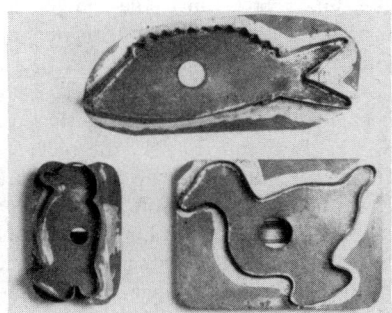

**Tin cutters: Fish, 3¼x4¼",
$28.00; Penguin, 2¾x1¾",
$20.00; Duck, 3¼x4¼",
20.00.**

Tulip (dbl) & leaf inset in oval, crimped rim, 3¾x2¾" **25.00**
Turkey w/tail wide, tin, flat bk, no hdl, 1870s, 4½" **55.00**
Wolf's head, tin, early 1900s, 4½" **32.00**

Cookie Jars

The appeal of the cookie jar is universal; folks of all ages, both male and female, love to collect 'em! The early thirties' heavy stoneware jars of a rather nondescript nature quickly gave way to figurals of every type imaginable. Those from the mid to late thirties were often decorated over the glaze with 'cold paint,' but by the early forties underglaze decorating resulted in cheerful, bright, permanent colors and cookie jars that still have a new look fifty years later.

Unmarked jars, unless properly identified and rare, bring the lowest prices, while cookie jars trimmed in gold are usually highly valued. The examples listed below were made by companies other than those found elsewhere in this book; see also specific manufacturers. Our advisors for this catgory are Fred and Joyce Roerig, authors of *The Collector's Encyclopedia of Cookie Jars;* they are listed in the Directory under South Carolina. For further study we also recommend *An Illustrated Guide to Cookie Jars* by Ermagene Westfall.

Albert Apple, Pitman-Dreitzer & Co **190.00**
Almost Home, 1986 Limited Ed of 20,000, Holiday Designs **65.00**
Apple, red, Treasure Craft **60.00**
Aunt Jemima, F&F **385.00**
Baby Elephant, unmk, American Bisque **110.00**
Balloon Lady, Pottery Guild **165.00**
Bartender, Fapco **175.00**
Bear, w/flasher, American Bisque **380.00**
Betsy Ross, Enesco **175.00**
Betsy Ross, Napco **165.00**
Boots, American Bisque **235.00**
Bull, Twin Winton **75.00**
Bull Dog Cafe, Treasure Craft **75.00**
Car, 1957 Chevy, Applause **110.00**
Century 21 ....**250.00**

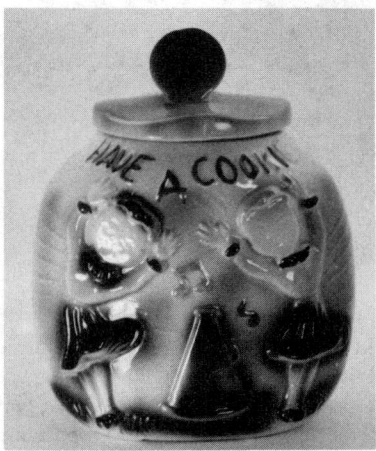

**Cheerleaders, corner jar,
American Bisque, $165.00.**

Chef, Nat'l Silver **325.00**
Chicken, Fredericksburg Art **30.00**
Christmas Tree, California Originals **390.00**
Clown, very lg, Maddux of California **325.00**
Clown, w/blackboard, American Bisque **310.00**
Clown on Stage, 805 USA, American Bisque **150.00**
Cookie Factory, Fitz & Floyd **95.00**
Cookie Shack, Twin Winton **60.00**
Cooky Chef, Pearl China **525.00**
Count, California Originals **675.00**
Dalmation, Treasure Craft **70.00**
Deer, in forest, American Bisque **260.00**
Dino, Flintstones, American Bisque **1,475.00**
Dog, w/toothache, very dk fur, American Bisque **740.00**
Donald Duck Turnabout, Leeds China **225.00**
Dutch Girl, Robinson-Ransbottom **240.00**
Elephant, Twin Winton **75.00**

Fire Truck, Twin Winton 125.00
Fireman, Robinson-Ransbottom 210.00
Fred, Flintstones, American Bisque 141.00
Friar Tuck, Goebel 310.00
Garage, Cardinal 135.00
Girl Bear, unmk, American Bisque, 1958 ....45.00
Gold Metal Cookies, tin 30.00
Goldilocks, Royal 265.00
Halo Girl, Deforest of California 1,200.00
Hen, Sierra Vista 65.00
Hobo, w/blackboard, American Bisque 410.00
Hootie Owl, Robinson-Ransbottom 95.00
Hound Dog, Doranne of California 90.00
Humpty Dumpty, Japan 80.00
Humpty Dumpty, Maddux of California 300.00
Indian, Lane 1,225.00
Ken-L-Ration Dog, F&F Die Works, Dayton Ohio 130.00
Koala Bear, California Originals 325.00
Little Bo Peep, Enesco 250.00
Little Red Riding Hood, Pottery Guild 150.00
Little Red Riding Hood, Weiss 375.00
Mammy, Gilner 2,025.00
Mickey/Minnie Mouse Turnabout, Leeds China 175.00

Monk, Cumberland Ware, 14",
$50.00.

Mr Rabbit, American Bisque 260.00
Mushroom, Treasure Craft 55.00
Nestle Toll House Cookies, unmk, Holiday Designs 95.00
Ol' King Cole, Robinson-Ransbottom 375.00
Olive Oyl, American Bisque 1,840.00
Oscar the Doughboy, w/gr hat, Robinson-Ransbottom 210.00
Oscar the Grouch, California Originals 75.00
Owl, Twin Winton 50.00
Panda Bear, Cumberland Ware 185.00
Peter Rabbit, Roman Ceramics 125.00
Pig, w/patch, American Bisque 150.00
Pinky Lee, pk hat, American Bisque 825.00
Pinocchio, Dayton Hudson 110.00
Pirate, Gonder 1,525.00
Police Chief Bear, Twin Winton 45.00
Polka Dot Witch, Fitz & Floyd 325.00
Poodle, deep maroon, American Bisque 125.00
Popeye, Vander 575.00
Puppy, USA, American Bisque, 1958 ....45.00
Rabbit, Maurice of California 90.00
Raccoon Bandit, Doranne of California 175.00
Rio Rita, Fitz & Floyd 120.00

R2-D2, Star Wars, Roman Ceramics 165.00
Sack of Cookies, American Bisque 55.00
Saddle, w/blackboard, American Bisque 250.00

Sailor, Robinson Ransbottom,
$150.00.

Sheriff, California Originals 45.00
Sid's Taxi, Appleman 425.00
Spaceship, Cookies Out of this World, American Bisque 375.00
Squirrel, Maddux of California 225.00
Squirrel, Vallona Star 75.00
Stagecoach, Sierra Vista 265.00
Strawberry, Treasure Craft 30.00
Treasure Chest, American Bisque 140.00
Truck, red, lg, Treasure Craft 925.00
Tugboat, w/bell in lid, USA, American Bisque 160.00
Umbrella Kids, USA 739, American Bisque 195.00
Victorian House, Fitz & Floyd 260.00
Whale, Robinson-Ransbottom 975.00
Wise Bird, Robinson-Ransbottom 75.00
3 Little Pigs, bl, Pamona 165.00

Cooper, Susie

    A 20th-century ceramic designer whose works are now attracting the attention of collectors, Susie Cooper was first affiliated with the A.E. Gray Pottery in Henley, England, in 1922 where she designed in lustres and painted items with her own ideas as well. (Examples of Gray's lustreware is rare and costly.) By 1930 she and her brother-in-law, Jack Beeson, had established a family business. Her pottery soon became a success and she was subsequently offered space at Crown Works, Burslem. In 1940 she received the honorary title of Royal Designer for Industry, the only such distinction ever awarded by the Royal Society of Arts solely for pottery design. Miss Cooper received the Order of the British Empire in the New Year's Honors List of 1979. She was the chief designer for the Wedgwood group from 1966 until she resigned in 1972. Since 1980 she has worked on a free-lance basis.

Bowl, Cockerel, 4-color w/copper lustre, Gray's Period, 9" 400.00
Chocolate pot, Crayon Line, red & brn, Kestrel shape, 7" 120.00
Coffeepot, Acorn, bl-gr wash, 7¾" 125.00
Coffeepot, orange & gray bands, Gray's Period, 8" 220.00
Coffeepot, yel wash, blk lines, 7¾" 150.00
Cup & saucer, Dresden Spray 40.00
Cup & saucer, gold-banded lily, Doric shape, 2¼" 60.00
Dish, gr & blk w/sgraffito design, oval, 8½" L 150.00
Egg cup, gray leaves, gr wash 75.00
Jam pot, Amaryllis, pk & gr, 4" 90.00

Jug, Crocus, turq, 6" 175.00
Meat dish, Nosegay, yel-wash border, oval, 14" 70.00
Mug, prancing unicorn, silver lustre, Kestral shape, 5" 150.00
Plaque, maroon leaves, 14" dia 175.00
Plate, Crayon Line, red, 10" 35.00
Plate, Gray Leaf, brn-wash border, 10" 30.00
Plate, Leaf & Vine, bl scroll border, 9" 40.00
Plate, Pear in Pompadour, gr/blk/red/yel, 6" 40.00
Vase, appl buttons at top, pk, 7½" 400.00

Coors

The firm that became known as Coors Porcelain Company in 1920 was founded in 1908 by John J. Herold, originally of the Roseville Pottery in Zanesville, Ohio. Though still in business today, they are best known for their artware vases and Rosebud dinnerware produced before 1939. Coors vases produced before the late thirties were made in a matt finish; by the latter years of the decade, high-gloss glazes were also being used. Nearly fifty shapes were in production, and some of the more common forms were made in three sizes. Typical colors in matt are white, orange, blue, green, yellow, and tan. Yellow, blue, maroon, pink, and green are found in high gloss. All vases are marked with a triangular arrangement of the words 'Coors Colorado Pottery' enclosing the word 'Golden.' You may find vases (usually 6" to 6½") marked with the Colorado State Fair stamp and dated 1939. For such a vase, add $10.00 to the suggested values given below. Our Rosebud advisor is Jo Ellen Winther. Advise for miscellaneous listings was provided by Jim and Carol Carlton; all are listed in the Directory under Colorado.

Rosebud, marmalade (no spoon), $100.00; Spoon (not shown), $75.00.

Ashtray, Rosebud, rare, 3½" 125.00
Baking pan, Rosebud, rectangular, 2x12x8" 30.00
Bowl, cereal; Rosebud, 6" 15.00
Bowl, mixing; Rosebud, hdld, 3½-cup 25.00
Cake knife, Rosebud, 10" 50.00
Casserole, Rosebud, str sides, 2-pt 30.00
Casserole, Rosebud, w/lid, 14-cup 45.00
Casserole, service; Rosebud, w/lid & underplate, 3½-pt 45.00
Creamer, Rosebud, 3" 15.00
Cup, custard; Rosebud, 4" 8.00
Egg cup, Rosebud, 6-oz 25.00
Honey pot, Rosebud, w/lid & ladle 175.00
Jar, utility; Rosebud, 2½-pt 45.00
Muffin set, Rosebud, 8" plate w/5½" dome lid 125.00
Pitcher, Rosebud, open, 4-pt 85.00
Plate, Rosebud, 7¼" 8.00
Plate, Rosebud, 9" 15.00
Platter, Rosebud, 12x9" 15.00
Shakers, Rosebud, str sides, 4½", pr 18.00
Shakers, Rosebud, 2½", pr 25.00

Teapot, Rosebud, 2-cup 85.00
Tumbler, Rosebud, ftd, no hdl, 12-oz 75.00
Tumbler, Rosebud, hdl, 8½-oz 75.00
Water server, Rosebud, corked stopper, 6-cup 65.00

Miscellaneous

Ashtray, Beer, Butter, Malted Milk, rnd, flat 95.00
Ashtray, ivory, common 3.00
Bank, clown, hanging 100.00
Bank, clown, sitting 100.00
Canasta tray card holder 45.00
Cookie jar, rope hdls 95.00
Crock, malted milk; porc, w/metal lid 150.00
Statue, buffalo 500.00
Vase, bl matt, bulbous urn form w/hdls, 6" 45.00
Vase, gr, bulbous, 8" 75.00
Vase, gr matt, bulbus urn form w/hdls, 10" 95.00
Vase, gr matt, Deco shape, rim-to-shoulder hdls, 8" 75.00
Vase, orange matt, Deco shape, rim-to-shoulder hdls, 10" 95.00
Vase, wht matt, bulbous, 6" 45.00
Vase, wht matt, bulbous urn form w/hdls, 8" 75.00
Vase, wht matt, Deco shape w/integral circular hdls, 6" 45.00
Vase, yel, bulbous, 10" 95.00
Whip, malted Milk 175.00

Copper

Handcrafted copper was made in America from early in the 18th century until about 1850, with the center of its production in Pennsylvania. Examples have been found signed by such notable coppersmiths as Kidd, Buchanan, Babb, Bently, and Harbeson. Of the many utilitarian items made, teakettles are the most desirable. Early examples from the 18th century were made with a dovetailed joint which was hammered and smoothed to a uniform thickness. Pots from the 19th century were seamed. Coffeepots were made in many shapes and sizes and along with mugs, kettles, warming pans, and measures are easiest to find. Stills ranging in sizes of up to fifty-gallon are popular with collectors today. Our advisor, Mary Frank Gaston, has compiled a lovely book, *Antique Brass and Copper*, with many full-color photos and current market values; you will find her address in the Directory under Texas.

Teakettle, swing handle, domed lid with brass urn finial, marked Hunneman, ca 1810, 11" diameter, $2,400.00.

Bed warmer, brass stopper w/ring hdl, lacquered, 12" dia 200.00
Bowl, centerpc; lion head w/ring hdls, plating gone, 10x11" 85.00
Clam steamer, mk Fried Loblich Wien (Austrian), 11x8" 175.00
Coal scuttle, ped base, tin lining, lacquered, 16" 225.00

Coffeepot, Deco shape w/wooden finial & angle hdl, 13" 145.00
Coffeepot, gooseneck spout, wood hdl & finial, 8½" 60.00
Coffeepot, hinged spout lid, wood hdl, Rome Metalware, 10", VG .40.00
Colander, tin lined, pierced floral-designed base, 26" L 250.00
Fire bk, emb peacock, mtd on wrought Nouveau fr, 28x17" 175.00
Funnel, triangular ring for hanging, 6" 20.00
Funnel, wide flat hdl w/rolled edge, 14x6" 35.00
Inkwell, hand cut & soldered, well made, Am 1870s, 4⅜" 275.00
Jardiniere & ped, overall repousse, Victorian, 28" 2,500.00
Kettle, dvtl work at top, Frankfort IN, 10½x8" 250.00
Kettle, preserving; iron hdls, mid-1800s, 4x8" 150.00
Kettle, wooden & brass hdl, brass finial, mk China, 9x6½" 175.00
Measure, tin lined, brass trim, unmk, 5½" 120.00
Measure, tin lined, mk Kreamer, 8" 80.00
Mug, dvtl, wrought copper hdl, early, 6" 140.00
Oil can, invt funnel top, strap hdl, curved spout w/brace, 9" 35.00
Pan, dvtl, wrought copper hdl, 9½" dia, +9" hdl 45.00
Pan, roasting; dmn shape, English, 1800s, 7x27x20" 425.00
Pan, sauce; copper w/CI hdl & lid, mk E Thomas & Co, 8" 45.00
Pitcher, tin lined, ca mid-1800s, 9" 90.00
Planter, appl brass lions' heads, brass paw ft, 15¼x13¼" 1,200.00
Planter, simple half-circle shape w/arched bk, 1930s, 5¼x6" 35.00
Plaque, dancing gypsy & faun in relief, Tinant, 10½x9" 175.00
Saucepan, dvtl, heart-shape hdl mt, 10", +5½" hdl 85.00
Sconce, hammered, w/wrought iron, 11", pr 48.00
Shoehorn, handmade from hammered sheet, ca 1800s, 8⅞" 55.00
Skillet w/tin lining, rolled rim, 16½" dia, +17" wrought hdl 135.00
Tray, emb berries & leaves in border, rectangular, 21x9" 125.00
Wash boiler, mk Canco, 14x27" 75.00
Wash tub, mk Perco Washer....Houston TX, Patent Pending 125.00

Copper Lustre

Copper lustre is a term referring to a type of pottery made in Staffordshire after the turn of the 19th century. It is finished in a metallic rusty-brown glaze resembling true copper. Pitchers are found in abundance, ranging from simple styles with dull bands of color to those with fancy handles and bands of embossed, polychromed flowers. Bowls are common; goblets, mugs, teapots, and sugar bowls much less so. It's easy to find, but not in good condition. Pieces with hand-painted decoration and those with historical transfers are the most valuable. Our advisor for this category is Richard Marden; he is listed in the Directory under New Hampshire.

Key: pw — pearlware

Creamer, figures & goat emb/mc in wide lt bl band, 4" 75.00
Creamer, girl w/horse, blk transfer, lustre trim, 4¾" 55.00
Goblet, blk transfer of Oriental band w/mc pnt, 4¼" 40.00
Loving cup, mc florals, scroll hdls, ped ft, beaded rim, 4⅝" 45.00
Mug, marbleized, 2¾" 60.00
Mug, yel & gr bands, beaded rim, 2¾x2⅜" 30.00
Pitcher, appl cherubs w/mc enamel & purple lustre, 8⅞" 220.00
Pitcher, Dmn Quilt, HP decor, 6½" 55.00
Pitcher, emb dancers, bl enameling, 6" 40.00
Pitcher, emb dancing woman & wheat, 3-color, 6½" 40.00
Pitcher, emb mc rose on wide dk bl band, 4" 40.00
Pitcher, emb rose & yel flowers w/gr leaves ea side, 8½" 135.00
Pitcher, floral decor w/bird, pw, 4¾" 165.00
Pitcher, house pattern band, 5⅞" 95.00
Pitcher, lady w/scythe, man w/flute, brn on wht band, 4½", EX ...45.00
Pitcher, Lafayette & Cornwallis on band, wear, 4" 465.00
Pitcher, marbleized pk band w/oval classical reserves, 7¾" 150.00

Pitcher, mc floral, lt wear, 7¼" 140.00
Pot, florals & bl bands, 6½" 72.50
Salt cellar, wide yel band, ftd, 2⅛x2⅞" 37.50
Teapot, bl & gold medallion trim, rectangular, 6-cup, 7" 225.00
Tumbler, floral band, beaded rim, 3¼x3½" 40.00

Vase, blue floral design with much gold on scalloped body, 8", $85.00.

Coralene Glass

Coralene is a unique type of art glass easily recognized by the tiny grains of glass that form its decoration. Lacy allover patterns of seaweed, geometrics, and florals were used, as well as solid forms such as fish, plants, and single blossoms. It was made by several glasshouses both here and abroad. Values are based to a considerable extent on the amount of beading that remains. Our advisors for this category are Betty and Clarence Maier; they are listed in the Directory under Pennsylvania.

Bottle, yellow seaweed on blue shaded to white, matching ball stopper, 6½", $200.00.

Pitcher, peachblow satin, seaweed motif, 8", +6 tumblers 1,300.00
Tumbler, bl shaded o/l, overall yel motif, 4" 185.00
Vase, bl w/yel wheat & leaf motif, 5" 135.00
Vase, lt bl Bristol, bird on branch motif, 1900, 5½" 210.00
Vase, peachblow w/yel seaweed motif, w/gold, Pat, Mt WA, 7½" .650.00
Vase, pk Dmn Quilt MOP, daisies/butterflies/bug motif, 8" 300.00

Coralene, Oriental

Ceramics decorated in the same manner as coralene glass were produced in Japan during the early 1900s. Many items are marked 'Patent Pending' or with a specific patent date.

Bowl, plums, purple on bl, 8" 180.00

Vase, pink roses on blue, green neck band, numbered, 4", $425.00.

Vase, gr & wht flowers w/gold on orange, 4¾" 375.00
Vase, iris, pk/lav on gr, cobalt & gold trim, 9x3½" 475.00
Vase, mc floral on yel shaded to burnt-orange, 4¾" 345.00

Cordey

The Cordey China Company was founded in 1942 in Trenton, New Jersey, by Boleslaw Cybis. The operation was small with less than a dozen workers. They produced figurines, vases, lamps, and similar wares, much of which was marketed through gift shops both nationwide and abroad. Though the earlier wares were made of plaster, Cybis soon developed his own formula for a porcelain composition which he called 'Papka.' Cordey figurines and busts were characterized by old-world charm, Rococo scrolls, delicate floral appliques, ruffles, and real lace which was dipped in liquified clay to add dimension to the work.

Although on rare occasions some items were not numbered or signed, the 'basic' figure was cast both with numbers and the Cordey signature. The molded pieces were then individually decorated and each marked with its own impressed identification number as well as a mark to indicate the artist-decorator. Their numbering system began with 200 and in later years progressed into the 8000s. As can best be established, Cordey continued production until sometime in the mid-1950s. Boleslaw Cybis died in 1957, his wife in 1958.

Key: ff — full figure

Man and lady, #300/ #301, 16", $175.00 for the pair.

Bird, #6004, bluebird on stump, lg 110.00
Bowl, #6034, appl rose w/leaves, gold trim, 5x4½" 15.00
Bowl, #7006, 2 appl roses, rtcl, gold trim, 8½x6" 32.00
Bowl, #8016, 3 appl roses, rtcl, gold trim, 5½x5" 24.00
Box, #6038, appl roses & leaves, gold trim, 5x5" 45.00
Bust, #5012, lady w/bl rose at bodice, flowers in hair 55.00
Cat, wht w/gr eyes & pk ears, script mk, 8½" 200.00
Catalog, factory's, 50-pg 50.00
Chinese wood duck, #325, intricate base, EX colors, rare 400.00
Clock, #909, bird & roses, rococo, wall hanging, 14½" 150.00
Clock, #914, 9½" 175.00
Courting group, man & lady on rnd base, #4129, lacy, rare 335.00
Cup & saucer, #624, appl pk roses, leaves on cup 55.00
Lady, #5061, Madame Dubarry, ff, rare, 14" 215.00
Lady, #5062, Godey lady, ff, 14" 110.00
Lady, #6405, flower-trimmed hat, pk & gray dress, 10½" 110.00
Lamp, #4004, bust on metal fr, orig shade, pr 90.00
Lamp, #4018/#4019, Colonial man & lady, no shades, pr 165.00
Man, #5041, ff, gray coat, rose & pk trim, 11½" 125.00
Man, #5042, ff, 11½" 125.00
Plaque, Primrose 200.00
Teapot, #631, appl pk roses & gr leaves, gold hdl, 7½" 285.00
Vase, #7094, Oriental figures & florals, gourd form, 9x8" 165.00
Wall shelf, #7028, nude encircling cornucopia bottom 100.00

Corkscrews

The history of the corkscrew dates back to the mid-1600s, when wine makers concluded that the best-aged wine was that stored in smaller containers, either stoneware or glass. Since plugs left unsealed were often damaged by rodents, corks were cut off flush with the bottle top and sealed with wax or a metal cover. Removing the cork cleanly with none left to grasp became a problem. The task was found to be relatively simple using the worm on the end of a flintlock gun rod. So the corkscrew evolved. Endless patents have been issued for mechanized models. Handles range from carved wood, ivory, and bone to porcelain and repousse silver. Exotic materials such as agate, mother-of-pearl, and gold plate were also used on occasion. Celluloid lady's legs are popular. Our advisor for this category is Roger Baker; he is listed in the Directory under California.

Anheuser-Busch, bottle shape, EX 45.00
Belgium, Challenge, common type, 1850s, EX 25.00
Carter's Ink, folding, Pat 1894 ......12.50
Champion, CI w/emb vines overall, wood hdl, bar mt 125.00
CJ Johnson Sheffield, horn hdl, steel blade, ca 1880, EX 75.00
England, brass shaft, Henshall-type button, wood hdl, EX 115.00
England, Farrow & Jackson Ltd..., sq shaft, wire helix, 1885 ......85.00
England, Lund Patentee London, rack & pinion, Pat 1855, EX ..285.00
England, picnic type, steel screw, ca 1800, EX 150.00
England, Sulgrave Manor, 2-finger style, bronze, EX 30.00
France, Laurent Sibet Rockport, grapevine hdl, EX 18.00
France, wooden dbl hdl w/figure cvg, rnd ft, NM 37.50
Germany, legs figural (gr stripes), ca 1910, EX 300.00
Germany, pocket style, plated lifter & worm, silver sleeve 88.00
Germany, spring bbl w/pin-type lock, wood hdl, EX 70.00
Germany, swivel-over collar style, rubber ring on fr, 1950s 25.00
Haff Pat, brass ring mk Pat Appl For, Apr/May 1885 ......85.00
Italy, barman figural, dbl lever, toasts on bk, 10½" 47.50
Italy, swivel-over collar type, NP brass, VG 25.00
Man w/straw hat figural, modern dbl-lever type, 8½" 20.00
Old Snifter, Senator Volkstead, thermoplastic w/mc pnt 225.00
Plastic duplex (dbl worm), picnic type, modern 5.00

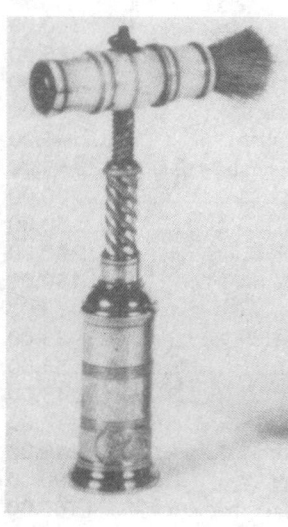

Thomason-type, patented, English, 19th century, 7⅜", $480.00.

Thomason, appl bronze crest tablet, bone hdl, Pat 1802, EX **425.00**
Unmk, dbl loop of wire finger hold, helical wire screw, 3" **3.00**
US, Hollwig 1891 Pat, Pabst Milwaukee advertising, EX **130.00**
US, NP steel worm, cap lifter & wire breaker, EX **150.00**
US, stag horn hdl, sterling silver cap, late 1800s, 8½" **80.00**
US Clough 1910 Pat, Hennessy advertising on wood sleeve **32.00**
Walrus tusk hdl w/sterling ends, SP worm & lifter, Pat 1906 ......**155.00**
Williamson's Pat 1897, self-pulling, EX **28.00**

Cosmos

Cosmos, sometimes called Stemless Daisy, is a patterned glass tableware produced from 1894 through 1915 by Consolidated Lamp and Glass Company. Relief-molded flowers on a fine crosscut background were painted in soft colors of pink, blue, and yellow. Though nearly all were made of milk glass, a few items may be found in clear glass with the designs painted on. In addition to the tableware, lamps were also made.

Butter dish, 6x8", $235.00.

Bottle, cologne; orig stopper, rare **150.00**
Condiment set, 3-pc in fr **350.00**
Creamer **150.00**
Lamp, banquet; kerosene, 24" **475.00**
Lamp, banquet; slender base, rnd globe, all orig, 16" **525.00**
Lamp, mini; 7" **325.00**
Lamp, 10" **400.00**

Pickle castor, dbl, mk SP fr **500.00**
Pickle castor, single, ftd SP fr **350.00**
Pitcher, milk; 5" **170.00**
Pitcher, syrup; 6" **200.00**
Pitcher, water **250.00**
Shakers, tall, orig lids, pr **100.00**
Spooner **125.00**
Sugar bowl, open **150.00**
Sugar bowl, w/lid **185.00**
Tumbler, 3¾" **65.00**

Cottageware

You'll find a varied assortment of novelty dinnerware items, all styled as cozy little English cottages or huts with cone-shaped roofs; some may have a waterwheel or a windmill. Marks will vary. English-made Price Brothers or Beswick pieces are valued in the same range as those marked Occupied Japan, while items marked simply Japan are considered slightly less pricey. Our advisor for this category is Grace Klender; she is listed in the Directory under Ohio.

Bowl, salad; English **65.00**
Butter dish, England **45.00**
Chocolate pot, English **135.00**
Cookie jar, pk/brn/gr, sq, Japan, 8½x5½" **65.00**
Cookie jar/canister, cylindrical, English **85.00**
Cookie or biscuit jar, Occupied Japan **85.00**
Creamer & sugar bowl, England, 2½", 4½" **45.00**
Cup & saucer, English, 2½", 4½" **45.00**
Demitasse pot, English **100.00**
Dish w/cover, Occupied Japan, sm **35.00**
Marmalade, English **40.00**

Price Brothers, England: marmalade and jelly, 2 houses cojoined, 4½", $85.00.

Mug, Price Bros **50.00**
Pin tray, English, 4" dia **20.00**
Pitcher, water; English **150.00**
Platter, oval, 11¾x7½" **45.00**
Sugar box, for cubes, English, 5¾" L **45.00**
Teapot, English or Occupied Japan, 6½" **50.00**
Toast rack, English **60.00**
Tumbler, Occupied Japan, 3½", set of 6 ....**60.00**

Coverlets

The Jacquard attachment for hand looms represented a culmination of weaving developments made in France. Introduced to America by the early 1820s, it gave professional weavers the ability to easily create complex patterns with curved lines. Those who could afford the new loom adaptation could now use hole-punched pasteboard cards to weave floral patterns that before could only be achieved with intense labor on a draw-loom.

Before the Jacquard mechanism, most weavers made their coverlets in geometric patterns. Use of indigo-blue and brightly colored wools often livened the twills and overshot patterns available to the small-loom home weaver. Those who had larger multiple-harness looms could produce warm double-woven, twill-block, or summer-and-winter designs.

While the new floral and pictorial patterns' popularity had displaced the geometrics in urban areas, the mid-Atlantic, and the Midwest by the 1840s, even factory production of the Jacquard coverlets was disrupted by cotton and wool shortages during the Civil War. A revived production in the 1870s saw a style change to a center-medallion motif, but a new fad for white 'Marseilles' spreads soon halted sales of Jacquard-woven coverlets. Production of Jacquard carpets continued to the turn of the century.

Rural and frontier weavers continued to make geometric-design coverlets through the 19th century, and local craft revivals have continued the tradition through this century. All-cotton overshots were factory produced in Kentucky from the 1940s, and factories and professional weavers made cotton-and-wool overshots during the past decade. Many Jacquard-woven coverlets have dates and names of places and people (often the intended owner — not the weaver) woven into corners or borders. In the listings that follow, examples are blue and white unless noted otherwise.

Jacquard

Exotic birds and floral medallions, blue and white, 2-piece, NM, $750.00.

Floral, corners sgn/dtd 1855, bl/gr/red/wht, 68x76"	450.00
Floral, dbl bird border, 2-pc, single weave, 66x86"	275.00
Floral, navy/natural, 2-pc, dbl weave, sm holes, 88x74"	75.00
Floral, 2-pc, dbl weave, 78x88", EX	350.00
Floral medallion, eagle borders, 1857, 1-pc, 85x96", EX	350.00
Floral medallion, eagle spandrels, 4-color, 1-pc, 77x77"	360.00
Floral medallion, red/navy/gold/natural, 1-pc, rpr, 86x80"	150.00
Floral medallions, single weave, 2-pc, 1855, 74x84"	250.00
Floral medallions, vintage borders, 2-pc, 1856, 92x82"	330.00
Floral medallions/pinwheels, red/gr/wht, 2-pc, 88x70"+fringe	470.00
Floral w/house & bird border, 2-pc, 1859, 72x88"	700.00
Florals, navy/red/wht, 2-pc, dbl weave, 76x82"	440.00

Flower urns & peafowl, Christian/Heathen border, 2-pc dbl	660.00
Geometric floral, navy/natural, 1-pc, single weave, 80x88"	300.00
Patriotic design, 3-color, Wm Ney, PA, 84x90", EX	660.00
Rose medallions, bird corners, 2-pc, 1844, 84x64"	395.00
Rose medallions/birds, red/bl/wht, 2-pc, sgn/1859, 84x72"	495.00
Star, birds/deer/buildings in corners, 5-color, 1-pc, 82x75"	695.00
Stars w/vining border, corners dtd 1843, 78x88"	850.00
Turkey/peacocks, vintage border, navy/wht, 2-pc, 84x78", G	650.00

Overshot

Bars w/circle devices at intersections, 3-color, 72x78", VG	295.00
Bl/natural, 2-pc, lt wear, 80x96"	135.00
Checks/sqs, geometric bands form stars at junctions, 4-color	275.00
Geometrics, linen & wool, bittersweet/natural, 2-pc, 86x92"	300.00
Optical pattern, bl/natural, 2-pc, 94x72"	140.00
Optical pattern, red/bl/natural, wear/stains, 88x96"	100.00
Optical pattern, rprs, 3-pc, 76x90"	200.00
Sqs in sqs, bl/red/wht, 2-pc dbl, rebound, 63x83"	325.00

Cowan

Guy Cowan opened a small pottery near Cleveland, Ohio, ca 1909, where he made tile and artware on a small scale from the natural red clay available there. He developed distinctive glazes — necessary, he felt, to cover the dark red body. After the war and a temporary halt in production, Cowan moved his pottery to Rocky River, where he made a commercial line of artware utilizing a highly-fired white porcelain. Although he acquiesced to the necessity of mass-production, every effort was made to insure a product of highest quality. Fine artists, among them Waylande Gregory, Margaret Postgate, and Viktor Schreckengost, designed pieces which were often produced in limited editions, some of which sell today for prices in the thousands. Most of the ware was marked 'Cowan' or 'Lakewood Ware,' not to be confused with the name of the 1930 mass-produced line called 'Lakeware.' Falling under the crunch of the Great Depression, the pottery closed in 1931. Our advisor for this category is Mark Bassett; he is listed in the Directory under Ohio.

Bookends, Sunbonnet, ivy, 7½", pr	275.00
Bowl, cream, gr int, 2x6"	45.00
Candlestick, floral scroll, mint gr, 3-light, pr+bowl	225.00
Charger, fox hunter on horse, mc, Schreckengost, 12"	1,250.00
Charger, man/golf bag, mc, Schreckengost, 11½"	1,500.00
Charger, tennis match, VS (Schreckengost) in motif, wht, 11"	1,000.00
Comport, sea horses on base, Special Ivory, ped ft, 3¼x6½"	45.00
Comport, tan, gr int, dmn shape, 2x7"	45.00
Jazz bowl, emb decor, blk on bl, sgn Schreckengost, 13½"	15,000.00
Lamp base, orange lustre, 12½"	80.00
Strawberry jar & underplate, mint gr, 7¾"	125.00

Vase, black and silver, designed by Waylande Gregory, fluted fan shape, 8", $350.00.

Vase, blk lustre, fluted, ftd, 5½" **100.00**
Vase, crystalline golden orange, 4" **85.00**
Vase, Oriental pheasant as body, flared neck, gr gloss, 11" **300.00**
Vase, sea horse, yel, fan form, 7⅛" **65.00**
Vase, sea horses on base, gr crystalline, fan form, 8" **150.00**

Cracker Jack

Kids have been buying Cracker Jack since it was first introduced in the 1890s. By 1912 it was packaged with a free toy inside. Before the first kernel was crunched, eager fingers had retrieved the surprise from the depth of the box — actually no easy task, considering the care required to keep the contents so swiftly displaced from spilling over the side! Though a little older, perhaps, many of those same kids still are looking — just as eagerly — for the Cracker Jack prizes. Point of sale, company collectibles, and the prizes as well have over the years reflected America's changing culture. Grocer sales and incentives from around the turn of the century — paper dolls, postcards and song books — were often marked Rueckheim Brothers (the inventors of Cracker Jack) or Reliable Confections. Over the years the company made some changes, leaving a trail of clues that often help collectors date their items. The company's name changed in 1922 from Reuckheim Brothers & Eckstein to The Cracker Jack Company. Their Brooklyn office was open from 1914 until it closed in 1923, and the first time the sailor Jack logo was used on their packaging was 1919. For packages and 'point of sale' dating, note that the word 'prize' was used from 1912 to 1925, 'novelty' from 1925 to 1932, and 'toy' from 1933 on. The first loose-packed prizes were toys made of wood, clay, tin, metal, and lithographed paper. Plastic toys were introduced in 1946. Paper wrapped for safety purposes in 1948, subjects echo the 'hype' of the day — Yo-Yos, tops, whistles, and sports cards in the simple, peaceful days of our country, propaganda and war toys in the forties, games in the fifties, and space toys in the sixties. Few of the estimated 15 billion prizes were marked. Advertising items from Angelus Marshmallow and Checkers Confections (cousins of the Cracker Jack family) are also collectible. When no condition is indicated, the items listed below are assumed to be in excellent condition. 'CJ' indicates that the item is marked. Note: An often-asked question concerns the tin Toonerville Trolley marked 'CJ.' No data has been found in the factory archives to authenticate this item; it is assumed that the 'CJ' merely refers to its small size. Our advisor for this category is Wes Johnson; he is listed in the Directory under Kentucky.

Cast Metal Prizes

Horse and wagon, marked CJ, 3-D, silver (also made in gold-washed cast metal), hollow center, 1910, 2½", $350.00.

Badge, shield, CJ Jr Detective, silver, 1931, 1¼" **35.00**
Badge, 6-point star, mk CJ Police, silver, 1931, 1¼" **35.00**
Button, stud bk, Me for Cracker Jack, boy & dog **26.00**
Button, stud bk, Xd bats & ball, CJ pitcher/etc series, 1928 ....**78.00**

Chair, T (Tootsie), 3 different sectional pcs, pnt, mini, ea **12.00**
Dollhouse items: lantern, mug, candlestick, etc; no mk, ea **6.50**
Pistol, soft lead, inked, CJ on barrel, early, rare, 2⅛" **180.00**
Ring, alphabet letter setting (series), unmk, ea **3.00**
Rocking horse, no rider, 3-D, inked, early, 1⅛" **12.00**
Rocking horse w/boy, 3-D, inked, early, 1½" **29.00**
Spinner, early pkg in center, 'More You Eat...,' CJ, rare **295.00**
TootsieToy series: boats, cars, animals; '31, ¾"-1½", ea **7.00**

Dealer Incentives

Blotter, CJ question mk box, yel, 7¾x3¾" **225.00**
Cart w/2 movable wheels, tin, wood dowel tongue, CJ **55.00**
Corkscrew/opener, metal plated, CJ/Angelus, 3" **75.00**
Corkscrew/opener, metal plated, CJ/Angelus, 3¾" tube case **75.00**
Jigsaw puzzle, CJ or Checkers, 1 of 4, 7x10", in envelope **35.00**
Magic puzzle, metal, CJ/Angelus, 1 of 15, '34, ea in envelope **14.00**
Mask, Halloween; paper, CJ, 10" or 12", ea **18.00**
Match holder, hinged, eng gold-tone case, CJ, 2½x1⅞" **650.00**
Palm puzzle, mirror bk, CJ, mk Germany/RWB, 1910-14, 1½" ...**110.00**
Pencil top clip, metal/celluloid, oval boy & dog logo **210.00**
Pencil top clip, metal/celluloid, tube shape w/pkg **190.00**
Postcard, bear, 1 of 16, CJ, 1907, ea **25.00**
Tablet, school; CJ, 1929, 8x10" **195.00**
Tape measure, celluloid, Angelus, 1½" oval **85.00**
Thimble, aluminum, CJ Co/Angelus, red pnt, rare, ea **165.00**

Packaging

Box, popcorn; red scroll border, CJ, ca 1920 ....**85.00**
Box, popcorn; store display, CJ, 1923, no contents **65.00**
Canister, tin, CJ Candy Corn Crisp, 10-oz **75.00**
Canister, tin, CJ Coconut Corn Crisp, 1-lb **55.00**
Canister, tin, CJ Coconut Corn Crisp, 10-oz **65.00**
CJ Commemorative canister, mc scene, 1990s, ea **9.00**
CJ Commemorative canisters, wht w/red scroll, 1980s, ea **6.50**
Crate, shipping; wood, CJ, Reuckheim Bros Eck, 1902-22, lg **175.00**

Paper Prizes

Baseball CJ score counter, 3⅜" L **145.00**
Book, Animals (or Birds), to color, Makatoy, 1949, mini **35.00**
Book, Bess & Bill on CJ Hill, series of 12, 1937, mini **85.00**
Book, Birds We Know, CJ, 1928, mini **75.00**
Book, drawing w/tracing paper, CJ, 1920s, mini **110.00**
Book, Twigg & Sprigg, CJ, 1930, mini **85.00**
Decal, cartoon or nursery rhyme figure, 1947-49, CJ **7.00**
Disguise, ears, red punch out (in carrier), 1950, pr **45.00**
Disguise, glasses, hinged, cellophane lenses, CJ, 1933 ....**110.00**
Disguise, mustache, blk/brn, in carrier, CJ, 1949 ....**45.00**
Fortune Teller, boy/dog on film in envelope, CJ, '20s, 1¾x2½" **55.00**
Fortune wheel, 2-pc litho, turn for fortune, CJ, 1¾" **68.00**
Game, Midget Auto Race, wheel spins, CJ, 1949, 3⅜" H **45.00**
Game spinner, ...baseball at home, rectangle, CJ, 2¾" W **125.00**
Game spinner, ...baseball at home, unmk, 1946, 1½" dia **40.00**
Hat, fold out, More You Eat/More You Want, CJ, early **75.00**
Hat, Indian headdress, CJ, early 1920s, 2½" **110.00**
Hat, Indian headdress, CJ, 1950s, 5⅜" **275.00**
Magic game book, erasable slate, series of 13, CJ, 1946, ea **27.00**
Movie, boy at blkboard, turn wheel: draws/erases, CJ, '31, 2" **185.00**
Movie, Goofy Zoo, turn wheel(s): change animals, 1939 ....**30.00**
Movie, pull tab for 2nd picture, series, CJ, 1943, 1¼", ea **90.00**
Movie, pull tab for 2nd picture, yel, early, 3", in envelope **145.00**
Riddle card, 2 series of 20, in pkg/from factory, CJ, ea **9.00**

Sand picture, sand pours for action, series of 14, 1967, ea 9.00
Top, golf game, wood stick center, CJ, 1933 ....47.00
Transfer, iron on, sport figure or patriotic, CJ, 1939, ea 20.00
Whistle, pressed paper, series of 10, 1948-49, CJ, 1¼x2", ea 38.00
Whistle, Razz Zooka, C Carey Cloud design, CJ, 1949 ....35.00

Plastic Prizes

Animals, standup, letter on bk, series of 26, Nosco, 1953, ea 3.50
Animals, standup on base, assorted, Nosco or CJ, 1947 on, ea 1.50
Badge, pin-bk, celluloid, pretty lady, CJ label, 1¼" 65.00
Baseball players, 3-D, bl or gray team, 1958, 1½", ea 7.00
Disc, emb comic character, series of 12, 1954, 1½" dia 9.00
Disc, emb fish plaque, oval, series of 10, 1956, ea 6.00
Dog, 3-D, hollow base, series of 10, CJCO, 1954, ea 4.50
Figure, circus; stands on base, 1 of 12, Nosco, 1951-54 ....1.75
Figure on rocking base, semi-flat, 1 of 9, Cloud design, 1956 ....3.00
Fob, alphabet letter w/loop on top, 1 of 26, 1954, 1½" 2.25
Magnifying glass, many designs/shapes, from 1961, ea 1.00
Palm puzzle, ball(s) roll into holes, plastic dome, from 1966 ....2.00
Pinball game, lever shoots ball/score in holes, 1964 to recent 2.00
Signs, road; Stop, Caution, etc, yel, series of 10, 1954-60, ea 3.00
Spinner, varied colors, 10 designs, from 1948, ea 1.50
Toys, take apart/assemble, variety, from 1962, assembled, ea 1.00
Toys, take apart/assemble, variety, from 1962, unassembled, ea 2.25
Whistle, tube w/animals on top, CJ, 1 of 6, 1950-53, 1⅜" 6.50

Premiums

Bat, baseball; wood, Hillerich & Bradsby, CJ, full sz 125.00
Book, pocket; jester on cover, CJ 62.00
Book, pocket; riddle/sailor boy/dog on cover, RWB, CJ 55.00
Harmonica, full scale, emb CJ, early, 5⅛" 385.00
Mirror, oval, Angelus (redhead or blond) on box 89.00
Pen, ink; w/nib, tin litho bbl, CJ 650.00
Recipe book, Angelus, 1930s 22.00
Wings, air corps type, silver or blk, stud-bk, CJ, 1930s, 3", ea 75.00

Tin Prizes

Badge, boy & dog, diecut, w/o tab at top 85.00
Badge, boy & dog, stand-up litho rectangle, est 1916, lg or sm, ea .145.00
Badge, emb/plated CJ officer, 2⅜" or 1⅝", early, ea 110.00
Badge, litho, red/wht/bl, boy/dog, CJ, 1920s, 1¼" dia 150.00
Bank, 3-D book form, red/gr/or blk, CJ Bank, early, 2" 95.00
Book mark, 4 different dogs, CJ, 2¾" ea....................................28.00
Boy & dog, diecut, complete w/bend-over tab, CJ 110.00
Brooch or pin, various design on card, CJ/logo, early, ea 125.00
Cash register, litho, More You Eat, CJ, early, 1⅞" 275.00
Clicker, 'Noisy CJ Snapper,' pear shape, aluminum, 1949 ....32.00
Doll dishes, tin plated, CJ, 1931, 1¾", 1⅞", & 2⅛" dia, ea 35.00
Fortune Wheel, 2-pc litho, CJ, 1939-41, 1¾" 55.00
Head nodder, leopard, rhino, goat, etc., litho, 1937, 1¾" ea 45.00
Helicopter, yel propeller, wood stick, unmk, 1937, 2⅝" 30.00
Horse & wagon, litho diecut, CJ & Angelus, 2⅛" 65.00
Horse & wagon, litho diecut, gray/red mks, CJ, 1914-23, 3⅛" 395.00
Model T Ford, license: NY 1915 #999, blk/wht, CJ, rare, 2" 410.00
Oval standup, Am flag, 1 of 4, unmk, 1936-46 ....37.00
Oval standup, comic character, 1 of 10, CJ, 1936-46 ....125.00
Pocket watch, silver of gold, CJ as numerals, 1931, 1½" 65.00
Sled, tin plated, CJ, 1931, 2" L 39.00
Small box shape: electric stove litho, unmk, 1⅛" 90.00
Small box shape: garage litho, unmk, 1⅛" 85.00
Small box shape: radio litho, bl, unmk, 1⅛" 80.00

Soldier, litho, die-cut standup, officer/private/etc, unmk, ea 22.00
Tall box shape: Frozen Foods locker freezer, '47, unmk, 1¾" 65.00
Tall box shape: grandfather clock, unmk, 1947, 1¾" 60.00
Tall box shape: radio, Tune in w/CJ, brn & yel, 1939, 1¾" 115.00
Tall box shape: Refrigerator Car, CJ 2006, 1947, 1¾" L 155.00
Tombstone shape: covered, clock, litho, 1931, ea 37.00
Train, engine & tender, litho, CJ Line/512, 2 versions, ea 125.00
Train, litho coach only, red, unmk, 1941 ....22.00
Train, litho engine only, red, unmk, 1941 ....17.00
Tray, emb, litho w/early pkg, smaller version 115.00
Tray, emb, litho w/early pkg, 2¼x1¾" 95.00
Wagon shape: Caterpillar tractor, unmk, 1931, 1¾" L 29.00
Wagon shape: CJ Shows, yel circus wagon, series of 5, ea 135.00
Wagon shape: Playtime Trailer (auto trailer), unmk, 1947 ....40.00
Wagon shape: tank, orange/red/gr camouflage, unmk 65.00
Wagon shape: Tank Corps No 57, gr & blk, 1941 ....30.00
Wheelbarrow, tin plated, bk leg in place, CJ, 1931, 2½" L 40.00

Miscellaneous

Ad, comic book, CJ, ea 9.00
Ad, Saturday Evening Post, mc, CJ, 1919, 11x14" 18.00
Hat, ball park vendor cap, CJ, 1930s 30.00
Lunch box, tin, 2 hdls, CJ, 1980s, 4½x5x6" 25.00
Lunch box, tin emb, CJ, 1970s, 4x7x9" 30.00
Medal, CJ salesman award, brass, 1939, scarce 125.00
Sign, bathing beauty, 5-color cb, CJ, early, 17x22" 300.00
Sign, boy or girl w/box of CJ, 5-color cb, early, 17x22", ea 300.00
Sign, Jack & Bingo, die-cut litho, easel standup, CJ, early 285.00
Sign, Santa & prizes, mc cb, Angelus, early, lg 245.00
Sign, Santa & prizes, mc cb, Checkers, early, lg 1,000.00
Sign, Santa & prizes, mc cb, CJ, early, lg 265.00
Sign, Santa & prizes, standing on early CJ pkg, mc cb, rare 345.00

Cranberry

Cranberry glass is named for its resemblance to the color of cranberry juice. It was made by many companies both here and abroad, becoming popular in America soon after the Civil War. It was made in free-blown ware as well as mold-blown. Today cranberry glass is being reproduced, and it is sometimes difficult to distinguish the old from the new. Ask a reputable dealer if you are unsure. See also Cruets; Salts; Sugar Shakers; Syrups.

Bottle, gold florals, clear bubble stopper, 7⅞x3¼" 145.00
Bowl, 3 crystal reeded ft, berry pontil, appl fans, 5½x6" 275.00
Creamer, frosted w/gold trim, clear hdl, 4x2½" 80.00
Decanter, eng leafy branches, flattened glass stopper, 11" 145.00
Decanter, mc fans/dots/etc, 3-petal top, bubble stopper, 8¾" 265.00
Decanter, 3-petal top, reed hdl, clear bubble stopper, 10" 125.00
Mug, Invt T'print, clear hdl, 4" 85.00
Pitcher, bl pansies & mixed flowers, clear loop hdl, 7" 475.00
Pitcher, mc floral, 8½" 350.00
Plate, 8" 24.00
Punch cup, HP florals, clear hdl 45.00
Rose rowl, threaded body w/ruffled rim, 3" 80.00
Shade, Dmn Quilt, 4x6x8" 250.00
Shakers, mc flowers, pewter lids, pr 135.00
Syrup, SP hdl & spout, 6¾" 350.00
Toothpick holder, Invt Baby T'print, bbl shape, satin 145.00
Urn, appl crystal flowers, hdls, w/lid, 8¾x5½" 550.00
Vase, appl crystal flowers & leaves, wishbone ft, 9¼x3½" 195.00
Vase, frosted center front w/HP lacy scrolls, ped ft, 14" 165.00

Vase, HP lilies of the valley w/gold leaves, 7½" 115.00
Vase, mc florals, bottle form, 9½x5½" 235.00
Vase, trumpet form, clear ft, 11¼", pr 360.00
Wine cruet, star cuttings, bulbous, faceted stopper, 9⅝" 145.00

Creamware

Creamware was a type of earthenware developed by Wedgwood in the 1760s and produced by many other Staffordshire potteries, including Leeds. Since it could be potted cheaply and was light in weight, it became popular abroad as well as in England, due to the lower freight charges involved in its export. It was revived at Leeds in the late 19th century, and the type most often reproduced was heavily reticulated or molded in high relief. These later wares are easily distinguished from the originals since they are thicker and tend to craze heavily. See also Leeds.

Charger, scalloped, emb feather edge, chips/wear, 19" 325.00
Cup & saucer, handleless; mc sprigs, brn bands, EX 65.00
Cup & saucer, handleless; Washington, blk transfer, mini, EX ...300.00
Cup & saucer, strawberries, brn vines/rims, VG 190.00
Figurine, bagpipers by column on mound base, bl/gr, 6", EX ...7,700.00
Pitcher, emb bands, bbl form, 6", EX 95.00
Pitcher, Washington & Lafayette, blk transfer, 5¼" 545.00
Plate, pk roses/yel thorns/bl flowers, 3-color border, 8½" 190.00
Plate, portrait of Prince Wm of Orange & verse, 10", EX 275.00
Plate, strawberries & floral sprays, pk band, shaped rim, 8" 145.00
Plate, strawberries & flowers, 6-color, drape/tassel border, 8" 200.00
Platter, basketweave, rtcl looping rim band, 9½" 140.00
Platter, bl feather & drapery rim, Oriental decor, 16½", EX 825.00
Platter, pnt crest, Prince of Wales feathers, 21", EX 350.00
Platter, rtcl rim w/molded foliage, 12¼", EX 125.00
Tall pot, mc florals, hairline/chip, 9¾" 220.00
Tea caddy, courting couple, blk transfer, no lid, 4⅛" 75.00
Teapot, purple rose/red & yel floral, emb rose finial, 5x8" 400.00

Crown Milano

Crown Milano was introduced in 1894 by the Mt. Washington Glass Company of New Bedford, Massachusetts. Along with Burmese, it was their best-selling line. The glass is very pale, almost ivory. It was blown, free-form or in molds, highly decorated with flowers and colored enamels, and fired. Made to compete with the English Porcelain Companies, Crown Milano required only about half as many steps to produce as the porcelain (for which it is often mistaken, especially when viewed from a distance). This enabled Mt. Washington to make very attractive pieces at competitive prices. Some of the very early pieces are referred to as 'Albertine'; these had a glossy finish. Satin pieces were marked 'CM,' and some were shipped with paper labels. One of the most outstanding Crown Milano decorators was Frank Guba, who preferred subjects such as flying ducks or other birds. Pieces decorated by him command very high prices. Our advisors for this category are Henry and Geneva Tyler; they are listed in the Directory under Florida. In the descriptions that follow, the glassware is assumed to be satin unless noted glossy.

Biscuit jar, Deco flowers w/jewels, SP rim & hdl, 6x5¼" 925.00
Biscuit jar, mums on shaded apricot, metal mts, 5½" dia 825.00
Biscuit jar, pansies & gold scrolls on cream, ruffled rim 650.00
Biscuit jar, pansies & gold scrolls on cream, 6x7" 925.00
Biscuit jar, pansies & medallions on wht, butterfly finial 800.00
Biscuit jar, rose panels, mc/wht on yel, SP mk lid, 6x7" 850.00
Biscuit jar, starfish, etc, jewels, SP rim & hdl, 5½x7¼" 1,725.00

Bowl, florals, mc w/gold on wht, hdls, w/lid, 5¾x9" 1,850.00
Box, collars & cuffs, poppies on top, bl bow appl to front 900.00
Box, ferns & scrolls, HP/blown out on gr, SP 4-ftd base, 6" 750.00
Box, mums, purple w/gold on cream, 12 blown-out swirls, 5x8" .700.00
Box, trinket; pansies & gold on shiny swirl, ftd, 3½" dia 400.00
Bride's bowl, floral/gold scrolls on pnt burmese, 2¾x10" ...1,250.00
Creamer & sugar bowl, violets on wht w/gold, 3½", 4½" dia 925.00
Creamer/sugar/jam jar, mums, gold on pk blush, ormolu mts ...1,100.00
Cup & saucer, pansies, gold trim, both w/rare paper label 2,400.00
Ewer, bl wisteria, dragon hdl, 8½x8" 3,650.00
Ewer, floral, wht w/gold leaves & vines on yel, bulbous, 12" ...1,400.00
Pitcher, tankard; gold floral/bow swags, 9", +4 tumblers 1,450.00
Rose bowl, mc pansies, gold flowers/trim on pnt burmese, 5" 675.00
Rose bowl, pansies on tan to yel, gold tracing, 4x5½" 400.00
Rose jar, florals w/in scrollwork, steeple stopper, 12x7" 3,200.00
Sweetmeat, jeweled starfish, SP rim/lid/hdl, 6" dia 1,650.00
Syrup pitcher, daisies, bee on pnt burmese, ribbed str sides 1,250.00
Vase, bats in flight, allover gold scrolls, label, 13" 3,500.00
Vase, ferns w/raised gold edges over pastel scrolls, 6x8" 700.00
Vase, flowers & gilt, melon shape base, slim neck, 13½x6¾" ..2,300.00

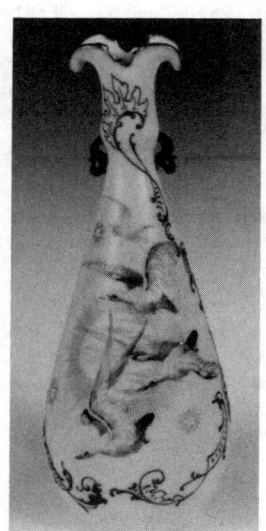

Vase, Guba ducks decoration, four small handles, 15", $4,200.00.

Vase, jack-in-pulpit; sm HP daisies, 14½x5½" 1,800.00
Vase, jeweled starfish w/cvd gilt goldfish, flared top, 10x8" 9,500.00
Vase, lotus blossoms/gilt/tan shadow leaves, 11x9" 1,400.00
Vase, spider mums, gold on cream, 11½" 1,200.00
Vase, wild rose/gold on cream, bulbous w/stick neck, 15" 1,300.00
Vase, wisteria/gold on melon form w/bulb neck, no mk, 9" 750.00

Cruets

Cruets, containers made to hold oil or vinegar, are usually bulbous with tall, narrow throats and a stopper. During the 19th century and for several years after, they were produced in abundance in virtually every type of glassware available. Those listed below are assumed to be with stopper and mint unless noted otherwise. Our advisor for this category is Elaine Ezell; she is listed in the Directory under Maryland.

Amazon, amethyst, matching hand-&-bar stopper 195.00
Argonaut Shell, wht opal 350.00
Beaded Circle, apple gr w/mc flowers, faceted stopper 185.00
Beaded Grape (California) 85.00
Beaded Grape (California), amber 165.00

Beaded Swag, etched, ruby stain w/EX gold 225.00
Beaded Swirl & Lens 125.00
Blazing Cornucopia, rpl stopper 135.00
Bluerina, Libbey 1,200.00
Broken Column 85.00
Bubble Lattice, bl satin, pressed faceted stopper 250.00
Cathedral, amber 95.00
Christmas Bead & Panel, wht opal base, rim hdl & beads 225.00
Circled Scroll, gr opal, faceted stopper, rare 575.00
Coin, amber, Fostoria 65.00
Coin Spot, cranberry opal 395.00
Cone, bl satin, clear faceted stopper 275.00
Cranberry moire satin, frosted hdl & stopper 295.00
Croesus, gr w/gold, sm 300.00
Crysanthemum Base Swirl, cranberry opal, cut stopper 625.00
Daisy & Button, amber stain 175.00
Daisy & Fern, Apple Blossom mold, bl opal 160.00
Daisy & Fern, Apple Blossom mold, wht opal, clear stopper 225.00
Daisy & Fern, cranberry satin 150.00
Dewey, gr, matching stopper 250.00
Dmn Quilt MOP, apricot/wht, triangular hdl, knobby stopper ..1,250.00
Empress, gr w/gold 315.00
Esther, gr w/gold, lg 285.00
Esther, gr w/gold, sm 250.00
Feather, emerald gr, gr faceted stopper 350.00
Fluted Scrolls, bl opal 225.00
Galloway, Maiden Blush 295.00
Georgia Gem, custard 245.00
Hearts, bl opal, Fenton 100.00
Hobnail, amber, French 245.00
Hobnail, bl, amber stopper & hdl 195.00
Hobnail, canary opal, Hobbs, matching faceted stopper 275.00
Hobnail, cranberry opal 375.00
Hobnail, vaseline 395.00
Invt T'print, amberina, cut w/eagle on arrow & stars, 5½" 900.00
Invt T'print, amberina, HP decor 450.00
Invt T'print, amberina, in Tufts SP fr 975.00
Invt T'print, amberina, petticoat shape, NE Glass, 6¾" 495.00
Invt T'print, amberina w/forget-me-nots, amber stopper 450.00
Invt T'print, cranberry 265.00
Invt T'print, cranberry, HP decor 450.00
Invt T'print, rubena, funnel shape 215.00
Invt T'print, rubena verde, wide base, vaseline hdl/stopper 485.00
Iris w/Meander, bl opal, clear paneled stopper 750.00
Iris w/Meander, vaseline opal 425.00
Jackson, custard, rpl stopper 95.00
Jackson, vaseline opal 225.00
Jewel & Flower, wht opal, flint 750.00
Jeweled Heart, gr 185.00
Leaf Mold, cranberry satin spatter, clear cut stopper 375.00
Louis XV, custard w/gold trim 280.00
Majestic, ruby stained, pressed faceted stopper 175.00
Mary Gregory, gr 100.00
Massachusetts 55.00
Medallion Sprig, cranberry, cut faceted stopper 350.00
Moon & Stars, amber 30.00
New Hampshire, rose stained 289.00
Palm Beach, red grapes/gr leaves on clear, clear stopper 135.00
Panelled Daisy & Button, amber stain 265.00
Panelled Sprig Lattice, wht opal 295.00
Polka Dot, vaseline, Fenton 100.00
Prize, emerald gr w/EX gold 250.00
Rib Optic, cranberry w/floral, clear bubble stopper, 8¾" 195.00
Ribbed Opal Lattice, clear opal, cut stopper 150.00

Shoshone, gr, ...120.00
Spangle, lt bl w/wht mottle & silver mica, Hobbs & Brockunier ..525.00
Stars & Bars, bl, Hobstar Block stopper 95.00
Swag w/Brackets, vaseline opal 350.00
Swirl, amberina, bulbous w/stick neck, 6" 395.00
Tokyo, bl opal, orig stopper 225.00
Tortoise Shell, swirled, dk amber stopper 345.00
Wheeling Drape, peachblow 650.00
Windows, cranberry opal, cut stopper 350.00
Winged Scroll, emerald gr w/gold, cut faceted stopper 315.00

Cup Plates, Glass

Before the middle 1850s, it was socially acceptable to pour hot tea into a deep saucer to cool. The tea was sipped from the saucer rather than the cup, which frequently was handleless and too hot to hold. The cup plate served as a coaster for the cup. It is generally agreed that the first examples of pressed glass cup plates were made about 1826 at the Boston and Sandwich Glass Co. in Sandwich, Cape Cod, Massachusetts. Other glassworks in three major areas (New England, Philadelphia, and the Midwest, especially Pittsburgh) quickly followed suit.

Antique glass cup plates range in size from 2⅝" up to 4¼" in diameter. The earliest plates had simple designs inspired by cut glass patterns, but by 1829 they had become more complex. The span from then until about 1845 is known as the 'Lacy Period,' when cup plate designs and pressing techniques were at their peak. To cover pressing imperfections, the backgrounds of the plates were often covered with fine stippling which endowed them with a glittering brilliance called 'laciness.' They were made in a multitude of designs — some purely decorative, others commemorative. Subjects include the American eagle, hearts, sunbursts, log cabins, ships, George Washington, the political candidates Clay and Harrison, plows, beehives, etc. Of all the patterns, the round George Washington plate is the rarest and most valuable — only three are known to exist today.

Authenticity is most important. Collectors must be aware that contemporary plates which have no antique counterparts and fakes modeled after antique patterns have had wide distribution. Condition is also important, though it is the exceptional plate that does not have some rim roughness. More important considerations are scarcity of design and color.

Our advisor for this category is John Bilane; he is listed in the Directory under New Jersey. The book *American Glass* by George and Helen McKearin has a section on glass cup plates. A more definitive book is *American Glass Cup Plates* by Ruth Webb Lee and James H. Rose. Numbers in the listings that follow (computer sorted) refer to the latter. When no condition is indicated, the examples listed below are assumed to have only minor rim roughness as is normal. See also Staffordshire; Pairpoint.

R-102, G 42.00
R-104, G+ 41.00
R-124-A, VG- 36.00
R-124-C, very rare, VG 110.00
R-126, very rare, VG 115.00
R-147, scarce, VG 45.00
R-174, thick, EX 45.00
R-177, VG+ 44.00
R-191-D, G 25.00
R-197, rare, G 55.00
R-199, rare, G 28.00
R-208, scarce, G 33.00
R-236, G 28.00
R-245, G 24.00

R-254, rare, VG 50.00
R-255, rare, VG 20.00
R-257, VG 29.00
R-258, VG 30.00
R-265, rare, VG+ 52.00
R-269, VG 30.00
R-270, rare, EX 60.00
R-271-A, VG+ 33.00
R-272-A, very rare, VG- 75.00
R-276, VG 36.00
R-285, VG 32.00
R-291, VG 26.00
R-313, VG 21.00
R-315, rare, VG 120.00
R-323, VG 18.00
R-326, G+ 17.00
R-327, G 12.00
R-332-B, G 12.00
R-334, VG 19.00
R-334-A, VG 15.00
R-339, VG 19.00
R-340, G 15.00
R-343-B, scarce, VG+ 35.00
R-367, G 10.00
R-369, VG+ 18.00
R-373, VG+ 16.00
R-379, VG+ 13.00
R-381, VG 13.00
R-388, G+ 11.00
R-390, G 9.00
R-390-A, VG 13.00
R-393, G 10.00
R-396, VG 13.00
R-402, VG 14.00
R-404, VG+ 13.50
R-41, scarce, VG+ 45.00
R-425, G+ 23.00
R-440, G+ 30.00
R-447, G 22.00
R-447-A, G 21.00
R-456, scarce, G 19.00
R-456-X-1, scarce, G 19.00
R-46, VG 26.00
R-465-H, VG 23.00
R-465-H-X-2, EX 26.00
R-465-N, G 16.00
R-47, G 25.00
R-476, G 13.00
R-501, G 11.00
R-535-A, G 21.00
R-54, scarce, EX 55.00
R-545, VG+ 17.00
R-564, VG 28.00
R-565, G 25.00
R-566-B, rare, VG 68.00
R-570, rare, G 81.00
R-574, extremely rare, VG 235.00
R-576, scarce, G 52.00
R-590, G 28.00
R-593, scarce, G+ 45.00
R-594, G 22.00
R-605-A, scarce, G 88.00
R-610-A, VG 34.00
R-610-C, VG 40.00

R-619, G+ 38.00
R-619-A, G 30.00
R-62-A, scarce, G 42.00
R-628, scarce, G 53.00
R-636, VG 42.00
R-637, very rare, VG 275.00
R-642, G+ 18.00
R-661, G 15.00
R-665-A, VG 36.00
R-666, G+ 32.00
R-674, scarce, VG 60.00
R-677-A, VG 36.00
R-679, VG 30.00
R-680-A, scarce, G 36.00
R-686, rare, VG+ 152.00
R-695, G 46.00
R-78, scarce, VG 60.00
R-79, G 32.00
R-89, rare, VG 135.00
R-95, opal opaque, rare, VG 138.00
R-98, rare, VG 68.00
R-99, rare, G 45.00

Currier & Ives by Royal

During the 1950s dinnerware decorated with transfer-printed scenes taken from prints by Currier and Ives was manufactured by Royal China and given as premiums through A&P stores. Though it was also made in pink, green and brown as well, the blue is by far the most popular. In addition to the dinnerware, a line of Fire-King baking pans and accessories was also available, as were vinyl placemats and various sizes of glass tumblers. Today it is readily available at reasonable prices, and it has become a very popular collectible at malls and flea markets around the country. Our advisors for this category are Treva and Jack Hamlin; they are listed in the Directory under Ohio.

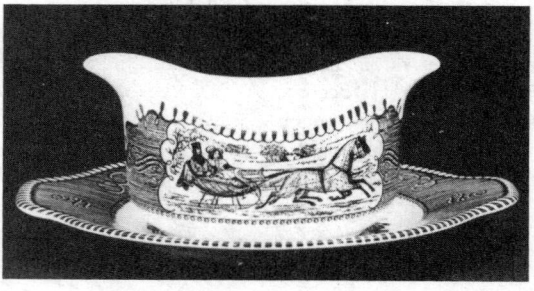

Gravy boat and undertray, $25.00.

Ashtray 10.00
Bowl, cereal; tab hdl, rare, 6⅜" 25.00
Bowl, cereal; 6⅜" 7.00
Bowl, fruit; 5½" 3.00
Bowl, lug soup; deep, tab hdl, 2¾x4¾" 20.00
Bowl, soup; flat, 8½" 7.50
Bowl, vegetable; 10" 20.00
Bowl, 9" 18.00
Butter dish, ¼-lb 25.00
Calendar plate, ca 1970s-85, ea 12.00
Candle lamp & globe, rare, tall, 3¾" base 30.00
Casserole, angle hdls, w/lid 60.00
Casserole, tab hdls, w/lid, old 100.00

Creamer	5.00
Cup & saucer	4.00
Gravy boat	13.00
Gravy boat, w/ladle & underplate	35.00
Gravy ladle	10.00
Mug, soup (or coffee); mk, 2¾x3¾"	18.00
Pie plate (6 decals made)	15.00
Plate, 10½"	4.00
Plate, 6"	2.50
Plate, 7⅜"	7.00
Plate, 9"	10.00
Platter, oval, 13"	22.00
Platter, rnd, mk, rare, 13" dia	40.00
Platter, rnd, mk, 11" dia	20.00
Platter, tab hdls, 10½"	18.00
Platter, 12" dia	25.00
Shakers, pr	15.00
Sugar bowl, w/lid	12.00
Teapot	75.00
Tumbler, juice	10.00
Tumbler, milk glass	7.00
Tumbler, old-fashioned, 3¼"	10.00
Tumbler, 13-oz, 5½"	12.00
Tumbler, 9-oz, 4¾"	12.00
Underplate, tab hdls, sm (for gravy boat)	12.00

Custard

As early as the 1880s, custard glass was produced in England. Migrating glassmakers brought the formula for the creamy ivory ware to America. One of them was Harry Northwood, who in 1898 founded his company in Indiana, Pennsylvania, and introduced the glassware to the American market. Soon other companies were producing custard, among them Heisey, Tarentum, Fenton, and McKee. Not only dinnerware patterns but souvenir items were made. Today custard is the most expensive of the colored pressed glassware patterns. The formula for producing the luminous glass contains uranium salts which imparts the cream color to the batch and causes it to glow when it is examined under a black light.

Argonaut Shell, bowl, master berry; gold & decor, 10½" L	265.00
Argonaut Shell, bowl, sauce; ftd, gold & decor	65.00
Argonaut Shell, butter dish, gold & decor	350.00
Argonaut Shell, butter dish, no gold	275.00
Argonaut Shell, compote, jelly; gold & decor, scarce	145.00
Argonaut Shell, creamer, gold & decor	135.00
Argonaut Shell, creamer, no gold	110.00

Argonaut Shell, creamer and sugar bowl, gold trim, $495.00.

Argonaut Shell, cruet, gold & decor	700.00
Argonaut Shell, pitcher, water; gold & decor	435.00
Argonaut Shell, spooner, gold & decor	135.00
Argonaut Shell, sugar bowl, w/lid, gold & decor	200.00
Argonaut Shell, tumbler, gold & decor	110.00
Bead Swag, bowl, sauce; floral & gold	50.00
Bead Swag, goblet, floral & gold	65.00
Bead Swag, tray, pickle; floral & gold, rare	260.00
Bead Swag, wine, floral & gold	60.00
Beaded Circle, bowl, master berry; floral & gold	245.00
Beaded Circle, butter dish, floral & gold	450.00
Beaded Circle, creamer, floral & gold	180.00
Beaded Circle, cruet, floral & gold, rare	1,175.00
Beaded Circle, pitcher, water; floral & gold	675.00
Beaded Circle, shakers, floral & gold, pr	800.00
Beaded Circle, spooner, floral & gold	175.00
Beaded Circle, sugar bowl, w/lid, floral & gold	275.00
Beaded Circle, tumbler, floral & gold, very rare	100.00
Cane Insert, berry set, 7-pc	450.00
Cane Insert, table set, 4-pc	450.00
Cherry & Scales, bowl, master berry; nutmeg stain	130.00
Cherry & Scales, butter dish, nutmeg stain	225.00
Cherry & Scales, creamer, nutmeg stain	115.00
Cherry & Scales, pitcher, water; nutmeg stain, scarce	325.00
Cherry & Scales, spooner, nutmeg stain, scarce	110.00
Cherry & Scales, sugar bowl, w/lid, nutmeg stain, scarce	125.00
Cherry & Scales, tumbler, nutmeg stain, scarce	50.00
Chrysanthemum Sprig, bowl, master berry; gold & decor	275.00
Chrysanthemum Sprig, bowl, master berry; no gold	175.00
Chrysanthemum Sprig, bowl, sauce; ftd, gold & decor	50.00
Chrysanthemum Sprig, butter dish, gold & decor	300.00
Chrysanthemum Sprig, celery vase, gold & decor, rare	375.00
Chrysanthemum Sprig, compote, jelly; gold & decor	135.00
Chrysanthemum Sprig, compote, jelly; no decor	95.00
Chrysanthemum Sprig, creamer, gold & decor	125.00
Chrysanthemum Sprig, cruet, gold & decor, 6¾"	350.00
Chrysanthemum Sprig, pitcher, water; gold & decor	470.00
Chrysanthemum Sprig, shakers, gold & decor, pr	300.00
Chrysanthemum Sprig, spooner, gold & decor	130.00
Chrysanthemum Sprig, spooner, no gold	75.00
Chrysanthemum Sprig, toothpick holder, gold & decor	300.00
Chrysanthemum Sprig, toothpick holder, no decor	165.00
Chrysanthemum Sprig, tumbler, gold & decor	55.00
Dandelion, mug, nutmeg stain	165.00
Delaware, bowl, sauce; pk stain	65.00
Delaware, creamer, breakfast; pk stain	70.00
Delaware, tray, pin; gr stain	75.00
Delaware, tumbler, pk stain	55.00
Diamond w/Peg, bowl, master berry; roses & gold	215.00
Diamond w/Peg, bowl, sauce; roses & gold	40.00
Diamond w/Peg, butter dish, roses & gold	235.00
Diamond w/Peg, creamer, ind; no decor	30.00
Diamond w/Peg, creamer, ind; souvenir	45.00
Diamond w/Peg, creamer, roses & gold	75.00
Diamond w/Peg, mug, souvenir	50.00
Diamond w/Peg, napkin ring, roses & gold, rare	150.00
Diamond w/Peg, pitcher, roses & gold, 5½"	260.00
Diamond w/Peg, shakers, souvenir, pr	175.00
Diamond w/Peg, sugar bowl, w/lid, roses & gold	160.00
Diamond w/Peg, toothpick holder, roses & gold	150.00
Diamond w/Peg, tumbler, roses & gold	60.00
Diamond w/Peg, water set, souvenir, 7-pc	650.00
Diamond w/Peg, wine, roses & gold	55.00
Diamond w/Peg, wine, souvenir	40.00

Everglades, bowl, master berry; gold & decor 215.00
Everglades, bowl, sauce; gold & decor 60.00
Everglades, butter dish, gold & decor 395.00
Everglades, creamer, gold & decor 155.00
Everglades, shakers, gold & decor, pr 375.00
Everglades, spooner, gold & decor 160.00
Everglades, sugar bowl, w/lid, gold & decor 235.00
Everglades, tumbler, gold & decor 100.00
Fan, bowl, master berry; good gold 135.00
Fan, bowl, sauce; good gold 55.00
Fan, butter dish, good gold 225.00
Fan, creamer, good gold 110.00
Fan, ice cream set, good gold, 7-pc 500.00
Fan, pitcher, water; good gold 275.00
Fan, spooner, good gold 100.00
Fan, sugar bowl, w/lid, good gold 150.00
Fan, tumbler, good gold 75.00
Fan, water set, good gold, 7-pc 700.00
Fine Cut & Roses, rose bowl, fancy int, nutmeg stain 100.00
Fine Cut & Roses, rose bowl, plain int 85.00
Geneva, bowl, master berry; floral decor, ftd, oval, 9" L 90.00
Geneva, bowl, master berry; floral decor, rnd, 9" 120.00
Geneva, bowl, sauce; floral decor, oval 45.00
Geneva, bowl, sauce; floral decor, rnd 45.00
Geneva, butter dish, floral decor 225.00
Geneva, butter dish, no decor 135.00
Geneva, compote, jelly; floral decor 95.00
Geneva, creamer, floral decor 100.00
Geneva, cruet, floral decor 465.00
Geneva, pitcher, water; floral decor 250.00
Geneva, shakers, floral decor, pr 280.00
Geneva, spooner, floral decor 100.00
Geneva, sugar bowl, open, floral decor 85.00
Geneva, sugar bowl, w/lid, floral decor 150.00
Geneva, syrup, floral decor 475.00
Geneva, toothpick holder, floral w/M gold 375.00
Geneva, tumbler, floral decor 50.00
Georgia Gem, bowl, master berry; good gold 135.00
Georgia Gem, bowl, master berry; gr opaque 115.00
Georgia Gem, butter dish, good gold 190.00
Georgia Gem, celery vase, good gold 145.00
Georgia Gem, creamer, good gold 100.00
Georgia Gem, creamer, no gold 60.00
Georgia Gem, mug, good gold 45.00
Georgia Gem, powder jar, w/lid, good gold 80.00
Georgia Gem, shakers, good gold, pr 160.00
Georgia Gem, spooner, souvenir 55.00
Georgia Gem, sugar bowl, w/lid, no gold 95.00
Grape (& Cable), bottle, scent; orig stopper, nutmeg stain 600.00
Grape (& Cable), bowl, master berry; nutmeg stain, ftd, 11" 375.00
Grape (& Cable), bowl, nutmeg stain, 7½" 60.00
Grape (& Cable), bowl, sauce; nutmeg stain, ftd 50.00
Grape (& Cable), butter dish, nutmeg stain 275.00
Grape (& Cable), compote, jelly; open, nutmeg stain 145.00
Grape (& Cable), compote, nutmeg stain, 4½x8" 300.00
Grape (& Cable), cracker jar, nutmeg stain 800.00
Grape (& Cable), creamer, breakfast; nutmeg stain 80.00
Grape (& Cable), humidor, bl stain, rare 950.00
Grape (& Cable), humidor, nutmeg stain, rare 900.00
Grape (& Cable), nappy, nutmeg stain, rare 60.00
Grape (& Cable), pitcher, water; nutmeg stain 400.00
Grape (& Cable), plate, nutmeg stain, 7" 50.00
Grape (& Cable), plate, nutmeg stain, 8" 65.00
Grape (& Cable), powder jar, nutmeg stain 350.00

Grape (& Cable), punch bowl, w/base, nutmeg stain 1,750.00
Grape (& Cable), spooner, nutmeg stain 145.00
Grape (& Cable), sugar bowl, breakfast; open, nutmeg stain 75.00
Grape (& Cable), sugar bowl, w/lid, nutmeg stain 195.00
Grape (& Cable), tray, dresser; nutmeg stain, scarce, lg 350.00
Grape (& Cable), tray, pin; nutmeg stain 135.00
Grape (& Cable), tumbler, nutmeg stain 75.00
Grape & Gothic Arches, bowl, master berry; pearl w/gold 200.00
Grape & Gothic Arches, bowl, sauce; pearl w/gold, rare 80.00
Grape & Gothic Arches, butter dish, pearl w/gold 235.00
Grape & Gothic Arches, creamer, pearl w/gold, rare 100.00
Grape & Gothic Arches, favor vase, nutmeg stain 80.00
Grape & Gothic Arches, goblet, pearl w/gold 75.00
Grape & Gothic Arches, pitcher, water; pearl w/gold 300.00
Grape & Gothic Arches, spooner, pearl w/gold 85.00
Grape & Gothic Arches, sugar bowl, w/lid, pearl w/gold 135.00
Grape & Gothic Arches, tumbler, pearl w/gold 65.00
Grape Arbor, vase, hat form 90.00
Heart w/T'print, creamer 85.00
Heart w/T'print, lamp, good pnt, scarce, 8" 435.00
Heart w/T'print, sugar bowl, ind 80.00
Honeycomb, wine 65.00
Horse Medallion, bowl, gr stain, 7" 80.00
Intaglio, bowl, master berry; gold & decor, ftd, 9" 250.00
Intaglio, bowl, sauce; gold & decor 50.00
Intaglio, butter dish, gold & decor, scarce 300.00
Intaglio, compote, jelly; gold & decor 125.00
Intaglio, creamer, gold & decor 125.00
Intaglio, cruet, gold & decor 475.00
Intaglio, pitcher, water; gold & decor 395.00
Intaglio, shakers, gold & decor, pr 235.00
Intaglio, spooner, gold & decor 125.00
Intaglio, sugar bowl, w/lid, gold & decor 165.00
Intaglio, tumbler, gold & decor 75.00
Inverted Fan & Feather, bowl, master berry; gold & decor 250.00
Inverted Fan & Feather, bowl, sauce; gold & decor 65.00
Inverted Fan & Feather, butter dish, gold & decor 350.00
Inverted Fan & Feather, compote, jelly; gold & decor, rare 500.00
Inverted Fan & Feather, creamer, gold & decor 150.00
Inverted Fan & Feather, cruet, gold & decor, scarce, 6½" 1,100.00
Inverted Fan & Feather, pitcher, water; gold & decor 600.00
Inverted Fan & Feather, punch cup, gold & decor 250.00
Inverted Fan & Feather, shakers, gold & decor, pr 600.00
Inverted Fan & Feather, spooner, gold & decor 145.00
Inverted Fan & Feather, sugar bowl, w/lid, gold & decor 225.00
Inverted Fan & Feather, tumbler, gold & decor 95.00
Jackson, bowl, master berry; good gold, ftd 135.00
Jackson, bowl, sauce; good gold 45.00
Jackson, creamer, good gold 85.00
Jackson, pitcher, water; good gold 250.00
Jackson, pitcher, water; no decor 175.00
Jackson, shakers, good gold, pr 195.00
Jackson, tumbler, good gold 50.00
Louis XV, berry set, w/nutmeg, 7-pc 375.00
Louis XV, bowl, master berry; good gold 165.00
Louis XV, bowl, sauce; good gold, ftd 47.00
Louis XV, butter dish, good gold 200.00
Louis XV, creamer, good gold 80.00
Louis XV, cruet, good gold 365.00
Louis XV, pitcher, water; good gold 225.00
Louis XV, spooner, good gold 80.00
Louis XV, sugar bowl, w/lid, good gold 150.00
Louis XV, tumbler, good gold 65.00
Maple Leaf, bowl, master berry; gold & decor, scarce 335.00

Maple Leaf, bowl, sauce; gold & decor, scarce 95.00
Maple Leaf, butter dish, gold & decor 350.00
Maple Leaf, compote, jelly; gold & decor, rare 455.00
Maple Leaf, creamer, gold & decor 150.00
Maple Leaf, cruet, gold & decor, rare 3,000.00

Maple Leaf, pitcher, green with gold trim, $465.00.

Vermont, toothpick holder, bl decor 155.00
Vermont, vase, floral decor, jeweled 95.00

Vermont, tumbler, painted flower and leaves, 4x3", $60.00.

Maple Leaf, pitcher, water; gold & decor 400.00
Maple Leaf, shakers, gold & decor, very rare, pr 800.00
Maple Leaf, spooner, gold & decor 155.00
Maple Leaf, sugar bowl, w/lid, gold & decor 230.00
Maple Leaf, tumbler, gold & decor 95.00
Panelled Poppy, lamp shade, nutmeg stain, scarce 800.00
Peacock & Urn, bowl, ice cream; nutmeg stain, sm 80.00
Peacock & Urn, bowl, ice cream; nutmeg stain, 10" 350.00
Punty Band, shakers, pr 175.00
Punty Band, spooner, floral decor 100.00
Punty Band, tumbler, floral decor, souvenir 65.00
Ribbed Drape, bowl, sauce; roses & gold 40.00
Ribbed Drape, butter dish, scalloped, roses & gold 375.00
Ribbed Drape, compote, jelly; roses & gold, rare 200.00
Ribbed Drape, creamer, roses & gold, scarce 180.00
Ribbed Drape, cruet, roses & gold, rare 650.00
Ribbed Drape, pitcher, water; roses & gold, rare 365.00
Ribbed Drape, shakers, roses & gold, rare, pr 360.00
Ribbed Drape, spooner, roses & gold 180.00
Ribbed Drape, toothpick holder, roses & gold 475.00
Ribbed Drape, tumbler, roses & gold 65.00
Ribbed Thumbprint, wine, floral decor 80.00
Ring Band, bowl, master berry; roses & gold 150.00
Ring Band, bowl, sauce; roses & gold 45.00
Ring Band, butter dish, roses & gold 250.00
Ring Band, compote, jelly; roses & gold, scarce 195.00
Ring Band, creamer, roses & gold 115.00
Ring Band, cruet, roses & gold 450.00
Ring Band, pitcher, roses & gold, 7½" 335.00
Ring Band, shakers, roses & gold, pr 155.00
Ring Band, spooner, roses & gold 110.00
Ring Band, syrup, roses & gold 465.00
Ring Band, toothpick holder, roses & gold 135.00
Ring Band, tray, condiment; roses & gold 200.00
Singing Birds, mug, nutmeg stain 75.00
Tarentum's Victoria, bowl, master berry; gold & decor 200.00
Tarentum's Victoria, butter dish, gold & decor, rare 300.00
Tarentum's Victoria, celery vase, gold & decor, rare 275.00
Tarentum's Victoria, creamer, gold & decor, scarce 135.00
Tarentum's Victoria, pitcher, water; gold & decor, rare 375.00
Tarentum's Victoria, spooner, gold & decor 135.00
Tarentum's Victoria, sugar bowl, w/lid, gold & decor 160.00
Tarentum's Victoria, tumbler, gold & decor 70.00
Vermont, butter dish, bl decor 195.00

Wide Band, bell, roses 195.00
Wild Bouquet, butter dish, gold & decor, rare 700.00
Wild Bouquet, creamer, no gold 145.00
Wild Bouquet, cruet, no decor, w/clear stopper 995.00
Wild Bouquet, sauce, gold & decor 60.00
Wild Bouquet, spooner, gold & decor 160.00
Wild Bouquet, tumbler, no decor 95.00
Winged Scroll, bowl, master berry; gold & decor, 11" L 175.00
Winged Scroll, bowl, sauce; good gold 45.00
Winged Scroll, butter dish, good gold 200.00
Winged Scroll, butter dish, no decor 150.00
Winged Scroll, celery vase, good gold, rare 400.00
Winged Scroll, cigarette jar, scarce 195.00
Winged Scroll, compote, ruffled, rare, 6¾x10¾" 495.00
Winged Scroll, cruet, good gold, clear stopper 375.00
Winged Scroll, hair receiver, good gold 135.00
Winged Scroll, pitcher, water; bulbous, good gold 350.00
Winged Scroll, shakers, bulbous, good gold, rare, pr 400.00
Winged Scroll, shakers, str sides, good gold, pr 195.00
Winged Scroll, sugar bowl, w/lid, good gold 150.00
Winged Scroll, syrup, good gold 395.00
Winged Scroll, tumbler, good gold 75.00

Cut Glass

The earliest documented evidence of commercial glass cutting in the United States was in 1810; the producers were Bakewell and Page of Pittsburgh. These first efforts resulted in simple patterns with only a moderate amount of cutting. By the middle of the century, glass cutters began experimenting with a thicker glass which enabled them to use deeper cuttings, though patterns remained much the same. This period is usually referred to as Rich Cut. Using three types of wheels — a flat edge, a mitered edge, and a convex edge — facets, miters, and depressions were combined to produce various designs. In the late 1870s, a curved miter was developed which greatly expanded design potential. Patterns became more elaborate, often covering the entire surface. The Brilliant Period of cut glass covered a span from about 1880 until 1915. Because of the pressure necessary to achieve the deeply cut patterns, only glass containing a high grade of metal could withstand the process. For this reason and the amount of handwork involved, cut glass has always been expensive. Bowls cut with pinwheels may be either foreign or of a newer vintage, beware! Identifiable patterns and signed pieces that are well cut and in excellent condition bring the higher prices on today's market.

Key:

dmn — diamonds	X-cut — crosscut
strw — strawberry	X-hatch — crosshatch

Basket, butterfly & flowers, sterling repousse hdl, 17x12" **1,100.00**
Basket, cosmos flowers & leaves, notched hdl, 15x10x5½" **275.00**
Basket, geometrics & florals, twisted hdl, 6½x7" **150.00**
Basket, strw dmns, notched hdl, 7x6x1½" **175.00**
Bottle, lay-down scent; dmns & swirls, sterling lid, 4½" **95.00**
Bowl, Alhambra, 4x9" **950.00**
Bowl, central star w/hobstars & flashed fans, 8" **60.00**
Bowl, Comet, 8" **235.00**
Bowl, fans/relief dmns/hobstars, folded-in rim, 9" **175.00**
Bowl, ferns & leaves w/X-hatches, rolled rim, 12" **50.00**
Bowl, flower; hobstars/dmns/strw dmns, notched rim, 3½x8½" ..**175.00**
Bowl, Harvard, rough rim, 8" **60.00**
Bowl, Harvard border, vesicas/flowers in base, canoe, 12½" L **90.00**
Bowl, hobstars & cane amid flashed/feathered stars, 9" **125.00**
Bowl, hobstars alternate w/Harvard, 8" **110.00**
Bowl, hobstars/starred hobs/X-hatches/fans, 8" **115.00**
Bowl, Honeycomb, SP rim, 8¼" **50.00**
Bowl, Hunt's Royal, 9" **375.00**
Bowl, Kohinoor center, curved miter splits, 9¼" **360.00**
Bowl, mint; pinwheels/hobstars/X-cut dmns, Clark, 5" **40.00**
Bowl, notched flash prisms & hobstars, clover shape, 8½" **160.00**
Bowl, nut; fan border, strw dmns/8 hobstars, 5" **135.00**
Bowl, pinwheels/hobstars/relief dmn, 8" **100.00**
Bowl, 3 prism fans/hobstars/relief dmn fields, 7½" **70.00**
Bowl, 6 panels alternate stars & dbl sqs, Maple City, 5" **75.00**
Butter dish, hobstar & button chain, faceted knob, 5½x8½" **350.00**
Butter dish, hobstars/X-cut dmns/fans, faceted knob, 7x9" **225.00**
Cake plate, hobstars/vesicas/fans/dmn points, 4-ftd **425.00**
Candy box, X-cut/dmns on ped w/base wafer, 6" dia **195.00**
Carafe, Hindoo step-cut neck & bodice, Hoare, 8½" **125.00**
Carafe, hobstars & nailhead vesicas, notched neck, 7" **75.00**
Card holder, intaglio rose ea side, 3½x2½" **100.00**
Celery tray, hobstars, 6-point star center, Eggington **160.00**
Celery vase, cane bars/hobstars/beading, Hoare, 5½x11½" **300.00**
Cheese & cracker set, geometrics & florals, 12" dia **150.00**

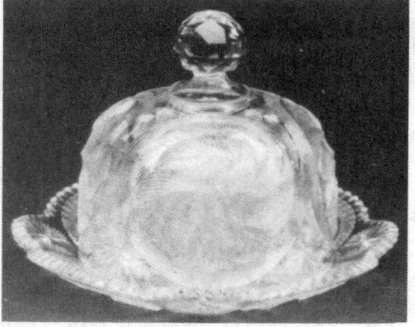

Cheese dish, brilliant swirling pattern, faceted knob finial, 8x10½", $550.00.

Claret, allover florals, metal hdl, 1800s, 11" **200.00**
Compote, chain of hobstars w/cane & star rim, Hoare, 7" H **250.00**
Compote, Harvard panels & flowers, star base, 11x7¾" **120.00**
Compote, hobstars in star, notched stem, 6x7" **150.00**
Compote, hobstars & buttoned vesicas, 6-sided, 8½" **175.00**
Compote, hobstars & fans, honeycomb stem/rayed base, 7½x6½" ..**100.00**
Compote, hobstars & fans/hobstars, rolled-in rim, 9½x6" **95.00**

Compote, jelly; hobstars/fans, spiral stick stem, 8½x6" **150.00**
Cookie server, butterflies & ferns, center hdl, Mortinsen, 10" **395.00**
Creamer & sugar bowl, hobstars & stars allover **195.00**
Creamer & sugar bowl, hobstars & X-hatches, cut hdls, 4½", 4" ...**300.00**
Creamer & sugar bowl, star flowers, notched hdls, 4", 3" **100.00**
Decanter, hobstars & fans, notched hdl & neck, 13" **500.00**
Decanter, hobstars/elongated stars/miters, w/stopper, 17" **110.00**
Decanter, nailhead, fluted shoulder, 3-tier neck, 12½" **95.00**
Decanter, Pineapple & Fan, notched hdl, faceted stopper, 13" ...**210.00**
Decanter, Strw Dmn & Fan, fluted neck, 3-notch hdl, 14" **170.00**
Decanter, 2 rows of punty, honeycomb neck, rayed base, 9½" **125.00**
Decanter, 4 bull's eye tears w/stars, teardrop stopper, 13½" **115.00**
Finger bowl, Dorian, 4½" **120.00**
Finger bowl, hobs/half-dmns/X-cut dmns, sgn Eggington **175.00**
Ice bucket, expanding stars, 6x6" **250.00**
Ice bucket, Russian, 5¼x6½" **350.00**
Jug, pinwheels/hobstars/fans/prisms, faceted stopper, 8" **175.00**
Jug, whiskey; tusks/vesicas w/hobstars/fans/dmn vesicas, 9½" **700.00**
Lamp, hobstars/dmn points/fans/X-hatching, 20" **2,350.00**
Nappy, #1 Spray pattern, sgn Illig, 6" **350.00**
Nappy, Harvard, step-cut ped ft, appl hdls, 8½x11" **400.00**
Pitcher, buttermilk; geometrics, notched hdl, 8" **300.00**
Pitcher, buttermilk; Pinwheel **150.00**
Pitcher, buttons & hobstars fr florals, bull's-eye hdl, 10" **135.00**
Pitcher, flashed hobstars, hobnails & fans, Hoare, 10½" **300.00**
Pitcher, milk; hobstars/dmn points/fans, 6" **225.00**
Pitcher, milk; hobstars/X-hatches/fans, 2-notch hdl, 6½" **225.00**
Pitcher, radiant daisies w/leaves & ferns, notched hdl, 10" **95.00**
Pitcher, St James, Hoare, 8" **250.00**
Pitcher, Sunburst, 3-notch hdl, fluted/notched spout, 11½" **525.00**
Pitcher, sunbursts over swag band, notched hdl, 7½" **150.00**
Pitcher, tankard; florals on leafy stems, 8½", +6 tumblers **150.00**
Pitcher, tankard; Harvard, notched hdl, 14" **625.00**
Pitcher, tankard; hobstars/fans/X-cut dmns, slim, 11" **250.00**
Pitcher, tankard; Pluto, Hoare, 14" **575.00**
Pitcher, tankard; Strw Dmn & Fan, 9" **40.00**
Plate, Arcadia w/Star, 7" **150.00**
Plate, hobstar fr in dbl sqs, silver rim, 9" **75.00**
Punch bowl, hobstars & X-hatching, 2-pc, 17x13" **2,250.00**
Punch bowl, Hunt's Royal, 12" **1,250.00**
Punch bowl, Pinwheel Variant, 12x12" **550.00**
Punch bowl, Russian/fans/hobstars, 2-pc, 8½x13"+base **2,250.00**
Ring dish, hobstars/dmn points/fans **225.00**
Rose bowl, cranberry to clear, Notched Prism & Zipper, 3" **350.00**
Salad fork, metal body w/hobstars on bulbous finial **200.00**
Salad fork & spoon, Russian hdls w/teardrops, Gorham mts, 11" ..**495.00**
Spooner, hobstars & fans, 4½" H **95.00**
Sugar & creamer, hobstars/dmn points/rays/feathers, ped ft **375.00**
Syrup, lg hobstar allover, rayed base, sterling hinged lid **250.00**
Tankard, prisms, emb florals, notched hdl, sterling trim, 12" **550.00**
Tazza, hobstar chain, teardrop stem, hobstar base, 7" dia **175.00**
Tray, Arcadia, Sterling Glass Co, 11x7" **375.00**
Tray, central 8-point star w/X-hatches/hobstars/fans, 7¼" **100.00**
Tray, ice cream; Stratford, notched hdls, 17½x10½" **600.00**
Tray, ice cream; 2 lg 24-point rosettes in center, 8x13½" **600.00**
Tray, pin; 3 hobstars w/4 dmns of X-hatching, 4x2¾" **125.00**
Tray, relish; hobstars/button/fans, oblong, 4¾x11½" **65.00**
Tray, Strauss Imperial, 14x8¾" **500.00**
Tumbler, juice; Russian, single star centers, att Hawkes **85.00**
Tumbler, juice; 12 hobstars/X-cut dmns/fans, 3½" **110.00**
Vase, bull's-eye panels/hobstar chains/X-cut dmns/fans, 14" **200.00**
Vase, columns of hobstars & bull's eyes, flared, 12" **370.00**
Vase, daisies on long leafy stems, corset shape, 12" **80.00**
Vase, flashed pinwheels & X-cut dmns, trumpet form, 17" **150.00**

Vase, floral cuttings, cylindrical w/bulging rim, 12" **50.00**
Vase, hobstars & sunbursts, heavy, 18¼" **1,000.00**
Vase, hobstars in vesicas, nailhead & fans, cylindrical, 14" **275.00**
Vase, hobstars/cane vesicas/fans, corset form, 12½" **100.00**
Vase, hobstars/fans/X-hatches, hobstar ft, trumpet form, 18½" ...**450.00**
Vase, intaglio primroses & buds among ferns, Signet, 8" **125.00**
Vase, pinwheels/hobstars/beading/fans, trumpet form, 13½" **185.00**
Vase, punty florals & ferns, rayed base, trumpet form, 16" **250.00**
Vinaigrette, Dbl Miter, cone shape, sterling mts, 5½" **175.00**

Cut Velvet

Cut Velvet glassware was made during the late 1800s. It is characterized by the effect achieved through the execution of relief-molded patterns, often ribbing or diamond quilting, which allows its white inner casing to show through the outer layer.

Butter dish, Honeycomb, shaded pk, cut amber finial, 6x7" **250.00**
Celery vase, Dmn Quilt, bl, box-pleated top, Mt WA, 6½" **725.00**
Rose bowl, Dmn Quilt, bl, 4-crimp top, 3¾x3⅜" **165.00**
Rose bowl, Dmn Quilt, gr, egg shape, 4⅛x3" **175.00**
Rose bowl, Dmn Quilt, lav-pk, egg shape, 4⅛x3" **175.00**
Sugar sifter, Dmn Quilt, bl **395.00**

**Vase, Diamond Quilted in blue, 7",
$250.00.**

Vase, Dmn Quilt, bl, frosted appl flower, 5½x3¼" **165.00**
Vase, Dmn Quilt, bl, 4¾x3¼" **145.00**
Vase, Dmn Quilt, bl, 6¼x2¾" **195.00**
Vase, Dmn Quilt, dk purple, bulbous w/long ruffled neck, 11" ...**825.00**
Vase, Dmn Quilt, lt gold, sm neck on dbl-gourd shape, 13½" **650.00**
Vase, Dmn Quilt, pk, crimped cylinder, 6" **150.00**
Vase, Dmn Quilt, pk, ruffled top w/clear edge, 10x4", pr **210.00**
Vase, Ribbed, bl, 6¼x3¼" **110.00**

Cybis

Boleslaw Cybis was a graduate of the Academy of Fine Arts in Warsaw, Poland, and was well recognized as a fine artist by the time he was commissioned by his government to paint murals in the Polish Pavillion's Hall of Honor at the 1939 World's Fair. Finding themselves stranded in America at the outbreak of WWII, the Cybises founded an artists' studio, first in Astoria, New York, and later in Trenton, New Jersey, where they made fine figurines and plaques with exacting artistry and craftsmanship entailing extensive handwork. The studio still operates today producing exquisite porcelains on a limited edition basis.

Ballerina on cue, wht on wood stand, 12½" **450.00**
Burro, Fitzgerald, 7¼" **250.00**
Calla Lily, #427, 16" **850.00**
Dahlia **685.00**
Deer mouse in clover, 1970 ....**135.00**
Duckling, 4" L **125.00**
Elephant **4,500.00**
Elizabeth Ann **245.00**
First Bouquet **600.00**
First in Flight **285.00**
Goldilocks & Panda Bears **800.00**
Great White Heron **1,500.00**
Hansel & Gretel, pr **1,000.00**
Heidi, 8" **400.00**
Holiday child clown, 1983 ....**400.00**
Holiday child w/panda, 1981 ....**400.00**
Holiday child w/teddy bear, 1982 ....**400.00**
Horse **1,675.00**
Juliet **2,000.00**
Kristina, ballerina, 6¾" **575.00**
Little Bo Peep, 10½" **600.00**
Little Boy Blue, 9" **450.00**
Little Miss Muffet, 7" **500.00**
Little Princess **415.00**
Little Red Riding Hood, 6¾" **200.00**
Madame Butterfly, #321, 13½" **2,000.00**

**Madonna Queen of Angels,
white, unglazed, 5",
$475.00.**

Magnolias, #391, 8" **350.00**
Male jogger, 14½" **350.00**
Noah **1,500.00**
Oriental boy head **600.00**
Pandora, girl sits w/box, 5" **700.00**
Performing dog, 8¼" **250.00**
Pollyanna, seated on chair, 7½" **350.00**
Queen Esther, #98, 13" **1,100.00**
Rebecca, kneeling girl w/flowers, 6½" **600.00**
Red Riding Hood **285.00**
Scarlett **1,350.00**
Skylarks, pr **1,550.00**
Turtle w/frog on bk, 5" L **100.00**
Wendy w/doll **550.00**
Wendy w/teddy bear **175.00**
Windflower **185.00**
Wood wren w/dogwood, 5½" **350.00**
Yankee Doodle Dandy, 9" **900.00**

Czechoslovakian Collectibles

Czechoslovakia came into being as a country in 1918. Located in the heart of Europe, it was a land with the natural resources necessary to support a glass industry that dates back to the mid-14th century. This ware has recently captured the attention of today's collectors, and for good reason. There are beautiful vases — cased, ruffled, applied with rigaree or silver overlay — fine enough to rival those of the best glasshouses. Czechoslovakian art glass baskets are quite as attractive as Victorian America's, and the elegant cut glass perfumes made in colors as well as crystal are unrivaled. There are also pressed glass perfumes, molded in lovely Deco shapes, of various types of art glass. Some are overlaid with gold filigree set with 'jewels.' Jewelry, lamps, porcelains, and fine art pottery are also included in the field.

More than seventy marks have been recorded, including those in the mold, ink stamped, acid etched, or on a small metal nameplate. The newer marks are incised, stamped 'Royal Dux Made in Czechoslovakia' (see Royal Dux), or printed on a paper label which reads 'Bohemian Glass Made in Czechoslovakia.' (Communist controlled from 1948, Czechoslovakia once again was made a free country in December 1989. Today it no longer exists; since 1993 it has been divided to form the world's two newest countries, the Czechoslovakian Republic and the Slovak Republic.) For a more thorough study of the subject, we recommend you refer to the book *Made in Czechoslovakia* by Ruth A. Forsythe; she is listed in the Directory under Ohio. Another fine book is *Czechoslovakian Glass & Collectibles* by Dale and Diane Barta. In the listings that follow, when one dimension is given, it refers to height; decoration is enamel unless noted otherwise. See also Erphila.

Candy Baskets

Cased 3-color mottle, blk rim & hdl, 7" 165.00
Gr varicolored stripes, lt gr hdl, flared rim, 8" 90.00
Red & yel mottle, ruffled rim, plain crystal hdl, 6½" 100.00
Red & yel mottle, twisted crystal thorn hdl, 7" 130.00
Red w/appl blk hdl & rim, ruffled edge, cased, 6½" 80.00
Streaky bl/yel/blk in red, clear hdl, 9½" 98.00
Varicolored, str Hobnail sides, squat, wide ruffled rim, 5½" 150.00

Cased Art Glass

Bowl, cameo-cut vine, dk gr on lt orange, ftd, 5½" 400.00
Bowl, mc mottle, inverted rim, sm ft, 4½" 60.00
Box, mc mottle w/blk buttressed ft, 8" dia 135.00
Candlestick, mc streaks, slim form w/saucer base, 8⅜" 80.00
Candlestick, orange w/mc mottle at base, 10¼" 45.00
Cocktail, mc rooster on gr, 3½" 35.00
Egg, mc mottle, 3" 65.00
Pitcher, exotic bird on orange, blk hdl, 11½" 130.00
Pitcher, mottled, ruffled rim, appl cobalt hdl, 9" 125.00
Tumbler, exotic bird on orange, 5¼" 48.00
Vase, bl pull-ups on bl, flared cylinder form, 7" 70.00
Vase, bud; orange w/6 clear ft, 8" 50.00
Vase, bud; silver-deposit bird & tree on yel, blk ft, 9½" 35.00
Vase, bud; wht enamel decor on orange, 8" 65.00
Vase, deep yel w/blk at rim & base, stick form, 10½" 37.50
Vase, gr bullet form w/3 bl buttress ft, 8¾" 60.00
Vase, gr w/brn swirl design, ball form, 6" 120.00
Vase, jack-in-the-pulpit; yel w/mc mottle at base, 7½" 60.00
Vase, maroon w/appl hdls, bulbous, flared rim, 7" 100.00
Vase, mc mottle, hexagonal, ftd, short neck, 4" 65.00
Vase, mc mottle w/appl cobalt hdls, ruffled rim, ftd, 4" 95.00
Vase, mottled, metal flower arranger, 5½" 50.00

Vase, mottled bullet form w/3 clear buttress ft, 7¼" 75.00
Vase, pk w/wht o/l swirling stripe, ruffled rim, ftd, 8½" 125.00
Vase, silver-deposit bird on blk, flared neck, 6½" 65.00
Vase, varicolored, bulbous, flared rim, 11½" 185.00
Vase, yel, appl blk serpentine decor, 9" 90.00
Vase, yel, slim w/ruffled blk rim, 8½" 40.00
Vase, yel mottle w/blk trim, ftd trumpet form, 6¾" 55.00
Vase, yel w/appl blk rim, classic form, 6¼" 60.00
Vase, yel w/mc mottle at base, short neck, ftd, 8" 48.00
Wine, yel, tall blk stem & base, 7½" 27.50

Cut Glass Perfume Bottles

Amber, 4 scrolling ft, frosted floral teardrop stopper, 8" 465.00
Amethyst, gold jewels, amethyst floral stopper, 5¾" 325.00
Bl, pyramidal, frosted florals in rectangular stopper, 6½" 135.00
Clear & frosted satin cut, lt bl drop stopper, 5½" 150.00
Crystal, dmn cuttings, red fan stopper, 3½" 70.00
Crystal, overall cuttings, crystal rectangular stopper, 4" 55.00
Crystal, stepped sides, bl shield-form stopper, 6½" 70.00
Crystal, wide base, crystal & frosted floral stopper, 7" 100.00
Crystal & frosted, frosted head in stopper, 5¾" 100.00
Gr, flared base, gr prism stopper, 5¼" 165.00
Gr, pyramid base, tall gr drop stopper, 6" 160.00
Gr, sq base, long tapered crystal stopper, 6¼" 135.00
Pk, stepped base, crystal triangular stopper, 5⅝" 135.00
Rose-amber, allover cuttings, fan stopper, 4¾" 85.00
Topaz, bulbous, crystal triangular stopper, 5" 115.00

Lamps

Art Deco geometrics, spherical, matching Deco cone shade, 9" . 800.00
Basket, crystal beads, glass fruit, metal trim, 10" 650.00
Desk, acid-cut counterbalance shade, slim/trn std, 10" 165.00
HP decor w/gold on milk glass, kerosene burner, 12¾" 125.00
Peacock figural, brass w/beaded tail, blk onyx base, 12" 565.00
Perfume, frosted glass w/HP dots, 6" 150.00
Table, dk bl lustre, classic form, rpl shade, 13" 90.00

Mold-Blown and Pressed Bottles

Perfume atomizer bottles, yellow opaline with black Art Deco-style floral decoration, 5½", $65.00; Electric blue, 3½", $26.00.

Amethyst & crystal, HP daisies, 7" 80.00
Clear & frosted w/gold trim, atomizer, 4¾" 65.00

Cranberry opal Hobnail, wht opal stopper, 5½" 90.00
Crystal, blk & red bands, slim, 7¾" 75.00
Gr, appl blk serpentine decor, atomizer, 8" 98.00
Mottled/cased, slim neck, puff-box base, blk stopper, 6⅜" 145.00
Orange cased, HP blk bands, bulbous, atomizer, 5" 60.00
Topaz tinted, pillow form, jet stopper, 5" 30.00

Opaque, Crystal, Colored Transparent Glass

Bottle, scent; blk opaque w/jewels, blk stopper, 3" 95.00
Bowl, cobalt w/silver-deposit decor & rim, 3¾" 70.00
Cruet, crystal, 5-sided, 6¼" 60.00
Pitcher, amber, yel o/l pull-ups, quilted, 11½" 170.00
Shakers, hen & rooster, crystal w/porc heads, 2¾", pr 45.00
Tumbler, crystal w/gr o/l at base, cobalt spiral threading, 5" 65.00
Tumbler, gr bubbly glass, HP coaching scene, 5¾" 65.00
Tumbler, orange & gr, stacked cone form, 4⅞" 25.00
Vase, cobalt cut to clear, floral etch, 10¼" 160.00
Vase, crystal w/allover intaglio cuttings, ball form, 5" 80.00
Vase, crystal w/alternating frosted panels, 10" 250.00
Vase, crystal w/bl variegated design, ball form, 8½" 175.00
Vase, crystal w/mottled o/l design, intagio flowers, 4¾" 80.00
Vase, frosted running horses in relief, ball form, 7" 90.00
Vase, golden topaz w/orange pull-ups, fan form, 8" 100.00
Vase, mauve, acid etched, ruffled rim w/blk trim, 5⅝" 115.00
Vase, pk frosted top, bl frosted bottom, enameling, 6½" 80.00
Vase, pk lustre, lustre threading at top, ftd, 9½" 400.00
Wine, gr bubbly glass, HP riding scene, 4¼" 45.00

Pottery, Porcelain, Semiporcelain

Vase, applied cherubs and flowers, marked Czechoslovakia Amphora, ca 1920s, 20½", $800.00.

Basket, blk & wht band on red, blk trim on rim & hdl, 4¼" 55.00
Basket, pearly wht w/emb braid at rim, blk trim, 4½" 35.00
Basket, purple lustre, 3¼" 35.00
Bowl, blk w/mc Deco-style floral vine, wht int, 3" 65.00
Candlestick, mc Deco florals on blk w/gold, wall mt, 9" 70.00
Candlestick, wht lustre w/dk bl bands, sq base, 4" 35.00
Canister, bl windmill scene on wht, sq, ftd, 7½" 35.00
Canister, mc Deco florals on wht, bl trim, 8½" 30.00
Clock, faux marble w/flower basket, German works, 7" 115.00
Creamer, moose head figural, mouth spout, 4½" 60.00
Creamer, parrot figural, mc, 4½" 32.50
Dinner set, rose floral, service for 8 ....550.00
Figurine, Deco lady w/hand to head, wht, 9¾" 185.00
Figurine, hound dog, brn & wht, 5" 50.00
Flower holder, bird on stump form, mc, 5⅜" 25.00

Kitchen set, scarlet w/flowers, complete, 15-pc 500.00
Pitcher, church scene, gr grass colors base, ornate hdl, 7¾" 55.00
Pitcher, emb HP fruit on maroon, angle hdl, 6½" 75.00
Pitcher, Peasant Art, flowers & fruit on bl, w/lid, 7" 95.00
Planter, mc roses on brn, emb decor at rim, ring hdls, 4¼" 45.00
Shakers, Mexican couple figurals, mc, 2¾", pr 22.50
Teapot, girl finial, skirt forms body of pot, mc pnt, 8" 110.00
Teapot, pk lustre, bulbous, 6⅛" 35.00
Tray, Peasant Art, floral, 14" dia 65.00
Vase, Egyptian figures in wide band, 9⅛" 315.00
Vase, lady's portrait on rust, brn at rim & hdls, 5⅝" 45.00
Vase, mc appl flowers on cream, brn trim & hdls, 8" 75.00
Vase, pearlescent wht w/orange rim & angle hdls, 5⅛" 25.00
Wall pocket, bird at side of pineapple form, 7" 85.00

D'Argental

D'Argental cameo glass was produced in France from the 1870s until about 1920 in the Art Nouveau style. Browns and tans were favored colors used to complement florals and scenic designs developed through acid cuttings. Our advisor for this category is Don Williams; he is listed in the Directory under Missouri.

Key: fp — fire polished

Cameo

Box, berry branches, wine/brn on lime, dome lid, 5½" dia 1,200.00
Lamp, desk; repeated '6s' on 6" dome shade/base, red on yel ...1,600.00
Lamp, long stylized leaves on 11" dome shade/vase std, 20" ...6,500.00
Vase, berries, gray on gray-cream, 6" 750.00
Vase, boat/man, sgn LS, 3½" 700.00
Vase, jack-in-pulpit; floral, red/wine on yel, 14x6" 1,750.00
Vase, lg palm trees/mtns/man in boat on opal, 8" 850.00
Vase, orchids, red on yel, baluster, 8" 750.00
Vase, roses, red/gr on lt gr to red, slim bottle form, 10" 1,500.00
Vase, trees/fence, dk brn/gr on rust, elongated/brn ft, 13" 1,600.00

Daum Nancy

Daum was an important producer of French cameo glass, operating from the late 1800s until after the turn of the century. They used various techniques — acid cutting, wheel engraving, and handwork — to create beautiful scenic designs and nature subjects in the Art Nouveau manner. Virtually all examples are signed. Our advisor for this category is Don Williams; he is listed in the Directory under Missouri.

Key: fp — fire polished

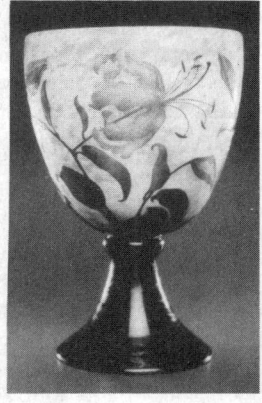

Vase, lilies, aubergine on gray mottle, chalice form on wide foot, 18¾x12", $3,500.00.

Cameo

Bottle, scent; mistletoe cut/pnt on lt gr, gilt mts, 8" **1,200.00**
Bowl, fuchsias cut/pnt on purple to wht, 2½x5½" **1,750.00**
Bowl, lake/trees/shrubs, 4-fold rim, 3¼x7¾" **1,350.00**
Chandelier, lg leaves/berries, umber on apricot/yel, 16" **5,700.00**
Compote, carnations, red/gr-blk on gr/pk, 6x7" **2,400.00**
Lamp, shade/base: winter trees on orange, 20x12" **18,000.00**
Lamp base, autumn leaves cut/pnt on mottle, 2-part, 26" **1,200.00**
Vase, autumn scene/lake/mtns, cut/pnt, cylindrical, 6½" **1,300.00**
Vase, banana leaves, gr/orange on wht mottle, slim, 24" **1,100.00**
Vase, blackberries, dk bl/gr on bl frost mottle, ftd, 15" **1,800.00**
Vase, bud; thistles cut/pnt on fiery amber, sqd ftd base, 6" **350.00**
Vase, ferns/etc, emerald/blk on gr mottle, slim, 21" **2,500.00**
Vase, floral, pk/wine on red/wine, fp, angle shoulder, 8" **3,100.00**
Vase, floral, rust/moss gr on orange, trumpet form, 23" **2,800.00**
Vase, floral branch, rust on clear, squat w/long neck, 12" **1,800.00**
Vase, grapevine, blk on yel/gr/rust, squat pill form, 4½" **900.00**
Vase, hyacinths, bl on bl/gr textured mottle, 4¾" **650.00**
Vase, hyacinths, red/purple/gr on mc mottle, 10½" **1,750.00**
Vase, lake scene, caramel on gold mottle, sgn, 16" **4,000.00**
Vase, lake/summer trees on bl/frost mottle, sqd form, 5" **1,600.00**
Vase, leaves/berries cvd/pnt on lt yel, bun ft, 19" **3,400.00**
Vase, lg iris, purple on purple to frost, fp, 13½x3½" **2,200.00**
Vase, lg leafy trees, gr on apricot to bl, cylinder, 13" **3,400.00**
Vase, lg trees before lake at sunset, umber on orange, 13" **2,800.00**
Vase, persimmons, gr/pk on pk/gr mottle, ftd cylinder, 15" **2,750.00**
Vase, prunus branch, pk w/gilt on clear, angular body, 7" **550.00**
Vase, rose hips/branches, amber/maroon, cylindrical, 4½" **770.00**
Vase, trees/lake, rust/brn/blk on rust mottle, disk ft, 9" **1,600.00**
Vase, vines w/florals, gr on apricot/rose, long neck, 15" **2,500.00**
Vase, woods/lake, brn on yel mottle, elongated, 12¾" **1,950.00**
Vase, 7 bats/landscape, gray-brn on yel/brn/amber, 7x9½" **5,300.00**

Miscellaneous

Bottle, scent; etched snowdrops on yel/rust; silver ft, 5" **1,265.00**
Bowl, brn/yel/wht mottle, 3x6" **125.00**
Bowl, etched/pnt flowers/wasps on yel/purple mottle, 5x8" **5,100.00**
Bowl, pk/cream mottle, 4-point rim, stepped ft, 6x12" **330.00**
Chandelier, 3 sm mottled orange/lav lily shades, metal mt **600.00**
Compote, gr w/metal inclusions, everted rim, 11" dia **230.00**
Decanter, etched cornflowers & bees w/gilt on lt bl, 4¾" **2,400.00**
Decanter, windmill/man in boat HP on wht opal, 9½x4½" **2,200.00**
Figurine, pate-de-verre, intaglio female, bk: male, bl, 12" L **800.00**
Salt cellar, autumn scene, etched/pnt on bl, bucket form **850.00**
Vase, band w/fighting dragons etched on blk, spherical, 6½" ..**1,500.00**
Vase, Berluze, gray & red mottle, pinched sides, 18½" **975.00**
Vase, bl, thick walls, rough frosted finish, U-form, 5½" **900.00**
Vase, bl, 4 rows hobs at shoulder, flared neck, 1925, 12" **3,000.00**
Vase, clear w/bubbles, invt bell form w/rope-twist rim, 7" **440.00**
Vase, cut deer on wine-brn, bk: stag, flattened, 1925, 11½" **2,700.00**
Vase, etched 'V's on topaz, faceted rnd ft, tumbler form, 7" **385.00**
Vase, etched deer/stylized foliage on emerald, 12" **3,500.00**
Vase, etched scales on lower half of topaz pear form, 18" **1,800.00**
Vase, etched trapezoids on gr, shouldered, 1930, 14" **1,100.00**
Vase, etched/gilt clematis vine on clear, angled sides, 13" **1,100.00**
Vase, etched/gilt lilies of the valley on opal, sqd, 4¾" **800.00**
Vase, etched/HP cornflowers on yel/pk mottle, 4" **1,150.00**
Vase, etched/HP cyclamen on mottle, sqd, 4¾" **1,200.00**
Vase, etched/HP floral on frost/lt bl, rectangle sides, 6" **1,600.00**
Vase, gr opal w/amethyst rim & ft, conical, 1930s, 7" **330.00**
Vase, lt bl w/turq inclusions, clear cased, 15" **1,725.00**
Vase, polished lt gr w/frosted flutes, flared U-form, 13" **2,750.00**

Vase, Soliflore, orange/yel mottle, rnd w/long neck, 12" **365.00**

Davenport

W. Davenport and Company were Staffordshire potters operating in that area from 1793 to 1887, producing earthenware, creamware, porcelain, and ironstone. Many different stamps, all with 'Davenport,' were used to mark the various types of ware. See also Mulberry; Flow Blue.

Compote, landscapes, multifoil rim, 1880, 9½", pr **250.00**
Cup & saucer, Adam's Rose-type floral, EX **225.00**
Jug, Japan pattern, serpent hdls, diaper border, 1820s, 4" **200.00**
Plate, foliate spray, swirled orange/brn/bl border, 8½" **150.00**
Plate, mc floral/brn bands, basketweave/rtcl border, mk, 7" **100.00**
Plate, orange reserves/pk & yel floral border, scalloped, mk, 9" **60.00**
Plate, pk/yel floral & bud, pk/gr foliage band, mk, 8½" **160.00**
Soup plate, pearlware, 3-color house, gr feather edge, 8" **425.00**
Tureen, sauce; Flute Player, bl transfer, anchor mk, EX **95.00**

De Vez

De Vez was a type of acid-cut French cameo glass produced by Cristallerie de Pantin in Paris around the turn of the century. Our advisor for this category is Don Williams; he is listed in the Directory under Missouri.

Cameo

Atomizer, seascape/boats, bl on lt pk, gilt-metal mts, 10" **1,500.00**
Bucket, fisherman scene, bl/gr on cased bl, hdls, 3¾" **875.00**
Compote, water/mtns/bldgs, rust/brn on yel, clear int, 4" **1,100.00**
Lamp, river/mtns/sailboats, 6" shade, baluster std, 18" **4,500.00**
Rose bowl, trees/water, blk on gold w/pk satin, 3" H **1,200.00**
Vase, lighthouse/boat/trees/mtns, grapes/leaves at top, 9½" **950.00**
Vase, maiden & 2 putto walk by lake, dbl o/l, sgn, 10½" **1,600.00**
Vase, mtn river scene in bl & gr, squat gourd form, 12" **1,200.00**
Vase, sailboat scenic, 3 cuts, 6" **885.00**
Vase, shepherds/mtns, pk/yel/bl, flattened pear form, 12" **1,500.00**
Vase, swans on mtn lake fr by trees, yel on gray, slim, 12" **2,000.00**
Vase, trees/lakes/mtns, gr/wine on yel, ftd, 9" **900.00**
Vase, woman in flowing scarves, bl/yel on rose, 18" **2,800.00**

De Vilbiss

Perfume bottles, atomizers, and dresser accessories marketed by the De Vilbiss Company are appreciated by collectors today for the various types of lovely glassware used in their manufacture as well as for their pleasing shapes. Various companies provided the glass, while De Vilbiss made only the metal tops. They marketed their merchandise not only here but in Paris, England, Canada, and Havana as well. Their marks were acid stamped, ink stamped, in gold script, molded in, or on paper labels. One is no more significant than another. For more information we recommend *Bedroom and Bathroom Glassware of the Depression Years* by Margaret and Kenn Whitmyer; their address is listed in the Directory under Ohio. Our advisor for this category is Randy Monsen; he is listed in the Directory under Virginia.

Atomizer, bl opal, Coin Spot, bulbous **65.00**
Atomizer, clear, threaded, 4" **70.00**
Atomizer, clear/wht cased, HP pk florals w/gold, complete, 8" ...**155.00**
Atomizer, gold, blk/orange twist stem, 9½" **150.00**

Atomizer, gold crackle, beaded flower on top, mk, 4¾" **65.00**
Atomizer, gold decor on smoked glass, orig label **75.00**
Atomizer, gold lined, 4-leaf clover shape, orig hardware **115.00**
Atomizer, gr enamel, much gold, orig cord & bulb, 7¾" **200.00**
Atomizer, penguin form, felt wings, Lenox **120.00**
Atomizer, turq-gr w/gold, Deco style, 7" **115.00**
Atomizer, wht cased satin w/gold & red holly **50.00**
Bottle, scent; gold, #500-92 .... **40.00**
Bottle, scent; irid, blk enamel top, stemmed ft, mk **85.00**
Box, blk matt w/gold decor, mk **88.00**
Ginger jar, Chinese red w/gold floral **95.00**
Lamp, perfume; moonlit scene, blk/orange on opal, slim, 8" **275.00**
Pin tray, blk matt w/gold trim **32.00**

Atomizer, alexandrite, Tiffin, mesh cord and bulb, 6", $250.00.

Decanters

Ceramic whiskey decanters were brought into prominence in 1955 by the James Beam Distilling Company. Few other companies besides Beam produced these decanters during the next ten years or so; however, other companies did eventually follow suit. At its peak in 1975, at least twenty prominent companies and several on a lesser scale made these decanters. Beam stopped making decanters in mid-1992. Now only a couple of companies are still producing these collectibles.

Liquor dealers have told collectors for years that ceramic decanters are not as valuable, and in some cases worthless, if emptied or if the federal tax stamp has been broken. Nothing is further from the truth. Following are but a few of many reasons you should consider emptying ceramic decanters:

1) If the thin glaze on the inside ever cracks (and it does in a small percentage of decanters), the contents will push through to the outside. It is then referred to as a 'leaker' and worth a fraction of its original value.

2) A large number of decanters left full in one area of your house poses a fire hazard.

3) A burglar, after stealing jewelry and electronics, may make off with some of your decanters just to enjoy the contents. If they are empty, chances are they will not be bothered.

4) It is illegal in most states for collectors to sell a full decanter without a liquor license.

Unlike years ago, few collectors now collect all types of decanters. Most now specialize. For example, they may collect trains, cars, owls, Indians, clowns, or any number of different things that have been depicted on or as a decanter. They are finding exceptional quality available at reasonable prices, especially when compared with many other types of collectibles.

We have tried to list those brands that are the most popular with collectors. Likewise, individual decanters listed are the ones (or representative of the ones) most commonly found. The following listing is but a small fraction of the thousands of decanters that have been produced.

These decanters come from all over the world. While Jim Beam owned its own china factory in the U.S., some of the others have been imported from Mexico, Taiwan, Japan and elsewhere. They vary in size from miniatures (approximately 2-oz.) to gallons. Values range from a few dollars to more than $3,000.00 per decanter.

Most collectors and dealers define a 'mint' decanter as one with no chips, no cracks, and label intact. A missing federal tax stamp or lack of contents have no bearing on value. All values are given for 'mint' decanters. A 'mini' behind a listing indicates a miniature. All others are fifth or 750 ml unless noted otherwise. Our advisor for this category is Roy Willis; he is listed in the Directory under Kentucky.

Aesthetic Specialties (ASI)

Cadillac, 1903, bl or wht **55.00**
Golf, Bing Crosby 39th **25.00**
Stanley Steamer, 1911 .... **45.00**
World's Greatest Hunter **30.00**

Ballantine

Knight **18.00**
Zebra **18.00**

Beam

Centennial Series, Colorado Centennial **10.00**
Centennial Series, Dodge City **7.00**
Centennial Series, Lombard **6.00**
Centennial Series, Washington Centennial **12.00**
Executive Series, 1987 Twin Doves **24.00**
Executive Series, 1988 Holiday Carolers **55.00**
Executive Series, 1989 Holiday Nutcracker **60.00**
Executive Series, 1990 Holiday Nutcracker **40.00**
Executive Series, 1991 Holiday Nutcracker **40.00**
Organization Series, Ahepa **5.00**
Organization Series, BPO Does **7.00**

Beam, Organization Series, Ducks Unlimited #15, Black Ducks, 1989, $85.00.

Organization Series, Ducks Unlimited #10, 1984 .... **70.00**
Organization Series, Ducks Unlimited #11, 1985 .... **45.00**
Organization Series, Ducks Unlimited #12, 1986 .... **40.00**
Organization Series, Ducks Unlimited #7, 1981 .... **45.00**
Organization Series, Ducks Unlimited #8, 1982 .... **45.00**
Organization Series, Ducks Unlimited #9, 1983 .... **40.00**
Organization Series, Fleet Reserve **10.00**
Organization Series, Pearl Harbor, 1972 .... **20.00**
Organization Series, Pearl Harbor Survivors' Assoc **10.00**
Organization Series, Shrine, Rajah Temple **28.00**
Organization Series, Sports Car Club of America **15.00**

Organization Series, Trout Unlimited 18.00
Organization Series, VFW 10.00
Organization Series, 101st Ariborne 15.00
People Series, Cowboy 25.00
People Series, Emmet Kelly 35.00
People Series, King Kamehameha 10.00
People Series, Paul Bunyan 8.00
People Series, Viking 15.00

Beam, Statue of Liberty, 12½",
$12.00.

Wheel Series, Caboose, red 70.00
Wheel Series, Cadillac, 1959 pk convertible 100.00
Wheel Series, Chevy, '57 Bellair blk hardtop 95.00
Wheel Series, Chevy, '57 Bellair turq convertible 60.00
Wheel Series, Chevy, Corvette, '63, silver-bl (NY plate) 125.00
Wheel Series, Chevy, Corvette, '68, bl or maroon 70.00
Wheel Series, Dodge, '70 Challenger, purple 60.00
Wheel Series, Dodge, '70 Challenger, yel hot rod 70.00
Wheel Series, Dump Truck 65.00
Wheel Series, Fire Engine, 1935 Pumper 75.00
Wheel Series, Ford, 1929 Pickup Parkwood 160.00
Wheel Series, Ford, 1929 Woodie station wagon 75.00
Wheel Series, Ford, 1935 Pickup, Clermont 60.00
Wheel Series, Golf Car 45.00
Wheel Series, Mercedes, 450 SL, bl, red or wht, ea 50.00
Wheel Series, Police Car, 1934 wht 95.00
Wheel Series, State Trooper Car, wht 55.00
Wheel Series, Train, Baggage Car 65.00
Wheel Series, Train, Caboose, red 70.00
Wheel Series, Train, Coal Tender 75.00
Wheel Series, Train, Dining Car 95.00
Wheel Series, Train, Grant Locomotive 90.00
Wheel Series, Train, Observation Car 55.00
Wheel Series, Train, Passenger Car 55.00

Brooks

Animal Series, Panda 18.00
Animal Series, Bengal Tiger..35.00
Animal Series, Northern Raccoon...45.00
Automotive & Transportation Series, Corvette, 1957 blk or yel ..110.00
Automotive & Transportation Series, Corvette, 1962 Mako Shark .30.00
Automotive & Transportation Series, Fire Engine 20.00
Automotive & Transportation Series, Snowmobile 12.00

Automotive & Transportation Series, Trail Bike 15.00
Bird Series, Canadian Loon..25.00
Bird Series, Snow Egret...25.00
Clown Series, #4, Keystone Cop 35.00
Clown Series, #5, Cuddles 30.00
Clown Series, #6, Tramp 30.00
Indian Series, Kachina #7, Mudhead 45.00
Indian Series, Kachina #8, Drummer 60.00
Indian Series, Kachina #9, Watermelon 30.00
People Series, Betsy Ross 10.00
People Series, Cigar Store Indian 8.00
People Series, Dakota Cowgirl 25.00
People Series, Fisherman 12.00
People Series, Jester 8.00
Sports Series, Georgia Bulldog 25.00
Sports Series, Man O' War 25.00
Sports Series, Razorback, 1969 ....15.00
Sports Series, Razorback, 1979 ....40.00
Sports Series, Tennis Player 12.00

Cyrus Noble

Dolphin 50.00
Elk, Bull 50.00
Gambler 45.00
Gambler, mini 12.00
Seal, Harp 50.00
South of the Border 40.00
Walrus Family 50.00
Walrus Family, mini 15.00

Double Springs

Bulldog, Georgia 12.00
Car, Excalibur Phaeton 15.00
Car, Mercedes Benz 25.00
Car, Rolls Royce 25.00
Car, Stanley Steamer 20.00

Famous Firsts

Duesenberg 90.00
Panda, Baby 90.00
Panda, Baby, mini 30.00
Phonograph 45.00
Phonograph, mini 20.00
Racer, National #8 ....60.00
Racer, National #8, mini 25.00

Grenadier

Billy Mitchell 40.00
General McArthur 35.00
Horse, Appaloosa 30.00
Horse, Arabian 30.00
Santa Claus 30.00

Hoffman

Mr Lucky Series, Mr Carpenter 35.00
Mr Lucky Series, Mr Carpenter, mini 15.00
Mr Lucky Series, Mr Dentist 30.00
Mr Lucky Series, Mr Dentist, mini 15.00
Mr Lucky Series, Mr Schoolteacher 30.00

Mr Lucky Series, Mr Schoolteacher, mini 15.00
Sports Series, Cheerleader, Dallas 30.00
Wildlife Series (Ohrman), Bear & Cub 40.00
Wildlife Series (Ohrman), Jaguar & Possum 30.00
Wildlife Series (Ohrman), Lion & Crane 30.00

Jack Daniels

Belle of Lincoln 25.00
Maxwell House 35.00
Silver Cornet 30.00
Tribute to Tennessee 30.00

Kontinental

Gandy Dancer 20.00
School Marm 30.00
Statue of Liberty 20.00

Lionstone

Automotive & Transportation Series, Johnny Lightning #2 ....65.00
Automotive & Transportation Series, STP Turbocar, red 45.00
Bird Series, Goldfinch 30.00
Bird Series, Owls 25.00
Bird Series, Quail 19.00
Bird Series, Robin 38.00
Bird Series, Robin, mini 18.00
Bird Series, Woodpecker 32.00
Bird Series, Woodpecker, mini 14.00
Old West Series, Bartender 30.00
Old West Series, Bartender, mini 16.00
Old West Series, Buffalo Hunter 30.00
Old West Series, Cowgirl 30.00
Old West Series, Gold Panner 45.00
Old West Series, Gold Panner, mini 15.00
Old West Series, Indian Tribal Chief 30.00

McCormick

McCormick, Frontiersman Series, Jim
Bowie, 14", $35.00.

Confederate Series, Jeb Stuart 60.00
Confederate Series, Jeb Stuart, mini 20.00

Confederate Series, Jefferson Davis 50.00
Confederate Series, Jefferson Davis, mini 20.00
Confederate Series, Robert E Lee 60.00
Confederate Series, Robert E Lee, mini 20.00
Confederate Series, Stonewall Jackson 50.00
Confederate Series, Stonewall Jackson, mini 20.00
Entertainer Series, Elvis, Designer #1 ....130.00
Entertainer Series, Elvis, Designer #2 ....180.00
Entertainer Series, Elvis, Designer #3 ....240.00
Entertainer Series, Elvis, Gold Encore #1 ....300.00
Entertainer Series, Elvis, Gold Encore #2 ....250.00
Entertainer Series, Elvis, Gold Encore #3 ....200.00
Great American Series, Alexander Graham Bell 25.00
Great American Series, Charles Lindbergh 30.00
Great American Series, Charles Lindbergh, mini 16.00
Great American Series, Henry Ford 25.00
Great American Series, Henry Ford, mini 15.00
Great American Series, Mark Twain 25.00
Great American Series, Mark Twain, mini 15.00

Mike Wayne

Christmas Tree, wht or gr 65.00
John Wayne, bust 75.00
John Wayne, portrait 40.00
John Wayne, statue, bronze 110.00
John Wayne, statue, gold 150.00

Mount Hope

American Legion Seaman 20.00
Fireman #1, PA Volunteer 85.00
Fireman #2, PA Volunteer, holding child 95.00

Old Bardstown

Delta Queen Riverboat 50.00
Foster Brooks 25.00
Surface Miner 20.00
Tiger 20.00

Old Commonwealth

Chief Illini #1 ....95.00
Chief Illini #2 ....70.00
Firefighter #2, Nozzleman 55.00
Firefighter #2, Nozzleman, mini 20.00
Firefighter #4, Fallen Comrade 55.00
Firefighter #4, Fallen Comrade, mini 28.00
Irish, Castles of Ireland 30.00
Irish, Flowers of Ireland 30.00
Irish, Happy Green 25.00
Irish, Irish Lore 25.00
Irish, Sons of Erin II 25.00

Old Fitzgerald

Irish, Charm 24.00
Irish, Luck 28.00
Irish, Songs of Ireland 18.00
Irish, Sons of Erin 18.00

Old Mr. Boston

Clown Head 15.00

Dan Patch 20.00
Paul Revere 10.00

Pacesetter

Tractor, Ford 100.00
Tractor, Ford, mini 50.00
Tractor, International 110.00
Tractor, International, mini 50.00

Ski Country

Bird Series, Cardinal 65.00
Bird Series, Cardinal, mini 40.00
Bird Series, Cardinal, 1991 Holiday 75.00
Bird Series, Cardinal, 1991 Holiday, mini 45.00
Bird Series, Duck, Ducks Unlimited Canvasback 55.00
Bird Series, Duck, Ducks Unlimited Canvasback, mini ...35.00
Bird Series, Duck, Ducks Unlimited Widgeon 60.00
Bird Series, Duck, Ducks Unlimited Widgeon, mini 30.00
Bird Series, Duck, Ducks Unlimited Widgeon, 1.75-litre ...200.00
Bird Series, Duck, Eider 70.00
Bird Series, Duck, Eider, mini 35.00
Bird Series, Duck, Mallard Family 75.00
Bird Series, Duck, Mallard Family, mini 40.00
Bird Series, Eagle on water 130.00
Bird Series, Eagle on Water, mini 50.00
Bird Series, Gamecocks, Fighting 150.00
Bird Series, Gamecocks, Fighting, mini 45.00
Bird Series, Owl, Screech Family 125.00
Bird Series, Owl, Screech Family, mini 85.00
Bird Series, Owl, Screech Family, 1-gal 475.00
Indian Series, Deer Dancer 120.00
Indian Series, Deer Dancer, mini 80.00
Indian Series, Wolf Dancer 85.00
Indian Series, Wolf Dancer, mini 40.00
Wildlife Series, Bobcat & Chipmunk 75.00
Wildlife Series, Bobcat & Chipmunk, mini 30.00
Wildlife Series, Moose 110.00
Wildlife Series, Moose, mini 45.00
Wildlife Series, Mountain Lion 75.00
Wildlife Series, Mountain Lion, mini 30.00
Wildlife Series, Skunk Family 65.00
Wildlife Series, Skunk Family, mini 30.00

Wild Turkey

Series III, No 10, Turkey & Coyote 85.00
Series III, No 10, Turkey & Coyote, mini 45.00
Series III, No 11, Turkey & Falcon 85.00
Series III, No 11, Turkey & Falcon, mini 45.00
Series III, No 12, Turkey & Skunk 85.00
Series III, No 12, Turkey & Skunk, mini 45.00
Series III, No 4, Turkey & Eagle 85.00
Series III, No 4, Turkey & Eagle, mini 85.00
Series III, No 5, Turkey & Raccoon 85.00
Series III, No 5, Turkey & Raccoon, mini 45.00
Series III, No 6, Turkey & Poults 85.00
Series III, No 6, Turkey & Poults, mini 45.00
Series III, No 7, Turkey & Fox 85.00
Series III, No 7, Turkey & Fox, mini 45.00
Series III, No 8, Turkey & Owl 90.00
Series III, No 8, Turkey & Owl, mini 45.00
Series III, No 9, Turkey & Bear Cubs 90.00

Series III, No 9, Turkey & Bear Cubs, mini 45.00

Decoys

American colonists learned the craft of decoy making from the Indians who used them to lure birds out of the sky as an important food source. Early models were carved from wood such as pine, cedar, balsa, etc., and a few were made of canvas or papier-mache. There are two basic types of decoys: water floaters and shorebirds (also called 'stick-ups'). Within each type are many different species, ducks being the most plentiful since they migrated along all four of America's great waterways. Market hunting became big business around 1880, resulting in large-scale commercial production of decoys which continued until about 1910 when such hunting was outlawed by the Migratory Bird Treaty.

Today decoys are one of the most collectible types of American folk art. The most valuable are those carved by such artists as Laing, Crowell, Ward, and Wheeler, to name only a few. Each area, such as Massachusetts, Connecticut, Maine, the Illinois River, and the Delaware River, produces decoys with distinctive regional characteristics. Examples of commercial decoys produced by well-known factories — among them Mason, Stevens, and Dodge — are also prized by collectors. Though mass-produced, these nevertheless required a certain amount of hand carving and decorating. Well-carved examples, especially those of rare species, are appreciating rapidly, and those with original paint are more desirable. Writer Carl F. Luckey has compiled a fully illustrated identification and value guide, *Collecting Antique Bird Decoys;* you will find his address in the Directory under Alabama. *The Collector's Guide to Decoys* by Sharon and Bob Huxford contains hundreds of photos (many in color) and gives values realized at auction during the past two years. It's available from your local bookstore or Collector Books. In the listings that follow, all decoys are solid-bodied unless noted hollow.

Key:
OP — original paint	RP — repaint
ORP — old repaint	WOP — worn original paint
OWP — original working paint	WRP — working repaint

Black Duck, Al McCormick, cork body, NM OP, pr 125.00
Black Duck, Dude Crane, hollow, WOP, hairline 125.00

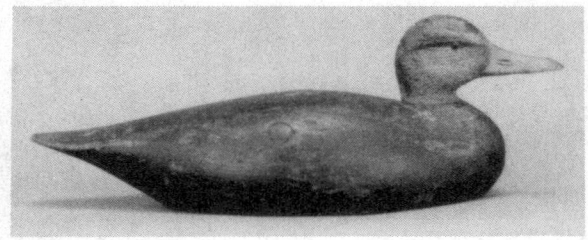

Black Duck, Elmer Crowell, slightly turned head, retains much original paint, lightly shot, oversize, $500.00.

Black Duck, J McLaughlin, sleeping, NM OP (flocked), ca 1940 .1,100.00
Black Duck, John Blair, hollow, ORP, sm cracks, rough bill ...1,250.00
Black Duck, John Blair, preening, ORP worn to OP, roughness .1,500.00
Black Duck, Rowley Horner, NM OP, EX detail & patina 2,850.00
Black Duck, Tom Fitzpatrick, low head, ORP, chips/scars 550.00
Black Duck, Walter Bush, hollow, ORP, structurally EX 350.00
Black Duck, Wildfowler Factory, sleeping, NM OP, sm dent 200.00
Black Duck pr, Jos Gigi, cork bodies, NM OP, '40s, oversized 300.00

Black Duck pr, Wildfowler Factory, unused, oversized, NM/M ...250.00
Bluebill Drake, Chas Birch, EX OP, sm separation at seam 550.00
Bluebill Drake, John English, ORP, thin crack in neck 550.00
Bluebill Drake, Mason Factory, Premier Grade, NM OP, shot mks ..1,600.00
Bluebill Hen, HM Shourds, hollow, EX OP, rpr chip, rpt bill 900.00
Bluebill Hen, Mason Factory, Std Grade, tack eyes, EX OP 350.00
Bluebill pr, Bob White, EX OP, structurally EX 1,000.00
Bluebill pr, Hurley Conklin, NM OP, structurally EX 900.00
Bluewing Teal Drake, Wm Finch, NM OP, fine combing, EX patina .1,300.00
Brandt, Wm Cranmer, NM OP, 1960s 300.00
Brant, Hurley Conklin, hissing head, hollow, NM OP 450.00
Brant, Hurley Conklin, swimming w/turned head, M 300.00
Canada Geese pr, Wildfowler Factory, NM OP, sm dents 500.00
Canada Goose, Madison Mitchell, EX OP, structurally EX, '60s ...350.00
Canvasback Drake, Madison Mitchell, dtd 1960, NM 200.00
Canvasback Drake, Mason Factory, Premier Grade, early WRP .350.00
Canvasback Drake, Ralph Reghi, ORP, hit by shot 225.00
Canvasback Drake, Ward Bros, wide body, EX OP, 1930s 5,200.00
Canvasback Hen, Mason Factory, Challenge Grade, hollow, NM OP ..2,750.00
Crow, Charles Perdew, EX OP, wear to top of bill 275.00
Curlew, unknown NJ carver, EX OP, lightly shot, ca 1890s 350.00
Dove, Don Vulcani, preening, lifted wing tips, M 450.00
Dove, Mason Factory, tack eyes, strong OP, rpl baleen bill 1,250.00
Dowitcher, att John Dilly, WOP, reglued cracks, hit by shot 400.00
Eider pr, Wildfowler Factory, EX OP, glass eyes, oversized 1,200.00
Golden Plover, Morton, NM OP, converted to use 1 stick 900.00
Goldeneye Hen, John English, ORP w/lt wear, ca 1880, EX 700.00
Goldeneye Hen, Wildfowler Factory, balsa body, stamped, NM ..160.00
Goldeneye pr, Ben Schmidt, EX cvg, NM OP, sm chip, dtd 1957 ..1,100.00
Great Horned Owl, RC Wilber, ORP, 1 eye missing, cracks 400.00
Greenwing Teal pr, Hurley Conklin, NM OP, structurally EX ...600.00
Mallard Drake, Dan English, low head, ORP, varnish, EX 750.00
Mallard Drake, Norman Hudson, NM OP w/scratch-pnt details ..1,250.00
Mallard Hen, Chas Allen, hollow, EX OP, relief cvd, 1959 ....400.00
Mallard pr, Wildfowler Factory, EX OP, dents, oversized 200.00
Mallard pr, Wildfowler Factory, NM OP, 1 w/crack in neck 500.00
Merganser Drake, Mason Factory, Premier Grade, WOP, scars ..800.00
Peep, Obediah Verity, full body, EX OP, rpl bill, hit by shot ...2,700.00
Pheasant, Jay Lapham, EX OP, chip/loose wings, mini 70.00
Pigeon, Austin Johnson, NM OP, metal bill, relief cvg, EX 150.00
Pigeon, Major MA Jones, relief wing cvg, NM OP w/EX detail ..250.00
Pintail Drake, Ben Schmidt, NM OP, metal inserted tail 1,200.00
Pintail Drake, James Holly, EX OP, sm rpr to neck 950.00
Pintail Drake, Miles Hancock, NM OP, hairline cracks 500.00
Pintail Drake, Ward Bros, cedar body, EX OP, sm chip, '54 ....2,750.00
Pintail Drake, Ward Bros, humpbk style, ORP, ca 1929 ....1,600.00
Redhead Drake, HV Shourds, RP in Shourds' manner, ca 1900 .600.00
Redhead Drake, Mason Factory, Std Grade, glass eyes, EX OP ...550.00
Redhead Drake, Nate Quillen, WOP, hit by shot, hairlines 1,100.00
Redhead Hen, Mason Factory, Premier Grade, EX OP, hit by shot .650.00
Redhead Hen, Zeke McDonald, ORP, hairline cracks, shot mks ..125.00
Ringneck Drake, Ben Schmidt, EX OP, wooden keel removed .1,350.00
Robin Snipe, Dodge Factory, EX OP, hit by shot, ca 1890 ....600.00
Sandpiper, Thos Gelston, NM OP, tack eyes, metal bill 200.00
Snow Goose, unknown carver, primitive, ORP, checks/lines 300.00
Widgeon Drake, Ward Brothers, NM OP, sm chip, ca 1940s ..4,100.00
Widgeon Drake, Wildfowler Factory, factory brand, M 100.00
Yellowlegs, att Joe Lincoln, raised wings, EX OP, rpl bill 1,200.00
Yellowlegs, Geo Boyd, NM OP, hairlines in neck, rpl bill 800.00
Yellowlegs, Rhodes Truex, EX OP, structurally EX, ca 1910 ....400.00

Dedham Pottery

Originally founded in Chelsea, Massachusetts, as the Chelsea
Keramic Works, the name was changed to Dedham Pottery in 1895
after the firm relocated in Dedham, near Boston, Massachusetts. The
ware utilized a gray stoneware body with a crackle glaze and simple
cobalt border designs of flowers, birds, and animals. Decorations were
brushed on by hand using an ancient Chinese method which suspended
the cobalt within the overall glaze. There were thirteen standard patterns, among them Magnolia, Iris, Butterfly, Duck, Polar Bear, and
Rabbit, the latter of which was chosen to represent the company on
their logo. On the very early pieces, the rabbits face left; decorators
soon found the reverse position easier to paint, and the rabbits were
turned to the right. In addition to the standard patterns, other designs
were produced for special orders. These and artist-signed pieces are
highly valued by collectors today.

Though their primary product was the blue-printed, crackle-glazed
dinnerware, two types of artware were also produced: crackle glaze and
flambe. Their notable volcanic ware was a type of the latter. The mark
is incised and often accompanies the cipher of Hugh Robertson. The
firm was operated by succeeding generations of the Robertson family
until it closed in 1943. Our advisor for this category is Dale MacLean;
he is listed in the Directory under Massachusetts. See also Chelsea
Keramic Art Works.

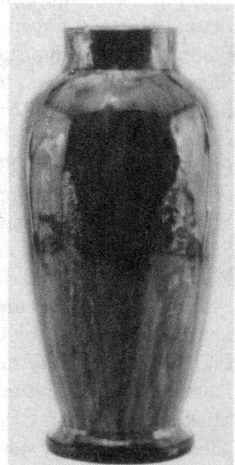

Vase, experimental drip glaze with dragon's blood, moss green, blue and rust highlights, signed HCR, old repair to foot, 15", $4,250.00.

Vase, gr dripping/mottled gloss, HCR, 9x5" 1,500.00
Vase, ivory/tan/mahog flambe, swollen shoulder, HCR, 9x8" ..1,200.00
Vase, mc mottled lustre, HCR, 8x5" 2,700.00
Vase, poppies/pods, bl on wht crackle, 8x5" 2,600.00
Vase, red/bl/gr Sang de Boeuf, mk Dedham/HCR #1, 3" 850.00
Vase, red/orange/gr lustred volcanic glaze, HCR, 6½x4¾" 2,800.00
Vase, red/orange/gr/bl/blk dripping flambe, HCR, 8½x5½" 3,000.00
Vase, thick brown drip over olive w/blisters, HCR, 10x5" 1,800.00

Dinnerware

Bacon rasher, Rabbit, stamped, 10x6¼" 375.00
Bowl, Azalea, stamped registered, 1½x5¾" 150.00
Bowl, Azalea, stamped registered, 3¾x9" 450.00
Bowl, Poppy, bl on wht crackle, pointed rim, 4x8¾" 600.00
Bowl, Rabbit, stamped, 1½x7½" 125.00
Bowl, Rabbit, stamped registered, 1⅞x5¼" 125.00
Bowl, vegetable; Rabbit, w/lid, imp/stamped, 3¼x10¾" 800.00
Candle snuffer, Rabbit, 2" 650.00
Creamer & sugar bowl, Rabbit, stamped registered, 2x4¼" 400.00
Egg cup, Rabbit, single, sgn DP, 2½x2" 150.00
Humidor, outlines of 2 elephants, dtd May 1917/#79, 7" 1,980.00
Marmalade, Azalea, stamped registered, 4x5" 250.00

Nappy, Rabbit, stamped registered, 2½x7½"	375.00
Nappy, Rabbit, stamped registered, 2x9¼"	425.00
Pitcher, Rabbit, stamped, 9x4¼"	600.00
Pitcher, Rabbit, stamped registered, 5x3"	325.00
Pitcher, Rabbit, 1 leaps over base of hdl, imp/stamped, 8½"	1,300.00
Plate, Azalea, imp only, 8½"	250.00
Plate, Azalea, imp/stamped, 10"	275.00
Plate, Birds in Potted Orange Tree, imp, 8½"	575.00
Plate, Butterfly w/Flower, stamped registered, 6¼"	375.00
Plate, Dolphin (upside down), imp, 8½"	850.00
Plate, Duck, imp/stamped, 10"	425.00
Plate, Duck, imp/stamped registered, 6¼"	200.00
Plate, Elephant, stamped registered, 10"	800.00
Plate, Golden Gate, Hugh Robertson, 10", EX	1,700.00
Plate, Grape, imp/stamped registered 1931, 6⅜"	200.00
Plate, Horse Chestnut, faintly stamped, rare variant, 8½"	950.00
Plate, Horse Chestnut, imp/stamped, 6"	165.00
Plate, Horse Chestnut, imp/stamped registered, 8⅜"	250.00
Plate, Horse Chestnut, stamped, 10"	275.00
Plate, Iris, imp/registered, 6"	195.00
Plate, Iris, imp/stamped, 8½"	245.00
Plate, Iris, M Davenport rebus, imp/stamped, 6"	275.00
Plate, Lobster, imp/stamped, 8¼"	575.00
Plate, Lobster, stamped registered, 6⅛"	400.00
Plate, Magnolia, imp/stamped registered, 10"	250.00
Plate, Moth w/Flower, imp/stamped, 8¼"	600.00
Plate, Owl w/Star & Moon, imp, 10"	2,500.00
Plate, Pineapple, imp cloverleaf w/CPUS, 8⅝"	800.00
Plate, Pond Lily, imp, 8¾"	250.00
Plate, Rabbit, imp/stamped registered, 10"	185.00
Plate, Rabbit, imp/stamped registered, 7¼"	150.00
Plate, Rabbit, M Davenport rebus, imp, 8½", set of 10	1,500.00
Plate, Snowtree, M Davenport rebus, imp/stamped, 6¼"	250.00
Plate, Turkey, imp/stamped, 8½"	350.00
Plate, wolfs & owls, dk bl, Robertson, ca 1900, 10"	6,000.00
Platter, Lobster, imp/stamped, glaze bursts, 12" dia	880.00
Platter, Rabbit, imp/stamped, 12" dia	375.00
Shaker, Rabbit, sgn DP, 3½"	250.00
Tile, Rabbit, faintly stamped, 5¾"	300.00

Degenhart

The Crystal Art Glass factory in Cambridge, Ohio, opened in 1947 under the private ownership of John and Elizabeth Degenhart. John had previously worked for the Cambridge Glass Company and was well known for his superior paperweights. After his death in 1964, Elizabeth took over management of the factory, hiring several workers from the defunct Cambridge Company, including Zack Boyd. Boyd was responsible for many unique colors, some of which were named for him. From 1964 to 1974, more than twenty-seven different moulds were created, most of them resulting from Elizabeth Degenhart's work and creativity, and over 145 official colors were developed. Elizabeth died in 1978, requesting that the ten moulds she had built while operating the factory were to be turned over to the Degenhart Museum. The remaining moulds were to be held by the Island Mould and Machine Company, who (complying with her request) removed the familiar 'D in heart' trademark. The factory was eventually bought by Zack's son, Bernard Boyd. He also acquired the remaining Degenhart moulds, to which he added his own logo. In general, slags and opaques should be valued 15% to 20% higher than crystals in color.

Beaded Oval Toothpick, Amethyst	17.50
Beaded Oval Toothpick, Bittersweet, 1976	35.00

Beaded Oval Toothpick, Crystal	15.00
Beaded Oval Toothpick, Fawn	22.50
Beaded Oval Toothpick, Lt Amberina, unmk	22.50
Beaded Oval Toothpick, Vaseline	20.00
Bird Salt & Pepper, Nile Green	37.50
Bird Salt & Pepper, Opalescent	37.50
Bird Salt w/Cherry, April Green	20.00
Bird Salt w/Cherry, Autumn	20.00
Bird Salt w/Cherry, Blue Fire	22.50
Bird Salt w/Cherry, Brownie	17.50
Bird Salt w/Cherry, Crown Tuscan	22.50
Bird Salt w/Cherry, Daffodil	20.00
Bird Salt w/Cherry, Ebony	27.50
Bird Salt w/Cherry, Emerald Green	17.50
Bird Salt w/Cherry, Forest Green	15.00
Bird Salt w/Cherry, Orchid	22.50
Bird Salt w/Cherry, Spring Green	22.50
Bird Salt w/Cherry, Teal	15.00
Bow Slipper, Cobalt, hand stamped	22.50
Bow Slipper, Custard, unmk	22.50
Bow Slipper, Milk Blue	22.50
Bow Slipper, Opal to Clear	20.00
Bow Slipper, Rose Marie	15.00
Bow Slipper, Ruby, unmk	32.50
Chick, Caramel, unmk, 2"	55.00
Chick, Crystal, 2"	15.00
Chick, Lemon Custard, unmk, 2"	60.00
Chick, Lt Powder Blue, 2"	25.00
Chick, Milk Blue, unmk, 2"	22.50
Colonial Drape Toothpick, Cobalt	20.00
Colonial Drape Toothpick, Lt Custard	25.00
Daisy & Button Salt, Amethyst	10.00
Daisy & Button Salt, Crystal, unmk	8.00
Daisy & Button Salt, Milk White, unmk	9.00
Daisy & Button Toothpick, Baby Blue Slag	27.50
Daisy & Button Toothpick, Lime Ice	22.50
Daisy & Button Toothpick, Milk Blue	16.00
Daisy & Button Toothpick, Vaseline	15.00
Forget-Me-Not Toothpick, Amberina	25.00
Forget-Me-Not Toothpick, April Green	25.00
Forget-Me-Not Toothpick, Blue & White Slag	25.00
Forget-Me-Not Toothpick, Brownie	15.00
Forget-Me-Not Toothpick, Buttercup Slag	30.00
Forget-Me-Not Toothpick, Crystal	13.00
Forget-Me-Not Toothpick, Daffodil	22.50
Forget-Me-Not Toothpick, Fog	20.00
Forget-Me-Not Toothpick, Grape	17.50
Forget-Me-Not Toothpick, Heatherbloom	27.50
Forget-Me-Not Toothpick, Ivory	20.00
Forget-Me-Not Toothpick, Misty Green	22.50
Forget-Me-Not Toothpick, Peach-Opaque	22.50
Forget-Me-Not Toothpick, Persimmon	17.50
Forget-Me-Not Toothpick, Royal Violet	22.50
Forget-Me-Not Toothpick, Sparrow Slag	25.00
Forget-Me-Not Toothpick, Spring Green	22.50
Forget-Me-Not Toothpick, Teal	20.00
Forget-Me-Not Toothpick, Toffee	25.00
Forget-Me-Not Toothpick, Tomato	37.50
Gypsy Pot Toothpick, Amethyst	15.00
Gypsy Pot Toothpick, Bittersweet, 1976	37.50
Gypsy Pot Toothpick, Bloody Mary	45.00
Gypsy Pot Toothpick, Bluebell	20.00
Gypsy Pot Toothpick, Crown Tuscan	25.00
Gypsy Pot Toothpick, Lavender Blue	35.00

Gypsy Pot Toothpick, Opalescent	22.50
Gypsy Pot Toothpick, Persimmon	20.00
Hand, Amethyst	10.00
Hand, Sapphire	10.00
Hand, Vaseline	10.00
Hat, Sapphire	15.00
Heart & Lyre Cup Plate, Amethyst, unmk	10.00
Heart & Lyre Cup Plate, Emerald Green, unmk	12.50
Heart & Lyre Cup Plate, Opalescent, unmk	15.00
Heart & Lyre Cup Plate, Pink, unmk	12.50
Heart Toothpick, Amberina	25.00
Heart Toothpick, Amethyst	17.50
Heart Toothpick, Buttercup	30.00
Heart Toothpick, Gray Tomato	27.50
Heart Toothpick, Milk Blue	22.50
Heart Toothpick, Opalescent	22.50
Hen Covered Dish, Caramel Custard, 3"	55.00
Hen Covered Dish, Forest Green, 3"	22.50
Hen Covered Dish, Sparrow, 3"	27.50

Hen Covered dish, Tomato, 3",
$65.00.

Hobo Shoe, Caramel Custard Slag	22.50
Hobo Shoe, Crown Tuscan	22.50
Owl, Amethyst	32.50
Owl, Apple Green	42.50
Owl, Blue Jay	47.50
Owl, Bluebird #2	55.00
Owl, Buttercup	47.50
Owl, Charcoal	47.50
Owl, Cobalt #2	35.00
Owl, Crystal	16.00
Owl, Daffodil	37.50
Owl, Fog	55.00
Owl, Ivorene	47.50
Owl, Lt Ivory	42.50
Owl, Milk Blue	32.50
Owl, Pearl Gray	42.50
Owl, Sahara Sand	52.50
Owl, Sapphire	22.50
Owl, Shell	45.00
Owl, Teal	27.50
Owl, Wanda Blue Opal	47.50
Pooche, Crystal	17.50
Pooche, Fawn	22.50
Pooche, Gray Tomato	35.00
Pooche, Gun-Metal Blue	25.00
Pooche, Ivory	22.50
Pooche, Sapphire	15.00

Portrait Plate, cobalt	50.00
Pottie Salt, Amethyst	10.00
Pottie Salt, Chocolate Creme	17.50
Pottie Salt, Honey	15.00
Pottie Salt, Milk Blue	15.00
Pottie Salt, Milk White	15.00
Pottie Salt, Nile Green	17.50
Skate Shoe, Persimmon, unmk	35.00
Skate Shoe, Sapphire	32.50
Texas Boot, Amethyst	17.50
Texas Boot, Baby Green	22.50

Delatte

Delatte was a manufacturer of French cameo glass. Founded in 1921, their style reflected the influence of the Art Deco era with strong color contrasts and bold design. Our advisor for this category is Don Williams; he is listed in the Directory under Missouri.

Cameo

Lamp, sea gulls, dk bl on olive, ships on base, 17"	3,500.00

Vase, irises, dark brown on orange and brown, 8", $900.00.

Vase, landscape along river, maroon/rose on wht, hdls, 9"	1,200.00
Vase, trumpet blossoms, red/wine on gray mottle, 16x6"	935.00
Vase, wisteria, bl tones on frost & bl, 10"	1,250.00

Delft

Old Delftware, made as early as the 16th century, was originally a low-fired earthenware coated in a thin opaque tin glaze with painted-on blue or polychrome designs. It was not until the last half of the 19th century, however, that the ware became commonly referred to as Delft, acquiring the name from the Dutch village that had become the major center of its production. English, German, and French potters also produced Delft, though with noticeable differences both in shape and decorative theme.

In the early part of the 18th century, the German potter, Bottger, developed a formula for porcelain; in England, Wedgwood began producing creamware — both of which were much more durable. Unable to compete, one by one the Delft potteries failed. Soon only one remained. In 1876 De Porcelyne Fles reintroduced Delftware on a hard white body with blue and white decorative themes reflecting the Dutch countryside, windmills by the sea, and Dutch children. This manufacturer is the most well known of several operating today. Their products are now produced under the Royal Delft label. Examples listed here are blue on white unless noted otherwise. See also specific manufacturers.

Bottle, English, Oriental coast, crimped rim, 1760, 9" 985.00
Bowl, barber's; Lambeth, floral garden, 1775, 6¾" H, EX 325.00
Bowl, barber's; wht, no decor, oval, ca 1700, 11" W 500.00
Bowl, English, floral, mc, 1765, 9", EX 300.00
Bowl, fruit; florals, bl cells, pierced gallery, 1760, 8⅝" 1,760.00
Bowl, fruit; Irish, rock garden/florals, 1750, 9¼" 495.00
Bowl, Lambeth, floral, leaf band, fluted, 1740, 9", EX 2,800.00
Bowl, Liverpool, florals/diapering, fish w/in, 1760, 7" 1,430.00
Bowl, punch; floral, fluted, 1740s, rstr, 9¾" 600.00
Bowl, Success to Trade, mc florals, 1750, 9", EX 660.00

Chargers: Basket of flowers with plume border, 14", pair, $750.00; Oriental style with floral medallion, lappet border, 14", $250.00.

Charger, Bianco Sopra Bianco, fence/garden, 1760, 13⅜", pr .2,100.00
Charger, Bristol, floral panels, ca 1740, 13¾" 360.00
Charger, castle & 3 swimming swans, 1700s, 12¼" 550.00
Charger, Dutch, fish/floral, 1700s, 12⅛" 825.00
Charger, Dutch, floral, ca 1790, 17¾" 660.00
Charger, Fazackerly, floral, mc, ca 1760, 13" 900.00
Charger, Fazackerly, floral, mc, ca 1760, 9" 330.00
Charger, floral medallions, mc, ca 1740, 13⅜", EX 935.00
Charger, Frankfort, Oriental decor, 1690, 13½", VG 975.00
Charger, William & Mary, titled portraits, 1690, 13½" 990.00
Colander & underplate, floral, scalloped, late 1700s, 9" 770.00
Dish, Dublin, flower vases, wide rtcl rim, 1760s, 11" L, EX 2,000.00
Figure, dog on base, puce/yel, 1780s, 4½" 450.00
Figurine, child on high chair, ca 1750, rstr, 4⅝" 200.00
Figurine, Dutch, cow w/milkmaid, wht/mc, 1780s, 8", EX, pr 985.00
Figurine, Dutch, dog on sq base, puce/yel, 1780s, 4½", EX 400.00
Figurine, Dutch, horse/rider, mc, 1700s, mc, 11", EX 985.00
Foot warmer, masks, molded scroll hdls, 1770, rstr, 9" 150.00
Ink pot, Dutch, floral, bl/manganese, sq, 1760s, 3½", EX 325.00
Jar, drug; Dutch, Macaginum/floral/peacock, Van Doyn, 8", EX ...650.00
Jar, drug; Neopolitan, classical figures, mc, 1750s, 6⅝" 600.00
Jar, Dutch, Oriental subject, brass lid, 1700s, 9½", EX 300.00
Jug, Lambeth, floral, bulbous, loop hdl, early 1700s, 5¼" 165.00
Jug, puzzle; Here Gentlemen Come Try...,1740, rstr, 7" 1,850.00
Pitcher, Oriental landscape, yel base/lip, 1700s, 9¼" 325.00
Plate, Bianco Sopra Bianco, mtn landscape, 1760, 8½", pr 825.00
Plate, Bristol, Oriental figural scene, mc, 1760, 9", VG 300.00
Plate, Bristol, 3-color rooster, 1740, rstr, 8½" 1,500.00
Plate, English, floral, bl/manganese, 1780s, 7", VG 100.00
Plate, English, garden/roosters, 1750, rstr/chips, 9" 100.00
Plate, Liverpool, floral, ca 1750, 8⅞", EX 200.00
Plate, Liverpool, Oriental coast, 1750, 8¾", EX 220.00
Plate, Oriental figures, ca 1760, 10", EX 525.00

Plate, William & Mary portraits, bl/yel, ca 1690, 8½" 3,025.00
Plate, William of Orange, verse, vine border, mc, 1700s, 9" 550.00
Platter, English, floral landscape, lattice rim, 1770, 19¾" 770.00
Posset pot, Bristol, Oriental man, bl/manganese, no lid, EX 1,400.00
Salt cellar, Dutch, man figural, mc, 1700s, 3¾", EX 1,750.00
Tile, farmer & animals, sgn Potter, 14x20" 465.00
Vase, bird/&floral panels, 6-sided, bird finial, 1700s, 9¾" 300.00
Vase, Dutch, goats scene, lid w/lion finial, LPK, 13", VG 800.00
Vase, Dutch, 6 bird/floral panels, squirrel finial, 10", VG 275.00
Vase, tulip; Dutch, floral, heart shape w/5 necks, 9", EX 875.00
Wall pocket, Lambeth, cornucopia w/mask head, wht, 8", VG ..465.00

Depression Glass

Depression Glass is defined by Gene Florence, author of several best-selling books on the subject, as 'the inexpensive glassware made primarily during the Depression era in the colors of amber, green, pink, blue, red, yellow, white, and crystal.' This glass was mass produced, sold through five-and-dime stores and mail-order catalogs, and given away as premiums with gas and food products.

The listings in this book are far from being complete. If you want a more thorough presentation of this fascinating glassware, we recommend *The Collector's Encyclopedia of Depression Glass, The Pocket Guide to Depression Glass, Elegant Glassware of the Depression Era,* and *Very Rare Glassware of the Depression Years* by Gene Florence, whose address is listed in the Directory under Kentucky.

Adam, bowl, cereal; pk, 5¾" 35.00
Adam, bowl, dessert; gr, 4¾" 13.50
Adam, bowl, pk, w/lid, 9" 50.00
Adam, butter dish, pk, w/lid 70.00
Adam, candy jar, gr, w/lid, 2½" 87.50
Adam, creamer, gr 18.00
Adam, lamp, gr 260.00

Adam, pitcher, pink, 32-oz, 8", $45.00.

Adam, plate, grill; pk, 9" 16.00
Adam, plate, salad; pk, sq, 7¾" 10.00
Adam, saucer, gr, sq, 6" 6.50
Adam, shakers, gr, 4", pr 90.00
Adam, sherbet, pk, 3" 25.00
Adam, tray, relish; pk, divided, 8" 16.00
Adam, tumbler, iced tea; pk, 5½" 50.00
Adam, tumbler, pk, 4½" 25.00
American Pioneer, bowl, console; gr, 10¾" 57.50
American Pioneer, bowl, pk, hdls, 5" 14.00
American Pioneer, bowl, pk, w/lid, 8¾" 85.00

American Pioneer, candlesticks, pk, 6½", pr 60.00
American Pioneer, candy jar, gr, w/lid, 1½-lb 110.00
American Pioneer, candy jar, gr, w/lid, 1-lb 90.00
American Pioneer, creamer, gr, 2¾" 19.50
American Pioneer, creamer, pk, 3½" 18.00
American Pioneer, goblet, water; pk, 8-oz, 6" 35.00
American Pioneer, ice bucket, pk, 6" 40.00
American Pioneer, pitcher, gr, covered urn, 7" 200.00
American Pioneer, pitcher, pk, covered urn, 5" 125.00
American Pioneer, plate, gr, 6" 14.00
American Pioneer, plate, pk, 8" 7.50
American Pioneer, sugar bowl, pk, 2¾" 17.50
American Pioneer, tumbler, gr, 8-oz, 4" 44.00
American Pioneer, whiskey, pk, 2-oz, 2¼" 40.00
American Sweetheart, bowl, berry; pk, flat, 3¾" 32.50
American Sweetheart, bowl, console; monax, 18" 350.00
American Sweetheart, bowl, soup; pk, flat, 9½" 50.00
American Sweetheart, pitcher, pk, 60-oz, 7½" 500.00
American Sweetheart, pitcher, pk, 80-oz, 8" 425.00
American Sweetheart, plate, luncheon; monax, 9" 9.00
American Sweetheart, plate, salver; pk, 12" 14.00
American Sweetheart, shakers, monax, ftd, pr 275.00
American Sweetheart, sherbet, pk, ftd, 3¾" 15.00
American Sweetheart, sherbet, pk, ftd, 4¼" 12.00
American Sweetheart, tumbler, pk, 10-oz, 4¾" 85.00
American Sweetheart, tumbler, pk, 5-oz, 3½" 65.00
American Sweetheart, tumbler, pk, 9-oz, 4¼" 60.00
Anniversary, bowl, berry; crystal, 4⅞" 3.00
Anniversary, bowl, fruit; pk, 9" 20.00
Anniversary, bowl, soup; pk, 7⅜" 14.00
Anniversary, cake plate, crystal, w/lid 15.00
Anniversary, cake plate, pk, 12½" 14.00
Anniversary, creamer, ftd, crystal 4.00
Anniversary, pickle dish, crystal, 9" 4.00
Anniversary, plate, dinner; pk, 9" 9.00
Anniversary, saucer, crystal 1.50
Anniversary, vase, pk, 6½" 25.00
Anniversary, wine, crystal, 2½-oz 7.00
Aunt Polly, bowl, berry; gr, 4¾" 7.50
Aunt Polly, butter dish, gr, w/lid 210.00
Aunt Polly, plate, sherbet; bl, 6" 11.00
Aunt Polly, sherbet, gr 8.00
Aunt Polly, sugar bowl, bl 30.00
Aunt Polly, vase, gr, ftd, 6½" 27.50
Beaded Block, bowl, celery; gr, 8¼" 12.50
Beaded Block, bowl, gr, deep, rnd, 6" 10.00
Beaded Block, bowl, gr, rnd, 6¼" 7.50
Beaded Block, bowl, gr, sq, 5½" 7.00
Beaded Block, bowl, opal, rnd, 6½" 16.00
Beaded Block, bowl, opal, 1-hdl, 5½" 12.00
Beaded Block, jelly, gr, stemmed, 4½" 9.00
Beaded Block, plate, gr, rnd, 8¾" 15.00
Beaded Block, plate, opal, sq, 7¾" 10.00
Beaded Block, sugar, bowl, opal 24.00
Beaded Block, vase, bouquet; gr, 6" 12.00
Block Optic, bowl, berry; gr, 4¼" 7.00
Block Optic, bowl, berry; gr, 8½" 24.00
Block Optic, bowl, cereal; pk, 5¼" 20.00
Block Optic, bowl, salad; gr, 7¼" 20.00
Block Optic, butter dish, gr, w/lid, 3x5" 45.00
Block Optic, cup, pk, 4 styles, ea 6.50
Block Optic, goblet, cocktail; pk, 4" 28.00
Block Optic, goblet, wine; gr, 4½" 30.00
Block Optic, ice bucket, pk 40.00

Block Optic, pitcher, gr, 54-oz, 8½" 32.00
Block Optic, pitcher, pk, 68-oz, 7⅝" 60.00
Block Optic, pitcher, pk, 80-oz, 8" 65.00
Block Optic, plate, dinner; pk, 9" 25.00
Block Optic, plate, luncheon; gr, 8" 5.00
Block Optic, plate, sherbet; pk, 6" 2.50
Block Optic, sherbet, gr, 6-oz, 4¾" 14.00
Block Optic, tumbler, gr, flat, 9-oz 15.00
Block Optic, tumbler, pk, flat, 10-oz 16.00
Block Optic, tumbler, pk, flat, 14-oz 19.00
Block Optic, tumbler, pk, ftd, 5-oz, 4" 13.00
Block Optic, tumbler, pk, ftd, 9-oz 14.00
Block Optic, vase, blown, gr, 5¾" 250.00
Block Optic, whiskey, gr, 2-oz, 2¼" 24.00
Bowknot, bowl, berry; gr, 4½" 13.00
Bowknot, bowl, cereal; gr, 5½" 16.00
Bowknot, plate, salad; gr, 7" 10.00
Bowknot, sherbet, gr, low ftd 13.00
Bowknot, tumbler, gr, 10-oz, 5" 16.00
Bubble, bowl, berry; bl, 4" 13.00
Bubble, bowl, berry; bl, 8⅜" 15.00
Bubble, bowl, cereal; crystal, 5¼" 5.00
Bubble, bowl, flat soup; bl, 7¾" 14.00
Bubble, bowl, fruit; crystal, 4½" 4.00
Bubble, cup, bl 3.00
Bubble, plate, bread & butter; bl, 6¾" 4.00
Bubble, plate, dinner; crystal, 9⅜" 5.00
Bubble, plate, grill; bl, 9⅜" 18.00
Bubble, platter, crystal, oval, 12" 5.00
Bubble, saucer, crystal 1.00
Cameo, bowl, cereal; gr, 5½" 28.00
Cameo, bowl, lg berry; gr, 8¼" 30.00
Cameo, bowl, salad; gr, 7¼" 47.50
Cameo, bowl, soup; gr, rimmed, 9" 40.00
Cameo, butter dish, yel, w/lid 1,300.00
Cameo, candy jar, gr, low, w/lid, 4" 65.00
Cameo, decanter, gr, w/stopper, 10" 125.00
Cameo, goblet, wine; gr, 4" 55.00
Cameo, pitcher, water; gr, 56-oz, 8½" 45.00
Cameo, plate, dinner; gr, 9½" 15.00
Cameo, plate, grill; yel, 10½" 6.00
Cameo, plate, luncheon; gr, 8" 9.00
Cameo, plate, sherbet; gr, 6" 3.50
Cameo, sherbet, gr, 3⅛" 12.00
Cameo, sherbet, yel, 4⅞" 37.50
Cameo, sugar bowl, gr, 4¼" 21.00
Cameo, tumbler, gr, flat, 11-oz, 5" 25.00
Cameo, tumbler, water; gr, 9-oz, 4" 22.00
Cameo, vase, gr, 5¾" 145.00

Cherry Blossom, pitcher, green, 42-oz, $50.00.

Cherry Blossom, bowl, berry; gr, 4¾" 15.00
Cherry Blossom, bowl, berry; pk, rnd, 8½" 40.00
Cherry Blossom, bowl, berry; pk, 4¾" 13.00
Cherry Blossom, bowl, cereal; gr, 5¾" 30.00
Cherry Blossom, bowl, fruit; pk, 3-legged, 10½" 67.50
Cherry Blossom, bowl, gr, 2-hdld, 9" 27.50
Cherry Blossom, bowl, soup; pk, flat, 7¾" 47.50
Cherry Blossom, bowl, vegetable; pk, oval, 9" 30.00
Cherry Blossom, cake plate, gr, 3-legged, 10¼" 24.00
Cherry Blossom, coaster, gr 10.00
Cherry Blossom, creamer, pk 16.00
Cherry Blossom, mug, gr, 7-oz 155.00
Cherry Blossom, pitcher, gr, ftd, floral at top, 36-oz, 8" 48.00
Cherry Blossom, plate, dinner; gr, 9" 20.00
Cherry Blossom, plate, grill; pk, 9" 20.00
Cherry Blossom, plate, salad; gr, 7" 18.00
Cherry Blossom, plate, sherbet; pk, 6" 6.00
Cherry Blossom, platter, gr, 13" 55.00
Cherry Blossom, platter, pk, oval, 11" 30.00
Cherry Blossom, saucer, pk 5.00
Cherry Blossom, sherbet, pk 14.00
Cherry Blossom, sugar bowl, gr 13.00
Cherry Blossom, sugar bowl lid, gr 15.00
Cherryberry, bowl, berry; pk or gr, deep, 7½" 19.50
Cherryberry, bowl, pk or gr, deep, 6¼" 42.50
Cherryberry, bowl, salad; pk or gr, deep, 6½" 17.50
Cherryberry, butter dish, pk or gr, w/lid 155.00
Cherryberry, olive dish, pk or gr, 1-hdl, 5" 14.00
Cherryberry, pickle dish, pk or gr 14.00
Cherryberry, plate, salad; pk or gr, 7½" 13.00
Cherryberry, plate, sherbet; pk or gr, 6" 8.00
Cherryberry, sherbet, pk or gr 8.00
Chinex Classic, bowl, cereal; ivory, 5¾" 5.00
Chinex Classic, bowl, salad; floral, 7" 20.00
Chinex Classic, bowl, soup; floral, flat, 7¾" 16.00
Chinex Classic, butter dish, ivory 52.50
Chinex Classic, creamer, floral 9.00
Chinex Classic, cup, ivory 4.50
Chinex Classic, plate, dinner; ivory, 9¾" 4.00
Chinex Classic, plate, sherbet; ivory, 6¼" 2.50
Chinex Classic, saucer, ivory 2.00
Chinex Classic, sherbet, floral, low ftd 10.00
Chinex Classic, sugar bowl, ivory 5.00
Christmas Candy, bowl, soup; crystal, 7¾" 6.50
Christmas Candy, creamer, teal 18.00
Christmas Candy, cup, teal 18.00
Christmas Candy, plate, bread & butter; crystal, 6" 3.00
Christmas Candy, plate, dinner; teal, 9⅝" 27.50
Christmas Candy, plate, luncheon; teal, 8¼" 16.00
Christmas Candy, plate, sandwich; crystal, 11¼" 13.50
Christmas Candy, saucer, crystal 2.00
Circle, bowl, pk or gr, 4½" 8.00
Circle, bowl, pk or gr, 8" 15.00
Circle, creamer, pk or gr 8.50
Circle, goblet, water; pk or gr, 8-oz 10.00
Circle, goblet, wine; pk or gr, 4½" 12.00
Circle, plate, dinner; pk or gr, 9½" 12.50
Circle, plate, sherbet; pk or gr, 6" 2.00
Circle, sherbet, pk or gr, 3⅛" 5.00
Circle, sherbet, pk or gr, 4¾" 6.00
Circle, tumbler, juice; pk or gr, 4-oz 8.00
Circle, tumbler, pk or gr, 10-oz 16.00
Circle, tumbler, pk or gr, 15-oz 18.00
Cloverleaf, bowl, cereal; yel, 5" 27.50

Cloverleaf, bowl, dessert; gr, 4" 17.50
Cloverleaf, bowl, gr, 8" 50.00
Cloverleaf, candy dish, yel, w/lid 95.00
Cloverleaf, cup, yel 9.00
Cloverleaf, plate, grill; gr, 10¼" 17.50
Cloverleaf, plate, luncheon; yel, 8" 13.00
Cloverleaf, plate, sherbet; gr, 6" 4.50
Cloverleaf, saucer, yel 4.50
Cloverleaf, sherbet, yel, ftd, 3" 10.00
Cloverleaf, tumbler, gr, flat, 9-oz, 3¾" 35.00
Colonial, bowl, berry; gr, 4½" 14.00
Colonial, bowl, cereal; gr, 5½" 77.50
Colonial, bowl, cream soup; pk, 4½" 55.00
Colonial, bowl, pk, 3¾" 40.00
Colonial, bowl, soup; pk, low, 7" 50.00
Colonial, bowl, vegetable; pk, oval, 10" 25.00
Colonial, butter dish, pk, w/lid 575.00
Colonial, goblet, claret; gr, 4-oz, 5¼" 24.00
Colonial, goblet, cocktail; gr, 3-oz, 4" 24.00
Colonial, goblet, cordial; gr, 1-oz, 3¾" 26.00
Colonial, goblet, water; gr, 8½-oz, 5¾" 28.00
Colonial, plate, dinner; pk, 10" 42.50
Colonial, plate, grill; pk, 10" 22.00
Colonial, plate, sherbet; pk, 6" 5.00
Colonial, platter, gr, oval, 12" 20.00
Colonial, shakers, pk, pr 125.00
Colonial, sherbet, gr 14.00
Colonial, spoon holder or celery dish, pk 115.00
Colonial, tumbler, juice; gr, 5-oz, 3" 23.00
Colonial, tumbler, lemonade; gr, 15-oz 65.00
Colonial, tumbler, pk, ftd, 5-oz, 4" 28.00
Colonial, tumbler, pk, 10-oz 33.00
Colonial, whiskey, pk, 1½-oz, 2½" 10.00
Colonial Block, bowl, pk or gr, 7" 16.00
Colonial Block, butter dish, pk or gr 42.50
Colonial Block, butter tub, pk or gr 32.50
Colonial Block, candy dish, pk or gr, w/lid, 8½" 32.50
Colonial Block, creamer, pk or gr 10.00
Colonial Fluted, bowl, berry; gr, 4" 5.00
Colonial Fluted, bowl, cereal; gr, 6" 7.50
Colonial Fluted, bowl, salad; gr, deep, 6½" 17.50
Colonial Fluted, creamer, gr 6.00
Colonial Fluted, plate, sherbet; gr, 6" 2.00
Colonial Fluted, saucer, gr 1.50
Colonial Fluted, sugar bowl, gr 5.00
Colonial Fluted, sugar bowl lid, gr 15.00
Columbia, bowl, cereal; crystal, 5" 14.00
Columbia, bowl, salad; crystal, 8½" 16.00
Columbia, bowl, soup; crystal, low, 8" 16.00
Columbia, butter dish, crystal, w/lid 15.00
Columbia, plate, luncheon; crystal, 9½" 8.50
Columbia, plate, snack; crystal 35.00
Columbia, saucer, crystal 3.00
Columbia, tumbler, crystal, 9-oz 22.00
Coronation, bowl, berry; pk, 4¼" 4.00
Coronation, bowl, nappy; pk, 6½" 6.00
Coronation, cup, pk 5.00
Coronation, pitcher, pk, 68-oz, 7¾" 200.00
Coronation, plate, sherbet; pk, 6" 1.50
Coronation, saucer, pk 2.00
Cremax, bowl, cereal; ivory, 5¾" 3.00
Cremax, creamer, ivory 4.50
Cremax, saucer, ivory 2.00
Cremax, sugar bowl, ivory 4.50

Cube, bowl, dessert; gr, 4½" 5.50
Cube, bowl, pk, deep, 4½" 6.50
Cube, bowl, salad; pk, 6½" 8.50
Cube, butter dish, pk, w/lid 55.00
Cube, candy jar, pk, w/lid, 6½" 25.00
Cube, coaster, gr, 3¼" 6.50
Cube, creamer, pk, 2" 2.00
Cube, creamer, pk, 3" 6.00
Cube, cup, gr 8.00
Cube, pitcher, gr, 45-oz, 8¾" 200.00
Cube, plate, luncheon; pk, 8" 5.00
Cube, plate, sherbet; pk, 6" 3.00
Cube, powder jar, pk, 3-legged, w/lid 22.00
Cube, saucer, gr 3.50
Cube, shakers, gr, pr 30.00
Cube, sugar bowl, pk, w/lid, 2" 2.00
Cube, tumbler, pk, 9-oz, 4" 55.00
Daisy, bowl, berry; amber, deep, 9⅜" 30.00
Daisy, bowl, berry; crystal, 4½" 4.50
Daisy, bowl, berry; crystal, 7⅜" 7.00
Daisy, bowl, cereal; amber, 6" 25.00
Daisy, bowl, cream soup; crystal, 4½" 4.00
Daisy, creamer, crystal, ftd 5.00
Daisy, plate, dinner; amber, 9⅜" 9.00
Daisy, plate, grill; crystal, 10⅜" 4.00
Daisy, plate, luncheon; crystal, 8¾" 4.00
Daisy, plate, salad; amber, 7¾" 7.00
Daisy, plate, sherbet; crystal, 6" 2.00
Daisy, relish dish, amber, 3-part, 8⅜" 30.00
Daisy, saucer, amber 2.00
Daisy, sherbet, crystal, ftd 4.50
Daisy, tumbler, amber, ftd, 12-oz 35.00
Daisy, tumbler, amber, ftd, 9-oz 18.00
Diamond Quilted, bowl, bl, crimped edges, 7" 15.00
Diamond Quilted, bowl, cereal; bl, 5" 13.00
Diamond Quilted, bowl, cream soup; gr, 4¾" 7.50
Diamond Quilted, bowl, gr, 1-hdl, 5½" 6.00
Diamond Quilted, compote, gr, w/lid, 11½" 65.00
Diamond Quilted, goblet, champagne; gr, 9-oz, 6" 9.00
Diamond Quilted, goblet, cordial; gr, 1-oz 10.00
Diamond Quilted, goblet, wine; gr, 2-oz 10.00
Diamond Quilted, ice bucket, bl 75.00
Diamond Quilted, plate, salad; gr, 7" 5.00
Diamond Quilted, plate, sandwich; gr, 14" 12.00
Diamond Quilted, plate, sherbet; bl, 6" 5.00
Diamond Quilted, punch bowl, gr, w/stand 380.00
Diamond Quilted, saucer, bl 5.00
Diamond Quilted, sherbet, gr 4.50
Diamond Quilted, tumbler, gr, ftd, 12-oz 14.00
Diamond Quilted, tumbler, gr, ftd, 6-oz 8.50
Diamond Quilted, tumbler, iced tea; gr, 12-oz 9.00
Diamond Quilted, tumbler, water; gr, 9-oz 8.00
Diana, bowl, console fruit; amber, 11" 12.00
Diana, bowl, cream soup; pk, 5½" 18.00
Diana, bowl, pk, scalloped edge, 12" 22.50
Diana, bowl, salad; pk, 9" 18.00
Diana, bowl cereal; pk, 5" 8.00
Diana, candy jar, pk, w/lid, rnd 35.00
Diana, creamer, pk, oval 10.00
Diana, plate, bread & butter; pk, 6" 4.00
Diana, plate, sandwich; amber, 11¾" 9.00
Diana, platter, pk, oval, 12" 25.00
Diana, saucer, pk 4.00
Diana, shakers, amber, pr 90.00

Diana, sherbet, pk 10.00
Diana, sugar bowl, pk, oval 7.00
Diana, tumbler, pk, 9-oz, 4⅛" 40.00
Dogwood, bowl, berry; gr, 8½" 90.00
Dogwood, bowl, cereal; pk, 5½" 22.00
Dogwood, bowl, fruit; pk, 10¼" 275.00
Dogwood, cake plate, pk, heavy solid ft, 11" 225.00
Dogwood, creamer, pk, thin, 2½" 15.00
Dogwood, pitcher, pk, 80-oz, 8" 525.00
Dogwood, plate, luncheon; pk, 8" 6.50
Dogwood, plate, salver; pk, 12" 23.00
Dogwood, platter, pk, oval, 12" 350.00
Dogwood, sherbet, pk, low ftd 85.00
Dogwood, sugar bowl, pk, thick, 3¼" 14.00
Doric, bowl, berry; gr, lg, 8¼" 15.00
Doric, bowl, berry; pk, 4½" 6.00
Doric, bowl, cereal; gr, 5½" 55.00
Doric, butter dish, gr, w/lid 75.00
Doric, cake plate, pk, 3-legged, 10" 20.00
Doric, candy dish, pk, w/lid, 8" 30.00
Doric, candy dish, pk, 3-part 5.00
Doric, coaster, gr, 3" 15.00
Doric, creamer, pk, 4" 10.00
Doric, cup, gr 8.00

**Doric, pitcher, green, 32-oz, 5½",
$37.00.**

Doric, pitcher, gr, flat, 36-oz, 6" 35.00
Doric, pitcher, gr, ftd, 48-oz, 7½" 750.00
Doric, plate, dinner; pk, 9" 10.00
Doric, plate, grill; gr, 9" 15.00
Doric, plate, salad; gr, 7" 16.00
Doric, plate, sherbet; gr, 6" 4.50
Doric, platter, gr, oval, 12" 20.00
Doric, relish tray, pk, 4x4" 8.00
Doric, relish tray, pk, 4x8" 10.00
Doric, saucer, pk 3.00
Doric, shakers, pk, pr 30.00
Doric, sherbet, gr, ftd 12.00
Doric, sugar bowl, gr 10.00
Doric, sugar bowl lid, gr 20.00
Doric, tray, gr, hdld, 10" 13.00
Doric, tray, serving; pk, 8x8" 18.00
Doric, tumbler, gr, flat, 9-oz, 4½" 85.00
Doric, tumbler, gr, ftd, 12-oz, 5" 95.00
Doric, tumbler, pk, ftd, 10-oz, 4" 50.00
English Hobnail, bowl, pk or gr, several styles, 6", ea ...12.00
English Hobnail, bowl, pk or gr, several styles, 8", ea ...23.00
English Hobnail, bowl, relish; pk or gr, oval, 12" 20.00

English Hobnail, candlesticks, pk or gr, 8½", pr 55.00
English Hobnail, celery dish, pk or gr, 12" 26.00
English Hobnail, cigarette box, pk or gr 30.00
English Hobnail, cologne bottle, pk or gr 30.00
English Hobnail, goblet, claret; pk or gr, 5-oz 20.00
English Hobnail, goblet, wine; pk or gr, 2-oz 22.00
English Hobnail, pitcher, pk or gr, 39-oz 175.00
English Hobnail, pitcher, pk or gr, 60-oz 210.00
English Hobnail, plate, dinner; pk or gr, 10" 22.50
English Hobnail, plate, pie; pk or gr, 7¼" 5.00
English Hobnail, tumbler, iced tea; pk or gr, 12-oz, 5" 24.00
English Hobnail, tumbler, pk or gr, ftd, 9-oz 16.00
English Hobnail, tumbler, pk or gr, 5- or 8-oz, 3¾" 14.00
Floragold, bowl, cereal; irid, rnd, 5½" 30.00
Floragold, bowl, fruit; ruffled, lg, 12" 6.50
Floragold, bowl, irid, ruffled, 9½" 7.50
Floragold, bowl, irid, sq, 4½" 5.00
Floragold, bowl, salad; irid, deep, 9½" 35.00
Floragold, butter dish, irid, rnd, w/lid 40.00
Floragold, coaster/ashtray, irid, 4" 5.00
Floragold, plate, sherbet; irid, 5¾" 10.00
Floragold, tumbler, irid, ftd, 11-oz 17.50
Floragold, tumbler, irid, ftd, 15-oz 85.00

Floral, bowl, vegetable; pink, with lid, 8", $42.50.

Floral, bowl, berry; pk, 4" 14.00
Floral, bowl, vegetable; pk, oval, 9" 15.00
Floral, butter dish, gr, w/lid 80.00
Floral, candlesticks, pk, 4", pr 65.00
Floral, candy jar, pk, w/lid 30.00
Floral, coaster, gr, 3¼" 8.00
Floral, lamp, pk 230.00
Floral, plate, grill; gr, 9" 155.00
Floral, plate, sherbet; gr, 6" 7.00
Floral, saucer, pk 9.00
Floral, shakers, pk, flat, 6", pr 45.00
Floral, sherbet, pk 14.00
Floral, sugar bowl, gr 10.00
Floral, sugar bowl lid, gr 15.00
Floral & Diamond Band, bowl, berry; pk, 4½" 7.00
Floral & Diamond Band, butter dish, pk, w/lid 125.00
Floral & Diamond Band, pitcher, gr, 42-oz, 8" 90.00
Floral & Diamond Band, sherbet, gr 7.00
Floral & Diamond Band, sugar bowl, gr, sm 10.00
Floral & Diamond Band, sugar bowl, gr, 5¼" 13.00
Floral & Diamond Band, sugar bowl lid, gr 55.00
Floral & Diamond Band, tumbler, iced tea; pk, 5" 30.00
Florentine No 1, ashtray, yel, 5½" 26.00
Florentine No 1, bowl, berry; gr, 5" 10.00

Florentine No 1, bowl, cereal; yel, 6" 20.00
Florentine No 1, butter dish, yel, w/lid 150.00
Florentine No 1, coaster/ashtray, yel, 3¾" 18.00
Florentine No 1, creamer, gr 9.00
Florentine No 1, plate, dinner; gr, 10" 14.00
Florentine No 1, plate, grill; yel, 10" 13.00
Florentine No 1, plate, salad; yel, 8½" 11.00
Florentine No 1, plate, sherbet; gr, 6" 5.00
Florentine No 1, platter, yel, oval, 11½" 19.00
Florentine No 1, saucer, gr 3.00
Florentine No 1, sherbet, yel, ftd, 3-oz 11.00
Florentine No 1, sugar bowl, gr 9.00
Florentine No 1, sugar bowl lid, gr 15.00
Florentine No 2, bowl, berry; gr, lg, 8" 19.00
Florentine No 2, bowl, cereal; yel, 6" 35.00
Florentine No 2, bowl, gr, 5¼" 30.00
Florentine No 2, butter dish, yel 135.00
Florentine No 2, candy dish, gr, w/lid 95.00
Florentine No 2, coaster/ashtray, gr, 3¾" 16.00
Florentine No 2, creamer, gr 7.50
Florentine No 2, cup, yel 8.00
Florentine No 2, pitcher, gr, 54-oz, 7½" 50.00
Florentine No 2, pitcher, yel, 76-oz, 8" 350.00
Florentine No 2, plate, dinner; gr, 10" 13.00
Florentine No 2, plate, grill; yel, 10¼" 10.00
Florentine No 2, plate, salad; gr, 8½" 7.00
Florentine No 2, platter, gr, oval, 11" 15.00
Florentine No 2, saucer, gr 3.00
Florentine No 2, sugar bowl, gr 8.00
Florentine No 2, sugar bowl lid, gr 13.00
Florentine No 2, tumbler, gr, ftd, 9-oz, 4½" 20.00
Florentine No 2, tumbler, juice; gr, 5-oz, 3½" 10.00
Flower Garden w/Butterflies, candlesticks, pk or gr, 8", pr 135.00
Flower Garden w/Butterflies, candy dish, pk, w/lid, 7½" 125.00
Flower Garden w/Butterflies, creamer, pk or gr 65.00
Flower Garden w/Butterflies, plate, dinner; pk or gr, 10" 40.00
Flower Garden w/Butterflies, powder jar, pk or gr, flat 60.00
Flower Garden w/Butterflies, powder jar, pk or gr, ftd 100.00
Flower Garden w/Butterflies, tray, pk or gr, oval, 5½x10" 50.00
Flower Garden w/Butterflies, vase, pk or gr, 10" 125.00
Forest Green, ashtray 3.50
Forest Green, bowl, salad; 7⅜" 12.50
Forest Green, bowl, soup; 6" 15.00
Forest Green, creamer, flat 6.00
Forest Green, plate, salad; 6⅝" 4.00
Forest Green, platter, rectangular 25.00
Forest Green, saucer 1.50
Forest Green, tumbler 5-oz 3.50
Forest Green, vase, 6⅜" 4.00
Forest Green, vase, ivy; 4" 3.00
Fortune, bowl, berry; pk, 4" 3.50
Fortune, bowl, dessert; pk, 4½" 4.00
Fortune, plate, sherbet; pk, 6" 2.50
Fortune, saucer, pk 2.50
Fortune, tumbler, water; 9-oz, 4" 8.50
Fruits, bowl, berry; gr, 8" 50.00
Fruits, cup, pk 6.00
Fruits, plate, luncheon; gr, 8" 6.00
Fruits, saucer, pk 4.00
Fruits, sherbet, pk 6.00
Fruits, tumbler, gr, 12-oz, 5" 95.00
Fruits, tumbler, juice; pk, 3½" 15.00
Georgian, bowl, berry; gr, 4½" 7.50
Georgian, bowl, berry; gr, 7½" 55.00

Georgian, bowl, cereal; gr, 5¾" 20.00
Georgian, bowl, vegetable; gr, oval, 9" 55.00
Georgian, hot plate, gr, center design, 5" 42.50
Georgian, plate, luncheon; gr, 8" 8.00
Georgian, saucer, gr 4.00
Georgian, sherbet, gr 11.00
Georgian, sugar bowl, gr, ftd, 4" 9.50
Georgian, sugar bowl lid, gr, 4" 82.00
Georgian, tumbler, gr, flat, 12-oz, 5¼" 97.50
Georgian, tumbler, gr, flat, 9-oz, 4" 47.50
Harp, ashtray/coaster, crystal 4.50
Harp, cup, crystal 12.50
Harp, plate, crystal, 7" 10.00
Harp, tray, crystal, rectangular 30.00
Heritage, bowl, berry; crystal, 5" 7.50
Heritage, bowl, berry; crystal, 8½" 27.50
Heritage, creamer, crystal, ftd 21.00
Heritage, cup, crystal 6.50
Heritage, plate, dinner; crystal, 9¼" 11.00
Heritage, plate, sandwich; crystal, 12" 12.50
Heritage, saucer, crystal 4.00
Hex Optic, bowl, berry; pk or gr, 7½" 7.00
Hex Optic, bucket reamer, pk or gr 50.00
Hex Optic, plate, luncheon; pk or gr, 8" 5.00
Hex Optic, plate, sherbet; pk or gr, 6" 2.00
Hex Optic, refrigerator dish, pk or gr, 4x4" 9.50
Hex Optic, saucer, pk or gr 2.00
Hex Optic, sherbet, pk or gr, ftd, 5-oz 4.00
Hex Optic, tumbler, pk or gr, ftd, 7" 11.00
Hex Optic, tumbler, pk or gr, 9-oz, 3¾" 4.50
Hex Optic, whiskey, pk or gr, 1-oz, 2" 7.50
Hobnail, bowl, cereal; crystal, 5½" 3.50
Hobnail, creamer, crystal, ftd 4.00
Hobnail, decanter, crystal, w/stopper, 32-oz 25.00
Hobnail, goblet, water; crystal, 10-oz 6.00
Hobnail, pitcher, milk; crystal, 67-oz 24.00
Hobnail, plate, sherbet; crystal, 6" 2.00
Hobnail, sherbet, crystal 3.00
Hobnail, tumbler, iced tea; crystal, 15-oz 7.00
Hobnail, tumbler, juice; crystal, 5-oz 4.00
Hobnail, tumbler, water; crystal, 9-oz or 10-oz, ea 5.00
Hobnail, tumbler, wine; crystal, ftd, 3-oz 6.50
Hobnail, whiskey, crystal, 1½-oz 6.00
Holiday, bowl, berry; pk, 5⅛" 11.00
Holiday, bowl, console; pk, 10¾" 87.50
Holiday, bowl, vegetable; pk, oval, 9½" 22.00
Holiday, candlesticks, pk, 3", pr 80.00
Holiday, creamer, pk, ftd 7.50
Holiday, pitcher, milk; pk, 16-oz, 4¾" 55.00
Holiday, pitcher, pk, 52-oz, 6¾" 30.00
Holiday, plate, chop; pk, 13¾" 85.00
Holiday, plate, sherbet; pk, 6" 4.50
Holiday, platter, pk, oval, 11⅜" 17.50
Holiday, sherbet, pk 6.00
Holiday, tumbler, pk, flat, 10-oz, 4" 18.50
Holiday, tumbler, pk, ftd, 4" 35.00
Holiday, tumbler, pk, ftd, 6" 12.50
Homespun, bowl, berry; pk, 8¼" 15.00
Homespun, bowl, cereal; pk, 5" 17.50
Homespun, butter dish, pk, w/lid 55.00
Homespun, cup, pk 10.00
Homespun, plate, dinner; pk, 9¼" 15.00
Homespun, plate, sherbet; pk, 6" 5.00
Homespun, saucer, pk 4.00

Homespun, tumbler, pk, ftd, 5-oz, 4" 6.50
Indiana Custard, bowl, berry; 4⅞" 7.50
Indiana Custard, bowl, berry; 8¾" 26.00
Indiana Custard, bowl, cereal; 5¾" 18.00
Indiana Custard, creamer 15.00
Indiana Custard, plate, dinner; 9¾" 20.00
Indiana Custard, plate, luncheon; 8⅞" 12.00
Indiana Custard, plate, salad; 7½" 10.00
Indiana Custard, platter, oval, 11½" 28.00
Indiana Custard, sherbet 85.00
Indiana Custard, sugar bowl lid 18.00
Iris, bowl, berry; crystal, beaded, 4½" 35.00
Iris, bowl, salad; irid, 9½" 11.00
Iris, bowl, sauce; irid, 5" 22.00
Iris, bowl, soup; crystal, 7½" 135.00
Iris, butter dish, crystal, w/lid 45.00
Iris, candlesticks, irid, pr 40.00
Iris, candy jar, crystal, w/lid 97.50
Iris, coaster, crystal 70.00
Iris, demitasse saucer, irid 140.00
Iris, goblet, irid, 4-oz, 5¾" 22.00
Iris, goblet, irid, 8-oz, 5¾" 110.00
Iris, goblet, wine; irid, 4" 30.00
Iris, plate, dinner; crystal, 9" 47.50
Iris, plate, luncheon; crystal, 8" 60.00
Iris, plate, sandwich; irid, 11 ....25.00
Iris, plate, sherbet; crystal, 5½" 12.00
Iris, saucer, crystal 10.00
Iris, sherbet, crystal, ftd, 2½" 21.00
Iris, sherbet, crystal, ftd, 4" 18.00
Iris, sugar bowl, crystal 10.00
Iris, tumbler, crystal, flat, 4" 100.00
Iris, tumbler, crystal, ftd, 6" 16.00
Iris, tumbler, crystal, ftd, 6½" 30.00
Iris, vase, irid, 9" 22.00
Jubilee, candlesticks, topaz, pr 150.00
Jubilee, cheese & cracker set, topaz 250.00
Jubilee, goblet, topaz, 12½-oz, 6⅛" 95.00
Jubilee, goblet, topaz, 6-oz, 5" 65.00
Jubilee, plate, luncheon; topaz, 8¾" 13.00
Jubilee, plate, sandwich; topaz, 13" 45.00
Jubilee, sherbet, topaz, 4¾" 45.00
Jubilee, sugar bowl, topaz 20.00
Jubilee, tray, sandwich; topaz, center hdl 185.00
Lace Edge, bowl, cereal; pk, 6⅜" 16.00
Lace Edge, bowl, salad; pk, 7¾" 18.00
Lace Edge, candlesticks, pk, pr 175.00

Lace Edge, candy dish, pink, $45.00.

Lace Edge, creamer, pk 20.00
Lace Edge, plate, dinner; pk, 10½" 24.00
Lace Edge, plate, luncheon; pk, 8¾" 15.00
Lace Edge, plate, salad; pk, 7¼" 19.00
Lace Edge, platter, pk, 12¾" 25.00
Lace Edge, sherbet, pk, ftd 75.00
Lace Edge, vase, pk, 7" 295.00
Laced Edge, bowl, bl or gr, divided oval, 11" 95.00
Laced Edge, bowl, fruit; bl or gr, 4½" 25.00
Laced Edge, bowl, vegetable; bl or gr, 9" 95.00
Laced Edge, creamer, bl or gr 32.50
Laced Edge, plate, dinner; bl or gr, 10" 65.00
Laced Edge, plate, salad; bl or gr, 8" 30.00
Laced Edge, platter, bl or gr, 13" 125.00
Laced Edge, tumbler, bl or gr, 9-oz 50.00
Lake Como, bowl, cereal; wht, 6" 20.00
Lake Como, bowl, soup; wht, flat 85.00
Lake Como, bowl, vegetable; wht, 9¾" 35.00
Lake Como, plate, dinner; wht, 9¼" 25.00
Lake Como, platter, wht, 11" 55.00
Lake Como, saucer, wht 10.00
Lake Como, sugar bowl, wht, ftd 25.00
Laurel, bowl, berry; ivory, 5" 7.00
Laurel, bowl, cereal; gr, 6" 7.00
Laurel, bowl, ivory, 11" 35.00
Laurel, cheese dish, gr, w/lid 50.00
Laurel, creamer, gr, short 9.00
Laurel, cup, gr 7.00
Laurel, plate, grill; ivory, 9⅛" 11.00
Laurel, plate, salad; gr, 7½" 9.00
Laurel, saucer, gr 3.00
Laurel, sugar bowl, ivory, short 9.00
Laurel, sugar bowl, ivory, tall 12.00
Lincoln Inn, ashtray, bl or red 16.00
Lincoln Inn, bowl, bl or red, ftd, 9¼" 30.00
Lincoln Inn, bowl, cereal; bl or red, 6" 12.00
Lincoln Inn, bowl, colors other than bl or red, ftd, 10½" 28.00
Lincoln Inn, bowl, finger; colors other than bl or red 12.00
Lincoln Inn, bowl, fruit; colors other than bl or red, 5" 9.00
Lincoln Inn, goblet, wine; colors other than bl or red 16.00
Lincoln Inn, nut dish, colors other than bl or red, ftd 11.00
Lincoln Inn, plate, bl or red, 6" 7.00
Lincoln Inn, plate, bl or red, 9¼" 25.00
Lincoln Inn, plate, colors other than bl or red, 8" 7.00
Lincoln Inn, shakers, bl or red, pr 195.00
Lincoln Inn, vase, color other than bl or red, ftd, 12" 85.00
Lorain, bowl, berry; yel, deep, 8" 125.00
Lorain, bowl, cereal; gr, 6" 32.50
Lorain, bowl, salad; gr, 7¼" 36.00
Lorain, plate, luncheon; yel, 8⅜" 25.00
Lorain, plate, sherbet; gr, 5½" 7.00
Lorain, platter, gr, 11½" 23.00
Lorain, sherbet, yel, ftd 28.00
Lorain, sugar bowl, gr, ftd 14.00
Madrid, ashtray, amber, sq, 6" 185.00
Madrid, bowl, berry; amber, 9⅜" 18.00
Madrid, bowl, cream soup; amber, 4¾" 14.00
Madrid, bowl, salad; amber, deep, 9½" 27.50
Madrid, bowl, salad; amber, 8" 14.00
Madrid, bowl, soup; amber, 7" 14.00
Madrid, cookie jar, amber, w/lid 42.50
Madrid, creamer, amber, ftd 8.00
Madrid, jam dish, amber, 7" 20.00
Madrid, plate, dinner; amber, 10½" 32.50

Madrid, plate, grill; gr, 10½" 15.00
Madrid, plate, luncheon; amber, 8⅞" 8.00
Madrid, plate, sherbet; gr, 6" 4.00
Madrid, saucer, amber 4.00
Madrid, sugar bowl, amber 7.00
Manhattan, bowl, sauce; crystal, 4½" 9.00
Manhattan, pitcher, pk, tilted, 80-oz 45.00
Manhattan, plate, salad; pk, 8½" 13.00
Manhattan, plate, sandwich; crystal, 14" 20.00
Manhattan, plate, sherbet; pk, 6" 45.00
Manhattan, relish tray insert, pk 6.00
Manhattan, sherbet, pk 12.00
Manhattan, wine, crystal, 3½" 5.00
Mayfair, bowl, cereal; pk, 5½" 20.00
Mayfair, bowl, pk, low, flat, 11¾" 48.00
Mayfair, bowl, vegetable; pk, 7" 22.00
Mayfair, celery dish, pk, 10" 35.00
Mayfair, creamer, bl, ftd 60.00
Mayfair, decanter, pk, w/stopper, 32-oz 130.00
Mayfair, goblet, wine; pk, 3-oz, 4½" 65.00
Mayfair, pitcher, bl, 37-oz, 6" 125.00
Mayfair, plate, dinner; pk, 9½" 45.00
Mayfair, plate, grill; bl, 9½" 45.00
Mayfair, plate, luncheon; pk, 8½" 22.00
Mayfair, sherbet, pk, ftd, 3" 15.00
Mayfair, whiskey, pk, 1½-oz, 2¼" 60.00
Mayfair Federal, bowl, cereal; gr, 6" 19.00
Mayfair Federal, bowl, cream soup; amber, 5" 17.50
Mayfair Federal, bowl, sauce; gr, 5" 11.00
Mayfair Federal, plate, dinner; amber, 9½" 12.00
Mayfair Federal, plate, grill; gr, 9½" 13.00
Mayfair Federal, plate, salad; amber, 6¾" 7.00
Mayfair Federal, saucer, amber 4.00
Mayfair Federal, sugar bowl, gr, ftd 15.00
Mayfair Federal, tumbler, amber, 9-oz, 4½" 22.50
Miss America, bowl, vegetable; pk, oval, 10" 25.00
Miss America, butter dish, pk, w/lid 500.00

**Miss America, celery tray, pink, 6½x10½",
$26.00.**

Miss America, coaster, pk, 5¾" 25.00
Miss America, compote, crystal, 5" 13.00
Miss America, goblet, juice; crystal, 5-oz, 4¾" 24.00
Miss America, goblet, water; pk, 10-oz, 5½" 38.00
Miss America, goblet, wine; pk, 3-oz, 3¾" 60.00
Miss America, pitcher, pk, 65-oz, 8" 110.00
Miss America, plate, dinner; crystal, 10½" 12.00
Miss America, plate, grill; pk, 10¼" 20.00
Miss America, plate, salad; pk, 8½" 20.00

Miss America, plate, sherbet; crystal, 5¾" 6.00
Miss America, platter, crystal, oval, 12" 14.00
Miss America, shakers, pk, pr 50.00
Miss America, sherbet, crystal 7.50
Miss America, sugar bowl, crystal 8.00
Moderntone, bowl, berry; cobalt, 5" 20.00
Moderntone, bowl, cereal; cobalt, 6½" 65.00
Moderntone, bowl, soup; cobalt, 7½" 90.00
Moderntone, plate, luncheon; amethyst, 7¾" 9.00
Moderntone, plate, salad; cobalt, 6¾" 10.00
Moderntone, platter, amethyst, oval, 11" 28.00
Moderntone, saucer, cobalt 5.00
Moderntone, sherbet, amethyst 10.00
Moderntone, sugar bowl, cobalt 10.00
Moderntone, tumbler, cobalt, 12-oz 85.00
Moderntone, tumbler, cobalt, 9-oz 30.00
Moderntone, whiskey, cobalt, 1½" 30.00
Moondrops, ashtray, colors other than red & bl 16.00
Moondrops, bowl, pickle; red & bl, 7½" 22.00
Moondrops, candy dish, colors other than red & bl, ruffled, 8" 19.00
Moondrops, plate, sherbet; red & bl, 6⅛" 6.00
Moondrops, saucer, red & bl 5.00
Moondrops, sherbet, red & bl, 2⅝" 15.00
Moondrops, sherbet, red & bl, 4½" 25.00
Moondrops, tumbler, red & bl, 12-oz, 5⅛" 26.00
Moonstone, bowl, berry; opal, 5½" 15.00
Moonstone, bowl, opal, crimped, 9½" 18.00
Moonstone, bowl, opal, flat, 7¾" 12.00
Moonstone, cigarette jar, opal, w/lid 20.00
Moonstone, creamer, opal 8.00
Moonstone, goblet, opal, 10-oz 18.00
Moonstone, plate, luncheon; opal, 8" 14.00
Moonstone, plate, sandwich; opal, 10" 22.50
Moonstone, plate, sherbet; opal, 6¼" 6.00
Moonstone, sherbet, opal, ftd 6.00
Moroccan Amethyst, bowl, amethyst, 10¾" 25.00
Moroccan Amethyst, goblet, juice; amethyst, 5½-oz, 4⅜" 8.50
Moroccan Amethyst, ice bucket, amethyst, 6" 27.50
Moroccan Amethyst, saucer, amethyst 1.00
Mt Pleasant, candlesticks, cobalt, single, pr 26.00
Mt Pleasant, leaf, cobalt, 8" 15.00
Mt Pleasant, mint dish, cobalt, center hdl, 6" 20.00
Mt Pleasant, sherbet, cobalt 15.00
Mt Pleasant, vase, cobalt, 7¼" 30.00
New Century, creamer, gr 8.00
New Century, goblet, wine; gr, 2½-oz 22.00
New Century, plate, dinner; gr, 10" 15.00
New Century, plate, grill; gr, 10" 10.00
New Century, plate, salad; gr, 8½" 8.00
New Century, plate, sherbet; gr, 6" 3.00
New Century, whiskey, gr, 1½-oz, 2½" 14.00
Newport, bowl, cereal; cobalt, 5¼" 30.00
Newport, plate, luncheon; cobalt, 8½" 12.00
Newport, plate, sherbet; cobalt, 6" 6.00
Newport, shakers, cobalt, pr 45.00
Newport, sherbet, cobalt 14.00
Newport, sugar bowl, amethyst 13.00
Newport, tumbler, amethyst, 9-oz, 4½" 30.00
No 610 Pyramid, bowl, pickle; yel, 9½" 50.00
No 610 Pyramid, bowl, pk, oval, 9½" 27.00
No 610 Pyramid, ice tub, yel 185.00
No 610 Pyramid, pitcher, pk 210.00
No 610 Pyramid, sugar bowl, yel 30.00
No 612 Horseshoe, bowl, berry; gr, 4½" 19.00

No 612 Horseshoe, bowl, berry; gr, 9½" 27.50
No 612 Horseshoe, bowl, cereal; yel, 6½" 20.00
No 612 Horseshoe, bowl, vegetable; yel, 8½" 25.00
No 612 Horseshoe, butter dish, gr, w/lid 600.00
No 612 Horseshoe, pitcher, gr, 64-oz, 8½" 220.00
No 612 Horseshoe, plate, dinner; gr, 10¾" 16.00
No 612 Horseshoe, plate, sandwich; yel, 11¼" 16.00
No 612 Horseshoe, plate, sherbet; gr, 6" 5.00
No 612 Horseshoe, platter, yel, oval, 10¾" 22.00
No 612 Horseshoe, saucer, gr 5.00
No 612 Horseshoe, tumbler, gr, 9-oz, 4½" 150.00
No 616 Vernon, cup, gr 14.00
No 616 Vernon, plate, luncheon; yel, 8" 8.50
No 616 Vernon, plate, sandwich; yel, 11" 24.00
No 616 Vernon, saucer, gr 5.00
No 616 Vernon, sugar bowl, gr, ftd 23.00
No 618 Pineapple & Floral, bowl, vegetable; crystal, oval, 10" 23.00
No 618 Pineapple & Floral, compote, amber, dmn shaped 7.00
No 618 Pineapple & Floral, creamer, amber, dmn shaped 10.00
No 618 Pineapple & Floral, cup, amber 9.00
No 618 Pineapple & Floral, plate, salad; amber, 8⅜" 8.00
No 618 Pineapple & Floral, plate, sandwich; amber, 11½" 15.00
No 618 Pineapple & Floral, platter, crystal, closed hdl, 11" 14.00
No 618 Pineapple & Floral, saucer, crystal 5.00
No 618 Pineapple & Floral, tumbler, crystal, 8-oz, 4¼" 32.50
No 622 Pretzel, bowl, berry; crystal teal, 9⅜" 15.00
No 622 Pretzel, bowl, celery; crystal teal, 10¼" 1.50
No 622 Pretzel, bowl, soup; crystal teal, 7½" 10.00
No 622 Pretzel, pitcher, crystal teal, 39-oz 150.00
No 622 Pretzel, plate, salad; crystal teal, 8⅜" 5.00
Normandie, bowl, berry; amber, 5" 5.00
Normandie, bowl, berry; pk, 8½" 20.00
Normandie, cup, amber 7.00
Normandie, plate, grill; amber, 11" 13.00
Normandie, plate, luncheon; pk, 9¼" 12.00
Normandie, plate, salad; pk, 8" 10.00
Normandie, platter, amber, 11¾" 15.00
Normandie, saucer, amber 4.00
Normandie, sherbet, pk 8.00
Old Cafe, bowl, berry; pk, 3¾" 3.00
Old Cafe, bowl, cereal; red, 5½" 9.00
Old Cafe, bowl, pk, hdl or hdls, 5" 4.50
Old Cafe, bowl, red, closed hdls, 9" 13.00
Old Cafe, lamp, pk 16.00
Old Cafe, pitcher, pk, 80-oz 80.00
Old Cafe, plate, dinner; pk, 10" 27.50
Old Cafe, plate, sherbet; pk, 6" 2.00
Old Cafe, tumbler, juice; pk, 3" 9.00
Old English, bowl, all colors, flat, 9½" 30.00
Old English, bowl, berry; all colors, 4" 15.00
Old English, creamer, all colors 17.00
Old English, tumbler, all colors, ftd, 5½" 30.00
Old English, vase, fan; all colors, 7" 45.00
Ovide, bowl, berry; blk, 4¾" 7.00
Ovide, bowl, berry; blk, 8" 14.00
Ovide, creamer, blk 6.00
Ovide, cup, blk 6.00
Ovide, shakers, gr, pr 26.00
Ovide, sugar bowl, gr 3.00
Oyster & Pearl, bowl, red, deep, hdl, 6½" 18.00
Oyster & Pearl, plate, sandwich; pk, 13½" 16.00
Parrot, bowl, berry; amber, 5" 15.00
Parrot, bowl, berry; gr, 8" 68.00
Parrot, bowl, soup; gr, 7" 35.00

Parrot, bowl, vegetable; amber, oval, 10" 55.00
Parrot, butter dish, amber, w/lid 1,100.00
Parrot, creamer, gr, ftd 32.50
Parrot, cup, gr 32.50
Parrot, hot plate, gr, 5" 650.00
Parrot, pitcher, gr, 80-oz, 8½" 1,300.00
Parrot, plate, dinner; amber, 9" 32.00
Parrot, plate, gr, sq, 10¼" 45.00
Parrot, plate, salad; gr, 7½" 30.00
Parrot, plate, sherbet; amber, 5¾" 16.00
Parrot, platter, amber, oblong, 11¼" 55.00
Parrot, saucer, gr 12.00
Parrot, shakers, gr, pr 200.00
Patrician, bowl, berry; amber, 5" 11.00
Patrician, bowl, berry; amber, 8½" 42.00
Patrician, bowl, cereal; gr, 6" 23.00
Patrician, bowl, cream soup; gr, 4¾" 18.00
Patrician, bowl, vegetable; gr, oval, 10" 30.00
Patrician, butter dish, gr, w/lid 96.00

Patrician, cookie jar, amber, $85.00.

Patrician, cup, amber 8.00
Patrician, pitcher, amber, 75-oz, 8" 100.00
Patrician, pitcher, amber, 75-oz, 8¼" 125.00
Patrician, plate, dinner; gr, 10½" 30.00
Patrician, plate, grill; amber,10½" 13.00
Patrician, plate, luncheon; 9" 11.00
Patrician, plate, salad; amber, 7½" 14.00
Patrician, plate, sherbet; amber, 6" 9.00
Patrician, platter, amber, oval, 11½" 30.00
Patrician, saucer, amber 9.00
Patrician, shakers, gr, pr 55.00
Patrician, sherbet, amber 12.00
Patrician, sugar bowl, amber, ...8.00
Patrician, tumbler, amber, 14-oz, 5½" 38.00
Patrician, tumbler, amber, 9-oz, 4½" 24.00
Patrick, bowl, console; yel, 11" 75.00
Patrick, bowl, fruit; pk, hdld......................................165.00
Patrick, candlesticks, yel, pr 75.00
Patrick, candy dish, pk, 3-ftd 148.00
Patrick, cup, pk 115.00
Patrick, goblet, juice; yel, 6-oz, 4¾" 45.00
Patrick, goblet, water; yel, 10-oz, 6" 65.00
Patrick, plate, salad; yel, 7½" 18.00
Patrick, saucer, pk 15.00
Patrick, sugar bowl, pk 120.00
Petalware, bowl, cereal; pk, 5¾" 8.00
Petalware, bowl, cream soup; monax, 4½" 9.00

Petalware, creamer, monax, ftd 6.00
Petalware, cup, monax 5.00
Petalware, plate, salad; monax, 8" 3.00
Petalware, plate, salver; pk, 11" 9.00
Petalware, saucer, pk 2.00
Petalware, sherbet, pk, low, ftd 6.00
Primo, bowl, yel or gr, 7¾" 18.00
Primo, creamer, yel or gr 10.00
Primo, plate, grill; yel or gr, 10" 9.00
Primo, plate, yel or gr, 7½" 7.00
Primo, sherbet, yel or gr 9.00
Primo, sugar bowl, yel or gr 10.00
Princess, ashtray, pk, 4½" 82.50
Princess, bowl, berry; pk, 4½" 20.00
Princess, bowl, cereal or oatmeal; gr, 5" 26.00
Princess, bowl, gr, hat shaped, 9½" 35.00
Princess, butter dish, pk or gr, w/lid 85.00
Princess, candy dish, pk or gr, w/lid 50.00
Princess, coaster, pk 60.00
Princess, creamer, pk, oval 13.00
Princess, cup, pk 10.00
Princess, pitcher, gr, 24-oz, 7⅜" 500.00
Princess, plate, grill; gr, 9" 12.00
Princess, plate, salad; gr, 8" 12.00
Princess, plate, sandwich; pk, hdld, 11½" 20.00
Princess, relish, pk, divided, 7½" 25.00
Princess, saucer, pk 9.00
Princess, sherbet, pk, ftd 18.00
Princess, sugar bowl, gr 10.00
Princess, tumbler, gr, ftd, 10-oz, 5¼" 28.00
Princess, tumbler, water; gr, 9-oz, 4" 24.00
Queen Mary, ashtray, crystal, oval, 2x3¾" 3.00
Queen Mary, bowl, berry; crystal, 8¾" 9.00
Queen Mary, bowl, crystal, 1 hdl or none, 4" 3.00
Queen Mary, butter dish, pk, w/lid 95.00
Queen Mary, celery or pickle dish, pk, 5x10" 20.00
Queen Mary, coaster, pk, 3½" 3.50
Queen Mary, creamer, crystal, oval 5.00
Queen Mary, plate, crystal, 6" or 6⅝", ea 3.00
Queen Mary, plate, dinner; pk, 9¾" 35.00
Queen Mary, plate, sandwich; pk, 12" 13.00
Queen Mary, relish tray, pk, 4-part, 14" 15.00
Queen Mary, sherbet, pk, ftd 6.00
Queen Mary, tumbler, juice; crystal, 5-oz, 3½" 4.00
Queen Mary, tumbler, pk, ftd, 10-oz, 5" 35.00
Radiance, bonbon, colors other than red or bl, ftd, 6" 10.00
Radiance, bonbon, red or bl, w/lid, 6" 45.00
Radiance, bonbon, red or bl, 6" 15.00
Radiance, bowl, cereal; red or bl, 10" 20.00
Radiance, bowl, colors other than red or bl, crimped, 10" 18.00
Radiance, bowl, pickle; other colors, 7" 12.00
Radiance, bowl, red or bl, flared, 10" 35.00
Radiance, bowl, red or bl, flared, 12" 37.50
Radiance, candlestick, other colors, 2-light, pr 55.00
Radiance, comport, colors other than red or bl, 6" 18.00
Radiance, comport, red or bl, 5" 25.00
Radiance, creamer, red or bl 20.00
Radiance, lamp, red or bl, 12" 95.00
Radiance, pitcher, red or bl, 64-oz 195.00
Radiance, plate, luncheon; red or bl, 8" 15.00
Radiance, punch bowl, red or bl 150.00
Radiance, punch ladle, colors other than red or bl 75.00
Radiance, saucer, red or bl 8.00
Radiance, sugar bowl, colors other than red or bl 12.00

Radiance, tray, colors other than red or bl, oval	22.00
Raindrops, bowl, cereal; gr, 6"	7.00
Raindrops, creamer, gr	7.00
Raindrops, plate, luncheon; gr, 8"	5.00
Raindrops, plate, sherbet; gr, 6"	2.50
Raindrops, saucer, gr	1.50
Raindrops, sherbet, gr	6.00
Ribbon, bowl, berry; gr, 4"	9.00
Ribbon, bowl, berry; gr, 8"	23.00
Ribbon, candy dish, gr, w/lid	35.00
Ribbon, cup, gr	4.50
Ribbon, plate, sherbet; gr, 6¼"	2.00
Ribbon, saucer, gr	2.00
Ribbon, sherbet, gr, ftd	4.50
Ribbon, sugar bowl, gr, ftd	12.00
Ribbon, tumbler, gr, 13-oz, 6½"	25.00
Ring, bowl, berry; crystal, 5"	3.50
Ring, bowl, berry; crystal, 8"	6.50
Ring, bowl, soup; crystal, 7"	8.00
Ring, cocktail shaker, crystal	17.50
Ring, creamer, gr, ftd	5.50
Ring, cup, crystal	5.00
Ring, ice tub, crystal w/decor	20.00
Ring, pitcher, crystal, 80-oz, 8½"	18.00
Ring, plate, luncheon; crystal, 8"	2.00
Ring, saucer, crystal	1.50
Ring, sugar bowl, crystal, ftd	4.00
Ring, tumbler, crystal, 12-oz, 5⅛"	5.50
Ring, tumbler, crystal, 5-oz, 3½"	3.00
Ring, vase, crystal w/decor, 8"	30.00
Rock Crystal, bowl, relish; red, 2-part, 11½"	60.00
Rock Crystal, candlesticks, red, tall, 8½", pr	325.00
Rock Crystal, candy dish, red, w/lid, rnd	150.00
Rock Crystal, compote, crystal, 7"	30.00
Rock Crystal, lamp, electric; red	600.00
Rock Crystal, pitcher, crystal, lg	150.00
Rock Crystal, roll tray, crystal, 13"	28.00
Rock Crystal, tumbler, juice; red, 5-oz	50.00
Rock Crystal, vase, crystal, ftd, 11"	45.00
Rose Cameo, bowl, cereal; gr, 5"	12.00
Rose Cameo, plate, salad; gr, 7"	9.00
Rosemary, bowl, berry; amber, 5"	5.00
Rosemary, bowl, cereal; amber, 6"	28.00
Rosemary, bowl, cream soup; gr, 5"	18.00
Rosemary, creamer, amber, ftd	8.00
Rosemary, plate, dinner; gr	12.00
Rosemary, plate, grill; amber	7.00
Rosemary, plate, salad; gr, 6¾"	8.00
Rosemary, saucer, gr	5.00
Roulette, bowl, fruit; gr, 9"	12.50
Roulette, pitcher, gr, 64-oz, 8"	32.00
Roulette, plate, sherbet; gr, 6"	4.00
Roulette, saucer, gr	3.00
Roulette, tumbler, water; pk, 9-oz, 4⅛"	18.00
Roulette, whiskey, pk, 1½-oz, 2½"	13.00
Round Robin, bowl, berry; gr, 4"	5.00
Round Robin, creamer, gr, ftd	6.50
Round Robin, domino tray, gr	30.00
Round Robin, plate, luncheon; gr, 8"	3.50
Round Robin, plate, sandwich; irid, 12"	6.00
Round Robin, plate, sherbet; irid, 6"	2.00
Round Robin, saucer, irid	1.50
Roxana, bowl, berry; yel, 5"	8.00
Roxana, bowl, cereal; yel, 6"	12.00
Roxana, plate, yel, 5½"	7.00
Royal Lace, bowl, berry; pk, rnd, 10"	25.00
Royal Lace, bowl, berry; pk, 5"	24.00
Royal Lace, bowl, cream soup; bl, 4¾"	33.00
Royal Lace, bowl, vegetable; bl, oval, 11"	50.00
Royal Lace, butter dish, bl, w/lid	525.00
Royal Lace, candlesticks, bl, str edge, pr	95.00
Royal Lace, cookie jar, bl, w/lid	300.00
Royal Lace, creamer, bl, ftd	50.00
Royal Lace, nut dish, bl	750.00
Royal Lace, pitcher, bl, 86-oz, 8"	200.00
Royal Lace, pitcher, pk, 68-oz, 8"	70.00
Royal Lace, pitcher, pk, 96-oz, 8½"	80.00
Royal Lace, plate, grill; bl, 9⅞"	38.00
Royal Lace, plate, luncheon; bl, 8½"	35.00
Royal Lace, plate, sherbet; pk, 6"	7.00
Royal Lace, platter, bl, oval, 13"	55.00
Royal Lace, saucer, pk	6.00
Royal Lace, sherbet, pk, ftd	15.00
Royal Lace, tumbler, bl, 10-oz, 4⅞"	95.00
Royal Lace, tumbler, pk, 5-oz, 3½"	22.00
Royal Ruby, ashtray, red, sq, 4½"	3.00
Royal Ruby, bowl, berry; red, 4¼"	5.00
Royal Ruby, bowl, berry; red, 8½"	16.00
Royal Ruby, bowl, salad; red, 11½"	30.00
Royal Ruby, bowl, vegetable; red, oval, 8"	35.00
Royal Ruby, card holder, red	50.00
Royal Ruby, creamer, red, flat	7.00
Royal Ruby, creamer, red, ftd	8.50
Royal Ruby, lamp, red	35.00
Royal Ruby, plate, luncheon; red, 7¾"	6.00
Royal Ruby, plate, salad; red, 7"	5.00
Royal Ruby, plate, sherbet; red, 6½"	3.00
Royal Ruby, punch bowl, red, w/stand	67.50
Royal Ruby, punch cup, red	2.50
Royal Ruby, tumbler, cocktail; red, 3½"	9.50
Royal Ruby, tumbler, water; red, 9-oz	6.00
Royal Ruby, tumbler, wine; red, ftd, 2½"	12.50
S Pattern, bowl, cereal; crystal, 5½"	3.50
S Pattern, creamer, amber, thick or thin	6.00
S Pattern, cup, crystal, thick or thin	3.00
S Pattern, plate, cake; crystal, 13"	55.00
S Pattern, plate, grill; amber	8.00
S Pattern, plate, luncheon; crystal, 8"	4.00
S Pattern, plate, sherbet; crystal, 6"	2.00
S Pattern, saucer, amber	2.00
S Pattern, sherbet, amber, ftd, low	7.00
S Pattern, tumbler, amber, 5-oz, 3½"	6.00
S Pattern, tumbler, crystal, 10-oz, 4¼"	4.50
Sandwich (Hocking), bowl, berry; crystal, 4⅞"	5.00
Sandwich (Hocking), bowl, crystal, oval, 8¼"	7.50
Sandwich (Hocking), bowl, salad; gr, 7"	50.00
Sandwich (Hocking), creamer, crystal	5.00
Sandwich (Hocking), cup, tea or coffee; crystal	2.00
Sandwich (Hocking), custard cup, crystal	3.50
Sandwich (Hocking), custard cup liner, gr	1.50
Sandwich (Hocking), pitcher, juice; gr, 6"	115.00
Sandwich (Hocking), plate, crystal, 8"	3.50
Sandwich (Hocking), plate, dessert; crystal, 7"	9.00
Sandwich (Hocking), plate, sandwich; crystal, 12"	20.00
Sandwich (Hocking), sherbet, crystal, ftd	7.00
Sandwich (Hocking), tumbler, crystal, ftd, 9-oz	21.00
Sandwich (Hocking), tumbler, water; gr, 9-oz	4.50
Sharon, bowl, berry; amber, lg, 8½"	6.00

Sharon, bowl, berry; pk, 5" 10.00
Sharon, bowl, cereal; amber, 6" 18.00
Sharon, bowl, cream soup; pk, 5" 36.00
Sharon, bowl, fruit; amber, 10½" 20.00
Sharon, bowl, vegetable; pk, oval, 9½" 25.00
Sharon, candy dish, amber, w/lid 40.00
Sharon, cheese dish, pk, w/lid 750.00
Sharon, creamer, amber, ftd 12.00
Sharon, jam dish, pk, 7½" 150.00
Sharon, plate, dinner; amber, 9½" 10.00
Sharon, plate, salad; pk, 7½" 20.00
Sharon, platter, amber, oval, 12½" 18.00
Sharon, sugar bowl, pk, ... 12.00
Sharon, tumbler, pk, ftd, 15-oz, 6½" 40.00
Sierra, bowl, berry; pk, 8½" 25.00
Sierra, bowl, cereal; gr, 5½" 12.00
Sierra, butter dish, pk, w/lid 55.00
Sierra, creamer, gr 19.00
Sierra, plate, dinner; gr, 9" 18.00
Sierra, platter, gr, oval, 11" 40.00
Sierra, saucer, pk 5.00
Sierra, serving tray, gr, 2-hdl 16.00
Sierra, sugar bowl, pk 15.00
Sierra, sugar bowl lid, pk 14.00
Spiral, bowl, berry; gr, 4¾" 4.50
Spiral, bowl, berry; gr, 8" 12.00
Spiral, creamer, gr, flat or ftd 7.00
Spiral, plate, sherbet; gr, 6" 2.00
Spiral, platter, gr 22.50
Spiral, preserve, gr, w/lid 30.00
Spiral, sandwich server, gr, center hdl 21.00
Spiral, saucer, gr 1.50
Spiral, sherbet, gr 3.50
Spiral, tumbler, juice; gr, 5-oz, 3" 4.00
Spiral, tumbler, water; gr, 9-oz, 5" 7.00
Starlight, bowl, cereal; crystal, 5½" 6.00
Starlight, creamer, crystal, oval 5.00
Starlight, plate, luncheon; crystal, 8½" 3.00
Starlight, plate, sandwich; crystal, 13" 12.00
Starlight, relish dish, crystal 12.00
Starlight, sherbet, crystal 11.00
Strawberry, bowl, berry; pk or gr, deep, 7½" 20.00
Strawberry, bowl, berry; pk or gr, 4" 8.00
Strawberry, bowl, pk or gr, 2" deep, 6¼" 60.00
Strawberry, bowl, salad; pk or gr, deep, 6½" 16.00
Strawberry, butter dish, pk or gr, w/lid 140.00
Strawberry, pickle dish, pk or gr 12.00
Strawberry, plate, salad; pk or gr, 7½" 12.00
Sunflower, creamer, pk 15.00
Sunflower, cup, gr 12.00
Sunflower, plate, dinner; gr, 9" 15.00
Sunflower, saucer, gr 8.00
Sunflower, sugar bowl, pk 15.00
Sunflower, tumbler, gr, ftd, 8-oz, 4¾" 28.00
Swirl, ashtray, pk, 5⅜" 6.00
Swirl, bowl, salad; pk, 9" 16.00
Swirl, bowl, ultramarine, closed hdls, ftd, 10" 30.00
Swirl, butter dish, ultramarine 245.00
Swirl, candy dish, ultramarine, w/lid 125.00
Swirl, creamer, pk, ftd 7.00
Swirl, plate, pk, 7¼" 6.00
Swirl, plate, salad; pk, 8" 8.00
Swirl, sherbet, pk, low ftd 10.00
Swirl, vase, ultramarine, ftd, 6½" 20.00

Tea Room, bowl, banana split; gr, 7½" 78.00
Tea Room, bowl, celery; pk, 8½" 25.00
Tea Room, bowl, finger; gr 45.00
Tea Room, bowl, salad; pk, deep, 8¾" 60.00
Tea Room, bowl, vegetable; gr, oval, 9½" 60.00
Tea Room, candlesticks, pk, low, pr 40.00
Tea Room, creamer, gr, 4" 25.00
Tea Room, goblet, gr, 9-oz 70.00
Tea Room, ice bucket, pk 50.00
Tea Room, mustard, gr, w/lid 135.00
Tea Room, parfait, pk 55.00
Tea Room, plate, luncheon; gr, 8¼" 32.00
Tea Room, sugar bowl, gr, flat, w/lid 175.00
Tea Room, sundae, pk, ruffled, ftd 65.00
Tea Room, tumbler, gr, ftd, 11-oz 40.00
Tea Room, tumbler, gr, ftd, 12-oz 50.00
Tea Room, tumbler, pk, ftd, 6-oz 30.00
Thistle, bowl, cereal; gr, 5½" 20.00
Thistle, bowl, fruit; pk, 10¼" 250.00
Thistle, plate, cake; pk, 13" 100.00
Thistle, plate, grill; pk, 10¼" 16.00
Thistle, plate, luncheon; pk, 8" 12.00
Twisted Optic, bowl, cereal; pk or gr, 5" 5.00
Twisted Optic, bowl, cream soup; pk or gr, 4¾" 10.00
Twisted Optic, creamer, pk or gr 7.00
Twisted Optic, pitcher, pk or gr, 64-oz 27.50
Twisted Optic, plate, salad; pk or gr, 7" 2.50
Twisted Optic, plate, sherbet; pk or gr, 6" 2.00
Twisted Optic, sherbet, pk or gr 5.50
Twisted Optic, tumbler, pk or gr, 9-oz, 4½" 6.00
US Swirl, bowl, berry; gr, 4⅜" 5.00
US Swirl, bowl, berry; pk, 7⅛" 15.00
US Swirl, bowl, gr, 1-hdl, 5½" 9.00
US Swirl, bowl, pk, oval, 8¼" 23.00
US Swirl, butter dish, gr, w/lid 65.00
US Swirl, butter dish lid, pk 15.00
US Swirl, plate, salad; gr, 7⅞" 5.00
US Swirl, plate, sherbet; gr, 6⅛" 2.00
US Swirl, shakers, gr, pr 40.00
Victory, bonbon, bl, 7" 19.00
Victory, bowl, bl, flat edge, 12½" 60.00
Victory, bowl, bl, rolled edge, 11" 45.00
Victory, bowl, cereal; bl, 6½" 26.00
Victory, bowl, console; pk, 12" 30.00
Victory, bowl, soup; pk, flat, 8½" 16.00
Victory, bowl, vegetable; pk, oval, 9" 30.00
Victory, candlesticks, bl, 3", pr 85.00
Victory, gravy boat, bl, w/underplate 290.00
Victory, plate, bread & butter; bl, 6" 15.00
Victory, plate, dinner; pk, 9" 18.00
Victory, plate, luncheon; pk, 8" 6.00
Victory, saucer, pk 4.00
Vitrock, bowl, berry; wht, 4" 4.00
Vitrock, bowl, cream soup; wht, 5½" 14.00
Vitrock, bowl, fruit; wht, 6" 5.00
Vitrock, creamer, wht, oval 4.00
Vitrock, plate, soup; wht, 9" 12.00
Vitrock, platter, wht, 11½" 25.00
Waterford, bowl, cereal; pk, 5½" 24.00
Waterford, creamer, crystal, oval 5.00
Waterford, pitcher, juice; crystal, tilted, 42-oz 22.00
Waterford, pitcher, pk, ice lip, tilted, 80-oz 130.00
Waterford, plate, dinner; crystal, 9⅝" 9.00
Waterford, plate, salad; crystal, 7⅛" 5.00

Waterford, saucer, pk 5.00
Waterford, sherbet, pk, ftd 12.00
Waterford, sugar bowl, pk, oval 22.00
Waterford, vase, crystal, 6¾" 8.50
Windsor, ashtray, crystal, 5¾" 12.50
Windsor, bowl, berry; pk, 8½" 15.00
Windsor, bowl, cream soup; crystal, 5" 5.00
Windsor, butter dish, crystal 25.00
Windsor, creamer, crystal 4.00
Windsor, pitcher, crystal, 52-oz, 6¾" 12.00
Windsor, pitcher, pk, 16-oz, 4½" 100.00
Windsor, plate, cake; pk, thick, 13½", pr 75.00
Windsor, plate, chop; crystal, 13⅝" 9.00
Windsor, plate, salad; pk, 7" 14.00
Windsor, plate, sherbet, pk, 6" 4.00
Windsor, relish platter, red, divided, 11½" 175.00
Windsor, saucer, crystal 2.00
Windsor, sherbet, crystal, ftd 3.00
Windsor, tray, pk, sq, 4" 10.00
Windsor, tumbler, pk, 9-oz, 4" 18.00

Derby

William Duesbury operated in Derby, England, from about 1755, purchasing a second establishment, The Chelsea Works, in 1769. During this period fine porcelains were produced which so impressed the King that in 1773 he issued the company the Crown Derby patent. In 1810, several years after Duesbury's death, the factory was bought by Robert Bloor. The quality of the ware suffered under the new management, and the main Derby pottery closed in 1848. Within a short time, the work was revived by a dedicated number of former employees who established their own works on King Street in Derby.

The earliest-known Derby mark was the crown over a script 'D'; however this mark is rarely found today. Soon after 1782, that mark was augmented with a device of crossed batons and six dots, usually applied in underglaze blue. During the Bloor period, the crown was centered within a ring containing the words 'Bloor' above and 'Derby' below the crown, or with a red printed stamp — the crowned Gothic 'D.' The King Street plant produced figurines that may be distinguished from their earlier counterparts by the presence of an 'S' and 'H' on either side of the crown and crossed batons.

In 1876 a new pottery was constructed in Derby, and the owners revived the earlier company's former standard of excellence. The Queen bestowed the firm the title Royal Crown Derby in 1890; it still operates under that name today. Our advisors for this category are Henry and Geneva Tyler; they are listed in the Directory under Florida. See also Royal Crown Derby.

Basket, floral encrusted sides/hdls, oval, 1825, 8¾" L 1,000.00
Cup & saucer, exotic bird, Kakiemon palette, 1815 ....220.00
Figurine, Falstaff, floral shirt, red pants, ca 1768, 10½" 650.00
Figurine, Mansion House Dwarf, ca 1780, 7" 800.00
Forks, Oriental scene on porc hdl, bl & wht, 6 in orig box 175.00
Vase, campana; View in Cumberland, snake hdls, 1820s, 6½" ...750.00
Vase, floral, gold trim, bulbous w/slim neck, 11½x4½" 900.00
Vase, rose panels, pk on gr, urn form w/hdls, ped ft, 9" 850.00
Vase, scenic reserves on dk bl, gilt hdls, 1850s, 7", pr 1,500.00
Waste bowl, stylized roots, leaf rim, bl w/gold, 1820, 6" 450.00

Desert Sands

As early as the 1850s, the Evans family living in the Ozark Moun-

tains of Missouri produced domestic clay products. Their small pot shop was passed on from one generation to the next. In the 1920s it was moved to North Las Vegas, Nevada, where the name Desert Sands was adopted. Succeeding generations of the family continued to relocate, taking the business with them. From 1937 to 1962 it operated in Boulder City, Nevada; then it was moved to Barstow where it remained until it closed in the late 1970s.

Desert Sands pottery is similar to Mission Ware by Niloak. Various mineral oxides were blended to mimic the naturally occuring sand formations of the American West. A high-gloss glaze was applied to add intensity to the colorful striations that characterize the ware. Not all examples are marked, making it sometimes difficult to attribute. Marked items carry an ink stamp with the Desert Sands designation. Paper labels were also used.

Vases: 4", $20.00; 2½", $15.00.

Bowl, swirled colors, 2¼x4½" 12.50
Bowl, swirled colors, w/lid, 4" 35.00
Butter dish 35.00
Candle holder vase, swirled colors, 5" 24.00
Mug, swirled colors, mk 28.00
Tumbler, swirled colors 10.00
Vase, swirled colors, 5" 22.50

Devon, Crown Devon

Devon and Crown Devon were trade names of S. Fielding and Company, Ltd., an English firm founded after 1879. They produced majolica, earthenware mugs, vases and kitchenware. In the 1930s they manufactured an exceptional line of Art Deco vases that have recently been much in demand.

Vase, String of Pearls, gold handles, footed, 10¼", $45.00.

Box, Scottish couple, Harry Lauder, musical, 2½x4¼x5¾" **175.00**
Jug, Irish Junting Cart, Killarny verse, musical, 7x4⅜" **165.00**
Jug, John Peel & hunt scene, musical, fox hdl, 7¾" **195.00**
Jug, Robert Burns, Auld Lang Syne, musical, 7x5¼" **195.00**
Mug, Auld Lang Syne, musical, 6¼x4½" **150.00**
Mug, John Peel, riding crop hdl, musical, 6⅛x4¼" **175.00**

Documents

Although the word 'document' is defined in the general sense as 'anything printed or written, etc., relied upon to record or prove something. . .,' in the collectibles market, the term is more diversified with broadsides, billheads, checks, invoices, letters and letterheads, land grants, receipts, and waybills some of the most sought after. Some documents in demand are those related to a specific subject such as advertising, mining, railroads, military, politics, banking, slavery, nautical, or legal (deeds, mortgages, etc.). Other collectors look for examples representing a specific period of time such as colonial documents, Revolutionary, or Civil War documents, early western documents or those from a specific region, state, or city.

Aside from supply and demand, there are five major factors which determine the collector-value of a document. These are:

1) Age — Documents from the eastern half of the country can be found that date back to the 1700s or earlier. Most documents sought by collectors usually date from 1700 to 1900. Those with 20th-century dates are still abundant and not in demand unless of special significance or beauty.

2) Region of origin — Depending on age, documents from rural and less-populated areas are harder to find than those from major cities and heavily populated states. The colonization of the West and Mid-West did not begin until after 1850, so while an 1870s billhead from New York or Chicago is common, one from Albuquerque or Phoenix is not, since most of the Southwest was still unsettled.

3) Attractiveness — Some documents are plain and unadorned, but collectors prefer colorful, profusely illustrated pieces. Additional artwork and engravings add to the value.

4) Historical content — Unusual or interesting content, such as a letter written by a Civil War soldier giving an eye-witness account of the Battle of Gettysburg or a western territorial billhead listing numerous animal hides purchased from a trapper, will sell for more than one with mundane information.

5) Condition — Through neglect or environmental conditions, over many decades paper articles can become stained, torn, or deteriorated. Heavily damaged or stained documents are generally avoided altogether. Those with minor problems are more acceptable, although their value will decrease anywhere from 20% to 50%, depending upon the extent of damage. Avoid attempting to repair tears with scotch tape — sell 'as is' so that the collector can take proper steps toward restoration.

Foreign documents are plentiful; and though some are very attractive, resale may be difficult. The listings that follow are generalized; prices are variable depending entirely upon the five points noted above. Values here are based upon examples with no major damage. Common grade documents without significant content are found in abundance and generally have little collector value. These usually date from the late 1800s and early 1900s. It should be noted that the items listed below are examples of those that meet the criteria for having collector value. There is little demand for documents worth less than $5.00. For more information we recommend *Owning Western History* by our advisor Warren Anderson. His address and ordering information may be found in the Directory under Utah.

Key:
illus — illustrated   vgn — vignette

Affidavit, CO Territory mining, work on Harsh Lode, 1864 ....**55.00**
Assay certificate, Silverton CO, preprinted, 1896, 5x8" **25.00**

Bill, for ship repairs, itemized, 1765, 3x4" **15.00**
Certificate, exchange; preprinted/filled in, 1864, EX **20.00**
Certificate/letter, VA, notification of soldier's death, 1863 ....**10.00**
Check, Big V Ranch, OK, preprinted, 1907, 3x8" **15.00**
Check, depository; US Depository, Phila, fancy eng, 1865 ....**7.50**
Check, Ouray Livery, CO, preprinted, 1904, 3x8" **20.00**
Check, treasurer; fancy eng, Liberty vignette, 1859 ....**5.00**
Commission, MN, sgn by Governor S Miller, dtd 1864, 11x15" ..**18.50**
Currency, 25¢ note, Washington portrait, gr overprint, 1863 ....**10.00**
Currency note, Hall & Sellers, Phila 1776, 30 shillings **32.50**
Deed, MA property, partially printed, 1801, 8x13" **17.50**
Discharge, Revolutionary War, sgn Brig Gen E Poor **225.00**
Discharge, Revolutionary War, sgn twice, 1780 ....**100.00**
Discharge, War of 1812, handwritten **24.00**
Draft, Carson City NV bank, Indian vignette, 1879 ....**18.50**
Draft orders, Richmond VA, calls for enlistment, 1864, 8x11" **28.00**
Exemption request & denial, Confederate captain, 1864, 2-pg **22.50**
Fractional note, 50¢, Edwin Stanton's portrait, 1866 ....**10.00**
Indenture, handwritten on vellum, 1700s, 18x12" **30.00**
Indenture, NJ, calligraphy, land by Maurice river, 1813, 3-pg **18.50**
Indenture, NJ, preprinted, fancy printed title, 1908 ....**15.00**
Indenture, NY State, lands in NY, 1815, 9½x16" **48.00**
Injunction, MS Territory, under penalty of $5000, 1806 ....**50.00**
Investigation, 79th VA Militia, possible theft, 1861-64, 8x12" **22.50**
Invoice, Boston, Depot of Army Clothing, clothing list, 1862 ....**6.00**
Invoice, Boston, ships vignette, printed by Loring, 1849 ....**10.00**
Invoice, KS, Armour Packing Co, 1905, 5x8" **10.00**
Last will & testament, MA, handwritten, 1819, EX **12.50**
Letter, Antietam Creek, battle news, descriptive, 1862 ....**35.00**
Letter, AZ, re: assignment of mining stock, 1905, 2-pg **10.00**
Letter, Dept of War, re: money to widows, 1816 ....**18.50**
Letter, IA, farm news/slave views/political comments, 1857 ....**35.00**
Letter, NC, battle needs/plans for life after war, 1863 ....**24.00**
Letter, VA, Mexican War news/colorful comments, 1845, 3-pg ...**30.00**
Letter, VA, news of Lincoln's death, 4-pg, Apr 1865 ....**95.00**
Letter, VA, war news/talks of Gen Jackson/etc, 4-pg, EX **75.00**
Letterhead, AK Territory, Office of Auditor (sgn), 1933 ....**20.00**
List of prisoners, 5th NH Volunteers, handwritten, 1863 ....**10.00**
Medical account sheet, treatment of wound/charges, 1790 ....**12.50**
Muster roll, NY St Volunteers, preprinted, 1863, lg **35.00**
Muster roll, preprinted, lists 38 soldiers/duties/etc, 1863 ....**28.00**

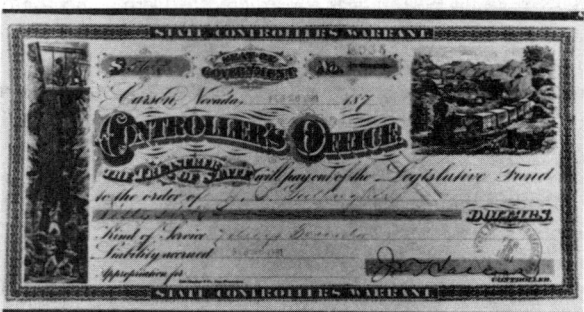

Nevada warrant to Senator J. Gallagher who received $56.00 for a week's work, mining and railroad illustrations, 1881, $25.00.

Notice, WY, proposals for water bonds, printed, 1893, 5x8" **25.00**
Order for arrest, VA, deserter, handwritten, 8x11" **22.50**
Orders, Manila, 8th Army Corps, imposed regulations, 1898 ....**6.50**
Orders, NH, Cavalry to report for duty, 1838 ....**8.00**
Pass, New Orleans LA, to rejoin command, preprinted, 1864 ....**28.00**

Pension request, Confederate widow, details of service, 1900 ....5.00
Pension request, MS, ex-slave/Confederate servant, 1915 ....25.00
Power of attorney, POW in Charleston, by attorney, 1864 ....10.00
Proclamation, details of B Harrison's death by McKinley, 1901 ...10.00
Promissory note, handwritten w/'Ye' Biblical style, 1776 ....12.50
Prospectus, NM, US Copper Co, ca 1916, 22-pg 30.00
Receipt, for 3 gun locks, handwritten, 1777 ....45.00
Receipt, Gen Johnson's brigade receives cattle, 1864 ....12.50
Receipt, minuteman's pay, preprinted, 1780 ....55.00
Receipt, N Pacific, preprinted, ticket purchase, 1897, 3x7" 10.00
Receipt, New Orleans, sale of cotton, details/charges, 1878 ....29.00
Receipt, Winchester VA, military food rations, 1863, 3x5½" 15.00
Recipe, for making saltpeter, handwritten, 1776 ....18.50
Record, return of deserter/dr's report/reprieve, 1781, EX 75.00
Request, NH, listing for ammunition, 1864, 8x11" 10.00
Request, VA, supplies needed for field hospital, Nov 1862 ....10.00
Request, VA, 6th US Cavalry supplies, sgn Lt Hutchins, 1862 ....10.00
Requisition, supplies for 11th US Colored Troops, 1864 ....12.50
Shipping release, from US Consulate, vignettes, 1863, 8x11" 10.00
Tax assessment, preprinted, listing slaves/values, 1860 ....12.50
Telegraph, from Gen McClellan to Gen Buell, by clerk, 1861 .....15.00
Voucher, Blk servant has paid debt to hospital, 1865 ....6.50
Warning, elections to be held, men must vote, MA, 1803 ....15.00
Warrant, MT, overprinted in red, Liberty vgn, 1893 ....10.00
Way bill, MS River steamboat, preprinted/filled in, 1867 ....15.00
Way bill, TN, Resolute Steamer...Passenger Packet, 1857 ....18.50
Writ, NH, summons for man, handwritten & printed, 1815 ....20.00

Dollhouses and Furnishings

Dollhouses were introduced commercially in this country late in the 1700s by Dutch craftsmen who settled in the East. By the mid-1800s they had become meticulously detailed, divided into separate rooms, and lavishly furnished to reflect the opulence of the day. Originally intended for the amusement of adults of the household, by the latter 1800s their status had changed to that of a child's toy. Though many early dollhouses were lovingly hand-fashioned for a special little girl, those made commercially by such companies as Bliss and Schoenhut are highly valued.

Furniture and furnishings in the Biedermeier style featuring stenciled Victorian decorations often sell for several hundred dollars each. Other early pieces made of pewter, porcelain, or papier-mache are also quite valuable. Certainly less expensive but very collectible, nonetheless, is the quality, hallmarked plastic furniture produced during the forties by Renwal and Acme, and the 1960s Petite Princess line produced by Ideal. In the listings that follow, dollhouses are litho paper on wood, unless otherwise noted. When no manufacturer or country of origin is noted, examples are German, turn of the century. Our advisor for this category is Barbara Rosen; she is listed in the Directory under New Jersey. See also Miniatures.

Furniture

Bed, filigree-cut head & ftbrds, w/linens, 5x10½x3", EX 200.00
Bed, oak, simple style, minor wear, EX 27.50
Bedroom suite, Deco style, bed+5 pcs, for 6" doll, EX 75.00
Birdcage w/bird, brass, Adrian Cook, VG 65.00
Blanket chest, pnt wood, Brittany, 3½x13¼x4", EX 150.00
Buggy, pnt CI, Kilgore, 2" 42.50
Candelabra, metal & glass, EX, pr 55.00
Carpet sweeper, pnt CI, Kilgore, 2¼" 40.00
Chair, red w/yel seat, Renwal 6.00
Chaise lounge, Little Hostess 14.00

Cupboard, kitchen; Petite Princess, EX 50.00
Fireplace, tin, pnt filigree, 4", G 100.00
Fireplace, tin litho, marble top, EX 40.00
Food, leg of lamb on tin plate 17.50
Food, loaf of bread on china plate 27.50
Food, red tart on china plate 2.75
Food, toast & muffin on paper plate 17.50
Grand piano, pnt CI, Arcade, 1920s, VG 65.00
Grandfather's clock, mk Brittany, 18x7x4½" 150.00
Lamp, banquet; brass, glass shade, EX 300.00

Living room set, Tootsietoy, 5-piece on cardboard rug, $65.00.

Organ, pnt wood, +7 brass accessories 275.00
Patio suite, bamboo, table+chairs+chaise, for 6" doll, 7-pc 85.00
Rack, towel; brass, G 75.00
Settee, pnt gilt mesh & wire, 6", +3 matching chairs....................125.00
Sideboard, Biedermeier, 6" 420.00
Stove, Eclipse, pnt CI, EX 195.00
Table, dining; w/picture, Petite Princess, NMIB 15.00
Table, drop leaf; gate-leg style, w/2 drws, Little Hostess 17.50
Table, gold metal, 3¾x3" sq, +4 mesh & wire chairs, EX 55.00
Table, rnd w/ped ft, Renwall 10.00
Television, Petite Princess 65.00
Vacuum cleaner, pnt CI w/cloth bag, 4¼", VG 60.00
Wash stand, filigree metal, w/chamber set & potty, 5½" 50.00
Wash stand, pnt tin, EX 40.00

Houses

American, kitchen, pnt tin, w/stove & accessories, 9x14x4" 95.00
American, 2-story/4-room, built-in cupboards, 60x23", EX 700.00

Bliss dollhouse, ca 1910, 9¾x6x3¼, VG, $400.00.

Bliss, 2-story/4-room, twin gables, 2 trn posts, 16½", EX 1,050.00
Bliss type, 2-story, pnt wood, lift-off roof, 14x6½", EX 220.00
Bliss type, 2-story/3-room, paper exterior, rpt/rpl, 18x12" 400.00
Cottage, dormer window, access through side, 8½x10" 220.00
Germany, kitchen, paper/pnt wood, pnt tin pcs, 13", EX 350.00
Germany, kitchen, pnt tin, w/stove/shelves/etc, 6⅜x5¾", G 135.00
Germany, Red-Roof Series, 3-story/8-room, rpt, 1920s, 40" 600.00
Log cabin, 2-story, Garrison type, 32x20", VG 250.00
Schoenhut, Colonial, 2-story/4-room, 16x17x11", EX 795.00
Schoenhut, farm, 2-story/6-room, clapboard, +furnishings 3,200.00
Schoenhut, pnt wood/fiberboard/cb, 6-room/2-hall, 27", EX 800.00
Swimming pool, pnt tin, +slide/sprinkler, 10x18x12", EX 150.00
Tootsietoy, 3-story/5-room, completely furnished, 26x23", EX ...750.00
Victorian, 3-story/3 room, 37x24x17", EX 600.00
Victorian, 3-story/3-room, columned porch, 25x22x14", EX 675.00

Dolls

Collecting dolls of any sort is one of the most rewarding hobbies in the United States. The rewards are in the fun, the search, and the finds — plus there is a built-in factor of investment. No hobby, be it dolls, glass, or anything else, should be based completely on investment; but any collector should ask: 'Can I get my money back out of this item if I should ever have to sell it?' Many times we buy on impulse rather than with logic, which is understandable; but by asking this question we can save ourselves a lot of 'buyer's remorse' which we have all experienced at one time or another.

Since we want to learn to invest our money wisely while we are having fun, we must become aware of defects which may devaluate a doll. In bisque, watch for eye chips, hairline cracks and chips, or breaks on any part of the head. Composition should be clean, not crazed or cracked. Vinyl and plastic should be clean with no pen or crayon marks. Though a quality replacement wig is acceptable for bisque dolls, composition and hard plastics should have their originals in uncut condition. Original clothing is a must except in bisque dolls, since it is unusual to find one in its original costume.

A price guide is only that — a guide. It suggests the average price for each doll. Bargains can be found for less-than-suggested values, and 'unplayed-with' dolls in their original boxes may cost more. Dealers must become aware of condition so that they do not overpay and therefore over-price their dolls — a common occurrence across the country. Quantity does not replace quality, as most find out in time. A faster turnover of sales with a smaller margin of profit is far better than being stuck with an item that does not sell because it is overpriced. It is important to remember that prices are based on condition and rarity. When no condition is noted, dolls are assumed to be in excellent condition with the exceptions of Armand Marseille, Madame Alexander, and Effanbee dolls, which are priced in mint condition. In relation to bisque dolls, excellent means having no cracks, chips, or hairlines, being nicely dressed, shoed, wigged, and ready to to be placed into a collection. For a more thorough study of the subject, we recommend you refer to the many lovely doll books written by authority Pat Smith, available at your favorite bookstore or public library.

Key:
bjtd — ball-jointed	o/m — open mouth
blb — bent limb body	p/e — pierced ears
bsk — bisque	pnt — painted
c/m — closed mouth	pwt — paperweight eyes
hh — human hair	RpC — replaced clothes
hp — hard plastic	ShHd — shoulder head
jtd — jointed	ShPl — shoulder plate
MIG — Made In Germany	SkHd — socket head
NC — no clothes	str — straight

o/c — open closed	trn — turned
OC — original clothes	

Armand Marseille

Alma, ShHd, 12"	185.00
Alma, ShHd, 15"	250.00
Alma, ShHd, 26"	600.00
AM, baby, flange neck, 1907, 16"	650.00
AM, Darling Baby, 1906, 12"	350.00
AM, Floradora, ShHd, 20"	375.00
AM, Floradora, ShHd, 23"	450.00
AM, Floradora, SkHd, 12"	185.00
AM, Floradora, SkHd, 15"	265.00
AM, Floradora, SkHd, 17"	325.00
AM, Floradora, SkHd, 27"	700.00
AM, Floradora 1374, ShHd, fur eyebrows, 21"	425.00
AM, Floradora 3748, ShHd, 21"	385.00
AM, Indian, SkHd, o/c, 1890s, 8"	450.00
AM, Kiddiejoy, ShHd, cloth body, c/m, girl, 20"	1,400.00
AM, Kiddiejoy, ShHd, 9"	225.00
AM, My Dearie, SkHd, 1908, 14"	265.00
AM, My Playmate (body), closed dome & c/m, 18"	1,800.00
AM, Rosebud, ShHd, 1902, 15"	300.00
AM, Roseland, 1910, 18"	450.00
AM, ShHd, boy, 14"	325.00
AM, SkHd, c/m, 14"	950.00
AM, SkHd, o/c eyes, 7"	125.00
AM, SkHd, o/m, blk, 12"	475.00
AM, SkHd, 16"	275.00
AM, SkHd, 17"	295.00
AM, SkHd, 26"	650.00
AM, SkHd, 8"	165.00
AM, Sunshine, ShHd, 1910, 24"	550.00
AM, trn ShHd, talks, 16"	500.00
AM 1894, ShPl, 26"	650.00
AM 1894, SkHd, blk, 12"	375.00
AM 1894, SkHd, wht, 12"	200.00
AM 1894, SkHd, wht, 16½"	325.00
AM 1894, SkHd, 14"	250.00
AM 200, SkHd, googly eyes, 11½"	2,600.00
AM 210, SkHd, googly eyes, 6"	1,750.00
AM 231, Fany, baby, c/m, 1913, 25"	8,400.00
AM 248, mk GB (Geo Borgfeldt), o/m, 1912, 10"	350.00
AM 250, mk GB (Geo Borgfeldt), SkHd, c/m, molded hair, 10½"	675.00

Armand Marseille, AM 251, marked GB, fully jointed toddler body, sleep eyes, open/closed mouth with molded tongue, 14", $1,600.00.

AM 252, SkHd, googly eyes, 10" 1,100.00
AM 252, SkHd, googly eyes, 1915, 9½" 1,100.00
AM 253, SkHd, googly eyes, 1915, 16" 1,900.00
AM 253, SkHd, googly eyes, 6½" 800.00
AM 253, SkHd, googly eyes, 8" 900.00
AM 254, SkHd, googly eyes, molded hair, 8" 950.00
AM 255, SkHd, intaglio eyes, 7½" 700.00
AM 257, baby, SkHd, 1914, 22" 550.00
AM 300n, adult, SkHd, 15½" 1,200.00
AM 315, Queen Louise, SkHd, 27" 850.00
AM 320, SkHd, c/m, googly eyes, 6½" 650.00
AM 3200, ShHd, some trn, 15" 275.00
AM 3200, ShHd, some trn, 1898, 14" 265.00
AM 3200, ShHd, some trn, 1898, 16" 265.00
AM 3200, ShHd, some trn, 22" 450.00
AM 3200, ShHd, some trn, 26" 600.00
AM 323, SkHd, googly eyes, 11" 1,000.00
AM 323, SkHd, googly eyes, 7½" 600.00
AM 324, googly eyes, 7" 465.00
AM 327, SkHd, baby, fur hair, 1914, 12" 350.00
AM 327, SkHd, 1914, 12" 325.00
AM 327, SkHd, 1914, 20" 450.00
AM 328, baby, SkHd, closed dome, 1922, 14" 245.00
AM 329, girl, SkHd, 9" 275.00
AM 341, My Dream Baby, flange, c/m, wht, 8" 265.00
AM 341, My Dream Baby, flange, c/m, 15" 550.00
AM 341, My Dream Baby, flange, c/m, 18" 700.00
AM 341, My Dream Baby, flange, c/m, 1924, 7" 245.00
AM 341, My Dream Baby, flange, c/m, 21" 775.00
AM 341, My Dream Baby, SkHd, c/m, 16" 650.00
AM 347, SkHd, 1909, 16" 550.00
AM 3500, ShHd, 17" 325.00
AM 351, My Dream Baby, flange, o/m, wht, 22" 850.00
AM 351, My Dream Baby, flange, o/m, 26" 1,000.00
AM 351, My Dream Baby, flange, o/m, 6" 165.00
AM 351, Wee One, rubber body, 1922, 7" 165.00
AM 352, Baby Love, flange, 1914, 19" 675.00
AM 3524, Baby Gloria, flange neck, 18" 1,000.00
AM 362, Teenie Weenie, baby, closed dome, wht, 15" 550.00
AM 370, fur eyebrows, 22½" 400.00
AM 370, 12" 185.00
AM 370, 15" 250.00
AM 370, 16½" 300.00
AM 370, 19½" 350.00
AM 370n, 12" 185.00
AM 372, Kiddiejoy, ShHd, molded hair, 1926, 9" 350.00
AM 375, Kiddiejoy, girl, SkHd, c/m, molded hair, 20" 2,600.00
AM 390, My Dearie, SkHd, 1908-22, 18½" 400.00
AM 390, My Dearie, 23" 465.00
AM 390, o/m, 7½" 175.00
AM 390, pnt bsk, 9" 145.00
AM 390, walks, 22" 575.00
AM 390, 16" 350.00
AM 390, 18" 400.00
AM 390, 21" 450.00
AM 390, 22" 485.00
AM 390, 24" 525.00
AM 390, 9½" 265.00
AM 390n, Louisa, 1915, 27" 650.00
AM 390n, Patrice, 18" 500.00
AM 390n, 1915, 11" 200.00
AM 395, Heidi, SkHd, 1920, 9" 250.00
AM 402, SkHd, pnt bsk, 14" 300.00
AM 450, SkHd, c/m, provincial attire, 19" 1,800.00

AM 500, Infant Berry, molded hair, 1908, 10" 500.00
AM 500, Infant Berry, molded hair, 1908, 5" 250.00
AM 500, Infant Berry, molded hair, 1908, 8" 300.00
AM 550, SkHd, c/m, 16" 2,000.00
AM 560a, Dorothy, 1912, 15" 475.00
AM 590, Hoopla Girl, o/c eyes & mouth, 16" 1,800.00
AM 600, SkHd, flange, c/m, 1910, 10" 1,000.00
AM 800, Baby Sunshine, 'Mama' talker in head, 1925, 16" 2,000.00
AM 917, Mobi, baby, Germany, Skhd, 1921, 16" 525.00
AM 95, trn ShHd, 20" 425.00
AM 966, baby, SkHd, flirty eyes, 14" 450.00
AM 970, Ladie Marie, Otto Gans, 1916, 20" 750.00
AM 975, Sadie, baby, Otto Gans, 1914, 17" 500.00
AM 975, Sadie, baby, SkHd, 1914, 24" 750.00
AM 975, Sadie, baby, SkHd, 1914, 9" 250.00
AM 980, baby, SkHd, 14" 400.00
AM 985, baby, SkHd, 13½" 400.00
AM 990, Happy Tot, baby, SkHd, 13" 400.00
AM 990, Happy Tot, baby, SkHd, 1910, 16" 450.00
AM 990, Happy Tot, baby, SkHd, 1910, 21" 625.00
AM 990, Happy Tot, baby, SkHd, 8" 200.00
AM 991, Kiddiejoy, baby, SkHd, 14" 400.00
AM 992, baby, SkHd, 1914, 22" 625.00
AM 995, baby, SkHd, 12" 350.00
AM 996, baby, SkHd, 15" 450.00
AM 997, Kiddiejoy, baby, SkHd, 14" 425.00
Columbia, ShHd, 1904, 24" 525.00
Lily, ShHd, 1913, 17" 350.00
Mabel, ShHd, 1898, 15" 300.00
Mabel, ShHd, 1898, 17" 345.00
Queen Louise, SkHd, 1910, 22" 450.00
Queen Louise, 100, Germany, SkHd, 1910, 12" 250.00
Queen Louise, 100, SkHd, 1910, 18½" 425.00
Wonderful Alice, SkHd, fur eyebrows, 26" 650.00

Automaton

Ballerina, bends at waist, stands on music box, Jumeau, 20" 9,500.00
Bsk head, o/m w/teeth, glass eyes, waltzes, J Steiner, 17" 9,600.00
Bsk ShHd flower seller w/garland, France, 18", EX 5,000.00
Papier-mache head, bamboo teeth, on cart, Theroude, 16" 3,600.00
Stands or sits w/instrument on music box, Jumeau, 14" 4,800.00
2 bsk headed clowns on bench, mk 44 Bavaria, 10½", EX 2,500.00

Barbie Dolls and Related Dolls

Though the face has changed three times since 1959, Barbie is still as popular today as she was when she was first introduced. Named after the young daughter of the first owner of the Mattel Company, the original Barbie had a white iris but no eye color. These dolls are nearly impossible to find, but there is a myriad of her successors and related collectibles just waiting to be found. When no condition is indicated, the dolls listed below are assumed to be in mint condition (without original box) unless otherwise specified. For further information we recommend *The World of Barbie Dolls* and *The Wonder of Barbie, 1976 — 1986*, by Paris, Susan, and Carol Manos; and *The Collector's Encyclopedia of Barbie Dolls and Collectibles* by Sibyl DeWein and Joan Ashabraner. *Barbie Fashion, Vol I, 1959 — 1967*, by Sarah Sink Eames, gives a complete history of the wardrobes of Barbie, her friends, and her family. Many of Patricia Smith's books contain chapters on Barbies as well as other dolls by Mattel.

Allen, 1964, 12" 95.00
Barbie, 1958-59, #1, doll only, 11½", M 2,500.00

Barbie dolls: Dressed in pink formal, Sears Exclusive, MIB, $175.00; Dressed in Magnificence gown, MIB, $150.00.

Barbie, 1958-59, #1, holes in ft, metal cylinders, 11½", MIB ...3,000.00
Barbie, 1959, #2, blond ponytail, 11½" 1,200.00
Barbie, 1960, #3, curved brows, mk, as nurse, 11½" 500.00
Barbie, 1961, #4, vinyl plastic, tan skin, 11½", MIB 350.00
Barbie, 1961, Friday Nite Date, 11½" 500.00
Barbie, 1962, Fashion Queen, 11½" 500.00
Barbie, 1963, Career Girl, 11½" 300.00
Barbie, 1963, Movie Date, 11½" 300.00
Barbie, 1963, Ski Queen, 11½" 350.00
Barbie, 1963, Swinging Easy, 11½" 300.00
Barbie, 1964, Drum Major, 11½" 400.00
Barbie, 1964, Guinevere, 11½" 450.00
Barbie, 1965, bendable legs, 11½", minimum value 300.00
Barbie, 1967-68, Twist 'N Turn, 11½" 300.00
Barbie, 1968, Spanish Talking 300.00
Barbie, 1969-70, Twist 'N Turn, 11½" 300.00
Barbie, 1970, Living, 11½" 175.00
Barbie, 1972, Growin' Pretty Hair, 11½" 295.00
Barbie, 1972, Miss America, 11½" 250.00
Barbie, 1974, Sweet 16, 11½" 75.00
Barbie, 1975, Deluxe Quick Curl 75.00
Barbie, 1975, Gold Medal Skater 95.00
Christie, 1968, Live Action 140.00
Christie, 1968-72, Blk, 11½" 85.00
Francie, w/grow-pretty hair, 1959, 11½" 150.00
Francie, 1964 ....125.00
Francie, 1969, Twist 'N Turn, 11½" 325.00
Jamie, 1959, Walking, Sears 175.00
Ken, Busy 150.00
Ken, flocked hair, non-bending knees, 12" 150.00
Ken, Live Action, 12" 95.00
Ken, Malibu, 12" 20.00
Ken, Talking, 12" 125.00
Ken, 1961, flocked hair, Campus Hero, 12" 225.00
Ken, 1962, in orig pajamas, 12" 150.00
Ken, 1962, pnt hair, OC, 12" 150.00
Ken, 1963, Ski Champion, 12" 250.00
Ken, 1972, Mod hair, 12" 150.00
Midge, 1963, Fancy Free 225.00
Midge, 1963, in raincoat outfit 150.00
Midge, 1964 ....150.00
PJ, 1959, Talking 125.00

PJ, 1972, Malibu, 11½" 30.00
Ricky, 1965, red hair & freckles 95.00
Skipper, 1955, Sledding Fun 150.00
Skipper, 1964 ....150.00
Skipper, 1965, Ship Ahoy dress 155.00
Skipper, 1981, Sensational Malibu 25.00
Skooter, 1963, minimum value 125.00
Stacey, 1968, Talking 275.00
Stacey, 1970, Maxie 'N Mini 250.00

Barbie Gifts Sets and Related Accessories

When no condition is indicated, the items listed below are assumed to be mint and in the original box.

Dress-Up Kit by Colorforms, M, $15.00.

Beach Party Play Set, w/doll, 1976-86, MIB 400.00
Case, Barbie in wht stole & long gown, vinyl, 1962 ....55.00
Clothes, Campus Sweetheart, 1964, M 250.00
Clothes, Fashion Fantasy, M 150.00
Clothes, Ice Empress, M 220.00
Clothes, Junior Prom, 1964 ....425.00
Clothes, Riding in the Park, 1965, M 150.00
Clothes, Riding in the Park, 1965, MIB 400.00
Clothes, Roman Holiday, 1958, M 600.00
Clothes, Roman Holiday, 1958, MIB, minimum value 1,500.00
Dressing table & bench, 1962 ....55.00
Dune buggy, M 85.00
Horse, Dancer, 3 leg joints, 1970, minimum value 100.00
Hot Rod, Irwin Corp, MIB 95.00
Knitting Pretty Set, 1963 ....65.00
Pink & Pretty Barbie Gift Set, England, minimum value 700.00
Roller Gift Set, Spain, minimum value 300.00
Ten Speeder, 1973, minimum value 40.00
Thermos Bottle, 1961, M 30.00
Walking Jamie Strollin' in Style Gift Set, 1972 ....500.00
Wardrobe, 1962, minimum value 55.00

Belton

Concave head, 2 or 3 hole, EX bsk, o/c or c/m w/wig, 10" 1,650.00
Concave head, 2 or 3 hole, EX bsk, o/c or c/m w/wig, 13" 2,000.00
Concave head, 2 or 3 hole, EX bsk, o/c or c/m w/wig, 15" 2,500.00
Concave head, 2 or 3 hole, EX bsk, o/c or c/m w/wig, 16" 2,600.00
Concave head, 2 or 3 hole, EX bsk, o/c or c/m w/wig, 17" 2,700.00

Concave head with three holes, EX bisque, open/closed mouth, set paperweight eyes, 17", $2,900.00.

Concave head, 2 or 3 hole, EX bsk, o/c or c/m w/wig, 20" 3,300.00
Concave head, 2 or 3 hole, EX bsk, o/c or c/m w/wig, 22" 3,500.00
Concave head, 2 or 3 hole, EX bsk, o/c or c/m w/wig, 23" 3,500.00
Concave head, 2 or 3 hole, EX bsk, o/c or c/m w/wig, 26" 4,100.00
Concave head, 2 or 3 hole, EX bsk, o/c or c/m w/wig, 8" 975.00

Bisque, Unmarked

French, ShHd, bl pwt eyes, c/m, brn wig, OC, 14", EX 1,500.00
French, ShHd, bl pwt eyes, c/m, p/e, kid body, OC, 12" 1,550.00
French, ShHd, bl pwt eyes, c/m, p/e, wig, OC, 15", EX 1,600.00
French, SkHd, bl stationary eyes, c/m, p/e, wig, OC, 14" 2,600.00
German, cup & saucer type, hh wig, kid body, OC, 23" 2,000.00
German, googly eyes, c/m, mohair wig, toddler body, 13½" 2,750.00
German, googly eyes, 5-pc body, OC, 5", EX 400.00

Bru

Closed mouth, all kid body, bsk lower arms, Bru, 13" 9,500.00
Closed mouth, all kid body, bsk lower arms; Bru, 16" 10,500.00
Closed mouth, all kid body, bsk lower arms; Bru, 18" 13,500.00
Closed mouth, all kid body, bsk lower arms; Bru, 21" 24,000.00
Closed mouth, all kid body, bsk lower arms; Bru, 26" 29,500.00
Closed mouth, kid/wood body, bsk lower arms; Bru Jne, 12" .23,000.00
Closed mouth, kid/wood body, bsk lower arms; Bru Jne, 14" .19,000.00
Closed mouth, kid/wood body, bsk lower arms; Bru Jne, 16" .24,500.00
Closed mouth, kid/wood body, bsk lower arms; Bru Jne, 20" .27,500.00
Closed mouth, kid/wood body, bsk lower arms; Bru Jne, 25" .39,000.00
Closed mouth, kid/wood body, bsk lower arms; Bru Jne, 28" .42,000.00
Closed mouth, kid/wood body, bsk lower arms; Bru Jne, 32" .46,000.00
Closed mouth, mk Bru, circle dot, 16" 23,000.00
Closed mouth, mk Bru, circle dot, 19" 26,000.00
Closed mouth, mk Bru, circle dot, 23" 29,000.00
Closed mouth, mk Bru, circle dot, 26" 33,000.00
Open mouth, comp walker's body, throws kisses, 18" 7,600.00
Open mouth, comp walker's body, throws kisses, 22" 8,300.00
Open mouth, comp walker's body, throws kisses, 26" 9,400.00
Open mouth, nursing (Bebe), high color, late SFBJ, 12" 2,600.00
Open mouth, nursing (Bebe), high color, late SFBJ, 15" 3,200.00
Open mouth, nursing (Bebe), high color, late SFBJ, 18" 3,500.00
Open mouth, nursing Bru (Bebe), early, EX bsk, 12" 5,400.00
Open mouth, nursing Bru (Bebe), early, EX bsk, 15" 8,200.00
Open mouth, nursing Bru (Bebe), early, EX bsk, 18" 9,800.00
Open mouth, socket head, compo body; Bru, R, 14", EX bsk ..6,500.00
Open mouth, socket head, compo body; Bru, R, 17", EX bsk ..7,400.00
Open mouth, socket head, compo body; Bru, R, 22", EX bsk ..8,300.00
Open mouth, socket head, compo body; Bru, R, 25", EX bsk ..10,000.00
Open mouth, socket head, compo body; Bru, R, 28", EX bsk ...11,500.00

China, Unmarked

Adelina Patti, center part, curls at temples, 1860s, 14" 350.00
Adelina Patti, center part, curls at temples, 1860s, 18" 450.00
Adelina Patti, center part, curls at temples, 1860s, 22" 525.00
Biedermeier or Bald Head, takes wig, RpC, 14" 925.00
Biedermeier or Bald Head, takes wig, RpC, 20" 1,400.00
Brown Eyes (pnt), any hairstyle or date, 16" 700.00
Brown Eyes (pnt), any hairstyle or date, 20" 1,200.00
Common Hairdo, blond or blk hair, RpC, after 1905, 12" 145.00
Common Hairdo, blond or blk hair, RpC, after 1905, 23" 285.00
Common Hairdo, blond or blk hair, RpC, after 1905, 8" 80.00
Covered Wagon Style, sausage curls, RpC, 1840s-70s, 12" 285.00
Covered Wagon Style, sausage curls, RpC, 1840s-70s, 24" 900.00
Curly Top, loose ringlet curls, RpC, 1845-60s, 16" 550.00
Curly Top, loose ringlet curls, RpC, 1845-60s, 20" 725.00
Dolly Madison, modeled ribbon & bow, RpC, 1870-80s, 14" 325.00
Dolly Madison, modeled ribbon & bow, RpC, 1870-80s, 18" 525.00
Dolly Madison, modeled ribbon & bow, RpC, 1870-80s, 21" 600.00
Flat Top, blk hair, mid-part/short curls, RpC, ca 1860, 17" 350.00
Flat Top, blk hair, mid-part/short curls, RpC, ca 1860, 20" 400.00
Glass Eyes, various hairstyles, RpC, 1840s-70s, 14" 1,200.00
Glass Eyes, various hairstyles, RpC, 1840s-70s, 22" 1,900.00
Japanese, blk or blond hair, mk or unmk, RpC, 1910-20s, 14" 185.00
Japanese, blk or blond hair, mk or unmk, RpC, 1910-20s, 17" 250.00
Man or Boy, glass eyes, side part, RpC, 14" 2,200.00
Man or Boy, pnt eyes, side part, RpC, 14", EX 1,200.00
Man or Boy, pnt eyes, side part, RpC, 16" 1,400.00
Man or Boy, pnt eyes, side part, RpC, 21½" 2,400.00
Peg Wood Body, early hairdo, 16", EX 3,400.00
Pet Name, molded shirtwaist w/name on front, RpC, 1905, 19" .285.00
Pet Name, molded shirtwaist w/name on front, RpC, 1905, 8" .135.00
Pierced Ears, various hairstyles, RpC, 14" 1,200.00
Pierced Ears, various hairstyles, RpC, 18" 1,800.00
Snood/Combs, any appl hair decor, RpC, 14" 650.00
Snood/Combs, any appl hair decor, RpC, 17" 800.00
Spill Curls, w/or w/out head band, RpC, 14" 475.00
Spill Curls, w/or w/out head band, RpC, 22" 950.00
Wood Body, articulated/slim hips, RpC, 1840s-50s, 12" 1,500.00
Wood Body, articulated/slim hips, RpC, 1840s-50s, 17" 3,200.00
Wood Body, jtd hips, covered-wagon hairdo, 1840s-50s, 12" 985.00
Wood Body, jtd hips, covered-wagon hairdo, 1840s-50s, 15" ..1,800.00

Cloth

Flip Wilson/Geraldine, talking (non-working), bright printed colors, ca 1970, EX, $35.00.

American, pnt features, oilcloth shoes, OC, 14½", M 500.00
Applause, Pippi Longstocking, yarn hair, 1988, 18", M 45.00
Bruckner, topsy-turvy, all cloth w/stiffened mask, 12", VG 265.00

Dolly Dear, litho, 7" 95.00
Foxy Grandpa, litho, 12" 130.00
France, stockinette face/hands, music box, OC, 15½", EX 225.00
Kamkin, molded & pnt face, swivel head, 5-pc body, OC, 18", VG .650.00
Knickerbocker, Raggedy Ann, printed, yarn hair, 1960s, 12" 165.00
Kruger, Popeye, well modeled, corn-cob pipe, 1930, 21½", EX ..850.00
Martha Chase, sateen body, mk on hip, 23", EX 1,600.00
Nurse Jane Fuzzy Wuzzy, 1920s, 20" 700.00
Pitti Sing, Arnold Printworks, uncut set of 4 ....175.00
Primitive oil-pnt face, wht w/blk cloth legs, RpC, 15", EX 750.00
Printed face, hair, undies, shoes, unmk, 17", EX 200.00
Uncle Mose, printed, mk on bk, 16", G 200.00
Uncle Wiggley, 1920s, 20" 800.00

Effanbee

Bernard Fleischaker and Hugo Baum became business partners in 1910, and after two difficult years of finding toys to buy and a retail market to sell them in, they decided to manufacture dolls of their own. Their lovely dolls were a decided success largely because of their dedication to their work and the mutual trust and respect they held for each other. This is reflected in the Effanbee trademark — Eff stands for Fleischaker and bee for Baum. The company still exists today.

Effanbee 'Central Park' 1978, and 'Charleston Harbor,' 1980, each 11" and from the Currier and Ives collection, $45.00 each.

Americana Collection, 1975-77, ea 50.00
Baby Cuddleup, vinyl-coated cloth & vinyl, 1953, 20" 50.00
Baby Evelyn, compo/cloth, 1925, 17" 300.00
Bedtime Story Collection, 1972, ea 40.00
Button Nose Betty, 1943, 8" 185.00
Candy Kid, compo, 1946, 12" 265.00
Charlie McCarthy, ShHd, blk dress suit, monocle, topper, 19" ..565.00
Cinderella, hp, 16", minimum value 425.00
Compo/cloth, ShHd, tin o/c eyes, human hair wig, 24" 250.00
Currier & Ives, plastic & vinyl, 12" 50.00
Dydee Baby, hp & vinyl, 1950 on, 15" 165.00
Eleanor Roosevelt, plastic & vinyl, 1985, 16" 65.00
Fluffy, vinyl, jtd neck/shoulders/hips, rooted hair, RpC, 10" 35.00
Half Pint, plastic & vinyl, 1966 on, 10" 35.00
Historical, compo, all orig, 14", NM 650.00
Honey, compo, OC, 14" 250.00
Honey Walker, hp, c/m, o/c eyes, saran wig, OC, 19" 350.00
Ice Queen, compo, o/m, OC, 17" 800.00
Lamkin, cloth & compo, 1930, 16" 500.00
Little Bo Peep, compo, pnt eyes, fully jtd, OC, 9" 250.00
Little Boy Blue, 1912, 12" 275.00
Little Girl, ShHd, compo/cloth, pnt eyes/hair, c/m, OC, 14" 165.00
Little Lady, compo/cloth, pnt eyes, 1944, OC, 27" 500.00
Lovums, o/c mouth smiling, molded hair, OC, 22" 350.00

Mae Starr, compo & cloth, o/m w/tongue & 2 teeth, OC, 30" ...450.00
Marilee, compo & cloth, o/m, 1920s, 14" 250.00
Marionnette, compo & wood, OC, 14" 175.00
Mary Ann, compo/cloth, o/m smiling, mk w/name, OC, 18" 285.00
Mary Jane, vinyl, flirty eyes, walker, RpC, 30" 285.00
Mickey, compo & cloth, flirty eyes, 1946, OC, 18" 325.00
Miss Chips, plastic & vinyl, 1965 on, 18" 40.00
Patricia, compo, o/c eyes, brn human hair wig, OC, 15" 395.00
Patricia, compo, OC, 14" 385.00
Patsy, compo, pnt eyes/hair, OC, 14" 365.00
Patsy Ann, compo, tin o/c eyes, RpC, 19" 465.00
Patsy Baby, compo, celluloid over tin o/c eyes, RpC, 10" 250.00
Patsy Babyette, compo, OC, 9" 245.00
Patsy Joan, compo, o/c eyes, molded hair, OC, 16" 450.00
Patsy Lou, compo, o/c eyes, bent left elbow, wig, 22" 485.00
Portrait doll, compo, 1940, 12", ea 265.00
Precious Baby, Limited Edition Club, 1975, M 550.00
Prince Charming, hp, OC, 16" 425.00
Rootie Kazootie, vinyl head/limbs, pnt eyes, RpC, 21" 185.00
Rosemary, compo/cloth, o/c eyes, orig wig, OC, 25" 400.00
Santa Claus, compo, molded hat & beard, late 1930s, 19" 1,000.00
Sister, compo/cloth, yarn hair, 1943, 12" 150.00
Skippy, compo, 1940s, 14" 445.00
Sugar Plum Fairy, plastic/vinyl, o/c eyes, OC, tag, 11" 40.00
Tommy Tucker, compo/cloth, flirty eyes, 22" 375.00
Victorian Lady, 1976-77, ea 85.00

Grace Putnam

Bsk, 1-pc, pnt eyes, 10/10/COPR, 6" 650.00
Bsk, 1-pc body & head, 1/COPR, 1923, 6" 650.00
Bye-Lo baby, 1360/30/COPR, RpC, 11" 750.00
Bye-Lo baby, 6 12/COPR, 1927, 16" 800.00
Bye-Lo baby, 6 12/COPR, 1927, 5" 650.00

Half Dolls

Half dolls, lovely porcelain figures awaiting attachment to secure bases, were never meant to be objects of play. Most of these lovely ladies were firmly sewn into pincushion bases that were beautifully decorated and served as the skirt of their gown. Other skirts were actually covers for items on milady's dressing table. Some were used for parasol or brush handles or for tops to candy containers or perfume bottles. Most popular from 1900 to about 1930, they will most often be found marked with the country of their origin — Bavaria, Germany, France, and Japan. You may also find some fine quality pieces marked Goebel, Dressel and Kester, and Heubach. For further information we recommend *The Collector's Encyclopedia of Half Dolls* by Frieda Marion and Norma Werner, available at your local bookstore or from Collector Books.

Germany, arms & hands attached, common type, 3" 30.00
Germany, arms & hands attached, common type, 5" 40.00
Germany, arms & hands attached, common type, 8" 55.00
Germany, arms & hands completely away, 12" 900.00
Germany, arms & hands completely away, 3" 135.00
Germany, arms & hands completely away, 5" 275.00
Germany, arms & hands completely away, 8" 600.00
Germany, arms extended, hands attached, 3" 65.00
Germany, arms extended, hands attached, 5" 75.00
Germany, arms extended, hands attached, 8" 95.00
Japan mk, 3" 20.00
Japan mk, 5" 30.00
Japan mk, 8" 50.00

Handwerck

#10, compo, bjtd, o/c eyes, p/e, 18" **475.00**
#109, brn o/c eyes, o/m w/4 teeth, long wig, RpC, 17" **500.00**
#109-7½, SkHd, compo, jtd, o/c eyes, o/m, p/e, RpC, 17" **500.00**
#1252/2, brn o/c eyes, o/m/4 teeth, wig, OC, 23", +box **1,600.00**
#79, bjtd, o/c eyes, o/m w/teeth, orig wig, 12" **1,400.00**

Bisque head, composition body, brown sleep eyes, open mouth, pierced ears, original human hair wig, original clothes, 20", $550.00.

Bsk ShHd, kid body, o/m, RpC, 15" **350.00**
Child, #d, bjtd, o/m, o/c eyes, after 1885, 24" **825.00**
Child, no #, bjtd, o/c eyes, wig, after 1885, 14" **400.00**
Germany, SkHd, compo, jtd, o/c eyes, o/m, RpC, 17½" **525.00**
Max Handwerck, SkHd, brn sleep eyes, o/m, orig wig, rprs, 22" .**300.00**
Max Handwerck, SkHd, compo, jtd, pwt eyes, lg ears, RpC, 15" ...**450.00**
Trn ShHd, full c/m, set eyes, unpierced ears, RpC, 15" **1,200.00**

Heubach

#1017, baby-faced toddler, o/m, 24" **1,950.00**
#119, character, molded braids, intaglio eyes, RpC, 16" **5,400.00**
#22-126, ShHd, jtd body, molded bonnet, o/c/m, RpC, 8" **1,200.00**
#2850, o/c mouth w/teeth, molded braided hair, 16" **9,500.00**
#4, SkHd, compo, fully jtd, intaglio eyes, c/m, RpC, 15" **1,600.00**
#5636, laughing child, intaglio pnt eyes, 9" **900.00**
#5689, smiling o/m, 15" **1,800.00**
#5730, Santa, 17" **2,500.00**
#5777, Dolly Dimples, bjtd, 15" **2,600.00**
#6, brn o/c eyes, o/m/4 teeth, wig, RpC, 29½" **950.00**
#6½, SkHd, 5-pc body, o/c eyes, teeth, RpC, 19" **750.00**
#6692, ShHd, smiling mouth, intaglio eyes, 16" **925.00**
#6736, laughing o/c mouth, molded lower teeth, 9" **850.00**
#6896, pouty mouth, jtd body, 20" **1,200.00**
#6969, pouty c/m, glass eyes, orig wig, 14" **2,500.00**
#7246, pouty boy or girl, jtd body, pnt eyes, 10", ea **950.00**
#7448, o/c mouth, half-shut eyes, 15" **2,700.00**
#7623, o/c mouth, intaglio eyes, molded hair, bent limbs, 11" **800.00**
#7644, SkHd or ShHd, laughing, intaglio eyes, 14", ea **850.00**
#7661, Blk, wide o/c mouth, molded hair, 13" **2,300.00**
#7669, laughing o/c mouth, glass eyes, walker, 13" **1,700.00**
#7684, screamer, 13" **925.00**
#7764, intaglio eyes, o/c mouth, molded hair, 5-pc body, 14" .**1,200.00**
#7768, Coquette, tilted head, molded hair, 10" **800.00**
#8420, pouty boy or girl, jtd, pnt eyes, 15" **750.00**
#8429, SkHd, glass eyes, c/m, RpC, 15" **5,400.00**

#8648, intaglio eyes, pouth c/m, 19" **2,800.00**
#9891, molded-on cap, intaglio eyes, 12" **1,200.00**
Baby, intaglio eyes, c/m, RpC, 8½" **550.00**
Coquette, tilted bsk ShHd, kid body, molded ribbon, RpC, 12" .**865.00**
Molded bonnet w/molded hair to front & sides of face, 10" **1,800.00**
SkHd, molded bonnet, holes at sides for ribbon, RpC, 9" **1,100.00**

Heubach-Koppelsdorf

#1092/0, ShHd, kid body, bsk arms, rpl wig, OC, 20" **365.00**
#242-14, baby, pnt bsk head, 5-pc bent-leg body, RpC, 11" **300.00**
#250, child, jtd, o/m, sleep eyes, 10" **225.00**
#250 3/0, SkHd, jtd compo, o/c eyes, 4 teeth, RpC, 16" **325.00**
#262, character child, molded hair, pnt eyes, after 1910, 12" **500.00**
#275, ShHd, kid body, compo arms, o/c eyes, o/m, RpC, 15" **285.00**
#300, baby, o/c eyes, 5-pc bent-limb body, after 1910, 6" **265.00**
#300 2/0, brn o/c eyes, o/m w/teeth, rpt limbs, wig, 14" **200.00**
#302, child, jtd, sleep or set eyes, o/m, 18" **400.00**
#320, baby, o/c eyes, o/m, 5-pc body, 25" **900.00**
#320, baby, 5-pc toddler body, after 1910, 15" **575.00**
#320 13/0, bsk head, jtd compo, bl o/c eyes, o/m, 11" **375.00**
#321, SkHd, o/c eyes, o/m w/2 teeth, OC, 14" **385.00**
#339, infant, brn pnt bsk head, 5-pc, o/c eyes, wig, 12" **525.00**
#339, infant, molded or pnt hair, o/c eyes, c/m, 12" **585.00**
Child, bsk ShHd, bsk limbs, kid body, RpC, 15" **250.00**

Ideal

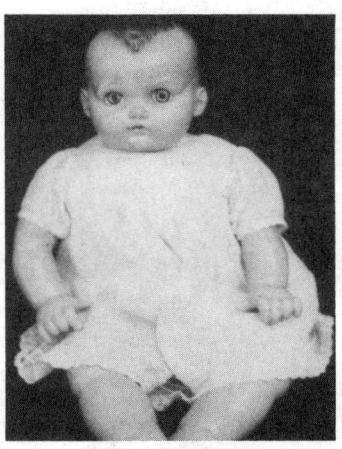

Ideal Doll, Made in USA, Pat. No. 2252077, composition head and limbs, stuffed cloth body, blue sleep eyes, painted hair, 1940s, redressed, 21½", $100.00.

Baby Belly Button, plastic & vinyl, OC, 1970, 9" **18.00**
Baby Crissy, pull string to make hair grow, 1973, OC, 24" **85.00**
Baby Snooks or other Flexy, wire & compo, 12", ea **275.00**
Bamm-Bamm, plastic & vinyl or all vinyl, 1963, 12" **15.00**
Betsy Wetsy, compo head, rubber body, after 1937, 16" **125.00**
Betty Jane, compo, o/m, o/c eyes, S Temple type, 1930s, 14" **185.00**
Bonnie Walker, hp, pin-jtd hips, o/m, flirty eyes, OC, 23" **85.00**
Compo, child, cloth body, str legs, OC, 14" **165.00**
Crissy, Look-a-Round, 1972, OC, 18" **45.00**
Deanna Durbin, compo, 1939, OC, 14" **475.00**
Dianna Ross, plastic & vinyl, OC, 18" **165.00**
Dorothy Hammill, 1977, OC, 11½" **30.00**
Dr Evil, jtd, w/face masks, 1965, OC, 11" **200.00**
Flossie Flirt, compo & cloth, flirty eyes, 1938-45, OC, 22" **300.00**
Goody Two Shoes, Walking & Talking, 1965, OC, 27" **225.00**
Honey Moon, magic skin body, wht yarn hair, 1965, OC, 15" **60.00**
Judy Garland, compo, 1939, OC, 14" **1,000.00**
King Little, compo & wood, 1940, OC, 14" **300.00**
Mary Jane, compo, o/m, o/c or flirty eyes, OC, 18" **250.00**

Miss Ideal, jtd, 1961, OC, 25" 375.00
Pepper, plastic & vinyl, freckles, OC, 9" 40.00
Sara Ann, hp, Saran wig, after 1952, OC, 14" 185.00
Snow White, compo, flirty eyes, blk mohair wig, OC, 22", EX ...600.00
Tabitha, cloth & vinyl, eyes pnt to side, 1966, 15" 50.00
Tickletoes, compo & cloth, 1930s, OC, 15" 150.00
Toni, mk P-92, OC, 17" 475.00

Jumeau

Emile Jumeau took over his father's doll company sometime in the 1870s. He brought many new innovations and ideas to the business. One fascination Jumeau had concerned dolls' eyes and led to the patents for eyelids that dropped over the eye itself; a second type allowed the doll to 'sleep.' Jumeau's distaste for German dolls is apparent in the booklets that were packaged with his dolls. These booklets referred to the German dolls as cheap and ugly and and as having 'stupid' faces. In reality, these less-expensive dolls were the downfall of the French doll manufacturers, and in 1899 the Jumeau company had to combine with several others in an effort to save the French doll industry from German competition.

Bsk SkHd, blond mohair, w/bottle/dog/music box, 18", VG 6,500.00
Closed mouth, mk EJ (incised) Jumeau, rpr ft, 24" 8,700.00
Closed mouth, mk EJ (incised) Jumeau, 10" 5,600.00
Closed mouth, mk EJ (incised) Jumeau, 14" 5,900.00
Closed mouth, mk EJ (incised) Jumeau, 16" 6,600.00
Closed mouth, mk EJ (incised) Jumeau, 19" 7,000.00
Closed mouth, mk EJ (incised) Jumeau, 21" 7,400.00
Closed mouth, mk Tete Jumeau, 10" 4,900.00
Closed mouth, mk Tete Jumeau, 14" 3,900.00
Closed mouth, mk Tete Jumeau, 16" 4,400.00
Closed mouth, mk Tete Jumeau, 19" 4,800.00

Closed mouth, marked Tete Jumeau, stationary eyes, pierced ears, blond wig, 20", EX, $4,900.00.

Closed mouth, mk Tete Jumeau, 21" 5,000.00
Closed mouth, mk Tete Jumeau, 23" 5,500.00
Closed mouth, mk Tete Jumeau, 25" 5,700.00
Closed mouth, mk Tete Jumeau, 28" 6,600.00
Closed mouth, mk Tete Jumeau, 30" 7,400.00
Depose/Tete Jumeau, swivel head, p/e, long curls, adult, 18" ...6,500.00
Depose/Tete Jumeau, swivel head, p/e, long curls, adult, 22" ..7,600.00
Depose/Tete Jumeau, swivel head, p/e, long curls, adult, 28" ..8,700.00
Jumeau 1907, SkHd, appl ears, o/m, 18" 2,400.00
Jumeau 1907, swivel head, o/m, o/c eyes, p/e, 18" 2,400.00
Jumeau 1907, swivel head, o/m, o/c eyes, p/e, 23" 2,800.00
Jumeau 1909, swivel head, o/m, inset eyes, p/e, 21" ...2,800.00
Long face, c/m, 21" 23,000.00
Long face, c/m, 30" 26,000.00
Mechanical/musical, c/m, p/e, pwt, hh, 12" on 4" box 4,800.00

Open mouth, mk Tete Jumeau, 10" 995.00
Open mouth, mk Tete Jumeau, 14" 1,700.00
Open mouth, mk Tete Jumeau, 16" 2,300.00
Open mouth, mk Tete Jumeau, 19" 2,600.00
Open mouth, mk Tete Jumeau, 21" 2,800.00
Open mouth, mk Tete Jumeau, 23" 3,000.00
Open mouth, mk Tete Jumeau, 25" 3,300.00
Open mouth, mk Tete Jumeau, 28" 3,600.00
Open mouth, mk Tete Jumeau, 30" 3,800.00
Open mouth, mk 1907 Jumeau, 14" 1,700.00
Open mouth, mk 1907 Jumeau, 17" 2,450.00
Open mouth, mk 1907 Jumeau, 20" 2,700.00
Open mouth, mk 1907 Jumeau, 25" 3,300.00
Open mouth, mk 1907 Jumeau, 28" 3,600.00
Open mouth, mk 1907 Jumeau, 32" 4,000.00
Phonograph in body, o/m, 20" 8,000.00
Phonograph in body, o/m, 25" 11,000.00
Portrait Jumeau, c/m, 16" 7,800.00
Portrait Jumeau, c/m, 20" 9,000.00

Kammer and Reinhardt

#100, baby, pnt hair & eyes, o/c mouth, 15" 700.00
#100/5, SkHD, bent leg, pnt eyes & hair, 20" 1,200.00
#101, boy or girl w/glass eyes, 12" 2,300.00
#101, boy or girl w/glass eyes, 16" 5,500.00
#101, boy or girl w/glass eyes, 20" 7,000.00
#101, boy or girl w/glass eyes, 9" 1,900.00
#101, boy or girl w/pnt eyes, 12" 2,000.00
#101, boy or girl w/pnt eyes, 16" 3,600.00
#101, boy or girl w/pnt eyes, 20" 5,000.00
#101, boy or girl w/pnt eyes, 9" 1,700.00
#107, Carl, pnt eyes, pouty mouth, orig mohair wig, 12½" 13,000.00
#109, rare, w/glass eyes, 15" 17,000.00
#109, rare, w/glass eyes, 18" 26,000.00
#109, rare, w/pnt eyes, 15" 14,000.00
#109, rare, w/pnt eyes, 18" 22,000.00
#112, rare, w/glass eyes, 15" 17,000.00
#112, rare, w/glass eyes, 18" 20,000.00
#112, rare, w/pnt eyes, 15" 10,000.00
#112, rare, w/pnt eyes, 18" 17,000.00
#114, rare, w/glass eyes, 15" 5,900.00
#114, rare, w/glass eyes, 18" 7,800.00
#114, rare, w/pnt eyes, 11" 3,200.00
#114, rare, w/pnt eyes, 15" 4,300.00
#114, rare, w/pnt eyes, 18" 5,500.00
#115 or #115a, c/m, 15" 4,500.00
#115 or #115a, c/m, 18" 4,900.00
#115 or #115a, c/m, 22" 5,300.00
#115 or #115a, o/m, 15" 1,400.00
#115 or #115a, o/m, 18" 2,300.00
#115 or #115a, o/m, 22" 2,600.00
#116 or #116a, c/m, 15" 3,000.00
#116 or #116a, c/m, 18" 3,500.00
#116 or #116a, c/m, 22" 4,600.00
#116 or #116a, o/m, 15" 1,400.00
#116 or #116a, o/m, 18" 2,300.00
#116 or #116a, o/m, 22" 2,600.00
#117, c/m, 18" 4,900.00
#117, c/m, 24" 6,900.00
#117, c/m, 30" 8,000.00
#117a, c/m, 18" 5,400.00
#117a, c/m, 24" 6,900.00
#117a, c/m, 30" 9,000.00

#126, brn o/c eyes, o/m w/teeth, 5-pc body, RpC, 17" 685.00
#126, sleeping/flirty glass eyes, o/m, silent, 28" 1,550.00
#126, toddler, sleeping/flirty eyes, o/m, 13½" 725.00
Dolly face, o/m, mold #400-403-109, etc, 16" 600.00
Dolly face, o/m, mold #400-403-109, etc, 20" 725.00
Dolly face, o/m, mold #400-403-109, etc, 24" 850.00
Dolly face, o/m, mold #400-403-109, etc, 28" 1,100.00
Dolly face, o/m, mold #400-403-109, etc, 38" 2,800.00
Dolly face, o/m, mold #400-403-109, etc, 40" 3,000.00

Kestner

Johannes D. Kestner made buttons at a lathe in a Waltershausen factory in the early 1800s. When this line of work failed, he used the same lathe to turn doll bodies. Thus the Kestner company began. It was one of the few German manufacturers to make the complete doll. By 1860, with the purchase of a porcelain factory, Kestner made doll heads of china and bisque as well as wax, worked-in-leather, celluloid, and cardboard. In 1895 the Kestner trademark of a crown with streamers was registered in the U.S. and a year later in Germany. Kestner felt the mark was appropriate since he referred to himself as the 'king of German dollmakers.'

#211, bisque sockethead, stationary brown eyes, JDK/MIG, dressed in christening gown, slip, booties, silk stockings and embroidered piece for neck, 19", EX, $1,200.00.

A, ShHd, o/m, MIG/Kestner, 19" 685.00
A/5, ShHd, o/c mouth, 23" 1,000.00
B/6, ShHd, kid w/bsk ½-arms, o/m w/teeth, o/c eyes, 19" 685.00
B/6, SkHd, jtd compo, o/m w/2 teeth, set eyes, 22" 900.00
Century Doll Co, flanged closed dome, c/m, 15" 685.00
C13/129, bsk SkHd, o/c eyes, o/m, 4 teeth, RpC, 22", G 900.00
D/8, SkHd & ShHd, kid w/bsk ½-arms, c/m, 15" 1,000.00
E/9, ShHd, o/m, MIG, 26" 1,000.00
E/9, SkHd, o/m, 1892, 26" 1,000.00
Excelsior Germany, SkHd, compo, o/m w/4 teeth, OC, 32" 1,800.00
G/11, Hilda, SkHd, o/c eyes, o/m w/2 teeth, 1920s, 15" 3,600.00
G/11, SkHd, brn, o/m, 16" 3,600.00
G/8, trn ShHd, o/m, MI/JDK, 19" 800.00
G11, SkHd, jtd, bl eyes, o/m, mohair wig, 19" 800.00
H 1/2, ShHd, o/m, 23" 900.00
H/12, SkHd, o/c mouth, JDK, 1892, 23" 3,400.00
Hilda, o/c eyes, o/m, orig wig, JDK, 15", EX 3,600.00
Hilda, toddler, jtd body, o/m, o/c eyes, 1914, rstr, 15" 4,800.00
I/13, SkHd, o/m, JDK, 1892, 16" 650.00
I/13, SkHd, o/m, JDK, 1892, 26" 985.00
J/13, SkHd, o/m, 1896, 27" 1,000.00
JDK, bsk head, glass eyes, c/m, appl ears, OC, 20", EX 4,800.00
JDK, bsk head, o/m w/teeth, o/c eyes, pnt hair, 15½" 600.00
JDK, bsk head on celluloid, R Gummi Co, turtle mk, 18" 650.00
JDK 12, SkHd, o/c eyes, o/m w/2 teeth, orig wig, RpC, 16" 600.00

JDK 12, SkHd, pwt, o/m, bent limbs, RpC, 15", VG 475.00
JDK 241, SkHd, jtd compo, o/m w/4 teeth, RpC, 21½", EX 5,800.00
K/12, ShHd, made for Century, o/c mouth, molded hair, 21" ..3,400.00
L 1/2/15 1/2, SkHd, c/m, 14" 1,900.00
L/15, SkHd, bsk ShPl, c/m, 21" 3,000.00
L/3, ShHd, o/c mouth w/molded teeth, 23" 3,600.00
N/17, SkHd, o/m, 1892, 17" 725.00
ShHd, o/c eyes, o/m, kid body & legs, bsk arms, 19", EX 600.00
SkHd, Oriental, o/m, JDK/Kestner, 14" 4,600.00
SkHd, pnt eyes, JDK/3 4/0, 8" 625.00
Trn ShHd, brn eyes, o/m, orig wig, kid body, 22", EX 750.00
Trn ShHd, Kidoline w/bsk ½-arms, o/c eyes, G/MIG, 16" 525.00
10, SkHd, bsk ShPl, c/m, 21" 2,900.00
10, SkHd, o/m mouth w/2 teeth, JDK/MIG, 12" 575.00
10/G, SkHd, c/m, JDK, 1912, 12" 600.00
1070, SkHd, o/m, G11/237 15/JDK Jr 1914 HILDA/GES, 16" ..3,600.00
11, SkHd, pnt eyes to side, o/c mouth, JDK/MIG, 11" 550.00
12, SkHd, 5-pc baby, o/c eyes, o/m/2 teeth, JDK/MIG, 15" 525.00
13, SkHd, o/m, JDK/MIG, 18" 700.00
143, ShHd, jtd compo, o/c eyes, o/m, mohair wig, 14", EX 1,000.00
143, ShHd, kid w/bsk ½-arms, o/m, 17" 1,300.00
143, ShHd, kid w/bsk ½-arms, o/m/teeth, 12" 700.00
145, ShHd, kid w/bsk ½-arms, o/c mouth, 15" 1,500.00
145, SkHd, c/m, MI/O/G/18, 14" 1,700.00
145, SkHd, c/m, 143/4/0/JDK, 11" 325.00
146, SkHd, swivel, on ShPl, o/m, JDK, 18" 825.00
147, trn ShHd, o/m, JDK, 25" 900.00
148, ShHd, kid w/bsk ½-arms, o/m, 7 1/2, 18" 500.00
148, ShHd, kid w/bsk ½-arms, o/m, 7 1/2, 21" 700.00
150, bsk, bl o/c eyes, o/m/4 teeth, mohair wig, RpC, 9" 550.00
150.1, bsk, Kestner seal on body, 8" 500.00
154, SkHd/ShHd, kid w/bsk ½-arms, o/m/teeth, DEP, 14" 650.00
154, SkHd/ShHd, kid w/bsk ½-arms, o/m/teeth, DEP, 17" 725.00
154, SkHd/ShHd, kid w/bsk ½-arms, o/m/teeth, DEP, 20" 800.00
154, SkHd/ShHd, kid w/bsk ½-arms, o/m/teeth, DEP, 21½" 750.00
154, SkHd/ShHd, kid w/bsk ½-arms, o/m/teeth, DEP, 26" 950.00
16, SkHd, o/m, JDK/MIG, 21" 650.00
16/GES#1, ShHd, o/c mouth, molded boy's hair, 16" 3,200.00
167, SkHd, jtd compo, o/m, p/e, F 1/2/MI6 1/2/G, 16" 675.00
167, SkHd, jtd compo, o/m, p/e, F 1/2/MI6 1/2/G, 20" 800.00
168, SkHd, o/m, MID/G7, 26" 950.00
169, SkHd, jtd compo, o/c eyes, c/m, B 1/2/BI6 1/2G, 16" 2,400.00
169, SkHd, jtd compo, o/c eyes, c/m, B 1/2/BI6 1/2G, 18" 2,700.00
171, SkHd, jtd compo, o/c eyes, o/m, 'Daisy,' F/M110, 15" 600.00
171, SkHd, jtd compo, o/c eyes, o/m, 'Daisy,' F/M110, 18" 700.00
171, SkHd, jtd compo, o/c eyes, o/m, 'Daisy,' F/M110, 22" 800.00
171, SkHd, jtd compo, o/c eyes, o/m, 'Daisy,' F/M110, 32" 1,300.00
180 12/Ox/Crown seal, SkHd, o/m, 16" 575.00
201, ShHd, celluloid on kid, o/m, set eyes/lashes, JDK, 19" 685.00
211, bent limbs, o/c eyes, o/m, orig mohair wig, 3DK, 12" 525.00
215, SkHd, jtd compo, fur eyebrows, o/m, MI9/GJDK, 21" 925.00
217A/Kestner, bsk, googly pnt eyes, c/m smile, 12" 4,600.00
221, c/m smile, googly eyes, wig, jtd compo, JDK, 15" 5,200.00
221/GES/GESCH, SkHd, googly eyes, c/m smile, G/JDK, 21" ..8,600.00
235, toddler, kid body, 16" 750.00
241, character, SkHd, o/c eyes, JDK, OC, 22" 5,900.00
245, SkHd, 5-pc baby, G/MIG/11/JDK Jr/1914 Hilda, 14" 3,300.00
245, SkHd, 5-pc baby, G/MIG/11/JDK Jr/1914 Hilda, 17" 3,800.00
257, SkHd, 5-pc baby, o/m, G/JDK, 10" 485.00
257, SkHd, 5-pc baby, o/m, G/JDK, 16" 700.00
257, SkHd, 5-pc baby, o/m, G/JDK, 20" 985.00
257, SkHd, 5-pc baby, o/m, G/JDK, 24" 1,500.00
260, flirty-eyed toddler, OC, 16" 1,800.00
7 1/2/B, ShHd, kid w/bsk ½-arms, o/c eyes, o/m/teeth, 14" 450.00

Lenci

Eleanora Scavani, separated from her husband who was in the service of Italy during WWI, found herself painfully alone after the death of her baby. With her brother as her partner, this talented artist began designing lovely felt-covered dolls with beautiful hand-painted features. These dolls became her children, and she regarded them as a tribute to her lost daughter.

Following the war, her husband returned and joined the firm as a partner. The Lenci firm (a name he used as a term of endearment for his wife) soon became well-known in the doll-making industry. Great care was taken in every detail. Characteristics of Lenci dolls include seamless, steam-molded felt heads, quality clothing, childishly plump bodies, and painted eyes that glance to the side. Fine mohair wigs were used, and the middle and fourth fingers were sewn together. Look for the factory stamp on the foot, though paper labels were also used. Dolls under 10" are known as mascots and usually sell for $125.00 to $150.00. The Lenci factory continues today, producing dolls of the same high quality.

Boy, pnt eyes, side-part hair, OC, 18" **1,600.00**
Boy, pouty mouth, pnt eyes, orig wig, OC, 17" **1,600.00**
Child, lg pnt eyes, mohair wig, bow in hair, OC, 15" **950.00**
Chinaman, brn pnt eyes, w/opium pipe, 1920s, 12½", M **1,650.00**
Christopher Robin, appl ears & mohair wig, OC, 17" **800.00**
Clown, pnt eyes, orig wig, OC, 18" **1,600.00**
Girl, brn eyes, tightly curled mohair wig, all orig, 17" **1,400.00**
Glass eyes, orig wig, OC, 17" **2,600.00**
Indian, brn pnt eyes, orig wig, OC, 17" **3,700.00**
Indian lady w/papoose, brn pnt eyes, jtd, OC, 18" **4,000.00**
Mascotte, pnt eyes, jtd, OC, 5" **250.00**
Shirley Temple type, pnt eyes, orig wig, OC, 28" **2,500.00**
Surprise eyes, very rnd pnt eyes, 'O'-shaped mouth, OC, 15" ..**1,500.00**

Madame Alexander

Beatrice Alexander founded the Alexander Doll company in 1923 using a lovely doll that was designed after her daughter Mildred. With the help of her three sisters, the company prospered; and by the late 1950s there were three factories with over six hundred employees making Madame Alexander dolls. The company still produces these lovely dolls today.

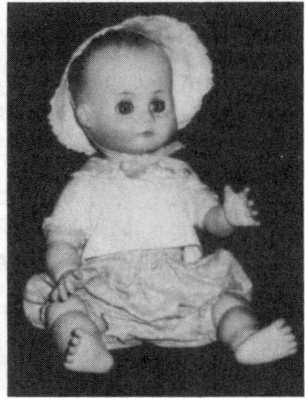

Kathy Tears, vinyl with painted hair, sleep eyes, open mouth/nurser, 1958, 15", M, $125.00.

Active Miss, hp, Violet/Cissy, 1954 only, 18" 875.00
Agatha, hp, Wendy Ann, 1953-54, blk top & floral gown, 8" .1,200.00

Alaska, Americana Series, Maggie, 1990, 8" 56.00
Alexander-kins, basic doll, str leg walker, 1955, 8" 200.00
Alexander-kins, Easter, hp, str leg non-walker, 1955, 8" 1,000.00
Alice in Wonderland, compo, Tiny Betty, 1930s, 7" 245.00
Altar Boy, hp, Americana Series, 1991, 8" 60.00
Amish Girl, hp, bend knee, Wendy Ann, 1966-69, 8" 400.00
Annabelle, hp, Maggie, 1951-52 only, 15" 475.00
Annie Laurie, compo, Wendy Ann, 1937, 14" 700.00
Armenia, Wendy Ann, 1989-90, 8" 52.00
Austria Girl, hp, str legs, Wendy Ann, mk Alex, 1973-75, 8" 60.00
Babs, hp, Maggie, 1949, 20" 650.00
Baby Lynn, cloth/vinyl, 1973-76, 20" 100.00
Baby Sister, cloth/vinyl, Mary Mine, 1977-79, 20" 75.00
Ballerina, compo, Little Betty, 1935-41, 9" 300.00
Ballerina, hp, bend knee, Wendy Ann, pk, 1962-72, 8" 200.00
Beauty Queen, hp, Cissette, 1961 only, 10" 225.00
Belle of the Ball, Portrette Series, Cissette, 1989 only, 10" 75.00
Betty Blue, str leg, Storybook Series, Maggie, 1987-88, 8" 60.00
Brazil, hp, str leg, Wendy Ann, mk Alex, 1973-75, 8" 60.00
Bride, compo, Wendy Ann, 1935-43, 18" 425.00
Bride, hp, Cissette, 1957-63, 10" 245.00
Bridesmaid, compo, Wendy Ann, 1939-44, 18" 450.00
Butch, compo/cloth, 1942-46, 12" 150.00
Camille, compo, Wendy Ann, 1938-39, 21" 2,000.00
Carmen, compo, Wendy Ann, 1937-40, 13" 465.00
Caroline, vinyl, 1961-62 only, 16" 300.00
Caroline Harrison, Presidents' Ladies, 1985-87 ....90.00
China, compo, Tiny Betty, 1936-40, 7" 250.00
Cinderella, compo, Princess Elizabeth, Sears, 1939, 14" 400.00
Cissette, hp, 1947-63, street dress, 11" 225.00
Clarabelle Clown, 1952-53, 19" 350.00
Country Christmas, Classic Series, Mary Ann, 1991, 14" 132.00
Cowgirl, hp, bend knee, Wendy Ann, 1967-79, 8" 350.00
Cuddly, cloth, 1942-44, 10½" 325.00
Czechoslovakia, compo, Tiny Betty, 1935-37, 7" 235.00
Daisy, Portrette Series, Cissette, 1987-89, 10" 85.00
December, Classic Series, Mary Ann, 1989 only, 14" 95.00
Dionne Quint, compo, toddler, 1937-38, 14" 425.00
Drum Majorette, hp, Wendy Ann, 1955 only, 7½" 900.00
Egypt, str leg, Wendy Ann, 1986-89, 8" 80.00
Elise, hp/vinyl, jtd ankles/knees, bouffant hair, 1963, 18" 250.00
Eliza, Classic Series, Louisa, 1991, 14" 155.00
Ellen Wilson, Presidents' Ladies, Louisa, 1988 ....85.00
Emily Dickinson, Classic Series, Mary Ann, 1989 only, 14" 90.00
Eva Lovelace, compo, Tiny Betty, 1935 only, 7" 245.00
Fairy Princess, compo, Wendy Ann, 1939-42, 15" 650.00
Fairy Queen, compo, Wendy Ann, 1940-46, 18" 900.00
Fashions of the Century, hp, Margaret, 1954-55, 18" 2,700.00
Florence Nightingale, Classic Series, 1986-87, 14" 700.00
Flower Girl, hp, Cissy, 1954 only, 18" 425.00
French Flower Girl, hp, Wendy Ann, 1956 only, 8" 650.00
Funny, cloth, 1963-77, 18" 55.00
Garden party, hp, Margaret, 1953 only, 18" 1,400.00
Geranium, early vinyl toddler, 1953, red dress/hat, 9" 95.00
Godey, hp, Glamour Girl Series, Maggie, 1953 only, 18" 1,400.00
Goldilocks, hp, Maggie, 1951 only, 18" 950.00
Grandma Jane, plastic/vinyl, Mary Ann, 1970-72, 14" 285.00
Gretel, compo, Tiny Betty, 1935-42, 7" 275.00
Groom, hp, Wendy Ann, 1953-55, 7½" 425.00
Hansel, hp, Margaret, 1948 only, 18" 675.00
Hiawatha, hp, Americana Series, Wendy Ann, 1967-69, 8" 365.00
Honeybun, 1951-52 only, 18" 120.00
Hyacinth, vinyl, toddler, 1953 only, bl dress/hat, 9" 95.00
Ida McKinley, Presidents' Ladies, Louisa, 1988 ....85.00

Indian, hp, bend-knee walker, Wendy Ann, 1965, 8" 365.00
Indian Boy, hp, bend knee, Wendy Ann, 1966 only, 8" 365.00
Isolde, Opera Series, Mary Ann, 1985-86 only, 14" 75.00
Italy, hp, str leg, mk Alex, 1973-75, 8" 60.00
Jacqueline Kennedy, Presidents' Ladies, Mary Ann, 1989-90, 14" 90.00
Jane Pierce, Presidents' Ladies, Mary Ann, 1982-84 ....95.00
Janie, toddler, 1964-66 only, 12" 300.00
Jasmine, Portrette Series, Cissette, 1987-88, 10" 85.00
Judy, compo, Wendy Ann, 1945-57, 21" 2,300.00
June Bride, compo, Portrait Series, 1939, 1946-47, 21" 2,000.00
Kate Greenaway, compo, Tiny Betty, 1938-43, 7" 285.00
Kathy Baby, vinyl, rooted or molded hair, 1954-56, 21" 100.00
Kelly, hp, Lissy, 1959 only, 12" 450.00
Kitten Kries, cloth/vinyl, 1967 only, 20" 85.00
Korea, hp, bend knee, Wendy Ann, 1968-70, 8" 450.00
Lady in Waiting, hp, Wendy Ann, 1955 only, 8" 1,400.00
Laurie of Little Men, hp, str leg, wht face, 1985-97, 8" 50.00
Lazy Mary, compo, Tiny Betty, 1936-38, 7" 275.00
Lila Bridesmaid, compo, Tiny Betty, 1938-40, 8" 265.00
Little Angel, latex/vinyl, 1950-57, 9" 145.00
Little Bo Peep, compo, Little Betty/Wendy Ann, 1936-40, 11" .325.00
Little Colonel, compo, c/m, Betty, 1935, 8½-9" 500.00
Little Madeline, hp, Madeline, 1953-54, 8" 525.00
Little Minister, hp, Wendy Ann, 1957 only, 8" 1,900.00
Little Southern girl, hp, Wendy Ann, 1953 only, 8" 975.00
Little Women, cloth, 1930-36, 16", ea 575.00
Little Women, hp, Margaret, 1947-56, 14-15", ea 425.00
Lively Kitten, knob makes limbs & head move, 1962-63, 18" 125.00
Lucy Bride, hp, Margaret, 1949-50, 14" 425.00
Madelaine Du Bain, compo, c/m, Wendy Ann, 1937, 11" 465.00
Maggie, hp, 1949-53, 18" 685.00
Maggie Teenager, hp, 1951-53, 18" 500.00
Maid of Honor, compo, Wendy Ann, 1940-44, 18" 700.00
Margaret O'Brien, compo, 1946-48, 24" 1,300.00
Margot, hp, Cissette, 1961 only, formal gown, 11" 400.00
Maria from Sound of Music, in sailor suit, 17" 400.00
Marlo Thomas, plastic/vinyl, Polly, 1967 only, 17" 600.00
Marm Liza, compo, Wendy Ann, 1938, 1946, 21" 2,300.00
Mary Ellen Playmate, plastic/vinyl, Mary Ann, 1965 only, 14" ..300.00
Mary Mine, cloth/vinyl, 1977-89, 21" 125.00
Mary Todd Lincoln, Presidents' Ladies, Louisa, 1982-84 ....275.00
Melanie, Cissette, 1959, pk tiered skirt, 10" 450.00
Melanie, hp, Wendy Ann, 1955-56, 8" 1,200.00
Mexico, compo, Tiny Betty, 1936, 7" 265.00
Michael, plastic/vinyl, Janie, 1969 only, 11" 365.00
Mistress Mary, compo, Tiny Betty, 1937-41, 7" 265.00
Mother Hubbard, Storyland Series, Wendy Ann, 1988-89, 8" 60.00
Muffin, cloth, 1966 only, 19" 95.00
Natasha, Jacqueline, #2255, 1989-90, 21" 375.00
Norwegian, compo, Tiny Betty, 1936-40, 8" 265.00
Oliver Twistail, cloth/felt, 1930s 700.00
Penny, cloth/vinyl, 1951 only, 34" 450.00
Peter Pan, hp, Margaret, 1953-54, 15" 950.00
Pip, cloth, Dickens character, early 1930s 800.00
Pollyana, rigid vinyl, Marybel, 1960-61, mk 1958, 16" 425.00
Portugal, hp, bend knee, Wendy Ann, 1968-72, 8" 125.00
Prince Charles, hp, Wendy Ann, 1957 only, 8" 825.00
Princess Elizabeth, compo, Tiny Betty, 1937-39, 7" 300.00
Princess Margaret Rose, hp, Margaret, 1949-53, 18" 775.00
Pussy Cat, Blk, reintroduced 1991, 14" 70.00
Queen, Elise, 1963 only, wht gown, 18" 750.00
Queen, hp, 1955 only, scarlet velvet robe, 8" 950.00
Red Boy, hp, bend knee, Wendy Ann, 1972, 8" 135.00
Red Riding Hood, hp, bend knee, 1965-72, 8" 135.00

Renoir, compo, Wendy Ann, 1946-46, 21" 2,200.00
Roller Skating, hp, Wendy Ann, 1953-55, 8" 500.00
Romeo, compo, Wendy Ann, 1949, 18" 1,400.00
Rosamund Bridesmaid, hp, Margaret, 1951 only, 15" 685.00
Rosebud, cloth/vinyl, 1952-53, 19" 150.00
Rosy, Mary Ann, 1988-90, 14" 70.00
Rumania, hp, bend knee, Wendy Ann, 1968-72, 8" 135.00
Sailorette, hp, Portrette Series, Cissette, 1988 only, 10" 85.00
Sandy McHare, cloth/felt, 1930s 650.00
Sarah Bernhardt, #2249, 1987 only, 21" 250.00
Scarlett O'hara, compo, Wendy Ann, 1939-46, 18" 1,100.00
Scarlett O'hara, hp/vinyl, Elise, 1963 only, 18" 900.00
School Girl, compo, Tiny Betty, 1936-43, 7" 285.00
Scots Lass, hp, bend-knee walker, Wendy Ann, 1963 only, 8" ...250.00
September, Classic Series, Mary Ann, 1989 only, 14" 80.00
Smarty, plastic/vinyl, 1962-63, 12" 365.00
Smiley, cloth/vinyl, Happy, 1971 only, 20" 265.00
Snow White, Walt Disney, limited edition, 1990, 12" 250.00
Soldier, compo, Wendy Ann, 1943-44, 14" 750.00
Sonja Henie, compo, Little Betty, 1940-41, 9" 400.00
South American, compo, Tiny Betty, 1938-43, 7" 300.00
Southern Girl, compo, Wendy Ann, 1940-43, 14" 475.00
Spanish Girl, hp, str leg, wht face, 1985, 8" 55.00
Suellen, compo, Wendy Ann, 1937-38, 17" 1,000.00
Sugar Tears, vinyl baby, Honey Bea, 1964 only, 12" 95.00
Suzy, plastic/vinyl, Janie, 1970 only, 12" 350.00
Sweet Tears, vinyl, 1965-74, 9" 45.00
Tiny Betty, compo, 1935-42, 7" 285.00
Tom Sawyer, hp, Storybook Series, Maggie Mixup, 1989-90, 8" ..85.00
Topsy-Turvy, compo, Tiny Betty heads, 1935 only 165.00
Turkey, hp, bend knee, Wendy Ann, 1968-72, 8" 125.00
Union Officer, Scarlett Series, Nancy Drew, 1990-91, 12" 80.00
Victoria, compo, Wendy Ann, 1939, 1941, 21" 2,200.00
Vietnam, hp, Wendy Ann, 1969-69, 8" 350.00
Violetta, Cissette, 1987-88, 10" 85.00
Wendy Ann, compo, 1935-48, 15" 325.00
Wendy Bride, compo, Wendy Ann, 1944-45, 22" 325.00
Yolanda, Brenda Starr, 1965 only, 12" 325.00

Papier-Mache

Clown, pnt features, o/c mouth, molded hair or wig, 12" 385.00
French, bald ShHd, pnt curls at face, bamboo teeth, RpC, 21" ..1,800.00
German, molded hair, pnt eyes, c/m, 1870s-1900s, RpC, 21" 500.00
German, ShHd, brn pnt eyes, molded hair, leather body, RpC, 7" .175.00
German, ShHd, brn pnt eyes, sausage curls, RpC, 8¼", EX 200.00
German, ShHd, brn pnt eyes, short curls, leather body, 7½" 200.00
German, ShHd, molded hair, pnt eyes, leather body, 11", EX 465.00
German, ShHd, wooden limbs, kid body, RpC, 10½", EX 550.00
German character, glass eyes, c/m, jtd, RpC, 15" 1,000.00
Greiner 1858-type ShHd, pnt eyes, sausage curls, RpC, 16", EX ...700.00
Motschmann type, glass eyes, c/m, wood & twill body, RpC, 15" .725.00
Pre-Greiner ShHd, bl set eyes, curly hair, cloth body, 20" 600.00
ShHd, molded beehive hair, cloth body/wood legs, OC, 10¼" ...800.00
Trn ShHd, solid dome, glass eyes, c/m, cloth body, RpC, 16" 650.00
1920s & later, cloth body, orig wig, RpC, 9" 90.00

Parian

Bald head, solid dome, w/wig, 1850s, RpC, 13" 775.00
Bsk, kid body, parian arms, pnt eyes w/red liner, 14" 450.00
Fancy hairstyle w/molded flowers/etc, cloth body, RpC, 18" ...1,800.00
German, ShHd, pnt eyes, c/m, p/e, molded hair, RpC, 24", EX ..550.00
Man or boy, part in hair, cloth body, RpC, 16" 900.00

Man or boy w/molded hat, RpC, 10" **2,000.00**
Molded braid wrapped around head, pnt eyes, p/e, RpC, 18" ..**1,400.00**
Molded head band, pnt eyes, p/e, called Alice, RpC, 13" **385.00**
Molded necklace or jewels, glass eyes, p/e, RpC, 18" **1,900.00**
Plain w/no decor in hair on on shoulders, 15" **350.00**
Swivel neck, glass eyes, cloth body, RpC, 18" **3,000.00**

Schoenhut

Albert Schoenhut left Germany in 1866 to go to Pennsylvania to work as a repairman for toy pianos. He eventually applied his skills to wooden toys and later designed an all-wood doll which he patented on January 17, 1911. These uniquely jointed dolls were painted with enamels and came with a metal stand. Some of the later dolls had stuffed bodies, voice boxes, and hollow heads; some were made with heads of imitation bisque. These innovations influenced the development of the popular Bye-Lo Baby which was introduced in 1924. Due to the changing economy and fierce competition, the company closed in the mid-1930s.

Maggie (missing a hand, one foot replaced) and Jigs of Bringing Up Father, original clothes, rare, 9" and 7", VG, $450.00 each.

Baby, bent limbs, decal eyes, o/c mouth, pnt hair, RpC, 16" **765.00**
Baby, bent limbs, pnt decal eyes, RpC, 12" **550.00**
Baby, regular body, pnt decal eyes, wig, 16" **825.00**
Boy, jtd, crazed face, 17", G **550.00**
Cap molded to head, RpC, 14" **2,500.00**
Child character, intaglio eyes, o/c mouth, wig, RpC, 14" **1,700.00**
Child w/cvd hair, comb mks, RpC, 21" **2,750.00**
Compo, molded curly hair, Patsy-style body, 1924, RpC, 14" **600.00**
Dolly face, decal eyes, o/c mouth w/teeth, 1915-30, RpC, 14" **775.00**
Girl, bl eyes, o/c mouth w/4 teeth, jtd, 15", G **800.00**
Girl w/cvd hair, molded ribbon, c/m, RpC, 14" **2,450.00**
Girl w/cvd hair, pouty mouth, RpC, 17" **2,650.00**
Man w/cvd hair, RpC, 19" **3,000.00**
Pouty boy, pnt hair, jtd, pnt touched up, 14", G **375.00**
Sleep eyes, o/c mouth w/teeth, RpC, 22" **1,500.00**
Sleep eyes, o/m w/teeth, OC, 14" **1,350.00**
Toddler, RpC, 15" **850.00**
Tootsie Wootsie, molded/pnt hair, o/c mouth w/teeth, RpC, 12" .**1,900.00**
Walker, pnt hair, bl eyes, c/m, spring-jtd, 16", VG **750.00**
Walker, 1-pc legs, pnt eyes, o/c or c/m, RpC, 15" **900.00**

SFBJ

By 1895 Germany was producing dolls of good quality at much lower prices than the French dollmakers because of lower wages in German factories. This was a serious threat to the French companies, and in a supreme effort to save the doll industry, several leading French manufacturers united to form one large company in the hope they could combine their strengths to save the French market. Bru, Raberry and Delphieu, Pintel and Godshaux, Fleischman and Bodel, and Jumeau united to form the company today known as SFBJ. Their dolls did well

while Germany was otherwise occupied with WWII, but after the war German doll production proved to be too strongly competitive, and SFBJ closed in 1958.

Bebe Parisiana, bsk head, c/m, inset eyes, 1902, 16" **2,600.00**
Celestine, bsk SkHd on papier-mache, o/m, inset eyes, 18" **900.00**
SkHd, jtd papier-mache/wood body, o/m, o/c eyes, 30" **1,600.00**
Tete Jumeau, p/e, o/m, o/c eyes/lashes, 18" **1,600.00**
Tete Jumeau, p/e, o/m w/teeth, o/c eyes, jtd wrists, 22" **2,000.00**
15, o/c eyes, o/m w/teeth, wood/compo body, RpC, 15", EX ...**1,650.00**
20, molded ptd shoes & eyes, 5-pc body, Paris/12, 10" **365.00**
203, 1900 bsk head on compo, o/c mouth, inset eyes, 20" **3,000.00**
215, bsk swivel on compo, c/m, inset eyes, 15" **2,000.00**
223, bsk, closed dome, o/m w/8 teeth, molded hair, 17" **2,000.00**
227, brn swivel closed dome head, animal skin wig, 15" **2,300.00**
227, brn swivel closed dome head, animal skin wig, 18" **2,500.00**
227, closed dome, o/m, inset eyes, pnt hair, 15" **2,100.00**
228, toddler, papier-mache body, c/m, inset eyes, 16" **2,200.00**
229, compo w/swivel head, o/c mouth, inset eyes, 18" **5,000.00**
229, wood walker, o/c mouth, inset eyes, 18" **4,000.00**
230, compo walker, p/e, o/m, inset eyes, 16" **1,600.00**
230, SkHd, p/e, o/m, o/c eyes, 23" **2,400.00**
235, closed dome, molded hair, o/c mouth & eyes, 16" **1,700.00**
235, closed dome, molded hair, o/c mouth & eyes, 8" **500.00**
236, laughing Jumeau, o/m, o/c eyes, dbl chin, 12" **1,300.00**
236, laughing Jumeau, o/m, o/c eyes, dbl chin, 17" **1,800.00**
236, laughing Jumeau, o/m, o/c eyes, dbl chin, 20" **2,200.00**
236, laughing Jumeau, o/m, o/c eyes, dbl chin, 22" **2,300.00**
238, compo w/swivel head, o/m, inset eyes, Paris 6, 15" **3,600.00**
239, Poulbot, c/m, street urchin, red wig, 14" **10,000.00**
239, Poulbot, c/m, street urchin, red wig, 17" **13,000.00**
245, boy, o/c mouth, lg glass eyes, googly, pnt shoes, 12" **2,600.00**
245, boy, o/c mouth, lg glass eyes, googly, pnt shoes, 8" **1,400.00**
247, toddler, o/c mouth/2 inset teeth, 16" **2,400.00**
247, toddler, o/c mouth/2 inset teeth, 20" **2,900.00**
247, toddler, o/c mouth/2 inset teeth, 24" **3,200.00**
247, Twirp, SkHd, o/c mouth & eyes/2 teeth, 21" **3,000.00**
251, toddler, 25" **2,600.00**
252, pouty, c/m, inset eyes, papier-mache body, 11" **2,800.00**
252, pouty, c/m, inset eyes, papier-mache body, 18" **6,200.00**
252, pouty, c/m, inset eyes, papier-mache body, 22" **7,800.00**
257, 1900 toddler, o/c mouth, inset eyes, 16" **2,500.00**
266, character, bsk head, closed dome, o/c mouth, 20" **4,200.00**
301, bsk SkHd on compo, o/m, inset eyes, 16" **725.00**
301, bsk SkHd on compo, o/m, inset eyes, 22" **1,200.00**
301, bsk SkHd on compo, o/m, inset eyes, 24" **1,400.00**
301, bsk SkHd on compo, o/m, inset eyes, 28" **1,700.00**
301, bsk SkHd on compo, o/m, inset eyes, 30" **1,900.00**
60, French WWI nurse, 5-pc body, SFBJ/13/0, 8½" **475.00**
60, kiss-blower, cryer/walker, 22" **2,300.00**
60, o/m w/teeth, o/c eyes, jtd body & wrists, 25½" **950.00**
60, SkHd, compo w/str legs, o/m, curved arms, 15" **650.00**
60, SkHd, papier-mache/compo, plunger cryer, o/m, 1-pc, 11" ...**575.00**

Shirley Temple

Bsk, Japan, 7½" **265.00**
Compo, 11", cowboy outfit, orig pin, EX **825.00**
Compo, 13", mk #1/13 on head & bk, 1934, OC **650.00**
Compo, 13", o/c eyes, o/m, orig wig, Little Colonel, EX **750.00**
Compo, 13", tagged bl/wht dress w/pin, 1930s, all orig **650.00**
Compo, 16", o/c eyes, o/m, handmade clothes, 1936, EX **485.00**
Compo, 16", red dotted dress, velvet coat/hat, all orig **675.00**

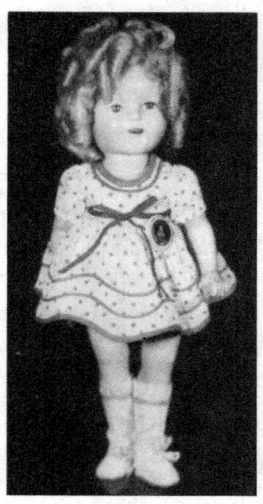

Composition, 17", Stand Up and Cheer, all original except shoes and wig, 1934, $725.00.

Compo, 18", o/c eyes, o/m, jtd, mohair wig, Ideal, '30s, VG 725.00
Compo, 18", o/c eyes, o/m, orig wig, RpC 500.00
Compo, 20", designed by Mollye, all orig, 1933 ....865.00
Compo, 20", tagged clothes, all orig, orig box 1,200.00
Compo, 25", red cotton dress, OC, 1935 ....1,000.00
Vinyl, 12", gr/wht dress, slip, complete, Ideal, 1957, MIB 200.00
Vinyl, 12", velveteen dress, rpl shoes, 1959 ....185.00
Vinyl, 15", flirty eyes, orig clothes, 1952, M 265.00
Vinyl, 15", Heidi outfit, w/pin & tag, 1957 ....300.00
Vinyl, 15", Rebecca, Ideal 300.00
Vinyl, 17", Heidi outfit, w/pin, MIB 400.00
Vinyl, 36", RpC, 1960 ....1,200.00
Vinyl, 8", Stowaway, Ideal, 1982 ....30.00

Simon and Halbig

Simon and Halbig was a large German doll firm that operated from ca 1870 until the 1930s. They were a popular supplier of bisque heads to French dollmakers of the 1870s and '80s. This company made dolls for such famous companies as Gimbel Bros., Jumeau, Kammer and Reinhardt, as well as many others. Halbig became the sole owner of the company in 1895 but did not register 'S&H' as his trademark until ten years later.

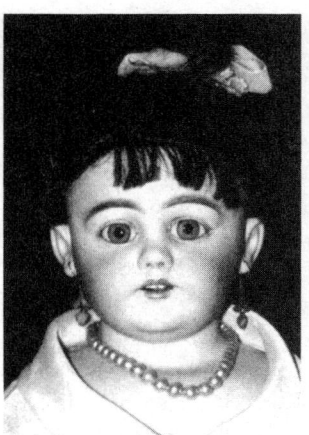

S&H 12/1010 DEP, shoulder head on adult-type kid body with bisque forearms, open mouth, pierced ears, 26", $825.00.

AW, SkHd, o/m, SH/13, 21" 850.00
Baby Blanche, SkHd, o/m baby, S&H, 16" 800.00

Baby Blanche, SkHd, o/m baby, S&H, 21" 950.00
CM Bergmann, SkHd, o/m, Simon & Halbig, 3 ½, 18" 625.00
CM Bergmann, SkHd, o/m, 1895, Halbig/S&H5, 30" 1,300.00
CM Bergmann, SkHd, o/m, 1897, S&H6, 12" 350.00
CM Bergmann, SkHd, o/m w/teeth, Simon & Halbig, RpC, 32" .1,500.00
Elenore, SkHd, o/m, CMB/Simon & Halbig, 18" 650.00
G68, SkHd, flirty eyes, 1908, S&H/K*R, 16" 550.00
Handwerck, SkHd, o/m, G/Halbig, 4, 26" 850.00
Handwerck, SkHd, o/m, o/c eyes, rpt jtd body, RpC, 33" 1,400.00
Handwerck, SkHd, o/m, S&H, 30" 1,100.00
Handwerck, SkHd, o/m, 1893, 16" 450.00
Handwerck, SkHd, o/m, 1895, G/S&H/1, 16" 450.00
Handwerck, SkHd, o/m w/teeth, o/c eyes, p/e, RpC, 38", EX ..1,700.00
Handwerck, SkHd, o/m w/teeth, Simon & Halbig, rpl wig, 32" .1,300.00
S&H3, all bsk, c/m, inset eyes, molded-on shoes, 6" 350.00
10, SkHd, o/m, G/Halbig/S&H, 16" 600.00
10, SkHd, o/m, G/Halbig/S&H, 19" 800.00
10, SkHd, o/m, G/Halbig/S&H, 22" 900.00
10 1/2, SkHd, o/m, flirty o/c eyes, S&H, 18" 900.00
100, SkHd, o/m, Simon & Halbig/S&C/G, 15" 500.00
100, SkHd, o/m, Simon & Halbig/S&C/G, 22" 725.00
1039, SkHd, flirty bl eyes, jtd walking body, p/e, wig, 22" 995.00
1039, SkHd, o/m w/teeth, p/e, jtd arms/wrists, hh, 22" 900.00
1078, SkHd, o/m, pwt, p/e, S&H, RpC, 18½" 725.00
1159, SkHd, adult, 1905, G/Simon & Halbig/S&H7, 14" 1,300.00
1159, SkHd, adult, 1905, G/Simon & Halbig/S&H7, 18" 1,800.00
1159, SkHd, adult, 1905, G/Simon & Halbig/S&H7, 24" 2,600.00
1159, SkHd, swivel on ShPl, wood w/kid fashion, o/m, 19" 2,400.00
1160, bsk ShHd, Little Women type, cloth body, S&H, 7" 400.00
1160, Louisa May Alcott, bsk head, cloth body, 7", EX 400.00
1249 Santa, bsk head, jtd compo, o/m, o/c eyes, p/e, 20" 1,300.00
1296, SkHd, 1911, FS&Co/Simon & Halbig, 14" 525.00
1329, SkHd, o/m, olive, G/Simon & Halbig/SH, 14" 1,900.00
151, SkHd, o/c mouth, pnt eyes, S&H/1, 16" 5,000.00
156, SkHd, 1925, S&H, 18" 625.00
156, SkHd, 1925, S&H, 22" 725.00
159, SkHd, o/m, Simon & Halbig, 16" 550.00
179, SkHd, o/m, Simon & Halbig S11H DEP, 20" 700.00
282, SkHd, o/m, SH, 14" 500.00
282, SkHd, o/m, SH, 18" 650.00
282, SkHd, o/m, SH, 22" 725.00
383, SkHd, flapper body, SH, 14" 1,200.00
409, SkHd, o/m, S&H, 24" 685.00
409, SkHd, o/m, S&H, 26" 850.00
409, SkHd, o/m, S&H, 30" 1,400.00
50, SkHd, c/m, Simon & Halbig, 16" 1,800.00
530, SkHd, o/m, G/Simon & Halbig, 21" 800.00
540, SkHd, o/m, G/Halbig/S&H, 16" 600.00
540, SkHd, swivel on bsk ShPl, o/m, S&H, G, 16" 600.00
550, SkHd, o/m, Simon & Halbig/S&H, 16" 600.00
570, SkHd, o/m, Halbig S&H/G, 18" 750.00
570, SkHd, o/m, walking, head turns, G/Halbig S&H, 18" 750.00
576, SkHd, o/m, Simon & Halbig, 16" 600.00
670, SkHd, o/m, Simon & Halbig, 16" 600.00
719, SkHd, bjtd, o/m, S12H/DEP, rpl wig, RpC, 20", EX 3,000.00
719, SkHd, c/m, S&H DEP, 16" 2,300.00
719, SkHd, swivel, ShPl, c/m, S&H, DEP, 20" 3,000.00
739, SkHd, c/m, brn, S 5 H DEP, 14" 1,600.00
739, SkHd, c/m, brn, S 5 H DEP, 18" 2,800.00
739, SkHd, o/m/4 teeth, brn stationary eyes, p/e, DEP, OC, 17" .1,300.00
759, SkHd, o/m, brn, S 10 H DEP, rare, 20" 10,000.00
769, SkHd, c/m, S&H DEP, 17" 2,600.00
905, SkHd, swivel on ShPl, c/m, SH, 21" 3,000.00
908, SkHd, swivel on ShPl, c/m, SH, 16" 2,700.00

929, SkHd, c/m, S&H, DEP, 20"	3,700.00
929, SkHd, c/m, S&H, DEP, 25"	4,900.00
939, SkHd, c/m, S 11H DEP, 17"	2,700.00
939, SkHd, c/m, S 11H DEP, 23"	3,500.00
939, SkHd, o/m, o/c eyes, S16H, 30"	4,600.00
940, SkHd, closed dome, o/c mouth, S 2 H, 26"	3,600.00
940, SkHd, swivel on ShPl, o/c mouth, S 2 H, 14"	1,500.00
945, SkHd, c/m, S 2 H DEP, 16"	2,200.00
949, ShHd, o/m, o/c eyes, S 10 H, bride clothes, 19½"	2,400.00

Steiner

Jules Nicholas Steiner established one of the earliest French doll manufactories in 1855. Having been a clockmaker, he began with mechanical dolls and his patents grew to include walking and talking dolls. In 1880 he registered a patent for a doll with moving eyes. This doll could be put to sleep by turning a rod that operated a wire attached to its eyes. Though these new innovations brought much acclaim to the Steiner company, it closed around 1910 because it could not compete with the less-expensive German dolls that were flooding the market at that time.

Three-face doll, bisque head, cloth body, composition arms, marked CB (Carl Bergner), ca 1899, frilly cap and gown, 16", $2,300.00.

A Series, c/m, wire eyes, jtd, RpC, 21"	6,100.00
A Series child, c/m, o/c eyes, jtd, cb pate, RpC, 28"	8,000.00
A Series child, c/m, pwt eyes, jtd, cb pate, RpC, 10"	3,200.00
A Series child, o/m, pwt eyes, jtd, cb pate, RpC, 14"	4,200.00
B Series, c/m, pwt eyes, jtd, RpC, 22"	5,000.00
Bourgoin, c/m, pwt eyes, jtd, 1870s, RpC, 25"	7,600.00
Bourgoin, c/m, pwt eyes, 1870s, RpC, 16"	5,500.00
Bsk head/shoulders/hips, Motschmann-style body, RpC, 18"	6,800.00
C Series, c/m, rnd face, pwt eyes, RpC, 21"	7,000.00
C Series, c/m, wire eyes, jtd, RpC, 17"	5,400.00
Cryer, ShHd, o/m w/teeth, mohair wig, RpC, 18", EX	2,400.00
Le Parisian, A Series, c/m, RpC, 14"	4,000.00
Le Parisian, papier-mache/wood jtd body, c/m, p/e, RpC, 14"	4,000.00
Mechanical, key wound, o/m w/teeth, RpC, 18"	1,800.00
Pk wash over eyes, jtd, RpC, 14"	4,200.00
Unmk, early wht bsk, rnd face, jtd, o/m w/teeth, RpC, 14"	4,200.00
Wht bsk, rnd face, o/m w/teeth, jtd, unmk, RpC, 14"	4,200.00
Wire eyes, c/m, flat glass eyes, jtd, RpC, 17"	5,250.00
Wire eyes, jtd compo w/str wrists, c/m, RpC, 25"	7,600.00

Vogue

Baby Dear, OC, 1960-61, 12"	60.00
Crib Crown Easter Bunny	1,400.00
Ginny, bend knee, 8"	145.00
Ginny, hp, o/c eyes, pnt lashes, strung, OC, 8"	325.00
Ginny Hawaiian, brn-blk, OC, 8"	725.00
Ginny International, vinyl, 1977	50.00

Ginny Toddles, compo, 1948-49, 8"	265.00
Hug-A-Bye Baby, OC, 1975, 16"	25.00
Wee Imp, red wig, OC, 8"	400.00

Wax, Poured Wax

Cuno & Otto Dressel, over compo, trn ShHd, squeaker, 16"	600.00
English, bsk limbs, trn ShHd, bl o/c eyes, kid body, 26"	1,200.00
English, leather arms, cloth body, glass eyes, 1830s, 25"	2,200.00
Montanari type, trn ShHd, inset bl eyes, OC, 17"	1,400.00
Over compo, bl o/c eyes, c/m, p/e, blond wig, RpC, 17", VG	325.00
Over compo ShHd, c/m, p/e, mohair wig in braids, RpC, 10"	150.00
Over compo ShHd, cloth body, kid hands, RpC, 33", VG	2,000.00
Over compo ShHd, molded hair, glass eyes, cloth body, 27"	600.00
Over papier-mache, cloth body, glass eyes, RpC, 1880s, 20"	575.00
Over papier-mache, cloth body, glass eyes, 1880s, RpC, 17"	450.00
Over papier-mache, cloth body, wood limbs, pnt eyes, 9"	300.00
Pompadour, over papier-mache, glass eyes, wig, 23"	700.00
Poured, molded blond curls, glass eyes, c/m, fits in egg, 6"	400.00
Poured, trn ShHd, cloth body, glass eyes, 1870s, RpC, 18"	675.00
Pumpkin head w/snood, wax over wood limbs, 1850s, RpC, 26"	1,800.00
Sonneberg Taufling, over compo, Motschmann baby, wig, 11", EX	550.00

Miscellaneous

Borgfeldt, ShHd, o/c eyes, o/m, orig wig, OC, 22"	475.00
Borgfeldt #329, bsk head, o/c eyes, o/m, blond wig, RpC, 15"	300.00
Chase, hospital baby, stockinette & cloth, oil pnt, 21", M	650.00
Cuno & Otto Dressel, Dutch girl, bsk head, o/c eyes, 23", VG	475.00
Fleisher, baby doll kit No F540, complete, 11", EX in box	90.00
Gesso over wood, glass eyes, pnt torso, English, RpC, 12"	1,400.00
JE Masson/A Lenternier, Lorraine character, bsk/compo, 11¼"	575.00
Martha Chase, baby, pnt cloth head/body, 16", G+	725.00
Sasha, 'Blond Gingham,' vinyl, blond hair, EX in box	250.00
Sasha, Blk boy 'Caleb,' vinyl, all orig, 16", M	285.00
Sasha, Blk girl 'Cora,' vinyl, all orig w/tag on wrist, 16", M	285.00
Sasha, boy, 'Gregor,' rigid vinyl, OC, 16"	200.00
Sasha, wht baby, rigid vinyl, pnt features, OC, 16"	185.00
Schmitt, bsk, pwt, c/m, short face, orig wig, OC, 15"	16,000.00
Schoenau Hoffmeister, bsk headed Polynesian, 5-pc compo, 9"	475.00
Tuck Comb, cvd wood, pnt hair/eyes, pegged body, OC, 11", EX	1,000.00

Door Knockers

Door knockers, those charming precursors of the door bell, come in an intriguing array of shapes and styles. The very rare ones come from England. Cast iron examples made in this country were often produced in forms similar to the more familiar doorstop figures.

Basket of flowers, pnt CI, EX	165.00
Bronze, lion, gr patina, 6¼"	105.00
Butterfly, 3-D, CI, EX pnt, oval bk	225.00
Deco design, brass, 6½"	50.00
Dragon, tooled wrought iron, w/strike, 6½"	115.00
Eagle, brass, England	55.00
Fox, brass, England	65.00
Lady's cameo-like profile, CI, EX pnt, oval bk	140.00
Lady's hand & ball, ruffled cuff & ring, brass	75.00
Lion's head, copper	48.00
Lion's head w/ring through nose, brass, 6"	35.00
Malvolio, full figure, brass, England	78.00
Rose, full blown, long stemmed, CI, EX pnt, oval bk	265.00
Sailing ship relief, CI, EX pnt, oval bk	105.00

Scottie dog, brass, England 48.00
Sir Walter Scott bust, brass, England 78.00
Viking, full figure, brass, England 78.00
Violin, brass, England 58.00

Highlander with bagpipes, brass, marked Made in Great Britain, 6", $185.00.

Doorstops

Although introduced in England in the mid-1800s, cast iron doorstops were not made to any great extent in this country until after the Civil War. Once called 'door porters,' their function was to keep doors open to provide better ventilation. They have been produced in many shapes and sizes, both dimensional and flat backed, and in the past few years have become a popular, yet affordable collectible. While cast iron examples are the most common, brass, wood, and chalk were also used. An average price is in the $40.00 to $50.00 range, though some are valued at more than $200.00. Doorstops retained their usefulness and appeal well into the thirties.

The prices below reflect market values in the East where doorstops are now at a premium. For other areas of the country, it may be necessary to adjust prices down about 25%. In the listings below, items are assumed flat backed unless noted full figured and cast iron unless noted otherwise. For further information we recommend *Doorstops, Identification and Values*, by Jeanne Bertoia.

Key:
B&H — Bradley & Hubbard   ff — full figured

Spanish Girl, painted cast iron, 9½", NM, $225.00.

Basket of Kittens, M Rosenstein, 1932, 3 kittens, 10x7" 350.00
Beagle Pup, ff, VG pnt, 8x7½" 350.00

Bobby Blake, Hubley #46, holds teddy bear, 9½x5¼" 400.00
Boston Bulldog, Greenblatt, glass eyes, 13x5½" 300.00
Boston Terrier, w/collar, EX pnt, 9⅝x11¾" 275.00
Butler, in blk tuxedo, arms akimbo, 12½x6" 400.00
Cape Cod, Albany-Nat'l, flowers around cabin, 5¾x8¾" 125.00
Cat, recumbent, rubber, cracked glaze, 8¾x4⅜" 130.00
Cat, Sculptured Metal, 1928, Halloween style, 13x9" 225.00
Chameleon, Sherwin Williams Pnt Co, worn pnt, 1¼x8" 125.00
Cherubs, 2 holding grapes, EX pnt, 10x6⅜" 350.00
Clown, hands on knees, EX pnt, 10x4½" 500.00
Cocker Spaniel, Metalcrafters, EX pnt, wedge, 1949, 9x7" 125.00
Conestoga Wagon, #100, yel top, red wheels, 8x11" 125.00
Cottage w/Fence, Nat'l #32, floral covering, 5¾x8" 125.00
Crocodile, ff, mouth open, tail flat, 2½x12" 100.00
Crocodile, mouth open, tail up, wedge, 5¾x11½", EX 100.00
Dachshund, Taylor Cook #8, orig pnt, 1930s, 5½x7¼" 350.00
Delphinium, Hubley #490, mc flowers in basket, 8¾x7¼" 145.00
Doberman Pinscher, Hubley, ff, EX pnt, 8x8½" 275.00
Doll on Base, ff, pk dress, 5½x4⅞", EX 100.00
Duck Head, brass, 11½x9", EX 125.00
Duck w/Top Hat, walking proud, EX pnt, 7½x4¼" 250.00
Dutch Girl, Hubley #10, flower baskets, 9¼x5½" 200.00
Elephant, S-117, EX pnt, 6½x8¼" 175.00
Elephant, w/circus blanket, EX pnt, 5x8" 125.00
English Bulldog, Hubley, ff, faces right, 5⅞x8½" 125.00
Fantail Fish, Hubley #464, 3 fish swimming, 9¾x5⅞" 165.00
Fox Terrier, Hubley, ff, VG pnt, 9½x11" 175.00
French Girl, Hubley #23, yel dress, 9¼x5½" 200.00
Fruits & Birds, 2 birds eating from bowl, 1929, 6½x5½" 165.00
Geisha Girl, Hubley, ff, in kimono, 10¼x3½" 350.00
German Shepherd, Hubley, ff, faces left, 9¼x10" 125.00
Giraffe, brass, wedge, S-110, 13½x5¼" 250.00
Giraffe, Hubley, EX pnt, 12½x9" 500.00
Heron, Albany #113, EX pnt, 7½x5⅛" 125.00
Horse Jumping Fence, Eastern Specialty #79, 7⅛x11¾" 325.00
Horse on Base, rearing over dog, 7¼x8½" 150.00
Huckleberry Finn, Littco, w/stick & bucket, 12½x9½" 475.00
Hummingbird, ff, worn pnt, 4x7" 225.00
Humpty Dumpty, #661, ff, seated on wall, 4½x3½" 275.00
Jill, Hubley #226, holding pail, 8¾x5¾" 350.00
Jonquil, Hubley #534, yel flowers, EX pnt, 7x6" 125.00
Lafayette, 1 hand in side, 1 w/sword, 11⅝x6⅜" 450.00
Lambs Under Tree, recumbent pr, orig pnt, 7¼x6⅜" 250.00
Lil Red Riding Hood, Hubley #95, worn pnt, 9½x5" 425.00
Little Colonial Lady, Nat'l, brn dress, 4⅝x3⅜" 80.00
Mayflower, Eastern Specialty Co, EX pnt, 8¼x9" 125.00
Old Woman, B&H #7796, yel dress, 11x7", EX 475.00
Owl, B&H #7797, brn w/blk eyes, 15½x5" 500.00
Owl on Stump, facing left, 10x6" 225.00
Parlor Maid, Hubley #268, holding tray, 9¼x3½" 375.00
Parrot, c Jo #1289, rubber knob, EX mc, on stump, 8x3⅞" 300.00
Parrot, Nat'l, glass eye, perched, EX pnt, 10⅜x6¾" 150.00
Parrot, Taylor Cook #4, 1930, EX pnt, 10½x4⅞" 315.00
Parrot in Ring, B&H, faces right, 13¾x7¼" 215.00
Peacock, bl bird w/feathers spread, EX pnt, 6¼x6¼" 165.00
Penguin w/Top Hat, Hubley, ff, EX pnt, 10½x3¾" 290.00
Persian Cat, Hubley, ff, faces left, 8½x6½" 150.00
Peter Rabbit, Hubley #96, eating carrot, 9½x4¾" 375.00
Pirate Girl, holding sword, EX pnt, 13⅞x7¼" 475.00
Polly on Perch, Hubley #180, EX mc pnt, 8⅛x5¼" 125.00
Puppies in Basket, M Rosenstein, 1932, 3 puppies, 7x7⅜" 325.00
Rabbit by Fence, Albany, EX pnt, 6⅞x8⅛" 325.00
Reclining Cat, Nat'l, ff, legs wide, 8⅛x4" 200.00
Rose Basket, Hubley #121, EX pnt, 11x8" 145.00

Saddled Horse, ff, gray w/purple saddle, 10x11½" 200.00
Setter, Hubley, ff, on point, EX pnt, 8¾x15⅞" 165.00
Ship, Nat'l, mc sails, EX pnt, 10x12" 150.00
Shore Bird, leaf in mouth, wings spread, EX pnt, 10x6½" 265.00
Show Horse, Hubley, ff, brn w/blk mane & tail, 8½x8" 150.00
Southern Belle, Nat'l #72, bl dress, 11¼x6" 125.00
Spaniel, chain from collar, EX pnt, 9x7" 300.00
Springer Spaniel, recumbent, EX pnt, 6¾x7" 125.00
Squirrel, eating nut on logs, worn pnt, 11x9½" 250.00
Squirrel, eats nut on stump, orig pnt, 9x6⅜" 165.00
St Bernard, Hubley, ff, lying down, faces left, 3½x10½" 225.00
Stagecoach, Hubley #376, man w/2 horses, 11¼x5⅞" 175.00
Swallows, Hubley #480, facing pr, EX pnt, 8½x7½" 315.00
Tiger, Hubley #269, wht coat w/top hat, 9⅜x 4¼" 500.00
Tropical Woman, holds fruit basket on head, 12x6¼" 200.00
Turkey, strutting gobbler, EX mc pnt, 13x11" 500.00
Uncle Sam, EX pnt, arms akimbo, knees spread, 12x5½" 500.00
Warrior, B&H #7795, holding staff, 13¼x7¼" 400.00
Witch, on broom, w/bat, 7x7" 275.00
Wolfhound, Spencer, EX blk & wht pnt, wedge, 6½x3½" 165.00
Woodsman, English, w/pipe & axe, dog beside, 13¼x9" 250.00
Zinnias, Hubley #316, in vase, VG pnt, 9¾x8½" 150.00

Dorchester Pottery

Taking its name from the town in Massachusetts where it was organized in 1895, the Dorchester Pottery Company made primarily utilitarian wares, though other types of items were made as well. By 1940 a line of decorative pottery was introduced, some of which was painted by hand with scrollwork or themes from nature. The buildings were destroyed by fire in the late 1970s and the pottery was never rebuilt. In the listings that follow, the decorations described are all in cobalt unless noted.

Bowl, Blueberry, stripe on hdls, incised mk, 4x6" 125.00
Bowl, centerpiece; Scallop Shell, 3-ftd, mk, 5x14¼" 45.00
Bowl, cereal; Pine Cone, 6" 40.00
Bowl, cereal; Scroll, 6" 40.00
Bowl, clown face, mk, 5¾" 110.00
Bowl, Flower, stamped mk, 1½x6¼" 110.00
Bowl, Grape, leaves on hdls, sgn, mk, 4x6" 135.00
Bowl, Poppy (int & ext), ftd, sgn, stamp mk, 2¾x8¼" 1,325.00
Bowl, Scroll, strip decor on hdls & rim, sgn, mk, 3½x6" 100.00
Bowl, Single Scroll, sgn, stamp mk, 2¼x5¾", pr 120.00
Candy dish, Daffodil, artist sgn, incised/stamped, 6½" 175.00
Casserole, Blueberry, mk, w/lid, rare 2½-qt, 5x8½" dia, EX 90.00
Casserole, Blueberry, w/lid, mk, 1-qt, 4x6" dia 200.00
Casserole, Scroll, w/lid, mk, 5x6½" 150.00
Chambersticks, Blueberry, mk, 5½", pr 150.00
Charger, Spiral, mk, 13" dia 275.00
Coffeecup, Blueberry 22.00
Coffeecup, Pine Cone 22.00
Cookie jar, Blueberry, bl int, incised/stamped, 5-qt, 9½x10" 700.00
Creamer, Blueberry 25.00
Creamer & sugar bowl, Blueberry, stamped, 4x4½" 150.00
Creamer & sugar bowl, Dbl Scroll, stamped, 3½x3" 120.00
Cup & saucer, Blueberry cup, Swirl saucer, mk, 3x3¼", 6¼" 200.00
Mug, Bell, striped hdl, paper label, 4½x3⅜" 130.00
Mug, Blueberry, stamped mk, 2¾x3¼" 40.00
Mug, Scroll, dtd 1775 & 1975, commemorative, mk, 4½", pr 120.00
Mug, Spouting Whale, striped hdl, sgn CAH, mk, 4½x3⅜" 90.00
Plate, Blueberry, sgn, stamped mk, 10½", set of 4 ....1,200.00
Plate, Fruit, strawberries & pear, sgn, 7½", EX 100.00

Plate, Thistle, incised pattern on dk brn, stamped, 9¾" 50.00
Sugar bowl, Blueberry, w/lid 45.00
Syrup, Grape, sgn CAH, stamped, 5½x5" 140.00
Syrup, Pine Cone, overall decor, mk, 4¼x3½" 100.00
Teapot & creamer, Scroll, sgn CAH, stamped, 4½x5", 4x5" 175.00

Dorflinger

C. Dorflinger was born in Alsace, France, and came to this country when he was ten years old. When still very young, he obtained a job in a glass factory in New Jersey. As a young man, he started his own glass-works in Brooklyn, New York, opening new factories as profits permitted. During that time he made cut glass articles for many famous people including President and Mrs. Lincoln, for whom he produced a complete service of tableware with the United States Coat of Arms. In 1863 he sold the New York factories because of ill health and moved to his farm near White Mills, Pennsylvania. His health returned, and he started a plant near his home. It was there that he did much of his best work, making use of only the very finest materials. Christian died in 1915, and the plant was closed in 1921 by consent of the family. Dorflinger glass is rare and often hard to identify. Very few pieces were marked — many only carried a small paper label which was quickly discarded.

Bottle, bitters; Oval & Split, scarce 175.00
Bowl, cranberry to clear, strawberry dmns, 7" 195.00
Bowl, X-Cut Dmn & Fan, curved rim, 5" dia 160.00
Champagne, cranberry to clear, Panel & Flute, clear stem 160.00

Cut glass decanter set, fitted wooden carrying case, metal handle impressed 'Dorflinger & Sons,' 12", $550.00.

Decanter, Asserian, att, 13" 1,000.00
Decanter, fans/oval punties/panels, hdl, ped ft, 13" 625.00
Plate, cranberry to clear, Vintage, 8" 495.00
Plate, Hob & Lace, dbl miter cane, 5" 85.00
Plate, Royal pattern, 32 pyramidal hobstars in center, 9" 395.00
Puff box, Arcola, faceted finial 150.00
Punch cut, gr to clear, Star, multirayed base, clear hdl 55.00
Sherbet, Calla Lily, 4x4½" 75.00
Tumbler, cranberry to clear, Thistles allover, ftd 195.00
Whiskey, cranberry to clear, Renaissance 150.00
Wine, cranberry to clear, Renaissance 185.00
Wine, cranberry to clear, X-cut dmns & fans, tulip shape 185.00
Wine, forest gr to clear, chain of X-cut dmns, clear punties 155.00
Wine, Kalana Lily, 5", set of 6 ....90.00

Dragon Ware

Dragon ware is fairly accessible and is still being made today. The 'new' Dragon ware is distinguishible by the lack of detail in the dragon. In the older pieces, much care is given to the slipwork dragon's eyes, scales, and wings. In the new ware, the dragon is 'flat' and lacks detail.

Colors are 'primary,' referring to background color, not the color of the dragon. The primary color of a 'new' piece has more shine than the older ware. Old colors are vibrant but for the most part not shiny (except for the lustre colors). 'New' colors include green, lavender, yellow, pink, blue, pearlized, and orange as well as the classic blue/black. Old colors include orange, green, yellow, blue, pearlized, and blue/black. In addition to lustre finishes, you will find some background colors that are applied unevenly (and without shine), producing a 'cloud' effect behind the dragon.

Many Dragon ware cups have lithophanes in the bottoms, often the face of a geisha girl. Nude lithophanes are more scarce but can sometimes be found in cups and saki cups. New pieces may also have lithophanes, but they are lacking in detail and tend to be flat. Items listed below are unmarked unless noted otherwise. Our advisor for this category is Suzi Hibbard; she is listed in the Directory under California.

Box, cigarette; +2 ashtrays 30.00
Box, egg form, ftd, mk Saji, 3" 30.00
Box, ruffled lid w/gold trim, 6½x5" 45.00
Castor set, 6-pc, on 10" tray 125.00
Cookie jar, gray, jeweled eyes, Nippon 200.00
Cup & saucer, bl, child's 12.50
Cup & saucer, bl & yel w/orange dragon 15.00
Cup & saucer, demitasse; bl, no lithophane 15.00
Cup & saucer, demitasse; gray cloud, MIJ 20.00
Cup & saucer, geisha lithophane 25.00
Cup & saucer, gr, no lithophane 17.50
Cup & saucer, gr w/lustre 25.00
Cup & saucer, nude lithophane 30.00
Cup & saucer, whistling; orange, mk MIJ 25.00
Cup & saucer & pie plate, bl cloud, lithophane 40.00
Incense burner, 3" 15.00
Nappy, brn, sq, mk MIJ, 6" 25.00
Nappy, wht beads, brn rim, mk MIJ, 5" 25.00
Pitcher, mini, 1¾" 10.00
Plate, luncheon; red w/lustre, w/cup, MIJ 45.00
Plate, mk Japan, 10" 40.00
Plate, wht beads & lav rim, 6" 20.00
Plate, wht beads & lav rim, 8" 25.00
Saki cup, whistling; gray 7.50
Saki set, +6 cups w/lithophanes 35.00
Saki set, +6 cups w/nude lithophanes 45.00
Saki set, gray, bbl dispenser, 6 saki cups 75.00
Snack set, gray, teapot+cr/sug+4 cups+4 plates 175.00
Snack set, 8½" L 45.00
Spoon holder, demitasse; bl 35.00
Tea set, bl cloud, lithophanes, Kutani, 21-pc 325.00
Tea set, child's, 5-pc, pot+cr/sug+cup & saucer 40.00
Tea set, gold dragons on cobalt, sgn Shofar on pot, 15-pc 425.00
Tea set, lithophane, 15-pc 150.00
Tea set, no lithophane, 15-pc 110.00
Teapot, gold hdl, 7" 45.00
Teapot, gr, child's 15.00
Teapot, wht w/gold dragon, child's 15.00
Teapot w/stand, gray, dragon spout, MIJ 45.00
Vase, ftd, integral hdls, sm neck w/ruffled rim, Nippon, 7" 200.00
Vase, gold trim, 6" 85.00
Vase, gray, jeweled eyes, Nippon, 6" 175.00
Vase, orange, 8" 60.00
Vase, orange lustre, hdls, 9" 95.00
Vase, pearlized, 6" 45.00

Vase, red & white, 6" 30.00
Vase, slender form, 6" 50.00
Vase, 3" 15.00
Vase, 4½", pr 40.00
Watering can, orange, 3" 10.00

Dresden

The term Dresden is used today to indicate the porcelains that were produced in Meissen and Dresden, Germany, from the very early 18th century well into the next. John Bottger, a young alchemist, discovered the formula for the first true porcelain in 1708 while being held a virtual prisoner at the palace in Dresden because of the King's determination to produce a superior ware. Two years later a factory was erected in nearby Meissen with Bottger as director. There fine tableware, elaborate centerpieces, and exquisite figurines with applied details were produced. In 1731, to distinguish their product from the wares of such potters as Sevres, Worcester, Chelsea, and Derby, the Meissen company adopted their famous crossed swords trademark. During the next century, several potteries were producing porcelain in the 'Meissen style' in Dresden itself. Their wares were often marked with imitations of Meissen's crossed swords.

The Carl Theime factory produced dinnerware as well as decorative pieces in the Meissen style from 1872 until 1972. Openwork pieces were their specialty. Their mark was an intertwined 'SP' with the word Dresden below. Other companies followed suit, and in 1883 began using the crown mark along with the Dresden indication. There were several variations of this mark employed over the years. Many of these companies produced Meissen-type wares well into the 20th century. See also Meissen; Pottschappel.

Candelabra, pk & yel appl roses on wht, 10", pr 400.00
Charger, mc sm floral on wht, rtcl rim, 3 dolphin ft, 10½" 395.00
Egg dish, mc floral w/gold, 8¾" 60.00
Figurine, bird, #1154H 98.00
Figurine, couple beneath tree, man looks on, 1870s, 15" 935.00
Figurine, dancer holds ruffled skirt wide, 10x10" 475.00
Figurine, lady sits w/fan, man w/mandolin, N mk, 4x4" 275.00
Figurine, lady w/flower holds pk bonnet, ruffled skirt, 6" 265.00
Figurine, peasant & sleeping lover, lamb/kid/children/bee, 10" ..650.00

Figurine, Presentation to Grandmother, 16x24", $2,500.00.

Figurine, 3 adults (1 seated)/3 children, 16x24" 2,500.00
Plaque, Fraumerai Tantler, peasant lady, wood fr, 4¾" 300.00
Plate, courting scene, rtcl border w/gold, 9", pr 340.00

Sweetmeat dish, man (or lady) reclining, flower decor, 4", pr **300.00**

Dresser Accessories

Dresser sets, ring trees, figural or satin pincushions, manicure sets — all those lovely items that graced milady's dressing table — were at the same time decorative as well as functional. Today they appeal to collectors for many reasons. The Victorian era is well represented by repousse silver-backed mirrors and brushes and pincushions that were used to display ornamental pins for the hair, hats, and scarves. The hair receiver — similar to a powder jar but with an opening in the lid — was used to hold the lovely strands of hair retrieved from the comb or brush. These were wound around the finger and tucked in the opening to be used later for hair jewelry and pictures, many of which survive to the present day. (See Hair Weaving.)

Celluloid dresser sets were popular during the late 1800s and early 1900s. Some included manicure tools, pill boxes, and buttonhooks, as well as the basic items. Because celluloid tends to break rather easily, a whole set may be hard to find today. (See also Plastics.) With the current interest in anything Art Deco, sets from the thirties and forties are especially collectible. These may be made of crystal, Bakelite, or silver, and the original boxes just as lavishly appointed as their contents.

Dresser set, celluloid with jewels, eight-piece set, $110.00.

Box, gr glass w/HP florals, hinged lid, 3½" **105.00**
Box, lime gr glass w/HP flowers & gold, jewel on top, 3¼" **110.00**
Box, sapphire bl glass, HP flowers/horseshoe, 3¼x3¼" **145.00**
Box, tortoise shell Bakelite, Deco-style dmn shape, 6" **30.00**
Brush & comb, silver, emb florals, mk Sterling **75.00**
Hair pin, sterling, 1893 on top, 4" **35.00**
Set, mirror/brush/jar/comb, silver, emb florals, mk sterling **195.00**

Dryden

James Dryden founded Dryden Pottery in July, 1946, in Ellsworth, Kansas. For ten years Dryden produced pottery from clay dug from the hills of Ellsworth County. Pieces were cast in molds and then glazed using processes Dryden learned while studying ceramics at the University of Kansas. Glazes were produced from volcanic ash, and recipes for them were a guarded secret. James Dryden is still numbered among the few potters who possessed the secret of decorative glazing with just one firing. Ellsworth Dryden was shipped to over six hundred retail outlets in forty different states. In the 1950s Dryden sold some pottery to Van Briggle to offset losses in counter sales. When I-70 opened, taking tourist traffic away from Dry-

den's plant, James Dryden moved to Hot Springs, Arkansas, in 1956. Since the late 1960s, most of the pottery has been wheel thrown.

It is easy to recognize those pieces produced in Kansas because they were made with a dark tan clay. Arkansas pottery pieces are pure white. Almost all of the pottery is marked with the Dryden signature. Kansas pieces may also show a mold number and a paper label. Of special interest to collectors are those pieces in animal shapes (elephants, panthers, and donkeys, for instance) and those sold as souvenirs (i.e., the K.U. jug). Our advisor for this category is Ralph Winslow; he is listed in the Directory under Kansas.

Ashtray, mauve, low bells, #17A **12.00**
Ashtray, yel, #7A **8.00**
Berry set, maroon, #C2, 7-pc **60.00**
Boot, cowboy; blk, #19 ....**15.00**
Bowl, Cheyenne Wyo, brn, #40, 6½" **25.00**
Bowl, gr, #72, 7½" **16.00**
Buffalo, Abilene Kans, brn **18.00**
Candle holders, maroon, #42, pr **15.00**
Cup, coffee; brn, #60 ....**8.00**
Flowerpot, gr, #6E, 3½" **12.00**
Jug, gr, #H4 ....**18.00**
Jug, Kanopolis Lake, #H3, 3" **19.00**
Jug, roadrunner, mauve, #8, 3¾" **18.00**
Jug, Salina Kans, #H1, 3½" **18.00**
Mug, Brookville Hotel 1870, aqua, #1 ....**15.00**
Mug, Clovis NM, gr, #6 ....**15.00**
Pitcher, fish, bl, #62 ....**45.00**
Pitcher, gr, #48 ....**12.00**
Pitcher, gr, bbl form, #8P **24.00**
Pitcher, Greensburg KS, yel, #102 ....**14.00**
Pitcher, Portsmouth O, gr, #12, 3½" **17.00**
Pitcher, Salina Kans, bl, #H5 ....**16.00**
Planter, mustard, #X, 10" **15.00**
Shakers, Chapman Grain Co, brn, #70 ....**15.00**
Spoon holder, Salina Kans, yel **14.00**
Tray, mauve, #7C, 9" **27.00**
Vase, bud; mustard, #97 ....**16.00**
Vase, Ellsworth County Tourney 1953, #18 ....**15.00**
Vase, mauve, #7R **15.00**

Duncan and Miller

The firm that became known as the Duncan and Miller Glass Company in 1900 was organized in 1874 in Pittsburgh, Pennsylvania, a partnership between George Duncan, his sons Harry and James, and his son-in-law Augustus Heisey. John Ernest Miller was hired as their designer. He is credited with creating the most famous of all Duncan's glassware lines, Three Face. (See Pattern Glass.) The George Duncan and Sons Glass Company, as it was titled, was only one of eighteen companies that merged in 1891 with U.S. Glass. Soon after the Pittsburgh factory burned in 1892, the association was dissolved, and Heisey left the firm to set up his own factory in Newark, Ohio. Duncan built his new plant in Washington, Pennsylvania, where he continued to make pressed glassware in such notable patterns as Bagware, Amberette, Duncan Flute, Button Arches, and Zippered Slash. The firm was eventually sold to U.S. Glass in Tiffin, Ohio, and unofficially closed in August 1955.

In addition to the early pressed dinnerware patterns, today's Duncan and Miller collectors enjoy searching for opalescent vases in many patterns and colors, frosted 'Satin Tone' glassware, acid-etched designs, and lovely stemware such as the Rock Crystal cuttings. Milk glass was made in limited quantity and is considered a good investment. Ruby glass, Ebony (a lovely opaque black glass popular during the twenties and thirties), and, of course, the glass animal and bird figurines are all highly valued examples of the art of Duncan and Miller.

Expect to pay at least 25% more than values listed for 'color' for ruby and cobalt and as much as 50% more in the Georgian, Pall Mall and Sandwich lines. Pink, green, and amber Sandwich is worth approximately 30% more than the same items in crystal. Milk glass examples of American Way are valued up to 30% higher than color, 50% higher in Pall Mall. Add approximately 40% to listed prices for opalescent items. Etchings, cuttings, and other decorations will increase values by about 50%. For further study we recommend *The Encyclopedia of Duncan Glass*, by Gail Krause; she is listed in the Directory under Pennsylvania. Also refer to *Glass Animals and Figural Flower Frogs of the Depression Era* by Lee Garmon and Dick Spencer; they are both listed under Illinois. See also Glass Animals.

Astaire, crystal; cocktail 7.00
Canterbury, amber; bowl, berry; 5" 11.00
Canterbury, amber; goblet, water 14.00
Canterbury, amber; plate, 8" 12.00
Canterbury, bl opal; bowl, crimped, 10½" 48.00
Canterbury, crystal; ashtray, 3½x2¾" 6.50
Canterbury, crystal; basket, 8x9" 36.00
Canterbury, crystal; bowl, hdls, 6" 8.00
Canterbury, crystal; bowl, oval, 10" 19.00
Canterbury, crystal; bowl, shallow, 14" 32.00
Canterbury, crystal; celery relish, 3-part, oval, 10½" ...16.00
Canterbury, crystal; creamer & sugar bowl, lg 24.00
Canterbury, crystal; goblet, water 10.00
Canterbury, crystal; pickle dish, 8½" 12.00
Canterbury, crystal; sherbet 8.50
Canterbury, crystal; tray, 2-part, for oil/vinegar, 8" ...10.00
Canterbury, crystal; vase, cloverleaf; 4" 13.00
Caribbean, bl; bowl, 5" 35.00
Caribbean, bl; champagne 45.00
Caribbean, bl; goblet, water 40.00
Caribbean, bl; mustard 75.00
Caribbean, bl; pitcher, milk 350.00
Caribbean, bl; pitcher, water 950.00
Caribbean, bl; plate, hdls, 6" 18.00
Caribbean, bl; relish, 2-part, 6" 30.00
Caribbean, crystal; mustard, w/lid 37.50
Caribbean, crystal; punch bowl 85.00
Caribbean, crystal/amber; punch cup 5.00
First Love, crystal; candle holders, 2-light, #30, pr ...40.00
First Love, crystal; candlesticks, 2-light, #41, pr 110.00
First Love, crystal; candy dish, 3-part, flat 75.00
First Love, crystal; creamer & sugar bowl, lg 45.00
First Love, crystal; goblet, champagne 25.00
First Love, crystal; goblet, cocktail 24.00
First Love, crystal; goblet, water; 6¾" 27.00
First Love, crystal; plate, sandwich; hdls, 11" 50.00
First Love, crystal; plate, torte; #111, 13" 65.00
First Love, crystal; relish, 2-part, #115, 8" 30.00
First Love, crystal; tumbler, ftd, 5-oz 24.00
First Love, crystal; vase, cornucopia; #117, 8" 85.00
First Love, crystal; vase/urn, ftd, sq, 6½" 45.00
Grecian, crystal; urn, ring hdl, sq, ftd, 5⅜" 37.50
Indian Tree, crystal; compote, tall 45.00
Indian Tree, crystal; plate, 8½" 16.00
Indian Tree, crystal; tumbler, ftd 24.00
Language of Flowers, crystal; compote, cheese 18.50
Language of Flowers, crystal; compote, ftd 28.00
Language of Flowers, crystal; mayonnaise 27.00

Language of Flowers, crystal; relish, 2-part 35.00
Lotus, blk; bonbon, decor, ftd 17.50
Mallard, crystal; decanter 95.00
Murano, crystal; candlesticks, ftd, pr 45.00
Murano, crystal; nappy, ruffled rim, 6" 20.00
Nautilus, bl opal; jar, cigarette; w/lid 250.00
Nautilus, gr; marmalade, SP lid 65.00
Nautilus, lt bl frost; marmalade, SP spoon & lid 110.00
Nautilus, lt bl; plate, hdls, 6" 60.00
Nautilus, lt bl; relish, 3-part, oval, 9¾" 65.00
Pall Mall, crystal; swan, silver o/l, 7½" 45.00
Pall Mall, crystal; swan, 10½" 45.00
Pall Mall, crystal; swan, 3½" 30.00
Pall Mall, crystal; swan, 7½" 35.00
Pall Mall, ruby; swan, 7" 45.00
Plaza, amber; tumbler, flat, 12-oz 15.00
Plaza, crystal; goblet, cocktail 12.00
Plaza, crystal; sugar bowl, w/lid 15.00
Sandwich, amberina; plate, 8" 15.00
Sandwich, crystal; ashtray, 2¼x3½" 12.50
Sandwich, crystal; basket, loop hdl, 6½" 90.00
Sandwich, crystal; bowl, float; 11¾" 40.00
Sandwich, crystal; bowl, fruit; flared rim, 12" 50.00
Sandwich, crystal; bowl, fruit; 6" 27.00
Sandwich, crystal; box, trinket; 3¾x5" 85.00
Sandwich, crystal; cake plate, ped ft, plain rim, 13" ...85.00
Sandwich, crystal; cake plate, ped ft, rolled edge, 11½" ...145.00
Sandwich, crystal; cheese & cracker set 75.00
Sandwich, crystal; coaster 11.00
Sandwich, crystal; compote, cheese 25.00
Sandwich, crystal; creamer & sugar bowl, ind, +tray ...28.00
Sandwich, crystal; cup & saucer 20.00
Sandwich, crystal; flower bowl, 11½" 47.00
Sandwich, crystal; flower/fruit epergne, 3-pc, 12" ...235.00
Sandwich, crystal; goblet, water 15.00
Sandwich, crystal; mint dish, flat, hdl, 5" 17.50
Sandwich, crystal; nut dish, 3½" 10.00
Sandwich, crystal; parfait 24.00
Sandwich, crystal; pitcher, water; ice lip 165.00
Sandwich, crystal; plate, deviled egg 85.00
Sandwich, crystal; plate, flat edge, 13" 45.00
Sandwich, crystal; plate, ice cream; rolled edge, 12" ...50.00
Sandwich, crystal; plate, 1-hdl, 7" 18.00
Sandwich, crystal; plate, 13" 47.00
Sandwich, crystal; plate, 7" 8.00
Sandwich, crystal; plate, 8" 12.00
Sandwich, crystal; plate, 9½" 60.00
Sandwich, crystal; relish, 3-part, ring hdl 35.00
Sandwich, crystal; syrup, w/lid 85.00
Sandwich, crystal; tray, divided, oval, 7" 15.00
Sandwich, ruby; goblet, wine 30.00
Spiral Flutes, amber; bowl, flat rim, 7" 8.00
Spiral Flutes, amber; bowl, grapefruit; 6¾" 7.00
Spiral Flutes, amber; bowl, 4¼" 5.00
Spiral Flutes, amber; plate, 6" 4.00
Spiral Flutes, amber; plate, 7½" 4.00
Spiral Flutes, amber; plate, 8¼" 4.00
Spiral Flutes, amber; sugar bowl 7.00
Spiral Flutes, amber; tumbler, 5⅛" 7.00
Spiral Flutes, crystal; cigarette holder/ashtray, ftd ...27.00
Spiral Flutes, crystal; cream soup 15.00
Spiral Flutes, crystal; goblet, cocktail, yel-flash rim ...9.00
Spiral Flutes, gr; bowl, grapefruit; ftd 9.00
Spiral Flutes, gr; cigarette holder/ashtray, ftd 30.00

Spiral Flutes, gr; compote, tall 25.00
Spiral Flutes, gr; cup, ftd 10.00
Spiral Flutes, gr; nut dish, ftd, ind 14.00
Spiral Flutes, gr; pickle dish, 8½" 15.00
Spiral Flutes, gr; plate, 6" 4.00
Spiral Flutes, gr; plate, 8½" 5.00
Spiral Flutes, gr; seafood sauce cup 22.50
Spiral Flutes, gr; sweetmeat, w/lid 125.00
Sylvan, crystal; swan, 7" 40.00
Sylvan, crystal/cobalt; relish, 3-part 40.00
Teardrop, crystal; ashtray, ind 5.00
Teardrop, crystal; bowl, ftd, 11½" 35.00
Teardrop, crystal; bowl, oval, 6" 7.00
Teardrop, crystal; bowl, salad; 12" 35.00
Teardrop, crystal; bowl, 3-compartment, 6" 6.00
Teardrop, crystal; celery, 3-part 22.00
Teardrop, crystal; claret, 5½" 16.00
Teardrop, crystal; creamer, 6-oz 6.00
Teardrop, crystal; cup & saucer, demitasse 16.00
Teardrop, crystal; goblet, cocktail; ftd, w/cutting 7.00
Teardrop, crystal; ice bucket, ftd, w/monogram 30.00
Teardrop, crystal; iced tea/hi-ball, flat 15.00
Teardrop, crystal; marmalade, w/lid 37.00
Teardrop, crystal; nut dish, 2-part, hdls, 6" 10.00
Teardrop, crystal; pitcher, water; ice lip 95.00
Teardrop, crystal; relish, 12" 20.00
Teardrop, crystal; sherbet, low 8.00
Teardrop, crystal; star centerpc, etched, hdls, 10" 36.00
Teardrop, crystal; tumbler, flat, 14-oz 18.00
Teardrop, crystal; tumbler, ftd, 12-oz 11.00
Teardrop, crystal/amber; punch mug 9.00
Terrace, cobalt; plate, hdls, 5" 75.00
Terrace, crystal; bowl, 5" 12.50
Terrace, crystal; cordial 45.00
Terrace, crystal; plate, 7½" 8.50

Durand

Durand Art Glass was a division of Vineland Flint Glass Works in Vineland, New Jersey. This division was geared toward the manufacture of fine hand blown art glass in the style of Tiffany and Steuben. Lustered glass and opal glass were used as a basis to create such patterns as King Tut, Heart and Vine, Peacock Feather and Egyptian Crackle. Crystal, cased and overlay glass were used to produce cut designs. Production began in 1924 and continued until 1931. Early art glass was unmarked. Later pieces were generally signed Durand, often written across a large 'V,' all in script. The numbers that sometimes appear along with the signature indicate shape and height of the object. Owner Victor Durand employed several employees as well as the owner of the failed Quezal Art Glass and Decorating Company, which explains why early Durand is often mistaken for Quezal. Our advisor for this category is Edward J. Meschi; he is listed in the Directory under New Jersey.

Bowl, Peacock Feather, bl & wht w/gold irid ft, 3x13" 600.00
Box, King Tut, gr on ambergris cased to opal, lid, 4x5" dia 770.00
Candlesticks, bl irid w/amber base, flange rim, #2044, 3", pr 650.00
Candlesticks, gold irid, mushroom form, 3½x4½", pr 350.00
Compote, hearts/vines, lt bl on royal irid, amber base, 5x7" 1,000.00
Goblet, Peacock Feather, bl & wht w/gold irid stem & base, 7" .200.00
Jar, bl irid, yel finial, sgn, w/lid, 7" 1,350.00
Jar, dresser; amber irid cut w/flowers & stems, w/lid, 3x4½" 250.00
Lamp, King Tut, bl on orange, metal mts, 13x7" 450.00
Rose bowl, airtraps in clear, #1995-4, 4" 220.00

Tumbler, Optic, ruby, ftd, 6" 75.00
Vase, amber irid w/threading o/l, 8" 325.00
Vase, amethyst, squatty, ribbed w/flared neck, #1986, 9x10" ...300.00
Vase, bl irid, classic form, 7" 525.00
Vase, bl irid, ribbed, bulbous w/stick neck, #1974, 12" 950.00
Vase, bl irid w/threading o/l, 10" 375.00
Vase, Egyptian Crackle, gr & wht on ambergris, 9" 875.00
Vase, floral, ruby o/l cut to crystal, 6½" 575.00
Vase, gold, ftd, #1721, 6¾" 325.00
Vase, gold irid, #1968-6, 6" 375.00
Vase, gr cased to opal, gold int, wide ribs, #1710-8, 8" 1,045.00
Vase, heart & vine, opal on bl irid, 9" 850.00
Vase, heart & vine, opal on gold irid, 12" 450.00
Vase, King Tut, amber hdls, slim, flared/hipped/ftd, 12" 1,025.00
Vase, King Tut, dk bl on orange, waisted rim, #161, 10" 800.00
Vase, King Tut, gold, orange & bl on opal, 10" 700.00
Vase, King Tut, gr on amber irid, #1706-8, 8" 600.00
Vase, King Tut, silver on apple gr, ftd, 10" 900.00
Vase, Lady Gay Rose w/gold King Tut design, 8" 1,300.00
Vase, opal/amber cased to ruby, gold int, 10-rib, 9" 1,500.00
Vase, pulled feathers, bl on opal w/gold o/l threading, 9" 650.00
Vase, Spanish yel, ribbed classic form, #1710, 6" 150.00

Durant Kilns

The Durant Pottery Company operated in Bedford Village, New York in the early 1900s. Its founder was Mrs. Clarence Rice; she was aided by L. Volkmar to whom she assigned the task of technical direction. (See also Volkmar.) The artware and tableware they produced was simple in form and decoration. The creative aspects of the were carried on almost entirely by Volkmar himself, with only minimal crew to help with production. After Mrs. Rice's death in 1919, the property was purchased by Volkmar, who chose to drop the Durant name by 1930. Prior to 1919 the ware was marked simply 'Durant' and dated. After that time a stylized 'V' was added.

Bowl, bl & purple, ftd, 3x6" 145.00
Bowl, blk drip, bl int, flared, dtd 1914, 6x4" 395.00
Bowl, Chinese plum, bl crackle int, oval, dtd 1917, 4x8x7" 295.00
Urn, wht gloss, goat-head hdls, mk, 21x10½" 375.00
Vase, bl/gr variegated matt, Volkmar, bulbous, #206, 9¾" 1,500.00
Vase, cobalt, exposed ft, flanged U-form, 1917, 6x7½" 175.00
Vase, eggplant matt, sgn Volkmar, 1937, 18½" 3,600.00

Easter

Eggs, bunnies, chicks, and baskets have all become basic elements of Easter celebrations, and the older, more interesting examples are being collected, often for nostalgic reasons, and displayed during the holidays to make the festivities brighter. For further information we recommend *A Guide to Easter Collectibles, Identification and Values*, by Juanita Burnett.

Eggs with chicks, painted tin, 3", $35.00 each.

Book, Tale of the Little Bunnies, ca 1914, EX 40.00
Candy container, Keystone cop on chick, compo, Germany, 5" .195.00
Chick in suit, compo, Germany, 4½", EX 145.00
Duck nodder, compo, yel w/mc clothes, 7" 135.00
Egg, cat, paper litho, 3", EX 35.00
Egg, children at play, paper litho, 5½", EX 30.00
Egg, milk glass, blown mold, HP decor, 6½" 35.00
Egg, papier-mache, gold decor, 6" 45.00
Plate, The Rabbit, Kevin Daniel, MIB 65.00
Pull toy, rabbit w/wheel barrow, paper/wood, Germany, 5½", EX .130.00
Rabbit, compo, wht w/glass eyes, Germany, 4½" 95.00
Rabbit in egg, compo, mc pnt, Germany, 5" 95.00
Rabbit w/carrot, brn/orange, compo, Germany, 6" 110.00

Elfinware

Made in Germany from about 1920 until the 1940s, these miniature vases, boxes, salt cellars, and miscellaneous novelty items are characterized by the tiny applied flowers that often cover their entire surface. Pieces with animals and birds are the most valuable, followed by
the more interesting examples such as diminutive grand pianos, candle
holders, etc. See also Salts, Open.

Basket, loop hdl, sm 35.00
Box, cologne; appl roses, gr lustre, 8½" 55.00
Box, lg appl flowers, 5" 95.00
Candlestick, sm ring hdl, 2½" 50.00
Dutch shoe, 4" 75.00
Inkwell, 3x3¾" 55.00
Place card holder, appl roses on fan shape, Germany 25.00

Shoe, 2¼x4½", $75.00.

Slipper, appl roses, Germany, 3" 45.00
Vase, 2¾" 40.00
Watering can, sm 30.00
Watering can, 6" 60.00

Epergnes

Popular during the Victorian era, epergnes were fancy centerpieces
often consisting of several tiers of vases (called lilies), candle holders, or
dishes, or a combination of components. They were made in all types of
art glass, and some were set in ornate plated frames.

Amethyst to frost, 1-lily in ruffled metal-ftd bowl, 17" 375.00
Aqua opal, 4 jack-in-pulpit vases w/gr rigaree in bowl, 17" 450.00
Bl, 1-lily, chrome-plated stand w/leaves, sm 45.00
Cranberry w/rigaree, 4 lilies w/folded rims in bowl, 20" 550.00

Cut, red to clear, 4 cones in gilt metal holder, 10¾" 550.00
Emerald w/clear rigaree, 3 lilies+2 baskets+12" bowl, 20" 1,150.00
Radiating flutes on lily+3 grad trays on invt lily base, 21" 400.00
SP, lg floriform+3 sm ones on scrolled arms, England, 12½" 300.00
Vaseline opal to clear w/appl spirals, 3-lily, 16½" 575.00

Diamond Quilted cut crystal
bowls, Victorian silverplated
frame with four scrollwork
arms, $1,900.00.

Erickson

Carl Erickson of Bremen, Ohio, produced hand-formed glassware from 1943 until 1960 in artistic shapes, no two of which were
identical. One of the characteristics of his work was the air bubbles
that were captured within the glass. Though most examples are
clear, colored items were also made. Rather than to risk compromis-
ing his high standards by selling the factory, when Erickson retired,
the plant was dismantled and sold.

Ashtray, turq, controlled bubbles, pipe form 55.00
Bowl, amber cased, bubbles & mica, 7" 45.00
Bowl, turq cased, controlled bubbles, oblong, 6½x8¾" 65.00
Candle holders, purple, controlled bubbles, 2", pr 100.00
Cruet, crystal, ground stopper, 9½" 70.00
Pitcher, smoke, appl hdl, heavy bottom, 13" 110.00

Erphila

Ebeling and Ruess, an importing company in Philadelphia, began
operations in 1886. The acronym (Erphila) was frequently substituted
for the manufacturer's mark on the imported items. It appears that the
Erphila mark was used through the late 1930s and then again after WW
II on products from U.S. Zone Germany as well as from other areas.
The company imported from factories such as Fustenberg, W. Goebel,
Villeroy and Boch, Heinrich, Keramos, and Schumann, to name a few.
Figurines, art pottery, and some utilitarian items can be found bearing
the Erphila mark. Examples are hard to find. Early German marks
(those prior to 1900) often contain the word (Fayence.) After the turn
of the century, a rectangular mark in green ink was used. Following
WWI, porcelain items were imported from Czechoslovakia. These
sometimes carried gold and silver labels. A small variety of marks were
used in the 1920s and '30s, but they all contained the name Erphila.
Sticker labels were also used. 'Bavaria,' 'Black Forest,' and 'Italy' are
sometimes found in combination with 'Erphila.'

Ebeling and Ruess continue the importing business, but it appears
that since the 1940s they are also using an 'E' and 'R' on a bell-shaped
mark. Because this mark does not contain the name 'Erphila,' we do not
consider it to be such. We assume that they stopped using this name
sometime in the 1950s.

Ashtray, Mrs Gamp, MIG 45.00
Basket, rust, sm, MIG, 4½" 29.00
Bookends, Colonial girl & boy, wht & pk, pr 43.00
Bookends, Dutch couple, pr 55.00
Bookends, man mending baskets, MIG, pr 55.00
Cake plate, carnations, MIG, 11" 28.00
Cookie jar, drinking scene on wht, 9½" 115.00
Cracker jar, orange poppy 60.00
Figurine, bird on stump, yel & gray, MIG, 4¾" 30.00
Figurine, birds (2), gr on wht base, MIG, 5" 30.00
Figurine, birds (2), wht w/gold trim, MIG 42.00
Figurine, man w/pipe, bl & wht, 6" 55.00
Figurine, pheasant, mc, MIG, 8x10" 68.00
Pitcher, cherries on wht w/bl trim, 7" 45.00
Pitcher, floral, mc on wht, 6½" 43.00
Pitcher, mc, bulbous bottom, narrow neck, 8½" 45.00
Sprinkling can, wht, orange & gr flowers, 6½" 40.00
Teapot, cat, gray & blk, MIG, 8" 90.00
Teapot, chicken, mc, MIG, 8" 75.00
Teapot, dog, gray & blk, MIG, 8" 90.00
Teapot, duck, mc, MIG, 8¼" 82.00
Teapot, rabbit, gray & blk, MIG, 8½" 110.00
Vase, wht w/yel rings, 3-leg, 4" 12.50

Eskimo Artifacts

While ivory carvings made from walrus tusks or whale teeth have been the most emphasized articles of Eskimo art, basketry and wood-working are other areas in which these Alaskan Indians excell. Their designs are effected through the application of simple yet dramatic lines and almost stark decorative devices. Though not pursued to the extent of American Indian art, the unique work of this northern tribe is beginning to attract the serious attention of today's collectors.

Basket, baleen, cvd ivory walrus head hdl on lid, 3x4" 700.00
Basket, coiled, dmn motif, w/lid, Ukon River area, 3x7" 200.00
Basket, mc baleen bands, ivory finial & disk, Inuit, 2½x4¼" 660.00
Cigarette holder, ivory w/cvd seal head, 1900, 3" 55.00
Cribbage brd, cvd ivory, salmon shape, orig pegs, 14" 175.00
Cribbage brd w/scrimshaw animals/people/birds/etc, 1910, 24" ..500.00
Cvg, ivory, polar bear, 1½x3" 21.00
Cvg, ivory & antler, man/4 seals/whale/igloo, 1960, 12x9x3" 125.00
Cvg, man w/seal, gray stone, 5⅝" 110.00
Doll, cvd wood face w/drawn features, fur clothes, 12½" 35.00
Knife, cvd stone & bone hdl, 6" 60.00
Knife, gr jade w/ivory hdl, built w/ivory pegs, 1860, 9x1½" 325.00
Necklace, 16 lg fossilized walrus teeth/trade beads on sinew 300.00

Fairings

Fairings, small chinaware figural groups that portray amusing (if not risque) scenes of courting couples, marital woes, and family feuds, were popular purchases and prizes at 19th-century English fairs. From 1840 through the 1850s, their bases were embossed with marks that identified the manufacturer as well as the artist who applied the polychrome enameling. From 1860 until 1870, they were no longer marked and became smaller in size. During the 1870s they retained their smaller size but once again were marked in relief, indicating manufacturer and artisan. Through the 1880s all marks were omitted; but the bases were much more shallow than those from the 1860s. About 1890 the Staffordshire potters sold the molds to German manufacturers who marked their product with the name of their country until about 1900. Examples from this period are most commonly encountered. Fairings made in Germany in the early 20th century often have two holes in their bases.

Generally, the more complex groups and those that are marked bring the higher prices. Earlier examples from the sixties and seventies are of better quality. Similar items such as small boxes and match holders with much the same type of theme and figural decoration are also listed here.

Baby & dog pull at doll, gold trim, 2¾x2½x5" 175.00
Bank, pk cottage w/Present From Scarborough in gold, 4" W 150.00
Before Marriage, couple on sofa 245.00
Box, baby in cradle, unmk German bsk, 2¾x4½" 165.00
Box, child in bed w/kitten, 4¼" 120.00
Box, child on sideboard taking grapes, 1880s 250.00
Box, child w/trumpet, doll in basket, Staffordshire, 3¾" 175.00
Box, girl w/mama dog & 2 puppies on lid, some gold, 4½" 150.00
Box, monkey playing instrument 200.00
Box, pigeon w/letter on lid, 2½x2½" 95.00
Box, reclining child w/basket of flowers, English, 3½" 150.00
Cat stands on gr base, 2½x3" 130.00
Girl peeking through bushes at rabbit 80.00
Happy Father, What 2?..., couple/twins, 1880s, 3½" 110.00
I Am Starting for a Long Journey, man w/satchel & book 175.00
Merry Widow, lady cat w/roses at ft 250.00
O Do Leave Me a Drop, 2 cats at box 175.00
Oysters Sir, lady at bench, w/match striker 255.00
Returning at One O'clock in the Morning, rare 150.00
Welsh Tea Party, mk Germany 275.00
Will We Sleep First or How?, 5¼x4" 195.00
12 Months of Marriage, unmk, 3½x3½" 265.00

Fans

The Japanese are said to have invented the fan. From there it went to China, and Portuguese traders took the idea to Europe. Though usually considered milady's accessory, even the gentlemen in 17th-century England carried fans! More fashionable than practical, some were of feathers and lovely hand-painted silks with carved ivory or tortoise sticks. Some French fans had peepholes. There are mourning fans, calendar fans, and those with advertising.

Fine antique fans (pre-1900) of ivory or mother-of-pearl have recently escalated in value. Those from before 1800 often sell for upwards of $1,000.00. Examples with mother-of-pearl sticks are most desirable; least desirable are those with sticks of celluloid. Our advisor for this category is Vicki Flanigan; she is listed in the Directory under Virginia.

Hand-painted vellum leaf with shepherdess and Cupid in landscape, carved mother-of-pearl sticks, artist signed, Continental, 10½", $800.00.

Brise, pierced horn, sticks: gilt/jewels/enamel, 1800s, 7" **600.00**
French paper, aristocratic scenes, rtcl, MOP sticks, 14x8" **265.00**
Fuchsia satin, HP pk flowers/bluebird, 19x13½" **125.00**
HP silk, tooled/gilt abalone shell ribs, 16x25" **440.00**
Lace & HP tulle, tortoise shell sticks, Fr, 26" W **165.00**
Ostrich feathers, bl on celluloid base, EX **45.00**
Pheasant feathers, tortoise shell sticks, 1910, 9" **115.00**
Pk feathers, celluloid splines, 15x20" **65.00**
Scene printed/HP on paper, rtcl MOP sticks, Europe, 1850s **425.00**
Watercolor Oriental landscape on paper, ivory ribs, 17", EX ..**1,300.00**
Wedding party HP, MOP/gilt floral sticks, sgn/Madrid, '05, 12" ...**265.00**

Farm Collectibles

Country living in the 19th century entailed plowing, planting, and harvesting; gathering eggs and milking; making soap from lard rendered on butchering day; and numerous other tasks performed with primitive tools of which we in the 20th century have had little first-hand knowledge. Our advisor for this category is Lar Hothem; his address is listed in the Directory under Ohio. See also Cast Iron; Woodenware; Wrought Iron.

Apple dryer, cherrywood fr, w/wire mesh center, 1890s **45.00**
Barrel opener, wooden w/metal tip, 1850s **22.50**
Book, Common Colic of the Horse, Alex Eger, 1907, EX **35.00**
Book, Dr D Robert's Practical Home Veterinarian, 1913, EX **5.00**
Book, Firestone Farm Guide, 1948 ....**10.00**
Book, Weeds of Farm & Garden, Pammell, 1920, 218-pg, EX **8.50**
Box, wagon feed, slant lid, iron hinges & hdls, 13x35x18⅝" **120.00**
Bull lead, CI **10.00**
Carrier, grain; homemade, wood w/bentwood hdl, primitive **75.00**
Corn husking peg, hand-cvd wooden peg w/leather strap **18.00**
Corn husking peg, iron w/brass fittings & leather strap **15.00**
Corn planter, wooden, hand type, 1870s **60.00**
Corn sheller, The Flower Pot **650.00**
Corn sheller, wooden hand type, 2-pc, 1800s, 17" L **210.00**
Cranberry rake, wooden, 10x20x21", EX **150.00**
Cream separator, De Laval, orig gold & blk pnt, 30x43", EX **100.00**

Flyswitch, horsehair on the hide on stick with wire wrap, ca 1860, $45.00.

Hook, iron, 4 prongs, w/hanging ring **25.00**
Hook, trammel; 2 str shafts w/hooks, wrought iron **200.00**
Implement seat, Deere & Mansur, deer logo, CI **35.00**
Implement seat, Jenkin, CI **125.00**
Lantern, pine w/natural finish, hinged doors & posts, 9½" **330.00**
Lard press, wood, heavy iron hinge, ca 1900 ....**125.00**
Manual, Fairbanks Morse Equipment, 1928 ....**10.00**
Measure, copper w/brass rim, Fairbanks & Co, cylindrical, 4x5" ...**325.00**
Mud shoes for workhorse, wood w/iron fittings, pr **200.00**
Picker, blueberry; orig gr pnt, flat bottom, 10x4¾" **75.00**
Planting tool, CI knife form w/pistol-like hdl, 9½x4x1¾" **36.00**
Rope maker, McMillan & Kant **175.00**
Rope maker, 3-strand, 1901 ....**100.00**
Rope maker, 5-strand **325.00**
Rope maker & wrench, dtd 1901 ....**55.00**
Sausage stuffer, pierced tin w/wooden plunger, 1870s, 29½" **125.00**
Sausage stuffer, Wagner #3, Salem Tool Co, 1900s, on board **45.00**
Scoop, cranberry; tin, 10½" **45.00**
Scythe, wrought, 1700s, 19" **45.00**
Seed grader, 2 tin grooved pcs w/varied hole szs in wood fr **55.00**
Seive, bean sorting; wooden slats, S Cloud, 1868, 18½" sq **195.00**
Shovel, forge; blacksmith's **30.00**
Strainer, milk; tin, on heavy wire stand **25.00**
Tobacco hiller, man-pushed, mule-pulled, dbl-blade, 1880s **45.00**
Wagon jack, wood w/wrought iron, simple tooling, 1860s, 19" ...**125.00**
Washtub, wood w/iron bands, pnt traces, 1850s, minimum **125.00**
Yoke, cow; bentwood, looped w/heavy wooden pc at bottom, 26" ..**50.00**
Yoke, goat; wooden U-shape, wooden pc at bottom, 14x9¼" **45.00**

Fenton

Frank and John Fenton were brothers who founded the Fenton Art Glass Company in 1906 in Martin's Ferry, Ohio. The venture, at first only a decorating shop, began operations in July of 1905 using blanks purchased from other companies. This operation soon proved unsatisfactory, and by 1907 they had constructed their own glass factory in Williamstown, West Virginia. John left the company in 1909 and organized his own firm in Millersburg, Ohio.

The Fenton Company produced over 130 patterns of carnival glass. They also made custard, chocolate, opalescent, and stretch glass. This company has always been noted for its various colors of glass and has continually changed its production to stay attune with current tastes in decorating. In 1925 they produced a line of 'handmade' items that incorporated the techniques of threading and mosaic work. Because the process proved to be unprofitable, the line was discontinued by 1927. Even their glassware made in the past twenty-five years is already regarded as collectible. Various paper labels have been used since the 1920s; only since 1970 has the logo been stamped into the glass. For information concerning Fenton Art Glass Collectors of America, Inc., see the Clubs, Newsletters, and Catalogs section of the Directory. See also Carnival Glass; Custard Glass; Stretch Glass.

Apple Blossom Crest, compote, #7228 ....**60.00**
Aqua Crest, bonbon, ruffled, 6" **12.50**
Aqua Crest, bowl, dbl-crimped, #7321, 11½" **75.00**
Aqua Crest, tidbit **65.00**
Aqua Crest, vase, #36, 4" **25.00**
Basketweave, basket, ruby, cupped bowl, 6" dia **24.00**
Basketweave, bowl, Mandarin red, shallow, 8" **88.00**
Beaded Melon, bottle, scent; gr cased, 3¼" **55.00**
Beaded Melon, creamer, gold o/l, #11 ....**38.00**
Beaded Melon, vase, gold o/l, tulip form, 9¼" **62.50**
Beaded Melon, vase, gr cased, tulip form, sm **35.00**

Beaded Melon, vase, lt gr o/l, dbl-crimped, 3¾" 42.00
Big Cookies, basket, jade gr, #1681 ....115.00
Black Rose, hurricane lamp, #7398 ....120.00
Blue Overlay, basket, #1924 ....42.00
Blue Overlay, jug, hdl, #192, 6" 40.00
Blue Overlay, rose bowl, #711, 4" 30.00
Blue Overlay, vanity set, 3-pc 90.00
Bubble Optic, vase, honey amber, 8¼" 62.50
Coin Dot, basket, cranberry opal, #1437, 7" 98.00
Coin Dot, basket, cranberry opal, #1925, 10½" 130.00
Coin Dot, bowl, cranberry opal, #1522, 10" 90.00
Coin Dot, bowl, cranberry opal, #203, 6" 65.00
Coin Dot, bowl, French opal, dbl-crimped, 10½" 45.00
Coin Dot, bowl, gr opal, 6" 75.00
Coin Dot, bowl, topaz opal, #203, 6" 58.00
Coin Dot, candy jar, cranberry opal, #1522 ....120.00
Coin Dot, creamer, bl opal, #1461 ....30.00
Coin Dot, creamer, cranberry opal, #1924, 4" 42.50

Coin Dot, hat, cranberry opalescent,
3½", $65.00.

Coin Dot, lamp, French opal, w/chimney, 11" 210.00
Coin Dot, lamp, student; honeysuckle opal, 21" 155.00
Coin Dot, pitcher, water; French opal 150.00
Coin Dot, top hat, Persian Bl opal, #1492 ....38.00
Coin Dot, vase, bl opal, hdls, #1353, 9" 90.00
Coin Dot, vase, cranberry opal, #194, 11" 110.00
Coin Dot, vase, cranberry opal, #194, 8½" 90.00
Coin Dot, vase, cranberry opal, dbl-crimped, #1450, 5" 78.00
Coin Dot, vase, topaz opal, #1440 ....78.00
Daisy & Button, basket, Colonial Bl, #1900, 7½" 52.50
Daisy & Button, bell, Lime Sherbet 18.00
Daisy & Button, bonbon, French opal, 5" 15.00
Daisy & Button, candlesticks, milk glass, 2-light, pr 40.00
Daisy & Button, goblet, water; amberina 20.00
Daisy & Button, slipper, pk opal, #1995 ....10.00
Daisy & Button, slipper, Provincial Bl opal, #1995 ....17.50
Daisy & Button, top hat, bl opal, #1900, 3¾" 40.00
Daisy & Button, vase, gr pastel, #1957, 8½" 45.00
Daisy & Button, vase, milk glass, ftd fan form, 10" 35.00
Daisy & Fern, pitcher, water; cranberry opal 255.00
Daisy & Fern, pitcher, water; vaseline, +6 tumblers 450.00
Daisy & Fern, pitcher, yel opal 250.00
Dancing Ladies, bowl, cobalt, #900, 12" 150.00
Dancing Ladies, vase, Mongolian Gr, flared rim, #901, 8½" ...185.00
Dancing Ladies, vase, ruby, #901, ca 1933, 9" 210.00
Diamond Lace, bowl, bl opal, #4824, 9½" 48.00

Diamond Lace, candlesticks, French opal, pr 40.00
Diamond Lace, compote, ftd, 1948 ....70.00
Diamond Lace, console set, French opal, #1948, 3-pc 80.00
Diamond Lace, epergne, milk glass, 4-pc, 10" 58.00
Diamond Lace, epergne, topaz opal, 4-pc, 10" 78.00
Diamond Optic, basket, mulberry, #192, 10½" 475.00
Diamond Optic, creamer & sugar bowl, rose, 3½" 40.00
Diamond Optic, jug, ruby o/l, hdl, #192, 8" 75.00
Diamond Optic, shakers, amber, pr 45.00
Diamond Optic, vase, cranberry opal, ca 1952-54, 7½" 80.00
Diamond Optic, vase, ruby, fan form, 31502, 8½" 40.00
Diamond Optic, vase, ruby o/l, dbl-crimped, 4¼" 24.00
Dogwood, vase, burmese, dbl-crimped, #7547, 5½" 85.00
Dolphin, bonbon, jade gr, sq 24.00
Dolphin, bonbon, ruby, #1621 ....38.00
Dolphin, bowl, console; jade gr, hdls, oval, ftd, 10½" 110.00
Dolphin, bowl, jade gr, hdls, #1504A 35.00
Dolphin, bowl, moonstone, oval, #1608, 10" 95.00
Dolphin, candlestick, ruby, 3½" 35.00
Dolphin, compote, ruby, crimped, hdls, 4" 70.00
Dolphin, vase, topaz stretch, fan form, 5" 65.00
Dot Optic, ivy ball, emerald gr, #1021 ....45.00
Dot Optic, pitcher, bl opal, 4" 37.50
Dot Optic, pitcher, water; gr opal 150.00
Dot Optic, top hat, cranberry opal, smooth rim, 6" 110.00
Dot Optic, vase, ruby o/l, 6" 35.00
Ebony, candy bowl, w/lid, #844, 6¼" 80.00
Ebony, candy jar, ca 1925, 9" 80.00
Emerald Crest, compote 35.00
Emerald Crest, creamer & sugar bowl 85.00
Emerald Crest, flowerpot w/attached saucer, #401, 4½" 80.00
Emerald Crest, jug, #711, 6" 42.00
Emerald Crest, vase, fan form, 6¼" 32.00
Emerald Crest, vase, 4½" 35.00
Flame Crest, cake plate, stem 150.00
Georgian, claret, ruby, #1611, 4½-oz 20.00
Georgian, cup, amber, #1611 ....12.50
Georgian, shakers, ruby, orig tops, 4½", pr 90.00
Georgian, tumbler, ruby, 2½" 6.00
Gold Crest, bonbon, tricorner, 5½" 15.00
Gold Crest, bowl, crimped, 8" 30.00
Gold Crest, bowl, 6" 10.00
Gold Crest, plate, 6¾" 14.00
Hearts & Flowers, cake plate, rose pastel, ftd 48.00
Hobnail, ashtray, topaz opal, fan form, 5½" 38.00
Hobnail, basket, bl opal, 4" 35.00
Hobnail, basket, bl opal, 7" 50.00
Hobnail, basket, gr opal, #3834, 7½" 98.00
Hobnail, basket, lime opal (rare), 4" 95.00
Hobnail, bell, Colonial Bl, #3667 ....12.50
Hobnail, bonbon, plum opal, 5½" 30.00
Hobnail, bonbon, yel opal, 5½" 30.00
Hobnail, bowl, berry; rose pastel, sq, #3928 ....18.00
Hobnail, bowl, plum opal, #3924, 9" 150.00
Hobnail, bowl, topaz opal, dbl-crimped, #3927, 7" 50.00
Hobnail, candle holder, topaz opal, cornucopia form, #3874 ....38.00
Hobnail, candle holders, milk glass, 6", pr 18.00
Hobnail, candlestick, cranberry opal, #3870 ....75.00
Hobnail, candlesticks, bl opal, cornucopia form, 6", pr 92.50
Hobnail, cigarette lighter, milk glass 20.00
Hobnail, compote, gr opal, ftd, w/lid 68.00
Hobnail, compote, plum opal, ped ft, low, 8" 90.00
Hobnail, creamer & sugar bowl, bl opal, star-shaped top 40.00
Hobnail, creamer & sugar bowl, topaz opal, #3900 ....36.00

Hobnail, creamer & sugar bowl w/tray, milk glass 25.00
Hobnail, cruet, bl opal, lg 65.00
Hobnail, cruet, bl opal, 4" 32.00
Hobnail, cruet, cranberry opal, 5" 100.00
Hobnail, cruet, milk glass, #3767, 7-oz 28.00
Hobnail, epergne, milk glass, 3-horn 25.00
Hobnail, epergne, pk opal, #3701, 4-pc 60.00
Hobnail, goblet, water; bl opal 35.00
Hobnail, goblet, water; milk glass, #3845 ....12.50

Hobnail, heart-shaped dish, plum opalescent, $85.00.

Hobnail, ivy bowl, milk glass, #3757 ....20.00
Hobnail, jam set, bl opal, #389, 3-pc 95.00
Hobnail, jardiniere, milk glass, #3994, 4½" 10.00
Hobnail, jug, cranberry opal, squat, #3965, 5½" 125.00
Hobnail, jug, lime opal, hdl, 6" 70.00
Hobnail, lamp, fairy; bl opal, 2-pc 18.00
Hobnail, lamp, fairy; Colonial Gr, #3608, 2-pc 12.50
Hobnail, lamp, table; cranberry opal 265.00
Hobnail, mayonnaise set, bl opal, 3-pc 60.00
Hobnail, mustard, bl opal, #3889 ....30.00
Hobnail, mustard, French opal, 3-pc 25.00
Hobnail, mustard, milk glass, w/underplate, 3-pc 12.50
Hobnail, pitcher, juice; yel opal, squat, +6 tumblers 195.00
Hobnail, pitcher, plum opal, ice lip, #3664, 70-oz 165.00
Hobnail, plate, French opal, 8" sq 40.00
Hobnail, relish, milk glass, heart form, #3733 ....22.50
Hobnail, rose bowl, gr opal, 4" 65.00
Hobnail, shakers, bl opal, pr 35.00
Hobnail, shakers, cranberry opal, #3806, pr 90.00
Hobnail, slipper, bl opal 24.00
Hobnail, tray, bl opal, fan form, 10½" 32.00
Hobnail, tumbler, gr opal, 6" 26.00
Hobnail, tumbler, juice; bl opal, flat 12.00
Hobnail, tumbler, milk glass, 8-oz 8.00
Hobnail, vase, bl opal, dbl-crimped, 8" 50.00
Hobnail, vase, bl opal, ftd fan form, 6" 35.00
Hobnail, vase, bud; Colonial Orange, #3756, 9½" 10.00
Hobnail, vase, bud; yel opal, ftd 40.00
Hobnail, vase, Colonial Bl, dbl-crimped, #3853, 3" 15.00
Hobnail, vase, cranberry opal, dbl-crimped, 3" 35.00
Hobnail, vase, cranberry opal, dbl-crimped, 8" 75.00
Hobnail, vase, emerald gr, dbl-crimped, #3850, 5½" 30.00
Hobnail, vase, gold o/l, #3856, 5½" 42.00
Hobnail, vase, lime gr opal, dbl-crimped, #389, 4½" 42.50

Hobnail, vase, Mandarin Red, flared rim, #621, 6" 60.00
Hobnail, vase, milk glass, pitcher form, #3760 ....44.00
Hobnail, vase, yel opal, ftd, 12" 60.00
Hobnail, wine, French opal, #3843, sm 20.00
Ivory Crest, bowl, 7" 60.00
Ivory Crest, candle holder, cornucopia form, 6¼" 35.00
Ivory Crest, plate, 11½" 75.00
Ivory Crest, plate, 8½" 40.00
Ivory Crest, vase, crimped, #711, 6" 30.00
Ivory Crest, vase, sq top, #201, 5" 45.00
Ivy, rose bowl, gr/wht, #711, 5" 58.00
Jade Green, candelabrum, #2318, 6" 50.00
Jade Green, candy dish, ftd 38.00
Jade Green, compote, 6" 25.00
Jade Green, ice bucket, hdld 50.00
Jade Green, sugar bowl 18.00
Jade Green, vase, flip; 9" 65.00
Jade Green, vase, str sides, 8" 35.00
Jamestown Blue, vase, 12" 90.00
Leaf, plate, milk glass, #5108, 11" 22.50
Leaf & Orange Tree, bowl, custard satin, 3-toed, #8223 ....25.00
Lilac, biscuit jar, #1681, rare 300.00
Lilac, shell bowl, #9020, 10" 95.00
Lily of the Valley, rose bowl, Sky Bl opal, #8453 ....28.00
Lily of the Valley, vase, Cameo opal, handkerchief form 18.00
Lime Satin, owl head fairy light 20.00
Lincoln Inn, compote, lt bl 42.50
Lincoln Inn, cup & saucer, aquamarine bl, #1700 ....38.00
Lincoln Inn, goblet, water; ruby 30.00
Lincoln Inn, tumbler, ruby, ftd, 5" 30.00
Lincoln Inn, wine, cobalt 25.00
Mandarin Red, ginger jar, #893, rare 285.00
Melon Rib, vase, pk o/l, 8" 60.00
Ming Green, bowl, octagonal, #750, 9", w/14" underplate 275.00
Ming Green, jar, macaroon; reed hdl 135.00
Ming Rose, bonbon, 3-toe, 6¾" 30.00
Ming Rose, macaroon jar, 6½" 78.00
Mongolian Gr, vase, crimped, #847, 5" 45.00
Orange Tree, candlesticks, custard satin, pr 37.50
Orange Tree, jelly compote, crystal 20.00
Peach Crest, basket, milk glass hdl, 1924, 7x5" 60.00
Peach Crest, basket, milk glass hdl, 6½" 58.00
Peach Crest, bowl, dbl-crimped, #7224, 10" 68.00
Peach Crest, powder jar, w/2 colognes 160.00
Peach Crest, top hat, 3¼" 32.00
Peach Crest, vase, crimped, #187, 6" 30.00
Peach Crest, vase, hand holds vase form, #193, 10¼" 150.00
Peach Crest, vase, tulip form, #7250, 8½" 65.00
Peach Crest/Beaded Melon, vase, #7156, 6" 48.00
Peacock, vase, burmese, #8257, 7½" 48.00
Pekin Blue, candlestick, #318, 3" 32.00
Periwinkle Blue, vase, flared, ca 1935, 8½" 60.00
Persian Medallion, basket, custard satin, #8238, 8½" 40.00
Persian Medallion, compote, Lime Sherbet, #8234 ....20.00
Persian Medallion, lamp, fairy; custard satin, #8408, 3-pc 32.00
Persian Medallion, lamp, fairy; rose burmese, #8408, 3-pc 90.00
Plymouth, champagne, ruby, 4" 22.00
Plymouth, ice bucket, crystal 45.00
Plymouth, sherbet, cobalt, 3½" 18.00
Plymouth, shot glass, ruby 15.00
Plymouth, wine, ruby 20.00
Polka Dot, butter dish, cranberry opal, milk glass base 120.00
Polka Dot, pitcher, cranberry opal, #2267, rare, 9" 400.00
Polka Dot, shakers, cranberry opal, 3¾", pr 55.00

Polka Dot, vase, cranberry opal, dbl-crimped, #2251, 7¾" 135.00
Polka Dot, vase, cranberry opal, tulip form, #2250, 8" 150.00
Reverse Melon, vase, amethyst, 7" 22.50
Rib Optic, creamer & sugar bowl, gr opal, #1604 ....88.00
Rib Optic, night set, gr opal, #401, ca 1927, 2-pc 55.00
Rib Optic, top hat, French opal, #1921, 10" 225.00
Rib Optic, vase, lime gr opal, #184, 11" 60.00
Rib Optic, wine, gr opal, #1647, 4" 35.00
Rosalene, candle holder, owl fairy light 48.00
Rosalene, swan, open, #5127 ....35.00
Rose Crest, basket, 10" 90.00
Rose Crest, vase, #192, 6½" 20.00
Rose Crest, vase, #192, 8" 50.00
Rose Crest, vase, dbl-crimped, #1924, 4" 25.00
Rose Crest, vase, 6½" 52.50
Rose Overlay, pitcher, #192, 8" 55.00
Rose Pattern, basket, pk opal, #9535, sm 18.00
Rose Pattern, basket, Provincial Bl opal, 8½" 30.00
Rose Pattern, vase, Provincial Bl opal, ftd, 9" 25.00
Ruby, tumbler, #1933, 4¼" 16.00
Ruby Overlay, bottle, scent; #192A 40.00
Ruby Overlay, vase, dbl-crimped, #192, 7½" 40.00
Scroll & Eye, compote, rose pastel, #9021 ....30.00
Scroll & Eye, plate, rose pastel, #9015 ....20.00
September Morn, flower frog, blk opaque 185.00
September Morn, flower frog, crystal 95.00
September Morn, flower frog, lt gr, blk base 140.00
September Morn, flower frog, red transparent 185.00
Sheffield, bowl, French opal, crimped, #1800, 12" 40.00
Sheffield, tumbler, amethyst, #1800, 4" 20.00
Silver Crest, banana boat, low 30.00
Silver Crest, bonbon, crimped, 5½" 10.00
Silver Crest, cake plate, ped ft, low, 13" 35.00
Silver Crest, candle holders, saucer base, 3¾", pr 55.00
Silver Crest, candlesticks, cornucopia; pr 55.00
Silver Crest, chip & dip set 65.00
Silver Crest, compote, ruffled & crimped, 8½" 17.50
Silver Crest, epergne, lg 145.00
Silver Crest, heart bowl, w/hdl 18.00
Silver Crest, ivy vase, crimped, #711 ....32.00
Silver Crest, relish, hdl 18.00
Silver Crest, tidbit tray, 3-tier 45.00
Silver Crest, tray, chrome center hdl, 5½" 18.00
Silver Crest, vase, dbl-crimped, #1924, 4½" 32.00
Snow Flake, rose bowl, cobalt opal, made for LG Wright 48.00
Spiral, vase, cranberry opal, #3160, 6½" 50.00
Spiral, vase, gr opal, 8" 48.00
Spiral Optic, bottle, bitters; cranberry opal, 9" 120.00
Spiral Optic, cruet, cranberry opal, clear twist reeded hdl 95.00
Spiral Optic, vase, cranberry opal, #3253, 6½" 68.00
Strawberry Pattern, basket, amethyst, #9433, 7" 28.00
Swan, bonbon, pk 27.50
Swan Lake, bowl, console; amber, lg 50.00
Swirl, cruet, ruby o/l, w/stopper 32.00
Swirl, ginger jar, cranberry opal, 10½" 178.00
Vasa Murrhina, basket, gr/bl, 7" 75.00
Vasa Murrhina, vase, Bl Mist, #6459, 14" 98.00
Vasa Murrhina, vase, gr/bl, dbl-crimped, #6454, 4" 48.00
Vasa Murrhina, vase, gr/bl, dbl-crimped, #6458, 11" 85.00
Vasa Murrhina, vase, Rose Mist, fan form, #6457, 7" 65.00
Velva Rose, vase, Spirit of St Louis, fan form, #562 ....130.00
Velvatone, compote, crimped, #574 ....35.00
Water Lily, basket, Lime Sherbet, #8434, 7" 35.00
Water Lily, candy dish, rosaline, ftd, #8480, w/lid 88.00

Water Lily, compote, Lime Sherbet, #8429, lg 27.50
Water Lily, jardiniere, custard satin, #8498 ....30.00
Water Lily, pitcher, custard satin, #8464, 30-oz 35.00
Water Lily, rose bowl, custard satin, #8429 ....20.00
Wistaria, candlesticks, purple irid, ca 1924-26, 8", pr 115.00
Wistaria, vase, wht satin, fan form, #349, 8" 40.00

Fiesta

Fiesta is a line of dinnerware produced by the Homer Laughlin China Company of Newell, West Virginia, from 1936 until 1973. It was made in eleven different solid colors with over fifty pieces in the assortment. The pattern was developed by Frederick Rhead, an English Stoke-on-Trent potter who was an important contributor to the art-pottery movement in this country during the early part of the century. The design was carried out through the use of a simple band-of-rings device near the rim. Fiesta Red, a strong red-orange glaze color, was made with depleted uranium oxide. It was more expensive to produce than the other colors and sold at higher prices. Today's collectors still pay premium prices for Fiesta Red pieces. During the fifties the color assortment was gray, rose, chartreuse, and dark green. These colors are relatively harder to find and along with Fiesta Red and medium green (new in 1959) command the higher prices.

Fiesta Kitchen Kraft was introduced in 1939; it consisted of seventeen pieces of kitchenware such as pie plates, refrigerator sets, mixing bowls, and covered jars in four popular Fiesta colors.

As a final attempt to adapt production to modern-day techniques and methods, Fiesta was restyled in 1969. Of the original colors, only Fiesta Red remained. This line, called Fiesta Ironstone, was discontinued in 1973.

Two types of marks were used: an ink stamp on machine-jiggered pieces and an indented mark molded into the hollowware pieces.

In 1986 HLC reintroduced a line of Fiesta dinnerware in five colors: black, white, pink, apricot, and cobalt (darker and denser than the original shade). Since then yellow, turquoise, and seafoam green have been added. Collectors have found that the new line poses no theat to their investments.

In the listings below, 'original colors' indicates only three of the original six — light green, turquoise, and yellow (or those remaining after specific original colors have been priced). Red, ivory and cobalt values are listed separately. For more information we recommend *The Collector's Encyclopedia of Fiesta, Harlequin, and Riviera* (values updated in 1994) by Sharon and Bob Huxford, available at your local bookstore or from Collector Books.

Dinnerware

Ashtray, '50s colors 65.00
Ashtray, orig colors 37.50
Ashtray, red or cobalt 45.00
Bowl, covered onion soup; cobalt or ivory 425.00
Bowl, covered onion soup; red 500.00
Bowl, covered onion soup; turq, minimum value 2,000.00
Bowl, covered onion soup; yel or lt gr 325.00
Bowl, cream soup; '50s colors 55.00
Bowl, cream soup; med gr, minimum value 2,600.00
Bowl, cream soup; orig colors 32.50
Bowl, cream soup; red, cobalt or ivory 46.00
Bowl, dessert; '50s colors, 6" 40.00
Bowl, dessert; med gr, 6" 250.00
Bowl, dessert; orig colors, 6" 30.00
Bowl, dessert; red, cobalt or ivory, 6" 40.00

Bowl, fruit; '50s colors, 4¾" 25.00
Bowl, fruit; '50s colors, 5½" 28.50
Bowl, fruit; med gr, 4¾" 270.00
Bowl, fruit; med gr, 5½" 60.00
Bowl, fruit; orig colors, 11¾" 130.00
Bowl, fruit; orig colors, 4¾" 22.00
Bowl, fruit; orig colors, 5½" 24.00
Bowl, fruit; red, cobalt or ivory, 11¾" 170.00
Bowl, fruit; red, cobalt or ivory, 4¾" 25.00
Bowl, fruit; red, cobalt or ivory, 5½" 27.00
Bowl, ftd salad; orig colors 190.00
Bowl, ftd salad; red, cobalt or ivory 230.00
Bowl, ind salad; med gr, 7½" 75.00
Bowl, ind salad; red, turq or yel, 7½" 57.50
Bowl, nappy; '50s colors, 8½" 40.00
Bowl, nappy; med gr, 8½" 85.00
Bowl, nappy; orig colors, 8½" 28.00
Bowl, nappy; orig colors, 9½" 35.00
Bowl, nappy; red, cobalt or ivory, 8½" 38.00
Bowl, nappy; red, cobalt or ivory, 9½" 45.00
Bowl, Tom & Jerry; ivory w/gold letters 215.00
Bowl, unlisted; red, cobalt, or ivory 250.00
Bowl, unlisted; yel 70.00
Candle holders, bulb; orig colors, pr 65.00
Candle holders, bulb; red, cobalt or ivory, pr 85.00
Candle holders, tripod; orig colors, pr 300.00
Candle holders, tripod; red, cobalt or ivory, pr 355.00
Carafe, orig colors 138.00
Carafe, red, cobalt or ivory 170.00
Casserole, '50s colors 225.00
Casserole, French; standard colors other than yel 450.00
Casserole, French; yel 200.00
Casserole, med gr 375.00
Casserole, orig colors 100.00
Casserole, red, cobalt or ivory 150.00
Coffeepot, '50s colors 210.00
Coffeepot, demi; orig colors 175.00
Coffeepot, demi; red, cobalt or ivory 225.00
Coffeepot, orig colors 125.00
Coffeepot, red, cobalt or ivory 165.00
Compote, orig colors, 12" 105.00
Compote, red, cobalt or ivory, 12" 130.00
Compote, sweets; orig colors 48.00
Compote, sweets; red, cobalt or ivory 60.00
Creamer, '50s colors 26.00
Creamer, ind; red 135.00
Creamer, ind; turq 215.00
Creamer, ind; yel 48.00
Creamer, med gr 48.00
Creamer, orig colors 16.00
Creamer, red, cobalt or ivory 22.00
Creamer, stick hdld, orig colors 30.00
Creamer, stick hdld, red, cobalt or ivory 35.00
Cup, demi; '50s colors 210.00
Cup, demi; orig colors 45.00
Cup, demi; red, cobalt or ivory 50.00
Egg cup, '50s colors 120.00
Egg cup, orig colors 40.00
Egg cup, red, cobalt, or ivory 50.00
Lid, for mixing bowl #1-#3, any color, minimum value 500.00
Lid, for mixing bowl #4, any color, minimum value 550.00
Marmalade, orig colors 135.00
Marmalade, red, cobalt or ivory 180.00
Mixing bowl, #1, orig colors 80.00

Mixing bowl, #1, red, cobalt, or ivory 110.00
Mixing bowl, #2, orig colors 65.00
Mixing bowl, #2, red, cobalt or ivory 75.00
Mixing bowl, #3, orig colors 72.50
Mixing bowl, #3, red, cobalt or ivory 80.00
Mixing bowl, #4, orig colors 82.50
Mixing bowl, #4, red, cobalt or ivory 90.00
Mixing bowl, #5, orig colors 92.50
Mixing bowl, #5, red, cobalt or ivory 100.00
Mixing bowl, #6, orig colors 112.50
Mixing bowl, #6, red, cobalt or ivory 132.50
Mixing bowl, #7, orig colors 152.50
Mixing bowl, #7, red, cobalt or ivory 175.00
Mug, Tom & Jerry; '50s colors 78.00
Mug, Tom & Jerry; ivory w/gold letters 55.00
Mug, Tom & Jerry; orig colors 45.00
Mug, Tom & Jerry; red or cobalt 60.00
Mustard, orig colors 115.00
Mustard, red, cobalt or ivory 160.00
Pitcher, disk juice; gray 1,100.00
Pitcher, disk juice; red 240.00
Pitcher, disk juice; yel 35.00
Pitcher, disk water; '50s colors 190.00
Pitcher, disk water; med gr, minimum value 550.00
Pitcher, disk water; orig colors 75.00
Pitcher, disk water; red, cobalt or ivory 110.00
Pitcher, ice; orig colors 75.00

Pitcher, ice; cobalt, $100.00.

Pitcher, ice; red 100.00
Pitcher, jug, 2-pt; '50s colors 90.00
Pitcher, jug, 2-pt; orig colors 47.50
Pitcher, jug, 2-pt; red, cobalt or ivory 65.00
Plate, '50s colors, 10" 38.50
Plate, '50s colors, 6" 7.00
Plate, '50s colors, 7" 10.00
Plate, '50s colors, 9" 16.00
Plate, cake; lt gr or yel 535.00
Plate, cake; red, cobalt or ivory 575.00
Plate, calendar; 1954 or 1955, 10" 32.00
Plate, calendar; 1955, 9" 37.50
Plate, chop; '50s colors, 13" 55.00
Plate, chop; '50s colors, 15" 70.00
Plate, chop; med gr, 13" 100.00
Plate, chop; orig colors, 13" 26.00
Plate, chop; orig colors, 15" 30.00
Plate, chop; red, cobalt or ivory, 13" 34.00
Plate, chop; red, cobalt or ivory, 15" 45.00

Plate, compartment; '50s colors, 10½" 42.00
Plate, compartment; orig colors, 10½" 25.00
Plate, compartment; orig colors, 12" 45.00
Plate, compartment; red, cobalt or ivory, 10½" 28.50
Plate, compartment; red, cobalt or ivory, 12" 40.00
Plate, deep; '50s colors 42.00
Plate, deep; med gr 82.50
Plate, deep; orig colors 27.50
Plate, deep; red, cobalt or ivory 40.00
Plate, med gr, 10" 75.00
Plate, med gr, 6" 12.00
Plate, med gr, 7" 22.50
Plate, med gr, 9" 35.00
Plate, orig colors, 10" 25.00
Plate, orig colors, 6" 4.00
Plate, orig colors, 7" 7.00
Plate, orig colors, 9" 8.50
Plate, red, cobalt or ivory, 10" 32.00
Plate, red, cobalt or ivory, 6" 6.00
Plate, red, cobalt or ivory, 7" 8.50
Plate, red, cobalt or ivory, 9" 15.00
Platter, '50s colors 40.00
Platter, med gr 80.00
Platter, orig colors 22.50
Platter, red, cobalt or ivory 32.00
Sauce boat, '50s colors 52.50
Sauce boat, med gr 87.50
Sauce boat, orig colors 32.00
Sauce boat, red, cobalt or ivory 48.00
Saucer, '50s colors 5.00
Saucer, demi; '50s colors 62.50
Saucer, demi; orig colors 12.00
Saucer, demi; red, cobalt or ivory 12.50
Saucer, med gr 8.00
Saucer, orig colors 3.00
Saucer, red, cobalt or ivory 4.00
Shakers, '50s colors, pr 34.00
Shakers, med gr, pr 65.00
Shakers, orig colors, pr 16.50
Shakers, red, cobalt or ivory, pr 23.00
Sugar bowl, ind; turq 250.00
Sugar bowl, ind; yel 72.50
Sugar bowl, w/lid; '50s colors, 3¼x3½" 45.00
Sugar bowl, w/lid; med gr, 3¼x3½" 90.00
Sugar bowl, w/lid; orig colors, 3¼x3½" 30.00
Sugar bowl, w/lid; red, cobalt or ivory, 3¼x3½" 40.00
Syrup, orig colors 192.50
Syrup, red, cobalt or ivory 225.00
Teacup, '50s colors 30.00
Teacup, med gr 45.00
Teacup, orig colors 22.00
Teacup, red, cobalt or ivory 26.00
Teapot, lg; orig colors 110.00
Teapot, lg; red, cobalt or ivory 145.00
Teapot, med; '50s colors 195.00
Teapot, med; med gr 400.00
Teapot, med; orig colors 110.00
Teapot, med; red, cobalt or ivory 125.00
Tray, figure-8; cobalt 55.00
Tray, figure-8; turq 180.00
Tray, figure-8; yel 180.00
Tray, relish; mixed colors, no red 160.00
Tray, utility; orig colors 28.00
Tray, utility; red, cobalt or ivory 32.00

Tumbler, juice; chartreuse, Harlequin yel or dk gr 275.00
Tumbler, juice; orig colors 27.50
Tumbler, juice; red, cobalt or ivory 32.00
Tumbler, juice; rose 38.00
Tumbler, water; orig colors 40.00
Tumbler, water; red, cobalt or ivory 50.00
Vase, bud; orig colors 45.00
Vase, bud; red, cobalt or ivory 60.00
Vase, orig colors, 10" 425.00
Vase, orig colors, 12" 500.00
Vase, orig colors, 8" 350.00
Vase, red, cobalt or ivory, 10" 475.00
Vase, red, cobalt or ivory, 12" 600.00
Vase, red, cobalt or ivory, 8" 400.00

Kitchen Kraft

Bowl, mixing; lt gr or yel, 10" 80.00
Bowl, mixing; lt gr or yel, 6" 55.00
Bowl, mixing; lt gr or yel, 8" 70.00
Bowl, mixing; red or cobalt, 10" 90.00
Bowl, mixing; red or cobalt, 6" 60.00
Bowl, mixing; red or cobalt, 8" 80.00
Cake plate, red or cobalt 48.00
Cake server, lt gr or yel 80.00
Cake server, red or cobalt 90.00
Casserole, ind; lt gr or yel 115.00
Casserole, ind; red or cobalt 130.00
Casserole, lt gr or yel, 7½" 70.00
Casserole, lt gr or yel, 8½" 85.00
Casserole, red or cobalt, 7½" 80.00
Casserole, red or cobalt, 8½" 95.00
Covered jar, lg; lt gr or yel 210.00
Covered jar, lg; red or cobalt 230.00
Covered jar, med; lt gr or yel 190.00
Covered jar, med; red or cobalt 210.00
Covered jar, sm; lt gr or yel 200.00
Covered jar, sm; red or cobalt 225.00
Covered jug, lt gr or yel 170.00
Covered jug, red or cobalt 180.00
Fork, lt gr or yel 70.00
Fork, red or cobalt 78.00
Metal frame for platter 22.00
Pie plate, lt gr or yel, 10" 38.00
Pie plate, lt gr or yel, 9" 35.00
Pie plate, red or cobalt, 10" 42.00
Pie plate, red or cobalt, 9" 40.00
Platter, lt gr or yel 65.00
Platter, red or cobalt 72.00
Platter, spruce gr 225.00
Shakers, lt gr or yel, pr 75.00
Shakers, red or cobalt, pr 85.00
Spoon, lt gr or yel 75.00
Spoon, red or cobalt 85.00
Stacking refrigerator lid, ivory 150.00
Stacking refrigerator lid, lt gr or yel 45.00
Stacking refrigerator lid, red or cobalt 52.00
Stacking refrigerator unit, ivory 150.00
Stacking refrigerator unit, lt gr or yel 32.00
Stacking refrigerator unit, red or cobalt 36.00

Fifties Modern

Postwar furniture design is marked by organic shapes and lighter woods and forms. New materials from war research such as molded ply-wood and fiberglass were used extensively. For the first time, design was extended to the mass and the baby-boomer generation grew up surrounded by modern shape and color, the perfect expression of postwar optimism. The top designers in America worked for Herman Miller and Knoll Furniture Company. These include Charles Eames, George Nelson and Eero Saarinen.

Italian glass from the fifties represents some of the most beautiful designs of the period. The color and expressive forms that came from the island of Murano during this time were the perfect expression of Italian style and flair.

This information was provided to us by Richard Wright.

Armchair, Alvar Aalto #51-1, molded birch 1-pc bk/seat **475.00**
Armchair, Gilbert Rohde, 1-pc metal fr w/curved bk/seat, VG ..**500.00**
Armchair, hotel; W McArthur, aluminum tube fr, no seat **1,500.00**
Armchair, K Weber, 3-banded D-form chrome side supports **2,900.00**
Armchair, W McArthur, club style, aluminum/naugahyde **1,900.00**
Bench, Geo Nelson, slats w/primavera top, blk legs, 56" L **800.00**
Bowl, Beatrice Wood, ceramic, red metallic over gr w/bl, 6" **450.00**
Bowl, Lovera, ceramic, dk red w/dk bl highlights, 4½x8½" **300.00**
Cabinet, A Aalto #206, 2 3-drw banks, step-bk base, 30x43".........**2,000.00**
Cabinet, Geo Nelson, 5-drw, teak w/chrome legs, 41x40x19" .**2,000.00**
Cabinet, W Hoffman, 2-door/4-drw, World's Fair brand **1,400.00**
Candlesticks, Dorothy C Thorpe, Lucite, pretzel shape, 7", pr ...**120.00**
Chair, 'grasshopper'; Eero Saarien, 1-pc arm/legs, VG **1,100.00**
Chair, antelope; Ernest Race, bent steel w/pierced wood seat **375.00**
Chair, coconut; Geo Nelson, uphl over shaped steel shell **3,750.00**
Chair, dining; Chas Eames, molded/curved plywood bk/seat **400.00**
Chair, dining; Paul McCobb, molded plywood seat, dowel bk **175.00**
Chair, J Risley, welded steel rods depict seated lady, 34" **1,400.00**
Chair, lounge; att Alf Svensen, birch w/retro uphl, adjusts **400.00**
Chair, lounge; Chas Eames LCW, molded dyed plywood, VG **700.00**
Chair, lounge; Geo Nelson, coral uphl, iron legs, birch fr **850.00**
Chair, lounge; Jens Risom, blk webbing on molded birch fr **230.00**
Chair, side; Alvar Aalto #68, molded birch, orig vinyl, 27" **150.00**
Clock, mantel; Kem Weber, multilevel, digital, Lawson, 14" ..**1,300.00**
Clock, mantel; Seth Thomas, bird's eye maple, Deco, 9", VG **375.00**
Clock, wall; Geo Nelson, glass w/blk design, brass face, 18" dia .**475.00**
Clock, wall; Geo Nelson, mc balls on brass spokes, 14" dia **350.00**
Clock, wall; Geo Nelson, orange steel 'asterisk,' 10" **350.00**
Clock, Zephyr; Kem Weber, chromium w/brass bars, Lawson Time .**900.00**
Desk, drop leaf; Geo Nelson, 3-drw, walnut w/brn trim **850.00**
Dresser, triple; Geo Nakashima, walnut, trapezoid top, 100" ..**2,000.00**
Lamp, floor; Geo Nelson, ovoid wire-cage 38" bubble shade **550.00**
Lamp, table; K Weber, tiered base, 2-tier 11" dia shade, VG **800.00**
Plaque, Desimone, ceramic w/cvd figures & donkey, 10x15" **125.00**
Plate, Desimone, ceramic, HP stylized birds, 10" **100.00**
Radio, Walter D Teague, bl mirror/chrome, Spartan, VG **1,200.00**
Rocker, Chas Eames, molded fiberglass body, Zenith Plastics **350.00**

Rocker, Vladamir Kagan, walnut, continuous-shaped seat and back with amorphic-shaped open sides, ca 1955, $1,500.00.

Stemware, Dorothy C Thorpe, airbrushed pk & gray, 16 pcs **400.00**
Stool, Able Sorensen, birch/nylon webbing, lift-off tray top **110.00**
Stool, Alvar Aalto #11, 13" dia birch top, 3 molded legs **290.00**
Storage system, Florence Knoll, burlap on doors, 29x72", VG **700.00**
Table, cocktail; Chas Eames, dished 34" dia birch top, VG **850.00**
Table, cocktail; free-form glass top/2-pc cut-out wood base **1,100.00**
Table, cocktail; Gilbert Rohde, glass w/leather legs, 34" dia **600.00**
Table, cocktail; Paul Laszlo, blk free-form top, walnut base **475.00**
Table, Frank Gehry, hollow laminated 17" cb cube **200.00**
Table, Geo Nelson, 30" L lift-off tray, U-form chrome base **800.00**
Table, Italian, hot air balloons on ivory wood top, 19" dia **400.00**
Table, night; Gilbert Rohde #3920, rosewood, ½-cylinder base .**475.00**
Tray, Machine Age, rvpt glass Deco graphic & chrome, 18" **325.00**
Vase, Beatrice Wood, ceramic, yel/ivory lustre w/mc spots, 5" **650.00**
Vase, Fantoni, ceramic, tan/brn, w/gr & blk cvg, sq, 10x9" **200.00**
Vase, Fantoni, gr/yel/brn, bulbous, for Raymor, 8x9" **140.00**
Vase, feelie; Cabat, bl drip over dk brn, tiny opening, 3" **260.00**
Vase, Italian, ceramic, orange/yel/gray, Raymor, 12½" **140.00**
Vase, Italian, unglazed terra cotta bottle w/cvd women, 17" **110.00**

Finch, Kay

Kay Finch and her husband, Braden, operated a small pottery in Corona Del Mar, California, from 1939 to 1963. The company remained small, employing from twenty to sixty local residents who Kay trained in all but the most requiring tasks, which she herself performed. The company produced animal and bird figurines, most notably dogs, Kay's favorites. Figures of 'Godey' type couples were also made, as were tableware (consisting of breakfast sets) and other artware. Most pieces were marked. Kay Finch died on June 21, 1993. Prices for her work have been climbing.

Our advisor for this category is Jack Chipman, author of *The Collector's Encyclopedia of California Pottery*; he is listed in the Directory under California. Original model numbers are included in the following descriptions — three-digit numbers indicate pre-1946 models. After 1946 they were assigned four-digit numbers, the first two digits representing the year of initial production. *Kay Finch Ceramics Identification Guide* (published in 1992), containing many reprints of original catalog pages, is available from Frances Finch Webb; she is also listed in the Directory under California.

Ashtray, Song of Sea, bl & ivory, Geo Finch design, 5x7" **15.00**
Console set, 2 ladies & vase, celedon gr, 10" **145.00**
Figurine, Afghan, playing, #5555, sm **275.00**
Figurine, Afghan, wht porc, #4830, sm **225.00**
Figurine, Afghan, windblown, #5757 ....**350.00**
Figurine, angels, 3 kneeling/1 standing, #4909/#4910, 4-pc **150.00**
Figurine, angels (harp/fiddle/horn), #5151/#5152/#5154, 3-pc........**125.00**
Figurine, Butch & Biddy (rooster & hen), pr **85.00**
Figurine, cat, imp Italian Tasia Nove **50.00**
Figurine, Chanticleer, rooster, #129, 10¾" **200.00**
Figurine, Christmas tree, #5150, 4" **95.00**
Figurine, Cocker Spaniel, #5260, 4½" **250.00**
Figurine, Cocker Spaniel, in-mold mk, 11" **275.00**
Figurine, cottontail rabbit, wht w/pk ears, 1946, 2½" **65.00**
Figurine, Cuddles, rabbit w/garland & hat, #4623, 10½" **650.00**
Figurine, Cuddles, rabbit w/purse & hat, #4623, 10½" **650.00**
Figurine, Dalmation, #159, 17" **575.00**
Figurine, Do & See No Evil, cats, #4834/#4835, 3", pr **125.00**
Figurine, donkey w/bells, 1941, 5" **135.00**
Figurine, elephant, 5" **75.00**
Figurine, girl w/bl pinafore, puffy sleeves, blond hair, 5¼" **65.00**
Figurine, Grandpa, pig, strawberries, #163, 10x16" **575.00**

Figurine, Hannibal, angry cat, wht w/bl/pk/blk details, 10¼" 100.00
Figurine, Harvey, rabbit, #4622, 21½" 450.00
Figurine, Jeep & Peep (ducks), 4", pr 80.00
Figurine, Joseph, #6054, 10" 85.00
Figurine, Little Angel, Afghan, gold, #4964, sm 75.00
Figurine, Mitzi, pomeranian, #465, 10" 425.00
Figurine, Monkeyshines, monkey, waving, #4952, 9½" 400.00
Figurine, Mr Tom, cat, orange/resist, 1960?, 17½" 650.00
Figurine, Polly, penguin, #467, 4¾" 120.00
Figurine, poodle, perky, #5419, 15" 575.00
Figurine, poodle, playful, #5203, 10" 250.00
Figurine, Puddin', Yorkie, #158, 12x12" 435.00
Figurine, rabbit, sitting, #120, 4" 85.00
Figurine, Sassy, pig, #166, 3½" 25.00
Figurine, skunks, #1774/#4775, 4", pr 225.00
Figurine, Sleepy, bear w/hat, #5004L, 5" 130.00
Figurine, Socko & Jocko, circus monkeys, #4541/#4841, pr 220.00
Figurine, squirrel, wht lustre, 1951, 10" 500.00
Figurine, Toot, owl, 5¾" 65.00
Figurine, turtle, sm glaze flake, 3½" 50.00
Figurine, Yorkie pup, #171, 5½" 200.00
Figurine, 3 Bears, #4351/#4352, 3", 2¼", 1½", set 120.00
Lapel pin, Afghan head, #5081 ....65.00
Mug, Missouri Mule 45.00
Planter, lady figural, lt gr w/gold, wall type, 15" 120.00
Plaque, pomeranian, #4955, 4¾" sq 35.00
Shakers, birds, bl & wht, pr 80.00
Shakers, ducks, white w/gr details, pr 65.00
Shakers, owls, wht w/bl trim, pr 70.00
Tumbler, Southern Comfort, mule figural, overglaze platinum 40.00
Vase, Santa figural, mk, 4¼" 45.00
Wall pocket, Santa face, 9½x8¾" 175.00

Findlay Onyx and Floradine

Findlay, Ohio, was the location of the Dalzell, Gilmore, and Leighton Glass Company, one of at least sixteen companies that flourished there between 1886 and 1901. Their most famous ware, Onyx, is very rare. It was produced for only a short time beginning in 1889 due to the heavy losses incurred in the manufacturing process.

Onyx is layered glass, usually found in creamy white with a dainty floral pattern accented with metallic lustre that has been trapped between the two layers. Other colors found on rare occasions include a light amber (with either no lustre or with gilt flowers), light amethyst (or lavender), and rose. Although old tradepaper articles indicate the company originally intended to produce the line in three distinct colors, long-time Onyx collectors report that aside from the white, production was very limited. Other colors of Onyx are very rare, and the few examples that are found tend to support the theory that production of colored Onyx ware remained for the most part in the experimental stage. Even three-layered items have been found (they are extremely rare) decorated with three-color flowers. As a rule of thumb, using white Onyx prices as a basis for evaluation, expect to pay two to five times more for colored examples.

Floradine is a separate line that was made with the Onyx molds. A single-layer rose satin glassware with white opal flowers, it is usually priced in the general range of colored Onyx.

Chipping around the rims is very common, and price is determined to a great extent by condition. Our advisors for this category are Betty and Clarence Maier; they are listed in the Directory under Pennsylvania.

Floradine

Bowl, fluted, squat bulbous base, 4" 775.00

Box, dresser; 5½" 800.00
Celery vase, fluted cylinder neck, bulbous body, 6½" 750.00
Creamer, bulbous, fluted neck, 4⅝" 750.00
Mustard pot, 3¾" 600.00
Sugar bowl, bulbous, w/lid, 5½" 850.00
Sugar shaker 600.00
Syrup pitcher 1,250.00
Toothpick holder, 2½" 800.00
Tumbler, slightly bulbous, 3⅝" 700.00

Onyx

Box, wht w/silver decor, 5½" dia 750.00
Celery, wht w/silver decor, 6½" 300.00
Creamer, wht w/silver decor, 4½" 350.00
Jam jar, wht w/silver decor 500.00
Mustard pot, wht w/silver decor, hinged metal top, 3" 650.00

Onyx pitcher, white with silver decoration, 8", $1,200.00.

Pitcher, wht w/silver decor, rim chips, flakes, 4½" 275.00
Spooner, wht w/silver decor, 4¼" 325.00
Sugar shaker, wht w/gold decor, 5" 485.00
Tumbler, wht w/silver decor, 3¾x2⅞" 325.00

Fire Marks

During the early 18th century, insurance companies used fire marks — signs of insurance — to indicate to the volunteer fire fighters which homes were covered by their company. Handsome rewards were promised to the brigade that successfully extinguished the blaze, so competition was fierce between rivals and sometimes resulted in an altercation at the scene to settle the matter of which brigade would be the one to fight the fire! Fire marks were originally made of cast iron or lead; later examples were sometimes tin or zinc. They were used abroad as well as in this country, and those from England tended to be much more elaborate. When municipal fire departments were organized in the mid- to late 1860s, volunteer departments and fire marks became obsolete.

Eagle Hose No 2, CI, lt rust, 11" H 35.00
Fire Assoc of Phila, pnt CI, hydrant, 7½x11" 135.00
Fire Assurance of Philadelphia, CI, oval, 11x7½" 85.00
Fire Department Insurance, CI w/mc pnt, 11½" L 375.00
Insured Mutual Hartford, brass 50.00
London Assurance Inc-AD 1720, tin 40.00
Protector Fire Ins Co London, copper, 1835, VG 50.00
Royal Exchange Assurance, lead, mtd on wood panel 50.00
Sun Ins Office, lead, sun w/16 rays, 7x7" 150.00
United Firemen's Ins Co Phila PA, CI, 11⅜x8¾", VG 100.00
4 clasped hands & #906, 7x10½" 365.00

Firefighting Collectibles

Firefighting collectibles have always been a good investment in terms of value appreciation. Many times the market will be temporarily affected by wild price swings caused by the 'supply and demand principle' as related to a small group of aggressive collectors. These collectors will pay well over market value for a particular item they need or want. Once their desires are satisfied, prices seem to return to their normal range. It has been noticed that during these periods of high prices, many items enter the marketplace that otherwise would remain in collections. This may (it has in the past) cause a price depression (due again to the 'supply and demand principle' of market behavior). But when all is said and done, the careful purchase of quality, well-documented firefighting items has been an enjoyable hobby and an excellent investment opportunity.

Today there is a large, active group of collectors for fire department antiques (items over 100 years old) and an even larger group seeking related collectibles (those less than 100 years old). Our advisors for this category (except grenades) are H. Thomas and Patricia Laun; they are listed in the directory under New York.

Fire grenades preceded the pressurized metal fire extinguishers used today. They were filled with a mixture of chemicals and water and made of glass thin enough to shatter easily when thrown into the flames. Many varieties of colors and shapes were used. Our fire grenades advisor is Lawrence Meyer; he is listed in the Directory under Illinois.

Key:
C&W — complete & working   SAFA — Superior American
NST — National Standard Thread   Alarm Co.
S&A — soda & acid

Adapter, suction; brass/chrome, NST, 4x4½", EX 25.00
Alarm box, aluminum, Gamewell Quick..., bull's eye door, EX 145.00
Alarm box, aluminum, SAFA, full-sz street box 85.00
Alarm box, aluminum, style 51, quick-acting door, complete 135.00
Alarm box, CI, Gamewell, instructional door, w/key guard 200.00
Alarm box, CI, Gamewell, telegraph door, slant fist, complete ..245.00
Alarm box, CI, Gamewell, telegraph door/key guard, complete .220.00
Alarm box, CI, Gamewell Excelsior, telegraph door/trap lock/key .325.00
Alarm box, CI, Utica...Alarm & Telegraph, full sz, complete 350.00
Alarm box, CI, Utica...Alarm..., Excelsior sz/style, complete 750.00
Alarm box, CI & brass, Holtzer Cabot, City of Boston, key, EX .125.00
Alarm box, CI & brass, Holtzer Cabot, 9½" dia 85.00
Alarm indicator, Gamewell, oak, no bell, C&W 2,000.00
Alarm indicator, Gamewell, vibrating bell on top, C&W 2,850.00
Alarm indicator, Gamewell, walnut, no bell, C&W 2,400.00
Alarm indicator, M Crane, walnut, flat-sided wheels, no bell 3,750.00
Axe, fireman's, 6-lb standard pick head 35.00
Axe, fireman's, 8-lb flat pick head, early 65.00
Axe, parade; Viking style, orig pnt, #2 on head, w/provenance ..125.00
Axe, Pompier (hatchet); wooden hdl, leather case 65.00
Badge, Albuquerque NM FD #118, bright nickel 35.00
Badge, Basking Ridge Fire Co No 1, NJ, silver metal 25.00
Badge, cap; Maltese Cross w/hose carriage, silver metal 15.00
Badge, Commissioner E Meadow Fire Dist, gold-tone metal 50.00
Badge, Flushing Fire Dept, Murry Hill Hose Co, silver metal 50.00
Badge, Harrisburg PA Driver, NP on brass, 1920s-30s, 2x2½" 45.00
Badge, Hudson Active 1 FD, silver metal 35.00
Ballot box, dvtl wood, sliding lid, w/blk & wht marbles, EX 100.00
Bell, alarm; brass, turtle type, center wind, 6", w/key 135.00
Bell, apparatus, 'after market' style, NP/brass, 12", C&W 450.00

Bell, apparatus, brass, swinging cradle type, 10" 650.00
Bell, apparatus, chrome/brass, Am LaFrance, eagle finial, 12" 575.00
Bell, apparatus, NP/brass, complete, 10" 375.00
Belt, parade; blk leather w/wht lettering: American, VG 65.00
Belt, parade; tooled leather, emb metal buckle, #1 in center 95.00
Bookends, firemen, 1 w/trumpet, 1 w/lantern, cvd wood, pr 70.00
Bracket, lantern; CI, bicycle clip, gooseneck, early 85.00
Bracket, lantern; NP brass, fits Dietz King, EX 100.00
Bucket, leather, old gr rpt, yel label dtd 1843, 13", EX 400.00
Bucket, leather, red w/gold Waltham VFA & CL in center, VG ..300.00
Bucket, metal, red pnt, mk Fire, round bottom, mop-pail sz 23.00
Bucket, rubberized canvas, overhaul type 65.00
Cape, oilcloth, red w/gold lettering, rstr 1,800.00
Clamp, hose; Akron, all metal, modern 45.00
Clamp, hose; aluminum or steel, mk Am LaFrance 95.00
Clamp, hose; Peerless, all CI 65.00
Extinguisher, Acme Dry Chemical, tin, 22", EX 30.00
Extinguisher, Am Eagle...Cinn O, Pat...1902, s+a, 2½-gal 150.00
Extinguisher, Badger, copper/brass, stored press, H20, pony sz 85.00
Extinguisher, Buffalo Jr, copper, emb label, s+a, pony sz, EX 150.00
Extinguisher, Eclipse, tin, EX 85.00
Extinguisher, Protection Sure Death to Fire, dry chemicals, EX ...65.00
Extinguisher, Pyrene, brass, pump type w/bracket, CCL4, 1-qt 25.00
Extinguisher, Stop Fire, Foamite-Childs, NP brass, CCL4, 1-qt ...50.00
Extinguisher, Underwriters Fire..., copper, s+a, 2½-gal 15.00
Frontispiece, high eagle, orig letters & #s, EX 85.00
Frontispiece, HP leather, Engineer/carriage in gold, 7¼" 500.00
Frontispiece, low front, emb #s, machine lettered, NM 20.00
Gong, Gamewell, flat-top oak case, common, 15" 2,300.00
Gong, Gamewell, Moses Crane style, walnut, 15" bell 2,450.00
Gong, Moses Crane, walnut w/feather & balls, 10" bell, C&W .1,800.00
Gong, Moses Crane, walnut w/feather & balls, 16" bell, C&W .2,850.00
Gong, Moses Crane, walnut w/feather & balls, 18" bell, C&W .3,750.00
Gong, Moses Crane, walnut w/feather & balls, 8" bell, C&W ...1,400.00
Gong, rotary, brass, dashbrd mt, ft operated, 10", C&W 350.00
Gong, rotary, New Departure, brass, pull chain op, 10" 275.00
Gong, rotary, New Departure, NP brass w/bracket, lever op, 10" ..475.00
Gong, Star Electric Binghamton, plain oak, 8" bell 450.00
Gong, Star Electric Binghamton NY, fancy oak case, 12" bell ...1,200.00
Gong, Star Gong, Boston, oak case, 12" 375.00
Gong indicator, fancy cvd oak case, 15" bell, C&W 7,500.00
Gong indicator, oak case w/trn posts, 18" bell, C&W 6,000.00
Gong indicator, plain oak case, 15" bell, C&W 5,300.00
Grenade, Firex, cobalt, unemb, orig metal hanger, 4", M 65.00
Grenade, Firex, cobalt, unemb, sealed in orig box, 3¾" 70.00
Grenade, Firex, deep turq, vertical ribs, 5½" 550.00
Grenade, Harden's, teal bl, full, sm chips, 6" 60.00
Grenade, Harden's Hand Grenade..., turq, smooth base, 6⅝" 210.00
Grenade, Harden's Star, bl, complete w/contents 60.00
Grenade, Harden's Star, deep cobalt, emb star, EX 90.00
Grenade, Harkness...Destroyer, sapphire w/blk streaks, 6" 425.00

Grenade, Hayward's Hand Fire Grenade, Patented August 8, 1871, bright green, original contents, 6¼", NM, $325.00.

Grenade, Imperial Grenade Fire Extinguisher, gr, EX 250.00
Grenade, Pat Aug 8th 1871...Improved 1881 on label, cobalt ...140.00
Grenade, Prevoyante Extincteur Grenade, amber, scarce 280.00
Halligan bar, sgn casting, Hugh Halligan, hexagon hdl, 1950s ...125.00
Handkerchief, presentational, fire scene, 1906, 22" sq, EX 250.00
Hat, parade; stovepipe type, red w/gold letters, VG 2,000.00
Helmet, aluminum, high eagle w/leather front, Cairns, EX 225.00
Helmet, aluminum, low, Cairns Senator Somerset FD, VG 110.00
Helmet, aluminum, low, Cairns Senator w/frontispc, EX 110.00
Helmet, brass, Sapeurs Pompiers D'Aunneuil on front, Fr, VG ..150.00
Helmet, fiberglass, blk w/leather frontispc, PFD 22, EX 25.00
Helmet, fiberglass, red w/leather frontispc, Tank 1 BVFD, EX 30.00
Helmet, leather, Gratacap, w/greyhound holder, 1858, NM 975.00
Helmet, leather, high eagle, America Hose frontispc, VG 350.00
Helmet, leather, high eagle, John Olson, rpt frontispc, EX 275.00
Helmet, leather, high eagle, Roulstone, Boston, VG 325.00
Helmet, leather, high eagle, Wilson, w/frontispc, EX 275.00
Helmet, leather, NYer, Cairns, Fire Chief, HP frontispc, EX 165.00
Helmet, leather, NYer low front, Cairns, Driver...1 WFD, EX ...135.00
Helmet, leather, NYer low front, Cairns, Lieut WFD, VG 125.00
Helmet, leather, NYer low front, Cairns, w/liner/shield, VG 125.00
Lantern, Dietz Chief, brass, cold-blast type, EX 650.00
Lantern, Dietz King, Am LaFrance, brass, NM 325.00
Lantern, Dietz King, brass, clear globe, EX 235.00
Lantern, Dietz King, tin w/copper tank, common, EX 125.00
Lantern, Dietz Queen, brass, EX 665.00
Lantern, Dietz Tubular, brass, w/slide-over cage, Pat 89 ....300.00
Lantern, Ham's (Rochester), NP/brass, +cage & shield, sz 39 .....300.00
Lantern, wrist type, brass, Kearsarge mk on clear globe, EX 750.00
Life net, rope, lg, VG 175.00
Life net, ¼-fold, canvas, lt stains/no mildew, '40s, complete 200.00
Nozzle, AJ Morse, brass, 20", complete w/tips & shut-off 75.00
Nozzle, Akro Ball Akron Wooster, brass, 8" 35.00
Nozzle, Allen, brass, open/close valve, 8½" 85.00
Nozzle, cellar distributor; Am Fire Equipment, Bresnan, 2½" 160.00
Nozzle, combination; Fog Nozzle Co, brass, 1½" 35.00
Nozzle, combination; Rockwood, aluminum, 2½" 35.00
Nozzle, Eastman, playpipe, leather hdls, complete 175.00
Nozzle, Eureka Fire Hose, brass, playpipe w/leather hdls 125.00
Nozzle, LaFrance, brass, playpipe, w/tips 225.00
Nozzle, Rockwood low velocity applicator, 1½" & booster szs 35.00
Nozzle, Santa Rosa, aluminum, 2½" 125.00
Nozzle, Santa Rosa, brass & chrome, 1½" 85.00
Nozzle, Silsby, brass, playpipe, complete, steamer sz 300.00
Nozzle, USR Co Eureka Division, brass, playpipe, leather hdls ...150.00
Photo, broadside, apparatus, mfr's delivery, post-1960 ....15.00
Photo, broadside, steamer fire engine, mfr's delivery photo 45.00
Photo, fireman w/helmet & trumpet, cabinet sz 10.00
Photo, horse-drawn fire wagon, 6x8"+mat & fr 35.00
Pin-bk, Prevent Forest Fires, cartoon creature, 1940s, ⅞" 12.50
Plaque, builder's, Jas Smith Builder NY, brass, 9", EX 350.00
Punch register, Gamewell, brass, 1" hole punch w/cup & key 225.00
Punch register, Gamewell, 1" arrow punch 150.00
Rattle, alarm; dbl reed w/weighted end, EX 75.00
Rattle, alarm; single reed, wooden w/War Alert label, 12", EX 50.00
Rattle, alarm; single reed, 11", EX 50.00
Rattle, alarm; single reed w/weighted end, 6½x7½", EX 105.00
Reel, take-up; brass, metronome type, ½", EX 275.00
Ribbon, convention; common variety, post-1900 ....15.00
Ribbon, convention; fancy, w/metal attachments, pre-1900, NM ...45.00
Ribbon, convention; pre-1900, VG to NM, from $18.00 up to 25.00
Sign, Firemen's Fund Ins Co, paper, fire scene, 26x10", VG 250.00
Staff, fire warden's, wooden, gold pnt, 58", EX 375.00
Telephone, Utica Fire Alarm Tel Co..., oak, wall type, 8" W 350.00

Torch, brass, spike end, wick pick, 14"+trn wood hdl, EX 450.00
Torch, parade, blk wood w/adjustable wick burner, 21", NM 75.00
Torch, parade; brass w/trn wood hdl, 18", EX 100.00
Transmitter, 4 rounds, Bliss Gamewell, 10x14" 175.00
Trophy, plastic, metal fireman w/lantern on top, 12" 10.00
Trumpet, presentation; SP, eng fire engine/flowers, 1887, 20" ...900.00
Trumpet, presentation; SP, eng steamer/equipment, 24", EX ..1,000.00
Trumpet, speaking; brass/nickel, 14" w/sash, C&W 325.00
Trumpet, speaking; octagonal, NP/brass, Cairnes & Bros 800.00
Wrench, spanner; Am LaFrance, Pat Feb 24, 1925 ....28.00

Fireglow

Fireglow is a type of art glass that first appears to be an opaque cafe au lait, but glows with rich red 'fire' when held to a strong source of light.

Ewer, landscape in brn tones w/in scroll, att Sandwich, 8" 175.00
Pitcher, wht flowers/orange leaves, ribbed, 8", +4 tumblers 275.00
Vase, birds/branches/florals, 11¾x5" 195.00
Vase, bl flowers w/brn leaves, stick neck, 7" 70.00
Vase, leaves/flowers, dbl gourd, 5" 70.00

Fireplace Implements

In the colonial days of our country, fireplaces provided heat in the winter and were used year round to cook food in the kitchen. The implements that were a necessary part of these functions were varied and have become treasured collectibles, many put to new use in modern homes as decorative accessories. Gypsy pots may hold magazines; copper and brass kettles, newly polished and gleaming, contain dried flowers or green plants. Firebacks, highly ornamental iron panels that once reflected heat and protected masonry walls, are now sometimes used as wall decorations. By Victorian times the cookstove had replaced the kitchen fireplace, and many of these early utensils were already obsolete; but as a source of heat and comfort, the fireplace continued to be used for several more decades. See also Wrought Iron.

Andirons, bell metal, urn top, 1820s, 26", EX 1,400.00
Andirons, brass, ball top, slipper ft, Am, 1800s, 15", pr 275.00
Andirons, brass & iron, urn top, Am, early 1800s, 23", pr 660.00
Andirons, brass finials on knife-blade shafts, 1900s, pr 330.00
Andirons, CI, heart stem, gooseneck finial, 14", pr 285.00
Andirons, wrought knife blade w/penny ft, brass urn finial, pr ...550.00
Bellows, orig yel pnt w/stenciling, brass nozzle, 18", EX 155.00
Bellows, turtle bk, orig red pnt, trn brass tip, 1800s, 18" 125.00

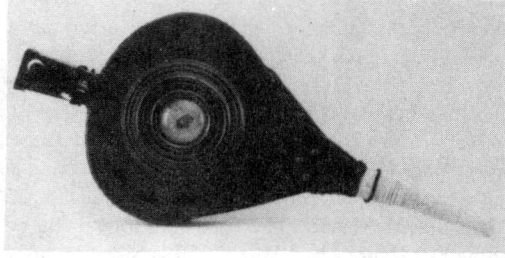

Bellows, walnut with black leaf and geometric inlays, raised turned panel with reverse-painted rose insert, America, 1800s, 22x19½", EX, $1,200.00.

Coffee roaster, sheet metal w/iron rod, wood hdl, 1800s, 51" **125.00**
Fender, CI D-form w/brass rim above wire screen, 1800s, 53" L ...**465.00**
Fender, Geo III, polished steel, late 1700s, 26x54" **275.00**
Fender, iron w/wire grill & brass top rail, 14x28x13" **300.00**
Fender, pierced brass, 1800s, 11x48½x15" **330.00**
Screen, brass mesh screen panels, 3-part, ea: 25x13½" **115.00**
Screen, Eastlake detail, needlepoint panel, Victorian, 52x28" ...**385.00**
Screen, English Sheraton, mahog w/rosewood graining, 40" **250.00**
Screen, tooled/pnt leather covering, 3 48x25½" sections **250.00**
Spit, brass & wrought iron, for roasting birds, 14" L **40.00**

Fishing Collectibles

Collecting old fishing tackle is becoming more popular every year. Though at first most interest was geared toward old lures and some reels, rods, advertising, and miscellaneous items are quickly gaining ground. Values are given for examples in excellent or better condition and should be used only as a guide. For more information contact our advisor Randy Hilst, an appraiser and collector whose address and phone number are listed in the Directory under Illinois.

Bucket, minnow; Falls City Angler's Choice ad, 1862, 8", EX **15.00**
Catalog, Abercrombie & Fitch, tackle, 1930, 68-pg, NM **60.00**
Catalog, Pflueger #61, 1941, 244-pg, NM **35.00**
Catalog, Von Lengerke & Detmold Inc, tackle, NY, '17, 188-pg **60.00**
Decoy, Brook Trout, unknown maker, pnt eyes, NM **250.00**
Decoy, red head/yel body, glass eyes & brass fins, 6½", EX **100.00**
Decoy, Yel Perch, Oscar Peterson, 2 weights, 7" L, EX **375.00**
Lure, Arbogast Weedless Sunfish, glass eyes, 1¾", NM **200.00**

Lure, Baby Jointed Pike Minnow, $12.00.

Lure, Bate's Patent Spinner, copper & SP, EX **400.00**
Lure, CB Hibbard, German silver, Pat Mar 25, 1984, 2" body, EX ..**25.00**
Lure, Creek Chub Giant Pikie, tack eyes, EX **20.00**
Lure, Creek Chub Jointed Darter, frog finish, pnt eyes **15.00**
Lure, Haskell Minnow, SP on copper w/brass tail, 1859, 4½" **6,000.00**
Lure, Heddon Coast Minnow, glass eyes, wood w/rubber tail **200.00**
Lure, Heddon Expert, wht w/red & bl, ca 1906, NM **190.00**
Lure, Heddon Midget Underwater, missing side hooks **25.00**
Lure, Henry C Brush's Floating Trolling Spoon, brass, EX **55.00**
Lure, K&K Minnowette, jointed body, metal tail, NM **325.00**
Lure, Shakespeare Frog Skin Bait, glass eyes, 3¾" **75.00**
Lure, Shakespeare Revolution, aluminum, 1906 style, 3¼" **100.00**
Lure, Walton Products Speed Bait, 12 propellers, NP, 1¼", NM ..**55.00**
Reel, Edward Vom Hofe #2, brass, Pat Jan 23, '83, 2¾", NM **300.00**
Reel, Hardy, Silex, quick-change spool, 4", M, +case **110.00**
Reel, Hardy, Uniqua, 2-screw latch, brass ft, 2⅞", MIB **90.00**
Reel, Hardy Bros, Perfect, hard rubber hdl, brass ft, 4¼" **150.00**
Reel, Heddon Automatic, free-stripping #87, MIB **30.00**
Reel, Islamurada, custom-built surf type, 3" side plate, EX **120.00**

Reel, James Heddon's Sons, level wind, German silver hdl **125.00**
Reel, Orvis, Gr Mtn, quick-change spool, 3½", M in bag **60.00**
Reel, Penn Senator, 1-pc cast spool, Star drag, chrome plated **50.00**
Reel, Pflueger Everlaster, plated over brass, surf caster, EX **55.00**
Reel, Shakespeare, Miller Autocrat Model HF, stainless **90.00**
Reel, spinning; Humphrey's Model #3A, stainless steel, EX **30.00**
Rod, Barney & Berry, trout fly, 3-pc, silver reel seat, 8½-ft **160.00**
Rod, Edward Von Hofe, saltwater, silver mts, 84", NM **75.00**
Rod, fly; South Bend, split bamboo w/cork hdl, 9-ft, EX **60.00**
Rod, HL Leonard Tournament, 3-pc, silver reel seat, 9½-ft **400.00**
Rod, Milward's Hexacane Deluxe, split cane, cork hdl, EX **75.00**
Rod, Orvis, 3-pc, screw-down reel band, cedar ft, 8½-ft **225.00**
Rod, spinning; Orvis Impregnated, cane, 2-pc, 7-ft **100.00**
Ruler, wooden, lists WI fish laws & limits, 1930s, 24" **6.50**

Flags of the United States

The brevity and imprecise language of the first Flag Act of 1777 allowed great artistic license for America's early flag makers. This resulted in a rich variety of imaginative star formations which coexisted with more conventional union patterns. In 1912 inviolate design standards were established for the new 48-star flag, but the banners of our past history continue to survive:

The 'Great Star' pattern — configured from the combined stars of the union, appeared in various star denominations for about 50 years, then gradually disappeared in the post-Civil War years.

The utilitarian 'scatter' pattern — created through the random placement of stars, is traceable to the formative years of our nation and remained a design influence through most of the 19th century.

The 'wreath' pattern — first appearing in the form of simple single-wreath formations, eventually evolved into the elegant double- and triple-wreath medallion patterns of the Centennial period.

Acquisition of specific star denominations is also a primary consideration in the collecting process. Pre-Civil War flags of 33 stars or less are very scarce and are typically treated as 'blue chip' items. Civil War-era flags of 34 and 35 stars also stand among the most sought-after denominations. Market demand for 36-, 37- and 38-star flags is strong but less broad-based, while interest in the unofficial 39-, 40-, 41- and 42-star examples is largely confined to flag aficionados. The very rare 43 remains in a class by itself and is guaranteed to attract the attention of the serious collector.

Row-patterned flags of 44, 45 and 46 stars still turn up with some frequency and serve as a source of more modestly priced vintage flags. Ordinary 48-star flags flood the flea markets and are priced accordingly, while the short-lived 49 is regarded as a legitimate collectible. 13-star flags, produced over a period of more than 200 years, surface in many forms and must be assessed on a case-by-case basis.

Many flag buffs favor sizes that are manageable for wall display. Extra-large flags may or may not be regarded as desirable, depending upon the beholder. Allowances are typically made for the normal wear and tear found on original period flags. Conversely, there is little or no collector demand for modern-day flag repros, regardless of condition.

The dollar value of a flag is by no means based upon age alone. The wide price swings in the listing below have been influenced by a variety of determining factors related to age, scarcity and aesthetic merit. In fact, almost any special feature that stands out as unusual or distinctive is a potential asset. Imprinted flags and inscribed flags; 8-point stars, gold stars, and added stars; extra stripes, missing stripes, tri-color stripes and war stripes are all part of the pricing equation. And while political and military flags may rank above all others in terms of prestige and price, any flag with a significant and well-documented historical connection has 'star' potential (pardon the pun).

Our advisor for this category is Robert Banks; he is listed in the Directory under Maryland.

13 stars, (4-5-4), sea captains, ca 1860s, 74x140" 280.00
13 stars, Betsy Ross flag, by grandaughter, 1903, 8x12" 550.00
13 stars, in semi-wreath, hand sewn, 1870s, 54x102" 180.00
13 stars, printed, w/advertisement, 1880s, 4x7" 40.00
13 stars, US Navy boat ensign, dtd Sept 1904, 44x78" 75.00
13 stars, 3rd MD pattern, hand sewn, 1840s, 32x45" 575.00
16 stars, naval ensign, hand sewn, CW era, 44x60" 600.00
19 stars, 16 orig+3, sewn scrap fabric, 39x66" 960.00
20 stars, hand-embr into Great Star, rare, 24x32" 1,050.00
23 stars, Civil War related, home-sewn muslin, 48x96" 200.00
24 stars, folk art, hand-tatted construction, 12x18" 225.00
25 stars, stenciled burlap on 24" wood tripod pole, 5x7" 220.00
26 stars, Great Star, embr on sewn silk, 30x43" 630.00
29 stars, entirely hand sewn, poor condition, 43x68" 410.00
30 stars, gold stars/fringe, silk, delicate, 52x68" 425.00
31 stars, Great Star, Lincoln related, printed, 11x14" 185.00
31 stars, Great Star, 14 stripes, hand sewn, 39x69" 600.00
31 stars, row pattern, hand-stitched bunting, 104x247" 580.00
32 stars, dbl wreath of inset stars, hand sewn, 36x48" 535.00
33 stars, hand-/machine-sewn wool bunting, 66x92" 475.00
33 stars, wreath w/10 stripes, hand sewn, 77x127" 450.00

34-Star, hand-sewn bunting, cryptic star arrangement forms rough-hewn federal shield when viewed from vertical position, 51x68", $600.00.

34 stars, dbl-wreath pattern, printed silk, 18x28" 225.00
34 stars, Great Star, mixed fabrics, sewn, 91x154" 670.00
34 stars, row pattern, pieced printed silk, 64x104" 390.00
34 stars form shield, all hand sewn, worn, 51x66" 600.00
34 stars in pentagonal clusters, hand sewn, 63x95" 620.00
35 stars, recruiting flag, sewn bunting, 50x116" 585.00
35 stars, row pattern, hand/machine sewn, 96x180" 510.00
36 stars, Civil War, 8-pointed, in sewn wreath, 78x90" 720.00
36 stars, in 6 rows, hand-sewn wool bunting, 71x114" 210.00
36 stars, sailing ship's, inscr & dtd, 75x142" 235.00
37 stars, printed silk, 32x40" 55.00
37 stars, row pattern, stitched bunting, 30x48" 180.00
37 stars, wreath pattern, hand-sewn cotton, 72x106" 290.00
37 stars, 6-pointed, hand-/machine-stitched cotton, 60x84" 375.00
38 stars, Blaine campaign, printed cotton, 17x27" 340.00
38 stars, Centennial 1876, printed cotton, 15x24" 70.00
38 stars, dbl-wreath pattern, sewn muslin, 87x128" 220.00

38 stars, from SS America, hand sewn, 68x108" 420.00
38 stars, Great Star, printed silk, gold fringe, 12x17" 65.00
38 stars, in rows, hand/machine-stitched bunting, 71x116" 145.00
38 stars, medallion-wreath pattern, printed cotton, 12x17" 55.00
38 stars, 1776-1876 pattern, printed linen, 27½x46" 330.00
39 stars, in rows, all machine-stitched bunting, 40x84" 150.00
39 stars, originally 34 Great Star, sewn, 69x129" 400.00
39 stars, row pattern variation, printed silk, 12x24" 45.00
39 stars, scatter pattern, hand sewn, 78x120" 185.00
39 stars, triple wreath, hand-sewn bunting, 60x108" 250.00
39 stars (6-5 pattern), printed gauze bunting, 19x34" 32.00
40 stars, unofficial, hand/machine sewn, 61x115" 110.00
40 stars, wreath-in-box pattern, hand sewn, 43x82" 160.00
41 star printed flags (17), uncut muslin, rare, 24x263" 300.00
42 stars, printed cotton, unhemmed, 18x24" 22.00
42 stars, sewn cotton, from Ft Hamilton NY, 120x177" 135.00
42 stars, Union scatter pattern, hand sewn, 48x72" 134.00
43 stars, machine-sewn bunting, extremely rare, 29x70" 425.00
43 stars (1 side only), 98989 pattern, homemade, 38x48" 175.00
44 stars, hand-sewn bunting, 70x144", EX 110.00
44 stars, machine-sewn cotton bunting, 53x82" 65.00
45 stars, hand-sewn wool bunting, 92x135" 55.00
45 stars, HP w/sewn muslin stripes, 38x70" 42.00
45 stars, machine-sewn cotton bunting, 80x108" 40.00
45 stars, printed silk w/red ribbon ties, 32x46" 38.00
45 stars, triple-wreath GAR flag, printed muslin, 11x16" 40.00
46 stars, machine-sewn wool bunting, 72x138" 40.00
46 stars, printed silk, in baton-type carrying tube, 12x17" 17.00
46 stars, random pattern, machine sewn, 40x100" 55.00
47 stars, unofficial, sewn bunting, 108x137" 170.00
48 stars, machine-sewn cotton bunting, 60x96" 25.00
48 stars, naturalization, sewn names, 1914, 14x24" 75.00
48 stars, sewn to form 'USA,' unauthorized WWI, 45x69" 175.00
48 stars, staggered rows (early), printed muslin, 13x23" 10.00
48 stars, Whipple Peace Flag, printed silk, 14x24" 220.00
48 stars, WWII liberation, from Liege, homemade, 68x93" 95.00
48 stars, 10-9 pattern, printed bunting, rare, 39x61" 55.00
49 stars, embr w/sewn stripes, gold fringe, 48x72" 60.00
49 stars, machine-sewn cotton, 36x60" 25.00
49 stars, 3 uncut flags, printed cottonsheet, 37x36" 18.00
50 stars, Carter campaign, printed plastic, 12x18" 15.00
50 stars, oddity, printed/sewn in gr & wht, 36x60" 65.00
52 stars, Spanish Am war era, home sewn, rare, 44x84" 215.00
56 stars, printed crepe paper, Oriental, 1920s, 9x9" 18.00

Florence Ceramics

Figurines marked 'Florence Ceramics' were produced in the forties and fifties in Pasadena, California. The quality of the ware and the attention given to detail are prompting a growing interest among today's collectors. The names of these lovely ladies, gents, and figural groups are nearly always incised into their bases. The company name is ink-stamped. Because this is a relatively new area of collecting and the rarity of many items has yet to be determined, examples are evaluated by size and intricacy of design. Our advisor for this category is Jack Chipman, author of *The Collector's Encyclopedia of California Pottery*; he is listed in the Directory under California.

Abigail, bl, 8½" 140.00
Amelia, brn, 9¼" 160.00
Angel 60.00
Ann 70.00
Ava, 10" 145.00

Belle, pk 65.00
Blossom Girl, planter 50.00
Camille, 8¼" 125.00
Charmaine, wht, 9" 135.00
Choir Boy 40.00
Clarissa, gold trim, 8" 100.00
Clarissa, gray 65.00
Clarissa, pk 75.00
Colonial Gentleman 140.00
David, wht 75.00
Dealer sign, emb roses, leaves & scrolling, mc w/gold, 8½" 195.00
Delia, gold trim, 8" 95.00
Douglas, gray 65.00
Elaine, 6" 50.00
Elizabeth, seated on settee, 8x7" 200.00
Emily, planter 45.00
Garr, salmon, pk, blk, & wht w/gold, 8½" 110.00
Irene, wht, 6" 60.00
Jim, 6¼" 65.00
Joy 60.00
June, planter 40.00
Kay, planter, 6" 50.00
King Louis XV 115.00
Lantern boy & Blossom girl, flower holders, 9", 8¼", pr 110.00
Lillian, pk, 8" 55.00
Louise, pk 45.00
Madeline 100.00
Madonna, wht w/gold 75.00
Marilyn, pk, 8½" 150.00
Matilda, rose, 8¼" 90.00
Melanie 60.00
Mimi, planter 45.00
Musetta, gr, 8½" 110.00
Nancy, bud vase 30.00
Oriental boy & girl, wht w/gold, 8½", pr 100.00
Pamela, pk 45.00
Patsy, planter, 6" 50.00

Pinky and Blue Boy, 12", $650.00 for the pair.

Plaque, lady w/parasol, 9x6½" 75.00
Polly, planter 40.00
Prima Donna, maroon 120.00
Rebecca, seated, 7½" 115.00
Sara, gray, 8" 100.00

Scarlet, 9" 100.00
Sue, wht w/gold 65.00
Sue Ellen 115.00
Suzette, wht/gr/pk, planter/vase, 6¾" 55.00
Vivian, gr, 9½" 145.00

Florentine Cameo

Although the appearance may look much like English cameo, the decoration on this type of glass is not wheel cut or acid etched. Instead a type of heavy paste — usually a frosty white — is applied to the face to create a look very similar to true cameo. It was produced in France as well as England; it is sometimes marked 'Florentine.'

Tumbler, floral, wht on apricot, 3¾" 65.00
Vase, 2 figures, wht on cranberry, sgn Cameo, 8x6" 200.00
Water set, cranberry w/wht tropical foliage & birds, 5-pc 550.00

Flow Blue

Flow Blue ware was produced by many Staffordshire potters; among the most familiar were Meigh, Podmore and Walker, Samuel Alcock, Ridgway, John Wedge Wood (who often signed his work Wedgewood), and Davenport. It was popular from about 1825 through 1860 and again from 1880 until the turn of the century. The name describes the blurred or flowing affect of the cobalt decoration, achieved through the introduction of a chemical vapor into the kiln. The body of the ware is ironstone, and Oriental motifs were favored. Later issues were on a lighter body and often decorated with gilt.

Our advisor, Mary Frank Gaston, has compiled a lovely book, *The Collector's Encyclopedia of Flow Blue China,* with full-color illustrations and current market values; you will find her address in the Directory under Texas.

Abbey, plate, Geo Jones, 6" 22.00
Abbey, plate, Geo Jones, 9½" 65.00
Alaska, butter pat, Grindley 35.00
Alaska, gravy boat, Grindley, ca 1891 ....90.00
Alaska, platter, Grindley, 16" 200.00
Alaska, sugar bowl, Grindley, w/lid, ca 1891-1914 ....185.00
Albany, butter dish, Johnson Bros 235.00
Albany, plate, Johnson Bros, 7½" 32.00
Aldine, bone dish, Grindley 35.00
Aldine, butter dish 225.00
Alexandria, plate, Hancock & Sons, 9½" 65.00
Alton, creamer, Grindley, 3½" 80.00
Amoy, cup plate, Davenport 125.00
Amoy, plate, Davenport, 10½" 120.00
Amoy, plate, Davenport, 7½" 90.00
Amoy, plate, Davenport, 8¼" 100.00
Amoy, plate, Davenport, 9¼" 110.00
Amoy, plate, dessert; Davenport 90.00
Amoy, soup bowl, Davenport, 10½" 155.00
Amoy, sugar bowl, Davenport 525.00
Arabesque, cup & saucer, Mayer 88.00
Arcadia, bowl, vegetable; Wilkinson, w/lid 215.00
Arcadia, plate, Wilkinson, 10" 95.00
Argyle, bowl, vegetable; Grindley, w/lid 345.00
Argyle, butter pat, Grindley 40.00
Argyle, creamer, Grindley 220.00
Argyle, plate, Ford & Sons, 7⅜" 60.00
Argyle, plate, Grindley, 8¾" 89.00

Argyle, platter, Grindley, 17" 245.00
Argyle, platter, unmk Grindley, 15" 225.00
Argyle, sauce dish, Grindley 32.00
Arundel, cracker jar, Doulton 250.00
Ashburton, bowl, soup; Grindley 85.00
Ashburton, bowl, vegetable; Grindley, w/lid 275.00
Ashburton, gravy boat, Grindley 95.00
Ashburton, soup ladle, Grindley 280.00
Astoria, butter pat, Johnson 35.00
Astoria, cup & saucer, Johnson 75.00
Astoria, pitcher, New Wharf Potteries, 6¾" 225.00
Astoria, plate, Johnson 75.00
Astral, gravy boat, Grindley, w/underplate 230.00
Astral, ladle, Grindley, sm 165.00
Astral, plate, Grindley, 9⅞" 88.00
Atlanta, bowl, vegetable; Wedgwood, lg 85.00
Atlanta, plate, Wedgwood, 9" 80.00
Atlas, toothbrush holder 60.00
Aurora, plate, Morley, 9¼" 65.00
Bamboo, plate, Bates & Walker, 10½" 35.00
Beaufort, bowl, vegetable; Grindley, lg 80.00
Beauties of China, MV&Co, 8½" 75.00
Belmont, bone dish, Meakin, 6x4½" 55.00
Belmont, butter pat, Meakin 45.00
Belmont, plate, Meakin, 6⅝" 50.00
Blue Rose, plate, Grindley, 6" 35.00
Brussels, platter, 14" 85.00
Burleigh, bowl, soup; Burgess & Leigh 88.00
Cambridge, butter pat, New Wharf Potteries 30.00
Cambridge, plate, Meakin, 9" 65.00
Cambridge, soup tureen, Meakin, w/lid 455.00
Candia, bowl, soup; Cauldon, 10⅛" 95.00
Candia, chocolate pot, Cauldon 465.00
Candia, cup & saucer, Cauldon 95.00
Candia, pitcher, melon ribs, Cauldon, cream sz 165.00
Canton, cup plate, Alcock 75.00
Carlton, bowl, vegetable; Alcock, 9¼" 250.00
Carlton, plate, Alcock, 8½" 100.00
Carlton, plate, Alcock, 9½" 125.00
Carlton, platter, Alcock, 11x8½" 250.00
Carlton, teapot, prof rpr 975.00
Carnation, chamber pot, Minton 250.00
Cashmere, plate, Morley, 8½" 115.00
Cashmere, plate, Morley, 9⅜" 125.00
Cavendish, biscuit jar, Keeling 337.50
Celeste, plate, 10½" 120.00
Celtic, platter, Grindley, 12⅞" 125.00
Celtic, platter, Grindley, 17½" 190.00
Chain of States, cup & saucer 95.00
Chapoo, bowl, berry; Wedge Wood 55.00
Chapoo, bowl, soup; Wedge Wood, 8⅜" 150.00
Chapoo, bowl, vegetable; Wedge Wood, w/lid 995.00
Chapoo, plate, Wedge Wood, 6⅜" 95.00
Chapoo, plate, Wedge Wood, 8⅜" 115.00
Chapoo, platter, Wedge Wood, 14" 350.00
Chapoo, teapot, Wedge Wood 600.00
Chen-Si, cup & saucer, handleless; Meir 150.00
Chen-Si, platter, Meir, 13⅝" 385.00
Chinese, cup & saucer, Dimmock 145.00
Ching, sauce dish, Davenport 52.00
Chusan, drainer, Wedgwood, 12¼" 450.00
Chusan, plate, Ashworth, 9¼" 135.00
Chusan, teapot, Fell 415.00
Clarence, sugar bowl, w/lid, Johnson Bros 100.00

Clayton, bacon dish, Johnson Bros 60.00
Clayton, bowl, vegetable; Johnson Bros, w/lid 235.00
Clayton, butter pat, Johnson Bros 35.00
Clayton, creamer, Johnson Bros 135.00
Clayton, cup & saucer, Johnson Bros 75.00
Clayton, gravy boat, Johnson Bros, w/underplate 135.00
Clayton, plate, Johnson Bros, 8" 38.00
Clayton, plate, Johnson Bros, 9" 50.00
Clifton, bowl, vegetable; lg 85.00

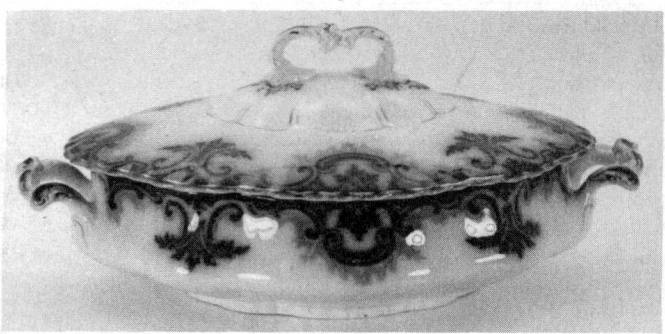

Clifton, casserole, gold trim, ruffled edge, with lid, 11½", $350.00.

Clover, cup & saucer, Grindley 65.00
Clover, plate, Grindley, 9" 48.00
Clytie, platter, Wedgwood, 18½" 685.00
Coburg, pitcher & bowl, Edwards 1,800.00
Coburg, plate, Edwards, 10¼" 150.00
Colonial, relish, Meakin, ca 1891 ....65.00
Colonial, sugar bowl, Meakin 45.00
Conway, bowl, soup; New Wharf Pottery, 9" 58.00
Corinthian, toothbrush holder, Wedgwood 80.00
Cyprus, honey dish, Davenport 85.00
Cyprus, teapot 495.00
Dainty, butter dish, Maddocks, w/lid 265.00
Dainty, cup & saucer, Maddocks 90.00
Dainty, egg cup, Maddocks 100.00
Davenport, teapot, Longport 465.00
Devon, bowl, vegetable; w/lid, Fell 195.00
Devon, platter, Grindley, 10" 55.00
Duchess, bowl, Grindley, w/lid, 5½x11" 165.00
Dundee, cup & saucer 75.00
Elgar, tureen, vegetable; Upper Hanley Potteries, w/lid 175.00
Excelsior, plate, Fell, 10½" 120.00
Fairy Villas, bowl, Adams, 10" 125.00
Fairy Villas, plate, Adams, 10¼" 95.00
Fairy Villas, plate, Adams, 11" 100.00
Ferrara, bowl, Wedgwood, 8⅛" 45.00
Ferrara, creamer & sugar bowl, Wedgwood 200.00
Ferrara, egg cup, Wedgwood 76.00
Floral, soup plate, Hughes, 8¾" 75.00
Florida, bowl, Grindley, 7½" 60.00
Florida, bowl, vegetable; oval, Grindley, 7" 75.00
Florida, plate, Johnson Bros, 10" 65.00
Formosa, plate, Mayer, 9¾" 135.00
Formosa, plate, Ridgway, 6¼" 88.00
Formosa, saucer, Mayer 85.00
Gainsborough, platter, Ridgway, scalloped, 16x12" 235.00
Geisha, creamer, Upper Hanley 100.00
Gem, butter pat, Maddocks 25.00

Geneva, pitcher, Doulton, 4" 125.00
Georgia, bowl, berry; Johnson Bros, ind 35.00
Gironde, bowl, berry; Grindley, 5" 35.00
Gironde, gravy boat, Grindley, w/underplate 225.00
Gironde, platter, Grindley, 15¼x10¾" 150.00
Glenmore, cup & saucer, Grindley 55.00
Glenmore, platter, Grindley, 12" 90.00
Glentine, plate, Grindley, 6" 30.00
Glentine, plate, Grindley, 9" 55.00
Glenwood, plate, Johnson Bros, 9" 50.00
Grace, butter pat, Grindley 32.00
Grace, platter, Grindley, 21" 350.00
Grecian Scroll, wash bowl & pitcher, Mayer 645.00
Grenada, cup & saucer, Alcock 85.00
Haddon, platter, Grindley, 14" 175.00
Hindustan, relish, Maddocks 275.00
Hindustan, saucer, Maddocks 50.00
Holland, platter, Johnson Bros, 14" 150.00
Hong Kong, bowl, soup; Meigh, 10¼" 165.00
Hong Kong, bowl, vegetable; Meigh, w/lid 280.00
Hong Kong, plate, Meigh, 8¾" 120.00
Hong Kong, platter, Meigh, 18x12" 665.00
Hong Kong, teapot 975.00
Horticultural, compote, ped ft, Wedgwood, 4x11¾x8" ...395.00
Horticultural, plate, Wedgwood, 9" 95.00
Idris, bone dish, Grindley 55.00
Indian, cup & saucer, handleless; Pratt 140.00
Indian, plate, Pratt, 7¼" 75.00
Indian, plate, Pratt, 9" 100.00
Indian, platter, Pratt, 13¼" 325.00
Indian Jar, platter, Furnival, 14" 400.00
Indian Jar, platter, 22" 1,200.00
Iowa, plate, Royal Staffordshire Pottery, 6" 35.00
Iris, gravy boat, Grindley 85.00
Janette, bowl, soup; Grindley, 9¼" 85.00
Janette, butter pat, Grindley 45.00
Japan, platter, Fell, 15" 325.00
Jenny Lind, bowl, vegetable; Wilkinson, 7½" 235.00
Kin Shan, plate, Challinor, 7¾" 90.00
Kyber, cup & saucer, handleless; Adams 135.00
Kyber, plate, Adams, 10" 110.00
Kyber, plate, Adams, 7" 55.00
Kyber, plate, Adams, 9" 90.00
La Belle, bowl, berry; Wheeling 55.00
La Belle, bowl, cereal; Wheeling 85.00
La Belle, bowl, soup; Wheeling, 9½" 80.00
La Belle, bowl, sq, Wheeling 245.00
La Belle, butter pat, Wheeling 42.00
La Belle, plate, Wheeling, 9½" 80.00
La Belle, platter, Wheeling, 11½" 95.00
La Francais, cup & saucer 20.00
Lahore, plate, Phillips & Son, 8½" 115.00
Lancaster, plate, New Wharf Pottery, 9" 55.00
Lancaster, sauce dish, New Wharf Pottery 32.00
Le Pavot, pitcher, milk; Grindley 275.00
Le Pavot, soup tureen, Grindley, 12" 145.00
Linda, platter, 13x9¼" 66.00
Lois, sugar bowl, Wood & Son 150.00
Lonsdale, plate, Ford, 10⅛" 85.00
Lorne, cup & saucer, demitasse; Grindley 75.00
Lorne, gravy boat, Grindley 85.00
Lorne, plate, Grindley, 8" 40.00
Lorne, plate, Grindley, 9" 65.00
Lorne, platter, Grindley, 16" 225.00

Lotus, gravy boat, Grindley, w/undertray 145.00
Lotus, plate, Grindley, 10" 50.00
Lotus, plate, Grindley, 9" 40.00
Lusitania, bowl, Wood & Sons, 9⅝" 95.00
Luzerne, bowl, soup; Mercer 72.50
Luzerne, plate, Mercer, 7⅜" 50.00
Luzerne, plate, Mercer, 9" 65.00
Mabelle, plate, Burgess & Leigh, 9" 35.00
Madras, pitcher, Doulton, 5" 125.00
Madras, plate, Doulton, 9⅛" 110.00
Madras, plate, Upper Hanley, 9" 100.00
Madras, saucer, Doulton 85.00
Magnolia, gravy boat, 2-spout, attached underplate, Johnson 165.00
Mandarin, plate, Pountney, 10" 75.00
Mandarin, plate, Pountney, 9¼" 70.00
Manhattan, butter pat, Alcock 45.00
Manhattan, cup & saucer, Alcock 65.00
Manilla, pitcher, water; Podmore Walker 495.00
Manilla, plate, Podmore Walker, 7⅜" 90.00
Manilla, plate, Podmore Walker, 8⅝" 125.00
Marechal Niel, butter pat, Grindley 35.00
Marechal Niel, platter, Grindley, 12½" 95.00
Marguerite, bone dish, Grindley 40.00
Marie, bowl, vegetable; rnd, Grindley, w/lid 165.00
Marie, butter pat, Grindley 32.00
Marie, plate, Grindley, 6" 55.00
Marlborough, bowl, vegetable; Grindley, w/lid 200.00
Marquis, plate, bread & butter; Grindley, 6" 32.00
Marquis, plate, Grindley, 10" 80.00
Marquis, plate, Grindley, 6" 30.00
Martha, bone dish, Bridgett & Bates 32.00
Melbourne, bowl, soup; Grindley, 8" 48.00
Melbourne, bowl, vegetable; Grindley, w/lid 275.00
Melbourne, bowl, vegetable; oval, Grindley 75.00
Melbourne, cup & saucer, Grindley 65.00
Melbourne, gravy boat, Grindley, 1891-1914 ....95.00
Melbourne, plate, Grindley, 10" 65.00
Melbourne, plate, 9" 45.00
Melbourne, platter, Grindley, 14x10" 195.00
Melbourne, platter, Grindley, 18½" 285.00
Melbourne, sauce tureen, Grindley 110.00
Mongolia, bowl, Johnson Bros, 3x8½" 75.00
Mongolia, platter, Johnson Bros, 11" 200.00
Mongolia, platter, Johnson Bros, 18½" 235.00
Nancy, bowl, vegetable; Grimwades, w/lid 300.00
Nancy, plate, Grimwades, 9½" 85.00
Nankin, cake plate, Ashworth 150.00
Nankin, platter, Doulton, 13½x10¾" 175.00
Navy, plate, Till, 9" 40.00
Ning-Po, soup bowl, 10½" 185.00
Non Pareil, bowl, berry; Burgess & Leigh 45.00
Non Pareil, bowl, cereal; Burgess & Leigh 70.00
Non Pareil, bowl, soup; Burgess & Leigh, 8⅝" 82.50
Non Pareil, bowl, vegetable; Burgess & Leigh 160.00
Non Pareil, bowl, vegetable; Burgess & Leigh, w/lid ...375.00
Non Pareil, butter pat, Burgess & Leigh 55.00
Non Pareil, plate, Burgess & Leigh, 6¾" 48.00
Non Pareil, plate, Burgess & Leigh, 7⅝" 75.00
Non Pareil, plate, Burgess & Leigh, 9¾" 105.00
Non Pareil, teacup & saucer, Burgess & Leigh 95.00
Normandy, bowl, cereal; Johnson Bros 30.00
Normandy, plate, Johnson Bros, 6¼" 42.50
Normandy, plate, Johnson Bros, 8" 65.00
Normandy, plate, Johnson Bros, 9⅜" 75.00

Normandy, platter, Johnson Bros, 10⅜" 185.00
Normandy, teacup & saucer, Johnson Bros 105.00
Olympia, butter dish, Grindley 115.00
Olympia, sugar bowl, Grindley, w/lid 95.00
Orchid, teapot, Maddocks 325.00
Oregon, bone dish 65.00
Oregon, cup & saucer, handleless; Mayer 120.00
Oregon, plate, Johnson Bros, 9" 60.00
Oregon, plate, Mayer, 9½" 125.00
Oregon, platter, Mayer, 13⅜" 375.00
Oregon, teapot, Mayer 600.00
Oriental, bowl, Ridgway, 6½" 65.00
Oriental, platter, Ridgway, 12¾" 250.00
Oriental, saucer, Alcock 50.00
Oriental, teapot, Ridgway 750.00
Osborne, cup & saucer, Grindley 98.00
Ovando, platter, Meakin, 12½" 165.00
Oxford, bowl, berry; Johnson Bros, 5⅜" 45.00
Oxford, butter pat, Johnson Bros 40.00
Oxford, gravy boat, Johnson Bros 55.00
Oxford, plate, Johnson Bros, 9⅞" 85.00
Oxford, sugar bowl, Johnson Bros, w/lid 110.00
Paisley, bowl, soup; Mercer, 8⅞" 80.00
Pekin, plate, Johnson Bros, 9" 80.00
Pekin, platter, 11½" 125.00
Pelew, plate, Challinor, 9¾" 125.00
Penang, platter, Ridgway, 13½x10½" 375.00
Persian Moss, bowl, berry; Utzschneider, 5" 35.00
Persian Moss, cracker jar, Utzschneider 235.00
Persian Moss, plate, Uzschneider, 7¾" 40.00
Persian Moss, soup plate, deep, Utzschneider 45.00
Poppy, bowl, Bennett, 8½" 55.00
Poppy, plate, Grindley, 9" 42.00
Princeton, plate, Johnson Bros, 10" 80.00
Renown, creamer & sugar bowl, w/lid, Staffordshire 110.00
Richmond, plate, Johnson Bros, 10" 50.00
Rock, plate, Challinor, 7½" 75.00
Rose, bone dish, Grindley 35.00
Roseville, bowl, vegetable; Maddocks, w/lid 315.00
Roseville, butter pat, Maddocks 45.00
Roseville, compote, Maddocks 255.00
Royal Blue, bowl, berry; Burgess & Campbell 45.00
Royal Blue, bowl, vegetable; Burgess & Campbell, ind 60.00
Royal Blue, cup & saucer, Burgess & Campbell 80.00
Royston, cup & saucer, demitasse; Royston 50.00
Ruins, platter, Copeland, ca 1848, 9⅛x6⅝" 225.00
Sabraon, creamer 215.00
Sabraon, plate, 10¾" 165.00
Sabraon, plate, 6¼" 95.00
Savoy, gravy boat, Stoke 100.00
Savoy, sugar bowl, Stoke, w/lid 120.00
Scinde, bowl, soup; Alcock, 10⅝" 60.00
Scinde, bowl, vegetable; Alcock, w/lid, sm rpr 750.00
Scinde, creamer, Podmore Walker 350.00
Scinde, plate, Alcock, 7¼" 95.00
Scinde, plate, luncheon 70.00
Scinde, platter, Alcock, 13x10" 395.00
Sefton, sauce tureen, Myott & Son, w/lid & ladle 265.00
Seville, plate, Wood & Sons, 6⅞" 55.00
Seville, sugar bowl, Wood & Sons 175.00
Shanghae, plate, Furnival, 10¼" 130.00
Shanghae, platter, Furnival, 13x10" 300.00
Shapoo, plate, Boote, 7⅜" 75.00
Shell, cup & saucer, handleless; Challinor 160.00

Shell, plate, Challinor, 8⅝" 75.00
Sloe Blossom, toothbrush holder, Ridgway, w/lid 265.00
Stanley, gravy boat, w/underplate, Johnson Bros 135.00
Temple, plate, Podmore Walker, 7¾" 110.00
Temple, plate, Podmore Walker, 8¾" 120.00
Temple, plate, Podmore Walker, 9¾" 130.00
Tivoli, gravy boat, Furnival 160.00
Togo, butter pat, Winkle 30.00
Tonquin, plate, Adams, 7½" 90.00
Tonquin, plate, Heath, 7¾" 95.00
Tonquin, platter, Adams, 15½x12" 625.00
Tonquin, sugar bowl, Heath 250.00
Touraine, bone dish, Stanley 80.00
Touraine, bowl, berry; Alcock 45.00
Touraine, butter pat, Stanley 55.00
Touraine, cup & saucer, Stanley 80.00
Touraine, plate, Alcock, 8⅞" 75.00
Touraine, plate, Stanley, 10" 85.00
Touraine, plate, Stanley, 7⅜" 40.00
Touraine, platter, Stanley, 12½x8½" 150.00
Turin, creamer & sugar bowl, Johnson Bros 225.00
Turin, sauce dish, Johnson Bros 18.00
Venice, bowl, berry; Johnson Bros 45.00
Venice, butter pat, Johnson Bros 45.00
Venice, toothbrush jar, Grimwades 85.00
Venus, gravy boat 65.00
Vermont, butter pat, Burgess & Leigh 35.00
Verona, butter pat, Burgess & Leigh 30.00
Verona, platter, Ford & Sons, 13½" 245.00
Verona, platter, Ford & Sons, 15" 275.00
Virginia, bowl, Maddocks & Sons, 6¼" 85.00
Virginia, butter pat, Maddocks & Sons 30.00
Waldorf, bowl, vegetable; New Wharf Pottery, rnd 120.00
Waldorf, plate, New Wharf Pottery, 9" 72.50
Waldorf, waste bowl, New Wharf Pottery 175.00
Warwick, saucer, Johnson Bros 25.00
Washington Vase, plate, 10" 60.00
Watteau, beaker, Doulton 70.00
Watteau, bowl, flanged rim, Doulton, 12½" 135.00
Watteau, compote, Doulton, 10¼" 375.00
Watteau, cup & saucer, Doulton 85.00
Watteau, cup & saucer, New Wharf Pottery 85.00
Watteau, plate, Doulton, 9½" 85.00
Watteau, plate, Staffordshire, 10⅛" 60.00
Waverly, butter pat, Maddocks 45.00
Waverly, pitcher, Maddocks, 6½" 235.00
Waverly, plate, Maddocks, 6¼" 40.00
Weir, soup tureen, Ford & Son, w/lid 395.00
Wheel, tea set, child's, 15-pc 950.00
Windsor, butter dish, Edwards & Sons, 3-pc 225.00
Windsor, gravy boat, CH&H 100.00
Windsor, platter, CH&H, 18" 250.00
Windsor Royal, butter pat, Edwards & Son 45.00
Windsor Royal, cup & saucer, Edwards & Son 100.00
Yedo, plate, Ashworth, 9¾" 75.00
Yedo, plate, dinner, Ashworth, 10⅜" 95.00
Yedo, platter, Ashworth, 15¼" 230.00
Yedo, soup, flanged rim, Ashworth, 10¼" 110.00
Yedo, tureen stand, Ashworth, 15" 300.00

Flue Covers

When spring housecleaning started and the heating stove was

taken down for the warm weather season, the unsightly hole where the stovepipe joined the chimney was hidden with an attractive flue cover. They were made with a colorful litho print behind glass with a chain for hanging. Although scarce today, some scenes were actually reverse painted on the glass itself. The most popular motifs were florals, children, animals, and lovely ladies. Occasionally flue covers were made in sets of three — one served a functional purpose, while the others were added to provide a more attractive wall arrangement. They range in size from 7" to 14", but 9" is the average. Our advisor for this category is Cara J. Washburn; her address is in the Directory under Wisconsin.

Brunette in jeweled dress and helmet, 8½", EX, $70.00.

Battle of Manila, May 1 1898, orig chain, 10x8", EX 50.00
Girl in pk dress, shoe advertising, orig chain, 6x8", EX.................50.00
Giving Thanks, crimped pewter edge, orig chain, 12", EX 35.00
Ladies (pr) in bl & gr on gray in gold fr, 9", G 22.50
Oriental boy w/bouquet, tin border, orig chain, 8½x7½" 50.00

Folk Art

That the creative energies of the mind ever spark innovations in functional utilitarian channels as well as toward playful frivolity is well documented in the study of American folk art. While the average early settler rarely had free time to pursue art for its own sake, his creative energy exemplified itself in fashioning useful objects carved or otherwise ornamented beyond the scope of pure practicality. After the advent of the Industrial Revolution, the pace of everyday living became more leisurely, and country folk found they had extra time. Not accustomed to sitting idle, many turned to carving, painting, or weaving. Whirligigs, imaginative toys for the children, and whimsies of all types resulted. Though often rather crude, this type of early art represents a segment of our heritage and as such has become valued by collectors.

Values given for drawings, paintings, and theorems are 'in frame' unless noted otherwise. See also Baskets; Decoys; Frakturs; Samplers; Trade Signs; Weathervanes; Wood Carvings.

Calligraphic drawing, dated 1861, unsigned, unframed, 8x10", $1,700.00.

Birdhouse, primitive, wood/roofing paper/worn pnt, 23x26x14" ...85.00
Calligraphy, pen & ink, Declaration of Independence, 22x18" 65.00
Calligraphy, pen & ink, landscape, 1900s, fr, 20x14" 30.00
Calligraphy, pen & ink, leaping stag, unsgn, 10x27" 800.00
Calligraphy, reward of merit, bird w/banner, dtd 1896, fr 175.00
Comb case, twig art, curved top pine board, 1900s, 8x14x11" 65.00
Engraving, bird, hand-colored, matted, fr, 17x13" 65.00
Painting, oil on academy brd, church landscape, fr, 11x16" 50.00
Painting, oil on brd, horse in stable, Burton, 183-, 28x22" 1,100.00
Painting, oil on brd, lady's portrait, cleaned/rstr, 23x15" 225.00
Painting, oil on canvas, lady's portrait, lacy cap, 30x25" 440.00
Painting, oil on canvas, man's portrait, primitive, 30x25" 1,980.00
Painting, oil on tin, primitive tulip still life, 14x18" 85.00
Theorem on paper, pen/ink/graphite, patriotic, 1870, 12x15" 275.00
Theorem on paper, rose, EX color, old fr, 14x11" 120.00
Theorem on velvet, fruit, pastels, matted, fr, 9¼x11½" 490.00
Theorem on velvet, lg mc parrot/flowers, gilt fr, 17x22" 500.00
Theorem on velvet, still life w/Canton bowl & fruit, 18x24" 265.00
Whimsey, china-head dolls in bottle, 1 at loom/1 at wheel, 16" .350.00
Whirligig, biplane, cvd wood, tin tail, worn pnt, 1930s, 27" 165.00
Whirligig, biplane, wood/metal, 3-D pilot, 1930s, 33" L 345.00
Whirligig, blksmith, pnt wood, 23x11x18" 495.00
Whirligig, canoe & 2 Indians, cvd wood, mc pnt, 1900, 11x21" ...660.00
Whirligig, Continental soldier, cvd/pnt, ca 1890, rstr, 24" 715.00
Whirligig, crow, cvd & pnt wood, 1800s, 25" 275.00
Whirligig, Dewey Boy, cvd & pnt wood, ca 1900, 12", EX 935.00
Whirligig, fiddler man/boy on fence on brd, 21x18x12" 990.00
Whirligig, horse, wood w/mc pnt, 1900s, 15" 220.00
Whirligig, man sawing wood, mc pnt on wood, 1900s, 57" 195.00
Whirligig, Roman soldier, pnt cvd wood, ca 1900, 12" 220.00
Whirligig, 2 figures, jtd wood, zinc flywheel, 1880s, 32" 1,300.00
Wreath, interlocking wood pcs, old blk pnt, 10x12" 75.00

Fostoria

The Fostoria Glass Company was built in 1887 at Fostoria, Ohio, but by 1891 it had moved to Moundsville, West Virginia. During the next two decades, they produced many lines of pressed patterned tableware and lamps. Their most famous pattern, American, was introduced in 1915 and was produced continuously until 1986 in well over two hundred different pieces. From 1920 to 1925, top artists designed tablewares in colored glass — canary (vaseline), amber, blue, orchid, green, and ebony — in pressed patterns as well as etched designs. By the late thirties, Fostoria was recognized as the largest producer of handmade glassware in the world. The company ceased operations in Moundsville in 1986.

Many items from both the American and Coin Glass lines are currently being reproduced by Lancaster Colony. In some cases the new glass is superior in quality to the old. Since the 1950s, Indiana Glass has produced a pattern called 'Whitehall' that looks very much like Fostoria's American, though with slight variations. Because Indiana's is not handmade glass, the lines of the 'cube' pattern and the edges of the items are sharp and untapered in comparison to the fire-polished originals. Three-footed pieces lack the 'toe' and instead have a peg-like foot, and the rays on the bottoms of the American examples are narrower than on the Whitehall counterparts. The Home Interiors Company currently offer several pieces of American look-alikes which were not even produced in the United States. Be sure of your dealer and study the books suggested below to become more familiar with the original line.

Coin Glass reproductions are flooding the market. Among items you may encounter are an 8" round bowl, 9" oval bowl, 8¼" wedding bowl, 4½" candlesticks, urn with lid, 6¼" candy jar with lid, footed comport, sugar and creamer; there could possibly be others. Colors in production are crystal, green, blue, and red. The red color is very good, but the blue is not the original color, nor is the emerald green. Buyer beware!

For further information see *Elegant Glassware of the Depression Era* by Gene Florence; and *Fostoria, the Popular Years, Third Edition Price Guide,* by Jo Ann Schliesman; and *Fostoria, An Identification and Value Guide of Pressed, Blown & Hand Molded Shapes* by Ann Kerr. *Glass Animals and Figural Flower Frogs of the Depression Era* by Lee Garmon and Dick Spencer offers an in-depth look at that particular aspect of Fostoria's production. (See also Glass Animals.) Their addresses are listed in the Directory under Illinois. Items with (+) at the end of the lines are currently being reproduced; prices are for original issues.

Arcady Footed iced tea, $17.50; Oyster cocktail, $12.00.

American, crystal, ashtray, sq, 2⅞" 7.50
American, crystal, bowl, boat form, 12" 22.50
American, crystal, bowl, floating garden; 11½" 55.00
American, crystal, bowl, fruit; shallow, 13" 60.00
American, crystal, bowl, nappy; 6" 20.00
American, crystal, bowl, oval, deep, 11¾" 52.50
American, crystal, bowl, vegetable; oval, 9" 35.00
American, crystal, bowl, wedding; w/lid, 6½" 100.00
American, crystal, butter dish, w/lid, oblong 42.50
American, crystal, candlestick, 3" 15.00
American, crystal, candlestick, 6" 37.50
American, crystal, cigarette box, w/lid, 4¾" 45.00
American, crystal, comport, jelly; w/lid, 6¾" 35.00
American, crystal, cookie jar, w/lid, 8⅞" 395.00
American, crystal, creamer, ind 8.50
American, crystal, cup, footed, 7-oz 10.00
American, crystal, decanter, w/stopper, 24-oz, 9¼" 95.00
American, crystal, hurricane lamp, complete, 12" 150.00
American, crystal, ice bucket, metal hdl 75.00
American, crystal, ice tub, 6½" 55.00
American, crystal, jam pot, w/lid, 4½" 45.00
American, crystal, ladle, mayonnaise 15.00
American, crystal, mayonnaise, 2-part, 6¼" 47.50
American, crystal, oil, 7-oz, 6¾" 47.50
American, crystal, pitcher, cereal; 5⅜" 40.00
American, crystal, pitcher, 2-pt, 7¼" 65.00
American, crystal, pitcher, 3-pt, 8" 75.00
American, crystal, plate, cake; ftd, 12" 47.50
American, crystal, plate, salad; 7" 10.00
American, crystal, plate, salad; 8½" 15.00
American, crystal, plate, torte; 14" 45.00
American, crystal, plate, torte; 18" 125.00
American, crystal, platter, oval, 12" 65.00
American, crystal, shakers, 3¼", pr 25.00
American, crystal, sugar bowl, w/lid, hdl, 5¼" 25.00
American, crystal, syrup, tea 90.00
American, crystal, vase, bud; flared, 6" 20.00
American, crystal, vase, bud; flared, 8½" 20.00
American, crystal, vase, bud; ftd, 6" 20.00
American, crystal, vase, flared, 10" 85.00
American, crystal, vase, flared, 7" 47.50
American, crystal, vase, flared, 9½" 75.00
American, crystal, vase, 8" 47.50
American Beauty, crystal, goblet, #6077/2, 10½-oz, 5⅝" 10.00
American Lady, crystal, tumbler; ftd, 5-oz, 4⅛" 11.00
Arlington, milk glass, ashtray; 9" 20.00
Arlington, milk glass, pepper mill, #2694, 6¼" 10.00
Autumn, crystal, goblet, #6068, 10-oz, 5¾" 10.00
Avalon, crystal, tumbler, iced tea; #6049, ftd, 15¼-oz, 6¼" 9.50
Baroque, bl, bowl, flared, 12" 45.00
Baroque, bl, bowl, rolled edge, 11" 65.00
Baroque, bl, bowl, salad; 10½" 47.50
Baroque, bl, candlesticks, dbl, 4½", pr 45.00
Baroque, bl, candlesticks, 4", pr 35.00
Baroque, bl, cheese & cracker set 95.00
Baroque, bl, plate, cake; hdld, 10" 40.00
Baroque, bl, plate, 7" 14.00
Baroque, bl, saucer 6.50
Baroque, crystal, bonbon, crystal, 3-toed, 7⅜" 12.00
Baroque, crystal, bowl, nappy; 5" 12.50
Baroque, crystal, bowl, serving; hdld, 8½" 20.00
Baroque, crystal, comport, 5½" 18.50
Baroque, crystal, creamer, ftd, 3¾" 10.00
Baroque, crystal, cup, ftd 8.50
Baroque, crystal, goblet, 9-oz, 6¾" 20.00
Baroque, crystal, plate, torte; 14" 25.00
Baroque, crystal, saucer 3.00
Baroque, crystal, sugar bowl, ftd, 3½" 8.00
Baroque, yel, bowl, hdld, 10½" 32.50
Baroque, yel, bowl, nappy; hdld, 5" 20.00
Baroque, yel, comport, 5½" 18.50
Baroque, yel, plate, cake; hdld 10" 20.00
Baroque, yel, saucer 4.00
Beacon, crystal, plate, #2337, 7" 7.50
Beloved, crystal, tumbler, juice; #6089/88, ftd, 5-oz, 4¾" 11.00
Betsy Ross, milk glass, plate, #2620, 8" 9.00
Bouquet, crystal, basket, #2630, reeded hdl, 10¼" 55.00
Bouquet, crystal, bowl, #2630, rolled edge, 11" 35.00
Bouquet, crystal, cheese & cracker set, #2630 ....45.00
Bouquet, crystal, ice bucket, #2630, chrome hdl 55.00
Bouquet, crystal, saucer, #2630 ....3.50
Bouquet, crystal, tray, lunch; #2630, hdld, 11¼" 27.50
Bouquet, crystal, vase, #4121, 5" 37.50
Bracelet, crystal, plate, #2337, 8" 6.50
Bridal Belle, crystal, tumbler, juice; platinum decor, ftd, 4⅞" 12.00
Bridal Wreath, crystal, goblet, claret; #6049, 5-oz, 5⅝" 22.50
Brighton, crystal, plate, #2337, 8" 8.00
Bristol, crystal, plate, #2337/550, 8" 5.00
Burgundy, crystal, tumbler, juice; #6092/88, ftd, 5½-oz, 4¾" 9.50
Buttercup, crystal, comport, #2364, 8" 45.00
Buttercup, crystal, plate, torte; #2364, 16" 55.00
Camellia, crystal, basket, #2630, reeded hdl, 10¼" 52.50
Camellia, crystal, plate, torte; #2630, 16" 45.00
Camellia, crystal, relish, #2630, 3-part, 11⅛" 37.50
Camellia, crystal, tumbler, juice; #6036, 5-oz, 4⅝" 13.50
Capri, crystal, goblet, cordial; #6045, 1½-oz, 2⅝" 10.00
Carousel, crystal, goblet, sherbet; #6080/11, 7-oz, 4¾" 10.00
Celeste, crystal, goblet, cordial; 1-oz, 3⅛" 10.00
Century, crystal, ashtray, ind, 2¾" 11.50
Century, crystal, bowl, cereal; 6" 18.00

Century, crystal, bowl, flared, 12" 37.50
Century, crystal, bowl, fruit; 5" 12.50
Century, crystal, bowl, nappy; hdld, 4½" 12.50
Century, crystal, bowl, salad; 8½" 42.50
Century, crystal, bowl, snack; ftd, 3½" 42.50
Century, crystal, candlesticks, trindle, 7¾", pr 75.00
Century, crystal, candy dish, w/lid 47.50
Century, crystal, comport, 4⅜" 18.00
Century, crystal, goblet, sherbet; 5½-oz, 5¾" 20.00
Century, crystal, goblet, wine; 5½-oz, 5¾" 31.50
Century, crystal, pitcher, 48-oz, 7⅛" 135.00
Century, crystal, plate, party; 8" 25.00
Century, crystal, plate, salad; crescent, 7½" 40.00
Century, crystal, plate, torte; 14" 27.50
Century, crystal, plate, 6" 10.00
Century, crystal, platter, oval, 12" 40.00
Century, crystal, relish, 2-part, 7⅜" 17.50
Century, crystal, relish, 3-part, 11⅛" 27.50
Century, crystal, saucer 3.00
Century, crystal, sugar bowl, ftd, 4" 9.50
Century, crystal, tumbler, ftd, 12-oz, 5⅞" 24.00
Chateau, crystal, plate, #2337/550, 8" 5.00
Chatham, crystal, goblet, parfait; #6036, 5½-oz, 5⅞" 11.00
Chintz, crystal, bowl, #2496, flared, 12" 45.00
Chintz, crystal, bowl, #2496, hdld, 10½" 40.00
Chintz, crystal, bowl, #6023, ftd 35.00
Chintz, crystal, bowl, bonbon, #2496, 7⅜" 25.00
Chintz, crystal, bowl, finger; #869, 4½" 40.00
Chintz, crystal, bowl, nappy; #2496, flared, hdls, 5" 12.50
Chintz, crystal, bowl, serving, #2496, hdls, 8½" 25.00
Chintz, crystal, candlesticks, #2496, 4", pr 35.00
Chintz, crystal, cheese & cracker set, #2496 ....62.50
Chintz, crystal, comport, #2496, 4¾" 35.00
Chintz, crystal, ice bucket, #2496 ....125.00
Chintz, crystal, plate, cracker; #2496, 11" 37.50
Chintz, crystal, saucer, #2496 ....6.00
Chintz, crystal, sugar bowl, #2496, ftd, 3½" 20.00
Christiana, crystal, goblet, sherbet; #6030, low, 4-oz, 3¾" 16.00
Circlet, crystal, creamer, #2666, ind 7.00
Circlet, crystal, goblet, #6055, 10-oz, 6⅛" 10.00
Circlet, crystal, relish, #2364, 2-part, 8¼" 15.00
Coin, amber, bowl, nappy; hdl, 5⅜" 20.00
Coin, amber, bowl, oval, 9" 30.00
Coin, amber, bowl, wedding; w/lid 70.00
Coin, amber, cake salver, ped ft, 6½" 110.00
Coin, amber, candle holders, 4½", pr 30.00

**Coin, candy jar, red, #1372/347, 6¼"
(has been reproduced), $70.00.**

Coin, amber, jelly compote 17.50
Coin, amber, lamp, coach; oil burner, 13½" 125.00

Coin, amber, pitcher, 32-oz 50.00
Coin, bl, ashtray, 5" 25.00
Coin, bl, bowl, oval, 9" 55.00
Coin, bl, bowl, ped ft, w/lid, 8½" 150.00
Coin, bl, pitcher, 32-oz 30.00
Coin, bl, vase, bud; 8" 40.00
Coin, crystal, ashtray, center coin, 7½" 18.00
Coin, crystal, bowl, oval, 9" 30.00
Coin, crystal, cake salver, ped ft, 6½" 90.00
Coin, crystal, candle holders, 8", pr 50.00
Coin, crystal, candy jar, #347, w/lid (+) 35.00
Coin, crystal, cruet, w/stopper, 7-oz 50.00
Coin, crystal, jelly compote 15.00
Coin, crystal, plate, 8" 20.00
Coin, crystal, punch cup 30.00
Coin, crystal, sugar bowl, w/lid 25.00
Coin, crystal, tumbler, 4¼" 27.50
Coin, crystal, urn, w/lid, 12¾" 75.00
Coin, crystal, vase, bud; 8" 20.00
Coin, emerald gr, ashtray, oblong, 4" 25.00
Coin, olive gr, bowl, nappy; 5⅜" 18.00
Coin, emerald gr, bowl, ftd, 8½" 100.00
Coin, olive gr, bowl, oval, 9" 30.00
Coin, olive gr, candle holders, 4½", pr 30.00
Coin, olive gr, candy box, w/lid, 4⅛" 30.00
Coin, olive gr, creamer 15.00
Coin, olive gr, sugar bowl, w/lid 30.00
Coin, olive gr, wedding bowl, w/lid 55.00
Coin, red, ashtray, 5" 22.50
Coin, red, bowl, rnd, 8" 45.00

Colony, vase, footed, 7½", $40.00.

Colony, crystal, ashtray, rnd, 3" 7.00
Colony, crystal, ashtray, rnd, 6" 17.50
Colony, crystal, bowl, cupped, 8" 32.50
Colony, crystal, bowl, hdls, 4¾" 8.00
Colony, crystal, bowl, salad; 9¾" 35.00
Colony, crystal, bowl, sq, 5½" 10.00
Colony, crystal, cheese & cracker set 35.00
Colony, crystal, creamer, 3¾" 6.00
Colony, crystal, ice bucket, plain edge 95.00
Colony, crystal, lamp, electric 125.00
Colony, crystal, plate, salver; ftd, 12" 50.00
Colony, crystal, plate, torte; 18" 65.00
Colony, crystal, stem, wine; 3¼-oz, 4¼" 22.00
Colony, crystal, tray, snack; 10½" 17.50
Colony, milk glass, butter dish, #2412, w/lid, oblong, 7½" 44.50
Contour, crystal, ashtray, 6½" 5.00
Contour, crystal, creamer, #2666, 3½" 7.00
Contour, crystal, plate, snack; #2666, 10" 11.50
Contour, crystal, tray, #2638, 7" 6.50

Coronet, crystal, bowl, fruit; 13" 15.00
Coronet, crystal, plate, lemon; 6¼" 6.00
Coronet, crystal, tray, lunch; hdld, 11½" 27.50
Cynthia, crystal, bowl, bonbon; #2560, 3-toed, 7¼" 17.50
Cynthia, crystal, goblet, claret; #6017, 4-oz, 5⅞" 22.50
Devon, crystal, plate, #2337/550, 8" 5.00
Devon, crystal, tumbler, iced tea; #6089/63, ftd, 13-oz, 6¼" 9.50
Diadem, crystal, goblet, sherbet; 6½-oz, 4" 3.50
Diamond, milk glass, sugar bowl, #679, 3⅜" 15.00
Duchess, crystal, goblet, cordial; #6068, 1¼-oz, 3" 12.50
Ebony, crystal, ashtray, #2667, 9" 17.50
Ebony, crystal, smoker set, #2496, 5-pc 27.50
Empress, crystal, plate, #2337, 8" 5.00
Enchantment, crystal, tumbler, juice; #6074/88, ftd, 5-oz, 4¾" 5.50
Engagement, crystal, goblet, sherbet; #6092/22, 7-oz, 5½" 10.00
Envoy, crystal, goblet, cordial; 1-oz, 2¾" 11.50
Evening Star, crystal, goblet, #6087/2, 8¼-oz, 7" 8.50
Evening Star, crystal, tumbler, juice; #6087/88, ftd, 11-oz, 6⅜" 7.00
Fairfax, amber, ashtray, 2½" 7.50
Fairfax, amber, baker, oval, 9" 15.00
Fairfax, amber, bonbon 9.00
Fairfax, amber, bowl, dessert; hdls, lg 10.00
Fairfax, amber, bowl, soup; 7" 12.00
Fairfax, amber, creamer, tea 7.00
Fairfax, amber, ice bowl liner 12.00
Fairfax, amber, ice bucket 30.00
Fairfax, amber, pitcher, #5000 ....110.00
Fairfax, amber, plate, salad; 7½" 3.00
Fairfax, amber, plate, whipped cream 8.00
Fairfax, amber, platter, oval, 12" 20.00
Fairfax, amber, saucer 2.50
Fairfax, amber, stem, wine; 3-oz, 5½" 18.00
Fairfax, amber, sugar bowl lid 20.00
Fairfax, amber, tumbler, ftd, 5-oz, 4½" 10.00
Fairfax, rose, bl or orchid; ashtray, 4" 17.50
Fairfax, rose, bl or orchid; bowl, cream soup; ftd 20.00
Fairfax, rose, bl or orchid; butter dish, w/lid 135.00
Fantasy, crystal, goblet, #6086/2, 11¾-oz, 6⅜" 12.00
Frisco, milk glass, candy jar, #1229, w/lid, 6½" 35.00
Gadroon, crystal, goblet, #6030, 10-oz, 7⅞" 15.00
Garland, crystal, goblet, cordial; #6077/29, 1-oz, 3" 10.00
Gold Coin, crystal, bowl, nappy; #1372/499, hdld, 5⅜" 15.00
Golden Flair, crystal, goblet, sherbet; #6087/11, 6½-oz, 5½" 5.00
Golden Grail, crystal, goblet, #6083/2, 11½-oz, 6¼" 9.00
Golden Lace, crystal, goblet, sherbet; #6085/11, 6-oz, 5¼" 15.00
Golden Love, crystal, plate, #2337/549, 7" 5.50
Gossamer, crystal, goblet, cordial; #6068, 1¼-oz, 3" 14.00
Gossamer, crystal, tumbler, juice; #6068, ftd, 5-oz, 4½" 10.00
Heather, crystal, candlesticks, #2630, trindle, 7¾", pr 85.00
Heather, crystal, cup, #2630, ftd, 6-oz 17.50
Heather, crystal, mustard, #2630, w/lid & spoon, 4" 52.50
Heather, crystal, preserve, #2630, ftd, w/lid, 6" 42.50
Heather, crystal, tidbit set, #2630, 3-pc, 10¼" 45.00
Heather, crystal, vase, bud; #2630, 6" 25.00
Heirloom, crystal, bowl, centerpiece; #2730/255, 12" 40.00
Heirloom, crystal, vase, bud; #1229/57, 6" 17.50
Heraldry, crystal, cup, #2666, 8-oz 11.50
Heraldry, crystal, plate, sandwich; #2364, 11" 17.50
Hermitage, amber, gr or topaz; bowl, finger; #2449½, 4½" 6.00
Hermitage, amber, gr or topaz; plate, #2449½, 8" 10.00
Hermitage, amber, gr or topaz; relish, pickle; #2449, 8" 11.00
Hermitage, crystal, ashtray, #2449 ....3.00
Hermitage, crystal, ashtray holder, #2449 ....5.00
Hermitage, crystal, bottle, oil; #2449, 3-oz 17.50

Hermitage, crystal, bowl, salad; #2449½, 7½" 8.00
Hermitage, crystal, coaster, #2449, 5⅝" 5.00
Hermitage, crystal, cup, #2449, ftd 6.00
Hermitage, crystal, mug, #2449, ftd, 9-oz 12.50
Hermitage, crystal, plate, #2449½, 7" 4.00
Hermitage, crystal, saucer, #2449 ....2.00
Hermitage, crystal, tumbler, #2449½, 2-oz, 2½" 4.00
Holiday, crystal, coaster, 4" 225.00
Holiday, crystal, tumbler, highball; 12-oz, 3¾" 5.00
Holly, crystal, cup, #2350½, ftd 16.50
Holly, crystal, relish, #2364, 3-part, 10" 37.50
Homespun, crystal, tumbler, iced tea; #4183/58, 15-oz, 5¾" 5.00
Horizon, crystal, bowl, salad; 8½" 11.50
Horizon, crystal, relish, #2650, 3-part, 12½" 17.50
Ingrid, crystal, plate, snack; #2666, 10" 14.00
Jenny Lind, amber, box, jewel; #833/293, 6" 60.00
Jenny Lind, amber, box puff; #829/580, 3⅛" 40.00
Jenny Lind, milk glass, box, handkerchief; #831/276, 5¼" sq 68.00
Jenny Lind, milk glass, pin tray, #826/544, 6" 35.00
Jenny Lind, milk glass, pomade, w/lid, #830/587, 2⅛" 30.00
Jenny Lind, milk glass, tray, dresser; #824/385, 11½" 48.00
Jenny Lind, ruby, cologne flask, w/stopper, #827/842, 10¾" 100.00
Jenny Lind, ruby, pin tray, #826/544, 6" 35.00
Juliet, crystal, plate, #2337/550, 8" 5.00
June, crystal, ashtray 23.00
June, crystal, bowl, finger; w/liner 32.50
June, crystal, candlestick, 2" 10.00
June, crystal, creamer, ftd 12.00
June, crystal, plate, cream soup; 7½" 4.00
June, crystal, sugar bowl lid 50.00
June, rose or bl, bowl, soup; 7" 100.00
June, rose or bl, creamer, tea 55.00
June, rose or bl, decanter 1,000.00
June, rose or bl, mayonnaise, w/liner 60.00
June, rose or bl, plate, grill; 10" 75.00
June, rose or bl, shakers, ftd, pr 165.00
June, topaz, comport, #2400, 5" 27.50
June, topaz, ice bucket 75.00
June, topaz, ice dish 40.00
Kashmir, bl, bowl, fruit; 5" 15.00
Kashmir, bl, candy dish, w/lid 95.00
Kashmir, bl, creamer, ftd 20.00
Kashmir, bl, plate, dinner; 10" 50.00
Kashmir, bl, saucer, rnd 10.00
Kashmir, yel or gr, bowl, finger 15.00
Kashmir, yel or gr, candlestick, 5" 22.50
Kashmir, yel or gr, pitcher, ftd 250.00
Kashmir, yel or gr, plate, cake; 10" 35.00
Kashmir, yel or gr, stem, wine; 2½-oz 32.00
Kashmir, yel or gr, sugar bowl, ftd 15.00
Kent, crystal, goblet, #6079, 11-oz, 6½" 6.00
Kimberly, crystal, goblet, cordial; #6071, 1-oz, 3¼" 17.50
Kimberly, crystal, relish, #2574/622, 3-part, 10" 15.00
Lacy Leaf, crystal, bowl, salad; #2630, 10½" 35.00
Laurel, crystal, goblet, #6017, 9-oz, 7⅜" 17.50
Laurel, crystal, tumbler, water; #6017, ftd, 9-oz, 5½" 14.00
Lido, crystal, cake plate, #2496, 10" 25.00
Lido, crystal, cheese & cracker set, #2496 ....47.50
Lido, crystal, goblet, wine; #6017, 3-oz, 5½" 19.50
Lido, crystal, tumbler, #6017, ftd, 12-oz, 6" 17.50
Mademoiselle, crystal, goblet, cocktail; #6033, 4-oz, 4¼" 8.00
Marilyn, crystal, goblet, #6055, 10-oz, 6⅛" 10.00
Marquis, crystal, goblet, #6045, 15¾-oz, 5⅞" 8.00
Marquis, crystal, goblet, #6055, 10-oz, 6⅛" 10.00

Marquis, crystal, tumbler, juice, #6045, 7¼-oz, 4⅝" 5.00
Mayflower, crystal, bowl, sweetmeat; #2560, 5½" 18.50
Mayflower, crystal, creamer, #2560, ftd, 7-oz, 4⅛" 17.50
Mayflower, crystal, goblet, sherbet; #6020, low, 6-oz, 5½" 15.00
Mayflower, crystal, saucer, #2560 ....3.50
Meadow Rose, crystal, bowl, serving; #2496, hdld, 8½" 47.50
Meadow Rose, crystal, candy box, #2496, w/lid, 3-part, 6¼" 125.00
Meadow Rose, crystal, goblet, cocktail; #6016, 3½-oz, 5¼" 25.00
Meadow Rose, crystal, plate, #2496, 8" 7.50
Meadow Rose, crystal, sugar bowl, #2496, ftd, 3½" 18.50
Melody, crystal, goblet, #6072/2, 10-oz, 6⅜" 9.00
Milkweed, crystal, candlesticks, #2630, duo, 7", pr 48.00
Milkweed, crystal, relish, pickle; #2630, 8¾" 21.50
Minuet, crystal, saucer, #2574 ....3.50
Minuet, crystal, 6025, 10-oz, 5½" 12.50
Moon Ring, crystal, goblet, cocktail; #6052, 3¾-oz, 3⅞" 6.00
Moonbeam, crystal, goblet, #6072, 10-oz, 6⅜" 8.00
Moonbeam, crystal, tumbler, iced tea; #6072, ftd, 13-oz, 6⅜" 9.00
Mount Vernon, crystal, goblet, #6031, 10-oz, 8⅛" 11.00
Mulberry, goblet, #6026, 9-oz, 7⅝" 22.50
Navarre, crystal, bell, dinner 30.00
Navarre, crystal, bowl, #2496, hdls, ftd, 10½" 60.00
Navarre, crystal, bowl, #2496, hdls, 4⅜" 11.00
Navarre, crystal, creamer, #2440, ftd, 6¾-oz, 4¼" 17.50
Navarre, crystal, cup, #2440 ....19.50
Navarre, crystal, plate, dinner; #2440, 9½" 39.50
Navarre, crystal, plate, torte; #2496, 14" 55.00
Navarre, crystal, relish, #2419, 5-part, 13¼" 85.00
Navarre, crystal, saucer, #2440 ....5.00
Navarre, crystal, sugar bowl, #2496, ind 17.50
Nordic, crystal, goblet, sherbet; #6077, 7-oz, 4¼" 4.00
Nosegay, crystal, goblet, claret/wine; #6051, 4-oz, 4½" 11.50
Nosegay, crystal, relish, #2666, 2-part, 7⅜" 17.50
Orleans, crystal, goblet, #6089/2, 11½-oz, 6¼" 9.00
Overture, crystal, goblet, wine/cocktail; #6086/27, 5½-oz, 4½" 8.50
Petite, crystal, goblet, cordial; #6085/29, 1¼-oz, 3½" 12.50
Pine, crystal, bonbon, #2666, 6⅞" 20.00
Pine, crystal, goblet, claret/wine; #6051, 4-oz, 4½" 8.50
Pine, crystal, goblet, cocktail; #6052, 3¾-oz, 3⅞" 18.50
Pine, crystal, relish, #2666, 6⅞" 20.00
Plume, crystal, plate, snack; #2666, 10" 11.50
Prelude, crystal, goblet, cocktail/seafood; #6071, 4½-oz, 5" 5.50
Priscilla, crystal, goblet, cordial; #6092/29, 1½-oz, 3½" 7.00
Raleigh, crystal, cake plate, #2574, hdld, 10" 12.50
Randolph, milk glass, creamer, #2675, ftd, 3⅝" 15.00
Randolph, milk glass, tumbler, #2675, ftd, 9-oz, 5¼" 15.00
Reflection, crystal, goblet, oyster cocktail; #6033, 4-oz, 3¾" 7.50
Reflection, crystal, tumbler, iced tea; #6033, ftd, 13-oz, 5⅞" 11.50
Regal, crystal, tumbler, iced tea; #6061, 12-oz, 6" 6.50
Revere, crystal, tumbler, juice; #6023, 5-oz, 4½" 8.00
Romance, crystal, bowl, #2364, flared, 12" 47.50
Romance, crystal, bowl, salad; #2364, 9" 37.50
Romance, crystal, candlestick, #2596, 5" 22.50
Romance, crystal, cheese & cracker set, #2364 ....75.00
Romance, crystal, plate, cracker; #2364, 11¼" 45.00
Romance, crystal, plate, sandwich; #2364, 11" 35.00
Romance, crystal, plate, torte; #2364, 14" 40.00
Romance, crystal, stem, claret; #6017, 4-oz, 5⅞" 30.00
Romance, crystal, vase, #4143, ftd, 7½" 57.50
Rondo, crystal, goblet, cordial; #6045, 1½-oz, 2⅝" 11.50
Rose, crystal, creamer, #2666, 3½" 19.50
Rose, crystal, sugar bowl, #2666, 2⅝" 18.50
Royal, amber or gr, bowl, #2324, ftd, 13" 45.00
Royal, amber or gr, bowl, soup; #2350, 7¾" 18.00

Royal, amber or gr, butter dish, #2350, w/lid 225.00
Royal, amber or gr, mayonnaise, #2315 ....25.00
Royal, amber or gr, pitcher, #1236 ....350.00
Royal, amber or gr, stem, sherbet; #869, low, 6-oz 12.50
Royal, amber or gr, stem, water; #869, 9-oz 20.00
Royal, amber or gr, vase, #2292, flared 90.00
Royal, bl, bowl, fruit; #2350, 5½" 16.50
Royal, bl, creamer, flat 21.00
Royal, blk, bowl, nappy; #2350, 8" 45.00
Royal, blk, ice bucket, #2378 ....70.00
Seascape, crystal, tray, mint; 7½" 19.50
Seville, amber, bowl, cereal; #2350, 6½" 16.00
Seville, amber, sugar bowl lid, #2350½ 75.00
Seville, gr, bowl, nappy; #2350, 9" 35.00
Seville, gr, plate, chop; #2350, 13¾" 35.00
Seville, gr, plate, luncheon; #2350, 8½" 6.50
Seville, gr, sauce boat, #2350 ....72.50
Seville, gr, stem, cocktail; #870 ....16.00
Seville, gr, stem, cordial; #870 ....70.00
Shirley, crystal, tray, tidbit; #2496, flat, 8¼" 17.50
Silver Flutes, crystal, goblet, parfait; 6-oz, 6⅛" 15.00
Skyflower, crystal, plate, #2666, 10" 17.50
Sonata, crystal, comport, 8" 11.50
Spinet, crystal, plate, #2337, 7" 5.50
Spray, crystal, goblet, sherbet; #6055, 6-oz, 4½" 11.00
Spray, crystal, tumbler, juice; #6055, ftd, 5½-oz, 4⅞" 11.00
Spring, crystal, tumbler, iced tea; #6060, 14-oz, 6¼" 7.50
Sprite, crystal, plate, #2337, 8" 7.50
Sprite, crystal, tumbler, juice; #6033, 5-oz, 4½" 10.00
Star Song, crystal, tumbler, iced tea; #6083/63, 13-oz, 6¼" ...11.50
Starflower, crystal, condiment set, #2630 ....115.00
Starflower, crystal, relish, pickle; #2630, 8¾" 22.50
Starflower, crystal, vase, #2630, hdld, 7½" 45.00
Sunglow, crystal, goblet, #6085/2, 8¾-oz, 6½" 9.00
Sylvan, crystal, bowl, #2666, oval, 8¼" 15.00
Sylvan, crystal, tumbler, iced tea; #6060, ftd, 14-oz, 6¼" ...11.00
Thistle, crystal, goblet, claret/wine; #6052, 4½-oz, 4⅜" 18.50
Trojan, pk, ashtray, #2350, lg 50.00
Trojan, pk, bowl, #2375, lemon form 18.00
Trojan, pk, bowl, #2395, 10" 85.00
Trojan, pk, bowl, cream soup; #2375, ftd 27.50
Trojan, pk, candy dish, #2394, w/lid, ¼-lb 250.00
Trojan, pk, plate, bread & butter; #2375, 6" 6.00
Trojan, pk, plate, salad; #2375, 7½" 9.00
Trojan, pk, sauce bowl, #2375 ....110.00
Trojan, pk, saucer, #2375 ....6.00
Trojan, yel, ashtray, #2350, sm 25.00
Trojan, yel, bowl, bonbon; #2375 ....13.00
Trojan, yel, ice bucket, #2375 ....65.00
Trojan, yel, sauce plate, #2375 ....40.00
Trojan, yel, vase, #2417, 8" 120.00
Versailles, bl, bowl, soup; #2375, 7" 60.00
Versailles, bl, creamer, tea; #2375½ 50.00
Versailles, bl, decanter, #2439, 9" 1,500.00
Versailles, bl, ice dish, #2451 ....40.00
Versailles, bl, plate, chop; #2375, 13" 60.00
Versailles, pk or gr, bowl, baker; #2375, 9" 50.00
Versailles, yel, bowl, #2394, 3-ftd, 6" 30.00
Versailles, yel, candlestick, #2395, 3" 20.00
Versailles, yel, ice bucket, #2375 ....75.00
Vesper, amber, bowl, #2371, oval, 13" 37.50
Vesper, amber, bowl, soup; deep, 8¼" 25.00
Vesper, amber, butter dish, #2350 ....750.00
Vesper, amber, creamer, #2350½, flat 20.00

Vesper, amber, egg cup, #2350 ....**35.00**
Vesper, amber, ice bucket, #2378 ....**62.50**
Vesper, amber, plate, luncheon; #2350, 8½" **8.50**
Vesper, amber, sugar bowl, #2350½, flat **20.00**
Vesper, amber, sugar bowl lid **150.00**
Vesper, amber, urn, lg **75.00**
Vesper, bl, platter, #2350, 15" **95.00**
Vesper, gr, ashtray, #2350, 4" **25.00**
Vesper, gr, bowl, fruit; #2350, 5½" **10.00**
Vesper, gr, candy jar, #2331, w/lid, 3-pt **90.00**
Victoria, crystal, goblet, cordial; 1¼-oz, 3" **10.00**
Wedding Ring, crystal, bowl, salad; #2364, 9" **17.50**
Willow, crystal, bowl, fruit; #2574, 13" **25.00**
Willow, crystal, plate, #2574, 8" **9.00**
Willowmere, crystal, cup, #2560, ftd, 5½-oz **15.00**
Willowmere, crystal, tumbler, #6024, ftd, 12-oz, 5¾" ...**22.00**

Frakturs

Fraktur is a German style of black letter text type. To collectors the fraktur is a type of hand-lettered document used by the people of German descent who settled in the areas of Pennsylvania, New Jersey, Maryland, Virginia, North and South Carolina, Ohio, Kentucky, and Ontario. These documents recorded births and baptisms and were used as bookplates and as certificates of honor. They were elaborately decorated with colorful folk-art borders of hearts, birds, angels, and flowers. Examples by recognized artists and those with an unusual decorative motif bring prices well into the thousands of dollars; in fact, some have sold at major auction houses in excess of $5,000.00. Frakturs made in the late 1700s after the invention of the printing press provided the writer with a prepared text that he needed only to fill in at his own discretion. The next step in the evolution of machine-printed frakturs combined woodblock-printed decorations along with the text which the 'artist' sometimes enhanced with color. By the mid-1800s, even the coloring was done by machine. The vorschrift was a handwritten example prepared by a fraktur teacher to demonstrate his skill in lettering and decorating. These are often considered to be the finest of frakturs. Those dated before 1820 are most valuable.

The practice of fraktur art began to diminish after 1830 but hung on even to the early years of this century among the Pennsylvania Germans ingrained with such customs. Our advisor for this category is Frederick S. Weiser; he is listed in the Directory under Pennsylvania.

Key:
brd — board
lp — laid paper
pr — printed
p/i — pen and ink
wc — watercolored
wp — wove paper

Birth Record

Birth and baptismal certificate, parrots, suns, tulips and vase enclose hearts and inscription, Friederich Krebs, Northampton Co, Pennsylvania, 1801, discoloration, 15x13", $1,100.00.

Block pr/wc, 1852, Beuvelle, Reading PA, 20x18" **175.00**
P, Berks Co, no coloring, 1801, 16x18" **110.00**

P/i/wc, angels/birds/eagle, 1853, fading, fr, 16½x14½" **80.00**
P/i/wc, compass star, 4-color, modern fr, 9½x8" **140.00**
P/i/wc, flower branches/birds/angels, 1836, modern fr, 17x13" **50.00**
P/i/wc, flowers, 5-color, 1824, minor damage, unfr, 12x7½" **1,430.00**
P/i/wc, flowers/birds/central heart, 1828, fr, 12x10" **700.00**
P/i/wc, flowers/birds/star, 1805, foxing/loss, 16½x19½" **75.00**
P/i/wc, ornate lettering/inscr/ABC, 1819, losses, 12x8" **95.00**
P/i/wc, Ritter, Reading PA, 1844, 19x16½" **95.00**
P/i/wc, stylized florals/birds/stars, 1825, damage, 16x10" **70.00**
P/i/wc/lp, flower border, 4-color, 1840, rprs, 16x18" **550.00**
P/i/wc/lp, flowers/foliage/3 birds, 1864, 15¼x11" **990.00**
P/i/wc/lp, geometric 3-color border, 1814, maple fr, 14x18" ...**1,320.00**
P/i/wc/lp, stylized 3-color floral, tears, fr, 6½x5¾" **215.00**
P/i/wc/wp, florals, English text, 5-color, 1840, 12x9⅝" **1,200.00**
P/wc, red & yel, 1812, Peters, Harrisburg PA, fr, 21x17" **110.00**
Pr/wc, angels/flowering vines/etc, 1818, PA, 20x16½" **220.00**
Pr/wc, 1843, Peters, Harrisburg PA, stains, 19x16" **165.00**
Pr/wc, 4-color, 1795, John Ritter, Reading PA, 18x15", EX **250.00**
Pr/wc, 5-color, 1839, John Ritter, Reading PA, 19x16" **150.00**

Miscellaneous

House blessing, p/hc, John Ritter, Reading PA, 18x16", VG **45.00**
P/i/wc/brn paper, drawing, birds/flowers, 1793, 7½x11½" **850.00**

Frames

Styles in picture frames have changed with the fashion of the day, but those that especially interest today's collectors are the deep shadow boxes made of fine woods such as walnut or cherry, those with Art Nouveau influence, and the oak frames decorated with molded gesso and gilt from the Victorian era. Our advisor for this category is Michael Hinton; he is listed in the Directory under Pennsylvania.

Brass filigree, gilt, 5" dia, pr **300.00**
Celluloid, emb ribbons & garlands, easel bk, 4⅛x3¼" **25.00**
Chip cvd, old red pnt & natural, easel bk, 7x5" **250.00**
Chip cvd, worn red pnt w/blk stripe, 4" molding, 18x21" **75.00**
Chip cvd, 3 openings: 4½x5¾", red varnish, 9½x31½" **110.00**
Empire, cherry, half-columns & corner blocks, old pnt, 17x13" .**425.00**

Mosaic floral design, easel back, 3x2⅛", $35.00.

Oak, gesso, emb florals, 18x24" **125.00**
Poplar, cross corners w/cvd & appl rosettes, 17x15" **110.00**
Sterling, etched flowers in ea corner, standing, 2x3" **75.00**
Walnut, oval liner, incised decor, dtd 1871, 20x30" **950.00**

Frances Ware

Frances Ware, produced in the 1880s by Hobbs, Brockunier and

Company of Wheeling, West Virginia, is either clear or frosted with amber-stained rim bands. The most often found pattern is Hobnail, but Swirl was also made.

Hobnail, clear; bowl, 7½" 65.00
Hobnail, clear; butter dish 95.00
Hobnail, clear; creamer 60.00
Hobnail, clear; finger bowl, 4" 35.00
Hobnail, clear; pitcher, 8½" 125.00
Hobnail, clear; spooner 40.00
Hobnail, frosted; bowl, ftd, berry pontil, 6x10" 150.00
Hobnail, frosted; bowl, oblong, 8" 75.00
Hobnail, frosted; bowl, sq, 7½" 70.00
Hobnail, frosted; bowl, 2½x5½" 40.00
Hobnail, frosted; bowl, 4½" 30.00
Hobnail, frosted; bowl, 8" 75.00
Hobnail, frosted; bowl, 9" 85.00
Hobnail, frosted; butter dish 120.00
Hobnail, frosted; celery vase 75.00
Hobnail, frosted; creamer 75.00
Hobnail, frosted; finger bowl, 4" 35.00
Hobnail, frosted; marmalade 125.00
Hobnail, frosted; pitcher, milk 150.00
Hobnail, frosted; pitcher, water; sq top 175.00
Hobnail, frosted; plate, sq, 5¾" 25.00
Hobnail, frosted; sauce dish, sq, 4" 28.00
Hobnail, frosted; shakers, very rare, pr 180.00

Hobnail, frosted; spooner, 4x4" diameter, $70.00.

Hobnail, frosted; sugar bowl, w/lid 80.00
Hobnail, frosted; syrup, pewter lid 165.00
Hobnail, frosted; toothpick holder 60.00
Hobnail, frosted; tray, cloverleaf, 12" 125.00
Hobnail, frosted; tray, oblong, 14" 150.00
Hobnail, frosted; tumbler, water 45.00
Swirl, clear; shakers, pr 55.00
Swirl, clear; syrup 90.00
Swirl, frosted; bowl, 3¾" H 40.00
Swirl, frosted; cruet 175.00
Swirl, frosted; cruet, orig stopper, miniature 260.00
Swirl, frosted; mustard jar 140.00
Swirl, frosted; shakers, pr 105.00
Swirl, frosted; sugar shaker, orig lid 125.00
Swirl, frosted; syrup, Pat dtd 145.00
Swirl, frosted; tumbler 35.00

Franciscan

Franciscan is a trade name used by Gladding McBean and Co.,

founded in northern California in 1875. In 1923 they purchased the Tropico plant in Glendale where they produced sewer pipe, gardenware, and tile. By 1934 the first of their dinnerware lines, El Patio, was produced. It was a plain design made in bright, attractive colors. El Patio Nouveau followed in 1935, glazed in two colors — one tone on the inside, a contrasting hue on the outside. Coronado, a favorite of today's collectors, was introduced in 1936. It was styled with a wide, swirled border and was made in pastels in both a satin and glossy finish. Before 1940 fifteen patterns had been produced. The first hand-decorated lines were introduced in 1937, the ever-popular Apple pattern in 1940, Desert Rose in 1941, and Ivy in 1948. Many other hand-decorated and decaled patterns were produced there from 1934 to 1984.

Dinnerware marks before 1940 include 'GMcB' in an oval, 'F' within a square, or 'Franciscan' with 'Pottery' underneath (which was later changed to 'Ware.') A circular arrangement of 'Franciscan' with 'Made in California USA' in the center was used from 1940 until 1949. At least forty marks were used before 1975; several more were introduced after that. At one time, paper labels were used.

The company merged with Lock Joint Pipe Company in 1963, becoming part of the Interpace Corporation. In July of 1979 Franciscan was purchased by Wedgwood Limited of England, and the Glendale plant closed in October, 1984.

Our advisors for this category are Mick and Lorna Chase (Fiesta Plus); they are listed in the Directory under Tennessee. Authority Delleen Enge has compiled an informative book, *Franciscan Ware*, with current values. You will find her address in the Directory under California. See also Gladding McBean.

Coronado

Bowl, cereal 12.00
Bowl, cream soup 23.00
Bowl, vegetable; serving, oval 20.00
Bowl, vegetable; serving, rnd 15.00
Butter dish 65.00
Candlesticks, pr 28.00
Casserole, w/lid 35.00
Cigarette box 40.00
Coffeepot, demitasse 95.00
Creamer & sugar bowl, w/lid 30.00
Cup & saucer 12.00
Cup & saucer, demitasse 22.00
Gravy boat, w/attached plate 28.00
Nut cup, ftd 16.00
Plate, chop; 12" 25.00
Plate, chop; 14" 35.00
Plate, 6½" 8.00
Plate, 7½" 10.00
Plate, 8½" 12.00
Platter, 11½" 25.00
Platter, 15½" 35.00
Saucer, cream soup 12.00
Shakers, pr 15.00
Sherbet 10.00
Teapot 65.00

El Patio

Bowl, cereal 12.00
Bowl, fruit 12.00
Bowl, salad; 3-qt 25.00
Bowl, vegetable; oval 30.00
Butter dish 35.00
Creamer 10.00

Cup	10.00
Cup, jumbo	18.00
Cup & saucer, demitasse	28.00
Gravy boat, w/attached underplate	27.00
Plate, bread & butter	7.00
Plate, 10½"	15.00
Plate, 8½"	12.00
Platter, 13"	17.50
Saucer	4.00
Saucer, jumbo	8.00
Sherbet	10.00
Sugar bowl, w/lid	18.00
Teapot, w/lid, 6-cup	45.00

Franciscan Fine China

The main line of fine china was called Masterpiece. There were at least four marks used during its production from 1941 to 1977. Almost every piece is clearly marked. This china is true porcelain, the body having been fired at a very high temperature. Many years of research and experimentation went into this china before it was marketed. Production was temporarily suspended during the war years. More than 170 patterns and many varying shapes were produced. All are valued about the same with the exception of the Renaissance group, which is 25% higher.

Bowl, vegetable; serving, oval	50.00
Cup	20.00
Plate, bread & butter	18.00
Plate, dinner	30.00
Plate, salad	25.00
Saucer	12.00

Hand-Painted Embossed Earthenware

Values listed here apply to the following: Apple, Desert Rose, Ivy, Meadow Rose, Forget-Me-Not, October, Strawberry, Fresh Fruit, and other hand-painted patterns. Daisy and Cafe Royal are both worth approximately 25% less, Poppy about 50% more. For Wildflower, double the listed values. Not all of the pieces described below were made in every pattern.

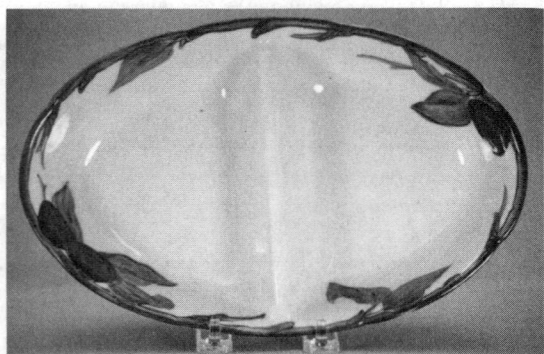

Apple, bowl, oval, 10½x7", $32.50.

Ashtray, ind; from $18.00 up to	25.00
Botl, cereal; ftd, from $28.00 up to	32.00
Bowl, batter	125.00
Bowl, bouillon; lug hdl, w/lid, sm, from $75.00 up to	95.00
Bowl, cereal	16.50
Bowl, fruit; sm	12.00

Bowl, rim soup; from $28.00 up to	38.00
Bowl, vegetable; sm	32.00
Casserole, ind	45.00
Coaster, 3¾", from $15.00 up to	20.00
Coffeepot, from $95.00 up to	125.00
Compote, lg	85.00
Creamer, ind	42.00
Creamer, reg	32.00
Cup & saucer, demitasse; from $45.00 up to	65.00
Cup & saucer, jumbo	65.00
Egg cup, from $25.00 up to	35.00
Goblet, ceramic, minimum value	75.00
Mug, 10- or 12-oz, ea	45.00
Mug, 7-oz	25.00
Napkin ring, from $25.00 up to	35.00
Pickle dish, 10¼"	35.00
Pitcher, milk; from $75.00 up to	95.00
Pitcher, water; from $85.00 up to	125.00
Plate, chop; 14"	75.00
Plate, grill/divided; 10¾", from $95.00 up to	125.00
Plate, 10½", from $15.00 up to	20.00
Plate, 6½", from $9.00 up to	12.00
Plate, 8½", from $18.00 up to	22.00
Plate, 9½", from $12.00 up to	18.00
Platter, 12½"	45.00
Platter, 14½"	65.00
Platter, 19½", from $250.00 up to	350.00
Relish, 3-part, 11"	65.00
Shaker & pepper mill, 6", pr, from $195.00 up to	225.00
Shakers, sm, pr	24.00
Shakers, tall, pr, from $45.00 up to	60.00
Sugar bowl, ind; open, sm	75.00
Sugar bowl, w/lid, lg, from $32.00 up to	45.00
Syrup pitcher, from $65.00 up to	80.00
Tray, 3-tier	75.00
Tumbler, juice; from $25.00 up to	35.00
Tumbler, water; from $25.00 up to	32.00

Frankart

During the 1920s Frankart, Inc., of New York City, produced a line of accessories that included figural nude lamps, bookends, ash trays, etc. These white metal composition items were offered in several finishes including verde green, jap black, and gun-metal gray. The company also produced a line of caricatured animals, but the stylized nude figurals have proven to be the most collectible today. With few exceptions, all pieces were marked 'Frankart, Inc.' with a patent number or 'pat. appl. for.' All pieces listed are in very good original condition unless otherwise indicated. Our advisor for this category is Walter Glenn; he is listed in the Directory under Georgia.

Ashtray, ballerina dances in center of 8" rnd onyx tray, 9"	325.00
Ashtray, nude on point, 3 trays form ballerina's tutu, 10"	410.00
Ashtray, nude on tiptoe arches bkward, holds tray, 10½"	425.00
Ashtray, nude stands atop stepped base, ashball at ft, 10"	390.00
Astray, nuds sits atop column, leg extends over sq tray, 9½"	450.00
Bookends, Indian chief & Indian lady w/child, 9½", pr	250.00
Bookends, nude dancing, frog on base, 10", pr	425.00
Bookends, nude standing, 'peek-a-boos' around books, 8", pr	325.00
Bookends, nymph sits atop mushrooms, 8", pr	285.00
Bookends, parrot (stylized) on arched perch, 7", pr	210.00
Lamp, combo ashtray: whale w/tray in mouth, 14"	250.00
Lamp, debutante sits/gazes into 3" crackle globe, 8½"	425.00

Lamp, nude, sits/holds 3" crackle globe in lap, 9" 525.00
Lamp, nude dancing silhouettes on rectangular glass panel, 11" .725.00
Lamp, nude sits/extends leg, 3" globes on sides, 7½" 650.00
Lamp, nudes (2) sit either side of glass skyscraper, 13" 700.00
Lamp, nudes (2) sit either side 5" crackle glass cube, 12" 525.00
Plaque, horse's head (stylized), 8" sq 175.00
Smoke set, nude holds cylindrical box, tray on base, 12" 525.00
Vase, nude embraces frosted glass vase, 10" 365.00

Frankoma

The Frank Pottery, founded in Oklahoma in 1933 by John Frank, became known as Frankoma in 1934. The company produced decorative figurals, vases, and such, marking their ware from 1936-38 with a pacing leopard 'Frankoma' mark. These pieces are highly sought. The entire operation was destroyed by fire in 1938, and new molds were cast — some from surviving pieces — and a similar line of production was pursued. The body of the ware was changed in 1954 from a honey tan (called 'Ada clay,' referring to the name of the town near the area where it was dug) to the to a red brick clay (known as Sapula), and this, along with the color of the glazes (over forty have been used), helps determine the period of production. A Southwestern theme has always been favored in design as well as in color selection.

In 1965 they began to produce a limited-edition series of Christmas plates, followed by a bottle vase series in 1969. Considered very collectible are their political mugs, bicentennial plates, Teenagers of the Bible plates, and the Wildfire series. Their ceramic Christmas cards are also very popular items with today's collectors.

Frankoma celebrated their 50th Anniversary in 1983. On September 26 of that same year, Frankoma was again destroyed by fire. Because of a fire-proof wall, master molds of all 1983 production items were saved, allowing plans for rebuilding to begin immediately.

Frankoma filed for Chapter 11 in April, 1990, and eventually sold to a Maryland investor in February of 1991, thereby ending the family-ownership era. For a more thorough study of the subject, we recommend that you refer to *Frankoma Treasures* by Phyllis and Tom Bess, our advisors; you will find their address in the Directory under Oklahoma.

Decanter, 10½", $40.00.

Ashtray, fish, #T-8, 1962-76, 7" 20.00
Bean pot, Barrel, #97V 35.00
Bookend, Charger Horse, Blk Onyx, Ada clay, #420, pr 195.00
Bookend, female figure, seated, w/Taylor name, #425, 5½" 500.00
Bookend, Mountain Girl, #420, pr 250.00
Bookend, Rearing Clydesdale, #431, pr 265.00
Bowl, 4-leaf clover, #223, 6" 10.00
Candle holders, Dusty Rose, Ada clay, dbl, #304, pr 45.00

Carafe, w/lid, any color 22.50
Christmas card, 1950-51, ea 75.00
Christmas card, 1954 ....75.00
Christmas card, 1955-56, ea 75.00
Christmas card, 1958 ....60.00
Christmas card, 1965 ....60.00
Christmas card, 1973-74, ea 45.00
Christmas card, 1975, bird in hand, Grace Lee, rare 115.00
Christmas plate, 1st ed, 1965 ....300.00
Christmas plate, 1966 ....80.00
Christmas plate, 1968 ....65.00
Dealer sign, Tepee 400.00
Donkey mug, 1976, Centennial Red 35.00
Donkey mug, 1978, Woodland Moss 30.00
Elephant mug, 1969, Nixon/Agnew, Flame 85.00
Elephant mug, 1972, Prairie Gr 50.00
Flower holder, boot, star on sides, Ada clay, #507, 3½" 12.00
Flower holder, elephant, #180 ....150.00
Honey jar, Beehive, Ada clay, #803, 12-oz 30.00
Honey jar, Beehive, Wisteria (lav), #803, 1983 ....25.00
Jug, Golda's Corn advertising, dtd 1951 ....35.00
Lazy susan, Wagon Wheel, Prairie Gr, #94FC 65.00
Mug, Plainsman, gr, 5CL, 12-oz 6.00
Mug, 1976 Bicentennial, Uncle Sam 15.00
Pitcher, Aztec, Ada clay, 2-qt 35.00
Pitcher, Wagon Wheel, Ada clay, #94-D, 2-qt 35.00
Planter, Madonna of Grace, Gracetone, #231-B, 6" 75.00
Plaque, Indian Maiden, Osage Brn, Ada clay, #132 ....60.00
Plaque, Indian's face, 3½x2" 15.00
Plate, Bob White Quail, 1972 ....100.00
Plate, Christmas 1969 ....40.00
Plate, Easter, Oral Roberts, 1972 ....12.50
Plate, Symbols of Freedom 22.00
Plate, Teenager of the Bible, Jesus the Carpenter 35.00
Plate, Wild Turkey, 1978 ....75.00
Sculpture, Amazon Woman, mk Frank Potteries, #101, 6¼x8" ..450.00
Sculpture, Bucking Bronco, no stepped base, #121, 5" 175.00
Sculpture, Circus Horse, Desert Gold, red clay 75.00
Sculpture, Cowboy Boot, mk Frankoma Pottery 15.00
Sculpture, Dreamer Girl 150.00
Sculpture, Gardener Boy, Prairie Gr 110.00
Sculpture, Greyhound, 6 petals on bk base, 1983 repro, 14" 75.00
Sculpture, Indian Chief, Ada clay, #142, 7½" 95.00
Sculpture, Prancing Colt, #117, 8" 600.00
Sculpture, Seated Puma, Ada clay, #114, 1934-63, 7½" 100.00
Sculpture, Swan, Peacock Bl, mini 40.00
Shakers, Aztec, brn, pr 12.00
Shakers, Snail, Desert Gold, Ada clay, #558-H, pr 12.50
Shakers, Tepee, gr, 3", pr 12.50
Sugar bowl, Wagon Wheel, w/lid 15.00
Tray, oval, #36, 1955-64, 12" 45.00
Trivet, Lazy Bones, 1957 only 60.00
Trivet, Sequoya's Alphabet, 5" 12.00
Trivet, Spanish Iron, 6" sq 12.00
Vase, Cactus, Red Bud 35.00
Vase, collector; V-1, Prairie Gr, 1969, 15" 100.00
Vase, collector; V-10, Morning-Glory Bl, wht int, 11½" 40.00
Vase, collector; V-12, 1980 ....40.00
Vase, collector; V-14, blk & Terra Cotta, 1972 ....80.00
Vase, collector; V-15, 2-pc, last of series 55.00
Vase, collector; V-3, red & blk, 1971, 12" 75.00
Vase, collector; V-4, blk & Terra Cotta, 1981, 13" 85.00
Vase, collector; V-8, Freedom Red & wht, 1976 ....70.00
Vase, ringed cylinder, #72, 10½" 12.50

Vase, scalloped top, str lines, #79, 7" 150.00
Wall pocket, cowboy boot, wht 10.00
Wall pocket, Phoebe, bsk, HP features & hair 185.00
Wall pocket, Phoebe, Prairie Gr, Ada clay 100.00

Fraternal Organizations

Fraternal memorabilia is a vast and varied field. Emblems representing the various organizations have been used to decorate cups, shaving mugs, plates, and glassware. Medals, swords, documents, and other ceremonial paraphernalia from the 1800s and early 1900s are especially prized. Our advisor for Odd Fellows is Greg Spiess; he is listed in the Directory under Illinois. Information on Masonic memorabilia has been provided by David Smies, who is listed under Kansas.

Masons

Apron, metallic embr on wht satin & bl velvet, 12x14"+fringe 20.00
Badge, Knights Templar, enameled, 2-pc, Denver, 1913 ....18.00
Badge, Order of E Star, brass, w/ribbon, Pittsburgh PA, 1929 ....6.00
Book, Encyclopedia of Freemasonry, Mackey, 2-volume set 60.00
Champagne, 1911 ....85.00
Cup, Syria Shrine, china, 3-hdl, 1905 ....85.00
Door knocker, brass, emblem, 1800s, rare 88.00
Emblem, brass horseshoe w/eye, eagle on top, 4x6", NM 65.00
Frame, cvd symbols, holding certificates, dtd 1860s, 31x22" 425.00
Hat, uniform; Knights Templar, blk wool, w/plume, EX 25.00
Match holder, aluminum, emblem at top, wall mt, 8½x5½" 75.00
Penny, copper, Manhattan KS, EX 15.00
Rug, emblem & Lodge name & #, Oriental type, 49x36" 265.00
Stamp holder, SP 25.00
Sword, heavily eng, Knights Templar, w/scabbard, EX 125.00

Odd Fellows

Badge, memorial; Rebeka Lodge, ornate, 1894 ....25.00
Block, cvd marble (for gavel) w/tassels, presented 1895, 12" sq ..165.00
Mask, pnt wire mesh w/cloth cap, ca 1900, EX 45.00
Medal, Grand Lodge, photo 9.00
Robe, blk & burgundy velvet w/'eye' symbol embr, 1890s 65.00
Staff, wooden, heart-in-hand finial, late 1800s, 10½" 375.00
Triptych, opens to 1833-1946 rosters, gessoed fr, 32¾" 990.00
Trivet, brass, 3 circles, hand w/heart, 3-circle hdl 85.00

Shrine

Frame, carved wood with gilt liner, with Masonic certificates dated 1865 and 1872, 31x22", $935.00.

Badge, enameled, 2-pc, MN, 1908 ....12.00
Cane, Smile w/Nile, Seattle, 1936 ....65.00
Chalice, cranberry glass w/silver sword hdls, 1908 ....175.00
Cup & saucer, glass, Los Angeles, 1906 ....70.00
Mug, glass, Atlantic City, 1904 ....75.00
Paperweight, spelter figure, 5" 40.00
Pendant, gold/silver scimitar, cross w/dmns 250.00

Fraunfelter

Charles Fraunfelter organized his company in Zanesville, Ohio, in 1915. It was known as the Ohio Pottery Company until 1923. During this period their main product was a line of utilitarian articles for chemical laboratories made of hard-paste porcelain. In 1918 they used the same body to produce a brown and white line called 'Petruscan.' By 1920 a line of hotel ware was added. The company organized in 1923 and became known as Fraunfelter China Company; but after the death of Fraunfelter in 1925, the business fell into hard times and eventually closed altogether in 1939.

Casserole, Deco motif on lid, 7¼" dia 55.00
Casserole, Petruscan, floral transfer, orig chrome holder 50.00
Teapot, brn/cream w/gold transfers, ribbed body 35.00
Teapot, gr/wht, flat lid, 3" 30.00
Vase, lovebirds, gold/silver details on gray, sgn/mk, 10" 165.00

Fruit Jars

As early as 1829, canning jars were being manufactured for use in the home preservation of foodstuffs. For the past twenty-five years, they have been sought as popular collectibles. At the last estimate, over four thousand fruit jars and variations were known to exist. Some are very rare, perhaps one-of-a-kind examples known to have survived to the present day. Among the most valuable are the black glass jars, the amber Van Vliet, and the cobalt Millville. These often bring prices in excess of $3,000.00 when they can be found. Aside from condition, values are based on age, rarity, color, and special features. Our advisor for this category is John Hathaway; he is listed in the Directory under Maine.

Acme Seal (script), regular mouth, pt 145.00
AGWL Pitts PA (base), aqua, wax sealer, qt 28.00
Amazon Swift Seal, bl, qt 12.00
American (eagle & flag) Fruit Jar, lt gr, ½-gal 138.00
American (NACGo), porc lined, aqua, midget 148.00
Anchor (block letters) below anchor emblem, clear, 1-qt 48.00
Atlas (erased) Mason Improved Pat'd, aqua, pt 18.00
Atlas E-Z Seal, aqua, ½-gal 7.00
Atlas E-Z Seal (in circle), cornflower bl, qt 38.00
Atlas Mason's Pat Nov 30th 1858, dk olive gr, ½-gal 33.00
Atlas Strong Shoulder Mason, apple gr, pt 23.00
Atlas Strong Shoulder Mason, aqua, pt 3.00
Ball (underlined) Perfect Mason, gripper ribs, bl, qt 7.00
Ball Ideal, bl, ½-pt 50.00
Ball Ideal, reverse: Ball 1976 Office Building, bl, pt 23.00
Ball Ideal Pat'd July 14th 1908, sq, qt 5.00
Ball Mason, lt olive gr, qt 22.00
Ball Mason Pat 1858, aqua, pt 10.00
Ball Perfect Mason, sq, bl, qt 14.00
Ball Special, bl, qt 6.00
Banner (circled) Pat Dates, aqua, ½-gal 98.00
Brockway Clear Vu Mason, qt 2.00
Buckey 3, aqua, lt lid stain, qt 198.00

Calcutt's Pat's Apr 11th Nov 7th 1893 (on lid), clear, qt 38.00
Chattanooga Mason (C in Circle), clear, pt 8.00
Cohansey (arched), aqua, ½-gal 38.00
Cohansey (arched), aqua, ½-pt 150.00
Cross Gem, aqua, midget 38.00
Crown Emblem Crown, gr, qt 22.00
Crown Emblem Imperial Heart Crown, aqua, qt 10.00
Cunningham & Co Pittsburgh PA (base), aqua, qt 33.00
Darling ADM (monogram), aqua, qt 38.00
Dexter (circled by fruit/vegetables), aqua, zinc lid, qt 58.00
DOC (base), aqua, wax sealer, ½-gal 23.00
Doolittle Pat Dec 3 1901 (on lid), clear, qt 23.00
Double Safety, clear, ½-pt 8.00
Drey Pat'd 1920 Improved Everseal, clear, ½-gal 15.00
Electric (script in circle), aqua, pt 10.00
Empire, aqua, qt 98.00
ET Cowdrey & Co Boston, amber, no closure, qt 73.00
Excelsior Improved, aqua, ½-gal 48.00
Franklin Dexter Fruit Jar, aqua, qt 30.00
Franklin No 1 Fruit Jar, aqua, qt 55.00
Gem, reverse: Hourglass, aqua, qt 18.00
Gem (Block G), aqua, midget 35.00
Genuine Boyd's Mason/Mason Shepherd's Crook, aqua, ½-gal 28.00
Gimbel Brothers Pure Food Store Philadelphia, clear, pt 48.00
Glassboro Trade 1 Mark Improved, aqua, ½-gal 18.00
Globe, amber, qt 53.00
Globe, amber, ½-gal 73.00
Handy Jar, clear, qt 58.00
Harvest Time Mason, clear, qt 10.00
Helme's Railroad Mills, amber, sm qt 23.00
Hilton Pat Mar 10th 1868, aqua, qt, repro clamp 745.00
Ideal, aqua, qt 18.00
Ideal Imperial, aqua, qt 23.00
Improved Corona Jar (made in Canada), clear, qt 3.00
Improved Gem Made in Canada, amber, clear lid, qt 58.00
Kerr Self Sealing Mason, US Bicentennial 1776-1976, red, qt 50.00
Knox (K in keystone), clear, ½-pt 10.00
L&W, aqua, no closure, qt 48.00
Leader, amber, qt 148.00
Leotric, sm mouth, aqua, ½-gal 12.00
Lynchburg Standard Mason, aqua, qt 18.00

Mason's (shield) Union, aqua, qt 125.00
Mason's Crystal Jar, clear, qt 28.00
Mason's GCCo Patent Nov 30th 1858, aqua, pt 14.00
Mason's Pat Nov 30th 1858, all 'N's reversed, aqua, qt 35.00
Mason's Pat Nov 30th 1858, olive gr, smooth lip, ½-gal 98.00
Mason's (lg) Patent Nov 30th 1858, aqua, midget 35.00
Mason's 21 (underlined)), Pat Nov 30th 1858, aqua, qt 22.00
Moore's Patent Dec 3d 1861, aqua, qt 78.00
Ohio Quality Mason, clear, qt 9.00
Pat'd March 26th 1867 BB Wilcox 17, aqua, qt 73.00
Pat Sept 18 1860, aqua, qt 98.00
Pint Standard, aqua, wax sealer, pt 75.00
Preserves (fancy letters), aqua, qt 98.00
Protector (arched), aqua, qt 48.00
Putnam Glass Works Zanesville O (base), aqua, qt 33.00
Queen, aqua, qt 22.00
Red (over key) Mason, aqua, qt 8.00
Safety Wide Mouth Mason Salem Glass Works NJ, aqua, qt 18.00
Schram Automatic Sealer (script), clear, qt 12.00
Simplex Mason, clear, pt 88.00
Standard (over shepherd's crook), aqua, qt 23.00
Standard (over shepherd's crook), aqua, wax sealer, qt 23.00
Star (below stippled star), lt aqua, qt 48.00
Stevens Tin Top Pat July 27, 1875, aqua, orig lid, ½-gal 125.00
Stevens Tin Top Pat July 27, 1875, aqua, wax sealer, qt 73.00
Swayzee's Improved Mason, aqua, pt 25.00
Trade Mark Lightning, amber, pt 75.00
Trade Mark the Dandy, aqua, clear lid, qt 35.00
Trade Mark the Dandy, lt amber, qt 98.00
Trademark Keystone Registered, clear, qt 7.00
Veteran (bust of veteran), sun-colored amethyst, pt 28.00
Victory in shield on lid, clear, qt 5.00
Weir Pat Mar 1st 92 April 16th 1902 No 2, stoneware, pt 38.00
Winslow Jar, aqua, qt 58.00
Woodbury, aqua, qt 38.00

Fry

Henry Fry established his glassworks in 1901 in Rochester, Pennsylvania. There, until 1933 when it was sold to the Libbey Company, he produced glassware of the finest quality. In the early years they produced beautiful cut glass; and when it began to wane in popularity, Fry turned to the manufacture of occasional pieces and oven glassware. He is perhaps most famous for the opalescent pearl glass called 'Foval.' It was sometimes made with blue or jade green trim in combination. Because it was in production for only a short time in 1926 and 1927, it is hard to find. For further study we recommend *The Collector's Encyclopedia of Fry Glassware* by the Fry Glass Society. Our advisor for this category is Ron Damaska; he is listed in the Directory under Pennsylvania. See also Kitchen Collectibles, Glassware.

Ashtray, Rose (pk), 4 buttressed ft 25.00
Baker, clear opal, oval, 1917, 6" 12.00
Basket, jade gr w/festooning, 12" 600.00
Bowl, cut w/hobstars & fans alternating w/Xd bars, 8" 100.00
Bowl, ivy; blk, clear swirl connector, blk ft 40.00
Bowl, opal w/bl festooning, bl ft, 4½" H 350.00
Bowl, salad; pearl opal w/jade gr rim & ft, 5½x9" 275.00
Cake pan, sq, 1947 ....20.00
Candle holder, amber, HP floral trim 15.00
Candle holder, Royal Blue 15.00
Candlesticks, Foval, opal w/bl wafers & spiral stem, 11", pr 375.00
Candy dish, pearl opal, bl ft & stem, 4¾" 160.00

Mason's (keystone) Improved, aqua, zinc band, glass insert, midget, M, $45.00.

Manufactured for JT Kinney Trenton NJ, aqua, qt 135.00
Mason Jar of 1872, aqua, qt 43.00

Casserole, floral etched lid, w/metal holder, 1938, 8" 25.00
Casserole, gr, w/lid, 1938, 7" 75.00
Casserole, ovenware, etched lid, silver-metal holder, 1954 ....35.00
Casserole, ovenware, wheel-cut leaf band, w/lid, #37 ....35.00
Cocotte, ovenware, str sides, 1926, 4½" 22.50
Comport, Foval, bl stem/trim/festooning, low, #2502, 5½" 250.00
Compote, cut, Pershing, invt trumpet form base, 8" 225.00
Creamer & sugar bowl, Vienna cutting, sawtooth rim 230.00
Cup & saucer, Azure Bl 20.00
Cup & saucer, coffee; Foval 75.00
Cup & saucer, Pearlware, tall, #9003 ....70.00
Egg cup, Foval, conical jade ft, #2300 ....55.00
Finger bowl, Rose (pk), etched floral band 25.00
Goblet, Quilted, Rose (pk), no connector, sm ft 15.00
Goblet, Vienna cutting, stemmed 90.00
Goblet, Wild Rose etch, cut stem 20.00
Jug, floral intaglio, scalloped rim, 4-pt 200.00
Jug, Foval, bl hdl & finial, #11 ....200.00
Jug, whiskey; Poppy cutting allover, orig cut stopper, 8" 345.00

Measure, 1-spout, #1933, 1-cup, $35.00.

Nappy, Wilhelm cutting, hdls 235.00
Percolator, Foval, glass insert 400.00
Pitcher, Leman cutting, tankard form, sgn hdl 285.00
Plate, Dmn Optic, Rose (pk), dinner sz 40.00
Plate, Foval, jade gr rim, 8½" 35.00
Plate, grill; amber, 3-compartment 25.00
Plate, luncheon; Dmn Optic w/blk reeding 75.00
Plate, Sunbeam cutting, 8" 175.00
Roaster, clear opal, w/lid, 1946, 14" L 75.00
Shaker, unnamed cut pattern, metal top 85.00
Spice tray, Rose (pk), 3-compartment, center hdl 35.00
Teapot, gold enamel bands, #2000, 6-cup 225.00
Tray, ice cream; Elsie cutting, 14" L 385.00
Tray, relish; Pershing Variant cutting 185.00
Tumble up, Thistle etch 60.00
Tumbler, floral cutting 55.00
Tumbler, iced tea; Grape etch, hdl 35.00
Tumbler, lemonade; Foval, jade hdl, #9416 ....75.00
Vase, Anemone etch, #804 line, 16" 50.00
Vase, azure bl reeding on crsytal, #2565 ....150.00
Vase, Foval, 3 jade ball ft, #828, 5" 3,235.00
Vase, Orion, classic form, scalloped rim 175.00
Vase, Poppy cutting on lower half, 4" 75.00
Vase, Rose (pk) festooning, cylindrical, 10" 400.00
Vase, violet; Foval, 3 bl ft, #823, 4" 250.00

Fulper

The Fulper Pottery was founded in 1899, after nearly a century of producing utilitarian stoneware under various titles and managements. Not until 1909 did Fulper venture into the art pottery field. Vasekraft, their first art line, utilized the same heavy clay body used for their utility ware. Although shapes were unadorned and simple, the glazes they developed were used with such flair and imagination (alone and in unexpected combined harmony) that each piece was truly a work of art. Graceful Oriental shapes were produced to complement the important 'famille rose' glaze developed by W.H. Fulper, Jr. Other shapes and glazes were developed in line with the Arts and Crafts movement of the same period.

During WWI, doll's heads and Kewpies were made to meet the demand for hard-to-find imports. Figural perfume lamps and powder boxes were made both in bisque and glazed ware. Examples prized most highly by collectors today are those made before a devastating fire destroyed the plant in 1929, resulting in an operations takeover by Martin Stangl later that same year.

Several marks were used: a vertical 'Fulper' in a line reserve, a horizontal mark, a Vasekraft paper label, 'Rafco,' 'Prang,' and 'Flemington.' Fulper values are to a major degree determined by the desirability of the glazes and forms. And, of course, larger examples command higher prices. Lamps with colored glass inserts are rare and highly prized. Our advisor for this category is Douglass White; he is listed in the Directory under Florida.

Ashtray, bl flambe, advertising, mk, 5" dia 100.00
Bookends, Mission bell tower form, taupe/mustard, 7", pr 550.00
Bookends, open books, pr 300.00
Bookends, Rameses II, gr matt, 10", pr 850.00
Bowl, bl/gr, semigloss drips on lt pepper-gray matt, 7½" 115.00
Bowl, cat's-eye glaze, ribbed ext, shaped edge, #472, 4x15" 260.00
Bowl, centerpc; drip glossy over oatmeal matt, mk, 5x11" 170.00
Bowl, copper o/l, hdls, 3" 395.00
Bowl, gr/gray crystalline, 3 candle-holder ft at rim, 6x8" 475.00
Candlesticks, mustard to dk gr crystalline, 16", pr 425.00
Chamberstick, gr gloss w/bl highlights, 7" 200.00
Chamberstick, gr/bl matt, shield bk, 7½" 225.00
Flower frog, gr crystalline on brn crystalline base, 4" 150.00
Flower frog, mushroom shape, gr/gun-metal gray, 3" 45.00
Jug, musical; gun-metal crystalline on gr flambe, 9½" 135.00

Vase, thick celadon green, strap handles, 9", $675.00.

Vase, gr crystalline drip, hexagonal, 11" 275.00
Vase, ashes-of-roses, bottle form, +4-ftd base w/gr, 19x7" 1,200.00
Vase, bl crystalline, sqd rim-to-shoulder hdls, #656, 7x7" 450.00
Vase, bl crystalline, vertical blk mk, miniature, 4" 150.00

Vase, bl-gr matt, hdls, ink stamp, 7½" 150.00
Vase, bl/gr/brn/yel flambe, 7-sided ovoid, #509, 10" 750.00
Vase, brn/bl flambe on cream, wide shoulder/angle hdls, 8" 300.00
Vase, bud; bl/brn flambe on bl speckled, #018, 5½", pr 275.00
Vase, bud; brn w/bl flambe drip over yel, 7" 170.00
Vase, butterscotch/aquamarine crystalline, hdls, mk, 7½" 200.00
Vase, butterscotch flambe, footed classical form, #661, 12" 475.00
Vase, cat's-eye flambe, cylindrical, #445, 8½x3" 290.00
Vase, cobalt drip over famille rose, sm hdls, #610, 10¾" 1,500.00
Vase, cobalt matt over rose w/lt bl, incised mk, 10½" 550.00
Vase, copper dust, rim-to-width akimbo Deco hdls, 5½" 325.00
Vase, cream over bl flambe, 3 'horn' hdls, teardrop form, 6" 350.00
Vase, cucumber crystalline, step-down w/A&C hdls, #T25, 7x9" .325.00
Vase, famille rose w/aqua drip, horizontal mk, 8" 190.00
Vase, gold crystalline on celedon gr at rim & base, 4" 275.00
Vase, gr crystalline, 3 lug hdls, 7" 295.00
Vase, gr/bl crystalline drip over bl, scroll hdls, #486, 12" 500.00
Vase, gr/tan/gun-metal/bl flambe, Chinese flask form, 10" 850.00
Vase, gun metal/gr drip, horizontal ribs, hdls, 18½" 650.00
Vase, lt gr crystalline, ring hdls, 13" 650.00
Vase, metallic bl flambe, flared ogee form, #563, 7" 475.00
Vase, mirror blk, hdls, horizontal mk, 7½" 85.00
Vase, Mission, brn, #23, 8x7" 675.00
Vase, navy/lt bl marbleized, #576, mk, 12x7" 450.00
Vase, olive/bl/gray flambe on speckled mustard, unmk, 5" 175.00
Vase, purple matt, early, 3½" 75.00
Vase, purple matt, ink stamp, 6½" 130.00
Vase, robin's egg bl matt, 4 curved hdls, #605, mk, 8½" 2,500.00
Vase, rose matt, vertical ink mk, 8" 170.00
Vase, roses in high relief on bl, mk, 6x6½" 180.00
Vase, streaky gr, 4 short angular bars at rtcl band, 13x8" 6,000.00
Vase, volcanic rust gloss, angle hdls, #27, Expo label, 11" 1,400.00
Vase, watermelon pk/gr matt, hdls, ink stamp, 7½" 145.00
Vase, wheat over mirror blk, ink stamp, 7½" 150.00
Vase, wisteria, mirror bl, emb mk, 6½" 120.00
Wall pocket, dbl, mirror blk, 3-hdl, 6½x8" 235.00
Wall pocket, Greek Key pattern, brn matt, 9" 220.00

Figurine, frog on base, 3½x7¼" diameter, $125.00.

Furniture

From the cabinetmaker's shop of the early 1800s with apprentices and journeymen who learned every phase of the craft at the side of the master carpenter, the trade had evolved by the mid-century to one with steam-powered saws and turning lathes and workers who specialized in only one operation. By 1870 the Industrial Revolution was in progress, and large factories in the East and Midwest turned out increasingly elaborate styles, ornately machine carved and heavily inlaid. Rococo,

Egyptian, and Renaissance Revival furniture adapted well to factory production. Eastlake offered a welcome respite from Victorian frumpery and a return to quality handcrafting. All of these styles remained popular until the turn of the century.

As early as 1880, factories began using oak; early mail-order catalogs offered oak furniture, simply styled and lighter in weight, since long-distance shipping was often a factor. Mission, or Craftsman, a style introduced around 1890, was simple to the extreme. Stickley and Hubbard were two of its leading designers. Other popular Victorian styles were Colonial Revival, Cottage, Bentwood, and Windsor. Prices are as variable as the styles.

Though the market is showing a slight recovery, some items are still selling below market value. Because of this, items that have sold at auction for at least 25% lower than their normal market values will be designated with an (*). Mahogany furniture, machine made, from the 1900s to the 1930s in traditional styling (Hepplewhite, Sheraton and Duncan Phyfe) is very popular right now, as is furniture decorated in the Chinoiserie and English Regency styles. On the down side, ordinary oak furniture is still selling well below its highs of a few years ago.

Learn to tell the difference between handmade and machine-made furniture. Condition is the most important factor to consider in determining value, and it's important to remember that *where* a piece sells, has a definite bearing on the price it will realize, due simply to regional preference. Our advisor for this category is Suzy McLennan Anderson, ISA, of Heritage Antiques, whose address is listed in the Directory under New Jersey. To learn more about furniture, we recommend *The Collector's Encyclopedia of American Furniture* by Robert and Harriet Swedberg.

Note: When only one dimension is given for blanket chests, dry sinks, tables, settees, and sofas, it is length.

Key:

Am — American	Geo — Georgian
brd — board	grpt — grainpainted
Chpndl — Chippendale	hdbd — headboard
Co — Country	hdw — hardware
cvd — carved	Hplwht — Hepplewhite
cvg — carving	mar — marriage
c&b — claw and ball	NE — New England
do — door	QA — Queen Anne
drw — drawer	trn — turning
Emp — Empire	Vict — Victorian
Fed — Federal	W/M — William and Mary
Fr — French	:— over (example: 1 do:2 drw —
ftbd — footboard	1 door over 2 drawers)
G — good	

Beds

Birch pencil post, rpl rails/canopy fr, old finish, 73x70x50" 1,500.00
Bird's-eye maple w/rosewood Vict, high hd/ftbd w/cartouches ...1,600.00
Day, Mission oak, worn leather pad, stepped post finials 525.00
Day, old hickory, orig caned fold-down bk/seat, 74", VG 475.00
Day, walnut early English, trn/cvd legs & posts, 37x67x22" 1,100.00
Half-tester, mahog Vict, trn finials, ornate hdbd, reduced 650.00
Half-tester, rosewood, att Mallard, elaborate cvg, 131" 12,000.00
Maple Co Fed, cvd tall post, New England, ca 1810, 71" 1,320.00
Oak w/appl decor & cvd head near top of hdbrd, 1900s, 79" H ..995.00
Rope, cannonball type, grpt, 44x69x52" 195.00
Rope, curly maple, trn posts/finials, scroll hdbd, 48x54x75" 1,800.00
Rope, maple w/curly head & ftbrds, trn posts, rfn, 46x53" 550.00
Rope, poplar, trn posts, 1-brd hd/ftbrds, rfn, 44x72x55" 225.00
Rope, poplar, trn posts w/ball & spire finial, rfn, 56x79x51" 335.00
Rope, poplar, trumpet finials, blanket bar, 40x75x51" 220.00
Rope, poplar Co, trn posts, high ft, old rpt, 33x57x42" 160.00

Rope, poplar/birch Co, short trn posts, red stain, 33x76x52" **65.00**
Rope, trundle, poplar, slat-type mattress rails, 40x59" **275.00**
Rope, trundle, walnut, ball post finials, castors, 16x63x42" **125.00**
Settle, pine w/red rpt & old brn grpt, folds out, 52x81x21" **175.00**
Tester, mahog Vict, fancy cornice/hdbd crown, 127" **1,500.00**
Walnut Renaissance Revival, burl cartouch, ornate hdbd, 89" **1,200.00**

Benches

Church, oak, cvd flower ea end, 1920s, 41x45x19" **325.00**
English, brn rpt, trn legs, plank seat, half-spindle bk **145.00**
Fireside, brass, vinyl reuphl, 65" **100.00**
Fr style w/cvd fr, old tapestry-weave uphl seat, 45" **415.00**
Limbert #566, even-arm settle, 8-slat bk, mk, 74", VG **3,250.00**
Mahog fr w/paw ft, lyre shape, velvet uphl, 36" **330.00**
Mission oak, solid bk/box seat, rnded arms, unmk, 52" **250.00**
Oak, shaped arms, splat bk, ca 1900, 37x50x20" **415.00**
Oak European style, bold overall cvg, much rstr/rpl, 83" **880.00**
Pine Co Hplwht, 1-brd, yel rpt, damaged corner, 21x99x14" **210.00**
Settle, mc stencil: birds/fruit, half spindles, some rpt, 73" **900.00**
Settle, oak Continental, ornate cvg, gr wash, dtd 1723, 87" **1,650.00**
Settle, oak/pine English, paneled, lift lid seat, rprs, 53" **300.00**
Settle, pine Co, shaped arms, panel bk, shoe ft, 55x61x16" **2,400.00**
Walnut fr, cabriole legs, c&b ft, needlepoint seat, 18x20x15" **330.00**
Water, PA pine/poplar, 2 panel do/1 shelf, 2-brd ends, 45" **2,750.00**
Water, pine Co, canted/dvtl legs, worn gr rpt, 12x32" **275.00**
Windsor, bamboo spindles/bowbk rail, trn legs, Phila, 73" **3,300.00**

Blanket Chests, Coffers, Trunks and Mule Chests

Country Federal grain and putty decorated blanket chest, Massachusetts, ca 1820, 41x38x17½", $4,290.00.

Curly maple Co, sq corner posts, paneled ends, rpl lid, 34" **660.00**
Immigrant's, oak English, wrought strapping, worn, 36¼" **300.00**
Immigrant's, pine w/orig pnt & stylized florals, 1815, 36" **715.00**
Mule, butternut Co, 2-drw/2 false drw, 2-pc, rpr, 43x44x21" ..**2,000.00**
Mule, maple Co, 1 dvtl/cockbeaded drw, 5-brd, 40x38x17" **440.00**
Mule, maple Co QA, 3-drw, 1-brd ends, old red traces, 46½" **825.00**
Mule, pine, brn vinegar-pnt drw, brn flame grpt, wear, 36x42" ..**750.00**
Mule, pine, 2-drw, 6-brd type, brn flame grpt, 38x41x37" **1,430.00**
Mule, pine Co Chpndl, 2-drw, 1 false drw, old red stain, 45" **990.00**
Mule, Southern yel pine, trn ft, sq posts, rpl hinges, 42" **560.00**
Mule, walnut Co, sq posts, 1-drw, lift lid, till, 39x41x19" **1,100.00**

Oak English coffer, paneled, relief cvg, rprs, w/till, 40" **385.00**
Oak primitive English coffer, simple panels, 30" **85.00**
PA German, brn mottle stain over red, dtd 1818, 37x49x21" **880.00**
Pine, orig flame grpt, dvtl, w/till, 25x38x20" **495.00**
Pine, 6-brd, staple hinges, old brn pnt, rprs, 16x29x12" **330.00**
Pine & walnut, paneled, w/till, worn red/gr rpt, 24x41x19" **385.00**
Pine Co, dvtl case, walnut till, rpl ft, 26x45x21" **115.00**
Pine Co, 6-brd, cut-out ft & till, old pnt, 21x37x17" **360.00**
Pine Co Hplwht, dvtl, Fr ft, strap hinges, grpt, 25x50x23" **660.00**
Pine/poplar, paneled sides/ends, w/till, grpt, 22x38x17" **465.00**
Pine/poplar PA w/flame grpt, dvtl, till, wrought straps, 50" **415.00**
Poplar, dvt, orig flame grpt, w/till, 1867, 23x44" **415.00**
Poplar, dvtl, 2-drw, old rpt, w/till, ca 1860, 31x50x21" **330.00**
Poplar Co Chpndl, 2 dvtl drw, moldings, till, gr pnt, 29x55" **275.00**
Poplar/walnut, paneled, w/till, orig red/blk grpt, 28x49x25" **350.00**
Walnut, paneled, trn ft, 1-brd lid, 2-part int, 23x37x16" **360.00**
Walnut Chpndl, dvtl, 2-drw, ogee ft, rpr, 32x53x24" **3,575.00**
Walnut Co, dvtl, bear trap lock, rpl strap hinges, 53" **685.00**
Walnut Co Chpndl, 3 dvtl drw, till w/3 drw, rprs, 28x50x23" .**1,100.00**
Walnut Co Sheraton, chip cvg, 2-drw, rope cvd legs, 32x38" .**3,000.00**
Walnut/poplar/maple, orig flame grpt w/yel grpt panels, 43" ...**1,100.00**

Bookcases

Limbert #356, 2 8-pane do, open end shelves, 48x52", EX **12,000.00**
Limbert #358, 2 do, corbels under extended top, 57x48", VG .**3,500.00**
Limbert #361, gallery top:2 do w/sm sq cutouts, 56x45", VG ..**4,750.00**
Mahog Traditional style w/inlay, glass do, 3-part, 73" **660.00**
Oak, folding (hinged sides), 8" gallery, 1920s, 48x30x11" **325.00**
Oak, 2 leaded/stained glass do, claw ft, 1900s, 65x48x13" **1,295.00**
Oak, 2-do, grotesques on stiles, bk rail, 1900s, 59x30x17" **850.00**
Oak, 4-unit sectional, 1920s, rstr/rfn **525.00**

Cabinets

Breakfront, mahog English style, beveled glass, 92x74" **800.00**
China, Fr style, gilt/HP, marble top/curved glass, 62x35" **715.00**
China, Fr style, gilt/HP scenes, curved glass, wear, 63x30" **600.00**
China, Mission oak, 2-do, 2" bk rail, 1920s, 57x42x15" **650.00**
China, oak, Arts & Crafts, 2-do, appl framing, 61x40" **1,200.00**
China, oak w/convex glass panels, claw ft, 1900s, 63x45" **1,100.00**
China, oak w/convex glass side panels, 1900s, 55x40x16" **1,000.00**
Corner, oak, beveled mirror bk, ldgl do, 3-leg, paw ft **1,250.00**
Curio, mahog Fr style, inlay & ormolu, marble top, 64x40x15" **415.00**
Curio, mahog Traditional style w/inlay, 1900s, 59x23x12" **300.00**
Curio, oak Vict, molding on crest/above base w/2 drw, 71" **750.00**
Hoosier, oak, 3-do:2-do:counter:lg do & 4 drw, 69x40x27" * **700.00**
Spice, pine, 3-drw, wooden knobs, 13x9x5"+4" curved bk **210.00**
Vitrine, English Adams style, mahog/satinwood/inlay, 31x24x18" **440.00**
Vitrine, mahog Traditional style, 20th C, 26x25x18" **85.00**

Candlestands

Birch, tripod base, snake ft, 1-brd, rfn, 26x18" **415.00**
Birch Co Chpndl, tripod base, snake ft, 1-brd, rprs, 16x15" **335.00**
Birch Co Hplwht, tripod base, scimitar legs, rfn, 26x21x14" **200.00**
Birch Co Hplwht, tripod base, spider legs, 1-brd, rprs, 39x17" **220.00**
Birch Co Hplwht, tripod base, 2-brd, 30x22x15" **385.00**
Bird's-eye maple Co Sheraton, 2-drw, rpl top, 29x18x21" **350.00**
Cherry Chpndl, tripod base, simple chip cvg, 1-brd, 26x15½" ...**2,200.00**
Cherry Co, tripod base, cut-out legs, 1-brd, 26" **660.00**
Cherry Co, tripod base, scimitar legs, 1-brd, 27x18x18" **330.00**
Cherry Co, tripod base, trn column, 2-brd, rprs, 28x18x17" **200.00**
Cherry Co Chpndl, walnut top, tripod base/snake ft, 25x17x18" ..**465.00**

Curly maple Co, tripod base, snake ft, gallery, 39x14x14" **1,500.00**
Curly maple Hplwht, tripod base w/spider legs, 2-brd, 26x16" **880.00**
Hardwoods w/copper pan, 2-socket, adjusts from 23", EX **470.00**
Mahog marquetry, tripod, trn column, rnd top, 28½x20" **440.00**
Maple Co Chpndl, tilt top, snake ft, 39x17" **1,450.00**
Oak Co, whittled legs, 1-brd 18" 8-sided top, early **675.00**
Wrought iron, tripod base, curved legs, oval ft, 1800s, 54" **1,760.00**

Chairs

Arm, Chpndl-style Martha Washington, old uphl, 36" **90.00**
Arm, mahog English Chpndl, reuphl, rprs, 41" **525.00**
Arm, mahog English Chpndl style, cvd fr, reuphl seat **525.00**
Arm, oak English Co Chpndl style, cvd crest, 1840s, 36½" **150.00**
Arm, Sheraton style, worn blk pnt, cane seat, 20th C, 33" **195.00**
Arm, Walnut German Rococo, acanthus/shell cvg, 1750s **700.00**
Bannister-bk side, mahog European, rush seat, worn, 43" **65.00**
Billiard, Limbert, Mission oak, high saddle seat/ft rest, EX **2,700.00**
Captain's, oak, continuous arm, 9-spindle, 1900s, 31x22" **220.00**
Corner, birch Co, trn legs/posts, rpl splint seat, rfn, 31" **275.00**
Corner, Co style, old blk pnt over gr, rpl seat, 33" **600.00**
Fruitwood Continental Baroque, balloon seat, rpr, 39" **750.00**
Highchair, captain's chair bk, old blk pnt stenciling, 32" **165.00**
Highchair, Co, natural finish, splint seat, 31" **250.00**
Host, mahog Sheraton, trn legs/EX reeded detail, rprs, 34" **400.00**
Ladderbk, Co English, rush seat, ft ended out, 42" **250.00**
Ladderbk arm, maple, 4 arched slats, shaped arms, rfn, 46" **770.00**
Ladderbk arm Co, simple cvg, 3-slat, splint seat, 41½" **75.00**
Ladderbk arm Co, slat seat, worn red pnt, 38½" **195.00**
Ladderbk arm Co, splint seat, old yel rpt, 41½" **300.00**
Ladderbk arm Co, trn legs/posts, splint seat, rpt, 46" **360.00**
Ladderbk arm Co, 5 grad slats, trn finials, rush seat, 44" **450.00**
Ladderbk side, 4-slat, trn finial, splint seat, 42¼" * **50.00**
Limbert, att; rocker, high bk w/6 slats, open arms, 41", EX **325.00**
Mahog Chpndl-style Martha Washington, cvd fr, reuphl, 43" **85.00**
Mahog English Chpndl, scroll bk, slip seat, rpr, 37" **275.00**
Oak, finger-hold bk rail, 5-spindle, cane seat, 1920s, 33" **50.00**
Quaint rocker #806, 4-slat bk, decal, orig finish, 37" **250.00**
Rocker, maple Co arm, trn posts, shaped arms, rush seat, 40" **110.00**
Rocker, nursing; 5-spindle bk, plank seat, rfn **50.00**
Rocker, oak, str crest over spindle bk, curved arms/legs **250.00**
Rocker, Old Hickory #23, 7-twig bk, 4 ea side, '20, 36", VG **475.00**
Rocker, sewing; blk & red grpt w/yel stripes & stencil, 29" **75.00**
Rosewood Am Rococo, cvd/laminated, att Belter, 1850s **11,500.00**
Rosewood Rococo Revival, floral-cvd/uphl bk/arms/seat, pr **1,300.00**

Savanarola-type chair, Baroque-carved oak with cherubs and foliage in relief on back, paw feet, $275.00.

Sheraton style, needlepoint uphl w/floral wreaths, 36" **165.00**
Side, arrow/spindle bk, plank seat, crest w/mc decor, worn **120.00**

Side, cherry Am Hplwht, rtcl/cvd bk, reuphl/rfn, 39" **330.00**
Side, cherry Co Chpndl, rtcl splat, yoke crest, rfn, 40" **300.00**
Side, Continental style, red/blk pnt w/mc florals, 42" **200.00**
Side, curly maple w/rstr blk/gold decor, trn crest rail, 34" **350.00**
Side, European style, cvd fr, worn leather seat, 1900s, 52" **140.00**
Side, fruitwood Co Hplwht, slip seat, old rprs, 34½" **165.00**
Side, mahog Chpndl ribbon-bk, sq molded legs, uphl seat, 39" * ..**550.00**
Side, mahog Chpndl style, c&b ft, 1900s, 37" **215.00**
Side, mahog English Chpndl, slip seat/rtcl splat/yoke crest * **125.00**
Side, mahog English Regency, slip seat, 34", EX **65.00**
Side, mahog Hplwht style, cvd slats, uphl seat, rfn, 36" **95.00**
Side, mahog veneer Am Emp, flame grpt, slip seat, 31" **75.00**
Side, mahog Vict, cvd crests:oval bks, balloon seat, 4 for **750.00**
Side, maple Co, trn legs/trifid ft, vase splat/rush seat, 41" **275.00**
Side, maple Co Chpndl, rtcl splat & crest, rush seat, 40" **385.00**
Side, oak, fancy tall bk w/uphl seat & bk panel, 1900s, 45" **185.00**
Side, oak W/M, trn front legs, shaped crest, rpl seat, 46" **715.00**
Side, Wallace Nutting #361, maple, vase splat, EX trn **550.00**
Side, walnut Gothic Revival, blk tapestry uphl, 48½" **145.00**
Side, walnut Renaisance style, European, worn reuphl, 36" **55.00**
Windsor, bamboo highchair, blk rpt over gr, adult sz, 47" **600.00**
Windsor, bamboo side, shaped seat, splayed base, rprs, 33" **385.00**
Windsor, bow-bk arm, blk rpt over rprs, 38" **250.00**
Windsor, bow-bk arm, old rpr, ca 1900, child's, 25" **195.00**
Windsor, bow-bk arm, splayed base, saddle seat, 35½" **1,400.00**
Windsor, bow-bk arm, 7-spindle, shaped seat, rprs, 33" **745.00**
Windsor, bow-bk side, 9-spindle, saddle seat, rfn, 34¼" **770.00**
Windsor, brace-bk side, Wallace Nutting, EX detail, 38½" **550.00**
Windsor, brace-bk w/shaped arms, 9-spindle, worn grpt, 37" ..**1,265.00**
Windsor, Co low-bk arm, rpl/rprs, old finish, 29" **385.00**
Windsor, comb-bk arm, splayed base, saddle seat, rpr, 48½" ...**1,500.00**
Windsor, comb-bk arm rocker, 7-spindle, modern pnt, 43¾" **625.00**
Windsor, continuous arm, splayed base, saddle seat, 38", EX ..**1,375.00**
Windsor, corseted bow-bk, 9-spindle, bamboo trn, VG **325.00**
Windsor, fan-bk Co side, 9-spindle, blk rpt w/gold striping **550.00**
Windsor, fan-bk w/added rockers, shaped crest, rpt, youth sz **665.00**
Windsor, writing arm (1-brd), drw, rprs, 44" **2,200.00**
Wing-bk arm NH Chpndl Co, chestnut legs, reuphl, 42" **1,650.00**

Chair Sets

Curly maple, sabre legs, rectangular crest+bar in bk, 8 for **1,200.00**
English Sheraton style, cvd mahog, 1900s, 38", 5 for **825.00**
European, bl & gold rpt w/silk uphl, rpr, 35", 4 for **2,400.00**
Grpt/2-color stripes/stencil on crest/slat, 6 for **1,650.00**
Half arrowbk, plank seat, flame grpt/stencil, 31", 6 for **825.00**
Mahog Chpndl-style, slip seats, rtcl bks, 37", 6 for **1,155.00**
Mahog Emp style, horsehair seats, 1800s, 37", 2 arm+6 sides ..**2,685.00**
Mahog Hplwht style, uphl seat, 1900s, 37", 2 arm+10 sides **5,950.00**
Mahog Traditional-style arm, low bk, leather uphl, 30", 4 for **725.00**
Oak, triple pressed bk, cane seat, trn legs, 39", 8 for **3,000.00**
Plank seat, old rpt w/foliage/stripe decor, 33", 6 for **560.00**
Pnt w/striping, roses in crest, ½-spindle bk, 33", 6 for **1,860.00**
Quaint, #377½ & 377, 1 arm+4 sides, tag, orig **825.00**
Rosewood w/classic inlay, velvet uphl, 34½", 4 for **220.00**
Walnut Biedermeier, curved bk w/rtcl splat, 1850s, 4 for **1,975.00**
Windsor, bamboo side, 16" seats, rfn, 31½", 4 for **285.00**
Windsor, pnt rod-bk side, sgn IC Tuttle, ca 1800, 34", 6 for ...**8,250.00**

Chests

Birch/pine Fed, 5-drw, cut-out ft, 1800s, 41x36x18" **2,500.00**
Butler's, cherry Chpndl, pull-out shelf:3 grad drw, 38x42" **1,375.00**
Butternut/maple Chpndl, New England, 1780s, 60x36x18" **4,400.00**

Cherry Chpndl, 4 dvtl/beaded drw, rpr ogee ft, 35x40x21" **2,650.00**
Cherry Chpndl, 4-drw, rstr bracket ft, rpl brasses, 34x40" **2,100.00**
Cherry Co, 6 dvtl drw, solid ends, rpl pulls, rfn, 44x38" **990.00**
Cherry Co, 6 dvtl/cockbeaded drw, paneled ends, rfn, 51x43" **800.00**
Cherry Co Emp, 4 dvtl drw, trn half columns, rpl pulls, 52" **385.00**
Cherry Co Emp, 4-drw, paneled ends, cvd pilasters, 47x42" **525.00**
Cherry Co Hplwht, 9 dvtl/beaded drw, banded inlay, 75x42" .**3,850.00**
Cherry Co Sheraton, 4 dvtl drw, X-banded veneer, 41x44" **600.00**
Cherry Co Sheraton, 4 dvtl/cockbeaded drw, 45x42x20" **825.00**
Cherry Fed, 5 dvtl/cockbeaded drw, reeded stiles, 44x43x20" **875.00**
Cherry Fed w/mahog veneer, New England, 1790s, 33x39x22" .**2,750.00**
Cherry Hplwht, w/inlay enclosing drw pulls, rstr/rpr, 47x40" ..**1,000.00**
Cherry Hplwht, 4 beaded drw, Fr ft, rpl brasses, 38x42" **1,750.00**
Cherry Hplwht, 4 dvtl/beaded drw, Fr ft, rpl hdw, 43x38" **2,200.00**
Cherry Sheraton, 4 dvtl/cockbeaded drw, trn legs, 29x26x16" ..**4,000.00**
Cherry Southern QA on fr, 2 sm dr:4, bandy legs, rstr, 54x41" ..**1,200.00**
Cherry/curly maple Co Emp, trn ft/pilasters, 2-do/5-drw, 49" ..**1,265.00**
Cherry/hardwoods Co Emp, 5-drw, paneled ends, trn ft, 48x42" ...**715.00**
Cherry/walnut Co Sheraton w/inlay, 4-drw, high trn ft, 48x40" .**1,200.00**
Cherry/walnut Co w/inlay, 4-drw, paneled ends, 45x45" **935.00**
Chest-on-Chest, mahog Chpndl, bonnet top, 10-drw, rprs, 87" .**3,650.00**

Classical Federal bow-front chest of drawers, four long drawers, capped animal paw feet, 37x42x21", $900.00.

Curly birch Co Sheraton, 4 cockbeaded drw/oxbow top, 38x42"..**3,000.00**
Curly maple Chpndl, 2 sm drw:5 grad, bracket ft, rfn, 47x36" .**4,180.00**
Curly maple Co Chpndl, 5-drw, never had hdw, 52x36", EX ..**1,700.00**
Curly maple Co Sheraton, 4 grad drw, inlaid stiles, 45x44" **1,800.00**
Curly maple/walnut Co Sheraton, 4 sm do:3, trn ft, 51x42" **1,700.00**
Curly walnut Hplwht w/inlay, 4 dvtl cockbeaded drw, 38x38" .**2,550.00**
Mahog Am Emp w/figured mahog veneer, 3-drw/stepbk top, 40" ..**425.00**
Mahog Emp, spiral columns, 6-drw, paw ft, 1840, 34" **1,200.00**
Mahog Emp style, 2 sm drw:4, trn pilasters, 46x46x23¼" **200.00**
Mahog English Chpndl, 3 serpentine drw, rprs, 22⅜x36" **2,530.00**
Mahog Fr Louis XV style, 3-drw, marble top, glass do, 46" **440.00**
Mahog veneer Emp, bowfront, 4-drw, stepbk top, 44x41x20" **850.00**
Mahog veneer English Hplwht w/inlay, bowfront, 3-drw, 35x41".**1,700.00**
Mahog veneer Italian bombe, lt wear, 20th C, 27x28x14", pr .**1,150.00**
Mahog w/flame veneer Sheraton, bowfront, 4-drw, 46x43x22" ..**990.00**
Mahog/cherry Emp, 3-drw, trn columns, paw ft, glass pulls, 44" **825.00**
Maple Co Chpndl, 4-drw, molded edge, rpl hdw, 34x37x19" **1,980.00**
Maple Co Chpndl, 6 grad/dvtl drw, molded cornice, 57x36" **5,600.00**
Oak, 3-drw, incised lines, str apron, 1920s, 32x40x28" **235.00**
Oak English QA on fr w/inlay, 5-drw, cabriole legs, 49" **550.00**
Poplar Co, brn flame grpt, solid ends, 4 dvtl drw, 42x39x18" **715.00**
Spool, walnut w/maple inlay, 4-drw, rpl pulls, 18x24x14" **495.00**

Stripped pine, 4-drw, panel side, shaped apron, 1880 ....**350.00**
Walnut Chpndl, 4-drw/dust shelves/rpl ogee ft, rfn, 36x37" ...**2,860.00**
Walnut Co Hplwht, 4 dvtl drw w/beading, rprs/rfn, 42x40x20" .**990.00**
Walnut Co Hplwht, 4 grad/dvtl/cockbeaded drw, Fr ft, 47x38" ..**825.00**
Walnut Co Hplwht, 4-drw, rpl hdw, rprs, 40x38x21" **1,155.00**
Walnut Co Hplwht, 5 dvtl/cockbeaded drw, bracket ft, 42x38" .**110.00**
Walnut Co Hplwht w/inlay, 4-drw, lion hdw, rstr, 39x42x20" ...**995.00**
Walnut Co Sheraton, trn ft w/castors, paneled sides, 31x44x22" ..**685.00**
Walnut Fed, 4-drw, paneled ends, rpl hdw, 43x40x20" **1,925.00**
Walnut Hplwht w/inlay, 4 dvtl/beaded drw, rpl/rpr, 40x38" **1,650.00**
Walnut PA Chpndl, 3 drw:2 drw:4 drw, ogee ft, rpl/rpr, 59x40" .**4,125.00**
Walnut PA on fr, 8-drw, molded cornice, rstr base, 57x23x42" **825.00**
Walnut QA w/burl veneer facade on fr, 8-drw, rstr, 62x39" **660.00**
Walnut/burl S German Baroque, serpentine, 4-drw, 35x44" ...**8,250.00**
Walnut/curly maple Am Emp, 9-drw, scroll ft & pilasters, 68" ...**600.00**

Cupboards (See Also Pie Safes)

Chimney, pine/poplar Co, dvtl, int drw, rpl ft, 70x24x18" **415.00**
Chimney, walnut & poplar, paneled do, grpt, 84x27x18" **440.00**
Corner, Cherry Co, 1 12-pane do:1 drw:2 panel do, 88x45" **5,500.00**
Corner, Cherry Co, 2 full-length raised panel do, 85x62" **990.00**
Corner, English, rfn oak, rstr cornice, 1800s, 46x29" **770.00**
Corner, pine Co, 4 panel do, appl molding/cornice, 82x45" **3,000.00**
Corner, pine English Co, folky detail, rstr, 87x50" **1,650.00**
Corner, pine Southern architectural, 2 full-length do, 96x58" ..**3,500.00**
Corner, poplar Co, 2 6-pane do:2 panel do, 2-pc, 79x55" **770.00**
Corner, poplar/cherry Co, 4 panel do, cornice, grpt, 80x48" ...**1,500.00**
Corner, walnut Co, panel do in simple 4" fr, 43x34" **225.00**
Corner, walnut Co, 1-pc, 2 6-pane do:2 drw:2 do, 84x59" **1,540.00**
Corner, walnut Co, 2 panel do:3 drw:2 panel do, 1-pc, 85x54" .**3,550.00**
Corner, walnut Co OH, 1 6-pane do:3 drw:2 panel do, 87x56" .**1,265.00**
Court, walnut, 2 drw/2 relief-cvd do, trn legs, 41x39x20" **275.00**
Hanging, oak English, cvd floral facade, 38½x36" **1,100.00**
Hanging, oak w/curly maple grpt, cvd arch in do, rpl, 38x28" **585.00**
Hanging, pine/poplar Co, panel do, base/crest molding, 42x25" .**300.00**
Hanging, Southwestern, old bl pnt w/gold trim, 16½x13" **525.00**
Hanging, walnut, 4-panel do, appl moldings, 32x24", EX **850.00**
Jelly, poplar, 1 panel do, 4-shelf, 1-brd type, 66x42" **2,600.00**
Jelly, Southern yel pine, dvtl, 2 panel do, rpr, 54x45" **1,100.00**
Jelly, walnut, 1 dvtl drw:2 panel do, 1-brd ends, 57x36" **600.00**
Jelly, walnut Co, cut-out ft, 1-drw, 2 panel do, 69x45x19" **1,540.00**
Linen press, English, oak w/inlay, 2 do:4 drw, 2-pc, 72x42" **660.00**
Linen press, mahog veneer English Hplwht, 4-drw, 2-do, 84" .**1,650.00**
Linen press, oak European style, panel do/2 sm dvtl drw, 61" **500.00**
Linen press, open top, 3 drw:2 panel do base, 82x59x21" **685.00**
Linen press, pine, 2 do:4 cockbeaded drw, rfn, 80x51x22" **990.00**
Oak, 2 glass do:3 drw:2 panel do, 2-pc step-bk, 83x41" **795.00**
Oak European, open top, 2 drw:2 do, cvd, 2-pc, 82x49x22" **440.00**
Pewter, pine Eng Co, open shelves:2 panel do/3 drw, 76x52" ..**1,750.00**
Pewter, walnut Co, open 3-shelf top:2 panel do, 1-pc, 86x47" ...**2,500.00**
Pewter, walnut Co, panel do, open shelves, no cornice, 71x47" .**800.00**
Pewter, walnut VA style, 2 1-brd do, open shelves, 77x41x19" .**1,150.00**
Pine Co, tall panel do: shorter do, 1-pc, rprs, 79x28x16" **1,325.00**
Pine Co, 2-pc, 2 6-pane do:step-bk w/3 drw & 2 do, 52" W **2,200.00**
Pine Co, 3-drw top:2 panel do, scalloped crest, 54x42x18" **1,760.00**
Pine Co Chpndl, 2 6-pane do:3-drw:2 do, pie shelf, 2-pc, 79" .**3,025.00**
Pine Co English, open top, 2-do:2-drw, 2-pc, rprs, 80x50x17" ...**300.00**
Pine Co English, 1-pc, open, rfn/rpr, 71x55x17" **1,705.00**
Pine Co English, 2 do:3 drw:2 panel do, 1-pc, rprs, 76" **385.00**
Pine Co English, 2-pc, mar, rfn, 84½x62½x23¼" **825.00**
Pine Southern type, 1 drw:2-drw:2 do, raised panels, 53x47x20" ..**700.00**
Poplar Co, 2 raised panel do, 3-shelf, bl traces, 72x50" **1,550.00**
Poplar Co, 4 panel do, 2-drw, 1-brd cornice, 1-pc, 71x40x20" ...**1,200.00**

Poplar Co step-bk, weathered old gray pnt, 3-do, 71x33" **1,100.00**
Store, pine Co English, 4 sliding do, molded cornice, 70x72" **250.00**
Walnut Co, 2 6-pane do:3 drws:2 do, H hinges, 85½x46½" **7,920.00**
Walnut/poplar Co Emp on fr, 1 panel do:1 drw, grpt, 58x40" **1,700.00**
Welsh, dk oak, 2 shelf:2 dvtl drw, 1890s, 72x54x18" **3,500.00**
Welsh, open top: 3 dvtl drw, ca 1900, mar, 80x60x21" **850.00**

Desks

Country Chippendale wavy birch slant-lid desk, New England, ca 1780, 39x38x19", $1,980.00.

Cherry Chpndl, slant lid, 3-drw, 1780s, 41x41x20" **4,125.00**
Curly maple Co Chpndl, slant front, 4-drw, fitted int, 42x36" ..**4,730.00**
Hardwood English Chpndl, 4-drw, slant lid, bracket ft, 42" **3,000.00**
Mahog Boston Chpndl block-front, slant top, shell cvgs etc .**10,750.00**
Mahog English Hplwht-style serpentine, 1850s, 30x51x26" * **660.00**
Mahog English Sheraton w/inlay, shaped top, 3-drw, trn legs .**1,650.00**
Mahog Hplwht w/inlay, 3-drw, fold-down top, 2-pc, rstr, 78" .**1,785.00**
Mahog Traditional style, leather insert & gilt, 30x24x48" **635.00**
Maple Chpndl, dvtl case, 4-drw, ogee ft, rprs, 43x40x19½" **1,950.00**
Oak, Arts & Crafts, sm drw ea side lg 1, lower shelves, 43" **330.00**
Oak, S-roll top, fitted int, 4 drw ea ped, 60" **1,200.00**
Pine Co, open top w/2 drw:slant lid:1-brd do, 1-pc, 57x24" **715.00**
Secretary, oak cylinder type w/spoon cvg, 1890s, 86x39x22" ...**1,500.00**
Tiger maple Co Chpndl, 4-drw, orig hdw, 1780s, 37½x35x18" .**4,840.00**
Walnut English Regency style, 5-drw, vinyl top, 30x51x28" **275.00**
Walnut PA Chpndl, fall front, reeded columns, 1770, 42" **4,000.00**
Wavy birch Co Chpndl, slant lid, New England, 1780s, 39x38" * .**1,980.00**

Dressers

Mahog Am Emp, 4-drw, flame grpt, ogee mirror, 75" **850.00**
Mahog English sea captain's, 5-drw/brass hdw/mirror, 40x42" * .**300.00**
Mahog Vict, serpentine marble top, bevel mirror, 1900, 79" **275.00**
Mahog Vict, shaped marble top, fancy crest, lg mirror, 88" **1,500.00**
Mahog w/cvg, shaped marble top, urn finials, candle shelves ..**1,400.00**
Oak, curved facade, swivel mirror, press/cvd decor **465.00**

Dry Sinks

Pine Co, 2 panel do, 2 dvtl drw, rprs, 30x61x18" **715.00**
Pine Co, 2-drw, 2 raised panel do, pnt int, 32x59x22" **935.00**
Poplar, 2 panel do/dvtl drw, porc knobs, grpt, PA, 33x46" **715.00**
Poplar Co, hutch top w/2 drw, 2-do/2-drw base, 51x62x22" **2,200.00**
Poplar Co, 2 paneled do, crest, trn ft, rfn/rpl, 34x49x22" **450.00**
Poplar/walnut Co, worn red rpt w/blk grpt, 2-do, 36x39x19" **650.00**

Primitive type, pine, 2 panel do, short ft, 30x41x24" **415.00**

Highboys

Curly maple QA CT, 5 grad drw:2 drw, cabriole legs, 74x36" .**13,750.00**
Mahog veneer on pine Am Chpndl style, 1900s repro, 86" **1,870.00**
Oak English Co QA, 5-drw top, 1-do base, rpr/rpl, 58x36" **660.00**
Tiger maple QA, flat top, scalloped apron, NE, 74" **15,500.00**
Walnut Co QA, 8 dvtl drws in top:3 in base, 70x38" **18,700.00**
Walnut English W/M, molded cornice, 2-pc, mar, 62" **4,400.00**

Lowboys

Cherry/birch/curly maple QA style, handmade repro, 30x20" **1,265.00**
Oak English Co QA, 1-drw, scalloped apron, rprs, 27¼" **1,155.00**
Walnut Chpndl style, 5-drw, cabriole legs, c&b ft, rstr, 30x35" .**880.00**
Walnut veneer English QA style, worn, 1800s, 29x36x18" **495.00**

Pie Safes

Butternut Co, 2 drw:2 drw, 12 punched tin panels, 51x38x18" ..**825.00**
Poplar Co, 12 tin panels, 1 dvtl drw, 54x39x16½", EX **500.00**
Poplar Co, 2 do:drw:2 do, 10 punched tin panels, 80x40" **575.00**
Poplar w/flame pnt, dbl do w/punched tin, 2-drw, 50x18x46" **980.00**
Walnut Co, dbl do, 12 punched tin panels, rpr, 50x40x18" **990.00**

Secretaries

Cherry Hplwht, mahog X-banding/maple stringing, 4-drw, 75" .**2,145.00**
Mahog Emp, 5 dvtl drws, fold-down top, 2-part, 86x45x22" ...**1,760.00**
Mahog Hplwht style lady's w/inlay, 3-drw, tambour top, 47x36" ..**770.00**
Mahog veneer European style, 2 do:2 drw:2 do, 2-pc, 82x47" **400.00**
Mahog/walnut veneer Continental style, mc florals, 76" **1,100.00**
Oak Vict, dbl do bookcase:cylinder:2 cupbrd do, 81x32" **850.00**

Settees

Arrow-back Windsor rocking settee with plank seat, completely original, refinished, New England, ca 1830, 32¾", $800.00.

Fr style, cvd fr, worn uphl, 58" **100.00**
Fr style, cvd fr w/antique ivory/gr finish, silk uphl, 51" **360.00**
Half-spindle bk w/scrolled armes, shaped crest, rfn, 72" **325.00**
Mahog Emp, cvd fr, paw/angel wing ft, lyre arms, uphl, 63" **775.00**
Mahog transitional Rococo, cvd crest, serpentine front, 82" **300.00**
Rosewood Rococo Revival, floral crest/curved bk, 1860, 72" ..**1,500.00**
Windsor, plank seat, spindle bk, rfn, 40" **800.00**

Windsor, 24-spindle rod-bk crest, curved arms, orig pnt, 77" ..**3,000.00**

Shelves

Corner, walnut, scrolled sides, 3 curved shelves, 27x17" **220.00**
Folding, pine w/breadbrd end, old wht pnt, 15x26" **195.00**
Pine European, mortar & pestle holder/spoon rack, 27" **135.00**
Plate rack, pine, 3-shelf, molded plate bars, 33x46" **415.00**
Walnut-color rfn, 3 scalloped shelves, trn posts, 25x23x7" **95.00**
Wooden thread spools w/5 graduated tiers, 59" **300.00**

Sideboards

Cherry Am Emp, flame grain mahog veneer, 3-do/3-drw, rfn, 61" **650.00**
Credenza, Louis XVI style, veneer, marble top, 35x47x22" **1,375.00**
Mahog Am Classical, flame grain veneers, 9-drw, 62x39x27" **990.00**
Mahog Am mixed styles, 3 drw:4 do, ornate cvg, 1800s, 42x72" **440.00**
Mahog English Hplwht, ebony inlay, 5-drw, step-bk top, 78" **1,575.00**
Mahog English Regency, 2 do flank 3 drw, rprs/damage, 36x67" ...**350.00**
Mahog Fed w/flame veneer, 2-do, 2 false do, 4-drw, 49x51" **1,700.00**
Oak, cvd w/dolphins' & ladies' heads, marble top, 75"L **3,500.00**
Oak English Arts & Crafts, 4 paneled do, 45x72x21½" **450.00**
Oak Vict, open & glass-do shelves, mirror, leaf/mask cvg **825.00**
Quaint, oak, mirror bk, 3-drw, 2-do, metal tag, 54x48" **1,100.00**
Quaint, shaped plate rail, do ea side bank of drw, rstr, 46" **2,000.00**

Sofas

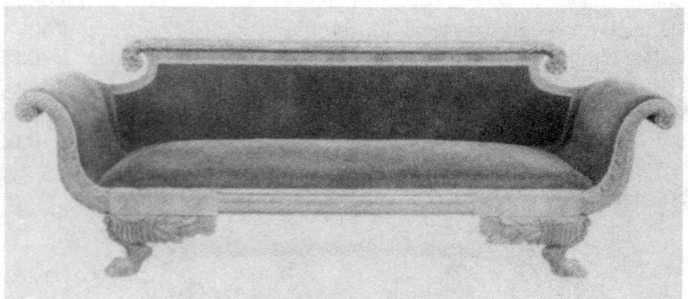

Classical Revival mahogany and mahogany veneer sofa, upholstered back, straight skirt, carved cornucopia and hairy paw feet, New England, ca 1830, 33x91", $1,500.00.

Chpndl-style camel-bk, cvd mahog base, damask uphl, 85" **875.00**
Emp, mahog lyre fr w/paw & wing ft, reuphl, 81" **2,300.00**
Mahog Am Emp, lyre fr, paw ft, floral cvgs, reuphl, 84" **660.00**
Mahog Fed, sq bk, reeded arm supports, no uphl, 37x79" **2,750.00**
Mahog MA Fed w/inlay, ca 1810, 35x71x24" **4,125.00**
Walnut Co, trn ft/posts/arms/finial, reuphl, 77" **525.00**
Walnut Vict, cvd walnut fr w/crest, reuphl, 65" **525.00**

Stands

Bamboo, old finish w/wear, Fr, 39½" **110.00**
Bedside, cherry, 1 nailed drw, 2-brd rpl top, rfn, 28x20x21" **300.00**
Bedside, cherry w/mahog veneer, 2 dvtl drw, rfn, 30x20x18" **440.00**
Bedside, cherry/poplar, 1 dvtl drw, rpl top, 38x19x16" **175.00**
Cherry, 2 dvtl drw w/bird's-eye veneer, drop leaves, 29x22x17" .**250.00**
Cherry Co, 1 dvtl drw, 2-brd, rfn, 29x19x19" **350.00**
Cherry Co Emp, G trnings, 30x21x23" **330.00**
Cherry Co Emp, trn column & drop, 2-brd, gr rpt, 27x20" **165.00**
Cherry Co Emp, 2 dvtl drw, relief cvg front/sides, 29x21x21" **880.00**

Cherry Co Hplwht, 2-drw, rfn/rstr/rpl, 29x17½x18" **440.00**
Cherry OH Co Emp, trn legs, scrolled drop on apron, 1-drw, 27" .**575.00**
Cherry/curly maple Co Emp w/burl veneer, 2-drw/2-brd, 22x19" ..**715.00**
Curly maple Co, 2 dvtl drw, trn legs, rfn, 39x20x20" **770.00**
Oak, rnd top:shaped base shelf, 4 trn splay legs **250.00**
Pine/poplar Co Sheraton, yel grpt, 3-drw, 33x19x17" **770.00**
Poplar Co, 1-drw, 1-brd, worn flame grpt, brass pull, 28x20x20" ..**275.00**
Poplar Co w/red stain, dvtl drw, trn legs, 1-brd 18x30" top **225.00**
Sewing, mixed hardwoods, 2-drw, 1-brd, 24x36x25" **195.00**
Walnut, slender trn legs, 1900s, 27½x14x14" **85.00**
Walnut Am Co Sheraton, 1 dvtl drw, gallery, towel bar, 31" **200.00**
Walnut Co Hplwht, 1-drw, sq tapered legs, rpl 2-brd 17" top **400.00**
Walnut Co Sheraton, 2-drw, trn/reeded legs, 2-brd, 39x23x21" ...**660.00**
Walnut w/figured veneer, checkerbrd drop-leaf top, 29x17x18" ...**135.00**
Walnut/cherry Sheraton w/inlay, 2-drw, cvd legs, 20x20x21" **550.00**

Stools

Footstool, cabriole legs, needlepoint top, 1900s, 16x10½" **95.00**
Footstool, hickory twigs, rpl wicker top, 1920, 11x12x16", G **230.00**
Footstool, lyre form, curly maple, red stain, 8x18½", pr **665.00**
Footstool, mahog, trn legs, uphl top, 20x17x17" **150.00**
Footstool, mahog Continental, uphl seat, rprs, 18x18x18" **350.00**
Footstool, pine, old red-brn pnt, cut-out ft, 8¾x24½x8" **135.00**
Footstool, pnt w/brn rpt over gr, scalloped brd legs, 8x10x19" **95.00**
Footstool, trn legs/rungs, twine top, old varnish, 6x9½" **25.00**
Footstool, Windsor, pnt mc florals, 6¾x11x6½" **1,151.00**
Organ, oak, rnd top adjusts, fluted/trn legs & column **175.00**

Tables

Card, cherry/curly maple Co Sheraton, mahog veneer apron **990.00**
Card, mahog Am Emp, reeded legs, folding swivel top, rfn **825.00**
Card, mahog Am Hplwht w/inlay, minor rprs, 21x37x17" **415.00**
Card, mahog Emp, ebony & gilt detail, swivel top, 39x36x18" **1,595.00**
Card, mahog English Chpndl, mortised/pinned apron, rfn **1,025.00**
Card, mahog Hplwht w/inlay, demilune folding top, 28x35x17" ..**990.00**
Coffee, rnd tooled Peruvian leather top, 1900s, 17½x34" **95.00**
Corner, oak English, gate-leg, rstr base/rpl top, 27x34x17" **415.00**
Demilune, walnut Am Hplwht, veneer apron w/inlay, 48x21" ...**880.00**
Dressing, mahog veneer Emp style, 28½x37¾x23"+mirror **165.00**
Dressing, pine/hardwood Co Sheraton, 2-drw, grpt, 37x36", EX ...**770.00**
Dressing, rosewood Rococo, rtcl crest on mirror, marble top ...**2,500.00**
Drop leaf, cherry Co, trn legs, 2-brd, 39x27x19"+13" leaves **360.00**
Drop leaf, cherry Co Sheraton, 1-dvtl drw, rfn, 20x36x17" **550.00**
Drop leaf, cherry Hplwht, rpl top, rfn, 29x42x18"+18" leaves **330.00**
Drop leaf, maple Co QA, swing leg/trifid ft, 39x39x13"+leaves **900.00**
Drop leaf, oak, trn legs, 1900s, 30x42x43"+2 13" leaves **200.00**
Drop leaf, walnut Co, 6 trn legs, 28x46x21"+18½" leaves **200.00**
End, mahog veneer Fr style, ormolu trim, 1900s, 29¼", pr **715.00**
EXtension, oak, lion's heads on legs, paw ft, 30x45"+4 leaves .**1,200.00**
Extension, oak w/split ped & paw ft, 1900s, 30x45" dia **1,000.00**
Game, mahog Em, swing top, drw in apron, 29x23x44", EX **440.00**
Game, mahog Geo II, rectangular hinged top:drw, sq legs **935.00**
Hall, mahog veneer English style, pull-out shelves, 12x36" **475.00**
Hutch, pine/poplar Co, oval top, 1-drw, rpt/rpr, 27x39x30" **880.00**
Library, mahog English Hplwht, 3 dvtl drw, leather top 56" **3,300.00**
Library, mahog English Regency, rope spiral legs, rprs, 28x54" ...**395.00**
Library, mahog veneer Italian style, cabriole legs, 60½" **250.00**
Limbert #112 console, hex top/face, 2-drw, 6-leg, 66", VG **4,500.00**
Limbert #146, oval top, 2 cutouts in ea side section, 45" **2,300.00**
Limbert #148, wide cut-out X-stretchers, mk, 30" dia, EX **2,900.00**
Limbert #158 occasional, base w/cutouts, 2 oval tiers, VG **4,250.00**
Oak English Co, sq tapered legs, 2-brd, 28x33x17" **150.00**

Old Hickory, 25" dia 5-brd pine top, woven bark skirt, shelf ...**1,100.00**
Parlor, mahog, turtle top, cabriole legs, stretchers w/finial **350.00**
Parlor, mahog Am Emp w/veneer, 4 scimitar legs, 30x35½" **250.00**
Parlor, walnut Vict, shaped marble top, shell-cvd frieze, 39" ...**1,600.00**
Pembroke, cherry Hplwht drop leaf, 1-drw, sq legs, 28x34x19" ..**825.00**
Pembroke, cherry/curly maple Co Sheraton, 29x18x36+leaves ..**440.00**
Pembroke, mahog, inlaid/cuffed/tapered legs, 1800s, rstr **2,600.00**
Pembroke, mahog English Co Chpndl, sq legs, 20x35"+leaves **400.00**
Pembroke, walnut Co Hplwht, dvtl drw, 2-brd, 42x20"+leaves **688.00**
Pier, mahog Chpndl, marble top/c&b ft/apron, rprs, 34x64" **1,430.00**
Quaint, dining, 48" dia, 4-legs w/X-stretcher, tag **935.00**
Sawbuck, chestnut/pine Co, 3-brd 30x65" worn top, rpr legs ..**1,600.00**
Tavern, birch/pine Co QA, 2-brd, rpl/rprs, 25½x32x24" **770.00**
Tavern, hardwood/hickory/pine Co Hplwht, 1-brd, 27x40x24" .**500.00**
Tavern, hardwoods Co QA, 1-drw, 2-brd breadbrd top, 41x26".......**1,540.00**
Tavern, pine Co Hplwht, reeded apron, breadbrd top, 31x23" **600.00**
Tea, cherry/maple Emp, tilt top, tripod base, 26x25½x17" **465.00**
Tea, mahog Chpndl, tilt top, tripod base/snake ft, rfn, 28x23" ...**900.00**
Tea, mahog Chpndl, tilt top/trn column/snake ft, rfn, 29x36" ...**2,250.00**
Tea, mahog Chpndl, 1-brd tilt top, snake ft, 35" dia * **700.00**
Tea, mahog Chpndl, 1-brd tilt top, trn column, rpr, 28x26" ...**1,200.00**
Tea, mahog Chpndl style, cabriole legs, c&b ft, 38x27x16" **550.00**
Tea, mahog Co English Chpndl, tilt top/tripod base, 27x25" **415.00**
Tea, mahog Traditional style, tilt-top, ped ft, 28x24" **330.00**
Tea, maple Chpndl, tilt top, tripod base, rfn, 27x36x35" **715.00**
Tea, maple Co Chpndl, tilt top, tripod base, 1-brd, 26x26½" ..**2,200.00**
Tea, maple/cherry Co Hplwht, tilt top, spade ft, rfn, 29x25" **525.00**
Tea, oak english, trn gate-leg, 2-drw, rpr, 28x40x12"+leaves * ...**385.00**
Work, Pine English Co, 1-drw (rpl), 2-brd, 31x72x29" **375.00**
Work, Pine English Co, 2-drw, base shelf, 2-brd, 31x57x24" **200.00**
Work, poplar, 2 dvtl drw, trn legs, 2-brd, rfn, 29x55x32" **600.00**
Work, walnut, H stretcher, 2-drw, 2-brd, PA, rprs, 20x73x36" ...**1,150.00**
Work, walnut Co Chpndl, beaded corners, 3-brd, rfn, 41x30" **825.00**
Work, walnut European style w/burl veneer, 1-drw, lift top **475.00**
Work drop leaf, mahog classical, 2-drw, 29x19x18+2 9" leaves ..**525.00**
Work drop leaf, mahog Co Sheraton, 1 drw/bin, 17x18"+leaves **4,125.00**
Work drop leaf, pine English Co, trn legs, rprs, 39x54x24" **200.00**
Writing, rosewood veneer Emp w/inlay, brass ft, 29x28x16" **660.00**

Wardrobes

Figured walnut & burl veneer, mirror in center do, 94x27" **1,980.00**
Mahog English Chpndl style, Chinese fretwork, 79" **550.00**
Mahog English Renaissance Revival, 3-section, 90x77" **1,700.00**
Pine Co, gr pnt over gr, beaded brds, batten do, 76x42x19" **350.00**
Pine/poplar, old red flame grpt, 1 panel do, 79x39" **400.00**
Tiger maple Classical, central drw: panel do, rfn, 74x47" **3,300.00**

Washstands

Cherry Sheraton bowfront, 1 dvtl drw, gallery, rprs, 38x24" **900.00**
Curly maple Sheraton style, 1-drw, gallery, 21x24x17" **250.00**
Mahog English Sheraton, trn legs/post, gallery, 42x24" **400.00**
Mahog Fed, 2 sm drws:1 lg drw, dvtl gallery, 38x18x16" **415.00**
Oak, bowfront, attached towel bar rack, appl decor, 55x34" **300.00**
Oak, sm mirror in lyre fr w/simple press-cvg, drw:2 do, sm **350.00**
Pine Co English, base shelf, low gallery, 31x21x18" * **75.00**
Pine Co English, base shelf, 1-drw, rstr, 39x35x15" **165.00**
Pine Co English, rpl gallery, damage/rfn, 42x31x15" **195.00**
Pine Co English, trn legs, 1-drw, gallery, 37x35x17" **275.00**
Pine Co Sheraton, 1-drw, gallery, yel grpt, 39x16x14" **360.00**
Poplar & hardwoods, orig brn grpt on yel, 38x30x15" **140.00**
Tiger maple Fed, shaped splashbrd, base stretcher, 30x18" **1,050.00**
Walnut Vict, rtcl panels, mirror, marble-top drw, 82" **650.00**

Miscellaneous

Armoire, bird's-eye maple w/rosewood Vict, mirror do, 93x46" .**3,400.00**
Armoire, mahog Vict, fancy crest, 2 mirrors/base drws, 91" **1,500.00**
Armoire, walnut Louis XV style, 3 mirror do, 106" W **2,600.00**
Bed steps, mahog, English, rpl needlepoint top, rfn, 16" **195.00**
Butler's tray & stand, dvtl mahog, gallery, 28¼x20¾" **500.00**
Cellarette, mahog Classical Revival w/veneer, 1825, 33x17x15" .**1,045.00**
Hall rack, mahog, flaring panel w/5 hooks & umbrella stand **985.00**
Hall tree, hardwood, brass hooks, old finish, 72" **150.00**
Hat rack, steer horn, dmn-shape mirror in velvet fr, 44x25" **200.00**
Magazine rack, mahog, V-shape, old finish, 21x18x14" **50.00**
Magazine stand, Limbert #304, slat sides, 4-shelf, 42" **900.00**
Pedestal, Classical column form, wood w/faux marble pnt, 38" ..**440.00**
Pedestal, mahog Am Emp w/figured veneer, 1 do/1 drw, 42" **365.00**
Pedestal, modern style w/open spiral column, 38" **175.00**
Pedestal, pine, mc marbleized pnt, MA, 14" **275.00**
Pedestal, walnut Vict, cvd/appl, 1870s, 35x15" sq **300.00**
Peg brd, 6 mushroom-shaped pegs, orig yel pnt, 32" L **220.00**
Pole screen, mahog Vict, scroll-cvd fr/ft, fluted stem, 77" **1,200.00**
Potty chair, spindle bk, rpt w/florals, ironstone pot, 39" **60.00**
Quilting fr, pine, old mc pnt w/yel striping, 30x95x41", EX **385.00**
Screen, emb leather, 6-section, worn/rpr, ea part: 19x85" **125.00**
Shoeshine stand, pine, CI ft rest w/horse ped, rfn, 20" **100.00**
Spoon rack, pine, orig rose-malled decor, 15¼" H **110.00**
Towel rack, mahog w/inlay, folding 2-section, 37x24" **150.00**
Towel rack, poplar, shoe ft, 3-part, folding, 26x32" **330.00**

Galle

Emile Galle was one of the most important producers of cameo glass in France. His firm, founded in Nancy in 1874, produced beautiful cameo in the Art Nouveau style during the 1890s, using a variety of techniques. He also produced glassware with enameled decoration, as well as some fine pottery — animal figurines, table services, vases, and other objects d' art. In the mid-1880s he became interested in the various colors and textures of natural woods and as a result began to create furniture which he used as yet another medium for expression of his artistic talent. Marquetry was the primary method Galle used in decorating his furniture, preferring landscapes, Nouveau floral and fruit arrangements, butterflies, squirrels, and other forms from nature. It is for his furniture and his cameo glass that he is best known today. All Galle is signed.

In the listings below, 'fp' indicates items that have been fire polished. Our advisor for this category is Don Williams; he is listed in the Directory under Missouri.

Cameo

Lamp, maroon cameo cut and wheel-finished floral motif on dome shade, baluster base (restored), 19½", $4,100.00.

Atomizer, river/trees, brn on frost/pk, flask form, 8½" **1,800.00**
Atomizer, sm floral, lav on shaded yel frost, wide base, 8" **1,250.00**
Box, floral, purple over yel/cream, w/lid, 2x4¼" **2,000.00**
Dish, leaves/berries, rose on yel/frost, canoe form, 7", EX **500.00**
Jar, leaf/berry on frost, lav dragonfly on lid, 2½" **1,000.00**
Lamp base, apple blossoms, dk red on yel, baluster, 11" **625.00**
Lamp base, lake/sailboats, purple on yel/wht, baluster, 13" **1,500.00**
Vase, berries on vine, purple on cream, fluted, 6½" **1,500.00**
Vase, bleeding hearts, red on yel, waisted rim, 6" **2,500.00**
Vase, bud; floral, purple on shaded pk frost, flared lip, 5" **800.00**
Vase, bud; river/trees, brn on yel/gr, 7¾" **1,200.00**
Vase, clematis, purple on wht/yel, ovoid, 18½" **2,500.00**
Vase, clematis, purple on wht/yel, rnd w/stick neck, 6¾" **920.00**
Vase, cracked-ice effect, ivory on bl, spherical, 9" **2,300.00**
Vase, crocuses, pk/lav on frost, ft w/appl amber ring, 10½" **985.00**
Vase, ferns/fronds, gr/brn on pk frost, 15½" **2,100.00**
Vase, floral, brn on gold, stick neck, 8" **900.00**
Vase, floral, lav on frosted, banjo shape, 6⅝" **700.00**
Vase, floral, lt brn on wht frost, stick neck, 6½" **600.00**
Vase, floral, orange-pk on cream, clover-shape top, 10½" **1,500.00**
Vase, floral, rust on yel frost, domical w/stick neck, 4" **800.00**
Vase, floral vines, violet on gray, wheel polished, 10" **2,500.00**
Vase, floral w/bees, mc, gold foil inclusions, verse, 13¾" **10,000.00**
Vase, floral w/vines, purple on citron, fluted, 8¼" **2,000.00**
Vase, floral/buds, brn/yel on rose to clear frost, slim, 15" **2,350.00**
Vase, floral/pods, gr/brn on gr/lav/brn, long neck, 10" **1,100.00**
Vase, flowering plants, gray/brn on yel, ovoid, 4¾" **770.00**
Vase, fuchsias, violet on yel frost, 4½x3½" **1,295.00**
Vase, grapevines, brn on orange-lined clear, 5" **700.00**
Vase, grapevines, brn on wht/yel, long cylinder neck, 13" **1,700.00**
Vase, hydrangeas, lav/gr on apricot/frost, can neck, 6" **900.00**
Vase, irises, amber on opal, fp, wide flat shoulder, 16" **3,200.00**
Vase, irises, lav/gr on yel/clear frost, 6" **770.00**
Vase, irises, purple on cream-gold, 15¾" **4,000.00**
Vase, lake/mtns/lg trees, dbl o/l on yel, ftd, 14" **9,750.00**
Vase, lake/mtns/trees, dk gr on brn to wht frost, 8" **1,600.00**
Vase, lake/woods, dbl o/l on frost, spherical, 6" **1,700.00**
Vase, lake/woods, gr/brn on wht/pk, dbl o/l, 12½", EX **2,400.00**
Vase, leaves/blossoms, mauve on pk-lined yel, 7" **660.00**
Vase, lilies, lav/olive on frost/pk, dbl o/l, hdls, 11½" **4,600.00**
Vase, lilies, lav/olive on wht/pk, hdld gourd form, 12" **3,650.00**
Vase, lilies, purple on cream-yel, 11¼" **3,000.00**
Vase, limbs/pods, lime/gr on gr/rust, tube w/bulb base, 18" **2,000.00**
Vase, man in boat/river, gr/brn on amber/gr, flat sides, 5x6" ...**1,650.00**
Vase, oak leaves/acorns, gr on orange/yel, cylindrical, 11" **1,150.00**
Vase, rambling roses, wine on yel frost, squat/bulbous, 8" **3,500.00**
Vase, roses, red on citron/clear, EX cutting, 8x6½" **3,500.00**
Vase, sailing ships, citron/lav on bl/brn, 4½" **850.00**
Vase, stylized leaves/berries, orange on wht mottle, 16x12" **3,000.00**
Vase, water lilies/pads, dk on lt bl, gr trees/yel sky, 12" **2,200.00**
Vase, wisteria pendants, violet & lav on yel frost, 16¼" **2,300.00**

Enameled Glass

Bowl, pond scene/lg flowers, blk/mc on opal, ruffled, 7½" **1,400.00**
Tumbler, fleur-de-lis, wht on amber, ribbed, 5" **150.00**
Vase, bleeding hearts, mc/gilt on lt gr, tricorn rim, 13" **2,500.00**
Vase, field flowers on topaz, ruffled U-form, 5" **2,200.00**
Vase, sunflowers superimposed on fishing scene, ribbed, 5" **990.00**

Marquetry, Wood

Table, daffodils, 14" sq top on 2 curved 3-part legs **1,400.00**
Table, 2-tier, floral/butterflies, curving legs, 29x25x16" **2,400.00**

Table, 2-tier, flowers/butterflies, 30x27x17" **2,400.00**
Table, 2-tier, jonquils/landscape, Y-shape legs, 30x20x30" **2,300.00**
Vitrine, flowers: top/sides/front panel, glass door, 53x24" **2,950.00**

Pottery

Ewer, poppies front/bk on dk bronze, bulbous/pinched, 7" **1,500.00**
Jar, molded as bag tied w/2 pk bows, bird atop, #113, 11x7" **1,100.00**
Pin tray, bachelor buttons, bl/purple/gr on emb wht, 6" L **200.00**
Pitcher, 2 men on bench, 3rd w/bagpipes on bronze C-shape, 8" .**1,500.00**

Plate, turned-up side with blue, gold and red surrealist design, $700.00.

Plate, floral/insects/inscription on wht, laced rim, 9", pr **935.00**
Vase, man's portrait, pillow form w/dbl ring hdls, sgn, 12" **900.00**
Vase, Oriental scene, bl/blk/gold on wht, trefoil, 10" **690.00**

Gambling Memorabilia

Gambling memorabilia from the infamous casinos of the West and items that were once used on the 'Floating Palace' riverboats are especially sought after by today's collectors.

Small horse race wheel with odds changer, reverse-painted glass front, restored, some replacements, 36x20", $770.00.

Caddy, poker chip; brn Bakelite, EX **15.00**
Card holder, Bakelite **40.00**
Chip, ivory, w/red & blk decor **15.00**
Chuck-a-luck cage, 10", w/3 dice, EX **25.00**
Chuck-a-luck cage, 13" **90.00**
Craps layout, Caesar's Palace, suede, unused **150.00**
Keno cage, nickeled CI & brass hourglass cage, 18x16x10", G ...**100.00**
Roulette wheel, Bakelite, 10" **65.00**
Spinner, brass w/blk lettering, EX **17.50**
Spinner, sterling w/red & blk letters, .12 troy oz, EX **35.00**
Wheel, pnt wood on CI upright base, 15¾" dia **365.00**
Wheel, pnt wood wheel on wood stand, 60" H, VG **175.00**

Game Calls

Those interested in hunting and fishing collectibles are beginning to take notice of the finer specimens of game calls available on today's market. Our advisor for this category is Randy Hilst; he is listed in the Directory under Illinois.

Crow, Charles Perdew, Pat 1900, 2⅞", EX 375.00
Crow, FA Allen, EX 75.00
Duck, AM Bowles, Olt-style toneboard, walnut bbl, early, EX ...150.00
Duck, Newt Rule, walnut, ca 1900-30, EX 200.00
Duck, Sharpie Shaw, burl walnut, EX 500.00
Duck, sm spittoon-shaped pc w/wire hdl, early 48.00
Duck, Tom Turpin, pintail whistle, rosewood, EX 125.00
Goose, Fuller's Goose Call Pat..., metal, ca 1890-1930, EX 200.00
Goose, LD Lothrop...1901, wood & brass, pump action, EX 350.00

Gameboards

Gameboards, the handmade ones from the 18th and 19th century, are collected more for their folk art quality than their relation to games. Excellent examples of these handcrafted 'playthings' sell well into the thousands of dollars; even the simple designs are often expensive. If you are interested in this field, you must study it carefully. The market is always full of 'new' examples. Well-established dealers are often your best sources; they are essential if you do not have the expertise to judge the age of the boards yourself.

Checkers, blk & red sqs mkd in yel, early 1900s, 15½" sq 700.00
Checkers, old red & wht pnt, 2-sided, early, 19x31" 200.00
Checkers, olive & red pnt over gray, 12x14" 330.00
Checkers, poplar, old red & blk w/mc decor, 19x18¾" 385.00
Checkers, poplar, rpt, 3-board, 39x18" 195.00
Checkers/cribbage, poplar, red/blk/brn/wht, 15x30" 195.00
Checkers/parcheesi, inlaid/pnt, 19x28" 2,350.00
Checkers/parcheesi, pnt wood, 6-color, lt wear, 16x16" 550.00
Cribbage, handmade/HP, 1890s, 7" L 660.00
Cribbage, mahog w/ivory inlay, 1800s, 10¾" 440.00
Cribbage, maroon Bakelite, NMIB 22.50
Fox & Geese, maple, rim holds 32 clay marbles, 10¼" dia 135.00

Games

Game collectors are finding it more difficult to find their treasures at shows and flea markets. Most of the action these days seems to be through specialty dealers and auctions. The appreciation of the art on the boards and boxes continues to grow. You see many of the early games proudly displayed as art, and they should be. The period from the 1850s to 1910 continues to draw the most interest. Many of the games of that period were executed by well-known artists and illustrators. The quality of their lithography cannot be matched today. The historical value of games made before 1850 has caused interest in this period to increase. While they may not have the graphic quality of the later period, their insights into the social and moral character of the early 19th century are interesting.

20th-century games invoke a nostalgic feeling among collectors who recall looking forward to a game under the Christmas tree each year. They search for examples that bring back those Christmas-morning memories. While the quality of their lithography is certainly less than the early games, the introduction of personalities from the comic strips, radio and later TV created new interest. Every child wanted a game that featured their favorite character.

The Great American War Game, J.H. Hunter, 1899, 25½x12", $1,100.00.

Amazing Game of Innocence Abroad, Parker Bros, 1888, EX 220.00
Arrest & Trial, board game, Transogram, 1963, EX 80.00
Babysitter, Ideal, 1966 ....45.00
Basket Making, 1940s, EX 18.00
Battle Line, board game, Ideal, 1964, NM 60.00
Bengalee Game of East, board game, ca 1945, EX in box 15.00
Bezique & Polish Bezique, Cavendish, ca 1910, EX in box 25.00
Blackout, Milton Bradley, 1939, EX 40.00
Book of Knowledge, Pressman, EX 15.00
Bow-L-Under, Cardinal, 1940s, VG 30.00
Chiromagica, McLoughlin Bros, 1870, complete, 11⅝" sq box ...300.00
Chutes & Ladders, Milton Bradley, 1956, EX 50.00
Climb the Mountain, Parker Bros, 1951, NM 20.00
Comical Game of Snap, Parker Bros, EX in box 15.00
Conflict, Parker Bros, 1960, NM 25.00
Discovery, Home Game, Lowell, 1960s, VG+ 15.00
Disneyland Pinball Game, Wolverine, 1960s, VG 40.00
Dragon's Teeth, Holyoke, 1948, EX 50.00
Eye Guess, Home Game, 2nd ed, NM 10.00
Fashionable English Game Sorry, Parker Bros 1st ed, 1934, VG .215.00
Ferrilude or Game of Beast, card game, West & Lee, 1873, EX 70.00
Flight Top, Louis Marx, EX 10.00
Game of Air Mail, marble game, Milton Bradley, ca 1927, EX ...195.00
Game of Birds, card game, Cincinnati Game Co, 1899, VG 48.00
Game of Cities, card game, 52 complete, Parker Bros, 1898 ....90.00
Game of State Capitals, Parker, 1952, EX in box 27.50
Game of the Mayflower, card game, AS Burbank, EX in box 48.00
Game of Who, Parker Bros, 1951, EX 75.00
Game of Yuneek, board game, McLoughlin Bros, 1889, EX 275.00
Great Game of Pit, Bull & Bear Edition, 1904, EX 22.50
Jr Weather Bureau, 1954 ....20.00
Kreskin ESP Game, Milton Bradley, 1966, EX in box 32.00
Magic Midway, board game, Cadaco, 1962, VG 20.00
Magnetic Jack Straws, Milton Bradley, 1920, EX in box 14.50
Modern Authors, card game, complete w/rules, M Bradley, EX 25.00
Monopoly, board game, Parker Bros, 1935, EX in box 185.00
Motorific Speed Trial Mark II, Ideal, 1969, M in lg box 15.00
Mr Bug Goes to Town, board game, Milton Bradley, 1955, NM ...60.00
Mysterious Planchette, board game, w/instructions, EX in box 90.00
Mystic Board, Haskelite Mfg, 1950s, VG 40.00
Nat'l Game of Am Eagle, board game, Ives, 1844, EX 4,125.00
Number Please, Home Game, Parker Bros, 1961, EX 40.00
Official NY World's Fair Game, Milton Bradley, 1964, NM 45.00
Outdraw the Outlaw Target Game, Mattel, 1959, NM 175.00
Park & Shop, Milton Bradley, 1950s, VG 25.00
Pigs in Clover, Milton Bradley, 1930, EX 35.00
Pirate & Traveler, Milton Bradley, 1953, 1st ed, EX 25.00
Pirate's Island, Corey Games, 1942, EX in box 250.00
Rambles, Am Publishing, geographical, 1881, G in box 195.00
Safari, Selchow & Righter, 1950, EX 50.00

Squashville County Fair, reading game, Parker Bros, '05, EX 25.00
Stagecoach, Milton Bradley, 1958, EX in G box 30.00

Starflight, table game, complete with playing pieces, EX graphics on box, 1931, 10¾x15½", $770.00.

Sunken Treasure, Parker Bros, 1948, VG in box 65.00
Super Winky Dink TV Game, Std Toycraft Prod, 1954, EX 75.00
Tiddledy Winks, Parker Bros, colorful litho box, pre-1900, EX 17.50
Turn Horse Racing, Delmar Derby, 1959 ....15.00
Veda, The Magic Answer Man, Pressman, 1950s, EX 30.00
Young Folks Historical Game, McLoughlin, EX 35.00
Zoom, airplane card game, Whitman, 1941, EX 27.50

Personalities, Movies, and TV Shows

$64,000 Question, Lowell, 1955, EX 40.00
Addams Family, card game, 1965, NM 23.00
Alley Oop, Royal Toy Co, 1937, rare, EX 80.00
Andy Griffith, card game, #1 series, Pacific Trading, MIB 30.00
Annie Oakley, board game, 1950s, M in VG box 30.00
Aquaman, Justice League America, Hasbro, 1960s, NM 60.00
Archie, Whitman, 1969, EX 40.00
Around the World in 80 Days, board game, Transogram, 1957, EX ..20.00
Art Linkletter, House Party, M 39.00
Babe Ruth's Baseball, Milton Bradley, ca 1926-28, EX 500.00
Babes in Toyland, WDP, Parker Bros, 1961, NM 40.00
Barney Google & Spark Plug, board game, Milton Bradley, 17", G .120.00
Batman, board game, Milton Bradley, 1966, EX 50.00
Batman & Robin Vs the Joker, board game, Hasbro, 1965, EX 60.00
Beat The Clock, Home Game; Milton Bradley, 1969, EX 20.00
Beat The Clock, Lowell, 1954, EX 50.00
Ben Casey, board game, Transogram, 1961, EX 40.00
Beverly Hillbillies Set Bk, card game, Milton Bradley, 1963, EX ..20.00
Bewitched, card game, Milton Bradley, 1965, EX 35.00
Bing Crosby's Call Me Lucky, board game, Parker Bros, 1954, EX ...30.00
Black Beauty, board game, Transogram, 1958, EX 30.00
Bobbsey Twins, 1953, MIB 30.00
Bonanza, Michigan Rummy, Parker Bros, 1964, EX 35.00
Break the Bank, Betty-B, 1955, EX 30.00
Buck Rogers, Interplanetary, VG 60.00
Bugs Bunny Adventure, board game, Milton Bradley, 1961, EX ...50.00
Bullwinkle, Electric Quiz, 1971, M on card 15.00
Bullwinkle's Hide & Seek, Milton Bradley, 1961, EX 60.00
Calling Superman, board game, Transogram, 1954, EX 125.00
Calvin & the Colonel, High Spirits, Milton Bradley, 1962, EX 70.00
Candid Camera, board game, Lowell, 1963, EX 50.00
Captain Gallant, Adventure, board game, Transogram, 1955, NM .90.00
Captain Kangaroo, Mr Green Jeans Rummy, 1950s, NM 15.00
Captain Midnight, Jumping Bean Target, 1939, M 30.00

Casper, board game, Milton Bradley, 1959, EX 20.00
Casper, ring toss, Milton Bradley, 1959, sealed, NM 40.00
Charlie McCarthy, Radio Party, complete w/envelope 30.00
Cherry Ames, Nursing, Parker Bros, 1959, VG 75.00
Cheyenne, board game, Milton Bradley, 1959, NM 85.00
Combat, board game, Ideal, 1963, EX 75.00
Dark Shadows, Mystery Maze, Whitman, 1968, EX 80.00
Davy Crockett, bagatelle type, Transogram, 1960, 4½", EX 30.00
Deputy, board game, Milton Bradley, 1960, EX 90.00
Dick Tracy, Selchow & Righter, 1961, G+ 30.00
Doc Holiday, Wild West, board game, Transogram, 1960, NM 60.00
Donald Duck, card game, Whitman, 1955, 44 cards, VG 25.00
Donald Duck's Party, Parker Bros, 1938, EX 95.00
Dr Kildare, board game, Ideal, 1962, NM 20.00
Eddie Cantor, board game, Parker Bros, 1940s, EX 45.00
Ellery Queen, Mystery, Ideal, 1967, EX 30.00
F-Troop, board game, Ideal, 1965, EX 175.00
Flintstones, Stone Age, board game, 1961, EX 25.00
Flying Nun, board game, Milton Bradley, 1968, EX 40.00
Garroway's Game of Possession, NBC, 1955, M 40.00
Gidget, board game, Standard ToyKraft, 1960s, EX 45.00
Green Ghost, Transogram, NM 25.00
Groucho Marx, TV Quiz, Pressman, 1950s, EX 65.00
Gunsmoke, Lowell, 1958, VG 35.00
Hagar the Horrible, Flag, MIB 10.00
Hanna-Barbera Break-A-Plate, Transogram, 1961, G+ 70.00
Have Gun Will Travel, board game, Parker Bros, 1959, EX 90.00
Hogan's Heroes, board game, no instructions, o/w complete 48.00
Hollywood Stars, Whitman, 1955, EX 20.00
Home Game, Pressman, 1950s, based on TV show, VG 55.00
Hopalong Cassidy, dart board, Toy Enterprises, '50, 14x17", NM ...45.00
Howdy Doody, Snap-A-Wink, Poll-Parrot premium, 1953, 13", NM .60.00
Howdy Doody, 3-Ring Circus, Gilmar, 1950s, EX 80.00
Huckleberry Hound, Western, Milton Bradley, 1959, EX 65.00
Kate Smith, America, board game, 1940, NM 38.00
Katzenjammer Kids, Hockey, 1950s, EX in box 36.00
Laramie, board game, Lowell, 1959, EX 50.00
Lassie, board game, Whitting, 1955, VG+ 40.00
Leave It to Beaver, Money Maker, NM 48.00
Lone Ranger, Pop-Up Target, darts, Transogram, '50s, NM 125.00
Lone Ranger, Target Board, color litho on metal, Marx, EX 140.00
Ludwig Von Drake, tiddlywinks, Whitman, 1961, EX 22.00
Man From UNCLE, board game, Ideal, 1965, EX 60.00
Man From UNCLE, Illya Kuryakin, card game, M Bradley, 1966, M .20.00
Match Game, Milton Bradley, 1963, M 20.00
McHale's Navy, board game, Transogram, 1962, EX 50.00
Mickey Mouse, Scatter Ball, Marx Bros, 1935, EX 265.00
Mickey Mouse, target game, board/gun/darts, Marx Bros, NM ...495.00
My Favorite Martian, board game, 1963, NM 140.00
Outer Limits, board game, Milton Bradley, 1964, EX 200.00
Perry Mason, board game, Transogram, 1959, VG 50.00
Peter Pan, board game, Transogram, 1953, NM 55.00
Peter Rabbit, rummy, Fairchild, 1950s, EX 15.00
Petticoat Junction, board game, EX 35.00
Popeye, Magnetic Fishing, Transogram, 1958, EX 50.00
Popeye, Pipe Toss, Rosebud, 1935, EX 50.00
Prince Valiant, Crossbow, 1948, EX in box 46.00
Quick-Draw McGraw, card game, 1961, MIB 11.50
Raggedy Ann, Magic Pebble, Milton Bradley, 1940, G 40.00
Red Ryder, Target, Whitman, 1939, EX 90.00
Robinson Crusoe, board game, Lowell Toy, 1960s, M 45.00
Romper Room, Wisk Off, TV game, no crayons, EX 20.00
Roy Rogers Lucky Horseshoe, Ohio Art Co, 1950s, VG 75.00
Sleeping Beauty, Parker Bros, 1958, EX 35.00

Soupy Sales, board game, Ideal, 1965, mini, sealed **95.00**
Speed Buggy, Hanna Barbera, 1973, EX **23.00**
Tom & Jerry, Tumble Race, Transogram, 1965, NM **30.00**
Tom Mix, Texas, board game, foreign, 1930, unused, cover VG ..**70.00**
Tom Seaver, Action Baseball, EX **26.00**
Uncle Wiggly, Milton Bradley, 1920s, EX in box **40.00**
Wild Bill Hickok, Breakfast, w/score card **14.00**
Wizard of Oz, Wonderful Game of Oz, Parker Bros, 1921, EX **350.00**

G. A. R. Memorabilia

The 'The Grand Army of the Republic' was first conceived by Chaplain W.J. Rutledge and Major B.J. Stephenson early in 1864 when they were tent-mates during our own Civil War. These men vowed to each other that if they were spared they would establish an organization that would preserve friendships and memories formed during this time. Shortly after the war ended, Rutledge and Stephenson made their desires a reality. The first National Convention of the Grand Army of the Republic was held in Indianapolis, Indiana, on November 20, 1866. The purpose of the organization was to provide aid and assistance to the widows and orphans of the fallen Union dead and to care for the hospitalized veterans as needed. The last comrade of the G.A.R. died in 1949.

Many items are surfacing from the early encampments which were held on both state and national levels, resulting in a wide variety of souvenir items having been made. Our advisor for this category is Richard Haussmann; he is listed in the Directory under Illinois.

Badge, 25th National Encampment, 1904, Warsaw-Winona, $32.00.

Badge, brass, wht ribbon, MA state seal, 1892 ....**15.00**
Badge, membership; Sons of Vets Auxiliary, bronze, w/ribbon **10.00**
Badge, 31st Nat'l Encampment, star & wreath, 2-pc, 1897 ....**15.00**
Book, Blue Book, Rules & Regulations, 1893, 330-pg, EX **30.00**
Book, GAR Ritual, hard cover, 1888, 30-pg, 6x8", VG **20.00**
Buckle, star in center, GAR above, on wht leather belt, EX **45.00**
Cabinet photo, vet in GAR uniform, slouch hat, 1904 ....**18.00**
Daily Program, Pan Am Expo, GAR Day, 1901, 6x9" **12.50**
Flag stand, CI, emb letters ea leg, 7x7x3" **20.00**
Insignia, hat; metallic gilt wreath, NP letters **10.00**
Lapel stud, bronze, w/logo **5.00**
Medal, Daughters of Union Vets Membership, 1861-65, MIB **12.00**
Medal, Gen Sheridan on front, 26th encampment, 1½" **12.50**
Medal, heavy bronze or brass, train at Pike's Peak, 1905 ....**28.00**
Medal, Post 5 Lynn MA, red ribbon, wht metal drop, 1902 ....**12.50**
Medal, Women's Relief Corps Officer, 1883 ....**12.50**
Miniature, canteen, logo & bl enamel, St Louis 1887, 1" dia **20.00**
Miniature, trophy cup, SP, trn wood base, 3½x2" **32.00**
Pamphlet, Memorial Day Address, 1889, 19-pg, 6x9" **12.00**
Pamphlet, Views of Lookout Mtn, battle signs, 1919, 72-pg **20.00**
Pin, celluloid, gold print, 1899, ⅞" **10.00**
Pin, Memorial Day, mc on celluloid, flag motif edge, 1¼" **12.50**

Postcard, child in uniform w/flowers, GAR above, Clapsaddle **5.00**
Postcard, Gen Meade's headquarters at Gettysburg, mc **4.00**
Ribbon, red silk, 19th Nat'l Encampment...NH, 1885, 9x2" **15.00**
Ribbon, 4th Reunion 1880 Weirs Landing, flag center, 6" **9.00**
Sheet music, Not Forgotten, CA White, 1872, EX **12.00**
Sheet music, They Died for You & Me, 1870, EX **12.50**
Shoulder strap, chaplain's, for vet's medal, Roman Cross **10.00**
Spoon, 29th Nat'l Encampment Louisville, eagle/shield hdl **25.00**
Ticket, Post #3 Relief Fund Fair, 1879, 3¼x2" **12.50**

Gas Globes and Panels

Gas globes and panels, once a common sight, have vanished from the countryside but are being sought by collectors as a unique form of advertising memorabilia. Early globes from the 1920s (some date back to as early as 1912), now referred to as 'one-piece globes,' were made of molded milk glass and were globular in shape. The gas company name was etched or painted on the glass. Few of these were ever produced, and this type is valued very highly by collectors today.

A new type of pump was introduced in the early 1930s; the old 'visible' pumps were replaced by 'electric' models. Globes were changing at the same time. By the mid-thirties a three-piece globe consisting of a pair of inserts and a metal body was being produced in both 15" and 16½" sizes. Collectors prefer to call globes that are not one-piece or plastic 'three-piece glass' (Type 2) or 'metal body, glass inserts' (Type 3). Though metal-body globes (Type 3) were popular in the 1930s, they were common in the 1920s, and some were actually made as early as 1915. Though rare in numbers, their use spans many years. In the 1930s Type 2 and Type 3 globes became the replacements of the one-piece globe. The most recently manufactured gas globes are made with a plastic body that contains two 13½" glass lenses. These were common in the fifties but were actually used as early as 1932.

Note: Standard Crowns with raised letters are one-piece globes that were made in the 1920s; those made in the 1950s (no raised letters), though one-piece, are not regarded as such by today's collectors. Both variations are listed below. Our advisor for this category is Scott Benjamin; he is listed in the Directory under Ohio.

Type 1, Plastic Body, Glass Inserts (Inserts 13½")
1931-1950s

Ashland Diesel **175.00**
D-X Marine, rare **450.00**
Dixie, plastic band **150.00**
DX Ethyl **250.00**
DX Lubricating Gasoline, tan body **200.00**
Falcon **450.00**
Frontier Gas, Rarin' To Go, w/horse **350.00**
Marathon, no runner **150.00**
Marine, sea horse, EX color **325.00**
Never Nox Ethyl **250.00**
Shamrock, oval body **175.00**
Spur, oval body **175.00**
Texaco Sky Chief **250.00**
Viking, pictures Viking ship **325.00**
66 Flite Fuel, Phillips, shield shape, all plastic **350.00**

Type 2, Glass Frame, Glass Inserts (Inserts 13½")
1926-1940s

American **350.00**
Champlin Preston, 3-pc glass **400.00**
Derby **375.00**

Esso 325.00
Frontier Gas, Double Refined 325.00
Gulf 375.00
Guyler Brand, milk glass, EX 650.00
Indian Gas, Red Dot 575.00
Kanotex, w/sunflower, gill body 425.00
Koolmotor, clover shape 750.00
Mobil Gas 400.00
Pure 400.00
Red Crown, milk glass 285.00
Sinclair Dino, milk glass, EX 250.00
Sinclair Pennant 650.00
Skelly Anomarx w/Ethyl 450.00
Standard Crown, bl 550.00
Standard Crown, gr or orange, ea 700.00
Standard Flame 300.00
Texaco Diesel Chief 600.00
Texaco Ethyl 1,000.00
Texaco Star, blk outline on 'T' 375.00
White Flash, gill body 375.00
White Rose, boy, glass body 1,000.00
WNAX, w/radio station pictured 900.00

Type 3, Metal Frame, Glass Inserts (Inserts 15" or 16½") 1915-1930s

Atlantic Ethyl, 16½" 600.00
Atlantic White Flash, 16½" 500.00
Blue Sunoco, 15" 425.00
Cities Services Oils, 15" fr, 1929 .... 450.00
Crown, crown figural, 16½", EX 950.00
Esso Extra, 15" 425.00
General Ethyl, 15" fr, complete 700.00
Mobil Gas, winged horse, 15" or 16½" metal fr, NM ... 600.00
Mobilfuel Diesel, lg horse, high profile 800.00
Pure, porc body, 15" 550.00
Purol Gasoline, w/arrow, porc body 850.00
Purol Pep, porc body 650.00
Red Crown Ethyl 600.00
Richfield, w/eagle 600.00
Rocor, w/eagle 650.00
Signal, old stoplight, 15", VG 2,800.00
Socony, milk glass inserts 850.00
Sunland Ethyl, 15" 550.00
Texaco Leaded, glass panels, pr 3,200.00
Tidex, 16½" 425.00
Tydol, 16½" 500.00
White Star, 15" fr, complete 750.00

Type 4, One-Piece Glass Globes, No Inserts, Co. Name Etched, Raised or Enameled — 1912-1931

Atlantic, chimney cap 2,400.00
Diamond 700.00
Dixie, etched 1,200.00
Iowa Gas 1,300.00
Musgo 3,000.00
Pierce Pennant, etched 2,500.00
Red Crown, rnd, etched 3,000.00
Republic, 3-sided 1,400.00
Shell, rnd, etched 650.00
Sinclair, etched, milk glass 1,000.00
Sinclair Aircraft, etched 3,500.00

Sinclair Aircraft, pnt 3,000.00
Sinclair H-C, pnt 1,000.00
Skelly 650.00
Super Shell, clam shape 1,300.00
Super Shell, rnd, etched 2,800.00
Texaco, milk glass, emb letters, brass collar ... 800.00
Texaco Ethyl 1,500.00
That Good Gulf..., emb, orange & blk letters, EX ... 800.00
White Rose, boy pictured, pnt 2,400.00

Gaudy Dutch

Inspired by Oriental Imari wares, Gaudy Dutch was made in England from 1800 to 1820. It was hand decorated on a soft-paste body with rich underglaze blues accented in orange, red, pink, green, and yellow. It differs from Gaudy Welsh in that there is no lustre (except on Water Lily). There are seventeen patterns, some of which are: War Bonnet, Grape, Dahlia, Oyster, Urn, Butterfly, Carnation, Single Rose, Double Rose, and Water Lily. For further information we recommend *The Collector's Encyclopedia of Gaudy Dutch & Welsh* by John Shuman, available from Collector Books. Values are given for mint condition examples unless otherwise.

Coffeepot, Single Rose, domed lid, 11⅛", NM, $3,200.00.

Butterfly, coffeepot, 11" 4,000.00
Butterfly, cup & saucer, butterfly on side ... 750.00
Butterfly, pitcher, milk; 4" 825.00
Butterfly, plate, butterfly in center, 9⅞" ... 1,700.00
Butterfly, plate, butterfly on side, 8¼" 900.00
Butterfly, sugar bowl 1,700.00
Carnation, cup plate 650.00
Carnation, pitcher, cream sz, 4⅛" 800.00
Carnation, plate, deep, sm feather border, 10" ... 775.00
Carnation, plate, 8" 600.00
Dahlia, creamer 900.00
Dahlia, plate, 8⅜" 900.00
Dahlia, tea bowl & saucer 750.00
Double Rose, creamer 600.00
Double Rose, plate, deep, hairline, 9¾" ... 290.00
Double Rose, plate, 10" 1,000.00
Double Rose, toddy plate, 4½" 750.00
Double Rose, waste bowl, 6" 625.00
Dove, cup & saucer, plain, broken band ... 485.00
Dove, plate, plain border, 6¼" 500.00
Dove, plate, 9¾" 800.00
Dove, teapot 1,000.00
Grape, pitcher, cream sz 695.00
Grape, plate, 6" 285.00
Grape, plate, 7⅛" 425.00
Grape, plate, 9¾" 600.00
Grape, teapot 700.00

Leaf, sugar bowl, w/lid 1,000.00
Oyster, cup & saucer, EX 285.00
Oyster, plate, 5⅝" 385.00
Oyster, plate, 8½" 475.00
Oyster, waste bowl, 6¼" 1,100.00
Primrose, plate, mk Riley, 8¾" 550.00
Primrose, sugar bowl 900.00
Primrose, waste bowl 750.00
Single Rose, cup plate 400.00
Single Rose, plate, 5¼" 375.00
Single Rose, plate, 6⅜" 475.00
Single Rose, plate, 9½" 550.00
Single Rose, teapot 1,500.00
Strawflower, plate, mk Riley, 10" 1,900.00
Strawflower, plate, soup 800.00
Strawflower, plate, 8½" 825.00
Sunflower, creamer 450.00
Sunflower, plate, 8¼" 600.00
Sunflower, tea bowl & saucer 800.00
Urn, creamer 350.00
Urn, cup & saucer 445.00
Urn, teapot 600.00
War Bonnet, coffeepot, rprs 900.00
War Bonnet, creamer 600.00
War Bonnet, plate, 8" 650.00
War Bonnet, teapot 2,000.00
War Bonnet, toddy plate, 8" 800.00
Zinnia, plate, 6⅜" 600.00

Gaudy Ironstone

Gaudy Ironstone was produced in the mid-1800s in Staffordshire, England. Some of the ware was decorated in much the same colors and designs as Gaudy Welsh, while other pieces were painted in pink, orange, and red with black and light blue accents. Lustre was used on some designs, omitted on others. The heavy ironstone body is its most distinguishing feature.

Key: ug bl — underglaze blue

Plate, Columbine, $90.00.

Bowl, Urn of Flowers, ug bl, w/lid, lt wear, 7¾x9½" 770.00
Coffeepot, Seeing Eye, Walley, Niagara shape, 11", EX 650.00
Creamer, Morning-Glory, ug bl w/gr, bl bands, 8-sided, 5½" 270.00
Creamer, Urn of Flowers, mc floral, pleated mold, 6½" 390.00
Cup & saucer, bl band/gr stripes/red & gr balls, mini, pr 55.00
Cup & saucer, handleless; Cabbage Rose, NM 145.00
Cup & saucer, Morning-Glory, ug bl w/gr 120.00
Cup & saucer, Seeing Eye, registry mk, NM 130.00
Cup & saucer, Strawberry, cobalt leaves w/lustre, EX 200.00
Pitcher, floral, bl/gr/yel/ochre/blk, hairline, 8" 135.00
Pitcher, molded design, ug bl w/bl highlights & lustre, 8" 165.00
Pitcher & bowl, floral, ug bl & mc enamel, mk, 10½", 14" 440.00
Plate, Morning-Glory, ug bl w/gr leaves, bl band, 8½", VG 85.00
Plate, Pinwheel, mk Ironstone, EX 50.00
Plate, Rose, red/gr/blk, stains, 7⅜" 85.00
Plate, Seeing Eye, mk Pearl White, 6½", EX 250.00
Plate, Seeing Eye, wear, 8½" 90.00
Plate, Seeing Eye, 7½" 150.00
Plate, Strawberry, cobalt leaves w/lustre, EX 130.00
Plate, Urn of Flowers, crazing, 8¾" 165.00
Plate, Urn of Flowers, ug bl, flaking, 9⅜" 250.00
Platter, flower basket center, mk Mason's, wear, 22¼" 360.00
Platter, Single Rose, 4-color, mk England, 13¼" L 138.00
Platter, Strawberry & Rose, 3-color, wear/stains, 14¾" 325.00
Sugar bowl, Morning-Glory, ug bl w/gr, 7" 510.00
Sugar bowl, Pinwheel, octagonal, mk Ironstone, 7¾", EX 310.00
Sugar bowl, Urn of Flowers, ug bl, stain, rprs, 7⅜" 225.00
Teapot, Morning-Glory, ug bl w/gr, 8-sided, mk D, 9" 875.00
Waste bowl, Grape Leaf, mc strawberry, 5½", EX 280.00
Waste bowl, Seeing Eye, emb foliage at rim, 5¼", EX 230.00

Gaudy Welsh

Gaudy Welsh was an inexpensive hand-decorated ware made in both England and Wales from 1820 until 1860. It is characterized by its colors — principally underglaze blue, orange-rust, and copper lustre — and by its uninhibited patterns. Accent colors may be yellow and green. (Pink lustre may be present, since lustre applied to the white areas appears pink. A copper tone develops from painting lustre onto the dark colors.) The body of the ware may be heavy ironstone, creamware, earthenware, or porcelain; even style and shapes vary considerably. Patterns, while usually floral, are also sometimes geometric and may have trees and birds. Beware! The Wagon Wheel pattern has been reproduced.

Our advisor for this category is Cheryl Nelson; she is listed in the Directory under Minnesota. For further information we recommend *The Collector's Encyclopedia of Gaudy Dutch and Welsh* by John Shuman, available from Collector Books.

Bryn Pistyll, jug, 5" 165.00
Buckle, cup & saucer 95.00
Cambrian Rose, jug, 7½" 365.00
Chain, jug, flow bl, 7¼" 385.00
Chinoiserie, mug, 2" 180.00
Columbine, cup & saucer 85.00
Columbine, teapot 275.00
Cosmos, cup & saucer 90.00
Feather, plate, mc, 9" 165.00
Floret, cup & saucer 80.00
Flower Basket, jug, 8" 295.00
Forget-Me-Not, jug, hydra hdl, 6" 215.00
Glamorgan, jug, 7" 325.00
Grape, jug, 7" 375.00
Grape, mug, child's, 2½" 150.00
Grape V, mug, child's, 2½" 195.00
Gwent, jug, 5" 295.00
Llanberis, jug, 8" 490.00
Nightingale, cup & saucer 95.00
Oyster, cup & saucer 80.00
Oyster, jug, 7" 100.00
Oyster, plate, 10" 125.00
Oyster, teapot 275.00
Pagoda, bowl, 7" 795.00

Pot de Fleurs II, urn 495.00
Rainbow, jug, 3½" 250.00
Rainbow, jug, 4" 295.00
Rosemary, cup & saucer 120.00
Sunflower, jug, 7" 315.00
Swansea Cottage, jug, gr, no bl, rare 565.00
Tulip, cup & saucer 90.00
Tulip, cup & saucer, Allerton 60.00
Tulip, plate, 10", from $75.00 up to 125.00
Tulip, teapot 225.00
Village, cake plate, gr, no bl 285.00

Geisha Girl

Geisha Girl Porcelain was one of several key Japanese china production efforts aimed at the booming export markets of the U.S., Canada, England, and other parts of Europe. The wares feature colorful, kimono-clad Japanese ladies in scenes of everyday Japanese life, surrounded by exquisite flora, fauna, and mountain ranges. Nonetheless, the forms in which the wares were produced reflected the late 19th- and early 20th-century Western dining and decorating preferences: tea and coffee services, vases, dresser sets, children's items, planters, etc.

Over a hundred manufacturers were involved in Geisha Girl production. This accounts for the several hundred different patterns, well over a dozen border colors and styles, and several methods of design execution. Geisha Girl Porcelain was produced in wholly hand-painted versions and those that were hand painted over stenciled outlines. Be wary of Geisha ware executed with decals. Very few decaled examples came out of Japan. Rather, most were Czechoslovakian attempts to hone in on the market. Czech pieces have stamped marks in broad, pseudo-Oriental characters. Items with portraits of Oriental ladies in the bottom of tea or sake cups are *not* Geisha Girl Porcelain, unless the outside surface of the wares are decorated as described above. These lovely faces are formed by varying the thickness of the porcelain body and are called lithophanes.

The height of Geisha Girl production was between 1910 and the mid-1930s. Some post-World War II production has been found marked Occupied Japan. The ware continued in minimal production through the 1980s, but point of origin for the reproductions is Hong Kong. Modern productions are discerned by the pure whiteness of the porcelain; even, unemotional borders; lack of background washes and gold enameling; and overall sparseness of detail.

For further information we recommend *The Collector's Encyclopedia of Geisha Girl Porcelain* by Elyce Litts, available at your local bookstore, from Collector Books, or directly from the author. She is listed in the Directory under New Jersey.

Key:
#2 — Torii	#68 — SGK China, Occupied
#4 — T in Cherry Blossom	Japan
#11 — diaper mk	J #1 — Yachi
#12 — Royal Kaga	J #6 — Tashiro
#16 — SNB	J #16 — Kutani
#19 — Japan	J #19 — Ozan
#20 — Made in Japan	J #36 — Made by Kato
#35 — Plum Blossom	J #46 — Yasutera
#42 — Vantine	

Basket vase, Bamboo Trellis, gr & brn trim w/gold, 8½", pr 150.00
Biscuit jar, Basket of Mums B, red w/gold, melon ribs, 3-ftd 65.00
Bowl, Garden Bench K, 9-lobed, gr w/gold, 2¼x8¾" 75.00
Bowl, master nut; Ribbon Parasol, red-orange w/gold 20.00
Bowl, Pointing D, red-orange w/gold buds, 5¼" 12.00

Box, Parasol D, egg form, red-orange, #20, 4½x3¾x3½" 35.00
Butter pat, Flower Gathering B, red-orange, 3¼" 8.00
Cake set, River's Edge, master+6 ind plates 75.00
Celery dish, Boat Festival, bl w/gold lacing, #35, 13" 32.00
Chocolate pot, Battledore, yel-gr, ribbed conical body, 9½" 65.00
Chocolate set, Chrysanthemum Garden, cobalt w/gold, #19, 9-pc ..85.00
Cup, Doll's Tea Party, Emery-Birel-Thayer, dtd 1916 ....10.00
Cup & saucer, AD; Torii & Parasol, red-orange w/gold, #19 ....20.00
Cup & saucer, chocolate; Garden Bench C, cobalt border 15.00
Cup & saucer, Peacock on a Flowered Stone Roof, cobalt/gold 25.00
Demitasse set, Geisha in Sampan B, pastels, #19, 11-pc 85.00
Egg cup, Cherry Blossom Ikebana, red, #20 ....10.00
Hair receiver, Bamboo Trellis, red-orange 25.00
Hatpin holder, Rendezvous, vine & leaves, J#16 ....100.00
Jar, condensed milk; Ikebana Party, cobalt w/gold, J#16, 3-pc 75.00
Mint dish, Seamstress, floral shape, hdls, #19, 5½x4" 14.00
Nappy, Mother & Daughter, dk turq w/gold, lobed 35.00
Pancake server, So Big, red w/gold lacing, J#16, 9½x3½" 150.00
Plate, Battledore, red-orange, swirled w/scalloped rim, 6¼" 20.00
Plate, Bird Cage, red-orange w/gold, 6" 12.00
Plate, Gardening, red-orange w/gold buds, 6" 10.00
Plate, Inside the Teahouse, apple gr, swirl fluted, 8½" 35.00
Salad set, Fan C, red w/gold buds, master+6 ind bowls 125.00
Sugar bowl, Boy w/Scythe, cobalt w/gold, #20 ....18.00
Sugar bowl, Mother & Daughter, 2 reserves, red w/gold 15.00
Teacup & saucer, Bicycle Race, red-orange w/gold 30.00
Teacup & saucer, Geisha in Sampan A, gold 15.00
Vase, Bamboo Trellis, red-orange, #14, 4½", pr 25.00

German Porcelain

Unless otherwise noted, the porcelain listed in this section is marked simply 'Germany.' Products of other German manufactures are listed in specific categories. See also Bisque; Pink Pigs; Elfinware.

Basket, appl flowers & cherubs, mc w/gilt, mk, 12x14x11¾" 165.00
Bowl, emb dogwood floral border, rose transfer, 10½" 85.00
Bowl, lady portrait/flowers transfer, rtcl sides, 3x8½" 200.00
Candlesticks, cherub stems, cornucopia sockets, 9⅝", pr 250.00

Figurine, 18th-Century figures on rocky knoll with flower garlands, late 1800s, chips, 17", $475.00.

Figurine, boy & girl in tan clothes, girl w/shoe, 11", pr 300.00
Figurine, Colonial man & lady, gold trim, 9½", pr 110.00
Figurine, dachshund, gr, humorous, 6¼x2x4" 65.00
Figurine, man & lady in pk & bl costumes, bsk, 18", pr 475.00
Figurine, monkey band, 1900s, 5-pc set 450.00
Figurine, soldier & lady w/appl flowers, 1860s, 13½", pr 795.00
Figurine, 2 nude children w/basket of flowers, 1800s, 5½" 200.00

Pin tray, hunter w/dogs, 2¼" **35.00**
Plaque, Cupid & umbrella, Jasper, bl, 4⅝" **55.00**
Plaque, lady's portrait, A Geyer, gold fr, 2½x3½" **200.00**
Plaque, Lohengrin & Elaine, Jasper, bl, 5⅞" **85.00**
Teapot, florals w/lav, ca 1800s, sm, EX **140.00**
Toothpick holder, nude in shell, NY souvenir, 3½" **35.00**
Tray, lady's portrait, St Kilian & beehive mk, 13¼" **225.00**
Vase, monkey holding gr basket figural, bsk, mk, 4x2½" **40.00**

Gladding McBean and Company

This company was established in 1875 in Lincoln, California. They first produced only clay drainage pipes, but in 1883 architectural terra cotta was introduced, which has been used extensively in the United States as well as abroad. Sometime later a line of garden pottery was added. They soon became the leading producers of tile in the country. In 1923 they purchased the Tropico Pottery in Glendale, California, where in addition to tile they also produced huge garden vases. Their line was expanded in 1934 to included artware and dinnerware.

At least fifteen lines of art pottery were developed between 1934 and 1942. For a short time they stamped their wares with the Tropico Pottery mark; but the majority was signed 'GMcB' in an oval. Later the mark was changed to 'Franciscan' with several variations. After 1937 'Catalina Pottery' was used on some lines. (All items marked 'Catalina Pottery' were made in Glendale.) For further information we recommend *The Collector's Encyclopedia of California Pottery* by our advisor for this category, Jack Chipman. He is listed in the Directory under California.

Bowl, Coronado Art Ware, ivory satin, bulbous, 8½" **35.00**
Candlestick, Coronado Art Ware, coral satin, 6½" **25.00**

Carafe, 8½", and four mugs, blue with wooden handles, $65.00 for the set.

Compote, Avalon Art Ware, turq & ivory, 8" **27.50**
Compote, Coronado Art Ware, ivory satin **30.00**
Lamp base, Ox Blood Art Ware, w/detached underplate **120.00**
Tile, angel fish, 6x6" **60.00**
Vase, bud; Encanto Art Ware, celadon **20.00**
Vase, Catalina Art Ware, coral satin, ribbed, 7¾" **37.50**
Vase, Coronado Art Ware, ivory satin, ftd, 10½" **45.00**
Vase, Encanto Art Ware, coral satin, cylindrical, 11½" **40.00**
Vase, Garden Ware, bl-gr w/bead relief at neck, 35" **525.00**
Vase, Ox Blood Art Ware, 11" **200.00**

Glass Animals and Figurines

These beautiful glass sculptures have been produced by many major companies in America; in fact, some are still being made today. Heisey, Fostoria, Duncan and Miller, Imperial, Paden City, Tiffin and Cambridge made the vast majority, but there were many others involved on a lesser scale. Some, but not all, marked their animals.

As many of the glass companies went out of business, molds were often sold to others still active who used them to reproduce their own line of animals. While some are easy to recognize, others can be very confusing. For example, Summit Art Glass now owns Cambridge's 6½", 8½", and 10" swan molds. We recommend *Glass Animals of the Depression Era* by Lee Garmon and Dick Spencer, if you're thinking of starting a collection or wanting to identify and evaluate the glass animals you already have. Both are our advisors for this category and are listed in the Directory under Illinois.

Cambridge

Bird, crystal satin, 2¾" L **30.00**
Blue jay, flower holder **125.00**
Bridge hound, ebony, 1¾" **35.00**
Buddha, amber, 5½" **225.00**
Eagle, bookend, 5½x4x4" **80.00**
Frog, crystal satin **25.00**
Heron, lg, 12" **125.00**
Heron, sm, 9" **75.00**
Lion, bookend, ea **125.00**
Owl, lamp, ivory w/brn enamel, ebony base, 13½" **1,000.00**
Pouter pigeon, bookend, milk glass, 5½" **70.00**
Scottie, bookend, hollow, pr **150.00**
Scottie, frosted, hollow, ea **75.00**
Sea gull, flower frog **50.00**
Swan, candlestick, milk glass, 4½" **175.00**
Swan, carmen, 6½" **200.00**
Swan, carmen, 8½" **250.00**
Swan, Crown Tuscan, 3½" **40.00**
Swan, Crown Tuscan, 8½" **95.00**
Swan, ebony, 10½" **250.00**
Swan, ebony, 12½" **300.00**
Swan, ebony, 3½" **60.00**
Swan, ebony, 8½" **125.00**
Swan, emerald, 3½" **35.00**
Swan, emerald, 8½" **125.00**
Swan, milk glass, 3½" **60.00**
Swan, milk glass, 6½" **125.00**
Swan, milk glass, 8½" **275.00**
Turkey, bl, w/lid **550.00**
Turkey, gr, w/lid **450.00**
Turkey, pk, w/lid **400.00**
Turtle, flower holder, ebony **225.00**

Duncan and Miller

Bird of paradise **700.00**
Donkey, cart & peon, 3-pc set **475.00**
Dove, head down, 11½" L **175.00**
Duck, ashtray, red, 7" **70.00**
Duck, cigarette box, red, 6" **170.00**
Goose, fat, 6x6" **275.00**
Heron, crystal satin, 7" **120.00**
Mallard duck, cigarette box, #30, w/lid, 3½x4½" **45.00**
Ruffled grouse, very rare **1,750.00**
Swan, ashtray, crystal w/bl neck, 4" **35.00**
Swan, bl opal, W&F, spread wings, 10x12½" **245.00**
Swan, candle holder, red w/crystal neck, 7" **70.00**
Swan, gr opal, W&F, spread wings, 10x12½" **225.00**
Swan, open, 7" **45.00**
Swan, solid, 3" **20.00**

Swan, solid, 5" 30.00
Swan, solid, 7" 75.00
Swan, wht milk glass w/red neck, 10½" 450.00
Swordfish 300.00
Swordfish, bl opal, rare 500.00
Sylvan swan, bl or pk, 6½" 125.00
Sylvan swan, vaseline opal, 6½" 185.00
Sylvan swan, yel opal, 7½" 100.00
Sylvan swan, 12" 85.00
Tropical fish, ashtray, pk opal, 3½" 50.00
Tropical fish, candle holder, 5" 500.00

Fenton

Alley cat, teal marigold, 11" 65.00
Bear, blk, sitting 16.00
Bear, carnival, sitting 20.00
Bear, wht irid, sitting 15.00
Boy, blk, praying 12.00
Bunny, lt bl 16.00
Bunny, pale yel 16.00
Butterfly, candle holder, ruby carnival, 1989 souvenir, 7½" 85.00
Cardinal head, ruby, 6½" 95.00
Donkey, custard, HP daisies, 4½" 45.00
Elephant, flower bowl, blk satin, 6½x9" 400.00
Elephant, whiskey bottle, periwinkle, 8" 450.00
Fish, paperweight, red carnival, ltd ed 55.00
Fish, red w/amberina tail & fins, 2½" 55.00
Fish, vase, milk glass w/blk tail & eyes, 7" 425.00
Happiness Bird, red, 6½" 28.00
Peacock, bookends, crystal satin, 5¾", pr 175.00
Turtle, flower block, amethyst, 4" L 85.00

Fostoria

Bird, candle holder, 1½" 15.00
Cardinal head, Silver Mist, 6½" 125.00
Cat, lt bl, 3¾" 35.00
Chanticleer, blk, 10¾" 600.00
Chinese Lute, ebony w/gold, 12½" 300.00
Colts, sitting 40.00
Colts, standing, Silver Mist 45.00
Deer, sitting or standing, crystal or bl 45.00
Deer, sitting or standing, milk glass 55.00
Deer, sitting or standing, Silver Mist 40.00
Dolphin, bl, 4¾" 25.00
Duck, mama 25.00
Duck w/3 ducklings, amber, set 50.00
Duckling, head bk (+) 20.00
Duckling, head down (+) 15.00
Duckling, walking (+) 15.00
Eagle, bookend, 7½" 90.00
Elephant, bookend, ebony, 6½", ea 65.00
Goldfish, horizontal, rare 125.00
Goldfish, vertical 95.00
Horse, bookend, 7¾", ea 45.00
Madonna, Silver Mist, orig issue, 10" (+) 50.00
Madonna, Silver Mist, w/base, orig issue, 11¾" (+) 80.00
Madonna, 10" (+) 60.00
Mermaid, 11½" 115.00
Pelican, amber, 1991 commemorative 55.00
Penguin, 4⅝" 75.00
Polar bear, topaz, 4⅝" 125.00
Polar bear, 4⅝" 65.00

Sea horse, bookend, 8", ea 115.00
Seal, topaz, 3⅞" 125.00
Squirrel 25.00
Squirrel, amber 35.00
Squirrel, frosted 25.00
St Francis, Silver Mist, orig issue, 13½" (+) ...325.00
Whale 20.00

Heisey

Airdale 500.00
Angelfish 120.00
Asiatic pheasant, 7½" L 300.00
Bull, sgn, 4x7½" 1,400.00
Bunny, head down, 2½" 200.00
Chick, head down or up, ea 65.00
Clydesdale, 7½x7" 400.00
Colt, kicking 185.00
Colt, kicking, amber 650.00
Colt, kicking, cobalt 950.00
Colt, rearing 195.00
Colt, rearing, amber 650.00
Colt, rearing, cobalt 950.00

Colt, standing, $90.00.

Colt, standing, amber 550.00
Colt, standing, cobalt 900.00
Cygnet, baby swan, 2½" 200.00
Doe head, bookend, 6¼" 800.00
Dolphin, candlesticks, #110, pr 250.00
Dolphin, candlesticks, Moongleam, #110, pr ...700.00
Donkey 275.00
Duck, ashtray 80.00
Duck, ashtray, Flamingo 160.00
Duck, ashtray, Marigold 195.00
Duck, flower block 140.00
Duck, flower block, Flamingo 200.00
Duck, flower block, Hawthorne 295.00
Elephant, amber, lg or med 1,850.00
Elephant, amber, sm 1,600.00
Elephant, lg or med 400.00
Elephant, sm 195.00
Filly, head bkward, 8⅛x5¼" 1,400.00
Fish, bookend, ea 135.00
Fish, bowl, 9½" 425.00
Fish, candlestick, 5" 150.00
Fish, match holder, 3x2¾" 150.00
Flying mare 2,800.00
Flying mare, amber 3,500.00

Frog, cheese plate, Flamingo, #1210 ....145.00
Frog, cheese plate, Marigold 285.00
Gazelle, 10¾" 1,500.00
Giraffe, head bk 185.00
Giraffe, head forward 200.00
Giraffe, head to side 200.00
Goose, wings down 425.00
Goose, wings half 95.00
Goose, wings up 100.00
Hen, 4½" 400.00
Horse, bookend 155.00
Horse head, bookend, frosted, ea 120.00
Horse head, box, 6½" 85.00
Horse head, cigarette box, #1489, 4½x4" 55.00
Horse head, cocktail shaker 85.00
Irish setter, ashtray 30.00
Irish setter, ashtray, Flamingo 45.00
Irish setter, ashtray, Moongleam 55.00
Kingfisher, flower block, Flamingo 175.00
Kingfisher, flower block, Moongleam 200.00
Mallard, wings down 325.00
Mallard, wings half 185.00
Mallard, wings up 150.00
Piglet, sitting 100.00
Piglet, standing 100.00
Plug horse 135.00
Plug horse, amber 600.00
Plug horse, cobalt 1,000.00
Pouter pigeon, 7½" L 700.00
Rabbit, paperweight, 2¾x3¾" 150.00
Rabbit mother, 4½x5½" 800.00
Ram head, stopper, 3½" 150.00
Ringneck pheasant, 11¾" 140.00
Rooster, amber, 5⅜" 2,500.00
Rooster, Fighting; crystal frost, 7½x5½" 200.00
Rooster, vase, 6½" 85.00
Rooster, 5½x5" 325.00
Rooster head, cocktail 50.00
Rooster head, cocktail shaker, 1-qt 65.00
Rooster head, stopper, 4½" 45.00
Scotty 100.00
Sea horse, cocktail 140.00
Show horse 1,250.00
Sow, 3x4½" 600.00
Sparrow 120.00
Swan, ind nut, #1503 ....20.00
Swan, master nut, #1503 ....45.00
Swan, pitcher 700.00
Swan, 7x8½" 800.00
Tiger, paperweight, 2¾x8" 1,100.00
Tropical fish, 12" 1,650.00
Wood duck 550.00

Imperial

Angelfish, bookend, amber (crystal or frosted), ea 150.00
Asiatic pheasant, amber 325.00
Bulldog-type pup, milk glass, 3½" 65.00
Champ terrier, caramel slag, 5¾" 95.00
Chick, head down, milk glass 10.00
Chick, head up, milk glass 10.00
Clydesdale, amber 325.00
Clydesdale, Verde Gr 150.00
Colt, balking, amber 140.00

Colt, balking, caramel slag 45.00
Colt, kicking, Horizon Bl 35.00
Colt, standing, amber 140.00
Colt, standing, Sunshine Yel 85.00
Cygnet, blk, 2½" 55.00
Cygnet, Horizon Bl 25.00
Dog, Airedale, caramel slag 95.00
Dog, Airedale, Ultra Bl 65.00
Donkey, caramel slag 55.00
Donkey, Meadow Gr Carnival 95.00
Duck, sitting, caramel slag, 4½" 45.00
Duck, standing, Ultra Bl, 2⅝" 45.00
Elephant, caramel slag, med 55.00
Elephant, Meadow Gr Carnival, #674, med 95.00
Elephant, Nut Brn, sm 120.00
Elephant Eminent, Meadow Gr Carnival, 4" 95.00
Filly, head bkward, Verde Gr 145.00
Filly, head forward, satin 75.00
Fish, candlestick, Sunshine Yel, 5" 40.00
Fish, match holder, Sunshine Yel satin, 3" 20.00
Gazelle, blk, 11" 400.00
Horse head, bookend, pk, rare, ea 300.00
Mallard, wings down, Horizon Bl, HCA, 4½" 75.00
Mallard, wings down, lt bl satin 22.50
Mallard, wings half, caramel slag 35.00
Mallard, wings up, caramel slag 35.00
Marmote Sentinel (woodchuck), caramel slag, 4½" 60.00
Owl, Hootless; caramel slag 50.00
Owl, jar, caramel slag, 16½" 65.00
Piglet, sitting, amber 75.00
Piglet, standing, amber 75.00
Piglet, standing, ruby, hole between legs 95.00
Plug horse, pk, HCA, 1978 ....40.00
Rabbit, paperweight, Horizon Bl, 2¾" 85.00
Rooster, amber 425.00
Rooster, fighting, pk 175.00
Scottie, milk glass, 3½" 45.00
Terrier pup, amethyst carnival, 3½" 45.00
Tiger, paperweight, caramel slag, 8" L 85.00
Tiger, paperweight, jade marbleized, 8" L 150.00
Wood duck, caramel slag 45.00
Wood duck, Ultra Bl satin 45.00
Wood duckling, floating, Sunshine Yel satin 15.00
Wood duckling, standing, Sunshine Yel satin 15.00

L.E. Smith

Camel, recumbent, amber, 4½x6" 60.00
Cock, Fighting; bl, 9" 45.00
Elephant, 1¾" 12.00
Goose, 2½" 12.00
Goose Girl, gr or flame, 6", ea 50.00
Goose Girl, orig, 6" 25.00
Horse, bookend, rearing, amber, ea 38.00
Horse, bookend, rearing, blk, ea 65.00
Horse, bookend, rearing, crystal, ea 20.00
Horse, bookend, rearing, emerald, ea 40.00
Horse, bookend, rearing, ruby, ea 40.00
Horse, recumbent, amberina, 9" L 125.00
King fish, aquarium, gr, 7¼x15" 265.00
Queen fish, aquarium, gr, 7x15" 225.00
Rooster, butterscotch slag, ltd ed, #208 ....85.00
Scottie, pipe rest, fired-on blk, 5½" L 10.00
Sparrow, head up, 3½" 15.00

Swan, milk glass, lg 45.00
Swan, milk glass w/decor, 8½" 45.00

New Martinsville

Bear, baby, head trn or str, 3" 60.00
Bear, mama, 4x6" 225.00
Bear, papa, 4x6½" 250.00
Chick, frosted, 1" 25.00
Duck, standing, Viking's Epic Line 35.00
Eagle, 8" 75.00

**Elephant, bookend, 5½",
$85.00 each.**

Gazelle, leaping, frosted base, 8¼" 65.00
German shepherd, 5" 75.00
Hen, 5" 65.00
Horse, head up, 8" 95.00
Nautilus shell, bookend, crystal frost, 6", ea 35.00
Piglet, standing 125.00
Porpoise on wave, orig 475.00
Rabbit, mama 350.00
Rooster w/crooked tail, 7½" 85.00
Seal, candlesticks, lg, pr 150.00
Seal w/ball, bookends, 7", pr 140.00
Seal w/ball, candle holder, 4½" 70.00
Starfish, 7¾" 80.00
Tiger, head down, frosted, 7¼" 200.00
Tiger, head up, 6½" 200.00
Wolfhound, 7" 95.00
Woodsman, sq base, 7⅜" 95.00

Paden City

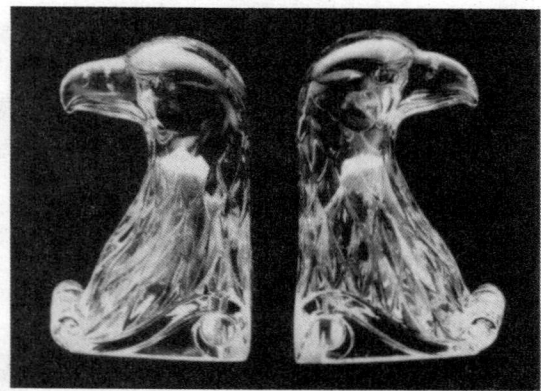

**American Eagle Head bookends, solid with flat back,
7½", $300.00 for the pair.**

Bunny, cotton-ball dispenser, ears bk, bl frosted 90.00
Bunny, cotton-ball dispenser, ears bk, crystal frosted 60.00
Bunny, cotton-ball dispenser, ears bk, milk glass 95.00
Bunny, cotton-ball dispenser, ears up, pk frosted 150.00
Dragon swan, 9¾" L 215.00
Goose, lt bl, 5" 115.00
Pheasant, Chinese; crystal, 13¾" 85.00
Pheasant, Chinese; med bl, 13¾" 150.00
Pheasant, head trn, lt bl, 12" L 175.00
Polar Bear on ice, 4½" 65.00
Pony, blk, 12" 350.00
Pouter pigeon, bookend, 6¼", ea 85.00
Rooster, Barnyard; 8¾" 85.00
Rooster, Chanticleer; lt bl, 9¼" 200.00
Rooster, Elegant; lt bl, 11" 225.00
Rooster, frosted 65.00
Rooster, head down, 8¾" 80.00
Squirrel on curved log, 5½" 65.00

Viking

Angelfish, blk, 6½" 150.00
Angelfish, milk glass, 6½" 70.00
Bird, med dk bl, 9½" 25.00
Bird, moss gr, 12" 25.00
Bird, Orchid, 9½" 30.00
Cat, gr, 8" 55.00
Duck, dk teal, Viking's Epic Line, 9" 30.00
Duck, fighting, head up or down, Viking's Epic Line 35.00
Duck, vaseline, 5" 25.00
Egret, orange, 12" 45.00
Horse, aqua bl, 11½" 95.00
Penguin, 7" 25.00
Rabbit, amber, 6½" 35.00
Rabbit (Thumper), 6½" 35.00
Rooster, Epic; red, 9½" (+) 60.00
Seal, persimmon, 9¾" L 15.00

Westmoreland

Bird in flight, Amber Marigold, wings out, 5" W 25.00
Bulldog, Crystal Mist, pnt collar, rhinestone eyes, 2½" ... 35.00
Butterfly, Gr Mist, 2½" 22.00
Butterfly, 4½" 27.00
Cardinal, Gr Mist 20.00
Owl, Crystal Mist, 5½" 30.00
Penguin on ice floe, Brandywine Bl Mist 35.00
Porky Pig, milk glass, hollow, 3" L 15.00
Pouter pigeon, any color, 2½", ea 25.00
Pouter pigeon, lilac, 1" 20.00
Robin, 3¼" L 20.00
Starfish, candle holders, milk glass, 5", pr 35.00
Turtle, flower block, gr, 7 holes, 4" L 55.00
Turtle, paperweight, Gr Mist, no holes, 4" L 22.00

Miscellaneous

Horse head, bookends, milk glass, Indiana, 6", pr 35.00
Lady's leg, bookends, custard, Mosser, pr 175.00
Mopey dog, Federal, 3½" 10.00
Panther, walking, bl, Indiana, 3x7" 250.00
Pouter pigeon, bookend, Indiana, 5½", ea 40.00
Turtle, amber, LG Wright, 10" L 85.00

Glass Knives

Glass knives were manufactured from about 1920 to 1950, with distribution at its greatest in the late thirties and early forties. Colors generally followed Depression Glass dinnerware: crystal, light blue, light green, pink (originally called rose), and more rarely amber, forest green and white (opal). Many glass knives were hand painted in fruit or flower designs. Knife blades were ground to a sharp edge. Today knives are usually found with blades nicked through years of use or bumping in silverware drawers or reground, which is acceptable to collectors as long as the original knife shape is maintained.

Many glass knives were engraved for gift-giving, personalized with the recipient's name and occasionally with a greeting. Originally presented in boxes, most glass knives were accompanied by a paper insert extolling the virtues of the knife and describing its care.

Boxes printed with World's Fair logos are fun to find, though not rare. Butter knives, which are smaller than other glass knives, typically were made in Czechoslovakia and sometimes match the handle patterns of glass salad sets. Knife lengths often vary slightly because the knives were snapped off the molded glass during manufacture.

Our advisor for this category is Adrienne Escoe; she is listed in the Directory under California. For information concerning the Glass Knife Collectors Club, see the Clubs, Newsletters, and Catalogs section of the Directory.

Values reflect knives with minor blade roughness or resharpening.

Aer-Flo (Grid), amber, 7½" 150.00
Aer-Flo (Grid), pk, 7½" 35.00
BK Co, crystal, 9¼" 22.00
BK Co, gr, 9¼" 40.00
BK Co, pk, 9¼" 150.00
Block, clear, 8¼" 15.00
Block, pk or gr, 8¼", ea 30.00
Block, vaseline, 8¼" 65.00

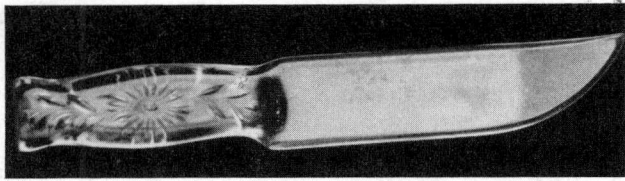

Dur-x 5-Leaf, small center, green, $30.00; Crystal, $14.00.

Dur-x 3-Leaf, lt amber, 9¼" 125.00
Dur-x 5-Leaf, crystal, 8½" 14.00
Dur-x 5-Leaf, gr, 8½" 30.00
Plain hdl, gr, 9" 40.00
Rose Spray, pk, 8½" 65.00
Star, bl, 8½" 24.00
Star, clear, 9½" 10.00
Star, pk, 8½" 20.00
Star, pk, 9½" 22.00
Stonex, gr, 8¼" 60.00
Thumbguard, no HP decor, 9¼" 15.00

Glidden

Genius designer Glidden Parker established Glidden Pottery in 1940 in Alfred, New York, having been schooled at the unrivaled New York State College of Ceramics at Alfred University. Glidden pottery is characterized by a fine stoneware body, innovative forms, outstanding hand-milled glazes, and hand decoration which make the pieces individual works of art. Production consisted of casual dinnerware, artware, and accessories that were distributed internationally.

In 1949 Glidden Pottery became the second ceramic plant in the country to utilize the revolutionary Ram pressing machine. This allowed for increased production and for the most part eliminated the previously used slip-casting method. However, Glidden stoneware continued to reflect the same superb quality of craftsmanship until the factory closed in 1957. Although the majority of form and decorative patterns were Mr. Parker's personal designs, Fong Chow and Sergio Dello Strologo also designed award-winning lines.

Glidden will be found marked on the unglazed underside with a signature that is hand incised, mold impressed, or ink stamped. Interest in this unique stoneware is growing as collectors discover that it embodies the very finest of Mid-Century High Style. Our advisor is David Pierce; he is listed in the Directory under Ohio.

Ashtray, Gr Mesa, #274-U, 5½" 30.00
Ashtray, High Tide, #2702-U, 10" 25.00
Ashtray, Loop Artware, #904-U, 6½x3¾" 60.00
Bowl, Engobe, Leaf, #27, 5¾" 15.00
Bowl, free-form, Charcoal & Rice, 7½x13" 85.00
Bowl, fruit; Feather, #271, 4½" 10.00
Bowl, lug soup; Viridian, #467, 3½x7½x6" 18.00
Bowl, salad; Sage & Sand, #17, 8" 15.00
Bowl, salad; Viridian, oval, #417, 4x9½x8" 20.00
Candlebench, Chi Chi Poodle, 8¾x3¾x2" 25.00
Candlebench, Mexican Cock, 8¾x3¾x2" 35.00
Casserole, Counterpane, #165, 8½x5½" 20.00
Casserole, Feather, #167, 4½x5¼" 12.00
Casserole, Pear, #165, 8½x5½" 30.00
Casserole, Turq Matrix, #163, 5x11x6½" 25.00
Casserole, Viridian, #163, 5x11x6½" 30.00
Charger, dk cobalt, Leaf pattern, #68, 15" dia 125.00
Creamer, Alfred Stoneware, #802, 4x5" dia 50.00
Creamer, Boston Spice, #1430, 6x3½x3½" 25.00
Creamer, Sage & Sand, #1430, 6x3½x3½" 12.00
Creamer & sugar bowl, Flourish, #144, #143 ....55.00
Cup & saucer, Flourish, #141, #142 ....20.00
Cup & saucer, Pear, #141, #142 ....10.00
Cup & saucer, Sage & Sand, #441A, #442 ....10.00
Cup & saucer, Turq Matrix, #141, #142 ....12.00
Cup & saucer, Viridian, #441A, #442 ....15.00
Pitcher, Feather, #617, 3-qt 40.00
Pitcher, Turq Matrix, #615, 1-qt 30.00
Planter, Ivy, bird form, Charcoal & Rice 75.00
Plate, Handsome Fish, #410, 8x7¼" 35.00
Plate, luncheon; Sage & Sand, #433, 10½" 8.00
Plate, salad; Plaid, #65, 7x7" 15.00
Teapot, Flourish, #140, 5¼x9x4¼" 45.00
Tumbler, Flourish, #1127, 5½" 20.00
Vase, Flourish, #5 ....40.00
Vase, Turq Matrix, #49, 6½x6" 30.00
Vase, Yellowstone, #86, 7¼x4¾x4¾" 25.00

Goebel

F.W. Goebel founded the Hummelwork Porcelain Manufactory in 1871, located in Rodental, West Germany. They produced porcelain figurines, plates, and novelties, the most famous of which are the Hummel figurines (these are listed in a separate section). There were many other series produced by Goebel — Disney characters, birds, animals, Art Deco figurines, and the Friar Tuck Monks that are especially popular. Our advisors for this category are Gale and Wayne Bailey; they are listed in the Directory under Georgia.

Bookends

Dutch boy & girl kissing, XS116-A&B, crown mk, pr 85.00
Franklin & Washington, LA5-A&B, 3-line mk, pr 75.00
Orange dogs, XS684-A&B, crown mk, pr 100.00

Cookie Jars

Cardinal Tuck, SD29, red monk, stylized bee mk, 9" 850.00
Friar Tuck, SD29, brn monk, full bee mk, 9" 350.00

Disney

Bambi, recumbent, Dis 21, stylized bee 35.00
Bambi ashtray, Dis 147, full bee mk 100.00
Thumper, sitting, Dis 36, full bee mk 65.00

Figurines

Charlot Byj Redhead, BYJ 9, E-E-E-K mk 50.00
Co-Boy, Pat the Pitcher, 17-529-16, trademk 6 (missing bee) 55.00
Holy Family, HX239, full bee mk, 6" 125.00
Madonna bust, HM52, full bee mk 65.00
Victorian couple, FR624-A&B, crown mk, pr 75.00

Miscellaneous

Ashtray, dwarf & bird, RF95, full bee mk 45.00
Ashtray, poodle, RT167, full bee mk 50.00
Ashtray, 3 dogs, RT133, crown mk 65.00

Bookends, Victorian couple, XS682 2/0, 5", $85.00 for the pair.

Eggcup, chicken, E165, dbl crown mk 85.00
Font, Holy water w/cross, HW99, stylized bee mk 35.00
Pitcher, parrot, S485, crown mk, 6" 65.00
Pitcher, penguin, S467, crown mk, 5½" 75.00
Pretzel holder, blk cat, KT123, full bee mk 50.00
Vase, flower, KL36, crown & full bee mk, 5½" 50.00

Goldscheider

The Goldscheider family operated a pottery in Vienna for many

generations before seeking refuge in the United States following Hitler's invasion of their country. They settled in Trenton, New Jersey, in the early 1940s where they established a new corporation and began producing objects of art and tableware items. In 1946 Marcel Goldscheider established a pottery in Staffordshire where he manufactured bone china figures, earthenware, etc., marked with a stamp of his signature. Larger artist-signed examples from either location are very valuable.

Lamp, dancer leans against a column, raised on square base, marked, 16¾", $1,100.00.

Figurine, baby giraffe, #754, paper label, 11" 150.00
Figurine, boy & girl, #7844 & #7845, pr 1,500.00
Figurine, gazelle's head, turq crackle, 9" 145.00
Figurine, lady in '30s plaid skirt by dog, Lorenzl, 11" 850.00
Figurine, lady w/dress parted to hip, sgn Lorenzl, 13" 1,150.00
Figurine, lady w/summer hat, sgn Bakon, #6940, 12" 1,050.00
Figurine, Madonna bust on wooden stand, USA 95.00
Figurine, Southern Belle, bl ruffled dress, w/hat, USA, 8" 75.00
Figurine, Victorian lady w/umbrella, USA, 8½" 95.00
Head of lady, red/orange hair & lips, yel flowers, 8" 350.00
Head w/hand holding apple, blk base, for Myotte Sone, 8" 250.00
Head w/hand holding orange eye mask, wht face, bl hair, 11" 375.00
Lamp base, belly-dancer stands by ornate post, Austria, 17" 1,100.00
Plaque, girl w/bonnet & flowers, 14½x9½" 275.00
Plaque, Madonna & Child, 15" 450.00

Gonder

Lawton Gonder grew up with clay in his hands and fire in his eyes. Gonder's interest in ceramics was greatly influenced by his parents who worked for Weller and a close family friend and noted ceramic authority, John Herold. In his early teens Gonder launched his ceramic career at the Ohio Pottery Company while working for Herold. He later gained valuable experience at American Encaustic Tile Company, Cherry Art Tile, and the Florence Pottery. Gonder was plant manager at the Florence Pottery until fire destroyed the facility in late 1941.

After years of solid production and management experience, Lawton Gonder established the Gonder Ceramic Art Company, formerly the Peters and Reed plant, in South Zanesville, Ohio. Gonder Ceramic Arts produced quality art pottery with beautiful contemporary designs which included human and animal figures and a complete line of Oriental pottery. Accentuating the beautiful shapes were unique and innovative glazes developed by Gonder such as flambe (flame red with streaks of yellow), 24k gold crackle, antique gold, and Chinese crackle.

All Gonder is marked with the company name and mold number. They include 'Gonder U.S.A' in block letters, 'Gonder' in script, 'Gonder Original' in script, and 'Gonder Ceramic Art' in block letters.

Paper labels were also used. Some of the early Gonder molds closely resemble RumRill designs that had been manufactured at the Florence Pottery; and because some RumRill pieces are found with similar (if not identical) shapes, matching mold numbers, and Gonder glazes, it is speculated that some RumRill was produced at the Gonder plant. In 1946 Gonder started another company which he named Elgee (chosen for his initials LG) where he manufactured lamp bases until a fire in 1954 resulted in his shifting lamp production to the main plant. Operations ceased in 1957. Our advisors for this category are Marilyn and John McCormick; they are listed in the Directory under Kansas.

Basket, no hdls, dk gr, pk int, H-36, 6¼x9¼" 15.00
Ewer, shell & starfish form, dk gr w/brn drip, #508, 13½" 35.00

Figure of lady water carrier, lime green, 14¼", $30.00.

Figurine, doe's head, mk, 9½" 35.00
Figurine, horse's head, bl & gr onyx, 13" L 45.00
Figurine, Oriental man & lady, 14", pr 75.00
Figurine, panther, blk, 12" 50.00
Planter, gondola, yel & pk 25.00
Planter, swan, gold crackle, E-44 ....30.00
Vase, flower form, E-3, 7½" 12.50
Vase, lav, hdls, H-5, 9" 18.00
Vase, ribbon candy design, yel w/brn streaking, #517, 10½" 18.00
Vase, scalloped shell, yel & bl mottle, J-60, 8" 15.00
Vase, twisted body, flesh w/gr mottle, E-64, 6¼" 6.50

Goofus Glass

Goofus was an inexpensive type of lustre-painted pressed glassware made by many companies during the first two decades of the 20th century. Bowls and trays are most common, and red and gold combinations are found more often than blues and greens. Our advisor for this category is Dan Gandolfo; he is listed in the Directory under Illinois.

Bonbon dish, strawberry, dome ft, orig pnt, 4" dia 42.50
Bowl, Dogwood, orig pnt, 3x9½", EX 48.00
Bowl, field flowers, crimped & ruffled, orig pnt, 3½x8" 47.50
Bowl, pears/cherries/plums, crimped rim, EX orig pnt, 4x7" 37.50
Bowl, reindeer in center, EX 20.00
Bowl, Wheel & Block, red/gold on opal, scalloped/crimped, 9" 37.50
Cake plate, La Belle, orig pnt, 11", EX 47.50
Coaster, flowers, orig pnt, rare, 3" dia 12.00
Lamp, oil; Nosegay, #2, EX orig pnt 155.00
Nut dish, cherries, orig pnt, scalloped rim, 6½" 42.50
Plate, Gibson Girl, red on gold, 8", EX 55.00
Plate, grapes in center, fancy gold rim, orig pnt, 8½" 45.00
Plate, monk drinking, rose edge, orig pnt, rare, 7", EX 38.00
Sugar shaker, grapes, gold on milk glass, orig pnt/top, 4½" 37.50

Tray, dresser; Cabbage Rose, sq, orig pnt, 6" 32.50
Tumbler, grapes, gold on crackle, orig pnt, 4", NM 50.00
Vase, Cabbage Rose, milk glass, pnt traces, 5½" 32.00
Vase, Chrysanthemums, orig pnt, 8", EX 37.50
Vase, dogwood blossoms, baluster, orig pnt, 15" 50.00
Vase, Irises, on bl glass, minor rstr, 6½" 30.00
Vase, Irises, orig pnt, 12", EX 70.00
Vase, Lovebirds, orig pnt, 10" 65.00
Vase, Statue of Liberty, rare, 12⅝" 98.00
Vase, Tree Rose, orig pnt, 12", M 55.00
Water bottle, grapes on crackle, no pnt, 7½" 35.00

Goss and Crested China

William Henry Goss received his early education at the Government School of Design at Somerset House, London, and as a result of his merit was introduced to Alderman William Copeland, who owned the Copeland Spode Pottery. Under the influence of Copeland from 1852-1858, Goss quickly learned the trade and soon became their chief designer. Little is known about this brief association, and in 1858 Goss left to begin his own business. After a short-lived partnership with a Mr. Peake, Goss opened a pottery on John Street, Stoke-on-Trent, but by 1870 he had moved to his business to a location near London Road. This pottery became the famous Falcon Works. Their mark was a spread-wing falcon (goss-hawk) centering a narrow, horizontal bar with 'W.H. Goss' printed below.

Many of the early pieces made by Goss were left unmarked and are difficult to discern from products made by the Copeland factory, but after he had been in business for about fifteen years, all of his wares were marked. Today unmarked items do not command the prices of the later marked wares.

Adolphus William Henry Goss (Goss's eldest son) joined his father's firm in the 1880s. He introduced cheaper lines, though the more expensive lines continued in production. Shortly after his father's death in 1906, Adolphus retired and left the business to his two younger brothers. The business suffered from problems created by a war economy, and in 1936 Goss assets were held by Cauldon Potteries Ltd. These were eventually taken over by the Coalport Group, who retained the right to use the Goss trademark. Messrs. Ridgeway Potteries bought all the assets in 1954 as well as the right to use the Goss trademark and name. In 1964 the group was known as Allied English Potteries Ltd. (A.E.P.), and in 1971 A.E.P. merged with the Doulton Group. Now it remains to be seen if Goss ware will ever be produced again. Our advisor for this category is Patrick Herley; he is listed in the Directory under New York.

Beer barrel, Burton 18.00
Beer bowl, dragon 18.00
Bowl, Acanthus Rose 40.00
Bucket, milk; Swiss 18.00
Bucket, Norwegian, Maldon 22.00
Bust, Dickens, parian, 8" 75.00
Candle snuffer, Aseroovy crest on wht, 2¼" 75.00
Cup & saucer, flags decor (war allies) 35.00
Ewer, Arundel, 4½" 20.00
First & Last House 115.00
Jug, Gloucester 15.00
Jug, Scarborough 15.00
Jug, Spanish, Eddyston 27.50
Look Out House 110.00
Manx Cottage 90.00
Mortar, Bideford 14.00
Mortar, Hythe Gromwellian 15.00
Night light, R Burns Cottage, 6" 150.00

Pot, Roman, Painswick	18.00
Rufus Stone	18.00
Shakespeare's House, sm	100.00
St Nicholas Chapel	170.00
Tobacco jar, terra cotta, 5½"	45.00
Tyg, 1-hdl	9.00
Urn, Nottingham	13.00
Vase, amphora, 1911 Coronation, 4"	42.50
Vase, bud; sm	10.00
Vase, Southport	15.00
Vase, Southwold, 6"	42.50
Yorick's Skull, sm	65.00

Crested China

Mother Shipton, Arcadian, $35.00; Caddie on golf ball, Arcadian, $55.00; Jovial monk holding glass, Arcadian, $25.00; Grotesque figure, German, $25.00; Bathing Bell on ashtray, Wilton, $80.00.

Arcadian, bottle, whiskey; '1 Special Irish,' Arms of Wicklow	25.00
Arcadian, ewer, Wembly	18.00
Arcadian, milk churn, Chippenham Ancient, 2¼"	10.00
Carlton, bust of Edward VII	75.00
Carlton, figurine, Fisher girl	50.00
Carlton, pot, hdls, w/lid	22.00
Savoy, tank, HMS Donner Blitzen, Portsmouth, 6"	45.00
Shelley, rose bowl, Stafford, silver, #147	32.50
Willow, figurine, Burns at the plough	75.00
Willow, model of Hay Castle, Debreos of Hay Castle, 3½"	45.00
Willow, pig, City of St Andrews, 3¼" L	28.00
Willow, Shakespeare Cottage	75.00

Gouda

Since the 18th century the main center of the pottery industry in Holland was in Gouda. One of its earliest industries, the manufacture of clay pipes, continues to the present day. The artware so easily recognized by collectors today was first produced about 1885. It was decorated in the Art Nouveau manner. Stylized florals, birds, and geometrics were favored motifs; only rarely is the scene naturalistic. The Nouveau influence was strong until about 1915. Art Deco was attempted but with less success. Though most of the ware is finished in a matt glaze, glossy pieces in both pastels and dark colors are found on occasion and command higher prices. Decoration on the glossy ware is usually very well executed. Most of the workshops failed during the Depression, though earthenware is still being made in Gouda and carries the Gouda mark. Until very recently Regina was still making a limited amount of the old Gouda-style pottery in a matt finish. Watch for the Gouda name, which is usually a part of the backstamp of the various manufacturers.

Bowl, Beek, mc design, house mk, 4x9"	135.00
Chamberstick, Danica, 5-color design, house mk, 2¾x5½"	88.00

Figurine, girl w/flowers in front of fence, rare, 6"	250.00
Ginger jar, vivid floral, high dome lid, mk Gouda, 16½"	900.00
Lamp base, sgn Kelor, 18"	295.00
Pitcher, Arco Royal, glossy, high hdl, 9½"	165.00

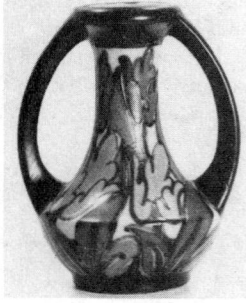

Vase, large stylized florals, blue and rose with green leaves on cream, handles, #7303, 10¼", $85.00

Vase, berries, orange on tan, bulbous, Zenigh, 2½"	30.00
Vase, continuous scene w/path, windmill, trees, Zuid, 9"	200.00
Vase, Deco flowers, Royal Zuid, 1930s, 3½", pr	95.00
Vase, floral, bulbous, 6"	130.00
Vase, iris, mini, 2"	60.00
Vase, mc band design on blk gloss, #814/Mero Plazuid, 11"	500.00
Vase, Nouveau design, high glaze, ca 1896, 11"	650.00
Vase, poppies, wine/purple/gr on lt & dk gr, sgn TR, 17"	350.00
Vase, starburst floral, Arnhem, blk matt, 2½"	35.00
Vase, stylized mc floral on wht clay, Arnhem, hdls, 11x11"	475.00

Graniteware

Graniteware, made of a variety of metals with enamel coatings, derives its name from its appearance. The speckled, swirled, or mottled effect of the vari-colored enamels may look like granite — but there the resemblance stops. It wasn't especially durable! Expect at least minor chipping if you plan to collect.

Graniteware was featured in 1876 at Phily's Expo. It was mass-produced in quantity, and enough of it has survived to make at least the common items easily affordable. Color, shape, and size are important considerations in evaluating an item; cobalt blue and white, green and white, brown and white, and old red and white swirled items are unusual, thus more expensive. Pieces of heavier weight, seam constructed, riveted, and those with wooden handles and tin or matching graniteware lids are usually older.

For further study we recommend *The Collector's Encyclopedia of Graniteware, Colors, Shapes, and Values*, Books I and II, by our advisor, Helen Greguire. Both are available from the author. For information on how to order, see her listing in the Directory under New York. For the address of the National Graniteware Society, see the section on Clubs, Newsletters, and Catalogs.

Ashtray, gray med mottle, red lettering, ⅜x4½", NM	225.00
Ashtray, red w/blk Polar Ware lettering, 1x4⅝" dia, M	185.00
Bean pot, cobalt & wht lg swirl, blk trim, 7x6⅞", EX	525.00
Bed pan, gray lg mottle, Nesco label, 4x19", M	95.00
Bread raiser, cobalt & wht med mottle, w/lid, 17¼" dia, EX	425.00
Bucket, bl & wht fine mottle, blk trim, label, w/lid, 5x4⅝", M	195.00
Bucket, blk & wht lg swirl int/ext, blk trim, w/lid, 7½", EX	495.00
Bucket, dinner; cobalt & wht lg swirl, 3-pc, Azurelite, VG	525.00
Bucket, slop; bl & wht med mottle w/cobalt, 10¼" dia, NM	195.00
Bucket, slop; red & wht lg mottle, red trim/wht int, 11¾", NM	495.00
Butter dish, solid yel, blk trim, French label, 7⅝" base, M	245.00
Can, cream; bl & wht lg swirl w/cobalt, Bl Dmn Ware, 7¾", NM	675.00
Can, cream; dk gr & wht lg swirl, blk trim, 7¾x4", EX	1,200.00

Can, cream; gray lg mottle, Made...USA by Savory label, 5¼", M .195.00
Can, cream; gray med mottle, lock lid, 5¾x3¼", NM 225.00
Can, milk; brn & wht lg swirl, blk trim, 9½x4¾", NM 995.00
Can, milk; dk bl & wht med mottled relish, wht int, 8⅞", NM ..250.00
Can, milk; lt bl & wht wavy mottle w/blk, Lee Mfg, 8¾", M ...1,095.00
Can, milk; red & wht lg swirl w/dk bl trim, 9¼x4⅞", EX 2,700.00
Candlestick, cobalt & wht lg swirl w/blk trim, 2¼", EX 1,100.00
Candlestick, solid red w/wht & navy trim, label, 1¾x5⅛", EX ...395.00
Candlestick, solid yel int/ext, blk hdl & trim, 5¾" dia, G 65.00
Canister, cobalt & wht lg mottle, cobalt trim, w/lid, 6⅝", EX 300.00
Canister, solid wht w/dk bl trim & lettering, 7½x5", M 85.00
Castor set, gray lg mottle, pewter trim, 6-pc, M 3,500.00
Chamber pot, bl & wht lg swirl w/blk, Azure label, 6½", EX 255.00
Coaster/ashtray, solid maroon, label, ¾x3" top dia, M 75.00
Coffee biggin, cobalt & wht lg swirl, 10⅛x3⅝", EX 725.00
Coffee biggin, mauve pk & wht lg swirl, blk trim, 10¾", NM 495.00
Coffee biggin, red & wht med mottle, red trim, 4-pc, 9¼", NM .595.00
Coffee biggin, solid yel, wht int & spreaders, 9", EX 90.00
Coffee boiler, gr & wht relish, cobalt trim, 11¼", EX 195.00
Coffee boiler, solid gray, EX 85.00
Coffeepot, bl & wht wavy mottle w/blk, 9¼", NM 375.00
Coffeepot, deep sea gr shaded to moss gr, wht int, 9", NM 325.00
Coffeepot, gr & wht lg swirl, Emerald Ware, NM 475.00
Coffeepot, gray med mottle, tin lid, Old Holland label, 7¾", NM ..135.00
Coffeepot, lt bl & wht lg swirl, wht int, seamless, 10½", M 495.00
Coffeepot, red & wht lg swirl, blk trim, seamed, 9½", EX 200.00
Coffeepot, red & wht med swirl, cobalt trim, 9½x5⅞", EX 1,650.00
Coffeepot, red int/ext, blk trim, bulbous, 9", NM 65.00
Cup, dk bl & wht med mottled relish, wht int, 2⅜x4", EX 55.00
Cup, yel & wht lg mottle int/ext, blk trim, 1960s, 2x3⅛", M 45.00
Cup & saucer, bl & wht lg splash-type mottle, 4" dia, EX 135.00
Cup & saucer, gray & wht med mottle, label, 4½", 15¾", M 125.00
Cuspidor, cobalt & wht lg swirl, cobalt trim, 2-pc, 11¼", EX 425.00
Cuspidor, lav-bl & wht lg swirl w/blk, 10⅝" dia, EX 295.00
Custard cup, bl & wht fine mottle, cobalt trim, 4¼" dia, NM 95.00
Custard cup, gr w/cream int, 2¼x3⅝" top dia, M 55.00
Dbl boiler, bl & wht lg swirl w/blk trim, 6⅝" dia, NM 395.00
Dbl boiler, blk & wht lg swirl int/ext, chrome lid, 8¼", NM 295.00
Dust pan, solid red, 10⅜x10½", NM 245.00
Egg cup, wht w/bl chicken wire, cobalt trim, 1½x1⅞", NM 135.00
Egg cup, wht w/blk trim, Polar Ware Co, M 110.00
Fry pan, bl & wht lg mottle, wht int, 10¼" dia, EX 195.00
Fry pan, lav-bl & wht lg swirl w/blk trim, 2x9⅞", EX 285.00
Funnel, bl & wht lg swirl w/blk trim, 4½x3¼" dia, EX 360.00
Funnel, wht w/blk trim & hdl, squat, 7½" dia, EX 45.00
Grater, solid dk gray, 11¾x4⅞", EX 235.00
Jug, batter; gray lg mottle, Primo Aluminum Enamel Ware, NM ...525.00
Kettle, cream w/gr trim, 16 ribs, 6x7⅜", NM 40.00
Kettle, gray lg mottle, seamless, w/lid, 6½x9", EX 110.00
Measure, aqua & wht lg swirl w/cobalt trim, strap hdl, 5", NM ..295.00
Measure, gray lg mottle, Royal Granite...Nesco label, 9½", M 250.00
Measure, lav-bl & wht swirl, blk trim, 9⅞x6½", EX 395.00
Measure, oyster; gray lg mottle, seamed, 4⅛x3½", EX 225.00
Mold, melon; solid bl, wht int, tin lid, 7¾" L, NM 155.00
Mold, tube; cobalt w/wht int, ribbed style, 8¼" dia, EX 95.00
Mug, brn & wht lg swirl, wht int, cobalt trim, 3⅛x4", EX 135.00
Mug, dk gr & wht lg mottle, Chrysolite, 2¾x2¾", EX 155.00
Mug, gray, mk US on bottom 65.00
Mug, red & wht lg mottle, wht int, blk trim, 3x3⅜", NM 40.00
Mug, red & wht lg swirl, cobalt trim, seamless, 3⅛x3¼", NM 525.00
Pail, water; solid gray, Royal Granite, salesman's sample, VG 350.00
Pan, drainer; brn & wht lg marbleized int/ext, 11" dia, NM 40.00
Pan, lady finger; gray lg mottle, Agate...L&G Mfg, 11½", NM ...395.00
Pan, muffin; cobalt w/sm wht flecks int/ext, 11-cup, 11" L, M 125.00

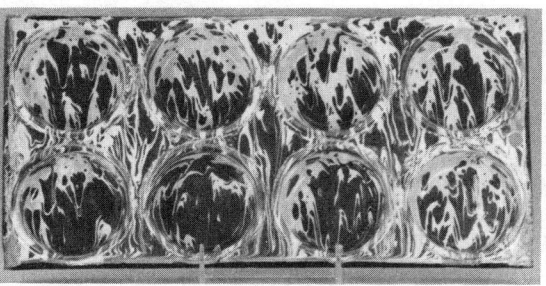

Muffin tin, cobalt and white large swirl, 8-cup, 7x14", EX, $525.00.

Pan, muffin; gray lg mottle, Turk's head style, 8-cup, NM 135.00
Pan, muffin; redipped brn & wht lg mottle, 8-cup, 14" L, NM ...285.00
Pan, muffin; solid gray, 12-cup, EX 55.00
Pan, pudding; red & wht lg swirl, cobalt trim, 3x8½", EX 400.00
Pan, pudding; solid wht w/cobalt trim, 7" dia, M 35.00
Pan, sauce; bl & wht lg mottle, blk trim, convex, 10" dia, EX 165.00
Pan, sauce; solid red-orange, wht int, blk trim, 6" dia, EX 20.00
Pan, tart; bl & wht fine mottle, cobalt trim, 5⅝" dia, M 75.00
Pan, tart; gray med mottle, La Fayette label, 1x6" dia, M 50.00
Pan, tube; gray, EX 45.00
Pickle castor, bl w/apple blossoms, pewter trim, 3-pc, M 2,500.00
Pie plate, deep sea gr shaded to moss gr, wht int, 9" dia, M 65.00
Pie plate, solid cobalt, wht int, ⅞x9" dia, G 25.00
Pitcher, milk; gray lg mottle, seamless, squat, 6⅞x4½", NM 185.00
Pitcher, milk; 5-color lg swirl, wht int, seamless, 9", EX 825.00
Pitcher, water; aqua & wht lg swirl, cobalt trim, 10¼", M 395.00
Pitcher, water; bl & wht lg swirl w/blk trim, 9", EX 525.00
Pitcher, water; gr & wht med mottle, Elite, VG 175.00
Pitcher, water; gray lg mottle, seamless, 10⅝x7", NM 185.00
Pitcher, water; mauve rose, wht int, blk trim, 9¼", NM 85.00
Pitcher & bowl, bl & wht lg swirl w/cobalt, Bl Dmn Ware, NM ..1,850.00
Plate, lt bl & wht med swirl int/ext, 10", EX 155.00
Platter, bl & wht lg swirl w/cobalt trim, Bl Dmn Ware, 14", NM .395.00
Roaster, blk bottom, Delft bl lid, seamless, 8½" dia, EX 65.00
Roaster, cream & gr int/ext, emb Savoy, 8x17", EX 85.00
Roaster, lt bl & wht lg swirl w/blk, w/lid, 11¾" dia, M 195.00
Roaster, solid red int/ext, bl trim, wire insert, 14¼", NM 110.00
Scoop, cobalt & wht lg swirl, wht int, 2⅜x6⅝", G 345.00
Scoop, solid wht, 9¼" L, EX 135.00
Soap dish, cobalt & wht lg swirl, EX 410.00
Soup tureen, white shaded to lt bl w/gold bands, Austria, NM ...275.00
Spoon, bl & wht lg mottle, blk hdl, wht int, 13", EX 110.00
Stock pot, bl & wht med swirl, wht int, w/lid, 13" dia, EX 125.00
Strainer, lt bl & wht lg mottle, wht int, 6⅝" dia, EX 315.00
Strainer, sink; dk cobalt & wht med mottle, teardrop form, EX .285.00
Sugar shaker, reddish-brn & wht med mottle, wht int, EX 285.00
Syrup, cobalt & wht lg swirl, Azurelite, 7½", NM 1,225.00
Tea strainer, gray & wht lg swirl int/ext, 4" dia, EX 165.00
Teakettle, bl & wht lg swirl, blk knob & trim, 9" dia, EX 575.00
Teakettle, cobalt & wht lg mottle, blk trim, 7½x10", EX 375.00
Teakettle, pk & wht marbleized, blk trim, 6¾x9" dia, NM 495.00
Teakettle, solid gray, NM 125.00
Teakettle, solid red, cobalt int, blk trim, label, 7x9", M 275.00
Teakettle, solid wht, blk trim & knob, wood bail, 8x8", NM 70.00
Teapot, bl & wht fine mottle, w/lid, Manning Bowman & Co, M .265.00
Teapot, bl cobblestones w/wht & brn chicken wire, 8", EX 495.00
Teapot, brn & wht lg swirl, NM 425.00
Teapot, cobalt & wht lg swirl w/blk, Belle shape, 7", EX 900.00
Teapot, cobalt w/wht veins, wht int, mk Pat, 5¾", EX 135.00

Teapot, deep red & wht lg swirl, blk trim, 1950, 7¾", NM 145.00
Teapot, gray med mottle, metal trim, 6¼x4" dia, EX 595.00
Teapot, lt gray lg mottle, seamed spout, 4x3⅛", EX 195.00
Teapot, robin's egg bl, gooseneck, squatty, EX 350.00
Teapot, wht & bl lg swirl 'Snow on the Mountain,' 9x5½", EX ..255.00
Teapot, wht w/violet band, pewter trim, squat, lg, M 275.00
Thermos, wht w/blk trim, VG 130.00
Tray, bl & wht lg swirl w/blk, oblong, 15⅝", EX 785.00
Tray, bl & wht med mottle, wht int, rectangular, NM 145.00
Tray, gray lg mottle, mk L&G Mfg, 13⅜x9½", NM 135.00
Tray, yel & wht lg swirl, blk trim, 1950s, 17¾" dia, M 85.00
Trivet, solid wht, fancy cutouts, 4-ftd, 7¾" dia, M 110.00
Tumbler, bl & wht fine mottle, blk trim, 2¾x2¾", NM 115.00
Tumbler, cobalt & wht lg swirl w/blk trim, VG 450.00
Wash basin, cobalt & wht lg mottle, salesman's sample, M 130.00
Wash basin, wht w/gold bands & blk trim, label, 12" dia, EX 60.00
Water cooler, lt bl & wht lg swirl, 2-pc, Lava Ware, EX 750.00

Green Opaque

Introduced in 1887 by the New England Glass Company, this ware is very scarce due to the fact that it was produced for less than one year. It is characterized by its soft green color and a wavy band of gold reserving a mottled blue metallic stain. It is usually found in satin; examples with a shiny finish are extremely rare.

Basket, ruffled Hobnail amber rim, amber hdl, 8¾x9⅛" 550.00
Bowl, everted lip, shallow, 7" 750.00
Bowl, waisted rim, 4x8" 600.00
Bowl, 3⅜x9" 700.00
Cruet, orig stopper 1,150.00
Punch cup 350.00
Shakers, squat, 2¾", pr 475.00
Spooner, 3¾" 850.00
Toothpick holder, gold trim 1,150.00
Tumbler, lemonade; w/hdl, 5" 900.00
Tumbler, 3¾" 850.00
Vase, flared, M gold & mottling, 6" 900.00

Greenaway, Kate

Kate Greenaway was an English artist who lived from 1846 to 1901. She gained worldwide fame as an illustrator of children's books, drawing children clothed in the styles worn by proper English and American boys and girls of the very early 1800s. Her book, *Under the Willow Tree,* published in 1878, was the first of many. Her sketches appeared in leading magazines, and her greeting cards were in great demand. Manufacturers of china, pottery, and metal products copied her characters to decorate children's dishes, tiles, and salt and pepper shakers as well as many other items. See also Napkin Rings.

Box, painted glass with boy and girl on lid, $450.00.

Almanac, 1886, wht leather, Sangorski/Sutcliffe 475.00
Almanac, 1892, Greenaway illus, EX 85.00
Book, Language of Flowers, leather cover, 1880s, EX 70.00
Book, Mother Goose, pre-1918, Frederick Warne, G 65.00
Book, paint; Little Folks, hardcover, early, EX 65.00
Book, Pied Piper of Hamlin, Greenaway illus, NM 65.00
Book, Under the Willow, Routledge, London, 1st ed, orig cloth .150.00
Bowl, Daisy & Button, amber; R&B SP holder w/girl & dog 515.00
Butter pat, children playing 40.00
Engraving, Harper's Bazaar, Jan 1879, full-pg 25.00
Match holder, ornate SP, girl in fancy clothes, Tufts 195.00
Paperweight, CI, girl in lg bonnet & Victorian dress, 3x2¾" 110.00
Pickle castor, bl; SP fr w/2 girls, blown-out florals 455.00
Pitcher, milk; bsk, girl figural, head is lid, 6½" 165.00
Stickpin holder, SP, girl figural, Meriden, 4" 125.00
Tea set, semiporc, floral motif, 3-pc 70.00
Toothpick holder, bsk, girl sits on stump, basket on bk 40.00
Toothpick holder, clear glass, 2 girls by basket 100.00

Greentown Glass

Greentown glass is a term referring to the product of the Indiana Tumbler and Goblet Company of Greentown, Indiana, ca 1894 to 1903. Their earlier pressed glass patterns were #11, a pseudo-cut glass design; #137, Pleat Band; and #200, Austrian. Another line, Dewey, was designed in 1898. Many lovely colors were produced in addition to crystal. Jacob Rosenthal, who was later affiliated with Fenton, developed his famous chocolate glass in 1900. The rich, shaded opaque brown glass was an overnight success. Two new patterns, Leaf Bracket and Cactus, were designed to display the glass to its best advantage, but previously existing molds were also used. In only three years Rosenthal developed yet another important color formula, golden agate. The Holly Amber pattern was designed especially for its production. The Dolphin covered dish with a fish finial is perhaps the most common and easily recognized piece ever produced. Other animal dishes were also made; all are highly collectible. There have been many repros — not all are marked! The symbol (+) at the end of some of the following lines was used to indicate items that have been reproduced.

Our advisors for this category are Jerry and Sandy Garrett; they are listed in the Directory under Indiana. See the Pattern Glass section for clear pressed glass; only colored items are listed here.

Animal dish, bird w/berry, emerald gr (+) 265.00
Animal dish, bird w/berry, Golden Agate 1,600.00
Animal dish, bird w/berry, teal bl 300.00
Animal dish, cat on hamper, canary, tall 475.00
Animal dish, cat on hamper, chocolate, low 600.00
Animal dish, cat on hamper, cobalt, tall 450.00
Animal dish, cat on hamper, Nile gr, tall (+) 1,400.00
Animal dish, dolphin, beaded, clear 290.00
Animal dish, dolphin, beaded, cobalt 600.00
Animal dish, dolphin, beaded, Golden Agate 900.00
Animal dish, dolphin, sawtooth, amber (+) 625.00
Animal dish, dolphin, sawtooth, canary 600.00
Animal dish, dolphin, sawtooth, cobalt 600.00
Animal dish, dolphin, smooth, chocolate 400.00
Animal dish, fighting cocks, amber 850.00
Animal dish, fighting cocks, canary 1,000.00
Animal dish, fighting cocks, cobalt 950.00
Animal dish, hen on nest, amber 170.00
Animal dish, hen on nest, Nile gr 1,400.00
Animal dish, hen on nest, teal bl 200.00
Animal dish, rabbit, amber (+) 165.00

Animal dish, rabbit, cobalt 450.00
Austrian, bowl, canary, rectangular, 8¼x5¼" 175.00
Austrian, butter dish, chocolate, child's 650.00
Austrian, cake stand, canary 290.00
Austrian, compote, canary, low ped 225.00
Austrian, cordial, emerald gr 235.00
Austrian, creamer, cobalt, child's 250.00
Austrian, goblet, canary 200.00
Austrian, punch cup, emerald gr 180.00
Austrian, sugar bowl, canary, w/lid, 4" 225.00
Austrian, vase, Nile gr, 6" 375.00
Austrian, wine, amber 275.00
Beehive, vase, bud; amber 275.00
Brazen Shield, bowl, bl, 7½" 135.00
Brazen Shield, compote, bl, w/lid, 6⅜" 185.00
Brazen Shield, pitcher, bl 250.00
Brazen Shield, spooner, bl 100.00
Brazen Shield, tumbler, bl 75.00
Cactus, bowl, chocolate, 8¼" 150.00
Cactus, cake stand, chocolate 1,250.00
Cactus, compote, chocolate, 9¼" 275.00
Cactus, sauce dish, chocolate, flat 140.00
Cactus, tumbler, iced tea; chocolate, 5" 95.00
Cord Drapery, bowl, cobalt, ftd, 6¼" 160.00
Cord Drapery, bowl, emerald gr, rectangular 190.00
Cord Drapery, creamer, amber, 4¼" dia 150.00
Cord Drapery, mug, amber, ftd 175.00
Cord Drapery, salt shaker, emerald gr 175.00
Cord Drapery, sugar bowl, cobalt, w/lid 195.00
Cord Drapery, syrup jug, chocolate 210.00
Cord Drapery, toothpick holder, amber 350.00
Cupid, butter dish, wht opaque 115.00
Cupid, spooner, Nile gr 325.00
Cupid, sugar bowl, chocolate, w/lid 450.00
Dewey, bowl, canary, 8" 85.00
Dewey, butter dish, cobalt, 4" 200.00
Dewey, creamer, chocolate, 4" 90.00
Dewey, creamer, Nile gr, 4" 150.00
Dewey, creamer, wht opaque, 4" 85.00
Dewey, pitcher, amber 150.00
Dewey, serpentine tray, amber, lg 75.00
Dewey, serpentine tray, emerald gr, lg 75.00
Dewey, sugar bowl, canary, w/lid, 2¼" dia 80.00
Dewey, tumbler, emerald gr 70.00
Diamond Prisms, tumbler, chocolate 600.00
Early Diamond, pitcher, amber 250.00
Early Diamond, tumbler, canary 165.00
Fleur-de-Lis, butter dish, chocolate 650.00
Fleur-de-Lis, nappy, chocolate, hdls 160.00
Fleur-de-Lis, pitcher, chocolate 1,000.00
Fleur-de-Lis, tumbler, chocolate 140.00
Greentown Daisy, butter dish, frosted emerald gr 115.00
Greentown Daisy, mustard pot, wht opaque, w/lid 65.00
Greentown Daisy, sugar bowl, chocolate, w/lid 195.00
Herringbone Buttress, bowl, amber, 5¼" 275.00
Herringbone Buttress, bowl, amber, 8¼" 325.00
Herringbone Buttress, bowl, emerald gr, 9¼" 235.00
Herringbone Buttress, cordial, emerald gr, 3⅜" 215.00
Herringbone Buttress, punch cup, emerald gr 140.00
Herringbone Buttress, vase, emerald gr, 6" 195.00
Holly, plate, cobalt, 7½" 3,000.00
Holly, spooner, rose agate 9,000.00
Holly, tumbler, wht agate 1,750.00
Holly Amber, bowl, 8½" 700.00

Holly Amber, butter dish, ped ft 2,600.00
Holly Amber, butter dish (+) 1,800.00

Holly Amber, compote, footed, 10¼x8¼", $2,500.00.

Holly Amber, cruet, w/stopper 2,000.00
Holly Amber, mug, 4" (+) 415.00
Holly Amber, pitcher 2,950.00
Holly Amber, relish, oval, 4½x7½" 450.00
Holly Amber, toothpick holder (+) 450.00
Holly Amber, vase, ped ft, 8" 2,000.00
Holly Amber, vase, 6" 750.00
Leaf Bracket, butter dish, cobalt 1,200.00
Leaf Bracket, cruet, chocolate 200.00
Leaf Bracket, pitcher, chocolate 450.00
Leaf Bracket, sugar bowl, chocolate 160.00
Mug, dog & child, Nile gr 375.00
Mug, Herringbone, chocolate 85.00
Mug, indoor drinking scene, chocolate, 5" 195.00
Mug, indoor drinking scene, Nile gr, 8½" 450.00
Mug, Serenade, chocolate, 4¾" 175.00
Mug, Serenade, emerald gr, 4¾" 110.00
Nappy, Leaf Bracket, triangular, hdls, 3-ftd, 3¾x5¾" 85.00
Novelty, Connecticut Skillet, chocolate 1,000.00
Novelty, corn vase, amber, 4⅝" 175.00
Novelty, creamer, Indian head, Nile gr, w/lid 800.00
Novelty, cuff set, amber 350.00
Novelty, hairbrush, Nile gr 575.00
Novelty, trunk, amber (+) 225.00
Pattern #11, bowl, emerald gr, 6¼" dia 65.00
Pattern #11, toothpick holder, emerald gr 80.00
Pattern #11, tumbler, iced tea; chocolate 375.00
Pitcher, Paneled, chocolate 575.00
Pitcher, Ruffled Eye, amber 175.00
Pitcher, Ruffled Eye, canary 285.00
Pleat Band, cordial, canary 200.00
Pleat Band, salt shaker, amber 85.00
Pleat Band, salt shaker, chocolate 225.00
Scalloped Flange, vase, Nile gr 325.00
Shuttle, bowl, chocolate, 8¼" 500.00
Shuttle, goblet, chocolate 800.00
Shuttle, mug, cobalt 325.00
Shuttle, salt shaker, chocolate 325.00
Shuttle, tumbler, chocolate 125.00
Teardrop & Tassel, butter dish, cobalt 225.00
Teardrop & Tassel, pitcher, emerald gr 250.00
Teardrop & Tassel, salt shaker, Nile gr 325.00
Teardrop & Tassel, spooner, cobalt 150.00
Teardrop & Tassel, spooner, emerald gr 135.00
Teardrop & Tassel, sugar bowl, Nile gr, w/lid 350.00

Toothpick holder, dog's head, frosted amber 300.00
Toothpick holder, picture fr, Nile gr 400.00
Toothpick holder, sheaf of wheat, amber 200.00
Toothpick holder, sheaf of wheat, teal bl 250.00
Tumbler, Sawtooth, chocolate 110.00
Tumbler, Uneeda Biscuit, chocolate, tall 150.00

Grueby

William Henry Grueby joined the firm of the Low Art Tile Works at the age of fifteen and in 1894, after several years of experience in the production of architectural tiles, founded his own plant, the Grueby Faience Company, in Boston, Massachusetts. Grueby began experimenting with the idea of producing art pottery and had soon perfected a fine glaze (soft and without gloss) in shades of blue, gray, yellow, brown, and his most successful, cucumber green. In 1900 his exhibit at the Paris Exposition Universelle won three gold medals.

Grueby pottery was hand thrown and hand decorated in the Arts and Crafts style. Vertically thrust stylized leaves and flowers in relief were the most common decorative devices. Tiles continued to be an important product, unique (due to the matt glaze decoration) as well as durable. Grueby tiles were often a full inch thick. Obviously incompatible with the Art Nouveau style, the artware was discontinued soon after 1910. The ware is marked in one of several ways: 'Grueby Pottery, Boston, USA'; 'Grueby, Boston, Mass.'; or 'Grueby Faience.' The artware is often artist signed. Our advisor for this category is David Rago; he is listed in the Directory under New Jersey.

Bowl, bsk, cvd/tooled leaves, shaped rim, #119, Post, 9", EX 825.00
Bowl, gr, cvd leaves & stylized flowers, squat, rare, 5x8" 3,520.00
Bowl, gr, leaves, inset neck/extended shoulder, #143/sgn, 4x9" .1,500.00
Bowl vase, teal bl, wide upright leaves, 5x3", EX 600.00
Frieze, Nouveau boat/waves, 6-color, 2-tile, 8½x17", EX 2,000.00
Lamp base, gr, long tooled/appl leaves, bbl shape, 12¼" 3,000.00
Tile, chamberstick & Grueby Tile, advertising pc, 6x4½" 900.00
Tile, galleon, brn/ivory on gr, sgn EA, 6" 450.00
Tile, tulip, yel/gr on gr, EX colors, no mk, 6x6" 500.00
Tile, yel rabbit/gr leaves on med gr, sgn CA, pewter fr, 6x6" 600.00
Tile, 3 emb/cvd elephants, natural colors, sgn FW, 5½x8½" ...4,100.00
Vase, bl, long wide-rib neck, bulbous base w/leaves, 12½" 2,200.00
Vase, curdled gr, hand thrown, long cylinder neck, 13", NM ..1,800.00
Vase, dk gr, sm/lg appl leaves alternate, squat body, rpr, 7" 1,100.00
Vase, dk gr, subtle leaves, tiny opening, 5¾x6¾" 800.00
Vase, gr, bulbous w/long can neck, 13" 1,650.00

Vase, green, two rows of wide tooled leaves on bulbous body, 19x12", $8,250.00.

Vase, gr, overlapping leaves, MA Seaman, #135, 9", NM 1,100.00
Vase, gr, ovoid, 2¾" 220.00
Vase, gr, 4 wide full-length appl leaves, 7¾x3¾" 1,100.00
Vase, gr, 5 lg upright leaves, scroll hdls, att Post, 11" 7,100.00
Vase, gr w/EX feathering, lg tooled leaves, sgn WP, 8" 5,000.00
Vase, gr w/yel buds, bronze rim, bulb base w/leaves, MS, 13" ..5,500.00
Vase, iris, red & bl, hdls, hole in base, 15x10" 20,000.00
Vase, lt gr, lg tooled leaves around body, Erickson, 7" 950.00
Vase, wht, tooled/appl short & long leaves, 9½x7¼" 1,600.00
Vase, yel, dbl-leaf rows, gourd shape, Kendrick, 11x7" 14,000.00
Vase, yel, ribbed gourd w/ 'stem' neck, 9x8" 4,000.00

Gustavsberg

Gustavsberg Pottery, founded near Stockholm, Sweden, in the late 1700s, manufactured faience, creamware, and porcelain in the English taste until the end of the 19th century. During the 20th century, the factory has produced some inventive modernistic designs, often signed by their artists. Wilhelm Kage (1889-1960) is best remembered for Argenta, a stoneware body decorated in silver overlay, introduced in the 1930s. Usually a mottled green, Argenta can also be found in cobalt blue and white. Other lines included Cintra (an exceptionally translucent porcelain), Farsta (copper-glazed ware), and Farstarust (iron oxide geometric overlay). Designer Stig Lindberg's work, which dates from the 1940s through the early 1970s, includes slab-built figures and a full range of tableware. Some pieces of Gustavsberg are dated.

Dish, fish shape, creamware, 13" 75.00
Figurine, girl holding cat, Lisa Larsen 175.00
Vase, bl, bottle shape, made by Friberg, ca 1950, 5" 300.00
Vase, cut-bk decor, dk bl over lt bl, sgn EE, 1913, 5" 275.00
Vase, ocean life, bl/dk gray on wht, Lindberg design, 6" 100.00

Hagen-Renacker

Best known for their line of miniature animal figures, Hagen-Renaker was founded in Monrovia, California, in 1946. In addition to the animals and under license from the Disney Studio, they made replicas of characters from several popular Disney films. The firm relocated in San Dimas in 1966, where they remain active to the present time. Their wares are sometimes marked with an incised 'HR,' a stamped 'Hagen-Renaker' or part of the name, or paper labels. For more information, we recommend *The Collector's Encyclopedia of California Pottery* by Jack Chipman.

Bank, Pig, from Disney Film: 3 Little Pigs, Fifties Series 300.00
Figurine, Arabian colt, 6¼x6¼" 120.00
Figurine, Arabian stallion, 9x11¼" 185.00
Figurine, baby Pegasus, Walt Disney line 150.00
Figurine, Bacchus, Fifties Series 175.00
Figurine, Carmencita, chihuahua pup begging, Masterson, 2" 75.00
Figurine, cottontail rabbit 60.00
Figurine, dodo bird, Blk Bsk line 65.00
Figurine, fox, flat face, Blk Bsk line, 4" 65.00
Figurine, goose, wht w/ornate bill & ft, standing, 6½" 45.00
Figurine, Miss Pepper, recumbent Morgan foal, '59, 2¾x4½" 175.00
Figurine, Pan on Greek column, 2-pc, Walt Disney line 220.00
Figurine, Pasha, baby elephant, Designers Workshop, '55, 3½" 65.00
Figurine, Peggy, squirrel, Designers Workshop, 4¼x4" 45.00
Figurine, rabbit baby, Designers Workshop, 2¼" 35.00
Figurine, unicorn, Walt Disney line 150.00
Figurine, 3 bears, ca 1950, papa: 2" 45.00

Plaque, prancing horses, 1950, 15x22" 150.00

Hagenauer

Carl Hagenauer founded his metal workshops in Vienna in 1898. He was joined by his son Karl in 1919. They produced a wide range of stylized sculptural designs in both metal and wood.

African child, stylized, copper neck ring, brass base, 5", EX 330.00
African hands & mask w/earring, surrealistic, 7x4x4" 475.00
Babies w/bronze collars, sits, crawls, stands (2"), set of 3 ....260.00
Cat, free-standing, slightly Cubist style, 3¾" L 220.00
Ducks, jtd wood, 1 w/inlaid eyes, 7½", 3", EX 700.00

Figure, carved wood dancing lady with curved brass leash attached to left thigh, marked, 22", $3,300.00.

Monkey, slightly Cubist style, 3¾" 400.00
Native, bronze w/dk patina, brass shield/upright spear, 8" 300.00
Native boy sitting on island w/palm tree, wood/bronze, 10" 850.00
Native throwing spear, bronze/brass, 5", EX 300.00
Nude dancer, dk bronze, on wood platform/bronze base, 12" ...1,100.00
Teddy bear w/outstretched arms, mini, 1", EX 200.00
2 bronze natives row wood canoe w/brass paddles, 7" L, EX 150.00

Hair Weaving

A rather unusual craft became popular during the mid-1800s. Human hair was used to make jewelry (rings, bracelets, lockets, etc.) by braiding and interlacing fine strands of hair into hollow forms with pearls and beads added for effect. Hair wreaths were also made, often using hair from deceased family members as well as the living. They were displayed in deep satin-lined frames along with mementoes of the weaver or her departed kin. The fad was abandoned before the turn of the century. Our advisor for this category is Steve DeGenaro; he is listed in the Directory under Ohio. See also Mourning Collectibles.

Wreath of hair, in 18x20" shadow box frame, $175.00.

Bracelet, 14k gold w/woven hair under crystal 245.00
Brooch, bow style, eng plaque, gold mts, 1850s 75.00
Brooch, woven loveknot w/eng center plaque, gold mts 150.00
Earrings, 3 woven acorns in dangle style, ca 1850, pr 165.00
Watch chain, braided hair w/2 sm garnets & moonstone, EX 75.00
Watch chain, 3 interwoven patterns, gold fittings, w/fob 60.00
Wreath, ornate design, lg, in pleated red satin shadow box 200.00

Hall

The Hall China Company of East Liverpool, Ohio, was established in 1903. Their earliest product was whiteware toilet seats, mugs, jugs, etc. By 1920 their restaurant-type dinnerware and cookingware had become so successful that Hall was assured of a solid future. They continue today to be one of the country's largest manufacturers of this type of product. Hall introduced the first of their famous teapots in 1920; new shapes and colors were added each year until about 1948, making them the largest teapot manufacturer in the world. These and the dinnerware lines of the thirties through the fifties have become popular collectibles. For more thorough study of the subject, we recommend *The Collector's Encyclopedia of Hall China* by Margaret and Kenn Whitmyer; their address may be found in the Directory under Ohio.

Blue Blossom, ball jug #4 ....75.00
Blue Blossom, casserole, Sundial #4 ....45.00
Blue Blossom, cookie jar, Sundial 275.00
Blue Bouquet, bowl, cereal; 6" 9.00
Blue Bouquet, bowl, fruit; 5½" 6.00
Blue Bouquet, bowl, salad; 9" 16.00
Blue Bouquet, bowl, Thick Rim, 7½" 16.00
Blue Bouquet, bowl, vegetable; rnd, 9¼" 22.00
Blue Bouquet, creamer, modern 10.00
Blue Bouquet, pie baker 25.00
Blue Bouquet, plate, 6" 5.00
Blue Bouquet, plate, 7¼" 7.00
Blue Bouquet, platter, oval, 11¼" 18.00
Blue Bouquet, teapot, Boston 95.00
Blue Garden, bowl, Thick Rim, 7½" 25.00
Blue Garden, water bottle, Zephyr style 250.00
Cactus, bowl, Five Band, 7¼" 35.00
Cactus, cookie jar, Five Band 175.00
Cactus, stack set, Radiance 75.00
Cameo Rose, bowl, oval, 10½" 18.00
Cameo Rose, bowl, soup; flat, 8" 15.00
Cameo Rose, plate, 9¼" 10.00
Cameo Rose, saucer 5.00
Cameo Rose, tidbit tray, 3-tier 45.00
Carrot/Golden Carrot, bean pot, New England #4 ....75.00
Carrot/Golden Carrot, bowl, Radiance, 7" 18.00
Carrot/Golden Carrot, syrup, Five Band 75.00
Clover/Golden Clover, batter bowl, Five Band 45.00
Crocus, bowl, fruit; 5½" 6.00
Crocus, bowl, oval 20.00
Crocus, bowl, soup; flat, 8½" 12.00
Crocus, coffeepot, Five Band 60.00
Crocus, creamer, Art Deco 17.50
Crocus, cup, St Denis 35.00
Crocus, jug, Simplicity 125.00
Crocus, leftover, rectangular 50.00
Crocus, mug, tankard style 45.00
Crocus, plate, 10" 30.00
Crocus, pretzel jar 100.00
Crocus, saucer 2.00

Crocus, shaker, hdl, ea	12.00
Crocus, sugar bowl, w/lid, Art Deco	27.50
Crocus, tidbit, 3-tier	45.00
Eggshell, bean pot, New England #4, Red Dot	65.00
Eggshell, host jug, Red Dot	50.00
Eggshell, mug, Tom & Jerry, Red Dot	10.00
Five Band, bowl, batter; red or cobalt	55.00
Five Band, coffeepot, red or cobalt	75.00
Five Band, jug, other colors, 5"	20.00
Heather Rose, bowl, salad; 9"	12.00
Heather Rose, coffeepot, Terrace	32.50
Heather Rose, creamer	6.00
Heather Rose, gravy boat, w/underplate	15.00
Heather Rose, platter, oval, 13¼"	13.00
Meadow Flower, casserole, Sundial #4	35.00
Medallion, jug, colors, ice lip, 5-pt	15.00
Mums, bowl, oval, 10¼"	15.00
Mums, creamer, Medallion	12.00
Mums, plate, 6"	4.00
No 488, bowl, Radiance, 9"	15.00
No 488, casserole, Sundial	35.00
No 488, custard	8.00
No 488, mug, Tom & Jerry	15.00
Orange Poppy, ball jug #3	45.00
Orange Poppy, bowl, fruit; 5½"	6.00
Orange Poppy, bowl, Radiance, 9"	17.50
Orange Poppy, bowl, soup; flat, 8½"	13.50
Orange Poppy, cake safe, metal	30.00
Orange Poppy, coffeepot, Great American	47.50
Orange Poppy, cup	8.00
Orange Poppy, leftover, loop hdl	40.00
Orange Poppy, plate, 7¼"	7.50
Orange Poppy, platter, oval, 13¼"	22.00
Orange Poppy, spoon	65.00
Orange Poppy, wastebasket, metal	37.50
Pastel Morning-Glory, bowl, fruit; 5½"	6.00
Pastel Morning-Glory, bowl, oval	17.50
Pastel Morning-Glory, bowl, salad; 9"	15.00
Pastel Morning-Glory, coffeepot, Terrace	50.00
Pastel Morning-Glory, drip jar, w/lid, Radiance	16.00
Pastel Morning-Glory, pie baker	20.00
Pastel Morning-Glory, platter, 13¼"	20.00
Pastel Morning-Glory, stack set, Radiance	65.00
Pert, jug, Chinese Red, 5"	12.00
Pert, sugar bowl, Chinese Red	8.00
Piggly Wiggly, baker, French, fluted	18.00
Piggly Wiggly, marmite, petite	30.00
Primrose, bowl, soup; flat, 8"	8.00
Primrose, plate, 9¼"	5.00
Radiance, bowl #2, ivory, 5¼"	4.00
Radiance, drip jar, red or cobalt	18.00
Red Poppy, bowl, cereal; D-style, 6"	12.00
Red Poppy, bowl, fruit; 5½"	5.00
Red Poppy, bowl, salad; 9"	15.00
Red Poppy, creamer, modern	12.00
Red Poppy, dust pan, metal	37.50
Red Poppy, gravy boat	20.00
Red Poppy, mixer cover, plastic	25.00
Red Poppy, pie baker	20.00
Red Poppy, plate, D-style, 8¼"	8.00
Red Poppy, platter, oval, D-style, 13¼"	20.00
Red Poppy, recipe box, metal	25.00
Red Poppy, sifter, metal	35.00
Red Poppy, sugar bowl, w/lid, Modern	15.00
Red Poppy, tablecloth, cotton	65.00
Red Poppy, tray, rectangular, metal	30.00
Red Poppy, waste can, rnd, metal	35.00
Ribbed, bean pot, russet or red	45.00
Royal Rose, bowl, salad; 9"	25.00
Royal Rose, casserole, Thick Rim	25.00
Sears' Arlington, bowl, fruit; 5¼"	5.00
Sears' Arlington, gravy boat, w/underplate	13.00
Sears' Arlington, platter, oval, 15½"	20.00
Sears' Monticello, bowl, fruit; 5¼"	4.50
Sears' Monticello, bowl, vegetable; w/lid	27.50
Sears' Monticello, pickle dish, 9"	6.00
Sears' Monticello, platter, oval, 13¼"	15.00
Sears' Mount Vernon, coffeepot, all-china	77.50
Sears' Mount Vernon, plate, 8"	4.00
Sears' Mount Vernon, saucer	2.00
Sears' Richmond, bowl, cereal; 6¼"	5.00
Sears' Richmond, bowl, vegetable; w/lid	25.00
Sears' Richmond, gravy boat, w/underplate	13.00
Sears' Richmond, platter, oval, 15½"	22.50
Serenade, bowl, Radiance, 6"	7.50
Serenade, coffeepot, drip; Medallion	25.00
Serenade, cup, D-style	7.00
Serenade, plate, 6"	3.00
Serenade, platter, D-style, 11¼"	15.00
Silhouette, bowl, fruit; 5½"	6.00
Silhouette, bowl, salad; 9"	15.00
Silhouette, coffee dispenser	75.00
Silhouette, coffeepot, Five Band	45.00
Silhouette, drip jar, w/lid, Medallion	20.00
Silhouette, match safe	45.00
Silhouette, sugar bowl, w/lid, Medallion	16.00
Springtime, ball jug #3	40.00
Springtime, bowl, rnd, D-style, 9¼"	15.00
Springtime, plate, D-style, 9"	6.00
Springtime, platter, oval, D-style	15.00
Teapot, Airflow, cobalt w/gold trim, 6-cup	50.00
Teapot, Aladdin, cobalt w/gold trim, oval infuser, 6-cup	85.00
Teapot, Albany, mahog w/gold trim, 6-cup	68.00
Teapot, Automobile, blk w/gold trim	600.00
Teapot, Automobile, red	700.00
Teapot, Baltimore, maroon, gold label, 6-cup	50.00
Teapot, Birdcage, maroon w/gold trim	250.00
Teapot, Boston, bl, gold label, 6-cup	35.00
Teapot, Carraway, bl, short spout, 6-cup	65.00
Teapot, Donut, red	250.00
Teapot, Football, maroon, 6-cup	600.00
Teapot, French, canary, flower decor, 4-cup	300.00
Teapot, French, emerald gr, flower decor, 4-cup	30.00
Teapot, Grape, ivory w/gold trim, 6-cup	85.00
Teapot, McCormick, maroon, w/infuser, 6-cup	35.00
Teapot, Melody, red, 6-cup	175.00
Teapot, Musical, bl, 6-cup	175.00
Teapot, New York, warm yel w/gold trim, 12-cup	50.00
Teapot, Parade, emerald gr w/gold trim, 6-cup	75.00
Teapot, Star, ivory w/gold, 6-cup	95.00
Teapot, Twinspout, maroon, 6-cup	65.00
Teapot, Windshield, blk w/gold trim, 6-cup	95.00
Teapot, Windshield, warm yel, 6-cup	75.00
Tulip, bowl, D-style, oval	19.00
Tulip, bowl, salad; 9"	18.00
Tulip, bowl, Thick Rim, 8½"	30.00
Tulip, custard	8.00
Tulip, plate, D-style, 6"	6.00

Tulip, platter, 13¼" 16.00
Tulip, saucer, D-style 2.00
Tulip, saucer, St Denis 6.00
Wild Poppy, coffeepot, Washington, 6-cup 175.00
Wildfire, bowl, salad; 9" 15.00
Wildfire, bowl, Thick Rim, 7½" 18.00
Wildfire, pie baker 30.00
Yellow Rose, bowl, cereal; 6" 8.00
Yellow Rose, creamer, Norse 11.00
Yellow Rose, plate, 8¼" 8.00

Zeisel Designs, Hallcraft

Bouquet, ashtray 10.00
Bouquet, bowl, celery; oval 16.00
Bouquet, casserole, 2-qt 27.50
Bouquet, gravy boat 17.50
Bouquet, percolator, electric 115.00
Bouquet, platter, 17" 25.00
Caprice, ashtray 5.00
Caprice, bowl, celery; oval 15.00
Caprice, butter dish 37.50
Caprice, casserole, 2-qt 22.00
Caprice, coffeepot, 6-cup 42.50
Caprice, jug, 1¼-qt 15.00
Caprice, onion soup, w/lid 17.50
Caprice, platter, 17" 22.00
Fantasy, ashtray 5.00
Fantasy, bowl, batter 37.50
Fantasy, bowl, celery; oval 12.50
Fantasy, bowl, vegetable; open, sq, 8¾" 15.00
Fantasy, casserole, Sundial 17.50
Fantasy, egg cup 17.50
Fantasy, platter, 15" 18.00
Fantasy, teapot, Streamline 250.00
Fern, ashtray 6.00
Fern, bowl, salad; 11¼" 11.00
Fern, plate, 6" 3.00
Fern, platter, 15" 17.50
Fern, sugar bowl, w/lid 13.00
Frost Flowers, cup 8.00
Frost Flowers, plate, 8" 6.50
Frost Flowers, vinegar bottle 22.00
Harlequin, coffeepot, 6-cup 29.00
Harlequin, vinegar bottle 22.00
Holiday, bowl, vegetable; open, sq, 8¾" 13.00
Holiday, butter dish 37.50
Mulberry, creamer 8.00
Mulberry, jug, 3-qt 17.50

Hallmark

Hallmark introduced a line of artplas (molded plastic) ornaments in 1973 that have quickly become popular with collectors. Since 1988 they have also produced miniature ornaments, which are very collectible as well, and a series of limited edition ornaments made for members of the Hallmark Keepsake Ornament Collectors' Club.

'Merry Miniatures' is a line of artplas 'Table Trimmers' made in 1973; collectors are avidly searching for these tiny figures in closets, children's toy boxes, and at flea markets.

The magazine, *The Ornament Collector*, edited by Rosie Wells, our advisor for this category, is available if you want more information on ornament collecting. Rosie also publishes a yearly official Secondary Market Price Guide on Hallmark Ornaments, Merry Miniatures, Stocking Hangers, Lapel Pins, Cookie Cutters, etc. Her address is listed in the Directory under Clubs, Newsletters, and Catalogs and again under Illinois. Values are for ornaments in mint condition and with their original boxes, while Merry Miniatures are assumed to be mint.

Ornaments

1975, Adorable Adornments-Santa, QX155-1, 3½" 235.00
1976, Nostalgia Ornaments-Drummer Boy, QX 130-1, 4¼" dia .150.00
1977, Old-Fashioned Customs Kissing Ball, QX 225-5, wht satin .145.00
1977, Yesteryears Collection-Reindeer, QX 173-5, 4¼" 135.00
1978, Panorama Ball, QX 145-6, 3⅝" dia 135.00
1979, Carousel Series-Christmas Carousel, QX 146-7, 3½" 185.00
1979, Holiday Scrimshaw, QX 152-7, angel form, 3½" 235.00
1980, Spot of Christmas Cheer, QX 153-4, teapot form, 2¾" 135.00
1981, Sailing Santa, QX 439-5, hot air balloon, 5" 190.00
1982, Holiday Wildlife-Cardinals, QX 313-3, wood/decofoam, 4" .425.00
1983, Christmas Wonderland, QX 221-9, glass ball, 3¼" 90.00
1983, 12 Days of Christmas, QMB415-9, musical, 3¾" 900.00
1984, Rocking Horse, QX 435-4, red & bl saddle, 4" W 75.00
1985, Little Red Schoolhouse, QLX 711-2, lighted, 2⅝" 90.00
1986, Jolly St Nick, QX 429-6, HP porc, 5½" 75.00
1987, Tin Locomotive, QX 484-9, 6th in series, 3½" 65.00
1988, Parade of Toys, QLX 719-4, light & motion, 3½" 45.00
1989, Animals Speak, QLS 723-2, lighted panorama ball, 3⅝" ..115.00

1989, Miniature, The Kringles, 1st in series, $35.00.

1989, Here Comes Santa-Christmas Caboose, QX 458-5, 3½" 40.00
1990, Baby's First Christmas, QLX 724-6, light & motion, 3¾" ...55.00
1990, Forest Frolics, QLX 723-6, light & motion, 4½" 55.00

Halloween

The origin of Halloween can be traced back to the ancient practices of the Druids of Great Britain who began their New Year on the 1st of November. The Druids were pagans, and their New Year's celebrations involved pagan rites and superstitions. They believed that as the old year came to an end the devil would gather up all the demons and evil in the world and take them back to Hell with him. Witches were women who had sold their souls to the devil and with their black cat in attendance, flew up through their chimneys on brooms. When the Roman Catholic Church came into power in 700 A.D., they changed the holiday into a religious event called 'All Saints Day,' or 'Allhallows.' The evening before, October 31, became 'Allhallow's Eve' or 'Halloween.' Today Halloween is strictly a fun time, and Halloween items are fun to collect. Pumpkin-head candy containers of papier-mache or pressed cardboard, noisemakers, postcards with black cats and witches, costumes, and decorations are only a sampling of the variety available. See also Candy Containers.

Candy container, blk cat w/jack-o'-lantern, plastic, Rosbro 25.00
Candy container, cat, papier-mache, arched bk, Germany 180.00
Candy container, Keystone Cat, heavy compo, Germany, '20s, 6" ..365.00
Candy container, pumpkin, cb, W Germany, 5" 130.00
Candy container, pumpkin, glass, rpt, early 90.00
Candy container, pumpkin lady, compo, Germany, 8½" 275.00
Candy container, pumpkin man, hard plastic, 5" 35.00
Candy container, vegetable person, compo, Germany, 3½" 150.00
Costume, polished red & blk cotton, devil's mask, 1920s, EX 60.00
Decoration, blk cat, foil, Am, 1940s, 14x8" 27.50
Decoration, blk cat & jack-o'-lantern, wax, 1940s, 3¼" 20.00
Decoration, devil's head, rubber, worn pnt, Japan, 2¾" 65.00
Decoration, scarecrow, cb & crepe paper, Beistle, 34", M 27.50
Decoration, skeleton, compo w/chenille legs & arms, Japan, 6" 48.00
Decoration, witch, cb, Merri-Lei, 20", NM 36.00
Diecut, blk cat, emb cb, Beistle, 5½x5½", M 22.50
Diecut, blk cat, emb cb, on orange honeycomb base, 12" 50.00
Diecut, blk cat, mice & quarter moon, Am, 1930s, 8½" 45.00
Diecut, blk cat face, cb, HE Luhrs, 8½x12", M 35.00
Diecut, cat w/instrument, HE Luhrs, 8½", EX 45.00
Diecut, Frankenstein, cb, life sz, EX 45.00
Diecut, scarecrow on pumpkin, 10" 35.00
Diecut, skull, Germany, 9", EX 55.00
Figurine, witch, bsk, Japan, 1930s, 3", M 110.00
Hat, blk Deco owl face w/orange border, crepe paper, 10x10" 22.00
Hat, cats & witches on orange, paper & red cellophane, 1950s 20.00
Hat, paper band, accordion-pleated tissue, HE Luhrs, 11½" L 25.00
Jack-o'-lantern, cb w/papier-mache wash, Germany, 1900, 5" 195.00
Jack-o'-lantern, celluloid, battery operated, Japan, 4¼" 110.00
Jack-o'-lantern, celluloid, w/arms & legs, MIB 145.00
Jack-o'-lantern, dbl-face, papier-mache, Germany, 8" 165.00
Jack-o'-lantern, hard plastic, w/bottom plug, 6" 55.00
Jack-o'-lantern, papier-mache, orig insert, Germany, 8½" 185.00
Jack-o'-lantern, papier-mache, orig insert, 5½" 135.00
Jack-o'-lantern, papier-mache, paper insert, Germany, 2¼" 110.00
Jack-o'-lantern, tin, orange & blk pnt, on 44" rod 775.00
Lantern, blk cat, papier-mache, 3½" 165.00
Lantern, cat, orange & blk papier-mache, w/insert, 7½" 135.00
Lantern, devil, pulp w/orig paper inserts, 1930s, 7", EX 465.00
Lantern, devil's head, celluloid on metal base, 3" 325.00
Lantern, skull, glass head on metal base, Hong Kong, NM 75.00
Marionette, devil, bsk legs, compo body & head, 8" 150.00
Mask, devil w/horns, papier-mache, 14x13", M 285.00
Mask, mobster, paper, Japan, 1950s, 7x5" 15.00
Noisemaker, cat paddle, heavy cb w/2 emb cat diecuts, 8" 45.00
Noisemaker, cat paddle, metal, M 45.00
Noisemaker, devil litho on cb, wood hdl, squeaker, Germany, 9" ..115.00
Noisemaker, Spanish dancer, tin, EX 45.00
Noisemaker, witch litho on cb, wood hdl, Germany, 11" 155.00
Tambourine, cat face, orig streamers, early 60.00

Hamada, Shoji

Shoji Hamada is the most famous of all Japanese potters. He was a former chemist who worked with Bernard Leach in the 1920s to rediscover the art of Oriental 'rural' pottery. All of Hamada's ceramics were fired in a wood-fired kiln. He used local clays, oxides, and ash glazes ground by hand. Hamada used a seal mark during the early 1920s when he was at St. Ives, England, After returning to Japan in 1923, his work was never signed. Instead he signed the wooden boxes he used for shipping.

Bottle, brn w/cobalt geometrics, sqd form, 1955, 7¾" 770.00
Bottle, gr trailings on tenmoku, sq sides, pressed, 7¾" 2,625.00

Dish, blk/wht trailings on dk ochre, press-mold, sq, 12" 850.00
Vase, buff on manganese matt, goblet form w/int funnel, 5½" ..6,400.00
Vase, gray over manganese, cup form on can ft, 4½" 4,500.00
Vase, iron-rich amber, ft unglazed, horizontal ribs, 3¾" 1,500.00
Vase, tenmoku trailings on tan w/brn blisters, sq sides, 7¾" 3,300.00
Vase, wht crackle, wide spade top on can body, 12¼" 10,400.00

Hampshire

The Hampshire Pottery Company was established in 1871 in Keene, New Hampshire, by James Scollay Taft. Their earliest products were redware and stoneware utility items such as jugs, churns, crocks, and flowerpots. In 1878 they produced majolica ware which met with such success that they began to experiment with the idea of manufacturing art pottery. By 1883 they had developed a Royal Worcester type of finish which they applied to vases, tea sets, powder boxes, and cookie jars. It was also utilized for souvenir items that were decorated with transfer designs prepared from photographic plates.

Cadmon Robertson, brother-in-law of Taft, joined the company in 1904 and was responsible for developing their famous matt glazes. Colors included shades of green, brown, red, and blue. Early examples were of earthenware, but eventually the body was changed to semiporcelain. Some of his designs were marked with an M in a circle as a tribute to his wife, Emoretta. Robertson died in 1914, leaving a void impossible to fill. Taft sold the business in 1916 to George Morton, who continued to use the matt glazes that Robertson had developed. After a temporary halt in production during WWI, Morton returned to Keene and re-equipped the factory with the machinery needed to manufacture hotel china and floor tile. Because of the expense involved in transporting coal to fire the kilns, Morton found he could not compete with potteries of Ohio and New Jersey who were able to utilize locally available natural gas. He was forced to close the plant in 1923.

Interest is highest on examples in the monochrome glazes, and it is the glaze, not the size or form, that dictates value. The souvenir pieces are not particularly of high quality and tend to be passed over by today's collectors.

Ashtray, green crystalline, lily pad rest at rim, M, $140.00.

Bowl, gr matt, emb Indian luck sign, 2½x6¾" 225.00
Candle holder, gr matt, hdl, #29, 6½" 175.00
Ewer, gr matt, 9x9" 250.00
Lamp, gr matt, #006, bent-panel glass shade, 19" 600.00
Lamp base, gr matt, leaves lap to right, Robertson, #03, 19" 600.00
Lamp base, gr matt, spiral cvd on front, MO/#007, 9½" 800.00
Pitcher, gr matt, emb leaves, sgn JS Keene, notched hdl, 7" 170.00
Pitcher, iris, purple on gr shaded w/blk trim, w/lid, 9½" 250.00
Sconce, gr matt, hooded 200.00
Vase, bl, emb stylized flowers, 7x4¾" 325.00

Vase, brn, cvd stylized upright leaves, 9x4¾" 250.00
Vase, chocolate brn mottle, mk, 5" 110.00
Vase, experimental bl volcanic on wht clay, conical, 3½" 250.00
Vase, gr matt, flaring base, sm rim hdls, 7x3¾" 150.00
Vase, teal matt w/cream drip & incised geometrics, 8" 450.00

Handel

Philip Handel was best known for the art glass lamps he produced at the turn of the century. His work is similar to the Tiffany lamps of the same era. Handel made gas and electric lamps with both leaded glass and reverse-painted shades. Chipped ice shades with a texture similar to overshot glass were also produced. Shades signed by artists such as Bailey, Palme, and Parlow are highly valued.

China and glassware decorated by Handel are rare and command high prices on today's market. Teroma is a term used to describe glassware decorated on the exterior with paint that has a sandy finish. Many of Handel's chinaware blanks were supplied by Limoges. Our advisor for this category is Daniel Batchelor; he is listed in the Directory under New York.

Key: chp — chipped/lightly sanded

Lamps

Base, bronzed metal gnarled tree trunk, unsgn, 14" 250.00
Base, bronzed metal inverted seed pod form, mk, 25" 600.00
Base, bronzed metal inverted trumpet form, mk, 22" 300.00
Base, bronzed metal vasiform w/vertical ribs, 23" 450.00
Base, copper pnt metal, baluster stem, floral ft, 24" 450.00
Boudoir, chipped ice 7" windmill/bldg/lake shade; trunk std ...2,750.00
Boudoir, rvpt 7" Deco floral shade mk Sample; base w/label ...1,200.00
Boudoir, rvpt 7" moon/ships ribbed dome shade; sgn std 2,300.00
Boudoir, rvpt 7" sqd/ribbed Teroma scenic shade #6460P; std .2,200.00
Boudoir, rvpt 7" tuck-under shade w/floral band; metal std 1,200.00
Boudoir, rvpt 8" winter chipped ice sgn shade; trunk std 1,700.00
Boudoir, rvpt/chp 7" bluebirds/branches dome shade; reed std .2,200.00
Boudoir, rvpt/chp 7" scenic dome shade #5601 (EX); gilt std ..1,100.00
Chandelier, ldgl 25" cone shape w/fruits on apron 3,680.00
Chandelier, rvpt 18" birds/trees unmk shade sgn Bedigie 5,000.00
Desk, slag w/Hawaiian o/l bell shade, harp fr, mk base, 18" ...1,200.00
Fluid burner, tam-o'-shanter 13" rose-band shade; sqd base 700.00
Piano, brn 7x10" #6132½ shade w/pine needles; base w/label 600.00
Piano, etch/pnt 8" dia brn shade; pivoting wht metal base 750.00
Piano, pnt 8" dia zigzag shade; pivoting copper base 1,700.00

Table, chipped ice 7" winter scene sgn shade; trunk std, EX ...3,250.00
Table, etch/rvpt 14" grapevine-band dome shade; slim std 1,100.00
Table, ext-pnt 18" Deco-band cased opal dome shade; mk std .1,800.00
Table, ldgl 12" sq pansy shade w/tulip border; petal-ft std 3,700.00
Table, ldgl 20" foliage-panel dome shade; vase std w/lg ft 2,000.00
Table, rvpt 10" mushroom trees shade #2871 sgn R; bamboo std .1,500.00
Table, rvpt 11" dragon/sunburst shade; std w/appl wire 1,600.00
Table, rvpt 15" rose-border cone shade #6300; foliate std 2,300.00
Table, rvpt 15" sunset forest dome shade; lappet-emb std 2,900.00
Table, rvpt 16" hydrangea dome shade; bronzed std #6739 .....9,600.00
Table, rvpt 16" moonlit scene dome shade; bronzed lobed std ..2,750.00
Table, rvpt/chp 10" scenic dome shade; bronzed sgn std, 14" ..1,800.00
Table, rvpt/chp 15" palms/dunes cone shade (EX); reeded std ..2,500.00
Table, rvpt/chp 16" poppy band on ochre shade w/emb border .6,750.00
Table, rvpt/chp 18" tree/sun shade sgn Broggi; 3-scroll std 7,600.00
Table, rvpt/chp 18" 3-parrot/floral shade sgn Bedigie; 25" 9,900.00
Table, Teroma 15" multiflora dome shade #7062BD; unmk std ..6,500.00
Table, Teroma 18" forest cone shade sgn R; Oriental std 3,700.00
Table, Teroma 18" rose-border dome shade #7013DM; unmk std .2,000.00
Table, Teroma 18" roses/butterflies dome shade #6688; mk std ..8,500.00
Table, 6-panel bent glass shade, ea fr w/gr leaves; urn std 990.00
Table, 7-panel 18" slag glass shade w/trees o/l; copper std 1,300.00
Torchiere, ext-pnt tumbler shade w/leaves; unmk std, 16" 600.00
Torchiere, rvpt tumbler shade w/mc flowers, rtcl mk std, 14" 850.00

Miscellaneous

Bookends, bronze, cast as paneled door w/window in arch, 7" 450.00
Bookends, bronze, classical architectural ruins, 7" 600.00
Bookends, bronze, Theodore Roosevelt bust, 6½", pr 475.00
Candle lamp, Teroma 9" hurricane shade, 10" mahog stick 5,500.00
Candlestick, Teroma, rocky landscape, 6-color, Guebisch, 8½" ..1,000.00
Chocolate pot, ferns, gr/gold/gray on beige, script mk, 11½" 450.00
Chocolate set, gold rings & hdls on beige, 15-pc 1,500.00
Cigarette holder, opalware, terrier by Bauer, metal mts, 3½" 450.00
Humidor, opalware, gr/red (no decor), pipe finial, 4x5½" 400.00
Smoking stand, brn/gr/tan opal, appl pipe, shield mk, M 750.00
Vase, china w/near-full length Nouveau maid, sgn Parlow, 16" .3,600.00
Vase, chipped ice w/floral medallion, gr & gold enamel, 13" ...1,050.00

Vase, Teroma glass with summer mountain landscape, marked, #4210, 8", $3,000.00.

Table lamp, reverse-painted 18" Elephantine Island (desert scene) shade, signed John Bailey, #6825; three-socket urn-form bronze standard, 23", $7,425.00.

Vase, Teroma, spring trees/birds, sgn Bedigie, 11x5½" 2,400.00
Vase, Teroma, trees/lake, sgn Gubisch, baluster, 10" 2,450.00
Vase, Teroma, wooded landscape, sgn Lockrow, #4219, 10¾" ..2,000.00

Harker

The Harker Pottery was established in East Liverpool, Ohio, in

1840. Their earliest products were yellowware and Rockingham produced from local clay. After 1900 whiteware was made from imported materials. The plant eventually grew to be a large manufacturer of dinnerware and kitchenware, employing as many as three hundred people. It closed in 1972 after it was purchased by the Jeannette Glass Company. Perhaps their best-known lines were their Cameo wares, decorated with white silhouettes in a cameo effect on contrasting solid colors. Floral silhouettes are standard, but other designs were also used. Blue and pink are the most often found background hues; a few pieces are found in yellow. For further information we recommend *The Collector's Guide to Harker Pottery* by Neva Colbert.

Bowl, Amy, deep, 9"	22.00
Bowl, Chesterton Gray, 5½"	6.00
Bowl, soup; White Rose	10.00
Bowl, utility; Deco Dahlia	9.00
Cake lifter, Pastel Tulip, crazed	32.00
Cake plate, Calico Tulip	16.50
Cake plate, Cameoware, bl, crazing	15.00
Creamer, Cameo Rose	10.00
Creamer & sugar bowl, Orange Tulip w/Wheat	14.00
Cup & saucer, Cameo Rose	6.00
Jug, Cameo Rose, rnd, w/lid, 6"	38.00
Lifter, Rose II	15.00
Mug, Cameoware, bl, child's	20.00
Pie plate, Cameo Rose, 9"	22.00
Pie plate, Petitpoint, 9"	15.00

Plate, Colonial Lady, gold trim, 9½", $10.00.

Plate, Cameo, 6"	3.00
Plate, Pastel Tulip, dinner sz	7.50
Plate, Pastel Tulip, salad sz	4.00
Platter, Apple & Pear, 13"	12.50
Platter, Cameo Rose, oval, 12"	24.00
Rolling pin, Fruit	78.00
Rolling pin, Mallo	80.00
Rolling pin, Modern Tulip	85.00
Rolling pin, Morning Glory	88.00
Rolling pin, Petit Point	70.00
Spoon & fork, Amy	34.00
Sugar scoop, Amy	36.00
Teapot, Apple II	30.00
Teapot, Modern Tulip	16.50
Tile, White Rose	25.00

Harlequin

Harlequin dinnerware, produced by the Homer Laughlin China Company of Newell, West Virginia, was introduced in 1938. It was a lightweight ware made in maroon, mauve blue, and spruce green, as well as all the Fiesta colors except ivory (see Fiesta). It was marketed exclusively by the Woolworth stores, who considered it to be their all-time best seller. For this reason they contracted with Homer Laughlin to reissue Harlequin to commemorate their 100th anniversary in 1979. Although three of the original glazes were used in the reissue, the few serving pieces that were made were restyled, and collectors found the new line to be no threat to their investments.

The Harlequin animals, including a fish, lamb, cat, penguin, duck, and donkey, were made during the early 1940s, also for the dime-store trade. Today these are very desirable to collectors of Homer Laughlin china.

In the listings that follow, use the values designated 'high' for all colors other than turquoise and yellow. For medium green, double the 'high' values on all items other than flat items and small bowls. *The Collector's Encyclopedia of Fiesta* (values updated in 1994) by Sharon and Bob Huxford contains a more thorough study of this subject. It is available from Collector Books or your local library.

Animals, mavericks, gold trim	32.00
Animals, non-standard colors	158.00
Animals, standard colors	85.00
Ashtray, basketweave, high	45.00
Ashtray, basketweave, low	30.00
Ashtray, regular, high	42.50
Ashtray, regular, low	32.00
Bowl, '36s oatmeal; high	17.00
Bowl, '36s oatmeal; low	11.50
Bowl, '36s; high	26.50
Bowl, '36s; low	17.00
Bowl, cream soup; high	20.00
Bowl, cream soup; low	16.00
Bowl, fruit; high, 5½"	9.00
Bowl, fruit; low, 5½"	6.00
Bowl, ind salad; high	26.50
Bowl, ind salad; low	17.00
Bowl, mixing; Kitchen Kraft, mauve bl, 8"	110.00
Bowl, mixing; Kitchen Kraft, red or spruce gr, 6"	72.00
Bowl, mixing; Kitchen Kraft, yel, 10"	110.00
Bowl, nappy; high, 9"	26.50
Bowl, nappy; low, 9"	16.50
Bowl, oval baker, high	25.00
Bowl, oval baker, low	18.00

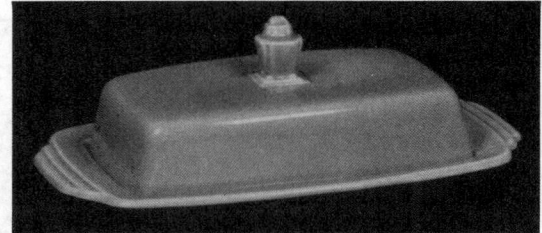

Butter dish, any color, low, ½-lb, 75.00.

Butter dish, high, ½-lb	90.00
Butter dish, low, ½-lb	75.00
Candle holders, high, pr	195.00
Candle holders, low, pr	162.00
Casserole, w/lid, high	95.00
Casserole, w/lid, low	58.00
Creamer, high lip, any color	72.00

Creamer, ind; high 17.00
Creamer, ind; low 12.50
Creamer, novelty, high 23.00
Creamer, novelty, low 16.00
Creamer, regular, high 13.50
Creamer, regular, low 8.00
Cup, demitasse; high 46.00
Cup, demitasse; low 27.50
Cup, lg, any color 92.00
Cup, tea; high 9.50
Cup, tea; low 7.50
Egg cup, dbl, high 20.00
Egg cup, dbl, low 14.00
Egg cup, single, high 21.00
Egg cup, single, low 16.50
Gravy boat, high 23.00
Gravy boat, low 16.00
Marmalade, any color 125.00
Nut dish, basketweave, orig color 8.00
Perfume bottle, any color 68.00
Pitcher, service water; high 55.00
Pitcher, service water; low 37.50
Pitcher, 22-oz jug, high 46.00
Pitcher, 22-oz jug, low 26.00
Plate, deep; high 20.00
Plate, deep; low 15.00
Plate, high, 10" 24.00
Plate, high, 6" 4.50
Plate, high, 7" 6.50
Plate, high, 9" 12.00
Plate, low, 10" 14.00
Plate, low, 6" 3.50
Plate, low, 7" 4.50
Plate, low, 9" 7.00
Platter, high, 11" 17.50
Platter, high, 13" 25.00
Platter, low, 11" 12.00
Platter, low, 13" 16.50
Saucer, demitasse; high 13.50
Saucer, demitasse; low 7.00
Saucer, high 3.50
Saucer, low 2.00
Saucer/ashtray, high 47.00
Saucer/ashtray, ivory 65.00
Saucer/ashtray, low 42.50
Shakers, high, pr 16.50
Shakers, low, pr 13.00
Sugar bowl, w/lid, high 17.00
Sugar bowl, w/lid, low 12.00
Syrup, any color 200.00
Teapot, high 88.00
Teapot, low 58.00
Tray, relish; mixed colors 200.00
Tumbler, high 40.00
Tumbler, low 30.00

Hatpin Holders

Most hatpin holders were made from 1860 to 1920 to coincide with the period during which hatpins were popularly in vogue. The taller types were required to house the long hatpins necessary to secure the large hats that were in style from 1890 to 1914. They were usually porcelain, either decorated by hand or by transfer with florals or scen-

ics, although some were clever figurals. Glass examples are rare, and those of slag or Carnival Glass are especially valuable.

If you are interested in collecting or dealing in hatpins or hatpin holders, you will find that authority Lillian Baker has several fine books available on the subject, including her most recent publication, *The Collector's Encyclopedia of Hatpins and Hatpin Holders*, complete with beautiful color illustrations and current market values. She is listed in the Directory under California. For information concerning the International Club for Collectors of Hatpins and Hatpin Holders, see the Clubs, Newsletters, and Catalogs section of the Directory. Our advisor for this category is Robert Larsen; he is listed in the Directory under Nebraska.

Celluloid, rnd base w/purple velvet pad, spindle center, 6", 60.00.

Benedict Curio Bronze, figures in medallion, 4¾" 85.00
Germany, china, mc roses on wht, simple flared shape 65.00
Germany, china, pk rose transfer on yel/gr, ftd cylinder, 4½" 65.00
Limoges, roses on wht w/gold, sq top, 5¼" 80.00
Nippon, storks around base on turq, gold top, lg 135.00
Pickard, floral w/gold trim at base & rim, 4½" 135.00
Royal Bayreuth, Goose Girl 325.00
Royal Bayreuth, penguin figural 895.00
Royal Bayreuth, Rose Tapestry 375.00
RS Germany, bluebird, simple shape, 4½" 85.00
RS Prussia, floral, 3-leg 250.00
Ruby glass w/HP daisies & gold sprays 110.00
Schafer & Vater, Egypto, jasperware, 6" 275.00
Shelly, Heather, 5¾" 98.00
Unmk china, figures & florals on cornucopia shape, 6½" 245.00
Unmk china, floral, pk on cream w/gold, 4¾x3⅞" 45.00

Hatpins

A hatpin was used to securely fasten a hat to the hair and head of the wearer. Hatpins, measuring from 4" to 12" in length, were worn from approximately 1850 to 1920. During the Art Deco period, hatpins became ornaments rather than the decorative functional jewels that they had been. The hatpin period reached its zenith in 1913 just prior to World War I, which brought about a radical change in women's headdress and fashion. About that time, women began to scorn the bonnet and adopt 'the hat' as a symbol of their equality. The hatpin was made of every natural and manufactured element in a myriad of designs that challenge the imagination. They were contrived to serve every fashion need and complement the milliner's art. Collectors often concentrate on a specific type: hand-painted porcelains, sterling silver, commemoratives, sporting activities, Carnival Glass, Art Nouveau and/or Art Deco designs, Victorian Gothics with mounted stones, exquisite rhinestones, engraved and brass-mounted escutcheon heads, gold and gems, or simply primitive types made in the Victorian parlor. Some collectors prefer the long pin-shanks while others select only those on tremblants or nodder-type pin-shanks.

If you are interested in collecting or dealing in hatpins, see the information in the Hatpin Holders introduction concerning reference books and a national collectors' club. For further study we recommend *The Collector's Encyclopedia of Hatpins and Hatpin Holders,* available at your local bookstore or from Collector Books. Our advisor for this category is Robert Larsen; he is listed in the Directory under Nebraska.

Key: cab — cabochon

Baroque MOP on gold mt w/faux rubies, 1½"	**90.00**
Brass, ornate filigree, vanity w/puff & mirror intact, 11½"	**900.00**
Carnival glass, butterfly, gr irid	**110.00**
Celluloid w/rhinestones	**25.00**
Eagle figural, nodder w/rhinestones, 1½" dia	**195.00**
Mercury glass, cased, Bohemia, ca 1905, 2¼"	**90.00**
Nouveau flower, enamel on copper, ca 1900, 1"	**55.00**
Porc ball w/HP figure, silver o/l, lg, 1½" dia	**275.00**

Satsuma hatpins, prices ranging from $175.00 up to $495.00.

Satsuma, HP robins, metallic mt, 1½", on 9" pin	**285.00**
Scorpion, brass on pearl & brass filigree, 3"	**165.00**
Sterling, cherub, ⅜"	**65.00**
Vanity, vinaigrette top, sterling	**695.00**

Haviland

The Haviland China Company was organized in 1840 by David Haviland, a New York china importer. His search for a pure white, nonporous porcelain led him to Limoges, France, where natural deposits of suitable clay had already attracted numerous china manufacturers. The fine china he produced there was translucent and meticulously decorated, with each piece fired in an individual sagger.

It has been estimated that as many as 60,000 chinaware patterns were designed, each piece marked with one of several company backstamps. 'H. & Co.' was used until 1890 when a law was enacted making it necessary to include the country of origin. Various marks have been used since that time including 'Haviland, France'; 'Haviland & Co. Limoges'; and 'Decorated by Haviland & Co.' Various associations with family members over the years have resulted in changes in management as well as company name. In 1892 Theodore Haviland left the firm to start his own business. Some of his ware was marked 'Mont Mery.' Later logos included a horseshoe, a shield, and various uses of his initials and name. In 1941 this branch moved to the United States. Wares produced here are marked 'Theodore Haviland, N.Y.' or 'Made In America.'

Though it is their dinnerware lines for which they are most famous, during the 1880s and 1890s they also made exquisite art pottery using a technique of underglaze slip decoration called Barbotine, which had been invented by Ernest Chaplet. In 1885 Haviland bought the formula and hired Chaplet to oversee its production. The technique involved mixing heavy white clay slip with pigments to produce a compound of the same consistency as oil paints. The finished product actually resembled oil paintings of the period, the texture achieved through the application of the heavy medium to the clay body in much the same manner as an artist would apply paint to his canvas. Primarily the body used with this method was a low-fired faience, though they also produced stoneware. Numbers in the listings below refer to pattern books by Arlene Schleiger.

Basket, HP violets, not factory decor, gold hdl, 1893-1930	**100.00**
Bowl, Clover, 6⅛"	**15.00**

**Bowl, Drop Rose, scalloped edge and foot, 10",
$350.00.**

Bowl, rice; Clover, 5⅝"	**20.00**
Bowl, soup; Rosalinde, w/underplate	**30.00**
Bowl, vegetable; Blackberry, sq, w/lid	**75.00**
Bowl, vegetable; scalloped, gold ribbon hdls & finial, 10x7¼"	**150.00**
Box, powder, florals w/gold & gr, Star form, 1893-1930, 4½"	**150.00**
Cake platter, birds & flowers w/gold, 16x10"+10 7¾" plates	**355.00**
Cake stand, Marseille form, ca 1876-1930, 2x9"	**95.00**
Celery dish, Clover, 12¼"	**25.00**
Chocolate pot, Diana form, salesman's sample, 9½"	**125.00**
Chocolate set, pk roses, 10" pot+4 cups & saucers	**450.00**
Coffeepot, floral w/gold, Pompadour form, 1888-96, 8½"	**175.00**
Coffeepot, Sandoz, bird figural, 1920-36, 4½"	**425.00**
Compote, center medallion, ormolu mts, 1893-1930, 7x5½"	**130.00**
Creamer & sugar bowl, gold bands on wht, 1850s-65, 7", 8"	**165.00**
Cup & saucer, Arbor	**38.00**
Cup & saucer, bouillon; floral, Crystal, w/lid, 1893-1930	**100.00**
Cup & saucer, Clover	**27.50**
Cup & saucer, Ladore	**26.00**
Cup & saucer, lav & pk roses w/gold, on blank #22	**22.50**
Cup & saucer, Princess	**27.50**
Cup & saucer, Rosalinde, French	**32.00**
Gravy boat, Clover, w/attached underplate	**80.00**
Gravy boat, Gotham	**40.00**
Knife rest, fishes joined at mouth, Sandoz, 5" L	**325.00**
Mayonnaise, gold trim on leaf shape, w/undertray, 1904-20	**85.00**
Pitcher, Moss Rose, gold trim, 1850s-65	**90.00**
Pitcher, pk roses w/gold, Burley, 8"	**165.00**
Pitcher, water; emb florals w/gold, 1850-65, 10"	**135.00**
Plate, Baltimore Rose, Ranson form, 1893-1930, 8½"	**65.00**
Plate, Clover, 7½"	**16.50**
Plate, Clover, 8"	**22.00**
Plate, Clover, 9¾"	**25.00**
Plate, Diana, 7½"	**32.00**
Plate, Ladore, 10"	**18.00**
Plate, Rosalinde, American, 10¼"	**20.00**
Plate, Silver Anniversary, 7½"	**22.00**
Platter, Autumn Leaf, 12"	**60.00**
Platter, Clover, 15¾"	**115.00**
Platter, Clover, 20"	**245.00**
Platter, lav & pk roses w/gold on blank #22, 14"	**45.00**

Platter, Princess, 12"	45.00
Platter, Princess, 16"	60.00
Platter, Silver Anniversary, 14"	90.00
Shaving mug, gold name & trim, 1876-78, 3¼"	110.00
Tray, floral, mk, 14½x9½"	75.00
Tureen, soup; Blackberry	150.00

Pottery

Ewer, stoneware, appl grapes/vines, gold accents, AD, 13"	1,400.00
Ewer, stoneware, cvd/appl pine cones, gold trim, 6½", NM	300.00
Ewer, stoneware, emb cherub, pnt/cvd flowers, #90, 8½"	800.00
Jardiniere, stoneware, brn w/tan/gr floral, att Dammouse, 7"	700.00
Pitcher, stoneware, cvd/appl flowers, att Dammouse, 6"	425.00
Pitcher, stoneware, cvd/pnt flowers, 1 appl flower, AD, 7"	425.00
Vase, Barbotine floral, dbl-mouth top, 4 sm ft, EDS, 4½"	850.00
Vase, Barbotine floral, rectangular, 1 sgn MB, 8½", pr	1,400.00
Vase, Barbotine floral, sgn MC, 7"	700.00
Vase, Barbotine floral, waisted w/3 sm ft, #L-30/GS, 4½"	325.00
Vase, Barbotine w/2 wildfowl, PLC, bulbous w/can neck, 11"	1,300.00
Vase, sculpted florals on terra cotta jug form, sgn, 14"	1,800.00
Vase, stoneware, appl/cvd leaves & grapes, AD, 15", NM	2,000.00
Vase, young fisherman (sgraffito), Chaplet mk, 11"	1,550.00
Vase, 2 baby ducks, bulbous w/lid, mk Limoges, 11x8", EX	900.00

Hawkes

Thomas Hawkes established his factory in Corning, New York, in 1880. He developed many beautiful patterns of cut glass, two of which were awarded the Grand Prize at the Paris Exposition in 1889. By the end of the century, his company was renowned for the finest in cut glass production. The company logo was a trefoil form enclosing a hawk in each of the two bottom lobes with a fleur-de-lis in the center. With the exception of some of the earlier designs, all Hawkes was signed.

Presentation pitcher, likeness of Thomas G. Hawkes, signed by W.H. Morse, coat of arms on reverse, extremely rare, 15", $4,000.00.

Bottle, Oil/Vinegar, etch floral, emb silver stopper, mk Pat	85.00
Bottle, scent; floral etch, melon ribs, ball stopper, 4½"	200.00
Bowl, Centauri, 8"	325.00
Bowl, Cetus, 4x9"	2,200.00
Bowl, floral vines, global, sq ft, 4x4"	40.00
Bowl, flower & berry vines, appl ft, 1½x5½"	145.00
Bowl, Gravic, intaglio florals, shallow, 8"	180.00
Bowl, hobstar chain & crosshatching, 4½x8x6"	160.00

Bowl, hobstars & fans, 24-point hobstar base, 8"	200.00
Bowl, hobstars w/spears on X-cut dmn variant, 7"	100.00
Bowl, Panel pattern, 8¼"	1,000.00
Celery tray, Festoon, 10½x5"	150.00
Compote, Gravic, baluster stem, 5" dia	140.00
Compote, hobstars, teardrop stem, 4-section, 7x8"	500.00
Compote, Radiant, heavy blank, teardrop stem, 7½x6"	200.00
Decanter, thistles intaglio, shot-glass top	275.00
Decanter, Waffle cutting, cut paneled stopper, sq, 9x3"	125.00
Dessert set, Chrysanthemum, 9" master bowl+8 5" ind	900.00
Highball, Thistle, sgn, 8"	50.00
Ice bucket, cut, hobstars/nailheads/fans, notched hdls, 5½"	400.00
Pitcher, Brunswick, 3-notch hdl, fluted spout, 9"	800.00
Pitcher, champagne; bull's eye & lattice/hobstars/fans, 16"	825.00
Plate, Gladys, 8"	150.00
Plate, X-cut dmn w/bull's eyes, floral swags, 10"	85.00
Server, floral wreaths, 2-tier, sterling hdl, 11"	225.00
Tankard, fine-cut ribbons w/floral neck band, 7½"	200.00
Tray, card; Middlesex variant, hobstars/fans/dmns, 5½" sq	135.00
Tray, ice cream; hobstars & stars, central petals, 10" dia	250.00
Tumble-up, verre de soie, etched swags/florals, 6½"	300.00
Tumbler, water; Iris	145.00
Vase, acid cut-bk gold dragon, sgn, 10"	400.00
Vase, China Aster, ped ft, 10x6"	400.00
Vase, exotic bird on branch, fan form, sterling base, 3¼x8"	250.00
Vase, fighting cocks etch, emb brass rim/base, str sides, 6"	300.00
Vase, floral intaglio, trumpet form, mk sterling, 11"	275.00
Vase, gold bowl, laurel leaf on wht flint, ftd ball base, 8"	50.00
Vase, Gravic, floral intaglio, trumpet form, 12"	160.00
Vase, Latticed Bull's Eye/cut ribs/hobstars, 12"	250.00
Vase, 2 intaglio irises on leafy stem, star base, 12"	225.00

Head Vases

Vases modeled as heads of lovely ladies, delightful children, clowns, Madonnas — even some animals — were once popular as flower containers. Today they represent a growing area of collector interest. Most of them were imported from Japan, although some American potteries produced a few as well.

For more information, we recommend *Head Vases, Identification and Values*, by Kathleen Cole.

Baby sucking finger, Relpo, #459B, 5"	42.50
Blk lady w/Afro hairdo, Relpo, #6673, 6½"	87.50
Child in pk hat holds gift in hands, Japan, 5½"	47.50
Clown, blk hat, red & wht bow tie, Inarco, #E2320, 5"	27.50
Geisha girl, Lee Wards label, 5"	25.00
Girl w/blond braids & wht bow, unmk, #4796, 5¾"	37.50
Girl w/blond flip, pearl necklace, R/B label, 5½"	37.50
Girl w/telephone in hand, Nancy Pew label, 6"	25.00
Lady in turban, pearl necklace, Napco, 5½"	20.00
Lady w/ flat-brimmed hat, hand to face, Lefton's, #2705, 6½"	42.50
Lady w/bonnet, winks & holds fan, unmk, 6"	42.50
Lady w/brn derby-style hat, pearl jewelry, unmk, 6½"	37.50
Lady w/feather in hat, pearl jewelry, Inarco, 5½"	42.50
Lady w/flat-brimmed bonnet holding poodle, unmk, 6"	25.00
Lady w/flat-brimmed hat & pearls, hands Xd, Rubens, 5¾"	42.50
Lady w/flower in hair, pearl jewelry, hand to face, Inarco, 7"	42.50
Lady w/flowers on bonnet, pearl jewelry, Japan label, 6"	42.50
Lady w/gr bow in hair, pearl jewelry, Napcoware, #6986, 9"	165.00
Lady w/hat, pearl jewelry, hand to face, Inarco, 7"	42.50
Lady w/hat, pearl jewelry, Inarco, 4¾"	32.50
Lady w/lacy hat, pearl jewelry, hand to face, Napco, 5½"	25.00

Lady w/lg flower at side of hair, pearl jewelry, Napco, 6½" **30.00**
Lady w/long blond hair, folded fan/pearl earrings, Inarco, 6" **30.00**
Lady w/long wht curls, bow on bodice, Relpo, #K1335, 8" **35.00**
Lady w/long wht hair to 1 side, pk kerchief, unmk, 5¼" **48.50**
Lady w/mc flowers in short hair, dangle earrings, unmk, 7½" **32.50**
Lady w/pk bonnet, pearl jewelry, unmk, 3½" **15.00**
Lady w/ribbon in hair, pearl jewelry, Rubens, #4104, 6½" **22.50**
Lady w/rose in hair, pearl jewelry, hand to face, Inarco, 6" **30.00**
Lady w/scarf over blond hair, unmk, 3" **15.00**
Lady w/side-swept hair, ruffled collar, pearls, unmk, 6½" **25.00**
Lady w/wide-rimmed hat w/appl flowers & gold, unmk, 5½" **15.00**
Mary & Child, pastels, unmk, 5½" **22.50**
Mother & child, pastels, Napcoware label, #R-7075, 5" **32.50**
Nun w/Bible in hands, eyes downward, unmk, #4155, 5½" **42.50**
Oriental lady in ornate headdress, unmk, 8½" **45.00**
Snow White, Walt Disney Productions, 5½" **225.00**
South Am lady w/turban & lg smile, unmk, 8" **150.00**
Teen girl, blond, pearl earrings/leaf pin, Napcoware, 4½" **27.50**
Teen girl in red hat, Brimm's label, 5" **20.00**
Teen girl w/blond curls, pearl jewelry, Napcoware, 9" **150.00**
Teen girl w/dk hair & yel bow, Enesco label, 4½" **27.50**
Teen girl w/lg pk bow in hair, pearl jewelry, unmk, 7½" **75.00**
Teen girl w/long flowing hair, Inarco, #E2967, 5½" **25.00**
Teen girl w/2 ponytails, thick lashes, unmk, 5½" **20.00**

Heisey

A.H. Heisey began his long career at the King Glass Company of Pittsburgh. He later joined the Ripley Glass Company which soon became Geo. Duncan and Sons. After Duncan's death Heisey became half-owner in partnership with his brother-in-law, James Duncan. In 1895 he built his own factory in Newark, Ohio, initiating production in 1896 and continuing until Christmas of 1957. At that time Imperial Glass Corporation bought some of the molds. After 1968 they removed the old 'Diamond H' from any they put into use. In 1985 HCA purchased all of Imperial's Heisey molds with the exception of the Old Williamsburg line.

During their highly successful period of production, Heisey made fine handcrafted tableware with simple, yet graceful designs. Early pieces were not marked. After November 1901 the glassware was marked either with the 'Diamond H' or a paper label. Blown ware is often marked on the stem, never on the bowl or foot. For information concerning Heisey Collectors of America, see the Clubs, Newsletters, and Catalogs section of the Directory. See also Glass Animals.

Charter Oak, crystal, finger bowl, #3362 ....**10.00**
Charter Oak, crystal, stem, cocktail; #3362, 3-oz **10.00**
Charter Oak, crystal, tumbler, #3362, flat, 12-oz **12.50**
Charter Oak, flamingo, stem, sherbet; #3362, low ft, 6-oz **15.00**
Charter Oak, moongleam, comport, #3362, low ft, 6" **55.00**
Charter Oak, moongleam, stem, goblet; high ft, 8-oz **35.00**
Chintz, crystal, bowl, mint; ftd, 6" **18.00**
Chintz, crystal, bowl, preserve; hdld, ftd, 5½" **15.00**
Chintz, crystal, mayonnaise, dolpin ft, 5½" **35.00**
Chintz, crystal, platter, oval, 14" **30.00**
Chintz, crystal, stem, oyster cocktail; #3389, 4-oz **10.00**
Chintz, crystal, tray, celery; 13" **18.00**
Chintz, crystal, tumbler, iced tea; #3389, 12-oz **14.00**
Chintz, sahara, bowl, jelly; 2-hdl, ftd, 6" **30.00**
Chintz, sahara, finger bowl, #4107 ....**15.00**
Chintz, sahara, plate, bread; sq, 6" **15.00**
Chintz, sahara, stem, cocktail; #3389, 3-oz **35.00**
Chintz, sahara, tray, celery; 10" **27.50**

Crystolite, crystal, ashtray, sq, 4½" **4.50**
Crystolite, crystal, basket, hdld, 6" **350.00**
Crystolite, crystal, bonbon, 2-hdld, 7½" **15.00**
Crystolite, crystal, bottle, bitters; w/short tube, 4-oz **175.00**
Crystolite, crystal, bowl, nut; ind, hdl, 3" **15.00**
Crystolite, crystal, bowl, preserve; 2-hdl, 6" **13.00**
Crystolite, crystal, bowl, preserve; 5" **12.00**
Crystolite, crystal, bowl, salad; rnd, 10" **47.50**
Crystolite, crystal, candy dish, w/lid, 5½" **50.00**
Crystolite, crystal, cheese dish, ftd, 5½" **20.00**
Crystolite, crystal, cigarette holder, oval **17.50**
Crystolite, crystal, ice tub, w/SP hdl **75.00**
Crystolite, crystal, jam jar, w/lid **50.00**
Crystolite, crystal, plate, cake salver; ftd, 11" **250.00**
Crystolite, crystal, plate, salad; 7" **9.00**
Crystolite, crystal, plate, sandwich; 14" **40.00**
Crystolite, crystal, plate, torte; 11" **24.00**
Crystolite, crystal, plate, torte; 14" **35.00**
Crystolite, crystal, sugar bowl, ind **15.00**
Crystolite, crystal, urn, flower; 7" **75.00**
Crystolite, crystal, vase, short stem, 3" **20.00**
Crystolite, crystal, vase, 12" **225.00**
Empress, gr, ashtray **190.00**
Empress, gr, bowl, nappy; 4½" **12.50**
Empress, gr, bowl, pickle or olive; 2-part, 13" **32.00**
Empress, gr, comport, ftd, 6" **65.00**
Empress, gr, creamer, ind **40.00**
Empress, gr, cup, bouillon; 2-hdl **33.00**
Empress, gr, plate, 8" **24.00**
Empress, gr, plate, 9" **40.00**
Empress, gr, tray, celery; 10" **26.00**
Empress, gr, tray, relish; 3-part, 10" **35.00**
Empress, pk, bowl, nappy; 8" **30.00**
Empress, pk, mustard, w/lid **60.00**
Empress, pk, plate, sq, 6" **10.00**
Empress, yel, bonbon, 6" **25.00**
Empress, yel, bowl, floral; flared, 9" **75.00**
Empress, yel, bowl, frappe; w/center **60.00**
Empress, yel, bowl, relish; triplex, 10" **55.00**
Empress, yel, bowl, relish; 3-part, triplex, 7" **30.00**
Empress, yel, bowl, vegetable; oval, 10" **45.00**
Empress, yel, jug, 3-pt, ftd **200.00**
Empress, yel, plate, sq, 2-hdl, 13" **40.00**
Empress, yel, plate, sq, 8" **22.00**
Empress, yel, plate, 12" **55.00**
Empress, yel, plate, 4½" **8.00**
Empress, yel, saucer **14.00**
Empress, yel, tray, celery; 13" **24.00**
Empress, yel, vase, ftd, 9" **110.00**
Greek Key, crystal, bottle, oil; w/#6 stopper, 6-oz **100.00**
Greek Key, crystal, bowl, almond form, ftd, 5" **35.00**
Greek Key, crystal, bowl, banana split; flat, 9" **27.50**
Greek Key, crystal, bowl, jelly; w/lid, 2-hdl, ftd **145.00**
Greek Key, crystal, bowl, nappy; shallow, 8½" **45.00**
Greek Key, crystal, bowl, nappy; 4½" **20.00**
Greek Key, crystal, bowl, nappy; 6" **25.00**
Greek Key, crystal, bowl, nappy; 7" **32.00**
Greek Key, crystal, bowl, orange; 12" **55.00**
Greek Key, crystal, bowl, punch; ftd, 12" **175.00**
Greek Key, crystal, butter/jelly dish, w/lid, 2-hdl **175.00**
Greek Key, crystal, comport, w/lid, 5" **85.00**
Greek Key, crystal, cup, punch; 4½-oz **20.00**
Greek Key, crystal, jar, crushed fruit; w/lid, 1-qt **300.00**
Greek Key, crystal, pitcher, 1-qt **85.00**

Greek Key, crystal, plate, 7" 17.00
Greek Key, crystal, plate, 9" 30.00
Greek Key, crystal, shakers, pr 90.00
Greek Key, crystal, sherbet, low ft, 6-oz 13.00
Greek Key, crystal, spooner, lg 75.00
Greek Key, crystal, stem, burgundy; 3½-oz 110.00
Greek Key, crystal, stem, cordial; ¾-oz 235.00
Greek Key, crystal, stem, 9-oz 125.00
Greek Key, crystal, straw jar, w/lid 300.00
Greek Key, crystal, tray, oblong, 13" 110.00
Greek Key, crystal, tumbler, flared rim or str sides, 12-oz 40.00
Greek Key, flamingo, bowl, punch; ftd, 12" 750.00
Ipswich, crystal, plate, sq, 8" 20.00
Ipswich, crystal, sherbet, 4-oz 9.00
Ipswich, crystal, stem, oyster cocktail; 4-oz 20.00
Ipswich, pk, candy jar, w/lid, ½-lb 225.00
Ipswich, pk, plate, sq, 7" 25.00
Ipswich, pk, sugar bowl 42.50
Ipswich, pk, tumbler, ftd, 12-oz 50.00
Ipswich, pk, tumbler, ftd, 8-oz 40.00
Ipswich, yel, pitcher, ½-gal 350.00
Lariat, crystal, ashtray, 4" 10.00
Lariat, crystal, basket, bonbon; 7½" 100.00
Lariat, crystal, basket, ftd, 10" 195.00
Lariat, crystal, bowl, camellia; 9½" 22.00
Lariat, crystal, bowl, fruit; 12" 20.00
Lariat, crystal, bowl, mayonnaise; 2-part, 7" 20.00
Lariat, crystal, candy box, caramel; w/lid 45.00
Lariat, crystal, candy dish, w/lid, 7" 50.00
Lariat, crystal, cheese dish, w/lid, ftd, 5" 40.00
Lariat, crystal, cigarette box 42.00
Lariat, crystal, jar, urn; w/lid, 12" 150.00
Lariat, crystal, lamp & globe, blk-out; 7" 100.00
Lariat, crystal, platter, oval, 15" 40.00
Lariat, crystal, shakers, pr 200.00
Lariat, crystal, stem, claret; blown, 4-oz 25.00
Lariat, crystal, tumbler, iced tea; ftd, 12-oz 18.00
Lariat, crystal, tumbler, juice; ftd, 5-oz 15.00
Lodestar, dawn, bowl, #1565, 6¾" 45.00
Lodestar, dawn, bowl, crimped, 11" 95.00
Lodestar, dawn, bowl, mayonnaise; 5" 55.00
Lodestar, dawn, creamer 50.00
Lodestar, dawn, pitcher, #1626, 1-qt 150.00
Lodestar, dawn, plate, 8½" 65.00
Lodestar, dawn, sugar bowl, w/hdls 85.00
Lodestar, dawn, vase, #1626, crimped, 8" 175.00
Lodestar, dawn, vase, #1626, 8" 140.00
New Era, crystal, bowl, floral, 11" 25.00
New Era, crystal, claret; 4-oz 15.00
New Era, crystal, creamer 35.00
New Era, crystal, plate, bread & butter; 5½x4½" 12.00
New Era, crystal, plate, 10x8" 35.00
New Era, crystal, saucer, after dinner 10.00
New Era, crystal, stem, champagne; 6-oz 12.50
New Era, crystal, stem, wine; 3-oz 35.00
New Era, crystal, tray, celery; 13" 30.00
New Era, crystal, tumbler, soda; ftd, 14-oz 15.00
New Era, crystal, tumbler, soda; ftd, 5-oz 7.00
New Era, crystal, tumbler, soda; ftd, 8-oz 10.00
Octagon, gr, plate, 14" 35.00
Octagon, orchid, bowl, soup; flat, 9" 30.00
Octagon, pk, bowl, mint; #1229, 6" 12.00
Octagon, pk, bowl, vegetable; 9" 20.00
Octagon, pk, sugar bowl, #500 ....20.00

Octagon, yel, basket, #500, 5" 170.00
Octagon, yel, bowl, #500, 6" 20.00
Octagon, yel, bowl, grapefruit; 6½" 22.00
Octagon, yel, bowl, jelly; #1229, 5½" 15.00
Octagon, yel, cup, after dinner 15.00
Octagon, yel, dish, frozen dessert; #500 ....15.00
Octagon, yel, plate, cream soup liner 7.00
Octagon, yel, plate, luncheon; 8" 10.00
Octagon, yel, plate, 10½" 30.00
Octagon, yel, platter, oval, 12¾" 30.00
Octagon, yel, tray, celery; 12" 17.00
Old Colony, crystal, bowl, vegetable; oval, 10" 34.00
Old Colony, crystal, creamer, ind 15.00
Old Colony, crystal, saucer, sq 4.00
Old Colony, crystal, stem, wine; #3390, 2½-oz 12.00
Old Colony, crystal, tumbler, juice; #3390, ftd, 5-oz 7.00
Old Colony, gr, saucer, rnd 10.00
Old Colony, gr, stem, cordial; #3390, 1-oz 165.00
Old Colony, gr, sugar bowl, ind 35.00
Old Colony, pk, bowl, dessert; oval, 2-hdl, 10" 40.00
Old Colony, pk, bowl, flared, ftd 35.00
Old Colony, pk, bowl, 2-hdl, ftd, 5" 17.50
Old Colony, pk, comport, oval, ftd, 7" 75.00
Old Colony, pk, finger bowl, #3390, ftd 16.00
Old Colony, pk, ice tub, dolphin ft 110.00
Old Colony, pk, shakers, pr 80.00
Old Colony, pk, stem, claret; #3380, 4-oz 50.00
Old Colony, pk, stem, sherbet; #3380, 6-oz 11.00
Old Colony, yel, bowl, grapefruit; #3380 ....18.00
Old Colony, yel, bowl, nappy; 8" 40.00
Old Colony, yel, bowl, triplex, 7" 25.00
Old Colony, yel, plate, rnd, 4½" 7.00
Old Colony, yel, plate, sq, 6" 15.00
Old Colony, yel, plate, sq, 7" 18.00
Old Colony, yel, stem, claret; #3380, 4-oz 27.50
Old Colony, yel, stem, cocktail; #3380, 3-oz 25.00
Old Colony, yel, stem, cordial; #3380, 1-oz 135.00
Old Colony, yel, sugar bowl, dolphin ft 45.00
Old Colony, yel, vase, ftd, 9" 150.00
Old Sandwich, cobalt, stem, claret; 4-oz 150.00
Old Sandwich, crystal, finger bowl 12.00
Old Sandwich, crystal, plate, sq, 7" 7.00
Old Sandwich, crystal, stem, sherbet; 4-oz 6.00
Old Sandwich, gr, beer mug, 18-oz 450.00
Old Sandwich, gr, candlestick, 6" 100.00
Old Sandwich, gr, parfait, 4½-oz 25.00
Old Sandwich, gr, pitcher, ice lip, ½-gal 180.00
Old Sandwich, gr, saucer 15.00
Old Sandwich, gr, stem, wine; 2½-oz 55.00
Old Sandwich, gr, tumbler, toddy; 6½-oz 22.00
Old Sandwich, pk, pilsner, 10-oz 32.00
Old Sandwich, pk, shakers, pr 65.00
Old Sandwich, pk, stem, low ft, 10-oz 25.00
Old Sandwich, pk, tumbler, iced tea; ftd, 12-oz 22.00
Old Sandwich, pk, tumbler, 10-oz 17.00
Old Sandwich, yel, beer mug, 12-oz 210.00
Old Sandwich, yel, creamer, 18-oz 190.00
Orchid, crystal, ashtray, 3" 27.50
Orchid, crystal, bell, dinner; #5022 or #5025 ....125.00
Orchid, crystal, bowl, flower; ftd, 11" 95.00
Orchid, crystal, bowl, fruit or salad; ftd, 9" 100.00
Orchid, crystal, bowl, gardenia; 13" 65.00
Orchid, crystal, bowl, oval, 4-ftd, 11" 80.00
Orchid, crystal, bowl, salad; deep, 10" 100.00

Orchid, crystal, bowl, salad; 7" 45.00
Orchid, crystal, candy box, w/lid, low ft, 6" 150.00
Orchid, crystal, cigarette holder, w/lid 125.00
Orchid, crystal, cocktail shaker, #4225, 1-pt 265.00
Orchid, crystal, comport, blown, 5½" 87.50

Orchid, Covered dish, horse finial, 4", $175.00.

Orchid, crystal, decanter, #4036½, 1-pt 235.00
Orchid, crystal, decanter, sherry; oval, 1-pt 225.00
Orchid, crystal, marmalade, w/lid 200.00
Orchid, crystal, mayonnaise, 1-hdl, 5½" 40.00
Orchid, crystal, oil, ftd, 3-oz 155.00
Orchid, crystal, pitcher, ice tankard; 64-oz 500.00
Orchid, crystal, plate, cake or salver; ftd, 14" 265.00
Orchid, crystal, plate, demitorte; 11" 50.00
Orchid, crystal, plate, salad; 7" 18.00
Orchid, crystal, plate, sandwich; 11" 50.00
Orchid, crystal, sugar bowl, ftd 25.00
Orchid, crystal, toast, w/dome 300.00
Orchid, crystal, tray, celery; 13" 47.50
Orchid, crystal, vase, bud; ftd, 8" 165.00
Orchid, crystal, vase, bud; sq, ftd, 8" 185.00
Orchid, crystal, vase, 14" 600.00
Plantation, crystal, bowl, celery; 2-part, 13" 35.00
Plantation, crystal, bowl, jelly; flared, 6½" 18.00
Plantation, crystal, bowl, nappy; 5" 15.00
Plantation, crystal, bowl, punch; 13" 500.00
Plantation, crystal, bowl, relish; rnd, 4-part 60.00
Plantation, crystal, bowl, salad; 9" 85.00
Plantation, crystal, butter dish, rnd, 5" 95.00
Plantation, crystal, candlestick, 1-light 75.00
Plantation, crystal, candlestick, 2-light 50.00
Plantation, crystal, cheese dish, w/lid, ftd, 5" 85.00
Plantation, crystal, comport, deep, w/lid, 5" 75.00
Plantation, crystal, creamer, ftd 25.00
Plantation, crystal, cup, punch 25.00
Plantation, crystal, marmalade, w/lid 100.00
Plantation, crystal, mayonnaise, rolled ft, 4½" 55.00
Plantation, crystal, plate, demitorte; 10½" 40.00
Plantation, crystal, plate, punch bowl liner, 18" 95.00
Plantation, crystal, plate, salad; 7" 15.00
Plantation, crystal, shakers, pr 45.00
Pleat & Panel, crystal, plate, dinner; 10¾" 15.00
Pleat & Panel, crystal, vase, 8" 20.00
Pleat & Panel, gr, bowl, grapefruit/cereal; 6½" 15.00
Pleat & Panel, pk, plate, bread; 7" 8.00
Pleat & Panel, pk, tumbler, ground bottom, 8-oz 12.00
Provincial, crystal, ashtray, sq, 3" 12.50
Provincial, crystal, bowl, flower; 12" 30.00
Provincial, crystal, bowl, punch; 5-qt 100.00
Provincial, crystal, butter dish, w/lid 85.00

Provincial, crystal, vase, pansy; 4" 25.00
Provincial, crystal, vase, sweet pea; 6" 35.00
Provincial, limelight gr, plate, buffet; 18" 165.00
Provincial, limelight gr, tumbler, ftd, 9-oz 65.00
Queen Ann, crystal, bottle, oil; 4-oz 35.00
Queen Ann, crystal, bowl, nappy; 8" 22.00
Queen Ann, crystal, candlestick, 3-ftd, 3" 45.00
Queen Ann, crystal, comport, sq, 6" 40.00
Queen Ann, crystal, ice tub, w/metal hdls 40.00
Queen Ann, crystal, jug, ftd, 3-pt 70.00
Queen Ann, crystal, tray, celery; 10" 12.00
Ridgeleigh, crystal, basket, bonbon 11.00
Ridgeleigh, crystal, bottle, cologne; 4-oz 85.00
Ridgeleigh, crystal, cheese dish, 2-hdl, 6" 11.00
Ridgeleigh, crystal, decanter, w/stopper, 1-pt 150.00
Ridgeleigh, crystal, pitcher, ½-gal 175.00
Ridgeleigh, crystal, stem, cocktail; pressed 22.00
Ridgeleigh, crystal, stem, wine; pressed 32.00
Ridgeleigh, crystal, vase, #1 ind, cuspidor form 25.00
Rose, crystal, bell, dinner; #5072 ....145.00
Rose, crystal, bowl, jelly; ftd, Waverly, 6½" 45.00
Rose, crystal, cocktail shaker, #4225, Cobel 125.00
Rose, crystal, plate, salad; Waverly, 7" 20.00

Stanhope, Creamer and sugar bowl, $50.00; Plate, 7", $7.50; Cup and saucer, $20.00.

Stanhope, crystal, ashtray, ind 20.00
Stanhope, crystal, bowl, salad; 11" 45.00
Stanhope, crystal, stem, claret; #4083, 4-oz 25.00
Stanhope, crystal, stem, goblet;, #4083, 10-oz 22.50
Stanhope, crystal, stem, wine; pressed, 2½-oz 20.00
Stanhope, crystal, vase, ball form, 7" 50.00
Twist, crystal, plate, relish; 3-part, 13" 17.00
Twist, gr, cocktail shaker, metal top 400.00
Twist, gr, tumbler, soda; ftd, 6-oz 20.00
Twist, pk, plate, utility; 3-ftd, 10" 30.00
Twist, pk, sugar bowl, ftd 30.00
Victorian, crystal, bottle, French dressing 50.00
Victorian, crystal, bowl, punch 225.00
Victorian, crystal, cigarette box, 4" 50.00
Victorian, crystal, plate, cracker; 12" 75.00
Victorian, crystal, stem, champagne; w/saucer, 5-oz 17.50
Victorian, crystal, tray, celery; 12" 25.00
Waverly, crystal, bowl, relish; oblong, 3-part, 7" 50.00
Waverly, crystal, bowl, salad; 7" 17.00
Waverly, crystal, comport, oval, low ftd, 7" 40.00
Waverly, crystal, honey dish, ftd, 6½" 22.00
Waverly, crystal, sandwich; 11" 18.00
Yeoman, crystal, plate, oyster cocktail; 8" 9.00
Yeoman, gr, bowl, banana split; ftd 35.00
Yeoman, gr, salver, low ftd, 12" 32.00
Yeoman, pk, plate, finger bowl underplate 5.00

Yeoman, yel, bowl, preserve; oval, 6" 17.00
Yeoman, yel, cruet, oil; 4-oz 50.00
Yeoman, yel, stem, soda; 5-oz 12.00
Yeoman, yel, tray, celery; 9" 16.00

Heubach

Gebruder Heubach is a German porcelain company that has been in operation since the 1800s, producing quality figurines and novelty items. They are perhaps most famous for their doll heads and piano babies, most of which are marked with the circular rising sun device containing an 'H' superimposed over a 'C.' Our advisor for this category is Grace Ochsner; she is listed in the Directory under Illinois.

Angry baby w/clenched hands sits before open eggshell, 5" 325.00
Baby, crawling, #8101, mk, 8" 450.00
Baby, crawling, molded hair, intaglio eyes, 7" L, NM 325.00
Baby, lying on bk, ft in air, 4" 200.00
Baby in highchair, molded clothes, sm 500.00

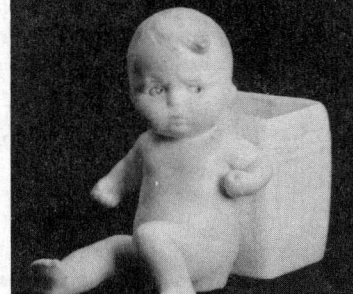

Baby seated before planter, 5½", $350.00.

Baby sits w/ice skates, night light, 3½" 475.00
Bicyclist, 11½" 350.00
Blond baby sits in tattered shoe, 12" 1,900.00
Blond boy sits astraddle bench blowing bubbles, 9" 400.00
Blond girl in pk pleated skirt w/gr sash, mk, 5¾" 325.00
Boy in red hat & eyeglasses sits w/arms Xd on chair bk, 7" 400.00
Boy w/monkey on arm, lav suit, 13" 450.00
Bust of Victorian girl leaning on log, mk, 6" 550.00
Dutch boy in wht suit pulls cap down w/both hands, 8" 425.00
Dutch children, sitting, mk, 7¼", pr 425.00
Dutch girl w/attached basket, flirty pose, mk, 7½" 325.00
Girl in bunny costume before lg pk egg, eyes to side, 7½" 525.00
Girl stands beside vase, mk, 6½" 175.00
Humidor, Jasper, gr, Indian chief on lid, 5" 150.00
Nude blond child sits w/hands to cheeks, 4" 225.00
Planter, shepherdess w/flock figural, mk, 4x10¾x2¾" 195.00
Plaque, Jasper, Indian on horse attacks bear, wht/lav, 9" L 215.00

Hickman, Royal Arden

Born in Willamette, Oregon, Royal A. Hickman was a genius in all aspects of design interpretation. Mr. Hickman's expertise can be seen in the designs of the lovely Heisey figurines, Kosta crystal, Bruce Fox aluminum, Three Crowns aluminum, Vernon Kilns, and Royal Haeger Pottery (as well as handcrafted silver, furniture, and paintings).

Because Mr. Hickman moved around during much of his lifetime, his influence has been felt in all forms of the media. Designs from his independent companies include 'Royal Hickman Pottery and Lamps' (sold through Ceramic Arts Inc., of Chattanooga, Tennessee), 'Royal Hickman's Paris Ware,' 'Royal Hickman — Florida,' and 'California Designed by Royal Hickman.' The following listings will give examples of pieces bearing the various trademarks. Our advisors for this category are Lee Garmon and Doris Frizzell; both are listed in the Directory under Illinois. See also Royal Haegar; Vernon Kilns, Melinda pattern.

Bruce Fox Aluminum

Banana leaf, sgn Royal Hickman-RH 6, 22½" L 25.00
Dish, lobster, lg 50.00
Dish, 3-point leaf, sgn Royal Hickman, 15½" L 25.00
Ivy tray, #362, 13" 20.00
Oak leaf, 2 acorns, 14½" L 20.00
Platter, fish, EX detail, sgn Royal Hickman-RH 3, 13x9" 50.00
2-acorn oak tray, 14½" 25.00
5-point leaf tray, 14" 25.00
7-point leaf tray, sgn Royal Hickman, 14" 25.00

California, Designed by Royal Hickman

Bowl, red w/blk highlights, #607, 9½" 15.00
Figurine, deer, apple gr w/wht spots, appl eyes, 15" 25.00
Figurine, giraffe & young, pk w/blk spots & vase, 11x7" 35.00
Punch bowl, Tom & Jerry, w/8 mugs 300.00
Swan, red w/blk highlights, #643, 17" 40.00

Miscellaneous Signatures

Sea horse vase, sgn Royal Hickman USA, #468, 8" 25.00
Vase, fish figurine, Petty Crystal Glaze, #467 ....25.00
Vase, lg heart, sgn Royal Hickman, Italy, #3774 ....35.00
Vase, rooster figurine, Petty Crystal Glaze, #565 ....95.00

Royal Hickman — Florida

Vase, free-form, #578, 14" 40.00
Vase, horse's head, gray w/wht mane, 13¾" 75.00
Vase, pouter pigeon, blk cascade, #599, 8½" 40.00
Vase, swan, head down, blk cascade, #624-R, 14" 60.00

Royal Hickman — Guadal La Jara, Mexico

Vase, 3 dolphin figurines, 13" 95.00

Higgins

Contemporary glass artists Frances and Michael Higgins have been designing high-quality glassware since the late 1940s. Their designs are often created by fusing layers of glass together, though sometimes colored ground glass is used to 'paint' the decoration onto the surface. Molds are used, and through a process called 'slumping,' the glass is fired to a very high temperature, causing it to soften and take on the predetermined shape. Their work is ultramodern and is more readily found in metropolitan areas.

The earliest mark was an embossed device collector's refer to as the Higgin's 'man' — an H formed with a cup-like top and bottom superimposed over a vertical line. Later production pieces such as the piece shown are always signed with 'Higgins' etched in gold on the surface. We were assisted in our research by Dennis Hopp; he is listed in the Directory under Illinois. Our advisor for this category is Judy Potter; she is listed in the Directory under Iowa.

Ashtray, abstracts in orange/blk/gold, 7x10" 60.00
Ashtray, lt gr w/lg stylized yel/gr/gilt flower, sq, 5x5" 40.00

Charger, lime blobs w/coral-like branches on clear, 14" 145.00
Plate, astors, gr w/gold trim, 12" 90.00

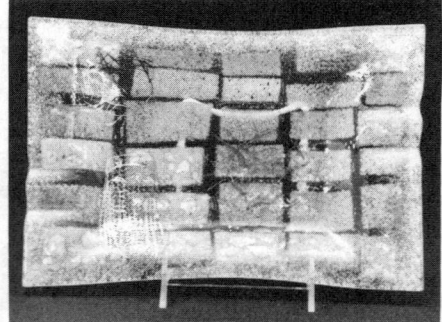

Tray, blue, lime, orange and green squares
with gold, 10", $65.00.

Tray, abstracts in bls & gold, 10x14" 190.00
Tray, lav irid w/long triangles in bl & gr, 10x10" 130.00

Historical Glass

Glassware commemorating particularly significant historical events became popular in the late 1800s. Bread trays were the most common form, but plates, mugs, pitchers, and other items were also pressed in clear as well as colored glass. It was sold in vast amounts at the 1876 Philadelphia Centennial Exposition by various manufacturers who exhibited their wares on the grounds. It remained popular well into the 20th century.

In the listings that follow, L numbers refer to a book by Lindsey, a standard guide used by many collectors. Our advisor for this category is Darlene Yohe; she is listed in the Directory under Arkansas. See also Bread Plates; Pattern Glass.

Bottle, Grant's Tomb, milk glass, no stopper 250.00
Bottle, Grover Cleveland bust, clear & frosted, L-318, lg 225.00
Bust, Dewey, Manila 1898, 5" 145.00
Bust, MJ Owens, frosted 55.00
Butter dish, American Shield 195.00
Calabash, Roosevelt-TVA, aqua, qt 60.00
Celery, Independence Hall 65.00
Covered dish, Battleship Maine, milk glass, L-466 ....95.00
Covered dish, Uncle Sam, milk glass, L-112 ....75.00
Cup, Harrison & Morton, bl 235.00
Cup plate, Bunker Hill 30.00
Dish, Flaming Sword, L-209 ....25.00
Flask, Grover Cleveland, etched, flat-side rectangle, 7" 475.00
Glass, ale; Centennial 55.00
Goblet, Pittsburgh Centennial 95.00
Lamp, oil; Goddess of Liberty, 1876 Centennial 125.00
Match holder, T Roosevelt, etched, top hat form 90.00
Mug, Christopher Columbus, L-1 ....45.00
Mug, Columbus & Geo Washington, L-2 ....45.00
Mug, Liberty Bell, snake hdl, Gillinder 300.00
Mug, Mephistopheles, milk glass 75.00
Paperweight, Director Goshorn, 1876, Gillinder, L-449 ....155.00
Paperweight, Plymouth Rock, L-18, sm 38.00
Paperweight, Washington Monument, milk glass, 5½" 175.00
Pickle dish, E Pluribus Unum 45.00
Pin tray, bust of McKinley, frosted base, L-297 ....110.00

Plate, Battleship Maine, openwork border, 5½" 16.00
Plate, Bunker Hill 85.00
Plate, Columbus, milk glass, 9½" 65.00
Plate, Dewey, frosted, L-392, 5½" 35.00
Plate, For President Winfield S Hancock, 8" 110.00
Plate, Garfield Star, frosted, L-299, 6" 45.00
Plate, Indian, milk glass, L-14, 7½" 60.00
Plate, Liberty Bell, 10½" 80.00
Plate, Old Glory, openwork border, 5½" 32.00
Plate, St Louis World's Fair, 1904, frosted, 7½" 40.00
Plate, Texian Campaign, lt bl, 9½" 195.00
Plate, unidentified lady, milk glass, L-453 ....95.00
Plate, Wm H Harrison, Tippecanoe, Fort Meigs, amber, 8" 225.00
Plate, Yankee Doodle, gr, openwork border, 5½" 35.00
Platter, Constitution, eagle & banner center 75.00
Shaker, Lighthouse 48.00
Syrup, Peace & Plenty, emb sailing ship & anchor, strap hdl 195.00
Toothpick holder, Preparedness, soldier figural, L-483 ....145.00
Tumbler, Admiral Dewey, L-396 ....48.00
Tumbler, America, L-48 ....25.00
Tumbler, Bust of McKinley in laurel wreath 75.00
Tumbler, Hobson, in laurel wreath, frosted 60.00
Tumbler, Louisiana Purchase, L-107 ....35.00
Tumbler, Philadelphia Sesquicentennial 18.00

Hobbs, Brockunier, & Co.

Hobbs and Brockunier's South Wheeling Glass Works was in operation during the last quarter of the 19th century. They are most famous for their peachblow, amberina, Daisy and Button, and Hobnail pattern glass. The mainstay of the operation, however, was druggist items and plain glassware — bowls, mugs, and simple footed pitchers with shell handles. See also Frances Ware; Peachblow.

Bowl, bl w/appl wht edge, clear int, ruffled, 3½x8" 495.00
Bowl, citron yel w/cranberry Candy Ribbon rim, 10" 120.00
Bowl, Daisy & Button, shallow, 7" 325.00
Cruet, Hobnail, vaseline, orig stopper, 7¾" 335.00
Cruet, Swirl, amber shaded to rust, polished pontil 350.00
Pitcher, Honeycomb, amber frost, ruffled rim, +4 tumblers 350.00
Pitcher, Honeycomb, bl opal, bl hdl, 9x7" 375.00
Tumbler, Hobnail, amber frost, 10-row, 4x2½" 75.00
Vase, Invt T'print, honey-amber, swirled ruffled top, 12" 125.00

Homer Laughlin

The Homer Laughlin China Company of Newell, West Virginia, was founded in 1871. The superior dinnerware they displayed at the Centennial Exposition in Philadelphia in 1876 won the highest award of excellence. From that time to the present, they have continued to produce quality dinnerware and kitchenware, many lines of which are becoming very popular collectibles. Most of the dinnerware is marked with the name of the pattern and occasionally with the shape name as well. The 'HLC' trademark is usually followed by a number series, the first two digits of which indicate the year of its manufacture. See also Fiesta; Harlequin; Riviera.

Amberstone, bowl, salad; jumbo 40.00
Amberstone, coffee server 50.00
Amberstone, mug, jumbo, rare 22.00
Amberstone, plate, pie 35.00
Amberstone, plate, 10" 7.00

Amberstone, sauce boat 22.00
Americana, bowl, w/lid, 9" 22.00
Americana, creamer 12.00
Americana, plate, 6" 4.00
Americana, platter, sq, 8" 12.00
Americana, teapot 65.00
Carnival, bowl, fruit; sm 7.00
Carnival, plate, 6½" 3.00
Casualstone, ashtray, rare 10.00
Casualstone, bowl, dessert 5.50
Casualstone, casserole 25.00
Casualstone, plate, bread & butter 3.00
Casualstone, platter, rnd 15.00
Conchita & Mexicana, fork 48.00
Conchita & Mexicana, jug, batter; w/lid 140.00
Conchita & Mexicana, plate, cake; 10½" 300.00
Dogwood, bowl, mixing; Kitchen Kraft, 6½" 25.00
Dogwood, cup & saucer 9.50
Dogwood, plate, 7" 7.00
Dogwood, platter, 13½" 20.00
Embossed Line, bowl, oval, 6½" 8.00
Embossed Line, casserole, 6" 28.00
Embossed Line, pitcher, batter 30.00
Embossed Line, plate, 10" 10.00
Epicure, bowl, vegetable; w/lid 45.00
Epicure, ladle, 5½" 25.00
Epicure, plate, 8" 10.00
Epicure, platter, lg 18.00
Epicure, shakers, pr 15.00
Harmony, bowl, fruit; 5½" 7.00
Harmony, casserole, Kitchen Kraft, 8" 32.00
Harmony, fork, Kitchen Kraft 40.00
Harmony, plate, 9" 7.00
Jubilee, bowl, fruit 5.00
Jubilee, coffeepot 35.00
Jubilee, plate, 6" 2.50
Jubilee, sauce boat 12.00
Oven-Serve, jar, w/lid, lg 60.00
Oven-Serve, platter 20.00
Pastel Nautilus, bowl, oatmeal; ftd, 6" 8.50
Pastel Nautilus, cup & saucer, after dinner 15.00
Pastel Nautilus, plate, 9" 7.00
Priscilla, bowl, vegetable; oval, 9" 18.00
Priscilla, coffeepot, Kitchen Kraft 75.00
Priscilla, pitcher, water; Kitchen Kraft 25.00
Priscilla, plate, 9" 8.00
Rhythm, bowl, nappy 12.00
Rhythm, casserole 50.00
Rhythm, creamer, 2¾" 7.00
Rhythm, plate, calender 12.00
Rhythm, plate, pie; Kitchen Kraft, 9½" 16.00
Rhythm, plate, 10" 12.00
Rhythm, platter, 13" 15.00
Rhythm Rose, plate, cake; Kitchen Kraft, 10½" 20.00
Serenade, bowl, lug soup 20.00
Serenade, plate, 7" 5.00
Serenade, teapot 65.00
Tango, bowl, oval, 9" 12.00
Tango, creamer 8.00
Tango, shakers, pr 12.00
Virginia Rose, bowl, deep, 5" 12.00
Virginia Rose, bowl, oatmeal; 6" 7.00
Virginia Rose, bowl, vegetable; scarce, 7½" 20.00
Virginia Rose, pitcher, milk; 5" 25.00
Virginia Rose, plate, 9" 8.00
Virginia Rose, platter (gravy liner), 9" 15.00
Wells Art Glaze, bowl, fruit; 5" 9.00
Wells Art Glaze, casserole 50.00
Wells Art Glaze, jug, w/lid & decals 45.00
Wells Art Glaze, nut dish/butter pat 9.00
Wells Art Glaze, sauce boat 18.00

Hull

The A.E. Hull Pottery was formed in 1905 in Zanesville, Ohio, and in the early years produced stoneware specialities. They expanded in 1907, adding a second plant and employing over two hundred workers. By 1920 they were manufacturing a full line of stoneware, art pottery with both airbrushed and blended glazes, florist pots, and gardenware. They also produced toilet ware and kitchen items with a white semiporcelain body. Although these continued to be staple products, after the stock market crash of 1929, emphasis was shifted to tile production. By the mid-thirties interest in art pottery production was growing, and over the next fifteen years, several lines of matt pastel floral-decorated patterns were designed, consisting of vases, planters, baskets, ewers, and bowls in various sizes.

The Red Riding Hood cookie jar, patented in 1943, proved so successful that a whole line of figural kitchenware and novelty items was added. They continued to be produced well into the fifties. (See also Little Red Riding Hood.) Through the forties their floral artware lines flooded the market, due to the restriction of foreign imports. Although best known for their pastel matt-glazed ware, some of the lines were high gloss. Rosella, glossy coral on a pink clay body, was produced for a short time only; and Magnolia, although offered in a matt glaze, was produced in gloss as well.

The plant was destroyed in 1950 by a flood which resulted in a devastating fire when the floodwater caused the kilns to explode. The company rebuilt and equipped their new factory with the most modern machinery. It was soon apparent that the matt glaze could not be duplicated through the more modern processes, however, and soon attention was concentrated on high-gloss artware lines such as Parchment and Pine and Ebb Tide. Figural planters and novelties, piggy banks, and dinnerware were produced in abundance in the late fifties and sixties. By the mid-seventies dinnerware and florist ware were the mainstay of their business. The firm discontinued operations in 1985.

Our advisor, Brenda Roberts, has compiled a lovely book, *The Collector's Encyclopedia of Hull Pottery*, with full-color photos and current values which has been recently reprinted. You will find her address in the Directory under Missouri.

Advertising plaque, The AE Hull Co Pottery, pk/bl, 5x11" 3,500.00
Alpine, pretzel jar, emb Alpine scene, brn, 9" 300.00
Alpine, tankard, emb Alpine scene, brn, 8½" 280.00
Blossom Flite, basket, T-4, 8½" 120.00
Blossom Flite, bowl, console; pk w/pk int, T-10, 16½" 135.00
Blossom Flite, candle holder, loop hdls, T-11, 3" 35.00
Blossom Flite, teapot, pk w/pk int, T-14, 8" 105.00
Bow-Knot, cornucopia, dbl; bl/turq, B-13, 13" 295.00
Bow-Knot, creamer, bl/turq, B-21, 4" 140.00
Bow-Knot, ewer, pk/bl, B-1, 5" 210.00
Bow-Knot, jardiniere, pk/bl, B-18, 5¾" 265.00
Bow-Knot, vase, bl/turq, hdls, flared rim, sq ft, B-8, 8½" 250.00
Bow-Knot, vase, pk/bl, B-2, 5" 160.00
Bow-Knot, vase, pk/bl, B-3, 6½" 140.00
Bow-Knot, wall pocket, pitcher form, turq/bl, B-26, 6" 210.00
Butterfly, ashtray, glossy, B-3, 7" 40.00
Butterfly, ewer, ivory w/bl int, B-11, 8¾" 175.00

Butterfly, lavabo, glossy, orig metal hanger, B-24/B-25, 16" 155.00
Butterfly, teapot, ivory w/bl int, B-18, 8½" 140.00
Calla Lily, bowl, console; pk/bl, 1-hdl, #590/32, 13" 140.00
Calla Lily, candle holder, leaf form, pk/bl, unmk, 2¼" 75.00
Calla Lily, cornucopia, bl/ivory, #570/33, 8" 110.00
Calla Lily, ewer, bl/pk, #506, 10" 365.00
Calla Lily, vase, bl, #530/33, 9" 360.00
Calla Lily, vase, bl/pk, angular hdls, #550/33, 7½" 145.00
Calla Lily, vase, turq, angular hdls, #501/33, 6½" 90.00
Camellia, basket, pk/bl, bow on front, #107, 8" 310.00
Camellia, cornucopia, cream, #101, 8½" 150.00
Camellia, ewer, pk/bl, #115, 8½" 285.00
Camellia, vase, bl/ivory, lamp shape, #139, 10½" 370.00
Camellia, vase, pk/bl, bulbous, sm hdls, #123, 6½" 90.00
Camellia, vase, pk/bl, swan shape, #118, 6½" 120.00
Camellia, vase, wht matt, fan shape, #143, 8½" 165.00
Capri, ewer, Seagreen, #87, 12" 110.00
Capri, planter, swan form, coral, #23, 8½" 65.00
Cereal Ware, canister, Golden Grecian, 8½" 75.00
Cereal Ware, jar, spice; Blue Star & Lattice, 4¾" 50.00
Cereal Ware, jar, spice; Flying Blue Bird 65.00
Cinderella Kitchenware, creamer, Blossom, #28, 4½" 36.00
Cinderella Kitchenware, pitcher, Bouquet, ice lip, #22, 64-oz 165.00
Continental, vase, bud; orange stripes, #66, 9½" 35.00
Continental, vase, candle holder/planter, bl stripes, #67, 4" 30.00
Continental, vase, gr stripes, #53, 8½" 45.00
Cook 'N Serve Ware, coffee server, brn/yel, #32, 11" 65.00
Dogwood, cornucopia, cream/bl, #522, 3¾" 75.00
Dogwood, vase, bl/bream, hdls, #509, 6½" 100.00
Dogwood, vase, cream, ornate hdls, flared rim, #510, 10½" 280.00
Dogwood, vase, pk/bl, low hdls, #515, 8½" 160.00
Dogwood, vase, suspended, pk/bl, #502, 6½" 235.00
Dogwood, window box, pk/bl, #508, 10½" 225.00
Early Art, candle holder, lav, lustre ware, unmk, 3" 75.00
Early Art, matt; vase, mc stripes, #26, H in circle, 8" 80.00
Early Art, vase, stoneware, blended bl, #39, 8" 90.00
Early Art, wall pocket, lustreware, unmk, 1927-30, 8½" 100.00
Early Banded Utility, bowl, stoneware, #428, H in circle, 5" 25.00
Early Banded Utility, casserole, yel ware, w/lid, #113, 7" 75.00
Early Utility, bowl, stoneware, gr, #421, 10" 75.00
Early Utility, pie plate, banded semiporc, unmk, 9" 45.00
Early Utility, pitcher, banded semiporc, E, 7" 60.00
Ebb Tide, ashtray, mermaid, E-8, 5" 135.00
Ebb Tide, cornucopia, fish & shell form, E-9, 11¾" 110.00
Ebb Tide, ewer, fish & shell form, E-10, 14" 250.00
Ebb Tide, teapot, E-14, 6½" 230.00
Imperial, ewer, Golden Mist, fish design, #482, 11" 128.00
Imperial, ewer, Golden Mist, swirl design, F-480, 10½" 85.00
Imperial, ewer, pk, #461, USA, 12" 40.00
Iris, basket, pk/cream, #408, 7" 300.00
Iris, candle holder, #441, 5" 90.00
Iris, ewer, rose/bl, #401, 13½" 525.00
Iris, jardiniere, cream, #413, 5½" 185.00
Iris, planter, pk/cream, rectangular, #412, 7" 224.00
Iris, vase, peach, hdls, #403, 4¾" 75.00
Iris, vase, pk/bl, #402, 7" 155.00
Iris, vase, rose/peach, petal rim, hdls, #407, 8½" 170.00
Lamp base, floral medallion on ivory, L-1, USA, 13" 340.00
Magnolia, glossy; bowl, console; bl floral on pk, H-23, 13" 130.00
Magnolia, glossy; creamer, pk floral on pk, H-21, 3¾" 30.00
Magnolia, glossy; vase, bl floral on pk w/gold, H-6, 6½" 52.00
Magnolia, matt; bowl, console; pk/bl, hdls, #26, 12" 180.00
Magnolia, matt; cornucopia, pk/bl, #19, 8½" 125.00
Magnolia, matt; ewer, dusty rose/yel, #5, 7" 165.00

Magnolia, matt; ewer, yel/rose, #14, 4¾" 45.00
Magnolia, matt; vase, dusty rose/yel, hdls, #11, 6¼" 68.00
Magnolia, matt; vase, pk/bl, #8, 10½" 165.00
Mardi Gras/Granada, ewer, pk/ivory, emb floral, #66, 10" 158.00
Mardi Gras/Granada, vase, suspended, ivory, ribbed, #215, 9" 66.00
Mirror Almond, bowl, divided; almond w/caramel rim, 11" 30.00
Mirror Almond, mug, almond w/caramel rim, 3¼" 4.00
Mirror Almond, plate, dinner; almond w/caramel rim, 10" 8.00
Mirror Brown, butter dish, brn w/ivory foam, 7½" 20.00
Mirror Brown, canister, flour; brn w/ivory foam, rnd, 9" 190.00
Mirror Brown, casserole, hen on nest, brn w/ivory foam, 8" 50.00
Mirror Brown, cookie jar, cylindrical, brn w/ivory foam, 8" 45.00
Mirror Brown, cookie jar, gingerbread man, brn w/ivory foam, 12" .165.00
Mirror Brown, jug/creamer, brn w/ivory foam, 4¼" 10.00
Mirror Brown, pig bank, Jumbo, brn w/ivory foam, #197 ....80.00
Mirror Brown, pig bank, sitting, brn w/ivory foam, #196, 6" 30.00
Mirror Brown, pitcher, ice lip, brn w/ivory foam, 7½" 36.00
Mirror Brown, plate, dinner; brn w/ivory foam, 10½" 8.00
Mirror Brown, plate, steak; oval, brn w/ivory foam, 12" 13.00
Mirror Brown, server, gingerbread man, brn w/ivory foam, 10" 70.00
Mirror Brown, spoon rest, brn w/ivory foam, oval, 6½" 30.00
Mirror Brown, teapot, brn w/ivory foam, 6" 32.00
Morning Glory, basket, ivory, #62, 8" 650.00
Novelty, ashtray/planter, wht w/blk foam, metal stand, #204 ....70.00
Novelty, band leader, unmk, 5" 95.00
Novelty, Basket Girl planter, pk, #954, 8" 46.00
Novelty, Crazy Horse planter, #959, 1938, 5" 40.00
Novelty, doorstop, cat, unmk, 7¼" 225.00
Novelty, figurine, dachshund, blk gloss, #120, 14" 195.00
Novelty, pig bank, Corky, yel, 5x7" 75.00
Novelty, planter, Bandana Duck, pk/gr, #74, 9" 82.00

Novelty planter, white lamb with blue bow, #965, 7½", $37.50.

Novelty, planter, knight on horsebk, pk/turq, #55, 8" 75.00
Novelty, telephone vase, pk/bl, #50, 9" 85.00
Novelty, vase, twin deer, pk/gray, #62, 11½" 60.00
Nuline Bak-Serve, bowl, mixing; Drape & Panel, D-1, 9½" 36.00
Nuline Bak-Serve, cookie jar, Fish Scale, C-20, 2-qt, 8" 90.00
Nuline Bak-Serve, Fr casserole, Drape & Panel, D-15, 4½" 30.00
Nuline Bak-Serve, jug, batter; Dmn Quilt, B-7, 5" 50.00
Orchid, basket, pk/cream, #305, 7" 800.00
Orchid, candle holder, pk/bl, #315, 4" 105.00
Orchid, jardiniere, bl/pk, #310, 4¾" 115.00
Orchid, lamp base, bl, unmk, 10" 400.00
Orchid, vase, bl, #302, 6" 100.00
Orchid, vase, ivory/pk/bl, #308, 4¾" 75.00
Orchid, vase, pk/bl, #301, 8" 170.00
Pagoda, vase, gr, 6-sided, P-5, 12½" 30.00
Pagoda, vase, Persimmon, 6-sided, P-3, 7¾" 18.00
Parchment & Pine, basket, Pine Gr & Pearl Gray, S-3, 6" 105.00

Parchment & Pine, instant coffee server, S-15, 8" 160.00
Pine Cone, vase, bl, hdls, #55, 6½" 130.00
Poppy, basket, pk/cream, #601, 9" 725.00
Poppy, bowl, low, bl/pk, hdls, ornate rim, #602, 6½" 225.00
Poppy, ewer, bl/pk, ornate rim, #610, 13½" 975.00
Poppy, jardiniere, pk/cream, #608, 4¾" 105.00
Rosella, basket, coral, R-12, 7" 280.00
Rosella, cornucopia, coral, R-13, 8½" 125.00
Rosella, ewer, ivory, R-7, 9½" 480.00
Rosella, lamp, ivory, unmk, foil label, 6½" 360.00
Rosella, sugar bowl, ivory, w/lid, R-4, 5½" 75.00
Rosella, vase, coral, classic form, R-2, 5" 40.00
Royal Imperial, window box, pk w/wht spatter, #82, 12½" 30.00
Royal Woodland, cornucopia, turq w/wht spatter, W-10, 11" 60.00
Royal Woodland, ewer, pk w/wht spatter, W-24, 13½" 215.00
Serenade, basket, Shell Pk, S-5, 6¾" 105.00
Serenade, candy dish, Regency Bl/Sunlight Yel, S-3, 8¾" 125.00
Serenade, casserole, Regency Bl/Sunlight Yel, w/lid, S-20, 9" 122.00
Serenade, ewer, shell pk, S-2, 6½" 105.00
Serenade, pitcher, Jonquil Yel/Willow Gr, S-21, 10½" 185.00
Serenade, vase, shell pk, S-11, 10½" 128.00
Sun-Glo, grease jar, pk, #53, 5¼" 35.00
Sun-Glo, pitcher, pk, ice lip, #55, 7½" 145.00
Sun-Glo, vase, pk, sm hdls, #100, 6½" 50.00
Thistle, vase, bl, #53, 6½" 100.00
Thistle, vase, pk, #51, 6½" 100.00
Tile, crest design, 6-color, Hull Faience, 6x6" 110.00
Tile, geometric design, bl/gold, 2¾x2¾" 30.00
Tile, ivory satin, emb Hull Tile, 4¼x4¼" 20.00
Tokay, consolette, lt gr/Sweet Pk, #14, 15¾" 195.00
Tokay, ewer, lt gr/Sweet Pk, twig hdl, #3, 8" 105.00
Tokay, planter, lt gr/Sweet Pk, #9, 8" 45.00
Tropicana, basket, Caribbean figure on wht, T-55, 12¾" 480.00
Tropicana, planter/vase, Caribbean figure on wht, T-57, 14½" ..340.00
Tulip, basket, pk/bl, #102/33, 6" 260.00
Tulip, ewer, yel/pk/bl, #109-33, 13" 340.00
Tulip, flowerpot, bl, attached saucer, #116-33, 6" 160.00
Tulip, jardiniere, pk/bl, #117-30, 5" 105.00
Tulip, vase, bl/pk, #111-33, 6" 110.00
Tulip, vase, bud; bl/pk, #104-33, 6" 90.00
Tulip, vase, pk/yel/bl, ring hdls, tulip form, #101-33, 9" ..240.00
Tuscany, candy dish, gr grapes on milk wht, #9, 8½" 130.00
Tuscany, ewer, gr grapes on Sweet Pk, #13, 12" 265.00
Tuscany, vase, gr grapes on milk wht, integral hdls, #12, 12" 92.00
Water Lily, bowl, console; walnut/apricot, #L-21, 13½" 230.00
Water Lily, jardiniere, walnut/apricot, #L-23, 5½" 105.00
Water Lily, lamp, ivory, unmk, 7½" 230.00
Water Lily, teapot, walnut/apricot, L-18, 6" 170.00
Water Lily, vase, turq/Sweet Pk, sm hdls, L-12, 10½" 175.00
Water Lily, vase, turq/Sweet Pk w/gold, #L-1, 5½" 52.00
Wild Flower (no series), candle holder, dbl; cream, #69, 4" 100.00
Wild Flower (no series), ewer, pk/russet, #55, 13½" 610.00
Wild Flower (no series), sugar bowl, pk/russet, #74, 4¾" ...135.00
Wildflower, basket, pk/bl, #16, 10½" 300.00
Wildflower, ewer, pk/bl, #2, 5½" 70.00
Wildflower, vase, pk/bl, #1, 5½" 45.00
Wildflower, vase, yel/rose, fan shape, angle hdls, #15, 10½" 210.00
Woodland, glossy; basket, chartreuse/rose, W-9, 8¾" 100.00
Woodland, glossy; teapot, chartreuse/rose, W-26, 6½" 135.00
Woodland, glossy; vase, bl/gr, W-8, 7½" 70.00
Woodland, glossy; vase, pk floral on ivory, W-1, 5½" 45.00
Woodland, matt; candle holder, Dawn Rose, W-30, 3½" 90.00
Woodland, matt; cornucopia, Dawn Rose, W-5, 6½" 105.00
Woodland, matt; ewer, Harvest Yel, W-6, 6½" 170.00

Woodland, matt; flowerpot, Dawn Rose, attached saucer, W-11, 5½" ..195.00
Woodland, matt; planter, Harvest Yel, W-19, 10½" 160.00
Woodland, matt; vase, Harvest Yel, hdls, W-18, 10½" 200.00
Woodland, matt; wall pocket, seashell, Harvest Yel, W-13, 7½" ..215.00

Hummel

Hummel figurines were created through the artistry of Berta Hummel, a Franciscan nun called Sister M. Innocentia. The first figures were made about 1935 by Franz Goebel of Goebel Art Inc., Rodental, West Germany. Plates, plaques, and candy dishes are also produced, and the older, discontinued editions are highly sought collectibles. Generally speaking, an issue can be dated by the trademark. The first Hummels, from 1934-1950, were either incised or stamped with the 'Crown WG' mark. The 'full bee in V' mark was employed with minor variations until 1959. At that time the bee was stylized and represented by a solid disk with angled symmetrical wings completely contained within the confines of the 'V.' The three-line mark, 1964-1972, utilized the stylized bee and included a three-line arrangement, 'c by W. Goebel, W. Germany.' Another change in 1970 saw the 'stylized bee in V' suspended between the vertical bars of the 'b' and 'l' of a printed 'Goebel, West Germany.' Collectors refer to this mark as the 'last bee' or 'Goebel bee.' The current mark in use since 1979 omits the 'bee in V.' For a more thorough study of the subject, we recommend *Hummel Figurines and Plates, A Collector's Identification and Value Guide*, by Carl Luckey, available at your local book dealer. Idiosyncrasies in the numerical order of the following listings are due to computer sorting. See also Limited Edition Plates.

Key:
ce — closed edition   GB — Goebel bee
CM — crown mark   SB — stylized bee
FB — full bee   LB — last bee

#17/0, Congratulations, stylized bee, 5½", $150.00.

#III/53, Joyful, candy box, CM, 6¼" 585.00
#III/57, Chick Girl, candy box, SB, 5¼" 310.00
#III/58, Playmates, candy box, SB, 5¼" 325.00
#III/63, Singing Lessons, candy box, SB, 5¼" 325.00
#III/69, Happy Pastime, candy box, FB, 6" 385.00
#1, Puppy Love, FB, 5" 375.00

#109/0, Happy Traveler, CM, 5"	350.00
#109/0, Happy Traveler, 3-line mk, 5"	110.00
#11/0, Merry Wanderer, FB, 4¾"	250.00
#1½/0, Merry Wanderer, 3-line mk, 4¼"	125.00
#110/I, Let's Sing, FB, 3⅞"	225.00
#110/0, Let's Sing, CM, 3¼"	325.00
#111/3/0, Wayside Harmony, SB, 3¾"	120.00
#112/I, Just Resting, FB, 5"	330.00
#118, Little Thrifty, FB, 5"	375.00
#119, Postman, SB, 5¼"	160.00
#12/I, Chimney Sweep, FB, 5½"	260.00
#123, Max & Moritz, 3-line mk, 5¼"	155.00
#125, Vacation Time, plaque, FB, 4⅜x5¼"	360.00
#126, Retreat to Saftey, plaque, FB, 4¾" sq	275.00
#128, Baker, CM, 4¾"	460.00
#128, Baker, LB, 4¾"	135.00
#13/2/0, Meditation, SB, 4¼"	135.00
#130, Duet, SB, 5¼"	220.00
#133, Mother's Helper, FB, 5"	260.00
#134, Quartet, plaque, CM, 6" sq	900.00
#134, Quartet, plaque, SB, 6" sq	275.00
#135, Soloist, 3-line mk, 4¾"	125.00
#136/I, Friends, LB, 5"	175.00
#141/I, Apple Tree Girl, CM, 6"	650.00
#141/I, Apple Tree Girl, LB, 6"	125.00
#142/X, Apple Tree Boy, LB, 29"	16,900.00
#142/3/0, Apple Tree Boy, LB, 4"	110.00
#144, Angelic Song, CM, 4¼"	400.00
#15/II, Hear Ye Hear Ye, FB, 7½"	660.00
#15/0, Hear Ye Hear Ye, FB, 5"	255.00
#15/0, Hear Ye Hear Ye, 3-line mk, 5"	160.00
#150/I, Happy Days, CM, 6"	1,100.00
#150/2/0, Happy Days, FB, 4¼"	275.00
#152/A/II, Umbrella Boy, CM, 8"	2,700.00
#152/A/0, Umbrella Boy, SB, 5"	480.00
#152/B/II, Umbrella Girl, FB, 8"	1,100.00
#152/B/0, Umbrella Girl, SB, 4¾"	480.00
#153/0, Auf Wiedersehen, CM, 5¼"	580.00
#153/0, Auf Wiedersehen, LB, 7"	240.00
#154/0, Waiter, SB, 6"	185.00
#16/1, Little Hiker, CM, 5½"	500.00
#163, Whitsuntide, FB, 7¼"	825.00
#164, Worship, font, FB, 2¾x4¾"	75.00
#165, Swaying Lullaby, plaque, FB, 4½x5¼"	750.00
#168, Standing Boy, SB, 4⅛x5½"	160.00
#17/2 or #17/II, Congratulations, FB, 8¼"	5,500.00
#170/I, School Boys, 3-line mk, 7½"	980.00
#170/III, School Boys, SB, ce, 10"	1,650.00
#171, Little Sweeper, 3-line mk, 4½"	110.00
#172/II, Festival Harmony, FB, 10¾"	980.00
#174, She Loves Me, She Loves Me Not, SB, 4¼"	200.00
#175, Mother's Darling, 3-line mk, 5½"	165.00
#176/I, Happy Birthday, FB, 6"	385.00
#177/I, School Girls, 3-line mk, 7½"	980.00
#177/III, School Girls, SB, ce, 9½"	1,650.00
#18, Christ Child, FB, 2x6"	135.00
#180, Tuneful Goodnight, plaque, FB, 4x4¾"	660.00
#182, Good Friends, FB, 4"	275.00
#183, Forest Shrine, CM, 7x9"	2,500.00
#185, Accordion Boy, LB, 5¼"	175.00
#186, Sweet Music, CM, 5¼"	525.00
#188, Celestial Musician, 3-line mk, 7"	225.00
#188/0, Celestial Musician, LB, 5"	175.00
#193, Angel Duet, candle holder, CM, 5"	550.00
#194, Watchful Angel, 3-line mk, 6½"	275.00
#196/0, Telling Her Secret, FB, 5¼"	400.00
#197, Be Patient, CM, 6¼"	875.00
#197/I, Be Patient, LB, 6¼"	225.00
#198/2/0, Home From Market, SB, 4¾"	110.00
#20, Prayer Before Battle, FB, 4¼"	275.00
#200, Little Goat Herder, FB, 5½"	700.00
#200/0, Little Goat Herder, FB, 4¾"	275.00
#201/2/0, Retreat to Saftey, LB, 4"	90.00
#203/2/0, Signs of Spring, FB, 4"	245.00
#206, Angel Cloud, font, LB, 2¼x4¾"	45.00
#207, Heavenly Angel, font, FB, 2x4¾"	75.00
#21/I, Heavenly Angel, LB, 6¾"	200.00
#217, Boy w/Toothache, FB, 5½"	300.00
#218, Birthday Serenade, FB, 5¼"	850.00
#218/2/0, Birthday Serenade, SB, 4¼"	490.00
#22/I, Angel w/Birds, font, CM, 3¼x4"	550.00
#224/I, Wayside Harmony, table lamp, 3-line mk, 7½"	285.00
#230, Apple Tree Boy, table lamp, FB, 7½"	825.00
#235, Happy Days, table lamp, SB, 7¾"	490.00
#24/I, Lullaby, candle holder, SB, 3¼x5"	150.00
#24/III, Lullaby, candle holder, SB, 6x8"	450.00
#240, Little Drummer, LB, 4¼"	110.00
#243, Madonna & Child, font, FB, 3¼x4"	65.00
#246, Holy Family, font, FB, 3x4"	135.00
#248, Guardian Angel, font, 3-line mk, 2¼x5½"	40.00
#255, A Stich in Time, 3-line mk, 6¾"	185.00
#256, Knitting Lessons, SB, 7½"	550.00
#261, Angel Duet, LB, 5½"	200.00
#262, Heavenly Lullaby, 3-line mk, 3½x5"	155.00
#27/III, Joyous News, FB, 4¼x4¾"	1,100.00
#28/III, Wayside Devotion, CM, 8½"	1,450.00
#29, Guardian Angel, font, SB, 2½x5⅝"	900.00
#3/I, Bookworm, CM, 5½"	825.00
#3/II, Bookworm, LB, 8"	840.00
#305, The Builder, LB, 5½"	190.00
#305, The Builder, SB, 5½"	6,600.00
#306, Little Bookkeeper, LB, 4¾"	220.00
#306, Little Bookkeeper, SB, 4¾"	1,650.00
#311, Kiss Me, LB, 6"	150.00
#311, Kiss Me, SB, 6"	1,100.00
#314, Confidentially, SB, 5½"	1,650.00
#317, Not For You, FB, 6"	6,600.00
#317, Not For You, LB, 6"	175.00
#319, Doll Bath, LB, 5¼"	190.00
#32/0, Little Gabriel, CM, 5"	350.00
#32/0, Little Gabriel, 3-line mk, 5"	125.00
#321, Wash Day, 3-line mk, 5¾"	190.00
#327, The Run-A-Way, 3-line mk, 5¼"	825.00
#328, Carnival, 3-line mk, 6"	180.00
#331, Crossroads, SB, 6¾"	1,650.00
#333, Blessed Event, SB, 5½"	2,200.00
#336, Close Harmony, SB, 5½"	225.00
#34, Singing Lesson, ashtray, SB, 3½x6¼"	150.00
#340, Letter to Santa Claus, SB, 7"	2,750.00
#342, Mischief Maker, 3-line mk, 5"	220.00
#344, Feathered Friends, FB, 4¾"	6,600.00
#346, The Smart Little Sister, LB, 4¾"	175.00
#348, Ring Around the Rosie, SB, 6¾"	2,200.00
#35/I, The Good Shepherd, font, FB, 2¾x5¾"	225.00
#353/0, Spring Dance, 3-line mk, 4¾"	4,500.00
#356, Gay Adventure, LB, 5"	165.00
#357, Guiding Angel, SB, 2¾"	75.00
#361, Favorite Pet, 3-line mk, 4¼"	275.00

#367, Busy Student, 3-line mk, 4¼" 140.00
#369, Follow the Leader, 3-line mk, 7" 820.00

#37, Herald Angels, candle holder, full bee, 2¾x4", $255.00.

#37, Herald Angels, candle holder, CM, 2½x4" 550.00
#374, Lost Stocking, LB, 4¾" 160.00
#378, Easter Greetings, 3-line mk, 5½" 380.00
#385/4, Chicken Licken, LB, 3¼" 100.00
#389, Girl w/Sheet Music, SB, 2½ to 2¾" 75.00
#392, Little Band, 3-line mk, 4¾x3" 200.00
#396, Ride Into Christmas, LB, 5¾" 350.00
#42/0, Good Shepherd, CM, 6¼" 340.00
#42/0, Good Shepherd, 3-line mk, 6¼" 210.00
#44/A, Culprits, table lamp, SB, 9½" 350.00
#44/B, Out of Danger, table lamp, SB, 9½" 340.00
#45/I, Madonna w/Halo, SB, 12" 100.00
#46/I, Madonna w/o Halo, FB, 11¼" 145.00
#47/II, Goose Girl, CM, 7½" 1,300.00
#47/3/0, Goose Girl, FB, 4" 220.00
#49/I, To Market, FB, 6¼" 825.00
#49/3/0, To Market, LB, 4" 165.00
#50/0, Volunteers, FB, 5½" 400.00
#52/I, Going to Grandma's, CM, 6" 1,100.00
#52/0, Going to Grandma's, FB, 4¾" 340.00
#54, Silent Night, candle holder, FB, 4¾x5½" 275.00
#55, St George, FB, 6¾" 375.00
#56/A, Culprits, SB, 6¼" 250.00
#58/I, Playmates, FB, 4½" 360.00
#6/I, Sensitive Hunter, SB, 5½" 185.00
#60 A/B, Farm Boy & Goose Girl, bookends, FB, 6", pr 660.00
#63, Singing Lesson, FB, 2¾" 150.00
#65, Farewell, CM, 4¾" 665.00
#65, Farewell, 3-line mk, 4¾" 240.00
#66, Farm Boy, FB, 5¼" 325.00
#69, Happy Pastime, SB, 3¼" 130.00
#71, Stormy Weather, CM, 6¼" 990.00
#73, Little Helper, FB, 4¼" 170.00
#74, Little Gardener, FB, 4¼" 170.00
#75, White Angel, font, FB, 1¾x3½" 55.00
#78/I, Infant of Krumbad, CM, 2½" 135.00
#78/II, Infant of Krumbad, 3-line mk, 3½" 50.00
#78/VIII, Infant of Krumbad, CM, 13½" 450.00
#8, Bookworm, FB, 4" 225.00
#81/0, School Girl, CM, 5¼" 475.00
#82/0, School Boy, SB, 5½" 175.00
#83, Angel Serenade, w/lamb, CM, 5" 640.00
#83, Angel Serenade, w/lamb, 3-line mk, 5" 215.00
#85/II, Serenade, FB, 7½" 600.00

#85/0, Serenade, FB, 4¾" 170.00
#86, Happiness, LB, 4¾" 135.00
#87, For Father, SB, 5½" 200.00
#9, Begging His Share, CM, 5½" 660.00
#91/A/B, Angel at Prayer, font, FB, 2x4¾", pr 115.00
#93, Little Fiddler, plaque, FB, 4¾x5⅛" 185.00
#94/3/0, Surprise, FB, 4¼" 200.00
#95, Brother, CM, 5½" 460.00
#95, Brother, LB, 5½" 195.00
#98/2/0, Sister, 3-line mk, 4¾" 200.00

Hutschenreuther

The Porcelain Factory C.M. Hutschenreuther operated in Bavaria from 1814 to 1969. After the death of the elder Hutschenreuther in 1845, his son Lorenz took over operations, continuing there until 1857 when he left to establish his own company in the nearby city of Selb. The original manufactory became a joint stock company in 1904, absorbing several other potteries. In 1969 both Hutschenreuther firms merged, and that company still operates in Selb. They have distributing centers in both France and the United States. Our advisor for this category is Jack Gunsaulus; he is listed in the Directory under Michigan.

Candlestick, cherub atop gold ball, 2-light, 6½x10" 185.00
Figurine, ballerina, soft gr, 9" 385.00
Figurine, ballerina, wht, orig label, 9" 225.00
Figurine, Glory of Christmas, ltd ed, boxed set of 4 ....210.00

Figurine, Grand Finale, leaping dancer, 9½", $345.00 (recast after the 1950s model).

Figurine, nude, arms up, 1 ft on gold ball, Tutter, 9" 375.00
Figurine, nude w/flowers, fawn at bk, Werner, 9" 395.00
Figurine, Thai dancer, snake about arm, mk RH, 9½" 150.00
Plate, Goldfinch, sgn Ruthven, ltd ed, 10½" 50.00
Plate, Roses of Redoute, set of 8 ....240.00
Platter, Kensington, 15x11" 50.00

Imari

Imari is a generic term which covers a broad family of wares. It was made in more than a dozen Japanese villages, but the name is that of the port from whence it was shipped to Europe. There are several types of Imari. The most common features a design with panels of birds, florals, or people surrounding a central basket of flowers. The colors used in this type are underglaze blue with overglaze red, gold, and green enamels. The Chinese also made Imari wares which differ from the Japanese type in several ways — the absence of spur marks, a thinner-type body, and a more consistent control of the blue. Imari-type wares were copied on the continent by Meissen and by English potters, among them Worcester, Derby, and Bow.

Bowl, floral reserves/dragons on base, shallow, Meiji, 12½" **660.00**
Bowl, vase of flowers, bronze mts, 2½x8½" **350.00**
Candlesticks, English, 5½", pr **385.00**
Carafe, late 1800s, 8" **400.00**
Charger, cranes in pine boughs, wht/red/gr/gold, Meiji, 18" **880.00**
Charger, floral reserves, dmn diapers, red/gr/rose, Meiji, 22" ...**1,045.00**
Charger, flower baskets & reserves, bl/red/gold, Meiji, 16" **1,000.00**
Charger, flowers in urn & floral panels, iron red/gr, 12" **300.00**
Charger, Japan, 18" **385.00**
Charger, mc florals, scalloped rim, 12¼" **275.00**
Ewer, floral meanders & garden panels, 5-color, 1700s, 6⅝" ...**1,045.00**
Plate, mc floral, late, 8¾" **77.50**
Plate, wedding; 3 friends/flower/etc, celadon rim, 1840s, 8½" **200.00**
Tea caddy, silver lid, 4¾" **325.00**
Umbrella stand, 1800s, 24½" **1,045.00**
Vase, phoenix in tree, mc reserves, baluster, Meiji, 18¼" **935.00**

Imperial Glass Company

The Imperial Glass Company was organized in 1901 in Bellaire, Ohio, and started manufacturing glassware in 1904. Their early products were jelly glasses, hotel tumblers, etc., but by 1910 they were making a name for themselves by pressing quantities of Carnival Glass, the iridescent glassware that was popular during that time. In 1914 NuCut was introduced to imitate cut glass. The line was so popular that it was made in crystal and colors and was reintroduced as Collector's Crystal in the 1950s. From 1916 to 1920 they used the lustre process to make a line called Imperial Jewels, now referred to as stretch glass. Free-Hand ware, art glass made entirely by hand using no molds, was made from 1922 to 1928.

The company entered bankruptcy in 1931 but was able to continue operations and reorganize as the Imperial Glass Corporation. In 1936 Imperial introduced the Candlewick line, for which it is best known. In the late thirties the Vintage Grape Milk Glass line was added, and in 1951 a major ad campaign was launched, making Imperial one of the leading milk glass manufacturers.

In 1940 Imperial bought the molds and assets of the Central Glass Works of Wheeling, West Virginia; in 1958 they acquired the molds of the Heisey Company and in 1960 the molds of the Cambridge Glass Company of Cambridge, Ohio. Imperial used these molds, and after 1951 they marked their glassware with an 'I' superimposed over the 'G' trademark. The company became a subsidiary of Lenox in 1973; subsequently an 'L' was added to the 'IG' mark. In 1981 Lenox sold Imperial to Arthur Lorch, a private investor (who modified the L by adding a line at the top angled to the left). He in turn sold the company to Robert F. Stahl, Jr., in 1982. Mr. Stahl filed for Chapter 11 to reorganize, but in mid-1984 liquidation was ordered, and all assets were sold. The few items that had been made in '84 were marked with an 'N' superimposed over the 'I' for 'New Imperial.' See also Candlewick; Carnival Glass; Stretch Glass.

Cathay Crystal

#5001, pagoda **550.00**
#5006, butterfly ash tray **25.00**
#5009, dragon candle holder, pr **400.00**
#5010, junk flower bowl **200.00**
#5017, egrette **300.00**
#5085, Pavillion tray **350.00**

Ashtray, purple slag, fancy, #150, 5" **35.00**
Basket, Cape Cod, hdld, #160/73, 11" **140.00**

Basket, purple slag w/milk glass hdl, #156, 5½" **35.00**
Bowl, baked apple; Tradition, bl **12.00**
Bowl, Collector's Crystal, cranberry, #737A, 8½" **45.00**
Bowl, Grape, purple slag, crimped, #62C, 9" **48.00**
Bowl, Grape, ruby slag, satin, crimped, #47C, 9" **54.00**
Bowl, Pillar Flute, bl, 10" **55.00**
Bowl, Rose, jade slag, crimped, 3-toed, #74C, 8" **48.00**
Bowl, Rose, milk glass, crimped, 3-toed, #1950/113C, 11½" **40.00**
Box, butter pat, #736 ....**18.00**
Box, flat iron, purple slag, w/lid, #971 ....**120.00**
Box, lion, caramel slag, w/lid, #159 ....**160.00**
Box, puff; Heart Leaf, purple slag, #312 ....**135.00**
Box, rooster, purple slag, w/lid, #158 ....**140.00**
Cake plate, Cape Cod, ftd, #160/67D, 10½" **50.00**
Cake plate, Collector's Crystal, Antique Bl, ftd, #505 ....**22.00**
Cake plate, Old Williamsburg, ftd, #341/67D, 11" **35.00**
Candle holder, Cape Cod, #160/80, 5" **25.00**
Candle holder, Corinthian, Azalea, #330, 7½" **30.00**
Candle holder, Dolphin, caramel slag, #779, 5" **40.00**
Candle holder, Hoffman House, amber, #46, 4¾" **20.00**
Candle holder, Provincial, Heather, #1506, 4½" **22.00**
Candle holders, Pillar Flute, bl, 2-light, pr **35.00**
Celery dish, Pillar Flute, ruby, oval **40.00**
Comport, Collector's Crystal, Verdi Gr, 7" **22.00**
Compote, Lace Edge, purple slag, crimped, 4-toed, #274C, 7" **45.00**
Creamer, Fancy Colonial, pk **15.00**
Creamer & sugar bowl, Grape, Rubigold Carnival, ftd, #831 ....**28.00**
Cup, bouillon; Cape Cod, #160/250 ....**35.00**
Cup & saucer, Pillar Flute, bl **35.00**
Decanter, Collector's Crystal, #612 ....**35.00**
Goblet, Cape Cod, Evergreen, #160, magnum, 14-oz **40.00**
Goblet, purple slag, #593 ....**32.00**
Goblet, Scroll, amber, #322, 11-oz **25.00**
Jar, America, Antique Bl, #282/1, sm **22.00**
Jar, Americana, amber, #282, lg **25.00**
Jar, purple slag, 4-toed, w/lid, #176 ....**35.00**
Jar, saddle, caramel slag, w/lid **85.00**
Lighter, Cape Cod, blk **32.00**
Mug, Eagle, ruby slag, satin, #154 ....**35.00**
Mug, Storybook, caramel slag, satin **35.00**

Pitcher, Cape Cod, ice lip, $65.00.

Pitcher, milk; Cape Cod, #160/240, 16-oz **55.00**
Plate, Coin, 1971 Kennedy Series **25.00**
Plate, Fancy Colonial, Reef Aqua, 7½" **14.50**
Plate, Pillar Flute, bl, 8½" **15.00**
Plate, Rose, milk glass, #1950/10D, 10½" **25.00**
Punch set, Collector's Crystal, low, #5, 14-pc **125.00**
Punch set, Peacock Carnival, #500, 15-pc **250.00**
Relish, Pillar Flute, bl, oval **16.50**

Shakers, Cape Cod, 160/213, 3-pc w/tray 42.00
Shakers, Salz & Pfeffer, Rubigold Carnival 50.00
Sherbet, Cape Cod, Azalea, #1602, tall 18.00
Sherbet, Grape, milk galss, gloss, #1950/473 ....10.00
Sherbet, Stamm House, Dewdrop Opal, #1886 ....12.00
Tumbler, Big Shot, ruby, 14-oz 18.00
Tumbler, iced tea; Cape Cod, ftd, #160, 12-oz 12.00
Tumbler, Smart Alec, 12-oz 8.00
Vase, dk bl w/inlaid lt bl drape, dk bl int, 10½" 475.00
Vase, Free-Hand, cobalt w/opal hearts & vines, 6½" 375.00
Vase, Free-Hand, gold w/stretched/ruffled top, waisted, 9" 160.00
Vase, Free-Hand, hearts/vines, bl on opal, 3-fold rim, 11" 400.00
Vase, Free-Hand, hearts/vines, hdls at neck, 11½" 660.00
Vase, Free-Hand, marbleized opal w/peacock bl liner, 10" 700.00
Vase, Free-Hand, marigold, dk bl leaves/vines, bulbous, 7" 400.00
Vase, Free-Hand, red w/stretched tan & opal int, ruffled, 8" 300.00
Vase, Loganberry, milk glass, 10" 30.00

Imperial Porcelain

The Blue Ridge Mountain Boys were created by cartoonist Paul Webb and translated into three-dimension by the Imperial Porcelain Corporation of Zanesville, Ohio, in 1947. These figurines decorated ashtrays, vases, mugs, bowls, pitchers, planters, and other items. The Mountain Boys series were numbered 92 through 108, each with a different and amusing portrayal of mountain life. Imperial also produced American Folklore miniatures, twenty-three tiny animals one inch or less in size, and the Al Capp Dogpatch series. Because of financial difficulties, the company closed in 1960.

American Folklore Miniatures

Cat, 1½" 40.00
Cow, 1¾" 35.00
Hound dogs 35.00
Plaque, store ad, Am Folklore Porcelain Miniatures, 4½" 400.00
Sow 30.00

Blue Ridge Mountain Boys by Paul Webb

Ashtray, #101, man w/jug & snake 75.00
Ashtray, #103, hillbilly & skunk 75.00
Ashtray, #105, baby, hound dog, & frog 110.00
Ashtray, #106, Barrel of Wishes, w/hound 75.00
Ashtray, #92, 2 men by tree stump, for pipes 125.00
Box, cigarette; #98, dog atop, baby at door, sq 115.00
Dealer's sign, Handcrafted Paul Webb Mtn Boys, rare, 9" 650.00
Decanter, #100, outhouse, man, & bird 75.00
Decanter, #104, Ma leaning over stump, w/baby & skunk 95.00
Decanter, man, jug, snake, & tree stump, Hispch Inc, 1946 .....75.00
Figurine, #101, man leans against tree trunk, 5" 90.00
Figurine, man on hands & knees, 3" 95.00
Figurine, man sitting, 3½" 95.00
Figurine, man sitting w/chicken on knee, 3" 95.00
Jug, #101, Willie & snake 75.00
Mug, #94, Bearing Down, 6" 95.00
Mug, #94, dbl baby hdl, 4¼" 95.00
Mug, #94, ma hdl, 4¼" 95.00
Mug, #94, man w/bl pants hdl, 4¼" 95.00
Mug, #94, man w/yel beard & red pants hdl, 4¼" 95.00
Mug, #99, Target Practice, boy on goat, farmer, 5¾" 95.00
Pitcher, lemonade 200.00
Planter, #100, outhouse, man, & bird 75.00

Planter, #105, man w/chicken on knee, washtub 110.00
Planter, #110, man, w/jug & snake, 4½" 65.00
Planter, #81, man drinking from jug, sitting by washtub 75.00
Shakers, Ma & Old Doc, pr 95.00

Miscellaneous

Items in this section that are designated 'IP' are miscellaneous novelties made by Imperial Porcelain; the remainder are of interest to Paul Webb collectors, though made by an unknown manufacturer. Prints on calendars and playing cards are signed 'Paul Webb.'

Artist board, babies or mtn women, sgn Paul Webb, 30x30" 275.00
Artist board, mtn boys only, sgn Paul Webb, 30x30" 225.00
Calendar, 1954, 12 sgn scenes, Brown & Bigelow, complete 48.00
Figurine, cat in high-heeled shoe, 5½" L 40.00
Hot pad, Dutch boy w/tulips, rnd, IP 30.00
Ink blotters, sgn scenes, ea 8.00
Mug, #29, man hdl, sgn Paul Webb, 4¾" 45.00
Planter, #106, dog sitting by tub, IP 75.00
Playing cards, ad: Rafe Oiling Gun, Brown & Bigelow, MIB 45.00
Shakers, pigs, 5", pr 95.00
Shakers, standing pigs, IP, 8", pr 95.00

Indian Tree

Indian Tree is a popular dinnerware pattern produced by various potteries since the early 1800s to recent times. Although backgrounds and borders vary, the Oriental theme is carried out with the gnarled, brown branch of a pink-blossomed tree. Among the manufacturers' marks, you may find represented such notable firms as Coalport, S. Hancock and Sons, Soho Pottery, and John Maddock and Sons.

Marked Maddock: Cup, $22.50; 6" plate, $5.00; 8" plate, $8.00; 10" plate, $12.50.

Bowl, rim soup; Maddock, 9" 20.00
Bowl, vegetable; Davidson & Son, oval, 10" 35.00
Bowl, vegetable; English, w/lid 75.00
Creamer, Maddock, 3" 20.00
Cup & saucer, AD; Minton 22.00
Gravy boat, Maddock 32.00
Gravy tureen, English, w/lid & ladle 85.00
Plate, Maddock, 7¾" 8.00
Platter, Maddock, 10½" 22.50
Teapot, Burgess & Lee 60.00

Inkwells and Inkstands

Receptacles for various writing fluids have been used since ancient times. Through the years they have been made from countless materials — glass, metal, porcelain, pottery, wood, and even papier-mache. During the 18th century, gold or silver inkstands were presented to royalty; the well-known silver inkstand by Philip Syng, Jr., was used for the signing of the Declaration of Independence, and impressive brass inkstands with wells and a pounce pot (sander) were proud possessions of men of letters. When literacy vastly increased in the 19th century, the dip pen replaced the quill pen; and inkwells and inkstands were widely used and produced in a broad range of sizes in functional and decorative forms from ornate Victorian to flowing Art Nouveau and stylized Art Deco designs. However, the acceptance of the ballpoint pen literally put inkstands and inkwells 'out of business.' But their historical significance and intriguing diversity of form and styling fascinate today's collectors.

Blown, dk olive gr, annular rings, 1½x2¼", NM 300.00
Blown, olive gr, conical, disk mouth, att Keene, 2¾" 275.00
Brass w/Deco designs, 2 glass inserts, 9¾" L, +sander 175.00
Brass w/2 hinged cut glass wells & lids, pen holder+dip pen 195.00
Bronze, cockatoo figural, Austria, worn pnt, 3½x4" 195.00
B3m, deep violet bl, 18 vertical ribs, orig cap, 1⅞" 300.00
B3m, lt olive yel, GII-15, att Mt Vernon, 1820s, 1¾" 2,600.00
B3m, yel-olive, disk mouth, Coventry Glass Works, 1⅞x2¼" 120.00

Carved wood with standing rooster and hen, two hen well covers at sides, flower carvings along front edge, 9x16", $350.00.

Champleve enamel & ormolu, Napoleon III, late 1800s, 20" L ..550.00
CI, man eating turkey figural, mc pnt, late 1800s, 5", EX 330.00
CI, mechanical, 3-D man/fence 2 wells w/aqua bottles, Newton ...1,125.00
Cut glass, Cane, Gorham sterling hinged lid w/eng 170.00
Fountain form, yel/wht stripes on clear, brass/marble base, 4" 350.00
Gilt bronze, Rococo style, English, late 1800s, 6½" 200.00
Glass, Memorial Hall 1876, NM 375.00
Latticinio, pk & wht stripes, orig pewter lid, 2½x3" 650.00
Metal, bell form w/incised decor, 3½x2½" 110.00
Pattern molded, aquamarine, 16-rib swirl, 2x1⅞" dia 1,000.00
Pewter, Nouveau emb w/enamel jewels, conical, English, 2x5" ..275.00
Pitkin, deep olive-yel, 36-rib swirl to left, 2⅛" dia 125.00
Pitkin, yel-olive, melon form, 28 vertical ribs, 2x2⅝" 1,800.00
Porc, cherubs in relief on tray, gilt trim, Germany, 8½" L 70.00
Porc, standing cat lady in yel dress, 5" 150.00
Sandwich type, irregular rectangle, ca 1830-60, 3x9½x6" 325.00
Silver-gilt w/lapis finials, 2 pots/dish on stand, Austria 660.00
Stoneware, cobalt w/incised Union & stars, N Boors...PA, 1½" ...880.00
Wht metal & brass, Queen Victoria bust, 1897 Jubilee, 7¼" 350.00

Insulators

The telegraph was invented in 1844. The devices developed to hold the electrical transmission wires to the poles were called insulators. The telephone, invented in 1876, intensified their usefullness; and by the turn of the century, thousands of varieties were being produced in pottery, wood, and glass of various colors. Even though it has been rumored that red glass insulators exist, none have ever been authenticated. Many insulators are embossed with patent dates.

Of the more than 3,000 types known to exist, today's collectors evaluate their worth by age and rarity of color. Aqua and green are the most common colors in glass, dark brown the most common in ceramic. Threadless insulators, (for example, CD #701.1) made between 1850 and 1865, bring prices well into the hundreds, if in mint condition.

In the listings that follow, the CD numbers are from an identification system developed in the late 1960s by N.R. Woodward.

Those seeking additional information about insulators are encouraged to contact Line Jewels-Insulators, whose address may be found in the Directory under Clubs, Newsletters and Catalogs) or attend a club-endorsed show. For information, contact Len Linscott, listed in the Directory under Florida.

Key:
* (asterisk) — Canadian   SDP — sharp drip points
CB — corrugated base   RB — rough base
CD — Consolidated Design   RDP — round drip points
SB — smooth base

CD 100.5, Pyrex, SB, clear 75.00
CD 102.3, KCGB, SB, aqua 20.00
CD 106.2, PSSA, SB, lt aqua 30.00
CD 109, Chicago, SB, aqua 800.00
CD 110.6, National, SB, lt gr 1,000.00
CD 114, Hemingray, SDP, ice bl 15.00
CD 122, Armstrong, SB, clear 1.00
CD 125, Hemingray, SDP, aqua 5.00
CD 128.5, Hemingray, SB, clear 35.00
CD 131.8, no name, SB, aqua 1,500.00
CD 132.4, no name, SB, lt gr 200.00
CD 135, Chicago, SB, bl-aqua 50.00
CD 136.7, no name, SB, off-clear 400.00
CD 140, Jumbo, SB, dk gr 150.00
CD 142, no name, SB, carnival 13.00
CD 143, CPR, SB, steel bl 15.00
CD 143*, CPR, SB, steel bl 15.00
CD 143*, no name (dbl thread), SB, gr 100.00
CD 145, HBR, SB, ice bl, aqua 15.00
CD 145, HI (entwined initials) Co, SB, aqua 2.00
CD 147, no name, SB, aqua 5.00
CD 152, (Diamond), SB, straw 10.00
CD 155, Kerr DP1, SB, bl tint 2.00
CD 160, 'B,' SB, aqua 5.00
CD 162, BGMCo, SB, lt purple 100.00
CD 183, Hemingray-71, CB, clear 5.00
CD 192-193, Am Tel & Tel Co, SB, aqua 30.00
CD 216, Armstrong's 51-U, SB, amber 3.00
CD 228, Brookfield, SB, dk aqua 400.00
CD 241, Hemingray-23, RDP or SDP, honey-amber 20.00
CD 245, TH-9200, SB, aqua 75.00
CD 252, Gayner No 620, SDP, aqua 25.00
CD 257, Hemingray/No 60, SDP, Hemingray Bl 10.00
CD 267, No 4 Cable, SB, emerald gr 200.00
CD 280, (Prism), SB, gr 40.00

CD 292.5, Boston-'Knowles 6,' SB, aqua 150.00
CD 338, Brookfield, SB, aqua 1,500.00
CD 701, no emb, threadless, SB, lt sage 350.00
CD 721*, no emb, threadless, SB, jade aqua milk 500.00
CD 728.7, no emb, threadless, SB, bl aqua 1,000.00
CD 732.2, LGT & Co, threadless, SB, lt aqua 900.00
CD 738, Chester NY, threadless, SB, root-beer amber 2,000.00

Irons

History, geography, art, and cultural diversity are all represented in the collecting of antique pressing irons. The progress of fashion and invention can be traced through the ages by relics left in the form of pressing devices used in earlier times. Goffering irons, once needed for the frills and ruffles of the Victorian age, have been out of use so long that they are seldom recognized today. The fluter, essential for producing the yards of crimped ruffles demanded by 19th-century ladies, is now a quaint curiosity. Industrial technology can be traced through records left by centuries of irons.

The native character of nations is reflected by the geography where irons are found. Some countries lacked iron, so they made their pressing devices of other materials. And because an iron foundry represents a high form of investment and technology, less wealthy societies frequently used the easier-to-work brass.

A culture's priorities are reflected in the tools in daily use. Some value innovation while others are content with a standard generic product. There are degrees of ornamentation, depending on the country, the people, and their approach to life.

At times, to the pleasure of today's collectors, the work trancends proficiency and rises into the realm of art. Using a variety of materials — iron, brass, or wood — artisans built a monument to their inner vision. Their work survives, testifiying to the care, love, and attention lavished on household implements, elevating them in status to something that delights the eye.

In the listing that follows, prices are given for examples in very good to excellent condition. Damage, repairs, plating, excessive wear, rust, and missing parts can dramatically reduce value. Our advisors for this category are Carol and Jimmy Walker, whose address is listed in the Directory under Texas. No appraisals. SASE required with correspondence.

Art Deco, electric, gr porc, single post hdl, Fr 150.00
Art Deco, electric, Proctor, Never Lift, center post 125.00
Art Deco, electric, Proctor, Never Lift, 1-prong 125.00
Art Deco, electric, Proctor, Never Lift, 2-prong 100.00
Art Deco, electric, Silver Streak, red, bl or gr, ea 1,300.00
Detachable hdl, AC Williams 35.00
Detachable hdl, Asbestos 35.00
Detachable hdl, Colebrookdale 35.00
Detachable hdl, Dover 45.00
Detachable hdl, Enterprise 35.00
Detachable hdl, Sensible, Pat 1887 ....55.00
Fluter, crank, American 100.00
Fluter, crank, Cole Prize Medal, Pat 06-12-1866 ....470.00
Fluter, crank, Companion, clamp on 225.00
Fluter, crank, Crown 125.00
Fluter, crank, Dudley 300.00
Fluter, crank, Manville 750.00
Fluter, crank, Mrs Cole's Pony, clamp on 500.00
Fluter, crank, Star 250.00
Fluter, hand, rocking, Geneva 55.00
Fluter, hand, rocking, The Best or The Star, ea 70.00
Fluter, hand, rolling, Clark 180.00
Fluter, hand, rolling, North Brothers 190.00

Fluter, hand, rolling, Norton, transverse 275.00
Fluter, hand, rolling, Shepard 190.00
Fluter, hand, rolling, Sundry 300.00
Gasoline, Am Gas Machine, side tank 95.00
Gasoline, Bl Coleman, 4A, USA 45.00
Gasoline, Comfort 50.00
Gasoline, Dmn, rnd tank 35.00
Gasoline, Dmn, triangle tank 50.00

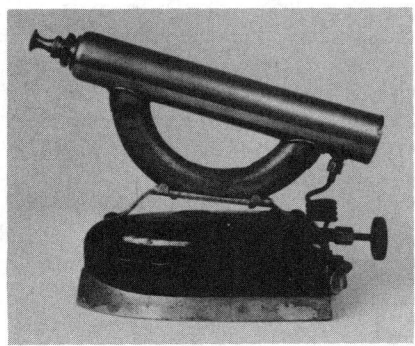

Gasoline iron, tank with pump forms handle, Acron Brass Mfg. Co. Chig. IL Pat May 13, 1913, $250.00.

Gasoline, Monitor 40.00
Gasoline, Red Coleman, 4A, Canada 300.00
Gasoline, Royal 40.00
Gasoline, Standard 160.00
Little, ACW, #1 ....50.00
Little, cross rib, #4 on hdl, 3⅝" 40.00
Little, detachable hdl, AC Williams, slide latch 225.00
Little, detachable hdl, Potts type w/trivet 85.00
Little, rope hdl, w/trivet, 2⅞" 35.00
Little, The Victor, #10 wooden hdl 195.00
Little, The Victor, #5 wooden hdl 225.00
Natural gas, Fairy Prince, bl porc, w/trivet, England 100.00
Natural gas, Imperial, w/trivet 100.00
Natural gas, IWANTU, dbl-point 45.00
Natural gas, Johnson, w/trivet 95.00
Natural gas, NU-STYL 150.00
Natural gas, Trent flip-over (reversible) 150.00
Natural gas, Vulcan, w/trivet 125.00
Sadiron, dolphin-form hdl 40.00
Sadiron, Enterprise, ventilated hdl 45.00
Sadiron, Ferris Cold Hdl, Pat Oct 16, 1891 ....190.00
Sadiron, mk only w/number 12.00
Sadiron, Monitor, dbl point 175.00
Sadiron, Ober, arched hdl 45.00
Sadiron, Salter, Silvester's Pat, England 25.00
Sadiron, Weida, Pat Mar 12, 1870 ....25.00
Travel, boudoir w/box of Meta Fuel 90.00
Travel, Clem, electric, in leather case, England 85.00
Travel, Elite, for gas jet 200.00
Travel, Gem, for gas jet 200.00
Travel, Sultana, w/trivet, for gas jet 275.00
Travel, Universal, electric, w/trivet & curling iron 60.00

Ironstone

During the last quarter of the 18th century, English potters began experimenting with a new type of body that contained calcinated flint and a higher china clay content, intent on producing a fine durable whiteware — heavy, yet with a texture that would resemble porcelain. To remove the last trace of yellow, a minute amount of cobalt was added, often resulting in a bluish-white tone. Wm and John Turner of Caughley, and Josiah Spode II were the first to manufacture the ware successfully. Others, such as Davenport, Hicks and Meigh, and Ralph and Josiah Wedgwood, followed with their own versions. The latter coined the name 'Pearl' to refer to his product and incorporated the term into his trademark. In 1813 a 14-year patent was issued to Charles James Mason, who called his ware Patented Ironstone. Francis Morley, G.L. Asworth, T.J. Mayer, and other Staffordshire potters continued to produce ironstone until the end of the century. While some of these patterns are simple to the extreme, many are decorated with in-mold designs of fruit, grain, and foliage on ribbed or scalloped shapes. In the 1830s transfer-printed designs in blue, mulberry, pink, green, and black became popular; and polychrome versions of Oriental wares were manufactured to compete with the Chinese trade. See also Mason's Ironstone. Our advise for this category comes from Home Place Antiques, whose address is listed in the Directory under Illinois.

Bowl, sauce; Sydenham, T&R Boote, 5⅜"	16.50
Bowl, soup; Full Ribbed, Pankhurst, 8¾"	32.00
Bowl, soup; Full Ribbed, Pankhurst, 9½"	36.00
Bowl, soup; Wheat, Turner Goddard & Co, 8¾"	32.00
Bowl, vegetable; Fig, Wedgwood, w/lid, med sz	125.00
Bowl, vegetable; Prize Bloom, Mayer, w/lid	125.00
Bowl, vegetable; Star Flower, Pankhurst, w/lid	125.00
Bowl, vegetable; Wheat & Blackberry, W Taylor, w/lid, 10¼" L	125.00
Bowl, waste; Lily of the Valley, Anthony Shaw, 4¾"	65.00
Butter dish, President, 3-pc	175.00
Chamber pot, Panelled Thistle, Bridgwood & Clarke, no lid	65.00
Chamber pot, President, J Edwards, w/lid	65.00
Coffee cup & saucer, Scotia, F Jones	60.00
Coffeepot, Lily, H Burgess	175.00
Coffeepot, Square Ridged, Johnson Bros, +cr/sug	275.00
Compote, New York, 9½" dia	175.00
Creamer, Square Ridged, Johnson Bros, 4⅝"	45.00
Creamer, Wheat & Clover, Turner & Tompkinson, 7⅜"	90.00
Cup plate, Fig, Davenport, 4¼"	35.00
Gravy boat, Sydenham, unmk	95.00
Ladle, sauce tureen; Boote's 1851, unmk, 7¼"	60.00
Mug, Ceres, unmk, 3⅜x3⅝"	80.00
Mug, Chinese, Anthony Shaw, 3½"	75.00
Pitcher, Gothic, JF, 9¾"	120.00
Pitcher, Olympic, Elsmore & Forster, 9⅜"	110.00
Pitcher, Panelled Leaves, Meakin, 8¾"	165.00
Pitcher, Portland, Elsmore & Forster, 9⅛"	130.00
Pitcher, Potomac, W Baker, 8½"	95.00
Pitcher, Victory, Edwards, 12¼"	90.00
Plate, Ceres, Elsmore & Forster, 9½"	27.50
Plate, Ivy Wreath, Meir & Son, 8¾"	20.00
Plate, Laurel Wreath, Elsmore & Forster, 9⅝"	36.00
Plate, Laurel Wreath, unmk, 4½"	20.00
Plate, Rolling Star, Edwards, 9½"	25.00
Plate, Sharon Arch, Davenport, 10½"	32.00
Plate, Sharon Arch, Wedgwood, 10⅝"	32.00
Plate, Sydenham, T&R Boote, 9⅛"	25.00
Platter, Ribbed Raspberry, J&G Meakin, 12"	65.00
Platter, well & tree; J&G Meakin, 16⅜"	85.00
Relish, Laurel Wreath, unmk	45.00
Soap dish, Block Optic, J&G Meakin, no insert, w/lid	68.00
Sugar bowl, Cable & Ring, Cockson & Chetwynd	45.00
Syrup, plain, pewter lid, unmk, 5⅜"	95.00
Tea saucer, Full Ribbed, Pankhurst, 6"	12.00

Teacup & saucer, Chelsea, Johnson Bros	17.50
Teacup & saucer, Leaf & Crossed Ribbon, Livesley Powell	32.00
Teacup & saucer, Wheat, Goddard & Burgess	50.00
Teapot, Ceres, Elsmore & Forster	195.00

Teapot, Meakin, #38, 9", $150.00.

Toothbrush holder, Victory, vase form, Edwards, 5¾" H	40.00
Toothbrush holder, Wheat & Blackberry, ST Jons	75.00
Tureen, sauce; Cable & Ring, Bridgwood & Son, +plate/ladle	125.00
Tureen, sauce; Sevres, Edwards, +underplate/lid	98.00
Wash bowl, Scalloped Decagon, Davenport, 13¼"	95.00
Wash bowl & pitcher, Chinese, T&R Boote	285.00
Wash bowl & pitcher, Fig, Wedgwood	365.00
Wash bowl & pitcher, Hanging Leaves, PB&H	300.00
Wash pitcher, Boote's 1851, T&R Boote, 12"	125.00
Wash pitcher, Corn & Oats, Davenport, 12½"	165.00
Wash pitcher, Forget-Me-Not, Wood, Rathbone & Co, 12"	125.00
Wash pitcher, Hebe, John Alcock, 11⅞"	150.00
Wash pitcher, Hyacinth, unmk, 13"	110.00
Wash pitcher, Panelled Thistle, Bridgwood & Clarke, 12¼"	130.00

Patterned Ironstone

Coffeepot, Challinor Ardennes, hexagonal, ftd, 10", EX	190.00
Cup & saucer, #2 Pattern, Elsmore & Forster, miniature, NM	80.00
Cup plate, Gipsy, bl transfer, 4"	35.00
Cup plate, Pomerania, brn transfer, 4", EX	20.00
Cup plate, Versailles, bl transfer, glaze wear, 4"	40.00
Cup plate, Zamara, purple transfer, yel/gr accents, 4"	50.00
Plate, Adalusia, pk/blk transfer, Adams, 7", NM	55.00
Plate, pastoral scene, floral border, dk bl transfer, 9½"	95.00
Plate, Pastoral 1790, 10½"	40.00
Platter, #2 Pattern, Elsmore & Forster, 16", EX	45.00
Platter, lustre band, cobalt leaves, Elsmore & Forster, 14"	50.00
Soup plate, #2 Pattern, Elsmore & Forster, 9¾"	25.00
Teapot, #2 Pattern, Elsmore & Forster, 8½", EX	120.00
Teapot, Columbia, mfg flaw, 9½"	190.00
Toddy plate, pk transfer w/dk bl accent, 5", EX	37.50
Wash bowl & 12" pitcher, #2 Pattern, Elsmore & Forster	210.00

Ivory

Technically, true ivory is the substance composing the tusk of the elephant; the finest type comes from Africa. However, tusks and teeth of other animals — the walrus, the hippopotamus, and the sperm whale, for instance — are similar in composition and appearance and have also been used for carving. The Chinese have used this substance for centuries, preferring it over bone because of the natural oil contained in its pores, which not only renders it easier to carve but also imparts a soft sheen to the finished product. Aged ivory usually takes on a soft caramel patina, but unscrupulous dealers sometimes treat new ivory to a tea bath to 'antique' it! A bill passed in 1978 reinforced a ban on the importation of whale and walrus ivory. All examples listed here are Oriental in origin unless noted otherwise.

Carved figural group, standing Chinese lady & man, 1900s, 9¾" on stand, $600.00.

Back scratcher, hand form, wooden hdl w/rpr, 16" 30.00
Brush pot, Eastern & Western scenes, octagonal, 1800s, 3⅝" 275.00
Busk, floral/geometrics/fish, sealing wax inlay, 1800s, 14" 825.00
Buttons, cvd flower form, set of 6 w/matching buckle, 1920s 85.00
Chess set, Oriental figures in natural & red, EX in case 220.00
Comb, cut-out circles & heart, 5¼" L 40.00
Concubine Xiang Fei in armor & helmet, mc stain, 1900s, 12" .1,045.00
Cribbage board, from walrus tusk, 3 pegs & end cap, 8" L 190.00
Cricket resting on cabbage, ca 1900, 6¼"+wood stand 330.00
Dr's lady, reclining, brocade-pattern tattoos, 8¼" 365.00
Dr's lady, 9½" L, w/rosewood settee 825.00
Glove duster, cvd & pnt detail, 5¼" 20.00
Glove stretcher, Chinese export, landscape scene, 1800s 770.00
Grasshopper on Chinese cabbage, 9⅜" on cvd teak stand 220.00
Guanyin standing w/crown & rosary, later gilding, 10" 660.00
Guardian w/jeweled diadem, mc pnt & gold, 24⅜" 825.00
Madonna w/rosary, European, 5½", M 195.00
Mirror, appl eagles/putti/feathers around oval, Dieppe, 31" 1,100.00
Official in belted robe & wood cap, Ming, rstr, 10¼" 1,200.00
Panel, birds & flowers in high relief, 1700s, 11½x3½" 1,870.00
Sage w/hands under long sleeves, smiling face, 8¼" 330.00
Shoe horn, cvd mouse on hdl, 5¼" L 20.00
Shoulao immortal w/peach, long beard, 11⅛" 475.00
Shoulao standing w/peach & staff, ca 1900, 4" 100.00
Tablet, tiger in landscape w/calligraphy, Korea, 1900s, 6¼" 50.00
Venus reclins w/Cupid at ft, Continental, 5" 200.00
Warror in ceremonial armor on knee w/sword, 1800s, 11" 440.00

Jack-in-the-Pulpit Vases

Popular novelties at the turn of the century, jack-in-the-pulpit vases were made in every type of art glass produced. Some were simple, others elaborately appliqued and enameled. They were shaped to resemble the lily for which they were named.

Bl Hobnail w/wine ruffled rim, 7x6½" 95.00
Lav w/purple fluted edge, 8x6" 100.00
Maroon & wht spatter, vaseline opal appl top, 11x6" 95.00
Red to opal, appl yel flower/leaves, appl ft, 8" 95.00
Rubena, appl vaseline ruffle, 11x5" 125.00
Wht o/l, gr int, 8x5" 85.00

Wht w/gr int, clear petal ft, 7x5¾" 95.00

Japanese Lustreware

Imported from Japan during the 1920s, novelty tableware items, vases ashtrays, etc. — often in blue, tan, and mother-of-pearl lustre glazes — were sold through five-and-dime stores or given as premiums for selling magazine subscriptions. The Occupied Japan Club is listed in the Directory under Clubs, Newletters, and Catalogs.

Ashtray, donkey pulling cart mk Ashes, 2½" W 5.00
Bottle, perfume; lay-down type 34.00
Bowl, console; bl w/wht flowers, rolled rim, 9", +frog 15.00
Clothes brush w/flapper half-doll, ribbon waistband 25.00
Creamer & sugar bowl, Deco florals, w/tray 25.00
Lamp, bird/leaves/lily base, rose decor on paper shade, 10" 30.00
Lamp, mc bird on blk tree trunk, parrot on paper shade, 10" 32.50
Lemon dish, flowers on bl, Occupied Japan 15.00
Shakers, Dolly Face, pr 12.50
Shakers, goose w/hat holds 2 'chick' shakers on oval tray 15.00
Shakers, house, bl & tan, pr on rectangular tray 10.00
Tea set, bluebird decor, child sz, 13-pc, serves 4 ....50.00
Wall pocket, fancy bird, lg 22.00

Jewelry

Jewelry as objects of adornment has always been regarded with special affection. Whether it be a trinket or a costly ornament of gold, silver, or enameled work, jewelry has personal significance to the wearer. The art of the jeweler is valued as is any art object, and the names of Lalique or Faberge on collectible pieces bring prices demanded by the signed works of Picasso. Once the province of kings and noblemen, jewelry now is a legacy of all strata of society. The creativity reflected in the jeweler's art has resulted in a myriad of decorative adornments for men and women, and the modern usage of 'lesser' gems and base metals has elevated the value and increased the demand for artistic merit, so that now it is considered by collectors to be on a par with intrinsic value. Luxuriously appointed pieces of Victorian splendor and Edwardian grandeur now compete with the unique, imaginative renditions of jewelry produced in the exciting Art Nouveau period as well as the adventurous translation of jewelry executed in man-made materials versus natural elements. Today prices for gems and gemstones crafted into antique and collectible jewelry are based on artistic merit, personal appeal, pure sentimentality, and intrinsic value. Note: Diamond prices vary greatly depending on color, clarity, etc. Values given here are for diamond jewelry with a standard commercial grade of diamonds that are most likely to be encountered.

Our advisor for this category is Rebecca Dodds; her address may be found in the Directory under Florida. If you are interested in collecting or dealing in jewelry, you will find that authority Lillian Baker has several fine books available on the subject — *100 Years of Collectible Jewelry: 1850-1950*; *Art Nouveau and Art Deco Jewelry*; and *Fifty Years of Collectible Fashion Jewelry: 1925-1975*. These books are complete with beautiful full-color illustrations and current market values. Mrs. Baker is listed in the Directory under California. See also Plastics.

Key:	
A/C — Arts and Crafts	comp — complementary
AD — Art Deco	ct — carat
AN — Art Nouveau	dmn — diamond
cab — cabochon	dwt — penny weight
cl — clear	Euro — European cut

fl — filigree
g'el-plt — gold electroplate
g-stn — gemstone
g-t — gold-tone
gf — gold filled
grad — graduated
gp — gold plated
gw — gold washed
k — karat

m/c — mine cut
plat — platinum
r/c — rose cut
r/stn — rhinestone
rdm — rhodium
stn — stone
tw — total weight
wg — white gold
yg — yellow gold

Bar pin, 14k wg fl, .02ct bl sapphire, yg bk, 1920s **75.00**
Bracelet, bangle; 14k yg, peacock opals & dmns (1ct tw) **950.00**
Bracelet, bangle; 14k yg, w/8 6x8mm opals+2 sapphires, hinged ..**485.00**
Bracelet, charm; 18k yg, 7 charms, some w/jewels, over 40 grams **800.00**
Bracelet, cultured pearls, 7½mm, 14k yg clasp, 8" **275.00**
Bracelet, Wm Spratling, sterling, 4 leafy links+domes, 8" **825.00**
Bracelet, yg open fl, Phi Kappa Alpha, inscr **40.00**
Bracelet, 18k yg, flexible, eng links, over ¼" W **195.00**
Bracelet, 18k yg, flexible geometric floral sections, 1¼" W **1,175.00**
Brooch, gw metal mt frames oval opal, tiny pearl drop, AN **440.00**
Brooch, ornate 800 silver w/enameled Romeo & Juliet, 2x1½" **90.00**
Brooch, yg, rope knot w/lg cab garnet, Victorian, 17.5dwt **450.00**
Brooch, 10k yg, arrow w/4 .02ct rubies & 4 tiny seed pearls **125.00**
Charm, 14k yg, baby shoes **75.00**
Clip, Mary Gage, silver/crystal leaf & berry clusters, pr **385.00**
Cuff links, 14k yg & blk onyx, heavy, lg, pr **235.00**
Earrings, 14k yg, repousse hoop, lg **90.00**
Earrings, 14k yg fl dangle type w/garnet **85.00**
Earrings, 14k yg w/rnd 17.5mm Mabe pearl **220.00**

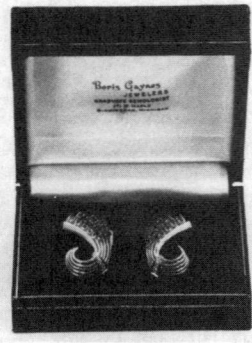

Earrings, Retro type, ruby and diamond on yellow gold, with original marked jeweler's box, $895.00 for the pair.

Locket, gilt & gf ornaments w/3 sm pearls, tintype inside **215.00**
Locket, sterling, on ¾" 3-section chain, 1840s **425.00**
Locket, 10k yg w/initials set in sm jewels, 12k chain **120.00**
Locket, 14k yg & enamel, 3 seed pearls in floral mt, 1½" **575.00**
Necklace, cultured pearls, 1-strand, 7mm, 16" **275.00**
Necklace, cultured pearls, 2-strand, grad, gold clasp, 18" **715.00**
Necklace, cultured pearls, 7.4 to 8mm, 14k gold clasp, 28" **935.00**
Necklace, Geo Jensen, thin rnd silver choker w/hook clasp **110.00**
Necklace, lapiz lazuli, 72 matched beads, 26" **385.00**
Necklace, yg chain, clasp mk 10k, 24" **110.00**
Pendant, gf, 9 leaves w/seed pearls+5 6mm garnets, 1920s **145.00**
Pendant, 14k, sapphire 3.5ct cushion & 3mm Baroque pearls **325.00**
Pendant, 14k yg, ½ct emerald **110.00**
Pendant, 14k yg w/red coral heart & seed pearl **125.00**
Pin, cvd coral flower & leaves in 14k yg mt, ½x2" **150.00**
Pin, G Jensen, stylized entwining bellflowers sgn CI, 1¾" **400.00**
Pin, sterling, fantailed goldfish, 2" **65.00**
Pin, 14k yg, cut-out flowers & garnets **150.00**
Ring, plat, 1.60ct Euro dmns+20 baguettes & rnds, sgn **4,000.00**

Ring, platinum, domed filigree, 1.65 carat European-cut diamond with four small bezel-set European diamonds, ca 1920, $3,600.00; Ring, platinum, filigree mount with two .70 carat European diamonds surrounded by ten small round diamonds, ca 1920, $2,200.00; Bar pin, platinum, floral filigree mount set with five graduated European-cut diamonds and seven small marquise and two triangular emeralds, ca 1930, $3,200.00.

Ring, plat fl, ½ct ruby solitaire **595.00**
Ring, wedding; 14k pk gold band **135.00**
Ring, wedding; 14k yg, .06ct solitaire dmn, +plain band **125.00**
Ring, 10k yg, .10ct rnd ruby w/6 .10ct bl opals, 1890s **135.00**
Ring, 10k yg w/blk enameling **50.00**
Ring, 14k, .33ct dmn, simple mt **285.00**
Ring, 14k plat w/old Euro .65ct dmn & 8 dmns (.60ct tw) **950.00**
Ring, 14k rose gold, .35ct sapphire+4 seed pearls, 1920s **275.00**
Ring, 14k wg, .15ct dmn+6 rnd sapphires (1.2ct tw) **250.00**
Ring, 14k wg, .30 Euro dmn in Tiffany mt **450.00**
Ring, 14k wg, .46ct yel sapphire, fl mt, 1910s **285.00**
Ring, 14k wg fl, 10mm Baroque cultured pearl, tiny emeralds **225.00**
Ring, 14k wg fl, 2 .20ct dmns+2 baguette sapphires **795.00**
Ring, 14k wg w/yg shank, .15ct dmn+9 sm brilliant-cut dmns **795.00**
Ring, 14k yg, .12ct dmn w/2 .09ct sapphires in oval, '30s **250.00**
Ring, 14k yg, .30ct dmn solitaire, hexagonal mt, '30s **500.00**
Ring, 14k yg, .70ct marquise gr dmn **750.00**
Ring, 14k yg, .85ct emerald & 2 full-cut dmns (.11 tw) **195.00**
Ring, 14k yg, baby's, M in orig box **45.00**
Ring, 14k yg, oval 4.85 andalucite+6 sm dmns (.95ct tw) **400.00**
Ring, 14k yg, raised 3-layer heart w/.18ct dmn **265.00**
Ring, 14k yg, ½" dia top w/.10ct r/c dmn & 8 sm r/c dmns **265.00**
Ring, 14k yg, 12mm amethyst in open mt w/lg petals, 1930s **200.00**
Ring, 14k yg, 2ct citrine encircled by snake, 1940s **140.00**
Ring, 14k yg, 9 sm dmns in floral mt **595.00**
Ring, 14k yg fl w/blk onyx & .25ct dmn **240.00**
Ring, 14k yg w/gr chalcedony cab & dmn chips **275.00**
Ring, 14k yg w/2 lg pearls & 2 rubies, Deco style **90.00**
Ring, 18k wg, .20ct dmn+4 sm dmns stair-stepping ea side **525.00**
Ring, 18k wg, 3 .12ct dmns+4 sm sapphires+2 .03ct dmns **650.00**
Ring, 18k wg fl, .25ct dmn, 4 baguette sapphires **825.00**
Ring, 18k wg w/5 dmns (.35ct tw) in long mt **285.00**
Ring, 18k yg, moss agate, Victorian **110.00**
Ring, 18k yg, 24 dmn baguettes (2.4ct tw)+.75ct faux ruby **575.00**
Ring, 18k yg w/7 cultured pearls **115.00**
Ring, 22k yg, basketweave dome, 7.09 grams **170.00**
Tie tack, 14k yg, .03ct Euro dmn, wht metal bk, 1920s **40.00**
Watch chain, mesh w/gf fob, 4" L **98.00**

Watch chain, 9k yg, 14" L +carnelian intaglio fob 485.00
Watch pin, gf, open loop pattern, ca 1910 ....78.00
Watch pin, Nouveau style, gf, ca 1900 ....82.50

Costume Jewelry

Bracelet, DeNicola, silver leaves 20.00
Bracelet, Eisenberg, r/stn on rhodium, flexible, 1960 ....125.00
Bracelet, Hobe, lg red stn, 1965 ....110.00
Brooch, Demaro, pearls & variegated color stns 85.00
Brooch, Kramer, chariot w/moving wheels, mc stns 85.00
Brooch, Kramer, mc fct stns, 1950s 40.00
Brooch, sterling frog w/HP body, r/stn legs & head 40.00
Earrings, blk plastic flowers, r/stn center 10.00
Earrings, Carnegie, pave set r/stns in rhodium, Art Modern 95.00
Earrings, Coro, enamel & r/stns 10.00
Earrings, Coro, gr r/stns 7.50
Earrings, dangle, blk plastic w/r/stns 10.00
Earrings, Eisenberg, cream & blk enamel, clip 40.00
Earrings, Hollycraft, pastel fct stns on g-t, 1960s 35.00
Earrings, Jomaz, bl glass cabs & r/stns, clip, 1940s 55.00
Earrings, Marvella, pearls & r/stns 7.50
Necklace, Haskell, pearl w/lg puffed heart, 26" 175.00
Necklace, lav plastic flowers w/r/stns, choker style 12.00
Necklace, Napier, gold braid, choker style 12.50
Necklace, Trifari, bl & wht enameling, choker style 18.00
Necklace, unmk, gilt & enamel fl w/Venetian ruby glass beads 95.00
Necklace, Van Dell, 18k gf, red stns, 1940s, +earrings 45.00
Necklace, Vendome, 3 strands of crystal beads & pearls 20.00
Pin, Boucher, clear r/stn & 4 bl teardrop stns 20.00
Pin, Boucher, pnt enamel fish form, 1955 ....50.00
Pin, Ciner, enamel strawberry 85.00
Pin, Coro, floral design topaz-color stns 38.00
Pin, Emmons, Rainbow Star, aurora borealis stns+cultured pearls 30.00
Pin, Joseff, oxidized brass bar w/tassel, 4½" 125.00
Pin, Reja, sterling w/purple stns, lg 125.00
Pin, S Coventry, gold leaf 6.50
Pin, Schreiner, orange & wht stns, mosaic center, lg 75.00
Pin, Trifari, gold bow 10.00

Josef Originals

Josef Original figurines were designed by Muriel Josef George of Arcadia, California, from 1946 until she retired in the late 1970s. They were made in California until the late 1960s, after which time she contracted them to a Japan manufacturer in order to be able to keep their prices low enough to remain competitive. All figures produced in Japan were made to her exact specifications, and the quality continued to be very high. After she retired, her partner, George Good, retained the Josef name and not only made figurines from the old molds but designed new ones as well. All Josef Originals are marked with an oval sticker, either with the California or Japan designation, and all (except the animals) carry either an incised or ink-stamped mark, 'Josef Originals'©. The company has been sold to Applause who continues to make Josef figurines, though not of the same good quality as the originals. Examples listed below are from the period of the 1940s through the 1970s (before Muriel's retirement) when the girls were all made with black eyes and the animals were all done in a glossy finish. More recent figures have brown-red eyes and the animals may have a flocked finish. Prices are for figurines in perfect condition; one with repair or damage is not considered collectible. Our advisors for this category are Jim and Kaye Whitaker (Eclectic Antiques), authors of a soon-to-be-released book on this subject, whose address is in the Directory under Washington.

Baby w/kitten, bl, pk or yel, Japan, 3", ea 30.00
Bear eating honey, Japan, 4" 25.00
Birthday Girl #1, bl & wht gown, blk eyes, Japan 30.00
Birthday Girl #16, bl gown, blk eyes, Japan 36.00
Birthday Girl #2, pk gown, blk eyes, Japan 30.00
Birthday Girl #3, bl gown, blk eyes, Japan 30.00
Birthstone Doll February, lav gown, purple stone, Japan 22.00
Birthstone Doll January, pk gown, red stone, Japan 22.00
Birthstone Doll March, aqua gown & stones, Japan 22.00
California Belle, Chapel Belle, pk gown, holding hymnal, CA 32.00
California Belle, Dinner Belle, bl gown, holding plate, CA 32.00
Chinese girl, wht kimono, blk fan (up or down), CA 45.00
Christmas Lady music box, fur collar, Japan, 6½" 90.00
Couple music box, mauve gown, bl cape, Japan, 5¼" 90.00
Doll of the Month, w/birthstones, CA, 3¼", ea 35.00
Duck family, dad, mom & baby, Japan, 2" to 4", set 58.00
Elephant w/flower, Japan, 5" 35.00
Gabrielle, bl gown & brn coat, 5¾" 60.00
Girl at piano music box, pk gown, ponytail, Japan 90.00
Jacques, pk suit & gray vest, 5¾" 60.00
January Doll, peach gown, w/muff & hat, CA 32.00
Lady music box, gr gown, w/hat, Japan, 6½" 90.00
Ladybug, Japan, 2½" 18.00
Little International, Africa, Blk girl, pk feather, Japan, 4" 33.00
Little International, America, Indian girl, Japan, 4" 33.00
Little International, France, pk, wht & bl clothes, Japan, 4" 33.00
Little International, Hungary, mauve/wht/bl/gold, Japan, 4" 33.00
Little International, Japan, pk kimono, gold trim, Japan, 4" 33.00
Little International, Sweden, gray gown, bl flowers, Japan, 4" 33.00
Love's Rendezvous, aqua gown & hat, Japan, 9" 125.00
Mama, pk gown, wht apron & candle, CA, 7¼" 85.00
Mice, various poses, costumes, glossy, Japan, ea 20.00
Monkeys, various poses & sizes, Japan, ea 20.00
Ostrich set, mom, dad & 2 chicks, Japan 150.00

Persian kitten with ball, Japan, 3", $24.00; Persian cat, Japan, 4", $26.00.

Pitty Sing, Chinese boy w/lg hat & kitten, CA, 4" 45.00
Prince, baby w/crown & cape, CA, 3¾" 45.00
Rabbits, various poses, Japan, 3" to 5", from $16.00 up to 20.00
School Belle, yel gown, w/apple & book, Japan, 3½" 30.00
Trousseau, bl gown, holds lav gown, pk roses, Japan, 9" 125.00
Turtle, laying on side, Japan, 2" 16.00

Judaica

The items listed below are representative of objects used in both the secular and religious life of the Jewish people. They are evident of a culture where silversmiths, painters, engravers, writers, and metal workers were highly gifted and skilled in their art. Most of the treasures shown in recently displayed exhibits of Judaica were confiscated by the Germans during the late 1930s up to 1945; by then eight Jewish synagogues and fifty warehouses had been filled with Hitler's plunder.

Judaica is currently available through dealers, from private collections, and the annual auction held in Israel.

Cache pot, Bezalel silver inlaid brass, 10-sided, 1912, 6" **1,000.00**
Chevra Kadisha tray, Austrian silver, eng foliage, 1896, 8½" **300.00**
Circumcision dish, Continental silver, repousse, 1900s, 8" **500.00**
Esther scroll, Continental silver cased, late 1800s, 11" **770.00**
Ethrog container, Continental silver, 4-ftd, 4¼" L **2,250.00**
Ethrog container, German silver, Georgian style, 5¼" **1,200.00**
Hanukkah lamp, Am SP, domed base, 8 sockets, 1910s, 15" **575.00**
Hanukkah lamp, Italian bronze, fan form, 8 oil pans, 6¼" **2,860.00**
Hanukkah lamp, Palestinian Limestone, 8 fonts, 7¼" **850.00**
Hanukkah lamp, Polish brass, trn stem, 8 oil fonts, 1800s **600.00**
Hanukkah lamp, Polish SP, canopy form, 8 fonts, 6¾" **385.00**
Havdallah plate, German porc, Star of David, 1900s, 5⅛" **300.00**
Kiddush beaker, Polish silver, eng vignettes, 1880s, 2½" **850.00**
Kiddush goblet, Bezalel silver, colored stones, 1920, 6¾" **660.00**
Kiddush goblet, Continental silver, 8-sided, 1800s, 4⅞" **935.00**
Marriage ring, Continental silver, inscr Mazal-Tov, 1900s **225.00**
Memorial candle holder, brass, tombstone shape, 1900s, 4½" **250.00**
Mezuah case, Continental brass, rectangular, 1600s, 6¾" **250.00**
Passover cloth, Palestinian silk, printed views, '20, 15x24" **200.00**
Passover dish, Continental porc, pnt & gold, 1800s, 9" **700.00**
Passover plate, Czechoslovakian pnt tin, 6-sided, 1900s, 15" ..**1,200.00**
Passover plate, Czechoslovakian porc, Karlsbad, 6½" **500.00**
Passover plate, German silver, repousse, floral rim, 6¼" **500.00**
Portal w/Hebrew Decalog w/in lintel fr, wood, 3¾" **350.00**
Purim dish, Hungarian porc, pnt scene, 1900s, 14" **850.00**
Rose water container, Persian silver, fruit form, 7½" **300.00**
Sabbath candelabrum, Bezalel silver, 2-arm, 1900s, 6" **800.00**
Sabbath knife, German silver w/MOP inlay, 1920s, 5½" **300.00**
Sewing box, Palestinian olive wood, book shape, 1900s, 5" **250.00**
Spice container, Continental silver, fish form, 1920s, 4" **300.00**
Spice container, Iraqui silver, fruit form, 1600s, 7" **1,320.00**
Spice container, Russian silver filigree, urn form, 4¾" **500.00**
Spice tower, Continental silver, removable spire, '20, 5" **150.00**
Vase, Bezalel brass, bulbous, vignettes, 1900s, 5" **200.00**
Vase, Bezalel silver-inlaid brass, baluster, 1914, 35" **935.00**
Wall hanging, Vision of Herzl/Star of David, 1900s, 44x25" ...**1,200.00**

Jugtown

The Jugtown Pottery was started about 1920 by Juliana and Jacques Busbee, in Moore County, North Carolina. Ben Owen, a young descendant of a Staffordshire potter, was hired in 1923. He was the master potter, while the Busbees experimented with perfecting glazes and supervising design and modeling. Preferred shapes were those reminiscent of traditional country wares and classic Oriental forms. Glazes were various: natural-clay oranges, buffs, 'tobacco-spit' brown, mirror black, white, 'frog-skin' green, a lovely turquoise called Chinese blue, and the traditional cobalt-decorated salt glaze. The pottery gained national recognition, and as a result of their success, several other local potteries were established. Jugtown is still in operation; however, they no longer use their original glaze colors which are now so collectible.

Bowl, Chinese bl, conical, 4x10" **125.00**
Bowl, redware, 7½" **32.00**
Bowl, redware w/orange glaze, low, open hdls, 15" **85.00**
Inkwell vase, Chinese bl **135.00**
Pie pan, orange, blk concentric-circled int, 9½" **42.50**
Pitcher, brn speckled, incised decor, 8½" **65.00**
Pitcher, gr w/bl, bulbous w/pinched spout, 5½" **55.00**
Pitcher, salt glaze w/dk bl lining & trim, strap hdl, 5" **65.00**

Pitcher with lid, redware, $40.00.

Plate, redware, mk, 10½" **25.00**
Vase, Chinese bl, red/turq, flat shoulder/short neck, 5" **425.00**
Vase, Chinese bl, red/turq, ovoid, 6x4½" **625.00**
Vase, cobalt, bulbous w/rim-to-width hdls, mk, 8" **195.00**
Vase, frogskin gr, ovoid, Ben Owen, 4" **135.00**

K. P. M. Porcelain

Under the tutelage of Frederick the Great, King of Prussia, porcelain manufacture was instituted in Berlin in 1751 by William K. Wegeley. In jealous competition with Meissen, hard-paste porcelain was produced (dinnerware, figurines, vases, etc.), some of which were undecorated while other pieces were hand painted in Watteau scenes, landscapes, or florals. It soon became evident that the factory was unable to offer serious competition. The King withdrew his support, and the factory failed in 1757. In 1761 Johann Ernst Gotzkowsky bought the rights and attempted a similar operation which soon failed due to financial difficulties. Still determined to gain the same recognition enjoyed by Meissen, the King bought the plant in 1763 and ruled the operation with an iron hand, often assuring his success by taking advantage of his position. The King died in 1786, but production has continued and quality tableware and decorative porcelains are still being made on a commercial basis. Earliest marks were simply 'G' or 'W,' followed by the scepter mark. After 1830 'K.P.M.' with an orb or eagle was adopted. Our advisor for this category is Don Williams; he is listed in the Directory under Missouri.

Cup & saucer, classical decor on bl/gold, winged figure hdl **140.00**
Figurine, boy holding tricorn hat, girl in bonnet, late, 14" **250.00**
Figurine, peasant girl w/basket of greens & cup of milk, 9" **500.00**
Figurine, Venus w/apple, cherubs/Paris at side, 1860-80, 8½" **600.00**
Gravy boat, gilt decor on wht, attached underplate, +ladle **100.00**
Plaque, Christ kneeling by rock, 5¾x8½" **1,750.00**
Plaque, cockatoo lands on maid's arm, 10x7", gesso fr **3,000.00**
Plaque, lady w/loose gown about her, sgn Wagner, oval, 5" **1,000.00**
Plaque, lady w/lute, sgn F Burfhardt, late 1800s, 6½x9" **2,750.00**
Plaque, lady w/red hair & laurel leaves, fr, 12½x10" **4,000.00**
Plaque, Madonna & Child, 8x6" **2,000.00**
Plaque, vestal virgin, EX/ornate fr, ca 1900, 21x17" **6,000.00**
Plaque, young boy, 1890s, 5½x4" **495.00**
Plateau mirror, 16-pc scrollwork sides remove, 1850s, lg **1,000.00**
Platter, Dresden flowers w/gold, scalloped, 13x9½" **500.00**
Vase, Napoleon's portrait, sgn Wagner, scepter mk, 7" **2,000.00**

Kayserzinn Pewter

J.P. Kayser Sohn produced pewter decorated with relief-molded

Art Nouveau motifs in Germany during the late 1800s and into the 20th century. Examples are marked with 'Kayserzinn' and the mold number within an elongated oval reserve. Items with dimensional animals, insects, birds, etc., are valued much higher than bowls, plates, and trays with simple embossed florals, which are usually priced at $100.00 to about $200.00, depending on size.

Bonbon, shell form w/Art Nouveau nude, sgn/#4136, 8x6¾" 185.00
Bowl, stylized floral, raised/shaped border, #4368, 17½" 260.00

Candelabra, shaped rectangular stems, four scroll branches with central light, impressed mark, #4485 and #4486, 18¾", $5,500.00 for the pair.

Egg dish, ftd sq base tray, dome lid, emb design, 10" W 300.00
Pitcher, floral in low relief, 9" 200.00
Pitcher, Mephistopheles, sgn/#d, 12" 355.00
Sugar bowl, Dragon Ship form, open, 8" L 150.00
Tray, fancy hdls, 14x11½", w/8" H Nouveau dome top 295.00
Vase, antelope skulls w/horns on chalice form, 14¼" 400.00
Vase, emb vintage, #49, 12" 200.00
Vase, fish & flower decor, 3-ftd, #53, 7" 60.00
Water can, fish relief, snail finial, leaf hdl, #7-4203, 11" 1,300.00

Keen Kutter

Keen Kutter was a brand name of E.C. Simmons Hardware, used from about 1870 until the mid-1930s. In 1923 Winchester merged with Simmons but continued to produce Keen Kutter marked knives and tools. The merger dissolved, and in 1940 the Simmons Company was purchased by Shapleigh Hardware. Older items are very collectible. For further study we recommend *Keen Kutter Collectibles*, an illustrated price guide by Jerry and Elaine Heuring, available at your favorite bookstore or public library.

Key: adj — adjustable

Auger, hand held 25.00
Auger bit set, KKSB13, 13-pc, NM 120.00
Axe, broad; Keen Kutter written out, no logo, NM 90.00
Axe, Dayton pattern, KKD301, NM 37.50
Axe, hand; boy's, Michigan pattern, NM 60.00
Axe, scout; w/sheath, KK20, NM 40.00
Bit, reamer; KK115, NM 15.00
Bit brace, KK112, 12", NM 25.00
Chisel, butt; KK5, 5-pc set, NM 90.00
Chisel, gouge; KK1B ¼, 11 szs, ¼"-2", NM 30.00
Chisel set, firmer; KKB12, 12-pc, NM 190.00
Drill, push; KK8, 9½", NM 30.00
Food chopper, K21, orig box & cookbook, NM 80.00
Hair clippers, #4, w/cover 30.00
Hammer, brick; KKB15, 24-oz, NM 40.00
Hammer, machinist's; KKM2, 24-oz, NM 25.00
Hammer, nail; KKP112, 14-oz, NM 25.00
Hammer, nail; KK411½, 16-oz, NM 25.00
Hatchet, claw; KKBC1, NM 30.00

Hatchet, half; KKBHO, NM 30.00
Hatchet, lathing; KKBAL1, NM 30.00
Hatchet, tobacco; KKBT2, NM 30.00
Hoe, garden mattock; KHW, Dig-ezy pattern, NM 42.50
Knife, butcher; K160, 6", orig box, NM 45.00
Knife, linoleum; 3" blade, NM 17.00
Knife, pocket; K254, brn bone hdl, 3¼", NM 70.00
Knife steel, K540, 8", NM 11.00
Kraut cutter, wooden, 1-blade, Pat 9/04, 8x26½", NM 70.00
Level, wooden, KKO, non-adj, brass top plate, 28", NM 25.00
Level, wooden, KK104, non-adj, brass top plate, 16", NM 40.00
Level, wooden, KK13, non-adj, brass top plate, 18", NM 45.00
Pipe cutter, K2, 3 wheel pattern, ¼"-2", NM 80.00
Pipe wrench, KK-14, Simmons 25.00
Plane, block; KK103, w/lever adj, 5½", NM 25.00
Plane, block; KK65, 7", NM 30.00
Plane, circular; KK115, 10", NM 230.00
Plane, combination; KK64, 21 cutters, NM 330.00
Plane, jointer; KK8, smooth bottom, 24", NM 70.00
Plane, smooth; KK22, 8", NM 40.00
Plane, smooth; KK4C, 9", NM 30.00
Pliers, channel lock; K507, 6½" 32.50
Pliers, flat nose, K86-6, ⅜" W, NM 32.50
Razor hone, Jr; aluminum box, instructions, NM 58.00
Razor hone, KK20, orig tin box, NM 25.00
Rosette iron, mk EG Simmons on lid, mini, 5", in mk box 150.00
Rule, folding, KK620, 4-fold, boxwood, 1" wide folded, 24" 40.00
Saw set, wide tooth for crosscut, NM 25.00
Scissors, S128AK, orig box, NM 70.00
Screwdriver, K50, 8", NM 18.00
Square, T bevel; fancy iron hdl, 6" 40.00
Straight razor, KK #49 ....35.00
Tap & die set, K31, 5 sz tap dies & guides, orig box, NM 575.00
Thermometer, indoor/outdoor, metal, wood bk, 2½x9" 165.00
Tool grinder, hand powered, NM 7.00
Waffle iron, 4-section, KK logo, EX 200.00
Weed cutter, KWCS-K, NM 37.50

Kelva

Kelva was a trademark of the C.F. Monroe Company of Meriden, Connecticut; it was produced for only a few years after the turn of the century. It is distinguished from the Wave Crest and Nakara lines by its unique Batik-like background, probably achieved through the use of a cloth or sponge to apply the color. Large florals are hand painted on the opaque milk glass; and ormolu and brass mounts were used for the boxes, vases, and trays. Most pieces are signed. Our advisors for this category are Dolli and Wilfred Cohen; they are listed in the Directory under California.

Box, daisies, bl on pk, ormolu ft, oval, 3¾x5½x4" 550.00
Box, floral, bl-gray on red, plain mold, 3½x5¾" dia 495.00
Box, floral, orange on gr, ftd base, sqd, 4" W 350.00
Box, floral, pk on bl-gray, mirror in lid, 3¾x4½" 595.00
Box, floral, wht on red, 3½x6" 525.00
Box, roses, pk on gr, fuchsia trim, wht dots, mk, 3½x6" 700.00
Box, watch; daisies, pk on bl 325.00
Box, wild roses, pk on gr, sq, hinged lid, 2¾x4" 425.00
Ferner, floral on pk, ogee sides, 7½" dia 550.00
Humidor, Cigars/floral on bl, oval 650.00
Humidor, Cigars/floral on rare brn, str sides, 4¾x3½" 695.00
Tray, Crown mold, floral on moss gr, 6" dia 275.00
Tray, daisies on maroon, rnd w/emb metal rim, rope hdl, 3½" 300.00

Vase, florals on light green, ormolu handles and base, 16½", $1,895.00.

Vase, floral, pk & wht on gr, ormolu top & hdls, 14½" 850.00
Vase, floral on rose, trumpet form w/4 ormolu ft, 6x2" 495.00
Whisk broom holder, floral on red, ornate ormolu bkplate 950.00

Kew Blas

Kew Blas was a trade name used by the Union Glass Company of Summerville, Massachusetts, for their iridescent, lustered art glass produced from 1893 until about 1920. The glass was made in imitation of Tiffany and achieved notable success. Some items were decorated with pulled leaf and feather designs, while others had a monochrome lustre surface. The mark was an engraved 'Kew Blas' in an arching arrangement.

Creamer, feathers, gold on opal, gold hdl/int, 3¼" 500.00
Pitcher, feathers, dk gr/gold on oyster wht, 4½" 700.00
Tumbler, gold w/bl highlights, pinched, 3½" 250.00
Vase, cvd bees on gold, scalloped/waisted cylinder, 9" 715.00
Vase, feathers, gold on opal, 5¼" 625.00
Vase, feathers on irid, trumpet form, att, 15½" 880.00
Vase, fishscales on diagonal, gold/gr irid, 7" 600.00
Vase, floriform; red w/purple highlights, 9" 300.00

King's Rose

King's Rose is a soft-paste ware that was made in Staffordshire, England, from about 1820 to 1830. It is closely related to Gaudy Dutch in body type as well as the colors used in its decoration. The pattern consists of a full-blown, orange-red rose with green, pink, and yellow leaves and accents. When the rose is in pink, the ware is often referred to as Queen's Rose. Our advisor for this category is Richard Marden; he is listed in the Directory under New Hampshire.

Coffeepot, red rose, pk band, sqd, mk J, 6", EX 350.00
Coffeepot, 4-color, ornate hdl, slim, 11" 1,550.00
Creamer, pk rose, vine border, mk Davenport/anchor, sq, 3½" ... 500.00
Creamer, Queen's, 4-color, molded ribs, 2⅝" 100.00
Cup & saucer, handleless; Queen's, 4-color, vine/rose rim, EX ... 150.00
Cup & saucer, red rose, vine border, EX 200.00
Cup & saucer, red rose, wide pk band, VG 95.00
Cup plate, vine border, 4⅜" 300.00
Plate, pk rose, vine border, shaped rim, 5¼", NM 130.00
Plate, pk rose, vine border, shaped rim, 7", NM 160.00
Plate, pk rose, vine border, 8", NM 170.00
Plate, solid border, flake, 8¼" 65.00
Plate, toddy; solid border, 5¼" 110.00
Soup plate, pk rose, vine border, 10", NM 270.00
Sugar bowl, Queen's, medallion, molded ribs, ring hdls, 4¾" 90.00

Kitchen Collectibles

During the last half of the 1850s, mass-produced kitchen gadgets were patented at an astonishing rate. Most were ingeniously efficient. Apple peelers, egg beaters, cherry pitters, food choppers, and such were only the most common of hundreds of kitchen tools well designed to perform only specific tasks. Today all are very collectible. Our advisor for Cast Kitchen Ware is Denise Harned, who is the author of *Griswold Cast Collectibles*. She is listed in the Directory under Connecticut. We also recommend *Kitchen Glassware of the Depression Years* by Gene Florence and *Kitchen Antiques, 1790-1940*, by Kathryn McNerney. See also Appliances; Glass Knives; Molds; Primitives; Reamers; Tinware; Wooden Ware.

Cast Kitchen Ware

Brownie cake pan, Griswold #9 .... 90.00
Bulged pot, Griswold #7, low 55.00
Cake mold, rabbit, Griswold 275.00
Cake mold, Santa, Griswold 495.00
Cornstick pan, Griswold #22 .... 40.00
Cornstick pan, Griswold #262, mini 95.00
Danish cake pan (aebleskiver)/egg poacher, Griswold #32 .... 38.00
Dutch oven, Griswold #7, w/trivet 135.00
Dutch oven, Griswold #8 Tite Top 38.00
Egg pan, Griswold #53 .... 55.00
Egg pan, Griswold #562 .... 75.00
Griddle, Griswold #12, lg logo, rnd 48.00
Griddle, Griswold #14, Erie 48.00
Griddle, Sultana, oval, 18" 40.00
Griddle, unmk, rectangular, 20" 40.00
Griddle, Wagner, rnd 20.00
Kettle, Griswold, Erie #812X 50.00
Muffin pan, Griswold #10 .... 45.00
Muffin pan, Griswold #9, golf ball 125.00
Patty bowl/hot pot, Griswold #871 .... 70.00
Patty set, Griswold #2, deep 25.00
Platter, Griswold #34 .... 20.00
Roaster, Griswold #5, oval 120.00
Roaster, Griswold #9 .... 275.00
Roll pan, Griswold #26 .... 45.00
Scotch bowl, Griswold #782, Erie 60.00
Skillet, Griswold #0 .... 150.00
Skillet, Griswold #3 .... 20.00
Skillet, Griswold #5, sm logo 20.00
Skillet, Griswold #7 .... 20.00
Skillet, Griswold #8, lg pattern 24.00
Skillet, Griswold #8, Victor 45.00
Skillet, Griswold #9, slant letters 36.00
Skillet, Griswold #9, Victor 45.00
Skillet, Mt Penn Stoves...& Ranges, Reading PA, 2½" dia 25.00
Skillet, Sidney, #0 sz 35.00
Skillet, unmk, old, 3½" dia+2¼" hdl 15.00
Skillet, unmk, 10" sq 30.00
Skillet, Wagner #8 .... 16.00
Spider skillet, unmk, 9½" dia+7" hdl 40.00
Teakettle, Geo Starrett NY, Pat July 14, 1868 .... 95.00
Waffle iron, EG Simmons, wooden hdls, child's 225.00
Waffle iron, Stover Jr #08, child's 225.00
Waffle iron, unmk, Am eagle design, 5½"+31" hdl 150.00
Waffle iron, unmk, dbl floral design, 10x5"+34" hdl 50.00
Waffle iron, unmk, dmn design, 8x7¾"+24" hdl, NM 225.00
Waffle iron, Wagner #8, tall stand, wood hdls, Pat 1910 .... 125.00

Wheat stick pan, Griswold #262, mini 95.00

Glassware

Bottle, water; dk amber 60.00
Bottle, water; forest gr, emb penguin 15.00
Bottle, water; red, plain or ribbed, Hocking 70.00
Bowl, batter, turq bl 50.00
Bowl, beater; Chalaine bl, w/spout, 4" H 40.00
Bowl, blk, 7⅜" 32.50
Bowl, blk fired-on, 10¼" 12.00
Bowl, Chalaine bl, 6" 35.00
Bowl, cobalt, LE Smith, 8¼" 45.00
Bowl, custard, 8" 16.50
Bowl, Delphite bl, horizontal ribs, 5½" 27.50
Bowl, Delphite bl, w/spout, 4¼" 45.00
Bowl, egg beater; Skokie gr, w/spout, McKee 12.00
Bowl, gr, 1-spout, 4½" 15.00
Bowl, gr clambroth, twist design, 4¾" 12.00
Bowl, gr Jadite, vertical ribs, Jeannette, 6" 10.00
Bowl, mixing; paneled, Hocking, 11½" 20.00
Bowl, mixing; pk, Federal, 9½" 15.00
Bowl, mixing; pk, Hex Optic, ruffled edge, 8¼" 22.00
Bowl, pk, concentric rings, slick hdl, 9" 22.00
Butter dish, amber, Federal, 1-lb 30.00
Butter dish, blk w/crystal top 65.00
Butter dish, cobalt, Butter Cover emb on lid, Hazel Atlas 165.00
Butter dish, Delphite bl, Jeannette 285.00
Butter dish, gr, Block Optic 37.50
Butter dish, gr, Hex Optic 65.00
Butter dish, gr Jadite (dk), Jeannette 37.50
Butter dish, gr or pk, Crisscross, 1-lb 35.00
Butter dish, pk, rectangular, bow-hdld lid 55.00
Butter dish, Red Ships on milk glass, McKee 22.00

Canister set, peacock blue with tin lids, 8-piece set in wire rack, rare, $1,100.00.

Canister, blk fleur-de-lis & Flour pnt on clear 15.00
Canister, blk fired-on, matching lid 25.00
Canister, blk lettering on custard, sq 45.00
Canister, Chalaine bl, rnd, w/bl lid, 10-oz 50.00
Canister, Coffee emb 18.00
Canister, Delphite bl, blk pnt Tea lettering, 20-oz 120.00
Canister, Delphite bl, rnd, McKee, 10-oz 45.00
Canister, dk amber, emb Coffee 85.00
Canister, forest gr, diagonal ridges, Owens-IL, 40-oz 22.50
Canister, gr Jadite, floral pattern in lid, Jeannette, 5½" 32.50
Canister, gr Jadite, rnd, screw-on lid, Jeannette, 40-oz 55.00
Canister, sugar; gr, globular, metal lid 95.00

Cheese dish, custard, rectangular, McKee 35.00
Cheese dish, dk amber 60.00
Cheese dish, gr clambroth, Hocking 65.00
Cocktail shaker, dk amber, pitcher shape 75.00
Coffeepot, w/lid, Silex, lg 95.00
Cookie jar, peacock bl, LE Smith 80.00
Cruet, chicken decal on frost 12.00
Cruet, forest gr 35.00
Decanter, gr, pinched-in sides, Hocking 35.00
Dispenser, custard, McKee 120.00
Dispenser, milk glass, McKee 100.00
Dripolater, Silex, lg 40.00
Egg cup, blk 12.50
Funnel, gr, Tufglas 80.00
Funnel, 11" 20.00
Funnel, 5" 10.00
Gravy boat, red, w/underplate, Imperial 165.00
Ice bucket, gr, Cambridge 30.00
Ice bucket, gr, w/metal lid 25.00
Ice bucket, gr clambroth, Fenton 45.00
Ice bucket, jade gr, Fenton 40.00
Jar, coffee; forest gr, emb Coffee on flip top, Owens-IL 60.00
Jug, batter; gr, Jenkins 120.00
Jug, batter; gr, New Martinsville 60.00
Ladle, blk, rnd hdl 25.00
Ladle, blk, wedge-shaped hdl 22.50
Ladle, gr, rnd bottom 12.00
Ladle, Moonlight bl 40.00
Ladle, pk, slim str hdl 9.00
Ladle, Primrose, Cambridge 25.00
Ladle, vaseline, knob ends in triangular shape 22.50
Ladle, yel, gr or pk, flat bottom, ea 12.00
Measure, amber, Federal, w/hdl 38.00
Measure, bl, 3-spout, Fire-King 18.00
Measure, cobalt, w/reamer top, Hazel Atlas, 2-cup 225.00
Measure, Delphite bl, Jeannette, 1-cup 45.00
Measure, dk amber 175.00
Measure, gr, no hdl, 3-spout, Federal 20.00
Measure, gr, tab hdl, Jeannette 26.00
Measure, gr, 20-oz 135.00
Measure, gr, 3-spout, Federal 35.00
Measure, Owens & Co 25.00
Measure, pk, 1-spout, US Glass 55.00
Measure, red fired-on, 3-spout, Hazel Atlas 40.00
Measure, Seville yel, ftd, w/hdl, 4-cup 65.00
Measure, Skokie gr, 2-spout, Mckee 140.00
Measure, stippled bottom, McKee unemb Glasbake 12.00
Measure, yel opaque, no hdl, McKee, 4-cup 275.00
Measure pitcher, Delphite bl, McKee, 4-cup 475.00
Measure pitcher, Delphite bl, sunflower base, Jeannette, 2-cup 50.00
Measure pitcher, gr, Hocking, 2-cup 20.00
Measure pitcher, pk, slick hdl 45.00
Measure pitcher, 1-qt 30.00
Mug, amber 37.50
Mug, blk 25.00
Mug, forest gr, Cambridge 42.50
Mug, gr, Hobnail 20.00
Mug, peacock bl 30.00
Mug, root beer; gr 30.00
Napkin holder, gr clambroth, Serv-All 145.00
Pitcher, gr, Hocking, 60-oz 15.00
Pitcher, milk; cobalt, Hazel Atlas 55.00
Pitcher, milk; pk, Hazel Atlas 20.00
Punch ladle, blk 60.00

Refrigerator dish, Chalaine bl, 7¼" sq	100.00
Refrigerator dish, gr clambroth, oval, Hocking, 8"	32.50
Refrigerator dish, lt bl, Glasbake, 4¼" sq	4.00
Refrigerator dish, milk glass, Breakstone's Fine Dairy Foods	12.50
Refrigerator dish, pk, Federal, 4x4"	7.50
Refrigerator dish, pk, Federal, 8x8"	32.00
Refrigerator dish, Vitrock, Hocking, 4x4"	10.00
Refrigerator dish, yel opaque, Hocking, 6x6"	20.00
Refrigerator jar, gr, rnd, w/lid, 9" dia	38.00
Refrigerator jar, red fired-on w/clear lid, Pyrex, 3½x4¾"	5.00
Rolling pin, clear w/cobalt hdls	185.00
Rolling pin, cobalt	80.00
Rolling pin, custard	185.00
Rolling pin, forest gr, blown	145.00
Rolling pin, gr Jadite	300.00
Rolling pin, lt amber, blown	120.00
Rolling pin, med amber, pontiled ends, ca 1860, 17¼"	130.00
Rolling pin, peacock bl	225.00
Rolling pin, wooden hdls, mk Silvers, NY	65.00
Salt box, gr Jadite, Jeannette	210.00
Server, wht clambroth, 7⅜" dia	12.00
Shaker, milk glass, Home Soap Company	12.50
Shaker, Vitrock, Hocking	8.00
Shakers, bl Dutch scene, 16-oz, pr	13.50
Shakers, blk, rnd, pr	18.00
Shakers, blk fired-on, metal top, pr	14.00
Shakers, blk lettering on custard, pr	24.00
Shakers, blk lettering on milk glass, lg, pr	85.00
Shakers, Chalaine bl, screw-on metal top, pr	100.00
Shakers, emb dots on sq shape, metal top, pr	12.00
Shakers, gr Jadite (dk), Jeannette, pr	25.00
Shakers, orange fired-on, Roman arch side panel, pr	20.00
Shakers, pk emb, Hazel Atlas, pr	95.00
Shakers, singing birds, blk & red on milk glass, pr	25.00
Shakers, Skokie gr, Roman arch side panel, Mckee, pr	25.00
Sherbet, gr clambroth	7.50
Soda glass, gr	12.00
Spoon holder, gr	185.00
Sugar shaker, amber, pinched-in sides, Paden City	145.00
Sugar shaker, blk, McKee, 3½"	15.00
Sugar shaker, gr, Beehive, Lancaster	135.00
Sugar shaker, West Sanitary Automatic Sugar	25.00
Sugar shaker, yel fired-on w/red top	20.00
Syrup, amber, hinged metal lid, Paden City #198, 8-oz	50.00
Syrup, blk, Fenton	50.00
Syrup, gr, floral cutting, w/underliner, Paden City	35.00
Syrup, gr, hinged metal lid, Paden City	30.00
Syrup, pk, Cambridge	50.00
Syrup, pk, hinged metal lid, Hazel Atlas	40.00
Toast holder	65.00
Trivet, red, rnd	45.00
Tumbler, blk, McKee	18.00
Tumbler, gr, Rena line, Paden City	10.00

Miscellaneous

Apple corer, tin, tubular hdl, 6"	15.00
Apple peeler, Geo R Thompson, CI, lever action	165.00
Apple peeler, Hudson, CI	65.00
Apple peeler, Rival #296, commercial type, 1889, weighs 37 lb	125.00
Apple peeler, Turntable '78, Reading Hdw, Pat 1878	100.00
Apple peeler, Turntable '98, Goodell& Co, Antrim NH	125.00
Apple peeler, Wht Mtn #3, Goodell Co...NH, CI, ca 1898	50.00
Apple peeler/corer/slicer, Tippecanoe, CI, 3-prong fork	95.00

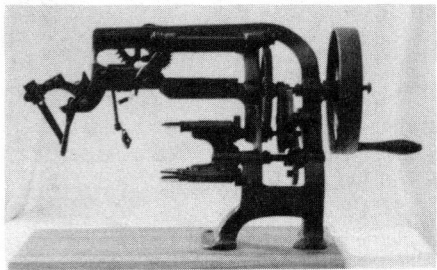

Apple peeler, D. Goodell, Antrim NH, cast iron, triple peeling action, $500.00.

Board, kraut; walnut w/cut-out heart on lollipop end, 10" L	350.00
Can opener, CI, bull's head on front at blades, tail is hdl	110.00
Can opener, Never-Slip, iron w/loop hdl, Pat Nov 12, '02	18.00
Can opener, Old Marvel, pnt CI, ca 1919, 7¼" L	45.00
Can opener, Pet Milk, tin	12.50
Cherry seeder, CI, mk Pat Date Apr 9, 1867	90.00
Cherry seeder, CI, 4-legged, ca 1860s, 7x10⅜"	85.00
Cherry seeder, Duke, Reading Hdw, Pat Pend, ca 1890, 11"	95.00
Cherry seeder, Enterprise, CI, 1903	65.00
Cherry seeder, Home Cherry Stoner, Pat Aug 7, 1917, 2-prong	58.00
Cherry seeder, Rollman, EX	35.00
Cherry seeder, Scott Mfg, lightweight CI, 3-legged, 7x12"	85.00
Chopper, Griswold #3, MIB	80.00
Chopper, sheet iron blade, forged nails, oak hdl, 1870s, 6½"	60.00
Chopper, wrought iron blade, wooden hdl	50.00
Chopper, 6 blades in bell shape, iron hdl	30.00
Churn, Dazey #40, Pat date, 1-gal	75.00
Churn, Lightning Butter Machine, Pat Feb 6, 1917, 2-qt	110.00
Churn, staved drum shape w/dk tin bands, crank hdl, 15x13"	135.00
Churn, wood w/old red pnt, wrought hdl, 13x12x12½"	175.00
Churn, wood w/orig red pnt, wrought crank hdl, 16¼"	225.00
Clothes sprinkler bottle, cat, ceramic w/marble eyes, 8"	75.00
Clothes sprinkler bottle, Chinaman, ceramic, yel & blk	30.00
Clothes sprinkler bottle, Dutch boy, ceramic, 8"	75.00
Clothes sprinkler bottle, Dutch girl, ceramic, 8"	75.00
Clothes sprinkler bottle, elephant, soft red plastic	18.00
Clothes sprinkler bottle, Myrtle, ceramic	80.00
Clothes sprinkler bottle, rooster, ceramic, 10"	65.00
Clothes sprinkler bottle, sadiron, ceramic, w/ivy	25.00
Crimper, bone wheel, wood hdl, 5½"	30.00
Crimper, brass, tamper end w/waffle design	50.00
Crimper, 2" wooden wheel, shaped hdl, 7½"	45.00
Cutter, biscuit; Forbes Quality Baking Powder, tin	10.00
Cutter, biscuit; Kreamer, strap hdl	8.00
Cutter, kraut; Disston & Morse	45.00
Cutter, kraut; pine, red finish, scratch cvd 1801, 19¼"	95.00
Cutter, slaw; walnut, slide box/CI blades/shaped hdl, 20"	250.00
Egg & cream beater, Dunlap Sanitary	20.00
Egg beater, A&J, Pat 1923	12.00
Egg beater, Art-Beck, rachet type, NMIB	38.00
Egg beater, coiled wire knob	18.50
Egg beater, Holts, Pat Aug 22, 1899-Apr 3, 1900, CI, 12"	40.00
Egg beater, Taplin, 1908	35.00
Egg beater, tin wheel w/6 wire loops, wooden hdl, 1900s	70.00
Egg beater, Turbine, 1910	40.00
Egg beater, Washburn Co, turbine type	25.00
Egg separator, Gem, rnd tin bowl w/slots, 1889, 3¼" dia	40.00
Egg separator, South Bend Malleable Range	15.00
Egg separator, Town Talk Flour, tin	15.00
Grater, hand-punched tin in wood fr, 1840s, 14x4¾"	85.00

Grater, heavy punched tin on oak board, 19" w/hdl **80.00**
Grater, ironstone, lt gray, curved top, 5½" **55.00**
Grater, nutmeg; Gem, Caldwell Mfg, tin/CI, mechanical, 1890s ..**125.00**
Grater, nutmeg; loop hdl, Pat 3/9/1866 ....**195.00**
Grater, nutmeg; The Standard, Pat 12/25/1887 ....**195.00**
Grater, pierced tin, pine bk w/cut-out hdl, 13½" L **135.00**
Grater, pierced tin in thick pine fr, 12¾x7" **48.00**
Grater, tin w/heavy wire fr, 3 surfaces, hinged door, 1910 ....**32.00**
Grinder, Standard Werk, brass & CI, late 1800s, 7½" L **40.00**
Grinder, Universal LFC Pat 1897, EX **35.00**
Grinder, wooden box shape w/knife-like spikes, 1860s, 11x7x7" ..**165.00**
Jar lifter/opener, Iron Hottongs, iron, lg **12.00**
Juicer, Dazey, metal, wall mt **30.00**
Masher, iron bottom w/holes, wood hdl, 16" **20.00**
Masher, wooden, 2⅝" dia w/5" fancy trn hdl, 9¾" **25.00**
Masher, zig-zag mashers work w/fulcrum action, 11½" **55.00**
Measure, Maytag, aluminum **12.00**
Mixer, Roberts Lightning, tin w/glass bottom, Pat...1913 ....**38.00**
Pan, angel food cake; Swans Down Cake Flour, tin **30.00**
Pan, cake; Calumet Baking Powder, tin, rnd **12.00**
Pitcher, MK Fairbanks Pure Refined Lard, tin, 2½" **28.00**
Potato peeler, unmk Hamlinite, tin bk, Pat July 20, 1920 ....**48.00**
Pricker, 1¼" iron prickers, fluted maple hdl, 1870s, 5¼" **85.00**
Raisin seeder, Everett, wood w/7 curved wires, 1889-93 ....**75.00**
Raisin seeder, EZ Raisin Seeder, Pat May 21, 1895, CI, 6" **250.00**
Raisin seeder, Gem, dtd Dec 24, 1895 ....**80.00**
Raisin seeder, unmk Lightning, orig blk pnt, 1895, 6¾" **65.00**
Rolling pin, curly maple, 15¼" **50.00**
Rolling pin, curly maple, 21" **150.00**
Rolling pin, maple, grooved hdl, mk Munsing **35.00**
Rolling pin, metal center w/oval cutouts, wooden hdls **32.00**
Rolling pin, wht stoneware, maple hdls, 19x3" dia **200.00**
Rolling pin, wood, bl & wht hdls, child's **20.00**
Scoop, flour; Jenny Wren Ready Mixed Flour, tin **10.00**
Sifter, Blood's Pat Sept 17, 1861 on paper label, wood **325.00**
Sifter, Duplex Sifter, Ullrich Tinware...1922, 5-cup **45.00**
Slicer, vegetable; WH Baldwin, Pat Oct 3, 1871, sm **34.00**
Slicer, vegetable; wooden w/wire pusher, dtd 1898, 3¾x21" **68.00**
Squeezer, lemon; maple w/lignum vitae cup, 11" **85.00**
Squeezer, lemon; Newman's Drum Squeezer...1883, 2x9x3½" **85.00**
Strawberry huller, Boston Huller, NP over brass, 1894 ....**7.00**
Sugar nippers, wrought iron, pliers type, lines/rings, 10" **200.00**
Whip, Fries, tin w/looped legs, side hdls, side crank **85.00**
Whip, mayonnaise; Universal, rare **400.00**
Wrench, fruit jar; Triumph, dtd Nov 3, '03 ....**9.00**

Knives

Knife collecting as a hobby began in earnest during the 1960s when government regulations required for the first time that knife companies mark their product with the country of origin. The few collectors and dealers cognizant of this change at once began stockpiling the older knives made before this law was enacted. Another impetus to the growing interest in this area came with the Gun Control Act of 1968, which severely restricted gun trading. Frustrated gun dealers transferred their attention to knives. Today there are collectors clubs in many of the states.

The most sought-after pocketknives are those made before WWII. However, Case, Schrade, and Primble knives of a more recent manufacture are also collected. Most collectors prefer knives 'as found.' Do not attempt to clean, sharpen, or in any way 'improve' on an old knife.

The prices quoted here are for knives in mint condition (except for those in the Miscellaneous section). If a knife has been used, sharp-

ened, or blemished in any way, its value decreases. The newer the knife, the greater the reduction in value. For further information refer to *The Standard Knife Collector's Guide* by Ron Stewart and Roy Ritchie and *Sargent's American Premium Guide to Knives and Razors, Identification and Values, 3rd Edition,* by Jim Sargent. Our advisor for this category is Charles D. Stapp; he is listed in the Directory under Indiana.

Key:
bd — blade   p/b — push button
Cut — Cutlery   s/b — switchblade
jack — jackknife   lp — long pull
w/b — winterbottom

Case, RM1097, Xmas tree hdl, 1-bd, Tested XX, 1920-30, 5" **420.00**
Case, R1094, candy stripe hdl, 1-bd, Tested XX, 1920-40, 4¼" ..**360.00**
Case, 05263SS, stag hdl, 2-bd, XX, 1940-64, 3⅛" **70.00**
Case, 32095F, fish scaler, yel hdl, 3-bd, Tested XX, 1920-40, 5" ..**70.00**
Case, 4103B&G, yel compo hdl, 1-bd, Tested XX, 1920-40, 3¼" .**180.00**
Case, 52024, stag hdl, 2-bd, Tested XX, 1920-40, 3" **240.00**
Case, 52087, stag hdl, 2-bd, XX, 1940-64, 3¼" **75.00**
Case, 61213½, Rogers bone hdl, 1-bd, Tested XX, 4" **720.00**
Case, 6165SAB, Rogers bone hdl, 1-bd, XX, 1940-64, 5¾" **420.00**
Case, 62027½, bone hdl, 2-bd, Tested XX, 2¾" **135.00**
Case, 62031, red bone hdl, 2-bd, XX, 1940-64, 3¾" **110.00**
Case, 62052, Congress, rough blk hdl, 2-bd, XX, 1940-50, 3½" **80.00**
Case, 6207, bone hdl, 2-bd, XX, 1940-64, 3½" **55.00**
Case, 6227, bone hdl, 2-bd, USA, 1965-69, 2¾" **40.00**
Case, 6246R, gr bone hdl, 2-bd, Tested XX, 1920-40, 4⅜" **240.00**
Case, 6269, gr bone hdl, 2-bd, Tested XX, 1920-40, 3" **165.00**
Case, 6318SPPU, gr bone hdl, 2-bd, Tested XX, 1920-40, 3½" ..**240.00**
Case, 7106, tortoise shell hdl, 1-bd, Tested XX, 1920-40, 2⅝" ...**270.00**

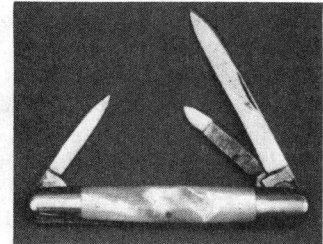

Case, #83063, 3-blade, mother-of-pearl handles, $225.00.

Case, 9151SAB, onyx hdl, 1-bd, Tested XX, 1920-40, 5¼" **560.00**
Case, 92042, cracked ice hdl, 2-bd, XX, 1940-64, 3" **35.00**
Keen Kutter, Bow Tie, bone hdl, 1-bd, EC Simmons, 3⅞" **140.00**
Keen Kutter, Coke bottle, bone hdl, 1-bd, EC Simmons, 5¼" **275.00**
Keen Kutter, Congress, brn bone hdl, 2-bd, EC Simmons, 3¾" ..**110.00**
Keen Kutter, premium stockman, plastic hdl, Keen Kutter, 3¼" ...**50.00**
Keen Kutter, Senators Pen, pearl hdl w/bail, EC Simmons, 2⅞" ...**45.00**
Keen Kutter, stockman, cracked ice hdl, Keen Kutter, 4" **110.00**
Keen Kutter, whittler, brn bone hdl, 3-bd, EC Simmons, 3⅝" **165.00**
Keen Kutter, whittler, swell center, bone hdl, EC Simmons, 3⅝" .**140.00**
Pal, penknife, bone hdl, 3-bd, (2 stamped), Pal Cutlery, 3" **55.00**
Pal, serpentine jack, bone hdl, 2-bd, Pal Cutlery, 3⅝" **65.00**
Pal, stockman, wht pyremite hdl, 3-bd, Pal Cutlery, 4" **90.00**
Queen, folding hunter, wb hdl, Q Stainless, 5¼" closed **110.00**
Queen, 21, sleeveboard, wb hdl, Queen steel, 1-bd, 5" **35.00**
Queen, 22, Barlow, brn bone hdl, 2-bd, 3½" **55.00**
Queen, 49, stockman, wb bone hdl, 3-bd, Queen, 4¼" **50.00**
Queen, 5, Senator, wb bone hdl, 2-bd, Queen Steel, 2½" **25.00**
Queen, 54, pearl hdl, 3-bd, Queen, 2⅝" **30.00**
Queen, 9, stockman, wb bone hdl, 3-bd, 4" **50.00**
Remington, R1163, jack, brn bone hdl, 2-bd, 4½" **450.00**

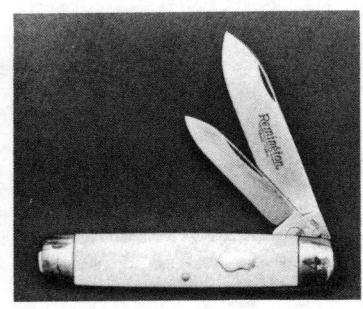

Remington, #R-1225, jack-knife, white composition handle, 2-blade, 4½", $200.00. (White handles are generally less desirable than others.)

Remington, R1383, fish scaler, lockbk, brn bone hdl, 4¼" 490.00
Remington, R1823, brn bone hdl, 2-bd, lp, 3⅝" 135.00
Remington, R238, cocobolo hdl, 2-bd, lp, 3⅝" 140.00
Remington, R3553, rnd bolsters, brn bone hdl, 3-bd, 4" 325.00
Remington, R365, jack, gold swirl pyremite hdl, 2-bd, 3¾" 225.00
Remington, R3843, utility, brn bone hdl, 6-bd, 3⅝" 380.00
Remington, R4273, sowbelly, brn bone hdl, 3-bd, 3¾" 650.00
Remington, R4703, Moose, brn bone hdl, 4¼" 325.00
Remington, R6563, swell center, brn bone hdl, 2-bd, lp, 3⅝" 140.00
Remington, R7124, sleeveboard, pearl hdl, 4-bd, lp, 3¼" 325.00
Remington, R7833, pinched brn bone bolsters, 2-bd, 4½" 780.00
Remington, R8065, pyremite hdl, dbl s/b, 2-bd, 3½" 480.00
Western States, 06245½, cigar, bone hdl, 2-bd, 3⅝" 95.00
Western States, 06256, swell center, bone hdl, 2-bd, 3" 35.00
Western States, 06265, bone hdl, 2-bd, 3⅜" 35.00
Western States, 1364, swell center, pyralin hdl, 3-bd, 3¼" 55.00
Western States, 16228½, peanut, bone hdl, 2-bd, 3" 75.00
Western States, 2175V, fish knife, toothpick, 1-bd, 5" 65.00
Western States, 2206, faux pearl hdl, 2-bd, 5⅛" 80.00
Western States, 6100L, lockbk, bone hdl, 1-bd, 5¾" 380.00
Western States, 6167, sleeveboard, bone hdl, 1-bd, 3½" 80.00
Western States, 6211R, Barlow, bone hdl, 2-bd+razor bd, 3⅜" ..165.00
Western States, 6342, stockman, bone hdl, 3-bd, 3⅝" 50.00
Western States, 742, stockman, bone hdl w/shield, 3-bd, 4" 65.00
Winchester, 1060, Texas jack, celluloid hdl, 1-bd, 4⅛" 240.00
Winchester, 1701, Barlow, bone hdl, 3½" 140.00
Winchester, 1703, Barlow, smooth bone, hdl, 1-bd, 5" 275.00
Winchester, 1905, jack, stag hdl, 1-bd, 4½" 165.00
Winchester, 1923, stag hdl, 1-bd, 4⅛" 230.00
Winchester, 1925, jack, stag hdl, 1-bd, 3½" 325.00
Winchester, 1936, toothpick, brn bone hdl, 1-bd, 5" 380.00
Winchester, 1937, jack, shell celluloid hdl, 3⅜" 185.00
Winchester, 2051, Senator, wht celluloid hdl, 1-bd, 2⅝" 170.00
Winchester, 2054, Senator, celluloid hdl, 1-bd, 3¼" 90.00
Winchester, 2067, serpentine pen, celluloid hdl, 1-bd, 3" 145.00
Winchester, 2069, jack, bl celluloid hdl, 1-bd, 3⅜" 190.00
Winchester, 2079, office, wht celluloid hdl, 3⅜" 170.00
Winchester, 2086, dog leg, celluloid hdl, 2-bd, 2¾" 150.00
Winchester, 2106, jack, bl abalone celluloid hdl, 2-bd, 3⅜" 185.00
Winchester, 2111, jack, celluloid hdl, 2-bd, 3½" 170.00
Winchester, 2113, peanut, celluloid hdl, 2-bd, 2¾" 140.00
Winchester, 2116, sleeveboard, celluloid hdl, 2-bd, 3⅜" 110.00
Winchester, 2215, jack, nickel silver hdl, 2-bd, 3½" 95.00
Winchester, 2302, Senator, pearl hdl w/bail, 2-bd, 2¼" 105.00
Winchester, 2306, Senator, pearl hdl, 2-bd, 2⅝" 115.00
Winchester, 2309, Senator, pearl hdl, 2-bd, 3" 150.00
Winchester, 2314, serpentine jack, pearl hdl, 2-bd, 3" 105.00
Winchester, 2320, sleeveboard, pearl hdl, 2-bd, 2⅞" 105.00
Winchester, 2335, Congress, pearl hdl, 2-bd, 3¼" 165.00
Winchester, 2345, Senator, pearl hdl, 2-bd, 3¼" 105.00
Winchester, 2356, lobster, pearl hdl, 2-bd, 2¾" 125.00
Winchester, 2361, dog leg, pearl hdl, 2-bd, 2¾" 135.00

Winchester, 2377, Senator, pearl hdl, 2-bd, 2⅝" 175.00
Winchester, 2613, sleeveboard, ebony hdl, 2-bd, 3⅜" 150.00
Winchester, 2640, Coke bottle, ebony hdl, 2-bd, 3¾" 280.00
Winchester, 2690, Texas jack, ebony hdl, 2-bd, 4½" 340.00
Winchester, 2991, peanut, brn bone hdl, 2-bd, 2⅞" 165.00
Winchester, 2999, dog leg jack, wht bone hdl, 2-bd, 3⅛" 190.00
Winchester, 3002, whittler, gr celluloid hdl, 3-bd, 3¾" 300.00
Winchester, 3022, whittler, faux tortoise hdl, 3-bd, 3¼" 280.00

Sheath Knives

Case, M3F, leather hdl, Case XX, 6¼" 35.00
Case, 161, gr bone hdl, Case's Tested XX, Case Bradford, 7½" ...115.00
Case, 223-6, blk compo hdl, Case XX USA, 10¼" 40.00
Case, 3 Finn, leather hdl, Case XX USA, 8¾" 35.00
Case, 323-5, leather hdl, rnd butt, Case XX, 9" 65.00
Case, 366, leather hdl, rnd butt, Case XX, 7¾" 40.00
Case, 523-6, stag hdl, Case XX, 10¼" 60.00
Case, 652-5, red bone hdl, saber bd, Case XX, 8¾" 115.00
Case, 666-4, early brn Rogers bone hdl, Case Tested XX, 7½" ...140.00
Queen, bird, yel scales hdl, Queen Steel, 3" bd, 6⅛" overall 40.00

Miscellaneous

Belt, spear bd: Barclay...Sheffield, 1880s, 7¾"+scabbard 40.00
Bowie, Civil War, D guard, 15½", EX 135.00
Bowie, clipped point, NP crossguard, compo grips, 1900, 16" 150.00
Bowie, German silver hilt, stag hdl, 9¼" bd, M 350.00
Bowie, Rogers Sheffield, 1860s, 13½", +leather scabbard 185.00
Bowie, spear-point bd, NP crossguard, 1870s, 10", EX 75.00
Dirk, Hart Bros Prussia hallmk on bd, 1880s, 10", EX 45.00
Dirk, US midshipman's, trn ivory hdl, etched bd, 1800s, 7½" 425.00
Plainsman's, dk worn blade, wood grip, 1880s, 8", VG 16.00
US Army 1887 Hospital Corps Type 1, wood hdl, 12" etch bd, EX ..875.00
US Model 1880 Hunting Type 2, brass hilt, 8½" bd, M 600.00
US N Diver's, wood hdl, 7" steel sawtooth bd, M 300.00

Kosta

Kosta glassware has been made in Sweden since 1742. Today they are one of that country's leading producers of quality art glass. Two of their most important designers were Elis Bergh (1929-1950) and Vicke Lindstrand, artistic director from 1950 to 1973. Lindstrand brought to the company knowledge of important techniques such as Graal, fine figural engraving, Ariel, etc. He influenced new artists to experiment with these techniques and inspired them to create new and innovative designs. Today's collectors are most interested in pieces made during the 1950s and '60s. Our advisor for this category is Abby Malowanczyk; she is listed in the Directory under Texas.

Bowl, bl & gr paisley decor, sgn Warff, 4x6" 325.00
Dish, gold/wht/brn swirls, free-form, 3x11x18" 300.00
Vase, clear, blk spiral cane, body w/2 holes, LH #1175, 12" 700.00
Vase, clear, red/blk/wht appl threads, Lindstrand #1099, 9" 750.00
Vase, etch fishermen, slanted rim, Lindstrand, #135, 6½" 400.00

Kutani

Kutani, named for the Japanese village where it originated, was first produced in the 17th century. The early ware, Ko Kutani, was made for only about thirty years. Several types were produced before

1800, but these are rarely encountered. In the 19th century kilns located in several different villages began to copy the old Kutani wares. This later, more familiar type has large areas of red with gold designs on a white ground decorated with warriors, birds, and flowers in controlled colors of red, gold, and black.

Charger, water/rocks/dwellings, ext: 3 peonies, 1800s, 13" 525.00
Crocus pot, blossom form, fish/shell fish decor, 1800s, 5½", pr ...625.00
Cup & saucer, people/floral/trees/clouds w/gilt, late 28.00
Dish, samurai & geisha in panels, red/blk/gold, ped ft, 7½" 400.00

Vase, festival scene with foliate borders, ovoid, 19th century, 18", $2,100.00.

Jar, warrior reserves, shishi finial, late 1800s, 21" 675.00
Plate, mandarins/floral reserve, 1875, 9½", set of 6 ....475.00
Vase, figures & flowers, on stand, 3½" 95.00
Vase, mums/birds on gilt & red, dbl gourd, Kinrande, 15" 700.00
Vase, peacocks/floral reserve, 3-toed gourd form, 18" 1,000.00

L. E. Smith

Perhaps best known for their line of black glass vases and novelty items, this 20th-century American glass company located in Mt. Pleasant, Pennsylvania, also made several patterns of colored Depression-type dinnerware as well as some glass animals. They reproduced the Moon and Star pattern during the 1960s which proved so successful that they continue to make a few pieces yet today, though the colors now in production (crystal, pink, cobalt, and teal green) are of no interest to collectors.

Bean pot, Greek Key, w/lid, 1920s-30s 47.50
Bonbon, cobalt, ftd, hdls, #2400 ....15.00
Bonbon, gr, #81 ....10.00
Bonbon, Mt Pleasant, cobalt, hdls, 7" 23.00
Bookends, rearing horse, amberina, pr 110.00
Bookends, rearing horse, pr 45.00
Bowl, blk, ftd, #515, 7" dia 20.00
Bowl, console; Moondrops, red, 3-ftd, 12" 85.00
Bowl, flower; Hobnail, blk, 6½" 28.00
Bowl, Mt Pleasant, blk, ftd, sq, 8" 30.00
Bowl, Mt Pleasant, blk, ftd, 9" 30.00
Bowl, vegetable; Moondrops, bl, oval, 9¾" 33.00
Butter dish, Moon & Star, amber, ¼-lb 15.00
Butter dish, Moon & Star, scalloped ft, patterned lid, 6x5½" 45.00
Cake plate, Mt Pleasant, gr, hdls, 10½" 16.00
Candy dish, Dresden floral, wht, rolled rim 18.00
Candy dish, rooster, 2-part, 9x7" 65.00
Compote, Moon & Star, scalloped, ftd, 5½x8" 30.00

Compote, Moondrops, blk, 4" 16.00
Cookie jar, gr transparent 35.00
Creamer, Scottie dog 12.50
Creamer & sugar bowl, Mt Pleasant, blk 37.50
Decanter, Moon & Star, bulbous, plain neck, 32-oz, 12" 50.00
Decanter, Moondrops, pk, 7¾" 38.00
Flowerpot, blk, ca 1930, 3" 12.50
Goblet, wine; Moon & Star, plain rim & ft, 4½" 9.00
Jardiniere, Greek Key, blk, 3-ftd, #23, 1930s 22.50
Loving cup, blk amethyst, 2-hdld, 8" 35.00
Mayonnaise, Mt Pleasant, cobalt, 3-ftd, 5½" 22.00
Mint dish, Mt Pleasant, blk, center hdl, 6" 22.50
Plate, Mt Pleasant, blk, 3-ftd 20.00
Plate, Mt Pleasant, blk, 7" 15.00
Plate, Mt Pleasant, pk, hdls, 7" 9.00
Rose bowl, Mt Pleasant, blk, ftd 27.50
Sandwich server, Mt Pleasant, amethyst, center hdl 38.00
Shaker, Snake Dance, blk opaque, emb figures, 3⅜" 105.00
Sherbet, Mt Pleasant, bl 16.00
Sherbet, Mt Pleasant, blk 16.00
Soap dish, Moon & star, allover pattern, 2x6" 12.00
Tray, cordial; blk, #381 ....10.00
Tray, cordial; gr or pk, #381 ....12.00
Tumbler, Moon & star, plain rim & disk ft, 7-oz, 4¼" 12.00
Tumbler, Mt Pleasant, amethyst, ftd 20.00
Urn, cobalt, #800/4, w/lid, 11" 115.00
Vase, blk, #1900, 7¼" 18.00
Vase, blk, #49, 6" 12.00
Vase, blk, urn form, late 1920s, 7¾" 22.50
Vase, cobalt, #711, 5½" 8.00
Vase, cobalt, stippled t'print, 5¾" 8.00
Vase, dancing nymphs, blk, hdls, 7" 30.00
Vase, Mt Pleasant, bl, 7¼" 35.00
Vase, silver leaf band on blk, #711, 6" 14.00
Vase, Snake Dance, blk, crimped top, hdls, ftd, #433 ....27.50
Window box, blk, #405, 7¾" 22.50
Window box, Pan & dancing girls, milk glass, 6¼" 12.00

Labels

Before the advent of the cardboard box, wooden crates were used for transporting products. Paper labels were attached to the crates to identify the contents and the packer. These labels often had colorful lithographed illustrations covering a broad range of subjects. Eventually the cardboard box replaced the crate, and the artwork was imprinted directly onto the carton. Today these paper labels are becoming collectible — primarily for the art, but also for their advertising appeal. Our advisor for this category is Cerebro; their address is listed in the Directory under Pennsylvania.

Apple, A Plus, olympic girl, 10¼x9" 5.00
Apple, Antler, 12-point buck, WA, 10¼x9" 45.00
Apple, Glacier Pack, snow-covered mountain, 10¼x9" 3.00
Apple, Grizzly Brand, bear, 9x11" 15.00
Apple, Hunter, red dog on farm 15.00
Apple, Independent, lg bell, 10¼x9" 4.00
Apple, Morjon, boy blowing horn 5.00
Apple, School Boy Brand, Paonia CO, 9x11" 18.00
Apple, Tasmania, bull's eye 2.00
Baking powder, Betty Ann, redheaded girl, NE 2.50
Baking powder, Colonial, plate of biscuits 1.00
Beer bottle, Chief, OshKosh, red/wht/bl 50
Beer bottle, WI Special IRTP, Dahlke, wht & gold 1.00

Broom, Hudson, steamboat, 3½x5" 2.00
Cigar box, Allright, man on a bicycle, M 8.00
Cigar box, Attracto, swans on moat, M 8.00
Cigar box, Bald Eagle, eagle on rock, M 15.00
Cigar box, Belle De Cuba, woman playing guitar, M 22.00
Cigar box, Canada, Indian & pilgrim, oval, M 8.00
Cigar box, Captain Corker, general smoking cigar, M ...30.00
Cigar box, Christy girl, woman, golf scene, M 8.00
Cigar box, Conewango, Indian in canoe, M 45.00
Cigar box, El Gaurdo, bulldog beside doghouse, M 12.50
Cigar box, El Recto, bearded man, M 3.00
Cigar box, Extra Fein, boy & dog, M 18.00
Cigar box, Golden Buck, deer & snow-covered mountain, M 55.00
Cigar box, John C Calhoun, Calhoun house, EX 8.50
Cigar box, Little Dan O'Brien, portrait, M 10.00
Cigar box, Mark Twain, portrait w/T Sawyer & H Finn, M 15.00
Cigar box, Snap Shot, lady's portrait, 1925, EX 25.00
Cigar box, Wht Cat, cat on cigar, Consolidated Litho, M 6.50
Cosmetic, Lady Luxury Perfume Box, lady & swan 2.00
Cranberry, Mayflower, pilgrims' ship, 7x10" 3.00
Cranberry, Peacock, bird w/wide-spread tail, 7x10" 3.00
Cranberry, Plymouth Rock, Indians coming ashore, 7x10" 8.00
Cranberry, Pointer, dog pointing, 7x10" 4.00
Cranberry, Turkey, Thanksgiving turkey, 7x10" 10.00
Egg, Farmer's Brand...Poached in...Middle West, 9½x11" 15.00
Firecracker pack, Am Way 100.00
Firecracker pack, Welcome 25.00
Grapefruit, Barbara Worth, cowgirl, 11x10" 70.00
Grapefruit, Linwood, red letters, 11x10" 2.00
Grapes, Air King, 4-prop plane, 13x4" 2.00
Grapes, Am Pride, eagle & shield, 13x4" 2.00
Grapes, Owl, lg owl on branch, 13x4" 2.00
Lemon, Cambria, eagle w/torches, 11x9" 3.00
Lemon, Collie, dog, 11x10" 45.00
Lemon, Honeymoon, castle on hill, 11x9" 45.00
Orange, Albion, red & pk roses, CA, 11x10" 17.00
Orange, Bird Rocks, gulls over ocean, 11x10" 30.00
Orange, Carmel, mission, 11x10" 55.00
Orange, Golden Trout, jumping fish, 11x10" 32.00
Peach, Fox, peach, fox & orchard 25.00
Peach, Stony Ridge, apples & peaches 4.00
Salmon, Capilano, mountains & totem poles 2.00
Sweet potato, Mary Agnes, girl w/straw hat 2.00
Tobacco, Cora 15.00
Vegetable, Castlewood, castle & tree 2.00
Vegetable, Plenti-Grand, girl in sunsuit 2.00
Whiskey bottle, Hunter Bourbon, hunter & dogs 2.00

Labino

Dominick Labino was a glass blower who until mid-1985 worked in his studio in Ohio, blowing and sculpting various items which he signed and dated. A ceramic engineer by trade, he was instrumental in developing the heat-resistant tiles used in space flights. His glassmaking shows his versatility in the art. While some of his designs are free-form and futuristic, others are reminiscent of the products of older glasshouses. Because of problems with his health, Mr. Labino became unable to blow glass himself; he died January 10, 1987. Work coming from his studio since mid-1985 has been signed 'Labino Studios, Baker,' indicating ware made by his protegee, E. Baker O'Brien. In addition to her own compositions, she continues to use many of the colors developed by Labino.

Bowl, clear/red swirls w/4 manipulated prunts, 1970, 3x6" 165.00

Bowl, gold ruby, sgn/1968, 7½" 850.00
Bowl, swirled bl/gold/red, str dimpled sides, 1967, 3x6" 165.00
Goblet, amber, int-twist air-trap stem, 1971, 6¾" 300.00
Paperweight, gr, controlled bubbles, 1970 ....300.00
Sculpture, clear over pk/gold, bubbles, 1976, 4½" 1,100.00
Sculpture, Emergence, bubble forms & veils, sgn/12-1974, 7" .2,300.00
Sculpture, Iris, cobalt, sgn/1975, 7½" 800.00
Sculpture, Lava, bl w/controlled folds on sides, 1979, 4" 1,200.00

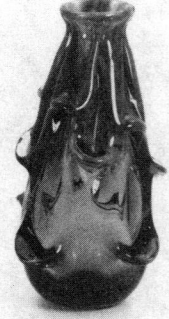

Vase, lava style with controlled folds, light burgundy, 1979, 7½", $1,400.00.

Vase, avocado gr w/bubbles, ovoid w/tiny opening, 1968, 4" 400.00
Vase, bl, blown & appl, vessel form, sgn/1965, 8¾" 1,700.00
Vase, copper ruby, continuous prunts, sgn/2-1971, 11½" 950.00
Vase, gr w/yel winged panels & swags, bottle shape, '80, 7" 500.00
Vase, ruby shading to gr, bottle form, 1971, 13" 800.00

Lace, Linens, and Needlework

It has been recorded that lace was found in the tombs of ancient Egypt. Lace has always been a symbol of wealth and fashion. Italian laces are regarded as the finest ever produced, but the differences between them and the laces of France are nearly indistinguishable. Needlework was revived during the 18th century and became the favorite of feminine pastimes. Examples of many forms (tatting, embroidery, needlepoint, and crochet, for instance) are available today; and though fragile in appearance, have withstood the ravages of time with remarkable durability.

Key:
embr — embroidered   ms — machine sewn
hs — hand sewn

Apron, crochet, lt gr & pk w/raised flower on pocket, 20" L 40.00
Bedspread, chenille, pk plush, ¾-sz, NM 135.00
Bedspread, chenille, wht roses, fringed, full sz 185.00
Bedspread, crochet, ecru lace, full sz 225.00
Bedspread, crochet, Star & Popcorn, scallops, twin sz 295.00
Bedspread, crochet, wht & dk gr, w/3" fringe, 80x100" 200.00
Bedspread, flocked velvet roses & vines, full sz 125.00
Bedspread, Marseilles lace, cutouts for bed posts, full sz 250.00
Bedspread, woven wht floral & dmn design, 72x84" 80.00
Blanket, baby's, tan twill, sateen bk, embr & ribbons, 36" sq 85.00
Blanket, bl & wht wool, center seam, 96x77" 130.00
Blanket, bl linsey-woolsey, coarse brn bking, 95x82" 150.00
Blanket, blk & red plaid wool, rolled hem, 88x82" 125.00
Blanket, homespun, bl/yel/natural/ecru, 1-pc, 91x44", VG 165.00
Blanket, homespun wool/linen, navy/natural, 2-pc, rpr, 86x68" .125.00
Blanket, western Indian scene woven in mc, 67x42" 195.00
Bolster cover, bl plaid linen, plain linen bk, 48x18" 125.00
Centerpc, crochet, initial encircled in flowers, 18x12" 65.00

Chair set, crochet, birds/bows/flowers, 3-pc	65.00
Curtains, lace, leaf pattern panels, 84x42", pr	150.00
Doily, crochet, ecru, 3 butterflies, 15½x9"	55.00
Napkin, damask, wide Greek Key w/sm fleur-de-lis, 18 for	80.00
Needlework, bird on floral branch, petit point, 14½" fr	95.00
Needlework, child & dog, 5-color, rpr, 27x34"	50.00
Needlework, crewel, man & horse scene, fr, 17x15"	220.00
Needlework, petit point, figures in garden, 33x26"	2,500.00
Needlework, stylized floral on blk, fading, 8x12"	195.00
Needlework, woman & child, English, 1800s, 21x16"	275.00
Needlework, 48-star flag, linen/ribbon, WWII, 20x20"	90.00
Needlework/watercolor on silk, lady in garden, fr, 23x33"	495.00
Pillowcase, crochet edge, pr	35.00
Pillowcase, hand embr, baby's	55.00
Pillowcase, homespun, 35x17"	45.00
Placemats, needlepoint lace, set of 10	150.00
Placemats & napkins, damask, orig labels, unused, set of 8	125.00
Runner, Battenburg lace, floral, scalloped, 14x38"	175.00
Runner, Battenburg lace, tapers to points, 25½" L	125.00
Runner, crochet, pinwheels, variegated lav, 18x48"	65.00
Runner, crochet, Statue of Liberty head, God Bless..., 17x23"	95.00
Runner, Pointe Venice lace, wht, 108"	125.00
Runner, Yo-Yo, 12x77"	55.00
Sheet, homespun linen, pk embr, rolled hem, 90x78", EX	65.00
Sheets, linen, cutwork, Edwardian, twin sz, pr	185.00
Show towel, cotton homespun w/wool embr, PA/1846, 57x18"	300.00
Show towel, homespun w/embr birds/flowers, PA/1825, 68x18"	415.00
Show towel, homespun w/3 cutwork panels, 53x15"	330.00
Show towel, PA German, homespun, pk X-stitch, fringe, 1834, 57"	140.00
Show towel, wht on wht woven dmns, red embr: EM 1847, 46x15"	135.00
Tablecloth, Battenburg, vintage pattern, 49" dia	175.00
Tablecloth, crochet, ecru, flower baskets & bows, 60x72"	100.00
Tablecloth, crochet, ecru floral, fringed border, 36" dia	55.00
Tablecloth, dbl damask, embr monogram, 68x108"	195.00
Tablecloth, dbl damask, 68x130", +12 napkins	250.00
Tablecloth, embr 2-color birds/etc, crochet border, 36x40"	175.00
Tablecloth, Irish linen, 5" crochet border, 36" dia	150.00
Tablecloth, linen, Cluny lace inserts, 68x138", +12 napkins	450.00
Tablecloth, linen, Cluny lace inserts & edge, 92" dia	325.00
Tablecloth, linen, drawnwork & embr, heavy, 76x82"	350.00
Tablecloth, linen, ecru, Cluny lace medallions, 136" L	225.00
Tablecloth, linen, ecru, cutwork, satin stitch, 120x70"	250.00
Tablecloth, Pointe Venice lace, 74x86"	350.00
Tablecloth, 4" filet lace border w/dancers, 18" dia	150.00
Tablecloth, 5" Cluny lace border, scalloped center, 22" dia	195.00
Tapestry, tavern courtyard scene, France, 27x52"	185.00

Lacy Glassware

Lacy glass became popular in the late 1820s after the development of the pressing machine. It was decorated with allover patterns — hearts, lyres, sheaves of wheat, etc. — and backgrounds were completely stippled. The designs were intricate and delicate, hence the term 'lacy.' Although Sandwich produced this type of glassware in abundance, it was also made by other eastern glassworks as well as in the midwest. By 1840 its popularity on the wane and a depressed economy forcing manufacturers to seek less expensive modes of production, lacy glass began to be phased out in favor of pressed pattern glass.

Our advisor for this category is Richard Marden; he is listed in the Directory under New Hampshire. Reference numbers correspond with *Sandwich Glass* by Ruth Webb Lee. When no condition is indicated, the items listed below are assumed to be without obvious damage; minor roughness is normal.

Bowl, Oak Leaf, minor rim roughages, 7", $85.00; Relish, Gothic Arch, 7¼", NM, $110.00.

Bowl, Hairpin rim, octagonal center, shallow, 5¾"	50.00
Bowl, L-80, 1¾"	50.00
Bowl, Lyre, oblong, Pittsburgh, L-102, 9"	165.00
Bowl, Peacock Eye, 7⅜"	65.00
Bowl, Pineapple Gothic, oblong, 9"	175.00
Bowl, Princess Feather, minor rim chips, 7½"	75.00
Bowl, Rayed Peacock Eye, rim nick, 7½"	75.00
Compote, Peacock Eye, L-139, 3⅝x7⅜"	485.00
Dish, L-81, oval, minor chips, 2⅞"	60.00
Plate, Beehive & Thistle, 8-sided, roughness, 9"	85.00
Plate, Fulton, sidewheeler in oval, scroll border, 6½", VG	20.00
Plate, Peacock Eye, 5¼"	25.00
Plate, Union, sailing ship facing right, 8-sided, 6½", VG	30.00
Sauce dish, Daisy, minor rim chip, 6"	75.00
Sauce dish, Peacock Eye, sm rim chips, 5¼"	75.00
Sauce dish, Peacock Eye variant, minor rim chips, 5"	75.00
Sauce dish, Stippled Bull's Eye, sm rim chip, 7"	75.00
Spooner, Horn of Plenty, minor roughness, 4¾"	25.00

Lalique

Beginning his lengthy career as a designer and maker of fine jewelry, Rene Lalique at first only dabbled in glass, making small panels of pate-de-verre (paste-on-paste) and cire perdue (wax casting) to use in his jewelry. He also made small flacons of gold and silver with his glass inlays, which attracted the attention of M.F. Coty, who commissioned Lalique to design bottles for his perfume company. The success of this venture resulted in the opening of his own glassworks at Combs-la-Ville in 1909. In 1921 a larger factory was established at Wingen-sur-Moder in Alsace-Lorraine. By the thirties Lalique was world renown as the most important designer of his time.

Lalique glass is lead based, either mold blown or pressed. Favored motifs during the Art Nouveau period were dancing nymphs, fish, dragonflies, and foliage. Characteristically the glass is crystal in combination with acid-etched relief. Later some items were made in as many as ten colors (red, amber, and green among them) and were occasionally accented with enameling. These colored pieces, especially those in black, are highly prized by advanced collectors.

During the twenties and thirties, Lalique designed several vases and bowls reminiscent of American Indian art. He also developed a line in the Art Deco style decorated with stylized birds, florals, and geometrics. In addition to vases, clocks, automobile mascots, stemware, and bottles, many other useful objects were produced. Most items made before his death in 1945 were marked 'R. Lalique'; later the 'R' was deleted even though some of the original molds were still used. Numbers found on the bases of some pieces are catalog numbers. Beware of fraudulent pieces that have began to surface in increasing numbers. Our advisor for this category is John Danis; he is listed in the Directory under Illinois.

Key:
cl/fr — clear and frosted   RL — signed R. Lalique
L — signed Lalique   RLF — signed R. Lalique, France

Ashtray, Irene, fr bird border, sgn, 3¾" dia 85.00
Bottle, atomizer, nuts, brn wash, sgn, rpl top, 7" 650.00
Bottle, scent; amber antique, brn stained, Grecian maidens, RL ...900.00
Bottle, scent; Amphytrite, shell, gr, w/nude stopper, L, 4" 3,500.00
Bottle, scent; Bouquet de Faunes, urn form w/4 masks, unsgn 350.00
Bottle, scent; Coeur des Calices, bl w/bee stopper, RL 1,500.00
Bottle, scent; Coral Rouge, red enamel coral, w/box 5,500.00
Bottle, scent; Cotes Bouchon Papillons, bl patina, L, 2" 1,800.00
Bottle, scent; Dans la Nuit, star motif, moon stopper, RL, 4" 700.00
Bottle, scent; draped lady as stopper, angled sphere, L, 4" 1,650.00
Bottle, scent; egg shape, for Worth, RL, w/box 2,200.00
Bottle, scent; grasshopper ea corner, RL, 5" 825.00
Bottle, scent; Le Jane, gr opal, snuff bottle form, w/box 1,800.00
Bottle, scent; Le Lilas, heart form, floral stopper, L, w/box 500.00
Bottle, scent; Le Long, blk enamel, chrome case, w/box 1,000.00
Bottle, scent; Les 5 Fleurs, for Forvil, blk rope, w/box 1,200.00
Bottle, scent; Molinard, 12 nudes, brn wash, RL, 5" 800.00
Bottle, scent; Mystere, lizards, blk, sq, w/red leather box 1,200.00
Bottle, scent; Palerme, beaded swags, blk stopper, RL, 4" 200.00
Bottle, scent; Panier de Roses, basket form, fr, RL, 4" 1,500.00
Bottle, scent; Paquerettes, tiara of daisies, sm, w/box 2,200.00
Bottle, scent; Phalene, amber, nude w/wings, w/box 1,800.00
Bottle, scent; Projects, sailboat motif, RL, w/box 500.00
Bottle, scent; Replique, acorn shape, w/box & ribbon 350.00
Bottle, scent; Sans Adieu, brn, brn tiered stopper, wood box 750.00
Bottle, scent; Serpent, classical snake design, blk stain, RL 900.00
Bottle, scent; Sirenes, 10 mermaids, gr wash, RL, 6¾" 1,300.00
Bowl, beaded circles, cl/opal, shallow, RLF, 10" 350.00
Bowl, Marguerites, flowers on rim, fr, L Cristal F, 14" 465.00
Bowl, Muguet, lily of valley, opal/bl wash, flared, RLF, 12" 1,265.00
Bowl, Nemours, recessed blossoms w/blk centers, cl, L, 10" 770.00
Bowl, Ondines Ouverte, mermaids/bubbles, opal, RL, 3x8" ...1,100.00
Bowl, Ondines Refermee, mermaids, opal/bl rim, RLF #381, 8" ..1,870.00
Bowl, Oursins #2, sea urchin shell, opal, RLF, 10" 575.00
Box, Cigales, cicadas, opal, RL, 2x10", w/compo box 1,100.00
Box, powder; Chantilly, deer/leaves, cl cab on lid, RL, 3½" 575.00
Box, puff; Houppes, milkweed, opal, RLF, lt wear, 5½" dia 350.00
Box, seminude/leaves, brn wash, L Depose Coty, 3" 385.00
Bracelet, Cerisiers, 13 leaf-emb ½-cylinder links, bl, RL 2,100.00
Brooch, Barrette Aubepines, floral, foil bkd, 2¾" L 700.00
Brooch, Sauterelles, grasshoppers, pk foil bkd, L, 1¾" dia 900.00
Carafe, Lotus, leaves overlap, enameled stopper, RLF, 6½" 385.00

Charger, Cote D'or, nudes in grape arbor, engraved Lalique France, 16", $3,250.00.

Clock, Hirondelles, birds/flowers, rnd dial, RLF, 6x6", EX 1,650.00
Clock, Inseparables, lovebirds ea side, opal, sq, RLF, 4½" 3,500.00

Crucifix, crystal, sgn L, silver metal base, 13" 600.00
Hat pin, Feuilles, spiral leaves, salmon wash, L, 10¾" 1,265.00
Lemonade set, oak leaves, cl/fr, LF, 9" pitcher+12 glasses 1,200.00
Mascot, Chrysis, kneeling nude on rnd base, fr, RLF, 5" 1,500.00
Mascot, Grande Libellule, dragonfly, gray-tone cl, RL, 8" 2,800.00
Mascot, Petite Libellule, dragonfly, RLF, 6" 1,100.00
Mascot, Tete D'Aigle, eagle's head on rnd base, RL, 4" 800.00
Mascot, Vitesse, nude lady, gray-tone cl/fr, RLF, 7" 5,500.00
Paperweight, St Christophe, St w/Child, fr intaglio, RL, 5" 300.00
Pendant, Fioret, nude/flowers, rose wash, RL 385.00
Pendant, Lys, lilies, dk red wash, triangular, RL, 2⅛" 685.00
Pendant, Tete, lady/flowers, bk set w/mirror, L, 3¼" L 1,265.00
Perfume burner, Sirenes, 10 nude mermaids, opal, RLF, 7" 825.00
Server, Pissenlit, radiating leaves, RLF, 12" dia 400.00
Sign, Cristal Lalique Paris, 3¾" sq, +blk plastic stand 250.00
Statue, Sirene, mermaid, opal, RL, 4" 1,950.00
Vase, Actina, spirals/swirls, opal/bl wash, U-form, RL, 9" 1,000.00
Vase, Airgrettes, birds/leaves, gray, U-form, RLF, 10" 9,750.00
Vase, Archers, 10 male hunters/birds, topaz/fr, RL, 11" 3,500.00
Vase, Avallon, birds/cherry tree, cl/fr, U-form, RLF, 6" 600.00
Vase, beaded tiers, flared cylinder, RL, 4¾" 220.00

Vase, Bresse, overall rooster motif, orange glass with white stain, 4½", $1,500.00.

Vase, Beautreillis, cl/opal, RLF/#989, 5½x7" 1,250.00
Vase, Canards, swirls bands/ducks, gr wash, ovoid, RLF, 5½" 975.00
Vase, Cerise, cherries on base, fr, RLF, 8" 1,100.00
Vase, Chardons, thistles ea corner, bulbous, RLF, 7" 475.00
Vase, Chevaux, base row of horses, opal, flared cone, RLF, 7" ...6,900.00
Vase, Chevreuse, 5 jutting rings of flowers, RLF, 6" 770.00
Vase, deer in forest, dk honey amber, RL, 7" 1,100.00
Vase, Domremy, high relief thistles, fiery opal, RLF, 8½" 1,200.00
Vase, Farandole, band of cherubs at base, bl, RLF, 7x10" 12,000.00
Vase, Formose, fish, fr, RL, 6¾x4¾" 900.00
Vase, Formose, fish, opal, RL 1,600.00
Vase, Graines, seed pod rows at base, alexandrite, RL, 8" 2,800.00
Vase, Malines, ribbed w/fern-like relief, opal, RLF, 5" 600.00
Vase, Marisa, 3 bands of fish, gray, spherical, RLF, 9½" 1,500.00
Vase, Milan, repeating leaves, gr, RLF, 10x11" 3,575.00
Vase, Moissac, frieze of leaves, opal, conical, RLF, 5" 1,700.00
Vase, Monnaie du Pape, leaves, red/fr, ovoid, RL, 9" 3,850.00
Vase, Mures, berries/thorns, opal w/bl wash, RL, 7½" 1,500.00
Vase, Ormeaux, leaves, fr w/amber wash, RLF, 7x7", EX 600.00
Vase, Ormeaux, leaves, smoky gray, RL, 7x7" 900.00
Vase, Palissy, snail shell mold, shiny w/matt int, RLF, 7" 750.00
Vase, Plumes, feathers, gray w/turq wash, bulbous, RLF, 8" 880.00
Vase, Sauterelles, grasshoppers, bl/fr, RLF, 11" 3,200.00
Vase, Sauterelles, grasshoppers, gr w/wht wash, RLF, 10½" 4,500.00
Vase, Tuileries, sparrows at bottom, bl-gr wash, RL, 11" 2,860.00
Vase, 6 Figurines et Masques, nudes/ovals, cased, RLF, 10" 4,500.00

Lamps

The earliest lamps were simple dish containers with a wick that hung over the edge or was supported by a channel or tube. Grease and oil from animal or vegetable sources were the first fuels used. Ancient pottery lamps, crusie, and Betty lamps are examples of these early types. In 1784 Swiss inventor Ami Argand introduced the first major improvement in lamps. His lamp featured a tubular wick and a glass chimney. During the first half of the 19th century, whale oil, burning fluid (a highly explosive mixture of turpentine and alcohol), and lard were the most common fuels used in North America. Many lamps were patented for specific use with these fuels.

Kerosene was the first major breakthrough in lighting fuels. It was demonstrated by Canadian geologist Dr. Abraham Gesner in 1846. The discovery and drilling of petroleum in the late 1850s provided an abundant and inexpensive supply of kerosene. It became the main source of light for homes during the balance of the 19th century and for remote locations until the 1950s.

Although Thomas A. Edison invented the electric lamp in 1879, it was not until two or three decades later that electric lamps replaced kerosene household lamps. Millions of kerosene lamps were made for every purpose and pocketbook. They ranged in size from tiny night or miniature lamps to tall stand or piano lamps. Hanging varieties for homes commonly had one or two fonts (oil containers), but chandeliers for churches and public buildings often had six or more. Wall or bracket lamps usually had silvered reflectors. Student lamps, parlor lamps (now called Gone-with-the-Wind lamps), and patterned glass lamps were designed to complement the popular furnishing trends of the day. Gaslight, introduced in the early 19th century, was used mainly in homes of the wealthy and public places until the early 20th century. Most fixtures were wall or ceiling mounted, although some table models were also used.

Few of the ordinary early electric lamps have survived. Many lamp manufacturers made the same or similar styles for either kerosene or electricity, sometimes for gas. Top-of-the-line lamps were made by Pairpoint, Phoenix, Tiffany, Bradley and Hubbard, and Handel. See also these specific sections.

Currently values of peg lamps are up by about 30% to 40%, and pattern glass lamps in some of the standard lines have jumped from 25% to 100%. When buying lamps that have been converted to electricity, inspect them very carefully for any damage that may have resulted from the alterations; such damage is very common, and when it does occur, the lamp's value may be lessened by as much as 50%. Lamps seem to bring much higher prices in some areas than others, especially the larger cities. Conversely, in rural areas they may bring only half as much as our listed values. One of our advisors for lamps is Ruth Osborne; she is listed in the Directory under Ohio.

Key:
ac — acorn burner   Ob — O burner
hb — hornet burner   pb — pinafore burner
nb — nutmeg burner   Vb — P&A Victor burner

Aladdin Lamps, Electric

From 1908 Aladdin lamps with a mantle became the mainstay of rural America, providing light that compared favorably with the electric light bulb. They were produced by the Mantle Lamp Company of America in over eighteen models and more than one hundred styles. During the 1930s to the 1950s, this company was the leading manufacturer of electric lamps as well. Still in operation today, the company is now known as Aladdin Industries Inc., located in Nashville, Tennessee. For those seeking additional information on Aladdin Lamps, we recommend *Aladdin — The Magic Name in Lamps*; *Aladdin Electric Lamps*; and *A Collector's Manual and Price Guide*, all written by our advisor for Aladdins, J. W. Courter; he is listed in the Directory under Kentucky. Mr. Courter has also published a book called *Angle Lamps, Collector's Manual and Price Guide*.

Bed, #2037 SS, flocked whip-o-lite shade, NM 75.00
Bed, #635-SS, whip-o-lite pleated shade, EX 200.00
Bedroom, M-62, metal, contemporary, EX 30.00
Bedroom, P-53, ceramic, NM 30.00
Boudoir, G-153, Moonstone, 1937, NM 75.00
Boudoir, G-36, Alacite spool design, 1948, NM 45.00
Bridge, #2050, swan base, EX 175.00
Bridge, #2093, NM 225.00
Bridge, #7092, swing arm, reflector, EX 125.00
Contemporary Metal, M-452, Cabana lamp w/ashtray, M 35.00
Figurine, G-130, Lulu, etched, crystal, minimum 1,000.00
Figurine, G-16, lady, Alacite, NM 500.00
Figurine, G-343, lady w/dog, NM 225.00
Figurine, G-46, Cupid, tall base, EX 100.00
Floor, #1062, candle arms, Junior sz, NM 175.00
Floor, #3349, Type A, EX 100.00
Floor, #3451, Type B, NM 150.00
Floor, #3533, reflector, NM 200.00
Floor, #3579, walnut, NM 250.00
Floor, #3952, Alacite ring, candle arms, night light, NM 300.00
Floor, #4504, Torchier, EX 200.00
Floor, #4556, Torchier, NM 200.00
Floor, #4898C, Circline, flourescent, trigger ring, EX 150.00
Floor, J-134, Junior sz (later known as lounge lamp), EX 100.00
Glass Urn, G-232A, Alacite, closed urn, NM 225.00
Glass Urn, G-378C, Hoppy Bullet, Alacite, w/decal 225.00
Magic Touch, MT-509, ceramic base, NM 300.00
Magic Touch, MT-520, cherry & brass base, EX 400.00
Pin-Up, G-353, Alacite, oval wall plate, EX 50.00
Pin-Up, M-350, cast wht metal, plated, NM 60.00
Ranch House, G-47C, Alacite Bullet, light in base, w/shade, EX .400.00
Table, E-205, Vogue Pedestal, ebony, NM 400.00
Table, G-16, EX 175.00
Table, G-173, Opalique, NM 125.00
Table, G-189, Tree Trunk, Opalique, EX 250.00
Table, G-236, Alacite, floral, EX 60.00
Table, G-291D, Alacite, decalcomania, illuminated base, NM 70.00
Table, G-67, Velvex, NM 375.00
Table, G-98, moonstone, EX 60.00
Table, M-2, bronze metal, EX 75.00
Table, P-408, planter, EX 60.00
Table, W-346, oak, EX 30.00
TV, M-469, metal, w/shade, M 30.00
TV, TV-387, ceramic base, modern design, EX 30.00

Aladdin Lamps, Kerosene

Aladdinette, metal chimney, NM 100.00
Caboose Model B, B-400, brass font, NM 125.00
Floor Model B, #1258, bronze, NM 125.00
Floor Model B, B-283, ivory & gold, EX 90.00
Model #12 Crystal Vase, #12U, ebony, 12", EX 250.00
Model #12 Crystal Vase, #1244, Bl Venetian Art-Craft, NM 250.00
Model #12 Florentine Vase, #1222, Rose Moonstone, 8½", EX .1,250.00
Table, Model #9, nickel, NM 120.00
Table Model A, #103 Venetian, Rose, EX 90.00
Table Model B, Beehive B-83, Ruby Crystal, NM 400.00
Table Model B, Cathedral B-111, Gr Moonstone, EX 200.00

Table Model B, Corinthian B-106, clear font, amber ft, NM **90.00**
Table Model B, Majestic B-122, Gr Moonstone, EX **300.00**
Table Model B, Queen B-98, Rose Moonstone, EX **325.00**
Table Model B, Quilt B-86, Gr Moonstone, EX **175.00**
Table Model B, Tall Lincoln Drape B-75, Alacite, EX **125.00**
Wall Bracket Model #1, NM **550.00**

Angle Lamps

The Angle Lamp Company of New York City developed a unique type of kerosene lamp that was a vast improvement over those already on the market; they were sold from about 1896 until 1929 and were expensive for their time. Our Angle lamp advisor is J.W. Courter; he is listed in the Directory under Kentucky. See the narrative for Aladdin Lamps for information concerning popular books Mr. Courter has authored.

Barn lantern, #115, complete w/clear chimney, EX **1,050.00**
Classic #1 table lamp, antique gold, NM **1,800.00**
Hanging, chandelier, 4-burner, polished brass, no glass, wired ..**3,750.00**
Hanging, Fleur-de-Lis, dbl, #252, polished brass, EX **350.00**
Hanging, Floral Garden, 3-burner, tin, wht opal shade, NM **925.00**
Hanging, Grape, dbl, #284, antique copper, milk glass shade, EX ..**575.00**
Wall, single, #103-NF, brass-plated tin, shaded ruby shade **800.00**
Wall, single, #163, polished brass, milk glass tulip shade **125.00**

Chandeliers

Brass fr w/cut crystal drops, 8-arm, electric candles, 40" **1,500.00**
CI, 3-arm, Lomax frosted star fonts w/10" milk glass shades **425.00**
Gilt brass, 2 glass inserts, 6 electric candles, 37" **660.00**
Wrought iron, 5-arm, simple style, 1800s, 27¼" **1,750.00**
3 rnd brass rings w/prisms, largest w/4 holders, 33x19" **400.00**

Decorated Kerosene Lamps

Cobalt cut to clear, clear base, NE Glass, 11" **1,650.00**
Cobalt cut to clear/frosted flowers, brass ft, 7" cut shade **900.00**
Dk bl cut to clear paw prints, brass stem/marble ft, 12" **700.00**
Red o/l w/4 flowers/reeding/ovals, att Sandwich, 11" **400.00**
Triple cut o/l w/butterflies, wht stem/marble base, Sandwich **900.00**
Vaseline w/opal swirls, finger lamp **335.00**
Wht cut to clear floral, mercury glass stem, slate ft, 8½" **425.00**
Wht cut to clear punties, brass stem, marble ft, 9" **250.00**
Yel cased satin, dmns/X motif, dome shade, 16" **975.00**

Fairy Lamps

Bl MOP satin, Clarke base **195.00**
Bl opaque w/emb beads, mk Clarke base, 5¼x2⅞" **85.00**

Burmese, clear marked Clarke base, unsigned Webb, 4x2¾", $175.00.

Burmese, tricorn crimped Webb Queen's base, Eden holder, 3" ...**550.00**
Burmese, 3½" dome shade on crimped 7" dia base, clear cup **475.00**
Burmese, 4-arm metal base w/4 ruffled holders, 3½" dome **1,200.00**
Burmese w/decor, decor base, Clarke burmese insert, Webb, 7" ..**2,700.00**
Burmese w/floral, clear Clarke cup, mk pottery base, 6", EX **1,300.00**
Burmese w/floral, on hdld gray Aladdin-style base mk Clarke .**1,050.00**
Chartreuse gr satin verre moire w/wht opaque pull-ups, 5⅛" **225.00**
Chartreuse satin Nailsea, pinched top base, mk cup, 4½" **600.00**
Chartreuse satin w/apple blossoms, crimped, Blumberg, 1½" **250.00**
Cranberry Nailsea, Clarke cup, candle insert, 4½" **500.00**
Cranberry Nailsea, 3" dome shade on 6" crimped-rim base **425.00**
Cranberry overshot, clear mk Clarke base, 3¾x3" **110.00**
Cranberry verre moire, ruffled base, Clarke cup, 5x6½" **650.00**
Daisy & Button, vaseline **75.00**
Dmn Quilt, rose MOP, clear Clarke base, 3½x3" **145.00**
Eyewinker, gr **35.00**
Gr o/l, dome shade, mk Clarke base, 4¾x4" **98.00**
Hobnail, emerald gr **50.00**
Owl head, cranberry satin, sgn Clarke base **195.00**
Owl head, frosted opal, clear Clarke base, 4½" **145.00**
Red Nailsea, unmk crystal peg base on Pairpoint ft, 7½" **250.00**
Rose Tiente Sunburst, mk Baccarat, saucer base, 4⅛x5⅜" **245.00**
Swirl, apple gr frost, clear Clarke base, 3¾x3" **110.00**
Swirl, candy stripe pk o/l, matching base, 3¾x2¾" **165.00**
Swirl, cranberry w/mica & gr threads, Clarke base, 3½" **165.00**
Swirl, pk satin, clear mk Clarke base, 4¼" **195.00**
Tartan, rainbow colors, clear Dmn Quilt base/Clarke cup, 6" ...**1,650.00**
Yel opaque & wht spatter, clear Clarke base, 3¾x3" **125.00**
2-Faced child's head shade, red satin, Clarke holder, 4½" **300.00**

Gone-with-the-Wind and Banquet Lamps

Artichoke, pnt milk glass shade/font, ormolu ft, 24", EX **250.00**
Cut/frosted pyriform shade, prisms, marble plinth, 30" **885.00**
Floral HP on shaded squat base/ball shade, orig, 22½" **375.00**
Floral HP on wht ball shade, rtcl brass column std, 29" **250.00**
Floral HP on yel/lt bl vase-form base/ball shade, orig, 30" **625.00**
Floral transfer on squat base/ball shade; Mt WA mkd metal, 24" ..**300.00**
Lt bl satin base/shade, brn eagle/World's Fair 1893, 20" **575.00**
Rose HP on yel/rose vase-form base/umbrella shade, orig, 24" **275.00**
Victoria, red satin, ball shade, ovoid font, ormolu ft, 27" **475.00**

Hanging Lamps

Cranberry T'print 14" shade/font, ornate brass fr, 3" prisms **800.00**
Peachblow melon-rib 14" shade/font, rtcl brass fr, Sandwich ..**2,000.00**
Porch, sq w/4 ruby glass panels, ornate CI mts, 22" **145.00**
Red 14" dome shade w/brass jewels, jeweled mt, amber prisms ...**600.00**
Ruby T'print 14" shade/chimney, clear font, prisms **800.00**
Store, The Rochester on yel brass font, pnt tin shade, 27" **200.00**
Wht font/ball shade w/mc bird in rushes, CI fr mk Pat 1875 ......**900.00**

Lanterns Lamps

Candle, gold/scrolls on tin, isinglass panels, folding, 5" **95.00**
NE Glass, tin w/pressed fixed globe, fluid burner, 1854, 13" **385.00**
Revere type, punched tin, conical top w/2nd candle socket, 13" ..**195.00**
Skater's, brass, dmn-form frwork, Pat 1867, 7½", NM **165.00**
Tin w/glass front/sides, brass collar/burner, reflector, 11" **170.00**
Tin w/onion glove, camphene burner, minor dents, 8", EX **285.00**

Lard Oil/Grease Lamps

Betty, iron, 7x5x3½" **135.00**

Betty, wrought iron, twisted hanger, 7¼" 330.00
Crusie, dbl, iron, EX hanger, sgn JB, 10½", NM 150.00
Crusie, dbl, iron w/lacy scrollwork, delicate hanger, 12½" 300.00
Crusie, overall pitting, rpr, 14" 75.00
Kettle, iron/brass, pencil std, 3-ftd saucer base, 9" 295.00
Pan, iron, orig trammel, 1700s, extends to 36", EX 235.00
Pan, orig trammel, extends to 18¾", NM 150.00
Rush light, iron, 3-leg, shoe ft, spring-operated, 9½" 465.00

Miniature Lamps, Kerosene

All Night wall lamp, brass hanger/reflector, 10" 95.00
Beaded Drape, red satin, ball shade, bulbous base, 11½" 250.00
Beaded Drape, wht opal w/lt bl t'prints, nb, 9½", NM 140.00
Beaded Heart, emerald gr, 5½" 295.00
Beaded Swirl, cranberry, chimney-shape shade, hb, 8" 250.00
Bl opaque, emb leaves/scrolls, flared sq w/ball shade, 10" 210.00
Brass w/emb scrolls on hdl, 4" mercury glass reflector, 8" 105.00
Burmese, crimped rim base w/tooled leaf hdl, 4¾x4" 775.00
Cranberry, HP lilies of the valley, 7¼" 1,075.00
Daisy & Button variant, milk glass, umbrella shade, nb, 10" 100.00
Evening Star, ER & Co emb in bottom, w/hdl, 2" 95.00
Gr & brn spatter, emb ribs & beads, 8½" 250.00
Gr opaque w/emb flowers on ball-shaped shade/base, nb, 8" 300.00
Lincoln Drape w/umbrella shade, clear w/HP floral, 6¾" 45.00
Little Buttercup, purple, w/hdl, ab, clear chimney, 6¾" 85.00
Log Cabin, amber, 3½", EX 650.00
Pk cased satin, melon-ribbed base, pansy ball shade, 6¾" 450.00
Pk satin Beaded Drape, ball shade/squat base, nb, 10½" 335.00
Sandwich, bl ped base w/clear font, Ob, 5" 260.00
Snail, milk glass w/pnt, umbrella shade/sqd base, nb, 10" 350.00
St Nicholas, full figure w/basket on bk, rare, 9" 1,500.00
Swirl, cranberry, bulbous shade/shaped font, clear petal ft 695.00
Swirl, spatter, bl ball shade, clear base, nb, 8" 220.00
Twinkle, amber w/stars on base, no shade, clear chimney, 7" 65.00
Twinkle, gr w/stars on base, ball shade, ab, 6¾", EX 170.00
Yel cased flute-top shade/urn-form base, crystal ft, 8" 695.00

Motion Lamps

Animated motion lamps were popular from the 1920s to the early 1960s. They are characterized by action created by heat from a light bulb which causes a cylinder to revolve and create the illusion of an animated scene. Some of the better-known manufacturers were Econolite Corp., Scene in Action Corp., and L.A. Goodman Mfg. Company. As with many collectible items, prices are guided by condition, availibility and collector demand, which seems to be more intense on the west and east coasts, often resulting in higher prices there than in the midwest. Values are given for lamps in mint condition. Any damage or flaws seriously reduce the price. Our advisors for motion lamps are Kaye and Jim Whitaker; they are listed in the Directory under Washington.

Antique cars, Econolite, gold wire base, 1957, 11" 140.00
Christmas tree, Econolite, many colors, paper, 1951, 15" 120.00
Eattle World's Fair, Econolite, gold wire base, 1962, 11" 150.00
Fireplace, Econolite, gold wire base, 1958, 11" 120.00
Forest fire, Econolite, gold wire base, 1955, 11" 120.00
Forest fire, Econolite (Roto-Vue Jr), gold, 1949, 10" 120.00
Forest fire, Scene in Action, glass & pot metal, 1931, 10" 195.00
Fountain of Youth, Econolite (Roto-Vue Jr), gold, 1950, 10" 130.00
Hopalong Cassidy, Econolite (Roto-Vue Jr), red, 1949, 10" 600.00
Mtn waterfall/campers, LA Goodman, gold wire base, 1956, 11" ..130.00
Niagara Falls, Econolite, gold wire base, 1955, 11" 110.00
Niagara Falls, Econolite (Roto-Vue Jr), gold, 1950, 10" 115.00

Niagara Falls, Scene in Action, glass & pot metal, 1931, 10" 195.00
Serenader, Scene in Action, glass & pot metal, 1932, 13" 225.00
Steamboats or riverboats, Econolite, gold wire base, '57, 11" 130.00
Truck & bus, Econolite, gold wire base, 1955, 11" 140.00

Pattern Glass Lamps

Acanthus Leaf, bl clambroth, wht stem (fractured), 11½" 400.00
Aquarius, amber, stem lamp, #2, 10" 125.00
Berkshire, appl hdl, 2¾" 70.00
Blackberry font, on brass stem & sq milk glass ft, #1, 8" 175.00
Bull's Eye, clear font, wht stem/ft, #1, 8¼" 250.00
Bull's Eye, clear font on emerald gr stem/ft, 9¼" 250.00
Coolidge Drape, cobalt, cobalt tulip-top chimney, ftd/hdl, 6" 225.00
Coolidge Drape, cobalt, stem lamp, #2, 9½", EX 225.00
Corn, stem lamp, #1, 7½" 225.00
Cranberry, ribbed, flared bottom w/'cap' top, clear hdl, 4" 135.00
Dmn Sawtooth & Sheath, w/hdl, 3⅜", EX 85.00
Feather Duster, amber, ftd, w/hdl, 5½", EX 75.00
Greek Key, matching chimney, stem lamp, 18½" 200.00
Heart, gr opaque, tall stem, 9¾" 175.00
Hobbs Blackberry, clear opal, stem lamp, #1, 8½" 250.00
Hobbs Snowflake, bl opal, clear stem, 8¾", EX 300.00
Invt T'print, clear opal, amber Fan stem, Ob/chimney, 7", EX ...125.00
Janice, bl, #1 pb/chimney, finger lamp, 5½", EX 120.00
Leaf & Jewel, ftd w/hdl, 5" 200.00
NY font, Chicago stem & ft, amber, stem lamp, #2, 10½" 55.00
Peacock Feather, amber, tall stem, #2, 9½" 225.00
Peacock Feather, amber, tall stem, 8" 190.00
Peacock Feather, bl, ftd/hdl, 6", EX 150.00
Princess Feather, cobalt, tall stem, #1, 8¼" 300.00
Princess Feather, ftd, w/hdl, 5⅝" 100.00
Princess Feather, gr opaque, stem lamp, #2, 9¾" 200.00
Ruffled Bull's Eye, amber w/molded collar, 4", EX 85.00
Sheldon Swirl, bl opal, clear ribbed stem, 8½", EX 325.00
Sheldon Swirl, vaseline opal, stem lamp, 8" 225.00
Triple Flute & Bar font, blk glass base, stem lamp, #1, 9¾" 150.00
Triple Swag & Dmn, bl Baroque base, stem lamp, #1, 10½" 200.00
Zipper Loop, marigold carnival, Ob/chimney, ftd/hdl, 5", VG 300.00
Zipper Loop, marigold, stem lamp, #2, 8" 300.00

Reverse-Painted Lamps

Forest landscape 17¾" helmet-shaped shade; baluster-formed gadrooned base, unsigned Pittsburgh, $2,800.00.

Jefferson, 14" 4-repeat flower shade; vasiform std 990.00
Moe Bridges 18" geese/moon/lake dome shade; sgn bronze std ..4,400.00

Moe Bridges 18" winter shaped-dome shade; gilt metal std **1,900.00**
Pittsburgh type, 16" cottage/mtns/lake dome shade; emb std **550.00**
Pittsburgh 18" scenic w/footbridge shade; bronzed metal std ...**1,100.00**
Unmk 10" fir trees dome shade; molded brass base, 16" **1,400.00**
Unmk 17" trees/cottage dome shade & rvpt cylinder base, 21" ..**750.00**

Student Lamps, Kerosene

Dbl, brass, horizontal, 1876 Spencer tank, wht shades, 21x14" ..**550.00**
Dbl, brass, repousse fluid font, Dardonville NY, 1850s **650.00**
Dbl, SP brass, milk glass shades, Argand/1871, 21x19", EX **800.00**
Dbl, yel brass w/gr cased shades, electrified, 27x23", EX **400.00**
Hanging, dbl, NP/ornate CI w/red cased shades, 47" **1,850.00**
Manhattan, NP brass, repro 7" milk glass shade, 21" **300.00**

Whale Oil/Burning Fluid Lamps

Alabaster gr font, figural wht metal stem, slate ft, 13" **150.00**
Blown, bulbous w/pressed lacy rnd base, Sandwich, 6" **350.00**
Blown, candlestick base w/knop stem, ball font, 10½" **280.00**
Blown, wht, base w/lion's head & flower basket, 7", EX **300.00**
Coin Dot, cranberry opal, Hobbs, w/hdl, 3" **650.00**
Cut Roman Key font/ball shade, spelter figural stem, 17" **400.00**
Cut/frosted Oregon shade/font, spelter figural stem, 22½" **400.00**
Flint, panels in ovals, ped base, hex ft. rnd shoulder, 7" **175.00**
Hoyt, floral etched panels, stem ft, gauffered chimney, 20" **275.00**
Mold blown, opal, paneled w/pressed hex base, 7½" **1,200.00**
Pressed, bl frost font w/floral medallion band, tin/CI std **65.00**
Pressed, bl opaque ribbed font on cobalt stem/ft, 9¼", EX **250.00**
Pressed, clear font on cobalt stem/ft, melon ribs, 7⅝" **175.00**
Pressed, cranberry Optic Rib w/clear hdl, wide disk ft, 4" **125.00**
Pressed, cup shape inverted in saucer, amber, 3⅜" **375.00**
Pressed, cup shape inverted in saucer, Ob/chimney, 3¼" **100.00**
Pressed, gr alabaster font, brass stem, marble base, 12" **200.00**
Pressed, hexagonal font/base w/sunbursts & ribs, 6¾", NM **75.00**
Pressed, loops on concave font, monument base, 11¾", EX **200.00**
Pressed, Ripley, sqd font w/canted corners, sqd stem, 11" **140.00**
Pressed, sapphire bl, molded collar, ftd finger lamp, 4½" **135.00**
Pressed, sapphire bl, vertical ribs, appl hdl, 3¼", EX **125.00**
Pressed, vaseline, hex base w/match holder, 8", EX **200.00**
Pressed, 8-side clear font on 8-side wht stem, Pat '73, 8" **95.00**
Ripley, ftd, dbl hdls, 5" **150.00**
Ruby/wht spatter, clear reed hdl, foreign burner, 4¾" **120.00**

Miscellaneous Lamps

Astral, brass, etched/cut shade on lotus font, marble base, 22" ...**500.00**
Astral, etch/cut shade, brass columnar std, marble base, 21" **275.00**
Bicycle, carbide, Solar Model CM Hall Lamp Co, NP brass **65.00**
Brass Rayo type, ped base, amber mushroom shade, 21" **165.00**
Electrolier, lady w/vase, bronze finish, 5-branch, 52½" **650.00**
Gunning light, tin, kerosene burner, worn orig wht pnt, 1910 ...**600.00**
Hurricane, 3-dolphin wht clambroth rnd-ft base, Sandwich ...**3,750.00**
Lace maker's, blown, baluster stem, spherical font, 6½" **330.00**
Peg, Bl swirl MOP ruffled shade/font, brass stick, 17" **650.00**
Piano, brass/iron w/yel cased 10" ball shade, adjusts to 61" **450.00**
Pocket Watch, NP brass, Folmer & Schwing, Pat '91, w/box **450.00**
Spelter, seated draped nude, Boston & Sandwich font **525.00**
Store, pressed, brass/wire fr, rnd tin blk-pnt shade, 24" **180.00**

Lang, Anton

Anton Lang was a German studio potter and an actor in the cast

of the Oberammergau Passion Plays early in the 20th century. Because he played the role of Christ three times, his pottery was purchased by tourists overseas and brought back to the U.S. in suitcases, which accounts for the prevalence of smaller examples today. During 1923 when the play was being threatened with extinction due to Germany's postwar Depression, Anton Lang and the other 'Passion Players' toured the U.S. performing scenes from the play and selling their crafts. Lang would occasionally throw pottery when the cast passed through a pottery center such as Cincinnati, where Rookwood was located. His pottery, marked with his name in script, is fairly scarce and highly valued for its artistic quality. Postcards, programs, and photographs depicting Lang are also collectible.

Bowl, yel gloss w/decor, sm **40.00**
Figure, goat, Deco style, wht translucent, handmade, 5" **150.00**
Flowerpot, ochre, ribbed, w/saucer, #" **45.00**
Jug, HP mc flowers on bl, ceramic stopper, 6" **95.00**
Pitcher, cobalt irid, HP Deco flowers & dots, yel int, 5" **150.00**
Sculpture, stylized man leaning into wind, 20" **1,000.00**
Urn, wheel thrown, bl mottled, 5½" **165.00**
Vase, bl w/stylized floral, 3" **65.00**
Vase, brn glossy, squeeze-bag edelweiss, Oberammergau, 4" **150.00**
Vase, brn w/decor, 6" **75.00**
Vase, stylized sunflowers, mc/incised, ovoid, 7" **250.00**

Le Verre Francais

Le Verre Francais was produced during the 1920s by Schneider at Epinay-sur-Seine in France. It was a commercial art glass in the cameo style composed of layered glass with the designs engraved by acid. Favored motifs were stylized leaves and flowers or geometric patterns. It was marked with the name in script or with an inlaid filigrane. Our advisor for this category is Don Williams; he is listed in the Directory under Missouri.

Key: fp — fire polished

Cameo

Veilleuse, birds in flight, blue to brown on yellow, peaked form on 3-legged wrought iron base, 6¾", $1,980.00.

Bowl, floral, 5x6", on tall ornate 3-ftd metal base, 14" **660.00**
Bowl vase, oleander limbs, orange on yel/orange frost, 7" **1,300.00**
Compote, Deco leafage, fp brn on yel-pk mottle, 5½x4" **350.00**
Ewer, sq Deco floral, brn/rust on yel, orange bun ft, 12" **800.00**
Lamp, butterflies on 9½" shade & base, label, 15" **3,000.00**
Lamp, Deco floral on closed-top 7" shade/base, bl/wht, 14" **1,650.00**

Lamp, stylized floral on orange 6" dome shade/vasiform std 1,400.00
Pitcher, lg flowerheads, orange on yel, amethyst hdl, 13" 500.00
Vase, berries on orange mottle, trumpet form, bun ft, 15" 700.00
Vase, exotic seed pods/stems, fp bl/orange on yel, ftd, 16" 825.00
Vase, fish band at shoulder, seaweed, gr/red/bl/frost, 8" 1,100.00
Vase, florals at shoulder, orange/wht, bun ft, Charder, 17" 770.00
Vase, lg overlapping leaf tips, rust/gr on amber tinge, 16" 650.00
Vase, shield-form/lozenges, orange/gr on orange, hdls, 8x6" 550.00
Vase, sq Deco floral, rust/brn on yel mottle, slim, 14" 850.00

Leeds, Leeds Type

The Leeds Pottery was established in 1758 in Yorkshire and under varied management produced fine creamware, often highly reticulated and transfer printed, shiny black-glazed Jackfield wares, polychromed pearlware, and figurines similar to those made in the Staffordshire area. Little of the early ware was marked; after 1775 the impressed 'Leeds Pottery' mark was used. From 1781 to 1820, the name 'Hartley Greens & Co.' was added. The pottery closed in 1898. Today the term 'Leeds' has become generic and is used to encompass all polychromed pearlware and creamware, wherever its origin. Thus similar wares of other potters (Wood for instance) is often incorrectly called 'Leeds.' Unless a piece is marked or can be definitely attributed to Leeds by confirming the pattern to be authentic, 'Leeds-Type' would be a more accurate nomenclature.

Key:

cw — creamware	sp — soft paste
pw — pearlware	ug — underglaze

Bowl, pw, gaudy floral, 3-color, hairline/chip, 4x10" 195.00
Candlestick, sq/rtcl, 12 sm rods support cup, mk, 9½" 550.00
Coffeepot, gr, emb leaves/arches/wicker, widow/child finial 600.00
Cup, pw, vertical ribbing, gr rim, 2x3¼", VG 50.00
Cup & saucer, handleless; gaudy floral, bl/wht, wear/stain 115.00
Dish, bl feather edge, mk Best Goods, rectangular, 5x4" 100.00
Dish, floral-rtcl lid w/flower finial, mk, 4¾x5½" L 525.00
Jug, bl & wht gaudy floral, leaf hdl, flakes, 8½" 715.00
Jug, Florizel & Perditta, ftd, ca 1800, 7½", EX 225.00
Jug, pw, floral/sheaf/farm tools/landscape, 5-color, 9⅜" 2,175.00
Jug, pw, gaudy floral, bl & orange, leaf hdl, flake, 6" 335.00
Plate, pw, lg ug bl rosette, floral rim, 10½" 425.00
Plate, pw, Returning Home, lady/boy, wear, 7½" 100.00
Plate, pw, ug bl floral sprig, bl scalloped/shell rim, 10" 125.00
Plate, pw, 4-color eagle, feather edge, 8-sided, 8¼", NM 660.00
Saucer, pw, gaudy floral, 4-color, 4¼" 85.00
Saucer, pw, gaudy floral, 5-color, flakes, 5⅜" 95.00
Soup plate, pw, 3-color floral, gr scallop/shell rim, 10" 260.00
Sugar bowl, pw, gaudy floral, 4-color, stain/wear, 4½" 330.00
Sugar bowl, tulip, 4-color, w/lid, chip/flake, 4¾x4¼" 415.00
Tea caddy, pw, floral, 3-color, 5¼", EX 1,010.00
Teapot, pw, gaudy floral, bl & wht, chip, 5¼" 165.00
Teapot, pw, gaudy floral, 4-color, leaf hdl, hairlines, 7½" 200.00
Tray, oval w/rtcl rim, mk, 10½x9½" 170.00
Tray, rtcl dmn shape, emb scrolls, twist hdl, 8" L 400.00

Lefton China

In 1940 the Lefton China Co. was founded by George Zoltan Lefton, a native of Hungary, who in the 1930s was in the designing and manufacturing of sportswear. His hobby of collecting fine porcelains led him to the creation of his own ceramic business. Today the company is a leading producer of ceramic giftware, and the products are found in gift shops thoughout the world.

Important to collectors are Lefton trademarks which aid in the dating of pieces. Most Lefton items are identified by a fired-on trademark or a paper label found on the bottom of each piece. These marks are found in both single and multicolor styles. Usually any number found below the marks are the item identification numbers and, if preceded by letters, will in fact be the factory identification numbers. Older and discontinued items such as a vase formed as hands, parakeets, Little Adorables (Limited Edition), flamingo with baby, cherubs on trees, Huckleberry Finn and dog set, Holy Family, Napoleon, and swan candy dishes are eagerly sought after by collectors. As with any antique or collectible, the prices vary, depending on location, condition, and availability. Our advisor for this category is Loretta DeLozier; she is listed in the Directory under Iowa.

Ashtrays, Wheat design, nested set w/holder, #20124 ....16.00
Bell, angel, #90283, 3½" 22.00
Bird, bobolink, #1290 ....35.00
Bookends, pheasants, #2230, 5", pr 70.00
Bowl, milk china, #822, 2½x5" 33.00
Candle holders, #363, pr 25.00

Candy bowl, applied cherub and roses, pastel green with bisque finish, #837, 7", $130.00.

Creamer, Bl Paisley, #2374 ....8.00
Creamer & sugar bowl, Bluebird, #290 ....25.00
Creamer & sugar bowl, Gr Hollyberry, #2047 ....16.00
Creamer & sugar bowl, 50th Anniversary 18.00
Cup & saucer, jumbo; Grandma or Grandpa, #2594 or #2596, ea ...25.00
Cup & saucer, Rose Chinz, #656 ....18.00
Egg cup, Bl Paisley, #2131 ....8.00
Figurine, Santa & Mrs Claus, #18 ....47.00
Pitcher & bowl, French Rose, #3383, 3¼", 5" 17.00
Planter, matt, #2707, 4½x5¼" 16.00
Plate, Brn Heritage Floral, #2222, 9" 25.00
Plate, Poinsettia, #4396, 9" 18.00
Shakers, Bluebirds, #282, pr 16.00
Shakers, Christmas trees, #54, pr 12.00
Teapot, Gr Hollyberry, #1357 ....45.00
Tray, tidbit; Rose Chinz, #651 ....16.00
Tray, tidbit; Rose Chinz, 2-tier, #649 ....38.00
Vase, flowers on bl ewer form, #2184, 5¾" 18.00
Vase, forget-me-nots, mc w/gold on pk porc, fluted rim, #7290 ....30.00
Vase, grapes, lt bl on wht bsk, #2186, 7½" 18.00
Vase, head form, matt, #1226, 6" 22.00
Vase, pk roses on pineapple form, #7283, 5" 50.00
Wall plaque, grapes, #455 ....13.00

Legras

Legras and Cie was founded in St. Denis, France, in 1864. Production continued until the 1930s. In addition to their enameled wares, they made cameo art glass decorated with outdoor scenes and florals executed by acid cuttings through two to six layers of glass. Their work is signed 'Legras' in relief. Our advisor for this category is Don Williams; he is listed in the Directory under Missouri.

Cameo

Bowl, berries cut/pnt on clear, 3x7" 300.00
Bowl, wide leaves cut/pnt on opal/amber, ogee sides, 5x7" 700.00
Vase, cherry blossoms cut/pnt on clear, bulbous, 8" 600.00
Vase, daisies in band w/brn stain on brn/wht mottle, 8x5½" 595.00
Vase, grapes/vines, amber on opaque opal, shouldered, 5" 500.00
Vase, grove of dk trees, peach/apricot sky, egg form, 5½" 725.00
Vase, leafy branches cascade from rim, purple on apricot, 6" 275.00
Vase, leaves & vines, cut/HP on pk frost, 9" 625.00
Vase, prunus blossoms, wine enamel on frost, ovoid, 8" 550.00
Vase, sea coast, gr on yel, bulbous w/rectangle neck, 2½" 365.00

Enameled Glass

Vase, shepherd/sheep/trees, HP scene & bkground, 11" 260.00
Vase, snow scene, blk/orange on clear, cylinder, 6" 350.00
Vase, snow scene w/peasant woman & village, orange sky, 17" ..900.00
Vase, trees/sailboats, orange/yel sky & water, 17" 350.00
Vase, winter scene w/lady & houses, HP on clear, 16" 275.00

Lenox

Walter Scott Lenox, former art director at Ott and Brewer, and Jonathan Coxon founded The Ceramic Art Company of Trenton, New Jersey, in 1889. By 1906 Cox had left the company and to reflect the change in ownership, the name was changed to Lenox Inc. Until 1930 when the production of American-made Belleek came to an end, they continued to produce the same type of high-quality ornamental wares that Lenox and Coxon had learned to master while in the employ of Ott and Brewer. Their superior dinnerware made the company famous, and since 1917 Lenox has been chosen the official White House China. Our advisor for this category is Mary Frank Gaston; she is listed in the Directory under Texas. See also Ceramic Art Company.

Ashtray, gold ship, Am Export 1960, 5½" 40.00
Bookend, stylized Trojan bust, incised mk, 7", pr 500.00
Bookends, Blk lady's torso, Deco, gr mk, pr 275.00
Bowl, fruit; Empress, sm 30.00
Bowl, vegetable; Eternal, oval 45.00
Bowl, vegetable; Kingsley, oval 135.00
Bowl, vegetable; Wyndcrest, oval 75.00
Bust, lady w/cascading hair, wht, gr mk, 8½" 275.00
Candlestick, wht ware, raised scalloped base, Belleek mk, pr 165.00
Chocolate pot, Autumn 225.00
Chocolate pot, mc daisies, Belleek, 11", +6 c/s 360.00
Creamer, Ming 60.00
Cup & saucer, Autumn 48.00
Cup & saucer, bouillon; Empress 45.00
Cup & saucer, Clarion 22.50
Cup & saucer, demitasse; Engagement, wht 95.00
Cup & saucer, demitasse; Lenox Rose 38.00
Cup & saucer, Fireflower 12.00
Cup & saucer, Rapture 25.00
Cup & saucer, Sachet 35.00
Cup & saucer, Westwind 25.00
Figurine, First Waltz, ltd ed, 1984 ....125.00
Figurine, vase, blue jay in tree, 5-color, ink stamp 300.00
Lamp, nude figural, 1929, 12½" 800.00

Pitcher, gold band w/6 red apples on olive, sgn McGrayhy, 6" ...200.00
Pitcher, silver o/l w/floral cameo, palette mk, 8" 500.00
Plate, bread & butter; Fairfield 18.00
Plate, bread & butter; Westwind 12.00
Plate, dinner; Autumn 50.00
Plate, dinner; Country Garden 35.00
Plate, dinner; Lenox Rose 30.00
Plate, dinner; Rapture 25.00
Plate, dinner; Westwind 25.00
Plate, mallard duck among rushes, gold trim, sgn Nosek, 10" 175.00
Plate, salad; Rapture 25.00
Plate, salad; Westwind 15.00
Platter, Empress, 19" 150.00
Platter, Kingsley, 17" 175.00
Punch bowl, bl plums on shaded ground, 2-part, Belleek, 15" 700.00
Relish plate, dbl, leaf-emb rim & int, center hdl, 15½" 75.00
Soup bowl, Lenox Rose, rimmed, 9" 45.00
Swan, bl mk, 8½" 75.00
Tea set, Virginian, gold hdls, 11" pot, 3-pc 350.00
Teapot, cobalt w/silver o/l, 7¾", +matching cr/sug 300.00
Teapot, Lenox Rose 225.00
Toby, William Penn, Indian hdl 190.00
Vase, brn w/fan-shaped Nouveau leaves, brn mk, 4x3½" 150.00
Vase, bud; multiflorals on porc, 6" 35.00
Vase, lady in long wht gown/pk floral, cylinder, Lenox, 12" 375.00
Vase, portrait medallions & florals w/gold, palette mk, 10" 350.00
Vase, stylized upright florals, mc on ivory, Belleek, 12x4" 175.00

Letter Openers

Made in a wide variety of materials and designs, letter openers make for an interesting collection that is easy to display and easy on the budget as well. Our advisor for this category is Ron Damaska; he is listed in the Directory under Pennsylvania.

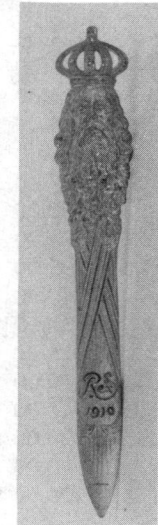

Gilded brass, King Rex head, Mardi Gras, dated 1910, $95.00.

Alligator w/Blk boy, Germany 35.00
Brass, gargoyle hdl, pierced work on blade, 10¼" 35.00
Celluloid, bust of Napoleon, lt tan, worn brn on hat, 7¾" 30.00
Chrome, fluted 12.50
Copper, bronco w/rider emb, 1940s 10.00
Ivory w/baleen trim, 8" 70.00
Ivory w/stanhope 60.00

Pewter, nude w/sword 9" , ...45.00
Plastic, Fuller Brush Man, clear or brn, ea 5.00
Plastic, Needham Oil, MA, gr 5.00
SP, Russian wolfhound figural hdl, Nouveau style, 11" 50.00
SP, San Francisco 1939 Expo, ornate hdl 27.50

Libbey

The New England Glass Company was established in 1818 in Boston, Massachusetts. In 1892 it became known as the Libbey Glass Company. At Chicago's Columbian Expo in 1893, Libbey set up a ten-pot furnace and made glass souvenirs. The display brought them world-wide fame. Between 1878 and 1918 Libbey made exquisite cut and faceted glass, considered today to be the best from the brilliant period. The company is credited for several innovations — the Owens bottle machine that made mass-production possible and the Westlake machine which turned out both electric light bulbs and tumblers auto-matically. They developed a machine to polish the rims of their tum-blers in such a way that chipping was unlikely to occur. Their glassware carried the patented Safedge guarantee. Libbey also made glassware in numerous colors, among them cobalt, ruby, pink, green, and amber. In 1935 it was bought by Owens-Illinois and remains a division of that company. See also Amberina and other specific types.

Bowl, cut, bottom w/5 flowers, dmn border w/basketweave, 9" ...150.00
Bowl, cut, dmn relief border, rayed center, 1¾x8" 50.00
Bowl, cut, Ellsmere, 9" 550.00
Bowl, cut, Senora, triangular, 3x10", EX 500.00
Candlesticks, cut, cornflowers/leaves, ribbed, 10", pr 425.00
Candlesticks, cut, thistle blossoms & leaves, 10", pr 350.00
Chalice, cut, gr/frost, deer & foliage allover, 5½" 295.00
Champagne, Menagerie, squirrel stem, 5½" 110.00
Compote, clear w/pk Optic Swirl, knop stem, sgn, 4x10" 225.00
Compote, cut, notched prism w/hobstars, trumpet form, 7½" 375.00

Cordial, greyhound stem, signed, 4", $125.00.

Cordial, crystal w/gr jade knop on stem, Nash, 5", set of 8 ....385.00
Creamer & sugar bowl, hobstars/prisms/strawberry dmns, 3" 110.00
Decanter, cut, Harvard, dbl spout, pyramid form, 15" 275.00
Flower center, cut, Express, cut ring near top, 13x8" 950.00
Maize, celery, clear w/amber staining & bl leaves, 6" 235.00
Maize, celery vase, gr husks on custard 180.00
Maize, condiment set, custard, 3 pcs on tray w/metal hdl 600.00
Maize, pitcher, bl husks on clear w/amber irid, clear hdl, 9" 585.00
Maize, shakers, gold-edged bl husks on custard, pr 250.00
Maize, sugar shaker, yel/gold leaves on custard, 5¾" 300.00
Maize, toothpick holder, gold-edged gr husks on custard 400.00
Maize, tumbler, bl husks on irid 235.00

Pitcher, Corinthian, triple-notched hdl, bulbous, 8½" 275.00
Pitcher, cut, Kingston, sgn, 9" 395.00
Pitcher, X-cut dmns w/vertical spears, 9", +5 tumblers 225.00
Plate, cut, Holly & Snowflake allover pattern, 7" 295.00
Plate, cut, Imperial, 7" 200.00
Saloon shaker, hobstars/X-hatching/fans, Honeycomb neck, 5" .165.00
Shakers, flowers & swags intaglio, Wilson sterling lid, pr 250.00
Sherbet, Menagerie, rabbit stem, 2½" 110.00
Spoon rest, cut, hobstar center w/8 cut panels, 7x5" 135.00
Tankard, sabres/hobstars/fans/nailheads, 9", +6 tumblers 425.00
Tazza, cut, hobstars/fans, notched stem, sabre mk, 8x7" 120.00
Tazza, intaglio flowers & leaves, twist stem, 5½x7½" 120.00
Tray, cut, button star w/flowers, hobstar border, 10¾" 150.00
Tray, cut, buttons fr in nailhead, ribbed oval, 13x10½" 850.00
Urn, fuchsias & sunflowers intaglio cuttings, 9x6½" 550.00
Vase, cut, cane bands alternate w/flutes, trumpet form, 9" 140.00
Vase, cut, punties/X-cut dmns, corset shape, Masonic sgn, 4" 125.00
Vase, cut, punty/strw dmns/fans, corset shape, 5" 125.00
Vase, cut, sabre, bands of cane & flutes, trumpet form, 9" 140.00
Vase, cut, thistle flowers & ferns, pattern ft, 12" 300.00
Vase, jack-in-pulpit; amberina, ruffled, 16" 900.00
Whiskey, wheat/fern/leaves, 2¼", pr 90.00
Wine, Menagerie, cat stem, 7" 110.00
Wine, Menagerie, kangaroo stem, 6" 110.00
Wine, Menagerie, polar bear stem, 5½" 125.00

Lightning Rod Balls

Used as ornaments on lightning rods, the vast majority of these balls were made of glass, but ceramic examples can be found as well. Their average diameter is 4½" but can vary from 3½" up to 5½". Only a few of the many available pattern-and-color combinations are listed here. The most common measure 4½" and are found in sun-colored amethyst and milk glass. Our advisor is Mike Bruner, who is currently working on a book on this subject. Anyone interested in receiving a hobby-related newsletter may write to him for more information; he is listed in the Directory under Michigan.

Amber, Hawkeye 80.00
Amber, Mast 125.00
Amber, RHF 200.00
Bl, ceramic, rnd 100.00
Clear, Swirl 100.00
Cobalt, plain, rnd 50.00
Gray-gr, D&S 65.00
Gray-gr, ribbed grape 175.00
Milk glass, Chestnut 45.00
Milk glass, Moon & Star 20.00
Orange, plain, rnd 300.00
Pk, rnd 425.00
Purple-blk, rnd 350.00
Red, Electra, cone 90.00
Red, Maher 190.00
Red, Moon & Star 125.00
Red, Thompson 70.00
Silver, National 400.00
Silver mercury, rnd 60.00
Teal bl, rnd 280.00

Limited Edition Plates

Currently values of some limited edition plates have risen dramatically while others have drastically fallen. Prices charged by plate dealers in the secondary market vary greatly; we have tried to suggest an average.

Bing and Grondahl

1895, Behind the Frozen Window	6,250.00
1896, New Moon	1,850.00
1897, Christmas Meal of Sparrows	1,100.00
1898, Roses & Star	685.00
1899, Crows Enjoying Christmas	1,500.00
1900, Church Bells Chiming	1,125.00
1901, 3 Wise Men	425.00
1902, Gothic Church Interior	365.00
1903, Expectant Children	370.00
1904, View of Copenhagen From Fredericksberg Hill	155.00
1905, Anxiety of the Coming Christmas Night	155.00
1906, Sleighing to Church	92.00
1907, Little Match Girl	105.00
1908, St Petri Church	65.00
1909, Yule Tree	95.00
1910, Old Organist	85.00
1911, Angels & Shepherds	77.00
1912, Going to Church	85.00
1913, Bringing Home the Tree	87.00
1914, Amalienborg Castle	77.00
1915, Dog on Chain Outside Window	125.00
1916, Prayer of the Sparrows	72.50
1917, Christmas Boat	72.50
1918, Fishing Boat	72.50
1919, Outside the Lighted Window	67.50
1920, Hare in the Snow	72.50
1921, Pigeons	65.00
1922, Star of Bethlehem	62.50
1923, Hermitage	60.00
1924, Lighthouse	70.00
1925, Child's Christmas	70.00
1926, Churchgoers	70.00
1927, Skating Couple	95.00
1928, Eskimos	60.00
1929, Fox Outside Farm	65.00
1930, Tree in Town Hall Square	80.00
1931, Christmas Train	80.00
1932, Lifeboat at Work	72.50
1933, Korsor-Nyborg Ferry	68.00
1934, Church Bell in Tower	65.00
1935, Lillebelt Bridge	68.00
1936, Royal Guard	75.00
1937, Arrival of Christmas Guests	80.00
1938, Lighting the Candles	150.00
1939, Old Lock-Eye, The Sandman	150.00
1940, Delivering Christmas Letters	150.00
1941, Horses Enjoying Meal	225.00
1942, Danish Farm on Christmas Night	185.00
1943, Ribe Cathedral	175.00
1944, Sorgenfri Castle	95.00
1945, Old Water Mill	115.00
1946, Commemoration Cross	75.00
1947, Dybbol Mill	95.00
1948, Watchman	75.00
1949, Landsoldaten	75.00
1950, Kronborg Castle at Elsinore	105.00
1951, Jens Bang	90.00
1952, Old Copenhagen Canals & Thorsvaldsen Museum	85.00
1953, Royal Boat	85.00

1954, Snowman	85.00
1955, Kaulundborg Church	85.00
1956, Christmas in Copenhagen	135.00
1957, Christmas Candles	145.00
1958, Santa Claus	95.00
1959, Christmas Eve	115.00
1960, Village Church	145.00
1961, Winter Harmony	98.00
1962, Winter Night	60.00
1963, Christmas Elf	80.00
1964, Fir Tree & Hare	39.00
1965, Bringing Home the Tree	42.00
1966, Home for Christmas	35.00
1967, Sharing the Joy	35.00
1968, Christmas in Church	32.00
1969, Arrival of Guests	24.00
1970, Pheasants in Snow	22.00
1971, Christmas at Home	19.00
1972, Christmas in Greenland	19.00
1973, Country Christmas	22.00
1974, Christmas in the Village	19.00
1975, The Old Water Mill	19.00
1976, Christmas Welcome	19.00
1977, Copenhagen Christmas	19.00
1978, A Christmas Tale	19.00
1979, White Christmas	21.00
1980, Christmas in the Woods	21.00
1981, Christmas Peace	24.00
1982, The Christmas Tree	37.00

M. I. Hummel

1972, Hear Ye, Hear Ye, $50.00.

1971, Heavenly Angel	525.00
1973, Globe Trotter	95.00
1974, Goose Girl	50.00
1975, Ride Into Christmas	50.00
1976, Apple Tree Girl	50.00
1977, Apple Tree Boy	60.00
1978, Happy Pastime	45.00
1979, Singing Lesson	30.00
1980, School Girl	40.00

Royal Copenhagen

1908, Madonna & Child	2,900.00
1909, Danish Landscape	160.00

1910, Magi 135.00	1974, Winter Twilight 28.00
1911, Danish Landscape 160.00	1975, Queens Palace 24.00
1912, Christmas Tree 160.00	1976, Danish Watermill 29.00
1913, Frederik Church Spire 145.00	1977, Immervad Bridge 24.00
1914, Holy Spirit Church 160.00	1978, Greenland Scenery 29.00
1915, Danish Landscape 165.00	1979, Choosing Tree 45.00
1916, Shepherd at Christmas 100.00	1980, Bringing Home Tree 37.50
1917, Our Savior Church 90.00	1981, Admiring Tree 39.00
1918, Sheep & Shepherds 90.00	1982, Waiting for Christmas 45.00
1919, In the Park 90.00	
1920, Mary & Child Jesus 90.00	

Limoges

From the mid-18th century, Limoges was the center of the porcelain industry of France, where at one time more than forty companies utilized the local kaolin to make a superior quality china, much of which was exported to the United States. Various marks were used; some included the name of the American export company (rather than the manufacturer) and 'Limoges.' After 1891 'France' was added. Pieces signed by factory artists are more valuable than those decorated outside the factory by amateurs. For a more thorough study of the subject, we recommend you refer to *The Collector's Encyclopedia of Limoges Porcelain* by our advisor, Mary Frank Gaston, who is listed in the Directory under Texas. Her book has beautiful color illustrations and current market values.

1921, Aabenraa Marketplace 85.00	
1922, 3 Singing Angels 75.00	
1923, Danish Landscape 75.00	
1924, Sailing Ship 100.00	
1925, Christianshavn Street Scene 85.00	
1926, Christianshavn Canal 85.00	
1927, Ship's Boy at Tiller 155.00	
1928, Vicar's Family 87.00	
1929, Grundtvig Church 87.00	
1930, Fishing Boats 115.00	
1931, Mother & Child 115.00	Basket, pk & red roses on cream, sgn DuVal, 9x5" 275.00
1932, Frederiksberg Gardens 110.00	Biscuit jar, couple reserve/florals on cream w/gold, mk, 8" 275.00
1933, Ferry & Great Belt 150.00	Biscuit jar, 2 cherubs w/dove, gold trim, 7½" 375.00
1934, Hermitage Castle 150.00	Bowl, fruit; sm pk roses center & rim, mk, 10½" 325.00
1935, Kronborg Castle 215.00	Bowl, punch; vintage decor, inscr on base, 15" 475.00
1936, Roskilde Cathedral 185.00	Bowl, punch; vintage decor, sgn LM Bockins, on stand 400.00
1937, Main Street of Copenhagen 230.00	Butter tub, HP raspberries w/gold, w/underplate 175.00
1938, Round Church of Osterlars 290.00	Chocolate pot, gold-paste floral on wht, mk, 7½" 100.00
1939, Greenland Pack Ice 375.00	Coffeepot, wht w/gold bands & trim, 9" 250.00
1940, Good Shepherd 375.00	Compote, rose-colored bands w/gold, mk, 4½x9" 550.00
1941, Danish Village Church 345.00	Cracker jar, floral, coral/yel/wht on gold & wht, 7½" 175.00
1942, Bell Tower 375.00	Cracker jar, pk & gr floral w/gold, mk, 6x8", +tray 325.00
1943, Flight Into Egypt 525.00	Dresser box, wht roses sides/lid, gold trim, mk, 6" 150.00
1944, Danish Village Scene 290.00	Egg dish, fluted edge, gold trim, mk, 9¼" 200.00
1945, Peaceful Scene 475.00	Ewer, mums & gold pods on cream, gold hdl & spout, 11", NM .265.00
1946, Zealand Village Church 175.00	Fish set, 23½" tray w/gold carp, +10 9½" plates/gravy 450.00
1947, Good Shepherd 245.00	Game set, exotic birds/florals, 18" platter+12 9" plates 800.00
1948, Nodebo Church 215.00	Jam jar, bl w/gold stencils, hdls, mk, w/underplate 250.00
1949, Our Lady's Cathedral 235.00	Mustache cup, demitasse; gold florals, mk 175.00
1950, Boeslunde Church 235.00	Picture frame, mc florals w/gold, ftd, mk, 10x6½" 325.00
1951, Christmas Angel 365.00	Pitcher, cider; roses, mc on bl w/gold, Merenlet, 6" 375.00
1952, Christmas in Forest 135.00	Plaque, classical women in meadow, 1900, 8x5½" 550.00
1953, Frederiksberg Castle 135.00	Plaque, courtship scene, couple in garden, sgn Lancy, 10" 450.00
1954, Amalienborg Palace 135.00	Plaque, duck flying over lake, Sena, 13½" 325.00
1955, Fano Girl 195.00	Plaque, Dutch scene, gold rococo border, 12½" 250.00
1956, Rosenborg Castle 185.00	Plaque, playful nymphs, sgn Ritter, 18" dia, fancy gesso fr 1,200.00
1957, Good Shepherd 105.00	Plaque, stag scene, artist sgn, gold rococo, 13¼" 425.00
1958, Sunshine Over Greenland 145.00	Plaque, trees/stream, sgn Ribes, 9½x12½", in fr 500.00
1959, Christmas Night 115.00	Plaque, windmill on river bank, E Vidal, 9" 175.00
1960, Stag 145.00	Plate, cavalier, mc costume, seated, gold border, 10" 275.00
1961, Training Ship 155.00	Plate, cavalier, yel tunic w/purple cape, Luc, 10", #42 ....225.00
1962, Little Mermaid 205.00	Plate, couple by wall, gold rococo rim, no mk, 12", pr 450.00
1963, Hojsager Mill 85.00	Plate, ducks in flight, sgn, gold rim, Coronet, 8⅝", pr 245.00
1964, Fetching the Tree 65.00	Plate, game birds, Roman gold edge, Coronet, 11⅛", pr 265.00
1965, Little Skaters 70.00	Plate, gobbler & hen, Melo, 9¾" 160.00
1966, Blackbird 38.00	Plate, hunter & his dog, artist sgn, mk, 13½", pr 650.00
1967, Royal Oak 40.00	Plate, roses, HP pk & gold, gold rim, Coronet, 7½" 30.00
1968, Last Umiak 39.00	Plate, 2 figures in sailboat, DuVal, 10" 250.00
1969, Old Farmyard 39.00	Platter, lg game birds, gold edges, oval, 16" L, pr 425.00
1970, Christmas Rose & Cat 39.00	
1971, Hare in Winter 24.00	
1972, In the Desert 24.00	
1973, Train Home Bound 24.00	

Powder box, mc floral w/gold trim, mk, 5½" **175.00**
Punch bowl, HP violets in & out, gold trim, T&V, 12½" **495.00**
Soap dish, Moss Rose, pierced lid, mk, 4½" **125.00**
Sugar bowl, Moss Rose, bl trim, mk, w/lid, 7½" **150.00**
Tankard, dragon shape gold hdl, pk roses w/gr leaves, 14" **1,100.00**
Tankard, stoneware, brn body w/blk & gold stars, 12" **1,500.00**
Teapot, silver o/l florals & scrolls on wht, 2¼x5½" **100.00**
Tray, Nouveau water lilies, sgn Crabb, gold rim, T&V, 1914 .....**185.00**
Tray, orange floral, gold scalloped/beaded edge, 10" **250.00**

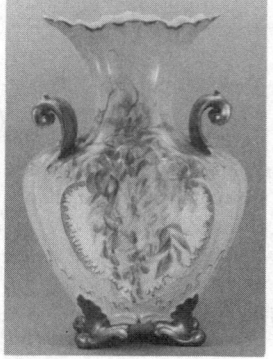

Vase, wisteria, signed Litch, gold feet and upturned handles, marked Elite, '97, 12", $325.00.

Vase, cavalier in landscape, baluster form, cabinet sz **225.00**
Vase, gold prunus/dragonfly on rose, facing pr, 5" **495.00**
Vase, ladies in oval panels, Chas Field, Haviland, 5½" **295.00**
Vase, lady's portrait reserve on turq lustre, 13" **500.00**
Vase, mums, purple/wht/yel/red on gr & yel, T&V, 6x7" **225.00**
Whiskey jug, pk & red roses w/gold, sgn Roby, T&V, 6⅜" **195.00**

Lithophanes

Lithophanes are porcelain panels with relief designs of varying degrees of thickness and density. Transmitted light brings out the pattern in graduated shading, lighter where the procelain is thin and darker in the heavy areas. They were cast from wax models prepared by artists and depict views of life from the 1800s, religious themes, or scenes of historical significance. First made in Berlin about 1803, they were used as lampshade panels, window plaques, or candle shields. Later steins, mugs, and cups were made with lithophanes in their bases. Japanese wares were sometimes made with dragons or geisha lithophanes. Our advisor for this category is Lucille Malitz; she is listed in the Directory under New York. See also Dragon Ware; Steins.

Candle holder, people/landscapes in 4 panels, brass mts, 9x6" **400.00**
Candle holder, 3 pastoral scenes, circular shape, 3½" **300.00**
Candle lamp, girl & dog by mtns, mk PPM #1198, 10x8" **500.00**
Lamp, oil; mountain landscape 4x5" shade, brass mts **400.00**
Lamp, open-top 13" dome shade w/3 panels, genre scenes **765.00**
Panel, girl carries child & leads lamp, sgn, KPM, 4¾x5" **200.00**
Panel, man talks to lady on bridge, brass, mk, Fr, 4x4½" **175.00**
Shade, 5-panel, scenics, mother/child/etc, 7x9½" dia **500.00**
Stein, couple dancing, deer transfer, ½-liter **150.00**
Stein, monk w/lady, nun figural, pewter mts, ½-liter, 7¼" **345.00**
Tea warmer, 4 mc scenic panels, ea 2¼x3", plated fr, 6" **450.00**
Tile, interior scene w/figs, KPM, 6x4½" **300.00**
Tile, tired shopkeeper, KPM, 6x4½", pr **400.00**

Little Red Riding Hood

Though usually thought of as a product of the Hull Pottery Com-

pany, research has shown that a major part of this line was actually made by Regal China. The idea for this popular line of novelties and kitchenware items was developed and patented by Hull, but records show that to a large extent Hull sent their whiteware to Regal to be decorated. Little Red Riding Hood was produced from 1943 until 1957. Values have risen sharply over the past several months. For further information we recommend *Collecting Hull Pottery's Red Riding Hood* by Mark Supnick. Watch for the announcement of another book on this subject by Joyce and Fred Roerig, authors of *The Collector's Encyclopedia of Cookie Jars*.

Bank, standing **635.00**
Butter dish **385.00**
Canister, salt **1,100.00**
Canister, sugar, flour, or coffee; ea **650.00**
Chocolate mug, blank **1,450.00**
Chocolate mug, decor **2,000.00**
Cookie jar, closed basket, minimum value **350.00**
Cookie jar, cold pnt red shoes/apron/bottom trim, no decals **185.00**
Cookie jar, open basket, minimum value **300.00**
Cookie jar, poinsettia **925.00**
Cookie jar, red trim **825.00**
Cookie jar, star apron, open basket **335.00**
Cracker jar, skirt held wide, 8½" **545.00**
Creamer, pour through head **275.00**
Creamer & sugar bowl, side pour **300.00**
Creamer & sugar bowl, tab hdls, crawling **495.00**
Lid, for sugar bowl **225.00**
Match holder, wall hanging **800.00**
Mustard jar, w/spoon **375.00**
Pitcher, batter **475.00**
Pitcher, milk; standing, 8" **265.00**
Shakers, rare, 4½", pr **850.00**
Shakers, 5½", pr **150.00**
String holder **2,950.00**
Teapot **350.00**
Wall pocket **475.00**
Wolf jar, red **1,200.00**
Wolf jar, yel **950.00**

Liverpool

In the late 1700s Liverpool potters produced a creamy ivory ware, sometimes called Queen's Ware, which they decorated by means of the newly perfected transfer print. Made specifically for the American market, patriotic inscriptions, political portraits, or other States themes were applied in black with colors sometimes added by hand. (Obviously their loyalty to the crown did not inhibit the progress of business!) Before it lost favor in about 1825, other English potters made a similar product. Today Liverpool is a generic term used to refer to all ware of this type. Our advisor for this category is Richard Marden; he is listed in the Directory under New Hampshire.

Jug, Amelia ship/flag, blk w/mc pnt, 10" **4,950.00**
Jug, Defence of Stonington CT/Eagle, blk, 10", EX **7,200.00**
Jug, eagle/shield/stars/wreath, blk, 9", EX **550.00**
Jug, Gallant Defense of Stonington Aug 9, 1814, 10⅜" **6,250.00**
Jug, Independence/Washington/etc, blk, 8" **1,650.00**
Jug, Plan of City of WA/Peace, Plenty..., blk, 1790s, 9⅛" **2,860.00**
Jug, Proscribed Heroes/Militia, blk w/mc pnt, 8¼", EX **3,850.00**
Jug, ship Majestic/Am flags/eagle crest, mc & gold, 1800s, 9" .**9,000.00**
Jug, ship/British flag/Susan's Farewell, blk, 9¼" **1,500.00**
Jug, Success to Trade/Am flag/ship/etc, w/gold, 8½" **7,700.00**

Jug, cartoon of cow pulled by Bunopart (sic) and John Bull being milked by Jefferson, back: American ship, black transfer with gilt border and initials 8", $8,500.00.

Jug, The Farmer's Arms/Am flag/etc, mc/gold, 8", EX 2,650.00
Jug, United We Stand.../eagle, blk w/mc pnt, 11½" 5,225.00
Jug, US Ship w/female figurehead, blk, 8¼" 1,750.00
Mug, Independence, flake, 5⅞" 1,550.00
Pitcher, milk; Weaver's Army...Truth w/Trust, 1800s, 6¾" 300.00
Plaque, Geo Washington portrait medallion, blk, 5x4" 1,980.00

Lladro

Lladro porcelains are currently being produced in Labernes Blanques, Spain. Their retired and limited edition figurines are popular collectibles on the secondary market.

All Aboard 150.00
Angel, Chinese, #4536 ....60.00
Angel w/Child, #34635 ....62.50
Can I Play 295.00
Clown w/Concertina, #1027 ....430.00
Coy, #5011 ....85.00
Dress Rehearsal, #5497 ....240.00
Elephant w/Calf, on base 250.00
Elizabeth, #5645 ....138.00
Fine Melody, #5585 ....175.00
Flower Song 400.00
Girl w/Cats, #1309 ....190.00
Girl w/Lamb, #1010 ....110.00
Girl w/Puppies in Basket, #1311 ....210.00
Girl w/Toy Wagon, #5044 ....140.00
Heavenly Chimes, #5732 ....75.00
Joy in a Basket, #5595 ....170.00
My Best Friend, #5401 ....155.00
My Buddy 320.00
Nativity Scene, impressed mk, 8½x5½" 155.00
New Playmates, #5456 ....132.00
Pierrot w/Concertina, #5279 ....105.00
School Days 375.00
Storytime, #5229 ....550.00
Sweet Dreams, #1535 ....130.00
Valencian Boy, #5395 ....320.00
Wedding, #4808 ....125.00

Lobmeyer

J. and L. Lobmeyer, contemporaries of Moser, worked in Vienna, Austria, during the last quadrant of the 1800s. Most of the work attributed to them is decorated with distinctive enameling; favored motifs are people in 18th-century garb.

Bowl, cobalt w/mc horses/nudes, 2 portraits ea side, ftd, 8" 500.00

Bowl, 18th-C people, fluted, oval, 5" L, +oval underplate 350.00
Tumbler, gold scrolls/mc beading, ftd, 5¼" 500.00

Locke Art

Joseph Locke already had proven himself many times over as a master glass maker, working in leading English glasshouses for more than seventeen years. He came to America where he joined the New England Glass Company. There he invented processes for the manufacture of several types of art glass — amberina, peachblow, pomona, and agata among them. In 1898 he established the Locke Art Glassware Co. in Mt. Oliver, Pittsburgh, Pennsylvania. Locke Art Glass was produced using an acid-etching process by which the most delicate designs were executed on crystal blanks. Most examples are signed simply 'Locke Art,' often placed unobtrusively near a leaf or a stem. Other items are signed 'Jo Locke,' some are dated, and some are unsigned. Most of the work was done by hand. The business continued into the 1920s. For further study we recommend *Locke Art Glass, Guide for Collectors*, by Joseph and Janet Locke, available at your local bookstore.

Bowl, Poppy, 2½x4½" 85.00
Pitcher, grapes/lines etching, waisted, 8½" 350.00
Sherbet, grapes/lines etching, 3½" 75.00
Vase, camphor frost w/stork in rushes, 6" 150.00
Vase, floral eng, ogee sides, flared rim, sgn, 8" 250.00
Vase, stork in rushes, amberina/milk glass/frosted camphor, 6" ...175.00
Wine, grape/lines etching, 4½" 75.00
Wine, grape etching, sgn, 5½", set of 4 ....275.00

Locks

The earliest type of lock in recorded history was the wooden cross bar used by ancient Egyptians and their contemporaries. The early Romans are credited with making the first key-operated mechanical lock. The ward lock was invented during the Middle Ages by the Etruscans of Northern Italy; the lever tumbler and combination locks followed at various stages of history with varying degrees of effectiveness. In the 18th century the first precision lock was constructed. It was a device that utilized a lever-tumbler mechanism. Two of the best-known of the early 19th-century American lock manufacturers are Yale and Sargent, and today's collectors value Winchester and Keen Kutter locks very highly. Factors to consider are rarity, condition, and construction. Brass and bronze locks are generally priced higher than those of steel or iron. Our advisor for this section is Joe Tanner; he is listed in the Directory under Washington.

Key:
bbl — barrel   st — stamped

Brass Lever Tumbler

Winchester stamped front and back, 2" wide, $125.00.

Ames Sword Co, Perfection stamped on shackle, 2¾" 60.00
Bingham's Best Brand, BBB emb on front, 3¼" 150.00
Cleveland 4 Way, Cleveland 4 Way emb on front, 3⅝" 90.00
Crusader, shield, swords emb on body, 2¾" 45.00
Eagle Lock Co, word Eagle emb on front, scrolled, 3" 60.00
Jackson's, stamped Jackson's on front, 2½" 20.00
Keen Kutter, shape of KK emblem, KK emb on front, 4¾" 125.00
Mercury, Mercury emb on body, 2¾" 75.00
Motor, Motor emb on body, 3¼" 35.00
Our Very Best, OVB emb on body, 2⅞" 150.00
Roeyonoc, Roeyonoc stamped on body, 3¼" 30.00
Romer & Co, Romer & Co stamped on dust cover, 3" 55.00
Ruby, Ruby emb in scroll on front, 2¾" 20.00
Safe, Safe emb in scroll on front, 2⅜" 20.00
Siberian, Siberian emb on shackle, 2½" 110.00
Sphinx, sphinx & pharaoh head emb on front, 2¾" 35.00
W Bohannan & Co, SW emb in scroll on front, 2⅜" 30.00
Winchester, Winchester emb on front, 3" 160.00

Combinations

Chicago Combination Lock Co, stamped on front, brass, 2¾" 60.00
Corbin Sesamee 4-Dial Brass Lock, stamped Sesamee, 2¾" 12.00
Edwards Mfg Co No-Key, stamped on lock, brass, 2¾" 60.00
Junkunc Bros Mfrs, all stamped on bk, brass, 1⅞" 25.00
Karco stamped on body, 2½" 50.00
Number or letter disk type (4 disks), brass, 2¾" 130.00
Sq lock case of steel, stamped Pat Germany, 4-wheel, 3¼" 110.00
Sutton Lock Co stamped on body, 3" 200.00
Your Own stamped on body, 3⅞" 325.00

Eight-Lever Type

Armory, brass, Armory 8-Lever stamped on front 25.00
Electric, steel, Electric stamped on front 25.00
Goliath, steel, Goliath 8-Lever stamped on front 20.00
Miller, steel, Miller 8-Lever stamped on front 18.00
Samson, brass, 8-Lever stamped on front 18.00

Iron Lever Tumbler

Beta, 2⅞", $15.00.

Bull, word Bull emb on front, 2⅝" 30.00
Bulldog, word Bulldog & face of dog emb on front, 2¾" 30.00
Dan Patch, Dan Patch emb on front, horseshoe on bk, 2¾" 130.00
Dragon, word Dragon & dragon emb on front, 2⅞" 25.00
Eagle, word Eagle emb on body, 4⅜" 40.00
Indian Head, Indian head emb on front, 3" 90.00
Jupiter, word Jupiter/star & moon emb on front, 3¼" 18.00
Karo, word Karo emb on front, CI, 3⅛" 25.00
King Korn, words King Korn emb on body, 2⅞" 40.00

Nineteen O Three, 1903 emb on front, iron, 3⅞" 90.00
Red Chief, words Red Chief emb on body, 3¾" 80.00
Rugby, football emb on body, 3" 20.00
Unique, word Unique emb on front, 3¼" 120.00
Yale & Towne, lion face emb on front, shackle mk Y&T, 3" 110.00

Lever Push Key

Champion, emb Champion 6-Lever, brass push-key type, 2¼" 25.00
Climax, emb Climax 6-Lever, iron push-key type, 2¼" 35.00
Columbia, emb Columbia 6-Lever, brass push-key type, 2¼" 35.00
Dash, emb Dash 6-Lever, iron push-key type, 2¼" 25.00
Excelsior, emb Excelsior 6-Lever, brass push-key type, 2¼" 25.00
Harvard, emb Harvard 4-Lever, brass push-key type, 2" 50.00
IXL, emb IXL on body, 2¼" 75.00
Keystone, emb Keystone 6-Lever, brass push-key type, 2¼" 40.00
McIntosh, emb McIntosh on body, 2¼" 90.00
SB Co, emb SB Co on body, 3¼" 60.00
Smith & Egge Mfg Co, Smith & Egge stamped on front, 3" 75.00
Ten Star, emb Ten Star 6-Lever, 2¼" 45.00

Logo — Special Made

Brass pancake push key emb US Internal Revenue, 2¼" 185.00
Heart-shape brass lever type emb Shults Co, bbl key, 2¾" 55.00
Heart-shape brass lever type st Board Education, bbl key, 3½" 60.00
Sq brass pin-tumbler case st Regd US Mail, int counter, 2¾" 140.00
Sq Yale-type brass pin tumbler, emb w/Texaco & star, 3" 25.00
Sq Yale-type brass pin tumbler, st Shell Oil Co on body, 3⅛" 20.00
Sq Yale-type brass pin tumbler, st US/A/tree/Forest Svc, 2⅞" 125.00

Pin-Tumbler Type

Corbin, brass, Corbin in oval stamped on body, 3⅝" 25.00
Eagle, brass, Eagle stamped on body, 2⅞" 20.00
Fulton, emb Fulton on body, 2⅝" 30.00
Hope, brass, emb Hope on body, 2½" 16.00
Il-A-Noy, emb Il-A-Noy on body, 2½" 40.00
Pearl, brass, emb Pearl on body, 2⅛" 16.00
Sargent, brass, emb Sargent on body, 3" 15.00
Segal, iron, emb Segal on shackle, 3¾" 40.00
Shapleigh, emb Shapleigh on body, 2⅝" 40.00
Yale, brass, emb Yale on body, Made in England on shackle, 3" ... 40.00
Yale, brass, emb Yale on body, Yale & Towne on shackle, 2⅝" 25.00

Scandinavian (Jail House) Type

JHW Climax Co, iron, 2⅞" 50.00
Star, emb line on bottom, iron, 3¾" 100.00
Star, iron, 2½" 70.00
99 Miller, emb 99, brass, 1¾" 80.00
999 Miller, emb 999, brass, 2½" 70.00

Six-Lever Type

Eagle, brass, Eagle 6-Lever stamped on body 15.00
Edwards, iron, Edwards stamped on body 15.00
Safe, brass, Safe stamped on body 18.00
Yale, brass, Yale emb on front 12.00

Story and Commemorative

AYPEX Seattle (Alaska Yukon Pacific Expo), emb tin/iron, 3" 225.00

Canteen, US emb on lock, lock: canteen shape, 2" 500.00
CI, emb ornate scroll motif throughout body of lock, 3½" 170.00
CI, emb skull/X-bones w/florals, NH Co on bk, 3¼" 200.00
CQD/sinking ship Titanic & SOS waves emb on brass, 2¾" 120.00
Eagle/stars/shield & stars, emb CI, Eagle Liberty, 2½" 300.00
Mail Pouch, emb on lock, lock in shape of a mail pouch, 3⅛" 225.00
1901 Pan Am Expo, brass, emb w/buffalo, 2⅝" 175.00

Warded Type

Army, iron pancake ward key, emb letters, 2½" 35.00
Globe, iron sq lock case, emb US on bk, 2⅜" 20.00
Hex, iron, sq lock case, emb US on bk, 2⅛" 95.00
Navy, iron pancake ward key, bk: scrolled emb letters, 2½" 35.00
Red Cross, brass sq case, emb letters, 2" 10.00
Rex, steel case, emb letters, 2⅝" 18.00
Safe, brass sq case, emb letters, 1⅞" 8.00
Safety First, brass pancake type, emb letters, 2¾" 15.00
Secure, iron pancake type, emb letters, 2⅝" 20.00
Sprocket, brass oval shape, emb letters, 2⅛" 50.00
Try Me, iron pancake type, emb letters, 2½" 25.00
Winchester, brass sq case, stamped letters, 2¾" 125.00

Wrought Iron Lever Type (Smokehouse Type)

DM&Co, bbl key, 4¼" 15.00
MW&Co, bbl key, 2⅝" 10.00
MW&Co, flat key, 3½" 20.00
S&Co, bbl key, 3" 8.00

Loetz

The Loetz Glassworks was established in Klostermule, Austria, in 1840. After Loetz's death the firm was purchased by his grandson, Johann Loetz Witwe. Until WWII the operation continued to produce fine artware, some of which made in the early 1900s bears a striking resemblance to Tiffany's, with whom Loetz was associated at one time. In addition to the iridescent Tiffany-style glass, he also produced threaded glass and some cameo. Our advisor for this category is Don Williams; he is listed in the Directory under Missouri.

Key:
att — attributed   o/l — overlay

Tazza, pale blue jade bowl with ribbed exterior on blue crackled iridescent turtle, applied blue drippings where joined, 5½x9", $1,450.00.

Biscuit jar, emerald w/gr embedded threads, silver mts, 7" 125.00
Bowl, centerpc; amber w/rainbow irid, Invt T'print, 5x11½" 675.00
Bowl, crystal w/rainbow lustre, gr threading, ribbed, 5x7" 250.00
Bowl, gold w/web pattern, dimpled, att, 2½x3" 95.00
Bowl, gr w/bl oil spots, folded/ruffled rim, 5x7" 650.00

Bowl, orange w/ruffled rim, in leaf-shape bl irid base, 6" 1,150.00
Bowl, silver o/l iris ea side, amber, ruffled, 4x5" 950.00
Bride's bowl, red & gr irid w/oil spots, 10½" 650.00
Chalice, yel w/bl oil spots, sq rim, 8" 600.00
Decanter, silver o/l scrolls on cobalt, bottle form, 11" 2,400.00
Ewer, frost w/pastel mums & gold floral band, 3-spout, 14" 1,500.00
Inkwell, gr irid w/drapes, brass lid w/bird finial 250.00
Inkwell, red irid, rtcl shoulder trim, metal lid, 2½x3¾" 425.00
Loving cup, gr w/threading, 3 prong hdls, brass rim, 5½" 150.00
Pitcher, gr irid, vertical 'branches,' rainbow hdl, 6" 200.00
Shell, nautilus shape, gold w/oil spots, 5½" 1,265.00
Smoke bell, opal irid w/yel & bl threads, metal cap, 5" 175.00
Tumbler, red irid w/amber flowing drips, reverse swirl, 4" 275.00
Vase, amber irid, lotus/pod metal mt, floral tripod ft, 11" 325.00
Vase, amber/yel w/int gr bars, fused gr speckles, 7" 400.00
Vase, amber/yel w/int red lines & fused red speckles, 10" 500.00
Vase, aqua & orange w/red feathers, orange int, 8x6" 3,250.00
Vase, bl irid w/oil spots, squatty w/distended neck, 7½" 900.00
Vase, bl texture on cobalt, ribbed/ruffled, 9¾" 675.00
Vase, bl w/gold irid oil spots, gourd shape, 5" 650.00
Vase, bl w/gr irid oil spots, 3-lobe top, 4x7" 750.00
Vase, blk, pinched sides, ribbed, 8½" 300.00
Vase, cobalt irid w/gold ribbons, squatty, 4" 350.00
Vase, dk amethyst, modernistic copper o/l, 10" 250.00
Vase, dk bl w/purple irid, Papillon, pinched sides, 3x3½" 550.00
Vase, dk bl w/turq irid crackle, 3 horn hdls, can neck, 8" 800.00
Vase, emerald irid w/bl vines, pulled scalloped rim, 4" 150.00
Vase, emerald w/ silver-bl oil spots, triple gourd, 9½" 600.00
Vase, gold, 'tree stump' w/holes on sides, scalloped, 10" 900.00
Vase, gold w/bl irid butterfly-wing mottling, 11x5" 750.00
Vase, gold w/raindrops, pinched, 5½" 250.00
Vase, gr irid, fan form w/7 necks atop inverted cone, 8" 300.00
Vase, gr irid, melon ribbed, att, 9½" 135.00
Vase, gr w/irid bl dimpled surface, 3½" 110.00
Vase, gr w/oil spots, wine threads, in sgn bronze hdld fr, 6" 400.00
Vase, jack-in-pulpit; amber irid w/bl spots, dimpled, 9" 700.00
Vase, lt gr irid frost w/bl striped long-stem pods, 10" 400.00
Vase, lt gr irid w/turq waves, 3-lobe w/pinched sides, 9" 550.00
Vase, pk irid, ribbed flower form w/tooled petal top, 9" 400.00
Vase, purple/bl irid, relief swirls, bulbous base, 10" 300.00
Vase, red w/pulled feathers, onion form, 10½" 1,500.00
Vase, red w/purple irid, lt gold floral tracery, 5½" 165.00
Vase, red-bronze w/purple & bl highlights, EX quality, 10" 1,250.00
Vase, ruby to lime w/invt spots, pulled/folded rim, 5" 300.00
Vase, ruby w/bl irid feathers, cylindrical, well mkd, 12" 1,500.00
Vase, salmon/dk bl w/3-color irid spots, wide ogee form, 7½" ..3,250.00
Vase, silver iris o/l, bl/salmon w/irid spots, slim, 6" 2,600.00
Vase, silver o/l dogwood & long stems on amber irid, 8" 1,500.00
Vase, silver o/l feathers on rainbow irid, 7¼" 1,500.00
Vase, silver o/l floral on bl, classic form, 4¼" 750.00
Vase, silver o/l floral on cobalt irid, cylindrical, 8" 1,350.00
Vase, silver o/l floral on peacock bl irid w/raindrops, 11" 2,450.00
Vase, silver o/l Nouveau swirls on amber w/irid swirls, 6" 1,700.00
Vase, silver o/l on lt gr w/irid swirls & raindrops, 7x5" 800.00
Vase, yel irid w/amber & opal loops, ruffled dbl gourd, 9½" 450.00
Vase, yel-gr w/gr feathers, flat top, 7¾x8" 1,900.00

Lomonosov Porcelain

Founded in Leningrad in 1744, the Lomonosov porcelain factory produced exquisite porcelain miniatures for the Czar and other Russian nobility. One of the first factories of its kind, Lomonosov pieces consisted largely of vases and delicate sculptures. In the 1800s Lomonosov became closely involved with the Russian Academy of Fine Arts, a connection which has continued to this day as the company continues to supply the world with these fine artistic treasures. In 1992 the backstamp was changed to read 'Made in Russia,' instead of 'Made in USSR.'

Bear, standing	16.00
Cat	37.50
Doe	95.00
Donkey, recumbent	18.50
Ermine, standing, #6432	25.00
Gazelle	10.00
Kazarka, #2157	30.00
Leopard cub	17.50
Moose	100.00
Otter	38.50
Raccoon, sitting, #6503	16.00
Raccoon, standing	12.50
Seal	18.50
Snowbird	12.00
Squirrel, #7404, mini	5.00
Terrier	25.00
Tiger cub, mini	14.00
Wild cat	42.50
Yakut woman w/fish	65.00
Young elk, #6111	82.50

Longwy

The Longwy workshops were founded in 1798 and continue today to produce pottery in the north of France near the Luxembourg-Belgian border under the name 'Societe des Faienceries de Lonswy et Senelle.' The ware for which they are best known was produced during the Art Deco period, decorated in bold colors and designs. Earlier wares made during the first quarter of the 19th century reflected the popularity of Oriental art, cloisonne enamels in particular. The designs were executed by impressing the pattern into the moist clay and filling in the depressions with enamels. Examples are marked 'Longwy,' either impressed or painted under glaze. Our advisor for this category is Wayne Kielsmeier; he is listed in the Directory under Arizona.

Bowl, bird, 7"	165.00
Box, floral, cvd/pnt, mc on wht & pk crackle, 6-sided, 7"	375.00
Charger, still life, Primavera, sgn Olesiwieg, 15"	1,200.00
Charger, 2 nudes, 1 blk/1 wht, in wine/bl landscape, 14½"	1,650.00
Plaque, Limoges-style floral w/gold on bl, sgn, 17" dia	875.00
Tea set, Deco floral, mc on wht, 3-pc+rpr 14" tray, 2 c/s	650.00
Tile, Deco lady/trees, Primavera, 8", NM	260.00
Trivet, sparrow on floral branch, metal fr, early mk, 6½"	150.00
Vase, Chinese style mc floral on bl, baluster, 6½x3", pr	225.00

Vases, exotic birds on cylindrical forms mounted on bases modeled as elephants, signed, #1035, 10½", $600.00 for the pair.

Vase, floral, cylinder on metal mt, 11"	295.00
Vase, shaped floral band at width of bell form, #5134, 13"	1,100.00

Lonsanti

Mary Louise McLaughlin, who had previously experimented in trying to reproduce Haviland faience in the 1870s and 'American faience' (a method of inlaying color by painting inside of the mold before the vessel was cast) in the mid-1890s, developed a type of hard-paste porcelain in which the glaze and the body fused together in a single firing. Her efforts met with success in 1900, and she immediately concentrated on glazing and decorating techniques. The ware she perfected was called Lonsanti, most of which was decorated with Nouveau florals, either carved or modeled. By 1906 she had abandoned her efforts. Examples are marked with several ciphers, one resembling a butterfly, another with the letters MCL superimposed each upon the other, and L McL in a linear arrangement. Other items were marked Lonsanti, sometimes in the Oriental manner.

Vase, ferns cvg, maroon on gr, bulbous, vertical mk, 5"	8,750.00
Vase, flowing gr/blk/red over wht, ML McLaughlin, 3"	1,400.00
Vase, mums cvg, pk & gr on taupe, sgn, 7½"	10,500.00

Lotton

Charles Lotton is a contemporary glass artist. He began blowing glass and developing original designs nearly thirty years ago. He now has work on display in many major glass museums and collections, among them the Smithsonian, the Art Institute of Chicago, the Museum of Glass, and the Chrysler Museum. He has become famous for his unique lamps. Each piece is signed and dated. His three sons, David, Daniel, and John, each work in their own studios. All four artists produce distinctive work. They sell their glass at antique shows and in their showroom in Lansing, Illinois. For further information read *Lotton Art Glass* by Charles Lotton and Tom O'Conner; see the Directory under Illinois.

Bottle, scent; pk pulled feathers, sgn Daniel, 1991, 6½"	225.00
Bowl, hooked feathers, dk bl/blk irid on opal, bl int, 8"	600.00
Bowl, irid texture, gr-gold pods & entwined vines, globular, 6"	400.00
Bowl, irid w/bl-gold irid split leaves on stems, 5x8"	700.00
Bowl, pulled feathers, gr on Prussian bl, 4¾"	365.00
Bowl, split leaves & vines, gr & blk on cranberry, 7¾x9"	850.00
Bowl, tangerine w/bl pulled feathers, 5½x8½"	900.00
Lamp, Multi-Flora, pk, 24"	3,400.00
Paperweight, azaleas & vines, gold/bl veiled core, 6x8"	1,750.00
Vase, bl textured irid w/bl lava rim, oviform, 6"	550.00
Vase, cranberry & opal leaves on blk stems, waisted, 6"	550.00
Vase, emerald gr w/mc leaves at shoulder, waisted neck, 5"	195.00
Vase, ferns, pk on bl, sgn Daniel, 1991, 6¾"	280.00
Vase, Gold Aurene w/pulled bl irid plumes, oviform, 7½"	375.00
Vase, gray-gr & opal leaves on frosted irid, waisted, 7"	550.00
Vase, hooked feathers on opal, red int, ovoid, 8"	800.00
Vase, jack-in-pulpit; Mandarin red, bl pulls on stem, '77, 12"	1,000.00
Vase, leaves & vines, pk on cobalt, bulbous, 5¼"	200.00
Vase, leaves & vines, pk/opal/gr on rose mottle, 9"	450.00
Vase, leaves & vines, silver & wht irid on red, 1991, 10"	700.00
Vase, leaves & vines on mottled cranberry & cobalt, 9¾"	550.00
Vase, Multi-Flora, emerald gr w/pk & bl flowers, '76, 5"	550.00
Vase, Multi-Flora, pk on verre-de-soie, ovoid, 10"	750.00
Vase, Multi-Flora, pk w/bl irid split leaves, bulbous, 8"	475.00

Vase, Multi-Flora, rose mottle, 4½" **500.00**
Vase, neodymium leaves & vines, cased, flared U-form, 8½" **400.00**
Vase, orange, opal & autumn gr leaves w/ruby vines, 8½" **450.00**
Vase, peacock feathers on cobalt, elongated, 9" **800.00**
Vase, peacock feathers on dk bl, cylinder w/top bulge, 12" **1,100.00**
Vase, red irid lava w/appl bl-gold irregular motif, 6½" **500.00**
Vase, split leaves & vines on cobalt, bulbous lip, 12" **750.00**
Vase, split leaves on gr irid, elongated, 10½" **600.00**
Vase, turq mottled Cypriot w/gold lava, cylindrical, 6" **375.00**
Vase, upright leaves, gold-bl irid on selenium red, 9" **650.00**
Vase, verre-de-soie, bl-gold drapes, ridged neck, 7½" **200.00**
Vase, webbing, lav-bl irid on ruby, ovoid, 8" **350.00**
Water sprinkler, Mandarin red w/bl feathers, '79, 12" **800.00**

Lotus Ware

Isaac Knowles and Issac Harvey operated a pottery in East Liverpool, Ohio, in 1853 where they produced both yellow ware and Rockingham. In 1870 Knowles brought Harvey's interests and took as partners John Taylor and Homer Knowles. Their principal product was ironstone china, but Knowles was confident that American potters could produce as fine a ware as the Europeans. To prove his point, he hired Joshua Poole, an artist from the Belleek Works in Ireland. Poole quickly perfected a Belleek-type china, but fire destroyed this portion of the company. Before it could function again, their hotel china business had grown to the point that it required their full attention in order to meet market demands. By 1891 they were able to try again. They developed a bone china, as fine and thin as before, which they called Lotus. Henry Schmidt from the Meissen factory in Germany decorated the ware, often with lacy filigree applications or hand-formed leaves and flowers to which he added further decoration with liquid slip applied by means of a squeeze bag. Due to high production costs resulting from so much of the fragile ware being damaged in firing and because of changes in tastes and styles of decoration, the Lotus Ware line was dropped in 1896. Some of the early ware was marked 'KT&K China'; later marks have a star and a crescent with 'Lotus Ware' added. Our advisor for this category is Mary Frank Gaston. She is listed in the Directory under Texas.

Bonbon, leaf-molded base & lid, appl pk bud & stem, 7x6" **3,400.00**
Bowl, floral branches, rtcl ovals, scalloped/beaded rim, 6" **200.00**
Bowl, 2 rtcl aqua medallions, mc roses, beaded oval rim, 4x6" ...**450.00**
Chocolate pot, gold floral/pods, lattice base, leaf hdl, 9" **300.00**
Cracker jar, fishnet/swirl, HP honeysuckles/gold leaves **250.00**
Cracker jar, paneled w/allover HP berries/flowers, 6½" **850.00**
Creamer, fishnet, bamboo hdl, 3¾" **160.00**
Cup, demi; lotus form, thorn hdl, on pod underplate, no mk **100.00**
Ewer, rtcl, melon ribs, beaded slim neck, 10" **1,850.00**
Jardiniere, 4 rtcl bosses, emb florals, wht, 4" **3,500.00**
Letter holder, multi-branch coral w/shell bk, leaf support **400.00**
Perfume, disk shape w/rtcl scrolls, 2-ftd, twig hdl, 3½" **300.00**
Pitcher, HP lilacs/gilt, gr bamboo hdl, squatty, 5½" **200.00**
Pitcher, lady w/harp & angel, pk/gr on spout, gold hdl, 5½" **275.00**
Pitcher, leaf texture, knotted bamboo hdl, squatty, 4" **175.00**
Pitcher, netting, bl/yel flowers, gold rim, bamboo hdl, 3½" **200.00**
Potpourri, HP violets, lg rtcl/mc-decor hdls & lid, ftd, 8" **800.00**
Potpourri, rtcl melon ribs w/mc decor, rtcl lid, ftd, 7½" **1,100.00**
Rose bowl, sm berries/leafy vines, cut-out leaf rim, ftd, 4" **400.00**
Rose jar, rtcl melon ribs, 6½x6½" **850.00**
Rose jar, 2 rtcl ovals, dbl-bead rim, rtcl lid, 4½" **550.00**
Rose jar, 4 rtcl ovals, bead/jewel swags, ftd egg form, 5½" **600.00**
Vase, pastel rtcl ribs, HP/gold-bead florals, ftd U-form, 8" **750.00**
Vase, 2 rtcl ovals, beaded florals, ftd/scroll hdls, 9½" **1,250.00**

Vase, 3 panels: gold net on bl, mc florals, 3 ball ft, 8x5" **550.00**

Lu Ray Pastels

Lu Ray Pastels dinnerware was introduced in the early 1940s by Taylor, Smith, and Taylor of East Liverpool, Ohio. It was offered in assorted colors of Persian Cream, Sharon Pink, Surf Green, Windsor Blue, and Gray in complete place settings as well as many service pieces. It was a successful line in its day and is once again finding favor with collectors of American dinnerware.

Demitasse set (ovoid sides): Pot, $95.00; Sugar bowl and creamer, $46.00; Cup and saucer, $18.00.

Bowl, cream soup **24.00**
Bowl, fruit; 5½" **4.50**
Bowl, mixing; lg **75.00**
Bowl, salad; lg **40.00**
Bowl, soup; 8" **12.50**
Bowl, tab hdl, 6" **13.50**
Bowl, vegetable; oval **15.00**
Bowl, vegetable; 9" **10.00**
Bowl, 36s **30.00**
Butter dish, w/lid, ¼-lb **25.00**
Casserole, w/lid **60.00**
Coffeepot, demi; ovoid, w/lid **95.00**
Coffeepot, demi; str sides, w/lid **150.00**
Creamer **5.00**
Creamer, demi; ovoid **22.00**
Creamer, demi; str sides **40.00**
Cup & saucer **7.50**
Cup & saucer, demi **18.00**
Cup & saucer, demi; str sides **25.00**
Egg cup **12.00**
Egg cup, Chatham Gray, rare color **15.00**
Epergne **95.00**
Muffin cover, w/8" underplate **80.00**
Nut dish **35.00**
Pitcher, bulbous w/flat bottom **40.00**
Pitcher, ftd **45.00**
Pitcher, juice; ovoid **110.00**
Pitcher, syrup **40.00**
Plate, cake **25.00**
Plate, Chatham Gray, rare color, 7" **10.00**
Plate, chop; 14" **27.50**
Plate, divided **25.00**
Plate, grill **15.00**
Plate, serving; tab hdl **25.00**

Plate, very rare, 8" 15.00
Plate, 10" 12.50
Plate, 6" 2.00
Plate, 7" 6.00
Plate, 9" 7.50
Platter, #1040, 9½" 8.00
Platter, oval, 11½" 10.00
Platter, oval, 12" 9.00
Platter, oval, 13" 10.00
Relish, 4-part 60.00
Sauce boat, fast-stand 17.50
Sauce pitcher 22.50
Saucer, cream soup 12.50
Shakers, pr 10.00
Sugar bowl, demi; ovoid, w/lid 24.00
Sugar bowl, demi; str sides, w/lid 40.00
Sugar bowl, w/lid 9.00
Teapot, w/lid, curved spout 40.00
Teapot, w/lid, flat-top spout 45.00
Tidbit, 2-tier 30.00
Tray, pickle 18.00
Tumbler, juice 22.50
Tumbler, water 45.00
Vase, bud; 2 styles, ea 175.00

Lunch Boxes

    Early 20th-century tobacco companies such as Union Leader, Tiger, and Dixie sold their products in square, steel containers with flat, metal carrying handles. These were specifically engineered to be used as lunch boxes when they became empty. (See Advertising, specific companies.) By 1930 oval lunch pails with colorful lithographed decorations on tin were being manufactured to appeal directly to children. These were made by Ohio Art, Decoware, and a few other companies. In 1950 Aladdin Industries produced the first 'real' character lunch box — a Hopalong Cassidy decal-decorated steel container now considered the beginning of the kids' lunch box industry. The other big lunch box manufacturer, American Thermos (later King Seely Thermos Company) brought out its 'blockbuster' Roy Rogers box in 1953, the first fully lithographed steel lunch box and matching bottle. Other companies (ADCO Liberty; Landers, Frary & Clark; Ardee Industries; Okay Industries; Universal; Tindco; Cheinco) also produced character pails. Today's collectors often tend to specialize in those boxes dealing with a particular subject. Western, space, TV series, Disney movies, and cartoon characters are the most popular. There are well over five hundred different lunch boxes available to the astute collector. These publications are of interest to lunch box collectors are a bimonthly newsletter, *The Pailentologist's Retort*, P.O. Box 3255, Burbank, CA 91508; *The Illustrated Encyclopedia of Metal Lunch Boxes* by Allen Woodall and Sean Brickell; and *A Pictorial Price Guide to Lunch Boxes and Thermoses* by Larry Aikins. Our advisor for this category is Allan Smith; he is listed in the Directory under Texas. In the following listings, lunch boxes are metal unless noted vinyl, and values include thermoses only when they are mentioned within the descriptions.

A-Team, w/thermos, 1985, NM 20.00
Annie, vinyl, w/thermos, 1982, EX 25.00
Archies, w/plastic thermos, Aladdin, 1969, VG 30.00
Barbie, vinyl, w/thermos, 1962, EX+ 130.00
Beany & Cecil, wht vinyl, 1962, VG 180.00
Berenstain Bears, w/thermos, American Thermos, 1983, EX 35.00
Bobby Soxer, vinyl, 1959, EX 600.00
Brady Bunch, w/thermos, 1970, EX 220.00

Brave Eagle, w/thermos, American Thermos, 1957, EX 350.00
Bullwinkle, vinyl, 1962, EX 300.00
Care Bears, w/thermos, 1983, NM 18.00
Charlie's Angels, w/thermos, Aladdin, 1978, EX 60.00
Chavo, w/thermos, 1979, NM 285.00
Chuck Wagon, w/thermos, American, 1958, EX 225.00
Civil War, plastic, 1961, EX 430.00
Cracker Jack, w/thermos, Aladdin, 1969, NM 70.00
Deputy Dawg, vinyl, 1961, EX 400.00

Disney Express, Aladdin, VG, $17.00.

Disney Magic Kingdom, w/thermos, 1980, NM 30.00
Donald Duck, tin litho, Cheinco, Disney, 1960, NM 120.00
Dr Suess, vinyl, w/thermos, 1970, EX 300.00
Emergency, metal dome, w/thermos, Aladdin, 1977, VG 50.00
Evil Knievel, w/thermos, 1974, EX 43.00
Flag-o-Rama, Universal, 1954, NM 800.00
Flipper, 1967, VG 45.00
GI Joe, w/thermos, King Seely, 1967, EX 170.00
Gigi, vinyl, w/thermos, 1962, EX+ 250.00
Gomer Pyle USMC, w/thermos, 1966, VG 100.00
Great Wild West, w/thermos, Universal, 1959, EX 700.00
Green Hornet, w/thermos, 1967, VG 150.00
Guns of Will Sonnet, VG 60.00
Gunsmoke, w/dbl LL's, w/thermos, Aladdin, 1959, EX+ 450.00
Happy Pow Wow, vinyl, 1970, EX 70.00
Highway Markers, 1972, VG 25.00
I Love a Parade, vinyl, 1970, EX 80.00
Jack & Jill, 1982, NM 450.00
James Bond, w/thermos, Aladdin, 1966, EX+ 260.00
Jetsons, metal dome, Aladdin, 1963, EX+ 850.00
Joe Palooka, tin litho, Ham Fisher, 1948, EX+ 100.00
Jr Nurse, vinyl, w/thermos, 1963, VG 110.00
King Kong, w/thermos, 1977, NM 75.00
Knight in Armor, NM 1,000.00
Kung Fu, w/thermos, 1974, EX 65.00
Linus the Lion Hearted, vinyl, w/thermos, 1965, EX 240.00
Little Dutch Miss, w/thermos, Universal, 1959, EX ...200.00
Lone Ranger, w/thermos, 1980, NM 45.00
Lone Ranger (bl band), Adco Liberty, 1954, VG 300.00
Man From UNCLE, w/thermos, King Seely, 1966, VG 190.00
Monkees, vinyl, w/thermos, 1967, EX 300.00
Monroes, w/thermos, 1967, VG 90.00
Moon Landing, vinyl, 1960, EX+ 200.00
Mork & Mindy, w/thermos, 1980, EX 25.00
NFL, w/thermos, Universal, 1962, VG+ 200.00
Partridge Family, w/thermos, 1971, M 100.00

Pele, w/thermos, King Seely, 1975, EX 100.00
Peter Pan, 1969, EX 75.00
Pigs in Space, w/thermos, M 40.00
Pink Panther, vinyl, w/thermos, 1980, NM 325.00
Pit Stop, Ohio Art, 1968, EX 280.00
Popeye, plastic, 3-D embossed, w/thermos, 1987, NM 25.00
Popeye, w/thermos, Universal, 1962, NM 600.00
Pro Sports, 1962, EX 65.00
Rambo, w/thermos, 1985, NM 18.00
Road Runner, w/thermos, 1970, EX 85.00
Robin Hood, w/thermos, Aladdin, 1965, EX 225.00
Robo Warriors, vinyl, 1970, EX+ 135.00
R2D2, vinyl, 1978, VG 200.00
Secret of Nimh, w/thermos, 1982, EX 25.00
Smokey Bear, vinyl, w/thermos, 1965, EX+ 325.00
Soupy Sales, vinyl, 1965, VG 120.00
Star Trek, dome, 1967, VG 300.00
Suburbanite Brunch Bag, vinyl, w/thermos, 1969, EX 70.00
Tammy, vinyl, w/thermos, 1984, NM 300.00
Tarzan, w/thermos, 1966, EX 150.00
Tom Corbett, space scenes, 1952, +thermos, EX 200.00
UFO, w/thermos, 1973, EX 90.00
Welcome Back Cotter, w/thermos, 1976, M 100.00
Westerner, vinyl, 1960, VG 175.00
Winnie the Pooh, w/thermos, 1967, EX+ 260.00
Yellow Submarine, w/thermos, King Seely, 1968, EX 395.00
Ziggy, vinyl, w/thermos, 1979, EX 150.00

Lutz

From 1869 to 1888, Nicholas Lutz worked for the Boston and Sandwich Glass Company where he produced the threaded and striped art glass that was popular during that era. His works were not marked, and since many other glassmakers of the day made similar wares, the term Lutz has come to refer not only to his original works but to any of this type.

Basket, pk threading, appl pk & clear tooled hdl, 6" 200.00
Bowl, Dmn Quilt, cranberry w/amber threads, ftd, 4x8" 200.00
Cup & saucer, bl/opal latticinio swirls 85.00
Finger bowl, opal threading w/gold mica, ftd/waisted, +plate 80.00
Finger bowl, pk/gold stripes, wht latticinio, baby-face hdls 165.00
Flask, red/wht/bl stripes, wht cased, 1870s, 8" 700.00
Tumbler, lemonade; cranberry threads, 2 appl berries 115.00
Wine, bl/wht opaque/clear swirl, att 130.00

Maddux of California

One of the California-made ceramics now so popular with collectors, Maddux was founded in the late 1930s and during the years that followed produced novelty items, TV lamps, figurines, planters, and tableware accessories. Our advisor for this category is Doris Frizzell; she is listed in the Directory under Illinois.

Ashtray, red or yel, metal caddy w/6 ind trays 20.00
Bull, red, head up/head down, #972 & #973, 11" L, pr 40.00
Cats, Deco style, blk matt, 12½", facing pr 45.00
Chinese pheasant, air-brushed colors, #912/#913, 11", pr 30.00
Cockatiel, 11" 25.00
Contempo bowl (set), wht satin, #1047, 16½" 15.00
Cookie jar, Humpty Dumpty, #2113 .... 500.00
Cookie jar, Raggedy Andy, #2108 .... 350.00
Doe, walnut, wht porc, tangerine, #907, 12½" 15.00

Ducklings, 3 on grassy base 20.00
Early Birds (pr), blk matt, tangerine, #969, 14½" 25.00

Flamingo line: double flamingo vase, 5", $40.00; single flamingo planter, 6", $40.00.

Flamingo, flying, natural, #970, 11" 45.00
Flamingo, winging, natural, #971, 12" 45.00
Green Pepper relish, #3275, w/lid 20.00
Horse head vase, aqua, #225, 12½" 18.00
Horse, prancing, #982 .... 20.00
Horses, rearing #925/charging #926, pr 20.00
Mallards, natural, #928 male/#929 female, 9½", pr 40.00
Planter, flamingo, pk, #515, 10½" 45.00
Planter, rearing horse, 10" 20.00
Rooster, #932, 10½" 30.00
Seashell bowl, wht, #3017 .... 15.00
Shell console bowl (set), pk, #1067, 16" 15.00
Stag, standing, natural colors, #924, 12½" 15.00
Swan console bowl (set), wht porc, #1019, 11½" 15.00
Swans (pr), blk matt, #923, 10½" 25.00
TV lamp, bassett hound, #896, 12½" 45.00
TV lamp, cockatiels (pr), #826 .... 50.00
TV lamp, Colonial ship, #892, 10½" 30.00
TV lamp, dbl deer, running, natural, #829, 10½" 35.00
TV lamp, head of Christ, 3-D planter, #841 .... 20.00
TV lamp, Malibu shell, Pearltone, #889, 10¼" 20.00
TV lamp, Mallard, flying, natural colors, #839 .... 30.00
TV lamp, mare & foal, wht porc, #897 .... 20.00
TV lamp, nativity scene, 3-D planter, #846, 12" 25.00
TV lamp, Persian Glory (horse head), #887, 11½" 20.00
TV lamp, prairie schooner (covered wagon), #844, 11" 40.00
TV lamp, stallion, prancing, on base, #810, 12" 30.00
TV lamp, swan planter, wht porc, #828, 12½" 20.00
TV lamp, Toro (bull), walnut, charging, #894, 11½" 20.00
TV lamp, Toro (bull), walnut, ft on mound, #859, 11½" 20.00
Vase, swan, wht, #221, 12" 20.00

Magazines

Magazines are collected for their cover prints and for the information pertaining to defunct companies and their products that can be gleaned from the old advertisements. See also Movie Memorabilia; Parrish, Maxfield.

Key:
 M — mint condition, in original wrapper
 EX — excellent condition, spine intact, edges of pages clean and straight
 VG — very good condition, the average as-found condition

Advertising Journal, 1922, April, VG 10.00

Air Tech, 1942, October, NM 15.00
Amazing Stories, 1930, July, EX 25.00
American Blacksmith, 1914, May, VG 12.00
American Heritage, 1954, December, 1st hardcover issue, VG 16.50
American Heritage, 1968, April, Mickey Mouse cover, VG 25.00
Atlantic, 1954, January, JFK as Senator cover, VG 15.00
Avant Garde, 1968, March, #2, Marilyn Monroe cover, NM 25.00
Bachelor, 1937, April, Vol 1, #1, VG 30.00
Baseball, 1937, Joe DiMaggio cover 30.00
Basketball, 1958, Wilt Chamberlain cover, EX 25.00
Collier's, 1905, September 23, Maxfield Parrish cover, VG 75.00
Collier's, 1912, May 18, Discovery of South Pole cover, VG 50.00
Collier's, 1912, May 4, Titanic article, VG 35.00
Cosmopolitan, 1899, September, Rose O'Neill illus, G+ 10.00
Cosmopolitan, 1952, November, Queen Elizabeth II cover, EX ...20.00
Cosmopolitan, 1953, May, Marilyn Monroe cover 25.00
Esquire, 1951, September, Marilyn Monroe fold-out, VG 25.00
Esquire, 1958, October, Silver Anniversary Issue, VG 15.00
Eye, 1951, April, Traffic in Souls, VG 10.00
Forms & Fantasies, 1898, May, Vol 1, #1, EX 17.00
Harper's Weekly, 1897, December 18, M Parrish cover, VG 175.00
Life, 1936, November, 30, West Point cadet cover, EX 27.50
Life, 1937, January 4, FD Roosevelt cover, EX 32.00
Life, 1938, August 22, F Astaire & G Rogers cover, VG 9.00
Life, 1938, July 11, Shirley Temple cover, EX 35.00
Life, 1938, May 23, Errol Flynn cover, VG 21.00
Life, 1939, May 29, Eleanor Roosevelt cover, EX 22.50
Life, 1943, January 25, Eddie Rickenbacker cover, EX 22.00
Life, 1952, April 7, Marilyn Monroe cover, EX 35.00
Life, 1959, November 9, Marilyn Monroe cover, EX 25.00
Life, 1964, August 28, Beatles cover, EX 20.00

Life, 1966, April 15, Louis Armstrong cover, EX, $35.00.

Look, 1949, April 26, Joe DiMaggio & Joe Jr cover 45.00
Look, 1950, August 29, Hopalong Cassidy cover, EX 28.00
Look, 1950, December 5, Esther Williams cover, EX 20.00
Mad Magazine, 1966, September, Batman & Robin cover, VG 20.00
McCall's, 1929, January, ad for Model A, VG 25.00
Motor Age, 1910, January 6, Madison Sq Garden Show, G+ 40.00
Nugget, 1957, July, The Date in Room 504, VG 10.00
NY Evening Graphic, 1932, April 23, Garbo/Gilbert cover, EX ...15.00
Outlook, 1901, June 1, Booker T Washington article, EX 9.00
Peek, 1938, January, Vol 1, #1, VG 15.00
People Today, 1955, Jayne Mansfield cover, pocket sz, EX 24.00
Picture, 1938, January, Vol 1, #1, VG 15.00

Playboy, 1st edition, Marilyn Monroe cover, VG, $1,500.00.

Playboy, 1954, September, Gina Lollabridgida, EX 135.00
Playboy, 1955, February, Jayne Mansfield centerfold, NM 135.00
Playboy, 1955, September, Marilyn Monroe centerfold, NM 100.00
Playboy, 1958, November, Brigitte Bardot centerfold, NM 25.00
Playboy, 1959, April, Tina Louise centerfold, EX 15.00
Playboy, 1960, January, Stella Stevens centerfold, EX 30.00
Playboy, 1967, December, Elke Summers centerfold, EX 15.00
Playgirl, 1974, June, Vol 1, #1, VG+ 40.00
Radio Guide, 1939, September 15, Baby Snooks (Brice) cover, EX ..12.50
Radio Romances, 1945, November, Joan Edwards, VG 8.00
Rolling Stone, 1981, January 22, John Lennon nude cover, VG ..40.00
Saturday Evening Post, 1901, February 9, H Fisher cover, EX 16.50
Saturday Evening Post, 1926, August, Rockwell cover, EX 18.00
Saturday Evening Post, 1933, April 8, N Rockwell cover, VG 12.00
Saturday Evening Post, 1933, December 2, Leyendecker cover, VG ...12.00
Saturday Evening Post, 1963, May, Leo Durocher cover, VG 22.00
Scientific American, 1916, November 4, 44th anniversary, VG ..10.00
Stars & Stripes, 1918, September 27, VG 18.00
Success, 1909, August, VG 10.00
Time, 1969, January 26, Fidel Castro, VG 8.00
True Confessions, 1934, June, Jean Harlow cover, VG+ 25.00
True Experiences, 1931, June, Cruel Lover, VG 8.00
TV & Radio Mirror, 1962, January, Rocky & Bullwinkle cover, VG ...55.00
Weird Tales, 1953, July, article by August Derleth, G 15.00
Who, 1941, April, Vol 1, #1, Winston Churchill, VG 20.00
Women's Home Journal, 1934, July, Mickey Mouse article, G 15.00
World's Events, 1906, February, EX 5.00
World's Work, 1928, January, KKK cover, VG 15.00

Majolica

Majolica is a type of heavy earthenware, design-molded and decorated in vivid colors with either a lead or tin type of glaze. It reached its height of popularity in the Victorian era; examples from this period are found in only the lead glazes. Nearly every potter of note, both here and abroad, produced large majolica jardinieres, umbrella stands, pitchers with animal themes, leaf shapes, vegetable forms, and nearly any other design from nature that came to mind. Few, however, marked their ware. Among those who did were Minton, Wedgwood, Holdcroft, and George Jones in England; Griffin, Smith and Hill (Etruscan) in Phoenixville, Pennsylvania; and Chesapeake Pottery (Avalon and Clifton) in Baltimore.

Color and condition are both very important worth-assessing factors. Pieces with cobalt, lavender, and turquoise glazes command the highest prices. For further information we recommend *The Collector's Encyclopedia of Majolica* by Mariann Katz-Marks (see Directory, Pennsylvania). Our advisor for this category is Hardy Hudson; he is listed in the Directory under Florida.

Basket, bamboo leaves on basketweave, Banks & Thorley 275.00
Basket, Bird in Flight, holds 6 egg cups, 9½" L 400.00
Basket, Luggage Strap, Cabbage Leaf & Daisy, 12½" L 400.00
Basket, shell, turq & lav, brn rope hdl, 8½" 350.00
Bowl, artichoke form w/bird finial on lid, 7¼" 350.00
Bowl, centerpc; wicker work & leafy garland, Wedgwood, 15" L ..800.00
Bowl, centerpc; 2 rabbits on ft below leafy bowl, Minton, 8" ..3,000.00
Bowl, chestnut leaf, gr on brn, prof rpr, 10" 150.00
Bowl, floral on turq, scalloped top, 4x9" 225.00
Bowl, holly & mistletoe, bird on rim, English mk, 4x8" 615.00
Bowl, Picket Fence, turq/brn/wht mottled int, 9" 200.00
Bowl, pk prunus blossoms on turq basketweave, 6-sided, 15" L ...375.00
Bowl, Pond Lily, ftd, Holdcroft, 11" 250.00
Bowl, sauce; Daisy, Etruscan, 8¼" L 295.00
Bowl, simple style w/floral int, ftd, twig hdls, 9" 175.00
Bowl, strawberries w/blossoms & leaves on wht, Wedgwood, 8" .250.00
Bowl, Sunflower, lav int, Wardle & Co, 10½" 300.00
Box, sardine; Cobalt & Seaweed, fish finial, 7½" 700.00
Box, sardine; fish & seaweed, duck finial, G Jones, 5¾" 1,000.00
Box, sardine; Floral & Fence, turq 'fence,' 7" 450.00
Box, sardine; much cobalt, dolphin ft, swan finial, 5¾" 800.00
Box, sardine; pointed leaves on cobalt, fish on lid, 9" 700.00
Box, sardine; yel basketweave, fish finial, 5½" sq 450.00
Box, tobacco; Blk boy w/melon lies on lg trunk, 6" L 425.00
Butter dish, Basketweave & Bamboo, Banks & Thorley, 8" 300.00
Butter dish, bl/brn/yel mottling, cow finial, Etruscan, rare, 7¾" ...1,200.00
Butter dish, Classical Urn, floral panels, Wedgwood, 8" L 575.00
Butter dish, Shell, Seaweed & Waves, 7" 350.00
Butter dish, Wild Rose, rope trim, twig hdl, 6½" 300.00
Butter pat, overlapping leaves 60.00
Butter pat, Pansy, mc petals, Etruscan, 3" 75.00
Butter pat, wicker pattern, Etruscan, 3" 75.00
Cake plate, Shell & Coral, open hdls, 11" 250.00
Cakestand, Astor, floral on wht, low ft, New England, 2x9" 300.00
Cakestand, fan on basketweave, low ft, 9" 250.00
Cakestand, lg gr 3-lobed leaf on turq, ftd, 9" 250.00
Cakestand, snail shell on turq fishnet, Fielding, 5¼x9½" 350.00
Cheese keeper, Dogwood, Geo Jones 2,500.00
Cheese keeper, floral w/basketweave base, Wedgwood, 10" 1,800.00
Cheese keeper, Lily, swan finial, Griffin, Smith & Hill, 7½" ..3,000.00
Cheese keeper, oak leaf on turq, acorn finial, Holdcroft, 5" 600.00
Cheese wedge, mc mottling, sheaf of wheat hdl, 5¾x9¾" 195.00
Cigarette urn, brn bear, basket on bk, pail between legs 1,350.00
Coffeepot, Hummingbird, Fielding, 9" 500.00
Compote, Bellflower, cobalt, ftd, 5x9½" 300.00
Compote, shell form, turq w/lav int, ftd, att Morley, 6x9" 325.00
Creamer, Blackberry, yel hdl & rim, English, 3½" 85.00
Creamer, Bow & Leaf, English Registry mk, 3¼" 135.00
Creamer, butterfly & floral, twig hdl, sq sides, 3½" 135.00
Creamer, Floral & Corn, rope hdl, 4½" 75.00
Cup, mustache; Shell & Seaweed, Etruscan, w/saucer, 8" dia 500.00
Cup & saucer, Bamboo & Floral, 6" 165.00
Cup & saucer, Pineapple, lav int, 5½" 175.00
Cup & saucer, Rose & Rope, brn bkground, lav int, 5½" 175.00
Cuspidor, Floral, canted corners, lav int, 5½" 250.00
Cuspidor, Floral & Basketweave, 7" 250.00
Cuspidor, Sunflower, cobalt w/lav int, Etruscan, 7" 750.00
Jar, bison head finial, mk Austria, 5" 145.00
Jardiniere, Blackberry, brn bkground, Wedgwood, 10" 600.00
Jardiniere, grotesque masks on intersecting bands, 8" 425.00
Match box, acorns & leaves on brn, lav int, G Jones, 4" 400.00
Match holder, drummer boy figural, Holdcroft, 3" 350.00
Mug, acorns & leaves on basketweave, Etruscan, 3½" 225.00
Mug, raspberries w/buds & leaves on yel, twig hdl, 3½" 175.00
Mug, shaving; pansies on turq, divided lav int, 3½" 250.00
Mug, sunflower on cobalt, lav int, twig hdl, 3½" 225.00
Pickle dish, Begonia Leaf, Griffin, Smith & Hill, 8" 125.00
Pitcher, Albino Shell, Etruscan, 5¾" 200.00
Pitcher, baseball players, monochrome, Etruscan, 7¾" 450.00
Pitcher, Basketweave & Bamboo, Banks & Thorley, 7½" 175.00
Pitcher, Basketweave & Fence, w/floral, 6" 100.00
Pitcher, Bird & Basketweave, 8½" 175.00
Pitcher, Bird & Fan, bamboo hdl, Wardle, 7¼" 350.00
Pitcher, Bird & Iris, sq sides, ftd, squat, Etruscan, 4" 150.00
Pitcher, birds & nest, wht ground, twig hdl, att Am, 9¼" 300.00
Pitcher, chickens at sides of wheat sheaf form, 7" 325.00
Pitcher, Corn, Etruscan, Griffin, Smith & Hill, 6" 300.00
Pitcher, Dogwood, brn ground, gr twig hdl, Holdcroft, 9" 250.00
Pitcher, Dogwood on Bark, twig hdl, lav int, unmk, 8" 200.00
Pitcher, duck figural, wing hdl, faience, Portugal, 11" 200.00
Pitcher, English cottage form, twig hdl, 7" 265.00
Pitcher, Fan, Butterfly & Cricket, lav int, 8¾" 250.00
Pitcher, Floral & Anchor, brn basketweave base, 8¼" 150.00
Pitcher, Floral & Basketweave, cobalt at top & hdl, 6½" 350.00
Pitcher, hummingbird & prunus blossom, stippled ground, 6¼" .250.00
Pitcher, Iris & Lily, turq int, Geo Jones, 6¾" 300.00
Pitcher, ivy on tree bark, gr on brn, U-form, English 145.00
Pitcher, lily form w/dragonflies, Adams & Bromley, 8" 250.00
Pitcher, Oak Barrel & Avocado, att Geo Jones, 5½" 300.00
Pitcher, owl figural, branch hdl, Morley, 8¼" 300.00
Pitcher, parrot figural, beak spout, French faience, 11" 150.00
Pitcher, Peas in Pod, basketweave base, pewter top, 5½" 275.00
Pitcher, Robin on Branch, pewter top, 4½" 250.00
Pitcher, Shell & Fishnet, seaweed hdl, turq int, Fielding, 7" 325.00
Pitcher, shell figural, waves at base, wht/bl, Fielding, 8" 350.00

Pitcher, spiraling conch shell form, Wedgwood, 10", $1,200.00.

Pitcher, Stork in Marsh, eel hdl, 9½" 450.00
Pitcher, syrup; Bow & Floral, 8¼" 250.00
Pitcher, syrup; Dogwood, str sides, Holdcroft, 4" 200.00
Pitcher, syrup; Sunflower on wht, Bennetts, 7¾" 225.00
Pitcher, underwater scene w/gulls on cobalt sky, G Jones, 8" 500.00
Pitcher, Water Lily & Dragonfly, bud on hdl, lav int, 7½" 250.00
Pitcher, wide floral band amid Oriental decor, S Lear, 9" 350.00
Planter, Picket Fence & Raspberry, lav int, 8" 395.00
Plate, begonia leaves overlapping, 8¾" 100.00
Plate, Bird & Fan, Wedgwood, 9" 250.00
Plate, Bird in Flight, turq ground, att Holdcroft, 8½" 300.00
Plate, Bow on Basketweave, turq ground, 6" 80.00

Plate, Cauliflower, bright colors, Etruscan, 9" 225.00
Plate, classical figures, Griffin, Smith & Hill, 8" 150.00
Plate, dessert; Fan & Bow, fan shape, 6½" 150.00
Plate, Fern & Bow, Banks & Thorley, 8" 125.00
Plate, geranium blossoms & gr leaves on brn, 9" 150.00
Plate, maple leaves on pk, Etruscan, 9" 175.00
Plate, Morning-Glory, red & gr on med bl, shaped rim, 9" 150.00
Plate, Morning-Glory & Picket Fence, deep, 9" 150.00
Plate, oyster; deep cobalt mottling, Minton, 10" 600.00
Plate, oyster; dolphins between ea of 5 shells, Wedgwood, 9" 500.00
Plate, oyster; seaweed & shells on cobalt, half-moon shape, 8" ...300.00
Plate, oyster; Shell & Seaweed, 7-shell, Minton, 9" 550.00
Plate, oyster; 5 sm & 1 lg fish, cobalt center, 10" 450.00
Plate, Parrot, Butterfly & Bamboo, English, 9" 150.00
Plate, Running Stag & Dog, floral & picket fence rim, 8" 125.00
Plate, Shell & Seaweed, Etruscan, 9" 245.00
Plate, Water Lily, lg leaf form, Geo Jones, 8" 250.00
Plate, Water Lily, no blossom, Minton, 9" 300.00
Platter, allover shells, Wedgwood, 21", M 2,500.00
Platter, banana leaves on basketweave, 14" L 250.00
Platter, basketweave, bl, swans w/wings wide as hdls, 13" 275.00
Platter, Begonia, leaves form corners, 11" L 250.00
Platter, Cattail & Fish, turq ground, Holdcroft, 25", M 2,500.00
Platter, Fan & Dragonfly, fan form, 10½" 250.00
Platter, Fish & Coral w/Waves, much cobalt, Wedgwood copy, 13" ..275.00
Platter, Floral & Besketweave, center medallion, turq, 11" 200.00
Platter, floral on dmn shape, 12" 175.00
Platter, mottled center, leafy border, oval, 14" 225.00
Platter, rose on basketweave, turq w/cobalt rim, hdls, 13" 250.00
Platter, Shell, Seaweed & Ocean Waves, oval, 13½" 250.00
Platter, Sunflower, twig hdls, att Wardle, 12½" 275.00
Relish, dogwood blossoms on 3-leaf form, Geo Jones, 12" 800.00
Relish tray, Grape Leaf, 8" 150.00
Strawberry server, blossoms, 2 side wells, 2 3-D birds, 15" 1,000.00
Sugar bowl, Leaf & Bow on bl basketweave, 4" 175.00
Sweetmeat server, deer's head figural, att Copeland, 4½" 450.00
Teapot, Basketweave & Floral, 6" 185.00
Teapot, Basketweave & Floral on turq, 6", +cr/sug 425.00
Teapot, Bird & Iris, Etruscan, 6", +cr/sug 700.00
Teapot, Blackberry, Clifton, 6" 250.00
Teapot, Cauliflower, Griffin, Smith & Hill, 5½" 350.00
Teapot, Chinaman on coconut figural, 7" 850.00
Teapot, Corn, corn finial, 6½" 245.00
Teapot, Floral & Basketweave on turq, 5" 250.00
Teapot, holly & berries on bl lattice, bark spout & hdl, 6" 225.00
Teapot, Melon & Bumps, brn bkground, 6½" 325.00
Teapot, Strawberry & Bow on turq basketweave, 6" 300.00
Teapot, Water Lily, bud finial, 4" 225.00
Toothpick holder, chick beside egg form, cobalt base, 4" 300.00
Tray, bread; Bamboo & Fern, cobalt center, Wardle, 13" 275.00
Tray, bread; Oak Leaf, twig hdl, Etruscan, 13" 300.00
Tray, 3 lg leaves w/dogwood, center twig hdl, G Jones, 12" 500.00
Umbrella holder, Nouveau flowers, 22x10", M 625.00
Vase, Bird in Flight & Pond Lily, cylindrical, 10" 350.00
Vase, songbird by trumpet flower figural, 6" 300.00
Wine cooler, Bacchanalian scene on wht, hdls, 10" 600.00

Malachite Glass

Malachite is a type of art glass that exhibits strata-like layerings in shades of green, similar to the mineral in its natural form. Some examples have an acid-etched mark of Moser/Carlsbad, usually on the base.

However, it should be noted that in the past fifteen years there have been reproductions from Czechoslovakia with a paper label.

Basket, woman & cherubs, loop hdl, 6x6½" 150.00
Box, nudes w/long hair on lid, nudes on bottom, 3½x2" 100.00
Cat, seated, tail around ft, 4½" 50.00
Vase, nude women & flowers, Moser/Carlsbad, 5", pr 175.00
Vase, nudes & grapes, Moser/Carlsbad, 9½" 200.00

Mantel Lustres

Mantel lustres are decorative vases or candle holders made from all types of glass, often highly decorated, and usually hung with one or more rows of prisms. In the listings that follow, values are given for a pair.

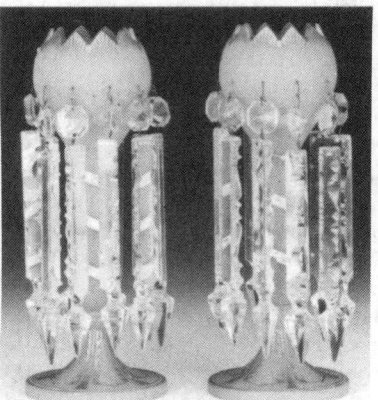

Blue satin with gilded sawtooth rim, notched spear prisms, late 1800s, 13½", $280.00 for the pair.

Bl opaque w/HP florals/much gold, scalloped, prisms, 9" 225.00
Cranberry w/HP floral, scalloped, long prisms, 14" 540.00
Pigeon blood w/enameling & gilt, cut prisms, 14" 355.00
Pk cased in wht w/gilt florals, 2 rows of prisms, 15" 400.00
Ruby glass w/HP floral & gold, Bohemian, 1800s, 14" 475.00
Wht cut to cranberry, gold decor, trumpet form w/prisms, 10" ...625.00

Maps and Atlases

Maps are highly collectible, not only for historical value but also for their sometimes elaborate artwork, legendary information, or data that since they were printed has been proven erroneous. There are many types of maps including geographical, military, celestial, road, and railroad. The most valuable are those made before the mid-1800s. Our advisor for this category is Murray Hudson; he is listed in the Directory under Tennessee.

Key:
hc — hand colored   p — publisher

Atlases

Colton's General, hc, 102 single or dbl folios, 1859, EX 1,500.00
Cram's Universal, geographical/astronomical, 1894, 560-pg, EX ..145.00
Gaskell's New & Complete Family...World, Chicago, 1886, EX ...160.00
Johnson's New Family, single & dbl sheets, hc, 1865, EX 450.00
Mitchell's New General, Phila, 1871, loose covers, complete 375.00
People's Popular...World, Tunison, Chicago, 1904, 316-pg, EX .175.00
Rand McNally Standard...World, Continental, Chicago, 1890, EX .195.00
Winn & Hammond New Family...World, Detroit, 1885, 124-pg, G ..85.00

Maps

AL, steamboat routes/etc, hc, Cowperthwait, 1850, 13x17"	40.00
Ancient world, hc, much text, dtd 1800, 14x20", EX	20.00
AR, survey of Cherokee & Chocktaw boundaries, 1845, 15x17"	12.50
Bentonsville NC, battlefield, Johnston, 1865, 9x10"	10.00
CA, hc, fancy flower border, Colton, 1858, 12x14"	22.50
CA, UT, NV, CO, NM, AZ, hc, Johnson, 1864, 18x26"	55.00
CA Coast, topographical, Jeff Davis, H Custer, 1855, 30x36"	30.00
Chatanooga & Chickamauga, topographical, 1864, 18x26"	12.50
Chicago, vertical print, hc, street guide, 1870, 15x23"	20.00
Eastern United States, hc, EX details, 1820, 10x12"	20.00
Greece, hc, J Barfield, lg text/history, 1800, 14x20", EX	20.00
Indianapolis, streets/parks/etc, Cram, Chicago, 1900, 14x22"	12.50
KY & TN, hc, shows some IN & OH, Colton, 1858, 12x14"	20.00
LA, hc, New Orleans inset, hc, Cowperthwait, 1850, 13x17"	40.00
LA, land districts/towns/etc, 1854, 17x18"	12.50
Mediterranean, hc, fancy cartouch, John Senex, 1710, 15x18"	35.00
MO, hc, Kansas City not colored, EX margins, Johnson, 11x14"	12.50
NB & KS Territory, 2 maps on 1 sheet, 1858, 11x14"	20.00
New England, RR lines/towns, pictorial cartouch, 1875, 22x34"	40.00
NY City, ferries/no bridges, hc, Cowperthwait, 1850, 13x17"	30.00
Port Royal & Beaufort, sailing map, 1862, 24x32"	20.00
Roman World, geographical Roman Empire, hc, 1800, 14x20"	20.00
Sierra Madre & Pima Villages, J Davis, 1854-55, 26x36"	45.00
South & New England, RR lines, hc, Watson, 22x26"	45.00
South West, RR/towns, hc, Watson, 1875, 22x26"	50.00
Southern & Northern & Frontier RR Systems, Lloyd, 1860, 40x48"	90.00
TX & OK, towns/RR/Indian territory/etc, litho, 1891, 14x21"	15.00
United States, huge AR & NW Territories, hc, 1820, 12x19"	90.00
United States, RRs/canals/Indians, Bradford, 1832, 10x13"	35.00
US Military RR, Southern states, J Bien, dtd 1866, 40x27"	65.00
Washington DC, Capitol inset, hc, Cowperthwait, 1850, 13x17"	30.00
Western States & Territories, RR, hc, Watson, 1875, 36x36"	50.00
World, as 2 globes, hc, Cowperthwait, 1850, 13x17"	30.00
WV & VA, towns & rivers, hc, floral border, 1867, 12x15"	20.00
13 Orig Colonies & NW Territory, hc, dtd 1879, 12x15"	15.00

Marblehead

What began as therapy for patients in a sanitarium in Marblehead, Massachusetts, has become recognized as an important part of the Arts and Crafts movement in America. Results of the early experiments under the guidance of Arthur E. Baggs in 1904 met with such success that by 1908 the pottery had been converted to a solely commercial venture. Simple vase shapes were often incised with stylized animal and floral motifs or sailing ships. Some were decorated in low relief; many were plain. Simple matt glazes in soft yellow, gray, wisteria, rose, tobacco brown, and their most popular, Marblehead blue, were used alone or in combination. The Marblehead logo is distinctive — a ship with full sail and the letters 'M' and 'P.' The pottery closed in 1936.

Vase, hand-painted frieze of fish swimming on gray, signed HT, ca 1910-15, 9x7", $3,500.00.

Bowl, stylized leaf/grape band, 5-color, EX art, 9"	1,700.00
Bowl vase, flowers, bl/gr/red on bl speckled, 3¾x4½"	750.00
Candlesticks, gr speckled, broad base, flared top, 14", pr	1,700.00
Cup, cider; dk bl w/dk gr band, 4"	185.00
Jar, lg oak trees, blk on dk gr, A Baggs, 4¼", NM	700.00
Jardiniere, wisteria, violet int, mk M & P, 6"	550.00
Lamp base, dk bl/gr drip glaze, cylindrical, 12x7"	700.00
Tankard, gr speckled, sgn AB, dtd Aug '07, 8", +4 mugs	1,100.00
Vase, bl, trumpet form, 4½"	245.00
Vase, bl to yel, ovoid w/flared lip, experimental (?), 8"	700.00
Vase, brn speckled, ovoid, 8¾x4½"	500.00
Vase, bud; gr, 3¾"	190.00
Vase, bud; lilac latticework on gr, 4¼"	375.00
Vase, dk bl, classic form, emb mk, 7"	400.00
Vase, dk bl, ovoid, 8½x4½"	500.00
Vase, dk bl speckled, widens toward base, 4½x4½"	200.00
Vase, elongated peacock feathers, blk/gr/brn on dk bl, 4x2"	650.00
Vase, feathered bl, shouldered cylinder w/inverted rim, 8½"	650.00
Vase, gr, wide incurvate top, 12x8"	1,800.00
Vase, gr, wide U-form w/flattened shoulder, 8x7"	850.00
Vase, gr speckled, flaring U-form, 5x5"	250.00
Vase, gr w/brn feathering, ovoid, 7x3¾"	425.00
Vase, leafy trees on pencil trunks, 3-color, EX art, 15"	16,000.00
Vase, leathery dk bl w/speckles, spherical, 6x7½"	500.00
Vase, navy bl matt, simple form & shape, 7"	375.00
Vase, ochre speckled, baluster, 9¼x5½"	650.00
Vase, ochre speckled shaded dk at rim, spherical, 5x5"	600.00
Vase, purple & bl mottle, 5"	450.00
Vase, stylized floral, 3-color on gray, H Tutt, 4½"	1,200.00
Vase, stylized floral, 3-color on yel, 5", NM	1,600.00
Vase, stylized leaf band, brn on gray-gr speckled, HT, 4½"	850.00
Vase, yel gloss w/purple & bl around bulbous top, 4x5"	300.00

Marbles

Marbles have been popular with children since the mid-1800s. They've been made in many types from a variety of materials. Among some of the first glass items to be produced, the earliest marbles were made from a solid glass rod broken into sections of the proper length which were placed in a tray of sand and charcoal and returned to the fire. As they were reheated, the trays were constantly agitated until the marbles were completely round. Other marbles were made of china, pottery, steel, and natural stones.

Below is a listing of the various types, along with a brief description of each. When size is not otherwise indicated, prices are listed for mint condition marbles of average size, ½" to 1".

Agates: stone marbles of many different colors — bands of color alternating with white usually encircle the marble; most are translucent.

Ballot Box: handmade (with pontils), opaque white or black, used in lodge elections.

Bloodstone: green chalcedony with red spots, a type of quartz.

China: with or without glaze, in a variety of hand-painted designs — parallel bands or bull's-eye designs most common.

Clambroth: opaque glass with outer evenly spaced swirls of one or alternating colors.

Clay: one of the most common older types; some are painted while others are not.

Comic Strip: a series of twelve machine-made marbles with faces of comic strip characters, Peltier Glass Factory, Illinois.

Crockery: sometimes referred to as Benningtons; most are either blue or brown, although some are speckled. The clay is shaped into a sphere, then coated with glaze and fired.

End of the Day: single-pontil glass marbles — the colored part often appears as a multicolored blob or mushroom cloud.

Goldstone: clear glass completely filled with copper flakes that have turned gold-colored from the heat of the manufacturing process.

Indian Swirls: usually black glass with a colored swirl appearing on the outside next to the surface, often irregular.

Latticinio Core Swirls: double-pontil marble with an inner area with net-like effects of swirls coming up around the center.

Lutz Type: glass with colored or clear bands alternating with bands which contain copper flecks.

Micas: clear or colored glass with mica flecks which reflect as silver dots when marble is turned. Red is rare.

Onionskin: spiral type which are solidly colored instead of having individual ribbons or threads, multicolored.

Peppermint Swirls: made of white opaque glass with alternating blue and red outer swirls.

Ribbon Core Swirls: double-pontil marble — center shaped like a ribbon with swirls that come up around the middle.

Rose Quartz: stone marble, usually pink in color, often with fractures inside and on outer surface.

Solid Core Swirls: double-pontil marble — middle is solid with swirls coming up around the core.

Steelies: hollow steel spheres marked with a cross where the steel was bent together to form the ball.

Sulfides: generally made of clear glass with figures inside. Rarer types have colored figures or colored glass.

Tiger Eye: stone marble of golden quartz with inclusions of asbestos, dark brown with gold highlights.

Vaseline: machine-made of yellowish-green glass with small bubbles.

For a more thorough study of the subject, we recommend *Antique and Collectible Marbles, Third Edition*, an identification and value guide by Everett Grist; you will find his address in the Directory under Tennessee.

Divided red, white and blue core surrounded by yellow and ribbon, alternating outer yellow and white swirls, ⅝", $25.00 (1¾", $100.00).

Agate, contemporary, carnelian, 1¾"	150.00
Banded Opaque, gr & wht, 2"	875.00
Banded Opaque, red & wht, 1¾"	775.00
Banded Opaque, red & wht, ¾"	85.00
Banded Transparent Swirl, bl, ¾"	50.00
Banded Transparent Swirl, lt gr, 1¾"	600.00
Bennington, bl, 1¾"	30.00
Bennington, bl, ¾"	1.00
Bennington, brn, 1¾"	15.00
Bennington, fancy, 1¾"	60.00
Bennington, fancy, ¾"	5.00
China, decorated, glazed, apple, 1¾"	800.00
China, decorated, glazed, rose, 1¾"	1,200.00
China, decorated, glazed, wht w/geometrics, 1¾"	45.00
China, decorated, unglazed, geometrics & flowers, ¾"	175.00
Clambroth, opaque, bl & wht, 1¾"	2,600.00
Clambroth, opaque, bl & wht, ¾"	250.00
Clambroth Swirl, red/wht, Germany, 1900, ⅞"	375.00
Clear Swirl Lutz-type, clear w/wht & gold swirls, 1¾"	750.00
Clear Swirl Lutz-type, clear w/wht & gold swirls, ¾"	110.00
Comic, Cotes Bakery, advertising	1,200.00

Comic, Kayo, rare	250.00
Comic, Little Orphan Annie	100.00
Comic, Moon Mullins	175.00
Comic, set of 12	1,350.00
Comic, Skeezix	100.00
Cork Screw, machine-made	5.00
End of Day, bl & wht, 1¾"	1,100.00
Goldstone, ¾"	35.00
Indian Swirl, 1¾"	3,500.00
Indian Swirl Lutz-type, gold flakes, ¾"	600.00
Line Crockery, clay, 1¾"	75.00
Mica, bl, ¾"	25.00
Mica, gr, 1¾"	400.00
Onionskin, w/mica, 1¾"	900.00
Onionskin, w/mica, ¾"	110.00
Onionskin, 16-lobe, unusual, 1¾"	1,800.00
Onionskin, ¾"	90.00
Onionskin, 4-lobe, 1¼"	450.00
Opaque Swirl, gr, ¾"	75.00
Opaque Swirl Lutz-type, bl, yel, gr, or vaseline, ¾"	325.00
Peppermint Swirl, opaque, red, wht, & bl, 1¾"	2,500.00
Peppermint Swirl, opaque, red, wht, & bl, ¾"	100.00
Pottery, 1¾"	45.00
Ribbon Core Lutz-type, red, 1¾"	1,800.00
Slag, machine-made, sm	3.00
Slag, machine-made, 1½"	150.00
Solid Opaque, gr, 1¾"	900.00
Solid Opaque, ¾"	50.00
Sulfide, angel, 1¾"	400.00
Sulfide, baboon playing bass fiddle, 2⅛"	700.00
Sulfide, bird, 2", EX	150.00
Sulfide, boar, 1⅞", EX	160.00
Sulfide, child sitting, 1¾"	400.00
Sulfide, child w/hammer, 1¾"	600.00
Sulfide, cow, 1¾"	150.00
Sulfide, crane w/fish, 1¾"	550.00
Sulfide, crucifix, 1¾"	600.00
Sulfide, dog, sitting, 1½", EX	110.00
Sulfide, dog, 1¾"	125.00
Sulfide, dog on cushion, wear, 2¼"	175.00
Sulfide, dog w/bird in mouth, 1¾"	750.00
Sulfide, dog w/open mouth, 1¾"	300.00
Sulfide, eagle, 1¾"	400.00
Sulfide, elephant, 1¾"	350.00
Sulfide, face of angel w/wings, 1¾"	400.00
Sulfide, figure-8, 1¾"	400.00
Sulfide, fish, 1¾"	175.00
Sulfide, goat, 1¾"	125.00
Sulfide, horse, rearing, clear w/gr swirl, 1⅞"	175.00
Sulfide, horse, 1¾"	150.00
Sulfide, lamb, lt amber, 1¾"	2,000.00
Sulfide, lamb, 1¾", NM	110.00
Sulfide, lion, 1¾"	200.00
Sulfide, Little Boy Blue, 1¾"	500.00
Sulfide, owl, 1¾"	150.00
Sulfide, owl w/wings spread, 1¾"	350.00
Sulfide, papoose, 1¾"	600.00
Sulfide, parrot, 1¾"	175.00
Sulfide, pig, 1¾"	150.00
Sulfide, pony, 1¾"	200.00
Sulfide, rabbit, 1¾"	150.00
Sulfide, razor-bk hog, 1½"	150.00
Sulfide, rooster, 1¾"	150.00
Sulfide, Santa Claus, 1¾"	1,200.00

Sulfide, sheep, lt amber, 1¾" **2,000.00**
Sulfide, sheep, 1¾" **110.00**
Sulfide, squirrel, standing, 1¾", EX **170.00**

Marine Collectibles

See also Steamship Collectibles; Telescopes; Scrimshaw; Tools.

Bailer, whale oil; mtd on wooden pole, 80" overall **400.00**
Beckets, rope w/wooden cleats, minor fraying, 10" L, pr **150.00**
Binnacle, brass, w/compass & burner, 9", VG **250.00**
Binnacle, brass w/mk Viking compass, 20" **50.00**
Binnacle, copper, liquid-filled compass, orig burner, 10" **225.00**
Binnacle, Kelvin & Hughes...London...Edinburg, wood/brass, 54" ..**650.00**
Box, document; pnt wood w/name, 8½x11½x12½", EX **150.00**
Chest, wood, pnt marine art, rope-work beckets, 17x40x18" **575.00**
Chronometer, Thomas Mercer, dbl-cased, 1915, EX **1,400.00**
Chronometer, Waltham USA, 3-tier brass/mahog case **525.00**
Clock, Chelsea, SS Marine Trade, brass, dtd 1943, 7½" dia **250.00**
Clock, ship's, Seth Thomas, brass, 8-day, inside bell, 6¾" **330.00**
Compass, CR Sherman...New Bedford, brass dry card, 1800s, EX ..**525.00**
Ditty bag, canvas, w/sailor's implements, Am, 1800s **495.00**
Fid, whalebone tip, wooden hdl w/silver band, early, 5" **50.00**
Figurehead, lady, full figure, cvd/rpt wood, 47", G **1,450.00**
Figurehead, lady w/EX detail, cvd/pnt wood, 1800s, 47½" **16,500.00**
Foghorn, EZ Blow Horn, Wilcox Crittenden, galvanized, 18" **125.00**
Foghorn, Lothrop's Pat...Gloucester MA, 13"+pump hdl, VG **175.00**
Helmet, diving; polished/lacquered, China, EX **1,000.00**
Inclinometer, phenolic, China **50.00**
Lamp, anchor, brass, 18¾" **160.00**
Lantern, anchor light, copper, clear lens, swing hdl, 16" **200.00**
Lantern, Perko, Perkins Marine...NY, brass/galvanized, 18" **175.00**
Light, mast head; copper, clear lens, missing burner, 26" **200.00**
Light, mast head; Perco, brass doors, red/gr lenses, 10" **95.00**
Light, ship's masthead; copper w/dbl lens, RC Murray, 1800s **200.00**
Octant, Solomon Mars 107..., brass w/silver scales, 1850s **350.00**
Octant, Spencer-Browning & Co, London, dbl-T, ebony/ivory .**675.00**
Octant, Walker Liverpool, brass mts, ivory plates, 1800s, EX **415.00**
Porthole, solid brass, 20" dia, EX **185.00**
Protractor, JW Strange Bangor ME, brass, 1876, 16" L **200.00**
Sextant, Spencer Barrett & Co London, brass & ebony, EX **440.00**
Sextant, Spencer Browning & Rust, London, 1800s, EX in box .**525.00**
Spade, sliver blubber; early whaling tool, 20½" L **200.00**
Spy glass, Blackford Emery London, 1800s, 24½", EX **225.00**
Telegraph, Chas Cory & Son...NY, brass, 11½", EX **375.00**
Telegraph, Engine Room on dial, brass, 34"+hdl **450.00**
Tooth, sperm whale, 4½" L **70.00**
Wheel, brass, 42" dia, EX **415.00**
Wheel, wood w/brass hub & banding, Brown Bros, 30" dia **325.00**

Martin Bros.

The Martin Bros. were studio potters who worked from 1873 until 1914, first at Fulham and later at London and Southall. There were four brothers, each of whom excelled in their particular area. Robert, known as Wallace, was an experienced stonecarver. He modeled a series of grotesque bird and animal figural caricatures. Walter was the potter, responsible for throwing the larger vases on the wheel, firing the kiln, and mixing the clay. Edwin, an artist of stature, preferred more naturalistic forms of decoration. His work was often incised or had relief designs of seaweed, florals, fish, and birds. The fourth brother, Charles, was their business manager. Their work was incised with their

names, place of production, and letters and numbers indicating month and year.

Bird, grotesque, bl/gray, 3" **735.00**
Bird, grotesque, brn/bl on ivory w/tan, 14", EX **12,800.00**
Bulldog, grotesque, ruffle around neck, rstr base, 11¼" **9,400.00**
Figurine, seated nude imp playing harp, ivory, 5½" **3,500.00**
Fish head, 'crest' atop, uptrn eyes, appl 'collar,' 6", EX **1,400.00**
Jug, bird form, bl/gray/tan/brn slip, 1898, rstr, 16⅝" **11,000.00**
Jug, grotesque sea creatures cvd on ivory, ovoid, 9¾" **1,850.00**
Jug, John Barleycorn face 1 side, bkground w/branches, 6¾" ...**1,200.00**
Jug, smiling face ea side, tan/brn/blk/wht slip, 1899, 7¼" **3,300.00**
Jug, smiling face w/exposed teeth ea side, brn/tan/wht, 9" **2,700.00**
Jug, 2 satyr masks/strapwork/leaves, wht/bl/gr, rstr, 6½" **450.00**

Lovebirds, multicolored slips, signed, dated 1902, 8¾", $7,500.00.

Pen holder, as man's head in wide-rim hat, brn/tan/bl, 3½" ...**1,150.00**
Spoon warmer, fins prop up open-mouth fish head, 6", EX **2,000.00**
Toothpick holder, head w/gaping mouth, mc/salt glaze, 2⅝" ...**1,100.00**
Vase, birds/floral twigs, tan/brn stoneware, #4-1887, 8" **2,300.00**
Vase, cvd honeycomb, brn on cream, 6 ogee panels, 10", EX **745.00**
Vase, dragons cvd on brn, 4 snake hdls, rstr, 9" **1,450.00**
Vessel, bird form, bl/brn/tan slip, 1894, rpr, 14" **9,350.00**
Vessel, bird form, mc on salt glaze, 1903, chip, 11" **6,050.00**

Mary Gregory

Mary Gregory glass, for reasons that remain obscure, is the namesake of a Boston and Sandwich Glass Company employee who worked for the company for only two years in the mid-1800s. Although no evidence actually exists to indicate that glass of this type was even produced there, the fine colored or crystal ware decorated with figures of children in white enamel is commonly referred to as Mary Gregory. The glass, in fact, originated in Europe and was imported into this country where it was copied by several eastern glasshouses. It was popular from the mid-1800s until the turn of the century. It is generally accepted that examples with all-white figures were made in the U.S.A., while gold-trimmed items and those with children having tinted faces or a small amount of color on their clothing are European. Though amethyst is rare, examples in cranberry command the higher prices. Blue ranks next; and green, amber, and clear items are worth the least. Watch for new glass decorated with screen-printed children and a minimum of hand painting. The screen effect is easily detected with a magnifying glass.

Biscuit jar, liliacs/gold lines on lt gr, SP mts, 8" W **300.00**
Bottle, scent; bl, girl in garden, w/stopper, 9½" **385.00**

Bottle, scent; sapphire, girl holds flowers in garden, 9½" 375.00
Box, amber, boy w/flowers by fence, hinged lid, 3½x3¾" 275.00
Box, amber, girl w/flower, 3-ftd metal base, 3½" dia 175.00
Box, cobalt, girl & birds, brass fr, hinged lid, 5¼" dia 400.00
Box, emerald gr, boy w/butterfly, gr finial, 6½x4" 225.00
Box, lt amethyst, girl w/bag of flowers/garden 2½x3½" 375.00
Box, sapphire bl, lady picks flowers, hinged lid, 5½" dia 375.00

Box, sapphire blue, girl in garden, ca 1875-1885, $400.00.

Centerpc, SP base w/3-D stork ea side wht-cased pk vase, 18" ...900.00
Hall lamp, gr Invt T'print, boy, bk: girl, 16x7", brass mts 1,295.00
Lustres, cranberry, girl, w/gold, 6 prisms, 10¼", facing pr 2,025.00
Mug, lime gr, girl w/flowers, Optic bkground, 4x2⅝" 70.00
Syrup, clear, girl in foliage, corset shape 225.00
Toothpick holder, citron, girl watching bird, ca 1890, rare 250.00
Tumbler, amber, girl w/basket, Optic bkground, 5x2½" 55.00
Tumbler, bl, girl, tint on face & hair, 6" 198.00
Tumbler, cranberry, boy & butterfly, gold trim, 5⅝" 135.00
Tumbler, sapphire bl, girl, bbl shape, 4½x2½" 55.00
Tumbler (for tumble-up), emerald gr, girl hangs wash, 4x2¾" 50.00
Vase, amber, girl/trees, bk: flowers, neck band, 6¾" 225.00
Vase, blk, girl by fence, in metal base w/storks, 8" 750.00
Vase, bud; honey-amber, girl w/leafy sprig, 4-petal top, 6½" 185.00
Vase, bud; lt amethyst, boy in foliage, 6" 110.00
Vase, chartreuse gr to clear frost, boy w/bird, 6x3¼" 135.00
Vase, cranberry, girl, 3½" 125.00
Vase, cranberry, leprechauns under toadstools smoking, 10", pr .600.00
Vase, gold-amber, boy, amber reeded snail hdls, gold trim, 7" 150.00
Vase, lime, girl, rtcl brass band/ft w/mc jewels, 7x2¼" 235.00
Vase, lt amber, girl in forest, flowers on bk, 6¾x3" 225.00

Mason's Ironstone

In 1813 Charles J. Mason was granted a patent for a process said to 'improve the quality of English porcelain.' The new type of ware was in fact ironstone which Mason decorated with colorful florals and scenics, some of which reflected the Oriental taste. Although his business failed for a short time in the late 1840s, Mason re-established himself and continued to produce dinnerware, tea services, and ornamental pieces until about 1852 at which time the pottery was sold to Francis Morley. Ten years later, Geo. L. and Taylor Ashworth became owners. Both Morley and the Ashworths not only used Mason's molds and patterns but often his mark as well. Because the quality and the workmanship of the later wares do not compare with Mason's earlier product, collectors should take care to distinguish one from the other. Consult a good book on marks to be sure. The Wedgwood Company now owns the rights to the Mason patterns and is reproducing the Vista pattern under its Franciscan trademark. Our advisor for this category is Susan Hirshman; she is listed in the Directory under Oregon.

Bowl, rimmed soup; Vista, pk 20.00
Bowl, vegetable; Vista, pk, oval 30.00

Bowl, vegetable; Vista, pk, w/lid 115.00
Butter dish, Vista, pk 35.00
Cheese dish, Vista, pk 50.00
Coffeepot, Vista, pk 65.00
Cup & saucer, demitasse; Vista, pk 25.00
Jug, milk; Vista, pk 45.00
Pitcher & bowl, gaudy ironstone, bl floral w/mc, 9", 12" 250.00
Plate, dinner; Vista, pk 20.00
Plate, salad; Vista, pk 10.00
Platter, Vista, pk, 15" 80.00
Platter, well & tree; Imari design, scalloped/canted, 21" 300.00
Soup plate, gaudy ironstone, mk Pat, 10½" 150.00
Sugar bowl, Vista, pk, w/lid 45.00
Tray, sandwich; Vista, pk 45.00
Wash set, snake hdl, bowl: 16", pitcher, 11", EX 550.00

Massier

Clement Massier was a French artist-potter who in 1881 established a workshop at Golfe Juan, France, where he experimented with metallic lustre glazes. (One of his pupils was Jacques Sicardo, who brought the knowledge he had gained through his association with Massier to the Weller Pottery Company in Zanesville, Ohio.) The lustre lines developed by Massier incorporated nature themes with allover decorations of foliage or flowers on shapes modeled in the Art Nouveau style. The ware was usually incised with the Massier name, his initials, or the location of the pottery. Massier died in 1917.

Bust of young woman, irid, hollow, mk A-4, att, 7½" 500.00
Plate, stylized leaves/vines on yel lustre, CM 1888, 8", EX 225.00
Vase, cloverleaves, 4½" 395.00
Vase, floral on irid, sqd rim, 4¾", NM 450.00
Vase, foliage at shoulder, mc irid, long neck, 9", EX 385.00

Match Holders

Before the invention of the safety match in 1855, matches were kept in matchboxes and carried in pocket-size match safes because they ignited so easily. John Walker, an English chemist, invented the match more than one hundred years ago, quite by accident. Walker was working with a mixture of potash and antimony, hoping to make a combustible that could be used to fire guns. The mixture adhered to the end of the wooden stick he had used for stirring. As he tried to remove it by scraping the stick on the stone floor, it burst into flames. The invention of the match was only a step away! From that time to the present, match holders have been made in amusing figural forms as well as simple utilitarian styles and in a wide range of materials. Both table-top and wall-hanging models were made — all designed to keep matches conveniently at hand. Our advisor for this category is Ron Damaska; he is listed in the Directory under Pennsylvania. See also Advertising.

Brass, Deco Porter, cigarette & book match holder, 10" 125.00
Brass, devil figural, scrolled wall mt, early 55.00
Bsk, girl in bonnet, Germany, EX 40.00
Bsk, skull form 32.00
China, gaudy decor, wall mt, Japan 25.00
China, shoe, striker on sole 25.00
CI, alligator form, EX details, 8" 125.00
CI, grapes & leaves, lacy openwork, old 55.00
CI, log cabin figural, hinged roof, orig pnt, 1860s, 4x2½" 140.00
CI, rooster finial, ped base, claw ft 95.00
CI, rtcl bkplate, 2-compartment, 7" 45.00

CI, turtle form, urn on bk, 1850s, 3⅜" L 125.00
CI, Venus & Cupid kissing, wall mt, V&M, 1915 ....85.00
Farmer's head, Iron Art, wall mt, 6x4½" 75.00
Glass, amber, hand holding container 80.00
Glass, Miss Liberty's head, 4½", EX 95.00
Hall china, box holder on tray 22.00
Haviland china, cone shape on tray, decal decor 98.00
Jasper, elephant head, hat & eyeglasses, chamberstick shape 95.00
NP CI, hatchet, wall hanging, 1908 ....42.50
Stafford owl by tree stumps, 4½" 85.00

Match Safes

Match safes, aptly named cases used to carry matches in the days before cigarette lighters, were used during the last half of the 19th century until about 1920. Some incorporated added features (hidden compartments, cigar cutters, etc.), some were figural, and others were used by retail companies as advertising giveaways. They were made from every type of material, but silverplated styles abound. Our advisor for this category is Ron Damaska; he is listed in the Directory under Pennsylvania. See also Advertising.

Bowler Bros Brewing, celluloid-wrapped NP brass, 2¾x1½", EX ..90.00
Brass, alligator form, hinged bk & head, EX pnt 150.00
Brass, birds, flowers & trees, Japan, ca 1900, 2" 60.00
Brass, hoof form, opening on base, 1x3" 125.00
Celluloid, Bergner & Ensel Brewing, girl/Phoenix logo, 2¾", G ...60.00
Copper & tin, florals & Cigars in relief, EX 40.00
Enterprise Brewing, emb NP brass, 2¾x1½", G 115.00
German silver, Nouveau lady w/flowing hair ea side 65.00
Indianapolis Brewing Co, emb winged girl, 2¾x1½", G 35.00
Joseph Stoeckle Dmn State Brewery, NP brass, 2¾x1½", VG 115.00
NP brass, buffalo in relief, EX, lt wear 42.50
Phoenix Brewery, emb Phoenix trademk on NP brass, G 65.00
Silveroine, Nouveau florals in relief, M 27.50

Silverplate, embossed fishing scene, 3", $45.00.

SP, Dr Meyer's & Co Specialists, w/stamp holder, Pat 1892 ....200.00
SP, walnut figural, top opens, striker on bk, 1¼x1¾" 125.00
SP, Willow Springs Brewing ad, souvenir, lt wear, 2¼" 85.00
Sterling, eng hunt scene, ornate 125.00
Sterling, Nouveau lady's head relief, 2⅛" 88.00
Sterling, plain w/monogram, 2½" 50.00

McCoy

The third generation McCoy potter in the Roseville, Ohio, area was Nelson, who with the aid of his father, J.W., established the Nelson McCoy Sanitary Stoneware Company in 1910. They manufactured churns, jars, jugs, poultry fountains, and foot warmers. By 1925 they had expanded their wares to include majolica jardinieres and pedestals, umbrella stands and cuspidors, and an embossed line of vases and small jardinieres in a blended brown and green matt glaze. From the late twenties through the mid-forties, a utilitarian stoneware was produced, some of which was glazed in the soft blue and white so popular with collectors today. They also used a dark brown mahogany color and a medium to dark green, both in a high gloss. In 1933 the firm became known as the Nelson McCoy Pottery Company. They expanded their facilities in 1940 and began to make the novelty artware, cookie jars, and dinnerware that today are synonomous with 'McCoy.' More than two hundred cookie jars of every theme and description were produced.

Stimulated by the high prices commanded by desirable cookie jars, a broad spectrum of 'new' cookie jars are flooding the marketplace in three categories: 1) Manufacturers have expanded their lines with exciting new designs to attract the collector market. 2) Limited editions and artist-designed jars have proliferated. 3) Reproductions, signed and unsigned, have pervaded the market, creating uncertainty among new collectors and inexperienced dealers.

More than a dozen different marks have been used by the company; nearly all incorporate the name 'McCoy,' although some of the older items were marked 'NM USA.' For further information consult *The Collector's Encyclopedia of McCoy Pottery* by Sharon and Bob Huxford, available at your local bookstore or public library. Numbers in listings below refer to this book.

Alert! It should be noted that the original Nelson McCoy Pottery has closed its doors. Now an entrepreneur has emerged and has adopted the McCoy Pottery name and mark. This company is reproducing old McCoy designs as well as some classic designs of other defunct American potteries. Their wares are signed 'McCoy' with a mark which very closely approximates the old McCoy mark. Our McCoy cookie jar advisor is Judy Posner; she is listed in the Directory under Pennsylvania.

Cookie Jars

Animal Crackers 95.00
Apollo Age, minimum value 1,000.00
Apple, 1950-64 ....50.00
Apple on Basketweave 45.00
Astronauts 400.00
Bananas 125.00
Barnum's Animals 350.00
Baseball Boy 195.00
Bear, cookie in vest, no 'Cookies' 75.00
Betsy Baker 250.00
Black Kettle, w/immovable bail, HP flowers 35.00
Black Vase, w/flowers on lid 165.00
Bobby Baker 85.00
Bugs Bunny, cylinder 225.00
Caboose 165.00
Cat on Coal Scuttle 150.00
Chairman of the Board, minimum value 400.00
Chef 125.00
Chiffoniere, Early American Chest 75.00
Chinese Lantern 55.00
Chipmunk 110.00
Christmas Tree, minimum value 750.00
Circus Horse 250.00
Clown Bust 125.00
Clown in Barrel 120.00
Clyde Dog 150.00
Coalby Cat 350.00
Coffee Grinder 35.00
Coffee Mug 30.00

Colonial Fireplace 95.00
Cookie Barrel 25.00
Cookie Boy 225.00
Cookie Cabin 125.00
Cookie Jug, dbl loop 30.00
Cookie Jug, single loop, 2-tone gr rope 22.00
Cookie Jug, w/cork stopper, brn & wht 22.00
Cookie Log 35.00
Cookie Safe 65.00
Cookstove 45.00
Corn 150.00
Covered Wagon 125.00
Cylinder, w/red flowers 35.00
Dalmations in Rocking Chair 375.00
Dog on Basketweave 85.00
Drum 75.00
Duck on Basketweave 75.00
Dutch Boy 55.00
Dutch Girl, boy on reverse, rare 150.00
Dutch Treat Barn 65.00
Elephant 225.00
Elephant w/Split Trunk, rare, minimum value 450.00
Engine, blk 175.00
Flowerpot, plastic flower on top, minimum value ...500.00
Football Boy 195.00
Forbidden Fruit 65.00
Freddy Gleep 500.00
Friendship 200.00
Frontier Family 45.00
Fruit in Bushel Basket 75.00
Gingerbread Boy 75.00
Globe 325.00
Grandfather Clock 85.00
Granny 85.00
Granny, gold trim 125.00
Hamm's Bear 225.00
Happy Face 65.00
Hen on Nest 95.00
Hillbilly Bear, rare, minimum value 900.00
Hobby Horse 150.00
Honey Bear 75.00
Indian 325.00
Jack-O'-Lantern, minimum value 500.00
Kangaroo, bl 300.00
Kettle, jumbo sz 35.00
Kissing Penguins 75.00
Kitten on Basketweave 85.00
Kittens (2) on Low Basket, minimum value 600.00
Kittens on Ball of Yarn 100.00
Kookie Kettle, blk 30.00
Lamb on Basketweave 65.00
Leprechaun, minimum value 1,200.00
Liberty Bell 40.00
Little Clown 85.00
Lollipop 85.00
Mac Dog 95.00
Mammy, Cookies on base 225.00
Mammy w/Cauliflower, G pnt, minimum value ...1,100.00
Modern 35.00
Monk 40.00
Mother Goose 150.00
Mr & Mrs Owl 125.00
Nursery, decal of Humpty Dumpty 125.00
Oaken Bucket 35.00

Old Churn 35.00
Pears on Basketweave 45.00
Pelican 175.00
Pepper, yel 35.00
Picnic Basket 75.00
Pineapple 60.00
Pineapple, Modern 45.00
Pirate's Chest 65.00

Planter, duck with umbrella, $125.00.

Popeye Cylinder 225.00
Potbelly Stove, blk 35.00
Puppy, w/sign 95.00
Quaker Oats, minimum value 1,000.00
Red Barn, cow in door, rare, minimum value 350.00
Rooster, wht, 1970-1974 ....65.00
Rooster, 1955-1957 ....125.00
Round w/HP Leaves 45.00
Sad Clown 75.00
Snoopy on Doghouse 295.00
Snow Bear 85.00
Stagecoach, minimum value 1,000.00
Strawberry, 1955-57 ....35.00
Strawberry, 1971-75 ....30.00
Teapot, 1971 ....40.00
Tepee, str top 325.00
Tilt Pitcher, blk w/roses 35.00
Tomato 30.00
Touring Car 125.00
Tudor Cookie House 125.00
Tulip on Flowerpot 150.00
Turkey, gr, rare color 300.00
Upside Down Bear, panda 75.00
WC Fields 225.00
Wedding Jar 110.00
Windmill 150.00
Wishing Well 40.00
Woodsy Owl 225.00
Wren House 150.00
Yosemite Sam, cylinder 225.00

Miscellaneous

Bean pot, Suburbia Ware, mk #7, 1964, 2-qt 18.00
Coffee server, turq, mk Eastman USA, late 1950s 22.50
Creamer & sugar bowl, angle hdls, mk #7, 1959 ....8.50
Cup bowl, yel, mk #5, 1940s 8.00
Custard cup, emb ribs, gr, unmk 3.50
Dripolator, 6-sided shape, mk #4, 1940s 22.50
Jardiniere, flying birds emb on green, #22, unmk, 7½" 30.00

Jug, frosted bl, 1967 ....**8.00**
Lamp, blk panther form, 1940s **32.00**
Mug, ivory shaded to brn, mk #7, 1956 ....**3.50**
Novelty, baseball glove, tan, no mk **10.00**
Novelty, duck on base, wht, no mk **10.00**
Novelty, rolling pin w/Boy Blue seated on top, no mk, 1952 ....**35.00**
Pitcher, chicken form, ivory, unmk, 1943 ....**20.00**
Pitcher, donkey form, mk #1, 1940s **40.00**
Pitcher, emb cloverleaves, mk #7, 1948 ....**20.00**
Pitcher, gr cloverleaf on cream, mk #4, 1940s **20.00**
Planter, cat w/gr bow, unmk, 1953 ....**12.50**
Planter, fish form, pk & gr, mk #7, 1955 ....**40.00**
Planter, goose w/card, mk #4, 1943 ....**14.00**
Planter, lamb w/bl flower at neck, pk ears, no mk **8.00**
Planter, lion form, mk #1, 1940 ....**28.00**
Planter, poodle dog, blk w/red bow, mk #7, 1956 ....**14.00**
Planter, rooster, gray w/red comb & waddle, mk #7, 1951 ....**17.50**
Planter, stork & basket, pk, wht & bl, mk #7, 1956 .....**14.00**
Sugar bowl, Sunburst gold, mk #4, 1957 ....**20.00**
Tea set, Ivy, brn on cream, mk #7, 1950, 3-pc **70.00**
Tea set, Pine Cone, gr, mk #4, 1946, 3-pc **60.00**

McCoy, J. W.

The J.W. McCoy Pottery Company was incorporated in 1899. It operated under that name in Roseville, Ohio, until 1911 when McCoy entered into a partnership with George Brush, forming the Brush-McCoy Company. During the early years, McCoy produced kitchenware, majolica jardinieres and pedestals, umbrella stands, and cuspidors. By 1903 they had begun to experiment in the field of art pottery and though never involved to the extent of some of their contemporaries, nevertheless produced several art lines of merit. Their first line was Mt. Pelee, examples of which are very rare today. Two types of glazes were used, matt green and an iridescent charcoal gray. Though the line was primarily mold formed, some pieces evidence the fact that while the clay remained wet and pliable it was pulled and pinched with the fingers to form crests and peaks in a style not unlike George Ohr.

The company rebuilt in 1904 after being destroyed by fire, and other artware was designed. Loy-Nel Art and Renaissance were standard brown lines, hand decorated under the glaze with colored slip. Shapes and artwork were usually simple but effective. Olympia and Rosewood were relief-molded brown-glaze lines decorated in natural colors with wreaths of leaves and berries or simple floral sprays. Although much of this ware was not marked, you will find examples with the die-stamped 'Loy-Nel Art, McCoy' or an incised line identification.

Loy-Nel-Art, jardiniere & pedestal, 22" **750.00**
Loy-Nel-Art, vase, tulips, #1050, 1912 ....**800.00**
Loy-Nel-Art, vase, 1912, #05, mk, 6" **200.00**
Mt Pele, ewer, blk irid, 7" **1,000.00**
Olympia, oil lamp, early 1900s **200.00**
Olympia, pitcher, mk as Olympia, 6¼" **200.00**
Olympia, tankard, 1902, 15¾" **600.00**
Rosewood, vase, emb decor, bulbous, #10, 1904, 10" ...**165.00**
Rosewood, vase, emb decor w/gold, #10, 9" **175.00**

McKee

McKee Glass was founded in 1853 in Pittsburgh, Pennsylvania. Among their early products were tablewares of both the flint and non-flint varieties. In 1888 the company relocated to avail themselves of a source of natural gas, thereby founding the town of Jeannette, Pennsylva-

nia. One of their most famous colored dinnerware lines, Rock Crystal, was manufactured in the 1920s. During the thirties and forties, colored opaque dinnerware and kitchenware, Sunkist reamers, and 'bottoms up' cocktail tumblers were produced as well as a line of black glass vases, bowls, and novelty items. All are popular items with today's collectors. The company was purchased in 1916 by Jeannette Glass, under which name it continues to operate. Our advisor for this category is Lisa Rastello; she is listed in the Directory under Illinois. See also Animal Dishes with Covers; Depression Glass; Kitchen Collectibles; Reamers.

Apple bowl, Jadite, rectangular, flowers, 3-ftd, ca 1920 ....**200.00**
Bottoms Up, butterscotch, opal, 3¼" **75.00**
Bottoms Up, Jadite, w/coaster **150.00**
Bulb bowl, Seville yel, 7" **38.00**
Candlestick, dolphin w/petticoat base, canary to opal, 6¾" **90.00**
Canister, Jadite, screw-on lid, 48-oz **125.00**
Clock, Tambour Art, amber or pk **335.00**
Compote, dolphin std, petticoat base, peacock bl w/opal, 5¾" H ..**100.00**
Egg cup, custard **15.00**
Lamp, Torchiere, crystal frost w/blk top **150.00**
Mug, Jadite, Bottoms Down **150.00**
Plate, Ray, flint, 1860s, rough rim **27.00**
Shakers, Fancy Arch, ruby stain, 2⅞", pr **90.00**
Shakers, Flower Panel, gr opaque, 2¾", pr **48.00**
Shakers, Interlocking Ovals, bl, 1⅞", pr **38.00**
Vase, nudes, blk amethyst, 3-sided, 3-ftd, 8" **175.00**

Medical Collectibles

The field of medical-related items encompasses a wide area from the primitive bleeding bowl to the X-ray machines of the early 1900s. Other closely related collectibles include apothecary and dental items. Many tools that were originally intended for the pharmacist found their way to the doctor's office, and dentists often used surgical tools when no suitable dental instrument was available. A trend in the late 1700s toward self-medication brought a whole new wave of home-care manuals and 'patent' medical machines for home use. Commonly referred to as 'quack' medical gimmicks, these machines were usually ineffective and occasionally dangerous. Our advisor for this category is Jim Calison; he is listed in the Directory under New York.

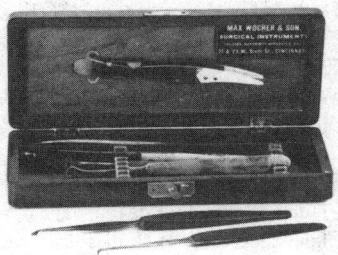

Surgical instrument set, Bakelite handles, Max Wocher & Son, 1860s, nine pieces in original wooden box, $295.00.

Bleeder, brass, 3 iron blades fold out, Norwick, 1840s **55.00**
Bleeding cup, glass, bell shape, ca 1810s, NM **25.00**
Blood pressure kit, mercury tube, Baum, NY **65.00**
Book, Developmental Anatomy, Leslie Brainerd Arey, 1926, EX .**10.00**
Book, Manual for Dental Assistants, Webster, 1932, 356-pg **8.00**
Book, Operative Surgery, Dr JJ McGrath, 1909, 650-pg, EX **10.00**
Book, Textbook of Nursing Technique, Kelley, 1935, EX **6.50**
Breast pump, brass plunger, Weiss & Son, 1880s, 2-pc, EX **295.00**
Dose glass, Hopkins Union Bitters, etched, gold trim, 2¼" **78.00**
Ear trumpet, brass, 1880s, 3½" **315.00**

Ear trumpet, gutta percha, 2-pc, collapsible 215.00
Eye cup, amberina 25.00
Eye cup, bl opal 25.00
Eye cup, cobalt 18.00
Eye cup, emerald gr 20.00
Eye cup, John Bull, clear, 1917 ....22.50
Gum mold, dentist's, for false teeth, CI, old 8.50
Infuser, porc, mk Berlin Germany 30.00
Nipple shield, glass, 1860s, EX 55.00
Pliers, tooth pulling; iron, early, EX 10.00
Quack instrument, electro-violet ray machine, VG 80.00
Spoon, medicine; mk Gibson, Inventor, ca 1837, EX 335.00
Sterilizer, copper, mk Arnold Steam...Pat May 9 82..., 21" H 200.00
Stethoscope, monaural, Bakelite, pocket type, 2-pc, 1880s 195.00
Stethoscope, monaural, ivory, 1-pc 550.00
Syringe, glass w/cotton string-wound plunger, 1860s 30.00
Syringe, infant; Goodrich, 1940s, NMIB 12.50
Tongue scraper, clear tortoise & ivory, 1840s 135.00
Tooth extractor, wooden hdl, EX 85.00
Tooth key, ebony X-hatched hdl, Weiss London, 1850s 395.00
Vaporizer, milk glass, 1920s, EX in orig box 25.00

Meissen

The Royal Saxon Porcelain Works was established in 1710 in Meissen, Saxony. Under the direction of Johann Freidrick Bottger, who in 1708 had developed the formula for the first true porcelain body, fine ceramic figurines with exquisite detail and tableware of the highest quality were produced. Although every effort was made to insure the secrecy of Bottger's discovery, others soon began to copy his ware; and in 1731 Meissen adopted the famous crossed swords trademark to identify their own work. The term 'Dresden ware' is often used to refer to Meissen porcelain, since Bottger's discovery and first potting efforts were in nearby Dresden. See also Onion Pattern.

Bust, girl in cap & gr scarf w/floral bouquet, 5½" 700.00
Candlestick, appl/HP flowers on Rococo vase stem, 9½", pr 650.00
Charger, wht w/emb gold foliage, Xd swords, 11" 300.00
Compote, rtcl woven border w/5 fruit medallions, 1880s, 7" 875.00
Cup & saucer, courting scenes on cobalt w/gilt, 3½" 300.00
Cup & saucer, emb wht/gr leaves w/gold tracery, 1800s 130.00
Desk set, harbor view/gilt, 1880s, 7x11" tray, bell, +2 pcs 950.00
Figurine, Apollo in chariot w/4 horses on plinth, 12x18" 7,000.00
Figurine, child kneels by fish trap, lobster in bag, 4¼" 475.00
Figurine, Cupid, Un Me Suffit, 1800s, 5¾" 695.00
Figurine, Cupid blksmith works on heart at anvil, 7½" 850.00
Figurine, Cupid finds 2 hearts under tree, 4¾" 550.00
Figurine, Cupid holds abalone shell, mk, 8" 650.00
Figurine, Cupid holds marriage contract & slipper 1,000.00
Figurine, Cupid on skull, mk, 8" 1,000.00

Figurine, Europa seated on Bull with two figures offering flowers, 9", $2,500.00.

Figurine, dog drinks from bowl, little girl sits beside, 3½" 495.00
Figurine, Europa & Bull, w/2 ladies offering flowers, 9" 2,500.00
Figurine, Europa & Bull w/2 attendants, rstr, 8½" 825.00
Figurine, huntsman on horsbk+4 dogs, Xd swords, 15x16" 2,500.00
Figurine, lady in lacy attire lays cards on table, 6", VG 500.00
Figurine, lovers/musicians/cherubs (7 figures), 14" 3,700.00
Figurine, nude child w/basket of flowers, 5½" 235.00
Figurine, nude w/Indian headdress on crocodile, 11" 1,800.00
Figurine, Venus & Adonis at pyre, she holds heart, 8½" 2,200.00
Figurine, Venus & Cupid w/Mercury behind, 9" 1,900.00
Figurine, Victorian lady on sofa w/emb florals, 6x6" 350.00
Figurine, Wind allegorical holds bird, cage aside, rpr, 5" 600.00
Figurine, woodpecker on stump, appl flowers & worm, 10" 950.00
Inkwell, floral & insect reserves on cobalt, 1800s, 2½" dia 235.00
Medallion, Madonna del Sedia in panel, after Raphael, 2¾" 250.00
Plate, botanical, rtcl basketweave rim, 1800s, 9½", pr 385.00
Plate, emb floral center w/gilt, cobalt border, 12¼" 300.00
Plate, mc floral centers w/basketweave borders, 9½", 6 for 600.00
Plate, 3 maidens & Cupid, blk & gold rim, 1800s, 8" 350.00
Slipper, pk/ruffled, cherubs/bl bow on toe, on pillow, 6x9" 280.00
Sweetmeat, figure seated by scalloped dish, wht, 10" L, pr 325.00
Tray, bl waves w/mermaid at edge, 3½" 300.00
Tray, floral reserve, emb & gilt border, hdls, 16" sq 895.00
Tray, modeled as mermaid emerging from ocean wave, 8½" L 450.00
Urn, pk & wht w/gold, flattened bulbous body, w/lid, 12¾" 800.00
Vase, HP fruit, snake hdls, fluted/gilt rim, 1880s, 11", pr 485.00
Vase, lovers reserve on cobalt, snake hdls, rtcl lid, 12" 1,500.00

Mercury Glass

Mercury glass was popular during the 1850s and enjoyed a short revival at the turn of the century. It was made with two thin layers, either blown with a double wall or joined in sections, with the space between the walls of the vessel filled with a mixture of tin, lead, bismuth, and mercury. The opening was sealed to prevent air from dulling the bright color. Though most examples are silver, blue, and gold can be found on occasion. Remember that the value of this type of glass hinges greatly upon condition of the mercury lining. In the listings that follow, all examples are silver unless noted another color.

Candlesticks, gold, dome base, 6", pr 80.00
Globe, 8" 95.00
Vase, gold, 5½" 30.00
Vase, floral sprays in panel, mc on silver, 10", pr 235.00
Witch ball, 18", +stand 165.00

Metlox

The Metlox Manufacturing Company was founded in 1927 in Manhattan Beach, California. Before 1934 when they began producing the ceramic housewares for which they have become famous, they made ceramic and neon outdoor advertising signs. The company went out of business in 1989.

Well-known sculptor Carl Romanelli designed artware in the late 1930s and early 1940s (and again briefly in the 1950s). His work is especially sought after today. Some pattern lines can be confusing. There are two 'rooster' lines, Red Rooster (red, orange, and brown) and California Provincial (dark green and burgundy), and there are two 'homestead' lines, Colonial Homestead (red, orange, and brown like the Red Rooster pieces) and Homestead Provencial (dark green and burgundy like California Provincial). For further information we recommend *The Collector's Encyclopedia of California Pottery* by our advisor, Jack Chipman; he is listed in the Directory under California.

California Aztec, carafe, w/lid, 18" 95.00
California Aztec, coffee server, tall 95.00
California Aztec, gravy boat 22.00
California Aztec, platter, oval, 9½" 18.00
California Contemporary, ewer, hourglass form 45.00
California Ivy, bowl, cereal; 7" 15.00
California Ivy, creamer 12.00
California Ivy, gravy boat 22.00
California Ivy, plate, 10¼" 15.00
California Ivy, sugar bowl, w/lid 15.00
California Mobile, coaster 10.00
California Mobile, cup & saucer 25.00
California Mobile, plate, 10" 20.00
California Provincial, canisters, set of 4 ....195.00
California Provincial, cup & saucer 22.00
California Provincial, gravy boat 22.00
California Provincial, match holder 65.00
California Provincial, pitcher, 1-qt 25.00
California Provincial, plate, 10" 18.00
California Provincial, plate, 9" 12.00
California Provincial, soup, flat 18.00
California Provincial, water can 27.50
California Strawberry, bowl, cereal; 5¾" 10.00
California Strawberry, bowl, vegetable; w/lid 45.00
California Strawberry, coffeepot 50.00
California Strawberry, creamer 10.00
California Strawberry, cup & saucer 15.00
California Strawberry, pitcher, 6" 22.00
California Strawberry, plate, 6" 5.00
California Strawberry, shakers, pr 12.00
California Strawberry, teapot 45.00
Golden Blossom, cup & saucer 12.00

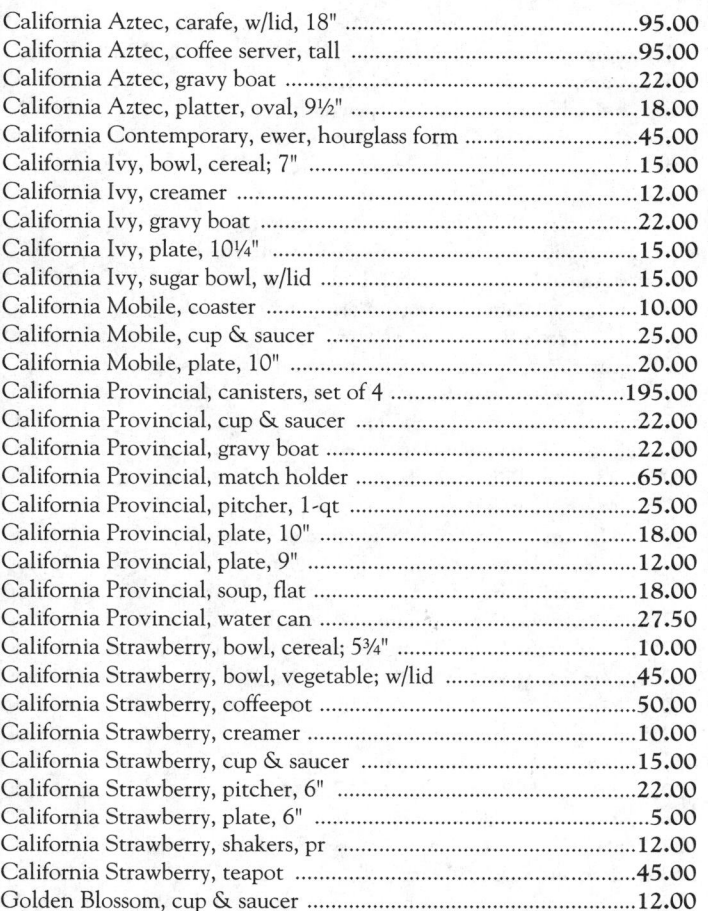

Homestead Provincial, creamer and sugar bowl, with lid, $22.00.

Homestead Provincial, bowl, cereal 10.00
Homestead Provincial, bowl, lug, 5" 15.00
Homestead Provincial, bowl, salad; 11" 25.00
Homestead Provincial, bowl, 10" 20.00
Homestead Provincial, bread tray 30.00
Homestead Provincial, coffeepot 40.00
Homestead Provincial, cup & saucer 20.00
Homestead Provincial, plate, 10" 10.00
Homestead Provincial, plate, 6" 6.00
Homestead Provincial, relish, divided 25.00
Homestead Provincial, teapot 35.00
Mosaic, vase, bud 20.00
Peach Blossom, plate, dinner 10.00
Provincial Blue, cup & saucer 15.00
Provincial Blue, plate, 10" 12.00
Provincial Blue, plate, 6½" 6.00

Provincial Blue, plate, 7½" 8.00
Provincial Blue, platter, 11" 22.00
Provincial Fruit, bowl, tab hdls, 5" 10.00
Provincial Fruit, butter dish 25.00
Provincial Fruit, coffeepot 45.00
Provincial Fruit, cup 10.00
Provincial Fruit, plate, 10½" 15.00
Provincial Fruit, platter, 14" 22.00
Provincial Fruit, shakers, pr 15.00
Red Rooster Provincial, bowl, berry; sm 8.00
Red Rooster Provincial, bowl, divided vegetable; hdls 45.00
Red Rooster Provincial, bread tray 27.50
Red Rooster Provincial, butter dish 35.00
Red Rooster Provincial, coffeepot 45.00
Red Rooster Provincial, cookie jar 75.00
Red Rooster Provincial, creamer 10.00
Red Rooster Provincial, cup 10.00
Red Rooster Provincial, plate, bread 6.00
Red Rooster Provincial, platter, 11" 22.50
Red Rooster Provincial, stein 45.00
Sculptured Daisy, bowl, deep, 7" 10.00
Sculptured Daisy, bowl, vegetable; tab hdls, 8" 22.00
Sculptured Daisy, canister, lg 50.00
Sculptured Daisy, cup & saucer 12.00
Sculptured Daisy, pitcher, milk; 6" 35.00
Sculptured Daisy, plate, salad 15.00
Sculptured Daisy, plate, 10½" 10.00
Sculptured Daisy, platter, 14" 30.00
Sculptured Daisy, soup, flat 18.00
Sculptured Grape, bowl, salad; lg 32.00
Sculptured Grape, bowl, vegetable; 9¼" 30.00
Sculptured Grape, chop plate, rnd, lg 40.00
Sculptured Grape, cup & saucer 20.00
Sculptured Grape, gravy boat & undertray 35.00
Sculptured Grape, pitcher, lg 45.00
Sculptured Grape, platter 35.00
Sculptured Grape, shakers, pr 15.00
Tropicana, bowl, low 35.00
Tropicana, vase, teardrop form 50.00
Yorkshire, bowl, ca 1939, 6" 15.00
Yorkshire, bowl, ca 1939, 9" 25.00
Yorkshire, plate, ca 1939, 6½" 15.00
Yorkshire, plate, ca 1939, 9" 22.00

Cookie Jars

Baby Bluebird on Pine Cone, Made in USA 75.00
Barrel of Apples 65.00
Bear, bl coat 75.00
Bear, sombrero 65.00
Bear, sweater & cookie 60.00
Black Topsy Girl, bl skirt, red belt 300.00
Blue Bird on Stump, Made in USA 50.00
Bubbles the Hippo, USA 225.00
Bucky Beaver, Made in USA 120.00
Circus Bear 165.00
Cow, w/butterfly & flowers 325.00
Dina (Stegasaurus) 130.00
Drum, bsk, mk 40.00
Dutch Boy, wht clothes w/bl trim 165.00
Fido 65.00
Frog, unmk 75.00
Frosty Penguin 75.00
Humpty Dumpty, mk 135.00

Lamb's Head, crier in lid 135.00
Mammy w/Mixing Bowl, red or bl dots, ea 200.00
Mona Dinosaur, mk 130.00
Orange, Made in USA 45.00
Panda Bear w/Lollipop, mk 185.00
Pinocchio, paper label 275.00
Raggedy Andy 150.00
Rose, Made in USA 285.00
Sir Francis Drake, unmk 55.00
Slenderella, mk 75.00
Space Rocket, minimum value 400.00
Uncle Sam Bear, minimum value 400.00
Wheat Shock 45.00

Romanelli Designs

Bookends, nude w/dogs, mc, pr 250.00
Figurine, deer, wht matt, Poppytrail, Deco, 7½" 75.00
Figurine, flamingo, 6" 40.00
Figurine, rooster, satin wht, 8¾" 75.00
Figurine, seminude cowgirl, mc, 9½" 175.00
Flower holder, draped nude before triple vase, ivory, 8¾" ...200.00
Miniature, bear, reclining 65.00
Miniature, crocodile 80.00
Miniature, cubistic dog 80.00
Miniature, elephant 95.00
Miniature, hippo 75.00
Miniature, horse 55.00
Miniature, Scottie dog 35.00
Miniature, seal 65.00
Miniature, turtle 60.00
Sculpture, Indian brave, naturalistic, ca 1940, 9" 250.00
Vase, angelfish form, 8½" 100.00
Vase, Leo, Zodiac, ca 1939, 8" 95.00
Vase, swordfish form, bl matt, 9" 150.00
Vase, Taurus, Zodiac, 8" 95.00

Mettlach

In 1836 Nicholas Villeroy and Eugene Francis Boch, both of whom were already involved in the potting industry, formed a partnership and established a stoneware factory in an old restored abbey in Mettlach, Germany. Decorative stoneware with in-mold relief was their specialty, steins in particular. Through constant experimentation, they developed innovative methods of decoration. One process, called chromolith, involved inlaying colorful mosaic designs into the body of the ware. Later underglaze printing from copper plates was used. Their stoneware was of high quality, and their steins won many medals at the St. Louis Expo and early world's fairs. Most examples are marked with an incised castle and the name 'Mettlach.' The numbering system indicates size, date, stock number, and decorator. Production was halted by a fire in 1921; the factory was not rebuilt. Our advisor for this category is Ron Fox; he is listed in the Directory under New York.

Key:
L — liter   PUG — print under glaze
POG — print over glaze   tl — thumb lift

#1044, plaque, HP: lady/bird/flowers, 17", EX 385.00
#1132, stein, etched: violinist/alligator, hdl chip, ½-L ...475.00
#1179/2327, beaker, PUG: boy w/dog & stein, ¼-L, M ...150.00
#1395, stein, etched: Fr cards, inlaid lid, ½-L, M 565.00
#1475, stein, etched: dwarfs dig ditch, inlaid lid, ½-L, M ...695.00

#1513, pitcher, couples dancing, Warth, 6¼", M 325.00
#1520, stein, etched: eagle/cavaliers, inlaid lid, ½-L, M ...790.00
#1526, stein, HP: crest, pewter lid, dent, 1-L 300.00
#1526, stein, HP: stein in shield, pewter lid, no tl, ½-L ...120.00
#1526/1078, stein, PUG: cavalier, pewter lid, ½-L, M 200.00
#1526/1109, stein, PUG: musicians, musical lid, 1-L, NM ...350.00
#1526/589, stein, PUG: drinking scene, pewter lid, ½-L, NM ...175.00
#1526/592, stein, PUG: man & lady, pewter lid, ½-L, NM ...100.00
#153, cup & saucer, relief: repeating early pattern, 3", M ...90.00
#1561, stein, etched/relief: dog, inlaid lid, rpr tl, ½-L ...515.00
#1607, plaque, Autumn Season, Warth, dtd 1885, mk, 11" ...535.00
#1645, stein, etched: tapestry, pewter lid, ½-L, M 400.00
#171, stein, relief: farming people, inlaid lid, ¼-L, NM ...125.00
#1737, stein, relief: vine decor, inlaid lid, .2-L, M 325.00
#1786, stein, etched/glazed: St Florian, dragon hdl, ½-L, M ...700.00
#1909, stein, HP: man w/lg hat, pewter lid, ½-L, NM 465.00
#1909/673, stein, PUG: dwarfs, pewter lid, dent, ½-L 200.00
#1909/747, stein, PUG: bowling drawfs, pewter lid, .3-L, M ...300.00
#1909/942, stein, PUG: rooster & watchman, pewter lid, ½-L, M ...250.00
#1932, stein, etched: fireman, Warth, fireman tl, ½-L, EX ...525.00
#1940, stein, relief: Yale University, pewter lid, 3-L, M ...900.00
#1946, stein, etched: lovers, inlaid lid, ½-L, M 550.00
#1947, stein, etched: cavalier/verse, inlaid lid, ½-L, M ...585.00
#2001, stein, etched/relief: doctor, inlaid lid, ½-L, M 590.00
#2002, stein, etched: Munich skyline, pewter lid, ½-L, NM ...365.00
#2028, stein, etched: drinking scene, inlaid lid, ½-L, M ...525.00
#2035, stein, etched: festive scene, inlaid lid, ½-L, M 450.00
#2052, stein, etched: Munich Child, inlaid lid, ¼-L, M 450.00
#2065, stein, etched/glazed: cavalier/lady, jewels, 1½-L, M ...1,600.00
#2080, plaque, etched: 4 Kurassiers, sgn Stocke, 15", NM ...1,300.00
#2082, stein, etched: Wilhelm Tell, inlaid lid, ½-L, M 1,265.00
#2089, stein, etched: man & barmaid, inlaid lid, ½-L, M ...875.00
#2090, stein, etched: man at table, Schlitt, .3-L, NM 565.00
#2091, stein, etched: St Lorian, inlaid lid, fireman tl, ½-L, M ...925.00
#2093, stein, etched: cards, inlaid lid, ½-L, M 800.00
#2097, stein, etched: musical notes, inlaid rim, ½-L 455.00
#2100, stein, etched: warrior & Roman, inlaid lid, ½-L, M ...900.00
#2130, stein, cameo: Gambrinus, inlaid lid, ½-L, M 600.00
#2134, stein, etched: dwarf in nest, inlaid lid, rpr, .3-L, ...660.00
#2140/952, stein, PUG: man/bicycle, inlaid lid, Am tl, ½-L, M ...635.00
#2177/959, stein, PUG: drunken knight, pewter lid, ¼-L, NM ...100.00
#2180/955, stein, PUG: cavalier panels, rpr hdl, .3-L 300.00
#2189, coaster, etched: drinking/smoking, 4½", NM 135.00
#2195/#2196, plaques, etched: Rheinsein/Stolzanfels, 18", pr ...1,600.00
#2205, stein, etched: hunters, squirrel lid, boar tl, .2-L, NM ...2,300.00
#2218, stein, transfer: Yale Boat House, no lid, .4-L, M ...160.00
#2227/900, stein, PUG: military scene, pewter rpr, .3-L ...1,100.00
#2238, stein, etched: 7th Regt Am Flags, inlaid lid, ½-L, NM ...1,100.00

#2277, stein, etched: Nurnberg, .3-liter, M, $260.00; #2093, stein, etched: suits of cards, firing flaw, ½-liter, $800.00.

#2327/1200, beaker, PUG: Stuttgart, ¼-L, EX 95.00
#2368/1091, beaker, PUG: cavalier, ¼-L, NM 150.00
#2384/1143, stein, PUG: cavaliers, pewter lid, ¼-L, NM ...465.00

#2430, stein, etched: cavalier, rpr, 3-L 700.00
#2442, plaque, Grecian soldiers in boat, sgn/dtd 1899, 18" 1,300.00
#2619/6075, vase, PUG: castle by water, rpr chip, 7½" 330.00
#2628, stein, cameo: bowling scene, inlaid lid, ½-L, M 865.00
#2715, stein, cameo: dancing scenes, inlaid lid, ½-L, M 1,000.00
#2716, stein, etched: festive scene, inlaid lid, ½-L, M 575.00
#2752, stein, etched: men at table, inlaid lid, ½-L, M 700.00
#2764, stein, etched: knight on wht horse, inlaid lid, ½-L, M .6,500.00
#2776, stein, etched: keeper of cellar, inlaid lid, ½-L, M 865.00
#2781, beaker, cameo: man & lady, ¼-L, M 415.00
#2815, beaker, cameo: dancers, ¼-L, M 300.00
#2832, stein, etched: lady in window, inlaid lid, ½-L, M 650.00
#2833, stein, etched: lovers, inlaid lid, ½-L, M 565.00
#2838, ashtray, etched: Art Nouveau, 2x4½" dia, M 300.00
#2869, stein, etched/glazed: Munich Child, inlaid lid, .9-L, M ..7,150.00
#2900, stein, etched: Quilmes Argentina, dtd 1930, ½-L, M 425.00
#2913, vase, Seccessionist floral & line design, 13½" 700.00
#2936, etched: elks, Nouveau style, inlaid lid, ½-L, NM 395.00
#2946, teapot, etched: Art Nouveau, sm rpr, 5½" 290.00
#2947, pitcher, stylized trees, bl/wht/tan, 6½", +7" tray 325.00
#3043, stein, etched/glazed: Munich scene, inlaid lid, ½-L, M ..1,735.00
#3057, stein, etched: festive scene, inlaid lid, .3-L 300.00
#3087, stein, etched/HP: lady w/stein, pewter lid, 1-L, M 800.00
#3089, stein, etched: Diogenes, Schlitt, inlaid lid, ½-L, M 1,275.00
#3091, stein, etched: knight drinking, inlaid lid, 1-L, M 1,400.00
#3092, stein, etched: bbl man, inlaid lid, ½-L, M 1,050.00
#3093, stein, etched: troll, Schlitt, inlaid lid, ½-L, M 2,195.00
#3173, stein, etched: man & lady, Hohlwein, inlaid lid, ½-L 695.00
#3321, creamer, etched: Art Nouveau, 4", M 120.00
#3358, vase, Art Nouveau feathers, shouldered, 12", M 235.00
#5006, stein, faience: Nurnberg castle, pewter lid, ½-L, M 550.00
#5062/1044, plaque, Delft-type scene, 17½", M 325.00

Microscopes

The microscope has taken on many forms during its 250-year evolutionary period. The current collectors' market primarily includes examples from England, those surplused from institutions, and continental beginner and intermediate forms which sold through Sears Roebuck & Company and other retailers of technical instruments. Earlier examples have brass maintubes which are unpainted. Later, more common examples are all black with brass or silver knobs and horseshoe-shaped bases. Early and more complex forms are the most valuable; these always had hardwood cases to house the delicate instrument and its accessories. Instruments were never polished during use, and those that have been polished to use as decorator pieces are of little interest to most avid collectors. Our advisor for this category is Dale Beeks; he is listed in the Directory under Idaho.

Acme, brass & iron, 14" case, EX 350.00
Baker, 224 High Holborn London, brass, 1840s, 17" 1,200.00
Bausch & Lomb, blk, horseshoe base, 1915, EX 150.00
Bausch & Lomb, blk base, brass tube, 1897, 14", EX 325.00
Bausch & Lomb, brass, tripod base, 1876, 16", EX, +case 375.00
Bausch & Lomb, brass, tripod base, 1885, 16", EX, +case 350.00
Bulloch, Chicago, brass, complex, Y base, 1880, 15", +case 950.00
English, professional, brass, 1876, 18", +case/accessories 900.00
English, student, brass, ca 1870, 12", +case/accessories 350.00
French, drum or furnace form, 5", EX, +case 55.00
French, student, ca 1910, 9", G, +case 65.00
German, student, rnd base, ca 1860, G, +case 150.00
Grunow, New Haven, iron & brass, 15", EX, +case 1,100.00
Grunow, New York, iron & brass, 15", EX, +case 900.00

Gundlach, brass, Y base, 1879, 14", EX 375.00
Gundlach Manhattan, student, all brass, 11", EX 250.00
Hand-held, simple form, 1890, 3", G 45.00
McAllister, brass, chain-drive focus, 14", G, +case 325.00
McIntosh Battery & Optical, brass & iron, 12", G 450.00
Queen, brass & iron, Y base, 14", G, +case 325.00
Spencer Lens Co, brass, horseshoe base, 13", EX 195.00
Stamp magnifier, brass, 3-leg, 1½", G 50.00
Tighe, brass, 12", EX, +case 450.00
Tolles, Boston, brass, Y base, ca 1880, 16", G, +case 750.00
Watson, English binocular form, 1880, 18", EX, +case 650.00
Zentmeyer, brass, complex, dbl pillar, tripod, base, 18", G 1,250.00

Midwestern Glass

As early as 1814, blown glass was made in Ohio. By 1835 glasshouses in Michigan were producing similar pattern-molded types that have long been highly regarded by collectors. During the latter part of the 19th century, all six of the states of the Northwest Territory were mass-producing the pressed glass tableware patterns that were then in vogue. Various types of art glass were produced in the area until after the turn of the century. Items listed here are attributed to the Midwest by certain physical characteristics known to be indigenous to that part of the country. See also Findlay Onyx; Greentown Glass; Libbey; Zanesville Glass. Our advisor for this category is Mark Vuono; he is listed in the Directory under Connecticut.

Bottle, club; aqua, broken swirl, stain, 8⅜" 138.00
Bottle, club; aqua, 30 broken-swirl ribs, 8" 165.00
Candlestick, hexagonal, open socket w/pewter insert, 9¾" 95.00
Cruet, sapphire bl, 16 swirled ribs, hollow hdl, 7" 2,310.00
Cruet, 13 vertical ribs, appl hollow hdl, 8¾" 195.00
Flask, chestnut; aqua, 21 vertical ribs, 6" 165.00
Flask, chestnut; pale gr, 18 swirled ribs, 6½" 195.00
Hat whimsey, amber w/clear rim, 6" 40.00
Pitcher, appl hollow hdl, 6⅞" 220.00
Pitcher, pale gr w/appl hdl, 16 swirled ribs, 6¼" 125.00

Militaria

Because of the wide and varied scope of items available to collectors of militaria, most tend to concentrate mainly on the area or areas that interest them most or that they can afford to buy. Some items represent a major investment and because of their value have been reproduced. Extreme caution should be used when purchasing Nazi items. Every badge, medal, cap, uniform, dagger, and sword that Nazi Germany issued is being reproduced today. Some repros are crude and easily identified as fakes, while others are very well done and difficult to recognize as reproductions. Purchases from WWII veterans are usually your safest buys. Reputable dealers or collectors will normally offer a money-back guarantee on Nazi items purchased from them. There are a number of excellent Third Reich reference books available in bookstores at very reasonable prices. Study them to avoid losing a much larger sum spent on a reproduction. Our advisor for this category is Ron Willis; he is listed in the Directory under Oklahoma.

Imperial German

Badge, Prussian Veteran's Assoc, shield shape w/eagle, EX 12.50
Badge, wound; WWI, Kriegsmarine, gold, hollow stamped 80.00
Badge, WWI, Army standard bearer, embr w/Xd flags, EX 150.00
Belt, WWI, brn leather, field-gray pnt buckle, EX 40.00

Buckle, WWI, stamped steel, field gray pnt, 1-pc, EX 18.00
Buckle, WWII, crown w/Cott Mit UNS Motto, brass, 2-pc 27.50
Cap, visor; WWI, Army officer, crush style, bl w/band, EX 90.00
Document, award for Kaiser Jubilee medal, 1898, EX 20.00
Epaulets, gold bullion, 2 silver rank pips, EX, pr 130.00
Grenade, WWI, wood hdl, steel head, EX 80.00
Helmet, spike; Baden Guard Grenadier, silver trim, EX 485.00
Helmet cover, officer's, for spike helmet, gray w/red, EX 70.00
Medal, Baden Veteran's Assoc Cross, 1914-18, w/ribbon 125.00
Medal, Bavaria War, Merit Cross, 3rd Class, bronze, EX 30.00
Medal, Franco-Prussian War, gilt bronze, w/ribbon 22.50
Medal, Iron Cross, 1st Class, domed, screwbk, w/case 150.00
Medal, pre-WWI, Baden Golden Erinnerungzeichen, cutouts 95.00
Medal, WWI, 1914 Iron Cross 2nd Class, w/ribbon, EX 42.00
Military pass, WWI, Kriegsmarine, 1917-18, EX 27.50
Plaque, Bismark portrait in relief, CI, 12½x17½" 95.00
Pocket, pocket; brass body, glass crystal, ca 1890, EX 25.00
Postcard, WWI, photo of soldier w/sweetheart, EX 6.00
Service bar, Landwehr 2nd Class, Xd swords, 1842-1913 ....17.50
Shoulderboards, medical staff, silver w/blk, slip-on, pr 32.00
Stein, crockery, Naval, dtd 1908, 1-liter, EX 925.00
Tunic, WWI, Air Service, field gray, concealed buttons, EX 485.00

Third Reich

Wall hanging, Nazi, eagle over swastika within wreath, heavy metal, 9x7½", $125.00.

Back pack, Army, olive canvas w/blk leather, 1940, EX 48.00
Badge, Infantry Assault, silver, stamped on bk, EX 65.00
Badge, Luftwaffe Flak Artillery Personel Specialty, cannon 10.00
Badge, Luftwaffe Ground, 2-pc, solid bk, hallmk, EX 42.00
Badge, Luftwaffe Paratrooper Combat, eagle & wreath, NM 155.00
Badge, Navy Destroyer, eagle & wreath, silver/gold, EX 115.00
Badge, Technical Specialist, silver embr, hammer/gear, EX 50.00
Boots, Army Mtn Troops, dk brn leather, cleats, EX, pr 95.00
Buckle, Army, aluminum, hallmk, 1937, EX 22.50
Buckle, Hitler Youth, NP, hallmk, EX 25.00
Canteen, aluminum, MKL 39, w/straps, EX 10.00
Canteen, Army, blk Bakelite cup, brn wool cover, EX 35.00
Canteen, Luftwaffe, wool cover, Bakelite cup, leather belting 27.50
Cap, visor; Luftwaffe, M43, gray wool, 1944, VG 40.00
Cap, visor; Luftwaffe, yel piping, eagle/wreath, EX 75.00
Cap, Waffen SS Officer, M43, gray twill embr eagle & skull, EX ...375.00
Chevron, Army Obergefreiter, silver bullion, gr wool 12.00
Collar tabs, Army Mtn Troop, gray embr on lt gr, pr 12.00
Collar tabs, Luftwaffe Flak Artillery Oberst, silver embr, pr 22.50
Collar tabs, Security & Rescue Service, silver embr on gr, pr 25.00
Flag, WWII, swastika, w/Iron Cross at corners, 112x187", EX 295.00

Hat, visor; Luftwaffe General, embr gold bullion eagle, EX 1,200.00
Helmet, Army, M34/40, field gray camo, VG 195.00
Helmet, Luftwaffe, M1935, gray camo, EX 165.00
Helmet, Luftwaffe Flight, brn leather, earphones, EX 75.00
Helmet cover, Waffen SS, summer camo, aluminum hooks, EX ..275.00
Insignia, cap; Waffen SS, joined skulls on tan camo, EX 70.00
Insignia, sleeve; Army Mtn Troops Edelweiss, gr wool, EX 90.00
Insignia, sleeve; German Youth, wht embr on red 6.00
Leaflet, propaganda, dropped on British, EX 10.00
Medal, Honor Cross, w/o swords, 1914-18, w/ribbon, EX 10.00
Medal, Russian Front, w/ribbon, EX 15.00
Medal, Shooting Assoc, silver w/gilt oak leaves, 1931, EX 65.00
Medal, War Service Cross 2nd Class, w/swords, EX 20.00
Scarf, neck; Africa Corps Desert, field gray, 1942, EX 60.00
Shoulder cord, Luftwaffe Marksmanship, eagle & wreath, EX 65.00
Shoulderboards, Army Panzer Oberstluetnant, gold pips, pr 42.50
Shoulderboards, Artillery Tropical, olive twill w/red, pr 65.00
Trousers, Army Assault, gray wool, flap pockets, EX 250.00
Trousers, Waffen SS, summer camo herringbone cotton, EX 300.00
Tunic, Army Administrative Oberintendanturrat, gray wool, EX .300.00
Tunic, Hunting Assoc, field gray, gr collar, insignias 35.00
Uniform, Army Mtn Troop Lieutenant, gray wool, EX 350.00
Uniform, Labor Corps, brn wool, Obertruppfuhrer shoulderboards .275.00

Japanese

Backpack, WWII, Army, roll pattern on khaki, EX 24.00
Badge, Army Pilot, silver bullion wings, yel wreath 30.00
Badge, WWII, Army Field Artillery Observer, gold mum/rams 80.00
Badge, WWII, Railway Police, silver w/red enamel, EX 48.00
Banner, mum/sun/flag, going into service, 9x33", EX 35.00
Blanket, WWII, Army, tan wool, issue tag, EX 38.00
Cape, WWII, Army Officer, olive-drab wool, Manchuria, EX 50.00
Chevrons, WWII, Police, Bevo-type embr wht mum on yel, pr 7.50
Collar tabs, WWII Fire Police Commander, cherry blossoms, pr ..12.00
Document, WWII, Declaration of War, 8-pg facsimile, 1941 .....700.00
Flag, pocket; w/collapsible pole & carrying bag, sm, EX 20.00
Foot locker, Army officer, wood, leather straps, lock & key 90.00
Grenade, WWII, type #97, inert, w/fuse assembly, EX 45.00
Helmet, Army, star on front, w/liner & tie straps 70.00
Helmet, Marine, anchor & mum on front, EX 135.00
Helmet, WWII, Navy Landing Forces, no liner, VG 80.00
Helmet cover, WWII, khaki cotton, drawstring, EX 60.00
Lapel rosette, Order of Golden Kite 5.00
Map, WWII, propaganda, land 'controlled,' 21x17", EX 25.00
Medal, Order of Golden Kite, 7th Class, w/ribbon, EX in box 160.00
Medal, Order of Rising Sun, 8th Class, incomplete ribbon 30.00
Medal, Order of Sacred Treasure, 6th Class, EX 65.00
Medal, Red Cross Special Membership, w/rosette, M in case 25.00
Medal, 1894-95 War, M 95.00
Medal, 1914-20 War, no ribbon, NM 40.00
Medal, 1931-4 China Incident, NM 45.00
Medallion, pre-WWII, military band member, bronze w/lion, M ..15.00
Raincoat, Army Officer, tan, waterproof, EX 22.00
Sandals, WWII, tropics, olive-drab web strap, brn leather, pr 45.00
Shirt, WWII, tropics, collarless, 2-pocket, EX 20.00
Sword knot, Samurai, bl & brn cord w/2 tassles, EX 18.00
Tunic, Army, tropics, khaki, Sergeant Major collar tabs, NM 45.00
Tunic, WWII, Army, M-1938, olive-drab wool, 4-pocket, EX 50.00
Uniform, WWII, Army, khaki cotton, wood buttons, EX 65.00

United States

Badge, WWI, Ship Building Identification, bronze, EX 15.00

Badge, WWII, Command Pilot, cloth, wht shield w/star, EX 12.50
Belt, cartridge, WWII, khaki web, 10-pocket, complete, M 8.00
Bible, Active Service Testament, New Testament, 1918, EX 8.00
Book, Soldiers of the Am Army 1775-1954, Todd, 1941, VG 10.00
Boots, flight; WWII, Army Air Forces, fleece lined, VG, pr 30.00
Boots, Navy Wave, blk leather, ankle height, 1959, M, pr 20.00
Box, tinder; Revolutionary War, steel, oval, 3x2½", EX 65.00
Button, Vermont State Seal, Scoville Mfg, 1880-1890 ....4.00
Canteen, Civil War, pnt bull's eye/bushes/bloody field, 7½" dia ...220.00
Canteen, Spanish-Am War era, canvas cover, w/stopper, EX 25.00
Canteen, WWI, khaki cloth cover, 'US' stencil, w/cup, EX 8.00
Canteen, WWII, aluminum, khaki canvas carrier, VG 12.50
Cap, WWII, Medical Corps Overseas, khaki, brn piping, EX 10.00
Carrier, grenade; Vietnam Era, 3-pocket type, w/belt hanger 6.50
Case, handcuff; Police, blk leather, belt loop, 1950s, EX 10.00
Certificate, wound; WWII, Infantry Corporal, 22x18" in fr 35.00
Chevron, Cavalry Sergeant, yel & khaki, ca 1900, EX 22.00
Cigarettes, WWII, Chesterfield, non-filters, unopened 22.50
Collar device, WWI, Army Prison Guard, bronze, EX 15.00
Collar disk, WWI, Infantry, crossed rifles, EX 8.00
Collar disk, WWI, Motor Transport Corps, hat on wheel 12.50
Cup, Civil War, tin, folding type in orig tin container, 3" 50.00
Flag, semaphore; WWI, Signal Corps, red & wht cotton 8.00
Gas mask, WWII, gr rubber, ca 1930s, EX 15.00
Great coat, WWII, Marine Corps, gr khaki blanket wool, EX 30.00
Hat, campaign; Signal Corps, khaki wool, leather sweatband, M .28.00
Helmet, Vietnam War, rpt Kelly gr shell w/camo cover, EX 25.00
Helmet, WWII, M5, bl-gray finish, w/ear flaps & liner, EX 25.00
Hood, field jacket; used w/model 1943 field jacket, khaki 7.50
Insignia, shoulder; Normandy Invasion, Am flags, M 42.50
Insignia, shoulder; WWII, Army Ground Forces, EX 8.00
Insignia, sleeve; WWI, Army Cook, cook's hat on tan khaki 7.50
Insignia, Spanish-Am War, Cavalry, crossed sabres, gilt 15.00
Insignia, visor hat; Commissary Sergeant, 1902 pattern, EX 25.00
Insignia, WWI, Bugler Specialist, khaki wool bugle on cotton 12.00
Insignia, WWII, Third Corps, bl embr caltrop on khaki wool 18.00
Jacket, flight; Vietnam War, Navy, brn leather, NM 185.00
Jacket, flight; WWII, A-2, brn leather, zipper front, EX 900.00
Jacket, flight; WWII, CBI, brn leather, zipper front, EX 1,200.00
Jacket, WWI, Ordnance Sergeant, w/76th Division patch, EX 60.00
Leaflet, propaganda; WWII, dropped on German forces, EX 12.00
Leaflet, propaganda; WWII, dropped on Japan, set of 3 ....35.00
Manual, WWII, Flight & Operational...Boeing B-29, EX 60.00
Map, WWII, Western Europe, cloth, dbl-sided, 27x27" 25.00
Map case, WWII, 4-pocket interior, khaki canvas, 1942, EX 15.00
Medal, Mexican Border Service, 5-sided fort, EX 25.00
Medal, WWI, Am Victory w/France bar, 1920, EX 22.00
Medal, WWII, City Service, bar pin & ribbon, MIB 18.00
Medal, WWII, Navy Good Conduct, EX 10.00
Medal, WWII, Town Service, top bar pin & ribbon, M in case 18.00
Pamphlet, US Army Recruiting, 1931, 36-pg, 6x9", EX 15.00
Paperweight, US Navy Factory WA DC, brass, 1860-75, 2½" 24.00
Religious statue, Civil War, St Joseph, lead, 1", in brass case 110.00
Sextant, WWI, Navy, brass fr, colored lenses, EX 235.00
Shirt, Korean War, Army insignia on tan khaki, 2-pocket, EX 7.50
Shirt, Vietnam War, Navy Seabees, khaki cotton, EX 12.00
Spoon, folding; Civil War officer's, brass w/bone hdl 35.00
Stove, field; Mtn Troop, Model 527, unissued, NM 150.00
Suspenders, ammunition belt; Model 1936 type, complete 8.00
Tunic, Vietnam Era, Staff Sergeant stripes, wool blend, EX 25.00
Tunic, WWI, Artillery, khaki wool, 4-pocket, bronze buttons 25.00
Tunic, WWII, Navy Commodore, bl wool, gold eagle buttons 50.00
Undershirt, WWII, Army, wht cotton, 1940s, M 8.00
Whistle, Civil War, soldered tin w/pea inside, EX 10.00

Miscellaneous

Austria, medal, Order of Malta, bronze, w/ribbon 45.00
Austria, medal, Signum Memoriae, bronze, w/ribbon 10.00
Britain, flight helmet, blk leather, quilted lining, EX 65.00
Britain, medal, Africa Star, bronze, w/ribbon 15.00
Britain, medal, Sudan Service, w/ribbon, mini 20.00
Britain, tricorner hat, blk wool w/gold border, ca 1900, EX 185.00
Britain, WWII, helmet, Pilot, type C, 1942 pattern, EX 150.00
Britain, WWII, smock, Paratrooper, Denison camo, 1942, EX ...125.00
France, insignia, Army Aviation Observer, hallmk, EX 10.00
France, jacket, Paratrooper, camo, 4-pocket, 1960s, M 95.00
France, medal, Croix de Guerre, bronze, 1914-18, w/ribbon 12.50
France, medallion, Free Czechoslovakia, bronze, M 25.00
France, WWII, britches, service; Engineer Officer, EX 85.00
France, WWII, greatcoat, bl blanket wool, silver buttons, VG 70.00
Poland, badge, 24th Infanty Regiment, silvered cross, 1918 ....48.00
Poland, medal, Cross of Merit, silver w/red enameling 95.00
Poland, medal, Order of Labor, silver starburst, enameling, EX ..145.00
Poland, medal, WWII, Battle of Warsaw, bronze, w/ribbon 48.00
Poland, medal, WWII, Home Army Cross, silver, scarce 80.00
Russia, badge, Imperial Guard, blk enamel cross w/silver fr 325.00
Russia, badge, Imperial State Militia, Czar Nicholas cypher 250.00
Russia, badge, Navy Commemorative, gold w/enamel, 1980s 32.00
Russia, binoculars, WWI, low power, brass & leather, EX 140.00
Russia, boots, Officer, blk leather, pull-on straps, EX, pr 130.00
Russia, cap, Army, brimmed, jungle fatigue, tan cotton, EX 45.00
Russia, cape, Army, rubberized canvas, dtd 1972, EX 125.00
Russia, fatigue tunic & breeches, star buttons, 1980s, M 95.00
Russia, greatcoat, Captain, gray wool, w/shoulderboards, M 450.00
Russia, hat, visor; bl-gray w/red piping, 1980s, EX 75.00
Russia, medal, Chaplain's Cross for War of 1812, bronze 450.00
Russia, medal, Good Conduct, 15 yrs of service, silver, EX 65.00
Russia, Sam Brown belt ensemble, brn leather, 1980s, M 100.00
Russia, wrist compass, WWII, Bakelite body, 1940, EX 48.00
Russia, wristwatch, Ministry of Defense, EX 145.00
West Germany, badge, Lufthansa Airlines Crew, ½-wing, recent .20.00
West Germany, Mauser Rifle cleaning kit canister, EX 8.00

Milk Glass

Milk glass is the current collector's name for milk-white opaque glass. The early glassmaker's term was Opal Ware. Originally attempted in England in the 18th century with the intention of imitating china, milk glass was not commercially successful until the mid-1800s. Pieces produced in the U.S.A., England, and France during the 1870-1900 period are highly prized for their intricate detail and fiery, opalescent edges.

Our advisor for this category is Rod Dockery; he is listed in the Directory under Texas. Several standard collectors' books have been referenced in our listings: Belknap (B), Ferson (F), Grist (G), Imperial's Vintage Milk Glass (I), Lindsey (L), Millard (M), and Warman (W). See also Animal Dishes with Covers; Bread Plates; Historical Glass; Westmoreland.

Ashtray, 3 Monks, M-57a 42.50
Birdhouse, wht w/red roof, F-223, +hanger 110.00
Bowl, Daisy & Tree of Life, Challinor-Taylor, B-106c 55.00
Box, Rabbit in Egg, F-131, 3¾" 95.00
Butter dish, Daisy & Tree of Life 115.00
Cake plate, 'H' pattern, Atterbury, 8" 45.00
Cake plate, Grape, ftd, Imperial, I-1950/375, 10" 40.00
Candle holders, Daisy & Button, ftd, 2½", pr 15.00
Candlesticks, Dolphin, hexagonal, Westmoreland, B-257a, 4", pr ..25.00
Compote, Basketweave, ped base, Atterbury, w/lid, F-351 ....115.00

Compote, Grape, Imperial, w/lid, I-195/859, 11½" 35.00
Compote, lattice edge, Challinor-Taylor, M-116a 55.00
Covered dish, Baseball, G-100c 25.00
Covered dish, Battleship, Wheeling, F-39, sm 65.00
Covered dish, Cabbage, Vallerysthal, F-212, EX 65.00
Covered dish, Cruiser Battleship, M-300b 90.00
Covered dish, Football, G-100 ....65.00
Covered dish, Little Red Schoolhouse, F-171, EX pnt 100.00
Creamer, Dahlia, ftd, M-152b, w/lid 25.00
Creamer, owl form w/glass eyes, F-587, sm 37.50
Creamer, Panelled Wheat, F-255 ....50.00
Creamer & sugar bowl, Blackberry, F-250/F-251, pr 100.00
Creamer & sugar bowl, Flat Dmn, F-195, mini 28.00
Egg cup, Chick, pnt details, B-274c 10.00
Flask, Klondyke, pewter screw cap, B-238b 78.00
Hat, Fedora, M-102a, EX pnt 75.00
Hat, Uncle Sam, M-198c 35.00
Inkwell, Minstrel Boy, W-15B 90.00
Jar, Owl, F-513 ....135.00
Lamp, Art Nouveau, nude w/harp, F-452 ....110.00
Match holder, Bible, M-222d 55.00
Match holder, Blk boy's head, EX pnt 100.00
Match holder, Hand & Fan, EX pnt, F-208 ....17.50
Match holder, Indian Head, B-204A, 5" 88.00
Match holder, Indian Head, mk K, W-25B 15.00
Match holder, Kettle, hanging, W-19B 10.00
Match holder, Pipe, F-532, worn pnt 24.00
Match holder, Uncle Sam's Hat, M-198c 30.00
Paperweight, Washington Monument, F-389 ....85.00
Pickle dish, Blackberry, dtd 1870, F-250 ....35.00
Pickle dish, Boat, Pat 1874, F-335, lg 35.00
Pickle dish, Heinz, gr & yel pnt, 4¾" L 38.00
Pitcher, Birds on Branch, F-519, EX 90.00
Pitcher, Fish, Atterbury, F-328, 7¼" 150.00
Pitcher, Fish, F-341, 4½" 135.00
Pitcher, Owl, F-587, 8" 150.00
Plate, ABCs, B-8e 50.00
Plate, Anchor & Belaying Pin, M-42 ....35.00
Plate, Anchor & Yacht (also known as Sailboat), B-13a 30.00
Plate, Angel w/Harp, B-11c 40.00
Plate, Apple Blossom, lattice edge, Atterbury, 10½" 80.00
Plate, California Bear, F-543 ....105.00
Plate, Chick & Eggs, B-21b, worn pnt 47.50
Plate, Columbus, M-11b 47.50
Plate, Contrary Mule, B-12b 40.00
Plate, Cupid & Psyche, B-6b 35.00
Plate, Eagle, Flag & Fleur-de-Lis, B-271 ....20.00
Plate, Eagle, Flag & Stars, B-6d 25.00
Plate, Easter Opening, B-70, 7½" 70.00
Plate, Owl Lovers, B-7b 45.00
Plate, Pie Crust, M-7a, 7⅞" 12.00
Plate, Rabbit & Horseshoe, M-43b 40.00
Plate, Rose, Imperial, I-1950/10D, 10½" 25.00
Plate, S-Triangle, B-5c 24.00
Plate, Shell & Grapes, B-4d 20.00
Plate, Spring Meets Winter 60.00
Plate, Woof Woof, B-13f 55.00
Plate, 3 Bears 40.00
Plate, 3 Kittens, B-10c 35.00
Plate, 3 Owls, F-500 ....35.00
Plate, 3 Puppies, B-20c 88.00
Platter, Retriever, after bird, lily pad border, B-53 ....95.00
Punch set, Grape, Imperial, I-1950/128, 15-pc 160.00
Shakers, Daisy, metal caps, pr 12.50

Sherbet, Rooster, red pnt details, B-274e 12.00
Spooner, Blackberry, dtd, F-253 ....40.00
Spooner, Ceres, B-217 ....65.00
Sugar bowl, Basketweave, w/lid, F-354 ....65.00
Sugar bowl, Chinese, W-53d, w/lid 48.00
Sugar bowl, Melon, F-360 ....85.00
Sugar shaker, Johnny Bull, Atterbury, F-340 ....80.00
Sugar shaker, Netted Oak, F-495 ....75.00
Swan, closed neck, basketweave base, B-155b 65.00
Syrup, Tree of Life, Challinor-Taylor 85.00
Toothpick holder, Horseshoe & Clover, F-186, EX pnt 40.00
Tray, Child & Shell, B-47 ....95.00
Tray, Chrysanthemum, 10x8" 25.00
Vase, Lily of the Valley, 7½" 15.00

Millefiori

Millefiori was a type of art glass produced during the late 1800s. Literally, the term means 'thousand flowers,' an accurate description of its appearance. Canes, fused bundles of multicolored glass threads such as are often used in paperweights, were cut into small cross sections, arranged in the desired pattern, refired, and shaped into articles such as cruets, lamps, and novelty items. It is still being produced, and many examples found on the market today are of fairly recent manufacture. See also Paperweights.

Basket, looped camphor hdl, 5½x5½" 275.00
Figurine, elephant w/trunk up, 4x4" 225.00

Lamp, red, blue, and white with gilt metal mounts, mushroom cap shade, 17", $1,200.00.

Lamp, boudoir; closed dome top w/berry, 3-arm spider, 12" 600.00
Lamp, egg-form 6½" shade on baluster stem w/bulge base, 17" 1,200.00
Pitcher, scroll hdl, petticoat shape, 6" 250.00
Rose bowl, scalloped, 4x4" 250.00
Vase, bulbous w/trumpet top, squatty, ftd, 7¾" 300.00
Vase, cupped rim, ftd, squatty, 7¾" 275.00
Vase, cupped rim on squatty body, ftd, 6¾" 150.00
Vase, dbl-waisted cylinder w/irregular flared rim, ftd, 8" 200.00
Vase, free-form hdls, ftd, 4½" 200.00

Miniatures

There is some confusion as to what should be included in a listing of miniature collectibles. Some feel the only true miniature is the salesman's sample; other collectors consider certain small-scale children's toys to be appropriately referred to as miniatures, while yet others believe a miniature to be any small-scale item that gives evidence to the craftsmanship of its creator. For salesman's samples, see specific category; other types are listed below. See also Dollhouses and Furnishings; Children's Things.

Armchair, rush seat, Am, early 1800s, 11½", EX	250.00
Bed warmer, copper w/trn hdl, 9" L	88.00
Blanket chest, dvtl cherry, tapered ft/brass escutcheon, 13"	715.00
Blanket chest, dvtl poplar, scroll apron, 1-drw, lift lid, 13"	2,800.00
Bureau, grpt, New England, 1830s, 9½x9x6", EX	660.00
Bureau, mahog, 3-drw, 6 ivory knobs, 6" W	150.00
Candle mold, 4-tube, tin, resoldered hdl, 6⅛"	325.00
Chest, blanket; poplar, red grpt, dvtl, 9½x12½x8"	550.00
Chest, cherry Sheraton, 4 grad drw, trn ft, 15x15"	880.00
Chest, cherry/walnut/curly maple, 4-drw, rstr, 25x22x13"	660.00
Chest, Chippendale style, mahog, 4-drw, repro, 30x26x16"	275.00
Chest, pine, 4-drw, trn ft, grpt, 14½x13½x7½"	715.00
Chest of drw, pine w/natural & red pnt, 2-drw, 4⅜x5½"	50.00
Cupboard, curly maple, open top, 1-pc, 21¼"	400.00
Dresser, 6-drw, trn legs, quarter columns, cvd skirt, 12x12"	450.00
Fire bucket, English leather w/brass hardware, 4½", VG	175.00
Flatiron, brass, trn wood hld, iron ingot, 3"	155.00
Hat, straw boater, Austin Co, NY, 5½"	135.00
Ladle, pewter, trn hdl, 6"	165.00
Mule chest, walnut w/red traces, trn ft, 3-drw, 16x20x11"	550.00
Rocker, Boston; orig grain finish & decor, 14½"	250.00
Sideboard, mahog Hplwht w/inlay, 8x13½x4¾"	1,500.00
Stand, mahog, drop leaf, 3 dvtl drw, trn pulls, 10¼"	360.00
Street light lamp, Westinghouse, wood base, brass top, 30", VG	150.00
Table, mahog, pie crust-edged top, trn column, 3-ftd, 8x6" dia	300.00
Table, Sheraton, mahog & veneer, tressel type, 2 peds, 30" L	195.00

Minton

Thomas Minton established his firm in 1793 at Stoke on Trent and within a few years began producing earthenware with blue-printed patterns similar to the ware he had learned to decorate while employed by the Caughley Porcelain Factory. The Willow pattern was one of his most popular. Neither this nor the porcelain made from 1798 to 1805 was marked (except for an occasional number series), making identification often impossible.

After 1805 until about 1816, fine tea services, beehive-shaped honey pots, trays, etc., were hand decorated with florals, landscapes, Imari-type designs, and neoclassic devices. These were often marked with crossed 'L's. It was Minton that invented the acid gold process of decorating (1863), which is now used by a number of different companies. From 1816 until 1823, no porcelain was made. Through the twenties and thirties, the ornamental wares with colorful decoration of applied fruits and florals and figurines in both bisque and enamel were usually left unmarked. As a result, they have been erroneously attributed to other potters. Some of the ware that was marked bears a deliberate imitation of Meissen's crossed swords. From the late twenties through the forties, Minton made a molded stoneware line (mugs, jugs, teapots, etc.) with florals or figures in high relief. These were marked with an embossed scroll with an 'M' in the bottom curve. Fine parian ware was made in the late 1840s, and in the fifties Minton experimented with and perfected a line of quality majolica which they produced from 1860 until it was discontinued in 1908. Their slogan was 'Majolica for the Millions,' and for it they gained widespread recognition. Leadership of the firm was assumed by Minton's son Herbert sometime around the middle of the 19th century. Working hand in hand with Leon Arnoux, who was both a chemist and an artist, he

managed to secure the company's financial future through constant, successful experimentation with both materials and decorating methods. During the Victorian era, M.L. Solon decorated pieces in the pate-sur-pate style, often signing his work; these examples are considered to be the finest of their type. After 1862 all wares were marked 'Minton' or 'Mintons,' with an impressed year cipher.

Many collectors today reassemble the lovely dinnerware patterns that have been made by Minton. Perhaps one of their most popular lines was Minton Rose, introduced in 1854. The company itself once counted forty-seven versions of this pattern being made by other potteries around the world. In addition to less-expensive copies, elaborate hand-enameled pieces were also made by Aynsley, Crown Staffordshire, and Paragon China. Solando Ware (1937) and Byzantine Range (1938) were designed by John Wadsworth. Minton ceased all earthenware production in 1939.

Dinnerware values given in the following listings are for items that were produced from 1870-1950. Current production pieces bring lower prices on the resale market. Advice for this category comes from Old China Patterns Ltd., they are listed in the Directory under Canada. See also Majolica; Minton; Pate-Sur-Pate.

Bowl, vegetable; Kent, oval	125.00
Cake plate, yel stylized flowers/leaves, silver edge, 12"	100.00
Cup & saucer, Gold Laurentian	90.00
Cup & saucer, Minton Rose, #A-4807	96.00

Lazy susan, Gothic design with shaped rim, 1867, rim restorations, 18¼", $800.00.

Mush cup & saucer, flowered bl w/Chinese red & mc	50.00
Plate, Cockatrice, turq	56.00
Plate, dinner; Adam, #S703 (new)	56.50
Plate, dinner; Gold Pandora; #H2530	56.50
Plate, dinner; Monarch, plain, #B1468	35.00
Plate, dinner; Windsor, bl, #K396	56.50
Platter, Ashton, 14"	125.00
Tile, Deco-style bird, EX	85.00
Vase, pond lilies/cattails on yel, gilt ring 'hdls,' 11"	1,400.00

Mirrors

The first mirrors were made in England in the 13th century of very thin glass backed with lead. Reverse-painted glass mirrors were made in this country as early as the late 1700s and remained popular throughout the next century. The simple hand-painted panel was separated from the mirrored section by a narrow slat, and the frame was either the dark-finished Federal style or the more elegant, often-gilded Sheraton.

Mirrors changed with the style of other furnishings; but whatever type you purchase, as long as the glass sections remain solid, even broken or flaking mirrors are more valued than replaced glass. Careful resilvering is acceptable if excessive deterioration has taken place. Our advisor for this category is Michael Hinton; he is listed in the Directory under Pennsylvania.

Key:
Chpndl — Chippendale   Fed — Federal
Emp — Empire   QA — Queen Anne

Adam's style gilt fr w/urn crest, 1900s 47x26" 450.00
Cherry w/old dk varnish, door in base, hanging, 39x26" 990.00
Chpndl mahog & giltwood, England, 1790s, 49x25" 13,200.00
Chpndl mahog scroll, rfn, rpr, 21x12" 300.00
Chpndl walnut scroll, orig glass, rpr, 21x13" 335.00
Chpndl-style bird's-eye & curly maple scroll, 38x18" 150.00
Classical, old gold rpt, rvpt lady w/flag, 2-part, 39x23" 165.00
Country QA pine, scrolled crest, rpt, 14½x8½" 525.00
Emp, gilt gesso/eagle cvg, convex mirror/candle arms, 32" 1,650.00
Emp, half-trnings, corner posts, rvpt, 2-part, rpt, 30x14" 220.00
Emp, wht pnt w/gilt, damaged floral gesso detail, 23x35" 300.00
Emp, worn gilt, old rvpt ship scene, 2-part, Am, 37x22" 375.00
Emp pier, wood & gesso, worn orig gilt, EX cvg, 59x28" 5,600.00
Fed gilt & rvpt, Am, 1815, 42½x25" 220.00
Fed gilt & rvpt, outset cornice w/urns, 1800s, 42x23" 715.00
Fed mahog/hardwood architectural, cornice, rvpt, 29x17" 300.00
Fed pine, 2-part architectural, rvpt house, 30x16" 415.00
Federal, mahog w/crest & cvd panels, ca 1810, 38" 350.00
Gesso on wood, English gilt (rpt), early, 18x20" 200.00
Gilt fr w/rnd top, ornate, 1900s, 41x34" 175.00
Giltwood cvd girandole, England, 1815, 35" 1,980.00
Hplwht mahog veneer scroll w/inlay, rpr, 33x19" 150.00
Hplwht mahog veneer-on-pine scroll w/inlay, 44x22", EX 1,045.00
Mahog veneer w/spiral edge mold, worn silvering, 10x8" 55.00
Plateau, Rococo scrolls, SP fr mk Depouse, 17½" L 195.00
QA style curly maple veneer, rstr, 35x20" 360.00
Shaving, Am Emp mahog veneer, 3 dvtl drw, 25x26x9" 360.00
Silver gilt, ornate cvg, oval, Made in Italy, 48x33" 135.00
SP fr w/raised brass crest, beveled, easel bk, 17x11" 85.00
Sunburst fr w/gilt, convex glass, 22½" dia 120.00

Mocha

Mocha Ware is utilitarian pottery made principally in England (and to a lesser extent in France) between 1780 and 1840 on the then prevalent creamware and pearlware bodies. Initially, only those pieces decorated in the seaweed pattern were called 'Mocha,' while geometrically decorated pieces were referred to as 'Banded Creamware.' Other types of decorations were called 'Dipped Ware.' During the last thirty to forty years the term 'Mocha' has been applied to the entire realm of 'Industrialized Slipware' — pottery decorated by the turner on his lathe using coggle wheels and slip cups.

Mocha was made in numerous patterns — Tree, Seaweed or Dandelion, Rope (also called Worm or Loop), Cat's-eye, Tobacco Leaf, Lollypop or Balloon, Marbled, Marbled and Combed, Twig, Geometric or Checkered, Banded, and slip decorations of rings, dots, flags, tulips, wavy lines, etc. It came into its own as a collectible in the latter half of the 1940s and has become increasingly popular as more and more people are exposed to the rich colorings and artistic appeal of its varied forms of abstract decoration.

The collector should take care not to confuse the early pearlware and creamware Mocha with the later kitchen yellow ware, graniteware, and ironstone sporting mocha-type decoration that was produced in America by such potters as J. Vodrey, George S. Harker, Edwin Bennett, and John Bell. This type was also produced in Scotland and Wales and was marketed well into the 20th century.

Bowl, earthworm 'waves,' some discoloration, 6" 550.00
Bowl, seaweed, bl & wht, cup shape, hairline, 4¼" 215.00
Chamber pot, seaweed, 3-color, 8⅜" 110.00
Flowerpot, blk seaweed w/pk stripes, chips, 7¼" 600.00
Flowerpot, earthworm, 4-color, tooled bl lip, 4¼", pr 3,200.00
Jar, seaweed, bl w/brn & wht stripes, rpl wooden lid, 7x5½" 105.00
Jar, stripes & wavy lines in wht & tan slip, 7¼", EX 250.00
Mug, bands, stripes & foliage, 4-color, hairline, 6" 220.00
Mug, brn & wht marbleized, firing crack, 4¼" 220.00
Mug, combed fine stripes, 4½", EX 880.00
Mug, earthworm, 3-color on bl w/brn bnds, leaf hdl, 4⅞" 165.00
Mug, earthworm, 4-color, leaf hdl, hairline, 3⅛" 300.00
Mug, earthworm on wide band w/striping, hairline, 6" 700.00
Mug, emb bands w/tan/gr/brn stripes, leaf hdl, chip, 6" 225.00
Mug, emb stripes, 4-color, leaf hdl, poor rpr, 4⅞" 165.00
Mug, fan-like designs, orange w/wht/tan/brn, leaf hdl, 4⅞" 2,200.00
Mug, geometric band, 3-color w/tan stripes, 5⅝", EX 160.00
Mug, gray band w/blk & bl dots, blk stripes on bl band, 5⅜", EX 425.00
Mug, seaweed, bl & wht band, leaf hdl, 3½" 415.00
Mug, seaweed, brn on pumpkin, 6", EX 465.00
Mug, seaweed, gr on sand-gray, 6½" 550.00
Mug, stripes, wht on tan w/brn band, 3½", EX 145.00
Mug, stripes, 4-color, leaf hdl, hairlines, 4⅝" 225.00
Mustard pot, 3-color stripes & emb gr band, rpr, 3⅝" 465.00
Pepper castor, earthworm & stripes, 4-color, rpr, 5⅛" 225.00
Pitcher, cat's eyes in 3 bands, bbl form, 6½", EX 1,200.00
Pitcher, earthworm, 3-color w/2-tone bl stripes, 6¾", EX 385.00
Pitcher, earthworm & stripes, 3-color, 7⅝", EX 435.00
Pitcher, lt gr & bl bands w/blk stripes & leaves, 7", EX 165.00

Pitcher, seaweed, green on mustard with blue and white rings, barrel shape, 7½", NM, $900.00.

Pitcher, seaweed, brn wht bands, hairline, 7½" 225.00
Pitcher, seaweed, 4-color, 1-pt, 4¾" 195.00
Pitcher, stripes, 5-color, leaf hdl, rpr, 7¾" 200.00
Pitcher, twigs, waves & cat's eyes, 4-color bands, 8" 2,750.00
Salt cellar, earthworms, 3-color bands, 2⅛x2¾" 250.00
Salt cellar, stripes, brn & wht, ftd, hairline, 2⅜" 110.00
Shaker, stripes, 3-color, 4⅜", NM 385.00

Molds

Food molds have become a popular collectible — not only for

their value as antiques, but because they also revive childhood memories of elaborate ice cream Santas with candy trim or barley sugar figurals adorning a Christmas tree. Ice cream molds were made of pewter and came in a wide variety of shapes and styles. Chocolate molds were made in fewer shapes but were more detailed. They were usually made of tin, copper, and occasionally of pewter. Hard candy molds were usually metal, although primitive maple sugar molds (usually simple hearts, rabbits, and other animals) were carved from wood. (Unless otherwise indicated, those in our listings are cast aluminum or stainless steel.) Cake molds were made of cast iron or cast aluminum and were most common in the shape of a lamb, a rabbit, or Santa Claus. Our advisors for this category are Dale and Jean Van Kuren; they are listed in the Directory under New York.

Chocolate Molds

Bear walking, 2-pc w/clamp, #3607, 5¾x2⅞" 80.00
Boy on bicycle, 9" 295.00
Bride or groom, 7½", ea 95.00

Chick in top hat, 5½", $65.00.

Dogs (3 Scotties), 4x10" 100.00
Duck swimming, 2-pc w/clamp, 4¼x3½" 80.00
Easter egg, Randle & Smith, 6½" 70.00
Father Christmas, 8" 90.00
Fish, mk GMT Co Germany, 10" 50.00
Fruit, oval, wire loop hanger, 4¼x6" 35.00
German Santa in sleigh, 2½x8" 125.00
Hen, folding, 2½" 100.00
Hen, sitting, lg 75.00
Horn of plenty, mk Germany, 7" 18.00
Jack-o'-lantern, mk USA, 3¼" 60.00
Pig standing, 2-pc w/clamp, 6½x3" 87.00
Rabbit, sitting, #37, 7¾x7½" 85.00
Rabbit, 11¼" 95.00
Rabbit in suit, 6" 40.00
Rabbit riding rooster, 10x5" 100.00
Rabbits (3), German, 5x8" 95.00
Rooster, 2-pc, w/clip, 3⅛x2¾" 45.00
Rooster, 3-part, USA, 5½x6½" 75.00
Santa, side hinge, 4½" 95.00
Santa, 7½" 95.00
Santas (2), 8x6" 95.00
Sheep, 4½" 68.00
Soccer player, 2-pc, w/clip 65.00

Hard Candy Molds

Castle w/flag, groove for stick, 1¾x1½" 75.00

Elephant, TM-138, groove for stick, 1¾x1¼" 60.00
Lion, 3-part, TM-40, groove for stick, 4x5" 115.00
Mary w/lamb, TM-244, groove for stick, 2x2" 80.00
Mouse, TM-37, groove for stick, 2¼x1¼" 90.00
Pipe, TM-88, groove for stick, 3½x¾" 42.50
Rat, TM-238, groove for stick, 2½x1" 80.00
Steamboat w/paddle wheel, groove for stick, 1¼x2¼" 88.00

Ice Cream Molds

Bell, #605 ....35.00
Christmas bells, 5 in mold, hinged 2-pc, 1900s 45.00
Cow, #659 ....20.00
Duck, 4" 65.00
Football, E-1159 ....25.00
Harp, aluminum, K-361, 1940s 32.00
Heart w/cupid, E&Co, 3¾" 45.00
Hen, 3¾" 85.00
Mum, E-355 ....22.00
O'possum, 5" L 115.00
Potato, K-154 ....35.00
Shriner's crescent shape, E&Co NY #1081, 5" 70.00
Soldier, 5⅝" 45.00
Stork w/baby, #631 ....40.00

Maple Sugar Molds

Beaver, hand cvd, EX detail, 5x9" 75.00
Birds, 5 in a row, EX details, ¾x11⅞x1¾" 50.00

Figure on horse, EX carving, $50.00.

Fruit & foliage, hardwood, 2-part, 5½x8" 28.00
Heart, stylized, 4¾x7½" 70.00
Hearts (2), varnished, 3x18" 125.00
Hearts (3), EX cvg on pegged 2-pc brd, 1¾x12x4¼" 110.00
House w/cvd-in windows & doors, separate sides & roof, 5½" 98.00
Rabbit sitting, EX cvg, 1¼x6½x5" 55.00

Miscellaneous

Cast iron, bird on branch, oval, 5" 225.00
Cheese, tin, heart shape, tubular ft, 2¾x5⅞x5¾" 170.00
Copper, swirl design, pinpoint holes, 6⅝" 85.00
Copper w/tin wash, ear of corn, worn, 6x4" 105.00
Copper w/tin wash, emb sheaf of wheat, 6x4½" 95.00
Pewter, 4-parts: grapes/eagles & swags/rabbit/basket, 5x6" 250.00
Pudding, tin, oval, domed lid w/wire hdl 38.00
Scottish shortbread, wood, cvd zigzag edge, 1¼x9½x7" 50.00

Tin, overlapping circles/fluted sides, center post, 4x7x5" 50.00
Tin, pear, lt rust, 5¼x3½" 75.00
Tin, 6-pointed star, tube center, 2½x9" 32.00
Tin/copper, cabbage rose, 4¼x5½x3¼" 125.00
Tin/copper, rose & leaves, fluted bottom, 4½x6⅝x4⅝" 125.00

Monmouth

The Monmouth Pottery Company was established in 1892 in Monmouth, Illinois. Their primary products were salt-glazed stoneware crocks, churns, jugs, Bristol, spongeware, and brown glaze. In 1906 they were absorbed by a conglomerate called the Western Stoneware Company. Monmouth became their #1 plant and until 1930 continued to produce stoneware marked with their maple leaf logo. Items marked 'Monmouth Pottery Co.' were made before 1906; after the merger, 'Co.' was dropped and 'Ill.' was substituted.

Cookie jar 50.00
Vase, Aztec, brn, 9" 95.00
Vase, emb floral neck band, lt bl/gr mottled matt, 18" 125.00
Vase, shaded tan textured matt, ring hdls, thrown, 10x10" 175.00

Monot and Stumpf

The firm of Monot and Stumpf was organized in 1868, the merger of the E.S. Monot and F. Stumpf glassworks. It was located in Pantin, France. They produced fine art glass of various types until ca 1892, when the company reorganized and became known as the Cristallerie de Pantin.

Bowl, pk opaline, in ormolu holder w/claw ft, 6" 425.00
Salt cellar, lav-pk opal, gold lustre int, fluted, 1⅝" 75.00
Salt cellar, pk opal, gold lustre int, 1¼x1⅞x2⅜" 65.00
Sauce dish, sq, EX color & opalescence, scarce, 4" 215.00
Shade, pk opal, swirled ribs, ruffled/flared, 6½x8½" 225.00
Vase, pk opal, ruffled fan-form top, 8x7¾" 265.00

Mont Joye

Mont Joye was a type of acid-cut French cameo glass produced by Cristallerie de Pantin in Paris around the turn of the century. It is accented by enamels. Our advisor for this category is Don Williams; he is listed in the Directory under Missouri.

Vase, iris and gold leaf spikes etched and painted on frosted textured crystal, 20", $2,000.00.

Dish, floral/buds, gold/wht/yel on gray texture, 4-lobe, 6" 400.00
Planter, gold decor on gr frost, 7½" 275.00

Vase, chestnuts/leaves, gold on crackle, mk France, 5" 600.00
Vase, floral, gold & gr on hammered amber ground, 6½" 595.00
Vase, irises on clear to amethyst, 12" 750.00
Vase, peonies on long stems, 4-sided, 8½" 650.00
Vase, poppies w/gold on textured clear, ovoid, 20" 935.00
Vase, thistles/scrolls on ice gr to opaque, shouldered, 12" 1,200.00
Vase, violets/gold on textured frost, ftd ribbed ovoid, 10" 650.00

Moorcroft

William Moorcroft began to work for MacIntyre Potteries in 1897. At first he was the chief designer, but very soon took over their newly created Art Pottery department. His first important design was the Aurelian Ware, part transfer and part hand-painted. Very shortly thereafter, around the turn of the century, he developed his famous Florian Ware with heavy slip, done in mostly blue and white. Since the early 1900s there has been a sucession of designs, most of them very characteristic of the company. Moorcroft left MacIntyre in 1913 and went out on his own. He had already well established his name, having won prizes and gold medals at the St. Louis World's Fair as well as in Paris. In 1929 Queen Mary, who had been collecting his pottery, made him 'Potter to the Queen,' and the pottery was so stamped up until 1949. William Moorcroft died in 1945, and his son Walter ran the company until recent years. The factory is still in existence. They now produce different designs but continue to use the characteristic slipwork. Moorcroft pottery was sold abroad in Canada, the United States, Australia, and Europe as well as in specialty areas such as the island of Bermuda.

Moorcroft went through a 'Japanese' stage in the early teens with his lovely lustre glazes, Oriental shapes and decorations. During the mid-teens he began to produce his most popular Pomegranate Ware, as well as Wisteria (often called 'Fruit'). Around that time he also designed the popular Pansy line as well as Leaves and Grapes. Soon he introduced a beautiful landscape series called variously Hazeldine, Moonlit Blue, Eventide and Dawn. These wonderful designs along with Claremont (Mushrooms) seem to be the most sought after by collectors today. It would be possible to add many other designs to this list.

During the 1920s and '30s, Moorcroft became very interested in highly fired Flambe (red) glazes. These could only be achieved through a very difficult procedure which he himself perfected in secret. He later passed the knowledge on to his son.

Dating of this pottery is done by knowledge of the designs, shapes, signatures and marks on the bottom of each piece; an experienced person can usually narrow it down to a short time frame. Prices escalated for this 'rediscovered' pottery in the late 1980s but has now leveled off. This is true mainly for the pre-1935 designs of William Moorcroft, which is the era most sought after by collectors. Advisors for this category are Wilfred and Dolli Cohen; they are listed in the Directory under California.

Ashtray, hibiscus, dk on flambe, 1953-78, 4" 35.00
Ashtray, pomegranates, red on cobalt, metal rim, '49-86, 2½" 60.00
Biscuit jar, Florian, lt/dk bl & wht, SP mts, 6x6", NM 900.00
Bowl, African lilies, pk & yel on cobalt, 1945-49, 4" 75.00
Bowl, anemones, pk on bl to gr, ca 1953-78, 4" 50.00
Bowl, anemones, pk on cobalt, 1949-86, 3" 45.00
Bowl, anemones, pk/purple on bl to gr, 1949-86, w/lid, 2x6" 100.00
Bowl, clematis, pk on wht, ca 1953-78, 7" 185.00
Bowl, clematis, purple & yel on bl-gr, 1949-86, 4" 65.00
Bowl, floral, cobalt & wht on aqua to cobalt, 1945-49, 2x5" 65.00
Bowl, grapes on med gr, ca 1928-53, 2½x5" 110.00
Bowl, lilies, mc on lt gr, ca 1949-86, 1x3" 65.00
Bowl, Pansy, 5¾" 350.00
Bowl, pomegranates, 6" 575.00

Box, floral, mc on teal gr, rectangular, ca 1945-49 ....140.00
Box, hibiscus, pk on gr, ca 1953-78, 4" dia 120.00
Box, pomegranates, mc on magenta, 1953-78, 2x4½" 245.00
Box, spring flowers, mc on bl shaded, ca 1953-78, 4" 130.00
Box, spring flowers, paper label, ca 1949-86, 4" 110.00
Candlesticks, clematis, unmk, 3", pr 180.00
Charger, fruit & leaves, mc on bl-gr, 1945-49, 14" 300.00
Charger, orchids, mc on lt gr, ca 1945-49, 12" 240.00
Charger, poppies, orange/cobalt/gr on flambe, 1949-86, 12" ...1,100.00
Charger, spring flowers, mc on bl matt, 1928-49, 12" 500.00
Compote, pansies, plum on cobalt, Tudric, pewter ft, 2½" H 230.00
Dish, anemones, pk on cobalt, ca 1949-86, 8½" L 110.00
Hair receiver, Flamminian Ware, gr w/purple, 1910s, 5" 210.00
Hot plate, MacIntyre, gr shaded w/gold rim, 1904-14, 5½" 295.00
Jar, jam; pomegranates, SP lid, 3" 475.00
Jar, pomegranates, w/lid, 7" 1,550.00
Jug, appl griffins on gr, WA Faience, MacIntyre, 1900s, 7" 425.00
Jug, dk gr & mint gr, pewter lid, MacIntyre, 1904-13, 7" 300.00
Lamp, anemones, red/wht/bl on gr to bl, 24" overall 400.00
Lamp, grapes, red/wht/purple, mk, ca 1929-49, 24" overall 550.00
Lamp, orchids, mc on ivory to cobalt, 1949-86, 24" overall 350.00
Lamp base, peacocks on orange to gr, ca 1945-49, 8" 650.00
Pitcher, Dura tableware, poppies, bl on gr, 1904-13, 6¼" 595.00
Pitcher, floral band on gr, bl hdl, Moorcroft, MacIntyre, 5" 595.00
Pitcher, gr on gr, Gesso Faience, MacIntyre, 1897-05, 6" 595.00
Tazza, apple blossoms on teal, pewter base, 1916-23, 5½" 750.00
Tazza, pansies, Tudric base, 7¼" 795.00
Tazza, pomegranates, Tudric base, 8½" dia 795.00
Teapot, Leaf & Berry 795.00
Vase, anemones, ca 1955, 6¼" 265.00
Vase, anemones, mc on cobalt, ca 1949-86, 4¾" 165.00
Vase, anemones, pk & bl on dk gr, 1949-86, 5" 120.00
Vase, anemones, red on copper-brn, 1953-78, 5" 210.00

Vase, red chrysanthemums on trumpet form, signed, dated 1913, 12", $3,000.00.

Vase, Claremont, ftd w/hdl ea side very wide body, 6½x4" 1,895.00
Vase, Claremont, mk Liberty, ca 1910, 5" 1,895.00
Vase, Claremont, mushroom, ca 1920, 6½" 2,950.00
Vase, Claremont, toadstools on brn/bl, #5, sgn WM, 3" 550.00
Vase, clematis, mc on cobalt, ca 1949-86, 4" 75.00
Vase, clematis, mc on gr to bl, ca 1945-49, 7" 225.00
Vase, clematis, mc on gr to bl, 1949-86, 5" 170.00
Vase, cornflowers, bl shades, drilled for lamp, rpr, 12" 950.00
Vase, Eventide Landscape, brn w/gr, bl & red, bulbous, 6" 1,900.00
Vase, floral, orange w/gr leaves on red flambe, 1928-53, 9¼" 450.00
Vase, Florian, pk w/gold & cobalt trim, 1904-13, 8" 1,495.00

Vase, Florian, 11½" 1,995.00
Vase, Florian (late), dk bl/red/yel flowers on red/bl, 6½x5½" ..1,750.00
Vase, fruit & leaves, flambe, 7" 1,250.00
Vase, fruit & leaves, mc on bl-gr, 1945-49, 8½" 500.00
Vase, fruit & leaves, mc on cobalt, ca 1945-49, 2½" 85.00
Vase, fruit & leaves, mc on cobalt, ca 1945-49, 5" 160.00
Vase, fruit & leaves, pk & purple on cobalt, 1953-78, 6" 180.00
Vase, fruit & leaves, yel & red on cobalt, 1953-78, 3" 100.00
Vase, grapes & leaves, pk/cobalt/yel on bl-gr, 1953-78, 12" 450.00
Vase, hibiscus, yel & red on gr to bl, ca 1949-86, 4" 80.00
Vase, iris & orchids, yel/lt gr/bl on gr, 1949-86, 3½" 90.00
Vase, landscape, gr, orange & bl on red flambe, rpr, 9¼" 675.00
Vase, landscape, repetitive trees, bl/gr/yel, can neck, 7x9" 4,250.00
Vase, lustre, purple w/gold & pk, hand thrown, 10½" 300.00
Vase, Moonlit Bl Landscape, #189, 6x4" 1,900.00
Vase, orchids, mc on cobalt, ca 1945-49, 6½" 350.00
Vase, orchids, mc on cobalt, ca 1949-86, 4" 285.00
Vase, orchids, mc on cobalt, mk, 1942, 12" 440.00
Vase, orchids, mc on wht to cobalt, 1945-49, 7" 385.00
Vase, pansies, cobalt & yel on bl-gr, ca 1949-53, 3½" 85.00
Vase, pansies, mc on wht to bl, lg script sgn, 8x4" 750.00
Vase, plums, mc on cobalt, mk, ca 1949-86, 5" 165.00
Vase, pomegranates, red in gr band on cobalt, 1953-78, 12" 650.00
Vase, pomegranates, red on cobalt, Burslem mk, 5½" 325.00
Vase, pomegranates, red on cobalt, ca 1928-53, 5" 210.00
Vase, pomegranates, red on cobalt, ca 1932, 7" 595.00
Vase, pomegranates, red on cobalt, mk, ca 1949-86, 3½" 120.00
Vase, pomegranates, red on cobalt, 1949-86, 7" 270.00
Vase, spring flowers, mc on lt to dk gr, 1953-78, 6" 255.00
Vase, wisteria, mc on cobalt, ca 1949-86, 12" 625.00
Vase, wisteria, mc on cobalt, ca 1949-86, 6½" 260.00
Vase, wisteria, mc on cobalt, ca 1949-86, 9½" 550.00
Vase, wisteria, mc on cobalt, Tudric base, 7" 895.00
Vase, wisteria, mc on cobalt, 3½" 315.00

Morgantown Glass

Incorporated in 1899, the Morgantown Glass Works experienced many name changes over the years. Today 'Morgantown Glass' is a generic term used to indicate all glass produced there. Purchased by Fostoria in 1965, the factory was permanently closed in 1971. Our advisor for this category is Jerry Gallagher, longtime researcher of the company and author of *A Collector's Handbook of Old Morgantown Glass, 1899-1971*. He is listed in the Directory under Minnesota. See Clubs, Newsletters, and Catalogs for information concerning Morgantown Collectors of America (a research society founded by Mr. Gallagher) and *The Morgantown Newscaster*, a quarterly M.A.C. journal with research updates and reports of current trends.

Adonis etch, crystal; stem, goblet; #7604½ Heirloom, 9-oz 45.00
Adonis etch, crystal/gr; stem, goblet; #7606½ Athena, 9-oz 95.00
Adonis etch, gr; stem, parfait; #7604½ Heirloom, 5-oz 55.00
Adonis etch, rose; stem, goblet; #7604½ Heirloom, 9-oz 60.00
Adonis etch, topaz; stem, goblet; #7604½ Heirloom, 9-oz 58.00
Am Beauty etch, crystal; jug, no lid, #19 Flemish, 34-oz 245.00
Am Beauty etch, crystal; jug, no lid, #2 Arcadia, 54-oz 310.00
Am Beauty etch, crystal; stem, champagne; #7668 Galaxy, 5-oz ..45.00
Am Beauty etch, crystal; stem, goblet; #7668 Galaxy, 10-oz 48.00
Am Beauty etch, crystal; stem, goblet; #7695 Trumpet, 10-oz 58.00
Am Beauty etch, rose; finger bowl, #2927, 4¼" 62.50
Am Beauty etch, rose; jug, no lid, #39 Milton, 54-oz 280.00
Am Beauty etch, rose; stem, goblet; #7565 Astrid, 10-oz 62.50
Am Beauty etch, rose-amber; jug, w/lid, #39 Milton, 54-oz 335.00

Aquaria etch, crystal/gr; champagne, #7634 Oceana, 6-oz 87.50
Aquaria etch, crystal/gr; goblet, #7643 Oceana, 9-oz 95.00
Art Moderne, cobalt w/crystal; candlesticks, #7640½, pr 335.00
Art Moderne, cobalt w/crystal; stem, cordial; #7640, 1½-oz 145.00
Art Moderne, cobalt w/crystal; stem, goblet; #7640, 9-oz 95.00
Art Moderne, crystal w/blk; stem, goblet; #7640, 9-oz 100.00
Art Moderne, crystal w/frost; stem, icer; sgnd DC Thorpe, 2-pc .245.00
Art Moderne, crystal w/pastel; stem, goblet; #7640, 9-oz 58.00
Art Moderne, pastel w/crystal; stem, goblet; #7640, 9-oz 90.00
Baden etch, blk filament; stem, goblet; #7606½ Athena, 9-oz 95.00
Barry #37, crystal/rose; jug, Palm Optic, 48-oz 335.00
Barry #37, Meadow Gr-cased Alabaster/gr; jug, 48-oz 595.00
Barry #37, Meadow Gr/Jade; jug, 48-oz 495.00
Barry #37AN, gr-cased Alabaster/gr; tumbler, ftd, 13-oz 95.00
Biscayne etch, crystal w/gold; bar tumbler, #9715, 2½-oz 68.00
Biscayne etch, crystal w/gold; goblet, #7587 Kingsley, 9-oz 57.50
Bramble Rose etch, crystal; champagne, #7577 Venus, 5½-oz 58.00
Bramble Rose etch, crystal; goblet, #7577 Venus, 9-oz 58.00
Bramble Rose etch, rose; plate, luncheon; #1500, 8½" 32.00
Carlton, platinum Marco; bowl, flared, #4355 Janice, 13" 215.00
Carlton, platinum Marco; stem, goblet; #7653 Cantata, 9-oz 78.00
Carlton etch, crystal/blk; goblet, #7606½ Athena, 9-oz 87.50
Carlton etch, crystal/blk; sherbet, #7606½ Athena, 5½-oz 65.00
Carlton Frostie etch, crystal; punch bowl, #21, 12" 465.00
Carlton Madrid, topaz/crystal; stem, goblet; #7665 Laura, 9-oz 65.00
Carlton Milan, crystal; stem, goblet; #7668 Galaxy, 10-oz 32.50
Cathay etch, crystal; stem, champagne; #7711 Callahan, 5½-oz ...50.00
Cathay etch, crystal; stem, goblet; #7711 Callahan, 9-oz 65.00

Continental Line baskets with crystal reeded handle (clockwise from top): Old Amethyst #4357 Trindle, 9", $360.00; Stiegel Green #4358 Patrick, 6", $275.00; Spanish Red #20 Jennie, 4½", $345.00.

Corinth etch, crystal w/gold; stem, goblet; #7654 Lorna, 9-oz 58.00
Corinth etch, crystal w/gold; stem, wine; #7654 Lorna, 3-oz 68.00
Crinkle, amberina; tumbler, water; flat, #1962, 10-oz 68.00
Crinkle, amethyst; tankard, lemonade; #1962, 64-oz, 9" 75.00
Crinkle, amethyst; tumbler, iced tea; ftd, #1962, 13-oz 27.50
Crinkle, crystal; pitcher, juice; #1962, 34-oz, 6½" 50.00
Crinkle, gr; Ockner jug, #1962, 54-oz 72.00
Crinkle, gr; tumbler, iced tea; ftd, #1962, 13-oz 24.00
Crinkle, lt bl; tumbler, flat, 20-oz, frosted, #1962 ....38.00
Crinkle, peacock bl; Ockner jug, #1962, 54-oz 98.00
Crinkle, peacock bl; tumbler, iced tea; ftd, #1962, 13-oz 27.50
Crinkle, peacock bl; tumbler, juice; flat, #1962, 6-oz 22.00
Crinkle, peacock bl; tumbler, water; flat, #1962, 10-oz 22.00
Crinkle, pink; sherbet, ftd, #1962, 6-oz 20.00
Crinkle, ruby; Ockner jug, #1962, 54-oz 135.00
Crinkle, ruby; Owl tumbler, highball; flat, #1969, 16-oz 85.00
Crinkle, ruby; tumbler, zombie; flat, #1962, 20-oz 38.00
Elizabeth, azure; stem, goblet; #7630 Ballerina, 9-oz 87.50
Elizabeth, azure; stem, goblet; #7664 Queen Anne, 9-oz 105.00
Elizabeth, crystal; stem, wine; #7630 Ballerina, 2¾-oz 65.00

Fairwin, bl filament; stem, goblet; #7673 Lexington, 9-oz 110.00
Fairwin, bl filament; stem, juice; #7673 Lexington, 5-oz 75.00
Faun etch, crystal/blk; champagne; #7640 Art Moderne, 5½-oz .160.00
Faun etch, crystal/blk; goblet, #7640 Art Moderne, 9-oz 185.00
Fernlee, blk filament; stem, goblet; #7672 Octette, 9-oz 78.00
Fernlee, crystal/blk; stem, goblet; #7640 Art Moderne, 9-oz 135.00
Florence etch, crystal; stem, cocktail; #300 Touraine, 3-oz 45.00
Florence etch, crystal; stem, goblet; #300 Touraine, 9-oz 42.50
Floret etch, crystal; stem, goblet; #7684 Yale, 9-oz 85.00
Floret etch, crystal; stemmed icer & insert, unknown # 65.00
Fontinelle, blk filament; candlesticks, low, #7620, pr 255.00
Fontinelle, blk filament; stem, goblet; #7620 Fontanne, 9-oz 150.00
Fontinelle, gr/crystal; stem, goblet; #7620 Fontanne, 9-oz 155.00
Golf Ball, cobalt/crystal; candlesticks, #7643 4", pr 195.00
Golf Ball, cobalt/crystal; candy dish, flat, #1212 Michael, 7" 300.00
Golf Ball, cobalt/crystal; stem, champagne; #7643, 5½-oz 47.00
Golf Ball, cobalt/crystal; stem, goblet; #7643, 9-oz 55.00
Golf Ball, crystal; pilsner, #7643, 10-oz, rare, 9" 145.00
Golf Ball, pastel/crystal; stem, goblet; from 48.00 up to 60.00
Golf Ball, rose/gr finial; candy dish, flat, #2938 Helga, 5" 660.00
Golf Ball, ruby/crystal; candy dish, #7858 Leora, 5½" 375.00
Golf Ball, ruby/crystal; candy dish, #9074 Maureen, 4½" 360.00
Golf Ball, ruby/crystal; candy dish, flat, #1212 Michael, 7" 275.00
Golf Ball, ruby/crystal; candy dish, flat, #2938 Helga, 5" 250.00
Golf Ball, ruby/crystal; compote, low, w/lid, #643 Celeste 350.00
Golf Ball, ruby/crystal; stem, goblet; #7643, 9-oz 48.00
Golf Ball, Stiegel/crystal; candy dish, LeRoy decor, #2938, 5" 290.00
Guest set, Anna Rose; Palm Optic, #25 Trudy, 2 pcs 60.00
Guest set, Azure; Festoon Optic, #25 Trudy, 2 pcs 80.00
Guest set, Azure; Peacock Optic, #24 Maria, 4 pcs, rare 465.00
Guest set, Baby Bl opaque; Hollyhock decor, #23 Margaret 165.00
Guest set, Golden Iris; hdld, pulled spout, #23 Margaret 250.00
Guest set, Jade Gr opaque; #25 Trudy, 2 pcs 78.00
Guest set, yel opaque bottle/blk tumbler, #25 Trudy 210.00
Hollywood, blk band; tumbler, highball; flat, #8701, 12-oz 38.00
Hollywood, red band; jug, cocktail; #548 Fairbanks, 36-oz 245.00
Labelle etch, crystal/blk; champagne, #7640 Art Moderne 68.00
Labelle etch, crystal/gold band; goblet, #7640 Art Moderne 95.00
LeMons, cobalt/gold; stem, goblet; #7640 Art Moderne, 9-oz 195.00
LeMons, cobalt/platinum; stem, goblet; #7640, 9-oz 145.00
LMX (El Mexicano), Hyacinth; Ockner jug, #1933, 54-oz 350.00
LMX (El Mexicano), Ice; candle holders, bulbous, 4", #1933, pr ..280.00
LMX (El Mexicano), Ice; sherbet, ftd, #1933 7-oz 25.00
LMX (El Mexicano), Rose Quartz; ice tub, #1933 ....295.00
LMX (El Mexicano), Rose Quartz; Ockner jug, #1933, 54-oz 340.00
LMX (El Mexicano), Rose Quartz; sherbet, ftd, #1933, 7-oz 57.00
LMX (El Mexicano), Rose Quartz; tumbler, ftd, #1933, 13-oz 68.00
LMX (El Mexicano), Seaweed; decanter, liquor; w/stopper, #1933 .225.00
LMX (El Mexicano), Seaweed; relish, 3-part, #1933 ....115.00
Mayfair etch, crystal; stem, champagne; #7668 Galaxy, 6-oz 27.00
Mayfair etch, crystal; stem, goblet; #7668 Galaxy, 10-oz 38.00
Melon, alabaster/cobalt; beverage set, #20069, 7-pc 850.00
Melon, frosted/blk; Aurora Etch; jug, #20069 ....695.00
Mikado etch, crystal; stem, champagne; #7711 Callahan, 6-oz 37.50
Mikado etch, crystal; stem, goblet; #7711 Callahan, 10-oz 48.50
Monroe #7690, cobalt or ruby/crystal; stem, champagne; 6-oz 75.00
Monroe #7690, cobalt or ruby/crystal; stem, goblet; 9-oz 87.50
Monroe #7690, Golden Iris/crystal; stem, cordial; 1½-oz 110.00
Monroe #7690, Old Amethyst/crystal; stem, cordial; 1½-oz 140.00
Monroe #7690, Old Amethyst/crystal; stem, goblet; 10-oz 110.00
Morgantown Square #77942, champagne, flared, 5½-oz 140.00
Morgantown Square #77942, goblet, flared, 10-oz 200.00
Morgantown Square #77943, champagne, DC Thorpe decor, 5-oz .195.00
Morgantown Square #77943, claret, DC Thorpe decor, 4½-oz ...255.00

Nantucket etch, crystal; stem, goblet; Queen Anne, 10-oz **95.00**
Nantucket etch, crystal/gr; stem, goblet; #7654 Lorna, 9-oz **78.00**
Nasreen, blk/filament; sherbet; #7606½ Athena, 5½-oz **75.00**
Nasreen, crystal/blk; tumbler, #9074 Belton, 9-oz **58.00**
Nasreen etch, topaz/crystal; stem, claret; #7665 Laura, 5-oz **95.00**
Old Bristol, cobalt w/opal; candlesticks, 4", pr **330.00**
Old Bristol, cobalt w/opal; plate, unknown #, 7½" **88.00**
Old English #7678, cobalt/crystal; stem, champagne; 6½-oz **50.00**
Old English #7678, cobalt/crystal; stem, goblet; 10-oz **62.00**
Old English #7678, ruby/crystal; stem, goblet; 10-oz **65.00**
Old English #7678, Stiegel Gr/crystal; stem, goblet; 10-oz **55.00**
Old English #7678, Stiegel Gr/crystal; stem, iced tea; 12-oz **55.00**
Old English #7678, Stiegel Gr/crystal; stem, sherbet; 6½-oz **45.00**
Palm Optic, alexandrite; iced tea, #7667 Georgian, 12-oz **165.00**
Palm Optic, Anna Rose; goblet; #7577 Venus, 9-oz **40.00**
Palm Optic, Anna Rose/gr; goblet; #7614 Hampton, 9-oz **87.50**
Palm Optic, Anna Rose/gr; goblet; #7646 Sophisticate, 9-oz **90.00**
Palm Optic, Anna Rose/gr; wine; #7614 Hampton, 3-oz **95.00**
Palm Optic, azure; champagne; #7536 Alycia, 9-oz **45.00**
Palm Optic, azure; goblet; #7536 Alycia, 5½-oz **50.00**
Palm Optic, azure; ice bucket, SP metal rim/bail **295.00**
Palm Optic, azure; salver, ftd, unknown #, 7" **145.00**
Palm Optic, crystal; goblet; #7577 Venus, 9-oz **38.00**
Palm Optic, crystal/Anna Rose; jug, #37 Barry, 48-oz **275.00**
Palm Optic, Venetian gr; goblet; #7577 Venus, 9-oz **48.00**
Palm Optic, 14k Topaz; goblet; #7577 Venus, 9-oz **38.00**
Paragon #77943½, crystal/blk; stem, goblet; 9-oz **145.00**
Paragon #77943½, crystal/blk; stem, sherbet; 5½-oz **85.00**
Peacock Optic, gr or rose; stem, goblet; #7638 Avalon, 9-oz **40.00**
Peacock Optic, gr; decanter, crystal stopper; #10½ Lynwood **355.00**
Peacock Optic, gr; tumbler, bar; flat, #9051, 1½-oz **85.00**
Picardy etch, crystal; champagne; #7646 Sophisticate, 5½-oz **35.00**
Picardy etch, crystal; goblet; #7646 Sophisticate, 9-oz **48.00**
Pineapple Optic, amber; goblet; #7644½ Vernon, 9-oz **45.00**
Pineapple Optic, gr; champagne; #7644½ Vernon, 5½-oz **38.00**
Pineapple Optic, gr; goblet; #7644½ Vernon, 9-oz **52.00**
Priscilla, blk filament; champagne, #7620 Fontanne, 6-oz **87.50**
Priscilla, blk filament; goblet, #7620 Fontanne, 9-oz **115.00**
Pygon #77942, crystal/blk; sherbet, 5-oz **65.00**
Pygon #77942, crystal/frosted; champagne, Thorpe, 5½-oz **135.00**
Pygon #77942, crystal/frosted; wine, sgn Thorpe, 3½-oz **150.00**
Pygon #77942, frosted; wine, Thorpe HP bird decor, 3½-oz **195.00**
Richmond, crystal; stem, goblet; #7570 Horizon, 10-oz **27.00**
Richmond, crystal; stem, goblet; #7589 Laurette, 9-oz **32.00**
Rosalie etch, crystal; bowl, console; #4355 Janice, 13" **185.00**
Rosalie etch, topaz/crystal; stem, goblet; #7662 Majesty, 10-oz **95.00**
Saranac etch, crystal; stem, champagne; #7690 Monroe, 5½-oz **48.00**
Saranac etch, crystal; stem, goblet; #7690 Monroe, 10-oz **68.00**
Sea Gulls, enamel decor; jug, #545 Pickford, 60-oz **395.00**
Sea Gulls, enamel decor; tumbler, ftd, #9093, 12-oz **75.00**
Sear's Lace Bouquet, crystal; champagne; #7668 Galaxy, 6-oz **38.00**
Sear's Lace Bouquet, crystal; goblet; #7668 Galaxy, 10-oz **47.50**
Sonoma etch, crystal; stem, goblet; #7659 Cynthia, 10-oz **65.00**
Sonoma etch, crystal; stem champagne; #7659 Cynthia, 6-oz **55.00**
Sonoma etch, topaz; stem, goblet; #7659 Cynthia, 10-oz **78.00**
Superba, blk/filament; champagne, #7664 Queen Anne, 6½-oz .**138.00**
Superba, blk/filament; goblet, #7664 Queen Anne, 10-oz **195.00**
Superba, crystal/blk; champagne; #7654½ Legacy, 6½-oz **135.00**
Superba, crystal/blk; goblet; #7654½ Legacy, 10-oz **185.00**
Tinker Bell, azure; tumbler, ftd, #9069, 12-oz **70.00**
Tinker Bell, crystal; goblet; #7631 Jewel, 10-oz **145.00**
Tinker Bell, crystal; guest set, #24 Maria, 4-pc, very rare **650.00**
Tinker Bell, gr; vase, bud; ftd, #53 Serenade, 10" **320.00**
Versailles, crystal; stem, goblet; #7688 Jamestown, 9-oz **48.00**

Versailles, crystal; stem, goblet; #7711 Callahan, 10-oz **48.00**
Victoria, crystal; goblet, #300 Touraine, 9-oz **45.00**
Victoria Regina, crystal/blk; goblet; #7640 Art Moderne, 9-oz **97.50**
Virginia etch, amber; stem, goblet; #7614 Hampton, 9-oz **50.00**
Virginia etch, crystal; stem, goblet; #7587 Hampton, 9-oz **40.00**
Virginia etch, crystal; stem, goblet; #7711 Callahan, 10-oz **48.00**
Yale #7684, cobalt or ruby; goblet, 9-oz **110.00**
Yale #7684, crystal; stem, goblet; 9-oz **90.00**
Yale #7684, Stiegel Gr; stem, goblet; 9-oz **98.00**

Continental Line

Ashley #4354, Stiegel/crystal; basket, ftd; 8-crimp, 10" dia **265.00**
Clayton #4357½, Ritz Bl/crystal; basket, canoe rim, 10" **325.00**
Electra #35½, Ritz Bl; vase, flower; hdld, 10" **285.00**
Irene #4356, amber/crystal; basket, 8-crimp, 10½" **315.00**
Irene #4356, Spanish Red/crystal; basket/bowl, 6-crimp, 10½" ...**285.00**
Janet #4355, Spanish Red/crystal; basket/bowl, 8-crimp, 13" **290.00**
Jennie #20, Anna Rose/crystal; basket, bonbon; 4½" dia **385.00**
Jupiter #71, Stiegel/crystal; vase, flower; Italian base, 6" **275.00**
Lyndale #64, Confetti; kerosene lamp, Italian base, 6" **450.00**
Naples #35½, Venetian Gr, vase, flower; Italian base, 12" **395.00**
Neapolitan #64, Ritz Bl; ivy ball, Italian base, 6" **235.00**
Patrick #4358, crystal; basket, flower; 8-crimp, 10" **345.00**
Patrick #4358, Randall Bl/crystal, basket, flower; 8-crimp, 8" **295.00**
Patrick #4358, Stiegel/crystal; basket, flower; 8-crimp, 8" **285.00**
Rima #68, Ritz Bl; vase, flower; Italian base, 10" **310.00**
Trindle #4357, Old Amethyst; basket, 8-crimp, 9" **340.00**
Vienna #71, Stiegel Gr; bowl, console; Italian base, 12" **785.00**
Ziegfield #61, Stiegel Gr; witch ball, Italian base, 8" **825.00**

Silk-Screen Color Printing on Crystal

Manchester Pheasant, champagne, #7664 Queen Anne, 6½-oz **148.00**
Manchester Pheasant, goblet, #7664 Queen Anne, 10-oz **210.00**
Manchester Pheasant, sherbet, #7664 Queen Anne, 6½-oz **135.00**
Queen Louise, crystal/rose; stem, cocktail; #7614 Hampton, 6-oz .**145.00**
Queen Louise, crystal/rose; stem, goblet; #7614 Hampton, 9-oz .**180.00**
Queen Louise, crystal/rose; stem, wine; #7614 Hampton, 6-oz ...**155.00**

Sunrise Medallion Etch

#37 Barry, azure; jug, ftd, 48-oz **585.00**
#37 Barry, crystal; jug, ftd, 80-oz **460.00**
#45 Catherine, azure; vase, bud; ftd, 10" **280.00**
#45 Catherine, gr or rose; vase, bud; ftd, 10" **270.00**
#53 Serenade, azure; vase, bud; bulbous, ftd, 10" **370.00**
#53 Serenade, rose; vase, bud; bulbous, ftd, 10" **360.00**
#7630 Ballerina, azure; stem, goblet; 9-oz **75.00**
#7630 Ballerina, crystal; stem, goblet; 9-oz **62.00**
#7630 Ballerina, green; stem, goblet; 9-oz **65.00**
#7630 Ballerina, rose; stem, goblet; 9-oz **70.00**
#7630 Ballerina, topaz; stem, goblet; 9-oz **62.00**
#7654½ Legacy, crystal w/moonstone; champagne, 6-oz **135.00**
#7654½ Legacy, crystal w/moonstone; cocktail, 3-oz **135.00**
#7654½ Legacy, crystal w/moonstone; goblet, 9-oz **190.00**
#7664 Queen Anne, azure; stem, goblet; 10-oz **90.00**
#7664 Queen Anne, crystal; stem, goblet; 10-oz **78.00**

Moriage

The term 'moriage' refers to certain Japanese wares decorated with applied slipwork designs. There are several methods used to achieve the characteristic relief effect. The decorative devices may be designed separately and applied to the vessel, piped on in narrow ribbons of clay (slip-trailed), or built up by brushing on successive layers of liquified slip. See also Dragon Ware; Nippon.

Box, floral reserves, 2x4" dia	125.00
Chocolate pot, heavy mauve moriage & mc florals, 12"	435.00
Cup & saucer, floral reserves, lav/rose/pk w/gold, mk	60.00
Ewer, floral medallions, mc slipwork, bulbous bottom, 12"	365.00
Planter, enamel & moriage florals, incurvate hdls, 8¼" W	245.00
Plaque, fronds & pods, ornate border, 8½"	210.00
Sugar shaker, roses on gr, bbl form	95.00
Vase, mc flowers in medallion on gr, unmk, 4½x2½"	65.00
Vase, Nouveau iris & lilies, beading, 12"	285.00
Vase, slipwork florals, mc bird-on-limb panels, 12½"	250.00

Mortars and Pestles

Mortars are bowl-shaped vessels used for centuries for the purpose of grinding drugs to a powder or grain into meal. The masher or grinding device is called a pestle.

Brass, 3¼x5½", w/7" brass pestle	100.00
Brass, 4½x4¾", w/pestle	75.00
Bronze, 2 sq side hdls, 1870s, sm, w/bronze pestle	20.00
Burl, half-trn/half irregular growth ft, 4¾", w/pestle	145.00
Burl, trn rings, old finish, 7", +plain wooden pestle	200.00
CI, chalice shape, 14", w/pestle	125.00
Free blown, gr, str sides, flared rim, 4⅜x4¾", w/pestle	350.00
Maple, 7½", w/pestle	110.00
Tiger maple, 7x6", w/ball-finial pestle	250.00
Wooden, lt wear, 7⅝x6", w/10" trn pestle	110.00
Wooden, trn, primitive, old varnish, 8", w/pestle	115.00

Mortens Studio

Oscar Mortens was already established as a fine sculptural artist when he left his native Sweden to take up residency in Arizona. During the 1940s he developed a line of detailed animal figures which were distributed through the Mortens Studios, a firm he co-founded with Gunnar Thelin. Thelin hired and trained artists to produce Mortens' line, which he called Royal Designs. More than two hundred dogs were modeled and over one hundred horses. Cats and wild animals such as elephants, panthers, deer, and elk were made, but on a much smaller scale. Bookends with sculptured dog heads were shown in their catalogs, and collectors report finding wall plaques on rare occasions. The material they used was a plaster-type composition with wires embedded to support the weight. Examples were marked 'Copyright by the Mortens Studio' either in ink or decal. Watch for flaking, cracks, and separations. Crazing seems to be present in some degree in many examples. When no condition is indicated, the items listed below are assumed to be in near-mint condition, allowing for minor crazing.

Afghan, tan/charcoal face, 7x7", M	90.00
Beagle, ivory/tan/blk, standing, paper label, 6x6"	70.00
Boston Terrier, ivory markings on blk, standing, 6x6", M	75.00
Chow pup, recumbent, tan & brn, 3x3"	50.00
Cocker Spaniel, #763D	55.00
Collie puppy	40.00
Dachshund, standing, lg	70.00
Dalmatian, #812, sm	45.00
Doberman, standing, 6x7"	70.00

English Setter, #848	65.00
German Shepherd, standing, 7"	85.00
German Shepherd pup, 3½x3½"	35.00
Great Dane, recumbent, blk details on tan, 7½x6½"	75.00
Horse, #701D, lg	68.00
Horse, rearing, 9"	75.00
Mexican chihuahua, sitting, tan w/blk details, 3x3½"	55.00
Persian cat	48.00
Pointer, sitting, ivory w/blk spots, 4x4¾"	65.00
Spaniel puppy, ivory w/blk spots, 3¾x3"	40.00
Springer Spaniel, 5"	65.00

Morton Pottery

Six potteries operated in Morton, Illinois, at various times from 1877 to 1976. Each traced its origin to six brothers who immigrated to America to avoid military service in Germany. The Rapp brothers established their first pottery near clay deposits on the south side of town where they made field tile and bricks. Within a few years, they branched out to include utility wares such as jugs, bowls, jars, pitchers, etc. During the ninety-nine years of pottery operations in Morton, the original factory was expanded by some of the sons and nephews of the Rapps. Other family members started their own potteries where artware, gift-store items, and special-order goods were produced. The Cliftwood Art Pottery and the Morton Pottery Company had showrooms in Chicago and New York City during the 1930s. All of Morton's potteries were relatively short-lived operations with the Morton Pottery Company being the last to shut down on September 8, 1976. For a more thorough study of the subject, we recommend *Morton's Potteries: 99 Years* by Doris and Burdell Hall; their address can be found in the Directory under Illinois.

Morton Pottery Works — Morton Earthenware Co. (1877-1917)

Coffeepot, brn Rockingham, 4 pcs, mini, 3"	75.00
Nappy, yel ware, plain, 10"	45.00
Nappy, yel ware, plain, 12"	60.00
Nappy, yel ware, plain, 4"	32.00
Nappy, yel ware, plain, 6"	36.00
Pie baker, brn Rockingham, 10"	100.00
Pie baker, brn Rockingham, 6"	60.00
Pie baker, brn Rockingham, 7"	70.00
Pie baker, brn Rockingham, 8"	80.00
Pie baker, brn Rockingham, 9"	90.00
Pitcher, cobalt, mini, 3¼"	55.00
Stein, brn Rockingham w/German motto, 6"	65.00

Cliftwood Art Potteries, Inc. (1920-1940)

Cliftwood Art Potteries, cardholder elephant with open basket each side, dark brown drip on light tan, 4x6", $70.00.

Bookends, lion & lioness on gr rocks, natural mc, 7¾", pr	100.00
Bookends, tree trunk w/appl birds, brn drip, pr	90.00
Bowl, console; wht matt, pk int, appl dolphin base, 8x5x14"	95.00

Chocolate set, tree trunk, brn drip, 7-pc (pitcher+6 mugs) 175.00
Compote, pk, appl dolphin base, 6x8" 85.00
Console set, tree trunk, brn drip, bowl+frog+2 candle holders 95.00
Figurine, billikin, brn, 11" 85.00
Figurine, billikin, brn, 8" 55.00
Figurine, billikin, cobalt, 11" 100.00
Figurine, billikin, cobalt, 8" 75.00
Vase, tree trunk, Herbage Gr 50.00
Vase, turq matt, appl dolphin base, 10" 65.00
Wall pocket, tree trunk form, brn drip 65.00

Midwest Potteries, Inc. (1940-1944)

Ashtray, hand w/appl saucer, 14k gold 22.00
Figurine, female dancer, wht w/gold, 8½" 25.00
Figurine, gazelle, brn & tan spray, 12¾" 35.00
Figurine, polar bear, wht, 6" 30.00
Figurine, police dog, wht w/gold, 6" 20.00
Figurine, road runner, mauve & bl spray, 8" 12.00
Figurine, spaniel, wht w/gold, 4" 16.00
Figurine, wild turkey on stump, natural colors spray, 12" 30.00
Lamp, urn w/tassel hdls, bl w/gold, 12" 25.00
Lamp/shadow box, wht, Deco style, holds 12" figurines, 20" 50.00
Planter, ducks, Mr & Mrs, wht w/gold, pr 24.00
Planter, mountain goat, gr 8.00
Planter, nest w/appl bird, bl 10.00
Vase, bud; hand form, tan matt, 4½" 14.00
Vase, bud; hand form, wht matt, 6" 18.00
Wall pocket, corner type, HP underglaze mums on wht, 5½" 14.00

Morton Pottery Company (1922-1976)

Au gratin dish, red & bl spatter on wht 50.00
Bank, hen, wht w/brushed blk trim 30.00
Bowls, mixing; red & bl spatter on wht, #600, nested set of 3 .....125.00
Christmas item, mug, natural colors 15.00
Christmas item, nut cup, natural colors 10.00
Christmas item, Santa plate, natural colors, 12" 45.00
Christmas item, Santa plate, natural colors, 8" 30.00
Christmas item, sleigh, wht w/HP underglaze holly 15.00
Coffeepot, Coffee Time w/clock face, yel 22.00
Cookie, turkey w/chick finial, brn w/red wattle 125.00
Cookie jar, hen w/chick finial, wht w/brushed blk trim 100.00
Cookie jar, turkey w/chick finial, wht w/burgundy wattle 150.00
Creamer & sugar bowl, hen & rooster, wht w/brushed blk trim 25.00
Pitcher, milk; red & bl spatter on wht, w/advertising 48.00
Salt, pepper or toothpick finial to hen cookie jar, rare, ea 45.00
Sauce warmer, blk candle holder w/yel sauce boat, 4-oz 15.00
Syrup, cobalt w/HP underglaze, Pat no-drip design 38.00
Syrup, floral w/gold decor 38.00
Syrup, gr, Pat no-drip design 20.00
Teapot, Teatime w/clock face, burgundy 22.00

American Art Potteries (1947-1961)

Figurine, squirrel, brn & gr spray 16.00
Flower bowl, rectangular w/frog or turtle frog, gr & yel spray 22.00
Lamp, TV; afghan hounds, blk, pr 55.00
Lamp, TV; conch shell, yel & brn 20.00
Lamp, TV; panther on log, blk 22.00
Planter, baby shoes on heart base, bl or pk 22.00
Planter, bunny at stump, natural colors 14.00
Planter, pheasant, natural colors 25.00
Wall pocket, apple on leaf, red & gr 15.00

Wall pocket, plum, lg 12.00

Moser

Ludwig Moser began his career as a struggling glass artist, catering to the rich who visited the famous Austrian health spas. His talent and popularity grew and in 1857 the first of his three studios opened in Karlsbad, Czechoslovakia. The styles developed there were entirely his own; no copies of other artists have ever been found. Some of his original designs include grapes with trailing vines, acorns and oak leaves, and richly enameled, deeply cut or carved floral pieces. Sometimes jewels were applied to the glass as well. Moser's animal scenes reflect his careful attention to detail. Famed for his birds in flight, he also designed stalking tigers — even elephants — all created in fine enameling.

Moser died in 1916, but the business was contined by his two sons who had been personally and carefully trained by their father. The Moser company bought the Meyr's Neffe Glassworks in 1922 and continued to produce quality glassware.

When identifying Moser, look for great clarity in the glass; deeply carved, continuous engravings; perfect coloration; finely applied enameling (often covered with thin gold leaf); and well-polished pontils. Our advisor for this category is Don Williams; he is listed in the Directory under Missouri. Items described below are enameled unless noted otherwise.

Bottle, scent; amethyst, faceted/angular, cut stopper, 4" 165.00
Bowl, avacado, octagonal on faceted ft, Hoffman design, 5" 250.00
Bowl, cranberry, gold insects/foliage, 2½x5", set of 6 ....800.00
Bowl, daisies/etc, 3 amber reeded ft w/lion masks, 5½" 150.00
Bowl, tulips intaglio, gr to clear, 5x9" 495.00
Box, amber, mc bird/bl & orange flowers, brass mts, 3x3½" 350.00
Box, amber, rabbit & trees w/gold, vintage band, 2½x7½" 575.00
Box, amber, wht lace w/purple & gold, hinged, 3½x5½" 375.00
Box, amethyst, butterfly/wheat on lid, ribbed, 2½" dia 225.00
Box, sapphire bl, daisies/apple blossoms, dots/scrolls, 3x5" 350.00
Compote, purple, eng Amazon female warriors band, 7x7" 350.00
Compote, purple w/eng band of Amazon female warriors, 7x7" ...350.00
Cruet, sapphire, seaweed, gr hdl, 7½" 225.00
Decanter, amber, mc/gold ferns, 12" L horn shape, metal ft 275.00
Decanter, amethyst to clear, intaglio floral, cut bands, 9" 400.00
Decanter, cranberry/clear w/gold grapes, 12", +tray/6 wines 1,500.00
Decanter, ruby panels/gilt decor, 8", +tray & 8 cordials 1,500.00
Decanter, smoky topaz, emb nudes, 10", +4 cordials, EX 250.00
Ewer, cranberry, gold/turq jewels, gold roses, 10x4" 250.00
Finger bowl, amethyst to clear, iris cutting, 4½", +plate 225.00
Goblet, lt gr, mc/gold allover floral, prunts on stem/ft, 8" 160.00
Jewel casket, ruby, elaborate gold floral, brass ft/hdl, 4" L 325.00
Nappy, cameo tulips, cranberry/crystal w/gold, hdl, 1¼x5½" 295.00
Pickle castor, amethyst w/gold warriors in band, SP fr 350.00
Pitcher, cranberry, allover pnt/gold, bladder form, 7x7" 550.00
Pitcher, rubena w/allover gold, bladder form, 3½x4" 365.00
Pitcher, tankard, apple gr to clear, poppies intaglio, 12¼" 765.00
Rose bowl, cranberry, floral branches w/gold, 3½x11" 175.00
Sugar shaker, clear w/cranberry panels, gold florals 265.00
Tazza, gr o/l, gold florals, cut/polished, 6x4" 100.00
Tumbler, amberina, Invt T'print, appl leaves/acorns/insects 650.00
Tumbler, juice; mc florals & gold on amber 85.00
Vase, alexandrite, ribbed goblet form, 9" 150.00
Vase, amber w/etched band of Amazon women & horses, 9" 465.00
Vase, aquamarine, 4 mc snakes/flowers, petal rim, 7" 400.00
Vase, cobalt w/gold etch character scene+5 animals, 16" 1,950.00
Vase, cranberry, gold flowers/leaves, ribbed, flared, 5" 150.00
Vase, cranberry, gold medallions/mc enamel beading, 9" 450.00
Vase, gr cut w/panels & gold warrior band, cylinder, 11" 250.00

Vase, Persian-style enameled floral decoration with four applied twisted glass bands enameled in gold, baluster form, 17½", $2,500.00.

Vase, mc leaves, appl acorns, 8x2½" 1,600.00
Vase, yel, cut w/2 rows of lg ovals, shouldered, 1930s, 6" 165.00
Vase, yel opal, grapes w/gr leaves, ftd, 5⅜x2" 345.00
Wine, amethyst over clear w/gold floral, cut/polished, 4" 60.00
1ase, cranberry, mc florals w/gold, 2¾" 225.00

Moss Rose

Moss Rose was a favorite dinnerware pattern of many Staffordshire and American potters from the mid-1800s. In America the Wheeling Pottery of West Virginia produced the ware in large quantities, and it became one of their bestsellers, remaining popular well into the nineties. See also Haviland.

Bone dish, unmk, gold edge 32.00
Bowl, vegetable; unmk, w/lid 50.00
Butter pat, Meakin, EX 15.00
Coffeepot, dolphin hdl, 7" 65.00
Creamer & sugar bowl, unmk 28.00
Gravy boat, Meakin 35.00
Mug, unmk, 3" 10.00
Plate, Powell Bishop, 9" 25.00
Plate, unmk, 7½" 9.00
Platter, rectangular, Meakin, 14x10" 35.00
Shaving mug, unmk 30.00
Tea set, American, 14-pc 125.00
Tea set, child's, 15-pc 275.00
Tea set, Japan, 16-pc+lids 60.00
Wash set, unmk, 11" pitcher+13½" bowl 295.00

Mother-of-Pearl Glass

Mother-of-Pearl glass was a type of mold-blown satin art glass popular during the last half of the 19th century. A patent for its manufacture was issued in 1886 to Frederick S. Shirley, and one of the companies who produced it was the Mt. Washington Glass Company of New Bedford, Massachusetts. Another was the English firm of Stevens and Williams. Its delicate patterns were developed by blowing the gather into a mold with inside projections that left an intaglio design on the surface of the glass, then sealing the first layer with a second, trapping air in the recesses. Most common are the Diamond Quilted, Raindrop, and Herringbone patterns. It was made in several soft colors, the most rare and valuable is rainbow — a blend of rose, light blue, yellow, and white. Occasionally it may be decorated with coralene, enameling, or

gilt. Watch for 20th-century reproductions, especially in the Diamond Quilted pattern. Our advisors for this category are Betty and Clarence Maier; they are listed in the Directory under Pennsylvania.

Basket, Herringbone, bl, fan shape, thorn hdl, 9¼x8¼" 625.00
Basket, Herringbone, pk, frosted hdl, ftd, 6½x3¾" 500.00
Bowl, Dmn Quilt, chartreuse, ruffled, 3 thorny ft, 3⅜" 425.00
Bowl, jack-in-pulpit; Moire, apricot to rose, star base 4x9" 385.00
Creamer & sugar bowl, Dmn Quilt, brn to gold, Webb, 3¼", 2½" ...650.00
Creamer & sugar bowl, Ribbon, bl, frosted wafer ft, 2¾" 395.00
Ewer, Dmn Quilt, pk, frosted thorn hdl, frosted rim, 14x5" 650.00
Lamp, table; Swirl, mauve, emb ribs, clambroth shade, 20¾" 950.00
Nut dish, Herringbone, rainbow, SP Pairpoint holder, 6" 675.00
Pitcher, Dmn Quilt, apricot, 7", +6 3⅝" tumblers 1,300.00
Pitcher, pk, Queen Anne's Lace & butterflies, +6 tumblers 2,250.00
Plate, Dmn Quilt, bl, mk Pat, 5¾" 275.00
Rose bowl, Dmn Quilt, pk, crimped, clear ft, 5½x5½" 365.00
Spooner, Dmn Quilt, bl, sq top, Mt WA, 5x3" 365.00
Sweetmeat, Ribbon, gr, rare color 595.00
Tumbler, Dmn Quilt, yel, 4" 145.00
Tumbler, Herringbone, bl, 4" 145.00
Tumbler, Swirl, gold to pale pk-wht, Mt WA, 9x3½" 425.00
Vase, Basketweave, bl, Webb, 7x5" 750.00
Vase, Coin Spot, cream, wht int, 8¼x4" 175.00
Vase, Dmn Quilt, bittersweet, triple-bulge neck, 9¼" 195.00
Vase, Dmn Quilt, bl, bottle form, 8¾x4" 135.00
Vase, Dmn Quilt, bl, cupid heads on ormolu ft, 6½x3½" 250.00
Vase, Dmn Quilt, bl, fluted 4-petal top, 6x3⅝" 155.00
Vase, Dmn Quilt, bl, ruffled top, 7x4" 200.00
Vase, Dmn Quilt, bl, Webb, 6½x4" 210.00
Vase, Dmn Quilt, deep apricot, 7" 225.00
Vase, Dmn Quilt, gr, opal int, mk Pat, 7½x4½" 475.00
Vase, Dmn Quilt, pk, 10¼x5⅜", pr 525.00
Vase, Dmn Quilt, pk to amber, stick neck, 7¼x3⅛" 335.00
Vase, Dmn Quilt, rainbow, 3-petal top, 6x3¾" 895.00
Vase, Dmn Quilt, yel, flowers & branches, ruffled, 7x4" 495.00
Vase, Drape, pk, ruffled rim, 5⅞x3½", pr 495.00
Vase, Herringbone, pk, fluted top, 7¼x4", pr 450.00
Vase, Peacock Eye, cream, 6½x3¾" 235.00
Vase, Raindrop, bl, 6-sided, frosted rim, Mt WA, 9x6" 395.00
Vase, Raindrop, butterscotch, camphor edge, Mt WA, 8" 375.00
Vase, Raindrop, butterscotch, frosted rim, 6¾x3⅞" 165.00
Vase, Ribbon, bl, pouch shape w/3-petal top, 4¾x6" 495.00
Vase, Ribbon, bl, 5x3½" 145.00
Vase, Swirl, orange, Stevens & Wms, 11x4⅝" 245.00
Vase, Wave, bl, ruffled w/clear edge, 6⅝x2⅞" 195.00

Mourning Collectibles

During the 18th and early 19th centuries, ladies made needlework pictures, samplers, paintings on ivory plaques, watercolor drawings, etc. to commemorate the death of a loved one. Elements contained in nearly all examples are the tomb, mourners, a weeping willow tree, and data relating to the deceased. Often plaits of hair were included. Today these are recognized and valued as a valid form of folk art. Our advisor for this category is Steve DeGenaro; he is listed in the Directory under Ohio. See also Hair Weaving.

Brooch, jet hand shape w/forget-me-nots, Victorian 85.00
Locket, appl gutta percha flowers on jet, holds 2 pictures 175.00
Locket, jet case w/3-D cvd gutta percha eagle, holds 1 photo 145.00
Memorial, die-cut/emb paper w/verse, rvpt trees, 1873, 22x26" 50.00

Memorial needlework, lady beside willow, inscr/1820, 29x26" ..**3,850.00**
Memorial needlework, lady by willow, inscr/1807, 16x22" **1,200.00**
Necklace, cvd jet beads, matt & polished, 2-strand, 24" **95.00**
Pin, gold & onyx w/plaited hair under crystal **195.00**
Pin, 14k gold w/onyx, blond hair under crystal, eng on bk **225.00**

Movie Memorabilia

Movie memorabilia covers a broad range of collectibles, from books and magazines dealing with the industry in general to the various promotional materials which were distributed to arouse interest in a particular film. Many collectors specialize in a specific area — posters, pressbooks, stills, lobby cards, or souvenir programs (also referred to as premiere booklets). In the listings below, a one-sheet poster measures approximately 27" x 41", three-sheet: 41" x 81", and six-sheet: 81" x 81". See also Autographs; Cartoon Art; Paper Dolls; Personalities.

Book, Gone w/The Wind, paperback, 1939 movie edition, NM ...**50.00**
Cigarette card, Gone w/Wind, Leigh/Gable, mc, 3x2½" **32.00**
Cigarette card, Gone w/Wind, Leigh/McDaniels, mc, 1⅜x2⅝" **27.50**
Cigarette card, Jezebel, Davis/Fonda, blk/wht, 4x2¾" **5.00**
Cigarette card, Plainsman, Cooper/Milan, blk/wht, 4x2¾" **4.00**
Cigarette card, Pygmalion, Howard/Hiller, blk/wht, 3x2½" **4.00**
Cigarette card, Riffraff, Harlow/Tracy, blk/wht, 4x2¾" **8.00**
Cigarette card, Thief of Bagdad, Sabu, 3x2½" **15.00**
Handbill, Regeneration, 4 scenes, 1923, 4⅝x7¼" **10.00**
Insert card, Chism, Wayne, Warner Bros, 1970, 14x36", EX **25.00**
Insert card, Search for Bridey Murphy, 1956, 14x36", NM **12.00**
Insert card, What's Up Doc?, Streisand/O'Neill, '72, 14x36", EX .**22.50**
Lobby card, Action in Arabia, Sanders/Bruce, 1944, 11x14", NM ..**5.00**
Lobby card, Baby Face Nelson, Rooney/Jones, 1947, 11x14", NM .**12.00**
Lobby card, Blk Sleep, Rathbone/Lugosi, 1956, 11x14", NM **16.00**
Lobby card, Cheyenne, Maynard, 1929, 11x14", EX **32.00**
Lobby card, Don't Fence Me In, Rogers/Evans, 1945, 11x14", NM ..**35.00**
Lobby card, His Private Secretary, Wayne/Knapp, 1933, 11x14", M .**90.00**
Lobby card, Jes Call Me Jim, Will Rogers, 1920, 11x14", EX **78.00**
Lobby card, Nevada Smith, Steve McQueen, 1965, 11x14", NM .**30.00**
Lobby card, Night Passage, Stewart/Murphy, 1957, 11x14", NM .**27.50**
Lobby card, Pirates of Monterey, Montez/Cameron, '47, 11x14", M ..**16.50**
Lobby card, Place in Sun, Cliff/Taylor, 11x14", EX **32.50**
Lobby card, Robe, Burton/Simmons, 1953, 11x14", EX **16.00**
Lobby card, Westbound Stage, Ritter, 1940, 11x14", NM **25.00**
Lobby card, 7-Yr Itch, Monroe/Ewell, 1955, 11x14", NM **75.00**
Magazine, Filmland, Jane Powell cover, 1954, VG **20.00**
Magazine, Hollywood Romances, Kim Novak cover, 1956, NM ..**30.00**
Magazine, Modern Screen, Jean Crain cover, May 1951, VG **22.00**
Magazine, Motion Picture, Esther Williams cover, 1948, EX **17.50**
Magazine, Motion Picture, Jane Powell cover, Feb 1951, VG **22.00**
Magazine, Motion Picture, Lauren Bacall cover, June 1945, VG ..**22.50**
Magazine, Movie Play, Gene Tierney cover, Nov 1954, NM **20.00**
Magazine, Movie Teen, June Allyson cover, July 1952, VG **20.00**
Magazine, Movie Time, Esther Williams cover, Aug 1954, NM ...**18.00**
Magazine, Movieland, Janet Leigh cover, Dec 1951, VG **25.00**
Magazine, Photoplay, Claudette Colbert cover, Dec 1945, VG **36.00**
Magazine, Photoplay, Debby Reynolds cover, Aug 1960, EX **40.00**
Magazine, Photoplay, Jean Harlow cover, Dec 1931, EX **95.00**
Magazine, Photoplay, Taylor/Burton cover, Oct 1973, EX **9.00**
Magazine, Screen Stories, Debby Reynolds cover, May 1960, NM ...**15.00**
Magazine, Screen Stories, Doris Day cover, Dec 1953, NM **20.00**
Magazine, Screenland, Betty Grable cover, Aug 1942, VG **40.00**
Magazine, Silver Screen, Constance Bennett cover, Apr 1932, NM ...**50.00**
Magazine, Silver Screen, June Allyson cover, Dec 1950, EX **17.50**

Magazine, TV Radio Mirror, Julia/Family Affair, 1969, EX **7.50**
Poster, Advise & Consent, Fonda/Laughton, 41x27", EX **32.00**
Poster, Alien, Weaver/Skerritt, 1979, 41x27", NM **35.00**
Poster, Ambush at Cimarron Pass, Eastwood, 1958, 41x27", M **42.00**
Poster, Animal Crackers, Marx Bros 1974 reissue, 41x27", EX **16.50**
Poster, Aristocats, cartoon, Disney, 1970, 41x27", NM **45.00**
Poster, Borrowed Trouble, Boyde/Clyde, 1948, 22x28", EX **22.00**
Poster, Bull Dogger, Bill Pickett, 1923, 1-sheet, NM **2,200.00**
Poster, Call It Murder, Bogart, 1946, 41x27", EX **100.00**
Poster, Charade, Grant/Hepburn, 1963, 41x27", EX **95.00**
Poster, Crime Doctor's Gamble, Baxter, 1947, 3-sheet, EX **155.00**
Poster, Day Earth Stood Still, alien scene, 1951, 1-sheet, EX ..**1,200.00**
Poster, Donovan's Reef, Wayne/Lamour/Martin, 1963, 41x27", EX .**100.00**
Poster, Fighting Frontiersman, Starrett, 1946, 41x27", VG **27.50**

Poster, *From Russia with Love,* Sean Connery, Italian version, United Artists, 1963, 55x39", $750.00.

Poster, Finian's Rainbow, Astaire/Clarke, 1968, 41x27", EX **42.50**
Poster, Giant, Dean/Taylor, 1956, 41x27", EX **300.00**
Poster, House of Wax, Vincent Price, 1953, 3-sheet, EX **425.00**
Poster, Hypnotic Eye, Bergerac/Anders, 1960, 41x27", EX **95.00**
Poster, Jayne Mansfield pinup, linen bk, 1960, 62x21" **300.00**
Poster, Johnny Cash, Cash/Carter, 1959, 41x27", EX **70.00**
Poster, Kiss of Araby, Alba/Byron/Windsor, 1933, 41x27", VG ...**75.00**
Poster, Let It Be, Beatles, 1970, 41x27", EX **120.00**
Poster, Mahogany, Ross/Williams/Perkins, 1975, 41x27", EX **32.00**
Poster, My Fair Lady, Hepburn/Harrison, 1964, 41x27", EX **165.00**
Poster, On the Waterfront, Marlon Brando, 1954, 1-sheet, EX ..**500.00**
Poster, Out of This World, Bracken/Lake, 1945, 41x27", EX **120.00**
Poster, Rachel Rachel, Woodward/Olsen, 1968, 41x27", EX **65.00**
Poster, Roaring Six Guns, Maynard, 1937, 41x27", EX **95.00**
Poster, Silver Bullet, Busey/McGill, S King, 1985, 41x27", EX **22.50**
Poster, Sons of Katie Elder, Wayne/Martin, 41x27", EX **75.00**
Poster, Summertime, Hepburn/Brazzi, 1955, 41x27", EX **95.00**
Poster, Taming of Shrew, Taylor/Burton, 1967, 41x27", NM **80.00**
Poster, Tomahawk Trail, Conners/Smith, 1947, 41x27", EX **37.50**
Poster, Twist Around Clock, Checker/Dion, 1961, 41x27", EX ...**48.00**
Poster, Yearling, Peck/Wyman, 1956, 41x27", EX **55.00**
Poster, 100 Rifles, Reynolds/Welch, 1959, 41x27", EX **22.50**
Poster, 3 Stooges in Orbit, 1962, 41x27", EX **75.00**
Program, Citizen Kane premier souvenir, RKO, 1941, 12x9", NM ..**650.00**
Program, Gone w/the Wind movie, orig 1939 ....**95.00**
Title card, Bad Day at Blk Rock, Tracy/Francis/Ryan, 11x14", EX ..**15.00**
Title card, Marauders, Boyd/Clyde, 1947, 11x14", M **22.00**
Title card, Night Creatures, Cushing/Romain, 1962, 11x14", NM .**22.50**
Window card, Aerial Gunner, Morris/Arlen, 1943, 14x22", M **36.00**
Window card, An Am Romance, Donlevy/Richards, 14x22", M ..**55.00**
Window card, Atlantic City, Moore/Taylor, 1944, 14x22", NM ..**55.00**
Window card, Dbl Exposure, Morris/Kelly, 1944, 14x22", NM **48.00**
Window card, Lover Come Back, Brent/Ball, 1946, 14x22", NM .**145.00**
Window card, Mr & Mrs North, Allen/Post, 1941, 14x22", NM ..**78.00**

Mt. Washington

The Mt. Washington Glass Works was founded in 1837 in South Boston, Massachusetts, but moved to New Bedford in 1869 after purchasing the facilities of the New Bedford Glass Company. Frederick S. Shirley became associated with the firm in 1874. Two years later the company reorganized and became known as the Mt. Washington Glass Company. In 1894 it merged with the Pairpoint Manufacturing Company, a small Brittania works nearby, but continued to conduct business under its own title until after the turn of the century. The combined plants were equipped with the most modern and varied machinery available and boasted a working force with experience and expertise rival to none in the art of blowing and cutting glass. In addition to their fine cut glass, they are recognized as the first American company to make cameo glass, an effect they achieved through acid-cutting methods. In 1885 Shirley was issued a patent to make Burmese, pale yellow glassware tinged with a delicate pink blush. Another patent issued in 1886 allowed them the rights to produce Rose Amber, or amberina, a transparent ware shading from ruby to amber. Pearl Satin Ware and Peachblow, so named for its resemblance to a rosy peach skin, were patented the same year. One of their most famous lines, Crown Milano, was introduced in 1893. It was an opal glass either free-blown or pattern-molded, tinted a delicate color and decorated with enameling and gilt. Royal Flemish was patented in 1894 and is considered the rarest of the Mt. Washington art glass lines. It was decorated with raised, gold-enameled lines dividing the surface of the ware in much the same way as lead lines divide a stained glass window. The sections were filled in with one or several transparent colors and further decorated in gold enamel with florals, foliage, beading, and medallions.

Our advisors for this category are Betty and Clarence Maier; they are listed in the Directory under Pennsylvania. See also Amberina, Cranberry; Salt Shakers; Burmese; Crown Milano; Royal Flemish; etc.

Biscuit jar, Napoli, Palmer Cox Brownies w/gold, 9x23" **5,500.00**
Biscuit jar, 6 wht sqs w/mc astors, silver mts mk Pairpoint, 7" **300.00**
Bowl, Ambero, rvpt water lilies, pk/yel/wht on amber, 3x13" **880.00**
Bowl, Dmn Quilt, mc florals/pk rim, pillow form, 4½x4x3¼" **295.00**
Box, bow-tied roses around emb gold floral on wht, sqd, 7" W ...**450.00**
Box, jewel; flower medallion, gold scrolls, SP rim, 3¼x7x4" **975.00**
Box, jewel; monk on opal, sgn Schindler, 3¼x5¼" **550.00**
Bride's bowl, apple blossoms on cranberry, SP fr, 10x8¼" **950.00**
Flower frog, florals on lt bl, mushroom shape, 3½" **195.00**
Lamp, scroll base sgn Miller; owl in landscape shade, 21" **675.00**
Mustard, roses/moss on yel-brn, melon ribs, SP lid/hdl/spoon **350.00**
Pickle castor, Albertine, HP floral/emb star, SP fr, 8½" **1,125.00**
Pitcher, mums & buds, 6x5½" **435.00**
Pitcher, tankard; pansies w/gold, pansy on hdl, 5" **400.00**
Pitcher, water; floral, mc on cranberry, 10¼", +6 mugs **1,050.00**
Rose bowl, florals & ivy w/gold on clear, 4x4½" **185.00**
Rose bowl, gold flowers & leaves, 6½" **295.00**
Rose bowl, pansies, lav on wht, yel rim w/12 'fingers,' 3x4" **285.00**
Shaker, Columbia 1893 Exhibition in gold, lay down **265.00**
Shakers, Cockel Shell, frosted w/floral, metal mt, 3", pr **1,200.00**
Shakers, egg form w/chick head metal tops, HP roses, 2½" L **850.00**
Shakers, floral on yel (or bl), stand-up egg shape, 2¼", pr **110.00**
Sugar shaker, asters, wht on yel to wht, egg shape, 4" **250.00**
Sugar shaker, daisies, wht on yel, egg shape, 4" **200.00**
Sugar shaker, daisies/dots, tomato form, emb butterfly top **380.00**
Sugar shaker, maiden hair fern, gr/brn on wht, egg shape, 4" **200.00**
Sugar shaker, raspberry vines on pnt burmese, egg shape, 5" **230.00**
Sugar shaker, violets on wht, egg form, 4" **175.00**
Tazza, Napoli, vintage, mc w/gold, 3¾x7½" **550.00**
Toothpick holder, bl violets on wht satin, ribbed, 2¼" **400.00**

Vase, signed Verona on base, 14", $1,500.00.

Vase, Albertine, leaves & feathers, mc on pnt burmese, 6¼" **375.00**
Vase, Dmn Quilt, HP florals, yel rim, pillow form, 4½" **275.00**
Vase, gold trees/gr cameo leaves on amber, sgn, 6½" **595.00**
Vase, Lava, bl/gr geometrics, opal spatter on blk, 6¼" **2,200.00**
Vase, Lava, mc sqs/gold on blk gloss, hdls, 5¾" **2,250.00**
Vase, mc flowers on red (rare) bkground, 11" **285.00**
Vase, Napoli, frog among bulrushes, 8 vertical ribs, 8½x5" **975.00**
Vase, Napoli, lilies, wht/pk/gr on dk gr, much gold, 10x6" **2,200.00**
Vase, Napoli, mums/gold sponging on lt yel T'print, 11¾" **1,600.00**
Vase, Opalware, Delft windmill scene on pk w/gold, 9x5½" **375.00**
Vase, seaweed HP on dk brn to gold, gourd shape, 11¼" **550.00**
Vase, Verona, lady & putti, 12" **1,250.00**
Vase, Verona, purple & wht iris, 12" **675.00**

Mulberry China

Mulberry china was made by many of the Staffordshire area potters from about 1830 until the 1850s. It is a transfer-printed earthenware or ironstone named for the color of its decorations, a purplish-brown resembling the juice of the mulberry. Some pieces may have faded out over the years and today look almost gray with only a hint of purple. (Transfer printing was done in many colors; technically only those in the mauve tones are 'mulberry'; color variations have little effect on value.) Some of the patterns (Corean, Jeddo, Pelew, and Formosa, for instance) were also produced in Flow Blue ware. Others seem to have been used exclusively with the mulberry color. Our advisor for this category is Mary Frank Gaston; she is listed in the Directory under Texas.

Abbey, creamer **175.00**
Athens, plate, 10" **40.00**
Bochara, gravy boat **250.00**
Brunswick, platter, w/polychrome, 17" **350.00**
Calcutta, cup & saucer, handleless **160.00**
Calcutta, plate, 8½" **48.00**
Castle Scenery, pitcher, 8" **375.00**
Chusan, platter, 18" **200.00**
Corean, bowl, potato; Podmore Walker, 9¼" **325.00**
Corean, bowl, vegetable; 8-sided, w/lid, lg **595.00**
Corean, creamer, Podmore Walker **325.00**
Corean, cup plate **50.00**
Corean, gravy boat **275.00**
Corean, pitcher, 1-qt **400.00**

Corean, plate, 7¾" 40.00
Corean, plate, 8¾" 50.00
Corean, plate, 9¾" 55.00
Corean, tureen, sauce; octagonal, Podmore Walker 425.00
Cyprus, honey dish, 4¼" 65.00
Cyprus, luncheon plate 45.00
Cyprus, plate, Davenport, 9" 55.00
Cyprus, sauce dish 35.00
Cyprus, toothbrush box 100.00
Cyprus, tureen, vegetable; Davenport, w/lid 175.00
Flora, soap dish, Walker, 3-pc 155.00
Hong, plate, 5" 37.50
Hyson, sugar bowl 155.00
Jeddo, bowl, vegetable; rectangular, loop hdl, Adams 275.00
Jeddo, pitcher, milk; 1-pt 95.00
Jeddo, pitcher, 12" 395.00
Jeddo, plate, Adams & Son, 10¼" 65.00
Jeddo, sugar bowl, w/lid 225.00
Madras, plate, 10" 130.00
Marble, pitcher, 8" 315.00
Nankin, creamer, Davenport 150.00
Neva, teapot, Challinor 250.00
Ning-Po, creamer, Hall 265.00
Palestine, plate, Adams, 9½", EX 50.00
Pelew, bowl, vegetable; Challinor, 11⅜x8¾" 250.00
Pelew, cup plate, Challinor 75.00
Pelew, plate, Challinor, 8" 35.00
Pelew, teapot, pumpkin shape, Challinor 620.00
Peruvian, pitcher, 8½" 385.00
Peruvian, plate, Wedgwood, 7½" 35.00
Peruvian, teapot, Wedgwood 280.00
Rhone Scenery, coffeepot, Podmore 375.00
Rhone Scenery, creamer 175.00
Rhone Scenery, plate, luncheon; TJ&J Mayer, 8⅝" 35.00
Rhone Scenery, platter, 15¾" 125.00
Rose, creamer, Walker 285.00
Savoy, platter, Walker, 15½" 285.00
Scinde, platter, Walker, 15½" 180.00
Shannon, plate, 8¼" 22.50
Singanese, toddy plate, J Wedgood, 5" 25.00
Temple, plate, Podmore Walker, 7¾" 38.00
Temple, tea bowl & saucer, Podmore Walker 75.00
Temple, tea tile, Podmore Walker 80.00
Tonquin, plate, 9¾" 50.00
Tonquin, platter, 10¾" 100.00
Tonquin, sauce bowl 40.00
Tonquin, sugar bowl, Heath, w/lid 170.00
Udina, cup & saucer, Clementson 65.00
Udina, teapot, Clementson 400.00
Vincennes, bowl, vegetable; Alcock, 7½x9¾" 220.00
Vincennes, platter, 15½" 175.00
Vincennes, sugar bowl, Alcock 250.00
Washington Vase, bowl, vegetable; 8" 100.00
Washington Vase, cup & saucer 65.00
Washington Vase, platter, 16x12" 190.00
Washington Vase, sugar bowl, Podmore Walker, w/lid, 9½" 275.00
Washington Vase, teapot 325.00
Washington Vase, waste bowl 195.00
Wreath, cup & saucer, handleless 60.00

Muller Freres

Henri Muller established a factory in 1900 at Croismare, France.

He produced fine cameo art glass decorated with florals, birds, and insects in the Art Nouveau style. The work was accomplished by acid engraving and hand finishing. Usual marks were 'Muller,' 'Muller Croismare,' or 'Croismare, Nancy.' In 1910 Henri and his brother Deseri formed a glassworks at Luneville. The cameo art glass made there was nearly all produced by acid cuttings of up to four layers with motifs similar to those favored at Croismare. A good range of colors was used, and some later pieces were gold flecked. Handles and decorative devices were sometimes applied by hand. In addition to the cameo glass, they also produced an acid-finished glass of bold mottled colors in the Deco style. Examples were signed 'Muller Freres' or 'Luneville.' Our advisor for this category is Don Williams; he is listed in the Directory under Missouri.

Vase, mountain landscape, salmon and brown on frosted yellow, 13", $3,500.00.

Cameo

Chandelier, thistles, wine on frost, 15", leafy metal mts 5,500.00
Lamp, desk; floral dome shade on branch-cast iron base, 14" ..2,000.00
Lamp, dome shade/slim std: birds/lake, wine on cream, 21x8" .13,500.00
Lamp, pastoral scene, dome on claw-ftd base, sgn, 12" 6,500.00
Plaque, lake w/man in boat, cobalt w/rainbow sky, 6½x12½" ..1,750.00
Vase, anemones, wine on pk/yel & amber streaky, bun ft, 11" ...1,500.00
Vase, birch trees, wht/gr on pk mottle, hdls, flattened, 14" 5,500.00
Vase, dahlias, purple on sky bl, Croismare, 14" 3,000.00
Vase, dk/mc winter trees on yel/purple mottle, 16½" 4,600.00
Vase, house/trees/mtns, bl on bl/pk/amber streaky, 12" 2,500.00
Vase, lake scene/2 figures, gr/orange/brn, sqd, 6½" 1,200.00
Vase, lg trees/lake/mtns, peach/brn on ivory, spherical 10" 2,900.00
Vase, lg trees/mtns/lake, salmon/brn on yel, ovoid, 13" 3,000.00
Vase, windmills/cottages, rust/brn on yel, sqd ovoid, 9" 1,750.00
Vase, woodland, dk red on yel, baluster w/disk ft, 17" 2,500.00
Vase, woodland, dk red on yel, baluster w/flared rim, 11½" 2,000.00
Vase, woods/lake, red on yel mottle, ovoid, 8" 1,500.00

Miscellaneous

Box, etched/HP currants, red on rust/purple mottle, 7" dia 1,600.00
Chandelier, mottled 14" dome shade+3 bell shades, metal mt ...1,000.00
Chandelier, orange/bl/red mottle, shallow bowl form, 16" 825.00
Chandelier, pine cones/birds emb on frost, globular, 10" 1,000.00
Lamp, gr/purple/wht dome shade, Nouveau base w/leaves, 15" ...550.00
Vase, berries, etched/HP on yel opal, baluster, 8½" 985.00
Vase, etched water fountains/birds on topaz, baluster, 15" 2,500.00
Vase, orange mottle w/bl & wht streaks, stepped neck, 7½x7" ...135.00

Muncie

Muncie Pottery, established in Muncie, Indiana, by Charles O. Grafton, was produced from 1922 until about 1935. It is made of a heavier clay than most of its contemporaries; the styles are sturdy and simple. Early glazes were bright and colorful. In fact, Muncie was advertised as the 'rainbow pottery.' Later most of the ware was finished in a matt glaze. The more collectible examples are those modeled after Consolidated Glass vases — sculptured with lovebirds, grasshoppers, and goldfish. Their line of Art Deco-style vases bear a remarkable resemblance to the Consolidated Glass company's Ruba Rombic line. Vases, candlesticks, bookends, ashtrays, bowls, lamp bases, and luncheon sets were made. A line of garden pottery was manufactured for a short time. Items were frequently impressed with MUNCIE in block letters. Letters such as A, K, E, or D and the numbers 1, 2, 3, 4, or 5 often found scratched into the base are finishers' marks.

Bookends, matt gr/rose, emb owls, pr 175.00
Canoe w/insert, matt bl/rose, 11½" 225.00
Lamp, matt gr/rose, 6" base 55.00
Pitcher, juice; orange peel, w/6 tumblers 235.00
Teapot w/music box, gloss gr, 6½" 165.00
Vase, pillow form, matt gr/rust, 9" 110.00
Vase, pillow form, matt rose/bl, 6" 75.00
Vase, pillow form w/hdls, gloss blk, 6" 85.00
Vase, Ruba Rombic star, gloss yel, 4" 155.00
Vase, ruffled top, gr/lav, 7" 55.00
Vase, ruffled top w/hdls, matt gr/rose, 6" 65.00

Musical Instruments

The field of automatic musical instruments covers many different categories ranging from watches and tiny seals concealing fine early musical movements to huge organs and orchestrions which weigh many hundreds of pounds and are equivalent to small orchestras. Music boxes, first made in the early 19th-century by Swiss watchmakers, were produced in both disk and cylinder models. The latter type employs a pinned cylinder with tiny pins that lift the teeth in the comb of the music box (producing a sound much like many individual tuning forks), and music results. The value of a cylinder music box depends on the length and diameter of the cylinder, the date of its manufacture, the number of tunes it plays (four or six is *usually* better than ten or twelve), and its manufacturer. Nicole Freres, Henri Capt, LeCoultre, and Bremond are among the most highly regarded, and the larger boxes made by Mermod Freres are also popular. Examples with multiple cylinders, extra instruments (such as bells or an organ section), and those in particularly ornate cabinets or with matching tables bring significantly higher prices. While smaller cylinder boxes are still being made, the larger ones (over 10" cylinders) typically date from before 1900. Disk music boxes were introduced about 1890 but were replaced by the phonograph only twenty-five years later. However, during that time, hundreds of thousands were made. Their great advantage was in playing inexpensive interchangeable disks, a factor that remains an attraction for today's collector as well. Among the most popular disk boxes are those made by Regina (USA), Polyphon, Mira, Stella, and Symphonion. Relative values are determined by the size of the disks they play, whether they have single or double combs, if they are upright or table models, and how ornate their cases are. Especially valuable are those that play multiple disks at the same time or are incorporated into tall case clocks.

Player pianos were made in a wide variety of styles. Early varieties consisted of a mechanism which pushed up to a piano and played on the keyboard by means of felt-tipped fingers. These use sixty-five note rolls. Later models have the playing mechanism built in, and most use eighty-eight note rolls. Upright pump player pianos have little value in unrestored condition because the cost of restoration is so high. 'Reproducing' pianos, especially the 'grand' format, can be quite valuable, depending on the make, the size, the condition, and the ornateness of the case. 'Reproducing' pianos have very sophisticated mechanisms and are much more realistic in the reproduction of piano music. They were made in relatively limited quantities. Better manufacturers include Steinway and Mason & Hamlin. Popular roll mechanism makers include Ampico, Duo-Art and Welte. The market for all types of player pianos has been weak for several years.

Coin-operated pianos (Orchestrions) were used commercially and typically incorporate extra instruments in addition to the piano action. These can be very large and complex, incorporating drums, cymbals, xylophones, bells, and hundreds of pipes. Both American and European coin pianos are very popular, especially the larger and more complex models made by Wurlitzer, Seeburg, Cremona, Weber, Welte, Hupfeld and many others. These companies also made automatically playing violins (Mills Violin Virtuoso, Hupfeld), banjos (Encore) and harps (Whitlock); these are quite valuable.

Mechanical organs range all the way from parlor pump organs and roll-operated reed organs, to band organs fround on carousels and giant fairground and dance hall organs. Pump organs made by Estey, Willcox and others are often very ornate but also very common and bulky; as a result, the market is very limited. The more sophisticated roll-playing reed organs are collectible but still find a limited market due to the cost of restoration. They are very undervalued and have been for a long time. Carousel-type band organs, especially those made by well-known manufacturers such as Wurlitzer and Artizan, continue to sell well. The highest values are reserved for the larger Welte, Gavioli, Bruder, and other organs used in fairgrounds, dance halls, and private residences that incorporate hundreds of pipes. With a harder-to-find larger instrument, a good supply of rolls contributes much to its value, since in many cases rolls cannot be found.

Unless noted, prices given are for instruments in fine condition, playing properly, with cabinets or cases in well-preserved or refinished condition. In all instances, unrestored instruments sell for much less, as do those with broken or missing parts, damaged cases, and the like. On the other hand, particularly superb examples in especially ornate case designs and those that have been particularly well kept will often command more. Our advisor for mechanical instruments is Martin Roenigk; he is listed in the Directory under Connecticut. Fred Oster advises us on non-mechanical instruments; he is listed under Pennsylvania.

Key:
c — cylinder   d — disk

Mechanical

Box, Bremond, Mandoline, 15" c, 6-tune 2,200.00
Box, Criterion, 12½" d, walnut case, +10 d in box 1,700.00
Box, Euphonia, 15" d, NM 3,600.00
Box, Jacot, 8-tune, 6 bells w/bee strikers, 12" c, EX 2,400.00
Box, Mermond, 6 18" cylinders, 6-tune, table model 9,500.00
Box, Mira, 18½" d, dbl comb, cvd, console 8,500.00
Box, Mira, 18½" d, dbl comb, table model 6,000.00
Box, Nicole, keywind, 12" c, 6-tune 1,800.00
Box, Nicole, keywind, 17x4" c, 4-tune 11,000.00
Box, Polyphon, 15½" d, dbl comb 3,200.00
Box, Polyphon, 19⅝" d, dbl comb, upright, rstr 5,600.00
Box, Regina, automatic changer, 15½" d, dbl comb 15,000.00
Box, Regina, automatic changer, 27" d, dbl comb 16,000.00
Box, Regina, tall clock, 15" d movement, dbl comb 12,000.00

Box, Regina, 15½" d, mahog, on stand, EX orig 3,960.00
Box, Regina, 15½" d, oak case, coin-op, table model, EX 3,200.00
Box, Regina, 15½" d, single comb 2,200.00
Box, Regina #50, 15½" d, table top, EX 4,000.00
Box, Reginaphone, 20¾" d, NP horn, matching base 8,000.00
Box, Stella, 17½" d, cvd front, drw, EX 4,750.00
Box, Swiss, grand piano form, EX 110.00
Box, Symphonion, dbl comb, w/grandfather clock, EX 9,500.00
Box, Symphonion, 7½" d 500.00
Box, Symphonion Eroica, 3-d player 26,000.00
Box, Thorens, 4½" d, +4 d 160.00
Box, 17" c, 12-tune, 5 bells w/bee strikers, rosewood box, EX .2,800.00
Nickelodeon, Cremona G, pipes, drum 36,000.00
Nickelodeon, Encore Banjo, automatic 32,000.00
Nickelodeon, Hupfeld Phonolist, 3 violins 18,500.00
Nickelodeon, Link, pictorial glass doors, 1900s, 77" L, EX 8,500.00
Nickelodeon, Mills Violano Virtuoso 15,000.00
Nickelodeon, Nat'l Horse Race, rare, EX orig 4,500.00
Nickelodeon, Seeburg B, leaded glass, EX 3,300.00
Nickelodeon, Seeburgh H, cvd columns, pipes 80,000.00
Nickelodeon, Weber Unica, pipes 14,000.00
Nickelodeon, Wurlitzer, leaded glass doors, 83" L, EX 8,000.00
Nickelodeon, Wurlitzer, piano only 2,400.00
Nickelodeon, Wurlitzer, 60 pipes, drums 16,000.00
Nickelodeon, Wurlitzer C, Grecian case, old rstr 23,500.00
Orchestrion, Coinola X, older rstr 12,000.00
Organ, Aeolian, Duo-Art, ornate, lg 2,800.00

Wurlitzer band organ, style #153, $40,000.00.

Organ, band; Wurlitzer #103, ca 1925, drums & cymbal added .12,000.00
Organ, band; Wurlitzer #125, all orig, rstr 20,000.00
Organ, band; Wurlitzer Military late model #146A, VG 22,000.00
Organ, fairground; Bruder, 52-key 42,000.00
Organ, fairground; Gavioli, 65-key 45,000.00
Organ, monkey; Bacigalupo, 42-key, 110 pipes 6,800.00
Organ, monkey; Harmonipan, EX orig 4,500.00
Organ, pump; Estey 350.00
Organ, street; Carl Frei, 78-key 32,000.00
Organ, street; Gasparini, Dutch, 52-key, EX orig 14,000.00
Organette, Artiston, 13" d 400.00
Organette, Celestina, roll operated 650.00
Organette, Concert Roller Organ, 6½" combs 600.00
Organette, Herophon, cb d 800.00
Organette, Rollmonica, mouth organ 80.00
Organette, Tanzbar, accordion, 4½" roll 900.00
Piano, baby grand; Franklin Ampico, EX orig 2,000.00
Piano, grand; Marshall-Wendall Ampico B, rstr 8,500.00
Piano, grand; Mason & Hamlin Model B Ampico, rstr, 84" ..17,500.00

Piano, grand; Steinway XR, Duo-Art, rstr, 74" 16,000.00
Piano, Louis Caspli/Gaston Fritch, bbl style, 10-tune, EX 700.00
Piano, Peerless, 44-note, oak cabinet w/fretwork, G 5,000.00
Piano, upright, Gulbransen, walnut, rstr 2,000.00
Symphonion, 14½" d, walnut case, EX orig, +7 d 1,525.00

Non-Mechanical

Alto Horn, French, NP, 3 piston valves, ca 1900, EX 70.00
Banjo, English, 7-string, Gothic-style neck, mid-1800s 450.00
Banjo, SS Stewart Universal Favorite, 5-string, 1890s, EX 350.00
Banjo, tenor, w/case 85.00
Bass viol, Wm Green, Medway MA, 1806 ....2,500.00
Bugle, Wurlitzer, military type, dvtl, silver mouthpc, 9" 100.00
Clarinet, Goldentone, EX 48.00
Concertina, M Hohner, squeeze box, old, EX 95.00
Concertina, Weidrich's Royal, old, EX 40.00
Dulcimer, handmade, walnut case, ca 1900, 48x15½x16½" 195.00
Fife, Am, stamped C, cocuswood, brass ferrules, 12", EX 55.00
Fife, Crosby, rosewood, nickel ferrules, 12", EX 60.00
Flugelhorn, PE Schmidt, brass/German silver, 1853-72, EX 750.00
Flute, Am, stained boxwood, bone mts, brass key, 1835, 17", EX .100.00
Flute, Firth Hall & Pond, boxwood, ca 1835, 21", EX 550.00
Flute, Geo Cloos, NY, grenadilla, nickel mts, ca 1900, 24" 250.00
French horn, AK Huttl, brass/German silver, 3 rotary valves 350.00
Guitar, CF Martin Model 4-21, ca 1880, EX in wood case 1,000.00
Guitar, Gibson J-45, flat top, script logo, 1947, VG, +case 1,400.00
Guitar, Martin D-28, flat top, 1952, EX, +G orig hard case 4,600.00
Guitar, Martin Model 0-18K, EX 1,200.00
Guitar, Martin 00-18, flat top, 1949, NM, +orig hard case 1,850.00
Guitar, steel; Harmony, lap type, pearloid body, EX, +case 140.00
Harmonica, Bandmaster Chromatic, 3 full octaves 35.00
Harmonica, Bluebird, Bohm System, Germany 45.00
Harmonica, Echo Harp, 6¾", EX in box 95.00
Harmonica, Hohner Marine Band, plastic, 1950s, 24½x6½", G ...50.00
Harmonica, Hohner Tremola Concert harp, 4 keys, 192 reeds, EX .145.00
Harmonica, M Hohner Germany Auto-Valve-Harp, 4½", MIB ...85.00
Harp, Erard, Paris, bird's-eye maple & giltwood, 1850s, EX 3,000.00
Piano, baby grand; Steinway & Sons, all orig, 1926, 70" 7,150.00
Piano, grand; Steinway, Empire-style, lyre pedal fr, 82", NM ..7,425.00
Piano, spinet; Wm Knabe & Co, mahog, 40½x59½", EX orig 100.00
Piano forte, Astor, mahog/ormolu Regency, line inlay, 58" L ..1,000.00
Piccolo, G Cloos NY, grenadilla, ivory head, 10", EX, +case 125.00
Piccolo, H Bettoney Boston, silver, closed G#, 1920s, 10" 175.00
Ukelele, Weymann, soprano, mahog, rprs 90.00
Violin, Stradivarius copy, ¾-size, w/bow, M 225.00
Zither, dtd 1893, EX 175.00
Zither, w/key, dtd 1893, VG 165.00

Mustache Cups

Mustache cups were popular items during the late Victorian period, designed specifically for the man with the mustache! They were made in silverplate as well as china and ironstone. Decorations ranged from simple transfers to elaborately applied and gilded florals. To properly position the 'mustache bar,' special cups were designed for the 'lefties.' These are the rare ones!

Floral, gold X-hatching & hdl, Limoges, ca 1908 ....95.00
Floral/bird transfer, ribbed, gold striping, Germany 35.00
Knights & angels w/gold, Royal Bavaria, wt/saucer 60.00

Lady w/flowers transfer, lg **40.00**
Oriental motif, HP, 2¾"x3", +saucer **50.00**
Pk lustre w/floral & Forget-Me-Not, rose-shape cup, Germany **65.00**
Roses, red on gr, Germany **55.00**
Rust & gr pattern, Paragon China, ca 1904 ....**70.00**
SP, cut/beaded decor, Eureka Silver, 1901, +saucer **115.00**
SP, floral eng, Barbour, EX **75.00**

Nailsea

Nailsea is a term referring to clear or colored glass decorated in contrasting spatters, swirls, or loops. These are usually white but may also be pink, red or blue. It was first produced in Nailsea, England, during the late 1700s but was made in other parts of Britain and Scotland as well. During the mid-1800s a similar type of glass was produced in this country. Originally used for decorative novelties only, by that time tumblers and other practical items were being made from Nailsea-type glass. See also Lamps; Witch Balls.

Bottle, gemel; clear w/rigaree & wht looping, bl rim, 8" **150.00**
Finger bowl, crimped, 5½", +matching underplate **180.00**
Flask, freeblown, red & bl loopings on milk glass, 6⅜" **300.00**
Flask, red loopings on wht glossy opaque, flattened, 7" **165.00**
Flask, red-amber w/irregular wht spirals, European, 4½" **225.00**
Lamp, pk & wht loopings, clear font w/berry pontil, 11½" **2,475.00**
Pipe, wht w/red loopings, 13½" **285.00**
Sweetmeat, pk/yel/opal swags, acid finish, silver mts, 4" **275.00**
Vase, bl opaque loopings on clear, scroll ft, rigaree, 5¾" **95.00**

Nakara

Nakara was a line of decorated opaque milk glass produced by the C.F. Monroe Company of Meriden, Connecticut, for a few years after the turn of the century. It differs from their Wave Crest line in several ways. The shapes were simpler; pastel colors were deeper and covered more of the surface; more beading was present; flowers were larger; and large transfer prints of figures, Victorian ladies, cherubs, etc., were used. Ormolu and brass collars and mounts complemented these opulent pieces. Most items were signed; however, this is not important since the ware was never reproduced. Our advisors for this category are Dolli and Wilfred R. Cohen; their address is listed in the Directory under California.

**Cigar humidor, transfer of lady, 7¾",
$1,000.00.**

Bonbon, floral, pk on bl, open type w/hdl **395.00**
Box, Bishop's Hat w/floral & beading, 4" dia **495.00**
Box, blown-out pansy on lid, unemb bottom, 3¾" dia **595.00**
Box, Collars & Cuffs; lilies on pnt 'burmese' **1,750.00**
Box, Crown Mold, roses on lid/base, mirror w/in, 5½x6" **825.00**
Box, Crown Mold, roses on pastel gr, sgn, 5x8" **1,350.00**
Box, Crown Mold, 6 roses on top, mirror inside, 5½x6" **1,100.00**
Box, floral, yel & pk on peach, 8-sided, 4½x6½", NM **985.00**

Box, flower bouquet on lid, wht on rose, 2x4½" dia **400.00**
Box, Kate Greenaway figures/beading, unemb form, 6" dia **800.00**
Box, 2 pk lilies/spiked leaves on turq, hinged, 4½" dia **475.00**
Jar, lady's portrait/dotted enamel on caramel, 4½" dia **425.00**
Tray, pin; scrolls & wht dots on pk, orig lining, 2¼x4¾" **175.00**
Vase, daisies in pk fr, lav/tan Nouveau decor, cylindrical, 11" **875.00**

Napkin Rings

Napkin rings became popular during the late 1800s. They were made from various materials. Among the most popular and collectible today are the large group of varied silverplated figurals made by American manufacturers. Recently the larger figurals in excellent condition have appreciated considerably. Only those with a blackened finish, corrosion, or broken and/or missing parts have maintained their earlier price levels. When no condition is indicated, the items listed below are assumed to be all original and in very good to excellent condition.

A timely warning: inexperienced buyers should be aware of excellent reproductions on the market, especially the wheeled pieces. However, these do not have the fine detail and patina of the originals and tend to have a more consistent, soft pewter-like finish. These are appearing at the large, quality shows at top prices, being shown along with authentic antique merchandise. Beware!

Key:
gw — gold washed   SH&M — Simpson, Hall, &
R&B — Reed & Barton   Miller

Baby in chair beside ring, rectangular base, Middletown #98 ......**365.00**
Baseball player with mitt ready to catch **250.00**
Belt-like ring w/buckle-form base, R&B #1627 ....**65.00**
Bird looks at eggs in nest, rnd base, Webster #178 ....**170.00**
Bird perched on leaves beside ring, logs base, Meriden #248 ....**90.00**
Birds on rnd base, bud vase in center of ring, Wilcox #1899 ....**85.00**
Boy by fence, hands out, ball-ftd oval base, Tufts #1593 ....**300.00**
Boy kicks on ea side of filigree ring, Meriden #332 ....**195.00**

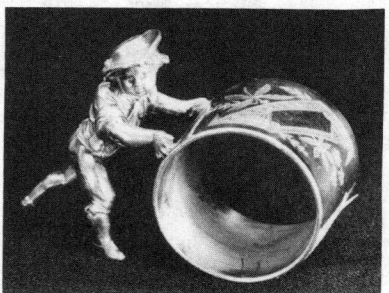

**Boy pushing ring, Meriden #161,
$265.00.**

Boy reclines on oval base & holds up ring, Wilcox #01540 ....**325.00**
Butterfly on hdl of cart holding ring, Meriden #211 ....**150.00**
Cat atop ring arches bk at dog, rnd base, Rogers #296 ....**275.00**
Cat w/glass eyes guards mouse, rnd base, Rogers #4377 ....**250.00**
Cherries & stems on leafy base, Acme **125.00**
Cherub kneels & holds ring, rectangular base, Tufts #1676 ....**250.00**
Cherub pushes ring up rock-like base, Elton #208 ....**120.00**
Cherub w/cymbals sits beside triangular ring, Meriden #246 ......**125.00**
Cherub w/oar rides astride dolphin, rstr, Meriden #157 ....**350.00**
Cherub w/ring on bk, scrolled base, ftd, Barbour #10 ....**265.00**
Cherubs hold ring ea side, rectangular base, Meriden #200 ....**135.00**

Cherubs sit ea side of ring, Meriden #147 ....150.00
Cockatoo ea side of ring, ball-ftd base, Pairpoint #13 ....235.00
Cockatoo rests on curved log base 75.00
Cow crouches by ring on elevated oval base, Rockford #173 ......185.00
Cupid blowning horn, floral rectangular base, SH&M #051 ....225.00
Cupid on ring pulled by bird, octagonal base, Rockford #151 .....250.00
Dachshund carries ornate ring on bk, rstr 295.00
Dog chases squirrel on top of ring, Meriden #0225 ....150.00
Dog on raised oval base seeks cat on ring, Meriden #275 ....235.00
Dog sits on sq ftd base chained to doghouse ring, SH&M #207 ..300.00
Dolphin w/ring on bk, Aurora #32, EX 265.00
Egyptian figure sits on base w/ring on wings, Meriden #202 ....70.00
Fan forms base for 2 butterflies holding ring 95.00
Fawn looks over fence that comes from ring, Meriden #0283 .....150.00
Fireman's helmet beside ring, rocky base, Pairpoint #81 ....165.00
Fox comes from side of ring, Meriden #217 ....50.00
Fox stalks on rnd base, fretwork, Dunham 195.00
Frog stands on lg jack-in-the-pulpit leaf, holds ring 295.00
Greenaway baby w/bonnet on chair, Middletown #98 ....300.00
Greenaway boy kneels & looks at nest of eggs, Meriden #269 ....300.00
Greenaway boy w/begging dog, Meriden #199, rstr 350.00
Greenaway girl holds ring, rectangular base, Toronto #1154 ......235.00
Greenaway girl w/dog, ball ftd base, Wm Rogers #244 ....300.00
Greenaway girl w/long coat & muffs, ring center, Meriden #380 ..500.00
Horse w/ring for stomach, R&B #1630 ....175.00
Hummingbird on flower, rnd base, Derby #365 ....100.00
Lady w/parasol, boy rolling ring, Tufts #1597 ....465.00
Leaves & logs ea side of bbl ring, R&B #625, EX 95.00
Lily pads w/ring resting on center, Meriden #166 ....75.00
Log-like ring rests w/logs ea side, R&B #1396 ....75.00
Monkey in man's clothes stands on rectangular base 250.00
Owl perched on leaves attached to ring, Middletown #112 ....65.00
Parrot w/glass eyes on loop hdl by ring, #4338 ....195.00
Peacock w/long plum on ring, ornate base, R&B #1327 ....115.00
Rabbit w/basket of eggs & milk bottle, Victor #169 ....235.00
Rabbits on sq grassy base, eng shells on ring, Pairpoint 450.00
Rip Van Winkle w/bbl on shoulder, rocky base, SH&M 750.00
Robin, chain looped around neck, fancy open base 225.00
Rooster crows over ring, no base, Pairpoint #58 ....75.00
Rooster w/3 leaves ea side of supported ring, unmk 95.00
Sailor boy stands by ring, lg anchor, SH&M #06 ....350.00
Scrollwork ea side of ring, oval base, Derby #344 ....65.00
Sheep beside ring on octagonal base, Aurora 35 ....200.00
Squirrel w/nut on lg ring, leafy base, Toronto #1102 ....125.00
Swan before ring on oval base, R Smith #312 ....225.00
Turkish dancer ea side of ring, Strictland #107 ....85.00
Turtle supports ring, circular base, Meriden #216 ....150.00
Wheelbarrow holds ornate ring, Pairpoint 215.00
Wolf baying at moon, fancy free-form Barbour base w/ball ft 250.00

Nash

A. Douglas Nash founded the Corona Art Glass Company in Long Island, New York. He produced tableware, vases, flasks, etc., using delicate artistic shapes and forms. After 1933 he worked for the Libbey Glass Company.

Bowl, bl w/silver mottling, red pull-ups, 4½x4½" 145.00
Vase, Chintz, dk bl w/silver irid, 8¾" 575.00
Vase, Chintz, peacock bl w/yel stripes, clear ft, #16S, 9½" 300.00
Vase, Chintz, red w/silver stripes, dbl ped ft, no mk, 16" 990.00
Vase, cobalt w/bl-gold swirled net motif, bulbous, 3¾" 575.00
Vase, dk amber, Cypriot type, GD-74, 9" 500.00

Vase, gold irid, ribbed body, bl ft, 13" 525.00
Vase, tomato red w/ruby ft, sgn, #RD84X, 9" 675.00

Natzler, Gertrude and Otto

The Natzler's came to the United States from Vienna in the late 1930s. They settled in Los Angeles where they continued their work in ceramics, for which they were already internationally recognized. Gertrude created the forms; Otto formulated a variety of interesting glazes, among them volcanic, crystalline, and lustre. Our advisor for this category is Abby Malowanczyk; she is listed in the Directory under Texas.

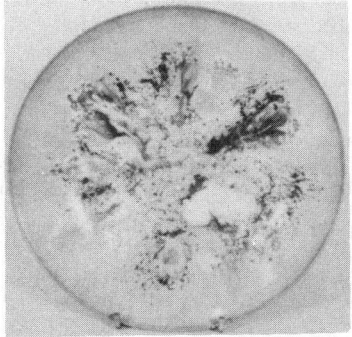

Bowl, multicolor floral and pebble interior, shallow, footed, 9½", $800.00.

Bowl, bl w/med to dk bl variations, ftd/flaring, 3½x8" 900.00
Bowl, indigo bl w/wht froth, curving sides, 2½x6" 700.00
Bowl, variegated mustard flambe w/rust rim & ft, 3x4" 600.00
Vase, yel/brn gloss, ftd, paper label/#d, 3½x5" 375.00

New England Glass Works

Founded in 1818 by Deming Jarves in Boston, Massachussetts, the New England Glass Company produced cut, blown three-mold, free-blown, and pressed glass of the highest quality. They were recognized for their fine decorative accomplishments, using etching, gilding, and engraving to emphasize their wares. For more than fifty years, they produced prize-winning pressed glass dinnerware sets. Because they refused to compromise the quality of their product by using the cheaper lime-based glass that flooded the market in the 1860s, the company fell into financial trouble and by 1877 was forced to close. However, William Libbey, who had been the sales manager there since 1870, leased the premises and resumed operations with his father, Edward Drummond Libbey, as full partner. In 1892 the firm became known as The Libbey Glass Company. See also Amberina; Libbey.

Bottle, bar; Flute, electric bl, lg doughnut lip, 10¾" 600.00
Bottle, bubbly gr, crudely appl lip, pontil scar, 1800s, 9⅝" 145.00
Bowl, Bigler, deep purple, polished pontil, 3x4¼" 550.00
Chestnut flask, blown, yel-olive, 1780-1830, 5¾" 120.00
Compote, Bellflower, fine rib, wafer attachment, 8¾", EX 125.00
Compote, Hairpin, loop pattern base, wafer attachment, 5¾" 140.00
Decanter, blown, yel-olive, flared mouth, 1800-40, 7⅝" 240.00
Decanter, ship's; cobalt bl, bulbous base, 8¼x6½", pr 250.00
Lamp, blown font on rolled/knopped stem, saucer base, 5½" 825.00
Salt cellar, cobalt, paneled & ftd 8-sided form, 3½" 150.00
Tumbler, dk gr tapering down to 6-sided stem & ft, 4¾" 200.00
Tumbler, lt gr paneled body on 6-sided ft, 5" 140.00
Vase, blown, cobalt, rolled-out lip, 1850s, 8", EX 575.00
Vase, canary, 3 printie block pattern, fluted rim, 9" 165.00

Vase, lav ruffled bowl w/rigaree, clear wafer, 16½" 1,200.00
Vase, sapphire bl, crimped tulip form, 9¼" 1,100.00
Vase, Three Printie Block, amethyst, 6-sided base, 9" 450.00
Vase, Three Printie Block, sapphire bl, 6-sided base, 10" 475.00
Wine, Rhine, apricot to clear, rayed base, 1890s 225.00

New Hall

The New Hall Company was established in the early 1780s in the Shelton district of England. In the early years, they produced hardpaste dinnerware typically decorated with simple floral sprays, often assigning a number rather than a name to their patterns. By 1812 a bone china body was favored and styles revised to suit the fashion. Decorations became more elaborate. Much of the ware was unmarked and is often attributed to Worcester. Occasionally a piece was marked 'New Hall' within a double circle. Production ceased by 1835.

Coffee can, Oriental 'Window' pattern, +5" dia saucer 150.00
Creamer, band w/pk flowers, yel/purple pansies, gilt, 6" 65.00
Cup & saucer, mc floral, yel rim, mk, set of 4 ....185.00
Cup & saucer, pk floral w/red buds & gr leaves, red rim 35.00

New Martinsville

The New Martinsville Glass Company took its name from the town in West Virginia where it began operations in 1901. In the beginning years, pressed tablewares were made in crystal as well as colored and opalescent glass. Considered an innovator, the company was known for their imaginative applications of the medium in creating lamps made entirely of glass, vanity sets, figural decanters, and models of animals and birds. In 1944 the company was purchased by Viking Glass, who continued to use many of the old molds, the animals molds included. They marked their wares 'Viking' or 'Rainbow Art.' Viking recently ceased operations and has been purchased by Kenneth Dalzell, President of the Fostoria Company. They, too, are making the bird and animal models. Although at first they were not marked, future productions are to be marked with an acid stamp. Dalzell/Viking animals are in the $50.00 to $60.00 range. Values for cobalt and red items are two to three times higher than for the same item in clear. See also Depression Glass; Glass Animals.

Mayonnaise, Radiance, 3-piece set, $35.00.

Banana boat, Janice, red, low ft, 12" 125.00
Basket, Janice, crystal w/red hdl, 4-ftd, 6½" 50.00
Bonbon, Janice, med bl, hdl, 7" 45.00
Bowl, nut; Florentine etch, center hdl, #4429, 11" 18.00
Candlestick, Prelude, single, 5" 24.00
Candlesticks, dbl; Florentine etch, #4429, pr 26.00

Cocktail, ruby w/platinum bands, #125 ....6.50
Compote, Princess, stemmed 20.00
Cordial, Prelude 20.00
Cordial, Radiance, amber, 1-oz 26.00
Creamer, Georgian, gr, 4" 15.00
Creamer, Radiance, ice bl 30.00
Cup, Janice, lt bl 15.00
Cup & saucer, Georgian, gr 12.50
Decanter, Mt Vernon, 11-oz, +8 ftd 1-oz cordials 195.00
Pitcher, Radiance, amber, 64-oz 125.00
Plate, Janice, lt bl, 8⅞" 20.00
Plate, luncheon; Radiance, amber, 8" 10.00
Plate, luncheon; Radiance; ice bl, 8" 16.00
Relish, Radiance, amber, 2-part, 7" 13.00
Server, Princess, center hdl 22.00
Shakers, Palmette Band, bl opaque, 2½", pr 60.00
Shakers, Radiance, red, pr 80.00
Shakers, Twenty Rib, ruby, ftd pillar shape, 3⅜", pr 110.00
Shot glass, red, 2¾" 16.00
Sugar bowl, Georgian, gr, w/lid, 3" 40.00
Tumbler, Hostmaster, ruby, 4¼" 11.00
Tumbler, Janice, ruby, ftd 30.00
Tumbler, Moondrops, red or cobalt, 4⅜" 35.00
Tumbler, Oscar, amber w/platinum trim 5.50
Tumbler, Radiance, amber, 9-oz 17.50
Vase/bookend, Nautilus, pr 60.00
Wine, Hostmaster, ruby, 4x2½" 11.00

Newcomb

The Newcomb College of New Orleans, Louisiana, established a pottery in 1895 to provide the students with first-hand experience in the fields of art and ceramics. Using locally dug clays — red and buff in the early years, white-burning by the turn of the century — potters were employed to throw the ware which the ladies of the college decorated. Until about 1910 a glossy glaze was used on ware decorated by slip painting or incising. After that a matt glaze was favored. Soft blues and greens were used almost exclusively, and decorative themes were chosen to reflect the beauty of the South. 1930 marked the end of the matt-glaze period and the art-pottery era.

Various marks used by the pottery include an 'N' within a 'C,' sometimes with 'HB' added to indicate a 'hand-built' piece. The potter often incised his initials into the ware, and the artists were encouraged to sign their work. Among the most well-known artists were Sadie Irvine, Henrietta Bailey, and Fannie Simpson.

Newcomb pottery is evaluated to a large extent by two factors: design and condition. In the following listings, items are assumed matt unless noted otherwise. Our advisor for this category is Dave Rago; he is listed in the Directory under New Jersey.

Bowl, berries, pk/gr on bl below gr band, Bailey/JM, 2½x8" 800.00
Bowl, dogwood at shoulder, S Irvine, 1919, EX cvg/color, 8" 950.00
Bowl, floral, bl matt, sgn F Simpson, 1912, 3½x9½" 700.00
Candle holder, Espanol pattern, S Irvine/#329, 3¾" 650.00
Creamer, stylized pineapple band on gloss, Urquhart, 3½" 850.00
Match holder, mossy oak trees, bl/gr on wht, S Irvine, 2x3" 675.00
Mug, stylized floral band on gloss, D Roman/JM, 4" 1,500.00
Pitcher, bluebells on gloss, SB Levy/JM, 7", NM 2,500.00
Plaque, moss/oak tree, S Irvine, 5½" 1,400.00
Tile, floral, L Nicholson, glossy, 4" sq 550.00
Vase, bl band w/dk pk floral on purple, S Irvine/J Hunt, 6x6" .1,500.00
Vase, blueberries on ivory band over dk gr-bl, Horner, 3¼" 750.00
Vase, clusters of wht flowers/gr foliage on bl, Simpson, 6" 1,800.00

Vase, trees, green and blue on white with light blue tree line beyond, Marie Hoe LeBlanc, CL-96, 9", $5,000.00.

Vase, cvd flower buds/lines at shoulder, Robinson, 5x5¾" **4,250.00**
Vase, encircling trees, bl/gr gloss, LeBlanc/JM, 9x4¾", NM **5,000.00**
Vase, floral, bl/lav/yel on bl & lav, S Irvine, 1918, 8x4" **1,900.00**
Vase, floral at shoulder, A Bailey, 1924, ovoid, 3¾x2½" **650.00**
Vase, floral at shoulder, glossy, MW Summey, 1909, 4x4½" **1,400.00**
Vase, floral band at wide shoulder, H Bailey/JM, 5" **1,300.00**
Vase, geometric bands relief, S Irvine, #245, 5" **600.00**
Vase, lg freesia, yel/gr on ivory & lt gr gloss, MWB, 6" **650.00**
Vase, lg oaks w/moss, pk sky, EX art, AF Simpson/JH, 4x4" **2,200.00**
Vase, moon/pine trees/shrubs, EX art, S Irvine/Meyer, 7x5½" .**3,750.00**
Vase, moss/trees, cvd/pnt, AF Simpson/JH, ovoid, 6" **1,500.00**
Vase, moss/trees, S Irvine/JM, ovoid, 5¾" **1,200.00**
Vase, pine cones, pk/gr on bl, H Bailey/J Meyer, #d, 8" **3,000.00**
Vase, pines against bl sky, gr shadow trees, AF Simpson, 16" ..**9,000.00**
Vase, repetitive floral on high gloss, EH Elliot, 3¾" **3,800.00**
Vase, repetitive pnt/cvd irises on gloss, H Bailey, 9" **13,000.00**
Vase, sang-de-boeuf lustre, stick neck, mk NC/JM, 5½x3" **650.00**
Vase, sm floral/lg leaves, H Bailey, 1926, 2½x3" **800.00**
Vase, upright leafy bands, gr on dk bl, S Irvine, 6x6" **1,000.00**

Newspapers

In addition to historic content, there are other factors that can add or take away from the value of an old newspaper. These factors are: whether or not the account is a 'first report' (the first time that the news appeared — a 'later-report' is a subsequent reporting); location of articles on the event (those with front-page articles are more highly valued); displayability (size of headlines, presence of photos or graphics to illustrate the event, etc.); whether the paper is from a small or large town; a daily or weekly; and charisma of the paper or event. Prices listed here are for a typical mid-sized town paper with front-page coverage and medium-size headlines.

Papers that do not cover a specific event are called 'atmosphere' newspapers. While these are not as valuable, they offer interesting insight into a particular era through ads for runaway slaves, ships' schedules, jobs wanted, etc. Many have interesting articles on topics such as mermaids, hangings, sea voyages, and a host of other topics.

For a more complete price guide and information on how to determine values as well as how to grade historic newspapers, detect reprints, where to buy and sell originals and much more, the Newspaper Collectors Society of America offers a *Free Mini-Course About Historic Newspapers*. To obtain your copy of the 24-page primer and extensive price guide, send $1.00 and an SASE to NCSA, Box 19134-S, Lansing, MI 48901. From it you will learn, for instance, how to recognize the original April 15, 1865, *New York Herald* version of the report of Lincoln's assassination from among the thousands of reprints which abound today. This booklet could save collectors from making bad investments and prevent dealers from loosing their honest reputation. Our advisor

for this category is Rick Brown; his name, address, and phone number are listed in the Directory under Michigan.

1784-1799, Atmosphere papers **30.00**
1800-1820, Atmosphere papers **8.00**
1821-1859, Atmosphere papers **6.00**
1861, Civil War opens, first Confederate reports **250.00**
1861, Civil War opens, first Union reports **125.00**
1861, Civil War opens, later Confederate reports **150.00**
1861, Civil War opens, later Union reports **40.00**
1861-1865, Atmosphere papers, Confederate **125.00**
1861-1865, Atmosphere papers, Union **8.00**
1861-1865, Major battles of Civil War, Confederate titles **250.00**
1861-1865, Major battles of Civil War, first Union reports **75.00**
1861-1865, Major battles of Civil War, later Union reports **35.00**
1862, Emancipation Proclamation **135.00**
1863, Battle of Gettysburg, first Union reports **125.00**
1863, Battle of Gettysburg, later Union reports **60.00**
1863, Gettysburg address **200.00**
1865, Capture & death of J Wilkes Booth **115.00**
1865, End of Civil War, first Union reports **125.00**
1865, End of Civil War, later Union reports **60.00**
1865, Fall of Richmond **175.00**
1865, Harper's Weekly, Apr 29 edition **350.00**
1865, Leslie's Illustrated Newspaper, Apr 29 edition **400.00**
1865, Lincoln assassination, NY Herald, Apr 15 ....**900.00**
1865, Lincoln assassination, other titles, first reports **200.00**
1865, Lincoln assassination, other titles, funeral reports **85.00**
1866-1900, Atmosphere papers **4.00**
1871, Chicago fire, Chicago paper, first reports **75.00**
1871, Chicago fire, later reports **35.00**
1876, Custer's Last Stand, first reports **200.00**
1876, Custer's Last Stand, later reports **75.00**
1881, Billy the Kid killed **200.00**
1881, Garfield assassinated **75.00**
1881, Gunfight at OK Corral **250.00**
1882, Jesse James killed, first reports **225.00**
1882, Jesse James killed, later reports **75.00**
1892, Lizzie Borden crime & trial **40.00**
1898, Sinking of Maine **40.00**
1898, Spanish American War begins **20.00**
1898, Spanish American War ends **30.00**
1900-1945, Atmosphere papers **3.00**
1901, McKinley assassinated **65.00**
1903, Wright Brother's flight **250.00**
1906, San Francisco earthquake, other titles **30.00**
1906, San Francisco earthquake, San Francisco paper **500.00**
1912, Sinking of Titanic, first reports **350.00**
1912, Sinking of Titanic, later reports **75.00**
1914, WWI begins **25.00**
1915, Lusitania sunk, first reports **125.00**
1917, US declares war **30.00**
1918, Armistice **40.00**
1927, Babe Ruth hits 60th home run **75.00**
1927, Lindbergh in Paris, first reports **75.00**
1927, Lindbergh in Paris, later reports **30.00**
1929, St Valentine's Day Massacre **135.00**
1929, Stock Market crash **100.00**
1931, Jack 'Legs' Diamond killed **28.00**
1932, Lindbergh baby found dead **65.00**
1933, Machine Gun Kelley captured **30.00**
1934, Baby Face Nelson killed **35.00**
1934, Bonnie & Clyde killed **135.00**
1934, Dillinger killed **100.00**

1934, Pretty Boy Floyd killed 30.00
1935, Will Rogers & Wiley Post in plane crash 35.00
1937, Hindenbergh explodes, first reports 65.00
1937, Hindenbergh explodes, later reports 35.00
1939-1945, Major battles in the war 25.00
1941, Pearl Harber attacked, Honolulu Star-Bulletin (+) 850.00
1941, Pearl Harbor attacked, Dec 8 issues, first reports 30.00
1941, Pearl Harbor attacked, other titles w/lg headlines 35.00
1944, D-Day 30.00
1945, FDR dies 20.00
1945, First atomic bomb dropped 30.00
1945, VE-Day or VJ-Day 30.00
1948, Dewey Defeats Truman, Chicago Daily Tribune 900.00
1950, US enters Korean War 20.00
1957, Soviets launch Sputnik 10.00
1958, Alaska joins Union 15.00
1959, Hawaii joins Union 15.00
1962, Death of Marilyn Monroe 30.00
1962, John Glenn orbits Earth 18.00
1963, JFK assassination, Nov 22, Dallas title 75.00
1963, JFK assassination, Nov 22 or 23, other titles 25.00
1968, Bobby Kennedy assassination 15.00
1968, Martin Luther King assassination 22.00
1969, Moon landing 18.00
1974, Nixon resigns 15.00
1977, Death of Elvis, Memphis paper 30.00
1986, Challenger explodes 6.00

Nicodemus

Chester Nicodemus moved from Dayton, Ohio, to Columbus in 1930 and started teaching at the Columbus Art School. During this time he made vases and commissioned sculptures, water fountains, and limestone and wood carvings. In 1941 Chester left the field of teaching to pursue pottery making full time, using local red clay containing a large amount of iron. Known for its durability, he called the ware Ferro-stone. He made teapots and other utility wares, but these goods lost favor, so he started producing animal and bird sculptures, nativity sets, and Christmas ornaments, some bearing Chester's and Florine's names as personalized cards for his customers and friends. Chester died in 1990.

His glaze colors were turquoise or aqua, ivory, green mottle, (pink) pussy willow, and golden yellow. The glaze was applied so that the color of the warm red clay would show through, adding an extra dimension to each piece. Examples are usually marked with his name incised in the clay, but paper labels were also used. Our advisor for this category is James Riebel; he is listed in the Directory under Ohio.

Ashtray, fraternity 25.00
Bookends, camel, pr 400.00
Bookends, dryad (kneeling nude), pr 250.00
Christmas card 100.00
Christmas decoration 40.00
Coffeepot, ind 100.00
Figurine, bull, 7" 200.00
Figurine, cardinal 250.00
Figurine, cat, 3" 85.00
Figurine, collie, 6" 150.00
Figurine, dachshund 150.00
Figurine, Madonna of the Flowers 150.00
Figurine, robin, 4½" 150.00
Figurine, St Francis, w/bowl 300.00
Figurine, St Francis, w/stand, no bowl, 14" 450.00
Nativity set, 9-pc 500.00

Pitcher, bl, 3" 20.00
Pitcher, mustard, sm 35.00
Pottery festival ornament, 1986-87, ea 50.00
Vase, hdls, 4" 125.00
Vase, w/fish & sea horse 400.00
Wall pocket, dbl, corn 350.00
Water fountain, boy w/frog, 21" 3,500.00

Niloak

During the latter part of the 1800s, there were many small utilitarian potteries in Benton, Arkansas. By 1900 only the Hyten Brothers Pottery remained. Charles Hyten, a second generation potter, took control of the family business around 1902. Shortly thereafter he renamed it the Eagle Pottery Company. In 1909 Hyten and former Rookwood potter Arthur Dovey began experimentation on a new swirl pottery. Dovey previously worked for the Ouachita Pottery Company of Hot Springs and produced a swirl pottery there as early as 1906. In March 1910 the Eagle Pottery Company introduced Niloak, kaolin spelled backwards. During 1911 Benton businessmen formed the Niloak Pottery corporation. Niloak, connected to the Arts and Crafts Movement and known as 'mission' ware, had a national representative in New York by 1913. Niloak's production centered on art pottery characterized by accidental, swirling patterns of natural and artificially colored clays. Many companies through the years have produced swirl pottery, yet none achieved the technical and aesthetic qualities of Niloak. Hyten received a patent in 1928 for the swirl technique. Although most examples have an interior glaze, some early Mission Ware pieces have an exterior glaze as well; these are extremely rare. Swirl/Mission Ware production continued steadily until the Depression when hard times and sagging sales caused Hyten to produce more traditional wares. In 1931 Niloak introduced Hywood Art Pottery, a glazed ware (sometimes similar in shape to Weller's Nile) of mostly hand-thrown vases. Soon thereafter, Niloak introduced castware as its primary production and renamed the line Hywood by Niloak. Throughout its existence, the company produced utilitarian items as well as artware. In 1934 Hyten's company found itself facing bankruptcy. Hardy L. Winburn, Jr., along with other Little Rock businessmen, raised the necessary capital and were able to provide the kind of leadership needed to make the business profitable once again. Both lines (Eagle and Hywood) were renamed 'Niloak' in 1937 to capitalize on this well-known name. The pottery continued in production until 1947 when it was converted to the Winburn Tile Company, which exists to this day in Little Rock. Be careful not to confuse the swirl production of the Evans Pottery of Missouri with Niloak. The significant difference is the dark brown matt interior glaze of Evans pottery.

Our co-advisors for this category are Lila and Fred Shrader (see the Directory under California) and David Edwin Gifford (see Arkansas), author of *The Collector's Encyclopedia of Niloak*.

Mission Ware

Ashtray/match holder, rnd, 5" 15.00
Bowl, cuspidor shape, 5" 95.00
Bowl, flat, rnd, 7½" 145.00
Bowl, mixing bowl shape, 4½x8" 245.00
Box, powder; w/lid, 3x4½" 145.00
Candlestick, flared base, 8" 175.00
Candlestick, squat, 2" 110.00
Chamberstick, cupped base, hdl, 4½" 165.00
Compote, ped ft, 5x8½" 295.00
Creamer, 3" 55.00
Decanter, cork-wrapped stopper, 10½" 450.00

Humidor, w/lid, 5x7" 340.00
Jar, cigarette; w/hdls & lid, 4x5" 200.00
Jar, cookies/crackers; w/lid, 6" 400.00
Mug, bbl shape, 5½" 150.00
Paperweight, flattened ball shape, 3½" 150.00
Pitcher, lemonade; 7½" 285.00
Pitcher, 9½" 285.00
Planter, flared lip, 5x6" 175.00
Rose jar, w/insert & lid, 9" 450.00
Tumbler, bbl shape 55.00
Tumbler, 4½" 50.00

Vases, 1st art mark, 8¼", $175.00 each.

Vase, bud; 6½" 100.00
Vase, cone shape, mini, 2¼" 95.00
Vase, cone shape, 9" 195.00
Vase, cylindrical, Pat Pend'g, 7½" 200.00
Vase, fan shape, 8" 145.00
Vase, rose bowl shape, 6½" 165.00
Wall pocket, 8¼" 235.00
Water bottle w/tumbler (tumble-up), 8¾" 350.00

Miscellaneous

Ashtray, bunny w/ears bk, 4" L 15.00
Ashtray, frog form, open mouth, 3½" 24.00
Basket, basketweave ext, 'woven' hdl, 7" 45.00
Bowl, scalloped & fluted, 6x8" 50.00
Bowl, scalloped & pierced, 3½x10" 60.00
Candlestick, flared base, 7½" 45.00
Figurine, bunnies, 5" 25.00
Figurine, camel, resting, 4" 20.00
Figurine, elephant, 2½" 20.00
Figurine, razor-bk hog, 4" 35.00
Flower frog, flying goose, 6½" 25.00
Jug, hand thrown, 7½" 50.00
Jug, 3½" 15.00
Pitcher, ball shape, 8" 35.00
Pitcher, petal shape, 8½" 40.00
Pitcher, w/lid, 6½" 45.00
Planter, camel w/HP highlights 35.00
Planter, circus elephant, 6½" 35.00
Planter, elephant, 4½" 20.00
Planter, goat, 4" 20.00
Planter, pelican w/HP highlights, 5½" 35.00
Planter, polar bear w/HP highlights, 4½" 35.00
Planter, swallow, 2½" 15.00
Plate, petal decor, 8½" 25.00
Shakers, bullet shape, 2½", pr 25.00
Shakers, penguins, 2½", pr 25.00
Tea set, pot+creamer & sugar bowl 100.00
Teapot, petal shape, 6½" 50.00

Toothpick holder, basket shape, 2" 22.00
Tumbler, 4½" 18.00
Vase, strawberry decor, hi-gloss blk, 10½" 40.00
Vase, swan hdls, 10¼" 45.00
Wall pocket, cup & saucer, 8" 38.00

Nippon

Nippon generally refers to Japanese wares made during the period from 1891 to 1921, although the Nippon mark was also used to a limited extent on later wares (accompanied by 'Japan'). Nippon, meaning Japan, identified the country of origin to comply with American importation restrictions. After 1921 'Japan' was the acceptable alternative. The term does not imply a specific type of product and may be found on items other than porcelains. For further information we recommend *The Collector's Encyclopedia of Nippon Porcelain* by our advisor, Joan Van Patten; you will find her address in the Directory under New York. In the following listings, items are assumed hand painted unless noted otherwise. Numbers included in the descriptions refer to these specific marks:

Key:
#1 — China E-OH   #5 — Rising Sun
#2 — M in Wreath   #6 — Royal Kinran
#3 — Cherry Blossom   #7 — Maple Leaf
#4 — Double T Diamond in   #8 — Royal Nippon, Nishiki
     Circle   #9 — Royal Moriye Nippon

Ashtray, Indian chief w/headdress in relief, #2, 6½" 900.00
Ashtray, sampan scene, 3 indents, #2, 5½" 100.00
Bookend, owl & tree trunk figural, gr #2, 9" 750.00
Bottle, scent; river scene, cobalt rim, gr #2, 5" 195.00
Bowl, Egyptian portrait reserve, blk/red rim, hdls, #2, 6½" 200.00
Bowl, gold leaf & berry o/l on wht, scalloped, #7, 9¾" 135.00
Bowl, peanuts in relief inside, hdls, gr #2, 7" 125.00
Bowl, pk roses & ornate gold border, scalloped, #7, 12" 250.00
Bowl, pk roses on wht, gold 6-scallop rim, #7, 7½" 100.00
Bowl, river scene, segmented sides, gold scallops, #7, 11" 375.00
Box, cigarette; camel rider in desert, gr #2, 4½" L 285.00
Box, powder; lady's portrait reserve on lid, #7, 5¼" dia 225.00
Cake plate, mc roses, ornate gold scalloped rim, #7, 11½" 250.00
Candlestick, floral w/heavy gold beads, bl #7, 10¾" 275.00
Candlestick, moriage trees in landscape, triangular, #2, 8" 300.00
Candy dish, hunt scene rim, 4-ftd, bl #7, 12" 250.00
Celery dish, celery stalk, gold hdls, #2, 13½", +6 salts 150.00
Cheese dish, Wedgwood, cream on bl, slant top, #2, 7¾" 400.00
Chocolate pot, silver o/l & cobalt on wht, mk, 11", +4 c/s 450.00
Cigar box, Deco floral reserve on lid, gr #2, 5½" L 225.00
Compote, woodland scene, hdls, gr #2, 5" 150.00
Compote, woodland scene, scalloped rim, #2, 3½x6½" 185.00
Condensed milk holder, gold o/l on wht, RC mk, 6", +tray 115.00
Cookie jar, florals w/moriage trim on wht, bl #7, 8" 325.00
Cookie jar, gold o/l florals on wht, bl #7, 8½" 250.00
Cookie jar, gold o/l on wht, gr mk, 8", +underplate 325.00
Cup, bouillon; roses & gold swags on wht, ftd, mk, 3¾" 25.00
Cup & saucer, Doll Face pattern, #5, 2⅛", 5" 60.00
Egg cup, Doll Face pattern, Morimura sticker, 3½" 75.00
Ewer, purple flowers over flared body, angle hdl, #6, 9½" 160.00
Ewer, swan scenic, moriage vintage at top, #7, 10" 375.00
Ewer, village & trees tapestry, bl #7, 10¾" 925.00
Ferner, moriage dragon, 4-ftd, ruffled rim, bl #7, 7½" 325.00
Ferner, Wedgwood, cream on bl, 4 columns, #2, 5" 450.00
Ginger jar, exotic bird reserve, Nippon mk, 7½" 300.00
Hatpin holder, gold o/l on wht, sq sides, open top, #7, 4⅞" 75.00

Hatpin holder, gold on cobalt & wht, undertray, #7, 4¾" 125.00
Humidor, Blk man's portrait, watermelon on lid, #2, 4" 600.00
Humidor, elk & trees at sunset, brn tones, #2, 5½" 375.00
Humidor, fox hunt scene, sq, bl #7, 6½" 600.00
Humidor, gold pine cones, gold squirrel finial, #7, 8" 650.00
Humidor, man on camel in relief, cylindrical, #2, 7½" 1,100.00
Humidor, monks/priests/animals in relief, #7, 7½" 1,400.00
Humidor, moriage playing cards on shaded brn, 3-hdl, #7, 6" 625.00
Humidor, mums on gold, w/gold beads, bl #7, 5½" 700.00
Humidor, portrait reserve, beaded bands on wht, #7, 7¾" 900.00
Humidor, windmill scene in relief, earth tones, #2, 6" 1,400.00
Incense burner, East Indian woman figural, mk, 8" 325.00
Jug, whiskey; mc roses, much gold, rose stopper, #7, 7" 500.00
Jug, whiskey; pine branches & cones, angle hdl, #2, 7½" 465.00
Jug, whiskey; river scene, gr base, angle hdl, #7, 8" 400.00
Jug, whiskey; scenic reserve on keg form, #2, 5½" 725.00
Jug, wine; lady & 2 children in river scene, #2, 9½" 800.00
Jug, wine; sampan reserve, geometric band, gr #2, 9½" 700.00
Lamp, sampan scenic reserve band on cobalt, mk, 17" 300.00
Matchbox holder/ashtray, Egyptian motif, gr #2, 3" H 200.00
Mug, sampan scene, gold hdl, #2, 5" 200.00
Mustard jar, river scene, earth tones, angle hdls, mk, 3½" 60.00
Nappy, pk flowers w/gold folded rim, 3-hdl, #7, 6¼" 110.00
Nut dish, Am Indian in canoe, 6-sided, hdls, #2, 5½" 150.00
Pitcher, florals on cobalt w/gold o/l, gr #7, 5¾" 365.00
Pitcher, lemonade; pk roses, mk, +4 tumblers 150.00
Pitcher, roses reserve, gold beads on gold, mk, 4" 150.00
Plaque, Blk man w/banjo, gr #2, 7¾" 350.00
Plaque, exotic bird on branch w/grapes, #7, 11" dia 285.00
Plaque, fruit still life, rectangular, #2, 10¼" W 575.00
Plaque, Indian on galloping horse relief, #2, 10½" 800.00
Plaque, man & running dogs in relief, gr #2, 12" 1,500.00
Plaque, swan scenic, intricate border, #2, 10" 235.00
Plaque, 2 dogs in relief, #2, 10½" 950.00
Plaque, 5 horses' heads in relief on shaded brn, #2, 10½" 1,100.00
Potpourri jar, sampan scene, gr #2, 5¾" 195.00
Relish, river scene at sunset, oval, #8, 8½" 150.00
Rose bowl, grapes in relief, gr #2, 3½" 350.00
Stein, floral, cloisonne on porc, #2, 7" 525.00
Stein, man w/wine smoking pipe, vintage border, #2, 7" 575.00
Stein, mug w/stein, vintage border, #2, 7" 525.00
Stein, pastoral scene, brn hdl w/decor, #2, 7" 525.00
Sugar bowl, lady's portrait reserve, gold o/l, hdls, #7, 6" 225.00
Tankard, moriage gulls, mk, 15¾" 675.00
Tea strainer, floral w/gold trim, #7, 6" L 135.00

Urn, floral reserve with much gold, 2-piece, L&Co., 7½", $170.00.

Urn, lady & peacock reserve, turq, gold o/l, w/lid, #7, 14" 1,300.00
Urn, portrait reserve, much gold beading, slim, #7, 10½" 875.00
Urn, river scenic band, gold beads/hdls/ft/lid, unmk, 9" 475.00
Urn, swan reserve on cobalt w/gold o/l, uptrn hdls, #7, 17" 2,500.00

Urn, swan scene, artist sgn, gold base/lid/hdls, gr #2, 19" **4,000.00**
Vase, bird on branch, coralene on wht, RS mk, 9½" 325.00
Vase, Countess Potocka in reserve, gold o/l, hdls, #7, 7½" 550.00
Vase, daffodils, ornate rope trim, ring hdls, gr #2, 9" 300.00
Vase, fisherman beside baskets in relief, hdls, #2, 8¼" 2,200.00
Vase, floral on tan shaded, gold ft & hdls, #2, 8½" 175.00
Vase, geisha scenic, gold angle hdls, #8, 9½" 150.00
Vase, leaves & berries in relief, flared cylinder, #7, 9¾" 675.00
Vase, lg pk roses, landscape beyond, cylindrical, #7, 12" 400.00
Vase, lg roses w/moriage trim, sm angle hdls, #7, 8" 250.00
Vase, man w/horse & cart scene, gold trim, dbl hdls, #2, 13" 850.00
Vase, mc florals & gold on basket form, unmk, 7" 350.00
Vase, mc florals on cobalt, long angle hdls, #6, 9½" 210.00
Vase, mc roses w/gold, 6-sided, shouldered, hdls, #2, 11" 275.00
Vase, moriage flowers, bulbous, hdls, gr #7, 5½" 200.00
Vase, moriage landscape, earth tones, bulbous, hdls, #7, 9" 425.00
Vase, moriage mtns & trees, uptrn hdls, #7, 10½" 450.00
Vase, moriage owl tapestry, much gold, ftd, hdls, #8, 12" 450.00
Vase, moriage trees in landscape, lobed, bl #2, 10" 400.00
Vase, orchids on lt bl shaded, gold hdls, gr #7, 10½" 200.00
Vase, orchids tapestry, gold ring hdls, mk #7, 9½" 500.00
Vase, phoenix bird reserve, elephant head hdls, #2, 5¾" 285.00
Vase, pk roses on tan mottle, slim pitcher form, mk, 11" 265.00
Vase, poppies w/gold on lav shaded, Royal mk, 12x5½" 130.00
Vase, red heart leaves on blk, cloisonne on porc, mk, 4" 300.00
Vase, river scene tapestry, integral hdls, #7, 6" 550.00
Vase, rose tapestry, gold o/l, hdls, bl #7, 6" 550.00
Vase, sampan reserve, florals on wht, ornate hdls, #2, 13¾" 500.00
Vase, scenic tapestry, sm mouth, cylindrical, #7, 6¼" 500.00
Vase, swan reserve, gold o/l on cobalt, bl #7, 9½" 525.00
Vase, Wedgwood, cream on bl, urn form, gr #2, 8" 500.00
Vase, windmill scene, 3-ftd, angle hdls, #2, 11" 300.00
Vase, yel roses on bl, shouldered, uptrn gold hdls, #2, 9¾" 200.00

Nodders

So called because of the nodding action of their heads and hands, nodders originated in China where they were used in temple rituals to represent deity. Early in the 18th century, the idea was adopted by Meissen and by French manufacturers who produced not only china nodders but bisque as well. Most nodders are individual; couples are unusual. The idea remained popular until the end of the 19th century and was used during the Victorian era by toy manufacturers.

Blk man, full figure, exaggerated features, 1930s 135.00
Chicken, papier-mache & wood w/metal legs 42.00
Donkey, celluloid 30.00
Dwight Eisenhower 38.00
Elephant, celluloid, red 30.00
Felix, pnt pot metal, Germany, 4¾", G+ 275.00
Friar w/snuff, ceramic, Portugal 125.00
Lady (homely) nursing baby, ceramic, Portugal 150.00
Peafowl, cvd wood, polychrome pnt, 5" 75.00
Santa, papier-mache, 10" 75.00

German Comic Characters

During the early 1930s, Germany produced a collection of small figure dolls, approximately 2" to 4" high, representing the most popular comic strip and cartoon characters of that time. They were made of bisque with brightly painted details and clearly stamped with their appropriate names and 'Germany' on their backs. Generally, their movable heads were attached with an elastic string going through their bodies, hence the name 'nodders', but there were some characters produced earlier that were frozen with no movable parts. The most popular ones came in boxed sets, but the lesser-known characters were sold separately, making them rarer and harder to find today. We have listed the most valuable characters from the series here; those not mentioned below are valued at $125.00 and under.

Ambrose Potts	350.00
Aunt Mamie or Uncle Willie, ea	350.00
Auntie Blossom	150.00
Bill, Dock, Avery, Max or Pop Jenks, ea	200.00
Buttercup	250.00
Chubby Chaney	250.00
Corky	475.00
Ferina	350.00
Grandpa Teen	350.00
Happy Hooligan	600.00
Harold Teen	150.00
Junior Nebbs	500.00
Lillums	150.00
Little Annie Rooney, arm only	250.00
Little Egypt	350.00
Lord Plushbottom	150.00
Ma or Pa Winkle, ea	350.00
Marjory, Patsy, Lilacs or Josie, ea	400.00
Mary Ann Jackson	250.00
Min Gump	150.00
Mr Bailey	150.00
Mr Bibb	400.00
Mr Wicker	250.00
Mushmouth	350.00
Mutt or Jeff, ea	250.00
Nicodemus	350.00
Old Timer	350.00
Pat Finnegan	400.00
Pete the Dog	150.00
Rudy or Fanny Nebbs, ea	250.00
Scraps	250.00
Widow Zander	400.00
Winnie Winkle	150.00

Noritake

The Noritake Company was first registered in 1904 as Nippon Gomei Kaisha. In 1917 the name became Nippon Toki Kabushiki Toki. The 'M' in wreath mark is that of the Morimura Brothers, distributors with offices in New York. It was used until 1941. The tree crest mark is the crest of the Morimura family.

The Noritake Company has produced fine porcelain dinnerware sets and occasional pieces decorated in the delicate manner for which the Japanese are noted. Their Azalea pattern was produced exclusively for the Larkin Company, who gave the lovely ware away as premiums to club members and their home agents. From 1916 through the thirties, Larkin distributed fine china which was decorated in pink Azaleas on white with gold tracing along edges and handles. Early in the thirties, six pieces of crystal hand painted with the same design were offered: candle holders, a compote, a tray with handles, a scalloped fruit bowl, a cheese and cracker set, and a cake plate. All in all, seventy different pieces of Azalea were produced. Some, such as the fifteen-piece child's set, bulbous vase, china ashtray, and the pancake jug, are quite rare. One of the earliest marks was the Noritake M in wreath with variations. Later the ware was marked 'Noritake, Azalea, Hand Painted, Japan.' Authority Joan Van Patten has compiled a lovely book, *The*

Collector's Encyclopedia of Noritake, with many full-color photos and current prices; you will find her address in the Directory under New York. Our advisor for Azalea is Alton Parker; he is listed in the Directory under Florida. In the following listings, examples are hand painted unless noted otherwise. Numbers refer to these specific marks:

Key:
#1 — Komaru #3 — N in Wreath
#2 — M in Wreath

Azalea

Basket, mint; Dolly Varden, #193	195.00
Bonbon, #184, 6¼"	50.00
Bowl, #12, 10"	42.50
Bowl, deep, #310	68.00
Bowl, fruit; shell form, #188, 7¾"	385.00
Bowl, oatmeal; #55, 5½"	28.00
Bowl, vegetable; divided, #439, 9½"	295.00
Bowl, vegetable; oval, #101, 10½"	60.00
Bowl, vegetable; oval, #172, 9¼"	58.00
Butter chip, #312, 3¼"	145.00
Butter tub, w/insert, #54	48.00
Cake plate, #10, 9¾"	40.00
Candy bowl, #185	195.00
Candy jar, #313	695.00
Casserole, gold finial, w/lid, #372	540.00
Casserole, w/lid, #16	125.00
Celery/roll tray, #99, 12"	55.00
Cheese/butter dish, #314	135.00
Child's set, #253, 15-pc	2,500.00
Coffeepot, AD; #182	595.00
Compote, #170	98.00

Condiment set, #14, 5-piece, $65.00.

Creamer & sugar bowl, #122	158.00
Creamer & sugar bowl, #449, ind	395.00
Creamer & sugar bowl, #7	45.00
Creamer & sugar bowl, AD; open, #123	140.00
Creamer & sugar bowl, gold finial, #401	155.00
Cruet, #190	195.00
Cup & saucer, #2	17.50
Cup & saucer, AD; #183	150.00
Cup & saucer, bouillon; #124, 3½"	24.50
Egg cup, #120	60.00
Gravy boat, #40	48.00
Jam jar set, #125, 3-pc	155.00
Match/toothpick holder, #192	130.00
Mayonnaise set, scalloped, #453, 3-pc	495.00
Mustard jar, #191	60.00
Pickle/lemon set, #121	24.50
Pitcher, milk jug; #100, 1-qt	195.00
Plate, #4, 7½"	10.00

Plate, bread & butter; #8, 6½" **10.00**
Plate, cream soup; #363 ....**175.00**
Plate, dinner; #13, 9¾" **28.00**
Plate, grill; 3-compartment, #338, 10¼" **165.00**
Plate, scalloped sq, salesman's sample **950.00**
Plate, soup; #19, 7⅛" **25.00**
Plate, sq, #315, 7⅝" **85.00**
Platter, #17, 14" **60.00**
Platter, #186, 16" **475.00**
Platter, #56, 12" **58.00**
Platter, cold meat; #311, 10¼" **215.00**
Refreshment set, #39, 2-pc **48.00**
Relish, #194, 7⅛" **85.00**
Relish, loop hdl, 2-part, #450 ....**425.00**
Relish, oval, #18, 8½" **20.00**
Relish, 2-part, #171 ....**58.00**
Relish, 4-part, #119, rare, 10" **150.00**
Saucer, fruit; #9, 5¼" **10.00**
Shakers, #126, ind, pr **27.50**
Shakers, bell form, #11, pr **30.00**
Shakers, bulbous, #89, pr **30.00**
Spoon holder, #189, 8" **115.00**
Spoon holder, #339, 2-pc **35.00**
Syrup, #97, w/underplate **135.00**
Tea set, child sz, 15-pc **2,500.00**
Tea tile, #169, 6" **48.50**
Teapot, #15 ....**110.00**
Teapot, gold finial, #400 ....**495.00**
Toothpick holder, #192 ....**130.00**
Vase, bulbous, #452 ....**1,150.00**
Vase, fan form, ftd, #187 ....**185.00**
Whipped cream set, #3, 3-pc **38.50**

Ashtray, Deco lady w/whippet, 6-sided, #2, 3½" **45.00**
Ashtray, Egyptian portrait, gr #2, 5" **95.00**
Ashtray, nude at rim of flower-form bowl, red #2, 7" **265.00**
Bowl, floral medallion, orange & bl lustre, hdls, #2, 9¼" ...**55.00**
Bowl, florals on bl, bird at rim, gr #2, 7½" **115.00**
Bowl, florals on wht, geometric bands, gold hdls, #2, 7" ...**40.00**
Bowl, flower form, arched hdl, ftd, red #2, 6¼" **80.00**
Bowl, leaves on bl, bluebird figure on rim, #3, 7½" L ...**110.00**
Bowl, red w/florals on wht int, #2, 10", +flower tray/spoons ...**115.00**
Bowl, winter scene, 3-lobed, 3 sm gold hdls, #2, 6½" ...**50.00**
Box, powder puff; red w/bl flower finial, #2, 3¾" **145.00**
Box, puff; Deco lady in tricorner hat, bouffant dress, sgn ...**190.00**
Box, trinket; Deco lady & whippet on cream, ftd, gr #2, 3" ...**55.00**
Cake plate, floral medallions on cream, hdls, #2, 11" ...**40.00**
Cake plate, sailboat & palms on bl & orange lustre, #2, 9¾" ...**40.00**
Candy dish, floral, wht int, gold center ring hdl, #2, 6" dia ...**55.00**
Celery set, river scene, #2, 12½" tray+6 3¾" salts **95.00**
Chamberstick, Egyptian decor on orange lustre, #2, 6½", pr ...**155.00**
Chamberstick, florals, orange lustre, ring hdls, #2, 2¼", pr ...**65.00**
Chocolate set, exotic bird on lustre, #2, 16-pc **260.00**
Chocolate set, pyramids near river, #2, 13-pc **195.00**
Compote, floral center, Greek Key gold border, hdls, #2, 9¾" ...**85.00**
Condiment set, Tree in Meadow, #2 ....**40.00**
Cookie jar, man on camel, cobalt & gold, #1, 7" **235.00**
Creamer, florals on cream w/orange lustre, gold hdl, #2, 5¾" ...**30.00**
Creamer, Tree in Meadow, 3" **12.00**
Cup & saucer, Tree in Meadow, #2 ....**18.00**
Egg cup, windmill scene, gold rim, gr #2, 3½" **25.00**
Flower holder, bird figural, bl w/orange lustre, #2, 4½" ...**185.00**
Gravy boat, Tree in Meadow, #2 ....**75.00**

Honey jar, hive form, appl figural bees, gr #2, 5½" **70.00**
Humidor, silhouette-type figure on cream, gr #2, 6½" ...**380.00**
Inkwell, clown figural, red #2, 4" **250.00**
Jam jar, floral medallion on yel w/gold, #2, 5" **55.00**
Jam jar, strawberries along sides, bud finial, gr #2, 5½" ...**55.00**
Jar, potpourri; bl top over wht, red bud finial, #2, 6" ...**70.00**
Lamp, house along river w/bridge, gr #2, 10" **110.00**
Lemon dish, lemons center, gold lustre rim, red #2, 6" ...**85.00**
Nappy, floral on shaded pastel, 1 hdl, gr #2, 5" **35.00**
Plaque, dog beside river, fancy rim, gr #2, 7½" **155.00**
Plaque, steamship, gold trim, #1, 10" **175.00**
Plate, Deco florals on blk, #2, 7½" **15.00**
Plate, sandwich; river scene, center hdl, #2, 8" **50.00**
Plate, Tree in Meadow, #2, 7" **13.00**
Plate, Tree in Meadow, dinner sz, #2 ....**95.00**
Punch bowl, peacock medallion w/gold, #2, 16", +8 cups ...**900.00**
Sauce dish, fruit int, ftd flower form, red #2, 4" **40.00**
Shell dish, Tree in Meadow, #2 ....**170.00**
Snack set, floral w/yel lustre, red #2, 7½" tray+cup **60.00**
Sugar bowl, parrots on red, gold hdls/finial, #2, 3¼" ...**25.00**
Tea caddy, Oriental man & horse on orange lustre, #2, 3¾" ...**215.00**
Tea set, snow scene w/gold trim, #2, 4¾" pot+20 pcs ...**225.00**
Tea tile, river scene, sq w/canted corners, gr #2, 5" **35.00**
Teapot, Tree in Meadow, #2 ....**90.00**
Toothpick holder, Tree in Meadow, #2 ....**65.00**
Tray, river scene, brns & pale bl, bl #1, 12" L **65.00**
Vase, Deco figure on red, slim, #2, 8½" **190.00**
Vase, floral, orange/bl lustre, 6 figural birds at rim, #2, 7" ...**275.00**
Vase, floral medallions on cream w/gold, angle hdls, #2, 7½" ...**265.00**
Vase, man on camel scene, gold angle hdls, #2, 8" **150.00**
Vase, river scene in leafy fr, orange lustre, hdls, #1, 6" ...**150.00**
Vase, river/house reserve on bl, scroll hdls, #2, 7¼", pr ...**325.00**
Vase, roses, mc on wht, gold at top, upright hdls, #2, 8½" ...**115.00**
Vase, Wedgwood type, bl & wht, bl #1, 9½" **335.00**
Wall pocket, appl butterfly & bee, red #2, 8¼" **85.00**
Wall pocket, Deco floral on red & yel, red #2, 8¼", pr ...**90.00**
Wall pocket, mc florals on cream, gold trim, #2, 8½" ...**90.00**

North Dakota School of Mines

The School of Mines of the University of North Dakota was established in 1890; but due to a lack of funding it was not until 1898 that Earle J. Babcock was appointed as Director, and efforts were made to produce ware from the native clay he had discovered several years earlier. The first pieces were made by firms in the east from the clay Babcock sent them. Some of the ware was decorated by the manufacturer; some was shipped back to North Dakota to be decorated by native artists. By 1909 students at the University of North Dakota were producing utilitarian items such as tile, brick, shingles, etc., in conjunction with a ceramic course offered through the Chemistry Department. By 1910 a ceramic department had been established, supervised by Margaret Kelly Cable. Under her leadership, fine artware was produced. Native flowers, grains, buffalo, cowboys, and other subjects indigenous to the state were incorporated into the decorations. Some pieces have an Art Nouveau — Art Deco style easily attributed to her association with Frederick H. Rhead, with whom she studied in 1911. During the twenties the pottery was marketed on a limited scale through gift and jewelry stores in the state. From 1927 until 1949 when Miss Cable announced her retirement, a more widespread distribution was maintained with sales branching out into other states. The ware was marked in cobalt with the official seal — 'Made at School of Mines, N.D. Clay, University of North Dakota, Grand Forks, N.D.' in a circle. Very early ware was sometimes marked 'U.N.D.' in cobalt by hand.

Bowl, cvd floral band on angle shoulder, CA Sorbo, 5x6¾" 225.00
Bowl, florals incised on lime gr to sand, sgn, 2½x6" 225.00
Bowl, Indian bird/flower symbols, 3-color, Kloster, 3½" H 800.00
Cookie jar, Aunt Susan (Blk), M Cable, #118 ....2,000.00
Humidor, Indian dancers, brn on rust, Mattson, 7" 1,300.00
Jardiniere, Arts & Crafts flowers cvd/pnt on gr, EWW, 6x6½" ..1,700.00
Pitcher, floral, Huck, 6" 195.00
Pot, brn w/mint gr int, Julia Mattson, 1940s, 4x5½" 135.00
Sugar bowl, cream w/cobalt, ink stamp decor on side, 3½" 480.00
Tile, cvd oxen & wagon, gr/brn, Flora Huckfield, 5" dia 250.00
Vase, brn tones, sgn Hovelson, 11" 190.00
Vase, cvd iris/leaves in brn on med gr, LM Barlow, 9x5½" 425.00

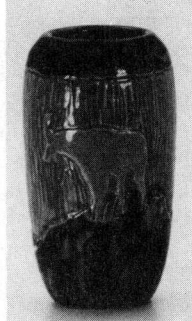

Vase, carved scene with mountain goat, signed Cable and C.K., blue and green gloss, 8", $1,100.00.

Vase, cvd ivy band, gr on buff, incurvate, Peterson, 6x6" 400.00
Vase, cvd shoulder band: children hold hands, brn, Peck, 5" 375.00
Vase, cvd stylized floral band, turq to ivory matt, 7x6" 250.00
Vase, cvd/pnt floral on pk/cream, Huck 'Apple Bloosoms,' 8½" .950.00
Vase, floral, Julia Mattson, 9" 595.00
Vase, lilac-bl, glossy, Julia Mattson, 1927 stamp, 4½" 135.00
Vase, prairie rose, mauve, Huck, 3" 250.00
Vase, prairie rose band at shoulder, lt bl/wht, Cable, 7" 800.00
Vase, wheat cvd on gr matt, FC Huckfield, 6¼x4½" 600.00
Vase, woodgrain cvd on 2-tone brn, can neck, Robinson, 7x8" ..260.00
Vase, 3 panels w/Conestoga wagon, Huckfield/Hammers, 5x4" .1,800.00

Northwood

The Northwood Company was founded in 1896 in Indiana, Pennsylvania, by Harry Northwood, whose father, John, was the art director for Stevens and Williams, an English glassworks. Northwood joined the National Glass Company in 1899 but in 1901 again became an independent contractor and formed the Harry Northwood Glass Company of Wheeling, West Virginia. He marketed his first carnival glass in 1908, and it became his most popular product. His company was also famous for its custard, goofus, and pressed glass. Northwood died in 1923, and the company closed. See also Carnival; Custard; Goofus; Opalescent; Pattern Glass.

Basket, pull-up, wht/wine/gold, clear florettes/ft, 12½" 1,200.00
Bowl, berry; Cherry T'print, ruby w/gold, 1 lg+4 sm 125.00
Bowl, berry; Peach, gr w/gold, 5" 35.00
Bowl, berry; Plum & Cherry, 9" 80.00
Bowl, berry; Regal, gr w/gold, 7-pc set 110.00
Bowl, berry; Royal Ivy, rainbow craquelle, lg+4 sm 450.00
Bowl, berry; Royal Ivy, rubena frost, 7-pc set 310.00
Bowl, berry; Royal Oak, rubena, 7-pc set 290.00
Butter dish, Royal Oak, frosted rubena, acorn finial, 5x5" 225.00
Celery vase, Leaf Umbrella, cased spatter 225.00
Creamer, Peach, gr w/gold 65.00

Creamer & sugar bowl, Royal Oak, rubena frost, w/lid, 6" 250.00
Cruet, Nestor, apple gr 200.00
Cruet, Nestor, sapphire bl, decor, orig stopper 135.00
Mug, Singing Birds, amethyst 105.00
Pitcher, Cherry T'print, cherries w/gold, water sz 125.00
Pitcher, HP lilies of the valley on bl w/gold trim, 12¾" 135.00
Pitcher, Invt Bull's Eyes, amber, reed hdl, 8¼" 75.00
Pitcher, Leaf Umbrella, cranberry, ca 1905, 9" 395.00
Pitcher, Nestor, amethyst 295.00
Pitcher, Plum & Cherry, ruby w/gold rim, water sz 125.00
Pitcher, Royal Ivy, rainbow craquelle 550.00
Pitcher, Royal Ivy, rainbow craquelle frost 595.00
Pitcher, Royal Oak, rubena, water sz 400.00
Plate, 3 Fruits, electric bl, stippled, ribbed ext, 9" 800.00
Rose bowl, mc pull-up design on wht, 8-crimp, thorn ft, 3" 275.00
Shakers, Circled Scroll, gr, bulbous, 2⅞", pr 150.00
Shakers, Intaglio, gr w/HP gold decor, 3", pr 150.00
Shakers, Leaf Umbrella, bl opaque, cased, 2⅞", pr 185.00
Shakers, Northwood's Cactus, cranberry opal, 3⅜", pr 295.00
Shakers, Quilted Phlox, gr pastel, cased, 3", pr 78.00
Shakers, Royal Ivy, cranberry rubena frost, 2⅝", pr 160.00
Shakers, Royal Ivy, rainbow craquelle, pr 400.00
Shakers, Royal Oak, pastel gr opaque, cased, 2⅝", pr 90.00
Spooner, Gothic Arches, gr w/gold 30.00
Spooner, Ovals in Sand, apple gr w/gold & HP flowers 75.00
Sugar bowl, Regal, bl opal, w/lid 275.00
Sugar bowl, Ribbed Pillar, cased spatter, w/lid 45.00
Sugar shaker, ring neck mold, cased spatter 150.00
Toothpick holder, Leaf Mold, cranberry & vaseline spatter 195.00
Toothpick holder, Leaf Mold, vaseline spatter 245.00
Toothpick holder, Royal Ivy, rubena 125.00
Tumbler, Cherry & Plum 22.00
Tumbler, Cherry Lattice, clear w/color stain 20.00
Tumbler, Grape & Cable, purple 55.00
Tumbler, Leaf Umbrella, bl cased 85.00
Tumbler, Oriental Poppy, gr w/gold 45.00
Tumbler, Peach, gr w/gold 30.00
Tumbler, Ribbed Pillar, cased spatter 45.00
Tumbler, Royal Ivy, cased spatter 70.00
Tumbler, Teardrop & Flower, bl w/gold 45.00
Vase, Leaf Umbrella, shiny yel, tall, rare 235.00
Vase, mc pull-up design on yel, 3-petal top, 3¼x3¾" 325.00
Water set, Golden Peach, gr w/gold, 7-pc 350.00
Water set, Memphis, gr w/gold, 7-pc 295.00

Norweta

Norweta pottery was made by the Northwestern Terra Cotta Company of Chicago, Illinois. It was made for approximately ten years, beginning sometime before 1907. Some was made with a crystalline glaze, and terra cotta vases were also produced. Not all was marked.

Paperweight, lg turtle, gr over bronze matt, 2½" 550.00
Pin tray, lg seal figure on side, bronze-like patina, 4½" 450.00
Vase, bl crystalline, very wide shoulder, 3½" 600.00
Vase, celadon crystalline, flaring cylinder, 9" 325.00

Nutcrackers

The nutcracker, though a strictly functional tool, is a good example of one to which man has applied ingenuity, imagination, and engineering skills. Though all were designed to accomplish the same end, hundreds of types exist in almost every material sturdy enough to withstand sufficient pressure to crack the nut. Figurals are popular collectibles, as are those with unusual design and construction. Patented examples are also desirable. Our advisor for this category is Earl MacSorley; he is listed in the Directory under Connecticut. For more information, we recommend *Ornamental and Figural Nutcrackers* by Judith A. Rittenhouse.

Alligator, CI, gr pnt, Am, 1950s, 14" **100.00**
Bearded man w/hat, cvd & lacquered, Swiss made, ca 1900, 8¾" ...**150.00**

Black man's head, carved wood, original paint and finish, ca 1900, 8½", $200.00.

Clown (Pierrot), dbl-faced, brass, ca 1900, 5¼" **75.00**
Crocodile, NP, faint pat #s on lower jaw, 8½" **30.00**
Dog, brass, 1930s, 9x3¾" **70.00**
Dog, CI, blk pnt, mk 24H on hdl, ca 1900, 10½" L **65.00**
Dragon, CI, old gold pnt, English, ca 1900, 14" **275.00**
Elephant, pnt CI, att Am, ca 1930s, 4¾x9¾" **150.00**
Elf w/beard, pnt CI, wood base, Am, late 1800s, 10" **400.00**
Fagin & Bill Sykes, dbl-sided, brass, late 1800s, 4¾" **50.00**
Fish, cvd olive wood, Greek, 1950s, 8" **25.00**
Frog, wrought w/glass eyes, mk Germany, 1900s, 6¼x8¾" **250.00**
Girl in hoop skirt, brass, MIE, Pat App'd..., 1956, 3¾" **125.00**
Jackdaw, wooden w/glass eyes, stain/pnt, English, 1850s, 8⅝" **525.00**
Jester figural, dbl-faced, brass, English, 1900s **50.00**
Lady's leg, cvd wood, 1950s, 7¼" **35.00**
Naughty Nellie, brass, unmk, 6" **75.00**
Peasant lady, cvd wood, Breton, ca 1930s, 8½" **75.00**
Snarling man, brn cvd hat, wooden hdl works jaw, 7½", EX **150.00**
Squirrel figural, brass, Made in Taiwan, recent repro **15.00**
Squirrel on base, CI, blk pnt, #1370 Emig, 1950s, 7¼" L **35.00**
Wolf's head, NP CI, Am, Pat 1920, 4⅞x10" **125.00**
Woodsman, cvd wood, fur hair, E Germany, recent, 10½" **150.00**

Occupied Japan

Items marked 'Occupied Japan' have become popular collectibles in the last few years. They were produced during the period from the end of World War II until April 18, 1952, when the occupation ended. By no means was all of the ware exported during that time marked 'Occupied Japan'; some was marked 'Japan' or 'Made In Japan.' It is thought that because of the natural resentment felt by the Japanese toward the occupation, only a fraction of these wares carried the 'Occupied' mark. Even though you may find identical 'Japan'-marked items, because of its limited use, only those with the 'Occupied Japan' mark are being collected

to any great extent. Values vary considerably, based on the quality of workmanship. Generally, bisque figures command much higher prices than porcelain, since on the whole they are of a finer quality.

For those wanting more information, we recommend *The Collector's Encyclopedia of Occupied Japan Collectibles* by Gene Florence; he is listed in the Directory under Kentucky. Our advisor for this category is Florence Archambault; she is listed under Rhode Island. She represents the Occupied Japan Club, whose mailing address may be found in the Directory under Clubs, Newsletters, and Catalogs. All items described in the following listings are assumed ceramic unless noted otherwise.

Ashtray, Am Indian chief's head form **12.50**
Ashtray, Florida, shape of state **15.00**
Ashtray, hand form, metal **12.50**
Ashtray, Huskie dog emb in center, Alaska on rim, metal **12.50**
Ashtray, Statue of Liberty emb in center, metal, 5" **15.00**
Bank, pig form, metal, 4" **20.00**
Bank, pig form, porc, 3" **12.50**
Binocular, full sz, in leather case **75.00**
Bookends, lady on upright L-form, 4½x5½", pr **40.00**
Box, piano form, metal, red velvet lined **15.00**
Box, ring; metal heart shape, emb florals, 3-ftd **12.50**
Candle holder, Mexican figural, 5" **35.00**
Chest, wood, 2-drw, natural finish w/red roses, 3x4½" **20.00**
Child's set, florals, 6-place, 23-pc **100.00**
Christmas item, reindeer, celluloid, 7x7½" **12.00**
Cigarette box, Oriental man carries box w/dragon finial, 6⅜" **25.00**
Cigarette box, pk floral on wht, 3¾x2¾", +4 trays **30.00**
Cigarette lighter, metal champagne bucket form **17.50**
Cigarette lighter, metal gun form w/pearl hdls **22.50**
Clock, cherubs & appl flowers, bsk, Ardalt Lenwile, 11½" **450.00**
Clock, regulator type, mahog, chimes, orig key, 18", EX **465.00**
Coaster, papier-mache, mk Alcohol Proof, Isco **4.00**
Creamer & sugar bowl on tray, tomato form, Maruhon **35.00**
Cup & saucer, demitasse; floral, hexagonal **15.00**
Cup & saucer, demitasse; floral medallion on rust, Kato **12.50**
Cup & saucer, demitasse; lacy flower on blk **12.50**
Cup & saucer, demitasse; mc florals on wht, gold trim **12.50**
Cup & saucer, demitasse; Oriental house scene **10.00**
Cup & saucer, floral on wht, ornate gold hdl, mini, ⅞" **8.00**
Cup & saucer, floral rim band on wht, Nasco Fine China **15.00**
Cup & saucer, gold horse/gray knight, ftd, Lamore China **20.00**
Cup & saucer, orange band, scalloped, Army-Navy souvenir, mini ...**10.00**
Cup & saucer, pk w/floral int, Jyoto **10.00**
Dinnerware, set for 12, w/gravy/4 platters/casserole, up to **450.00**
Dinnerware, set for 4, w/creamer & sugar bowl, up to **200.00**
Dinnerware, set for 6, w/gravy boat & sm platter, up to **250.00**
Dinnerware, set for 8, w/gravy & 3 platters, up to **300.00**
Doll, celluloid, Kewpie, 2¾" **15.00**
Easter basket, woven wicker, 7x7" **35.00**
Figurine, angel musician, pk bsk, 2½", pr **25.00**
Figurine, ballerina, bsk, gr net tutu, 6" **42.50**
Figurine, ballerina w/porc skirt, 7" **50.00**
Figurine, Blk boy holding pot, 3" **27.50**
Figurine, Blk fiddler, 5" **35.00**
Figurine, boy, mc clothes, 7" **27.50**
Figurine, boy & girl watering lg sunflower, Paulux, 5½" **75.00**
Figurine, boy playing accordion for chicken, 4⅛" **10.00**
Figurine, boy sits on fence, Hummel type, 4" **15.00**
Figurine, boy w/scottie dog, Hummel type, 5½" **30.00**
Figurine, bulldog, brn & wht, sm **15.00**
Figurine, cherub on boot, bsk, Ugaco, 6x4" **65.00**
Figurine, cherub on butterfly, bsk, 3" **30.00**
Figurine, cherub plays violin, Ardalt, bsk, 5" **65.00**

Figurine, Colonial couple at piano, gold mk, 5½" 50.00
Figurine, Colonial couple in bl, 4¾" 15.00
Figurine, Colonial couple w/sled on base, 5¾" 60.00
Figurine, Colonial dancing couple, 3⅛" 10.00
Figurine, Colonial lady w/basket, man w/flowers, 8", pr 48.00
Figurine, Colonial lady w/fan, 12" 85.00
Figurine, Colonial man & lady, bsk, 11", pr 145.00
Figurine, Colonial musicians, 11", pr 140.00
Figurine, Colonial soldier, 5" 20.00
Figurine, cowboy w/rifle, 3" 15.00
Figurine, cowgirl, mc clothes, 4¼" 15.00
Figurine, Dalmatian dog, blk & wht, 2x3", MIB 12.00
Figurine, dog playing bass horn, 3½" 8.50
Figurine, Dutch boy (or girl) w/bucket on string, 4¼", pr 25.00
Figurine, Dutch boy w/buckets, bl clothes, 4" 15.00
Figurine, Dutch girl w/basket, Delft style, HP, 5" 20.00
Figurine, Dutch lady w/flowers, Ucagco, 10⅛" 65.00
Figurine, French peasant, bsk, 10", pr 120.00
Figurine, frog playing mandolin, bsk, 3½" 15.00
Figurine, gaucho w/guitar, 6½" 25.00
Figurine, gazelles, bk to bk, Deco styling, 3¾" 8.50
Figurine, girl in wht robe plays accordion, 5¾" 15.00
Figurine, girl playing accordion, dog at side, on base, 3⅞" 12.50
Figurine, girl playing mandolin, Hummel type, 4" 20.00

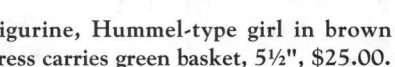
Figurine, Hummel-type girl in brown dress carries green basket, 5½", $25.00.

Figurine, girl w/long apron, 8¼" 35.00
Figurine, girl w/terrier, bl bonnet, 6" 27.50
Figurine, gnome, mc, 5⅛" 15.00
Figurine, hula girl, 4½" 15.00
Figurine, Indian in canoe w/plastic flowers 20.00
Figurine, lady holding skirt wide, 5" 12.50
Figurine, lady in fancy dress holds mirror, 6" 20.00
Figurine, lady in low-cut gown w/fan, 9¾" 50.00
Figurine, lady in 3-tier net skirt & hat, 6" 50.00
Figurine, lady standing & playing stringed instrument, 4" 12.50
Figurine, lady stands & reads book, 8⅜" 35.00
Figurine, lady w/children on emb floral shoe, Chikusa, 5" 65.00
Figurine, lady w/crown & scepter, 8⅛" 45.00
Figurine, lady w/fan & man w/hat on base, HP, 6⅜" 50.00
Figurine, man seated, mc clothes, 3" 15.00
Figurine, man w/accordion, bl mk, 4" 10.00
Figurine, man w/balloons, Doulton like, 4" 22.50
Figurine, man w/hand to mouth, well dressed, 4" 15.00
Figurine, Oriental dancer, bl R in shield, 14½" 125.00
Figurine, Oriental girl reclines on rug, 3¼x3½" 12.00
Figurine, peasant lady w/basket, yel & bl, 5" 17.50
Figurine, seated courting couple w/lambs, bsk, mk ST, 8x9" 300.00
Figurine, villain & lady captive, bl mk, 7½" 65.00
Figurine, youthful gentleman, Florence look-alike, 9" 40.00

Figurine, 2 beagles on base, 3" 24.00
Figurine, 2 natives in outhouse, '1 Moment Please,' 3" 32.00
Figurine, 3 people by horse-drawn coach, 6x7" 75.00
Furniture, chair, tiny appl roses on wht, 3" 10.00
Furniture, chest, red w/wht trim, 1½" 7.50
Furniture, china cabinet w/dishes, 2¼" 15.00
Furniture, dresser, gold trim on wht, 2" 10.00
Furniture, refrigerator, wht w/red trim, 3½" 15.00
Lamp base, courting couple, 6½", pr 60.00
Lamp base, lady in pk hat, 8¼" 35.00
Lamp base, musician & singer, 11½", pr 75.00
Linen, tablecloth, red plaid w/yel & bl, sewn-in tag, 48" 50.00
Mug, bbl form, man in nightshirt hdl, 4¼" 27.50
Mug, face of winking man, 4" 35.00
Pitcher, ladies, cream on bl, Wedgwood style, 4¼" 15.00
Planter, bird beside house, 3" 7.50
Planter, Blk boy w/watermelon, 5" 45.00
Planter, boy beside cherry tree, 3⅝" 10.00
Planter, boy w/cat at feet beside basketweave planter 15.00
Planter, cradle w/baby form, 4" 18.00
Planter, frog in weeds, 3⅝x3" 15.00
Planter, girl w/arms spread to hold basket for flowers, 5" 20.00
Planter, girl w/cart, 2⅝" 6.00
Planter, Indian boy w/lg bowl, 7⅛" 25.00
Planter, Oriental boy w/rickshaw, HP 12.50
Planter, Oriental girl w/shell, red mk, 6⅛" 25.00
Planter, Oriental man w/shoulder yoke holding 2 buckets, 6¾" 22.50
Planter, Scottie figural, 7" 37.50
Plaque, Colonial man & lady, 6", pr 48.00
Purse, crocheted oval w/straps & lid, cloth label, 9" L 75.00
Shakers, bride & groom, pr 25.00
Shakers, coolies w/pumpkins, pr 25.00
Shakers, graduates, pr 20.00
Shakers, silver-tone metal, ftd, hdls, 2¼", pr 17.50
Shakers, tomato form, 3½", pr 20.00
Shoe, lady's high-heel shoe w/appl flower, 2⅜" 8.00
Slide rule, MIB 25.00
Stein, people sitting at table, bl tones, 6" 20.00
Sweater, baby's, shell-stitch crochet in bl & wht 45.00
Teapot, aluminum, 9" 32.00
Teapot, tomato form, +matching creamer & sugar bowl 65.00
Toby mug, General McArthur, 5" 50.00
Toy, stork, celluloid, 9" 50.00
Tray, metal, souvenir of United Nations, 2x4¾" 10.00
Tray, metal, 2 rnd compartments, Statue of Liberty in 1 ....15.00
Tray, pin; ballerina w/porc skirt stands at side, 4" 40.00
Vase, carriage scene, classic form, 3" 8.00
Vase, emb mc floral on wht, sm angle hdls, 4¼" 15.00
Vase, lg appl rose on bulbous form, 4¼" 15.00
Vase, mc floral on bl, mk Meiko China, 3⅛" 15.00
Vase, Nouveau form w/appl leaves, gilt, 10" 60.00
Vase, pagoda in relief, ftd, sm hdls, 5¼" 24.00
Vase, Wedgwood style, 2¾" 10.00
Vase, wht w/lg appl rose, Andrea, 4¾" 15.00

Ohr, George

George Ohr established his pottery around 1893 in Biloxi, Mississippi. The unusual style of the ware he produced and his flamboyant personality earned him the dubious title of 'the mad potter of Biloxi.' Though acclaimed by some of the critics of his day to be perhaps the most accomplished thrower in the history of the industry, others overlooked the eggshell-thin walls of his vessels, each a different shape and contortion, and saw only that their 'tortured' appearance contradicted their own sedate preferences.

Ohr worked alone. His work was typically pinched and pulled, pleated, crumpled, dented, and folded. Lizards and worms were often applied to the ware, each with detailed, expressive features. He was well recognized, however, for his glazes, especially those with a metallic patina. The ware was marked with his name, alone or with 'Biloxi' added. Ohr died in 1918. Our advisor for this category is Fer-Duc, Inc.; whose address is listed in the Directory under New York.

Bowl, gr/gun metal, pinched-in face in front/dimples, 3x5" **1,300.00**
Bowl, gr/pk/bl/red froth, closed-in rim, 4x6" **950.00**
Bowl, lt brn/gr gloss w/brn specks, tortured top, 2x5" **650.00**
Bowl, rust/brn bsk, deeply folded/pinched free-form, 6", EX **1,700.00**
Bowl vase, tan bsk, deep twist, 1 side rim ruffled, 3½x6" **700.00**
Cup, gun-metal drip/brn-gr, asymmetrical hdls, 4½x6¼" **1,800.00**
Mug, puzzle; dk brn speckled/gun metal, 4x5" **550.00**
Pen holder, long-eared mule on flat base, 2½", NM **600.00**
Pitcher, puzzle; gulf shore cvg on tan, holes at top, 8" **2,700.00**

Vase, olive, sienna and burnt umber, indented bulbous base with pleated and flared rim, stamped mark, 5⅞", $1,980.00.

Vase, bl gloss w/gr splashes over red clay, folded rim, 5" **1,800.00**
Vase, blk, tan int, waisted w/row of dimples, rim folds, 4½" **1,100.00**
Vase, blk matt, folded lip/crimped neck, symmetrical, 3½x4" .**2,500.00**
Vase, blk to brn gloss, crimped rim, 4¾" **900.00**
Vase, brn gloss w/dk brn & yel spots, bulbous bottom, 3x3½" **400.00**
Vase, brn speckled, deep long folds/dimples, 5x5" **2,800.00**
Vase, dk gr drip on leathery dk bl, lg dimples, crimped, 6" **1,800.00**
Vase, dk purple above purple semi-matt, waisted/crimped, 5" .**2,400.00**
Vase, feathered gr/gun metal on tan, cone w/bulb top, 8x3" **850.00**
Vase, gr gloss w/matt gun-metal mottle, squat gourd, 3x4" **1,200.00**
Vase, gr/gun-metal mottle, rolded rim, cvd band, 5x3" **900.00**
Vase, lt bsk w/sm glaze drops, deep twist/cvg in body, 7x5" **750.00**
Vase, lt gr/purple volcanic, can neck/angle shoulder, 4" **1,900.00**
Vase, marbleized gun metal/rust/clear, ripped/folded rim, 4" ...**1,000.00**
Vase, red mottle, cup form above angle shoulder, ped ft, 5" **2,300.00**
Vase, red/gr/dk bl/wht mottle, baluster w/flared rim, 5½" **1,600.00**
Vase, red/tan bsk w//blk highlights, pinched/folded, 5x7" **3,750.00**
Water jug, bsk, ring hdl atop, ovoid, 9x6" **325.00**

Old Ivory

Old Ivory dinnerware was produced during the late 1800s by Herman Ohme, of Lower Salzbrunn in Silesia. The patterns are referred to by the numbers stamped on the bottom of many items. (Though not every piece is numbered, the vast majority bears the tiny blue fleur-de-lis/crown mark with Silesia or Germany beneath. Handwritten numbers signify something other than pattern.) Patterns #16 and #84 are the easiest to find and come in a wide variety of table items. Values are about the same for both patterns. Other floral designs include pink, yellow, and orange roses; holly; and lavender flowers — all on the same

soft ivory background. The ware was not widely distributed; its two main distribution points were in Maine and, to a lesser extent, Chicago. Our prices are intended to represent a nationwide average, though you may have to pay a little more in some areas. Novice collectors should be aware of copy-cat versions from the turn of the century that are much heavier and of a coarser material. They are marked 'Old Ivory' without the blue trademark. They are not included in this listing.

Basket, #201, 3½x8½x5" **250.00**
Bowl, #122, poppies, dbl hdls, oval, 12½x8" **150.00**
Bowl, #75, 9½" **115.00**
Bowl, berry; #15, master+6 sm **295.00**
Bowl, berry; #75, 5½" **38.00**
Bowl, vegetable; #22, Holly, 9½" **195.00**
Cake plate, #6, 10" **75.00**
Cake plate, Clarion, pk & yel roses, hdld **165.00**
Celery tray, #10, daisies, 11½" **85.00**
Celery tray, #15, 11½" **95.00**
Celery tray, roses, #16, 11½" **95.00**
Chocolate pot, #16 or #84 ....**450.00**
Chocolate set, #11, pot+6 c/s **800.00**
Chop plate, #11, 13" **185.00**
Chop plate, #15, 13" **250.00**
Chop plate, #16 or #84, 13" dia **325.00**
Cracker jar, #16 or #84, squatty, hdls **425.00**
Creamer, #118 ....**85.00**
Creamer & sugar bowl, #16 or #84 ....**225.00**
Demitasse set, #28, pot+6 c/s+cr & sug **975.00**
Jam jar, #200 ....**295.00**
Mayonnaise, #16 or #84, w/undertray, gold & floral border **285.00**
Muffineer, #16 or #84 ....**395.00**
Pickle dish, #15, oval, 6½x4¼" **45.00**
Plate, #16 or #84, 6¾" **27.50**
Plate, #16 or #84, 7½" **50.00**
Platter, cold meat; #15, extended self hdls, 11¼x8" **200.00**
Relish, #8, rectangular **85.00**
Shakers, #16 or #84, pr **125.00**
Shakers, #75, pr **135.00**
Spoon rest, #200, flat, cutout for hanging **95.00**
Tea tile, #16 or #84 ....**225.00**
Toothpick holder, #16 or #84 ....**200.00**

Old MacDonald's Farm by Regal

Located in Antioch, Illinois, the Regal China Company has been in business since 1938. Products of interest to collectors are James Beam Decanters, cookie jars, salt and pepper shakers and similar novelty items. The Old MacDonald's Farm series listed below is becoming especially collectible. Our advisor for this category is Joyce Roerig, author of *The Collector's Encyclopedia of Cookie Jars;* she is listed in the Directory under South Carolina.

Butter dish, cow's head **235.00**
Canister, Cookies, lg **350.00**
Canister, flour, cereal, coffee, or cookie; med, ea **235.00**
Canister, pretzels, peanuts, popcorn, chips, tidbits; lg, ea **350.00**
Canister, salt, sugar, or tea, med, ea **235.00**
Canister, soap, lg **350.00**
Cookie jar, barn **275.00**
Creamer, rooster **110.00**
Grease jar, pig **185.00**
Jar, spice; sm **125.00**

Pitcher, milk	450.00
Shakers, boy & girl, pr	80.00
Shakers, churn, pr	80.00
Shakers, feed sacks w/sheep, pr	165.00
Sugar bowl, hen	125.00
Teapot, duck's head	275.00

Old Paris

Old Paris porcelains were made from the mid-18th century until about 1900. Seldom marked, the term refers to the area of manufacture rather than a specific company. In general, the ware was of high quality; characterized by classic shapes, colorful decoration, and gold application.

Compote, openwork fruit, flared rim, gold trim, 1850s	100.00
Creamer, boy's portrait, pk & bl	150.00
Cup & saucer, garden flowers w/gold, scroll hdl, 3½", 4 for	160.00
Figurine, dancing maid, gilt-decor gown, scroll base, 12"	130.00
Pitcher, neoclassical w/roses & gold scrolls, 1830s, 9¼"	325.00
Plate, stag & doe in landscape, sgn Rihouet, ca 1830, 9"	425.00
Platter, fish; forget-me-nots, gold trim, 1840s, 25¼"	200.00
Platter, gold & wht, oval	200.00
Punch bowl, British ship oval reserve w/gold, 1800s, 11"	190.00
Scenter, cavalier on floral Rococo base, 1850s, 12½"	475.00
Tea set, Queen's pattern, ca 1870, 19-pc	250.00
Teapot, gold & wht, ca 1850, 8½"	180.00
Urn, figure scene, bsk cherub faces in sunrays on base, 10½"	400.00
Vase, allegorical, old man carries young lady, 1820, 12½"	900.00
Vase, cupids/maids on blk, ormolu mts, now lamp, 32", pr	650.00
Vase, floral reserves, pear shape, 3 rocaille arms, 1840, 7"	800.00
Vase, potpourri; Rococo form w/florals, w/lid, 1830s, 12½"	1,300.00
Vase, scene on bl, ftd ovoid, 1800s, 10", pr	495.00
Veilleuse, tower form w/mc florals & gold, 1830s, 9½"	450.00

Old Sleepy Eye

Old Sleepy Eye was a Sioux Indian chief who was born in Minnesota in 1780. His name was used for the name of a town as well as a flour mill. The Sleepy Eye Milling Company of Sleepy Eye, Minnesota, contracted the Weir Pottery Company of Monmouth, Illinois, to make steins, vases, salt crocks, and butter tubs which the company gave away to their customers in each bag of their flour. A bust profile of the old Indian and his name decorated each piece of the blue and gray stoneware. In addition to these four items, the Minnesota Stoneware Company of Red Wing made a mug with a verse which is very scarce today.

In 1906 Weir Pottery merged with six others to form the Western Stoneware Company in Monmouth. They produced a line of blue and white ware using a lighter body, but these pieces were never given as flour premiums. This line consisted of pitchers (five sizes), steins, mugs, sugar bowls, vases, trivets, and mustache cups. These pieces turn up only rarely in other colors and are highly sought by advanced collectors. Advertising items such as trade cards, pillow tops, thermometers, paperweights, letter openers, postcards, cookbooks, and thimbles are considered very valuable. The original ware was made sporadically until 1937. Brown steins and mugs were produced in 1952.

Barrel, flour; orig paper label, 1920s	935.00
Barrel, grapevine-effect banding	1,500.00
Bread scraper	450.00
Butter crock, Flemish	625.00
Calendar, 1904, NM	375.00
Calendar, 1904, VG	150.00

Cookbook, EX	185.00
Cookbook, Indian on cover, Sleepy Eye Milling Co, 4¾x4"	70.00
Cookbook, loaf of bread shape, EX	115.00
Cookbook, loaf of bread shape, NM	310.00
Cookbook, sq	100.00
Coupon, for ordering cookbook	60.00
Dough scraper, tin/wood, To Be Sure, EX	435.00
Fan, Indian chief, die-cut cb, 1900	220.00
Flour sack, cloth, mc Indian, red letters	345.00
Flour sack, paper, Indian in blk, blk lettering, NM	125.00
Ink blotter	125.00
Label, barrel end; mc Indian portrait, 16", NM	160.00
Label, egg crate; Indian chief in color, 1930s, 9x11"	32.00
Label, egg crate; unused	22.50
Letter opener, bronze	900.00
Match holder, pnt	1,875.00
Match holder, wht	1,050.00
Milk carton	22.50
Mirror, advertising, 1935	45.00
Mug, bl & wht, 4¼"	220.00
Mug, verse, Red Wing, EX	1,625.00
Paperweight, bronzed company trademk	560.00
Pillow cover, Sleepy Eye & tribe meet President Monroe	750.00
Pillow cover, trademk center w/various scenes, 22", NM	750.00
Pitcher, #1, 4"	185.00
Pitcher, #2	250.00
Pitcher, #3, rare	315.00
Pitcher, #3, w/bl rim	1,375.00
Pitcher, #4	400.00
Pitcher, #5	435.00
Pitcher, bl & gray, 5"	235.00
Pitcher, bl on cream, 8", M	345.00
Pitcher, gold & brn, 1981	160.00
Pitcher, standing Indian, good color, #5 size	1,560.00
Plaque, plaster bust of Old Sleepy Eye in wood fr, 33x25"	385.00
Postcard, colorful trademk, 1904 Expo Winner	185.00
Ruler, wooden	500.00
Salt crock, Flemish, 4x6½"	560.00
Sign, self-fr tin, Old Sleepy Eye Flour, 20x24"	2,500.00
Sign, tin litho die-cut Indian, ...Flour & Cereals, 13½"	1,650.00
Spoon, demitasse; emb roses in bowl, Unity SP	105.00

Indian-head spoons, set of six, $150.00 each with original wrapping.

Spoon, Indian-head hdl	125.00
Stein, bl & wht, 7¾"	625.00
Stein, brn, 1952, 22-oz	435.00

Stein, brn & wht	1,125.00
Stein, brn & yel, Western Stoneware	1,125.00
Stein, cobalt	1,000.00
Stein, Flemish	595.00
Stein, ltd edition, 1979-84, ea	125.00
Sugar bowl, bl & wht, 3"	750.00
Thermometer, front rpl	400.00
Tumbler, etched, 1979 commemorative	32.00
Vase, bl & wht, good color, 9"	530.00
Vase, brn on yel, rare color	1,000.00
Vase, Indian & cattails, Flemish, 8½"	470.00
Watch fob, Sleepy Eye Mills, Indian, M	62.50

O'Neill, Rose

Rose O'Neill's Kewpies were introduced in 1909 when they were used to conclude a story in the December issue of *Ladies' Home Journal.* They were an immediate success, and soon Kewpie dolls were being produced worldwide. German manufacturers were among the earliest and also used the Kewpie motif to decorate chinaware as well as other items. The Kewpie is still popular today and can be found on products ranging from Christmas cards and cake ornaments to fabrics and wallpaper.

Our advisor for this category is Denis C. Jackson who is listed in the Directory under Washington. In the following listings, 'sgn' indicates that the item is signed Rose O'Neill. Unsigned items are of little interest to collectors. Items marked 'Germany' are sometimes reproductions.

Bell, Kewpie figural, brass	85.00
Book, Biography of a Boy, O'Neill illus, 1910	45.00
Book, Hickory Limb, Fillmore John Lane, NY, 1910	25.00
Book, Kewpie Primer, Rose O'Neill illus, 118-pg, EX	10.00
Book, Sing a Song of Safety, B&WS	35.00
Booklet, Jell-O Girls Entertain, O'Neill illus, 1920s, EX	30.00
Card, Christmas; Kewpie, lacy, fold-out, pre-1920	18.00
Clock, jasper, Kewpie, sgn O'Neill	325.00
Color book, Kewpies, Saalfield, 1962, M	25.00
Cookbooklet, Jell-O, What 6 Famous Cooks Say, 1912	45.00
Kewpie, bean bag body, 10"	45.00

Kewpie, bisque, Hero, attired as the Kaiser, molded clothes, very rare, 7", $2,000.00.

Kewpie, bsk, Blk Hottentot, 5"	500.00
Kewpie, bsk, Blunderboo, on stomach, sgn, 4"	400.00
Kewpie, bsk, Confederate Soldier, sgn, 4½"	700.00
Kewpie, bsk, Farmer, sgn, 4"	495.00
Kewpie, bsk, Guitar Player, sgn, 3½"	400.00
Kewpie, bsk, Japan, 2"	45.00

Kewpie, bsk, Japan, 5"	95.00
Kewpie, bsk, jtd shoulders & hips, pnt shoes & socks, 5"	545.00
Kewpie, bsk, jtd shoulders & hips, 4"	465.00
Kewpie, bsk, jtd shoulders only, 1-pc body, bl wings, 1½"	125.00
Kewpie, bsk, jtd shoulders only, 1-pc body, bl wings, 6"	200.00
Kewpie, bsk, sgn on ft, eyes to right, 9"	330.00
Kewpie, bsk, Thinker, sgn, 4"	425.00
Kewpie, bsk, Traveler, tan or blk suitcase, sgn, 3½"	325.00
Kewpie, bsk, w/dog Doodle, sgn, 3½"	2,200.00
Kewpie, bsk, w/drawstring bag, sgn, 4½"	600.00
Kewpie, bsk, w/outhouse, sgn, 2½"	1,200.00
Kewpie, bsk, w/Teddy bear, sgn, 4"	750.00
Kewpie, bsk, w/umbrella & dog, sgn, 3½"	2,300.00
Kewpie, bsk head, glass eyes, cloth body, mk, 12", minimum	2,700.00
Kewpie, bsk head, jtd toddler, glass eyes, O'Neill/JDK, 10"	4,200.00
Kewpie, bsk head, pnt eyes, cloth body, mk, 10"	2,400.00
Kewpie, bsk shoulder head, cloth body, 6"	600.00
Kewpie, celluloid, jtd shoulders, w/sticker, 3"	60.00
Kewpie, celluloid, w/sticker, 22"	900.00
Kewpie, celluloid, w/sticker, 5"	90.00
Kewpie, cloth, clothes form body, face mask, Krueger, 8"	165.00
Kewpie, cloth, 1-pc, clothes, Krueger, 12"	265.00
Kewpie, cloth, 1-pc, Cuddles Kewpie, Krueger, 7", M	165.00
Kewpie, cloth, 1-pc stuffed body & limbs, Krueger, 15"	165.00
Kewpie, compo, jtd shoulders, hips & neck, 9"	200.00
Kewpie, compo, jtd shoulders only, 9"	135.00
Kewpie, hard plastic, jtd shoulders, neck & hips, 1950s, 12"	250.00
Kewpie, red plush w/vinyl mask, Knickerbocker, 1960s, 6"	60.00
Kewpie, vinyl, jtd shoulders, hip & neck, 12"	125.00
Kewpie, vinyl, jtd shoulders only, 9"	55.00
Kewpie, vinyl, Ragsy, 1-pc, molded-on clothes, 1964, 8"	60.00
Kewpie, vinyl, Thinker, 1-pc, sitting, 1971, 4"	15.00
Kewpie, vinyl head & limbs, cloth body, 16"	200.00
Letter opener, Kewpie figural hdl	65.00
Magazine, Puck, O'Neill 'Sure to Enjoy It' mc cover, 1901	95.00
Match holder, 3 Kewpies, scrolls, bsk &/or pot metal, sgn	400.00
Note paper, Kewpie, sgn Rose O'Neill, MIB	20.00
Ornament, wedding cake; Kewpie couple, musical base, 1930s	275.00
Paperweight, sulfide, Kewpie	100.00
Plate, Kewpies, sgn Rose O'Neill, Royal Rudolstadt, 6¼"	125.00
Soap, Kewpie figural, 4", M	85.00
Talcum container, Kewpie, celluloid or tin, 7" to 8", ea	225.00
Tea set, Kewpies, c Mrs Rose O'Neill Wilson, Bavaria, 6-place	745.00
Tie tac, Kewpie	25.00
Valentine, Kewpie, fold-out, lacy, sgn, pre-1930	15.00

Onion Pattern

The familiar pattern known to collectors as Onion acquired its name through a case of mistaken identity. Designed in the early 1700s by Johann Haroldt of the Meissen factory in Germany, the pattern was a mixture of earlier Oriental designs. One of its components was a stylized peach, which was mistaken for an onion; as a result, the pattern became known by that name. Usually found in blue, an occasional piece may also be found in pink and red. The pattern is commonly associated with Meissen, but it has been reproduced by many others including Villeroy and Boch and Royal Copenhagen.

Blue Danube is a modern line of Onion-patterned dinnerware produced in Japan and distributed by Lipper International of Wallingford, Connecticut. 125 items are available in porcelain; it is sold in most large stores with china departments.

Bouillon cup & saucer, Meissen	45.00

Bowl, berry; Xd swords, 5¼" **40.00**
Bowl, notched corners, Xd swords, sq, 9" **275.00**
Bowl, sq, Meissen in oval, #19, 8½", pr **200.00**
Cache pot, gold borders, Meissen, 1890s, 5½" **225.00**
Cake plate, 10" dia **150.00**
Canister, Zucker, stenciled, ped base **65.00**

Casserole, Johnson Bros., England, with lid, $165.00.

Coffeepot, graniteware **50.00**
Coffeepot, 1800s, 9½" **375.00**
Compote, rtcl bowl, Meissen, 8½x9½" **325.00**
Creamer, Meissen, 3½" **50.00**
Dish, leaf shape, w/hdls, Xd swords, 3½" **75.00**
Dish, shell shape, Meissen, 1900, 7¾", pr **220.00**
Jar, instant coffee; Japan **20.00**
Letter opener, brass blade, Germany **35.00**
Masher, lg **165.00**
Pestle **145.00**
Plate, dinner; 1900s, 10½" **70.00**
Plate, lattice edge, Meissen, 11½" **165.00**
Plate, Meissen, 6¼" **28.00**
Plate, Meissen, 9½" **59.00**
Plate, sq, Meakin, 7" **30.00**
Platter, scalloped oval, 1880s, Xd swords, 23x18" **500.00**
Reamer, red, old, unmk Germany **100.00**
Salt box, rnd, wood lid, wall mt, Made in Japan, 7" **95.00**
Sauce boat, Hutschenreuther **30.00**
Shaving mug, w/matching brush **75.00**
Spoon, 10" **85.00**
Sugar bowl, Xd swords **190.00**
Tea set, doll sz, 10-pc **165.00**
Tureen, leaf finial & hdls, Meissen, w/lid, 13½" **600.00**
Tureen, rnd, w/liner, Japan, 9" **30.00**
Tureen, shell hdls, dome lid, 1900, 10½" H **650.00**
Utensil holder, hanging, 15-slot, 5½x12x10" **495.00**
Whisk **100.00**

Opalescent Glass

    First made in England in 1870, opalescent glass became popular in America around the turn of the century. Its name comes from the milky-white opalescent trim that defines the lines of the pattern. It was produced in table sets, novelties, toothpick holders, vases, and lamps.

Acorn Burrs (& Bark), bowl, sauce; bl **40.00**
Alaska, banana boat, vaseline **260.00**
Alaska, butter dish, vaseline **225.00**

Alaska, creamer, bl **75.00**
Alaska, creamer, emerald **55.00**
Alaska, creamer, vaseline **65.00**
Alaska, cruet, emerald **195.00**
Alaska, pitcher, water; bl **385.00**
Alaska, pitcher, water; vaseline **370.00**
Alaska, shakers, bl, pr **100.00**
Alaska, shakers, bl w/HP decor, pr **110.00**
Alaska, shakers, vaseline, pr **90.00**
Alaska, spooner, bl **75.00**
Alaska, spooner, vaseline **65.00**
Alaska, sugar bowl, bl, w/lid **160.00**
Alaska, sugar bowl, vaseline, w/lid **135.00**
Alaska, tray, bl **180.00**
Alaska, tumbler, vaseline **65.00**
Arabian Nights, pitcher, water; bl **275.00**
Arabian Nights, pitcher, water; vaseline **265.00**
Arabian Nights, pitcher, water; wht **210.00**
Arabian Nights, tumbler, cranberry **100.00**
Argonaut Shell, butter dish, bl **295.00**
Argonaut Shell, compote, jelly; vaseline **85.00**
Argonaut Shell, cruet, wht **150.00**
Argonaut Shell, spooner, bl **150.00**
Argonaut Shell, sugar bowl, bl, w/lid **225.00**
Argonaut Shell, tumbler, vaseline **125.00**
Beaded Ovals in Sand, butter dish, bl **270.00**
Beaded Ovals in Sand, creamer, gr **70.00**
Beads & Bark, vase, gr, ftd **55.00**
Beatty Rib, creamer, ind; wht **25.00**
Beatty Rib, sugar bowl, bl **125.00**
Beatty Swirl, butter dish, bl **160.00**
Beatty Swirl, mug, bl **50.00**
Beatty Swirl, pitcher, water; vaseline **170.00**
Beatty Swirl, tray, water; bl **80.00**
Beatty Swirl, tumbler, vaseline **45.00**
Blown Drape, tumbler, gr **40.00**
Boggy Bayou, vase, amethyst **45.00**
Bubble Lattice, butter dish, gr **150.00**
Bubble Lattice, cruet, vaseline **160.00**
Bubble Lattice, finger bowl, gr **30.00**
Bubble Lattice, sugar bowl, wht **65.00**
Bubble Lattice, toothpick holder, gr **240.00**
Bubble Lattice, tumbler, cranberry **95.00**
Buttons & Braids, bowl, wht **35.00**
Buttons & Braids, pitcher, water; bl **175.00**
Buttons & Braids, pitcher, water; gr **175.00**
Buttons & Braids, tumbler, bl **40.00**
Buttons & Braids, tumbler, cranberry **135.00**
Christmas Pearls, shakers, gr, pr **90.00**
Christmas Snowflake, tumbler, bl **85.00**

Christmas Snowflake (Northwood), tumbler, white, $70.00.

Christmas Snowflake, tumbler, cranberry 100.00
Chrysanthemum Base Swirl, bowl, sauce; wht 25.00
Chrysanthemum Base Swirl, butter dish, bl 300.00
Chrysanthemum Base Swirl, pitcher, water; bl 495.00
Chrysanthemum Base Swirl, straw holder, bl 450.00
Chrysanthemum Base Swirl, sugar shaker, bl 190.00
Chrysanthemum Base Swirl, tumbler, bl 80.00
Circle Scroll, compote, jelly; bl 145.00
Circle Scroll, spooner, gr 80.00
Circle Scroll, sugar bowl, gr 210.00
Circle Scroll, tumbler, bl 90.00
Coin Spot, bowl, cranberry, master 60.00
Coin Spot, celery vase, gr 110.00
Coin Spot, compote, bl 50.00
Coin Spot, pitcher, water; gr 130.00
Coin Spot, pitcher, water; rubena 170.00
Coin Spot, pitcher, water; wht 90.00
Coin Spot, sugar shaker, gr 95.00
Coin Spot, tumble-up, cranberry 235.00
Coin Spot, tumbler, bl 40.00
Criss Cross, pitcher, water; cranberry, Consolidated 1,200.00
Criss Cross, sauce, wht, Consolidated 45.00
Daisy & Fern, bottle, scent; cranberry 240.00
Daisy & Fern, creamer, cranberry 195.00
Daisy & Fern, mustard pot, bl 85.00
Daisy & Fern, pitcher, water; bl 225.00
Daisy & Fern, pitcher, water; wht 135.00
Daisy & Fern, shakers, cranberry, 2¾", pr 170.00
Daisy & Fern, sugar bowl, bl 125.00
Daisy & Fern, tumbler, gr 50.00
Daisy & Fern, vase, cranberry 135.00
Diamond Spearhead, celery vase, wht 90.00
Diamond Spearhead, compote, gr, tall 125.00
Diamond Spearhead, compote, jelly; vaseline 100.00
Diamond Spearhead, creamer, bl 90.00
Diamond Spearhead, cup & saucer, vaseline 80.00
Diamond Spearhead, mug, cobalt 70.00
Diamond Spearhead, pitcher, water; bl or vaseline 395.00
Diamond Spearhead, pitcher, water; wht 275.00
Diamond Spearhead, spooner, gr 100.00
Diamond Spearhead, sugar bowl, bl 200.00
Dolly Madison, creamer, gr 90.00
Dolly Madison, spooner, bl 70.00
Dolly Madison, spooner, wht 55.00
Dolly Madison, sugar bowl, bl, w/lid 125.00
Dolly Madison, tumbler, gr 80.00
Double Greek Key, butter dish, wht 210.00
Double Greek Key, celery vase, bl 120.00
Double Greek Key, creamer, bl 110.00
Double Greek Key, shakers, wht, pr 150.00
Double Greek Key, spooner, bl 75.00
Double Greek Key, sugar bowl, bl, w/lid 155.00
Double Greek Key, tumbler, bl 65.00
Drapery, creamer, bl 65.00
Drapery, pitcher, water; bl 175.00
Everglades, bowl, sauce; bl, oval 40.00
Everglades, butter dish, bl 250.00
Everglades, butter dish, vaseline 280.00
Everglades, compote, jelly; gr 125.00
Everglades, compote, jelly; vaseline 115.00
Everglades, creamer, bl 125.00
Everglades, pitcher, water; vaseline 375.00
Everglades, shakers, vaseline, pr 220.00
Everglades, sugar bowl, bl 135.00

Everglades, tumbler, bl 70.00
Fan, butter dish, gr 350.00
Fan, gravy boat, wht 35.00
Fern, finger bowl, bl 55.00
Fern, mustard pot, bl 130.00
Fern, pitcher, bl 225.00
Fern, shakers, wht, pr 90.00
Fern, toothpick holder, cranberry, rare 450.00
Fern, tumbler, cranberry 90.00
Fern, tumbler, wht 30.00
Flora, butter dish, wht 160.00
Flora, compote, jelly; vaseline 115.00
Flora, creamer, vaseline 80.00
Flora, cruet, bl 650.00

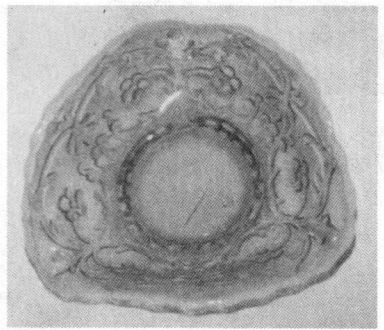

Flora novelty bowl, cobalt, $50.00.

Flora, pitcher, water; bl 475.00
Flora, shakers, vaseline, pr 320.00
Flora, shakers, wht, pr 250.00
Flora, spooner, vaseline 90.00
Flora, sugar bowl, bl, w/lid 120.00
Flora, toothpick holder, vaseline 310.00
Flora, toothpick holder, wht 200.00
Flora, tumbler, bl 75.00
Fluted Scrolls, butter dish, bl 160.00
Fluted Scrolls, cruet, bl 150.00
Fluted Scrolls, pitcher, water; bl 200.00
Fluted Scrolls, pitcher, water; vaseline 195.00
Fluted Scrolls, puff box, vaseline 50.00
Frosted-Leaf & Basketweave, butter dish, vaseline 240.00
Frosted-Leaf & Basketweave, creamer, vaseline or canary 125.00
Frosted-Leaf & Basketweave, spooner, bl 130.00
Frosted-Leaf & Basketweave, sugar bowl, bl 170.00
Gonterman Swirl, butter dish, amber 325.00
Gonterman Swirl, celery vase, bl or amber 185.00
Gonterman Swirl, creamer, bl 80.00
Gonterman Swirl, cruet, bl 300.00
Hobnail, butter dish, bl 250.00
Hobnail, butter dish, cranberry 290.00
Hobnail, creamer, vaseline 95.00
Hobnail, finger bowl, cranberry 90.00
Hobnail, syrup, rubena 325.00
Hobnail, tray, water; bl 160.00
Hobnail, tumbler, cranberry 85.00
Honeycomb, cracker jar, bl 265.00
Honeycomb, pitcher, amber 350.00
Honeycomb & Clover, bowl, master berry; bl 60.00
Honeycomb & Clover, bowl, novelty, wht 26.00
Honeycomb & Clover, butter dish, bl 325.00
Honeycomb & Clover, tumbler, gr 75.00
Idyll, butter dish, gr 365.00
Idyll, creamer, gr 85.00

Idyll, spooner, bl 130.00
Idyll, sugar bowl, gr 160.00
Idyll, toothpick holder, bl 275.00
Idyll, tumbler, bl 80.00
Intaglio, bowl, novelty, bl 45.00
Intaglio, butter dish, bl 400.00
Intaglio, compote, jelly; wht 30.00
Intaglio, creamer, bl 60.00
Intaglio, cruet, vaseline 285.00
Intaglio, shakers, bl, pr 150.00
Intaglio, spooner, wht 35.00
Intaglio, sugar bowl, wht 85.00
Intaglio, tumbler, wht 50.00
Inverted Fan & Feather, creamer, bl 140.00
Inverted Fan & Feather, shakers, bl, pr 250.00
Inverted Fan & Feather, tumbler, bl 85.00
Iris w/Meander, bowl, master berry; gr 80.00
Iris w/Meander, butter dish, bl 300.00
Iris w/Meander, compote, jelly; bl or vaseline 45.00
Iris w/Meander, creamer, bl or vaseline 75.00
Iris w/Meander, pickle dish, wht 50.00
Iris w/Meander, pitcher, water; bl 375.00
Iris w/Meander, spooner, bl 75.00
Iris w/Meander, sugar bowl, gr, w/lid 125.00
Iris w/Meander, toothpick holder, wht 45.00
Iris w/Meander, tumbler, wht 55.00
Iris w/Meander, vase, vaseline 60.00
Jackson, candy dish, vaseline 40.00
Jackson, creamer, bl 75.00
Jackson, pitcher, water; bl 275.00
Jackson, spooner, vaseline 60.00
Jackson, sugar bowl, bl 115.00
Jackson, sugar bowl, vaseline 110.00
Jackson, tumbler, wht 60.00
Jewel & Flower, bowl, novelty, bl 35.00
Jewel & Flower, butter dish, bl 350.00
Jewel & Flower, creamer, wht 55.00
Jewel & Flower, cruet, vaseline 585.00
Jewel & Flower, pitcher, water; bl 650.00
Jewel & Flower, pitcher, water; vaseline 450.00
Jewel & Flower, spooner, bl 95.00
Jewel & Flower, tumbler, vaseline 70.00
Jeweled Heart, bowl, sauce; wht 25.00
Jeweled Heart, butter dish, bl 300.00
Jeweled Heart, compote, gr 120.00
Jeweled Heart, plate, bl, sm 40.00
Jeweled Heart, sugar bowl, gr, w/lid 155.00
Jeweled Heart, tumbler, gr 55.00
Lords & Ladies, butter dish, bl 85.00
Lords & Ladies, creamer, bl 55.00
Lustre Flute, bowl, sauce; bl 25.00
Lustre Flute, butter dish, bl 285.00
Lustre Flute, pitcher, bl 325.00
Lustre Flute, spooner, bl 90.00
Lustre Flute, tumbler, wht 40.00
Over-All Hob, creamer, bl 50.00
Over-All Hob, pitcher, water; vaseline 175.00
Palm Beach, pitcher, water; vaseline 350.00
Palm Beach, spooner, vaseline 125.00
Palm Beach, sugar bowl, bl 175.00
Palm Beach, tumbler, bl 95.00
Palm Beach, wine, vaseline, rare 350.00
Paneled Holly, bowl, master berry; bl 85.00
Paneled Holly, butter dish, bl 300.00

Paneled Holly, shakers, bl, pr 105.00
Paneled Holly, spooner, wht 60.00
Paneled Holly, sugar bowl, bl 225.00
Paneled Holly, tumbler, wht 45.00
Paneled Sprig, cruet, wht 115.00
Paneled Sprig, toothpick holder, wht 70.00
Poinsettia, bowl, fruit; bl 70.00
Poinsettia, pitcher, water; bl, either shape 275.00
Poinsettia, sugar shaker, gr 200.00
Poinsettia, syrup, cranberry 350.00
Poinsettia, tumbler, bl 95.00
Polka Dot, pitcher, water; cranberry 995.00

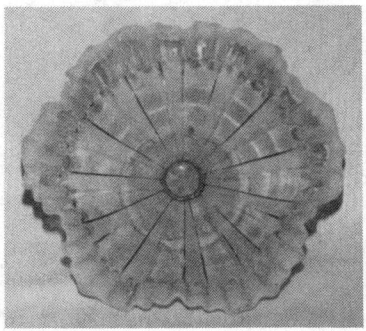

Popsicle Sticks, bowl, blue, footed, $35.00.

Princess Diana, butter dish, bl 90.00
Princess Diana, compote, bl, metal base 120.00
Princess Diana, pitcher, water; vaseline 90.00
Regal, butter dish, bl 245.00
Regal, celery vase, bl 165.00
Regal, celery vase, gr 140.00
Regal, pitcher, gr 285.00
Regal, sugar bowl, bl 195.00
Reverse Swirl, bottle, water; bl 140.00
Reverse Swirl, butter dish, vaseline 165.00
Reverse Swirl, cruet, cranberry 450.00
Reverse Swirl, custard cup, bl 45.00
Reverse Swirl, lamp, cranberry, mini 290.00
Reverse Swirl, pitcher, water; bl 195.00
Reverse Swirl, sugar shaker, vaseline 135.00
Reverse Swirl, tumbler, wht 26.00
Ribbed Spiral, creamer, vaseline 55.00
Ribbed Spiral, pitcher, water; bl 600.00
Ribbed Spiral, shakers, bl, pr 195.00
Ribbed Spiral, toothpick holder, bl 160.00
Ribbed Spiral, vase, vaseline, lg 35.00
Ruffles & Rings, bowl, nut; gr 42.00
Ruffles & Rings, rose bowl, bl 45.00
Scroll w/Acanthus, bowl, master berry; bl 40.00
Scroll w/Acanthus, butter dish, bl 350.00
Scroll w/Acanthus, compote, jelly; gr 40.00
Scroll w/Acanthus, pitcher, water; gr 360.00
Scroll w/Acanthus, shakers, gr, pr 80.00
Scroll w/Acanthus, sugar bowl, gr 135.00
Scroll w/Acanthus, toothpick holder, bl 200.00
Scroll w/Acanthus, tumbler, gr or vaseline 70.00
Seaweed, butter dish, cranberry 350.00
Seaweed, pitcher, water; bl 310.00
Seaweed, syrup, wht 115.00
Shell, Beaded; sugar bowl, bl 185.00
Shell, Beaded; toothpick holder, gr 500.00
Shell, Beaded; tumbler, gr 85.00

Spanish Lace, bottle, scent; bl 175.00
Spanish Lace, bride's basket, cranberry, either sz 160.00
Spanish Lace, creamer, bl 80.00
Spanish Lace, cruet, bl 230.00
Spanish Lace, jug, liqueur; cranberry 750.00
Spanish Lace, pitcher, water; cranberry 500.00
Spanish Lace, rose bowl, vaseline 45.00
Spanish Lace, shakers, vaseline, bulbous, 2⅞", pr 160.00
Spanish Lace, sugar shaker, cranberry 180.00
Spanish Lace, tumbler, vaseline 60.00

Spokes and Wheels, square plate, aqua (rare color), $100.00.

Stars & Stripes, pitcher, water; cranberry 975.00
Stars & Stripes, tumbler, wht 60.00
Stripe, pitcher, bl 250.00
Stripe, shakers, vaseline, pr 95.00
Stripe, tumbler, bl 45.00
Sunburst on Shield, bowl, master berry; bl 60.00
Sunburst on Shield, cruet, bl, rare 500.00
Sunburst on Shield, pitcher, water; bl 500.00
Sunburst on Shield, spooner, bl 125.00
Sunburst on Shield, sugar bowl, vaseline 175.00
Sunburst on Shield, tumbler, bl 100.00
Swag w/Brackets, bowl, novelty, vaseline 40.00
Swag w/Brackets, bowl, sauce; gr 26.00
Swag w/Brackets, butter dish, bl 195.00
Swag w/Brackets, compote, jelly; bl 48.00
Swag w/Brackets, creamer, bl 75.00
Swag w/Brackets, creamer, vaseline 70.00
Swag w/Brackets, shakers, vaseline, pr 175.00
Swag w/Brackets, spooner, bl 85.00
Swag w/Brackets, toothpick holder, gr 270.00
Swag w/Brackets, tumbler, gr 60.00
Swirl, pitcher, water; bl 125.00
Swirl, pitcher, water; cranberry 595.00
Swirl, sugar bowl, bl, w/lid 85.00
Swirl, toothpick holder, gr 100.00
Tokyo, compote, jelly; bl 40.00
Tokyo, plate, wht 30.00
Tokyo, sugar bowl, bl 110.00
Tokyo, vase, gr 45.00
Water Lily & Cattails, bowl, master berry; bl 55.00
Water Lily & Cattails, relish, gr, hdls 75.00
Water Lily & Cattails, spooner, amethyst 65.00
Water Lily & Cattails, sugar bowl, gr 140.00
Water Lily & Cattails, tumbler, bl 55.00
Wild Bouquet, bowl, sauce; bl 35.00
Wild Bouquet, butter dish, bl 450.00
Wild Bouquet, compote, jelly, gr 135.00
Wild Bouquet, compote, jelly; bl 150.00
Wild Bouquet, creamer, gr 70.00
Wild Bouquet, shakers, bl, pr 135.00

Wild Bouquet, toothpick holder, gr 400.00
Wild Bouquet, tumbler, bl, rare 125.00
Wild Bouquet, tumbler, wht 22.00
Windows (Swirled), celery vase, bl 75.00
Windows (Swirled), mustard, cranberry 100.00
Windows (Swirled), pitcher, water; cranberry 695.00
Windows (Swirled), plate, cranberry, either sz 200.00
Windows (Swirled), toothpick holder, bl 275.00
Wreath & Shell, bowl, master berry; bl 85.00
Wreath & Shell, bowl, novelty; vaseline 50.00
Wreath & Shell, bowl, sauce; bl 30.00
Wreath & Shell, butter dish, bl 225.00
Wreath & Shell, celery vase, bl 165.00
Wreath & Shell, pitcher, water; wht 170.00
Wreath & Shell, rose bowl, bl 80.00
Wreath & Shell, sugar bowl, cranberry, w/lid 130.00

Opaline

A type of semiopaque opal glass, opaline was made in white as well as pastel shades and is often enameled. It is similar in appearance to English bristol glass, though its enamel or gilt decorative devices tend to exhibit a French influence.

Bottle, scent; bl, gold & wht allover decor, 5" 75.00
Bottle, scent; gr, alabaster base w/gilt mts & Paris litho, 7" 325.00
Bottle, scent; pk, 6⅝", +cut & enameled stopper 125.00
Box, bl w/gold prunus, not hinged, 1½x1½" 60.00
Box, clambroth, egg form w/gilt brass 'nest,' 4" 195.00
Box, pk, gold scrolls, scenic hinged lid, 1¾x2½" 95.00
Compote, clambroth, fancy brass mts, lion finial, 6x4" 245.00

Orientalia

The art of the Orient is an area of collecting currently enjoying strong collector interest, not only in those examples that are truly 'antique' but in the 20th-century items as well. Because of the many aspects involved in a study of Orientalia, we can only try through brief comments to acquaint the reader with some of the more readily available examples. We suggest you refer to specialized reference sources for more detailed information. Our advisor for this category is Clarence Bodine; he is listed in the Directory under Pennsylvania.

See also Canton; Champleve; Cloisonne; Coralene, Oriental; Dragon Ware; Geisha Girl; Imari; Ivory; Kutani; Moriage; Nippon; Noritake; Peking Cameo Glass; Rose Medallion; Satsuma; Soapstone; Thousand Faces.

Key:
Ch — Chinese	FV — Famille Verte
ctp — contemporary	E — export
cvg — carving	hdwd — hardwood
do — door	Jp — Japan
drw — drawer	Ko — Korean
Dy — Dynasty	lcq — lacquer
FJ — Famille Juane	rswd — rosewood
FN — Famille Noire	tkwd — teakwood
FR — Famille Rose	

Blanc de Chine

Bowl, lotus form, 1700s, 3½" 125.00
Figure, Guanyin, goddess on dragon's head w/scepter, 10" 600.00

Figure, Guanyin, goddess w/jeweled garlands, 1800s, 10½" 800.00
Wine cup, jue form, vertical posts, 3 slub ft, 6" 600.00

Blue and White Porcelain

Box, dragon chases flaming pearl, 4-tier, w/lid, 8¾" H 400.00
Jar, dragon encircles tapered ovoid form, 1800s, 12½" 400.00
Pilgrim flask, bats among peach branches, ca 1900, 9⅝" 715.00
Plate, dragon chases jewel amid cloud scrolls, 1800s, 10⅜" 500.00
Plate, E, fisherman/pine/crane in landscape, 1600s, 9¾" 400.00
Tureen, peony/pine/etc, bombe form, pierced lid, 1700s, 11½" H ..770.00
Vase, birds in continuous panel, baluster form, 1800s, 18½" 990.00
Vase, figures in country, scrolling hdls, ca 1900, 12" 650.00
Vase, figures in river landscape, baluster, 1800s, 7¼" 500.00
Vase, figures/dwellings in landscape, baluster, 1800s, 22¾" 415.00
Vase, floral/bird panels, lion finial, Kangxi, 10¼", EX 400.00
Vase, florals/much foliage, globular bottle form, 1900, 8¼" 440.00
Vase, lotus blossoms, slender ovoid form, 1900s, 12⅛", pr 350.00
Vase, scholars in garden, baluster form, 1800s, 17¼" 500.00

Bronze

Abumi, silver inlay dragon & clouds, Tokugawa, 11" L, pr 770.00
Bowl, Koryo style, coin-shaped roundel, low, Ko, 6¼" 500.00
Censer, archaistic cicadas, animal-head hdls, 1800s, 12" 525.00
Censer, lotus form w/raised veins, rtcl lid, Meiji, 7¼" 825.00
Incense burner, Ming style, silver inlay scenes, Meiji, 19" 1,875.00
Suiban, 4 cloud supports, animal-mask hdls, Meiji, 18" 440.00
Vase, baluster form w/mixed metal inlay, Meiji, 9½" 330.00
Vase, gold inlay flecks, waisted, 4 ring hdls, 1800s, 9½" 825.00
Vase, hu shape, waisted neck, tubular hdls, 1800s, 14⅜" 400.00
Vase, trumpet neck, animal-head loop hdls, Ch, 13½" 550.00

Celadon

Celadon, introduced during the Ching Dynasty, is a green-glazed ware developed in an attempt to imitate the color of jade. Designs are often incised or painted on over glaze in heavy enamel applications.

Bowl, blk & wht florals, wht floral int, Koryo Dy, 5¼" 550.00
Bowl, floral medallion, deep, short ring ft, Ming Dy, 12½" 1,000.00
Bowl, imp/inlay florals, octagonal, Koryo Dy, 4½" 385.00
Bowl, lotus, blk & wht slip on gray-gr, rpr, Ko, 8¼" 550.00
Bowl, lotus & flowering leaf scrolls, Ko, rpr, 7⅛" 800.00
Cup, Anhua decor on bell shape, ring ft, Qianlong, 4" 415.00
Dish, bl, dragon panel, key fret band, Qianlong mk, 10⅝" 500.00
Figure, crane stands on fungus, brn/bl trim, 1900s, 16", pr 1,800.00
Incense burner, olive, glossy, tripod base, Ming Dy, 14" 1,200.00
Pot lid holder, octagonal w/4 cabriole legs, 1700s, 3" 110.00
Shrimp dish, FR, bird & butterfly decor, 9¾", EX 440.00
Vase, figures in garden, raised hdls, 1800s, 17½", pr 1,045.00
Vase, floral panels, scepter hdls, Qianlong mk, 9⅛" 825.00
Vase, scenic reserves (2), stick neck, 1800s, 15½" 1,100.00

Furniture

Armchair, Huanghuali yoke-bk w/calligraphic decor, 44", pr ..4,950.00
Bench, rswd, cvd crest w/lotus, medallion marble inset bk, 65" ..1,000.00
Cabinet, pnt deer in landscape, 3-drw, 2-door, Ko, 25x25" 335.00
Cabinet, 2 full-length doors, Jachimu, 1700s, 57x32x17" 1,650.00
Cabinet, 3 spindle tiers, X-braces, 2-door/2-drw, Ch, 66" 1,875.00
Commode, coromandel style, lcq/cvd giltwood, 1800, 44½" 1,000.00
Cupboard, 2 lg doors, flanged apron, red lcq, 1900, 80x43" 6,000.00

Desk, 8 panel doors, ped ends w/fretwork, 1800s, 32x53x25" ..2,500.00
Screen, 6 cvd figural panels w/calligraphy, lcq wood, 66x97" 700.00
Shelf, tkwd w/nacre inlay around base, Ch, 22x16x7" 160.00
Stand, cvd tkwd, Ch, wear, 28½x19¾x14½" 165.00
Stool, cane seat in molded fr, Huanghuali, 20x24x24", pr 4,125.00
Table, cvd tkwd, Ch, 28¼x19¾x14", nesting set of 4 ....330.00
Table, mah jong; wood, rotating top, Hung Mu, 36" sq 200.00
Table, rswd/tkwd, abalone shell inlay, Ch, 16x48x18" 125.00
Table, tkwd, cvd apron, claw & ball ft, 20x28"+4 stools 325.00
Table, tkwd, much cvg, 3-drw, dk finish, Ch, 32x30x38" 360.00

Hardstones

Green jade bowl carved as a lotus leaf with ducks, late 19th century, 6½" long, on hardwood stand, $750.00.

Jade, gr, plaque, ethereal landscape, 11"+rtcl wood stand 1,750.00
Jade, lt gr w/dk gr patches, vase, hu shape, 1800s, 5¼" 1,200.00
Jade, milky-wht w/brn inclusions, Guanyin w/vial, 1900, 7" 500.00
Jade, wht, pendant, axe form w/cvd dragon crest, 1700s, 2½" 495.00
Jade, wht, plaque, landscape in clouds, rtcl, 1800s, 3" W 300.00
Jade, wht opaque, plaque, archaistic blade form, 5¼", pr 330.00
Jadeite, gr, pin, phoenix form w/gold clasp, 2⅜" 415.00
Jadeite, lav, vase, mask & ring hdls, w/lid, 4¾" 1,045.00
Nephrite, celadon w/dk gr inclusions, tray, flower form, 9½" 360.00
Nephrite, lt gr w/brn inclusions, phoenix w/peach branch, 5" 770.00
Nephrite, wht, plaque, convex oval w/relief-cvd gourds, 4¾" 385.00
Rock crystal, phoenix w/head over wings, 1800s, 7⅝", pr 440.00
Rose quartz, vase, temple jar form, ca 1900, 5¼" 330.00

Inro

Lcq, blk, landscape reserves, 4-case, Meiji, 3" 220.00
Lcq, gilt & silver, hawk on prunus tree, 4-case, 1800s, 3⅛" 800.00
Lcq, gold, continuous landscape, 2-case, 1800s, 2¾" 750.00
Lcq, gold & silver, flying bird, 3-case, Meiji, 2¾" 1,650.00
Lcq, gold & silver, landscape, 5-case, 1800s, 2¾" 935.00
Lcq, gold & silver, mums, canted corners, 4-case, 1800s, 2¾" 770.00
Wood, ebonized, sages in landscape, 3-case, 1800s, 3" 650.00
Wood, legend front panels, wave border, 1-case, 1800s, 2" 800.00

Lacquer

Lacquerware is found in several colors, but the one most likely to be encountered is cinnabar. It is often intricately carved, sometimes involving hundreds of layers built one at a time on a metal or wooden base. Later pieces remain red, while older examples tend to darken.

Basin, multi-dmn family crest, gilt hiramaki-e, 1800s, 24" 550.00
Bowl, gilt, lozenge diaper lattice, w/lid, Meiji, 8¾" 2,000.00
Box, dragons/snake/tortoise MOP inlay on red, 4¼x10" 175.00

Box, gold, temple buildings in landscape, Jp, 2¼x4x5¼" 2,500.00
Box, letter; gilt scenes on blk, early 1800s, EX 450.00
Box, peacock & paulownia MOP inlay on blk, int tray, 16x14" .250.00
Box, tamabuchi form, silver-inlay reserve, Meiji, 2x5⅜x4" 5,500.00
Karabitsu, blk, ribbed sides, 4-ftd, w/lid, Meiji, 13¼" 500.00
Screen, blk w/ivory inlay, figures in garden, Jp, 38x48x16" ...3,000.00
Sword stand, gold & silver, floral diapering, Meiji, 20" L 1,650.00
Tea caddy, E, genre scenes in gilt panels, 1830s, 4x8¾" 935.00
Tray, cranes in landscape, blk/gold/silver, Meiji, 17x16" 1,000.00

Netsukes

A netsuke is a miniature Japanese carving made with two holes
called the Himitoshi, either channeled or within the carved design. As
kimonos (the outer garment of the time) had no pockets, the Japanese
man hung his pipe, tobacco pouch, or other daily necessities from his
waist sash. The most highly valued accessory was a nest of little drawers
called an Inro, in which they carried snuff or sometimes opium. The
netsuke was the toggle that secured them. Although most are of ivory,
others were made of bone, wood, metal, porcelain, or semiprecious
stones. Some were inlaid or lacquered. They are found in many forms;
figurals the most common, mythological beasts the most desirable.
They range in size from 1" up to 3", which was the maximum size
allowed by law. Many netsukes represented the owner's profession, religion, or hobbies. Scenes from the daily life of Japan at that time were
often depicted in the tiny carvings. The more detailed the carving, the
greater the value.

Careful study is required to recognize the quality of the netsuke.
Many have been made in Hong Kong in recent years; and even though
some are very well carved, these are considered copies and avoided by
the serious collector. There are many books that will help you learn to
recognize quality netsukes, and most reputable dealers are glad to assist
you. Use your magnifying glass to check for repairs. In the listings that
follow, netsukes are ivory unless noted otherwise; 'stain' indicates a
color wash.

Cicada w/wings folded bk, boxwood, blk pigment, 1800s, 1¾" ...220.00
Elder grooming, long kimono, boxwood, Ryukei, late 1800s, 1" .330.00
Hotei exposing stomach, holds lg sack, 1800s, 1½" 385.00
Karashishi beast w/paw on ball, curly mane, 1¼" 495.00
Karashishi perches on bearded sage, 1800s, 2¾" 465.00
Laozi in flowing robe sits on ox, legs form Himitoshi, 2¾" 3,850.00
Rat w/chestnut, tail curled over body, boxwood, 1⅛" 385.00
Turtle w/smaller turtle on bk, boxwood, Meiji, 1½" 550.00
Youth kneels & lifts Okame mask, stain, Ryo, 1800s, 1⅛" 1,650.00

Porcelain

Chinese export ware was designed to appeal to Western tastes and
was often made to order. During the 18th century, vast amounts were
shipped to Europe and on westward. Much of this fine porcelain consisted of dinnerware lines that were given specific pattern names. Rose
Mandarin, Fitzhugh, Armorial, Rose Medallion, and Canton are but a
few of the more familiar.

Bowl, Ch'ien Lung, hunt scenes, old rstr, 6½x16" 10,750.00
Bowl, E, mc grapes/staff/hat/horn/medallions/flag, 6¼" 75.00
Bowl, E, mc Oriental figures, prof rstr, 9¼" 200.00
Bowl, E, mc urn & flowers, 3 repeats, rstr, 10⅜" 350.00
Bowl, FR Narcissus, Daoist immortals on turq, Daoguang, 8" .1,650.00
Bowl, FV, animal-head loop hdls, tripod base, w/lid, 10½" 550.00
Bowl, salad; Bl Fitzhugh, hairline, 9¾" 990.00
Candlestick, E, bl & red armorial decor w/gold, 6⅜" 400.00
Figure, E, rooster on base, turq/violet yel, 1900s, 15", pr 500.00

Hot water pot, E, Arms of Smale, ca 1800, 9¼" 650.00
Jar, E, Oriental scenes, baluster form, 15½", pr, EX 400.00
Jar, FR, lotus petals/peony/vines, w/lid, 1900s, 18½", pr 880.00
Jardiniere, FR, flowering plants, lappet border, 1800s, 12" 825.00
Jardiniere, FR, genre scene, hexagonal, 6 sm ft, 8" 550.00
Mug, E, 8 figures in scene, mc, prof rpr, 1-pt 175.00
Pitcher, orange bird & butterfly, 1800s, 9¾" 880.00
Plate, Bl Fitzhugh, 9¾" 110.00
Plate, E, romantic landscape, sepia w/gold, 7⅝" 250.00
Plate, Fitzhugh, armorial, rtcl rim, unicorn crest, 10¼" 470.00
Plate, Rose Canton, 1800s, 9¾", pr 550.00
Plate, soup; Bl Fitzhugh, 9", 9 for 600.00
Platter, Bl Fitzhugh, pierced inset liner, gold trim, 17¾" 1,100.00
Platter, Bl Fitzhugh, 13½" 300.00
Platter, Bl Fitzhugh, 18", EX 475.00
Platter, Bl Fitzhugh, 1800s, 17" 800.00
Platter, Bl Fitzhugh, 21", EX 825.00
Punch bowl, Canton FR, gilt-metal mts, 1800s, 15" on stand .1,200.00
Punch bowl, E, FJ w/medallions, Rose Canton border, 15½" ...1,650.00
Punch bowl, E, orange bird & butterfly, CH, 1800s, 14¼" 1,870.00

Segmented condiment tray, Chinese Export, late 1700s, held in wooden stand, 12¼" diameter, $1,450.00.

Tea caddy, E, gilt decor w/cypher, 1800s, 5" 360.00
Teapot, Rose Canton, w/butterfly, orig basket & lid, 6½" 175.00
Tureen, Bl Fitzhugh, armorial crest of Beale, 1800s, 10¾" 1,980.00
Tureen, Canton FR, alternating reserves, w/lid, 1800s, 13" 350.00
Undertray, Canton Rose, butterfly, 8½", EX 100.00
Vase, FN Rouleau, mythical animals, sq, rnd rim, 1800s, 20" ..3,300.00
Vase, FN Rouleau, songbirds on branches, tubular neck, 18" ..1,045.00
Vase, FR, court scenes/birds/etc, trumpet form, 1800s, 15" 1,050.00
Vase, FR, landscape panels, iron red & gilt ground, 9⅝" 600.00
Vase, FR, peony in peach branch, stick neck, ftd, 20" 5,225.00

Pottery

Figure, Earth Guardian on haunches, Sancai glaze, Tang Dy, 29" ..880.00
Figure, horse on plinth, unglazed, Tang Dy, 13½" 2,500.00
Jar, bl souffle, short neck, metal mts, w/lid, 1700s, 25" 1,100.00
Jar, gr w/silver irid, ovoid, wide rim, Han Dy, 4¾" 715.00
Jar, storage; gr, rolled rim, sloped shoulder, Han Dy, 12¼" 1,100.00
Tile, roof; Quan Ti on horse in clouds, late 1800s, 23" 550.00
Vase, Banko, contorted face form, gray ware, 1920s, 2½" 115.00
Vase, bl souffle, waisted, ovoid, flared ft, drilled, 17½" 330.00
Vase, sang de boeuf, baluster form, red to wht, 15" 440.00

Rugs

The 'Oriental' or Eastern rug market has enjoyed a renewal of interest in recent years as collectors have become aware of the fact that some of the semiantique rugs (those sixty to one hundred years old) may be had at a price within the range of the average buyer.

Key:
mdl — medallion   dmn — diamond

Afshar, flowerheads on navy, red border, 1870s, 72x56" 1,100.00
Afshar, mc boteh on red, ivory meander border, 1900s, 104x53" ...825.00
Baluch, dmn lattice on mc geometrics, boteh border, 75x38" 660.00
Baluch, mc tree of life on apricot, red border, 64x33" 330.00
Baluch, octagons/rosettes on bl, red crab border, 72x42", EX 550.00
Bidjar, mdl/spandrels, rosette border, 1890s, 84x50" 1,450.00
Chinese, floral design & ivory border on med bl, 36x138" 220.00
Gendje, mc mdls on red, star border, 1890s, 75x46" 1,320.00
Heriz, floral columns on red, floral border, 1930s, 105x29" 1,045.00
Heriz, hexagonal mdls on rust, bl border, 134x112" 3,500.00
Heriz, mc mdls/pendants on red, turtle border, 128x98" 1,760.00
Heriz, mc palmettes on red, bl spandrels/border, 79x54" 1,200.00
Heriz, mdl on red, dk bl border, early 1900s, 144x96" 2,975.00
Heriz, mdl on terra cotta, dk bl border, 1900s, 141x116" 3,025.00
Heriz, polygon columns on brn-red, gold border, 108x31" 715.00
Karabagh, mdl on rust-red, bl-gr border, l890s, 86x60" 1,650.00
Karabagh, 4 mdls/mc animals on bl, leaf border, 136x60" 900.00
Karachoph Kazak, 8-sided mdls/sqs on teal, 1890s, 92x66" 450.00
Karadja, mc mdls on rust-red, bl border, 1930s, 46x38" 715.00
Karadja, mdls on rust-red, bl border, 1930s, 126x34" 660.00
Kazak, bl sqs inset w/dmns on red, bl polygon border, 84x48" .1,200.00
Kazak, mc hexagonal mdls on navy, dmn border, 104x44" 990.00
Khamseh, mdls on rust, star border, ca 1900, 74x63" 500.00
Kuba, mc mdls on navy bl, aubergine border, 1900s, 74x48" 550.00
Kurd, mdl columns, 5-color, 1900s, 110x64" 500.00
Kurd, stepped mdl on navy, lt bl border, 78x52" 935.00
Kurd, 8-sided mdls on tan, rosette/leaf border, 75x42" 550.00
Marasali, abrashed red w/striped boteh border, 1890s, 57x46" 990.00
Qashqai, mdls/animals/birds on bl, leaf border, 106x56" 715.00
Serapi, mc floral mdl on rust, turtle border, 150x84" 2,650.00
Shirvan, gold field w/lattice, ivory border, 54x40" 880.00
Shirvan, Lesghi stars on bl, ivory border, 1870s, 60x38" 660.00
Shirvan, mc lattice/rosettes on violet w/leaf border, 50x42" 600.00
Tekke, mc columns & guls on rust, octagon border, 44x38" 715.00

Snuff Bottles

The Chinese were introduced to snuff in the 17th century, and their carved and painted snuff bottles typify their exquisite taste and workmanship. These small bottles, seldom measuring over 2½", were made of amber, jade, ivory, and cinnabar; tiny spoons were often attached to their stoppers. By the 18th century, some were being made of porcelain, others were of glass with delicate designs tediously reverse painted with minuscule brushes sometimes containing a single hair. Copper and brass were used but to no great extent.

Agate, blossoming peony branches in deep relif, lapis stopper 500.00
Agate, tan w/swirling dk brn, gr quartz stopper, 1800s 220.00
Amber w/eng figure, horn top, 3½" 130.00
Clear glass overlaid w/woven straw, ivory collar, screw top 330.00
Cloisonne, lotus blossoms, flattened ovoid, jade stopper 500.00
Copper, HP Oriental scenes, 2½" 125.00
Cvd agate, gr jade top, 2⅞" 286.00
Gr jadeite, flattened vasiform w/parrot hdls, duck stopper 225.00
Gr tourmaline, cvd as fish w/boy on bk, amethyst stopper 440.00
Hornbill, landscape panel w/pavilions, w/stopper, 1800s 825.00
Malachite, cvd trees & figures, 2½" 215.00

Molded porc, dragon & flaming jewel, red/blk, red stopper 715.00
Molded porc, lotus leaf/buds, 4-color, purple glass stopper 400.00
Moss agate, ovoid, gr glass stopper, 1800s 660.00
Peking glass, red o/l, carp swimming, gr glass stopper, 1800s ...1,100.00
Peking glass, red o/l, sages on bridges, gr glass stopper 990.00
Peking glass, wht opaque w/Oriental relief, loose cap, 3" 300.00
Peking glass, wht w/mottled gr & tan, 2¾" 95.00
Peking glass bl o/l, birds on prunus branches, 1880s, 5⅞" 300.00
Porc, dragon/cranes/clouds HP w/gold, gr glass stopper 400.00
Porc, monkeys in trees, underglaze bl & red, glass stopper 400.00
Rock crystal, bat cvgs, ovoid form, gr hardstone stopper 330.00
Rvpt acrobats on stage, glass stopper, 1750-1850 ....335.00
Soapstone, brn shaded to wht w/relief cvg, 3" 60.00

Textiles

Badge, rank; flowers/bats/scrolls embr, 1800s, 12x12" 440.00
Cape, priest's, cranes/clouds embr on peach silk, 1900, 57" 800.00
Cover, silk brocade w/dragons chasing pearls, lined, 54x49" ...1,500.00
Jacket, florals & butterflies embr on bl silk, 1800s, 40" 700.00
Jacket, Kesi dragon & jewel amid clouds embr, 1800s, 29" 1,540.00
Needlework picture on silk, young lady/old man, 12x12", EX 75.00
Panel, alter; dragon & peonies embr on red silk, 1800s, 70¼" 400.00
Panel, lohan/tiger/tree embr, brocade border, 1800s, 61x35" 495.00
Panel, pine tree & flowered foliage embr on bl silk, 37x37" 500.00
Robe, dragon & jewels embr on purple brocade, 1800s, 56" 440.00
Robe, dragon & pearls embr on bl gauze, 1800s, 54" 1,450.00
Robe, dragon embr & gold couched on red-brn, 1800s, 43" 1,200.00
Robe, dragon/jewel/bats, gold couched on red, 1880s, 44" 1,550.00
Robe, floral-pattern rondels embr on silk gauze, 1800s 660.00

Robe, gilt embroidery dragon and pearl on blue silk with phoenix birds, bats and other symbols, Chinese, late 1800s, $1,000.00.

Robe, priest's, Buddha on throne embr on satin, 1700s, 95" 660.00
Vest, dragons/jewels embr on satin, Kesi mandarin sqs, 1800s .1,450.00

Woodblock Prints, Japanese

Carp amid waterweeds, Taito II, oban tate-e 440.00
Crane stands on pine in silhouette, Hiroshige, kakemono-e 715.00
Hawk feeding young in pine, Kunyoshi, kakemono-e 1,500.00
Nude arranging hair before window, Hakuho, neo ukiyo-e 600.00
Okubi-e of a bijin, Kiyochika, oban tate-e triptych 330.00
Peacock preening on rock amid peonies, Hiroshige, kakemono-e ..880.00
Pontoon Bridge at Sano, Hokusai, oban yoko-e, trimmed 330.00
Waterfall in Mtns of Izu, Hiroshige, oban tate-e 1,750.00
Woman w/umbrella in snow storm, att Kunisada, 9½x14" 135.00

Miscellaneous

Bowl, copper w/brass rim/ft, mc dragons, gr int, 3⅞x9" 85.00
Cvg, wood, dbl dragons, EX detail, China, 1920s, 13x18½" 250.00

Okimono, ivory, ball form w/12 cvd animals, Meiji, 2⅛" **660.00**
Okimono, ivory, Chinese sage at wine bbl, 4½", EX **275.00**
Okimono, ivory, Jo (spirit) disguised as old man, 1950s, 5¾" **275.00**
Tsuba, CI w/gold o/l of insects, 1800s, 2½" oval **1,100.00**
Tsuba, silver o/l, 2 karako by riverbank, sgn, Meiji, 2¼" **1,500.00**

Orrefors

Orrefors Glassworks was founded in 1898 in the Swedish province of Smaaland. Utilizing the expertise of designers such as Simon Gate, Edward Hald, Vicke Lindstrand, and Edwin Ohrstrom, it produced art glass of the highest quality. Various techniques were used in achieving the decoration. Some were wheel engraved; others were blown through a unique process that formed controlled bubbles or air pockets resulting in unusual patterns and shapes. Our advisor for this category is Abby Malowanczyk; she is listed in the Directory under Texas.

Bowl, male nudes, ftd, sgn/#d, 5" **285.00**
Bowl, 4 panels w/nudes, Gate, #107, 7¾", +underplate **1,800.00**
Decanter, Susanna bathing, Old Men watching, #1230 ....**690.00**
Vase, amber, GUX1460/3, 1936 ....**125.00**
Vase, Ariel, gr, geometrics, Ingeborg Lundin, 1970, 6" **1,200.00**
Vase, Ariel, 2 lg trees, lime/gr, Alberius, U-form, 8" **1,430.00**
Vase, Graal, diver/mermaid in gr, #301-B, lt stain, 5½" **415.00**
Vase, Graal, fish/seaweed, E Hald, spherical, 5" **690.00**
Vase, gray, PU3634, 1960 ....**125.00**
Vase, gray, Sven Palmquist, #2632/128, 1960, 6½x4½" **150.00**

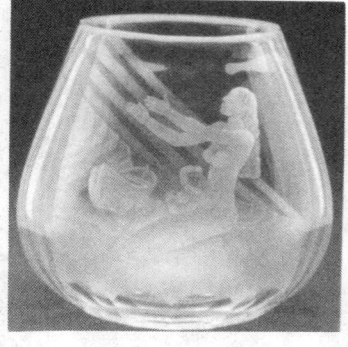

Vase, engraved nude mother and child, boat beyond, signed Gate, #2632, D9 (1970 revision of a 1941 design) A.S., 8¾", $850.00.

Vase, nude diver/waves/bubbles, blk ft, Lindstrand, 11" **935.00**
Vase, nude male diver, Lindstrand, #1348, 12" **1,950.00**
Vase, nude/2 birds, Palmquist/#2327RB-5, 11x6x3¾" **200.00**
Vase, sailboat/waves, Lindstrand, #1402, 11" **1,495.00**

Ott and Brewer

The partnership of Ott and Brewer began in 1865 in Trenton, New Jersey. By 1876 they were making decorated graniteware, parian, and 'ivory porcelain' — similar to Irish belleek though not as fine and of different composition. In 1883, however, experiments toward that end had reached a successful conclusion, and a true belleek body was introduced. It came to be regarded as the finest china ever produced by an American firm. The ware was decorated by various means such as hand painting, transfer printing, gilding, and lustre glazing. The company closed in 1893, one of many that failed during that depression. In the listings below, the ware is belleek unless noted otherwise. Our advisor for this category is Mary Frank Gaston; she is listed in the Directory under Texas.

Bouillon, Cactus, gold thistles & hdls, w/underplate, mk **400.00**

Bowl, gold florals & leaves, scalloped, 2 mks, 2x4¾" **195.00**
Cake plate, Tridacna, gold decor, rare, 9½" **300.00**
Creamer, gold florals, branch hdl, 4" **225.00**
Cup & saucer, gold paste flowers, thin **145.00**
Cup & saucer, gold paste flowers, 2½", 5½" dia **220.00**
Egg fr, gold paste flowers/sponged gold, ped ft, dolphin finial **950.00**
Ewer, gold stylized leaves, cactus hdl, 8½" **1,100.00**
Pitcher, mc morning-glories, gold leaves, mk, 5¼x10½" **1,800.00**
Pitcher, pk w/gold water lilies & leaves, mk, 8¼x6½" **1,400.00**
Plate, pk lustre w/gold rim, 6¾" **125.00**
Shoe, appl bow, sponged gold, 7½" **700.00**
Teapot, Tridacna, yel w/gold, wht loop hdl, mk, 4" **300.00**
Vase, gold paste florals on matt, short ped ft, 6½" **585.00**
Vase, gold paste leaves & butterfly on matt, hdls, 5½" **585.00**

Overbeck

The Overbeck Studio was established in 1911 in Cambridge City, Indiana, by four Overbeck sisters. It survived until the last sister died in 1955. Early wares were often decorated with carved designs of stylized animals, birds, or florals with the designs colored to contrast with the background. Others had tooled designs filled in with various colors for a mosaic effect. After 1937, Mary Frances, the last remaining sister, favored handmade figurines with somewhat bizarre features in fanciful combinations of color. Overbeck ware is signed 'OBK,' frequently with the designer's and potter's initials under the stylized 'OBK.'

Brooch, blond in full skirt, 4-color, 2" dia **250.00**
Figurine, Colonial girl, hoop skirt, mc **310.00**
Figurine, robin w/wings spread, feeding 4 chicks in nest **1,100.00**
Figurine, squirrel w/nut, floral base, 2½" **195.00**
Jardiniere, repetitive flowers, gr-brn on tan, 5x7", NM **4,400.00**
Vase, floral panels, gr on tan, sgn E&F, cylindrical, 5¾" **1,500.00**
Vase, people carrying flowers, yel/bl on pk, MF, 8", EX **3,100.00**
Vase, wide stylized cloud/rain band on speckled brn, 8¾x5" ...**4,600.00**
Vase, 4 panels w/sharp geometrics, bl/grn matt, sgn, 5x6" **1,400.00**

Overshot

Overshot glass is characterized by the beaded or craggy appearance of its surface. Earlier ware was irregularly textured, while 20th-century examples tend to be more uniform.

Basket, amethyst to clear, ruffled, clear twist hdl, 6¼x5" **120.00**
Basket, apricot to clear, crimped, Sandwich, 6x6" **150.00**
Basket, yel opaque w/gold trim, emb swirls, 5½x4" **95.00**
Pitcher, dbl rope hdl, 3-crimp mouth, Sandwich, 1870s, 13" **250.00**
Pitcher, ice bladder, rope hdl, Sandwich, 1870s, 12⅝" **200.00**
Pitcher, Sandwich, 1870-87, 10¼x6" **75.00**
Pitcher, tankard, cranberry, clear reed hdl, rnd mouth, 7¾" **140.00**
Pitcher, tankard, cranberry, clear reed hdl, rnd mouth, 9⅛" **175.00**
Pitcher, wrap-around twist hdl, 12¾" **225.00**
Rose bowl, rubena w/tooled opal flower, gr vine, 5x6½" **150.00**
Vase, pk, appl random amber threading, 5½" **225.00**

Owens Pottery

J.B. Owens founded his company in Zanesville, Ohio, in 1891, and until 1907, when the company decided to exert most of its energies in the area of tile production, made several quality lines of art pottery. His first line, Utopian, was a standard brown ware with underglaze slip decoration of nature studies, animals, and portraits. A similar line, Lotus, utilized lighter background colors. Henri Deux, introduced in 1900, featured incised Art Nouveau forms inlaid with color. (Be aware that the Brush McCoy Pottery acquired many of Owens' molds and reproduced a line similar to Henri Deux, which they called Navarre.) Other important lines were Opalesce, Rustic, Feroza, Cyrano, and Mission, examples of which are rare today. The factory burned in 1928, and the company closed shortly thereafter. Values vary according to the quality of the artwork and subject matter. Examples signed by the artist bring higher prices than those that are not signed.

Henri Deux, vase, Nouveau-style face, 8½" 500.00
Matt Gr, mug, sgn Chilcote, #662-10, 6" 150.00
Matt Gr, vase, bud; cherries & leaves, sgn H, 10" 250.00
Matt Gr, vase, classic form w/4 tab ft, integral hdls, 7" 300.00
Matt Gr, vase, floral w/Indian profile on bk, 12" 450.00
Matt Gr, vase, squat bottle in 4 conforming buttresses, 6" 500.00
Mission, vase, Santa Barbara Mission, w/oak stand: 13" 1,750.00

Utopian, vase, shaped rim, 4-footed, #821, 5¼x4½x3⅛", $165.00.

Utopian, vase, daisies, bottle shape, #112, 6" 125.00
Utopian, vase, floral, 3-hdl, 6½" 225.00
Utopian, vase, Indian portrait, pillow form, 12", EX 3,000.00
Utopian, vase, pansies, bulbous, squat, 5" 150.00
Utopian, vase, pansies, paneled, matt, sgn MC, 4x4" 200.00
Utopian, vase, 2 chicks after worm, Timberlake, 16", EX 2,500.00

Pacific Clay Products

The Pacific Clay Products Company got its start in the 1920s as a consolidation of several smaller southern California potteries. The main Los Angeles plant had been founded in 1890 to make kitchen stoneware, ollas, and similar items. Terra cotta and brick were later produced.

In 1932 Hostess Ware, a vividly colored line of dinnerware, was introduced to compete with Bauer's Ring Ware. Coralitos, a lighter-weight, pastel-hued dinnerware line was first marketed in 1937, and a similar but less expensive line called Arcadia soon followed. Art ware including vases, figurines, candlesticks, etc., was produced from 1932 to 1942, at which time the company went into war-related work and pottery manufacture ceased. A limited amount of hand-decorated dinnerware was also made. For further information we recommend *The Collectors Encyclopedia of California Pottery* by our advisor, Jack Chipman; he is listed in the Directory under California.

Coaster, Ring-style 10.00
Cocktail cup 35.00
Coffee cup, Ring-style, lg 25.00
Custard cup, early design 30.00
Egg cup, early design, flat ft 45.00
Goblet 65.00
Jar, w/lid, 5" 75.00

Pie plate, delphinium bl, wood hdl, 11" 80.00
Pitcher, ball jug form, early 60.00
Pitcher, Ring-style, 2-qt 65.00
Plate, child's feeding; 3-compartment, emb bunny border, 9" 80.00
Plate, Plaid, dinner sz 35.00
Plate, Spiral, salad sz 25.00
Shakers, Ring-style, pr 15.00
Teacup & saucer, Ring-style 25.00
Teapot, apricot, ftd, early 150.00
Teapot, long spout, ftd 100.00
Tray, Ring-style, 15" 65.00
Tumbler, 4" 22.00
Vase, bird motif, HP, ca 1939, 8¼" 40.00
Vase, bud; 7" 22.00
Vase, low hdls, 5" 65.00

Paden City

The Paden City Glass Company began operations in 1916 in Paden City, West Virginia. The company's early lines consisted largely of the usual pressed tablewares, but by the 1920s production had expanded to include colored wares in translucent as well as opaque glass in a variety of patterns and styles. The company maintained its high standards of handmade perfection until 1949, when under new management much of the work formerly done by hand was replaced by automation. The Paden City Glass Company closed in 1951; its earlier wares, the colored patterns in particular, are becoming very collectible.

Paden City Glass is not always easily recognized by collectors or dealers, as it was almost never marked. It is believed this was so the glass could be sold to decorating companies. The company assigned both line numbers and names to many of its blanks or sets of glassware. Colors were sometimes given more than one name, and etchings were named as well. All this makes identification of items offered for sale through mail order difficult, and labels prepared by dealers are often confusing.

A review of literature available on Paden City reveals the following names for the company's plate etchings: Ardith; California Poppy; Cupid; Delilah Bird (Peacock Reverse); Eden Rose; Frost; Gazebo; Gothic Garden; Lela Bird; Nora Bird; Orchid (three variations); Peacock and Rose (Peacock and Wild Rose); Samarkand; Trumpet Flower; Utopia. Names given to cuttings made on Paden City blanks are Yorktown and Lazy Daisy. It is not clear whether the names originated with Paden City or with secondary decorating companies.

Our advisors for this category are George and Mary Hurney; they are listed in the Directory under Illinois. (Note: their interest is only in Paden City glassware, not the pottery.) See also Glass Animals; Kitchen Collectibles, Glass.

This list gives company line numbers with corresponding line names:

#69, #69½ — Georgian
#191 — Party
#210 — Regina
#215 — Hotcha
#220 — Largo
#221 — Maya
#300 — Wotta
#411 — Mrs B
#412 — Crow's Foot Square
#890 — Crow's Foot Round
#895 — Lucy
#991 — Penny
#994 — Popeye and Olive
#1503 — Trance

And, finally, a listing of colors with alternate names or descriptive phrases:

Amber — (dull)	Mulberry — amethyst
Cheriglo — (delicate) pink	Opal — opaque white
Cobalt Blue — Royal Blue	Primrose — (amber with reddish
Crystal — (clear, no tint)	tint)
Dark Green — forest green	Red — ruby
Dark Amber — (honey color)	Rose — (dark pink)
Light Blue — Copen, Neptune	Yellow — (pale, soft)

Basket, Trance, #1503, Forest Gr, 7½" 22.00
Bowl, berry; Crow's Foot, red, 5" 5.00
Bowl, console; Blk Forest, pk, rolled edge, +2 candlesticks 255.00
Bowl, console; Crow's Foot, amber, 3-ftd, 11½" 30.00
Bowl, console; Hotcha, amber, 3-ftd, 11½" 35.00
Bowl, console; Maya, bl, 3-ftd, 11½" 55.00
Bowl, Peacock & Wild Rose, pk, rolled edge 80.00
Bowl, vegetable; Crow's Foot, red, oval 29.00
Candlesticks, #117, amber, pr 65.00
Candlesticks, Crow's Foot, cobalt, mushroom, pr 95.00
Candlesticks, Gazebo etch, 2-light, pr 55.00
Candlesticks, Nora Bird, pk, pr 120.00
Candy dish, Cupid, pk, ftd 170.00
Candy dish, Cupid, 3-part 150.00
Candy dish, Vale, #900 ....70.00
Cheese & cracker, Crow's Foot, red 225.00
Compote, Crow's Foot, red, 6⅝" 60.00
Compote, Cupid, pk 80.00
Compote, Luli, red, 7½" 75.00
Compote, Peacock & Wild Rose, gr 75.00
Compote, Peacock & Wild Rose, pk, 6¼" 65.00
Creamer & sugar bowl, Mrs B, red 25.00
Cup & saucer, Crow's Foot, amber 5.00
Cup & saucer, Crow's Foot, red, rnd 17.00
Cup & saucer, Crow's Foot, red, sq 10.00
Cup & saucer, Mrs B, red 10.00

Dresser set, #191 Party, cobalt: Perfume, $65.00 each; Puff box, $35.00; Tray, $30.00.

Ice bucket, Peacock & Wild Rose, gr 95.00
Pitcher, Blk Forest, crystal, 8", 62-oz 175.00
Plate, Crow's Foot, amber, sq, 10¾" 19.00
Plate, Crow's Foot, amber, 6" 2.00
Plate, Crow's Foot, amber, 8" 5.00
Plate, Crow's Foot, red, sq, 6" 4.00
Plate, Crow's Foot, red, sq, 8½" 10.00
Plate, Crow's Foot, red, 6" 8.00
Plate, Crow's Foot, red, 9¼" 33.00
Plate, Mrs B, red, 8¼" 8.00

Platter, Crow's Foot, amber, oval 10.00
Salver, cake; Cupid, pk, ftd 140.00
Salver, cake; Orchid, ftd 27.00
Shakers, Penny Line, amber, pr 10.00
Stem, cordial, Penny Line, red 24.00
Stem, goblet, Penny Line, gr, 6" 12.00
Stem, goblet, Penny Line, red, 4¾" 10.00
Stem, goblet, water; Penny Line, red 19.00
Stem, wine, Fortune, red, #836, 3-oz 12.00
Tray, Ardith, gr, center hdl 60.00
Tray, Crow's Foot, red, center hdl 72.00
Tray, Peacock & Wild Rose, pk, center hdl 90.00
Tray, Swan Neck, Gazebo etch, center hdl 50.00
Tumbler, water; Crow's Foot, amber 35.00
Tumbler, water; Crow's Foot, cobalt 55.00
Tumbler, water; Crow's Foot, red 75.00
Vase, Blk Forest, blk, 10" 110.00
Vase, Blk Forest, gr, 6½" 75.00
Vase, Crow's Foot, red, 8½" 55.00
Vase, Orchid etch, pk, 12" 130.00
Vase, Peacock & Wild Rose, pk, 12" 135.00
Vase, Peacock & Wild Rose, pk, 8½" 140.00
Water set, Crow's Foot, red, pitcher+6 tumblers 350.00

Paintings on Ivory

Miniature works of art executed on ivory from the 1800s are assessed by the finesse of the artist, as is any fine painting. Signed examples and portraits with an identifiable subject are usually preferred.

Marie Antoinette and Beethoven, both in Boulle-style frames, 3¼x2½", $1,000.00 for the pair.

Baby in eyelet dress resting on pillow, metal fr, 3x3½" 225.00
Boudoir scene, sgn Bonnia, 1770, 3½x4⅝" 675.00
Child, cased in gold locket fr, ⅞x1" 250.00
Interior scene, HP, sgn, in ivory fr, 1860s, 5x6" 275.00
Lady, cast metal fr, 3½x2¾" 220.00
Lady, locks of hair on reverse, fr, 2¼x1⅞" 500.00
Lady, oval molded wood fr, 4¾x4⅛" 245.00
Lady, roses in hair, sgn Brun, in gold-filled locket, 2x1½" 200.00
Lady, sgn CT, 16k gold & pearl fr, 1907, 3⅛x2½" 350.00
Lady, sgn Drea, rectangular gilt metal fr 175.00
Lady, watercolor, oval, in leather case, 3¼x2½" 660.00
Lady in bl, att L Sully, early 1800s, 2⅜x1⅞" 350.00
Lady in Empire dress/fancy hair/pearls, sgn, lacy fr, 5⅜" 350.00
Lady in fancy gown & hat before red curtain, fr, 4⅜x3¾" 225.00
Lady in lacy collar, in gold-filled pendant, 1700s, 2½x2" 400.00
Lady in lacy hat, brass fr, 3¾x3" 325.00
Lady in wht gown, sgn Taussins, gutta percha fr, 4½x5" 225.00

Lady on celluloid ivory, wood fr, Mallet, 5x4¾" **40.00**
Lady w/red feather in hair, gold-filled fr, 1700s, 2⅛x1¾" **600.00**
Lady writing letter, Cupid at shoulder, Thamerette, rnd fr **180.00**
Man, eglomise glass, gilt fr, 5x4½" **245.00**
Man, identified, in gold pendant case w/hair, 2½" **5,500.00**
Man, identified, sgn/dtd 1803, in gold-plated fr, 3x2½" **990.00**
Man, watercolor, sgn Ladd, 1800s, 2⅛x1¾" **300.00**
Man, watercolor, unsgn, in gold locket fr, 1¼x⅞" **385.00**
Man, watercolor, unsgn, in leather case, 3¾x3" **525.00**
Man in bl coat, brass locket fr, ca 1800, 2⅞x2" **200.00**
Man in bl coat, 1700s, 2⅝x2" **425.00**
Man in blk coat, rectangular, fr, 1800s, sm **100.00**
Man in brn coat, old blk fr, 6¼x5½" **220.00**
Man in ermine cape, sgn Lagarde, gilt metal fr **400.00**
Man in mc coat & lace jabot, 1700s, 3⅛x2½" **450.00**
Man in uniform, sgn, gilt brass filigree fr, 5½x4¼" **185.00**
Nellie Pye, in scarf w/pearls, sgn Plyman, ivory fr, 3x3½" **150.00**
Nobleman, sgn Donz, wood fr, 1700s, 3⅛x2⅜" **210.00**
Washington, Fr-made for Am, 1860-70, fr **400.00**

Pairpoint

The Pairpoint Manufacturing Company was built in 1880 in New Bedford, Massachusetts. It was primarily a metalworks whose chief product was coffin fittings. Next door, the Mt. Washington Glassworks made quality glasswares of many varieties. (See Mt. Washington for more information concerning their artware lines.) By 1894 it became apparent to both companies that a merger would be to their best interest.

From the late 1890s until the 1930s, lamps and lamp accessories were an important part of Pairpoint's production. There were three main types of shades, all of which were blown: puffy — blown-out reverse-painted shades (usually floral designs); ribbed — also reverse painted; and scenic — reverse painted with scenes of land or seascapes (usually executed on smooth surfaces, although ribbed scenics may be found on occasion). Cut glass lamps and those with metal overlay panels were also made. Scenic shades were sometimes artist signed. Every shade was stamped on the lower inside or outside edge with 1) The Pairpoint Corp., 2) Patent Pending, 3) Patented July 9, 1907, or 4) Patent Applied For. Bases were made of bronze, copper, brass, silver, or wood and are always signed.

Because they produced only fancy, handmade artware, the company's sales lagged seriously during the Depression; and as time and tastes changed, their style of product was less in demand. As a result, they never fully recovered; consequently part of the buildings and equipment was sold in 1938. The company reorganized in 1939 under the direction of Robert Gundersen and again specialized in quality hand-blown glassware. Isaac Babbit regained possession of the silver departments, and together they established Gundersen Glassworks, Inc. After WWII, because of a sharp decline in sales, it again became necessary to reorganize. The Gundersen-Pairpoint Glassworks was formed, and the old line of cut, engraved artware was reintroduced. The company moved to East Wareham, Massachusetts, in 1957. But business continued to suffer, and the firm closed only one year later. In 1970, however, new facilities were constructed in Sagamore under the direction of Robert Bryden, sales manager for the company since the 1950s.

In 1974 the company began to produce lead glass cup plates which were made on commission as fund-raisers for various churches and organizations. These are signed with a 'P' in diamond and are becoming quite collectible. Our advisor for Pairpoint lamps is Daniel Batchelor; he is listed in the Directory under New York. See also Napkin Rings.

Glass

Bowl, floral/fern cutting on amber, ribbed, 11", +4" sticks **325.00**

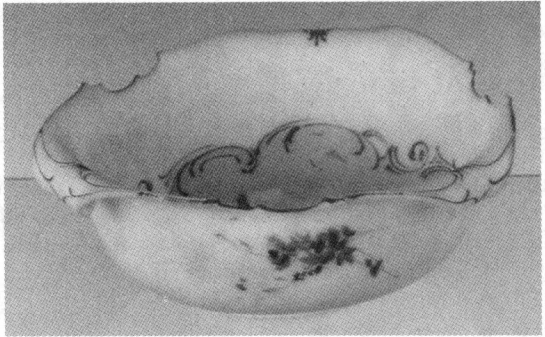

Bowl, painted as Delft, signed, 9½", **$300.00.**

Candlesticks, canary yel w/appl spirals, 10", pr **150.00**
Candlesticks, cobalt, 16", pr **275.00**
Candlesticks, grapes eng on gr, 10½", pr **275.00**
Candlesticks, Venitti design, rosaria & wht spirals, 10", pr **1,500.00**
Tazza, dk amethyst w/vintage etch, w/lid, 6½x8", pr **275.00**
Vase, cobalt lily form, clear bubble knob stem, 13" **235.00**
Vase, lg gold ruby swirls in clear, bubble ball ft, 7x12" **300.00**
Vase, mums, pk & red on gr, 8½" **185.00**
Vase, ruby cornucopia w/clear bubble ball base, Gundersen **435.00**

Lamps

Etch/pnt 12" roses/gilt drape gr Berlin unmk shade; unmk std ...**1,300.00**
Ext/rvpt 16" orchids 8-scallop Murano shade; gilt metal std **2,500.00**
Puffy 13" roses shade; grapes/vines as arms & emb on base **8,200.00**

Puffy 14" squared Devonshire shade hand painted with yellow and red roses on blue and white lattice ground with two hummingbirds in flight; silverplated 2-socket base with foliate designs, 21½", $3,575.00.

Puffy 14" butterfly/roses shaped shade w/gold; mk std **6,500.00**
Puffy 14" floral shade; pyramid base w/4 floral supports **15,400.00**
Puffy 18" Ravena Pilgrims Landing shade; emb SP mk std **8,000.00**
Puffy 8" rose/butterfly shade; SP mk base w/4 paw ft, 16" **4,400.00**
Puffy 8½" Stratford flower shade; silver lotus bud base **2,800.00**
Puffy 9" Stratford roses shade w/blk border; lappet gilt std **2,500.00**
Rvpt 10" swag/urn bottom-flared shade; mahog std w/gilt mts ...**1,100.00**
Rvpt 12" Directorie windmill/houses shade; mk candle base ...**2,200.00**
Rvpt 14" palm trees/sailboat Berkeley shade; hdld urn std **2,300.00**
Rvpt 15" castle/mtns/people cone shade; #3067 'copper' std ...**1,900.00**
Rvpt 15" scenic Carlisle shade; sqd 4-paw mk std **2,250.00**
Rvpt 16" multifloral Directorie shade; unmk candelabrum std ..**5,750.00**
Rvpt 17½" jungle bird Carlisle cone shade; 3-part SP std **6,000.00**

Rvpt 18" shepherd/flock Copley shade sgn Gifford; mahog std ..**3,500.00**

Pairpoint Limoges

Limoges china china blanks were imported from France in strict accordance with Pairpoint specifications. They were decorated by Pairpoint in designs that ranged from simple to elaborate florals and scenics. These are easily identified. Look for the Pairpoint name over a crown with the Limoges name below. You may also find similar ware marked 'Pairpoint Minton.'

Box, jewel; roses, pk & wht on gr, kidney shape, 7½" L **195.00**
Ewer, fuchsia & chrysanthemums, gold scrolls & hdl, 15½" **500.00**
Gravy boat, mc flowers/emb scrolls on wht, ornate hdl, +tray **180.00**
Pitcher, pk rose near hdl on beige w/lt & dk gr, 6½" **600.00**
Plate, oyster; mc floral w/much gold on wht, 6 for **650.00**
Vase, poppies, pk & wht on gr mottle, 2-part, 24" **950.00**
Vase, spider mums, red & pk on gr, 8½" **195.00**

Paper Dolls

No one knows quite how or when paper dolls originated. One belief is that they began in Europe as 'pantins' (jumping jacks) and were frequently worn as part of the costume. By the late 1790s, they were being mass-produced. During the 19th century, most paper dolls portrayed famous dancers and opera stars such as Fanny Elssler and Jenny Lind. In the late 1800s, the Raphael Tuck Publishers of England produced many series of beautiful paper dolls; retail companies used them as advertisements to further the sale of their products. Around the turn of the century, many popular women's magazines began featuring a page of paper dolls.

Most familiar to today's collectors are the books with dolls on cardboard covers and clothes on the inside pages. These made their appearance in the late 1920s and early thirties. The most collectible (and the most valuable) are those representing celebrities, movie stars, and comic-strip characters of the thirties and forties.

Authority Mary Young has compiled an informative book, *Collector's Guide to Paper Dolls*, with current prices; you will find her address in the Directory under Ohio. When no condition is indicated, the dolls listed below are assumed to be in mint, uncut, original condition. Cut sets will be worth about half price if all dolls and outfits are included and pieces are in very good condition. If dolls were produced in die-cut form, these prices reflect such a set in mint condition with all costumes and accessories.

Amy Carter, MIB **20.00**
Ann Sheridan, cut, EX **30.00**
Annie Oakley, 1947, complete **40.00**
Baby Sparkle Plenty, uncut, 1948, NM **65.00**

Betty Grable Paper Dolls — A Look Thru Book, Merrill, 1953, book: 10½x14", cut, EX, $45.00.

Barbie & Friends, All Sports Tournament, Whitman, 1981, NM ...**12.50**
Blondie in the Movies, Whitman #979, book type, 1941, EX **95.00**
Bob Hope & Dorothy Lamour, uncut **225.00**
Buffy, uncut, 1969, M **40.00**
Career Girls, flocked, uncut, 1944, NM **30.00**
Carmen Miranda, cut, EX **60.00**
Clarke's Minuet Series, 9 dolls & piano, EX **95.00**
Deanna Durbin, Spanish, 1940s, EX **55.00**
Deanna Durbin, uncut, 1940s, M **185.00**
Dinah Shore, cut, EX **32.00**
Dionne Quints, complete, uncut **225.00**
Double Wedding, Merrill #3472, partially punched/cut, 1939, EX ..**75.00**
Elizabeth Taylor, cut, EX **65.00**
First Ladies of the White House, Saalfield #2164, 1937, EX **75.00**
Gilda Radner, NM **25.00**
Gone w/the Wind, Merrill #3405, complete/cut clothes, '40, EX ...**165.00**
Gone w/the Wind, uncut, #3405, 1940, M **350.00**
Grace Kelly, uncut, M **195.00**
Greer Garson, uncut, NM **90.00**
Gulliver's Travels, Walt Disney, 1940s, M **135.00**
Hedy Lamar, cut, EX **45.00**
Hollywood Fashion, cut, Saalfield #2242, 1939, EX **25.00**
Jeanette MacDonald, cut, EX **30.00**
Judy Garland, Whitman #999, complete, 1940, EX **120.00**
Lana Turner, uncut, NM **130.00**
Laugh-In, 1969, M **35.00**
Lennon Sisters, cut, 1957, EX **35.00**
Liberty Military Uniforms, WWII, M **55.00**
Margaret O'Brien, uncut, NM **145.00**
Marilyn Monroe, uncut, M **285.00**
Mary Poppins, uncut, 1964, M **30.00**
Munsing Miss Molly, 1909, 16x11", M **35.00**
My Doll Family w/Their Own Home, 1955, NM **65.00**
Nurses Three, 1964, M **15.00**
Oklahoma, uncut, NM **85.00**
Partridge Family, M **25.00**
Patti Page, cut, EX **18.00**
Raggedy Ann, uncut, 1980, M **5.00**
Rhonda Fleming, uncut, M **75.00**
Ricky Nelson, uncut, M **150.00**
Rock Hudson, uncut, M **75.00**
Roy Rogers Corral, uncut **95.00**
Shirley Temple, #1761, uncut, 1937, NM **275.00**
Shirley Temple, uncut, 1942, M **250.00**
Shirley Temple, uncut, 1959, M **40.00**
Shirley Temple, uncut, 1970s, NM **20.00**
Sleeping Beauty, partially cut, 1959, EX **35.00**
Snow White & 7 Dwarfs, 1939, M **200.00**
Sweetheart Paper Dolls, uncut, 1943, NM **25.00**
Three Sisters, Whitman #969, Sally, Sue & Dot, complete, VG ..**25.00**
Trudy in Her Teens, Merrill #4829, 1941, mini sz, M **75.00**
Tyrone Power & Linda Darnell, Merrill, 1941, EX **70.00**
Waltons, Whitman, uncut, 1975, M **15.00**
Welcome Back Kotter, MIB **30.00**
Whopper, Whitman, 16 dolls in orig box, 1940s, complete **25.00**
1964 World's Fair, uncut, M **35.00**

Paperweights

All paperweights listed here are made totally of glass (including the lampwork flowers, fish, birds, snakes, lizards, and millefiori rods). The only elements that are not glass are the clay sulfides encased within some of the Baccarat and St. Louis weights. Today, antique weights (1845 to ca 1870s) and those made by contemporary artists attract the most attention and are the most expensive. Lower-priced 'gift' weights come from American glasshouses and studios, China, Murano, Italy, and Scotland. But because of the expenses involved in their manufacture (fuel, material, and labor), even they are not cheap. There is an international association of paperweight collectors with many state and regional chapters. (For information see Clubs, Newsletters, and Catalogs in the Directory.) Many books are currently available on the subject of paperweights. For the beginner we recommend *All About Paperweights* by L.H. Selmen.

Probably inspired by the work of Pierre Bigaglia (Venice), the French factories of Baccarat, Clichy, and St. Louis turned their attention to paperweight-making in the 1840s. They first made millefiori paperweights, the technique a revival of methods used in Alexandria, Damascus, Rome, and Byzantium before the time of Christ. (This art form had faded out but had been revived in 16th-century Venice.) The French Classic period was 1845 to 1860; English (Whitefriars and Bacchus) and American (Sandwich and New England) glasshouses followed their lead about ten years later. Gradually, as the paperweight's popularity declined, production began to wane; Clichy closed in the 1880s, as did a couple American factories. Baccarat made weights as late as 1910; in the '20s and '30s, a worker by the name of Dupont revived the art. Then in the 1950s St. Louis and Baccarat sparked a renewal of interest in weight-making that is still going strong today. Some of the most desirable weights from American artists were made by the Banfords, Randall Grubb, Rick Ayotte, Chris Buzzini, Ken Rosenfeld, Gordon Smith, Paul Stankard, Charles Kaziun (d), Del (d) and Debbie Tarsitano, and the Trabuccos. From Scotland, Paul Ysart (d), Perthshire and Caithness/Whitefriars were also well known.

Note: Prices do not reflect the usual 10% buyer's fee charged by most auction houses. Furthermore, there are many factors which determine value, particularly of antique weights. Auction-realized prices of contemporary weights are usually other than issue price; 'list price' may be for weights issued earlier and reduced for clearance or influenced by market demand and other factors. The competition for antique weights has been increasing dramatically over the last five years. New collectors entering the field have greatly influenced prices. As the numbers of collectors increase, available antique weights decrease per capita, forcing prices upwards. Since the 1930s antique paperweights have steadily increased in value making them one of today's best investments. The dimension given at the end of the description is diameter.

Key:
con — concentric	latt — latticinio
fct — faceted	mill — milleflori
gar — garland	o/l — overlay
grd — ground	pwt — paperweight
jsp — jasper	sil — silhouette

Ayotte, Rick

Berry bouquet on clear grd, 3½"	850.00
Mallard ducks & chick in water w/grass/mushrooms, etc, 4⅜"	1,450.00
Peace rose bouquet w/bluish leaves, 3¾"	900.00
Roses & buds on clear grd, 3¾"	950.00

Baccarat, Antique

Buttercup w/gars, clear star-cut base, 1⅞"	3,400.00
Gridel deer, goat & dog sils on clear, 3⅛"	2,450.00
Louis Napoleon sulfide in clear star-cut base, 2¾"	1,100.00
Mill circles surround center canes w/arrowheads, 3"	1,050.00
Mill w/stars, animals & B/1848, Gridel, 3"	2,200.00

Napoleon III etched into amber-flash base, fct, 3¼"	450.00
Pansy w/bud & leaves on clear star-cut base, 2¾"	900.00

Baccarat, Modern

Butterfly on teal grd, 1971, 3¼"	675.00
Clematis flowers (2) fct on cobalt grd, 1969, 3⅛"	685.00
Dahlia on cobalt grd, 1970, 3⅛"	885.00
Mt Rushmore, fct dbl o/l sulfide, 1976, 4⅛"	600.00
Queen Elizabeth & Prince Philip sulfide on amethyst grd, '53	125.00
12 zodiac sil canes on carpet grd, 1969, 3⅛"	675.00

Banford, Bob

Cherries on branch w/wht latt pcs, 3 to 4"	600.00
Pears & cherries on muslin grd w/2-color torsade, 3 to 4"	800.00
Pk dahlia on wht muslin grd w/pk & bl torsade, 3 to 4"	800.00
Upright flower on latt grd w/torsade, 3"	825.00
2 pears on branch w/veined leaves on latt grd, 3 to 4"	600.00
3 pears on branch w/veined leaves, fct star-cut base, 3 to 4"	750.00
5 mc flowers surround pansy, dmn-cut base, 3 to 4"	2,000.00

Banford, Bobby

Bl & wht complex flower w/3 buds on clear grd, 3¾"	600.00
Bouquet of 2 turq flowers, yel buds & yel knotweed, 3 to 4"	600.00
Cardinal on branch w/buckeye flowers on lt bl grd, 3 to 4"	450.00
Dahlia & buds on dk purple grd, 3¼"	625.00
Flowers, buds & knotweed, amethyst & yel w/blk, 3 to 4"	600.00
Hawthorn bouquet w/6 blossoms+buds, 3 to 4"	600.00
Pk foxgloves w/honeycomb fct on cobalt, 3 to 4"	600.00
3 amethyst flowers, 2 buds, 2 pk knotweeds, 3¾"	700.00
3 butterfly fish w/coral & shell, compound, 3 to 4"	600.00
3 flowers, yel & orange on blk grd, 3 to 4"	600.00

Banford, Ray

Amethyst iris in yel & wht o/l basket, 3 to 4"	1,400.00
Yel iris & buds w/gr leaves on clear grd, 3 to 4"	800.00
Yel-orange iris & buds w/gr leaves on blk, 3 to 4"	800.00
5 pk & wht roses on cobalt grd, 3 to 4"	850.00

Clichy, Antique

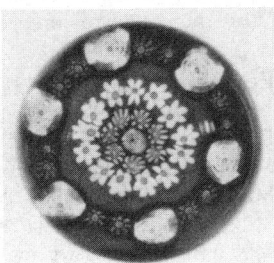

Clichy, patterned concentric millefiori on red ground, 2½", $2,000.00.

Red/wht/bl/gr mill canes in bl & wht stave basket, 2⅞"	1,450.00
Spaced con mill w/red/wht/gr/yel canes on bl grd, 2⅝"	1,200.00
Spaced mill, 2 wht/pk Clichy roses w/in complex canes, 2⅝"	900.00
9 pk roses, con mill on clear, 1¾"	1,400.00

Grubb, Randy

Bl, purple & red dahlia bouquet on clear grd, 3⅜"	375.00

Plum flowers in pk/wht fct o/l, flute cutting on lower half 800.00
Purple dahlia, 1987 ....375.00
Purple grape cluster on clear grd, 1991, 3" 265.00
Red dahlia w/bud, mill gar & star-cut base, 1993 ....700.00
3 grape clusters w/gr leaves in clear w/purple/wht dbl o/l 750.00

Kaziun, Charles

Bl & wht flower & buds on red & wht jsp grd, K cane, 2¼" 320.00
Initial cane amid 7 complex, torsade, turq grd w/mica, 1⅞" 985.00
Purple 5-petal flower & buds on wht grd, K cane, 2¼" 320.00
Roses, w/bud & gold bee on cobalt grd, 2¼" 880.00
Yel & blk ribbon snake on muslin grd, K cane, 2½" 1,050.00
Yel & orange snake on dk gr on opaque w/goldstone, 2¼" 900.00

Lundberg Studios

Lundberg, S; cherry dahlia w/gr stem & leaves on dk bl grd 290.00
Lundberg, S; Japanese bl iris w/sword-like leaves 320.00
Lundberg, S; nasturtium w/bud & leaves on bl & wht grd, 3¼" ..340.00
Lundberg, S; pk & bl fish, plant life on pebble grd 290.00
Lundberg, S; salmon hibiscus w/stamen & leaves on clear 250.00
Lundberg, S; Shamrock Oxalix w/heart-shaped leaves on bl grd ...320.00
Lundberg, S; 2 fish in natural habitat 320.00
Salazar, D; lady slipper on bl grd 285.00
Salazar, D; lady slipper on clear grd, 1991, 3¼" 285.00
Salazar, D; tropical fish, gr sea life, jelly fish on bl grd 290.00
Salazar, D; wht crane & bl sky, 2½" 275.00
Salazar, D; yel Peace rose w/ruffled petals & gr leaves 320.00

New England Glass, Antique

Nosegay w/3 complex canes & 4 leaves w/stem in clear, 1⅞" 375.00
Pear, blown, on clear 'cookie' base, 2¾" 1,175.00
Scramble type w/some complete canes 175.00
Wht cane w/set-ups of aqua/red canes, dbl swirl wht latt grd 400.00
5 pears/4 cherries on latt grd, 3" 850.00
5 pears/4 cherries/leaves in latt basket, sm bubbles, 2½" 650.00

Parabelle

Mc mill in con pattern, 1989, 3" 265.00
Pansy w/in 5 cane rings on cobalt grd, 1991, 2¾" 140.00
Rooster sil cane in con mill w/bl & wht torsade, 1988, 3⅜" 295.00
Wht Clichy-type rose in pattern mill on lime gr grd, 2¾" 165.00

Perthshire

Dragonfly over bouquet, fct, compound, waffle base, '74, 3½" 500.00
Mc butterfly sil cane centers pattern mill, 3⅛" 95.00
Mill, fct dbl o/l close pack, 1981, 2⅝" 450.00
Mill close pack w/in 20 latt twists, 2½" 235.00
Mixed fruits on dbl swirling latt basket, 1980, 1½" 525.00
Pansy, fcts & gars on latt grd, 1971, 2¾" 575.00
Penguin, fct, lt bl o/l, hollow 450.00
Snowflake pattern close-pack canes on wht latt on gr grd, 3½" ..245.00
Wild pansies gars/fct on bl grd, 1985, 3⅛" 325.00

Rosenfeld, Ken

Bouquet, red/violet/bl/yel flowers, plaque type, 3⅜" 800.00
Coleus bouquet of yel & bl on clear grd, 3⅝" 500.00
Floral bouquet on clear grd, 1987, 3" 325.00

Flowers, yel & bl w/lav blooms on earth grd, 3½" 550.00
Flowers & buds, purple w/yel stamens on clear grd, 3¼" 625.00
3 raspberries on stem w/leaves 300.00
5 mc flowers on earth grd w/roots & gr foliage 550.00

Smith, Gordon

Coral snake in complex foliage & grd, 3½" 900.00
Lipstick Tang fish among coral on reef 800.00
Royal Tang fish among coral & helpora, much color 800.00
2 blk raspberries & gr berry w/pk blossom, 3¼" 800.00
2 yel Skunk Anemones among sea anemones & coral on bl grd .800.00
3 dogwood blossoms w/leaves & stem on gr grd 800.00
5 strawberries w/blossoms, earth grd w/straw 1,000.00

St Louis, Antique

Bouquet fct upright, w/torsade on clear star-cut base, 3" 3,550.00
Fruits on dbl latt basket, 2⅝" 2,100.00
Mushroom con pattern w/torsade on clear star base, 3⅛" 3,500.00
Pattern mill on latt grd w/gr/red/yel/bl/wht canes, 2¼" 800.00
Pk dbl clematis w/yel match-head stamen, gr leaves, 2½" 1,450.00
Scramble w/devil cane, 2½" 650.00

St. Louis, Modern

Doily mill on orange grd, rare color, 1972, 3" 485.00
Flower w/5 wht cane petals & 5-leaf bud, pistachio grd, '73 ....350.00
Pear w/2 gr leaves on wht grd, fct top, 1993 ....250.00
Strawberry w/leaves on clear grd, fct star-cut base, 1993 ....250.00
Yel & red apple w/leaves on lt bl grd, top fct, '93, 2½" 250.00
2 cherries & leaves on stem on lt bl grd, fct top, 1993 ....250.00
2 plums on branch w/4 leaves, star-cut base w/top fct 250.00
5 flowers on pk grd, fct 'armour' sulfide, 1979, 3⅛" 450.00

Trabucco, Jon and David

Cherries, buds & blossoms, roots on earth grd, 3¼" 550.00
Con mill of red, wht & bl canes, 3" 350.00
Pk rose & 4 buds w/6 lt bl blooms, 3" 300.00
Raspberries, flowers & buds on clear grd, 3¼" 425.00
Yel 5-petal flower w/2 buds & 5 pk cherries, 3" 300.00
2 upright blk & wht orchids, 3⅛" 400.00

Trabucco, Victor

Butterfly, flowers, buds & berries on clear grd, 4" 950.00
Citron flower w/2 buds, pk & wht on clear grd, 3⅛" 600.00
Raspberries & wht buds on clear grd, 4" 950.00
Yel rose & buds on cobalt, 3⅜" 600.00
2 lg citron flowers & buds in clear, 4" 950.00

Ysart, Paul

Mc mill canes on lt bl jsp grd, early, att, 3" 400.00
Orange fish w/purple fins on bl & wht jsp grd, H cane, 3" 475.00
Wht flower gar on dk gr, 2⅞" 825.00
5 lg complex mill canes spaced w/6 sm on dk bl grd, att, 3" 425.00

Miscellaneous

D'Albret, JF & Mrs Kennedy sulfide, gr o/l w/gold, cut base 250.00
Daum, France; crystal shield w/blk demonic mask, 4x3½" 150.00

Daum, France; snail form, gr/gold-brn mottle, 4¼" 175.00
Ebelhare, Drew; mill canes in pk/lime stave basket, moss grd 185.00
Ebelhare, Drew; Piedouche w/mill & torsades, 2½" 600.00
Hansen, Ron; ring tree, bl poinsettia/gr leaves on tan, 4" 145.00
Manson, Wm; 3 Xmas candles/leaves/mill gar on amethyst, 3½" ..375.00
Maul, Grant; water lily in S Jersey style, 3½" 350.00
Orient & Flume, pk dogwoods, compound design on clear irid, 3" ...300.00
Stankard, P; chokeberry on clear grd, compound, 1976, 1¾" ..1,550.00
Stankard, P; St Anthony's fire, clear ground, compound, 2¾" ...1,275.00
Tarsitano, Debbie; dahlia on clear grd, 3½" 2,150.00
Tarsitano, Delmo; Lizard & flower on sandy grd, 3¼" 1,250.00
Union Glass, red flower w/2 sm bl flowers, inscr/1916, 2¾" 250.00
Whitefriars, mill fct in close pack, 3¼" 300.00
Whitefriars, mill in con pattern, ca 1900, 3½" 215.00

Papier-Mache

The art of papier-mache was mainly European. It originated in Paris around the middle of the 18th century and became popular in America during Victorian times. Small items such as boxes, trays, inkwells, frames, etc., as well as extensive ceiling moldings and larger articles of furniture were made. The process involved building layer upon layer of paper soaked in glue, then coaxed into shape over a wood or wire form. When dry it was painted or decorated with gilt or inlays. Inexpensive 20th-century 'notions' were machine processed and mold pressed. See also Christmas; Candy Containers.

Tray, serpentine molded with painted hunt scene, English, 1800s, on modern stand with serpentine apron, cross stretcher, 20x31x23" overall, $3,000.00.

Box, octagonal, holds 9 sm trays, red & blk w/MOP inlay, 12" 65.00
Cigar case, HP w/dancing couple & flute player, pouch w/in, 5½" L ..185.00
Duck, orig mc pnt, mk Germany on wood base, 4⅝", EX 40.00
Fire screen, painted, butterfly form, 1860, 57" 350.00
Grasshopper, worn mc pnt, glass eyes, leg missing, 7", VG 260.00
Owl, worn orig pnt, edge damage, 14", G 35.00
Rooster, tin tail, mc pnt, EX details, 7½x7½x3⅜" 350.00

Parian Ware

Parian is hard-paste unglazed porcelain made to resemble marble. First made in the mid-1800s by Staffordshire potters, it was soon after produced in the United States by the U.S. Pottery at Bennington, Vermont. Busts and statuary were favored, but plaques, vases, mugs, and pitchers were also made.

Bust, girl w/scarf around head, inscr 'Winter' & J&TB, 8" 95.00
Bust, lady, mk C Delpech Art Union of London 1855, 13", EX .330.00
Bust, maid w/curly hair, low-cut dress, separate base, 22" 600.00
Bust, Shakespeare, circular base, unmk, 7¼x5½" 85.00
Ewer, leaf & grain emb, gr/yel enamel, pewter lid, mk, 9⅛" 185.00
Jug, hunters, wht/lav, April 1847, Alcock, 4½" 100.00
Nude seated on cloth, fish below, Copeland, 12" 535.00

Pitcher, allover emb figures, Jones & Walley, 1842, 8" 100.00
Vase, emb ferns, appl vintage on shoulders, 9" 60.00

Parrish, Maxfield

Maxfield Parrish was a painter and illustrator who began his career in the last decade of the 19th century. His work remained prominent until the early 1940s. His most famous painting, *Daybreak*, was published in print form in 1923 and since then has sold in huge volumn. All prices are for framed prints except for those from the 1960s.

Ad, Broadwater County Creamery..., Sunrise, print, 8½x7" 100.00
Ad, Djer-Kiss, lady among flowers, 1921, fr, 11x15" 145.00
Ad, Fisk Tires, Literary Digest, 1918, 10½x7½", VG+ 25.00
Ad, Hire's Root Beer, Century Magazine, 1921, 8½x6", EX 50.00
Ad, Jello, King & Queen Might Eat..., 1921, 6¾x10", EX 60.00
Ad, Peter Pumpkin for Ferry Seeds, from magazine 135.00
Ad, Royal Baking Powder, blk & red, 8½x6", VG 65.00
Ad, Swift's Ham, Jack Sprat, 1921, fr, 12x14" 150.00
Blotter, for billboard company, scene by MP, 3½x6", EX 40.00
Book, Arabian Nights, Scribner's, 1st edition, 1904, EX 200.00
Book, Arabian Nights, volume w/9 plates, 1941, VG+ 150.00
Book, Coy Ludwig, w/many plates w/sz & numbers, EX 55.00
Book, Golden Age, volume w/18 plates, blk & wht, 1900, EX ...175.00
Book, King Albert's, Dieserai, EX 40.00
Book, Knickerbocker's History NY, Parrish illus, 1915, EX 175.00
Book, Poems of Childhood, Parrish illus, Scribner's, 1904, EX ...200.00
Book, Tanglewood Tales, Wonderbook, 1910, EX 150.00
Book plate, End, last from Knave of Hearts, fr, 1925, EX 75.00
Book plate, Pool, Villa d'Esta..., Italian Gardens, 8x5", EX 35.00
Calendar, businessman's; Cadmus Sowing, fr, 7x6½", EX 190.00
Calendar, Contentment, complete, 1928, sm, VG+ 250.00
Calendar, Golden Hours, fr, lg, 22x14½", EX 850.00
Calendar, New Moon, complete, 1958, 24x17, NM+ 465.00
Calendar, Solitude, Mazda, complete, 1932, 20x11" 750.00
Calendar, Sunlit Road, Dodge, 1929, 8x5¾", EX 95.00
Calendar, Thy Rocks & Rills, ad/Dental Supply, 15x12", VG 130.00
Calendar, Venetian Lamplighter, complete, 1924, sm, VG+ 250.00
Calendar, Village Brook, complete, ad/J Helwig, 7x6", VG+ 45.00
Calendar print, Dreamlight, fr, 1925, 25x15", NM 620.00
Calendar print, Egypt, fr, 1922, sm, EX 250.00
Calendar print, Mill Pond, 1948, 15x12", EX 130.00
Calendar print, Primitive Man, fr, 1922, sm, EX 200.00
Calendar print, Solitude, antique fr, 1932, sm, EX 200.00
Calendar print, Waterfall, fr, 1931, sm, EX 225.00
Figure, Bandmaster, no baton, GE advertising item 700.00
Magazine cover, Ladies' Home Journal, July 1896, VG+ 75.00
Magazine cover, Wht Birch-Winter, Yankee Magazine, 1935, VG ..35.00
Poster, Thy Templed Hills, 29½x21", NM 430.00
Poster stamp, Brill Brothers, Get the Habit, 1915, 5x6" 65.00
Print, Aladdin, standing w/wizard, 1909, 11x13" 160.00
Print, Atlas, fr, 12x9", VG+ 100.00
Print, Canyon, Rienthal & Newman, orig fr, 15x12", NM 250.00
Print, Cassim in the Caves..., orig label, 11x8¾", EX 120.00
Print, Circe's Palace, 1908, 15½x12½" 125.00
Print, Contentment, ladies on rocks, Mazda, 1928, 9x13" 275.00
Print, Daybreak, orig fr, 18x30", NM 150.00
Print, Dinkey Bird, nude on swing, 1905, 13x17" 250.00
Print, Dreaming, House of Art, orig fr & title, 6x10", EX+ 250.00
Print, Dreaming, nude beneath tree by waterfall, 1928, 22x24" .500.00
Print, Dreamlight, lady on swing, fr, 1925, lg, NM 625.00
Print, Early Autumn, fr, 1939, 16½x13", EX 125.00
Print, Enchantment, lady in moonlight, Mazda, '25, 8½x12" 300.00

Print, Entrance...King of Hearts, fr, 1925, EX 85.00
Print, Evening, nymph by lake at dusk, 1922, 14x17" **265.00**
Print, Evening, 1924, ornate Nouveau fr, 12½x16½" **250.00**
Print, Evening Shadows, farm scene, 1953, 19x23" **475.00**
Print, Florentine Fete, fr, 1916, 8½x14", EX 80.00
Print, Frog Prince, knave & gr frog, 1925, 8x12" 85.00
Print, Golden Hours, Edison/Mazda, 1929, 16x23" **595.00**
Print, Harvest, orig fr & label, 7½x5½", NM 70.00
Print, Hilltop, fr, 12x17½", EX **350.00**
Print, King Pompdebile, w/guards/etc, 1925, 12x14" 90.00
Print, Knave, under oaks near waterfall, '25, 12x14" **220.00**
Print, Lady Violetta, blond lady in long dress, 1925, 12x14" **100.00**
Print, Love's Pilgrimage, couples below balustrade, '12, 8x16" 95.00
Print, Lute Players, c House of Art, fr, 6 10", EX **250.00**
Print, Night in the Desert, 500 made, blk & wht, 18x14", NM **220.00**
Print, Old Glen Mill, mill scene, 1954, 16x19" **375.00**
Print, Path to Home, wintery farm scene, 1950, 11x14" **250.00**
Print, Peace at Twilight, winter scene, 8½x11", EX 130.00
Print, Perfect Day, pond & meadow landscape, 1943, 15x19" **300.00**
Print, Pierrot's Serenade, mandolin player, 1908, 12x14" 140.00
Print, Pierrot's Serenade, 11¼x9¾", EX 90.00
Print, Queen Sulnair summoning her relatives, fr, 12x10" 150.00
Print, Quiet Solitude, woodland scene, 1962, 17x14", EX **210.00**
Print, Romance, antique fr, 14x24", M **550.00**
Print, Rubaiyat, orig fr, 1917, 8x30", EX **450.00**
Print, Sandman, gnome w/sack, castle/moon beyond, '05, 8x11" 115.00
Print, Song of Sixpence, king & queen, 1911, 7x11" 85.00
Print, Spirit of Transportation, orig fr & label, 16x20", EX **650.00**
Print, Stars, 12x20", NM **300.00**
Print, Sunup, farmhouse & pond, 1956, 11x11" 150.00
Print, Thy Templed Hills, 1938, 4x5", EX 50.00
Print, Twilight, old barn, fr, 16x12", EX 150.00
Print, Village Church, fr, 18x9", EX 160.00
Print, Waterfall, fr, 7x10", EX **200.00**
Print, When Day Is Dawning, village scene, 1954, 12x15" 150.00
Print, Winter Sunrise, 8½x11", EX 150.00

Pattern Glass

Pattern Glass was the first mass-produced fancy tableware in America and was much prized by our ancestors. From the 1840s to the Civil War, it contained a high lead content and is known as 'flint glass.' It is exceptionally clear and resonant. Later glass was made with soda lime and is known as non-flint. By the 1890s pattern glass was produced in great volume in thousands of patterns, and colored glass came into vogue. Today the highest prices are often paid for these later patterns flashed with rose, amber, canary, and vaseline; stained ruby; or made in colors of cobalt, green, yellow, amethyst, etc. Demand for pattern glass declined by 1915, and glass fanciers were collecting it by 1930. No other field of antiques offers more diversity in patterns, prices, or pieces than this unique and historical glass that represents the Victorian era in America.

Our advisor for this category is Darlene Yohe; she is listed in the Directory under Arkansas. For a more thorough study on the subject, we recommend *The Collector's Encyclopedia of Pattern Glass*, by Mollie Helen McCain, available from Collector Books. See also Bread Plates; Cruets; Historical Glass; Salt and Pepper Shakers; Salts, Open; Sugar Shakers; Syrups; specific manufacturers such as Northwood.

Note: Values are given for open sugar bowls and compotes unless noted 'w/lid.'

Actress, bread plate, HMS Pinafore scene, 7x12" 75.00
Actress, compote, high std, 10" 95.00
Actress, marmalade, w/lid 115.00

Actress, sauce bowl, frosted, ftd, 5" 20.00
Actress, shakers, orig tops, pr 90.00

Actress

Admiral Dewey, see Dewey; See Also Greentown Dewey
Alabama, celery tray 35.00
Alabama, creamer 42.50
Alabama, shakers, pr 60.00
Almond Thumbprint, goblet, non-flint 15.00
Almond Thumbprint, tumbler, ftd 38.00
Amazon, claret, etched 32.00
Amazon, egg cup 12.50
Amazon, tumbler, etched 22.50
Amberette, see Klondike
Apollo, compote, w/lid, 8¾x4¾" 50.00
Apollo, goblet 30.00
Apollo, plate, sq, 9½" 27.50
Apollo, salt cellar 20.00
Arched Ovals, shakers, gr, pr 48.00
Arched Ovals, wine 15.00
Argus, celery vase, plain base 85.00
Argus, egg cup 25.00
Argus, wine, cut 48.00
Art, bowl, 9¾" 40.00
Art, creamer, regular 48.00
Art, goblet 65.00
Ashburton, decanter, canary yel, flint, orig stopper 950.00
Ashburton, tumbler, ale; flint, 5" 87.50
Ashburton, wine, flint 45.00
Atlas, bowl, 6" 37.50
Atlas, butter dish 48.00
Atlas, sauce bowl, ftd, 4" 15.00
Atlas, tumbler 27.50
Atlas, wine 30.00
Aurora, butter dish, ruby stained 87.50
Aurora, waste bowl 30.00
Austrian, creamer, emerald gr 110.00
Austrian, goblet 38.00
Aztec, champagne 16.00
Aztec, goblet 34.00
Baby Thumbprint, see Dakota
Balder, see Pennsylvania
Baltimore Pear, creamer 28.00
Baltimore Pear, pitcher, water 98.00
Baltimore Pear, plate, 9" 36.00
Bar & Diamond, shakers, orig tops, pr 50.00
Bar & Diamond, tumbler 22.50
Barberry, compote, high std, 8" 37.50
Barberry, tumbler, ftd 22.50
Barley, compote, high std, w/lid, 6" 48.00
Barley, relish, 8½" L 18.00
Barley, wine 38.00

Barred Forget-Me-Not, goblet 40.00
Barrel Huber, see Huber
Basket Weave, creamer, bl 32.00
Basket Weave, mug, 3" 20.00
Beaded Acorn Medallion, sugar bowl, w/lid 42.50
Beaded Band, butter dish 37.50
Beaded Band, relish, sm 15.00
Beaded Grape, bowl, gr, sq, 7¼" 35.00
Beaded Grape, bowl, vegetable; gr, 7⅜" 35.00
Beaded Grape, butter dish, gr, sq 85.00
Beaded Grape, sauce dish, hdls 15.00
Beaded Grape Medallion, celery vase 70.00
Beaded Grape Medallion, goblet, buttermilk 32.00
Beaded Grape Medallion, goblet, lady's 32.00
Beaded Grape Medallion, wine 52.00
Beaded Medallion, butter dish 42.50
Beaded Medallion, compote, low std, w/lid, 8¼" 88.00
Beaded Medallion, egg cup 24.00
Beaded Mirror, see Beaded Medallion
Beaded Swirl, cake stand, emerald gr 48.00
Beaded Swirl, creamer, flat 25.00
Beaded Swirl, pitcher, water; gr 60.00
Beaded Tulip, bowl, oval, 9½" 22.50
Beaded Tulip, goblet 32.50
Beaded Tulip, tray, water 50.00
Bearded Head, see Viking
Bellflower, butter dish, single vine 98.00
Bellflower, champagne, single vine, knob stem 100.00
Bellflower, compote, 4½x8½" 95.00
Bellflower, cordial, single vine, bbl shape 122.50
Bellflower, goblet, single vine 55.00
Bellflower, mug, single vine 235.00
Bellflower, spooner, single vine 45.00
Bellflower, wine, single vine, bbl shape, knob stem 115.00
Bent Buckle, see New Hampshire
Bigler, champagne 98.00
Bigler, decanter, bar lip, 1-pt 60.00
Bird & Fern, see Hummingbird
Bird & Strawberry, butter dish, w/lid 98.00
Bird & Strawberry, creamer 55.00
Bird & Strawberry, cup, w/color stains 37.50
Bird & Strawberry, sugar bowl, w/lid 68.00
Bleeding Heart, goblet, knob stem 32.50
Bleeding Heart, pitcher, water 95.00
Bleeding Heart, spooner 32.00
Bleeding Heart, wine, knob stem 165.00
Block & Fan, carafe 48.00
Block & Fan, finger bowl 50.00
Block & Fan, plate, 10" 40.00
Block & Fan, relish, 11⅛" L 42.50
Blue Jay, see Cardinal Bird
Bohemian, bowl, berry; boat shape, gr 50.00
Bohemian, mug, rose stained w/gold 80.00
Bohemian, tumbler, rose stained 45.00
Bouquet, sugar bowl, w/lid 32.00
Bow Tie, compote, 6½x8¼" 55.00
Bow Tie, creamer 55.00
Bow Tie, pitcher, water 55.00
Bow Tie, salt cellar, master 36.00
Bow Tie, tumbler 60.00
Broken Column, banana stand 115.00
Broken Column, carafe 80.00
Broken Column, tumbler 45.00
Buckle, salt cellar, flat, flint 32.00

Buckle, sugar bowl, w/lid, flint 95.00
Buckle w/Star, celery vase 27.50
Buckle w/Star, compote, 7x8¼" 65.00
Buckle w/Star, pitcher, water 75.00
Buckle w/Star, sauce bowl, flat, 4½" 12.00
Bull's Eye, celery vase, flint 125.00
Bull's Eye, mug, appl hdl, 3½" 100.00
Bull's Eye, wine 60.00
Bull's Eye & Daisy, tumbler, emerald gr 15.00
Bull's Eye & Fan, custard cup 10.00
Bull's Eye & Fan, relish 22.50
Bull's Eye & Fan, tumbler, pk stained 67.50
Bull's Eye Band, see Reverse Torpedo
Bull's Eye in Heart, see Heart w/Thumbprint

Bull's Eye with Diamond Point

Bull's Eye w/Diamond Point, honey dish 32.00
Bull's Eye w/Diamond Point, sugar bowl, w/lid 128.00
Bull's Eye w/Diamond Point, wine 125.00
Button Arches, pitcher, milk; ruby stained 105.00
Button Arches, salt cellar, ind 17.50
Button Panel, pitcher, water 48.00
Cabbage Rose, basket, 12" 130.00
Cabbage Rose, butter dish 65.00
Cabbage Rose, egg cup 40.00
Cabbage Rose, wine 40.00
Cable, celery vase 95.00
Cable, egg cup 45.00
Cable, plate, 6" 75.00
California, see Beaded Grape
Canadian, goblet 55.00
Canadian, wine 55.00
Cane, goblet, amber 35.00
Cane, goblet, vaseline 40.00
Cane, tray, water; bl 55.00
Cape Cod, creamer 36.00
Cape Cod, goblet 48.00
Cape Cod, wine 36.00
Cardinal Bird, goblet 35.00
Cardinal Bird, honey dish, 3½" 35.00
Cardinal Bird, sauce bowl, ftd 17.50
Carnation, pitcher, water; ruby stained w/gold 265.00
Cathedral, compote, amber, ruffled, 7½x9½x6½" 70.00
Cathedral, creamer, amber, flat, sq 48.00
Cathedral, sauce bowl, bl, flat, 4" 25.00
Cathedral, sugar bowl, w/lid 65.00
Centennial, see Liberty Bell
Chain, relish, 7½x5¼" 22.50
Chain, sugar bowl, w/lid 35.00
Chain & Shield, creamer 32.00

Chain & Shield, pitcher, water 55.00
Chain w/Diamonds, see Washington Centennial
Chain w/Star, goblet 22.50
Chain w/Star, jelly compote 18.00
Chain w/Star, relish 12.50
Chain w/Star, tumbler 20.00
Chandelier, celery vase 45.00
Chandelier, creamer 32.00
Chandelier, tumbler, water; etched 42.50
Checkerboard, compote, 8" 27.50
Checkerboard, wine 20.00
Classic, bowl, hexagonal, open log ft, 8" 115.00
Classic, celery vase 120.00
Classic, plate, 10" 185.00
Classic Medallion, marmalade, w/lid 125.00
Coin, see US Coin
Colonial, tumbler, ftd, flint 75.00
Colorado, bowl, flared rim, 5" 20.00
Colorado, calling card tray 27.50
Colorado, mug 20.00
Colorado, salt cellar, master 32.00
Colorado, vase, trumpet form, 14" 58.00
Columbian Coin, butter dish, frosted coins 175.00
Columbian Coin, compote, w/lid, frosted coins, 8" 165.00
Columbian Coin, lamp, frosted coins, 12" 185.00
Columbian Coin, syrup, frosted coins 190.00
Comet, butter dish 185.00
Comet, goblet 88.00
Comet, whiskey, hdl 260.00
Compact, see Snail
Connecticut, celery vase 27.50
Connecticut, pitcher, water 50.00
Cord & Tassel, egg cup 38.00
Cord & Tassel, goblet 38.00
Cord & Tassel, wine 45.00
Cord Drapery, creamer, bl 127.50
Cord Drapery, sugar bowl, gr, w/lid 175.00
Cordova, banana stand 88.00
Cordova, punch cup 8.00
Cordova, syrup, pewter top 100.00
Cottage, champagne 70.00
Cottage, goblet, bl 50.00
Cottage, plate, 7" 22.50
Croesus, butter dish, gr w/gold 165.00
Croesus, condiment tray 30.00
Croesus, salt cellar, amethyst, ftd 40.00
Croesus, sugar bowl, gr, w/lid 80.00
Crow's Foot, see Yale
Crown Jewels, see Chandelier
Cryptic, see Zippered Block
Crystal Wedding, creamer, etched 57.50
Crystal Wedding, goblet 45.00
Cube w/Fan, see Pineapple & Fan
Cupid & Venus, celery vase 42.50
Cupid & Venus, champagne 65.00
Cupid & Venus, goblet 78.00
Cupid & Venus, mug, 3" 60.00
Cupid & Venus, sugar bowl, w/lid 68.00
Currant, goblet, buttermilk 20.00
Currant, wine 35.00
Currier & Ives, creamer 32.00
Currier & Ives, cup & saucer, bl 82.50
Currier & Ives, pitcher, milk 36.00
Currier & Ives, spooner 20.00

Currier & Ives, sugar bowl, w/lid 42.50
Currier & Ives, waste bowl 40.00
Currier & Ives, wine 16.00
Curtain, butter dish 65.00
Curtain, compote, 8" 45.00
Curtain, creamer 30.00
Curtain, spooner 25.00
Curtain Tie-Back, goblet, flat base 27.50
Curtain Tie-Back, relish 12.50
Cut Log, cake stand, 10" 65.00
Cut Log, goblet 60.00
Cut Log, sugar bowl, w/lid 65.00
Cut Log, tankard 75.00
Dahlia, cordial, amber 50.00
Dahlia, creamer 20.00
Dahlia, pitcher, milk; bl 50.00
Daisy & Button, celery vase, amber 42.50
Daisy & Button, dust pan whimsey, lt bl 40.00
Daisy & Button, egg cup, bl 22.50
Daisy & Button, sauce bowl, bl, sq, 4" 15.00
Daisy & Button, tray, apple gr 60.00
Daisy & Button, tumbler, bl 32.00
Daisy & Button, tumbler, vaseline 32.50
Daisy & Button w/Crossbar, cake stand, bl 82.50
Daisy & Button w/Crossbar, creamer, bl 32.00
Daisy & Button w/Crossbar, goblet 27.50
Daisy & Button w/Crossbar, mug, 3" 12.50
Daisy & Button w/Thumbprint Panels, butter dish, w/lid 185.00
Daisy & Button w/Thumbprint Panels, shaker, amber stained 78.00
Daisy & Button w/Thumbprint Panels, tumbler, bl panels 40.00
Daisy & Button w/V Ornament, creamer, bl 55.00
Daisy & Button w/V Ornament, pitcher, water; vaseline 95.00
Daisy & Button w/V Ornament, tumbler 15.00
Daisy & Button w/V Ornament, tumbler, amber 30.00

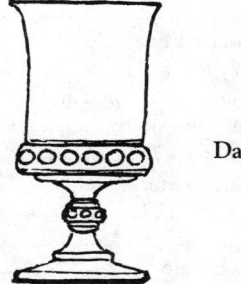

Dakota

Dakota, cake stand, etched, 9½" 65.00
Dakota, goblet, etched 38.00
Dakota, sugar bowl, etched, w/lid 65.00
Dakota, tray, condiment; metal hdls 80.00
Dakota, tumbler, etched 30.00
Dakota, wine 25.00
Dart, goblet 27.00
Dart, tumbler 18.00
Deer & Dog, creamer 88.00
Deer & Dog, sugar bowl, frosted dog finial 125.00
Deer & Dog, wine 80.00
Deer & Log, butter dish, ped ft, frosted dog finial 135.00
Deer & Pine Tree, bowl, 5x8" 25.00
Deer & Pine Tree, cake stand 98.00
Deer & Pine Tree, sugar bowl, w/lid 60.00

Delaware, banana bowl 40.00
Delaware, bowl, gr, gold trim, 8" 50.00
Delaware, dresser tray 32.00
Delaware, sugar bowl 60.00
Dew & Raindrop, bud vase, 6" 25.00
Dew & Raindrop, pitcher, water 50.00
Dewdrop, mug 28.00
Dewdrop, relish 17.50
Dewdrop w/Star, sugar bowl, w/lid 60.00
Dewey, see also Greentown, Dewey
Dewey, tumbler 48.00
Diagonal Band, cake stand 32.00
Diagonal Band, creamer 30.00
Diagonal Band, sugar bowl 16.00
Diagonal Band, wine 25.00
Diagonal Band & Fan, wine 27.50
Diamond Cut w/Leaf, creamer 24.00
Diamond Horseshoe, see Aurora
Diamond Medallion, see Grand
Diamond Point, champagne, flint 125.00
Diamond Point, goblet, amber 26.00
Diamond Point, pitcher, water; flint 450.00
Diamond Point, sugar bowl, w/lid, flint 98.00
Diamond Point, wine, flint 65.00
Diamond Quilted, bowl, bl, 7¼" 30.00
Diamond Quilted, creamer, amber 38.00
Diamond Quilted, relish, vaseline, leaf shape, 8" 15.00
Diamond Quilted, sauce bowl, amber, ftd, 4" 17.50
Diamond Thumbprint, cordial, 4" 315.00
Diamond Thumbprint, decanter, orig patterned stopper, 1-pt 175.00
Diamond Thumbprint, whiskey, flint 150.00
Dinner Bell, see Cottage
Doric, see Feather
Double Leaf & Dart, see Leaf & Dart
Drapery, butter dish 40.00
Drapery, goblet 27.50
Drapery, sugar bowl, w/lid 45.00
Egg in Sand, creamer 27.50
Egg in Sand, relish 12.50
Egg in Sand, sauce bowl 12.50
Egg in Sand, tumbler, amber 32.50
Egyptian, butter dish 75.00
Egyptian, creamer 45.00
Egyptian, relish, 5½x8½" 21.00
Elephant, see Jumbo
Emerald Green Herringbone, see Florida
Empress, butter dish 60.00
Empress, sugar bowl, gr w/gold, w/lid 125.00
Empress, tumbler, gr w/gold 50.00
English Hobnail Cross, see Klondike
Esther, bowl, 8" 75.00
Esther, cracker jar, amber stained 235.00
Esther, creamer, gr 120.00
Esther, ice cream tray, gr w/gold 150.00
Esther, pitcher, gr w/gold, 10" 195.00
Esther, plate, 10¼" 28.00
Esther, tumbler, gr 47.50
Etched Dakota, see Dakota
Eureka, cordial 42.00
Eureka, wine 32.00
Excelsior, cologne bottle, faceted stopper 98.00
Excelsior, cordial 45.00
Excelsior, creamer, molded hdl 85.00
Excelsior, egg cup 27.50

Eyewinker, banana stand 130.00
Eyewinker, cake stand, 9½" 68.00
Eyewinker, cracker jar 130.00
Eyewinker, tumbler 24.00
Fairfax Strawberry, see Strawberry

Feather

Feather, cake plate 55.00
Feather, goblet 75.00
Feather, honey dish 15.00
Feather, tumbler, water; gr 80.00
Feather, wine, scalloped rim 45.00
Festoon, creamer 38.00
Festoon, marmalade 34.00
Festoon, tumbler 32.50
Fine Cut, cake stand 36.00
Fine Cut, pitcher, water; amber 78.00
Fine Cut, plate, amber, 10" 22.50
Fine Cut, tray, ice cream; lion's head hdls, amber 42.50
Fine Cut & Block, goblet, pk blocks 48.00
Fine Cut & Block, pitcher, water; amber blocks 90.00
Fine Cut & Diamond, see Grand
Fine Cut & Feather, see Feather
Fine Cut & Panel, celery vase 32.50
Fine Cut & Panel, creamer, amber 32.00
Fine Cut & Panel, plate, bl, 6" 32.00
Fine Cut & Panel, plate, vaseline, 6" 22.50
Fine Cut & Panel, relish, vaseline, 7x3½" 21.50
Fine Cut & Panel, tumbler, vaseline 37.50
Fine Cut & Panel, wine, amber 35.00
Fine Rib, champagne, flint 125.00
Fine Rib, egg cup, dbl, flint 36.00
Fine Rib, goblet, flint 75.00
Fine Rib, whiskey, hdld, flint 145.00
Fine Rib, wine, flint 45.00
Fingerprint, see Almond Thumbprint
Fishscale, celery vase 32.00
Fishscale, creamer 25.00
Flamingo Habitat, creamer 40.00
Flamingo Habitat, goblet 32.00
Flamingo Habitat, tumbler 32.00
Flamingo Habitat, wine 45.00
Florida, goblet 22.50
Florida, plate, 7½" 12.00
Florida Palm, cake stand, 9½" 25.00
Florida Palm, creamer 17.50
Florida Palm, tumbler 30.00
Flower Pot, creamer, vaseline 8.80
Flower Pot, goblet 45.00
Flute, claret 25.00

Flute, whiskey, hdld 60.00
Frosted Circle, plate, 7" 22.50
Frosted Circle, tankard 85.00
Frosted Leaf, celery vase 120.00
Frosted Leaf, egg cup 87.50
Frosted Leaf, tumbler, ftd 98.00
Frosted Lion, see Lion
Frosted Ribbon, see Ribbon
Frosted Roman Key, champagne 75.00
Frosted Roman Key, sugar bowl, w/lid 85.00
Frosted Stork, bread plate 57.50
Frosted Stork, goblet 62.50
Frosted Stork, tray, 11x15⅛" 98.00
Galloway, basket, twisted hdl 80.00
Galloway, creamer 25.00
Galloway, egg cup, clear w/gold 32.00
Galloway, pitcher, water; rose stained 175.00
Galloway, relish 15.00
Galloway, sauce bowl, flat, 4¼" 17.50
Garfield Drape, cake stand, 9½" 78.00
Garfield Drape, goblet 40.00
Garfield Drape, spooner 30.00
Gem, see Nailhead
Georgia, goblet 27.50
Georgia, mug 30.00
Georgia, tumbler 35.00
Good Luck, see Horseshoe
Gothic, compote, flint, 7" 70.00
Gothic, creamer, flint 195.00
Gothic, egg cup, flint 55.00
Grand, bowl, oval, 9" 12.50
Grand, cake stand, 10" 34.00
Grand, pitcher, water 42.00
Grand, sugar bowl, w/lid 38.00
Grape & Festoon w/Shield, goblet, w/Am shield 45.00
Grape & Festoon w/Shield, mug, sapphire bl, 2½" 50.00
Grape & Festoon w/Shield, mug, 1⅞" 17.50
Grape & Festoon w/Stippled Leaf, sugar bowl, w/lid 60.00

Grasshopper

Grasshopper, butter dish, amber 100.00
Grasshopper, salt cellar 48.00
Grasshopper, sugar bowl, w/insect, w/lid 75.00
Greek Key, celery tray, 9" L 40.00
Greek Key, goblet 88.00
Greek Key, punch cup 16.50
Greek Key, tumbler 78.00
Guardian Angel, see Cupid & Venus
Hairpin, celery vase, flint 60.00
Hairpin, champagne, flint 72.50
Hairpin, tumbler 55.00
Hairpin, wine, flint 55.00
Halley's Comet, creamer 40.00

Hamilton, egg cup 45.00
Hamilton, goblet 40.00
Hamilton w/Leaf, tumbler, clear leaf 50.00
Hamilton w/Leaf, whiskey, hdl, clear leaf 95.00
Hawaiian Lei, cake stand, 9¼" 35.00
Hawaiian Lei, cup & saucer 40.00
Heart w/Thumbprint, goblet 60.00
Heart w/Thumbprint, mustard jar, gr 90.00
Heart w/Thumbprint, tumbler, clear w/gold 67.50
Heart w/Thumbprint, wine, gr w/gold 140.00
Heavy Panelled Fine Cut, wine 20.00
Herringbone, jelly compote, gr 42.50
Herringbone Band, see Ripple
Herringbone Buttress, see Greentown, Herringbone Buttress
Hickman, creamer, gr 37.50
Hickman, goblet 42.00
Hidalgo, goblet 20.00
Hidalgo, sugar bowl, w/lid 42.50
Hidalgo, waste bowl 26.00
Hinoto, egg cup 38.00
Hinoto, tumbler, ftd 47.50
Holly, butter dish 135.00
Holly, cake stand, 11" 125.00
Holly, egg cup 58.00
Holly, tumbler 115.00
Holly, wine 150.00
Holly Amber, see Greentown, Holly Amber
Honeycomb, claret, flint 32.00
Honeycomb, egg cup, flint 35.00
Honeycomb, honey dish, w/lid, non-flint 24.00
Honeycomb, vase, flint, 7½" 42.50
Hops & Barley, see Wheat & Barley
Horn of Plenty, bowl, flint, 8½" 135.00
Horn of Plenty, butter dish, acorn finial, flint 130.00
Horn of Plenty, decanter, w/Dmn Point stopper, flint, 1-qt 175.00
Horn of Plenty, egg cup, flint 45.00
Horn of Plenty, goblet, flint 75.00
Horseshoe, butter dish 95.00
Horseshoe, creamer 45.00
Horseshoe, goblet, knob stem 40.00
Horseshoe, plate, 10" 75.00
Horseshoe, wine 160.00
Huber, celery vase 38.00
Huber, egg cup 30.00
Huber, sugar bowl, w/lid 65.00
Hummingbird, creamer 45.00
Hummingbird, tumbler, bar; amber 65.00
Hummingbird, wine 95.00
Idaho, see Snail
Illinois, doughnut stand, sq, 7½" 60.00
Illinois, pitcher, milk; rnd, SP trim 180.00
Illinois, relish 15.00
Inverted Fern, goblet 24.00
Inverted Fern, sugar bowl, w/lid, flint 95.00
Iowa, carafe 32.00
Iowa, decanter 38.00
Iowa, pitcher, water 48.00
Iowa, punch cup 15.00
Iowa, tumbler 24.00
Iris Column, see Broken Column
Iris w/Meander, see Opalescent Glass
Ivy in Snow, creamer 20.00
Ivy in Snow, mug, ruby stained 48.00
Jacob's Ladder, cake stand, 12" 55.00

Jacob's Ladder, creamer 35.00
Jersey Swirl, salt cellar, bl, ind 22.00
Jersey Swirl, salt cellar, canary, ind 22.50
Jewel Band, goblet 36.00
Jewel w/Dewdrop, bowl, 8½" 36.00
Jewel w/Dewdrop, compote, 12x7" 130.00
Jewel w/Dewdrop, mug 15.00
Jewel w/Dewdrop, tumbler 24.00
Jewel w/Festoon, creamer 25.00
Jewel w/Festoon, punch cup 20.00
Jewel w/Festoon, sugar bowl, w/lid 35.00
Jewel w/Moondrop, cake plate 50.00
Jewel w/Moondrop, tumbler 42.50
Jewelled Moon & Star, butter dish 68.00
Jewelled Moon & Star, carafe 45.00
Jewelled Moon & Star, goblet 45.00
Jewelled Moon & Star, tumbler 24.00
Job's Tears, see Art
Jumbo, creamer 155.00
Jumbo, goblet 695.00
Jumbo, pitcher, elephant in base 700.00
Jumbo, spooner 98.00
Kentucky, cake stand, 9½" 40.00
Kentucky, punch cup, gr 20.00
Kentucky, wine, gr 40.00
King's Crown, butter dish 40.00
King's Crown, cordial 30.00
King's Crown, creamer, clear w/gold, ind 30.00
King's Crown, cup & saucer 65.00
King's Crown, punch bowl, ftd 265.00
Klondike, butter dish, amber stained 295.00
Klondike, butter pat, amber stained 35.00
Klondike, celery vase, amber stained 135.00
Klondike, goblet, frosted & amber stained 255.00
Klondike, tumbler, frosted 150.00
Kokomo, goblet 25.00
Kokomo, tumbler 20.00
Kokomo, wine 20.00
La Clede, see Hickman
Lace, see Drapery

Lady Hamilton

Lady Hamilton, sauce dish, flat, 4" 6.00
Lady Hamilton, tumbler, bar 36.00
Lawrence, see Bull's Eye
Leaf, see Maple Leaf
Leaf & Dart, egg cup 22.50
Leaf & Dart, pitcher, milk 135.00
Leaf & Dart, wine 28.00
Leaf Bracket, see Greentown, Leaf Bracket
Leaf Medallion, see Northwood, Leaf Medallion
Liberty Bell, creamer 127.50
Liberty Bell, pitcher, water 845.00
Liberty Bell, plate, closed hdls, 6" 78.00

Liberty Bell, spooner, mini 300.00
Lily of the Valley, honey dish 12.50
Lily of the Valley, pitcher, water 165.00
Lily of the Valley, sugar bowl, 3-ftd, w/lid 85.00
Lincoln Drape, egg cup 70.00
Lincoln Drape, sugar bowl, w/lid 120.00
Lincoln Drape w/Tassel, salt cellar, master 120.00
Lincoln Drape w/Tassel, spill holder 55.00
Lion, cordial, frosted 165.00
Lion, egg cup, frosted 65.00
Lion, spooner 55.00
Lion, wine 215.00
Log Cabin, butter dish 300.00
Log Cabin, pitcher, water 350.00
Long Spear, see Grasshopper
Loop, champagne, non-flint 16.00
Loop, cordial, non-flint 36.00
Loop, goblet, flint 22.50
Loop, salt cellar, master; flint 30.00
Loop, wine, flint 32.00
Loop & Dart, goblet 32.00
Loop & Dart, sugar bowl, w/lid 45.00
Loop & Dart w/Round Ornament, creamer 38.00
Loop w/Stippled Panels, see Texas
Magnet & Grape, champagne, frosted leaf, flint 125.00
Magnet & Grape, compote, stippled leaf, non-flint, 7½" 60.00
Maine, butter dish 60.00
Maine, compote, gr, 8" 60.00
Maine, creamer 28.00
Maine, pitcher, water 100.00
Maine, wine, gr 67.50
Manhattan, creamer 50.00
Manhattan, plate, 6" 12.00
Manhattan, salt shaker, orig top 25.00
Manhattan, violet bowl 22.50
Maple Leaf, bowl, oval, ftd, 6x10" 55.00
Maple Leaf, butter pat 15.00
Maple Leaf, compote, vaseline, log ft, 7" 105.00
Maryland, butter dish, ruby stained 98.00
Maryland, pitcher, milk, clear w/gold 45.00
Maryland, relish, ruby stained 50.00
Maryland, wine 32.50
Mascotte, butter pat 12.00
Mascotte, cheese dish 67.50
Mascotte, shaker, etched 25.00
Massachusetts, bar bottle, 11" 60.00
Massachusetts, codial 58.00
Massachusetts, wine 45.00
Medallion, cake stand, amber 48.00
Medallion, goblet, amber 45.00
Medallion, pitcher, water; bl 78.00
Medallion, relish, amber, 7x5" 22.00
Melrose, compote, 5¾x7½" 25.00
Melrose, plate, 8" 12.00
Melrose, wine 20.00
Michigan, bowl, 10" 37.50
Michigan, egg cup 25.00
Michigan, goblet 37.50
Michigan, punch cup, HP decor 12.50
Minerva, butter dish 95.00
Minerva, compote, 8½x8" 90.00
Minerva, honey dish 20.00
Minnesota, carafe 40.00
Minnesota, cup 17.50

Minnesota, sauce bowl 12.00
Minnesota, tumbler, water 20.00
Minor Block, see Mascotte
Mirror, see Galloway
Missouri, butter dish 57.50
Missouri, celery vase 30.00
Missouri, pitcher, milk; gr 88.00
Missouri, tumbler, gr 36.00
Missouri, wine 75.00
Moon & Star, bowl, berry; 8¼" 32.00
Moon & Star, butter dish 48.00
Moon & Star, claret 45.00
Moon & Star, relish, oblong 17.50
Morning Glory, compote, flint, 5x7¾" 295.00
Morning Glory, salt celler, ped ft, flint, master 230.00
Nail, goblet, ruby stained 85.00
Nail, pitcher, water 80.00
Nail, sauce bowl, flat, 4½" 10.00
Nailhead, bowl, 6" 17.50
Nailhead, goblet 20.00
Nailhead, spooner 20.00
Nailhead, wine 35.00
Nestor, butter dish, clear w/gold 67.50
Nestor, sauce dish, gr w/HP decor 38.00
Nestor, shaker, purple, orig top 58.00
Nestor, tumbler, gr 32.00
New England Pineapple, creamer, flint 275.00
New England Pineapple, goblet, flint 70.00
New England Pineapple, salt cellar, master; flint 45.00
New England Pineapple, wine, flint 245.00
New Hampshire, sugar bowl, rose stained, 3" 27.50
New Jersey, carafe, water 80.00
New Jersey, olive dish 17.50
New Jersey, plate, 8" 14.00
Notched Rib, see Broken Column
O'Hara Diamond, goblet 22.50
O'Hara Diamond, jelly compote, ruby stained 140.00
O'Hara Diamond, sugar shaker, ruby stained 145.00
Oaken Bucket, see Wooden Pail
One Hundred & One, goblet 50.00
One Hundred & One, sugar bowl, w/lid 45.00
One-O-One, see One Hundred & One
Oregon #1, compote, w/lid, 11" 45.00
Oregon #1, mug, ftd 40.00
Oregon #1, tumbler 28.00
Orion, see Cathedral
Palmette, cake stand 70.00
Palmette, goblet 38.00
Palmette, sauce bowl, flat, 4" 16.00
Panelled Daisy, celery vase 36.00
Panelled Daisy, goblet 27.50
Panelled Daisy, sugar bowl, w/lid 47.50
Panelled Forget-Me-Not, pitcher, milk 57.50
Panelled Forget-Me-Not, relish, hdls 22.50
Panelled Herringbone, see Florida
Panelled Star & Button, mug, mini 17.50
Panelled Star & Button, salt cellar, master 15.00
Panelled Thistle, butter dish, w/bee 65.00
Panelled Thistle, champagne, w/bee, flared 40.00
Panelled Thistle, sugar bowl, w/lid 42.50
Panelled Thistle, wine, no bee 27.50
Pavonia, pitcher, lemonade 115.00
Pavonia, pitcher, lemonade; ruby stained 135.00
Pavonia, salt cellar, master 18.00

Pavonia, tankard, etched 48.00
Pavonia, tumbler, etched 22.50
Peerless, see Lady Hamilton
Pennsylvania, butter dish, clear w/gold 60.00
Pennsylvania, cordial 88.00
Pennsylvania, goblet, clear w/gold 25.00
Pennsylvania, pitcher, water 75.00
Pennsylvania, wine 60.00
Pillow Encircled, sauce dish 12.00
Pillow Encircled, sugar bowl, w/lid 35.00
Pineapple & Fan, tumbler, water; gr 55.00
Pineapple & Fan, vase, trumpet form, 10" 32.00
Pineapple Stem, see Pavonia
Pioneer, see Westward Ho
Pleat & Panel, cake stand, sq, 10" 60.00
Pleat & Panel, goblet 35.00
Pleat & Panel, sugar bowl 25.00
Plume, bowl, w/lid, 8" 45.00
Plume, butter dish 45.00
Plume, celery vase 35.00
Polar Bear, tray, water; frosted, 16" 215.00
Polar Bear, waste bowl, frosted 115.00
Popcorn, butter dish, w/lid 50.00
Popcorn, celery vase 20.00
Popcorn, wine 32.00
Portland, goblet 37.50
Portland, pitcher, pk stained, 11" 175.00
Portland, toothpick holder 24.00
Portland, wine 30.00
Powder & Shot, egg cup, flint 48.00
Powder & Shot, honey dish, flint 12.00
Powder & Shot, sugar bowl, w/lid, flint 88.00
Prayer Rug, see Horseshoe

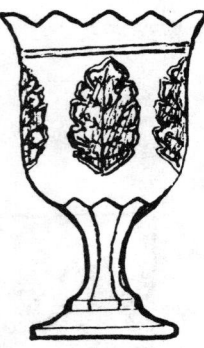

Pressed Leaf

Pressed Leaf, sugar bowl, w/lid 40.00
Pressed Leaf, wine 40.00
Primrose, pickle dish 20.00
Primrose, plate, amber, 7" 22.50
Primrose, tray, water; 11" dia 32.00
Princess Feather, creamer 40.00
Princess Feather, pitcher, water 78.00
Priscilla, bowl, shallow, 9" 40.00
Priscilla, creamer 40.00
Priscilla, syrup, orig pewter lid 130.00
Prism, egg cup 27.50
Prism, pitcher, water 110.00
Prism, tumbler, buttermilk 37.50
Psyche & Cupid, creamer 65.00
Psyche & Cupid, pitcher, water 80.00

Pygmy, see Torpedo
Raindrop, compote, amber, 4x8" 55.00
Recessed Pillared Red Top, see Nail
Red Block, decanter, 12" 165.00
Red Block, pitcher, tankard 125.00
Red Block, wine 38.00
Red Top, see Button Arches
Reverse Torpedo, basket 68.00
Reverse Torpedo, creamer 72.00
Reverse Torpedo, tumbler 32.00
Ribbed Ivy, egg cup 40.00
Ribbed Ivy, goblet 45.00
Ribbed Palm, champagne, flint 75.00
Ribbed Palm, compote, flint, 8¼x8¾" 125.00
Ribbed Palm, spooner, flint 65.00
Ribbed Palm, wine, flint 75.00
Ribbon, butter dish 75.00
Ribbon, champagne, frosted 98.00
Ribbon, pomade jar, w/lid 38.00
Ribbon, sugar bowl, frosted, w/lid 55.00
Ribbon Candy, bowl, 8½" 25.00
Ribbon Candy, cordial 44.00
Ribbon Candy, plate, 11" 42.00
Ripple, ice tub 55.00
Ripple, wine 35.00
Ripple Band, see Ripple
Rochelle, see Princess Feather
Roman Key, sugar bowl, w/lid, flint 120.00

Roman Rosette

Roman Rosette, butter dish 47.50
Roman Rosette, creamer 30.00
Roman Rosette, goblet 40.00
Roman Rosette, wine, ruby stained 50.00
Rose in Snow, goblet, bl 47.50
Rose in Snow, pitcher 125.00
Rose in Snow, sauce bowl, flat, 4" 16.50
Rose Sprig, bowl, ftd, 10" 50.00
Rose Sprig, cake stand, amber, sq, 10" 85.00
Rose Sprig, compote, 8" L 45.00
Rose Sprig, plate, sq, hdls, 6" 27.50
Rose Sprig, relish boat, bl 22.00
Rosette, goblet 37.50
Rosette, jelly compote 20.00
Rosette, pitcher, milk 57.50
Royal Ivy, see Northwood, Royal Ivy
Royal Oak, see Northwood, Royal Oak
Ruby Thumbprint, see King's Crown
S-Repeat, sauce bowl, apple gr w/gold 30.00
S-Repeat, tumbler, amethyst 42.50

Sandwich Star, compote, low std, 8½" 60.00
Sandwich Star, decanter, bar lip, 1-pt 75.00
Sawtooth, champagne, knob stem, flint 60.00
Sawtooth, cordial, ruby stained 40.00
Sawtooth Band, see Amazon
Scalloped Daisy Red Top, see Button Arches
Scroll w/Flowers, mustard jar 45.00
Scroll w/Flowers, sugar bowl, w/lid 55.00
Sedan, creamer 25.00
Sedan, mug, mini 16.50
Sedan, see Panelled Star & Button
Seneca Loop, see Loop
Sequoia, see Heavy Panelled Fine Cut
Shell & Jewel, bowl, 8" 32.00
Shell & Jewel, pitcher, milk; bl 78.00
Shell & Jewel, pitcher, water; bl 85.00
Shell & Jewel, tumbler, amber 35.00
Shell & Tassel, compote, sq, w/lid, 5¼" 68.00
Shell & Tassel, creamer, sq 57.50
Shell & Tassel, goblet, knob stem 65.00
Shell & Tassel, ice cream tray 62.50
Sheraton, pitcher, milk 32.00
Sheraton, pitcher, water 48.00
Sheraton, relish, hdld, bl 22.50
Shoshone, carafe 42.00
Shoshone, spooner, amber 48.00
Shoshone, toothpick holder, ruby stained 90.00
Shoshone, wine, ruby stained 58.00
Shrine, pickle dish 18.00
Shrine, sugar bowl, w/lid 50.00
Shuttle, butter dish 115.00
Shuttle, mug, amber 325.00
Shuttle, tumbler 48.00
Skilton, compote, 7" 27.50
Skilton, pitcher, water 45.00
Snail, butter dish, ruby stained 150.00
Snail, celery vase 50.00
Snail, custard cup 30.00
Snail, goblet, ruby stained 90.00
Snail, wine 68.00
Spades, see Medallion
Spirea Band, cake stand, bl, 10½" 85.00
Spirea Band, goblet, vaseline 38.00
Spirea Band, platter, amber, 10½x8½" 26.00
Sprig, cake stand 45.00
Sprig, goblet 40.00
Sprig, pitcher, water 55.00
Sprig, wine 38.00
Star & Feather, plate, amber, 7" 18.00
Star Rosetted, creamer 32.00
Star Rosetted, goblet 32.00
Star Rosetted, plate, 7" 12.00
Stars & Stripes, creamer 22.00
Stars & Stripes, wine 17.50
States, goblet, clear w/gold 38.00
States, nappy, hdls, clear w/gold 25.00
Stedman, champagne 40.00
Stedman, spooner 15.00
Stippled Chain, egg cup 30.00
Stippled Chain, goblet 22.50
Stippled Forget-Me-Not, cup & saucer 40.00
Stippled Forget-Me-Not, sugar bowl, w/lid 40.00
Stippled Grape & Festoon, compote, low dtd, 8" 40.00
Stippled Grape & Festoon, pitcher, water 100.00

Stippled Grape & Festoon, sugar bowl 22.50
Stippled Ivy, egg cup 27.50
Stippled Ivy, sugar bowl, w/lid 38.00
Stippled Panelled Flower, see Maine
Strawberry, spooner 35.00
Strawberry, wine 100.00
Strigil, bowl, flared rim, 9" 26.00
Strigil, plate, 11" 27.50
Sunk Honeycomb, cheese dish, ruby stained 175.00
Sunk Honeycomb, cup & saucer, ruby stained 37.50
Sunk Honeycomb, mug, ruby stained, souvenir 42.00
Sunken Primrose, see Florida
Swan, creamer, amber 50.00
Swan, goblet, canary yel 75.00
Swan, sugar bowl 45.00
Swan, sugar bowl, w/lid 195.00
Tarentum's Thumbprint, pitcher, water; etched 45.00
Teardrop & Diamond Block, see Art
Teardrop & Tassel, creamer 40.00
Teardrop & Tassel, goblet 145.00
Teardrop & Tassel, pitcher 75.00
Teardrop & Tassel, sugar bowl, w/lid 65.00
Tennessee, celery vase 35.00
Tennessee, mug 38.00
Texas, creamer, clear w/gold, ind 22.00
Texas, goblet, clear w/gold 68.00
Texas, toothpick holder, rose stained 95.00
Theatrical, see Actress
Thousand Eye, cordial 25.00
Thousand Eye, goblet, apple gr 45.00
Thousand Eye, mug, apple gr, 3½" 30.00
Thousand Eye, pitcher, water 75.00
Thousand Eye, plate, 10" 35.00
Thousand Eye, plate, 6" 20.00
Three Face, biscuit jar 900.00
Three Face, butter dish 145.00
Three Face, celery vase 125.00
Three Face, champagne, saucer type 150.00
Three Face, compote, 7½x6" 75.00
Three Face, creamer 100.00
Three Face, marmalade jar 225.00
Three Face, pitcher, water 325.00
Three Face, sugar bowl, w/lid 130.00
Three Face, wine 175.00
Three Panel, compote, bl, 4x8" 40.00
Three Panel, goblet, vaseline 42.00
Thumbprint, see Argus
Thumbprint Band, see Dakota
Thumderbird, see Hummingbird
Torpedo, banana stand 57.50
Torpedo, compote, w/lid, 7¼x7" 67.50
Torpedo, creamer, ftd 32.50
Torpedo, sugar bowl, w/lid 67.50
Torpedo, wine 50.00
Tree of Life, see Portland
Tree of Life w/Hand, butter dish 130.00
Tree of Life w/Hand, celery vase 48.00
Tree of Life w/Hand, creamer, w/hand & ball hdl 67.50
Triangular Prism, spooner, flint 55.00
Triple Triangle, butter dish 60.00
Tulip w/Sawtooth, compote, 5½x8" 65.00
Tulip w/Sawtooth, creamer, flint 85.00
Tulip w/Sawtooth, egg cup, flint 20.00
Tulip w/Sawtooth, salt cellar, petal rim 45.00

Tulip w/Sawtooth, wine 36.00
Two Panel, bowl, bl, oval, 7¾" 25.00
Two Panel, butter dish, vaseline 60.00
Two Panel, goblet, amber 30.00
Two Panel, wine, vaseline 35.00

US Coin

US Coin, bowl, frosted, 6" 225.00
US Coin, bread tray, frosted 300.00
US Coin, butter dish, frosted 425.00
US Coin, compote, frosted, low std, w/lid, 6" 300.00
US Coin, compote, frosted, str top, 8½" 400.00
US Coin, compote, frosted, w/lid, 7" 450.00
US Coin, compote, frosted, w/lid, 8" 500.00
US Coin, compote, high std, flared rim, frosted, 9½" 400.00
US Coin, creamer, frosted 595.00
US Coin, epergne, frosted 700.00
US Coin, goblet, frosted, 6½" 300.00
US Coin, sauce bowl, frosted, ftd 185.00
US Coin, spooner, frosted 250.00
US Coin, sugar bowl, frosted 350.00
US Coin, toothpick holder 175.00
US Coin, tumbler, frosted 225.00
Utah, butter dish 36.00
Utah, creamer 30.00
Utah, tumbler 17.50
Valencia Waffle, pitcher, water 44.00
Valencia Waffle, relish, amber, 9x5⅜" 22.50
Valencia Waffle, salt cellar, master 25.00
Vermont, basket, clear w/gold 32.00
Vermont, basket, gr w/gold 42.50
Vermont, pitcher, water; gr w/gold 130.00
Viking, butter dish 85.00
Viking, celery vase 40.00
Viking, pitcher, water 95.00
Viking, sugar bowl, w/lid 85.00
Waffle, celery vase, flint 135.00
Waffle, egg cup, flint 45.00
Waffle, goblet, flint 95.00
Waffle, whiskey, flint 80.00
Waffle, wine, flint 115.00
Waffle & Thumbprint, bar bottle, 1-qt 75.00
Waffle & Thumbprint, bowl, 5x8¼" 52.50
Waffle & Thumbprint, goblet, flint 95.00
Waffle & Thumbprint, whiskey, hdld, 3" 285.00
Washington, celery vase 90.00
Washington, decanter, orig stopper 155.00
Washington, wine 120.00
Washington Centennial, butter dish, ftd 95.00
Washington Centennial, egg cup 42.00
Washington Centennial, sugar bowl 25.00

Wedding Bells, goblet 45.00
Wedding Ring, goblet, flint 85.00
Wedding Ring, sugar bowl, w/lid 78.00
Wedding Ring, syrup 97.50
Westward Ho, butter dish 145.00
Westward Ho, goblet 75.00
Westward Ho, platter, 13" 165.00
Westward Ho, wine 230.00
Wheat & Barley, compote, amber, 8¼" 80.00
Wheat & Barley, jelly compote 20.00
Wheat & Barley, shakers, pr 37.50
Wheat & Barley, sugar bowl, bl, w/lid 72.50
Wildflower, celery vase, apple gr 85.00
Wildflower, creamer, amber 32.00
Wildflower, creamer, vaseline 50.00
Wildflower, goblet, bl 45.00
Willow Oak, creamer 34.00
Willow Oak, creamer, bl 48.00
Willow Oak, goblet 45.00
Willow Oak, plate, bl, 9" 48.00
Willow Oak, tumbler 36.00
Windflower, butter dish 52.50
Windflower, creamer 37.50
Windflower, sauce bowl 15.00
Wisconsin, creamer 50.00
Wisconsin, cup & saucer 48.00
Wisconsin, tumbler 42.50
Wooden Pail, creamer 32.00
Wooden Pail, pitcher 95.00
Wooden Pail, pitcher, vaseline 135.00
Wooden Pail, sugar bowl, amethyst, mini 24.00
Wyoming, butter dish 55.00
Wyoming, creamer 48.00
Wyoming, tumbler 58.00
Wyoming, wine 85.00
X-Ray, celery vase, emerald gr 50.00
X-Ray, marmalade, emerald gr w/gold 70.00
X-Ray, sugar bowl, w/lid, regular 37.50
Yale, butter dish 47.50
Yale, goblet 35.00
Yale, sugar bowl, w/lid 42.50
Yale, tumbler 20.00
Zipper, butter dish 42.00
Zipper, cheese dish 50.00
Zipper, creamer 20.00
Zippered Block, creamer, ruby stained

Paul Revere Pottery

The Saturday Evening Girls were a social group of young Boston
ladies who met to pursue various activities, among them pottery making. Their first kiln was bought in 1906, and within a few years it
became necessary to move to a larger location. Because their new quarters were near the historical Old North Church, they chose the name
Paul Revere Pottery. With very little training, the girls produced only
simple ware. Until 1915 the pottery operated at a deficit; then a new
building with four kilns was constructed on Nottingham Road. Vases,
miniature jugs, children's tea sets, tiles, dinnerware, and lamps were
produced, usually in soft matt glazes often decorated with incised,
hand-painted designs from nature. Occasional examples in a dark high
gloss may also be found.

Several marks were used: 'P.R.P.'; 'S.E.G.'; or the circular device,
'Boston, Paul Revere Pottery' with the horse and rider.

The pottery continued to operate; and, even though their product
sold well, the high production costs of the handmade ware caused the
pottery to fail in 1946.

Bowl, gr/gold crystalline flambe, PRP, 9" dia, NM 250.00
Bowl, gun metal, blk-on-bl int, PRP, 7½" 150.00
Box, bl semimatt, cylinder w/dome lid, SEG/11-22, 2½x4" 140.00
Box, gun-metal gray matt, mk, w/lid, 5" dia 85.00
Candle holders, bl/gr mottle, PRP, rpr, 7½x4", pr 125.00
Creamer, bl w/brn line & wht at top, bl int, SEG/5-21/ECT, 3¼" 100.00
Cup & saucer, rabbit medallion, bl bands, SEG 11-21 SG 200.00
Luncheon service, tree band, gr/bl/blk on cream, SEG, 3-pc 550.00
Mug, trees/bird/verse, SEG/1915/SG, 4" 1,400.00
Pitcher, lg tulips, yel/brn/blk on yel, SEG/AM, 8", VG 650.00
Pitcher, purple flambe, 3" 85.00
Pitcher, tankard; snowy mtns at top on bl-gr, 5" 325.00

Plate, trees landscape with moon and
lakeside cottage in Arts and Crafts
style, signed Sara Galner, SEG/SG/11-
15, 12¼", $1,100.00.

Plate, HOS in center, pigs on 3-color bands, SEG/FL, 8½" 1,800.00
Plate, landscape border on lt bl, PRP, 8" 240.00
Plate, Sammy His Plate, SEG, 8", +mug, Sammy His Mug, ducks .795.00
Tile, cottage/lake scene in center, 6-color, SEG, 5¾" dia 400.00
Vase, band of flying ducks, 4-color on lt bl, PRP, 8½" 1,300.00
Vase, bl matt, paper label, bulbous, 7" 200.00
Vase, blk-lined trees, brn on gray-gr, SEG, cylindrical, 7" 440.00
Vase, bud; bl gloss, bulbous base, PRP, 8" 95.00
Vase, chrome yel matt, mk, 8¾" 140.00
Vase, gray/bl gloss w/dk specks, bowl form, #924, 3½x4½" 95.00
Vase, silver crystals on speckled brn, PRP, 6" 250.00
Vase, teal drip on bl gloss, PRP, 10½x5½" 350.00
Vase, tulips, yel on dk/lt/teal bl mottle, PRP, 9x4¾" 200.00

Peachblow

Peachblow, made to imitate the colors of the Chinese Peachbloom
porcelain, was made by several glasshouses in the late 1800s. Among
them were New England Glass; Mt. Washington; Webb; and Hobbs,
Brockunier and Company (Wheeling). Its pink shading was achieved
through action of the heat on the gold content of the glass. While New
England's peachblow shades from deep crimson to white, Mt. Washington's tends to shade from pink to blue-gray. Many pieces were enameled and gilded. While by far the majority of the pieces made by New
England had a satin (acid) finish, they made shiny peachblow as well.

Wheeling glass, on the other hand, is rarely found in satin. In the 1950s Gundersen-Pairpoint Glassworks initiated the reproduction of Mt. Washington peachblow using an exact duplication of the original formula. Though of recent manufacture, this glass is very collectible. Our advisors for this category are Betty and Clarence Maier; they are listed in the Directory under Pennsylvania.

Basket, Hobnail, w/amber hdl, Sandwich, 6½x6" **250.00**
Bottle, scent; allover gold netting, floral emb, Webb, 4½" **500.00**
Bowl, gold leaves/int decor, scalloped/folded rim, Webb, 7" **250.00**
Bowl, gold pine needles & flowers, Webb, 2⅝x9x7" **295.00**
Bowl, low ped ft, Webb, 4x7⅜" **495.00**
Bowl, sq frosted briar hdls, Sandwich, 4x9¼" **450.00**
Celery vase, acid, NE Glass, crimped, 6" **500.00**
Celery vase, Hobnail, Sandwich, 7x4" **475.00**
Celery vase, pie crust crimped, NE Glass, 3¾" **175.00**
Condiment, ribbed pillar, HP floral, Webb, 3-pc, SP fr **475.00**
Creamer, amber hdl, Wheeling, 3" **575.00**
Cup & saucer, acid, reeded hdl, Gundersen, poor color, 3½x5" **50.00**
Cup & saucer, Gundersen, EX color **275.00**
Darner, NE Glass, 6" **155.00**
Ewer, acid, gold floral/berries/butterfly, Webb, 6¾", pr **350.00**

Morgan vase, Wheeling, 8¾", $1,100.00.

Pitcher, appl clear branch hdl w/leaf Xs body, cased, 9" **200.00**
Pitcher, conical top on 2-ball pinched body, NE Glass, 7" **400.00**
Pitcher, Drape, amber hdl, ruffled lip, Wheeling, 8" **800.00**
Pitcher, duckbill spout, Wheeling, rare, 6¾x4" **3,500.00**
Pitcher, quadrefoil top, amber hdl, Wheeling, 7¼" **1,250.00**
Pitcher, 10-row Hobnail, frosted hdl, Sandwich, 6¾" **550.00**
Plate, luncheon; Gundersen, 8" **150.00**
Rose bowl, gold flowers & butterfly, Webb, 2½" **385.00**
Rose bowl, NE Glass, 4x4" **485.00**
Rose bowl, ribbed, NE Glass, 2½x3" **350.00**
Shaker, EX color, Wheeling, 2¾" **485.00**
Shaker, tubular, 2-pc top, NE Glass, 3⅝" **535.00**
Spooner, crimped top, NE Glass, 4½x3¼" **750.00**
Spooner, Wheeling, 4½" **375.00**
Sugar shaker, orig metal top, Wheeling, 5¾x3½" **1,750.00**
Syrup pitcher, flares toward bottom, orig top, Wheeling **2,750.00**
Tumbler, Gundersen, 3¾" **140.00**
Tumbler, Hobbs & Brockunier, 4" **250.00**
Tumbler, NE Glass, 3¾" **250.00**
Tumbler, Wheeling, 3½" **325.00**
Urn, acid, gold/HP ferns, ornate metal base/lid, Webb, 23" **600.00**
Vase, acid, bulbous, Wheeling, 3½" **500.00**
Vase, acid, cylindrical w/3-lobe rim, NE Glass, 11" **300.00**
Vase, acid, dimpled body, stick neck, Webb, 8" **120.00**

Vase, acid, gold daisies/butterflies, stick neck, Webb, 9" **300.00**
Vase, acid, stick neck, Webb, 11" **175.00**
Vase, acid, swirl mold, ruffled, Sandwich, 5" **75.00**
Vase, bulbous, Wheeling, 6½x6½" **850.00**
Vase, chalice shape, Gundersen, 12" **350.00**
Vase, cornucopia; ruffled top, Gundersen **525.00**
Vase, deep color, pale cream int, Stevens & Wms, 13¼x6" **725.00**
Vase, gold branches/silver flowers, Webb, 5¼x3½" **265.00**
Vase, gold floral vines/butterfly, stick neck, Webb, 10" **450.00**
Vase, gold florals & dragonfly, Webb, 5½x2½" **500.00**
Vase, lily; acid, Mt WA, 7" **3,000.00**
Vase, lily; bird-on-branch SP fr, 5½" **675.00**
Vase, lily; Gundersen, 9x3¼" **425.00**
Vase, Mat-Su-Noke florals, crimped, Stevens & Wms, 4¾x2¾" ...**350.00**
Vase, mc birds & flowers w/gold, Webb propeller mk, 5x3½" **495.00**
Vase, Morgan; in amber griffin holder, Wheeling, 7¾" **1,750.00**
Vase, pk band encircles shoulder, Gundersen, 6½x3¾" **145.00**
Vase, Roman Key bands/Grecian lady, sqd hdls, Webb, 8" **700.00**
Vase, stick neck, Wheeling, 8" **850.00**
Vase, tapered, Wheeling, 3½" **350.00**
Vase, Wheeling, 13" **1,250.00**

Pearlware

Developed by Wedgwood in the late 1770s primarily for their dinnerware lines, pearlware was soon being made by many other Staffordshire potteries as well. Much of it was made for export to America. It is characterized by its blue-white body, similar in appearance to true porcelain. During the first decade of the 1800s, pearlware with chinoiserie decorations and hand-painted flowers became popular.

Bowl, bl feather edge, underglaze bl/yel daisies, Wood, 7½" **365.00**
Coffeepot, 4-color springs encircle floral, dome lid, 10", EX **650.00**
Creamer, bl & wht molded design, lt stain, 3¼" **385.00**
Creamer, floral, yel/gr/ocher, bl band, leaf hdl, 4⅜", EX **116.00**
Creamer, underglaze bl floral/leaf/striping, emb hdl, 3" **210.00**
Figure, man w/bottle in hand, ca 1795, 5½", EX **300.00**
Mug, satyr face, brn & gr, ca 1795, 4⅛" **350.00**
Mug, wide 5-color floral band, brn striping/band, 6", NM **825.00**
Obelisk, appl classical medallions on bl, rprs, 1800s, 11½" **495.00**
Plate, Adam's Rose type, Wood, 6¾" **35.00**
Plate, bl & wht Oriental decor on emb rim, flakes, 4¾" **165.00**
Plate, lg red flower w/yel & blk, lt bl border, scalloped, 9" **100.00**
Plate, 4-color floral, brn rim stripe, lt wear, 8¼" **115.00**
Plate, 4-color leaf band, sprig center, 8-sided, 6½" **140.00**
Platter, bl feather edge, lg underglaze bl floral, 13½", NM **575.00**
Platter, bl feather edge, mk Best Goods, 12½" **85.00**
Sauce boat, duck form, gr/bl/yel/gray, ca 1790, 7¾" **500.00**
Sugar bowl, yel/bl leaves, bl buds, acorn finial, 5", VG **325.00**
Tea bowl & saucer, bl 5-petal floral w/yel & gr, Davenport, NM ...**180.00**
Tea bowl & saucer, floral, bl & wht, flake **155.00**
Tea bowl & saucer, lg bl flower w/4-color leaf, mk #5, EX **260.00**
Tea bowl & saucer, peafowl, 5-color, EX **700.00**
Tea bowl & saucer, sepia scene, red rim, EX **40.00**
Teapot, floral wreaths, 3-color, acorn finial, 7½", EX **400.00**
Teapot, mc floral band, emb floral hdl, 5½", NM **325.00**
Teapot, rose, mc, hairline/crazing, 5⅞" **240.00**

Peking Cameo Glass

The first glasshouse was established in Peking in 1680. It produced glassware made in imitation of porcelain, a more desirable medium to the Chinese. By 1725 multilayered carving that resulted in a cameo effect lead to the manufacture of a wider range of shapes and colors. The factory was closed from 1736 to 1795, but glass made in Po-shan and shipped to Peking for finishing continued to be called Peking glass. See also Orientalia.

Bowl, deep aubergine, hexagonal w/everted rim, 5¼" **2,000.00**
Bowl, forest gr, flower form, ca 1900, 5½" **78.00**
Bowl, milk wht, scrolled hdls, pewter mts, 1800s, 5¼" **88.00**
Cup, egg-yolk yel, flared rim, ca 1800, 2¼" **400.00**
Plate, forest gr, 12-sided, late 1800s, 10½" **125.00**
Plate, milk wht, pewter trim, late 1800s, 6¾" **75.00**
Plate, pale gr, late 1800s, 9¾" **115.00**
Vase, phoenixes & masks form band, yel, 1800s, 5½" **1,000.00**
Vase, vibrant lime gr globular form, 6⅞" **2,000.00**

Cameo

Bowl, bird on flower branch, gr on wht, 1900, 6⅛", pr **1,400.00**
Ginger jar, crane & lotus on pk, globular form, 1800s, 8" **1,000.00**
Vase, bird on floral branch, bl on wht, stick neck, 1800s, 8" **700.00**
Vase, bird on fruited branch, red & gr on wht, 9" **800.00**
Vase, birds & flowering lotus plants, gr on wht, 1900, 8", pr ...**1,000.00**
Vase, figural landscape, blk on wht, 1800s, 8½", pr **2,500.00**
Vase, floral scrolls, lappet band, bl on clear, 1800s, 8¾" **3,200.00**
Vase, florals & bird, yel on wht, 8" **300.00**

Peloton

Peloton glass was first made by Wilhelm Kralik in Bohemia in 1880. This unusual art glass was produced by rolling colored threads onto the transparent or opaque glass gather as it was removed from the furnace. Usually more than one color of threading was used, and some items were further decorated with enameling. It was made with both shiny and acid finishes.

Pitcher, overshot frosted, mc strings, 8", +4" tumbler **300.00**
Rose bowl, mc coconut strings on wht, petal ft, 3¾x2½" **295.00**
Rose bowl, rim w/3 pulls, clear rigaree/ft, ribbed, 4x3½" **325.00**
Vase, clear, bl strings, bulbous, 6¾x5⅛" **145.00**
Vase, clear, gr strings & hdls, 6¾x5⅜" **195.00**
Vase, clear over lav, mc strings, corset shape, crimped, 6" **450.00**
Vase, dk lav to wht, mc strings, 5½" **350.00**
Vase, lav to cream, clear cased, mc strings, ribbed, 6x5" **450.00**
Vase, pk cased, mc strings, ruffled rim, 3½x3" **195.00**
Vase, wht, mc strings, ruffled, 5 wishbone ft, 6½x4" **450.00**
Vase, wht cased, mc strings, ruffled, 5¼x4¼" **225.00**
Vase, wht w/mc pastel strings, ribbed, 5 appl ft, ruffled, 7" **450.00**

Pennsbury

Established in the 1950s in Morrisville, Pennsylvania, by Henry Below, the Pennsbury Pottery produced dinnerware and novelty items, much of which was sold in gift shops along the Pennsylvania Turnpike. Henry and his wife, Lee, worked for years at the Stangl Pottery before striking out on their own. Lee and her daughter were the artists responsible for many of the early pieces, the bird figures among them. Pennsbury pottery was hand painted, some in blue on white, some in multicolor on caramel. Pennsylvania Dutch motifs, Amish couples, and barbershop singers were among their most popular decorative themes. Sgraffito (hand incising) was used extensively. The company marked their wares 'Pennsbury Pottery' or 'Pennsbury Pottery, Morrisville, PA.'

In October of 1969 the company closed. Contents of the pottery were sold in December of the following year, and in April of 1971, the buildings burned to the ground. Items marked Pennsbury Glenview or Stumar Pottery (or these marks in combination) were made by Glenview after 1969. Pieces manufactured after 1976 were made by the Pennington Pottery. Several of the old molds still exist, and the original Pennsbury Caramel process is still being used on novelty items, some of which are produced by Lewis Brothers, NJ. Production of Pennsbury dinnerware was not resumed after the closing. Our advisor for this category is Shirley Graff; she is listed in the Directory under Ohio. Note: prices may be higher in some areas of the country — particularly on the East Coast, the southern states, and Texas.

Advertising sign, 4½" long, $145.00.

Ashtray, Amish 20.00
Ashtray, Doylestown Trust 25.00
Ashtray, Outen the Light 20.00
Ashtray, Rotary Club, Levittown, 8" 15.00
Ashtray, Such Schmootzers 18.00
Bowl, Folkart, rnd, 11" 30.00
Bowl, pretzel, Gay Nineties 85.00
Bowl, Revere, ftd, 9" 30.00
Butter dish, Blk Rooster 40.00
Cake stand, Blk Rooster 75.00
Candle holder, Red Rooster 40.00
Candy dish, Hex, 6" 30.00
Canister, Blk Rooster, wooden lid, 4-pc set, minimum value 385.00
Coaster, Fish, pretzel form 15.00
Cookie jar, hummingbird, wht, #119 ....150.00
Creamer & sugar bowl, Red Rooster 40.00
Cruet, Amish head, pr 100.00
Cruet, Gay Nineties, pr 150.00
Cup & saucer, Blk Rooster 30.00
Cup & saucer, Hex 20.00
Dish, fish form, gr & wht, 10" L 30.00
Gravy boat, Blk Rooster 30.00
Mug, Barbershop Quartet 25.00
Mug, beer; Eagle, 5" 20.00
Mug, coffee; Amish 30.00
Pitcher, Amish lady, mini 17.50
Pitcher, Amish man, 4" 20.00
Pitcher, Folkart, 3¾" 22.50
Pitcher, Hex, 4" 20.00
Plaque, Bucks Country Week commemorative 40.00
Plaque, Nat'l Newark & Essex 30.00
Plate, Courting Buggy, 8" 25.00
Plate, Daily Bread, 8" 55.00
Plate, Mother's Day, 1971 ....22.50
Plate, Red Rooster, factory fr, 11" 65.00
Plate, Red Rooster, 10" 40.00

Shakers, Red Rooster, pr 20.00
Teapot, Red Rooster, 4-cup 55.00
Tile, Amish, 4" 20.00
Tile, basket of flowers, 6" 35.00
Tile, Don't Be Doppish 25.00
Tile, Picking Apples, 6" 35.00
Wall pocket, Blk Rooster 42.00

Pens and Pencils

The first metallic writing pen was patented in 1809, and soon machine-produced pens with steel nibs gradually began replacing the quill. The first fountain pen was invented in 1830; but, due to the fact that a suitable metal for the tips had not yet been developed, they were not manufactured commercially until the 1880s. The first successful commercial producers were Waterman in 1884 and Parker with the Lucky Curve in 1888.

The self-filling pen of 1890 featured the soft, interior sack which filled with ink as the metal bar on the outside of the pen was raised and lowered. Variations of the pumping mechanism were tried until 1932 when Parker introduced the Vacumatic, a sackless pen with an internal pump. Our advisors for this category are Judy and Cliff Lawrence; they are listed in the Directory under Florida. For those seeking additional information, a catalog is published monthly by the Pen Fancier's, whose address can be found in the Directory under Clubs, Newsletters, and Catalogs. In the listings that follow, all pens are lever-filled unless otherwise noted.

Key:

AF — aeromatic filler	GPT — gold-plated trim
BF — button filler	HR — hard rubber
CF — cartridge filler	NPT — nickel-plated trim
CPT — chrome-plated trim	PF — plunger filler
ED — eyedropper filler	TD — touchdown filler
GFT — gold-filled trim	VF — vacumatic filler
GPM — gold-plated metal	

Ballpoint Pens

Everhard Faber, 1946, brn/GF cap, EX 65.00
Eversharp, CA, 1946, bl/GF cap, M 95.00
Eversharp, CA, 1947, GFM, EX 125.00
Eversharp, Skyline, CA, 1944, maroon w/striped cap, EX 50.00
Eversharp, Skyline, CA, 1948, brn/gold striped cap, M 50.00
Reynold's, Internat'l, 1945, aluminum, GF clip, EX 125.00
Sheaffer, Stratowriter, 1946, GFM, M 95.00

Dip Pens

ES Johnson, MOP & GFM (seamless), #4 nib, EX 165.00
Grieshaber, orange & wht glass holder & GFM, worn nib holder .65.00
HM Smith, 1867, retractable, pencil combo, blk HR, GFT, EX .125.00
LeRoy W Fairchild Regal, reverse holder, blk HR, GFT, EX 150.00
Spencer, MOP & GFM (seamless), #3 nib, EX 150.00

Fountain Pens

Conklin, Crescent Filler, 1925, GFM filigree, EX 800.00
Conklin, Crescent Filler #20P, 1924, blk chased HR, GFT, EX .150.00
Eversharp, #64, 1944, maroon, solid gold cap & trim, LF, EX 350.00
Eversharp, Silver Seal Doric, 1940, silver pearl, NPT, LF, G 125.00
Eversharp, Skyline, 1942, brn, GFT, LF, G 69.00
Eversharp, Skyline, 1944, blk, silver striped cap, GFT, LF, EX 99.00

John Holland, Royal, 1926, ivory w/red ends, GFT, LF, EX 149.00
John Holland, 1922, GFM, LF, EX 179.00
Moore, Fingertip, 1947, maroon, chrome cap, GFT, LF, EX 99.00
Parker, #25½ Jack Knife Safety Lucky Curve, 1919, BF, EX 995.00
Parker, #51, 1951, gr, Lustraloy cap, CPT, AF, EX 52.00
Parker, #61, 1956, turq, Lustraloy cap, CPT, M 125.00
Parker, #75, 1965, sterling silver, GFT, EX 129.00
Parker, Bl Dmn Duofold, 1941, pearl/blk stripes, GFT, VF, EX 95.00
Parker, Bl Dmn Maxima Vacumatic, 1939, stripes, GFT, VF, EX ..500.00
Parker, Bl Dmn Slender Maxima Vacumatic, 1940, VF, EX 350.00
Parker, Bl Dmn Vacumatic, 1946, gold stripes, GFT, VF, EX 95.00
Parker, Bl Dmn 51, 1945, mustard brn, GF cap, GFT, VG, EX ..145.00
Parker, Challenger, 1939, blk, GFT, BF, EX 99.00
Parker, Duofold, 1941, gold-gr pearl/blk stripes, GFT, BF, EX 105.00
Parker, Duofold Jr, 1933, burgundy/blk marbleized, GFT, BF, EX ..165.00
Parker, Duofold Sr Big Red, 1925, GFT, BF, EX 325.00
Parker, No 2½ Lucky Curve, 1918, blk chased HR, GFT, BF, EX ..145.00
Parker, No 2½ Lucky Curve DQ, 1922, blk-lined HR, BF, EX ...135.00
Parker, Parkette, 1938, red marbled, GFT, alloy nib, G 55.00
Parker, Slender Maxima, 1942, silver stripes, NPT, VF, EX 325.00
Parker, True Bl Ring, 1929, GFT, BF, EX 115.00
Parker, True Bl Ring, 1930, GFT, BF, G 99.00
Parker, Vacumatic Jr, 1947, bl stripes, GFT, VF, EX 85.00
Pick, 1926, blk chased HR, red ends, GFT, LF, M 129.00
Sheaffer, Admiral Snorkel, 1954, gr, GFT, M 39.00
Sheaffer, Lifetime, 1926, blk, GFT, initialed, LF, EX 325.00
Sheaffer, Lifetime, 1934, pearl & blk marbleized, GFT, LF, EX ..165.00
Sheaffer, Lifetime #875, 1937, silver stripes, NPT, LF, EX 119.00
Sheaffer, Triumph Lifetime Masterpc, 1942, 14k gold, LF, EX ..1,500.00
Sheaffer, Wht Dot Crest Triumph TM, 1951, gr, GFT, TD, EX ...75.00
Sheaffer, Wht Dot Imperial IV, 1965, blk, GFT, TD, EX 59.00
Wahl, #2, 1921, blk chased HR, NPT, LF, EX 149.00
Wahl, Oxford, 1933, pearl & blk marbleized, GFT, LF, G 99.00
Wahl, 1927, red mottled HR, GFT, LF, EX 149.00
Wahl-Eversharp, Gold Seal Doric, 1932, blk, GFT, LF, EX 900.00
Waterman, Hundred Year, 1944, blk, GFT, LF, std sz, EX 260.00
Waterman, Ideal, 1939, blk, globe clip, GFT, LF, EX 350.00
Waterman, Ideal #452, 1927, sterling filigree, LF, EX 600.00
Waterman, Ideal #454, 1925, sterling, initialed, LF, EX 650.00
Waterman, Ideal #52V, 1925, red HR, GFT, LF, EX 200.00
Waterman, Supersz Hundred Year, 1942, blk, GFT, LF, EX 899.00

Mechanical Pencils

Conklin, 1930, blk, GFT, EX 79.00
Eversharp, Presentation Skyline Repeater, 1945, gr, GFT, M 99.00
Eversharp, 1938, gr jade marbleized, GFT, initialed, EX 95.00
Gold Medal, 1927, red HR, GFT, M 229.00
Parker, Duofold Jr, 1927, gr jade, GFT, EX 125.00
Parker, Pastel, 1927, magenta moire, GFT, M 95.00
Parker, 51, 1948, blk, GF top, EX 79.00
Parker, 51 Liquid Lead, 1954, blk, GF top, GFT, M 49.00
Parker, 51 Repeater, 1951, gr, Lustraloy top, CPT, M 42.00
Sheaffer, Lifetime, 1925, blk, GFT, EX 35.00
Sheaffer, Wht Dot, 1967, sterling silver, G 69.00
Wahl-Eversharp, Gold Seal, 1929, rosewood, GFT, EX 125.00
Wahl-Eversharp, lady's, 1920, eng vine pattern, sterling, EX 149.00
Waterman, Ideal, 1925, sterling, EX 300.00
Waterman, Ideal, 1928, olive ripple HR, GFT, EX 165.00

Sets

Parker, Bl Dmn Major Vacumatic & Repeater, 1939, red, GFT, EX ...295.00
Parker, 61, 1956, aqua, GF caps, GFT, capillary filler, EX 195.00

Parker, 61 Presidential, 1960, 14k gold, capillary filler, EX 1,200.00
Parker, 61 1st Edition Heritage, 1956, turq, GFM caps, EX 395.00
Pelikan-Gunther Wagner, Man, 1952, blk, gr stripes, GFT, M ...259.00
Sheaffer, Admiral Snorkel, 1954, maroon, GFT, M 49.00
Sheaffer, Lifetime #2000, 1946, blk w/14k gold trim, LF, NM 275.00
Sheaffer, Wht Dot Clipper Snorkel, 1952, gray, GFT, TD, EX 79.00
Waterman, Hundred Year, 1942, ruby red, GFT, LF, std sz, EX ..399.00

Personalities, Fact and Fiction

One of the largest and most popular areas of collecting today, if tradepaper ads and articles be any indication, is character-related memorabilia. Everyone has favorites, whether they be comic-strip personalities or true-life heroes. The earliest comic strip dealt with the adventures of the Yellow Kid, the smiling, bald-headed Oriental boy always in a nightshirt. He was introduced in 1895, a product of the imagination of Richard Fenton Outcault. Today, though very hard to come by, items relating to the Yellow Kid bring premium prices.

In 1902 Buster Brown and Tige, his dog and constant companion (more of Outcault's progenies), made it big in the comics as well as in the world of advertising. Shoe stores appealed to the younger set through merchandising displays that featured them both. Today items from their earlier years are very collectible.

Though her 1923 introduction was unobtrusively made through only one newspaper, New York's *Daily News,* Little Orphan Annie, the vacant-eyed redhead in the inevitable red dress, was quickly adopted by hordes of readers nationwide; and before the demise of her creator, Harold Gray, in 1968, she had starred in her own radio show. She made two feature films, and in 1977 'Annie' was launched on Broadway.

Other early comic figures were Moon Mullins, created in 1923 by Frank Willard; Buck Rogers by Philip Nowlan in 1928; and Betty Boop, the round-faced, innocent-eyed, chubby-cheeked Boop-Boop-a-Doop girl of the early 1930s. Bimbo was her dog and KoKo her clown friend.

Popeye made his debut in 1929 as the spinach-eating sailor with the spindly-limbed girlfriend, Olive Oyl, in the comic strip *Thimble Theatre,* created by Elzie Segar. He became a film star in 1933 and had his own radio show that during 1936 played three times a week on CBS. He obligingly modeled for scores of toys, dolls, and figurines, and especially those from the thirties are very collectible.

Tarzan, created around 1930 by Edgar Rice Burroughs, and Captain Midnight, by Robert Burtt and Willfred G. Moore, are popular heroes with today's collectors. During the days of radio, Sky King of the Flying Crown Ranch (also created by Burtt and Moore) thrilled boys and girls of the mid-1940s. Hopalong Cassidy, Red Rider, Tom Mix, and the Lone Ranger were only a few of the other 'good guys' always on the side of law and order.

But of all the fictional heroes and comic characters collected today, probably the best loved and most well known is Mickey Mouse. Created in the late 1920s by Walt Disney, Micky (as his name was first spelled) became an instant success with his film debut, Steamboat Willie. His popularity was parlayed through wind-up toys, watches, figurines, cookie jars, puppets, clothing, and numerous other products. Items from the 1930s are usually copyrighted 'Walt Disney Enterprises'; thereafter, 'Walt Disney Productions' was used.

For those interested in Disneyanna, we recommend *Stern's Guide to Disney Collectibles; Character Toys and Collectibles* (there are two volumes); and *The Collector's Encyclopedia of Disneyana.* All are available from Collector Books. Our advisors for this category are Cathy and Norm Vigue; they are listed in the Directory under Massachusetts. See also Autographs; Banks; Big Little Books; Cartoon Books; Children's Books; Comic Books; Cookie Jars; Dolls; Games; Lunch Boxes; Movie Memorabilia; Paper Dolls; Pin-Back Buttons; Posters; Puzzles; Rock 'N Roll Memorabilia; Toys.

Addams Family, Gomez hand puppet, NM 130.00
Addams Family, Haunted House model kit, Aurora/Filmways, EX ..595.00
Alfred E Newman, model, unbuilt, Aurora, 1965, NMIB 185.00
Alice in Wonderland, paint book, bright cover, 1951, M 55.00
Andy Panda, Fast Action book, 1942, EX 40.00
Atom Ant, Tricky Trapeze, M 28.50
Baby Huey, hand puppet, M 45.00
Barney Google & Spark Plug, figure, bsk, 1922, 3x3", EX 110.00
Barney Rubble, doll, vinyl, 1960, 10", M 30.00
Batman, Batchute, 1966, M 30.00
Batman, bull horn, plastic, Bayshore Ind, 1966, M 42.00
Batman, glasses, 1966, M 8.00
Batman, hand puppet, cloth body, M 40.00
Batman & Robin, talking alarm clock, MIB 120.00
Beany, hat w/2-propellers, NM 45.00
Beany & Cecil, Colorforms set, 1961, MIB 125.00

Betty Boop nodder, celluloid, Made in Japan, copyright Fleischer Studios, 7", NMIB, $1,500.00.

Betty Boop, figure, jtd wood, orig blk dress, Kallus, EX 850.00
Betty Boop, figure, jtd wood & compo, 1930s, 12", NM 525.00
Betty Boop, socks, 1930s, orig label, rare, pr 95.00
Betty Grable, color book, 1953, unused 45.00
Big Bird, alarm clock, animated, tin litho, 1960, NM 18.50
Billy the Kid, cap gun, metal w/buffaloes on hdls, 8", MIB 135.00
Bonzo, toothpick holder, porc figural, 1930s 45.00
Bozo the Clown, slide puzzle, illus card 19.50
Buck Jones, badge, Jr Sheriff, EX 22.00
Buck Jones, horseshoe pin, EX 20.00
Buck Rogers, badge, Solar Scout, 1935, NM 95.00
Buck Rogers, figure, solid lead, Cocomalt premium, M 15.00
Buck Rogers, flying saucer, 1940s, NM 90.00
Buck Rogers, pin-bk button, Whitehead & Hoag, 1935, M 65.00
Buck Rogers, pocket watch, Ingraham, 1935, NM 495.00
Buck Rogers, Pop pistol, 1930s, NM 188.00
Buck Rogers, sweater emblem, Solar Scout, M 60.00
Buck Rogers, uniform, M 250.00
Buck Rogers, Walkie Talkie, 1950s, M 75.00
Buck Rogers, Wilma, lead figure, solid, M 15.00
Buckwheat, wristwatch, 1988, MIB 65.00
Buffy & Jody (Family Affair), alarm clock, Sheffield, CBS, NM ...65.00
Bugs Bunny, Soaky, 10", NM 15.00
Bullwinkle, balancing toy, 1969, M on card 15.00
Bullwinkle, color book, 1972, M 15.00
Buster Crabbe, TV Week guide, BC on cover, 1950, NM 12.50
Buzz Corey, wristwatch, Time Co, M w/tag in 5" worn box 500.00
Captain Marvel, Billy Batson magic box, NM 60.00
Captain Marvel, button, club membership, 1947, NM 80.00
Captain Marvel, club letter/envelope, 1944 ....28.00
Captain Marvel, Magic whistle, 1947, NM 75.00

Captain Marvel, tie clip, figural, 1944, NM on VG illus card 80.00
Captain Marvel, toss bag, NM 41.00
Captain Midnight, badge, Flight Patrol Wings, 1941, M 65.00
Captain Midnight, manual for decoder, 1941, M 120.00
Captain Midnight, manual for Silver Dart decoder, 1957, M 240.00
Captain Midnight, ring, Mystic Eye Detector, 1942, M 145.00
Captain Midnight, service ribbon pin, 1944, M 65.00
Captain Midnight, spy scope, 1947, M 75.00
Carmen Miranda, color book, 1942, unused 40.00
Casper, color book, Casper & Ghostly Trio, 1966, unused, M 18.00
Casper, color book, Spooky & Casper, 1966, unused, M 13.50
Casper, Harveyland Read & Do album, '72, unused, M 20.00
Casper & Wendy, kite, paper, unused, M 13.50
Cat in Hat, music box, Dr Seuss, 1970, M 45.00
Cecil, costume, Ben Cooper, M 55.00
Cecil, disguise kit, Mattel, 1962, NM 52.00
Charlie Chaplin, figure, celluloid, 4", NM 1,350.00
Charlie Chaplin, Funny Stunts comic book, 1917, EX 50.00
Charlie McCarthy, doll, rubber, Effanbee, NM 68.00
Charlie McCarthy, figure, Elastolin, scarce, 1930, NM 115.00
Charlie McCarthy, paint book, 1938, EX 75.00
Charlie McCarthy, paper money, M, ea pc 5.00
Charlie McCarthy, spoon, metal, figural hdl 5.00
Cisco Kid, bread label, EX 5.00
Cisco Kid, comic album, 1953, EX 12.50
Cisco Kid, hobby horse, EX 90.00
Cisco Kid, western outfit, 1950, NM 90.00
Cisco Kid & Pancho, cereal bowl, blk on milk glass, M 20.00
Cisco Kid & Pancho, color book, Saalfield, oversz, unused 20.00
Dale Evans, cowgirl outfit, illus box, '40, unused, VG+ 72.00
Dale Evans, holster outfit, NM 135.00
Dale Evans, Lucky Horseshoe pendant necklace, M on card 20.00
Dale Evans, wash mit, cloth 20.00
Davy Crockett, Alamo ID bracelet, MIB 50.00
Davy Crockett, bank, Pony Express saddle bag, M in pkg 30.00
Davy Crockett, gun & holster set, MIB 75.00
Davy Crockett, lamp, DC figural, coppery metal, orig shade 125.00
Davy Crockett, night light, cb conestoga, Cactus Craft, M 110.00
Davy Crockett, pistol, flintlock type, Marx, 11", NM 40.00
Davy Crockett, plate, Oxford China 50.00
Davy Crockett, powder horn, compass & belt, M on card 10.00
Davy Crockett, wristwatch, NM in 2x5" box w/Liberty Bell 635.00
Deanna Durbin, color book, 1940, unused 40.00
Dennis the Menace, squirt gun, figural, 1954, MIB 60.00
Deputy Dawg, Soaky, M 18.00

Dick Tracy pop-up book, vivid color, NM, $175.00.

Dick Tracy, badge, Honor, M 42.00
Dick Tracy, Cine-Vue camera, plastic, Acme, '47, EX, +3 films 115.00
Dick Tracy, click pistol, Marx #36, NM 90.00
Dick Tracy, doll, Little Honeymoon, 1965, NMIB 185.00

Dick Tracy, electronic wrist radio, M 105.00
Dick Tracy, figure, pnt compo, mouth moves, 13½", M 375.00
Dick Tracy, hat ring, NM 185.00
Dick Tracy, jackknife, illus hdl, authorized, 1940, EX 50.00
Dick Tracy, penlight, 1940s, M 60.00
Dick Tracy, Sparkle Plenty, soap figure, MIB 39.00
Dick Tracy, telephone, Marx, 1967, M 35.00
Dick Tracy, water pistol, plastic, 1955, M 30.00
Dionne Quints, fan, cb, N Haledon Bus Lines, 1935, EX 35.00
Dionne Quints, scrapbook, over 150 clippings, EX 75.00
Don McNeill's Breakfast Club, 1954 Yearbook, 48-pg, EX 15.00
Don Winslow, flashlight gun, NM 105.00
Donald Duck, ashtray, ceramic, Italy, 3½x5x4", NM 25.00
Donald Duck, bank, tin litho bldg, Chein, WDP, 7" L, NM 185.00
Donald Duck, letter opener, HP celluloid, 5" 65.00
Donald Duck, planter, ceramic, Italy, 1950s, 6½x7x3", EX 15.00
Donald Duck, pocket watch, Ingersoll, 1939, scarce, EX 325.00
Donald Duck, Soaky 15.00
Dopey, bank, WD, American Pottery, NM 125.00
Dr Doolittle, costume, Emma Fairfax, 1963, unused, MIB 38.00
Dr Doolittle, hand puppet, talking, 1967, M 70.00
Dr Doolittle, model kit, The Flounder, Aurora, sealed, M 145.00
Dukes of Hazzard, slot car, electric, Ideal, 1981, M on card 14.00
Dumbo, figural planter, American Pottery, NM 32.00
Elmer Fudd, Soaky, 1960, 10", M 15.00
Felix the Cat, bud vase, Made in Japan, 5", NM 550.00
Felix the Cat, candy pail, tin litho, w/lid, 8x7" dia, EX 850.00
Felix the Cat, china set, NM 90.00
Felix the Cat, cigarette lighter, 1930s, 2", EX 85.00
Felix the Cat, creamer, porc figural, blk/wht/bl, 4", NM 85.00
Felix the Cat, figure, CI, 1923, 2", NM 90.00
Felix the Cat, figure, HP compo, stands up, 1920s, 4½", EX 150.00
Felix the Cat, figure, lead, 2½", M 120.00
Felix the Cat, figure, wood, 12", M 600.00
Felix the Cat, mustard or condiment pot, 3¾", NM 600.00
Felix the Cat, pep pin, NM 31.00
Felix the Cat, squeeze toy, rubber, 6½", M 75.00

Ferdinand the Bull, child's purse, Walt Disney Enterprises, ca 1938, $100.00.

Fiddler Pig, toothbrush, ceramic, WD, 4¼", EX 50.00
Flash Gordon, kite, jet-propelled, M 70.00
Flash Gordon, Pep pin, NM 30.00
Flash Gordon, 2-way telephone, Marx, 1940s, NM 150.00
Flintstones, Bam Bam figure, Ideal, 12½", NMIB 75.00
Flintstones, Pebbles bank, vinyl, orig label, 1973, M 19.00
Flintstones, Pebbles doll, vinyl, jtd, 7", NM 56.00
Foghorn Leghorn, figural liquor bottle, HP, Italy, NMIB 28.00
Fonzie, paint set, sealed, 1979, MIB 14.50
Fonzie, wristwatch, Time Trends, 1976, NM 65.00

Frankenstein, costume, Universal Monsters, 1980, NM 26.00
Frankenstein, lamp, plastic, head form, 1960, EX 75.00
Frankenstein, picture kit, copper plaque, K&B, 11x8", VG+ 100.00
Frankenstein, Soaky, M 150.00
Gabby Hayes, Shooting Cannon ring, 1951 premium 175.00
Gene Autry, cap gun, CI, faux pearl hdls, w/GA signature, 7" ...275.00
Gene Autry, cap pistol, red grips, signature on fr, 6½", EX 30.00
Gene Autry, photo postcard, M 12.00
Gene Autry, wristwatch, Wilane, w/papers, NMIB 300.00
Gene Autry, 6-Shooter wristwatch, New Haven, EX in photo box .450.00
Gene Autry, 79 rpm record set, Okeh Records, set of 4, NM 30.00
Green Hornet, costume, Ben Cooper, 1966, EX 150.00
Green Hornet, hand puppet, Ideal, NMIB 300.00
Green Hornet, Kato drinking glass, M 75.00
Green Hornet, kite, well illus, 1950s, M in unopened pkg 35.00
Green Hornet, ring, secret compartment, hornet seal, M 450.00
Green Hornet, stickers, Gower/Greenway, 1966, EX 250.00
Happy Hooligan, candy dish, HH on rabbit, compo, 7½", NM .1,350.00
Happy Hooligan, notebook pad, colorful, 1928 ....12.50
Hector Heathcote, Wonder book, 1961, NM 10.00
Herman & Katnip, kite, paper, unused, M 13.50
Herman Munster, doll, Mattel, NM 168.00
Hoot Gibson, lariat, NM 60.00
Hopalong Cassidy, Automatic Shooting Gallery, tin w/up, EX ..280.00
Hopalong Cassidy, briefcase, Hoppy on Topper, M 195.00

Hopalong Cassidy camera, Galter Products, $35.00. Same, MIB (with illustration), $200.00.

Hopalong Cassidy, color photo, inscr, Bond Bread, 1950s 15.00
Hopalong Cassidy, field glasses, metal, 1940, NM 82
Hopalong Cassidy, wristwatch, mtd on saddle, VG in box 300.00
Hopalong Cassidy, wristwatch, US Time, orig band, EX 140.00
Horace Horsecollar, figure, wood, orig ears, WDE, 6½", EX 500.00
Howdy Doody, Circus color book, 1951, unused, M 21.00
Howdy Doody, Clock-A-Doodle clock, tin litho, 9", EX 2,750.00
Howdy Doody, Doodle slate, 1950s, unused, M 24.00
Howdy Doody, Fun Book, bright colors, 1951, NM 45.00
Howdy Doody, Mr Bluster & Dilly Dally lapel pins, EX 38.00
Howdy Doody, mug, HD on lid, Century Plastic, 3½", EX 75.00
Howdy Doody, pencil w/Howdy's head, Kagran, M 11.50
Howdy Doody, sales catalog, 1947, 20-pg, EX 55.00
Howdy Doody, swimming tube, HD & friends, 16" dia, M 60.00
Howdy Doody, wristwatch, 50th Anniversary, NMIB 50.00
I Dream of Jeannie, doll, fully dressed, 20", EX 145.00
Inch High Private Eye, mini gun set, 1973, M on card 9.00
James Bond, Code-O-Matic Machine, Multiple, '60, EX+ 105.00
Jerry Mahoney, ventriloquist dummy, compo head, all orig, 23" ...175.00
Jiggs, stick puppet, 12", M 160.00
Jimmy Allen, flight wings, Richfield, 1934 premium 25.00
Jimmy Allen, photo w/stewardess 15.00
Joe Palooka, punching bag, 1950s, NM 60.00

Jr G-Men of Am, badge, gold-plated tin, 1930, M 18.00
Lady & the Tramp, figures, ceramic, Japan, 1960, M, pr 38.00
Li'l Abner, Baby Barry hand puppet, M 70.00
Li'l Abner, Shmoo doll, inflatable vinyl, 1940, 15", NM 90.00
Little Beaver, archery set, illus cb holder, Slesinger, '51 ....45.00
Little Lulu, doll, felt, 10", NM 150.00
Little Lulu, 3-D Valentines, unpunched set of 4, 1940, M 40.00
Little Orphan Annie, decoder, radio premium, 1940, EX 28.00
Little Orphan Annie, figure, jtd wood, pnt, Jaymar, 5", NM 75.00
Little Orphan Annie, Pep pin, NM 25.00
Little Orphan Annie, Soaky, M 75.00
Little Orphan Annie, stove, 4⅜", NM 15.00
Little Orphan Annie, water pistol, NM 105.00
Little Orphan Annie, wristwatch, New Haven, VG in 7" box ...325.00
Lone Ranger, badge, Deputy, secret compartment, 1949, NM 95.00
Lone Ranger, badge, Silver Cup Bread Safety Scout membership .20.00
Lone Ranger, camera, De-luxe Cine-Vue, +3 films, Acme, '40, EX ..125.00
Lone Ranger, Cheerios box, portrait on front, NM 85.00
Lone Ranger, Deputy kit, Cheerios premium, 1980, M in pkg 18.50
Lone Ranger, Deputy secret folder, 1949 ....36.00
Lone Ranger, globe, Round-Up Show, glass, Drier, '40s, 4", EX ...65.00
Lone Ranger, gum cards, 12 different, mainly G 60.00
Lone Ranger, neckerchief, mk TLR inc, NM 60.00
Lone Ranger, pin, Hi-Yo Silver, 1938, NM 15.00
Lone Ranger, pocketknife, red, silver bullet, EX 75.00
Lone Ranger, ring, Atom Bomb, common, NM 80.00
Lone Ranger, ring, flashlight, NM 53.00
Lone Ranger, Tonto biscuit tin, on Scout, 1950, 5" dia, NM 70.00
Lone Wolf, arrowhead membership pin, 1932 ....16.00
Lucille Ball, writing tablet, color portrait cover, EX 35.00
Lum & Abner, Pine Ridge News letter & mailer, 1936, NM 16.50
Magilla Gorilla, figure, twist & pose, Ideal, 1964, M 35.00
Major Matt Mason, Callisto alien w/accessories, '69, M on card ...190.00
Melvin Pervis, ring, Law & Order, NM 40.00
Mickey Mouse, alarm clock, wood fr, Phinney Walker, EX 35.00
Mickey Mouse, bowl, red enamel European MM, 1930s 65.00
Mickey Mouse, bread wrapper band, paper, red/blk, WDE, NM ...25.00
Mickey Mouse, bubble gum cards, 1930, lot of 8, EX 90.00
Mickey Mouse, cereal spoon, Post Toasties premium, M in pkg ...75.00
Mickey Mouse, clock, Ingersoll, electric, 4¼", G 375.00
Mickey Mouse, Dakin vinyl figure, 1977, 6", M in pkg 27.50
Mickey Mouse, doll, rubber w/movable head, WDP, 10½", VG ...25.00
Mickey Mouse, doll, WDP, Charlotte Clark, 8½", EX 900.00
Mickey Mouse, dye packet, Spain, early 1930s, M 13.00
Mickey Mouse, figure, bsk, in tuxedo & top hat, WD, 4", NM ...400.00
Mickey Mouse, figure, celluloid, rpt, loose string, 5" 150.00
Mickey Mouse, gear shift lever knob, cased in plastic, WDP 45.00
Mickey Mouse, magic slate, WDE, 4x2½", EX 45.00
Mickey Mouse, pencil box, cb figural, Dixon, 8½", EX 225.00
Mickey Mouse, planter, china figural, 4½", EX 375.00
Mickey Mouse, premium picture, Congoleum Rugs, WDE, 12x9", NM .60.00
Mickey Mouse, sand pail, Treasure Island, OH Art, '35, 4", EX .190.00
Mickey Mouse, school ink pen, wooden, early Mickey, 6½" 55.00
Mickey Mouse, sewing kit, Soreng-Manegold, 5" dia, NM 250.00
Mickey Mouse, soap figure, DH&Co of London, 5", NM w/tag ..175.00
Mickey Mouse, teaspoon, stainless, Bunny Japan, WDP 8.50
Mickey Mouse, Transfer-O-S for Easter Eggs, Paas, '30, NM 85.00
Mickey Mouse, wristwatch, bracelet band, 1933, NMIB 695.00
Mickey Mouse Club, LP record, WDP, 26 songs, 1962, EX 20.00
Mickey Mouse Club, pin-bk button, WDE, 1928-30, 1¼", NM 45.00
Mighty Mouse, Soaky, M 30.00
Mighty Mouse, sticker book, unused, '54, M 40.00
Mighty Mouse, Teach Time Pendulum clock, 1981, M in VG box ...18.50
Mighty Mouse, wristwatch, Territoons, 1979 ....85.00

Minnie Mouse, figure, celluloid, loose string, 4¾", EX 150.00
Minnie Mouse, pencil box, cb figural, WD, 8½", EX 85.00
Mr Ed, talking hand puppet, 1962 ....65.00
Mr Magoo, vacuform sign, for Stag beer, 1959, M 45.00
Mr Magoo, Waldo ring, M on illus card 25.00
Mr T, wristwatch, Bradley, 1980, NMIB 60.00
Mutt, dancing doll, wooden, M 80.00
Mutt, figure, bendable, 1946, NM 210.00
Mutt & Jeff, figural pitcher, porc, Germany, 1930s 125.00
Olive Oyl, hand puppet, Gund, 1938, NM 40.00
Olive Oyl, Pep pin, M 15.00
Pappy Yokum, hand puppet, M 40.00
Partridge Family, gum cards, 20 different, M 20.00
Peabody & Sherman, flicker pictures, cereal premium, '60s, M 9.50
Peter Pan, storybook & LP record, WDP, 1969, EX 25.00
Pinocchio, advertising sign, cb, WDP, 21x13", EX 55.00
Pinocchio, bank, compo figural, WDE, 1939, 6", EX 130.00
Pinocchio, Walt Disney's Pinocchio Coloring Book, WDP, 1939, EX ..25.00
Pluto, figure, bsk, 3", EX 45.00
Popeye, belt, brass buckle, Star Suspender & Belt, '29, NM 160.00
Popeye, Bifbat paddle toy, 1929, NM 90.00
Popeye, Brutus mask, cb, 1940s, NM 60.00
Popeye, figure, bl soft plastic, Marx, 60mm, M 12.00
Popeye, figure, CI, 1930s, 3½", NM 150.00
Popeye, hand puppet, M 28.00
Popeye, Jeep figure, jtd wood, pnt, 1930s, 7½", NM 600.00
Popeye, jewelry pins, Bakelite, 10 on orig display card, M 250.00
Popeye, lamp, figural base, orig shade, rstr, 1937, 14½" 400.00
Popeye, mask, cb, 1940s, M 60.00
Popeye, pencil sharpener, hand crank, Irwin, 1919, 3", NM 200.00
Popeye, Times Star Newsboy apron, King Features, 1929, 21", EX ..100.00
Popeye, Yazoo pipe, Northwestern Productions, 1934, NM 45.00
Porky Pig, bank, HP metal, PP beside barrel, 1940s, M 100.00
Porky Pig, hand puppet, 1950s, 8", M 30.00
Porky Pig, liquor bottle, pnt figural, Italy, NMIB 25.00
Porky Pig, Soaky, 1960, 9", M 15.00
Prince Valiant, shield, tin litho, M 60.00
Prince Valiant, sword & tin scabbard, Mattel, 1950s, NM 75.00
Red Ryder, holster, leather, no gun, EX 20.00
Red Ryder, lucky coin, Penney's, M 10.00
Red Ryder, molding set, 1948, M 80.00
Red Ryder, pin, Victory Patrol, NM 125.00
Red Ryder, salesman's case for gloves 125.00
Rin Tin Tin, button, Name the Puppy, w/mailer, M 20.00
Rin Tin Tin, figure, plush & vinyl, name on collar, 12", NM 38.00
Robin, bank, porc figural, 1966, MIB 65.00
Roy Rogers, book, Trigger to the Rescue, Whitman, '50, EX 19.00
Roy Rogers, cap pistol, gold w/plastic hdls, 8", NM on card 240.00
Roy Rogers, crayon set, Roy & Trigger on box, Toykraft, EX 65.00
Roy Rogers, figure, Tootsietoy, 1¾", NM 56.00
Roy Rogers, Fix It Chuck Wagon & Nellie Belle Jeep, +3 figures ..245.00
Roy Rogers, gun, Tuck-A-Way, M on card 50.00
Roy Rogers, gun set w/leather holsters, logo buckle, Schmidt, EX ..495.00
Roy Rogers, movie theater giveaway photo, 1950s, 5x7", M 12.50
Roy Rogers, paint set, 1950s, NM 13.50
Roy Rogers, ring, Branding Iron, NM 60.00
Roy Rogers, ring, Silver Hat, NM 27.00
Roy Rogers, wall bank, RR & Trigger in horseshoe, 6x8", EX 65.00
Roy Rogers, wristwatch, Ingraham, 1951, EX 100.00
Sad Sack, doll, vinyl, 1950s, 15", NM 125.00
Secret Agent X-9, gun & billy club, NM 18.00
Secret Squirrel, push puppet, Kohner, M 28.50
Shirley Temple, book, Stars & Films of '37, Daily Express, NM ...30.00
Shirley Temple, color book, Little Princess, '39, 15x11", EX 110.00

Shirley Temple, doll buggy, pnt wood, Whitney, 32x29", NM ...400.00
Shirley Temple, embroidery set, Gabriel #311, 1960, NMIB 20.00
Shirley Temple, figure, bsk, as Captain January, 6½" 65.00
Shirley Temple, School Set pencil box, NM 35.00
Shirley Temple, scrapbook, Saalfield #1714, 1935, NM 25.00
Shirley Temple, sheet music, I'll Be Seeing You, EX 25.00
Shirley Temple, ST & Her House playhouse, NM in G box 95.00
Six Million Dollar Man, model kit, 1974, sealed, M 18.50
Sky King, microscope, Detecto, NM 38.00
Sky King, ring, Electronic TV, 1949 premium 125.00
Sky King, ring, Navajo Indian, NM 90.00
Sky King, signal scope, NM 75.00
Smokey Stover, figure, hard plastic, 1960s, 3", NM 18.00
Smokey the Bear, doll, rubber body, lithoed box, Ideal, 15", EX ...125.00
Smokey the Bear, Soaky 12.00
Snoopy, bank, ceramic, Snoopy on lemon, 1960, EX 19.50
Snoopy, bank, ceramic baseball player figural, late 1960s, M 17.50
Snoopy, doll, astronaut, vinyl, 1969, 9½", NM 11.25
Snow White, lamp, compo figural, WDE, 1938, NM 195.00
Snow White, rug, Alexander Smith of NY, 60x45", EX 400.00
Snow White, wristwatch, 1950, MIB 250.00
Snow White, 3-D viewer & 6 slides, 1950, MIB 110.00
Snow White & 7 Dwarfs, Big Golden Book, 1952, EX 6.00
Snow White & 7 Dwarfs, bsk 8-pc set, she: 3¼", Borgfeldt, MIB ..500.00
Snow White & 7 Dwarfs, wall lamp, WDE, 1938, 17", NM 110.00
Space Patrol, binoculars, 1950s, NM 53.00
Space Patrol, Smoke gun, 1950s, NM 188.00
Spiderman, hand puppet, Ideal, 1967, NM 45.00
Stan Musial, bkpack, official, sealed, 1964, M 65.00
Steve Canyon, jet helmet, 1959, NM 75.00
Super Heroes, gum card packs, stickers, unopened 28.00
Superman, Adventures of Superman game, M Bradley, 1940s, NM .140.00
Superman, costume, Ben Cooper, 1948, NMIB 145.00
Superman, Cut-Out Adventure book, M 120.00
Superman, figural water pistol, 1950s, M 40.00
Superman, hand puppet, Ideal, 1965, M 35.00
Superman, movie viewer, 1965, NM 18.50
Superman, Pep pin, NM 35.00
Superman, rub-ons, illus box, 1964, M 32.00
Superman, secret code, 1939, NM 36.00
Superman, Sparkle Paint set, illus card, 1965, EX 20.00
Superman, tie, 1950, M on unpunched illus display card 250.00
Tarzan, model kit, w/booklet, EX pnt, Aurora, '67 ....45.00
Tennesse Jed, Look Around ring, 1940s, NM 45.00
Three Stooges, Curly hand puppet, cloth body, G 58.00
Tom & Jerry, bowl & mug, ceramic, mc, 1970s, NM 45.00
Tom & Jerry, color book, 1952, M 20.00
Tom Corbett, badge, Space Cadet, 1950, NM 38.00
Tom Corbett, Space Cadet Rocketship, tin litho, Marx, '40, VG+ .235.00
Tom Mix, bag of marbles, NM 23.00
Tom Mix, baseball bat, NM 31.00
Tom Mix, baseball cap, NM 31.00
Tom Mix, branding iron, TM brand, NM 95.00
Tom Mix, bullet flashlight, M 78.00
Tom Mix, compass/magnifying glass, brass, '39, NM 60.00
Tom Mix, cowboy shirt, NM 78.00
Tom Mix, cowgirl skirt, NM 95.00
Tom Mix, periscope, Ralston Straight Shooters, M in mailer 90.00
Tom Mix, ring, initials, 1935, NM 75.00
Tom Mix, ring, Look Around, 1946 premium 100.00
Tom Mix, ring, Magnet, 1945, NM 72.00
Tom Mix, secret code manual, M 66.00
Tom Mix, spinner, Good Luck, NM 27.00
Tom Mix, telegraph set, red, battery-op, 1940, NM 180.00

Tom Mix, watch fob, Gold Ore, premium 20.00
Uncle Wiggily, Painting Fun book, 1924, EX 65.00
Walter Lantz, ink stamp set, rubber, stamps, set of 12, M 24.00

Wimpy mechanical tricycle with revolving bell, tin litho with celluloid arms, Linemar, King Features Syndicate, 4x3½", NMIB, $3,000.00.

Wimpy, cb mask, 1940s, M 20.00
Wimpy, figure, hard plastic, '60, 3", M 24.00
Wimpy, hand puppet, Gund, NM 28.00
Wolfman, Soaky, NM 60.00
Wonder Woman, wristwatch, 1977, MIB 65.00
Woody & Winnie Woodpecker, hand puppets, '62, 22", M, pr 40.00
Woody Woodpecker, Soaky, M 22.00
Woody Woodpecker, spoon, WW figural.....................5.00
Woody Woodpecker, TV Color-By-# set, Conn Pencil, '58, NM .25.00
Yogi Bear, Head Ring, inflatable, 1963, MIB 29.00
Yogi Bear, spoon, YB figural 5.00
Yogi Bear, True-Vue Magic Eyes, viewer & card, 1960s, M on card ..20.00
Zorro, gum cards, 1¢ packs, unopened 100.00
Zorro, magic skate, 1964, NM 12.50
Zorro, wristwatch, Ingersoll, 1950, EX 50.00

Peters and Reed

John Peters and Adam Reed founded their pottery in Zanesville, Ohio, just before the turn of the century, using the local red clay to produce a variety of wares. Moss Aztec, introduced about 1912, has an unglazed exterior with designs molded in high relief and the recesses highlighted with a green wash. Only the interior is glazed to hold water. Pereco (named for Peters, Reed and Company) is glazed in semi-matt blue, maroon, or cream. Orange was also used very early, but such examples are rare. Shapes are simple with in-mold decoration sometimes borrowed from the Moss Aztec line. Wilse Blue is a line of high-gloss medium blue with dark specks on simple shapes. Landsun, characterized by its soft matt multicolor or blue and gray combinations, is decorated either by dripping or by hand brushing in an effect sometimes called Flame or Herringbone. Chromal, in much the same colors as Landsun, may be decorated with a realistic scenic, or the swirling application of colors may merely suggest one. (Brush-McCoy made a very similar line called Chromart. Neither will be marked; and due to the lack of documented background material available, it may be impossible make a positive identification. Collectors nearly always attribute this type of decoration to Peters and Reed.) Shadow Ware is a glossy, multicolor drip over a harmonious base color. When the base is black, the effect is often iridescent.

Perhaps the most familiar line is the brown high-glaze artware with the 'sprigged'-type designs. Although research has uncovered no positive proof, it is generally accepted as having been made by Peters and Reed. It is interesting to note that many of the artistic shapes in this line are recognizable as those made by Weller, Roseville, and other Zanesville area companies. Other lines include Mirror Black, Persian, and an unidentified line which collectors call Mottled Colors. In this high-gloss line, the red clay body often shows through the splashed-on multicolors.

In 1922 the company became known as the Zane Pottery. Peters and Reed retired, and Harry McClelland became president. Charles Chilcote designed new lines, and production of many of the old lines continued. The body of the ware after 1922 was light in color. Marks include the impressed logo or ink stamp 'Zaneware' in a rectangle.

Bookends, Pereco, section of fluted columns w/leaves, 5" 75.00
Bowl, Moss Aztec, emb fans, #402, 4" 35.00
Bowl, Pereco, 3x6" 30.00

Brown Ware vases: 3¼x5½", $60.00; 4x4½", $45.00.

Doorstop, cat, yel 500.00
Flower frog, Landsun, lily pad form, 6½" W 30.00
Jardiniere & pedestal, Moss Aztec, floral band, 32" 550.00
Pitcher, tankard; Brn Ware, grapes & leaves, scalloped, 18" 265.00
Vase, bud; Marbleized, petticoat base, 6½" 55.00
Vase, Chromal, 3-color landscape, 7¾" 350.00
Vase, emb floral, terra cotta, 10½" 125.00
Vase, Landsun, brn w/blk, 6" 55.00
Vase, Moss Aztec, daisies, 8" 70.00
Vase, Shadow Ware, tan w/bl & yel runs, bulbous, 8" 90.00
Wall pocket, Egyptian Ware, Pharoah profile on gr matt, 8" 150.00
Wall pocket, Zaneware, yel, 10½" 60.00

Pewabic

The Pewabic Pottery was formally established in Detroit, Michigan, in 1907 by Mary Chase Perry Stratton and Horace James Caulkins. The two had worked together since 1903, firing their ware in a small kiln Caulkins had designed especially for use by the dental trade. Always a small operation which relied upon basic equipment and the skill of the workers, they took pride in being commissioned for several important architectural tile installations.

Some of the early artware was glazed a simple matt green; occasionally other colors were added, sometimes in combination, one over the other in a drip effect. Later Stratton developed a lustrous crystalline glaze. (Today's values are determined to a great extent by the artistic merit of the glaze.) The body of the ware was highly fired and extremely hard. Shapes were basic, and decorative modeling, if used at all, was in low relief. Mary Stratton kept the pottery open until her death in 1961. In 1968 it was purchased and reopened by Michigan State University. Several marks were used over the years: a triangle with 'Revelation Pottery' (for a short time only); 'Pewabic' with five maple leaves; and the impressed circle mark.

Bowl, blk to gr irid w/allover irid highlights, 3x8" 290.00
Bowl, silver-gr irid w/blk int, rnd logo, 1½" H 200.00
Bowl, translucent over yel-brn clay, 3-ft, hand thrown, 5½" 275.00
Tile, Detroit skyline, red/gr irid, 1933, 3" dia 225.00
Vase, bl lustre w/pk & gold highlights, 4" 700.00
Vase, bl-gray mottle/gold irid, short flaring rim, 5x5½" 650.00
Vase, dk gold-pk metallic w/bl & silvery drips, sgn EJP, 6x4½" ..475.00
Vase, dk gray-gr w/red lustre patches, 3¾x4½" 400.00
Vase, gold/bronze/gr/bl/purple lustre, hand thrown, 6½x4½" 500.00
Vase, gold/pk metallic w/EX irid, shouldered, sm flake, 4" 240.00
Vase, gr/purple metallic w/gold & pk highlights, 5x4" 600.00
Vase, gray irid w/turq drippings, 2½" 250.00
Vase, metallic bl, gold irid drip, gr highlights, 8½x7", EX 2,300.00
Vase, pk/yel metallic w/bright bl drip, conical, mk, 6x5" 950.00
Vase, silver-gr w/bright pk & purple highlights, 12", NM 1,200.00
Vase, silver/gray/purple/bl irid, rnd logo, 2¼" 200.00
Vase, turq w/brn specks & fine crystals, glossy, bulbous, 6" 375.00

Pewter

Pewter is a metal alloy of tin, copper, very small parts of bismuth and/or antimony, and sometimes lead. Very little American pewter contained lead, however, because much of the ware was designed to be used as tableware, and makers were aware that the use of lead could result in poisoning. (Pieces that do contain lead are usually darker in color and heavier than those that have no lead.) Most of the fine examples of American pewter date from 1700 to the 1840s. Many pieces were melted down and recast into bullets during the American Revolution in 1775; this accounts to some extent why examples from this period are quite difficult to find. The pieces that did survive may include buttons, buckles, and writing equipment as well as the tableware we generally think of.

After the Revolution makers began using antimony as the major alloy with the tin in an effort to regain the popularity of pewter, which glassware and china was beginning to replace in the home. The resulting product, known as britannia, had a lustrous silver-like appearance and was far more durable. While closely related, britannia is a collectible in its own right and should not be confused with pewter.

Key: tm — touch mark

Basin, angel tm w/Erlangen 1827, wear, 3⅛x12" 185.00
Basin, English tm (faint), 11⅞" 270.00
Basin, faint angel tm, Continental, wear/dents, 2½x9¾" 125.00
Basin, IM tm, wide flat rim, 3½x10¾" 110.00
Basin, Thomas Danforth eagle tm, minor wear/dents, 2¾x10" ...360.00
Basin, Townsend & Compton tm, normal wear, 2¾x11" 300.00
Basin, Townsend & Compton tm, normal wear, 13" 220.00
Bowl, baptismal; LL Williams, ftd, 4¾x6¾" 350.00
Bowl, Danforth rampant lion tm, wear, shallow, 13¼" 275.00
Bowl, Love tm, 1⅜x11" 400.00
Bowl, unmk, lt wear, 2⅞x11½" 110.00
Candle holder, unmk Am, saucer base w/hdl, 4" dia 175.00
Candlestick, Flagg & Homan tm, 7¾" 200.00
Candlestick, unmk, ribbed detail, 10¾" 85.00
Candlestick, unmk Am, 7" 115.00
Candlesticks, unmk, w/push-ups, 8", pr 220.00
Charger, angel tm, lt wear, 16½" 370.00
Charger, angel tm, minor wear/dents, 14" 250.00
Charger, Continental fleur-de-lis tm, wear/scratches, 15" 230.00

Charger, crowned rose tm w/London, wear/scratches, 17" 350.00
Charger, crowned rose tm w/WH, lt wear, 16½" 385.00
Charger, English tm (faint), minor wear/pitting, 18" 385.00
Charger, Georg Kling angel tm, scalloped rim, lt wear, 12½" 200.00
Charger, John Watts, minor wear, 13½" 220.00
Charger, T Danforth tm, rprs, 13" dia 400.00
Charger, unmk, wear/scratches, 13½" 175.00
Charger, unmk English, wear/sm rim split, 16½" 300.00
Coffeepot, Rufus Dunham tm, scroll hdl, ped ft, rpl lid, 12" 150.00
Coffeepot, unmk Am, cast fruit finial, battered/soldered, 10" 115.00
Creamer, Flagg & Homan Pewter tm, cast floral finial, 5½" 95.00
Cup, unmk, dents, 2⅝" 50.00
Flagon, German eagle tm, w/thumb pc, eng GOP 1842 on lid, 10" .225.00

Hair tonic bottle, HT embossed on front, 9", $150.00.

Inkwell, unmk, hinged lid, missing insert, 2¼" 85.00
Invalid feeder, MAW Aldersgate ST, 5" 40.00
Ladle, unmk, battered bowl, trn hdl, 15½" 30.00
Lamp, chamber; unmk, dbl-spout burning fluid burner, 6", EX ...165.00
Lamp, Sellew & Co Cincinnati, burning fluid burner, 8¾" 415.00
Lamp, unmk Am, saucer base w/hdl, pewter cap, 4x3½" 125.00
Lavabo, Continental, old rpr, rpl bowl, 18" 120.00
Measure, Birmingham tm, 1-pt, 5", EX 100.00
Measure, English tm, ftd, ear hdl, monogram, 1-pt, 6¼" 100.00
Measure, English tm, tankard form, 4¾", EX 160.00
Measure, Irish tm, fleur-de-lis thumb pc, basin form, w/lid, 6" 165.00
Measure, John Warne tm, brass rim, rpr, 1-qt, 5¾" 95.00
Measure, Watts & Harton London tm, tankard form, 1-pt, 5¼" ...95.00
Muffineer, mk English Pewter, hammered, 6⅛" 95.00
Pitcher, ale; English tm, domed lid & thumb pc, lt wear, 8" 335.00
Pitcher, unmk, wear & soldered rpr, 7⅝" 150.00
Pitcher, unmk Am, eng letter, 6½" 220.00
Pitcher, water; Am tm, hinged lid, 10½", EX 215.00
Pitcher, water; R Gleason tm, hinged lid, 8½" 300.00
Plate, angel tm, eng rim initials, 8⅜" 85.00
Plate, angel tm (partial), scalloped, wear/scratches, 9½" 85.00
Plate, David Melville tm (faint), rprs, 8⅛" 250.00
Plate, eagle tm, minor wear/pitting, 7⅞" 100.00
Plate, Geo Lightner tm, 8¾" 310.00
Plate, hot water; Henry & Richard Joseph tms, 8" dia, EX 165.00
Plate, John Townsend London tm, 9¼", EX 65.00
Plate, London tm, 6", pr 130.00
Plate, London tm, 9½", pr 145.00
Plate, Love tm, minor scratches, 7⅞" 300.00
Plate, Love tm, minor wear/corrosion, 7⅞" 245.00
Plate, Richard Austin tm (partial), scratches, 7⅞" 200.00
Plate, Samuel Ellis tm, wear, 7¾" 200.00

Plate, Samuel Pierce tm, battered, 8"	275.00
Plate, Samuel Pierce tm, ca 1792-1830, 11¼"	395.00
Plate, Thos Townsend & Compton tm, 8½"	160.00
Plate, unmk Am, minor wear/pitting, 8⅜"	88.00
Porringer, faint tm, resoldered cast flowered hdl, 5½" dia	200.00
Porringer, GS tm, cast crown hdl, 5½"	330.00
Porringer, unmk Am, tab hdl w/hanging hole, 7"	500.00
Pot, Sheffield tm, side spout, wood hdl, 8"	120.00
Tall pot, H Homan tm, floral eng, cast floral finial, 11"	115.00
Tall pot, H Homan tm, soldered rprs, 11¼"	65.00
Tall pot, J Danforth tm, wooden finial, 10", EX	250.00
Tea caddy, BGS&Co tm, almond shape, bright-cut designs, 3¾"	330.00
Teapot, Am tm (indistinct), finial wafer missing, 6½"	175.00
Teapot, Dixon & Smith tm, wooden hdl & finial, 7¾"	200.00
Teapot, James Dixon & Sons tm, reeding, fruit finial, 5½"	75.00
Teapot, James Dixon tm, soldered rpr, 5⅛"	85.00
Teapot, Putnam tm, some battering/rprs, 7¾"	110.00
Teapot, unmk Am, soldered rprs, 8¼"	140.00
Tumbler, unmk (att Boardman), 3⅛"	60.00

Phoenix Bird

Blue and white Phoenix Bird china has been produced by various Japanese potteries from the early 1900s. With slight variations the design features the Japanese bird of paradise and scroll-like vines of Kara-Kusa, or Chinese grass. Although some of their earlier ware is unmarked, the majority is marked in some fashion. More than one hundred different stamps have been reported, with 'Made in Japan' the one most often found. Coming in second is Morimura's wreath and/or crossed stems (both having the letter 'M' within). The cloverleaf with 'Japan' below very often indicates an item having a high-quality transfer-printed design. Among the many categories in the Phoenix Bird pattern are several shapes; therefore (for identification purposes), each has been given a number, i.e. #1, #2, etc. Newer items, if marked at all, carry a paper label. Compared to the older ware, the coloring of the new is whiter and the blue more harsh; the design is sparse with more ground area showing. Although collectors buy even 'new' pieces, the older is of course more highly prized and valued. For further information we recommend *Phoenix Bird Chinaware, Books I — IV*, written and privately published by our advisor, Joan Oates; her address is in the Directory under Michigan. Join Phoenix Bird Collectors of America (PBCA) and receive the *Phoenix Bird Discoveries* newsletter, an informative publication that will further your appreciation of this chinaware. See Clubs, Newsletters and Catalogs for ordering information.

Creamer and sugar bowl, marked Nippon, $50.00.

Bouillon & saucer	25.00
Cake tray, rnd w/hdls, #3	55.00

Coffeepot, post-1970	45.00
Cup & saucer, chocolate; scalloped	25.00
Cup & saucer, tea/coffee	9.00
Gravy boat, #2, Nippon	75.00
Hot water pot & cover, #1	65.00
Ice cream dish, oval w/inverted scallops	35.00
Mustard pot, w/lid, #2	55.00
Pitcher, lemonade; bulbous	145.00
Pitcher, water; bell shape	135.00
Plate, bread & butter; 6"	7.00
Plate, dessert; 7¼"	9.00
Plate, dinner; 9¾"	45.00
Plate, luncheon; 8"	18.00
Shakers, #3 or #7, ea pr	28.00
Sugar bowl, Nippon, #11	30.00
Syrup, no lid intended, #9, sm	18.00
Tea set, child's, #1, 3-pc	135.00
Teapot, w/lid, #10	55.00
Water tankard, bell shape	135.00

Phoenix Glass

Founded in 1880 in Monaca, Pennsylvania, the Phoenix Glass Company became one of the country's foremost manufacturers of lighting glass by the early 1900s. They also produced a wide variety of utilitarian and decorative glassware, including art glass by Joseph Webb, colored cut glass, Gone-with-the-Wind style oil lamps, hotel and bar ware, and pharmaceutical glassware. Today, however, collectors are primarily interested in the 'Sculptured Artware' produced in the 1930s and 1940s. These beautiful pressed and mold-blown pieces are most often found in white milk glass or crystal with various color treatments or a satin finish.

Phoenix did not mark their 'Sculptured Artware' line on the glass; instead, a silver and black or gold and black foil label in the shape of the mythical phoenix bird was used.

Quite often glassware made by the Consolidated Lamp and Glass Company of nearby Coraopolis, Pennsylvania, is mistaken for Phoenix's 'Sculptured Artware.' Though the style of the glass is very similar, one distinguishing characteristic is that perhaps 80% of the time Phoenix applied color to the background leaving the raised design plain in contrast, while Consolidated generally applied color to the raised design and left the background plain. Also, for the most part, the patterns and colors used by Phoenix were distinctively different from those used by Consolidated.

In 1970 Phoenix Glass became a division of Anchor Hocking which in turn was acquired by the Newell Group in 1987. Phoenix has the distinction of being one of the oldest continuously operating glass factories in the United States. For more information refer to *Phoenix and Consolidated Art Glass, 1926-1980*, written by our advisor, Jack D. Wilson, who is listed in the Directory under Illinois. See also Consolidated Glass.

Bowl, Tiger Lily, pk frosted, 11½"	275.00
Candle holders, Strawberry, gr over milk glass, 4¼", pr	130.00
Compote, Lacy Dewdrop, bl on milk glass, orig label	150.00
Unbrella vase, Thistle, tan pearlized, 18"	450.00
Vase, Aster, slate gray pearlized, 7"	95.00
Vase, Bittersweet, Reuben Line, lt bl wash, 9½"	175.00
Vase, Bluebell, lt pk pearlized, 7"	85.00
Vase, Fern, crystal on bl, 7"	85.00
Vase, Fern, lt gr pearlized, 7"	125.00
Vase, Fern, wht on gray-gr, 7"	80.00
Vase, Freesia, milk glass on brn, fan shaped, 8¼"	170.00

**Vase, Freesia, blue and frosted, 8",
$295.00.**

Vase, Katydid, Reuben Line, amber, orig label, 8¼" **275.00**
Vase, Lily, yel wash, tri-crimp, 8½" **295.00**
Vase, Madonna, tan pearlized **200.00**
Vase, Philodendron, bl, ormolu hdls & ftd base, 14" **400.00**
Vase, Philodendron, brn shadow finish, 11½" **175.00**
Vase, Philodendron, tan pearlized, 11½" **175.00**
Vase, Primrose, frosted design on bl, 8¾" **475.00**
Vase, Wild Geese, lt gr pearlized, pillow form, 10" **175.00**
Vase, Wild Geese, red pearlized, 10" **275.00**
Vase, Wild Rose, aqua wash on frosted design, 10½" **250.00**
Vase, Zodiac, slate bl over milk glass, rare, 10½" **650.00**
Vase, Zodiac, wht figures on peach, rare, 10½" **700.00**

Phonographs

The phonograph, invented by Thomas Edison in 1877, was the first practical instrument for recording and reproducing sound. Sound wave vibrations were recorded on a tinfoil-covered cylinder and played back with a needle that ran along the grooves made from the recording, thus reproducing the sound. Other companies further improved Edison's invention: Victor, Edison, Columbia, Zonophone, Vitaphone, and there were others. Wooden-horn phonographs with outside horns are the most valuable. Spring models were produced until 1929 (and later); after 1929, most were electric (though some electric motor models were produced as early as 1910.) Our advisor for this category is J.R. Wilkins; he is listed in the Directory under Texas. Unless another condition is noted, prices are for complete, original phonographs in at least fine to excellent condition. Note: Edison coin-operated cylinder players start at $7,000.00 and may go up to $20,000.00 each.

Key:
mg — morning-glory   rpd — reproducer
NP — nickel plated

Aretino, disk player, 3" center spindle, gr mg horn, 1902 .... **750.00**
Berliner Trademark, disk player **3,000.00**
Busy Bee, disk player, 8-petal red horn w/decal, EX **400.00**
Columbia AB Graphophone, cylinder player w/2 mandrels **1,250.00**
Columbia AH, brass bell front-mt horn, EX **1,000.00**
Columbia AK, oak case, 15" brass bell horn, EX **775.00**
Columbia AQ, 2-min, key wind, sm horn, EX **350.00**
Columbia AR Graphophone, EX **1,700.00**
Columbia AZ, cylinder player **400.00**
Columbia BC Graphophone 20th-C Premier, Higham rpd, 1906 .**1,100.00**
Columbia BF (Peerless) Graphophone, long mandrel, NP horn, EX .**925.00**
Columbia BI, oak case, red rear-mt horn, EX **775.00**
Columbia BI Sterling, pillared case, EX **1,500.00**
Columbia BK, cylinder player, no horn, incomplete rpd **225.00**
Columbia BN, disk player, blk horn, table model **475.00**

Columbia Grafonola Mignon, floor model, 190-102, EX **150.00**
Columbia Grand AG Graphophone, 5" mandrel, 56" horn, +stand .**1,400.00**
Edison Amberola X, EX **400.00**
Edison Amberola 30, oak, w/stand **400.00**
Edison D Red Gem, 2/4-min, K reproducer, 2-part horn, EX ..**1,200.00**
Edison Fireside, H rpd, EX **650.00**
Edison Fireside, 2/4-min, C rpd, metal cygnet horn **950.00**
Edison Fireside B, lg diaphragm Amberola rpd, cygnet horn **975.00**
Edison Gem B, banner decal, C rpd, sm horn, EX **500.00**
Edison Home, C rpd, 14" brass bell horn, EX **425.00**
Edison Home, cylinder player, mg horn, suitcase type **625.00**
Edison S-19, dmn disk, floor model **250.00**
Edison Standard, cylinder player, brass bell horn **475.00**
Edison Standard, 2/4-min, cylinder player **475.00**
Edison Triumph, 2/4-min, oak case, cygnet oak horn, EX **2,350.00**
Edison Triumph E, 33" horn **850.00**
Eldridge R Johnson M-4132, Victor type, rare, EX **2,800.00**
Excelda Cameraphone, EX **80.00**
Little Wonder, iron base, horn w/rpd in middle, EX **625.00**
Pathe, disk player, 2 heads, table model **200.00**
Premier, music notes on rpd, 12" turntable, floor model **275.00**
Silvertone, floor model, EX **100.00**
Standard Talking Machine Model A, rear mt, red horn **525.00**
Standard Talking Machine X2, front mt, blk horn **525.00**
Standard-X, disk player, EX **575.00**
Talkaphone Brooke, EX **600.00**
Victor Credenza VV-8-30X Orthophonic, EX **1,000.00**
Victor E, Exhibition rpd, rear mt, brass bell horn, EX **1,000.00**
Victor I, disk player, 9½" dia brass bell horn, 1903, EX **1,150.00**
Victor II, disk player, brass bell horn, EX **1,175.00**
Victor II, Exhibition rpd, oak horn, EX **2,500.00**
Victor III, disk player, brass bell horn, EX **1,400.00**
Victor III, disk player, Exhibition rpd, oak outside horn **2,250.00**
Victor M, disk player, bk mt, EX **1,150.00**
Victor Monarch Special, 24" front-mt brass bell horn, 1901 ...**1,500.00**
Victor MS, Exhibition rpd, oak horn, EX **2,400.00**
Victor P, disk player, brass bell horn, EX **1,050.00**
Victor R, brass bell horn, EX **1,050.00**
Victor R Royal, wooden tone arm, Exhibition Jr rpd, 1902-04, EX ..**900.00**
Victor V, w/Exhibition rpd, oak horn, EX **3,100.00**
Victor Victrola #100, mahog, NP trim, EX orig **250.00**
Victor Z, Exhibition rpd, EX **1,400.00**
Victrola VV-IX, oak case, table model **175.00**
Yankee Prince, rear mt, w/horn, G label, ca 1904 .... **400.00**
Zonophone Grand Opera, rpd, brass horn, EX **1,100.00**

Photographica

Photographic collectibles include not only the cameras and equipment used to 'freeze' special moments in time but also the photographic images produced by a great variety of processes that have evolved since the daguerrean era of the mid-1800s. For the most part, good quality images have either maintained or increased in value. Poor quality examples (regardless of rarity) are not selling well. Interest in cameras and stereo equipment is down, and dealers report that often average-priced items that were moving well are often completely overlooked. Though rare items always have a market, collectors seem to be buying only if they are bargain priced. Our advisor for this category is John Hess; he is listed in the Directory under Massachusetts.

Albumens

#149 Pacific Ave Santa Cruz CA, street car, Webb, 7x10", NM ..**30.00**

Cabinet card, Indian portrait, DF Barry, 1880s, 5x4" **440.00**
Incidents of the War, O'Sullivan & Gardner, 1863, 6¾x8¾" **385.00**
Joseph Brant Chief of Mohawks, from Duke of Warwick painting ..**48.00**
Portrait of Lincoln, A Hesler, oval, GB Ayers, 1890s, 8x6" **600.00**
Redwood tree in Santa Cruz, Reese, dtd 1886, 7x10" **15.00**
Soldier w/amputated leg, Dr Wm Bell, 1865, 9½x7½" **550.00**
Storefront w/2 men & dog in doorway, 1850s, 6½x8½", NM **22.00**
Traveler's Boat at Ibrim, Frith, 1862, 5x6½" **220.00**
Union soldier, full-length, WL Germon...Phila, in 17x20" fr **120.00**
11 firemen & horse-drawn hook & ladder, MA, 1859, 8x10" **32.50**

Ambrotypes

An ambrotype is a type of photograph produced by an early wet-plate process whereby a faint negative image on glass is seen as positive when held against a dark background.

Half plate, couple pose before Niagara Falls, 1850s, +case **525.00**
Half plate, farmhouse, clothes on line, ME, MOP case **200.00**
Half plate, 1st Congregational Church, MA, EX, +leather case .**715.00**
Whole plate, Gen Barnard Elliot, ruby, 1850s, +period fr **800.00**
Whole plate, 8-member missionary family, Hawaii **300.00**
4th plate, drummer boy w/mother & sister, +case **145.00**
4th plate, horse & sleigh, driver w/buffalo skins, EX **135.00**
6th plate, Japanese man & boy in formal attire, 1870s, +case .**1,650.00**
6th plate, married couple seated w/dog in laps, +case **20.00**
6th plate, policeman, hand-tinted, 1850s, +leather case **300.00**
6th plate, post mortem, baby in wht, 1850s, +case **150.00**
6th plate, twin sisters, in 2-tone leather case, EX **30.00**
6th plate, Union soldier kneels w/rifle, +case **265.00**
6th plate, US Marine, frock coat, metal mat/surround, early **150.00**
9th plate, Blk boy in jacket & plantation-style hat, cb case **70.00**
9th plate, Confederate soldier in gray uniform, EX, +case **95.00**
9th plate, gentleman's portrait in profile, from painting, EX **14.00**
9th plate, John Brown portrait, +period fr **715.00**
9th plate, Zouave drummer boy w/cartridge case, ruby, +case **285.00**

Cabinet Photos

Allistair Mac Wilkie, Man w/11-Ft Beard, Wendt, NJ, VG **16.00**
Bearded Lady Grace Gilbert, 32 yrs, 20" beard, Wendt, NJ, VG ...**15.00**
Blk gentleman w/beard, well-dressed, Alley, VG **7.50**
Comanche woman, bare-breasted, Buehman, 1875 ....**125.00**
Construction of Olcott Falls Dam, NH, partially completed **10.00**
Dirigible w/Am flag attached, early 1900s, EX **40.00**
Edgar Allen Poe, bust portrait **16.00**
Ethel Barrymore, profile in feathered hat, Morrison, Chicago **20.00**
First Passenger Train on Pike's Peat Summit, Hiestand #320 ....**20.00**
Fraternal officer seated w/sword in lap, feather in hat, EX **6.00**
Frontiersman in buckskins w/SS Ballard rifle, 1889 ....**95.00**
Frontiersman w/Winchester & lady w/SS F Wesson rifle, 1893 ....**95.00**
Ganges River Looking Towards a Decrepid Wooden Village, 1870s ..**12.50**
Henry Ward Beecher, bust pose, Warren, Boston, VG **7.00**
Horse-drawn hay rake w/CI seat, ca 1875 ....**10.00**
James A Garfield, semiprofile, 1880 ....**16.00**
Maricopa man, bare-chested, shell necklace, Buehman, 1875 ......**97.50**
Marksmen stand w/Spencer & Stevens rifles, VG **40.00**
Marshall Pass, Big Bend Near Shirley, Jackson #1003 ....**26.00**
Maurice Barrymore as Captain Swift, standing in tux, Falk **20.00**
McKee's Cottages, Ojai Valley, Ventura CA, Hayward & Muzzall ..**12.50**
Militiaman w/M1881 Helmet, stands in uniform, 9-button coat ..**10.00**
Mother & 3 daughters, 1 w/bsk-headed doll, Call, NH **8.50**
Pat Fitzgerald, full-length boxing pose, Fox, VG **16.00**
Pike's Peak RR, Summit & Donkey; WE Hook, VG **20.00**

Pima woman w/water jug on head, Buehman, 1875 ....**88.00**
Policeman in dbl-button coat, w/helmet, ¾-view, 1880s **10.00**
Spanish Am War sailors next to cased brass sextant **10.00**
Spanish Am War soldiers around Civil War cannon monument, VG ..**12.50**
Sufter Jung's Tomb, Delhi, Cades, 1870s **12.50**
Teacher & Indian students, Wrensted, Pocatello, 1900 ....**22.50**
Uma Indian maiden, bare-breasted, H Buehman, 1875 ....**150.00**
Ute Pass & Rainbow Falls, Hiestand #20, Manitou CO, EX **20.00**
2 Indian women & child, Grangeville ID **35.00**

Cameras

Among the earliest daguerrean cameras was the sliding box-on-a-box camera. It was focused by sliding one box in and out of the other, thus adjusting the distance of the lens to the ground glass. This was replaced on later models with leather bellows. These were the forerunners of the multilens cameras developed in the late 1870s, which were capable of recording many small portraits on a single plate. Double-lens cameras produced stereo images which, when viewed through a device called a stereoscope, achieved a 3-dimensional effect. In 1888 George Eastmann introduced his box camera, the first to utilize roll film. This greatly simplified the process, making it possible for the amateur to enjoy photography as a hobby. Detective cameras, those disguised as books, handbags, etc., are among the most sought after by today's collectors.

Voightlander Bessa 6x6 (Baby Bessa), ca 1936-49, $40.00.

Adams Adlake Repeater, box style, side crank, EX **55.00**
Adox Blitz, Bakelite box type, ca 1950, NM **25.00**
Agfa Speedy Compur, Compur shutter, ca 1934-42, EX **45.00**
Am Buckeye Special, roll film or glass plates, ca 1897, EX **90.00**
Ansco #3 Folding Buster Brown, ca 1914, NM **20.00**
Anthony Klondike, fixed-focus box type, 1898, NM **80.00**
Balda Glorina, folding type, ca 1936, EX **42.50**
Blair Baby Hawk-Eye, box type, ca 1896-98, EX **185.00**
Canon Seiki S-11, metal bady, 1946-47, NM **400.00**
Conley, holds 5x7" plates, w/Wallensack lens, 1901, EX **95.00**
Conley Snap #2, folding strut-type, EX **22.50**
E&HT Anthony, 8x10" dry plate, B French lens, 1870s, +tripod ..**350.00**
Eastman Kodak Brownie Cresta, blk plastic, box type, 1955-58 ....**12.50**
Expo Watch Camera, SP, detachable lens, 1890s, NM **300.00**
Genos Special, blk Bakelite, box type, 1953, NM **30.00**
Graflex Graphic Sr, red bellows, brass trim, 1904, NM **165.00**
Kodak Duoflex, w/cover, 1930, EX **15.00**
Kodak Target Hawkeye XIX-16, NM **18.00**
Krauss Peggy II, coupled range finder, ca 1934, EX **425.00**
MarVette, Bakelite case, 127 half-frames, EX **20.00**
Nikon S2, chrome w/blk dials, 1954-58, EX **225.00**
Olympus Wide II, lever advance, folding crank, 1958-61, NM **55.00**
Polaroid Big Shot, fixed focus lense, 1971-75, M **15.00**
Polaroid 95A, aluminum body, folding bed style, 1950s, EX **20.00**
Rochester Folding Premo, folding plate type, 1893-94, EX **125.00**
Universal Uniflash, plastic, 1940, +orig flash & box, NM **22.50**

Univex Model A, NM in orig box w/instructions **30.00**
Voigtlander Vito, folding type, yel hinged filter, 1939-48, NM **48.00**
Zeiss Ikon Contessa LK, no range finder, 1963-65, NM **55.00**

Carte De Visites

Among the many types of images collectible today are carte de visites, known as CDVs, which are 2¼" x 4" portraits printed on paper and produced in quantity. The CDV fad of the 1800s enticed the famous and the unknown alike to pose for these cards, which were circulated among the public to the extent that they became known as 'publics.' When the popularity of CDVs began to wane, a new fascination developed for the cabinet photo, a larger version measuring about 4½" x 6½". Note: A common portrait CDV is worth only about 50¢ unless it carries a revenue stamp on the back; those that do are valued at about $1.00 each.

Bella Coola Indian in Wild West Show, Germany, 1887 ....**125.00**
Boston Corbett of 16th NY Cavalry Who Killed JW Booth, EX ...**200.00**
Caleb Cushing, bust portrait, Warren, Boston **7.50**
Charles Dickens seated at writing desk, VG **12.50**
Chester A Arther US President, bust portrait, VG **10.00**
Civil War drummer w/regimental drum, full-length, EX **150.00**
Civil War Navy engineer w/dress hat & M1852 sword, ¾-view **16.50**
Civil War soldier leans on M1842 musket, full-length **70.00**
Dwarf holding cane, well dressed, RB Lewis, MA **12.50**
Frederick Douglass seated, in suit & vest, VG **125.00**
Gateway of Billenoor Temple, S India, Chase, 1866 ....**12.50**
Gen Geo H Thomas Rock of Chickamauga, Anthony **50.00**
Gen James McPherson, Killed at Atlanta 1864; IL bk mark **85.00**
Gen Nathaniel Lyon, Killed at Wilson's Creek..., Anthony **60.00**
General AP Hill, Anthony **90.00**
Girl in lg shoe w/27 or so dolls on ladders, VG **10.00**
John Greenleaf Whittier the Quaker Poet, bust pose, Currier **12.50**
John Wilkes Booth & the Devil **125.00**
John Wilkes Booth seated in studio chair, VG **45.00**
Lady seated w/sheep's head in lap, VG **12.50**
Lincoln, mourning, 1865 ....**150.00**
MA Sergeant w/stripes showing, 1860s **28.00**
Major SE Houghton, 19 Yrs Old, Height 31"..., EX **12.50**
Man sits beside stereo viewer & cards on table, Low, MA **12.50**
Military 1870s musician playing piccolo, swallow-tail coat, EX **20.00**
Miss Suzie Doll, Age 7 Yrs; midget, Chas Eisenmann, VG **10.00**
Museum of Fine Arts, Boston, building w/Gothic spires, 1870s **10.00**
Postmortem, baby under knit blanket, rattle in hand **10.00**
Pulpit rock, Sand Stone, 40-Ft High, Saint Croix...WI, Ransom ..**10.00**
Seth Kinman in buckskins w/percussion rifle, Gardner, 1864 ....**85.00**
Stephen A Douglas, ½-length, in suit coat & vest, EX **30.00**
Theatrical queen seated in blk & wht fur robe, 1864 ....**10.00**
Thomas Nast, Sorony **125.00**
Tombstone of Ludwig Von Beethoven, Albin Mutterer's, Germany ..**8.50**
Union Infantryman w/bayonetted musket in full uniform, Walzl .**30.00**
Union Officer leaning on M1850 sword, frock coat, kepi, etc **35.00**
Union Private seated, 4-button sack coat, Keeley, PA **22.50**
Union Private w/Bowie knife & cartridge revolver in belt **60.00**
Union soldier in 9-button coat, MA mk **27.50**
US Grant, VA City NV, 1879 ....**85.00**
View of Temple at Challumberum S India, Chase, NY, 1865 ....**12.50**
Wagon Train East of Beaver Dam, Echo, UT Territory, Carter **70.00**
Washington embracing Lincoln in heaven **32.00**
Wm A Wheeler Vice President of US..., bust portrait, EX **10.00**

Daguerreotypes

Among the many processes used to produce photographic images are the daguerreotypes (made on a plate of chemically treated metal) — the most-valued examples being the 'whole' plate which measures 6½" x 8½". Other sizes include the 'half' plate, measuring 4½" x 5½", the 'quarter' plate at 3¼" x 4¼", the 'sixth' plate at 2¾" x 3¼", the 'ninth' at 2" x 2½", and the 'sixteenth' at 1⅜" x 1⅝". (Sizes may vary slightly, and some may have been altered by the photographer.)

Half plate, child w/toy ram, Fontayne & Porter, Cincinnati OH ..**850.00**
Half plate, man's portrait, Hayes NY, 1850s, +case w/MOP inlay ..**300.00**
Half plate, mason w/apron & neck devices, gold tint, +case **650.00**
Whole plate, postmortem, identified abolitionist, EX **1,100.00**
16th plate, man w/long hair in suit & tie, bust view, +case **20.00**
4th plate, carriage driver occupational, 1840s, +leather case ...**1,045.00**
4th plate, Greek Revival house, 1850s, +leather case **660.00**
4th plate, lady's portrait, gold-toned/hand tinted, +preserver **185.00**
4th plate, lady w/baby in lap, Cooley, Springfield, +case **25.00**
4th plate, lady w/bonnet & overcape, seated by table, +case **20.00**
4th plate, man & dog seated on fancy couch, 1850s, +case **1,100.00**
4th plate, matronly lady, lace bonnet, bust view, North, OH **25.00**
4th plate, mulatto lady & Blk man, gilt details, 1850s, +case **770.00**
4th plate, officer seated, wife stands w/arm at shoulder, EX **125.00**
4th plate, unfinished building, 1850s, +leather case **440.00**
4th plate, well-dressed young couple, matted, 1840s, EX **70.00**
6th plate, boy & girl w/long-haired dog, EX **185.00**
6th plate, butcher at work, hand tinted, 1840s, sealed, +case ..**1,045.00**
6th plate, cobbler at work, 1850s, +leather case **660.00**
6th plate, girl w/lilacs, hand tinted, 1850s, +case **550.00**
6th plate, Jenny Lind, tinted close-up, +Jenny Lind case **625.00**
6th plate, lady in blk dress knitting, wht bonnet, EX **45.00**
6th plate, lady w/arm on books, holds open dag case, early **45.00**
6th plate, man & 2 ladies w/arms entwined, horizontal **22.50**
6th plate, man seated by flower basket, Phila, +case **20.00**
6th plate, mother & son holding hands, +case **22.50**
6th plate, mother & son w/book, Troy NY, +case **15.00**
6th plate, postmortem, man, couple stand behind, 1850s, +case ...**550.00**
6th plate, sisters w/doll, +full case **55.00**
6th plate, timber mill in Strongsville OH, 1840s, +case **2,600.00**
6th plate, tinsmith at work w/tools at table, EX **325.00**
6th plate, 1-eyed lady dwarf knitting, 1850s, +leather case **825.00**
9th plate, giant w/family members, 1850s, in brass preserver **220.00**
9th plate, well-dressed boy, SD Carleton, +case **18.00**

Photos

**Salt print of Sam Houston, 7x5",
$200.00.**

Bromide, 2 hunters w/guns/early auto/4 deer, 9¾x7¾" **35.00**
Charles Lindbergh, formal portrait, Paris 1927 ....**85.00**
Orotone, Floridian landscape w/cypress & palms, 1900, 10x11½" ...**660.00**
Photochrome, Apache Chief James Garfield, ca 1900, 11½x9" ..**715.00**
Photogravure, Walpi Indian Village, Ansel Adams, 1939-40 ....**10.00**
Platinum print, Chief Hollow Horn Bear, Rinehart, 9⅜x7½" .**1,045.00**

Platinum print, Esther Chamberlain, Ben-Usuf, Zaida, 8x3½" ...550.00
Salt print, boy & dog stand before house, 1840s, 8½x6½" 220.00
Salt print, Brevet Gen Geo V Stannard of VT, 1864, on orig mt ...600.00
Salt print, girl w/patriotic dress & flag, 1860s, 18x13" 825.00
Salt print, nude before mirror, D'Olivier, 1850s, 2¾x2¼" 575.00
Salt print, painter/tools/skull, Lloyd, 4¾x3½" 300.00
Salt print, President Millard Fillmore, oval, 1850s, 8x5" 715.00
Silver print, Beatles w/Order of British Empire Medals, 8x10" ..1,320.00
Silver print, Blk man's portrait, Eickemeyer, 1898, 9½x7½" 715.00
Silver print, Buzz Aldrin Jr by Lunar module, Armstrong, 8x10" .1,760.00
Silver print, Hindenberg disaster, Becker, 1937, 13½x10½" 880.00
Silver print, Hiroshima after bomb, S Troutman, 1945, 7x9" 385.00
Silver print, Reichstag in ruins, 1933, 8x10" 440.00

Stereoscopic Views

Stereo cards are photos made to be viewed through a device called a stereoscope. The glass stereo plates of the mid-1800s and photo prints produced in the darkroom are among the most valuable. In evaluating stereo views, the subject, date, and condition are all-important. Some views were printed over a thirty- to forty-year period; 'first generation' prices are far higher than later copies. Right now, quality stereo views are at a premium.

Battle of Chattanooga, directing troops, HL Roberts...Phila 60.00
Blackfoot women & papoose at home, Ingersol, 1895 ....7.50
Chief Blackhawk & family, blk/wht, Cosmopolitan 8.00
Chipewyan lady making birch canoe, Ingersol 8.00
Cliff Palace in the Mesa Verde, Keystone 10.00
Crow Indians doing Ghost Dance, Griffith 9.00
De Pick of De Hull Roost, boy steals chicken, Keystone, VG 8.50
Gold Mining at Cape Nome AK, Griffith & Griffith Series 1906 ...32.50
Interior of Fort Stedman, Petersburgh VA, Brady 65.00
Learning to Coast-The Start, Griffith & Griffith, 1902 ....5.00
Libby Prison, Kilburn #891 ....65.00
Moki maiden's morning toilet, Underwood, 1901 ....17.00
Panoramic View of Johnsonville on Tennessee River, VG 70.00
Plains Indian talks to cowboy in sign language, Keystone 25.00
Ruins of Secession Hall, Charleston SC, Brady 80.00
Sioux rider & pony, Ingersol 6.00
Skeleton of Famous Fairmont Hotel, San Francisco CA, EX 20.00
Soldiers' Home view of dining room, Marion IN, 1898 ....17.50
Souix warriors leaving camp, Keystone 17.50
Victory or Death Battle of Gettysburg, Kilburn #7721 ....15.00
View from Lynchburg Canal, Richmond VA 70.00
View of Outer Trenches Last Day of Battle, Nashville, 1864 ....80.00

Tintypes

Tintypes, contemporaries of ambrotypes, were produced on japanned iron and were not as easily damaged.

Half plate, 3 men in band uniforms, 1 w/major's staff, EX 65.00
4th plate, Indian lady w/baby, gold touches, EX 150.00
4th plate, 4 seamstresses w/articles of their trade, NM 12.50
6th plate, Confederate w/bugle & revolver, +Union case 220.00
6th plate, dog on table w/man in chair beside, 1860s, +case 45.00
6th plate, fraternal member w/vestments, tricorner hat, VG 5.50
6th plate, lady w/book on table, tinted cheeks, +full case 40.00
6th plate, tennis player w/racquet, ca 1870s, EX 40.00
6th plate, Union soldier w/7 gilt buttons, unarmed, +case 75.00
6th plate, 19th century New England church w/spire 20.00
6th plate, 2 ladies seated in 1905 auto, studio pose, VG 10.00
9th plate, infant's portrait, +leatherette case w/gilt 22.50

9th plate, Union soldier seated w/Colt pistol, EX 80.00

Union Cases

From the mid-1850s until about 1880, cases designed to house these early images were produced from a material known as thermoplastic, a man-made material with an appearance much like gutta percha. Its innovator was Samuel Peck, who used shellac and wood fibers to create a composition he called Union. Peck was part owner of the Scoville Company, makers of both papier-mache and molded leather cases, and he used the company's existing dies to create his new line. Other companies, among them A.P. Critchlow & Company, Littlefield, Parsons & Company, and Holmes, Booth & Hayden soon duplicated his material and produced their own designs. Today's collectors may refer to cases made of this material as 'thermoplastic,' 'composition,' or 'hard cases,' but the term most often used is 'Union.' It is incorrect to refer to them as gutta percha cases.

Sizes may vary somewhat, but generally a 'whole' plate case measures 7" x 9⅛" to the outside edges, a 'half' plate 4⅞" x 6", a 'quarter' plate 3¾" x 4¾", a 'sixth' 3⅛" x 3⅝", a 'ninth' 2⅜" x 2⅞", and a 'sixteenth' 1¾" x 2". Clifford and Michele Krainik and Carl Walvoord have written a book, *Union Cases*, which we recommend for further information.

Angel w/flower cornucopia, 9th plate, VG 70.00
Beehive & farm tools, Littlefield-Parsons, 9th plate, VG 60.00
Catching butterflies, Littlefield-Parsons, 9th plate 75.00
Chess players, Littlefield-Parsons, 1856, 9th plate 125.00
Children at stile, sm, G 150.00
Church window, Critchlow, 6th plate, VG 55.00
Church window, Critchlow, 9th plate, EX 45.00
Farmer w/scythe up ladder in tree, 1857, 6th plate, EX 100.00
Floral & scrollwork, 4th plate, EX 60.00
Landing of Columbus, whole plate, 7¼x9¼" 2,400.00
Monk meditating, Littlefield-Parsons, oval, sm 160.00

Eagle at Bay, Rinhart #70, 3¾x3¼", EX, $115.00.

Moses among bulrushes, oval, 9th plate, EX 100.00
Roses & scrolls, S Peck, 9th plate, VG 60.00
Single pear, 9th plate, VG 50.00
Spray of flowers, Littlefield-Parsons, 9th plate, VG 50.00
Strawberry, 9th plate, G 50.00
Tiny heads in oval, Critchlow, 4th plate, VG 110.00
Union on scroll w/flag & shield, 6th plate, EX 135.00
Washington bust, First in Peace etc, 3⅜x3¾" 330.00
Washington Monument/eagles/angels/etc, 5x6¼" 250.00

Viewers and Slides

Brewster, walnut, scalloped mirror flat, in fitted box, EX 300.00
Claudet, maroon leather, brass bbl lenses, late 1840s, EX 525.00
Enterprise, slide projector, tin/cast metal, Pat 1899 ....50.00
Keystone, 2 Bausch & Lomb-lens bellows, 1904 ....200.00
Keystone Telebinocular, collapsible, book-form box 60.00

Magic lantern, pnt tin/brass, w/12 slides, Plank, EX in box **100.00**
Pervescope, Pat 1895, EX **35.00**
Sawyers Jr Projector, stereoscope viewer, 26 reels, M **30.00**
Slides, Pacific Coast Views, Watkins, 10 for **200.00**
View-Master Stereoscope, +80 View-Master reels, 1950s, EX **75.00**
Witte Moviescope, 4-in-1, cb, Zeotrope design, w/strips, VG **275.00**
Zeotrope, sees movies through slots, 9½" dia, EX **475.00**

Miscellaneous

Album, brn emb cover, celluloid leaves, 28 tintypes, 42-pg **85.00**
Book, Art & Technique of Color Photography, Lieberman, 1951 ..**65.00**
Book, Fotygraft Album, F Wing, Relly & Britton, 1916, EX **12.50**
Book, Popular Mechanics Photo Handbook, 1948, VG **9.00**
Case, MOP, floral, 6th plate **200.00**
Manual, New Leica, Morgan & Lester, 1951, EX in jacket **37.50**
Movie projector, Pathex, +reels (1 Lindbergh reel) & case **225.00**
Stanhope, alabaster bbl, Niagara Falls scene **30.00**
Stanhope, binoculars, bone, Statue of Liberty view **50.00**
Stanhope, binoculars, ivory **65.00**
Stanhope, inkwell, ivory, chalet form, German views **50.00**
Stanhope, pen, rhinestones, Lord's Prayer **45.00**
Stanhope, pipe, cvd wood, 6 Port Erin views, 1" L, EX **50.00**
Stanhope, scent bottle, brass, w/neck chain, 6 views, EX **155.00**
Stanhope, tape measure, bbl form w/ivory finial, 1 view **65.00**

Piano Babies

A familiar sight in Victorian parlors, piano babies languished atop shawl-covered pianos in a variety of poses: crawling, sitting, on their tummies or on their backs playing with their toes. Some babies were nude, and some wore gowns. Sizes ranged from about 3" up to 12". The most famous manufacturer of these bisque darlings was the Heubach Brothers of Germany, who nearly always marked their product; see Heubach for listings. Watch for reproductions

Blk, on tummy & elbows, w/top hat, terra cotta **495.00**
Crawling boy, hands on book, floral gown, #5540, 16", NM **525.00**
Girl, umbrella in left hand, skirt in right, fancy hat, 17" **195.00**
Half reclining, holding ft, 11" **165.00**
On bk plays w/toy sheep, Germany, #11290, 5x10" **550.00**
On side, rabbit under arm, cat on bk, lt bl floral gown, 9" **225.00**
On stomach, str arms raise chest, cat on bk/under arm, 9" **230.00**
On stomach, thumb raised to mouth, ft raised, Germany, 9x7" ..**250.00**
On tummy, knee bent as if to crawl, pk roses on dress, 10" **250.00**
On tummy holding puppy, 8" **175.00**
Seated, dog in crook of right arm, floral gown, bonnet, 8" **250.00**
Seated, playing w/toes, pk gown, 4½" **175.00**

Pickard

Founded in 1893 in Edgerton, Illinois, the Pickard China Company was originally a decorating studio, importing china blanks from European manufacturers. Some of these early pieces bear the name of those companies as well as Pickard's. Trained artists decorated the wares with hand-painted studies of fruit, florals, birds, and scenics and often signed their work. In 1915 Pickard introduced a line of 23k gold over a dainty floral-etched ground design. In the 1930s they began to experiment with the idea of making their own ware and by 1938 had succeeded in developing a formula for fine translucent china. Since 1976 they have issued an annual limited edition Christmas plate. They are now located in Antioch, Illinois.

The company has used various marks. The earliest (1893-1894) was a double-circle mark, 'Edgerton Hand Painted' with 'Pickard' in the center. Variations of the double-circle mark (with 'Hand Painted China' replacing the Edgerton designation) were employed until 1915, each differing enough that collectors can usually pinpoint the date of manufacture within five years. Later marks included the crown mark, 'Pickard' on a gold maple leaf, and the current mark, the lion and shield. Work signed by Challinor, Marker, and Yeschek is especially valued by today's collectors. Our advisor for this category is Milt Steinfeld; he is listed in the Directory under New Jersey.

Bowl, fruit; gooseberries, sgn Mullen, ftd, 3½" **175.00**
Bowl, nut; nuts & leaves w/gold, sgn Vokral, scalloped, 8" **185.00**
Bowl, pk & wht poppies & daisies w/gold, sgn Gasper, 7¼" **140.00**
Bowl, pk clovers & gr leaves & gold, sgn Reury, 7½" **145.00**
Bowl, pk roses w/gold, sgn Brauer, scalloped, 8⅞" **165.00**
Bowl, red & bl grapes, sgn Beutlich, leaf form w/hdl, 9½" **215.00**
Bowl, red cherries & pk flowers, ornate gold border, 10¼" **155.00**
Bowl, red gooseberries w/in & w/out, sgn Kruesche, 5¾" **150.00**
Cake plate, wht azaleas & gr leaves w/much gold, sgn, 11" **120.00**
Creamer & sugar bowl, currants, gold trim & hdls, sgn, w/lid **325.00**
Creamer & sugar bowl, floral w/much gold, w/lid & shakers **150.00**
Creamer & sugar bowl, Italian gardens, sgn Vabornic **165.00**

Lemonade pitcher, chrysanthemums on orange with much gold, signed Reau, 7", $450.00.

Mayonnaise, bl cornflowers w/gold, sgn CK, +7¼" underplate ...**165.00**
Mug, currants, sgn Vokral, gold rim/base/hdl, 6" **300.00**
Pitcher, Antique Chinese Enamel, sgn Tolpin, much gold, 10" .**325.00**
Pitcher, cider; acorns/branches w/gold on cream, 1894-1904 mk .**395.00**
Pitcher, grapes & leaves, dk red w/gold, sgn Vokral, 8" **325.00**
Pitcher, water lilies, gold hdl, 1898, 7" **300.00**
Plate, farm & stream scene, gold trim, hdls, Challinor, 10½" **150.00**
Plate, peaches, gold trim, sgn Heap, scalloped, 8½" **85.00**
Plate, red currants, sgn Gasper, gold rim, 8½" **85.00**
Plate, strawberries, sgn Comyn, gold rim, 8⅜" **75.00**
Plate, trees & pond, sgn Challinor, 9½" **100.00**
Plate, wht snowdrop flowers, Leach, wide gold border, 8¾" **65.00**
Plate, yel daffodils, sgn Goess, gold border, 8¾" **85.00**
Plate, Yosemite, sgn Marker, 8" **100.00**
Platter, grapes & leaves w/much gold, sgn Coufall, 12¼" **210.00**
Sugar bowl, hummingbird & orchids, sgn Challinor, w/lid **60.00**
Syrup jug, tulips, sgn Hessler, gold rim, 6¼" **160.00**
Tile, apple blossom w/gold, sgn Marker, 1895 mk, 6¾" dia **225.00**
Tray, dresser; Italian garden, sgn Gasper, hdls, 16x10" **155.00**
Tray, dresser; roses w/gold edge, sgn Challinor, 12x9¼" **200.00**
Vase, hollyhocks, sgn Challinor, gold rim, 11½" **500.00**
Vase, mc landscape, Chlinder, hdls, 4-ftd, leaf mk, 4x2½" **275.00**
Vase, scenic, sgn E Challinor, matt, 7½" **395.00**

Pickle Castors

Pickle castors, which were both functional and decorative, became popular after the Civil War, reaching their peak about 1885. By 1900 they had virtually disappeared from factory catalogs. Numerous styles were available. They consisted of a decorated, silverplated frame that held either a fancy clear pressed-glass insert or one of decorated colored art glass — the latter being popular in the more affluent Victorian households and more desirable with collectors today.

In the listings below, the description prior to the semicolon refers to the jar (insert), and the remainder of the line describes the frame. When no condition is indicated, the silverplate is assumed to be in very good to excellent condition; glass jars are assumed near-mint.

Key:
rsl — resilvered   3-D — three-dimensional

Amberina with painted birds and flowers, dog finial; silverplated frame with pickles and leaves, 10", with tongs, $675.00.

Amberina, swirled ribs, Libbey; ftd Meriden fr 465.00
Baby Invt T'print, cranberry, HP floral; Wilcox flower fr 425.00
Bead & Drape, red satin; ftd SP fr, +tongs 325.00
Bl, rows of dmn prisms/faceted blocks; fr w/emb birds etc 185.00
Block Variant; Pairpoint fr w/griffins, +tongs 195.00
Cerulean bl, HP floral; tall ornate ftd fr, SHM mk 495.00
Cranberry, HP florals; tall ftd R&B fr, rstr 425.00
Cranberry, Invt T'print, M Gregory boy; Rockford #611 foxes fr ...500.00
Cranberry, Panelled Sprig; ornate mk fr, +tongs 495.00
Cranberry, ribbed, bulbous bottom; ftd fr 375.00
Cranberry, vertical ribs; ftd Tufts fr w/side bail 350.00
Cranberry satin w/gold dmns & florals; ornate Pairpoint fr 400.00
Cranberry T'print w/HP flowers; mk Webster fr w/many leaves .425.00
Crown Milano w/Timothy Canty floral; Pairpoint fr, +tongs 800.00
Daisy & Button, sapphire bl; orig ftd SP fr 295.00
Daisy & Button w/V Ornament, bl; mk Rogers fr 295.00
Dbl, frosted bbl, leaf finials; leafy fr, twist bail, rstr 350.00
Dmn Point, clear; ornate ftd Meriden fr, +tongs 125.00
Dmn Quilt, rubena w/mc coralene florals; Tufts fr, EX 525.00
Frosted birds on clear; ball ftd rstr SP fr, 14", +tongs 135.00
Invt T'print, bl, lavish HP floral, scalloped; SHM fr, rstr 550.00
Invt T'print, cranberry, gold trim/HP flowers; Tufts fr 450.00
Invt T'print, cranberry, HP florals; short ornate fr 375.00
Invt T'print, gr, HP, gold trim, appl rope/floral; Meriden fr 485.00
Leaf Mold, cranberry & vaseline satin spatter; SP fr, rstr 395.00
Peachblow w/floral; fr w/emb birds, ornate finial, 9" 425.00
Pineapple & Fan, Holbrook; SP fr, +tongs 85.00
Pk shaded cased satin, ovoid; fancy fr w/ped base 395.00
Pk to rose shaded, blown-out shells, HP florals; sgn SP fr 350.00
Royal Ivy, rainbow craquelle; cucumber leaf fr mk Aurora 500.00
Shaded peach satin, gilt acorns, Mt WA; Pairpoint griffins fr .1,100.00
Shell & Tassel; orig Tufts sq fr w/sq lid, +tongs 165.00
Swirl, cranberry w/HP florals; Benedict fr 395.00
Swirl Optic, yel, HP floral; ornate fr, pelican finial, rstr 495.00
Wht opal swirl stripes, hourglass shape; sgn ornate SP fr 295.00
Yel satin quilt, cased, HP decor; orig ornate SP fr, EX 765.00

Pie Birds

A pie bird (also known as a pie vent or pie funnel) is placed in the middle of a pie to serve the dual purpose of supporting the pastry (to prevent sogginess) and to act as a vent that allows the steam to escape, thus avoiding runover. They are open-bottomed, hollow, and glazed inside and out. They are designed with a top vent, and most have two arches around the base. The steam enters the pie bird via the arches and exits through the top vent. In Victorian times pie funnels were first used in deep-dish meat pies. Bird-shaped vents were made as early as 1910 in England and from 1930 until the '60s in America. Later, figural pie vents were made in England. In the past two years, over 100 new U.S.-made pie vents have flooded the collectibles market, only one of which was made by a commercial pottery. Incense burners, one-hole pepper shakers, and a dated brass toy bird whistle should not be mistaken for pie vents.

Our advisors for this category are Alan Pedel (representing the English market; see England in the Directory) and Lillian Cole (listed under New Jersey).

Bear holding honey jar, ceramic 28.00
Benny Baker, w/utensils, mk Pat Pend, by Cardinal China, 5½" ..65.00
Bird, bl & wht on wht base, 2-pc 65.00
Bird, lt mustard, mk Sun Glow, England, 4½" 30.00
Blackbird on wht base, mk Royal Worcester England, 2-pc 45.00
Blk man in wht chef's clothes holds rabbit by ears, ceramic 50.00
Blue Willow, rooster, goose, birds, new, ea 15.00
British Bobby, vents from helmet, ceramic 38.00
Canary, yel w/pk lips 18.00
Chick, yel w/pk beak, Josef Original 18.00
Cow, ceramic 22.00
Dragon, gr w/spines & horns, ceramic 40.00
Elephant, gray, mk Nutbrown, English Reg No 65.00
Funnels, cream, unmk, from England, various heights, ea 15.00
Granny (Little Baker), no arches, imported, 1970s 20.00
Humpty Dumpty 22.00
Mammy, ceramic, 5" 45.00
Repros from Taiwan, Chef or Mammy, red, yel & wht, ea 10.00
Repros from Taiwan, Cleminson or Shawnee styles, tan bases, ea ..10.00
Rooster, mc, Cleminson 23.00
Snowman w/pie, dressed in hat/scarf/mittens, ceramic 45.00
Songbird, bl, pk or cinnamon, 4½", ea 20.00
Songbird, bl w/blk speckles, heavy ceramic, 4¾" 20.00
Songbird, blk or cream w/gold trim, ea 35.00
Witch in blk w/long gray hair holds pie w/bird flying out 48.00

Pierce, Howard

Howard Pierce opened a studio in Claremont, California, in the mid-1940s where he produced small ceramic models of birds and animals, figurines, and vases, making his molds and decorating his ware with no outside help except for his wife and more recently his daughter. He was best known for his skill at sculpting his models, which he decorated entirely with the airbrush. Early items were incised 'Howard Pierce, Claremont, California' or stamped 'Howard Pierce Porcelain.' Not all of his ware is marked, however, and some pieces carry only his initials. For more information we recommend *The Collector's Encyclopedia of California Pottery* by Jack Chipman, whose address may be found in the Directory under California.

Ashtray, high-style, lt gray lava w/cobalt int 45.00
Bowl, gondola shape, brn on wht, 5x9½" 20.00

Bust, lady, stylized, brn agate, ca 1956, 10½" **195.00**

Figurines, giraffes, brown agate, in-mold marks, 1950s, 10½", $80.00 for the pair.

Figurine, goose, blk & gray speckled, 8¼" **55.00**
Figurine, native man & woman, brn on wht, 7", 7½", pr **145.00**
Figurine, owls in tree, lg **75.00**
Figurine, pigeon, wht w/brn head & base, 1950s, 7½" **35.00**
Figurine, polar bear, brn on wht, 4½" **45.00**
Figurine, quail family, 1 lg: 5½"+2 sm **85.00**
Figurine, water bird, wht w/brn bill & ft, 14" **65.00**
Vase, gr mottle, glossy, cylindrical, 7¼" **35.00**
Vase, 3-color jasper, Huck Finn & dog, disk type, 4" **65.00**
Wall pocket, 3-color jasper, plants, Claremont, 2½x4½" **40.00**

Pigeon Blood

Pigeon blood glass, produced in the late 1800s, may be distinguished from other dark red glass by its distinctive orange tint.

Butter dish, Venecia, HP decor **150.00**
Goblet, gold scrolls, lady & gent in oval, Venetian, 8" **75.00**
Pitcher, Bulging Loops, water sz **395.00**
Plate, ca 1900, 8" **135.00**
Rose bowl, floral w/gold, 5" **62.50**
Shakers, Ada, orig lids, pr **150.00**
Shakers, Flower Band, orig tops, pr **165.00**
Syrup pitcher, Torquay **275.00**
Toothpick holder, Fine Rib **65.00**
Vase, florals, 10½" **180.00**
Vase, 5x6" **50.00**
Wine, 6" **40.00**

Pilkington

Founded in 1892 in Manchester, England, the Pilkington pottery experimented in wonderful lustre glazes that were so successful that when they were diplayed at exhibition in 1904, they were met with critical acclaim. They soon attracted some of the best ceramic technicians and designers of the day who decorated the lustre ground with flowers, animals, and trees; some pieces were more elaborate with scenes of sailing ships and knights on horseback. Each artist signed his work with his personal monogram. Most pieces were dated and carried the company mark as well. After 1913 the company became known as Royal Lancastrian.

Their Lapis Ware line was introduced in the late 1920s, featuring intermingling tones of color under a matt glaze. Some pieces were very simply decorated while others were painted with designs of stylized leafage, scrolls, swirls, and stripes. The line continued into the thirties. Other pieces of this period were molded and carved with animals, leaves, etc., some of which were reminescent of their earlier wares.

The company closed in 1938 but reopened in 1948. During this period their mark was a simple P within the outline of a petaled flower shape. Our advisor for this category is David Erhard; he is listed in the Directory under California.

Bookends, dolphin, 5½", pr **300.00**
Figurine, bear, by Richard Joyce, 3½" **225.00**
Tile, Apache dancer, set of 3 ....**130.00**
Vase, Aventurine bl, 7" **250.00**
Vase, bud; Prussian Bl, 5" **175.00**
Vase, Deco design, grs & bls, matt, 6½x6½" **275.00**
Vase, gold lustre w/mc highlights, long bottle neck, 7" **300.00**
Vase, matt gr, gourd shape, 7" **175.00**
Vase, matt orange, 10" **200.00**

Pillin

Polia Pillin was born in Poland in 1909; many of her family were artisians and craftsmen. Except for a few weeks of formal instruction at the Hull House in Chicago, Pillin is self-taught in the arts. Her work has been shown in many exhibits, and she has received awards from the Los Angeles County Art Institute, Syracuse Museum, Los Angeles County Fair, and the California State Fair. First interested in oils and watercolors, she has carried the same Byzantine quality over to her pottery. All of her work is signed 'Pillin' or 'W&P Pillin,' both with the loop of the P extended in an arc over the remaining letters of her name.

Bowl, bust portraits & birds on bl, 5½x10½" **450.00**
Bowl, bust portraits on blk, 6½x5½" **425.00**
Bowl, lady & tree, 3¾x5" **325.00**
Bowl, punch; mc yel, rare, 16" **1,600.00**
Bowl, women's portraits, brn/blk, bulbous, 4x7" **450.00**
Charcoal, Southwest scene, fr, 19x12" **675.00**
Lamp base, 12 figurals, rare, 14" **1,750.00**
Painting, abstract, paper, fr, 15x11" **750.00**
Pendant, horse on bl, 2" **55.00**
Plaque, farm scene, 12x12" **1,050.00**
Plate, children w/balloons on yel, 7½" **135.00**
Plate, frolicking horses on gr, 7½" **125.00**
Plate, ochre tones, 9" sq **250.00**

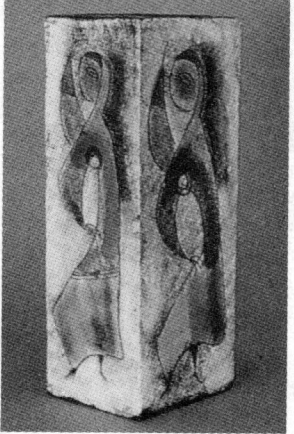

Vase, abstract figure in green, blue and pink on sponged gray and black background, 11½x3¾", $850.00.

Vase, abstract figure on all 4 sides, 11½x3¾" 975.00
Vase, Bentonite, abstract, 6" 375.00
Vase, Bentonite, fish decor, 4" 475.00
Vase, birds on gr w/pastels, 5¼" 225.00
Vase, birds on yel, 1½" 90.00
Vase, bust portraits on blk, bulbous, 9½" 475.00
Vase, figure on blk, 11" 900.00
Vase, fish, pk & gr, squat, 2" 90.00
Vase, gr/pastel, bottle form, 11½" 225.00
Vase, horse/2 ladies, wht on peacock & rust, 9x7" 850.00
Vase, horses, 7" 395.00
Vase, horses (2), 2" 150.00
Vase, horses on pastels, 5¾" 195.00
Vase, lady w/birds, ball form, 6" 425.00
Vase, lady w/flower & bird, 6" 425.00
Vase, nudes on red, 12x6", NM 1,250.00
Vase, 3 nudes on bl, 9¼" 600.00
Vase, 3 nudes on pastels, 4½" 250.00

Pin-Back Buttons

Buttons produced up to the early 1920s were made of a celluloid covering held in place by a ring (or collet) to the back of which a pin was secured. Manufacturers used these 'cellos' to advertise their products. Many were of exceptional quality in both color and design. Buttons in sets were produced that featured a variety of subjects. These were given away by tobacco, chewing gum and candy manufacturers, who often packed them with their product as premiums. Usually the name of the button maker or the product manufacturer was printed on a paper placed in the back of the button. Often these 'back papers' are still in place today. Much of the time the button maker's name was printed on the button's perimeter, and sometimes the copyright was added. Beginning in the 1920s, a large number of buttons were lithographed on tin; these are referred to as tin 'lithos.' Nearly all pin-back buttons are collected today for their advertising appeal or graphic design. There are countless categories to base a collection on.

The following listing contains non-political buttons representative of the many varieties you may find. All are celluloid unless described otherwise. Values reflect buttons in excellent, well-centered condition, with bright color and only the very slightest of wear, if any.

Acorn Stoves & Ranges, Used by Millions, acorn, mc, ⅞" 18.00
Andy Gump for Congress, blk & wht, ⅞" 12.00
Ascalion Commandery, Knights Templar, bird, mc, 1906, 1¾" 45.00
Ball RR Watches, GAR medal, mc on gold, 1901, ⅞" 10.00
Balloon Route Trolley Trip, Pacific Electric Ry, mc, 1¼" 35.00
Be Sunny, Sunny Jim (of Force cereals), sepia, 1¼" 10.00
Buster Brown Bread, BB & Tige, mc w/gray rim, 1½" 30.00
Buster Brown Bread, BB & Tige, mc w/yel rim, 1½" 25.00
CD Kenny Co, Welcome Home, knight w/shield, mc, 1¾" 60.00
Ceresota Flour, boy slices bread, mc w/dk brn rim, 1¼" 60.00
Chessie C&O Ry, sleeping cat, blk/pk/gray, 1½" 25.00
Chevrolet, Watch the Leader, tin litho, mc, ⅞" 10.00
Concord State Fair, lady in red, mc, 1901, 1¼" 40.00
Crown Mfg Co, Phelps NY, farm drill, mc, 1" 75.00
Dead Shot Smokeless Powder, duck, mc, ⅞" 50.00
Deering Harvester Co, Chicago, farming scene, mc, 1¼" 65.00
Ducks Unlimited, duck flying over marsh, mc, 1950, 1¼" 50.00
Gen J Haller, True Son of Poland, blk & wht, 1923, 1¼" 8.00
General Foch, blk & wht, 1¼" 12.00
Giant Seesaw, Trans-Miss Expo, Omaha, sepia, 1898, 1½" 30.00
Gold Dust Washing Powder, Blk twins in yel tub, ⅞" 50.00
Indian, Meet Me at the Redpath Chautauqua, mc on red, 1" 24.00

Iver Johnson Cycles, lady pops up through wheel, mc, ⅞" 35.00
Iver Johnson Cycles, Major Taylor (Blk cyclist), mc, ⅞" 50.00
Koveralls, mules try to pull pants apart, blk/red/wht, ⅞" 10.00
LeRoys Home Made Mayonnaise, mc jar on dk bl, ⅞" 25.00
Let's 'Lect Lum Edwards for Pres (radio), brn & wht, 1" 15.00
Little Orphan Annie, Some Swell Sweater, sgn, mc, 1¼" 70.00
Majestic Ranges, range on ship's flag, mc, ⅞" 10.00
MIA? Missing or Prisoner (Vietnam War), wht on blk, 1¾" 7.00
Montgomery Ward & Co, Chicago building, mc w/dk bl rim, 1¼" 20.00
Montgomery Ward Electric Horseless Carriage, mc, 1¼" 95.00
Old Musty, Van Norstrands Ale, owl & keg, mc, 1¼" 75.00
Page, fence around world globe, mc, ⅞" 12.50
Palmer Method Writing, for merit, gr/pk/wht on gold, ⅞" 3.00
Parrot Brand ABC Soda Crackers, parrot, Pat 1896, mc, ⅞" 15.00
Rumely Oil Pull, tractor, gr/blk/red/wht, 1¼" 70.00
Save Old Ironsides 1797-1925, ship, bl/blk/red/wht, ⅞" 12.00
Snow White Jingle Club Member, red/bl letters on wht, 1¼" 50.00
Square Deal Fence, Keystone Co wire, blk/wht on red, 1½" 15.00
State Seal, Iowa, bl on wht, 1¼" 4.00
Struby-Estabrook Merc Co, Welcome Arch, mc, 1¼" 35.00
The New Huber, steam engine tractor, mc w/bl rim, 1½" 75.00
Tiffin Wagon Co, The Best Yet Produced, wagon, mc, 1¼" 85.00
Tim McCoys Vigilantes, tin litho, bl on wht, ⅞" 45.00
Welcome Boardman, pilot & plane, blk/yel/wht, 1931, 1¼" 35.00
Yellow Kid #22, w/paint & brush, blk/red/yel/wht, 1¼" 25.00

Pink Lustre Ware

Pink lustre was produced by nearly every potter in the Staffordshire district in the 18th and 19th centuries. The application of gold lustre on white or light-colored backgrounds produced pinks, while the same over dark colors developed copper. The wares ranged from hand-painted plaques to transfer-printed dinnerware. Design features in the phrase immediately following the item (i.e. cup, plate, etc.) are in pink lustre unless otherwise specifically described within the line.

Tea bowl and saucer, $75.00.

Coffeepot, lady/flowers transfer, dome lid, 12", EX 275.00
Creamer, rim/base band, Oriental transfer w/mc, 3½" 170.00
Creamer & sugar bowl, leaves, 5-color floral, w/lid, 5¾", EX 120.00
Cup & saucer, band, 4-color foliage/floral 55.00
Cup & saucer, bands, arched mc sunrise/sunset design 50.00
Cup & saucer, bands, Victoria & Albert purple transfer 110.00
Cup & saucer, blk transfer cottage w/lustre trim, worn 65.00
Cup & saucer, border panel w/red & gr floral, EX 25.00
Cup & saucer, sprigs/stems/stripes, 5-color floral, w/hdl 40.00
Cup & saucer, stripes/rosettes, red/gr floral, NM 75.00
Pitcher, floral, emb mc strawberries, 7" 85.00
Pitcher, house pattern on pearlware, prof rpr, 7" 195.00

Pitcher, Mariner's Compass w/ship, transfer/mc, 9", NM 390.00
Pitcher, vintage w/bl stripes, chip, 4½" 220.00
Plate, banding, King's Rose-type 4-color floral, 7½", NM 65.00
Plate, blk transfer: Duke of Wellington, mk Scott, 9½", NM 200.00
Plate, leaves/rim band, Adam's Rose-type floral border, 7½" 80.00
Plate, stripes/bands, blk transfer genre scene, scalloped, 8" 55.00
Platter, house/flowers, pk, stains, 18" 220.00
Teapot, house pattern, hairline, 8" 125.00

Pink Paw Bears

These charming figural pieces are very similar to the Pink Pigs described in the following category. They were made in Germany during the same time frame. The cabbage green is identical; the bears themselves are whitish-gray with pink foot pads. You'll find some that are unmarked while others are marked 'Germany' or 'Made in Germany.' In theory, the unmarked bears are the oldest, made prior to 1890 when the McKinley Tariff Act required imports to be marked with the country of origin. Those marked 'Made In' were probably produced after the revision of the Act in 1914.

1 by bean pot 135.00
1 by graphophone 135.00
1 by honey pot 125.00
1 by top hat 110.00
1 in roadster (car identical to pk pig car) 145.00
1 on binoculars 135.00
1 peeking out of basket 115.00
1 peering in hand mirror 135.00
1 sitting in wicker chair 150.00
2 in purse 135.00
2 in roadster 150.00
2 on pin dish 120.00
2 peering in floor mirror 150.00
2 sitting by mushroom 125.00
3 on pin dish 130.00

Pink Pigs

Pink Pigs on cabbage green were made in Germany around the turn of the century. They were sold as souvenirs in train depots, amusement parks, and gift shops. 'Action pigs' (those involved in some amusing activity) are the most valuable, and prices increase with the number of pigs. Though a similar type of figurine was made in white bisque, most serious collectors prefer only the pink ones. They are marked in two ways: 'Germany' in incised letters, and a black ink stamp 'Made in Germany' in a circle.

Pigs on cotton bale, one at top, other peering through hole, $95.00.

1 beside gr drum, wall-mt match holder 60.00
1 beside stump, camera around neck, toothpick holder 120.00

1 coming out of cup 65.00
1 coming out of suitcase 85.00
1 coming through gr fence, post at sides, open for flowers 95.00
1 driving touring car 145.00
1 in case looking through binoculars 125.00
1 in gr Dutch shoe 50.00
1 in gr suitcase bank, head 1 side, bk other, gold trim 75.00
1 in Japanese submarine, Japan imp on both sides 125.00
1 in jaws of trap, rare, unmk, 5" L 125.00
1 in money sack bank 85.00
1 in roadster 145.00
1 lg pig sitting behind 3" trough 75.00
1 napping on side, Schlite Patent, 5" L 98.00
1 on binoculars, gold trim 115.00
1 on gr trinket dish, leg caught in lobster claw 65.00
1 on horseshoe-shaped dish w/raised 4-leaf clover 75.00
1 on keg playing piano 150.00
1 on shoulder of gr ink bottle 75.00
1 plays accordion on side of tray, wht bear ea side 125.00
1 pushing head through wooden gate 75.00
1 putting letter in mail box 85.00
1 reclining on horseshoe ashtray 70.00
1 riding train, 4½" 150.00
1 sits, holds orange Boston Baked Beans pot match holder 65.00
1 sits by high-top boot 75.00
1 sitting in bathtub 95.00
1 sitting on log, mk Germany 80.00
1 standing in gr tub 95.00
1 w/attached toothpick holder 65.00
1 w/front ft in 3-part dish containing 3 dice, 1 ft on dice 75.00
1 w/tennis racket stands beside vase, Lawn Tennis, 3¾" 95.00
1 wearing chef's costume, holds frypan, w/basket 95.00
2, mother & baby in bl blanket in tub, rabbit on board atop 85.00
2, mother in tub gives baby a bottle, lamb looks on, 4x3½" 85.00
2, 1 at telephone booth, 1 inside, 4½" 95.00
2 at confession, 4½" 90.00
2 behind trough, unmk 75.00
2 by eggshell 80.00
2 dancing, in top hat, tux & cane 110.00
2 holding hands in roadster, 4½" L 160.00
2 in basket, Merry Squealers, 3½x3" 90.00
2 in bed, Good Night on footboard, 4x3x2½" 145.00
2 in carriage 95.00
2 in love sit on lg log, 2 openings on tree stump, 7" L 75.00
2 in open trunk, 3¾" 95.00
2 in purse 75.00
2 on basket, head raising lid, plaque on front 80.00
2 on binoculars, gold trim 140.00
2 on cotton bale, 1 peers from hole, 1 over top 95.00
2 on seesaw on top of pouch bank 75.00
2 on top hat 95.00
2 on tray hugging, 3x4½" 65.00
2 sitting at table playing card game 'Hearts' 170.00
3, 1 on lg slipper playing banjo, 2 dancing on side 145.00
3, 2 sit in front of coal bucket, 3rd inside 125.00
3 at trough, 4½" L 98.00
3 sm pigs behind oval trough, mk, 2¾x2½x1¾" 90.00
3 w/baby carriage, father & 2 babies, Wheeling His Own 95.00
3 w/carriage, mother & 2 babies, Germany 95.00

Pisgah Forest

The Pisgah Forest Pottery was established in 1920 near Mount Pisgah in Arden, North Carolina, by Walter B. Stephen, who had worked in previous years at other locations in the state — Nonconnah and Skyland (the latter from 1913 until 1916). Stephen, who was born in the mountain region near Asheville, was known for his work in the Southern tradition. He produced skillfully-executed wares exhibiting an amazing variety of techniques. He operated his business with only two helpers. Recognized today as his most outstanding accomplishment, his Cameo line was decorated by hand in the pate-sur-pate style (similar to Wedgwood Jasper) in such designs as Fiddler and Dog, Spinning Wheel, Covered Wagon, Buffalo Hunt, Mountain Cabin, Square Dancers, Indian Campfire, and Plowman. Stephen is known for other types of wares as well. His crystalline glaze is highly regarded by today's collectors.

At least nine different stamps mark his wares, several of which contain the outline of the potter at the wheel and 'Pisgah Forest.' Cameo is sometimes marked with a circle containing the line name and 'Long Pine, Arden, NC.' Two other marks may be more difficult to recognize: 1) a circle containing the outline of a pine tree, 'N.C.' to the left of the trunk and 'Pine Tree' on the other side; and 2) the letter 'P' with short uprights in the middle of the top and lower curves. Stephen died in 1961, but the work was continued by his associates. Our advisor for this category is R.J. Sayers; he is listed in the Directory under North Carolina.

Bowl vase, turq & pk crackle, Stephen, 1942 ....35.00
Creamer & sugar bowl, turq w/pk, demi, 1941 ....50.00
Jug, plum w/cream int, hdl, 1942, 8" 70.00
Lamp base, Cameo, pioneer scene, wht on lt bl, Stephen, 11" 150.00
Pitcher, Cameo, wagon train, gr band, sgn Stephen, 1962, 6" 120.00
Teapot, gr, high glaze, 6x8½" 60.00

Vase, blue crackle, 6x6½", $125.00.

Vase, aqua, bulbous, Stephen, 1937, 10" 60.00
Vase, Cameo, wagon train/dogs/etc, wht on bl, 5" 150.00
Vase, crystalline, bl/ivory, pk int, Stephen, 1949, 5½" 200.00
Vase, crystalline bl, 9" 250.00
Vase, crystalline bl w/pk int, bulbous, dtd 1938, 4" 150.00
Vase, crystalline solid wht, dtd 1953, 6½" 200.00
Vase, Nonconnah, bridge/forest relief on gr, Stephen, 11½" ...1,000.00
Vase, turq, corset form, dtd 1941, 4½" 50.00
Vase, turq to plum, bulbous, dtd 1950, 5½" 65.00

Pittsburgh Glass

As early as 1797, utility window glass and hollowware were being produced in the Pittsburgh area. Coal had been found in abundance, and it was there that it was first used instead of wood to fuel the glass furnaces. Because of this, as many as 150 glass companies operated there at one time. However, most failed due to the economically disastrous effects of the War of 1812. By the mid-1850s those that remained were producing a wide range of flint glass items including pattern-molded and free-blown glass, cut and engraved wares, and pressed

tableware patterns. Our advisor for this category is Mark Vuono; he is listed in the Directory under Connecticut.

Ale glass, dk amethyst, flint, free-blown clear base, 7¼" 50.00
Bottle, bar; Pillar mold, cranberry cased in clear, 11" 715.00
Candlestick, amber, dolphin w/clear petal top, 11" 525.00
Candlestick, hexagonal stem, open socket, 9¾" 55.00
Candlestick, yel opal, rnd base, hexagonal stem, 9⅜" 165.00
Celery vase, festoon & floral eng, 20-rib swirl, 8¼" 325.00
Creamer & sugar bowl, cobalt rim, 1820s, 3½" 450.00
Cruet, yel-amber, 8-Pillar mold, appl neck ring & hdl, 6½" 4,550.00
Decanter, cut panels/strawberry dmns/fans/roundels, 8⅛" 275.00
Decanter, Pillar mold, appl ring, flared lip, 10¾" 50.00
Decanter, Pillar mold w/8 amethyst vertical ribs, 10¾" 1,450.00
Inkwell, olive-amber, b3m, 3¼" 150.00
Jigger, sapphire bl, 6-panel, 2¼" 20.00
Jigger, violet bl, arched panels, 2⅜", pr 30.00

Pillar Mold pitcher, cranberry with clear-cased cranberry blown handle, pontil scar, 9½", $8,800.00; Bar bottle, flute pattern, amethyst, doughnut lip, polished pontil, 11", $650.00.

String holder, clear w/appl electric bl trim, 4½x4¾" 140.00
Tumbler, amber, 6-panel, 3⅜" 160.00
Tumbler, aqua, 6-panel, 3½" 40.00
Tumbler, bl & brn swirl, 6-panel w/horizontal steps, 3⅛" 250.00
Tumbler, cobalt, 20-panel, 3⅛" 75.00
Tumbler, cobalt, 6-panel, 6 arches, 3⅜" 85.00
Tumbler, cobalt, 7-panel, 7 arches, 3⅜" 110.00
Tumbler, cobalt, 8-panel, flake, 3¼" 95.00
Tumbler, deep amethyst, 8-panel, 3½" 260.00
Tumbler, deep sapphire bl, 7-panel, 4" 138.00
Tumbler, electric bl, 6-panel, 2¼" 75.00
Tumbler, fiery opal, 5-panel, 3¾" 225.00
Tumbler, grass gr, T'print, ground bottom, 3½" 75.00
Tumbler, lt bl, 6-panel, 3" 105.00
Tumbler, lt gr, 8-panel, 3⅝" 200.00
Tumbler, red-violet, 3⅜" 160.00
Tumbler, sapphire bl, 7-panel, 3⅛" 66.00
Tumbler, sapphire bl, 8-panel, 4" 120.00
Tumbler, violet, 8-panel, 3¼" 170.00
Tumbler, yel, wide & narrow panels, 3½" 140.00
Vase, cobalt, 8-Pillar mold, appl low ft, flared rim, 10⅜" 1,050.00
Vase, free-blown, std, 8" 70.00
Vase, Pillar mold, simple cut notches/pillars, 10¼" 195.00
Vase, Pillar mold & drape, appl ft, scalloped rim, 10¼" 500.00
Vase, 8-Pillar mold, scalloped rim, 9¾", pr 375.00
Wine, cut strawberry dmns & fans, 4" 36.00

Plastics

The term 'collectible plastics' is defined as those types produced between 1868 (when synthetic plastics were invented) and the period immediately following WWII. There are several, and we shall mention each one and attempt briefly to acquaint you with their characteristics:

1) Pyroxylin (Celluloid, Loalin, French Ivory, Pyralin). Chemical name: cellulose nitrate. Earliest form, invented in 1868 by John Wesley Hyatt; highly flammable; yellows with age; much used in toiletry articles. Fairly lightweight, many articles of pyroxylin were made by heating and molding thin sheets.

2) Cellulose Acetate (Tenite, Similoid). Made in attempt to produce a product similar to cellulose nitrate but without the flammability. Had limited use in the costume jewelry trade; most often encountered as car knobs and handles of the thirties and forties. Surfaces tend to crack with age and exposure to light. Always molded, never cast. Colors varied; imitation horn and marble were most popular.

3) Casein Plastics (Ameroid, Galalith, Dorcasine, Casolith). Invented in 1904 using milk proteins. Use limited to buttons and buckles due to warping and lengthy curing time. Made in a wide range of colors; very easy to laminate or to carve from stock rods or sheets, but never molded.

4) Phenol Formaldehyde (Bakelite, Catalin, Marblette, Agatine, Gemstone, Durite, Durez, Prystal). Invented by L.H. Baekland in 1908; used extensively in the thirties. There are two major types: cast and molded. Molded types include Durez and Bakelite, dark-toned, wood flour-filled plastics that were used extensively for early telephones (still used when non-conductivity of heat and electricity is vital). The most popular name in cast phenolics was Catalin, trade name of the American Catalin Corporation of New York. Made in a wide range of colors; widely used for costume jewelry, cutlery handles, decorative boxes, lamps, desk sets, etc. Heavyweight material with a slightly 'greasy' feel; very hard but can be carved with files, grinding tools, and abrasive cutters. Buffs to high, durable polish. Cast phenolics were used primarily from 1930 to around 1950 when they proved too labor-intensive to be economical.

5) Urea Formaldehyde (Beetleware, Plaskon, Duroware, Hemocoware, Uralite). Invented around 1929, this was lighter in color than phenol formaldehyde, thus used for injection-molded products in pastel colors. Lightweight, not strong; shiny rather than glossy. It cannot be carved and was used mainly for cheap radio and clock cases, never for jewelry.

The period between the two World Wars produced acrylic resins such as Lucite and vinyl. Polystryene made its appearance then, and furfural-phenols were in use in industrial applications. Though a great future was predicted for ethyl cellulose, by the late thirties it was still in the experimental phase. For most purposes the field of decorative plastics from the first half of the century can be narrowed down to the five major types listed above. Of these, cellulose acetate is rarely encountered. Casein is limited to button and belt buckle manufacture; urea is easily identifiable as a cheap, brittle material. Pyroxylin is the celluloid of which so many vanity sets were made. Molded phenolics such as Bakelite were dark in color and used for utilitarian objects; cast phenolics such as Catalin were used most notably for jewelry (please don't call it Bakelite), cutlery handles, desk sets, and novelties.

Dealers and collectors should be aware of '70s reproduction Marblette animal napkin rings (they have no eye rods and no age patina) and molded acrylic bracelets in imitation of carved Catalin ones (look for a seam line or lack of definition in carved areas). As prices rise, copies become more common. 1986 saw the mass-production of inlaid polka-dot bracelets using old-stock findings but without the precision fit (or patina) of the originals.

In 1988 and continuing to the present, a large number of 'collage' pieces appeared in vintage clothing and antique stores on the West and East Coasts. These are over-sized, glued-together assemblages of old Catalin stock parts including buttons with the shanks filed off, poker chips, etc. made into brooches or pendants, sometimes hung on necklaces of re-strung Catalin beads. They can be recognized by their aesthetically jumbled, 'put-together' look; and although some may claim they are old, they are not.

Our advisor for this category is Catherine Yronwode, who also publishes an informative newsletter, *The Collectible Plastics;* she is listed in the Directory under California. Our thanks to Benjamin Rose for help with radio prices.

Bakelite

Cigarette box, half-cylinder, rotates open, dk brn 40.00
Clock, electric, alarm, Deco design, blk or dk brn 65.00
Clock, mantel, wind-up alarm, Deco design, dk brn 60.00
Inkwell, streamlined, blk, w/lid 25.00
Penholder, streamlined, blk 22.50
Radio, Majestic #55, dk brn, 1939 ....250.00
Radio, Silvertone Compact, Sears, dk brn, 1936-37 ....250.00
Radio, Stewart Warner Varsity College, dk brn, 1938-39 ....250.00
Roulette wheel, dk brn, 1930s 80.00
Roulette wheel, mc Catalin chips, wood rack, w/box, 1930s 200.00
Watch, lady's handbag; Westclox, blk, 2¾" dia 70.00

Catalin

Ashtray, marbleized lt gr, sq, 4½" 30.00
Barometer, Taylor, amber & dk gr, rectangular, 4" 40.00
Blotter, Carvacraft, Great Britain, amber & blk 45.00
Bottle opener, chrome plate, red, gr, or amber hdl 10.00
Bracelet, bangle; apple-juice clear, figural bk-cvg 175.00
Bracelet, bangle; apple-juice clear, floral bk-cvg 150.00
Bracelet, bangle; apple-juice clear, geometric bk-cvg 130.00
Bracelet, bangle; deep cvg, w/rhinestones 80.00
Bracelet, bangle; elaborate floral cvg, narrow 40.00
Bracelet, bangle; elaborate floral cvg, wide 65.00
Bracelet, bangle; lt geometric cvg, narrow 28.00
Bracelet, bangle; lt geometric cvg, wide 45.00
Bracelet, bangle; novelty, mc, figural or animal cvg 250.00
Bracelet, bangle; scratch cvd, narrow 18.00
Bracelet, bangle; scratch cvd, w/rhinestones 25.00
Bracelet, bangle; scratch cvd, wide 25.00
Bracelet, bangle; stylized floral cvg, narrow 28.00
Bracelet, bangle; stylized floral cvg, wide 45.00
Bracelet, bangle; uncvd, narrow 6.00
Bracelet, bangle; uncvd, wide 10.00
Bracelet, bangle; 12 inlaid polka dots, wide 180.00
Bracelet, bangle; 2-color stripes 70.00
Bracelet, bangle; 3-color stripes 90.00
Bracelet, bangle; 4-color (or more) stripes 125.00
Bracelet, bangle; 6 inlaid polka dots, narrow 180.00
Bracelet, cellulose acetate chain, 7 cvd figural charms 250.00
Bracelet, clamper; figural, animal, or novelty applique 225.00
Bracelet, clamper; inlaid geometric designs 150.00
Bracelet, clamper; stylized floral cvg 52.00
Bracelet, clamper; w/inlaid rhinestones 40.00
Bracelet, curved/flat links, deeply cvd 60.00
Bracelet, curved/flat links, uncvd 45.00
Bracelet, stretch; orig elastic, Catalin & metal 48.00
Bracelet, stretch; orig elastic, deeply cvd 60.00
Bracelet, stretch; orig elastic, mc, uncvd 50.00
Buckle, latch type, mc, novelty or figural applique 40.00
Buckle, latch type, mc, stylized floral or geometric, cvd 40.00

Buckle, latch type, mc, uncvd 25.00
Buckle, latch type, 1-color, novelty or figural applique 25.00
Buckle, latch type, 1-color, stylized floral or geometric 10.00
Buckle, latch type, 1-color, uncvd 5.00
Buckle, latch type, 1-color w/rhinestones, Deco 25.00
Buckle, slide type, mc, stylized floral or geometric, cvd 35.00
Buckle, slide type, mc, uncvd 12.50
Buckle, slide type, 1-color, stylized floral or geometric, cvd 8.00
Buckle, slide type, 1-color, uncvd 4.00
Butter mold, gr/amber/brn, floral cvg, 2½" 32.00
Buttons, card of 6, red or blk laminated, 1½" rod 18.00
Buttons, card of 6, scotty, fruit, or cvd floral figural 28.00
Buttons, card of 6, uncvd octagonal, amber, 1" dia 10.00
Cake breaker, CJ Schneider, red, gr, or amber hdl 4.00
Carving set, knife, fork, steel 30.00
Carving set, 3-pc w/wood wall rack 40.00
Checkers, red & blk, full set, in box 32.00
Cheese slicer, scotty hdl, wood & chrome base 15.00
Chess set, hand cvd, red & blk, leather box 250.00

Chip holder with chips, dice, dice cups and checkers. See listings below for values.

Chopsticks, ivory, pr 3.00
Cigarette box, chrome inserts, cylindrical, 4½" 40.00
Cigarette box, lt gr, wood bottom, rectangular, 5½x3¾" 30.00
Cigarette holder, imitation amber, sterling tip, orig case 25.00
Cigarette holder, long, mc or w/rhinestones 25.00
Cigarette lighter, Arco-Lite devil's head, red or blk 175.00
Cigarette lighter, mc stripes or inlay 45.00
Clock, New Haven, wind-up alarm, amber, Deco, 3⅝" 52.00
Clock, Sessions, electric alarm, scalloped case, 4¼" dia 52.00
Clock, Seth Thomas, wind-up alarm, maroon case, 3½" 42.00
Clock, Westclox, Moonbeam, electric flashing light alarm 60.00
Clothesline, Jigger, red anchors, 10 pins, metal box 10.00
Cocktail recipes, Ben Hur, mtd on drunk, red w/blk base 45.00
Cocktail recipes, Ben Hur, mtd on fighting roosters 45.00
Cork, Ben Hur, w/red fighting roosters, blk base 20.00
Corkscrew, chrome, red, gr, or amber hdl 12.50
Corn holder, Kob Knobs, diamond shape or lathe trn, 8 +box ...40.00
Crib toy, Tykie Toy, boy, girl, clown, kitten, etc, ea 100.00
Crib toy, Tykie Toy, clown, loalin head/Catalin body 60.00
Crib toy, Tykie Toy, elephant, laolin head/Catalin body 60.00
Crib toy, Tykie Toy, 11 mc spools on string, 1940s 50.00
Crib toy, Tykie Toy, 12-1½" rings on 2⅞" ring, 1940s 50.00
Crib toy, Tykie Toy catalog, 1946 ....25.00
Crib toy, Tykie Toy Tales (book about these toys), 1946 ....35.00
Dice, ivory or red, 2½", pr 15.00

Dice, ivory or red, ¾", pr 2.00
Dice cage, metal/red Catalin, blk Lucite base, w/dice 75.00
Dice cup, leather or cork lined 30.00
Dominoes, ivory or blk, full set, w/wood box 30.00
Dominoes, red or gr, full set, w/wood box 40.00
Drawer pull, 1-color, w/pnt inlay stripe 2.00
Drawer pull, 2-color, octagon, w/inlaid dot 3.00
Dress clip, mc inlaid Deco design 20.00
Dress clip, novelty, figural, animal, or vegetable 50.00
Dress clip, scratch cvd 14.00
Dress clip, stylized floral cvg 20.00
Dress clip, 1-color, w/rhinestones, Deco design 20.00
Earrings, lg drop style, pr 10.00
Earrings, novelty, figural, animal, or vegetable, pr 35.00
Earrings, stylized floral cvg, pr 15.00
Earrings, uncvd disks, pr 6.00
Egg beater, red, gr, or amber hdl 16.00
Flatware, chrome plate, 1-color hdl 1.50
Flatware, chrome plate, 3-pc matched place setting 6.00
Flatware, stainless, 1-color hdl 2.00
Flatware, stainless, 1-color hdl, leatherette box, 36-pc 180.00
Flatware, stainless, 1-color hdl, 3-pc matched place setting 7.50
Flatware, stainless, 2-color hdl 3.50
Flatware, stainless, 2-color hdl, wood box, 36-pc 225.00
Flatware, stainless, 2-color hdl, 3-pc matched place setting 12.00
Gavel, lathe turned, ivory 18.00
Gavel, lathe turned, red, blk, & ivory 25.00
Gavel, lathe turned, red, w/presentation box, dtd 1946 ....28.00
Ice cream scoop, stainless, red hdl 19.00
Inkwell, Carvacraft Great Britain, amber, dbl well 90.00
Inkwell, Carvacraft Great Britain, amber, single well 70.00
Knife, cvd red, gr, or amber hdl 6.00
Lamp base, brass & amber, Deco design, 10" 30.00
Lamp base, red, amber, & blk, Deco design, 8" 44.00
Letter opener, blk & amber stripes, Deco design 20.00
Letter opener, chrome/Catalin, Deco design 14.00
Letter opener, marbleized gr, dagger shape 20.00
Mah-Jong set, tiles, rails, 6-color, complete, w/box 45.00
Memo pad, Carvacraft Great Britain, amber 45.00
Nail brush, Ducky, duck shape, translucent eye rod 32.00
Nail brush, marbleized lt gr, 2½x1½" 8.00
Nail brush, Masso, amber octagon, 2" dia 8.00
Nail brush, turtle shape, dark amber, 3½" 16.00
Napkin ring, amber, red, or gr, 2" dia band 8.00
Napkin ring, animal or bird, no inlaid eye or ball on head 25.00
Napkin ring, elephant w/ball on head 35.00
Napkin ring, lathe turned, amber, red, or gr, 1¾" dia 8.00
Napkin ring, Mickey Mouse or Donald Duck shape w/decal 58.00
Napkin ring, rabbit w/inlaid eye rod 35.00
Napkin ring, rocking horse or camel w/inlaid eye rod 66.00
Napkin ring, scotty, w/inlaid eye rod 38.00
Napkin ring set, 6-colors, 2" band, orig box 40.00
Necklace, cellulose acetate chain, animal figurals 250.00
Necklace, cellulose acetate chain, Deco dangling pcs 175.00
Necklace, cvd red & amber beads, 18" 65.00
Necklace, uncvd gr beads, 20" 40.00
Ozone generator, Air-Clear, dk amber, streamlined case 70.00
Pencil sharpener, Disney character decal, silhouette shape 38.00
Pencil sharpener, gun, tank, or plane shape w/decal 30.00
Pencil sharpener, orange, no decal, ¾x1" 8.00
Pencil sharpener, red, Mickey Mouse decal, ¾x1" 30.00
Pencil sharpener, scotty, red, cvd details, blk base 30.00
Pencil sharpener, scotty, yel, silhouette shape 20.00
Pencil sharpener, Trylon & Perisphere, 1939 World's Fair 50.00

Penholder, amber & blk striped, Deco design 35.00
Penholder, marbleized amber, Deco design 25.00
Penholder, Scotty dog, red w/blk base 45.00
Picture frame, amber & red Deco design, 6x7" 45.00
Picture frame, red, gr, or amber, sq, 6" 35.00
Pin, animal, resin wash w/glass eye, lg 110.00
Pin, animal, resin wash w/glass eye, sm 75.00
Pin, animal or vegetable, inlaid or appl in several colors, lg 170.00
Pin, animal or vegetable, inlaid or appl in several colors, sm 95.00
Pin, animal or vegetable, 1-color, lg 80.00
Pin, animal or vegetable, 1-color, sm 60.00
Pin, mc Deco design, lg 60.00
Pin, mc Deco design, sm 40.00
Pin, novelty or patriotic figural, resin wash/inlay/appl, lg 185.00
Pin, novelty or patriotic figural, resin wash/inlay/appl, sm 120.00
Pin, novelty or patriotic figural, 1-color, lg 95.00
Pin, novelty or patriotic figural, 1-color, sm 65.00
Pin, stylized floral cvg, lg 40.00
Pin, stylized floral cvg, sm 32.00
Pin, w/danglers, animal or vegetable, resin wash/inlay/appl 195.00
Pin, w/danglers, animal or vegetable, 1-color 100.00
Pin, w/danglers, geometric form, mc 60.00
Pin, w/danglers, geometric form, 1-color 45.00
Pin, w/danglers, novelty or patriotic, resin wash/inlay/appl 210.00
Pin, w/danglers, novelty or patriotic, 1-color 110.00
Pipe, amber & gr, bowl lined w/clay 28.00
Pitcher, glass, red, gr, or amber hdl, syrup size 18.00
Pocket watch, Debonaire, yel Deco case, 1⅞" dia 60.00
Poker chip rack, cylindrical, w/50 chips, 2½" 85.00
Poker chip rack, rectangular, w/200 chips, 4" 120.00
Powder box, amber & blk fluted cylinder, 2½" 45.00
Powder box, amber & gr fluted cylinder, 4" 56.00
Radio, AMC 'Peaktop,' amber, maroon trim 2,500.00
Radio, Emerson Cathedral (AU190), amber 1,200.00
Radio, Emerson Cathedral (AU190), bright red, very rare 13,000.00
Radio, Emerson Cathedral (AU190), gr marbled 2,200.00
Radio, Emerson College model, amber or gr, 1938 ....950.00
Radio, Emerson College model, red, 1938 ....1,200.00
Radio, Fada Streamliner, amber, amber knobs/bezel, 1941 ....950.00
Radio, Fada Streamliner, amber, red knobs/bezel, 1941 ....1,100.00
Radio, Fada Streamliner, red, amber knobs/bezel, 1941, rare ...9,800.00
Radio, Kadette Klockette, amber, gr, or maroon, 1937 ....1,200.00
Radio, Kadette Klockette, red, 1937 ....1,500.00
Ring, inlaid Deco stripe design, 2-color 45.00
Ring, stylized floral cvg, 1-color 35.00
Ring, uncvd, 1-color 15.00
Ring, uncvd, 2-color 25.00
Ring case, hinged-lid style, amber or maroon 100.00
Ring case, open-top style, amber, red, or blk, Deco design 85.00
Safety razor, Schick Injector, amber hdl 12.00
Safety razor, Schick Injector, extra blades, orig box, 1939 ....40.00
Salad servers, Chase chrome, ivory, blk, or brn, pr 30.00
Salad servers, chrome, red, gr, or amber hdls, pr 12.00
Shakers, ball shape or half-cylinder shape, 1½", pr 25.00
Shakers, glass, in 3⅛" Catalin holder, pr 19.00
Shakers, mushroom shape, amber & ivory, 1⅞", pr 25.00
Shakers, stepped cylinder shape, 3½", pr 25.00
Shakers, Washington Monument, 3¼", pr 25.00
Shaving brush, red, gr, or amber 18.00
Shaving brush, red, gr, or amber, w/holder 30.00
Spatula, stainless, red, gr, or amber hdl 4.50
Spoon, iced tea, chrome, w/Catalin knob, 6-pc set 18.00
Spoon, slotted, stainless, red, gr, or amber hdl 4.50
Steering knob, chrome clamp 18.00

Stirrer, iced tea; Chase, chrome ball/mint leaf, 6-pc set 26.00
Stirrer, iced tea; shovel blade, Catalin hdl, 6-pc set 36.00
Strainer, red, gr, or amber hdl, 2¾" dia 4.00
Strainer, red, gr, or amber hdl, 5" dia 6.00
Swizzle stick, baseball-bat shape, amber or red 4.00
Swizzle stick holder, amber or red, Rheingold Lager decal 70.00
Thermometer, BT Co, amber & blk, 2¾" dia 38.00
Thermometer, Taylor, amber & dk gr, rectangular, 4" 45.00
Writing set, blk, amber, or gr marble, Deco, 5-pc, orig box 150.00

Celluloid

Bracelet, imitation tortoise w/inlaid rhinestones 40.00
Bracelet, snake w/inlaid rhinestones 48.00
Bridge marker, pnt ivoroid animal or figure, France 20.00
Bridge pencil holder, animal, pearlescent ivory on blk 60.00
Buttons, ivoroid or pearlescent, ¾" dia, card of 6 ....8.00
Carving set, ivoroid, knife/fork/steel, eng blade 30.00
Clock, Greek temple facade, wind-up alarm, ivoroid 45.00
Dresser set, amberoid & gr marbleized, 7-pc 70.00
Dresser set, ivoroid, 10-pc, w/9" bevel glass mirror 100.00
Dresser set, ivory pearlescent or amberoid, 5-pc 50.00
Flatware, gr pearl on blk hdl, 3-pc set 9.00
Flatware, ivoroid hdl, table knife, fork, or spoon, ea 1.00

Giraffe rattle, marked Japan, 12½",
$130.00.

Hair receiver, ivoroid, pearlescent or amberoid, w/2-part lid 10.00
Manicure set, ivoroid, pearlescent or amberoid, 10-pc, +case 30.00
Manicure set, 4 mini-tools in coral-color tube, Germany 22.00
Manicure set, 4 mini-tools in tube holder w/pnt florals 35.00
Mirror, dresser; ivoroid, cut-out hdl, bevel glass, 8" 18.00
Mirror, dresser; ivoroid, oval bevel glass, 13" 28.00
Mirror, dresser; pearlescent or amberoid, bevel glass, 12" 20.00
Picture frame, easel bk, ivoroid, 2" dia 12.00
Shaving stand, ivoroid, 5-pc, w/razor 75.00

Lucite

Bottle, perfume; w/atomizer, rose inclusion 10.00
Bracelet, stretch, orig elastic, clear, bk-cvd 25.00
Picture frame, Deco, clear, sq, 6" 14.00
Purse, box style, clear, pearl, ivory, or tortoise 45.00
Shakers, translucent red, 4", pr 12.00

Playing Cards

Playing cards can be an enjoyable way to trace the course of history. Knowledge of the art, literature, and politics of an era can be gleaned from a study of its playing cards. When royalty lost favor with the people, Kings and Queens were replaced by common people. During the periods of war, generals, officers, and soldiers were favored. In the United States, early examples had portraits of Washington and Adams as opposed to Kings, Indian chiefs instead of Jacks, and goddesses for Queens.

Tarot cards were used in Europe during the 1300s as a game of chance, but in the 18th century they were used to predict the future and were regarded with great reverence.

The backs of cards were of no particular consequence until the 1890s. The marble design used by the French during the late 1800s and the colored wood-cut patterns of the Italians in the 19th century are among the first attempts at decoration. Later the English used cards printed with portraits of royalty. Eventually cards were decorated with a broad range of subjects from reproductions of fine art to advertising.

Although playing cards are becoming popular collectibles, prices are still relatively low. Complete decks of cards printed earlier than the first postage stamp can still be purchased for less than $100.00. Our advice for this category comes from the American Antique Deck Collectors Club, 52 Plus Joker; see Directory under Clubs, Newsletters, and Catalogs.

Key:
C — complete	OB — original box
cts — courts	SC — score card
hc — hand colored	std — standard
J — joker	XC — extra card

Advertising

Am Hoist & Derrick, wide, '07, 52+special J, NM in torn box ...**150.00**
Anheuser-Busch Spanish Am War, USPC 1898, 52+J, EX, OB **460.00**
Cornell University, silver/blk/red bks, 1935, 52+XC, MIB **23.00**
Dobbs Hats, hunt scene bks, 1929, 52+J+SC, VG, OB **75.00**
Dr Daniels Vet Medicine, wide, 1900, 52+bulldog J, G in OB **66.00**
Edison Mazda Lamps, wide, bl/gold bks, '12, 52+J+2XC, EX, OB ..**115.00**
El Kusto Cigars, wide, red ad bks, special A, 52C, G, OB **20.00**
Franklin Cigars, B Franklin bks, 1908, 52+special J+XC, MIB **60.00**
General Electric, refrigerator bks, special A, 52C, G, OB **6.00**
Grant's Whiskey, non-std, 1938-40, 52+2J+2XC, MIB **32.00**
Kelly Springfield Tires, Lotta Miles bk, 1915, 52+2XC, MIB **50.00**
Modern Woodmen of Am, red/gr bks, 1931, 52+SC, VG, OB **85.00**
Old English Pipe Tobacco, wide, '06, 52+J+SC, EX, broken box .**42.50**
Patent Cereals, Old Man Rex bks, wide, 52C, NM, OB **22.50**
Peter Schulyer Cigars, 52+J, EX, OB **160.00**
Portina Cigars, 52+J, EX, OB **295.00**
Union United Brewery, 52+J, EX, OB **300.00**

Modern Decks

Aircraft Spotter, wide, red rider bks, 1942, 52+J+XC, MIB **35.00**
Amma, non-std, service branch suits, 52+2XC, MIB **68.00**
Bannister Babies, photo bks, dbl deck, 1954, 52+J, EX/VG **12.00**
Butch, Too Hot/Too Cold, dbl deck, Staehle, 104C, EX, OB **16.50**
Dallas Cowboys' Cheerleaders, wide, 1982, M in sealed OB **11.00**
Deland's Daisy, mk magic deck, baseball ace, 52+J, EX, OB **50.00**
Elvgren, Number to Remember, pinup bks, 52+J, NMIB **20.00**
Elvgren, 52 Am beauties, all different, 52C, M in cellophane **55.00**
Esquire, pinups, canasta dbl deck, ea: 52+2J, VG, OB **22.00**
Hollywood, Aces/Js as star caricatures, 52+3J+XC, M in G box ...**16.50**
Kennedy Kards, Kennedy family cts, 1963, M in cellophane **30.00**
Mythological Zoo, D Martin, creature bks, 1971, M in wrap **50.00**
Salvador Dali, Dali design bks, Fr, 1959, NMIB **115.00**
Vargas, Vanities, woman faces, 52+J+bio J, 1950, MIB **145.00**

Vargas, 52 different pinups on faces, 1953, 52+2XC, MIB **155.00**
Victory, non-std cts, WWII, 52+2J, NM in EX, OB **165.00**

Older Decks, Narrow, Odd Sizes or Shapes

Arrco, Colonial couple dancing bks, 52+J+XC, M in wrapper **8.00**
Chicago USPC issue, Bubbles, 1931, 52+J+2XC, NMIB **16.50**
Congress USPC, Antonio, 1926, 52+J+XC, MIB **18.00**
Congress USPC, Comet/Papillon, dbl deck, 1929, NM in case **16.00**
Congress USPC, Harbor, 52+J, G, OB **2.50**
Dondorf Patience #165, fantasy cts, Nazi stamp, 1936, EX, OB **15.00**
Dondorf Whist #184, fantasy cts, 52+J, MIB **76.00**
Dougherty, Indicator #50, red bks, 52C, EX, OB **15.00**
Dougherty, 2 34-star reversible flags on bks, 52C, EX **130.00**
Globe, IW Richardson, circular, 1880s, 52+J, VG, broken box **82.50**
Little Duke #24, USPC, very sm, 52+J, NM in taped box **11.00**
New Era Concave, Deco-style bks, 1929, 52+J+SC, NMIB **45.00**
Russell, April Showers, 52+J, G+, OB **5.00**
Standard, Aviator J, 1920s, 52+J+XC, M in wrapper **16.50**

Older Decks, Wide

Army & Navy #303, bl angel bks, 1885, 47 of 52, G **30.00**
Bicycle #808, Cupid, red bks, ca 1910, 52+XC, EX-, OB **85.00**
Bicycle #808, Motorette #1, ca 1900, 52C, VG **118.00**
Bicycle #808, New Fan, ca 1895, 52+J, EX in broken box **44.00**
Bird's Duplicate Whist, Johnson, 1893, 52, VG, broken box **145.00**
Congress, Regal Series, Geo V bks, Downey, 52+J, EX-, OB **95.00**
Congress #606, At Sea, tan border, 1919, M in sealed box **35.00**
Dante & Beatrice, Piatnik, ca 1924, 52+J+EC, M in torn box ...**125.00**
Dougherty, Tudor, rural scene bks, 1900, 52+J, EX, broken box ...**40.00**
Goodall Clan Tartan, Mackay, 52+J, MIB **20.00**
Handa, fantasy cts, Denmark, 1944, 52+J+XC, MIB **38.00**
Nat'l Aladdin #1001, red bks, 1910s, 52+J, MIB **80.00**
Russell, NY Girl, cream border, pinochle, NM, OB **27.50**
Squared Faro #366, USPC #366, 1-way cts, 1887, 52C, EX- **275.00**
Treasury #89, bl Dragon Bird bks, fortune on ea, 1910, VG, OB ..**18.00**
Union PCC Sporting, fisherman bks, 52+J, much wear, G- **140.00**

Souvenir and Expositions

Alaska, wide, totem pole bks, 1926, 52+bear J+XC, MIB **200.00**

American Indian Souvenir Playing Cards, Lazarus & Melzer, 1900, 53 good cards in fair case, $495.00.

California, M Rieder, oranges on bks, ca 1912, 52+J+XC, NMIB ...**75.00**
Canada, Montreal & Quebec, wide scenic, 53+map card, VG, OB ...**12.00**
Century of Progress, Electrolite Products/53 views, 1934, MIB **26.00**

Century of Progress, narrow, scenic bks, 1933, 52+J+XC, EX **15.00**
Columbian Expo, Clark, landing bks, 1893, 52+J+XC+blank, MIB .**200.00**
Columbian Expo, Winters, 1893, 52+Uncle Sam J, NM in case ..**245.00**
Cuba, wide scenic views, 1915, 52+J, MIB **66.00**
Florida E Coast, state seal bks, ca 1900, 52+J, MIB **60.00**

Homes of Henry Wadsworth Longfellow and Ralph Waldo Emerson, 2 complete decks, EX in VG box, $15.00.

Niagara Falls, 4 corner indices, 52+Maid J+XC, VG, torn box **25.00**
Oregon, Mt Hood, outdoor scenes, 1902, 52, M in taped box **38.50**
Pan Am Expo, Buffalo, Expo scene faces, ca 1901, 52+J **100.00**
Paris Expo, NYCC, 'Royalty Deck,' 1878, 52+J, EX, OB **495.00**
Paris Expo, Tom Beaver, statue bks, ca 1900, 52+J, M, OB **175.00**
Paris Expo, Tom Jones, wide, fair scenes, 1900, 52+J, MIB **150.00**
Rocky Mtns, Tom Jones, Columbine bks, 52+special J+XC, MIB ..**60.00**
St Louis, Meyer Bro, Louis XVI portrait bks, 1901, 52C, MIB **110.00**
Wht Mtns, Old Man of Mtns bks, photo faces, '10, 52+J+XC, MIB ...**80.00**
Yellowstone, Bl Rays/gold edges, 1925, 52+J, M in broken box **27.50**

Tarot and Fortune Telling

Fortune Telling #3013, Whitman, 1936, 45C+instructions, NMIB ..**30.00**
Madam Morrow's, McLoughlin, 1886, 36C+instructions, VG, OB ..**55.00**
Military, doves/bells/stars/hearts suits, 56C, ca 1918, MIB **110.00**
New Art Tarot, Knapp, EX color, 1929, 78C, MIB **195.00**
Revelation #357, fortune margins, 1919, 52+J+booklet, EX, OB .**22.00**

Transformations

Art for Earth, rain forest theme, 54C+booklet, MIB **30.00**
French, Grimaud, cts/pips/Aces transform, 1870s, 44 of 53 ....**150.00**
Harlequin, Tiffany & Co, Carryl, 1879, 52C, EX, partial OB **700.00**
Harlequin #2, Kinney, cts & pips transform, 1889, 13 of 52, EX ...**67.00**
Kinney Tobacco, pips transform, 52+J, 1889, EX, OB..............**1,430.00**
Murphy Varnish, cartoons on pips, 1883, 52+J, M, EX, OB **3,600.00**
Vanity Fair, pips/aces/cts transform, 1895, 52+J, EX- **425.00**
Ye Witches #62, USPC, faces transform, 1896, 52+J, EX- **130.00**
Ye Witches #62, USPC, faces transform, 1896, 52+J, M, VG, OB .**300.00**

Transportation: Airline, Steamship, Railroad

Air Canada, 7x11 pattern gold logo on blk, 1966, sealed, MIB **8.00**
Alaska Air, Sky's the Limit, B-727 bks, 1978, MIB **11.00**
Am Air, lt bl bks, special Aces, 1962, 52C, EX, OB **9.00**
Ethiopian Air, mc bks, special cts/J, 1971, MIB **33.00**

Hamburg Am Steamship, Pocker, Army & Navy ace, 52C, EX, OB ..**100.00**
Hamburg Amerika Steamship, wide, Goodall, 52+2XC, EX- **85.00**
Kerr-Silver Fleet, Waddington, 1930s, 52+2J, VG, OB **22.00**
Milwaukee RR, wide scenic souvenir, 1 track, 1915, VG, OB **45.00**
New England Transportation, bus/truck bks, dbl deck, 52/52, G ..**12.00**
Northern Pacific, vertical lines/logo on blk, 52+2XC, G, OB **40.00**
Norwegian America Steamship, wide, 52C, VG, OB **175.00**
NY Central, Palisades, scenic bks, 1932, 52+J+XC, VG, OB **27.50**
Pan-Am, World Series USA bk, sealed, MIB **8.00**
Santa Fe RR, train in desert bks, 1952, sealed, MIB **22.00**
Southern Pacific, wide, red logo, 52+J, M, OB **18.00**
Steamboat Dbl Heads, USPC, 52, EX, OB **195.00**
Steamboat 7-11, Russel, 52+J, EX, VG, OB **235.00**
Trans Caribbean, purple-tone photo of DC-8, 1960s, EX, OB **35.00**
Union Pacific Overland Route RR, ca 1900, 52+J+XC, NMIB ..**220.00**
White Pass & Yukon RR, ca 1910, 52+J+XC+map card, EX, OB .**187.00**
White Pass & Yukon RR, repro, wide scenic, 52+J+XC, MIB **24.00**

Political

The most valuable political items are those from any period which relate to a political figure whose term was especially significant or marked by an important event or one whose personality was particularly colorful. Posters, ribbons, badges, photographs, and pin-back buttons are but a few examples of the items popular with collectors of political memorabilia.

Political campaign pin-back buttons were first mass-produced and widely distributed in 1896 for the president-to-be William McKinley and for the first of three unsuccessful attempts by William Jennings Bryan. Pin-back buttons have been used during each presidential campaign ever since and are collected by many people. The most scarce are those used in the presidential campaigns of James Davis in 1924 and James Cox in 1920. Our advisor for this category is Paul J. Longo; he is listed in the Directory under Massachusetts. See also Autographs; Broadsides; Historical Glass; Watch Fobs.

Ad card, Garfield/Hancock, mechanical, 5x4", EX **20.00**
Badge, G Cleveland, Am's Tariff Reform Champion, w/ribbon **40.00**
Badge, McKinley/Hobart inaugural, heavy, 1897, EX, w/ribbon ...**75.00**
Badge, McKinley/Roosevelt, celluloid, 1900, 1¼" **30.00**
Badge, Republican Alternate Delegate, 1928, NM **40.00**
Badge, Republican Nat'l Convention, FD Roosevelt, 1936 ....**40.00**
Badge, Union & Liberty...Abram (sic) Lincoln, paper, EX **400.00**
Book, Republican Party, Pictorial History, 1980, M **15.00**
Booklet, Lincoln/McClellan election, for McClellan, 1864 ....**40.00**
Booklet, Little Blk Master, anti-alcohol & coffee, 110-pg, EX **25.00**
Bottle opener, donkey figural, pnt CI, 1933, 3½" **25.00**
Bust, FD Roosevelt, gold-pnt plaster, Rucci, 1933, 10" **60.00**
Button, clothing; Cleveland/Hendricks emb, brass **22.00**
Campaign book, Bryan/Sewell jugate, 1896, 328-pg, EX **25.00**
Cane, McKinley Our Next President, figural hdl, wood staff **100.00**
Cane, Wm Jennings Bryan campaign, metal figural hdl, 35", EX ..**125.00**
Charm, Ike on 4-leaf clover shape, brass **6.00**
Charter certificate, Socialist Party chapter, 1917, lg, EX **50.00**
Cigar band, Judge Taft, early portrait, M **30.00**
Clicker, Click w/Dick, Nixon portrait **20.00**
Cuff links, LBJ on cowboy hat form, brass, pr **15.00**
Doll, 1988 Republican Team elephant, NM **8.00**
Earrings, I Like Ike/Dick, celluloid, red/wht/bl, pr, M **20.00**
Envelope, Gen McClellan 1864 Presidential Campaign, EX **30.00**
Ferrotype, Douglas/Johnson, dbl-sided, 1860, EX **250.00**
Flag, McKinley portrait, Patriotism...Prosperity, 12x18", EX **150.00**
Handbill, Anti Woman Suffrage, 9 reasons against, 10x8" **20.00**

Handkerchief, Stevenson/Sparkman jugate, bl, faded 20.00
Handout, Warren Harding, shows electorial ticket, cb, EX 12.00
Horn, Truman, Vote Straight Democratic Nov 2, 1948, orange, EX .35.00
Invitation, Kennedy inaugural, official, eng & emb gold 15.00
Jigsaw puzzle, Spiro Agnew as Superman, MIB 20.00
License plate, Hoover, blk letters on cream, EX 30.00
License plate, LBJ for the USA, red/wht/bl, EX 15.00
Luggage tag, President Nixon, Now More Than Ever, plastic 10.00
Match safe, Admiral Dewey emb bust on blk, NM 150.00
Match safe, Brewery Workmen, anti-prohibition, celluloid/metal .100.00
Mug, James G Blane, Knights of Labor, glass, 1884, 6" 50.00
Paperweight, Garfield bust, frosted glass, 3½x4½" 45.00
Pennant, Fidel Castro portrait/26 de Julio on cloth, 1959, EX 40.00
Pennant, James M Cox for Governor, paper, red/wht/bl, rare, EX ..300.00
Phone dialer, Nixon for President, plastic 25.00
Pin, Al Smith, red/wht/bl enamel top bar, wht elephant, 1928 ....12.50
Pin, elephant head w/glasses (Goldwater) 10.00
Pin, FD Roosevelt portrait w/sm donkey suspended below, 1936 ..12.50
Pin, Goldwater, w/pearl 8.50
Pin, Ike, cobalt or lav jewels 8.00
Pin, Ike in flower shape, sequined cloth, red/wht/bl 12.00
Pin, T Roosevelt portrait, celluloid, as Rough Rider, ⅞" 25.00
Pin, Wm J Bryan, celluloid, flag motif edge, ⅞", EX 15.00
Pin, Woodrow Wilson portrait, celluloid, ⅞", EX 15.00
Pin holder, T Roosevelt, CI, Acme Die, 2x4", EX 35.00
Pin-bk, Clean House w/Dewey, bl & wht, EX 5.00
Pin-bk, Dewey/Bricker jugate 15.00
Pin-bk, Dwight D Eisenhower, portrait 10.00
Pin-bk, Gen John Pershing Welcome home, portrait, red/wht/bl .15.00
Pin-bk, McKinley/Roosevelt, mc celluloid, EX 25.00
Pin-bk, Mondale/Ferraro jugate, West Virginia's Choice 5.00
Pin-bk, NAACP, brn & wht, 1948, EX 15.00
Pin-bk, T Roosevelt, celluloid, brn & wht, EX 20.00
Pin-bk, T Roosevelt, Preparedness..., celluloid, red/wht/bl, EX 37.50
Plate, Eisenhower color portrait 12.00
Plate, JF Kennedy & family, mc on wht, 9¼" 10.00
Plate, WH Taft portrait, Serres China, 1908, 7" 25.00
Plate, Wm J Bryan, ceramic, sepia portrait w/gold, 8½" 50.00
Plate, Wm McKinley/Hobart jugate, gold rim, 8", EX 75.00
Pocket mirror, Draft Dewey for President, bl & wht, EX 50.00
Pocket mirror, RF Kennedy Destined To Become President, mc ..25.00
Postcard, McKinley Memorial, Temple of Music, mc, EX 5.00
Postcard, Mr & Mrs H Taft in carriage, photo, 1909 ....5.00
Postcard, T Roosevelt 1904 campaign, EX 12.00
Postcard, What's in the Glass, temperance poem, EX 8.00
Poster, CW Fairbanks, VP under T Roosevelt, 1904, VG 75.00
Poster, FD Roosevelt a Gallant Leader, matted/fr, 12x17", EX 45.00
Poster, JF Kennedy campaign, color, 1963, 28x41" 25.00
Program, Carter Wht House Christmas party, gold eng 12.50
Ribbon, Al Smith notification, gold letters on blk, EX 85.00
Ribbon, Elect Dewey & Warren, eagle portrait, EX 25.00
Ribbon, Freedom Protection, Yours Truly A Lincoln, printed, fr ..700.00
Ribbon, Polk portrait amid flags, silk, NM 750.00
Ribbon, Republican Railroad Club, blk & wht, 1892, VG 25.00
Ribbon, Vote McKinley Citizen's Ticket, paper, 3x8", VG 75.00
Ribbon, Woodrow Wilson Our Choice, red/wht/bl, NM 75.00
Ring, Al Smith 1928, NP w/mc enameling, NM 35.00
Silk, Buckingham, CT's Civil War governor, 1884, 7½", EX 25.00
Stereo card, Hayes/Wheeler jugate, floral border, 1876 ....25.00
Stereo card, T Roosevelt taking oath, mc, 3½x7", EX 12.00
Sticker, Kennedy for US Senator (John), red/wht/bl, NM 25.00
Sticker, Willkie Regardless of Party, red/wht/bl, NM 8.00
Stickpin, Al Smith, plastic derby form 30.00
Stickpin, Benjamin Harrison, 1888 campaign 25.00

Stickpin, Big Stick figural, mk TR, brass, NM 75.00
Stickpin, T Roosevelt, Our Choice, brass, 1904 ....40.00
Studs, FD Roosevelt, portrait, pr 14.00
Studs, Hoover, elephant, pr 12.50
Thimble, Alfred E Smith for President, bl enameling 22.50
Thimble, Coolidge & Dawes, bl enameling, M 15.00
Ticket, Democratic Nat'l Convention, 1924, complete 15.00
Ticket, Republic Nat'l Convention 1896, 1st day only, NM 25.00
Tie bar, Goldwater, gold-pnt metal 8.00
Tile, McKinley portrait, info on bk, bl ceramic, 3x3", EX 65.00
Token, Blaine/Logan jugate, Republican mottos, 1884, 1" 25.00
Token, Gen US Grant/wreath, I Propose To Fight..., 1868 ....35.00
Token, Henry Clay, Farmer of Ashland, copper, 1832 ....45.00

Tray, William McKinley portrait, painted tin, chips, EX, 17x12", $125.00.

Watch, Nixon caricature, shifting eyes, Honest Time, M 50.00
Watch fob, Bryan holding key to White House lock, brass, '08 ....55.00
Watch fob, Grover Cleveland for President, wht metal 75.00
Watch fob, Roosevelt/Fairbanks, brass, sq, 1904 ....35.00
Window hanger, FD Roosevelt 1932 campaign, cloth, 6x6", EX ..25.00

Pomona

Pomona glass was patented in 1885 by the New England Glass Works. Its characteristics are an etched background of crystal lead glass often decorated with simple designs painted with metallic stains of amber or blue. The etching was first achieved by hand cutting through an acid resist. This method, called first grind, resulted in an uneven feather-like frost effect. Later, to cut production costs, the hand-cut process was discontinued in favor of an acid bath which effected an even frosting. This method is called second grind. Our advisors for this category are Betty and Clarence Maier; they are listed in the Directory under Pennsylvania.

Pitcher, 1st grind, oak leaves and acorns, amber stain, 7½", $500.00.

Bowl, 1st grind, NM amber stain, 3x4½" 275.00
Celery, 1st grind, bl cornflowers, pinched rim, petal ft, 7" 485.00
Celery, 2nd grind, Invt T'print, bl cornflowers, ftd, 6¾" 225.00
Creamer, 2nd grind, bl cornflowers, ruffled, 3x6" 250.00
Creamer & sugar bowl, 1st grind, ruffled, amber stain hdls 585.00
Creamer & sugar bowl, 1st grind, wishbone ft, 4", 4", pr 675.00
Finger bowl, 2nd grind, bl cornflowers, 10-crimp, 5½" 150.00
Finger bowl, 2nd grind, blueberries, ruffled, 2½x5" 90.00
Goblet, 1st grind, no decor, 6" 115.00
Pitcher, 2nd grind, bl cornflowers, 7" 200.00
Pitcher, 2nd grind, Inv't Dmn, 7" 95.00
Pitcher, 2nd grind, pansies/butterflies, 7½" 275.00
Punch cup, 1st grind, bl cornflowers, M 145.00
Rose bowl, 2nd grind, bl cornflowers, 3¾" 120.00
Shaker, 1st grind, bl cornflowers, amber stain, 3⅝" 635.00
Shaker, 1st grind, blueberries, w/stain, 2-pc top, 3⅝" 315.00
Toothpick holder, 1st grind, cornflowers, tricorner, no color 175.00
Tumbler, lemonade; 2nd grind, Rivulet, w/hdl 185.00
Tumbler, 1st grind, bl cornflowers, 3¾" 145.00
Tumbler, 2nd grind, bl cornflowers 95.00
Tumbler, 2nd grind, blueberries, amber stain/gold trim, 3¾" 175.00
Vase, 1st grind, cornflowers, scalloped fan shape, 3x6" 235.00
Vase, 1st grind, flared/ruffled, wishbone ft, 3½x5" 350.00
Vase, 2nd grind, Invt T'print, EX stain, fan form, 3x6" 135.00

Postcards

Postcards are distinguished from almost any other collectible due to the fact that nearly any topic can be found represented on cards! For this reason, postcard collecting is considered the 'all-encompassing hobby'! A German by the name of Emmanuel Herrman is credited for inventing the postcard, first printed in Austria in 1869. They were eagerly accepted by the Continentals and the English alike, who saw them as a more economical way to send written messages.

The first to be printed in the United States were on U.S. government postals. The Columbian Exposition of 1892-1893 served as the spark that ignited the postcard phenomenon. Souvenir cards by the thousands were sent to folks back home — expo scenes, transportation themes, animals, birds, and advertising messages became popular. There were patriotic themes, Black themes, and cards for every occasion and holiday. Scenics, cards with small-town railroad depots, and views of U.S. towns (especially photos) are very sought after.

Some of the earliest postcard publishers were Raphael Tuck, Nister, and Gabriel. Early 20th-century illustrators such as Frances Brundage, Rose O'Neill, and Ellen Clapsaddle designed cards that are especially collectible today.

Although the postcard rage waned at the onset of WWI, they rank today among the most sought-after type of ephemera, second only to stamps.

Even though postcards may be sixty to ninety years old, they must be in excellent condition. As a worth-accessing factor, condition is second only to subject matter. When no condition is indicated, the items listed below are assumed to be in excellent condition whether used or unused, and are representative of cards with strong collector appeal. Many postcards are worth much less.

Key:
p/ — publisher   s/ — signed

Advertising, Hershey's Cocoa, cows in pasture 4.00
Advertising, Varro Cigars, 2 men w/mules in village 7.00
Airplane, First Flying Machine, blk & wht 17.00
Airplanes, International Aviation Meet, Chicago, early 17.00

Betty Grable pinup, El Rancho Vegas 25.00
Black, Pick the Pickaninnies, folding puzzle, Ullman, 1907 ....75.00
Black, Watermelon Into Coon, #977 ....99.00
Brundage, Frances; Indian in daily activity, set of 3 ....145.00
Christmas, golliwog figure w/wishes 28.00
Christmas, Greetings, horseshoe/holly/etc, Clapsaddle, '07, EX 6.50

Christmas, Santa with tree and sack of gifts, 1908, NM, $12.00.

Christmas, Santa in red & bl trimming tree, Sander, 1906 ....12.50
Dionne Quints in lacy dresses, about 5 years old, blk & wht 8.00
Expo, CA Midwinter, Electric Tower, Hergert/Schmidt, 1894 ...120.00
Expo, Rio de Janiero, chromolitho view, 1908, set of 5 ....88.00
Fantasy, An Elfin Serenade, 2 elves around flowers 20.00
Fantasy, Just Arrived, baby in cabbage head 10.00
Fantasy, vegetable people 10.00
Fantasy subjects & fairies, C Symonds, set of 6 ....66.00
Halloween, Blk Art, Clapsaddle Series #1393, 1912, EX 10.00
Halloween, girl/boy/candles/jack-o'-lanterns, Griggs, 1911 ....10.00
Halloween, Ye Halloween Greeting, S Carpenter #98, 1921 ....5.00
Happy New Year, 1908 in snow caps, 1908, NM 6.50
Hold-to-light, Crystal Palace, London, EX 25.00
Hold-to-light, Easter greetings, unused set of 5 ....90.00
Hold-to-light, Gates Circle, Delaware Park, Buffalo NY, EX 26.00
Hold-to-light, Koehler views of NY state, 1900s, set of 6 ....78.00
Hold-to-light, Luna Park, Coney Island NY, EX 30.00
Hold-to-light, Town Hall & Castle St, Liverpool 25.00
NY Zoological society, unused, 12 for 25.00
Photo, Am Indian Kil-So-Quah & son, 1810-1911 ....4.00
Photo, Am Indian Red Eagle, 1773 ....4.00
Photo, Arch & Lily Bridge, Galveston TX, railroad scene 5.00
Photo, Calvin Coolidge & Garibaldi Sargent, P&A Photos Inc 6.50
Photo, Captain John, Chief of Indians, AW Erics, 1906 ....25.00
Photo, Chalmers Motor Company, Detroit MI 14.00
Photo, Cherry St Looking West, Macon GA, 1924, EX 5.00
Photo, Cincinnati Northern RR Bridge, Franklin OH 6.00
Photo, City Hall, Perth Amboy NJ 2.50
Photo, Courthouse, Hastings NE 2.50
Photo, CRI & PRR Station, Ottawa IL 5.00
Photo, Crow lady dressed for cold on prairie 4.00
Photo, Ferris wheel, Paris 15.00
Photo, Ferry Between Davenport IA & Rock Island IL 3.00
Photo, Flags of 39th Division, Pershing in Trier, 1919, EX 8.00
Photo, General Pershing reviewing troops, EX 8.00
Photo, Genuine Native Daughters of Golden West, 1910 ....27.50
Photo, Giant Jetties at Aransas Harbor 1.50
Photo, Lake Shore and B&O Depot, Gary IN 5.00
Photo, Lillian Russell in Victorian-style portrait 5.00
Photo, Maid of the Mist, ship's portrait, Niagara Falls 3.00
Photo, Maude Adams dressed for role in Peter Pan 5.00
Photo, men dressed as women, ca 1910 ....15.00

Photo, New Miami County Courthouse, Peru IN 3.00
Photo, Pershing Sq, New York City, street scene, 1923, EX 5.00
Photo, Pipe Organ of Presbyterian Church, Marion IN 1.50
Photo, Reid's Memorial Hospital, Richmond IN 2.50
Photo, Sonja Henie in slacks, 1930s, unused, NM 15.00
Photo, St Paul's Chapel, NY City 1.50
Photo, State Capitol, Augusta Maine 2.00
Photo, State Capitol, Montgomery AL 2.00
Photo, State Capitol, Springfield IL 2.00
Photo, Teddy Roosevelt & Hoxley in biplane, Cole, 1910, EX ..195.00
Photo, Union Depot, Springfield IL 5.00
Photo, US Battleship New Hampshire 3.00
Photo, USS Titanic steamship, US Publishing, unused 50.00
Photo, Wabash RR Station Decater IL 5.00
Photo, whaling scene, 1920 ....10.00
Sepia, Blanche Bates in scene from Girl of Golden West 5.00
Sepia, Margaret Anglin & Henry Miller in Great Divide 4.50
Sepia, Wm Faversham in scene from Squaw Man 5.00
Smith, J Wilcox; Garden Series #100, set of 6 ....195.00

Souvenir, Coney Island Mall, Cincinnati, Ohio, 1950 postmark, $12.00.

Thanksgiving, Peace & Prosperity, turkey/pumpkin, 1910, EX 8.00
Thanksgiving, sleigh/horses/family/farm scene, 1908, EX 12.50
Thanksgiving, turkey on hill, R Veen Fiet, 1909, EX 6.50
Tuck, Halloween, witch/cat/pumpkin-head man, 1909, EX 15.00
Tuck, Teddy Bear Series #118, set of 12 ....100.00
Valentine, Curtis, 1906, M 5.00
Wain, Louis; cat, Busy Fluffkin Family Series, set of 6 ....165.00
Wain, Louis; Santa w/tree & bag of toys, unused 75.00
Winsch, child holding Teddy bear, EX 42.00
Winsch, Thanksgiving Indian maiden, VG 22.00
Winsch, valentine, spider web/blond/hearts, VG 37.50

Posters

Advertising posters by such French artists as Cheret and Toulouse-Lautrec were used as early as the mid-1800s. Color lithography spurred their popularity. Circus posters by the Strobridge Lithograph Co. are considered to be the finest in their field, though Gibson and Co. Litho, Erie Litho, and Enquirer Job Printing Co. printed fine examples as well. Posters by noted artists such as Mucha, Parrish, and Hohlwein bring high prices. Other considerations are good color, interesting subject matter and, of course, condition. The WWII posters listed below are among the more expensive examples; 80% of those on the market bring less than $50.00. See also Movie Memorabilia; Political.

Key:
B&B — Barnum and Bailey   RB — Ringling Bros.

Advertising

Aultman & Taylor Farm Machinery, barnyard scene, 15x36", G ...350.00
Barker's Liniment, animals, ca 1883, 24x30", VG 525.00
BF Goodrich, Aida portrait, ca 1901, 29x18"+fr, EX 175.00
Black Valley RR, temperance ad/stagecoach/train, 23x17", VG .900.00
Bloomer Club Cigar, 2 women in bloomers, 20½x15", EX 1,500.00
Cleveland Bicycles, couple, sepia tones, Niagara, 24x17", EX 750.00
Duke's Mixture, military men, Best in War..., 30x20", G 200.00
Firestone Rims, people in touring car, 40x20½", VG 850.00
Hamilton Brown Shoes, Am Lady of 1904, metal fr, 30x20½", VG .120.00

Harper's February, Edward Penfield, 1897, 19x14", VG, $850.00.

Hartford Tires, racing trio, Gies Litho, 22x28", G 350.00
Hellman Brewing Co, blk & wht, fr, 24x18", VG 25.00
Howard Dustless-Duster, lady in sailor outfit, 28x19", NM 400.00
Hygienic Water Cure Sanitorium, Our Home on Hillside, 24x36", G .100.00
Lakeside Maple Syrup, winter scene, Forbes, 23x20", NM 850.00
Motorcycle Assoc of America, race scene, Donaldson, 21x40", EX .1,300.00
Pierce Arrow Cycles, couple on veranda, 52x36", G 700.00
Rice's Seeds, girl looks over vegetables, mc, 28x20", NM 1,050.00
Voyt Milling Co, toy honoring Lindbergh's flight, 22x16", VG .225.00

Circus

B&B, Rare Zoological Features, 4 giraffes, 1909, 27x37", EX 675.00
Barnum Startles the World Again..., vignettes, 1882, 28x10½" ..1,760.00
Christiani Bros, circus parade, 28x42", w/attached streamer 300.00
Cole Bros, elephants perform, Erie Litho, 28x41", VG 80.00
Cole Bros, Miss Christiani, color, 28x21", EX 55.00
Cole Bros, Mrs Clyde Beatty & animals, Erie Litho, 41x28", G .100.00
Cole Bros, 24 performing elephants, 28x42", NM 300.00
Downie Bros, action scenes, Epic Litho, 41x28" in metal fr 400.00
Hoews' & Cushing's US Circus, vignettes, 1875, 28x9½" 275.00
Miller Bros, girl shot from cannon, Temple Litho, 28x41" 250.00
NY Circus, vignettes, Boston, 1872, 24x8½" 275.00
RB B&B, Great Yacopi Troupe acrobats, color, 38x42" 125.00
RB B&B, Marcellus Troupe posed as statue, color, 28x21" 150.00
RB B&B, trainers & seals, torn border, 42x28", G 60.00
Seils Sterling, chariots pulled by dogs, 14x41" 150.00

Exposition

Brussels, World of Science, Art & Industry, 1897, 41x60" 700.00

Paris, king/queen/joker cards, color, 1900, 24x16" 385.00
Paris, lady's head against flags, Jules Simon, 1927, 24x16" 330.00
Velencia, boat at sea, Ortega, 1944, 26x17" 275.00

Magic

Alexander the Man Who Knows, 1930s-40s, 42x28", VG 90.00
Ask Alexander, mind reader, 27x41", EX 200.00
Fak Hongs, hooded mystic, 1910, 28x37", VG 450.00
Houdini Water Torture Escape, Doug Henning, 1971, 30x46" 60.00
Selvaggio, full portrait in bl & wht, 1920s, 31x23", VG 225.00
The Marvellous Chinese Conjurer, magician's portrait, EX 850.00
The Wizard, portrait of witchery, 1915, 42x79", VG 850.00

Theatrical

Ah la Pepinier Revue, 1898 ....80.00
Blue Jeans, drama by Joseph Arthur, 1890s, 42x29", EX+ 175.00
Davy Crockett, w/woman on horse, 1870, 27¾x20", VG 700.00
Julia Arthur, actress w/jewels around neck, 19x23½", M 200.00
Little Eva's Temptation, Blk girl & sunflower, 27x18", VG 300.00
Mammoth Pavilion, tent scene, Ackermann Quigley, 42x28", VG .100.00
New Fogg's Ferry, comedy/drama, 1890s, 40x28", VG 80.00
Uncle Tom's Cabin, cabin scene, Donaldson, 1885, 25x31", VG ..225.00
Uncle Tom's Cabin, Uncle Tom & Eva, mc, ca 1900, 21x28", EX ..200.00
3 Penny Opera, portrait of James Julia, 1976, 41x81", EX 650.00

Travel

Air France, plane flies across European sights, 1950, 20x12" 450.00
Algeria pictured at edge of desert, 1932, 40x25", EX 450.00
American Line, sm ship passes lg ship, ca 1900, 36x40", EX ...1,500.00
Cunard Line, fleet at sea, 44x32", VG 650.00
Red Star Line, ocean liner w/star behind, ca 1950, 20x26" 375.00
Swiss Air, Winter Sports, family skis, 1950s, 40x25", EX 200.00

War

Civilian Exclusion Order #36, Japanese-Am instructions 1,100.00
WWI, American All, color litho, 1918, EX 250.00
WWI, Clear the Way, naval crew behind girl, color, 20x30" 275.00
WWI, Eat More Corn..., color, 1917, 21x29", M 175.00
WWI, Fight, color litho, 40½x19¾", EX 200.00
WWI, Fight or Buy Bonds, HC Christy, 40x30" 275.00
WWI, Greatest Mother..., red/blk/grey, 41½x27", VG 45.00
WWI, I Want You, Uncle Sam pointing finger, fr, EX 1,200.00
WWI, I Want You for the Navy, color litho, 1917, 40x26½" 400.00
WWI, Keep Him Free, proud eagle, 1918, 20x30", M 250.00
WWI, Red Cross nurse/wounded soldier, H Fisher, 20x34", EX .330.00
WWI, Victory Liberty Bonds, HC Christy, 1917, 40x27", VG ...170.00
WWI, Victory Liberty Bonds, Naval ships/submarine, 30x39", VG ...135.00
WWI, You Buy Liberty Bond Lest I Perish!, 1917, 20x18", EX ..195.00
WWII, Back 'Em Up!, Gen Eisenhower, 1944, 28x20", EX 75.00
WWII, Fly w/the Marines, 1942, 37x28", EX 230.00
WWII, Save Rubber, GIs in jeep, 40x28", EX 100.00
WWII, She's Ready...Buy War Bonds, blond walking, 14x11", EX ..55.00
WWII, Tell It to Marines, red/wht/bl, 1942, 37x28", EX 175.00
WWII, US Red Cross truck, 31x41", VG 75.00
WWII, We Have Just Begun To Fight, GI charging, 27x21", EX .75.00

Miscellaneous

Boxing, Sammy Harris, Blk boxer, ca 1920s, 1-sheet 125.00
Carnival, Am's Greatest Monkey Contest, Donaldson, 29x22", EX .350.00

Man on the Moon, Apollo II, Peter Max, 1969, 24x36", M 150.00
Minstrel, FS Walcott Rabbit Foot Minstrel, ca 1935, 1-sheet 195.00
Wanted, John Dillinger, Dept of Justice, 8x8" card stock 300.00

Pot Lids

Pot lids were pottery covers for containers that were used for hair dressing, potted meats, etc. The most desirable were decorated with colorful transfer prints under the glaze in a variety of themes, animal and scenic. The first and probably the largest company to manufacture these lids was F & R Pratt of Fenton, Staffordshire, established in the early 1800s. The name or initials of Jesse Austin, their designer, may sometimes be found on exceptional designs. Although few pot lids were made after the 1880s, the firm continued into the 20th century.

American pot lids are very rare. Most have been dug up by collectors searching through sites of early gold rush mining towns in California. Minor rim chips are expected and normally do not detract from listed values.

American

Jules Hauel & Co. Perfumers, The Queen, God Bless Her, Pratt scene of men toasting, repairs and chips, 4¾", $400.00.

Holloway's Ointment, brn transfer, 3⅛" 50.00
Purified Charcoal...Paste, blk transfer, X Bazin, 3⅝x2¼" 80.00
Queen, God Bless Her; Jules Hauel Perfumers, mc, rpr, 4¾" 400.00
Rose Vegetable Tooth Paste...Hauel..., red transfer, 2¾" 475.00
7 Highest...Worlds Fair 1851, blk, HP&WC Taylor, 4¼" 120.00

English

Cherry Tooth Paste...John Gosnell, blk transfer, 1¼" 140.00
Square in Strasburg, mc transfer, Pratt, 3", EX 150.00
Victor Emmanuel & Garibaldi, mc transfer, Pratt, 4¼", NM 175.00
Village Wedding, mc transfer, Pratt, 4", EX 100.00
Woods Areca Nut Tooth Paste, blk transfer, 1860-80, 2⅝" 30.00

Potschappel

In the town of Potschappel in 1872, Carl Thieme began a porcelain factory called the Saxonian Porcelain Factory. His work was of excellent quality and consisted of figures, vases, urns, lamp bases, birds, bowls, and animals, the work being similar to Dresden-Meissen and

Sitzendorf. After World War II the company was incorporated and became Saxonian Porcelain Factory Dresden. There are four or five marks assigned to his work.

Figurine, bird of paradise, 15x9½", pr 1,200.00
Figurine, couple w/flower baskets, 9½", pr 650.00
Figurine, monkey seated w/apple, tan & wht, 16" 775.00
Figurine, pug dogs, tan & wht, male & female, 7x7", pr 570.00
Lamp base, figural reserves/encrusted florals, w/shade, 30" 1,500.00
Pillow perfumer, cherubs & flowers, umbrella cork, 4½x4½" 85.00
Tea set, molded heads & flowers, 15-pc 495.00
Urn, appl florals, bird finial, w/lid, 19" 2,750.00
Vase, figures in garden reserve, floral panels, 1880s, 12" 450.00

Powder Horns and Shot Flasks

Though powder horns had already been in use for hundreds of years, collectors usually focus on those made after the expansion of the United States westward in the very early 1800s. While some are basic and very simple, others were scrimshawed and highly polished. Especially nice carvings can quickly escalate the value of a horn that has survived intact to as high as $400.00. Those with detailed maps, historical scenes, etc., bring even higher prices.

Metal flasks were introduced in the 1830s; by the middle of the century they were produced in quantity and at prices low enough that they became a viable alternative to the powder horn. Today's collector regards the smaller flasks as the more desirable and valuable, and those made for specific companies bring premium prices.

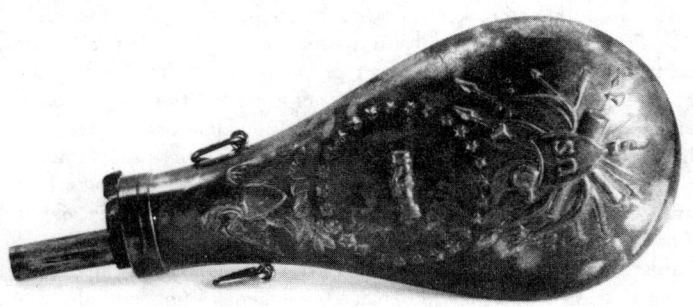

Brass flask, eagle above pair of clasped hands, US shield over flags, arrows and weapons at the bottom, 9", $185.00.

Flask, brass, hunter by gate w/dogs, 8½", EX 75.00
Flask, brass, hunting scenes/1775, sporting sz, VG 90.00
Flask, brass, pharoah's horses, G&JW Hawksley 265.00
Flask, copper, brass spout, Pease, dtd, 1856, EX 250.00
Flask, copper, open game bag, sitting dogs, Hawksley, 8" 355.00
Flask, leather w/brass fittings, emb forest scene, EX 150.00
Flask, tin, gr pnt, brass cap, label: Hazard Powder Co, 7" 85.00
Flask, tin w/brass cap, flat cylinder, cone top, 1860s, 4½" 45.00
Horn, brass base & ring, eng neck & body, dtd 1820, EX 400.00
Horn, coat of arms/birds/animals/hunters, EX 200.00
Horn, eagle & shield, inscr, crack, 8" 135.00
Horn, English ships & marine decor, dtd 1829, 15" 275.00
Horn, Fr & Indian War, NY scenes, dtd 1759, 13½" 8,250.00
Horn, hearts & scallops, wood cap, 1850s, 15", EX 115.00
Horn, hearts/stars/birds, sgn/1883, 7", EX 450.00
Horn, lion/unicorn/hunter/dogs/deer, 12", VG 2,000.00
Horn, sailing scenes, silver mts, 8", EX 435.00

Horn, ship/flowers/name/1758, minor damage, 14" 2,400.00
Horn, 2-tier pouring end, wood w/6-point star, 17" 185.00

Pratt

Prattware is a type of relief-molded earthenware with polychrome decoration. Scenic motifs with figures were popular; sometimes captions were added. Jugs are most common; but teapots, tableware, even figurines were made. The term 'Pratt' refers to Wm. Pratt of Lane Delph, who is credited with making the first of this type, though similar wares were made later by other Staffordshire potters.

Figurine, cat, brn & yel on gr cushion, hollow, 1780s, 3" 1,100.00
Figurine, cow w/farmer, Yorkshire-type palette, 1810s, 6" 1,650.00

Figurines, Elijah and Widow of Zarephath, titled 'Eliga' and 'Wido' on bases, late 1700s, 9½", $660.00 for the pair.

Figurine, farmer w/shovel, dog aside, cow behind, 6", EX 1,650.00
Figurine, man holds bottle, sq base, 5½", EX 300.00
Figurine, shepherd w/shovel, cow behind, 2 lambs aside, 5¾" .2,300.00
Figurine, standing milkmaid, cow behind, calf aside, 5¾" 2,300.00
Jar, Middle Eastern city mc scene on ironstone, 3¼" 155.00
Pipe, coiled, Admiral's head bowl, rstr stem/neck, 8¾" 1,000.00
Pipe, puzzle; red & bl stripes/dots, 1790s, rpr, 9½" 1,500.00
Pitcher, 3 mc peafowl in reserve on wht, vine at rim, 8" 1,400.00
Plate, Chinese musicians, emb mc floral/swag border, 5½" 70.00
Plate, flower vase transfer w/mc, emb mc floral border, 7" 135.00
Plate, genre transfer w/mc, emb mc floral/swag border, 7", EX 70.00
Plate, mother/child transfer w/mc, emb mc floral border, 7" 100.00
Plate, Oriental transfer scene w/mc, figural/vine border, 7" 125.00
Sauce boat, duck form, gr/bl/yel/gray spots, 8" L, EX 495.00
Sauce boat, fish form, orange & gr, ca 1790, 6", EX 350.00
Soup plate, floral transfer w/mc, emb mc floral border, 8" 175.00

Precious Moments™

Known as 'America's Hummels,' Precious Moments™ are a line of well-known collectibles created by Samuel J. Butcher and produced by Enesco, Inc. These pieces have endeared themselves to many because of the inspirational messages they portray. Over 300,000 have joined the National Club in thirteen years.

The collection was fifteen years old in 1993. Each piece is produced with a different mark each year. This mark, not the date, is usually the link to the value of the piece. Most mold changes result in increased values; and when a piece is retired or suspended, its price increases as well. As an example, 'God Loveth a Cheerful Giver' retailed for $9.50 in 1980; it was retired in 1981 and has a secondary market price now of $750.00. The majority of the collection has increased in value from its original retail.

Rosie Wells Enterprises, Inc., our advisor for this category, has published the Precious Moments™ collector magazine, *Precious Collectibles*®, as well as a secondary market price guide. She has hosted International Conventions for Precious Moments™ collectors since 1983. Her address is in the Directory under Clubs, Newsletters, and Catalogs. Items listed below are assumed to be in mint condition with the original box.

Baby's 1st Christmas, boy w/block, E-2372, Fish mk 70.00
Bethany, girl angel doll, #12432, Olive Branch mk 140.00
Blessed Are Pure in Heart, baby in cradle, E-3104, Dove mk 30.00
Come Let Us Adore Him, boy at manger, E-2011, no mk 265.00
God Bless You w/Rainbows, night light, #16020, Dove mk 115.00
God Is Love, girl w/goose in lap, E-5213, Hourglass mk 80.00
His Name Is Jesus, shepherds at manger, E-5381, Cross mk 125.00
I Get a Bang Out of You, clown w/balloons, #12262, Dove mk 70.00
I'm Nuts About You, squirrel ornament, #520411, G Clef mk 30.00
Isn't He Wonderful, angel w/harp, E-5639, Triangle mk 65.00
Jesus Is Born, children actors, musical, E-2809, Fish mk 105.00

Jesus Is the Light, E-1373G, no mark, $130.00.

Jesus Loves Me, boy w/teddy frame, E-7170, Hourglass mk 55.00
Joy to the World, angel w/trumpet, E-2343, Triangle mk 55.00
Lord Bless You & Keep You, bride & groom bell, E-7179, no mk .55.00
Love Is Sharing, girl w/lollipop, E-3110G, no mk 100.00
O Come Let Us Adore Him, 4-pc nativity, #111333, Cedar Tree mk ..255.00
Peace on Earth, choirboys, E-4725, Cross mk 70.00
Prayer Changes Things, boy & girl pray, E-1375B, Triangle mk .165.00
Press On, girl ironing, E-9265, Fish mk 75.00
Reindeer, ornament, #102466, Dove mk 190.00
Ringbearer, Bridal Party series, E-2833, Cross mk 28.00
This Land Is Our Land, Columbus in ship, #527386, Vessel mk .350.00
Thou Art Mine, children tracing in sand, E-3113, Fish mk 55.00
To Thee w/Love, girl w/kittens, E-0534, Cross or Dove mk, ea 55.00
We Saw a Star, angels making star, musical, #12408, Fish mk 110.00
Wee Three Kings, plate, E-0538, no mk 55.00

Pre-Columbian Artifacts

The term 'pre-Columbian' loosely refers to some time prior to 1492, when Columbus arrived in America. In particular, it indicates pre-1492 artifacts of Central and South America, some of which can be dated as early as 4000 B.C. Artifacts representing the cultures of the Inca, Maya, and Aztec Indians are avidly sought by the collector. These

may be made of precious metals and hardstones or pottery. Some were used in rituals and religious rites; some such as bowls and other utensils, though strictly utilitarian, nevertheless convey through form and decoration the craftsmanship of these early tribes.

Bird point, blk obsidian, triangular, ⅝" **4.50**
Bowl, Jalisco pottery, brn w/int glaze, 2x3½" **35.00**
Bowl, Nyarit, pottery, diagonals/dots, 2½x5" **60.00**
Cvg, gr jadite human w/hands together, 6x3½" **125.00**
Cvg, jadite human w/clasped hands, Mexican, 9½" **100.00**
Cvg, jadite long-tailed lizard, pouncing, Mexican, 3x11" **85.00**
Cvg, Toltec, stone face w/headdress, containing frog, 6" **250.00**
Dagger, brn flint, 7" **45.00**
Figurine, Colima warrior, seated, redware, 8x4" **125.00**
Incense burner, dk gray basalt, 4" **65.00**

Primitives

Like the mouse that ate the grindstone, so has collectible interest in primitives increased, a little bit at a time, until demand is taking bites instead of nibbles into their availability. Although the term 'primitives' once referred to those survival essentials contrived by our American settlers, it has recently been expanded to include objects needed or desired by succeeding generations — items representing the cabin-n'-cornpatch existence as well as examples of life on larger farms and in towns. Through popular usage, it also respectfully covers what are actually 'country collectibles.'

From the 1600s into the latter 1800s, factories employed carvers, blacksmiths, and other artisans whose handwork contributed to turning out quality items. When buying, 'touchmarks,' a company's name and/or location and maker's or owner's initials, are exciting discoveries.

Primitives are uniquely individual. Following identical forms, results more often than not show typically personal ideas. Using this as a guide (combined with circumstances of age, condition, desire to own, etc.) should lead to a reasonably accurate evaluation. For items not listed, consult comparable examples. Authority Kathryn McNerney has compiled several lovely books on primitives and related topics: *Primitives, Our American Heritage; Collectible Blue and White Stoneware;* and *Antique Tools, Our American Heritage.* You will find her address in the Directory under Florida. See also Butter Molds and Stamps; Boxes; Copper; Farm Collectibles; Fireplace Implements; Kitchen Collectibles; Molds; Tinware; Weaving; Woodenware; and Wrought Iron.

Bed warmer, brass, astronomical eng, star cutouts, iron hdl **250.00**
Bed warmer, brass, eng flowers, trn cherry hdl, 42½", EX **360.00**
Bed warmer, brass, eng rooster on lid, trn cherry hdl, 44½" **440.00**
Box, dough; poplar w/old red traces, trn legs, 28x42x20" **675.00**
Candle mold, 12-tube, tin, battered, 11" **120.00**
Candle mold, 24-tube, pine fr, 16¼x19½x7" **1,100.00**
Candle mold, 3-tube, tin, ear hdl, 10¼" **120.00**
Candle mold, 36-tube, tin, dbl-ear hdls, 10", VG **350.00**
Candle mold, 4-tube, tin, strap hdl, 1790-1810, 6" **100.00**
Candle mold, 6-tube, tin, ear hdl, 10¾" **125.00**
Candle mold, 6-tube, tin, oblong top & base, 9½" **115.00**
Candle mold, 8-tube, tin, ear hdl, curved base, 9¾" **165.00**
Candle mold, 8-tube, tin, w/hdl, 11" **110.00**
Candle screen, gilt brass w/needlepoint on wool, 20½" **145.00**
Cheese drainer, tin heart shape, punched decor, 2½x14x14" **770.00**
Cheese ladder, wood, mortised & pegged, 26x20" **135.00**
Coal hod, mahog w/brass trim, English, 20" L, EX **195.00**
Coat rack, pine, 7 cut-out pegs w/rnd ends, 1800s, 44" L **75.00**
Cookie roller, wood pegged roller in 9" yoke, 1910s, EX **98.00**
Dough scraper, wrought blade, wooden grip, 1870s, 4½" **75.00**

Dough scraper, wrought iron, half-rnd blade, 1-pc, 5½" **78.00**
Fly swatter, leather w/wood hdl, ca 1900, 15" **30.00**
Foot warmer, copper, oval, brass cap & ring **80.00**
Foot warmer, punched tin, butternut fr, trn posts, 6x7½x9" **250.00**
Foot warmer, punched tin in mortised wooden fr, 8x14x14" **300.00**
Foot warmer, wooden, old red pnt, door slides/bail hdl, 10½" **295.00**
Peel, tin & iron, flat rivets, 17¾" **55.00**

Pine spoon rack, incised initials, old blue-gray paint, 1800s, 12x12x7", $600.00.

Pump, pine, wood hdl & spigot, handmade, 38" **225.00**
Rack, drying; pine, 2 mortised/pinned bars, old gr rpt, 33x20" ...**150.00**
Rack, drying; poplar, old blk pnt, shoe ft, 3-bar, 31x24" **165.00**
Rack, drying; walnut, folding, mortised/pinned, 62x30" **75.00**
Roaster, chestnut; tin hinged skillet w/iron hdls, 1870s **55.00**
Rum horn, eng animals/birds/man w/tail/etc, 8¾", EX **88.00**
Skimmer, tallow; punched tin dipper on iron hdl **60.00**
Skimmer, wrought iron & brass, starflower punched bowl, 25" ..**175.00**
Skis, crudely cvd, rivets form ft rests, 1900s, 70½", pr **100.00**
Spigot, sap; wood & pewter **12.00**
Stocking dryer, wire, child's, pr **30.00**
Stocking stretchers, Fairway Store...Boston, wooden, pr **55.00**
Sugar cutter, hand-forged iron w/wood hdl, 12½" **140.00**
Sugar nipper, wrought iron, pliers type, scrolls/circles **150.00**
Wagon jack, wooden, handmade, old **60.00**
Washboard, aluminum in wooden fr, sm **25.00**
Washboard, cvd grooves, lg hand hold on side, 1850s, 26x11" ...**120.00**
Washboard, handmade, cvd grooves, child's, 9¼x6¼" **48.00**
Washboard, Little Darling, wood & tin, 17½x8¼" **35.00**
Washboard, reversible tin mk Pail in wood fr, sm **25.00**
Washboard, wooden, mk Victory, Nat'l Washboard Co, std sz **60.00**
Washer, clothes; copper funnel type w/wood hdl, Pat...'09 ....**40.00**
Wig duster, wood w/leather bellows, cork stopper, Victorian **60.00**

Prints

The term 'print' may be defined today as almost any image printed on paper by any available method. Examples of collectible old 'prints' are Norman Rockwell magazine covers and Maxfield Parrish posters and calendars. 'Original print' refers to one achieved through the efforts of the artist or under his direct supervision. A 'reproduction' is a print produced by an accomplished print maker who reproduces another artist's print or original work. Thorough study is required on the part of the collector to recognize and appreciate the many variable factors to be considered in evaluating a print. Prices vary from one area of the country to another and are dependent upon new findings regarding the scarcity or abundance of prints as such information may arise. Although each collector of old prints may have their own varying criteria by which to judge condition, for those who deal only rarely in this area or newer collectors, a few guidelines may prove helpful. Staining, though unquestionably detrimental, is nearly always present in some degree and should be weighed against the rarity of the print. Professional cleaning should improve its appearance and at the same time help preserve it. Avoid tears that affect the image; minor margin tears are another matter, especially if the print is a rare one. Moderate 'foxing' (brown spots caused by mold or the fermentation of the rag content of old paper) and light stains from the old frames are not serious unless present in excess. Margin trimming was a common practice; but look for at least ½" to 1½" margins, depending on print size.

For further study see *Huxford's Fine Art Value Guide*, available from your local bookstore or Collector Books. When no condition is indicated, the items listed below are assumed to be in very good to excellent condition. See also Parrish, Maxfield.

Audubon, John J.

Audubon is the best known of American and European wildlife artists. His first series of prints, 'Birds of America,' was produced by Robert Havell of London. They were printed on Whitman watermarked paper bearing dates of 1826 to 1838. The Octavo Edition of the same series was printed in seven editions, the first by J.T. Bowen under Audubon's direction. There were seven volumes of text and prints, each 10" x 7", the first five bearing the J.J. Audubon and J.B. Chevalier mark, the last two, J.J. Audubon. They were produced from 1840 through 1844. The second and other editions were printed up to 1871. The Bien Edition prints were full size, made under the direction of Audubon's sons in the late 1850s. Due to the onset of the Civil War, only 105 plates were finished. These are considered to be the most valuable of the reprints of the 'Birds of America Series.'

In 1971 the complete set was reprinted by Johnson Reprint Corp. of New York and Theaturm Orbis Terrarum of Amsterdam. Examples of the latter bear the watermark G. Schut and Zonen. In 1985 a second reprint was done by Abbeville Press for the National Audubon Society.

Although Audubon is best known for his portrayal of birds, one of his less-familiar series, 'Vivaparous Quadrupeds of North America,' portrayed various species of animals. Assembled in corroboration with John Bachman from 1839 until 1851, these prints are 28" x 22" in size. Several octavo editions were published in the 1850s. In the following listing, all measurements are actual print size unless stated otherwise.

Am Crow, Bien **2,000.00**
Am Magpie, #357, Havell, 1837, 38¾x26" **4,500.00**
Arctic Fox, #121, JT Bowen, 1844, 21x25" **2,500.00**
Brazilian Caracara Eagle, #156, Havell, 39x26" **7,500.00**
Burgomaster Gull, #396, Havell, 26x28½" **2,900.00**
Cayenne Tern, #273, Havell, 1835, 14¾x20½" **1,050.00**
Common Am Skunk, Female/Young; #42, Bowen, 1844, 27x21¼" ...**3,500.00**
Cougar, Male; #96, Bowen, 1846, 21½x27⅛" **4,500.00**
Florida Comorant, #252, Havell, 1835, 19½x26½" **975.00**
Gannet, #326, Havell, 1836, 26x39½" **8,000.00**
Golden Eagle, #181, Havell, 39x26" **7,500.00**
Great Am Cock Male, #1, 39½x26¾" sheet **45,000.00**
Great Am Hen & Young, #6, 26¾x39¾" sheet **25,000.00**
Great Auk, #465, Bien, NY, 1860, 26½x39¾" **2,000.00**
Key-West Dove, #167, Havell, 25x38" **5,000.00**
King Duck, #276, Havell, 1835, 26¼x38½" **4,500.00**
Maryland Marmot, wood duck, lg folio **900.00**
Moose Deer, Bowen, lg folio **3,000.00**
Musk Ox, Males; #111, Bowen, 1847, 21⅝x27⅛" **2,000.00**

Red-Breasted Sandpiper, #315, Havell, 1836, 12¼x19½" **750.00**
Trumpeter Swan, #376, Havell, 1837, 25½x38½" **30,000.00**
Velvet Duck, Male & Female; #247, Havell, 1835, 24x38⅛" ..**3,500.00**
Virginian O'possum Female/Young Male, #66, Bowen, 21x27" **4,500.00**
White Ibis, #222, Havell, 1833, 26x28" **7,800.00**
Whooping Crane, #261, Havell, 38¾x26¼" **20,000.00**

Currier and Ives

Nathaniel Currier was in business by himself until the late 1850s when he formed a partnership with James Merrit Ives. Currier is given credit for being the first to use the medium to portray newsworthy subjects, and the Currier and Ives views of 19th-century American culture are familiar to us all. In the following listings, 'C' numbers correspond with a standard reference book by Cunningham. Values are given for prints in very good condition; all are colored unless indicated black and white. Unless noted 'NC' (Nathaniel Currier), all prints are published by Currier and Ives. Our advisors for this category are John and Barbara Rudisill (Rudisill's Alt Print Haus); they are listed in the Directory under Maryland.

Abigail, NC, 1846, C-9, sm folio **75.00**
Accomodation Train, 1876, C-32, sm folio **400.00**
Alnwick Castle/Scotland, undtd, C-87, med folio **125.00**
Am Country Life, October Afternoon; NC, 1855, C-122, lg folio ..**2,700.00**
Am Farm Scenes/No 3, NC, 1853, C-133, lg folio **4,000.00**
Am Farm Yard, Morning; 1857, C-139, lg folio **2,750.00**
Am Fireman, Prompt to the Rescue; 1858, C-154, med folio ..**1,200.00**
Am Forest Game, 1866, C-156, lg folio **1,000.00**
Am Game, 1866, C-163, lg folio **1,000.00**
Am Nat'l Game of Baseball, 1866, C-180, lg folio **25,000.00**
Am Prize Fruits, 1862, C-183, lg folio **1,900.00**
Among the Pines, A First Settlement; undtd, C-214, sm folio ...**300.00**
Andrew Jackson, 7th President of US; NC, undtd, C-216, sm ...**150.00**
Arguing the Point, NC, 1855, C-265, lg folio **4,500.00**
Arkansas Traveler, 1870, C-270, sm folio **250.00**
Autumn, 1871, C-312, sm folio **125.00**
Autumn on Lake George, undtd, C-324, sm folio **225.00**
Barefoot Boy, 1872, C-368, sm folio **175.00**
Battle of Gettysburg, undtd, C-407, sm folio **235.00**
Bear Hunting, Close Quarters; undtd, C-447, sm folio **750.00**
Beautiful Persian, undtd, C-457, sm folio **65.00**
Beg Sir, undtd, C-476, sm folio **135.00**
Benjamin Franklin, Statesman...; NC, 1847, C-499, sm folio **500.00**
Between Two Fires, 1879, C-511, sm folio **235.00**
Blue Fishing, undtd, C-578, sm folio **950.00**
Boss of the Track, 1881, C-619, sm folio **200.00**
Bound To Smash, 1877, C-633, sm folio **200.00**
Brave Wife, undtd, C-651, sm folio **100.00**
Brook Trout Fishing, 1872, C-704, sm folio **900.00**
Brush on the Homestretch, 1869, C-711, lg folio **1,900.00**
Burning of Chicago, 1871, C-738, sm folio **450.00**
Camping in the Woods, Laying Off; 1863, C-774, lg folio **4,000.00**
Canal Scene, Moonlight; undtd, C-781, sm folio **300.00**
Capturing the Whale, NC, undtd, C-812, sm folio **1,500.00**
Cares of a Family, NC, 1856, C-814, lg folio **4,000.00**
Caught on the Fly, 1879, C-864, sm folio **300.00**
Cause & Effect, A Natural Result; 1887, C-866, sm folio **225.00**
Central Park, The Drive; 1887, C-951, med folio **2,200.00**
Champion Pacer Direct, 1891, C-966, sm folio **350.00**
Chicago in Flames, undtd, C-1027, sm folio **600.00**
Chicky's Dinner, undtd, C-1029, sm folio **150.00**
Choice Bouquet, 1874, C-1041, sm folio **150.00**
Christ Walking on the Sea, undtd, C-1071, sm folio **30.00**

Christening, undtd, C-1078, sm folio **90.00**
City of New York, NC, 1855, C-1102, lg folio **3,000.00**
Clearing on the Am Frontier, undtd, C-1131, sm folio **300.00**
Clipper Ship in a Hurricane, 1855, C-1154, med folio **2,000.00**
Clipper Ship in a Snow Squall, undtd, C-1157, sm folio **1,100.00**
Clipper Yacht Am of NY, NC, undtd, C-1176, sm folio **700.00**
Cork Castle & Black Rock Castle, undtd, C-1253, sm folio **90.00**
Crack Sloop in Race to Windward, 1882, C-1281, lg folio **2,000.00**
Crack Team at a Smashing Gait, 1869, C-1282, lg folio **1,700.00**
Custer's Last Charge, 1876, C-1333, sm folio **350.00**
Daisy & Her Pets, 1876, C-1346, sm folio **90.00**
Daughters of the Regiment, NC, 1849, C-1451, sm folio **150.00**
Day Before Marriage, NC, 1847, C-1459, sm folio **100.00**
Death Shot, undtd, C-1523, sm folio **195.00**
Declaration Committee, 1876; 1876, C-1530, sm folio **300.00**
Disputed Heat, Claiming Foul; 1878, C-1587, lg folio **1,800.00**
Dutchman & Hiram Woodruff, 1871, C-1640, sm folio **700.00**
El Capitan, From Mariposa Trail; undtd, C-1681, sm folio **650.00**
Emma, NC, 1849, C-1727, sm folio **90.00**
English Winter Scene, undtd, C-1745, sm folio **600.00**
Enoch Arden, The Lonely Isle; 1869, C-1749, lg folio **300.00**
Express Train, NC, 1870, C-1792, sm folio **2,200.00**
Family Pets, NC, undtd, C-1840, sm folio **100.00**
Farmer's Home, Autumn; 1864, C-1889, lg folio **2,000.00**
Favorite Horse, NC, undtd, C-1922, sm folio **250.00**
First Ride, NC, 1849, C-1987, sm folio **130.00**
Flower Vase, NC, 1848, C-2047, sm folio **135.00**
Fording the River, NC, undtd, C-2081, sm folio **550.00**
Forest Scene, Summer; undtd, C-2086, sm folio **225.00**
Fox Chase, Gone Away; NC, 1846, C-2103, sm folio **325.00**
Fox Hunting, The Find; undtd, C-2112, med folio **600.00**
Fruit & Flowers Piece, 1863, C-2160, med folio **375.00**
Fruits, Summer Varieties; 1871, C-2190, sm folio **175.00**
Fruits of Temperance, 1870, C-2195, sm folio **185.00**
Fruits of the Season, 1870, C-2198, sm folio **150.00**
Gem of the Atlantic, NC, 1849, C-2228, sm folio **800.00**
Gen Lewis Cass, NC, 1846, C-2288, sm folio **80.00**
Gen Tom Thumb, Smallest Man Alive; NC, 1849, C-2305, sm folio .**150.00**
Georgie, Quite Tired; undtd, C-2359, sm folio **90.00**
Glen at Newport, undtd, C-2383, sm folio **250.00**
God Bless Our Home, undtd, C-2392, sm folio **200.00**
Going to Pasture, Early Morning; undtd, C-2403, sm folio **200.00**
Going to the Trot, Good Day; 1869, C-2409, lg folio **2,200.00**
Got the Drop on Him, 1881, C-2455, sm folio **250.00**
Grand National Whig Banner, NC, 1844, C-2511, sm folio **200.00**
Great Bartholdi Statue, 1882, C-2570, lg folio **1,200.00**
Great Salt Lake, Utah; undtd, C-2649, sm folio **400.00**
Group of Lilies, undtd, C-2670, sm folio **130.00**
Happy Family, NC, undtd, C-2708, sm folio **130.00**
Harbor for the Night, undtd, C-2724, sm folio **325.00**
Harvesting, The Last Load; undtd, C-2750, sm folio **325.00**
Haunted Castle, undtd, C-2756, sm folio **75.00**
High Bridge at Harlem NY, NC, 1849, C-2810, sm folio **550.00**
Home in the Wilderness, 1870, C-2861, sm folio **650.00**
Home of the Deer, undtd, C-2867, med folio **500.00**
Home on the Mississippi, 1871, C-2876, sm folio **500.00**
Home Sweet Home, 1874, C-2878, sm folio **250.00**
Hooked!, 1874, C-2928, sm folio **500.00**
Horse Fair, undtd, C-2940, sm folio **325.00**
Hues of Autumn on Racquet River, undtd, C-2982, sm folio **300.00**
Husking, 1861, C-2008, lg folio **9,800.00**
Hyde Park on the Hudson River, NC, undtd, C-3010, sm folio ..**300.00**
Idlewild, On the Hudson; undtd, C-3026, sm folio **250.00**
In the Mountains, undtd, C-3071, sm folio **225.00**

Ingleside Winter, undtd, C-3112, sm folio	600.00
Inviting Dish, 1870, C-3124, sm folio	150.00
James Buchanan, 15th President of US, NC, undtd, C-3151, sm	175.00
Jane, undtd, C-3181, sm folio	80.00
John, NC, 1845, C-3250, sm folio	150.00
John Adams, 2nd President of the US; NC, undtd, C-3251, sm	175.00
Jolly Dog, 1878, C-3287, sm folio	125.00
Just Married, undtd, C-3321, sm folio	95.00
Kiss Me Quick, NC, undtd, C-3349, sm folio	600.00
Kitties Among the Roses, 1873, C-3352, sm folio	150.00
Lady of the Lake, NC, undtd, C-3384, sm folio	75.00
Lake George, NY; undtd, C-3407, sm folio	250.00
Lake in the Woods, undtd, C-3409, sm folio	225.00
Lakeside Home, 1869, C-3423, med folio	350.00
Landing of the Pilgrims, NC, undtd, C-3422, sm folio	300.00
Leaders, 1888, C-3471, lg folio	1,000.00
Liberty, 1876, C-3486, sm folio	200.00
Life in the Woods, Returning; 1860, C-3513, lg folio	3,000.00
Life of a Fireman, Ruins; NC, 1854, C-3520, lg folio	3,000.00
Life of a Hunter, Catching a Tartar; 1861, C-3521, lg folio	6,000.00
Life on the Prairie, Buffalo Hunt; 1862, C-3527, lg folio	5,500.00
Little Bo-Peep, undtd, C-3577, sm folio	150.00
Little Ellen, undtd, C-3614, sm folio	95.00
Little Jamie, undtd, C-3642, sm folio	95.00
Little Mary & Her Lamb, 1877, C-3670, sm folio	150.00
Little Red Riding Hood, undtd, C-3696, sm folio	150.00
Little Sisters, 1875, C-3710, sm folio	95.00
Loss of Steamship Swallow, NC, 1845, C-3779, sm folio	425.00
Low Water on the Mississppi, 1868, C-3824, lg folio	4,800.00
Lucy, NC, undtd, C-3835, sm folio	95.00
Maiden's Rock, Mississippi River; undtd, C-3891, sm folio	500.00
Mama's Rosebud, 1858, C-3949, med folio	140.00
Maple Sugaring, Early Spring; 1872, C-3975, sm folio	1,250.00
Marriage Certificate, NC, 1848, C-4000, sm folio	125.00
Martha Washington, undtd, C-4022, sm folio	80.00
May Queen, NC, undtd, C-4089, sm folio	90.00
Men That Kept the Bridge, 1881, C-3964, sm folio	200.00
Midnight Race on Mississippi, 1860, C-4116, lg folio	5,000.00
Mill-Cove Lake, undtd, C-4123, sm folio	350.00
Mink Trapping, Prime; 1862, C-4139, lg folio	12,500.00
Mixed at the Finish, 1880, C-4162, sm folio	250.00
Moonlight in the Tropics, undtd, C-4176, sm folio	100.00
Moose & Wolves, A Narrow Escape; undtd, C-4185, sm folio	300.00
Moosehead Lake, undtd, C-4186, sm folio	250.00
Mother's Wing, 1866, C-4239, med folio	200.00
Mountain Ramble, undtd, C-4244, sm folio	195.00
My Boyhood's Home, 1872, C-4276, sm folio	200.00
My Dear Little Pet, 1877, C-4289, sm folio	100.00
My Highland Boy, NC, undtd, C-4305, sm folio	95.00
My Little Wht Kitties, Dominos; undtd, C-4336, sm folio	135.00
My Three Wht Kittens, Their ABCs; undtd, C-4357, sm folio	135.00
Narrows From Staten Island, NC, undtd, C-4380, sm folio	375.00
Naval Heroes of the US, Plate 3; NC, 1846, C-4399, sm folio	550.00
New England Home, undtd, C-4417, sm folio	220.00
New Palace Steamer Pilgrim, 1883, C-4427, med folio	800.00
New Suspension Bridge, Niagara Falls; undtd, C-4432, sm folio	300.00
Newport Beach, undtd, C-4453, sm folio	300.00
Niagara Falls, From Goat Island; undtd, C-4458, med folio	350.00
Night by the Campfire, 1861, C-4472, med folio	550.00
Nip & Tuck, 1878, C-4481, sm folio	275.00
October Landscape, undtd, C-4529, med folio	550.00
Old Farm Gate, 1864, C-4555, lg folio	1,300.00
Old Farm House, 1872, C-4557, sm folio	1,300.00
Old Homestead in Winter, 1864, C-4563, lg folio	8,000.00
Old Mill in Summer, undtd, C-4571, sm folio	275.00
Old Oaken Bucket, 1872, C-4577, sm folio	225.00
On a Point, 1855, C-4592, med folio	600.00
On the Coast of California, undtd, C-4598, sm folio	350.00
On the St Lawrence, Indian Encampment; undtd, C-4609, sm folio	300.00
Outward Bound, NC, 1845, C-4663, sm folio	600.00
Pacing for a Grand Purse, 1890, C-4677, lg folio	1,500.00
Pacing Wonder Sleeping Tom, 1879, C-4687, sm folio	350.00
Peaceful River, undtd, C-4736, sm folio	150.00
Perry's Victory on Lake Erie, NC, undtd, C-4754, sm folio	650.00
Popping the Question, NC, 1847, C-4846, sm folio	95.00
Preparing for Market, NC, 1856, C-4870, lg folio	3,500.00
Pride of the Garden, 1873, C-4914, sm folio	175.00
Progressive Democracy, Prospect...; 1860, C-4960, med folio	300.00
Puzzled Fox, 1872, C-4984, sm folio	300.00
Quail Shooting, NC, 1852, C-4989, lg folio	3,250.00
Quails, NC, undtd, C-4992, sm folio	350.00
Rafting on the St Lawrence, undtd, C-5051, med folio	425.00
Raspberries, 1870, C-5065, sm folio	150.00
Remember the Sabbath Day..., undtd, C-5112, med folio	50.00
Rising Family, 1857, C-5151, lg folio	5,000.00
Roadside Mill, 1870, C-5175, sm folio	350.00
Robinson Crusoe..., 1874, C-5189, sm folio	175.00
Rocky Mountains, undtd, C-5195, sm folio	900.00
Rose of May, 1870, C-5215, sm folio	95.00
Safe Sailing, undtd, C-5292, sm folio	175.00
Sale of the Pet Lamb, undtd, C-5368, med folio	500.00
Scenery of the Catskills, undtd, C-5419, sm folio	300.00
See-Saw, undtd, C-5457, med folio	300.00
Silver Cascade, Wht Mtns; undtd, C-5521, sm folio	300.00
Snowshoe Dance, undtd, C-5579, med folio	1,500.00
Soldier's Adieu, NC, 1847, C-5593, sm folio	125.00
Soldier's Memorial, 1863, C-5600, med folio	200.00
Southern Beauty, undtd, C-5630, sm folio	75.00
Southern River Scenery, 1870, C-5633, sm folio	200.00
Spaniel, NC, 1842, C-5637, sm folio	250.00
Sperm Whale in a Furry, NC, 1852, C-5648, sm folio	1,200.00
Split Rock, St Johns River; NC, undtd, C-5663, sm folio	275.00
Squall Off Cape Horn, undtd, C-5680, sm folio	275.00
Stable, No 1; undtd, C-5683, med folio	1,200.00
Stag at Bay, undtd, C-5687, sm folio	150.00
Steamer Penobscot, 1883, C-5736, lg folio	1,350.00
Strawberries, 1863, C-5838, sm folio	150.00
Striped Bass, 1872, C-5844, sm folio	250.00
Summer Gift, 1870, C-5860, sm folio	150.00
Summer Time, undtd, C-5878, med folio	400.00
Sunnyside on Hudson, undtd, C-5893, sm folio	225.00
Sunrise on Lake Saranac, 1860, C-5895, lg folio	3,000.00
Sylvan Lake, undtd, C-5940, sm folio	200.00
Three Sisters, 1871, C-6045, sm folio	100.00
Through to the Pacific, 1870, C-6051, sm folio	1,200.00
Tom Paddock, undtd, C-6093, sm folio	175.00
Trolling for Bluefish, 1866, C-6158, lg folio	11,000.00
Trotting Cracks at the Forge, 1869, C-6169, lg folio	9,000.00
Under Cliff, on the Hudson; undtd, C-6282, sm folio	250.00
Under the Rose, 1872, C-6283, sm folio	100.00
Valley Forge VA, undtd, C-6355, sm folio	250.00
Vase of Flowers, undtd, C-6363, sm folio	125.00
Velocipede, 1869, C-6365, sm folio	1,900.00
View of Hudson River...Ruggle's House, 1846, C-6421, sm folio	250.00
View on Housatonic, 1867, C-6443, lg folio	1,200.00
View on Hudson, Crow's Nest; undtd, C-6447, sm folio	275.00
View on Rondout, undtd, C-6451, med folio	600.00
View on St Lawrence, Indian Encampment, undtd, C-6452, sm	300.00

Village Blacksmith, 1864, C-6462, lg folio 2,400.00
Village Street, 1855, C-6464, med folio 500.00
Washington as a Mason, undtd, C-6512, sm folio 200.00
Washington at Prayer, NC, undtd, C-6517, sm folio 125.00
Washington Crossing Delaware..., undtd, C-6523, sm folio 400.00
Washington's Reception by Ladies, NC, 1845, C-6554, sm folio ..125.00
Water Rail Shooting, NC, 1855, C-6567, sm folio 800.00
Whale Fishery, Laying On; NC, 1852, C-6626, sm folio 1,500.00
Wild Duck Shooting, On the Wing; 1870, C-6671, sm folio 600.00
Wild West in Darktown, Buffalo Chase; 1893, C-6679, sm folio ..250.00
William Tell, Son's Head; undtd, C-6712, sm folio 95.00
Winter in the Country, Cold Morning; 1864, C-6736, lg folio .10,000.00
Winter Morning, 1861, C-6740, med folio 2,000.00
Woodcock, 1871, C-6770, sm folio 300.00
Woodcock Shooting, 1870, C-6775, sm folio 550.00
Wooding Up on the Mississippi, 1863, C-6776, lg folio 9,500.00
Yo-Semite Falls, California; undtd, C-6829, sm folio 350.00
Young Brood, 1870, C-6840, sm folio 250.00
Young Sailer, NC, 1849, C-6867, sm folio 175.00

Fox, R. Atkinson

A Canadian who worked as an artist in the 1880s, R. Atkinson Fox moved to New York about ten years later, where his original oils were widely sold at auction and through exhibitions. Today he is best known, however, for his prints, published by as many as twenty printmakers. More than thirty examples of his work appeared on Brown and Bigelow calendars, and it was used in many other forms of advertising as well. Though he was an accomplished artist able to interpret any subject well, he is today best known for his landscapes. Fox died in 1935. Our advisor for Fox prints is Pat Gibson whose address is listed in the Directory under California.

Andrew Jackson, 1923 calendar, #742, 8x5" 80.00
Benjamin Franklin, 1923 calendar, #744, 8x5" 80.00
Dawn, #1, 18x10" 125.00
Day Dreams, #138, in orig oval fr, 16x20" 150.00
Good Ship Adventure, #17, 16x10" 125.00
Grover Cleveland, 1923 calendar, #711, 5x3½" 80.00
Harvesting, 1912 calendar, #451, unfr, 6x8" 195.00
Mirror Lake, #488, 5¼x3½" 95.00
Monarch of the North, polar bears, #613, 14½x10" 250.00
Mount Shasta, #486, 5¼x3½" 95.00
On The Meadows, #359, 6½x10" 125.00
Prize Stock, cow at water's edge, #479, 8x10" 150.00
Spirit of Youth, #4, 18x10" 75.00
Sunset Dreams, #23, 18x10" 90.00
The Day's Work Done, 2 horses at stream, #626, 9x7", M 185.00
Tom & Jerry, horses, #583, 9x12" 165.00
When Evening Calls Them Home, cows by stream, #353, med folio ..125.00

Gutmann, Bessie Pease

Delicately tinted prints of appealing children sometimes accompanied by their pets, sometimes asleep, often captured at some childhood activity are typical of the work of Gutmann; she painted lovely ladies as well and was a successful illustrator of children's books. Her career spanned the earlier decades of this century. Our advisor for this category is Earl MacSorley; he is listed in the Directory under Connecticut.

Always, #774, 1913, 18½x13½" 950.00
Awakening, #664 ....75.00
Baby's 1st Christmas, #158 ....150.00
Bedtime Story, #712 ....250.00

Daddy's Coming 300.00
Fairest of the Flowers, #659 ....300.00
Goldilocks, #771 ....400.00
Harmony, #802 ....125.00
In Disgrace, #792 ....150.00
Kitty's Breakfast, #805 ....85.00
Little Bit of Heaven, #650 ....75.00
Message of the Roses, #641 ....250.00
Mischief, #729 ....175.00
Reward, #794 ....150.00
Rosebud, #780 ....125.00
Sonny Boy, #784 ....100.00
Thank You God, #822 ....60.00
Touching, #210 ....85.00

Icart, Louis

Louis Icart was a Parisian artist who immortalized the women of France through his etchings, which were widely produced in the 1920s. During the thirties and forties, his popularity waned, and etchings from this period are harder to find. He also produced a few lithographs and about four hundred oils. Most etchings made after 1925 have Icart's embossed 'windmill' seal at the lower left. Be skeptical of watercolors and sketches that look similar in subject to one of the etchings. Prices appear to be stabilizing, as the art market adjusts to American recession and Japanese lethargy. Our Icart advisor is William Holland, author of *Louis Icart: The Complete Etchings;* and *The Collectible Maxfield Parrish;* he is listed in the Directory under Pennsylvania.

Youth, etching and drypoint in colors, 1930, 24x15¾" (margins trimmed), $3,300.00.

Basket of Apples, 1924, 17x12", VG 1,200.00
Bathers, 1926, 21½x18", EX 1,850.00
Belle Rose, 1933, 16x21" 2,000.00
Carmen, 1927, 21x14", VG 990.00
Cigarette Memories, 1931, 14½x17½" 3,500.00
Coursing II, 1929, 16x25¾", EX 3,575.00
Fallen Nest, Estampe Moderne, 1924, 15x19" 1,150.00
Fanny & Cat, 1926, 15x13¾", EX 2,000.00
Gay Senorita, 1939, 17½x21½", VG 1,495.00
Gossip, 1926, 17½x13¾", EX 1,500.00
Hydrangeas, 1929, trimmed oval, 16¾x21" 990.00
Joan of Arc, 1929, 19x15" 1,500.00
Joy of Life, on plastic, 1970 ....75.00
La Lettre, lithograph, 1928 ....95.00
Lady of the Camelias, 1927, 17x21" 1,500.00

Laughing, 1930, 12x17", EX 1,650.00
Laziness, 1925, 15x19" 1,800.00
Leaving Home, 1929, 15½x19", EX 1,400.00
Lilies, 1934, 27¾x18¾" 3,500.00
Love Letters, 1926, 14½x19", EX 1,500.00
Love's Blossom, 1937, 17½x25" 3,500.00
Meditation, 1928, 12½x17", VG 1,800.00
Minuet, 1929, 21x14", EX 1,200.00
Modern Eve, 1933, 21x16½" 5,000.00
Orchids, 1937, 28x19½" 4,100.00
Pink Slip, 1939, 19x11" 3,000.00
Salome, 19¾x13¾" 1,400.00
Scheherezade, 1927, 14x20½" 1,840.00
Sleeping Beauty, 1927, 15x18½" 1,650.00
Symphony in Blue, pencil sgn, 22¼x18¾", EX 1,600.00
Thais, 1927, 16x20¾" 1,850.00
Venetian Nights, 1926, 20x13" 1,100.00
Winter Bouquet, 1924, 16½x11¾" 1,900.00
2 Beauties, Browner Art Co, 1975, 18x25" 45.00

Nutting, Wallace

Born in 1862, Nutting pursued many careers. His hand-tinted photographs of landscapes and interior scenes are prized by collectors today. He was also a writer, minister, farmer, and a furniture maker, designing reproductions of early American pieces. Collectors of his prints should be aware of rosy-hued, inconsistently bright or dark examples — especially large prints of An Elaborate Dinner and A Chair for John; these have been reproduced. Prices for large interior prints have recently been on the increase. Those with animals have risen at least 50% in the past few years, and prints with men are commanding extremely high prices. Those with babies and/or adolescent children bring very high prices as well. Our advisor for this category is Milt Steinfeld; he is listed in the Directory under New Jersey.

Apple Tree Bend, 11x13" 105.00
Cold Day, girl cores apples, sits by fireplace, 10x12" 175.00
Corner Cupboard, girl gets china from cupboard, 11x17" 175.00
Highland Brae, stream runs past trees, 11x14" 125.00
Home Room, girl in rocker sips tea, 13x16" 195.00
New Hampshire Road, bridge reflected in stream, 13x16" 110.00
Newton Autumn, 15x16½" 135.00
Old Drawing Room, girl in bl dress plays piano, 11x17" 225.00
Old Time Romance, lady reading, 1914, in orig 12x15 fr 195.00
Over the Teacups, girl sets tea table in parlor, 14x17" 275.00
Patriarch in Bloom, trees over wall in country, 10x13" 110.00
Petaled Way, 13½x17½" 95.00
Quilting, 3 ladies in bedroom, 12x16" 215.00
Shower Petal, tree beside wall on country road, 14x16" 145.00
Solitude Moments, 21x25½" 170.00
Stitch in Time, girl sits & sews by fireplace, 11x14" 175.00
Tea for Two, 2 seated girls have tea in house, 11x14" 175.00
Untitled, girl braids rug by fire, 5x7" 75.00
Untitled, girl in bed looks in mirror, 5x7" 75.00
Untitled, girl in bed looks in purse, 7x9" 95.00
Untitled, girl sews by fire, 7x9" 110.00
Untitled, girl writes letter by fireplace, 7x9" 95.00
Untitled, road along stream, 8x10" 48.00
Untitled, 2 girls talk sitting by fire, 8x10" 110.00
Vines & Thatch, cottage stands by canal, Holland, 11x14" 175.00
Yosemite Waters, orig 13x11" fr 215.00

Warhol, Andy

Campbell's Soup II: Vegetarian Vegetable, 1969, 32x19" 3,200.00

Flash-November 22, 1963, silkscreen, sgn, 1963, fr, 21" sq 920.00
Flowers, wove paper, sgn, 1970, fr, 36"sq 3,800.00
Mao, wove paper, sgn, 1972, fr, 40x19½" 3,500.00
Mick Jagger, sgn, 1975, fr, 44x29" 5,200.00
Reigning Queens: Q Beatrix...Netherlands, sgn, 1985, 39x32" ...2,000.00
Reigning Queens: Q Elizabeth II...UK, sgn, 1985, 39x32" 2,200.00

Yard-Longs

Values for yard-longs are given for examples in very good to excellent condition, full length, nicely framed, and with the original glass. To learn more about this popular area of collector interest, we recommend Those Wonderful Yard-Long Prints and More, and More Wonderful Yard-Long Prints by our advisors W.D. and M.J. Keagy, and C.G. and J.M. Rhoden. They are listed in the Directory under Indiana and Illinois respectively. A word of caution: watch for reproductions; know your dealer.

American Beauty Roses, Paul DeLongpre, c 1896 ....150.00
Barbara, sgn C Allan Gilbert, c 1912 ....185.00
Battle of the Chicks, Ben Austrian, ca 1920 ....150.00
Carnation Symphony 140.00
Carnations, Grace Barton Allen 130.00
Kittens w/Mother, 1 turning pg of book 175.00
Pompeian art panel, Alluring, sgn Bradshaw Krandall 185.00
Selz Good Shoes, sgn Earl Chambers, 1920 calendar 200.00
Selz Good Shoes, sgn Haskell Coffin, 1920 calendar 225.00
Study of Sweet Peas, Grace Barton Allen, c 1900 ....150.00
Swallows over Lily Pads, J Hoover & Son, c 1897 ....200.00
Water Lilies w/Dragonfly, Fisher 140.00
Yard of Cherries & Flowers, LeRoy 150.00
Yard of Chrysanthemums, Maud Stumm 130.00
Yard of Pansies, Maud Stumm 130.00
Yard of Tulips, Paul DeLongpre 175.00
1904 Pabst Extract calendar, different baby ea month 250.00

Purinton

Founded in 1936 in Wellsville, Ohio, Purinton Pottery relocated in 1941 in Shippenville, Pennsylvania, and began producing hand-painted wares that are today attracting the interest of collectors of 'country-type' dinnerware. Using bold brush strokes of vivid color, simple yet attractive patterns such as Apple, Fruits, Tea Rose, and Pennsylvania Dutch were manufactured in tableware sets and accessory pieces.

Bank, Uncle Sam 25.00
Bowl, fruit; Maywood, 12" 50.00
Bowl, spaghetti; Apple, 14½" 50.00
Bowl, vegetable; Fruit, 8" 12.00
Butter dish, Ivy, ¼-lb 50.00
Canister, Palm Tree 100.00
Coffee server, Tulip 75.00
Coffeepot, Plaid, 8-cup 50.00
Cookie jar, Fruit 50.00
Cookie jar, Humpty Dumpty 250.00
Cookie jar, Intaglio 65.00
Creamer, Plaid 10.00
Cruet, Plaid, sq 20.00
Jam & jelly dish, Chartreuse 20.00
Jug, Kent, souvenir 50.00
Jug, Maywood, Kent, 1-pt 50.00
Lazy Susan, scalloped lid 150.00
Mug, beer; Plaid, 16-oz 50.00

Mug, Intaglio, jug form, 8-oz **40.00**
Mug, juice; Intaglio, 5-oz **14.50**
Pickle dish, Pennsylvania Dutch, 6" **25.00**
Plate, chop; Apple, 12" **40.00**
Platter, Apple, 12" **30.00**
Platter, Plaid, 11" **20.00**

Ribbon Flower: Fruit bowl, 12", $50.00; Dutch jug, $45.00.

Range set, Maywood, 3-pc **60.00**
Server, Intaglio, rectangular, 11" **35.00**
Shakers, Chartreuse, jug form, pr **15.00**
Teapot, Plaid, 6-cup **30.00**
Tumbler, Apple, short **14.00**
Tumbler, Apple, 12-oz **12.00**

Purses

Beaded purses and bags represent an area of collecting interest that is very popular today. Purses from the early 1800s are often decorated with small, brightly colored glass beads. Cut steel beads were popular in the 1840s and remained stylish until about 1930. Mesh purses are also popular. In the 1820s mesh was woven. Chain-link mesh came into usage in the 1890s, followed by the enamel mesh bags carried by the flappers in the 1920s. Purses are divided into several categories by (a) construction techniques — whether beaded, embroidered, or a type of needlework; (b) material — fabric or metal; and (c) design and style. Condition is very important. Watch for dry, brittle leather or fragile material. For those interested in learning more, we recommend *Antique Purses, A History, Identification, and Value Guide, Second Edition*, by Richard Holiner; *More Beautiful Purses*, and *Combs and Purses*, both by Evelyn Haertigi of Carmel, California. Our advisor for this category is Veronica Trainer; she is listed in the Directory under Ohio.

Key: WD — Whiting & Davis

Beaded, blk & gold geometric design, thin fr, 5¾x7¼" **70.00**
Beaded, blk w/sequins allover, cocktail clutch type **38.00**
Beaded, floral tapestry, drawstring, 6x8¾" **60.00**
Beaded, floral tapestry, ornate fr, chain hdl, fringe, 8x14" **350.00**
Beaded, scenic tapestry, ornate fr w/jewels, 6¼x6" **65.00**
Brocade, satin lined, fitted w/compact & lipstick, 1940s **105.00**
Cloth, blk silk, ornate 800 silver fr, Germany, 9½x9¼" **150.00**
Leather, alligator, clutch style, 8x15", NM **120.00**
Leather, brn reptile, clutch, 1940s, 6x10", EX **30.00**
Leather, tooled decor, clutch style, Meeker, 5¼x9¼" **55.00**

Leather, tooled decor, metal fr, strap hdl, Jemco, 9x7½" **85.00**
Lucite, marble-like w/rhinestones in lid, pail shape, 7x6" **425.00**
Lucite, tortoise, box shape, 7¾x5" **300.00**
Lucite w/woven brass base, resembles basket **35.00**
Mesh, check pattern, W&D El Sah-style fr, 5x6½" **65.00**
Mesh, fine, gold w/HP porc top w/violets, W&D, 1920s, M **425.00**
Mesh, gold, clutch type w/rhinestone clasp, EX **60.00**
Mesh, gold, Deco-style W&D fr, 5x5¾" **45.00**
Mesh, mc, bl satin lining, orig mirror, bl enamel on Deco fr **425.00**
Mesh, mc geometric florals, Mandalian fr, fringe, 4½x8¾" **125.00**
Mesh, mc geometrics, ornate W&D jeweled fr, 4x7" **80.00**
Mesh, red, ornate red W&D fr, 5½x7½" **75.00**
Mesh, spider-web design, W&D fr, 5½x6¾" **95.00**
Mesh, 3-color stripes, ornate W&D fr, 2½x3" **30.00**
Mesh, 800 silver, 7 garnets set on fr, +coin purse **400.00**
Needlework on canvas, heavy beadwork, Lucite hdls **28.00**
Suede w/needlework portrait scene, clutch type **75.00**
Tapestry, scenic reserve/florals, jeweled fr, Austria, 8x7" **175.00**

Puzzles

'Jigsaw' puzzles have been around almost as long as games. The first examples were handcrafted from wood, and they are extremely difficult to find. Most of the early examples featured moral subjects just as the board games did. By the 1890s jigsaw puzzles had become a major form of home entertainment. During the Depression years jigsaw puzzles were set up on card tables in almost every home. The early wood examples are the most valuable.

Cube puzzles, or blocks, were often made by the same companies as the board games. Again, early examples display the finest quality lithography. While all subjects are collectible, some (Such as Santa blocks) often command prices higher than games from the same period. Our advisors for this category are Norm and Cathy Vigue; they are listed in the Directory under Massachusetts.

Animal Antics Scroll, McLoughlin, 1894, EX **465.00**
Changeable Charlie, dtd 1943 ....**12.50**
Children of Am History, All Fair #680, 1940s, pr in box, EX **15.00**
First Ringing of Liberty Bell, wood, 200-pc, 1880s, 9x12", NM **85.00**
Flying Family, jigsaw, 1932, M in envelope **35.00**
Four-Footed Friends, cubes, McLoughlin, EX in box **465.00**
Keep Going w/Kellogg's, boy w/baseball, 1933, 6x8", NM **32.00**
Old Grist Mill, Fairco #1535, 1940s, 14x19", M in NM box **10.00**
Pretty Country Picture, cb, Parker Bros, 3 in 9½x16" box **78.00**
Santa, McLoughlin Bros **850.00**
Sliced Animals, Selchow & Righter, NY, 1900, EX in box **110.00**
Sweet Innocence, Tuco, cb, EX **8.00**

Personalities, Movies, and TV Shows

Andy Panda, fr-tray, 1962, VG **5.00**
Batman, jigsaw, Whitman, 1966, EX **45.00**
Beverly Hillbillies, jigsaw, Family Portrait, 1963 ....**28.00**
Beverly Hillbillies, jigsaw, Granny & Elly Mae, 1963 ....**28.00**
Bozo the Clown, jigsaw, on high wire, Whitman, 1969, EX **15.00**
Bugs Bunny, fr-tray, Whitman, 1964, water-skiing, NM **15.00**
Captain Marvel, Picture Puzzle, Fawcett Pub, 1941, G **50.00**
Captain Universe, Space Puzzle, fr-tray, EX '50s graphics, M **18.00**
Casper, fr-tray, 1950s, EX **15.00**
Cinderella, Puzzle Box, cb, M Bradley, 3 in 9½x16" box **35.00**
Deputy Dawg, jigsaw, Whitman, 1972, NM **20.00**
Flash Gorden, fr-tray, Milton Bradley, 1951, NM **35.00**

Flintstones, fr-tray, Fred w/ice cream, 1962, VG 20.00
Fury, fr-tray, Whitman, 1955, 3 boys on Fury, VG 10.00
Gabby Gator, fr-tray, 1963, VG 10.00
Hopalong Cassidy, fr-tray TV puzzles (4), Milton Bradley, NM 75.00
Hopalong Cassidy, picture puzzle, #2983, ca 1940, in fr 40.00
Howdy Doody, fr-tray, 1-man band, 1954, EX 20.00
Howdy Doody, illus envelope, Poll Parrot, 8x8", NM 100.00
Huckleberry Hound, fr-tray, 1960s, EX 15.00
Huckleberry Hound, slide puzzle, M on card 25.00
Huckleberry Hound w/Pixie & Dixie, fr-tray, 1960, EX 13.50
Lady & The Tramp, Whitman, 1954, VG 15.00
Lassie, jigsaw, fends off puma, Whitman, 1966, NM 20.00
Munsters, fr-tray, family in lab, Whitman, 1965, VG 45.00
Peter Pan, fr-tray, dueling w/Hook, Jaymar, 1950s, VG 20.00
Popeye, jigsaw, picnic scene, Jaymar, 1960s, VG 10.00
Raggedy Ann, set of 6 forms train, Milton Bradley, '44 ....88.00
Roy Rogers, fr-tray, 1952, 15x11", NM 25.00
Star Trek, Beaming Down, 1974, EX 10.00
Superman, jigsaw, 1966, EX in box 16.50
Tom & Jerry, fr-tray, 1969, EX in box 10.00
Wizard of Oz, jigsaw, Jamar, 1940s, NMIB 45.00
Woody Woodpecker, fr-tray, 1962, NM 12.00
Zorro, fr-tray, 1964, M 15.00

Quezal

The Quezal Art Glass and Decorating Company of Brooklyn, New York, was founded in 1901 by Martin Bach. A former Tiffany employee, Bach's glass closely resembled that of his former employer. Most pieces were signed 'Quezal,' a name taken from a Central American bird. After Bach's death in 1920, his son-in-law, Conrad Vohlsing, continued to produce a Quezal-type glass in Elmhurst, New York, which he marked 'Lustre Art Glass.' See also that specific category. Examples listed here are signed unless noted otherwise.

Candlestand, emerald gr w/irid bl, hollow, 7½" 300.00
Chandelier, brass w/4 arms, 5 gold 7" tulip shades 1,350.00
Lamp, cherub figural on Fr bronzed-metal base, gold shade 350.00
Lamp, feathered burgundy/gold bell shade; dragonfly on base .1,000.00
Sconce, 2 scroll arms w/3 gr & gold feathered lilies 495.00
Shade, feathers, opal on ribbed gold irid, 4¾", pr 300.00
Shade, feathers on gold, 6" 250.00
Taster, gold, oval w/4 dimples, 2¾" 135.00

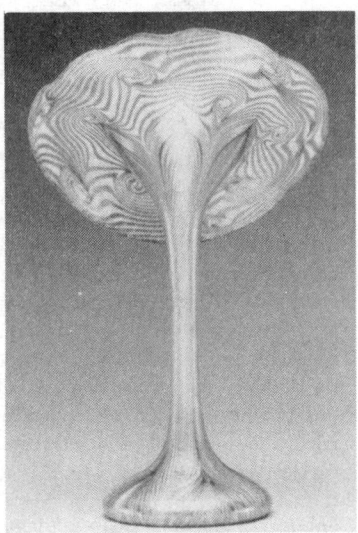

Jack-in-the pulpit vase, green and gold feathers, gold throat, 8¾", $2,400.00.

Vase, bl irid, trumpet neck, 6½" 500.00
Vase, bl irid, weighted base, 10" 625.00
Vase, bl irid, wide shoulder & base, flared rim, 8" 550.00
Vase, feathers, gold/gr on wht, gold links at shoulder, 6½" 1,400.00
Vase, feathers, gr on opal, gold int, ruffled trumpet form, 6" 825.00
Vase, feathers, heart band, wht/gr/gold, trumpet form, 10" 1,250.00
Vase, gold, squatty w/stick neck, #K-947, 9" 400.00
Vase, jack-in-pulpit; allover feathers, 3-color+gold, 12x8" 4,000.00
Vase, leaves, gold/gr on opal, gold rolled rim, att, 3½" 650.00

Quilts

Quilts, while made of necessity, nevertheless represent an art form which expresses the character and the personality of the designer. During the 17th and 18th centuries, quilts were considered a necessary part of a bride's hope chest; the traditional number required to be properly endowed for marriage was a 'baker's dozen'! Quilts were used not only for bed coverings but for curtains, extra insulation, and mattresses as well. The early quilts were made from pieces salvaged from cloth items that had outlived their original usefulness and from bits left over from sewing projects. Regardless of shape, these scraps were fitted together following no organized lines. The resulting hodge-podge design was called a crazy quilt.

In 1793 Eli Whitney developed the cotton gin; as a result, textile production in America became industrialized. Soon inexpensive fabrics were readily available, and ladies were able to choose from colorful prints and solids to add contrast to their work. Both pieced and appliqued work became popular. Pieced quilts were considered utilitarian, while appliqued work was shown with pride of accomplishment at the fair. Today many collectors prize pieced quilts and their intricate geometric patterns above all other types. Many of these designs were given names: Daisy and Oak Leaf, Grandmother's Flower Garden, Log Cabin, and Ocean Wave are only a few. Appliqued quilts involved stitching one piece — carefully cut into a specific form such as a leaf, a flower, or a stylized device — onto either a large one-piece ground fabric or an individual block. Often the background fabric was quilted in a decorative pattern.

Amish women scorned printed calicos as 'worldly' and instead used colorful blocks set with black fabrics to produce a stunning pieced effect. During the Victorian era, the crazy quilt was revived, but the ladies of the 1870s used plush velvets, brocades, silks, and linen patches and embroidered along the seams with feather or chain stitches.

Another type of quilting, highly prized and rare today, is trapunto. These quilts were made by first stitching the outline of the design onto a solid sheet of fabric which was backed with a second having a much looser weave. White was often favored, but color was sometimes used for accent. The design (grapes, flowers, leaves, etc.) was padded through openings made by separating the loose weave of the underneath fabric; a backing was added and the three layers quilted as one.

Besides condition, value is judged on intricacy of pattern, color effect, and craftsmanship. Examine the stitching. Quality quilts have from ten to twelve stitches to the inch. In the listings that follow, examples rated excellent have minor defects. Values given here are auction results; retail may be somewhat higher.

Key:
dmn — diamond	hq — hand quilted
embr — embroidered	mp — machine pieced
hs — hand sewn	ms — machine sewn

Amish

Blk rectangle in borders of purple & blk, purble binding, lg 635.00

Bow Tie, bright colors, ms binding, EX hq, 72x88", EX **1,600.00**
Center Dmn, rich colors, feather/dmn quilting, 1900, NM **2,750.00**
Crosses & Losses, wht/bl/lav, 1935, 79x90", EX **600.00**
Fence Row Vt, band border, sawtooth edge, '10, 82x64, EX **1,100.00**
Octagons & 9-Patch, bl shades w/gr border, full sz, EX **500.00**
Squares, wine/gr/olive w/blk grid, blk border, lg, EX **425.00**
Star center, blk on orange, contemporary, 89x94", M **725.00**
9-Patch, 24 blocks, vine/diagonal stitching, 1900, lg **635.00**

Appliqued

Basket of flowers, reds and greens, slightly faded, 94x89", $850.00.

Butterfly Charm, mc on wht, hs, 1920s, 75x61" **350.00**
Carolina Lily, red/gr/wht, mp/hq & appliqued, 1900s, 82x61", EX .**400.00**
Colonial Lady, mc on wht, gr border, hs, 1975, 104x78", M **435.00**
Eagle, yel on wht, hs, hq grid, ca 1930, 94x78", EX **350.00**
Floral, bold/intricate, 5-color on wht, trapunto, 86x102" **2,975.00**
Floral Medallion, 12 repeats, mc calicos, 76x98" **500.00**
Floral Medallion, 4-color on wht, hs/embr, 1930s, 86x74" **1,400.00**
Florals (bold) in grid, 4-color on wht, ms, 72x84", NM **1,100.00**
Flower Patch, wht/gr/yel/orange/pk/bl, hs, 1986, 84x98" **575.00**
Flowers & Fans, 5-color, scalloped edge, 84x84", EX **660.00**
Garden Bouquet, mc prints/wht, hs, ltweight, '30s, 74x62" **465.00**
Love Apple Vt, gr/red/gold, hs, EX quilting, 1860, 85x83", EX .**1,150.00**
Maple Leaf, mc leaves in gr grid, hs, 1979, 99x79" **350.00**
North Carolina Rose, 4-color, hs, top ca 1938, 80x65", M **575.00**
Oal Leaf Medallion, sawtooth border, red/gr/wht, PA, 82x82" ...**525.00**
Plume pinwheels w/star centers in grid, 4-color on wht, 80x83" .**600.00**
Roses & vining border, gr calico/solid red, hs, 96x96" **495.00**
Tulips, red & gr on yel calico w/gr piping, 98x96", NM **995.00**
Vining florals & swags, 4-color calico, dtd 1851, 84x84", EX ..**1,750.00**

Mennonite

Bars, tan on bl-gr, feather quilting, 74x78", EX **1,500.00**
Log Cabin Vt, stars & blades, 1860s, 79" sq, EX **1,200.00**
Pinwheels, goldenrod/navy on dk brn, bk: bars, 90" sq **575.00**
Ribbon Star, 8-point, dk w/muted brights, ca 1910, EX **465.00**
Weathervane, 5-color, bl & wht check bk, 82x78" **1,200.00**
9-Patch, mc prints/pk calico/gr border, PA, 83x84" **850.00**

Pieced

Amish Bars, bls/blk cotton & polyester, mp/hq, '87, 34x44" **160.00**

Baskets, gr/yel/wht, mp/hq, 1950, primitive, 78x78", EX **235.00**
Cathedral Window, mc cottons, sawtooth edge, hs, 96x80", NM ...**1,495.00**
Country String, mc cotton, mp/hq, 1930s, 82x54", EX **235.00**
Crazy, pks/brns, cotton, calico border, 1930s, 88x86" **400.00**
Crazy, satin & velvet w/much embr, 1880s, 66x54", VG **440.00**
Crazy, silk/velvet, w/appl & embr devices, 1885, 78x74", EX **450.00**
Crazy, silks/satins/velvet, flower embr, 1884, 68x68", EX **1,400.00**
Dbl Wedding Ring, mc, bright, ca 1920s, full sz, NM **350.00**
Dbl Wedding Ring, purple/lav/mc prints, ms/hq, 107x85" **350.00**
Drunkard's Path, gr & yel, cotton, mp/hq, 1930s, 92x78", EX **575.00**
Fan, mc on wht, pk & turq, striping, mp/hq, '40s, 35x29" **125.00**
Flower Basket, yel & bl, sm stitches, ca 1908, 84x96", EX **250.00**
Flower Garden, mc, ca 1915, 72x92", EX **350.00**
Flyfoot (Catch Me If You Can), bl/wht, hs, 1930, 84x75", EX ...**300.00**
Grandmother's Flower Garden, prints/solids, hs, 1945, 82x63" ..**200.00**
Hole in Barn Door, gr/wht/red, hs, fading, 1900, 80x66", EX **525.00**
Indian Wedding Ring, trundle sz, early 1900s, VG **395.00**
Irish Chain w/3-stripe border, mc/wht, 1894, 75x76", EX **350.00**
Jacob's Ladder, red/wht/bl, hs, 1940s, 72x69", NM **500.00**
Jacob's Ladder Vt, purple/wht, mp/EX hq, 88x74" **465.00**
Log Cabin, mc prints/solid red, 78x89", EX **450.00**
Lone Star, pks, cotton, hs, 1940s, 79x71", EX **500.00**
Lone Star, 4-color on wht, mp/hq, 1974, 114x101", M **475.00**
Lone Star, 5-color on wht, hq, 1930s, 68x66", EX **550.00**
Monkey Wrench, brn & gold prints, hs, 1880s, 85x72", EX **525.00**
Monkey Wrench, mc calicos & prints on wht, ca 1900, 78x67" .**375.00**

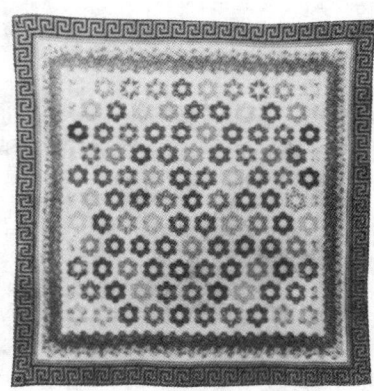

Mosaic patchwork, various calicos, Greek Key outer border, mid-1800s, some staining, 42x44", EX, $1,200.00.

Ohio Star, gold/wht cotton, hs, 1920s, 86x76", EX **500.00**
Patchwork, mc solids & prints, hs, 1940, 84x74", NM **395.00**
Pennsylvania Dutch, pk/wht, hs, ca 1900, 84x80", EX **500.00**
Philadelphia Pavement, mc prints/calico/wht, 74x77", EX **365.00**
Puss in the Corner, 3-color, bound 3 sides, hs, 1800, 73x51" **395.00**
Schoolhouse, mc calico in pk & wht grid, PA, 72x83", EX **500.00**
Seven Sisters, mc on pk, cotton, hs, 1800s, 78x62", EX **400.00**
Single Irish Chain Vt, mc on yel, mp/hq, ca 1940, 94x66" **350.00**
Spools, mc prints, 1890s, sm stain, 73x83" **395.00**
Star Bouquet, mc prints/solids, hs/hq, 1989, 87x75", NM **230.00**
Stars, bl/wht, scalloped border, feather quilted, 100x86", NM ...**1,500.00**
String Star, mc on pk, 1940s top, newly hq, 82x66", NM **185.00**
String Star, mc prints on wht, hs, '30s, new border, 81x60" **350.00**
Stylized crosses, mc calicos on wht & blk print, 72x85", EX **220.00**
Sunburst, oranges/golds/wht, hs, EX quilting, '40s, 89x88", NM ...**925.00**

Thousand Pyramid Medallion, mc prints, 1912, 75x75", EX **450.00**
Trip Around the World, solids/prints, hs, 1930s, 77x65" **350.00**
Trumpet Vine, red/gr/orange calico on wht, hs, 1880s, 80x78" ..**350.00**
US Flag Hostage, red/wht/bl/gold, hs, detailed, '80, 118x108" ...**1,500.00**
Variable Stars, bl/beige/rust, mp/hand tied, '50s, 82x62", M **175.00**
Whirligig, mc scraps on yel, mp/hq, 1940s, 87x72", EX **500.00**
Windmill Blades, red & mc calicos, ca 1890, 72x70", EX **450.00**
9-Patch Vt, peach/yel/wht, ms/hq, 1940s, 83x65" **350.00**

Quimper

Quimper is a type of pottery produced in Quimper, France. A tin enamel-glazed earthenware pottery with hand-painted decoration, it was first produced in the 1600s by the Bousquet and Caussy Factories. Little of this early ware was marked. By the late 1700s, three factories were operating in the area, all manufacturing the same type of pottery. The Grande Maison de HB, a company formed as a result of a marriage joining the Hubaudiere and Bousquet families, was a major producer of Quimper pottery. They marked their wares with various forms of the 'HB' logo; but of the pottery they produced, collectors value examples marked with the 'HB' within a triangle most highly.

Francois Eloury established another pottery in Quimper in the late 1700s. Under the direction of Charles Porquier, the ware was marked simply 'P.' Adolph Porquier replaced Charles in the 1850s, marking the ware produced during that period with an 'AP' logo. 'PB' (for Porquier-Beau) was used ca 1875 until 1900.

Jule HenRiot began operations in 1886, using molds he had purchased from Porquier. His mark was 'HR,' and until the 20th century he was in competition with The Grande Maison de HB. In 1926 he began to mark his wares 'HenRiot Quimper.' In 1968 the two factories merged. They are still in operation under the name Les Faenceries de Quimper. The factory sold in the fall of 1983 to Sarah and Paul Janssens from the United States, making it the first time the owners were not French. For those interested in learning more about Quimper, we recommend *Quimper Pottery: A French Folk Art Faience* by Sandra V. Bondhus, our advisor for this category, whose address can be found in the Directory under Connecticut.

Banette, Breton mother & girl spin flax, PB, 9½" **925.00**
Banette, piper, mc florals, 1800s, HRQ, 8¼" **405.00**
Bookends, boy w/bagpipes/girl on bench, HBQ, 6¾", pr **150.00**
Bowl, barber's, peasant lady/garlands, HB, late 1800s, 11¼" L **475.00**
Bowl, Breton man, floral garland, HBQ, 2½x7¼" **80.00**
Bowl, nut; Breton man & lady, floral border, HRQ, 2¾", pr **70.00**
Box, lute player, gr sponged trim, HQ, prof rpr, 2¼x5" **240.00**
Celery, Ivoire Corbeille, lady's protrait, boat shape, HQF, 10" ...**130.00**
Coffee cup, Breton lady & floral sprays, ca 1900, HBQ, rstr **20.00**
Compote, Breton man w/walking stick, mc, ped ft, HBQ, 5x9¾" .**210.00**
Creamer & sugar bowl, Ordinaire, man/lady, HQF/HQF, 3", 4¼" ..**80.00**
Figurine, ladies & man dancing, Modern Movement, mc, HQF, 3" ...**100.00**
Figurine, lady, wht coif/pk apron/cobalt skirt, HQFJE, 3¼" **110.00**
Font, holy water; ermine tail form, man by cross, HQF, 9¼" **250.00**
Goblet, peasant man w/bird, mc, clover shape, ped ft, HQF, 5" **45.00**
Ink stand, lady w/basket, dbl decor riche, HQ/HQF, 7¼x6" **300.00**
Jar, jam; peasant lady, garland on bk & lid, mc, HBQ, 4½" **95.00**
Jardiniere, peasant children & piglet, decor riche, PB, 5x9¾" **340.00**
Jardiniere, swan form, lady seated on breast, HRQ, 6¾x8" **250.00**
Mustard jar, Breton lady, florals, mc, HRQ, 4¼" **120.00**
Piggy bank, men w/roses & birds ea side, hairlines/rstr, 8" L **190.00**
Pipe rest, duck figural, mc, HF, 3¼x5¾" **25.00**
Plaque, Les Filets Bleus, central decor, 12½" **350.00**
Plate, biniou player, mc, floral sprays, HB, 9¾" **300.00**
Plate, Breton fisherman & daughter, mc, PB, 9¼" **825.00**

Plate, Breton lady in breeze, mc, 1800s, HB, 9¾" **300.00**
Plate, Ivoire Corbeille, daisies, mc, HQ, 9½" **32.00**
Plate, lady knits, girl holds yarn, mc, wire hanger, HR, 8" **550.00**
Plate, man, arms folded, mc, flower rim, late 1800s, HB, 9¾" **350.00**
Plate, man w/walking stick, Malicorne, 1800s, 5" **30.00**
Plate, Mayflower, bl & red border, HQF, 9⅝" **325.00**
Plate, Modern Movement, mc floral, HBQ, 9", pr **50.00**
Plate, Ordinaire, Breton lady, scalloped, HQF, 4½" **40.00**
Plate, Ordinaire, Breton man & lady, HQF, 6", pr **55.00**
Plate, WWI commemorative, soldier by cannon, HQ, 1917, 9" .**700.00**
Platter, Breton lady, sprig border, scalloped, HBQ, 12x9" **230.00**
Platter, Broderie Breton couple, HBQ, 14¾x11¼", NM **350.00**

Platter, Naive, fisherman and lady drawing water, unsigned HB, 1880s, 19½x14½", NM, $1,000.00.

Platter, peasant girl w/parasol, HR, 14¼x11" **525.00**
Salt cellar, bagpipe form, lady's portrait, mc, HQF, 4½" **60.00**
Salt cellar, dbl; lady sits w/2 baskets, HBQ, 4½x6" **70.00**
Salt cellar, dbl; swan form, man & lady, HQF, 3½" **95.00**
Sconce, man's head form w/shell bk plate, late 1800s, unmk **210.00**
Smoker figurine, pelican figure, holds smoker's needs, mc, HBQ ..**350.00**
Snuff box, pansies/peasant lady, mc, heart shape, unmk HBQ, 3" .**140.00**
Snuff box, watch face/man on flower form, mc, 1800s, unmk **325.00**
Sugar bowl, Breton man & lady, gr sponged hdls, HRQ, 6½" **110.00**
Teapot, Ordinaire, man on front/floral on bk, HQF, 7¾", NM .**150.00**
Tureen, Breton lady, floral border, mc, AP, 1800s, 5¼x9¼" **200.00**
Vase, Breton man, floral sprays, ftd fan form, HQF, 8¼" **180.00**
Vase, Breton man w/striped pants, sunflowers, hdls, HQ, 8¼" **300.00**
Vase, Breton musicians, decor riche, flower spray, HQ, 15" **925.00**
Vase, Broderie Breton couple, 4 sunflower panels, HBQ, 10" **315.00**
Vase, quintel; man playing flute, garlands, HQF, 4" **75.00**
Vase, triple cornucopia; Modern Movement style, HBQ, 13½" ..**200.00**

Radford

Pottery associated with Albert Radford (1882-1904) can be categorized by three periods of production. Pottery produced in Tiffin, Ohio, (1896-1899) consists of bone china (no marked examples known) and high-quality jasperware with applied Wedgwood-like cameos. Tiffin jasperware is often impressed 'Radford Jasper' in small block letters. At Zanesville, Ohio, Radford jasperware was marked only with an incised, two-digit shape number, and the cameos were not applied but rather formed within the mold and filled with a white slip. Zanesville Radford ware was produced for only a few months before the Radford pottery was acquired by the Arc-en-Ciel company in 1903.

Production in Zanesville was handled by Radford's father, Edward (1840-1910), who remained in Zanesville after Albert moved to Clarksburg, West Virginia, where the Radford Pottery Co. was completed shortly before Albert's death in 1904. Jasperware was not produced in Clarksburg, and the molds appear to have been left in Zanesville, where some were subsequently used by the Arc-en-Ciel pottery. The Clarksburg, West Virginia, pottery produced a standard glaze, slip-decorated ware, Ruko; Thera and Velvety, matt glazed ware often signed by Albert Haubrich, Alice Bloomer, and other artists; and Radura, a semimatt green glaze developed by Albert Radford's son, Edward. The Clarksburg plant closed in 1912. Our advisor for this category is James L. Murphy; he is listed in the Directory under Ohio.

Jardiniere, matt pea green, impressed Radura, 10", $150.00.

Jasper

Bowl, muses & vintage, bl, fluted rim, imp mk	295.00
Ewer, appl grapes & raspberries, Old Man Winter hdl, 9"	350.00
Letter holder, lady w/bow & target scene, bark trim, #61	500.00
Mug, appl grapes	275.00
Mug, floral relief, lt bl, 4½"	150.00
Pitcher, grapes, Old Man Winter hdl, #17, 9"	600.00
Pitcher, tankard, vintage, lt bl, #28, 12"	200.00
Vase, bust of Washington, reverse: eagle, bark trim, #12, 7"	265.00
Vase, cupids on flying eagles, #23, 9½"	475.00
Vase, cupids w/flower garland; reverse: cupid; #57, 5½"	150.00
Vase, flask shape, Grecian lady & man, bark trim, #21, 9"	600.00
Vase, flat & twisted, running girl, deep bl, #53, 3½"	100.00
Vase, horses (3) in clouds w/chariot, bark trim, #16, 7"	300.00
Vase, kneeling lady, arms up, bird in hand, bark trim, #24, 9"	600.00
Vase, lady, arm raised w/flowing robe, #19, 9"	600.00
Vase, lady w/dog, bk: Roman kneels, bark trim, #18, 7"	350.00
Vase, lady w/fire beside her, grapes reverse, #55, 3½"	100.00
Vase, sitting lady, trees & dog, bark trim, #22, 9"	600.00
Vase, 2 children & lion, wht & lt brn, #15, 7"	225.00

Miscellaneous

Candlestick, Ruko, floral, brn streaked, imp mk, 6"	125.00
Jardiniere, Ruko, tulips, 8½x9"	250.00
Jardiniere & ped, winged creatures/foliage, streaky gr, 34"	500.00
Vase, Radura, matt gr, 4-hdld, 10"	150.00
Vase, Thera, gr bsk w/pk floral, 8", NM	160.00
Vase, Thera, gr w/nasturtium decor, cylindrical, 12"	250.00
Vase, Velvety, gr w/nasturtiums, sgn AB, #1452, 14"	500.00
Vase, Velvety, matt gr w/wild roses, #7463, 10"	200.00
Vase/lamp base, bulbous, std glaze, dogwood decor, 10x13"	350.00

Radios

Vintage radios are becoming very collectible. There were thou-sands of styles and types produced, the most popular of which today are the breadboard and the cathedral. Consoles are usually considered less saleable, since their size makes them hard to display and store. For those wishing to learn more about antique radios, we recommend *The Collector's Guide to Antique Radios, Volume I and II*, by Sue and Marty Bunis, available from your local bookstore or Collector Books. They are also the authors of *A Collector's Guide to Transistor Radios*. Values are given for radios in near mint to mint condition.

Key:
phono — phonograph   tbl/m — table model

A-C Dayton XL-5, wood, 3-dial panel, battery, tbl/m	100.00
Addison B2E, plastic, Deco style, 2 pinwheel knobs, tbl/m	300.00
Admiral 5G22, plastic, sq dial, alarm clock, 4 knobs, tbl/m	30.00
Admiral 8D15, wood, blk dial, 3 knobs, phono, console, 1949	80.00
Air Castle, G-521, leatherette, tambour top, portable, 1949	45.00
Air-Way #61, walnut, window dials, 6 tubes, tbl/m, 1925	150.00
Airline, #62-606, telephone dial, grill bars, tbl/m, 1938	85.00
Airline #15BR-1544A, plastic, lattice grill, tbl/m, 1951	35.00
Arvin #568A Phantom Blonde, lower rnd dial, tbl/m, 1938	65.00
Atwater Kent #456, Tombstone, wood, cloth grill, 1936	250.00
Atwater Kent #90, Cathedral, wood, half-rnd dial, 1931	450.00
Belmont #8A59, wood, push buttons, phono, console, 1946	75.00
Bendix #110, walnut plastic, slide rule dial, tbl/m, 1948	65.00
Bendix #55P3, walnut plastic, wood-grained grill, tbl/m, '49	45.00
Bremer-Tully #7-71, wood, highboy, upper grill, console, '28	175.00
Concord #1-516, plastic, airplane dial, tbl/m, 1949	35.00
Coronado #35RA-43-9856A, crisscross grill, portable, 1953	30.00
Crosley #11, plastic, right front dial, louvers, tbl/m	45.00
Crosley #146, Cathedral, wood, cloth grill, fluted columns	240.00
Crosley #401 Bandbox Jr, metal, window dial, tbl/m, 1928	80.00
Crosley #51-S Special, wood, blk Bakelite panel, tbl/m, '24	115.00
Crosley #6H2, Tombstone, wood, rnd dial, cloth grill, 1933	110.00
Day-Fan Dayroyal, mahog, storage/doors, desk console, '26	150.00
Delco R-1233, plastic, vertical bars, tbl/m, 1948	90.00
Detrola #383, cloth cover, sq dial, 2 knobs, portable, '41	30.00
Dewald #551, walnut, center grill, 2 knobs, tbl/m, 1933	85.00
Eagle A, wood, rectangular, 3 dials, battery, tbl/m, '23	110.00
Emerson #25A, wood, curved top, cloth grill, tbl/m, 1933	95.00
Emerson #409 Mickey Mouse, Mickey w/cello on grill, tbl/m, '33	1,250.00
Emerson #553A, leatherette, slide rule dial, portable, '47	35.00
Emerson #569A, plastic, flip-up front, portable, 1948	60.00
Emerson #810B, plastic, pointer over lg grill, tbl/m, 1955	40.00
Emerson AU-190, Tombstone, yel Catalin, gold dial, 1938	1,000.00
Emerson CH-246, plastic, wrap-around louvers, tbl/m, 1939	60.00
Fada #20, 2-tone metal, rectangular, window dial, tbl/m, 1929	110.00
Fada #260V, ivory plastic, airplane dial, tbl/m, 1936	85.00

Fada 845, plastic Deco-style case, AC/DC table model, 1950, $135.00.

Fairbanks-Morse #6AC-7, 2-tone wood, tuning eye, chairside	120.00
Farnsworth CT-60, fold-down luggage-type portable, 1941	30.00
Firestone #4-A-89, plastic, half-moon dial, tbl/m, 1950	35.00
Freshman #5-F-5, mahog, 3 dials, built-in speaker, tbl/m, '25	145.00

General Electric #136, plastic, recessed bars, tbl/m, '50 ....**40.00**
General Electric #453, plastic, checked grill, tbl/m, 1956 ....**20.00**
General Electric F-63, walnut, gold dial, tbl/m, 1937 ....**95.00**
General Electric H-530, Tombstone, wood, sm case, 1939 ....**95.00**
General Electric P-672, plastic, logo on bars, portable, '58 ....**20.00**
General Television #25B5, 2-tone, battery, portable, 1947 ....**30.00**
Globe #553, plastic, half-moon dial, tbl/m, 1947 ....**75.00**
Gloritone #24, Cathedral, wood, window dial, 2 knobs, 1933 ....**225.00**
Grebe Challenger 5, plastic, sq dial, 5 tubes, tbl/m, 1938 ....**50.00**
Hallicrafters #5R24, rnd dial, woven grill, portable, 1952 ....**35.00**
Hoffman C-1007, wood, pull-out phono, 23 tubes, console, '49 .**180.00**
Howard #472F, wood, pull-out phono, console, 1948 ....**85.00**
Kadette #44 Jewel, red plastic, plastic cutouts, tbl/m, '35 ....**300.00**
Kellogg #521, wood, lowboy, stretcher base, console, 1928 ....**175.00**
Knight #4G-420, slide rule dial, 3 knobs, phono, 1950 ....**25.00**
Kolster #8B, wood, window dial, loop antenna, console, 1926 ...**225.00**
Majestic #7C432, wood, slide rule dial, tubular ft, tbl/m, '47 ....**40.00**
Meck CE-500, wood, sq dial, 3 knobs, lift top, tbl/m, 1948 ....**30.00**
Midwest #18-35, wood, Deco style, 18 tubes, console, 1935 ......**275.00**
Monitor M-403, wood, picture on grill, tbl/m, 1947 ....**40.00**
Motorola #5T11M, plastic, rnd dial, 2 knobs, tbl/m, 1959 ....**20.00**
Motorola #52C1, plastic, alarm clock, 4 knobs, tbl/m, 1953 ....**20.00**
Motorola B-150, mts on bike hdlbars, w/battery pack, 1940 ....**85.00**
Olympic #7-925, wood, slide rule dial, phono, console, 1948 ....**70.00**
Packard-Bell #531, plastic, perforated grill, tbl/m, 1954 ....**25.00**
Philco #17-D, wood, highboy, dbl doors, 6 legs, console, '33 ......**165.00**
Philco #39-70, Tombstone, wood, rnd shoulders, battery, '39 .....**100.00**
Philco #41-844, louvers, tambour door, portable, 1941 ....**40.00**

**Philco 42-PT96 Transitone, wood with plastic
escutcheon, table model, 1942, $45.00.**

Philco #46-350, wood/leatherette, tambour cover, portable, '46 ...**45.00**
Philco #49-902, plastic, recessed front, louvers, tbl/m, '49 ....**40.00**
Philco #53-563 Transitone, plastic, 2-band, tbl/m, 1953 ....**50.00**
Philco #70, Cathedral, walnut, window dial, 7 tubes, 1931 ....**350.00**
Philharmonic #149-C, wood, phono, lift top, console, 1949 ....**55.00**
Pilot E-20, burl walnut, Deco style, tbl/m, 1934 ....**90.00**
RCA #1R81, plastic, rnd center dial, side knobs, tbl/m, '52 ....**35.00**
RCA #280, wood, lowboy, window dial, 12 tubes, console, '33 ..**175.00**
RCA #5T, Tombstone, wood, center dial, cloth grill, 1936 ....**140.00**
RCA #55U, wood, slide rule dial, 2 knobs, tbl/m, 1946 ....**30.00**
RCA #8X72, ivory plastic, slide rule dial, tbl/m, 1949 ....**40.00**
RCA #85E, walnut finish, Deco style, chairside, 1937 ....**120.00**
RCA #9TX, Catalin, dial knob, horizontal louvers, tbl/m, '39 ...**700.00**
RCA Radiola II, mahog, 2 dials, front removes, portable, '23 .....**300.00**
RCA U-119, wood, tall case, push buttons, tbl/m, 1939 ....**40.00**
Regal #575, plastic, slide rule dial, louvers, tbl/m, 1953 ....**45.00**
Roland #5C2, plastic, alarm clock, vertical bars, tbl/m, '53 ....**25.00**
Sentinel #11, walnut, lowboy, 8-sided grill, console, 1930 ....**165.00**
Sentinel Duotrola, wood, phono, 2-pc chairside, 1930 ....**225.00**

Silvertone #3068, wood, slide rule dial, console, 1955 ....**55.00**
Silvertone #6002, medal, 2 knobs, midget tbl/m, 1946 ....**75.00**
Silvertone #9006, plastic, twin speakers, tbl/m, 1959 ....**15.00**
Sonora D-12, wood, slide rule dial, louvers, tbl/m, 1938 ....**60.00**
Sparton #10, Tombstone, wood, half-moon dial, 3 knobs, '31 ....**125.00**
Sparton #557, bl or peach mirror glass w/chrome, tbl/m, '36 ...**2,500.00**
Sterling #5 Concertone, Tombstone, wood, cloth grill, 1931 .....**135.00**
Stewart Warner #91-531, walnut, upright tbl/m, 1938 ....**75.00**
Stewart-Warner #07-5R3, ivory plastic, louvers, tbl/m, 1940 ....**75.00**
Stromberg-Carlson #22, wood, window dial, console, 1931 ....**190.00**
Stromberg-Carlson #230-H, wood, left grill bars, tbl/m, '37 ....**75.00**
Symphony #260, striped grass cloth w/pnt palms, tbl/m, '48 ....**150.00**
Temple G-521, slide rule dial, antenna extends, portable, '47 ......**35.00**
Trav-Ler #550, wood, rnd dial, 3 knobs, tbl/m, 1937 ....**65.00**
Truetone D-2020, plastic, slide rule dial, tbl/m, 1950 ....**40.00**
Truetone D-2963, plastic, slide rule dial, tbl/m, 1949 ....**30.00**
Western Electric #4B, wood w/blk front panel, tbl/m, 1923 ....**450.00**
Westinghouse WR-205, Tombstone, wood, upper grill, 1935 .....**135.00**
Zenith 4-K-402Y, cloth covered, battery, portable, 1940 ....**35.00**
Zenith 5-G-636, wood, boomerang dial, 2 knobs, tbl/m, 1942 ......**75.00**

Novelty

If you would like more information on novelty radios, we recommend *Collector's Guide to Novelty Radios*, by Marty Bunis and Robert F. Breed.

Alligator figural, eyes show settings, GE, Hong Kong, 11½" L **35.00**
Cabbage Patch Kids on yel rectangle, plastic, '81, Hong Kong **15.00**
Cabin cruiser, plastic & metal, Japan, 11½" L **70.00**
Cadillac convertible, plastic, Hong Kong, ca 1963, 10" L **42.50**
Cracker Jack box, Borden, Hong Kong, 1968, 1974, 5" **35.00**
Elephant figural, bl plastic, pk details, Hong Kong, 5¼" **16.00**
Faultless Spray Starch can, Hong Kong, 6½x2⅝" dia **35.00**
Gas pump, blk plastic, 1930s style, Synanon, 9½" **25.00**
He-Man/Skeletor (dbl-faced), plastic, Mattel, 1984, 5x4" **20.00**
High-heeled shoe, plastic, China, Columbia Telecom, 9¾" **30.00**
Jukebox, resembles Wurlitzer #1015, AM/FM, Windsor, 7x4" **30.00**
Mickey Mouse in car, plastic, Hong Kong, 4¼x6¼" **75.00**
Miracle Whip jar, plastic, Hong Kong, 5x3" dia **30.00**
Mork From Ork Eggship, plastic egg form, Hong Kong, 1979 ....**35.00**
My Little Pony on rectangle, plastic, Hasbro, 1983, 5" **20.00**
Owl figural, plastic w/brass-plated trim, Japan, 6½x4" **60.00**
Phonograph, 'Gramy-Phone' on side, lg horn, Japan, 7x6½" **40.00**
Pillsbury Doughboy figural, walkman type, Hong Kong, 6½" **45.00**
Raisin man figural, plastic, CalRab, Applause, 1988, 7" **50.00**
Ray-O-Vac Battery form, Hong Kong, 4¼x2¾" dia **35.00**
Sheep figural, wht plastic w/blk & yel, Hong Kong, 4x6" **16.00**
Snoopy pointing, plastic, red/wht/blk, w/mike, Hong Kong **40.00**
Space capsule, red & blk plastic, Magnavox, Hong Kong, 4" **20.00**
Starroid IR12 (robot form), plastic, Hong Kong, 1977, 8¼" **60.00**
Tennis ball, soft cover, Hyman, Hong Kong, 1987, 4½" **25.00**

Transistor

Post-World War II baby boomers, now approaching their fiftieth year, are rediscovering prized possessions of youth, their pocket radios. The transistor wonders, born with rock 'n roll, were at the vanguard of miniaturization and futuristic design in the decade which followed their introduction to Christmas shoppers in 1954. The tiny receiving sets launched the growth of Texas Instruments and shortly to follow abroad, Sony and other Japanese giants.

The most desirable sets include the 1954 four-transistor Regency TR-1 and colorful early Sony and Toshiba models. Certain pre-1960 models by Hoffman and Admiral represented the earliest practical use of solar technology and are also highly valued. To avoid high tariffs, scores of two-transistor sets, boys' radios, were imported from Japan with names like Pet and Charmy. Many early inexpensive transistor sets could be heard only with an earphone. The smallest sets are known as shirt-pocket models while those slightly larger are called coat pockets. Early collectible transistor radios all have civil defense triangle markings at 640 and 1240 on the frequency dial and nine or fewer transistors. Very few desirable sets were made after 1963. Model numbers are most commonly found inside sets. Our advisor for this category is Mike Brooks; he is listed in the Directory under California and welcomes questions. Please include a SASE.

Admiral #7L12, w/Sun Power Pack	300.00
Automatic TT-600 'Tom Thumb,' 2-tone plastic	125.00
Bulova #742 Super 6	50.00
Champion, 2-transistor, boy's	40.00
Emerson #888 Atlas, w/random-pattern grill	100.00
General Electric P-715-D, leather & metal	45.00
Harpers #2TP-110, earphone only	60.00
Hit Parade, boy's, earphone only	50.00
Hoffman, various sets mk Solar, ea	200.00
Lafayette FS-91, w/fold-out stand	50.00
Magnavox AM-22	40.00
Miniman TK-2, earphone only	65.00
Motorola #8X-26S	30.00
Pet, 2-transistor, boy's	40.00
Raytheon T-100-3, blk & red	175.00
Realistic Hi-Fiver	45.00
Regency TR-1, mandarin red	300.00
Regency TR-1, mottled mahog	500.00
Regency TR-1, 1st transistor, blk	200.00
Regency XR-2A, earphone only	125.00
Roland All Transistor #66	50.00
Sony TR-620	60.00
Standard Micronic Ruby	80.00
Toshiba TR-193, lace-pattern grill	200.00
Yuko, earphone only	50.00
Zenith, Royal #500D, maroon	100.00

Railroadiana

Collecting railroad-related memorabilia has become one of America's most popular hobbies. The range of collectible items available is almost endless, considering the fact that more than 175 different railroad lines are represented. Some collectors prefer to specialize in only one, while others attempt to collect at least one item from every railway line known to have existed. For the advanced collector, there is the challenge of locating rarities from short-lived railroads; for the novice there are abundant keys, buttons, passes, and playing cards. Among the most popular specializations are dining-car collectibles — flatware, glassware, dinnerware, etc., in a wide variety of patterns and styles.

Almost anything from the Rock Island Line has become very collectible, and good lanterns are appreciating on today's market. The Denver & Rio Grande Railroad lantern manufactured by Handlan-Buck, top marked and with a red cast (embossed) melon globe now commands about $1,400.00. Lantern prices are based on the scarcity of the railroad, the color and shape of the globe, and whether the railroad name is embossed rather than being simply acid etched. Note: Two-color lantern globes are now being reproduced.

For a more thorough study, we recommend *Railroad Collectibles, Third Revised Edition*, by Stanley L. Baker, available at your local library or bookstore. Because prices are so volatile, the best pricing sources are often monthly or quarterly 'For Sale' lists. Two you may find helpful may be ordered from Golden Spike, P.O. Box 422, Williamsville, NY 14221, and Grandpa's Depot and Caboose, P.O. Box 480030, Denver, CO 80248-0030. Our advice for the dinnerware section comes from Shrader's Antiques (see Directory, California), while Grandpa's Depot (see Colorado) advises us for the remainder.

Key:
BL — bottom logo	SL — side logo
BS — bottom stamped	SM — side marked
NBS — no bottom stamp	TL — top logo
R&B — Reed and Barton	TM — top marked

Dinnerware

Ashtray, SP, cobalt w/logo, NBS	125.00
Bowl, baker; WP, Feather River, NBS, 5½" dia	155.00
Bowl, berry; ATSF, California Poppy, NBS	35.00
Bowl, berry; B&O, Capitol, NBS, 5¼"	45.00
Bowl, berry; CMStP&P, Peacock, NBS, 5"	32.00
Bowl, berry; CMStP&P, Traveler, NBS, 5"	30.00
Bowl, berry; GN, Oriental, NBS, 5¼"	50.00
Bowl, berry; N&W, Dogwood, NBS, 5"	25.00
Bowl, berry; Southern, Peach Blossom, NBS, 5¼"	125.00
Bowl, bouillon; B&O, Centenary, BS	75.00
Bowl, Bouillon; C&O, George Washington, BS	175.00
Bowl, bouillon; CMStP&P, Traveler, w/lid, NBS	85.00
Bowl, cereal; B&O, Capitol, NBS, 6½"	55.00
Bowl, cereal; CMStP&P, Traveler, BS, 6½"	85.00
Bowl, cereal; GN, Glacier, BS, 6¼"	110.00
Bowl, cereal; PRR, Keystone, NBS, 6½"	65.00
Bowl, cereal; UP, Circus, NBS, 6"	245.00
Bowl, rimmed soup; B&O, Centenary, BS, 9"	165.00
Bowl, rimmed soup; CMStP&P, Peacock, NBS, 9"	55.00
Bowl, rimmed soup; CN, Queen Elizabeth, NBS, 9¼"	55.00
Bowl, rimmed soup; PRR, Liberty, BS, 9¼"	125.00
Bowl, rimmed soup; SP, Sunset, BS, 9½"	175.00
Bowl, rimmed soup; UP, Cheyenne, BS, 9"	135.00
Bowl, salad; MStP&SStM, Logan, BS, 8½"	110.00
Bowl, vegetable; B&O, Capitol, BS, 6x5"	85.00
Bowl, vegetable; CMStP&P, Galatea, BS, 6x5"	85.00
Bowl, vegetable; CRI&P, Golden State, BS, 6½x5"	77.00
Bowl, vegetable; N&W, Cavalier, NBS, 5½x4½"	35.00
Butter pat, A&WP, Montgomery, NBS	35.00
Butter pat, ATSF, Bleeding Blue, NBS	195.00
Butter pat, ATSF, California Poppy, NBS	35.00
Butter pat, B&O, Centenary, BS	65.00
Butter pat, CMStP&P, Traveler, NBS	75.00
Butter pat, CRI&P, Golden State, NBS	100.00
Butter pat, D&RGW, Blue Adam, NBS	25.00
Butter pat, KCS, Roxbury, NBS	25.00
Butter pat, L&N, Green Leaf, NBS	45.00
Butter pat, MKT, Katy Ornaments, NBS	35.00
Butter pat, NYC, Commodore, BS	65.00
Butter pat, P&LE, Monogram, NBS	300.00
Butter pat, PRR, Liberty, NBS	110.00
Butter pat, Pullman, NBS	135.00
Butter pat, SP, Harriman Blue Hospital, NBS	185.00
Butter pat, UP, Harriman Blue, NBS	28.00
Butter pat, UP, Winged Streamliner, NBS	35.00
Chocolate pot, ATSF, Mimbreno, BS	250.00
Chocolate pot, CP, Bows & Leaves, BS	125.00
Compote, SP, Hotel Del Monte, BS	200.00
Creamer, ACL, Flora of the South, BS, 3½"	195.00

Creamer, B&O, Centenary, BS 195.00
Creamer, B&O, Centenary, Shenango, 4" 55.00
Creamer, C&O, Charlottesville, 3¼" 110.00
Creamer, CMStP&P, Galatea, 3¼" 85.00
Creamer, CP, Halifax, 3" 35.00
Creamer, CRI&P, Golden State, no hdl 85.00
Creamer, DRGW, Blue Adam, no hdl 35.00
Creamer, GN, Empire, no hdl 55.00
Creamer, N&W, Dogwood, 3" 35.00
Creamer, SP, Sunset, no hdl 110.00
Creamer, UP, Harriman Blue, no hdl 55.00
Cup, bouillon; SP, Prairie Mtn Wildflowers 150.00
Cup & saucer, ATSF, Adobe, BS 140.00
Cup & saucer, ATSF, Black Chain 35.00
Cup & saucer, B&O, Capitol 195.00
Cup & saucer, CB&Q, Chuck Wagon 165.00
Cup & saucer, CMStP&P, Traveler 135.00
Cup & saucer, CP, Tremblant 65.00
Cup & saucer, D&RGW, Prospector 185.00
Cup & saucer, demitasse; ATSF, Mimbreno, BS 385.00
Cup & saucer, demitasse; B&A, Aroostook 55.00
Cup & saucer, demitasse; C&O, George Washington 210.00
Cup & saucer, demitasse; FH, Webster 85.00
Cup & saucer, demitasse; GN, Glory of the West 145.00
Cup & saucer, demitasse; SP, Prairie Mtn Wildflowers 175.00
Cup & saucer, FH, Southwest, BS 195.00
Cup & saucer, GM&O, Rose 255.00
Cup & saucer, L&N, Green Leaf 135.00
Cup & saucer, NYC, DeWitt Clinton 95.00
Cup & saucer, SP, Prairie Mtn Wildflowers 85.00
Cup & saucer, UP, Challenger, BS 55.00
Cup & saucer, UP, Winged Streamliner, NBS 55.00
Egg cup, CMStP&P, Peacock, NBS 85.00
Egg cup, dbl; CMStP&P, Traveler, NBS 62.00
Egg cup, SP, Prairie Mtn Wildflowers, NBS 110.00
Egg cup, UP, Desert Flower, BS 60.00
Egg cup, UP, Portland, Rose, NBS 285.00
Egg cup, UP, Winged Streamliner, NBS 45.00
Gravy boat, ATSF, California Poppy, BS 165.00
Gravy boat, C&O, George Washington, NBS 85.00
Gravy boat, CP Foliage, BS 75.00
Gravy boat, D&RGW, Exposition, NBS 55.00
Gravy boat, DL&W, St Albans, NBS 65.00
Gravy boat, PRR, Purple Laurel, NBS 75.00
Gravy boat, Pullman, Indian Tree, SL 145.00
Gravy boat, UP, Desert Flower, BS 95.00
Hot food cover, WP, Feather River, SL 235.00
Ice cream shell, ATSF, California Poppy, NBS 79.00
Ice cream shell, CMStP&P, Galatea, NBS 135.00
Ice cream shell, NP, Garnet, BS 225.00
Matchbox holder/ashtray, CN, Green-Gold, SL 95.00
Matchbox holder/ashtray, N&W, Dogwood, NBS 75.00
Mustard pot, ATSF, Mimbreno, w/lid, BS, 3" 195.00
Mustard pot, N&W, Coach & Four, w/lid, NBS, 3" 150.00
Mustard pot, UP, Harriman Blue, no lid, NBS, 2¾" 35.00
Pitcher, ATSF, Bleeding Blue, SL, 6" 400.00
Pitcher, B&O, Centenary, BS, 5" 195.00
Pitcher, CRI&P, Sage Green, inside logo, 4½" 225.00
Plate, Alaska, McKinley, NBS, 5½" 295.00
Plate, Amtrak, National, NBS, 6½" 25.00
Plate, ATSF, Adobe, TL, 9½" 85.00
Plate, ATSF, California Poppy, NBS, 9½" 85.00
Plate, ATSF, Mimbreno, BS, 9½" 125.00
Plate, B&O, Centenary, BS, 8½" 110.00

Plate, B&O Railroad, Lamberton China, 10¼",
$290.00; Cup and saucer, B&O Railroad, The Philip
E. Thomas 1838, $150.00.

Plate, Boston & Albany, Berkshire, NBS, 9" 275.00
Plate, C&O, Chessie, NBS, 9½" 235.00
Plate, C&O, George Washington, BS, 8" 75.00
Plate, CMStP&P, Traveler, NBS, 9½" 165.00
Plate, CN, Continental, BS, 9" 35.00
Plate, CN, Ottawa, BS, 7½" 55.00
Plate, CP, Empress, NBS, 9¼" 110.00
Plate, CRI&P, Empress, NBS, 9¼" 110.00
Plate, CRI&P, Golden State, NBS, 9½" 175.00
Plate, CRI&P, LaSalle, BS, 9½" 145.00
Plate, D&H, Canterbury, NBS, no TL, 9" 125.00
Plate, DRGW, Prospector, NBS, 9½" 110.00
Plate, Erie, Susquehanna, BS, 8" 150.00
Plate, FEC, Carolina, BS, 7½" 65.00
Plate, GM&O, Rose, NBS, 6" 125.00
Plate, GN, Mtns & Flowers, BS, 9½" 195.00
Plate, GN, Oriental, BS, 6" 85.00
Plate, KCS, Roxbury, NBS, 9" 45.00
Plate, L&N, Green Leaf, NBS, 9½" 45.00
Plate, MKT, Alamo, cobalt border, BS, 10½" 475.00
Plate, MP, St Albans, NBS, 9" 75.00
Plate, N&W, Coach & Four, NBS, 9" 95.00
Plate, N&W, Dogwood, legend on reverse, BS, 10½" ...145.00
Plate, N&W, Yellowbird, NBS, 5½" 60.00
Plate, NP, Yellowstone, NBS, 7½" 95.00
Plate, NYC, DeWitt Clinton, BS, 9½" 75.00
Plate, NYC, Mercury, BS, 9" 75.00
Plate, PRR, Broadway, BS, 9" 75.00
Plate, Pullman, Indian Tree, TL, NBS, 7" 50.00
Plate, service; C&O, George Washington, BS, 10½" ...525.00
Plate, SP, Imperial, BS, 8" 125.00
Plate, SP, Prairie Mtn Wildflowers, BS, 9½" 75.00
Plate, SP, Sunset, BS, 9½" 210.00
Plate, SPS, American, NBS, 9" 85.00
Plate, UP, Circus, NBS, 9½" 265.00
Plate, UP, Historical, NBS, 7½" 165.00
Plate, UP, Winged Streamliner, NBS, 6½" 35.00
Plate, UP, Zion, NBS, 9½" 195.00
Plate, Wabash, Banner, NBS, 9½" 210.00
Plate, WP, Feather River, NBS, 7" 75.00
Platter, ACL, Flora of the South, BS, 11½x7½" 225.00
Platter, ATSF, Mimbreno, BS, 9½x6" 225.00
Platter, CB&Q, Violets & Daisies, NBS, 7½x5" 45.00
Platter, Erie, Gould, bow shape, NBS, 9x6" 75.00
Platter, NP, Monad, NBS, 8½x7" 85.00

Platter, NYC, Hyde Park, bow shape, BS, 11½x7½" 110.00
Platter, SP, Sunset, BS, 9x6" 125.00
Platter, T&P, Eagle, BS, 12½x9" 125.00
Platter, UP, Challenger, NBS, 10x8" 65.00
Relish, ACL, Flora of the South, BS, 10x5" 185.00
Relish, ATSF, Mimbreno, BS, 10½x4" 210.00
Relish, B&O, Capitol, TL, 11½x6" 155.00
Relish, MP, Bismark, NBS, 10x5" 225.00
Relish, N&W, Yellowbird, NBS, 7½x4" 75.00
Sherbet, ATSF, Mimbreno, ped ft, BS 75.00
Sugar bowl, C&O, Greenbrier, w/lid, NBS 55.00
Teapot, CP, Verde Green, SL, NBS 195.00
Teapot, Pullman, Verde Green, SL, NBS 225.00

Glassware

Ashtray, McCloud RR, red logo, 3½" dia 17.50
Ashtray, N&W, gr w/red logo, 4¼" dia 15.00
Ashtray, NP, red Yellowstone Park logo, 4" dia 12.50
Champagne, AT&SF, cut banner w/Santa Fe, 3½" 150.00
Cordial, AT&SF, script logo 25.00
Cruet, SP, Daylight w/ball & wing logo 180.00
Martini set, UP, frosted logo, mixer+2 roly polys+stirrer 50.00
Shot glass, D&H in shield, 2¾" 20.00
Shot glass, UP, frosted logo 15.00
Shot glass, UP, modern shield, frosted, 1½-oz, NM 10.00
Tumbler, Burlington Rte, 4½" 12.00
Tumbler, C&O, bl Chessie cat logo, 4½" 10.00
Tumbler, juice; NYC, wht enameling, 3" 30.00
Tumbler, MP, eagle logo, 4¼" 8.00
Tumbler, Santa Fe, bl cross logo, 4½" 10.00
Wine, CN, etched logo, 4½" 38.00
Wine, IC, dmn logo, stemmed 20.00

Lamps

Berth, Pullman, steel/porc, egg shape, NM, pr 48.00
Caboose, Adlake, sq top, oil, 1 red/3 amber lenses, EX 140.00
Caboose bunk, UP, steel/brass, pebbled top globe 42.50
Marker, NYCS, Adlake, sq top, oil, complete, NM, pr 200.00
Semaphore, UP, Adlake, electric, dbl bull's-eye lens, NM 90.00
Switch, Adlake, red/wht lenses, unissued, M 150.00
Switch, PRR, Adlake, SM PRR Keystone, 1909, EX 165.00

Lanterns

Before 1920 kerosene brakemen's lanterns were made with tall globes, usually 5⅜" tall. These are the most desirable and are usually found at the top of the price scale. Short globes from 1921 through 1940 normally measure 3½" in height, except for those manufactured by Dietz, which are 4" tall. (Soon thereafter, battery brakemen's lanterns came into widespread useage; these are not popular with collectors and are generally not railroad marked.)

All should be marked with the name or initials of the railroad. Look on the top, the top apron, or the bell base (if it has one). Globes may be found in these colors (listed in order of popularity): clear, red, amber, aqua, cobalt, and two-color.

C&A, bell bottom, tall cast globe 65.00
C&O, Adlake Kero, clear etched globe w/Erie dmn, no font, G ...65.00
C&O, bell bottom, short cast globe 30.00
Conductor's, P Gray & Sons, brass, gr-over-clear globe, EX 500.00
Conductor's, Pullman style, Adams & Westlake, unmk globe, G .300.00
CTA, Adlake Kero, red unmk globe, dtd 2-27, EX 50.00

D&RG, Handlan, TM on apron, tall clear globe, G 300.00
D&SL, Adlake Reliable, TM, Pat 1923, EX 500.00
Dietz #6, B&A, bell bottom, tall clear cast globe 175.00
DNW&P, clear tall mk globe, brass burner, Pat 1909, EX 750.00
Dominion Tubular Lamp Works, Grand Trunk, clear cast globe ..325.00
K&ITRR, bell bottom, tall cast globe 80.00
L&N, Armspear, tall clear mk globe, dtd 1895, TM, complete ...165.00
MC, Armspear, clear mk globe, Pat 1889, VG 145.00
MOPAC, Handlan, TM on apron, short red mk globe, complete, G ...65.00
NYCS, Handlan, TM on apron, short red etched globe, G 60.00
PC&S, bell bottom, brass top 900.00
Pere Marquette, Adlake Reliable, tall clear mk globe, M 195.00
PRR, bell bottom, brass top 700.00
PRR, bell bottom, tin top 130.00
Reliable, Erie RR, tall red mk globe 150.00
Reliable, Santa Fe, slick top, tall clear cast logo globe 160.00
T&P, Adlake Kero, short red etched globe, TM, complete, G 85.00
TTRR, Adlake 1923 Reliable, tall red mk globe, single guard 150.00
WT Co, Casey, unmk globe 100.00

Linens

Apron, Amtrak cook's, string ties, 31x34" 15.00
Blanket, BR, lt bl, lap sz 45.00
Blanket, Burlington Northern, mottled brn, full sz 50.00
Blanket, Empire builder, orange on gr, lg 275.00
Blanket, NP, lt tan w/brn letters, North Star wool, EX 165.00
Blanket, Pullman, cinnamon color, EX 80.00
Blanket, UP, blk letters on gray, NM 85.00
Headrest cover, SR, brn w/gr circle logo, button-down 17.50
Headrest cover, UP, yel w/red Streamliner logo, button-down 20.00
Napkin, Amtrak, royal bl, stamped letters, 18x10" 4.00
Napkin, GN, wht-on-wht leaf design, gr script, 20x20" 10.00
Napkin, Rio Grande, wht embr on plum, 18" sq 10.00
Napkin, Rock Island, floral design on ecru, 18" sq 7.00
Napkin, Santa Fe, wht-on-wht leaf motif, 18x20" 12.50
Napkins, C&O, bl sewn-in letters on wht, 18" 7.00
Pillowcase, CA Zephyr, stamped logo, regular sz, EX 6.50
Sheet, Pullman, stamped logo, dtd 1924, twin sz, EX 14.00
Sheet, Rio Grande, wht, sewn-in speed letters in orange 12.00
Tablecloth, CA Zephyr, wht-on-wht logo, 46" 10.00
Tablecloth, CN, maple leaf logo, 44x48", EX 12.00
Tablecloth, Rio Grande, speed letters, 45", G 15.00
Tablecloth, Rock Island, wht-on-wht floral, 43x58" 30.00
Towel, BN, sewn-on gr letters, 20x22", M 8.50
Towel, CA Zephyr, wht w/red woven stripe, 16x22" 7.50
Towel, GN, wht-on-wht Puritan Dundee, red stripe, VG 12.00
Towel, Pullman, wht w/bl stripe, 16x22" 10.00
Towel, SF, red stripes, cross logo, 14x22", VG 4.50
Towel, UP, orange stripe on wht, EX 10.00

Locks

Brass switch locks (pre-1920) were made in two styles: heart-shaped and Keen Kutter style. Values for the heart-shaped locks are determined to a great extent by the railroad represented and just how its name appears on the lock. Most in demand are those with large embossed letters; if the letters are small and incised, demand is minimal. For instance, one from the Union Pacific line (even with heavy embossed letters) may go for only $45.00, while the same from the D&RG railroad could go easily sell for $250.00. Old Keen Kutter styles (brass with a 'pointy' base) from Colorado & Southern and Denver & Rio Grande could range from $600.00 to $1,200.00.

Steel switch locks (circa 1920 on) with the initials of the railroad incised in small letters — for example BN, L&H, and PRR — are usually valued at $12.00 to $15.00.

DL&W, brass, heart shape, 1955 on reverse, w/chain, G **30.00**
Road & bridge, UP, brass, Adlake on drop, heart shape **40.00**
Service, D&RG, brass, heart shape, switch sz, Fraim, 1908 ....**150.00**
Signal, D&RG, brass, 6-lever, pancake style **40.00**
Signal, DL&W, brass, emb on drop: Remove Key When Locking, G .**40.00**
Switch, B&O, brass, heart shape, F&S Hdw, w/chain **90.00**
Switch, D&RG, brass, heart shape, G drop, complete w/chain ..**600.00**
Switch, D&RG, brass, Keen-Kutter style, emb letters ea side **450.00**
Switch, DL&W, pressed brass, ET Fraim **25.00**
Switch, IOC, Slaymaker, brass, heart shape, no chain, EX **55.00**
Switch, JL Howard, Maine Central, brass, heart shape **125.00**
Switch, Long Island, steel, Adlake, lg head & bbl, w/chain **35.00**
Switch, UP, Adlake on drop, brass, heart shape, w/chain **35.00**
Switch, VGN, Yale, heart shape, steel hasp dtd 1903, EX **110.00**

Silverplate

The value of a hollowware item is affected by where the logo and/or railroad name was stamped; a side-marked piece is much preferred to one with the mark on the bottom. Note: Some railroad silver from early private cars has recently surfaced. Marks such as Denver & Salt Lake car 101 (called the 'Pheasant') and FECRy's 'Alicia' (Henry Flagler's car) are good examples and might today be considered 'museum quality' by railroadiana buffs.

Butter pat, NYC, BS, Reed & Barton **15.00**
Coffeepot, Burlington Rte, SM, Reed & Barton, 1-pt **95.00**
Creamer, D&RG, pagoda finial, Reed & Barton, 8-oz **175.00**
Creamer, NHNH&HR, BS, Reed & Barton, 8-oz **45.00**
Crumber, GN, Hutton, TM **85.00**
Crumber, SR, Pattern #172, Reed & Barton **85.00**
Crumber, UP, Westfield, TM, lt wear **75.00**
Finger bowl, CA Zephyr, Deco style, BS, 1952 ....**75.00**
Finger bowl, GN, Deco style, pierced sides, BS, 1949 ....**35.00**
Fork, cocktail; SP, Broadway, BS, Daylight logo **25.00**
Fork, dinner; ACL, Zephyr **10.00**
Fork, dinner; ATSF, TM, Made in Taiwan **5.00**
Fork, dinner; C&NW, Windsor, TM, lt wear **15.00**
Fork, ice ceam; CCC&ST, Commonwealth, TM, Reed & Barton .**20.00**
Fork, place; NYC, Century, BM **10.00**
Fork, place; SCL, Zephyr, TM **10.00**
Gravy boat, UP, dtd 1954, 4-oz **65.00**
Ice tongs, D&RG, Belmont, TM, Reed & Barton, 7½" **275.00**
Ice tongs, SF, Albany, 7½" **150.00**
Knife, butter; ACL, Zephyr, TM **12.00**
Knife, dinner; SR, Century, SM **12.00**
Knife, fish; Pullman, Roosevelt **15.00**
Knife, steak; Fred Harvey, Albany **18.00**
Ladle, soup; D&RG, Belmont, TM, Reed & Barton, 7½" **225.00**
Menu holder, GN, pierced sides, Deco style, G **85.00**
Plate, steak; MoPac, BS, 10", w/lid **250.00**
Spoon, demitasse; Burlington Rte, Belmont, BS **25.00**
Spoon, iced tea; B&O, Cromwell **7.00**
Spoon, iced tea; Burlington Rte, Belmont, BS, Reed & Barton **18.00**
Spoon, iced tea; NYC, Century, BM **10.00**
Spoon, iced tea; Pullman, Roosevelt, BS, Internat'l **20.00**
Spoon, iced tea; SP, Broadway, BS **25.00**
Spoon, iced tea; SR, Century **12.00**
Spoon, place; ACL, Zephyr, TM **10.00**
Spoon, place; CCC&ST, Alden, TM, Reed & Barton **20.00**
Spoon, place; Fred Harvey, Albany **18.00**

Spoon, place; Fred Harvey, Cromwell, TM **18.00**
Spoon, place; Seaboard, Century, BM **10.00**
Spoon, place; SR, Century, BM **12.00**
Spoon, serving; B&O, Cromwell, TM **7.00**
Spoon, serving; Fred Harvey, Albany **18.00**
Spoon, serving; Pullman, Roosevelt **15.00**
Spoon, soup; PARR, Broadway **10.00**
Spoon, souvenir; NP, NP Depot Bismark ND in bowl, 5" **40.00**
Sugar bowl, NP, BS, Reed & Barton, 12-oz **45.00**
Sugar bowl, NYNH&HR, BS, Reed & Barton **45.00**
Sugar tongs, C&NW, Broadway, fancy cup ends, TM **65.00**
Sugar tongs, Rock Island, TM, Internat'l **75.00**
Sugar tongs, UP, Sierra, claw ft, TM, Reed & Barton **50.00**
Teaspoon, Fred Harvey, Albany, BS, MIE **18.00**
Tray, GN, well for lid inset, TM, BS, 1948-51, 6¾x5¼" **35.00**
Tureen, D&RG, pagoda finial, Reed & Barton, 1-pt, +tray **295.00**

Miscellaneous

Switch keys are brass with a hollow barrel and a round head with a hole in the center. The initials or the name of the railroad company that used it are incised on the head. Examples representing common railroads are valued at $15.00 and up, while those from the Colorado & Southern Ry are now selling for $65.00, as are some of the early predecessors.

Annual passes are skyrocketing in popularity (as opposed to trip or one-time passes, which are not very desirable in the field of pass collecting). Their values are contingent upon the specific railroad, its length of run (whether it was a short one or a major line), and their appearance. Many were tiny works of art lettered with fancy calligraphy and decorated with vignettes.

Timetables are climbing rapidly in popularity, and pins with the names of railroad companies are very good right now. On the other hand, 'Brotherhood' pins (or any item) hold little interest for collectors. Watch for reproductions signs; most are small in size, about 5" x 12", on aged cardboard under glass in black frames. These will read 'Public Telephone,' 'Waiting Room,' etc.

Ashtray, Pullman, emb logo on tin, 4" dia **6.50**

Badge, Berkshire Street Railway 25, blue enameling on nickel silver, $65.00.

Badge, Dallas Ry & Terminal Company operator **35.00**
Badge, FJ&G Motorman, brass, peaked top, EX patina, scarce ...**110.00**
Badge, hat; D&RG Conductor, silver w/blk emb letters, M **85.00**
Badge, hat; Pullman Sleeping Car Porter, blk on silver **50.00**
Badge, hat; Santa Fe Porter, bl logo on silver, VG **65.00**
Badge, Lackawanna RR Collector emb on gold, lt wear **85.00**
Badge, Long Island Asst Conductor, bl logo, M **40.00**
Badge, Pullman, Maltese cross shape, M **225.00**
Badge, Rock Island Conductor, brass, EX patina **95.00**
Book, Hear the Train Blow, Beebe & Cleg, 1952, w/dust jacket ...**40.00**
Book, register; C&NW freight Conductor, 1906, EX **5.50**
Booklet, C&NW, Summer Tours, canyon cover, 1941, 7x10" **10.00**
Booklet, SP, Inside Track, 1914 ....**50.00**
Box, cigar; PRR, wood, streamliner on curve, 2x9¼x6", EX **25.00**

Box, flare; red pnt metal, complete w/red signal flag & hdl 15.00
Box, ticket; Pullman, golden oak, brass knob, 9½x7½x12" 75.00
Broadside, Norris Locomotive Works, ca 1831, 17x13", VG 300.00
Brochure, Cripple Creek, color, timetable sz 10.00
Brochure, D&H, Lake George, Girl on Palisades cover, 1910 ....8.00
Brochure, Pullman, Folding Bed, interior views, 1931, 12" 10.00
Builder's plate, Pullman, emb brass, 1½x18" 60.00
Calendar, perpetual, MoPac, diesel engine pictured, M 165.00

Calendar, Rock Island Route, cardstock, partial pad, 22x14", 1889, $135.00.

Chair, folding; Pullman, conductor's, ca 1895 ....100.00
Clothes brush, Pullman, porter's, maple hdl, EX 25.00
Coat, CA Zephyr steward, Meier, bl w/embr logo, lg 50.00
Coat, MKT conductor's, 3 gold 'Katy' coat buttons, VG 40.00
Cuff protector, B&O, Chessie System, Safety First, pr 6.50
Gauge, NY Air Brake Co, red hand 95.00
Gauge, Westinghouse, brass, red & blk hand, 3x6" dia 95.00
Grenade, B&O Fire Extinguisher, Star in emb star, yel-gr, 8" 425.00
Hat, Amtrak Conductor, gold badge & buttons, modern style 60.00
Hat, Reading Lines & dmn logo, summer wicker, blk visor 65.00
Key, berth; cross shape w/T hdl in center, 6" 45.00
Key, berth; T-shaped, lg, scarce 40.00
Key, caboose; ACL, Adlake, long solid bbl, EX 20.00
Key, switch; NYCS, Adlake 22.50
Key, switch; UP, JHW Climax Co, Newark NJ 28.00
Ladder, upper berth; Pullman, oak, metal ft, 6½x22" 95.00
Magazine, Kansas City Southern Current Events, Jan 1914 ....12.00
Map, WP System, San Jose to Pit River, 9x15", EX 5.00
Pass, annual; ATSF, Western Lines, hard stock, 1910, G 10.00
Pass, annual; Brotherhood of...Firemen & Enginemen, 1907 ....2.50
Pass, annual; C&NW, issued to dining car inspector, 1945 ....42.50
Pass, annual; Fred Harvey, hard stock, 1920, EX 15.00
Pass, annual; GN, lt bl, 1942 ....4.50
Pass, annual; NYC&StL, 1957-58 ....7.00
Pass, annual; NYCS, center logo, 1934, VG 5.00
Pass, annual; Wabash, bl flag logo, 1926, EX 7.50
Pass, SP, sunset logo, 1948-49 ....7.00
Pay stub, D&RG Western, 1940 ....4.00
Photo, Burlington Rte, Zephyr winding through mtnside, 9x12" 4.00
Pin, lapel; Burlington Rte Veterans Assoc, ½" dia 15.00
Pin, lapel; Pullman, 25 Years of Service, ½x¾" 35.00
Playing cards, PC, logo, dbl deck, EX in box 15.00
Playing cards, UP, shield in right corner, single deck, EX 15.00
Postcard, D&RG, In the Clouds, folding, postmk 1916, EX 15.00
Sign, American Express Co, enameled, 13x17", VG 175.00
Sign, Canadian Pacific Express, tin, 13x20", G 350.00

Sign, Coach Snack Bar, dbl sided, 10" sq, sticks to window, M 5.00
Sign, No Smoking Permitted..., steel, red & blk pnt, 6x9", EX 10.00
Sign, NY Subway, sheet metal, 14 brass grommets, 19x44" 195.00
Sign, Reserved for Train Crew, cb, dk bl on wht, 8x12", VG 5.00
Sign, Ry Express, tin, locomotive & truck, 13x19", G 300.00
Sign, Shenandoah Valley, rvpt on glass, 21x28"+fr, G 1,150.00
Sign, Soo Line, metal, emb wht letters on blk, 4x22", NM 85.00
Stamper, Government Freight US 12.00
Sticker, baggage; Burlingon Rte, silver & bl Zephyr, 1940 ....4.50
Stool, MP, silver pnt, Morton nameplate, older sz: 9½x14" 195.00
Stove, caboose; PRR, EX 150.00
Timetable, Boston & Maine, blk & wht, 1920, 3x5" 15.00
Timetable, Burlington, red w/blk, 1914, VG 17.50
Timetable, C&NW, shows passenger terminal, 1914 ....15.00
Timetable, CCC&ST, Suburban, 1895, 2½x6" 15.00
Timetable, CM&STP, New Olympian, 1920 ....20.00
Timetable, D&RG, red, Moffat Tunnel bk cover, 1930, EX 10.00
Timetable, GN, yel cover, lists stations/etc, 1893, 70-pg 100.00
Timetable, IL Central, 1910, VG 5.00
Timetable, Lehigh Valley, red flag logo, lg map, 1898, EX 100.00
Timetable, ME Central, brn cover, 1881, EX 25.00
Timetable, MKT, bl cover w/red logo, 1899, EX 55.00
Timetable, MoPac, yel cover, 1891, EX 25.00
Timetable, NYC, West Shore RR, red/wht/blk, 1914, EX 30.00
Timetable, NYNH&H, blk & wht, 1894 Local, G 15.00
Timetable, OR Short Line, blk & wht, 1919, EX 18.00
Timetable, PA RR, blk & wht, Service to South, 1947, EX 7.50
Timetable, Soo Line, blk & wht, 1920, EX 17.50
Timetable, UP, red cover, 1910, VG 15.00
Timetable/brochure, CD&MRy, full-page system map, 1936, 9x12" .20.00
Timetable/brochure, GN, 2-pg, 1902 ....15.00
Uniform, IL Central waiter's, wht w/orange piping, EX 35.00
Waybill, CP, filled out for extra baggage, 1879 ....35.00
Wrench, monkey; GN, metal, Trimo, 11" 20.00

Razors

As straight razors gain in popularity, prices increase. And with the lure of investment appreciation, the novice or the speculator sometimes find themselves making purchases that later prove to be unwise. It is important to be able to recognize the material of which the handle is made. This has a great bearing on value, and imitations abound. Learn to distinguish between celluloid and genuine ivory. Razors with plain celluloid handles are practically worthless unless the blade carries a desirable trademark. Those with decorations of scrollwork, leaves and vines, or decorative metal on each end fall into the $8.00 to $12.00 price range. Even plain ivory-handled razors are not especially valuable unless the blade is well marked and from a good manufacturer. On a more positive note, celluloid-handled razors with designs such as castles, windmills, nudes, deer, alligators, automobiles, horses, cowboys, peacocks, and various kinds of birds, etc., are very desirable (some more than others) and are usually worth from $25.00 to $50.00 to collectors. Those with a figural handle such as a fish, shotgun, eagle, or a barber pole might be worth in excess of $100.00 for an especially nice example. Ivory, on the other hand, is rarely found; if the carvings are well done, clean, undamaged specimens should start at about $100.00 and escalate according to the intricacy of the design.

Buffalo horn is sometimes mistakenly called bone. It is usually black, translucent tan, or gray. Though plain handles are worth very little, the early heat-molded examples with a motif such as mentioned above often sell for more than $100.00. In the same range are mother-of-pearl and stag (deer horn) handles; very elaborate designs go even higher, but watch for imitations.

There is one imitation, however, that is highly desirable. That is jigged bone made to look like stag. This material is rough textured and dyed a handsome tan or brown; usually examples with these handles sell in the $40.00 to $75.00 range. Razors with wooden handles are very rare, but even those from the 1800s are worth only about $35.00, since they are usually very plain. 20th-century examples are only valued at around $15.00. Don't be fooled by buffalo horn colored in imitation of tortoise — and you'll find celluloid imitations, too. Genuine tortoise handles are worth from $25.00 to $100.00 depending on age, condition, and workmanship. Sterling razors are valued at $75.00 and up, but make sure they are marked 'sterling.' Even if you were to mistake aluminum for silver, those with relief-cast designs are worth $50.00 to $75.00, but only $20.00 or so if the design is incised.

Corn razors were made to pare troublesome corns on the feet. They are a bit smaller and if plain worth a little more than plain full-size razors. Fancy examples are generally not worth as much as their full-size couterparts.

The older blades are wedge-shaped (flat-sided) in cross-section; hollow-ground blades (made after 1880) are concave. Generally speaking, those etched with words are only worth a little more than a plain, common blade. Try to find those with people, places, and things — the more famous, the better.

Key:
cell — celluloid   gw — gold washed
bd — blade

Benito, faux ivory hdl: Mussolini bust inlay, EX 42.50
Case Bros, candy-stripe hdl, sq point, Tested XX, EX 230.00
Case Bros, slick blk hdl, hollow point, Tested XX, EX 170.00
Case Bros, tortoise bamboo hdl, sq point, EX 160.00
Case MFG CO, inlaid blk hdl & tang, sq point, EX 275.00
Cattaraugus Cutlery Co, bl hdl, wht liners, sq point, EX 30.00
Clements, Sheffield, hollow-ground bd, ivory hdl 45.00
Crawick, Picadilly, ivory hdl, hollow-ground bd 95.00
Curtain & Clark Cutlery, gr-yel hdl, owl & scroll, EX 45.00
Curvfit the Woman's Razor, gold plate, Pat 1945, NMIB 15.00
Diamondine Germany, blk cell hdl, stamped horse/fish logo, VG ...12.00
Durham Duplex, ivory cell hdl, May 28, 1907, EX 5.00
Durham Omino, ivory cell hdl, May 28, 1907, VG 9.00

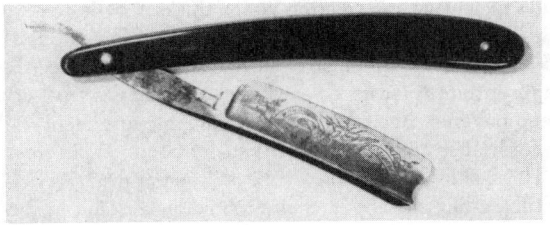

Early black plastic handle, blade etched E Pluribus Unum with eagle, John Smith, Sheffield, England, $35.00.

Ern, etched bd: Mignon, MOP hdl w/11 panels ea side, EX 200.00
Eversharp Schick Injector, gold plated, wht & tan hdl, 4½", EV ..12.50
Eversharp Schick Injector, wht hdl, 4⅞", NM in case 80.00
Garfield memorium & death dates etch on bd, 6", EX 150.00
Gem, gold plated w/wht hdl, 1940s, 5⅛", EX in plastic case 10.00
Genco Heavy Geneva, NY USA, blk hard rubber hdl, VG 11.00
Geneva Cutlery Co Geneva NY, red & pk Bakelite hdl, EX 12.00
Geo Fleissner...NY, spotted horn hdl, EX 20.00
Gillette Big Fellow, EX lg, NM in dvtl box 50.00

Gillette Bl Band, bl w/blk letters, 1930s, VG 10.00
John D Case, hollow point, gr pearl hdl, travel sz, EX 400.00
John D Case, Ringleader, br & red mottled hdl, EX 150.00
Joseph Elliot Fine Indian Steel, wedge bd, blk horn hdl 40.00
Kane Cutlery, red transparent hdl, hollow point, EX 40.00
Kinfolks Bl Steel Special, mk wht hdl, NM 35.00
King...Indiana PA, striped hdl w/silver caps, EX 40.00
Laurel, vest pocket, complete in tin box 20.00
Liliput, corn razor, MIB 20.00
Mooney & Moyer, blk hard rubber hdl: lady w/flowing hair 35.00
Oxford, etched bd, faux ivory hdl: windmill scene, EX colors 65.00
Pep, faux tortoise shell hdl, MOP escutcheon & brass trim 65.00
Red Point, Utica Knife & Razor Co, rubber inlaid hdl, VG 12.00
Robeson Premier, yel mottled cell hdl, EX 40.00
Robeson Shuredge, hollow-ground bd, blk cell hdl 36.00
Sha-Ve-Zee, Pat 1918, EX, +box of blades 15.00
Shumate, faux jigged bone hdl, EX 42.00
Simplex Military, 4⅛", NMIB 15.00
Smith, Lyon & Field, etched bd, faux ivory hdl, ear of corn 65.00
SR Droescher, scroll hdl, etched bd, Our Star, EX 55.00
Standard Knife Co, slick blk hdl, sq point, EX 120.00
Star, government issue, 1940s, 4", MIB 15.00
Valet Auto Strop Model C, w/strop, 4⅛", NM 15.00
Wade & Butcher, ground bd, 3-pc MOP cvd hdl w/brass liners ..375.00
Washington, hollow ground-bd, aluminum hdl, Nouveau lady ..165.00
Weck Bantam E Wick & Co NY, red over ivory hdl, EX 12.00
Worthington, Cleveland, faux ivory hdl: German silver inlay 45.00
Wostenholm, Geo & Son, IXL Sheffield, fancy blk cell hdl, EX ..11.00
Yankee Cutlery...Magnetized, bamboo pattern, EX 35.00

Reamers

Reamers have been made in hundreds of styles and colors and by as many manufacturers. Their purpose is to extract the juices from lemons, oranges, and grapefruits. The largest producer of glass reamers was McKee, who pressed their products from many types of glass — custard; delphite and Chalaine blue; opaque white; Skokie green; black; caramel and white opalescent; Seville yellow; and transparent pink, green, and clear. Among these, the black and the caramel opalescents are the most valuable.

The Fry Glass Company also made reamers that are today very collectible. The Hazel Atlas Crisscross orange reamer in pink often brings in excess of $250.00; the same in blue, $275.00. Hocking produced a light blue orange reamer and, in the same soft hue, a two-piece reamer and measuring cup combination. Both are considered rare and very valuable with currently-quoted estimates at $400.00 and up for the former and $800.00 and up for the latter. In addition to the colors mentioned, red glass examples — transparent or slag — are rare and costly.

Among the most valuable ceramic reamers are those made by American potteries. The Spongeband reamer by Red Wing is valued in excess of $500.00; Coorsite reamers with gold or silver trim are worth $200.00 and up. Figurals are popular — Mickey Mouse and John Bull may bring $300.00 to $400.00. Others range from $45.00 to $150.00. Fine china one- and two-piece reamers are also very desirable and command very respectable prices.

A word about reproductions: A series of limited edition reamers is being made by Edna Barnes of Uniontown, Ohio. These are all marked with a 'B' in a circle. Other repoductions have been made from old molds. The most important of these are: Anchor Hocking 2-piece 2-cup measure and top, Gillespie 1-cup measure with reamer top, Westmoreland with flattened handle, Westmoreland 4-cup measure embossed with orange and lemons, Duboe (hand-held darning egg), and Easley's diamonds 1-piece.

Our advisor for this category is Dee Long; she is listed in the Directory under Illinois. For more information concerning reamers and reproductions, contact our advisor or the National Reamer Collectors Association (see Clubs, Newsletters, and Catalogs). Be sure to include an SASE when requesting information.

Ceramic

Clown baby, red and green hat, yellow lemon bowl with green handle, 4½", $70.00. (With matching lid: $90.00.)

Clown figural, gr/orange/blk/wht, Japan, 7½"	60.00
Clown figural, lt gr/orange/wht, Japan, 6½"	55.00
Clown figural, maroon/gr/blk/wht, Japan, 6½"	55.00
Clown figural, purple/bl/wht, 6"	50.00
Cottage form, bl/gr/maroon, Japan, 5¾"	65.00
Cottage form, tan w/gr trim, Japan, 5½"	65.00
Mexican face, yel hat, 4¾"	46.00
Mexican w/cactus figural, Japan	200.00
Moss Rose	50.00
Pear figural, Japan, 4½"	40.00
Pear figural, tan w/brn hdl & gr leaves	40.00
Pear figural, wht w/gr leaves & gold	58.00
Pitcher form, mc flowers on beige, tan trim on top	35.00
Pitcher form, rust leaves, dk bl trim, 3½"	35.00
Saucer form w/Negro head reamer, Japan, 3½"	275.00
Simple 2-spout style, wht, France, 3¼"	20.00
Windmill form, Japan, 4½"	50.00

Glass

Anchor Hocking, gr, pitcher, form, ftd, 4-cup	35.00
Cambridge, dk amber, long spout, lg	725.00
Cambridge, gr, ftd, sm	400.00
Clambroth, boat shape	200.00
Federal, amber, ribbed, loop hdl	25.00
Federal, pk, ribbed loop hdl	35.00
Fenton, sun-colored amethyst, 2-pc, baby sz	75.00
Fry, Azure bl, str sides, open tab hdl	1,250.00
Glasbake, crystal, McKee on hdl	125.00
Hazel Atlas, fired-on red 2-cup measure w/milk glass reamer	50.00
Hazel Atlas, gr, Crisscross, tab hdl, lg	12.00
Hazel Atlas, yel, 2-cup measure w/reamer top	265.00
Hocking, gr, 4-cup pitcher, flat, w/reamer top	25.00
Hocking, Vitrock, loop hdl, orange reamer	20.00
Indiana, amber, spout opposite hdl, lg	260.00
Indiana, dk amber	300.00
Jeannette, crystal, loop hdl, lg	10.00
Jeannette, Delphite bl, sm	65.00
Jeannette, gr, tab hdl, 5⅞"	15.00
LE Smith, pk, 2-pc, baby sz	200.00

McKee, blk, grapefruit reamer	900.00
McKee, custard, emb McK, 6"	35.00
McKee, yel opaque, grapefruit reamer	200.00
Orange Juice Extractor, pk, unemb	55.00
Saunders, blk	1,200.00
Sunkist, caramel	300.00
Sunkist, Jadite	35.00
Sunkist, ultramarine	625.00
Tufglas, gr	90.00
US Glass, gr, insert near top of cup, slick hdl	35.00
US Glass, pk, tub form w/reamer top	200.00
US Glass, slick hdl, grapefruit reamer	425.00
US Glass, yel, pitcher form	700.00
Westmoreland, amber, 2-pc, baby's sz	195.00

Records

Records of interest to collectors are often not the million-selling hits by 'superstars.' Very few records by Bing Crosby, for example, are of any more than nominal value, and those that are valuable usually don't even have his name on the label! Collectors today are most interested in records that were made in limited quantities, early works of a performer who later became famous, and those issued in special series or aimed at a limited market. Vintage records are judged desirable by their recorded content as well; those that lack the quality of music that makes a record collectible will always be 'junk' records in spite of their age, scarcity, or the obsolescence of their technology.

Records are usually graded visually rather than by audio quality, since it is seldom if ever possible to first play the records you buy at shows, by mail, at flea markets, etc. Condition is one of the most important value-assessing factors. For example, a truly mint-condition Elvis Presley 45 of Milk Cow Blues (Sun 215) has a potential value of over $1,000.00. If that same 45 had a sticker on it that was one-eighth of an inch square, it could lose up to half of that value! To be judged mint, a record and sleeve must be in original, unsealed condition. It may have been played but has no visual or audible deterioration. Excellent condition is a rating applied to a record that may show slight signs of wear and use but will have almost no audible defect.

While the value of most 78s does not depend upon their being in appropriate sleeves or jackets (although a sleeveless existence certainly contributes to damage and deterioration!), this is not the case with many 45s, most EPs (extended play 45s) and LPs (long-playing 33⅓s). Often, common and otherwise minimally valued 45s might be collectible if they are in appropriate 'picture sleeves' (special sleeves that depict the artist/group or other fanciful or symbolic graphic and identify the song titles, record label and number), e.g. many common records by Elvis Presley, The Beatles and The Beach Boys. In order for most EPs and LPs to be saleable, they *must* be in their original jackets and in nice condition — indeed, excellent or better — unless they are very scarce and sought-after. Sleeves may show marginal deterioration but no repairs, pen or pencil marks, stickers, or physical damage. A Good record has both visual and audible distractions but is still playable. Sleeves will show ring wear but will not be physically damaged, and Fair indicates a record that is both visually and audibly distracting, one that has obvious damage — no skips, but possible 'play through' scratches. It can still be usable. Sleeves will show heavy ring wear and some minor physical damage. A Poor record may or may not play. Sleeves are faded, torn, marked, or otherwise damaged beyond pleasurable viewing.

Many promo records being discarded by radio stations today are finding their way into collections. These may say 'Not for Sale,' 'Audition Copy,' 'D.J.,' etc. These radio station versions are sometimes different than commercial issues and usually more sought after than their commercial twins.

Our advisor for this category is L.R. Docks, author of *American Premium Record Guide*, which lists 60,000 records by over 7,000 artists, now in its fourth edition. He is listed in the Directory under Texas. In the listings that follow, prices are suggested for records that are in excellent condition.

Key:
Bru — Brunswick
Ch — Champion
Col — Columbia
Edi — Edison
Para — Paramount
Orch — Orchestra
Vi — Victor
Vo — Vocalion

Edison long-playing (24 minutes at 36 rpm!), ca 1927, $25.00.

Blues, Rhythm and Blues, Rock 'N Roll, Rockabilly

Academics, Too Good To Be True, Ancho 101, 45 rpm 10.00
Ace, Johnny; Saving My Love for You, Duke 118, 45 rpm 12.50
Adams, Faye; Say a Prayer, Herald 423, 45 rpm 6.50
Beatles, Do You Want To Know a Secret, Vee Jay 587, 45 rpm ...10.00
Berry, Chuck; Sweet Little Rock & Roll, Chess 1709, 78 rpm 25.00
Bonds, Lee; I'm Lookin' for...Lovin', Decca 29338, 45 rpm 6.50
Brooks, Sonny; I'm So Downhearted, Tip Top 1008, 45 rpm 10.00
Brown, Richard (Rabbit); James Alley, Vi 20578, 78 rpm 200.00
Cadets, Don't Be Angry, Modern 956, 45 rpm 17.50
Campbell, Glen; Turn Around Look At Me, Crest 1087, 45 rpm ...8.50
Cline, Patsy; Walkin' After Midnight, Decca 30221, 78 rpm 25.00
Coasters, Charlie Brown, Atco 6132, 78 rpm 35.00
Cochran, Eddie; Sittin' in Balcony, Liberty 55056, 78 rpm 20.00
Dubs, Could This Be Magic, Gone 5011, 45 rpm 6.50
El Dorados, Tears on My Pillow, Vee Jay 250, 45 rpm 17.50
Fabulous Four, Why Do Fools Fall..., Chancellor 1078, 45 rpm 12.50
Falcons, Sent Up, Silhouette 521, 78 rpm 30.00
Five Keys, Glory of Love, Aladdin 3099, 78 rpm 60.00
Five Keys, With a Broken Heart, Aladdin 3085, 78 rpm 60.00
Five Notes, You Are So Beautiful, Josie 784, 45 rpm 45.00
Forehand, AC; Mother's Prayer, Vi 20547, 78 rpm 30.00
Four Tunes, Wishing You Were Here..., RCA Vi 4102, 45 rpm ...10.00
Gents, Melo; Baby Be Mine, Warner Bros 5056, 45 rpm 12.50
Gibbs, Georgia; Great Balls of Fire, RCA Vi 7098, 45 rpm 6.50
Guitar, Sonny; Betty Lou, Yucca 136, 45 rpm 10.00
Hall, Roy; See You Later Alligator, Decca 29786, 45 rpm 20.00
Harlem Stars, All Right Baby, E&W 100, 78 rpm 60.00
Harrison, Wilbert; Good Bye Kansas City, Fury 1028, 78 rpm 50.00
Hayes, Henry & Band; Bowlegged Angeline, Swing 414 ....40.00
Hightower, Willie; If I Had a Hammer, Fury 5002, 45 rpm 6.50
Hollywood Flames, Strollin' on the Beach, Ebb 144, 45 rpm 6.50

Interiors, Darling Little Angel, Worthy 1008, 45 rpm 10.00
Jackson, Handy; Trouble, Sun 177, 78 rpm 150.00
James, Bill; School's Out, Mun Rab 104, 45 rpm 12.00
Jay, Bobby; Sweet Little Stranger, Imperial 5590, 45 rpm 12.50
Jets, Heaven Above Me, Gee 1020, 45 rpm 100.00
Keynotes, Wish You Were Here, Apollo 493, 45 rpm 25.00
Lancers, Royal; Angel in My Eyes, Citation 5004, 45 rpm 10.00
Lewis, Jerry Lee; Great Balls of Fire, Sun 281, 78 rpm 40.00
Lewis, Jerry Lee; Whole...Shakin' Going On, Sun 267, 45 rpm 6.50
Little Cool Breezes, Won't You Come In, Ebony 1015, 45 rpm 40.00
Luman, Bob; I Know My Baby Cares, Capitol 2972, 45 rpm 6.00
Mac & Jake, Yakety Yak, Meteor 5022, 78 rpm 30.00
Mello-Kings, Shirley, Imperial 5105, 78 rpm 35.00
Muddy Waters, Train Fare Home, Aristocrat 1306, 78 rpm 30.00
Nelson, Ricky; You're My One & Only Love, Verve 10070, 78 rpm .25.00
Nichols, Manny; Walkin-Talkin' Blues, FBC 125, 78 rpm 100.00
Oliver, Bobby; Where Do Dreams Go, Lucky Four 1004, 45 rpm ...6.50
Pacers, I Found a Dream, Calico 101, 45 rpm 6.50
Presley, Elvis; Good Rockin' Tonight, Sun 210, 78 rpm 200.00
Presley, Elvis; I Beg of You, RCA Vi 20-7150, 78 rpm 50.00
Presley, Elvis; Love Me Tender, RCA Vi 6643, 45 rpm 6.50
Presley, Elvis; Shake, Rattle & Roll, RCA Vi 6642, 78 rpm 42.50
Price, Lloyd; Hello Little Girl, KRC 303, 45 rpm 6.50
Red Jacks; Big Brown Eyes, Apt 25006, 45 rpm 8.50
Riley, Billy; Red Hot, Sun 277, 78 rpm 40.00
Rivieras, A Night To Remember, Algonquin 718, 45 rpm 6.50
Rupert, Ollie; Ain't Gonna Be Your...Dog, Vi 20577, 78 rpm 100.00
Salvo, Sammy; Marble Heart, Imperial 5615, 45 rpm 6.50
Scott, Jack; My Special Angel, Jubilee 5606, 45 rpm 5.50
Sensations, A Part of Me, Argo 5391, 45 rpm 6.50
Sheiks, Walk That Walk, Cat 116, 45 rpm 8.50
Sims, Frankie Lee; Home Again Blues, Bl Bonnet 147, 78 rpm 60.00
Strong, Barret; Money, Anna 1111, 78 rpm 200.00
Sweeney, Jim; The Midnight Hour, Date 1001, 45 rpm 6.50
Tan, Roy; I Don't Like It, Dot 15551, 45 rpm 5.50
Temptations, Letter of Devotion, Goldisc 3007, 45 rpm 8.50
Thompson, Junior; Raw Deal, Meteor 5029, 78 rpm 40.00
Tomerlin, Kenny; Crazy Little Teen, Teen Ager 1001, 45 rpm 6.50
Volumes, Teenager Paradise, Jubilee 5446, 45 rpm 5.50
Walker, Jackie; Peggy Sue, Imperial 5473, 45 rpm 15.00
Warren, Baby Boy; Mattie Mae, Bl Lake 106, 78 rpm 35.00
Watson, Jimmy; Daisy, Bru 55079, 45 rpm 6.50
Willis, Don; Boppin' High School Baby, Satellite 101, 45 rpm ..150.00
Yelvington, M; Drinkin' Wine Spodee-O-Dee, Sun 211, 78 rpm .40.00

Country and Western

Allard, Weldon; Too Late You Say, Imperial 8117, 78 rpm 10.00
Armstrong & Jacobs; Let Me Call You..., Supertone 9661, 78 rpm .7.50
Arthur, Charline; I've Got Boogie Blues, Bullet 707, 78 rpm 6.50
Blue, Bud; Blind Mother's Prayer, Okeh 45254, 78 rpm 8.50
Borton, Godfrey; Don't Forget Me...Darling, Bell 1186, 78 rpm ...6.50
Caldwell Bros, Somebody's Waiting..., Supertone 9343, 78 rpm ...8.50
Carter Family, You've Been a Friend..., Decca 5283, 78 rpm 6.00
Cash, Johnny; Luther Played the Boogie, Sun 316, 78 rpm 50.00
Chase, Chezz; Log Cabin Blues, Para 3178, 78 rpm 6.50
Cobb & Underwood, Blk Sheep Blues, Ch 16144, 78 rpm 40.00
Cross, Ballard; The Wabash Cannon Ball, Vo 5377, 78 rpm 12.50
Delmore Bros, Leavin' On That Train, Bluebird 7913, 78 rpm 7.50
Foley, David; I'll Never Be Yours, Challenge 393, 78 rpm 10.00
Ford, Jack; That's All You Gotta Do, Chess 4858, 78 rpm 6.50
Godwin, Shorty; Turnip Greens, Col 15411-D, 78 rpm 10.00
Hadley, Red; Brother That's All, Meteor 5017 ....15.00
Hall, Roy; I Wonder Where You Are..., Bluebird 8959, 78 rpm 6.50

Harper Bros, Dreamy Rock Mountain Moon, Bru 469, 78 rpm 8.00

Henslee, Gene; Rockin' Baby, Imperial 8277, 78 rpm 20.00

Hess, Bennie; Texas Stars, Opera 1019, 78 rpm 10.00

Honeycutt, Glenn; I'll Be Around, Sun 264, 78 rpm 15.00

Horton, Johnny; Birds & Butterflies, Abbott 103, 78 rpm 15.00

Hughey, Dan; Sweet Kitty Wells, Ch 15502, 78 rpm 6.00

Hutchens, John; I Got Mine, Ch 15503, 78 rpm 6.00

Johns, Whitey; The Farm Relief Song, Challenge 852, 78 rpm 5.00

Jones, Gene; Stop, Look & Listen, Gold Star 1382, 78 rpm 6.50

Jones Bros, Little Gr Valley, Melotone 12179, 78 rpm 6.50

Kincaid, Bradley; On Top of Old Smoky, Superior 2770, 78 rpm .25.00

Leake County Revelers, Lazy Kate, Col 15767-D, 78 rpm 35.00

Mack, Bill; Forever I'll Wait for You, Imperial 8192, 78 rpm 6.50

Marshall, Charlie; The Old Hitchin' Rail, Vo 03045, 78 rpm 12.50

Marvin, Johnny; I'm Gonna Yodel My Way..., Vi 23691, 78 rpm ...12.50

Mattox, Jimmie; Good Bye Mama, Gennett 7227, 78 rpm 50.00

McClendon Bros, Free As I Can Be, Bluebird 7339, 78 rpm 10.00

Miller, David; Lonesome Valley, Ch 15317, 78 rpm 6.50

Moatsville String Ticklers, Moatsville Bls, Col 15491-D, 78 rpm .30.00

Morris Bros, Let Me Be Your Salty Dog, Bluebird 7967, 78 rpm ...10.00

Nix, Hoyle; Big Ball's in Cowtown, Star Talent 709, 78 rpm 15.00

Oakley, Jesse; I Got Mine, Supertone 9256, 78 rpm 6.50

Oklahoma Wranglers, I Can't Go On...Way, Sterling 202, 78 rpm ..25.00

Peck, Bert; Over Hills to Poor House, Bru 522, 78 rpm 10.00

Penewell, Jack; Last Night I Was Dreaming, Para 3131, 78 rpm 6.50

Pickard Family, Down in Arkansas, Banner 6283, 78 rpm 5.00

Pierce, Webb; In the Jailhouse, Pacemaker 1015, 78 rpm 12.50

Pine Ridge Boys, Lonesome for You, Bluebird 8940, 78 rpm 6.50

Plye, Peter; Talking the Blues, Bullet 602, 78 rpm 6.50

Price, William; Little Birdie, Challenge 332, 78 rpm 6.50

Reinhart, Dick; Rambling Lover, Bru 386, 78 rpm 12.50

Revelers, Dear Old Dixieland, Vo 04441, 78 rpm 6.50

Roberts, Kenny; Out Where West Winds Blow, Vogue R736, 78 rpm ...60.00

Rodgers, Jimmie; Treasures Untold, Bluebird 5838, 78 rpm 6.50

Rogers, Ernest; Willie, Chimney Sweeper; Vi 20502, 78 rpm 5.00

Scott County Trio, Silvery Bell, Supertone 9308, 78 rpm 6.50

Sprague, Carl T; Bad Companions, Vi 19747, 78 rpm 5.00

Steen, Joe; Railroad Jack, Ch 16258, 78 rpm 20.00

Stokes, Leonard; There's Gr Hill..., Bluebird 7401, 78 rpm 6.50

Taggart, Charles Ross; Sister Sorrowful, Edi 51001, 78 rpm 8.50

Texas Rhythm Boys, Benzedrine Blues, Royalty 600, 78 rpm 20.00

Three Musketeers, Chattanooga Mama, Bluebird 8129, 78 rpm 6.50

Walker, Dave; Someone Owns a Cottage, Superior 2688, 78 rpm ..20.00

Watson, George P; Love's a Magic Spell, Edi 51530, 78 rpm 6.50

White, John; Strawberry Roan, Romeo 5066, 78 rpm 5.00

Wiggins, Pete; Everybody Does It in Hawaii, Okeh 45412, 78 rpm ...6.50

Williams, Hank; I Wish I Had a Nickel, MGM 12244, 78 rpm 12.50

Williams, Marc; My Blue Heaven, Decca 5216, 78 rpm 6.50

Winfield, Justin; Say, Darling, Say, Gennett 6733, 78 rpm 32.50

Zack & Glenn, Love's Old Sweet Song, Okeh 45240, 78 rpm 6.50

Jazz, Dance Bands, Personalities

Al Friedman & His Orch, My Blue Heaven, Edi 52128, 78 rpm ...10.00

Arnold Johnson & His Orch, Georgie Porgie, Bru 4080, 78 rpm ...6.50

Astaire, Fred; Let's Call Whole Thing Off, Bru 7857, 78 rpm 8.50

Badgers, Just a Little Way From Home, Broadway 1180, 78 rpm ...6.50

Baker, Belle; Cheer Up, Bru 4843, 78 rpm 8.00

Barnes, Walter; My Kinda Love, Bru 4187, 78 rpm 50.00

Beale Street Five, Waitin' Around, Lincoln 2219, 78 rpm 6.50

Beale Street Seven, Sweet Papa Joe, Lincoln 2190, 78 rpm 10.00

Beery, Noah; One Little Drink, Bru 4828, 78 rpm 7.50

Bennie Krueger & His Orch, Steppin' Out, Bru 2563, 78 rpm 6.50

Billy James' Dance Orch, Muddy Water, Oriole 829, 78 rpm 10.00

Blue Room Orch, Pretty Little Thing, Broadway 1268, 78 rpm 6.50

Bluebirds, Let's Misbehave, Vo 15652, 78 rpm 10.00

Bob Green's Dance Orch, When I Found You, Oriole 1700, 78 rpm ..6.50

Bob Howard & His Orch, It's Unbelievable, Decca 347, 78 rpm ..10.00

Bobby's Revelers, Heebie Jeebies, Silvertone 3551, 78 rpm 75.00

Bostonians, I've Found a New Baby, Vo 15298, 78 rpm 8.50

Broadway Broadcasters, Oh How I Miss You..., Cameo 738, 78 rpm .5.50

Broadway Syncopaters, House of David Blues, Vo 14670, 78 rpm ..8.50

Brunies, Merritt; Angry, Autograph 610, 78 rpm 60.00

Buffalodians, Baby Face, Banner 1776, 78 rpm 8.00

Campus Boys, Lovable & Sweet, Banner 6483, 78 rpm 10.00

Carolina Club Orch, Sweet Child, Perfect 14551, 78 rpm 6.50

Carolina Collegians, Before the Rain, Banner 6319, 78 rpm 8.50

Caroliners, I'm Happy, Banner 0847, 78 rpm 10.00

Casa Loma Orch, Smoke Rings, Bru 6289, 78 rpm 6.50

Charleston Chasers, One Sweet Letter..., Col 911-D, 78 rpm 10.00

Checker Box Boys, It Goes Like This, Broadway 1209, 78 rpm 6.50

Clevelanders, She Belongs to Me, Bru 3279, 78 rpm 6.50

Collegians, Crying for the Carolines, Broadway 1349, 78 rpm 6.50

Columbo, Russ; Time on My Hands, Bluebird 6503, 78 rpm 8.00

Conway's Band, Ragtime in a Toy Shop, Okeh 4208, 78 rpm 6.50

Cook, Ann; Mamma Cookie, Vi 20579, 78 rpm 75.00

Cotton Pickers, Hot Lips, Bru 2292, 78 rpm 6.50

Crosby, Bing; She Reminds Me of You, Bru 6853, 78 rpm 6.50

Detroiters, Dream Dream Dream, Romeo 500, 78 rpm 4.00

Dickerson, Carroll; Missouri Squabble, Bru 3990, 78 rpm 35.00

Dixie Daisies; I've Got a Song for Sale, Cameo 414, 78 rpm 6.50

Dixie Devils, Miss Golden Brown, Van Dyke 71805, 78 rpm 17.50

Dixie Jazz Band, Cat's Kittens, Jewel 5488, 78 rpm 6.50

Dodds, Johnny; After You've Gone, Bru 3568, 78 rpm 35.00

Dubin's Dandies, She Stole My Heart, Banner 0623, 78 rpm 8.50

Ellington, Duke; Louisiana, Bru 4110, 78 rpm 30.00

Emperors, Go, Joe, Go, Harmony 383-H, 78 rpm 12.50

Essex Club Orch, A Little Bit Bad, Vo 15170, 78 rpm 6.50

Etting, Ruth; Easy Come, Easy Go, Bru 6892, 78 rpm 10.00

Evans, Edith; My Kinda Love, Bru 4291, 78 rpm 10.00

Fields, Shep; Atlanta GA, Vogue R712, 78 rpm 50.00

Frankie Masters & Orch, I'm Walkin' on Air, Vi 21102, 78 rpm 6.50

Garland, Judy; Sleep, My Baby Sleep, Decca 1796, 78 rpm 6.50

Geer, Gloria; Bye Bye Blackbird, Cameo 963, 78 rpm 5.50

Georgians, Without You Sweetheart, Cameo 8111, 78 rpm 6.50

Golden Gate Orch, Southern Rose, Edi 52162, 78 rpm 15.00

Golden Gate Orch, Tell Me Little Daisy, Edi 52162, 78 rpm 50.00

Gotham Stompers, Did Anyone...Tell You, Variety 541, 78 rpm .10.00

Happiness Boys, I Wish't I Was in Peoria, Col 534-D, 78 rpm 6.50

Happy Six, Shake Your Little Shoulder, Col A2929, 78 rpm 6.50

Harmonians, Say It Again, Harmony 127-H, 78 rpm 6.50

Harris, Lillian; Baby...Please Come Home, Regal 9497, 78 rpm 25.00

Henry Halstead & Orch, Sweet Little You, Vi 19406, 78 rpm 8.50

Hotel PA Music, Lucky Little Devil, Harmony 1082-H, 78 rpm 6.50

Imperial Dance Orch, Lady Luck, Banner 0532, 78 rpm 6.50

Jackson, Mike; Just Too Bad, Victor 20181, 78 rpm 15.00

Jim-Dandies, Shake That Thing, Harmony 55-H, 78 rpm 15.00

Jungle Band, Dog Bottom, Bru 4450, 78 rpm 20.00

Jungle Band, Rockin' Chair, Bru 6732, 78 rpm 10.00

Kane, Helen; My Man Is on the Make, Vi 22475, 78 rpm 10.00

Kay, Dolly; A Good Man Is Hard To Find, Vo 15664, 78 rpm 35.00

Kentucky Serenaders, Gypsy Blues, Regal 9143, 78 rpm 6.50

Kirk, Andy; Loose Ankles, Bru 4803, 78 rpm 25.00

Kirk, Andy; Saturday, Bru 6027 ....35.00

Kopp, Howard; One Step More, Col A2376, 78 rpm 10.00

KXYZ Novelty Band, I Never Knew, Bluebird 5832, 78 rpm 12.50

Lumberjacks, I Found My Sunshine...Rain, Cameo 9020, 78 rpm ...10.00

Lynch's Rhythm Aces, She's My Baby..., Challenge 742, 78 rpm ...8.50

Majestic Dance Orch, I've Seen My Baby, Banner 0596, 78 rpm **6.50**

Mann, Marion; You Took Advantage of Me, Vogue R731, 78 rpm .**45.00**

Melody Sheiks, Behind the Clouds, Okeh 40560, 78 rpm **8.00**

Melrose, Kansas City Frank; Pass the Jug, Bru 7062, 78 rpm **60.00**

Midnight Ramblers, Ain't Misbehavin', Broadway 1302, 78 rpm ...**6.50**

Napoleon, Phil; Mary Dear, Edi 51996, 78 rpm **35.00**

New Orleans Jazz Band, Some of...Days, Regal 9839, 78 rpm **12.50**

NY Syncopators, Dream Little Dream..., Odeon 36206, 78 rpm ...**25.00**

Okeh Syncopators, Nobody's Sweetheart, Okeh 40072, 78 rpm ...**10.00**

Original Memphis Five, Shufflin' Mose, Edi 51204, 78 rpm **20.00**

Original Six, She's a Mean Job, Okeh 4546, 78 rpm **6.50**

Palace Dance Orch, I'm Following You, Broadway 1330, 78 rpm ...**6.50**

Piccadilly Players, Someday Sweetheart, Edi 52167, 78 rpm **55.00**

Putney Danridge & His Orch, Double Trouble, Vo 3082, 78 rpm ..**8.50**

Ramblers, She Knows Her Onions, Romeo 266, 78 rpm **6.50**

Rose Room Orch, It Must Be Love, Banner 6206, 78 rpm **12.50**

Roy Carlson's Dance Orch, In Springtime, Banner 6419, 78 rpm ..**8.00**

Savoy Bearcats, Stampede, Vi 20460, 78 rpm **30.00**

Sissle, Noble; Loveless Love, Bru 6073, 78 rpm **20.00**

Six Jumping Jacks, More We Are Together, Bru 3524, 78 rpm **6.50**

Southerners, My Bundle of Love, Gennett 3265, 78 rpm **12.50**

Stomp Six, Everybody Loves My Baby, Autograph 626, 78 rpm .**300.00**

Taft, William Howard; Our Army & Navy, Vi 16143, 78 rpm **6.50**

Ted Russell & Orch, You Took...Breath Away, Ch 40072, 78 rpm ..**8.50**

Troubadours, Ipana; Side By Side, Col 1009-D, 78 rpm **5.00**

University Six, Rosy Cheeks, Harmony 399-H, 78 rpm **6.50**

Varsity Eight, I Like You Best of All, Cameo 695, 78 rpm **6.50**

Ward, Billy; Squeeze Me, Oriole 4472, 78 rpm **20.00**

Washingtonians, Rainy Nights, Pennington 1437, 78 rpm **87.50**

White, Willy; Try & Play It, Perfect 11175, 78 rpm **10.00**

Williams, Mary Lou; Clean Pickin', Decca 1155, 78 rpm **10.00**

Williamson's Beal St Frolic Orch, Bear Wallow, Vi 20555, 78 rpm .**75.00**

Wilson, Lena; I Don't Love Nobody, Emerson 10745, 78 rpm **12.50**

Young, Margaret; Mama Goes...Papa Goes, Bru 2514, 78 rpm **6.50**

Red Wing

The Red Wing Stoneware Company, founded in 1878, took its name from its location in Red Wing, Minnesota. In 1906 the name was changed to the Red Wing Union Stoneware Company after a merger with several of the other local potteries. For the most part they produced utilitarian wares such as flowerpots, crocks, and jugs. Their early 1930s catalogs offered a line of art pottery vases in colored glazes, some of which featured handles modeled after swan's necks, snakes, or female nudes. Other examples were quite simple, often with classic styling. After the addition of their dinnerware lines in the 1935, 'Stoneware' was dropped from the name, and the company became known as Red Wing Potteries, Inc. They closed in 1967. For further study we recommend *Red Wing Stoneware, An Identification and Value Guide*, and *Red Wing Collectibles* by Dan and Gail DePasquale and Larry Peterson, available at your bookstore or from Collector Books. Our advisor for the general dinnerware lines is Doug Podpeskar; he is listed in the Directory under Minnesota. Karen Silvermintz (see Texas) and Charles Alexander (see Indiana) advise on the Town and Country dinnerware.

Key:

c/s — cobalt on stoneware   RW — Red Wing

MN — Minnesota   RWUS — Red Wing Union

NS — North Star   Stoneware

Commercial Art Ware and Miscellaneous

Ash receiver, donkey figural w/open mouth, bl **60.00**

Ashtray, red wing form, emb feathers **38.00**

Bust, President McKinley, sgn bk **295.00**

Clock, Mammy figural, wall hanging **125.00**

Figurine, cow w/nursing calf on base, brn **475.00**

Figurine, lady w/tambourine, cinnamon, 10" **175.00**

Figurine, reclining draped lute player w/doe, #2507, maroon **195.00**

Jug, Egyptian, brn, mini **40.00**

Pitcher, Monk, dark brown, 8½", $175.00.

Sewer pipe, advertising **50.00**

Toothpick holder, gopher on stump form **130.00**

Vase, cherubs & garlands, Brushware, mk **95.00**

Vase, elephant-head hdls, mustard gloss, 6x5" **24.00**

Vase, gr, Deco style, #1359 ....**50.00**

Vase, Roman scene emb, gr gloss, 2-hdld jug shape, 10" **65.00**

Cookie Jars

Bob White, unmk **80.00**

Carousel, unmk **350.00**

Crock, wht **25.00**

Dutch Girl, yel w/brn trim **60.00**

Friar Tuck, cream w/brn trim, mk **60.00**

Friar Tuck, gr, mk **150.00**

Friar Tuck, yel, unmk **60.00**

Grapes **70.00**

Grapes, cobalt or dk purple, ea **80.00**

Jack Frost, unmk **600.00**

King of Tarts, mc, mk **500.00**

King of Tarts, pk w/bl & blk trim, mk **350.00**

King of Tarts, wht, unmk **350.00**

Peasant design, emb/pnt figures on brn **60.00**

Pierre (chef), brn, unmk **60.00**

Pierre (chef), gr, unmk **200.00**

Pierre (chef), pk, mk **250.00**

Pineapple **100.00**

Dinnerware

Bob White, beverage server & stand, 14" **95.00**

Bob White, bowl, divided vegetable **25.00**

Bob White, butter dish, ¼-lb **75.00**

Bob White, casserole, 2-qt **25.00**

Bob White, cookie jar **140.00**

Bob White, hors d'ouvres bird **30.00**

Bob White, Lazy Susan **125.00**

Bob White, pitcher, water; 60-oz **35.00**

Bob White, plate, 11" **11.00**

Bob White, tumbler, rare, 4-oz **125.00**

Bob White, vinegar & oil cruets, pr **150.00**

Bob White, water cooler, w/lid & stand, 2-gal, M 450.00
Brittany, buffet bowl 42.00
Capistrano, bowl, divided vegetable 20.00
Capistrano, plate, dinner; 10" 10.00
Capistrano, platter, 15" 15.00
Country Garden, bread tray 48.00
Country Garden, gravy boat 20.00
Country Garden, plate, 10½" 15.00
Country Garden, plate, 8" 10.00
Driftwood, bowl, divided vegetable 12.50
Driftwood, creamer 12.00
Driftwood, plate, dinner 10.00
Driftwood, plate, salad 7.50
Frontenac, creamer 10.00
Frontenac, plate, dinner 8.00
Frontenac, trivet 50.00
Lanterns, cup & saucer 10.00
Lotus, plate, 10½" 12.50
Lotus, plate, 7½" 7.00
Lotus, relish, 3-part 20.00
Lotus, teacup 7.50
Lute Song, bowl, cereal; 6¾" 8.00
Lute Song, bowl, vegetable; 8" 16.00
Lute Song, cup & saucer 10.00
Lute Song, nappy 15.00
Lute Song, platter, 13" 20.00

Magnolia, tray, metal handle, $15.00.

Magnolia, plate, 10" 12.00
Magnolia, rim soup 9.50
Morning-Glory, creamer & sugar bowl 12.00
Morning-Glory, plate, 6½" 6.50
Morning-Glory, platter, 13" 16.00
Orleans, pitcher, water 68.00
Pepe, beverage server, w/lid 45.00
Pepe, bowl, divided vegetable 25.00
Pepe, cup & saucer 12.00
Pepe, plate, 10" 12.00
Random Harvest, casserole, w/lid 28.00
Random Harvest, coffeepot, tall 27.50
Random Harvest, plate, 10" 12.50
Random Harvest, platter, 13" 15.00
Round-Up, bowl, salad; sm, 6" 40.00
Round-Up, bowl, salad; 12" 125.00
Round-Up, bowl, salad; 9½" 80.00
Round-Up, casserole, lg 195.00
Round-Up, casserole, sm 130.00
Round-Up, cup & saucer 40.00

Round-Up, plate, dinner 30.00
Round-Up, plate, salad 17.50
Round-Up, teapot 220.00
Smart Set, bowl, salad 100.00
Smart Set, butter dish 200.00
Smart Set, cocktail tray 45.00
Smart Set, cruets, pr 150.00
Smart Set, marmite, hdld, w/lid 28.00
Tampico, casserole, w/lid 60.00
Tampico, cup & saucer 12.50
Tampico, mug, coffee 45.00
Tampico, plate, 10½" 12.50
Tampico, platter, 13¼" 20.00
Village Green, bean pot, 2-qt 25.00
Village Green, bowl, cereal 15.00
Village Green, bowl, rimmed soup 16.00
Village Green, bowl, salad; ind, 6" 14.00
Village Green, bowl, sauce 8.50
Village Green, butter dish, w/lid 25.00
Village Green, casserole stand, 8" 12.50
Village Green, coffee server, w/metal stand, 1-gal 55.00
Village Green, gravy boat, w/tray 25.00
Village Green, plate, bread & butter 5.50
Village Green, plate, salad; 8" 8.50
Village Green, shakers, pr 20.00
Village Green, warmer, sm 20.00
Zinnia, chop plate, 12½x11" 10.00
Zinnia, plate, 10" 10.00

Stoneware

Bean pot, Albany slip, Boston style, MN, ½-gal 125.00
Bean pot, Albany slip, Boston style, NS, 1-gal 125.00
Bean pot, Albany slip, Boston style, RWUS, 1-gal 200.00
Bean pot, Albany slip & wht, bail hdl, RWUS, 1-qt 75.00
Bowl, cap; full panel & ridges, red & bl sponging on wht, 5" 175.00
Bowl, mixing; bl bands on wht, lg 70.00
Bowl, paneled, bl sponging on wht, rare 225.00
Bowl, paneled, red & bl sponging on wht, 5" 275.00
Bowl, red & bl sponging on saffron 75.00
Bowl, shoulder; Albany slip, RW, 1-pt 50.00
Bowl, wht w/bl bands at rim 70.00
Casserole, Spongeband, RWU, med or lg, ea 225.00
Chamber pot, Albany slip, fancy hdl, RW 100.00
Chamber pot, bl bands on wht, unsgn 125.00
Chamber pot, wht, fancy hdl, RW, 7" 100.00
Churn, birch leaves/#8, c/s, unsgn, 8-gal 350.00
Churn, butterfly/#6, c/s, RW, 6-gal 800.00
Churn, leaf/#3, c/s, molded, MN, 3-gal 650.00
Churn, P/#4, c/s, RW, 4-gal 650.00
Churn, red wing/#2 on wht, RWUS, 2-gal 225.00

Cooler, Sanitary School Appliances, 8-gallon, $375.00.

Cooler, butterfly/#6, c/s, RW, 6-gal 1,700.00
Cooler, daisy/#5, c/s, RW, 6-gal 1,600.00
Cooler, Ice Water/#3/red wing, c/s, RW, 3-gal 425.00
Cooler, Ice Water/#6/flower, c/s, RW, 6-gal 4,500.00
Cooler, Water Cooler/red wing on wht, bl bands, RWUS, 2-gal ..1,300.00
Crock, birch leaf/#10, c/s, MN, 10-gal 375.00
Crock, birch leaves/#25, c/s, MN, 25-gal 450.00
Crock, butter; wht, low style, RW, 10-lb 75.00
Crock, butterfly/#10, c/s, RW, 10-gal 400.00
Crock, butterfly/#20, c/s, RW, 20-gal 450.00
Crock, dbl P/#4, c/s, MN, 4-gal 350.00
Crock, drop-8 design/#3, c/s, 3-gal 275.00
Crock, lily/#30, c/s, RW, 30-gal 1,100.00
Crock, red wing/#12 on wht, RWUS, 12-gal 80.00
Crock, target/#2, c/s, RW, 2-gal 125.00
Crock, 2 elephant-ear leaves/#10, c/s, RWUS, 10-gal 80.00
Crock, 2 elephant-ear leaves/#4, c/s, RWUS, 4-gal 70.00
Crock, 2 sets of leaves/#10, c/s, RWUS, 10-gal 275.00
Cuspidor, molded seam, bl & wht sponging, RW, 10" 600.00
Cuspidor, molded seam, wht w/Albany slip top, unsgn 125.00
Cuspidor, no seam, bl & wht sponging, unsgn 500.00
Jar, butter; Albany slip, high style, NS, ½-gal 40.00
Jar, butter; Albany slip, low style, MN, 10-lb 40.00
Jar, butter; Albany slip, low style, RW, 1-lb 80.00
Jar, butter; wht, low style, MN, 10-lb 40.00
Jar, butter; wht, low style, NS, 2-lb 40.00
Jar, fruit; Stone Mason, c/s, Pat Jan 24, 1899, 1-gal ...375.00
Jar, packing; wht, bail hdl, MN, 3-lb 80.00
Jar, preserve; Albany Slip, wall stamp, RW, 1-gal 375.00
Jar, preserve/snuff; Albany slip, MN, 2-gal 150.00
Jar, preserve/snuff; wht, RW, 1-gal 200.00
Jar, wax sealer; Albany slip, MM, ½-gal 40.00
Jar, wax sealer; Albany slip, MN, 1-qt 65.00
Jar, wax sealer; Albany slip, RW, 1-qt 55.00
Jug, beehive threshing; birch leaves/#5 on wht, RW, 5-gal 450.00
Jug, beehive; #5 etched on Albany slip, hand-trn, RW, 5-gal 700.00
Jug, beehive; birch leaf/#5, c/s, RW, 5-gal 1,300.00
Jug, beehive; birch leaves/#4, c/s, hand-trn, RWUS, 4-gal 400.00
Jug, beehive; red wing/#3 on wht, RWUS, 3-gal 250.00
Jug, bl bands on wht, cone top, RW, 1-qt 425.00
Jug, common, Albany slip, ball top, MN, 1-gal 50.00
Jug, common, Albany slip, ball top, NM, ½-gal 150.00
Jug, common, Albany slip, funnel top, MN, 1-gal 85.00
Jug, common, Albany slip, standard top, MN, ½-gal 60.00
Jug, common, wht, ball top, MN, 1-gal 60.00
Jug, fancy, wht w/bl band & brn top, MN, 1-pt 650.00
Jug, fancy, wht w/brn ball top, MN, ⅛-pt 225.00
Jug, fancy, wht w/brn ball top, RW, 1-gal 175.00
Jug, fancy, wht w/brn ball top, RW, ½-gal 200.00
Jug, fancy, wht w/brn ball top, RW, ½-pt 175.00
Jug, fancy, wht w/brn ball top, unmk, 1-pt 50.00
Jug, molded seam, Albany slip, bail hdl, MN, ½-gal 225.00
Jug, molded seam, Albany slip, ball top, MN, 2-gal 450.00
Jug, molded seam, bl sponging on wht, bail hdl, MN, 1-gal 950.00
Jug, molded seam, wht, bail hdl, MN, 1-qt 125.00
Jug, molded seam, wht, bail hdl, MN, ½-gal 100.00
Jug, molded seam, wht, bail hdl, RW, 1-gal 150.00
Jug, molded seam, wht, bail hdl, RW, 1-qt 125.00
Jug, molded seam, wht, wide mouth, RW, 1-qt 45.00
Jug, shoulder; Albany slip, cone top, RW, 2-gal 500.00
Jug, shoulder; birch leaves/#3 on wht, molded, MN, 3-gal 100.00
Jug, shoulder; brn & salt glaze, cone top, 2-gal 275.00
Jug, shoulder; brn & salt glaze, dome top, 1-gal 75.00
Jug, shoulder; brn & salt glaze, dome top, 2-gal 125.00

Jug, shoulder; brn & salt glaze, funnel top, 1-gal 80.00
Jug, shoulder; brn & salt glaze, funnel top, ½-gal 125.00
Jug, shoulder; brn & salt glaze, funnel top, 2-gal 125.00
Jug, shoulder; brn & salt glaze, pear top, ½-gal 300.00
Jug, shoulder; brn & salt glaze, standard top, 1-gal 125.00
Jug, shoulder; brn top, red wing on wht, 1930s, 2-gal 350.00
Jug, shoulder; red wing/#3 on wht, molded, RWUS, 3-gal 70.00
Jug, shoulder; wht, cone top, RW, 1-gal 60.00
Jug, shoulder; wht, cone top, RW, ½-gal 95.00
Jug, shoulder; wht, dome top, MN, 1-gal 75.00
Jug, shoulder; wht, funnel top, MN, 2-gal 75.00
Jug, shoulder; wht, standard top, MN, 1-qt 80.00
Jug, shoulder; wht, standard top, MN, 2-gal 50.00
Jug, shoulder; wht, standard top, RW, 1-gal 35.00
Jug, shoulder; wht, standard top, RW, 1-qt 80.00
Jug, shoulder; wht, standard top, short, MN, 1-qt 80.00
Jug, shouldered; wht, standard top, wide mouth, MN, 1-gal 75.00
Jug, syrup; wht, cone top, MN, ½-gal 70.00
Jug, syrup; wht, standard top, MN, 1-gal 60.00
Pan, milk; Albany slip, NM 85.00
Pipkin, Albany slip, unsgn 85.00
Pipkin, wht w/Albany slip lower half, MN, 1-pt 195.00
Pitcher, Albany slip, bbl form, RW 125.00
Pitcher, bl & wht mottle, fancy hdl, RWUS, ½-gal 325.00
Pitcher, Cherryband, bl on wht, ca 1915 ....200.00
Pitcher, dk gr matt, emb Minn SW Co on top 350.00
Pitcher, Dutch boy & girl, bl & wht, RW, 1920s, sm 650.00
Pitcher, milk; Albany slip, Russian style, 1-gal 90.00
Pitcher, mustard; wht, MN, 1-qt 80.00
Pitcher, Spongeband & Saffron, RWUS, sm 200.00
Spittoon, Albany slip, MN, lg 475.00
Spittoon, bl bands on salt glaze, German style, MN 650.00
Spittoon, bl bands on salt glaze, German style, unsgn 400.00
Spittoon, salt glaze, unsgn 200.00
Wash bowl & pitcher, emb lily, lt bl & wht 650.00

Town and Country

Produced by Red Wing for one year only in the late 1940s, Town and Country was designed by Eva Zeisel as an informal or semiformal dinnerware. Irregular, often eccentric shapes characterize the line, as handles of pitchers and serving pieces are usually extensions of the rim. Bowls and platters are free form comma shapes or appear tilted, with one side slightly higher than the other. Although the ware is unmarked, it is recognizable by its distinctive shapes and glazes. White is often used to complement interiors of bowls and cups, Bronze (metallic brown) enjoys favored status, while gray is unusual. Other colors include rust, dusk blue, sand, chartreuse, peach, and forest green.

Teapot, sand, $250.00; Syrup, chartreuse, $95.00.

Bean pot, rust, w/lid	350.00
Bowl, mixing; dusk bl	95.00
Bowl, vegetable; sand, 8"	35.00
Casserole, marmite, chartreuse, ind	25.00
Casserole, peach, stick hdl	95.00
Creamer, rust	35.00
Cruets, oil & vinegar; mixed colors, orig stoppers, sm, pr	150.00
Cup & saucer, forest gr w/wht int	27.50
Pitcher, peach, 3-pt	125.00
Pitcher, sand, 2-pt	85.00
Plate, bronze, 10"	45.00
Plate, chartreuse, 6"	5.00
Plate, gray, 8"	15.00
Plate, rust, 10"	25.00
Plate, 6½"	5.00
Platter, peach, comma shape, 9"	35.00
Shakers, Schmoo shape, mixed colors, pr	65.00
Sugar bowl, bronze, w/lid	65.00
Syrup, chartreuse	95.00
Teapot, sand	250.00

Redware

The term redware refers to a type of simple earthenware produced by the Colonists as early as the 1600s. The red clay used in its production was abundant throughout the country, and during the 18th and 19th centuries redware was made in great quantities. Intended for utilitarian purposes such as everyday tableware or use in the dairy, redware was simple in design and decoration. Glazes of various colors were used, and a liquid clay referred to as 'slip' was sometimes applied in patterns such as zigzag lines, daisies, or stars. Plates often have a 'coggled' edge, similar to the way a pie is crimped or jagged, which is done with a special tool. In the following listings, EX (excellent condition) indicates only minor damage. Our advisor for this category is Barbara Rosen; she is listed in the Directory under New Jersey.

Charger, 3-line yellow slip waves on red-orange, finely notched rim, PA, 12¾", $800.00.

Bank, apple form, realistic red & yel pnt, 3¼"	140.00
Bank, castle form, brn mottle, 2½x3⅝x2⅛"	120.00
Bank, hen & chicks in basket, mc pnt, flaking, 3¼"	195.00
Bird house, wheel thrown, worn red pnt on roof, 11"	95.00
Boot, orange w/blk specks, sgn HR Diehl on sole, 2½" L	90.00
Bottle, brn, sloped shoulder, flared mouth, 4⅞x3⅜"	60.00
Bottle, Geo WA sitting on stump shape, pnt decor, 13", EX	160.00
Bottle, gr w/brn flecks & gr stripes, IS Stahl, 1939, 5¾"	55.00

Bowl, brn splotches, cup shape w/strap hdl, 3½x5¼"	110.00
Bowl, brn sponging, worn/flakes, 4x10"	95.00
Bowl, dk brn mottle, ear hdls, 2⅝x4⅜"	130.00
Bowl, milk; rim spout, EX color, 8"	145.00
Bowl, orange-brn, crimped/folded rim, incised lines, 3x6"	180.00
Bowl, sgraffito/eagle/flowers/1827, late 1800s, 2½x12½"	415.00
Bowl, worn yel slip, worn int, 5½"	75.00
Bowl, 3-color detailed slip decor, 2x10"	1,450.00
Bowl, 3-line yel slip, coggled rim, chip, 6½" dia	105.00
Chamber pot, brn int, unglazed ext, 4½x8½"	30.00
Charger, 3-line yel slip, coggled rim, 11¾"	700.00
Charger, 3-line yel slip waves, coggled edge, 14½", EX	285.00
Coffeepot, engine-trn bands, 1770s, England, 11", EX	600.00
Creamer, brn, sgn HS Shofield, 3", EX	135.00
Creamer, dk brn, 3"	120.00
Crock, brn w/mica flecks, incised lines, 6¼x6½"	95.00
Crock, brn w/mica flecks, incised lines on shoulder, 6x4"	75.00
Crock, brn-gr, flared rim & base, 5¼x4⅛"	110.00
Crock, dk brn, incised line decor, 4⅝x4⅝"	50.00
Crock, dk brn, sgn John Bell, 5⅜x4⅞"	210.00
Crock, lt brn w/manganese splotches, strap hdl, 5⅝x4¾"	95.00
Crock, orange-brn w/manganese splotches, flared rim, 6x5⅛"	130.00
Cup, dk brn, flared rim, incised hdl, 2⅜x3"	110.00
Cup, orange, tapered sides, incised line decor, 5x4⅞"	75.00
Cup, yel w/brn mottle, 3¾x5⅛"	260.00
Dish, brn mottle, scalloped, imp rosettes/beading, 8½", EX	300.00
Figure, chicken, amber & gr, cole slaw base, EX tooling, 12"	470.00
Figure, rooster, orange w/manganese breast, red comb, 6½"	275.00
Figurine, poodle, glazed, Am, 4½x4"	400.00
Flowerpot, brn sponging, tooled/crimped rim, w/saucer, 8¾"	220.00
Flowerpot, brn w/gr slip splotches, w/underplate, 4⅝x5⅝"	160.00
Flowerpot, orange mottle w/gr & yel slip, coggled rim, 5⅜"	180.00
Flowerpot, orange w/manganese splotches, w/underplate, 4½x6"	65.00
Flowerpot, orange w/yel slip splotches, 4¾x5½"	150.00
Flowerpot, yel w/brn mottle, crimped, saucer base, 5½", EX	160.00
Herb pot, brn splotches on ochre, Am, 1800s, 4¼"	275.00
Hot plate, rust w/brn spots, swirled design, 8-ftd, 6", EX	210.00
Jar, amber w/brn splotches, ribbed strap hdl, old rpr, 6"	50.00
Jar, blk/brn/amber mottle, ovoid, 5½"	60.00
Jar, brn mottle, incised lines on shoulder, 6x4⅝"	190.00
Jar, brn w/mottling, cylinder w/sloped shoulder, 8", VG	200.00
Jar, dk brn, ovoid, lt wear, 9¼"	85.00
Jar, dk brn, ovoid, rnded shoulder, 10½", EX	115.00
Jar, dk brn, sgn John Bell, 8¼x5¼"	190.00
Jar, dk brn mottle, bulbous, 6⅛x4⅛"	70.00
Jar, dk w/brn splotches, cylindrical, w/lid, 6¾", EX	220.00
Jar, int glaze, hairline, 5¾"	30.00
Jar, manganese splotches, Am, 1800s, 9½"	400.00
Jar, preserve; gr mottle w/brn, Southern US, 1800s, 4⅝"	285.00
Jar, red-orange w/dk brn alkaline decor, ovoid, 1-gal	250.00
Jar, yel, sgn John Bell, 7⅜x4⅞"	280.00
Jug, amber, ovoid, appl strap hdl, wear/flakes, 11½"	115.00
Jug, puzzle; glazed, dtd 1789, 7½", EX	330.00
Jug, yel, ovoid, 4½"	140.00
Loaf pan, 4-line yel slip decor, coggled rim, rprs, 17½"	100.00
Mold, lamb, recumbent, orange int, unglazed ext, 4½x7x3¼"	475.00
Mold, swirled/scalloped, orange w/manganese mottle, 3¼x4¼"	275.00
Mold, Turk's head, amber w/brn flecks, 9"	60.00
Mold, Turk's head, brn irid, center funnel, 3¾x6½"	75.00
Mold, Turk's head, orange w/manganese splotches, 2½x7½"	60.00
Mold, Turk's head, yel slip wavy line & polka dots, 9½"	155.00
Mug, shaving; dk brn, strap hdl, 4¼", EX	80.00
Pie plate, brn w/manganese mottle, 1⅝x6¼"	40.00
Pie plate, coggled edge, chips/hairlines, 6¼"	140.00

Pie plate, dk amber, incised distlefink w/flowers, inscr, 10½" 195.00
Pie plate, dk brn flecks, 7⅞" 75.00
Pie plate, gr-brn, 1⅝x5⅞" 40.00
Pie plate, lt gr, coggled decor, flake, 8¾" 100.00
Pie plate, orange, EX color, hairline, 7⅝" 145.00
Pie plate, orange, 8¼" 30.00
Pie plate, orange w/yel slip sprig, coggled rim, 12½" 375.00
Pie plate, plaid 3-color slip, wear, 8" 580.00
Pie plate, simple yel slip decor, coggled rim, 10¼" 385.00
Pie plate, yel w/gr mottling, sgraffito decor, Troxel, 11" 975.00
Pie plate, 3-line yel slip on dk brn, coggled rim, chips, 8" 225.00
Pie plate, 4-line yel slip, coggled rim, flakes, 9½" 220.00
Pitcher, brn, appl strap hdl, tooled shoulder & lip, 10", EX 75.00
Pitcher, dk brn, molded floral w/cherub heads, Sellers, PA, 8" ...150.00
Pitcher, dk brn mottled metallic, 6⅛" 55.00
Pitcher, gr w/orange spots, ovoid, flakes, 7⅞" 85.00
Pitcher, gr-amber, ribbed strap hdl, wear, 8¼" 225.00
Pitcher, lt brn w/dk brn mottling, 8¼" 500.00
Plate mold, sgn L&J, 7¾ dia, EX 110.00
Pot, dk w/brn splotches, strap hdl, pouring spout, rpl lid, 5" 75.00
Pot, gr, ribbed body, New England, 1800s, 8½" 800.00
Salt, master; dk brn, crock shape, 1½x2" 85.00
Teapot, overall manganese, beaded band, reeded hdl, 9¾" 125.00
Whistle, bird form, brn slip eyes, lead glaze, 1755, 10" 3,000.00

Relief-Molded Jugs

Early relief-molded pitchers (ca 1830s-40s) were made in two-piece molds into which sheets of clay were pressed. The relief decoration was deep and well defined, usually of animal or human subjects. Most of these pitchers were designed with a flaring lip and substantial footing. Gradually styles changed, and by the 1860s the rim had become flatter and the foot less pronounced. The relief decoration was not as deep, and foliage became a common design. By the turn of the century, many other types of pitchers had been introduced, and the market for these early styles began to wane.

Watch for recent reproductions; these have been made by the slip-casting method. Unlike relief-molded ware which is relatively smooth inside, slip-cast pitchers will have interior indentations that follow the irregularities of the relief decoration. Our advisor for this category is Kathy Hughes; she is listed in the Directory under North Carolina.

Apostle, wht, Meigh, 1842, 9⅞" 525.00
Bacchanalian Dance, wht, Meigh, 1844, 7⅝" 425.00
Eglinton Tournament, buff, Ridgway, 1840, 7¼" 375.00
Gipsy, lav on parian, Alcock, 1842, 4¾" 195.00
Julius Caesar, gray, appl laurel wreath, Meigh, 1839, 8¼" 450.00
Naomi & Daughter-in-Law, lav on parian, Alcock, 1847, 8¾" ..375.00
Pan (w/lid), buff, Wm Ridgeway, 1830s, 7¼" 250.00
Silenus, gr, Minton, 1845, 9" 425.00
Tam O'Shanter, glazed bl, Ridgeway, 1835, 8¼" 295.00
Tulip, bl & wht, Dudson, 1860, 7" 175.00
Two Drivers, gray, Minton, ca 1849, 7⅞" 575.00

Restraints

Since the beginning of time, many things from animals to treasures have been held in bondage by hemp, bamboo, chests, chains, shackles, and other constructed devices. Many of these devices were used to hold captives who awaited further torture, as if the restraint wasn't torturous enough. The study and collecting of restraints enables one to learn much about the advancement of civilization in the country or region from which they originated. Such devices at various times in history were made of very heavy metals — so heavy that the wearer could scarcely move about. It has only been in the last sixty years that vast improvements have been made in design and construction that afford the captive some degree of comfort. Our advisor for this category is Joseph Tanner; he is listed in the Directory under Washington.

Key:
bbl — barrel
d-lb — double lock button
K — key
Kd — keyed
lc — lock case
NST — non-swing through
ST — swing through
stp — stamped

Foreign Handcuffs

Adams, teardrop lc, bbl Kd, NST, usually not stp 170.00
Australian, Saf Lock, ST, takes pin-tumbler K in side, stp 140.00
Deutsche Polizei, ST, middle hinge, folds, takes bbl-bit K 80.00
East German, aluminum, single lg hinge, bbl key 40.00
East German, heavy steel, NP single lg hinge, NST, bbl key 60.00
English, Chubb, NST, hi-security 10-slider lock mechanism 275.00
English, Chubb Arrest, steel, ST, multi-bit solid K 225.00
English, Latrobe, aluminum alloy, center chain, ST, dbl-bit K ...160.00
French Lapegy, ST, aluminum alloys, takes flat bitted K 75.00
German, 3-lb steel set, 2⅝" thick, center chain, bbl K 175.00
German Clejuso, oval design, ST, dbl-cuff weight, 22-oz 100.00
German Clejuso, sq lc, adjusts/NST, d-lb on side, bbl K 100.00
German Darby, adjusts, well finished, sm 120.00
German Hamburg 8, non-adjust NST, center bar/post w/K-way ...250.00
Hiatt, English Darby, like US CW Darby, stp Hiatt & #d 65.00
Hiatt, solid state, 2 separate cuffs joined bk to bk, stp/#d 165.00
Hiatt English non-adjust screw K Karby style, uses screw K 100.00
Hiatt Figure 8, swings open to insert/withdraw wrists 125.00
Italian, stp New Police, modern Peerless type, ST, sm bbl K 35.00
Plug 8, remove plug before inserting external threaded K 200.00
Spanish, stp Alcyon/Star, modern Peerless type, flat K 65.00
Spanish, stp Alcyon/Star, modern Peerless type, ST, sm bbl K 45.00

Foreign Leg Shackles

East German, aluminum, lg hinge, cable amid 4 cuffs, bbl key 65.00
German Clejuso, sq lc, adjusts/NST, d-bl on side, bbl K 125.00
German Clejuso Darby type, adjusts/NST/plated, uses screw K ..160.00
Hiatt English combo manacles, handcuff/leg irons w/chain 275.00
Hiatt English non-adjust screw K Darby style, uses screw K 100.00
Hiatt Plug leg irons, same K-ing as Plug-8 cuffs, w/chain 225.00

U.S. Handcuffs

American Munitions, modern/rnd, sm bbl Kd, ST bow, stp 45.00
Bean Giant, sideways figure 8, solid center lc, dbl-bit K 400.00
Bean Patrolman, kidney-bean form, d-lb on lc, NST, stp T 100.00
Bean-Cobb, sm rnd lc, removable cylinder, d-lb, NST, 1899 .....80.00
Cavenay, looks like Marlin Daley but w/screw K, NST 160.00
Civil War padlocking type, various designs w/loop for lock 170.00
Colt, modern ST bow, sm bbl Kd, stp w/Colt & co name 150.00
Flash Action Manacle, like Bean Giant w/ST, K-way center 200.00
Flexibles, steel segmented bows, NST Darby type, screw K 150.00
H&R Super, NST, shaft-hinge connector takes hollow titted K 100.00
Harvard, takes sm bbl K, ST, stp Harvard Lock Co 65.00
Judd, NST, used rnd/internally triangular K, stp Mattatuck 100.00
Lilly Hand Iron, 2" strap iron (8" L), oval bands, NST, sq K 400.00
Marlin Daley, NST, bottle-neck form, neck stp, dbl-titted K 175.00
Mattatuck, NST, propeller-like K-way, stp Mattatuck/etc 85.00

Palmer, 2" steel bands, 2 K-ways (top & center), NST stp **300.00**
Peerless, ST, takes sm bbl K, stp Mfg'ered by Peerless Co **40.00**
Peerless, ST, takes sm bbl K, stp Mfg'ered by S&W Co **75.00**
Phelps, NST, twist chain between cuffs, Tower Look-alike **200.00**

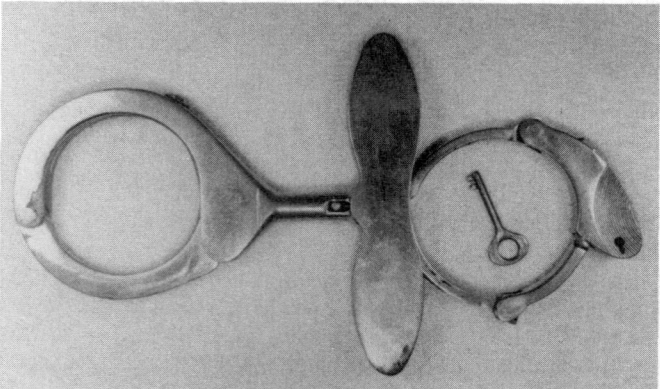

Pratt combo, one cuff connects with nipper/claw, swing through, marked Pratt, $225.00.

Rankin, steel NST, mk screw K **200.00**
Romer, NST, takes flat K, resembles padlock, stp Romer Co **250.00**
S&W 94 Maximum Security, ST, takes Ace-type K, stp S&W **80.00**
Strauss, ST, takes lg solid bitted K, stp Strauss Eng Co **85.00**
Tower, NST, bottom K, solid/flat fitted K goes in cuff edge **100.00**
Tower bar cuffs, cuffs separate by 10-12" steel bar **120.00**
Tower Dbl Lock, NST, takes bbl-bitted K, usually stp Tower **60.00**
Tower Detective Pinkerton, NST, sq lc, bbl-bitted K, no stp **110.00**
Tower Single Lock, NST, bbl-bit K, K-way slanted on lc, sm **70.00**
Tower-Bean, NST, sm rnd lc, takes tiny bbl-bitted K, stp **75.00**
Tri-lock, heavy polymer & stainless steel, triple lock **60.00**
Walden 'Lady Cuff,' NST, takes sm bbl K, lightweight, stp **250.00**

U.S. Leg Shackles

American Munitions, as handcuffs **55.00**
Civil War or prison ball & chain, padlocking or rivet type **250.00**
Cloc spike, 30" L opening for ankle w/padlock & 2 spikes **500.00**
H&R Supers, as handcuffs **400.00**
Harvard, as handcuffs **75.00**
Judd, as handcuffs **135.00**
Leg lock brace, metal brace, ankle to knee, lever locked **225.00**
Oregon boot, break-apart shackle on above ankle support **400.00**
Palmer, as handcuffs but w/detachable chain, NST **400.00**
Strauss, as handcuffs **125.00**
Tower, bottom K, as handcuffs **90.00**
Tower ball & chain, leg iron w/chain & 6-lb to 50-lb ball **200.00**
Tower Dbl-Lock, as handcuffs **80.00**
Tower Detective, as handcuffs **150.00**

Various Other Restraining Devices

African slave Darby-style cuffs, heavy iron/chain, handmade **130.00**
African slave Darby-style leg shackles, heavy/hand forged **160.00**
African slave padlocking or riveted forged iron shackles **135.00**
Darby neck collar, rnd steel loop opens w/screw K **150.00**
English figure-8 nipper, claws open by lifting top lock tab **65.00**
Gale finger cuff, knuckle duster, non-K, mk GFC **125.00**
German nipper, twist hdl opens/closes cuff, stp Germany/etc **75.00**
Jay Pee, thumb cuffs, mk solid body, bbl K **15.00**

Mighty-Mite, thumb cuffs, solid body, ST, mk, bbl K **65.00**
Tower Lyon, thumb cuffs, solid body, NST, dbl-bit center K **150.00**

Reverse Painting on Glass

Verre eglomise is the technique of painting on the underside of glass. Dating back to the early 1700s, this art became popular in the 19th century when German immigrants chose historical figures and beautiful women as subjects for their reverse glass paintings. Advertising mirrors of this type came into vogue at the turn of the century.

Abraham Lincoln portrait attributed to Mathew Prior, large size in original frame, $450.00.

Flowers in base, on tinsel, mc on blk, grpt fr, 12x17" **350.00**
Lady's portrait, noted 'Adelle,' orig fr, 13½x10½" **425.00**
Lady's portrait, titled, flakes/wear, fr, 10⅛x7⅝" **140.00**
Lady's portrait, titled, mc on gr ground, fr, 9⅛x6½" **415.00**
Landscape w/crane & deer, Chinese, 1800s, 18x25" **325.00**
Man's portrait, noted 'Frederike,' orig fr, 13½x10⅝" **385.00**
Man's portrait, unsgn, 1800s, fr, 10½x15¼", VG **165.00**

Richard

Richard, who at one time worked for Galle, made cameo art glass in France during the 1920s. His work was often multilayered and acid cut with florals and scenics in lovely colors. The ware was marked with his name in relief. Our advisor for this category is Don Williams; he is listed in the Directory under Missouri.

Cameo

Atomizer, leaves, raspberry/pk, wafer ft, sgn, 7" **775.00**
Vase, bud; floral, purple on bl, 7", NM **350.00**
Vase, cottage/trees/mtns/lake, yel to lav, 13¾" **1,900.00**
Vase, hyacinth/vines, bl on orange, ftd, 8½" **475.00**
Vase, lake/bldgs/mtns fr by lg trees, ftd/scalloped, 16" **2,000.00**
Vase, trees/houses/mtns, purple to med/lt purple, 8x6" **900.00**

Ridgway

As early as 1792, the Ridgway brothers, Job and George, produced fine quality earthenwares in Shelton, Staffordshire, marking their products 'Ridgway, Smith, & Ridgway' and later 'Job & George Ridgway.' Around 1800 the brothers split, and each had his own firm, both in Shelton. They were joined in the business by various members of the Ridgway family, and in fact their descendants still operate there today.

The two firms created by the split were the Bell Works and the Cauldon Pottery. Bell produced stone china and earthenware decorated with blue transfer printing. Their mark was 'J. & W. Ridgway' or 'J. & W.R.' (John and William) until 1848 when 'William Ridgway' was used. The Cauldon Pottery made earthenware, stone china, and high-quality porcelains fine enough to win them the distinction of being appointed potters to the Queen. From 1830 their wares attest to this fact, bearing the Royal Arms mark with 'J.R.' within the crest. In 1840 '& Co.' was added. Most examples of Ridgway's wares found today are transfer-printed historical scenes. See also Staffordshire, Historical; and Flow Blue.

Biscuit jar, Coaching Days, brn rattan hdl, 6½" 230.00
Bowl, Coaching Days, 10" 50.00
Cup & saucer, Royal Vista 20.00
Mug, Coaching Days, 4" 35.00

Mug, Columbus Cathedral, Havana Cuba, 4¾", $35.00; Tray, Racing the Mail, 6¾" square, $35.00.

Mug, Mormon Sq, Salt Lake City, 4½" 45.00
Pitcher, Coaching Days, 5½" 60.00
Pitcher, stoneware, bl w/emb band, HP flowers, 1835, 11" 160.00
Plaque, Taking Up the Mails, yel, 12" 130.00
Plate, Coaching Days, Waiting for the Stage Coach, 9" 35.00
Teapot, Coaching Days, 5½" 165.00
Tray, Coaching Days, oval, 12½" 80.00

Rie, Lucie

Lucie Rie was born in 1902. She moved to London in 1938 and shared her studio with Hans Coper from 1946 to 1958. Her ceramics look modern; however, they are based on shapes from many world cultures dating back to Roman times. Lucie Rie is best known for the use of metallic oxides in her clay and glazes. She specializes in the hand throwing of thin porcelain bowls, which is a very difficult process. her works are in the world's best museums. All of her ceramics are impressed with a seal mark on the bottom, a cojoined 'R & L' within a rectangular reserve.

Bottle, creamy gr, cylindrical w/cone neck, 7¾" 865.00
Bottle, turq/ochre mottle, cylinder w/flared rim, 15¾" 8,600.00
Bowl, bsk w/cvd cobalt bands, manganese int, conical, 4¾" 2,575.00
Bowl, lt gr w/cvg on manganese band, can ft, 5¼" 1,865.00

Bowl, manganese matt, cvd ft/int band on cobalt, can ft, 6" ...2,600.00
Bowl, manganese runs from rim over lt yel, short base, 2½" 1,450.00
Bowl, uranium yel, on short can base, 3¼" 1,050.00
Vase, manganese matt in X-hatching on sage gr, can form, 4" 450.00

Riviera

Riviera was a line of dinnerware introduced by the Homer Laughlin China Company in 1938. It was sold exclusively by the Murphy Company through their nationwide chain of dime stores. Riviera was unmarked, lightweight, and inexpensive. It was discontinued sometime prior to 1950. Colors are mauve blue, red, yellow, light green, and ivory. On rare occasions, dark blue pieces are found, but this was not a standard color. For further information we recommend *The Collector's Encyclopedia of Fiesta* (now with 1994 values) by Sharon and Bob Huxford, available from Collector Books.

Batter set, complete 215.00
Batter set, ivory, w/decals, complete 145.00
Bowl, baker; 9" 18.00
Bowl, cream soup; w/liner, ivory 80.00
Bowl, fruit; 5½" 9.00
Bowl, nappy, 9¼" 18.00
Bowl, oatmeal; 6" 26.00
Butter dish, cobalt, ¼-lb 200.00
Butter dish, colors other than cobalt & turq, ¼-lb 95.00
Butter dish, turq, ¼-lb 185.00
Butter dish, ½-lb 90.00
Casserole 80.00
Creamer 8.00
Cup & saucer, demitasse; ivory 50.00
Jug, open, ivory, 4½" 80.00
Jug, w/lid 100.00
Pitcher, juice; mauve bl 175.00
Pitcher, juice; yel 90.00
Plate, deep 16.00
Plate, 10" 32.00
Plate, 6" 7.00
Plate, 7" 8.00
Plate, 9" 12.50
Platter, closed hdls, 11¼" 18.00
Platter, cobalt, 12" 48.00
Platter, 11½" 14.00
Sauce boat 17.50
Saucer 3.00
Shakers, pr 16.00
Sugar bowl, w/lid 16.00
Syrup, w/lid 110.00
Teacup 8.50
Teapot 100.00
Tidbit, ivory, 2-tier 70.00
Tumbler, hdl 55.00
Tumbler, hdl, ivory 115.00
Tumbler, juice 42.00

Robertson

Fred H. Robertson, clay expert for the Los Angeles Brick Company and son of Alexander Robertson of the Roblin Pottery, experimented with crystalline glazes as early as 1906. In 1934 Fred and his son George established their own works in Los Angeles, but by 1943 they had moved operations to Hollywood. Though most of their early wares were turned by hand, some were also molded in low relief. Fine crackle glazes and crystallines were developed. Their ware was marked with 'Robertson,' 'F.H.R.,' or 'R.,' with the particular location of manufacture noted. The small pottery closed in 1952.

Bowl, bl drip over wht crackle, 4" 55.00
Lamp, HP floral on wht crackle, 1945, 11½", Hollywood 200.00
Plate, antelope silhouette, HP, 10½", Hollywood 175.00
Tile, children & goose, blk on wht, 4x4" 85.00
Vase, crystalline, bl flakes on gold-yel, Los Angeles, 5" 1,300.00

Robj Bottles

Robj was the name of a retail store that operated in Paris for only a few years, from about 1925 to 1931. Robj solicited designs from the best French artisans of the period to produce decorative objects for the home. These objects were produced mostly in porcelain but also in glass and earthenware. The most well known are the figural bottles which were particularly popular in the United States. However, Robj also produced tea sets, perfume lamps, chess sets, ashtrays, bookends, humidors, powder jars, cigarette boxes, figurines, lamps, and milk pitchers. Robj objects tend to be whimsical, and all embody the Art Deco style. Our advice for this category comes from Randall Monsen and Rod Baer, their address is listed in the Directory under Virginia.

Bottle, French priest, blk hat forms stopper, 10½x4" 365.00
Bottle, in the form of a man in gray coat/blk hat, 10" 325.00
Bottle, scent; sitting Oriental, no lid 50.00
Cocktail shaker, golfer figural, bl & wht 1,200.00
Condiment jars as people, 1 cleric, 1 veggie man, 3 pcs, EX 750.00
Decanter, musical, Russian man, hat forms stopper, 12" 350.00
Decanter, preacher, pnt flakes 175.00
Inkwell, Blackamoor in gold/wht robe holds well, no lid, 6" 275.00
Perfume burner, wht-robed Oriental, X-legged on steps, 8" 550.00

Rock 'N Roll Memorabilia

Memorabilia from the early days of Rock 'n Roll recalls an era that many of us experienced firsthand; these listings are offered to demonstrate the many and various aspects of this area of collecting. Values are for mint condition examples. Our advisor for Elvis memorabilia is Rosalind Cranor, author of *Elvis Collectibles* and *Best of Elvis Collectibles* (Overmountain Press); she is listed in the Directory under Virginia. The remainder is under the advisement of Bojo (Bob Gottuso); see Pennsylvania.

Beatles, Disk Go Case, plastic, NM, $85.00.

Beatles, assignment book, Select-O-Pack, vinyl w/2 pads, EX 225.00
Beatles, balloon, various colors, sealed in pkg, ea 45.00
Beatles, belt, vinyl, made in a variety of colors, EX, ea 80.00

Beatles, binder, vinyl, 3-ring, various colors, ea 85.00
Beatles, blanket, wool & fiber, portraits, Whitney, 80", EX 450.00
Beatles, bongo drums, Mastro, EX 600.00
Beatles, bracelet, portrait medallion on chain, EX 65.00
Beatles, cap, Ringo cap label, many colors, EX, ea 150.00
Beatles, cartoon colorforms, w/instructions, complete in box 275.00
Beatles, character glasses w/decal & gold rim, UK, EX, 4 for 500.00
Beatles, color book, group on yel cover, Saalfield, EX 60.00
Beatles, Disk Go case, plastic 45 rpm record holder 85.00
Beatles, doll, John or George w/guitar, vinyl, Remco, 4", ea 75.00
Beatles, doll, vinyl, Paul or Ringo, Remco, 4", ea 55.00
Beatles, dolls, bobbin' head, set of 4, EX 325.00
Beatles, dolls, inflatable, set of 4, EX 325.00
Beatles, drum, Ringo, w/stand, sticks, etc, UK 350.00
Beatles, flasher ring, EX 18.00
Beatles, Flip Your Wig game, complete, EX in box 75.00
Beatles, guitar, 4 pop, Mastro, EX 250.00
Beatles, guitar (toy), Red Jet, electric, Selcol, 31", M 1,400.00
Beatles, hair spray, Bronson Products, 8", EX 700.00
Beatles, Halloween costume, w/mask, ea 200.00
Beatles, hatbox, vinyl (red or blk), Air-Flite, EX 500.00
Beatles, litter holder, vinyl, Air-Flite, VG 300.00
Beatles, lunch box, bl, EX 250.00
Beatles, lunch box, Yel Submarine, EX 225.00
Beatles, magnetic hair game, w/wand, UK, EX 450.00
Beatles, model kit, Ringo, Revell, EX in box 150.00
Beatles, napkin, paper, set of 50 in orig package, M 725.00
Beatles, pennant, portraits, red & blk on wht, Irwin, 22", NM ...125.00
Beatles, phonograph, group pictures on top & inside, EX 1,200.00
Beatles, pillow, group protrait, Nordic House, 12", EX 130.00
Beatles, pin-bk button, portraits, 3" dia, EX 20.00
Beatles, plate, Hard Days Night scene, Bamboo...Co, M, 12" 125.00
Beatles, plate, portraits on china, Washington Pottery, 7", M 100.00
Beatles, record case, heavy cb, Air-Flite, holds 33 rpms, NM 225.00
Beatles, ring binder, purple variation, VG 150.00
Beatles, shoulder bag, vinyl, portraits in blk on wht, VG 375.00
Beatles, Soaky bottle, Paul or Ringo, ea 60.00
Beatles, tablecloth, continuous pattern, EX 325.00
Beatles, talcum powder, Margo of Mayfair, UK, EX 390.00
Beatles, tennis shoes, WingDings, low cut, EX 300.00
Beatles, trading cards, Hard Day's Night, sealed pack of 5, EX 50.00
Beatles, Yel Submarine, diecast, Corgi, 5", EX 200.00
Billy Joel, concert pass, Stormfront Tour, 1990, autographed 35.00
Bob Dylan, concert poster, blk & wht, 1979, 20½x14", M 45.00
Elvis Presley, belt buckle, brass, 1956, EX 195.00
Elvis Presley, board game, w/8x10" photo, 1956, MIB 1,350.00
Elvis Presley, Christmas card, mc, 1966, 8x5", NM 50.00
Elvis Presley, dog tag key chain, no card, NM 75.00
Elvis Presley, dog tag key chain, w/card, NM 160.00
Elvis Presley, handkerchief, bl border, 1956, NM 460.00
Elvis Presley, necklace, Love Me Tender, gold heart, no card, NM .100.00
Elvis Presley, necklace, Love Me Tender, gold heart, w/card, NM .175.00
Elvis Presley, photo, blk & wht, RCA giveaway, wallet sz, NM 66.00
Elvis Presley, pin-bk, ...for President, celluloid, 3⅜", NM 80.00
Elvis Presley, postcard, blk & wht portrait, Nat'l Press, NM 10.00
Elvis Presley, record player, gold signature, table model, EX ...1,000.00
Elvis Presley, ring, picture on metal, mid-1970s, NM 18.00
Elvis Presley, scrapbook, 1956, 14½x12", EX 450.00
Elvis Presley, sheet music, Scratch My Back, NM 15.00
Elvis Presley, skirt, irid figures, etc on felt, 1956, NM 1,125.00
Elvis Presley, teddy bear, w/pin & ribbon, 1957, 24", NM 450.00
Elvis Presley, ticket stub, early concert, from $75.00 up to 150.00
Hermann's Hermitts, charm bracelet, 5 photos on chain, 1950s 40.00
Jimi Hendrix, concert poster, Santa Barbara CA, 1967, 23x18" .100.00

Jimi Hendrix & Moby Grape, concert poster, 1967, 34x18", EX ..100.00
Kiss, bedspread, sealed in bag w/insert 100.00
Kiss, board game, complete, EX 40.00
Kiss, Colorforms, 1979, unused, M 45.00
Kiss, dolls, Mego, set of 4, EX 225.00
Kiss, guitar, plastic, 24", EX 75.00
Kiss, Halloween costume, w/mask, EX in box 45.00
Kiss, Kiss Your Face make-up kit, sealed 80.00
Kiss, pencils, 4 in package 35.00
Kiss, record player, Tiger 125.00
Kiss, transistor radio 50.00
Kiss, trash can, EX 80.00
Led Zeplin, concert poster, bright colors, 1979, 18x22", EX 100.00
Led Zeplin, concert poster, Santa Barbara CA, 1969, 23x18", VG ..100.00
Mick Jagger, poster, Performance, 1970, 41x27", EX 70.00
Monkees, board game, MIB 95.00
Monkees, Hey-Hey jigsaw puzzle set, MIB 35.00
Monkees, More of the Monkees gum card pack, unopened 15.00
Monkees, 45 rpm record holder, M 110.00
Otis Rush, poster, psychedelic images, 1967, 14x20", M 75.00
The Byrds/Fleetwood Mac, poster, 1969, 14x22", M 250.00

Rockingham

In the early part of the 19th century, American potters began to favor brown- and buff-burning clays over red because of their durability. The glaze favored by many was Rockingham, which varied from a dark brown mottle to a sponged effect sometimes called tortoise shell. It consisted in part of manganese and various metallic salts and was used by many potters until well into the 20th century. Over the past two years, demand and prices have risen sharply, especially in the East. See also Bennington.

Bottle, flower urn relief ea side, EX detail, 10⅜" 350.00
Bottle, shoe form, sole has old gold pnt, 9" 100.00
Bowl, shallow, 2¼x9¼" 95.00
Bowl, shallow, 3¼x11½" 125.00
Bowl, tan & wht stripes & brn sponging, 4½x9½" 135.00
Cuspidor, molded shells, 7½" 50.00
Jug, Duke of Wellington figural, ca 1850, 7½x4¾" 265.00
Mold, tulips, 9" dia, EX 175.00
Mug, 3½" 100.00
Pie plate, 9⅝" 100.00
Pitcher, emb eagle/boar/stag/etc, hound hdl, 10" 195.00
Pitcher, hunt scene, 9⅞" 150.00
Pitcher, molded peacock, 8½" 150.00
Platter, sm chip, 15" L 170.00
Soap dish, oval, 4⅞" L 85.00
Teapot, molded leaf decor, chips, 8" 175.00
Teapot, molded leaves, 1800s, 10" 450.00
Teapot, Rebecca at well 150.00

Rogers, John

John Rogers (1829-1904) was a machinist from Manchester, New Hampshire, who turned his hobby of sculpting into a financially successful venture. From the originals he meticulously fashioned of red clay, he had bronze master molds made from which plaster copies were cast. He specialized in five different categories: theatrical, Shakespeare, Civil War, everyday life, and horses. His large detailed groupings portrayed the life and times of the period between 1859 and 1892. When no condition is indicated, examples are assumed to be in very good to

excellent condition. Our advisor for this category is George Humphrey; he is listed in the Directory under Maryland.

Balcony 1,500.00
Bubbles 2,000.00
Charity Patient 650.00
Checkers Players, sm 1,500.00
Chess 825.00
Courtship in Sleepy Hollow, Pat date 550.00
Fairy's Whisper, ca 1881 ....1,400.00
Faust & Marguerite, Leaving the Garden 1,200.00
First Ride 725.00
Going for the Cows 450.00
Hide & Seek 2,000.00
Mail Day 2,000.00

Matter of Opinion, $600.00.

Neighboring Pews 475.00
Parting Promise 475.00
Peddler at the Fair 800.00
Picket Guard 750.00
Playing Doctor 500.00
Politics 700.00
Polo 2,000.00
Referee 600.00
Rip Van Winkle on Mountains, Pat July 25, 1871, 21" 450.00
Slave Auction 2,000.00
Tap on the Window 525.00
Traveling Magician, ca 1877 ....750.00
Washington 1,250.00
Weighing the Baby, Pat 1875, 21" 600.00
Wounded Scout, ca 1864 ....750.00

Rookwood

The Rookwood Pottery Company was established in 1879 in Cincinnati, Ohio. Its founder was Maria Longworth Nichols Storer, daughter of a wealthy family who provided the backing necessary to make such an enterprise possible. Mrs. Storer hired competent ceramic workers who through constant experimentation developed many lines of superior art pottery. While in her employ, Laura Fry invented the airbrush-blending process for which she was issued a patent in 1884. From this, several lines were designed that utilized blended backgrounds. One of their earlier lines, Standard, was a brown ware decorated with underglaze slip-painted nature studies, animals, portraits, etc. Iris and Sea Green were introduced in 1894 and Vellum, a transparent mat-glaze line, in 1904. Other lines followed: Ombroso in 1910 and Soft Porcelain in 1915. Many of the early artware lines were signed by the artist. Soon after the turn of the 20th century, Rookwood manufactured 'production' pieces that relied mainly on molded designs and forms rather than freehand decoration for their esthetic appeal. The Depression brought on financial difficulties from which the pottery never recovered. Though it continued to operate, the quality of the ware deteriorated, and the pottery was forced to close in 1967.

Unmarked Rookwood is only rarely encountered. Many marks may be found, but the most familiar is the reverse 'RP' monogram. First used in 1886, a flame point was added above it for each succeeding year until 1900. After that a Roman numeral added below indicated the year of manufacture. Impressed letters that related to the type of clay utilized for the body were also used — G for ginger, O for olive, R for red, S for sage green, W for white, and Y for yellow. Artware must be judged on an individual basis. Quality of the artwork is a prime factor to consider. Portraits, animals, and birds are worth more than florals; and pieces signed by a particularly renowned artist are highly prized. Our advice for this category comes from Fer-Duc Inc., whose address is listed in the Directory under New York.

Bisque

Ewer, floral, butterfly hdl, AB Sprague, #461, 1889, 4" 375.00
Jar, wild roses, G Young, bulbous w/can neck, 1889, 6" 600.00
Jardiniere, magnolia on wht, A Valentien, 1886, 16" 2,400.00
Pilgrim flask, cvd outlines of Oriental figures etc, 8x5" 850.00
Potpourri jar, apple blossoms, MA Daly, #282, 1887, 7½" 800.00
Potpourri jar, mums, wht/gold on gray, A Van Briggle, 6" 825.00

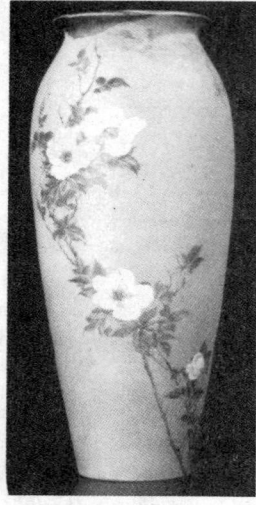

Vase, wild roses on light blue, Shirayamadani, 'S' mark, 1887, 21½", $3,500.00.

Vase, crabs/seaweed, brn on med brn, #94B, 1884, 7½x7" 700.00
Vase, floral on peach, cvd/gilt accents, MA Daly, 1887, 11" 550.00
Vase, vines/berrries, cvd/pnt, H Wenderoth, 1881, 10", NM 425.00
Vase, wild roses on lt peach, EX art, unsgn, 1888, 8x7" 900.00

Cameo

Bowl, hollyhocks, pointed/shaped rim, W7/#228, 1887, 3x13" ...300.00
Coffeepot, roses, wht on dk peach, G Young, 1889, 9" 425.00
Creamer, floral spray on peach/wht, S Toohey, #47, 1887, 2" 150.00
Pitcher, wild rose spray on lt yel, MA Daly, #182, 1887, 7" 800.00
Pitcher, wild roses, A Sprague, pear form, 1889, 7" 275.00
Plate, floral spray, MA Daly, sqd, #317, 1886, 10" 325.00
Plate, roses, H Wilcox, 1890, 8½" 475.00

Rose jar, roses, Artus Van Briggle, rtcl/gilt stopper, 8x6" 850.00

Iris

Vase, blkberries on lt gr to blk, K Van Horne, '09, 8½" 1,800.00
Vase, daffodils on pk to gr, EN Lincoln, 1910, 6½x3½" 1,100.00
Vase, dogwood on bl shaded to gray, S Sax, #935C, '07, 9x5" .1,500.00
Vase, ducks by moonlit lake, Shirayamadani, #1358B, 12¾" ...38,000.00
Vase, floral, wht w/pk buds on shaded gr, C Baker, '01, 7½" 880.00
Vase, floral, wht/yel on shaded gray, I Bishop, 1908, 5½" 550.00
Vase, floral at shoulder, G Reed, #919, 1901, 4" 495.00
Vase, grape/vines, F Rothenbusch, 1903, 7¾" 825.00
Vase, grapes/vines on bl to pk, L Asbury, 1907, 7¾x3¾" 800.00
Vase, grapes/vines on wht to purple, S Sax, #909, '02, 9" 1,300.00
Vase, hydrangea, wht/gr on cream, E Diers, #892, '04, 8½" 2,400.00
Vase, jack-in-pulpit on blk to gray-gr, S Sax, 1902, 10x4½" 3,100.00
Vase, Japanese irises on blk to bl, Schmidt, '11, #1655, 8" 10,250.00
Vase, lg poppies, wht/gr on lav to lt gr, L Asbury, '08, 11" 2,300.00
Vase, lg thistles, pk/gr on gr to lt pk, S Coyne, '08,9½" 1,400.00
Vase, maple leaves, yel/tan on dk gray, K Van Horne, '09, 8" .1,200.00
Vase, orchids, AR Valentien, #940B, 1903, 12" 2,200.00
Vase, poppies on lt gray, AR Valentien, #922B, 1902, 11" 3,450.00
Vase, roses on ivory to gray, SE Coyne, 1906, 9¾x3¾" 1,100.00
Vase, tulips, rust/celadon on blk, S Sax, 1906, 5½x3¾" 1,900.00
Vase, 4 geese in flight on lt bl/gr, ET Hurley, '04, 9½" 4,600.00

Jewel Porcelain

Vase, fish/flowers, brn/taupe on ivory, J Jensen, '46, 7x5" 900.00
Vase, floral wreath at shoulder, L Epply, 1919, 5½x6½" 1,000.00
Vase, lg cvd poppies on brn to orange, H Wilcox, 1929, 8x4" .1,200.00
Vase, lg parrot, Shirayamadani, 1930, 9" 2,750.00

Limoges

Bowl, floral, hammered texture, LA Fry, #166, 1882, 3½x7¾" ...770.00
Candlestick, trumpet vines, HR Strafer, #S-1022, 1892, 6" 250.00
Jug, cvd/gilt Moorish patterns, HP roses/bugs, 1883, 9¾x7" 600.00
Jug, swallows in flight, W McDonald, 1883, 4½" 550.00
Lamp, grasses/birds, A Valentien, #225, bulbous, 1883, 7½" ...2,500.00
Pitcher, apple blossoms on bl, AR Valentien, 1881, 9" 550.00
Pitcher, birds/bats/owls/etc, EG Winslow, 1882, rpr, 7" 550.00
Pitcher, sm florals on branch, A Valentien, 1881, 9" 850.00
Plate, grasses/sm bird, A Bookprinter, fluted, 1886, 6½" 275.00
Tea jar, grasses/2 birds, A Valentien, 1885, w/lid, 6½" 925.00
Vase, grasses/sm birds, H Horton, #126, 1883, 8¾" 825.00
Vase, 5 bats/cattails/clouds on dk gr, AR Valentien, 10" 1,900.00

Mat

Bowl, geometrics/linear rim band emb, turq w/gr speckles, 7" 220.00
Bowl, incurvate w/rtcl ferns, gr to pk, #1288, 2¾x6½" 275.00
Mug, cvd Arts & Crafts design on gr, #345C, 1902 ....150.00
Mug, cvd circles on lt gr, #354C, 1902 ....150.00
Vase, A&C leaves/flowers emb on gr/brn, #2129, 1927, 9" 300.00
Vase, berries on ivory band on purple, C Steinle, 1916, 5" 375.00
Vase, crocuses, mc on lav to bl, HE Wilcox, 1926, 7x3½" 1,200.00
Vase, cvd floral, red/gr on gr matt, A Pons, 1907, 3x4¾" 375.00
Vase, cvd floral/leaves, mc on purple, CS Todd, 1916, 9x5" ...1,000.00
Vase, emb floral, rose w/gr overglaze, angle hdls, 1915, 4" 150.00
Vase, floral, cvd/inlaid, Wm Hentschel, #904CC, 1914, 10" ..1,100.00
Vase, floral, red on brn/turq butterfat, E Lincoln, '30, 6" 400.00
Vase, floral, yel/bl on turq, CS Todd, 1914, 6x3¼" 350.00

Vase, lg orchids, gold/wine on gr, AR Valentien, '01, 8x6" 2,300.00
Vase, peacock feathers emb on lt bl, #2404, 1927, 6" 260.00
Vase, stylized floral/molded buttresses, yel, #2431, 1902, 9" 220.00

Porcelain

Bowl vase, mum border, bl on wht, pk int, A Conant, 4¾" 1,400.00
Flowerpot, tulips, pk/yel on bl gloss, Shirayamadani, 1946 ....750.00
Ginger jar, birds/butterflies on gr, ET Hurley, 1924, 15" 2,600.00
Vase, deer outlines, brn/bl/gray, Jens Jensen, 1945, 8x4" 1,300.00
Vase, floral, mc on purple to gray, Shirayamadani, 1926, 9" 1,400.00
Vase, floral band, pk/blk/wht on bl, H Wilcox, #1278F, 7" 650.00
Vase, pansies, ET Hurley, spherical, 1946, 4x5" 450.00
Vase, wht 'clouds' on blk bsk, L Holtkamp, 1952, 6" 225.00

Sea Green

Vase, bl irises, M Nourse, #907-DD, 1904, 10½" 65.00
Vase, copper o/l foliage, lotus/pads, JD Wareham, 5x5" 11,000.00
Vase, lobster/sea grasses, ET Hurley, #745-B, 1898, 7¾" 550.00
Vase, palm leaves on blk in sea gr, Rothenbusch, 1900, 5½" ...2,500.00
Vase, yel jonquils, S Toohey, #589-D, 1898, 11" 4,600.00
Vase, 5 fish, ET Hurley, #907D, 1903, 10", NM 2,200.00

Standard

Bowl, roses, E Noonan, #214C, 1903, 2¾x5½" 300.00
Ewer, fruit blossoms, EP McDonald, #471B, 1893, 12", EX 550.00
Ewer, lg rose, A Van Briggle, #S871, 1889, 7½" 750.00
Jardiniere, wild roses, A Sprague, hdls, 1889, 7x8" 700.00
Jug, silver o/l scrolls on corn, AR Valentien, 1892, 8" 3,000.00
Mug, Black Eye (Indian), J Swing, 1900, 4½" 1,100.00
Mug, Chief Goes to War, Sioux; ER Felton, 1900, 5" 1,150.00
Pitcher, cherries, C Baker, U-form, 1892, 4½x6" 150.00
Vase, Am Indian (titled), G Young, 1901, #787C, 11⅛" 17,000.00
Vase, blackberries, E Lincoln, 1903, 8x4½" 425.00
Vase, cherry blossoms, S Markland, ornate pointed hdls, 5" 300.00
Vase, forget-me-nots, Olga Reed, 1895, 7x5½" 300.00
Vase, fruit/floral branch, Shirayamadani, #535Y, 1890, 7" 850.00
Vase, Japanese mums/seascape on bl, A Conant, 1918, 9x6½" ..5,500.00
Vase, lg irises, AM Valentien, trumpet neck, 1896, 14¾x6" ...1,200.00
Vase, lg narcissus, L Van Briggle, flared/bulbous, 1902, 7½" 450.00
Vase, pine cones, tan/gr on shaded brn, C Duell, '03, 8x4" 375.00
Vase, shoulder portrait of lad, MA Daly, hdls, 1897, 9" 1,750.00
Vase, silver o/l scrolls, berries, S Toohey, 1893, 7" 2,100.00
Vase, Stars Come Out, Sioux; AD Sehon, 1901, 7½" 2,500.00
Vase, tulips/foliage, C Lindeman, 1908, 9¼x4½" 500.00
Vase, wild roses, E Lincoln, 1894, 5½x4" 300.00
Whiskey jug, ear of corn/wheat, M Nourse, 1899, 8" 400.00

Vellum

Plaque, Autumn, houses/trees, Rothenbusch, 1929, 7x12", +fr .4,600.00
Plaque, lake viewed through trees, SE Coyne, 1900, 12x14" ...4,300.00
Plaque, Point Loma, seascape, L Asbury, 1916, 5x8", +gilt fr ..1,900.00
Plaque, trees shadowed in water, C Schmidt, fr, 5x9½", EX 1,700.00
Plaque, trees/snow/pk & bl sky, S Coyne, 10x15", +oak fr 9,000.00
Vase, apple blossoms on turq, L Asbury, bulbous, '28, 10" 1,400.00
Vase, boats in purple on gr ocean, S Coyne, 1912, 9x4¾" 1,500.00
Vase, cherry blossoms on bl to pk, C Steinle, 1919, 4½" 300.00
Vase, cvd irises, gray/wht on lt gray, K Van Horne, 7½", NM 600.00
Vase, daffodils, C Steinle, 1907, 9" 650.00
Vase, floral branches, ET Hurley, #9040, 1910, 8¾" 770.00

Vase, lg birch trees/lake, ET Hurley, 1930, 10½x5½" 2,600.00
Vase, lg iris on whiplash stem, L Asbury, 1905, 9" 1,600.00
Vase, lt trees/twilight, F Rothenbusch, 1917, 7½x3½" 1,250.00
Vase, pansies on shaded gray/pk, EN Lincoln, #942D, 1900, 6" .500.00
Vase, roses, pk on shaded bl/gr/pk, MH McDonald, 1913, 6x3½" .600.00
Vase, trees/birds/winter sunset, ET Hurley, hairline, 8" 1,200.00
Vase, Venetian harbor, C Schmidt, #1882, 1919, 9¾" 3,100.00
Vase, wide cvd grapevine band on dk bl-gr, S Sax, 1915, 9¾" 850.00

Wax Mat

Bud vase, floral on bl to gr butterfat, SE Coyne, 1927, 7" 300.00
Stein, cvd abstract floral, sgn AP, #1014D, 1907, 7" 300.00
Vase, blueberries on turq/bl, E Lincoln, 1929, 10¾x4½" 1,100.00
Vase, daffodils on pk shaded, EX art/glaze, S Coyne, 12x5" 1,400.00
Vase, floral, mc on mustard, L Abel, 1927, 17x8" 2,000.00
Vase, floral, purple/gr on brn, MH McDonald, 1925, 8½x3½" ...350.00
Vase, floral, yel/purple on dk bl, C Abel, 1925, 7½x4" 450.00
Vase, floral on butterfat turq/navy, Shirayamadani, '31, 5" 650.00
Vase, floral vines/leaves on lt ground, #2639E, 1924, 8" 350.00
Vase, flowers, red/brn on purple to red, E Lincoln, '25, 15" 1,400.00
Vase, peonies on pk to bl, E Lincoln, #1369C, 1928, 11" 985.00
Vase, tulips, bl-lined red & yel on rose, sgn, 1925, 8" 500.00

Miscellaneous

Advertising sign, 1947, scroll ends/1 in front, wht, 3¾x5" 1,175.00
Ashtray, 1949, rook on side, Bengal Brn, #1139, 4" 125.00
Bookends, 1918, Oriental woman in lotus position, McDonald .200.00
Bookends, 1922, seated Oriental, bl/blk, W McDonald, 8" 825.00
Bookends, 1943, rook on open book, taupe/dk bl, 6½" 200.00
Bookends, 1945, rook, red/gr mottle, #2275, 5", NM 325.00
Bowl, 1927, seminude at ea end, wht w/bl int, mk LA, 7" 550.00
Paperweight, 1940, Potter at the Wheel on bk, 3½" dia 175.00

Sign, tan and brown mat, 1924, 4x13¼", $1,200.00.

Plaque, Faience, trees/mtns/lake, wide oak fr, tile: 13" sq 2,500.00
Tea set, 1919, gr gloss w/dk bl bands, #2469, pot: 5½" 325.00
Vase, 1883, lg cvd peonies on brick red & gilt, CVM, 12x14" ...1,900.00
Vase, 1922, flat blk crystalline, maroon int, #1123, 6" 375.00
Vase, 1927, leaf design at top on bl crystalline, 5½" 200.00
Vase, 1930, iris relief on turq gloss, cast HW, #6171, 15¾" 600.00
Vase, 1932, pk/bl drip on tan, pk int, #6306, 7" 300.00
Vase, 1943, coromandel glaze, ribbed, mk S, 5¾", NM 275.00
Vase, 1945, lt/dk bl drip glaze, ftd sqd form w/hdls, 10" 125.00
Vase, 1946, lg orchids, cvd/pnt, Shirayamadani, sqd, 7½" 900.00
Vase, 1946, lt cvg, brn scallops/sm floral on ochre, 6" 125.00
Vase, 1953, woven uprights & horizontals, bl & blk, sgn, 7" 750.00
Vase, 1960, blk bsk w/thick wht glossy drip, #6614, 4" 70.00

Vase, 1960, Venini handkerchief shape, brn & bl drip, 9x8" **240.00**

Rose Mandarin

Similar in design to Rose Medallion, this Chinese Export porcelain features the pattern of a robed mandarin, often separated by florals, ladies, genre scenes, or butterflies in polychrome enamels and often having gold trim. Elaborate in decoration, this pattern was popular from the late 1700s until the early 1840s.

Water bottle and wash basin, wear and rim chips, $1,200.00.

Bowl, fruit; late 1800s, 10" L, +undertray **1,850.00**
Bowl, rice; w/lid & ring-type undertray, EX, pr **150.00**
Cache pot, 4½", w/underplate **525.00**
Chamberstick, 3½", w/prof rpr snuffer **300.00**
Coffeepot, w/lid, 1800s, 11" **1,100.00**
Dish, serving; shaped, 10½" L **365.00**
Garden seat, 18½" **2,975.00**
Hot water dish, gold trim, wear, 9¼" **525.00**
Platter, gilt trim, rpr, 17" **525.00**
Platter, 12¾", pr **715.00**
Punch bowl, 15½" **4,850.00**
Shrimp dish, shaped rim, extended on 1 side, 1800s, 10½" **550.00**
Temple jar, w/gold, foo dog finial, 1800s, 16¾" **1,870.00**
Temple jar, 24" **3,850.00**
Tureen, sauce; 15" dia, EX **1,750.00**
Vase, 23", pr **3,850.00**

Rose Medallion

Rose Medallion is one of the patterns of Chinese export porcelain produced from before 1850 until the second decade of the 20th century. It is decorated in rose colors with panels of florals, birds, and butterflies that form reserves containing Chinese figures. Pre-1850s ware is unmarked and is characterized by quality workmanship and gold trim. From about 1850 until circa 1860, the kilns in Canton did not operate, and no Rose Medallion was made. Post-1860 examples (still unmarked) can often be recognized by the poor quality of the gold trim or its absence. In the 1890s the ware was often marked 'China'; 'Made in China' was used from 1910 through the 1930s.

Bowl, chamber; flat rim, prof rpr, 15½", EX **275.00**
Bowl, 4½x11¾" **495.00**
Bowl, 5½x13½" **1,045.00**
Box, dresser; w/lid, rim chip, 3⅞" dia **600.00**

Candlesticks, appl dragons, 7½", pr **935.00**
Candlesticks, chip, 8", pr **775.00**
Candlesticks, lt wear, 9½", pr **1,045.00**
Charger, 14¾" **105.00**
Cone, 13½" **1,320.00**
Hot water dish, 10" **600.00**
Jardiniere, 12x14½" **775.00**
Pitcher, gold trim, base chip, 16" **1,045.00**
Pitcher, paneled, 7½" **825.00**
Platter, Made in China, ca 1910-20, 16" **350.00**
Platter, orange peel, 15" L **415.00**
Punch bowl, gold trim, wear, 11½" **715.00**
Shrimp dish, cypher in butterfly reserve, gold trim, 10½" **425.00**
Teapot, Cadogan, rpr, 5½" **525.00**
Teapot, cylindrical, twig hdl, berry finial, 6x4¾" **200.00**
Umbrella stand, 24" **1,550.00**
Urn, 15½" **490.00**
Vase, classic form, 1800s, 12", pr **600.00**
Vase, gold dragons & foo dogs, old rpr, 14", pr **715.00**
Vase, Ku form, 14" **715.00**

Roselane

Founded in California in 1938 by William and Georgia Fields, the Roselane company at first produced only figurines for the local florist. But by the forties they offered candle holders, wall pockets, vases, and a line of modernistic animals mounted on wooden bases. In the fifties their 'Sparklers' became popular — small stylized animal and bird figures with rhinestone eyes. (Today these are worth from $5.00 to $15.00, depending on size.) The company closed in 1977. A variety of marks was used; all incorporate the Roselane name.

Planter, coolie atop, $22.00.

Bowl, fish design, turq & blk, w/stand, 13" dia **65.00**
Dealer sign, Roselane, deep aqua, glossy, 3x12½" **175.00**
Figurine, Bali dancer male, 11" **35.00**
Figurine, boy w/dog, brn on wht, 5½" **10.00**
Figurine, deer, brn & wht w/sparkler eyes, 4x3½" **12.00**
Figurine, deer, head up, 8" **15.00**
Figurine, pheasant, brn on wht matt, tail up, 7¾" **22.50**
Figurine, Siamese cat, sparkler eyes, pk studded collar, 4" **12.00**
Figurine, Siamese cat, sparkler eyes, 7½" **15.00**
Sculpture, elephant, stylized, brn lustre, wood base, 8" **125.00**
Vase, Chinese modern, emb decor base, ftd, 9¾" **25.00**

Rosemeade

Rosemeade was the name chosen by Wahpeton Pottery Company

of Wahpeton, North Dakota, to represent their product. The founders of the company were Laura A. Taylor and R.J. Hughes, who organized the firm in 1940. It is most noted for small bird and animal figurals, either in high gloss or a Van Briggle-like matt glaze. The ware was marked 'Rosemeade' with an ink stamp or carried a 'Prairie Rose' sticker. The pottery closed in 1961. Our advisor for this category is Bryce L. Farnsworth; he is listed in the Directory under North Dakota.

Ashtray, Equitable Life Assurance..., emb mother/child/angel **36.00**
Ashtray, Minnesota state, Lake of the Woods **65.00**
Ashtray, North Dakota state, Kiwanis **55.00**
Ashtray, Northern Pike **135.00**
Bank, fish **420.00**
Bell, tulip form **175.00**
Bookend, bear, ea **250.00**
Bookend, NDAC Bison, ea **345.00**
Cotton receiver, rabbit form **150.00**
Ewer, Minnesota Centennial **115.00**
Figurine, duck, mini **85.00**
Figurine, fighting cocks, mini, pr **150.00**
Figurine, finches, mini, pr **135.00**
Figurine, fox, recumbent **190.00**
Figurine, pony, Art Deco style, 4¾" **290.00**
Flower frog, pheasant **95.00**
Hors d'oeuvres, fish **55.00**
Hors d'oeuvres, turkey on tray **115.00**
Incense burner, elephant **200.00**
Lamp, TV; horse **490.00**
Lamp, TV; pheasant **500.00**
Paperweight, Minnesota Centennial, 3¾" dia **90.00**
Planter, pheasant **310.00**
Planter, swan **30.00**
Plaque, fish **130.00**
Shakers, badger, pr **500.00**
Shakers, bluebird, pr **175.00**
Shakers, cow, purple, pr **260.00**
Shakers, deer, leaping, pr **160.00**
Shakers, dog's head, Greyhound, pr **40.00**
Shakers, dog's head, Scottie, pr **40.00**
Shakers, dove, pr **650.00**
Shakers, duckling, pr **70.00**
Shakers, elephant, pr **75.00**
Shakers, Fort Lincoln Blockhouse, pr **205.00**
Shakers, Indian's head, pr **650.00**
Shakers, muskie, pr **210.00**
Shakers, pheasant, tail up, pr **47.50**
Shakers, pig, standing upright, lg, pr **150.00**
Shakers, raccoon, pr **150.00**
Shakers, roadrunner, pr **200.00**
Shakers, robin, pr **180.00**
Shakers, rooster, strutting, pr **155.00**
Shakers, sailboat, pr **460.00**
Spoon rest, rooster **75.00**
Vase, bird on nest on stump, 6" **40.00**
Vase, blk, Art Deco, 10" **45.00**
Vase, boot, bl matt, 6½" **50.00**
Vase, HP violets, sgn AK, rare, 5" **500.00**
Vase, lovebirds **40.00**
Wall pocket, deer **40.00**

Rosenthal

In 1879 Phillip Rosenthal established the Rosenthal Porcelain

Factory in Selb, Bavaria. Its earliest products were figurines and fine tablewares. The company has continued to operate to the present decade, manufacturing limited edition plates.

Bowl, lady's portrait, scalloped edge with heavy gold trim, 10¾", $135.00.

Bowl, fruit; White Velvet, platinum trim **5.00**
Bowl, White Velvet, platinum trim, 9½" **30.00**
Figurine, Airedale Terrier **140.00**
Figurine, angel, pk & wht, 5½" **145.00**
Figurine, angelfish, sgn Heidenreich, 16" **750.00**
Figurine, bird, #1648 ....**160.00**
Figurine, dove, #1500 ....**98.00**
Figurine, ducks, #153 ....**98.00**
Figurine, fox **135.00**
Figurine, horse, #1136 ....**198.00**
Figurine, Pan recoiling from a crocodile, 26" **1,600.00**
Figurine, rooster & hen, pr **195.00**
Figurine, terrier, standing, Karner **295.00**
Platter, White Velvet, platinum trim, 13" **32.00**
Platter, White Velvet, platinum trim, 15" **37.00**
Relish, White Velvet, platinum trim, oval, 9½" **18.00**
Tray, Monbijou, woodland scene w/deer, hdls, 1898, 15x10" **99.00**

Roseville

The Roseville Pottery Company was established in 1892 by George F. Young in Roseville, Ohio. Finding their facilities inadequate, the company moved to Zanesville in 1898, erected a new building, and installed the most modern equipment available. By 1900 Young felt ready to enter into the stiffly competitive art pottery market. Roseville's first art line was called Rozane. Similar to Rookwood's Standard, Rozane featured dark blended backgrounds with slip-painted underglaze artwork of nature studies, portraits, birds, and animals. Azurean, developed in 1902, was a blue and white underglaze art line on a blue blended background. Egypto (1904) featured a matt glaze in a soft shade of old green and was modeled in low relief after examples of ancient Egyptian pottery. Mongol (1904) was a high-gloss oxblood red line after the fashion of the Chinese Sang de Boeuf. Mara (1904), an iridescent lustre line of magenta and rose with intricate patterns developed on the surface or in low relief, successfully duplicated Sicardo's work. These early lines were followed by many others of highest quality: Fudjiyama and Woodland (1905-06) reflected an Oriental theme; Crystalis (1906) was covered with beautiful frost-like crystals. Della Robbia, their most famous line (introduced in 1906), was decorated with designs ranging from florals, animals, and birds to scenes of Viking warriors and Roman gladiators. These designs were accomplished by sgraffito with slip-painted details. Very limited but of great importance to collectors today, Rozane Olympic (1905) was decorated with scenes of Greek mythology on a red ground. Pauleo (1914) was the last of the artware lines. It was varied — over two hundred glazes were recorded — and some pieces were decorated by hand, usually with florals.

During the second decade of the century until the plant closed forty years later, new lines were continually added. Some of the more popular of the middle-period lines were Donatello, 1915; Futura, 1928; Pine Cone, 1931; and Blackberry, 1933. The floral lines of the later years have become highly collectible. Pottery from every era of Roseville production — even its utility ware — attest to an unwavering dedication to quality and artistic merit.

Examples of the fine art pottery lines present the greatest challenge to evaluate. Scarcity is a prime consideration. The quality of artwork varied from one artist to another. Some pieces show fine detail and good color, and naturally this influences their values. Studies of animals and portraits bring higher prices than the floral designs. An artist's signature often increases the value of any item, especially if the artist is one who is well recognized. For further information consult *The Collector's Encyclopedia of Roseville Pottery, First and Second Series*, by Sharon and Bob Huxford, available at your local library or bookstore. Our advisors for this category are Jeanette and Marvin Stofft; they are listed in the Directory under Indiana.

Apple Blossom, basket, twig hdl, #310, 10" 135.00
Apple Blossom, bowl, sm twig hdls, #326-6, 2½x6½" 55.00
Apple Blossom, vase, twig hdls, #387, 9" 85.00
Autumn, pitcher, landscape on brn shaded, unmk, 8½" 365.00

Autumn shaving mug, 4", $275.00.

Autumn, wash bowl & pitcher, landscape on brn, 14½", 12½" ..800.00
Aztec, vase, geometrics on bl, shouldered, slim, unmk, 10½" 265.00
Aztec, vase, geometrics on brn, slightly waisted, 11" 375.00
Azurean, vase, floral, bl & wht, shouldered, #822/7, 15½" 1,050.00
Azurean, vase, landscape, bl on wht, bulbous, unmk, 9" 1,850.00
Baneda, bowl, foliate band on gr, hdls, unmk, 3½x10" 175.00
Baneda, vase, foliate band on gr, 6" 200.00
Bank, cat's head, unmk, 4" 165.00
Bank, pig, gr & wht, unmk, 2½x5½" 115.00
Bittersweet, basket, #807-8, 8½" 65.00
Bittersweet, basket, #808, 6" 65.00
Bittersweet, teapot, #871S, +cr/sug 225.00
Bittersweet, vase, twig hdls, #885-10, 10" 90.00
Blackberry, candle holders, flared base, 4½", pr 300.00
Blackberry, jardiniere, sm hdls, unmk, 7" 345.00
Blackberry, vase, ring hdls, 8" 325.00
Blackberry, vase, sm hdls, 4" 185.00
Bleeding Heart, candlestick, long hdls, #1139-4½", 5" 60.00
Bleeding Heart, plate, 6-sided, #381-10, 10½" 115.00
Bushberry, bowl, twig hdls, #411, 4" 55.00
Bushberry, cornucopia, dbl, 6" 100.00
Bushberry, ewer, #2, 10" 135.00
Bushberry, vase, integral hdls, #38-12, 12½" 225.00
Carnelian I, vase, drip glaze, angle hdls, ink stamp, 10" 100.00
Carnelian I, vase, drip glaze, fan form, ink stamp, 6" 37.50

Carnelian II, urn, mottled glaze, ornate hdls, unmk, 8" 165.00
Carnelian II, vase, drip glaze, angle hdls, 7" 115.00
Chloron, vase, emb grapes, integral hdls, ink stamp, 9" 275.00
Clemana, bowl, floral, bl wash, #281-5, 4½x6½" 85.00
Clemana, vase, floral, gr & wht on brn, hdls, #759-14, 14" 350.00
Clematis, candle holders, gr, hdls, #11, 4½", pr 60.00
Clematis, cookie jar, gr, #3, 10" 200.00
Clematis, vase, floral, gr, 8" 60.00
Columbine, basket, bl, #367, 10" 115.00
Columbine, ewer, bl, angle hdl, #18, 7" 70.00
Columbine, vase, angle hdls, #17-7, 7½" 85.00
Cornelian, pitcher, corn emb on bl, unmk, 6" 85.00
Cornelian, pitcher, Wild Rose emb, unmk, 9" 80.00
Cosmos, console bowl, low hdls, #374-14, 15½" 150.00
Cosmos, vase, floral, bl, 6" 100.00
Crystalis, candlestick, flared ft, Rozane Ware Mongol seal, 9" 850.00
Crystalis, vase, cream w/bl crystals, shouldered, unmk, 11" 1,300.00
Crystalis, vase, flaring cylinder w/3 futuristic arms, 12" 2,400.00
Crystalis, vase, yel/tan mottle, cylinder w/3 emb heads, 15" 2,000.00
Dahlrose, vase, floral, sm angle hdls, paper label, 6" 80.00
Dahlrose, window box, floral band, rectangular, 6x16" 150.00
Della Robbia, mug, landscape, Rozane Ware seal, 4½" 475.00
Della Robbia, tankard, tall trees in landscape, 10½" 1,650.00
Della Robbia, teapot, inscription, Rozane Ware seal, 5½" 1,050.00
Della Robbia, vase, floral, rtcl rim, Rozane Ware seal, 14" 3,625.00
Della Robbia, vase, floral panels, rtcl neck band, 15½" 26,000.00
Della Robbia, vase, grapes & leaves, lt on med bl, 11½", EX 800.00
Della Robbia, vase, Nouveau flowers/swirls, 15" 13,500.00
Dogwood I, jardiniere, floral on gr, ink stamp, 8" 105.00
Dogwood I, vase, floral on gr, ink stamp, 7" 115.00
Dogwood II, tub, floral on gr, hdls, unmk, 4x7" 65.00
Donatello, basket, cherubs in band, 7½" 115.00
Donatello, compote, cherubs in band, mk, 4" 80.00
Donatello, jardiniere, cherubs in band, 8½" 85.00
Donatello, plate, cherubs in center, unmk, 8" 215.00
Donatello, vase, cherubs in panel, gray (rare), unmk, 8½" 165.00
Dutch, pitcher, children, unmk, 7½" 130.00
Dutch, tumbler, girl, unmk, 4" 105.00
Earlam, bowl, unmk, 3x11½" 85.00
Early Pitcher, Boy, unmk, 7½" 300.00
Early Pitcher, Bridge, unmk, 6" 115.00
Early Pitcher, Cow, unmk, 7½" 275.00
Early Pitcher, Landscape, blended glaze, unmk, 7½" 115.00
Early Pitcher, utility, feathery leaves, unmk, 6½" 55.00
Egypto, lamp base, 3 men on elephants, trunk hdls, unmk, 10" ..550.00
Egypto, vase, emb medallions, sq sides, Egypto seal, 12½" 315.00
Falline, vase, pea pods, gourd shape, low hdls, 12½" 450.00
Falline, vase, pea pods, loop hdls, unmk, 6" 250.00
Ferella, bowl, red & gr, ftd, 12" 325.00
Ferella, lamp base, non-standard bl & gr, unmk, 10½" 450.00
Ferella, vase, angle hdls, 4" 185.00
Florentine, vase, reserves & draped florals, angle hdls, 8" 70.00
Foxglove, flower frog, cornucopia shape, 4" 35.00
Foxglove, tray, 1-hdl, 8½" 65.00
Foxglove, vase, angle hdls, #42, 4" 30.00
Freesia, flowerpot/saucer, 5½" 75.00
Freesia, vase, angle hdls, #121-8, 8" 67.50
Fuchsia, vase, #896-8, 8½" 175.00
Fuchsia, vase, loop hdls, #892-6", 6" 135.00
Fudji, vase, stylized florals, bl on cream, unmk, 9" 1,325.00
Fujiyama, jardiniere, stylized butterflies, ink stamp, 9" 1,100.00
Fujiyama, vase, floral, cylindrical, ink stamp, 15" 950.00
Futura, candle holders, ivory & gr, 4", pr 150.00
Futura, jardiniere, stylized florals, angle hdls, unmk, 6" 175.00

Futura, vase, lt/dk bl triangle panels, pillow form, 5x6" 135.00
Gardenia, bowl, ring hdls, ruffled rim, #641-5, 5" 50.00
Gardenia, vase, low hdls, #687-12, 12" 120.00
Holland, pitcher, Dutch figures, unmk, 12" 250.00
Holly, creamer, unmk, 3" 115.00
Holly, teapot, unmk, 4¼" 225.00
Imperial, basket, #7, 9" 90.00
Imperial, planter, unmk, 14x16" 100.00
Imperial II, vase, flattened gourd shape, unmk, 4½" 115.00
Iris, console bowl, #362-10, 3½x12½" 115.00
Ivory II, figurine, nude, unmk, 9" 350.00
Ivory II, jardiniere, unmk, 6" 47.50
Ixia, vase, floral, gourd form, low uptrn hdls, #857-8, 8½" 65.00
Jonquil, bowl, floral, low hdls, unmk, 3" 85.00
Jonquil, vase, floral, hdls, paper label, 8" 150.00
Juvenile, creamer, Santa Claus, 3½" 135.00
Juvenile, cup & saucer, ducks, gr band, unmk, 2", 5½" 85.00
Juvenile, egg cup, rabbit & bl band, ink stamp, 3" 200.00
Juvenile, mug, fat puppy, gr band, unmk, 3½" 115.00
Juvenile, pudding dish, chicks, gr band, unmk, 3½" 50.00
Juvenile, sugar bowl, nursery rhyme motif, 3" 115.00
Lombardy, vase, bl, 3 sm buttressed ft, unmk, 6" 150.00
Luffa, vase, floral, sm angle hdls, unmk, 8½" 120.00
Magnolia, pitcher, cider; #132, 7" 200.00
Magnolia, planter, #388-6, 8½" 65.00
Magnolia, vase, dbl bud; #186, 4½" 65.00
Mara, vase, emb foliage, gourd shape, ring hdls, unmk, 5½" 1,600.00
Matt Green, basket, emb decor, hanging, unmk, 9" 135.00
Matt Green, jardiniere, 4 sm ft, unmk, 6" 80.00
Matt Green, planter & liner, emb decor, #510, 4" 135.00
Ming Tree, bowl, tub form, twig hdls, #526-9, 4x11½" 50.00
Ming Tree, candle holders, twig hdls, #551, pr 50.00
Ming Tree, vase, twig hdls, #582, 8" 55.00
Moderne, candle holder, triple; #1112, 6" 125.00
Moderne, comport, ftd, #295, 5" 115.00
Mongol, mug, 3-hdl, 6" 775.00
Mongol, vase, candle holder form, 3 upright hdls, 3½", NM 450.00
Mongol, vase, gourd form, 8" 850.00
Morning Glory, candlestick, flared ft, sm hdls, unmk, 5" 140.00
Morning Glory, vase, angle hdls, unmk, 15" 600.00
Morning Glory, vase, angle hdls, 12" 400.00
Morning Glory, vasse, urn form, 6" 225.00

Moss, vase, 7½", $185.00.

Moss, vase, pillow form, sm hdls, #781-8, 8" 135.00
Mostique, bowl, stylized florals, unmk, 7" 40.00
Mostique, jardiniere, stylized florals, unmk, 8" 115.00
Mug, floral decal, unmk, 5" 85.00
Mug, FOE, Liberty, Truth, Justice, Equality, unmk, 5" 110.00
Mug, Loyal Order of Moose, moose portrait, unmk, 5" 100.00

Mug, Roosevelt portrait, Our Choice, 1908, unmk, 5" 250.00
Normandy, basket, grapevines form band, unmk, hanging, 7" 185.00
Novelty Stein, This Is So Sudden, 4½" 200.00
Novelty Stein, Try It on the Dog, 5" 200.00
Olympic, pitcher, Ulysses at table of Circle, 7" 2,125.00
Pauleo, vase, berries & leaves on shaded gray lustre, unmk, 17" .950.00
Pauleo, vase, gray/gr/bl separated glaze, bulbous, unmk, 9" 400.00
Pauleo, vase, purple/lav/pk separated glaze, 18½" 950.00
Peony, bookend, #11, 5½" 125.00
Peony, vase, low hdls, #681-4, 14" 200.00
Persian, jardiniere, stylized floral on cream, ink mk, 5" 165.00
Pine Cone, centerpiece/candle holder, gr, #324, 6" 275.00
Pine Cone, jardiniere, brn, 5¼" 145.00
Pine Cone, vase, urn form, twig hdls, , gr, #908-8, 8" 175.00
Poppy, ewer, ornate rim, #880-18, 18½" 300.00
Poppy, jardiniere, ring hdls, #335-6, 6½" 115.00
Rosecraft Black, comport, ftd, unmk, 4x11" 115.00
Rosecraft Black, vase, gourd form, hdls, paper label, 9" 135.00
Rosecraft Blended, vase, bud; cylindrical, #36-6 ....55.00
Rosecraft Hexagon, bowl, sm angle hdls, ink stamp, 7½" 85.00
Rosecraft Panel, jar, gr, w/lid, ink stamp, 10" 325.00
Rosecraft Vintage, vase, grapes band, sm angle hdls, 8½" 145.00
Rozane, letter holder, floral, rectangular, 3½" 185.00
Rozane, Light; bowl, floral, incurvate rim, hdls, 3" 165.00
Rozane, Light; tankard, ears of corn on shaded ground, 10" 375.00
Rozane, Light; vase, floral, slim, flared base, sm hdls, 14" 850.00
Rozane, mug, ears of corn, artist sgn, ornate hdl, 6" 215.00
Rozane, tankard, floral, cylinder w/flared base, #821, 10½" 265.00
Rozane, vase, dog's portrait, classic shape, 17" 2,750.00
Rozane, vase, floral, angle hdls, #7, 11" 250.00
Rozane, vase, floral, artist sgn, long neck & hdls, 7" 225.00
Rozane, vase, floral, gourd shape, 9" 165.00
Rozane, vase, floral, slim cylinder form, 10½" 375.00
Rozane, vase, raspberries, W Myers, ovoid, 9x6" 550.00
Rozane 1917, basket, floral on bl, ink stamp, 11" 120.00
Rozane 1917, bowl, floral, tub hdls, ftd, ink stamp, 5" 75.00
Rozane 1917, vase, floral on yel, 10" 75.00
Russco, cornucopia, triple; paper label, 8x12½" 80.00
Russco, vase, trumpet form, sm uptrn hdls, unmk, 7" 65.00
Savonia, console bowl, salmon pk, unmk, 4x10" 65.00
Savonia, vase, emb floral, salmon pk, unmk, 9" 135.00
Snowberry, bowl, console, hdls, #1-BL-1, 10" 65.00
Snowberry, vase, pillow form, #1-FH-6, 6½" 50.00
Sunflower, bowl, sm hdls, unmk, 4" 210.00
Sunflower, vase, sm hdls, unmk, 10" 500.00
Teasel, vase, low hdls, #887-10, 10" 150.00
Thornapple, vase, dbl bud; #1119, 5½" 65.00
Thornapple, vase, ftd, sm hdls, #820-9, 9½" 135.00
Topeo, bowl, graduated pearl decor at rim, unmk, 3x11½" 60.00
Tourist, window box, pastoral landscape, unmk, 8½x19" 1,150.00
Tourmaline, candlestick, streaky bl, flared rim, 5" 45.00
Tuscany, flower arranger, integral hdls, unmk, 5½" 37.50
Velmoss Scroll, vase, floral on tan, bulbous, unmk, 5" 105.00
Velmoss Scroll, vase, floral on tan, ftd slim form, unmk, 10" 125.00
Vista, basket, floral, unmk, 12" 275.00
Vista, vase, floral, sm hdls, #121-15, 15" 350.00
Volpato, candlesticks, emb floral, ivory, 9½", pr 185.00
Water Lily, basket, stylized rim, integral hdl, #382, 12" 150.00
Water Lily, bowl, angle hdls, #663, 3" 35.00
Water Lily, ewer, #11, 10" 125.00
Water Lily, vase, hdls, flared ft, #78-9, 9" 115.00
Wincraft, basket, floral on yel, #209, 12" 85.00
Wincraft, dealer sign, unmk, 4½x8" 700.00
Wincraft, vase, floral on turq, ftd cylinder, #285, 10" 80.00

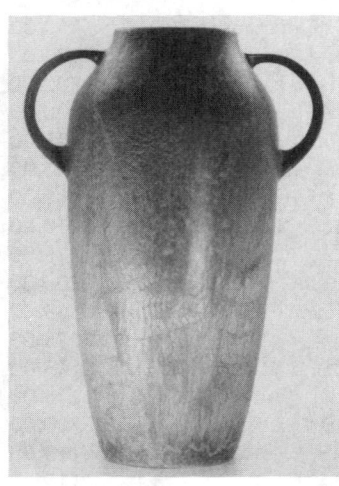

Windsor, vase, 16", $1,500.00.

Windsor, basket, integral hdl, paper label, 4½" 200.00
Windsor, candlesticks, hdls, 4½", pr 185.00
Windsor, lamp base, globular, integral hdl, unmk, 7" 315.00
Windsor, vase, floral on bl, hdls, paper label, 9" 325.00
Wisteria, vase, floral, waisted, low angle hdls, 10" 425.00
Woodland, vase, floral on cream, classic form, 19" 1,625.00
Woodland, vase, floral on cream, shouldered, unmk, 6½" 565.00
Zephyr Lily, vase, fan form, low hdls, #105-6, 6½" 60.00
Zephyr Lily, vase, urn form, #202-8, 8½" 85.00

Rowland and Marsellus

Though the impressive back stamp seems to suggest otherwise, Rowland and Marsellus were not Staffordshire potters but American importers who commissioned various English companies to supply them with the transfer-printed historical ware that had been a popular import item since the early 1800s. Plates (both flat and with a rolled edge), cups and saucers, pitchers, and platters were sold as souvenirs from 1890 through the 1930s. Though other importers — Bawo & Dotter, and A. C. Bosselman & Co., both of New York City — commissioned the manufacture of similar souvenir items, by far the largest volume carries the R. & M. mark, and Rowland and Marcellus has become a generic term that covers all 20th-century souvenir china of this type. Their mark may be in full or 'R. & M.' in a diamond. Though primarily made with blue transfers on white, other colors may occasionally be found as well. Our advisor for this category is David Ringering; he is listed in the Directory under Oregon.

Key:
r/e — rolled edge   v/o — view of
s/o — souvenir of

Cup & saucer, Chicago, s/o 65.00
Cup & saucer, Niagara Falls NY, s/o 65.00
Cup & saucer, Provincetown MA, s/o 65.00
Cup & saucer, Yale, s/o, AF Wylie 65.00
Plate, Albany (NY), s/o, State Capital, r/e, 10" 50.00
Plate, Biltmore House, Asheville NC, fruit & flower border 50.00
Plate, Bunker Hill Monument, Ye Olde Historical Pottery, 9" 30.00
Plate, Cincinnati OH, s/o, State Capital, r/e, 10" 45.00
Plate, coupe; Chicago, v/o, Marshall Field & Co, 6" 30.00
Plate, coupe; Denver, v/o, 10" 50.00
Plate, coupe; Early Missions of CA, s/o, Parmelee & Dorhman, 6" ..30.00
Plate, coupe; Miami, s/o, Chief Osceola, 10" 50.00
Plate, coupe; Salem, v/o, witch & 5 scenes, Daniel Low, 6" 30.00

Plate, Denver, Co, s/o, Capitol Building, r/e, 10" 50.00
Plate, Haverhill MA, Whittier's Birthplace, 9" 30.00
Plate, Hermitage, fruit & flower border 45.00
Plate, Jackson, MS, s/o, New Capital Building, r/e, 10" 55.00
Plate, Lookout Mtn, TN, s/o, Moccasin Bend & Lookout, r/e, 10" ...50.00
Plate, Marblehead MA, Old Town House Built 1777, 9" 30.00
Plate, Nashville, v/o, State Capitol, r/e, 10" 60.00
Plate, Plymouth Rock, fruit & flower border 40.00
Plate, Portland OR, s/o, Mt Hood, r/e, 10" 55.00
Plate, St Paul Minn, s/o, State Capitol, r/e, 10" 50.00
Plate, Waltham Watch Factory, fruit & flower border 50.00
Tumbler, Fall River MA, v/o 65.00
Tumbler, Montreal PQ, s/o 65.00
Tumbler, Thousand Islands, v/o 65.00

Royal Bayreuth

Founded in 1794 in Tettau, Bavaria, the Royal Bayreuth firm originally manufactured fine dinnerwares of superior quality. Their figural items, produced from before the turn of the century until the onset of WWI, are highly sought after by today's collectors. Perhaps the most abundantly produced and easily recognized of these are the tomato and lobster pieces. Fruits, flowers, people, animals, birds, and vegetables shapes were also made. Aside from figural items, pitchers, toothpick holders, cups and saucers, humidors and the like were decorated in florals and scenic motifs. Some, such as the very popular Rose Tapestry line, utilized a cloth-like tapestry background. Transfer prints were used as well. Two of the most popular are Sunbonnet Babies and Nursery Rhymes (in particular, those decorated with the complete verse).

Caution: Many pieces were not marked; some were marked 'Deponiert' or 'Registered' only. While marked pieces are the most valued, unmarked items are still very worthwhile. Our advisors for this category are Larry Brenner from New Hampshire and Dee Hooks from Illinois; they are listed in the Directory under their home states.

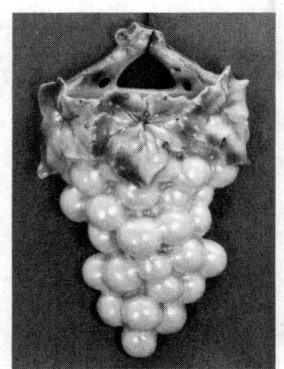

**Wall pocket, grapes, white, 9",
$350.00.**

Figurals

Ashtray, Devil, red, bl mk 325.00
Ashtray, elk, bl mk 300.00
Bowl, pansy, bl mk, 9" 295.00
Bowl, poppy, red, bl mk, 6" 150.00
Bowl, salad; lobster, bl mk 225.00
Box, tomato, w/plate, bl mk, sm 65.00
Candle holder, poppy, red, bl mk 575.00
Candy dish, lettuce leaf, bl mk 40.00
Candy dish, lobster, bl mk, 5½" 180.00
Cup, demitasse; Devil & Cards, bl mk 265.00
Cup & saucer, demitasse; rose, bl mk 385.00

Marmalade, orange, bl mk 375.00
Match holder, chimp, wall hanging, bl mk 800.00
Mug, beer; Devil & Cards, commemorative, bl mk 250.00
Mustard, grapes, pearlized, bl mk 285.00
Nut dish, poppy, red, bl mk 50.00
Pitcher, apple, bl mk, cream sz 215.00
Pitcher, bull, blk, bl mk, cream sz 195.00
Pitcher, butterfly, open wings, bl mk, cream sz 275.00
Pitcher, cat, blk, bl mk, cream sz 165.00
Pitcher, clown, red, bl mk, cream sz 215.00
Pitcher, coachman, bl mk, cream sz 215.00
Pitcher, coral shell, hdl, unmk, cream sz 145.00
Pitcher, crow, bl mk, cream sz 150.00
Pitcher, dachshund, bl mk, cream sz 255.00
Pitcher, Devil & Cards, bl mk, cream sz 200.00
Pitcher, Devil & Cards, commemorative, bl mk, water sz ...250.00
Pitcher, duck, bl mk, cream sz 200.00
Pitcher, eagle, bl mk, cream sz 200.00
Pitcher, eagle, bl mk, water sz 700.00
Pitcher, elk, bl mk, cream sz 155.00
Pitcher, elk, bl mk, milk sz 285.00
Pitcher, elk, bl mk, water sz 675.00
Pitcher, fish, open mouth, bl mk, milk sz 300.00
Pitcher, frog, unmk, cream sz 175.00
Pitcher, girl w/basket, bl mk, rare, cream sz 750.00
Pitcher, lamplighter, bl mk, cream sz 300.00
Pitcher, lobster, bl mk, cream sz 105.00
Pitcher, low shell, bl mk, cream sz 100.00
Pitcher, mountain goat, bl mk, cream sz 300.00
Pitcher, oak leaf, pearlized, bl mk, cream sz 285.00
Pitcher, Old Man of Mtn, bl mk, cream sz 65.00
Pitcher, Old Man of Mtn, unmk, cream sz 45.00
Pitcher, orange, bl mk, cream sz 200.00
Pitcher, pansy, bl mk, cream sz 225.00
Pitcher, pelican, bl mk, cream sz 300.00
Pitcher, rose, bl mk, cream sz, 3½" 395.00
Pitcher, tomato, bl mk, cream sz 75.00
Pitcher, tomato, bl mk, water sz 395.00
Pitcher, water buffalo, blk, bl mk, cream sz 200.00
Pitcher & sugar bowl, grapes, purple, bl mk 300.00
Plate, poppy, red, bl mk, 7½" 120.00
Shakers, apple, unmk, pr 150.00
Shakers, grapes, pearlized, bl mk 95.00
Shakers, tomato, bl mk, 2½", pr 90.00
Sugar bowl, apple, yel, bl mk 150.00
Sugar bowl, elk, low, bl mk 300.00
Sugar bowl, lobster, bl mk, w/lid 180.00
Sugar bowl, poppy, bl mk 150.00
Sugar bowl, tomato, bl mk 75.00
Teapot, tomato, bl mk, lg 195.00
Toothpick holder, elk, bl mk 200.00
Waste bowl, lobster, bl mk 200.00

Nursery Rhymes

Bell, Jack & the Beanstalk, unmk 295.00
Candlestick, Jack & Jill, bl mk, ring hdl 215.00
Chamberstick, Little Jack Horner, bl mk 185.00
Coffeepot, Jack & Jill, bl mk 315.00
Cup & saucer, Jack & the Beanstalk, bl mk 195.00
Pitcher, Jack & Jill, bl mk, cream sz 195.00
Pitcher, Little Miss Muffet, bl mk, milk sz 200.00
Pitcher, Ring Around the Rosie, bl mk, cream sz 185.00
Plate, Little Bo Peep, bl mk, 6¼" 95.00

Plate, Little Jack Horner, bl mk, 7¾" 115.00
Sugar bowl, Little Boy Blue, bl mk 195.00
Sugar bowl, Little Miss Muffet, bl mk 215.00

Scenics and Action Portraits

Ashtray, hunt scene, sq shape, bl mk 100.00
Ashtray, penguin scene, bl mk 155.00
Basket, cows, bl mk, 4½" 220.00
Bell, hunt scene, bl mk 230.00
Bowl, Blk Corinthian, bl mk, 6" 95.00
Bowl, Snow Babies, ruffled rim, bl mk, 6" 200.00
Box, man w/checkers, dome-shaped lid, bl mk 165.00
Box, woman & geese, club shape, bl mk 95.00
Candle holder, cows, bl mk 235.00
Candle holder, pastoral scene, ring hdl, bl mk 265.00
Candle holder, sheep grazing, bl mk 150.00
Candlesticks, Blk Corinthian, ring hdl, bl mk, pr 200.00
Candlesticks, Red Corinthian, bl mk, pr 200.00
Celery tray, goats, bl mk 95.00
Clock, hunt scene, bl mk 400.00
Compote, mtn sheep, bl mk 175.00
Cup & saucer, Beach Babies, bl mk 195.00
Cup & saucer, stag & doe, bl mk 200.00
Cup & saucer, tavern scene, bl mk 98.00
Flower arranger, hunt scene, bl mk 265.00
Hair receiver, sheep, dome top, bl mk 175.00
Hair receiver, stag & doe, bl mk 200.00
Hatpin holder, lady riding/couple at croquet, bl mk, 5" ...150.00
Mug, Oriental bird, bl mk 125.00
Nappy, Brittany Girl, hdls, 3" 95.00
Nappy, girl w/geese, bl mk, scalloped, 3" 315.00
Nappy, stag & doe, hdl, bl mk 135.00
Pitcher, Beach Babies, bl mk, cream sz 175.00
Pitcher, bird of paradise, bl mk, cream sz 100.00
Pitcher, Blk Corinthian, bulbous, bl mk, cream sz 75.00
Pitcher, Brittany Girl, yel, bl mk, 4" 100.00
Pitcher, goats, pinched spout, bl mk, milk sz 215.00
Pitcher, Gr Corinthian, bulbous, bl mk, cream sz 75.00
Pitcher, hunt scene, bl mk, water sz 195.00
Pitcher, hunt scene, sq shape, bl mk, cream sz 110.00
Pitcher, hunt scene, yel, bl mk, milk sz, 6" 100.00
Pitcher, man & horses, bl mk, milk sz 215.00
Pitcher, mtn goats, pinched spout, bl mk, cream sz, 4" ...195.00
Pitcher, mtn sheep grazing, bl mk, cream sz, 4" 355.00
Pitcher, Snow Babies, bl mk, cream sz 215.00
Pitcher, tavern scene, bl mk, milk sz 180.00
Plate, Brittany Girl, bl mk, 7" 85.00
Plate, mtn goat, bl mk, 8" 100.00
Rose bowl, hunt scene, bl mk, 3" 120.00
Salt cellar, mtn goats, ped ft, bl mk 70.00
Shakers, Blk Corinthian, bl mk, pr 100.00
Sugar bowl, Brittany Girl, bl mk 75.00
Sugar bowl, man w/chickens, bl mk, w/lid 100.00
Sugar bowl, Snow Babies, bl mk 235.00
Teapot, Blk Corinthian, bl mk 215.00
Teapot, hunt scene, bl mk, mini 195.00
Toothpick holder, courting couple, bl mk 100.00
Toothpick holder, mtn goat, bl mk 125.00
Tray, dresser; Red Corinthian, bl mk 200.00
Tray, mountain & castle, bl mk, 11" 475.00
Vase, Blk Corinthian, bl mk, 5½" 95.00
Vase, Brittany Girl, hdls, SP rim, bl mk, 5" 120.00
Vase, bud; castle, bulbous, bl mk 225.00

Vase, cattle, bl mk, 5" 95.00
Vase, chickens & rooster, tumbler shape, bl mk 95.00
Vase, courting couple, bl mk, 4" 345.00
Vase, cows, bl mk, 3½" 100.00
Vase, girl w/turkeys, hdls, bl mk, 3" 115.00
Vase, Gr Corinthian, bl mk, 9" 315.00
Vase, hunt scene, hdls, bl mk, 4" 110.00
Vase, ladies w/sheep, 3-hdl, bl mk 100.00
Vase, Red Corinthian, bl mk, 4½" 75.00
Vase, stag & doe, hdls, mini 130.00
Vase, turkey w/man, bl mk, 4½" 100.00
Vase, Yel Corinthian, bl mk, 5½" 95.00

Sunbonnet Babies

Ashtray, washing, bl mk 185.00
Bowl, bl mk, 10" 415.00
Bowl, cereal; sweeping, bl mk, 5¼" 335.00
Bowl, washing, bl mk, 9" 400.00
Cake plate, washing, bl mk, 10¼" 295.00
Candlestick, cleaning, shield bk, bl mk 500.00
Chamberstick, sewing, ring hdl, bl mk 415.00
Cup & saucer, demitasse; washing, bl mk 325.00
Cup & saucer, fishing, bl mk 350.00
Cup & saucer, sweeping, bl mk 300.00
Ferner, babies washing, bl mk, 3" 350.00
Hair receiver, sewing, bl mk 385.00
Hair receiver, washing, 4-leg, bl mk 425.00
Heart dish, bl mk 185.00
Nappy, sq, bl mk 200.00
Pitcher, cleaning, bl mk, cream sz, 3" 275.00
Pitcher, cleaning, bl mk, 4" 335.00
Pitcher, fishing, blm k, 3½" 350.00
Pitcher, ironing, bl mk, 4" 345.00
Pitcher, scrubbing floor, bl mk, cream sz 345.00
Pitcher, sweeping, bl mk, 3½" 350.00

Pitcher, Sunbonnet Babies sewing, 4½", $395.00.

Pitcher, washing, bl mk, 4½" 335.00
Plate, ironing, bl mk, 6" 125.00
Rose bowl, fishing, bl mk 395.00
Sugar bowl, fishing, open, bl mk 235.00
Sugar bowl, washing, bl mk, w/lid 385.00
Tumbler, cleaning, bulbous, 3½" 450.00
Vase, sewing, bl mk, ewer shape 325.00

Tapestries

Ashtray, Rose Tapestry, 4 corners, bl mk 300.00
Bottle, scent; floral, bl mk, sterling cap, 2" dia ..275.00
Box, trinket; mtn/buildings/waterfall, unmk, 2½x4x2¾" ...150.00
Ferner, cows, bl mk 275.00

Hair receiver, courting scene, bl mk 325.00
Hair receiver, goat scene, bl mk 225.00
Hair receiver, Rose Tapestry, bl mk 225.00
Hair receiver, turkeys, bl mk 300.00
Hatpin holder, Rose Tapestry, bl mk 485.00
Humidor, lady leaning on horse, bl mk, 6½" 850.00
Leaf dish, courting scene, bl mk 215.00
Nappy, girl w/geese, bl mk, 3" 325.00
Nappy, Rose Tapestry, yel, leaf shape, bl mk 265.00
Pin dish, courting scene, bl mk, w/lid 325.00
Pin dish, Rose Tapestry, bl mk, 4½" 225.00
Pitcher, bird of paradise, bl mk, cream sz 125.00
Pitcher, goat scene, pinched spout, bl mk, cream sz, 4" ...210.00
Pitcher, goats, bl mk, 4" 355.00
Pitcher, Rose Tapestry, pinched spout, bl mk, milk sz, 5" ...425.00
Pitcher, Rose Tapestry, pinched spout, blk mk, 4½" ..240.00
Pitcher, Rose Tapestry, pk & yel on gr, bl mk, 3¾" ..225.00
Plaque, peacock & mtn scene, bl mk, 9½" 850.00
Plate, Rose Tapestry, bl mk, 4½" 95.00
Plate, Rose Tapestry, bl mk, 6" 185.00
Powder box, castle scene, bl mk 275.00
Powder box, courting scene, bl mk 350.00
Powder box, Rose Tapestry, 3-color, bl mk 385.00
Relish, courtship scene, open hdl, bl mk, 8¼x4" 200.00
Relish, Rose Tapestry, bl mk 350.00
Ring tree, Rose Tapestry, 3-color, bl mk 485.00
Sugar bowl, courting scene, bl mk 350.00
Sugar bowl, Rose Tapestry, bl mk 350.00
Toothpick holder, lady w/horse, ball shape, bl mk ...295.00
Tray, dresser; Rose Tapestry, 3-color w/gold 225.00
Vase, castle scene, bl mk, 4" 325.00
Vase, Rose Tapestry, pk & yel, bl mk, 4¼" 325.00
Vase, Rose Tapestry, 3-color, bl mk, 2½" 345.00
Vase, Rose Tapestry, 3-color, bl mk, 4½" 365.00

Royal Bonn

Royal Bonn is a fine-paste porcelain, ornately decorated with scenes, portraits, or florals. The factory was established in the mid-1800s in Bonn, Germany; however, most pieces found today are from the latter part of the century.

Clock, mantel; HP flowers, exposed escapement, Ansonia, 14" .695.00
Ewer, floral tapestry, brass base/rim/spout, snake hdl, 19" ...535.00
Ewer, mc flowers w/much gold, scrolled hdl, 10½x4" ..155.00
Umbrella stand, iris, red on gr to yel to bl 375.00
Vase, floral w/gold outlines, gold hdls/scalloped top, 12" ...165.00
Vase, gold floral on shaded brn, in 3-leg brass stand, 7" ...395.00
Vase, iris, pk on bl to gr w/gold, 11" 115.00
Vase, mc flowers w/raised gold, hdls, 20x5" 350.00
Vase, mc pansies on maroon to yel, old mk, 5½" 75.00

Royal Copenhagen

The Royal Copenhagen Manufactory was established in Denmark in about 1775 by Frantz Henrich Muller. When bankruptcy threatened in 1779, the Crown took charge. The fine dinnerware and objects of art produced after that time carry the familiar logo, the crown over three wavy lines. See also Limited Edition Plates.

Charger, silhouettes, blk on ivory, HC Anderson, 13½" ...75.00
Cup & saucer, demitasse; half-covered w/lacy pattern ...40.00

Egg cup, bl lace pattern	40.00
Figurine, boy at lunch, #865	175.00
Figurine, boy w/calf, #772	290.00
Figurine, boy w/gourd, #4539	225.00
Figurine, boy w/horn, #3689	105.00
Figurine, farm girl, #815	375.00
Figurine, girl seated w/doll, #1938	200.00
Figurine, girl w/basket & jug, #815	200.00
Figurine, girl w/calf, #779	280.00
Figurine, Goat Lady, #694	350.00
Figurine, Goose Girl, #527	250.00
Figurine, Gossips, 2nd version, #1319	400.00
Figurine, Icelandic Falcon, #263	300.00
Figurine, koala bear, #5402$575 in 11th edition	275.00
Figurine, lady knitting, #1317	275.00
Figurine, lady w/wool sweater, #1251	120.00
Figurine, man w/2 calves, #1858	375.00
Figurine, milkmaid, #2017	195.00
Figurine, milkmaid, #899, 11½"	425.00
Figurine, October, #4532	275.00
Figurine, Pan on ped, #433	285.00
Figurine, Pan playing pipes, #1736	235.00
Figurine, Pan riding bear, #1804, rare	585.00
Figurine, Pan w/goat, youthful, #1012/498, 5"	262.00
Figurine, Pardon Me, #2372	295.00
Figurine, polar bear, #320	50.00
Figurine, polar bear, #729	120.00
Figurine, rabbit, #4676	245.00
Figurine, robin, fat, #1166, 2¾"	75.00
Figurine, rooster, #1127, 3¾"	50.00
Figurine, Sandman, #1145	165.00
Figurine, 2 children, #1761	625.00
Figurine, 2 girls in garden, #1316	325.00
Platter, Flora Danica	1,250.00
Teapot, bl, fluted, plain, sm	125.00
Teapot, Flora Danica	1,475.00
Vase, Taaske 1927, 7"	75.00

Royal Copley

Royal Copley is a decorative type of pottery made by the Spaulding China Company in Sebring, Ohio, from 1942 to 1957. They also produced two other major lines — Royal Windsor and Spaulding. Royal Copley was primarily marketed through five-and-ten cent stores; Royal Windsor and Spaulding were sold through department stores, gift shops, and jobbers. Items trimmed in gold are worth 25% to 50% more than the same item with no gold trim.

For more information we recommend *Royal Copley* and *More About Royal Copley* by Leslie and Marjorie Wolfe, edited by our advisor for this category, Joe Devine; he is listed in the Directory under Iowa. These books have been brought back by popular demand and include updated values.

Bank, rooster, Chicken Feed on base, 7½"	50.00
Bank, Teddy bear, paper label only, 7½"	50.00
Blade bank, barber pole figural, gold trim, paper label, 6¼"	35.00
Bowl, sm bird perched at rim, gr stamp mk, 4"	12.00
Figurine, hen, paper label only, 7"	24.00
Figurine, lark (or skylark), full body, 6½"	16.00
Figurine, Mallard duckling bending head, paper label, 5"	15.00
Figurine, parrot, any color combination, 8"	32.00
Figurine, thrush, full body, paper label, 6½"	16.00
Lamp, Oriental boy figural base, orig shade	35.00

Lamp base, cocker spaniel figural, rare, 10"	45.00
Pitcher, floral decal on wht, gold stamped mk, 6"	12.00
Pitcher, Pome Fruit on bl, 8"	35.00
Planter, appl dogwood blossoms, pk on brn, 8¼"	16.50
Planter, Balinese girl, paper label only, 8½"	20.00
Planter, Big Blossom, red & bl, stamp mk, 3"	12.00
Planter, Blackamoor, sgn w/emb letters on bk, 8"	35.00
Planter, blk cat, pk bow at neck, 8"	36.00
Planter, clown figural, opening at bk of pants, 8¼"	45.00
Planter, cocker spaniel's head, emb mk, 5"	15.00
Planter, dog pulling wagon, 'Flyer' on side of wagon, 5¾"	28.00
Planter, Dutch boy w/bucket, paper label, 6"	20.00
Planter, elephant w/front ft on ball, paper label only, 6"	25.00
Planter, farm boy w/fishing pole (or farm girl), 6½", ea	24.00
Planter, girl w/wheelbarrow, paper label, 7"	25.00
Planter, hat w/flower band form, hangs or rests on table, 7"	24.00
Planter, hen plaque, made to hang or set on table, 6¾"	35.00
Planter, kitten & birdhouse, paper label, rare, 8"	65.00
Planter, kitten w/ball of yarn, paper label only, 8¼"	27.00
Planter, Oriental child w/lg vase, paper label, 4¾"	12.00
Planter, pup in basket, paper label, 7"	28.00
Planter, rooster walking, any color but wht, 5½"	28.00
Planter, salmon (3) jumping, pk on teal waves, 6½x11½"	45.00
Planter, salt box, 'Salt' in scrolling reserve, 5½"	30.00
Planter, tanager beside stump, gr stamp mk, 6¼"	20.00
Planter, teddy bear w/concertina, paper label, 7½"	60.00
Planter, 3-section, 2½x6½"	9.00
Planter/wall pocket, boy w/wide brim hat, 7½"	28.00
Planter/wall pocket, Chinese girl, 7½"	28.00
Sugar bowl, leafy flower form, hdls, stamped mk	15.00
Vase, bud; parrot on stump figural, 5"	16.00
Vase, cornucopia; rose decal on wht, gold trim, 8¼"	19.00
Vase, fish form, paper label only, 6"	35.00
Vase, Floral Beauty, emb flowers, bl on pk, 8"	24.00
Vase, ivy, gr on ivory, ftd, paper label only, 7"	9.00
Vase, ivy, gr on ivory, ftd pillow form, paper label, 6¼"	10.00
Vase, rose decal on wht, hdls, gold stamp mk, 8"	14.00
Vase, roses decal, closed scroll hdls, 7"	12.00
Vase, stylized leaf emb on sq shape, 8¼"	10.00
Vase/planter, bamboo, oval, paper label, 4½"	10.00
Vase/planter, deer head, ears bk, paper label, 7⅛"	20.00
Vase/planter, deer head in relief on side w/opening, 7½"	19.00

Royal Crown Derby

The Royal Crown Derby company can trace its origin back to 1848. It first operated under the name of Locker & Co. but by 1859 had became Stevenson, Sharp & Co. Several changes in ownership occured until 1866 when it became known as the Sampson Hancock Co. The Derby Crown Porcelain Co. Ltd. was formed in 1876, and these companies soon merged. In 1890 they were appointed as a manufacturer for the Queen and began using the name Royal Crown Derby.

In the early years considerable 'Japan ware' decorated in Imari pattern using red, blue, and gold in Oriental patterns was popular. They excelled in their ability to use gold in the decoration, and some of the best flower painters of all time were employed. Nice vases or plaques signed by any of these artists will bring thousands of dollars: Gregory, Mosley, Rouse, Gresley, and D'esir'e Leroy. We have observed porcelain plaques decorated with flowers signed by Gregory selling at auction for as much as $12,000.00. If you find signed pieces and are not sure of your values, it would be best if possible to have it appraised by someone very knowledgable regarding current market values.

As is usual among most other English factories, nearly all of the vases produced by Royal Crown Derby came with covers. If they are missing, deduct 40% to 45%. There are several well-illustrated books available from antique book sellers to help you learn to identify this ware. The back stamps used after 1891 will date every piece except dinnerware. The company is still in business producing outstanding dinnerware and Imari-decorated figures and serving piecs. They also produce custom (one only) sets of table service for the wealthy of the world. The advisors for this category are Henry and Geneva Tyler, who are listed in the Directory under Florida.

Animal (pheasant, turtle, cat), Imari decor, ca 1985, ea	100.00
Coffepot, red Ayes pattern	200.00
Cup & saucer, Imari, 1910	90.00
Ewer, gilt on teal gr, #4540/877, 1883, 8x5½"	950.00
Plate, Imari, 1909, 6"	45.00
Plate, Imari, 1912, 10¼"	100.00
Plate, service; roses at rim, sgn Gregory	650.00
Potpourri, florals on ivory, w/lid, #544/2658, ca 1885	850.00
Tureen; soup; Imari fruit finial, 12¾"	1,600.00

Vase, Persian style with reticulated handles, gilt and blue designs on yellow, #322, c 1844, $2,750.00.

Vase, mc gilt & decor, melon shape, w/lid, #2409/408, 1886	5,000.00
Vase, mums on ivory, #2747/542, 1888	650.00
Vase, peacocks, gilt on yel, 1882, 9½x13"	785.00

Royal Doulton, Doulton

The range of wares produced by the Doulton Company since its inception in 1815 has been vast and varied. The earliest wares produced in the tiny pottery in Lambeth, England, were salt-glazed pitchers, plain and fancy figural bottles — all utility-type stoneware geared to the practical needs of everyday living. The original partners, John Doulton and John Watts, saw the potential for success in the manufacture of drain and sewage pipes and during the 1840s concentrated on these highly lucrative types of commercial wares. Watts retired from the company in 1854, and Doulton began experimenting with a more decorative style of product. As time went by, many glazes and decorative effects were developed, among them Faience, Impasto, Silicon, Carrara, Marqueterie, Chine, and Rouge Flambe. Tiles and architectural terra cotta were an important part of their manufacture. Late in the 19th century at the original Lambeth location, fine artware was decorated by such notable artists as Hannah and Arthur Barlow, George Tinworth, and J.H. McLennan. Stoneware vases with incised

animal drawings, gracefully shaped urns with painted scenes, and cleverly modeled figurines rivaled the best of any competitor.

In 1882 a second factory was built in Burslem which continues even yet to produce the famous figurines, character jugs, series ware, and table services so popular with collectors today. Their Kingsware line, made from 1899 to 1946, featured flasks and flagons with drinking scenes, usually on a brown-glazed ground. Some were limited editions, while others were commemorative and advertising items. The Gibson Girl series, twenty-four plates in all, was introduced in 1901. It was drawn by Charles Dana Gibson and is recognized by its blue and white borders and central illustrations, each scene depicting a humorous or poignant episode in the life of 'The Widow and Her Friends.' Dickensware, produced from 1911 through the early 1940s, featured illustrations by Charles Dickens, with many of his famous characters. The Robin Hood series was introduced in 1914; the Shakespeare series #1, portraying scenes from the Bard's plays, was made from 1914 until World War II. The Shakespeare series #2 ran from 1906 until 1974 and was decorated with featured characters. Nursery Rhymes was a series that was first produced in earthenware in 1930 and later in bone china. In 1933 a line of decorated children's ware, the Bunnykins series, was introduced; it continues to be made to the present day. About 150 'bunny' scenes have been devised, the earliest and most desirable being those signed by the artist Barbara Vernon.

Factors contributing to the value of a figurine are age, color, and detail. Those with a limited production run and those signed by the artist or marked 'Potted' (indicating a pre-1939 origin) are also more valuable. After 1920 wares were marked with a lion — with or without a crown — over a circular 'Royal Doulton.' Our advisor for this category is Nicki Budin; she is listed in the Directory under Ohio.

Animals and Birds

Cat, character	225.00
Dog, Airedale, #1023, med	175.00
Dog, Boxer, #2643, 6½"	150.00
Dog, Bulldog, brindle, #1043, med	575.00
Dog, Bulldog, brn & wht, #1046, med	520.00
Dog, Bulldog, w/flag, lg	650.00
Dog, Bulldog, wht, #1072, lg	900.00
Dog, Bulldog, wht, #1074, sm	155.00
Dog, Bulldog pup, K-2	100.00
Dog, Cairn, #1033, lg	595.00
Dog, Cairn, #1034, med	250.00
Dog, Cocker Spaniel, blk & wht, #1108, lg	300.00
Dog, Cocker Spaniel, blk & wht, #1109, med	135.00
Dog, Cocker Spaniel, liver & wht, #1002, lg	300.00
Dog, Cocker Spaniel w/pheasant, #1029, 2½"	75.00
Dog, Collie, #1057	645.00
Dog, Corgi, #1559, sm	110.00
Dog, Corgi, #2557, lg	1,100.00
Dog, Dachshund, #1139, lg	575.00
Dog, Dachshund, #1140, med	275.00
Dog, Doberman Pinscher, #1117, sm	175.00
Dog, English Pointer, #2624, lg	415.00
Dog, English Setter, #1049, lg	650.00
Dog, English Setter, #1050, med	145.00
Dog, English Setter, #1051, sm	150.00
Dog, Foxhound, K-7, 2½"	75.00
Dog, French Poodle, #2631, med	185.00
Dog, German Shepherd, #1115, med	130.00
Dog, Great Dane, #1601, lg	900.00
Dog, Irish Setter, #1055, med	150.00
Dog, Irish Setter, #1056, sm	145.00
Dog, Irish Setter, #1057, lg	965.00

Dog, Pekingese, HN1012 ....90.00
Dog, Scottish Terrier, #1008, lg 715.00
Dog, Scottish Terrier, #1016, sm 140.00
Dog, Terrier w/ball 75.00
Dog, Terrier w/bone in mouth 75.00
Dog, Welsh Corgi, #2558, med 465.00
Dog chewing slipper, #2654, 3¼" 75.00
Elephant, #2644, 5½" 100.00
Pig, recumbent, head up, #2648, 1¾" 175.00

Bunnykins

Cup & saucer, Feeding the Baby 85.00
Cup & saucer, Leapfrog 85.00
Cup & saucer, Santa Claus 95.00
Figurine, Bedtime, yel, #103 ....85.00
Figurine, Harry the Herold 40.00
Figurine, Jogging, #22 ....45.00
Figurine, Knockout Bunny 40.00
Figurine, Milkman, #125, limited edition 75.00
Figurine, Soccer Player, #116 ....75.00
Mug, Asleep in the Open Air 85.00
Mug, Family at Breakfast 85.00
Mug, Family w/Pram 85.00
Mug, Gardening 85.00
Plate, baby's, Convalescing 115.00
Plate, baby's, Toast for Tea Today 120.00
Plate, Letterbox, 7½" 70.00
Plate, oatmeal; Going Shopping 70.00
Plate, oatmeal; Mr Piggly's Store 67.50
Plate, oatmeal; Watering the Flowers 85.00
Plate, Playing on River, 6½" 60.00
Plate, Visiting the Cottage, 6½" 60.00
Plate, Watering the Flowers, 7½" 85.00

Character Jugs

Anne of Cleves, D6754, mini 130.00
Anthony & Cleopatra, D6728, lg 145.00
Antique Dealer, D6807, limited ed, lg 185.00
Apothecary, D6567, lg 135.00
Ard of 'Earing, D6588, lg 1,150.00
Arry, D6207, lg 165.00
Auld Mac, D5823, lg 110.00
Auld Mac, D6253, mini, A 55.00
Bill Sykes, D6684, mini 40.00
Blacksmith, D6571, lg 135.00
Captain Henry Morgan, D6469, sm 55.00

Captain Hook, D6597, large, 7", $525.00.

Catharine Howard, D6645, lg 145.00
Catharine of Aragon, D6643, lg 130.00
Catharine Parr, D6664, lg 145.00
Cavalier, D6114, lg, A 165.00
Chelsea Pensioner, D6817, lg 125.00
City Gent, D6185, lg 110.00
Collector, D6796, lg 180.00
Davy Crockett & Santa Ana, D6729, lg 145.00
Dick Turpin, D6485, gun hdl, 1st version, lg ...150.00
Falstaff, red, D6795, lg 130.00
Falstaff, yel, D6795, limited edition, lg 135.00
Farmer John, D5788, lg 160.00
Fat Boy, D6142, tiny 95.00
Fortune Teller, D6523, mini 250.00
Gardener, D6634, sm 80.00
George III & George Washington, D6749, limited edition, lg 135.00
Gladiator, D6556, mini 325.00
Gone Away, D6531, lg 120.00
Granny, D5521, toothless, lg 800.00
Granny, D6520, mini 55.00
Groucho Marx, D6710, limited edition 115.00
Gulliver, D6563, sm 350.00
Henry VIII, D6642, lg 110.00
Izaac Walton, D6404, lg 110.00
Jane Seymour, D6646, lg 135.00
Jarge, D6288, lg 300.00
Jarge, D6295, sm 180.00
Johnny Appleseed, D6372, lg 365.00
London Bobby, D6744, lg 110.00
Long John Silver, D6386, sm 55.00
Lumberjack, D6613, lg 68.00
Mad Hatter, D6790, limited edition, sm 125.00
Mae West, D6688, lg 130.00
Mr Micawber, D6138, mini 55.00
Napoleon & Josephine, D6750, limited edition, lg 135.00
Neptune, D6548, lg 100.00
North American Indian, D6665, mini 50.00
North American Indian, D6786, limited edition, lg 100.00
Paddy, D5768, sm 55.00
Pearly King, D6760, lg 100.00
Porthos, D6516, mini 45.00
Regency Beau, D6559, lg 950.00
Rip Van Winkle, D6517, mini 45.00
Robinson Crusoe, D6539, sm 45.00
Robinson Crusoe, D6546, mini 40.00
Romeo, D6670, lg 110.00
Sairey Gamp, D5451, lg 110.00
Sairey Gamp, D5528, sm 55.00
Sam Weller, D6064, lg, A 150.00
Sam Weller, D6147, tiny 95.00
Santa w/Wreath, D6794, lg 285.00
Scaramouche, D6561, sm 435.00
Shakespeare, D6689, lg 100.00
Tam O'Shanter, D6632, lg 130.00
Tam O'Shanter, D6636, sm 55.00
Tony Weller, X-lg 200.00
Town Crier, D6530, lg 180.00
Town Crier, D6544, mini 135.00
Veteran Motorist, D6633, lg 115.00
Walrus & Carpenter, D6600, lg 145.00

Figurines

A La Mode, HN2544 ....165.00

Abdullah, HN2104	450.00
Affection, HN2236	125.00
Ajax, HN2908	450.00
Alexandra, HN2398	140.00
Alexandra, HN3286	175.00
All Aboard, HN2940	125.00
Angela, HN2389, wht dress, tiara	98.00
Annette, HN1550, gr skirt	495.00
Ascot, HN2356	185.00
Auctioneer, HN2988	195.00
Autumn Breezes, HN1911	235.00
Baba, HN1244, yel & gr pants	765.00
Bachelor, HN2319	225.00
Ballerina, HN2116	225.00
Beachcomber, HN2487, matt	165.00
Beat You to It, HN2871	350.00
Bedtime Story, HN2059	200.00
Bess, HN2002	225.00
Blacksmith, HN2782	185.00
Blithe Morning, HN2065	200.00
Blue Bird, HN1280	675.00
Bluebeard, HN2105	375.00
Boatman, HN2417	150.00
Bon Appetit, HN2444	165.00
Boy From Williamsburg, HN2183	125.00
Breezy Day, HN3162	120.00
Bride, HN2166, pk & wht gown	225.00
Bride, HN2873, gold trim	130.00
Bridesmaid, HN2196	135.00
Bridesmaid, HN2874	110.00
Bridget, HN2070	325.00
Bunny, HN2214	155.00
Captain, HN2260, 9½"	250.00
Carpet Seller, HN1464, hand closed	275.00
Catherine of Aragon, HN3233	450.00
Cavalier, HN2716, 2nd version	250.00
Cellist, HN2226	365.00
Centurion, HN2726	185.00
Charlotte, HN2421	150.00
Charmian, HN1568	675.00
Christine, HN2792	275.00
Christmas Morn, HN1992	235.00
Christmas Time, HN2110	365.00
Cissie, HN1809	115.00
Clarissa, HN2345	175.00
Clockmaker, HN2279	250.00
Clown, HN2890	235.00
Cobbler, HN1706	250.00
Collinette, HN1999, red cloak	550.00
Country Lass, HN1991	125.00
Daffy Down Dilly, HN1712	335.00
Dancers of the World, Mexican Dancer, HN2866	550.00
Deidre, HN2020	345.00
Detective, HN2359, 9½"	250.00
Doctor, HN2858	295.00
Dreamweaver, HN2283	185.00
Drummer Boy, HN2679	350.00
Dulcie, HN2305	175.00
Elegance, HN2264	150.00
Eliza, HN2543	190.00
Embroidering, HN2855	175.00
Empress Dowager, HN2391	750.00
Fair Maiden, HN2211	175.00
Favourite, HN2249	185.00

Fiddler, HN2171	765.00
Fiona, HN2694	125.00
Flower Seller's Children, HN1342	650.00

Fortune Teller, HN2159, $450.00.

Gay Morning, HN2135	275.00
Genevieve, HN1962	250.00
Genie, HN2989	150.00
Giselle, HN2139	395.00
Gollum, HN2913	125.00
Good Catch, HN2258	140.00
Goody Two Shoes, HN1905	455.00
Grace, HN2318	135.00
Grand Manner, HN2723	185.00
Gypsy Dance, HN2230, 2nd version	300.00
Harvestime, HN3084	130.00
Helmsman, HN2499	225.00
Her Ladyship, HN1977	300.00
Hilary, HN2335	155.00
Honey, HN1909, pk dress	325.00
Huckleberry Finn, HN2927	100.00
Innocence, HN2842	155.00
Ivy, HN1768	125.00
Jack, HN2060	165.00
Jane, HN2806	150.00
Janine, HN2461	185.00
January, HN2697	110.00
Jersey Milkmaid, HN2057	200.00
Jill, HN2061	165.00
Joan, HN2023	225.00
Jovial Monk, HN2144	200.00
Judge, HN2443	165.00
Judith, HN2089	300.00
Judith, HN2313, limited edition	160.00
Karen, HN2388	430.00
Kate Hardcastle, HN2028	650.00
Kathy, HN2346, Greenaway	145.00
Kirsty, HN2381	145.00
Lady April, HN1958, red & purple	315.00
Lady Diana Spencer, HN2885	350.00
Lambing Time, HN1890	195.00
Laura, HN3136, bl, limited edition	150.00
Leisure Hour, HN2055	375.00
Lifeboat Man, HN2764	180.00
Lobster Man, HN2317	180.00
Loretta, HN2337	130.00
Lori, HN2801	125.00
Lunchtime, HN2485	155.00
Lynne, HN2329	160.00

Margery, HN1415 ....350.00
Master Sweep, HN2205, 8⅝" 450.00
May, HN2711 ....130.00
Meditation, HN2330 ....295.00
Melanie, HN2271 ....150.00
Memories, HN2030 ....365.00
Mendicant, HN1365 ....275.00
Merry Christmas, HN3096 ....115.00
Midinette, HN2090 ....295.00
Milkmaid, HN2057 ....150.00
Musicale, HN2756 ....80.00
Nana, HN1766 ....475.00
Nanny, HN2221 ....185.00
Negligee, HN1219, bl hair band, rare 1,400.00
New Companions, HN2770 ....175.00
News Vendor, HN2891, limited edition 145.00
Nicola, HN2804, limited edition 160.00
Nina, HN2347, matt 150.00
Officer of the Line, HN2733 ....225.00
Old King, HN2134 ....450.00
Old King Cole, HN2217 ....495.00
Old Meg, HN2494 ....215.00
Olga, HN2463 ....165.00
Omar Khayyam, HN2247 ....150.00
Once Upon a Time, HN2047 ....500.00
Orange Lady, HN1953, 8¾" 265.00
Orange Vendor, HN1966 ....750.00
Pamela, HN1469, gr dress 825.00
Patricia, HN2715 ....155.00
Paula, HN2906 ....125.00
Pearly Boy, HN2035 ....165.00
Pillow Fight, HN2270 ....235.00
Polka, HN2156 ....335.00
Polly Peachum, HN549 ....385.00
Pope John Paul II, HN2888 ....125.00
Potter, HN1493 ....450.00
Premiere, HN2343 ....165.00
Pretty Polly, HN2768 ....115.00
Pride & Joy, HN2945 ....225.00
Prince of Wales, HN1217 ....1,200.00
Puppet Maker, HN2253 ....415.00
Queen Elizabeth II, HN3440, limited edition 400.00
Rag Doll Seller, HN2944 ....150.00
Repose, HN2272 ....225.00
Rosabell, HN1620 ....750.00
Rowena, HN2077 ....600.00
Royal Governor's Cook, HN2233 ....365.00
Sheikh, HN3083 ....95.00
Shephard, HN3160 ....115.00
Silks & Ribbons, HN2017 ....165.00
Simone, HN2378 ....145.00
Sleeping Beauty, HN3079 ....155.00
Sleepy Darling, HN2953 ....235.00
Snake Charmer, HN1317 ....1,475.00
Sonata, Enchantment series, HN2438 ....90.00
Sophie, Greenaway, HN2833 ....135.00
Stitch in Time, HN2352 ....200.00
Stop Press, HN2683 ....160.00
Summer's Day, HN2181 ....325.00
Sweet Violets, HN3175 ....90.00
Tea Time, HN2255 ....155.00
Tinkle Bell, HN1677 ....100.00
Toymaker, HN2250 ....350.00
Traveler's Tale, HN3185 ....95.00

Tulips, HN1334 ....1,600.00
Veronica, HN1517 ....355.00
Victoria, HN2417 ....175.00
Vivienne, HN2073 ....250.00
Votes for Women, HN2016 ....200.00
Wigmaker of Williamsburg, HN2239 ....185.00
Young Master, HN2872 ....225.00

Flambe

Alligator, rare 1,500.00
Cat, #9, 4¾" 130.00
Confucious, #3314 ....195.00
Dog of Fo, Collector's Club 175.00
Duck, #395, 2½" 125.00
Duck, floating, 7¼" 400.00
Elephant, sgn Noke, lg 300.00
Elephant, trunk raised, Sung, 5½" 195.00
Fox, crouching, lg 565.00
Genie, #2999 ....195.00
Hippo, 3¼x6¾" 1,250.00
King Penguin, #84, 6" 130.00
Monkeys, hugging pr, #486, rouge 325.00
Mouse on cube, #1164 ....575.00
Owl, #2249 ....200.00
Penguin on base, 9" 1,000.00
Rabbit, ear up, #113 ....70.00
Rabbit, ears tucked, #43, old 465.00
Rhinoceros, 9¾x17" 550.00
Rhinoceros, half seated, #615, 9x17" 1,275.00
Salmon, 12¼" 500.00
Tiger, #809, 6" 450.00
Tiger, crouching, rouge, #111 ....700.00
Tortoise, #101, 1x3" 545.00
Wolf, sitting, tail around legs, 5" 100.00
Vase, fish, Sung, sgn FM, 8½" 765.00
Vase, landscape, 14" 565.00
Vase, red/dk bl, mk Flambe Veined #1618, bottle form, 10" 250.00
Vase, Sung, mc veining/mottling, Noke/FM, 1930, 7" 565.00
Vase, veined, #1618, 13¼" 265.00
Vase, woodcut, #1613, 6½" 110.00
Vase, 1619 Country House, #31, 11" 200.00
Wizard, #3121 ....120.00

Series Ware

Ashtray, Dutch People, mk, 3⅝" dia 37.50
Ashtray, witches at cauldron, mk, 3½" 42.50
Biscuit jar, Coaching Days 250.00
Bowl, Bobby Burns, 7½" 150.00
Box, Nursery series, girl by shore 55.00
Box, Robin Hood, rectangular, 2x3½x4½" 150.00
Cheese dish, Coaching Days 325.00
Coffeepot, Moorish Gate, mk, 6¾" 150.00
Comport, Sunset Cottage, sgn Morrey, porc, 3¾x5⅛" 175.00
Cup & saucer, Dickensware, Poor Jo/Bill Sykes, 3rd mk 110.00
Cup & saucer, Don Quixote 50.00
Cup & saucer, Mad Hatter 125.00
Cuspidor, Isaac Walton, 7" 985.00
Jardiniere, Shakespeare, Ophelia & Hamlet, 9x10" 300.00
Match holder, Dutch People, sterling rim 195.00
Match holder, Monks, profile, 2½" 95.00
Mug, Dutch People, 3 girls, yel & gr trim, mk, 2x1¾" 40.00
Mug, Moreton Hall, court scene, D1898 ....135.00

Mug, shaving; Kingsware, sterling rim 565.00
Pitcher, Coaching Days, 6" 195.00
Pitcher, Dickensware, Old Curiosity Shop, sq 175.00
Pitcher, Egyptian, geometric border, mk, 6⅜" 100.00
Pitcher, hot water; Shakespeare, Orlando, 7" 200.00
Pitcher, Night Watchman, 8" 105.00
Pitcher, Welsh Ladies, pinched spout, 2¼" 115.00
Plate, Arabian Nights, Arrival of Unknown Princess, 10⅜" 85.00
Plate, Automobile series, Deaf, scarce, 10⅜" 365.00
Plate, Dickensware, Fat Boy, 2nd mk, 10½" 125.00
Plate, Dickensware, Sam Weller, 1st mk, 10½" 125.00
Plate, Eglington Tournament, knights, 10" 95.00
Plate, Gibson Girl, Miss Babbles Brings the Paper 130.00
Plate, Gibson Girl, They Take a Morning Run 125.00
Plate, Old English Sayings 55.00
Plate, Town Officials, night watchman, 10" 65.00
Plate, Windsor Castle, 10½" 55.00
Sugar bowl, Fox Hunting, John Peel, hunters w/horses 75.00
Teapot, Reynard the Fox 265.00
Toothpick holder, sunset scene, hdls 90.00
Tray, Dickensware, Bill Sykes, rectangular, mk, 11x5⅝" 95.00
Tray, Under the Greenwood Tree, 11x5" 110.00
Vase, Babes in Woods, flow bl, gold trim, hdls, 8" 365.00
Vase, Babes in Woods, flow bl, gold trim, 6⅜x4⅜" 265.00
Vase, Dickensware, Sydney Carton, hdls, 7" 185.00
Vase, Dunolly Castle, sgn Hughes, mk, 4⅜x2¾" 175.00
Vase, Dutch People, hdls, 5½x5" 165.00
Vase, Gleaners & Gypsies, 2" 80.00
Vase, Welsh People, mini 175.00

Stoneware

Beaker, horses, H Barlow, dtd 1877, 5½" 550.00
Humidor, hunting figures in relief, mk, 5x4⅛" 155.00
Jardiniere, frieze of coach/horses/sheep/cattle, Barlow, 8" 1,875.00
Jardiniere, horse scenes, H Barlow, 1882, 6½x6½" 1,500.00
Lawn fountain, pelican figural, 15" 325.00
Pitcher, horse scene, H Barlow, 1878, 9¼" 1,100.00
Pitcher, incised Islamic leaves, bl/brn on brn, 5", NM 180.00
Pitcher, pate-sur-pate birds & leaves, Barlow, 7" 465.00
Pitcher, tan tapestry w/red, gold & wht trim, 3⅜" 45.00
Ring dish, owl figural, brn & tan, 4x3¼" 170.00
Teapot, frieze of goats, eagle spout, Barlow, 5½" 1,500.00
Umbrella stand, HP decor/appl floral medallions, 1910, 24" 500.00
Vase, app cherry blossoms/birds/fish, wht/brn on tan, 6" 300.00
Vase, emb flowers, bl on bl-gr mottle, Lambeth, 6½" 85.00
Vase, frieze of kangaroos, leaf borders, H Barlow, 12" 1,100.00
Vase, frieze of pigs & flowers, foliage border, Barlow, 11" 1,000.00
Vase, horses, scrolled leaves, H Barlow, Lambeth, 11" 1,150.00
Vase, horses/sheep, fleur-de-lis band, Hanna Barlow, 16" 1,550.00

Toby Jugs

Best Is None Too Good, D6107, 4½" 350.00
Cap'n Cuttle, D6266, 4½" 185.00
Charrington, One Toby Leads to Another 350.00
Cliff Cornell, bl, med, 5½" 325.00
Cliff Cornell, tan, 9" 435.00
Falstaff, D6063, sm 75.00
Falstaff, 8½" 145.00
Happy John, D6031, lg 145.00
Happy John, D6070, 5½" 90.00
Honest Measure, D6108, 4½" 85.00
Jolly Toby, D6109, 6½" 90.00

Sairey Gamp, D6263 ....200.00
Sherlock Holmes, D6661 ....145.00
Sir Francis Drake, D6660, 9" 145.00
Sir Winston Churchill, D6172, 5½" 95.00
Sir Winston Churchill, D6175, 4" 75.00
Squire, D6319 ....265.00

Miscellaneous

Ash bowl, Parson Brown, D6008 ....110.00
Ashtray, John Barleycorn, D5602 ....110.00
Ashtray, Parson Brown, D5600 ....110.00
Basin, Secessionist design w/stylized flowers on wht, 8x14" 700.00
Beaker, Wedding, Princess of Wales, 1981 ....40.00
Bust, Tony Weller, D6051 ....85.00
Cigarette lighter, Bacchus, D6505 ....250.00
Cigarette lighter, Beefeater, D6233 ....145.00
Cigarette lighter, Long John Silver, table type 100.00
Jardiniere, cvd/pnt floral, bl/wht on tan, Lambeth, 7x9" 300.00
Jug, Paddy, musical 550.00
Pitcher, Am Indian: as hdl/spout/emb on sides, 5½" 250.00
Pitcher, daisies w/gold tracery, openwork rim, Burslem, 9¼" 175.00
Pitcher, Oliver Twist, emb figures, tankard form, D6286 ....185.00
Umbrella stand, leafy limbs, brn/tan/bl, sgn, Lambeth, 13" 425.00
Vase, cherry blossoms, spherical w/bottle neck, Burslem, 10" 125.00

Vases, cobalt flowers and gold trim on red-orange, 9", $350.00 each.

Vase, floral on cloth texture, Slater's mk, slim, 16½" 350.00
Vase, stylized palmette trees, squeezebag, dk bl/brn, 11" 315.00
Wall mask, Sweet Anne, HN1590 ....445.00

Royal Dux

    The Duxer Porzellan Manufactur was established by E. Eichler in 1860. Located in what is now Duchcov, Czechoslovakia, the area was known as Dux, Bohemia, until WWI. The war brought about changes in both the style of the ware as well as the mark. Prewar pieces were modeled in the Art Nouveau or Greek Classical manner and marked with 'Bohemia' and a pink triangle containing the letter 'E.' They were usually matt glazed in green, brown, and gold. Better pieces were made of porcelain, while the larger items were of pottery. After the war the ware was marked with the small pink triangle but without the Bohemia designation; 'Made in Czechoslovakia' was added. The style became Art Deco, with cobalt blue a dominant color.

Bowl, boy on branch over pool, appl flowers, pk mk, 9½" **495.00**
Bust, Victorian lady, parian, pastels, much lace, 16" **850.00**
Chalice, cherubs on front, hdls, ped ft, 15" **450.00**
Comport, cobalt bowl, maid & children as stem, rnd base, 20" ..**950.00**
Figurine, boy leads oxen pr, gr/pk/cream matt, ca 1905, 15" L **795.00**
Figurine, cockatoo, wht w/pk, 7" **75.00**
Figurine, German shepherd dog, 8" **110.00**
Figurine, girl at waterfall, gr hue, pk triangle mk, 12½" **995.00**
Figurine, Harlequin couple dancing, sgn, #204/72, 20x15" **850.00**
Figurine, lady filling jug from running water, 9" **350.00**
Figurine, lady looks into pond, 11x12" **525.00**
Figurine, lady sits & feeds pigeons, 9x10" **395.00**
Figurine, lady w/2 turkeys & basket, pk triangle mk, 10" **595.00**
Figurine, polar bear, 10½x12½" **450.00**
Figurine, sheepherder, pk triangle mk, 16½" **895.00**
Figurine, shell on ped w/lady atop, 2nd at side, 17½" **895.00**
Figurine, Spanish dancer w/tambourine, 8" **295.00**
Figurine, woman & child, early pk triangle mk, 16" **695.00**
Pitcher, HP florals, maroon & cream, triangle mk, 1918, 22" **495.00**
Vase, emb branches swirl to form 2 levels of hdls, ftd, 16" **425.00**
Vase, Nouveau form w/appl grapes, gr on cream w/gilt, 19" **400.00**

Royal Flemish

Royal Flemish was introduced in the late 1880s and was patented in 1894 by the Mt. Washington Glass Company. Transparent glass was enameled with one or several colors and the surface divided by a network of raised lines suggesting leaded glasswork. Some pieces were further decorated with enameled florals, birds, or Roman coins. Our advisors for this category are Betty and Clarence Maier; they are listed in the Directory under Pennsylvania.

Vase, snow geese against rising sun, pale blue panels with stars, maroon top with stylized dragons, 14½x5", $8,300.00; Biscuit jar, gold Roman coins on maroon, beige, and brown, 8x5½", $3,200.00.

Biscuit jar, mc panels, lion in shield, gold scrolls, 5x7½" **3,750.00**
Ewer, gold leaves/helmet/shield/lion, 3-fold rim, 12" **5,000.00**
Ewer, lad spears winged creature, much gold, rnd body, 11" **4,950.00**
Vase, gold cherub fights dragon, bk: boy & griffin, 13½" **3,000.00**
Vase, gold dragon/stars, ornate collar, muted reds, 8" **2,750.00**
Vase, gold pansies on clear frost, 7½x7½" **1,385.00**
Vase, griffin/scrolls on 'stained glass,' bulbous, 4" **1,200.00**
Vase, pansies, wine on frost, much gold, bulb neck, 8x8" **1,385.00**

Royal Haeger, Haeger

In 1871 David Henry Haeger, a young son of German immigrants, purchased a brick factory at Dundee, Illinois, and began an association with the ceramic industry that his descendants have pursued to the present time. David's bricks had rebuilt Chicago after their great fire in 1871. By 1914 they had ventured into the field of commerical artware. Vases, figurines, lamp bases, and gift items in a pastel matt glaze carried the logo of the company name written over the bar of an 'H.' From 1929 to 1933, they produced a line of dinnerware which they marketed through Marshall Fields. Ware produced before the mid-thirties sometimes is found with a paper label; these are of special interest. 'Royal Haeger,' their premium line designed in 1938 by Royal Hickman, is highly desirable with collectors today. The mark 'Royal Haeger' (in raised lettering) was used during the thirties and forties; later a paper label in the shape of a crown was used.

Fast becoming popular with today's collectors is the Earth Graphic Wraps line, first introduced in the mid-'70s. These one-of-a-kind pieces consist of rough, raised formations on backgrounds of marigold, white, fern, and brown, in both matt and glossy finishes.

The Macomb plant, built in 1939, primarily made ware for the florist trade. A second plant, built there in 1969, produces lamp bases. For those interested in learning more about the subject, we recommend *Collecting Royal Haeger* by our advisors, Lee Garmon and Doris Frizzell; both are listed in the Directory under Illinois.

Bookends, R-700, lion's head, 7½", pr **30.00**
Bowl, R-293, violin, 17" L **30.00**
Candle holders, R-173, dbl branch, 9" W, pr **75.00**
Candle holders, R-183, fish (single), 5", pr **45.00**
Figurine, F-16, wild goose, wings straight, 7" **8.00**
Figurine, F-17, wild goose, wings up, 6½" **8.00**
Figurine, R-1179, garden girl, 14" **35.00**
Figurine, R-1224, gypsy girl, 16½" **150.00**
Figurine, R-1225, girl w/2 bowls, 13" L **35.00**
Figurine, R-1231, St Francis, 10½" **20.00**
Figurine, R-1442, cocker spaniel, standing, 7½" **25.00**
Figurine, R-155, angelfish, head up, 5¼" **10.00**
Figurine, R-161, race horse w/jockey, 9" **45.00**
Figurine, R-233, pouter pigeon, 7" **35.00**
Figurine, R-287, birdhouse w/2 birds, 9½" **20.00**
Figurine, R-313, tigress, 8" **125.00**
Figurine, R-314, tiger, 11" **125.00**
Figurine, R-375A, polar bear cub, sitting, 3" **20.00**
Figurine, R-376A, polar bear cub, walking **20.00**
Figurine, R-390, South Am girl, from neck up, 11" **45.00**
Figurine, R-411, girl w/doe, 10½" **40.00**
Figurine, R-472, Russian lady's head, 12" **65.00**
Figurine, R-896, cat, sleeping, 7" **20.00**
Figurine, R-897, cat, standing, 7" **15.00**
Figurine, R-898, cat, sitting, 6" **15.00**
Figurine, R-975, figure running, 12" **15.00**
Flower block, R-125, sea gull w/wings up, 17½" H **95.00**
Flower block, R-138, 3 leaping fish, 10" H **95.00**
Flower block, R-169B, trout leaping, 7" **30.00**
Flower block, R-189, nude sitting w/knees up, 6" **40.00**
Flower block, R-673, Mongolian woman, 13" **30.00**
Gondola, R-812, no inserts, 15½" **12.00**
Lamp, Earth Graphic Wrap, 34" **95.00**
Planter, R-1146, stag, 5½" **15.00**
Planter, R-1331, greyhound, 12" L **35.00**
Planter, R-1462, wheelbarrow, 10" L **8.00**
Planter, R-983, giraffe, 16" L **50.00**
Planter/bowl, R-1192, sailfish, 11" L **25.00**
Pot, #8207, Earth Graphic Wrap, 9" dia **35.00**
TV lamp/planter, #6202, greyhound, 13" L **35.00**
Vase, bud; R-603, Goldi Locks, 5½" **7.50**
Vase, cornucopia; R-298, shell, 11" **20.00**

Vase, floor; R-144, floral base, 20" **200.00**
Vase, R-100, cylindrical, cut-out floral band at top, 14" **95.00**
Vase, R-170, ram's head, curling horns, 11" **35.00**
Vase, R-174, horse's head (down, laughing), 10" **50.00**
Vase, R-190, squid decor, 4-sided, ftd, 8" **30.00**
Vase, R-243, cylindrical w/sq ped ft, 12" **50.00**
Vase, R-425, macaw, 16" **250.00**

Royal Rudolstadt

The hard-paste porcelain that has come to be known as Royal Rudolstadt was produced in Thuringia, Germany, in the early 18th century. Various names and marks have been associated with this pottery. One of the earliest was a hay fork symbol associated with Johann Frederich von Schwarzburg-Rudolstadt, one of the first founders. Variations, some that included an 'R,' were also used. In 1854 Earnst Bohne produced wares that were marked with an anchor and the letters 'EB.' Examples commonly found today were made during the late 1800s and early 20th century. These are usually marked with an 'RW' within a shield under a crown and the words 'Crown Rudolstadt.' Items marked 'Germany' were made after 1890.

Ewer, floral w/gold on yel, gold hdl about neck, 10½" **135.00**
Ewer, flowers w/gold beads, gold dragon hdls, 12" **140.00**
Figurine, girl in rocker, HP pastels, crown mk, 7½" **135.00**
Plate, Merry Surprise, lady/cherub in garden, 9½" **150.00**
Tea set, golliwogs dancing, child's, 13-pc **295.00**
Vase, floral on lt gr w/gold, ornate hdls/ft, 12½" **110.00**

Royal Vienna

In 1719 Claude Innocentius de Paquier established a hard-paste porcelain factory in Vienna where he made highly ornamental wares similar to the type produced at Meissen. Early wares were usually unmarked; but after 1744, when the factory was purchased by the Empress, the Austrian shield (often called 'beehive') was stamped on under the glaze. In the following listings, values are for hand-painted items unless noted otherwise. Decal-decorated items would be considerably lower.

Note: An influx of Japanese reproductions on the market have influenced values to decline on genuine old Royal Vienna. Buyer beware! On new items the beehive mark is over the glaze, the weight of the porcelain is heavier, and the decoration is obviously decaled. Our advisor for this category is Madeleine France; she is listed in the Directory under Florida.

Vase, lady's portrait reserve on green with gold trim, 11½", $950.00.

Bowl, Constance, gr & gold border, mk, 2x10x8" **800.00**
Bowl, Marie Antoinette/Grafin Potocka, w/gold, hdls/lid, 3" H **225.00**
Candlesticks, scenic medallions, Kauffmann, mk, 5½", pr **550.00**

Charger, Venus & Aeolus, nymphs/peacocks/etc, 12" **2,000.00**
Cup & saucer, lady's portrait, ornate hdl, ftd, set of 4 ....**950.00**
Demitasse pot, ladies on dk rose, heavy gold, +tray/9-pcs **550.00**
Jug, floral bouquets, w/lid, 5" **130.00**
Plaque, Guten Marsen, portrait of a girl, Leidel, fr, 10x8" **375.00**
Plate, lady w/garland of grapes, mc/gilt border, 1880s, 9½" **500.00**
Plate, musical scene w/figures, bl w/gold, F Koller, 9½" **450.00**
Plate, Punishment of Cupid, 14½" **700.00**
Tray, Hector's Abschied, dk red w/rtcl rim, 11½" **475.00**
Urn, lady & cherub reserve on red w/gold, hdls, 10½" **170.00**
Urn, lady on rocky shore, landscape on bk, gold trim, 24¼" **1,700.00**
Vase, children as 4 seasons, 3" **225.00**
Vase, Coquetterie, lady in plumed hat, sgn Tenner, lid, 8½" **750.00**
Vase, Gibson girl, cylindrical Nouveau mold w/hdls, 8" **150.00**
Vase, lady's portrait, gold hdls & trim, ca 1900, 10¼" **895.00**
Vase, lady's portrait reserve, bl/gr/gold ground, mk, 8½" **595.00**
Vase, lady's portrait/gilt flowers/turq beads on maroon, 9¾" **795.00**
Vase, Lemiramis reserve on red & blk, much gold, ca 1880, 7" ..**775.00**
Vase, Madame LeBrun, sgn Wagner, 8" **900.00**
Vase, Meditation (lady) on bl/lav, w/gold, stick neck, 7" **375.00**
Vase, Ruth's profile/allover gold lines, teal, ftd/hdls, 4" **250.00**

Roycroft

Near the turn of the century, Elbert Hubbard established the Roycroft Printing Shop in East Aurora, New York. Named in honor of two 17th-century printer-bookbinders, the print shop was just the beginning of a community called Roycroft, which came to be known worldwide. Hubbard became a popular personality of the early 1900s, known for his talents in a variety of areas from writing and lecturing to manufacturing. The Roycroft community became a meeting place for people of various capabilities and included shops for the production of furniture, copper, leather items, and a multitude of other wares which were marked with the Roycroft symbol, an 'R' within a circle below a stylized cross. Hubbard lost his life on the Lusitania in 1915; production in the community continued until the Depression.

Interest is strong in the field of Arts and Crafts in general and in Roycroft items in particular. Copper items are evaluated to a large extent by the condition of the original patina that remains. Our advisor for this category is Bruce Austin; he is listed in the Directory under New York.

Armchair, GPI in crest rail, orig leather seat, EX **1,600.00**
Ashtray, #639, hammered, brass balls accent rests, 5x8" dia **170.00**
Ashtray, hammered copper, 4x2" **100.00**
Book, Little Journeys, 14-volume set, 1916, VG **100.00**
Book, Maude, Tennyson, EX **375.00**
Book, White Hyacinths, Hubbard **140.00**
Bookcase, #085, 3-door, sgn, orig finish, 66" W **12,000.00**
Bookends, tooled florals, copper, dk patina, 3½x2", pr **165.00**
Candelabrum, 6 cups on 12" bar w/scroll supports, 14", VG **375.00**
Candlestick, #412, orig med patina, 12" **600.00**
Candlestick, bobeche w/sm curled hdl, flaring base, 2x4" **90.00**
Candlesticks, brass-washed copper, 4x4" dia base, VG, pr **130.00**
Candlesticks, long sq stems, Princess, K Kipp, no mk, 8", pr **400.00**
Candlesticks, thin std w/base twist, dk wash, lt wear, 12", pr **500.00**
Chair, Morris; #045, 4-slat sides, rnded arms, EX **1,600.00**
Chamberstick, brass-washed copper, 1½x5", VG **115.00**
Chamberstick, hammered copper, 1x6" dia, EX **120.00**
Crumber set, copper w/emb floral, dk patina, 2-pc, 8", 9" L **300.00**
Framed prayer, grapevine border, hand-illumined, 12½x9", EX ..**300.00**
Inkwell, copper, hinged top/glass insert, mk, 2x3" sq **200.00**
Lamp, desk; #C-901, copper stick base/7" dome shade, VG **750.00**

Lamp, desk; #906, hammered copper, helmet shade, rfn, 13x7" .1,000.00
Lamp, ldgl 18" cone shade, vase std: riveted band/hdls, 22" 6,000.00
Smoking set, hammered copper w/brass finish, urn on 16" tray 20.00
Softball, dk leather w/tan stitching, mk, rare, 4", EX 800.00
Table, library; like #075, 2-drw, rfn top, 48" W 1,300.00
Tray, fruit; hammered int w/triangular leaf, 8", VG 200.00
Tray, hammered copper w/riveted hdls & cvd border, wear, 16" ...300.00
Vase, gr patina, tall/flared neck, flat wide body, 16" 2,100.00
Vase, hammered brass w/banded design, 5", VG 140.00
Vase, hammered copper, squat base/flare neck, M patina, 4½x6" .550.00
Vase, hammered copper w/inlaid stylized band, cylinder, 6½", EX .750.00
Vase, heavy hammered copper, emb rose band at rim, rfn, 6x3" .550.00
Vase, wood-grain copper, 4 silver sqs, 4 long open hdls, 8" 2,200.00
Vase, 2 rows open sqs on sqd/flaring form, 7" 3,250.00

Rozenburg

Some of the most innovative and original Art Nouveau ceramics were created by the Rozenberg factory at The Hague in The Netherlands between 1885 and 1916. Some pieces are similar to Gouda. Rozenburg also made highly prized eggshell ware, so called because of its very thin walls; this is eagerly sought after by collectors. T.A.C. Colenbrander was their artistic leader, with Samuel Schellink and J. Kok designing many of the eggshell pieces.

Key: eg — eggshell

Charger, stylized flowers in earth tones, ca 1890s, 18" 1,900.00
Jar, eg, roses/butterflies, pointed lid w/2 holes, rstr, 16" 2,100.00
Jug, Nouveau butterflies/florals, sgn VW, #614, mks, 7" 500.00
Plate, eg, roses, red/brn/wht/gr on wht, Hartgring, 6½" 700.00
Tile, windmill, pastoral, pictoral fr, sgn Gabriel 465.00
Vase, abstract batik flowers, yel/dk bl on wht, #786, 9" 850.00

Vase, butterflies and florals on dark blue-green, J.L. Verhoog, arched handle, 1898, 13", $1,600.00.

Vase, exotic birds/etc, wht/dk bl/red/gold, W 59G, 6x8" 550.00
Vase, Nouveau-style HP decor, brns/bls/yels, D Haag, 13" 1,600.00

Rubena

Rubena glass was made by several firms in the late 1800s. It is a blown art glass that shades from clear to red. See also Art Glass Baskets; Cruets; Sugar Shakers; Salts; specific manufacturers.

Biscuit jar, Invt T'print w/HP daisies, SP lid, 7" 200.00
Bottle, scent; ACB, gold trim, cut stopper, 7¼x3" 110.00
Bottle, scent; cut crystal stopper, 6¼x2½" 88.00
Celery vase, HP flowers, SP fr 295.00
Cheese dish, 7x10½" 195.00
Cruet, Invt T'print, 6¾" 400.00
Finger bowl, hobnail, ruffled, 4½" 85.00
Jelly dish, crimped lid, threading, vaseline rigaree, SP fr 215.00
Pitcher, frosted, Hobnail, 7x7" 375.00
Pitcher, Invt T'print, Hobbs & Brockunier, miniature, 4" 200.00
Pitcher, tricorner lip, HP florals, bulbous, 8" 400.00
Toothpick holder, Invt T'print, bulbous 95.00
Vase, HP lilies of the valley, 10½" 135.00
Vase, pansies/leaves, scalloped, 4½" 150.00

Rubena Verde

Rubena Verde glass was introduced in the late 1800s by Hobbs, Brockunier, and Company of Wheeling, West Virginia. Its transparent colors shade from red to green. Our advisor for this category is Mike Roscoe; he is listed in the Directory under Michigan. See also Art Glass Baskets; Cruets; Sugar Shakers; Salts.

Cruet, tepee shape, trefoil spout, faceted stopper, 7" 485.00
Cup, wht floral, ribbed, 2¾" 120.00
Rose bowl, Coin Spot, 3x4" 140.00
Vase, crystal appl spiral rigaree, 8¼x1⅞" 95.00
Vase, deep color, clear base, flared ribbed trumpet form, 5" 275.00
Vase, gr rigaree & ft, 8¼x3" 95.00
Vase, HP pk & wht florals w/gold, unsgn Moser, 11½" 395.00
Vase, Invt T'print w/HP flowers, sq top, 3½" 100.00
Vase, jack-in-the pulpit; appl hdls, 8x5½" 245.00
Wine, Invt T'print, 4¼" 135.00

Ruby Glass

Produced for over one hundred years by every glasshouse of note in this country, ruby glass has been used to create decorative items such as one might find in gift shops, utilitarian bottles and kitchenware, figurines, and dinnerware lines such as were popular in the Depression era. For further information and study, we recommend *Ruby Glass of the 20th Century* by our advisor, Naomi Over; she is listed in the Directory under Colorado.

Basket, Blenko, yel hdl on 4½" H body 65.00
Bottle, beer; Royal Ruby, Anchor Hocking, 1950, 32-oz 27.50
Bowl, Oyster & Pearl, Anchor Hocking, 1938-40, 6½" 20.00
Cake plate, Sandwich, Indiana, 1960s-70s, 13" 88.00
Candlestick, Viking, swan neck, 6¼" 27.50
Candy dish, Sweetheart, fluted, LG Wright, 1976, 3¾" 22.50
Comport bonbon, Dmn Optic, #1502, 7½" 38.00
Creamer & sugar bowl, Anchor Hocking 20.00
Cup, measuring; unknown maker, 16-oz 27.50
Cup & saucer, Anchor Hocking, ca 1940s 10.00
Figurine, bird, Swedish Glass, 4" 17.50
Figurine, elephant, Swedish Glass, ca 1980, 5" 18.00
Lamp, fairy; Sweetheart, LG Wright, 1974-81, 4½" 30.00
Marmalade, Eyewinker, LG Wright, 1974-81, 8¾" 40.00
Nappy, Royal Ruby, Anchor Hocking, 6½" 10.00
Pickle dish, Royal Ruby, Anchor Hocking, 1940s, 7" 18.00
Pitcher, Blenko, #3750, 16-oz 22.00

Pitcher, Blenko, #939P, ca 1952, 14" **65.00**
Pitcher, High Point, Anchor Hocking, 1940s, 80-oz **45.00**
Pitcher, hostess; Roly Poly, Macbeth-Evans, 1932, 32-oz **70.00**
Pitcher, Royal Ruby, Anchor Hocking, 1940s, 80-oz **45.00**
Pitcher, tan & gold scrolls, appl ruby hdl, 2¼x2¼" **110.00**
Plate, Oyster & Pearl, Anchor Hocking, 13½" **42.50**
Plate, Royal Ruby, Anchor Hocking, 9" **8.00**
Swan, Summit Art Glass (Cambridge mold), 1986, 13" **80.00**
Tumbler, Georgian, Anchor Hocking, 1940s, 9-oz **7.50**
Tumbler, Hobnail, Anchor Hocking, 1930s, 4½" **6.50**
Tumbler, iced tea; Provincial (Bubble), Anchor Hocking, 16-oz ..**17.50**
Vase, Blenko, #404M, 11x8¼" **57.50**
Vase, Duncan & Miller, Swirl cornucopia, #121, 14" **135.00**
Vase, Elite, Westmoreland, 1981, 8½" **28.00**
Vase, fan form, ca 1925, 8½" **45.00**
Vase, Rachel, Anchor Hocking, 1940s, 10" **45.00**
Vase, swan hdls, Venetian, 12" **130.00**

Ruby-Stained Souvenirs

Ruby-flashed or ruby-stained glass was made through the application of a thin layer of color over clear. It was used in the manufacture of some early pressed tableware and from the Victorian era well into the 20th century for souvenir items which were often engraved on the spot with the date, location, and buyer's name.

Bell, St Louis, 7" **80.00**
Creamer, Block & Star **37.50**
Creamer, Gettysburg PA, 1863 ....**28.00**
Cruet, Sunken Honeycomb, Mother, World's Fair 1893 ....**95.00**
Hatchet, Montana **70.00**
Mug, Button Arches, St Louis Exposition, 1904 ....**45.00**
Mug, Heart Band, Oxford MI **42.00**
Pin dish, heart shape **35.00**

Spooner, Button Arches, Sister 1897, $40.00.

Toothpick holder, Beaded Swag, Heisey **55.00**
Toothpick holder, Button Arches, name & 1903, 2¼x2" **30.00**
Toothpick holder, scalloped Swirl **40.00**
Toothpick holder, Trophy **25.00**
Tumbler, Atlantic City 1898 ....**50.00**

Rugs

Hooked rugs are treasured today for their folk-art appeal. It was a craft that was introduced to this country in about 1830 and flourished its best in the New England states. The prime consideration is not age

but artistic appeal. Scenes with animals, buildings, and people; patriotic designs; or whimsical themes are preferred. Condition is, of course, also a factor. Marked examples bearing the stamps of 'Frost and Co.,' 'Abenakee,' 'C.R.,' and 'Ouia' are highly prized. Note: the rugs listed here are rag unless noted otherwise.

9th Regt US Infantry, eagle & shield, late 1800s, 20x34", $1,100.00.

Beaver/tree/butterfly, 4-color, late, 20x39", NM **55.00**
Bird medallion, red/bl/yel/gr on wht/beige, early, 29x42" **660.00**
Blk panther in tree, 4-color on gray, 1940s, 43x24" **90.00**
Brn & wht w/mc stripes, PA, 173x188", EX **165.00**
Cat & kittens, grays & yel on beige, mc border, 27x51" **550.00**
Cat & leafy flower border, mc on gray, 1800s, 39x46" **3,850.00**
Child w/wagon & dog before blksmith's shop, 32x34", NM **300.00**
Deer w/button eye in mc landscape, 23x38" **275.00**
Floral, mc on olive-beige w/brn & red stripes, rpr, 34x55" **65.00**
Floral, 4-color on gray, hooked/sheared, 31x20" **50.00**
Floral, 6-color on beige, 72x38", EX **450.00**
Floral (stylized) in brns/bls/grs, 30x80" **600.00**
Floral design w/sculptured details, mc pastels, 18x28" **160.00**
Flower wreath w/in flower border, 8-color wool, 72x107" **2,650.00**
Geometric dot pattern, mc on taupe, Am, 1900s, 18½x38" **165.00**
Geometrics, mc cotton & wool, Am, ca 1900, 30x58" **350.00**
Gray stripe w/oak leaf & acorn borders, 5-color, 28x92" **465.00**
Grenfell, Canadian geese above evergreens, 1900s, 27x40" **400.00**
Horse & buggy w/driver, mc on gray, late, 14x27" **65.00**
Penny, wool, dmns & flowers, 5-color, wear/rprs, 28x46" **200.00**
Rectangular twining bands in earth tones, 1900, 100x35" **385.00**
Ribbon-like stripes in basketweave pattern, ca 1920, 33x29" **115.00**
Tree of life/butterfly/florals/squirrel, mc, 1940s, 61x88" **1,750.00**
Trout, 7-color, Am, late 1800s, 18½x32", EX **475.00**
Welcome on variegated field, late 1800s, 19½x30" **425.00**

RumRill

George Rumrill designed and marketed his pottery designs from 1933 until his death in 1942. During this period of time, four different companies produced his works. Today the most popular designs are those made by the Red Wing Stoneware Company from 1933 until 1936 and Red Wing Potteries from 1936 until early 1938. Some of these popular lines include Trumpet Flower, Classic, Manhattan, and Athena, the Nudes.

For a period of months in 1938, Shawnee took over the production of RumRill pottery. This relationship ended abruptly and the Florence Pottery took over and produced his wares until the plant burned down. The final producer was Gonder. Pieces from each individual pottery are easily recognized by their designs, glazes, and/or signatures. It is interesting to note that the same designs were produced by all three companies. They may be marked RumRill or with the name of the specific company that made them. Our advisors for this category are Wendy and Leo Frese; they are listed in the Directory under Texas.

Candlesticks, bl & tan, #397, 5½", pr 10.00
Candlesticks, cream, #231-C, 7", pr 20.00
Candlesticks, cream, #357, 2½", pr 7.00
Candlesticks, turq, #240, 9", pr 30.00
Ewer, Dutch Bl, #295, 10" 50.00
Ewer, gr to orange, #184, 7" 20.00
Ewer, ivory, #220, 10" 30.00
Vase, blended bl & tan, #401, 12" 60.00

Vase, green shading to brown, 4-handled, 9½", $75.00.

Vase, blended bl & tan, #423, 13" 60.00
Vase, gr, #275, 8" 20.00
Vase, ivory & gr, #400, 11½" 60.00
Vase, jade, #569, 11½" 350.00
Vase, wht, #568, 11½" 275.00
Vase, yel & gr, #567, 8½" 150.00

Ruskin

This English pottery operated near Birmingham from 1989 until 1935. Its founder was W. Howson Taylor, and it was named in honor of the reknown author and critic, John Ruskin. The earliest marks were 'Taylor' in block letters and the initials 'WHT,' the smaller W and H superimposed over the upright leg of a larger T. Later marks included the Ruskin name.

Jar, bl flambe, bruise to int of lid, 4½x3" 275.00
Vase, feathered gray/sange-de-boeuf, flattened shoulder, 4" 350.00
Vase, feathered sang-de-boeuf, can neck, bulbous body, 9x9½" ..750.00
Vase, peach shaded to coral, w/lid, #1920, 14" 175.00

Russel Wright Dinnerware

Russel Wright, one of America's foremost industrial designers, also designed several lines of ceramic dinnerware, glassware, and aluminum ware that are now highly sought-after collectibles. His most popular dinnerware then and with today's collectors, American Modern, was manufactured by the Steubenville Pottery Company from 1939 until 1959. It was produced in a variety of solid colors in assortments chosen to stay attune with the times. Casual (his first line sturdy enough to be guaranteed against breakage for ten years from date of purchase) is relatively easy to find today — simply because it has held up so well. During the years of its production, the Casual line was constantly being restyled, some items as many as five times. Early examples were heavily mottled, while later pieces were smoothly glazed and patterned. The ware was marked with Wright's signature and 'China by Iroquois.' It was marketed in fine department stores throughout the country. After 1950 the line was marked 'Iroquois China by Russel Wright.'

To calculate values for items in American Modern, add 100% to the suggested prices in the following listings for examples in these colors: White, Bean Brown, Cantaloupe, and Glacier Blue. In Casual, Brick Red and Aqua items go for around 200% more than any other color, while those in Avocado Yellow are priced lower than suggested values. Values are given for glassware in coral and seafoam; other colors are 10% to 15% less. For those wanting to learn more about the subject, we recommend *The Collector's Encyclopedia of Russel Wright Designs* (with updated values) by our advisor, Ann Kerr. She is listed in the Directory under Ohio.

American Modern

Advertising brochure 35.00
Ashtray coaster 15.00
Bowl, divided vegetable 75.00
Bowl, lug fruit 15.00
Bowl, salad 75.00
Bowl, vegetable 22.00
Bowl, vegetable; w/lid 45.00
Butter dish 160.00
Carafe 160.00
Casserole, w/lid, 12" 45.00
Celery dish 24.00
Chop plate 30.00
Coffeepot, AD 65.00
Coffeepot, 8x8½" 150.00
Creamer 10.00
Cup & saucer 15.00
Cup & saucer, AD 25.00
Gravy boat, 10½" 20.00
Lug soup 15.00
Mug (tumbler) 60.00
Pickle dish 15.00
Pitcher, water 100.00
Pitcher, water; w/lid 175.00
Plate, salad; 8" 12.00
Platter, 13¼" 25.00
Ramekin, ind; w/lid 150.00
Refrigerator jar 165.00
Relish, divided 175.00
Salad fork & spoon 55.00
Shakers, pr 14.00
Sugar bowl, w/lid 14.00
Teapot, 6x10" 75.00
Tumbler, child's 60.00

Casual

Bowl, cereal; orig or restyled, 5", ea 8.00

Bowl, divided vegetable; 10"	45.00
Bowl, fruit; restyled, 5¾"	8.00
Bowl, salad; 52-oz, 10"	30.00
Butter dish, ½-lb	65.00
Carafe	125.00
Casserole, 10"	50.00
Casserole lid, for 4-qt casserole	20.00
Creamer, lg family sz	30.00
Creamer, restyled	15.00
Cup & saucer, restyled	10.00
Cup & saucer, tea	15.00
Gravy stand (becomes lid), 7½"	100.00
Mug, 13-oz	75.00
Percolator	125.00
Plate, luncheon; 9½"	8.00
Plate, salad; 7½"	10.00
Platter, 14½"	30.00

Restyled water pitcher, $125.00; Family size creamer, $30.00; After dinner coffeepot, $75.00.

Shakers, stacking, pr	12.50
Sugar bowl, lg family sz	18.00
Teapot, restyled	130.00

Glass

American Modern, chilling bowl, 12-oz, 3x5½"	100.00
American Modern, cocktail, 3-oz, 2½"	25.00
American Modern, cordial, 2"	38.00
American Modern, dbl old-fashioned	45.00
American Modern, dessert dish, 2"	40.00
American Modern, goblet, 4"	40.00
American Modern, pilsner, rare, 7"	100.00
American Modern, sherbet, 2½"	25.00
American Modern, tumbler, iced tea; 13-oz	30.00
American Modern, tumbler, juice; 4"	30.00
American Modern, tumbler, water; 4½"	30.00
American Modern, wine, 3"	25.00
Eclipse, old-fashioned	15.00
Eclipse, shot glass	10.00
Flair, tumbler, iced tea; 14-oz	65.00
Flair, tumbler, juice; 6-oz	50.00
Flair, tumbler, water; 11-oz	65.00
Pinch, tumbler, iced tea; 14-oz	35.00
Pinch, tumbler, juice; 6-oz	35.00
Pinch, tumbler, water; 11-oz	35.00
Snow glass, bowl, salad/vegetable; rnd	165.00
Snow glass, candle holders, pr	200.00

Snow glass, shakers, pr	65.00
Snow glass, tumbler, iced tea; 14-oz	125.00
Snow glass, tumbler; juice; 5-oz	125.00

Highlight

Bowl, vegetable; White, Pepper, or Blueberry, oval	65.00
Butter dish, Citron or Nutmeg	275.00
Casserole (Baine Marie), Wht, Pepper, or Blueberry	100.00
Cup, Citron or Netmeg	18.00
Cup, Wht, Pepper, or Blueberry	20.00
Gravy boat, Wht, Pepper, or Blueberry	35.00
Mug, Citron or Nutmeg	30.00
Plate, dinner; Citron	25.00
Plate, dinner; Pepper, Blueberry, Nutmeg or Gr	30.00
Platter, Citron or Nutmeg, rnd, sm	55.00
Relish server, Wht, Pepper or Blueberry	60.00
Shakers, Wht, Pepper or Blueberry, pr	50.00

Spun Aluminum

Russel Wright's aluminum ware may not have been especially well accepted in its day — it tended to damage easily and seems to have had only limited market appeal — but today's collectors feel quite differently about it, as is apparent in the suggested values noted in the following listings.

Baine Marie, server	400.00
Candelabrum, rare, 18x14"	200.00
Casserole	110.00
Cheese board	85.00
Flower ring	125.00
Gravy boat	125.00
Hot relish server	175.00
Humidor, sandwich	160.00
Ice bucket	75.00
Muffin warmer, wire insert, w/lid	100.00
Old-fashioned set, 20-pc	450.00
Pitcher, sherry	250.00
Portable bar/serving cart	2,000.00
Punch set	1,500.00
Relish rosette, sm	125.00
Serving accessory, sm	100.00
Smoking stand	650.00
Spaghetti set, 3-pc	400.00
Tea set, 4-pc	500.00
Tray, tidbit	110.00
Vase, 12"	110.00
Vase or flowerpot, sm, ea	85.00
Wastebasket	110.00

Sterling

Ashtray	75.00
Bowl, bullion, 7-oz	12.00
Bowl, onion soup; 10-oz	20.00
Coffee bottle	85.00
Pitcher, water; restyled	60.00
Pitcher, water; 2-qt	55.00
Plate, bread & butter; 6¼"	5.00
Plate, dinner; 10¼"	12.00
Plate, salad; 7½"	7.00
Platter, oval, 13⅝"	20.00
Sauce boat, 9-oz	20.00

Teapot, 10-oz 65.00

Miscellaneous

Bauer, bowl, mantelpiece; #9A, 24" L 825.00
Bauer, vase, #2A, 8½" 375.00
Bauer, vase, oval, #18A, 12" 900.00
Circus animals, from $500.00 up to 650.00
Flair, bowl, vegetable; shallow, oval 12.00
Flair, creamer & sugar bowl, w/lid 25.00
Flair, plate, salad 5.00
Frosted Oak, bowl, serving 300.00
Harker White Clover, bowl, cereal/soup; clover decor 14.00
Harker White Clover, bowl, vegetable; 7½" 20.00
Harker White Clover, gravy boat, clover decor 25.00
Harker White Clover, plate, dinner; clover decor, 9¼" 14.00
Home Decorator, bowl, vegetable; oval, deep 13.00
Home Decorator, cup & saucer 8.00
Home Decorator, lug soup 12.00
Home Decorator, tumbler 15.00
Hull cutlery, ea pc 50.00
Ideal Ware, butter dish 45.00
Ideal Ware, child's boxed set 165.00
Ideal Ware, freezing dish 20.00
Ideal Ware, jug, water; lg 25.00
Knowles, bowl, serving; 12¼" 28.00
Knowles, plate, dinner; 10¾" 15.00
Knowles, platter, 13" L 18.00
Knowles, teapot 125.00
Mary Wright, wooden cheese board 150.00
Mary Wright Country Garden serving items, from $165.00 up to .200.00
Meladur, bowl, fruit; 6-oz 8.00
Meladur, cup & saucer 10.00
Meladur, plate, compartmented, 9½" 10.00
Oceana, nut bowl 250.00
Residential, bowl, fruit 12.00
Residential, covered onion soup, ea pc 12.00
Residential, plate, dinner 5.00
Residential, platter 18.00
Swan, nut cup 125.00
Theme Informal, mug 75.00
Wave, bowl, salad 550.00

Russian Art

Before the Revolution in 1917, many jewelers and craftsmen created exquisite marvels of their arts, distinctive in the extravagant detail of their enamel work, jeweled inlays, and use of precious metals. These treasures aptly symbolized the glitter and the romance of the glorious days under the reign of the Tsars of Imperial Russia. The most famous of these master jewelers was Carl Faberge (1852-1920), goldsmith to the Romanovs. Following the tradition of his father, he took over the Faberge workshop in 1870. Eventually Faberge employed more than 500 assistants and set up workshops in Moscow, Kiev, and London as well as in St. Petersburg. His specialties were enamel work, clockwork automated figures, carved animal and human figures of precious or semiprecious stones, cigarette cases, small boxes, scent flasks, and his best-known creations, the Imperial Easter Eggs — each of an entirely different design. By the turn of the century, his influence had spread to other countries, and his work was revered by royalty and the very wealthy. The onset of the war marked the end of the era. Very little of his work remains on the market, and items that are available are very expensive. But several of his contemporaries were goldsmiths whose

work can be equally enchanting. Among them are Klingert, Ovchinnikov, Smirnov, Ruckert, Loriye, Cheryatov, Kuzmichev, Nevalainen, Adler, Sbitnev, Third Artel, Wakewa, Holmstrom, Britzin, Wigstrom, Orlov, Nichols, and Plincke. Most of them produced excellent pieces similar to those made by Faberge between 1880 and 1910.

Perhaps the most important bronze Russian artist was Eugenie Alexandrovich Lanceray (1847-87). From 1875 until 1887, he modeled many equestrian groups of falconers and soldiers ranging in height from about 20" to 30". Some of them bear the Chopin foundry mark; they are presently worth from $4,000.00 up. Other excellent artists were Schmidt Felling (19th century), who specialized in mounted figures of cossacks wearing military uniforms, and Nicholas Leiberich (late 19th century), who also specialized in equestrian groups. Most of the pieces made by the above artists were signed and had the foundry mark (Chopin, Woerfell, etc.).

Russian porcelain is another field where Imperial connections have undoubtedly added to the interest of collectors and museums worldwide. The most important factories were: Imperial Russian Porcelain, St. Petersburg (or Petrograd or Leningrad, 1744-1917); Gardner, Moscow (1765-1872); Kuznetsoff, St. Petersburg and Moscow (1800-1900); Korniloff, St. Petersburg (1800-1900); and Babunin, St. Petersburg (1800-1900).

Bowl, champleve, Khlebnikov, 1883, sm 200.00
Box, Neillo, eng w/bldgs, assayer Dubronin, 1822-55 ....180.00
Cigarette case, silver, Ivanov, 1873 ....260.00
Cordial, mc floral on textured gold enamel, 3½" 425.00
Cup, christening; glass, etched Peter the Great/1905, 5½" ...330.00
Cup w/lid & saucer, porc, samovar shape, Kuznetsov, 5", EX ...200.00
Dish, porc, as grape cluster on leaf, Kuznetsov, 8", EX 385.00
Egg, enameled, Kuzmichev, 1908-17, lg 1,300.00
Egg, porc w/HP floral on lt gr, Imperial Porc Factory, 1890 ...700.00
Figurine, man in wht tunic leaning on stump, 1700s, 9½" ...750.00
Group, patinated iron, cossack rider embraces woman, 15" ...525.00
Plate, porc, portrait Empress Elizabeth, Safronov, 8", EX ...300.00
Podstakan, silver filigree, Ozeritsky, 1908-17 ....875.00
Salt cellar, enameled, Ovchinikov, 1895 ....200.00
Salt cellar, scroll & star champleve, red/gr/wht, mk NK, 2½" ...425.00
Spoon, champleve enamel, red/blk/3 bls, 5¼", pr in case ...550.00
Spoon, enameled, JV Aarne, assayer Lebedkin, 1896-03, 3¾" ...170.00
Spoon, enameled, mk CK, Gustav Klingert, 1896, 4½" 115.00
Spoon, enameled, mk MC, Semenova, assayer Lebedkin, 1896, 4½" ...175.00
Spoon, enameled, mk NO, Ovchinnikov, 1880, 4½" 130.00
Spoon, enameled, Semenova, assayer Lyapunov, 1896-03, 6½" ...175.00
Spoon, salt; enameled, mk Moscow #84, ca 1880, 3" 120.00
Teapot, enamel w/fighting cocks, onyx set in hdl, #84, 6" ...900.00
Vase, porc, HP figure scenes, gilt hdls/ft, Gardner, 10", pr ...2,000.00
Water pipe, porc, floral/portraits on magenta, 5-part, 1800s ...165.00

Sabino

Sabino art glass was produced by Marius-Ernest Sabino in France during the 1920s and '30s. It was made in opalescent, frosted, and colored glass and was designed to reflect the Art Deco style of that era. In 1960 using molds he modeled by hand, Sabino once again began to produce art glass using a special formula he himself developed that was characterized by a golden opalescence. Although the family continued to produce glassware for export after his death in 1971, they were never able to duplicate Sabino's formula.

Bottle, scent; Frivolites, ladies & swans, 6¼" 85.00
Box, powder; Petalia, med sz 110.00
Figurine, Argentina 900.00

Figurine, branch of birds	875.00
Figurine, cherub	25.00
Figurine, dragonfly	125.00
Figurine, Egyptian goddess	65.00
Figurine, elephant group	2,500.00
Figurine, Isadora Duncan	625.00
Figurine, La Carpe	2,500.00
Figurine, lady & doves	350.00
Figurine, Madonna, sq base, med sz	85.00
Figurine, nude w/graceful cloak, 9½"	400.00
Figurine, nude w/long hair falling to ft, 1 arm above, 7"	500.00
Figurine, pekingese	25.00
Figurine, rooster, lg	365.00
Mask, Triton	2,275.00
Plaque, oval w/cherubic head, in wood stand, 17½"	2,600.00
Tray, sea urchin, lg	85.00
Tray, swallow, sm	40.00
Vase, Algues Marines	365.00
Vase, amber, curved leaf tips/disks, partial polish, 12"	1,500.00
Vase, Beehive	195.00
Vase, Columbes, opal	525.00
Vase, La Danse	1,500.00
Vase, Manta Ray	300.00
Vase, Ovals & Pearls	265.00
Vase, Paradis	750.00
Vase, rows of jutting sqs, opal, tumbler form, 5½", EX	385.00
Vase, sparrow band, stylized feathers on body, opal, 8"	975.00

Salesman's Samples and Patent Models

Salesman's samples and patent models are often mistaken for toys or homemade folk art pieces. They are instead actual working models made by very skilled craftsmen who worked as model-makers. Patent models were made until the early 1900s. After that, the patent office no longer required a model to grant a patent. The name of the inventor or the model-maker and the date it was built is sometimes noted on the patent model. Salesman's samples were occasionally made by model-makers, but often they were assembled by an employee of the company. These usually carried advertising messages to boost the sale of the product. Though they are still in use today, the most desirable examples date from the 1800s to about 1945.

Many small stoves are incorrectly termed a 'salesman's sample'; remember that no matter how detailed one may be, it must be considered a toy unless accompanied by a carrying case, the indisputable mark of a salesman's sample.

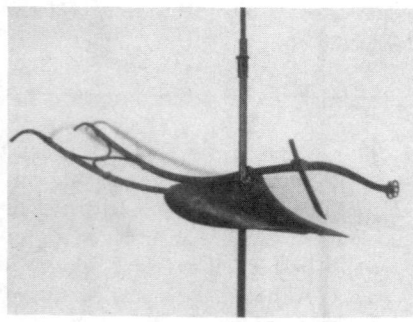

Single-bottom plow, cast iron, mounted on wooden base, 1800s, 37x30", $1,000.00.

Boiler, Humphrey, CI & brass, orig pnt, 10½x3" dia, EX	400.00
Boots, maroon leather, calf height, 4", EX	45.00
Cedar chest, Lane Cedar Chests, Altavista VA, 4½x9x4½"	48.00
Chemical toilet, porc & oak, complete in metal case	350.00

Fence, wooden, cattle type, 14", VG	200.00
Fencing, cast metal base w/chicken wire, Pace, 6x11½", EX	75.00
Garden swing, wood slats, 2 loveseats on tripod, 19x19x14"	650.00
Generator, Colt Standard, carbide feed, 1910, M in case	685.00
Harness, farm type for horse, 1¾x5x6", VG	200.00
Ice cream freezer, Peerless	150.00
Lectern, blk pnt on pine, 13¾x7¾x9¾"	135.00
Light, gas; brass fixture screws to wall outlet, glass cover	150.00
Lunch pail, miner's; NP brass, Lisk	390.00
Pans, cast aluminum, 2 roasters/skillet/2 sauce pans/2 lids	180.00
Post hole digger, wood & brass, 3x29x3", EX	200.00
Rifle case, leather & brass, Moose Brand, 5½x16¼x3", VG	200.00
Safe, Mosler, CI, front loading, 17x12x6¼", VG in case	1,000.00
Screen door, Winioski ME, 18½x8", VG	125.00
Table, quartered oak, extension type, ped base, 23x10¼", VG	300.00
Toilet seat, purple plastic, 2x7x9", EX	65.00
Washing machine, Dexter, copper/brass/wood, 12", G	600.00
Washing machine, Kraut, wood & iron, Pat 1888, 14", G	770.00

Salt Glaze

As early as the 1600s, potters used common salt to glaze their stoneware. This was accomplished by heating the salt and introducing it into the kiln at maximum temperature. The resulting gray-white glaze was a thin, pitted surface that resembles the peel of an orange.

Basket, emb/shaped/rtcl rim, emb fruit/nuts, +11" (EX) stand	2,800.00
Bowl, fruit; emb dots & diaper, basketweave panels, 11½"	700.00
Candle snuffer, as a standing lady in frilly cap, rstr, 3¾"	1,900.00
Cup, HP Chinaman seated in garden, 2-hdl, ftd, 4¾", EX	2,400.00
Dish, intricately emb shaped border, allover emb, 12", NM	1,000.00
Dish, shaped/emb rtcl rim, allover intricate emb, 10½"	935.00
Figurine, cat, seated, looking left, bl eyes, 1760s, 6"	9,350.00
Figurine, squirrel, seated/nut in paws, emb scrolls, 4", EX	3,000.00
Pitcher, classical figures, wht on brn, pewter lid, mk, 8¼"	110.00
Pitcher, drabware w/appl wht floral, pear form, lid, 6", VG	3,500.00
Plate, Success to the King of Prussia emb on rim, 9"	1,870.00
Pounce pot, waisted, trn decor, 1¾", NM	990.00
Sauce boat, emb pineapple/wheat in basket, allover emb, 6" L	770.00
Tankard, mc inscription/scrolling foliage, dtd 1763, 5", EX	1,500.00
Teapot, emb bamboo branches w/birds, bamboo hdl, 7"	175.00
Teapot, emb leaves/bell flowers, scroll hdl, 5x7½"	180.00
Teapot, vintage body, lion mask & paw ft, bird finial, 7¼"	500.00
Teapot, 3 lion-mask/paw ft, emb vines, bird finial, 7", VG	465.00
Teapot stand, on 4 high pierced bracket ft, 6" dia	4,400.00

Salt Shakers

The screw-top salt shaker was invented by John Mason in 1858. In 1871 when salt became more refined, some ceramic shakers were molded with pierced tops. 'Christmas' shakers, so called because of their December 25, 1877, patent date, were fitted with a rotary agitator designed to break up any lumps in the salt. There are four types: Christmas Barrel (rare in cranberry and amethyst); Christmas Panel (rare in colors); Christmas Pearl (opaque, pearly white with painted decor); and Octagon Waffle (clear, thick glass made in three sizes with a rotary agitator, sometimes having undated tops). The dated tops and patented agitators were produced by Dana K. Alden of Boston, who contracted with various glasshouses to make the glass bodies. The Christmas Barrel and Christmas Panel patterns were produced by Boston and Sandwich (though the Christmas Barrel was made elsewhere as well). Alden contracted with Mt. Washington to make the Christmas Pearl pattern, and Waffle Octagon was made by several glass factories, McKee and Federal among them. Both of the latter patterns were made as late as 1900. Identical shakers which have no agitator or dated top are the companion peppers; these fetch about 30% less than the salts on today's markets.

Today's Victorian salt shaker collectors' interest primarily encompasses art glass, decorated cranberry and ruby, and custard and colored opalescent examples. (See also specified categories.) If you would like to learn more abut Victorian glass salt shakers, we recommend *The World of Salt Shakers, Second Edition,* by Mildred and Ralph Lechner; their address may be found in the Directory under Virginia. In the following listings, prices are for single shakers unless noted 'pair.' Values are for old, original shakers. Some of these have been reproduced, and this will be noted in the description.

Ada, cranberry, 2⅞" 70.00
Atterbury Twin, wht opaque Cryolite, Pat Oct 28, 1873, 3⅛" ...140.00
Banded Shells, gr opaque, ca 1890, 1⅞" 45.00
Bead & Panel, crystal to wht opal base, Peterson, 2¾" 45.00
Beaded Lattice & Frame, wht opal, 3½" 34.00
Beaded Oval Mirror, bl opaque, ca 1890, 3¼" 60.00
Beaded Vertical, wht opal, 2⅞" 19.00
Beatty Honeycomb, bl opal, ca 1888-90, 2⅝" 70.00
Big Grape, wht opaque opal w/gold goofus pnt, 4" 25.00
Billiken, wht opal, ca 1908, 4" 190.00
Block Hexagon, ruby stain, US Glass, 2⅞" 55.00
Bow & Flower, wht opaque w/EX gold, 2¾" 21.50
Broken Rib, bl opaque, ca 1897, 2⅞" 45.00
Bubble (Bubble Lattice), cranberry opal satin, 2⅞" 110.00
Bulge Bottom, wht opaque opal w/HP poppies & leaves, 2¼" ...50.00
Bulging Cloud, bl opaque, bulbous, 3" 35.00
Bulging Fleur-de-Lis, custard opaque w/fired-on pk, 1½" 65.00
Bulging Leaf, bl opaque, Consolidated, 1894-96, 2" 35.00
Bulging 9-Leaf Vt, wht opaque, 1897-1900, 3" 30.00
California (Beaded Grape), gr, US Glass, 2¾" (+) 65.00
Cambridge #1035, pressed octagon w/intaglio flowers, 3⅛" ...20.00
Christmas Barrel, amber, w/lid (dtd) & agitator, Dana K Alden ...100.00
Christmas Barrel, apple gr, w/lid & agitator 110.00
Christmas Barrel, cobalt, w/lid & agitator, +pepper, pr 200.00
Christmas Barrel, cranberry, w/lid & agitator 325.00
Christmas Barrel, cranberry, w/lid & agitator, +pepper, pr 550.00
Christmas Barrel, dk amethyst, w/lid & agitator 100.00
Christmas Barrel, gr, w/lid & agitator, 2½" 70.00
Christmas Barrel, lt gr, w/lid & agitator, 2½" 70.00
Christmas Barrel, peacock bl, w/lid & agitator, +pepper, pr ...250.00
Christmas Panel, amethyst, w/lid & agitator 225.00
Christmas Panel, cranberry, w/lid & agitator 300.00
Christmas Panel, dk amethyst, w/lid & agitator 275.00
Christmas Panel, sapphire bl, w/lid & agitator 225.00
Clover & Rosette, wht opal, pillar shape, 3⅜" 20.00
Co-op's Royal Vt, ruby stain, ca 1894, 2⅞" 38.00
Columbian Coin, gold trim, ca 1891, 2⅞" 55.00
Concave Beaded Panel, wht opal w/HP florals, 3" 38.00
Consolidated's Princess Swirl, pk cased, 1896-1900, 3" 60.00
Corn, custard opaque, tapered ear form, 3⅛" 55.00
Corner Rib, wht opaque opal w/worn gold, 2¾" 10.00
Cottage, bl, ca 1874, 2⅛" 75.00
Curved Klondike (Amberette), clear frost w/amber stain, 3" ...180.00
Dbl Cord & Tassle, pk opaque, Consolidated, 1894-1900, 2" ...60.00
Dbl Fan Band, pk opaque, 1894-1900, 3⅜" 40.00
Delaware (Four Petal Flower), rose flashing & gold, 2⅝" 140.00
Dogwood, red & gilt goofus pnt, 1901-06, 3¾", EX 45.00
Empress, emerald gr w/EX gold, 3¼" 70.00
English Barrel, coral opaque cased w/HP floral, 2⅜" 250.00
Eye-Winker, 1889-95, 3" (+) 30.00
Fandangle, gr opaque, WV Glass, 2⅝" 40.00

Fenton Swirl, lt pk opaque, ca 1954, 3⅛" 24.00
Fern Leaf, wht opaque opal w/EX gold, 1901-07, 3" 20.00
Flared Rib, bl opaque, ca 1894-1900, 3" 35.00
Flora, emerald gr w/gold, ca 1895, 3⅛" 78.00
Floral Neck, wht opaque opal w/red & gilt goofus pnt, 3⅛" ...25.00
Flower Band, pigeon blood satin, 1901-02, 1⅝" 60.00
Forget-Me-Not, bl 30.00
Frances Ware Swirl, clear frost w/amber-stained top, 3⅜" 150.00
Gaudy Scroll, wht opaque opal, ca 1900-08, 2½" 15.00
Georgia Gem, HP floral on custard, 2½" 58.00
Grape & Leaf, wht opaque opal w/goofus gold, ftd, 3⅛" 20.00
Hobnail, cranberry opal, Fenton, 1955-67, 3⅛" 35.00

Intaglio, green with gold trim, Northwood, ca 1900-03, $90.00.

Iowa, clear w/EX gold, US Glass, 2¾" 40.00
Iris w/Meander (Iris), gr, 3¼" 90.00
Josephine's Fan, Robinson, 2⅝" 20.00
Lacy Medallion (Jewel), gr w/EX gold, US Glass, 3" 45.00
Little Acorn, bl opaque, US Glass, 6¼" 30.00
Little Shrimp, gr opaque, ca 1895-1901, 1½" 65.00
Long Petal Daisy, gr opaque, Consolidated, 1904, 3½" 75.00
Matted Leaf, wht opal HP yel to wht, Phoenix, ca 1897, 2½" ...50.00
Minnesota, bulbous, US Glass, 2¾" 37.00
Octagon Panel, blk opaque, US Glass, 3⅜" 25.00
Octagon Waffle, w/agitater & dtd 1877 lid, 3" 50.00
Panelled Shell, pk, triple cased, 1894-1900, 3" 60.00
Petticoat, vaseline w/EX gold, 3" 50.00
Pleated Skirt, gr opaque, ca 1891, 1¾" 42.00
Radiant, worn gold, Pat 1887 top, ca 1887, 3" 90.00
Reverse Swirl, cranberry opal, Model Flint, 3¼" 110.00
Ribbed Melon, wht opaque opalware, ca 1890-97, 2⅝" 38.00
Ribbon Swirl, vaseline opal, 1886-1890, 2¾" 80.00
Ring Neck, pk & wht translucent w/gold mica, 3" 135.00
Roman Rosette, clear w/ruby stain, US Glass, 3" 80.00
Rose, wht opaque, fire-polished top, Fenton, ca 1967, 3⅜" 25.00
Scrolled Rib, bl opaque, 12 ribs, 1891-99, 2½" 34.00
Six Beaded Panels, bl opaque, 1897-1901, 3⅝" 40.00
Sunset, pk opaque, 1894-97, 2⅞" 45.00
Tall Pansy, bl opaque, ca 1894-1900, 3⅝" 35.00
Tarentum's Atlanta (Dmn & Teardrop), 3" 25.00
Tarentum's Thumbprint, HP decor on custard, 2⅝" 80.00
Tarentum's Victoria, gr opaque, 2⅝" 50.00
Texas, US Glass, 2¾" 30.00
Thousand Eye, vaseline, ca 1875-80, 2¾" 50.00
Three Face, clear frosted, 2⅝" 125.00
Triple Rib, bl translucent, Consolidated, 1895-1902, 3" 55.00
Triple Shell, wht opal w/HP mc decor, 1⅞" 75.00
Vertical Opal Ribbon, clear w/wht opal stripes, 2½" 36.00
Winsome, 6 concave vertical panels, Riverside, 3⅛" 20.00

Novelty

Those interested in novelty shakers will enjoy *Salt and Pepper Shakers, Volumes I-IV,* by Helene Guarnaccia, and *The Collectors Encyclopedia of Salt and Pepper Shakers, Figural and Novelty, Volumes I and II,* by Melva Davern. Both are available at your local library or from Collector Books. Note: 'Mini' shakers are no taller than 2". Instead of having a cork, the user was directed to 'use tape to cover hole.' Our advisor for Novelty Salt Shakers is Judy Posner; she is listed in the Directory under Pennsylvania.

Goofy in car, Walt Disney, $495.00.

Advertising, Campbell Kids, pr	59.00
Advertising, Chicken of the Sea Tuna, pr	32.00
Advertising, Colonel Harland Sanders, hard plastic, pr	95.00
Advertising, Elsie Cow, head stacks on shoulders, pr	110.00
Advertising, Esso plastic gas pump, pr, MIB	28.00
Advertising, Estinger beer bottle, pr	25.00
Advertising, Fairyland Farms milk bottle, pr	49.00
Advertising, Glenshaw ABCB Convention, 1962, 5½", pr	10.00
Advertising, Glenshaw Glass 80th Anniv, bottle, 5½", pr	40.00
Advertising, Greyhound bus, ceramic, pr	75.00
Advertising, Hershey Ice Cream soda, pr	45.00
Advertising, Hershey's Baking Chocolate, pr	55.00
Advertising, Idaho King 'Spud,' pr	85.00
Advertising, Kellogg's Snap & Pop, pr	75.00
Advertising, Ken L Ration cat & dog, plastic, pr	15.00
Advertising, Magic Chef, milk glass, pr	75.00
Advertising, Mr Peanut, ceramic w/glass eyes, pr	125.00
Advertising, Pillsbury Poppin' Fresh Poppy, plastic, pr	25.00
Advertising, Sympathetic Ear Restaurant, pr	55.00
Advertising, Tee & Eff, Tastee Freeze, pr	45.00
Anthropomorphic, bug couple, dressed up, he w/cigar, pr	24.00
Anthropomorphic, cactus sheriff & outlaw, pr	35.00
Anthropomorphic, fish-face couple wearing hats, pr	28.00
Anthropomorphic, fork & spoon running, pr	22.00
Anthropomorphic, frying pan & spatula heads, pr	23.00
Anthropomorphic, ink bottle & blotter-head couple, pr	75.00
Anthropomorphic, lobster couple, dressed up, pr	24.00
Comic, Bonzo pup, pr	24.00
Comic, Bonzo pup condiment set	95.00
Comic, Heckle & Jeckle, pr	125.00
Comic, Kayo (from Moon Mullins), pr	55.00
Comic, Pixie & Dixie (mice), pr	65.00
Comic, Splinter & Knothead, Walter Lantz, pr	150.00
Comic, Stan Laurel & Oliver Hardy, Beswick, 3-pc set	185.00
Comic, Sylvester & Bugs Bunny, Lego, pr	150.00
Comic, Woody Woodpecker, pr	95.00
Disney, Alice in Wonderland, ivory w/gold, Regal, pr	495.00
Disney, Baby Dumbo in flight, Japan, pr	95.00

Disney, castle, metal, 2-pc on tray	95.00
Disney, Donald & Daisy Duck shaking hands, pr	85.00
Disney, Donald Duck, ivory w/M gold, Leeds, pr	95.00
Disney, Dumbo's Crows, Blk stereotypes, pr	135.00
Disney, Ferdinand the Bull, pr	85.00
Disney, Figaro, Nat'l Porc, 1941, pr	85.00
Disney, Hop Lo mushrooms, Fantasia, Vernon Kilns, '40, pr	225.00
Disney, Mickey & Minnie Mouse, Leeds, pr	45.00
Disney, Mickey Mouse, Dan Brechner Imports, pr	225.00
Disney, Mowgli & baby elephant, Enesco, Jungle Book, pr	225.00
Disney, Pinocchio & Stromboli's girl marionette, pr	95.00
Disney, Silly Synphony pigs, full color, pr	75.00
Disney, Thumper, Leeds, pr	45.00
Mini, baby bottle & booties, pr	24.00
Mini, bellows & coal scuttle	24.00
Mini, blueberry pie & coffee, pr	28.00
Mini, cowboy hat & gun in holster, M on card	42.00
Mini, drum & trumpet, pr	42.00
Mini, mailbox & package, pr	35.00
Mini, pipe & slippers, pr	19.00
Mini, sled & ice skates, pr	32.00
Mini, straw holder & ice cream soda, pr	45.00
Nodder, bears, sitting, regular base, pr	25.00
Nodder, camel w/monkeys, pr	165.00
Nodder, deer, pr	29.00
Nodder, flamingo, regular base, pr	50.00
Nodder, hen & rooster condiments, hand-painted base, pr	59.00
Nodder, Indians in drum, pr	79.00
Nodder, kangaroo w/baby, pr	95.00
Nodder, Mexico bullfight condiment, pr	145.00
Nodder, nude Blk lady & watermelon, pr	185.00
Nodder, pig couple, walking, pr	135.00
Nodder, skull, lavender base, pr	35.00
Nude or naughty, his & hers nude sunbathers, pr	42.00
Nude or naughty, nude, reclining, 3-pc	39.00
Nude or naughty, nude, 3 red stones, 3-pc set	39.00
Nude or naughty, nude on barrel, Japan, pr	19.00
Nude or naughty, nude on barrel, sgn Kindel, pr	35.00
Nude or naughty, outhouse couple, Hurry I Can Hardly Wait, pr	48.00
Nursery Rhyme/Fairy Tale, Aladdin w/jewels & gold lamp, pr	35.00
Nursery Rhyme/Fairy Tale, Babar the Elephant & wife, pr	65.00
Nursery Rhyme/Fairy Tale, blkbird in pie, pr	32.00
Nursery Rhyme/Fairy Tale, cat (gray) & fiddle, pr	24.00
Nursery Rhyme/Fairy Tale, Goldilocks, Relco, pr	45.00
Nursery Rhyme/Fairy Tale, Humpty Dumpty & Woman in Shoe, pr	29.00
Nursery Rhyme/Fairy Tale, Humpty Dumpty stacks on wall, pr	32.00
Nursery Rhyme/Fairy Tale, Little Boy Blue in haystack, pr	65.00
Nursery Rhyme/Fairy Tale, Mary Had a Little Lamb, pr	35.00
Nursery Rhyme/Fairy Tale, Paul Bunyon (seated) & Babe, pr	55.00
Nursery Rhyme/Fairy Tale, Tortoise & Hare, pr	32.00
Plastic, carafe on burner, pr	19.00
Plastic, champagne bottle on ice, pr	27.00
Plastic, dream house, pr	23.00
Plastic, electric mixer, pr	22.00
Plastic, fruit bowl, pr, MIB	25.00
Plastic, lawn mower, pr	22.00
Plastic, pearl in oyster, pr	16.00
Plastic, Strum a Guitar, MIB	30.00
Plastic, toaster, Niagara Falls, pr, MIB	22.00
Vegetable people, celery people, pr	28.00
Vegetable people, corn teapot people, pr	29.00
Vegetable people, eggplant fellow, pr	85.00
Vegetable people, Idaho King Spud, pr	85.00
Vegetable people, pea pod girl waving, pr	28.00

Vegetable people, pear head, pr 19.00

Salts, Open

Before salt became refined, processed, and free-flowing as we know it today, it was necessary to serve it in a salt cellar. An innovation of the early 1800s, the master salt was placed by the host and passed from person to person. Smaller individual salts were a part of each place setting. A small silver spoon was used to sprinkle it onto the food.

If you would like to learn more about the subject of salts, we recommend 5,000 Open Salts, written by William Heacock and Patricia Johnson, with many full-color illustrations and current values. Our advisor for this category is Chris Christensen; he is listed in the Directory under California. In the listings below, the numbers refer to Open Salts by Johnson and Heacock and Pressed Glass Salt Dishes by L.W. and D.B. Neal. Lines with 'repro' within the description reflect values for reproduced salts.

Key:
EPNS — electroplated nickel silver   HM — hallmarked

Animals, Figurals, and Novelties

Bird & Berry, McKee, amber or bl vase, #997, ea 55.00
Bird & Berry, sgn Degenhart, #998 ....40.00
Bird & Berry, unsgn Degenhart, #933 ....35.00
Coach, bl or amber, #417, ea 110.00
Dog pulling cart, amber, #2102, M 95.00
Dresser, salt & pepper, #7472 ....150.00
Duck, heavy crystal, European, #4677, 2¾" 45.00
Duck on nest, Staffordshire, #1008 ....65.00
Figural hdl, dbl, clear, European, #3777 ....35.00
Horseshoe, 'Good Luck,' #3742, master 65.00
Novelty, chickens, dbl, milk glsss, sgn Vallerystahl, #4447 ....55.00
Novelty, horseshoe, #3741, ind 20.00
Rabbit, covered, signed Vallerystahl, #3750 ....45.00
Sleigh, amber glass, ca 1900, #3734 ....85.00
Sleigh, Fostoria, ca 1940, #3735 ....45.00
Squirrel on tree, #3735, ind 45.00
Swan, gr, sgn Cambridge, #935 ....45.00
Turtle, clear, #3758 ....40.00
Wagon, clear, ca 1890, #3739 ....50.00
Wildflower on turtle base, amber, #506 ....125.00

Art Glass

Cased, pk & wht, ruffled top, #126 ....125.00
Cranberry glass, ruffled rigaree, tulip top, SP holder 150.00
Crown Milano, shiny, unsgn, #46 ....175.00
Daum Nancy, cameo, rain scene 1,000.00
Daum Nancy, floral, sgn, #7 ....500.00
Daum Nancy, windmill scene, sgn, #10 ....600.00
English, William & Mary, yel vaseline, #69 ....55.00
Legras, floral, sterling gold-washed base, sgn, #12 ....450.00
Monot & Stumpf, ormolu holder 175.00
Monot & Stumpf, rnd, #19-22 ....110.00
Quezal, #18, 1" dia 175.00
Steuben, calcite, ped ft, #34 ....195.00
Tiffany, bl, ruffled top edge, sgn, #3 ....300.00
Tiffany, ruffled top edge, sgn, #32 ....125.00
Webb, cameo, w/spoon 600.00
Webb, cranberry, clear rigaree, berry pontil, SP holder 275.00
Webb, vaseline, clear rigaree, berry pontil, SP fr, #96 ....250.00

China

Austria, HP, rnd, sgn, #1272, ind 18.00
Celery salt, HP, EX quality, #1720 ....15.00
Elfinware, Germany, basket shape, #1253 ....20.00
Elfinware, Germany, bird hdls, #1261 ....40.00
Elfinware, Germany, swan, ornate, #1039 ....40.00
Elfinware, Japan, #1222 ....15.00
German Dresden, appl flowers, sgn, #1689, ind 55.00
Haviland, pattern decor, 31400, ind 30.00
Japan, HP, #1443, ind 15.00
Limoges, HP china, rnd, sgn, #1275, ind 15.00
Meissen, sgn, ca 1890, #1812-1814 ....175.00
Nippon, celery salt, #1714 ....15.00
Nippon, HP, rnd, 3 legs, #1423-1425 ....15.00
Nippon, HP, rnd, 3-ftd, #1365, ind 15.00
Royal Bayreuth, ped ft, HP scenic, sgn, #1666 ....85.00
Royal Copenhagen, ca 1890, #1201 ....75.00

Cut Glass

Cranberry, etched, ped, ca 1890, #123 ....110.00
Dmn Point, #3101 ....10.00
Faceted, #2919 ....10.00
Hawkes, sgn, #3064 ....45.00
Heart/club/dmn/spade, #3034-3035, set of 4 ....100.00
J Hoare, sgn, #3166 ....40.00
Ped ft, sgn Clark, #3009 ....25.00
Ped ft, sgn Waterford, ca 1970, #3698 ....55.00
Ped ft, Waterford type, ca 1860, #3699 ....75.00
Ped ft, Waterford type, gr, ca 1860, #601 ....125.00
Zippered, #3088 ....15.00

Lacy Glass

American, non-flint repro, ca 1920-40, VG 45.00
Avon, repro 5.00
Neal-BF-1, basket of flowers, VG 100.00
Neal-BF-1B, basket of flowers, opal, chip on leg 125.00
Neal-BT-8, Lafayette boat, cobalt, sgn Sandwich, VG 950.00
Neal-DI-8, dbl, roughage on bottom 175.00
Neal-EE-3B, eagles on 4 corners, VG 150.00
Neal-EE-8, eagle, rnd, M 280.00
Neal-GA-2, cathedral windows, cobalt, leg chip 125.00
Neal-HN-18A, opaline, ftd, VG 375.00
Neal-NE-1A, wht opaque, sgn NE Glass Co Boston, EX 300.00

Pottery

Figural, condiment w/spoons, German, #1119 ....110.00
Quimper, ca 1920, #1729 ....25.00
Quimper, dbl, figural hdl, ca 1890, #1129 ....125.00
Quimper, dbl, hdl, HP, #1132 ....95.00
Royal Doulton, sterling hallmk rim, ca 1873, #1870 ....125.00
Royal Doulton, sterling hallmk rim, ca 1900, #1851 ....65.00
Royal Worcester, dbl wall, ca 1862, #1861, ind 125.00
Wedgwood, sterling hallmk rim, ca 1897, sgn, #1850 ....150.00

Pressed Glass, Clear

Alexis, Fostoria, #2631 ....10.00
Applied Bands, #2934, ind 25.00
Arched Leaf, master 18.00
Atlanta (Lion), #2758, ind 45.00

Atlanta (Lion), master 45.00
Beatty Rib, old, #3387 ....10.00
Buckle, #3608, master 35.00
Butterfly & Cattails, #3568 ....35.00
Diamond Point Disc, #2930 ....15.00
Diamond Rosette, #3407, master 25.00
Diamond Shield, #3600 ....25.00
Grasshopper, #3573 ....35.00
Harp, #3601, master 45.00
Heisey Pillows, sgn, #2697 ....35.00
Illinois, plain, #2760, ind 15.00
Jacob's Ladder, #3580 ....35.00
King's Crown, plain, #2776 ....25.00
Lincoln Drape, #3619 ....45.00
Medallion Sunburst, #2543 ....10.00
Open Plaid, #3567 ....20.00
Plain Band, Heisey, #2560 ....22.00
Sawtooth Circle, #3540 ....30.00
Serrated Rib & Fine Cut, #2535, ind 10.00
Snail, #2656, ind 30.00
Tree of Life, 'Salt,' #3582, master 75.00
Washington, #2504, ind 27.00
Washington Centennial, #2518, ind 20.00
Washington State, #2518, ind 20.00
3-Panel, master 15.00

Pressed Glass, Colored

Beatty Rib, bl 35.00
Beatty Rib, opal 30.00
English Hobnail, gr, bl, etc, old, ea 20.00
English Hobnail, Wright repro, ea 5.00
Fine Cut & Block, amber flashed, #837, master 65.00
Fine Cut & Block, bl, pk, (etc) flashed-on, ea 45.00
Heisey Tub, cobalt, sgn 75.00
Heisey Tub, unsgn, #374 ....25.00
Hobnail, opal, amber, or bl, ea 25.00
Jersey Swirl, bl, #426 ....25.00
Leaf & Rib (Maple Leaf), vaseline or bl, ea 25.00
Panel w/Dmn Point, apple gr, #372 ....45.00
Wreath & Shell, bl or vaseline, ea 125.00
3-Panel, bl, vaseline, amber or gr, #554, ea 18.00

Silverplate

Clear glass liner, #3918, Victorian 65.00
Oblong, ftd, Meriden Co, #4050, worn 20.00
Overshot glass in holder, #4215-4217 ....75.00
Ped ft, Meriden Co, #3948, worn 20.00
Ruby liner, Derby hallmk holder, #319 ....75.00
Salt & pepper, English, ca 1890, #4134 ....25.00

Sterling

Albert Cole Medallion, ca 1850, #4208 ....225.00
American, lattice w/glass liner, ca 1900, ind 25.00
English, David Hannel, ca 1875, #4232, sm dents, pr ...250.00
English, Dixon & Son, oblong, 4 ft, #3965, ind 55.00
English, gr liner, ca 1920, ind 65.00
English, shell, 3 ball ft, #4279, ind 25.00
English, tureen shape, heavy Baroque, ca 1890 ....85.00
English trencher, Rockefeller repro, spoon, #4227 ...75.00
European, cobalt in 800 silver holder, ca 1850, #676 ...125.00
European, reindeer pulling sleigh, #4748 ....375.00

French, cobalt, dbl, ped ft, ca 1850, #761 ....150.00
French, ornate, ca 1800, master 150.00
French, ornate, ca 1845, #3935, w/spoon, ind 125.00
French, ornate, ca 1890, #3937, w/spoon, ind 125.00
French, sq w/glass insert, #3946, w/spoon, ind 100.00
German, glass insert, ca 1880, #3938, ind 35.00
German, ped ft, figural hdls, ca 1822, #4286, pr ...500.00
German, swan liner, 800 silver, ca 1890, #4294, w/spoon ...95.00
German, wheelbarrow, 800 silver, ca 1800, #4229 ...135.00
German, 3 swans hold salt, ca 1890, #714 ....175.00
Gorham, ped ft, gold wash, ca 1900, #4248 ....65.00

Master salt, sterling with gold wash, repousse animals, animal figural feet, 5" wide, $500.00.

Reed & Barton, ca 1890, #4226, master, pr 190.00
Rnd, plain, #3997-4000, sm 70.00
Rnd, plain, hallmk, ca 1920, #4237 ....25.00
Russian, #3936, not old, w/spoon 45.00
Russian enamel, ca 1896, #2022 ....450.00
Russian enamel, ca 1970, #2008, w/spoon 75.00
Swan, glass w/sterling wings, ca 1920, #4289 ....45.00
Towle, modern, #4238, w/spoon, ind 35.00
Viking ship, 830 silver, not old, #4260, w/spoon 45.00

Other Types

Amethyst glass, ca 1880, Pairpoint, #416 ....85.00
Amethyst glass, grape leaf, Fostoria, ca 1940 ....25.00
Amethyst glass, tub shape, sgn Sowerby, #413 ....50.00
Amethyst glass, tureen shape, Chpndl hdl, sgn Sowerby, #385 ...75.00
Blue glass, rnd, cut & faceted, #3891 ....20.00
Blue glass, tub shape, sgn Vallerystahl, #501 ....55.00
Blue glass, tureen shape, Chpndl hdl, sgn Sowerby, #385 ...85.00
Celluloid, Viking ship, ivory, w/pepper, #207 ....35.00
Cobalt glass, ped ft, ca 1860, #629, master 125.00
Cranberry glass, rnd, 3 clear appl ft, #280, sm 30.00
Cranberry glass, sterling o/l, #271 ....125.00
Green glass, opal, sgn Baccarat, ca 1885, #360 ....65.00
Intaglio, cut & beveled, clear, #3418 ....20.00
Intaglio, cut & beveled, color, #227 ....25.00
Intaglio, in jeweled holder, any 90.00
Intaglio, pnt animal center, butterfly, sgn, #156 ......60.00
Intaglio, pressed, clear, #3426 ....20.00
Intaglio, pressed, color, #219 ....15.00
Mercury glass, cobalt, #655, master 55.00

Samplers

American samplers were made as early as the the colonial days;

even earlier examples from 17th-century England still exist today. Changes in style and decorative motif are evident down through the years. Verses were not added until the late 17th century. By the 18th century, samplers were used not only for sewing experience but also as an educational tool. Young ladies, who often signed and dated their work, embroidered numbers and letters of the alphabet and practiced fancy stitches as well. Fruits and flowers were added for borders; birds, animals, and Adam and Eve were popular subjects. Later, houses and other buildings were included. By the 19th century, the American Eagle and the little red schoolhouse had made their appearances.

Fanny Marks record and sampler wrought the age of 15, 1825, multicolor threads on linen, some fading and fiber loss, framed, 24¼x16¼", $2,475.00.

ABCs, homespun bound in ribbon, sgn/1829, 9x18" 275.00
ABCs & rows of stitches, homespun, sgn/not dtd, 18x9" 145.00
ABCs/dogs/strawberry border, homespun, sgn, unfr, 19x13", EX ..400.00
ABCs/flowers, homespun, worn, modern fr, 13x11" 250.00
ABCs/flowers/animals/etc, homespun, sgn/1820, fr, 22x18" 330.00
ABCs/flowers/buildings/birds, homespun, stain, 9½x13" 380.00
ABCs/flowers/verse/vines, linen, sgn/1876, matted/fr, 17x16" 275.00
ABCs/numbers, homespun, initials/1827, unfr, 8x8", EX 165.00
ABCs/numbers/flowers/verse, homespun, sgn/1820, unfr, 16x17" .550.00
ABCs/numbers/strawberries, homespun linen, fr, 18½x8½" 330.00
ABCs/numbers/verse/flowers, homespun, fr, 22x20" 990.00
ABCs/numbers/vines, wool on punched paper, sgn/1853, 26x21" ..400.00
ABCs/trees/flowers/etc, homespun, sgn/1802, stain, 16x13" 440.00
ABCs/verse, EX stitching, homespun, sgn/1732, unfr, 16x9" 935.00
ABCs/verse/birds/heart, homespun, sgn/1842, 15x11" 600.00
ABCs/verse/buildings/bird/trees, homespun, rprs, 18x18" 165.00
ABCs/verse/flower baskets, linen, sgn/1817, fr, 14x17" 2,100.00
ABCs/verse/flowers, homespun, sgn/1827, stains, unfr, 21x16" ..550.00
ABCs/verse/flowers/dog, homespun, fr, 15¼x13½" 250.00
ABCs/verse/flowers/trees, homespun, sgn/1835, 18x19", EX 385.00
ABCs/verse/landscape, mc on linen, sgn/1818, fr, 27x17" 1,100.00
ABCs/verse/trees/flowers/animals, homespun, sgn/1839, 17x11" ..500.00
ABCs/verse/trees/flowers/etc, homespun, sgn/1826, fr, 14x11" ..1,200.00
Birds/flowers/houses/windmill, homespun, sgn/1842, 22x18" ..3,300.00
Family register w/vining florals, homespun, 1814, 21x19" 880.00
Family register/flowers, linen, sgn/1832, fr, 18x17" 880.00
Flower baskets, flower border, Spanish inscr/sgn/1846, 22x22" ..495.00
House/garden/trees/flower border, linen, sgn/1830, 20x19" ...1,400.00
Let Me Live in House..., house/roof/trees, mc, 1920s, 15x12" 60.00
Map of England & Wales, homespun, fr, 26x23" 440.00
Verse/cottage/farm scene, EX color, sgn/1817, fr, 17x13" 1,500.00
Verse/flower baskets/bouquets, homespun, sgn/1860, 18x15" 400.00
Verse/flowers/birds/animals/etc, homespun, sgn/1835, 25x30" ..665.00
Verse/patterned bands/inscr, sgn/1768, unfr, 7¼x6" 1,100.00
Verse/trees/buildings/birds, homespun, sgn/1788, 19x15" 465.00
2-story house, mc, punched paper, fr, 7¾x9¾" 195.00

Sandwich Glass

The Boston and Sandwich Glass Company was founded in 1820 by Deming Jarves in Sandwich, Massachusetts. Their first products were simple cruets, salts, half-pint jugs, and lamps. They were attributed as being one of the first to perfect a method for pressing glass, a step toward the manufacture of the 'lacy' glass which they made until about 1840. Many other types of glass were made there — cut, colored, snakeskin, hobnail, and opalescent among them. After the Civil War, profits began to dwindle due to the keen competition of the Western factories which were situated in areas rich in natural gas and easily accessible sand and coal deposits. The end came with an unreconcilable wage dispute between the workers and the company, and the factory closed in 1888. Our advisor for this category is Richard Marden; he is listed in the Directory under New Hampshire. See also Cup Plates; Salts, Open; specific types of glass.

Basin, bl, pressed, ca 1850s, 1x3" 275.00
Bell, smoke; free-blown, wht opal w/bl rim & top ring, 9x6" 80.00
Bottle, scent; bright amethyst, 12-sided, 1860-80, 6⅛" 180.00
Bottle, scent; cobalt, 12-sided, flared mouth, att, 4¾" 190.00
Bottle, scent; gr, oval panels, orig stopper, 5½" 275.00

Bowl, lacy, octagonal shape, 9¼", $125.00.

Bowl, Nailhead Dmn w/hobstars/vesicas/X-hatching, 6" dia 175.00
Bowl, peachblow w/sqd frost hdls, pinched/ruffled rim, 4x9" 450.00
Bowl, pk to clear, oval punties/feathered stars, sm 95.00
Bowl, tomato, sqd w/folded crystal-edge rim, rope hdl, 4x10" 225.00
Candlestick, Acanthus Leaf, bl & wht opaque, 10¾" 475.00
Candlestick, bl, columnar std, petal socket & wafer, 9½" 600.00
Candlestick, clambroth, columnar std, 9¼" 200.00
Candlestick, Petal & Loop, 7¼" 125.00
Candlestick, pressed flint, hexagonal base & wafer, 7¾" 90.00
Candlesticks, canary yel, columnar std, 9⅞", NM, pr 350.00
Candlesticks, canary yel, dolphin w/step base, 10½", EX, pr 450.00
Candlesticks, clambroth, dolphin w/dbl-step base, 9¾", pr 650.00
Candlesticks, Petal & Loop, bl over wht, 7", pr 1,350.00
Candlesticks, Petal & Loop, canary yel, lt roughness, 7⅛", pr 250.00
Candlesticks, Petal & Loop, clambroth, 7", NM, pr 525.00
Compote, Petal & Loop, flint, 7x9½" 110.00
Cup & saucer, lacy, BK #3337, 1835-50 ....220.00
Decanter, b3m, cobalt, tam-o'-shanter stopper, ½-pt 425.00
Decanter, Horn of Plenty, back-bar type, 1-pt, 8¾" 135.00
Epergne, overshot, appl gr snakes w/gold, 2-pc, 9½" dia 400.00
Inkwell, GI-7, b3m, dk cherry puce, vertical ribs, 1⅞" 325.00
Lamp, fluid; canary yel, waisted, 6-sided base, 9¼" 275.00
Lamp, fluid; Four Printie Block, canary yel, 11½" 450.00
Lamp, fluid; frosted bl, brass fluted font, 21" 500.00
Lamp, fluid; Loop, sapphire bl, 8-sided std, sq base, 8½" 600.00

Lamp, oil; clambroth, acanthus leaf form, base roughage, 12" 400.00
Pitcher, bl overshot w/appl amber reeded hdl, 1870-80, 8x6" 220.00
Pitcher, GIII-12, b3m, clear, incurvate rim, 2" 850.00
Sugar bowl, Gothic Arch, clambroth, rim roughage, 5½x4½" 525.00
Sweetmeat, Petal & Loop, flint, w/lid, 8½x6" 200.00
Tray, ice cream, 4 sunbursts, dmns, hobstars & X-hatching 685.00
Tumbler, b3m, sheared rim, pontil scar, 1820-40, 4⅜" 160.00
Vase, cobalt bl, hyacinth form, 6¾" 75.00
Vase, Fleurette, fireglow satin, fluted, 4⅞x3⅞" 110.00
Vase, Loop, wafer joined to rnd base, 10" 170.00
Vase, T'print, canary yel, petal top, 6-side stem, 12", pr 800.00
Vase, wht w/red rim, blown, on pressed Baroque base, 11" 110.00

Sarreguemines

Sarreguemines, France, is the location of Utzschneider and Company, founded in 1770, producers of majolica, transfer-printed dinnerware, figurines, and novelties which are usually marked 'Sarreguemines.'

Bowl, Cabbage Leaf, gr, 6½" 30.00
Ewer, Deco figures, 13" 140.00
Pitcher, face; brn w/bl int, 7" 75.00
Plate, character, sgn Fenault 35.00
Plate, French song, 7½" 28.00
Platter, fruit on gold-leaf bkground, 12" 85.00
Tray, dancing peasants, mk 55.00
Vase, amber to rich brn, bl int, mk, 6½" 60.00

Satin Glass

Satin glass is simply glassware with a velvety matt finish achieved through the application of an acid bath. This procedure has been used by many companies since the 20th century, both here and abroad, on many types of colored and art glass. See also Mother-of-Pearl.

Shell pattern, pink with hand-painted floral decoration, left to right: Biscuit jar, $200.00; Creamer and sugar bowl, $225.00.

Atomizer, opal w/floral, 6" 100.00
Biscuit jar, pk to wht, mc carnations w/gold, SP, 7½" 225.00
Biscuit jar, pk w/mc flowers & scrolls, SP mts, 6" 175.00
Biscuit jar, tan w/wine flowers, metal rim, twist bail, 6" 125.00
Ewer, bl w/floral, folded ruffled rim, 10" 135.00
Ewer, pk w/mc floral, camphor thorn hdl, 3-spout rim, 7½" 95.00
Rose bowl, pk o/l, basket shape w/frosted hdl, 5⅜x3½" 125.00
Vase, bl o/l, HP florals, frosted ruffled rim, 9½x3½" 125.00
Vase, bl verre moire, wht opaque pull-ups, fluted rim, 3¾" 150.00
Vase, bl w/floral, melon ribs, ruffled, 9", pr 185.00

Vase, bl w/silver flowering branches/rim/base, ftd, 6½" 100.00
Vase, butterscotch to wht, stick-neck gourd form, 15" 175.00
Vase, deep bl to lt bl, wht int, English, 10½x5½" 265.00
Vase, pk o/l w/allover pnt: birds/gold apples/etc, 12" 265.00

Satsuma

Satsuma is a type of fine cream crackle-glaze pottery or earthenware made in Japan as early as the 17th century. The earliest wares, made at the original kiln in the Satsuma province, were enameled with only simple florals. By the late 18th century, a floral brocade (or nishikide design) was favored, and similar wares were being made at other kilns under the direction of the Lord of Satsuma. In the early part of the 19th century, a diaper pattern was added to the florals. Gold and silver enamels were used for accents by the latter years of the century. During the 1850s, as the quality of goods made for export to the western world increased and the style of decoration began to evolve toward becoming more appealing to the Westerners, human forms such as Arhats, Kannon, geisha girls, and samurai warriors were added. Today the most valuable pieces are those marked 'Kinkozan,' 'Shuzan,' 'Ryuzan,' and 'Kozan.' The genuine Satsuma 'mon' or mark is a cross within a circle — usually in gold on the body or lid, or in red on the base of the ware. Character marks may be included.

Caution: Much of what is termed 'Satsuma' comes from the Showa Period (1926 to the present); it is not true Satsuma but a simulated type, a cheaper pottery with heavy enamel.

Bowl, butterflies & flowers, gilt diapering, Ryuzan, 6⅛" 770.00
Bowl, figures in landscape, cobalt & gold trim, Shuzan, 9¾" 300.00
Box, beauties/scholars, foo dog finial, 3¾x3" 650.00
Box, musicians/samarai/dancing geisha, Yoshigawa, 4¼" dia ...1,500.00
Box, 2 men w/palanquin in village, mc w/gold, Ninzan, 4⅜" 525.00
Censer, flowers & basketwork, fret border, ftd, Shuzan, 4" 825.00
Charger, 3 shaped medallions w/figures, 8¾" 500.00
Dish, 16 Arhats & dragon, scalloped, 7¾" 1,000.00
Jar, allover figures/faces/goldwork, emb figures, lid, 19" 2,500.00
Jar, immortals & dragon, immortals int, w/lid, 2" 150.00
Jar, man w/maid, bk: children, allover pnt/gold, 16x13" 1,300.00
Plate, rakkan & dragons between mon, sgn, 6¾" 470.00
Tea set, autumn branches & geometrics, Satsuma mon, 15-pc ...300.00
Tea set, scenic panels, dragon hdls/finials, Kinkozan, 15-pc 2,475.00
Vase, children in band, florals/gilt dots, earthenware, 8¼" 2,500.00
Vase, figures in scenic reserves, bottle form, Shuzan, 7½" 385.00
Vase, samurai & geisha in panels, baluster form, 12" 1,300.00

Scales

In today's world of pre-measured and pre-packaged goods, it is difficult to imagine the days when such products as sugar, flour, soap, and candy first had to be weighed by the grocer. The variety of scales used at the turn of the century was highly diverse; at the Philadelphia Exposition in 1876, one company alone displayed over three hundred different weighing devices. Among those found today, brass, cast iron, and plastic models are the most common. Fancy postal scales in decorative wood, silver, marble, bronze, and mosaic are also to be found. Those seeking additional information concerning antique scales are encouraged to contact the International Society of Antique Scale Collectors, whose address can be found in the Directory under Clubs, Newsletters, and Catalogs.

Key:
bal — balance
g — gram
lb — pound
NP — nickel plated

Am Implement, spring bal, brass face, up to 25 lbs 30.00
Butter, wooden, old red pnt, hanging, 1850s, 34" beam 185.00
Chatillon Milk Scale, 8" brass dial, up to 150 lbs, EX 45.00
CT Fairbanks...VT, Pat Nov 8, 1859, counter type, sm 145.00
Dairy type, hangs, 7" dia dial, 11½"+lg hook at bottom 38.00
Doyle & Son Borough London SE #1, merchant's 200.00
Doyle & Son London, brass, bal, 20" 220.00
European, bal, wood & brass, brass weights, 9" L 200.00
French, bal, brass on walnut base, 11" L 250.00
Fulton's Quality, counter type, CI, Pat 1869, up to 25-lb, VG 165.00
Honest Weight, counter type, brass pan, rpl decals, 16" L 95.00
Imperial, Gilfillan Scale & Hdw Co Chicago, brass, 9½" 125.00
J Hart Maker Birmingham, merchant's, mid-1800s 350.00
Jacobs Brooklyn, grocer's, scoop-type pan, all orig 50.00
Landers Improved Spring Bal Warranted 150-lbs, brass/iron, 23" .125.00
London, brass & iron bal, incomplete, rpl pans/arm, 21" 55.00
Mascot, egg weighing, EX orig bl-gray pnt 18.50
Medical/gold, all brass, complete w/weights, 1850s, +orig box 65.00
Merchant's, CI base w/gr pnt, tin pan, ca 1885, To Weigh 7 Lbs ..125.00
Merchant's, copper pan, iron weights, mk To Weigh 14 lbs, 8" ..225.00
P Rogers & Co, CI bal, pnt decor, 27", VG 150.00
Postage, brass, illegible mk 90.00
Royal, spring bal, brass face, up to 50-lbs 35.00
Salter's, brass, spring bal, hanging 18.00
Store, lg rnd dial, dk tin scoop shape pan, hanging 110.00
Swedish Mace, brass, measure fits into cylinder, 9x6½" 125.00
Triner, postal, 1952, 16-oz 35.00
Triner, postal, 1958, 4-lb 55.00
Troemner, bal, mahog case, 1940s, 8½x13", EX 150.00
W&T Avery Ltd Birmingham, brass, 13" L 175.00

Schafer and Vater

Established in 1890 by Gustav Schafer and Gunther Vater in the Thuringia, a region of southwest Germany; by 1913 this firm employed two hundred workers. The original factory burned in 1918, but production and export continued until WWII. It is unlikely that they exported after the Wall was built.

Schafer & Vater's range was wide, and not all pieces are marked with the nine-point star (with 'R' inside) under a crown, but the collector soon learns to recognize their styles, color washes and wonderful sense of whimsy. The pieces without the marks are often impressed with a four-digit mold number and a two-digit artist mark. Although often marked 'Made in Germany' with blue or black ink, it is rare to find a piece with a crown and star mark in ink. Pieces that are ink-marked in this manner also have a splotch of glaze over the mark to protect it. None of the impressed-marked pieces are glazed underneath.

Another hallmark of this pottery is the fine texture of the clay used in production. Mined locally, it was rich with kaolin and resulted in a finished product with velvety texture and very fine grain. The glazed bisque pieces may be multicolored, decorated in brown and blue washes, and occasionally left entirely white. The glazes may be clear, iridescent or Tiffany type. Jasper items come in may colors, often layered for effect. Blue, green, pink, and lavenders are common, but brown, gray, ivory and other colors were used as well. Some items are decorated in more than one of these colors and may have white insets reminiscent of the traditional cameo (or one with an intricate floral or whimsical animals), Grecian scenes, comic characters and more. The light slip wash over some of the jasper items hugs the details and highlights intricate features of their fine modeling. Any jasper container is invariably glazed on the inside, and many of the dresser pieces and vases are 'jeweled' with spots of richly colored glaze applied as accents.

Many Schafer and Vater items find a place with cross-over col-

lectibles such hatpin holders, dresser sets, match strikers, shaving mugs, razor banks, toothpick holders, tea sets, cups and saucers, and animal figures. The company was an authorized manufacturer of Rose O'Neill Kewpies. They made naughties and nudes well as 'nippers' or 'give-aways,' small glazed bottles used at the turn of the century to hold gifts of liquor for hotel and restaurant patrons. The giveaway bottles and the figural pitchers are very collectible. Many were made in a multitude of sizes ranging from 3" to 11". The liquor bottles were often sold with trays and shot glasses that would complement the figure.

The market for Schafer and Vater is highly volatile at this writing. As new collectors continue to enter the market, supply and demand definitely drive the price structure. Our advisor for this category is Dawn Ricker; she is listed in the Directory under Michigan. Anyone interested in the formation of a collector's society is welcome to contact her.

Ash pot, match holder, bug-eyed man, mouth moves, mc, mk ...175.00
Ash pot, miner's bust, How Are You Off for Coals?, 3⅝" 185.00
Ashtray, long-haired women smoking, lav jasper w/wash 155.00
Atomizer, Nouveau face, pk jasper w/jewels, gr wash 110.00
Bottle, Apache dancers, mc, mk 185.00
Bottle, Carrie Nation, Thank Heaven for Prohibition, 11" 300.00
Bottle, couple in formal attire 'tango,' mc, mk 225.00
Bottle, cruet type, gr w/red medal, held by German boy 150.00
Bottle, dancers, Turkey Trot, mc, mk 200.00
Bottle, English doctor, musical, 11", w/tray & 5 shots 850.00
Bottle, English doctor w/lg syringe, bl, mk, 5½" 250.00
Bottle, flowers on gr bsk, stem hdl, mc, mk 65.00
Bottle, Foo Dog, orange, Deco style, unmk 190.00
Bottle, hunter w/rifle & bottle, mc, mk 150.00
Bottle, man w/lady on lap, Dr Ordered, mc 210.00
Bottle, Merry Christmas, Santa w/tree, mc, mk 200.00
Bottle, monk, brn wash, mk, 11", w/tray & 5 shots 700.00
Bottle, monk pouring drink, bl wash, mk, 5" 135.00
Bottle, monk pouring drink, brn wash, mk, 5" 110.00
Bottle, monk pouring drink, mc, mk, 5" 165.00
Bottle, Pagliaccio carry woman, legs are stopper, bl, mk 325.00
Bottle, Pan hugging smiling moon, bl, mk, 11½" 475.00
Bottle, robed skeleton, mk, 7", w/tray & 4 shots 450.00
Bottle, robed skeleton, 8", w/Poison tray & 4 skull shots 550.00
Bottle, Scotch Whiskey, brn w/mc Scotsman, mk, 6" 125.00
Bottle, smiling pear figural, mc, mk 190.00
Bottle, Ticklish Time, man's head w/fly on nose 175.00
Bottle, Uncle Sam sitting on bbl, brn, mk, 8" 350.00
Bottle, woman kneels w/turkey on bk, Hitchy-Koo, mc, mk 275.00
Bowl, roses on gr bsk, unglazed, mc, mk 45.00
Bowl, sugar; parrots, wht bsk w/roses, mc, mk 90.00
Box, lady w/rose w/in wreath, bl jasper 1¾x3¼" 95.00
Brush hdl, smiling head in top hat, lt gr, unmk 50.00
Candlestick, cameo, pk, bl & gr jasper 125.00
Candlestick, Indian head figural, brn bsk, gr wash, unmk 185.00
Candlestick, 2 cameos, pk & bl jasper, mk 135.00
Candy container, pig playing flute, Pig'n Whistle, mc, mk 245.00
Card holder, elephant 100.00
Clock, dresser; cherubs w/instruments, bl & wht jasper 225.00
Clock, dresser; lady dancing & florals, bl & wht jasper 180.00
Clock, dresser; Rose O'Neill, bl & wht jasper, MIG, mk 350.00
Cup & saucer, pk bsk, cameo, scrollwork 150.00
Cup & saucer, rose, tinted, bl crown & star mk, MIG 110.00
Figurine, googly-eyed girl w/puppy, mc, unmk, 2½" 100.00
Figurine, Mr Tenor, man in tuxedo, comic, bsk, unmk, 7⅝" 185.00
Figurine, topsy-turvy, man & pig's head, mk, rpr 65.00
Figurine, woman sitting in dress & lg hat w/bird, rpr 110.00
Figurine, 3 girls at piano, wht & gr 95.00
Hair receiver, mc jewels on lav, sgn, 3¼" 50.00

Hair receiver, 3-color jasper 65.00
Hatpin holder, Art Nouveau head, pk bsk w/gold trim 295.00
Hatpin holder, Egyptian heads, pk bsk, 4½" 275.00
Hatpin holder, geisha, lav jasper w/gold wash, mk 225.00
Hatpin holder, Kewpies, bl & wht jasper, R O'Neill, mk 425.00
Humidor, English tea party cameo, gr/bl/wht jasper, mk 200.00
Incense burner, elephant heads w/snake charmer, mk 110.00
Jar, Victorian lady w/parasol on royal bl, 3½" dia 55.00
Match holder, floral on lt gr, attached tray, mk 50.00
Match holder, lady w/legs in air, Here's a Scrape, mc 145.00
Match holder, Sherlock Holmes, A Bid Draw, mc, mk 175.00
Match holder, smiling man w/chin on hands, mc, mk 125.00
Match striker, farmer, His Country Seat, 3½" 185.00
Match striker, lg blk cat/kitten, Don't Scratch Me, 3¾" 165.00
Mug, shaving; stag's head emb ea side, mk, 3¼x3" 75.00
Mustard set, 3 different heads, dk bl, mk, jar/shakers/tray 235.00
Mustard set, 3 Dutch heads, bl, mk, jar/shakers/tray 210.00
Necklace, Nouveau lady's head, jewels & pearl on pk jasper 600.00
Nodder, Blk banjo player, bsk, 3", EX 225.00
Nodder, chubby Dutch girl holding 2 geese, mc, mk 145.00
Nodder, What a Night, windswept man in coat w/cigar, mc 125.00
Pin dish, heart shape, cameo, Tiffany int, mc, mk 95.00
Pin dish, heart w/figural wht rose on gr bsk 30.00
Pin dish, lady cradling aardvark, naughty, lav jasper 195.00
Pin dish, Nouveau face, jasper, jeweled, mk 125.00
Pin dish, Oriental lady, Yel Peril, lav jasper 160.00
Pin dish, stylized rooster, bl & wht jasper, unmk 125.00
Pin tray, skeleton holds coffin open, If You Please, 1912 ....135.00
Pitcher, bear in coat & coat, mc, mk, 5" 200.00
Pitcher, bear in coat & muff, bl, mk, sm chip, 3¾" 45.00
Pitcher, bear w/muff, 6½" 250.00
Pitcher, Blk w/bulging eyes, claw hands, mc, mk, 3½" 210.00
Pitcher, Blk w/bulging eyes, claw hands, mc, mk, 4½" 275.00
Pitcher, bulbous shape w/crowing cock hdl, brn, mk, 4½" 135.00
Pitcher, clown, cream sz 135.00
Pitcher, clown w/mandolin, mc, mk, 5½" 185.00
Pitcher, devil in suit w/wings, kneeling, mc, mk, 4" 195.00
Pitcher, Dutch girl, cream sz 110.00
Pitcher, girl in red & gr dress, comic, mk, 3⅞" 125.00
Pitcher, goat w/boutonniere, mc, mk, 5½" 210.00
Pitcher, kneeling Oriental w/crying baby, mc, mk, 6½", EX 100.00
Pitcher, maid w/jug & keys, mc, 3½" 98.00
Pitcher, man's head, smoking cigar, lg 150.00
Pitcher, Mother Goose, bl, mk, 3½" 100.00
Pitcher, orangutan, all red, w/coat, hat & cane, mc, mk, 4" 125.00
Pitcher, orangutan, in coat w/hat & cane, mc, mk, 4" 150.00
Pitcher, screaming Oriental w/monkey on bk, mc, mk, 4" 120.00
Pitcher, screaming Oriental w/monkey on bk, mc, mk, 4½" 145.00
Pitcher, screaming Oriental w/monkey on bk, mc, mk, 5½" 205.00
Pitcher, screaming Oriental w/monkey on bk, mc, mk, 6½" 255.00
Pitcher, smiling apple w/lg leaves, mc, mk, 4" 135.00
Pitcher, smiling boy w/umbrella on bk, mc, mk, 5½" 155.00
Pitcher, smiling Dutch girl w/jug & keys, mc, mk, 5½" 135.00
Pitcher, smiling Oriental w/flapping goose, bl, mk, 4" 85.00
Pitcher, smiling Oriental w/flapping goose, mc, mk, 6½" 225.00
Powder jar, bust of lady on half-circle shape, 4½x3" 55.00
Tea set, cherubs & children, bl & wht jasper, child's, no c/s ...145.00
Tea set, Cupid, flowers, lady w/mandolin, pk jasper, mk 475.00
Tea set, figural English man & woman, pk jasper, complete 1,200.00
Tea set, lady cameos, bl & wht jasper, rectangular pot 800.00
Tea set, smiling yel apples, mc, child's, no c/s 325.00
Teapot, lady's head, spout is nose, pk jasper w/brn wash 200.00
Toothpick holder, baby devil, winged, stick legs w/gr ft 135.00
Toothpick holder, chubby elf, pk bsk w/gr wash, mk, 4½" 140.00

Toothpick holder, fat pk pig asleep on bl pillow, mk 85.00
Toothpick holder, frog in gown w/mandolin, by basket, mk, #d ...175.00
Toothpick holder, pig head on dog body, pk jasper, gr wash 125.00
Toothpick holder, sailor holding lg bathing beauty, mc, mk, 3" ...60.00
Toothpick holder, sailor holding lg bathing beauty, mc, mk, 4" ...95.00
Toothpick holder, thin man racing fat man, mc, unmk 245.00
Vase, cherubs, Greek lady & birds on brn bsk, mk, 12" 175.00
Vase, Classical woman in wht on gr jasper, 6" 45.00
Vase, cowboy on horse in reserve, royal bl, 3-prong mk, 6" 200.00
Vase, Cupid, bl & wht jasper, half-rnd, mk, 6" 65.00
Vase, ewer form, Nouveau women form hdl 225.00
Vase, farmer w/dog & scythe on brn bsk, mk, 11" 160.00
Vase, geisha sits before fan-shape vase, mk, 4¼x5¼" 160.00
Vase, googly-eyed girl w/bear, mc, mk, 3½" 60.00
Vase, Japanese woman w/fan & goose, egg shape 145.00
Vase, lady's head emb, gold trim, mk, 4¾x3" 55.00
Vase, Pan w/pipes, bl & wht jasper, half-rnd 85.00
Vase, Tiffany glaze, cavorting boys insert, mk, 6" 185.00

Scheier

The Scheiers began their ceramics careers in the late 1930s and soon thereafter began to teach their craft at the University of New Hampshire. After WWII they cooperated with the Puerto Rican government in establishing a native ceramic industry, an involvement which would continue to influence their designs. In the fifties they retired and moved to Mexico; they currently reside in Arizona.

Vase, double-headed creatures in primitive style, ca 1955, 7x6", $180.00; Vase, sgraffito figures on matt ground, ca 1948, 7x10", $550.00.

Bowl, cvd figures/fish, bl band on brn, 5¾x6" 600.00
Vase, cvd 'fish-people' all around, bl-tan ground, 8x3¼" 400.00
Vase, cvd 'fish-people' on tan to dk bl, ftd egg form, 5x4" 400.00
Vase, cvd pregnant women/4-leg animals, wht on blk, 18½x7" ...1,200.00
Vase, cvd/appl men, bl/turq on gun metal, ftd U-form, 9x7" 950.00
Vase, medallions w/relief figures, charcoal, ftd, 7½x7½" 500.00

Schiebe-Alsbach

Founded in Thuringia in the 1840s and still in production today, the Schiebe-Alsbach factory was the first in the area to make porcelain figures on a large scale. Their earliest were devotional Madonnas, though Rococo figures were soon included in their line as well. In 1890 they were producing Meissen-style figures, lace figures, and historial figures and groups. Now nationalized and incorporated into a larger firm, the factory is Europe's largest manufacturer of this types of ware. Their mark is an 'S' with superimposed crossed lines, today slightly modified from the original.

Bust of Napoleon, gr tunic w/medals, blk hat, N on base, 10½" .250.00
Dancing couple, Dutch boy & girl, 6" 160.00
Lovers, lady in gold, Cupid at base, man on knee, 12½", pr 850.00
Marshal DeBeauharnais, in uniform, 10½" 175.00
Marshal Dumoriez, wht pants, long bl coat, 10" 175.00
Marshal Kellerman, bl coat jacket, wht cockade hat, 10" 175.00
Marshal Lannes, bl coat w/red sash, 10" 175.00
Marshal Murat, long gr coat, red cockade on hat, 10" 175.00
Marshal Murat, on prancing horse, 11x9" 450.00
Napoleon, wht uniform, gr jacket, long gray coat, 10" 175.00
Napoleon Coronation Preparation, 3 figures at table, 9x12" 950.00
Napoleon Corssing Alps, gr coat, rearing wht horse, 10½" 325.00
Napoleon Crossing Berezina, rides horse over bridge, 11" 475.00
News Vendor, bl coat/brn hat, papers in arm, 1860s mk, 5½" 95.00
Othello, on balcony before man & lady, 10x15" 1,350.00
Swan, appl pk & bl flowers, 8¼" 115.00
Pully on Horse, Napoleon aide on wht horse, plumed hat, 11" ...450.00
4 children at tea table, Kister, parian, ca 1850, 6½x10" 350.00

Schlegelmilch Porcelain

Authority Mary Frank Gaston, who is our advisor, has completed three volumes of *The Collector's Encyclopedia of R.S. Prussia* with full-color illustrations and current values. Mold numbers appearing in some of the listings refer to these books. You will find Mrs. Gaston's address in the Directory under Texas.

Key:
BM — blue mark   SM — steeple mark
GM — green mark   RM — red mark

E.S. Germany

Fine chinaware marked 'E.S. Germany' or 'E.S. Prov. Saxe' was produced by E.S. Schlegelmilch at his Suhl factory in the Thuringia region of Prussia from sometime after 1861 until about 1925.

Basket, lady & child reserve w/gold & lustre, mk, 7" 125.00
Bowl, bird on floral branch, mk, 7", +underplate 45.00
Bowl, boat scene, dmn shape, hdls, mk, 6½x6½" 55.00
Cake plate, calla lilies, wht w/gr clovers, 10¼" 165.00
Cake plate, Gibson girl portrait on bl w/gold, mk, 10½" 435.00
Cup & saucer, demitasse; lady w/daisy crown mk 80.00
Ewer, lady smelling rose, mk, 17" 695.00
Pitcher, maiden w/cupid, raised florals w/gold, 7½" 195.00
Plate, lady & cherub, turq & gold rim, open hdls, mk, 10" 195.00
Plate, peacock center, floral border, orange lustre hdls 80.00
Plate, portrait w/flowers & gold, scalloped, hdls, mk, 9½" 145.00
Vase, lady & peacock, lav & wht w/gold, mk, 12" 245.00
Vase, lady's portrait, gold tub hdls, mk, 7½" 300.00
Vase, lady's portrait on pearlized ground, dbl hdls, RM, 12" 350.00
Vase, lady w/roses portrait, much gold & beading, 11½", pr 750.00
Vase, mythological scene, MOP & gold, hdls, mk, 7½" 155.00

R.S. Germany

In 1869 Reinhold Schlegelmilch began to manufacture porcelain in Suhl in the German province of Thuringia. In 1894 he established another factory in Tillowitz in upper Silesia. Both areas were rich in resources necessary for the production of hard-paste porcelain. Wares

marked with the name 'Tillowitz' and the accompanying 'R.S. Germany' phrase are attributed to Reinhold. The most common mark is a wreath and star in a solid color under the glaze. Items marked 'R.S. Germany' are usually more simply decorated than R.S. Prussia. Some reflect the Art Deco trend of the 1920s. Certain hand-painted floral decorations and themes such as 'Sheepherder,' 'Man with Horses,' and 'Cottage' are especially valued by collectors — those with a high-gloss finish or on Art Deco shapes in particular. Not all hand-painted items were painted at the factory. Those with an artist's signature but no 'Hand Painted' mark indicate that the blank was decorated outside the factory.

R.S. Germany plate, Indian decoration, 8", $375.00.

Basket, HP florals, 3-section, mk, 8x6¾" 125.00
Bowl, apple blossoms, gr & wht, cabbage mold, mk, 9½" 450.00
Bowl, floral int, lettuce leaf mold, mk, 7" 30.00
Bowl, flowers & leaves, open hdls, ftd, mk, sm 25.00
Bowl, peach roses int, 3-ftd, mk, 2¾x5¼" 72.50
Bowl, roses, 4 openwork areas at rim, mk, 7" 55.00
Bowl, snowballs, unmk, 9¾" 75.00
Cake plate, basket of flowers, open hdls, mk, 10" 60.00
Cake plate, Queen Louise portrait, floral mold, hdls, SM, 10" 700.00
Cake plate, snowballs, mk, 10" 80.00
Celery vase, bird of paradise, mk, 10½" 350.00
Cheese & cracker dish, orchids, mk, 8¾" 125.00
Cheese & cracker dish, roses, gold rim, BM 110.00
Condensed milk holder, floral on wht w/gold, mk, 5" 165.00
Creamer & sugar bowl, floral, lav & wht on brn w/gold, mk 45.00
Creamer & sugar bowl, peach roses, mk 45.00
Creamer & sugar bowl, tulips on tan to gray, gold trim, mk 50.00
Cup & saucer, mustache; floral, mk 85.00
Hatpin holder, roses, hexagonal ft, mk 95.00
Mug, scuttle; poppies, mk, 3½" 110.00
Mustard pot, pk roses, 4-scallop mold, mk 78.00
Napkin ring, floral on wht w/gold, mk 135.00
Pin box, roses, pk on gr, scalloped dmn shape, BM 100.00
Plate, flamingos & roses, smooth gold rim, mk, 8" 175.00
Plate, lilacs, pk & gr on wht w/gr & gold, mk, 11¼" 115.00
Plate, palm tree, orange in sky & water, gold trim, mk, 8½" 95.00
Plate, tulips w/gold leaves, Nouveau style, mk, 10½" 60.00
Toothbrush holder, violets w/gold, wing mk, 4½x3" 200.00
Tray, floral, mc w/gold tracery, RM, 11½x7½" 115.00
Vase, windmill scene, salesman's sample, gr wreath mk, 4" 195.00

R.S. Poland

'R.S. Poland' is a mark attributed to Reinhold Schlegelmilch's factory in Tillowitz, Silesia. It was in use for a few years after 1945.

Bowl, berry; crowned cranes, mk, 5¾" 800.00
Bowl, dahlias, mk, 9" 175.00

Bowl, lav & orange roses, center hdl, mk, 8x11" 525.00
Bowl, poppies, heart mold, mk, 3x10¼" 265.00
Bowl, Rembrandt's Night Watch, on gray-bl, mk, 5⅜" 145.00
Cake plate, floral, floral border, hdls, 10" 135.00
Planter, floral band w/gold, ped ft, mk, 6¾x6½" 245.00
Planter, floral medallions, mk, 5½x7½" 235.00
Plate, lav & orange roses on shell shape, mk, 8¼" 150.00
Server, lav & orange roses, center hdl, mk, 11" dia 515.00
Vase, cavaliers, mk, 4" 300.00
Vase, lady, sheep & cottage scene, ornate gold hdls, mk, 10" 635.00
Vase, Melon Boys, flared sides, mk, 7½" 1,500.00
Vase, mill scene & ladies w/sheep, gold hdls, mk, 10" 635.00
Vase, poppies, wht on cream to brn, mk, 12x6¼" 375.00
Vase, Rembrandt's Night Watch, dk gr, mk, 4½" 235.00
Vase, rose, wht on tan & yel, bottle form, mk, 4" 65.00
Vase, yel roses, mk, 3⅝x1½" 100.00
Wall plaque, daisies, 10½" 125.00

R.S. Prussia

Art porcelain bearing the mark 'R.S. Prussia' was manufactured by Reinhold Schlegelmilch from the late 1870s to the early 1900s in a Germanic area known until the end of WWI as Prussia. The vast array of mold shapes in combination with a wide variety of decorations is the basis for R.S. Prussia's appeal. Themes can be categorized as figural (usually based on a famous artist's work), birds, florals, portraits, scenics, and animals.

R.S. Prussia plate, 3-color roses, white ivy leaves at rim, red mark, 10½", $285.00.

Bowl, berry; fruit, leaf mold border, mk, 5½" 70.00
Bowl, berry; mill scene, mk, 5½" 110.00
Bowl, berry; roses, acorn mold, RM, 10½", +6 5" bowls 575.00
Bowl, berry; water lilies, RM, lg, +6 sm 285.00
Bowl, centerpc; floral, carnation mold, mk, 15" 1,750.00
Bowl, Diana the Huntress w/6 portrait medallions, RM, 11" ...1,500.00
Bowl, floral, cattail mold, unmk, 10½" 450.00
Bowl, floral, mc on pearlized, mk, 10½" 250.00
Bowl, floral, purple & wht on gr satin irid w/gold, mk, 10" 225.00
Bowl, fruit, gold trim, icicle mold, RM, 8½" 295.00
Bowl, hanging flower basket, medallion mold, RM, 11" 165.00
Bowl, magnolias, RM, 10½" 275.00
Bowl, masted schooner, jewels, lustre finish, RM, 3x10½" 1,000.00
Bowl, ostrich, mk, 10¾" 3,000.00
Bowl, pk poppies & daisies reflecting, flower mold, 6" 135.00
Bowl, pk roses, iris mold, mk, 10½" 300.00
Bowl, poppies, pk/gr/brn w/cobalt, unmk, 3x10¼" 475.00
Bowl, roses, pk on pk, carnation mold, unmk, 1¾x6¼" 195.00
Bowl, roses & daisies, RM, 8" 65.00
Bowl, roses & lily of valley, plume mold, RM, 8" 225.00

Bowl, sheepherder, RM, 10¾" 795.00
Bowl, snow birds, icicle mold, 3-ftd, mk, 2¾x7½" 885.00
Bowl, swan in evergreens, elongated, RM, 13" 500.00
Bowl, winter season, iris mold, RM, 10" 2,200.00
Cake plate, barnyard scene, icicle mold, steeple mk 575.00
Cake plate, basket of flowers, gold trim, RM, 11½" 275.00
Cake plate, Diana the Huntress, mk, 10½" 495.00
Cake plate, Dice Players, jewels, open hdls, RM, 10" 1,350.00
Cake plate, Dice Players, point & clover mold, RM, 11" 1,100.00
Cake plate, floral, mc w/gold, unmk, 10½" 165.00
Cake plate, floral w/gold on wht to dk gr, mk, 11", +6 plates 300.00
Cake plate, hidden image, iris mold, 11" 265.00
Cake plate, mill scene, sawtooth mold, mk, 10" 500.00
Cake plate, roses, pk on bl, carnation mold, mk, 11" 225.00
Cake plate, roses, pk on bl, clover mold, mk, 11" 175.00
Cake plate, wheat w/cobalt, floral mold, steeple mk 450.00
Celery tray, roses, crimped rim, open hdls, mk, 12" 185.00
Celery tray, Snow Bird, w/medallions, RM, 12" 2,450.00
Celery vase, Dice Players, point & clover mold, RM, 12" 950.00
Chocolate pot, floral, iris mold, unmk 350.00
Chocolate pot, floral & gold overall, ornate dbl hdl, mk 395.00
Chocolate pot, poppies, carnation mold, RM, +cr/sug 1,200.00
Chocolate pot, roses, pk & red on wht, RM, 10½" 375.00
Chocolate pot, roses, pk w/gr lustre trim, RM, +4 c/s 560.00
Chocolate pot, roses & snowballs, point & clover mold, RM, 10" .265.00
Chocolate pot, swans & evergreens, mk, +6 c/s 2,400.00
Coffeecup & saucer, swan, satin, RM 95.00
Coffeepot, floral, fancy mold, unmk, 9" 375.00
Cracker jar, floral, sunflower mold, ftd, RM, 6½" 275.00
Cracker jar, lilies, wht on wht, RM 250.00
Cracker jar, poppies, carnation mold, mk 365.00
Cracker jar, roses on satin, corset shape, RM, 6¾" 250.00
Creamer, hidden image, mk, 5" 245.00
Creamer, roses & lily of valley, ribbon hdl, unmk 55.00
Creamer & sugar bowl, floral, molded petal ft, RM 285.00
Creamer & sugar bowl, floral, plume mold, RM 235.00
Creamer & sugar bowl, fruit, grape mold, RM 195.00
Creamer & sugar bowl, lilacs on turq & wht, unmk 150.00
Cup & saucer, lilacs, ped ft, mk 125.00
Cup & saucer, lily, wht w/aqua trim, mk 100.00
Finger bowl, Angelica Kauffmann medallion, mk, 2¾x5" 195.00
Flower bowl, tulips, mc on gr, +2-tier frog, RM, 4½x5" 195.00
Jar, biscuit; castle scene, brns & lavs, mk, 5x8½" 600.00
Jar, dresser; bell-shaped flowers, mk, 2½x4" 165.00
Loving cup, roses, pk on gr & cream, 3-hdld, mk 165.00
Mug, scuttle; iris, w/mirror, prof rpr 425.00
Mug, shaving; floral, mk 175.00
Mustard pot, Dogwood, mk, w/spoon 130.00
Mustard pot, flowers & glass bowl, point & clover mold, RM 190.00
Pitcher, cider; flowers in bowl, point & clover mold, RM, 6½" ..395.00
Pitcher, floral, fancy mold, 8 ball ft, tankard, mk, 14" 695.00
Pitcher, lemonade; fruit, mold #655, unmk, 6½" 675.00
Pitcher, Ribbon & Jewel, opal jeweling, RM, 9¼" 495.00
Pitcher, roses w/gold, mk, 5" 175.00
Pitcher, Summer season, carnation mold, tankard, RM, 14" ...6,250.00
Plate, cottage scene, blown-out lily mold, unmk, 8" 295.00
Plate, Fall season, 6 medallions, red & gold, RM, 10" 1,500.00
Plate, magnolias, scalloped rim, RM, 7½" 165.00
Plate, pk flowers & gold carnations, carnation mold, RM, 8½" ..125.00
Plate, poppies w/much gold, iris mold, RM, 9½" 275.00
Plate, roses, pk on pk, carnation mold, unmk, 7½" 185.00
Plate, scattered flowers on satin, RM, 8" 175.00
Plate, swan & castle, RM, 9" 145.00
Plate, swans, raindrop mold, RM, 8" 295.00

Relish, roses on lav shaded, opal jewels, mk, 9½x4¾" 235.00
Relish, sheepherder, RM, 12" 695.00
Relish, swans among lilies, gold beads & hdls, RM, 9½x4½" 250.00
Sugar shaker, courting scene, RM 465.00
Tea set, florals on turq w/pk & wht panels, ribbed, RM, 3-pc 325.00
Teapot, gr & wht floral w/raised gold, RM, 5" 125.00
Tray, cottage scene on pearlized, carnation mold, hdls RM 800.00
Tray, dresser; fruit on tan, iris mold, RM 225.00
Tray, dresser; gazebo & swan, RM 400.00
Tray, swans, icicle mold, unmk 475.00
Vase, boy & girl, hdls, RM, 4½" 450.00
Vase, castle scene, pillow form, RM, 7" 800.00
Vase, castle scene, RM, 4¼" 375.00
Vase, Colonial courting couple, dk gr & gold, hdls, mk, 4½" 325.00
Vase, Melon Boys, RM, 4½" 495.00
Vase, ostrich, hdls, RM, 9½" 3,500.00
Vase, roses w/gold on cobalt, mk, 5" 450.00
Vase, Spring season, hdls, RM, 10" 1,350.00
Watering can, church on cobalt, mk, 5¾" 495.00

R.S. Suhl, E.S. Suhl

Porcelains marked with this designation are attributed to Reinhold Schlegelmilch's Suhl factory.

Box, floral, w/beveled mirror, mk 200.00
Ewer, floral on gr, gold hdl, mk, 13¼" 250.00
Teapot, Dogwood, w/cr & sug 310.00
Tray, relish; cavaliers, oval, hdls, mk, 9½x4½" 300.00
Vase, Melon Boys, mk, 9" 800.00
Vase, night watchman on shaded brn, gold uptrn hdls, mk, 6" ...600.00
Vase, sunflowers on brn, hdls, mk, 6¾" 110.00
Wall plaque, daisies, 10½" 125.00

R.S. Tillowitz

R.S. Tillowitz-marked porcelains are attributed to Reinhold Schlegelmilch's factory in Tillowitz, Silesia.

Cake set, fuchsia on gr w/tan shadows, open hdls, 7-pc 350.00
Cup & saucer, demitasse; wht flowers, mk 60.00
Mint dish, floral, mk, 7½x5" 100.00
Pitcher, lemonade; poppies, mk 125.00
Plate, cherries, mk, 11" 60.00
Plate, stylized butterfly border w/gold, gold hdls, mk, 7" 35.00
Tray, magnolias, w/gold, mk, 8¾x4" 55.00

Schneider

The Schneider Glass Company was founded in 1914 at Epinay-sur-seine, France. They made many types of art glass, some of which sandwiched designs between layers. Other decorative devices were applique and carved work. These were marked 'Charder' or 'Schneider.' During the twenties commercial artware was produced with Deco motifs cut by acid through two or three layers and signed 'LeVerre Francais' in script or with a section of inlaid filigrane. Our advisor for this category is Don Williams; he is listed in the Directory under Missouri. See also Le Verre Francais.

Bowl, etched geometrics on topaz/clear, everted/ftd, 5¾" 625.00
Chalice, bl w/appl prunts, pk mottled ft, ruffled rim, 7" 3,675.00
Compote, clear orange bowl on purple mottle ft, 5x14" 750.00
Compote, etched leaf band on topaz, rnd/ftd, cvd bosses, 7" ...2,700.00

Compote, lime gr bowl on dbl-knob amethyst ped, sgn, 8½" 595.00
Compote, lt purple mottle, dk streaky purple ft, 5x14" 685.00
Compote, yel/orange on elongated purple ft, 7½" 1,000.00
Compote, yel/rust mottle, stepped sides, CI ft w/3 'jewels,' 6" 900.00
Lamp, table; hammered bronze w/4 arms, ea w/shades, 17" 1,300.00
Light fixture, single 10¼" globe in wrought iron 500.00
Vase, appl wavy purple lacing on etched clear/pk mottle, 20" .1,600.00
Vase, clear w/int bubbles, appl swirls, flat sides, 9½" 685.00
Vase, crackled yel mottle, clear cased, conical/ftd, 5½" 575.00
Vase, Deco berries, orange cut to frost, candy cane mk, 24" 1,300.00
Vase, etched leaf band on topaz, hdls, bulbous/ftd, 7" 2,700.00
Vase, jade w/int bubbles, purple hdls, cylinder neck, 4" 475.00
Vase, orange-yel mottle to dk red w/mustard streaks, 12½" 750.00
Vase, pk/clear mottle w/appl irregular bands, bulbous, 11½" 900.00
Vase, pk/yel mottle w/3 prunts, bulbous w/long neck, 20" 900.00
Vase, topaz w/int bubbles, appl drops ea side, ftd, 8" 675.00

Schoolhouse Collectibles

Schoolhouse collectibles bring to mind memories of a bygone era when the teacher rang her bell to call the youngsters to class in a one-room schoolhouse where often both the 'hickory stick' and an apple occupied a prominent position on her desk. Our advisor for this category is Kenn Norris; he is listed in the Directory under Texas.

Bell, brass, blk wooden hdl, 5" 48.00
Book, Descriptive Astronomy, Steele, 1872, EX 45.00
Book, Dick & Jane, Scott Foresman, wraps, VG+ 60.00
Book, Eclectic Geography, R Hinman, 1888, EX 9.50
Book, Elementary Geology, R Tarr, illus, 1907, 490-pg, EX 10.00
Book, High-School Dictionary, Webster, 1868, 420-pg, EX 10.00
Book, N American Arithmetic, F Emerson, Boston, 1838, VG 12.50
Book, Plane Geometry, Wentworth, 1889, EX 25.00
Book, Town's New Speller & Definer, 1863, EX 12.50
Book, Zanerian Manual of Alphabets, EX 75.00
Desk, schoolmaster's, rfn cherry, 2 dvtl drw, 32x39x30" 525.00
Desk, soft wood, slant lid, pegged, top gallery, 36x30x24" 195.00
Diploma, ornate lettering, PA College, Gettysburg PA, 1930, fr ..17.50
Globe, floor standing, 16" globe in mahog stand, 39" 225.00
Globe, Joslin's Six Inch Terrestrial, Boston 1854, CI base 1,275.00
Intercom, wall; Western Electric, brass & Bakelite 95.00
Lab manual, General Zoology, 1944 ....10.00

Pencil sharpener, Planetary Pencil Pointer, A.B. Dick Co., Pat 1896, EX, $45.00.

Slate, dbl; wood frs w/laced string/red felt edge, 11x8" 60.00
Slate, in wooden fr w/mc florals & gr scrolls, 8¾x6¾" 55.00
Slate, mk Nall School Slate Co...Penn USA, pine edge, 11x8" 18.00
Spelling board, heavy red cb, letters & #s, 1916, 14" dia 115.00

Pencil Boxes

Among the most common of school-related collectibles are the many classes of pencil boxes. Generally from the period of the 1870s-1940s, these boxes were made in many hundred different styles. Materials included tin, wood (thin frame and solid hardwood) and leather; later fabric and plastics were used. Most pencil boxes were in a basic, rectangular configuration, though rare examples were made to resemble other objects. These included rolling pins, ball bats and nightsticks. Pencil boxes are still to be found at reasonable prices, though collectors have lately noticed this field. All boxes listed below are in very good to near-mint condition. Our advisors for pencil boxes are Sue and Lar Hothem, authors of *School Collectibles of the Past*; they are listed in the Directory under Ohio.

Ball bat, trn wood, World's Champion, 11x1¼" **45.00**
Dbl-level, pull & twist top, wood, 9⅛x2¼x1⅝" **28.00**
Dbl-level, wood, Pan Am, 1901, 9¼x2¼x1¾" **50.00**
Fabric, slide drw, Am, 1940s, 8¼x5x⅞" **15.00**
Four-level, pull & twist top, wood, scarce, 9¼x2⅛x2¼" **70.00**
Framed wood, Jack & Jill, 7⅞x2⅜x1½" **20.00**
Multiplier, tin, cylindrical, Pat 1896, 8¾x1½" **95.00**
Oak w/EX grain, lift lid, heavy, 8x2¾x1⅜" **15.00**
Plain, wooden litho, lift lid, Germany, 8½x2¼x1⅜" **18.00**
Plastic, pistol shape, 8x4⅝x½" **28.00**
Single-level, slide top, wood, 9¼x1½x⅞" **24.00**
Single-level, slide top, wood w/shoe store advertising, 9x2x⅞" **32.00**
Tin, Jackie Coogan, smiling face, 7⅞x2¼x1⅝" **40.00**
Tin, Red Goose Shoes, school scene, 7¾x2⅛x¾" **45.00**
Tin, Scholar's Companion, Pat 1874, 7¼x3x1" **70.00**
Wood, pencil form, Atlantic City, 11¼x1⅛" **32.00**

Schoop, Hedi

Swiss-born Hedi Schoop started her ceramics business in North Hollywood in 1940. With a talented crew of about twenty decorators, she produced figurines, figure-vases, console sets, TV lamps, and other decorative housewares — much of which was accented with gold or platinum trim. Schoop's pottery closed after a fire destroyed the building in 1958. Marks are impressed or printed. For further information we recommend *The Collector's Encyclopedia of California Pottery* by our advisor, Jack Chipman; he is listed in the Directory under California.

Ashtray, HP florals **25.00**
Bowl, shell form, pk w/gold trim, 12" **30.00**
Candle holder, dbl; peasant lady, 12½" **45.00**
Candle holder, mermaid holding 2 shells aloft, 13½" **225.00**
Figurine, clown w/cello, platinum overglaze, 1943, 12½" **95.00**
Figurine, girl w/accordion, 11" **45.00**
Figurine, Josephine, holds flower bowl, 1943, 13" **85.00**

Figurines, Oriental boy and girl, green and black clothing with gold trim, 10½", $95.00 for the pair.

Figurine, Oriental figure w/lantern, much gold, 12½", pr **100.00**
Figurine, peasant girl w/bowl over head, 14" **60.00**
Figurine, Tiny, flower girl, late 1940s, 7" **40.00**
Planter, girl w/eyes open, 8" L **65.00**
Planter, hobby horse, wht w/lav, 7x8" **65.00**
Planter, lady dancing w/basket on head, 13" **65.00**
Plate, French poodle, sq **30.00**
Tray, Queen of Hearts, sq **35.00**
Vase, stylized chicken, 9", pr **85.00**

Scouting Collectibles

Boy Scouts

Scouting was founded in England in 1907 by a retired Major General, Lord Robert Baden-Powell. Its purpose is the same today as it was then — to help develop physically strong, mentally alert boys and to teach them basic fundamentals of survival and leadership. The movement soon spread to the United States, and in 1910 a Chicago publisher, William Boyce, set out to establish Scouting in America. The first World Scout Jamboree was held in 1911 in England. Baden-Powell was honored as the Chief Scout of the World. In 1926 he was awarded the Silver Buffalo Award in the United States. He was knighted in 1929 for distinguished military service and for his scouting efforts. Baden-Powell died in 1941. For more information you may contact our advisor, R.J. Sayers, author of *Guide to Scouting Collectibles*, whose address (and ordering information regarding his book) may be found in the Directory under North Carolina.

Binoculars, BSA, Fr made, slip lens, 1920s, +case **50.00**
Book, Cub Scouting, Baden-Powell, yel cover, 1920 ....**22.00**
Book, Cubbing the Boy's Cubbook, Wolf Rank, Part 1, '30-35 .....**10.00**
Book, Den Mother's Denbook, 1st/proof edition, 1937 ....**22.00**
Camera, BSA, Kodak, bellows type, gr, 1930s **50.00**
Cigarette card, Baden-Powell, Adkin & Sons **7.50**
Coin, BSA, Civic Good Turn, brass, 1974 ....**2.00**
Coins, BSA, 1977 Nat'l Jamboree Souvenir set, 1937-77 (+) **5.00**
Cuff links, BSA, 1964 Nat'l Jamboree, enamel logo **10.00**
Greeting card, Baden-Powell's African Home, sgn, 1921 ....**60.00**
Handbook, BSA, 4th edition for Boys, Rockwell cover, 1940s **7.50**
Jacket, BSA, 4 billows pockets, #583, 1918-24 era **50.00**
Knife, BSA, Remington, RH-54 type, 1925-32, 7" blade, +sheath ..**50.00**
Medal, BSA, 1920 World Jamboree US Contingent, 3-color ribbon .**300.00**
Mess kit, BSA, 7-pc, #1535, 1925-32, lg **22.00**
Patch, BSA, Air Scout Scribe, Xd quills, 1958-68 ....**20.00**
Patch, BSA, Eagle, Sea Scout on bl, type I, 1924-32 ....**230.00**
Patch, BSA, Explorer Apprentice, wings & anchor, 1948-58 ....**5.00**
Patch, BSA, Tenderfoot Bugler, gold embr on tan sq, 1918-24 ..**200.00**
Patch, BSA, 1929 World Jamboree, woven, silk bk **90.00**
Patch, BSA, 1981 Nat'l Jamboree, Wide Game **2.00**
Patch, jacket; BSA, 1960 Nat'l Jamboree, 6" **13.00**
Patch, Nat'l Order of Arrow Conference, 1963 ....**20.00**
Patch, Patrol Leader, 2 gr felt bars on tan sq, 1918-24 ....**10.00**
Pin, BSA, Press Club, #347, 1937-45 ....**10.00**
Pin, Eagle Scout Ribbon Bar; w/device, wide bar, 1934 ....**25.00**
Pin, lapel; Explorer Silver Award, sterling, 1958-68 ....**35.00**
Pin, LSA, Lone Scout monogram, 1915-24 ....**50.00**
Pocketknife, Be Prepared, stag hdl, 4-blade, 1911-15 ....**150.00**
Pocketknife, Cub Scout Official, blk hdl, emb emblem **10.00**
Pocketknife, Remington, oval shield, 4-blade+tool, 1925 ....**80.00**
Pocketknife, Remington, 4-blade+opener, bone hdl, 1927-28 ......**70.00**
Pocketknife, Ulster, Pal Cutlery, 4-blade, stag hdl, 1940s **45.00**
Pocketknife, Ulster, 4-blade, stag hdl w/shackle, 1925-41 ....**20.00**

Pocketknife, Ulster, 5-blade, wht delrin hdl, 1980-81 ....**4.50**
Poster, BSA, 1935 Nat'l Jamboree, Rockwell, 20x30" **100.00**
Ring, BSA, sterling, rope fretwork, 1925-32 ....**20.00**
Ring, Eagle Scout, 14k gold **100.00**
Statuette, BSA, scout, ivory finish, 1918-24, 17" **50.00**
Uniform, BSA leader, dress jacket/pants/belt/socks, '37-45 ....**50.00**

Girl Scouts

Collecting Girl Scout memorabilia is a hobby that is growing nationwide. When Sir Baden-Powell founded the Boy Scout Movement in England, it proved to be too attractive and too well adaped to youth to limit its great opportunities to boys alone. The sister organization, known in England as the Girl Guides, quickly followed and was equally successful. Mrs. Juliette Low, an American visitor to England and a personal friend of the father of Scouting, realized the tremendous future of the movement for her own country, and with the active and friendly cooperation of the Baden-Powells, she founded the Girl Guides in America, enrolling the first patrols in Savannah, Georgia, in March 1912. In 1915 National Headquarters were established in Washington, DC, and the name was changed to Girl Scouts. The first National Convention was held in 1914, and each succeeding year has shown growth and increased enthusiasm in this steadily growing army of girls and young women who are learning in the happiest ways to combine patriotism, outdoor activities of every kind, skill in every branch of domestic science and high standards of community service. Today there are over 400,000 Girl Scouts and more than 22,000 leaders. Mr. Sayers is also our Girl Scout advisor.

Armband, GSA, embr GSM on khaki, pre-uniform **100.00**
Badge, GSA, General Profiency, 1917 era **5.00**
Belt buckle, GSA, 1936 ....**10.00**
Calendar, GSA, 1919, complete **50.00**
Camera, GSA, Brownie, box type, 1957 ....**15.00**
Camera, GSA, Kodak, bellows type, 1930 ....**60.00**
Camera, GSA, Univex, bellows type, 1938 ....**50.00**
Cross, GSA Life Savings, 1916 era **200.00**
Cup, collapsible; GSA, aluminum, 1950 ....**5.00**
Diary, GSA, 1st issue, 1928 ....**10.00**
Diary, GSA, 1929 ....**15.00**
Doll, GS uniform, gr shorts, Uneeda, 1960-64, 15" **30.00**
Doll, GSA, Sylvia, 1940 era **50.00**
Doll, GSA, Terri Lee, 1949 ....**40.00**
Emblem, GSA, Hospital Aide **20.00**
Game, GSA Troup, 1939, in box **15.00**
Medal, GSA, Honorable Mention, 1920 era **100.00**
Pin, GSA, Mariner, 1940 ....**15.00**
Plantation Cookie container, GSA, litho **40.00**
Postcard, GSA, outdoors type, 1928, set of 6 ....**25.00**
Postcard, GSA, silhouette, 1922, set of 6 ....**30.00**
Poster, GSA, 'Jingle,' 1920 ....**75.00**
Poster, GSA, girl saluting, 1917 ....**100.00**
Poster, GSA, 25th Anniversary, 1937 ....**40.00**
Ring, GSA, gold-tone metal w/gr stone **10.00**
Uniform, GS Brownie, middy & bloomers, 1918 ....**200.00**
Uniform, GSA, full dress, lt gr, 1930 era **50.00**

Scrimshaw

The most desirable examples of the art of scrimshaw can be traced back to the first half of the 19th century to the heyday of the whaling industry. Some voyages lasted for several years, and conditions on board were often dismal. Sailors filled the long hours by using the tools of

their trade to engrave whale teeth and make boxes, pie crimpers (jagging wheels), etc., from the bone and teeth of captured whales. Eskimos also made scrimshaw, sometimes borrowing designs from the sailors who traded with them.

Beware of fradulent pieces; fakery is prevalent in this field. If you're in doubt, it's best to deal with reputable people who guarantee the items they sell. There are also many carved teeth that are actually made of plastic. A listing of these plastic items has been published by the Kendall Whaling Museum in Sharon, Massachusetts. Our advisor for this category is John Rinaldi; he is listed in the Directory under Maine. See also Powder Horns.

Blocks, whalebone, fitted w/dbl sheaves, slotted, 1¾x3x2", pr **875.00**
Bodkin, whale ivory, wood & shell inlay, 1840s, 3½", EX **275.00**
Busk, rising sun/mourning scene/bird/promise, 13" **465.00**
Clenched fish w/full sleeve cuff, whale ivory, 1840s, 2½" **1,275.00**
Clock tower, 2 6" fitted teeth w/ships eng, 1840s, 7½x9½" **5,875.00**
Crimper, cut-out hearts & pierced decor, 1840s, 5" **1,200.00**
Crimper, lady's leg, 3-tined fork, ca 1850, 5", 1¾" wheel **2,400.00**
Crimper, pierce-cvd hearts in hdl, ca 1850, 6", 1¾" wheel **1,790.00**
Ditty box, open-cvd whalebone/wood, 1840s, 5x10x7" **5,600.00**
Ditty box, wood/ivory/MOP inlay lid, 1850s, 4x8x6", EX **3,985.00**

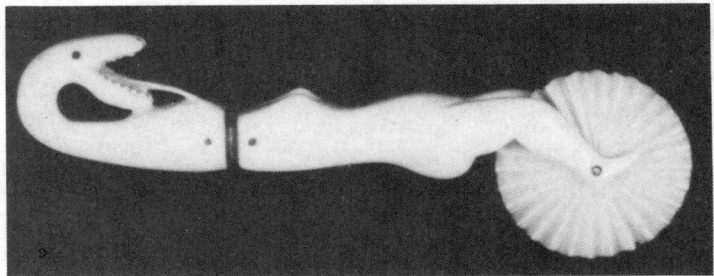

Jagging wheel, female body forms handle, legs hold wheel, serpent's head at opposite end, mid-1800s, 6⅝", $3,250.00.

Jagging wheel, classical lady form, 1800s, 6½" **1,980.00**
Ossik, polar bear & walrus cvgs, baleen separators, 21" **425.00**
Panbone, whaling scenes/Union Jack/pennants/etc, 5x7½" **1,050.00**
Pendant, whale tooth, clenched fist cvg, 1800s, 3½" **895.00**
Rolling pin, wood w/trn whale ivory hdls, 1840s, 16x2" **675.00**
Swift, tortoise & MOP inlays, ca 1840, 22½x20" dia (open) ...**3,950.00**
Tambua, whale tooth, bored hole ea end, Figian, 6x3" **975.00**
Teeth, full length man & lady, blunt tips, 1840s, 5¾", pr **3,690.00**
Tooth, Am ship/man battling lion, 1830s, 6x2⅜" **2,450.00**
Tooth, basket of flowers, faded red & gr stain, 4½" **195.00**
Tooth, Godey lady/New England building, red/blk stain, 7½" **600.00**
Tooth, lady in fancy dress w/flower, 1800s, 5½x2½" **890.00**
Tooth, lady w/children & dog, lady w/flowers, mc, 1840, 7¾" ...**1,985.00**
Tooth, mother & daughter/soldiers on horsebk, ca 1850, 7x3" ..**1,790.00**
Tooth, sailing ship from port side, ca 1850, 5½x1¾" **895.00**
Tooth, whaling scene w/longboat & men, ca 1850s, 6½x2¾" .**2,450.00**
Tooth, whaling scene/tent & palm, w/fr border, 6½" **2,200.00**
Tooth, whaling scene/whales/gulls/flag/etc, EX patina, 7" **1,750.00**
Tooth, 15 figures (men/women/children/animals), ca 1880s, 6" ..**1,800.00**
Tusk, walrus, Am flag/ship/ladies' portraits, mc, 13" **2,800.00**
Tusk, walrus, Victorian children, mc, 1850s, 14½" **550.00**

Sebastians

Sebastian miniatures were first produced in 1938 by Prescott W.

Baston in Marblehead, Massachusetts. Since then more than six hundred have been modeled. These figurines have been sold through gift shops all over the country, primarily in the New England states. In 1976 Baston withdrew his Sebastians from production. Under an agreement with the Lance Corporation of Hudson, Massachusetts, one hundred designs were selected to be produced by that company under Baston's supervision. Those remaining were discontinued. In the time since then, the older figurines have become very collectible. Price is determined by three factors: 1) in production/out of production; 2) labels — color of oval label, i.e. red, blue, green, etc.; Marblehead label, a green and silver palette-shaped label used until 1977; or no label; 3) condition. If there is no label and the varnish coat is quite yellowed, then it is considered to be of the Marblehead era. Dates are merely copyright dates and have no particular significance in regard to value. (Signed) 'P.W. Baston' should only have impact on price when the signature is an actual autograph. Most pieces are manufactured with an imprinted 'P.W. Baston' on the base. Baston died in 1984; the miniatures are now being done by P.W. Baston, Jr.

Aerial Tramway	150.00
America Remembers Family Sing	100.00
America Salutes Desert Storm, pnt	150.00
Ben Franklin	60.00
Chiquita Banana	200.00
Clown, #130A	75.00
Colonial Glass Blower	25.00
Dachshund	150.00
Davy Crockett	150.00
Dilemma, #82	150.00
Gardener Man	200.00
Gardener Woman	200.00
George & the Hatchet	300.00
Great Stone Face	300.00
Hannah Dustin	200.00
Horizontal Girl	200.00
IBM 305 RAMAC	275.00
J Warren at Bunker Hill	75.00
Jamestown Ships	200.00
Jesse Buffin	125.00
John Hancock, #1211 or #121F, ea	100.00
John Smith & Pocahontas	115.00
Jordan Marsh Observer, #113	125.00
Merchants Warren Sea Captain, #329	150.00
Mr & Mrs Beacon Hill, #79 & #80, pr	100.00
Mr Obocell, #164	75.00
Mr Sheraton	200.00
Nathaniel Hawthorne	150.00
Old Powder House, pen stand, #212A	200.00
Patrick & Sarah Henry, #125 & #126, pr	100.00
Phoebe	125.00
Robin Hood & Little John	300.00
Romeo & Juliet, pr	100.00
Royal Bengal Lancer	200.00
Santa, Jell-O	300.00
Scrooge, Marblehead	45.00
Self-Portrait	35.00
Shoemaker Haverhill, pen stand, #292C	175.00
Sitzmark	100.00
Slalom	100.00
St Jude Thaddeus	250.00
St Piux X	300.00
Statue of Liberty, AT&T	75.00
Toll House, Town Crier	125.00
Uncle Mistletoe	125.00

Sevres

Fine-quality porcelains have been made in Sevres, France, since the early 1700s. Rich ground colors were often hand painted with portraits, scenics, and florals. Some pieces were decorated with transfer prints and decalcomania; many were embellished with heavy gold. These wares are the most respected of all French porcelains. Their style and designs have been widely copied, and some of the items listed below are Sevres-type wares.

Box, nudes/scrolls/gilt on cobalt, sgn Froger, 7½" H	950.00
Cachepot, floral panels, ogee sides, hdls, 4¼x7¾"	200.00
Figurine, dying man below head of Athena, bsk, 19x24"	350.00
Lamp, banquet; courting scenes, roses, gold trim, 21"	450.00

Plaque, nude cherubs with mountain goat on wooded cliff, gold and blue border, 20", $1,550.00.

Plate, wreath/cherubs/Louis Phillipe insignia, 1844 mk, 9½"	250.00
Urn, figural scene, sgn Fuchs, ormolu mts, w/lid, 21"	2,500.00
Urn, maid/cupid 1 side sgn Rolli, cobalt w/ormolu mts, 15"	1,200.00
Urn, wht ovals w/mc floral on dk bl, gold ram hdls, 16", pr	1,750.00
Vase, gallant & village w/gold, sgn, brass base, 1850s, 9¾"	200.00
Vase, lady & cupid portrait, sgn, bl & gold, ormolu mts, 15"	495.00
Vase, lovers reserve on cobalt, baluster, 11½"	300.00
Vase, scenic reserves on Celeste Bl, mask hdls, 12⅜"	900.00

Sewer Tile

Whimsies, advertising novelties, and other ornamental items were sometimes made in potteries where the primary product was simply tile.

Birdhouse, tooled bark-like surface, 8½"	525.00
Brick w/Lincoln bust in relief, unglazed, 8x4"	180.00
Camel on rectangular base, sgn EJE, 5½"	335.00
Cat, tooled decor, rpr tail, 7⅜"	75.00
Dog, EX mold & tooling, firing crack, 11½"	770.00
Dog, EX mold & tooling, sm chips on ft, 13"	1,100.00
Dog, molded front, simple tooling, flat bk, mk Arnold, 9½"	110.00
Dog, recumbent, on rectangular base, flake on muzzle, 7¼"	220.00
Dog, seated, flat bk, EX molded detail, 11¾", EX	110.00
Dog, seated, simple tooled details, 10½"	330.00
Frog, blk glass marble eyes, old rpt, 5¼"	165.00
Frog, EX detail, 7" L	250.00
Horse head, hand molded & tooled, 7"	240.00
Lady's high-top boot, EX molding, 4"	40.00
Lady's high-top shoe, EX molding & tooling, 5"	140.00
Lion, on rectangular scalloped-edge base, EX detail, 10" L	385.00
Lion, rectangular base, LE Sr, #15, dtd 1954, 8½"	275.00
Man in shoe, hand formed & tooled, 3"	195.00

Minerva head, advertising paperweight, Nelsonville, 4⅜", EX ...185.00
Owl on stump, mk Ross Clay Plant, 12¼", EX 80.00
Pig, inscised ER, heavy, 9" 165.00
Pig w/molded flowers on bk, 6⅝" 360.00
Rabbit bank, 10½" L 415.00
Scottie dog, sm chip, 3" 50.00
Squirrel w/nut, hand molded & tooled, pnt eyes, 11" 300.00
Stump planter, CCP Co Uhrichesville, sm chips, 24" 220.00
Stump planter, unmk, 33" 110.00
Turtle, primitive, hand molded, 7½" L 300.00

Sewing Items

Sewing collectibles continue to intrigue collectors, and fine 19th-century and earlier pieces are commanding higher prices due to increased demand and scarcity. Complete needlework boxes and chatelaines in original condition are rare. But even though they may be incomplete, as long as boxes contain fittings of the period and the chains of the chatelaine are intact and contemporary with the style and the individual holders original and matching the brooch, they should be considered prime additions to any collection. As 19th-century items become harder to find, new trends in collecting develop. Among them are needlebooks, many of which were decorated with horses, children, beautiful ladies, etc. Some were giveaways printed with advertisements of products and businesses. Even early pins are collectible; the earliest were made in two parts with the round head attached separately. Pin disks, pin cubes, and other pin holders make interesting additions to a sewing collection as well.

Tape measures are now popular. Victorian figurals command premium prices. Early wooden examples of transferware and Tunbridge ware have gained in popularity as have figurals of vegetable ivory, celluloid, and other early plastics. From the 20th century, tatting shuttles made of plastics as well as bone, brass, sterling, and wood decorated with Art Nouveau, Deco, and more modern designs are in demand; so are darning eggs, stillettos, and thimbles. Because of the decline in the popularity of needlework after the 1920s (due to increased production of machine-made items), many novelty-type items were made in an attempt to regain consumer interest, and many collectors today find them appealing.

Watch for reproductions. Sterling thimbles are being made in Holland and in the U.S. and are available in many designs from the Victorian era. But the originals are usually plainly marked, either in the inside apex or outside on the band. Avoid testing gold and silver thimbles for content; this often destroys the inside marks. Instead, research the manufacturer's mark; this will often denote the material as well. Even though the reproductions are well finished, they do not have the manufacturers' marks. Many thimbles are being made specifically for the collectible market; reproductions of porcelain thimbles are also found. Prices should reflect the age and availability of these thimbles.

Basket, sweetgrass, flying saucer form, orig turq dye, 10" 30.00
Basket, yarn; sweetgrass, 2-hdl, 7½" dia 45.00
Book, Adventure Book of Needlework, 1958 ....9.00
Box, mahog veneer, inlaid ivory dmn in lid, fitted int, 9" 50.00
Box, rosewood veneer, brass escutcheon, ivory knobs, 11" 75.00
Box, wooden, old red pnt, cvd hdl, dbl lid, 1800s, 10x11x9" 70.00
Catalog, Barbours Lace Making & Needlework, color, 1896, 97-pg .30.00
Darner, bl & gold herringbone on milk glass, ca 1910, 5⅝" 500.00
Darner, emb Amster Stocking Darner..., cobalt, 5¼" 165.00
Darner, mc spatter, inside coated w/chalk, 1900s, 11½" 125.00
Darner, mc spatter cased, sheared end, ca 1900, 6½" 90.00
Darner, mc spatter/clear, chalk-like coating inside, 9" .:..............100.00
Darner, mica flecks in milk glass, amber cased, 5⅜" 225.00

Darner, nailsea, wht loopings on violet, ca 1900, 6" 525.00
Darner, sapphire bl, bulb form, orig screw-on cap, 6½" 75.00
Darning egg, yel-amber w/dk amber spatter, 3¼" 110.00
Jar, burl wood, pincushion in lid, 4½x4" 95.00
Kit, wht metal, bullet form w/red tassels, w/contents 25.00
Lamp, Riverside clinch collar, domed base, 11½" 55.00
Magazine, Needlecraft, 1916, EX 5.00
Measure, brass, turtle, tail winds, EX 95.00
Measure, metal, iron figural 40.00
Measure, metal, owl sitting on limb, Germany 45.00
Measure, Stanhope, bbl form 75.00
Pincushion, shoe shape, mk Sterling, cloth insert, 3½" 115.00
Sewing bird, brass, Pat 1853 ....175.00
Sewing bird, CI, scroll top w/red silk pincushion, 6" 380.00
Shuttle, tatting; SP, Germany 40.00
Shuttle, tatting; sterling 65.00
Shuttle, tatting; sterling, NM in orig flowered box 100.00
Stand, 5 chrome upright sections on 5x4" stand 20.00
Thimble, aluminum, Regal Lumber & Coal 7.50
Thimble, plastic, Holsum Bread 3.00
Thimble, 18k gold 78.00
Thread holder, CI w/pincushion/pin dish, ftd base, Pat 70, 7" 150.00

Sewing Machines

The fact that Thomas Saint, an English cabinetmaker, invented the first sewing machine in 1790 was unknown until 1874 when Newton Wilson, an English sewing machine manufacturer and patentee, chanced on the drawings included in a patent specification describing methods of making boots and shoes. By the middle of the 19th century, several patents were granted to American inventors, among them Isaac M. Singer, whose machine used a treadle. These machines were ruggedly built, usually of cast iron. By the 1860s and '70s, the sewing machine had become a popular commodity, and the ironwork became more detailed and ornate.

Though rare machines are costly, many of the old oak treadle machines (especially these brands: Davis, Home, Household, National, New Home, Singer, Weed, Wheeler & Wilson, and Wilcox & Gibbs) have only nominal value. Our advisors for this category are Sandra and Peter Frei; they are listed in the Directory under Massachusetts.

Wilcox and Gibbs sewing machine, dated 1861, $295.00

Atwater, Pat May 5, 1857 ....1,200.00
Child's, Baby Brother, electric motor, Japan 125.00
Child's, Betsy Ross, EX in case 60.00
Child's, blk enamel w/red & gold on NP body, Germany, 1900s ..150.00

Child's, Ideal, japanned & NP, 25x18x12" **125.00**
Child's, Jet Sew-O'Matic, metal/plastic, Straco, Germany, 9" **37.50**
Child's, Kayanee, hardwood base, batteries, Germany **125.00**
Child's, Pretty Maid, tin **35.00**
Child's, Sewmaster, flower decals, Germany, after WWII **150.00**
Child's, Singer, electric, complete w/carrying case **65.00**
Child's, Singer Featherweight #221, portable, EX **285.00**
Child's, Singer, tan metal, w/clamp, 6", w/instructions, NMIB ..**150.00**
Child's, Singer Sewhandy #20, EX in box **115.00**
Child's, unmk, chain driven **125.00**
Child's, Vulcan, metal, EX **30.00**
Grover & Baker, latest Pat May 27, 1856 ....**1,200.00**
Nettleton & Raymond, Pat April 14, 1857 ....**5,000.00**
Shaw & Clark, CI, fluted column, ped base, 1865, VG **75.00**
Watson, Pat March 11, 1856 & Dec 8, 1857 ....**850.00**
Wheeler Wilson, 625 Broadway, EX **125.00**
Wilcox & Gibbs, rpl wheel hdl, 11½x8x6", G **40.00**
Wilcox & Gibbs, 1871 ....**95.00**

Shaker Items

The Shaker community was founded in America in 1776 at Niskeyuna, New York, by a small group of English 'Shaking Quakers.' The name referred to a group dance which was part of their religious rites. Their leader was Mother Ann Lee. By 1815 their membership had grown to more than one thousand in eighteen communities as far west as Indiana and Kentucky. But in less than a decade, their numbers began to decline until today only a handful remain. Their furniture is prized for its originality, simplicity, workmanship, and practicality. Few pieces were signed. Some were carefully finished to enhance the natural wood; a few were painted.

Although other methods were used earlier, most Shaker boxes were of oval construction with overlapping 'fingers' at the seams to prevent buckling as the wood aged. Boxes with original paint fetch triple the price of an unpainted box; number of fingers and size should also be considered.

Although the Shakers were responsible for weaving a great number of baskets, their methods are not easily distinguished from those of their outside neighbors, and it is nearly impossible without first-hand knowledge to positively attribute a specific example to their manufacture. They were involved in various commercial efforts other than woodworking — among them sheep and dairy farming, sawmilling, and pipe and brick making. They were the first to raise crops specifically for seed and to market their product commercially. They perfected a method to recycle paper and were able to produce wrinkle-free fabrics. Our advisor for this category is Nancy Winston; she is listed in the Directory under New Hampshire. Standard two-letter state abbreviations have been used throughout the following listings.

Key:
bj — bootjack   PH — Pleasant Hill
CB — Canterbury   ML — Mt. Lebanon
EF — Enfield   SDL — Sabbathday Lake
NL — New Lebanon   WV — Watervliet

Basket, berry; dk tin bands, New Haven CT, dtd 1859, 1-cup **110.00**
Basket, blk ash, hickory hoop hdl, dbl-wrapped rim, 16x14" ...**1,050.00**
Basket, laundry; blk ash, dbl hdls, EF, 1840s, 22x28" dia **300.00**
Basket, wool; blk ash, wrapped rim, cvd hdl, 1850s, 19x33x20" .**500.00**
Bench, pine, classic form, half-moon cutout, 1820s, 40" L **8,000.00**
Bonnet, palm leaf, brn taffeta, purple velvet trim **200.00**
Box, blanket; pine, dvtl, wrought hdls, 1915, 20x32x20" **1,300.00**
Box, dome top, paper-covered brd, CB, 1890s, 5x9x6" **450.00**
Box, maple, 1-drw, hinged lid, rectangular, rpr, 7½x11½" **195.00**

Box, pine, drw in base, early 1800s, 32x37½x21" **600.00**
Box, poplarware, kid trim, pk satin lining, 5" sq **250.00**
Box, sewing; rfn pine, w/drw & spool compartment, 6¼" **195.00**
Box, storage; pine, red pnt, dvtl, iron hdls, WV, 46" L **1,300.00**
Box, tool; walnut & bird's-eye maple, fitted tray, 13x25x14" ..**1,200.00**
Box, work; pine, compartments, red stain, 1850s, 17x30x12" ..**1,550.00**
Box, 2-finger, red pnt, inscr/dtd 1852 lid, 6½" **5,225.00**
Box, 2-finger, varnished, ca 1850s, oval, 7¼" **880.00**
Box, 3-finger, maple/pine, varnished, copper tacks, oval, 3x7" ...**400.00**
Box, 3-finger, varnished, oval, 8¾" **715.00**
Box, 4-finger, maple/pine, NL, 1830s, 4¾x11½" **500.00**
Box, 4-finger, ochre pnt, cvd ER in base, oval, 5½" **3,575.00**
Box, 4-finger, tiger maple/pine, lt water stain, 4½x11½" **350.00**
Box, 4-finger, 1800s, 13½" dia **990.00**
Bucket, pine, dk varnish, orig lid, EF, 7¾x9¾", EX **325.00**
Bucket, pine, orig mustard pnt, 71 on lid/77 on base, 6x7" **1,200.00**
Candlestand, cherry, snake leg, sq top, NL, 24x17x17" **2,000.00**
Carrier, maple/hickory/pine, red stain, swing hdl, 1850s, 4x12" .**600.00**
Carrier, sewing; cherry/pine/maple, 4-finger, satin int, 8x9" **450.00**
Carrier, sewing; 3-finger, SDL, 1900s, 8" **300.00**
Chair, arm #0; maple, dk stain, rpl tape seat, 22¾" **1,600.00**
Chair, arm #6; maple, tape seat, shawl bar, ML, 1880-1920 ....**880.00**
Chair, arm #6; maple/oak, tape seat, ML, 1860s, 42" **900.00**
Chair, arm rocker #0; NL, 1900, EX **3,000.00**
Chair, arm rocker #6; maple, tape seat, ML, 1880-1920 ....**880.00**
Chair, arm rocker; old blk rpt, rpl tape seat/bk, ML, 34" **495.00**
Chair, arm rocker; trn posts, shaped arms, rpl tape seat, 37" **715.00**
Chair, elder's rocker; tiger maple, tape seat, NL, 44" **7,500.00**
Chair, maple, slat bk, old rfn, early 1800s, 40½" **415.00**
Chair, maple & birch, slat bk, tilters, 1850s, rfn, 40¾" **550.00**
Chair, rocker #0; maple, gr velvet seat, ML, 1880s, 23" **1,750.00**
Chair, rocker #3; rpl tape seat, ML, 1890s, 33¾" **250.00**
Chair, rocker #3; maple, red stain, tape seat, ML, 34½" **1,000.00**
Chair, rocker #3; maple, tape seat, ML, 1880s, 33" **600.00**
Chair, rocker #4; maple, rpl splint seat, ML, 1890s, 34" **450.00**
Chair, rocker #6; maple, fabric bk/seat, 1890s, 41" **700.00**
Chair, rocker #7; maple, tape seat & bk, ML, 1880-1920 ....**825.00**
Chair, rocker #7; maple, walnut stain, ML, 1880s, 42" **900.00**
Chair, side #3; shawl bar, rpl seat, rfn, ML, 1890s, 32⅝" **195.00**
Chair, side; birch, orig stain, cane seat, tilters, EF, 41" **4,000.00**
Chair, side; maple, dk stain, tilters, NL, 1850s, 39" **700.00**
Chair, side; maple, tape seat, NL, 1840s, 36" **400.00**
Chair, side; maple/figured cherry, tape seat, WV, 41" **550.00**
Chair, side; tiger maple, rush seat, EF, 1830s, child's **11,000.00**
Chair, tiger maple, tilters, slat bk, early 1800s, 41" **4,675.00**
Chest, butternut/poplar, 7-drw, dvtl, 52" **2,000.00**
Chest, pine, 7-drw, NH, early 1800s, 74x36x19¼", EX **4,400.00**
Chest, sewing; red mahog, 4-drw, dvtl, 38x35x24" **15,000.00**
Chest, walnut, 5-drw, shaped apron, OH, 1850s, 55x44x23" ..**9,350.00**
Cloak, bl wool w/mc print tie, CB, 1900s, EX **650.00**
Cupboard, hanging; pine, wash traces, ML, 1932, 33x17x18" **800.00**
Cupboard, pine, orig red stain, panel door, 40x34x10" **900.00**
Cupboard, walnut, 1 panel door over 4 drw, OH, 1832, 97" ..**11,000.00**
Cupboard, 1 panel door over 2 drw, Swain, 1845, 78x44" **2,850.00**
Cupboard, 2 panel doors over 6 sm dvtl drw, CB, 57x39" **4,125.00**
Desk, school; pine/maple/ash, dbl slant lid, Am, 1800s **660.00**
Desk, variegated woods, upper drw, Hold...1875, 32x28x17" ..**1,000.00**
Desk, writing; maple & poplar, w/added gallery, early 1800s **350.00**
Dipper, wooden, ochre pnt, 5½", EX **220.00**
Dust pan, maple/tin, long tapered hdl, EF, 1850s, 37x12" **600.00**
Foot warmer, oak, dvtl, iron bail hdl, NL, 1820s, 6¼x8x8" **1,800.00**
Ladder, pnt wood, LA Shepard CB NH label, 109x12" **1,650.00**
Lap robe, mc fabric lined w/patterned cotton, att, 54x69", VG ..**900.00**
Lectern, pine, bl pnt, breadboarded/nailed, 1900s, 29x34x19" ...**550.00**

Photograph, blk/wht portrait, brother in workshop, fr, 23x17" ...250.00
Pillow fluffer, bentwood loop, wooden hdl, 20½" L 110.00
Pincushion, stuffed gr velvet on maple screw stand, 10½" 770.00
Rug, mc abstract rag type sewn on bed ticking, 25x45" 300.00
Rug, mc wool yarn, sewn, 46x28" 250.00
Shovel & tongs, CI, NL, 1840, 23", 21" 300.00
Sieve, wood & horsehair, 1800s, 9¾", EX 137.50
Spinning wheel, walking; birch/maple/hickory, 58x73" 475.00
Stand, birch & maple, rfn, EF, early 1800s, 24½x19¼" 2,300.00
Stool, maple, red tape seat, ML, 1880s, 19x14x14" 400.00
Stove, CI, NL, 1800s, 18¾x31x11" 550.00
Stove, CI, str tapered leg, 18x39x13" 900.00
Sugar tub, wood, 1-finger lap on lid/2 on base, 1860s, 11¼" 295.00
Table, birch, 1-drw, NH, 1825-1850, 26½x17x16½" 935.00
Table, cherry, 1-drw, CB, 1800s, old rfn, 29x36x24" 1,650.00
Table, cherry, 1-drw, old finish, mid-1800s, 28x22x30", EX 7,700.00
Table, dressing; rfn hardwood, 1-drw, CB, 1920s, 30x37x21" 550.00
Table, maple & birch, 1-drw, CB, old rfn, 1800s, 26x30x18" ..2,400.00
Table, pine, 1-drw, orig red pnt, CB, 1800s, 28x28x18" 2,425.00
Table, work; cherry/curly maple, 2-drw, 1 drop leaf, 55" 11,500.00
Table, work; pine/maple, orig pnt, trn legs, 1850s, 23x26x18" ...500.00

Shaving Mugs

Between 1865 and 1920, the personalized shaving mug became very popular, with the occupational shaving mugs enjoying their greatest popularity. Most men having occupational mugs would frequent the barber shop several times a week where their mugs were clearly visible for all to see in the barber's rack. As a matter of fact, this display was in many ways the index of the individual town or neighborhood.

During the first twenty years, blank mugs were almost entirely imported from France, Germany and Austria and were hand painted in this country. Later on, some china was produced by local companies. It is noteworthy that American vitreous china is inferior to the imported Limoges and is subject to extreme crazing.

Artists employed by the American barber supply companies were for the most part extremely talented and were capable of executing any design the owner required, depicting his occupation, fraternal affiliation or sport. When the mug was completed, the name was always added (as was the gold trim) in varying degrees, depending on the price paid by the customer. This price was determined by the barber who added his markup to that of the barber supply company. As mentioned above, the popularity of the occupational shaving mug diminished with the advent of World War I and the introduction by Gillette of the safety razor, later followed by the blue laws forcing barber shops to close on Sundays, thereby eliminating the political and social discussions for which the barber shops were so well noted.

Occupational shaving mugs are the most sought after of the group which would include those with sport affiliations. Fraternal mugs, although desirable, do not command the same price as the occupationals. Occasionally, you will find the owner's occupation together with his fraternal affiliation. This combination could add anywhere between 25% to 50% to the price. Price is dependent on the execution of the painting, rarity of the subject and detail. Some subjects can be done very simply; others can be done in extreme detail, commanding substantially higher prices. It is fair to say, however, that the rarity of the occupation will dictate the price. Mugs which have lost the gold through wear lose between 20% and 30% of their value immediately. This would not apply to the gold trim around the rim, but to the loss of the name itself. Our advisor for this category is Burton Handelsman; he is listed in the Directory under New York.

Civil War era, dk gray tin, side brush holder, strap hdl 110.00

Fraternal, Civil War Sons Assoc, medals, gilt band, VG 125.00
Fraternal, compass & ruler surrounding eye, Shaw, G 60.00
Fraternal, Crown of Life & cross, EX gold, rpr 200.00
Fraternal, eagle w/shield, Freedom/Charity/Friendship, T&V 85.00
Fraternal, FOE, lg eagle flying, 6-color, crack 50.00
Fraternal, Knights of Columbus, EX gold decor & name 50.00
Milk glass, Viking, dtd 1867 ....75.00

Occupational, Made for Geo. W. Stockwell, horse-drawn ice wagon, multicolored paint with gold trim, T&V Limoges France, ca 1890-1920, NM, $700.00.

Occupational, baker w/loaves of bread, 3½x3¼", G 350.00
Occupational, bartender, 5 people at bar, 8-color, worn gold 600.00
Occupational, bartender & 2 customers, 4x3¾", VG 450.00
Occupational, baseball catcher w/equipment, 3½x3½", G 1,500.00
Occupational, blacksmith, man at forge, worn gold, NM 450.00
Occupational, blacksmith, man shoeing horse, Germany, G 750.00
Occupational, bookkeeper, man w/ledger at desk, Germany, EX ..600.00
Occupational, bricklayer, tools, much gold & name 200.00
Occupational, butcher, cow head & tools, gold name & trim 150.00
Occupational, carpenter, man w/tools, EX gold, Germany 450.00
Occupational, engineer, train w/man driving, 5-color, G gold 400.00
Occupational, farmer, man w/horse-drawn harrow, worn gold, 4" ..450.00
Occupational, foundry man, men working, M gold, T&V Limoges ..1,475.00
Occupational, furniture maker, man working, EX gold, M 650.00
Occupational, general store owner, man at counter, 4x3¾", EX .475.00
Occupational, grocer, horse-drawn wagon, 3¾", VG 300.00
Occupational, hunter w/dog & ducks, 3¾x4" dia, VG 350.00
Occupational, ice man, man & horse-drawn ice wagon, EX 425.00
Occupational, jockey, seated on horse, 3¾x3½" dia, VG 550.00
Occupational, lathe operator, TV France, VG 400.00
Occupational, man w/quill pen writing, 3½x3½" dia, VG 650.00
Occupational, milk man, horse-drawn milk wagon, T&V, EX ...650.00
Occupational, minister, open Bible, CA Smith Supplies, EX ..1,600.00
Occupational, paper hanger, man at work, 4x3¾", EX 1,250.00
Occupational, pharmacist, mortar & pestle, Austria, G 130.00
Occupational, piano salesman, upright piano, Austria, VG 700.00
Occupational, salesman, w/customer & new boots, 3¾", EX 750.00
Occupational, tailor, man sewing at table, VG 225.00
Occupational, tinsmith, smelting, worn gilt, Germany, VG 1,200.00
Occupational, trainman, red box car, mc florals, NM 320.00
Occupational, trolley operator, man & trolley, Limoges, NM .1,750.00
Occupational, whiskey distiller, bottle, mc flowers/gold, EX 500.00
Occupational, writer's hand & pen on paper, worn gold 275.00
Patriotic, eagle & flags, mc w/gold, mk P Germany, NM 200.00
Rabbit in man's overcoat & glasses, gold name & trim 100.00
Scenic, mtn scene w/church & lake, 5-color, EX 100.00

Shawnee

The Shawnee Pottery Company operated in Zanesville, Ohio,

from 1937 to 1961. They produced inexpensive novelty ware (vases, flowerpots, and figurines) as well as a very successful line of figural cookie jars, creamers, and salt and pepper shakers.

They also produced three dinnerware lines, the first of which, Valencia, was designed by Louise Bauer in 1937 for Sears & Roebuck. A starter set was given away with the purchase of one of their refrigerators. Second and most popular was the King Corn line. It was produced from 1946 to 1954, when the colors were changed to a lighter yellow for the kernels and darker green for the shucks. This variation was called Queen Corn. Their third dinnerware line, produced after 1954, was called Lobsterware. It was made in either black, brown, or gray; lobsters were usually applied to serving pieces and accessory items.

For further study we recommend these books: *The Collector's Guide to Shawnee Pottery* by our advisors, Janice and Duane Vanderbilt, who are listed in the Directory under Indiana; and *Shawnee Pottery, An Identification and Value Guide,* by Jim and Bev Mangus, who are listed in Ohio.

Cookie Jars

Basketweave, hexagon form, gold trim w/decals, mk USA 100.00
Beanpot, Snowflake, bl & gr, mk USA 50.00
Cottage, mk USA 6 ....400.00
Drum Major, gold trim, mk USA 10 ....450.00
Dutch Boy, gold w/decals, HP flowers on bk, mk USA 225.00
Dutch Boy, Great Northern, mk Great Northern 1025 ....200.00
Dutch Girl, gold trim w/decals, mk USA 200.00
Dutch Girl, tulip on dress, mk USA 225.00
Elephant, pk, mk Shawnee 60 ....150.00
Fernware, octagonal, mk USA 75.00
Fruit Basket, gold trim, mk Shawnee 84 ....200.00
Jack Tar, blk or blond hair, gold trim, mk USA 400.00
Jo Jo the Clown, gold trim, mk Shawnee 12 ....300.00
Jug, bl/yel/gr, mk USA 75.00
Little Chef, wht w/gold trim, mk USA 150.00
Muggsy, gold trim, no decals, mk Pat Muggsy USA 600.00
Owl, gold trim, mk USA 225.00
Puss-n-Boots, gold w/decals, mk Pat Puss-n-Boots 350.00
Puss-n-Boots, tail over foot, mk Pat Puss-n-Boots 200.00
Sitting Elephant, gold trim w/decals, mk USA 350.00
Smiley, apples, mk USA 250.00
Smiley the Pig, bl bib, cold pnt, mk USA 150.00
Smiley the Pig, gold & decals, flies pnt on head, mk USA 325.00
Smiley the Pig, shamrocks on bottom, mk USA 150.00
Smiley the Pig, strawberries, gold trim, mk USA 700.00
Winnie the Pig, peach collar, mk Pat Winnie USA 225.00
Winnie the Pig, red collar, gold trim, mk USA 300.00

Corn Line

Cookie jar, $185.00.

Bowl, cereal; mk #94 ....45.00
Bowl, mixing; mk #6, 6" 30.00
Bowl, vegetable; mk #95 ....35.00
Butter dish, mk #72 ....50.00
Creamer, gold trim, mk USA 60.00
Creamer, mk #70 ....25.00
Cup, #90 ....30.00
Mug, #69 ....45.00
Pitcher, mk #71 ....65.00
Pitcher, wht corn, gold trim, mk USA 100.00
Pitcher, wht corn, mk USA 70.00
Plate, mk #68, 10" 30.00
Plate, mk #93, 8" 25.00
Platter, mk #96, 12" 45.00
Relish dish, mk #79 ....17.00
Saucer, King, mk #91 ....12.00
Shaker, Indian corn 65.00
Shakers, lg, pr 25.00
Sugar bowl, w/lid, mk #78 ....30.00
Sugar shaker, wht corn 60.00
Teapot, mk #65, 10-oz 120.00
Teapot, wht corn, gold trim, mk USA, 30-oz 120.00

Kitchenware

Creamer, elephant, gold trim, flower decals, mk Pat USA 200.00
Creamer, Puss-n-Boots, gold trim, Shawnee 85 ....225.00
Creamer, Sunflower, mk USA 45.00
Lobster, bowl, batter; w/lid 80.00
Lobster, butter dish 80.00
Lobster, mug 135.00
Lobster, plate, compartments 150.00
Lobster, shakers, claw, pr 20.00
Lobster, spoon holder, dbl 165.00
Pitcher, Bo Peep, gold trim, mk Pat Bo Peep 250.00
Pitcher, Fernware, octagon jug, mk USA 75.00
Pitcher, Little Bo Peep, mk Shawnee 47 ....150.00
Shakers, Dutch Boy & Girl, gold & decals, pr 125.00
Shakers, fruit, mk Shawnee 82, pr 25.00
Shakers, Muggsy, sm, pr 50.00
Shakers, Puss 'n Boots, gold trim, pr 60.00
Shakers, Smiley & Winnie, sm, pr 50.00
Teapot, cookie house, mk USA 7 ....320.00
Teapot, Granny Anne, mk USA 100.00
Valencia, ashtray 16.50
Valencia, bowl, dessert; 6" 12.00
Valencia, bowl, mixing; 10" 25.00
Valencia, bowl, vegetable; w/lid, 9½" 55.00
Valencia, coffeepot, AD 60.00
Valencia, egg cup 12.00
Valencia, pie plate, 10½" 22.00
Valencia, plate, 9¾" 14.00
Valencia, spoon, 9½" 45.00
Valencia, vase, 12" 22.00

Miscellaneous

Bank, bulldog, mk w/paper label 160.00
Bank, Smiley the Pig, chocolate bottom, mk Shawnee Smiley 60 ..200.00
Bank, Winnie the Pig, butterscotch, mk Shawnee Winnie 61 ....200.00
Figurine, deer 75.00
Figurine, donkey & cart, gloss finish, mk USA 538 ....14.00
Figurine, duck, gold trim, stamped Shafer, mk USA 720 ....32.00
Figurine, high-heel shoe, mk USA 15.00

Figurine, hound w/jug, mk Shawnee 610 ....**15.00**
Figurine, little elephant, mk USA 759 ....**15.00**
Figurine, pekingese **65.00**
Figurine, puppy **65.00**
Figurine, rabbit, mk w/paper label **75.00**
Figurine, teddy bear **65.00**
Ice server, elephant, mk Shawnee 60 ....**150.00**
Planter, boy w/wheelbarrow, mk USA 750 ....**20.00**
Planter, bull, mk 668 ....**15.00**
Planter, doe & fawn, gold trim, mk Shawnee 669 ....**24.00**
Planter, doe & fawn, mk Shawnee 721 ....**24.00**
Planter, elf shoe, gold trim, mk Shawnee 765 ....**20.00**
Planter, gazelle, mk USA 613 ....**24.00**
Planter, grist mill, gold trim, mk Shawnee 769 ....**32.00**
Planter, locomotive, mk USA 550 ....**32.00**
Planter, squirrel, gold trim, mk Shawnee 664 ....**15.00**
Planter, stagecoach, mk Shawnee 733 ....**34.00**
Planter, toy horse, mk Shawnee 660 ....**20.00**
Planter, Uncle Sam top hat, mk USA **8.00**
Vase, tulip, mk USA 1115 ....**10.00**
Wall pocket, birds at birdhouse, mk USA 830 ....**24.00**

Shearwater

Since 1928 generations of the Peter, Walter, and James McConnell Anderson families have been producing figurines and artwares in their studio at Ocean Springs, Mississippi. Their work is difficult to date. Figures from the twenties and thirties won critical acclaim and have continued to be made to the present time. Early marks include a die-stamped 'Shearwater' in a dime-sized circle, a similar ink stamp, and a half-circle mark. Any older item may still be ordered in the same glazes as it was originally produced, so many pieces on the market today may be relatively new. However, the older marks are not currently in use. Currently produced Blacks and pirates figurines are marked with a hand-incised 'Shearwater' and/or a cypher formed with an 'S' whose bottom curve doubles as the top loop of a 'P' formed by the addition of an upright placed below and to the left of the S. Many are dated, '93, for example. These figures are generally valued at $35.00 to $50.00 and are available at the pottery or by mail order. New decorated and carved pieces are very expensive, starting at $400.00 to $500.00 for a 6" pot.

Bowl, bl w/rings, 3½x6½" base, 3½" opening **45.00**
Cup & saucer, Oriental decor, gr **35.00**
Pot, gun-metal gr, flared rim, 2¼x5" **50.00**
Vase, cvd ducks encircle body, yel/turq, 6½x6½" **1,000.00**
Vase, cvd fish on bl gloss, sgn Anderson, 1930, 9" **1,350.00**
Vase, gr matt, bulbous, 6" **68.00**
Vase, Ming gr, early mk, 8x5¼" **88.00**
Vase, pelicans emb, Deco style, lav/brn flecks, 7" **515.00**
Vase, stylized birds/trees, bls on wht gloss, U-form, 1940, 4" **400.00**

Sheet Music

Sheet music is often collected more for its colorful lithographed covers, rather than for the music itself. Transportation songs (which have pictures or illustrations of trains, ships, and planes), Ragtime and Blues; Comic characters (especially Disney), Sports, Political, and Expositions are eagerly sought after. Much of the sheet music on the market today is valued at under $5.00; some of the better examples are listed here. Our advisor for this category is Jeannie Peters; she is listed in the Directory under Ohio.

Key: SP — facsimile signed photo

Annie Doesn't Live Here..., Guy Lombardo cover, 1933, M **3.00**
Anywhere I Wander, Danny Kaye photo cover, 1951, EX **4.00**
April in Portugal, Vic Damone cover, 1953, M **3.00**
Blood & Sand, Judy Garland cover, EX **30.00**
Boy Scouts on Parade, march, 1912, EX **15.00**
Come On Say Hello, cover by Pfeiffer, 1910, EX **12.00**
Early Bird, Shirley Temple photo cover, 1936, NM **15.00**
Gee I Wish I Was Back..., Movie: White Christmas, 1942, M **10.00**
I Hate Men, Musical: Kiss Me Kate, 1948, EX **4.00**
I Have Eyes, Movie: Paris Honeymoon, 1938, EX **8.50**
I Left My Heart in San Francisco, Tony Bennett SP cover **5.00**
I Live In Turkey, Musical: Ziegfield Follies, 1920, EX **8.50**
I'll Be Thinking of You, Merv Griffin photo cover, M **3.00**
I'll Have Vanilla, Eddie Cantor photo cover, 1934, EX **8.50**
I'll Hold You in My Heart, Eddy Arnold photo cover, 1947, NM ...**3.00**
I'll Walk Alone, Dinah Shore photo cover, 1944, NM **3.00**
I Love Paris, Musical: Can Can, 1953, M **4.00**
It Looks Like Big Night Tonight, L Ashley SP cover, 1908, M **10.00**
It Might As Well Be Spring, Movie: State Fair, 1945, M **3.00**
It's a Hap-Hap-Happy Day, Movie: Gulliver's Travels, 1939, M **7.50**
It's All So New to Me, Shirley Temple photo cover, 1935, EX **15.00**
Left Right Out of Your Heart, Patti Page photo cover, '43, M **3.00**
Let It Snow, Perry Como photo cover, 1945, M **3.00**
Let's Get Lost, Movie: Happy Go Lucky, 1943, NM **7.00**
Let This Be Your Mother's Day, E Morton photo cover, '15, EX **3.50**
Little Ford Rambled Right Along, 1914, EX **12.50**
Marianne, Easy Riders photo cover, 1955, M **5.00**
Marry the Man Today, Musical: Guys & Dolls, 1950, M **5.00**
No Letter Today, Gene Autry photo cover, 1943, M **3.00**
No Star Is Lost, Sammy Kaye photo cover, 1939, M **3.00**
Nobody's Heart, Movie: All's Fair, 1942, M **5.00**
Nobody's Knows Trouble I've Seen, Cadets photo cover, 1935, M .**5.00**

Oh! Mother I'm Wild, by Howard Johnson, Harry Pease, and Eddie Nelson, 1920, $10.00.

Old Master Painter, Gordon MacRae photo cover, 1949, EX **3.50**
Our Love Affair, Movie: Strike Up the Band, 1940, NM **9.00**
Out in Great Open Spaces, Kate Smith photo cover, 1932, EX **4.00**
Over the Top, WWI march, 1917, EX **6.50**
Pink Elephants on Parade, Movie: Dumbo, 1941, NM **15.00**
Pipe Dreaming, Movie: Around the World, M **5.00**
Please, Movie: Big Broadcast, 1932, EX **12.00**
Please Learn To Love, Musical: Buddies, 1919, NM **9.00**
Polly-Wolly Doodle, Shirley Temple photo cover, 1935, EX **8.50**
Rose of My Dreams, Mrs C Chaplin photo cover, 1919, EX **12.00**
Russian March, pre-1900 march, 1861, EX **17.00**
Scotch Lassie, litho cover by JH Bufford, 1873, EX **45.00**
Second Hand Rose, Barbara Streisand photo cover, 1965, NM **3.00**
Secret Love, D Day SP cover, Movie: Calamity Jane, 1953, EX **5.00**
Seventeen, Boyd Bennett photo cover, 1955, NM **3.00**

Sew the Buttons On, Musical: Riverwind, 1963, NM 3.00
Shaking the Blues Away, Movie: Easter Parade, 1947, NM 5.00
Soon, Bing Crosby & Joan Bennett photo cover, 1935, M 3.50
Sound of Music, Movie: same title, 1959, NM 3.50
Speaking Confidentially, Movie: Every Night at Eight, 1935, M 5.00
Sunny Boy, Al Jolson photo cover, 1928, NM 6.50
Sunny Side of the Street, Movie: same title, 1930, M 5.00
That Lucky Old Sun, Frankie Laine photo cover, 1949, NM 3.00
That's Amore, Movie: same title, D Martin SP cover, '53, EX 5.00
That's Music to Me, cover by Pfeiffer, 1939, EX 8.50
That Was Before I Met You, cover by Pfeiffer, 1911, EX 8.00
Thrilled, Guy Lombardo photo cover, 1935, NM 3.00
Thunder Over Paradise, Movie: Rose of the Rancho, 1935, NM 4.50
Ting-A-Ling, Paul Ash photo cover, 1926, NM 3.00

Shelley

In 1872 Joseph Shelley became partners with James Wileman, owner of Foley China Works, thus creating Wileman & Co. in Stoke-on-Trent. Twelve years later James Wileman withdrew from the company, though the firm continued to use his name until 1925 when it became known as Shelley Potteries, Ltd. Like many successful 19th-century English potteries, this firm continued to produce useful household wares as well as dinnerware of considerable note. In 1896 the beautiful Dainty White shape was introduced, and it is regarded by many as synonymous with the name Shelley. In addition to the original Dainty 6-Flute design, other lovely shapes were produced: 12-Flute, 14-Flute, Oleander, Queen Anne, and the more modern shapes of Vogue, Regent, and Eve.

Though often overlooked, striking earthenware was produced under the direction of Frederick Rhead and later Walter Slater and his son, Eric. Many notable artists contributed their talents in designing unusual, attractive wares: Rowland Morris, Mabel Lucie Attwell, and Hilda Cowham, to name but a few.

In 1966 Allied English Potteries acquired control of the Shelley Company, and by 1967 the last of the exquisite Shelley China had been produced to honor remaining overseas orders. In 1971 Allied English Potteries merged with the Doulton group. Our advisors for this category are Lila and Fred Shrader; they are listed in the Directory under California.

Ashtray, Blue Rock, Dainty shape, 5" dia 35.00
Ashtray, Blue Rock, 3½" sq 20.00
Ashtray, Harmony, 5" dia 39.00
Ashtray, RAF, scenes & insignia, 5" dia 35.00
Bowl, cereal; Bridal Rose, 6½" 35.00
Bowl, cereal; Dainty White, 6½" 29.00
Bowl, cereal; Harebell, Oleander shape, 6½" 35.00
Bowl, cream soup; Dainty Blue, w/underplate 78.00
Bowl, cream soup; Drifting Leaves, w/underplate 55.00
Bowl, fruit; Rose Pansy Forget-Me-Not, 6-flute, 5½" 32.00
Bowl, fruit; Rosebud, Oleander shape, 5½" 32.00
Bowl, soup; Sheraton, rimmed, 8" 25.00
Bowl, soup; Violets, rimmed, 6-flute, 8¼" 65.00
Bowl, vegetable; Begonia, oval, 6-flute, 9½" 85.00
Bowl, vegetable; Bowl of Fruit, Queen Anne shape, hdls, w/lid ..175.00
Bowl, vegetable; Campanula, oval, 6-flute, 9½" 95.00
Bowl, vegetable; Duchess, hdls, w/lid, 9" 165.00
Bowl, vegetable; Heavenly Blue, 6-flute, hdls, w/lid, 9½" 225.00
Bowl, vegetable; Regency, 6-flute, hdls, w/lid, 9½" 195.00
Bowl, vegetable; Serenity, 9½" 65.00
Box, Dainty Pink, w/lid, 4x5½" 125.00
Butter dish, Campanula, oblong, 6-flute, w/lid 100.00

Butter dish, Harmony, oblong, w/lid 120.00
Butter dish, Primrose, Oleander shape, w/lid 110.00
Butter pat, Bridal Rose, 6-flute 55.00
Butter pat, Campanula 45.00
Butter pat, Dainty Blue 59.00
Butter pat, Mayfair w/gr border 45.00
Butter pat, Wildflower, 6-flute 55.00
Butter tub, Harmony, w/lid & underplate 135.00
Cake plate, Blue Poppy, tall ped, 6-flute, 8" 175.00
Cake plate, Bridal Rose, Oleander shape, tab hdls 85.00
Cake plate, Cloisonne, Queen Anne shape, 9" sq 150.00
Cake plate, Forget-Me-Not, 6-flute, tab hdls, 9" sq 85.00
Candle holder, Cloisello, 9" 195.00
Candle holder, Dainty Green, w/metal insert 95.00
Candle holder, Moresque, 7" 245.00
Candle holder, Tulips on blk matt, 7" 155.00
Candy dish, Campanula, 6-flute, tab hdls, 5" sq 32.00
Candy dish, Crochet, pk, 5¼" dia 25.00
Candy dish, Daffodil, 14-flute, 5½" dia 35.00
Candy dish, Dainty Pink, 5" dia 45.00
Candy dish, Pomegranate on bl & gold bkground, w/lid 165.00
Chamber set, Cloisonne, pitcher+bowl+candle holder+soap dish .365.00
Chamber set, Dainty Mauve, pitcher & bowl, 6-flute 650.00
Cheese dish, Blue Rock, 6-flute, w/lid 195.00
Cheese dish, Harmony, w/lid 150.00
Children's ware, bowl, Hilda Cowham, Teddy Bears, 8½" 125.00
Children's ware, bowl, Mabel Lucie Attwell, 5½" 95.00
Children's ware, cup & saucer, Mabel Lucie Attwell pixies 145.00
Children's ware, egg cup, Mabel Lucie Atwell pixies 75.00
Children's ware, jug, zoo animals, 6" 95.00
Children's ware, plate, Hilda Cowham, ABCs w/animals 55.00
Children's ware, plate, Mabel Lucie Attwell, Boo Boos, 8" 145.00
Children's ware, plate, zoo animals, 8½" 45.00
Chocolate pot, Rosebud, 5½" 155.00
Chocolate pot, Vogue shape w/red & wht stripes, 6½" 275.00
Cigarette holder, Blue Rock 39.00
Cigarette holder, Lilac, 6-flute 42.00
Coffeepot, Garland of Flowers, pk, Queen Anne shape, 8-cup ...225.00
Coffeepot, Harmony, 6-cup 125.00
Coffeepot, Hibiscus, 6-flute, 8-cup 245.00
Coffeepot, pk & gold, Stanley shape, 4-cup 150.00
Coffeepot, Rosebud, 6-flute, 6-cup 225.00
Comport, Intarsio, w/ped & 3 S-curve supports, 8" 395.00
Comport, Oriental flowers w/rich gold, w/ped, 8" 275.00
Condiment set, Blue Rock, shakers+mustard w/lid+tray 210.00
Condiment set, Harmony, shakers+mustard w/lid+tray 155.00
Creamer & sugar bowl, Begonia, 6-flute, med 65.00
Creamer & sugar bowl, Bowl of Fruit, Queen Anne shape 125.00
Creamer & sugar bowl, DuBarry, w/lid 50.00
Creamer & sugar bowl, Rose & Red Daisy, 6-flute, w/lid, med 95.00
Creamer & sugar bowl, Violets, 6-flute, w/lid, lg 110.00
Creamer & sugar bowl, Wild Anenome, 6-flute, ind 65.00
Creamer & sugar bowl w/tray, Wildflower, 6-flute, w/lid, med ...150.00
Cup & saucer, alternating blk & gold panels, 6-flute 65.00
Cup & saucer, Archway of Roses, Queen Anne shape 62.00
Cup & saucer, Begonia, Oleander shape 52.00
Cup & saucer, Black Leafy Tree, Queen Anne shape 75.00
Cup & saucer, Blue Rock, mini 125.00
Cup & saucer, Blue Rock, 14-flute 55.00
Cup & saucer, Bluebell Wood, 6-flute, tall 56.00
Cup & saucer, Dainty Blue, 6-flute 56.00
Cup & saucer, demitasse; Autumn Leaves, Queen Anne shape 59.00
Cup & saucer, demitasse; Campanula, 14-flute 52.00
Cup & saucer, demitasse; Dainty Mauve, 6-flute 57.00

Cup & saucer, demitasse; Old Mill, 14-flute 52.00
Cup & saucer, demitasse; Pansy Spray, 6-flute 52.00
Cup & saucer, demitasse; pk matt w/gold int, Vogue 62.00
Cup & saucer, demitasse; Serenity, Gainsborough shape 52.00
Cup & saucer, demitasse; Windflower, 6-flute 55.00
Cup & saucer, DuBarry, Henley shape 42.00
Cup & saucer, Duchess, Henley shape 40.00
Cup & saucer, English Lakes, Henley shape 45.00
Cup & saucer, Gladiola, Eve shape 56.00
Cup & saucer, Glorious Devon, 6-flute 59.00
Cup & saucer, gr dots on Dainty White 60.00
Cup & saucer, Hedgerow, Gainsborough shape 47.00
Cup & saucer, heraldic shield on Dainty White 50.00
Cup & saucer, Iris, 6-flute 57.00

Cup and saucer, Lily of the Valley, 6-flute, $56.00.

Cup & saucer, Maytime, Oleander shape 60.00
Cup & saucer, Maytime, Ripon shape, gold ped 60.00
Cup & saucer, Melody Chintz, Oleander shape 60.00
Cup & saucer, Morning-Glory, 6-flute 57.00
Cup & saucer, Old Bow, Gainsborough shape 49.00
Cup & saucer, Primrose, 14-flute 55.00
Cup & saucer, Regency, 6-flute 49.00
Cup & saucer, Scenics, Chester shape 52.00
Cup & saucer, Sunrise & Tall Trees, Queen Anne shape 65.00
Cup & saucer, Thistle, 6-flute 55.00
Cup & saucer, Wild Anenome, Henley shape 54.00
Egg cup, Blue Rock, 6-flute, sm 49.00
Egg cup, Dainty White, 6-flute, sm 45.00
Egg cup, gr dots on Dainty White, 6-flute, lg 68.00
Egg cup, Harmony, sm 42.00
Egg cup set, Blue Rock, 4 sm cups on indented 6x6" tray 335.00
Egg cup set, Harmony, 4 sm ped cups on indented 6x6" tray 225.00
Gravy boat, Georgian, w/underplate 85.00
Gravy boat, Harebell, Oleander shape, w/underplate 140.00
Gravy boat, Heavenly Blue, 6-flute, w/underplate 185.00
Gravy boat, Rosebud, 6-flute, w/underplate 175.00
Horseradish container, Dainty Blue, 6-flute, w/lid & tray 150.00
Horseradish container, Harmony, w/lid & tray 70.00
Jam container, English Bouquet, 6-flute, w/lid & underplate 135.00
Jam container, Harebell, Oleander shape, w/lid 75.00
Kitchen reminder, Mabel Lucie Attwell vegetable people, 6x8" ...110.00
Lamp base, Harmony Drip Ware, 9" 175.00
Lamp base, Jazz circles on blk matt, 9" 135.00
Menu plaque, colonial couple decor, 5x7" w/support 110.00
Muffin, covered; Stocks, 6-flute, 9" 155.00
Mug, Dainty Mauve, 6-flute, 4¾" 85.00
Mug, Rambler Rose, 4¾" 55.00
Mug, Violet, 4¾" 50.00
Mustard container, Harmony, w/lid & underplate 85.00
Mustard container, Pansy Spray, w/lid & underplate 85.00

Mustard container, Regency, 6-flute, w/lid & underplate 95.00
Napkin ring, Begonia 60.00
Pitcher, Dainty Pink, 6-flute, 6½" 125.00
Pitcher, Harmony, 7" 97.00
Pitcher, Hunting Scene (Wileman), 7½" 225.00
Plate, Autumn Leaves, Queen Anne shape, 7½" 45.00
Plate, Begonia, 6-flute, 10½" 55.00
Plate, Begonia, 6-flute, 6" 28.00
Plate, Begonia, 6-flute, 8" 35.00
Plate, Dainty Blue, 6-flute, 10½" 78.00
Plate, Dainty Blue, 6-flute, 6" 30.00
Plate, Dainty Blue, 6-flute, 8" 40.00
Plate, Heraldic ware: Coronation of Elizabeth II, 6-flute, 8" 45.00
Plate, Indian Peony, 8" 35.00
Plate, Melody Chintz, Henley shape, 10½" 75.00
Plate, Melody Chintz, Henley shape, 6" 30.00
Plate, Melody Chintz, Oleander shape, 10½" 85.00
Plate, Melody Chintz, Oleander shape, 8" 50.00
Plate, Moire Antique, 8" 85.00
Plate, Rose Arches, Queen Anne shape, 8" 48.00
Plate, Rosebud, 6-flute, 9" 75.00
Plate, Vase of Flowers, Queen Anne shape, 10¼" 75.00
Platter, Begonia, 6-flute, 11x8½" 135.00
Platter, Dainty Pink, 6-flute, 12x10" 165.00
Platter, Drifting Leaves, 11x8½" 65.00
Platter, DuBarry, 16x14" 95.00
Platter, Forget-Me-Not, 6-flute, 14x12" 225.00
Platter, Pink Scroll, Queen Anne shape, 14x12" 185.00
Platter, Wildflower, 6-flute, 16½x14" 245.00
Pudding mold, geometric shape, 7½x5" 78.00
Relish, Bridal Rose, 6-flute, 5x8" 78.00
Relish, Old Sevres, fluted, 5x9" 45.00
Relish, Rose & Red Daisy, 6-flute, divided, 5x9" 95.00
Shakers, Dainty Blue, 6-flute, cylindrical, 3½", pr 85.00
Shakers, Drifting Leaves, pear shape, 4", pr 45.00
Shakers, Honeysuckle, 6-flute, pear shape, 3½", pr 85.00
Snack set, Rosebud, cup+indented 8" sq plate 75.00
Snack set, Windflowers, 6-flute, cup+indented 8" dia plate 85.00
Tankard, Festival of Empire Series, 7" 195.00
Tea & toast set, Forget-Me-Not, 6-flute, cup+6x9" tray 75.00
Tea & toast set, Heavenly Pink, 6-flute, cup+6x9" tray 85.00
Teapot, Begonia, Gainsborough shape, 6-cup 145.00
Teapot, Drifting Leaves, 8-cup 145.00
Teapot, Heavenly Blue, 6-flute, 8-cup 225.00
Teapot, Lily of the Valley, 6-flute, 2-cup 195.00
Teapot, Phlox, Regent shape, 6-cup 160.00
Teapot, Stocks, Gainsborough shape, 8-cup 155.00
Teapot, Wildflowers, 6-flute, 4-cup 195.00
Toast rack, Harmony, 5-bar 85.00
Toast rack, Shamrock, 3-bar 75.00
Toothpick holder, Dainty Blue, 6-flute 55.00
Tray, dresser; Cloisonne, 6x9" 75.00
Tray, triple; Regency, 6-flute, w/hdl, lg 195.00
Tray, triple; Thistle, 6-flute, w/hdl, sm 175.00
Tureen, Begonia, 6-flute, hdls, w/lid 395.00
Tureen, Blue Rock, Oleander shape, hdls, w/lid 350.00
Vase, Cloisonne, 6" 45.00
Vase, Harmony, cylindrical, 7½" 90.00
Vase, Indian Peony, 5½" 55.00

Silhouettes

Silhouette portraits were made by positioning the subject between a bright light and a sheet of white drawing paper. The resulting shadow was then traced and cut out, the paper mounted over a contrasting color and framed. The hollow-cut process was simplified by an invention called the Physiognotrace, a device that allowed tracing and cutting to be done in one operation. Experienced silhouette artists could do full-length figures, scenics, ships, or trains freehand. Some of the most famous of these artists were Charles Peale Polk, Charles Wilson Peale, William Bache, Doyle, Edouart, Chamberlain, Brown, and William King. Though not often seen, some silhouettes were completely painted or executed in wax. Examples listed here are hollow-cut unless noted.

Key:
bk — backing
c/p — cut and pasted
fl — full length

p — profile
wc — watercolor

Girl with flower basket and sprig, mounted on watercolor background, Auguste Edouart, Boston, 1842, later frame, 11½x9½", $1,430.00.

Lady, fl, brushed gilt/mc gouache details, sgn, fr, 15x11" 880.00
Lady, p, EX ink details, stains/tears, cloth bking, fr, 5x4" 60.00
Lady, p, hollow cut, blk cloth bking, G fr, 6¾x6⅜" 75.00
Lady, p, pen & ink detail, stain, fr, 5x4" 220.00
Lady w/book sits in chair, ink w/gilt, 1840s, fr, 14x10" 300.00
Lady w/wood-block printed torso, identified, 1831, 5½" 195.00
Man, fl, faint gold highlights, fr, 13x7" 275.00
Man, fl, wht brushed details, ink landscape, ornate fr, 16x14" 525.00
Man, p, cloth bking, in orig cb folding case, 5¾x4½" 400.00
Man, p, gold highlights, gilt fr, 5½x4½" 650.00
Man, p, hollow cut, inlaid fr, 4⅛x3½" 195.00
Man, p, hollow cut, molded fr, 3½x2¼" 175.00
Man, p, identified, dtd 1848, fr, 4⅝x4⅜" 200.00
Man, portrait, ink/wc, primitive, gilt fr, 6x5" 285.00
Man & lady, fl, hollow cut, modern, old ogee veneer fr, 10x12" ...65.00
Man & lady, p, hollow cut, poor paper, single fr: 8⅝x12" 165.00
Parents/2 children grouping, fl, ink wash details, fr, 12x16" 470.00

Silver

Coin Silver

The mark 'Coin Silver' was used after the 1830s to indicate items made with 900 parts of silver to every 1,000 parts of content.

C Stewart, NY; tablespoon, appl hdl 45.00
Crane & Co, St Louis; tablespoon, beaded edge, ca 1850 ....30.00
David Kinsey, spoon, eng hdl, 9", 3 for 90.00
Duhme & Co, spoon, bright cut hdl, 6", 7", pr 25.00
E&D Kinsey, ladle, rattail hdl, eng name, 9" 110.00
Goblet, cast garland swags, inscr, 3.8-t-oz, 5⅛" 205.00
H Bryant Jr, spoon, rattail hdl, 8½", pr 30.00

HB Standwood, water pitcher, eng grapevines/foliage, 13" **1,400.00**
I Bartlet, tablespoon **37.50**
Lincoln & Reed, Boston; sugar urn, inscr/dtd 1845, 16-t-oz **247.50**
McCarty & Hurlburt, teaspoon, rattail hdl, 5⅝", 6 for **80.00**
PB&C, tumbler, cast wreath, inscr/1841, 4.3-t-oz, 4⅛" **248.00**
R Strickland, teaspoon, 5¾" **15.00**
Rasch, vessel, Minerva-head hdl, basketweave band, 23.8-t-oz ..**685.00**
Robert & Wm Wilson, Phila; mug, autographed R Woods, 1825..**375.00**
Wm Tenney, NYC; tablespoon, Threaded Fiddle, 1840s **40.00**

Flatware

Silver flatware is being collected today either to replace missing pieces of heirloom sets or in lieu of buying new patterns, by those who admire and appreciate the style and quality of the older ware. Prices vary from dealer to dealer; some pieces are harder to find and are therefore more expensive. Items such as olive spoons, cream ladles, lemon forks, etc., once thought a necessary part of a silver service, may today be slow to sell; as a result, dealers may price them low and make up the difference on items that sell more readily. Many factors enter into evaluation. Popular patterns may be high due to demand though easily found, while scarce patterns may be passed over by collectors who find them difficult to reassemble. See also Tiffany, Silver.

Key:
FH — flat handle
gw — gold washed

HH — hollow handle
t-oz — troy ounce

Alhambra, egg spoon, Whiting 28.00
Antique Lily Engraved, berry spoon, Whiting, 9" 145.00
Antique Lily Engraved, oyster ladle, Whiting, 11½" 235.00
Arabesque, demitasse spoon, JR Wendt 20.00
Arabesque, ice cream spoon, JR Wendt 40.00
Arabesque, serving spoon, gw bowl, Whiting, sm 95.00
Arabesque, tablespoon, Whiting 50.00
Berkshire, cocktail fork 15.00
Bridal Rose, citrus spoon, Alvin 45.00
Bridal Rose, gravy ladle, Alvin 110.00
Buttercup, ice cream fork, Gorham 40.00
Buttercup, master butter spreader, Gorham, 7¾" 30.00
Buttercup, pierced nut spoon, Gorham 55.00
Byzantine, soup ladle, Wood & Hughes 450.00
Cambridge, ice cream fork, Gorham 32.00
Canterbury, bouillon spoon, Towle 30.00
Canterbury, short iced teaspoon, Towle 35.00
Celestial, sugar shell, Wood & Hughes 85.00
Chantilly, bouillon spoon, Gorham 22.00
Chantilly, carving set, Gorham, sm 65.00
Chantilly, demitasse spoon, Gorham 15.00
Chantilly, flat butter spreader, Gorham, ind 7.00
Chantilly, parfait spoon, Gorham, 8¼" 37.50
Chantilly, punch ladle, Gorham 350.00
Chantilly, salad fork, Gorham 20.00
Chantilly, sardine fork, Gorham 85.00
Chantilly, seafood fork, Gorham 22.00
Chantilly, sugar tongs, Gorham 50.00
Chantilly, teaspoon, Gorham 15.00
Charles II, preserve spoon, Dominick & Haff, 7¼" 80.00
Chrysanthemum, butter pat, Tiffany 135.00
Chrysanthemum, dinner fork, Tiffany 85.00
Colonial, salad fork, Tiffany 48.00
Colonial, sardine fork, Gorham 60.00
Cordova, master salt cellar, Towle 50.00
Cordova, olive spoon, Towle 55.00

Corinthian, dinner fork, Reed & Barton	30.00
Cupid, teaspoon, Reed & Barton	20.00
Diamond, pickle fork, Reed & Barton	25.00
Diamond, serving fork, Reed & Barton, 8¼"	85.00
Diamond, sugar shell, Reed & Barton	30.00
Diamond, sugar tongs, Reed & Barton	35.00
Dresden, cucumber server, Whiting	120.00
Eglantine, berry spoon, repousse strawberry, gw bowl, Gorham	425.00
Egyptian, mustard spoon, Whiting	77.00
Empress, cheese scoop, Gorham	70.00
English King, fish slice, Tiffany	350.00
Fairfax, demitasse spoon, Gorham	15.00
Fairfax, jelly server, Durgin	20.00
Fairfax, sardine serving fork, 5-tined, Durgin	125.00
Fairfax, sugar Tongs, Durgin	55.00
Federal Cotillion, olive spoon, Frank Smith	40.00
Fiddle Thread, bouillon spoon, Frank Smith	20.00
Fiorito, salad fork, Reed & Barton	50.00
Fiorito, teaspoon, Reed & Barton	25.00
Florence, soup ladle, Internat'l, 13½"	450.00
Florentine, asparagus fork, Gorham, 9"	300.00
Florentine, cold meat fork, Gorham, 8½"	175.00
Florentine, salad fork, Tiffany	50.00
Fontainebleau, master salt spoon, Gorham	40.00
Fontainebleau, sugar spoon, Gorham	65.00
Fontenac, cold meat fork, Internat'l	950.00
Fontenac, sugar spoon, Internat'l	55.00
Georgian, cheese scoop, Towle, sm	95.00
Grande Baroque, luncheon fork, Reed & Barton	30.00
Grande Baroque, teaspoon, Reed & Barton	22.00
Grecian, gravy ladle, Gorham	110.00
Grecian, ice cream server, Gorham	85.00
Gypsy, luncheon fork, Shiebler	25.00
Hamilton, olive spoon, Alvin	36.00
Heraldic, mustard ladle, Whiting	80.00
Holly, sardine fork, Tiffany, 5⅝"	235.00
Honeysuckle, sugar sifter, Whiting	125.00
Imperial Chrysanthemum, fried oyster server, Gorham, 8¼"	300.00
Imperial Chrysanthemum, ice cream knife, Gorham, 10⅝"	250.00
Imperial Chrysanthemum, oyster fork, Gorham	20.00
Imperial Chrysanthemum, sugar tongs, Durgin	85.00
Imperial Queen, ice cream slicer, Whiting, 10½"	250.00
Imperial Queen, luncheon fork, Whiting	25.00
Imperial Queen, master butter spreader, Whiting	55.00
Ivory, pea spoon, Whiting, 8¼"	350.00
Jack & Jill, spoon, Tiffany	175.00
King Edward, dinner fork, Whiting	45.00
King Edward, luncheon fork, Whiting	35.00
King Edward, tablespoon, Whiting	60.00
King George, ice tongs, Gorham, 6¾"	375.00
King George, sauce ladle, Gorham	60.00
La Marquise, citrus spoon, Reed & Barton	35.00
La Parisienne, berry spoon, gw, Reed & Barton, lg	230.00
La Parisienne, bouillon, Reed & Barton	25.00
La Parisienne, egg spoon, Reed & Barton	24.00
La Parisienne, luncheon knife, Reed & Barton	35.00
La Parisienne, punch ladle, twist hdl, Reed & Barton, 16¼"	350.00
La Parisienne, teaspoon, Reed & Barton	20.00
Labors of Cupid, strawberry fork, Dominick & Haff	80.00
Lancaster, cold meat fork, Gorham	65.00
Lancaster, gravy ladle, Gorham	85.00
Lancaster, master butter knife, Gorham	25.00
Lancaster, punch ladle, Gorham	350.00
Legato, butter spreader, flat hdl, Towle	18.00
Legato, cream soup, Towle	35.00
Legato, gravy ladle, Towle	65.00
Legato, luncheon fork, Towle	28.00
Legato, pickle fork, Towle	28.00
Legato, salad fork, Towle	30.00
Les Cinq Fleurs, master butter spreader, Reed & Barton	50.00
Les Cinq Fleurs, teaspoon, Reed & Barton	25.00
Les Six Fleurs, butter pick, Reed & Barton	85.00
Les Six Fleurs, cold meat fork, Reed & Barton	195.00
Les Six Fleurs, dinner fork, Reed & Barton	65.00
Lily, berry spoon, Whiting, lg	325.00
Lily, berry spoon, Whiting, sm	225.00
Lily, bouillon spoon, Whiting	40.00
Lily, butter fork, Whiting	85.00
Lily, dinner fork, Whiting	77.00
Lily, dinner knife, Whiting	78.00
Lily, ice cream slice, Whiting, 9¾"	350.00
Lily, luncheon fork, Whiting	48.00
Lily, preserve spoon, Whiting	135.00
Lily, sugar shell, Whiting	65.00
Lily, tablespoon, Whiting	85.00
Lily, teaspoon, Whiting, sm	19.00
Lily of Valley, demitasse spoon	20.00
Lily of Valley, luncheon knife	55.00
Louis XV, bonbon, pierced, Whiting	25.00
Louis XV, butter fork, Whiting	35.00
Louis XV, butter spreader, flat hdl, Whiting	15.00
Louis XV, cold meat fork, Whiting, 7½"	50.00
Louis XV, dessert spoon, Whiting	25.00
Louis XV, dinner fork, Whiting	25.00
Louis XV, egg spoon, gw, Whiting	48.00
Louis XV, olive spoon, Whiting	30.00
Louis XV, sardine fork, Whiting	35.00
Lucerne, sugar tongs, Wallace	40.00
Lucerne, teaspoon, Reed & Barton	18.00
Luxenburg, fish fork, Gorham	68.00
Madame Royal, salad serving spoon, Durgin	125.00
Majestic, cocktail fork, Alvin	30.00
Majestic, dinner knife, Alvin	28.00
Marechal Niel, ice or nut spoon, Durgin	220.00
Marguerite, cucumber server, Gorham	65.00
Marguerite, tablespoon, Wood & Hughes	45.00
Marlborough, luncheon fork, Reed & Barton	20.00
Mary Chilton, teaspoon, Towle	10.00
Maryland, breakfast knife, Gorham	20.00
Maryland, sugar spoon, Gorham	35.00
Mazarin, cheese/jelly scoop, Dominick & Haff	65.00
Meadow Rose, master butter spreader, Towle	30.00
Meadow Rose, steak carving set, Towle	60.00
Medallion, dbl-lipped sauce ladle, Dominick & Haff	195.00
Medallion, sardine fork, Gorham	185.00
Medallion, teaspoon, Wood & Hughes	30.00
Milan, ice cream knife, Gorham, 9⅝"	100.00
Minuet, cucumber server, Internat'l	40.00
Minuet, poultry shears, Internat'l	60.00
Mt Vernon, horseradish spoon, Lunt	65.00
Murillo, teaspoon, Wood & Hughes	20.00
Mythologique, pie fork, Gorham	110.00
Mythologique, serving fork, Gorham, 8⅞"	195.00
New Art, berry spoon, Durgin, heavy, lg	350.00
New Queens, tablespoon, Gorham	50.00
Newcastle, olive spoon, Gorham, 8¼"	35.00
Nuremberg, egg spoon, Alvin	25.00
Old Colonial, dessert spoon, Towle	30.00

Old Colonial, luncheon fork, Towle 30.00
Old English, pastry fork, Towle 25.00
Old Medici, tablespoon, Gorham 65.00
Old Medici, teaspoon, Gorham 25.00
Old Newbury, beef fork, Towle, lg 60.00
Old Newbury, bouillon ladle, Towle 160.00
Old Newbury, butter spade, Towle 70.00
Old Newbury, cocktail fork, Towle 20.00
Old Newbury, sauce ladle, Towle 40.00
Old Orange Blossom, berry spoon, Alvin, sm 110.00
Old Orange Blossom, demitasse spoon, Alvin 30.00
Old Orange Blossom, seafood fork, Alvin 25.00
Olympian, berry spoon, Tiffany, 9⅛" 325.00
Orange Blossom, cold meat fork, Alvin 165.00
Orange Blossom, demitasse spoon, Alvin 22.00
Palm, chocolate ladle, Gorham 135.00
Pansy, butter spreader, flat hdl, Internat'l 20.00
Pansy, dinner fork, Internat'l 28.00
Paul Revere, gravy ladle, Towle 55.00
Paul Revere, lettuce fork, Towle 85.00
Paul Revere, preserve server, Towle 45.00
Persian, fish server, eng, Tiffany, 11" 38.00
Persian, ice cream spoon, Tiffany 80.00
Persian, tablespoon, Tiffany 100.00
Plymouth, soup ladle, Gorham, lg 250.00
Pointed Antique, luncheon fork, Reed & Barton 28.00
Pointed Antique, salad fork, Reed & Barton 33.00
Pointed Antique, tablespoon, Reed & Barton 75.00
Pomona, ice cream spoon, Towle 30.00
Pompadour, dinner fork, Whiting 35.00
Prelude, butter spreader, flat hdl, Internat'l 18.00
Radiant, dinner fork, Whiting 35.00
Radiant, seafood fork, Whiting 23.00
Radiant, soup ladle, gw bowl, Whiting, 14" 425.00
Radiant, teaspoon, Whiting 20.00
Renaissance, citrus spoon, Dominick & Haff 45.00
Renaissance, cream ladle, Dominick & Haff 195.00
Renaissance, soup ladle, Dominick & Haff, 14½" 450.00
Repousse, ice tongs, Kirk 200.00
Repousse, lettuce fork, Kirk 65.00
Repousse, pie server Kirk 145.00
Richelieu, bouillon, Tiffany 35.00
Richelieu, sugar sifter, Tiffany, 5¾" 225.00
Rococo, berry spoon, Dominick & Haff 75.00
Rococo, mustard ladle, Dominick & Haff 50.00
Rose Point, bowl, Wallace, 10" 195.00
Rose Point, grapefruit, Wallace 18.00
Rose Point, iced teaspoon, Towle 22.50
Rosette, master butter spreader, Gorham, 7¾" 35.00
Sandringham, demitasse spoon, Shiebler 20.00
Sandringham, oyster server, gw, Reed & Barton 400.00
Sandringham, pie knife, Shiebler 185.00
Saratoga, coffee spoon, Tiffany 37.50
Saratoga, fish knife, flat hdl, Tiffany 110.00
Seville, ice cream fork, Towle 25.00
Shell & Thread, ice cream spoon, Tiffany 80.00
St Cloud, dessert spoon, Gorham 25.00
St Cloud, soup ladle, gw bowl, Gorham 500.00
St Cloud, teaspoon, Gorham 25.00
St Dunstan Chased, fish fork, Gorham 30.00
St Dunstan Chased, fish knife, HH, Gorham 50.00
Strasbourg, ice cream spoon, Gorham 28.00
Strasbourg, luncheon fork, Gorham 18.00
Strasbourg, master salt spoon, Gorham 35.00

Venetian, fish knife, flat hdl, Wood & Hughes 40.00

Versailles, flatware service, Gorham, 130 pieces totalling 163 troy ounces of weighable silver, $4,400.00.

Versailles, egg spoon, Gorham 20.00
Versailles, ice cream fork, Gorham 40.00
Viking, sugar tongs, Alvin, 3¾" 35.00
Vintage, cream soup 12.00
Vintage, dinner fork 16.00
Vintage, dinner knife, HH 18.00
Vintage, individual butter spreader 14.00
Vintage, luncheon fork, HH 12.00
Vintage, luncheon knife, HH 14.00
Vintage, salad fork 24.00
Violet, dinner fork, Wallace 32.00
Violet, luncheon fork, Whiting 25.00
Violet, soup ladle, Wallace 350.00
Violet, teaspoon, Towle 22.50
Watteau, gravy ladle, Durgin 90.00
Watteau, ice cream spoon, Durgin 35.00
Watteau, master salt spoon, Durgin 40.00
Watteau, sugar shell, Durgin 40.00
Wave Edge, conch berry spoon, Tiffany, 9⅜" 400.00
Waverly, horseradish spoon, Wallace 45.00
Waverly, sardine tongs, Wallace 120.00
Waverly, sugar sifter, Wallace 250.00
Winthrop, ice cream slice, Tiffany, 11⅜" 375.00
Zephyr, gravy ladle, Wood & Hughes 50.00

Hollow Ware

Until the middle of the 19th century, the silverware produced in America was custom made on order of the buyer directly from the silversmith. With the rise of industrialization, factories sprung up that manufactured silverware for retailers who often added their trademark to the ware. Silver ore was mined in abundance, and demand spurred production. Changes in style occurred at the whim of fashion. Repousse decoration (relief work) became popular about 1885, reflecting the ostentatious preference of the Victorian era. Later in the century, Greek, Etruscan, and several classic styles found favor. Today the Art Deco styles of this century are very popular with collectors. In the listings that follow, manufacturer's name or trademark is noted first; in lieu of that information, listings are by country. Weight is given in troy ounces. See also Tiffany, Silver.

AE Warner, sugar basket, repousse, base dent, 4½" 330.00
Apollo, tazza, 4-post std, stepped rnd base, 6x10½" 385.00
Arthur Stone, bowl, lt hammering, rnd ft, 3¼x7¼" 600.00
Arthur Stone, tray, rnded sq, 12½" 825.00
Bailey & Co, vase, Greek Key border, w/lid, 8" 400.00
Cartier, tray, cast foliage rim, 30-t-oz, 14" 415.00
Cellini Craft Sterling, bowl, oval quatrefoil, ftd, 6.6-t-oz 105.00
Duhme, tea set, 109-t-oz, 5-pc 1,925.00
Durgin, tea/coffee set, Colonial Revival, 5-pc, 87-t-oz, EX 1,400.00
EA Tyler New Orleans, presentation mug, 5-t-oz, 3⅝" 1,875.00
Edward Oakes, porringer, hammered, appl leaves on hdl, 4½" 935.00
Exemplar, bowl, trifid scroll ft, scalloped, 3.0-t-oz, 5⅞" 85.00
Frank Smith, compote, rtcl/shaped rim, emb leaves, 10" 825.00
G Hindmarsh, salver, scrolled border/ft, eng armorial, 16" 2,500.00
Geo Jensen, bowl, Blossom, open stem of leaves/berries, 8" H ...2,100.00
Geo Jensen, bowl, openwork blossoms set on rim, 8" L 3,200.00
Geo Jensen, bowl, plain, leaf/seed openwork base, #19A, 7" ...2,200.00
Geo Jensen, cigarette box, bud finial w/in dmn on lid, 9" 2,300.00
Geo Jensen, creamer/sugar, leaf/bead hdls, by Neilsen, 4½" 1,600.00
Geo Jensen, cruet stand, rtcl foliate sides, 2 bottles, 9" 9,200.00
Geo Jensen, fish platter, rtcl blossom hdls, 13½" L 5,700.00
Geo Jensen, pitcher, can neck, ebony/silver hdl, 7" 1,150.00
Geo Jensen, pitcher, Grape, raised ft, ebony hdl, 9½" 5,700.00
Geo Jensen, pitcher, baluster w/rope-twist ft rim, 9" 3,200.00
Geo Jensen, salad serving fork & spoon, Acorn, 5-t-oz 525.00
Geo Jensen, sugar castor, grapevine eng, 7" 2,100.00
Geo Jensen, tea/coffee set, plain/leaves base, 5-pc, 106-t-oz 9,350.00
Geo Jensen, tray, scallop at ea corner chased w/floral, 9" 2,500.00
Geo Jensen, vegetable dish, beaded border, reed finial, 11" 3,000.00
Gorham, compote, Medallion, oval w/loop hdls, 10" L 700.00
Gorham, creamer & sugar bowl, 7.5-t-oz 85.00
Gorham, pitcher, Greek Revival motif, slight dent, 10" 825.00
Gorham, sauce boat, baluster w/acanthus leaf border, 4½" 275.00
Gorham, tea service, oval shapes, 3-pc, 39-t-oz 500.00
Gorham, tea/coffee set, flattened baluster from, 5-pc, 80-t-oz ...1,000.00
Gorham, tray, molded border, 29-t-oz, 14" 240.00
Gorham, tray, oval w/molded rim, 25" L 1,200.00
Gorham, vase, hammered w/appl & eng prunus, trumpet form, 15" .365.00

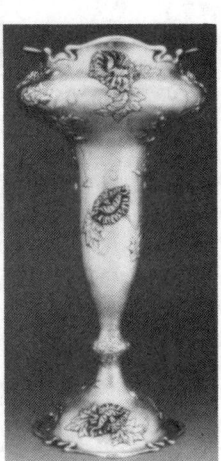

Graff, Washbourne & Dunn, Art Nouveau vase, flared top with raised serpentine rim and repousse poppies on dome foot, 120 troy ounces, 24", $6,600.00.

Grogan Co, pitcher, floral tooling, 30-t-oz 385.00
Hawksworth-Erye & Co, candlesticks, stepped base, 6", pr 500.00
Internat'l, punch bowl, rtcl bellflower rims, 6", +tray 1,700.00
Internat'l, tea set, Prelude, 47-t-oz, 3-pc 525.00
Ivar Petersen, vegetable dish, rtcl leaf/grape finial, 10" 1,800.00
JA/JS, sugar castor, quatrefoil, 1884-85, 9" 200.00
Jacobi, chamberstick, repousse, 5½" dia 385.00

Jacobi & Jenkins, platter, repousse, oval, 14" 330.00
Jas Young, teapot, oval cylinder w/eng arms, Geo III, 5" 6,600.00
Karl Lenione, tray, hammered, banded rim, 12" 495.00
Kirk, goblet, w/monogram, 6¼", set of 8 ....800.00
Kirk, plate, floral repousse rim, 12½-t-oz, 20" 300.00
Kirk & Son, bowl, repousse, rnd w/monogram, 9" 200.00
Kirk Sterling, bowl, ftd, 2.3-t-oz, 4x9¼" 105.00
London hallmks, bowl, flared rim, 1763, 4½-t-oz 275.00
London hallmks, shakers, cobalt glass inserts, 1915, 3", pr 75.00
R&S Hennell, tea set, eng design/crest, 4-pc, 37-t-oz 825.00
Redlich, dish, leaf form w/vine hdls, 9", pr 770.00
Reed & Barton, bowl, Francis I, 11" dia 990.00
Robert & Wm Wilson, porringer, ca 1825-46, 6-t-oz, 1¾" 385.00
Shreve Crump & Low, candlesticks, Queen Anne, 7", pr 550.00
SM&Co, dish, Rococo-style relief, 1894-95, 6" L, pr 495.00
T Starr, bowl, shaped rim chased/rtcl w/carnations, 11" 660.00
Theo Barr, tea/coffee set, scalloped, paw ft, 6-pc, 126-t-oz 1,900.00
Towle, hot water kettle on stand, 40-t-oz, 13" 400.00
Tuttle, tea/coffee set, globular w/shell ft, 6-pc, 83-t-oz 1,650.00
W Hutton & Son, candlesticks, stop flutes, columnar, 5½", pr ...600.00
Wallace, coffeepot, Princess Mary, 20.7-t-oz, 10½" 248.00
Wallace, tray, roll; octagonal, plain, 19-t-oz, 12" 200.00
Watson, bride's basket, rtcl foliage, 14" 300.00
Whiting, bread tray, Nouveau irises, 14" L 400.00
Wood & Hughes, bowl, as leaf w/appl grapevines at rim, 13" ..6,000.00
800 mk, tea set, animal head spouts/foliage/Rococo, 68-t-oz ...1,375.00

Silver Overlay

The silver overlay glass made during the 1800s was decorated with a cut-out pattern of sterling silver applied to the surface of the ware.

Basket, cranberry w/lattice o/l, silver hdl, 5½x6" 600.00
Bottle, scent; emerald w/abstract scroll o/l, mk/#d, 6x4" 600.00
Bud vase, gr w/stylized floral o/l, cylindrical, 7" 100.00
Cruet, gr cut to clear w/floral & scroll o/l, mk Alvin, 7" 750.00
Decanter, cranberry cut to clear w/roses o/l, Alvin/#d, 13" 1,850.00
Flask, clear w/scroll o/l, hinged lid, flattened, 5" 275.00
Inkwell, bright gr w/wild roses, scrolls & lattice o/l, 4x3" 650.00
Rose bowl, emerald w/allover rose & scroll o/l, mk Alvin 725.00
Vase, blk satin w/cattail & flower o/l, att Cambridge, 5½" 300.00
Vase, bright bl, wht int w/simple flower o/l, bulbous, 4½" 110.00
Vase, clear w/Deco roses o/l, silver top/base band, 12x7" 575.00
Vase, cranberry w/mums, leaves & stems o/l, 12½x5" 300.00
Vase, cranberry w/roses & monogram crests o/l, Alvin, 4½" 150.00
Vase, emerald w/carnation & arch o/l, disk ft, 8x3" 600.00
Vase, emerald w/floral o/l, 2½x3" 275.00
Vase, turq w/floral & scroll o/l, mk Fine 900/1000, 2¾" 500.00

Silverplate

Silverplated hollow ware is fast becoming the focus of attention for many of today's collectors. See also Railroadiana, Silverplate.

Key: gw — gold wash

Flatware

Alhambra, cocktail fork 8.00
Alhambra, fruit knife 9.00
Alhambra, ladle, 10¾" 65.00
Ambassador, cream soup 4.00

Ambassador, iced tea 6.50
Arbutus, salad fork 12.50
Argosy, ice cream fork 9.00
Avalon, luncheon fork 6.00
Avon, orange knife 15.00
Ballad, gravy ladle 15.00
Berkshire, cream ladle 24.00
Cardinal, dinner fork, Wallace 8.00
Cardinal, salad fork, Wallace 7.50
Carnation, cocktail fork 10.00
Carnation, dinner fork 12.00
Carnation, luncheon fork 10.00
Charter Oak, salad fork 30.00
Chatauqua, iced teaspoon 3.00
Chatsworth, berry spoon, gw 35.00
Columbia, crumber 45.00
Eternally Yours, pickle fork, Internat'l 12.00
Eternally Yours, 3-light candle holder 70.00
Fair Oak, salad fork 5.00
Flair, coffee spoon 7.50
Flair, dinner knife 8.50
Flair, slotted tablespoon 19.00
Floral, salad fork, Wallace 20.00
Floral, seafood fork, Wallace 14.00
Floral, teaspoon, Wallace 8.00
Grenoble, carving set, med sz, 3-pc 30.00
Grosvenor, bouillon 5.50
Grosvenor, fruit spoon 5.50
Grosvenor, pickle fork 8.00
Grosvenor, seafood 6.00
Holly, gravy boat 55.00
Holly, seafood fork 25.00
Holly, tomato server 85.00
Lady Hamilton, iced tea 6.00
Lido, tomato server 14.00
Lovely Lady, berry spoon, Holmes & Edwards, lg 10.00
Lovely Lady, cocktail fork, Holmes & Edwards 7.00
Lovely Lady, salad fork, Holmes & Edwards 9.00
Marcella, pastry fork 12.50
Modern Baroque, pickle fork, Internat'l 10.00
Monarch (1889), sugar tongs 25.00
Nenuphar, ladle, 10" 60.00
New Century, berry spoon, gw 34.00
New Century, pie server 35.00
Old Colony, gravy ladle 20.00
Old Colony, pickle fork, long hdl 14.00
Oxford, gravy ladle 15.00
Patrician, bouillon 6.00
Poppy, cream ladle 18.00
Poppy, gravy ladle 20.00
Queen Bess, teapot 55.00
Queen Bess, tray, lg 85.00
Rex (1894), berry spoon 30.00
Roman (1884), punch ladle 175.00
Rondel, pastry fork 9.00
Sheraton, fruit spoon 5.50
Sheraton, seafood 5.50
Starlight B, cold meat fork, Internat'l 12.00
Vintage, cold meat fork, 8¾" 40.00
Vintage, demitasse cream ladle 30.00
Vintage, fruit spoon 15.00
Vintage, gravy ladle 20.00
Vintage, oyster ladle, 12¼" 85.00
Vintage, serving fork 35.00

Vintage, twisted butter knife 13.00
Wildwood, seafood 6.50
Yale (1894), pie server 45.00
Yale (1894), salad serving fork 55.00

Hollow Ware

Bowl, allover emb foliage, squirrel on rim, Derby, 9" 330.00
Bowl, console, rtcl rim, gadrooned edge, 12¼" 45.00
Bowl, down-trn rim, ca 1920, Reed & Barton, 13" 45.00
Bowl, lg scrolling foliate hdls, paw ft, cobalt liner, 20" 200.00
Butter dish, ornate, ped ft, revolves, Simpson, Hall & Miller 350.00
Candlesticks, acanthus socket, rtcl bobeche, 11", pr 375.00
Candlesticks, fluted shafts, Continental, 1800s, 8½", pr 150.00
Candlesticks, Wm IV style, 1800s, 12½", pr 660.00
Chip & dip, eng platter w/gadrooned attached cup, 12" 45.00
Coffeepot, demitasse; vase shape eng w/florals, Barbour, 8¾" 180.00
Coffeepot, Fairmont Hotel, Reed & Barton 38.00
Compote, fruit; ribbed base, griffin/floral eng, hdls, 1850s 150.00
Entree dish, gadrooned finial, eng crest, French, 8" 200.00
Epergne, stem/4 scroll arms w/foliage, cut glass bowl, 21" 1,100.00
Match holder, 2 cherubs support holder, Rogers, Smith & Co ...395.00
Nut bowl, squirrel on branch hdl, Reed & Barton 395.00
Pitcher, classical style, lg lip/scroll hdl, rnd base, 10" 380.00
Pitcher, eng floral band around rim, garlands on sides, 8" 150.00
Pitcher, ice water; baluster w/lg hdl, lid, Wilcox, 13" 125.00

Tazza, fluted brim with applied frog on a stem support over a circular foot, Derby, ca 1880s, 5¾x7", $200.00.

Tazza, glass, base: Indians/buffalo hunt, Reed & Barton, 9" 175.00
Tea set, grape design, 3-pc 275.00
Tea urn, neoclassical style, Wm Hutton & Sons, 1920s 220.00
Teapot, goat finial, eng fishing scene, Waters & Thorp 180.00
Tray, eng crest, oval, Mapin & Webb, 23½" 200.00
Trophy, figural dog & Xd rifles, Simpson, Hall & Miller 450.00
Tureen, bowl form, cylinder legs, C Dresser, 1880s, 8" W 3,200.00
Tureen, rnd w/symetrical stepped hdls, cylinder finial, 7" 460.00
Tureen, soup; Roman soldier band, steer-head hdls, 1800s, 16" ..475.00

Sheffield

Bowl, ruffled floral edge, rtcl body, 4x11" 50.00
Bowl, vegetable; cast vintage rim, lion & unicorn mk, 11¼" 40.00
Bowl, vegetable; interchangable liner & lid, 14" 310.00
Candle snuffer & tray, worn plating on tray, EX 350.00
Candlesticks, classical column design, 5¼", pr 95.00
Candlesticks, Corinthian column design, 10½", pr 375.00
Candlesticks, telescoping style, EX detail, 8", 4 for 770.00
Hot water urn, Geo II, vasiform w/hdls, 18", EX 350.00
Punch bowl, 12¾", +12 cups 235.00
Tea caddy, tooled rose details, lt wear, 5" 120.00
Tea set, classical bright-cut detail, 4-pc 125.00
Tea set, 3-pc, 8½" 110.00

Tray, tea; classical openwork, garland gallery, hdls, 19¾" 220.00
Urn, hot water; claw ft, ball finial, 1800s, 12½" 150.00

Silver Resist

The process for decorating pottery with the silver-resist method involved first coating the design or that portion of the pattern that was to be left unsilvered with a water-soluble solution. The lustre was applied to the entire surface of the vessel and allowed to dry. Before the final firing, the surface was washed, removing only the silver from the coated areas. This type of ware was produced early in the 1800s by many English potteries, Wedgwood included.

Bowl, vintage decor, lt wear, 4¼x9¼" 165.00
Creamer, bird in tree, lt wear, 4⅝" 180.00
Pitcher, birds & flowers, 6⅝", VG 100.00
Pitcher, floral, wear/flakes, 6¼" 165.00
Pitcher, vintage & farmer's arms, wear, 5½" 140.00

Sinclaire

In 1904 H.P. Sinclaire and Company was founded in Corning, New York. For the first sixteen years of production, Sinclaire used blanks from other glassworks for his cut and engraved designs. In 1920 he established his own glass-blowing factory in Bath, New York. His most popular designs utilize fruits, flowers, and other forms from nature. Most of Sinclaire's glass is unmarked; items that are carry his logo: an 'S' within a wreath with two shields.

Basket, cut cornflowers, 6" dia 160.00
Bowl, cranberry rim cut w/leaves & berries, hex std, 13" dia 475.00
Bowl, flute & panel border, tricornered, 9" 150.00
Candlesticks, amber, tulip cups, 10-prism bobeche, 9" 295.00
Jam jar, florals/leaves cutting, 3½" 100.00
Plate, Adam, 5¾" 150.00
Tray, bread; frosted dahlias intaglio, dotted rim, 13½x6" 350.00
Vase, eng florals, mk, 12½" 105.00
Vase, ribbed cutting, rose etching at top, 12½" 200.00

Sitzendorf

The Sitzendorf factory began operations in East Germany in the mid-1800s, adopting the name of the city as the name of their company. They produced fine porcelain groups, figurines, etc., in much the same style and quality as Meissen and the Dresden factories. Much of their ware was marked with a crown over the letter 'S' and a horizontal line with two slash marks.

Figurine, 8 figures surrounding piano, each with enameling, gold decoration and lace trim, 19¼" long, $770.00.

Candelabra, 2-light, floral branches, cherubs base, 13½", pr 400.00
Candelabra, 5-light, appl flowers, 2 cherubs, 21", pr 1,250.00

Compote, cherub support, rtcl lattice bowl w/mc roses, 17" 900.00
Compote, rtcl, tree trunk std w/maid+2 cherubs, 20" 450.00
Figurine, apple pickers, boy & girl w/dog, 9½x7" 650.00
Figurine, boy & girl w/lambs, 10", pr 395.00
Figurine, gardener w/watering can, lady w/flowers, 9", pr 450.00
Figurine, 3 maids in appl/pnt floral chariot w/griffins, 15" 900.00
Inkstand, Rococo scrolls, appl florals, 2 wells, 9½" 425.00
Mirror, cupids relief, appl flowers, easel bk, ball ft, 12" 385.00
Vase, maidens, Kauffmann, floral panels, Voigt, 3-hdl, 8" 225.00

Slag Glass

Slag glass is a marbleized opaque glassware made by several companies from about 1870 until the turn of the century. It is usually found in purple or caramel (see Chocolate Glass), though other colors were also made. Pink is rare and very expensive.

Blue, basket, cherries/leaves in relief, crimped/ruffled, 9" 75.00
Blue, humidor, drum shape, cap-shaped finial, 6½x5¼" 250.00
Pink, Invt Fan & Feather, butter dish, ftd, 6x8" 1,200.00
Pink, Invt Fan & Feather, creamer & sugar bowl, 4½", 6½" 1,200.00
Pink, Invt Fan & Feather, cruet 1,400.00
Pink, Invt Fan & Feather, jelly compote 550.00
Pink, Invt Fan & Feather, pitcher, water 1,500.00
Pink, Invt Fan & Feather, punch cup 300.00
Pink, Invt Fan & Feather, sauce dish, 4" 265.00
Pink, Invt Fan & Feather, shakers, rare, pr 1,200.00
Pink, Invt Fan & Feather, spooner 375.00
Pink, Invt Fan & Feather, toothpick holder 650.00
Pink, Invt Fan & Feather, tumbler 400.00
Purple, Beads & Bark, vase, novelty 50.00
Purple, Fluted Shell, bowl, pie-crust rim, 8½" 75.00
Purple, Jenny Lind, compote, 7¾x8½" 165.00
Purple, Oval Medallion, spooner 85.00
Purple, Panel & Waffle mold, compote, w/lid, 8x8" 80.00
Purple, plate, lattice edge, 13" 85.00
Purple, Scroll w/Acanthus, creamer & sugar bowl 100.00
Purple, vase, paneled sides, 8" 90.00
Red, vase, mc/gold decor at top, 7" 60.00

SMF (Schramberg/Wheelock Black Forest)

Since 1918 the Schramberger Majolica Factory in Schramberg, Wurttemberg, Germany, has produced majolica, stoneware, and porcelain. Various marks were used (Schramberg, and Wheelock 'Black Forest' Hand Painted Pottery), but the common link is the SMF insignia. They produced a number of hand-painted pieces, but those of most interest to collectors are painted in gaudy colors in bizarre designs on equally bizarre shapes. As a result it is often referred to as the 'poor man's Clarice Cliff.' Collectors will note that most pieces bear an incised mold number, a painter's number, and the SMF mark. Of special note are the pieces marked Gobelin, followed by a number (or simply G and the number). Gobelin wares have a gray background with as many as ten colors used in the design. The number denotes particular color combinations. For example, Gobelin 3 pieces will be painted in green and orange leaves and yellow eyes, along with other colors specific to that design. Expect to find Gobelin-numbered pottery in various unusual shapes. It is not uncommon to find pieces that are chipped, and a perfect piece should be valued by its owner. Our advisor for this category is Ralph Winslow; he is listed in the Directory under Kansas.

Ashtray, Deco style, G-5, SMF Wheelock 48.00
Basket, G-5, SMF-W, #2706 ....40.00

Boat, 4-color, SMF, #2390 ....45.00
Bowl, G-2, Mepoco Ware 45.00
Candle holder, G-2, SMF-W, #6932 ....45.00
Inkwell, 3-color, G-3, SMF-W 50.00
Planter, G-3, SMF-W, 3118 ....55.00
Plate/plaque, leaves, G-6, SMF-W 48.00
Vase, blk & orange leaves, SMF, #2822 ....85.00
Vase, floral, 3-color, SMF, 6½" 35.00
Vase, floral, 4-color, SMF, #2604 ....42.00
Vase, G-3, SMF, 9" 52.00
Vase, gray w/blk hdls, G-4, 9" 55.00
Vase, 4-color, SMF, 7½", pr 45.00
Vase, 8-color, bulbous, G-1, 7" 65.00

Smith Bros.

Alfred and Harry Smith founded their glassmaking firm in New Bedford, Massachusetts. They had been formerly associated with the Mt. Washington Glass Works, working there from 1871 to 1875 to aid in establishing a decorating department. Smith glass is valued for its excellent enameled decoration on satin or opalescent glass. Pieces were often marked with a lion in a red shield. Our advisors for this category are Betty and Clarence Maier; they are listed in the Directory under Pennsylvania.

Biscuit jar, daisies ea side, emb rim, sq, 5½" W 300.00
Biscuit jar, daisies on cream, SP trim, rampant lion mk, 7" 375.00
Biscuit jar, Persian-style jeweled circles & fans, rare 995.00
Bowl, pansies on off-wht, gold beaded rim, melon ribs, 2x3½" ...250.00
Box, ivy leaves/emb gold on ivory, melon ribs, 5½" dia 375.00
Box, sm bl floral on wht, melon ribs, 5½" dia 250.00
Creamer & sugar w/lid, gold floral/bl swirls, melon ribs, 4" 500.00
Jar, florals & berries, mc on lt bl mottle, melon ribs, 3¼" 365.00
Plate, Santa Maria, mc on bl sea, World's Fair 1893, 7¾" 965.00
Vase, bird on branch on salmon pk, 5⅞x2⅛" 175.00
Vase, birds on floral limb, cone shape, 6" 385.00
Vase, floral, bl w/gold, rampant lion mk, 6⅞" 550.00
Vase, lily, wht w/bl-gr & blk leaves on pk, ca 1870s, 7" 185.00
Vase, violets, pinched, beaded rim, 4½" 395.00
Vase, 2 circles, 1 w/2 red birds, widens toward base, 6" 385.00

Snow Babies

During the last quarter of the 19th century, snow babies — little figurals in white snowsuits — originated in Germany. They were made of sugar candy and were often used as decorations for Christmas cakes. Later on they were made of marzipan, a confection of crushed almonds, sugar, and egg whites. Eventually porcelain manufacturers began making them in bisque. They were popular until WWII. These tiny bisque figures range in size from just over 1" up to 7" tall. Quality German pieces bring very respectable prices on the market today. Beware of reproductions. Our advisor for this category is Linda Vines; she is listed in the Directory under New Jersey.

Babies, 2 holding Santa's hands, Germany, 2" 125.00
Babies, 2 sliding down brick wall, Germany, 2½" 125.00
Baby, jtd at shoulders & hips, Germany, 3½" 200.00
Baby, sitting or standing, Germany, 1" 40.00
Baby hiding under iceberg, snow bear on top, Germany, 2" 125.00
Baby hugging brn bear, Germany, 2" 110.00
Baby in sled pulled by huskies, Germany, 3" 150.00
Baby inside igloo, Santa on top, Germany, 2½" 150.00
Baby inside igloo, Santa on top, Japan, 2½" 65.00

Baby with red ball, Germany, 2", $110.00. (Photo courtesy of Linda L. Vines.)

Baby playing musical instrument, Germany, 2" 90.00
Baby riding on snow bear, Germany, 2½" 125.00
Baby sitting, fine quality, snowed hands & ft, Germany, 2" 125.00
Baby standing, googly-eyed, oversz head, open bk, Germany, 3¾" .175.00
Baby standing on lg snowball, Japan, 2½" 25.00
Baby w/seal & red ball, Germany, 2" 110.00
Baby w/seal & red ball, recent, B Shackman, unmk, 2" 25.00
Carollers, 3 w/snow hats & lantern on snow base, Germany, 2" ...90.00
Child, no-snow boy or girl, pushing lg snowball, Germany, 2" 90.00
Child on sled, snow hat & sweater, pastel pants, Germany, 2" 90.00
Santa atop gray elephant, Germany, 2½" 165.00
Santa in boat by snow-topped lighthouse, Germany, 3" 110.00
Santa in silver car, toys in bk, Germany, 1½" 90.00
Snow bear standing or walking, Germany, 2½" 75.00
Snow dog, standing or recumbent, Germany, 3½" 90.00
Snow mother pushing twins in red carriage-sled, Germany, 2¼" ..165.00
Snow-topped house, Santa on top, Germany, 3" 110.00
Snowman w/top hat & cane, looks like WC Fields, Japan, 1½" 30.00

Snuff Boxes

As early as the 17th century, the Chinese began using snuff. By the early 19th century, the practice had spread to Europe and America. It was used by both the gentlemen and the ladies alike, and expensive snuff boxes and bottles were the earmark of the genteel. Some were of silver or gold set with precious stones or pearls, while others contained music boxes. In the following listings, the dimension noted is length. See also Orientalia, Snuff Bottles.

Castle HP on wood, Germany, 1890s, 4x2¼" 150.00
Chinese ivory, gourd w/flowers, 1930s, 3¼" 195.00
Enamel, figures in landscape, hinged lid, 1700s, 2⅝" 435.00
Horn w/ivory & wood inlays on top, 3⅜" 95.00
Papier-mache, HP girl's portrait, 3¾" dia, EX 165.00
Papier-mache shoe, blk lacquer w/floral, wire inlay, 5" 125.00
Papier-mache w/pnt eng of woman & parrot, 3" 95.00
Silver, Geo III, bright cut border w/monogram, 1790s, unmk 180.00
Silver, Geo III, vermeil int, sgn IB, ca 1800 ....325.00
Silver, sq form w/emb tavern scene, Continental 80.00
Silver w/enameling, lobed ends, 950 std, 2½-troy oz 265.00
Tortoise shell, lady's portrait on ivory, 1800s, 2¾" dia 325.00
Wooden shoe form, hinged lid, 2¾x8" 75.00

Soapstone

Soapstone is a soft talc in rock form with a smooth, greasy feel from whence comes its name. In colonial times it was extracted from out-croppings in large sections with hand saws, carted by oxen to mills, and fashioned into useful domestic articles such as footwarmers, cooking utensils, inkwells, etc. During the early 1800s, it was used to make heating stoves and kitchen sinks. Most familiar today are the carved vases, bookends, and boxes made in China during the Victorian era.

Censer, dragon-mask/ring hdls, dragon finial, 3-leg, 8"	150.00
Figure, Lohan w/dbl-gourd bottle, 1800s, 2"	80.00
Figure, old man w/walking staff, 10"	100.00
Foot warmer, oblong, heavy wire bail, EX	45.00
Seal, oxen, head bent down, brn, rstr, 2½"	165.00
Vase, daisies/leaves, vintage rim, blk soapstone base, 11"	80.00
Vase, dbl; brn, joined by floral cvg, 3x6"	110.00
Wax seal, foo dog, 12", pr	200.00

Soda Fountain Collectibles

As the neighborhood ice cream parlor becomes a thing of the past, soda fountain memorabilia from fancy backbars to ice cream advertising is becoming a popular field of collecting. One area of interest is the glassware used to serve the more elaborate ice cream concoctions. A sundae glass is familiar to us all, but there was also a 'lucky mondae' glass, narrow at the bottom and flaring to a top dimension equal to one scoop. There are footed banana split dishes and soda pop glasses with the name or logo of the beverage company painted on them.

Syrup dispensers, especially those from the teens, today command high prices. These had spherical or urn-shaped dispensers and carried names such as Jersey Creme, Buckeye, Cherry Smash, etc.

It is estimated that ice cream dippers may be found in approximately two hundred different styles — some bowl shaped or cylindrical, some for making ice cream sandwiches, and even a very rare heart-shaped dipper. (This one was used along with matching heart-shaped ice cream dishes.)

Glass straw holders are very collectible. Clear is the most common color, but they are also found in green and pink; some are made of frosted glass. Early examples were pattern molded; some had matching glass lids — these are the most desirable. Our advisors for this category are Joyce and Harold Screen; they are listed in the Directory under Maryland. See also Advertising.

Bottle, Cleary Root Beer, stoneware	45.00
Bottle holder, for rnd-bottom bottle	50.00
Bowl, syrup; Hire's Root Beer, Villeroy & Boch, 12x17½", NM	20,000.00
Box, Mother Goose straws, bright color, NM	20.00
Button, pin-bk; Arctic Ice Cream	20.00
Button, pin-bk; Tellings Ice Cream	20.00
Cone holder, clear glass, metal lid, NP base, 13½", EX	425.00
Cone holder, glass, emb cones on base, ind	25.00
Cup, Orange Crush, porc	300.00
Dipper, banana split; Gilchrist	365.00
Dipper, banana split; United	550.00
Dipper, Benedict, 1¾", EX in box	40.00
Dipper, Dover Slicer, single trigger	350.00
Dipper, Gilchrist #31, NP brass, wood hdl	25.00
Dipper, Gilchrist #33, 2" bowl, EX	100.00
Dipper, Guaranteed Disher, 'worm' drive	400.00
Dipper, heart shape	3,000.00
Dipper, Indestructo #4, sz 8-30	25.00
Dipper, Keiner-Williams Conical, Pat 1905	20.00
Dipper, Pi-Alamoder	700.00
Dipper, Safe-T Cone, aluminum, 7½"	24.00
Dipper, sandwich; Meyers, curved	175.00

Dish, banana split; frosted, flat	5.00
Dish, banana split; pk, ftd	60.00
Dish, ice cream; heart shape, ftd	400.00
Dispenser, Cardinal Cherry, VG on wrought iron stand, 58"	500.00
Dispenser, Cherry Julep, red & wht, no pump, 11", EX	400.00
Dispenser, Concord Punch, frosted glass, 19", VG	150.00
Dispenser, Dr Pepper, urn shape, glass holder, 18x9", G	10,000.00
Dispenser, Eskimo Pie, Magic Jar, glass lined, NPCI ft, 15½"	1,000.00
Dispenser, Grape Kola, gold lettering, rpl lid, 19x9", VG	900.00
Dispenser, Green River, milk glass, metal base, 14", G	200.00

Dispenser, Hires, hourglass shape with original pump, 15x7", EX, $425.00.

Dispenser, Hires, spigot type, complete, 11¼"	800.00
Dispenser, Hires, w/pump, 12½", G	275.00
Dispenser, iced tea; clear glass, NP spigot, pnt hdl, 19", EX	100.00
Dispenser, Jersey Creme, red & gr w/gold, no pump, 11¾", G	425.00
Dispenser, Jersey Creme, red & gr w/gold, w/pump, 15", VG	550.00
Dispenser, Liberty Root Beer, spigot, decals, 27x16" dia, G	975.00
Dispenser, Mission Grapefruit, gr crackle, chromed base, EX	225.00
Dispenser, Prall's Root Beer, frosted glass, 19½", G	210.00
Dispenser, Texberry, bbl shape, worn silver bands, 11¾", G	80.00
Dispenser, Ward's Lemon Crush, lemon form, no pump, 11", VG	450.00
Dispenser, Ward's Lemon Crush, lemon form, rpl pump, EX	500.00
Dispenser, Ward's Lemon Crush, lemon form, w/pump, 11", EX	800.00
Dispenser, Ward's Lime Crush, lime form, rpl pump, 10", VG	800.00
Dispenser, Ward's Orange Crush, orange form, no pump, 10", G	400.00
Dispenser, Ward's Orange Crush, orange form, orig pump, 12", EX	600.00
Fan, hand held, fountain scenes, pre-1290	27.50
Fan, hand held, 1920-40	20.00
Fan, hand held, 1940 on	7.50
Flavor board, ca 1900	425.00
Flavor board, rvpt, 1930s	150.00
Fountain glass, Dr Pepper, 1st script logo, flared, 6", EX	1,100.00
Fountain glass, Hires, Enjoy Nature's Delicious Drink	45.00
Fountain glass, ice cream soda; gr, Tea Room pattern	60.00
Fountain glass, ice cream soda; pk, Tea Room pattern	90.00
Fountain glass, Mah-Tay, syrup line	15.00
Fountain glass, Moxie, Drink, orange band	22.50
Fountain glass, Seven-Up, gr	16.50
Ice shaving machine, pnt CI, filigree top, 35"	825.00
Jar, crushed fruit; clear glass, 10-sided, Heisey mk, 10", EX	200.00
Jug, syrup; crockery, John Matthews Co, NY, 1-gal	100.00
Magazines, bound volumes of 'Druggist Circular...,' ca 1865	250.00
Malted milk container, Bordens, aluminum	32.50
Malted milk container, Thompson's, enamel	350.00
Mixer, AC Gilbert, EX	65.00
Mixer, Arnold's, wht porc base, EX	80.00
Mixer, Coles Shaker, CI, dbl shaker, hand crank, 24", EX	825.00

Mixer, Hamilton Beach, single head, 2-speed 125.00
Mixer, Hamilton Beach, triple head, EX 275.00
Mixer, hand-cranked floor model 800.00
Mixer, Horlick's, glass platform, rvpt/NP base, 17", G 200.00
Mixer, Horlick's, porc on steel base, NP mechanism, 17", G 180.00
Mug, Armour's Veribest Root Beer, stoneware, 5⅞", G 20.00
Mug, Buckeye Root Beer, stoneware, figural hdl, 6", VG 70.00
Mug, Buckeye Root Beer, stoneware, plain hdl 60.00
Mug, Chelmsford Spring Ginger Beer, stoneware, 4¾", EX 35.00
Mug, Dr Swett's Root Beer 185.00
Mug, Dr Swett's Root Beer, stoneware, 4¾", VG 100.00
Mug, Hires Root Beer, boy toasting, Mettlach, 4¼" 175.00
Mug, Hires Root Beer, Join Health & Cheer, 5", VG 225.00
Mug, Hires Root Beer, Villeroy & Boch, 4½", G 250.00
Mug, root beer; Jim Dandy, crockery 125.00
Photo, int view of soda fountain, ca 1900, 5x7" 50.00
Photo, stereo view card showing soda fountain, ca 1900 ....90.00
Postcard, interior view of fountain, blk/wht, pre-1920 ....12.50
Postcard, interior view of fountain, color, pre-1920 ....18.00
Pump, syrup; rnd 4" NP lid, fits most dispensers 20.00
Sign, Buckeye Root Beer, cb, mug & dancing satyrs 300.00
Sign, Grape Ola, tin, 20x14" 175.00
Sign, trolley car; Just Because, cherry sundae, cb, 20x10" 150.00
Sign, True Fruit, self-fr tin, 38x24" 400.00
Soda apparatus, Arctic, marble, holds 8 dispensers, Tufts, EX .1,500.00
Stool, wooden seat, brass ftrest, CI base, 27x11" dia, EX 125.00
Straw dispenser (or straw jar), Grape Smash, w/lid 750.00
Straw holder, clear glass, 'cut' Illinois pattern, glass lid 350.00
Straw holder, clear glass, 'cut' Illinois pattern, no lid 100.00
Straw holder, clear glass, metal lid, common, 10" 150.00
Straw holder, clear glass, metal top/base, Bloomfield, 13½" 25.00
Straw holder, clear glass, sq, Near Cut 700.00
Straw holder, clear glass, sq w/emb stars, no top, 9½", EX 100.00
Straw holder, clear glass NP base & lid, 11", VG 140.00
Straw holder, faceted glass, brass inserts, 12x4" dia, EX 135.00
Straw holder, gr glass, 'cut' Illinois pattern, no lid 300.00
Straw holder, gr glass, 'cut' Illinois pattern, w/glass lid 500.00
Straw holder, gr glass, metal lid, 12" 500.00
Straw holder, gr glass, w/lid, 10" 450.00
Straw holder, horizontal, Heisey 600.00
Syrup bottle, Cherry Smash, label under glass, w/lid 150.00
Syrup bottle, Ginger Ale label, glass, orig cap, 11" 75.00
Table, CI, glass display top, swing-out seats 725.00
Table, wood top, +4 wire chairs 135.00
Tape measure, Abbotts Ice Cream 25.00
Watch fob, A Health Food, ice cream brick shape 100.00

Spangle Glass

Spangle glass, also known as Vasa Murrhina, is cased art glass characterized by the metallic flakes embedded in its top layer. It was made both abroad and in the United States during the latter years of the 19th century, and it was reproduced in the 1960s by the Fenton Art Glass Company.

Vasa Murrhina was a New England distributor who sold glassware of this type manufactured by a Dr. Flower of Sandwich, Massachusetts. Flower had purchased the defunct Cape Cod Glassworks in 1885 and used the facilities to operate his own company. Since none of the ware was marked, it is very difficult to attribute specific examples to his manufacture. See also Art Glass Baskets; Fenton.

Basket, gr & wht spatter w/mica, clear thorn hdl, 6¼" 120.00
Bowl, gold shaded w/mica, wht int, clear ruffle, 2¾x8" 95.00

Candlestick, blk amethyst, hollow baluster stem, 18" 220.00
Ewer, dk wine, wht int, clear rim/thorn hdl, dbl bulb, 8" 375.00
Rose bowl, rose w/silver mica, egg shape, 8-crimp, 3½x2¾" 75.00
Rose bowl, rose w/silver mica, 8-crimp, 3½x3½" 105.00
Sweetmeat, pk w/silver flecks, HP leaves/flowers, 6" dia 110.00

Vase, cased turquoise with mica, 7", $165.00.

Vase, amber & pk opaque stripes w/mica, hdls, 10½", pr 165.00
Vase, jack-in-pulpit; mc spatter w/silver mica, fluted, 7" 85.00
Vase, mc spatter w/silver mica, ruffled, 8¾x3¾" 90.00
Vase, orange w/mica, wht int, ewer form, 3-petal top, 8½" 125.00
Vase, pk w/silver mica, wht int, ruffled, 9x3½" 100.00
Vase, yel w/crystal rim, wht cased, allover silver mica, 4" 95.00

Spatter Glass

Spatter glass, characterized by its multicolor 'spatters,' has been made from the late 19th century to the present by American glass houses as well as those abroad. Although it was once thought to have been made entirely by workers at the 'end of the day' from bits and pieces of leftover scrap, it is now known that it was a standard line of production. See also Art Glass Baskets.

Basket, 4-color, ruffled, clear twist hdl, 6x5x4" 85.00
Candlesticks, deep amethyst & wht, clear ft, 8½x4⅜", pr 85.00
Candlesticks, 5-color, wht int, 8¾x3⅞", pr 125.00
Creamer & sugar bowl, 5-color, 3-petal top, 3¼", 6" 110.00
Pitcher, yel opaque & orange, emb swirls, clear hdl, 6¾" 175.00
Sugar shaker, cobalt/orange/wht cased, orig collar & lid 145.00
Tumbler, pk & wht, Invt T'print, 3¾x2⅝" 45.00
Vase, mc, appl clear hdl, 8" 65.00
Vase, mc w/HP flowers & butterfly, ewer form, 11x3¾" 120.00
Vase, yel & wht w/mc HP flowers & bird, clear hdls, 7¼" 195.00

Spatterware

Spatterware is a general term referring to a type of decoration used by English potters beginning in the late 1700s. Using a brush or a stick, brightly colored paint was dabbed onto the soft-paste earthenware items, achieving a spattered effect which was often used as a border. Because much of this type of ware was made for export to the United States, some of the subjects in the central design — the schoolhouse and the eagle patterns, for instance — reflect American tastes. Yellow, green, and black spatterware is scarce and highly valued by collectors.

In the descriptions that follow, the color listed after the item indicates the color of the spatter. The central design is identified next, and the color description that follows that refers to the design.

Key:
cs — cut sponge   ds — design spatter

Bowl & pitcher set, peafowl, 4-color, red rim, Adams, EX 550.00
Creamer, bl, Fort, 3-color, hairline/wear, 4⅜" 300.00
Creamer, brn/blk, rose, 3-color, 4" 245.00

Creamer, red and yellow with green hand-painted flower, ca 1850, 3⅞x5⅜", $325.00.

Creamer, red/bl, flower cluster, red & gr, 3½" 170.00
Creamer, red/bl, rose, 4-color, stain/hairline, 5⅜" 145.00
Cup, bl, wigwam, NM 85.00
Cup, yel, tulip, rivet rpr 45.00
Cup plate, bl, brn Am Eagle & Shield transfer, 3¾" 375.00
Pitcher, bl, wht reserves, blk stripes, 4-color flower, 7⅝" 350.00
Pitcher, rainbow, 5-color, molded details, shaped hdl, 7½", EX ..275.00
Pitcher, transfer print w/chinoiserie panel, 1800s, 10", EX 250.00
Plate, bl, acorn & oak leaf, 4-color, hairline, 8¼" 660.00
Plate, bl, Am Eagle & Shield, 7" 165.00
Plate, bl, Am Eagle & Shield, 8¼" 185.00
Plate, bl, Chinese transfer, 9¼" 110.00
Plate, bl, plain center, 10-sided, 7¼" 65.00
Plate, gr, columbine, red striping, 8⅜" 100.00
Plate, purple, columbine/rose bud/thistle, 4-color, 6⅝", EX 125.00
Plate, purple, 6-pointed star, gr/red/bl, rpr, 9" 120.00
Plate, red, bl flower transfer, 12-sided, 8" 225.00
Plate, red, bull's-eye, 10-sided, 9¼" 225.00
Plate, red, columbine/rose bud/thistle, 8⅜", EX 125.00
Plate, red/gr, flower, red/gr, 8½" 190.00
Plate, toddy; bl, bull's eye, 5¼" 110.00
Plate, 3-color, sm chip, 7¾" 105.00
Platter, bl, rose, 3-color, old rpr, 13⅓" 220.00
Saucer, gr, peafowl, 4-color, sm stain 185.00
Saucer, rainbow, peafowl, 4-color 125.00
Sugar bowl, bl, Adam's Rose, flared rim, rpr, 3¾", EX 300.00
Tea bowl & saucer, bl, red striping, Tunstall, mini 72.50
Tea bowl & saucer, bl, tulip, mk M w/anchor, rpr 125.00
Tea bowl & saucer, bl, tulip, 3-color 375.00
Tea bowl & saucer, gr, peafowl, 4-color 425.00
Tea bowl & saucer, purple, Adam's Rose, EX 140.00
Tea bowl & saucer, purple, red/gr/blk rose 105.00
Tea bowl & saucer, rainbow, red/gr, Davenport anchor mk 250.00
Tea bowl & saucer, red/gr, floral, red/gr, mk M w/asterisk, NM 90.00
Tea bowl & saucer, schoolhouse, red/gr/brn, rpr 470.00
Tea bowl & saucer, water bug, 5-color 325.00

Cut-Sponge

Bowl, blk, red/bl flowers w/red cs florets, Adams, 9" L 250.00
Creamer, bl, snowflakes, 4", NM 180.00
Pitcher, bl cs border/florets, red flowers, Aul Heather, 5½" 210.00
Plate, bl, Am Eagle on shield/E Pluribus Unum, 8¾" 160.00
Plate, blk, red/bl flowers w/red cs florets, Adams, 9" 210.00
Platter, blk, red/bl flowers, red cs florets, Adams, 12½" L 250.00

Design Spatter

Creamer, Adam's Rose, alternating red/gr daisy band, 4" 210.00

Creamer, bands of yel bow knots & gr no-center daisies, 4½" 220.00
Creamer, purple/gr holly, minor wear, 4" 95.00
Plate, dogwood, purple bow knot border, 9¾", NM 200.00
Plate, gr daisies, purple/red columbine, bluebells, 6½" 110.00
Plate, purple thistles, red bow knots, bl flowers, 10" 225.00
Plate, purple/yel pansy, gr bow knot border, 10", NM 225.00
Plate, rabbit transfer, gaudy ds mc floral rim, 9⅛" 330.00
Plate, red columbine w/red buds & bluebells, 9½", NM 180.00
Platter, purple/gr holly, 11" 190.00
Sugar bowl, purple/red columbine, bluebells, grapes finial, 8" 250.00
Tea bowl & saucer, Adam's Rose, bl no-center daisy border 230.00
Tea bowl & saucer, Adam's Rose w/gr bow knot border, VG 95.00

Spectacles

Collectors of Americana are beginning to appreciate the charm of antique optical items, and those involved in the related trade find them particularly fascinating. Anyone, however, cannot help but notice the evolution of technology apparent when viewing a collection of old eye ware and at the same time admire the primitive ingenuity involved in its construction. Our advisor for this category is Dale Beeks; he is listed in the Directory under Idaho.

Lorgnette, openwork case w/marcasites, blk velvet ribbon 85.00
Lorgnette, sterling, on long sterling chain 225.00
Lorgnette, 10k yel gold w/short heart-shaped hdl 175.00
Lorgnette, 14k gold plated, long hdl 180.00
Lorgnette, 14k wht gold, folding, EX in leather case 110.00
Opera glasses, bl enamel w/HP florals, gold ormolu mts, rare 415.00
Opera glasses, MOP, 1800s, EX in orig leather case 95.00
Opera glasses, MOP & red enameling 150.00
Opera glasses, telescoping hdl, gilt/inset shell, Paris 225.00
Spectacles, faux tortoise shell, early 24.00
Spectacles, folding, 1700s, 5½", w/shagreen case, EX 935.00

Spelter

Spelter figurines are cast from commercial zinc and coated with a metallic patina. The result is a product very similar to bronze in appearance, yet much less expensive.

Candelabra, 2-light, putti std, base w/3 kneeling boys, 17" 550.00
Clock, mantel; modeled as horse w/attendent, GE, 17" 125.00
Figure, Richard I, 13x10½" 285.00
Figure, young shepherd, recumbent, w/staff & horn aside, 13" ...210.00
Figurine, dancer, scantily clad, w/tambourine, 27" 495.00
Lamp, peasant girl w/flower basket on head, oil burner, 13" 65.00

Spode-Copeland

The Spode Works was established in 1770 and continued to operate under that title until 1843. Their earliest products were typical underglaze blue-printed patterns. After 1790 a translucent porcelain body was the basis for a line of fine enamel-decorated dinnerware. Stone china was introduced in 1805, often in patterns reflecting an Oriental influence. In 1833 Wm Taylor Copeland purchased the company, continuing business in much the same tradition. During the last half of the 19th century, Copeland produced excellent parian figures and groups with such success that many other companies attempted to reproduce his work. He employed famous paintresses to decorate plaques, vases, and tablewares, many examples of which were signed by the artist. Most of the Copeland wares are marked with one of several variations that incorporate the firm name. Today the company is owned by Royal Worcester, Ltd., and operates under the name of Royal Worcester Spode, Ltd. Our advisor for this category is Don Haase; he is listed in the Directory under Washington.

Bowl, cereal; Patricia	28.00
Bowl, cream soup; Fairy Dell, w/underplate	35.00
Bowl, rim soup; Patricia, earthenware, 7"	30.00
Bowl, vegetable; Chelsea Garden, bone china, oval, 8"	145.00
Bowl, vegetable; Florence, earthenware, oval	55.00
Bowl, vegetable; Patricia, oval, 10"	85.00
Bowl, vegetable; Tower, bl, ftd, w/lid, Spode, 10x8"	265.00
Butter dish, Buttercup, rectangular, w/lid	45.00
Butter pat, Tower, pk	25.00
Cake plate, Florence, hdls, 9"	85.00
Cake plate, Patricia, hdls, 9"	85.00
Chop plate, Patricia, 13"	145.00
Coffeepot, Chelsea Bird, earthenware, 6-cup	145.00
Cup & saucer, bouillon; Patricia	35.00
Cup & saucer, Bridal Rose, bone china	69.00
Cup & saucer, Christmas Tree, gr trim	39.00
Cup & saucer, demitasse; Old Salem	35.00
Cup & saucer, Irene, bone china	69.00
Egg cup, Gainsborough	32.00
Egg cup, Patricia	32.00
Lazy susan, Tower, pk	495.00
Mug, George Washington, Copeland	135.00
Pitcher, Churchill Toby, mc, mk Copeland Spode England, 8½"	55.00
Pitcher, Herrings Hunt, gr trim, 8"	135.00
Pitcher, Tower, bl & wht, 8"	225.00
Plate, bread & butter; Buttercup	25.00
Plate, bread & butter; Chelsea Garden, bone china	39.00
Plate, dinner; Chelsea Garden, bone china	69.00
Plate, dinner; Mayflower	39.00
Plate, dinner; Patricia	39.00
Plate, dinner; Tower, bl w/o wht rim	45.00
Plate, luncheon; Famille Rose	35.00
Plate, luncheon; Patricia	35.00
Plate, salad; Buttercup	28.00
Plate, salad; Chelsea Garden, bone china	49.00
Plate, salad; Patricia	28.00
Platter, Chelsea Garden, bone china, 17"	295.00
Platter, Florence, 17"	155.00
Platter, Patricia, 13"	110.00
Platter, Tower, bl, 17"	245.00
Platter, Wild Flower, 17"	165.00
Sugar bowl, Christmas Tree, gr trim, w/lid	45.00
Syrup, Tower, bl, pewter lid, S-10288, 6"	120.00
Teapot, Buttercup	155.00
Teapot, Tower, bl, 8-cup	225.00
Tureen, soup; Tower, bl, w/lid, lg, +ladle & underplate	595.00
Tureen, soup; Tower, bl, w/lid, sm, +lid & underplate	495.00
Tureen, soup; Venetian scene, 19th C, 14"	715.00
Vase, gr w/bird reserves, emb shell/scroll ft, 7"	265.00

Spongeware

Spongeware is a type of factory-made earthenware that was popular during the last quarter of the 19th century. It was decorated by dabbing color onto the drying ware with a sponge, leaving a splotched design at random or in simple patterns. Sometimes a solid band of color was added. The vessel was then covered with a clear glaze and fired at a high temperature. Blue on white is the most preferred combination, but green on ivory, orange on white, or those colors in combination may also occasionally be found.

Bowl, bl on yel ware, dome lid, bail hdl, glazed int, 13"	155.00
Bowl, bl/wht, rnd ft, 2x5"	130.00
Bowl, bl/wht, 10"	175.00
Bowl, brn/bl on cream, 4¼"	60.00
Bowl, brn/bl/red on cream, 5x9½"	75.00
Casserole, bl & rust on cream, sm	90.00
Creamer, bl/wht, 4", EX	125.00
Creamer, gr/bl on cream, 3"	90.00
Cuspidor, bl bands rim & base, concave sides, 5x10"	75.00
Ink pot, bl/wht, bulbous w/tapered base, 4"	110.00
Jar, bl/wht, bail hdl, w/lid, 6"	265.00
Mush cup, flowing bl sponging, 5x8", w/8" saucer	200.00
Pitcher, bl/wht, slightly bulbous bottom, 9"	215.00
Pitcher, brn/gr on yel, 4½"	65.00
Pitcher, gr/wht, 8"	100.00
Pitcher, pattern sponging, emb rose on side, 9"	285.00
Plate, bl/wht, 9½", M	110.00
Platter, bl/wht, 12¼x8"	175.00

Soap dish, plain clay center with raised bars, 6x4", $110.00.

Soap dish, bl/wht, 3½x4½"	85.00
Wash pitcher, bl banding, 11"	195.00
Waste bowl, bl/wht, 5" dia	100.00

Spoons

Souvenir spoons have been popular remembrances since the 1890s. The early hand-wrought examples of the silversmith's art are especially sought and appreciated for their fine craftsmanship. Commemorative, personality-related, advertising, and those with Indian busts or floral designs are only a few of the many types of collectible spoons. In the following listings, spoons are entered by city, character, or occasion.

Key:
B — bowl	FF — full figure
BR — bowl reverse	GW — gold wash
emb — embossed	H — handle
eng — engraved	HR — handle reverse

Alaska on shaft of totem pole FF/enameled H; plain B; JM Co	75.00
Albany & patriot H; fish-form shaft; shell B	46.00
Baltimore 1901 on H; plain B; demitasse	12.50
Brooklyn Bridge, bridge in B; ornate H; 5½"	25.00
Bunker Hill & monument on H; plain B; demitasse	24.00
California on shaft; fruit basket finial H; Santa Ana in B	47.50

Cambridge OH in GW B; state seal & flags emb on H 30.00

Chicago & buildings on H; Art Institute emb in B; Watson 48.00

Christmas on shaft; Santa finial H; scenic B; hallmk 125.00

Cincinnati emb on scroll H; monument eng in B 20.00

Cleveland, Soldiers & Sailors monument finial H; scenic B 47.50

Columbian Expo shaft; portrait finial H; scenic B; hallmk 58.00

Des Moines on HR; lady's face emb on finial; plain B; Towle 48.00

Fruit basket/initials on H; plain B; coin silver, Wm S Willis 62.00

Galveston TX on shaft; lg fish emb on H; sailboat in GW B 55.00

Golden Gate Bridge on H; plain B 25.00

Grand Canyon on H w/scenic finial; plain B 27.50

Honolulu on shaft; cut-out scenic H; plain B 37.50

Indian FF H; emb scene in B; English hallmks 110.00

Iron Maiden on H; opens/shows spikes; view in B; 800 mk 110.00

Jacksonville etch in B; palm tree FF H 38.00

Jacksonville stylized letters on H; plain B 25.00

John Alden finial H; Speak for Yourself... on shaft; plain B 50.00

Lewis & Clark Expo, skyline & salmon form H; building in B 35.00

Longfellow's home in B; pine cones emb on H 46.00

Louisville on shaft; Daniel Boone finial H; plain B; Watson 47.50

Madison WI eng in GW B; Blk boy w/watermelon emb on H 80.00

Marineland in B; cut-out dolphin on H; demitasse 10.00

Missouri seal & scenes emb on H; red enamel St Louis in GW B .65.00

Narrangansett Pier RI emb in B; Indian chief finial H 55.00

New East River scene etch in B; golfer emb on H; mk CB&H 70.00

Niagara Falls view emb in B; Indian FF H; 5¾" 155.00

Old Senate House Kingston NY in B; Viking pattern H 37.00

Philadelphia, FF Colonial man on H; plain B; Caldwell 75.00

Richardson Grove CA & cut-out tree on H, plain B 15.00

Rock Island stylized letters on H; etch scenic B 37.50

Roseville OH eng in B; vine pattern H; Gorham 30.00

Salem & witch emb on H; plain B; Durgin 75.00

Salem MA on shaft w/witch finial H; plain B; Whiting-Davis 47.50

San Gabriel Mission on H; Catalina Island scenic B 48.00

Santa Cruz CA & natural bridge in B; fish finial H 50.00

St Petersburg on shaft w/stork cut-out finial H; plain B 36.00

Stork figural H; birth dates in B 40.00

Sumter SC eng in B; cut-out holly H; 5⅝" 35.00

Texas & symbols on H; Alamo scenic B; P&B 45.00

Uncle Sam FF H; capitol scene emb in B 85.00

University of IL Library building B; graduate FF H; Watson 75.00

Vancouver etch in B; miner FF H; Rogers 60.00

Washington Monument & wreaths on H; capitol building in B .120.00

Washington Monument H; capitol scene emb in GW B 32.00

Washington on shaft of H w/eagle finial; capitol building in B 46.50

Waterfall etch in B; heavily emb floral H; Rogers 32.00

William Penn FF H; Liberty Bell emb in B 95.00

Wisconsin & state seal on H; Grand Ave scene in B; Watson 52.50

Yellowstone Park shaft, elk/bear on H; Old Faithful Inn in B 40.00

1933 Century of Progress on H; plain B; Watson 40.00

Sporting Goods

When sports cards became so widely collectible several years ago, other types of related memorabilia started to interest sports fans. Now they search for baseball uniforms, autographed baseballs, game-used bats and gloves, and all sorts of ephemera. Although baseball is America's all-time favorite, other sports have their own groups of interested collectors. Our advice for this category comes from Paul Longo Americana, Box 490, Chatham Rd., South Orleans, Cape Cod, Massachusetts 02662. See also Target Balls.

Banner, 1932 Olympic Games, CA, cloth, 30x30", EX 400.00

Baseball, sgn by 1929 Athletics, 21 signatures, EX 600.00

Baseball, sgn by 1950 Dodgers, 27 signatures, VG 300.00

Baseball, sgn by 1957 Braves, 24 signatures, EX 250.00

Baseball, sgn by 1968 Cardinals, 23 signatures, EX 120.00

Baseball, sgn Jimmy Fox 800.00

Bat, Cooperstown, autographed by 60 Hall of Famer's 3,000.00

Bat, Schoolboy Rowe, HOF, mini, M 50.00

Bat, sgn Nolan Ryan 150.00

Bat, Ty Cobb 'Georgia Peach' decal, ca 1908, NM 700.00

Beanie, World Series, Pittsburgh, felt, rare, 1950, NM 70.00

Blanket, Ty Cobb, brn felt, NM 200.00

Book, Baseball Complete, Hodges, Grosset & Dunlop, 1952, EX .15.00

Book, fact; Major League Baseball, Musial cover, 1944, EX 30.00

Book, How To Play Your Best Golf, Armour, EX 10.00

Book, Spalding's Ice Hockey Guide, 1937, EX 35.00

Book, 1945 Major League Baseball Facts, Whitman, 1945, 144-pg .12.50

Booklet, America's Cup, illus, 1899, EX 75.00

Booklet, How To Play Baseball, Spaulding, 1932, EX 25.00

Button, M Mantle retirement day, mc, 1969, NM 15.00

Card, cigarette; Bridwell, Coupon Cigarettes, 1909, VG 20.00

Card, cigarette; Tinker, Sweet Caporal Cigarettes, 1909, NM ...125.00

Catcher's mitt, Gus Mancuso model, Pat 1925, EX 70.00

Glove, baseball; Nellie Fox, EX 50.00

Glove, baseball; Ted Williams model, 1950s, EX 60.00

Guide, boxing; Scientific Boxing, James Corbett, 1912, EX 100.00

Jersey, Lakers #33, worn by Kareem Abdul-Jabaar 3,000.00

Magazine, Sport, Willy Mays baseball cover, 1964, EX 25.00

Pass, Nat'l League of Professional Baseball Clubs, 1918, EX 100.00

Pass, season; St Louis Nat'l Baseball Club, 1934, EX 50.00

Pennant, Chicago Bears, felt, ca 1950, 28", EX 45.00

Pennant, Hank Aaron All Time Home Run Champion, 1974, EX ...30.00

Pennant, Indianapolis Motor Speedway, yel felt, 1940, 17", EX .100.00

Pennant, New York Yankees, felt, 1950s, EX 40.00

Periscope, PGA Spectator, 1930s 40.00

Photo, Cleveland Indians team, blk & wht, 1936, fr, 9x33" 200.00

Photo, Ted Williams in uniform, blk & wht, inscr/sgn, 1957 .....125.00

Plate, 1968 Olympics, Staffordshire, gold leaf, 7" dia 60.00

Postcard, Cardinals team photo, 1926, EX 45.00

Postcard, Chicago Cubs ball park, 1910 ....60.00

Postcard, photo US Olympic track team, 1912 ....25.00

Program, Army-Navy football game, 1939 ....35.00

Program, East-West Classic football game, 1946, EX 35.00

Program, Harlem Globetrotters official souvenir, 1952 ....35.00

Program, Pebble Beach lady's golf championship, 1940 ....25.00

Program, Spartans Vs Hoosiers football game, 1950, EX 25.00

Program, St Louis Vs Yankees, 1926 World Series, EX 500.00

Program, 1946 World Series, Cardinals Vs Red Sox, NM 150.00

Program from 1956 World Series, Yankee Edition, $125.00.

Scorebook, Wilson Official, endorsed by Ray Schalk, 1922, EX ...75.00
Scorecard, baseball; Pirates & Dodgers, 1937, EX 35.00
Tennis balls, Macy's, 1930s, sealed can 65.00
Ticket, Internat'l Boxing Club, Sugar Ray Robinson/Graziano 90.00
Tumbler, Indianapolis 500, 1954 ....25.00
Uniform, baseball; made by Maynard Athletic, M unused 100.00
Uniform, Rangers #34, worn by Nolan Ryan 8,000.00
Uniform, Yale, wool, Spalding, w/cap & undershirt 200.00
Wristwatch, Al Kaline of face, orig leather band, EX 100.00
Yearbook, Blk pictorial, 1944, rare, EX 450.00
Yearbook, Harlem Globetrotters, 1960, EX 30.00
Yearbook, Negro Baseball, Robinson on cover, 1946, EX 500.00

St. Clair

The St. Clair Glass Company began as a small family-oriented operation in Elwood, Indiana, in 1941. Most famous for their lamps, the family made numerous small items of carnival, pink and caramel slag, and custard glass as well. Later, paperweights became popular production pieces; many command considerably high prices on today's market. Weights are stamped and usually dated, while small production pieces are often unmarked. Our advisor for this category is Bonnie Pruitt, author of the *St. Clair Glass Collector's Book*. Her listing is in the Directory under Indiana; it includes information about how to order her book.

Ash bowl, aqua flowers, paperweight base, Joe St Clair 45.00
Ashtray, flower, sm 70.00
Bell, Christmas, lg 115.00
Bell, mc flowers, paperweight base, Joe St Clair, 4½" 35.00
Bicentennial Bell, bl carnival, sm 22.50
Bird, yel & clear, sm 35.00
Bottle, scent; carnival glass 95.00
Candle holder, mc floral, sulfide 80.00
Lamp, boudoir; wht lilies in paperweight base, 14", pr 115.00
Lamp, kerosene; pk slag 225.00
Owl ring tree, chocolate slag 45.00
Paperweight, bl flowers, Joe St Clair 44.00
Paperweight, butterfly, sulfide, controlled bubble & etched 325.00
Paperweight, cameo, sulfide, windowed & etched 325.00
Paperweight, elephant, sulfide 155.00
Paperweight, flower, windowed, Ed St Clair 275.00
Paperweight, flowers, Paul St Clair, X-lg 115.00
Paperweight, Kennedy, sulfide, etched & windowed 225.00
Paperweight, Kewpie, sulfide, non-windowed 165.00
Paperweight, Kewpie, sulfide, windowed 185.00
Paperweight, strawberry form 185.00
Pear, carnival glass 95.00
Plate, Bicentennial, cobalt, Joe St Clair 25.00
Plate, Lyndon B Johnson portrait center 22.50
Plate, 1889 coin, cobalt, Joe St Clair, sm 25.00
Ring holder, teapot form 80.00
Salt cellar, gr carnival, oblong 30.00
Scottie, custard 135.00
Toothpick holder, Fan & Feather, marigold 27.50
Toothpick holder, flower, weighted 70.00
Toothpick holder, Holly, gr carnival, sgn Joe St Clair 45.00
Toothpick holder, Indian, Joe St Clair 45.00
Toothpick holder, Indian Maiden, caramel 115.00
Toothpick holder, Nixon/WA/Indian, 1776-1976, red, Bob St Clair .45.00
Toothpick holder, swans, gr carnival 40.00
Toothpick holder, tan & gray slag, Joe St Clair 45.00
Toothpick holder, witch, ice bl 45.00
Tumbler, Grape & Cable, red carnival 35.00

Vase, wht w/silver irid, sgn Tom St Clair, 3½" 28.00
Wheelbarrow, chocolate glass, Joe St Clair 40.00
Whiskey/toothpick, cobalt, cut pattern (rare), Joe St Clair 35.00

Staffordshire

Scores of potteries sprang up in England's Staffordshire district in the early 18th century; several remain to the present time. (See also specific companies.) Figurines and groups were made in great numbers; dogs were favorite subjects. Often they were made in pairs, each a mirror image of the other. They varied in heights from 3" or 4" to the largest, measuring 16" to 18". From 1840 until about 1900, portrait figures were produced to represent specific characters, both real and fictional. As a rule these were never marked.

The Historical Ware listed here was made throughout the district; some collectors refer to it as Staffordshire Blue Ware. It was produced as early as 1820, and because much was exported to America, it was very often decorated with transfers depicting scenic views of well-known American landmarks. Early examples were printed in a deep cobalt. By 1830 a softer blue was favored, and within the next decade black, pink, red, and green prints were used. Although sometimes careless about adding their trademark, many companies used their own border designs that were as individual as their names.

This ware should not be confused with the vast amounts of modern china (mostly plates) made from early in the century to the present. These souvenir or commemorative items are usually marketed through gift stores and the like. (See Rowland and Marsellus.) Our advisor for this category is Richard Marden; he is listed in the Directory under New Hampshire. See also specific manufacturers.

Key:
blk — black   l/b — light blue
gr — green   m/b — medium blue
d/b — dark blue   m-d/b — medium dark blue

Historical

Basket, Dorney Court, d/b, rtcl, Wood's, 11", +9¼" tray 1,350.00
Bowl, Lake, Regents Park, d/b, beaded rim, Wood, 10½" 385.00
Bowl, Little Falls NY, l/b, Ridgway, 10" 265.00
Bowl, Near Fort Miller Hudson River, l/b, Clews, 11½" 575.00
Bowl, Oriental scene w/zebra, d/b, Rogers, 9" sq, VG 85.00

Platter, View of Greenwich, dark blue, 15", $495.00.

Bowl, pudding; Wadleigh House, d/b, beaded rim, Hall, 11", EX ..225.00
Bowl, sauce; scene at Tivoli, d/b, Wood, 6¼" 175.00

Bowl, Sea Shell, d/b, hdls, w/lid, Stubbs & Kent, 8¾" 600.00
Bowl, soup; St Peters, Wood's Italian Scenery, 10¼" 195.00
Bowl, tea dregs; fisherman/English village, d/b, 5½" 175.00
Bowl, tea dregs; Rebecca at Well, d/b, 4¾" 235.00
Coffeepot, Wadsworth Tower, Hartford, d/b, Wood, 11½" 2,000.00
Condiment bowl, Osterly Park, d/b to l/b, rtcl, Riley, 11½" 650.00
Creamer, Oxford Angelican, pk 175.00
Creamer, sheep, d/b 325.00
Cup & saucer, apples, d/b, scalloped 155.00
Cup & saucer, Christmas Eve, d/b, Wilkie series, Clews 225.00
Cup & saucer, Commodore MacDonnough's Victory, d/b, Wood ...375.00
Cup & saucer, dragons, d/b, flatiron hdl, NM 135.00
Cup & saucer, eagle on rock, purple, Wood 165.00
Cup & saucer, lovers in tropical forest, d/b 165.00
Cup & saucer, man & dog walking, m/b, appl hdl, X-lg 145.00
Cup & saucer, men/bridge/Indians, English engraver's view 145.00
Cup & saucer, Rebecca at Well, d/b, Clews 225.00
Cup & saucer, Wadsworth Tower, d/b, Wood, NM 325.00
Cup plate, arched stone bridge, d/b, Wood's Fr series, 3⅝" 195.00
Cup plate, Batalha Portugal, d/b, 3⅞" 145.00
Cup plate, Battery, d/b, Wood's Shell border, 3½" 250.00
Cup plate, Cottage in Woods, d/b, Wood, 3⅝" 235.00
Cup plate, Hudson River View, blk, Clews, 3¾" 85.00
Cup plate, John Wesley portrait, commemorative, blk, 4" 165.00
Cup plate, NY from Weehawken, l/b, coats-of-arms border, 4" ..185.00
Cup plate, sailboat, brn, 3⅞" 45.00
Cup plate, View Near Conway NH, l/b, Wood, 4⅛", NM 225.00
Custard cup, grape clusters, d/b, flared sides, appl hdl 165.00
Pitcher, Albany, l/b, Meigh, 8¾" 175.00
Pitcher, Lafayette at Franklin's Tomb, d/b, Wood, rpr, 5¾" 350.00
Pitcher, NY City Hall/Hospital, d/b, Stevenson, 6" 750.00
Plate, American Villa, d/b, 10" 225.00
Plate, archers shooting birds, pk, 6" 45.00
Plate, Arms of Rhode Island, d/b, Mayer, 8¾" 475.00
Plate, beehive, d/b, Stevenson, 8¾" 185.00
Plate, British Views, d/b, Henshall, 9¾" 75.00
Plate, Cadmus, d/b, Wood, 10" 595.00
Plate, Canon Hall Yorkshire, m-d/b, Riley, 8¾" 145.00
Plate, Cascade de Gresy, d/b, Wood, 7¾" 155.00
Plate, Castle of Lavenza, d/b, 10" 185.00
Plate, Christ Church Oxford, m/b, Ridgway, 9¾", EX 65.00
Plate, City Hall NY, brn, Jackson, 10½", NM 85.00
Plate, City Hall NY, d/b, Ridgway, 9¾" 275.00
Plate, Courthouse Baltimore, d/b, Henshall, 9½" 375.00
Plate, Dreghorn House Scotland, d/b, Hall, 6½" 175.00
Plate, Erie Canal, d/b, medallions in border, 10" 450.00
Plate, Erie Canal at Buffalo, blk, Stevenson, 10¼" 65.00
Plate, Falls of Killarny, m-d/b, 6⅝" 65.00
Plate, family & cathedral, d/b, Panoramic Scenery, 10¼" 165.00
Plate, Finsbury Chapel, d/b, 5½" 85.00
Plate, Fisherman's Hut, d/b, 10" 145.00
Plate, Fountain Abbey, d/b, Clews, 10" 95.00
Plate, fruit & flowers, d/b, Stubbs, 10" 195.00
Plate, Gen Jackson Hero of New Orleans, blk, Wood, 6½" 250.00
Plate, Guys Cliff Warwickshire, m-d/b, Wood, 10⅛" 98.00
Plate, Harvard College, brn w/wht emb rim, Wood, 10½" 145.00
Plate, Harvard Hall, Jackson, brn, 6¾" 90.00
Plate, Kent East Indiaman, d/b, Wood's Shell border, 9", NM ...185.00
Plate, lady & child in river scenic, l/b, 9¾" 45.00
Plate, Landing of the Fathers, m/b, Wood, 10" 165.00
Plate, Landing of the Fathers, m/b, Wood, 5½" 65.00
Plate, man on horse/buildings, d/b, wht rim, Rogers, 10¼" 165.00
Plate, man/lady/donkey/sheep/ruins, c/b, Davenport, 8¾" 160.00
Plate, Marine Hospital, Louisville, d/b, Shell border, 8½" 325.00

Plate, Masion de Raphael, d/b, Wood, 6½" 185.00
Plate, Mastoke Castle Warwickshire, d/b, Wood, 8½" 165.00
Plate, Midnight Race on Mississippi, gray, ironstone, 10¼" 85.00
Plate, Mohamedan Mosque & Tomb, d/b, Hall, 9¾" 95.00
Plate, Montreal Steamship British Am, sepia, Davenport, 7" 195.00
Plate, New York, pk, Adams, 6" 65.00
Plate, otter, d/b, Hall's Quadruped series, 8¾" 85.00
Plate, Palestine, d/b, wht scalloped rim, 9½" 145.00
Plate, Park Theatre NY, d/b, acorn & oak leaf, Stevenson, 10" ..395.00
Plate, Pass in Catskills, d/b, Wood, 7½" 350.00
Plate, Peace & Plenty, d/b, Clews, 8" 325.00
Plate, Peace & Plenty, d/b, Clews, 9" 375.00
Plate, Penn's Treaty, m/b, T Green, 8¼" 125.00
Plate, Pittsfield Elm, d/b, Clews, 10½" 425.00
Plate, Ponte Rotto, d/b, Wood's Italian series, 10", M 165.00
Plate, Quebec, d/b, Clews' Cities series, prof rpr, 9" 135.00
Plate, Sea Shells, d/b, Stubbs, 10" 245.00
Plate, Season (March), dk pk, Adams, 9½" 55.00
Plate, Shannondale Springs VA, pk transfer, Adams, 7⅛" 85.00
Plate, Sheltered Peasants, m-d/b, 10", EX 85.00
Plate, soup; Arms of NY, d/b, Mayer, 10" 695.00
Plate, soup; Chateau du Ermononville, d/b, Wood, 9¼" 180.00
Plate, soup; Hartford, pk, Jackson, 10½" 150.00
Plate, soup; Indian Temple on River, d/b, 8½" 65.00
Plate, soup; lady & children milking, d/b, 10" 185.00
Plate, soup; ship w/Am flag, d/b, Henshall, 9¾" 325.00
Plate, soup; Warwick Castle, d/b, Wood, 9¾" 175.00
Plate, St Catherine's Hill, d/b, Clews, 7¾", NM 95.00
Plate, Swiss chalet/men in mtns, d/b, 10¼", NM 155.00
Plate, Table Rock Niagara, d/b, Wood, 10" 495.00
Plate, Transylvania University, Lexington KY, d/b, Wood, 9" ...350.00
Plate, Trenton Falls, d/b, Wood's Shell border, 7½" 350.00
Plate, View Near Conway NH, pk, Adams, 9½" 85.00
Plate, Villa in Regents Park London, d/b, Adams, 8¾" 185.00
Plate, Vue du Ancienne Abbaye, d/b, Wood, 9½" 180.00
Plate, Vue du Chateau Ermenonville, d/b, Wood, 10¼" 195.00
Plate, Vue Prise en Savoie, d/b, Wood's French series, 7⅝" 155.00
Plate, West Point, Hudson River, blk, Clews, 8" 100.00
Plate, Wild Rose, l/b, 8¾" 45.00
Platter, Conway Castle, d/b, Hall's Select Views, 15" 675.00
Platter, Court House Boston, d/b, Hall, 10½" 1,350.00
Platter, Diorama View of Houghton Conquest House, d/b, 21½" ...1,050.00
Platter, Harper's Ferry, red, Adams' US Views, 15½" 325.00
Platter, Hermitage en Dauphine, d/b, Wood, 14¾" 695.00
Platter, Moose, d/b, Hall's Quadruped series, 15¼" 1,400.00
Platter, Newburgh Hudson River, l/b, scalloped, Clews, 17¾" 375.00
Platter, Niagara Falls From Am Side, d/b, Wood, 15" 800.00
Platter, St George's Chapel..., d/b, Wood, 16¾" 795.00
Platter, Tomb of Emperor Shah Jehan, d/b, Hall, 18" 975.00
Sauce boat, Batalha Portugal, d/b 195.00
Sauce boat, fisherman on bank, boats in water, d/b 195.00
Shaker, birdcage, d/b, Adams, 4¼" 325.00
Sugar bowl, Floral & Urn, d/b 175.00
Sugar bowl, Lafayette at Franklin's Tomb, d/b, Wood, rpr 475.00
Sugar bowl, Oriental ladies by river, d/b 325.00
Sugar bowl, Rural Estates, d/b, eagle head hdls 495.00
Teapot, Castle in Argyllshire Scotland, d/b, Hall, 11", EX 575.00
Teapot, Commodore McDonnough's Victory, d/b, 11", EX 675.00
Teapot, Rural Estates, d/bl, 11", NM 495.00
Teapot, shepherds w/sheep & dogs, d/b, 11¼" 495.00
Tureen, Castle, d/b, Clews, 11¼x13¼", +lid/ladle/tray 2,450.00
Tureen, gravy; Eagle & Shield, l/b, d/b border, rare 395.00
Tureen, Haughton Hall, Norfolk, d/b, Stevenson, w/lid, 16" L ...995.00
Wash bowl & pitcher, family picnicking/fishing, d/b 1,275.00

Wash bowl & pitcher, Lafayette at Franklin's Tomb, d/b, Wood .2,350.00
Wine cup, fruit & flowers, d/b, flared rim 185.00

Miscellaneous

Bust of George Washington, 7⅞",
$400.00.

Bottle, scent; HP cherub in wooded landscape, 2¼" 200.00
Bust of Madonna, pearlware, after E Wood, 1790-1800, 15" 625.00
Covered dish, hen on brn basket, bsk, 6¾x6¾x5" 250.00
Creamer, cow, yel & blk splashes, milkmaid, 1800, 6½" L 900.00
Cup plate, red rose, bl & yel flowers, red striping, Wood 100.00
Figurine, boy riding goat, EX color, 1860s, 12½" 675.00
Figurine, boy sits beside dog, lt wear, mini, 2¾" 120.00
Figurine, Britannia w/lion, silver lustre trim, 9½", EX 500.00
Figurine, cat, yel & blk splashes, orange collar, 1800s, 3½" 325.00
Figurine, cockerel, gaudy decor, 1835, 6" 775.00
Figurine, couple by well, she w/ewer, he w/wheat, 10" 275.00
Figurine, cow, red & wht, 'Milk Sold Here,' 1855-65, 14½" 2,000.00
Figurine, cow & calf, EX color, 1870s, 4¾x6" 485.00
Figurine, dalmatian sits on oval base w/gilt bands, 5", pr 325.00
Figurine, dog, recumbent, tan & blk splashes, 1780s, 3½" 145.00
Figurine, draped figure, jug at ft, on sq plinth, 9" 250.00
Figurine, exotic bird beside eggs in nest, mc, rpr, 8" 500.00
Figurine, giraffe seated by palm tree, 1840, 8" 665.00
Figurine, girl beside baby in cradle, 7" 55.00
Figurine, girl sits sidesaddle on rearing pony, 6½" 98.00
Figurine, greyhound seated on grassy knoll, 8¾", NM 365.00
Figurine, groom on leaping horse, mc, 1850s, 9½" 595.00
Figurine, Highlander w/bagpipes, resting hound, 1850, 11" 165.00
Figurine, lady, pearlware w/worn mc enamel, prof rpr, 9" 165.00
Figurine, lamb, free standing, sanded coat, 2¼" 260.00
Figurine, lamb, recumbent, curly coat, early, 2½" 250.00
Figurine, lion, standing, 3¼", EX 110.00
Figurine, lion & lamb, both recumbent, 1840s, 3¾x4¾" 200.00
Figurine, Little Red Riding Hood, 1800s, 15½" 500.00
Figurine, man or lady on horsebk, 12", EX, pr 200.00
Figurine, poodle, sanded coat, pk purse in mouth, 3", EX 95.00
Figurine, poodle w/yel basket, stands on plinth, 2" 145.00
Figurine, Prince & Princess, 9½" 215.00
Figurine, rabbit, 4-color on gr cole slaw grass base, 3½" 250.00
Figurine, Royal Children, 12" 265.00
Figurine, Scotsman & lass on clock, 14", NM 175.00
Figurine, Scotsman w/cocker spaniel, 8½" 135.00
Figurine, spaniel, copper lustre spots, rpr, 9½", pr 440.00
Figurine, spaniel, copper lustre spots, 7" 175.00
Figurine, spaniel, gold lustre & wht w/mc, 9¾", pr 275.00
Figurine, spaniel, red & blk splashes, yel collar, 3½" 175.00

Figurine, spaniel, red & wht, chips, 2⅞", pr 165.00
Figurine, spaniel, red & wht, EX details, ca 1855, 10", pr 1,000.00
Figurine, spaniel, rust spatter, lg wht & gold locket, 9½" 75.00
Figurine, spaniel w/flower basket, red spots, 8", EX, pr 845.00
Figurine, Vicar & Moses, early version, ca 1840, 9½" 660.00
Figurine, whippet, brn & wht, sits on gr base, 4½" 350.00
Figurine, whippet seated on bl pillow base, 4¾" 185.00
Figurine, 2 milkmaids, mc enamel, lt wear, 8½" 240.00
Inkwell, dog & pup on pillow, scroll-leg base, rpr, 4" L 135.00
Inkwell, poodle w/flower basket, well in base, early, pr 785.00
Mug, mc on blk transfer: birth inscription, 1834, 3", NM 100.00
Mustard pot, man figural, hat forms lid, 1840s, 5" 435.00
Pitcher, floral neck/body, 4-color, pearlware, 7" 300.00
Pitcher, peacock on pearlware, 1810, 6½" 600.00
Pitcher, 2 women at fountain, red transfer, 10¾", NM 90.00
Plate, Birds in Their Little Nests, emb floral rim, 6½" 80.00
Plate, flower center, wide mc rim band, mk W & Wood, 6¾" 70.00
Plate, gaudy mc floral, eagle mk, 10", EX 95.00
Plate, Those Who Dainties Love Shall..., mc, emb rim, 5" 50.00
Platter, peacock on creamware, feather edge, 1810, 16" 575.00
Platter, 3 terriers, after Armfeld, by Ferryhough, 1895, 9" 215.00
Pot, lady figural, hat forms lid, 1840s, rprs, 4½" 320.00
Spill vase, cow & boy figural, mc, ca 1850s 535.00
Spill vase, dog beside tree, mc w/gilt, 6½" 225.00
Tea bowl & saucer, Caledonia, gr & blk 115.00
Tea bowl & saucer, gaudy 4-color swags, NM 155.00
Wash bowl & pitcher, tulips in mc on pearlware, 1830s 825.00
Waste bowl, gaudy rose, lt wear, 5½" 135.00

Stained Glass

There are many factors to consider in evaluating a window or panel of stained glass art. Besides the obvious factor of condition, intricacy, jeweling, beveling, and the amount of selenium (red, orange, and yellow) present should all be taken into account. Remember, repair work is itself an art and can be very expensive. Our advisor for this category is Carl Heck; he is listed in the Directory under Colorado.

Lamps

Bigelow Kennard, shade, 12" brickwork dome, pk pearl sqs 875.00
Chicago Mosaic, 24" dome w/flowers, bronze tree trunk base ..3,000.00
Duffner-Kimberley, floral band, conical, 20" 3,500.00
Duffner-Kimberley, poppies, irreg edge, bronze base, 27x20" ...18,000.00
Unmk, chandelier, 22" irreg floral border shallow shade, 22" ..1,250.00
Unmk, shade, vintage border, brickwork/crown above, 24" 1,100.00
Wilkinson, 22" 4-repeat floral cone shade; att metal std 3,000.00

Windows

Am shield center, red/wht/bl/yel, ca 1875, 34x28" 1,000.00
Geometrics, Prairie School style, 33x34", pr 750.00
La Farge, radiating flowers, sgn/dtd center panel, 50x38" 690.00

Stanford

The Stanford Pottery Co. was founded in 1945 in Sebring, Ohio. One of the founders was George Stanford, a former manager at Spaulding China (Royal Copley). They continued in operations until the factory was destroyed by a fire about 1961. They produced a Corn Line, similar to that of the Shawnee Company, that is today becoming very collectible. Most examples are marked (either Stanford Sebring Ohio or with a paper label), so there should be no difficulty in distinguishing one from the other.

In addition to their Corn line, they produced planters and figurines, many of which were black trimmed with gold, made to be sold as pairs or sets. Wall pockets and vases were made as well. In 1949 they introduced a line called Tomatoe Ware, consisting of a cookie jar, grease jar, salt and pepper shakers, creamer and sugar bowl, mustard jar, marmalade jar, etc. These were shaped as bright red tomatoes with green leaves and stems (often used as lid finials) and were marketed under the name 'The Pantry Parade.' Our advisor for this category is Joe Devine; he is listed in the Directory under Iowa.

Corn Line, butter dish **45.00**
Corn Line, cookie jar **85.00**
Corn Line, creamer & sugar bowl **45.00**
Corn Line, pitcher, 7½" **55.00**
Corn Line, relish tray **35.00**
Corn Line, shakers, pr **25.00**
Corn Line, spoon rest **25.00**
Corn Line, teapot **60.00**
Planter, drum major or majorette, ea **15.00**
Planter, Dutch boy or girl by tulip, blk w/gold trim, ea **15.00**
Tomatoe Ware, cookie jar **50.00**
Tomatoe Ware, creamer **25.00**
Tomatoe Ware, grease jar **25.00**
Tomatoe Ware, marmalade jar **25.00**
Tomatoe Ware, mustard jar **25.00**
Tomatoe Ware, sugar bowl **25.00**
Wall pocket, bird, bl & cobalt w/gold trim **28.00**

Stangl

Stangl Pottery was one of the longest-existing potteries in the United States, having as its beginning in 1814 the Sam Hill Pottery, becoming the Fulper Pottery which gained eminence in the field of art pottery (ca. 1860), and then coming under the aegis of Johann Martin Stangl. The German-born Stangl joined Fulper in 1910 as chemical engineer, left for a brief stint at Haeger in Dundee, Illinois, and rejoined Fulper as general manager in 1920. He became president of the firm in 1928. Although Stangl's name was on much of the ware from the late twenties onward, the company's name was not changed officially until 1955. J.M. Stangl died in 1972; the pottery continued under the ownership of Wheaton Industries until 1978, then closed. Stangl is best known for its extensive Birds of America line, styled after Audubon; its brightly colored, hand-carved, hand-painted dinnerware; and its great variety of giftware, including its dry-brushed gold lines. For more information we recommend *Stangl Pottery* by Harvey Duke; for ordering information refer to the listing for Nancy and Robert Perzel, Popkorn Antiques (our advisors for this category), in our Directory under New Jersey.

Birds

#3250D, Grazing Duck, antique gold **60.00**
#3250E, Drinking Duck **75.00**
#3273, Rooster, 5¾" **400.00**
#3276, Bluebird **85.00**
#3276D, Bluebirds, 8" **150.00**
#3286, Hen, brn & blk, early, 3¼" **75.00**
#3400, Lovebird **55.00**
#3401, Wren **50.00**
#3402, Oriole, 3¼" **60.00**
#3402D, Orioles, old **200.00**
#3405, Cockatoo, 6" **55.00**

#3405D, Cockatoos, early 175.00
#3406, Kingfisher, paper label 70.00
#3408, Bird of Paradise, 5½" 100.00
#3443, Flying Duck, antique gold 135.00
#3444, Cardinal, red matt, 6½" 110.00
#3445, Rooster 125.00
#3446, Hen, speckled, 7" 130.00
#3447, Prothonatary Warbler 75.00
#3448, Bl Headed Vireo 65.00
#3452, Painted Bunting, 5" 100.00
#3454, Key West Quail Dove, single wing up 275.00
#3456, Cerulean Warbler, 4½" 65.00
#3457, Pheasant, 7¼x15" 800.00
#3490D, Redstarts 175.00
#3491, Hen Pheasant 200.00
#3492, Cock Pheasant, 6¼x11" 200.00
#3499, Parrot, 5½" 140.00
#3580, Cockatoo, 8½" 125.00
#3581, Group of Chickadees, 5¾" 185.00
#3582D, Parakeets 175.00
#3583, Parula Warbler, dk bl 50.00
#3584, Cockatoo, 11½" 225.00
#3585, Roufous Hummingbird, 3" 55.00
#3589, Indigo Bunting 65.00
#3590, Carolina Wren 120.00
#3591, Brewers Blackbird 125.00
#3592, Titmouse 55.00
#3593, Nuthatch, 2½" 50.00
#3594, Red-Faced Warbler 60.00
#3596, Gray Cardinal 75.00
#3597, Wilson Warbler, yel, 3½" 50.00
#3598, Kentucky Warbler, 3" 55.00
#3599D, Hummingbirds 240.00
#3626, Broadtail Hummingbird 150.00
#3627, Rivoli Hummingbird 150.00
#3628, Reifers Hummingbird 120.00
#3629, Broadbill Hummingbird 125.00
#3634, Allen Hummingbird, 3½" 60.00
#3635, Goldfinches, group 180.00
#3715, Blue Jay, w/peanut 550.00
#3722, European Finch 300.00
#3746, Canary, w/rose flower 200.00

#3750D, Western Tanagers, $350.00.

#3751, Red-Headed Woodpecker, red matt 150.00
#3757, Scissor-Tailed Flycatcher, 11" 525.00
#3810, Blackpoll Warbler 130.00
#3811, Chestnut-Backed Chickadee, 5" 100.00
#3812, Chestnut-Sided Warbler 95.00
#3813, Evening Grosbeak 120.00
#3848, Golden Crowned Kinglet 95.00

#3849, Goldfinch 95.00
#3850, Yellow Warbler, 4" 90.00
#3851, Red-Breasted Nuthatch 65.00
#3868, Summer Tanager 400.00
#3924, Yel-Throated Warbler 275.00

Miscellaneous

Amberglo, bowl, 8" 20.00
Amberglo, coffer server 50.00
Amberglo, gravy boat w/undertray 20.00
Animal, dog, sitting, #3280, 5¼" 300.00
Animal, elephant, #3249, 3" 200.00
Animal, elephant, Antique Gold, 5" 100.00
Animal, rabbit match holder, #3245 ....250.00
Antique Gold, candlesticks, #5138, pr 25.00
Antique Gold, horn of plenty, #5065 ....30.00
Antique Gold, server, center hdl, 10" 10.00
Antique Gold, vase, bud; #3981, 6½" 15.00
Apple Delight, snack plate, 8¼" 3.50
Ashtray, pansy form, 4" 12.00
Basket w/bow, matt bl, #3252 ....65.00
Blueberry, bowl, fruit; 5½" 15.00
Blueberry, bowl, 10" 30.00
Blueberry, bowl, 12" 50.00
Blueberry, candle warmer 18.00
Blueberry, cup & saucer 12.00
Blueberry, plate, 10" 15.00
Colonial, candlesticks, single, pr 25.00
Colonial, custard cup 7.50
Colonial, plate, 12½" 15.00
Country Garden, bowl, divided vegetable 25.00
Country Garden, bowl, 8" 25.00
Country Garden, coaster 9.00
Country Garden, cup 10.00
Country Garden, plate, 10" 15.00
Country Garden, plate, 8" 10.00
Dealer sign, bl & wht mottle, 3x7" 100.00
Dealer sign, gr lettering & red cherries on wht, 3x7" ...150.00
Deco Delight, creamer, silver-gr 40.00
Deco Delight, sugar bowl, Persian yel, w/lid 65.00
Deco Delight, teapot, Colonial bl 145.00
Fairlawn, server, center hdl 10.00
First Love, bowl, tab hdls, 5¼" 8.50
First Love, bowl, 5½" 7.50
First Love, butter dish 25.00
First Love, plate, chop; 12¼" dia 20.00
First Love, plate, 6" 5.00
First Love, plate, 8" 8.00
First Love, platter, oval, 14¾" 20.00
First Love, relish, curved, ftd, 11¼" L 15.00
Flowerpot, tulip, bl, 4" 15.00
Fruit, bowl, salad; 10" 40.00
Fruit, bowl, soup; 7½" 20.00
Fruit, bowl, 8½" 25.00
Fruit, cup & saucer, w/peach 17.00
Fruit, pitcher, ½-pt 15.00
Fruit, plate, 10" 18.00
Fruit, plate, 8" 12.00
Golden Blossom, plate, 8" 8.00
Golden Harvest, coffee warmer 12.00
Golden Harvest, lug soup 10.00
Golden Harvest, pitcher, lg 25.00
Golden Harvest, plate, 10" 10.00

Kiddieware, bowl, Little Boy Blue 50.00
Kiddieware, bowl, Little Quackers 65.00
Kiddieware, cup, Five Little Pigs 60.00
Kiddieware, cup, Little Bo Peep 45.00
Kiddieware, divided dish, ABCs 100.00
Kiddieware, divided dish, Five Little Pigs 200.00
Kiddieware, plate, Indian Campfire 175.00
Kiddieware, plate, Little Boy Blue 75.00
Lyric, pitcher, 11" 75.00
Magnolia, shakers, pr 12.00
Miniature, ashtray, pig form, med bl, 3" 40.00
Miniature, cornucopia, Colonial bl, #3209, 2¼" 10.00
Miniature, jug, tangerine, #1388, 2¼" 12.00
Orchard Song, mug, tall 25.00
Orchard Song, plate, 8" 10.00
Orchard Song, server, center hdl 8.00
Sculptured Fruit, bowl, 10" 35.00
Sportsman's Ware, ashtray, mallard, #3926, 10½" 38.00
Stoby mug, chief, w/orig hat, tan w/blk trim 100.00
Stoby mug, Cry Baby w/orig hat, natural colors 200.00
Terra Rose, pitcher, 1-pt 15.00
Terra Rose, vase, pitcher form, #3214, 8" 25.00
Terra Rose, warmer, gr 10.00
Thistle, bowl, 8" 25.00
Thistle, cup & saucer 8.50
Thistle, plate, bread & butter 6.00
Wig stand, lady's head, brunette, wood base, 16" 200.00
Wild Rose, butter dish 35.00

Stanley Tools

The Stanley company was founded in Connecticut in 1854, and over the years has absorbed more than a score of tool companies already in existence. By the second decade of the 20th century, having long since solidified their position as the source for tools of the highest grade, the company boasted worldwide prestige. Through both World Wars, they were recognized as one of the nation's premier producers of wartime goods. Industrial arts classes introduced baby boomers to Stanley tools and provided yet another impetus to expansion and recognition. Overall, the company's growth and development has kept an easy pace along with the economy of the nation, and it continues today as a leader in the field of tool production.

Two factors to consider when evaluating a tool are these: age and condition. One of their earliest trademarks (1854-1857) is 'A. Stanley.' In the early twenties, their now-familiar 'sweetheart' trademark, the letters SW and a heart shape within the confines of a modified rectangle, was adopted. They continued to use this trademark until it was discontinued in 1933. Many other variations were used as well, some of which contain a patent date. A study of these marks will help you determine the vintage of your tools. Condition is extremely important, and though a light cleaning is acceptable, you should never attempt to 'restore' a tool by sanding, repainting or replacing parts that may be damaged or missing. Tools listed below are for those in average as found condition, ranging from very good to excellent.

For more information, we recommend *Antique and Collectible Stanley Tools*, written by our advisor, John Walter, who is listed in the Directory under Ohio.

Brace, bit; #813 ....15.00
Brace, corner bit; #982 ....45.00
Brace, Spofford, #8 ....25.00
Chisel, socket; #760 ....15.00
Chisel set, Everlasting, #70 ....375.00
Drill, breast; #731 ....30.00

Drill, hand; #614	22.50
Gauge, dbl; #172	45.00
Gauge, marking; #62	7.50
Gauge, mortise; #77	30.00
Hammer, tack; magnetic, #1	100.00
Level, carpenter's, #1097, 12"	300.00
Level, carpenter's, #14	45.00
Level, hexagon, #31	25.00
Mallet, #15	30.00
Plane, bull nose rabbet; #90	60.00
Plane, circular; Defiance, #9	500.00
Plane, dado; #39-1	150.00
Plane, jack; #27½	45.00
Rule, architect's, #53½	55.00
Rule, blacksmith's, #17	30.00
Rule, scholar's, #173	450.00
Screwdriver, jackknife; #1022	150.00
Spoke shave, adjustable, #152	37.50
Square, combined try & mitre; #2, manufactured in 1874 only	75.00
Square, triangular mitre	500.00

Statue of Liberty

Long before she began greeting immigrants in 1886, the Statue of Liberty was being honored by craftsmen both here and abroad. Her likeness was etched on blades of the finest straight razors from England, captured in finely detailed busts sold as souvenirs to Paris fairgoers in 1878, and presented on colorfully lithographed trade cards, usually satirical, to American shoppers. Perhaps no other object has been represented in more forms or with such frequency as the universal symbol of America. Liberty's keepsakes are also universally accessible. Delightful souvenir models created in 1885 to raise funds for Liberty's pedestal are frequently found at flea markets, while earlier French bronze and terra cotta Liberties have been auctioned for over $100,000.00. Some collectors hunt for the countless forms of 19th-century Liberty memorabilia, while many collections were begun in anticipation of the 1986 Centennial with concentration on modern depictions. Our advisor for this category is Mike Brooks; he is listed in the Directory under California.

Coffeepot, bright enameling on metal, 11", $250.00; Photograph album, multicolor celluloid-covered image on front, velvet back, 8x10", EX, $275.00.

Coffeepot, mc image on enameled metal pot, 11"	250.00
Cup, pewter, Germany, ca 1904	60.00
Engraving, dedication ceremony, Am Bank Note Co, 1883, 5½x4"	110.00
Invitation to inauguration, by President Cleveland	150.00
Lamp base, wht metal figural, clock in base, 1885, 20", EX	300.00
Medal, Tasset, Paris, 1876 (earliest known)	100.00
Model, CI figural w/nickeled silver flame, rare, 40", EX	11,000.00
Model, plaster figural, Max Voit, 1918, 72", EX	880.00
Photo album, celluloid image on front, velvet bk, 10x8", EX	275.00
Photograph, August Bartholdi, Falk Studio	125.00
Photograph, Liberty nearing completion, 1886	85.00
Radio speaker stand, cast wht metal, Palcone Palradio, 17"	175.00
Spoon, Liberty figural hdl, SP, 5¾", EX	77.00
Watercolor, View of Liberty, JW Goppard, 21x15", EX	220.00

Steamship Collectibles

For centuries, ocean-going vessels with their venturesome officers and crews were the catalyst that changed the unknown aspects of our world to the known. Changing economic conditions, unfortunately, have now placed the North American shipping industry in the same jeopardy as the American passenger train. They are becoming a memory. The surge of interest in railroad collectibles and the railroad-related steamship lines has lead collectors to examine the whole spectrum of steamship collectibles. Our advisors for this category are Lila and Fred Shrader; they are listed in the Directory under California.

Dinnerware

Creamer, New England Steamship Co	38.00
Cup & saucer, demitasse; Alaska SS	48.00
Cup & saucer, GNPSS	135.00
Cup & saucer, Puerto Rico Line	45.00
Gravy boat, Am Mail	50.00
Ice cream shell, Alaska SS	55.00
Mug, coffee; Holland Am Line, SS Noordaam, striped border	8.50
Pitcher, Canadian Nat'l, Maritime, 6"	52.00
Plate, American Mail, 7"	28.00
Plate, Cunard White Star, 9", well used	75.00
Plate, Matson, floral border, bottom stamp, 8"	28.00
Plate, New England SS, 5½"	45.00
Plate, Prudential Lines, geometric border, 9½"	29.00
Platter, Standard Oil, 6x9½"	110.00
Teapot, Cunard, tan & blk pinstripes on Cuba shape	125.00
Teapot, Matson, teal gr 'M,' 2-cup	85.00

Miscellaneous

Button, uniform; Cunard, brass	7.50
Cuff links, Am President Lines, brass, eng, lg, pr	25.00
Hat ribbon, French Lines, SS Ile de France	45.00
Key chain, France III, portrait, bk: Joan of Arc, 1" dia	10.00
Launch book, Cunard Line, Queen Elizabeth, 1938, EX	110.00
Map, Arctic Ocean, routes shown, ca 1900, 15x14", EX	45.00
Paperback book, Picture History of SS Normandie, Braynard	18.00
Passenger list, Constitution, 1965	6.00
Pin, Queen Elizabeth II, HP brass figural, NM	20.00
Playing cards, Concordia Lines Norway, EX	20.00
Playing cards, Holland Am Line, dbl deck, EX	25.00
Playing cards, Swedish Am Lines, slip case, VG	18.00
Postcard, Cunard Lines, RMS Queen Mary, mc, lg	12.00
Postcard, White Star Lines, RMS Titanic, blk & wht, reissue	20.00
Publication, RMS Mauretania Cruise News, loose-leaf, 1954, VG	20.00
Schedule, Great Lakes, SS Missouri	8.50
Sign, Canadian Pacific Royal Mail, porc, red/wht, rare	600.00
Spoon, demitasse; Holland Am Lines, SS Noordaam, SP	16.00
Stationery, Holland Am Line, flag logo/watermk, 1 sheet, M	3.00
Stationery, Michelangelo, portrait, 1 sheet	3.00
Timetable, Burns Laird, colored photo+3 blk & whts, 1957	5.00
Timetable, Niagara to Sea, Canada, 1917	15.00
Towel, state room; Cunard Lines, RMS Caronia	32.00

Steins

Steins have been made from pottery, pewter, glass, stoneware, and porcelain, from very small up to the four-liter size. They are decorated by etching, in-mold relief, decals, and occasionally they may be hand painted. Some porcelain steins have lithophane bases. Collectors often specialize in a particular type — faience, regimental, or figural — while others limit themselves to the products of only one manufacturer. Our advisor for this category is Ron Fox; he is listed in the Directory under New York. See also Mettlach.

Key:
L — liter
lith — lithophane
POG — print over glaze
PUG — print under glaze
tl — thumb lift

Blown, Hobnail, copper inlaid lid, eagle tl, ½-L, M 145.00
Blown, transfer/HP: eagle w/crown, no lid, ½-L, NM 140.00
Blown & cut, Circle, red stain/gold trim, glass lid, ¼-L, NM 215.00
Blown & cut, elaborate/fine-cut pattern, glass lid, 1-L, NM 375.00
Blown & cut, floral pattern, pewter lid, ½-L, M 175.00
Blown & cut, repeating pattern, pewter lid & tl, ½-L, EX 60.00
Blown & cut, SP lid w/coin design (worn), .3-L 65.00
Character, alligator, porc, Schierholz, ½-L, NM 1,000.00
Character, bowling pin, pottery, loose strap, ½-L, NM 200.00
Character, bowling pins, pottery, inlaid lid, 1-L, M 230.00
Character, Chinaman, pottery, Merkelbach & Wick, ½-L, M 410.00
Character, devil, porc, Bohne/Sohne, inlaid lid, ½-L, M 800.00
Character, Duley, mk Ceramarte LTDA Webco, ½-L, M 98.00
Character, Funnel Man w/verse, pottery, ½-L, M 445.00
Character, Hops Lady, pottery, pewter lid, rpr, ½-L 250.00
Character, LAW Bicycle, porc, Schierholz, ½-L, EX 200.00
Character, monk, porc, lith, ½-L, EX 140.00
Character, monk, pottery, Goebel stylized bee, ½-L, M 335.00
Character, monk, pottery, inlaid lid, ¼-L, NM 250.00
Character, monk, stoneware, Merkelbach & Wick, ½-L, M 245.00
Character, monkey, pottery, rpl tl, ½-L 195.00
Character, Munich Child, pottery, inlaid lid, ½-L, EX 150.00
Character, Munich Child, pottery w/pottery lid, ½-L, EX 250.00
Character, Munich Child, Reinemann, inlaid lid, .2-L, M 275.00
Character, Mushroom Lady, porc, Schierholz, porc lid, ½-L, M ...2,550.00
Character, Nurnberg Tower, pewter, flag finial, 6¼", EX 165.00
Character, sleeping hunter, porc, G Bauer, rpr, ½-L 1,250.00
Character, soldier, pottery, #1577, Hanke, rpr strap, ½-L 375.00
Character, tower, pottery, inlaid lid, rpr, ½-L 525.00
Character, Wendelstein mtn, stoneware, Pauson, ½-L, EX 285.00
Character, woman, pottery, Merkelbach & Wick, ½-L, M 300.00
Copper & pewter, eng, mk Manning Bowman, 1-L, EX 75.00
Copper plated, relief: Capo di Monte-style scene, 10½", EX 230.00
Metal, relief: floral, w/wood panels, St Louis Silver, 1-L, EX 175.00
Military, porc, 32 Signal...Corps 1955, eagle finial, ½-L, M 380.00
Military, porc, 4 Allied...Air Force...1955-56, lith, ½-L, M 100.00
Military, porc, 540 Engineer Group, gate finial, ½-L, M 235.00
Military, pottery, relief: Bavarian Commemorative, ½-L, NM ...525.00
Nazi, pottery, transfer/HP: Landespolizei..., rpr, ½-L, EX 275.00
Nazi, stoneware, transfer/HP: 11 Battr II...1937, ½-L, EX 550.00
Occupational, pewter, eng: butcher, ca 1900, 3-L, EX 465.00
Occupational, porc, transfer/HP: porter, lith, ½-L, M 825.00
Occupational, porc, transfer: baker, lith, ½-L, NM 300.00
Occupational, porc, transfer: blksmith, lith, ½-L, EX 350.00
Occupational, porc, transfer: brewer, lith, ½-L, M 500.00
Occupational, porc, transfer: brewer, rpl lid, ½-L 200.00
Occupational, porc, transfer: carpenter, lith, ½-L, EX 300.00
Occupational, porc, transfer: hunter, lith, ½-L, M 250.00
Pewter, Budweiser, mk Shirley Wmsburg VA, eagle finial, ½-L, M ..88.00
Pewter, eng: Aiken Tennis Court 1902, Reed & Barton, 1-L, EX ..150.00
Pewter, eng: floral, lid dtd 1801, 1-L, EX 300.00
Pewter, relief: Boston scenes, pewter lid, ½-L, EX 110.00
Pewter, relief: couple dancing, ½-L, EX 100.00
Pewter, relief: drinking scene, musical lid & tl, ½-L, EX 100.00
Pewter, relief: eagle, bust of lady on spout, ½-L, EX 150.00

Pewter, relief: festive scene, pewter lid, ½-L, EX 150.00
Pewter, relief: knight, crest finial, rpr, 2-L, EX 300.00
Pewter, relief: Roman scene, lg ram tl, 1-L, EX 175.00
Pewter, relief: scenic, barmaid on lid, ½-L, VG 140.00
Pewter over nickel, relief: party scene, figural hdl, ½-L, EX 400.00
Porc, etch: soldier, copper & silver lid, ½-L, NM 500.00
Porc, HP: birds, lith, pewter lid, ½-L, EX 215.00
Porc, HP: monk w/wine, gold trim, no lid, Lenox, ½-L 140.00
Porc, transfer/HP: hunter, lith, old rpr, ½-L, VG 115.00
Porc, transfer/HP: man & lady at window, lith, ½-L, M 165.00
Porc, transfer: bicyclists, inlaid lid, ½-L, M 745.00
Pottery, Apostle body style, pewter lid, ca 1900, 1-L, NM 450.00
Pottery, etch: drinking scene, pewter lid, JWR #1010, ½-L, M ...150.00
Pottery, etch: Gambrinus, inlaid lid, 1-L, NM 245.00
Pottery, etch: knight & maiden, JWR #11070, rpr, 1-L 200.00
Pottery, etch: man & cherub, inlaid lid, JWR #130, .3-L, M 135.00
Pottery, etch: man & lady, silver wear on lid, ½-L, EX 150.00
Pottery, etch: men at tavern, inlaid lid, Gerz #1229, ½-L, M 165.00
Pottery, etch: men paying bill, Marzi & Remi #1617, ½-L, M 300.00
Pottery, etch: merry people, new pewter lid, 1-L, EX 90.00
Pottery, etch: party scene, Merkelbach & Wick #2002, 1-L, M ..300.00
Pottery, etch: picnic, Thewalt #425, ½-L, EX 100.00
Pottery, etch: Souvenir of FL..., alligator hdl, no lid, ½-L, M 245.00
Pottery, etch: 2 ladies, pewter lid, #427, .4-L, M 120.00
Pottery, heavy relief: people w/donkey, 1-L, M 200.00
Pottery, HP: cherubs/brewers, pewter lid, lion tl, 1-L, EX 300.00
Pottery, HP: Munich Child scene, pewter lid, 1-L, M 750.00
Pottery, HP: shell w/sail & torch, Merkelbach & Wick, .2-L, NM ...165.00
Pottery, relief: animals hunted, fox hdl, no tl, .3-L, EX 65.00
Pottery, relief: apostles, Kruessen, pewter lid, ¼-L, EX 250.00
Pottery, relief: Art Nouveau, pewter lid, ½-L, M 250.00
Pottery, relief: cavalier & maiden, pewter lid, 1-L, M 130.00
Pottery, relief: couple dancing, rpl pewter lid, 1-L, NM 50.00
Pottery, relief: Dr Swett's...Root Beer, no lid, .3-L, M 200.00
Pottery, relief: drinking scene, pewter lid, ½-L, M 75.00
Pottery, relief: lady w/beer, 2 dwarfs on lid, ½-L, M 130.00
Pottery, relief: man & lady, dwarfs on lid, ½-L, M 150.00
Pottery, relief: mandolin player, barmaid lid, 1-L, EX 150.00
Pottery, relief: monkeys, monkey hdl, no lid, ½-L, M 120.00
Pottery, relief: Munich Child on bbl, pewter lid, 1-L, EX 150.00
Pottery, relief: pig & bowling pins, pewter lid, ½-L, EX 150.00
Pottery, relief: soccer game, ball finial, ½-L, M 600.00
Pottery, relief: trumpeter of Sackingen, pewter lid, 1-L, M 130.00
Pottery, relief: 2 cavaliers drinking, dwarf on lid, ½-L, M 150.00
Pottery, relief: 20 coins, inlaid lid, eagle tl, ½-L, NM 250.00
Pottery, transfer/HP: Englishman, pewter lid, ½-L, EX 135.00
Pottery, transfer/HP: fireman, tools on pewter lid, ½-L, EX 120.00
Pottery, transfer/HP: lady, pewter lid, ½-L, EX 110.00
Pottery, transfer: Festival Hannover 1924, pewter lid, ½-L, M 75.00
Pottery, transfer: Nouveau wheat, SP lid, ½-L, NM 365.00
Pottery, transfer: US Life Saving Station..., ¼-L, M 120.00
Pressed glass, floral pattern, pewter lid, 4½", M 60.00
Regimental, glass, transfer: Betriebs Komapgnie...1905, ½-L, M ...950.00
Regimental, porc, Garde du Corps 1906-09, Schierholz, ½-L, EX .2,750.00
Regimental, porc, transfer: artillery scene, 1950s, ½-L, M 195.00
Regimental, porc, 109 Infantry...1904-07, lith, ½-L, M 435.00
Regimental, porc, 125 Infantry 1904-06, roster, lith, ½-L, M 400.00
Regimental, porc, 16 Infantry...1904-06, lith, lion tl, ½-L, NM .315.00
Regimental, porc, 17 Dragoon...1903-06, lith, ½-L, NM 350.00
Regimental, porc, 172 Infantry...1909-11, lith, ½-L, M 325.00
Regimental, porc, 2 Jager...1906-09, lith, eagle tl, 12", NM 1,200.00
Regimental, porc, 49 Fld Artillery...1899, lith, ½-L, M 345.00
Regimental, porc, 9 Infantry...1897-99, lith, ½-L, M 275.00
Regimental, pottery, ...1909-12, stanhope in eagle tl, 13", EX ..1,700.00

Regimental, stoneware, transfer: 12 Infantry...1912-14, ½-L, M .550.00
Stoneware, combed, porc girl inlay lid, pewter base, 1-L, EX 95.00
Stoneware, etch: Art Nouveau, Gerz, pewter lid, .3-L, EX 150.00
Stoneware, etch: country scene, Marzi & Remy, ½-L, M 425.00
Stoneware, etch: horse, pewter lid w/crest, 1820, .3-L, EX 300.00
Stoneware, etch: Lowenbrau Keller, pewter lid, 1-L, M 215.00
Stoneware, etch: party scene, Marzi & Remy #1638, ½-L, M 200.00
Stoneware, etch: Pschorr Brau, combed, pewter lid, 1-L, EX 185.00
Stoneware, etch: Unions Brau, Munich Child pewter lid, 1-L, NM ..465.00
Stoneware, faience, mk 1842 Schafer Beer, pewter lid, ½-L, EX ...125.00
Stoneware, glazed relief: floral, metal lid, ½-L, NM 75.00
Stoneware, relief/etch: Allgemaner Schnauferl Club, '05, 1-L, M .230.00
Stoneware, relief: Art Nouveau, pewter lid, ½-L, NM 200.00
Stoneware, relief: drinkers/dwarfs, Regensburg, 1-L, EX 115.00
Stoneware, relief: dwarfs, porc lid, Regensburg, ½-L, EX 100.00
Stoneware, relief: Gambrinus, mermaid tl, Regensburg, ½-L, EX .85.00
Stoneware, transfer/etch: mtn scene, pewter lid, ½-L, M 230.00
Stoneware, transfer/HP: Crest of Bremen, ½-L, NM 235.00
Stoneware, transfer/HP: Munich Child, Thewalt, ½-L, M 150.00
Stoneware, transfer/HP: Spaten Brau, pewter lid, ½-L, NM 200.00
Stoneware, transfer: Eye Bar Club 1909, pewter lid, ½-L, NM 75.00
Stoneware, transfer: Lemps Special Brew, pewter lid, ½-L, M 565.00
Stoneware, transfer: Otto Huber NY, pewter lid, ½-L, NM 250.00
Wood, burned: cavalier, leafy trim, rpr hdl, .2-L, EX 100.00
Wood, burned: florals, partly colored, wood lid, 1-L, EX 150.00
Wood, cvd: Oriental-type decor, wood hdl & lid, ½-L, EX 80.00

Steuben

Carder Steuben glass was made by the Stueben Glass Works in Corning, New York, while under the direction of Frederick Carder from 1903 to 1932. Perhaps the most popular types of Carder Steuben glass are Gold Aurene which was introduced in 1904 and Blue Aurene, introduced in 1905. Gold and Blue Aurene objects shimmer with the lustrous beauty of their metallic iridescence. Carder also produced other types of 'Aurenes' including Red, Green, Yellow, Brown, and Decorated, all of which are very rare. Aurene also was cased upon Calcite glass. Some pieces had paper labels.

Other types of Carder Steuben include Cluthra, Cintra, Florentia, Rosaline, Ivory, Ivorene, Jades, Verre de Soie; there are many more.

Frederick Carder's leadership of Steuben ended in 1932, and the production of colored glassware soon ceased. Since 1932 the tradition of fine Steuben art glass has been continued in crystal.

Our advisor for this category is Thomas P. Dimitroff; he is in the Directory under New York. In the following listings, examples are signed unless noted otherwise.

Key: ACB — acid cut back

Basket, Verre de Soie, V hdl, 10½x10" 350.00
Bottle, perfume; Oriental Poppy, #547, 9⅞" 2,800.00
Bottle, scent; Bl Aurene, conical stopper, #1414, 7½" 800.00
Bottle, scent; Bl Aurene, flame stopper, ftd, #1414, 7⅞" 700.00
Bottle, scent; Gold Aurene, sgn, #2833, orig stopper 650.00
Bottle, scent; Verre de Soie, Lt Bl Jade stopper, #1455, 5" 500.00
Bottle, scent; Verre de Soie, slender, teardrop stopper, 8" 350.00
Bowl, ACB Canton pattern, Plum Jade, #2928, 4x8" 2,500.00
Bowl, amethyst, spittoon shape, 10" 225.00
Bowl, Dk Bl Jade, like #6962, 6½x9½" 1,600.00
Bowl, Dmn Quilt, red threading on crystal, #6772, 2¾x12" 225.00
Bowl, Florentia, cinnamon, #6782, 4x12" 2,500.00
Bowl, Florentia, pk, 5-petal flower w/in, flat rim, 4x12" 2,200.00
Bowl, Gold Aurene, ftd, #6106, 11½" 350.00

Bowl, Gold Aurene, w/purple irid, petaled, #204, +7" plate 300.00
Bowl, Gold Aurene & Calcite, in irid blk hollow holder, 4x13" ...300.00
Bowl, Gold Aurene & Calcite, mk, 6" 230.00
Bowl, Gold Aurene & Calcite, shallow, 10¼" 295.00
Bowl, Gold Aurene & Calcite, 3x5" 250.00
Bowl, Gr Jade, wide flat rim, 3x12" 250.00
Bowl, Grotesque, ivory, 6½x12" 450.00
Bowl, Grotesque, ruby, sqd, #7277, 7x11" 375.00
Bowl, Ivorene, oblong/ruffled, #7563, 6½x13½x10½" 425.00
Bowl, Ivorene w/bl irid int, unsgn, 3x5¾" 325.00
Bowl, lt topaz w/bl rim, #5061, 2x12" 40.00
Bowl, Mat Su Noke, Amethyst Cintra, Oriental hdls, 4x8", NM .650.00
Bowl, nut; Gold Aurene, 4 reeded ft, #139, 4" 525.00
Bowl, punch; Gold Aurene, stretched rim, sgn/#2852, 12", EX ..750.00
Bowl vase, Grotesque, Bl Jade, 7x6¼x12" 3,500.00
Candle holder, Bl Aurene, twisted stem, 8" 325.00
Candle holder, Rosaline w/Alabaster, sgn Carder, 1¼", pr 500.00
Candlesticks, Celeste Bl, ribbed w/crystal wafers, #2596, 12" 150.00
Candlesticks, Gold Aurene, twisted stem, sgn/#686, 10", pr 880.00
Candlesticks, Pomona Gr, gr spirals on clear stems, 10", pr 350.00
Candlesticks, random threading w/bubbles on antique gr, 14", pr ..675.00
Candlesticks, Selenium Red, Burlington eng, mk, 7", pr 725.00
Champagne, Bristol Yel, ball stem, sgn/#7336, 5½" 85.00
Chandelier, brass dome w/7 Gold Aurene bell shades, chained .1,600.00
Chandelier, Gold Aurene, 3 lilies, scroll arms, 23" H 700.00
Chandelier, urn-form hanger w/2 Gold Aurene lilies, 14" H 300.00
Compote, Bl Aurene, twist stem, sgn Steuben/Aurene, #367, 6" ..750.00
Compote, bonbon; Verre de Soie, bl finial/twist stem, 6" 825.00
Compote, Cyprian, bl rim, stick stem, 3½x8" 250.00
Compote, dk amethyst, #2848, 8" 145.00
Compote, floral eng on lt gr, crystal ft, #7032, 7", pr 300.00
Compote, Verre de Soie, appl peach on lt gr w/bl rim, 8x6" 1,250.00
Cup & saucer, Gr Jade, unsgn 175.00
Cup & saucer, Rosalene, unsgn 175.00
Figurine, gazelle & calf, #7399, pr 460.00
Fish bowl, Celeste Bl, 7x13½" 175.00
Flower bowl, Verre de Soie, Optic panels, 4¼x6½" 110.00
Goblet, ACB Alicia pattern, Gr Jade on Alabaster, #7443, 6" ...350.00
Goblet, Oriental Jade, swirled w/half-twist stems, #2361 ....400.00
Goblet, Rosaline w/Alabaster twist stem, #3551, 8½" 225.00
Goblet, topaz w/Celeste Bl reeding, #5193 ....85.00
Lamp base, ACB mums/leaves, Yel Jade, rectangular, 6" 400.00
Lamp base, Cintra, wheat stalks, opal on gr, w/metal: 33" 1,200.00
Lamp base, Gr Jade, blk rigaree hdls, slim, Carder, 25", EX 300.00
Lamp base, Moss Agate, mc/silver-speckled dk amethyst, 25" .1,700.00
Luminor, Pineapple, controlled bubbles, glass base, #6971, 9¾" .600.00
Nut dish, Bristol Yel w/blk threading, ped base, 3x5" 195.00
Paperweight, cranberry int w/controlled bubbles, 4½x5" 450.00
Pitcher, Gold Aurene, bl highlights, monogram, 10" 1,350.00
Pitcher, Gr Jade on Alabaster 550.00
Planter bowl, Bl Aurene, 3 prunt ft, sgn/#2586, 12" 770.00
Plate, amethyst w/opal, 8¼", pr 100.00
Plate, luncheon; Gold Ruby w/wht rim 85.00
Plate, Oriental Jade, 8½" 60.00
Salt cellar, Bl Aurene, sgn/#564, 8-rib 375.00
Salt cellar, Gold Aurene w/EX irid, incurvate, #567 ....250.00
Shade, bl-gold irid, ribbed, #2306, 4¼", set of 4 ....780.00
Shade, Gr Aurene, appl platinum border, 10" dia 1,290.00
Sherbet, Gold Aurene, #2361, 3½", set of 5 ....700.00
Sherbet, Gold Aurene on Calcite, unsgn, +underplate 195.00
Sherbet, Gr Jade w/Alabaster ft, unsgn 85.00
Sherbet, Van Dyke, amber stem, +underplate 120.00
Tazza, Gold Aurene w/Calcite half-twist stem, #402, 7x7" 525.00
Tumbler, Verre de Soie, monogrammed, 4¼", set of 6 ....175.00

Urn, Gold Aurene, pink irid band, flared rim, 5½x7" 675.00
Vase, ACB, Plum Jade, Chang, 10" dia 4,900.00
Vase, ACB carnations, Gr Jade on wht, 10" 900.00
Vase, ACB flowers, gr on rose quartz/yel, drilled, 14" 575.00
Vase, Alabaster/Gr Jade, dbl 'M' appl hdls, #2939, 10¾" 1,000.00
Vase, amber, ribbed, #6031, 7" 125.00
Vase, amber, ribbed, cylindrical, folded rim, sgn, 10¼" 140.00
Vase, Aqua Marine, swirls, #6031, 6¾" 200.00
Vase, Aurene, gold feathers, Alabaster/gr petals, #548, 6" 3,000.00

Vases, left to right: Blue Aurene with heart shapes and pulled designs in white and gold iridescence, wide mouth tapers to slender foot, signed/#8300, 12", $2,600.00; Blue Aurene with pale green highlights, flared cylinder form, signed/#6127, 10", $1,100.00.

Vase, Bl Aurene, #2683, mk, 11" 2,350.00
Vase, Bl Aurene, classic form, 10" 2,500.00
Vase, Bl Aurene, collar neck, #2845, 10½" 2,000.00
Vase, Bl Aurene, flared 10-rib body, 6x7" 600.00
Vase, Bl Aurene, flattened fan form, ped ft, sgn/#2697, 8½" ...1,500.00
Vase, Bl Aurene, opal/gold vines, fan form, #6297, 9x7" 2,500.00
Vase, Bl Aurene, ribbed, flared, 6½" 650.00
Vase, Bl Aurene, squat w/wide flared top, lt ribbing, 5" 715.00
Vase, Bl Aurene, trumpet form w/ruffled rim, label, 6" 600.00
Vase, Bl Aurene on Calcite, ruffled trumpet form, 12½" 1,100.00
Vase, Celeste Bl, 6x3½" 90.00
Vase, Cluthra, amethyst, classic form, 10" 1,000.00
Vase, Cluthra, Amethyst, opal 'M' appl hdls, #2959, 11" 1,800.00
Vase, Cluthra, etched archer/gazelles, gr-cased pk/gr, 14" 7,700.00
Vase, Cluthra, gr, #2863, 8" 850.00
Vase, Cluthra, wht, classic form, 8½" 725.00
Vase, Controlled Cintra, lt gr & wht, 6½x8x7½" 950.00
Vase, Flemish Bl, fan form, sgn 250.00
Vase, Flemish Bl, ftd, ribbed, like #442, 12" 200.00
Vase, Gold Aurene, flared rim, mk, 4" 295.00
Vase, Gold Aurene, lt Dmn Quilt, #243, 8½" 700.00
Vase, Gold Aurene, ruffled, bluish knop stem/base, #312, 13" 850.00
Vase, Gold Aurene, ruffled trumpet neck, pinched sides, 4¾" 600.00
Vase, Gold Aurene, sqd ball top, ped base, sgn/#150, 5", pr 770.00
Vase, gr, blown molded w/ribs, ped ft, 9x5½" 275.00
Vase, gr, 3-prong stump form, #2744, 6" 250.00
Vase, Gr Aurene, gold vines/leaves, like #1210, 9½" 4,500.00
Vase, Gr Cintra & Alabaster, Chrysanthemum etch, #6589, 13¼" .4,500.00
Vase, Gr Jade, spherical, 7x7" 330.00
Vase, Gr Jade w/Alabaster, 2-prong, 9¼x5¼" 675.00

Vase, Grotesque, gr to clear, 11" 475.00
Vase, Grotesque, Rosaline to Alabaster, 4½" 350.00
Vase, Intarsia, rose vines/scrolls on crystal, #5070, 8x7" 4,700.00
Vase, Ivorene, classic form, 9" 475.00
Vase, Ivorene, classic urn shape, 8x7" 395.00
Vase, Ivorene, ribbed, flared, #368, 4" 275.00
Vase, Lt Bl Jade w/Alabaster ft, like #1979, 8" 1,800.00
Vase, lt pk w/cobalt threading, ribbed fan form, 9x9", pr 500.00
Vase, Moss Agate, 11⅞" 6,500.00
Vase, Selenium Red, ribbed, 7" 450.00
Vase, Spanish Gr, threaded border, fan form, sgn Carder, 9" 400.00
Vase, Spanish Gr, V-form fan on ped ft, 8½" 220.00
Vase, topaz, ribbed, flared, #7185, 9x10" 100.00
Vase, topaz, wheel-cut floral swags, fan form, 11x9" 250.00
Vase, Verre de Soie, Dmn Quilt, pk threaded rim, 10" 275.00
Vase, Wisteria, 12 pillar ribs, #7228, 8" 850.00
Vase, Yel Bristol, airtrap bubbles/threading, U-form, 8" 220.00
Wine, Selenium Red, molded twisted stems, 4½" 100.00

Stevengraphs

A Stevengraph is a small picture made of woven silk resembling an elaborate ribbon, created by Thomas Stevens in England in the latter half of the 1800s. They were matted and framed by Stevens, usually with his name appearing on the mat or, more commonly, the trade announcement on the back of the mat. He also produced silk postcards and bookmarks, all of which have 'Stevens' woven in silk on one of the mitered corners. Anyone wishing to learn more about Stevengraphs is encouraged to contact the Stevengraph Collectors' Association, whose address can be found in the Directory under Clubs, Newsletters, and Catalogs.

Called to the Rescue, M 250.00
Dick Turpin's Last Ride on His Blk Bess, Hogarth, VG 150.00
First Point, EX 150.00
For Life or Death (2 horses), G 300.00
God Speed the Plough, G 150.00
Good Old Days, sgn front, orig label on bk, orig ornate fr, NM ..175.00
Lady Godiva Procession, M 275.00
Meet, unmk, VG 165.00
Mrs Cleveland, G 100.00
Niagara, EX 450.00
Panel, Benjamin Harrison, G 100.00
Present Time (60 Miles an Hour), EX 175.00
President Grover Cleveland, G 100.00
Start, NM 175.00
Victoria Queen of Empire on Which Sun Never Sets, VG 150.00

Miscellaneous

Bookmark, Birthday Gift, G 50.00
Bookmark, Centennial USA, Father of Our Country, VG 100.00
Bookmark, Ever Dearest Ever Nearest, G 50.00
Bookmark, Home Sweet Home, VG 65.00
Bookmark, Last Rose of Summer, G 50.00
Bookmark, My Dear Mother, G 40.00
Bookmark, Present From Crystal Palace, G 50.00
Bookmark, Robert Burns, VG 70.00
Bookmark, To My Son, G 40.00
Bookmark, Wish, G 50.00

Stevens and Williams

Stevens and Williams glass was produced at the Brierly Hill Glassworks in Stourbridge, England, for nearly a century, beginning in the 1830s. They were credited with being among the first to develop a method of manufacturing a more affordable type of cameo glass. Other lines were also made — silver deposit, alexandrite, and engraved rock crystal, to name but a few. Our advisor for this category is Don Williams; he is listed in the Directory under Missouri.

Basket, pk w/mica flakes, emb ribs, amber scallops, 7½x5" **275.00**
Bowl, Gr Jade, Alabaster disk base, mk Brierly, 8" **250.00**
Creamer, wht opaque w/mc appl flowers, pk int, 2⅞x2¾" **245.00**
Fairy lamp, Sombrero intaglio, amber, fluted base, 6¼" **595.00**
Pitcher, rainbow stripe swirl, reeded crystal hdl, 8x7" **475.00**
Pitcher, rust pull-ups, clear/yel/wht opaque/pk layers, 9" **750.00**
Rose bowl, brn o/l, gold flowers at top, pleated rim, 5x3½" **450.00**
Rose bowl, pk emb basketweave o/l, cream int, pleated, 6x4½" ..**425.00**
Vase, bl swirl MOP satin, mk, 6⅜x3½" **495.00**
Vase, bl to yel MOP satin swirl, stick neck, 12" **1,000.00**
Vase, floral intaglio, pk on wht satin, ruffled, 5x3" **295.00**
Vase, gilt floral on gr satin w/stripes, clear ft, 3" **250.00**
Vase, gold over pk-red MOP satin swirl, stick neck, 9" **900.00**
Vase, lime satin, emb swirls, bulbous w/high cone ft, 10½" **600.00**
Vase, pk o/l, amber ruffled top, HP florals, sgn, 5¾x4" **235.00**
Vase, pk o/l w/appl amber leaf & cranberry acorns, 10" **595.00**
Vase, pk o/l w/appl mc fruit, amber hdl & branch, 8x3½" **750.00**
Vase, pk o/l w/lg appl opal leaves/rim, 12" **395.00**
Vase, rainbow cameo flowers on wht opaque satin, 5¾x8" **2,500.00**
Vase, shiny ruby/yel/opal pull-up design, can neck, 8" **325.00**
Vase, turq opal swirl, clear petal ft, ruffled fan top, 6" **165.00**
Vase, wht w/pk int, amber rim, amber/red leaves, 6¾" **165.00**
Vase, wht w/pk int, appl pastel-stripe leaves, amber rim, 8" **245.00**

Stickley

Among the leading proponents of the Arts and Crafts Movement, the Stickley brothers — Gustav, Leopold, Charles, Albert, and John George — were at various times and locations separately involved in designing and producing furniture as well as decorative items for the home. (See Arts and Crafts for further information.) The oldest of the five Stickley brothers was Gustav; his work is the most highly regarded of all. He developed the style of furniture referred to as Mission. It was strongly influenced by the type of furnishings found in the Spanish missions of California — utilitarian, squarely built, and simple. It was made most often of oak, and decoration was very limited or non-existent. The work of his brothers display adaptations of many of Gustav's ideas and designs. His factory, the Craftsman Workshop, operated in Eastwood, New York, from the late 1890s until 1915, when he was forced out of business by larger companies who copied his work and sold it at much lower prices. Among his shopmarks are the early red decal containing a joiner's compass and the words 'Als Ik Kan,' the branded mark with very similar components, and paper labels.

The firm known as Stickley Brothers was located first in Binghamton, New York, and then Grand Rapids, Michigan. Albert and John George made the move to Michigan, leaving Charles in Binghamton (where he and an uncle continued the operation under a different name). After several years John George left the company to rejoin Leopold in New York. (These two later formed their own firm called L. & J.G. Stickley.) The Stickley Brothers Company under Albert's sole direction produced furniture that featured fine inlay work, decorative cutouts, and leaned strongly toward a style of Arts and Crafts with an English influence. It was tagged with a paper label 'Made by Stickley Brothers, Grand Rapids' or with a brass plate or decal with the words 'Quaint Furniture,' an English term he chose to refer to his product. In addition to his furniture, he made metal furnishings as well.

The workshops of the L. & J.G. Stickley Company first operated under the name 'Onondaga Shops.' Located in Fayetteville, New York, their designs were often all but copies of Gustav's work. Their products were well made and marketed, and their business was very successful. Their decal labels contained all or a combination of the words 'Handcraft' or 'Onondaga Shops,' along with the brothers' initials and last name. The firm continues in business today. Our advisor for this category is Bruce Austin; he is listed in the Directory under New York. Note: When only one dimension is given for tables, it is length.

Gustav Stickley

Gustav Stickley copper and leaded glass table lamp, curvilinear handles at each side, 16" with 26½" diameter shade, $1,750.00.

Armchair, #318, 1904 mk, EX orig finish, 38x27" **750.00**
Armchair, #344, child's, horizontal bk slats, rpl seat, mk **375.00**
Armchair, #345, 5-slat V-bk, orig uphl, cleaned, decal, EX **2,400.00**
Armchair, arched seat rails, 1 lg slat ea side, mk, 40", VG **3,000.00**
Armchair, V crest rail, 5-slat bk, open sides, decal, 37", VG **800.00**
Book stand, #72, overhanging top, 3-shelf, Ellis design, 42" **4,000.00**
Book stand, #79, plank sides w/D-hdl cutouts, mk, 39x14", EX ...**1,900.00**
Bookcase, #510 (1-door), 12 mullioned panes, no mk, 53x30" ..**6,000.00**
Bookcase, #715, 1 16-pane door, EX orig blk finish, mk, 56" ..**6,000.00**
Bookcase, #718, 2 doors w/16 panes, decal/label, 54x56", VG ...**3,750.00**
Bookshelf/cabinet, #722, side door, Ellis design, mk, 45x38" ...**6,000.00**
Chair, Morris; #332, 5 slats under flat arms, mk, 41", VG **4,500.00**
Chair, side; #306½, ladderbk w/rpl seat, decal, 36", VG **200.00**
Chair, side; #352, 4-slat bk (arched top), orig seat, 6 for **6,000.00**
Chair set, #270, drop-in leather seat, brand, 6 for **2,800.00**
Chair set, #306½ (6 ladderbks)+#310½ (2 armchairs), EX **2,900.00**
Charger, #345, hammered copper w/emb pods, EX patina, 20" ..**5,250.00**
Daybed, #220, 6-slat head/ftbrds, new pads, mk, 82", EX **5,000.00**
Desk, #709, 5-drw w/oval pulls, mk, rstr top, +#306 chair **2,000.00**
Desk, #729, fall front, 2 drws+3, decal/label, 45x37", VG **2,800.00**
Floor lamp, #500, 4 ft arranged as X, mk, rpl shade, 57" **1,900.00**
Footstool, #301, tapered ft, red decal, rpl rush top, 18x20" **550.00**
Footstool, #395, spindle sides, orig tacked leather, 15x20" **2,900.00**
Hall tree, #52, sq post w/orig hooks, mk rpr/rfn, 71", G **750.00**
Lamp, shoe-ft trestle base, gabled glass/copper 10" W shade **6,000.00**
Lantern, #304, iron w/heart cutouts, rpl glass, hanging, 10" **900.00**
Lantern, #830, copper grid over amber glass, no mk, 11x6" **550.00**
Lantern, #830, copper grid over amber glass, w/chain, 11x6" ..**1,500.00**
Lantern, att, iron w/4 glass trapezoids & triangles, 17", VG **850.00**
Letter case, #96, mk, orig leather on bottom, 7x12", EX **800.00**
Light, hammered copper cap/Tiffany lily shade, hanging, EX **650.00**
Music stand, #674, 4-tier, 5-spindle sides, label, 42x20", VG ..**2,900.00**

Paper clip, hand-wrought copper, stylized spade form, mk, EX ...**400.00**
Rocker, #317, arms, 1904 mk, EX orig finish, 39x27x23", EX **650.00**
Rocker, #323, curved bk, 5-slat bk/sides, orig finish, sgn **2,700.00**
Rocker, #337, Ellis design, decal, 35", EX **200.00**
Rocker, #359A, 11-spindle bk, open arms, new seat, 37", VG ...**1,600.00**
Rocker, #365, 3-slat bk, open arms, orig seat, mk, 29", VG **550.00**
Server, #970, dbl-key tenons, iron hdw, early, 37x44", EX **7,000.00**
Settle, #225, crib type, 5-slat sides, mk, cleaned, 78" **4,750.00**
Shaving mirror, free-standing, red decal, 21½x24x7", M **1,400.00**
Stand, #604, 20" dia top, arched X-stretchers, decal, 26" **750.00**
Stand, #642 (similar), 2 sm drw over 1, backsplash, 22" W, VG ..**1,600.00**
Stand, #654, 24" dia top, arched X-stretchers, decal, EX **850.00**
Stand, #660, 18" sq top w/canted corners, overhang top, 20" ..**1,200.00**
Table, #26, 23" top/shelf cvd as flower face, foliate legs **6,000.00**
Table, #440, thru-tenon top/X-stretchers, mk, rfn, 30" dia **3,000.00**
Table, #441, thru-tenons/stacked stretchers, 36" dia, VG **2,400.00**
Table, #603, notched X-stretchers, label, 20x18" dia, VG **850.00**
Table, #611, 24" sq top w/canted corners, base shelf, mk **1,600.00**
Table, #624, 48" hexagonal tacked leather top, 6-leg, EX **10,000.00**
Table, #671, drop leaf, shoe ft, rfn, partial label, 32" dia **1,400.00**
Table, dining; #634, massive posts, 54" dia, +6 leaves, VG **7,500.00**
Table, library; #619, 3-drw, decal/label, recoated, 66", VG **4,500.00**
Table, library; #653, extended top, 1 drw, decal, 48", VG **1,500.00**
Table, luncheon; #647, overhanging 30x28" top, no mk, EX ..**1,600.00**
Wastebasket, #94, slat sides, tapered form, mk, 14", EX **1,900.00**

L. & J.G. Stickley

Bed, #114, 7-slat head/ftbrds, stretcher crest rail, dbl **2,700.00**
Bed, 5 broad slats under V rail, rnded posts, mk, full sz **3,100.00**
Book stand, #46, 4-tier, 3-slat sides, decal, 42x21", EX **1,900.00**
Bookcase, #641, 16-pane door/thru tenons, decal, 55x30", EX ..**3,300.00**
Chair, Morris; #410 (similar), 7-slat sides, decal, 40", VG **4,500.00**
Chair, Morris; #471, 6-slat sides, spring seat, 41x32", VG **2,000.00**
Chair, Morris; #830, bk adjusts, flat arms, decal, reuphl **3,500.00**
Chair, side; #330, 8-spindle bk, tacked leather seat, decal **600.00**
Chiffonier, #102, 2 cabinet doors over 4 drw, 50x36" **2,000.00**
China cabinet, #746, 2 glass doors, ea w/6 sm panes, 44x16" ..**3,200.00**
Dresser, 2 sm drw over 2, backsplash, no mk, 39x42x21" **1,600.00**
Dresser, 2 sm drw over 2, w/lg sq mirror, no mk, 67x42" **2,300.00**
Footstool, #397, orig spring pad/uphl, decal, 20" W, EX **465.00**
Mirror, #98, arched fr, 26x35" **975.00**
Night stand, #105, 2-drw, 4-leg, 29x19x14" **1,495.00**
Rocker, #461 (similar), 7-slat sides, decal, 36", VG **1,600.00**
Secretary, #662, 12 pane doors, fall front, mk, 72x21", EX **4,500.00**
Settle, #221, 16-slat bk, 7-slat sides, decal, 60", EX **7,500.00**
Settle, #738, 13 canted bk slats, 4-slat arms, no mk, 76" **4,500.00**
Stand, #558, 15" 8-side top, X-stretchers, decal, rfn, 17" **650.00**
Table, #381, 36" dia top, arched X-stretchers, no mk, EX **1,500.00**
Table, #559, 19½" octagonal top, X-stretcher base, 20" **1,300.00**
Table, #573, rnd base shelf on X-stretchers, decal, 29x18" **1,500.00**
Table, #593, 48x30" top overhangs, divided sides, mk, varnish ..**750.00**
Table, #713, 54" dia top on ped base, decal, +6 11" leaves **2,750.00**
Table, library; #531, dbl-key tenon shelf, 1-drw, 48", VG **900.00**

Stickley Bros.

Armchair, #312½, 5-slat bk, old leather seat/finish, decal **750.00**
Bed, #308, 3 slats ea side broad slat, high posts, twin sz **1,300.00**
Book stand, #4702, 3-tier, 3-slat sides, 31x26", EX **1,000.00**
Book stand, #4703, 4-tier, 3-slat sides, label, 40", VG **850.00**
Box, cigar; #64, copper w/cedar lining, brass trim, 12" L **935.00**
Magazine stand, #4600 (similar), 4-shelf/slat sides, tag, 36" **600.00**
Pedestal, #133, 13" sq top, reverse-tapered base, 34", VG **1,300.00**

Plant stand, 3 spindles on 2 sides, Quaint tag, 17" sq, EX **1,200.00**
Rocker, cube w/4 wide slats ea side, cushion, att, 27x29x31" ..**1,400.00**
Settle, #3504, low open arms, 12-slat bk, cushion, #d, 49" **750.00**
Stand, extended 18" sq top, splay legs, shelf, tag, 32", VG **1,200.00**
Table, library; #2660, 1-drw, MacMurdo ft, tag, 42", EX **850.00**
Table, 27" hex top, ea apron panel w/bud inlay, 6-leg, mk **4,000.00**

Stiegel

Baron Henry Stiegel produced glassware in Pennsylvania as early as 1760, very similar to glass being made concurrently in Germany and England. Without substantiating evidence, it is impossible to positively attribute a specific article to his manufacture. Although he made other types of glass, today the term Stiegel generally refers to any very early ware made in shapes and colors similar to those he is known to have produced — especially that with etched or enameled decoration. It is generally conceded, however, that most glass of this type is of European origin. Our advisor for this category is Mark Vuono; he is listed in the Directory under Connecticut.

Bottle, purple with hand-painted birds over central heart within floral border, German inscription on back, ca 1770, minor repair to lip, 6", $850.00.

Bottle, HP bird & floral, 6-color, pewter threaded top, 5¾" **500.00**
Bottle, overall ornate eng, pewter collar, 1780-1830, 7" **300.00**
Flip glass, eng repeating motif at top, paneled 5⅞" **175.00**
Mug, eagle & flower, 5-color, 4½x3¼" **1,000.00**
Tumbler, eng flower baskets, sheared rim, pontil scar, 5⅛" **300.00**

Stocks and Bonds

Scripophily (scrip-awfully), the collecting of 'worthless' old stocks and bonds, gained recognition as an area of serious interest around the mid-1970s. Today there are an estimated 5,000 collectors in the United States and 15,000 worldwide. Collectors who come from numerous business fields mainly enjoy its hobby aspect, though there are those who consider scripophily an investment. Some collectors like the historical significance that certain certificates have. Others prefer the beauty of older stocks and bonds that were printed in various colors with fancy artwork and ornate engravings. Even autograph collectors are found in this field, on the lookout for signed certificates.

Many factors help determine the collector value: autograph value, age of the certificate, the industry represented, whether it is issued or not, its attractiveness, condition, and collector demand. Certificates from the mining, energy, and railroad industries are the most popular with collectors. Other industries or special collecting fields include banking, automobiles, aircraft, and territorials. Serious collectors usually prefer only issued certificates that date from before 1910. Unissued certificates are usually worth one-fourth to one-eighth the value of one that has been issued. Inexpensive issued common stocks and bonds dated between the 1940s and 1980s usually retail between $1.00 to $10.00. Those dating between 1890 and 1930 usually sell for $10.00 to $50.00. Those over one hundred years old retail between $25.00 and $100.00 or more, depending on the quantity found. Autographed stocks normally sell anywhere from $100.00 to $1,000.00. A formal collecting organization for scripophilists is known as The Bond and Share Society with an American chapter located in New York City.

Our advisor for this category is Warren Anderson; he is listed in the Directory under Utah. In many of the following listings, two-letter state abbreviations immediately follow company name. All are in fine condition unless noted otherwise.

Key:
cp — coupon   U — unissued
I/C — issued/cancelled   vgn — vignette
I/U — issued/uncancelled

AK Exploration & Mining, AK Territory/1935, I/C 25.00
Alabama/Chattanooga RR, 1896, 3 RR vgns, I/U 155.00
Am Voting Machine Co, ME/1917, torch vgn, I/U 20.00
Anglo-CA Gold Mining Co, England/1852, blk on wht, I/U 75.00
Bedford Gold Mining, CO/1903, gold seal/EX artwork, I/U 22.00
Cedar Hollow Line, PA/1856, train/smelters vgn, I/C 55.00
Central Transportation, PA/1873, train vgn, I/C 12.50
Champlain Construction, 1899, 3 RR vgns, U 15.00
Cincinnati, WA & Baltimore RR, 1st mortgage bond, ABNCo ...10.00
Comet Mining of UT, France/1883, 2 6" vgns, I/U, 13x18" 85.00
Commercial Motor Body Corp, DE/1917, emb seal, I/U 25.00
Conway's Theatre Ticket Offices, DE/1919, angel vgn, I/U 25.00
Death Valley-Arcalvada Consolidated Mines, WY/1907, vgn, I/U ...35.00
Early Silver Mining, CO/1880s, miners vgn, U 20.00
Golden Streak Mining & Milling, Nevada/1868, miners vgn 165.00
Golf, CO & SF Ry, TX/1928, train vgn, ABNCo, I/C 30.00
Gray Eagle Gold Mining, AZ Territory/1909, eagle vgn, I/U 25.00
Home Insurance, NY/1930, 3 vgns, ABNCo, I/C 15.00
Ingersoll Warner Mercantile, KS/1906, Indians/train vgn, I/U 30.00
Internat'l RR, TX/1874, $1000 w/coupons, sgn G Grow, I/U 150.00
MA & NM Consolidated Mining, MA/1882, $100, eagle vgn, I/U ..60.00
Mohawk & Malone Ry, NY/1902, elk & deer vgns, ABNCo, I/U ..35.00
Nat'l Gold & Silver Mining, SD/1919, 3 vgns, I/U 25.00
Nat'l Mines & Products, WY/1921, eagle vgn, SBNCo, I/U 15.00
New Viola Co Ltd, England/ID/1890, ornate print, I/U 32.50
Old Colony RR, 1845-49, bl w/red corporate seal, I/C 55.00
Park City Mining & Smelting, CO/1922, goddess vgn, ABNCo, I/C ..25.00
Rico Mining, CO/1915, brn print, RBNCo, I/C 20.00
Rosco Stock, UT Territory/1890, bull vgn, U 18.00
Sierra Consolidated Gold Mining, WV/1906, 20 coupons, I/U 25.00
Tamarack Gold Mining & Milling, AZ/1906, train vgn, I/U 20.00
Texas Crude Oil Co, TX/1919, 5" gusher vgn, gr seal, I/U 25.00
Tonopah & Mt Butler Gold Mining, AZ Territory/1903, vgn, I/U ..30.00
Treasure Gold Mining, AZ Territory/1910, 3 vgns, I/U 25.00
United Petroleum, CO/1917, train w/oil cars vgn, RBNCo, I/U ...15.00
Upper Potomac Steamboats, VA/1875, steamer vgn, I/U 55.00
Wells Fargo, 1863, sgn by founders, sm folio, I/C 1,300.00
Whtwater Oil Mining & Refining, CO/1902, 5 tax stamps, I/U ...25.00
Woodburn Oil Corp, DE/1932, eagle vgn, ABNCo, I/U 7.00
Yosemite Dredging & Mining, NV/1912, photo vgn, seal, I/U 30.00
1st Nat'l Bank of Bend, OR/1926, eagle vgn, 20 shares, I/U 32.50

Stoneware

There are three broad periods of time that collectors of American

pottery can look to in evaluating and dating the stoneware and earthenware in their collections. Among the first permanent settlers in America were English and German potters who found a great demand for their individually turned wares. The early pottery was produced from red and yellow clays scraped from the ground at surface levels. The earthenware made in these potteries was fragile and coated with lead glazes that periodically created health problems for the people who ate or drank from it. There was little stoneware available for sale until the early 1800s, because the clays used in its production were not readily available in many areas and transportation was prohibitively expensive. The opening of the Erie Canal and improved roads brought about a dramatic increase in the accessibility of stoneware clay, and many new potteries began to open in New York and New England.

Collectors have difficulty today locating earthenware and stoneware jugs produced prior to 1840, because few have survived intact. These ovoid or pear-shaped jugs were designed to be used on a daily basis. When cracked or severely chipped, they were quickly discarded. The value of handcrafted pottery is often determined by the cobalt decoration it carries. Pieces with elaborate scenes (a chicken pecking corn, a bluebird on a branch, a stag standing near a pine tree, a sailing ship, or people) may easily bring $1,000.00 to $12,000.00 at auction.

After the Civil War there was a need and a national demand for stoneware jugs, crocks, canning jars, churns, spittoons, and a wide variety of other pottery items. The competition among the many potteries reached the point where only the largest could survive. To cut costs, most potteries did away with all but the simplest kinds of decoration on their wares. Time-consuming brush-painted birds or flowers quickly gave way to more simply executed swirls or numbers and stenciled designs. The coming of home refrigeration and Prohibition in 1919 effectively destroyed the American stoneware industry. In the following listings, all decorations are executed in cobalt on salt glaze unless noted. See also Bennington, Stoneware.

Bottle, bl top, J Chester, Lemon Beer, EX 55.00
Bowl, milk; flower, S Fayette & Co, Utica, 2-gal, EX 240.00
Bowl, milk; foliage, brushed, str sides, 4x9" dia 300.00
Butter crock, floral/feather leaves, brushed, 5x9½" 350.00
Churn, #3, brushed cobalt, appl hdls, wooden lid, 15¼" 335.00
Churn, bust of General w/mustache, ER Evans, 6-gal, EX 11,500.00
Churn, fan-tail bird & wreath, Whites Utica, rpr, 4-gal 175.00
Churn, impressed #2, cobalt slip decor, 14", EX 325.00
Churn, stylized floral/#5, brushed, ovoid, stains, 18" 220.00
Churn, 3 flowers & leaves, WE Welding, Ont, 5-gal, EX 250.00
Churn, 4 squiggled bands, White Utica NY, rpr, 6-gal 150.00
Crock, #6, bird on branch, Weston & Gregg, Ellenville NY, EX ..550.00
Crock, bird & dots (bold), Edmands & Co, crack, 3-gal 375.00
Crock, bird on leafy branch, base chip, 1½-gal, EX 250.00
Crock, bird on 2 lg flowers (bold), John Burger, 6-gal, EX 5,250.00
Crock, bird/leaves (folky/bold), J Burger Jr...NY, 5-gal, NM ...1,900.00
Crock, bluebird, Whites Utica NY, flaking, 1-gal 200.00
Crock, butter; allover tulip decor, att PA, EX 375.00
Crock, butter; floral, brushed, appl hdls, w/lid, 11" dia 735.00
Crock, cake; revolving flowers w/bl band, rim chip, 1-gal 140.00
Crock, cobalt quillwork label: 6 Butter 1870, hdls, 13¾" 385.00
Crock, face in 8-pointed star, T Harrington, 3-gal, EX 3,750.00
Crock, fish (dotted/ribbed), W Hart, Ogdensburgh, 5-gal, EX 850.00
Crock, floral, ovoid, 1-gal, EX 90.00
Crock, floral (bold), NA White & Son, 2-gal, EX 110.00
Crock, floral (dotted), Haxstun Ottman/Ft Edward NY, 1-gal, EX ..150.00
Crock, floral spray (dotted), Ft Edward Stoneware, 3-gal, EX 210.00
Crock, leaf/#2, John Burger, Rochester, 2-gal, NM 160.00
Crock, man & lady (names/detailed), Fulper Bros, 4-gal, EX ..10,000.00
Crock, tulip/leaves (lg), Burger & Lang...NY, 2-gal, EX 230.00
Crock, wreath/#3, Burger & Co, Rochester NY, 3-gal, EX 225.00

Dog, seated, wht clay, clear w/gr spots, Ohio, 6¼" 220.00
Jar, Anshovis incised in bl, bl band, 1-qt, M 190.00
Jar, floral, (dbl/leafy/bold), Lyons, 3-gal, EX 225.00
Jar, floral, brushed, N Clark, ovoid, hdls, 13", EX 255.00
Jar, floral (triple, bold), HN Ballard, Burlington VT, 3-gal, EX ..200.00
Jar, gray salt glaze w/brushed cobalt design, ovoid, 8¾" 160.00
Jar, leaves, Nichols & Boynton...VT, w/lid, 1½-gal, EX 500.00
Jar, med brn w/gr highlights, appl hdls, sm chips, 3½" 35.00
Jar, parrot on plume (bold), FB Norton...MA, rpr, 3-gal 325.00
Jar, pine tree, NA White & Son, Utica NY, 1-gal, EX 140.00
Jar, revolving flower & leaf design, 2-qt, NM 130.00
Jar, wreath (bold)/#2, Harrington & Burger, 2-gal, NM 600.00
Jar, wreath (bold)/#4, Burger & Co, Rochester NY, 4-gal, EX 250.00
Jar, wreath/floral at neck, ovoid, minor chips, 15" 125.00
Jar, 2-tone gray & gr, ovoid, Boston 1804, chips, 9½" 1,200.00
Jug, amber, molded lady's leg hdl, 8¼", EX 250.00

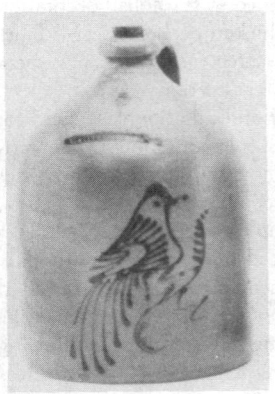

Jug, bird on branch, cobalt on salt glaze, Whites Utica, ca 1880, 2-gallon, EX, $500.00.

Jug, bird on branch (long tail), Whites, 3-gal, EX 425.00
Jug, bird on leaf (bold/ribbed), CW Brawn, ovoid, 3-gal, NM .2,900.00
Jug, bird on ribbed stump (vivid), OL & AK Ballard, 2-gal, NM .2,200.00
Jug, Chollar Darby & Co, Homer, ovoid, tight line, 1-gal 90.00
Jug, cobalt imp label: IM Mead & Co #2, ovoid, 13", EX 160.00
Jug, fan-tail bird w/ribbed body, Whites Utica, 1-gal, EX 450.00
Jug, feather (ribbed/bold), W Hart, Ogdensburg, 2-gal, EX 120.00
Jug, fish/tree/flower, SH Addington, Utica, ovoid, 3-gal, NM .3,750.00
Jug, floral, brushed, ovoid, WE Welding Brantford 3, 16¼" 385.00
Jug, floral w/dotted heart, 1-gal, EX 125.00
Jug, floral/#3, brushed, 15¼" 375.00
Jug, flourish/#2, N Clark & Co, ovoid, 13" 335.00
Jug, gray salt glaze, incised slipwork fish, chip, 10" 450.00
Jug, leaf design, West Troy Pottery, 2-gal, EX 90.00
Jug, orchid (bold ribs), Whites Utica, 1-gal, EX 250.00
Jug, pine tree, NA White, Utica NY, 1-gal, NM 120.00
Jug, pumpkin-head man/leaves, brushed, 14", EX 900.00
Jug, ship's anchor in water, West Troy Pottery, 5-gal, NM 4,500.00
Jug, stencil: HJ Miller, hairline/chip, 12" 225.00
Jug, sunflower (lg/brushed), CH Harris, 11½", VG 450.00
Jug, tree on brushy ground, Haxtun Ottman & Co, 3-gal, NM .1,150.00
Jug, tulip w/ribbed leaves, John Burger, Rochester, 2-gal, EX 160.00
Jug, 2 birds on 3 flowers, Whites Utica, dbl hdls, 5-gal, EX 1,100.00
Pitcher, floral, brushed, gray w/brn mottle, ovoid, 9" 55.00
Pitcher, floral, brushed, J Burger Rochester, rpr, 9½" 300.00
Pitcher, floral/foliage/daubs, brushed, 10½", G 475.00
Pitcher, flower & leaf, ½-gal, NM 290.00
Pitcher, incised vines, bl band, pewter lid, EX 170.00
Pitcher, leaves/#2, hdl stripes, brushed, 13" 375.00
Salt cellar, brushwork, 2½", NM 85.00
Wash board, w/flint enamel scrubber 400.00

Store

Perhaps more more than any other yesteryear establishment, the country store evokes the most nostalgic feelings for folks old enough to remember its charms — barrels for coffee, crackers, and big green pickles; candy in a jar for the grocer to weigh on shiny brass scales; beheaded chickens in the meat case outwardly devoid of nothing but feathers. Today mementos from this segment of Americana are being collected by those who 'lived it' as well as those less fortunate! Our advisor for this category is Charles Reynolds; he is listed in the Directory under Virginia. See also Advertising.

Display cabinet, octagonal oak frame revolves on fancy painted aluminum base with ball and claw feet, 66", VG, $475.00.

Bag, burlap; Goldfinch Potatoes, bird, #100 sz 10.00
Bag holder, heavy wire, folds up 140.00
Bin, apple; slatted wood, stenciled letters, 35x31x31", EX 495.00
Bin, spice; Empire Hdw Co NY, 6 drawers, 13x24x13" 600.00
Cabinet, cheese display; glass & oak, 22x20x22", VG 350.00
Canister, tin, Loverin & Brown...Chicago on lid, 10⅝x5½" 48.00
Case, display: pine, glass window, lift-off lid, 13x12x8" 195.00
Ceiling fan, CI/wood, 4-blade, Western Electric, 66", G 125.00
Corset form, w/sample corset attached, 30x8" dia, EX 125.00
Counter, grain; oak & curved glass, 6-compartment, 33x72x9" .3,500.00
Counter, 27 glass-front drawers in wood case, 36x120x25" 700.00
Credit coin, Finder Please Return to...PA emb on German Silver ..10.00
Cutter, cheese; pnt CI, dial adjustment on bk, Enterprise, 30" ...330.00
Dispenser, brass/tin/glass, w/measuring spout, 41x17x15", G 175.00
Dispenser, ribbon; oak, w/21 metal spools, Lokner, 39x24" dia ..525.00
Dispenser, wrapping paper; CI/wood, counter top type, 9x12x6" ...300.00
Jar, candy; glass, 4-sided ovoid shape, pyramid cap, 26x6x6" 475.00
Mannequin, lady, cvd wood, worn orig pnt, rprs, 48" 2,500.00
Rack, baseball bat display; stenciled letters, 65" H, EX 1,100.00
Rack, broom display; CI, on casters, Pat 1885, 28x12", EX 245.00
Rack, buggy whip display; ornate CI, Pat 1900, 37x28" dia, EX .200.00
Scoop, rnd at top & hooded, tin w/shaped wooden hdl, 16" 45.00
Secretary, storekeeper's, open top, 2-pc, old pnt, 65x36x36" 575.00
Stand, umbrella; CI, locking levers & keys, 1860, 40", EX 270.00
String & bag holder, wire pyramid shape, self standing 195.00

Stoves

Antique stoves' desirability is based on two criteria: their utility and their decorative value. It's the latter that adds an 'antique' premium to the basic functional value that could be served just as well by a modern stove. Sheer age is usually irrelevant. Decorative features that enhance desirability include fancy, embossed ornamentation, nickel-plated trim, mica windows, ceramic tiles, and (in cooking stoves) water reservoirs and high warming closets rather than mere high shelves. The less sheet metal and the more cast iron, the better. Look for crisp, sharp designs in preference to those made from worn or damaged and repaired foundry patterns. Stoves with a pastel porcelain finish can be very attractive; blue is a favorite, white is least desirable. Chrome trim, rather than nickel, is the mark of a stove too recent to be interesting. Among stove types, base burners (with self-feeding coal magazines) are the most desirable. Then come the upright, cylindrical 'oak' stoves, kitchen ranges, and wood parlors. Potbellies approach the margin of undesirability; laundries and gasoline stoves plunge through it.

In judging condition look out for deep rust pits, warped or burnt-out parts, unsound firebricks, poorly fitting parts, poor repairs, and empty mounting holes indicating missing trim. Search meticulously for cracks in the cast iron. Our listings reflect auction prices of completely restored, safe, and functional stoves, unless indicated otherwise.

There's a thin but continuing stream of desirable antique stoves going to the high-priced Pacific Coast market. Interest in antique stoves is least in the Deep South. Demand for wood/coal stoves is strongest in areas where firewood is affordable and storage of it is practical. Demand for antique gas ranges has become strong, especially in metropolitan markets, and interest in antique electric ranges is starting to surface. The market for antique stoves is so limited and the variety so bewildering that a consensus on a going price can hardly emerge. They are only worth something to the right individual, and prices realized depend very greatly on who happens to be in the auction crowd. Even an expert's appraisal will usually miss the realized price by a substantial percent.

Base Burners

Art Amherst #15, NP trim, tiles, 11" urn, 50x25x28" 1,875.00
Burdett-Smith #44, swivel top, tiles, 38" 1,185.00
Detroit Emerald Jewel #14, NP/CI, 54"+15" brass urn 1,550.00
Favorite #30, Piqua OH, ornate CI, mica windows, 52"+14" urn .2,000.00
Michigan Stove, Art Garland #400, gargoyles/NP/mica, 1889, rstr ...9,800.00
Ransom Art Denmark #15, Albany NY, tiles/NP/mica, 1887, VG ..4,500.00
Thos Caffney Waverly #12, Boston MA, 40x20x22" 1,875.00
Weir Glenwood #6, NP trim, mica windows, 1909, 68" 875.00

Box Stoves

A Belanger Barge #34, scrollwork, CI, 1905, sm 187.50
BF&M Co #1, front load, early legs, 1800s, 17x13x24" 125.00
E Eaton #24, Amherst NH, schoolhouse type, 24x38x16" 435.00
Shaker, 1-pc cast body, wrought latch, 1800s, 21x35x14" 345.00
Unknown, parlor type, reeded column sides, 1830s, 25x37x17" .500.00
Walker & Pratt Laconia, ornate CI, NP footrail, 1860s, 35" 125.00

Franklin Stoves

Acme #18 Orient 1890, 6 tiles, mica windows, fancy 375.00
Iron Foundry...NH, ornate CI, grate missing, 1820s, 37x26x32" ...200.00
Magee Ideal #3, CI fireplace, 2 side trivets, 1892, 32x28" 250.00
Muzzy & Co Villa Franklin, folding doors, 1830s, 30"+4" urn 175.00
Noyes & Nutter Kineo #16, fireplace, 1870s, 32x23x20" 185.00
Southard Robertson Sunny Hearth #2, 1850s, 35x20x29½" 275.00
Tyson #1, 2 sheet metal columns, swing doors, 36x17x25" 350.00
Walker & Pratt Good Cheer #22, fireplace, 1850s, 32x27x31" ..300.00
Wyer & Noble, CI/brass-trim fireplace, old 2,000.00

Parlor Stoves

AJ Coffin #4, ornate CI, 4-column, 1840s, 47"+10" urn 1,450.00

Albany NY, ornate CI, 4-column, paw ft, 1820s, 42"+15" urn ..1,600.00
Bangor Comfort #23, oval w/dome top, Pat 1875, 33"+10" urn ..185.00
Bangor Foundry & Machine, cook top, 3 mica windows, 30" 165.00
Barstow Gem #3, oven under dome, Pat 1892, 30x21x27" 325.00
Burdett Smith & Co #44, sq, tiles, mica door, 38"+8" urn 350.00

Co-Op Foundry Silven Red Cross #31, four small decorative tiles, gargoyle heads on legs, Pat 1888-89, 37"+6" urn, $300.00.

GW Eddy Forest #3, ornate CI, Pat 1854, 28"+6" urn 275.00
Ilion #3, ornate CI, rnd body, claw ft, 1853, 27"+11" urn 600.00
Ilion #5, ornate CI, ca 1853, 33"+13" 2-pc urn 500.00
JC Fletcher, Fuller Warren & Morrison, Troy NY, Pat 1853, 45" ..850.00
JH Shear #2, Albany NY, CI, column style, 56" 850.00
Johnson, Geer & Carr #4, CI, 4-column, 56" 1,000.00
Joliet Moores Air Tight Heater #402B, Pat 1883, 45"+14" urn ..900.00
JS&M Peckham Rosedale #23, 1870s, 33"+10" swivel top dome ..250.00
Low & Hicks Revere Air-Tight #4, cathedral front, 29"+11" urn ...325.00
Low/Hicks Gothic #4, 4 slide front doors, 1840s, 36"+6" urn 425.00
Modern Glenwood Wood Parlor, slide top, 1900s, 45x28x24½" ...325.00
Morison & Manning (att), column type, 1830s, 42x21x32" 2,300.00
Perry Dandy #12, swivel dome top w/8" lid, 46"+7" urn 200.00
Pratt & Wentworth Peerless, tip-up dome, 1840s, 37x19x25" 135.00
Rathbone Sard & Co Floral Acorn #38, ca 1894, 37"+9" urn 725.00
SH Ransom, ornate CI, rnd air intake, Pat 1846, 26"+14" urn ...275.00
SH Ransom Parlor #3 Gem, ornate CI, Pat 1855, 32"+6" urn ...625.00
SH Ransom Peruvian, 2 slide front doors, 1853, 27"+13" urn ...300.00
Somersworth #20, tip-up dome top, 1850s, 39x30x29" 300.00
Unknown, ornate CI, 2-column, missing urn, ca 1830s, 40" 725.00
Vose & Co #5 Temple, CI, Pat 1854, 44" 800.00
Warnick & Leibrandt Union Airtight, ornate CI, 1851, 26" 250.00
Weir Modern Glenwood Oak #116, mica windows, 1908, 68x25x25" ..375.00
Wood/Bishop Ideal 23 Clarion, flat top, 1880s, 36x27x25" 900.00
Wood/Bishop Royal Clarion #14, mica door, oven, 1890s, 50" ..225.00

Ranges (Gas)

Cribben-Sexton Univ, 4-burner, gr/cream, high oven, '27, VG ..375.00
Detroit Jewel, 4-burner, blk/NP, glass oven door, 1918, VG 500.00
Magic Shef, 6-burner/2-oven, warming closet, 1932, EX 2,500.00
Weir Insulated Glenwood, 6-burner/2-oven, wht, 1932, rstr ..4,125.00

Ranges (Wood and Coal)

Laundry, Welker & Pratt #14, holds irons, Pat 1874, 25x24x24" ...500.00
Noyes & Nutter Kineo C, roll top, water tank, 1900-15 ....650.00
Portland Ideal Atlantic 8-20, ornate CI, bk shelf, 1850s 1,550.00

Stoves

Portland Queen Atlantic, unadorned, 19½x19½x12" 625.00
Taunton Quaker Standard #8-20, NP trim, trivets, shelf, 1890s .850.00
Walker & Pratt Billage Crawford Royal, swing trivets, 1900s 725.00
Weir Glenwood C #280, dbl-shelf bk, no trivets, 1900s 1,000.00
Wood/Bishop Imperial Clarion #8-20, warming closet, dtd 1898 ..1,800.00
Wood/Bishop Popular Clarion, scrolling, trivets, 1890s 1,050.00

Miscellaneous

Fireplace, unknown mfg, claw ft, early 1800s, 30x28x40" 300.00
Griswold, space heater, sheet steel, iron base & top, 27" 110.00
Laundry, Stamford Laundry #20, 4-ring lid, 21½x21x26" 188.00
Oil burning, Monitor #20, cookstove, dtd 1887, 29x21x23" 125.00
Sears & Roebuck Signal Oak #22, coal burning, 42½" 138.00

Stove Manufacturers' Toy Stoves

Buck's Jr Range, St Louis MO, new body/pnt/recast parts, 26" ...850.00
Charter Oak #503, GF Filley, St Louis MO, 14x12x25", EX ...2,050.00
Dainty, Reading Stove Works, PA, 7x13x8", VG 150.00
Great Majestic Jr, Majestic Mfg, 31x16x23, M 5,650.00
Karr, Qualified, bl porc w/NP, Belleville IL, 1925, EX 2,500.00
Karr Range, Belleville IL, bl porc, old model, 21½x13x9" 3,100.00
Karr repro, Qualified, bl porc w/NP, 1950s, EX 2,500.00
Little Eva T Southard, NYC, 8½x14x11", G 350.00
Little Fanny, CI, minor rust, EX 300.00
Little Willie, CI, EX 75.00
Royal American, Bridgeford, Louisville KY, 14x12x10", G 950.00

Toy Manufacturers' Toy Stoves

Eagle, Hubley, Lancaster PA, NP, recast parts 450.00
Eclipse, CI, EX 175.00
Little Giant, unmk/unidentified, 7½x8½x11", EX orig 675.00
Novelty, Kenton Hdwe, bl pnt/NP trim, rfn, 13x6½x8½" 600.00
Pet, The; Young Bros, Albany NY, 10½x6x8½" 165.00
Queen, The; unmk/unidentified, copper o/l, 23½", M 2,400.00
Rival, J&E Stevens, Cromwell CT, 14x9x16", M, +2 kettles ..1,350.00
Rival, J&E Stevens, Cromwell CT, 1895, 13x7½x18½", G 240.00
Triumph, Kenton Hdwe, OH, 14x8½x19", G 195.00

Strawberry Soft Paste and Lustreware

Strawberry lustre is a general term for pearlware and semiporcelain decorated with hand-painted strawberries, veins, tendrils, and pink lustre trim. Strawberry soft paste is decorated creamware without the pink lustre trim. Both types were made by many manufacturers in England in the 19th century, most of whom never marked their ware.

Key: pw — pearlware

Bowl, pw, scalloped, pk/red bands w/in, hairlines, 3½x6" 500.00
Cup & saucer, pw, pk/red int bands, EX 325.00
Plate, pw, wide pk/red rim bands, #8, 8" 425.00
Teapot, baluster form, 11¼" 850.00

Stretch Glass

Stretch glass, produced from 1916 until after 1930, was made in an effort to emulate the fine art glass of Tiffany and Carder. The glassware was sprayed with a special finish while still hot, and a reheating process caused the coating to contract, leaving a striated, crepe-like iridescence. Northwood, Imperial, Fenton, Diamond, Lancaster, and the United States Glass Company were the largest manufacturers of this type of glass. See also specific companies.

Candle holders, blue, Central Glass, 7", $56.00 for the pair.

Bowl, amber, flared rim, 12" 35.00
Bowl, amber, Jeannette, 3⅞x10" 40.00
Bowl, bl, flared rim, Imperial, 10" 40.00
Bowl, bl, ribbed int, ftd, 9½" 35.00
Bowl, bl opaque, ribbed, flared, Northwood, 3x9½" 42.50
Bowl, gr, flared rim, 10" 32.00
Bowl, gr, rolled edge, Fenton, 10" 45.00
Bowl, olive gr, ftd, 9½" 35.00
Bowl, vaseline, gold band, 2¼x12¾" 42.00
Bowl, vaseline, Northwood, 3x13" 50.00
Bowl, vaseline, US Glass, #806, 2¼x11" 40.00
Bowl, wht, HP florals, Lancaster, 3x9¾" 35.00
Cake plate, gr, center hdl, sq top 35.00
Candlesticks, bl, Northwood, 8½", pr 75.00
Candlesticks, Dmn, gr, hollow, 9¾", pr 45.00
Candlesticks, olive gr, Colonial style, 8½", pr 65.00
Candlesticks, pk, Fenton, #316, 3½x4¼", pr 35.00
Compote, Dmn, bright gr, zipper notch stem, 5½x6½" 60.00
Compote, gray, Imperial, 7x8¼" 47.50
Compote, wht, HP florals, Lancaster, 4¼x6¾" 35.00
Guest set, pk, Fenton #200 ....125.00
Lemon server, gr, Fenton 28.00
Plate, gold rim, 7½" 10.00
Plate, vaseline, 8" 12.00
Plate, wht, Colonial panel, 7" 8.00
Server, amber, center hdl, 10½" dia 35.00
Sherbet, amberina, ribbed, ftd, 3⅜x4" 40.00
Sugar bowl, vaseline, Fenton #3 ....26.00
Vase, pk, Fenton, #573 ....38.00

String Holders

Today, if you want to wrap and secure a package, you have a variety of products to choose from: cellophane tape, staples, etc. But in the 1800s, string was about the only available binder; thus the string holder, either the hanging or counter type, was a common and practical item found in most homes and businesses. Chalkware and ceramic figurals from the 1930s and 1940s contrast with the cast and wrought iron examples from the 1800s to make for an interesting collection. Our advisor for this category is Charles Reynolds; he is listed in the Directory under Virginia.

Apple & berries, chalkware, EX pnt 32.00
Brass, ornate, for desk, DM Read Co Fair Week, 1909, 3x2" 25.00

Cat's face, Hold Howard China, 1958 ....15.00
Chef's face, ceramic, gold trim, lg 65.00
Dutch boy w/pipe, chalkware, EX pnt 45.00
Group of 3 girls, ceramic, Japan 50.00
Mammy head, plaster, orange bandana 270.00
Mechanical, ball runs on track, CI 365.00
Post Toasties, tin, circular, 4½x11½" dia, G 725.00
Postem Beverages, tin, 4-color pnt, Pat 1916, 11½" dia, VG 600.00
Sailor, eyes to side, w/pipe, chalkware 35.00
SSS for the Blood, CI w/rtcl insert, EX pnt, 4⅞" 195.00
Strawberry w/face, chalkware, EX 40.00
Tabby, CI, mc pnt, 1880s, 5⅝" 385.00
Top hat w/face, chalkware, EX pnt 45.00
Treen, EX trn/detail, lid w/hole & finial, metal cutter, 3" 185.00

Sugar Shakers

Sugar shakers (or muffineers, as they were also called) were used during the Victorian era to sprinkle sugar and spice onto breakfast muffins, toast, etc. They were made of art glass, in pressed patterns, and in china. See also specific types and manufacturers.

Apple Blossom, Northwood 165.00
Argus Swirl, peachbloom 265.00
Beauty, red flashed, orig ornate lid 325.00
Block & Fan 85.00
Bulging Loops, bl cased 500.00
Chrysanthemum Base Swirl, wht speckled 175.00
Coin Spot, Cranberry opal, wide waist 235.00
Coin Spot, rubena, 4½" 175.00
Cone, bl opaque 145.00
Cone, pk satin, squat 135.00
Flower & Pleat, clear/frosted 135.00
Invt T'print, amber w/decor, pewter collar & lid 225.00
Invt T'print, cranberry, tapered form, 5½" 185.00
Invt T'print, rubena, 5½" 200.00
Lattice, ribbed cranberry opal 450.00
Optic Panel, honey amber, HP florals, orig collar & lid 175.00
Parian Swirl, wht opaque, decor 135.00
Raindrop, apricot MOP w/floral, 2-pc lid, Mt WA, 5½" 875.00
Reverse Swirl, canary yel opal 250.00
Strawberry, Dmn & Fan cut w/rayed base, sterling lid 165.00
Waterford style, allover dmns, SP top, 5¾x3" 75.00
Wht satin w/gr shamrocks & bl dots, Dithridge 175.00

Sunderland Lustre

Sunderland lustre was made by various potters in the Sunderland district of England during the 18th and 19th centuries. It is characterized by a splashed-on application of the pink lustre, which results in an effect sometimes referred to as the 'cloud' pattern. Some pieces are transfer printed with scenes, ships, florals, or portraits.

Punch bowl, hunting scenes, 12", M, $725.00.

Bowl, vegetable; almond shape, 10¼" 50.00
Bowl, vegetable; rectangular, w/lid, 8" 290.00
Chamber pot, verse 'Marriage'/other blk transfers w/mc, EX 565.00
Mug, 2½" 60.00
Pitcher, Iron Bridge at Sunderland, brn transfer, 7⅛", EX 385.00
Pitcher, Sailor's Farewell/Mariner's Compass, blk, 7", VG 100.00
Plaque, Thou God Seest..., blk transfer, wear, 6" dia 185.00
Platter, 12½" L 385.00
Wine, wht band w/mc florals, copper lustre trim, wear, 4" 125.00

Surveying Instruments

The practice of surveying offers a wide variety of precision instruments primarily for field use, most of which are associated with the recording of distance and angular measurements. These instruments were primarily made from brass; the larger examples were fitted with tripods and protective cases. These cases also held accessories for the instruments, and these can sometimes play a key part in their evaluation. Instruments in complete condition and showing little use will have much greater values than those that appear to have had moderate or heavy use. Instruments were never polished during use, and those that have been polished as decorator pieces are of little interest to most avid collectors. Our advisor for this category is Dale Beeks; he is listed in the Directory under Idaho.

Compass, John Bliss...NY, brass, orig pnt, 2" dia, EX, +case 150.00
Compass, RS Burrough Providence, wooden bowl, 18th C, EX ..375.00
Compass, Thomas Greenough Boston N England, wood, 1750s, 13" .1,200.00
Compass, W&LE Gurley, brass, w/level, EX in box, +tripod ...1,200.00

Syracuse

Syracuse was a line of fine dinnerware and casual ware which was made for nearly a century by the Onondaga Pottery Company of Syracuse, New York. Early patterns were marked O.P. Company. Collectors of American dinnerware are focusing their attention on reassembling some of their many lovely patterns. In 1966 the firm became officially known as the Syracuse China Company in order to better identify with the name of their popular chinaware. Many of the patterns were marked with the shape and color names (Old Ivory, Federal, etc.), not the pattern names. By 1971 dinnerware geared for use in the home was discontinued, and the company turned to the manufacture of hotel, restaurant, and other types of commercial tableware. Our advisor for this category is Mary Delucchi; she is listed in the Directory under California.

Arcadia, demitasse cup & saucer 30.00
Arcadia, plate, 7" 18.00
Avalon, cup & saucer, gold trim 32.00
Avalon, plate, 10" 25.00
Bombay, creamer & sugar bowl, ivory w/gold trim 70.00
Briarcliff, bowl, vegetable; w/lid, 8" dia 85.00
Clover, bowl, cereal; 5½" 16.00
Clover, bowl, vegetable; rnd, w/lid, 8" 85.00
Clover, cup & saucer 24.00
Clover, plate, dinner; 10" 20.00
Clover, plate, salad; 8" 16.00
Clover, platter, 12" 30.00
Coralbel, cup & saucer 24.00
Coralbel, plate, bread & butter 15.00
Coralbel, plate, dinner 30.00
Coralbel, plate, salad 15.50
Coralbel, soup 25.00
Coronet, cup & saucer 32.00
Jefferson, gravy boat 65.00

Jefferson, rimmed soup 25.00
Lady Mary, plate, 9¾" 20.00
Lady Mary, platter, 8" 30.00
Lyric, cup & saucer 32.00
Orchard, plate, dinner 25.00
Orleans, bowl, vegetable; w/lid 125.00
Orleans, creamer & sugar bowl, w/lid 65.00
Orleans, cup, bouillon 12.00
Orleans, cup & saucer 25.00
Orleans, gravy boat 65.00
Orleans, platter, 12" 50.00
Orleans, platter, 14" 55.00
Rosalie, plate, dinner; 10" 30.00
Silhouette, plate, 10½" 30.00
Silhouette, plate, 8" 20.00
Stansbury, cream soup, w/underplate 30.00
Stansbury, cup & saucer 32.00
Stansbury, plate, salad; 8" 16.00
Stansbury, platter, 12x9" 50.00
Symphony, plate, dinner 22.00
Victoria, plate, dinner; 10" 30.00
Victoria, platter, 12x9" 70.00

Syrups

Values are for old, original syrups. Beware of reproductions! See also various manufacturers and specific types of glass.

Artichoke, frosted, orig pewter hinged lid 165.00
Banded Shells, milk glass, 5½" 95.00
Block Band, marigold flashed, Geo Duncan, 1880s 250.00
Catherine Ann, milk glass, orig lid & hdl 125.00
Chrysanthemum Base Swirl, wht speckles 245.00
Coin Spot, bl opal, ring neck, dtd lid 215.00
Cone, pk cased 235.00
Cord & Tassel 130.00
Coreopsis, EX decor 265.00
Flower & Pleat, clear & frosted 150.00
Geneva, custard w/gr & gold decor 495.00
Guttate, pk cased, metal lid 315.00
Heart & T'print, 4" 95.00
Hercules Pillar, bl 250.00
Jacob's Ladder, knight's head finial 150.00
Kokomo, orig spring lid 95.00
Maine, orig spring lid 125.00
Missouri 85.00
Optic, rubena, Hobbs 185.00
Peachblow, flaring toward base, orig top, Wheeling 2,750.00
Priscilla, Findlay, orig pewter lid 145.00
Priscilla, gr w/gold, scarce 450.00
Ribbed Pillar, pk spatter 295.00
Seneca Loop, flint, appl strap hdl, dtd pewter lid 150.00
Shoshone, yel flashed, rare 350.00
Strawberry Patch, milk glass 95.00
Torquay, pigeon blood 935.00
Venetian Dmn, bl spatter 275.00
Wildflower, bl 350.00
X-Ray, gr w/EX gold, rare 500.00
Zipper, squat, metal lid & hdl 85.00

Tamac Pottery

At the close of World War II, jobs were almost impossible to find for homecoming military men. Leonard Tate and Allen Macauley were two such men. The state of Oklahoma, at that time, was trying to encourage industry and was offering free factory sites for new businesses. As a result of economic necessity, the two young men and their wives, Marjorie Tate and Betty Macauley, moved from New Jersey to the town of Perry, Oklahoma. The two women were already acquainted and had worked together in the design department at Congoleum Nairn in New Jersey. The foursome decided to combine efforts and past experiences and thus formed 'Tamac' pottery, a conglomeration of the two last names.

The company was first organized in September 1946, in the garage of Leonard Tate's parents in Perry, Oklahoma. Although it was a twenty-four hour job, only a few pieces of pottery were produced daily. The plant expanded in 1948 with over three hundred pieces of earthenware manufactured in a single day.

The Tates and Macauleys were directly responsible for all phases of Tamac production: designing and making the molds, mixing the Oklahoma and Kansas clays, final processing and shipping. The pottery process took approximately ten days to complete. All of the phases were carried out in the Perry, Oklahoma, plant. All four took turns in the retail store and conducted tours. The business had customers from every state in the union and from several foreign countries.

Approximately seventy various pieces of Tamac pottery were produced, mainly consisting of buffet/dinnerware. Other 'specialty' pieces included candle holders, ashtrays, vases, and table centerpieces. One of their most popular sellers was the barbeque line which consisted of tray-like plates with unique coffee mugs having non-traditional handles. The barbeque sets were designed with the idea that more casual backyard dining and entertaining would be done in the postwar era.

Six colors were produced, each with a 'frosted' rim of a different color. The six colors were: Frosty Pine, Avocado, Frosty Fudge, Honey, Raspberry, and Beige. The Frosty Pine and Avocado (both with dark green bases) are the most readily available. Few items, mainly 'specialty' pieces, were manufactured in Raspberry.

By 1950 the Macauleys became homesick for the East and sold their shares to the Tates. Around 1952 the Tamac business had expanded and required bank financing. Bankers didn't understand the manufacturing business and refused to give the Tates the backing they needed. Consequently the plant was sold. Although others took over the plant, they too encountered the same difficulties. The plant was permanently closed in the early 1970s.

Tamac pottery can easily be identified by its unique design and the stamp on the bottom of each piece: 'TAMAC Perry, Okla USA.' Some earlier pieces carry the etched 'TAMAC' mark.

Our advisors for this category are Bob and Dondee Klein. They are listed in the Directory under Oklahoma.

Ashtray, bridge 8.00
Ashtray, Oklahoma 15.00
Ashtray, rnd 15.00
Ashtray, 3-corner 8.00
Bird, 3-dimensional, ea 30.00
Bowl, centerpc; dish garden 20.00
Bowl, centerpc; S-shape 17.50
Bowl, gourd shape, 22" 25.00
Bowl, serving; 2-qt 18.00
Bowl, serving; 4-qt 30.00
Butter dish, no lid 9.00
Candle holder, dbl 25.00
Candle holder, single 18.00
Casserole, w/lid, 2-qt 30.00
Coffee mug, w/finger insert 9.00

Coffeecup, hdls	5.00
Creamer, 8-oz	8.00
Creamer & sugar bowl, demitasse	15.00
Cup, demitasse	12.00
Decanter, wine; w/no stopper	20.00
Decanter, wine; w/stopper	60.00
Goblet, wine; 6-oz	13.00
Pitcher, juice; 24-oz	15.00
Pitcher, 2-qt	25.00
Pitcher, 4-qt	35.00
Planter vase, w/no tray, 5x6" dia	20.00
Planter vase, w/tray, 5x6" dia	25.00
Planter vase, w/tray & drain hole	15.00
Plate, barbeque; 15"	12.00
Plate, dinner; 10"	8.00
Platter, turkey; 18"	35.00
Saucer	3.00
Saucer, demitasse	7.00
Shakers, pr	10.00
Spoon holder	15.00
Sugar bowl, open	7.00
Sugar bowl, w/lid	10.00
Teapot, short & squat	50.00
Teapot, tall & thin	55.00
Toothpick holder	7.00
Tumbler, juice; 4-oz	10.00
Tumbler, 16-oz	8.00
Vase, free form, 5½"	25.00
Violet planter, w/tray & drain hole	17.00
Wall vase/pocket, 5"	12.50

Target Balls

Prior to 1880 when the clay pigeon was invented, blown glass target balls were used extensively for shotgun competitions. Approximately 2¾" in diameter, these balls were hand blown into a three-piece mold. All have a ragged hole where the blowpipe was twisted free. Target balls date from approximately 1840 (English) to World War I, although they were most widely used in the 1870-1880 period. Common examples are unmarked except for the blower's code — dots, crude numerals, etc. Some balls are embossed in a dot or diamond pattern so they were more likely to shatter when struck by shot, and some have names and/or patent dates. When evaluating condition, bubbles and other minor manufacturing imperfections are acceptable; cracks are not. The prices below are for mint condition examples.

English target ball, shooter embossed in two panels, $300.00.

Amber w/emb ribs, horizontal or vertical	150.00
Bogardus' Glass Ball Pat'd April 10 1877, amber, Am	350.00
Bogardus' Glass Ball Pat'd April 10 1877, other than amber, Am	800.00
CTB Co, blk pitch, Pat dates on bottom, Am	250.00

Dmn Quilt w/plain center band, ground top, Am	150.00
Dmn Quilt w/shooter emb in 2 panels, clear, English	300.00
Dmn Quilt w/shooter emb in 2 panels, gr or purple, English	300.00
For Hockey's Pat Trap, gr, English	500.00
Great Western Gun Works, Pittsburgh, amber, Am	900.00
Gurd & Son, London, Ontario, amber, Canadian	500.00
Ilmenau (Thur) Sophiehutte, amber, Dmn Quilt, Germany	425.00
Ira Paine's Filled Ball Pat Oct 23 1877, amber, Am	250.00
Ira Paine's Filled Ball Pat Oct 23 1877, other than amber, Am	800.00
NB Glass Works Perth, other than pale gr, English	200.00
NB Glass Works Perth, pale gr, English	100.00
Plain, amber w/mold mks	65.00
Plain, clear w/mold mks	1,000.00
Plain, cobalt w/mold mks	150.00
Plain, purple w/mold mks	150.00
T Jones, Gunmaker, Blackburn, pale bl, English	150.00
WW Greener, St Mary's Works, various colors, English, ea	250.00

Related Memorabilia

Ball thrower, dbl; old red pnt, ME Card, Pat...78, 79, VG	900.00
Clay birds, Winchester, Pat May 29 1917, 1 flight in box	100.00
Pitch bird, blk DUVROCK	1.00
Shell, dummy, w/single window, any brand	35.00
Shell, dummy shotgun, Winchester, window w/powder, 6"	125.00
Shell set, dummy, Gamble Stores, 2 window shells, 3 cut out	125.00
Shell set, dummy, Winchester, 5 window shells	175.00
Shell set, dummy shotgun, Peters, 6 window shells+full box	175.00
Shot shell loader, rosewood/brass, Parker Bros, Pat 1884	50.00
Target, blk japanned sheet metal, Bussy Patentee, London	50.00
Target, BUST-O, blk or wht breakable wafer	20.00
Trap, DUVROCK, w/blk pitch birds	150.00
Trap, MO-SKEET-O, w/birds	150.00

Tea Caddies

Because tea was once regarded as a precious commodity, special boxes called caddies were used to store the tea leaves. They were made from various materials: porcelain, carved and inlaid woods, and metals ranging from painted tin or tole to engraved silver. Our advisor for this category is Tina Carter; she is listed in the Directory under California.

Burl wood, brass bound, domed lid, England, 1800s	270.00
Faience, fleur-de-lis decor w/griffins & shield	265.00

Figured walnut and rosewood with silver and mother-of-pearl inlay, canted corners, brass ball feet, fitted interior, English, 7x11x6", $1,200.00.

Mahog & rosewood w/inlay, fitted int w/2 compartments, 12¾" **325.00**
Mahog veneer w/inlay, Am or England, 1800s, 3¾x4¾x4½" **250.00**
Mahog veneer w/int lids, rpl ivory-like escutcheon, 7¾" **225.00**
Mahog veneer w/wood inlay musical marquetry top, 8" L **415.00**
Mahog w/inlaid knight on lid, loose seams, 13" L **175.00**
Mahog w/inlaid top & ivory escutcheon, 1800s, 5x4x5" **195.00**
Oriental porc, mc enameling & gilt, rim rpr, 6" **30.00**
Rosewood veneer w/inlaid MOP, rpl bowl, 11¾" **250.00**
Silver, repousse floral festoons, etc, hallmk **395.00**
Sterling, Georgian style, urn finial, Sheffield, 10 troy-oz **300.00**
Toleware, mc plums on dk japanning, 6⅞x3" **35.00**
Tortoise shell, Geo III, ormolu paw ft, hipped lid, 5x6" **850.00**
Tortoise shell veneer w/ivory inlay, SP ball ft, 5¼" **745.00**
Zebrawood, rectangular, twin compartment & mixing bowl, 1890s ..**260.00**

Tea Leaf Ironstone

Tea Leaf Ironstone became popular in the 1880s when middle-class American housewives became bored with the plain white stone china that English potters had been exporting to this country for nearly a century. The original design has been credited to Anthony Shaw of Longport, who decorated the plain ironstone with a hand-painted copper lustre design of bands and leaves. Originally known as Lustre Band and Sprig, the pattern has since come to be known as Tea Leaf Lustre. It was produced with minor variations by many different firms both in England and the United States. By the early 1900s, it had become so commonplace that it had lost much of its appeal.

Items marked Red Cliff are reproductions made from 1950 until 1980 for this distributing and decorating company of Chicago, Illinois. Hall China provided many of the blanks.

Our advice for this category comes from Home Place Antiques, whose address is listed in the Directory under Illinois.

Baker, rectangular, Meakin, 8¾x6½" **35.00**
Bone dish, scalloped, Meakin **75.00**
Bowl, rectangular, Wilkinson, 9½x6¾" **55.00**
Bowl, soup; Wedgwood, 9" **30.00**
Bowl, vegetable; Fish Hook, bracket ft, w/lid, Meakin, 11x7" **165.00**
Bowl, vegetable; Octagonal/Ribbed Pagoda, w/lid, 11x7" **195.00**
Butter dish, sq, w/drain, Wedgwood, 5½" **165.00**
Butter pat, Alfred Meakin **14.00**
Butter pat, rnd, unmk, 3" **12.00**
Butter pat, sq, ribbed at corners, Meakin **12.50**
Cup & saucer, Chelsea shape, Johnson Bros, 2⅝", 3½" **85.00**
Cup & saucer, handleless; Lily of the Valley **135.00**
Cup & saucer, handleless; Meakin, 3", 3½" **90.00**
Cup & saucer, handleless; NY shape, Teaberry **120.00**
Cup & saucer, str sides, Alfred Meakin **85.00**
Cup plate, Meakin, 3½" **50.00**
Cup plate, unmk, 3½" **50.00**
Gravy boat, Fish Hook, Meakin, 2¾x8" **75.00**
Gravy boat, Meakin, +undertray **120.00**
Gravy boat, Ribbed, Wedgwood **75.00**
Ladle, sauce; unmk **265.00**
Pitcher, milk; Bamboo, Meakin, 8½x7¾" **295.00**
Plate, gold lustre, Bridgewood, 7" **10.00**
Plate, Meakin, 6¾" **10.00**
Plate, Meakin, 9" **20.00**
Plate, Meakin, 9¾" **30.00**
Plate, Red Cliff, 8" **12.00**
Plate, Wedgwood, 8¼" **14.00**
Plate, Wedgwood, 9" **30.00**
Platter, Chinese, 14x10" **85.00**

Platter, rectangular, Alfred Meakin, 11x8" **42.00**
Platter, rectangular, Meakin, 12¾x9⅛" **52.50**
Platter, rectangular, Mellor-Taylor, 13¾x10" **75.00**
Platter, rectangular, Wedgwood, 10" **45.00**
Platter, Wilkinson, 11" **50.00**
Relish tray, Bamboo, Alfred Meakin **40.00**
Sauce bowl, sq, ribbed corners, Meakin, 4¼" **12.50**
Shaving mug, emb berries, 12-panel mold, sgn Shaw **175.00**
Shaving mug, Shaw, lg sz, 3½x3⅜", EX **195.00**
Shaving mug, Teaberry Variant, Clementson **235.00**
Sugar bowl, Fish Hook, Meakin, 6½x6" **85.00**
Sugar bowl, Lily of the Valley, Shaw, 5½x6½" **150.00**

Teapot, A.J. Wilkinson, 10", $265.00.

Teapot, Chinese shape, Shaw, 10" **225.00**
Teapot, Fish Hook, Meakin **195.00**
Toothbrush holder, Meakin, 5" **175.00**
Toothbrush holder, Mellor-Taylor **155.00**
Tray, service; Anthony Shaw, pierced hdls **125.00**
Tureen, sauce; Bamboo, Meakin, +lid/ladle/underplate **375.00**

Teapots

The custom of drinking tea has resulted in the production of many tea-related collectibles; the most popular is the teapot. The first teapots were manufactured in the Chinese village of Yixing during the late 16th century and were no bigger than the tiny cups previously used for tea drinking. Amazingly these same tiny teapots are still being used today.

A wide range of teapots can be found by the avid searcher; those most readily available today were produced from about 1870 to the present. Almost every pottery and porcelain manufacturer in Europe as well as in America have produced teapots. Some are purely functional, others decorative and whimsical. Refer to various manufacturers' names for further listings. Our advisor for this category is Tina Carter; she is listed in the Directory under California. Watch for her forthcoming book called *Collector's Guide to Teapots*, soon to be released.

Automobile, gr glaze, no mk, 8" L **300.00**
Barge, brn, emb mk, S Derbyshire, England, lg **75.00**
Bone china, bl/wht/gold, SYP, Wedgwood, England, ca 1905-06 ..**125.00**
Brn floral transfer w/gold, Hammersly Bone China, 8" **75.00**
Bunny, mk England, ca 1950, 6-cup **45.00**
Cat figural, paw spout, blk/gray/cream, US Zone Germany, 9" **45.00**
Charles & Diana, brn pottery, Wales CM, 2½" **78.00**
China w/rooster & hens transfer, oval body, Victoria, 9" L **110.00**
Coralene dragon, DM mk, Japan, 6-cup **28.00**

Dbl spout, earthenware, slip decor, ca 1890 ....85.00
Dmn shape, brn w/HP flowers in formal rows, England, #405097 .35.00
Dog figural, sitting on haunches, upraised legs form spout 45.00
Ellgreave, Wood & Sons, England, ironstone w/floral 35.00
Fitz & Floyd, Christopher Columbus, ltd ed, recent 90.00
Flow bl, man seated, legs outstretched, conical hat, 8x9" 50.00
Flowers on pk, mk Sadler, 6-cup 35.00
Gr lustre, HP, Royal Hanover, Germany, 6½" 75.00
Horizontal lines, bulbous, Susie Cooper, England 65.00
HP decor, mk Wade, +matching cr/sug 55.00
HP floral, Bonn, Germany, 4-cup 45.00
Iced Tea dispenser, 2-pc, brn, USA 175.00
Jasperware, bl/wht, Wedgwood, England, ca 1784, 2-cup 210.00
John Bull figural, wht porc 90.00
Majolica, wooded scene, mk Weller & USA, ca 1930, VG 48.00
Ming Tea Co, made in Japan, w/label, 1½-cup 18.00
Old English Sampler, H&K, England, 6-cup, EX 45.00
Pyrex mk, blown glass, etched flowers, 6-cup 48.00

Raised floral design on brown, 'A Present From a Friend,' 19th century, 10", $1,000.00.

Rococo style, HP gold, appl flowers, mk Italy, 10" 38.00
Rooster w/gold specks, head creamer, neck sugar, Japan, 9" 28.00
Rudolph the Red Nosed Reindeer, Japan, w/creamer & sugar 65.00
Silver lustre, Sutherland, England, 6-cup 60.00
Snow White w/Dwarfs, musical, Walt Disney Productions 50.00
Spode's Tower, bl/wht transfer, London shape, England, VG 45.00
Tank, gr w/silver details, Made in England, 8½" L 200.00
Torquay, scene & motto, Watcombe, England, 1½-cup 45.00
WWII, Esc to US by Royal Navy or Allied Fleets, England, brn ..38.00

Teco

Teco artware was made by the American Terra Cotta and Ceramic Company, located near Chicago, Illinois. The firm was established in 1886 and until 1901 produced only brick, sewer tile, and other redware. Their early glaze was inspired by the matt green made popular by Grueby. 'Teco Green' was made for nearly ten years. It was similar to Grueby's yet with a subtle silver-gray cast. The company was one of the first in the United States to perfect a true crystalline glaze. The only decoration used was through the modeling and glazing techniques; no hand painting was attempted. Favored motifs were naturalistic leaves and flowers. The company broadened their lines to include garden pottery and faience tiles and panels. New matt glazes (browns, yellows, blue, and rose) were added to the green in 1910. By 1922 the artware lines were discontinued; the company was sold in 1930.

Values are dictated by size and shape, with architectural and organic forms being more desirable. Teco is usually marked with a vertical impressed device comprised of a large 'T' to the left of the remaining three letters.

Ashtray, grumpy 'troll' figure, head/ft either side, 5½" 250.00
Bowl, gr, repeating slanted Nouveau-style protrusions, 10" 600.00
Bowl, gr, rolled rim, 2x6" 325.00
Bowl, gr, saucer shape on Xd ft, 2½x10½" 1,400.00
Bowl, gr w/blk, flat shoulder w/wide flutes, 2½x8" 425.00
Coaster, oatmeal w/Cubs team insignia, 4¼" dia 135.00
Vase, bl, body in base of 3 pointed buttresses, Moreau, 7" 6,000.00
Vase, brn, gourd form w/4-petal top, Albert design, #233, 5" 325.00
Vase, brn, 4 bar hdls at pinched-in neck, Mundie, #269, 11" ..1,400.00
Vase, gr, #51, 3½" 330.00
Vase, gr, can neck on bulb body, angle hdls, 3¾x3¼" 425.00
Vase, gr, cylinder w/in 2 long upright buttresses, 5½" 600.00
Vase, gr, flared rim, ovoid w/closed angular hdls, Gates, 9" 800.00
Vase, gr, gourd form w/in 4 integral buttresses, Mundie, 7" 2,000.00
Vase, gr, megaphone shape w/in 4 long uprights, 7", NM 750.00
Vase, gr, ogee sides w/hdls, WD Gates design, #407, 9" 850.00
Vase, gr, pear shape w/2 sqd rim-to-body hdls, 6¾x4" 700.00
Vase, gr, swirling dome shape, Albert, #319, 6¼" 2,800.00
Vase, gr, 4 bar hdls at incurvate neck, WB Mundie, 11", EX- .1,000.00
Vase, gr, 4 C-shape rim extensions about waisted neck, 4½" 900.00
Vase, gr matt, 4x4" 325.00
Vase, gr w/blk, petal top, buttress base, Moreau #420, 14" 2,000.00
Vase, gr w/gray, 4 buttresses hold cone form, sm rpr, 6x12" 6,000.00
Vase, gr w/gun metal, hdld amphora shape, 9½x5" 750.00
Vase, gr w/veins, bulbous, #246, 3½x4" 350.00
Vase, gr w/veins, ovoid w/tiny opening, 4½" 425.00
Vase, leathery yel, 4 strap hdls at recessed neck, rpr, 14" 1,700.00
Vase, metallic crystalline, red/gold/blk, stick neck, 8½" 750.00
Vase, moss gr mottle gloss over metallic burgundy, #64B, 11½" .225.00
Vase, rose, buttressed flower form, F Moreau #423, rpr, 12" 600.00

Teddy Bear Collectibles

The story of Teddy Roosevelt's encounter with the bear cub has been oft recounted with varying degrees of accuracy, so it will suffice to say that it was as a result of this incident in 1902 that the teddy bear got his name. These appealing little creatures are enjoying renewed popularity with collectors today. To one who has not yet succumbed to their obvious charms, one bear seems to look very much like another. How to tell the older ones? Look for long snouts, jointed limbs, large feet and felt paws, long curving arms, and glass or shoe-button eyes. Most old bears have a humped back and are made of mohair stuffed with straw or excelsior. Cute expressions, original clothes, a nice personality, and, of course, good condition add to their value. Some Steiff bears in mint condition may go as high as $100.00 per inch. These are easily recognized by the trademark button within the ear. For further information we recommend *Teddy Bears, Annalee's & Steiff Animals*, by Margaret Fox Mandel, available from Collector Books. See also Toys, Steiff.

Key: jtd — jointed

Bears

Am, jtd, button eyes, embr face, 1910, 18", G 495.00
Am, jtd, gold mohair, glass eyes, embr nose, 1910s, 8", EX 325.00
Am, jtd, gold mohair, sleep eyes, 1920s, 13", EX 675.00
Am, jtd, hump, glass eyes, fiber filled, 1916, 19", VG 300.00
Am, jtd, mohair, glass eyes, hump, 1920s, 21", M 495.00
Am, jtd, mohair, glass eyes, straw filled, 1908, 33", EX 1,600.00
Chad Valley, jtd, long gold mohair, 23", EX 825.00
Character, jtd, cinnamon plush, plastic eyes, 1960s, 15", NM 75.00
Character, jtd, tan mohair, button eyes, 1950s, 13", EX 80.00
Clemens, growler, mohair, dressed as lifeguard, w/tag, 15", NM .300.00

Clemens, jtd, cinnamon mohair, glass eyes, 1940s, 17", EX **325.00**
Clemens, jtd, tan mohair, felt mouth, 1950s, 10" **225.00**
Cramer, Dicky Bear, wht mohair w/tan inset nose, 1920s, 16", EX ..**950.00**
England, jtd, hump, glass eyes, embr nose, 1920s, 20", VG **250.00**
England, jtd, yel mohair, glass eyes, embr nose, 17", EX **400.00**
German, growler, dk brn w/tan, straw filled, '50s, 18", VG **195.00**
German, jtd, gold mohair, button eyes, embr face, '06, 16", EX ..**695.00**
German, jtd, gold mohair, button eyes, embr face, '06, 21", EX ..**2,090.00**
German, jtd, gold mohair, 13", M **495.00**
Growler, jtd, brn mohair, straw filled, 25", EX **375.00**
Hermann, cheerleader, jtd, 8", M **95.00**
Hermann, jtd, brn mohair, open mouth, 12", EX **125.00**
Hermann, jtd, gold mohair, sheared nose, 1930, 16", EX **425.00**
Hermann, jtd, gold mohair, 3-claw paws, 1950s, 12", VG **300.00**
Hermann, squeaker, mohair, hump, straw filled, '55, 17", M **215.00**
Hermann, wht mohair, plastic eyes, embr nose, 1950s, 6" **150.00**
Ideal, gold mohair, button eyes, 1906, 16", EX **865.00**
Ideal, jtd, cinnamon plush, glass eyes, 1940s, 14", NM **150.00**
Ideal, jtd, gold mohair, button eyes, ca 1907, 16", EX **895.00**
Ideal, jtd, tan cotton plush, ca 1923, 15", VG **450.00**
Japan, Winnie the Pooh, 1950s, 5½", NM **87.50**
Knickerbocker, jtd, wht mohair, glass eyes, 1930s, 17", EX **325.00**
Knickerbocker, jtd, wht plush, plastic eyes, ca 1950s, 11", EX **120.00**
Petz, growler, jtd, honey melange, US Zone, 16", EX **350.00**
Schuco, jtd, mohair, 2½" **395.00**
Schuco, orange mohair, for perfume, 3", M **600.00**
Schuco, wht mohair w/felt paws, 2½", NM **365.00**
Schuco, yes/no, mohair, linen pads, 1920s, 12", NM **1,200.00**
Steiff, air-brushed mohair, plastic eyes, button, '50s, 29", G **150.00**
Steiff, blond mohair, jtd, button eyes, w/book, 9½", G **525.00**
Steiff, blond mohair, jtd, steel eyes, embr snout, 8½", EX **525.00**
Steiff, cinnamon mohair, hump, jtd, w/button, 1907, 13" **1,750.00**
Steiff, growler, iron & rubber-wheel base, button, 27", VG **900.00**
Steiff, long curly mohair, w/button, 1950s, 30", NM **350.00**
Steiff, mohair, hump, w/button, ca 1935-40, 13½", M **1,250.00**
Steiff, tan mohair, button eyes, rprs, w/button, '08, 15", NM **850.00**
Steiff, wht mohair, glass eyes, rpl pads, button, 11", VG **525.00**
Steiff, yel mohair, jtd, glass eyes, embr snout, 1910s, 18", VG **995.00**

Telephones

Since Alexander Graham Bell's first successful telephone communication, the phone itself has undergone a complete evolution in style as well as efficiency. Early models, especially those wall types with ornately carved oak boxes, are of special interest to collectors. Also of value are the candlestick phones from the early part of the century and any related memorabilia.

Oak wall phone, ringer at top, ear piece intact, light wear, 20½x9½", $190.00.

Am Electric, oak dbl box, swivel mouthpc, 31x12", NM **625.00**
Am Telephone & Telegraph, candlestick, 1915, EX **125.00**
Automatic Electric, beige, 3-slot pay phone, 1950s, EX orig **150.00**
Automatic Electric, chrome, 3-slot pay phone, 1950s, EX orig ...**225.00**
Automatic Electric #50, EX **65.00**
Cradle style, off-wht plastic, 1930s, 6x8x5" **100.00**
Kellogg, candlestick & box, no dial **145.00**
Kellogg Switchboard, Supply Signal Crops, US Army, in case ...**35.00**
North Electric, Cleveland, oak, wall type **265.00**
Oak, 2-box wall type, center iron-bk transmitter, 32x10x9", G ..**250.00**
Swedish Am, wood, wall type, EX **250.00**
Table model, golden oak w/glass panel, 40", EX orig **2,600.00**
Trimline, rotary dial, push button, 1968, M **10.00**
Vought Berger Co, LaCross WI **400.00**
Western Electric, cradle-type #102, dial **145.00**
Western Electric, operator's, candlestick type, EX **90.00**
Western Electric, oval base, non-dial cradle style **45.00**
Western Electric, wall type, space saver, non-dial, 1920s **35.00**
Western Electric, walnut, wall type, 1880s, 13x6x4½", EX **600.00**
Western Electric #205, blk variation, 1938, EX **115.00**
Wood, crank style, wall type, unmk, EX **190.00**

Blue Bell Paperweights

First issued in the early 1900s, these bell-shaped glass weights were used as giveaways and by telephone company executives to prevent stacks of papers from blowing off their desks in the days of overhead fans. Over the years they have all but vanished — some taken by retiring employees, others accidently broken. The weights came to be widely used as advertising by individual telephone companies; and as the smaller companies merged to form larger companies, more and more new weights were created. They were widely distributed with the opening of the first transcontinental telephone line in 1915. The weight embossed 'Opening of Trans-Pacific Service, Dec. 23, 1931,' in peacock blue glass is very rare, and the price is negotiable. In 1972 the first Pioneer bell paperweights were made to sell to raise funds for the charities the Pioneers support. This has continued to the present day. These bell paperweights have also become 'collectibles.' For further study we recommend *Blue Bell Paperweights, 1992 Revised Edition*, by Jacqueline Linscott; she is listed in the Directory under Florida.

Bell System Ches & Pot Tel Company & Assoc Companies, ice bl .**450.00**
Bell Telephone System, cobalt **225.00**
Break-Up of the Bell System, opaline bl swirl **50.00**
Compliments of Millville Kiwanis Club, ice bl **800.00**
Missouri & Kansas Telephone Company, peacock **125.00**
Nebraska Telephone Company, peacock **325.00**
New York Telephone, cobalt **110.00**
Pays 7% Mountain States Telephone, peacock **200.00**
Region 10 Assembly, bl **100.00**
Southern Bell Telephone & Telegraph Company, cobalt w/gold ...**175.00**
Western Electric Company, cobalt **200.00**

Related Memorabilia

Rasp, Bell System **10.00**
Sign, dbl-sided, Bell System, enamel, lollipop type **750.00**
Sign, Federal Telephone, dbl-sided porc, flanged, 17x18", EX **225.00**
Sign, Public Telephone, flanged porc on steel, 12" sq, G **65.00**

Telescopes

Old telescopes are still appreciated for the quality of the workmanship and materials that went into their production. Large telescopes were mounted on tripod stands; spyglasses were hand held. Most were made of brass and wood.

E Vion Paris, brass/leather, 4-draw, w/lens covers 330.00
Harris & Son London, brass, 3-draw, late 1800s, EX 225.00
JB Adkins-Beal, brass w/wooden bbl, 2-draw, 17½", EX 250.00
Lord Bury Telescope JH Steward...London, brass, 3-draw, EX 250.00
Pinkham R Smith Co, Boston, brass case, 1-draw, 26", EX 360.00
Unmk, brass, 3-draw, w/lens covers, 33", EX 180.00
Unmk, wooden bbl, 1-draw, 48", EX 210.00

Televisions

Many early TVs have escalated in value in the last few years. Pre-1943 sets (usually with only one to five channels) are often worth $500.00 to $5,000.00. Unusually styled small-screen wooden 1940s TVs are 'hot'; but most metal, Bakelite, and large-screen sets are still shunned by collectors. 1950s color TVs with 16" or smaller tubes are valuable; larger color sets are not. Our advisor for this category is Harry Poster; author of *Poster's Radio & Television Price Guide 1920-1990, 2nd Edition*; he is listed in the Directory under New Jersey.

Admiral, #20B1, 12" 75.00
Air King, A-2000, 10" tabletop 80.00
Andrea, KTE-5, 5" pre-war kit chassis w/front, minimum 1,500.00
Ansley, projecting set, end-table style 75.00
Automatic, #1649 & similar 16" sets 45.00
Belmont, #10DX21, X22, pull-out tube console 175.00
Bendix, #2000 Series, 10" & 12" tabletops 75.00
CBS-Columbia, 1950s blk & wht, 12" & larger 45.00
Crosley, #9-420, #424, 12" console, ea 80.00
Emerson, Model #527, early, 10" 135.00

Emerson #639, 7" tabletop, 1949, $200.00.

Emerson #654 & sq 12" consoles, ea 45.00
Garod, #1220, #1230TVP, 12" combos, ea 65.00
General Electric, #15CL100, 15" color console, 1954 ....650.00
General Electric, #800, or similar Bakelite tabletop, ea 185.00
Meck, XC-703, 7" portable 165.00
Motorola, #7-VT-2, Bakelite 7" tabletop 135.00
Philco, #48-1001, #1002, 10" tabletop, ea 135.00
Philco, Safari, Model H-2010, 1st transistor type, w/hood 185.00
RCA, #721-TS, 10" rnd tabletop 120.00
RCA, metal, lightweight 1950s portable, ea 75.00
Scott, #800BT, projection combo 500.00
Sparton, #4920 or similar 12" console, ea 45.00
Teleking, #210, #310, 10", ea 75.00

Westinghouse, H-242, H-251, or similar electric magnifier 135.00
Zenith, mid-1950s lightweight metal portable, ea 75.00
Zenith, 1948-50 combination set, 'porthole' screen 80.00

Teplitz

Teplitz, in Bohemia, was an active art pottery center at the turn of the century. The Amphora Pottery Works was only one of the firms that operated there. (See Amphora.) Art Nouveau and Art Deco styles were favored, and much of the ware was hand decorated with the primary emphasis on vases and figurines. Items listed here are marked 'Teplitz' or 'Turn,' a nearby city. Our advisor for this category is Jack Gunsaulus; he is listed in the Directory under Michigan.

Bust of lady in lacy bonnet, pastel blues and greens, signed Stellmacher, 18½", $500.00.

Bust of Ophelia, RS&K, 24" 1,200.00
Figure, Mercury & Sea Goddess, pastels w/gold, 18½", pr 800.00
Tray, high-relief eagle/snake on rim, rectangular, 5x16" 270.00
Vase, copper-gr, lower part w/vertical panels, 11½" 660.00
Vase, florals & butterflies, wht on cobalt, Wahliss, 15" 585.00
Vase, florals w/gold, RS&K Turn Teplitz, 7" 150.00
Vase, florals w/gold on cream, bulbous, 8½" 195.00
Vase, florals w/gold on gr & cream, gold hdl, 13" 155.00
Vase, mother/child reserve on bl mottled w/gold, hdls, 7" 245.00
Vase, Nouveau form w/rtcl top, poppies/gilt, Wahliss, 9" 275.00
Vase, Nouveau girl sits on stump, Wahliss, cream ground, 6" 495.00
Vase, stylized iris, bl/wht on gr w/gold, RS&K, 9" 385.00
Vase, sun/trees, insect/floral band, stick neck, RS&K, 12" 465.00

Terra Cotta

Terra cotta is a type of earthenware or clay used for statuary, architectural facings, or domestic articles. It is unglazed, baked to durable hardness, and characterized by the color of the body which may range from brick red to buff.

Humidor, blk Greek figures, lid w/NP hinge, 4¾" 55.00
Jar, grisaille hunt scenes, Registry mk, 4" 35.00
Plaque, Ages of Love classical frieze, Ipsen, 1800s, 17½x7" 130.00
Umbrella stand, dragon decor, 23½" 85.00

Thermometers

Few objects man has invented have been so eloquently expressed both functionally and artistically as the ubiquitous thermometer. Developed initially by Galileo as a scientific device, thermometers slowly evolved into decorative objet d'art, functional household utensils, and eye-catching advertising specialties. Most American thermometers manufactured early in the 20th century were produced by Taylor (Tycos), and today their thermometers remain the most plentiful on the market. Decorative thermometers manufactured before 1800 are now ensconced in the permanent collections of approximately a dozen European museums. Because of their fragility, few devices of this era have survived in private collections. Nowadays most antique thermometers find their way to market through estate sales.

Insofar as sheer beauty, uniqueness, and scientific accuracy, decorative thermometers are far superior to the ordinary and inexpensive versions which carry advertising. Decorative thermometers run the gamut from plain tin household varieties to the highly ornate creations of Tiffany and Bradley and Hubbard. They have been manufactured from nearly every conceivable material — oak, sterling, brass, and glass being the favorites — and have tested the artistry and technical skills of some of America's finest craftsmen. Ornamental models can be found in free-hanging, wall-mounted, or desk/mantel versions.

Thermometer prices are based on age, ornateness, and whether mercury or alcohol is used as the filler in the tube. A broken or missing tube will cut at least 40% off the value. (Only one company in the world makes replacement tubes.) Virtually all American-made thermometers available today as collectors' items were made between 1875 and 1940. The Golden Age of decoratives ended in the early 1940s as modern manufacturing processes and materials robbed them of their natural distinctiveness.

Key:
br — brass	mrc — mercury
F&C — Fahrenheit & Celsius	pmc — permacolor
F&R — Fahrenheit & Reamer	sc — scales
hyg — hygrometer	stl — stainless

Adams, G; hanging, mahog/br bulb cap, lg sc, red spirit, 9x2" **225.00**
Alexandre, desk, scimitar figural, brass sc/mrc, 9" **280.00**
Alexandre, folding, F&R sc, mrc, 1850s **320.00**
Amadio, F, Corn Hill, desk, ivory pillar/compass, mrc, 1890, 10" .**1,300.00**
Anonymous, desk, brass conquistador figural, brass sc/mrc **430.00**
Anonymous, desk, dogs figural, brass sc/mrc, 1915, 9" **300.00**
Anonymous, desk, frog on ladder, cb sc/alcohol, 6" **260.00**
Anonymous, desk, picture fr w/glass, mrc, 1902, 7" **180.00**
Army & Navy (Westminster), travel, ivory sc, 1875, 5", +case ..**300.00**
Bargess Reversible Box, br sc, oak case, mrc, 5½" **125.00**
Bearskin Ltd, wall, metal clip, rnd mcr, 1930, 3x4" **300.00**
Blk/Starr/Frost, desk, barometer, stl, F&C, mrc, '10, 11" **2,300.00**
Bradley & Hubbard, desk, br/ornate lion, br sc/mrc, 9", VG **280.00**
Capendium, desk, handmade br/porc fr, F&C sc, rnd mrc, 4" **850.00**
Carpenter & Westley, desk, ivory w/glass dome mrc, 1880, 6" ...**800.00**
Casella London, wall, maxi/minimum, 2 units, wood, plastic sc .**260.00**
Cheshire Silversmiths, desk, br candelabra, mrc, 1875, 10" **4,500.00**
Chester, desk, stl sc, sterling bezel, mrc, 2x6" **350.00**
Clark, desk, ivory ped, crown, mrc, 1904, 7" **295.00**
Cloister, inkwell, stl bk & base w/angels at side, 1901 ....**975.00**
Creswel, travel, ivory case/mirror, removable sc, mrc, 2½" **2,800.00**
CW Wilder...NH, bear & billboard br figural, mrc, 6½" **200.00**
CW Wilder...NH, desk, Deco women, br F sc, mrc, 8" **750.00**
Desk, cvd walrus tusk, 2-tier disk base, inlay sc, 1860, 9" **300.00**
Desk, Spirit of St Louis, dragon, F br sc/mrc, '01, 6" **1,500.00**
Diamond, wall, br F sc on wood, rare, 7½x1½" **400.00**
Dixie, W (London); desk, gilt/br, Gothic, SP sc, mrc, 8" **710.00**
Dolland London, hanging, mahog fr, sterling sc/mrc, 1810, 18" .**4,600.00**
Dollard London, desk, sterling, br sc, mrc, 1908, 6" **750.00**

Dring & Fage, desk, marble, ivory sc, mrc, 1880, 6" **1,500.00**
English, desk, trn ivory, glass dome, mrc, 1860, 11" **475.00**
Freeborn, desk, bronze w/lead decor/br sc, mrc, 8" **130.00**
G Cooper, desk, bell shape w/cupola, sterling, dial, 2x3" **150.00**
Gilbert & Co, travel, silver eng sc, mrc, 1850, 8" **630.00**
Gloucester Scientific, sterling case, glass front, pmc, 42" **1,200.00**
Haris, P & Co (Birmingham); desk, boxwood, 3-tube, mrc, 12" .**410.00**
Heath & Wing, figural calendar, br w/porc sc, mrc, 1870 ....**1,000.00**
Hiergelsell Bros, indoor, cabinet/oak bk, bl liquid, #159 ....**160.00**
Honeywell, desk, Bakelite bell base, dial sc, 1935, 3" dia **300.00**
J Waldstein, wall, br R sc on wood, mrc, 1900s, 10½" **650.00**
Pairpoint, desk, sterling picture fr, mrc, 1907, 5" **600.00**
Pairpoint, mantel, br, w/angel, sterling sc/mrc, 1904 ....**325.00**
Reau, desk, sq incline base, floral top, mrc, 1895 ....**180.00**
Rowley & Sons, travel, ivory sc, mrc, 1894, 4", +case **180.00**
Short & Mason, recording drum, copper case, 1910 ....**75.00**
Slouche, desk, alabaster ped, paper sc inset, mrc, 8x2½" **95.00**
Somalvico, Jos; desk, figural, flared base, br sc, mrc, 10" **480.00**
Standard, for Fairbanks & Co, rnd, br case, 1886, 7" **160.00**
Standard, wall, br case, dial counterbalance, 1885, 9" **210.00**
Standard, wall, ivory F sc on ebony, mrc, 1880, 9" **375.00**
Taylor, hanging, ornate wood bk, br sc, 10x7" **80.00**
Taylor Castle..., w/hyg, mahog fr, sterling sc/mrc, 1785, 12" ..**3,800.00**
Therm-O-Dial, hanging, brass, beehive shape, dial, 1915, rare ..**315.00**
Thermindex, Switzerland, desk, Bakelite stand, F sc, 5" **430.00**
Thomas Wright, desk, octagon, pot metal, F&C sc, 5x3" **190.00**
Tiffany, amber glass w/grapes, gold mt, brass/mrc, '06, 8x12" ..**2,250.00**
Tiffany, desk, horoscope, bronze, mrc, 1907, 4x7" **375.00**
Tiffany, gr glass w/pine needles, brass sc/mrc, '02, 8x12" **2,800.00**
Tiffany & Co, desk, sterling, br sc/mrc, 3x5", 1900, rare **1,600.00**
Tycos, maxi/minimum, japanned tin/br, mrc, T-5452, 8" **125.00**
Tycos-Taylor, outdoor wall, wood fr, red liquid, 27x5" **55.00**
VJD Inc, wall, clip, F br sc, mrc tube, 1895, 4" **700.00**
W Pratt, desk, wood inlays, ivory sc, mrc, 1900, 6" **90.00**
Wall, Fr gilt, wood fr, silver eng, F&R sc, mrc, 1776, 10x14" ..**3,600.00**
Warren Foundries, wall, umbrella w/dragon hdl, br sc, mrc, 12" .**220.00**
West, desk, Gothic design, br, 1900, 12" **1,250.00**
White & Westall, wall, wht Bakelite F sc, mrc, 7" **450.00**
Whitehead & Hoag, Lambrecht's Polymeter, wall, mrc, 9" **890.00**
Wise, desk, Tunbridge, twin columns, mrc, 1870, 5" **1,750.00**

1000 Faces China

So named because of its many hand-painted faces, much of this chinaware was made during the '30s through the '50s (some even earlier). Though many pieces are unmarked, others are marked 'Made in Japan.' There are two primary patterns, 'Black Face' and the 'Gold' pattern, and variations exist. Both designs employ many colors. Dinner plates usually are decorated with an outer-most 'ring of color' (two or three hues) containing a simple design which is often flowers. The inner ring is usually comprised of many colors radiating from the center circle which may be done in a primary color (red, for instance) with a design such as a dragon or clouds painted in gold. 'Black Face' is distinguishable by its range of colors — primarily red, white, and yellow with some green and blue — and the black hand-painted faces. The 'Gold' pattern is also multicolored but is dominated by the gold throughout the design, and the faces themselves are gold as well. Other variations include '1000 Men in Robes' and '1000 Faces' with black or blue rims on the saucers and cups. These pieces seem to be very scarce. In the listings that follow, all items are marked 'Made in Japan' (MIJ) unless noted otherwise. Our advisor for this category is Suzi Hibbard; she is listed in the Directory under California.

Cup & saucer, blk faces **40.00**

Cup & saucer, demitasse; gold **25.00**
Cup & saucer w/pie plate, blk faces **50.00**
Plate, blk, 10" **45.00**
Shakers, pr **18.00**
Snack set, 8½" L **45.00**
Soup set, blk faces, 3-pc **75.00**
Sweetmeat set, w/lcq box, 9-pc, 12" **125.00**
Tea set, gold, 15-pc, serves 6 ....**125.00**
Teapot, gold, w/dragon spout, 7" **50.00**

Tiffany

Louis Comfort Tiffany was born in 1848 to Charles Lewis and Harriet Young Tiffany of New York. By the time he was eighteen, his father's small dry goods and stationery store had grown and developed into the world-renowned Tiffany and Company. Preferring the study of art to joining his father in the family business, Louis spent the next six years under the tutelage of noted artists. He returned to America in 1870 and until 1875 painted canvases that focused on European and North African scenes. Deciding the more lucrative approach was in the application of industrial arts and crafts, he opened a decorating studio called Louis C. Tiffany and Co., Associated Artists. He began seriously experimenting with glass, and eschewing traditionally painted-on details, he instead learned to produce glass with qualities that could suggest natural textures and effects. His experiments broadened, and he soon concentrated his efforts on vases, bowls, etc., that came to be considered the highest achievements of the art. Peacock feathers, leaves and vines, flowers and abstracts were developed within the plane of the glass as it was blown. Opalescent and metallic lustres were combined with transparent color to produce stunning effects. Tiffany called his glass Favrile, meaning handmade.

In 1900 he established Tiffany Studios and turned his attention full time to producing art glass, leaded-glass lamp shades and windows, and household wares with metal components. He also designed a complete line of jewelry which was sold through his father's store. He became proficiently accomplished in silverwork and produced such articles as hand mirrors embellished with peacock feather designs set with gems and candlesticks with Favrile glass inserts.

Tiffany's work exemplified the Art Nouveau style of design and decoration, and through his own flamboyant personality and business acumen he perpetrated his tastes onto the American market to the extent that his name became a household word. Tiffany Studios continued to prosper until the second decade of this century when due to changing tastes his influence began to diminish. By the early 1930s the company had closed.

Serial numbers were assigned to much of Tiffany's work, and letter prefixes indicated the year of manufacture: A-N for 1896-1900, P-Z for 1901-1905. After that, the letter followed the numbers with A-N in use from 1906-1912; P-Z from 1913-1920. O-marked pieces were made especially for friends of relatives; X indicated pieces not made for sale.

Our listings are primarily from the auction houses in the East where Tiffany sells at a premium. All pieces are signed unless noted otherwise. Our advisor for Tiffany lamps is Carl Heck; he is listed in the Directory under Colorado.

Key: c-b — counter-balance

Glass

Bowl, Aqua Pastel, herringbone leaf pattern, 3¾x12½" **650.00**
Bowl, bl/purple irid, expanded dmn, 12", +2-tier flower frog ...**1,500.00**
Bowl, gold w/EX color, swirled prunts, 4⅜", +5½" plate **400.00**
Bowl, gold w/purple-bl highlights, purple-gr int, 3x10½" **500.00**
Bowl, irid gold millefiori, ruffled, 1½x6¼" **700.00**
Bowl, lily pads, gr on gold, #128, 2x15" **1,250.00**

Bowl, lily pads/vines on gold w/EX highlights, 10", +frog **850.00**
Bowl, Tel El Amarna, 3 reeded scroll ft, 11" **1,250.00**
Candle holder, Pk Pastel, cupped ped ft, #1817, 4¼" **440.00**
Candlestick, gold, twist stem, 9" **400.00**
Champagne, gold, dbl-knop stem, #F-1774, 8" **600.00**
Compote, gold w/irid, flared cone body, ped ft, label, 5x8" **425.00**
Compote, Lav-Pk Pastel, clear knop ft w/lt scallops, 2x6" **600.00**
Cordial, amber irid, tall slim std, 4¾", set of 6 ....**800.00**
Decanter, gold, pinched sides, #514, 10x4½" **1,800.00**
Decanter, lt citron, pinched sides/stopper, narrow neck, 10" **450.00**
Finger bowl, gold millefiori, 4", +underplate **1,250.00**
Goblet, gold, dbl-bubble stem, 7", set of 4 ....**1,200.00**
Goblet, gold, wheel-cut grapevine borders, set of 12 ....**1,800.00**
Paperweight, 4 goldfish/bubbles in gr, dragonfly atop, 5½" **8,000.00**
Parfait, Aqua Pastel, ribbed, 6¼" **500.00**
Parfait, gold w/bl highlights, clear ft, 5" **295.00**
Pitcher, 3-petal leaves, gr on gold irid, 4" **1,275.00**
Plate, 5-petal flower, gold on opal, #K2357, 8" **700.00**
Salt cellar, bl irid, ruffled, 1½x2⅝", pr **825.00**
Salt cellar, gold, bowl shape, #1308, 2¼" dia **150.00**
Salt cellar, gold, rnd w/prunts, #W-1719, 1" dia **175.00**
Shade, gas light; gold irid, ribbed, 5" **300.00**
Shade, Morrish, feathers, gr/gold on opal, 8-sided rim, 6" **875.00**
Sherbet, gold, prunts on cup & base, 4¾" **300.00**
Shot glass, gold w/bl highlights, pinched, 1½" **150.00**
Taster, gold, swirled prunt, 2¼", set of 6 ....**1,400.00**
Toothpick holder, gold irid, dimpled sides, 2" **210.00**
Vase, Amethyst Pastel, optic ribs, shaped V-form, ftd, 6½" **275.00**
Vase, bl irid, lt ribs, pulled nubs at shoulder, 4" **880.00**
Vase, bl w/purple & pk irid, tube neck/shouldered, 9" **1,700.00**
Vase, bud; 5 pointed gr leaves on gold, 12" **935.00**
Vase, cobalt irid, 18-rib ruffled trumpet form, 10" **990.00**
Vase, cvd flower garlands on gold, scroll hdls, #1159, 9" **1,150.00**
Vase, Deco foliate motif eng on gold, angle shoulder, 18" **3,900.00**

Vase, feathers, blue gold on iridized red Favrile, #9356A, 3½", $4,500.00.

Vase, feathers, pk/gr on peach irid, waisted cylinder, 6" **900.00**
Vase, feathers at base on gold, jeweled ormolu top, 9" **1,100.00**
Vase, feathers on gold irid, lily form in bronze ft, 13" **1,250.00**
Vase, feathers on gold trumpet form, bronze base, #1043, 12" **800.00**
Vase, floriform; bl irid, ribbed body, rnd ft, #2468, 10½" **1,375.00**
Vase, floriform; bl irid, stretched/ruffled, stick stem, 4½" **1,100.00**
Vase, floriform; feathers, gr on opal, gold ft/int, 4x5" **1,175.00**
Vase, floriform; feathers on ft/bowl, gr on gold & gr, 14" **2,600.00**
Vase, floriform; feathers on gold, flat top, slim std, 10" **1,800.00**
Vase, floriform; gold, trumpet shaped, rnd ft, #5780, 11" **690.00**
Vase, gold, classic form, ribbed scroll hdls, #1068, 10" **1,100.00**
Vase, gold, elongated neck, bulb body, ped ft, #1835, 7" **440.00**
Vase, gold trumpet form, in 14-rib bronze base, #160, 15" **700.00**
Vase, gold w/bl & pk irid, #9161B, mini, 2x2" **425.00**
Vase, gold w/EX highlights, classic form, #4785H, 17x9" **2,400.00**
Vase, gold w/pk & bl highlights, ftd ribbed cylinder, 12" **850.00**

Vase, hearts & vines, gr on gold, #5516, 2¾x3½" **1,250.00**
Vase, jack-in-pulpit; amber irid, slim std, dome ft, 19" **9,000.00**
Vase, leaves, gr on lt apricot, cupped base, #8975, 10½" **2,200.00**
Vase, leaves on gold, flanged rim, slim, ftd, 9" **775.00**
Vase, lt gold, baluster, #3902M, 10½" **1,000.00**
Vase, paperweight, jonquils, gr/yel on frost, slim, 17½" **8,000.00**
Vase, purple to wht w/stripes, clear base, trumpet form, 12" **1,500.00**
Vase, red damascene, ftd, #E-2313, 3½" **47,000.00**
Vase, red w/gold waves, wide shoulder, disk ft, #3918P, 1½" ...**1,800.00**
Vase, Tel el Amarna, emerald gr/wht int, shoulder band, 9" ...**4,000.00**
Vase, waves, gold on gr, waves/dots at base, lt ribbing, 6" **1,300.00**
Wax stamp, gold w/EX highlights, 3 scarabs, no mk, 2", NM **180.00**
Wine, med gr w/opal stem & bowl, 4x3¼" **325.00**

Lamps

Base, Cypriote, bl w/opal & amber mottle, amphora form, 23" ...**700.00**
Base, tree trunk on disk ft, 6-socket, gilt, #553 ....**12,500.00**
Base w/pods, slim shaft w/flower buds, harp arms, #670, 55" ...**1,250.00**
Candle, amber irid shade/twist base, feathered stem, 14", EX .**1,300.00**
Candle, gold emb shade/twist stick w/gold candle, 14", EX **1,300.00**
Chandelier, 6-light, sm gold shades hang from C-scrolls, 15" ..**3,800.00**

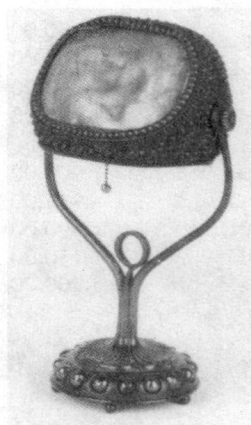

Desk lamp, two gold iridescent turtle-back tiles mounted in beaded bronze single-socket shade on molded platform base with sixteen glass jewels, #D801, 14", EX, $3,500.00.

Desk, bl pastel 6" shade; dore harp-shape base **2,850.00**
Desk, bronze 7" star-cut shade w/glass liner; #417 std, EX **2,500.00**
Desk, damascene 7" dome shade on c-b std #415 ....**3,200.00**
Desk, lav irid 8" dome shade w/gr waves, c-b #415 base **6,900.00**
Desk, gilt-bronze 8" dia shade w/geometric band; #417 w/c-b .**2,000.00**
Desk, gr dome shade w/irid waves; harp std, tripod ft, #438 .....**4,000.00**
Desk, gr turtlebk tile in bronze shade; Zodiac base w/harp **4,250.00**
Desk, ldgl nautilus form shade; lappet-emb std #1543, 14" **5,000.00**
Desk, silver dome w/gr waves shade in harp std, #569 ....**6,900.00**
Floor, bl 10" dome shade w/wavy band, c-b std #681, 53" **9,750.00**
Floor, gold 10" dome shade; gilt knopped std #619, 53" **4,600.00**
Floor, gold 10" shade (EX) on 5-leg c-b std #468, 55" **5,050.00**
Floor, ldgl 25" brickwork shade; std #277, 80" **17,500.00**
Floor, linenfold-band 20" shade; #379 6-light std, 63" **11,500.00**
Lantern, 4 turtlebk tiles w/openwork crown, ea panel: 8x6" **6,700.00**
Lily, 10-light, gold sgn shades; lily pad std #381 ....**21,850.00**
Lily, 7-light, rainbow irid shade (6 sgn), lily pad base, 20" **13,800.00**
Lily, 7-light (2 cracked), 7-arm tree-trunk std #29721, 26" **5,900.00**
Oil, 10" globe shade w/vertical pulls; converted #D-435 base .**2,800.00**
Sconce, bronze 3-arm mt w/cvd acorn, gold lilies, 6x9" **2,200.00**
Shade, Dmn Quilt, amber irid, lily form w/bulbous base, 5" **650.00**
Student, dbl; gr glass blown into shade fr; std #25574, 29" **12,100.00**
Student, dbl; 10" gr/irid wht-lined shades; Pine Needle can ..**11,000.00**
Table, damascene 10" gr/gold dome shade; matching base, 18" ..**5,600.00**

Table, damascene 16" gold/opal shade; #25882 ftd std **4,400.00**
Table, damascene 16" gr/gold shade; 4-leg urn base #6816 ......**3,500.00**
Table, feathered 10" gr/cream cased shade; #325 std, 18" **3,200.00**
Table, gold w/waves 9¾" dome shade; rnd pottery base, 16" **4,400.00**
Table, ldgl 16" acorn-band shade (EX); acorns on #26872 std ...**3,200.00**
Table, ldgl 16" apple blossoms dome shade; 4-ftd bun std **6,300.00**
Table, ldgl 16" Colonial geometric shade; Hampshire base **6,000.00**
Table, ldgl 16" dogwood band shade; #25778 std **12,000.00**
Table, ldgl 16" pansy dome shade; ftd std #26877 w/bun base ..**28,750.00**
Table, ldgl 16" pansy shade; 4-ftd bun-shape std #9939 ....**11,000.00**
Table, ldgl 17" 6-dragonfly cone shade; #533 std **19,500.00**
Table, ldgl 18" lemon-leaf band shade; simple std #532 ....**6,500.00**
Table, ldgl 18" peony shade; 4-leg #1475 paw-ft std **60,000.00**
Table, ldgl 18" swirl leaf brickwork-band shade; std #533 ....**6,500.00**
Table, ldgl 20" daffodil w/narcissus band shade; std #26619 ..**66,300.00**
Table, ldgl/turtlebk 18" brickwork shade; 6-panel #533 std ...**10,000.00**

Metal Work

Items are bronze unless noted otherwise.

Ash stand, griffin atop slim std supports urn in beak, 31" **2,990.00**
Ash stand, rnd bowl atop slim std, rnd ft, #1648, 28" **1,200.00**
Bookends, Bookmark, gilt, #1056, 6" **550.00**
Bookends, Buddha in arch, copper patina, 6" **350.00**
Bowl, w/insert, #1727, 2¾x8" **500.00**
Box, cigarette; Grapevine, #8, 5" **385.00**
Box, emb/cloisonne band on lid, gilded, 4 ball ft, #130 ....**600.00**
Box, glove; Grapevine, gr glass int, #827, 13¾" L **2,500.00**
Box, Grapevine, gr glass liner, 6¾" L **440.00**
Box, Greek Key on lid corners, wood lined, #1114, 5" W, EX **500.00**
Candelabra, 2-light, gold favrile cups, central snuffer, 15" **4,300.00**
Candlestick, dbl, gr 'jewels,' on heart-shape base, #6075, 4" ...**3,800.00**
Candlestick, jeweled cup, vine hdl/stem, leaf ft, #1203, 8" **2,000.00**
Candlestick, 3-stem base, feathered glass cup, #1228, 11" **2,800.00**
Candlestick, 3-stem ft, bronze cup, #S786, 12" **1,300.00**
Clock, Grapevine, amber/wht liner, #878, 9¾x6½" **4,000.00**
Clock, Venetian, dk patina, #1679, 4¼x3¾x3" **700.00**
Desk set, Bookprinter, bookends/inkwell/scissors/tray+2 pcs ...**1,500.00**
Desk set, Pine Needle, calendar/letter opener/rack+4 pcs **880.00**
Figure, lion, brn patina, sgn/#d, 4¾" L **775.00**
Frame, Adam, gilt patina, #1786, 9½" **2,300.00**
Frame, Am Indian, dk brn patina, #1187, 6x7½", EX **750.00**
Frame, Chinese, dk brn patina, #1761, 8¾" **1,150.00**
Frame, Grapevine, gr/wht glass liner, gr/brn patina, 9" **2,400.00**
Frame, Pine Needle, gr glass liner, #946, 10" **2,880.00**
Frame, Pine Needle, gr glass liner, oval reserve, 12" **3,900.00**
Frame, Pine Needle, mottled amber glass, #948, 7½" **1,000.00**
Frame, Venetian, mc enamel/gilt, #1682, 11¾" **3,900.00**
Inkstand, Chinese, dk brn patina, #1753, 5" **465.00**
Inkwell, hammered w/geometric scrolls, no liner, #1112 ....**275.00**
Inkwell, 3 nude men pull rope-tied chest, gilt, 11" L **4,600.00**
Inkwell, 3-leg pot w/6 'jewels,' turtlebk in lid, 4" **1,875.00**
Magnifying glass, Abalone, gilt, MOP inlay, #1178, 9" **575.00**
Paperweight, dog's head form, inscr Shando, 2¼x3½" **220.00**
Pot, cast metal, relief robed men/bldgs, From Antique, 4" **465.00**
Smoking stand, telescopic base emb w/leaves, #1651, 26½" **465.00**
Tazza, Abalone, 8" dia **165.00**

Pottery

Compote, lily pad & lotus mold w/frogs, tan/wht mottle, 6¾" ..**11,000.00**
Pitcher, golden-bl irid, 3-spout, butterfly hdl, 6" **2,000.00**
Vase, Bronze Ware, o/l w/tulips & stems, bl int, 7x2½" **1,650.00**

Vase, Bronze Ware, textured leaves/vines, #E-72, 14" **4,500.00**
Vase, dk bl/mustard mottle, flaring cylinder, 14½" **1,875.00**
Vase, poppies emb on gr crystalline, tiny rpr, 11x9" **2,800.00**
Vase, silver-clad bronze w/emb poppies, #BP3M, 9", NM **4,250.00**

Silver

Water pitcher, lily of the valley blossoms and leaves on hammered ground, Paris Exhibition mark, 1891-1902, 52-troy-oz, 12", $8,525.00.

Bowl, chased C-scrolls, everted rim, brass insert, 12" **1,150.00**
Bowl, egg & dart molded rim, 12" L **525.00**
Compote, appl/rtcl chrysanthemum rim, low ftd, 35-oz **1,980.00**
Compote, everted rim w/flowers & rtcl lattice, 4", pr **1,200.00**
Dish, vegetable; rnd w/molded dome lid, monogram, 9½" L **880.00**
Pitcher, neoclassical band, 1865, 22-oz, 9" **935.00**
Punch ladle, Wave Edge, monogram, 13" **440.00**
Vase, violet etch on melon form, monogram, 1891-02, 3" **600.00**

Tiffin Glass

The Tiffin Glass Company was founded in 1887 in Tiffin, Ohio, one of the many factories composing the U.S. Glass Company. Its early wares consisted of tablewares and decorative items such as lamps and globes. Among the most popular of all Tiffin products was the black satin glass produced there during the 1920s. In 1959 U.S. Glass was sold, and in 1962 the factories closed. The plant was re-opened in 1963 as the Tiffin Art Glass Company. Products from this period were tableware, hand-blown stemware, and other decorative items.

Those interested in learning more about Tiffin glass are encouraged to contact the Tiffin Glass Collectors' Club, whose address can be found in the Directory under Clubs, Newsletters, and Catalogs. See also Black Glass.

Ashtray, Fuchsia, w/cigarette rest, 2¼x3¾" 20.00
Bell, Fuchsia, 6" 65.00
Bell, table; Cherokee Rose 50.00
Bottle, oil; Flanders, yel, w/stopper 175.00
Bowl, bonbon; Flanders, pk, 2-hdl 40.00
Bowl, bonbon; Fuchsia, #5831, 2-hdl 35.00
Bowl, centerpiece; Cherokee Rose, 13" 65.00
Bowl, console; Cadena, yel, 12" 45.00
Bowl, console; Fuchsia, flared, 11⅞" 65.00
Bowl, cream soup; Cadena 20.00
Bowl, finger; Cadena, yel, ftd 22.50
Bowl, finger; Cherokee Rose, 5" 17.50
Bowl, finger; Flanders, w/liner 17.00
Bowl, finger; Fuchsia, #041, ftd, 4" 40.00
Bowl, finger; Fuchsia, w/#8814 liner, 4½" 50.00
Bowl, fruit or nut; Cherokee Rose, 6" 17.50
Bowl, grapefruit; Cadena, ftd 20.00

Bowl, pickle; Cadena, 10" 12.50
Bowl, salad; Cherokee Rose, deep, 10" 40.00
Bowl, salad; Cherokee Rose, 7" 27.50
Bowl, salad; Fuchsia, #5902, deep, 9¾" 50.00
Bowl, salad; Fuchsia, #5902, 7¼" 30.00
Bowl, whipped cream; Fuchsia, #310, 3-ftd 30.00
Cake plate, Cherokee Rose, center hdld, 12½" 35.00
Cake plate, Fuchsia, #5831, 2-hdl, 10½" 50.00
Candlestick, Cadena, pr 17.50
Candlestick, Cherokee Rose, dbl branch, pr 75.00
Candlestick, Flanders, pk, pr 120.00
Candlestick, Fuchsia, #348, pr 65.00
Candlestick, Fuchsia, ball center, 2-light, 5", ea 55.00
Candlestick, Rosalind, yel, blown, pr 90.00
Candy jar, Flanders, pk, w/lid, flat 125.00
Candy jar, Flanders, w/lid, ftd 75.00
Celery, Flanders, 11" 25.00
Celery, Fuchsia, #5831, oval, 10" 32.50
Champagne, Adam, pk 30.00
Champagne, Athens-Diana 20.00
Champagne, Cadena, 6½" 17.00
Champagne, Carillon 10.00
Champagne, Casual 3.00
Champagne, Chardonnay 17.00
Champagne, Cherokee Rose, #17399 ....24.00
Champagne, Classic 22.50
Champagne, Empire 20.00
Champagne, Eternally Yours 10.00
Champagne, Flanders, pk, saucer form 30.00
Champagne, Fontaine, gr 30.00
Champagne, June Night, #17392 ....24.00
Champagne, Linda, cut 13.00
Champagne, Mansard 12.00
Champagne, Nouvelle 20.00
Champagne, Persian Pheasant, #17538 ....25.00
Cheese & crackers, Flanders, pk 85.00
Cigarette holder, Copen Bl 65.00
Claret, Cherokee Rose, 4-oz 40.00
Claret, Flanders 40.00
Claret, Julia, amber, 6⅛" 35.00
Cocktail, Cadena, 5¼" 17.50
Cocktail, Cerice 22.00
Cocktail, Cherokee Rose, #17403 ....24.00
Cocktail, Classic 35.00
Cocktail, Flanders 15.00
Cocktail, Fuchsia, #17453, 3½-oz, 4⅝" 32.50
Cocktail, June Night, #17392 ....27.00
Cocktail, oyster; Cadena 15.00
Cocktail, oyster; Flanders, pk 30.00
Cocktail, oyster; Fuchsia 28.00
Cocktail, Princess etch, #643 ....12.00
Cocktail, Rambler Rose, #188 Line, pk 40.00
Comport, cheese; Sylvan, gr 15.00
Comport, Cherokee Rose, 6" 60.00
Comport, Flanders, pk, 6" 100.00
Comport, Flanders, yel, 3½" 55.00
Comport, Palais Versailles, gold trim 100.00
Cordial, Byzantine 35.00
Cordial, Cadena, ¾-oz, 5¼" 50.00
Cordial, Cherokee Rose, 1-oz 55.00
Cordial, Flanders, yel 65.00
Cordial, June Night, #17403 ....45.00
Cordial, Persian Pheasant 45.00
Cordial, Wistaria, #17477 ....45.00

Cornucopia, Kilarney, 11½" 225.00
Creamer, Cadena, yel 25.00
Creamer, Cerice, ftd 25.00
Creamer, Cherokee Rose 30.00
Creamer, Flanders, pk, flat 115.00
Creamer, Flanders, pk, ftd 100.00
Creamer, Fuchsia, #5831, ind, 2⅞" 35.00
Cup & saucer, Athens-Diana 22.00
Cup & saucer, Rosalind, yel, blown 18.00
Cup & saucer, Sylvan, pk 35.00
Decanter, Athens-Diana, #185 ....135.00
Decanter, Flanders 150.00
Goblet, water; Cadena, yel, 7½" 35.00
Goblet, water; Camelot 10.00
Goblet, water; Cerice, #3075 ....24.00
Goblet, water; Cherokee Rose 22.50
Goblet, water; Eternally Yours 15.00
Goblet, water; Flanders 25.00
Goblet, water; Flanders, pk 40.00
Goblet, water; Fuchsia, tall 25.00
Goblet, water; Heirloom 10.00
Goblet, water; Huntington 15.00
Goblet, water; June Night, #17392 ....24.00
Goblet, water; La Fleur, topaz, crystal stem, 8" 32.00
Goblet, water; Manchester 22.00
Goblet, water; Palais Versailles 55.00
Goblet, water; Renaissance, gold trim 30.00
Goblet, water; Roselyn, yel 18.00
Goblet, water; Wistaria, #17394 ....25.00
Grapefruit, Flanders, yel, w/liner 40.00
Mayonnaise, Cadena, yel, w/liner, ftd 45.00
Mayonnaise, Cherokee Rose, w/liner & ladle 45.00
Mayonnaise, Flanders, pk, w/liner 75.00
Nut cup, Flanders, blown, ftd 30.00
Parfait, Cherokee Rose, 4½-oz 40.00
Parfait, Classic 45.00
Parfait, Flanders, yel 50.00
Parfait, Flying Nun 38.00
Parfait, Fontaine, Twilight w/crystal stem 45.00
Pitcher, Cadena, w/lid, ftd 225.00
Pitcher, Cherokee Rose 295.00
Pitcher, Fuchsia, #194, w/lid 325.00
Pitcher, tankard, Swedish Modern, #5935, blown, 11½" 65.00
Plate, Byzantine, 10½" 35.00
Plate, Cadena, yel, 7¾" 12.00
Plate, Cadena, 6" 5.00
Plate, Cadena, 9¼" 30.00
Plate, Classic, 7½" 17.50
Plate, Flanders, 6" 10.00
Plate, Flanders, 8" 12.00
Plate, Fuchsia, #5831, 2-hdl, 6⅜" 12.50
Plate, Julia, amber, 10" 20.00
Plate, La Fleure, yel, 7¼" 15.00
Plate, Roselyn, yel, 10½" 35.00
Plate, sandwich; Cherokee Rose, 14" 30.00
Plate, sandwich; Fuchsia, #8833, 14¼" 35.00
Plate, sherbet; Cherokee Rose, 6" 5.00
Relish, Cherokee Rose, 3-part, 6½" 25.00
Relish, Flanders, yel, 3-part 35.00
Relish, Fuchsia, sq, 3-part, 9¼" 35.00
Rose bowl, Cerulean Bl, #17430 ....80.00
Saucer, Cadena, yel 12.50
Saucer, Flanders, yel 8.00
Saucer, Fuchsia, #5831 ....7.50

Saucer, La Fleure, yel 5.00
Shakers, Fuchsia, pr 75.00
Sherbet, Cadena, yel 22.00
Sherbet, Classic, pk 30.00
Sherbet, Flanders, pk 25.00
Sherbet, Fuchsia, #15083, 4⅛" 12.00
Sherbet, Huntington, tall 12.00
Sherry, Cherokee Rose, 2-oz 30.00
Sherry, Classic 60.00
Sherry, Persian Pheasant, wide mouth 25.00
Sugar bowl, Cadena 15.00
Sugar bowl, Cerice 25.00
Sugar bowl, Cherokee Rose 30.00
Sugar bowl, Flanders, pk, flat 110.00
Sugar bowl, Flanders, yel, ftd 50.00
Sugar bowl, Fuchsia, #5831, ind, 2⅞" 35.00
Sugar bowl, La Fleure, yel 37.50
Sundae, Cerice, #071 ....18.00
Sundae, Flanders 15.00
Sundae, Rambler Rose, #188 Line, pk 35.00
Tumbler, bar; Fuchsia, #506, 2-oz, 2½" 50.00
Tumbler, iced tea; Cherokee Rose, ftd, 10½-oz 26.00
Tumbler, iced tea; Classic Shawl Dancer, cone shape 20.00
Tumbler, iced tea; Flanders, ftd, 12-oz 20.00
Tumbler, iced tea; Fontaine, Twilight, ftd 48.00
Tumbler, iced tea; June Night, #17358, 6½" 28.00
Tumbler, iced tea; Rosalind, yel, ftd 22.00
Tumbler, juice; Cadena, ftd, 4¼" 17.50
Tumbler, juice; Cerice, #071, ftd 18.00
Tumbler, juice; Cherokee Rose, ftd, 5-oz 25.00
Tumbler, juice; Coronada, #185 ....45.00
Tumbler, juice; Fuchsia, #15083, ftd, 5-oz, 4¼" 22.00
Tumbler, juice; Wistaria, #17394 ....25.00
Tumbler, water; Cadena, ftd, 5¼" 20.00
Tumbler, water; Cherokee Rose, ftd, 8-oz 25.00
Tumbler, water; Flanders, pk, ftd, 9-oz 30.00
Tumbler, water; Fuchsia, #15083, 9-oz, 5¼" 25.00

Vase, Tiffin Optic, cranberry flashed cut to clear, 1947, cut by Lucien Delevenne, 12", $250.00.

Vase, bud; Cherokee Rose, 10" 35.00
Vase, bud; Cherokee Rose, 11" 40.00
Vase, bud; Cherokee Rose, 6" 25.00
Vase, bud; Cherokee Rose, 8" 45.00
Vase, bud; Flanders, yel 45.00
Vase, bud; Fuchsia, #14185, 6½" 30.00
Vase, bud; Fuchsia, #14185, 8¼" 35.00

Vase, Cherokee Rose, flared, 12" 75.00
Vase, Cherokee Rose, tub form, 9¼" 60.00
Vase, Cherokee Rose, urn form, 11" 75.00
Vase, cornucopia; Copen Bl, 8¼" 75.00
Vase, Fuchsia, #15082, beaded stem, 10⅞" 65.00
Vase, Fuchsia, #5872, bulbous bottom, 10¾" 125.00
Vase, Princess, 4" 22.50
Vase, Swedish Modern, #17350, blown, 11½" 55.00
Whiskey, Flanders 32.00
Wine, Cadena, yel, 6" 40.00
Wine, Cherokee Rose, 3½-oz 35.00
Wine, Eternally Yours 15.00
Wine, Flanders, yel 37.50
Wine, Fuchsia 35.00
Wine, Jefferson 10.00
Wine, Manchester 25.00
Wine, Riveria 24.00

Tiles

Though originally strictly functional, tiles were being produced in various colors and used as architectural highlights as early as the Ancient Roman Empire. By the 18th century, Dutch tiles were decorated with polychrome landscapes and figures. During the 19th century, there were over a hundred companies in England involved in the manufacture of tile. By the Victorian era, the use of decorative tiles had reached its peak. Special souvenir editions, campaign and portrait tiles, and Art Nouveau motifs with lovely ladies and stylized examples from nature were popular. Today all of these are very collectible. See also specific manufacturers.

Low, shepherd and flock in village street, glossy teal blue, signed AO (Arthur Osbourne), late 1800s, 18x10", EX, from $700.00 to $750.00.

AE Tile, Simple Simon, 9-color, fr, mk, 6" sq 295.00
AE Tile, sunflower w/dragonfly, brn, 6", 5-pc set, 1882 ....310.00
AE Tile, windmill & birds, bl Delft type, mk, 6" 45.00
Batchelder, lion, brn bsk w/bl highlights, mk, 3¾" 95.00
California Art Tile, knight & castle, mc, SP fr, mk, 6¼" 175.00
California Faience, Ave Maria w/illus, 5-color, mk, 4x4⅛" 135.00
Claycraft, Persian vine, 6-color enamel, mk, 5¾" 110.00
Claycraft, spider web, books, etc, 5-color, mk, 4" 60.00
Delft, rook in winter scene 60.00
Eastwood, Lincoln portrait, commemorative, inscr bk, 6x9"+fr ..450.00
Grueby, galleon, 5-color, mk HMCX, 8" 1,750.00
Gustavsberg, scenic 35.00
J&JG Low, clock, figure/cranes, brass fr, 1884, 4⅜x9⅛" 1,100.00
Minton, sailing ship/people on land, gr/pk/brn, 5½x2½", fr 175.00
Mosaic, Boaster, mc cartoon, sgn, C68/BB/28, fr, 6" 260.00

Mosaic, Lincoln bust, wht on bl, hexagonal, mk, 3" 95.00
Mosaic, olive crystals on bl, paper label, 6x3" 65.00
Mosaic, 6-point star & cross, brn/gray/gr crystals, mk, 3" 45.00
Newcomb, geometric cvg, bl & brn, felt bk, mk, 6" dia 870.00
Owens, leaf in high relief, 2-tone matt gr, mk, 6" 160.00
Pewabic, plant in high relief, irid lav/gr/gold, 4x8½x1½" 265.00
Pilkington, Deco Apache dancer, set of 3 ....135.00
Rookwood, parrot, 7-color, ftd, #3077, 1930, 5½" 175.00
Strong, Harris; abstract, 1960, 6x6" 70.00
Unmk, lady's portrait in 3 sections, yel craquelle, 18x6" 95.00
Unmk, portrait of man (lady), brn, 6x6", pr 110.00
Van Briggle, poppies, wht/gr/blk, VBPCo #14, fr, 6" 185.00
W DeMorgan & Co, floral, purple/gr/bl on wht, 6" 350.00
W DeMorgan & Co, floral sprays, bl/gr/purple on wht, 9" 400.00
Walrich, poppies, bl/yel/gr, mk, 4⅞" 210.00

Tinware

In the American household of the 17th and 18th centuries, tinware items could be found in abundance, from food containers to foot warmers and mirror frames. Although the first settlers brought much of their tinware with them from Europe, by 1798 sheets of tin plate were being imported from England for use by the growing number of American tinsmiths. Tinwares were often decorated either by piercing or painted designs which were both freehand and stenciled. (See Toleware.) By the early 1900s, many homes had replaced their old tinware with the more attractive aluminum and graniteware.

In the 19th century, tenth wedding anniversaries were traditionally celebrated by gifts of tin. Couples gave big parties, dressed in their wedding clothes, and reaffirmed their vows before their friends and family who arrived bearing (and often wearing) tin gifts, most of which were quite humorous. Anniversary tin items may include hats, cradles, slippers and shoes, rolling pins, etc. See also Primitives and Kitchen Collectibles.

Anniversary, bonnet, cloth trim, tin flowers/feathers, 8" 770.00
Anniversary, bouquet of 8 flowers, 16" 550.00
Anniversary, gavel filled w/noise-making rattles, 14½" 55.00
Anniversary, hair comb, 1800s, 9" 360.00
Anniversary, invitation, dtd 1875, 3x5", EX in orig envelope 75.00
Anniversary, top hat, lt rust, 8" 350.00
Anniversary, top hat, 6¼" 275.00
Can, milk; w/lid & bail hdl, 1-gal 30.00
Candle snuffer, cone shape, stationary ring at top 55.00
Coffeepot, EX punched PA German floral, strap hdl, sgn, 11" ..3,400.00
Coffeepot, side strap hdl, 8" 48.00
Cutter, biscuit; heavy wire hdl 48.00
Cutter, doughnut; handmade, flat top w/hold, 2⅞" dia 15.00
Dinner horn, orig red & bl japanning, 17" 55.00
Dinner horn, oval strap hdl, 54½" L 100.00
Dipper, trn wooden hdl, 14" 50.00
Dishpan, handmade, slant sides, 6x10½" 40.00
Funnel, soldered strap hdl, sm holes for straining, 6½x6¼" 25.00
Grater, soap; rolled edges, 13x5½" 50.00
Kettle lifter/pourer, iron wire hdls adjust, Pat 1898, 16x10" 48.00
Ladle, rnd stick hdl w/hook end, 3½" dia, 11½" hdl 32.00
Letter holder, gold stencils, 3 sections, 6½x12x4¼" 68.00
Lunch pail, oval, hinged hdl, wood finial, 4½x6⅜x4⅜" 55.00
Match holder, emb fisherman/ship/etc, hanging 65.00
Measure, emb rings, 1-gal 40.00
Measure, emb rings, 1-qt 30.00
Mug, strap hdl, brass plaque stamped Half-Pint 25.00
Oil lamp filler, squatty funnel shape, shaker type 75.00
Pan, bread; dbl, oval, dtd Aug 3, '97 ....28.00

Pan, steamer; pie-pan shape, hooks on kettle, mk Mar 11, '11	**30.00**
Pie crimper, wooden hdl, 6¾"	**35.00**
Rack, potato baking; rnd points hold 6, hangs, '09, 14x2¼"	**44.00**
Rake, blueberry; CH Drisko & Brother...ME, orig pnt, 9½"	**90.00**
Sausage stuffer, wooden plunger, 23½x3½" dia	**40.00**
Sconce, scroll strap arms, saucer base, oval bk, 3½", pr	**260.00**
Scoop, cheese; rnd tin blade, maple hdl, 10¾"	**60.00**
Spatula, smithy made, 1-pc	**50.00**
Strainer, soldered seams, brass screen, 3" legs, 6x9½"	**56.00**
Strainer pan, oval, ftd, 3¼x9½x6¾", EX	**25.00**
Teakettle, stick spout, strap hdl, handmade, early, 5½" dia	**65.00**
Toddy/ale warmer, funnel-shape cup, saucer base, 1800s	**150.00**

Tobacciana

Tobacciana is the generally accepted term used to cover a field of collecting that includes smoking pipes, cigar molds, cigarette lighters, humidors — in short, any article having to do with the practice of using tobacco in any form. Perhaps the most valuable variety of pipes is the meerschaum, hand carved from hydrous magnesium, an opaque white-gray or cream-colored mineral of the soapstone family. (Much of this is today mined in Turkey which has the largest meerschaum deposit in the world, though there are other deposits of lesser significance around the globe.) These figural bowls often portray an elaborately carved mythological character, an animal, or a historical scene. Amber is sometimes used for the stem. Other collectible pipes are corn cob (Missouri Meerschaum) and Indian peace pipes of clay or catlinite. (See American Indian Art.)

Chosen because it was the Indians who first introduced the white man to smoking, the cigar store Indian was a symbol used to identify tobacco stores in the 19th century. The majority of them were hand carved between 1830 and 1900 and are today recognized as some of the finest examples of early wood sculptures. When found they command very high prices. Our advisor for this category is Chuck Thompson; he is listed in the Directory under Texas. See also Advertising; Snuff Boxes.

Album, Geo Washington, premium, Allen & Ginter	**250.00**
Ashtray, glass w/deer cuttings, metal top, 2½x4½" dia	**35.00**
Book, The Story of Lucky Strike, 1939 World's Fair, EX	**15.00**
Box, cigarette; 14k rose & yel gold, sapphire clasp, 1920s	**800.00**
Cheroot holder, meerschaum, nude woman, amber stem, 8"	**150.00**
Cigar box opener, Pennant Cigars, NY, EX	**4.50**
Cigar holder, banded agate, in velvet-lined leather box, M	**45.00**
Cigar holder, meerschaum, girl/spinning wheel, cased, 6"	**565.00**
Cigarette case, brn enamel, sterling center w/marcasites	**37.50**
Cigarette case, Deco-style blk enamel & chrome, Ronson, 1930	**65.00**
Cigarette case, ivory, EX cvg, Caldwell, 1850s, 2¼x6¼x5"	**1,300.00**
Cigarette case, MOP inlay, MIE, 4⅜x3⅜x½", M	**100.00**
Cigarette dispenser, elephant figural, CI	**150.00**
Cigarette holder, amber, cvd, 3½", NM in case	**45.00**
Cigarette holder, Bakelite & amber, unused	**30.00**
Cigarette holder, ivory & cloisonne, 3"	**30.00**
Cigarette holder, meerschaum, dragons	**35.00**
Cutter, cigar; Brunhoff Mfg, emb CI, dual arms, 7¼", G	**200.00**
Cutter, cigar; Cubanola, NP & pnt CI, 6¾", G	**275.00**
Cutter, cigar; Keystone, key wind	**195.00**
Cutter, cigar; meerschaum, St George & dragon, in case, 6"	**465.00**
Cutter, cigar; Pico Grande 5¢ Cigars, dtd 1902	**250.00**
Cutter, cigar; pistol shape, Bakelite bbl	**65.00**
Cutter, cigar; rvpt glass, tin body, wood base, 8"	**65.00**
Cutter, cigar; Traveler, CI, label under glass, 1910s, NM	**385.00**
Cutter, cigar; wood & CI bbl form, w/striker, 7", EX	**100.00**
Cutter, plug; Climax	**65.00**

Cutter, plug; Drummond, Good Luck/cloverleaf on CI, 17", G	**65.00**
Cutter, plug; Prize Cutter by S Lee, w/cork former	**60.00**
Cutter, plug; Star	**55.00**
Cutter/lighter, cigar; CI, counter type, Pat 1897	**225.00**
Figure, Indian, cvd wood, EX patina, Sullivan, 36", EX	**10,450.00**
Figure, Indian Chief, chalkware, 24x12x9", G	**200.00**
Humidor, French Louis XVI style, mahog w/ormolu trim	**165.00**
Humidor, hen figural, mc pnt, pottery, 10"	**80.00**
Humidor, La Palina Cigars ad on brass	**75.00**
Humidor, La Paloma, glass	**22.50**
Humidor, man's face, pottery, rattan hdl	**125.00**
Humidor, milk glass w/HP florals, ornate Nouveau brass lid	**90.00**
Humidor, monkey w/pipe, pottery, 1910s, 6"	**110.00**
Jar, Copenhagen, stoneware, emb Pittsburgh PA	**20.00**
Lighter, baseball figure, wht metal, 1913, 5"	**330.00**
Lighter, brass w/red pnt (worn), Austria...1912, 2¾"	**22.00**
Lighter, cigar; boy figural, cast metal, 1900, 15½", NM	**500.00**
Lighter, cigar; man w/keg, gun & dog, cast metal, 1900s, EX	**715.00**
Lighter, cigar; Midland Model Jump Spark, oak case, 15", EX	**300.00**
Lighter, cigar; tiered oak case w/NP works, 15", VG	**110.00**
Lighter, cigar; Wrigley Jr & Co Chicago, 1910, 9x9", VG	**500.00**
Lighter, football, silvery metal, Occupied Japan, 3"	**50.00**
Lighter, gold heart shape, hangs from chain, Japan, 1½"	**17.50**
Lighter, gold-plated w/leather, Evans, MIB	**40.00**
Lighter, golf club head figural, chrome, 5"	**25.00**
Lighter, hammered copper/silver, Chinese style, Gorham	**500.00**
Lighter, mc flowers on red case, Penguin, 1⅝"	**30.00**
Lighter, Ronson Maximus, 3⅛x1¾x⅝", MIB	**65.00**
Lighter, roulette wheel on side, Manor, Japan, NM	**75.00**
Lighter, terrier dog on lt gr, Manor, Japan, M	**35.00**
Lighter, yel & brn decor on caramel, Brite, Japan, 2"	**30.00**
Pipe rack, molded compo w/baseball batter, holds 2, 6", VG	**275.00**
Pipe tamper, trn ivory hdl, brass base, early, 2⅜"	**70.00**
Spittoon, brn scrolls, mk Medalta	**37.50**
Spittoon, red & bl flowers on wht porc	**55.00**
Tamper, lady's leg, cvd ivory, 1700s	**225.00**
Tamper, whalebone, geometric cvg, EX	**45.00**

Pipes

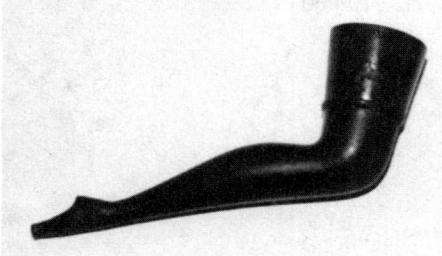

Amber Cigarillo, lady's leg shape, high-top laced boot as mouthpiece, $175.00. (Photo courtesy of Chris Rossiter; see Directory under Wisconsin.)

Amber bowl & stem, skull shape w/18k gold band, 8½"	**750.00**
Blown glass, cranberry, England	**125.00**
Blown glass bowl & stem, HP floral pattern	**50.00**
Bone & wood, hag in bonnet cvg	**135.00**
Burled wood bowl & reservoir, stem w/NP trim, Czech	**45.00**
Clay, French lady w/lg hat, 1860s, 4¼"	**45.00**
Clay, General Pershing in cape forms bowl, England, 7"	**12.00**

Clay, Punch (as w/Judy) shaped bowl, Dutch made, 1920s, 7½" ...30.00
Meerschaum, animals fighting, amber stem, rpr, 20" 1,000.00
Meerschaum, bearded Arab's head, in case, 4¼", EX 165.00
Meerschaum, cottage & horse, dtd 1816 ....185.00
Meerschaum, dog, 1½x3", in case 90.00
Meerschaum, eagle holding egg, amber mouthpc, 6½" 175.00
Meerschaum, head of Pan, in case, 6⅝" 385.00
Meerschaum, horn stem, Bakelite mouthpc, 8½" 75.00
Meerschaum, horse's head cvg, amber stem 275.00
Meerschaum, man's head w/glass cigarette, 1½x4" 245.00
Meerschaum, relief horses against flower, 8", EX 115.00
Meerschaum, Winston Churchill bust bowl, amber stem, '40s ...375.00
Porc, monkey's head bowl, mc, birch stem 375.00
Porc, 16th-C lady on bowl, red mouth pc, flex hose 175.00
Wood, bull's head cvg, ivory horns, amber eyes, 1950s 65.00
Wood, stag cvg, tin lid, German, 1800s 165.00

Toby Jugs

The delightful jug known as the Toby dates back to the 18th century, when factories in England produced them for export to the American colonies. Named for the character Toby Philpots in the song *The Little Brown Jug*, the Toby was fashioned in the form of a jolly fellow, usually holding a jug of beer and a glass. The earlier examples were made with strict attention to details such as fingernails and teeth. Originally representing only a non-entity, a trend developed to portray well-known individuals such as George II, Napoleon, and Ben Franklin. Among the most-valued Tobies are those produced by Ralph Wood I in the late 1700s. By the mid-1830s Tobies were being made in America. See also Doulton, Lenox, and Occupied Japan.

Creamware, holds jug/cup, 1 in ea hand, pipe at ft, 9", EX 1,100.00
Falstaff, Staffordshire, 1800s, 9" 190.00
King in striped suit, Staffordshire, 1800s, 9¾" 210.00
Man in bl coat, gold vest, lustreware, 1800s, 9¾" 240.00
Man in bl coat, lustreware, 1800s, 6½" 140.00
Man in bl coat, spotted vest, Staffordshire, 1800s, 8½" 260.00
Man in bl coat, yel vest, Staffordshire, 1800s, 9¾" 180.00
Man in brn coat, gr vest, N&NF Co, 1800s, rpr, 10" 75.00
Man in brn coat, spatterware hat/base, Staffordshire, 10" 325.00
Man in gr coat, caryatid hdl, Staffordshire, 1800s, 9½" 230.00
Man in gray coat, yel hat, blk vest, Staffordshire, 10" 275.00
Man in lav coat, striped vest, dolphin hdl, 1800s, 6¾" 150.00
Man in pk coat, mc vest, carries snuff box, Staffordshire, 10" 300.00
Man in red coat, Hearty Good Fellow, Staffordshire, 11½" 240.00
Man in yel & bl, Staffordshire, 1800s, 8½" 150.00
Man in yel coat, spotted vest, Staffordshire, 1800s, 7⅛" 110.00
Man on keg mk Home Brewed Ale, Staffordshire, 1800s, 11¼" .350.00
Man standing, Bennington type, 1800s, 9½" 100.00
Napoleon, mc w/gold, A Evans, Phila PA, 9¾" 250.00
Watchman, Staffordshire, early 1800s, 9½" 300.00

Toleware

The term 'toleware' originally came from a French term meaning 'sheet iron.' Today it is used to refer to paint-decorated tin items, most popular from 1800 to 1850s. The craft was very popular in Pennsylvania, Connecticut, Maine, and New York state. Early toleware has a very distinctive look. The surface is dull and unvarnished; background colors range from black to cream. Geometrics are quite common, but florals and fruits were also popular motifs. Items made after 1850 were often stenciled, and gold trim was sometimes added.

American toleware is usually found in practical, everyday forms — trays, boxes, and coffeepots are most common — while French examples might include candlesticks, wine coolers, jardinieres, etc. Be sure to note color and design when determining date and value, but condition of the paint is the most important worth-assessing factor. Our advisors for this category are Barbara and Frank Pollack; they are listed in the Directory under Illinois. In the listings that follow, the dimension given for boxes and trays indicates length.

Box, candle; floral, mc on red, blk striping, dents, 9" 75.00
Box, deed; commas/florals, mc on dk japanning, dome top, 8" ...300.00
Box, deed; floral, mc on dk japanning, dome top, 5x9x5" 470.00
Box, deed; foliage, red & gr on brn japanning w/wht band, 4¼" ...40.00
Box, deed; mc bronze powder stencil on brn japanning, 8¼" 35.00
Box, spice; gold stencil on orig brn japanning, 7¼" dia 115.00
Canister, tea; commas & stars, red & gr on gr & yel, 8" 35.00
Coal scuttle, floral bouquets, grapevine hdls, ca 1900, 24½" ...1,100.00
Coal scuttle, red & gold decor on blk, lt wear, 23½" 125.00

Coffeepot, stylized flowers in the Pennsylvania Dutch style on red ground, cylindrical with hooked spout, 10¾", $2,800.00.

Creamer, floral, 3-color on blk, minor dents, 4⅛" 220.00
Creamer, floral, 5-color on dk brn japanning, lt wear, 4" 165.00
Fire screen, CI/steel, old red rpt w/decor, adjusts, 55½" 440.00
Fire screen, mc flower baskets on blk rpt, CI base, 53" H 250.00
Match safe, early, 7½" 300.00
Scissors wick trimmers, floral on blk, w/tray 50.00
Syrup, commas, red on dk bl japanning, Molasses stencil, 5½" 40.00
Syrup, old red rpt w/birds & flowers, 5⅝" 75.00
Tea caddy, floral, 3-color on dk japanning, 5¾" 165.00
Tea caddy, floral, 4-color on blk japanning, lt wear, 4½" 110.00
Tray, bread; floral, 5-color on dk japanning, lt wear, 13" 195.00
Tray, bread; fruit stencil, mc w/yel striping, wear, 14x8" 55.00
Tray, peacocks on branches, mc on dk japanning, 22x30" 300.00
Tray, stenciled leaves & cones surround HP landscape, 20x15" .330.00
Urn, landscape reserve on gr w/gold, lion head hdls, Fr, 16" 300.00

Tools

Before the Civil War, tools for the most part were handmade. Some were primitive to the point of crudeness, while others reflected the skill of those who took pride in their trade. Increasing demand for quality tools and the dawning of the age of industrialization resulted in tools that were mass-produced. Factors important in evaluating antique tools are scarcity, usefulness, and portability. Those with a manufacturer's mark are worth more than unmarked items. When no condition is indicated, the items listed here are assumed to be in excellent condition. Our advisor for this category is Jim Calison; he is listed in the Directory under New York. See also Keen Kutter; Stanley; Winchester.

Axe, grubbing; 2-head, hand forged **38.00**
Calipers, bronze, sgn TJ Smith, 1800s, 12¾" **110.00**
Carrier, carpenter's, cvd center hdl w/oval cutout, 3½x18x14" **55.00**
Cutter, burley tobacco **40.00**
Drill, bow; brass w/rosewood hdl, ivory spool, 13" **300.00**
Gauge, mortising; cherry w/brass mts **65.00**
Hacksaw, iron; brass color, wood hdl, cuts iron & wood **68.00**
Hatchet, earliest factory-made type, 1845 ....**45.00**
Jack, carriage; oak, iron teeth **100.00**
Knife, hoof; natural, bone hdl, 1890-99 ....**28.00**
Level, cherry, brass throat, 1867 ....**80.00**
Level, dark wood, brass top plate & trim, 6" **50.00**
Level, Davis, #9, 24" **85.00**
Maul, burl; wht oak hdl, 18th C **55.00**
Measure, cloth, 50-ft in brass case **10.00**
Measure, Lufkin #066D **7.50**
Measure, Master #306 ....**10.00**

Molding plane, wood with brass screws, handle to side, 12", $85.00.

Plane, coach maker's, 7" **75.00**
Plane, thumb; mahog, sm, 3¾" **60.00**
Plane, wooden, adjustable gate & depth **60.00**
Saw, dovetail; brass backed, turned wooden hdl, 10½" **50.00**
Saw, trenching; maple, 1840 ....**75.00**
Scraper, cooper's, pull type, maple hdl, brass ferrule **40.00**
Square, rosewood w/brass insert, EX **15.00**
Square, try; cherry, polished iron, brass bindings & inlays **30.00**
Tongs, button; handmade **35.00**
Trammel, wood & brass, 1890 ....**98.00**
Witchet, hardwoods, brass-lined throat, dbl blade, 1840 ....**225.00**
Wrench, steamboat engineer's, factory made **55.00**

Toothbrush Holders

Most of the collectible toothbrush holders were made in prewar Japan and were modeled after popular comic strip and Disney characters. Since many were made of bisque and decorated with unfired enamel, it's not uncommon to find them in less-than-perfect paint, a factor you must consider when attempting to assess their values. Our advisor for this category is Marilyn Cooper; she is listed in the Directory under Texas.

Baker **65.00**
Butcher, Candlestick Maker, ea **85.00**
Calico Dog, toothbrush through mouth **65.00**
Cat, blk, standing on paws **140.00**
Clown, hanging **60.00**
Dog, blk, holding flowers **120.00**
Dog, Bonzo **100.00**

Dog, not Bonzo **80.00**
Ducky Dandy, bsk **95.00**
Humpty Dumpty, bsk, Disney **350.00**
Humpty Dumpty, not Disney **125.00**
Octopus, plastic **30.00**
Old King Cole **80.00**
Old Woman in Shoe **75.00**
Peter Rabbit **115.00**
Rabbit, gr, Norwood **90.00**
Red Riding Hood **120.00**
2 boys in car, EX pnt **75.00**
2 boys in car, no pnt **45.00**
3 Bears **115.00**
3 Bears, holding porridge bowls **195.00**
3 Pigs, playing drum, fiddle & flute, Disney **225.00**

Three Little Pigs, prewar Japan, copyright Walt Disney, ca 1930, 3½", M, $225.00.

3 Pigs, standing, not Disney **125.00**
3 Scottie dogs holding cards **95.00**

Toothpick Holders

Once common on every table, the toothpick holder was relegated to the china cabinet near the turn of the century. Fortunately, this contributed to their survival. As a result, many are available to collectors today. Because they are small and easily displayed, they are a very popular collectible. They come in a wide range of prices to fit every budget. The rare ones have been reproduced and, unfortunately, are being offered for sale right along with the originals. These 'repros' should be priced in the $10.00 to $30.00 range. Unless you're sure of what you're buying, choose a reputable dealer. In addition to pattern glass, you'll find examples in china, bisque, art glass, and various metals. Toothpick holders in the listings that follow are glass unless noted otherwise. Those that have been reproduced are designated with a (+), however values are for the originals. Our advisor for this category is Judy A. Knauer; she is listed in the Directory under Pennsylvania.

Alabama **70.00**
Amberina, sq rim, in Tuft's holder w/Greenaway girl, 5½" **575.00**
Amberina, Venetian Dmn, 2¼" **175.00**
Apollo **20.00**
Banded Barrel **20.00**
Beaded Grape, emerald gr w/worn gold **50.00**
Beatty Honeycomb, bl opal **60.00**
Beatty Honeycomb, lav opal **65.00**
Beatty Rib, bl opal, sm **40.00**
Beatty Rib, clear opal **30.00**
Block, Wheeling **35.00**
Box in Box **35.00**
Box in Box, gr **75.00**
Buckingham **30.00**
Bull's Eye & Fan, clear w/worn gold **30.00**
Burmese, sq top, Mt WA, 2½" **350.00**

Cactus, chocolate (+)	90.00
Carnation, Fostoria	75.00
Champion, gr	55.00
Coiled Serpent, milk glass	45.00
Colorado, clear w/worn gold (+)	20.00
Cordova, ruby stained	45.00
Daisy, frosted	20.00
Daisy & Button, amber	30.00
Daisy & Button, urn form	20.00
Dbl Circle, variant gr, rare	70.00
Dmn Point Heart (+)	45.00
Dmn Quilt, burmese, sq top	345.00
Dmn Spearhead, cobalt opal	195.00
Dmn Spearhead, vaseline opal	65.00
Dog & Basket, Tufts SP	65.00
Domino	35.00
Esther, gr w/gold	95.00
Eureka	32.00
Eureka, ruby stained	65.00
Fancy Loop, gr, Heisey	145.00
Fancy Loop, Heisey	65.00
Fashion, Imperial (+)	20.00
Florette, bl opaque, 2⅛"	65.00
Florette, pk opaque	60.00
Four Ladders	30.00
Georgia Gem, custard, HP florals	85.00
Gonterman Swirl, amber w/frosted base	180.00
Gonterman Swirl, frosted, bl ruffled rim	195.00
Hartford	60.00
Harvard, custard	35.00
Hobb's Hobnail, vaseline	60.00
Iris w/Meander, bl opal	110.00
Iris w/Meander, gr opal	65.00
Kansas	50.00
Kemple Daisy, pnt, #1160	25.00
King's Crown	20.00
Krystol-Kradle	35.00
Lower Manhattan, gr stained	35.00
Madora	30.00
Majestic, ruby stained	125.00
Manhattan, yel stain	45.00
Mardi Gras	40.00
Michigan, bl stain w/decor (+)	80.00
Mikado, yel	20.00
Nestor, bl, no decor	75.00
New Hampshire	25.00
New Hampshire, rose	55.00
Ohio Star	60.00
Owl w/wings spread figural, carnival glass (+)	10.00
Paddle Wheel	45.00
Paneled Grape (+)	45.00
Pennsylvania, gr	150.00
Pleating, ruby grapes	50.00
Polished Mirror, Duncan	22.50
Portland	25.00
Prince of Wales, ruby stained, Heisey	275.00
Priscilla, Heisey	50.00
Prize, emerald gr w/gold	125.00
Queen's Necklace	60.00
Radiant, etch decor	36.00
Reverse Swirl, bl & wht speckles	95.00
Ribbed Pillar, pk frost	65.00
Ribbed Spiral, bl opal	90.00
Ribbed Spiral, canary opal	80.00

Ruby Thumbprint, etched	48.00
Ruby Thumbprint	30.00
Scalloped Six Point	36.00
Scroll w/Cane Band, amber stained	70.00
Simplicity Scroll	20.00
Simplicity Scroll, gold tint	20.00
Spearpoint Band, ruby stained	45.00
Swinger (+)	30.00
Tarentum T'print, custard	150.00
Tepee, Duncan	40.00
Texas	35.00
Thousand Eye, canary	40.00
Tiny Thumbprint, HP mums on custard	80.00
Tree of Life, gr	50.00
Truncated Cube, ruby stained	40.00
US Coin, 1892 (+)	95.00
US Rib, clear w/worn gold	25.00
US Rib, emerald gr	35.00
Venetian Dmn, amberina	165.00
Vermont, gr (+)	50.00
Washington (State series), custard	55.00
Wedding Bells, Fostoria	50.00

Torquay 'Devon Motto' Ware

Torquay is a unique type of pottery made in the South Devon area of England as early as 1867. At the height of productivity, at least a dozen companies flourished there, producing simple folk pottery from the area's natural red clay. The ware was both wheel-turned and molded and decorated under the glaze with heavy slip resulting in low-relief nature subjects or simple scrollwork. Three of the best-known of these potteries were: Watcombe (1867-1962); Aller Vale (in operation from the mid-1800s, producing domestic ware and architectural products); and Longpark (1890 until 1957). Watcombe and Aller Vale merged in 1901 and operated until 1962 under the name of Royal Aller Vale and Watcombe Art Pottery.

Perhaps the most famous type of ware potted in this area was Motto Ware, so called because of the verses, proverbs, and quotations that decorated it. This was achieved by the sgraffito technique — scratching the letters through the slip to expose the red clay underneath. The most popular patterns were Cottage, Black Cockerel, Multi-Cockerel, and a scrollwork design called Scandy. Other popular decorations were Kerswell Daisy, ships, kingfishers, and many other birds on blue ground. Aller Vale ware may sometimes be found marked 'H.H. and Company,' a firm who assumed ownership from 1897 to 1901. 'Watcombe Torquay' was an impressed mark used from 1884 to 1927.

Our advisors for this category are Jerry and Gerry Kline; they are listed in the Directory under Ohio. If you're interested in joining a Torquay club, the address of The North American Torquay Society is given under Clubs, Newsletters, and Catalogs.

Ashtray, Cottage, Royal Watcombe, 'Mind the Carpet,' 4¾"	48.00
Ashtray, fish, Blk Cockerel, Longpark, 'A Place for Ashes'	90.00
Basket, Sailboat, 'Tell No Tales...,' mini, 2¼"	95.00
Beaker, Scandy, Aller Vale, 'Du Zummat...,' 3¾"	46.50
Bowl, Blk Cockerel, Royal Torquay, 'Du'ee Ave...,' 4¾"	100.00
Bowl, Cottage, 'Many Friends, Few Helpers,' 2¼x3½"	50.00
Bowl, Cottage, Babbacombe, 'Too Many Cooks Spoil...,' 4½"	70.00
Bowl, Cottage, Watcombe, 'There's More in the Kitchen...,' 6"	100.00
Bowl, Scandy, 'A Stitch in Time Saves Nine,' 4¼"	75.00
Butter dish, Cottage, 'Be Aisy w/the Butter,' 4½" dia	115.00
Candlestick, Kingfisher, 'Sleep Falls Sweetly...,' 4"	85.00

Candlestick, Cockerel, 'Last in Bed Put Out the Light,' 4½", $250.00.

Chamberstick, 'Many Are Called...,' 6x5" dia 125.00
Chamberstick, Parrot, Royal Torquay, 'Good Night,' 2x3½" 78.00
Chamberstick, Scandy, Longpark, 'Many Are Called...,' 6" 175.00
Cheese dish, Cottage, Watcombe, 'Help Yourself...,' 6½x5¼" 225.00
Coffeepot, Cottage, w/motto, 5" 150.00
Creamer, Blk Cockerel, Longpark, 'Be Aisy...,' 2¼" 48.00
Creamer, Cottage, w/motto, 2½x2¾" 45.00
Cup, Scandy, Longpark, 'Guid Folks Are...,' 3-hdl, TYG, 5" 98.00
Cup & saucer, Cottage, Babbacombe, 'First Things First' 50.00
Cup & saucer, Cottage, Babbacombe, 'Waste Not...,' 3" dia 50.00
Cup & saucer, Cottage, Watcombe, 'Hope Well & Have Well' ...50.00
Cup & saucer, Cottage, Watcombe, 'Say Little But Think Much' .50.00
Egg cup, Blk Cockerel, Longpark, w/motto, 2½"+ped/saucer 50.00
Egg cup, Cottage, Babbacombe, 'Fresh Laid,' 1¾" 27.50
Egg cup, Cottage, Burns Cottage, 1¾" 35.00
Egg cup & saucer, Cottage, Watcombe, 'Still Waters Run Deep' ...45.00
Hair receiver, Scandy, Watcombe, 'Save While...,' 6½" 100.00
Hatpin holder, Primrose, unmk Am, 'I'll Take Care...,' 4¼" 90.00
Hatpin holder, Shamrock, Aller Vale, 4¾" 200.00
Hot water pot, Blk Cockerel, Longpark, 'May the Hinges...,' 5" .125.00
Hot water pot, Cottage, Longpark, 'Hear All...,' 6" 165.00
Inkwell, Forget-Me-Not, 'We're Aye Prood...,' 2¾" 80.00
Inkwell, Scandy, Longpark, 'Daunt'e Keep Talkin...,' 3" 80.00
Inkwell, Shamrock, Aller Vale, w/motto, 1¾" 75.00
Jar, jam; Cottage, 'Time Ripens All Things,' 4¼x3" 58.00
Jug, Sailboat, Southenden Sea, 'Stracht Frae the Coo,' 2¾" 45.00
Mug, Cottage, 'Every Blade of Grass...,' 5x3¾" 70.00
Mug, Cottage, 'Guid Volks Be Scarce...,' 3⅞x3⅛" 50.00
Mug, Cottage, Dartmouth, 'Daunee Be Fraid...,' 4" 45.00
Mug, shaving; Sailboat, Longpark, 'Rolling Stone...,' 4" 230.00
Mustard jar, Cottage, Watcombe, 'Hope Well...,' w/lid, 4" 55.00
Pin dish, Scando, w/motto, 4¾" 50.00
Pitcher, Apple, Royal Torquay, 'Truth Is a Gem...,' 5½" 137.50
Pitcher, Blk Cockerel, 'Good Morning...,' 3½" 60.00
Pitcher, Cottage, 'Take a Wee Drop,' mini, 1¾" 72.50
Pitcher, Cottage, 'To Thine Own Self Be True,' 3" 45.00
Pitcher, Cottage, MIE, 'Straight From the Cow,' mini, 2" 70.00
Pitcher, Cottage, Royal Watcombe, 'Fresh Cream Today,' 2½" 42.50
Pitcher, Cottage, St Mary Church, 'Take a Little Cream,' 3" 37.50
Pitcher, Cottage, Watcombe, 'Give Every Man Thy Ear...,' 4½" ..95.00
Pitcher, Cottage, Watcombe, 'He Soars Not High...,' 3½" 52.50
Pitcher, Cottage, Watcombe, 'There's Gladness in...,' 3½" 48.00
Pitcher, Drum, 'Drink Like a Fish, Water Only,' 4½" 55.00
Pitcher, Primrose, unmk Am, 'Be Canny w/the Cream,' 2¾" 65.00
Pitcher, Sailboat, 'Stracht Frae the Coo,' 2¾" 45.00
Pitcher, Scandy, 'Fresh From the Dairy,' unmk, 3¼" 42.00
Pitcher, Scandy, Aller Vale, 'Stracht Frae the Coo,' 2½" 50.00
Pitcher, Scandy, Aller Vale, 'Take a Little Cream,' 3" 47.50
Plate, Cottage, Dartmouth, 'Be Like the Sundail...,' 10" 60.00

Plate, Cottage, Royal Watcombe, 'Enough's As Good...,' 6½" 75.00
Shakers, Cottage, 'Help Yourself.../Take a Little...' 2¾", pr 65.00
Shakers, Cottage, 'Pass the Salt,' 2¾", pr 65.00
Sugar bowl, Blk Cockerel, Longpark, 'Be Aisy...,' 3¾" 50.00
Sugar bowl, Cottage, 'Remembered Joys Are Never Past,' NM 45.00
Sugar bowl, Tormohun, Long Park, 'Be Aisy w/the Sugar,' 4" 35.00
Teapot, Cottage, Babbacombe, 'Do What You Can...,' 4¼x5" ...225.00
Teapot, Scandy, Aller Vale, 'Droon Yer Sorrows...,' 4½" 175.00
Teapot, Two Cottages, showpiece, Watcombe, w/motto, 9x11" .1,200.00
Tile, Cottage, faience, 'Come & Zee Us in Summer,' 5" dia 85.00
Tile, Cottage, Watcombe, When You Finish Pouring...,' 6" dia 82.50
Tile, curling iron; Scandy, Longpark, w/motto, 7½x5" 200.00
Tile, Scandy, w/motto, 4½" dia 70.00
Tile, tea; Scandy, 'Striving To Better Oft...,' 5½" 85.00
Toast rack, Watcombe, 'Help Yourself to Toast,' 5x3½" 155.00
Tray, dresser; Cottage, Watcombe, unusual motto, 7½x11" 300.00
Tray, dresser; Kingfisher, Watcombe, 10½x7½" 225.00
Tray, dresser; Scandy, Longpark, unusual motto, 7½x11" 275.00
Vase, Hart & Moist, 'Keep Good Company & You Shall...,' 3½" .60.00
Vase, Ship, 'East or West Home Is Best,' unmk, 3½" 60.00
Vase, udder; Passion Flower, 'Guid Folks Are Scarce...,' 3½" 95.00

Tortoise Shell Glass

By combining several shades of glass — brown, clear, and yellow — glass manufacturers of the 19th century were able to produce an art glass that closely resembled the shell of the tortoise. Some of this type of glassware was manufactured in Germany. In America it was made by several firms, the most prominent of which was the Boston and Sandwich Glass Works.

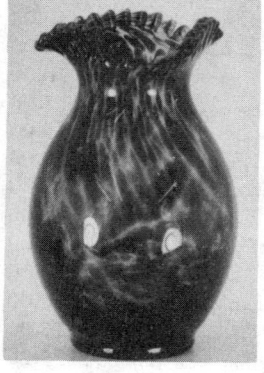

Vase, crimped rim, 9", $135.00.

Bowl, amber base/ft, 4x7¾" 125.00
Jar, ftd, w/lid, 8½" 70.00
Pitcher, tall gas can shape w/2 appl rings, 10" 200.00
Plate, free-blown, 11¾" 85.00
Vase, random fluted top, 10" 130.00

Toys

The prices shown in this edition reviews auction reports, known sales, and sales lists. We have shown prices of toys in various conditions and noted which toys sold with boxes. To get the most out of this guide, when you see the same toys with different prices, you must consider these important factors. On occasion, a toy will bring a much higher than normal price at auction. This is 'auction fever.' Sometimes a collector simply wants to add a toy to his collection, and to him price is not as important as availability.

Toys can be classified into at least two categories: early collectible toys with an established history and the newer toys. The antique toys are easier to evaluate. A great deal of research has been done on them, and much data is available. The newer toys are just beginning to be studied; relative information is only now being published, and the lack of production records makes it difficult to know how many may be available. Often warehouse finds of these newer toys can change the market. This has happened with battery-operated toys and to some extent with robots. Review past issues of this guide. You will see the changing trends for the newer toys. All toys become more important as collectibles when a fixed period of manufacture is known. When we know the numbers produced and documentation of the makers is established, the prices become more predictable.

The best way to learn about toys is to attend toy shows and auctions. This will give you the opportunity to compare prices and condition. The more collectors and dealers you meet, the more you will learn. There is no substitute for holding a toy in your hand and seeing for yourself what they are. If you are going to be a serious collector, buy all the books you can find. Read every article you see. Knowledge is vital to building a good collection. Study all books that are available. These are some of the most helpful: *American Toy Cars and Trucks* by Lillian Gottschalk; *Toy Autos 1890-1939*, the Peter Ottenheimer Collection; *Collecting the Tin Toy Car, 1950-1970*, by Dale Kelley; *Arcade Toys* by Al Aune; *The Art of the Tin Toy* by David Pressland; *Lehmann Toys* by Cieslik; *The History of Martin Mechanical Toys* by Marchand; *Mechanical Toys* by Spilhaus; *American Antique Toys* by Barenholtz, McClintock, and Holland; *American Clockwork Toys* by Whitton; *The George Brown Sketchbook* by Edith Barenholtz; *Toy Dreams* by Kitahara; *Collecting Toys, Collecting Toy Soldiers* and *Collecting Toy Trains, An Identification & Value Guide #3*, by Richard O'Brien; *Occupied Japan Toys with Prices* by David Gould and Donna Crevar Donaldson; *Evolution of the Pedal Car and Other Riding Toys, 1844-1970*, by Neil Wood; *Toys of the Historical, Rarity & Value Guide, 1931-1963*, by John Murray and Bruce Fox. Other informative books (published by Collector Books) are *Stern's Guide to Disney Collectibles* by Michael Stern; *Modern Toys, American Toys, 1830-1980* by Linda Baker; *Character Toys and Collectibles* and *Toys, Antiques & Collectibles* by David Longest; *Collectors Guide to Tootsietoys* by David Richter; *Collectible Male Action Figures* by Paris and Susan Manos; and *Matchbox Toys, 1948-1993* by Dana Johnson. If you still seek information we further recommend *Toys of the Sixties, a Pictorial Guide* by Bill Bruegman, and *Fisher-Price, a Historical, Rarity, Value Guide, 1931-1963* by John Murray and Bruce Fox. *The Dictionary of Toys Sold in America, Vol. I & II*, by Earnest and Ida Long are good for identification and dating. The Longs are our advisors for all toys except Farm Toys, Steiff, Toy Soldiers, and Trains; they are listed in the Directory under California. In the listings that follow, toys are listed by manufacturer's name if possible, otherwise by type. Condition is given when known. Measurements are given when appropriate and available; if only one dimension is noted, it is the greater one — height if the toy is vertical, length if it is horizontal. See also Children's Things; Personalities. For toy stoves, see Stoves.

Key:
b/o — battery operated   NP — nickel plated
jtd — jointed   w/up — wind-up

Cast Iron

Cast iron toys were made from shortly before the Civil War until the 1940s. They are evaluated to a large extent by scarcity, complexity, design, and detail. See next section for examples of cast iron toys listed by company name.

Bus, dbl decker, worn pnt, 8", G	175.00
Cannon, red & blk pnt, lt wear, 8½"	115.00
Coal cart w/donkey & driver, worn mc pnt, 13½"	415.00
Dump truck, red & gr chipped pnt, 7", VG	260.00
Fire pumper, orig flaking pnt, NP trim, 20", G	275.00
Fire pumper, pnt CI, NP trim, minor flakes/pits, 21½", VG	1,400.00
Fire pumper, red & blk pnt, NP pumper trim, rubber tires, 6", G	125.00
Hook & ladder truck, pnt CI, 3 ladders, worn figures, 28", G	1,200.00
Ice wagon w/horse & driver, mc pnt, rpl wheel, 16"	275.00
Milk truck, worn pnt, windshield post missing, 4"	130.00
Railroad cars, NY Central & Hudson RR, 8" to 9½", set of 3	165.00
Roadster, blk pnt, rpl figure, 8", G	150.00
Roadster, rpt, rubber tires (2 spares), 5", G-	20.00
Sedan, orange & blk pnt, lt wear, 4½"	88.00
Sidewheeler, rpt, articulated, 10½", G	95.00
Stanley surrey w/fringe, worn pnt, 11½", VG	110.00
Steam shovel, chipped red pnt, NP shovel, 4½", G	30.00
Touring car, driver missing, VG mc pnt, 9½"	165.00
Touring car, 3-color pnt, wht rubber wheels, 5", EX	185.00
Tractor, chipped pnt, NP wheels, 3½", VG	25.00
Train set, NP finish, MCRR on flat car, 5-pc, 31" L, EX	95.00
Trolley, orange pnt, integral figures, 7½", VG	275.00
1-horse coach, w/driver & passenger, 3-color pnt, 16", VG	200.00
1-horse milk wagon, 3-color pnt w/silver, 12", VG+	140.00
1-horse sleigh, pnt chips & wear, lt rust, 14½", G	900.00
2-horse fire patrol wagon, mc pnt, rpt figures, 19", VG	350.00

Company or Country of Manufacturer

Bliss, horse-drawn sand and gravel wagon, lithographed paper on wood, wagon dumps, 9¾x21", VG, $325.00.

Akro Agate, Popeye Marble Shooter, complete set, NM in box	500.00
Alps, Boardwalk Delight, tin/celluloid, clockwork, 10", VG	240.00
American Flyer, Uncle Sam on Bicycle, tin litho, 8", EX	150.00
American Toy, Auto Wheel Coaster, wooden wagon, 1918, 40", G	135.00
American Toy, Blk Jiggers, pnt wood/compo/cloth, 10½", VG	800.00
Amsco, Doll-E-Detecto Scales, working, MIB	100.00
Arcade, Andy Gump & 348 car, pnt CI, 7", VG	2,100.00
Arcade, Century of Progress Bus, pnt CI, lt rust, 12", G	185.00
Arcade, convertible, pnt CI, driver missing, 6¾", G	700.00
Arcade, Ford Weaver Wrecker, pnt CI, 1919, 8⅜", G	800.00
Arcade, Mack Stake Truck, pnt CI, lt surface rust, 12", G	1,800.00
Arcade, McCormick-Deering wagon w/2 horses, pnt CI, 12", EX	275.00
Arcade, NY World's Fair Bus, pnt CI, 8¼", EX	150.00
Arcade, Pontiac Sedan, pnt CI, NP, 6", G	325.00
Arcade, Railroad Wrecker, pnt CI, 10¼", G	300.00
Arcade, sedan, CI w/blk pnt, lt rust, 6½", G	60.00
Arcade, Showboat, pnt CI & metal, w/label, 10½", G	475.00
Arcade, tractor & wagon, pnt CI, rpr to shaft, 9", G	60.00
Arcade, Trailways Bus, pnt CI, NP trim, 9", G	375.00
Arcade, World's Fair Trolley, pnt CI, 6¾", VG	325.00

Arcade, wrecker, CI, VG red pnt, 6", VG 275.00
Arcade, wrecker, CI, worn bl pnt, 6½", G 90.00
Bing, Ford Model-T Touring Car, lady driver, w/up, 6¼", EX 250.00
Bing, gunboat, pnt metal, clockwork, ca 1910, 10¼", VG 475.00
Bing, Model-T coupe, tin litho w/up, 6", EX 295.00
Bing, Model-T sedan, 4-door, tin litho w/up, 6", EX 285.00
Bing, speed boat, twin propellers, clockwork, 1910, 7½", EX 330.00
Borgfeldt, Donald Duck Carousel, celluloid/tin, 8", NMIB 4,500.00
Borgfeldt, Felix, wood jtd, w/paper label, 4½", VG 170.00
Borgfeldt, Henry & Brother, celluloid/tin w/up, 6½", EX in box ..1,900.00
Borgfeldt, Henry Motoring, celluloid & tin w/up, 6", NMIB ...4,600.00
Borgfeldt, Mickey Mouse, decaled wood, 1928, 6½", EX 1,075.00
Borgfeldt, Mickey Mouse Express Wagon, wood, 1931, 12", EX .750.00
Borgfeldt, Mickey Mouse Whirligig, celluloid, 10", NMIB 7,000.00

Bramwell-Smith & Co., painted tin sidewheeler, Pat May 7, 1872, 10½", EX in poor box, $5,500.00.

Buddy L, Express Truck, pressed steel, worn pnt, 23½", G 275.00
Buddy L, Flivver Model-T Truck, tin litho, 11", EX 1,500.00
Buddy L, Ice Delivery Truck, pnt steel, rpt, 26", G 500.00
Buddy L, Railway Express Truck, pnt steel, rpt, 25", G 575.00
Buddy L, Texaco Gasoline Truck, pnt steel, decals, 23½", VG ...200.00
Buffalo, Red Streak Racer, pnt steel, 20½", G 150.00
Buffalo, Silver Dash Auto Racer, litho/pnt tin, '25, 12½", VG ...300.00
Carette, gunboat, pnt metal, clockwork, ca 1910, G 1,045.00
Carpenter, fire pumper, pnt CI, missing figures, 19", G 550.00
Chad Valley, Mickey Mouse Table Tennis Set, EX- 375.00
Chein, Aero Swing #265, tin litho, musical, 1930s, 9½", EX 225.00
Chein, Broadway Trolley, tin litho, 8¼", VG 375.00
Chein, Disneyland Ferris Wheel, tin litho w/up, 17", NM 650.00
Chein, Drum Major, tin litho, clockwork, 9", VG 200.00
Chein, Ferris Wheel, tin litho, clockwork, 16½", EX 400.00
Chein, Hercules Storage Truck, tin litho, 7¾", VG 425.00
Chein, Ignatz Mouse on Tricycle, tin/wood, 1932, 9", EX 550.00
Chein, Mechanical Drummer, tin litho, clockwork, 9", EX 230.00
Chein, Musical Roundabout, tin litho, lever action, 10¼", EX ..225.00
Chein, Popeye Floor Puncher, tin litho, 1932, 7½", NMIB 4,000.00
Chein, Popeye Overhead Puncher, tin, 1932, 9½", VG in box ..2,750.00
Chein, Popeye Sparkler, later version, 4", NMIB 375.00
Chein, Popeye Walker, tin litho w/up, 1932, 6¼", NM 450.00
Chein, Roller Coaster, tin litho w/up, 2 cars, 19½", VG 210.00
Chein, Traffic Cop, tin litho w/up, 5½", VG 70.00
Converse, farm set, wood litho barn & animals, 1890s, EX 495.00
Corgi, Army Fuel Tanker #1134, NMIB 40.00
Courtland, Ice Cream Cart, tin litho, mechanical, 6½", VG 225.00
Cowdery, Flivver Center-Door Sedan, pnt steel, 11", MIB 450.00
Cragstan, Ford Fairlane Skyliner, b/o, 11", MIB 400.00
Cragstan, Happy Santa, celluloid/tin/cloth, b/o, 12", VG+ 125.00
Cragstan, Mr Robot, w/orig inserts, MIB 1,300.00
Dayton, fire truck, tin litho, friction, 1920s, 12½", VG 375.00

Doepke, cement mixer, pnt metal, G 195.00
E Trask, Salem Witch Fortune Teller, lever action, 1867, 6" ..1,450.00
England, ladder truck, tin litho, clockwork, no figures, 9", G 110.00
Fallows, train, tin, engine+boiler+tender+2 cars, 1885, 22" 450.00
Fallows, 1-horse cart, pnt (worn) & emb tin, 10¼", G 165.00
Fallows, 2-horse trolley, pnt tin, late 1800s, 10", G 357.00
Fisher-Price, Barky Puppy, #103, EX 250.00
Fisher-Price, Big Bill Pelican, w/fish, #794, 1961-69, NM 55.00
Fisher-Price, Chatter Monk, #798, EX 45.00
Fisher-Price, Doctor Doodle, #477, 1940, EX 165.00
Fisher-Price, Musical Push Chime, #722, 1950-68, EX 20.00
Fisher-Price, Push Bunny Cart, #401, 1942, VG 75.00
Fisher-Price, Rooster Cart, #469, 1938-41, EX 95.00
Fisher-Price, Safety School Bus, #983, 1959-61, EX 95.00
Fisher-Price, Snoopy Sniffer, #181, NM 25.00
Fisher-Price, Sonny Duck Cart, #410, NM 120.00
Fisher-Price, Streamline Express, #215, 1935, NM 300.00
Fisher-Price, Talking Donald Duck, #764, NM 80.00
Fisher-Price, Teddy Tucker, #711, NM 115.00
Fisher-Price, Teddy Xylophone, #752, 1946-48, EX 95.00
Fisher-Price, Woofy Wagger, #447, EX 45.00
Fleishmann, Passenger Liner, tin, clockwork, 12½", EX 300.00
Fleishmann, steamer, pnt steel w/up, w/flags/key, 7½", VG 225.00
France, open touring car, litho & pnt tin, 13", VG 850.00
France, sedan, tin litho, clockwork, 6¼", G 40.00
George Brown, horse & cart, pnt tin, 8", VG 1,000.00
George Fisher, limousine, tin litho, clockwork, 1900, 7¾", EX ..525.00
Germany, boy pushes girl on swing, tin w/up, 7", G 450.00
Germany, Carrette Limo, pnt tin, working, 16", EX 8,200.00
Germany, Charlie Chaplin Dancer, tin litho, crank, 6½", NM ..1,500.00
Germany, Chinaman on stump w/mandolin, tin w/up, 1880s, 8", G ..450.00
Germany, Felix Riding His Scooter, tin litho w/up, 8", NM 1,250.00
Germany, Felix Sparkler, tin litho, 5", G 200.00
Germany, Felix Walker, tin w/up, c 1922-34, 7", EX 350.00
Germany, Ferris Wheel, 6 gondolas/12 passengers, tin, 15¾", G ...375.00
Germany, girl on potty, tin litho, squeeze action, 5x4", EX 165.00
Germany, Grandma Sparkler, tin litho, missing spring, 5", G 60.00
Germany, Harold Lloyd on Telephone, bell-ringer, 6", NM 300.00
Germany, Lady Bug, tin litho, mechanical, 5", VG 130.00
Germany, limousine, litho & pnt tin, 10½", VG 650.00
Germany, Mickey Mouse Sax Player, tin litho, 1931, 6", VG ..1,250.00
Germany, open touring car, tin litho, mechanical, 10½", G 450.00
Germany, Peacock, tin litho, orig comb, EX colors, 9", VG 70.00
Germany, Racing Car #5, tin litho, 8¼", G 1,800.00
Germany, Strolling Woman, pnt tin, clockwork, 7", G 300.00
Germany, Toonerville Trolley, tin litho, 7", G 450.00
Germany, touring car, litho & pnt tin, working, 9", VG 950.00
Germany, trolley car, tin w/up, 6", EX 150.00
Germany, trotter & sulky, pnt compo/tin/plastic, 6½", VG 35.00
Gilbert, Erector Amusement Park Set, 1930s, VG 500.00
Girard, handcar, litho & pnt tin, mechanical, 6", VG 160.00
Girard, Spirit of St Louis, stenciled tin w/up, 13", G 250.00
Girard, Whiz Sky Fighter, stenciled tin, clockwork, 9", VG 350.00
Guntherman, Carousel, tin litho, 3-D figures, working, 6", VG .750.00
Guntherman, Clown Musician & Juggler, pnt tin w/up, 8", G ...950.00
Guntherman, Flying Machine, pnt tin w/up, 5½", EX 770.00
Guntherman, Tango, tin litho w/up, 8", EX in box 1,870.00
Happynak, Mickey & Minnie Mouse Sand Pail, tin litho, 4½", M..175.00
Harris, Triple-Team Water Tower, pnt CI, 1900, 30", VG 700.00
Hartland, Babe Ruth, EX 175.00
Hartland, Canadian Mounted Police, complete, NM 75.00
Hartland, Chris Colt, standing gunfighter, complete, NM 175.00
Hartland, Cochise, complete, M w/tag 125.00
Hartland, Dale Evans, complete, M w/tag 165.00

Hartland, Dan Troop, standing gunfighter, complete, NM 150.00
Hartland, Eddie Matthews, baseball player, NM 135.00
Hartland, General Lee, complete, NM 95.00
Hartland, George Washington, complete, NM 65.00
Hartland, Hank Aaron, baseball player, NM w/bat 200.00
Hartland, Hobie Gillman, complete, NM 150.00
Hartland, Indian brave, complete, M 95.00
Hartland, Jim Hardie, complete, NM w/tag 145.00
Hartland, Johnny McKay, standing gunfighter, complete, NM ..200.00
Hartland, Matt Dillon, complete, NM w/tag 125.00
Hartland, Mickey Mantle, baseball player, M w/bat & tag 265.00
Hartland, Paladin, standing gunfighter, complete, NM 135.00
Hartland, Stan Musial, w/o bat, otherwise NM 150.00
Hartland, Willy Mays, baseball player, NM 250.00
Hartland, Yogi Berra, EX 150.00
Hasbro, Walt Disney's Loony-Kins Set, 15½", VG in box 25.00
Hoge, Fire Chief Car, pnt steel, clockwork, 14½", VG 275.00
Hubley, Air Compressor Truck, pnt pot metal, 7", EX in box ...130.00
Hubley, Indian Motorcycle, pnt CI, NP trim, 9", G 625.00
Hubley, Indian Traffic Car, pnt CI, ca 1929, 8¾", VG 1,100.00
Hubley, Piston Racer, CI, orig bl pnt, lt rust, 7", G 225.00
Hubley, Popeye on Motorcycle, pnt CI, ca 1938, 9", EX 3,575.00
Hubley, Popeye Spinach Wagon, pnt CI, 3x5", EX 650.00
Hubley, racer, pnt CI, NP driver (rpl), 6¾", VG 130.00
Hubley, Roman Chariot, pnt CI, cracked shaft, 10", G 425.00
Hubley, Royal Circus Cage Wagon, pnt CI, gold trim, 16", VG .950.00
Hubley, Santa Sleigh, CI, recast parts, 14", G 700.00
Hubley, sedan, pnt CI, spare tire on bk, 6", G 325.00
Hubley, 2-horse drawn fire pumper, CI, mc pnt, 20", VG 275.00
Hull & Stafford, locomotive, pnt tin, mc pnt, 10¼", G 660.00
Ives, Dancing Lady, clockwork, 1882, 12⅝", EX 5,850.00
Ives, horse on wheels, CI, worn pnt, ca 1895-1910, 7½" 600.00
Ives, horse-drawn cart, tin clockwork, 15½", G- 4,500.00
Ives, Steam Launch Neptune, pnt brass, 9½", VG in box 1,325.00
Ives, train, mc pnt on CI, 1890, 21¼" L, 3-pc 425.00
Ives, train set, CI, locomotive: 8½", 1900s, 4-pc, VG 200.00
Japan, Answer Game Robot, b/o, working, 14", VG 250.00
Japan, Bear Golfer, tin litho w/up, 5", VG 150.00
Japan, Blk Henry's Cart, pnt tin/celluloid w/up, 5¼", G 200.00
Japan, Blue Bird Plane, tin litho, 10¼", VG 175.00
Japan, Boy on Tricycle, tin/celluloid, clockwork, 6", G 110.00
Japan, Bristol Bulldog Airplane, tin litho, b/o, 12", VG 200.00
Japan, Cary the Crow, tin litho, clockwork, 3¾", EX in G box ..110.00
Japan, Chevy Dump Truck, tin litho, friction, 9", EX in box 80.00
Japan, Dolly Seamstress, tin/plastic, b/o, 5¾", VG 120.00
Japan, Donald Duck Waddler, tin w/up, 5½", NMIB 1,800.00
Japan, Donald Pulled by Pluto, celluloid/tin, 5½", NM 1,600.00
Japan, Drummer, compo/celluloid/cloth, clockwork, 11", G 200.00
Japan, Donald Duck pulled by Pluto, celluloid, 8", EX 1,100.00
Japan, Electromobile, pnt tin, b/o, 8", EX in box 120.00
Japan, Fishing Polar Bear, tin litho/fabric, b/o, 10¾", VG 100.00
Japan, Ford Convertible, litho & pnt tin, friction, 12", VG 275.00
Japan, girl pushes carriage, celluloid/tin, clockwork, 5", G 110.00
Japan, Greyhound Bus, tin litho, friction, 13", EX in box 90.00
Japan, Interstate Express, tin litho, 12¾", EX in box 120.00
Japan, Kay Tee Glider, tin litho, friction, 10½", G in box 70.00
Japan, Military Cycle, tin litho w/up, 5½", VG 160.00
Japan, Monkey Basketball Player, tin litho w/up, 7¼", VG 150.00
Japan, Municipal Railway Trolley, tin litho, friction, 7", G 30.00
Japan, Percy Penguin, tin litho, friction, 5", VG in G box 120.00
Japan, Poor Pete, pnt celluloid, clockwork, 6", VG 300.00
Japan, Rocking Dog, tin litho, clockwork, 5½", EX 95.00
Japan, Santa Claus, tin litho w/up, rings bell/waves, 6", VG 120.00
Japan, Sparky Robot, pressed tin w/up, 7½", G in box 225.00

Japan, Strutting Duck, tin litho w/up, 7", VG in box 60.00
Japan, Talking Robot, litho & pnt tin/plastic, b/o, 11", VG 550.00
Japan, Tom & Jerry Cart, tin litho, w/o, 8¼", VG 150.00
Japan, 588 Isetta Car, tin litho, friction, 6¾", VG 275.00
Jean Schoenner, locomotive, tin w/up, 13¾", EX 165.00
Jorikawa, Super Astronaut Robot, tin/plastic, 11¾", EX 145.00
Kellerman, Dump Truck, pnt tin, clockwork, 10", VG 140.00
Kenton, automotive hose & ladder wagon, pnt CI, 9", G 500.00
Kenton, buckboard, CI, some pnt crazing, 14½", G 120.00
Kenton, hay wagon w/2 horses, pnt CI, stake body, 14½", G ...100.00
Kenton, horse-drawn farm wagon, pnt CI, 15", EX 275.00
Kenton, Overland Circus Cage Wagon w/polar bear, pnt CI, 14" ..250.00
Kenton, Sight Seeing Auto, pnt CI, ca 1900, 10¼", VG 9,000.00
Keystone, Kingsbury Rapid Fire Monoplane, steel, 23½", EX ..1,200.00
Keystone, Mickey Mouse Movie Projector, 11", EX in box 525.00
Keystone, wrecker, pnt steel w/decals, 1920s, 25", G 200.00
Kilgore, roadster w/rumble seat, pnt CI, 6", G 325.00
Kingsbury, Golden Arrow Racer, pnt metal, 1930s, 20", VG 220.00
Kingsbury, ladder wagon, pnt steel/CI/wood, 28", VG 140.00
Kingsbury, Taxi Plane, dbl wings, w/pilot, tin, 1925, 16", G 450.00
Knickerbocker, Minnie Mouse Cowgirl, w/accessories, 13", EX ..2,000.00
Knickerbocker, Roly Poly Popeye Target, paper/plastic, 20", VG ..135.00
Kyosho, car, gas driven, Futuba 2-channel radio control, 18", EX .100.00
Lehmann, Adam, litho & pnt tin w/up, 8", VG 900.00

Lehmann, Ajax, Roman gladiator with clubs moves backwards and does flip flops, clockwork, 10", NM in original box, $2,000.00.

Lehmann, Autobus, tin litho, lt pitting, 8", G 725.00
Lehmann, Balky Mule, tin litho, ca 1903, 6¾", EX in box 500.00
Lehmann, Balky Mule, tin litho & cloth, mechanical, 8", G 150.00
Lehmann, Dare Devil, zebra w/cart & driver, tin w/up, 7", EX ...375.00
Lehmann, Express, tin litho, flywheel, early version, 6", G 400.00
Lehmann, Na-Nu, tin litho w/up, 7", EX 275.00
Lehmann, Na-Ob, tin litho, mechanical, 5", VG 575.00
Lehmann, New Century Cycle, tin litho, 2nd version, 5¼", G ..335.00
Lehmann, Oh-My, Blk man on platform, tin w/up, 10", EX 525.00
Lehmann, Paddy & the Pig, 1900s, 5⅞", EX 1,045.00
Lehmann, Rad Cycle, litho & pnt tin, mechanical, 5", VG 700.00
Lehmann, Rad Cycle & Anxious Bride, litho & pnt tin, 9", VG .1,700.00
Lehmann, sailor, tin w/up, rpl clothes, 8", G 400.00
Lehmann, Sea Lion, tin litho w/up, whiskers gone, 7½", VG 85.00
Lehmann, Tut Tut, litho & pnt tin, 6¾", VG 700.00
Lehmann, Zeppelin EPL 11, tin/plastic w/up, 11½", EX 950.00
Lehmann, Zulu, tin litho w/up, 6½", G 425.00
Linemar, Bubble Blowing Popeye, tin litho, b/o, 12", NMIB ...2,050.00
Linemar, Donald Duck Jalopy, tin litho w/up, 5½", VG 350.00
Linemar, Ham 'N Sam, tin litho w/up, 5¼", NM 1,650.00
Linemar, Knitting Minnie Mouse, tin litho w/up, 6¾", EX 770.00

Linemar, Mickey Mouse & Driver, tin w/up, 6⅝", EX 825.00
Linemar, Mickey Mouse Hi-Wheeler Bike, 7", EX 425.00
Linemar, Mickey Mouse Roller Skater, tin litho w/up, 6", NM ...2,100.00
Linemar, Mickey's Delivery, tin/celluloid, friction, 6", VG 450.00
Linemar, Olive Oyl Sports Roadster, tin, friction, 8", NMIB ..2,300.00
Linemar, Olive Oyl Tricycle, tin litho w/up, 4", NMIB 2,450.00
Linemar, Playful Pluto & Goofy, tin litho w/up, 5½", NM 1,200.00
Linemar, Pluto Drum Major, tin litho, clockwork, 6½", G 110.00
Linemar, Popeye & Olive Oyl Playing Ball, 19", NMIB 1,500.00
Linemar, Popeye & Olive Oyl Stretchy Hand Car, 6½", NMIB ..3,500.00
Linemar, Popeye Bank, tin litho, clockwork, 3¾", VG 230.00
Linemar, Popeye Lantern, tin litho, 7½", NMIB 900.00
Linemar, Popeye Sports Roadster, tin, friction, 8", EX 1,200.00
Linemar, Popeye Transit Hauler & Trailer, friction, 13", NMIB ..3,200.00
Linemar, Popeye Turnover Tank, tin litho w/up, EX 600.00
Linemar, Running Pluto, tin litho, friction, 4¼", VG 180.00
Linemar, Smoking Popeye, tin litho, b/o, 8½x6", NMIB 1,750.00
Linemar, Tramp, tin litho, friction, 3¾", EX in VG box 210.00
Linemar, Tumbling Popeye, mechanical, 4½" 1,900.00
Linemar, Wimpy Nodder, tin litho w/up, 5", EX 1,050.00
Linemar, Wimpy Tricycle w/Revolving Bell, tin w/up, 4", NMIB .3,000.00
Lionel, Donald Duck Rail Car, 10x7", EX in box 1,000.00
Lionel, Electric Stove, enameled steel, 1932, 30x26x11", EX 935.00
Lionel, Mickey Mouse Stoker, 0-gauge, tin litho, 3⅞", EX 195.00
Lionel, Peter Rabbit Chick-Mobile, pnt compo, clockwork, 9½", G ..185.00
Marx, #12 Racer, tin litho w/up, 16", VG 120.00
Marx, Airplane Hangar, tin litho, clockwork, 6", EX 250.00
Marx, Amos 'N Andy Fresh Air Taxi, tin litho, 8", G 550.00
Marx, Amos 'N Andy Fresh Air Taxi, tin litho, 8", NM 1,550.00
Marx, Amos Walker, tin litho, clockwork, rpl arms, 11½", G 375.00
Marx, Andy Walker, tin litho, clockwork, 12", VG/EX 650.00
Marx, Atomic Pistol Flashlight, extra lenses, 8", EX in box 85.00
Marx, Auto Transport Truck, pnt steel, 13¾", +2 sm cars, EX ...140.00
Marx, BO Plenty, tin litho, clockwork, 8½", EX 270.00
Marx, boy on tricycle, tin litho w/up, 1930s, 9", G 220.00
Marx, Busy Miners, tin litho w/up, 16½", VG 210.00
Marx, Campus Jalopy, tin litho w/up, lt rust, 5¾", G 160.00
Marx, Charlie McCarthy in Benzine Buggy, tin w/up, 7¾", EX ..775.00
Marx, Charlie McCarthy Walker, tin litho, clockwork, 8¾", VG ..300.00
Marx, Chompy the Beetle, tin w/up, 6", NM 210.00
Marx, City Airport, pressed steel, b/o, 2 planes, 17", G 160.00
Marx, City Airport, tin litho, b/o, lt dents, 17", G 50.00
Marx, Climbing Fireman, tin litho w/up, 23", EX 225.00
Marx, Crazy Car, tin litho w/up, worn, 7¼", G 160.00
Marx, Derrick Loader, tin litho, hand crank, 8", EX in box 85.00
Marx, Dumbo, tin litho, clockwork, 4½", VG in VG box 375.00
Marx, Falcon sports car, tin litho/vinyl, friction, 20", G 150.00
Marx, Fanny Farmer Truck, plastic, stencils, 9½", NM 130.00
Marx, Ferdinand, tin litho, clockwork, 7¼", G 100.00
Marx, Figaro, tin litho, clockwork, rpl ears, 5", G 110.00
Marx, Filling Station, tin litho, rubber hose, b/o, 9½", VG 180.00
Marx, Fire Chief Car, tin litho w/up, 7", VG 80.00
Marx, Fred Flintstone on Dino, tin w/up, 8", EX 225.00
Marx, George Drummer Boy, tin litho, clockwork, 9¼", EX 290.00
Marx, Home Dairy Truck, tin litho, 11", EX in box 160.00
Marx, Hopalong Cassidy Rocker, tin litho, clockwork, 10", VG ...325.00
Marx, Iceman, tin litho w/up, 8½", NMIB 2,200.00
Marx, Joe Penner, tin litho, clockwork, 8", VG 320.00
Marx, King Racer, tin litho, 8½", EX in box 1,050.00
Marx, Knockout Champs, celluloid/tin litho w/up, 7⅛", EX 500.00
Marx, Magic Barn & Tractor, tin litho, clockwork, 10½", EX 250.00
Marx, Marine Corps Truck, tin litho, w/marine figures, 13", EX ...150.00
Marx, Merry Makers Band, tin litho w/up, 7", EX in torn box ...1,200.00
Marx, Mickey Mouse Express, tin litho, clockwork, 9¼", VG 250.00

Marx, Mickey Mouse Piano, paper litho on wood, 10", EX 1,450.00
Marx, Midget Racer, tin litho, clockwork, 5", VG 160.00
Marx, Mortimer Snerd, tin litho, clockwork, 8¾", G 250.00
Marx, Northwest Plane, tin/plastic, b/o, 15", VG in box 100.00
Marx, Peter Pan tea set, 13-pc, EX 45.00
Marx, Pinocchio, tin litho, clockwork, 8¾", G 325.00
Marx, Pinocchio the Acrobat, tin litho w/up, 1939, 16½", VG ..500.00
Marx, Popeye & Olive Oyl Jiggers, 1934, 9", NMIB 4,000.00
Marx, Popeye Dippy Dumper, celluloid/tin, 9", NMIB 2,200.00
Marx, Popeye Express (honeymoon type), 9½" dia, NMIB 2,250.00
Marx, Popeye Jigger, tin litho, 1935, 10", EX in box 1,250.00
Marx, Popeye w/Parrot Cage, tin litho, 8", NMIB 1,400.00
Marx, Popeye w/Parrots, tin litho, clockwork, 7½", G 230.00
Marx, Range Rider, tin litho, clockwork, 10", VG 210.00
Marx, Rocket Racer, tin litho w/up, 16½", G 300.00
Marx, Sheriff Pat Garrett Best of West figure, M in G box 90.00
Marx, Sheriff Sam Whoopee Car, tin/plastic, clockwork, 6", VG .110.00
Marx, Siren Police Patrol, pnt/stenciled steel, 15", G 110.00
Marx, Speed King racer, tin litho w/up, 16½", VG in box 225.00
Marx, Speedboy Delivery truck, tin litho, 10", EX 300.00
Marx, Toy Down Dairy Wagon, tin litho w/up, 10¼", VG 180.00
Marx, tractor & trailer, tin litho, clockwork, rstr, 11", G 140.00
Marx, Wise Pluto, tin litho w/up, 8¼", VG 375.00
Mason Parker, buckboard, pnt steel, articulated horse, 29", G 525.00
Mattel, Popeye in the Music Box, tin litho, 5½", NM 200.00
Mengel, Mickey Mouse Rocker, decal on seat, 36" long, EX 500.00
Metalcraft, Shell Motor Oil Stake Truck, pnt steel, 12", G 450.00
Metalcraft, Sunshine Biscuit truck, pnt steel, 12¼", VG 725.00
Nifty, Barney Google on Spark Plug, tin w/up, 7", VG 500.00

Nifty, Felix the Movie Cat platform pull toy, lithograph on tin, 7½", NM in EX box, $5,750.00.

Nifty, Krazy Kat on platform, tin litho, 7½", NMIB 1,300.00
Nifty, Mickey & Minnie Mouse Acrobats, 17", NMIB 2,200.00
Nifty, Mickey Mouse Jazz Drummer, tin, squeeze, 6½", NM 3,800.00
Nifty, Toonerville Trolley, tin litho w/up, 7½", EX 750.00
NN Hill Brass, Mickey Mouse Toy Telephone, upright, 7", EX ..450.00
Occupied Japan, Circus Tricycle, celluloid/tin, 4¼", VG 40.00
Occupied Japan, Dancing Couple, celluloid, clockwork, 4¾", VG ..80.00
Occupied Japan, Running Mickey on Pluto, WDP, 5", NMIB 5,000.00
Ohio Art, Mickey Mouse Carpet Sweeper, early, 2x7x4", NM ...200.00
Ohio Art, Mickey Mouse Drum, tin litho, 4x9" dia, EX 275.00
Ohio Art, Mickey Mouse Sand Set, tin litho, 3-pc, NMIB 1,100.00
Ohio Art, Mickey Mouse Washing Machine, WDE, 7½", NM ..425.00
Ohio Art, Mickey Mouse Watering Can, WDE, 6x4" dia, NM ..175.00
Orkin, Battleship New Mexico, tin, clockwork, 25", G 2,100.00

Orkin, Battleship New York, tin litho, clockwork, 25", G 2,300.00
Orobor, open touring car, tin litho, mechanical, 5", G 350.00
Paradise Novelty, Donald Duck Cyclist, 5½", NMIB 1,850.00
Peter Puppet Playthings, Flub-a-Dub Marionette, 12", VG 100.00
Remco, Captain America utility set, 1977, M 20.00
Republic, Ladder Fire Truck, pnt tin, friction, 1921, G 150.00
Saunders, Marvelous Mike Tractor, metal/plastic, b/o, 13", VG .275.00
Schneider, Mickey Mouse Racing Car, Disney, w/up, 4", NM ...1,350.00
Schuco, BMW Sport Car #4001, red pnt, clockwork, 5⅝", EX...195.00
Schuco, Charlie Chaplin, tin w/up, 6½", NMIB 1,200.00
Schuco, Dancing Rabbit, mohair/fabric/wood/metal, 8", EX 275.00
Schuco, Racing Motorcycle #5, tin litho w/up, 5", G 325.00
Seiberling Rubber, Mickey Mouse figure, 3½", NM 75.00
Spear, Donald Duck jack-in-box, compo/cloth/wood, 10", VG ..140.00
Steelcraft, Army Scout Plane, pnt steel w/decals, '30s, 22", G 360.00
Steelcraft, Marion steam shovel, pnt steel, 14", VG 65.00
Strauss, Continental Flyer, tin litho, mechanical, 11½", VG ..1,000.00
Strauss, Dandy Jim Clown Dancer, tin litho w/up, 10", VG 450.00
Strauss, Ham 'N Sam Minstrel Team, tin litho w/up, 6½", VG ..500.00
Strauss, Ham 'N Sam Minstrel Team, tin litho w/up, 6⅝", EX ...700.00
Strauss, Interstate Bus, tin litho, 10¾", G 240.00
Strauss, Jenny Balking Mule, tin litho w/up, 9¼", VG in box 250.00
Strauss, Jitney Bus #66, tin litho w/up, 9½", EX 1,250.00
Strauss, Red Star Van, tin litho w/up, 7½", G 150.00
Strauss, Travel Chicks, tin litho w/up, 7½", G 135.00
Strauss, Yell-O-Taxi, tin litho w/up, 7½", VG+ 550.00
Structo, dump truck, pnt steel, 18", G 60.00
Structo, rug loom, wood fr, complete w/partial rug, 1920s 200.00
Sun Rubber, Mickey's Fire Truck, pnt rubber, 6½", G 90.00
Taiwan, F-14 Jet Fighter, tin litho/plastic, b/o, 14", EX 100.00
Tonka, Allied Moving Van, pressed steel, decal, 27", G 110.00
Tonka, Ford Fire Truck, w/fire hydrant, 1956, NM 325.00
Tonka, gas truck, pnt metal, EX 495.00
Tonka, grain hauler, pnt metal, VG 125.00
Tonka, hook & ladder truck, steel, rubber tires, EX 125.00
Tonka, log truck, pnt metal, NM 175.00
Tootsietoy, Freight Train #5550, 1930s, complete, EX in box 200.00
Tootsietoy, Midnight Flyer, pnt cast metal, 14", 5-pc, VG 210.00
Tootsietoy, Standard Oil Truck, red, 6" 40.00
Tootsietoy, tow truck, yel, 6" 40.00
Unique Art, Dogpatch Band, tin litho w/up, 8", G 375.00
Unique Art, GI Joe & Jouncing Jeep, tin litho w/up, 7", VG 110.00
Unique Art, GI Joe & K-9 Pups, tin litho, clockwork, 9", G 150.00

Unique Art, Kiddy Cyclist, lithograph on tin, wind-up, 8½", EX, $185.00.

Unique Art, Kiddie Cyclist, tin litho, clockwork, 9", NM 375.00
Unique Art, Li'l Abner Band, tin litho w/up, 10½", EX 725.00
Unique Art, Sky Rangers Airplane Tower, tin litho w/up, 10", VG .325.00
US Zone Germany, Bell Hop, tin litho/compo, 3½", EX 140.00
US Zone Germany, Equestrian, tin litho/compo w/up, 4", VG 60.00

W Germany, Carnival Ride, tin litho w/up, 8¼", VG in box 220.00
W Germany, Thunderbird Car, tin litho, 12", VG 200.00
Wells, Cabriolet w/driver, tin litho, mechanical, 9¼", VG 600.00
Wells, coupe w/driver, tin litho, mechanical, 8½", VG 220.00
Wolverine, Bake-A-Cake cooking set, NM 100.00
Wolverine, battleship, tin litho w/up, 1930s, 14⅜", EX 175.00
Wolverine, Merry-Go-Round, tin litho, lever action, 12½", G ..200.00
Wolverine, No 27 Drum Major, tin litho, clockwork, 13¾", G ..130.00
Wolverine, Snow White ironing board, metal, 21x27x8", EX 145.00
Wolverine, Streamline Railway, tin litho/wood, b/o, 17½", G 50.00
Wolverine, Sunny Suzy flatiron, chrome, electric, M 20.00
Wolverine, Zilotone, steel/tin litho w/up, 1930s, G 700.00
Wyandotte, dump truck, pnt steel, 21", VG 200.00
Yone, Corvair Convertible, tin litho friction, 9", EX in box 400.00

Farm Toys

Arcade, tractor and trailer, cast iron, worn red paint, 2x9", $150.00.

Baler, Ertl, diecast, w/4 bales, 1/16 scale, NMIB 40.00
Combine, Reuhl, Massey Harris, VG 485.00
Corn sheller, Ertl #4968, 1/8 scale, MIB 17.00
Plow, Carter, Case, 2-bottom, tin, 1/16 scale, EX 100.00
Plow, Ertl #525, John Deere, 1/16 scale, MIB 14.00
Shed & Barn w/Silo Sound Set, Ertl #4219, MIB 43.00
Thresher, Arcade, pnt CI, 1930, sm, EX 500.00
Tractor, Arcade, Allis Chalmers, 12½", +trailer 275.00
Tractor, Arcade, Fordson, pnt CI, 1928, 6", EX 125.00
Tractor, Arcade, McCormick Deering, rpl driver, lg, G 275.00
Tractor, Corgi, Ford, w/hydraulic scoop, #74, MIB 100.00
Tractor, Ertl, John Deere #3010, 3-point hitch, 1961-64, VG 150.00
Tractor, Ertl, Minneapolis-Moline, wht wheels, VG 180.00
Tractor, Hubley, Farmall M, 1952 model, 1/12 scale, EX 95.00
Tractor, Hubley, Huber, pnt CI, 7½", VG 600.00
Tractor, John Deere, cast aluminum, w/high lift, 1960 ....145.00
Tractor, John Deere, diecast, w/high lift, 1950s, 13" 150.00
Tractor, Lesney, Massey Harris #745D, M 450.00
Tractor, Marx, Sparkling, tin w/up, 1940s, MIB 195.00
Tractor & dump trailer, Arcade, Allis Chalmers, pnt CI, 8", EX ..75.00
Wagon, Arcade, McCormick-Deering, gr & red pnt, 12½", G 85.00
Wagon, John Deere, pnt wood/CI, 43", VG 225.00

Guns and Cap Bombs

Though toy guns were patented as early as the 1850s, the cap pistol was not invented until 1870, when paper caps that were primarily developed to detonate muzzleloaders became available. Some of the earlier models were very ornate and were occasionally decorated with figural heads. Most are marked with the name of their manufacturer; Ace, Daisy, Bulldog, Victor, and Excelsior are the most common.

Abe Lincoln cap bomb, nickeled CI, 2-pc, 2", EX 325.00
Admiral Dewey Cap Bomb, nickeled CI, 2½", VG 35.00
Big Scout cap gun, CI, NM 50.00

Chinaman cap bomb, CI, 1¾", VG 130.00
Cleve O cap bomb, CI, 3½", EX 250.00
Daisy Buck Rogers Atomic Pistol, metal, 9½", G, +holster 110.00
Daisy Superman Krypto Ray Gun, b/o, 7", VG 170.00
Hero cap gun, CI 50.00
Hubley Flintlock Jr cap gun, red & wht box 50.00
Hubley Rodeo cap gun, wht grips, tin box 50.00
Kilgore Buck cap gun, MIB 50.00
Kilgore Hawkeye #4, MIB 50.00
Kilgore Hawkeye automatic cap gun 25.00
Marx G-Man Machine Gun, plastic & tin litho, w/up, 25", VG ...80.00
Marx Popeye Pirate Pistol, tin litho, 10", EX in 6-color box 475.00
Marx Tom Corbett Space Gun, tin litho, 10", EX in mc box 225.00
National by Mason, automatic cap gun, brn grips 40.00
Nichols Dyna-Mite derringer cap gun, M in presentation box 20.00
Yel Kid cap bomb, CI, reverse: Say!, 2", VG 110.00

Pedal Cars and Ride-On Toys

Aerial Ladder Truck #79, ride-on, Keystone, 30½", G 600.00
Airplane, Steelcraft, slight rust & pnt loss, 50", G 900.00
Airplane, Toledo Mfg, pressed steel, EX orig pnt, 60" 3,000.00
American Nat'l Pumper, celluloid windshield, 1928, 60", EX .15,000.00
Boat, pressed steel, bl w/wht striping (rpt), 42", VG 300.00
Chrysler Air Flo, Steelcraft, rstr 3,600.00
Clicker crank front, wood rprs, worn pnt, ca 1914, 42", G 700.00
Convertible, '50s style, Rosca name plate, minor rstr, 44" 250.00
Convertible 'hot rod,' balloon-type wheels mk Trying, 36", G ...400.00
Convertible, 1950s style, minor dents, rpt, 37", G 325.00
Convertible resembling '50s Chevy, sheet metal, rpt, 44", VG ...475.00
Fire engine w/hose & ladders, Am Nat'l, rstr, 64", M 3,500.00
Packard, running boards, spot-light, headlights, siren, 50", G .5,000.00
Pumper, Toldeo Co, tin boiler, hand crank, rpt, 60", EX 2,000.00
Race car-style w/pointed nose, worn orig pnt, 1930s, 40", G 300.00
Renault, sloping front, mk Ferbedo on tires, 1930s, 42", VG 700.00
Roller derby-type auto, all wood, ca 1930, 53", G 300.00
Skippy Desoto, Pioneer, ca 1935-36, orig pnt, 38", VG 900.00
Steam roller, ride-on, red & blk pnt w/decals, Keystone, 20" 300.00

Penny Toys

Rabbit on wheeled base, marked Gesch, 3¼", $285.00.

Army tank, US Army WWI, June 20th 1916 on tin, 2½", NM ..125.00
Blk dancer, tin, Germany, ca 1900, 3⅝", EX 600.00
Carousel w/3 children on chairs, tin w/up, 4", EX 425.00
Chinaman w/twirling parasol, mc pnt, Distler, 3⅜", VG 1,300.00
Donkey-drawn cart w/driver, tin litho, 6½", G orig 250.00
Fire pumper, tin litho, 5½", EX 335.00
Girl in stroller, Germany, ca 1900, 2¾" 360.00
Hansom Cab, Germany, 4½", EX 385.00
Horse-drawn coach, mc pnt, 4½", VG 240.00
Horse-drawn delivery wagon, tin litho, mc, 5", EX 175.00
Horseless carriage, friction flywheel, mc int, 2⅞", VG 500.00

Limousine, tin litho, bright colors, Germany, 3¼", VG 300.00
Motorcycle, 3 wheels w/driver, mk CRO, 3½", G 325.00
Pool player at table w/rack & steel ball, tin, 1916 ....165.00
Porter, tin litho, lt rust, Germany, 4", VG 130.00
Race car w/driver, tin, boxy style, Fischer, 4½", EX 200.00
Taxicab, friction flywheel, red, wht & bl, Distler, 3⅛", VG 375.00
Touring car w/chauffeur, tin w/up, Germany, 4½", EX 125.00
Zeppelin, yel & blk balloon, bl propellers, red basket, 3", G 250.00

Pipsqueaks

Pipsqueak toys were popular among the Pennsylvania Germans. The earliest had bellows made from sheepskin. Later cloth replaced the sheepskin, and finally paper bellows were used.

Bird, papier-mache, mc pnt, spring legs, squeaks, 3½" 72.50
Bird, papier-mache/felt/crepe paper, squeaks, Germany, 5", EX 95.00
Cat on haunches, furry surface, Germany, 1870s, 9x5x3½" 325.00
Chicken, papier-mache, worn mc pnt, rprs/silent, 8¾" 50.00
Child, bsk head, cloth cap, flannel-covered base, silent, 5½" 40.00
Dog, seated, chalk, blk spotted, bl base, silent, 3½" 150.00
Goose, papier-mache, mc pnt, spring legs, squeaks, rprs, 6" 150.00
Rooster, cloth/wood/paper/feathers, silent, 7", G- 60.00
Rooster, on springs, mtd on squeak box, 12", EX 200.00
Rooster, papier-mache, minor pnt chips, rpl leather, 7", VG 200.00
Rooster, spring legs, 4" cage, pops out when door opens, EX 95.00
Rooster in wooden cage, felt & feather covering, silent, 4½" 78.00
Sheep, papier-mache w/orig mc pnt, squeaks, 4¼" 170.00
Sheep in cage, wood/paper, silent, 5¾" 150.00

Pull Toys

Camel, off-set wheel action, A Bergman, pnt tin, 9¼", EX 1,650.00
Duck, papier-mache on wooden base w/cb wheels, mc pnt, 4" ...115.00
Geese (3), papier-mache on spring legs, CI wheels, mc pnt, 10" L ..825.00
Horse, blk mohair, steel eyes, leatherette tack, 7¾", EX 150.00
Horse, wood w/CI wheels, worn pnt, mane/tail traces, 16x20" ...195.00
Horse on oversz chair cart, worn mc pnt on tin, 5" 165.00
Horse-drawn CI wagon w/heart-shaped wheels & bell, 13", VG ...550.00
Sheep, wood/wool/papier-mache, tin wheels, lt wear, 7¼" 360.00
Turkey, pnt tin, wings flap, 1800s, 5¼", G 165.00

Schoenhut

Acrobat lady, bsk head, long neck, 8", EX 425.00
Alligator, glass eyes, EX 500.00
Alligator, pnt eyes, regular, EX 300.00
Ball, EX 65.00
Barney Google, fabric clothes, 7", VG 150.00
Chair, EX 12.50
Chinese acrobat, wooden pressed head, EX 435.00
Deer, glass eyes, VG 650.00
Dollhouse, sm, EX 265.00
Donkey, pnt eyes, reduced, EX 50.00
Felix the Cat, paper label, 4", EX 165.00
Felix the Cat, paper label, 4", NM 225.00
Foxy Grandpa, Rolly Dolly, lg, EX 550.00
Golfer girl, EX 625.00
Gorilla, cvd ears, EX 1,500.00
Gorilla, pnt eyes, EX 1,450.00
Happy Hooligan, VG 950.00
Hobo, wooden pressed head, VG 260.00
Kangaroo, pnt eyes, EX 725.00

Ladder, NM 18.00
Lion tamer, bsk head, orig clothes, EX 285.00
Lion tamer, wooden pressed head, EX 250.00
Negro dude, wooden pressed head, reduced, EX ...435.00
Polar bear, pnt eyes, VG 625.00
Ringmaster, plaster face, reduced, EX 225.00
Table, EX 32.00
Teddy Roosevelt, VG 1,250.00
Tiger, pnt eyes, reduced, EX 295.00
Zebra, glass eyes, EX 800.00

Steiff

Margaret Steiff began making her felt stuffed toys in Germany in the late 1800s. The animals she made were tagged with an elephant in a circle. Her first teddy bear, made in 1903, became such a popular seller that she changed her tag to a bear. Felt stuffing was replaced with excelsior and wool; when it became available, foam was used. In addition to the tag, look for the 'Steiff' ribbon and the button inside the ear. For further information we recommend *Teddy Bears and Steiff Animals*, a full-color identification and value guide by Margaret Fox Mandel, available from Collector Books or your public library. See also Teddy Bears.

Bear, mohair, hump, w/button, ca 1935-40, 13½", M 1,250.00
Beaver, Bucky, mohair & felt, wooden teeth, '50s, 38", EX 725.00
Cat, Susi, brn mohair, complete ID, 4" 60.00
Cow on wheels, mohair, glass eyes, felt hoofs, '50s, 21", EX 395.00
Cow w/udders, collar & bell, w/button & tag, 10" 275.00
Deer, brn mohair, w/button & tag, 6½", M 68.00

Dog, Molly, orange tag, 4", NM, $125.00.

Dog, Scotty, blk mohair, w/chest tag, 4", M 185.00
Elephant, Jumbo, w/button & chest tag, 9", NM 200.00
Giraffe, plush, glass eyes, on platform, w/ID, 1950s, 98" 2,500.00
Hedgehog, Mecki, all ID, 6½", M 120.00
Horse on wheels, felt, button eyes, 1913, 9x9½", VG 385.00
Kaola bear, script button, stock tag, 5" 200.00
Kitten, striped plush, w/button & tag, 2½", M 65.00
Lamb, woolly blk, w/wht tag, 5", NM 25.00
Lobster, red mohair, complete ID, 11", NM 575.00
Mallard duck, w/chest tag, 4½", NM 100.00
Mickey Mouse, bright colors, w/2 tags, 7" 1,900.00
Mouse, woolly gray, w/button & tag, 1½", M 25.00
Owl, Wittie, brn mohair, complete ID, 4", M 60.00
Raccoon, Raccy, w/tag, 6", NM 150.00
Raven, woolly blk, metal ft, script button, stock tag, 3" 32.00
Seal, Robby, complete ID, 9", M 350.00
Skunk, Phuey, begging, script button/stock tag, 8", NM 300.00
Teddy baby, wool plush, linen pads, w/collar/bell, '30s, 12" 545.00
Teddy Clown, jtd, mohair, glass eyes, 1928, 18", M 1,450.00

Tiger, Bengal; open mouth w/teeth, w/button, 9", M 450.00
Tiger, reclining, complete ID, 10x19", NM 325.00
Vulture, mohair/felt/plastic, w/button, 1950s, 22½", EX 715.00

Toy Soldiers

Unique to this country are what are called 'Dimestore' soldiers; they were made by various companies from the 1930s and until sometime in the 1950s. The most common are Barclay, Manoil, and Jones (hollow cast lead); Grey Iron (cast iron); and Auburn (rubber). They're about 4 to 4½" high. They were sold in Woolworth and Kresge's 5 & 10 Stores (most for just five cents), hence the name 'Dimestore.' Marx made tin soldiers for use in target gun games; these sell for about $4.00. Condition is most important as these toys were made to play with. They're most often found with much of the paint worn off. In the listings that follow, prices are for examples in excellent condition which means they show very little wear. Please remember that these pieces are only representative. There were over 600 made, plus a number of others by minor makers such as Tommy Toy and All-Nu, all of which are higher priced. Serious collectors should to refer to *Collecting Toys* (1993) or *Toy Soldiers* (1992), both by Richard O'Brien, Books Americana, Inc. Reference numbers are those used in O'Brien's books and are considered the standard for the hobby. Another very popular toy soldier has been made by Britains of England since 1893. They are smaller and more detailed than 'Dimestores,' and variants number in the thousands. O'Brien's Toy Soldier book has over 200 pages devoted to Britains and other foreign makers. Our advisor for this category is Tim O'Callaghan; he is listed in the Directory under Michigan.

Auburn, A002, infantry private 12.00
Auburn, A006, Foreign Legion private 18.50
Auburn, A014, Red Cross doctor 32.50
Auburn, A022, sniper, crawling, rifle on bk 70.00
Auburn, A036, motor scout 40.00
Barclay, B005, flagbearer, short stride, tin helmet 24.00
Barclay, B010, machine gunner, long stride, kneeling 20.00
Barclay, B013, sniper, long stride, tin helmet, firing 22.50
Barclay, B023, officer w/sword, short stride 26.50
Barclay, B029, soldier w/gas mask charging, cast helmet 28.00
Barclay, B030, bugler, long stride, tin helmet 17.50
Barclay, B035, West Point officer, short stride 18.00
Barclay, B041, Italian officer 200.00
Barclay, B054, Naval officer, short stride 95.00
Barclay, B067, telephone operator 17.50
Barclay, B071, sentry 16.50
Barclay, B086, sharpshooter, short stride 20.00
Barclay, B104, wounded, tin helmet 16.50
Barclay, B111, cook peeling potatoes 24.00
Barclay, B132, w/field phone, cast helmet 65.00
Barclay, B146, surgeon & soldier 115.00
Barclay, B211, marching 24.00
Barclay, B236, bugler 12.50
Barclay, B256, wounded head & arm 20.00
Grey Iron, G003, Colonial color bearer, rare 365.00
Grey Iron, G005, cadet, early version 16.50
Grey Iron, G023, doughboy w/bayonet 22.50
Grey Iron, G024, cavalryman, early 35.00
Grey Iron, G029, doughboy charging 15.00
Grey Iron, G043, Royal Canadian mounted policeman 45.00
Grey Iron, G061, machine gunner 15.00
Grey Iron, G066, sailor, wht uniform 16.50
Grey Iron, G098, wounded, on crutches 42.50
Grey Iron, G111, Foreign Legion bomber 38.00
Jones, J012, seated, w/rifle 75.00

Jones, J020, flag bearer; J013, officer pointing, $225.00 each.

Jones, J018, ammunition carrier, scarce	385.00
Jones, J028, doctor w/medical bag	78.00
Jones, J032, marching, carrying rifle	112.50
Manoil, M001, flag bearer, hollow base	77.50
Manoil, M010, officer, 2nd version	20.00
Manoil, M015, drummer	36.00
Manoil, M023, sailor, hollow base	45.00
Manoil, M025, marine, hollow base	70.00
Manoil, M039, machine gunner, seated	25.00
Manoil, M048, sniper	20.00
Manoil, M058a, stretcher carrier w/medical kit	95.00
Manoil, M062, soldier charging w/bayonet	37.50
Manoil, M066, kneeling w/bayonet	65.00
Manoil, M080, motorized machine gunner	45.00
Manoil, M088, parachute jumper	22.50
Manoil, M101, lineman & telephone pole w/oval base	90.00

Trains

Electric trains were produced as early as the late 19th century. Names to look for are Lionel, Ives, and American Flyer.

The following listings were prepared by our advisor, Bruce C. Greenberg (see the Directory under Maryland), and are taken from his comprehensive publications on Lionel, American Flyer, and Ives trains. The prices presented are the most common versions of each item. In many cases, there are several other variations often having a substantially higher value. Identification numbers given in the listings below actually appear on the item.

American Flyer 283, S Gauge engine w/tender, EX	65.00
American Flyer 332DC, S Gauge engine w/tender, EX	380.00
American Flyer 332DC, S Gauge engine w/tender, G	80.00
American Flyer 360, 361 S Gauge diesels, EX	175.00
American Flyer 360, 361 S Gauge diesels, G	45.00
Ives 11, O Gauge steam engine w/tender, EX	250.00
Ives 11, O Gauge steam engine w/tender, G	110.00
Ives 1118, O Gauge Steam engine w/tender, EX	150.00
Ives 1118, O Gauge steam engine w/tender, G	75.00
Ives 1132, Wide Gauge steam engine w/tender, 1921-26, EX	900.00
Ives 1132, Wide Gauge steam engine w/tender, 1921-26, G	450.00
Ives 3240, 1 Gauge electric engine, 1912-20, EX	800.00
Ives 3240, 1 Gauge electric engine, 1912-20, G	400.00
Ives 3241, Wide Gauge electric engine, 1921-25, EX	200.00
Ives 3241, Wide Gauge electric engine, 1921-25, G	100.00
Ives 3243, Wide Gauge electric engine, 1921-28, EX	600.00
Ives 3243, Wide Gauge electric engine, 1921-28, G	350.00

Lionel 1668, O Gauge steam engine w/tender, 1937-41, EX	130.00
Lionel 1668, O Gauge steam engine w/tender, 1937-41, G	70.00
Lionel 2037, O Gauge steam engine/tender, 1954-55, 57-63, EX	90.00
Lionel 2037, O Gauge steam entine/tender, 1954-55, 57-63, G	50.00
Lionel 224, O Gauge steam engine w/tender, 1938-42, EX	100.00
Lionel 224, O Gauge steam engine w/tender, 1938-42, G	80.00
Lionel 2343, O Gauge diesels, 2 units, EX	500.00
Lionel 2343, O Gauge diesels, 2 units, G	200.00
Lionel 252, O Gauge electric engine, 1926-32, EX	150.00
Lionel 252, O Gauge electric engine, 1926-32, G	100.00
Lionel 380, Std Gauge electric engine, 1923-27, EX	400.00
Lionel 380, Std Gauge electric engine, 1923-27, G	200.00
Lionel 400E, Std Gauge steam engine, 1931-40, EX	2,300.00
Lionel 400E, Std Gauge steam engine, 1931-40, G	1,200.00
Lionel 408E, Std Gauge electric engine, 1927-36, EX	1,400.00
Lionel 408E, Std Gauge electric engine, 1927-36, G	700.00
Lionel 42, Std Gauge electric engine, 1913-23, rnd hood, EX	600.00
Lionel 42, Std Gauge electric engine, 1913-23, rnd hood, VG	250.00
Lionel 50, 027 Gauge gang car, 1954-64, EX	60.00
Lionel 50, 027 Gauge gang car, 1954-64, G	30.00
Lionel 58, 027 Gauge rotary snowplow, 1959-61, EX	625.00
Lionel 58, 027 Gauge rotary snowplow, 1959-61, G	275.00
Lionel 60, O Gauge trolley, 1955-58, EX	125.00
Lionel 60, O Gauge trolley, 1955-58, G	60.00

Lionel 681, O Gauge steam engine, with tender (not shown), 1950, NM, $200.00.

Lionel 700E, O Gauge steam engine w/tender, 1937-42, G	2,000.00
Lionel 726, O Gauge steam engine w/tender, 1946-49, EX	400.00
Lionel 726, O Gauge steam engine w/tender, 1946-49, G	200.00
Lionel 773, O Gauge steam engine w/tender, 1950, 64-66, EX	750.00
Lionel 773, O Gauge steam engine w/tender, 1950, 64-66, G	375.00
Lionel 8, Std Gauge electric engine, 1925-32, EX	200.00
Lionel 8, Std Gauge electric engine, 1925-32, G	110.00

Miscellaneous

Noah's ark, pine, worn pnt, wire nails, 19½"+14 animals	580.00
Noah's ark, pnt wood, flat figures etc, 15½", G	150.00
Push toy, clown on unicycle, articulated, pnt wood, 23¼"	325.00
Puzzle blocks, farm animals, Germany, VG in box	35.00
Puzzle blocks, zoo animals, Germany, Victorian, EX in box	95.00
Rocking horse, cloth covered, w/saddle, swivel base, 30x34", EX	500.00

Trade Signs

Trade signs were popular during the 1800s. They were usually made in an easily recognizable shape that one could mentally associate with the particular type of business it was to represent, especially appropriate in the days when many customers could not read!

Apothecary, mortar & pestle, zinc, 3-D, 36x23" dia, VG 650.00
Barber, wooden pole, blk & silver pnt, 74", VG 150.00
Doctor, Dr Chas H Higgins..., silver pnt on blk, wood, 12x36" ..400.00
Glasses Fitted, rvpt letters on glass, brass fittings, 28", EX 675.00
J&P Coats, cabinet, oak, ribbed roll opening, 24x31x11", EX 550.00
Keene Ice Skates, ice skate form, NP CI, 8x10x37½", VG 7,250.00
Key form, 2-sided cast metal, EX 85.00
Optometrist, CI fr w/glass lenses, worn pnt, 18", G 500.00
Painter, palette form, mc pnt on wood, ca 1880, 32x29", EX ..1,320.00
Pretzel form, compo, used in barroom, 14x20x2", G 150.00
Shotgun, pnt wood, rpl triggers, 22x167x8", VG 1,900.00
Stable, horse's head, cvd/laminated wood, 30", VG 990.00
Valley Shoe Service, 3-D shoe form, pnt wood, 60" L, VG 300.00
Watchmaker, pocket watch, CI fr, rpt dial, 37x20x2", G 100.00
Watchmaker, pocket watch, pnt/cvd wood, 29x21" dia 1,555.00
Watchmaker, pocket watch, rvpt on convex glass/gold rpt, 13" .250.00
Watchmaker, pocket watch, wood w/mat brd face, gold pnt, 24" ..330.00

Tramp Art

Today considered a type of American folk art, tramp art was primarily made from the end of the Civil War until the 1930s. Often produced by tramps and hobos from wooden materials which could be scavenged (crates and cigar boxes, for instance), articles such as jewelry boxes and picture frames were usually decorated by chip carving and then stained. Some of them were painted; the best were polychromed. Our advisors for this category are Matt Lippa and Elizabeth Schaaf; they are listed in the Directory under Alabama.

Sewing box, chip carved, double pedestal, five drawers, 1900s, 18x11x17", EX, $795.00.

Box, appl dbl horseshoes & birds, chip cvd, hinged, 7x10x6", EX ..240.00
Box, chip cvd, dk gr pnt, hinged top, 1900s, 7x9x5½", EX 200.00
Box, chip cvd (10-layer), ftd, dk lacquer, 1890s, 14x12x10", VG ..475.00
Box, chip cvd (5-layer), 4-drw, from cigar boxes, 1900, 35x7x6" ..385.00
Box, sewing; chip cvd, dbl ped, 5-drw, 1900s, 18x11x7", EX 745.00
Clock case, church form, 4 to 7 layers, lacquer, 1880s, 13" 525.00
Comb case, chip cvd (10 to 15 layers), brn pnt, 1900s, 36x18" ...1,650.00
Comb case, chip cvd (5-layer), mc pnt, 1920s, 18x12½x5" 425.00
Cradle, softwoods, sq & rnd nails, varnish, crude, 1870s, 16" 595.00
Dresser, chip cvd (5 to 6 layers), 4-drw, wht pnt, 1910 ....2,000.00
Dresser, chip cvd (5 to 8 layers), porc pulls, 1900s, 28x12" 400.00
Frame, chip cvd, heart shapes, fence-like border, 20x18" 350.00
Frame, simple chipping (8-layer), silver pnt, 1920, 12x13" 275.00
Lodge, 4-story Bavarian, w/fretwork, pnt/stain, 48x24x8" 4,000.00
Match box holder/ashtray, chip cvd, gold pnt, '20s, 9½x3x3" 85.00
Mirror frame, simple notched bands, 12x13" 95.00
Planter, 16-layer ped base, 8-sided (9-layer), 1900, 10x8" 350.00

Traps

Though of interest to collectors for many years, trap collecting has gained in popularity over the past ten years in particular, causing prices to appreciate rapidly. Traps are usually marked on the pan as to manufacturer, and the condition of these trademarks are important when determining their value. Grading is as follows:

Good: one-half of pan legible.
Very Good: legible in entirety, but light.
Fine: legible in entirety, with strong lettering.
Mint: in like-new, shiny condition.
Our advisor for this category is Boyd Nedry; he is listed in the Directory under Michigan. Prices listed here are for traps in fine condition.

Acme, mousetrap, wood snap 18.00
Adirondack, trip wire 300.00
Alexander, sz C 250.00
All-Steel #2, dbl long spring 50.00
Arrow #4, underspring 85.00
Austin Humane 22.00
Auto-Set, mousetrap, wood snap 8.00
Beaten Path, rat trap, metal 25.00
Bell Spring #1¼, single long spring 125.00
Bergs Automatic Mousetrap, tin 18.00
Bigelow Killer, #1 ....12.00
Blake & Lamb, #1, single long spring 3.00
Bonafied Mousetrap, wood snap 18.00
Buffalo Bill Rat Trap, wood snap 15.00
Bullock Jump, Self Setter #1 ....225.00
Cabela's #3, dbl coil spring 8.00
Catchemalive, live mousetrap, tin 125.00
Champion #1, single long spring 5.00
Chasse Mousetrap, wood, 3-hole choker 40.00
Cinch Mole 20.00
Clipper Killer 50.00
Cobra, mousetrap, metal snap 4.00
Cooper Clutch, dbl jaws 45.00
Cortland #2, dbl long spring 125.00
Cosey's Killer, pan type 30.00
Crago Clutch #7 ....225.00
Dauffer Killer 30.00
Dearborn #1½, single long spring 200.00
Delusion Live Mouse, wood & tin 45.00
Diamond #21½, single long spring 6.00
E-Z-K #2, mousetrap, Pratt Mfg Co, wood snap 10.00
Eclipse #2, dbl underspring 45.00
Economy #3, dbl long spring 45.00
Electrocuter, mouse killer, blk plastic 25.00
Elenchik #1½, dbl coil spring 12.00
End-O-Mice, throwaway mousetrap 10.00
Evans Fish & Mousetrap, brass 225.00
Ezy Set Mouse, metal snap 20.00
Fairy Mousetrap, live trap by H&R 75.00
Funsten Flotrap, metal 350.00
Gabriel Game & Fish Trap 250.00
Gibbs #0, coil spring 20.00
Gibbs Dope Trap #3, dbl long spring 300.00
Gibbs Gladiator Mousetrap, metal snap 20.00
Gibbs Live Muskrat 350.00
Gomber Beaten Path, mousetrap, metal 18.00
Half Moon Mousetrap, tin, choker 40.00
Hawley & Norton #3, dbl long spring 35.00
Hector #0, single long spring 30.00

Helfrich #750, dbl coil spring 65.00
Hell Cat Mouse Trap, metal, auto set 18.00
Hero Mouse Trap, wood snap, Scotland 10.00
Herter's #4, dbl coil spring 10.00
Hibbard Rat Trap, wood snap 10.00
Hotchkiss-Sons #2, dbl long spring 60.00
Hunter Killer 15.00
Jack Frost Killer 15.00
Jillson Mole Trap, spear type 135.00
Ketch 2, preset wht plastic mousetrap 6.00
Ketchum #1, runway trap 30.00
Kitty-Got-Cha, mousetrap, plastic 40.00
Kleflock #1, killer 18.00
Knapp #1½, dbl coil spring 8.00
Last Gasp, mousetrap, wood snap 10.00
Little Champ, mousetrap, plastic, choker 16.00
Lohmar #3, dbl coil spring 20.00
Manning #9, dbl coil spring 95.00
Montgomery #2, dbl coil spring 6.00
Nash Mole Choker 6.00
Newhouse #1, single long spring 20.00
Newhouse #4, dbl long spring 35.00
Newhouse #6, bear trap, Animal Trap Co 750.00
Oberto #3, dbl underspring 30.00
Out-O-Sight Mole 20.00
Pioneer #1, single long spring 5.00
Prott #1¼, single long spring 35.00
PS Mfg Co #2, dbl long spring 35.00
PS&W #1, single long spring 8.00
Quigly, rat trap, wood snap 15.00
Rice Sq Jaw Killer 22.00
Runway Mousetrap, metal 16.00
Sabo-Den Trap 95.00
Safe Set, mousetrap, metal 25.00
Sargent #2, dbl long spring 35.00
Shene #3, coil spring 75.00
Stephens Snow Trap 450.00
Sure Catch, rat trap, wood snap 6.00
Taylor FC Special #2, dbl long spring 18.00
Thumb set, mousetrap, metal 18.00
Trailzend #5, dbl long spring 500.00
Triumph #2, dbl long spring 14.00
Triumph #2XK, dbl coil spring 14.00
Triumph #34X, master grip, dbl coil spring 90.00
True Value #1, single long spring 6.00
U-Neek, mousetrap, glass, by Otto Kamphne 85.00
Union Hardware #2, dbl long spring 70.00
Victor #0, single underspring 8.00
Victor Dbl Shot #2 ....18.00
Webley #2, dbl long spring 15.00
Western Exterminator, rat trap, wood snap 5.00
Winona Mouse Trap, metal snap 8.00
Wood & Waters Killer 8.00

Trivets

Although strictly a decorative item today, the original purpose of the trivet was much more practical. They were used to protect table tops from hot serving dishes, and irons heated on the kitchen range were placed on trivets during use to protect work surfaces. The first patent date was 1869; many of the earliest trivets bore portraits of famous people or patriotic designs. Florals, birds, animals, and fruit were other favored motifs. Watch for remakes of early original designs. Some of these are marked Wilton, Emig, Wright, Iron Art, and V.M. for Virginia Metalcrafters. However, many of these reproductions are becoming collectible in the '90s. Expect to pay considerably less for these than for the originals, since they are abundant.

Brass

Cutouts, ped ft, 9½x7" dia 100.00
Flatiron shape, open center, 10x3¼" 95.00

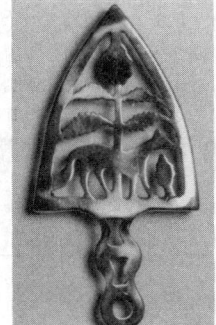

Fox and tree openwork on flatiron shape, 7¼", $150.00.

Heart form w/greyhound cut-out center, 3 cutouts in hdl, 9" 95.00
Horse in center, 3-leg fireplace type, 3½x6" dia 85.00
Outer ring contains lg star, 6" 95.00
Repousse w/hand stippled ground, Arts & Crafts era, 7" sq 75.00
Scalloped border, smooth top, early 1800s, 3½x8" 150.00
Star eng on octagonal shape, 4 short ft, 6½" 60.00
6-point star in hexagon, 3-ftd, 8½" 85.00
8-petal center, wrought iron legs, trn wood hdl, 12½" 125.00

Cast Iron

Cathedral pattern, 3¾x1⅝" 15.00
Circular, 3 rod ft, 1800s, lg 80.00
Geo Washington portrait relief on flatiron shape, 9¼" L 300.00
Hearts, flatiron shape, ftd, 8" 95.00
Open star & fan, Cleveland Foundry, for flatiron 28.00
Pineapple & Scroll, Wilton 12.00
Scalloped rnd form w/7 open concentric hearts, 7½" 115.00
Star in circle w/in flatiron shape, 8¼" 40.00
Strauss Comfort Gas Iron, ornate, w/legs, lg 25.00

Wrought Iron

Adjustable pot rest, rnd w/3 legs, 6x25x9" dia 165.00
Dbl heart, shoe ft, blk pnt, 4½" 165.00
Heart & compass starflower cutouts, boot ft, horn hdl, 11¼" L ..525.00
Heart shape, penny ftd, wood hdl, 1700s, 11½" 235.00
Rnd, 3 penny ft, 2¼x4½" dia 65.00
Rope twist open quatrefoil, matching legs, shoe ft, 4½" 95.00
Tiny curls at tips of ft, wood hdl, 1½x5¾x4" 95.00

Trolls

The modern-day version of the troll was designed in 1952 by Helena and Marti Kuuskoski of Tamperee, Finland. Those made by Dam and those marked with a horseshoe are among the most valuable, since both are made from the original Kuuskoski design. Many copies have been produced, the best of which are the Wishniks, made by the Uneeda Doll Company. These were first marketed in 1963 and are currently still available. Troll animals are scarce, and values are rising. New Dam animals are easily distinguished from the old ones, and though they are popular sellers, it's the old issues that hold their value and collectors' interest. Our advisor for this category is Roger Inouye; he is listed in the Directory under California.

Ballerina, red hair, gr eyes, felt clothes, Thomas Dam, 5½" 55.00
Batman, red fur hair, gr eyes, mask, bat on chest, unmk, 3" 20.00
Boy or girl bank, felt clothes, any coloring, Thomas Dam, 6" 25.00
Boy or girl pirate bank, red hair, gr eyes, Thomas Dam, 8" 35.00
Carrying case, troll on lid, 'Niks & Naks,' 4x6" 15.00
Clothes, Uneeda Wishnik, 3", M in orig 5x5" header card 20.00
Cow, wht hair, brn eyes, Design Dam, 1964, 3½" 45.00
Devil w/horns, any coloring, Reisler of Denmark, 3½" 15.00
Dog, spacesuit or business suit, Royalty Designs of FL, 3½" 25.00
Donkey, any coloring, finger puppet, Dam Things, 3" 45.00
Elephant, any coloring, finger puppet, Dam Things, 3" 45.00
Elephant, flesh-color skin, brn hair & eyes, Dam Things, 7" 125.00
Eskimo, brn hair & eyes, pnt clothes, Dam Things, 1965, 5½" 75.00
Horse, gray hair, brn eyes, Dam Things, 3" 45.00
Judge, orange eyes, gray hair, Uneeda Wishnik, 5½" 20.00
Lion, Dam Things, wht hair, brn eyes, 6" 75.00
Nude, any color hair & eyes, unmk, 3" 8.00
Nude, any color hair & eyes, unmk, 5½" 10.00
Nude, any hair & eyes, red lips, unmk, 13" 85.00
Nude pencil topper, any coloring, Scandia House, 1½" 12.00
Playboy Bunny, bl hair & eyes, Dam Things, complete, 12" 135.00
Playboy Bunny, clip hands, felt clothes, unmk, 3½" 15.00
Sailor, bl & wht outfit, Dam Things, 11" 100.00
Teddy bear, gr plush body, unmk, 18" 55.00
Troll House, molded furnishings, Standard Plastics, 9x12" 15.00
Troll Village, Marx, MIB 150.00

Trunks

In the the days of steamboat voyages, stagecoach journeys, and railroad travel, trunks were used to transport clothing and personal belongings. Some, called 'dome top' or 'turtle backs,' were rounded on top to better accommodate milady's finery. Today some of the more interesting examples are used in various ways in home decorating. For instance, a flat-topped trunk may become a coffee table, while a smaller dome style may be 'home' for antique dolls or a teddy bear collection. In the listings that follow, when one dimension is given, it is length.

Camphorwood, Chinese export, late 1800s, 15x34x16" 500.00
Dome top, blk splotches pnt on red, 1800s, 10x34x12" 600.00
Dome top, dvtl pine, orig brn grpt, European, 35" 85.00
Dome top, iron butt hinges, bl sponge pnt, dvtl, 13x24x12" 180.00
Dome top, pine, wrought iron straps/hinges/hdls, German, 51" ..500.00
Dome top, wire hinges, mc pnt w/flower decor, 12x25x13" 300.00

Tuthill

The Tuthill Glass Company operated in Middletown, New York, from 1902 to 1923. Collectors look for signed pieces and those in an identifiable pattern. Condition is of utmost importance, and examples with brilliant cutting and intaglio (natural flowers and fruits) combined fetch the highest prices.

Bowl, allover brilliant cuttings, 8-sided, 2x9¼x6½" 390.00

Bowl, floral wreath intaglio w/berries & fern, 2¼x9¼" 75.00
Candy dish, floral intaglio, hobstar cutting, 5½" 225.00
Compote, cherries intaglio (unpolished), 7" 225.00
Compote, vintage intaglio, rolled rim, 4x8" 450.00
Creamer & sugar bowl, Rosemere, dbl notched hdls, 4" 250.00
Creamer & sugar bowl, wheel-cut flowers & stems, squat, 2½" ...200.00
Cruet, Primrose, orig teardrop stopper, sgn 265.00
Mayonnaise set, Phlox, 2-pc, 3" 300.00
Olive dish, Primrose & Geometric, 3½x7½" 235.00
Plate, hobstars & fan, sgn, 6" 70.00
Shakers, flowers/vines cutting, hobstar neck band, 3½", pr 120.00
Shot glass, Primrose 40.00
Tazza, vintage intaglio, sgn, 4x6" 225.00
Tray, heavy brilliant cuttings & floral pattern, sgn, 8x5" 300.00
Tray, Rosemere & Geometric, 7½x3" 225.00
Tray, vintage intaglio, 7½x5½" 425.00
Tray, Woodlily cutting, 12" dia 475.00
Vase, bud; Phlox, 6" 150.00
Vase, poppies & leaves intaglio, rolled shoulder, 5x6" 300.00
Vase, sweet pea; vintage intaglio, ruffled, sgn, 4½" 325.00

Typewriters

The first commercially successful typewriter was the Sholes and Glidden, introduced in 1874. By 1882 other models appeared, and by the 1890s dozens were on the market. At the time of the First World War, the ranks of typewriter-makers thinned, and by the 1920s only a few survived.

Collectors informally divide typewriter history into the pioneering period, up to about 1890; the classic period, from 1890 to 1920; and the modern period, since 1920. There are two broad classifications of early typewriters: (1) Keyboard machines, in which depression of a key prints a character and via a shift key prints up to three different characters per key. (2) Index machines, in which a chart of all the characters appears on the typewriter; the character is selected by a pointer or dial and is printed by operation of a lever or other device. Even though index typewriters were simpler and more primitive than keyboard machines, they were none-the-less a later development, designed to provide a cheaper alternative to the standard keyboard models that were selling for upwards of $100.00. Eventually second-hand keyboard typewriters supplied the low-price customer, and index typewriters vanished except as toys. Both classes of typewriters appeared in a great many designs.

It is difficult, if not impossible, to assign standard market prices to early typewriters. Unlike collectors of postage stamps, carnival glass, etc., few people collect typewriters, so there is no active marketplace from which to draw stable prices. Also, condition is a very important factor, and typewriters can vary infinitely in condition. A third factor to consider is that an early typewriter achieves its value mainly through the skill, effort, and patience of the collector who restores it to its original condition, in which case its purchase price is insignificant. Some unusual-looking early typewriters are not at all rare or valuable, while some very ordinary-looking ones are scarce and could be quite valuable. No general rules apply. When no condition is indicated, the items listed below are assumed to be in excellent, unrestored condition. Our advisor for this category is Mike Brooks; he is listed in the Directory under California.

Am Typewriter...NY, blk enamel mechanism, mahog base, G 250.00
Blickensderfer #5, orig case, EX 135.00
Boston, index 1,500.00
Corona #3, folding, w/case 55.00
Duplex 500.00
Fitch, EX 500.00

Hall, index, EX 700.00
Hammond Multiplex, folding keyboard, orig cover, EX 100.00
Jewett, #1 ....400.00
Keystone 1,200.00
Lambert, index, w/case 600.00
Merritt, index, wood cover, instruction label in lid, EX 395.00
New Century Caligraph 300.00
Oliver #5 Standard Visible 75.00
Oliver #9, EX decals, VG 60.00
Postal 350.00
Remington, #Z 150.00
Royal, Hebrew letters, ca 1920, EX 350.00
Sholes & Glidden, 1st mass-produced, ca 1874, EX 1,000.00
Underwood, Hebrew-character keys, 1900s, EX 250.00
Victor, index, rare, EX 500.00

Uhl Pottery

Founded in Evansville, Indiana, in 1849 by German immigrants, the Uhl Pottery was moved to Huntingburg, Indiana, in 1908 because of the more suitable clay available there. They produced stoneware — Acorn Ware jugs, crocks, and bowls — which were marked with the acorn logo and 'Uhl Pottery.' They also made mugs, pitchers, and vases in simple shapes and solid glazes marked with a circular ink stamp containing the name of the pottery and 'Huntingburg, Indiana.' The pottery closed in the mid-1940s. Those seeking additional information about Uhl pottery are encouraged to contact the Uhl Collectors' Society, whose address is listed in the Directory under Clubs, Newsletters, and Catalogs.

Ashtray, brn, #140 ....50.00
Ashtray, pig, wht 175.00
Bowl, batter; bl, mk, 8" 80.00
Bowl, mixing; basketweave, brn, 8" 45.00
Bowl, mixing; reverse pyramid, bl, 7" 60.00
Bowl, Tulip, bl, #122, 8½" 75.00
Candle holder, w/shield, hand trn, gr 225.00
Casserole, bl, mk, #529, 3-pt 60.00
Casserole, bl, stick hdl, #200 ....70.00
Cookie jar, globe, yel 65.00
Cookie jar, pk, mk, #522 ....190.00
Feeder, chicken, UCO, tank & base, #9-A 125.00
Feeder, dog, yel, #145, 7½" 75.00
Feeder, Scottie dog, bl, #129, 5" 125.00
Jar, Acorn Ware, ice water, 5-gal 275.00
Jar, Acorn Ware, preserve, brn on wht, 1-gal 85.00
Jar, Acorn Ware, steam table, wht, 8½" 60.00
Jar, Acorn Ware, 12-gal 90.00
Jar, Acorn Wares, 2-gal 35.00
Jar, butter; wht, mk, 2-lb 40.00
Jar, grease; pk 75.00
Jug, Acorn Ware, brn on wht, 2-gal 45.00
Jug, Acorn Ware, harvest, w/air vent, wire bail, 1-gal 135.00
Jug, Acorn Ware, sorghum, dbl hdls, brn on wht, 10-gal 140.00
Jug, Acorn Ware, wht, 5-gal 70.00
Jug, baseball, wht, mini 60.00
Jug, bellied, bl, #176, ½-pt 45.00
Jug, canteen, brn, ½-pt 35.00
Jug, Egyptian, bl, #141, 16-oz 50.00
Jug, Grecian, bl, #162 ....75.00
Jug, Merry Christmas, brn on wht, 1942, mini 225.00
Jug, shoulder, Great Smoky Mtns advertising, mini 175.00
Mug, coffee; pk, 8-oz 50.00

Pitcher, acid, brn, mk, ½-gal 60.00
Pitcher, bellied, bl & wht sponging, ½-gal 380.00
Pitcher, ice restrainer, pk, 5-pt 85.00

Pitcher, Lincoln portrait embossed on blue, 1-pint, $295.00.

Pitcher, Lincoln, bl, incised mk, 2-qt 500.00
Pitcher, Lincoln, bl, incised mk, 3-qt 650.00
Pitcher, Lincoln, bl, 1-qt 375.00
Pitcher, Lincoln, bl, ½-pt 225.00
Pitcher, rustic, brn, bbl form, 100-oz 60.00
Plate, bl, mk, 6" 50.00
Plate, pk, mk, 10" 70.00
Porch pedestal, brn, mk C-15, 16" 65.00
Porch pot, brn, mk C-14, 14" dia 50.00
Shoe, baby, tied shoestrings, wht, mk 55.00
Shoe, Dutch, pk, #-6 ....65.00
Shoes, lady's slippers, wht, mk, mini, pr 90.00
Stein, bl, flagon, 16-oz 45.00
Stein, bl, grape, 12-oz 100.00
Stein, tan, bbl form, mk, 16-oz 15.00
Stein, tan, bbl form, Rhinegold advertising, 20-oz 80.00
Stein, yel, bbl form, mk, mini, 3-oz 90.00
Vase, bl, #158, 5" 75.00
Vase, bud; bl, #22, mini, 3" 75.00
Vase, bud; wht, mk, #24, mini, 3½" 125.00
Vase, cemetery; bl, 5" dia 55.00
Vase, cut flower, bl, mk, #116, 5" 60.00
Vase, cut flower, blk, #114, 10" 35.00
Vase, orange blossom, pk, #118, 4" 85.00
Vase, yel, #153, 5" 40.00
Wren house, terra cotta, #525 ....285.00

Ungemach Pottery Company

Fred Ungemach began his career as a boy, jiggering for the Nelson McCoy Pottery of Roseville, Ohio. Later he worked for Thomas Watt in Hawthorne, Pennsylvania, then he returned to Roseville to work for the Ransbottom Pottery. In 1938 with the help of his daughter Mary, who was an employee of the Brush Pottery, he opened his own company in Roseville. The business was first known as the South Fork Pottery, but after several years and a number of expansions, the name was changed to the Ungemach Pottery Company (UPCO).

In June 1950 a flood demolished the plant, but it reopened in three weeks and continued to expand. In April 1966 the plant was struck by lightening and was destroyed again, but by September of the same year they were back in production. Then in 1984 the pottery was sold to the Friendship Pottery of Roseville, Ohio.

Ungemach produced a full line of wares including kitchen items, planters, vases, and novelty pieces and during the 1940s and '50s obtained an exclusive contract with Walt Disney Productions, Burbank, California, to produce Disney character planters. These pieces were marked with Disney copyrights only. Their other production pieces are marked in a variety of ways 'Ungemach, UPCO, Roseville,' and a few are not marked at all. Our advisors for this category are Brenda and Jerry Siegel; they are listed in the Directory under Missouri.

Bowl, fluted, rnd, brn, #762 ....**7.00**
Bowl, fruit; yel, #779, 7" **8.00**
Bread server, brn, mk Roseville #630, 10" **8.00**
Bread server, rust & brn, oval, #797 ....**9.00**
Candy server, bl, 10" **11.00**

Lamp, snowman's head, with black, red and green paint, no mark, 8½", $24.00.

Planter, bonsai, wht, #289, 9x6x3½" **10.00**
Planter, cactus, yel, 8" **8.00**
Planter, chalice, brn, mk Flora Plant UPCO, rare, 8" **16.00**
Planter, fluted star, tan, 5" **6.00**
Planter, hand thrown, gr, #489, 8" **9.00**
Planter, octagonal, tan, #755 ....**6.00**
Planter, rnd, tan, 6½" **4.00**
Planter, rnd, wht, #610, 4½" **4.00**
Strawberry pot, gr, 4" **6.00**

Unger Brothers

The Art Nouveau silver produced by Unger Brothers, who operated in Newark, New Jersey, from the early 1880s until 1909, is fast becoming very popular with today's collectors. In addition to tableware, they also made brushes, mirrors, powder boxes, and the like for milady's dressing table as well as jewelry and small personal accessories such as match safes and flasks. They often marked their products with a circle seal containing an intertwined 'UB' and '925 fine sterling.' In addition to sterling, a very limited amount of gold was also used. Note: This company made no pewter items; Unger designs may occasionally be found in pewter, but these are copies. Items dated in the mark or signed 'Birmingham' are English (not Unger).

Box, hinged lid, mk Unger/#B-2649, 1x4½" L, EX **180.00**
Box, very plain, #B2649, 3x5" **160.00**
Butter pick, Duvaine **100.00**
Cream ladle, Duvaine **65.00**
Cuff links, lady's head, pr **110.00**
Doll mirror, cupids, mini **350.00**
Doll rattle, w/bells, mini **295.00**
Glove stretcher, poppies & maidenhair fern **235.00**
Hairbrush, Lily **95.00**
Jelly cake server, Passaic **295.00**
Ladle, cream; Duvaine **95.00**
Ladle, mustard; Duvaine **125.00**

Nut scoop, Duvaine **165.00**
Pickle fork, Duvaine, 6¼" **65.00**
Sardine fork, Duvaine, lg **185.00**
Spoon, demitasse; Duvaine, gilt bowl **30.00**
Sugar spoon, Duvaine **60.00**
Teaspoon, Duvaine **35.00**
Tomato server, Duvaine **195.00**

Universal

Universal Potteries Incorporated operated in Cambridge, Ohio, from 1934 to 1956. Many lines of dinnerware and kitchen items were produced in both earthenware and semiporcelain. In 1956 the emphasis was shifted to the manufacture of floor and wall tiles, and the name was changed to the Oxford Tile Company, Division of Universal Potteries. The plant closed in 1976. Our advisor for this category is Ted Haun; he is listed in the Directory under Indiana.

Ballerina, bowl, vegetable; w/lid **12.00**
Ballerina, bowl, vegetable; 9" **6.00**
Ballerina, creamer & sugar bowl, w/lid **15.00**
Ballerina, gravy boat **10.00**
Ballerina, relish, 7" **5.00**
Calico Fruit, water jug **28.00**
California Fruit, bowl, w/lid, 5" **20.00**
California Fruit, custard **5.00**
Cattail, bowl, deep, 6" **10.00**
Cattail, bowl, vegetable; oval, 9" **12.00**
Cattail, butter dish, 1-lb **35.00**
Cattail, creamer & sugar bowl, w/lid **16.00**

Cattail, cup & saucer, $10.00.

Cattail, grease jar, stain **12.00**
Cattail, jug, water; w/stopper **30.00**
Cattail, pie plate **15.00**
Cattail, pie server **12.00**
Cattail, plate, dinner; 9" **12.00**
Cattail, plate, sherbet; 6" **5.00**
Cattail, platter, tab hdls, 11½" **14.00**
Cattail, soup, tab hdl, 6" **10.00**

Val St. Lambert

Since its inception in Belgium at the turn of the 19th century, the Val St. Lambert Cristalleries has been involved in the production of high quality glass, specializing in cameo. The factory is still in production. Our advisor for this category is Don Williams; he is listed in the Directory under Missouri.

Cameo

Bottle, scent; amber to clear, dmn & arch pattern **50.00**
Box, bl opaque w/fiery opal, basketweave, sgn, 3¾x4" **85.00**
Pitcher, tankard; daisies, bl on frost, metal rim, 12" **125.00**
Tumbler, acid-cut/gilt band w/ladies, cranberry bands, 5" **225.00**
Tumbler, classic figures, cranberry on clear w/gold, 5¼" **225.00**
Vase, fish/lotus, red on aqua, etched/gilt lobster, 9", EX **1,350.00**
Vase, leaves & pendants, cut/HP in violet on frost, 12½" **675.00**
Vase, poppies, lav on frost, waisted, 8" **450.00**
Vase, poppies, wine frost on frost, glossy wavy collar, 7" **300.00**

Valentines

Handmade Valentines date back to the mid-1700s in the United States; as time went on, increased interest resulted in other types of Valentine cards being made. Today Valentine collectors are not the only ones who buy; Valentines are often considered a desirable addition to other collections as well — Black memorabilia, advertising, transportation memorabilia, Walt Disney, cartoon and movie characters, etc. Besides examples representing these areas, 3-dimensionals and mechanical Valentines (1860s to the present) are becoming highly prized by many collectors. There are six qualifying specifications to consider when evaluating a Valentine card: age, size, category, manufacturer, artist signature, and condition. Our advisor for this category is Katherine Kreider; she is listed in the Directory under California.

Key: HCPP — honeycomb paper puff

Honeycomb paper puff, gazebo, 3 child musicians, Made in Germany, 10½x8¼", M, $125.00.

Airplane, 2-D, chromolitho, MIG, 1920s, 4⅜x3½x3" **30.00**
Airplane, 3-D, lobster on wing, MIG, 1920s, 9x8", NM **125.00**
Ambassador, 3-D, train, 1960, 7x10", EX **35.00**
Angel amid flowers, 2-D, chromolitho, MIG, 1900s, 3x4x2", NM ..**25.00**
Ballerina, chromolitho, HCPP tutu, MIG, 1927, 5¼x4½", EX **30.00**
Big-eyed boy, litho, cobweb center, 1900s, EX **75.00**
Big-eyed child rides mechanical duck, 5½x7", VG **35.00**
Big-eyed children in 1920s car w/dog, 2-D, 7x8x3", VG **75.00**
Big-eyed girl in bonnet, mechanical, litho, MIG, '23, 8x5", EX **45.00**
Big-eyed kids on HCPP atomizer, tab stand, '20s, 8x7½", NM ...**150.00**
Black child under sprinkling can, USA, 1940s, 5½x3½", NM **35.00**
Black harmonica player, USA, 1900s, 3¾x2¾", NM **40.00**
Brownie & Cub Scout, USA, 1950s, 6x3¼", EX **15.00**
Buster Brown, mechanical, chromolitho, MIG, 9¼x6½", NM ...**175.00**
Cagney, James; USA, 1935, 5⅞x3½", EX **45.00**
Cherub on HCPP base of 3-D windmill, chromolitho, 5½", NM ..**35.00**

Cherub w/butterfly net, 2-D, litho, MIG, 4x2½x1½", NM **55.00**
Choked to Death, dtd 1909, 7½x6", NM in orig box **175.00**
Cinderella-type coach, 3-D w/HCPP, 1900s, 11¼x13x6", VG **95.00**
Clapsaddle, cherub in cart w/hearts, 3-D, 4¼x6¼x2½", NM **75.00**
Cobweb, HP orig, 1850, 8x9", EX **250.00**
Dirigible, HCPP top, child in basket, tab stand, MIG, 4", EX **50.00**
Dopey, mechanical, Walt Disney Enterprises, 4¼x3", NM **75.00**
Drayton, Grace; 3-D, children w/pony, USA, 9⅜x7½", NM **125.00**
Dutch boy w/orig pc of Wrigley's gum, 6½x3½", NM **75.00**
Elephant w/clown, USA, 1940s, 4½x3½", NM **10.00**
Geppetto on raft, mechanical, Walt Disney Productions, '39, EX ...**65.00**
Girl & boy at piano, 2-D, MIG, 3⅜x4x1", EX **45.00**
Goat & cart, girl delivers milk, tab stand, USA, 10x7", VG **35.00**
Hallmark, 3-D, castle, 1948, 9x14", NM **50.00**
Halls Bros, dog w/felt ears, 1940s, 8½x6¾", VG **15.00**
Hanging, litho hearts, 4 tiers w/orig ribbon, 12", EX **75.00**
Harp, litho stands w/tab accented w/Victorian scraps, 7", EX **75.00**
HCPP, apple core w/2 litho children, USA, '20s, 10¼", NM **125.00**
HCPP basket & hearts, litho cherubs, ca 1925, 8½", EX **85.00**
Hold-to-light, 3-D children w/pk flowers, MIG, 8¼", NM **150.00**
Hot air balloon, litho w/orig ribbon, MIG, 9½x4", NM **150.00**
Howland, Esther; orig, 1845, EX, w/HP envelope **350.00**
Kautz, artist paints portrait, mechanical, '25, 6x4½", EX **35.00**
Kautz, boy in winter garb, mechanical, tab stand, 7⅜", EX **25.00**
Kautz, cat, mechanical, tab stand, USA, 1925, 4½x3½", NM **35.00**
Kautz, cowboy on horse, mechanical, tab stand, USA, 6¾", EX ...**45.00**
Loverville Telephone Card, cast-metal phone, 4x3¼", EX **75.00**
Manuscript type w/HP litho, 1845, 5x8", EX **100.00**
Mechanical, airplane, 1940s-50s, 3¼x4½", EX **8.00**
Mechanical, baseball player, USA, 1940s, 5½x3", NM **20.00**
Mechanical, bear on stump, Stecher Litho, tab stand, 5", EX **25.00**
Mechanical, chubby child on scales, MIG, 6¼x3¼", NM **25.00**
Mechanical, cow, head & neck moves, USA, '40s, 7¼x4¾", NM ..**20.00**
Mechanical, girl w/slate, litho, tab stand, 1924, 6x4", EX **20.00**
Mechanical, gypsy, USA, 6½x2¼", NM **15.00**
Mechanical, lobster, tab stand, MIG, 1927, 6¾x4½", EX **35.00**
Mechanical, miner panning for gold, Canada, 5½x3", EX **15.00**
Mechanical, parrot, chromolitho, tab stand, MIG, 6¾", EX **35.00**
Mechanical, Russian bear & child, tab stand, MIG, 8½", EX **55.00**
Native American w/orig feather, USA, 7x4", EX **35.00**
Nister, boy & girl, litho, Bavaria, 1900s, 4¾x3", EX **35.00**
Nister, mother & children, hanging litho, #114, 13x6½", VG **80.00**
Olive Oyle & Popeye, USA, 1940s, 5¾x5", EX **45.00**
Pinocchio, mechanical, Walt Disney Enterprises, 1938, 5", NM ..**75.00**
St Bernard dog, w/orig chain to doghouse, MIG, 10", VG **75.00**
Steamship, 4-D, all orig, MIG, 10½x6x3", 1900s, NM **250.00**
Tuck, Artistic Series, carriage/Blk Child/3-D flowers, 7", VG **95.00**
Tuck, girl w/orig ribbon in hair, Series #1557, 5x2", NM **75.00**
Tuck, horse-drawn carriage, 3-D, 6½x10⅜x4½", EX **175.00**
Uncle Sam, Made in USA, 1943, 5x6", VG **15.00**
3-D Victorian scene in open heart, To My..., MIG, 3½", NM **75.00**

Van Briggle

The Van Briggle Pottery of Colorado Springs, Colorado, was established in 1901 by Artus Van Briggle, whose early career had been shaped by such notables as Karl Langenbeck and Maria Nichols Storer. His quest for several years had been to perfect a completely flat matt glaze, and, upon accomplishing his goal, he opened his pottery. His wife, Anne, worked with him, and they, along with George Young, were responsible for the modeling of the wares. Their work typified the flow and form of the Art Nouveau movement, and the shapes they designed played as important a part in their success as their glazes.

Some of their most famous pieces were Despondency, Lorelei, and Toast Cup. Increasing demand for their work soon made it necessary to add to their quarters as well as their staff. Although much of the ware was eventually made from molds, each piece was carefully trimmed and refined before the glaze was sprayed on. Their most popular colors were Persian Rose, Ming Blue, and Mustard Yellow.

Van Briggle died in 1904, but the work was continued by his wife. New facilities were built; and by 1908, in addition to their artware, tiles, gardenware, and commercial lines were added. By the twenties the emphasis had shifted from art pottery to novelties and commercial wares. As late as 1970, reproductions of some of the early designs continued to be made. Until about 1920 most pieces were marked with the date and shape number; after that the AA mark was used.

Ashtray, Indian kneels/grinds corn, turq, sgn AB, '20s, 6" **125.00**
Bowl, pine cones, purple w/bl highlights, 1915, 5x9" **750.00**
Bowl vase, arrowroot leaves at shoulder, 2-tone bl, 5x9" **550.00**
Bowl vase, heart leaves, brn mottle, 1914, 3½x6¼" **450.00**
Bud vase, no emb, veined lime, long neck/squat base, '02, 6" **500.00**
Bud vase, swirling leaves, feathered teal, #129, '03, 7" **700.00**
Figurine, burro, turq, 3½" **65.00**
Figurine, nude w/shell in lap, Persian Rose, 7" **250.00**
Lamp, girl w/urn on shoulders, aubergine/gr, orig shade, 10" ...**1,000.00**
Lamp, girl w/urn on shoulders, bl-gr matt, orig shade, 10" **1,000.00**
Lamp, gourd form, bl-gr matt, orig floral shade, 7½" **600.00**
Vase, columbines at shoulder, dk bl w/maroon, 1916, 10" **700.00**

Vase, columbines on yellow, gourd form, #188, 1903, 6", $1,000.00.

Vase, crocuses, frog-skin gr, EX emb, #145, '08, 3½x4½" **1,200.00**
Vase, curving leaves, Persian Rose w/bl base, #26, 1916, 5" **350.00**
Vase, daffodils, bl crystalline w/red touches, 1903, 8", NM **1,300.00**
Vase, daisies, turq mottle, EX emb, #145, 1907-12, 12x5" **1,800.00**
Vase, floral, 4 hdls at recessed neck, #761, ca '08, 6" **550.00**
Vase, floral neck w/3 open hdls, lt bl w/purple, 1905, 9½" **800.00**
Vase, floral top, brn/yel w/gray crystalline, 1916, 11", EX **450.00**
Vase, irises/stems, gr/brn, 2 hdls at wide base, '20s, 13" **225.00**
Vase, Lady of the Lily, reclining nude, turq/bl, '20s, 11" **900.00**
Vase, leaves at wide top, fluted body, red w/gr, 1903, 7" **1,600.00**
Vase, long-stem floral, gr, #649, ca 1907-1912, 10" **500.00**
Vase, Lorelei, turq, pre-1935, 10" **700.00**
Vase, mistletoe, bl w/some crystalline, 1902, III, 5½" **1,600.00**
Vase, morning-glories, olive gr w/dk highlights, 1905, 6x5" **750.00**
Vase, narcissus/swirled relief stems, tan/gr, #40, '02, 11" **2,300.00**
Vase, no design, mustard yel, #269, 1906, 7¾" **700.00**
Vase, no design, wht w/gr & red highlights, 1906, X, 7" **400.00**

Vase, Nouveau lilies, tobacco w/yel mottle, #289, 1905, 10" ...**3,250.00**
Vase, Nouveau poppies, lt bl over red clay, #173, '05, 9½" **1,000.00**
Vase, peacock feathers, lt bl on bsk, #407, 1907, 16x8" **3,500.00**
Vase, peacock feathers, wht to purple, #231, '03, 5½x6" **2,000.00**
Vase, peacock feathers on shoulder, gr mottle, #231, '04, 5" **900.00**
Vase, pendant floral, curdled lime w/some red, #197, '03, 6" **900.00**
Vase, poppies on whiplash stems, gr/purple, 1908-11, #694, 7" ..**1,400.00**
Vase, poppy pods above long stems, lav/bl, ca '08, 7x4" **550.00**
Vase, poppy pods at rim/stems, dk bl, #830, ca 1911, 7½" **700.00**
Vase, spider in ring on front, gr/yel, #15, III, 4½" **700.00**
Vase, stylized floral, red/gr, #164, dtd 1904, 8½x7" **1,100.00**
Vase, stylized floral at rim, gr mottle w/red, 1902, 3x6" **700.00**
Vase, stylized hearts, gr variegated, bulbous, 1904, 4" **800.00**
Vase, stylized neck band, bl-gray mottle, 1907-12, 5x4½" **500.00**
Vase, stylized trefoils, bl-gray, EX emb, '02, 3½x3½" **900.00**
Vase, stylized tulips, EX emb, teal bl, #829, ca '08, 6x6" **900.00**
Vase, 3-tulip stem ea side, bl/gr, cone shape, '05, 17" **2,600.00**
Vase, 5 flowers at shoulder, stems, gr/tan, #836, 1913, 6" **465.00**

Vaseline

Vaseline, a greenish-yellow colored glass produced by adding uranium oxide to the batch, was produced during the Victorian era. It was made in smaller quantities than other colors and lost much of its popularity with the advent of the electric light. It was used for pressed tablewares, vases, whimseys, souvenir items, oil lamps, perfume bottles, drawer pulls and doorknobs. Pieces have been reproduced, and some factories still make it today in small batches. Vaseline glass will flouresce under an ultraviolet light. Our advisor for this category is Terry Fedosky; she is listed in the Directory under Kentucky.

Bottle, scent; oval panels, cut/faceted stopper, 4½" **110.00**
Bottle, scent; Ribbed Pillar Mold, blown stopper, 1850s, 6" **1,200.00**
Bottle, scent; w/vaseline Maltese Cross-like stopper, 4" **65.00**
Bowl, fruit; Dmn Quilt, 8" **60.00**
Creamer, Block, bulbous, ribbed top, scalloped rim, 2¼" **55.00**
Creamer, Daisy & Button w/Crossbar **42.50**
Creamer, Hobnail, sq mouth, 4¼x3¼" **225.00**
Cup, Dog & Cat, children's **28.00**
Hat, Daisy & Button, plain brim **38.00**
Paperweight, cut book shape, 1¾x4¼x2¼" **195.00**
Rose bowl, Button Panels **35.00**
Salt cellar, Two Panel, oval **18.00**
Tray, dresser; ca 1900, 8¾" **70.00**
Tumbler, Daisy & Button w/T'print Panel **35.00**

Venetian Glass

Venetian glass is a thin, fragile ware usually made in colors, often with internal gold or silver flecks. It was produced on the island of Murano, near Venice, as early as the 13th century. 20th-century glassware is always heavier and thicker than the older ware. Note: Only special 1920s pieces are commanding high prices. The '50s pieces have come down in price, because many of these companies are still in business today and are reissuing '50s designs. Ribbon-glass scent bottles with flower stoppers; small leaf-shape compotes with bird head finials; figural pieces such as fish and roosters; and handkerchief vases are among 'new' items currently on the market. Most carry the Murano label.

Basket, ruby, dmn pattern, scalloped, gold trim, 8x5½" **175.00**
Bottle, clear, yel/orange appl murrines, Ermanno Toso, 12½" **230.00**
Bowl, red w/silver, folded flower-like rim, 5" **60.00**

Bowl, ruby w/metallic bubbles, hexagonal free-form, 3x11" 27.50
Box, clear, yel/orange appl murrines, Ermanno Toso, 7" dia 115.00
Clown holding ball, mc w/gold mica, 11¾" 125.00
Clown w/guitar, mc w/gold, 8¾" 80.00
Clown w/umbrella, mc w/gold, 8½" 90.00
Console set, swirl w/gold flecks, leaf prunts on sticks, 3-pc 295.00
Cordial, gr, gold tracery, emb floral medallion, set of 5 ....15.00
Decanter, cobalt w/much gold, pastel flowers, 9"+6 cordials 48.00
Decanter, smoke w/wht mermaid inside, 9", +6 figural stems 385.00
Dish, heart shape, wht cased, gold flecks, Murano, 5½" 15.00
Duck, clear w/int gold layer, tallest 12", pr 130.00
Goblet, wine; gold vines w/purple & gr foliage, gr stem, 7¾" 82.50
Lady in bl gown, gold in hands & hair, Murano, 12" 235.00
Paperweight, whale form, millefiori, 6" 125.00
Penguin, blk/wht body, gold leaf on clear base, 8½" 290.00
Rooster, yel/red/gr/bl & clear w/gold, Avem, 1950s, 7½" 110.00
Salt cellar, open swan, amethyst w/gold flecks, 3¼" 150.00
Squirrel, amber & clear w/copper flecks, Murano, sm 50.00
Squirrel, red/gr/clear w/silver mica, Murano, 11" 85.00
Swan, ruby, Invt T'print body, appl gold flecks, 4½" 65.00
Vase, amethyst swirls, rim fused to form 2 openings, 10x9" 150.00
Vase, bud; gold medallion, lattice & scrolling, 8" 20.00
Vase, clear w/red int decor, purple swirl, Murano, 8x4" 185.00
Vase, heavy bl bottom w/int purple decor & top, 10x6" 325.00
Vase, mc canes in red cased to clear, sqd, 7¾" 550.00
Vase, mc swirls over wht, att Toso, Murano, 1950, 9" 450.00
Vase, 2 shades of deep bl, teardrop form, Murano, 6½x3" 110.00

Venini Glass

Fine contemporary art glass signed Venini (sometimes with Murano added) has been commanding high prices in some of the Eastern auction galleries. Art Deco items and those from the fifties are the most sought after.

Sculptures, chickens, amber with applied green opaque decoration and black eyes, designed by Bianconi, Murano, ca 1950, 7", $6,500.00 for the pair.

Bottle, amber w/plum band & stopper, Bianconi, 1955, 14½" .1,500.00
Bottle, grape top, yel mid strip, gr bottom, Wirkkala, 17" 1,045.00
Bottle, upright areas of colors, Bianconi/Vignelli, 10" 2,800.00
Bowl, heavy lt gr w/int bubbles, sqd form, Scarpa, 1940s, 5" 400.00
Bowl, lt amber stripes alternate w/brn & wht latticinio, 6" 220.00
Bowl, shell; plum irid, Scarpa, 1940s, 10" W 1,800.00
Chicken, amber w/appl gr & blk, Bianconi, 1950, 7", EX, pr ..6,500.00
Cowboy hat, blown in 1 pc, att, 7x16" 440.00
Dove, gr w/clear irid casing, Lundgren, Murano, 5", pr 900.00
Egg shape, appl wht/clear glass spirals, base opening, 7" 165.00

Farmer w/spade, Barovier, 1937, 11" 375.00
Hourglass, turq/cobalt, Paolo Venini, 1950s, 11½" 475.00
Light, wht globe w/irregular wide orange band, 19" dia 275.00
Plate, dk violet/purple off-rnd canes, de Santillana, 11" 3,800.00
Vase, amber w/lt ribs, ovoid w/flat rim & ft, Zecchin, 11½" 60.00
Vase, amethyst, ribbed onion w/trumpet neck, Zecchin, 9½" 550.00
Vase, handkerchief; clear w/wht latticinio, Bianconi, 5" 230.00
Vase, handkerchief; opaque wht, Bianconi, 6" 190.00
Vase, handkerchief; turq bl-gr cased to wht, 6" 250.00
Vase, patchwork design, Bianconi, 1955, 9" 7,500.00
Vase, red, bulbous shoulder, paper label, 1930s, 10½" 1,900.00
Woman, hands at waist, clear/latticinio/stars, Bianconi, 10" ...6,500.00

Verlys

Verlys art glass, produced in France after 1931 by the Holophane Company of Verlys, was made in crystal with acid-finished relief work in the Art Deco style. Colored and opalescent glass was also used. In 1935 an American branch was opened in Newark, Ohio, where very similar wares were produced until the factory ceased production in 1951. French Verlys was signed with one of three mold-impressed script signatures, all containing the company name and country of origin. The American-made glassware was signed 'Verlys' only, either scratched with a diamond-tipped pen or impressed in the mold. There is very little, if any, difference in value between items produced in France and America. Though some seem to feel that the French should be higher priced (assuming it to be scarce), many prefer the American-made product.

In June of 1955, about sixteen Verlys molds were leased to the A.H. Heisey Company. Heisey's versions were not signed with the Verlys name, so if an item is unsigned it is almost certainly a Heisey piece. The molds were returned to Verlys of America in July 1957. Our advisor for this category is Don Frost; he is listed in the Directory under Oregon.

Bowl, Birds & Bees, clear & frosted, 2¼x11⅝" 250.00
Bowl, Chrysanthemum (known as Casket), opal, 6¼x10" 385.00
Bowl, Pine Cone, bl, mk, 6" 150.00
Bowl, Poissons, fish, bl & opal, fish form hdls, 3¾x19¼" 1,500.00
Bowl, Poppies, clear & frosted, 13½" 250.00
Charger, Birds & Dragonflies, 12" 300.00
Disk, gull & carp decor on molded crystal, 13¾" 230.00
Vase, Alpine Thistle, opal, shouldered, 9" 625.00
Vase, Butterflies, 5" 225.00
Vase, Lovebirds, clear & frosted, paper label, 4¾x7" 225.00
Vase, Lovebirds, clear & frosted, 4¾x7" 145.00
Vase, mermaid, shouldered, Directoire bl, 1 of 2 forms, 11" 1,350.00
Vase, Thistle, topaz, 9¾" 795.00

Vernon Kilns

Vernon Potteries Ltd. was established by Faye G. Bennison in Vernon, California, in 1931. The name was later changed to Vernon Kilns; until it closed in 1958, dinnerware and figurines were their primary products. Among its wares most sought after by collectors today are items designed by such famous artists as Rockwell Kent, Walt Disney, Don Blanding, Jane Bennison, and May and Vieve Hamilton. Authority Maxine Nelson has compiled a lovely book, *Collectible Vernon Kilns*, with full-color photos, current prices and an index; you will find her listed in the Directory under California.

Barkwood, bowl, vegetable; 9" 12.00
Barkwood, creamer & sugar bowl, w/lid 20.00

Barkwood, plate, 10"	10.00
Barkwood, platter, 13½"	14.00
Brown-Eyed Susan, chop plate, 12"	18.00
Brown-Eyed Susan, teapot	45.00
Burkwood, pitcher, ½-pt	15.00
Calico, syrup	65.00
Chatelaine, plate, dinner; 1-leaf, bronze	17.00
Chatelaine, teacup & saucer, jade	30.00
Coral Reef, plate, bl, 10½"	45.00
Coral Reef, plate, maroon, Don Blanding, 9¾"	40.00
Dreamtime, plate, 6"	7.00
Early California, casserole, turq, w/lid	35.00
Early California, chop plate, 13"	25.00
Early California, cup & saucer, orange	15.00
Early California, egg cup	15.00
Early California, lug soup, open	12.00
Early California, pitcher, 1-qt	30.00
Fantasia, bowl, mushroom, lt gr, #120	150.00
Fantasia, bowl, Satyr, #124, wht w/turq int	250.00
Fantasia, bowl, Sprites, HP, #125, 11½"	350.00
Fantasia, bowl, winged nymph, pk, #122, 2½x12"	200.00
Fantasia, coffeepot, Nutcracker, 6-cup	550.00
Fantasia, figurine, Baby Blk Pegasus, #19	450.00
Fantasia, figurine, Baby Weems, Disney, 1941	265.00
Fantasia, figurine, Centaurette, #18, 7½"	750.00
Fantasia, figurine, Centaurette, #22, 8"	800.00
Fantasia, figurine, elephant in pk, #25, 5"	400.00
Fantasia, figurine, satyr, #3, 4½"	250.00
Fantasia, figurine, sprite, #12, 4¾"	225.00
Fantasia, plate, Nutcracker, 9"	150.00
Fantasia, shakers, Milk Weed, pr	75.00
Fantasia, shakers, mushroom, pr	125.00
Fantasia, vase, goldfish, c 1940 Walt Disney, #121	300.00
Gingham, bowl, divided vegetable	22.00
Gingham, bowl, mixing; 9"	35.00
Gingham, bowl, vegetable; 9"	16.00
Gingham, casserole, w/lid	25.00
Gingham, coffee carafe	28.00
Gingham, cup & saucer	10.00
Gingham, pitcher, bulb base, 1-pt, 7"	20.00
Gingham, pitcher, streamlined, ½-pt	18.00
Gingham, pitcher, 2-qt	45.00
Gingham, plate, 6¼"	3.00
Gingham, plate, 9½"	9.00
Gingham, sugar bowl, w/lid	12.00

Harvest, teapot, 6-cup, $65.00.

Hawaiian Flowers, bowl, chowder; tab hdls, w/lid	50.00
Hawaiian Flowers, bowl, fruit	12.00

Hawaiian Flowers, plate, 9"	25.00
Hawaiian Flowers, soup, coupe	35.00
Heavenly Days, creamer	8.00
Heavenly Days, mug	15.00
Homespun, bowl, vegetable; 9"	15.00
Homespun, chop plate, 12"	18.00
Homespun, chop plate, 14"	25.00
Homespun, creamer & sugar bowl, w/lid	25.00
Homespun, cup & saucer	12.00
Homespun, egg cup	15.00
Homespun, plate, 6¼"	4.00
Homespun, plate, 7½"	8.00
Homespun, plate, 9½"	10.00
Homespun, platter, oval, 10¼"	15.00
Homespun, platter, oval, 12½"	17.00
Homespun, platter, oval, 14¼"	20.00
Lei Lani, chop plate, 12"	95.00
Lei Lani, chop plate, 14"	145.00
Lei Lani, creamer, sgn Blanding	35.00
Mayflower, creamer & sugar bowl	35.00
Mayflower, cup & saucer	18.00
Mayflower, plate, 6"	6.00
Mayflower, platter, oval, 14"	35.00
Mayflower, sauce boat	45.00
Mayflower, shakers, pr	18.00
Moby Dick, plate, bl, 9½"	65.00
Modern California, egg cup	20.00
Modern California, teapot, orchid	65.00
Monterey, bowl, chowder	12.00
Monterey, creamer & sugar bowl, w/lid	22.00
Monterey, cup	12.00
Monterey, shakers, pr	12.00
Native California, chop plate, 14"	30.00
Native California, shakers, pr	16.00
Organdie, bowl, fruit; 5½"	4.00
Organdie, chop plate, 12"	15.00
Organdie, creamer & sugar bowl, w/lid	20.00
Organdie, cup & saucer	12.50
Organdie, pepper shaker	5.00
Organdie, plate, 10"	12.00
Organdie, plate, 6½"	4.50
Organdie, plate, 7½"	8.00
Organdie, plate, 9½"	10.00
Organdie, platter, oval, 12"	15.00
Organdie, sauce boat	18.00
Organdie, shakers, pr	12.00
Organdie, teapot, ind	20.00
Organdie, tidbit tray, 1-tier, 7½"	15.00
Planter, bird, decor, #134	65.00
Plate, Baker's Chocolate	35.00
Plate, Colorado, red	10.00
Plate, Down on the Levee, Bits of Old South, 1940, 8½"	45.00
Plate, Hollywood	25.00
Plate, Indiana, bl	10.00
Plate, Kentucky, red	12.00
Plate, Oklahoma map, bl	18.00
Plate, Old Mill, Bits of Old South, 1940, 8½"	45.00
Plate, Pennsylvania, mc	15.00
Plate, Purdue University	12.50
Plate, San Francisco cable cars	20.00
Platter, Down on the Levee, Bits of Old South, 14"	85.00
Rhythmic, cup & saucer	45.00
Rhythmic, plate, 10½"	35.00
Rippled, cup & saucer	35.00

Rippled, plate, 10½" 30.00
Salamina, chop plate, 14" 450.00
Salamina, cup & saucer 50.00
Salamina, plate, 9½" 95.00
Salamina, sugar bowl, w/lid, regular 95.00
Salamina, tumbler 100.00
Tam O'Shanter, bowl, divided vegetable 30.00
Tam O'Shanter, butter dish, ¼-lb 35.00
Tam O'Shanter, casserole, hdls, w/lid 50.00
Tam O'Shanter, casserole, w/lid, 1½-qt 35.00
Tam O'Shanter, chop plate, 12" 35.00
Tam O'Shanter, coaster 18.00
Tam O'Shanter, coffee server, w/stopper 45.00
Tam O'Shanter, flowerpot, w/saucer, 3" 35.00
Tam O'Shanter, platter, 11" 15.00
Tam O'Shanter, platter, 13" 19.00
Tickled Pink, bowl, divided 25.00
Tickled Pink, relish dish, 3-section 22.00
Tweed, plate, 6¼" 5.00
Ultra California, bowl, Buttercup, 1-pt 20.00
Ultra California, bowl, chowder; Carnation 15.00
Ultra California, cup & saucer, Ice Gr 20.00
Ultra California, demitasse pot 75.00
Ultra California, plate, luncheon; Aster 12.00

Villeroy and Boch

The firm of Villeroy and Boch, located in Mettlach, Germany, was brought into being by the 1841 merger of three German factories — the Wallerfangen factory, founded by Nicholas Villeroy in 1787; the Mettlach factory, founded by Jean Francis Boch 1809; and Boch's father's factory in Septfontaines, established in 1767. Villeroy and Boch produced many varieties of wares, including earthenware with printed under-glaze designs which carried the well-known castle mark with the name 'Mettlach.' See also Mettlach.

Companion chargers, Rheinstein Castle on cliff, #2195; Stolzenfels Castle on cliff, #2196, each 17½", $1,900.00 for the pair.

Beaker, bowler, ¼-L, M 82.50
Beaker, soccer player, ¼-L 95.00
Beaker, young woman, V&B Dresden mk, ¼-L 75.00
Charger, Meissen castle on Elbe, 12" 195.00
Ewer, cupid figure under spout, scroll hdl, 13" ...200.00
Mug, Wekara, relief, terra cotta bkground, #3487, ¼-L 40.00
Pitcher, bowler, 7⅛" 120.00
Pitcher, horse rider, 7⅛" 105.00
Pitcher, 2 soccer players, 7⅛" 198.00
Plaque, Wallerfangen, #3163, 15" 85.00
Plaque, Wallerfangen, #3192, 15" 50.00

Plaque, Wallerfangen, bl, #23054, 10" 50.00
Stein, Mercedes automobile, chromolitho, modern, ½-L 150.00
Tile, Oriental fish, 6" 45.00
Tray, holds 6 egg cups, lt platinum wear, 1852-73 mk, 10" L 685.00
Tray, lovers in garden, wood fr, 12½x18½" 250.00
Vase, gun metal/blk gloss, Deco shape, 4" 95.00
Vase, stoneware, gr/tan crystalline, spherical, 10½" 210.00
Vase, stylized bear, brn/bl on cream matt, bulbous, '25, 9" 275.00

Vistosa

Vistosa was produced from about 1938 through the early forties. It was Taylor, Smith, and Taylor's answer to the very successful Fiesta line of their nearby competitor, Homer Laughlin. Vistosa was made in four solid colors: mango red, cobalt blue, light green, and deep yellow. 'Pie crust' edges and a dainty five-petal flower molded into handles and lid finials made for a very attractive, yet nevertheless, commercially unsuccessful product. Our advisor for this category is Ted Haun; he is listed in the Directory under Indiana.

Bowl, salad; ftd 95.00
Bowl, 5¾" 8.00
Bowl, 8½" 24.00
Chop plate, 11" 15.00
Chop plate, 13" 18.00
Chop plate, 15" 35.00
Creamer 10.00
Cup & saucer 15.00
Egg cup 22.50
Gravy boat 78.00
Pitcher, cobalt 75.00
Pitcher, red 75.00
Plate, salad; 7" 8.00
Plate, 7" 7.00
Plate, 9" 10.00
Shakers, pr 18.00
Sugar bowl, w/lid 15.00
Teapot 95.00

Volkmar

Charles Volkmar established a workshop in Tremont, New York, in 1882. He produced artware decorated under the glaze in the manner of the early barbotine work done at the Haviland factory in Limoges, France. He relocated in 1888 in Menlo Park, New Jersey, and together with J.T. Smith established the Menlo Park Ceramic Company for the production of art tile. The partnership was dissolved in 1893. From 1895 until 1902, Volkmar located in Corona, New York, first under the name Volkmar Ceramic Company, later as Volkmar and Cory, and for the final six years as Crown Point. During the latter period he made art tile, blue under-glaze Delft-type wares, colorful polychrome vases, etc. The Volkmar Kilns were established in 1903 in Metuchen, New Jersey, by Volkmar and his son. Wares were marked with various devices consisting of the Volkmar name, initials, or 'Crown Point Ware.'

Tile, leaves allover 110.00
Vase, dk bl mottled matt, 3 rim-to-shoulder angle hdls, 7x6" 375.00
Vase, gr mottle on brn, widens toward base, rim chip, 10x5½" ...275.00

Volkstedt

There were several porcelain factories in and around Volkstedt,

Province of Thuringia, the original and earliest one established in 1762 by George Heinrich Macheleid. Others soon followed, producing many fine porcelain figures and groups in the Sheib-Alsbach, Potschappel, and Sitzendorf style. The 'crossed hayforks' mark was used from 1787 to 1800 by Christian Nonne; it was later modified with the addition of a crown by R. Ekhart (1906-08). An 'M' crossed by a 'V' with a crown was used from 1907-47 by Muller, who used an oval-shaped diamond with an 'M,' 'V' and a crown from 1910-1960. The Greiner Bros. mark was a double-crossed 'G' and a crown, in use from 1850-1920.

Two girls precede bride and groom, page with train, 9x13", $1,250.00.

Figurine, couple by rail watching 2 swans, 9x8½"	550.00
Figurine, girl in floral gown w/goose, after Canova, 6"	150.00
Figurine, lady carries basket, 5"	150.00
Figurine, lady in red top, torch in hand, Canova, 6"	165.00
Figurine, lady sits w/lute, man w/music book at side, 9x9"	1,100.00
Figurine, Victorian gent escorts lady, 5½"	200.00
Figurine, 2 girls precede bride & groom, page w/train, 9x13"	1,250.00
Plaque, gr jasper w/wht floral Baroque fr, ca 1874, 9x10½"	450.00
Vase, floriform w/HP maid, 3-D nymph on base, 1910, 18"	300.00

Wade

The Wade Group of Potteries originated in 1810 with a small, single-oven pottery near Chesterton, just west of Burslem, England. This pottery, first owned by a Henry Hallen, was eventually taken over by George Wade who had opened his own pottery (also in Burslem) in 1867. Both the Hallen pottery and the original Wade pottery specialized in ceramic and pottery items for the textile industry, then booming in northern England. By the early 20th century, the two potteries were merged, taking the name of George Wade Pottery, which in 1919 became George Wade & Son Ltd.

George Wade's brother, Albert, had interests in two potteries, A.J. Wade Ltd. and Wade Heath & Co. Ltd. which manufactured decorative tiles, teapots, and other related dinnerware. In 1938 Wade Heath took over the Royal Victoria Pottery, also in Burslem, and began producing a wide range of figurines and other decorative items. In 1947 a new pottery was opened in Portadown, Northern Ireland, to produce both industrial ceramics and Irish porcelain giftware. In 1958 all the Wade potteries were amalgamated, becoming the Wade group of Potteries. The most recent addition to the group is Wade (PDM) Limited, a marketing arm for the advertising ware made by Wade Heath at the Royal Victoria Pottery. Wade (PDM) Limited was incorporated in 1969. In 1989 the Wade Group of Potteries was bought out by Beauford Engineering. With this takeover, Wade Heath and George Wade & Son Ltd. were combined to form Wade Ceramics. Wade (Ireland) Ltd. and Wade (PDM) Ltd. became subsidiaries of Wade Ceramics. In 1990 Wade (Ireland) Ltd. changed its name to Seagoe Ceramics Limited. For those interested in learning more about Wade pottery, we recommend

The World of Wade by Ian Warner and Mike Posgay; Mr. Warner is listed in the Directory under Canada.

Blow-up Disney, Dachie, 1961-65	270.00
Blow-up Disney, Scamp, 1961-65	130.00
Blow-up Disney, Thumper, 1961-65	250.00
Blow-up Disney, Tramp, 1961-65	215.00
Blow-up Disney, Trusty, 1961-65	160.00
Hanna-Barbera, Huckleberry Hound, 1959-60	85.00
Hanna-Barbera, Mr Junks, 1959-60	90.00
Hanna-Barbera, Yogi Bear, 1959-60	85.00
Nursery Favourite, Goosey Gander, 1976	85.00
Nursery Favourite, Goosey Gander, 1991	33.00
Nursery Favourite, Mary Mary, 1974	40.00
Nursery Favourite, Mary Mary, 1990	34.00
Nursery Favourite, Polly Kettle, 1973	30.00
Nursery Favourite, Polly kettle, 1990	23.00
Nursery Favourite, Tom Piper, 1973	34.00

Piggy bank family, Annabel, $45.00.

Nursery Favourite, Tom Piper, 1990	27.00
Sailor, 1949-58	150.00
Sea Lion corkscrew, 1960	80.00
Snow White & the 7 Dwarfs, ca 1981-86, complete set	900.00
Soldier, 1949-58	150.00
Tailor, 1949-58	150.00
Thomas the Tank Engine miniature, 1985-87	55.00
Thomas the Tank Engine money box, 1958-87	155.00
Tinker, 1949-58	150.00
TV Pet, Bengo, 1959	46.00
TV Pet, Mitzi, 1959	46.00

Wallendorf

The Wallendorf Porcelain Factory has operated from the mid-1700s in the area of East Germany known as Thuringia up to the present day.

Figurine, ballerina w/arms out & leg extended, 1950, 9"	225.00
Figurine, lady on bench looking in mirror, 7"	275.00
Figurine, male & female ballet dancers, ca 1950, 9"	250.00

Wallace China

Dinnerware with a Western theme produced by the Wallace China Company, who operated in Caifornia from 1931 until 1964, has become very popular. Artist Till Goodan designed three lines, Rodeo,

Pioneer Trails, and Boots and Saddle, which they marketed under the package name Westward Ho. When dinnerware with a western theme became so popular just a few years ago, Rodeo was reproduced, but the new trademark includes neither 'California' or 'Wallace China.'

Our advisor for this category is Marv Fogleman; he is listed in the Directory under California. If you'd like to learn more about this company, we recommend *The Collector's Encyclopedia of California Pottery* by Jack Chipman.

Boots & Saddle, ashtray	**55.00**
Boots & Saddle, creamer	**95.00**
Boots & Saddle, plate, 9"	**125.00**
El Rancho, bowl, vegetable; rnd, 10"	**150.00**
El Rancho, platter, oval, 13½"	**125.00**
Little Buckaroo, 3-pc set	**350.00**
Pioneer Trails, ashtray, Sam Houston	**55.00**
Pioneer Trails, bowl, 3x9"	**200.00**
Pioneer Trails, chop plate, 13"	**200.00**
Pioneer Trails, creamer & sugar bowl	**225.00**
Pioneer Trails, platter, oval, 15½"	**175.00**
Rodeo, ashtray	**55.00**
Rodeo, bowl, chili; 5¾"	**65.00**
Rodeo, bowl, salad; 13"	**450.00**

Rodeo: Bowl, 13", $450.00; Plate, 13½", $200.00.

Rodeo, creamer	**125.00**
Rodeo, cup & saucer, 11-oz, 7½"	**90.00**
Rodeo, pitcher, water; 72-oz	**350.00**
Rodeo, plate, chop; 13"	**200.00**
Rodeo, plate, 10½"	**90.00**
Rodeo, plate, 7¼"	**60.00**
Rodeo, platter, oval, 15½"	**200.00**
Rodeo, shakers, 5", pr	**150.00**
Westward Ho (brands only), bowl, mixing; nested set of 5	**450.00**

Walrath

Frederick Walrath was a studio potter who worked from around the turn of the century until his death in 1920. He was located in Rochester, New York, until 1918 when he became associated with the Newcomb Pottery in New Orleans, Louisiana.

Candle holder, cherub seated atop tree trunk, sgn MI, 12"	**1,000.00**
Figurine, nude kneeling, outstretched arm, supports bowl, M	**450.00**
Vase, lg soft pk flowers on dk gr, wide base, 4½", EX	**1,200.00**

Walrich

This small pottery operated in Berkeley, California, from 1922 until about 1930. They designed their own molds and developed their own glazes and are well known for their formula for a particularly outstanding shade of blue. Porcelain as well as earthenware clays were utilized, and in addition to artware vases, figurines were also made. Their trademark was a vase enclosed within a circle with the name of the pottery and its location in letters around the inner perimeter.

Bowl, med aqua matt, sgn GR Wall, 2x5½"	**115.00**
Candle holder, gr crystalline, 2x5"	**122.00**

Walter, A.

Almaric Walter was employed from 1904 through 1914 at Verreries Artistiques des Freres Daum in Nancy, France. After 1919 he opened his own business where he continued to make the same type of quality objets d'art in pate-de-verre glass as he had earlier. His pieces are signed A. Walter, Nancy H. Berge Sc.

Bowl, abstract lotus, shades of gr, 3¾"	**625.00**
Salver, amber/orange mottle, hdls, 10"	**350.00**
Tray, beetle inside, wine/blk on yel mottle, 5½" L	**2,200.00**
Tray, yel-gold w/gr moth on scrolled ends, 3x9x4"	**4,000.00**
Vase, overlapping leaves & flowers at base, gr on lime, 4½"	**3,500.00**

Warwick

The Warwick China Company operated in Wheeling, West Virginia, from 1887 until 1951. They produced both hand-painted and decaled plates, vases, teapots, coffeepots, pitchers, bowls, and jardinieres featuring lovely florals or portraits of beautiful ladies done in luscious colors. Backgrounds were usually blendings of brown and beige, but ivory was also used (and on rare occasion, pink). Various marks were employed, all of which incorporate the Warwick name. For a more thorough study of the subject, we recommend *Warwick, A to W*, a supplement to *Why Not Warwick* by our advisor, Donald C. Hoffmann; his address can be found in the Directory under Illinois. In an effort to inform the collector/dealer, Mr. Hoffmann now has a video available that identifies the company's decals and their variations by number. These numbers are contained within the following listings.

Mug, brn, Dickens, sq hdl, VT #1 & #2, 4"	**75.00**
Mug, brn, dogs, rnd hdl, VT #10, 4"	**90.00**
Mug, brn, fraternal, rnd hdl, VT #4, 4"	**80.00**
Mug, brn, fraternal, sq hdl, VT #2, 4"	**70.00**
Mug, brn, friar, finger-hole hdl, VT #4 & #5, 3"	**50.00**
Mug, brn, friar, finger-hole hdl, VT #6, 3"	**60.00**
Mug, brn, friar, finger-hole hdl, VT #7 & #9, 3"	**55.00**
Mug, brn, friar, sq hdl, VT #1 & #2, 4"	**70.00**
Mug, brn, Indians, rnd hdl, VT #6, 4"	**100.00**
Mug, brn, Indians, rnd hdl, VT #8, 4"	**85.00**
Mug, brn, monk, rnd hdl, monk, VT #3, 4"	**60.00**
Mug, charcoal, friar, rnd hdl, VT #10, 4"	**90.00**
Mug, brn matt, fraternal, rnd hdl, VT #4, 4"	**80.00**
Mug, tan-brn matt, fisherman, sq hdl, VT #2, 4"	**80.00**
Mug, tan-brn matt, monks, sq hdl, VT #1 & #2, 4"	**75.00**
Mug, pk/gr, monks, sq hdl, VT #1 & #2, 4"	**95.00**
Mug, red, fisherman, sq hdl, VT #1 & #2, 4"	**75.00**
Mug, red, monk, ring hdl, VT #2, 5"	**80.00**
Plate, brn to cream, friar, VG #12 & #16, 10"	**95.00**
Plate, brn to yel, dog, VT #7, 10"	**115.00**
Plate, gr to cream, friar, VT #14, 10"	**100.00**
Spirit jug, brn, fisherman, VT #2	**235.00**

Spirit jug, brn, floral, VT #9 ....290.00
Spirit jug, brn, Indian, VT #9 ....250.00
Spirit jug, matt tan-brn, VT #12 ....280.00
Stein, brn, Dickens, ring hdl, VT #1, 5" 75.00
Stein, brn, friar, ring hdl, VT #7, 5" 90.00
Stein, brn, Indian, ring hdl, VT #6, 5" 115.00
Stein, brn, monk, ring hdl, VT #1, 5" 70.00
Stein, charcoal, friar, ring hdl, VT #15, 5" 95.00

Tankard, brown with F.O.E. and
eagle, red mark, A-34, $220.00;
Matching mug, $50.00.

Tankard, brn, Dickens, ring hdl, VT #1, 15" 260.00
Tankard, brn, dog, rnd hdl, VT #7, 10" 250.00
Tankard, brn, fraternal, ring hdl, VT #3, 15" 230.00
Tankard, brn, friar, ring hdl, VT #10, 13" 230.00
Tankard, brn, friar, rnd hdl, VT #11, 10" 240.00
Tankard, brn, friar, rnd hdl, VT #15, 10" 200.00
Tankard, brn, fruit, ring hdl, VT #8, 13" 265.00
Tankard, brn, Indian, ring hdl, VT #4, 15" 295.00
Tankard, brn, portrait, ring hdl, VT #23, 15" 300.00
Tankard, brn, portrait, ring hdl, VT #4, 13" 245.00
Tankard, matt bl, fraternal, sq hdl w/bar, VT #1, 10" 300.00
Tankard, matt brn, fisherman, sq hdl w/bar, VT #1, 10" 300.00
Vase, A Beauty, 15" 300.00
Vase, Albany, 7" 235.00
Vase, Alexandria, 12½" 295.00
Vase, Bonnie, 10¼" 320.00
Vase, Bouquet #1, brn, lady w/poppy, VT #21, 11½" 265.00
Vase, Bouquet #1, brn, lady w/red roses, VT #16, 11½" 250.00
Vase, Bouquet #1, matt, portrait, w/lg hat, VT #12, 11½" 300.00
Vase, Bouquet #1, red, LeBrun as child, VT #37, 11½" 265.00
Vase, Bouquet #1, red, orchid, VT #4, 11½" 285.00
Vase, Bouquet #1, wht, birds, VT #3, 11½" 290.00
Vase, Bouquet #2, brn, blond's portrait, VT #14 or #15, 10½" ...260.00
Vase, Bouquet #2, brn, Bonfits #1 w/rose, VT #39, 10½" 270.00
Vase, Bouquet #2, brn, Bonfits #2, pillbox hat, VT #40, 10½" ...285.00
Vase, Bouquet #2, brn, Bonfits #4, lg hairdo, VT #42, 10½" 330.00
Vase, Bouquet #2, brn, lady w/gold earrings, VT #27, 10½" 240.00
Vase, Bouquet #2, brn, LeBrun as adult, VT #36, 10½" 245.00
Vase, Bouquet #2, brn, Madame ReCamier, VT #38, 10½" 270.00
Vase, Bouquet #2, charcoal, nude, VT #29 & #30, 10½" 380.00
Vase, Bouquet #2, cream-tan, floral, VT #16, 10½" 290.00
Vase, Bouquet #2, gr, portrait, VT #37, 10½" 295.00
Vase, Bouquet #2, matt, tan, pine cones, VT #14, 10½" 290.00
Vase, Bouquet #2, matte, tan-gr, portrait, VT #43, 10½" 280.00

Vase, Bouquet #2, pk, portrait, VT #6, 10½" 325.00
Vase, Bouquet #2, red, portrait, VT #25, 10½" 275.00
Vase, Bouquet #2, red, portrait, VT #35, 10½" 285.00
Vase, Bouquet #2, red, portrait, VT #37 & #38, 10½" 280.00
Vase, Bouquet #2, wht, portrait, VT #17, 10½" 300.00
Vase, Bouquet #2, wht, portrait, VT #47, 10½" 315.00
Vase, Bouquet #2, yel-gr, portrait, VT #9, 10½" 350.00
Vase, Carnation, brn, floral, VT #15, 9" 120.00
Vase, Carnation, charcoal, floral, VT #13, 9" 155.00
Vase, Carnation, gr, floral, VT #20, 9" 175.00
Vase, Carnation, yel-gr, portrait, VT #9, 9" 250.00
Vase, Carol, matt, pine cones, VT #14, 8" 255.00
Vase, Carol, pk, portrait, VT #9, 8" 300.00
Vase, Chicago, pk, portrait, VT #6, 8" 300.00
Vase, Chrys #1, brn, floral, VT #4, 15" 180.00
Vase, Chrys #2, brn, floral, VT #15, 15" 170.00
Vase, Chrys #2, charcoal, floral, VT #13, 15" 185.00
Vase, Clematis, matt, nut, VT #12, 10½" 280.00
Vase, Clematis, red, portrait, VT #15, 10½" 290.00
Vase, Clematis, wht, birds, VT #3, 10½" 300.00
Vase, Clytie, red, floral, VT #2, 6½" 320.00
Vase, Clytie, red, portrait, VT #36, 6½" 325.00
Vase, Dahlia, brn, portrait, VT #37, 8½" 275.00
Vase, Dahlia, matt, nut, VT #12, 8½" 270.00
Vase, Dainty, pk, portrait, VT #6, 4½" 300.00
Vase, Duchess, brn, floral, VT #10, 8" 190.00
Vase, Duchess, wht, bird, VT #2, 8" 230.00
Vase, Egyptian, brn, floral, VT #9, 11¾" 325.00
Vase, Egyptian, charcoal, floral, VT #13, 11¾" 335.00
Vase, Flower, brn, floral, VT #15, 10" 135.00
Vase, Flower, brn, floral, VT #8, 12" 145.00
Vase, Flower, matt, floral, VT #6, 10" 145.00
Vase, Flower, red, floral, VT #2, 10" 150.00
Vase, Flower, red, floral, VT #3, 12" 165.00
Vase, Gem, brn, floral, VT #10, 12" 225.00
Vase, Gem, brn, portrait, VT #38, 12" 240.00

Wash Sets

Before the days of running water, bedrooms were standardly equipped with a wash bowl and pitcher as a matter of necessity. A 'toilet set' was comprised of the pitcher and bowl, toothbrush holder, covered commode, soap dish, shaving dish, and mug. Some sets were even more elaborate. Through everyday usage, the smaller items were often broken, and today it is unusual to find a complete set.

Porcelain sets decorated with florals, fruits, or scenics were produced abroad by Limoges in France; some were imported from Germany and England. During the last quarter of the 1800s and until after the turn of the century, American-made toilet sets were manufactured in abundance. Tin and graniteware sets were also made.

Alhambra, flow bl, Meakin, pitcher+bowl+soap dish+pot 1,000.00
Bl/wht spongeware w/bl band, pitcher, 12", +bowl, EX 550.00
Burford's Porc, gr floral/gilt, pitcher+bowl+5 pcs 2,000.00
English, bl-gr florals, pitcher+bowl+toothbrush holder+pot 350.00
Festoon, med bl transfer, Wedgwood, pitcher + bowl, EX 135.00
Homer Laughlin, gold floral/sprigs, pitcher+bowl+5 pcs 500.00
Homer Laughlin, pk & yel roses on bl w/gold, pitcher+bowl 185.00
Ironstone, wht w/gold trim, pitcher+bowl 165.00
Knowles-Taylor-Knowles, child's, wht w/gold, pitcher+bowl 85.00
Mason's Ironstone, bl dragon transfer, 16" pitcher+bowl, EX 350.00
Mercer Pottery, Trenton NJ, wht w/gold trim, 5-pc, EX 385.00
Minton, child's, gr ivy on cream, 7" pitcher+9½" bowl 250.00

Old Paris, floral & scrollwork panels on wht, pitcher + bowl **575.00**
Rosetti, Royal Doulton, pitcher + bowl **235.00**

Watch Fobs

Watch fobs have been popular since the last quarter of the 19th century. They were often made by retail companies to feature their products. Souvenir, commemorative, and political fobs were also produced. Of special interest today are those with advertising, heavy equipment in particular. Some of the more pricey fobs are listed here, but most of those currently available were produced in such quantities that they are relatively common and should fall into a price range of from $3.00 to $10.00. Our advisor for this category is Tony George; he is listed in the Directory under California.

Allis-Chalmers, emb tractor, bronze, NM **6.50**
Baker's Steam Tractor **75.00**
Caterpillar The Nation's Road Maker, brass, Holt, w/strap, EX ..**115.00**
Dartboard motif, Sterling, dtd 1905 ....**85.00**
DeLaval, enamel, EX **98.00**
El Paso Saddlery, 1889, saddle shape **140.00**
Euclid Dozer, early **25.00**
Euclid Earth Moving Equipment, emb machine, silver, 1950s **20.00**
FOE, Liberty, Truth, Justice..., bronze, 1918, EX **10.00**
Hammey's Roundup, saddle shape **175.00**
Heraldry on bloodstone seal, 18k gold w/etruscan work, 4½" **200.00**
Horse's head, cvd MOP **30.00**
Huber Farm Tractor, 1800s **100.00**
John Deere, bl porc, oval **175.00**
John Deere JD 690 Excavator, silver, 1970 ....**7.50**
Keystone Watch Case, souvenir of 1893 World's Fair **35.00**

Lima (steam shovel), Move the Earth With a Lima, brass, 1950, $30.00.

Litchfield Mfg Waterloo IA, bulldog **85.00**
Los Angeles Saddlery, saddle shape **135.00**
Maine, emb eagle, Spanish-Am War **22.00**
New Castle Centennial 1825-1925, bronze, Whitehead & Hoag .**20.00**
Nouveau-style lady, gold filled **145.00**
Ohio Machinery Co, Cleveland, silver, 1970s, EX **10.00**
Parson's Heavy Duty McIlhany Equipment, NP, EX **15.00**

Red Dmn Overalls & Shirts, celluloid, red/wht/bl, EX **35.00**
Remington 100th Anniversary **195.00**
Shell Oil, metal w/yel enamel **60.00**
Shield w/fleur-de-lis, Sterling **98.00**
SP brass, emb 1920 airplane, auto & bicycle, unmk **20.00**
Swastika motif on gold-plated brass, 1890s **70.00**
United Serum Co, Kansas City KS, We Save 'Em, bronze, 1912 ..**37.50**
United States Horseshoe Co **45.00**
Van Pattens Flying Vee Eff Ranch, saddle shape **140.00**
Wallis, tractor **78.00**
William Jennings Bryan, leather & celluloid **135.00**
Worthington Blue Brute Hand Held Rock Drills, silver, 1930s **40.00**

Watch Stands

Watch stands were decorative articles designed with a hook from which to hang a watch. Some displayed the watch as the face of a grandfather clock or as part of an interior scene with figures in period costumes and contemporary furnishings. They were popular products of Staffordshire potters and silver companies as well.

Architectural, wooden, mc pnt, Austrian, 1800s, 13" **250.00**
Bronze, maiden w/2 doves beside cartouche-shaped holder **325.00**
Building facade, mahog/whale ivory/bone, dtd 1839, 11x7" **1,350.00**
CI, emb helmets/armor, 4 ivory boar tusks, 10½" **95.00**
Domed base holds wood/papier-mache doll, chalk, 14", VG **400.00**
Father Time stands by aperatur, giltwood, 1800s, 10" **450.00**
Micro mosaic plaque & holder w/mosaic scene, Italian **660.00**

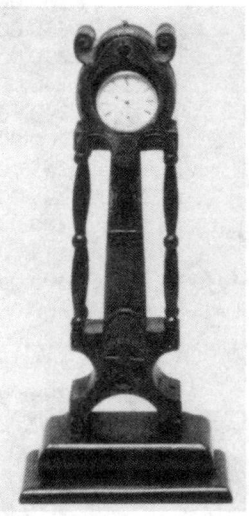

Moses Burnam, tall clock form, carved and painted, ca 1840, with Elgin National Watch Co. pocket watch, 13", $1,300.00.

Neoclassical giltwood, Chronos figure, Austrian, 1800s, 10" **350.00**
Neoclassical giltwood, 2 seated figures, Austrian, 1800s, 11" **220.00**
Neoclassical pnt/gilt, crest/columns, dbl, Austrian, 12½" **465.00**
Neoclassical pnt/parcel gilt, columns/swags, Austrian, 13" **330.00**
Oak w/allover cvd punched design, circle fr in top, rpr, 7" **175.00**
Prisoner of war, bone gazebo w/arched roof, 1820s, 10x7" **975.00**

Watches

First made in the 1500s in Germany, early watches were actually small clocks, suspended from the wrist or belt. By 1700 they had become the approximate shape and size we know today. The first watches produced in America were made in 1810. The well-known

Waltham Watch Company was established in 1850. Later, Waterbury produced inexpensive watches which they sold by the thousands.

Open-face and hunting-case watches of the 1890s were often solid gold or gold-filled and were often elaborately decorated in several colors of gold. Gold watches became a status symbol in this decade and were worn by both men and women on chains with fobs or jeweled slides. Ladies sometimes fastened them to their clothing with pins often set with jewels. The chatelaine watch was worn at the waist, only one of several items such as scissors, coin purses, or needle cases, each attached by small chains.

Most turn-of-the-century watch cases were gold-filled; these are plentiful today. Sterling cases, though interest in them is on the increase, are not in great demand. Our advisors for this category are The Sandlers (Maundy International Watches), Antiquarian Horologists, price consultants, and researchers for many watch reference guides and books on Horology. Their firm is a leading purveyor of antique watches of all kinds. They are listed in the Directory under Kansas. For character-related watches, see Personalities.

Key:

adj — adjusted	k/s — key set
brg — bridge plate design	k/w — key wind
d/s — double sunk dial	l/s — lever set
fbd — finger bridge design	mvt — movement
g/f — gold-filled	o/f — open face
g/j/s — gold jewel setting	p/s — pendant set
h/c — hunter case	r/g/p — rolled gold plate
HCI#P — heat, cold,	s — size
isochronism & position	s/s — single sunk dial
adjusted	s/w — stem wind
j — jewel	w/g/f — white gold-filled
k — karat	y/g/f — yellow gold-filled

Am Watch Co, 0s, 7j, #1891, 14k, h/c, Am Watch Co 450.00
Am Watch Co, 12s, 17j, #1894, 14k, o/f, Royal 275.00
Am Watch Co, 12s, 21j, #1894, 14k, h/c 575.00
Am Watch Co, 16s, 11j, #1872, p/s, silver, h/c, Park Road 425.00
Am Watch Co, 16s, 15j, #1883, y/g/f, 2-tone, Railroad King 650.00
Am Watch Co, 16s, 15j, #1899, y/g/f, h/c 190.00
Am Watch Co, 16s, 16j, #1884, 5-min, coin silver, Repeater .4,250.00
Am Watch Co, 16s, 17j, #1888, Railroader 495.00
Am Watch Co, 16s, 19j, #1872, 14k, h/c, Am Watch Co 2,650.00
Am Watch Co, 16s, 21j, #1888, o/f, 14k, Riverside Maximus .1,475.00
Am Watch Co, 16s, 21j, #1899, y/g/f, l/s, o/f, Crescent St 265.00
Am Watch Co, 16s, 21j, #1908, y/g/f, o/f, Grade #645 ....195.00
Am Watch Co, 16s, 23j, #1908, o/f, 18k, Premier Maximus 8,000.00
Am Watch Co, 16s, 23j, #1908, y/g/f, o/f, adj, RR, Vanguard 285.00
Am Watch Co, 16s, 23j, #1908, y/g/f, o/f, Vanguard Up/Down ..565.00
Am Watch Co, 18s, #1857, silver h/c, Samuel Curtiss k/w 2,700.00
Am Watch Co, 18s, 11j, #1857, k/w, 1st run, PS Barlett 950.00
Am Watch Co, 18s, 11j, #1857, silver, h/c, k/w, DH&D 1,425.00
Am Watch Co, 18s, 11j, #1857, silver, h/c, k/w, s/s, Ellery, EX ..275.00
Am Watch Co, 18s, 15j, #1877, k/w, RE Robbins 395.00
Am Watch Co, 18s, 17j, #1883, y/g/f, o/f, Crescent Street 175.00
Am Watch Co, 18s, 17j, #1892, HC, Canadian Pacific Railway .1,350.00
Am Watch Co, 18s, 17j, #1892, y/g/f, o/f, Sidereal, rare 1,950.00
Am Watch Co, 18s, 17j, 25-yr, y/g/f, o/f, s/s, PS Bartlett 140.00
Am Watch Co, 18s, 21j, #1892, y/g/f, o/f, d/s, Crescent St 325.00
Am Watch Co, 18s, 21j, #1892, y/g/f, o/f, Grade #845 ....250.00
Am Watch Co, 18s, 21j, #1892, y/g/f, o/f, PA Special 1,945.00
Am Watch Co, 18s, 7j, #1857, k/w, CT Parker, scarce 2,650.00
Am Watch Co, 6s, 7j, #1873, y/g/f, h/c, Am Watch Co 195.00
Auburndale Watch Co, 18s, 7j, k/w, l/s, Lincoln 1,250.00
Aurora Watch Co, 18s, 11j, o/f, k/w, h/c 425.00

Aurora Watch Co, 18s, 15 ruby j, k/w, h/c 1,250.00
Ball (Elgin), 18s, 17j, silver, o/f, Official RR Standard 525.00
Ball (Hamilton), 16s, 21j, #999, g/f, o/f, l/s 365.00
Ball (Hamilton), 16s, 23j, #998, y/g/f, o/f, Elinvar 825.00
Ball (Hamilton), 18s, 19j, #999, g/f, o/f, l/s 450.00
Ball (Hampden), 18s, 17j, o/f, adj, RR, Superior Grade 1,375.00
Ball (Illinois), 12s, 19j, w/g/f, o/f 250.00
Ball (Waltham), 16s, 17j, y/g/f, o/f, Commercial Std 190.00
Ball (Waltham), 16s, 21j, o/f, Offical Standard 325.00
Columbus, 18s, 11-15j, k/w, k/s 440.00
Columbus, 18s, 15j, o/f, l/s 175.00
Columbus, 18s, 15j, y/g/f, o/f, Jay Gould 650.00
Columbus, 18s, 21j, y/g/f, h/c, train on dial, Railway King 495.00
Columbus, 18s, 23j, 14k, h/c, Columbus King 2,250.00
Columbus, 6s, 11j, 14k, h/c 495.00
Cornell, 18s, 15j, s/w, JC Adams 595.00
Cornell, 18s, 15j, silver, h/c, k/w, John Evans 465.00
Dudley, 12s, #1, 14k, o/f, flip-bk case, Masonic 3,450.00
Elgin, 10s, 18k, h/c, k/w, k/s, s/s, Gail Borden 675.00
Elgin, 12s, 15j, 14k, h/c 450.00
Elgin, 12s, 17j, 14k, h/c, GM Wheeler 495.00
Elgin, 16s, 15j, doctor's, 4th model, 14k, 2nd sweep hand 1,650.00
Elgin, 16s, 15j, 14k, h/c 575.00
Elgin, 16s, 21j, g/f, 3 fbd, grade #72-91, scarce 1,850.00
Elgin, 16s, 21j, y/g/f, g/j/s, o/f, BW Raymond 285.00
Elgin, 16s, 21j, y/g/f, g/j/s, 3 fbd 395.00
Elgin, 16s, 21j, y/g/f, o/f, l/s, RR, Father Time 295.00
Elgin, 16s, 23j, up/down indicator, BW Raymond 850.00
Elgin, 17s, 7j, k/w, orig silver case, Leader 250.00
Elgin, 18s, 11j, silver, h/c, k/w, gilded, MG Odgen 250.00
Elgin, 18s, 15j, o/f, d/s, k/w, silveroid, RR, BW Raymond 250.00
Elgin, 18s, 15j, silver, h/c, PA RR dial, BW Raymond k/w mvt .1,500.00
Elgin, 18s, 15j, 14k, h/c, k/w, k/s, HL Culver 1,245.00
Elgin, 18s, 17j, silveroid, BW Raymond 230.00
Elgin, 18s, 21j, y/g/f, o/f, Father Time 325.00
Elgin, 18s, 23j, y/g/f, o/f, 5-position, RR, Veritas 425.00
Elgin, 6s, 11j, 14k, h/c 400.00
Elgin, 6s, 15j, 20-yr, y/g/f, h/c, s/s 150.00
Fredonia, 18s, 11j, y/g/f, h/c, k/w 350.00
Hamilton, #4992B, 16s, 22j, o/f, steel case 250.00
Hamilton, #910, 12s, 17j, 20-yr, y/g/f, o/f, s/s 125.00
Hamilton, #912, 12s, 17j, y/g/f, o/f, adj 125.00
Hamilton, #920, 12s, 23j, 14k, o/f 495.00
Hamilton, #922MP, 12s, 18k case, Masterpiece (sgn) 1,200.00
Hamilton, #925, 18s, 17j, y/g/f, h/c, s/s, l/s 190.00
Hamilton, #928, 18s, 15j, y/g/f, o/f, s/s 160.00
Hamilton, #933, 18s, 16j, NP, h/c 1,200.00
Hamilton, #938, 18s, 17j, 10k, y/g/f, adj 495.00
Hamilton, #940, 18s, 21j, NP, coin silver, o/f 285.00
Hamilton, #946, 18s, 23j, y/g/f, o/f, g/j/s, EX 625.00
Hamilton, #947, 18s, 23j, 14k, h/c, orig/sgn, EX 6,450.00
Hamilton, #950, 16s, 23j, y/g/f, o/f, l/s, sgn d/s 550.00
Hamilton, #965, 16s, 17j, 14k, h/c, p/s, brg, scarce 995.00
Hamilton, #972, 16s, 17j, y/g/f, g/j/s, o/f, d/s, l/s, adj 175.00
Hamilton, #974, 16s, 17j, 20-yr, y/g/f, o/f, s/s 125.00
Hamilton, #992, 16s, 21j, y/g/f, o/f, adj, d/s, dbl roller 265.00
Hamilton, #992B, 16s, 21j, y/g/f, o/f, l/s, Bar/Crown 325.00
Hampden, 12s, 17j, w/g/f, o/f, thin model, Aviator 125.00
Hampden, 16s, 17j, o/f, adj 70.00
Hampden, 16s, 17j, y/g/f, h/c, s/w 180.00
Hampden, 16s, 21j, g/j/s, y/g/f, NP, h/c, Dueber, ¾-mvt 240.00
Hampden, 16s, 21j, o/f, adj, dbl roller, Special Railway 275.00
Hampden, 16s, 7j, gilded, NP, ¾-mvt 60.00
Hampden, 18s, 15j, k/w, mk on mvt, Railway 950.00

Hampden, 18s, 15j, s/w, gilded, JC Perry 250.00
Hampden, 18s, 15j, silver, h/c, k/w, Hayward 215.00
Hampden, 18s, 15j, y/g/f, damascened, h/c, Dueber 200.00
Hampden, 18s, 21j, y/g/f, g/j/s, h/c, New Railway 280.00
Hampden, 18s, 21j, y/g/f, o/f, d/s, l/s, N Am Railway 270.00
Hampden, 18s, 23j, y/g/f, d/s, adj, New Railway 365.00
Hampden, 18s, 23j, 14k, h/c, Special Railway 950.00
Hampden, 18s, 7-11j, k/w, gilded, Springfield Mass 150.00
Howard, E; 16s, 15j, 14k, h/c, s/w, Series V, L sz 1,400.00
Howard, E; 18s, 15j, silver, h/c, k/w, Series I, N sz 1,950.00
Howard, E; 18s, 15j, 14k, h/c, k/w, Series II, N sz 1,950.00
Howard, E; 18s, 15j, 18k, h/c, k/w, Series II, N sz 3,400.00
Howard, E; 18s, 17j, 25-yr, y/g/f, o/f, orig case 495.00
Howard, E; 6s, 15j, 18k, h/c, s/w, Series VI, G sz 1,650.00
Howard (Keystone), 12s, 23j, 14k, h/c, brg, Series 8 ....940.00
Howard (Keystone), 16s, 17j, y/g/f, o/f, Series 9 ....295.00
Howard (Keystone), 16s, 21j, y/g/f, o/f, RR Chronometer II ...450.00
Howard (Keystone), 16s, 23j, y/g/f, o/f, Series 0, jeweled bbl ...695.00
Illinois, 0s, 7j, 14k, h/c, l/s 325.00
Illinois, 12s, 17j, y/g/f, o/f, d/s dial 95.00
Illinois, 16s, 17j, silver, h/c, RR King 750.00
Illinois, 16s, 17j, y/g/f, o/f, d/s, Bunn, EX 385.00
Illinois, 16s, 19j, y/g/f, o/f, d/s, 60-hr, Sangamo Special ...1,095.00
Illinois, 16s, 21j, g/j/s, h/c, Burlington 250.00
Illinois, 16s, 21j, o/f, d/s, Santa Fe Special 395.00
Illinois, 16s, 21j, y/g/f, o/f, s/s, Bunn Special 325.00
Illinois, 16s, 23j, y/g/f, o/f, d/s, RR, Bunn Special 700.00
Illinois, 16s, 23j, y/g/f, stiff bow, o/f, Sangamo Special 795.00
Illinois, 18s, 11j, #1, silver, k/w, Alleghany 340.00
Illinois, 18s, 11j, #3, o/f, s/w, l/s, Comet 250.00
Illinois, 18s, 11j, Forest City 225.00
Illinois, 18s, 15j, #1, adj, k/w, k/s, Stuart 1,550.00
Illinois, 18s, 15j, #1, y/g/f, h/c, k/w, gilt, Bunn 1,600.00
Illinois, 18s, 15j, k/w, k/s, gilt, Railway Regulator 675.00
Illinois, 18s, 15j, silveroid , s/w 95.00
Illinois, 18s, 17j, g/j/s, adj, B&O RR Special 1,625.00
Illinois, 18s, 17j, NP, coin silver, h/c, s/w, Bunn 425.00
Illinois, 18s, 17j, silveroid, o/f, d/s, adj, Lakeshore 325.00
Illinois, 18s, 17j, o/f, s/w, 5th pinion, Miller 325.00
Illinois, 18s, 21j, g/j/s, g/f, o/f, A Lincoln 340.00
Illinois, 18s, 21j, g/j/s, o/f, adj, B&O RR Special 2,250.00
Illinois, 18s, 21j, 14k, h/c, g/j/s, Bunn Special 1,575.00
Illinois, 18s, 23j, g/j/s, Bunn Special 495.00
Illinois, 18s, 24j, g/j/s, o/f, adj, Chesapeake & Ohio 3,450.00
Illinois, 18s, 24j, g/j/s, Bunn Special 775.00
Illinois, 18s, 26j, g/j/s, o/f, Ben Franklin USA 6,500.00
Illinois, 18s, 26j, 14k, Penn Special 6,500.00
Illinois, 18s, 7j, #3, Interior 240.00
Illinois, 18s, 7j, #3, silveroid, America 225.00
Illinois, 18s, 9-11j, silveroid, o/f, k/w, s/s, Hoyt 275.00
Illinois, 8s, 13j, ¾-mvt, Rose LeLand, scarce 450.00
Ingersoll, 16s, 7j, wht base metal, Reliance 45.00
Lancaster, 18s, 7j, o/f, k/w, k/s, eng case 275.00
Marion US, 18s, h/c, k/w, k/s, ¾-plate, Asa Fuller 495.00
Marion US, 18s, 15j, NP, h/c, s/w, Henry Randel 675.00
Melrose Watch Co, 18s, 7j, k/w, k/s 495.00
New York Watch Co, 18s, 7j, silver, h/c, k/w, Geo Sam Rice ...375.00
New York Watch Co, 19j, low sz #, wolf's teeth wind 2,500.00
Patek Philippe, 12s, 18j, 18k, o/f 2,400.00
Patek Philippe, 16s, 20j, 18k, h/c 3,400.00
Rockford, 16s, 17j, y/g/f, h/c, brg, dbl roller 225.00
Rockford, 16s, 21j, #515, y/g/f 275.00
Rockford, 16s, 21j, g/j/s, o/f, grade #537, rare 1,650.00
Rockford, 16s, 23j, 14k, o/f, mk Doll on dial/mvt 2,250.00

Rockford, 18s, 15j, silver, o/f, k/w 175.00
Rockford, 18s, 17j, silveroid w/mc dial, fancy mvt/hands 275.00
Rockford, 18s, 17j, y/g/f, o/f, Winnebago 275.00
Rockford, 18s, 21j, o/f, King Edward 425.00
Seth Thomas, 18s, 17j, #2, g/j/s, adj, Henry Molineux 950.00
Seth Thomas, 18s, 17j, Edgemere 150.00
Seth Thomas, 18s, 25j, g/j/s, g/f, Maiden Lane 3,250.00
Seth Thomas, 18s, 7j, ¾-mvt, bk: eagle/Liberty model 275.00
South Bend, 12s, 21j, dbl roller, Grade #431 ....225.00
South Bend, 12s, 21j, orig o/f, d/s, Studebaker 325.00
South Bend, 18s, 21j, g/j/s, h/c, Studebaker 925.00
South Bend, 18s, 21j, 14k, h/c 995.00
Swiss, 18s, 18k, h/c, 1-min, Repeater, High Grade 4,250.00

Waterford

The Waterford Glass Company operated in Ireland from the late 1700s until 1851 when the factory closed. One hundred years later (in 1951) another Waterford glassworks was instituted that produced glass similar to the 18th century wares — crystal glass, usually with cut decoration. Today Waterford is a generic term referring to the type of glass first produced there.

Vase, exquisite cutting with scalloped top, 9", $280.00.

Brandy, Lismore 49.00
Carafe, Lismore 150.00
Claret, Colleen 48.00
Cocktail, Colleen, 4½" 48.00
Compote, Egyptian figures in bronze, 9¼x13" 450.00
Compote, fruit; Masterpiece Collection 695.00
Decanter, Baltray, crisscross miters/Xs, fluted, 10½" 165.00
Decanter, Inverted Arches w/T'print & fine rays, 10¼" 165.00
Decanter, Kenmore 200.00
Decanter, ship's; Alana 335.00
Flute champagne, Colleen 46.00
Flute champagne, Kylemore 55.00
Goblet, water; Colleen 48.00
Goblet, water; Lismore 39.00
Lamp, Masterpiece Collection 595.00
Liquor, Lismore 28.00
Old-fashioned, dbl; Comeragh 50.00
Sherbet, Colleen, 4⅜x4½" 48.00
Tumbler, highball; Colleen, 13-oz, 5½" 44.00
Tumbler, water; Colleen, 4½" 45.00
Tumbler, water; Comeragh 50.00
Tumbler, water; Lismore 34.00
Wine, Colleen, 3⅞" 42.50

Wine, Colleen, 5¾" 45.00
Wine, Kylemore 45.00
Wine, Lismore, tall stem 37.00

Watt Pottery

The Watt Pottery Company was established in Crooksville, Ohio, on July 5, 1922. From approximately 1922 until 1935, they manufactured hand-turned stone containers — jars, jugs, milk pans, preserve jars, and various sizes of mixing bowls, usually marked with a cobalt blue acorn stamp. In 1936 production of these items was discontinued, and the company began to produce kitchen utility ware and ovenware such as mixing bowls, spaghetti bowls and plates, canister sets, covered casseroles, salt and pepper shakers, cookie jars, ice buckets, pitchers, bean pots, and salad and dinnerware sets. Most Watt ware is individually hand-painted with bold brush strokes of red, green, or blue contrasting with the natural buff color of the glazed body. Several patterns were produced: Apple, Autumn Foliage, Cherry, Dutch Tulip, Morning-Glory, Pansy, Rooster, Tear Drop, Starflower, and Tulip, to name a few. Much of the ware was made for advertising premiums and is often found stamped with the name of the retail company.

Tragedy struck the Watt Pottery Company on October 4, 1965, when fire completely destroyed the factory and warehouse. Production never resumed, but the ware they made has withstood many years of service in American kitchens and is today highly regarded and prized by collectors. The vivid colors and folk art-like execution of each cheerful pattern create a homespun ambiance that will make Watt pottery a treasure for years to come.

For further study we recommend *Watt Pottery, An Identification and Value Guide*, by Sue and Dave Morris; she is listed in the Directory under Iowa. For the address of the *Watt's News* newsletter, see the section on Clubs, Newsletters, and Catalogs.

Apple, bowl, #24 ....225.00
Apple, bowl, mixing; #63 ....55.00
Apple, bowl, mixing; #8 ....65.00
Apple, casserole, French hdl, w/lid, #18, ind 265.00
Apple, casserole, w/lid, #601 ....165.00
Apple, cookie jar, w/lid, #503 ....550.00
Apple, creamer, #62 ....110.00
Apple, mug, #121 ....225.00
Apple, pie plate, #33 ....150.00
Apple, pitcher, #15 ....85.00
Apple, pitcher, w/ice lip, #17 ....300.00
Apple, shakers, hourglass form, pr 275.00
Apple, sugar bowl, w/lid, #98 ....425.00
Autumn Foliage, bowl, mixing; #07 ....45.00
Autumn Foliage, mug, #121 ....225.00
Autumn Foliage, platter, #31 ....150.00
Autumn Foliage, shakers, hourglass form, pr 250.00
Autumn Foliage, sugar bowl, open, #98 ....150.00
Banded, boxl, mixing; bl & wht bands, 6" 35.00
Brown glaze, dog dish, #7 ....145.00
Cherry, bowl, cereal; #52 ....55.00
Cherry, bowl, spaghetti; #39 ....175.00
Cherry, pitcher, #15 ....125.00
Dogwood, bowl, serving; 15" 150.00
Double Apple, casserole, w/lid, #96 ....325.00
Dutch Tulip, bowl, mixing; #7 ....125.00
Dutch Tulip, bowl, salad; #73 ....250.00
Dutch Tulip, bowl, w/lid, #05 ....250.00
Dutch Tulip, cheese crock, w/lid, #80 ....850.00
Dutch Tulip, pitcher, sq shape, #69 ....600.00

Eagle, casserole, w/lid, #601 ....450.00
Esmond, Happy & Sad Face cookie jar, w/lid 500.00
Goodies jar, w/lid, #59 ....475.00
Kitch-N-Queen, bowl, mixing; ribbed, #8 ....45.00
Kitch-N-Queen, ice bucket, w/lid, #9 ....125.00
Kla-Ham'rd, pie plate, #43-13 ....35.00
Moonflower, casserole, pk or gr starflower, w/lid, 8¾" 150.00
Morning-Glory, pitcher, w/ice lip, #96 ....550.00
Morning-Glory, sugar bowl, open, #98 ....250.00
Open Apple, bowl, mixing; #8 ....185.00
Rio Rose, bowl, mixing; 8" 65.00
Rio Rose, bowl, spaghetti; 13" 75.00
Rio Rose, casserole, stick hdl, w/lid, ind 125.00
Rio Rose, cup & saucer 85.00
Rooster, baking dish, rectangular 800.00
Rooster, bowl, spaghetti; #39 ....375.00
Rooster, bowl, w/lid, #67 ....225.00

Rooster, cheese crock, #80, $750.00.

Rooster, creamer, #62 ....250.00
Rooster, pitcher, #16 ....150.00
Rooster, shakers, bbl form, pr 400.00
Silhouette, cookie jar, gr on brn starflower, w/lid, #21 .....165.00
Starflower, bean pot, w/lid, #76 ....175.00
Starflower, bowl, #04 ....65.00
Starflower, bowl, mixing; #8 ....50.00
Starflower, casserole, tab hdld, w/lid, #18, ind 150.00
Starflower, grease jar, w/lid, #47 ....250.00
Starflower, pie plate, #33 ....250.00
Starflower, pitcher, #15 ....65.00
Tear Drop, bean pot, w/lid, #76 ....125.00
Tear Drop, pitcher, #15 ....65.00
Tear Drop, shakers, bbl form, pr 300.00
Tulip, bowl, #64 ....75.00
Tulip, bowl, mixing; #63 ....135.00
Tulip, casserole, ribbed, w/lid, #601 ....265.00
Tulip, cookie jar, w/lid, #503 ....450.00
Tulip, creamer, #62 ....185.00
Tulip, pitcher, #16 ....200.00
White Daisy, pitcher, 7" 200.00
Woodgrain, cookie bbl, w/lid, #617W 125.00

Wave Crest

Wave Crest is a line of decorated opal ware (milk glass) patented in 1892 by the C.F. Monroe Co. of Meriden, Connecticut. They made a full line of items for every room of the house, but they are probably best known for their boxes and vases. Most items were hand painted in various levels of decoration, but more transfers were used in the later years prior to the company's demise in 1916. Floral themes are common; items with the scenics and portraits are rarer and more highly prized. Many pieces have ornately scrolled ormolu and brass handles, feet and rims attached. Early pieces were often signed with a black mark; later a red banner mark was used, an occasionally a paper label may be found. However, the glass is quite distinctive and has not been reproduced, so even unmarked items are easy to recognize. Our advisors for this category are Dolli and Wilfred Cohen; they are listed in the Directory under California. Note: There is no premium for signatures on Wave Crest. Values are given for hand-decorated pieces that are *not* worn.

Ash receiver, daisies, bl on peach & wht, metal base **195.00**
Biscuit jar, floral, HP/brn transfer, emb mold, 11½x5¼" **295.00**
Biscuit jar, floral transfer, molded lattice, 12½x5" sq **295.00**
Biscuit jar, Rococo, HP florals on beige, SP mts, mk, 9x5" **495.00**
Biscuit jar, Swirl, pansies, HP on cream, unmk, rstr SP, 7¾" **495.00**
Bowl, trinket; Swirl, floral, bl & wht on yel shaded, 3" **100.00**
Box, Baroque Shell, w/florals, 4x7" dia **750.00**
Box, Christmas Holly, irid int, 7" dia **975.00**
Box, clock insert in lid, pk daisies in bl fr, sqd **1,795.00**
Box, Collars & Cuffs, Puffy, bl/wht floral, sq, 7" W **950.00**
Box, cut glass, lg hobstar/prism cuts, mirror w/in, 6" dia **795.00**
Box, morning-glories on gr w/webbing & pk enamel, 6" dia **595.00**
Box, Niagara Falls transfer on lt bl, mk, 2¼x3" sq **325.00**
Box, pansies, mc on lt pk to yel, blk mk, 6¾x7½" **1,495.00**
Box, pansies on emb pk, dk gr/gold drips, hinged, 3x8" dia **600.00**
Box, Puffy, pk wild roses on lid, 3" dia **225.00**
Box, Puffy, w/red clover/wht daisies, sqd, 7" W **595.00**
Box, Swirl, autumn leaves/florals on peach, 5½" dia **225.00**
Box, Swirl, erratic blk ribbon/sm flowers on wht, 7" dia **885.00**
Box, Swirl, lily of valley on lt bl, no mk, 3" dia **250.00**
Box, Swirl w/floral, 7" **595.00**
Box, Swirl w/sm flowers, ormolu ftd base, 6x7" **750.00**
Box, wild roses/leaves fr red daisies on emb lt gr, 5½" dia **350.00**
Card holder, Puffy, florals, ornate rim, 4¼x2¾x1½" **350.00**
Cigarette/match holder, emb scrolls/daisies, ormolu ft, 3x6" **450.00**
Ferner, floral, bl on lt bl, brass liner, 4¼x7½" **395.00**
Ferner, Puffy, floral, pk on bl, metal rim, insert, 7" dia **395.00**
Humidor, Cigars/forget-me-nots, Indian/horse on lid, mk **660.00**
Humidor, Puffy w/mc flowers & scrolls, metal mts **950.00**
Humidor, Swirl w/scroll & wild rose panels, 7" **650.00**
Photo holder, clovers, pk on lt bl, ftd, orig lining, label **550.00**
Shakers, Erie Twist, solid wht, pr **150.00**
Shakers, Swirl, floral, bl on pk to wht, pr **185.00**
Sugar shaker, Swirl, yel flowers & bl scrolls **495.00**
Tray, floral, pk on bl, open, w/mirror, 4¾x4" dia **575.00**
Tray, jewel; Swirl, floral, mc on pk & wht panels, 2¼x6¾" **275.00**
Vase, floral, mc on yel to cream, emb decor, str sides, 6" **275.00**
Vase, floral, pk on wht w/gr scrolls, dolphin mts/hdls, 17" **1,295.00**
Vase, lg spray of mc mums on wht w/emb scrolls, slim, 10" **595.00**
Vase, mums, pk/wht/orange on lt pk, beaded rim, 10" **595.00**
Vase, violets on yel to wht, str w/ormolu base & ft, 6¼" **395.00**

Weapons

Among the varied areas of specialization within the broad category of weapons, guns are by far the most popular. Muskets are among the earliest firearms; they were large-bore shoulder arms, usually firing black powder with separate loading of powder and shot. Some ignited the charge by flintlock or caplock, while later types used a firing pin with a metallic cartridge. Side arms, referred to as such because they were worn at the side, include pistols and revolvers. Pistols range from early single-shot and multiple barrels to modern types with cartridges held in

the handle. Revolvers were supplied with a cylinder that turned to feed a fresh round in front of the barrel breech. Other firearms include shotguns, which fired round or conical bullets and had a smooth inner barrel surface, and rifles, so named because the interior of the barrel contained spiral grooves (rifling) which increased accuracy. For further study we recommend *Modern Guns, Tenth Edition*, by Russell Quertermous and Steve Quertermous, available at your local bookstore. Our advisor for swords is Steve Hess; he is listed in the Directory under Florida. All other weapons are under the advisement of Steve Howard, see the Directory under California. See also Militaria.

Key:
bbl — barrel
cal — caliber
conv — conversion
cyl — cylinder
f/l — flintlock
f/s — full stock
ga — gauge
hdw — hardware
h/s — half stock

mag — magazine
mgn — magnum
mod — modified
oct — octagon
o/u — over/under
p/b — patch box
perc — percussion
/s — stock

Astra presentation grade semiautomatic pistol, 32 ACP caliber, plastic grips, engraved scroll pattern, pre-WWII, 3¾" barrel, NM, $2,000.00.

Carbines

Burnside Civil War, 54 cal, orig sights, complete w/ring, VG **500.00**
Burnside Civil War, 54 cal, sight & ring missing, 21" bbl, G **375.00**
Colt Lightning Trapper, 44/40 cal, full mag, 16" bbl, EX **1,900.00**
German military, G33/40, full-length stock, 20" bbl, G **400.00**
Kruger Mini-14, 223 cal, stainless, pistol grip/s, 18" bbl, M **425.00**
Marlin 1893, 30/30 cal, full mag, 20" bbl, G **150.00**
Poutney & Trimble, 50 cal, military sights, 21⅝" bbl, M **2,350.00**
Remington 760, 30/06 cal, bead front, pistol grip, 19" bbl, VG ..**225.00**
Ruger #3, 22 Hornet cal, single shot, 22" rnd bbl, M **275.00**
Ruger 10/22, 22 LR cal, flip-down sights, w/scope, 18" bbl, EX ..**125.00**
Sharps 1863, 52 cal, carbine butt, missing ring, 22" bbl, G **1,550.00**
Sharps 1863SRC, 52 cal, orig sights, w/ring & bar, 22" bbl, G **1,325.00**
Smith Civil War, 52 cal, complete w/ring & bar, 21½" bbl, EX ..**1,000.00**
Spencer 1865, 50 cal, w/Stabler cutoff, 20" bbl, EX **1,600.00**
Springfield 1855 pistol-type perc, 58 cal, 12" bbl, VG **1,600.00**
US M1 (Inland Mfg), 30 M1 carbine cal, pistol grip, 18" bbl, EX .**400.00**
Winchester Pre-64 94, 32 cal, peep sight/full mag, 20" bbl, EX ..**200.00**
Winchester 1866, 44 cal rimfire, full mag, w/ring, 20" bbl, VG .**4,500.00**
Winchester 1873, 44/40 cal, full mag, 20" bbl, saddle ring, G **400.00**

Winchester 1886, 45/70 cal, full mag, w/ring, 22" bbl, EX 7,500.00
Winchester 1892, 38/40 cal, rpl sight, 2/3-mag, 20" bbl, VG 900.00
Winchester 1894 Pre-War, 32/40, full mag, 20" bbl, EX 275.00
Winchester 94, 30/30 cal, button mag, w/ring, 20" bbl, rstr 450.00
Winchester 94 Eastern, 32 special cal, full mag, 20" bbl 300.00
Winchester 94 Trapper, 30/30 cal, full mag, w/ring, 16" bbl, M .250.00

Muskets

Austrian Military, perc, 70 cal, brass bbl bands, 42" bbl, VG 425.00
Brown-Bess 3rd Model, f/l, 75 cal, f/s, brass hdw, 39" bbl, G 800.00
Colt 1863, mk lock, bbl dvtl for sight, G 350.00
European military, bolster perc conv, 70 cal, 44" bbl, G 200.00
European military perc, 75 cal, brass hdw, 39¼" bbl, VG 400.00
Francotte (Belgium) perc, 70 cal, oct breech, 40" bbl, VG 450.00
Harper's Ferry 1812, bbl mk US & Ohio, dtd 1816, VG 625.00
Remington 1858, lock/bbl dtd 1858, bbl stamped NJ, VG 475.00
Savage 1863 Civil War, 58 cal, f/s, NP, 40" bbl, NM 750.00
Spanish, perc, 58 cal, lock mk Madrid/1861, 33" bbl, VG 165.00
Springfield, bolster perc conv, 69 cal, f/s, 42" bbl, G 500.00
Tower, perc, 58 cal, f/s, brass trigger guard, 39" bbl, G 550.00
Tower 1862, 61 cal, 39½" bbl, VG 225.00
Tower-Brn-Bess 2nd Model, perc conv, 75 cal, 42½" bbl, EX 895.00
US Springfield 1842, 69 cal, 42" rnd bbl, NM+bayonet 4,000.00
US Springfield 1861, 48 cal, f/s, rpl sight, 39" cut bbl, G 200.00
US Springfield 1863, 58 cal, 40" bbl, EX+bayonet & sling 2,800.00
US Springfield 1885, 58 cal, f/l stock, CI hdw, 40" bbl, G 675.00
US Springfield 1896 (Krag), 30 US cal, w/ring, 22" bbl, G 400.00
US/Norfolk 1861, 48 cal, lock mk & dtd 1863, 40" bbl, VG 350.00
Winchester Hotchkiss, 45/70 cal, bolt action, 28" bbl, VG 500.00
Winchester low-wall winder, 22 short cal, 28" bbl, EX 500.00

Pistols

British Sea Service f/l, 55 cal, f/s, mk RE, 12" bbl, VG 1,100.00
Colt Camp Perry Target, 22 cal, single shot, 10" bbl, VG 600.00
Colt Government, 45 ACP cal, rpl grips, 5" bbl, G 275.00
Colt 1st Model Derringer, 41 cal, CI, 2½" bbl, VG 800.00
Colt 1902 Sporting Automatic, 38 rimless cal, 6" bbl, G 350.00
Colt 1903 Pocket, 32 ACP cal, rubber grip, 3¾" bbl, EX 300.00
Colt 1911 Army, 45 ACP cal, walnut grips, 5" bbl, VG 300.00
CZ 27, 7.65 cal, compo grip w/monogram, 3¾" bbl, VG 85.00
Fr 1763 f/l, 70 cal, brass hdw, 8⅛" mk bbl, VG 1,600.00
Harrington & Richardson, 32 cal, self-loading, 3½" bbl, EX 250.00
Hi-Standard H-E, 22 LR cal, walnut grips, 4½" bbl, VG 300.00
J Tarrat perc, 45 cal, single shot, 4¼" damascus oct bbl, G 125.00
Kentland & Co f/l, 65 cal, brass hdw, 9⅛" steel bbl, VG 925.00
Mauser, 32 ACP cal, wood grips, pocket type, 3¼" bbl, VG 75.00
Nock perc conv, 65 cal, single shot, 6" damascus oct bbl, G 175.00
Philadelphia derringer, 44 cal, much eng, 2½" bbl, 5½", EX ...2,000.00
Remington derringer, 32 cal, ring trigger, 4-shot, 3⅜" bbl, G 175.00
Ruger RST-4-S, 22 LR cal, stainless, plastic grips, 4¾" bbl, M ...285.00
Smith & Wesson 61-2, 22 LR cal, plastic grips, 2" bbl, VG 200.00
Springfield Armory 1911 Army, 45 ACP cal, 5" bbl, VG 550.00
Stevens Tip-Up #41, 22 cal, wood grips, 3½" rnd/oct bbl, EX 500.00
US Army WWII (Remington Rand), 45 cal, wood grips, 5" bbl, M .575.00
US Property Colt 1903 Officer's, 32 ACP cal, 5" bbl, M 1,750.00
US R Johnson Marshal f/l, 54 cal, single shot, 8½" bbl, EX 2,050.00
Walther PTK, 7.65 cal, marbleized grips w/banner, 3¼" bbl, G ..125.00

Revolvers

Brevet, 32 cal, folding trigger, dbl action, 3¾" bbl, EX 100.00
Colt (2nd Generation), 38 cal, single action, 5½" bbl, EX 800.00

Colt Bisley, 38/40 cal, single action, 7½" bbl, EX 4,000.00
Colt New Line, 22 cal, flute cyl, ivory grips, 2¼" bbl, G 375.00
Colt New Service, 45 cal, ivory grips, 7½" bbl, EX 600.00
Colt Officer's Model Target, 22 LR cal, wood grips, 6" bbl, EX ..325.00
Colt Official Police, 38 special cal, wood grips, 6" bbl, EX 175.00
Colt Police Positive, 32/20 cal, rubber grips, 6" bbl, VG 200.00
Colt Shooting Master Target, 38 cal, wood grips, 6" bbl, EX 925.00
Colt 1862 Police, 36 cal, 5-shot cyl, wood grips, 6" bbl, VG ...1,150.00
Colt 1878, 41 cal, dbl action, rubber grips, 4½" bbl, VG 550.00
FIE Model E15, 22 LR cal, single action, 4¾" bbl, NM 100.00
Iver Johnson, 38 S&W cal, dbl action, rubber grips, 5" bbl, M ...155.00
Nagant, 44 cal, dbl action, wood grips, 6" oct bbl, EX 375.00
Nagant Brevet, 38 cal, dbl action, 6" oct bbl, +bayonette 1,200.00
Remington Army perc, 44 cal, wood grips, 8" oct bbl, G 250.00
Ruger New Model Single Six, 22 LR & 22 mgn cal, 5½" bbl, EX .225.00
Ruger Redhawk Mgn, 44 cal, stainless, 7½" bbl, M 375.00
Smith & Wesson, 45 L Colt conv, triple lock, 6½" bbl, VG 375.00
Smith & Wesson #2 Army, 32 long cal rimfire, 6" oct bbl, EX ...900.00
Smith & Wesson Safety DA, 38 cal, pearl grips, rare 2" bbl, M ..775.00
Smith & Wesson 1st Model, 3rd issue, 22 cal, 3¼" bbl, EX 300.00
Smith & Wesson 1917 Army, 45 ACP cal, rpl grips, 5½" bbl, VG .225.00
Smith & Wesson 27-2, 357 mgn cal, wood grips, 8⅜" bbl, M 275.00
Smith & Wesson 38/44 Outdoorsman, 38 special cal, 6½" bbl, M ..675.00
Smith & Wesson 48, 22 mgn cal, wood grips, 8⅜" bbl, M 250.00
Smith & Wesson 48-4, 22 mgn cal, factory eng, 8⅜" bbl, M 550.00
Smith & Wesson 57 Mgn, 41 cal, target trigger, 8⅜" bbl, EX 500.00
Smith & Wesson 57 Mgn, 44 cal, red ramp front, 8⅜" bbl, M 350.00
Webly Mark VI, 45 cal, rubber grips, 6" bbl, EX 250.00
Winchester 70 XPR Featherweight, 257 cal, 22" bbl, M 475.00

Rifles

Browning Grade 2, 22 LR cal, eng action, 19½" bbl, M 625.00
Colt Burgess, 44/40 cal, lever action, 25½" oct bbl, VG 975.00
Colt Lightning, 38/40 cal, full mag, 26" rnd bbl, EX 1,200.00
E Loomis Plains perc, 38 cal, h/s, 30½" bbl, G 275.00
Enfield 1887, 45 cal, single shot, f/s, 33" bbl, G 225.00
George Fay KY, 50 cal, f/s, brass hdw, 41" oct bbl, VG 1,500.00
German 98 Sniper's, 8mm cal, 24" bbl, VG, +M scope in case ...600.00
Johnson Automatic 1941, 30-06 cal, 22" bbl+sling & bayonet ...1,800.00
KY f/l, 60 cal, smooth bore, brass hds, f/s, 39" oct bbl, G 800.00
Lee Arms USN 1879, 45/70 cal, mk breech, f/s, 29" bbl, VG 700.00
Marlin GA22, 22 LR cal, full mag, ltd ed, 22" rnd bbl, EX 150.00
Marlin 1881 Standard, 40/60 cal, 38" oct bbl, G 450.00
Marlin 1892, 32 cal rimfire, full mag, 24" oct bbl, G 175.00
Remington 1863 Zouave perc, 58 cal, f/s, 33" bbl, EX 1,800.00
Remington 700 Safari, 375 mgn cal, bolt action, 24" bbl, M 400.00
Ruger 10/22 Deluxe, 22 LR cal, pistol grips, 18½" bbl, EX 135.00
Sharp's New Model 1863, 52 cal, military sights, 30" bbl, G 800.00
Smith & Wesson Sporting, 30-06 cal, bolt action, 21" bbl, NM ...300.00
Springfield 1870 USN, 50 cal, single shot, 32⅝" bbl, G 400.00
Springfield 66, 50/70 cal, military sights, 28½" bbl, G 200.00
US Harper's Ferry MS, rebored to 58 cal, 33" bbl, G 875.00
US Smith Corona 08-43, 30-06 cal, peep sights, f/s, 24" bbl, VG .175.00
US Springfield M-1 Garand, 30-06 cal, f/s, 24" bbl, M 550.00
US Springfield 1888 trap door, 45/70 cal, 32⅝" bbl, NM 900.00
US Springfield 1898 (Krag), 30 cal, f/s dtd 1902, 30" bbl, EX 525.00
US Springfield 1903-A1, 30-06 cal, 24" rpl bbl dtd 1942, NM ...300.00
US 1819 JH Hall breech-loading f/l, 52 cal, 32⅝" bbl, NM 3,250.00
Weatherby 3000L, 30-06 cal, left-hand bolt action, 22" bbl, M .500.00
Whitney Arms, 32/20 cal, lever action, 24" oct bbl, G 350.00
Winchester 1895, 30-06 cal, rpl bead, 24" rnd bbl, G 300.00
Winchester 1906, 22 cal, full mag, grip stock, 20" rnd bbl, G 175.00
Winchester 52 Target, 22 cal, 28" med-weight bbl, EX 400.00

Winchester 54, rare 22 hornet cal, 14" rnd bbl, EX 800.00
Winchester 61, 22 special cal, pistol grips, 24" rnd bbl, EX 300.00
Winchester 70 XPR Featherweight, 257 cal, 22" bbl, M+scope ..475.00
Winchester 92, 44/40 cal, str grip stock, 24" oct bbl, G 425.00

Shotguns

Baretta S680 o/u, 12-ga, 29½" ventilated rib bbls, M 800.00
Browning A-5, 12-ga, mod choke, 26" bbl, EX 350.00
Browning A-5 auto loading, 16-ga, full choke, 28" bbl, EX 650.00
Browning A-5 Light, 20-ga, full choke, pistol grip, 26" bbl, M ...550.00
Browning Lightning o/u, 12-ga, full/mod choke, 28" bbl, NM 900.00
Colt Damascus dbl bbl hammerless, 12-ga, 30" bbl, EX 850.00
Darne pre-WWI, 16-ga, eng action, 24" dbl bbls, VG 700.00
Fox Sterlingworth by Savage, 12-ga, 30" full/mod bbls, G 225.00
Francotte dbl bbl, 12-ga, eng action, 30" steel bbls, G 400.00
Ithaca Deluxe Grade 3, 10-ga, 32" dbl steel bbls, VG 350.00
Ithaca hammerless, 12-ga, 25" dbl damascus bbls, reblued, EX ...250.00
Ithaca 37 Steel Grade, 12-ga, mod choke, 28" bbl, M 300.00
Joseph Child o/u perc, 29" oct 40 cal rifle bbl/12-ga bbl, G 625.00
Joseph Manton perc, 12-ga, 30" damascus dbl bbls, VG 350.00
Parker hammer, 10-ga, top lever, 32" damascus dbl bbls, VG 350.00
Parker Trogan Grade, 20-ga, full/mod choke, 28" dbl bbls, VG ..800.00
Remington Sportsman A-5, 16-ga, 2¾" chamber, 28" bbl, VG ..400.00
Savage 311, 410-ga, full chokes, 26" dbl bbls, M 175.00
Smith LC A2 Grade, 12-ga, full/mod chokes, 30" dbl bbl, NM .4,000.00
Weatherby Centurion semiautomatic, 12-ga, 30" bbl, NM 325.00
Winchester Super X Model 1, 12-ga, 3 30" bbls, EX 325.00
Winchester 1100, 20-ga, poly-choke, 27" bbl, EX 150.00
Winchester 1300 Ranger, 21-ga, winchoke set, 28" bbl, M 350.00
Winchester 42 Deluxe, 410-ga, mod choke/fancy grip, 26" bbl, NM ..1,300.00
Winchester 42 Field Grade, 410-ga, full choke, 26" bbl, EX 850.00
WW Greener hammerless, 16-ga, 28" damascus dbl bbls, G 400.00
Zoli o/u, 12-ga, box lock action, pistol grip, 28" bbl, M 350.00

Swords

All swords listed below are priced 'with scabbard.'

Am horseman's saber, brass guard, dbl-edged 31½" blade, G 700.00
Ames US Civil War 1841, brass D guard, 21¼" mk blade, EX 575.00
Artillery officer's, eagle head type, 30" blade, 1830s, EX 375.00
Confederate officer's, leather-covered grip, 36" blade, EX 1,500.00
European court, iron hilt, wood hdl, 39" Coulichimard blade 700.00
Fr Artillery short broad sword, brass hilt, 19¼" blade, VG 100.00
NCO saber, wood hdl, brass grip, 28" blade, ca 1810, VG 150.00
Non-regulation Civil War officer's, ornate etch, 34" blade, EX ..900.00
Samari, CI suba w/gold inlay, 27" blade, VG 300.00
US 1860 Cavalry, brass guard/hilt, 35¼" curved blade, G 325.00
USN 1917, pierced hand guard/compo hdl, 24¾" steel blade, EX ..225.00

Weathervanes

The earliest weathervanes were of handmade wrought iron and were generally simple angular silhouettes with a small hole suggesting an eye. Later copper, zinc, and polychromed wood with features in relief were fashioned into more realistic forms. Ships, horses, fish, Indians, roosters, and angels were popular motifs. In the 19th century, silhouettes were often made from sheet metal. Wooden figures became highly carved and were painted in vivid colors. E.G. Washburne and Company in New York was one of the most prominent manufacturers of weathervanes during the last half of the century. Two-dimensional sheet metal weathervanes are increasing in value due to the already

heady prices of the full-bodied variety. Originality, strength of line, and patination help to determine value. When no condition is indicated, the items listed below are assumed to be in excellent condition.

Key:
fb — full-bodied   f/fb — flattened full-bodied

Stag, molded copper, attributed to Harris & Co., Boston, 19th century, bullet holes, 25x31", $4,675.00.

Banner, iron, cut-out letter A, gold pnt, Am, 1800s, 40" 330.00
Butterfly, sheet metal, mc pnt, late 1800s, 16½x23" 1,550.00
Eagle, copper & zinc, full bodied, 1900s, 15x34½" 550.00
Eagle, molded copper, Am, early 1900s, 40x55" 2,300.00
Eagle, molded copper, EX details, old gilt rpt, 1900s, 32½" 880.00
Eagle, molded copper, gold pnt, 1900s, 19x25" 495.00
Eagle w/wings wide, tin, 21½" H on CI arrow 160.00
Grasshopper, sheet copper, verdigris, Am, 1900s, 35" L 770.00
Grasshopper, zinc, worn gold pnt, Am, 1900s, 20¼" 360.00
Half Moon (Hudson's ship) form w/inscr, molded copper, 44x45" ..1,875.00
Horse, Morgan; sheet metal, ca 1900, 28½x33", EX 600.00
Horse, sheet copper & zinc, Am, 1800s, 24", EX 1,325.00
Horse, sheet metal, old mc pnt, 30", on wooden arrow, VG 250.00
Horse & sulky on arrow, sheet iron, blk pnt, 39" 245.00
Horse prancing, pnt wood, rpr, 1800s, 24" on modern base 75.00
Horse running, cast & sheet copper, EX patina, 33" on rpl base .2,300.00
Horse running, CI, Am, 1900s, 30x23½" 2,650.00
Horse running, copper & zinc, gold pnt, Jewell, 1800s, 18x27" .1,450.00
Horse running, molded copper, verdigris, 1800s, 32" 1,650.00
Horse running, molded copper & zinc, gold rpt, 1800s, 31" 880.00
Horse running, molded copper/cast zinc, verdigris, 1880s, 28" 880.00
Horse running, sheet metal, 2-pc w/rivets, old pnt, 24x38" 2,000.00
Horse running, tin & CI, 2-part, 9½x8" on 24" CI arrow 185.00
Horse running w/rider, molded copper & zinc, 1800s, Am, 41" 1,550.00
House silhouette, galvanized sheet metal, 27" on 77" stand 250.00
Mariner w/spy glass, sheet metal, blk pnt, Am, 1800s 600.00
Merino sheep, molded copper, verdigris, 1800s, 28½" 4,125.00
Moose, zinc & copper, wooden base, 1900s, 28½x39" 700.00
Nude, molded copper, recumbent, flowing hair, 44x60x23" 1,650.00
Ox, molded zinc & copper, gold rpt, 1850s, 19½x34½" 3,850.00
Peacock, wood & wire silhouette, mc pnt, 1900s, 14x49" 935.00
Pig, tin, old silver-gray pnt, 5x9¼x¾"+21" CI arrow 185.00
Rooster, cast & sheet iron, gold rpt, 37" 1,550.00
Rooster, copper, worn gilt, late 1800s, 18x20" 2,400.00
Rooster, sheet copper, verdigris, ca 1800, old rpr, 23x42" 3,300.00
Rooster, sheet metal, 2-pc, mc pnt, lt rust, 32½", VG 600.00

Sailing ship, wood & metal, EX pnt, Am, 1930s, 16x25" **715.00**
Schooner, tin/wood/wire, EX pnt, 1900s, 31", EX **1,100.00**
Scroll, copper, zinc & iron, gold pnt, 1800s, 47x55x7" **935.00**
Shorebird, metal, old gilt pnt, 1900s, 18½x24" **1,200.00**
Stag leaping, copper & zinc, att Harris, Boston, rprs, 30x31" ..**9,900.00**
Steer, molded copper, verdigris, cast horns, 11½x26" **1,750.00**
Touring car, copper, Am, 1910, 13x31", EX **3,000.00**
Weaver's shuttle, molded copper, verdigris, Am, 1800s, 64" ...**2,750.00**

Weaving

Early Americans used a variety of tools and a great amount of time to produce the material from which their clothing was made. Soaked and dried flax was broken on a flax brake to remove waste material. It was then tapped and stroked with a scutching knife. Hackles further removed waste and separated the short fibers from the longer ones. Unspun fibers were placed on the distaff on the spinning wheel for processing into yarn. The yarn was then wound around a reel for measuring. Three tools used for this purpose were the niddy-noddy, the reel yarn winder, and the click reel. After it was washed and dyed, the yarn was transferred to a barrel-cage or squirrel-cage swift and fed onto a bobbin winder.

Today flax wheels are more plentiful than the large wool wheels since they were small and could be more easily stored and preserved. The distaff, an often-discarded or misplaced part of the wheel, is very scarce. French spinners from the Quebec area painted their wheels. Many have been stripped and refinished by those unaware of this fact. Wheels may be very simple or have a great amount of detail, depending upon the owner's ethnic background and the maker's skill.

Hatchel, mixed hardwoods, sheet metal trim, steel spikes, 16" **85.00**
Hatchel, wood base & lid, punched tin sheath, 1773, 5x14x3" ..**170.00**
Loom light, wrought, sawtooth ratchet, rushlight holder **880.00**
Swift, maple w/cup finial, iron clamp, 24x26" expanded **195.00**
Wheel, corner type, tripod base, trn legs/etc, +2 distaffs **425.00**
Wheel, hardwood, Alfred ME, rpl treadle arm, 33" **300.00**
Wheel, hardwoods, incomplete bobbin assembly, 43" dia, 60" ...**200.00**
Wheel, Saxony style, orange & blk striping, complete, IA Fox ..**425.00**
Wheel, Saxony style, trn legs/spokes, complete, EX **350.00**
Winder, bench-type base, 4 trn legs, cvd 1781, EX **200.00**
Winder, hardwoods, geared counter mechanism, 36", EX **150.00**
Winder, 6 trn arms, flattened finial, orig pnt, 30½" dia **400.00**

Webb

Thomas Webb and Sons have been glassmakers in Stourbridge, England, since 1837. Besides their fine cameo glass, they have also made enameled ware and pieces heavily decorated with applied glass ornaments. The butterfly is a motif that has been so often featured that it tends to suggest Webb as the manufacturer. Our advisor for this category is Don Williams; he is listed in the Directory under Missouri. See also specific types of glass such as Alexandrite, Burmese, Mother of Pearl, and Peachblow.

Bowl, aqua to cream o/l, clear snail ft/rigaree/prunts, 4½" **265.00**
Bowl, burnt orange satin w/ecru int, crimped/petal top, 3½" **200.00**
Bowl, Dmn Quilt pk MOP satin, pleated, frosted base, 3½x10" .**750.00**
Bowl, pk w/yel int, 3 appl clear ft & leaf, 8-crimp, 3½x4" **145.00**
Ewer, 3 apples, gold leaves/branches on bl satin, 9x4" **425.00**
Jar, sweetmeat; florals/acorns on deep bl MOP satin, SP lid ...**1,125.00**
Pitcher, tankard; orange satin w/gold roses & insects, 11" **400.00**
Pitcher, tankard; peachblow, sgn, 9" **385.00**

Rose bowl, blown-out floral on gr to wht satin, 4" dia **275.00**
Rose bowl, florals on ivory, egg shape, 8-crimp, 3½x2½" **95.00**
Rose bowl, gold leaves/mc geometrics on cream, ftd, 3½x3" **75.00**
Vase, cased amethyst, allover dk raised leafy vines, 5¾" **190.00**
Vase, cream, cranberry threads/clear rigaree, egg shape, 4½" **95.00**
Vase, dotted flowers, red/bl/yel on opal, stick neck, 10½' **450.00**
Vase, florals on lt to dk pk satin, 4 emb shells, 3¼x4½" **125.00**
Vase, florals/bird/butterfly, yel on bl shaded satin, 8x6" **425.00**
Vase, gold fern/butterfly on orange shaded, hdls, 7", pr **495.00**
Vase, gold foliage/butterflies/monkey on red cased, 6" **325.00**
Vase, gold prunus on bl shaded, sqd/dimpled, 4" **245.00**
Vase, gold prunus/butterfly on yel satin, cream int, 6½" **325.00**
Vase, gold prunus/pine needles on brn satin, cream int, 6x6" **595.00**
Vase, Nouveau-style tulips, yel-gr on crystal, flared, 9x6½" **675.00**
Vase, orange cased w/much gold, bronzy sq hdls, 7¼", pr **500.00**
Vase, pk & wht stripes, not cased, frilly top, 8x4" **425.00**
Vase, yel to wht satin, wht int, gourd shape, 10½" **285.00**

Cameo

Bottle, lay-down, floral/grass, wht on bright bl, 6½" **2,000.00**
Bowl, daisies, bk: wisteria, floral rim, wht on red, 4½" **1,400.00**
Bowl, gooseberry vines, wht on red, 2¾x5" **1,400.00**
Bowl, lilies, bk: lily of valley, wht on bl, 3x4" **2,200.00**
Bowl, pk o/l cut w/leaves & flowers, clear ft, crimped, 5½" **1,200.00**
Lamp, base/shade w/floral, bk: bee, wht/red on citron, 12½" ...**7,000.00**
Vase, bleeding hearts, wht/red on citron, bulbous, 6½" **2,300.00**
Vase, clematis, who on red, ovoid, att, 8" **1,200.00**

Vase, dianthus blossoms and grasses, blue and white on pale amber, applied cobalt layered in white elbow-shaped 'bamboo' handles, Gem, 6", $8,500.00.

Vase, ferns/grass, pk on wht, ruffled stick neck, 4¾" **300.00**
Vase, fish/bird bands, simulated ivory, bulbous neck, 6¾" **1,500.00**
Vase, floral, bk: butterfly, wht on citron, bulbous, 10" **2,200.00**
Vase, floral, wht on red, detailed leaves & buds, 5" **1,250.00**
Vase, floral/bk: butterfly, wht on amber, cupped rim, 5" **750.00**
Vase, geraniums, bk: butterfly, wht on red, bulbous, 9" **3,300.00**
Vase, lilies/buds, wht on brn, 6" **1,400.00**
Vase, rose bush/butterflies, wht on citron, bottle form, 13" **3,500.00**
Vase, sunflowers/leaves, geometric band, wht on red, 7¾" **2,500.00**

Wedgwood

Josiah Wedgwood established his pottery in Burslem, England, in 1759. He produced only molded utilitarian earthenwares until 1770 when new facilities were opened at Etruria for the production of ornamental wares. It was there he introduced his famous Basalt and Jasperware. Jasperware, an unglazed fine stoneware decorated with classic figures in white relief, was usually produced in blues; but it was also made in ground colors of green, lilac, yellow, black, or white. Occasionally three or more colors were used in combination. It has been in continuous production to the present day and is the most easily recognized of all the Wedgwood lines. Jasper-dip is a ware with a solid-color body or a white body that has been dipped in an overlay color. It was introduced in the late 1700s and is the type most often encountered on today's market.

Though Wedgwood's Jasperware was highly acclaimed, on a more practical basis his improved creamware was his greatest success. Due to the ease with which it could be potted and because its lighter weight significantly reduced transportation expenses, Wedgwood was able to offer 'chinaware' at affordable prices. Queen Charlotte was so pleased with the ware that she allowed it to be called 'Queen's Ware.' Most creamware was marked simply 'Wedgwood.' ('Wedgwood & Co.' and 'Wedgwood' are marks of other potters.) From 1769 to 1780, Wedgwood was in partnership with Thomas Bentley; artwares of the highest quality may bear the 'Wedgwood & Bentley' mark indicating this partnership. Moonlight Lustre, an allover splashed-on effect of pink intermingling with gray, brown, or yellow, was made from 1805 to 1815. Porcelain was made, though not to any great extent, from 1812 to 1822. Bone china was produced before 1822 and after 1872. These types of wares were marked 'WEDGWOOD' (with a printed 'Portland Vase' mark after 1872). Stone china and Pearlware were made from about 1820 to 1875. Examples of either may be found with a printed or impressed mark to indicate their body type. During the late 1800s, Wedgwood produced some fine parian and majolica. Creamware, hand painted by Emile Lessore, was sold from about 1860 to 1875. From the 20th century, several lines of lustre wares — Butterfly, Dragon, and Fairyland (designed by Daisy Makeig-Jones) — have attracted the collector and, as their prices suggest, are highly sought after and admired.

Nearly all of Wedgwood's wares are clearly marked. 'WEDGWOOD' was used before 1891, after which time 'ENGLAND' was added. Most examples marked 'MADE IN ENGLAND' were made after 1905. A detailed study of all marks is recommended for accurate dating. See also Majolica.

Key:
WW — Wedgwood   WWE — Wedgwood England

Plaque, Sacrifice to Hymen, 3-color Jasper, wooden frame, 5¾x9½", $1,200.00.

Ashtray, Jasper, terra cotta, WWE, ca 1958, 3½" dia	50.00
Basket, Creamware, bell flowers, WW, w/lid & ladle	800.00
Basket, Creamware, rust linear decor, raffia hdl, WW, 1840s	235.00
Biscuit barrel, Jasper, buff & blk, WWE	450.00
Biscuit barrel, Jasper, dk bl, WWE, 6x6"	235.00
Biscuit barrel, Jasper, lt gr, rstr SP trim, WW	275.00
Bowl, Basalt, incurvate rim, shallow, WW, 9¾"	225.00
Bowl, bone china, heavy gold & cobalt decor, WW, 1890s	215.00
Bowl, Butterfly Lustre, Melba center, MIE, #Z-4832, 8"	550.00
Bowl, Butterfly Lustre, Oriental landscape int, 8"	565.00
Bowl, Dragon Lustre, orange w/bl int, 1910, 9"	555.00

Bowl, Dragon Lustre, orange/red, bone china, MIE, 6½"	500.00
Bowl, Fairyland Lustre, Empire, Elves, MIE, #Z-4968, 4¼"	2,500.00
Bowl, Fairyland Lustre, fairy in lg hat, WW, #Z-4968, 3x7"	2,500.00
Bowl, Hummingbird Lustre, geese borders, WW, 4½x10"	425.00
Bowl, Jasper, blk, Dancing Hours, MIE, ca 1961, 10"	1,000.00
Bowl, Jasper, blk, Imperial shape, MIE, 10"	335.00
Bowl, Jasper, lt bl, MIE, 2½x4¾"	50.00
Bowl, Jasper, lt bl, WWE, 2x4¾"	75.00
Bowl, punch; Fairyland Lustre, Thumbelina, WWE, #Z-5200, 11"	3,000.00
Box, Jasper, dk bl, WWE, 3¾x4¾"	110.00
Box, Jasper, med bl, heart shape, WWE, 1948, sm	98.00
Box, Jasper, olive gr, heart shape, WWE, 2x4½x3½"	185.00
Brooch, Jasper, lt bl, sterling mt, WW, 1½" dia	235.00
Brooch/pendant, Jasper, lt bl, WW, in 14k gold oval fr	350.00
Bust, Basalt, Mercury, WW, 17"	1,200.00
Candlesticks, Jasper, dk bl, WW, ca 1860, 5½", pr	400.00
Candlesticks, Jasper, dk bl, WWE, 5", pr	225.00
Cigarette lighter, Jasper, med gr, MIE, ca 1955	60.00
Clock, Jasper, lav/gr/wht, seated figures, Tempus Fugit, WW	1,500.00
Clock, Jasper, lt gr, Fr movement, brilliants, WWE	1,200.00
Comport, Gr Glaze, Victorian	225.00
Console set, Jasper, primrose/terra cotta, WWE, 3-pc	250.00
Cracker jar, bone china, Imari colors, SP mts, WW, 5" dia	265.00
Creamer, Basalt, checkered pattern, helmet shape, WW, 3⅛"	275.00
Creamer, Drabware, salt glazed, Egyptian decor, WW, ca 1805	350.00
Creamer, Drabware, wht florals, WW, 1830s	200.00
Creamer, Jasper, dk bl, WWE, 2½"	75.00
Creamer, Jasper, lt bl, St Louis shape, WWE, 2¼x3½"	100.00
Creamer, Jasper, lt bl, WWE	65.00
Creamer, stoneware, cobalt vintage decor on wht, WW, 1810s	235.00
Creamer & sugar bowl, Jasper, lt bl, WWE	130.00
Cup, Basalt, arabesques & foliage, WW, ca 1800, 4½"	385.00
Cup & saucer, Basalt, Niagara Falls, WWE	100.00
Cup & saucer, Creamware, gr, floral, WW, ca 1882	25.00
Cup & saucer, Drabware, lt bl int, gold trim, WW	125.00
Cup & saucer, Jasper, bl, infants playing, WW, ca 1800	550.00
Flower frog, Creamware, tree trunk form, WWE, 1919, 6" dia	75.00
Flowerpot, Jasper, dk bl, lion's head, WWE, 3⅝x4"	175.00
Jardiniere, stoneware, olive gr, flared top, 7½"	550.00
Loving cup, Jasper, lt bl, 3-hdl, WWE, 4½"	170.00
Matchbox holder, Jasper, dk bl, WW, 2¼x1½"	125.00
Matchbox holder, Jasper, lt bl, WW, 3¾x6" dia	130.00
Matchbox holder/striker, Jasper, dk bl, WWE, 2½x2" dia	125.00
Medallion, Jasper, Elizabeth, MIE, 1953, 4¼x3¼"	150.00
Mug, bone china, Shakespeare's 400th Anniversary	55.00
Pepper shaker, Jasper, lt bl, lighthouse form, MIE, 3¾"	95.00
Pitcher, Basalt, clover/thistle/rose/harp, WW, 3¾"	235.00
Pitcher, Basalt, Victoria, BC, WWE, 3½"	110.00
Pitcher, Capriware, terra cotta/enamel, WW, 8½"	715.00
Pitcher, Copper Lustre, Fallow Deer, bone china, WWE	140.00
Pitcher, Creamware, dk bl-gr, WW, 7"	235.00
Pitcher, Creamware, lt bl, fruit & flowers, WW, 6½"	275.00
Pitcher, Jasper, dk bl, WWE, 4½"	130.00
Pitcher, Jasper, Etruscan shape, MIE, ca 1960	235.00
Pitcher, Jasper, gr, Classical figures, WWE, 4½"	165.00
Pitcher, tankard; Jasper, dk bl, WWE, 4"	80.00
Pitcher, tankard; Jasper, lt gr, WW, 4"	100.00
Plaque, bone china, Enchanted Palace, WWE, ca 1976	1,500.00
Plaque, Fairyland Lustre, Elves in Pine Tree, MIE	4,500.00
Plaque, Fairyland Lustre, Picnic by River, WWE, 5x10½"	4,400.00
Plaque, Fairyland Lustre, Stuff...Dreams..., WWE, 11½x16"	13,200.00
Plaque, Jasper, bl, Flora, WW, 10x7"	375.00
Plaque, Jasper, lt bl, Fall, oval, WW, 1810, 4x5"	550.00
Plaque, Jasper, lt bl, Four Seasons, WW, 3x6"	450.00

Plaque, Jasper, lt bl, Pegasus, WWE, fr, 4" dia 135.00
Plaque, Jasper, tri-color, Blind Man's Bluff, 6x12" 1,900.00
Plate, Creamware, Art Nouveau w/lustre, WWE, ca 1907 ....125.00
Plate, Creamware, Bl Willow w/HP decor, WWE 100.00
Plate, Creamware, ca 1800, 8" sq 110.00
Plate, Creamware, Carmel Mission, WWE, 1930s 100.00
Plate, Creamware, leaf hdl, ca 1800 ....110.00
Plate, Creamware, shell shape w/Japan decor 45.00
Plate, Drabware, gold rim, WW, ca 1830, 9¾" 75.00
Plate, Dragon Lustre on MOP, #X-4831, 1925, 9", pr 500.00
Plate, Gr Glaze, Grapeleaf, WW, 8" 78.00
Plate, Gr Glaze, Sunflower, WW, 8" 100.00
Plate, Jasper, Christmas 1969, 1st edition 100.00
Plate, Jasper, dk bl, Aurora, WW, 8" 165.00
Plate, Jasper, dk bl, WWE, 6" 75.00
Plate, Jasper, lt bl, Cupid, WWE, 8" 80.00
Plate, Silver Lustre, M Taplin, bone china, WWE, 8", set of 4 ...360.00
Potpourri jar, Jasper, dk bl, WWE, mini 225.00
Ring tree, Jasper, lt gr, WW, 2¾x3" 175.00
Salt cellar, Jasper, lt bl, 2x2½" 98.00
Sugar bowl, Basalt, widow finial, twig hdls, WW, ca 1840 ....245.00
Sugar bowl, Jasper, dk bl, WWE, w/lid, 5½" dia 150.00
Sugar caster, Jasper, dk bl, SP top, MIE 235.00
Sweetmeat jar, Jasper, sage gr, WW, rstr SP lid, 4½" 195.00
Syrup, Jasper, dk bl, pewter lid, WWE 200.00
Tea caddy, Jasper, 3-color, WWE, 5¼" 500.00
Tea set, stoneware, platinum over copper, WWE, 3-pc 750.00
Teapot, Basalt, Capri, WW, ca 1840, lg 550.00
Teapot, Jasper, dk bl, Classical figures, WWE, 6¼" 250.00
Teapot, Jasper, dk bl, rnd w/flat top, WWE 365.00
Teapot, Jasper, dk bl, WWE, 4½x6¼" 110.00
Tile, calendar, WW, 1903 ....100.00
Tile, stoneware, Etruria, brn foliage, wire fr, WW, 6" sq 125.00
Tray, Fairyland Lustre, Garden of Paradise I, #Z-4968, 11" dia ..2,300.00
Tray, Jasper, blk, spade form, WW, ca 1890 ....50.00
Tray, Jasper, Portland bl, WWE, 4⅜" dia 30.00
Vase, Basalt, Canada coat of arms, WWE, 6" 100.00
Vase, bone china, Imari colors, hexagonal, WW, 7" 220.00
Vase, bone china, lt bl, Daventry, WWE, 14" 2,000.00
Vase, Dragon Lustre, bl mottle, Portland mk/MIE, 13" 995.00
Vase, Dragon Lustre, lt bl, bone china, WWE, 8½" 545.00
Vase, Fairyland Lustre, Argus Pheasant, WWE, #Z-5486, 11¾" ..3,025.00
Vase, Fairyland Lustre, Imps on Bridge, WWE, #Z-5481, 11¾" ...6,600.00
Vase, Fairyland Lustre, Temple on Rock, WWE, #Z-29468, 19" ...17,600.00
Vase, Jasper, blk, Muses, w/lid, WWE, 11½", pr 2,800.00
Vase, Jasper, dk bl, classical figures, WW, 4⅞x3¾" 125.00
Vase, Jasper, dk bl, man w/dog, WW, 5¼x2½" 125.00
Vase, Jasper, dk bl, WWE, mini, 1¼" 95.00
Vase, Jasper, lilac, WWE, ca 1960, 3⅜" 125.00
Vase, Jasper, lt bl, ovoid, ca 1825, 9½" 1,500.00
Vase, Jeweled Tree Lustre, flame, #Z-3150, 8" 2,250.00
Vase, spill; Jasper, dk bl, Muses, WW, 5" 375.00
Vase, Victoria Ware, brn/cream gloss, gold trim, hdls, 7½" 400.00

Weil Ware

Max Weil came to the United States in the 1940s, settling in California. There he began manufacturing dinnerware, figurines, cookie jars, and wall pockets. American clays were used, and the dinnerware was all hand decorated. Weil died in 1954; the company closed two years later. The last backstamp to be used was the outline of a burro with the words 'Weil Ware — Made in California.' Many unmarked pieces found today originally carried a silver foil label, but you'll often find a four-digit handwritten number series, especially on figurines. For further study we recommend *The Collector's Encyclopedia of California Pottery* by our advisor, Jack Chipman. He is listed in the Directory under California.

Ashtray, Bamboo, 5" 7.50
Bowl, dogwood, wht on gray, oval, 10" 12.00
Bowl, salad; Rose, sm 4.00
Bowl, shell form, pk w/pale gr int 12.00
Butter dish, Blossom, ¼-lb 20.00
Cup & saucer, Rose 6.00
Dish, Dogwood, divided, sq, 10½" 8.00
Figurine, boy w/wheelbarrow, #4005 ....22.00
Figurine, girl, lifted chin, sgraffito floral on skirt, lg 35.00

Figure of a girl, rose dress with flower decoration, 11", $30.00.

Figurine, girl w/bowl, 11" 30.00
Figurine, lady's head w/fan, HP flowers, 8" 35.00
Shelf sitter, Oriental girl 25.00
Vase, bud; Ming Tree, w/coralene, #946, 6" 20.00
Vase, Ming Tree, w/coralene, 8½" 30.00
Vase, mint gr w/pk int, ribbed, 8" 25.00
Vase, sailor boy w/flowers before wht vase, 10¾" 35.00

Weller

The Weller Pottery Company was established in Zanesville, Ohio, in 1882, the outgrowth of a small one-kiln log cabin works Sam Weller had operated in Fultonham. Through an association with Wm. Long, he entered the art pottery field in 1895, producing the Lonhuda Ware Long had perfected in Steubenville six years earlier. His famous Louwelsa line was merely a continuation of Lonhuda and was made in at least five hundred different shapes until 1924. Many fine lines of artware followed under the direction of Charles Babcock Upjohn, Art Director from 1895 to 1904: Dickens Ware (1st Line), under-glaze slip decorations on dark backgrounds; Turada, featuring applied ivory bands of delicate openwork on solid dark brown backgrounds; and Aurelian, similar to Louwelsa, but with a brushed-on rather than blended ground. One of their most famous lines was 2nd Line Dickens, introduced in 1900. Backgrounds, characteristically caramel shading to turquoise matt, were decorated by sgraffito with animals, golfers, monks, Indians, and scenes from Dickens novels. The work is often artist signed. Sicardo, 1903, was a metallic lustre line in tones of rose, blue, green, or purple with flowing Art Nouveau patterns developed within the glaze.

Frederick Hurten Rhead, who worked for Weller in 1903 to 1904, created the prestigious Jap Birdimal line decorated with geisha girls, landscapes, storks, etc., accomplished through application of heavy slip forced through the tiny nozzle of a squeeze bag. Other lines to his credit are L'Art Nouveau, produced both in high-gloss brown and matt pastels, and 3rd Line Dickens, often decorated with Cruikshank's illustrations in relief. Other early artware lines were Eocean, Floretta, Hunter, Perfecto, Dresden, Etched Matt, and Etna.

In 1920 John Lessel was hired as Art Director, and under his supervision several new lines were created. LaSa, LaMar, Marengo, and Besline attest to his expertise with metallic lustres. The last of the artware lines and one of the most sought-after by collectors today is Hudson, first made during the early 1920s. Hudson, a semimatt glazed ware, was beautifully artist decorated on shaded backgrounds with florals, animals, birds, and scenics. Notable artists often signed their work, among them Hester Pillsbury, Dorothy England Laughead, Ruth Axline, Claude Leffler, Sarah Reid McLaughlin, E.L. Pickens, and Mae Timberlake.

During the thirties Weller produced a line of gardenware and naturalistic life-sized figures of dogs, cats, swans, geese, and playful gnomes. The Depression brought a slow, steady decline in sales, and by 1948 the pottery was closed. For a more thorough study we recommend *The Collector's Encyclopedia of Weller Pottery* by Sharon and Bob Huxford, available at your local library or from Collector Books.

Ardsley, vase, bud; cattails w/lilies at base, 7½" 55.00
Ardsley, vase, cattails, fan form, 8" 100.00
Art Nouveau, ewer, floral, 4-sided, ornate hdl, 14½" 365.00
Art Nouveau, Glossy; vase, classic lady, slim, unmk, 12½" 375.00
Art Nouveau, vase, floral, stick neck, 8" 150.00
Art Nouveau, vase, grapes, 16" 400.00
Athens, vase, swags & medallions, ummk, 10" 450.00
Aurelian, jardiniere & pedestal, floral, unmk, 38" 2,500.00
Aurelian, lamp, grape clusters, sgn E Roberts, hand mk, 29" ...1,700.00
Aurelian, tankard, cavalier, sgn Fouts, slim, 16½" 1,300.00
Aurelian, vase, dog w/game in mouth, pillow form, 7½x8" 1,375.00
Aurelian, vase, floral, sgn HM, silver o/l flared rim, 11½" 1,375.00
Auroro, vase, goldfish, sgn Hattie Mitchell, hand mk, 9" 1,100.00
Baldin, Blue; vase, apples, unmk, 11" 325.00
Baldin, vase, apples, bulbous, unmk, 5½" 145.00
Barcelona, candle holders, geometric florals, 2x5", pr 100.00
Barcelona, vase, geometric florals, waisted, hdls, 6½" 150.00
Besline, candlestick, floral, w/lustre, unmk, 10½" 135.00
Besline, vase, leaves & berries, paper label, 11" 535.00
Blue Drapery, planter, floral, rectangular, 4" 40.00
Blue Drapery, wall pocket, floral, unmk, 5½" 150.00
Blue Ware, jardiniere, 4 angels, 9" 185.00
Blue Ware, vase, classical figure, 8½" 185.00
Bonito, candle holders, floral on cream, 1½", pr 60.00
Bonito, vase, floral on cream, sgn NC, sm angle hdls, 10" 215.00
Brighton, parrot, unmk, 12½" 900.00
Brighton, penguins, unmk, 5" 700.00
Brighton, swan flower frog, unmk, 4½" 250.00
Brighton, woodpecker, unmk, 5" 200.00
Burntwood, urn, floral on tan, brn rim & base, unmk, 6½" 135.00
Burntwood, vase, floral on tan, brn rim & base, unmk, 7" 135.00
Camelot, vase, geometric design on gourd shape, unmk, 8" 135.00
Cameo Jewell, jardiniere, 11" 275.00
Cameo Jewell, jardiniere & pedestal, 22" 550.00
Candis, candle holders, gr w/gr wash on wht, 1½", pr 35.00
Chase, vase, fox hunt scene in silver o/l, ftd, 12" 475.00
Chase, vase, fox hunt scene on bl, bulbous, 6½" 235.00
Chengtu, ginger jar, Chinese Red, 12" 215.00
Chengtu, urn, Chinese Red, 3½" 75.00
Claywood, mug, floral on tan, brn rim & hdl, unmk, 5" 85.00
Claywood, umbrella stand, floral panels on tan w/brn, 19½" 200.00
Claywood, vase, floral panels, 8½" 85.00
Cloudburst, vase, brn/rust/wht w/lustre, bulbous, unmk, 10½" ...225.00
Cloudburst, vase, lav/wht/rose w/lustre, unmk, 4½" 70.00
Coppertone, ashtray, frog on rim, 6½" 165.00

Coppertone, figure, frog w/banjo, 7½" 1,050.00
Coppertone, vase, emb florals, twig hdls, unmk, 8½" 250.00
Coppertone, vase, frog hdls, 8" 600.00
Creamware, Decorated; mug, decalcomania, unmk, 5" 65.00
Creamware, Decorated; vase, floral, HP, 11½" 325.00
Dickens I, jardiniere, floral, 8" 260.00
Dickens I, lamp, floral, loop hdls, 3-ftd, 11" 1,000.00
Dickens I, loving cup, floral, sgn, 3-hdl, 5½" 350.00
Dickens I, mug, floral, sgn MM, 4½" 135.00
Dickens II, ewer, fish, sgn EL Pickens, 11½" 650.00
Dickens II, ewer, mermaid, unmk, 10½" 575.00
Dickens II, humidor, Captain, head figural, 7" 950.00
Dickens II, humidor, Turk, head figural, 7" 975.00
Dickens II, mug, Black Bird portrait, sgn UJ, 6" 700.00
Dickens II, vase, cavalier, sgn, glossy bl on bl, unmk, 13½" 1,050.00
Dickens II, vase, Chief Hollowhorn Bear, sgn AD, 13" 1,925.00
Dickens II, vase, Dombey & Son, sgn W Gibson, 10½" 850.00
Dickens II, vase, Don Quixote & Sancho, Pickens, 16" 2,000.00
Dickens II, vase, hunting dog, sgn EL Pickens, 9" 1,375.00
Dickens II, vase, Indian portrait, sgn HS, cylindrical, 11" 900.00
Dickens II, vase, man fishing, hand mk, 15½" 1,500.00
Dickens II, vase, Old North Church, pillow form, 7x8" 1,625.00
Dickens II, vase, rabbit in landscape, sgn, slim, 17" 1,350.00
Dickens II, vase, swordsmen, sgn LJB, hdls, 5½" 650.00
Dickens III, teapot, Captain Cuttle, F Dombey, #5055, 7" 750.00
Dresden, vase, windmill scene, bl on bl, sgn LJB, 10½" 575.00
Dupont, vase, flower baskets, cylindrical, 10" 115.00

Eocean, Late Line; vase, yellow roses, 8", $215.00; Hudson, vase, yellow florals on matt ground ground shading from pink to green, 12", $425.00; Dresden, windmill scene on blue shaded to green, signed Matt Weller, 5", $425.00.

Eocean, basket, floral, flared ft, unmk, 6½" 250.00
Eocean, Late; vase, bud; floral, unmk, 6½" 85.00
Eocean, vase, floral, cylindrical, sm loop hdls at top, 16" 500.00
Eocean, vase, floral, sgn EP, 4 sm high hdls, 10½" 450.00
Eocean, vase, owl on branch before full moon, sgn EB, 10½" ..1,350.00
Etna, vase, Beethoven medallion, 12" 400.00
Etna, vase, floral, pk on shaded ground, 5½" 110.00
Etna, vase, lizard on gourd shape, brn to pk shaded, 4½" 450.00
Evergreen, candlesticks, 1½", pr 35.00
Flask, Dust Remover, unmk, 6" 160.00
Flask, PAP Loyal Order of Moose, unmk, 4½" 120.00
Flask, Take a Plunge, unmk, 6" 120.00
Flemish, tub, floral, tub hdls, 4" 65.00

Flemish, umbrella stand, fruit trees, 22" 600.00
Flemish, vase, floral, unmk, 7½" 135.00
Floretta, ewer, grapes on dk brn, 10½" 120.00
Floretta, Matt; tankard, fruit on branch, sgn CD, unmk, 13½" ...400.00
Floretta, vase, floral on brn shaded, uptrn hdls, 6½" 110.00

Forest, jardiniere and pedestal, 29x12½", from $950.00 to $1,200.00.

Forest, pitcher, woodland scene, glossy, 5" 175.00
Forest, vase, florest scene, flared cylinder, unmk, 13½" 250.00
Fruitone, vase, 6-sided, sm rolled rim, 8" 125.00
Fruitone, wall pocket, 5½" 110.00
Glendale, vase, bird in landscape, classic form, 12" 450.00
Glendale, vase, bird in landscape, unmk, 6" 250.00
Glendale, vase, birds at nest, bulbous, 9" 450.00
Glendale, vase, birds at nest, cylindrical, slim, 12" 450.00
Hudson, jardiniere, floral, bl & wht on bl, sgn RS, 8x10" 325.00
Hudson, vase, bud; floral, mc on bl, 7¼" 90.00
Hudson, vase, cottage & trees, sgn Timberlake, rpr, 8¼" 700.00
Hudson, vase, cottage/lg poplar, M Timberlake, 8¾" 2,000.00
Hudson, vase, daisies, yel on bl, M Ansel, slim, 8½" 250.00
Hudson, vase, dogwood, cream on bl-gr, S Timberlake, 7" 220.00
Hudson, vase, dogwood, lt gray on gray, hexagonal, 11½" 250.00
Hudson, vase, dogwood on bl to yel, Davis, 6¾" 325.00
Hudson, vase, floral, bl & brn on bl to pk, LBM, 7¼" 240.00
Hudson, vase, floral, maroon & gr on wht, 6½" 190.00
Hudson, vase, floral, mc on gr to mauve, Timberlake, 9½" 275.00
Hudson, vase, floral, mc on pk to bl, sgn ST, 7" 175.00
Hudson, vase, floral, mc on teal, sgn Pillsbury, 11¾" 950.00
Hudson, vase, floral, pk & gr on bl, sgn McLaughlin, 10" 250.00
Hudson, vase, floral, pk on bl to yel, sgn ST, 7 /12" 175.00
Hudson, vase, floral, rose & pk on bl, unmk 140.00
Hudson, vase, flowers & twigs, red & blk on wht, 7" 120.00
Hudson, vase, flowers on lav band, block mk, 11" 160.00
Hudson, vase, hangng leaves/berries, C Leffler, 7" 550.00
Hudson, vase, irises, lav/bl on lav to gr, LBM, 15x7" 1,100.00
Hudson, vase, lg iris, pk/bl on gray, McLaughlin, 14¾" 1,300.00
Hudson, vase, lg parrot/flowering branch, Timberlake, 14" 6,250.00
Hudson, vase, lilacs, pk & bl, McLaughlin, 13¼" 480.00
Hudson, vase, rose of Sharon, SR McLaughlin, 12x8" 900.00
Hudson, vase, roses, cream on dk gr to mauve, 12½" 450.00
Hudson, vase, roses on bl to mauve to yel, Pillsbury, 8" 300.00
Hudson, vase, sailboats/mtns/trees, Pillsbury, 9½" 2,000.00
Hudson, vase, sm pendant floral, sgn Hood, cylindrical, 7" 275.00
Hudson, vase, water lily, wht & gr, sgn D England, unmk, 10¾" ..300.00
Hudson Light, vase, dogwood on gray to gr to yel, 11" 145.00
Hudson Light, vase, floral, mauve on bl-gray to cream, 10" 325.00

Hudson Light, vase, floral, on gray-gr to yel, 11½" 160.00
Hudson Light, vase, tulips, pk & gr on pastel, rpr, 12" 110.00
Hudson Perfecto, vase, lg peonies, Leffler, 9x9" 750.00
Hunter, ewer, duck, ruffled top, X357 on base, 11" 625.00
Hunter, vase, duck swimming, squat ewer form, 7" 500.00
Hunter, vase, elk, integral hdls, #343, 6½" 650.00
Ivoris, ginger gar, emb decor, uptrn hdls, 8½" 80.00
Ivoris, vase, ornate hdls, 6" 35.00
Ivory, jardiniere, squirrels in tree, unmk, 6½" 115.00
Ivory, jardiniere & pedestal, classic figures, 36" 1,050.00
Ivory, vase, floral swag on 4-lobe shape, unmk, 8½" 70.00
Ivory, vase, vine panels on cylindrical form, 10" 67.50
Jap Birdimal, vase, bird in flight, wht on gray, unmk, 7" 400.00

Jap Birdimal, vase, geisha in colorful robes, green grass and trees on aqua background, signed Rhead, #462, 12", $1,250.00.

Jap Birdimal, vase, landscape, bl on pk shaded, 14" 700.00
Jap Birdimal, vase, Oriental lady, sgn VMH, 13" 1,800.00
Jap Birdimal, vase, Oriental lady, unmk, 4" 575.00
Klyro, basket, floral, 4 sm ft, unmk, 7" 85.00
Klyro, planter, floral, sq sides, 4 sm ft, 4" 55.00
Knifewood, bowl, daisies, 3" 85.00
Knifewood, vase, swan scenic, 5" 165.00
Knifewood, wall pocket, daisies on brn, 8" 165.00
La Sa, lamp, palm trees in landscape, 14½" 425.00
La Sa, vase, water landscape, 6½" 225.00
Lamar, vase, water scenic, flared rim, unmk, 11½" 350.00
Lamar, vase, water scenic, sm ring ft, 14½" 500.00
Lorbeek, candle holders, lav-pk w/stepped base, 2½", pr 45.00
Louwelsa, Blue; vase, floral, sgn LM, short narrow neck, 10" 675.00
Louwelsa, Blue; vase, floral, 1 integral hdl, 3" 350.00
Louwelsa, candle holder, floral, sgn MH, 4½" 130.00
Louwelsa, ewer, floral, bulbous, long slim neck, 10" 275.00
Louwelsa, ewer, floral, 5" 120.00
Louwelsa, ewer, floral w/silver o/l, slim form, 9" 1,750.00
Louwelsa, Green; vase, floral, cylindrical, 6½" 600.00
Louwelsa, humidor, floral, sgn CA, 5½" 485.00
Louwelsa, jardiniere, floral, ruffled rim, 9½" 275.00
Louwelsa, lamp, floral, sgn, 3-ftd, 10" 775.00
Louwelsa, mug, floral, sgn MM, 5½" 175.00
Louwelsa, mug, portrait, sgn Ferrell, #432, 6½" 850.00
Louwelsa, tankard, grapes, sgn Ferrell, 17" 575.00
Louwelsa, vase, fish, sgn L Blake, classic form, 7" 1,350.00

Louwelsa, vase, floral, sgn H Pillsbury, bulbous, unmk, 24½" ..1,950.00
Louwelsa, vase, floral, sgn JB, bulbous, flared rim, 7" 200.00
Louwelsa, vase, floral, sgn M, pillow form, unmk, 4" 135.00
Louwelsa, vase, floral, sgn MH, integral hdls, 3-ftd, 5" 155.00
Louwelsa, vase, floral, 4½" 120.00
Louwelsa, vase, grapes on vine, sgn CJ Dibowsky, 25" 2,000.00
Louwelsa, vase, Indian, Levi Burgess, #602, 10½" 950.00
Louwelsa, vase, Indian girl's portrait, integral hdls, 10" 1,750.00
Louwelsa, vase, pansies w/silver o/l, bulbous, 6½" 2,250.00
Malverne, jardiniere & pedestal, floral, 34" 550.00
Malverne, vase, leaves, gourd shape, 5½" 35.00
Malverne, wall pocket, leaves, unmk, 11" 135.00
Mammy Line, creamer, nude child forms hdl, 3½" 275.00
Mammy Line, syrup pitcher, Mammy figural, 6" 400.00
Mammy Line, teapot, Mammy figural, 8" 625.00
Marbleized, vase, bulbous, 4½" 55.00
Marbleized, vase, flared cylinder, 10½" 115.00
Marbleized, vase, shouldered form, 9½" 115.00
Marvo, bowl, foliage, gr wash on brn, unmk, 5" 45.00
Marvo, vase, dbl bud; foliage, gr, unmk, 4½" 65.00
Melrose, basket, grape clusters on pk, brn twig hdl, 10" 175.00
Melrose, vase, floral on pk, ruffled rim, hdls, 5x7" 95.00
Minerva, vase, cranes, cylindrical, 8½" 425.00
Mirror Black, bowl, faintly scalloped rim, 11" 55.00
Mirror Black, bud vase, flared rim, unmk, 5½" 35.00
Mirror Black, wall pocket, unmk, 8" 130.00
Modeled Etched Matt, vase, rose on long stem, sq sides, 10" 235.00
Montego, vase, gr runs on brn, flared rim & ft, 9½" 125.00
Muskota, boy fishing, unmk, 6½" 300.00
Muskota, fence, 5" 165.00
Muskota, geese flower frog, unmk, 6" 225.00
Muskota, powder jar, lady figural, unmk, 7" 275.00
Noval, comport, ivory w/blk trim, fruit hdls, unmk, 5½" 65.00
Noval, vase, floral, pk on cream, blk trim & hdls, unmk, 6" 60.00
Novelty, wall vase, pitcher form, wht, 7½" 75.00
Paragon, vase, floral, bl wash on wht, bulbous, 6½" 75.00
Paragon, vase, floral, bulbous, 7½" 85.00
Pearl, candle holders, pearls & florals on cream, 8½", pr 135.00
Pearl, wall vase, pearls & florals on cream, 8" 175.00
Perfecto, ewer, floral, unmk, #580/2, 12" 475.00
Perfecto, vase, floral, sgn HP, unmk, #436, 17" 700.00
Pumila, bowl, flower form, 3½" 22.50
Pumila, console plate, flower form, unmk, 3x12" 45.00
Roma, candlestick, floral bands, 11½" 80.00
Roma, comport, floral, 3 integral hdls on base, 5½" 85.00
Roma, console, grapes on vines, w/liner, unmk, 6½x18" 165.00
Roma, jardiniere, flower basket reserves, unmk, 10½" 225.00
Roma, vase, bud; floral, unmk, 6½" 55.00
Rosemont, jardiniere, bird on floral branch on cream, 7" 250.00
Sabrinian, vase, shells on body, sea horse hdls, 12" 275.00
Sabrinian, window box, shells form sides, 3½x9" 175.00
Sicardo, vase, crashing waves, mc irid on red, 27", NM 8,750.00
Sicardo, vase, emb poppies, 11" 3,500.00
Sicardo, vase, floral, cylindrical, 9" 875.00
Sicardo, vase, floral, horn-like hdls, 6" 750.00
Sicardo, vase, floral, pillow form, 6½x10" 900.00
Sicardo, vase, floral, shouldered, 6" 500.00
Sicardo, vase, floral, trumpet neck, 15½" 1,425.00
Sicardo, vase, irises/kingfishers, gold/mc irid, 25" 8,000.00
Sicardo, vase, leaves/grasses, gr irid, ovoid, 7½" 950.00
Sicardo, vase, maple leaves, dk irid, teardrop w/hdls, 8", NM ..2,100.00
Sicardo, vase, shamrocks, gr irid, bulging base, 6" 900.00
Sicardo, vase, stars, gold on orange to gr, broad base, 6" 1,000.00
Sicardo, vase, stars, silver/bl on burgundy, waisted, 6" 550.00

Sicardo, vase, gold daisies and petals on
purple lustre, horn-like handles, 9",
$750.00.

Sicardo, vase, swirling floral, bl irid, 9½", NM 1,400.00
Silvertone, basket, floral, twig hdl, 13" 250.00
Silvertone, vase, floral, ruffled rim, hdls, 8½" 300.00
Suevo, humidor, geometric design on brn, 6" 250.00
Tivoli, vase, classic form on ftd base, unmk, 9½" 115.00
Tivoli, vase, cylindrical w/flared rim & ftd base, unmk, 8½" 105.00
Trellis, wall shelf, turq, unmk, 10½" 115.00
Turada, humidor, appl filigree, no lid, 5½" 300.00
Turada, lamp base, appl filigree, ftd, 8" 825.00
Turada, mug, appl filigree, #562/7 on base, 6" 285.00
Tutone, bowl, console; floral, w/frog, 3½", 1½" 110.00
Tutone, vase, floral, 4 sm ft, 4" 40.00
Velva, vase, floral on brn, uptrn hdls, 9½" 62.50
Velva, vase, floral on gr, uptrn hdls, 6" 42.50
Velvetone, batter jug, blended pastels, 10" 150.00
Velvetone, pitcher, blended pastels, 10" 135.00
Voile, vase, fruit-filled tree, fan form, unmk, 7" 40.00
Voile, vase, fruit-filled tree, unmk, 9" 90.00
Woodcraft, bowl, rtcl 'woven branch' rim, 3½" 70.00
Woodcraft, candle holder, tree trunk form, 8½" 60.00
Woodcraft, vase, foliage on flared cylinder, unmk, 13" 150.00
Woodcraft, vase, owl perched on branch of stump form, 16" 850.00
Woodcraft, wall vase, bird at nest & flowers, 14½x12½" 625.00
Zona, baby plate, squirrels, ABC rim, unmk, 7½" 85.00
Zona, jardiniere, floral rim band w/blk trim, unmk, 7" 135.00
Zona, pitcher, exotic bird reserve, twig hdl, 8" 185.00
Zona, plate, fruit branch along rim, unmk, 10" 21.00

Western Americana

The collecting of Western Americana encompasses a broad spectrum of memorabilia and collectibles. Examples of various areas within the main stream would include the following fields: weapons, bottles, photographs, mining/railroad artifacts, cowboy paraphernalia, farm and ranch implements, maps, barbed wire, tokens, Indian relics, saloon/gambling items, and branding irons. Some of these areas have their own separate listings in this book. Western Americana is not only a collecting field but is also a collecting *era* with specific boundaries. Depending upon which field the collector decides to specialize in, prices can start at a few dollars and run into the thousands.

Our advisor for this category is Bill Mackin, author of *Cowboy and Gunfighter Collectibles* (order from the author); he is listed in the Directory under Colorado.

Bit, Crockett, lady's legs, nickeled, silver mts 250.00

Bit, silver inlay, prison-made in Canyon City 400.00
Boots, thigh high, Wild West Show, 1890s, pr 2,700.00
Branding iron, hand forged, socket type w/early twist, 20" 35.00
Branding iron, wrought iron, self-standing, 17¾" 38.00
Bridle, horsehair, ca 1900, prison-made, EX 1,200.00
Buckle, bucking bronco, mk Nickel Silver 28.00
Bull whip, braided leather, swivel hdl 125.00
Chair, steer horns, ca 1900, EX 1,500.00
Chaps, batwing style, over 2000 nickel studs, unmk, EX 5,600.00
Chaps, shotgun type, fringed, AJ Stevenson, Helena MT, EX ...4,400.00
Chaps, wooly, wht, Hamley, EX 2,500.00
Chaps, wooly, wht, worn 450.00
Cuff, cowboy's, leather, pr 135.00
Holster, half-flap style, Spangenburg, Tombstone AZ Territory ..4,500.00
Horseshoe, copper, 1898 inscr on inside, 5" 35.00
Saddle, cowboy's, blk leather w/lg & sm NP mts 375.00
Saddle, half-seat style, unmk, NM 950.00
Saddle, parade, much silver, Licthenberger & Ferguson 6,500.00
Skull, cow bone, weathered, 13½x12½x7½" 110.00

Spurs, Bohlin, silver and gold overlay, with straps, 1930, EX, $2,800.00 for the pair.

Spurs, Buermann, Hercules Bronze, str shank, pr 225.00
Spurs, Buermann, OK style, ca 1877, pr 210.00
Spurs, Buermann, Star, dropped shank, pr 165.00
Spurs, Civil War officer's, brass, 1848 model, pr 290.00
Spurs, Colonial singles, 1800s, pr 200.00
Spurs, Crockett, lady's legs, silver mtd, blued, pr..........................675.00
Spurs, Eureka, pr 135.00
Spurs, GS Garcia, fancy silver inlay hearts, Elko NV, 1910, pr ..6,600.00
Spurs, Qualey, silver inlay, very fancy, pr 7,000.00
Spurs, silver mtd, drop shank, CA, unmk, pr 425.00
Tie slide, steer head w/turq stone eyes 45.00

Western Pottery Manufacturing Company

This pottery was originally founded as the Denver China and Pottery Company; William Long was the owner. The company's assets were sold to a group who in 1905 formed the Western Pottery Manufacturing Company, located at 16th Street and Alcott in Denver, Colorado. By 1926 there were 186 different items being produced, including crocks, flowerpots, kitchen items, and other stoneware. The company dissolved in 1936.

Seven various marks were used during the years, and values may be higher for items that carry a rare mark. Numbers within the descriptions refer to specific marks, see the line drawings. Prices may vary depending on demand and locale. Our advisors for this category are Cathy Segelke and Pat James; they are listed in the Directory under Colorado.

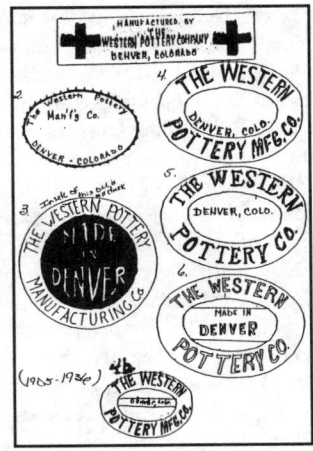

Crock, 2-gallon, mark #6, NM, $30.00.

Churn, #2, hdl, 4-gal, M 75.00
Churn, #2, hdl, 5-gal, M 65.00
Churn, #2, no lid, 5-gal, G 80.00
Crock, #4, bail lip, 4-gal, G 55.00
Crock, #4, hdl, no lid, 8-gal, M 90.00
Crock, #4, ice water; bl/wht sponge pnt, 3-gal, NM 30.00
Crock, #4, 2-gal, M 32.00
Crock, #4, 6-gal, EX 72.00
Crock, #4b, 20-gal, M 200.00
Crock, #4b, 22x17½", 15-gal, NM 150.00
Crock, #4b, 30-gal, NM 225.00
Crock, #5, bail lip, 1½-gal, M 45.00
Crock, #5, no lid, 6-gal, M 70.00
Crock, #5, no lid, 6-gal, M 70.00
Crock, #6, wire hdl, 10-gal, NM 100.00
Crock, #6, 3-gal, M 40.00
Crock, #6, 4-gal, M 50.00
Crock, #6, 5-gal, NM 60.00
Crock, water; #6, brn/wht, 5-gal, NM 200.00
Foot warmer, #6, M 50.00
Jug, #6, brn/wht, 1-gal, EX 25.00
Jug, #6, brn/wht, 5-gal, M 75.00
Rabbit feeder, #1, EX 25.00
Rabbit waterer, #1, M 25.00

Westmoreland

Originally titled the Specialty Glass Company, Westmoreland began operations in East Liverpool, Ohio, producing utility items as well as tableware in milk glass and crystal. When the company moved to Grapeville, Pennsylvania, in 1890, lamps, vases, covered animal dishes, and decorative plates were introduced. Prior to 1920 Westmoreland was a major manufacturer of carnival glass and soon thereafter added a line of lovely reproduction art glass items. High-quality milk glass became their speciality, accounting for about 90% of their production. Black glass was introduced in the 1940s, and later in the decade ruby-stained pieces and items decorated in the Mary Gregory style became fashionable. By the 1960s colored glassware was being produced, examples of which are very popular with collectors today. Early pieces were marked with a paper label; by the 1960s the ware was embossed with a superimposed 'WG.' The last mark was a circle containing 'Westmoreland' around the perimeter and a large 'W' in the center. The company closed in 1985. See also Animal Dishes with Covers; Carnival Glass. Note: Though you may find pieces very similar to Westmoreland's, their Della Robbia has no bananas among the fruits relief.

Basket, Della Robbia, color stain, 12" 150.00
Bowl, Beaded Grape, milk glass, ftd, 9" 45.00
Bowl, Beaded Grape, milk glass w/HP roses, sq, flat, w/lid 65.00
Bowl, Della Robbia, gold fruit, rolled rim, 13½" 65.00
Bowl, Della Robbia, w/color stain, 12" 65.00
Bowl, Dolphin & Shell, ped ft, Antique Bl Mist, 8" 45.00
Bowl, Dolphin & Shell, ped ft, Antique Bl Mist, 12" 125.00
Bowl, English Hobnail, amber, 4⅜" 15.00
Bowl, English Hobnail, crystal, 4¾" 8.50
Bowl, fruit; Old Quilt, milk glass, ftd, 9" 45.00
Bowl, Lattice, milk glass, low, flared rim, 11" 26.50
Bowl, Panelled Grape, milk glass, low ftd, 9" 45.00
Bowl, Princess Feather, crystal, 4½" 12.00
Bowl, Thousand Eye, ruby & marigold flashed, 11½" 30.00
Box, Old Quilt, milk glass, sq, w/lid, #41 ....35.00
Cake plate, Ring & Petal, milk glass 37.50
Cake salver, Old Quilt, crystal 45.00
Candle holders, Beaded Grape, milk glass, pr 25.00
Candlesticks, Dolphin, Antique Bl Mist, sm, pr 40.00
Candlesticks, Dolphin, milk glass, 4", pr 30.00
Candlesticks, Dolphin, milk glass, 9", pr 85.00
Candlesticks, Panelled Grape, milk glass, 4", pr 25.00
Candy dish, Beaded Grape, milk glass, ped ft, 4" 20.00
Candy dish, Panelled Grape, gr satin, lacy 20.00
Candy dish, Panelled Grape, milk glass, low ftd, 6½" 22.00
Cocktail, English Hobnail, amber 15.00
Compote, English Hobnail, milk glass, hdls, 8" 35.00
Compote, Princess Feather, Golden Sunset 42.00
Compote, Sawtooth, ruby, tall ped, w/lid 65.00
Creamer, English Hobnail, crystal 7.50
Creamer & sugar bowl, Della Robbia, milk glass 22.00
Creamer & sugar bowl, Old Quilt, milk glass, lg 28.00
Creamer & sugar bowl, Panelled Grape, milk glass, w/lid, sm ...25.00
Creamer & sugar bowl, Peacock, milk glass 40.00
Cruet, English Hobnail, milk glass, sm 18.00
Cup, Fruit, strawberry, milk glass 12.00
Cup & saucer, American Hobnail, milk glass 10.00
Cup & saucer, Panelled Grape, milk glass 20.00
Epergne, Panelled Grape, mint gr, 3-pc 200.00

Fairy lamp, ruby stained, $65.00.

Fruit cocktail, Panelled Grape, milk glass 30.00
Goblet, water; Ashburton, gr 6.00
Goblet, water; Della Robbia, milk glass 20.00
Goblet, water; Della Robbia, w/color stain 35.00
Goblet, water; Old Quilt, milk glass 20.00
Goblet, water; Panelled Grape, milk glass 20.00
Goblet, water; Princess Feather, crystal 15.00
Goblet, water; Wakefield, HP w/ruby accent 38.00

Gravy boat, Panelled Grape, milk glass, w/underplate 65.00
Hat, English Hobnail, milk glass 18.00
Honey dish, Roses & Bows, milk glass, w/lid 40.00
Ice tub, English Hobnail, crystal 65.00
Ivy ball, English Hobnail, milk glass, 6½" 25.00
Jardiniere, Panelled Grape, milk glass, ftd, 5" 25.00
Jug, Panelled Grape, milk glass, 1-qt 35.00
Mayonnaise, Panelled Grape, milk glass, w/underplate 30.00
Mustard, English Hobnail, milk glass, w/lid & spoon 30.00
Pickle jar, Panelled Grape, milk glass 125.00
Pitcher, juice; Old Quilt, milk glass 35.00
Planter, Panelled Grape, milk glass, 5x9" 35.00
Plate, Della Robbia, crystal, 10½" 15.00
Plate, National, milk glass, 6" 25.00
Plate, Panelled Grape, milk glass, luncheon sz 32.00
Plate, Princess Feather, crystal, 8" 15.00
Punch cup, Paneled Grape, milk glass 10.00
Punch set, Princess Feather, crystal 350.00
Saucer, Fruit, grape, milk glass 8.00
Shakers, Panelled Grape, milk glass, pr 18.00
Shakers, Princess Feather, crystal, pr 24.00
Sherbet, English Hobnail, amber 12.50
Sherbet, Thousand Eye, crystal, 4¼" 12.00
Sherbet, Thousand Eye, purple & marigold stain 15.00
Sherbet, Thousand Eye, ruby/marigold/bl stain, 4¼" 15.00
Sugar bowl, Beaded Grape, milk glass 15.00
Sugar bowl, English Hobnail, crystal 12.50
Sugar bowl, Panelled Grape, milk glass, ftd, sm 10.00
Tumbler, Beaded Edge, milk glass, ftd 10.00
Tumbler, Della Robbia, crystal, ftd, 4¾" 15.00
Tumbler, iced tea; Della Robbia, milk glass 16.00
Tumbler, Old Quilt, milk glass, 9-oz 15.00
Vase, Beaded Grape, milk glass, tall 45.00
Vase, bl satin, Mary Gregory style, dtd 1974, 7" 88.00
Vase, bud; Panelled Grape, pastel fruit, 16" 25.00
Vase, bud; Roses & Bows, milk glass, 10" 30.00
Vase, fan; English Hobnail, milk glass, 5" 15.00
Wine, Thousand Eye, ruby/marigold/bl stain, 5" 18.50

Wheatley, T. J.

In 1880 after a brief association with the Coultry Works, Thomas J. Wheatley opened his own studio in Cincinnati, Ohio, claiming to have been the first to discover the secret of under-glaze slip decoration on an unbaked clay vessel. He applied for and was granted a patent for his process. Demand for his ware increased to the point that several artists were hired to decorate the ware. The company incorporated in 1880 as the Cincinnati Art Pottery, but until 1882 it continued to operate under Wheatley's name. Ware from this period is marked 'T.J. Wheatley' or 'T.J.W. and Co.,' and it may be dated.

Lamp base, floral spray, Limoges style, dtd 1880, 9½", NM 325.00
Mug, gr matt, pretzel twist hdl, advertising 165.00
Vase, dogwood in slip relief, pk on gr, sq form, 9x7x3½" 165.00
Vase, gr matt, 4 bar hdls around recessed coiled neck, 7" 700.00
Vase, lg appl poppies/leaves, mc on cobalt, rstr, 14½x12" 250.00
Vase, relief leafage, gr matt, unmk, 13" 1,750.00

Whieldon

Thomas Whieldon was regarded as the finest of the Staffordshire potters of the mid-1700s. He produced marbled and black Egyptian wares as well as tortoise shell, a mottled brown-glazed earthenware accented with touches of blue and yellow. In 1754 he became a partner of Josiah Wedgwood. Other potters produced similar wares, and today the term Whieldon is used generically.

Basket, blue, green, and ochre splashed on brown mottled ground, overall reticulation on oval form with two handles, ca 1760, with 9⅝" wide stand, $6,000.00.

Box, gr/brn/ochre/gray mottle, hinged lid, 2½" dia	990.00
Coffeepot, tortoise shell, no lid, ca 1760, 7"	475.00
Figurine, cat, seated on gr plinth, ca 1800, 2½"	425.00
Mustard pot, gr/ochre/bl/brn mottle, twisted C-hdl, 3", VG	700.00
Plate, brn mottle, milled edge, octagonal, 8½"	235.00
Plate, mc on mottled gray, reeded border, octagonal, 8½"	750.00
Plate, tortoise shell, molded feather rim, crazing, 9½"	220.00
Plate, yel/gr/gray on brn, emb feather edge, 1770s, 10", VG	200.00
Platter, brn mottle w/gray & bl spots, ribbed border, 10½"	825.00
Platter, gr/ochre/gray on brn, shaped/emb rim, 18"	7,700.00
Platter, tortoise shell w/bl & gr, emb rim, rpr, 10⅜"	300.00
Soup plate, ochre/brn/gray/gr, shaped/panel border, 9", EX	1,900.00
Tea caddy, emb Chinese people/landscape, canted corners, 5"	2,200.00
Tea canister, cauliflower, 1765, int rstr chip, 4"	325.00
Teapot, clouded ware, brn/yel/gr tortoise shell, 1750s, 5¼"	385.00
Teapot, pectin shell, cream/bl/brn marbleized, 1745, 5"	6,000.00
Vase, brn/bl/gray splashes, baluster w/collar rim, 6½", EX	3,500.00
Wall vase, brn mottle, cornucopia w/bust of lady, rstr, 11"	825.00

Wicker

Wicker is the basket-like material used in many types of furniture and accessories. It may be made from bamboo cane, rattan, reed, or artificial fibers. It is airy, lightweight, and very popular in hot regions. Imported from the Orient in the 18th century, it was first manufactured in the United States in about 1850. The elaborate, closely-woven Victorian designs belong to the mid- to late 1800s, and the simple styles with coarse reedings usually indicate a post-1900 production. Art Deco styles followed in the twenties and thirties. The most important consideration in buying wicker is condition — it can be restored, but only by a professional. Age is an important factor, but be aware that 'Victorian-style' furniture is being manufactured today.

Key:
HB — Heywood Brothers   H/W — Heywood-Wakefield
WR — Wakefield Rattan Co.

Armchair, oversz wing type, dk stain, WR, 48", pr	1,500.00
Armchair, tight weave, continuous arms, str apron, 1910s	375.00
Armchair, tight weave seat, birdcage legs, curlicues, 1890s	565.00
Armchair, tight weave w/scrolls, rolled arms & bk, 1900s	465.00
Basket, arched hdl, early 1900s, 7½x9x5¾"	55.00
Basket, sewing; tight weave, 2-door, wht pnt, EX	200.00
Carriage, hearts & curlicues, wire wheels, 1880s	825.00
Carriage, metal fr, 4 metal wheels, 35x32", VG	325.00
Chair, photographer's, tight weave, birdcage details, 1910s	485.00

Chair, side; ornate fan bk, pressed seat, fancy apron	200.00
Cradle, swings in fr, ca 1900, EX	1,250.00
Footstool, sq base, rnd top w/uphl insert, 9½x12"	100.00
Lamp, table; tight weave, natural finish	250.00
Lamp, tight weave base, ornate weave dome shade, 1890s, 16"	325.00
Lounge, tight weave, bk & armrest, cushioned	425.00
Music stand, scroll ft, oak shelf, WR, 1890s	325.00
Rocker, high bk, ornate arms & apron, 1890s, 38"	725.00
Rocker, platform, ornate-patterned bk, H/W, 48"	990.00
Settee, loose weave, half-cushioned bk & cushioned seat	300.00
Settee, tight weave, sturdy, for 2 children, 22½x31"	800.00
Sofa, tight weave w/dmn patterns, 3-cushion, flat arms, 1910s	1,800.00
Stand, tight weave, blk & orange pnt, sq w/shelf	275.00
Tea caddy, tight weave, wht pnt, EX	325.00
Tea cart, tight weave, bottom shelf, front wheels, top tray	275.00
Tea cart, tight weave, child sz	300.00
Tray, breakfast; w/cup holder, paper rack on side, 1920s	120.00
Vanity, tight weave, wht pnt, child sz	175.00

Willets

The Willets Manufacturing Company of Trenton, New Jersey, produced a type of belleek porcelain during the late 1880s and 1890s. Examples were often marked with a coiled snake that formed a 'W' with 'Willets' below and 'Belleek' above. Not all Willets is factory decorated. Items painted by amateurs outside the factory are worth considerably less. In the listings below, all items are belleek unless noted otherwise. Our advisor for this category is Mary Frank Gaston. You will find her address in the Directory under Texas.

Bowl, HP flowers & berries, sq, 7½"	250.00
Bowl, roses, artist sgn, ruffled, shallow, 8¾"	295.00
Chalice, roses in pk/ruby, wide gold rim/int, Royston, 11"	450.00

Mugs, each with dog portraits and dragon-form handles, signed G.Y. Houghton, 1904, 5¾", $825.00 for the pair.

Pitcher, lemonade; mc lilies w/gold trim & scrolls, 7x8"	250.00
Pitcher, tankard; seated gent w/glass, sgn Doering, 14"	500.00
Salt cellar, HP, gold crimped rim, mk, pr	110.00
Vase, HP pansies, 13½"	285.00
Vase, lilacs, mk, 15"	350.00
Vase, red hollyhocks, cylindrical, 13½"	180.00
Vase, stylized flowers, bl on pearlized, gold trim, 2¾"	145.00
Vase, 2 egrets on pk & blk, tapering shape, 11⅝"	325.00

Willow Ware

Willow Ware, inspired no doubt by the numerous patterns of the blue and white Nanking imports, has been popular since the late 18th century and has been made in as many variations as there were manufacturers. English transfer wares by such notable firms as Allerton and Ridgway are the most sought after and the most expensive. Japanese potters have been producing Willow-patterned dinnerware since the late 1800s, and American manufacturers have followed suit. Although blue is the color most commonly used, mauve, black, and even multi-color Willow Ware may be found. Complementary glassware, tinware, and linens have also been made. In addition to 'Allerton' and 'Ridgway,' both companies used the possessive forms of their names in marking their wares (i.e. Allerton's, Ridgway's). For further study we recommend the book *Blue Willow*, with full-color photos and current prices, by Mary Frank Gaston. You will find her address in the Directory under Texas. In the following listings, if no manufacturer is noted, the ware is unmarked. See also Buffalo.

Bowl, berry; Homer Laughlin Co, sm 8.00
Bowl, pk, unmk, 10" 18.00
Bowl, rice; Ridgway, 5" 25.00
Bowl, soup; Ridgway 22.00
Bowl, unmk, 5½" 3.50
Bowl, vegetable; Dbl Phoenix, w/lid 58.00
Bowl, vegetable; unmk, 9" 15.00
Cheese dish, England 185.00
Coaster, Schwepps Sparkling Grapefruit 65.00
Coaster, Yorkshire Relish 50.00
Creamer, ind 8.00
Creamer & sugar bowl, demitasse; w/lid, Japan 45.00
Cup & saucer, demitasse; Geisha lithophane in base, eggshell 25.00
Cup & saucer, demitasse; Japan 12.00
Egg cup 10.00
Gravy boat & ladle, unmk 30.00
Jug, batter; w/lid 128.00
Mug, Japan 10.00
Pitcher, Ridgway, 3¼" 35.00
Plate, grill; Sterling, pk 10.00
Plate, Japan, blk mk, dinner sz 9.00
Plate, Japan, 6" 5.00
Plate, Maastricht, 6" 10.00
Plate, pk, Ridgway, 7¾" 10.00
Plate, Ridgway, 10½" 18.00
Plate, Ridgway, 7" 13.00
Plate, Ridgway, 8¼" 20.00
Plate, Shenango, 13" 35.00
Plate, toddy; Staffordshire, scalloped, wear, 4½" 40.00
Plate, unmk, 9" 5.00
Platter, Homer Laughlin Co, 12" 25.00

Platter, Willam A. Adderly, 10x8", $65.00.

Platter, Ridgway, 11½" 65.00
Platter, Wedgwood, 11x9" 95.00
Reamer & pitcher, Moriyama 289.00
Shakers, Japan, bbl form, pr 20.00
Snack set, cup on sq plate 68.00
Soup spoon 6.00
Sugar bowl, Ridgeway 30.00
Teapot, unmk 45.00
Tidbit, 3-tier, pk, unmk 45.00
Toothpick holder 18.00
Wall pocket, pitcher form 40.00

Winchester

The Winchester Repeating Arms Company lost their important government contract after WWI and of necessity turned to the manufacture of sporting goods, hardware items, tools, etc., to augment their gun production. Between 1920 and 1931, over 7,500 different items, each marked 'Winchester Trademark U.S.A.,' were offered for sale by thousands of Winchester Hardware stores throughout the country. After 1931 the firm became Winchester-Western. See also Knives. Our advisor for this category is James Anderson; he is listed in the Directory under Minnesota.

Advertising card, dtd 1952, sm 20.00
Auger bit, #6, 8½" 20.00
Auger bit set, 13-pc, #WSR13, NM 190.00
Axe, broad; single bevel, trademk USA 75.00
Axe, camp; w/sheath, #W20, NM 85.00
Baseball glove, boys 325.00
Bevel, sliding T; #W125/8, 8", NM 70.00
Bit brace, #W210, 10", NM 55.00
Bit brace, ball bearings, #WBB12, 12", NM 75.00
Book, Gun That Won West, Williamson, 1st edition, EX 25.00
Bottle, gun oil; M in yel box 40.00
Bullet mold, .44WCF, wood hdls, G 45.00
Butt plate, hard blk plastic 20.00
Calendar, store; 1927 ....300.00
Can, gun oil; red 20.00
Catalog, Winchester Repeating Arms, 1919, 208", G 120.00
Catalog, World Standard Guns & Ammo, 1934, 152-pg 50.00
Chisel, flat cold; 8 szs, ¼"-1", #W14, NM 20.00
Cotter pin puller, #W8, NM 30.00
Diploma, Jr Rifle Corps 75.00
Drill set, 9-pc, #W109M, NM 115.00
File, G 30.00
Flashlight, solid 22k copper, bullet end 20.00
Flashlight, 5-cell, EX 75.00
Hammer, machinist's, 28-oz, #WM3, NM 60.00
Hammer, nail; 14-oz, #W512, NM 50.00
Hammer, nail; 20-oz, #W1, NM 50.00
Hat, straw, mk Winchester Store, NM 150.00
Hatchet, lathing; #WP420, NM 45.00
Hatchet, rig builder's, #WRBG, NM 45.00
Hatchet, shingling; #WBS1, NM 60.00
Headlamp, 30-cell, rectangular belt battery case+cord, NM 60.00
Level, pocket; #W31/3, 3", NM 90.00
Level, wooden; #WO/28, 28", NM 90.00
Level, wooden; #W30/24, 24", NM 120.00
Padlock, brass 100.00
Paperweight, glass, 1910 ....70.00
Pencil, carpenter's, #W1915, NM 25.00
Pin-bk button, Jr Rifle Corps 30.00

Plane, block; 6", #W9½, NM 70.00
Plane, corrugated bottom, #3026 ....60.00
Plane, dado; 8", #W39-1, NM 120.00
Plane, fillister; #W39-1, 8½", NM 120.00
Plane, jointer; 21", #W31, NM 120.00
Plane, router; #W171, 8", NM 100.00
Plane, smooth; 9", #W4C, NM 90.00
Pliers, electrician's, #W14, 3 szs, NM 30.00
Punch, center; #W115, ⅜", NM 20.00
Rasp, wood; #WHRW10, NM 30.00
Razor, straight; #8536, MIB 125.00
Razor strap 135.00
Rod, fishing; steel, #5360, G 60.00
Rod, fly; bamboo, G 135.00
Roller skates, #10, MIB 85.00
Roller skates, child's, MIB, pr 85.00
Ruler, folding; #W18, 24", NM 90.00

Salute cannon, Model #98, 10-gauge blank
caliber, 12" barrel, mounted on iron carriage
with rubber tires, pre-WWII, NM, $750.00.
(Also made in 12-gauge.)

Saw, coping; #W50, NM 60.00
Saw, crosscut; #W2015, NM 70.00
Saw, hand; #W13, G 60.00
Saw, NM 125.00
Saw, wood; #W75, NM 70.00
Screwdriver, offset; #W0S6, NM 45.00
Sign, standup, shows Model 55 & 77 guns, EX 100.00
Spoke shave, #W91, 10", NM 70.00
Square, steel; #W3, 24", NM 45.00
Tennis racquet 200.00
Tent, 84x108", w/poles 100.00
Token, tool checkout, brass 75.00
Tool cabinet, #W7, 42 tools, NM 22.50
Wrench, monkey; #WB10, 10", NM 75.00
Wrench, open end; #W125, 5 szs, NM 30.00
Wrench, open end; curved, #1837 ....30.00
Wrench, pipe; #WSP14, 14", NM 55.00
Wrench, pipe; wood hdl, #1022 ....50.00

Windmill Weights

Windmill weights were used to protect the windmill's plunger rod from damage during high winds by adding weight that slowed down the speed of the blades.

Bull, Fairbury, blk & wht spots, 38-lb, 24½x18¼x1⅛" 700.00

Eclipse Moon, Fairbanks Morse, CI, 27-lb, 10x6½x3½" 225.00

Elgin rooster with ribbed
rainbow tail, 18x16x3",
$1,500.00.

Horse, bob-tailed, Demster, CI, G wht pnt, 16⅝x17¼x¾" 265.00
Horse, long-tailed, Demster, old blk pnt, 37-lb, 21½" 1,000.00
Rooster, Hummer, CI, old mc pnt, ca 1900, 9⅞x8⅞x1¾" 425.00
Spear, Challenge, CI, no pnt, 35-lb, 24" 800.00
Star, Flint & Walling, pnt CI, 31-lb, 7½x3½" 765.00

Winfield

The Winfield Pottery was founded in 1929 in Pasadena, California. The artware and giftware items they made were marked Winfield, Pasadena, sometimes with the date added. In 1946 the line of more than 400 shapes was licensed to the American Ceramic Products Company of Santa Monica who began using the Winfield trade name on their semi-porcelain dinnerware. The Winfield Pottery from then on marked their output 'Gabriel.' Both companies closed during the early 1960s.

Bottle, wht w/emb decor, red stopper, 6¾" 35.00
Bowl, serving; Primitive Pony, 9" sq 40.00
Cheese dish, Bl Pacific 30.00
Chocolate pot, gr w/ivory int, +6 hdld mugs 185.00
Coffeepot, Bird of Paradise 35.00
Cup & saucer, Desert Dawn 12.00
Figurine, deer, recumbent, 4¼x4¾" 85.00
Honey jar, bear finial 60.00
Plate, Bird of Paradise, 10" 10.00
Plate, chop; Desert Dawn, 14" sq 30.00
Plate, Dragon Flower, 10" 10.00
Plate, Geranium, HP, 8½" 20.00
Vase, lt bl, cylindrical, 4¼" 20.00
Vase, lt gr, shouldered form, 4¾" 25.00

Wire Ware

Two thousand years B.C. wire was made by cutting sheet metal into strips which were shaped with a mallet and file. By the late 13th century, craftsmen in Europe had developed a method of pulling these strips through progressively smaller holes until the desired gauge was obtained. During the Industrial Revolution of the late 1800s, machinery was developed that could produce wire cheaply and easily; and it became a popular commercial commodity. It was used to produce large items such as garden benches and fencing as well as innumerable small pieces for use in the kitchen or on the farm. Beware of reproductions. Our advisor for this category is Rosella Tinsley; she is listed in the Directory under Kansas.

Basket with majolica insert, Victorian, unusual shape, 13" long, $125.00.

Basket, petal-shaped sides, scalloped bottom, folds, 4½x7"	48.00
Basket, potato; sm dmn designs, bail hdl, ½-bushel	48.00
Bucket, heavy wire in dmn design, bail hdl, 12x12"	55.00
Carpet beater, braided design, oval shape w/wood hdl	21.00
Carpet beater, heavy wire, wood hdl	22.00
Carrier, bottle; holds 6, twisted hdl, 4x9x14"	45.00
Compote, fancy, sm rnd scalloped base, lg bowl top	125.00
Condiment holder, 3 rnd deep 'cups,' ftd, center loop hdl	60.00
Drainer, wavy dmn design, wire hdls, 4 loop ft, 15" dia	42.00
Egg holder, holds 4, center hdl w/loop, 4-ftd	40.00
Fly cover, screen wire, wooden knob, 6½"	50.00
Fork, heavy twisted wire, long loop on hdl, 1880s	22.00
Glove, butcher's, woven wire mesh	20.00
Hanger, curved ends w/spiral wire for puffed sleeves, 1880s	28.00
Hanger, heavy wire & wood, PA advertising	48.00
Pie lifter, V-shaped wires move up & down wire loop	42.00
Pie rack, 4-tier	85.00
Pot scrubber, wire rings, old	28.00
Rack, bacon; heavy gauge, 8-prong	18.00
Rack, utensil; fancy bk, 6 heavy wire hooks, hangs, 21¼" L	135.00
Scrubber, wire ringlets, twisted wire hdl	30.00
Skewer set, heavy twisted stem, 1870s, 10½"	125.00
Soap dish, twisted, fancy wire bk w/hanging loop	60.00
Soap saver, oblong screen wire, wire & wood hdl	18.00
Tea ball, screen wire, tin banding, lock fastener, 2¼" dia	28.00
Toaster, Maltese cross design, wood hdl	40.00
Toaster, 3-ftd, 2" between racks, 1860s, 8x8"	110.00
Tongs, 2 hinged parts, 4 finger-shaped ends	26.00
Tray, cutlery; heavy screen w/tin banding & corners, 3x11x8"	58.00
Trivet, tea; twisted wire, 6½" dia	35.00
Trivet, woven dmn center, 8" dia	16.00
Whisk, fancy twisted stem, target-shaped base, 1870s, 11½"	65.00

Witch Balls

Witch balls were a Victorian fad touted to be meritorious toward ridding the house of evil spirits, thus warding off sickness and bad luck. Folklore would have it that by wiping the dust and soot from the ball, the spirits were exorcised. It is much more probable, however, considering the fact that such beautiful art glass was used in their making, that the ostensive Victorians perpetrated the myth rather tongue-in-cheek while enjoying them as lovely decorations for their homes.

Free-blown, cranberry, sheared mouth, Am, 1850-80, 4¼"	325.00
Free-blown, gr opaque, sheared mouth, Am, 1850-80, 5"	160.00
Free-blown, teal bl, tooled mouth, Am, 1850-80, 3¾"	155.00
Free-blown, yel-gr opaque, tooled mouth, Am, 1850-80, 5"	100.00

Nailsea, bl-wht loopings on aqua, Am, 1850-80, 4½"	300.00
Nailsea, cranberry loopings on clear, 1830-60, 4"	200.00
Nailsea, gr opaque loopings on milk glass, Am, 1850-80, 4¾"	750.00
Nailsea, pigeon blood red loopings on milk glass, Am, 4½"	900.00
Nailsea, pk & wht opaque loopings on clear, Am, 1850-80, 5"	650.00
Nailsea, rose loopings on milk glass, Am, 1850-80, 4½"	825.00
Nailsea, wht loopings on clear, matching stand, 14" overall	950.00
Nailsea, wht loopings on clear, 1830-60, 7½"	200.00
Nailsea, wht loopings on cobalt, tooled mouth, 3⅛"	800.00
Nailsea, wht opal loopings on clear, 5½"	150.00
Nailsea, wht opal loopings on smoky clear, 1830-60, 6"	175.00
Pattern molded, electric bl, 16-rib swirl, 1850-80, 6¾"	365.00
Pattern molded, 12 vertical ribs, Am, 1850-80, 3½"	200.00

Wood Carvings

Wood sculptures represent an important section of American folk art. Wood carvings were made not only by skilled woodworkers such as cabinetmakers, carpenters, etc., but by amateur 'whittlers' as well. They take the form of circus-wagon figures, carousel animals, decoys, busts, figurines, and cigar store Indians. Oriental artists show themselves to have been as proficient with the medium of wood as they were with ivory or hardstone. See also Carousel Animals; Decoys; Tobacciana.

American eagle, multicolor paint with gold lettering and details, ca 1900, 24½x73", $8,250.00.

Bald eagle, stylized, EX detail & pnt, 30"	275.00
Bear, sitting w/head up, EX details, old finish, 8"	75.00
Bearded man, primitive, mc pnt, wear, 10½"	55.00
Bird, old natural patina, label: Canton OH 1880, sm	50.00
Bird, 3-D, stylized, mc pnt, button eyes, on base, 17"	220.00
Blk man & lady, humorous, 1900s, 69", pr	800.00
Boston terrior, pnt, '30s, 15x14x¾"	35.00
Eagle feeding young, old worn mc pnt & gilt, 7½"	135.00
Hobo w/pack, mc pnt, 10", EX	65.00
Horse, orig wht pnt w/mc trim, leather harness, 7¾"	95.00
Horse, standing, naturally darkened, ca 1900, 9½x10x2"	125.00
Horse on base, mc pnt, 1900s, 8⅛"	50.00
Lady's head, worn/flaking pnt, 1 glass eye missing, 10"	350.00
Man (short) embracing nude lady (tall), natural patina, 12½"	115.00
Man w/sad face, worn patina, 10"	195.00
Match holder, cat form, hangs by tail, 1930s	45.00
Novelty, snake, jtd, mc pnt w/articulated jaws, 29"	160.00
Plaque, eagle, 1800s, 9½x18¼", EX	250.00
Rooster w/fan-shaped tail on oval base, mc pnt, 5⅛"	360.00
Wellington Victor at Waterloo, man on horse, mc rpt, 74"	1,980.00
Woodpecker on tree w/fruit, EX patina, 12"	50.00

Woodenware

Woodenware (or treenware, as it is sometimes called) generally refers to those wooden items such as spoons, bowls, food molds, etc., that were used in the preparation of food. Common during the 18th and 19th centuries, these wares were designed from a strictly functional viewpoint and were used on a day-to-day basis. With the advent of the Industrial Revolution which brought it new materials and products, many of the old woodenwares were simply discarded. Today original hand-crafted American woodenwares are extremely difficult to find.

Board, cheese; cheese cvd at top, w/knife, 7/8x10¼x11½" 110.00
Board, cookie; cat on 1 side, equestrians on verso, 10x6½" 78.00
Board, cookie; man & dog, 27½x9" 100.00
Board, cookie; poplar, old finish, 25½" dia 200.00
Board, cookie; poplar, 1-pc w/cut-out hdl, 19x23" 160.00
Board, cookie; springerle, 6 designs, 6x3⅞" 95.00
Board, cookie; 14 cvd animals, elongated, dk patina, 20x5" 360.00
Board, cookie; 9 cvd designs, rectangular, 6¾x5¼" 250.00
Board, corn cutting; yel pine, tin blade, bootjack ft, 28x6" 65.00
Board, cutting; butternut, worn surface, 17½x10" 25.00
Board, cutting; pegged sq hdl, 15¼x11½"+4¾" hdl 48.00
Board, cutting; pine, red pnt edge, 1¼x20x9" 40.00
Board, cutting; walnut, curved shoulders, slot, 10x10"+hdl 45.00
Board, dough; pine (1-pc), edges on 3 sides, 1¾x25x21" 58.00
Board, noodle; pine, 19½" dia+3¼" hdl 85.00
Board, pie; ear hdls, 12" dia+2½" hdl 48.00
Bowl, ash burl, cut-out hdls, G figure, 4¼x11¾x16¼", EX 800.00
Bowl, ash burl, G old finish, 3x8½" 480.00
Bowl, ash burl, G scrubbed finish, 4¼x13" 500.00
Bowl, burl, Am, 1800s, rim split, 20" dia 900.00
Bowl, burl, EX figure & end hdls, oblong, 4½x16¾" 1,265.00
Bowl, burl, oblong w/irregular edge, 4¾x12x14" 365.00
Bowl, burl, primitive, open knothole, 6x12½" 200.00
Bowl, chopping; pine, oblong, Am, 1800s, 26½" L 195.00
Bowl, ltweight, EX patina, 1¾x7" 115.00
Bowl, maple, cvd finger notches ea end, 2½x17x9¼" 120.00
Box, knife scouring; pine, sq nails, 2½x13x8¼" 68.00
Breadboard, Our Daily Bread, 11½" dia 68.00
Bucket, staved, tin bands, wire bail w/wood grip, 7x9" 54.00
Bucket, sugar; staved, dk rpt, 9½", EX 125.00
Bucket, sugar; staved, dk tin bands, early 48.00
Bucket, sugar; staved, lt gr rpt, 12" 275.00
Bucket, sugar; staved, old pnt, 8¾" 145.00
Butter curler, curved base w/cvd grooves, 1850s, 1-pc 70.00
Butter paddle, burl, EX figure, mini, 4¾" 335.00
Butter paddle, chestnut or ash burl, 12¼" L 150.00
Butter paddle, curly maple, hook hdl, age cracks, 11" 75.00
Butter paddle, cvd star flower, scrubbed hardwood, 6½" 300.00
Butter paddle, maple, inlay ivory heart, 1924, 10" 330.00
Butter print wheel, scrubbed, 5½" 175.00
Butter scoop, burl, lg blade, curved hdl, EX figure, 11½" L 585.00
Cake print, fireman w/trumpet, bk: floral medallions, 11" 700.00
Canteen, staved, old red pnt, rope hdl, 1850s, 5x8½" dia 295.00
Cheese drainer, pine, dvtl, mortised dowels, sq nails, 18" 275.00
Cheese ladder, maple, mortised & pinned, 1700s, 11x31" 110.00
Cheese ladder, mortised & pinned crossbars, 25¾x9¾" 88.00
Compote, treenware, worn 3-color pnt, 5¾x12" 400.00
Cookie rolling pin, 1-pc, 12" 48.00
Cream/butter stirrer, 1-pc, long open cutout in paddle, 25" 48.00
Curd breaker, wood drum w/blades, crank hdl, orig pnt, 1850s 235.00
Dipper, maple w/some burl, deep bowl, short/well-shaped hdl 465.00
Doughnut cutter, EX patina 75.00
Jar, Pease, ftd, w/lid, worn varnish, 4½" 245.00
Jar, Pease, ftd, w/lid & wire bail hdl, worn varnish, 2¾" 300.00
Jar, Pease, orig varnish, EX color, 6¼" 360.00
Jar, Pease, w/lid, 1½" 280.00

Jar, bulbous with small foot, iron and wooden bail handle, original D.M. Pease paper label, $550.00.

Measure, dbl; staved, tin bands, peck & half peck 110.00
Measure, iron bands & hdl, 1816 cvd in side, 9x14" dia 125.00
Mold, maple sugar; maple wood, cvd heart/dmn/spade, 17¾" L ..150.00
Muddler, hand cvd, 1-pc, 2¼" bottom, 13" hdl 36.00
Noggin, 1-pc, hand-cvd maple, 8" 145.00
Pastry roller, cvd cow/flowers/leaves 375.00
Pastry roller, cvd leaves/strawberry on wheel, 5" L 185.00
Rack, spoon; pine, rnd grooves for 6 spoons, fancy bk, 17x10" ...130.00
Scoop, apple butter; hand cvd, slant sides, open-D hdl, 15½" 85.00
Scoop, cranberry; flat bottom, 15¼x10½x5" 225.00
Sieve, bentwood, no bottom band, laced, fine screen, 13" dia 42.00
Spile, maple sap 10.00
Spoon, curly maple, 17", EX 95.00
Spoon, eng decor in bowl, shaped hdl, 6¼" 60.00
Spoon, hand cvd, tablespoon sz 18.00
Spoon, 4½x3¼" bowl+13½" hdl 65.00
Spuntle (butter scraper), cvd w/thin blade 30.00
Teapot, Pease, wire bail hdl, 2⅞x5" 350.00
Trencher, old scorp mks, oval, 4x18¾x10½" 145.00
Trencher, primitive cvg, lt wear, 3x17½x9⅛" 140.00
Trencher, trn, late 1700s, 14¼", EX 195.00
Wine, Pease, red & gr bands, 3½" 55.00
Wine, Pease, red sponging, 3¼" 110.00

Woodworking Machinery

Vintage cast iron woodworking machines are monuments to the highly skilled engineers, foundrymen, and machinists who devised them, thus making possible the mass production of items ranging from clothespins, boxes, and barrels to decorative moldings and furniture. Though attractive from a nostalgic viewpoint, many of these machines are bought by the hobbyist and professional alike, to be put into actual use — at far less cost than new equipment. Many worth-assessing factors must be considered; but as a general rule, a machine in good condition is worth about 65¢ a pound (excluding motors). A machine needing a lot of restoration is not worth more than 35¢ a pound, while one professionally rebuilt and with a warranty can be calculated at $1.10 a pound. Modern, new machinery averages over $3.00 a pound. Two of the best sources of information on purchasing or selling such machines are *Vintage Machines — Searching for the Cast Iron Classics*, by Tom Howell, and *Used Machines and Abused Buyers* by Chuck Seidel from *Fine Woodworking*, November/December 1984. Prices quoted are for machines in good condition, less motors and accessories. Our advisor for this category is Mr. Dana Martin Batory; he is listed in the Directory under Ohio. No phone calls, please.

American Saw Mill Machinery Company, 1890s

Band saw, Monarch Line, #X25, 30" built-in ball bearing motor ..770.00

Band saw, tilting table, 36" 850.00
Jointer, Monarch Line, #XII, ball bearing, 12" 1,040.00
Jointer, Monarch Line, #XII, ball bearing, 16" 1,200.00
Jointer, Monarch Line, ball bearing bench, 8" 475.00
Lathe, Monarch Line, manual training, 12x24" 535.00
Mortiser, Monarch Line, #XI, hollow chisel, motorized 345.00
Planer, Monarch Line, single surface, 30" 2,600.00
Planer/matcher/moulder, Triumph, dbl surface, 24" ...1,700.00
Sander, Monarch Line, #X8, ball bearing drum & disk 560.00
Table saw, Monarch Line, #X24, tilting arbor, 16" 425.00
Table saw, Monarch Line, Universal, ball bearing, 14" 1,140.00

Blue Star Products, 1939

Band saw, #1200, 12" floor model 85.00
Drill press, #500, 12" bench model 30.00
Lathe, #1002, 72" bed, 10" swing 60.00
Table saw, #800, 8" 95.00

Boice-Crane Power Tools, 1937

Band saw, #800, 14" 100.00
Belt sander, #1136, hand stroke 125.00
Drill press, #1600, 15" 75.00
Jointer, #950, 4" 50.00
Lathe, #1100, gap bed 50.00
Scroll saw, #900, 24" 75.00
Spindle sander, #560 ....100.00
Table saw, #1500, tilting arbor, 10" 100.00

Crescent Machine Company, 1921

Band saw, 36" 975.00
Jointer, bench; 4" 50.00
Mortiser, hollow chisel 525.00
Table saw, cut off; 16" 550.00
Universal Wood-Worker #59, 5 machines in 1 ....2,050.00

Defiance Machine Works, 1910

Band saw, 28" 520.00
Planer, 4-roll, single surface, 24" 1,300.00
Shaper, #4, dbl spindle, upright 1,430.00
Table saw, #2, hand feed, 20" 650.00
Table saw, #2, power feed, 20" 1,100.00

Gallmeyer & Livingston Company, 1927

Band saw, Union, 20" 390.00
Borer, Union, vertical 270.00
Combination, Union #86, Universal 8" saw/6" jointer 340.00
Jointer, Union, motor on arbor, 8" 370.00
Jointer, Union, 6" 190.00
Shaper, Union, dbl spindle 780.00
Table saw, Union #7, 7" 210.00

G.N. Goodspeed Company, 1876

Boring maching, upright 225.00
Planer, New & Improved, Pony, 24" 900.00
Sawing & boring machine 200.00
Table saw, 12" 200.00

Greenlee Bros. & Company, 1925

Borer, #355, single spindle, vertical 520.00

Mortiser, #225, hollow chisel 750.00
Rip saw, #405, heavy, 36" 2,115.00
Swing saw, #445, belt-driven, heavy, 40" 975.00
Table saw, #478, dbl arbor, 18" 1,750.00
Tenoner, #530, sash, door & cabinet, ball bearing 1,530.00

Hoyt & Brother Company, 1888

Band scroll & resawing machine, #1194, 20" 1,700.00
Boring machine, horizontal 390.00
Boring machine, Universal, vertical, single spindle 360.00
Cutoff saw, overhung, traversing, 14" 650.00
Cutoff saw, swing, 14" 260.00
Dovetailing machine, 13" 490.00
Flooring & ceiling machine, TW Harvey, #3, 6" 2,600.00
Jointer, Perfection, 8" 450.00
Mortiser & borer, #2 ....780.00
Mortising machine, hollow chisel, Giant 295.00
Moulding machine, 4-headed, 10" 2,400.00
Planer, matcher & surfacer, New Combined, #2, 24" 5,200.00
Planer & polishing machine, 42" 2,600.00
Planing & matching machine, #7, 13" 3,250.00
Resawing machine, circular, 50" 2,860.00
Sandpapering machine, The Boss, #5, 24" 1,595.00
Scroll saw, #1 ....300.00
Shingle machine, Grand Mogul, 2-block, automatic feed 2,210.00
Surfacer & sizer, dbl cylinder, endless bed, #2, 30" 6,825.00
Table saw, #2, 14" 800.00
Tenoning machine, #2 ....650.00
Universal Wood-Worker, 5 machines in 1 ....1,500.00
Wood shaper, dbl spindle 850.00

Ober Manufacturing Company, 1889

Rip saw, self feed, 14" 725.00
Saw, swing cutoff, 18" 275.00
Shaper, saw & jointer combination 400.00

Oliver Machinery Company, 1912

Band saw, #17, 30" 925.00
Lathe, #24, dbl end, 8-ft bed, 16" 1,175.00
Sander, vertical & disk, #34, 24" 1,475.00
Shaper, #483, high speed, dbl spindle 1,300.00
Table saw, #32, Variety, 12" 500.00

Parks Ball Bearing Machine Company, 1925

Parks 'Endurance' 20" single surface planer, ca 1925, $950.00.

Band saw, H-62, Jewel, 22" 250.00
Jointer, H-133, Ideal, 12" 400.00

Planer, H-117, Endurance, 20" 950.00
Sander, H-139, Peerless, flexible belt 650.00
Sanding machine, H-165, Economy, 24" 230.00
Saw, H-97, swing cutoff, Alert, 12" 225.00

P.B. Yates Machine Company, 1917

Jointer, #199, 12" 1,235.00
Planer, #160, dbl surface, 20" 5,000.00
Rip saw, #255, self feed, circular, 20" 1,235.00
Sander, #232, swing cutoff, 16" 260.00

L. Power & Co., 1888

Mortiser & borer, #2 ....780.00
Planer & matcher (combined), #5, 24" 5,525.00
Rip saw, #2, self feed, 24" 1,040.00
Shaper, single spindle, reversible 585.00
Table saw, self feed, 14" 715.00

S.A. Woods Machine Company, 1876

Circular resawing machine, Joslin's Improved, 50" ...2,275.00
Molding machine, #1, 2-roll, 12" 2,275.00
Planer, panel; Improved, 20" 520.00
Planer, Pat Improved, shop surface, 30" 1,430.00

Sprunger Power Tools, 1950s

Band saw, 14" 60.00
Jigsaw, 20" 40.00
Lathe, gap bed, 10" 50.00
Table saw, tilt arbor, 10¼" 75.00

Worcester Porcelain Company

The Worcester Porcelain Company was deeded in 1751. During the first or Dr. Wall period (so called for one of its proprietors), porcelain with an Oriental influence was decorated in underglaze blue. Useful tablewares represented the largest portion of production, but figurines and decorative items were also made. Very little of the earliest wares were marked and can only be identified by a study of forms, glazes, and the porcelain body, which tends to transmit a greenish cast when held to light. Late in the fifties, a crescent mark was in general use, and rare examples bare a facsimile of the Meissen crossed swords. The first period ended in 1783, and the company went through several changes in ownership during the next eighty years. The years from 1783-1792 are referred to as the Flight period. Marks were a small crescent, a crown with 'Royal,' or an impressed 'Flight.' From 1792-1807 the company was known as Flight and Barr and used the trademark 'F&B' or 'B,' with or without a small cross. From 1807-1813 the company was under the Barr, Flight, and Barr management; this era is recognized as having produced porcelain with the highest quality of artistic decoration. Their mark was 'B.F.B.' From 1813-1840 many marks were used, but the most usual was 'F.B.B.' under a crown to indicate Flight, Barr, and Barr. In 1840 the firm merged with Chamberlain, and in 1852 they were succeeded by Kerr and Binns. The

firm became known as Royal Worcester in 1862. The production was then marked with a circle with '51' within and a crown on top. The date of manufacture was incised into the bottom or stamped with a letter of the alphabet, just under the circle. In 1891 Royal Worcester England was added to the circle and crown. From that point on each piece is dated with a code of dots or other symbols. After 1891 most wares had a blush color ground. Prior to that date it was ivory. Most shapes were marked with a unique number.

During the early years they produced considerable ornamental wares with a Persian influence. This gave way to a Japanesque influence. James Hadley is most responsible for the Victorian look. He is considered the 'best ever' designer and modeller. He was joined by the finest porcelain painters. Together they produced pieces with very fine detail and exquisite painting and decoration. Figures, vases and tableware were produced in great volume and are highly collectible. During the 1890s they allowed the artists to sign some of their work. Pieces signed on the face by the Stintons, Baldwyn, Davis, Raby, Austin, Powell, Sedgley and Rushton (not a complete list) are in great demand. The company is still in production. There is an outstanding museum on the company grounds in Worcester, England.

The advisors on this category are Henry and Geneva Tyler in Florida. Note: most pieces had lids or tops (if there is a flat area on the top lip, chances are it had one), if missing deduct 30 to 40%.

Biscuit jar, flowers on blush, w/underplate, 5½x5" 475.00
Bowl, floral on blush, ftd, #1459, 6½x11¾" 525.00
Candle snuffer, owl, #67 ....190.00
Ewer, floral on blush, #1309, 16¼x8" 2,100.00
Ewer, flying swans on bl, sgn Baldwyn, #1309, 16¼x8" 7,500.00
Figurine, Bathers Surprise, modeled by Hadley, blush, 26½" ...3,250.00
Figurine, bird, sgn Doughty, #d 1,200.00
Figurine, Bringaree Indians, #1243, 9", pr 1,900.00
Figurine, camel, #209, 7x9½" 1,000.00
Figurine, cattle, sgn Linder, #d, ea 850.00
Pitcher, floral, blush, flat bk, #1094, 5¼x4" 135.00
Urn, floral, blush, hdls, crown lid, 12½x9" 2,000.00
Vase, flowers w/gilt tracery, blush, #1398, 21x9" 5,400.00
Vase, cattle on ivory, #2192, 10½x5½" 1,300.00
Vase, flying swans on bl, sgn Baldwyn, #1572, 10½x7¼" ...3,750.00
Vase, metallic birds on ivory, #784, ca 1883, 14½x6", pr 2,150.00
Vase, pastoral scene on dk bl, H Davis, #1937, 25½x11½" ...19,500.00
Vase, raised gold florals, w/lid, #1428, 13x11½" 2,850.00
Vase, roses on blush, #2260, 5¾" 375.00

World's Fairs and Expos

Since 1851 and the Crystal Palace Exhibition in London, World's Fairs and Expositions have taken place at a steady pace. Many of them commemorate historical events. The 1904 Louisiana Purchase Exposition, commonly known as the St. Louis World's Fair, celebrated the 100th anniversary of the Louisiana Purchase agreement between Thomas Jefferson and Napoleon in 1803. The 1893 Columbian Exposition, known as The Chicago World's Fair, commemorated the 400th anniversary of the discovery of America by Columbus in 1492. (Both of these fairs were held one year later than originally scheduled.) The multitude of souvenirs from these and similar events have become a growing area of interest to collectors in recent years. Many items have a 'crossover' interest into other fields: i.e., collectors of postcards and souvenir spoons eagerly search for those from various fairs and expositions. For additional information collectors may contact World's Fairs Collectors Society (WFCS), whose address is in the Directory under Clubs,

Newsletters, and Catalogs, or our advisor, D.D. Woollard, Jr. His address is listed in the Directory under Missouri.

Key:
T&P — Trylon & Perisphere   WF — World's Fair

1876 Centennial, Philadelphia

Ad card, Machinery Hall, PH Taylor..., groceries/etc, 4½x3" **17.50**
Bandana, linen, printed brn buildings, red border, 26x25" **150.00**
Book, Centennial Exhibition, emb medal on covers, Fry, +insert .**17.50**
Medallion, wood, Gen JR Hawley bust in relief, 2½", EX **75.00**
Stud, brass, emb building, Art Gallery 1876, 1" dia **25.00**
Ticket, lady w/sword/eagle/cornucopia, Phila Bank Note, 3¾" **12.50**

1893 Columbian, Chicago

Book, Century WF Book for Boys & Girls, hardbk, 245-pg, NM ..**35.00**
Book, World's Columbian..., Illus, Campbell, Jan 1892, 32-pg, NM ..**17.50**
Book, Youth's Companion, WF view on soft cover, VG **20.00**
Booklet, World Is Mine, Simmons Saw & Mfg Co, 5x3¼", NM ..**12.50**
Card, Old Times Distillery building diecut, 3½x2¼" **20.00**
Paperweight, sepia Ferris wheel view in glass, 3" dia **60.00**
Playing cards, Columbian Souvenir, Clark, 54 in worn box **100.00**
Razor, buildings etch on blade, Vulcan, blk hdl, 6¼", NM **85.00**
Ribbon, landing scene/flag, Nat'l...School Celebration, mc **22.50**
Spoon, building view in bowl, floral hdl, Leonard SP, 6" **12.50**
Ticket, Chicago Day, w/stub **17.50**
Tray, Columbus & buildings w/floral border, SP, ftd, 7" dia **75.00**

1898 Trans-Mississippi

Match safe, NP, female figure, Expo buildings **48.00**
Pin-bk, Iowa Day Sep 21-98, celluloid, 1¼" **30.00**
Spoon, SP, Government building in bowl **24.00**
Tray, building emb on pot metal, slight wear, 3½" **20.00**

1901 Pan American

Ad card, Heide's Licorice Pastiles..., boy in fancy clothes **10.00**
Book, Enterprising Housekeeper, soft cover, 80-pg, 4¼x6½" **17.50**
Book, Souvenir of Pan-Am Expo, Bayne, soft cover, 9x7" **20.00**
Booklet, Singer machines, fair buildings/etc, 4½" dia **17.50**
Doll, Kewpie type, mk Pan-Am on ft, celluloid, all orig, 3" **50.00**
Elongated cent, Electric Tower, M **12.50**
Envelope, buffalo on globe/Electric tower, Niagara, 3½x6" **12.50**
Letter opener, partially flattened nail, Pan-Am...1901, 5½" **20.00**
Medal, nude lady, Gold Medal Highest Award, brass, worn, 1¼" ...**5.00**
Mug, ladies as N&S Am, Expo mk, Columbian Art Pottery, 5" ...**85.00**
Paperweight, McKinley & Temple of Music, glass, 4x2¼x1" **25.00**
Pin-bk, ladies in shape of N&S Am, mc, celluloid, 1¼" **20.00**
Pocket mirror, Castle Copal, celluloid, Expo mk/1901, 2⅛" **50.00**
Shot glass, When You Drink-Do of Me Think, buffalo/etc, 2½" ...**30.00**
Spoon, sterling, McKinley bust enameled on hdl **90.00**
Spoon, US Govt Building in bowl, Indian on hdl, USSC, 4½" **15.00**

1904 St. Louis

Book, Phila Souvenir-St Louis, bl/wht soft cover, VG **17.50**
Booklet, Universal Expo, illus, 80-pg, 9x12", EX **27.50**
Elongated cent, Festival Hall & Central Cascades, NM **12.50**
Napkin ring, emb fair building on metal **35.00**
Paperweight, Central Cascades view in glass, 4x2¼" **25.00**

Paperweight glass, enclosed sea shells, 3" **17.50**
Pitcher, ruby-stained glass, 4½" **45.00**
Pitcher, US Govt Building, porc, 3", NM **40.00**
Plate, Festival Hall & Cascade Gardens pressed in glass, 7" **17.50**
Postcard, Palace of Transportation, NM **3.00**

Silk ribbon, Festival Hall and Central Cascades, 9x5", $220.00.

Tray, Education & Electrical Buildings, mc, steel, 5x3¼", EX **20.00**
Tumbler, buildings emb on metal, 3½" **35.00**
Tumbler, buildings emb on milk glass, 5" **15.00**
Tumbler, triple scene on china, 4" **45.00**

1905 Lewis and Clark

Pin-bk, 2 frogs under umbrella, mc on celluloid, WF mk, 1¾" **40.00**
Plate, Miss Liberty, Lewis & Clark, porc, unmk, 8½" **55.00**
Postcard folder, mc views, Wolff & O'Brien, set of 24 ....**20.00**
Tray, Foreign Exhibit Buildings emb, aluminum, 6½x4" **20.00**

1907 Jamestown

Badge, ships of 1607 & 1907, brass, 2¼", +inscr hanger **16.00**
Book, view; Jamestown Expo Co, 18-pg+2 maps, 5½x7" **17.50**
Cent, Lucky Penny Pocket Piece, aluminum, encased **10.00**
Medal, Indian chief/Landing of...Captain J Smith, copper, 2" **12.50**
Napkin ring, 3 views on copper plate over base metal, 2" dia **15.00**
Plate, building view, red-brn on wht, Rowland & Marsellus, 6" ...**45.00**
Tray, Expo views, copper plate over base metal, scalloped, 7" **15.00**

1915 Panama Pacific

Ad card, panoramic view, folding, Traveler's Ins, 13x3¼" **5.00**
Book, Views of..., sepias, soft cover, CTCo, 24-pg, 10x8" **17.50**
Book, What We Saw at..., hardbk, Gordon, 86-pg, 7x9½" **20.00**
Book, 13th Labor of Hercules, soft cover, 56-pg, 7x10", EX **20.00**
Mailing folder, 22 color views in strip, 4x6" **12.50**
Pin-bk, PPIE San Francisco 1915, bl/gold/wht, 1" dia, NM **20.00**

1926 Sesquicentennial

Ashtray, Liberty Bell emb on heavy metal, oval, 5½x3¼" **15.00**
Brooch, Liberty Bell medallion, copper metal in gr fr, 1x1¼" **20.00**

Folder, NY City Day Itinerary, Nov 12, 1926, 4x6", NM 10.00
Key, head in shape of Liberty Bell, WF mk, metal, 2¼", NM 12.50
Mailing folder, Official Souvenir, 18 mc views in strip, 6" L 12.50
Medal, WA bust/Liberty Bell on gold metal, 1⅜" 10.00
Paperweight, Liberty Bell figural, heavy metal, 3x3x1½" 15.00
Pencil case, Liberty Bell on leather, 3x8", NM 25.00
Pin-bk, Liberty Bell 1776/1926, mc, celluloid, 1" dia 12.50
Postcard, fair views, set of 7 (all different) 20.00
Program, Official...Daily, July 20, 1926 (Ohio Day), 32-pg, M 12.50

1933 Chicago

Ashtray, Sky Ride & Fort Dearborn emb on brass, 5" sq 7.50
Bank, mc fair buildings litho on tin, Am Can, 3½x2", NM 25.00
Bookmark/letter opener, comet design, brass-tone metal, 4½" 10.00
Candle holders, emb buildings on silver metal, 1934, 4", pr 30.00
Cigar pack, Wht Owl, ...Produced at CWF 1933, unopened, M ...50.00
Crumb tray, floral design on wood, comet sticker on bk, 7¼" 10.00
Fan, fair views, cb, 3-part, 8½x13" (open), EX 40.00
Handkerchief, comet logo, gr & wht, silk, 11x11", NM 15.00
Key, Keep Me for Good Luck, Master Lock Co, 2", NM 12.50
Mailing case, 20 photos, Davis, 1934, complete 10.00

Miniature globe with building views in base, B&D Products, EX, $50.00.

Napkin ring, comet logo on gold w/red trim, metal, 1½" dia 15.00
Needle folder, mc buildings ea side, lt wear, 6½x4½" 5.00
Pin-bk, comet & I Was There, red/wht/bl, tin litho, NM 10.00
Plaque, blk & silver metallic on wood, emb buildings, 3x5" 40.00
Plate, Carillon Tower, gr & wht, Pickard, 7½" 30.00
Spoon, emb designs/Century of Progress...on hdl, mk Sterling 30.00
Spoon, Fort Dearborn in bowl, SP, 6" 7.50
Ticket, mc, to Fort Dearborn w/attached Gen Admission stub 12.50

1939 New York

Bandana, Boy Scout 1939 Service Camp, 30" sq, EX 100.00
Bank, book shape, metal w/T&P on leather cover 40.00
Bank, T&P, glass w/emb center, 3½x3¼x2" 60.00
Book, Official Guide, 1st ed, 1939, 256-pg 20.00
Bookends, T&P design, marble, 4½", M, pr 200.00
Booklet, Futurama, minor staining, 20-pg 10.00
Catalog, Masterpieces of Art, 1940, 258-pg 20.00
Collar clip, T&P design, 2" 30.00
Folder, mailing; 18 mc views of fair 15.00
Hot pad, Administration Building emb, 8x6" 15.00
Pin-bk, I Was There, T&P, celluloid, 1939, ⅝" 12.50

Plate, ceramic, potter at wheel, lt bl, 7" 25.00
Seal, Boy Scout Camp, gummed 5.00
Seal, Greyhound Bus, gummed, 1939, 3½x3" 5.00
Spoon, souvenir; various bowl designs, SP, Wm Rogers, ea 12.50
Tie clip, T&P design, 2½" 22.50
Tray, T&P design, metal, some wear, 18x11" 50.00
Watering can, T&P design, ceramic, mini 50.00

1939 San Francisco

Book, Famous Guide to San Francisco & WF, 144-pg, 5x7", NM ...15.00
Folder, general fair info, dtd 1939, 3½x6", NM 5.00
Folder, Kirkland Travel Service, 2 tours shown, folded: 4x9" 7.50
Ice pick, WF mk on wooden hdl, 8", NM 20.00
Mailing folder, Treasure Island Night & Day, 14 mc views, NM ..10.00
Medal, locomotives of Union Pacific, alumimum, NM 10.00
Medal, Petroleum Exhibit, brass, 1⅜", NM 7.50
Plate, Golden Gate Internat'l Expo, Homer Laughlin, 10" 90.00
Postcard, Sunken Gardens, Exhibit Palaces, Expo Tower, M 2.50
Ticket, Cavalcade of Golden West, 2x1¼" 3.00
Ticket folder, WF Premiere, 2½x6", +pin-on badge, M 35.00

1962 Seattle

Book, Century 21, illus, Morgan, 1959-pg 30.00
Brochure, w/map of grounds & week's schedule of events, NM 3.00
Certificate, from One Million Silver Dollar display, NM 10.00
Dish, Space Needle & fairgrounds on china, 11" dia 20.00
Dish, Space Needle on china, 4" dia 7.50
Lapel pin, Century 21 Expo, silver on bl 10.00
Tumbler, Space Needle, red & wht w/gold, 5½" 14.00

1964 New York

Booklet, From Savage to Citizen, Wycliff Bible Translators, NM ...4.50
Booklet, Let's Go to Fair & Futurama, 32-pg, 5¼x8½", NM 7.50
Magazine, NY Vacation Lands 1965 WF Edition, 80-pg, 7x10½" .10.00
Map, Tri-State Road Map WF Issue, Tidewater Oil, NM 8.00
Postcard, Travelers Ins Co Pavilion, mc, NM 2.50
Puzzle, fair scene, fits in fr tray, M Bradley, EX color, NM 15.00
Sticker, New Jersey Tercentenary Pavilion, paper, 1¾" dia 3.00
Tray, Heliport & top of Fair Restaurant, mc on metal, 5x7", EX 5.00

Wright, Frank Lloyd

Born in Richland Center, Wisconsin, in 1869, Wright became a pioneer in architectural expression, developing a style referred to as 'prairie.' From early in the century until he died in 1959, he designed houses with whose rooms were open, rather than divided by walls in the traditional manner. They exhibited low, horizontal lines and strongly projecting eaves, and he filled them with furnishings whose radical aesthetics complemented the structures to perfection. Several of his homes have been preserved to the present day, and collectors who admire his ideas and the unique, striking look he achieved treasure the stained glass windows, furniture, chinaware, lamps, and other decorative accessories made by Wright.

Armchair, oak, 15-spindle sides, ca 1895, 39" 16,000.00
Block, terra cotta, angular geometric recesses, 13x12x12" 1,300.00
Book, Future of Architecture, NY, 1953, 326 pgs, M 175.00
Ceiling grille, oak, geometrically arranged slats, 37x7" 2,700.00
Chair, side; mahog, low bk, spindles extend below drop seat ...30,000.00

Door knob/escutcheon, bronze, ornate scrolls/florals, 14" **1,600.00**
Frieze, CI, berry/acanthus leaf repeats, 7x87" **3,200.00**
Frieze, pine wood, joined Xs in shaped ovals, pnt, 10x39" **450.00**
Library table, oak, trestle form w/medial shelf, 65" **16,000.00**
Print, int drawing of Coonley House on brn paper, 12x21" **700.00**
Skylight, grille work, sqs/bars, 20x36" **2,600.00**
Sofa section, angled, brn tweed, loose cushions, 90", VG **900.00**
Sofa section, Taliesin, wood base w/cvg, brn tweed, 64", VG ..**2,000.00**
Table, coffee; Taliesin, extended top, plank sides, 60", VG **4,000.00**
Table, serving; oak, 2nd tier extends, 1-drw, 41x36, 22" **11,000.00**
Vase, gr, hexagon w/stylized flower ea corner, Teco, 23" **40,000.00**
Window, geometrics/sm 'tulips,' wht/red on clear, 49x31", EX .**5,500.00**
Window, ldgl, simple geometrics, nearly all clear, 36x26" **3,600.00**

Wrought Iron

Until the middle of the 19th century, almost all the metal hand forged in America was made from a material called wrought iron. When wrought iron rusts it appears grainy, while the mild steel that was used later shows no grain but pits to an orange-peel surface. This is an important aid in determining the age of an ironwork piece.

Box lock, for house door, oval brass knob, latch/hdl, sgn **55.00**
Broiler, rotary type, scroll details, 32" L **150.00**
Broiler, rotary type, twisted/scrolled detail, 1763, 26" L **450.00**
Broiler, rotary type, well-shaped hdl, 13" dia, 24" L **115.00**
Broiler, tripod base, penny ft, adjusts, 28" H **300.00**
Broiler, 7½x7½" w/11" hdl **125.00**
Candle snuffer, scissors type **60.00**
Dipper, brass inlay in hdl, 14¾" **150.00**
Fork, 3 silver inlays, eng eagle & Liberty, 16¼" **165.00**
Fork, 3 tines form basket-like cup, tooling, brass hdl, 5" **160.00**
Hasp, for Conestoga wagon tool box, fleur-de-lis, 15", VG **90.00**
Hook, meat; loop w/teardrop opening, 2 tines, 1870s, 21" **65.00**
Hook, meat; twisted hdl, 4 hooks, 14½" **75.00**
Hook, pot; dbl, 1820s, 15½" **45.00**
Ladle, early, 19⅜", EX **50.00**
Nippers, sugar, 8" **140.00**
Pan, 3-legged, 12½" dia+31" hooked hdl **145.00**
Pan, 3-legged, 6½"+11" hdl **200.00**
Pike, boatman's, 1700s, 15" L **55.00**
Rack, utensil; European style, 1800s, 26x31" **90.00**
Rack, utensil; tooled bar, tree-like tooled finials, 12½" L **385.00**
Spatula, keyhole type, early, 19", EX **100.00**
Spatula, 3 brass inlays w/eng heart, dtd 1827, 22" **300.00**
Toaster, spiral arch design, ca 1700s, 16" **250.00**
Toaster, twisted design, 5½x19"+19" hdl **125.00**
Tongs, looped hdls end in tight curl, 1865, 16½" **55.00**
Trammel, primitive, 2 hooks, 12¾" **95.00**

Yellow Ware

Ranging in color from buff to deep mustard, yellow ware which almost always has a clear glaze can be slip banded, plain, Rockingham decorated, flint enamel glazed, or mocha decorated. Mocha-decorated pieces are usually the most expensive and desirable. The majority of pieces are plain and do not bear a manufacturer's mark. Yellow ware which was primarily produced in the United States, England, and Canada was popular from the mid-19th century to the early 20th century. A utilitarian ware, it was first domestically produced in New York, New Jersey, Pennsylvania, and Vermont. With more than thirty active potteries, East Liverpool, Ohio, became the center for yellow ware pro-

duction. After experiencing several years of dramatic price increases, the market has begun to stabilize. For further information we recommend *Collecting Yellow Ware, An Identification and Value Guide*, written by our advisor, John Michel, and Lisa S. McAllister. Mr. Michel's address is in the Directory under New York.

Bowl, mixing; seaweed, brn on yellow ware, 6½x13½" **275.00**
Bowl, mixing; slip decor, common type, up to **95.00**
Bowl, tea; 2 wide wht bands, 6" **125.00**
Bowl, wide bl band between narrow wht bands, 4½" **75.00**
Chamber pot, brn & wht slip bands, open, 1850s-1920s, 7" **97.50**
Colander, milk pan shape, lg holes, 1880s, 11" **550.00**
Cookie jar, emb floral decor, ca 1900-40, lg **135.00**
Creamer, cow, plain yel, minimum value **2,000.00**
Crock, emb bands, fancy hdls, English, 1870-90, 10" dia **285.00**
Custard cup, rnd shape, common type, 4" **22.00**
Custard cup, 3 wht rings, ca 1880-1930 ....**50.00**
Flask, fish form, English, 1850-90, 10½", minimum value **950.00**
Flowerpot & saucer, 1900-30 ....**150.00**
Jar, preserve; wax sealer type, 7½" **185.00**
Ladle, plain yel, 10", minimum value **750.00**
Mold, bunch of grapes, fluted sides, 8x7x4", VG **130.00**
Mold, ear of corn, scalloped, gallery base, 9x8x4", EX **140.00**
Mold, ear of corn, 4" **95.00**
Mold, fish, 1850-1900, 12" **500.00**
Mold, fruit, rectangular, sm **195.00**
Mold, melon shape, 1850-80, 8" **200.00**
Mold, parrot on branch, 10x8" **500.00**
Mold, rabbit, 1880-1920, 8" **145.00**
Mold, rose w/buds & leaves, 1850-80, 5" **285.00**
Mold, turtle form, late 1800s, 6x8" **550.00**
Mug, narrow wht bands, Am **200.00**
Mustard pot, incised lines filled in w/bl slip, 1850-1900 ....**350.00**
Pepper pot, bl bands, English, 1870-1900 ....**575.00**
Pipkin, mk Jeffords Pottery **425.00**

Pitcher, three bands, six rings of colored slip each, 7", $400.00.

Pitcher, basketweave & morning glory emb, ca 1900 ....**175.00**
Pitcher, bl sponging, ca 1920, 6" **120.00**
Pitcher, blk floral seaweed over rust & wht bands, 8½" **1,050.00**
Plate, 10¾", EX **60.00**

Platter, canted corners, plain, 1850-90 ....465.00
Rolling pin, wht bands, wooden hdls, ca 1880-1920 ....550.00
Salt cellar, master; bl bands 325.00
Salt crock, bl & wht bands, wooden lid, hanging 265.00
Shaving mug, light application of Rockingham, 1860-90 ....425.00
Soap dish, plain yel, rectangular, 6½x3½" 335.00
Teapot, basketweave emb, Jeffords 465.00
Teapot, leaves & stars emb, England, 1840s, 1-cup 445.00

Zanesville Glass

Glassware was produced in Zanesville, Ohio, from as early as 1815 until 1851. Two companies produced clear and colored hollowware pieces in five characteristic patterns: 1) diamond faceted, 2) broken swirls, 3) vertical swirls, 4) perpendicular fluting, 5) plain, with scalloped or fluted rims and strap handles. The most readily identified product is perhaps the whiskey bottles made in the vertical swirl pattern, often called globular swirls because of their full, round bodies. Their necks vary in width; some have a ringed rim and some are collared. They were made in several colors; amber, light green, and light aquamarine are the most common. Our advisor for this category is Mark Vuono; he is listed in the Directory under Connecticut.

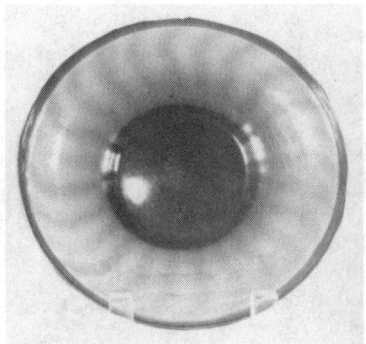

Pan, amber, twenty-four swirled ribs, shallow with folded rim, 7¼", $725.00.

Bottle, club; aqua, 24 swirl ribs to right, wide mouth, 8½" 175.00
Bottle, globular; aqua, 24 swirl ribs, lt stain, 8" 300.00
Bottle, globular; aqua, 24 swirl ribs to left, 9½" 465.00
Bottle, globular; citron, 24 swirl ribs, EX impression, 7½" 2,200.00
Bottle, globular; gold-amber, 24-rib, lt impression, 7¾" 975.00
Bottle, nursing; aqua, 24 vertical ribs, 7", NM 115.00
Creamer, cobalt bl lead glass, trumpet neck, petal ft, 5" 400.00
Flask, chestnut; dk amber, 24 swirl ribs, 5" 325.00
Flask, chestnut; gold-amber, 24 swirl ribs, lt wear, 5" 220.00
Inkwell, gr-aqua, 24 vertical ribs, funnel well, 2½" 145.00

Zsolnay

Only until the past decade has the production of the Zsolnay factory become more correctly understood. In the beginning they produced only cement; industrial and kitchen ware manufacture began in the 1850s, and in the early 1870s a line of decorative architectural and art pottery was initiated which has continued to the present time.

The city of Pecs (pronounced Paach) is the major provincial city of southwest Hungary close to the Yugoslav border. The old German name for the city was Funfkirchen, meaning 'Five Churches.' (The 'five-steeple' mark became the factory's logo in 1878.)

Although most Americans only think of Zsolnay in terms of the bizarre, reticulated examples of the 1880s and '90s and the small 'Eosine' green figures of animals and children that have been produced since the 1920s, the factory went through all the art trends of major international art potteries and produced various types of forms and decorations. The 'golden period,' circa 1895-1920, is when its Art Nouveau (Sezession in Austro-Hungarian terms) examples were unequaled. Vilmos Zsolnay was a Renaissance man devoted to innovation, and his children carried on the tradition after his death in 1900. Important sculptors and artists of the day were employed (usually anonymously) and married into the family, creating a dynasty.

Nearly all Zsolnay is marked, either impressed 'Zsolnay Pecs' or with the 'five steeple' stamp. Variations and form numbers can date a piece fairly accurately. For the most part, the earlier ethnic historical-revival pieces do not bring the prices that the later Sezession and second Sezession (Deco) examples do. Our advisor for this category is John Gacher; he is listed in the Directory under Rhode Island.

Ewer, satyr & maid sit/stand on shoulder, wine irid, 18" 4,000.00
Figurine, seated boy w/cat on shoulder, bl irid, 6" 400.00
Jug, intricate floral w/star-rtcl appl disks, #962, 12x10" 550.00
Urn, mc Persian floral, braid hdls, rstr/hairlines, 12", pr 250.00

Vase, peony, butterflies and leaves on spotted ground with gilding, #872, 14¾", $1,725.00.

Vase, intricate floral w/butterflies, mc/gold, #872, 15" 1,725.00
Vase, intricate floral w/4 rtcl melon ribs, #1063, 4x7", NM 55.00
Vase, peacock irid, baluster w/can neck, 10" 600.00
Vase, red irid on 'crackled mud' texture, 5½" 210.00
Vase, 3 appl medallions w/rtcl, yel/blk/red, 3-hdl 9½" 115.00
Vase, 3-D mermaid/man on shoulder, emb fish, bl irid, 9x11" .1,600.00
Vase, 4 mice on red/ochre irid, dbl gourd w/4 hdls, 7" 900.00

Advisory Board

The editors and staff take this opportunity to express our sincere gratitude and appreciation to each person who has in any way contributed to the preparation of this guide. We believe the credibility of our book is greatly enhanced through their efforts. See each advisor's Directory listing for information concerning their specific areas of expertise.

You will notice that at the conclusion of some of the narratives the advisor's name is given. This is optional and up to the discretion of each individual. Simply because no name is mentioned does not indicate that we have no advisor for that subject. Our board grows with each issue and now numbers over 350; if you care to correspond with any of them or anyone listed in our Directory, you must send a SASE with your letter. If you are seeking an appraisal, first ask about their fee, since many of these people are professionals who must naturally charge for their services. Because of our huge circulation, every person who allows us to publish their name runs the risk of their privacy being invaded by too many phone calls and letters. We are indebted to every advisor and very much regret losing any one of them. By far, the majority of those we lose give this reason. Please help us retain them on our board by observing the simple rules of common courtesy. Take the differences in time zones into consideration; some of our advisors tell us they often get phone calls in the middle of the night. For suggestions that may help you evaluate your holdings, see the Introduction.

Charles and Barbara Adams
Middleboro, Massachusetts

Jay Adams
Clifton, New Jersey

Geneva D. Addy
Winterset, Iowa

Charles Alexander
Indianapolis, Indiana

Margaret Alves
Shelton, Connecticut

James Anderson
New Brighton, Minnesota

Suzy McLennan Anderson
Holmdel, New Jersey

Tim Anderson
Provo, Utah

Warren R. Anderson
Cedar City, Utah

Dorothy Malone Anthony
Fort Scott, Kansas

John Apple
Racine, Wisconsin

Dick and Ellie Archer
St. Augustine, Florida

Una Arnbal
Ames, Iowa

Bruce Austin
Pittsford, New York

Rod Baer
Vienna, Virginia

Wayne and Gale Bailey
Dacula, Georgia

Mrs. Lillian Baker
Fellow IBA, Cambridge, England
Gardena, California

Roger Baker
Woodside, California

Robert Banks
Brookeville, Maryland

Jim Barker
Bethlehem, Pennsylvania

Kit Barry
Brattleboro, Vermont

Henry Bartsch
Rockaway, Oregon

Mark Bassett
Lakewood, Ohio

Daniel J. Batchelor
Oswego, New York

Dana Martin Batory
Crestline, Ohio

Joyce Bee
Sandy, Oregon

D.R. Beeks
Coeur d'Alene, Idaho

Scott Benjamin
Elyria, Ohio

Phyllis and Tom Bess
Tulsa, Oklahoma

Robert Bettinger
Mt. Dora, Florida

John E. Bilane
Union, New Jersey

Dale Blann
Wheatland, Indiana

Clarence H. Bodine, Jr.
New Hope, Pennsylvania

Sandra V. Bondhus
Unionville, Connecticut

Clifford Boram
Monticello, Indiana

Dick and Waunita Bosworth
Kansas City, Missouri

Jeff Bradfield
Dayton, Virginia

Tom Bradshaw
Ventura, California

Larry Brenner
Manchester, New Hampshire

William J. Brinkley
McLeansboro, Illinois

Mike Brooks
Oakland, California

Jim Broom
Effingham, Illinois

David L. Brown
Victoria, British Columbia,
Canada

Rick Brown
Newspaper Collector's Society of
America
Lansing, Michigan

Mike Bruner
West Bloomfield, Michigan

Nicki Budin
Worthington, Ohio

Robert C. Butz
Newbury Park, California

Jim Calison
Wallkill, New York

Carol and Jim Carlton
Englewood, Colorado

Fran Carter
Coos Bay, Oregon

Tina M. Carter
El Cajon, California

Sally S. Carver
Chestnut Hill, Massachusetts

Cerebro
East Prospect, Pennsylvania

Jackie Chamberlain
Wickenburg, Arizona

Mick and Lorna Chase
Crookeville, Tennessee

Pat and Chris Christensen
Costa Mesa, California

Jack Chipman
Redondo Beach, California

Wilfred and Dolli Cohen
Santa Ana, California

Richard Cohn
St. Paul, Minnesota

Auction Houses

We wish to thank the following auction houses whose catalogs have been used as sources for pricing information. Many have granted us permission to reproduce their photographs as well.

A-1 Auction Service
P.O. Box 540672, Orlando, FL 32854; 407-841-6681. Specializing in American antique sales

America West Archives
Anderson, Warren
P.O. Box 100, Cedar City, UT 84721; 801-586-9497; publishes 26-page illustrated catalog 6 times a year that includes auction section of scarce and historical early western documents, letters, autographs, stock certificates, and other important ephemera. Subscription: $15 per year

Andre Ammelounx
The Stein Company
P.O. Box 136, Palatine, IL 60078; 708-991-5927 or (Fax) 708-991-5947. Specializing in steins, catalogs available

Annual Perfume Bottle Auction
Monsen & Baer
310 Maple Ave., West #270, Vienna, VA 22180; 703-938-2129

Anthony J. Nard & Co.
US Rt. 220, Milan, PA 18831; 717-888-9404 or (Fax) 717-888-7723

Arman Absentee Auctions
16 Sixth St, Stamford, CT 06905; 203-928-5838. Specializing in American glass, Historical Staffordshire, English soft paste, paperweights

Bertoia & Brady Auctions
2413 Madison Ave., Vineland, NJ 08360; 609-692-4092

Bider's
241 S. Union St., Lawrence, MA 01843; 508-688-4347 or 508-683-3944. Antiques appraised, purchased, and sold on consignment

Brian Riba Auctions Inc.
P.O. Box 53, Main St., S. Glastonbury, CT 06073; 203-633-3076

Butterfield & Butterfield
220 San Bruno Ave., San Francisco, CA 91043; 415-861-7500 or (Fax) 415-861-8951. Also located at:
7601 Sunset Blvd., Los Angeles, CA 90046; 213-850-7500 or (Fax) 213-850-5843. Fine Art Auctioneers and Appraisers since 1865

C.E. Guarino
Box 49, Denmark, ME 04022

Charles E. Kirtley
P.O. Box 2273, Elizabeth City, NC 27096; 919-335-1262. Specializing in World's Fair, Civil War, political, advertising and other American collectibles

Cincinnati Art Gallery
635 Main St., Cincinnati, OH 45202; 513-381-2128. Specializing in American art pottery, American and European fine paintings, watercolors

Col. Doug Allard
P.O. Box 460, St. Ignatius, MT 59865-0460; 406-745-2951 or (Fax) 406-745-2961

Collectors Auction Services
326 Seneca St., Oil City, PA 16301; 814-677-6070. Specializing in advertising, oil and gas, toys, rare museum and investment-quality antiques

David Rago
P.O. Box 3592, Station E, Trenton, NJ 08629; 609-397-9374
Gallery: 17 S. Main St., Lambertville, NJ 08530. Specializing in American art pottery and Arts & Crafts

Doyle Auctioneers & Appraisers
109 Osborne Hill Rd., Fishkill, NY
12524; 914-896-9492. Thousands
of collectibles offered: call for free
calendar of upcoming events

Dunbar's Gallery
Leila and Howard Dunbar
76 Haven St., Milford, MA
01757; 508-634-8697 or (Fax)
508-634-8698.

Dynamite Auctions
Franklin Antique Mall & Auction Gallery
1280 Franklin Ave., Franklin, PA
16323; 814-432-8577 or 814-786-
9211

Du Mouchelles
409 Jefferson Ave., Detroit, MI
48226

Early Auction Co.
123 Main St., Milford, OH 45150

Garth's Auctions Inc.
2690 Stratford Rd., Box 369,
Delaware, OH 43015; 614-362-4771

Glass-Works Auctions
James Hagenbuch
102 Jefferson, East Greenville,
PA 18041; 215-679-5849. America's leading auction company in
early American bottles and glass

Greenberg Auctions
7566 Main St., Sykesville, MD
21784. Specializing in trains: Lionel,
American Flyer, Ives, Marx, Ho

Guernsey's
136 E. 73rd St., New York, NY
10021; 212-794-2280. Specializing
in carousel figures

Hake's Americana & Collectibles
Specializing in character and personality collectibles along with all
artifacts of popular culture for
over 20 years. To receive a catalog for their next 3,000-item
mail/phone bid auction, send $5
to Hake's Americana, P.O. Box
1444M, York, PA 17405

Horst Auctioneers
Horst Auction Center
50 Durlach Rd. (corner of Rt. 322
& Durlach Rd., West of Ephrata),
Ephrata, Lancaster County, PA
17522; 717-859-1331 or 717-738-
3080. Voices of Experience

Jack Sellner
Sellner Marketing of California
P.O. Box 308, Fremont, CA
94536; 415-745-9463

James D. Julia
P.O. Box 210, Showhegan Rd.,
Fairfield, ME 04937

James R. Bakker Antiques, Inc.
James R. Bakker
370 Broadway, Cambridge, MA
02139; 617-864-7067. Specializing in American paintings, prints
and decorative arts

John Toomey Gallery
818 North Blvd., Oak Park, IL
60301; 708-383-5234 or (Fax) 708-
383-4828. Specializing in furniture
and decorative arts of the Arts &
Crafts, Art Deco and Modern
Design movements; Modern Design
Expert: Richard Wright

Joy Luke Fine Arts Brokers and
Auctioneers
The Gallery
300 East Grove St., Bloomington,
IL 61701; 309-828-5533

Ken Farmer Realty & Auction
Company
1122 Norwood St., Radford, VA
24141; 703-639-0939 or (Fax)
703-639-1759

L.R. 'Les' Docks
Box 691035, San Antonio, TX
78269-1035. Providing occasional
mail-order record auctions, rarely
consigned; the only consignments
considered are exceptionally
scarce and unusual records

Litchfield, Auction Gallery
425 Bantam Rd., P.O. Box 1337,
Litchfield, CT 06759; 203-567-
3126 or (Fax) 203-567-3266

Lloyd Ralston Toys
447 Stratford Rd., Fairfield, CT
06432

Manion's International Auction
House, Inc.
P.O. Box 12214, Kansas City, KS
66112

Maritime Auctions
R.R. 2, Box 45A, York, ME
03909; 207-363-4247

McMasters Doll Auctions
P.O. Box 1755, 5855 Glenn
Highway Rd., Cambridge, OH
43725; 614-432-4320 or (Fax)
614-432-3191

Mid-Hudson Auction Galleries
One Idlewild Ave., Cornwall-on-
Hudson, NY 12520; 914-534-
7828 or (Fax) 914-534-4802

Monsen & Baer
Monsen, Randall; and Baer, Rod
310 Maple Ave. West, Suite
#115, Vienna, VA 22180; 703-
938-2129. Cataloged auctions of
perfume bottles. We purchase,
sell, and accept consignments.
Specializing in commercial,
Czechoslovakian, Lalique, Baccarat, Victorian, crown top, fac-
tices, miniatures

Noel Barrett Antiques & Auctions
P.O. Box 1001, Carversville, PA
18913; 215-297-5109 or (Fax)
215-297-0457

Nostalgia Co.
21 S. Lake Dr., Hackensack, NJ
07601; 201-488-4536

Nostalgia Galleries
657 Meacham Ave., Elmont, NY
11003; 516-326-9595. Auction-
ing items from almost every area
of the collectible field, catalogs
available

Phillips
406 E. 79th St., New York, NY
10021

The Political Gallery
1325 W. 86th St., Indianapolis,
IN 46260; 317-257-0863. Publishes quarterly catalogs

Postcards International
P.O. Box 2930, New Haven, CT
06515-0030; 203-865-0814 or
(Fax) 203-495-8005

Refinders
737 Barberry Rd., Highland Park,
IL 60035; 708-831-1102 or 708-
831-1160. Refinders will find your
wants from 1860-1960

Rex Stark Auctions
49 Wethersfield Rd., Bellingham,
MA 02019

Richard A. Bourne Co. Inc.
Estate Auctioneers & Appraisers
Box 141, Hyannis Port, MA
02647; 617-775-0797

Richard Opfer Auctioneering, Inc.
1919 Greenspring Dr., Timo-
nium, MD 21093; 301-252-5035

Roan, Inc.
Box 118, R.D. 3, Cogan Station,
PA 17728

Robert W. Skinner, Inc.
Auctioneers & Appraisers
Rt. 117, Bolton, MA 01740; 617-
779-5528

Ron Fox Auctions
Ron Fox
83 Morris St., Brentwood, NY
11717; Telephone and Fax: 516-
952-7719. Specializing in steins;
auctions with illustrated catalogs
and video tapes

Soldiers Trunk
60 Craigs Rd., Windsor, CT
06095; 203-688-0580. Specializing
in American and foreign military
items; 4 catalog issues for $20.00.

Sotheby Parke Bernet, Inc.
980 Madison Ave., New York,
NY 10021

Treadway Gallery, Inc.
2029 Madison Rd., Cincinnati,
OH 45208; 513-321-6742 or (Fax)
513-871-7722. Specializing in
American Art Pottery; American
and European art glass; European
ceramics; Italian glass; fine American and European paintings and
graphics; and furniture and decorative arts of the Arts & Crafts, Art
Nouveau, Art Deco and Modern
Design Movements. Modern
Design expert: Thierry Lorthioir.
Members: National Antique Dealers Association, American Art Pottery Association, International
Society of Appraisers, American
Ceramic Arts Society, Ohio Decorative Arts Society, Art Gallery
Association of Cincinnati.

Weschler's
Adam A. Weschler & Son
905 E. St. N.W., Washington,
DC 20004

Willis Henry Auctions
22 Main St., Marshfield, MA
02050

Directory of Contributors

When contacting any of the buyers/sellers listed in this part of the Directory by mail, you must include an SASE (stamped, self-addressed envelope) if you expect a reply. As hectic as our lifestyles are, the time it saves them is probably worth more to them than the price of a stamp. Not only that, but trying to decipher someone's handwritten name and address can be very frustrating. Sometimes even zip codes are unreadable, and even more time is required to double check zip code numbers. And in the end, if 'Rosen' becomes 'Rirer' and 'Ave. 5' becomes 'Ave. S,' even if the person you contacted was gracious enough to answer you, you probably won't ever know he did. Many of these people are professional appraisers and there will be a fee for their time and service. Find out up front. Include a clear photo if you want an item identified. Most items cannot be described clearly enough to make an identification without a photo.

If you call and get their answering machine, when you leave your number so that they can return your call, tell them to call back collect. And please take the differences in time zones into consideration. 7:00 AM in the midwest is only 4:00 AM in California! And if you're in California, remember that even 7:00 PM is too late to call the east coast. Most people work and are gone during the daytime. Even some of our antique dealers say they prefer after-work phone calls. Don't assume that a person who deals in a particular field will be able to help you with related items. They may seem related to you when they are not.

Please, we need your help. This book sells in such great numbers that allowing their names to be published can create a potential nightmare for each advisor and contributor. Please do your part to help us minimize this, so that we can retain them on our board and in turn pass their experience and knowledge on to you through our book. Many of our people tell us that even with the occasional problem, they feel that the good outweighs the bad and makes all their hard work worthwhile.

Alabama

Dole, Pat
9825 Red Mill Rd.
Birmingham, 35215; 205-833-9853. Specializing in Purinton pottery

Lippa, Matt; and Schaaf, Elizabeth
Artisans
R.R. 1, Box 20-C, Mentone, 35984; 205-634-4037. Specializing in folk art, quilts, painted and folky furniture, tramp art, whirligigs, windmill weights

Luckey, Carl
Carl F. Luckey Communications
R.R. 4, Box 301, Lingerlost Tr., Killen, 35645. Freelance writer specializing in art, antiques, and collectibles. No telephone calls will be accepted.

Arizona

Chamberlain, Jackie
Jackie Chamberlain Antiques
P.O. Box 20842, Wickenburg, 85358. Specializing in holiday collectibles, antique reference books, pewter ice cream molds, rare out-of-print books. Holiday slide program available for rent

Chase Collectors Society
c/o Barry L. Van Hook
2149 Jibsail Loop, Mesa, 85202-5524; 602-838-6971. Publishes (6 issues per year) newsletter *Art Deco Reflections*; Membership: $10, newsletter sample copy: $1

Ellwood, J.M.
7077 E. Main #4, Scottsdale, 85251; 602-947-9679. Specializing in cast iron banks, toys, irons, trivets, doorstops and miscellaneous cast iron

Kielsmeier, Wayne B.
Covington Fine Arts Gallery, Inc.
4951 E. Grant, Rd. 107, Tucson, 85712; 602-326-6111. Specializing in 19th- and 20th-century American and European paintings, prints, watercolors, and art pottery

Arkansas

Gifford, David Edwin
Arkansas Pottery Research
P.O. Box 7617, Little Rock, 72217. Historian/author/collector of Arkansas art pottery from 1905 to 1932. Seeking all information and company literature on the Ouachita Pottery, Niloak Pottery, and Camark Pottery companies as well as quality pieces marked Ouachita Hot Springs, Niloak Patent Pend'G, LeCamark or Hywood Art Pottery, will answer queries — LSASE please

Hall, Doris and Burdell
B&B Antiques
P.O. Box 1501, Fairfield Bay, 72088 or 210 W. Sassafras Dr., Morton, IL 61550. Authors of *Morton's Potteries: 99 Years* Specializing in Morton pottery, American dinnerware, early American pattern glass, historical items

Musgrave, Marge
Look Nook Antiques
R.R. 3, Box 352, Mountain Home, 72653; 501-499-5283. Specializing in art glass and colored Victorian glass

Whysel, Steven
Antique & Art Galleries Ltd., Inc.
109 N. Main, Bentonville, 72712; 501-273-7770. Specializing in Art Nouveau, full line, books and art

Yohe, Darlene
Timberview Antiques
P.O. Box 343, Stuttgart, 72160; 501-673-3437. Specializing in American pattern glass, historical glass, Victorian pattern glass, carnival glass, and custard glass

California

Baker, Mrs. Lillian
15237 Chanera Ave., Gardena, 90249; 213-329-2619. Author Collector Books on antique, collectible, and high-fashion costume jewelry, hatpins and hatpin holders, miniatures

Baker, Roger
Baker's Lady Luck Emporium
Box 620417, Woodside, 94062. Specializing in Saloon Americana — advertising, gambling, bar bottles, cigar lighters, match safes, bowie knives, dirks, daggers, cowboy hats, spurs, chaps, saddles, barber items: bottles, shaving mugs, razors

Berman, Joanne
6130 Rampart Dr., Carmichael, 95608; 916-966-3490. Specializing in decorative (non-advertising) thermometers

Bradshaw, Tom
325 Carol Dr., Ventura, 93003; 805-653-2723. Specializing in antique Bohemian glass

Brooks, Mike
7335 Skyline, Oakland, 94611; 510-339-1751. Specializing in typewriters, transistor radios, early televisions, Statue of Liberty

Butz, Robert C.
Collector's Wedgwood
P.O. Box 462, Newbury Park, 91319; 805-496-7805. Specializing in Wedgwood

Carter, Tina M.
882 S. Mollison, El Cajon, 92020; 619-440-5043. Specializing in teapots, tea-related items, tea tins, children's and toy tea sets, coffeepots, etc.; forthcoming book in 1994, contact for details

Chipman, Jack
California Spectrum
Box 1429, Redondo Beach, 90278. Specializing in California ceramics; author of *Collector's Encyclopedia of California Pottery*, autographed copies available from author for $24.95+$3.50 postage and handling+(CA) tax of $2.35

Christensen, Pat and Chris
1067 Salvador St., Costa Mesa, 92626. Specializing in open salts

Cohen, Wilfred and Dolli
Antiques & Art Glass
P.O. Box 27151, Santa Ana, 92799; 714-545-5673 (best to phone after 6:00 p.m. Pacific time). Specializing in Wave Crest (C.F. Monroe); Victorian Era art and pattern glass (salt shakers, toothpick holders, syrups, cruets, sugar shakers, tumblers, biscuit jars, table and pitcher sets); art and cameo glass open salts; custard and ruby stain glass; burmese, peachblow and amberina glass; pottery by Moorcroft (pre-1935 only); Buffalo (Deldare and Emerald ware); and Polia Pillin. Please include SASE for reply.

Delucchi, Mary
Classic Tableware
P.O. Box 4265, Stockton 95204; 209-956-4645 (Shop: 1868 Country Club Blvd.). Specializing in discontinued patterns: china, earthenware, crystal and silver

Ehrhard, J. David
Psycho-Ceramic Restorations
c/o Showcase Antiques, 4405 Fair Oaks Ave., Pasadena. 91105; Specializing in restoration of ceramics, collects Susie Cooper and British pottery, Mabel Lucie Attwell

Enge, Delleen
Franciscan Dinnerware Matching Service
323 E. Matilija, Ste. 112, Ojai, 93023

Escoe, Adrienne S.
Glass Knife Collectors Club
P.O. Box 342, Los Alamitos, 90720; 310-430-6479. Specializing in glass knives

Fogleman, Marv
Marv's Memories
1914 W. Carriage Dr., Santa Ana, 92704; 714-751-24663. Specializing in Western Dinnerware, Metlox, Mikasa, and Franciscan

George, Tony
22431-B160 Antonio Pkwy., #252, Rancho Santa Margarita, 92688; 714-589-6075. Specializing in watch fobs

Gibson, Pat
38280 Guava Dr., Newark, 94560; 510-792-0586. Specializing in R.A. Fox

Harrison, Gwynne
P.O. Box 1, Mira Loma, 91752-0001; 909-685-5434. Specializing in Autumn Leaf (Jewel Tea)

Hibbard, Suzi
WanderWares
2570 Walnut Blvd. #20, Walnut Creek, 94596; 510-947-1076. Specializing in Dragonware, 1000 Faces china, Oriental china. Inquiries should be accompanied by SASE

Howard, Steve
101 1st St., Suite 404, Los Altos, 94022; 510-484-4488. Specializing in antique American firearms, bowie knives, Western Americana, old advertising and vintage gambling items

Inouye, Roger
2622 Valewood Ave., Carlsbad, 92008-7925. Specializing in Trolls.

Kreider, Katherine
Kingsbury Productions
4555 N. Pershing Ave., Suite 33-138, Stockton, 95207; 209-467-8438. Specializing in Valentines

Long, Earnest and Ida
Long's Americana
P.O. Box 90, Mokelumne Hill, 95245; 209-286-1348. Specializing in children's items: toys, banks, games, etc.; publishers of *Dictionary of Toys, Vol. I & II*; *Dictionary of Still Banks*; and *Penny Lane*, a history of antique mechanical toy banks

MacKie, Jim and Linda
P.O. Box 1419, Soquel, 95073; 408-475-8049. Specializing in all advertising and (Linda's specialty) early lithography citrus and cigar labels

Maurer, Oveda L.
Oveda Maurer Antiques
34 Greenfield Ave., San Anselmo, 94960; 415-454-6439. Specializing in 18th-century and early 19th-century American furniture, lighting, pewter, and hearthware

Nelson, Maxine
873 Marigold Ct., Carlsbad, 92009. Specializing in Vernon Kilns; author of *Collectible Vernon Kilns*; autographed copies available from the author for $24.95+$2.50 postage & handling (CA sale tax: $1.93); SASE appreciated for inquiries

Paper Pile Quarterly
Ada Fitsimmons, Editor
P.O. Box 337, San Anselmo, 94979; 619-322-3525. Sales and features magazine serving paper collectors and dealers since 1980, quarterly cataloged sales, large advertising section; Subscription: $17 per year (shipped 1st class)

Pardini, Dick
3107 N. El Dorado St., Dept. SAPG, Stockton, 95204-3412; 209-466-5550 (recorder may answer). Specializing in California Perfume Company items dating from 1886 to 1928: buyer and information center. Not interested in items that have Avon, Perfection, or Anniversary Keepsake markings. California Perfume Company offerings must be accompanied by a photo, Xerox copy, or sketching along with a condition report and, most important, price wanted. Inquiries require large SASE; not necessary if offering items for sale

Sanford, Steve and Martha
230 Harrison Ave., Campbell, 95088; 408-978-8408. Specializing in Brush McCoy

Shrader, Fred and Lila
Shrader Antiques
2025 Hwy. 199, Crescent City, 95531; 707-458-3525. Specializing in railroad, steamship, and other transportation memorabilia; Shelley, Buffalo, and select Americana

Stella's Collectibles
Memory Lanes Antique Mall
20740 S. Figueroa St, Carson, (Space 214) 90745; 310-316-7198; PCH Antique Mall Long Beach (Space 129); Santa Monica Antique Market (Space 113); Westchester Faire Mall (Space 320-326); Nana's Antiques and Collectibles, Temecula. Specializing in quality glass, china, figurines, and plates

Yronwode, Catherine
6632 Covey Rd., Forestville, 95436; 707-887-2424. Specializing in pre-1950 collectible plastic

Zeder, Audrey
6755 Coralite St. S., Long Beach, 90808 (appointment only). Specializing in British Royal Commemorative Souvenirs (mail-order catalog available). Author (Wallace-Homestead) of *British Royal Commemoratives*

Canada

Brown, David L.
Stevengraph Collectors Assn.
2103-2829 Arbutus Rd., Victoria, British Columbia, V8N 5X5; 604-477-9896. Specializing in Stevengraphs

Melis, Mirko
Marcelle Antiques
4589 Longmoor Rd., Mississauga, Ontario, L5M 4H4; 905-820-8066. Specializing in American and European art glass, Russian works of art (enamels, porcelains, silver, etc.), English and Continental glass and china, member of Antique Appraisal Association of America, Inc., and AADA (Associated Antique Dealers of America, Inc.)

Old China Patterns Limited
1560 Brimley Rd., Unit 1, Scarborough, Ontario, MIP369; 416-299-8880 or (Fax) 416-299-4721. Specializing in discontinued china dinnerware, matching service (since 1966), charter member I.A.D.M.

Warner, Ian
P.O. Box 93022, 499 Main St. S., Brampton, Ontario, L6Y 4V8; 905-453-9074 or (Fax) 905-453-2931. Specializing in Wade porcelain and Swankyswigs, author of *The World of Wade*, Co-author: Mike Posgay

Colorado

Carlton, Carol and Jim
8115 S. Syracuse St., Englewood, 80112; 303-773-8616. Specializing in Broadmoor, Coors, and other Colorado pottery

Heck, Carl
Carl Heck Decorative Arts
Box 8416, Aspen, 81612; 303-925-8011. Specializing in original Tiffany lamps, art glass, windows, and chandeliers. Also reverse-painted and leaded glass table lamps, stained and beveled glass windows, bronzes, paintings, etc.; Buy and sell. Please include SASE for reply

Mackin, Bill
Author of *Cowboy and Gunfighter Collectibles*; available from author: P.O. Box 70, Meeker, 81641; 303-824-6717, paperback: $22; 1993-94 updated Price Guide: $9. Specializing in old and fine spurs, guns, gun leather, cowboy gear, Western Americana (Collection in the Museum of Northwest Colorado, Craig)

Over, Naomi L.
8909 Sharon Lane, Arvada, 80002; 303-424-5922. Specializing in ruby glassware

Segelke, Cathy; and James, Pat
Hillrose, 303-847-3758 (Cathy) or 308-847-3759 (Pat). Specializing in crocks, Western Pottery Mfg. Co. (Denver, CO)

Toohey, Marlena
703 S. Pratt Parkway, Longmont, 80501; 303-678-9726. Specializing in black glass; book available from author for $20 (includes shipping and handling)

White, John 'Grandpa'
Grandpa's Depot
Denver Union Station, 1616 17th St., Denver, 80202; 303-892-1177 or (Fax) 303-573-5505. Specializing in railroad-related items, catalogs available

Winther, Jo Ellen
8449 W. 75th Way, Arvada, 80005; 800-872-2345 or 303-421-2371. Specializing in Coors

Connecticut

Alves, Margaret
84 Oak Ave., Shelton, 06484; 203-924-4768. Specializing in spoons: plated, sterling, silver, pre-1920s

Bondhus, Sandra V.
Box 100, Unionville, 06085; 203-678-1808. Author of *Quimper Pottery: A French Folk Art Faience*; specializing in Quimper pottery

Harned, Denise
P.O. Box 330373, Elmwood, 06133-0373. Author of *Griswold Cast Collectibles*. Specializing in Griswold cast iron and aluminum

Kilbride, Mrs. Richard J.
81 Willard Terrace, Stamford, 06903; 203-322-0568. Has available for sale: *Art Deco Chrome, The Chase Era*, and *Art Deco Chrome, Book 2, A Collector's Guide, Industrial Design in the Chase Era*

MacSorley, Earl
823 Indian Hill Rd., Orange, 06477; 203-387-1793 (after 7:00 p.m.). Specializing in nutcrackers, Bessie Pease Gutmann prints, figural spittoons

Postcards International
Shapiro, Marty
P.O. Box 2930, New Haven, 06515-0030; 203-865-0814 or (Fax) 203-495-8005. Specializing in vintage picture postcards

Rivera, Ted
Box 163, Torrington, 06790; 203-489-4325. Specializing in inkwells and inkstands; co-author of *Inkstands and Inkwells: A Collector's Guide*

Roenigk, Martin
Mechantiques
26 Barton Hill, E. Hampton, 06424; 203-267-8682. Specializing in mechanical musical instruments, music boxes, band organs, musical clocks and watches, coin pianos, orchestrions, monkey organs, automata, mechanical birds and dolls, etc.

Thalberg, Bruce
Mountain View Dr., Weston, 06883; 203-227-8175. Specializing in canes and walking sticks: novelty, carved, and Black

Van Deusen, Hobart
28 The Green, Watertown, 06795; 203-945-3456. Specializing in Canton, SASE required when requesting information

Vuono, Mark
306 Mill Rd., Stamford, 06903; 203-357-0892 (10 a.m. to 5:30 p.m. EST). Specializing in historical flasks, blown 3-mold glass, blown American glass

Delaware

Davis, Patricia M.
700 Greenhill Ave., Wilmington, 19805; 302-658-2992

District of Columbia

Durham, Ken and Jackie (By appointment)
909 26 St. N.W., Washington, DC 20037. Specializing in counter-top arcade machines, trade stimulators, and vending machines; 16-page illustrated list: $2; Send SASE for free list of books on coin-operated machines

England

Pedel, Alan
Hidden Treasures
Marwood Lee, Barnstaple, Devon, EX31 4EB; 011-44-271-75166 (anytime). Specializing in pie birds and most other collectibles

Florida

Archer, Dick and Ellie
Artiques
419 Sevilla Dr., St. Augustine, 32086; 904-797-4678. Specializing in Victorian silverplate: figurals, fancy hollowware, and collectibles

Bettinger, Robert
P.O. Box 333, Mt. Dora, 32757; 904-735-3575. Specializing in American art pottery

Cohen, Joel
Cohen Books & Collectibles
P.O. Box 810310, Boca Raton, 33481; 407-487-7888. Specializing in Disneyana

deCourtivron, Gael
Cocaholics
4811 Remington Dr., Sarasota, 34234; 813-355-2652 or 813-359-2652. Specializing in Coca-Cola memorabilia.

Dodds, Rebecca
Silver Flute
Box 39644, Ft. Lauderdale, 33339. Specializing in jewelry

Donnelly, Ron
Saturday Heroes
Box 7047, Panama City Beach, 32413. Specializing in Big Little Books, movie posters, premiums, western heroes, character collectibles, early Disney. For inquiries include SASE

France, Madeleine
P.O. Box 15555, Ft. Lauderdale, 33318; 305-584-0009. Specializing in top-quality perfume bottles: Rene Lalique, Steuben, Czechoslovakian, DeVilbiss, Baccarat, Commercials

Harry, Pauline
Pauline Harry Paper Collectibles
11493 Spring Hill Dr., Spring Hill, 34609; 904-686-9418. Specializing in pinups, illustrators, Rockwell, Leyendecker, etc., old magazines

Hess, Steve
Confederate Swords
P.O. Box 3476; Deland, 32723; 904-254-1809 or 904-736-1067. Specializing in Confederate swords

Hudson, Hardy
Our Antiques Market
5453 Lake Howell Rd., Winter Park, 32792; 407-657-2100 from 11:00 a.m. to 6:00 p.m. Specializing in majolica, American art pottery;

Lawrence, Judy and Cliff
1169 Overcash Dr., Dunedin, 34698; 813-734-4742. Specializing in fountain pens, dip pens, and mechanical pencils

Linscott, Jacqueline C.
3557 Nicklaus Dr., Titusville, 32780. Specializing in Blue Bell paperweights; author of *1992 Revised Edition, Blue Bell Paperweights*, complete with history, illustrations, and price guide; Available from author for $12

Linscott, Len
Line Jewels-Insulators
3557 Nicklaus Dr., Titusville, 32780. Specializing in glass and porcelain insulators. Also glass insulator books by CD number (LSASE required)

McNerney, Kathryn
118 Creek Hollow Lane, Middleburg, 32068. Author (Collector Books) on blue and white stoneware, primitives, tools

Parker, Alton B.
Box 110, 5030 W. 14 St., Bradenton, 34207; 813-756-0386. Specializing in Azalea china, Depression Glass, Roseville pottery

Supnick, Mark
8524 N.W. 2 St., Coral Springs, 33065; 305-755-3448. Author of *Collecting Hull Pottery's Little Red Riding Hood*. Specializing in American pottery

Tyler, Henry and Geneva
13 Bellevue Dr., Treasure Island, 33706.

White, Douglass
Classic Interiors & Antiques
2042 N Rio Grande Ave, Suite E, Orlando, 32804; 407-839-0004. Specializing in Fulper, Arts & Crafts furniture

Georgia

Bailey, Wayne and Gale
P.O. Box 173, Dacula, 30211; 404-963-5736. Specializing in Goebels (Friar Tuck)

Glenn, Walter
Geode Ltd.
3393 Peachtree Rd., Atlanta, 30326; 404-261-9346. Specializing in Frankart

Hartley, Glenn, Sr.
Fire Mark Circle of the Americas 2859 Marlin Dr., Chamblee, 30341-5119; 404-451-2651. Specializing in fire marks, Methodist, Masonic, Foremost Dairies, Goodyear

Joiner, John R.
52 Jefferson Parkway, Apt. D, Newman, 30263; 404-502-9565. Specializing in commercial aviation collectibles

Idaho

Beeks, D.R.
P.O. Box 2515, Coeur d'Alene 83814; 208-667-0830. Specializing in instruments of early science, technology, and medicine. Also surveying instruments, microscopes

Illinois

Ammelounx, Andre
The Stein Auction Company
P.O. Box 136, Palatine, 60078; 708-991-5927 or (Fax) 708-991-5947. Specializing in steins, catalogs available

Brinkley, Wm. J.
Brinkley Galleries
401 S. Washington Ave., McLeansboro, 62859. Specializing in Meissen, Dresden, European porcelains, American porcelains (Cybis)

Broom, Jim
Box 65, Effingham, 62401. Specializing in opalescent pattern glassware

Danis, John
11028 Raleigh Ct., Rockford, 61115; 815-963-0757 or (Fax) 815-877-6042. Specializing in R. Lalique

Feldman, Arthur M.
Arthur M. Feldman Gallery
1815 St. Johns Ave., Highland Park, 60035; 708-432-8858. Specializing in Judaica and antiques

Frizzell, Doris
Doris' Dishes
5687 Oakdale Dr., Springfield, 62707; 217-529-3873. Specializing in Royal Haeger, and Depression Glass; Co-author (Collector Books) of Royal Haeger book

Gandolfo, Dan
The Goofus Connection
3 So. 577 Elizabeth, Warrenville, 60555; 708-393-9115. Specializing in goofus glass

Garmon, Lee
1529 Whittier St., Springfield, 62704; 217-789-9574. Specializing in Royal Haeger, Royal Hickman, glass animals; co-author (Collector Books) of Glass Animals and Figural Flower Frogs of the Depression Era

Griffith, Woody
Chicago, 312-975-1957. Specializing in Jewel Tea, Noritake, Hall, perfumes

Grubb, Elmer
Pleasant Hill Antique Mall, Booth #83
99 Kerfoot, East Peoria, 61611; 309-699-4389. Specializing in Illinois Hutch sodas

Hall, Doris and Burdell
B&B Antiques
210 W. Sassafras Dr., Morton, 61550 or P.O. Box 1501, Fairfield Bay, AR 72088. Authors of Morton's Potteries: 99 Years; specializing in Morton pottery, American dinnerware, early American pattern glass, historical items

Haussmann, Richard A., Past President, Aurora Historical Society
Aurora, 60507

Hilst, Randy
1221 Florence #4, Pekin 61554; 309-346-2710. Specializing in general line including fishing and hunting collectibles

Hoffmann, Pat and Don, Sr.
1291 N. Elmwood Dr., Aurora, 60506; 708-859-3435. Authors of Warwick, A to W, a supplement to Why Not Warwick? China Collector's Guide; video regarding Warwick decals currently available. Specializing in Warwick china

The Home Place Antiques
Durham, William; Galaway, William
615 S. State St., Belvidiere, 61008; 815-544-0577. Specializing in Tea Leaf ironstone and white ironstone

Hooks, Dee
Dee's China Shop
P.O. Box 142, Lawrenceville, 62439; 618-943-2741. Specializing in R.S. Prussia, Royal Bayreuth, Haviland, other fine china

Hopp, Dennis Carl
Chicago, 312-935-7872. Specializing in Higgins glass

Hurney, George and Mary
Glass Connection (mail-order only)
312 Babcock Dr., Palatine, 50067; 708-359-3839. Specializing in Depression Glass and Paden City glass (not advising on pottery)

International Society of Antique Scale Collectors
Bob Stein, President
176 W. Adams, Suite 1706, Chicago, 60603; 312-263-7500. Publishes Equilibrium, quarterly magazine; Quarterly President's Newsletter; annual membership directory; out-of-print catalogs. Holds annual convention

John Toomey Gallery
818 N. Blvd, Oak Park, IL 60301

Long, Dee
112 S. Center, Lacon, 61540. Specializing in reamers

Lotton, Charles
Lotton Art Glass
1938 177th St., Lansing, 60438; 708-474-4022. Specializing in art glass

Lubliner, Larry
Refinders mail/telephone auction
737 Barberry Rd., Highland park, IL 60035; 708-831-1102 or 708-831-1160. Refinders will find your wants from 1860-1960

Meyer, Larry
4001 Elmwood, Stickney, 60402; 708-749-1564. Specializing in fire grenades

Miller, Larry; and Strickfaden, Dick
218 Devron Circle, E. Peoria, 61611-1605. Specializing in German and Czechoslovakian Erphila

Ochsner, Grace
Grace Ochsner Doll House
R.R. 1, Box 95, Niota, 62358; 217-755-4362. Specializing in piano babies, bisque German dolls

Owen, Larry and Sally
Specializing in Morten Studio dogs, etc.

Pollack, Frank and Barbara
(Appointment only)
1214 Green Bay Rd., Highland Park, 60035; 708-433-2213. Specializing in American country antiques and art

Pustelniak, Mary
Mary's Antiques
Paris, 217-465-5185.

Randy's Ol' Time Collectibles
Illinois Antique Center
100 Walnut St., Peoria, 61602; 309-346-2710. Specializing in general line, including hunting and fishing collectibles

Rastello, Lisa
Milkweed Antiques
5N531 Ancient Oak Lane, St. Charles, 60175; 708-377-4612. Specializing in Depression-Era collectibles

Rhoden, Joan and Charles
Memories/Rhoden's Antiques
605 N. Main, Georgetown, 61846; 217-662-8046. Specializing in Heisey and other Elegant Glassware, general line antiques. Co-authors of Those Wonderful Yard-Long Prints and More, and More Wonderful Yard-Long Prints, illustrated value guides

Rodrick, Tammy
Stacey's Treasures
R.R. 2, Box 163, Sumner, 62466. Specializing in antiques and collectibles

Spencer, Dick
Glass and More (Shows only)
1203 N. Yale, O'Fallon, 62269; 618-632-9067. Specializing in Cambridge, Fenton, Fostoria, Heisey, etc.

Spiess, Greg
230 E. Washington, Joliet, 60433; 815-722-5639. Specializing in Odd Fellows lodge items

Stifter, Donna & Craig
P.O. Box 6514, Naperville, 60540; 708-717-7949. Specializing in Pepsi-Cola, Coca-Cola and other soda-pop brand collectibles

Weldi-Skinner, Mary
1656 W. Farragut Ave., Chicago, 60640. Specializing in American and European art pottery, designer collectibles

Wells, Rosalie J. 'Rosie'
R.R. 1S, Canton, 61520; 1-800-445-8745. Publishes magazines and annual price guides for Precious Moments Collectibles, Hallmark Ornament Collectibles and Hallmark Merry Miniatures. She hosted the International Convention for Precious Moments Collectors each year since 1984 and hosts the Annual Midwest Collectibles Fest in St. Charles, IL. Write for free literature. She also offers a touch-tone 900 line for collectors 18 years and older to leave their Voice Ad for collectors of over 26 collectibles and antiques across the USA to buy or sell through. (1-900-740-7575) $2 per minute. For more information, call 1-800-445-8745.

Wilson, Jack D.
P.O. Box 81974, Chicago, 60681-0974; 312-282-9553. Specializing in Phoenix and Consolidated glass; buying Ruba Rombic; Author of *Phoenix & Consolidated Art Glass: 1926-1980*. Secretary of Phoenix and Consolidated Glass Collectors' Club. Editor of *Phoenix & Consolidated Glass Collectors' News & Views* newsletter (published bimonthly); Membership: $25 (single), $35 (couple) per year

Yester-Daze Glass
c/o Illinois Antique Center
100 Walnut St., Pekin, 61554; 309-347-1679. Specializing in Cambridge, Fostoria, Depression Glass and '50s glass

---

Indiana

Alexander, Charles
221 E. 34th St., Indianapolis, 46205; Specializing in American dinnerware.

Anbrose, Don & Susan
Gilley's Antique Mall
R. R. 2, Box 298A, Monrovia, 46157; 317-996-2514. Specializing in graniteware, Hoosier cabinets, oak furniture

Armstrong, Dale
Downstairs Attic
7307 N. State Road 39, Lizton, 46149; 371-994-5125. Specializing in glassware, collectibles and antique furniture

Blann, Dale
President of Uhl Collectors' Society
R.R. 1, Box 136, Wheatland, 47597; 812-321-4141. Contact for membership and newsletter information

Boram, Clifford
Antique Stove Information Clearinghouse
Monticello; Free consultation by phone only: 219-583-6465

Brown, Linda
P.O. Box 525, Lebanon, 46052; 317-325-2419. Specializing in Black Americana along with general line antiques and collectibles

Clark, Marion
R.R. 1, Box 412, Monrovia, 46157; 317-996-3403. Specializing in glassware & collectibles

Croan, Etta R.
R.R. 1, Box 30, Filmore, 46128; 317-246-6741

Crossroads Antique Mall
311 Holiday Square, Seymour, 47274; 812-522-5675. Open 7 days a week

Daniels, Dottie
Dottie's Antiques & Collectibles
7502 Higdon Ct., Indianapolis, 46214; 317-271-5507. Specializing in primitives

Dunn, Keith L.
Dunn in the Past
9101 E. Co. Rd. 200 So., Kirkland, 46050; 317-758-6282. Specializing in pottery: Watt, Purinton, Roseville, Fiesta

Earl, Jesse
330 Junkin St., Connersville, 47331; 317-825-9875. Specializing in science fiction and monsters

Edwards, Bill
620 W. 2nd, Madison, 47250. Author (Collector Books) on Carnival Glass

Faulkner, Joan
Doll Adoption Agency, Etc.
1149 Buchanan St., Plainfield, 46168; 317-839-6092. Specializing in dolls, jewelry, miscellaneous smalls

Fisher, Todd
Crossroads Antique Mall
311 Holiday Square, Seymour, 47274; 812-522-5675. Open 7 days a week

Fred, James A.
Antique Radio Labs
R.R. 1, Box 41, Cutler, 46920; 317-268-2214. Specializing in radios made from 1922 to 1950

Galliher, David A.
2500 W. Berwyn Rd., Muncie, 47304; 317-284-6668. Specializing in powder horns (pre-1820) and flasks, decoys

Garrett, Jerry and Sandi
Jerry's Antiques (Shows only)
1807 W. Madison St., Kokomo, 46901; 317-457-5256. Specializing in Greentown glass, old postcards

Gilley, Betty
Gilley's Antiques
1209 W. Main St., Plainfield, 46168; 317-839-8779. Specializing in pottery, china, furniture

Gilley's Antique Mall and Collectibles
1209 W. Main (US 40), Plainfield, 46168; 317-839-8779. Open daily from 10 a.m. to 5 p.m., features booths with over 250 dealers; outdoor summer weekend flea market

Haisley, Gary
Old Tyme Toy Mall
542 Circle Dr., Fairmount, 46928; 317-948-5479. Specializing in farm toys of the '40s through '70s, cast iron farm toys, Vindex and Arcade

Haskett, Don and Sandy
Red House Antiques, located at Gilley's Mall, 1209 W. Main (US 40), Plainfield, 46168; 317-852-4518. Specializing in furniture, glassware, advertising, watches, knives, and miscellaneous

Haun, Ted
2426 N. 700 East, Kokomo, 46901; 317-628-3640. Specializing in American pottery and china, '50s items, Russel Wright designs

Heiss, Virginia
7777 N. Alton Ave., Indianapolis, 46268; 317-875-6797. Specializing in Muncie, AMACO, Brandt Steele, Marblehead, Kenton Hills

Hufferd, Suzan
6625 Sunbury Dr., Indianapolis, 46241. Specializing in vinyl advertising, Dakin characters and fast food

Hulse, Bill
Uncle Munchies Antiques Inc.
1173 E. Buchanan St., Plainfield, 46168; 317-839-4947. Specializing in general line

Hunt, Michael
Old Country Store
9016 Greenlee Circle, Indianapolis, 46234; 317-271-5602. Specializing in antique advertising

Keagy, William and June
P.O. Box 106, Bloomfield, 47424; 812-384-3471. Co-authors of *Those Wonderful Yard-Long Prints and More*, and *More Wonderful Yard-Long Prints*, illustrated value guides

Knotts, P.L.
Knotts Collectibles
6150 S. 800 E., Zionsville, 46077-9020; 317-873-6499. Specializing in really neat stuff!

Lawyer, Eddie L.
E.L. Lawyer Antiques & Collectibles
Gilley's Antique Mall
317-839-8952. Specializing in Nippon, World's Fair souvenirs, the unusual, general line

McMullen, John and Jan
Curio Shop
3521 Brewer Dr., Indianapolis, 46222; 317-291-0536

Mendenhall, Mary R.
285 N. Mill St., Plainfield, 46168. Specializing in general line

Mills, Joe and Sharon
Glean 'N' Gather Antiques
390 E. Washington St., Martinsville, 46151; 317-342-0391

Mueller, Hilda
317-888-7842
Specializing in china, glassware, and silverplate

Nichols, Rita
Danville, 46122. Specializing in antiques and collectibles

Old Storefront Antiques
P.O. Box 357, Dublin, 47335; 317-478-4809. Specializing in country store items, tins, primitives, pharmaceuticals, advertising, etc. Active in mail order with catalogs available. Information requires LSASE

Percell, Ron
Webb's Antiques Mall
106 E. Main St., Centerville, 47330;
317-855-5733 or 317-855-5551.
Specializing in folk art and country
collectibles

Pruitt, Bonnie
B & W Bargain Barn
3350 W. 700 N., Anderson, 46011;
317-754-7010. Author of *St. Clair
Glass Collector's Book*, available for
$15 each from author

Renner, Dave and Penny
P.O. Box 312, Granger, 36530; 219-
293-1881. Specializing in Depression glass

Schroeder, Lowell
Unique Antiques & Memorabilia
107 S. Vine St., Plainfield,
46168; 317-856-7139. Specializing in general merchandise

Scowden, Virgil
Williamsport, 47993; 317-762-
3408 or 317-762-3178. Antiques
museum, general line, tours

Slater, Thomas D.
The Political Gallery
1325 W. 86th St., Indianapolis,
46260; 317-257-0863. Specializing
in political and sports memorabilia

Stapp, Charles Dennis
7037 Haynes Rd., Georgetown,
47122. Specializing in jackknives,
hunting knives, military knives,
straight and safety razors

Stofft, Marvin and Jeanette
Marnette Antiques
Tell City, 47586; 812-547-5707.
Specializing in Ohio art pottery,
buy and sell

Swayzee Antique Mall
115 N. Washington St., Swayzee,
46986; 317-922-7903

T.J.'s Collectibles Etcetera
Olde Tyme Toy Mall
105 S. Main St., Fairmount, 46928;
317-948-3150. Specializing in Disneyana and Raggedy Ann and Andy

Tucker, Doris
Brownsburg

Vanderbilt, Duane and Janice
4040 W. Over Dr., Indianapolis,
46268; 317-875-8932. Authors
(Collector Books) of *Collector's
Guide to Shawnee Pottery*

Webb's Antique Mall
over 400 Quality Dealers
200 W. Union St., Centerville, 47330

White, Lloyd and Peggy
Toy Time
515 Joe Martin Rd., Lowell, 46356;
219-696-7324. Specializing in Hopalong Cassidy, Black dolls, Black collectibles, advertising items

Iowa

Addy, Geneva D.
Winterset, 50273; 515-462-3027

Arnbal, Una
Woodland Antiques
236 Trail Ridge Rd., Ames, 50010;
515-292-1005. Specializing in
china, glass, Lomonosov figurines

DeGood, Hal and Meredith
The Baggage Car
3100 Justin Dr., Suite B, Des
Moines, 50322; 515-270-9080. Specializing in Hallmark collectibles;
publishers of Hallmark newsletter

DeLozier, Loretta
1101 Polk St., Bedford, 50833.
Specializing in Lefton china

Devine, Dennis; Norman; and Joe
D & D Antique Mall
1411 3rd St., Council Bluffs, 51503;
712-323-5233 or 712-328-7305.
Specializing in furniture, phonographs, collectibles, general line. Joe
Devine: Royal Copley collector

Jaarsma, Ralph
De Pelikaan Antieks
812 Washington St., c/o Red Ribbon Antique Mall, Pella, 50219.
Specializing in Dutch antiques

Morris, Susan
P.O. Box 708, Mason City, 50402.
Specializing in Watt pottery and
Purinton pottery; Author of *Watt
Pottery — An Identification and
Value Guide* and *Purinton Pottery —
An Identification and Value Guide*

Nichols, Harold J.
632 Agg, Ames, 50010; 515-292-
9167. Author of *McCoy Cookie Jars
from the First to the Last*. Specializing in Roseville, Weller, McCoy

Picek, Louis
Main Street Antiques
110 W. Main St., Box 340, West
Branch, 52358. Specializing in folk
art, country Americana, the unusual

Westmoreland Glass Society
Jim Fisher, President
513 5th Ave., Coralville, 52241;
319-354-5011. Membership: $15
for a single, $25 per household

Kansas

Anthony, Dorothy Malone
World of Bells Publications
802 S. Eddy, Fort Scott, 66701;
316-223-3404. Specializing in
publishing and selling books on
all types of small bells

McCormick, John and Marilyn
P.O. Box 3174, Shawnee, 66226;
913-441-0793. Specializing in
Gonder pottery

Robison, Joleen A.
502 Lindley Dr., Lawrence,
66044. Author (Collector Books)
on advertising dolls

The Sandlers'
Maundy International
P.O. Box 13028-PG, Shawnee Mission, 66282; 1-800-235-2866. Specializing in watches — antique
pocket and vintage wristwatches

Smies, David
Pops Collectibles
Box 522, 315 So. 4th, Manhattan, 66502; 913-776-1433. Specializing in coins, stamps, cards,
tokens, Masonic collectibles

Tinsley, Rosella
105 15th St., Osawatomie, 66064;
913-755-3237. Specializing in
primitives, kitchen, farm, woodenware, and miscellaneous
(phone calls only)

Winslow, Ralph
4008 W. 100th Terrace, Overland Park, 66207. Specializing in
Dryden and Shramberg pottery

Kentucky

Courter, J.W.
3935 Kelley Rd., Kevil, 42053; 502-
488-2116. Specializing in Aladdin
lamps; Author of *Aladdin — The
Magic Name in Lamps*, softbound,
180 pages; and *Aladdin Electric
Lamps*, hardbound, 229 pages

Fedosky, Terry
R.R. 1, Box 118, Symsonia, 42082.
Specializing in vaseline glass

Florence, Gene
Box 7186H, Lexington, 40522.
Author (Collector Books) on
Depression Glass, Occupied Japan

Johnson, Wes, Sr.
106 Bauer Ave., Louisville, 40207;
502-899-3030 (Ext. #228). Specializing in Cracker Jack: toys,
point of sale, packages, etc.;
Checkers Confection, Schoenhut
toys, Victor Toy Oats, Universal
Theatre (Chicago), old toys

Willis, Roy M.
Heartland of Kentucky Decanters
and Steins
P.O. Box 428, Lebanon Jct., 40150;
Huge selection of limited edition
decanters and beer steins — open
showroom. Include large self-
addressed envelope (two stamps)
with correspondence. Fee for
appraisals. Decanter price guide (listings only, no pictures): $5 PPD.

Maine

Hathaway, John
Hathaway's Antiques
Upper Main St., Bryant Pond,
04219; 207-665-2124. Specializing
in fruit jars; mail order a specialty

Rinaldi, John
Nautical Antiques and Related
Items
Box 765, Dock Square, Kenneb-
unkport, 04046; 207-967-3218.
Specializing in nautical antiques,
19th- & 20th-century American
paintings; Annual Fall catalog: $3

Maryland

Banks, Robert
18901 Gold Mine Court,
Brookeville, 20833. Specializing in
American flags of historical significance and exceptional design

Ezell, Elaine; & Newhouse, George
Cruets Cruets Cruets
P.O. Box 1609, Pasadena, 21122-
1609; 410-255-6777. Specializing in
cruets, glass, porcelain, and pottery

Greenberg, Bruce C., Ph. D.
Greenberg Publishing Company, Inc.
7566 Main St., Sykesville, 21784.
Specializing in toy trains; author
and publisher of comprehensive
publications on Lionel, American
Flyer, and Ives trains

Humphrey, George C.
4932 Prince George Ave., Beltsville, 20705; 301-937-7899. Specializing in John Rogers groups

Michels, John
Jamm Enterprises
1658 Hardwick Rd., Baltimore, 21286; 410-825-3636. Specializing in watch holders and small clocks

Meadows, John, Jean and Michael
Meadows House Antiques
919 Stiles St., Baltimore, 21202; 410-837-5427. Specializing in antique wicker; rustic, twig, and old hickory furniture; quilts; tramp art

Rudisill's Alt Print Haus
Rudisill, John and Barbara
24305 Waterview Dr., Worton, 21678; 410-778-9290. Specializing in Currier & Ives

Screen, Harold and Joyce
2804 Munster Rd., Baltimore, 21234; 410-661-6765. Specializing in soda fountain 'tools of the trade' and paper: catalogs, *Soda Fountain* magazine, etc.

Massachusetts

Adams, Charles and Barbara
Middleboro, 02346; 508-947-7277. Specializing in Bennington (brown only)

Dunbar's Gallery
Leila and Howard Dunbar
76 Haven St., Milford, 01757; 508-634-8697 or (Fax) 508-634-8698. Specializing in advertising and toys

Frei, Peter and Sandra
P.O. Box 500, Brimfield, 01010; 1-800-942-8968. Specializing in sewing machines, adding machines, and hand-powered vacuum cleaners; SASE required with correspondence

Hess, John A.
Fine Photographic Americana
P.O. Box 3062, Andover, 01810; 508-470-0327. Specializing in 19th-Century photography

Longo, Paul J.
Paul Longo Americana
Box 490, Chatham Rd., South Orleans, Cape Cod, 02662; 508-255-5482. Specializing in political pins, ribbons, banners, autographs, old stocks and bonds, baseball and sports memorabilia of all types

MacLean, Dale
Dale's
593 High St., Dedham, 02026; 617-326-3010. Specializing in Dedham pottery

Morin, Albert
668 Robbins Ave. #23, Dracut, 01826; 508-454-7907. Specializing in miscellaneous Akro Agate and Westite

Owings, K.C., Jr.
Antiques Americana
Box 19, N. Abington, 02351; 617-857-1655. Specializing in Civil War, Revolutionary War, autographs, documents, books, antiques

Vigue, Norm and Cathy
62 Bailey St., Stoughton, 02072; 617-344-5441. Buying and selling TV, western, and cartoon-show collectibles

Wellman, BA
9 Cottage St., Southboro, 01772. Specializing in all areas of American ceramics with video book. Identification and price guides available on Ceramic Arts Studio

Michigan

Brown, Rick
Newspaper Collectors' Society of America
Box 19134-S, Lansing, 48901; 517-887-1255 or (Fax) 517-887-2194. Specializing in newspapers

Bruner, Mike
Mike's Americana
6980 Walnut Lake Rd., West Bloomfield, 48323; 313-661-2359. Specializing in lightning rod balls

Gunsaulus, Jack
Gray's Gallery/Jack's Corner Bookstore
583 W. Ann Arbor Trail, Plymouth, 48170; 313-455-2373. Specializing in porcelain, books, jewelry, glass

Marsh, Linda K.
1229 Gould Rd., Lansing, 48917. Specializing in Degenhart glass

Nedry, Boyd W.
728 Buth Dr., Comstock Park, 49321; 616-784-1513. Specializing in traps (including mice, rat, and fly traps) and trap-related items

Newbound, Betty
4567 Chadsworth, Commerce, 48382. Author (Collector Books) on Blue Ridge dinnerware. Specializing in collectible china and glass

Nickel, Mike
A Nickel's Worth
P.O. Box 456, Portland, 48875; 517-647-7646. Specializing in Roseville, Weller, Rookwood and other important American art pottery, Venetian/Murano glass, Art Deco

O'Callaghan, Tim
46878 Betty Hill, Plymouth, 48170; 313-459-4636. Specializing in dimestore soldiers, also Ford Motor Co., and 'Old Ironsides' (USS Constitution) memorabilia

Oates, Joan
685 S. Washington, Constantine, 49042; 616-435-8353. Specializing in Phoenix Bird chinaware

Ricker, Dawn V.
39145 Marne, Sterling Heights, 48313; 801-566-0891. Schafer & Vater collector

Roscoe, Mike
Lane St. Antiques
106 S. Lane St., Blissfield, 49228; 517-486-4243. Specializing in toys, advertising, coin-operated machines, furniture, and miscellaneous

Minnesota

Anderson, James
Box 12704, New Brighton, 55112; 612-484-3198. Specializing in old fishing lures and reels, also tackle catalogs, posters, calendars, Winchester items

Gallagher, Jerry
420 1st Ave. N.W., Plainview, 55964; 507-534-3511. Specializing in Morgantown research; matching service for Morgantown, Heisey, Fostoria, Cambridge, Duncan, and Tiffin. Publisher of Morgantown 1931 Catalog Reprint (out of print), *A Collector's Handbook of Morgantown Glass, 1899-1971*; *Morgantown Colors* placard; and *The Morgantown Newscaster*, quarterly journal of the Morgantown Collectors of America, Inc. (subscription: $15 per year)

Harrigan, John
1900 Hennepin, Minneapolis, 55403; 612-872-0226. Specializing in Battersea (English enamel) boxes

Ketcham, Steve
Steve Ketcham Antiques (Shows and mail order only)
Box 24114, Edina, 55424; 612-920-4205. Specializing in early American bottles; early Red Wing stoneware (no art pottery or dinnerware); advertising signs, trays, and trade cards

Nelson, C.L.
Box 222, Spring Park, 55384; 612-473-5625. Specializing in 18th-, 19th- and 20th-century pottery and porcelain, among others: Gaudy Welsh, ABC plates, relief moulded jugs

Podpeskar, Doug
624 Jones St., Eveleth, 55734-1631; 218-744-4854. Specializing in Red Wing dinnerware

Schoneck, Steve
P.O. Box 56, Newport, 55055; 612-459-2980. Specializing in American art pottery, Arts & Crafts, Handicraft Guild of Minneapolis

Missouri

Bosworth, Dick and Waunita
Kansas City Trade Winds
7307 N.W. 75th St., Kansas City, 64152. Specializing in American art pottery, Parrish prints, art glass

Clapp, Barbara J.
301 N. Main, Mt. Vernon, 65712; 417-466-2515. Specializing in dinnerware and pottery

International Rose O'Neill Club
Contact Karen Stewart
P.O. Box 668, Branson, 65616. Dues: $7 (single) or $10 (family) includes newsletter *Kewpiesta Kourier*, published quarterly

MidweSterling-Replacement Division
4311 NE Vivion Rd., Kansas City, 64119; 816-454-1990. Specializing in sterling flatware replacement; having the largest inventory nationwide of active and discontinued silver patterns

Old World Antiques
1715 Summit, Kansas City, 64108
Branch Location: 4436 State Line
Rd., Kansas City, 66103. Specializing in 18th- and 19th-century
furniture, paintings, accessories,
clocks, medical and scientific
instruments, chandeliers, sconces,
Sabino, and much more

Our McCoy Matters
Lynch, Kathy
McCoy Publications, P.O. Box
14255, Parkville, 64152; 816-587-
9179. Subscription: $24 per year
(6 issues)

Ridley, Thomas J.
MidweSterling
4311 N.E. Vivion Rd, Kansas City,
64119-2890; 816-454-1990 or (Fax)
816-454-1605. Specializing sterling
silver flatware. Closed Wednesday,
Sunday

Roberts, Brenda
Country Side Antiques
R.R. 2, Marshall, 65340. Specializing in Hull pottery and general line.
Author of *Roberts' Ultimate Encyclopedia of Hull Pottery*, with companion price guide; SASE required

Roeder, Jim
715 Catalpa, Webster Groves,
MO 63110-4205

Siegel, Brenda and Jerry
Tower Grove Antiques
3308 Meramec, St. Louis, 63118;
314-352-9020. Specializing in
Ungemach pottery

Smith, Pat
Independence
Author (Collector Books) of doll
book series

Stout, Elizabeth M.
152 Highway F., Defiance, 63341;
314-987-2223. Specializing in
Calendar Plates

Wiesehan, Doug
D & R Farm Antiques
4535 Hwy. H, St. Charles, 63301.
Specializing in salesman's samples
and patent models, antique toys,
farm toys, metal farm signs

Williams, Don
P.O. Box 147, Kirksville 63501.
Specializing in art glass; SASE
required with all correspondence

Woollard, D.D., Jr.
11614 Old St. Charles Rd.,
Bridgeton, 63044; 314-739-4662.
Specializing in World's Fair & Exposition memorabilia

Nebraska

Larsen, Robert V.
3214 19th St., Columbus, 68601.
Specializing in old hatpins and
hatpin holders

New Hampshire

Brenner, Larry L.
Brenner Antiques
1005 Chestnut St., Manchester,
03104; 603-625-8203. Specializing in Royal Bayreuth

Marden, Richard G.
Box 524, Elm St., Wolfeboro,
03894; 603-569-3209

Winston, Nancy
Willow Hollow Antiques
R.F.D. 1, Box 550, Northwood,
03261; 603-942-5739. Specializing
in Shaker baskets, primitives, country smalls, paper Americana, toys

New Jersey

Adams, Jay (Mail order only)
245 Lakeview Ave., Suite 208,
Clifton, NJ 07011; 201-365-5907.
Specializing in Depression-era
china and glass

Anderson, Suzy McLennan
Heritage Antiques & Appraisal
Services
65 E. Main St., Holmdel, 07733;
908-946-8801 or (Fax) 908-946-
1036. Specializing in American
furniture and decorative accessories

Bilane, John E. (Mail order only)
2065 Morris Ave., Apt. 109,
Union, 07083. Specializing in
antique glass cup plates

Cole, Lillian M., Editor of *Piebirds
Unlimited* newsletter
14 Harmony School Rd., Flemington, 08822; 908-782-3198. Specializing in pie birds, pie funnels, pie vents

Dezso, Doug
864 Paterson Ave., Maywood,
07607-2119; 201-488-1311. Specializing in candy containers, nodders, pep pins, glass figural inkwells

Doorstop Collectors of America
Doorstopper newsletter
Jeanie Bertoia
2413 Madison Ave., Vineland,
08630; 609-692-4092. Membership $20 per year, includes 2
newsletters and convention.
Send 2-stamp SASE for sample

Litts, Elyce
P.O. Box 394, Morris Plains,
07950; 201-361-4087. Author
(Collector Books) of *Collector's
Encyclopedia of Geisha Girl Porcelain*

Meschi, Edward J.
129 Pinyard Rd., Monroeville,
08343; 609-358-7293 or (Fax)
609-358-7293. Specializing in
Durand art glass, fine arts

Perzel, Robert and Nancy
Popkorn
4 Mine St. (near Main St.), P.O.
Box 1057, Flemington, 08822;
908-782-9631. Specializing in
Stangl dinnerware, birds, and artware; Depression Glass

Poster, Harry
Vintage TVs
Box 1883, S. Hackensack, 07606;
Days: 201-794-9606; 24-Hour Fax:
201-794-9553; Phone: 201-410-
7525. Writes *Poster's Radio and
Television Price Guide*. Specializes
in vintage TV's, transistor radios,
3-D stereo cameras

Rago, David
9 S. Main St., Lambertville,
08530; 609-397-9374. Specializing in Arts & Crafts, art pottery

Rosen, Barbara
6 Shoshone Trail, Wayne, 07470.
Specializing in figural bottle
openers and antique dollhouses

Steinfeld, Milt
633 Westfield Ave., Box 457,
Westfield, 07091. Specializing in
collectible glass and china, Victorian silverplate, and other small
collectibles

Vines, Linda L.
Yesterday Once More
P.O. Box 721, Upper Montclair,
07043; 201-746-5206. Specializing in Snow Babies, all holidays
(Christmas, Easter, Halloween),
dolls and toys

Visakay, Stephen
Vintage Cocktail Shakers
P.O. Box 1517, W. Caldwell,
07007-1517. Specializing in barware.

New Mexico

Hardisty, Don
Artistic Restorations: Specializing
in Bossons and Hummels
3020 E. Majestic Ridge, Las
Cruces, 88011; 505-522-3721 or
800-BOSSONS (267-7667); Fax
available (call first): 505-522-
7909

Nelson, Scott H.
Box 6081, Santa Fe, 87502. Specializing in African art

New York

Austin, Bruce A.
1 Hardwood Hill Rd., Pittsford,
15434; 716-387-9820 (days). Specializing in clocks and Arts &
Crafts furnishings and accessories

Batchelor, Daniel J.
R.R. 10, Box 1010, Oswego, 13126.
Specializing in Pairpoint, Handel,
Bradley and Hubbard lamps; Photo
and SASE required with all correspondence

Calison, Jim
Tools of Distinction
Wallkill, 12589; 914-895-8035.
Specializing in antique and collectible tools, buying and selling

Dimitroff, Thomas P.
Dimitroff's Antiques (Appointment only)
140 E. First St., Corning, 14830;
607-962-6745. Specializing in
Steuben and cut glass

Doyle, Robert A.
Doyle Auctioneers & Appraisers
109 Osborne Hill Rd., Fishkill,
12524. Thousands of collectibles
offered, call for free calendar of
upcoming auctions

Fer-Duc Inc.
Ferrara, Joseph
Box 1303, Newburgh, 12550;
914-565-5990. Specializing in
American art pottery (Ohr,
Rookwood, Zanesville), 19th-
and 20th-century American
paintings

Fox, Ron
Ron Fox Auctions
83 Morris St., Brentwood, 11717; Telephone and Fax: 516-952-7719. Specializing in steins; auctions with illustrated catalogs and video tapes

Gerson, Roselyn
P.O. Box Letter S, Lynbrook, 11563; 516-593-8746. Author/collector specializing in unusual, gadgetry, figural compacts and vanity bags/purses

Greguire, Helen
Helen's Antiques
103 Trimmer Rd., Hilton, 14468; 716-392-2704. Specializing in graniteware (any color), Carnival Glass lamps and shades, Carnival Glass lighting of all kinds; Author (Collector Books) of *The Collector's Encyclopedia of Graniteware, Colors, Shapes & Values*, (updated values) for $27.95 (including postage and handling); Second book on graniteware now available (same price); Also available is *Carnival in Lights*, featuring Carnival Glass, lamps, shades, etc., for $11.95+$1.50 postage and handling; all available from author at above address. Also interested in unusual and rare toasters

Handelsman, Burton
18 Hotel Dr., White Plains, 10605; 914-428-4480 (Home) and 914-761-8880 (office). Specializing in occupational shaving mugs, accessories

Herley, Patrick J.
P.O. Box 606, E. Setauket, 11733; 516-928-6052. Specializing in Goss china

Jordan, Ruth E.
Meridale, 13806; 607-746-2082. Specializing in cut glass, American Brilliant period

Laun, H. Thomas and Patricia
Little Century
215 Paul Ave., Syracuse, 13206; 315-437-4156. Summer residence: Box 69-A, Cape Vincent, 13618; 315-654-3244. Specializing in firefighting collectibles

Malitz, Lucille
Lucid Antiques
Box KH, Scarsdale, 10583; 914-636-7825. Specializing in lithophanes, medical antiques, stanhopes, antique kaleidoscopes

Manns, William
P.O. Box 47, Millwood, 10546; 914-245-2926 or (Fax) 914-962-1945. Co-author of *Painted Ponies*, deluxe hard-bound edition (226 pages), available from author for $39.95+$4 shipping. Specializing in carousel art and western antiques

Meisel, Louis K. and Susan P.
Meisel Decorative Arts Gallery
133 Prince St., New York City, 10012. Specializing in Clarice Cliff and 20th-century designs in jewelry, watches, toys, unusual vintage bicycles, and model sailboats

Michel, John and Barbara
Americana Blue
200 E. 78th St., 18E, New York City, 10021; 212-861-6094. Specializing in yellow ware and cast iron

Owens, Lowell
Owens' Collectibles
12 Bonnie Ave., New Hartford, 13413. Specializing in beer advertising

Pisello, Faye
577 Lake St., Wilson, 14172. Specializing in Brownies by Palmer Cox

Rifken, Blume J.
Author of *Silhouettes in America — 1790-1840 — a Collector's Guide*. Specializing in American antique silhouettes from 1790 to 1840

Safir, Charlotte F.
1349 Lexington Ave., 9-B, New York City, 10128; 212-534-7933. Specializing in cookbooks, children's books (out-of-print only)

Schleifman, Roselle
Ed's Collectibles/The Rage
16 Vincent Rd., Spring Valley, 10977; 914-356-2121. Specializing in Duncan & Miller and elegant glass

Steinbock, Nancy
Nancy Steinbock Posters & Prints
518-438-1577. Specializing in posters: travel, war, literary, advertising

Tuggle, Robert
105 W. St., New York City, 10023; 212-595-0514. Specializing in John Bennett, Anglo-Japanese china

Van Kuren, Jean and Dale
Ruth's Antiques, Inc.
9060 Main St., Clarence, 14031; 716-632-1630. Specializing in Buffalo pottery, general line

Van Patten, Joan F.
Box 102, Rexford, 12148. Author (Collector Books) of books on Nippon and Noritake

North Carolina

Degenhardt, Richard K.
Sugar Hollow Farm
124 Cypress Point, Hendersonville, 28739; 704-696-9750. Author of *Belleek, The Complete Collectors' Guide and Illustrated Reference*. Specializing in Belleek (The only Belleek is the Irish. Established by legal action in 1929)

Hughes, Kathy (Mrs. Paul)
Tudor House Galleries
1401 E. Blvd., Charlotte, 28203; 704-377-4748. Specializing in Relief-Moulded Jugs, 18th- and 19th-century English pottery and 19th-century oil paintings

Kirtley, Charles E.
P.O. Box 2273, Elizabeth City, 27096; 919-335-1262. Specializing in monthly auctions and bid sales dealing with World's Fair, Civil War, political, advertising, and other American collectibles

Sayers, R.J.
Southeastern Antiques & Appraisals
P.O. Box 629, Brevard, 28712. Specializing in Boy Scout collectibles, Pisgah Forest pottery, primitive American furniture; Author of *Guide to Scouting Collectibles*, available from author for $24.95+$4.00 postage

North Dakota

Farnsworth, Bryce
1334 14½ St. South, Fargo, 58103; 701-237-3597. Specializing in Rosemeade pottery

Ohio

Baker, Shirley
Shirley's Collectibles
673 W. Twp. Rd. 118, Tiffin, 44883; 419-447-9875. Specializing in Tiffin glass

Bassett, Mark
P.O. Box 771233, Lakewood, 44017. Specializing in Cowan, American and European art pottery, Art Deco.

Batory, Mr. Dana Martin
402 E. Bucyrus St., Crestline, 44827. Specializing in antique woodworking machinery, old and new woodworking machinery catalogs. In order to prepare a difinitive history on American manufacturers of woodworking machinery, Dana is interested in acquiring by loan, gift, or photocopy, any and all documents, catalogs, manuals, photos, personal reminiscences, etc., pertaining to woodworking machinery and/or their manufacturers. NO phone calls please.

Benjamin, Scott
P.O. Box 611, Elyria, 44036; 216-365-9534. Specializing in gas globes; Co-author of *Gas Pump Globes*, listing nearly 4,000 gas globes with over 400 photos, book includes prices, rarity guide, histories and reproduction information. Currently available from author

Blair, Betty
Golden Apple Antiques
216 Bridge St., Jackson, 45640; 614-286-4817. Specializing in art pottery, Watt, cookie jars, chocolate molds, general line

Briggs, Karen
Toledo, Specializing in glass, china, pottery, knives

Budin, Nicki
Curio Cabinet
679 High St., Worthington, 43085; 614-885-1986. Specializing in Royal Doulton

China Specialties, Inc.
19238 Dorchester Circle, Strongsville, 44136; 216-238-2528. Specializing in Autumn Leaf

Cincinnati Auction Gallery
635 Main St., Cincinnati, 45202; 513-381-2128. Specializing in American art pottery (especially Rookwood), American and European fine paintings, watercolors

Collectors of Findlay Glass
P.O. Box 256, Findlay, 45840. An organization dedicated to the study and recognition of Findlay glass, *The Melting Pot* newsletter published quarterly, convention held annually, membership: $10 per year

DeGenaro, Steve
P.O. Box 5662, Youngstown, 44504. Specializing in post-mortem photos, mourning collectibles

De Luca, Mary A.
Red Barn Antiques
5510 W. Lakeshore Dr., Port Clinton. 43452; 419-635-2045. Specializing in general line

Distel, Ginny
Distel's Antiques
4041 S.C.R. 22, Tiffin, 44883; 419-447-5832. Specializing in Tiffin glass

Ebner, Rita and John
Cracker Barrel Antiques
4540 Helen Rd., Columbus, 43232. Specializing in door knockers, cast iron bottle openers, doorstops, general line

Ferguson, Maxine
Wayside Antiques
2290 E. Pike, Zanesville, 43701. General line, furniture, dolls, pottery, glass

Forsythe, Ruth A.
Box 327, Galena, 43021. Author of *Made in Czechoslovakia*, books I and II

Garen, David R.
308 Melody Lane, Defiance; 43512. Specializing in milk bottles

Graff, Shirley
4515 Grafton Rd., Brunswick, 44212. Specializing in Pennsbury pottery

Guenin, Tom
Box 454, Chardon, 44024. Specializing in antique telephones and antique telephone restoration

Hamlin, Jack & Treva
R.R. 4, Box 150, Kaiser St., Proctorville, 45669. Specializing in Currier and Ives by Royal China Co.

Harnish, Jerry
Old Tyme Toy Mall/Booth #3
110 Main St., Bellville, 44813; 419-886-4782. Specializing in G.I. Joe

Hothem, Lar
Hothem House
Box 458, Lancaster, 43130. Specializing in books about Indians and artifacts

Kao, Fern Larking
Lustre Pitcher Antiques
P.O. Box 312, Bowling Green, 43402; 419-352-5928. Specializing in jewelry, sewing implements, ladies' accessories

Kerr, Ann
P.O. 437, Sidney, 45365; 513-492-6369. Author (Collector Books) of *Collector's Encyclopedia of Russel Wright Designs*. Specializing in work of Wright, interested in 20th-century decorative arts

Kitchen, Lorrie
Toledo, 419-478-3815 or Tavares, FL (winter), 904-742-2638. Specializing in Depression-era Glass, Hall china, Fiesta, Blue Ridge, Shawnee

Klender, James and Grace
Town & Country Antiques & Collectibles
P.O. Box 447, Pioneer, 43554; 419-737-2880. Specializing in Depression Glass, and general line

Kline, Mr. and Mrs. Jerry and Gerry
Members of North American Torquay Society and Torquay Pottery Collectors' Society
604 Orchard View Dr., Maumee, 43537; 419-893-1226. Specializing in collecting Torquay pottery

Mangus, Jim and Bev
5147 Broadway NE, Louisville, 44641; 216-455-8785. Specializing in Shawnee pottery

Mathes, Richard
P.O. Box 1408, Springfield, 45501-1408; 513-324-6917. Specializing in Buttonhooks

Mondloch, Dee
Precious & Few
709 N. Union St., Fostoria, 44830; 419-435-2987. Specializing in Tiffin glass

Moore, Carolyn
445 N. Prospect, Bowling Green, 43402. Specializing in primitives, yellow ware, graniteware

Murphy, James L.
1023 Neil Ave., Columbus, 43201; 614-297-0746. Specializing in Radford, Vance, Avon

National Heisey Glass Museum
Heisey Collectors of America Inc.
6th & Church Sts., P.O. Box 4367, Newark, 43055; 614-345-2932

National Imperial Glass Collectors' Society, Inc.
P.O. Box 534, Bellaire 43906. Dues: $12 per year (plus $1 for each additional member in the same household), quarterly newsletter, convention every June

Nelson, Norman
2267 E. Erie, Lorain, 44052; 216-288-4977. Specializing in jukeboxes

Osborne, Ruth
Box 85, Higginsport, 45131. Specializing in vintage clothing, lamps, jewelry. Please, no phone calls.

Peggy & Tom's Antiques
(Appointment only)
17902 Landeur Rd., Cleveland, 44119; 216-486-5767. Specializing in militaria, jewelry (fine and costume) and accessories

Peters, Jeannie L.
Mt. Washington Antiques
3742 Kellogg, Cincinnati, 45226; 513-231-6584. Specializing in sheet music

Pierce, David
27544 Black Rd., P.O. Box 248, Danville, 43014; 614-599-6394. Specializing in Glidden pottery

Radel, Erle and Janice
Rapids Renovations & Antiques
Grand Rapids. Specializing in furniture and fine jewelry, (collectors only) Labino art glass

Rees, Debbie
Zanesville.
Specializing in Watt, blue and white stoneware, Steiff, cookie jars, Roseville pottery

Riebel, James; Krause, Terry
Pottery Peregrinators
Zanesville, 614-452-7687. Specializing in American art pottery, Nicodemus, and Carnival Glass

Rodgers, Joanne
Stretch Glass Society
P.O. Box 770643, Lakewood, 44107. Specializing in Stretch Glass

Roscoe, Mike
3351 Lagrange, Toledo, 43608; 419-244-6935. Specializing in toys, art glass, general line

Trainer, Veronica
Bayhouse
Box 40443, Cleveland, 44140; 216-871-8584. Specializing in beaded and enameled mesh purses

Tucker, Dan
Toledo, 419-478-3815 or Tavares, FL (winter), 904-742-2638. Specializing in Depression-era glass, Hall china, Fiesta, Blue Ridge, Shawnee

Vroman, Bill & Judy
739 Eastern Ave., Fostoria, 44830; 419-435-5443. Collectors of Jewel Tea or Autumn Leaf, Buying-Selling all types of fine antiques

Walker, Bunny
Box 502, Bucyrus, 44820; 419-562-8355. Specializing in Steiff teddy bears, penny toys, pottery

Walter, John
The Old Tool Shop
208 Front St., Marietta, 45750; 614-373-9973. Specializing in all types of antique tools

Whitmyer, Margaret and Kenn
Box 30806, Gahanna, 43230. Author (Collector Books) on children's dishes. Specializing in Depression-era collectibles

Wilkins, Juanita
The Bird of Paradise
Lima, 419-227-2163. Specializing in R.S. China, Old Ivory china, colored pattern glass, lamps, and jewelry

Young, Mary
1040 Greenridge Dr., Kettering, 45429. Author (Collector Books) of *Collector's Guide to Paper Dolls*

Oklahoma

Bess, Phyllis and Tom
Authors of *Frankoma Treasures*,
14535 E. 13th St., Tulsa, 74108;
918-437-7776. Specializing in
Frankoma pottery

Klein, Bob and Dondee
1002 Walnut Court, Guthrie,
73044; 405-282-6545. Specializing in Tamac pottery

Moore, Art and Shirley
2145 S. Norfolk Ave., Tulsa,
74114; 918-747-4164. Specializing
in Lu Ray Pastels, Depression Glass

Willis, Ron L.
2110 Fox Ave., Moore, 73160.
Specializing in militaria

Oregon

Bartsch, Henry
Antique Registers
2050 N. Hwy. 101, Rockaway
Beach, 97136; 503-355-2932.
Specializing in antique cash regis-
ters, co-author of *Antique Cash
Registers 1880-1920*

Bird, Leah and Walt
Bird's Nest
P.O. Box 4502, Medford, 97501;
503-779-3028. Specializing in
vintage clothes, purses, lace, ribbon, half-dolls

Brady, Glen
P.O. Box 3933, Central Point,
97502; 503-772-0350. Specializing in metal trucks (Tonka, Ertl),
Smokey Bear, cookie jars, wash-
boards, Autumn Leaf, Campbell
Kids

Brown, Marcia
Sparkles
6959 Pinehurst, Central Point,
97502; 503-826-3039. Specializing in rhinestones

Buzan, James
Antique Workshop
17935 Monticello Dr., Gladstone,
97027-1338; 503-655-7686
(evenings). Specializing in fine art
tile and decorative arts

Carter, Fran (Appointment only)
Box 3220, Coos Bay, 97420; 503-
888-5780. Specializing in estate
sales

Cox, Billy & Thelma, Owners
Medford Antique Mall
1 West 6th St., Medford 97501;
503-773-4983

Crandall, Peter B.
Oregon General Store Museum
P.O. Box 561, Eagle Point,
97524; 503-826-3746. Specializing in primitives, general store,
early Americana, etc.

Fitzpatrick, Sarah
Box 2025, White City, 97503;
503-826-3748. Specializing in
Star Trek, Star Wars, Shenango
china, books

Frost, Donald M.
Country Estate Antiques
(Appointment only)
17875 N.W. Tillamook Dr., Portland, 97229; 503-531-3563. Specializing in fine glass and porcelain

Geddes, Marjorie
Beaverton, 503-649-1041. Specializing in sewing items, butter
pats, egg cups, miscellaneous
small and elegant collectibles

Hinderer, Gloria
1947 Old Military Rd., Center
Point, 97502; 503-772-6858. Specializing in general antiques

Hirshman, Susan and Larry
Everyday Antiques
542 Siskiyou Blvd., Ashland,
97250; 503-482-9411. Specializing in china, glassware, kitchenware

Main Antique Mall
30 N. Riverside, Medford, 97501;
503-779-9490. Quality products
and services for the serious collector, dealer or those just browsing

Miller, Don and Robby
P.O. Box 508, Talent, 97504;
503-535-1231 Specializing in
milk bottles, TV Siamese cat
lamps, seltzer bottles, red cocktail
shakers.

Morris, Thomas G.
Prize Publishers
P.O. Box 8307, Medford, 97504;
503-779-3164. Author of *The
Carnival Chalk Prize*, a pictorial
price guide on carnival chalkware
figures with brief histories and
values for each

Moss, Cindy
557 Daniel St., Central Point,
97502; 503-664-2689. Specializing in Schillings Brand Spice &
Extracts bottles, green handled
kitchen tools

Ringering, David
Belle Ringer Antiques
1480 Tamale Dr. SE, Salem, 97301;
503-585-8253. Specializing in Rowland & Marsellus and other sou-
venir/historical china with scenes of
buildings, parks, and other tourist
attractions of the 1890s-1930s. Feel
free to contact David if you have
any questions about Rowland &
Marsellus or other souvenir china.
He will be happy to answer questions about souvenir china.

Pennsylvania

Atkinson, Phil and Karol
903 Apache Trail, Mercer, 16137;
412-475-2490. Specializing in
antique advertising, country store
collectibles

Barker, Jim
Toastermaster Antique Appliances
P.O. Box 41, Bethlehem, 18016;
610-861-7706. Specializing in
electric toasters and appliances

Barrett, Noel
Rosebud Antiques
P.O. Box 1001, Carversville,
18913; 215-297-5109. Specializing in toys

Bodine, Clarence H., Jr., Proprietor
East/West Gallery
41B Ferry St., New Hope, 18938;
908-782-3430 (evenings). Specializing in antique Japanese wood-
block prints, netsuke, inro, tsuba

Cerebro
P.O. Box 327, East Prospect,
17317; 717-252-2400 or 800-69-
LABEL. Specializing in antique
advertising labels, especially cigar
box labels, cigar bands, food
labels, firecracker labels

Damaska, Ron
738 9th Ave., New Brighton,
15066; 412-843-1393. Specializing in Fry cut glass, match holders, oil lamps, silver; SASE
required when requesting information

DLK Nostalgia & Collectibles
P.O. Box 5112, Johnstown, 15904.
Specializing in corkscrews and
openers, Art Deco, clocks, toys,
breweriana, football cards, radios,
militaria, antique guns, robots, battery-operated toys, miscellaneous

Garvin, Joann
P.O. Box 182, Beaver Falls,
15010; 412-843-3999. Specializing in Fiesta

Gottuso, Bob
Bojo
P.O. Box 1203, Cranberry Town-
ship, 16033-2203; Phone/Fax:
412-776-0621. Specializing in
Beatles, toys and Rock 'N Roll
memorabilia

Hagenbuch, James
Glass-Works Auction
102 Jefferson, East Greenville,
18041; 215-679-5849. America's
leading auction company in early
American bottles and glass

Hain, Henry F., III
Antiques & Collectibles
2623 N. Second St., Harrisburg,
17110; 717-238-0534. Lists available of items for sale

Hinton, Michael C.
246 W. Ashland St., Doylestown,
18901; 215-345-0892. Owns/oper-
ates Bucks County Art & Antiques
Company and Chem-Clean Furniture Restoration Company. Specializing in quality restorations of a
wide range of art and antiques from
colonial to contemporary. Catalog
of paintings and frames available

Holland, William
William Holland Fine Arts
1708 E. Lancaster Ave., Paoli,
19301; 610-648-0369 or (Fax) 610-
647-4448. Specializing in Louis Icart
etchings and oils, Art Nouveau and
Art Deco items; Author of *Louis
Icart: The Complete Etchings* and *The
Collectible Maxfield Parrish*

Kamm, George
George Kamm Paperweights
24-SP Townsend Ct., Lancaster,
17603; 717-872-7858. Specializing
in antique and contemporary
paperweights — color brochure
published bimonthly. $5 annual fee
(refundable). Sample on request
(#10 SASE required)

Knauer, Judy A.
National Toothpick Holder Collectors' Society
1224 Spring Valley Lane, West Chester, 19380; 610-431-3477. Specializing in toothpick holders and Victorian glass

The Krauses
Krause, Gail
97 W. Wheeling St., Washington, 15301; 412-228-5034. Author of book on Duncan glass

Lindsay, Ralph
P.O. Box 21, New Holland, 17557. Specializing in target balls. SASE required with correspondence

Maier, Clarence and Betty
Mail order: The Burmese Cruet
Box 432, Montgomeryville, 18936; 215-855-5388. Specializing in Victorian art glass.

Marks, Mariann Katz
1416 Main, Honesdale, 18431. Author (Collector Books) of *Majolica Pottery, Second Series*. Specializing in collecting, buying, and selling American and English majolica of the Victorian period; LSASE required for mail order list. Enclose photo and price wanted with offers to sell

Oster, Frederick
Frederick W. Oster Fine Violins
1529 Pine St., Philadelphia, 19102; 215-545-1100 or (Fax) 215-735-3634. Specializing in rare and antique instruments of the violin family, as well as antique stringed and wind instruments

Posner, Judy
R.D. 1, Box 273, Effort, 18330; 717-629-6583. Specializing in figural pottery, cookie jars, salt and peppers, Black memorabilia, Disneyana, character, and advertising collectibles

Rosso, Philip J. and Philip Jr.
Wholesale Glass Dealers
1815 Trimble Ave., Port Vue, 15133; 412-678-7352. Specializing in Westmoreland glass

Weiser, Pastor Frederick S.
55 Kohler School Rd., New Oxford, 17350; 717-624-4106. Specializing in frakturs and other Pennsylvania German documents

Rhode Island

Dumont, Louise
579 Old Main St., Coventry, 02816; 401-828-2799. Winter address: 319 Hawthorne Blvd, Leesburg, FL 34748; 904-787-6060. Specializing in cookie jars, Abingdon

Gacher, John
The Zsolnay Store
152 Spring St., Newport, 02840; 401-841-5060. Specializing in Zsolnay, Fischer, Amphora, and Austro-Hungarian art pottery

The Occupied Japan Club
c/o Florence Archambault
29 Freeborn St., Newport, 02840. Publishes bimonthly newsletter, *The Upside Down World of an O.J. Collector*. SASE required when requesting information

South Carolina

Roerig, Fred and Joyce
R.R. 2, Box 504, Walterboro, 29488; 803-538-2487. Specializing in cookie jars; authors of *Collector's Encyclopedia of Cookie Jars, an Illustrated Value Guide*, publishers of *Cookie Jarrin' with Joyce: The Cookie Jar Newsletter*

Tennessee

Chase, Mick and Lorna
Fiesta Plus
380 Hawkins Crawford Rd, Crookeville, 38501; 615-372-8333. Specializing in Fiesta, Franciscan, other American dinnerware

Grist, Everett
6503 Slater Rd., Suite H, Chattanooga, 37412-3955; 615-855-4032. Specializing in covered animal dishes and marbles

Hudson, Murray
Murray Hudson Antiquarian Books & Maps
109 S. Church St., Box 163, Halls, 38040; Fax & phone: 900-836-9057 or phone 800-748-9946. Specializing in antique maps, globes, and books with maps, atlases, explorations, travel guides, geographies, surveys, etc.

Texas

Cooper, Marilyn
8408 Lofland Dr., Houston, 77055; 713-465-7773. Specializing in figural toothbrush holders, Pez

Dockery, Rod
4600 Kemble St., Ft. Worth, 76103; 817-536-2168. Specializing in milk glass; SASE required with correspondence

Docks, L.R. 'Les'
Shellac Shack; Discollector
Box 691035, San Antonio, 78269-1035. Author of *American Premium Record Guide*. Specializing in vintage records

Frese, Leo and Wendy
Three Rivers Collectibles
Box 551542, Dallas, 75355; 214-341-5165. Specializing in Rum-Rill, Red Wing pottery and stoneware, Hull

Gaston, Mary Frank
Box 342, Bryan, 77806. Author (Collector Books) on china and metals

Malowanczyk, Abby and Wlodek
Collage-20th Century Classics
3017-B Routh St., Dallas, 75201; 214-880-0020 or (Fax) 214-351-6208. Specializing in architect-designed furniture and decorative arts from the modern movement

Norris, Kenn
Schoolmaster Auctions
P.O. Box 4830, 208 Kerr St., Sanderson, 79848; 915-345-2640. Specializing in school-related items and barbed wire

Potter, Judy
Collector's Gallery/Megan's
4511 McKinney Ave., Dallas, 75206; 214-520-7579 or 1540 8th Ave., Marion, IA 52302; 319-377-1206. Specializing in Higgins, Bellaire, Vernon Kilns

Pringle, Joyce M.
Chip & Dale Collectables
3500 S. Cooper St., Arlington, 76015. Specializing in Boyd, Summit, and Mosser glass

Silvermintz, Karen
5254 Vanderbilt, Dallas, 75206; 214-821-4028. Specializing in American pottery, Russel Wright American dinnerware

Smith, Allan
1806 Shields Dr., Sherman, 75090; 903-893-3626. Specializing in children's lunch boxes and all types of advertising, especially Coca-Cola, Dr. Pepper, Pepsi Cola, RC Cola, Red Goose, Buster Brown Shoes, character tin wind-up toys, and western stars' items

Thompson, Chuck
Chuck Thompson & Associates
P.O. Box 11652, Houston, 77293. Send LSASE for free list of Chuck's tobacciana publications; Thompson specializes in smoker's, ashtrays with and without advertising imprints. His research includes ashtrays designed for homes, automobiles, ocean liners, hotels, trains, and any place where 'ash receivers' were provided to accomodate smokers.

Tucker, Richard and Valerie
Argyle Antiques
P.O. Box 262, Argyle, 76226; 817-464-3752 or (Fax) 817-464-7293. Specializing in windmill weights, shooting gallery targets, figural lawn sprinklers, and cast iron advertising paperweights

Waddell, John
2903 Stan Terrace, Mineral Wells, 76067. Specializing in buggy steps

Walker, Jimmy and Carol
The Iron Lady
501 N. 5th, Waelder, 78959; 512-665-7166. Specializing in pressing irons. LSASE required when requesting information; No Appraisals

Wilkins, James R.
Olden Year Musical Museum
Box 381951, Duncanville 75138; 214-298-5587. Specializing in music boxes, phonographs, grind organs, nickelodeons

Utah

Anderson, Tim
Box 461, Provo, 84603; 801-226-1787. Specializing in autographs; Buys single items or collections — historical, movie stars, US Presidents, sports figures, and pre-1860 correspondence

Anderson, Warren R.
America West Archives
P.O. Box 100, Cedar City, 84721;
801-586-9497. Specializing in old
stock certificates and bonds, western
documents and books, financial
ephemera, autographs, maps, photos.
Author of *Owning Western History*,
with over 75 photos of old documents and recommended reference
guide. Available ($18.00 soft cover
or $28.00 hardback, postpaid) from
author at above address

Vermont

Barry, Kit
143 Main St., Brattleboro, 05301;
802-254-3634. Author of *The
Advertising Trade Card*. Specializing in advertising trade cards and
ephemera in general

Virginia

Bradfield, Jeff
Jeff's Antiques
90 Main St., Dayton, 22821; 703-
879-9961. Also located in Rocky's
Antique Mall (I-81), Exit 60, Wey-
ers Cave. Specializing in postcards,
candy containers, sugar shakers,
toys, pottery, furniture, lamps, and
advertising items

Cranor, Rosalind
P.O. Box 859, Blacksburg, 24063.
Specializing in Elvis collectibles,
author of *Elvis Collectibles* and
Best of Elvis Collectibles (each at
$19.95+$1.75 shipping & handling), available from author

Flanigan, Vicki
Flanigan's Antiques
P.O. Box 1662, Winchester, 22601.
Specializing in antique dolls and
hand fans

Friend, Terry
R.R. 4, Box 152-D, Galax, 24333;
703-236-9027 after 9:30 p.m.
EST. Specializing in coffee mills;
SASE required

Haigh, Richard
P.O. Box 29888, Richmond,
23242; 804-741-5770. Specializing in art glass (Locke Art,
Steuben)

Harold, James P.
2200 Columbia Pike, Arlington,
22204-4422. Specializing in pink
lustre ware

Lechner, Mildred and Ralph
Box 554, Mechanicsville, 23111;
804-737-3347. Author (Collector
Books) on glass salt shakers. Specializing in art and pattern glass
salt shakers circa 1870-1940.
Directors of Antique and Art
Glass Salt Shakers Society Club,
1991-92

Monsen, Randall; and Baer, Rod
Monsen & Baer
310 Maple Ave. West, #270,
Vienna, 22180; 703-938-2129.
Specializing in perfume bottles,
Roseville pottery, Art Deco

Reynolds, Charles
Reynolds Toys
2836 Monroe St., Falls Church,
22042; 703-533-1322. Specializing in limited edition mechanical
and still banks, figural bottle
openers

Tutton, John
R.R. 4, Box 929, Front Royal,
22630; 703-635-7058. Specializing in milk bottles

Washington

Haase, Don (Mr. Spode)
D&D Antiques
P.O. Box 818, Mukilteo, 98275;
206-348-7443. Specializing in
Spode china

Jackson, Denis C., Editor
The Illustrator Collector's News
P.O. Box 1958, Sequim, 98382;
206-683-2559. Copy of recent
sample: $3. Specializing in old
magazines & illustrations such as:
Rose O'Neill, Maxfield Parrish,
pinups, Marilyn Monroe, Norman
Rockwell, etc.

Rothe, Linda
Seattle. Specializing in Black
Americana

Wheeler-Tanner Escapes
Tanner, Joseph and Pamela
3024 E. 35th Ave., Spokane,
99223; 509-448-8457. Specializing in handcuffs, leg shackles,
balls and chains, restraints and
padlocks of all kinds (including
railroad) locking and non-locking
devices; Also Houdini memorabilia: autographs, photos, posters,
books, letters, etc.

Whitacker, Jim and Kaye
Eclectic Antiques
P.O. Box 475S, Lynnwood,
98046; 206-774-6910. Specializing in Josef Originals and motion
lamps

West Virginia

Fostoria Glass Society of America,
Inc.
Box 826, Moundsville, 26041.
Specializing in Fostoria glass

Wisconsin

Apple, John
John Apple Antiques
1720 College Ave., Racine,
53403; 414-633-3086. Specializing in brass cash registers and
parts

Fortney, Daniel
Suite 713, Chalet at the River,
823 N. 2nd St., Milwaukee,
53203. Specializing in china and
glass

Knapper, Mary
Phoneco, Inc.
207 E. Mill Rd., P.O. Box 70,
Galesville, 54630; 608-582-4124.
Specializing in telephones, antique
to modern

Matzke, Gene
Gene's Badges & Emblems
2345 S. 28th St., Milwaukee, 53215;
414-383-8995. Specializing in police
badges, leg irons, old police photos,
fire badges (old), patches, old handcuffs, and memorabilia

Rice, Ferill J.
302 Pheasant Run, Kaukauna,
54130. Specializing in Fenton art
glass

Rossiter, Chris
Box 264, Cleveland, 53015; 414-
693-8086. Specializing in pipes
(especially porcelains) also collecting toys and English military

Washburn, Cara
Washburn Antiques
751 E. Thomas St., Osseo 54758;
715-597-2666 (M-F). Specializing
in glass (over 3,000 pieces), tools,
toys, furniture, general merchandise

Clubs, Newsletters, and Catalogs

Akro Agate Collectors Club and *Clarksburg Crow* quarterly newsletter
Roger Hardy
10 Bailey St., Clarksburg, WV 26301-2524; 304-624-4523. Annual membership fee: $15

America West Archives
Anderson, Warren
P.O. Box 100, Cedar City, UT 84721; 801-586-9497; 26-page illustrated catalogs issued 6 times a year. Has both fixed-price and auction sections offering early western documents, letters, stock certificates, autographs, and other important ephemera. Subscription: $15 per year

American Antique Deck Collectors
52 Plus Joker Club
Clear the Decks, quarterly publication
Ray Hartz, President
P.O. Box 1002, Westerville, OH 43081; 614-891-6296. Specializing in antique playing cards

American Bell Association, Int., Inc.
c/o The Bell Tower
P.O. Box 19443, Indianapolis, IN 46219. Dorothy Malone Anthony, Past President

Antique & Art Glass Salt Shaker Collectors' Society (AAGSSCS)
2832 Rapidan Trail, Maitland, FL 32751

Antique & Collectors Reproduction News
Antiques Coast to Coast
c/o Lorna Bambrook
Box 71174, Des Moines, IA 50325; 515-270-8994 or (subscriptions only) 800-227-5531. Monthly newsletter, subscription: $32 per year in US; $41 in Canada.

Antique Purses Catalog: $4
Bayhouse
P.O. Box 40443, Bay Village, OH 44140; 216-871-8584. Includes colored photos of beaded and enameled mesh purses.

Antique Radio Club of America
81 Steeplechase Rd., Devon, PA 19333

Antique Souvenir Collectors' News
Gary Leveille, Editor
P.O. Box 562, Great Barrington, MA 01230

Antique Stove Association
Clifford Boram, Secretary
417 N. Main St., Monticello, IN 47960. Inquiries should be accompanied by SASE and marked 'Urgent' in red

Antique Trader Weekly
Kyle D. Husfloen, Editor
P.O. Box 1050, Dubuque, IA 52004. Featuring news about antiques and collectibles, auctions and events; listing over 165,000 buyers and sellers in every edition. Subscription $32 (52 issues) per year

Antique Wireless Association
Ormiston Rd., Breesport, NY 14816

Appraisers National Association
120 S. Bradford Ave., Placentia, CA 92670; 714-579-1082. Founded in 1982 by Dr. David Long, Ph.D, President of the College for Appraisers, to provide for a standardization of educational requirements for certification of its appraiser members and assure the public that A.N.A. appraisers not only have a broad range of knowledge in personal property valuation, but are held to the highest ethical and professional standards in the industry.

Arkansas Pottery Collectors' Society
P.O. Box 7617, Little Rock, AR 72217

Arts & Crafts Quarterly
9 S. Main St., Lambertville, NJ 08530; 609-397-9374

Ashtray Collectors' Club International
Chuck Thompson
Box 11652, Houston, EX 77293; Club is for collectors of smoker's ashtrays, from inexpensive advertising ashtrays to valuable works of art; Members receive free ads in bimonthly newsletter; Membership: $9.95 per year

Autographs of America
Anderson, Tim
P.O. Box 461, Provo, UT 84603. Free sample catalog of hundreds of autographs for sale

Avon Times (National Newsletter Club)
c/o Dwight or Vera Young
P.O. Box 9868, Dept P., Kansas City, MO 64134. Inquiries should be accompanied by large SASE.

Black Memorabilia Catalog
Judy Posner
R.D. 1, Box 273 SC, Effort, PA 18330. Send $2 and LSASE

Boyd's Art Glass Collectors Guild
P.O. Box 52, Hatboro, PA 19040-0052. Books available: *Boyd's Crystal Art Glass, The Tradition Continues*, P.O. Box 127, Cambridge, OH 43725; and *Boyd's Art Glass Production 1978-1991*, P.O. Box 11806, Kansas City, MO 64138

British Royal Commemorative Souvenirs Mail Order Catalog
Audrey Zeder
6755 Coralite St. S, Long Beach, CA 90808

California Perfume Company
For information contact Dick Pardini
3107 North El Dorado St., Dept. SAPG, Stockton, CA 95204-3412. Information requires large SASE; not necessary when offering items for sale

Candy Container Collectors of America
P.O. Box 8708, Canton, OH 44711-8708
Or contact: Jeff Bradfield
90 Main St., Dayton, VA 22821

The Cane Collector's Chronicle
Linda Beeman
15 2nd St. N.E., Washington, D.C. 20002; $30 for 4 issues

The Carousel News & Trader
87 Parke Ave. W., Suite 206, Mansfield, OH 44902. A monthly magazine for the carousel enthusiast. Subscription: $22 per year, sample: $3

The Carousel Shopper Resource Catalog
Box 47, Dept PC, Millwood, NY 10546. Only $2 (+50¢ postage). A full-color catalog featuring dealers of antique carousel art offering single figures or complete carousels, museums, restoration services, organizations, full-size reproductions, books, cards, posters, auction services, and other hard-to-find items for carousel enthusiasts.

Central Florida Insulator Collectors
557 Nicklaus Dr., Titusville, FL 32780

Ceramic Arts Studio Collector's Association
P.O. Box 46, Madison, WI 53701

Character Collectibles Catalog
Judy Posner
R.D. 1, Box 273 SC, Effort, PA 18330. Send $2 and LSASE

Chase Collectors Society
c/o Barry L. Van Hook
2149 W. Jibsail Loop, Mesa, AZ 85202-5524; 602-838-6971. Publishes newsletter *Art Deco Reflections*, Membership: $10, Sample copy of newsletter: $1

Chicagoland Antique Amusements Slot Machine & Jukebox Gazette
Ken Durham, Editor
P.O. Box 2426, Dept. S, Rockville, MD 20852. 20-page newspaper published twice a year. Subscription: 4 issues for $10; sample: $5

Coin-Op Newsletter
Ken Durham, Publisher
909 26th St. N.W., Washington, D.C. 20037. Subscription (10 issues): $24 per year, Sample: $5

The Cola Clan
Alice Fisher, Treasurer
2084 Continental Drive N.E., Atlanta, GA 30345

Collectors of Findlay Glass
P.O. Box 256, Findlay, OH 45840. An organization dedicated to the study and recognition of Findlay glass, newsletter *The Melting Pot*, published quarterly, convention held annually; Membership: $10 per year

The Compact Collectors
Roselyn Gerson
P.O. Box S, Lynbrook, NY 11563.
Publishes *Powder Puff* newsletter,
which contains articles covering
all aspects of compact collecting,
restoration, vintage ads, patents,
history, and articles by members
and prominent guest writers.
Seeker and sellers column offered
free to members

Cookie Jar Catalog
Judy Posner
R.D. 1, Box 273 SC, Effort, PA
18330. Send $2 and LSASE

*Cookie Jarrin' with Joyce: The
Cookie Jar Newsletter*
R.R. 2, Box 504, Walterboro, SC
29488

*The Copley Connection: Royal
Copley Collectors' Newsletter*
Joe Devine
1411 3rd St., Council Bluffs, IA
51503; or
Barbara Burke
4213 Sandhurst Dr., Orlando, FL
32817. Bimonthly publication,
Subscription: $12 per year

Currier & Ives Catalog
Rudisill's Alt Print Haus
P.O. Box 199, Worton, MD
21678. Please include LSASE

The Cutting Edge, quarterly publication of the Glass Knife Collectors Club
Adrienne S. Escoe, Editor
P.O. Box 342, Los Alamitos, CA
90720. Subscription: $5 per year,
Sample: $1.25

*The Dedham Pottery Collectors
Society Newsletter*, published quarterly
Jim Kaufman, Publisher
248 Highland St., Dedham, MA
02026; 800-283-8070. Subscription: $18

Depression Glass Daze
Teri Steel, Editor/Publisher
Box 57, Otisville, MI 48463; 313-
631-4593. The nation's market
place for glass, china, and pottery

Disneyana Catalog
Judy Posner
R.D. 1, Box 273 SC, Effort, PA
18330. Send $2 and LSASE

Docks, L.R. 'Les'
Shellac Shack
Box 691035, San Antonio, TX
78269-1035. Send $2 for a 72-
page catalog of 78s that Docks
wants to buy, the prices he will
pay, and shipping instructions

Doorstop Collectors of America
Doorstopper newsletter
Jeanie Bertoia
2413 Madison Ave., Vineland,
NJ 08630; 609-692-4092; Mem-
bership: $20 per year, includes 2
newsletters and convention.
Send 2-stamp SASE for sample

Doyle Auctioneers & Appraisers
Doyle, Robert A.
109 Osborne Hill Rd., Fishkill, NY
12524; 800-551-5161. Newsletter:
Auction Opportunities, Inc., for $25
per year

Dragonware Club
c/o Suzi Hibbard
2570 Walnut Blvd. #20, Walnut
Creek, CA 94596; 510-947-1076.
Inquiries should be accompanied by
SASE. All contributions are welcome.

Drawing Room of Newport
Gacher, John
152 Spring St., Newport, RI 02840;
401-841-5060. Book on Zsolnay
available

The Elegance of Old Ivory newsletter
Box 1004, Wilsonville, OR 97070

Fiesta Club of America
P.O.Bos 15383
Loves Park, IL 61132-5383
$20 per year

Fenton Art Glass Collectors of
America, Inc.
Williamstown, WV 26187
Fiesta Collector's Quarterly Newsletter
19238 Dorchester Circle,
Strongsville, OH 44136. Subscrip-
tion: $12 per year

Figural Bottle Opener Collectors
c/o Craig Dinner
Box 251, Townsend, VT 05353.
Please include SASE

Fire Mark Circle of Americas
Glen Hartley, Sr.
2859 Marlin Dr., Chamblee, GA
30341-5119; 404-451-2651. Specializing in fire marks, Methodist,
Masonic, Foremost Dairies, Goodyear

Fostoria Glass Society of America, Inc.
P.O. Box 826, Moundsville, WV
26041

Frankoma Collectors Newsletter
244 Fox Lane, Belvidere, IL
61008; 815-544-5620

Friar Tuck Collectors Club
P.O. Box 173, Dacula, GA 30211;
404-963-5736. Quarterly newsletter, annual convention, write or
call for membership application
and information

H.C. Fry Society
P.O. Box 41, Beaver, PA 15009.
Founded in 1983 for the sole purpose of learning about Fry glass; Publishes quarterly newsletter *Shards*

GAR Post 20 Illinois
Richard A. Haussman, Chaplain
P.O. Box 1865, Aurora, 60507

George Kamm Paperweights
24-SP Townsend Court, Lancaster,
PA 17603; 717-872-7858. Specializing in antique and contemporary
paperweights; Color brochure published bimonthly, $5 annual fee
(refundable); Sample on request
(requires #10 SASE)

Glass Knife Collector's Club
Adrienne S. Escoe
P.O. Box 342, Los Alamitos, CA
90720

*Gonder Pottery Collectors' Newslet-
ter*
c/o John and Marilyn McCormick
P.O. Box 3174, Shawnee, KS
66226

Grandpa's Depot & Caboose
John 'Grandpa' White
Denver Union Station, 1616 17th
St. Denver, CO 80202; 303-892-
1177 or (Fax) 303-573-5505.
Publishes catalogs on railroad-
related collectibles

Hake's Americana & Collectibles
Specializing in character and personality collectibles along with artifacts of popular culture for over 20
years. To receive a catalog for their
next 3,000-item mail/phone bid
auction, send $3 to:
Hake's Americana
P.O. Box 1444M, York, PA 17405

Ice Screamer
c/o Duvall Sollers
P.O. Box 132, Monkton, MD
21111. Published bimonthly,
dues: $15 per year; annual con-
vention late June

The Illustrator Collector's News
(*TICN*)
Denis C. Jackson, Editor
P.O. Box 1958, Sequim, WA 98382;
Fax (206-683-2559. Subscription:
$17 per year; $3 for sample copy of
bimonthly publication. Publishes
price and identification guides on
various illustrators and magazines,
write for further information.

Indiana Historical Radio Society
245 N. Oakland Ave., Indianapolis, IN 46201

International Association of Calculator Collectors/*International
Calculator Collector Newsletter*
Guy Ball, Co-Editor
14561 Livingston St., Tustin, CA
92680-2618. Subscription: $8 per
year ($12 foreign), published
quarterly

International Club for Collectors
of Hatpins & Hatpin Holders
(ICC of H&HH)
Lillian Baker, Founder
15237 Chanera Ave., Gardena,
CA 90249; 213-329-2619.
Monthly *Points* newsletter and
Pictorial Journal

International Perfume and Scent
Bottle Collectors Association
Randall B. Monsen, Membership
Secretary
310 Maple Ave. W. #270,
Vienna, VA 22180

International Rose O'Neill Club
Contact Karen Stewart
P.O. Box 668, Branson, MO
65616 Publishes quarterly
newsletter *Kewpiesta Kourier*.
Dues: (includes newsletter) $7
(single) or $10 (family)

International Society of Antique
Scale Collectors
Bob Stein, President
176 West Adams, Suite 1706,
Chicago, IL 60603; 312-263-7500.
Publishes *Equilibrium*, quarterly
magazine; Quarterly President's
Newsletter; Annual membership
directory and out-of-print scale cat-
alogs. Holds annual convention

Kitchen Antiques & Collectibles News newsletter
Publication of KOOKS (Kollectors of Old Kitchen Stuff)
Dana & Darlene DeMore, Editors
4645 Laurel Ridge Dr., Harrisburg, PA 17110; 717-545-7320. Subscription: $24 per year for 6 issues

The Lady's Gallery, publication of fashion, decorative arts, and collectibles
Subscription: $23.95 (US, 6 issues) per year; Call 800-622-5676 for further information

The Laughlin Eagle
Joan Jasper, Publisher
Richard Racheter, Editor
1270 63rd Terrace S., St. Petersburg, FL 33705; Subscription: $14 (4 issues) per year; sample issue: $4

Line Jewels-Insulator
3557 Nicklaus Dr., Titusville, FL 32780. Books/price guides (not sold separately) available: *Most About Glass Insulators*, 455-page and price guide, 159-page, for $43 US funds; *Insulators Vol.1*, 180-page, *Vol.II*, 325-page and price guide, 116-page, for $63 US funds. For information, send LSASE.

Mabel Lucie Attwell Catalogs
c/o Showcase Antiques
4405 Fair Oaks Ave., Pasadena, CA 91105; 818-577-9660

Majolica Mail Order Catalog
Items from the collection of Mariann Katz Marks
P.O. Box 750, Honesdale, PA 18431. Please send LSASE for majolica listing

Marble Collectors' Society of America
P.O. Box 222, Trumbull, CT 06611
Claire Block, Secretary
Publishes *Marble Mania*, gathers and disseminates information to further the hobby of marbles and marble collecting. $12 adds your name to the contributor mailing list ($21 covers 2 years)

Mike's General Store
52 St. Anne's Rd., Winnepeg, Manitoba, Canada R2M 2Y3; 204-255-3464. Catalog subscription: $6 per issue or next 4 issues for $20

Morgantown Collectors of America
Jerry Gallagher
420 1st Ave. N.W., Plainview, MN 55964; 507-534-3511. *The Morgantown Newscaster*, quarterly journal for research of Morgantown Glass only; affiliated with no club. Subscription: $15 per year. Morgantown 1931 Catalog Reprint (presently out of print). *Morgantown Colors* placard: $4 postpaid. *A Collector's Handbook of Morgantown Glass, 1899-1971*, call for price and shipping information. Please send SASE for answers to queries.

Mt. Washington Art Glass Society
P.O. Box 24094, Fort Worth, TX 76124-1094. Publishes MWAGS *Review*, to educate, inform and provide helpful information to anyone interested in art glass; holds annual convention. Subscription/membership: $20 per individual or $25 for two persons in one household.

Mystic Lights of the Aladdin Knights bimonthly newsletter
c/o J.W. Courter
3935 Kelley Rd., Kevil, KY 40253; 502-488-2116. Information requires LSASE

National Association of Avon Collectors
c/o Connie Clark
6100 Walnut, Dept. P, Kansas City, MO 64113. Information requires large SASE

National Association of Miniature Enthusiasts (N.A.M.E.)
Box 2621, Anaheim, CA 92804-0621; 714-871-NAME

National Autumn Leaf Collectors' Club
c/o Gwynne Harrison
P.O. Box 1, Mira Loma, CA 91752-0001; 909-685-5434

National Blue Ridge Newsletter
Norma Lilly
144 Highland Dr., Blountville, TN 37617. Subscription: $15 per year (6 issues)

National Cambridge Collectors, Inc.
P.O. Box 416, Cambridge, OH 43725

National Graniteware Society
P.O. Box 10013, Cedar Rapids, IA 52410

National Greentown Glass Association
1807 W. Madison, Kokomo, IN 46901

National Imperial Glass Collectors' Society, Inc.
P.O. Box 534, Bellaire, OH 43906. Dues: $12 per year (plus $1 for each additional member in same household), quarterly newsletter, convention every June

National Insulator Association
1315 Old Mill Path, Broadview Heights, OH 44147

National Milk Glass Collectors' Society and *Opaque News* quarterly newsletter
c/o Helen D. Storey
46 Almond Dr., Cocoa Townes, Hershey, PA 17033. Please include SASE.

National Reamer Association
c/o Larry Branstad
R.R. 3, Box 67, Frederic, WI 54837

National Toothpick Holder Collectors' Society
Joyce Ender, Treasurer
Box 246, Sawyer, MI 49125. Dues: $15 (single) or $20 (couple) per year (includes monthly *Toothpick Bulletin*.) Annual convention held in August

National Valentine Collectors Association
Evalene Pulati
P.O. Box 1404, Santa Ana, CA 92702; 714-547-1355. Specializing in Valentines and love tokens

New England Society of Open Salt Collectors
Mimi Waible, Membership Chairman
P.O. Box 177, Sudberry, MA 01776; 508-443-3613. Dues: $5 per year

New York Decorative Ceramic Society
9 S. Main St., Lambertville, NJ 08530. Meetings held 4-6 times a year in New York and New Jersey, at museums, galleries, and collectors' homes

Newspaper Collector's Society of America
Rick Brown
Box 19134-S, Lansing, MI 48901; 517-887-1255 or (Fax) 517-887-2194

North American Torquay Society
Jerry and Gerry Kline, Archivists
604 Orchard View Dr., Maumee, OH 43537. Quarterly newsletter sent to members; Information and membership form requires #10 SASE

North American Trap Collectors' Association
c/o Tom Parr
P.O. Box 94, Galloway, OH 43119-0094. Dues: $15 per year; Publishes bimonthly newsletter

The Occupied Japan Club
c/o Florence Archambault
29 Freeborn St., Newport, RI 02840. Publishes *The Upside Down World of an O.J. Collector*, a bimonthly newsletter. Information requires SASE

Old Storefront Antiques
P.O. Box 357, Dublin, IN 47335; 317-478-4809. Publishes catalogs on store items, primitives, advertising, profession-related, etc. Each is available for $1.50 or all 17 for $17 postpaid. Include LSASE

Old Stuff
Donna and Ron Miller, Publishers
336 N. Davis, P.O. Box 1084, McMinnville, OR 97128; 503-434-5386. Published 6 times annually; Copies by mail: $3 each; Annual subscription: $12 ($20 in Canada)

On the LIGHTER Side bimonthly newsletter
International Lighter Collectors
Judith Sanders, Editor
136 Circle Dr., Quitman, TX 75783; 903-763-2795 or (Fax) 903-763-4953. Annual convention held in different cities in the US; Subscription fees: Overseas rate, US and Canada rate, and a Junior & Senior Citizen rate. Please include SASE when requesting information.

Open Salt Collectors of the Atlantic Regions (O.S.C.A.R.)
Lee Anne Gommer, Secretary
56 Northview Dr., Lancaster, PA 17601. Dues: $5 per year

Open Salt Seekers of the West, Northern California Chapter
Sarah Kawakami, Secretary
2005 Pitnam St., Antioch, CA 95409; 510-757-9603. Dues: $5 per year

Open Salt Seekers of the West, Southern California Chapter
Pat and Chris Christensen, Newsletters
1067 Salvador, Costa Mesa, CA 92626; 714-540-1225. Dues: $5 per year

Our McCoy Matters
Kathy Lynch, Editor
McCoy Publications, P.O. Box 14255, Parkville, MO 64152; 816-587-9179. Subscription: $24 for 6 issues

Paper Pile Quarterly magazine
Ada Fitzsimmons, Editor
P.O. Box 337, San Anselmo, CA 94979; 619-322-3525. Sales and features magazine serving paper collectors and dealers since 1980, quarterly cataloged sales, large advertising section. Subscription: $17 per year (shipped 1st class)

Paperweight Collectors' Association, Inc
P.O. Box 1059, Easthampton, MA 01027; 413-527-2598. Membership: $15 per person or $25 per couple. Publishes 5 newsletters a year; Biannual conventions to promote and study paperweights. Annual Bulletin not included with dues

Pen Fancier's Club
1169 Overcash Dr., Dunedin, FL 34698. Publishes monthly catalog of pens and mechanical pencils. Subscription: $36 per year, Sample: $3

Perfume & Scent Bottle Collectors
Jeane Parris
2022 E. Charleston Blvd., Las Vegas, NV 89104; 702-385-6059. Membership: $15 USA or $30 Foreign (includes quarterly newsletter). Information requires SASE.

Phoenix and Consolidated Glass Collectors' Club
Jack D. Wilson, Secretary/Editor (club newsletter)
P.O. Box 81974, Chicago IL 60681-0974; 312-282-9553. Membership: $25 for single, $35 for couple per year

Phoenix Bird Discoveries newsletter
Joan Oates
685 S. Washington, Constantine, MI 49042; 616-435-8353. Subscription: $8 per year (2 issues)

Pie Birds Unlimited Newsletter
Lillian M. Cole
14 Harmony School Rd., Flemington, NJ 08822; 908-782-3198. Specializing in pie birds, pie funnels, pie vents

The Political Gallery
Thomas D. Slater
1325 W. 86th St., Indianapolis, IN 46260; 317-257-0863. Specializing in political and sports memorabilia

Precious Collectibles magazine for Precious Moments figurine collectors, *The Ornament Collector* magazine for Hallmark ornaments and other ornaments, and the *Collectors' Bulletin* magazine for all Limited Edition collectibles

Rosie Wells Enterprises, Inc.
R.R. 1S, Canton, IL 61520. Write for free literature. Rosie also has informational secondary market price guides for Precious Moments collectibles, Hallmark Ornaments and Hallmark Merry Miniatures. She also has a Buy-Sell-Trade Ad telephone line for collectors across the USA for over 42 collectibles and antiques, 1-900-740-7575. For additional information, call 800-445-8745

Purinton Pastimes
P.O. Box 9394, Arlington, VA 22219. Newsletter for Purinton pottery enthusiasts; Subscription: $10 per year

R. Lalique
John Danis
11028 Raleigh Ct., Rockford, IL 61115; 815-963-0757 or (Fax) 815-877-6042

Roseville's of the Past newsletter
Jack Bomm, Editor
P.O. Box 681117, Orlando, FL 32868-1117. $19.95 per year for 6 to 12 newsletters

Salt & Pepper Catalog
Judy Posner
R.D. 1, Box 273 SC, Effort, PA 18330. Send $2 and LSASE

Salt & Pepper Novelty Shakers Club
Irene Thornburg
581 Joy Road, Battle Creek, MI 49017; 616-963-7953. Publishes quarterly newsletter, holds annual convention, dues: $20 per year in US, Canada and Mexico ($5 extra for spousal membership)

Shawnee Pottery Collectors' Club
P.O. Box 713, New Smyrna Beach, FL 32170-0713. Monthly nationwide newsletter. SASE (c/o Pamela Curran) required when requesting information. Optional: $3 for sample of current newsletter

Southern Folk Pottery Collectors Society
Roy M. Thompson, Jr., Founder
1828 N. Howard Mills Rd. Robbins, NC 27325; 910-464-3961

Southern Oregon Antiques & Collectibles Club
P.O. Box 508, Talent, OR 97540; 503-535-1231 Meets 1st Wednesday of the month, promotes 2 shows a year in Medford, OR

Spoonville Scoop
Alves, Margaret
84 Oak Ave., Shelton, 06484; 203-924-4768. Specializing in spoons: plated, sterling, silver, pre-1920s. Subscription: $8 per year (published bimonthly)

Stanley Tool Collector News
c/o The Old Tool Shop
208 Front St., Marietta, OH 45750. Features articles of interest, auction results, price trends, classified ads, etc. Subscription: $20 per year; Sample: $6.95

Stevengraph Collectors Assn.
David L. Brown
2103-2829 Arbutus Rd., Victoria, British Columbia, Canada, V8N 5X5; 604-477-9896

Stretch Glass Society
P.O. Box 770643, Lakewood, OH 44107. Membership: $10; quarterly newsletter, annual convention

Surveyors Historical Society Identification Committee
D.R. Beeks
P.O. Box 2515, Coeur d'Alene, ID 83814; 208-667-0830

Susie Cooper Catalogs
J. David Ehrhard
c/o Showcase Antiques
4405 Fair Oaks Ave., Pasadena, CA 91105; 818-577-9660

Swan Seekers Network
4118 E. Vernon Ave., Phoenix, AZ 85008-2333; Telephone and Fax: 602-957-6294. The source for buyers and sellers of Swarovski crystal

Table Toppers
1340 West Irving Park Rd., P.O. Box 161, Chicago, IL 60613; 312-769-3184. Membership: $18 (single) per year, which includes *Table Topics*, a bimonthly newsletter for those interested in table-top collectibles

The Tanner Restraints Collection
3024 E. 35th, Spokane, WA 99223; 509-448-8457. 40-page catalog of magician/escape artist equipment from trick and regulation padlocks, handcuffs, leg shackles, straight jackets to picks, and pick sets. Books on all of the above and much more. Catalog: $3

Tea Leaf Club International
222 Powderhorn Dr., Houghton Lake, MI 48629. Publishes *Tea Leaf Readings* newsletter for members. Membership: $20 (single) or $25 (couple) per year

Tea Talk
Tina M. Carter, teapot columnist
Diana Rosen and Lucy Roman, Editors
419 N. Larchmont Blvd., Los Angeles, CA 90004; 213-659-9650. Subscription: $17.95 per year, sample: $2

Thermometer Collectors' Club of America
Warren D. Harris, President
6130 Rampart Dr., Carmichael, CA 95608; 916-966-3490

Thimble Collectors International
6411 Montego Rd., Louisville, KY 40228

Three Rivers Depression Era Glass Society
Meetings held 1st Monday of each month at DeMartino's Restaurant, Carnegie, PA. For more information call: Edith A. Putanko at John's Antiques & Edie's Glassware
Rte 88 & Broughton Rd, Bethel Park, PA 15102; 412-831-2702

Tiffin Glass Collectors
P.O. Box 554, Tiffin, OH 44883. Meetings at Seneca Cty. Museum on 2nd Tuesday of each month

Tobacco Antiques and Collectibles Market
Chuck Thompson, Publisher
P.O. Box 11652, Houston, TX 77293. Subscription: $9.95 (12 issues); $19.95 in Canada and Mexico; all other foreign countries: $30 for 6 issues

Tops & Bottoms Club (Rene Lalique perfumes only)
c/o Madeleine France
P.O. Box 15555, Ft. Lauderdale, FL 33318

Toy Gun Collectors of America Newsletter
Jim Buskirk, Editor & Publisher
175 Cornell St., Windsor, CA 95492; 707-837-9949. Published quarterly, covers both toy and BB guns. Dues: $15 per year

The Trade Card Journal
Kit Barry
143 Main St., Brattleboro, VT 05301. A quarterly publication on the social and historical use of trade cards

UHL Collectors' Society
Dale Blann, President
R.R. 1, Box 136, Wheatland, IN 47597; 812-321-4141.
Tom Eubelhor, Secretary/Treasurer
233 E. Timberlin Lane, Huntingburg, IN 47542; 812-482-9575.
Tim Hodges, Newsletter
1378 W. Andrew Lane, Jasper, IN 47546; 812-482-3016. For membership and newsletter information contact any of the above.

Vaseline Glass Newsletter
Jerry Chambers
2163 Pomona Place, Fairfield, CA 94533; 707-425-6166 after 4:30 p.m. P.S.T.

Vernon Views newsletter
P.O. Box 945, Scottsdale, AZ 85252. Published quarterly beginning with the spring issue, $10 per year

Vintage Fashion & Costume Jewelry newsletter/club
P.O. Box 265, Glen Oaks, NY 11004; 718-969-2320 or 718-939-3095. Year's subscription (4 issues): $15 in US; $20 in Canada; $25 International. Back issues available at $5 each

Walking Stick Notes
Cecil Curtis, Editor
4051 E. Olive Rd., Pensacola, FL 32514. Quarterly publication with limited distribution

Watt's News, newsletter for Watt pottery enthusiasts
c/o Watt Collectors Association
P.O. Box 184, Galesburg, IL 61402-0184. Subscription: $10 per year; quarterly newsletter, annual convention

Westmoreland Glass Society
Jim Fisher, President
513 5th Ave., Coralville, IA 52241; 319-354-5011. Membership: $15 for a single & $25 per household

The Whimsey Club
c/o Christopher Davis
522 Woodhill, Newark, NY 14513. *Whimsical Notions*, quarterly newsletter; dues: $5 per year. Annual meeting in Rochester, NY, in April during Genessee Valley Bottle Collectors' Show

The Willow Word
Mary Lina Berndt, Publisher
P.O. Box 13382, Arlington, TX 76094. Each bimonthly issue contains 20 pages of articles, photographs and full-color 'centerfold.' Subscription: $20 in US, $22 in Canada, $25 overseas (US funds only)

World's Fair Collectors' Society, Inc.
Fair News, monthly newsletter (for members)
Michael R. Pender, Editor
P.O. Box 20806, Sarasota, FL 34238; 813-923-2590. Dues: $17 per year in USA, $18 in Canada, and $27 for overseas members

The Zsolnay Store
152 Spring St., Newport, RI 02840; 401-841-5060. Zsolnay book available

Index

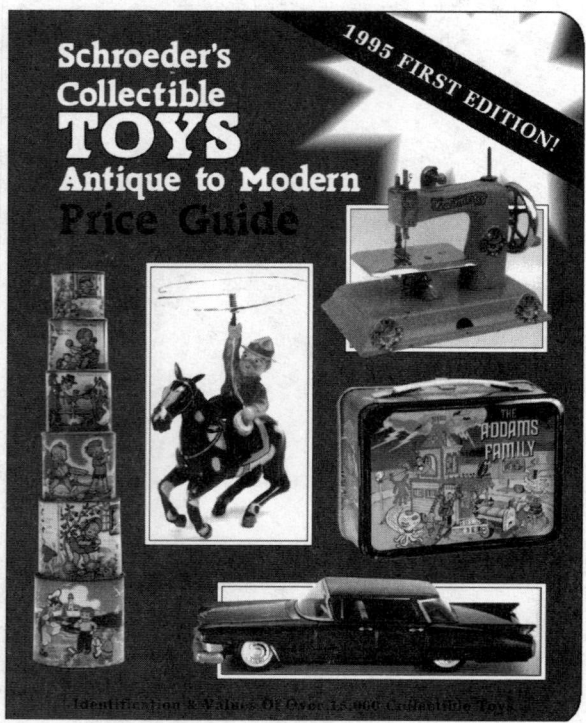